June 22–27, 2014
Snowbird, UT, USA

Association for Computing Machinery

Advancing Computing as a Science & Profession

SIGMOD'14

Proceedings of the 2014 ACM SIGMOD International Conference on Management of Data

Sponsored by:

ACM SIGMOD

Supported:

Goldman Sachs, Microsoft, Oracle, AT&T, Baidu, Facebook, Google, IBM Research, Pivotal, SAP, Tableau, WalmartLabs, Intel, NEC, Yahoo! Labs, Morgan & Claypool Publishers, Elsevier, & Springer

Association for
Computing Machinery

Advancing Computing as a Science & Profession

The Association for Computing Machinery
2 Penn Plaza, Suite 701
New York, New York 10121-0701

Notice to Past Authors of ACM-Published Articles
ACM intends to create a complete electronic archive of all articles and/or other material previously published by ACM. If you have written a work that has been previously published by ACM in any journal or conference proceedings prior to 1978, or any SIG Newsletter at any time, and you do NOT want this work to appear in the ACM Digital Library, please inform permissions@acm.org, stating the title of the work, the author(s), and where and when published.

ISBN: 978-1-4503-2376-5 (Digital)

ISBN: 978-1-4503-3176-0 (Print)

Additional copies may be ordered prepaid from:

ACM Order Department
PO Box 30777
New York, NY 10087-0777, USA

Phone: 1-800-342-6626 (USA and Canada)
+1-212-626-0500 (Global)
Fax: +1-212-944-1318
E-mail: acmhelp@acm.org
Hours of Operation: 8:30 am – 4:30 pm ET

Printed in the USA

Welcome Message from the SIGMOD Chairs

We are delighted to welcome you to SIGMOD 2014, the 2014 edition of the ACM SIGMOD International Conference on Management of Data, at Snowbird, Utah, in the Rocky Mountains of the United States. Snowbird is a mountain ski and summer resort. Many attractions, parks, and recreational areas – including the Yellowstone, Zion, Bryce Canyon, Capitol Reef, Great Basin, Canyonlands, and Arches national parks – are within a day's drive. The mountain scenery of Snowbird is also adjacent to the urban environment of Salt Lake City.

SIGMOD 2014 hosts an exciting technical program, with two keynote talks, by Maurice Herlihy (Brown University) and Eric Sedlar (Oracle Labs); a panel session on "Should we all be teaching 'Intro to Data Science' instead of 'Intro to Databases'?," by Bill Howe (University of Washington), Michael Franklin (University of California, Berkeley), Juliana Freire (New York University), James Frew (University of California, Santa Barbara), Tim Kraska (Brown University), and Raghu Ramakrishnan (Microsoft Corporation); an industrial panel on "Are We Experiencing a Big Data Bubble?," by Fatma Özcan (IBM Almaden Research Center), Daniel Abadi (Yale University), Marcel Kornacker (Cloudera), C Mohan (IBM Almaden Research Center), Karthik Ramasamy (Twitter), and Janet Wiener (Facebook, Inc.); 107 research paper presentations; 6 tutorials; 30 demonstrations; and 15 industrial presentations selected from among 44 submissions. In addition to having 25-minute presentation slots, research papers are included in one of two Research Plenary Poster Sessions. One of these sessions is jointly for PODS and SIGMOD research papers, to deepen the ties between the two conferences.

SIGMOD 2014 includes several technical and social events designed specifically for student attendees. The SIGMOD/PODS 2014 Ph.D. Symposium, the Undergraduate Research Poster Competition, and the New Researcher Symposium are all established components of the SIGMOD program and are all part of SIGMOD 2014. The conference also hosts a session dedicated to highlighting the finalists of the SIGMOD Programming Contest. (This year's task is to implement a multidimensional, high-throughput, in-memory indexing system.) In addition, the conference includes a Sponsor Session for our industry partners to present the cool things they have done and introduce career opportunities in industry. This helps bring student attendees together with our Gold, Platinum, and Diamond sponsors. A "vis-à-vis" meeting aimed at helping Ph.D. students meet internationally recognized researchers in their research areas, will also be organized to exchange ideas and receive guidance in a relaxed social setting.

We are immensely grateful to the many researchers who have shaped the conference program. In particular, we thank the Keynotes Chair Gustavo Alonso (ETH Zürich), the Panels Chairs Susan Davidson (University of Pennsylvania) and Sunita Sarawagi (IIT Bombay), the Tutorial Chairs Chris Jermaine (Rice University) and Yufei Tao (Chinese University of Hong Kong), the Industrial Program Chairs Fatma Özcan (IBM Almaden) and Nesime Tatbul (Intel Labs and MIT), together with the 13 members of the Industrial Program Committee, the Demonstrations Chairs Wolfgang Lehner (Technische Universität Dresden) and Bettina Kemme (McGill University), together with the 53 members of the Demonstration Program Committee, the Workshops Chair Anastasia Ailamaki (EPFL), the Undergraduate Research Program Chairs Mario Nascimento (University of Alberta) and Anastasios Kementsietsidis (IBM TJ Watson Laboratories), the New Researcher Symposium Chairs Anish Das Sarma (Google Research) and Alexandra Meliou (University of Massachusetts, Amherst). We also express our enormous gratitude to the 13 Program Committee "area coordinators," Lei Chen (Hong Kong University of Science and Technology), Michael Franklin (University of California, Berkeley), Alfons Kemper (Technical University of Munich), Laks Lakshmanan (University of British Columbia), Ioana Manolescu (Inria Saclay), Tova Milo (Tel Aviv University), Elke Rundensteiner (Worcester Polytechnic Institute), Ken Salem (University of Waterloo), Dennis Shasha (New York University), Divesh Srivastava

(AT&T Labs-Research), Kian-Lee Tan (National University of Singapore), Patrick Valduriez (Inria Sophia-Antipolis Méditerranée), and Xiaokui Xiao (Nanyang Technological University) along with the 111 members of the SIGMOD 2014 Program Committee.

This year we had two submission cycles for SIGMOD research papers – one in mid-September and the second one in mid-December. We received 421 research paper submissions across two cycles. As usual, each paper was reviewed by at least three program committee members, followed by a discussion led by the area coordinators. We followed a review process that resembles journal reviewing – papers went through multiple rounds of reviews until a final decision was taken. Out of 421 submissions, 29 were directly accepted, 102 went through a major revision process, and 290 were rejected. Out of the 102 that went through a major revision 56 were accepted, a further 22 were accepted following a third round of "minor revisions," and 24 were rejected. Since the review process resembled journal-style, the acceptance rates are also similar to top journals.

We also acknowledge all members of the SIGMOD 2014 organizing committee, as well as the SIGMOD Executive Committee, for invaluable help and guidance throughout the many months leading to the conference. The strong organizing team for SIGMOD 2014 includes proceedings chairs Xiang Lian (University of Texas - Pan American) and Florin Rusu (University of California Merced), finance chair Nikolaus Augsten (University of Salzburg), publicity chairs Guoliang Li (Tsinghua University) and Ashwin Machanavajjhala (Duke University), social media chair Ming Hua (Facebook), sponsorship chairs Yi Chen (New Jersey Institute of Technology) and Nick Koudas (University of Toronto), exhibit chairs Rui Zhang (University of Melbourne) and Peixiang Zhao (Florida State University), local arrangements chair Ryan Johnson (University of Toronto), registration chairs Tingjian Ge (University of Massachusetts, Lowell) and Gabriel Ghinita (University of Massachusetts, Boston), demonstration and workshop local arrangement chair Jeff Phillips (University of Utah), web chairs Huiping Cao (New Mexico State University) and Bin Yao (Shanghai Jiao Tong University), travel award committee chairs Alexandra Meliou (University of Massachusetts, Amherst) and Cong Yu (Google Research), and programming contest chairs Sam Madden (MIT) and Jeong-Hyon Hwang (University of Albany). The success of this conference is impossible without their hard work and persistent dedication. K. Selçuk Candan deserves special thanks for providing us with his advice and SIGMOD institutional memory, as well as for his help with logistics throughout the conference planning. We are also grateful to the Microsoft Research Conference Management Toolkit (CMT) team for their extremely prompt and helpful support throughout the complex conference reviewing process. (We used CMT for the submission and reviewing of research papers, demonstrations, and industrial presentations.) We also extend our appreciation to the student volunteers.

We thank the many SIGMOD 2014 supporters, whose contributions helped to maintain the conference registration fees low, most significantly for student attendees: Platinum Level: Goldman Sachs, Oracle, and Microsoft; Gold Level: AT&T, Baidu, Facebook, Google, IBM Research, Pivotal, SAP, Tableau, and @WalmartLabs; and Silver Level: Intel, NEC and Yahoo! Labs. University of Utah and the Utah State University have also extended their generous support to SIGMOD 2014. Finally, the National Science Foundation and the SIGMOD Executive Committee have financially supported the SIGMOD 2014 student travel award program.

We welcome you to Snowbird and we sincerely hope that you will enjoy SIGMOD 2014!

Curtis Dyreson
General Chair

Feifei Li
General Chair

M. Tamer Özsu
Program Chair

Xiang Lian
Proceedings Chair

Florin Rusu
Proceedings Chair

Table of Contents

Research Session 8: Data Cleaning

Session Chair: Bogdan Cautis *(Université Paris Sud)*

Research Session 9: Data Exploration

Session Chair: Dennis Shasha *(New York University)*

Industry Session 3: Storage Management

Session Chair: Hakan Hacigumus *(NEC Labs)*

Keynote 2

Session Chair: Gustavo Alonso *(ETH Zurich)*

Research Session 10: Crowdsourcing

Session Chair: Timos Sellis *(RMIT University)*

Research Session 11: Parallel Graph Processing

Session Chair: Xin L. Dong *(Google)*

Research Session 12: Potpouri

Session Chair: Feifei Li *(University of Utah)*

Demo A

Tutorial 2

Research Session 13: Data Management over Modern Hardware

Session Chair: Ryan Johnson *(University of Toronto)*

Research Session 14: Non-Traditional Data

Session Chair: Florin Rusu *(University of California, Merced)*

Research Session 15: MapReduce Processing

Session Chair: Konstantinos Karanasos *(IBM Almaden Research Center)*

Demo B

Panel

Research Session 16: Distributed and Parallel Data Management

Session Chair: Alfons Kemper *(Technical University of Munich)*

Industry Session 4: Big Data Systems

Session Chair: Shel Finkelstein *(SAP Labs)*

Tutorial 3

Research Session 22: Query Processing and Optimization 2

Session Chair: Nikolaus Augsten *(University of Salzburg)*

Research Session 23: Processing Dynamic Graphs

Session Chair: Ambush Singh *(University of California, Santa Barbara)*

Research Session 24: Cloud Computing

Session Chair: Sudipta Das *(Microsoft Research)*

Research Session 28: Big Data

Session Chair: Selcuk K. Candan *(Arizona State University)*

Undergraduate Abstracts

SIGMOD 2014 Conference Organization

General Chairs: Curtis Dyreson *(Utah State University, USA)*
Feifei Li *(University of Utah, USA)*

Program Chair: M. Tamer Özsu *(University of Waterloo, Canada)*

Panels Chairs: Susan Davidson *(University of Pennsylvania, USA)*
Sunita Sarawagi *(IIT Bombay, India)*

Proceedings Chairs: Xiang Lian *(University of Texas - Pan American, USA)*
Florin Rusu *(University of California Merced, USA)*

Local Arrangements Chair: Ryan Johnson *(University of Toronto, Canada)*

Publicity Chairs: Guoliang Li *(Tsinghua University, China)*
Ashwin Machanavajjhala *(Duke University, USA)*

Registration Chairs: Tingjian Ge *(University of Massachusetts, Lowell, USA)*
Gabriel Ghinita *(University of Massachusetts, Boston, USA)*

Tutorial Chairs: Chris Jermaine *(Rice University, USA)*
Yufei Tao *(Chinese University of Hong Kong, China)*

Keynotes Chair: Gustavo Alonso *(ETH Zürich, Switzerland)*

Industrial Program Chairs: Fatma Özcan *(IBM Almaden Research Center, USA)*
Nesime Tatbul *(Intel Labs and MIT, USA)*

Demonstrations Chairs: Wolfgang Lehner *(Technische Universität Dresden, Germany)*
Bettina Kemme *(McGill University, Canada)*

Workshops Chair: Anastasia Ailamaki *(EPFL, Switzerland)*

Undergraduate Research Chairs: Mario Nascimento *(University of Alberta, Canada)*
Anastasios Kementsietsidis *(IBM TJ Watson Labs, USA)*

Finance Chair: Nikolaus Augsten *(University of Salzburg, Austria)*

Social Media Chair: Ming Hua *(Facebook, USA)*

Sponsorship Chairs: Yi Chen *(New Jersey Institute of Technology, USA)*
Nick Koudas *(University of Toronto, Canada)*

Exhibit Chairs: Rui Zhang *(University of Melbourne, Australia)*
Peixiang Zhao *(Florida State University, USA)*

Demonstration and Workshop Local Arrangements Chair: Jeff Phillips *(University of Utah, USA)*

Web/Information Chairs: Huiping Cao *(New Mexico State University, USA)*
Bin Yao *(Shanghai Jiao Tong University, China)*

Travel Awards Chairs: Alexandra Meliou *(University of Massachusetts, Amherst, USA)*
Cong Yu *(Google Research, USA)*

Programming Contest Chairs: Sam Madden *(MIT, USA)*
Jeong-Hyon Hwang *(University of Albany, USA)*

New Researcher Symposium Chairs: Alexandra Meliou *(University of Massachusetts, Amherst, USA)*
Anish Das Sarma *(Google Research, USA)*

Program Committee Group Leaders: Lei Chen *(Hong Kong University of Science and Technology, China)*
Michael Franklin *(University of California, Berkeley, USA)*
Alfons Kemper *(Technical University of Munich, Germany)*
Laks Lakshmanan *(University of British Columbia, Canada)*
Ioana Manolescu *(Inria Saclay, France)*
Tova Milo *(Tel Aviv University, Israel)*
Elke Rundensteiner *(Worcester Polytechnic Institute, USA)*
Ken Salem *(University of Waterloo, Canada)*
Dennis Shasha *(New York University, USA)*
Divesh Srivastava *(AT&T Labs – Research, USA)*
Kian-Lee Tan *(National University of Singapore, Singapore)*
Patrick Valduriez *(Inria Sophia-Antipolis Méditerranée, France)*
Xiaokui Xiao *(Nanyang Technological University, Singapore)*

Program Committee: Daniel Abadi *(Yale University, USA)*
Ashraf Aboulnaga *(QCRI, Qatar)*
Pankaj Agarwal *(Duke University, USA)*
Divyakant Agrawal *(University of California, Santa Barbara, USA)*
Anastasia Ailamaki *(EPFL, Switzerland)*
Reza Akbarinia *(INRIA, France)*
Gustavo Alonso *(ETH Zürich, Switzerland)*
Walid Aref *(Purdue University, USA)*
Michael Armbrust *(Google, USA)*
Philip Bernstein *(Microsoft, USA)*
Angela Bonifati *(Université Lille 1, France)*
Philippe Bonnet *(IT University of Copenhagen, Denmark)*
Stephane Bressan *(National University of Singapore, Singapore)*
Michael Böhlen *(University of Zurich, Switzerland)*
Ceren Budak *(Microsoft Research, USA)*
K. Selçuk Candan *(Arizona State University, USA)*
Bogdan Cautis *(Telecom ParisTech, France)*
Sharma Chakravarthy *(University of Texas at Arlington, USA)*
Badrish Chandramouli *(Microsoft Research, USA)*
Wei Chen *(Microsoft Research Asia, China)*
Yi Chen *(New Jersey Institute of Technology, USA)*
Rada Chirkova *(North Carolina State University, USA)*

Program Committee (continued):

Dario Colazzo *(Université Paris-Dauphine, France)*
Bin Cui *(Beijing University, China)*
Carlo Curino *(Microsoft Research, USA)*
Gautam Das *(University of Texas at Arlington, USA)*
Sudipto Das *(Microsoft, USA)*
Khuzaima Daudjee *(University of Waterloo, Canada)*
Amol Deshpande *(University of Maryland, USA)*
Alin Deutsch *(University of California, San Diego, USA)*
Yanlei Diao *(University of Massachusetts, Amherst, USA)*
Jens Dittrich *(University of Saarlands, Germany)*
Alin Dobra *(University of Florida, USA)*
Xin Luna Dong *(Google, USA)*
Alan Fekete *(University of Sydney, Australia)*
Peter Fischer *(Universität Frieburg, Germany)*
Juliana Freire *(Polytechnic Institute of NYU, USA)*
Johann-Christoph Freytag *(Humboldt-Universität zu Berlin, Germany)*
Bugra Gedik *(Bilkent University, Turkey)*
Johannes Gehrke *(Cornell University, USA)*
Lukasz Golab *(University of Waterloo, Canada)*
Amit Goyal *(Twitter, USA)*
Goetz Graefe *(HP Labs, USA)*
Torsten Grust *(Technische Universität Tübingen, Germany)*
Dimitrios Gunopulos *(University of Athens, Greece)*
Chetan Gupta *(Hitachi America, USA)*
Wook-Shin Han *(POSTECH, South Korea)*
Jeong-Hyon Hwang *(SUNY Albany, USA)*
Ihab Ilyas *(University of Waterloo, Canada)*
Christian S. Jensen *(Aalborg University, Denmark)*
Theodore Johnson *(AT&T Labs – Research, USA)*
Konstantinos Karanasos *(IBM Almaden Research Center, USA)*
Martin Kersten *(CWI, Netherlands)*
Daniel Kifer *(Penn State University, USA)*
Masaru Kitsuregawa *(University of Tokyo and NII, Japan)*
George Kollios *(Boston University, USA)*
Tim Kraska *(Brown University, USA)*
Harumi Kuno *(HP Labs, USA)*
Alexandros Labrinidis *(University of Pittsburgh, USA)*
Guoliang Li *(Tsinghua University, China)*
Ninghui Li *(Purdue University, USA)*
Xuemin Lin *(University of New South Wales, Australia)*
Eric Lo *(Hong Kong Polytechnic University, China)*
Jiaheng Lu *(Renmin University, China)*
Ashwin Machanavajjhala *(Duke University, USA)*
David Maier *(Portland State University, USA)*
Nikos Mamoulis *(Hong Kong University, China)*

Program Committee *(continued)*: Stefan Manegold *(CWI, Netherlands)*
Marta Mattoso *(Federal University of Rio de Janeiro, Brazil)*
Gerome Miklau *(University of Massachusetts, Amherst, USA)*
Thomas Neumann *(Technische Universität München, Germany)*
Beng Chin Ooi *(National University of Singapore, Singapore)*
Ippokratis Pandis *(IBM Almaden Research Center, USA)*
Dimitris Papadias *(Hong Kong University of Science & Technology, China)*
Yannis Papakonstantinou *(University of California, San Diego, USA)*
Aditya Parameswaran *(Stanford University, USA)*
Jignesh Patel *(University of Wisconsin, Madison, USA)*
Andy Pavlo *(Carnegie Mellon University, USA)*
Dino Pedreschi *(Università di Pisa, Italy)*
Jian Pei *(Simon Fraser University, Canada)*
Peter Pietzuch *(Imperial College London, UK)*
Fabio Porto *(LNCC, Brazil)*
Krithi Ramamritham *(IIT Bombay, India)*
Vijayshankar Raman *(IBM Almaden Research Center, USA)*
Christopher Re *(Stanford University, USA)*
Mirek Riedewald *(Northeastern University, USA)*
Tore Risch *(Uppsala Universitet, Sweden)*
Kenneth Ross *(Columbia University, USA)*
Senjuti Basu Roy *(University of Washington, Tacoma, USA)*
Sudeepa Roy *(University of Washington, USA)*
Dimitris Sacharidis *(Athena Research Center, Greece)*
Russell Sears *(Startup, USA)*
Timos Sellis *(RMIT University, Australia)*
Kyuseok Shim *(Seoul National University, South Korea)*
Ambuj Singh *(University of California, Santa Barbara, USA)*
Yannis Sismanis *(IBM Almaden Research Center, USA)*
S. Sudarshan *(IIT Bombay, India)*
Jens Teubner *(Technische Universität Dortmund, Germany)*
Alexander Thomson *(Google, USA)*
Anthony Tung *(National University of Singapore, Singapore)*
Vasilis Vassalos *(Athens University of Economics and Business, Greece)*
Gottfried Vossen *(Westf. Wilhelms-Universität Münster, Germany)*
Song Wang *(Hitachi America, USA)*
Kyu-Young Whang *(KAIST, South Korea)*
Steven E. Whang *(Google Research, USA)*
Sai Wu *(Zhejiang University, China)*
Jun Yang *(Duke University, USA)*
Carlo Zaniolo *(University of California, Los Angeles, USA)*
Meihui Zhang *(National University of Singapore, Singapore)*
Xiaofang Zhou *(University of Queensland, Australia)*

Demonstrations Program Committee:

Alberto Aabelló *(Universitat Politècnica de Catalunya, Spain)*
Mohamed Ali *(Microsoft, USA)*
Klaus Berberich *(Max-Planck Institute, Saarbrücken, Germany)*
Christof Bornhoevd *(SAP, Palo Alto, USA)*
Michael Cafarella *(University of Michigan, USA)*
Fei Chiang *(McMaster University, Hamilton, Canada)*
Ugur Demiryurek *(University of Southern California, USA)*
Aaron Elmore *(University of California Santa Barbara, USA)*
Johann Gamper *(Free University of Bozen-Bolzano, Italy)*
Rainer Gemulla *(Max-Planck Institute, Saarbrücken, Germany)*
Boris Glavic *(IIT Chicago, USA)*
Martin Grund *(Exascale Infolab, Fribourg, Switzerland)*
Thomas Heinis *(EPFL, Switzerland)*
Bijit Hore *(University of California, Irvine, USA)*
Yan Huang *(University of North Texas, USA)*
Claudia Ignat *(INRIA, France)*
Dmitri V. Kalashnikov *(University of California, Irvine, USA)*
Verena Kantere *(University of Geneva, Switzerland)*
Raghav Kaushik *(Micrsoft Research, USA)*
Sang-goo Lee *(Seoul National University, South Korea)*
Alexandra Meliou *(University of Massachusetts, Amherst, USA)*
Bernhard Mitschang *(University of Stuttgart, Germany)*
Guido Moerkotte *(University of Mannheim, Germany)*
Mohamed Mokbel *(University of Minnesota, USA)*
Atsuyuki Morishima *(Tsukuba University, Japan)*
Barzan Mozafari *(University of Michigan, USA)*
Mario Nascimento *(University of Alberta, Canada)*
Rimma Nehme *(Grey Systems Lab, USA)*
Themis Palpanas *(University of Trento, Italy)*
Athanasios Papaioannou *(EPFL, Switzerland)*
Torben Bach Pedersen *(Aalborg University, Denmark)*
Ilia Petrov *(Technische Universität Darmstadt, Germany)*
Rachel Pottinger *(University of British Columbia, Canada)*
Jeff Pound *(University of Waterloo, Canada)*
B. Aditya Prakash *(Virginia Tech, USA)*
Louiqa Raschid *(UMCP Maryland Business School, USA)*
Frank Renkes *(SAP, Germany)*
Uwe Roehm *(University of Sidney, Australia)*
Heiko Schuldt *(University of Basel, Switzerland)*
Junho Shim *(Sookmyung Women's University, South Korea)*
Michal Shmueli-Scheuer *(IBM, USA)*
Yasin Silva *(Arizona State University, USA)*
Knut Stolze *(IBM Lab, Böeblingen, Germany)*
Shirish Tatikonda *(IBM Almaden Research Center, USA)*
Jaideep Vaidya *(Rutgers University, USA)*

Demonstrations Program Committee (continued):

Florian Waas *(Datometry, USA)*
Till Westmann *(Oracle Labs, USA)*
Robert Wrembel *(Poznan University of Technology, Poland)*
Fei Xu *(Microsoft, USA)*
Xiaochun Yang *(Northeastern University, China)*
Demetris Zeinalipour *(University of Cyprus, Cyprus)*
Kamal Zellag *(McGill University, Canada)*
Roger Zimmermann *(National University of Singapore, Singapore)*

Industrial Program Committee:

Peter Bonzc *(CWI, Netherlands)*
Shel Finkelstein *(SAP, USA)*
Hakan Hacigumus *(NEC Labs, USA)*
Sam Madden *(MIT, USA)*
Renee Miller *(University of Toronto, Canada)*
Satish Nadathur *(Intel, USA)*
Vivek Narasayya *(Microsoft, USA)*
Chris Olston *(Google, USA)*
Lin Qiao *(LinkedIn, USA)*
Mary Roth *(IBM, USA)*
Swami Sivasubramanian *(Amazon, USA)*
Garret Swart *(Oracle, USA)*
Hans Zeller *(HP, USA)*

SIGMOD 2014 Sponsor & Supporters

Sponsor:

Platinum Supporters:

Gold Supporters:

Silver Supporters:

Platinum Publisher:

Silver Publishers:

Demonstration of the Myria Big Data Management Service

Daniel Halperin, Victor Teixeira de Almeida, Lee Lee Choo, Shumo Chu, Paraschos Koutris, Dominik Moritz, Jennifer Ortiz, Vaspol Ruamviboonsuk, Jingjing Wang, Andrew Whitaker, Shengliang Xu, Magdalena Balazinska, Bill Howe, and Dan Suciu
Computer Science & Engineering and eScience Institute, University of Washington

ABSTRACT

In this demonstration, we will showcase Myria, our novel cloud service for big data management and analytics designed to improve productivity. Myria's goal is for users to simply upload their data and for the system to help them be self-sufficient data science experts on their data – *self-serve analytics*. From a web browser, Myria users can upload data, author efficient queries to process and explore the data, and debug correctness and performance issues. Myria queries are executed on a scalable, parallel cluster that uses both state-of-the-art and novel methods for distributed query processing. Our interactive demonstration will guide visitors through an exploration of several key Myria features by interfacing with the live system to analyze big datasets over the web.

Categories and Subject Descriptors

H.2.4 [**Database Management**]: Systems—Distributed databases, Query processing, Relational databases

Keywords

Myria; data management; distributed database; query visualization

1. INTRODUCTION

Over the past year and a half, our group at the University of Washington has developed a new online service for managing big data. Our service, called Myria, now runs on 100-node Amazon EC2 deployments and processes terabytes of data from applications in astronomy, oceanography, social media, and cybersecurity, as well as standard benchmarks. More importantly, Myria is set up as a cloud service that users access directly from their browsers, dramatically reducing the "activation energy" required to be productive with big data. This demonstration will showcase the overall Myria service and system and several of its specific novel features.

Myria motivation: The analysis of massive-scale datasets has become an important capability both in industry and in the sciences and many systems have recently emerged to support it. But deep data analytics today is a high-touch business: it requires a highly specialized expert who thoroughly understands both the application domain and a growing ecosystem of complex distributed systems and advanced statistical methods, and who needs to perform repeatedly a series of data exploration steps to prepare the data for machine learning and other analyses. Myria aims to make data management and analysis a pleasant and productive experience. Our project started from a re-examination of the foundations of big data management with the ultimate goal of significantly improving *productivity* in big data management and analytics.

SIGMOD'14, June 22–27, 2014, Snowbird, UT, USA.

ACM 978-1-4503-2376-5/14/06 ...$15.00.
http://dx.doi.org/10.1145/2588555.2594530.

How can we improve productivity in the analysis of big data? We identify three key challenges that need to be overcome, which, in ensemble, are not met by any system available today, and we describe how Myria tackles these challenges head on.

• **Cloud service deployment.** For many of today's systems, users must still purchase and administer physical or virtual computers; even with a pre-configured cluster, the setup instructions on the Hadoop, Spark, or GraphLab project websites take hours to days to execute successfully the first time. For many users, the complexity and cost of startup and continual administration and maintenance are prohibitive. Some data management systems are also available as cloud services, but these services often offer obscure black-boxes that make it difficult for users to predict and debug performance or to predict and control costs.

In contrast to existing systems, Myria is designed as a cloud service from the ground up. The primary interface is a web browser that uses the same programmatic REST interface as any low-level system tools. From innovative service level agreements and resource management, to multi-language query support, to graphical query debugging, Myria reinvents the interface between users and cloud services. Myria's goal is for users to simply upload their data and for the system to help them be self-sufficient data science experts on their data – *self-serve analytics*.

• **Programmability.** SQL is perceived as ill-suited for analytics tasks, motivating a number of extensions — window functions, pivoting, UDAs, UDFs, in-database analytics packages such as MADlib, etc. But analytics remain a second-class feature in these RDBMS-based solutions, requiring significant expertise by both users and algorithm designers. Hadoop, GraphLab, Spark, and related systems require users to develop algorithms in low-level imperative languages, reducing opportunities for algebraic optimization and reuse. Language layers on top of these runtimes (Pig, Hive, Shark, etc.) limit expressiveness to that of the language.

Myria strikes a balance between these extremes: we adopt a core programming model that extends relational algebra with iteration that affords rich, iteration-aware optimization without sacrificing expressive power. Guided by prior experience in delivering database-as-a-service capabilities to scientists [3], we aim to support both "users" and "algorithm designers" with a common set of web-based interfaces, languages, and APIs that scale gracefully from simple SPJ queries to advanced application-specific analytics tasks. Like Hyracks, we emphasize the use of core parallel query processing concepts as a first-class concern, but we place less emphasis on supporting legacy code written for Hadoop or Pregel and more emphasis on empowering non-specialists, especially scientists. Myria currently supports SQL, a variant of Datalog, and a new hybrid declarative/imperative analytics language called MyriaL.

• **Efficient processing.** Finally, users want good performance, so our system must be able to optimize and scale queries. Myria puts a strong emphasis on efficient query processing, by combining state-of-the-art and novel ideas in both theory and systems.

With its foundation in relational algebra, we understand well how to optimize and parallelize many Myria queries. However, opti-

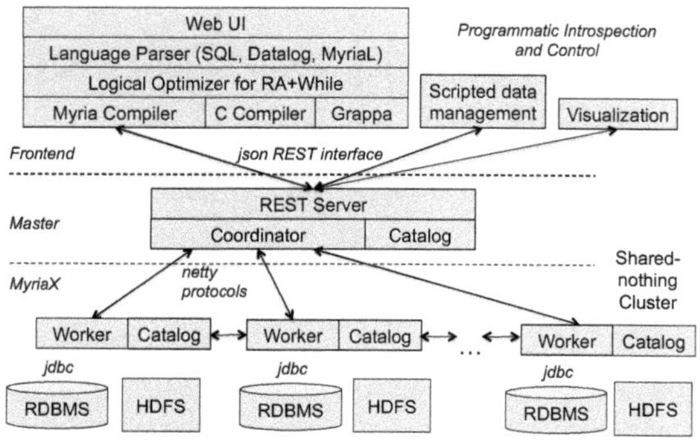

Figure 1: Myria System Architecture

mizations for queries that combine basic algebra, recursion, and aggregations are still not well understood. The Myria team is developing new techniques for large distributed query processing [2], and we are validating and leveraging them using the system itself.

For scalability and efficiency, Myria's execution layer, MyriaX adopts state-of-the-art system design principles. MyriaX uses a parallel, pipelined, possibly cyclic graph of dataflow operators with built-in support for asynchronous evaluation of recursive queries. Our research extends the system in many important directions including lightweight failure handling in iterative computations and dynamic resource allocation for elastic scalability.

In this demonstration, we will showcase Myria's capabilities both as a cloud service and a big data management system. We will do so through a coordinated set of high-level and low-level demonstrations on multiple laptops. The demonstrations will use a 64-instance Myria deployment and be driven by real queries from domain scientists in astronomy, oceanography, and social science.

2. MYRIA OVERVIEW

In this section, we present a brief overview of Myria as context for understanding the novel features we will demonstrate, which are described in subsequent sections. Figure 1 shows the overall architecture of the Myria system.

The primary interface to Myria is a frontend website hosted on Google App Engine, with software components as shown above the dashed line in Figure 1. The screenshot in Figure 2 shows the main query editor. For our supported languages, Myria provides a set of sample queries (left) as a starting point for query authoring (right top). Myria parses the query to basic relational algebra (right middle) and produces an optimized, parallel, distributed physical plan for a shared-nothing cluster (right bottom). The user can visualize a query plan via the pop-out links, and can submit the query. Other panels let users examine datasets in the system, previously submitted and running queries, and provide other features.

The center component in Figure 1 is the master. It hosts the REST interface used by the web UI and other tools, maintains metadata about system resources and datasets (e.g., used by the query optimizer and web UI), and it mediates access to the cluster.

The bottom part of Figure 1 shows the architecture of Myria's query execution engine, MyriaX. MyriaX is a pipelined, parallel, distributed dataflow evaluation system that takes a (possibly cyclic) graph of operators and executes it efficiently on a shared-nothing cluster. This pipeline is divided into fragments, which are trees of operators that can operate on a single compute node in a single thread; fragment leaves and roots are typically system I/O operators that read, write, or transfer data. MyriaX can incorporate data from many sources, such as relational DBMS, Hadoop FS, Amazon S3, public data on the Internet, etc. Additionally, MyriaX can scale the cluster up and down dynamically as the system workload changes.

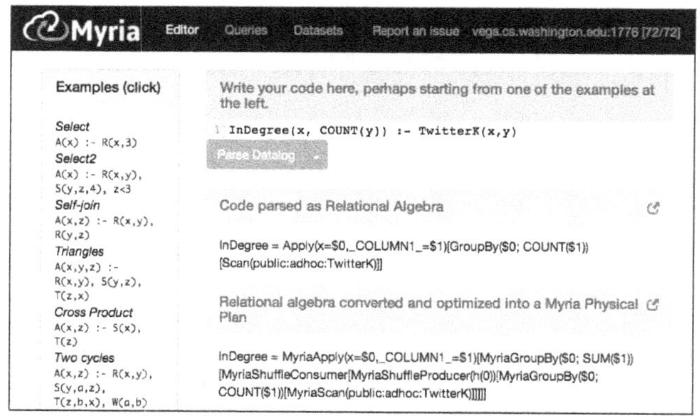

Figure 2: Myria Browser-based Front-End

3. DEMONSTRATED FEATURES

We divide our demonstrations of Myria features into three phases: 1) Myria to its users, 2) Myria's execution engine and algorithms, and 3) Myria as a service. Combined, these features show how Myria comprises a system designed from the ground up to improve productivity for both nascent and experienced data scientists (1 and 2) in an efficient and scalable, and hence sustainable way (2 and 3).

3.1 Myria to its Customers

In this phase of the demonstration, the visitor will act as a scientist analyzing a big dataset.

3.1.1 How users access Myria

The website described in §2 is the principal way that most users will access Myria, but this is not the only way to use Myria. We designed the REST interface to Myria—the same interface used by the website—to be sufficiently flexible to support an entire ecosystem of clients that connect with Myria programmatically. Supplemental clients provide tools for: data management tasks such as uploading a folder of related datasets and automatically building a union for entire-corpus analysis; downloading data for offline analysis in domain-specific tools; and exploring data visually.

3.1.2 Supported query languages

Myria accepts queries written in SQL, Datalog, or a new Pig Latin-like language we call MyriaL. Based on our experience with SQLShare [3], we believe that science users can write data analysis tasks in SQL. We expect Datalog's declarative style to have similar appeal, especially for recursive queries. Myria's Datalog compiler has support for stratified negation and a variety of simple aggregates. Myria uses semi-naive evaluation to efficiently compute recursive results, using asynchronous computation when possible.

MyriaL is a hybrid imperative/declarative language, similar to Pig Latin [7] extended with iteration. We developed MyriaL because certain iterative programs—in which facts from one iteration are aggregated to produce the facts in the next iteration, e.g., PageRank—are cumbersome to express in Datalog and hard for the query execution engine to optimize. MyriaL lets users directly express efficient execution strategies, such as custom variants of standard semi-naive evaluation that overwrite facts rather than accumulate them, when aggregation is used (e.g., for connected components). Users can also encode optimizations that incorporate domain-specific knowledge. Each line of a MyriaL program corresponds to a declarative query comprising one or more relational algebra operations, expressed in a comprehension syntax. MyriaL iteration employs a simple do/while construct, in which the continuation condition is a singleton boolean relation. Figure 3 shows the MyriaL program for semi-naive evaluation of graph reachability.

```
Edge = SCAN(user@uw.edu:edges_table);
Reachable = [1 AS addr]; Delta = Reachable;
DO
  NewNodes = [FROM Delta, Edge WHERE Delta.addr = Edge.src
              EMIT Edge.dst AS addr];
  Delta = DIFF(DISTINCT(NewNodes), Reachable);
  Reachable = UNIONALL(Delta, Reachable);
WHILE [*COUNTALL(Delta) > 0];
```

Figure 3: Graph reachability in MyriaL.

3.1.3 *What the user will see and do*

For the demonstration, Myria will be pre-loaded with scientific datasets including an n-body simulation that models matter in the evolving early universe, flow cytometry measurements of ocean microorganisms, and the Twitter social network graph [5]. The user can tour the datasets in the system and learn their relationships by inspecting provenance trees generated from the Myria query log.

The user will be presented with sample queries in the three languages. The system will automatically translate user-generated SQL or Datalog queries into MyriaL to aid in comprehension.

Finally, the user will examine the standard sigma-clipping outlier removal algorithm [6] to see how it admits domain-specific algorithmic optimizations for incremental evaluation. Specifically, we will guide the user through authoring a sequence of MyriaL programs which refine the algorithmic and relational algebra algorithms for noticeable, orders-of-magnitude speedups in query processing time.

3.2 Myria Engine and Algorithms

In the second phase of the demonstration, the visitor will learn about Myria's query execution and monitoring features.

3.2.1 *Query Execution in MyriaX*

As described in §2, Myria's physical query plans take the form of pipelined, possibly cyclic, dataflow graphs of operators. In Myria's execution engine, MyriaX, data flow between operators takes the form of batches of tuples, aggregated to amortize per-operator-invocation overheads. MyriaX uses both standard techniques and novel algorithms for evaluation of relational algebra. Execution proceeds in parallel both within a node—multiple independent or pipelined parts of a query plan can be executed concurrently in separate threads—and across nodes, in the common case of data-level parallelism in query evaluation.

MyriaX natively supports iterative and recursive computations. For some classes of programs (e.g., reachability, connected components, or PageRank), MyriaX provides asynchronous query processing capabilities using incremental variants of physical operators with stream-oriented computation. For the general case, iterative queries are optimized and executed as a series of synchronous jobs.

3.2.2 *Query Monitoring and Debugging*

Myria provides extensive visual query monitoring and debugging functionalities to aid in self-serve data exploration. Myria uses modern data visualization techniques built on d3.js combined with Myria's analytics capabilities to let users interactively explore query execution profiles. Our in-browser tool provides a suite of visualizations to enable query execution profiling from various perspectives; Figure 4 shows an example Myria visualization that shows the execution of a parallel join. We found these views to be critical for performance debugging: (1) The *query plan* visualization shows a line chart of cluster utilization for each query fragment, measured as the fraction of workers executing it. In this view, a long tail identifies a query bottleneck. (2) The user can visualize *communication* between workers in a communication matrix and request more details on the communication between pairs of workers over time. (3) Finally, the *operator level* visualization (Figure 4) shows a Gantt chart of operators executing a specific query fragment across

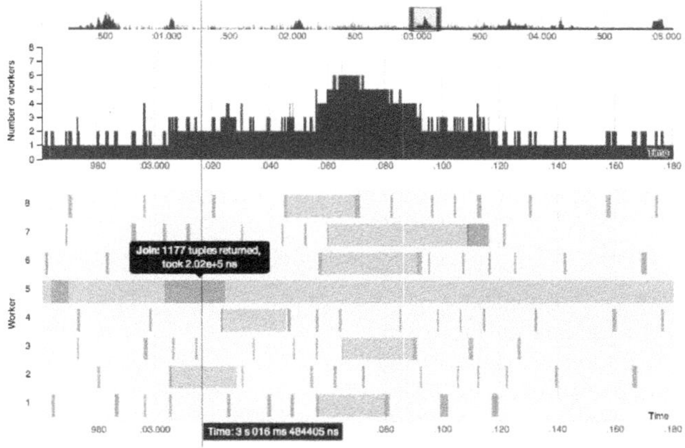

Figure 4: Visualization of 100 ms (x-axis, zoomed via the mini-map on top) of a query fragment performing a join in parallel on 8 workers. An operator is visible in the bottom chart if it is computing at a point in time on the specified worker.

workers. Operators of the specified fragment are shown in unique colors in separate lanes for each worker. This view serves to identify or explain low-level implementation problems.

3.2.3 *Distributed Join Algorithms*

In Myria, we are pushing the bounds of algorithmic understanding of efficient distributed query execution and putting these ideas into practice in our optimizer and executer.

To illustrate these novel techniques [1, 2], consider triangles:

`Triangles(x,y,z) :- R(x,y), S(y,z), T(z,x).`

A typical parallel database might decompose the computation into two pipelined hash-joins:

`A(x,y,z) = R(x,y)` $\bowtie_y$ `S(y,z)` and then

`Triangles(x,y,z) = A(x,y,z)` $\bowtie_{xz}$ `T(z,x).`

However, such a query plan is highly inefficient if the intermediate result A is large, since A is shuffled and sent to the next join. For the Twitter follower graph [5], A contains 9 trillion tuples.

Myria can instead apply the HYPERCUBE algorithm [2], which computes the triangles using a *single* shuffling step. The algorithm assigns each worker node a virtual coordinate in a 3-dimensional hypercube, (p_x, p_y, p_z), and hashes each tuple involving x, y, or z to the corresponding space. $R(x, y)$ is sent to the xy subspace containing all nodes of the form $(h(x), h(y), *)$. Correspondingly, the tuples of S and T are sent to the yz and xz subspaces. Each node finally performs a local join to discover those triangles (x, y, z) that are hashed to its coordinates (p_x, p_y, p_z). Myria uses a simplified Leapfrog Triejoin [9] to compute triangles locally in a single multiway join step without computing the large intermediate results.

This single-step algorithm transfers only the input datasets rather than large intermediate results, at the cost of data replication: tuples are hashed to multiple workers, whereas the pipelined hash-join approach sends each tuple to only one worker. For skewed datasets, this replication has further gains, because "hot" vertices with high degree are balanced across multiple workers.

Myria optimizes for the right combination of join techniques given the input data statistics and the structure of the joins.

3.2.4 *Failure Handling During Iteration*

MyriaX provides intra-query failure handling: During query execution, without blocking the main data flow, each worker records the data sent to downstream workers in an in-memory buffer, spilling to disks if necessary. When a worker fails, the master starts a recovery worker as the replacement. The live workers send the buffered out-

Tier 1: $0.10/hour

Within 20 seconds:
SELECT <up to 10 attributes>
FROM <Fact | Dimension>
WHERE <up to 100% of data>

Within 1 minute:
SELECT <up to 5 attributes>
FROM <Fact JOIN 4 Dimensions>
WHERE <up to 10% of data>

Within 10 minutes:
SELECT <up to 10 attributes>
FROM <Fact JOIN 8 Dimensions>
WHERE <up to 100% of data>

Tier 2: $0.25/hour

Within 5 seconds:
SELECT <up to 10 attributes>
FROM <Fact | Dimension>
WHERE <up to 100% of data>

Within 2 minutes:
SELECT <up to 10 attributes>
FROM <Fact JOIN 8 Dimensions>
WHERE <up to 100% of data>

Tier 3: $0.50/hour

Within 1 second:
SELECT <up to 10 attributes>
FROM <Fact | Dimension>
WHERE <up to 100% of data>

Figure 5: A PSLA only shows improvements across tiers

going information to the new worker, and the new worker catches up using these data directly.

Most modern engines provide this or other failure-handling methods during query execution. The novelty in Myria lies in our study of failure-handling methods for iterative queries. Iterative applications have special properties that we can exploit: First, data often includes inherent structural redundancy. For instance, we can discover that a vertex is reachable in the presence of data loss as long as any incoming edge from any reachable neighbor is known. Second, many iterative computations incrementally build or refine their states and outputs. Together, these factors facilitate state compression and accelerate recomputation using more recent data when state is lost. Myria exploits these properties when possible.

Depending on the iterative query, Myria uses different state buffering strategies: 1) Simple buffers (default): keep data in FIFO queues. 2) Replacement buffers: In many iterative computations, new messages overwrite or update old ones—stale labels in connected components—so only updated results need be retained. 3) Prioritized buffers: By ordering messages with a query-specific objective function, MyriaX can propagate "good" tuples (e.g., weights of high-degree vertices in PageRank) earlier when recovering, leading to faster convergence.

3.2.5 What the user will see and do

The user will begin with a triangular query on a Twitter dataset representing the following-followee relation. The user will choose between two query plans for the query: (1) a traditional query plan consisting of two pipelined distributed hash joins, and (2) Myria's novel query plan consisting of one HyperCube shuffle step and a local multiway join step. Myria's visualizer will serve to compare and analyze the performance of the two query plans.

As a second step, the user will execute a connected-components query over the Twitter dataset using either synchronous or asynchronous iterative processing. The user will be invited to kill a worker during the query execution and see how the system recovers automatically under different fault-tolerance strategies. The focus will be on the performance implications of each combination of failure-handling and execution methods.

3.3 Myria as a Service

We aim to run Myria as a sustainable, publicly available resource for big data analytics. This goal leads us to a research agenda in cost-effective cluster management and better customer-provider relationships, which we will demonstrate in the third phase.

3.3.1 Personalized Service Level Agreements

We have developed a new type of relationship between customers and cloud service providers, the *personalized* service level agreement (PSLA) [8] illustrated in Figure 5. The goal of a PSLA is to switch from a resource-centric approach—in which users lease CPU, memory, disk, or network resources—and instead focus on allowing the user to think directly about query capabilities (in the form of query templates) and performance versus service price. Given a user's data, our approach automatically generates sample queries and a PSLA. The key challenge is to generate PSLAs that are both concise (few tiers with few query templates) and precise (time thresholds are close to expected query runtimes).

3.3.2 Elastic Scalability

Myria can scale its resource usage and performance as query workloads change and to satisfy its customer PSLAs. First, Myria can dynamically add or remove *compute nodes*—worker instances that process queries, but do not store data. Compute nodes can be added or removed from query processing even while queries execute. Second, data in Myria can be partitioned across *storage nodes* using consistent hashing [4]. This enables Myria to rebalance storage workloads with minimal data transfer when *storage nodes* are added or removed. Third, consistent hashing is also used for data *replication* in Myria. Replicas provide resilience to storage node loss and increase the system's overall data parallelism by providing concurrent reads and distributed writes. Our research focuses on how best to leverage these techniques when operating Myria as a service in a public cloud.

3.3.3 What the user will see and do

The user will start by exploring the N-body universe simulation dataset. N-body simulations are widely used tools in astrophyics, that help astronomers understand how gravity influences dark, star and gas particles across time. The user will be able to select any subset of tables from the dataset and change the table sizes (different simulations produce different dataset sizes). She will then observe how changing the input changes the generated PSLA. Finally, the user will be able to execute queries at the different service tiers in the PSLA and will compare the observed performance across these tiers. As the queries execute, we will also demonstrate how Myria can add and remove data and compute resources on the fly and how doing so affects performance.

4. CONCLUSION

Our Myria service aims to improve productivity for data scientists by accelerating the bottleneck steps in data management and exploration, and to make these capabilities accessible to a new class of users – *self-serve analytics*. This demonstration shows the three key aspects of Myria: Myria's interface to users, its system internals, and its as-a-service features.

Acknowledgments. This work was supported in part by the National Science Foundation grant IIS-1247469 and by the Intel Science and Technology Center for Big Data. We thank Ginger Armbrust, Sophie Clayton, Fabio Governato, Sarah Loebman, Tom Quinn, and Francois Ribalet for providing scientific data and queries.

5. REFERENCES

[1] F. N. Afrati and J. D. Ullman. Optimizing joins in a Map-Reduce environment. In *EDBT*, 2010.

[2] P. Beame, P. Koutris, and D. Suciu. Communication steps for parallel query processing. In *PODS*, pages 273–284, 2013.

[3] B. Howe et al. Collaborative science workflows in SQL. *Computing in Science & Engineering, Special Issue on Science Data Management*, 15(2), May/June 2013.

[4] D. Karger et al. Consistent hashing and random trees: Distributed caching protocols for relieving hot spots on the World Wide Web. In *STOC*, 1997.

[5] H. Kwak, C. Lee, H. Park, and S. Moon. What is Twitter, a social network or a news media? In *Intl. Conference on World Wide Web (WWW)*, 2010.

[6] M. Moyers et al. A demonstration of iterative parallel array processing in support of telescope image analysis. *PVLDB*, 6(12):1322–1325, 2013.

[7] C. Olston, B. Reed, U. Srivastava, R. Kumar, and A. Tomkins. Pig Latin: A not-so-foreign language for data processing. In *SIGMOD*, 2008.

[8] J. Ortiz, V. Teixeira de Almeida, and M. Balazinska. A vision for personalized service level agreements in the cloud. In *SIGMOD DanaC Workshop*, 2013.

[9] T. L. Veldhuizen. Leapfrog Triejoin: a worst-case optimal join algorithm. *CoRR*, abs/1210.0481, 2012.

DataSift: A Crowd-Powered Search Toolkit

Aditya Parameswaran
Stanford and U. Illinois (UIUC)
Urbana, IL
adityagp@illinois.edu

Ming Han Teh
Stanford University
Stanford, CA
minghan@cs.stanford.edu

Hector Garcia-Molina
Stanford University
Stanford, CA
hector@cs.stanford.edu

Jennifer Widom
Stanford University
Stanford, CA
widom@cs.stanford.edu

ABSTRACT

Traditional search engines are unable to support a large number of potential queries issued by users, for instance, queries containing non-textual fragments such as images or videos, queries that are very long, ambiguous, or those that require subjective judgment, or semantically-rich queries over non-textual corpora. We demonstrate DataSift, a crowd-powered search toolkit that can be instrumented over any corpus supporting a keyword search API, and supports efficient and accurate querying for a rich general class of queries, including those described previously. Our demonstration will allow conference attendees to issue live queries for image, video, and product search, as well as "play back" the results of a wide variety of prior queries issued on DataSift. Attendees will also be able to perform a side-by-side comparison between DataSift and traditional retrieval schemes.

1. INTRODUCTION

While information retrieval systems have come a long way in the last two decades, modern search engines still have quite limited functionality. For example, they have difficulty with:

- Non-textual queries or queries containing both text and non-textual fragments: For instance, a query *"cables that plug into <IMAGE>"*, where <IMAGE> is a photo of a socket, cannot be handled by any current search engine.
- Queries over non-textual corpora: For instance, a query *"funny pictures of cats wearing hats, with captions"* cannot be handled adequately by any image search engine. Typical image search engines only perform keyword search over image tags, which may not be sufficient to identify if an image satisfies the query.
- Long queries: For instance, a query *"find noise canceling headsets where the battery life is more than 24 hours"* cannot be handled adequately by a product search engine, e.g., Amazon (`www.amazon.com`). Search results are often very noisy for queries containing more than 3-4 keywords.
- Queries involving human judgment: For instance, a query *"apartments that are in a nice area near Somerville"* cannot be handled adequately by an apartment search engine, e.g., Craigslist (`www.craigslist.com`).
- Ambiguous queries: For instance, a query *"running jaguar images"* cannot be handled adequately by an image search engine. Search engines cannot tease apart queries which have multiple or ambiguous interpretations, e.g., the car vs. the animal.

For all of these types of queries, currently the burden is on the user to attempt to express the query using the search interfaces provided. Typically, the user will try to express his or her query in as few textual keywords as possible, try out many possible reformulations of the query, and pore over hundreds or thousands of search results for each reformulation. For some queries, e.g., *"buildings that look like <IMAGE>"*, identifying a formulation based solely on text is next to impossible.

Additionally, there are cases where the user does not possess the necessary knowledge to come up with query reformulations. For instance, for the query *"cables that plug into <IMAGE>"*, a particular not-so-technologically-savvy user may not be able to identify that a socket is of a particular type, say a USB 2.0 socket.

To reduce the burden on the user, both in terms of labor (e.g., in finding reformulations and going through results) and in terms of knowledge (e.g., in identifying that a socket is indeed a USB 2.0 socket), we turn to humans (i.e., the crowd) for assistance. We have developed DataSift, a powerful general-purpose search toolkit that uses humans (i.e., crowd workers) to assist in the retrieval process. Our toolkit can be connected to any traditional corpus with a basic keyword search API. DataSift then automatically enables rich queries over that corpus. Additionally, DataSift produces better results by harnessing human computation to filter answers from the corpus.

We propose to demonstrate DataSift in action, both with prerecorded queries as well as with live queries that are handled by Amazon Mechanical Turk (`mturk.com`) workers. The demonstration will illustrate how DataSift works, how it can outperform traditional approaches, and some of the remaining challenges. The rest of this proposal is divided into two parts: We first give an overview of DataSift and its components. In the second part, we describe the proposed demonstration.

The first part of the proposal is a brief summary of a companion paper [8] that appeared at the HCOMP Conference in November 2013. In the companion paper, we additionally describe in detail the different ways DataSift can be built, their pros and cons, and a thorough performance evaluation of these ways or schemes versus each other and versus traditional retrieval schemes. We also studied how DataSift parameters may be tuned to achieve even higher accuracy for fixed cost.

Figure 1 shows a high-level overview of DataSift: The user provides a rich search query Q of any length, that may include textual

SIGMOD'14, June 22–27, 2014, Snowbird, UT, USA.
Copyright 2014 ACM 978-1-4503-2376-5/14/06 ...$15.00.
http://dx.doi.org/10.1145/2588555.2594510.

and/or non-textual fragments. DataSift uses an internal pipeline that makes repeated calls to a crowdsourcing marketplace, specifically, Mechanical Turk (`mturk.com`), as well as to the keyword search interface to the corpus. When finished, a ranked list of results is presented back to the user, like in a traditional search engine. As an example, Figure 2 depicts the ranked list of results for the query Q = *"type of cable that connects to <IMAGE: USB B-Female socket of a printer>"* over the Amazon products corpus. The ranked results provide relevant USB 2.0 cables with a B-Male connector.

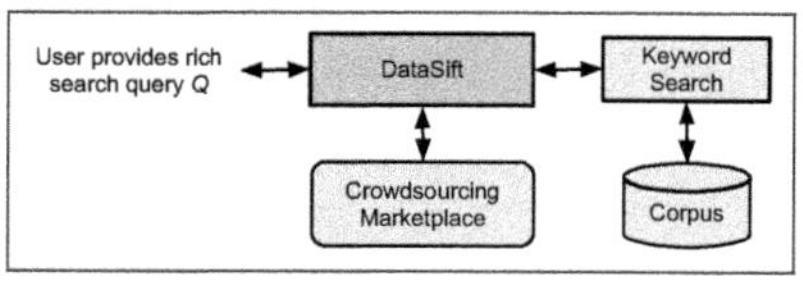

Figure 1: DataSift **Overview**

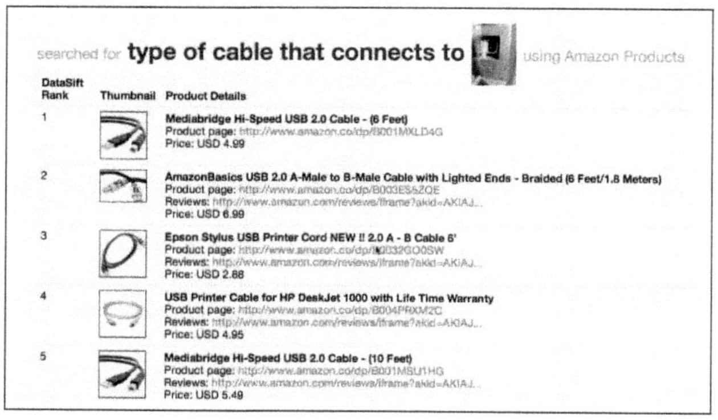

Figure 2: DataSift **Example**

A disadvantage of our approach is that the response time will be substantially larger than with a traditional search engine. Thus, our approach is only applicable when the user is willing to wait for higher quality results, especially when the user himself does not know whether the results are correct (for example, in the USB cable case), or when he is not willing or capable of putting in the effort to find items that satisfy his query. Our experience so far is that the wait times are of the order of twenty minutes to an hour. (Note that users can see partial results as they come in.) We discuss mechanisms for addressing this issue for our demonstration scenarios in Section 3.

We now present some challenges in building DataSift, using our earlier example: Q = *"type of cable that connects to <IMAGE>"*. We assume that we have a product corpus (e.g., Amazon products) with a keyword search API. Consider the following three (among others) possible configurations for DataSift:

- **Gather:** Provide Q as is to a number of human workers and ask them for one or more reformulated textual keyword search queries, e.g., *"USB 2.0 Cable"* or *"printer cable"*. Then retrieve products using the keyword search API for the reformulated keyword search queries and present the results to the user.
- **Gather-Filter:** The same configuration as **Gather**, but in addition ask human workers to filter the retrieved products for relevance to the query Q, e.g., whether they are cables that plug into the desired socket, before presenting the results to the user.
- **Iterative Gather-Filter:** The same configuration as **Gather**, but in addition first ask human workers to filter a small sample of retrieved products from each reformulated textual query for relevance to Q, allowing us to identify which reformulations produce better results. Then, retrieve more from the better reformulations, e.g., more from *"USB 2.0 printer cable"* instead of *"electronic cable"*. Finally, ask human workers to filter the retrieved results before presenting the results to the user.

In addition to determining which configuration we want to use, each of the configurations above has many parameters that need to be tuned. For instance, for the last configuration, DataSift needs to make a number of decisions, including:

- How many human workers should be asked for reformulated keyword search queries? How many keyword search queries should each worker provide?
- How many items should be retrieved initially for each reformulation? How many should be retrieved later (once we identify which reformulations produce better results)?
- How do we decide if a reformulation is better than a different one?
- How many human workers should be used to filter each product for relevance to Q?
- How should the cost be divided between the steps?

Our current implementation of DataSift is powerful enough to be configured to match all of the configurations we have described, plus others. We achieve this flexibility by structuring the toolkit as six plug-and-play components that can be assembled in various ways.

To the best of our knowledge, we are the first in addressing the problem of designing a rich general-purpose search toolkit augmented with the power of human computation. By themselves, traditional information retrieval techniques are insufficient for our human-assisted retrieval task. On the other hand, existing crowd-powered systems, such as Turkit [5], and CrowdPlan [4] do not address the problem of improving information retrieval. CrowdQ [2] tackles the problem of using humans to detect common patterns in search queries, and could be used in conjunction with DataSift to detect and cater for the more popular patterns. Unlike DataSift, CrowdQ does not support rich queries containing images or videos. Unlike social or collaborative search, e.g., [3, 1, 6], we do not leverage the social network, and the system moderates the interaction using reformulations and filtering to ensure high quality results.

2. ARCHITECTURE

A user enters a query into DataSift, which could contain textual and non-textual fragments. The corpus of items I (products, images, or videos) over which DataSift is implemented has a keyword search API: it accepts a textual keyword search query and a number k, and returns the top k items (products, images, or videos) along with their ranks. The crowdsourcing marketplace M may be used to recruit multiple human workers to attempt each task independently, and returning the answers to DataSift. DataSift makes repeated calls to both I and M, and then eventually provides the user with n items in ranked order.

2.1 Components

Next, we describe the components internal to DataSift. Components are categorized into: (1) Crowdsourced Components: components that interact with the crowdsourcing marketplace, and (2) Automated Components: components that function independent of the crowdsourcing marketplace. The function signatures and specifications of these components can be found in our companion paper [8].

Crowdsourced Components

- **(G) Gather Component**: The Gather Component G asks human workers for fully textual reformulations for Q, asking human workers to respond to the task "Please provide reformulated keyword search queries for the following query: Q". This component provides DataSift a mechanism to retrieve items (using the keyword search API) for Q when Q contains non-textual fragments.

- (F) **Filter Component**: The input to the Filter Component F is a set of items. For each item, F determines whether the item satisfies the query Q or not, by asking human workers to respond to the following task: "Does the item i satisfy query Q: (Yes/No)". Since human workers may be unreliable, multiple workers may be asked to respond to the same task on the same item i. The number of humans asked is determined by designing a filtering strategy [7] using the overall accuracy threshold t (set by the application designer).

Automated Components

- (R) **Retrieve Component**: The Retrieve Component R uses the keyword search API to simultaneously retrieve items for multiple textual queries T from the corpus. For each textual query T, items are retrieved along with their keyword search result ranks for T (as assigned in the output of the keyword search API call by the corpus).
- (S) **Sort Component**: The Sort Component S merges rankings, providing a rank for every item based on how well it addresses Q. If preceded by the F component, then S returns a rank for every item based on the difference between the number of YES and NO answers for each item. If preceded by the R component, then S simply merges the ranks arising from the results of the textual retrieval.
- (W) **Weighting Component**: For Iterative Gather-Filter (Section 1), the weighting component is the component that actually evaluates reformulations. The component always follows F, using the results from F to compute weights corresponding to how good different reformulations are in producing items that address Q.

  Component W receives as input items from the Filter Component F and the textual query T that generated the items. For each textual query T, given the output of the filtering component F, the weighting component returns a weight based on how useful the textual query is in answering Q. These weights are then used by the R component in preferentially retrieving more items from better reformulations.

2.2 Configurations

We now describe the configurations that DataSift can support, among others. (We focus on those that we think are the most interesting and important.) We will allow conference attendees to examine the performance for each of these configurations.

- RS: (Only possible if Q is textual) This configuration refers to the traditional information retrieval approach: component R uses the query Q to directly retrieve the top n items with ranks using the keyword search API. In this case, component S does nothing, simply returning the same items along with the ranks.
- RFS: (Only possible if Q is textual) From the items retrieved by component R, component F uses humans to better identify which items are actually relevant to the query Q. Component S then uses the output of F to sort the items in the order of the difference in the number of Yes and No votes for an item as obtained by F, and return n items along with their ranks.
- GRS: (Gather from Section 1) Component G gathers textual reformulations for Q, asking human workers for reformulations. Subsequently, R retrieves the top items along with ranks for each of these reformulations. Then, S sorts the items by simply merging the ranks across the reformulations, with ties being broken arbitrarily. Items are returned along with their ranks.
- GRFS: (Gather-Filter from Section 1) Component G gathers textual reformulations, after which component R retrieves items with ranks for each of the reformulations. Then, component F filters the items using human workers. Subsequently, the items are sorted by component S based on the difference in the number of Yes and No votes for each item, and the top n are returned along with their ranks; ties are broken arbitrarily.
- GRFWRFS: (Iterative Gather-Filter from Section 1) Component G gathers textual reformulations, after which component R retrieves a few items from each of the reformulations. Component F then filters the set of retrieved items. The output of F provides us with an initial estimate as to how useful each reformulation is in answering the query Q.

  Subsequently, component W computes a weight for each of the textual reformulations based on the results from F. These weights are then used by component R to preferentially retrieve additional items from reformulations in proportion to the weight. Component F filters the retrieved items once again. Eventually, the component S sorts the items in the order of the difference between the number of Yes and No votes, and returns the items along with their ranks.

Easy Queries (5)
funny photo of barack obama eating things
bill clinton waving to crowd
matrix digital rain
eiffel tower, paris
5 x 5 rubix cube
Hard Queries (5)
tool to clean laptop air vents
cat on computer keyboard with caption
handheld thing for finding directions
the windy city in winter, showing the bean
Mitt Romney, sad, US flag
Selected Others
funny photos of cats wearing hats, with captions
the steel city in snow
stanford computer science building
database textbook

Table 1: Sample textual queries

3. DEMONSTRATION SCENARIOS

A challenge in demonstrating DataSift is that DataSift takes much longer than traditional web search (producing higher quality human-curated results). While users will be able to see partial results for queries as they come in and see how their query is progressing, typical DataSift queries take twenty minutes to an hour to complete. These inherent delays means that we need to be creative in demonstrating the system.

We consider two demonstration scenarios: the first scenario involves browsing pre-recorded queries. For a large set of queries (described below) issued to DataSift, we have recorded every action taken within DataSift to produce results for the queries (e.g., when DataSift moves from component G to F, or when it decides to get an additional human opinion on an item in F) and outside DataSift (i.e., responses from human workers), and allow atten-

Rich Queries (5)
buildings around <IMAGE: UC Berkeley's Sather Tower>
device that reads from <IMAGE: Iomega 100MB Zip Disk>
where to have fun at <IMAGE: Infinity Pool at Marina Bay Sands hotel in Singapore>
tool/device that allows me to do hand gestures such as in: <VIDEO: motion sensing demonstration using fingers >
type of cable that connects to <IMAGE: USB B-Female socket of a printer>

Table 2: Sample Rich Queries

dees to "play back" every step of the action. This scenario is analogous to videos that show how to bake a cake: you begin by showing how to mix the ingredients; but then, instead of waiting, you fast forward through the intermediate steps to the finished product.

The second scenario involves attendees issuing live queries to DataSift, viewing progress of live queries issued by other attendees, and lastly, but certainly not the least, acting as human workers and answering tasks generated by queries issued by other attendees. Due to the challenges described earlier, we will encourage attendees to (a) fill out an email address field to have the results for the queries they issued sent to them when complete, and/or (b) return within half an hour to check the results of their queries. (Alternatively, if demo sessions are split between two days, attendees will be able to view the results of the queries they issued the previous day.)

3.1 Scenario 1: Pre-recorded Queries

In this scenario, we will allow conference attendees to play back, for a broad variety of queries, how they were addressed by various DataSift configurations. This will allow attendees to get a better intuition for the design choices and challenges underlying DataSift. For example, will allow attendees to view:

- how each search query was broken down into questions asked to humans;
- how, in the case of ambiguity in F, additional human workers were asked the same question;
- what kinds of interfaces were used to ask questions to human workers, and why they were designed that way;
- how, even though some human workers were answering questions incorrectly, DataSift was able to recover and reduce the impact of workers with poor ability;
- how GRFWRFS ends up giving better results than GRFS due to the reweighting component; and
- the cases where DataSift gave less-than-perfect results, and why.

The list of textual queries that we plan to allow attendees to peruse include the ones shown in Table 1, while the list of "rich media" queries (i.e., queries containing non-textual fragments such as images or videos) that we plan to allow attendees to peruse include the ones shown in Table 2.

We will also allow conference attendees to study side-by-side comparisons between the same queries addressed by various crowd-powered DataSift configurations and the traditional fully-automated retrieval scheme (RS). Since rich media queries are simply not supported by traditional retrieval approaches, for the side-by-side comparison, we can only support fully textual queries. We will demonstrate to the attendees that GRFWRFS clearly outperforms all other configurations, with up to 200% higher precision than RS on average. Furthermore, we will demonstrate that GFRWRFS significantly outperforms the simpler configurations such as GRFS and GRS, because GFRWRFS preferentially retrieves more from the better reformulations.

3.2 Scenario 2: Live Queries

In this scenario, we will allow conference attendees to pose queries to DataSift. DataSift supports four keyword search corpora: Youtube Videos (`youtube.com`), Amazon Products (`amazon.com`), Google Images (`images.google.com`), and Shutterstock Images (`www.shutterstock.com`). Attendees will be able to issue queries on-the-fly to any of these corpora, and view the progress of queries issued by other attendees.

We will support two crowdsourcing marketplaces for live queries: first, Amazon's Mechanical Turk, and second, the marketplace of SIGMOD conference attendees — that is, we will allow conference attendees to act as workers, and complete tasks generated from queries issued by other attendees. To support the latter interaction, we will have two laptops set up, one with the DataSift query interface, and one with the conference attendee marketplace interface.

Consider the following trace of attendees interacting with DataSift and the conference attendee marketplace:

- Attendee X issues two queries Q1 and Q2.
- Attendee Y issues two queries Q3 and Q4 of their own, then logs onto the conference attendee marketplace, answers tasks generated by (say) component G for Q1 and Q2
- Attendee Z logs into the conference attendee marketplace, answers tasks generated by (say) component F for Q1 and Q2, and by (say) component G for Q3 and Q4
- ...

As the above trace indicates, as part of this scenario, conference attendees will be able to play the role of both the potential users of DataSift, as well as the human workers working on tasks generated by DataSift. This scenario will demonstrate that, perhaps somewhat surprisingly, even though some conference attendees may suggest poor reformulations for the G component or answer filtering questions incorrectly for the F component, DataSift is resilient enough to ensure that the final results returned are unaffected by individual incorrect responses and still have a high degree of precision.

4. REFERENCES

[1] L. A. Adamic, J. Zhang, E. Bakshy, and M. S. Ackerman. Knowledge sharing and yahoo answers: everyone knows something. In *WWW*, 2008.

[2] G. Demartini, B. Trushkowsky, T. Kraska, and M. J. Franklin. Crowdq: Crowdsourced query understanding. In *CIDR*, 2013.

[3] D. Horowitz and S. D. Kamvar. The anatomy of a large-scale social search engine. In *WWW*, 2010.

[4] E. Law and H. Zhang. Towards large-scale collaborative planning: Answering high-level search queries using human computation. In *In AAAI*, 2011.

[5] G. Little, L. B. Chilton, M. Goldman, and R. C. Miller. Turkit: tools for iterative tasks on mechanical turk. In *HCOMP*, 2009.

[6] M. R. Morris and J. Teevan. Collaborative web search: Who, what, where, when, and why. *Synthesis Lectures on Information Concepts, Retrieval, and Services*, 1(1):1–99, 2009.

[7] A. Parameswaran, H. Garcia-Molina, H. Park, N. Polyzotis, A. Ramesh, and J. Widom. Crowdscreen: Algorithms for filtering data with humans. In *SIGMOD*, 2012.

[8] A. Parameswaran, M. H. Teh, H. Garcia-Molina, and J. Widom. Datasift: An expressive and accurate crowd-powered search toolkit. In *HCOMP*, 2013.

Reactive and Proactive Sharing Across Concurrent Analytical Queries

Iraklis Psaroudakis Manos Athanassoulis Matthaios Olma Anastasia Ailamaki
École Polytechnique Fédérale de Lausanne
{iraklis.psaroudakis, manos.athanassoulis, matthaios.olma, anastasia.ailamaki}@epfl.ch

ABSTRACT

Today an ever increasing amount of data is collected and analyzed by researchers, businesses, and scientists in data warehouses (DW). In addition to the data size, the number of users and applications querying data grows exponentially. The increasing concurrency is itself a challenge in query execution, but also introduces an opportunity favoring synergy between concurrent queries. Traditional execution engines of DW follows a *query-centric* approach, where each query is optimized and executed independently. On the other hand, workloads with increased concurrency have several queries with common parts of data and work, creating the opportunity for sharing among concurrent queries. Sharing can be *reactive* to the inherently existing sharing opportunities, or *proactive* by redesigning query operators to maximize the sharing opportunities.

This demonstration showcases the impact of proactive and reactive sharing by comparing and integrating representative state-of-the-art techniques: *Simultaneous Pipelining (SP)*, for reactive sharing, which shares intermediate results of common sub-plans, and *Global Query Plans (GQP)* for proactive sharing, which build and evaluate a single query plan with shared operators. We visually demonstrate, in an interactive interface, the behavior of both sharing approaches on top of a state-of-the-art storage engine using the original prototypes. We show that pull-based sharing for SP eliminates the serialization point imposed by the original push-based approach. Then, we compare, through a sensitivity analysis, the performance of SP and GQP. Finally, we show that SP can improve the performance of GQP for a query mix with common sub-plans.

Categories and Subject Descriptors

H.2.4 [**Database Management**]: Systems—*Query processing*

General Terms

Design, Experimentation, Performance

Keywords

Data Warehouses, Query Processing, Data Sharing, Work Sharing, Simultaneous Pipelining, Shared Pages List, Global Query Plans, Reactive Sharing, Proactive Sharing, QPipe, CJOIN

SIGMOD'14, June 22–27, 2014, Snowbird, UT, USA.

ACM 978-1-4503-2376-5/14/06 ...$15.00.
http://dx.doi.org/10.1145/2588555.2594514.

1. INTRODUCTION

Today, in the era of big data, organizations are called to process an ever-increasing mass of data to deduce valuable information. To meet their needs, organizations employ data warehouses (DW), which are specialized databases for serving online analytical processing (OLAP) workloads. OLAP queries are mostly ad-hoc, long-running, and scan-heavy queries.

The execution engine of a traditional DW typically evaluates the mix of concurrent analytical queries using a query-centric model: each query is optimized and evaluated independently of the other queries in the system. This approach misses opportunities of sharing common parts of data and work across the query mix. Taking advantage of these opportunities can further enhance the performance of highly-concurrent DW, by reducing contention for I/O, CPU, and RAM resources, and freeing up resources.

Our study shows the performance benefits from state-of-the-art sharing techniques. We explore how and when these techniques should be employed, we make a head-to-head comparison and we combine them. The first study and implementation was presented at VLDB 2013 [8]. In this work, we demonstrate the sharing techniques in a unified system, and provide to the audience the opportunity to visually assess the effect of the sharing techniques on performance, and trigger various workload parameters for an interactive sensitivity analysis.

Overview of the sharing techniques. The demonstration evaluates two fundamental strategies for sharing: (a) *reactive sharing* which acts using the sharing opportunities that inherently exist in the workload (e.g. common sub-plans) and (b) *proactive sharing* which maximizes work and data sharing (e.g, by analyzing the workload and building synergistically shared operators in a global query plan). Throughout our experimentation and analysis we use two representative state-of-the-art techniques. For reactive sharing we use Simultaneous Pipelining (SP) by integrating its original research prototype QPipe [5], and for proactive sharing we use using Global Query Plans (GQP) with shared operators, by integrating the original research prototype CJOIN [2]. Both techniques use shared scans. In the remainder of the paper we refer to the sharing strategies using the respective techniques: SP for reactive sharing and GQP for proactive sharing.

SP identifies common sub-plans among concurrent queries at run-time, evaluates only one and pipelines the results to the rest simultaneously. Figure 1a shows an example of two queries that share a common sub-plan below the join operator (along with any selection and join predicates), but have a different aggregation operator above the join. SP evaluates only one of them, and pipelines the results to the other aggregation operator.

Though SP is limited to common sub-plans with identical predicates, a shared operator in a GQP can handle multiple concurrent

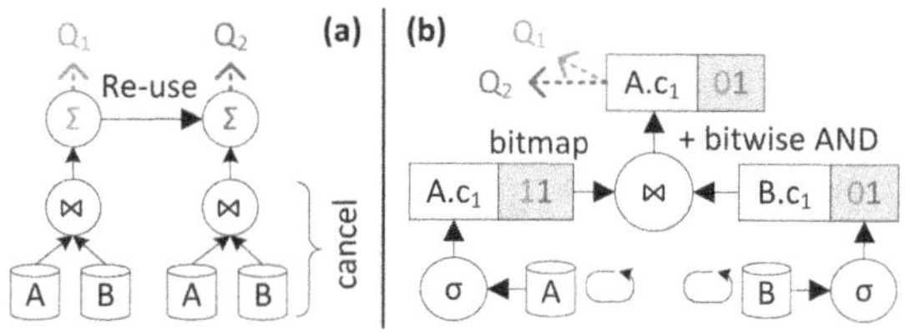

Figure 1: (a) SP on two queries having a common sub-plan below a join. (b) Example of shared scans and a shared join operator in a GQP. The GQP evaluates two queries with the same join predicate but possibly different selection predicates.

queries with similar plans but potentially different predicates. The basic technique for enabling them is sharing tuples among queries and correlating each tuple to the queries, e.g. by annotating tuples with a bitmap, the bits of which signify whether the tuple is relevant to one of the queries. Figure 1b gives an example of two queries that join two relations using the same join predicate, but have different selection predicates for both relations. The shared scans attach a bitmap to each scanned tuple, calculated after evaluating the selection predicates of the queries, and the shared join operator performs a bitwise AND operation between the bitmaps of the joined tuples to preserve their correlation to the queries.

Improving SP. In order to overcome the negative effects of aggressive sharing with SP [6] we study the mechanism of copying common results among operators. We show that the push-based model for SP creates a serialization point during sharing, and we address this bottleneck by introducing the novel Shared Pages List (SPL) data structure which implements a pull-based model of SP [8], allowing a single producer and multiple consumers accessing the data. The demonstration allows the audience to verify the serialization point of the push-based model, and dynamically trigger the usage of SPL to evaluate its impact (see Section 4.3).

Comparing SP vs. GQP. We integrate the original research prototypes that introduced SP and GQP into one system: we integrate the CJOIN operator as an additional stage of the QPipe execution engine (see Section 3) on top of the Shore-MT storage manager [7]. Thus, we can dynamically decide whether to evaluate multiple concurrent queries with the standard query-centric operators of QPipe (with or without SP) or the shared operators of the GQP of CJOIN. The demonstration allows the audience to dynamically choose which technique to use when evaluating an analytical workload, under a combination of adjustable parameters, and visually assess the differences between the two sharing techniques (see Section 4.4). The live comparison gives the audience the opportunity to validate the rules of thumb presented in the experimental comparison of SP vs. GQP [8]. Shared operators enhance performance for workloads with high concurrency, but their high book-keeping overhead in comparison with query-centric operators, overwhelms performance for workloads with low concurrency. On the other hand, SP enhanced by SPL is beneficial for both low and high concurrency.

Combining SP and GQP. SP and GQP are orthogonal sharing techniques that can be combined to get the best of the two worlds. SP can be applied on the shared operators of a GQP (e.g., aggregations), further improving the performance of a GQP in a query mix with common sub-plans, as it avoids reevaluating them through the GQP, and instead it reuses the common intermediate results. The demonstration showcases an analytical workload where the audience can dynamically trigger the number of common sub-plans in the mix and assess the effect of SP on GQP.

Visual experience. This demonstration includes a graphical interface that allows the audience to change system and workload characteristics in order to assess the effect of the different techniques of sharing on the execution performance of concurrent analytical queries. Workload parameters, such as the number of concurrent queries or their similarity, affect performance, and the audience can explore different combinations of parameters. The output is shown with a set of dynamically generated graphs, accompanied by system measurements (e.g. CPU times).

2. RELATED WORK

Sharing in the I/O layer. By sharing data, the accesses of queries in the I/O layer are coordinated. The typical DW uses buffer pool management techniques and eviction policies. More recently, shared scans [8] have been proposed to better co-ordinate multiple queries that scan the same relation, reducing buffer pool contention and avoiding unnecessary I/O. Both QPipe and CJOIN use a simple form of shared scans, circular scans [5].

Sharing in the execution engine. By sharing work among queries, we refer to techniques that avoid redundant computations inside the execution engine. A typical DW uses query caching, materialized views, or Multi-Query Optimization (MQO) techniques. These techniques, however, do not exploit sharing opportunities among in-progress queries. Both SP and GQP provide deeper and more dynamic forms of sharing at run-time. The main aim of our demonstration is to showcase these sharing techniques.

For both techniques, we use their original research prototype systems: QPipe for SP, and the CJOIN operator for GQP. CJOIN is restricted to the evaluation of star queries, with a GQP composed of shared scans and shared hash-joins. After CJOIN, more recent research prototypes (DataPath [1] and SharedDB [4]) have advanced GQP to more general schemas and operators. Without loss of generality, we restrict our evaluation of GQP with CJOIN to star schemas, which are very common in relational DW, and correlate our observations to more general schemas and operators [8].

3. DEMONSTRATED SYSTEMS

In this section, we give quick overview of the original systems that implemented SP and GQP: the QPipe execution engine and the CJOIN operator respectively. We also explain how we improve QPipe with a pull-based model of SP, and how we integrate the CJOIN operator into the QPipe execution engine to take advantage of both sharing techniques.

The QPipe execution engine. In QPipe, each relational operator is encapsulated into a self-contained module called a *stage*, which has a queue for work requests and employs a local thread pool for processing them. A query plan is converted to a series of interdependent *packets*, dispatched to the relevant stages. Data flow between packets is implemented through FIFO buffers and page-based exchange, following a push-only model with pipelined execution (as shown in [3]). SP is implemented at execution time at any stage, when an incoming packet has a common sub-plan with an ongoing packet, by copying the results of the ongoing packet to the FIFO buffer of the incoming packet. SP may not be activated for certain cases of relational operators and query inter-arrival delays [5].

Shared Pages List. The push-based model using intermediate FIFO buffers involves a serialization point during SP when the single producer forwards the common intermediate results to multiple consumers. This bottleneck makes SP beneficial only for cases of high concurrency, where sharing proves better than not sharing by avoiding contention for resources [6]. A pull-based model for SP

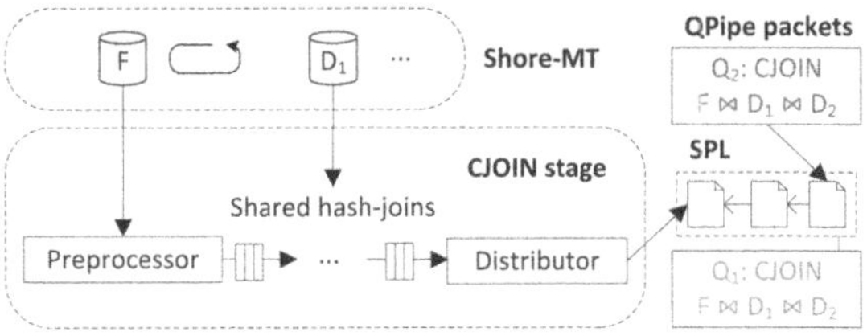

Figure 2: Integration of CJOIN into QPipe for the evaluation of star queries joining the fact table with dimension tables.

virtually eliminates this serialization point, by sharing intermediate results instead of forwarding them [8]. To achieve this, an intermediate data structure, the *Shared Pages List* (SPL), replaces FIFO buffers, allowing a single producer and multiple consumers.

The CJOIN operator. CJOIN evaluates the joins of concurrent star queries, using a GQP with shared scans, shared selections and shared hash-joins. Due to the semantics of star schemas, the directed acyclic graph of the GQP takes the form of a chain [8]. CJOIN exploits this form and evaluates a single pipeline: the *preprocessor* uses a circular scan of the fact table, and flows fact tuples through the pipeline. The shared hash-joins in-between join the fact tuples with the corresponding dimension tuples and additionally perform a bitwise AND between their bitmaps. At the end of the pipeline, the *distributor* examines the bitmaps of the joined tuples and forwards them to the relevant queries.

Integration. We integrate the CJOIN operator into the QPipe execution engine as a new stage, using Shore-MT [7] as the underlying storage manager. CJOIN supports only shared hash-joins, hence, any subsequent operators are query-centric. Having CJOIN integrated into QPipe, we can enable SP for the CJOIN stage, combining the two sharing techniques. Figure 2 shows the new stage that encapsulates the CJOIN pipeline, and how two star queries, having a common sub-plan under their CJOIN packets, share the intermediate results with a SPL. Only Q_1 is evaluated by CJOIN, saving admission costs and unnecessary book-keeping costs for Q_2.

4. DEMONSTRATION WALKTHROUGH

The demonstration will be executed using a poster, and an interactive graphical application. The application will showcase a number of predefined scenarios, that are executed on the spot, to demonstrate the advantages of the sharing techniques, their various aspects and trade-offs. Apart from the predefined scenarios, the audience will be able to modify the parameters to create custom scenarios, and get an insight on the effect of the parameters on the overall performance of analytical workloads.

4.1 Poster

We use a poster to introduce the audience to the traditional query-centric model, SP, and GQP. We explain how the query-centric model misses sharing opportunities across concurrent analytical queries, and how SP and GQP can take advantage of sharing opportunities. We also introduce the user to the general design of the original prototype systems QPipe and CJOIN, how we integrate the CJOIN operator as an additional stage in QPipe, and how the SPL data structure supports a pull-based version of SP. Finally, we include key plots of the predefined scenarios (detailed in the following sections) and explain their implications.

4.2 System setup

The graphical web interface runs on a dedicated virtual machine in our lab and can be accessed by a laptop at the conference, where

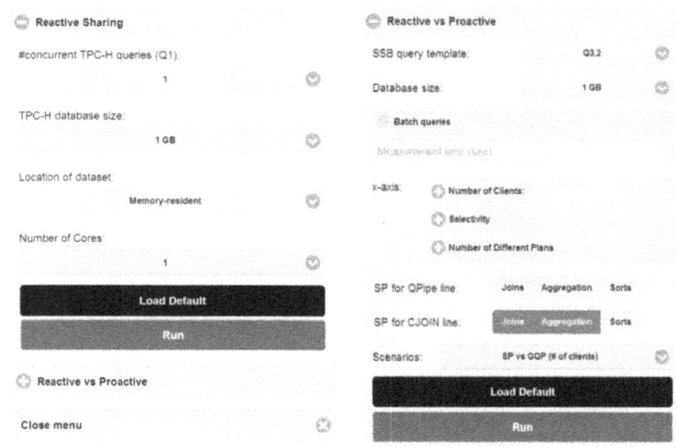

(a) Scenario I (b) Scenario II-IV

Figure 3: Execution options

the audience can define the parameters for the scenarios, and visualize the results. The experiments run remotely on multiple machines hosting multiple instance of our database server at EPFL. We use three machines, in parallel, to measure the response time or throughput of the different configurations required for the following scenarios. Each machine has two 8-core Intel Xeon E5-2660 processors (with hyper-threading enabled), 128GB RAM, and seven 300GB 15kRPM SAS 3.5" hard disks. The O/S is a 64-bit SMP Linux (Red Hat), with a 2.6.32 kernel.

4.3 Scenario I: Push-based vs. Pull-based SP

The aim of this scenario is to show the advantages of a pull-based model of SP, using our new SPL data structure, versus the original push-based model of SP. Sharing intermediate results with push-based SP proves to be beneficial when executing concurrent queries, only when the system does not have available parallelism to execute each query independently because the overhead to copy the results dominates the response time. Pull-based sharing with SPL, however, minimizes the copying overhead and is beneficial even when the system has available parallelism. The audience can see this behavior by plotting the response time of concurrent queries and binding the database server process to a minimum of 1 and a maximum of 32 cores. In addition, the interactive interface allows to experiment with different database sizes, with memory-resident and disk-resident databases, with different number of concurrent queries, and with different buffer-pool sizes for the case of the disk-resident database.

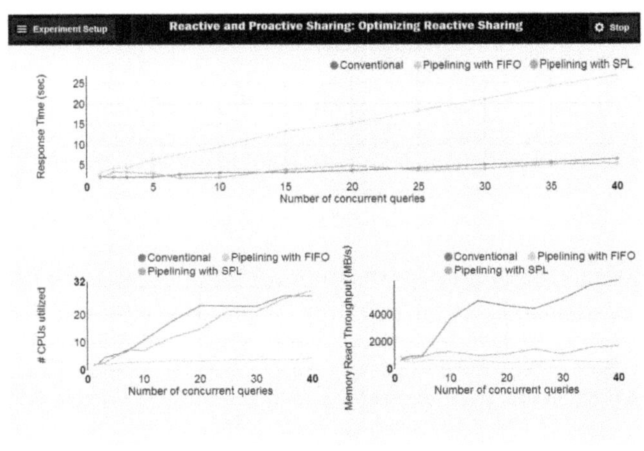

Figure 4: GUI for Scenario I

The default scenario demonstrates the performance of the two models using an experiment which evaluates SP for the table scan stage with a memory-resident database [8]. Specifically, we use identical TPC-H Q1 instances, submitted at the same time. Figure 3(a) shows an example of the GUI for the default scenario where the user can alter the parameters of the experiment, and Figure 4 shows how the experiment execution will be monitored by showing for each level of concurrency (i) the response time of the workload, (ii) the CPU utilization, and (iii) the I/O (memory bus) throughput for the disk-resident (memory-resident) dataset.

The serialization point of the push-based SP (FIFO) increases the response time with additional concurrent queries, while CPU load does not increase significantly. The pull-based SP (SPL) overcomes the serialization point, and is able to fully use CPU resources. The query-centric execution has marginally lower response time than the pull-based approach when the available parallelism is lower than the concurrency of the workload, but pull-based sharing improves performance for higher concurrency.

4.4 Scenarios II-IV: SP vs GQP

The rest of the scenarios explore the trade-offs of the two sharing techniques, SP and GQP. The workload now consists of queries issued concurrently by a number of clients following instantiations of a Star Schema Benchmark (SSB) template. Each client submits queries iteratively. We present performance in terms of throughput. Figure 3(b) shows the GUI that the user can alter the different starting parameters building different execution scenarios. Figure 5 shows the output of a sample execution for these scenarios.

The dark blue line shows the performance of the QPipe execution engine and query-centric relational operators. On the configuration pane, the user can enable SP for the different stages of QPipe. Without SP for any stage, the QPipe engine is similar to a query-centric execution engine with shared scans. The light blue line shows the performance of the QPipe execution engine with the CJOIN operator evaluating the hash-joins of all concurrent star queries in the workload. By enabling SP for the CJOIN stage, the user can assess the performance of the combination of the two sharing techniques.

The rest of the configuration parameters allow the audience to differentiate from the default scenarios II-IV, and create custom ones. The x-axis can be selected among the number of concurrent clients, the selectivity of the queries, and the number of possible different plans for the selected query template (affecting the number of common sub-plans in the query mix for SP). The user can also modify which SSB query template to be used, the scale factor of the dataset, whether the database is memory-resident or disk-resident, whether clients should co-ordinate to submit their queries in batches (ensures maximal SP sharing and decreases admission costs for GQP), and the throughput measurement duration for each point of the selected x-axis.

Scenario II: Impact of concurrency. This scenario fixes selectivity to 1%, randomizes the template's parameters to decrease the efficiency of SP, and modifies the number of concurrent clients (x-axis). The database is disk-resident, and SP is enabled for all stages for both lines. Here we show that shared operators in a GQP are more efficient in evaluating a high number of concurrent queries in comparison to standard query-centric operators.

Scenario III: Impact of selectivity. This scenario randomizes the template's parameters to decrease the efficiency of SP, fixes the number of concurrent clients to a low concurrency value, and modifies the parameters' selectivity (x-axis). The database is memory-resident, and SP is enabled for all stages for both lines. The aim of this scenario is to show that shared operators in a GQP have a high bookkeeping overhead in comparison to query-centric operators.

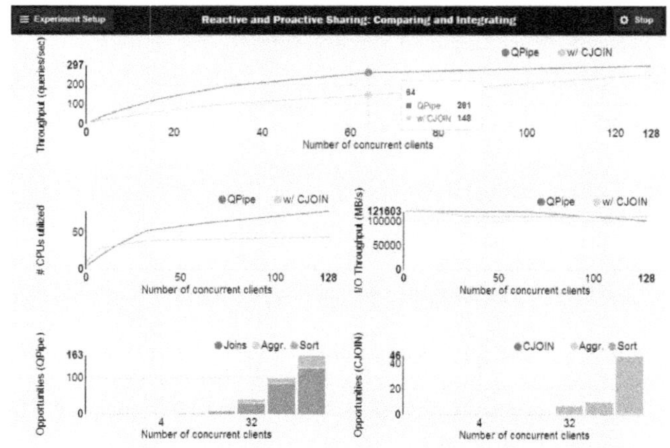

Figure 5: GUI for Scenarios II-IV

Scenario IV: Impact of similarity. This scenario fixes the number of concurrent clients to a high concurrency value, fixes the selectivity, and modifies the number of possible different plans (x-axis) to restrict their randomness. Fewer available plans translates to more common sub-plans for the same number of clients, while a higher number of available plans translates to fewer common sub-plans and fewer SP opportunities. The database is disk-resident, and SP is enabled for all stages for both lines. Batching is used to maximize SP opportunities. The aim of this scenario is to show that we can combine SP with a GQP to improve the performance of shared operators for a query mix with common sub-plans. The measurements with regards to the number of SP opportunities exploited for each stage comprise the most significant metric for this scenario.

5. CONCLUSIONS

In this demonstration, we show how and when reactive and proactive work sharing outperforms query-centric execution in the context of analytical workloads. The demonstration is composed of a poster and an interactive graphical user interface that allows the audience to assess the performance benefits of the sharing techniques, how they compare against each other, and how they can be combined to exploit both techniques.

Acknowledgments. This work was supported by the FP7 project BIGFOOT (grant n. 317858).

6. REFERENCES

[1] S. Arumugam, A. Dobra, C. M. Jermaine, N. Pansare, and L. Perez. The DataPath system: a data-centric analytic processing engine for large data warehouses. *SIGMOD*, 2010.

[2] G. Candea, N. Polyzotis, and R. Vingralek. Predictable performance and high query concurrency for data analytics. *VLDBJ*, 2011.

[3] K. Gao, S. Harizopoulos, I. Pandis, V. Shkapenyuk, and A. Ailamaki. Simultaneous Pipelining in QPipe: Exploiting Work Sharing Opportunities Across Queries. *ICDE*, 2006.

[4] G. Giannikis, G. Alonso, and D. Kossmann. SharedDB: Killing One Thousand Queries with One Stone. *VLDB*, 2012.

[5] S. Harizopoulos, V. Shkapenyuk, and A. Ailamaki. QPipe: a simultaneously pipelined relational query engine. *SIGMOD*, 2005.

[6] R. Johnson, S. Harizopoulos, N. Hardavellas, K. Sabirli, I. Pandis, A. Ailamaki, N. G. Mancheril, and B. Falsafi. To share or not to share? *VLDB*, 2007.

[7] R. Johnson, I. Pandis, N. Hardavellas, A. Ailamaki, and B. Falsafi. Shore-MT: a scalable storage manager for the multicore era. *EDBT*, 2009.

[8] I. Psaroudakis, M. Athanassoulis, and A. Ailamaki. Sharing data and work across concurrent analytical queries. *VLDB*, 2013.

SLQ: A User-friendly Graph Querying System

Shengqi Yang[1] Yanan Xie[2] Yinghui Wu[1] Tianyu Wu[2]
Huan Sun[1] Jian Wu[2] Xifeng Yan[1]
[1]University of California Santa Barbara [2]Zhejiang University
{sqyang, yinghui, huansun, xyan}@cs.ucsb.edu
{xyn, tywu, wujian2000}@zju.edu.cn

ABSTRACT

Querying complex graph databases such as knowledge graphs is a challenging task for non-professional users. In this demo, we present SLQ, a user-friendly graph querying system enabling schemaless and structureless graph querying, where a user need not describe queries precisely as required by most databases. SLQ system combines searching and ranking: it leverages a set of transformation functions, including abbreviation, ontology, synonym, etc., that map keywords and linkages from a query to their matches in a data graph, based on an automatically learned ranking model. To help users better understand search results at different levels of granularity, it supports effective result summarization with "drill-down" and "roll-up" operations. Better still, the architecture of SLQ is elastic for new transformation functions, query logs and user feedback, to iteratively refine the ranking model. SLQ significantly improves the usability of graph querying. This demonstration highlights (1) SLQ can automatically learn an effective ranking model, *without* assuming manually labeled training examples, (2) it can efficiently return top ranked matches over noisy, large data graphs, (3) it can summarize the query matches to help users easily access, explore and understand query results, and (4) its GUI can interact with users to help them construct queries, explore data graphs and inspect matches in a user-friendly manner.

Categories and Subject Descriptors

H.2.4 [**Database Management**]: Systems—*Query processing*

Keywords

schemaless graph querying; keyword query; graph databases

1. INTRODUCTION

Graph querying is widely adopted to retrieve information from emerging graph databases, *e.g.,* knowledge graphs, information and social networks. Given a query, it is to find reasonable top answers from a data graph. Searching real-life graphs, nevertheless, is not an easy task especially for non-professional users. (1) Either no standard schema is available, or schemas become too complicated for users to completely possess. (2) Graph queries are hard to write and interpret. Structured queries (*e.g.,* XQuery [4] and SPARQL [5,7]) require the expertise in complex grammars, while keyword queries [8,10] can be too ambiguous to reflect user search intent. Moreover, most of these methods adopt predefined ranking models [5,8], which is barely able to bridge the gap between queries and their desired matches. (3) Moreover, it is a daunting task for users to inspect a large number of matches produced from querying large-scale heterogeneous graph data.

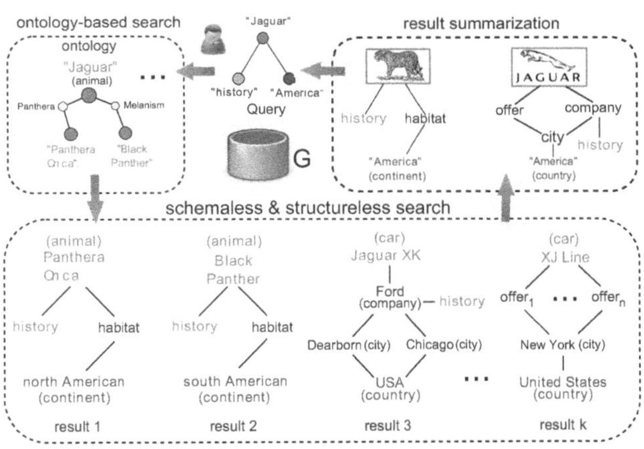

Figure 1: Searching a knowledge graph

Example 1: Consider a query asking "tell me about the history of Jaguar in America". The query can be presented as either a keyword query "Jaguar history America", or a small graph in Fig. 1. To find answers for such a simple query is, nevertheless, not easy. (1) A keyword *e.g.,* "Jaguar" may not have identical matches, but instead can be matched with entities that are semantically close, *i.e.,* luxury cars or animals. *How to find matches that are semantically related to the query?* (2) A large number of possible answers can be identified by various matching mechanisms. For example, "Panthera Onca" is closely related with "Jaguar" as its scientific name, while "Jaguar XK" is another match obtained simply by string transformations. *Which one is better?* A ranking model should be employed and tuned with or without manual tuning effort. (3) There are a large number of good results, *e.g.,* different species related to Jaguar (result

SIGMOD'14, June 22–27, 2014, Snowbird, UT, USA.

http://dx.doi.org/10.1145/2588555.2594516.

1 and result 2), or various car prototypes (result 3 to result k). *How to help users better understand results without inspecting them one by one?* This kind of complexity contrasts to the impatience of web users who are only interested in finding good answers in a short time. □

To answer these questions, we propose SLQ, a novel graph querying system for schemaless and structureless querying [13]. (1) To better understand search intent, SLQ interprets queries with external ontologies to find semantically close matches. (2) It automatically supports multiple mapping functions, namely, *transformations*, *e.g.*, synonym, abbreviation, ontology, to identify reasonable answer via learning to rank, and works with both (a) a cold-start strategy that requires no manual effort for system tuning, and (b) a warm-start strategy to adjust the ranking model with available user feedback and query logs. (3) To help users better understand results and refine queries, it supports concise result summarization. Users may inspect small summaries, and then decide to (a) drill-down for details, or (b) interactively refine queries with interesting summaries. To the best of our knowledge, these features are not seen before in any previous graph querying systems (*e.g.*, [4–8]).

SLQ system is among the first efforts of developing a unified framework for schemaless and structureless querying. Designed to help users access complex graphs in a much easier and powerful manner, it is capable of finding high-quality matches when structured query languages do not work.

Queries and datasets. SLQ supports a wide range of queries. Users may issue (1) a keyword query as a set of keywords, where each keyword describes an entity; or (2) a (not necessarily connected) graph query, where each query node has a set of labels as conditions, and an edge between two nodes, if any, specifies the relation constraints posed on two query nodes by users. We demonstrate SLQ over three major knowledge graphs, *i.e.,* DBpedia, YAGO2 and Freebase as described in the table below. A single such knowledge graph could have more than 10K types of entities, making it difficult for users to fully grasp.

Graphs	entities	relations	node types	relation types
DBpedia [1]	3.7M	20M	359	800
YAGO2 [5]	2.9M	11M	6,543	349
Freebase [2]	40.3M	180M	10,110	9,101

Table 1: Knowledge graphs

We next introduce SLQ and its features in detail.

2. ONTOLOGY-BASED QUERYING

In contrast to conventional graph querying systems, SLQ does not limit itself with single, fixed search semantic. Instead, it employs a set of matching functions that are more capable to find good matches in heterogeneous graphs [13]. We start by demonstrating *ontology-based search*, as an example for various matching mechanisms integrated in SLQ.

One of the challenges is to find the semantically related matches. SLQ leverages ontology-based search [12] to bridge the entities from queries and data graphs via a set of ontology closeness metrics. Given external ontology graphs (*e.g.,* DBPedia Ontology [1]), SLQ finds the semantically related entities (specified by a closeness measure) in the ontology graphs for each entity (keyword) in a query [12]. A straightforward "substituting-and-querying" method may next interpret the query by substituting the keywords with their related entities, which in turn have matches in the data graph. Top matches can then be extracted by processing each new query. However, it may yield a tremendous number of queries. Instead, SLQ leverages an effective ontology index [12]. In a nutshell, it computes several sketches of the data graph using the ontology graph. Each sketch is induced by grouping the nodes that are semantically close. Upon receiving a query, SLQ can efficiently identify the top matches by querying on these small sketches only.

Example 2: While there are no similarly labeled entities for "Jaguar" in the data graph (Fig. 1), SLQ checks an ontology graph, and identifies its two semantically related matches (as a type of animal): "Panthera Onca", its scientific name and "Black Panther", its melanistic color variant. These can hardly be found by conventional IR metrics or string similarity, or by using the query and data graph alone. □

SLQ wraps ontology-based searching with (a) an ontology transformation function that maps a keyword to a set of valid entities, and (b) an ontology index. These are seamlessly integrated in the query processing of SLQ (Section 3).

3. QUERYING PROCESSING MODULE

SLQ does not require a user to describe a query precisely as required by most search applications. To render this high flexibility to the users, in the core of the framework is a mechanism of *transformation*: given a query, the query evaluation is conducted by checking if its matches in a graph database can be reasonably "transformed" from the query through a set of transformation functions.

Transformations. To characterize query matches, SLQ adopts transformations defined on the attributes and values of both nodes and edges of the query [13]. A query node (or edge) has a match if it can be converted to the latter via a transformation. For example, a query node "IBM" shall be matched to a node with label "International Business Machines." The table below summarizes several common transformations supported by SLQ.

Category	Transformations
String	First token, Last token, Abbreviation, Prefix, Acronym, Drop word, Bag of words
Semantic	Ontology, Synonym (WordNet [3])
Numeric	Unit conversion, Date gap, Date conversion, Numeric range
Topology	Distance, Labeled path

Better still, SLQ exposes a generic interface abstracted for any transformation. New transformations complying with the interface can be readily plugged in.

Example 3: Recall the query in Fig. 1. SLQ captures the matches for the keyword "Jaguar" as follows. (1) The matches "Panthera Onca" and "Black Panther" can be identified by ontology transformation (Section 2). (2) The match "Jaguar XK" can be matched by "First token", a String transformation. (3) The match "XJ Line" can be captured by "Bag of words", indicating that "Jaguar" appears in its text description. For edge ("Jaguar", "America"), an topology transformation "Distance" maps it to a path from "Panthera Onca" to "north America" in result 1. □

Matching Quality Measurement. To measure the quality of the matches induced by various transformations, SLQ adopts a ranking function of *weighted transformations*. The function incorporates two types of score functions: node matching and edge matching score function. Each score function aggregates the contribution of all the possible transformations with corresponding weights. More specifically, by harnessing the probabilistic graphical model, we define the ranking function with *Conditional Random Fields* [9], since it satisfies two key considerations: using training data, its *formulation* could optimize the weights of the transformations for good ranking quality; the *inference* on the model provides a mechanism to search top-k matches quickly.

Ranking model learning. A key issue is how to select a ranking function by determining reasonable weights for the transformations. Instead of assigning equal weights or calibrating the weights by human effort, SLQ automatically *learns* the weights from a set of *training instances*. Each instance is a pair of a query and one of its relevant (labeled as "good") answers. The learning aims to identify for each transformation a weight, such that if applied, the model ranks the good answers as high as possible for each instance.

SLQ begins with a cold-start stage where no manual effort is required for instances labeling, and can be "self-trained" in the warm-start stage, using user feedback and query logs. (Cold-start) When no user query log is available, SLQ randomly extracts a set of subgraphs from the data graph as "query templates." It then injects a few transformations to the template and generates a set of training queries. Intuitively, each training query should have the corresponding templates as its "good matches," since the query can be transformed back to the template.

Query Processing. SLQ efficiently finds top matches, leveraging *approximate inferencing* [9]. It treats a query as a graphic model and the matches as assignment to its random variables (query nodes). By propagating messages among the nodes in the graphical model, the inference can identify top assignments (matches) that maximize the joint probability (ranking score) for the model. Together with a graph sketch data structure, this technique dramatically reduces the query processing time, with only small loss of match quality (less than 1% in our validation).

4. RESULT SUMMARIZATION

Due to the sheer volume of data, graph querying usually generates a lot of results that are too many to inspect. This not only makes the understanding of the results a daunting task, but also frustrates the users to continue refining the search. The result summarization feature of SLQ addresses the two challenges in a "two-birds-with-one-stone" way by leveraging [11]. (1) Given a query and a set of matches, SLQ effectively describes all the matches (as graphs) with a few *summary graphs*. A summary graph preserves the connectivity of the keyword pairs. By reviewing the summary graphs, users easily get intuitive "big pictures" of all the matches. (2) The summary graphs can further be used to refine the search by suggesting new query nodes or edges, or be issued directly as new queries.

Example 4: SLQ provides two intuitive summaries for the matches in Fig. 1. The first summary indicates that "Jaguar" refers to animals living in America continents with evolution history. The second shows that it refers to a certain type of cars sold by dealers and companies in major cities of USA, with the company history in car industry. In addition, new nodes or keywords, *e.g.,* "offer", are suggested to users to inspire queries with new interests. □

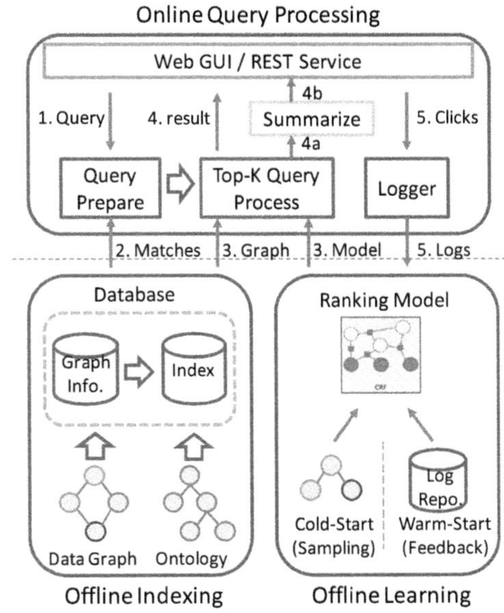

Figure 2: SLQ: Architecture

5. SYSTEM DESIGN

The system SLQ consists of back-end and front-end modules, as illustrated in Fig. 2. For the back-end, SLQ integrates (1) a full fledged indexing module (the lower left part in Fig. 2) which implements all the indices in Section 3, and (2) an offline learning module for the ranking model (the lower right part in Fig. 2). Each module in the back-end can be maintained dynamically in response to data updates, without affecting the front-end, *i.e.,* online query processing. We also separate the information for graph structure and its node and edge content, and store the latter in the database. This enables SLQ to perform fast graph traversal by only loading much smaller graph structure into the memory, while accessing richer content, *e.g.,* attribute values, documents, pictures in the database.

The front-end modules reside in the application layer (online query processing), as shown in the upper level in Fig. 2. Upon receiving a query, (1) the "`query prepare`" module first interprets the query to an internal format, and prepares the match candidates by looking up the indices; (2) SLQ next invokes "`top-k query process`" using the ranking model to find accurate matches; (3) once the top-k results are generated, SLQ directly renders the results to the user through our "`GUI/REST service`"; (4) SLQ can also provide the users with the summarized views of the results via "`summarize`"; and (5) the user queries and result preferences are memorized by "`Logger`" to improve the ranking model.

SLQ is designed with elasticity. It can be scaled up easily by duplicating a module without affecting the others. For example, when there are intensive query requests, we can duplicate the application layer in multiple servers and then evenly distribute the queries among the servers.

6. DEMONSTRATION OVERVIEW

Setup. We will demonstrate SLQ over the knowledge graphs in Table 1. The system is implemented in Java and is deployed on an Intel Core i7 2.8GHz, 32GB server.

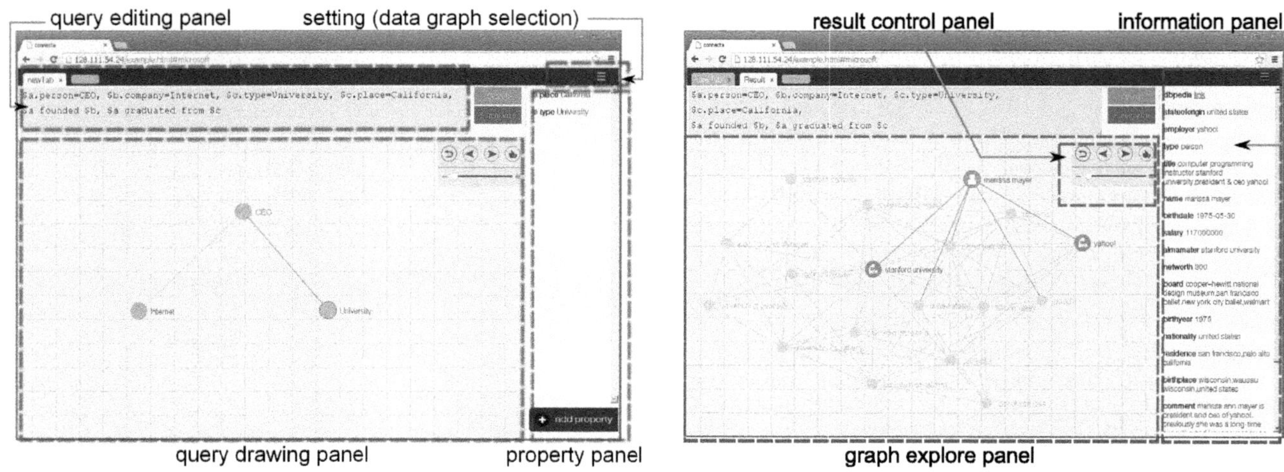

(a) Query formalization interface

(b) Graph exploration interface

Figure 3: SLQ: User interface

Demo Scenario. SLQ provides user interfaces for *query formalization* and *query result exploration* (Fig. 3). We invite users to experience (1) how to easily form a query without prior training in query languages or graph databases, (2) how the results, summaries and even the data graph can be conveniently navigated and viewed.

As shown in Fig 3(a), the query formalization interface renders the users with two major *query panels* to form queries. (1) Users can conveniently draw a graph query in the **`query drawing panel`**, and can freely add and edit the properties and values in the the **`property panel`** for each query node or edge. (2) Alternatively, users are invited to use our built-in query language SLQL in the **`query editing panel`**. SLQL is designed for simplicity. It consists of two types of statements: (1) the *node statement*, "$\$x$.*property* = *value*", where "$\$x$" denotes a query node with a label constraint "*property* = *value*", and (2) the *edge statement*, "$\$x$ *predicate* $\$y$", where "$\$x$" and "$\$y$" are the query nodes as in (1) and "*predicate*" indicates the relationship between the two nodes. A graph query and its SLQL representation is shown in Fig. 3(a).

The second demonstration scenario invites users to run their queries and inspect the results. A user can also run the query on various knowledge graphs, *e.g.,*Freebase, chosen from **`setting`**. The results of the query in Fig. 3(a) are shown in the graph exploration interface (Fig 3(b)). The **`graph explore panel`** renders top-1 result (the highlighted part) as well as its peripheral structure (the dim part) in the data graph. The user can then inspect the detail information of a node/edge shown in the **`information panel`**. By double-clicking a node, users are able to explore the one-hop neighbors of the node from the data graph. Moreover, the **`result control panel`** enables the user to navigate the next/previous result or return to the top-1 result. The user feedback will be recorded if they click the **`like button`** on specific results. We also invite users to try the **`summarize`** button to view the summarized results from a large collection of returned matches, and drill down to find details.

7. ACKNOWLEDGMENTS

This research was sponsored in part by the Army Research Laboratory under cooperative agreements W911NF-09-2-0053, NSF IIS-0954125 and NSF IIS-0905084. The views and conclusions contained herein are those of the authors and should not be interpreted as representing the official policies, either expressed or implied, of the Army Research Laboratory or the U.S. Government.

8. REFERENCES

[1] Dbpedia. *dbpedia.org*.

[2] Freebase. *freebase.com*.

[3] Wordnet. *wordnet.princeton.edu*.

[4] D. Chamberlin et al. XQuery 1.0: An XML Query Language. W3C Working Draft, June 2001.

[5] J. Hoffart, F. M. Suchanek, K. Berberich, E. Lewis-Kelham, G. de Melo, and G. Weikum. Yago2: Exploring and querying world knowledge in time, space, context, and many languages. In *WWW*, 2011.

[6] D. Mottin, M. Lissandrini, V. Yannis, and T. Palpanas. Exemplar queries: Give me an example of what you need. In *VLDB*, 2014.

[7] J. Pérez, M. Arenas, and C. Gutierrez. Semantics and complexity of SPARQL. *TODS*, 34(3), 2009.

[8] J. Pound, I. F. Ilyas, and G. Weddell. Expressive and flexible access to web-extracted data: a keyword-based structured query language. In *SIGMOD*, 2010.

[9] C. Sutton and A. McCallum. An introduction to conditional random fields for relational learning. *Introduction to statistical relational learning*, 93:142–146, 2007.

[10] H. Wang and C. Aggarwal. A survey of algorithms for keyword search on graph data. *Managing and Mining Graph Data*, pages 249–273, 2010.

[11] Y. Wu, S. Yang, M. Srivatsa, A. Iyengar, and X. Yan. Summarizing answer graphs induced by keyword queries. *VLDB*, 6(14), 2013.

[12] Y. Wu, S. Yang, and X. Yan. Ontology-based subgraph querying. In *ICDE*, 2013.

[13] S. Yang, Y. Wu, H. Sun, and X. Yan. Schemaless and structureless graph querying. *VLDB*, 7(7), 2014.

TAREEG: A MapReduce-Based Web Service for Extracting Spatial Data from OpenStreetMap*

Louai Alarabi, Ahmed Eldawy, Rami Alghamdi, Mohamed F. Mokbel

KACST GIS Technology Innovation Center, Umm Al-Qura University, Makkah, KSA
{larabi,eldawy,rghamdi,mmokbel}@gistic.org
University of Minnesota, Minneapolis, MN 55455, USA
{louai,eldawy,alghamdi,mokbel}@cs.umn.edu

ABSTRACT

Real spatial data, e.g., detailed road networks, rivers, buildings, parks, are not really available in most of the world. This hinders the practicality of many research ideas that need a real spatial data for testing experiments. Such data is often available for governmental use, or at major software companies, but it is prohibitively expensive to build or buy for academia or individual researchers. This demo presents TAREEG; a web-service that makes real spatial data, from anywhere in the world, available at the fingertips of every researcher or individual. TAREEG gets all its data by leveraging the richness of OpenStreetMap dataset; the most comprehensive available spatial data of the world. Yet, it is still challenging to obtain OpenStreetMap data due to the size limitations, special data format, and the noisy nature of spatial data. TAREEG employs MapReduce-based techniques to make it efficient and easy to extract OpenStreetMap data in a standard form with minimal effort. TAREEG is accessible via `http://www.tareeg.org/`

1. INTRODUCTION

Taking advantage from the explosion in the number of GPS-enabled smart devices and the ubiquity of location services, there has been an increasing interest from industry and academia to advance the state of the art in location-based services that include shortest path queries, k-nearest-neighbor queries, range queries, spatial keyword search, and others (e.g., [9, 4, 10]). However, a major obstacle in progressing this kind of research is the difficulty in getting hands on real spatial data. While this may not be a problem for major industries, who can afford buying actual and accurate spatial data from specialized companies (e.g., NavTeq), this is prohibitively expensive for small startups and academia.

*This work is supported in part by KACST GIS Technology Innovation Center at Umm Al-Qura University, under project GISTIC-13-14, and was done while the first, second, and fourth authors were visiting the center.

SIGMOD'14, June 22–27, 2014, Snowbird, UT, USA.
Copyright 2014 ACM 978-1-4503-2376-5/14/06 ...$15.00.
http://dx.doi.org/10.1145/2588555.2594528.

To fill in this gap, OpenStreetMap [6] has been launched in 2004 to allow volunteers to combine their efforts in building an exhaustive and trustworthy map for the whole planet with an increased focus given to road networks. OpenStreetMap whole world dataset is free and accessible as a file called *Planet.osm* in an XML format that is updated on daily basis, where its current size is 435 GB. Despite its richness, using this data is not an easy task due to its huge size and non-standard format. For example, to extract the road network of Istanbul, Turkey, one needs to parse the whole 435 GB file, and extract the parts that are related to Istanbul. Furthermore, in these parts, one needs to parse records carefully, to extract the XML tags that are related to road networks and exclude everything else. Also, we need to overcome the noisy data as many of the data there are contributed from volunteers. As a result, several attempts were proposed to extract data from OpenStreetMaps. For example, the GeoFabrik project [3] allows users to download a predefined area from OpenStreetMaps, yet it does not provide any kind of extraction of specific map features (e.g., road network). It is basically a range query service over existing data without any attempt to read the noisy format. Also, OSMOSIS [8] and OSM2PGSQL [7] are two proposed tools that attempt to process the whole *Planet.osm* by loading it on spatial databases. However these tools may take up to several days for loading the entire *Planet.osm* file. For instance, in [5], the authors report that they spent 305 hours (approximately 12 days) for loading and analyzing the data for their experiment. In another benchmark of OSM2PGSQL, importing the *Planet.osm* to database takes up to 7 days of processing [7].

In this demo, we present TAREEG; an easy and efficient web service tool to extract spatial data from OpenStreetMaps. TAREEG users can: (1) extract geographical information through a nicely designed web service with the daily updated geographical data on any arbitrary region on world map, (2) Export the extracted data in CSV, KML, and shapefile formats, and (3) Visualize the geographical data on the map using four different mapping engines, which are OpenStreetMap, Google Maps, Google Hybrid Maps, and Esri Maps. All TAREEG services are done very efficient and online. For most of the requests, it takes only few second to receive the extracted data via email.

The key idea behind the performance of TAREEG is that it uses the MapReduce paradigm to speed up data extraction, indexing, and querying from Planet.osm file. In particular, TAREEG is powered by SpatialHadoop [2]; an ex-

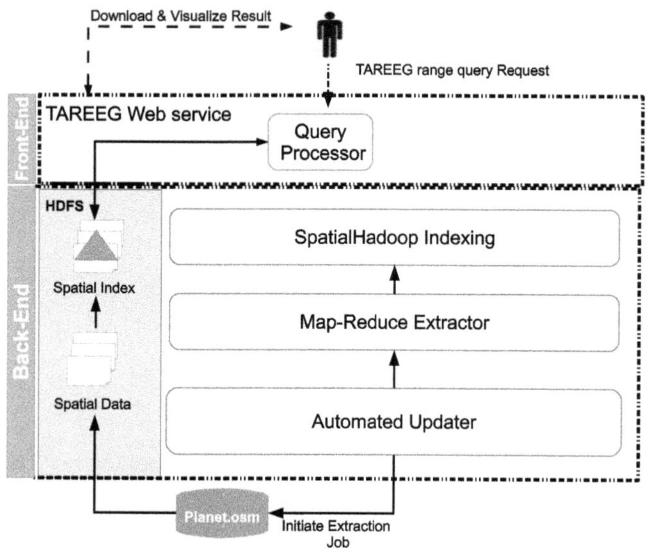

Figure 1: System Overview

tended MapReduce framework that deals efficiently with spatial data. In terms of data extraction and indexing, TAREEG takes advantage of SpatialHadoop and its distributed nature in the following: (1) each machine independently downloads part of the Planet.osm file that needs to be processed on that machine, decompress and process it on the fly. (2) TAREEG employs a special *file splitter* and *record reader* components that are capable of efficiently parsing the whole file and extracting its data in a distributed manner, and (3) TAREEG uses the indexing capabilities of SpatialHadoop to build efficient spatial indices for extracted data which allows user queries to run instantly on very large datasets. As a result, downloading and indexing the whole OpenStreetMap with all its spatial features takes few hours instead of few days. Then, querying this data takes few seconds instead of hours. The idea is that SpatialHadoop partitions this data over computing nodes using a spatial partitioning scheme, where spatially close by features are stored in the same file block.

2. SYSTEM OVERVIEW

Figure 1 gives the system overview of TAREEG. A map-reduce framework is used to handle a large scale dataset. A user interacts with TAREEG via its front-end that includes a web interface allowing users to submit their requests of any arbitrary region on the world map. Users may also visualize the extracted information via TAREEG front-end. Internally, TAREEG processes user requests by fetching the spatial information from spatial indexed files. TAREEG system back-end processes user requests through several processing stages: (1) Extraction stage, which is responsible for categorizing the contents of *Planet.osm* into bunch of homogeneous information stored separately, (2) Indexing stage, which is responsible for building spatial indexes on the extracted data, and (3) Querying stage, which is responsible on querying the indexed data.

As OpenStreetMap is updated on a daily or weekly basis, TAREEG employs an automatic updater module that is responsible for downloading the latest *Planet.osm* file and trigger the extraction and indexing stages. Automated module runs automatically daily once a new dataset is updated.

3. DATA EXTRACTION

Extracting information from OpenStreetMap is not a trivial task. OpenStreetMap dataset stores all data types sequentially in one large volume file in a semi-structured XML format. The XML file starts with nodes, then ways, and finally, relations. Tags are nested in each of these data types. The challenge of extracting information from Open StreetMap depends on identifying the annotation (i.e., tags) that imply categorized spatial data. We basically run a map-reduce job which takes the URL of the compressed Planet.osm file as an input. The output of data extraction will be several categorized files. Each file contains a homogeneous spatial information, e.g., road network data will be stored in one file and lakes in another one. In this phase, we implement a map-reduce program to extract information from the large scale OpenStreetMap data. We retrieve the URL of the latest version of *Planet.osm* and trigger a map-reduce job with the following three main components, namely splitter, Record Reader, and Mapper, described briefly below:

- **Splitter**: The *splitter* component breaks the input *Planet.osm* file into chunks of 64 MB (the default block size in HDFS). Since the file is compressed in *block zip* format, it is possible that each chunk is downloaded and decompressed separately to extract part of the XML file. Such splitting will cause inconsistent XML structures in each split which is handled later by the *Record Reader*. Thus, splitting the *Planet.osm* will parallelize and distribute the processing load into several map tasks, which is much faster than processing on a single node machine.

- **Record Reader**: Basically, default record reader in Hadoop processes text files line-by-line, so we can not process the data of *Planet.osm* inline. Due to the inconsistent representation of each split, we implemented an XML element reader instead of the default line reader provided by Hadoop framework. The output of this component is an XML *element* which will be sent later to the mapper. In addition, record reader is responsible for completing inconsistent elements in each split. To elaborate more, if a split has some missing information about one concise type such as *buildings*, the record reader will fetch these missing information from the next split. Then the element(s) are passed to the mapper.

- **Mapper**: This component receives *elements* sent by the Record Reader and classifies each element based on its annotation (i.e., tags), and then writes the result into separate files, based on the type of the extracted data, to HDFS, i.e., all road networks are written in one file, while lakes are written in another file, and so on. These data are stored randomly as a set of nodes N, which consists of $N = \{node\_id, longitude, latitude, tags\}$ and another set of extracted data R that consists of $R = \{edge\_id, node1\_id, node2\_id, tags\}$. R described as any type of geographical data, such as road network, lakes, buildings, or zip code, state, and national boundaries.

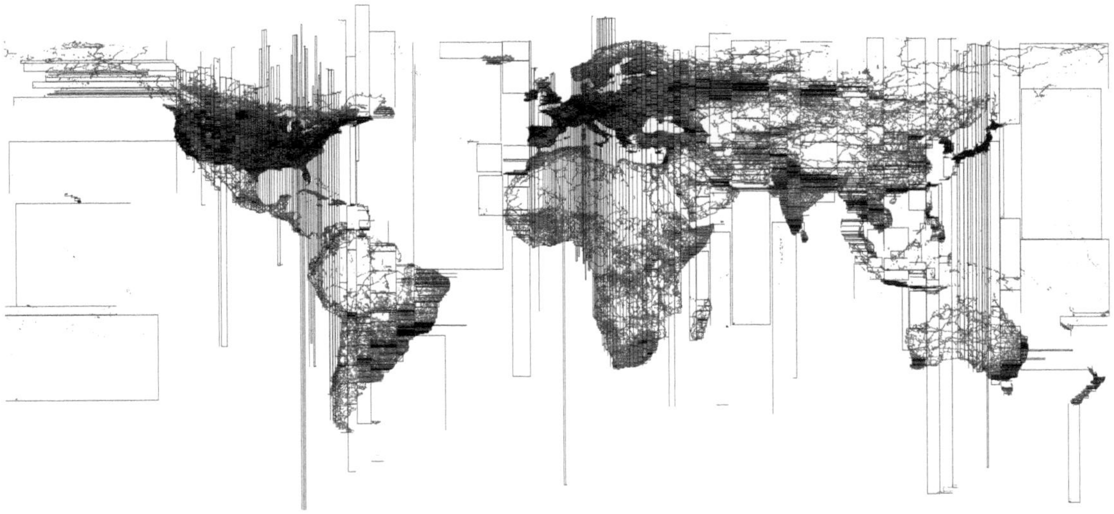

Figure 2: Spatial Data Partitioned

We use Pig [1] to combine the extracted data R with its spatial information (i.e., geolocation) from nodes N in a way similar to the join operation in any relational database. The output of the Pig program is a spatial set R' that consists of $R' = \{edge\_id, node1\_id, longitude1, latitude1, node2\_id, longitude2, latitude2, tags\}$. Each record $r' \in R'$ is now associated with the corresponding geo-location and neither sparsely nor spatially stored in HDFS.

4. INDEXING

Files generated by the extractor are heap files which are not organized in a specific order. This means that a range query executed to extract data in a specific region would have to scan the whole file to retrieve the result. This will considerably slow down the system, especially for larger datasets such as road network which has a total size of 130 GB. To speed up the processing of extracted datasets, we need to build spatial indexes for each dataset that efficiently supports range queries. One method to index datasets is to store each one as a relation in a spatial DBMS (e.g., PostGIS), and build a spatial index such as an R-tree on that relation. Once the relation is indexed, range queries can be expressed in SQL and executed efficiently inside the spatial DBMS. Unfortunately, this technique rendered infeasible due to the long time consumed to build the indexes.

To be able to construct the indexes efficiently in a timely manner, we use SpatialHadoop [2] to take advantage of its spatial indexing techniques. SpatialHadoop supports different types of spatial indexes including Grid file, R-tree, and R+-tree. Once datasets are extracted from the *Planet.osm* file, we use the SpatialHadoop '`index`' command on each file separately to build an index for it. The partition size is set to 64 MB (default for Hadoop). Each index is stored as one *master* file that stores the boundaries of each partition, and multiple data files with each file containing line segments overlapping with one partition.

Figure 2 gives the main reason behind the efficiency of spatial data indexing and querying in TAREEG. The figure shows an R+-tree partitioning scheme for the whole road network file. All road networks are depicted in blue lines, while the black rectangles in indicate partition boundaries. While some road segments cross multiple partitions, partition boundaries remain disjoint due to the properties of the R+-tree. As each partition is sufficient for only 64 MB worth of data, we can see that dense areas (e.g., Europe) are contained in very small partitions, while sparse areas (e.g., oceans) are contained in very large partitions. One way to look at this figure is that this is the way that SpatialHadoop divides a dataset of 455 GB into small chunks, each of 64 MB. Recall that in Hadoop, this 455 GB file will be divided into chunks of 64 MB as sequential heap file, which definitely does not fit spatial operations.

5. QUERY PROCESSING

Queries sent to TAREEG are basically range queries that request extracting a certain type of spatial data (e.g., road networks, lakes, buildings, borders) within a certain area of interest, presented as a rectangular area. When a range query is sent to TAREEG, it first executes that query on the master file to retrieve partitions that overlap the range query. For each matching partition, the records in the corresponding data file are compared to the query range and all matching records are stored as part of the answer. Since in R+-tree some records overlapping multiple partitions are replicated, a post processing duplicate avoidance step is executed to ensure the correctness of the answer as described in [2].

6. DEMONSTRATION SCENARIO

Conference audience can interact with TAREEG through two main functionalities: (1) *Data extraction request*, where audience can submit extraction requests through nicely designed web interface, by selecting any arbitrary region of world map and the type of spatial data they want to extract. (2) *Spatial data download and visualization*, where audience can download and visualize exported data on either OpenStreetMap, Google Maps, Google Hybrid Maps (i.e., hybrid satellite images with labels), and Esri Maps (i.e National Geographic map). A first version of TAREEG is currently accessible online at: `http://www.tareeg.org`

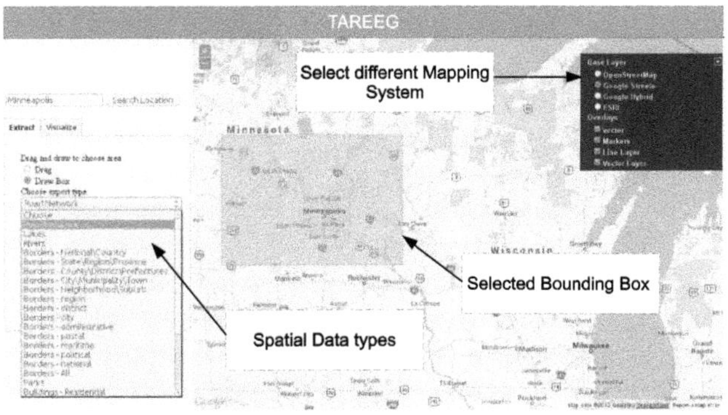

Figure 3: TAREEG Web Interface

6.1 Spatial Data Extraction Request

Initially, audience interact with TAREEG system by requesting different spatial data type as shown in Figure 3, following few steps: (1) the user selects any arbitrary region from the world map, either by zooming and draging the map to the geographical area of interest, or by searching the area of interest using the search bar, (2) the user specifies a boundary rectangle of the selected region, (3) the user provides an email address, in which TAREEG will send an email when the request is satisfied with links to download the requested data, and (4) the user submits the request by hitting the 'Extract button'.

Once a request is received, TAREEG processes this request by querying the requested spatial data from the back-end of the system, and notifies the requester through email once the data is available. It is important to note here that all requests to TAREEG are satisfied from its own local data, as there is no need to contact OpenStreetMap servers, and hence requests are usually satisfied within a few seconds. Once the requested data is available, the user will receive an email from TAREEG with hyperlinks to download the requested data. The time of processing the request depends on the size of the selected region and complexity of the requested dataset.

6.2 Spatial Data Download & Visualization

TAREEG users receive their extracted data in three common standard formats, a Comma Separated Values (CSV) files, Google Keyhole Markup Language (KML), and Esri geospatial vector (shapefile) formats . TAREEG only supports visualizing (CSV) format, where KML and shapefile can be already visualized through various applications (e.g QGIS, Google Earth). The CSV format has the following structure:

```
Node < Node_id , Latitude , Longitude >
Edge <Edge_id , Start_Node_id ,  End_Node_id ,  [Tags] >
```

Figures 4 and 5 give two examples of the visualization tool of TAREEG, where an extracted set of lakes and road networks are visualized, respectively. TAREEG visualizer shows the spatial data on the map by uploading the CSV files, that were sent to the user as hyperlinks in an email. TAREEG visualizer supports four different mapping engines, where audience can experience the easiness of switching the gear between these mapping engines.

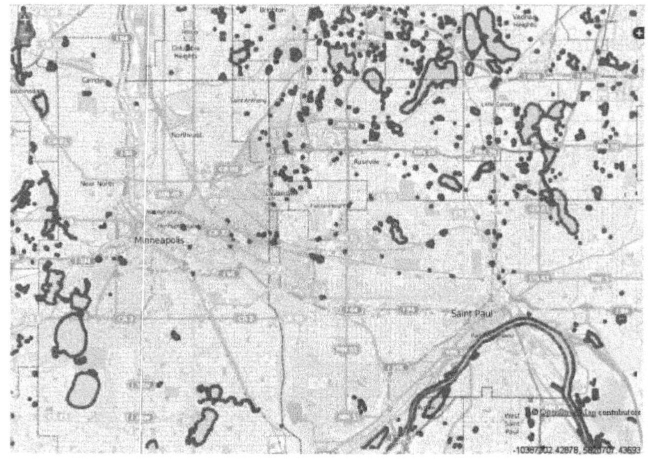

Figure 4: Extracted lakes

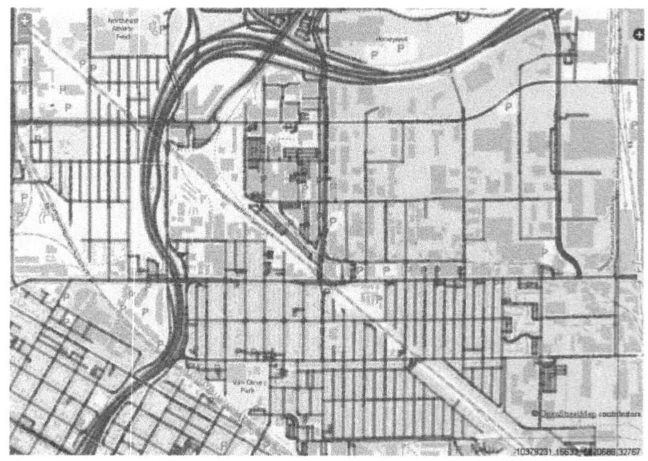

Figure 5: Extracted Road Networks

7. REFERENCES

[1] Apache. Pig http://pig.apache.org/, June 2013.

[2] A. Eldawy and M. F. Mokbel. A demonstration of spatialhadoop: An efficient mapreduce framework for spatial data. *PVLDB*, 2013.

[3] geofabrik. http://download.geofabrik.de/, Dec. 2013.

[4] S. Luo, Y. Luo, S. Zhou, G. Cong, and J. Guan. DISKs: a system for distributed spatial group keyword search on road networks. 5(12):1966–1969, 2012.

[5] P. Mooney and P. Corcoran. Characteristics of heavily edited objects in openstreetmap. *Future Internet*, 2012.

[6] OSM. http://www.openstreetmap.org, Dec. 2013.

[7] osm2pgsql. Benchmarks jun 2012 http://wiki.openstreetmap.org/wiki/Osm2pgsql/benchmarks.

[8] Osmosis. 2013 http://wiki.openstreetmap.org/wiki/Osmosis.

[9] J. R. Thomsen, M. L. Yiu, and C. S. Jensen. Effective caching of shortest paths for location-based services. SIGMOD, 2012.

[10] A. D. Zhu, H. Ma, X. Xiao, S. Luo, Y. Tang, and S. Zhou. Shortest path and distance queries on road networks: towards bridging theory and practice. SIGMOD, 2013.

Searching with XQ: the eXemplar Query Search Engine

Davide Mottin
University of Trento
Trento, Italy
mottin@disi.unitn.eu

Matteo Lissandrini
University of Trento
Trento, Italy
ml@disi.unitn.eu

Yannis Velegrakis
University of Trento
Trento, Italy
velgias@disi.unitn.eu

Themis Palpanas
Paris Descartes University
Paris, France
themis@mi.parisdescartes.fr

ABSTRACT

We demonstrate *XQ*, a query engine that implements a novel technique for searching relevant information on the web and in various data sources, called *Exemplar Queries*. While the traditional query model expects the user to provide a set of specifications that the elements of interest need to satisfy, XQ expects the user to provide only an element of interest and we infer the desired answer set based on that element. Through the various examples we demonstrate the functionality of the system and its applicability in various cases. At the same time, we highlight the technical challenges for this type of query answering and illustrate the implementation approach we have materialized. The demo is intended for both researchers and practitioners and aims at illustrating the benefits of the adoption of this new form of query answering in practical applications and the further study and advancement of its technical solutions.

Categories and Subject Descriptors

H.3.3 [**Information Storage and Retrieval**]: Information Search and Retrieval—*Query formulation*

Keywords

Query paradigms; Exemplar queries; Labeled graphs

1. INTRODUCTION

Highly structured query languages are typically used by expert users that know well what they are looking for and how to express it using the constructs of the query language. Nowadays, a large number of users are technically novice or have no clear idea of the item they are looking for, thus, they are producing simple, vague, and most of the time, ambiguous queries. This has led into a large amount of work on trying to discover what the user had in mind when formulating the query. Techniques such as interactive query relaxation [6], semantic enhancement, or related queries using log-analysis [7], are only some examples among the many.

We demonstrate here a novel query technique we have recently introduced [5], in which the user knows an element among those expected to be in the desired result set, but cannot provide a set of specifications that actually describe all the elements in that desired set. In other words, the user "query" works as an example of what the user is looking for. We call this novel query paradigm *exemplar queries* to emphasize its different nature from those mentioned previously and the new evaluation methods it requires.

Although the idea of exemplar queries looks very similar to the well-known notion of query by example (QBE), it is fundamentally different. In QBE, the user query is used simply to communicate to the query evaluation engine the conditions that the elements in the result set should satisfy. In some sense, QBE works like a wild-card query, and is simply a more user-friendly method to describe the query conditions. In an exemplar query, on the other hand, the information provided by the user is a sample from the desired set, which means that the conditions characterizing all the elements in the desired answer may not even be explicitly stated in the user query.

Exemplar queries may attract considerable attention from many different types of end users. They are particularly suitable for users that need to investigate a topic in a field in which they have none or limited experience, which means that they do not know the terminology to formulate the right search queries, but instead they know of a specific instance (sample) of what they are looking for. For example, a student asked to investigate a new topic may be given a paper on that topic as a starting point. The challenge is that many aspects of the topic may not be explicitly stated in the provided paper, thus, they have somehow to be inferred. A different example is the one of a lawyer or a reporter that may have a specific case in their hands and are looking to find other similar cases.

Exemplar queries may also attract considerable attention from the search engine community since they can significantly advance the field with novel functionalities.

In particular, in parallel to the query evaluation that a search engine performs, the user query can also be seen as an exemplar query and be evaluated as such. The results of this evaluation can be appended to the results the search engine generates, increasing the probability to capture the user's intent. For instance, a query on the World War II will typically return documents related to this war. Evaluating

SIGMOD'14, June 22–27, 2014, Snowbird, UT, USA.

http://dx.doi.org/10.1145/2588555.2594529.

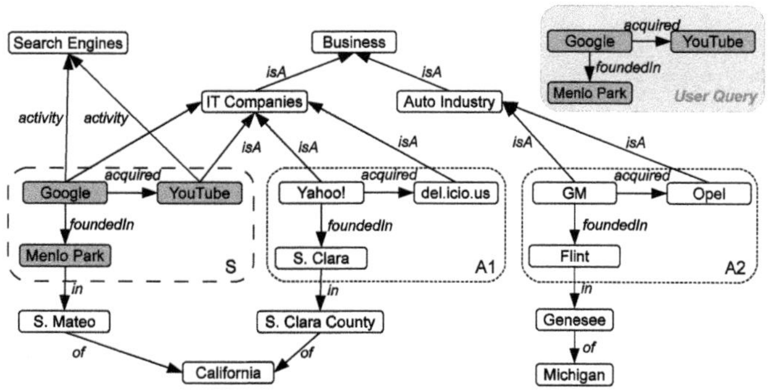

Figure 1: Exemplar Query Example

the query as an exemplar query will result to many other big wars in history. Exemplar queries can also be used to enhance the "related information" sections that existing search engines are currently offering, like for instance, the related entities or the queries other users have also searched that Google provides on the side bar. In the query about World War II, for example, the side bar may contain also link on information about World War I, or the Roman Empire wars.

This demonstration is about XQ, a system that implements this new search paradigm of exemplar queries, and can complement to existing search engines and significantly enrich the current user experience.

2. RUNNING EXAMPLE

The demonstration will not be around a single running example, but the participants will have the opportunity to try many different searches, either proposed by the demonstrators or by the participants themselves. The principal running example illustrating the functionality of the system, however, and the one that will be first presented is the one of the exemplar query of *Google* and *YouTube*. Consider the case of a university student who has been given an assignment to perform a study on company acquisitions in California. The student is not really an expert in the field, and not familiar with the related terminology. Writing a query with the terms "acquisitions" and "California" will in the best case return documents talking about the topic of acquisitions, that are also mentioning California. An article on the takeover of *del.icio.us* by *Yahoo!* may not be returned if the actual words of acquisition and California are not explicitly mentioned in the text. The student knows that a good case of the type of acquisition she is looking for is the one of *YouTube* by *Google*. Thus, she issues the query: *"Google founded in Menlo Park acquired YouTube"*. The search engine typically responds with results related to *Google*, *Menlo Park*, and *YouTube*, but will not return anything related to an acquisition of *del.icio.us* by *Yahoo!*. The same query without the geographic specification place is still valid, but any further specification in the example is useful to restrict the search space. If there is a significant number of users that have performed similar searches in the past, an analysis of the query logs may reveal that information and the search engine may be able to propose, in the related searches section, queries on *Yahoo!* and *del.icio.us*. (A simple test in existing search engines reveals that this is not actually happening.) Relaxing one or more of the query conditions does not help in a significant way, since the results are still focused around the *Google* case. Nevertheless, XQ is able to perform the right reasoning and return the *Yahoo!-del.icio.us* case.

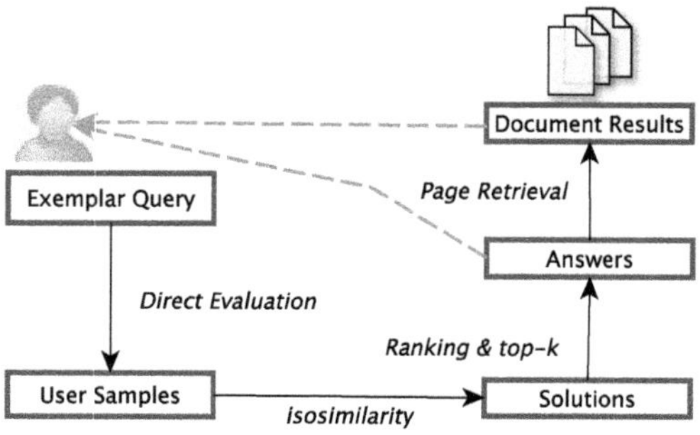

Figure 2: Exemplar Query Evaluation Steps

Consider now a second candidate answer for the user query: *Opel* that was acquired by *General Motors* (*GM*). Among the *Yahoo!-del.icio.us* and *GM-Opel*, it is more likely that the former is among the company acquisitions that the user is interested in, and not the latter. This is because even though *Yahoo!* was founded in a different city than *Google*, that city is still in California (just like *Google*), while the city that *GM* was founded is in Michigan. Furthermore, the example of *Google*-YouTube is about IT companies, and so are the *Yahoo!-del.icio.us*, while *GM-Opel* belong to the automotive industry. XQ is able to also discover and return *GM-Opel* as an answer to the exemplar query but will rank it lower than the one of *Yahoo!-del.icio.us*.

Figure 1 illustrates a portion of the data repository with the information described previously, the exemplar query (top left) and the relationships that lead to the inference of the respective exemplar query answers.

Given the case of *Google-YouTube*, our system is able to identify not only that both the cases of *Yahoo!-del.icio.us* and *GM-Opel* are related to the case of *Google-YouTube* but also that the former is more related to it than the latter.

3. TECHNICAL DESCRIPTION

Figure 2 illustrates the individual steps of an exemplar query evaluation task. It is assumed that data is modeled using a graph based data model in which an element of interest is represented as a node and its characteristic attributes as edges. The model is generic enough to capture data in many different application scenarios.

[Direct Evaluation] Given the user query, the first step is to identify in the data repository the structure to which the user is referring, i.e., those representing the example that the user already knows to be part of the desired result set. We refer to that structure as the *user sample*. The reason we consider that structure as the example and not what the user has actually provided in query expression is two-fold. The first is that what the user provides may be vague and imprecise since it is typically expressed in some user friendly language such as a set of keywords. The second is that in order to construct the exemplar query answers, we need to find similar elements to the element the user knows about (the one specified in the user query), but to do so we need to know as much information as possible about that element. Unfortunately, most of the time the user query contains only the information necessary to identify the required element and is not intended for providing a full description of the element. Thus, in order to obtain as much information as possible, there is a need to recognize it in the data repository and retrieve all the information that is available for it.

For this task there is already a large volume of literature on methods that can be used. In our system we are based on some semantic-based technique we have recently developed [1], but this is not the focus of our current demonstration, so we will not elaborate on it.

[IsoSimilarity] Once the user sample has been identified, we search in the database elements similar to it. Note that the previous step may generate more than one sample. If this happens, then the current step is repeated for each of the samples identified. Checking for similar elements is a challenging task due to the number of similarity checkings that need to be done, a solution that does not scale well.

To reduce the number of similarity searches that need to take place, XQ uses an intelligent pruning and similarity evaluation technique. The idea is to remove in advance nodes that are unlikely to be of interest to the user. The first intuition is that nodes in the graph that are located far from the user sample will be also semantically distant from the user's intention as expressed in the query. Conversely, the portion of the graph that is likely to contain relevant answers is called *Relevant Neighborhood*, and it is constructed from the subset of nodes with higher proximity, in terms of path length, to the nodes of the user sample. For this reason XQ uses a principled way of measuring the relative distance and for pruning the graph, which builds upon the well known concept of the Personalized PageRank (PPV) [2]. In XQ, user preferences are expressed through the nodes and edges in the exemplar query. Hence, the XQ algorithm does not treat all edges equally as it happens for links between webpages, instead it adapts to the various edges and their labels, and assign weights proportional to the amount of information carried by each edge compared to other edges. Thus the main difference between the original PPV model and the one XQ uses, i.e., the Adaptive Personalized PageRank Vector (APPV), lays on the fact that we build the adjacency matrix $\boldsymbol{A}$ of the database D in order to take into account also the different importance of the edges. The APPV $\boldsymbol{v}$ is then defined as for the PPV and is computed over the weighted matrix $\boldsymbol{A}$ with: $\boldsymbol{v} = (1-c)\boldsymbol{A}\boldsymbol{v} + c\boldsymbol{p}$. In the computation of the vector $\boldsymbol{v}$, $\boldsymbol{p}$ is the vector that represents the starting probability in the PPV algorithm and which is conveniently biased towards the nodes in the user sample. In order to obtain higher performance XQ approximates the computation of the APPV vector by implementing an iterative function that does not need to traverse the entire graph but guesses the value of the PageRank using an approach similar to the *weighted particle filtering procedure* proposed in [4]. The final values contained in the APPV vector $\boldsymbol{v}$ represent an estimate of the distances of the nodes in the graph from the subset of nodes in the user sample. The distance values in $\boldsymbol{v}$ are then seen as a *relevance* measure, and we keep those nodes with a value higher than a threshold.

For similarity, XQ uses a method based on graph isomorphism on edge labels. Sub-graph isomorphism is known to be an NP-complete problem. To improve the performance, XQ uses an effective way to prune the search space even further than what was pruned by the relevance measure, and restricts the list of database nodes that have to be matched to the nodes of the user sample in order to find isomorphic structures. For this, it uses an efficient technique for comparing nodes, and an algorithm for effectively rejecting pairs of nodes that are bound to not participate in any isomorphic mapping. For each node we store a signature precomputing the set of edge-labels of the edges at a fixed distance from the node. The verification process matches the query node signatures with each node signature in the Relevant Neighborhood and prunes the non-matching nodes. The effectiveness of the method is further improved by exploiting the concept of simulation, which is a computationally tractable notion of graph matching. Although this technique may lead to false positives, the schema is effective and reduces further the search space and time. The false positives are subsequently removed by running the traditional isomorphic verification algorithm on them. A more detailed description of this step can be found in the conference version of this work [5].

[Ranking] Once the set of solutions of the user samples have been computed, they need to be ranked according to the likelihood that they are of interest to the user. Finding the right ranking function requires taking into consideration the various factors that may affect such a list. We claim that such a decision depends on two main parameters: the structural similarity and the importance of the label structures. For the first, we have adopted a metric that is based on a vectorial representation of nodes using its neighborhood [3] extended to capture the differences among nodes that emerge when taking into account the edge-labels of the neighbors. For the second, XQ uses the Personalized Page Rank (computed in the previous step) that among others embeds the distance information in that score to take into consideration the distance of a node from the user sample. As the final ranking score we take the linear combination

$$\rho(n_s, n) = \lambda \mathcal{S}(n_s, n) + (1-\lambda)\boldsymbol{p}[n]. \tag{1}$$

where $\boldsymbol{p}[n]$ is the APPV score and $\mathcal{S}(n_s, n)$ is the structural similarity. λ is a diversification parameter that depends on the user and on the data. A value close to 1 favors results similar to the neighbor nodes of the user sample, while a value close to 0 favors solutions close to the sample.

[Page Retrieval] The ranked solutions are elements in the data repository that are related to the user sample. They can be used as already mentioned in the side bar of existing search engines to provide other related information to the user query. For instance, they can form a section (or enhance an existing one) on related queries, or related entities. However, it may be of interest to actually retrieve pages about these elements and merge them into the existing search results of a traditional search engine. For this, an optional step is the one of page creation that retrieves pages from a search engine related to each of the solutions generated in the previous step.

4. SYSTEM DESCRIPTION

The interface of the XQ System looks similar to the interface of known search engines, with the typical search field and the list of results below it (see Figure 3). However, the results are fundamentally different than those search engines typically provide since it implements the exemplar query evaluation task of Figure 2. Apart from the system functionality that can be observed on this main page, the system offers the interested researcher the opportunity to dig into the individual steps and observe the results. For instance, given an exemplar query and the generated result answer, the option "Samples" at the top leads the user into a different panel that illustrates the samples that have been found

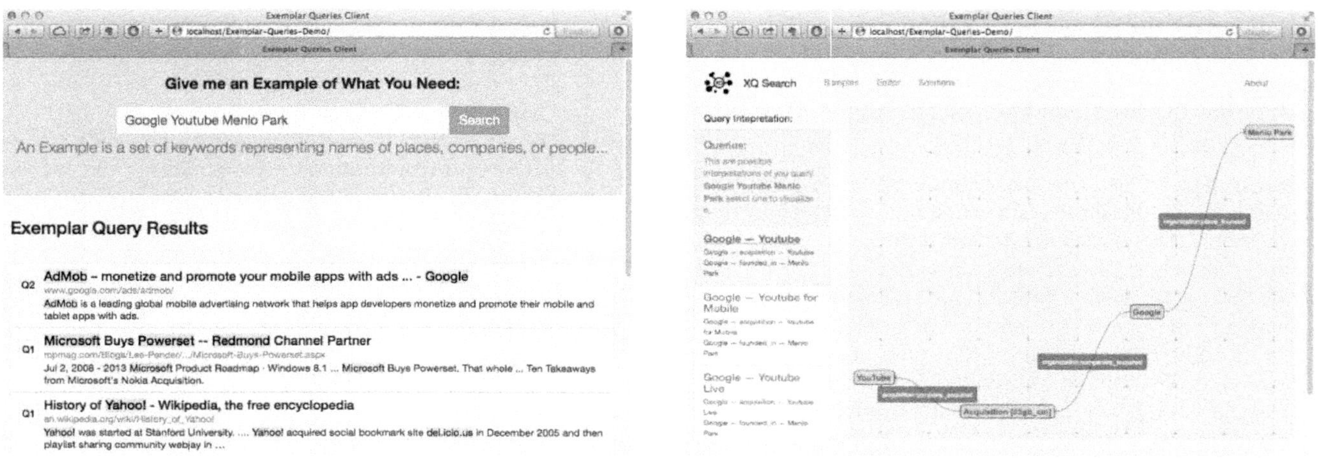

Figure 3: The XQ System Interface: The main panel (left) and the sample panel (right).

for the provided exemplar query. This panel is illustrated on the right-hand side of Figure 3. The left part of this panel is the list of the found samples and by clicking on one of them, the canvas part illustrates its properties and neighbors in the data repository. This can help in understanding why a structure in the repository is considered as a sample.

Selecting a sample from the list and then the option "Solutions" from the top menu-bar, the user can observe all the solutions that the system has generated for the selected sample, i.e., the structures that are considered related to the sample. The list of solutions is ranked according to the believed relevance to the sample. Clicking a solution in the list displays in the canvas its structure, so that a participant can understand why a specific solution has been selected.

Retrieving documents related to each of these solutions generates the set of documents returned as an answer to the exemplar query and are shown on the main page (Figure 3 left-hand side) under the search text field.

5. DEMONSTRATION SCENARIO

The demo will start with a very brief introduction on the idea of exemplar queries followed by a series of exemplar query executions and the explanation of the retrieved results. This will be done mainly on the main screen of the XQ Engine. The first exemplar queries to be executed will be proposed by the demonstrators (with the very first being the one described in Section 2) and will be particular queries that will help the audience in quickly and fully understanding the notion of exemplar queries. Then, the audience will have the opportunity to try their own queries and evaluate the quality of the retrieved results.

As a dataset for the demonstration, we will be using freebase, which is a knowledge base modeled as an RDF graph containing around 53 million nodes and 213 million edges. All the queries tried during the demonstration will be executed at real-time, with no pre-computed results used.

For every query executed in our system, we will be able to show the computation that has taken place in each of the processing steps of the exemplar query evaluation algorithm. This will be done through the panels "Samples" and "Solutions" described in the previous section.

Statistics about execution time and data characteristics will also be available to the demonstration audience to show the challenging performance issues ands solutions. The participant will be able to change the λ parameter of the ranking function and observe the behavior of the algorithms.

In a separate window, we will also send the user queries to be executed by one or more search engines (either semantic or traditional), and look at the results they return alongside other complementary information they provide such as related searches or related entities. We will compare this cumulative information to the results that our system returns as an answer to the exemplar queries, and highlight the differences between the two approaches.

[Demonstration Goals] The main goal of the demonstration is to introduce the SIGMOD community to this new form of query answering and highlight its benefits. Through the executed queries the participant will realize the opportunities that this new form of query answering has to offer.

Furthermore, through the direct comparison with existing search engines, it will be shown how hard, or even impossible, is to obtain these results using existing technologies.

At the same time, the current demonstration has a highly educational goal. It aims at raising awareness of the technical challenges that this form of query answering brings on the table, how they have been solved in the current version of the system, initiate interesting discussions and exchange of ideas, and, hopefully, stimulate a number of researchers on working on the topic.

6. REFERENCES

[1] S. Bergamaschi, E. Domnori, F. Guerra, R. Trillo Lado, and Y. Velegrakis. Keyword search over relational databases: a metadata approach. In *SIGMOD*, pages 565–576, 2011.

[2] G. Jeh and J. Widom. Scaling personalized web search. In *WWW*, pages 271–279, 2003.

[3] A. Khan, N. Li, X. Yan, Z. Guan, S. Chakraborty, and S. Tao. Neighborhood based fast graph search in large networks. In *SIGMOD*, pages 901–912, 2011.

[4] N. Lao and W. W. Cohen. Fast query execution for retrieval models based on path-constrained random walks. In *KDD*, pages 881–888, 2010.

[5] D. Mottin, M. Lissandrini, Y. Velegrakis, and T. Palpanas. Exemplar queries: Give me an example of what you need. *PVLDB*, 7(5), 2014.

[6] D. Mottin, A. Marascu, S. B. Roy, G. Das, T. Palpanas, and Y. Velegrakis. A probabilistic optimization framework for the empty-answer problem. *PVLDB*, 6(14):1762–1773, 2013.

[7] D. Mottin, T. Palpanas, and Y. Velegrakis. Entity Ranking Using Click-Log Information. *IDA Journal*, 17(5):837–856, 2013.

MeanKS: Meaningful Keyword Search in Relational Databases with Complex Schema

Mehdi Kargar[1], Aijun An[1], Nick Cercone[1], Parke Godfrey[1], Jaroslaw Szlichta[*2] and Xiaohui Yu[1]
[1] Department of Computer Science and Engineering, York University
{kargar,aan,nick,godfrey,}@cse.yorku.ca and xhyu@yorku.ca
[2] University of Ontario Institute of Technology
jaroslaw.szlichta@uoit.ca

ABSTRACT

Keyword search in relational databases was introduced in the last decade to assist users who are not familiar with a query language, the schema of the database, or the content of the data. An answer is a join tree of tuples that contains the query keywords. When searching a database with a complex schema, there are potentially many answers to the query. Therefore, ranking answers based on their relevance is crucial in this context. Prior work has addressed relevance based on the size of the answer or the IR scores of the tuples. However, this is not sufficient when searching a complex schema.

We demonstrate MeanKS, a new system for meaningful keyword search over relational databases. The system first captures the user's interest by determining the roles of the keywords. Then, it uses schema-based ranking to rank join trees that cover the keyword roles. This uses the relevance of relations and foreign-key relationships in the schema over the information content of the database. In the demonstration, attendees can execute queries against the TPC-E warehouse and compare the proposed measures against a gold standard derived from a real workload over TPC-E to test the effectiveness of our methods.

1. INTRODUCTION

Keyword search, a well known mechanism for retrieving relevant documents in information retrieval, has recently been used for extracting information from relational databases. Users usually do not have sufficient knowledge about the structure of data nor query languages such as SQL [2, 3]. Keyword search over databases can bridge this gap. An answer to the query is a set of tuples from the database that *cover* the keywords of the query, and a natural *structure* —a tree from the database's schema— that spans those tuples. Previous work restricts answers over *minimal* trees [2, 1], meaning there is no answer over a sub-tree of the tree in question. However, there is another aspect of an answer: relevance to the query. By restricting answers to a minimal structure, some relevant answers may be missed.

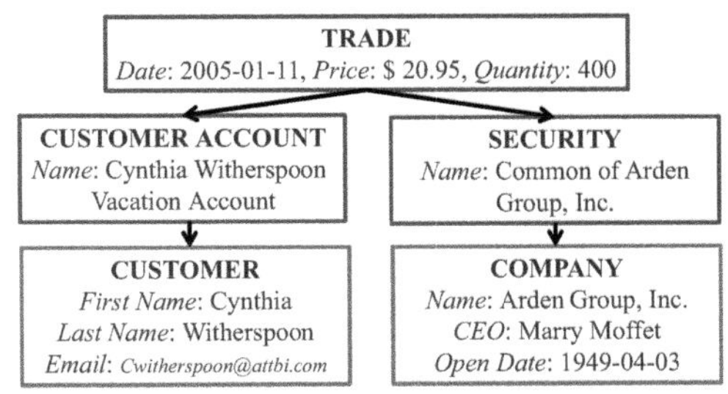

Figure 1: A non-minimal answer by DISCOVER [2].

Consider the keyword query *"Cynthia Arden"* over the TPC-E[1] schema. The TPC-E benchmark simulates the *online transaction processing* (OLTP) workload of a brokerage firm.[2] The keywords *Cynthia* and *Arden* may appear in different relations. Each could refer to the name of a *customer*, *broker*, *company*, CEO of a *company*, or be in the title of a *news item*. Of course, each of these different relations for *Cynthia* and for *Arden* potentially lead to rather different answers. For example, Figure 1 shows an answer for the keyword query *"Cynthia Arden"* on TPC-E, which says that a customer *Cynthia* buys the stocks of a company named *Arden Group*. This is an interesting and relevant relationship between *Cynthia* and *Arden* assuming, the user wants to find out the relationship between customer *Cynthia* and company *Arden Group*. However, such an answer would be missed if we restrict the answer to be structurally minimal while covering all the query keywords (This happens in the previous works such as DISCOVER [2].) This is because *Cythia* also appears in an intermediate node of the tree and thus the *customer* node is pruned. This also arises for *Arden*.

Another issue in keyword search is to score answers for *relevance*. The relevance of an answer depends on many factors: the tuples in the answer and how the keywords appear in them; the bridging tuples that do not contain keywords; and the join tree. How to measure the value of each of these is open to question. Prior work has addressed relevance. In [2], a simplistic solution of scoring relevance as the reciprocal of the number of edges in an answer's tree was proposed. This heuristic assumes that fewer joins involved mean the tuples are related more closely. This approach might work for a small and simple schema, but it fails to return relevant

*Szlichta is also a Fellow at IBM Centre for Advanced Studies in Toronto.

[1] http://www.tpc.org/tpce/

[2] The TPC-E has a reasonably complex schema and contains 33 tables.

SIGMOD'14, June 22–27, 2014, Snowbird, UT, USA.

http://dx.doi.org/10.1145/2588555.2594533.

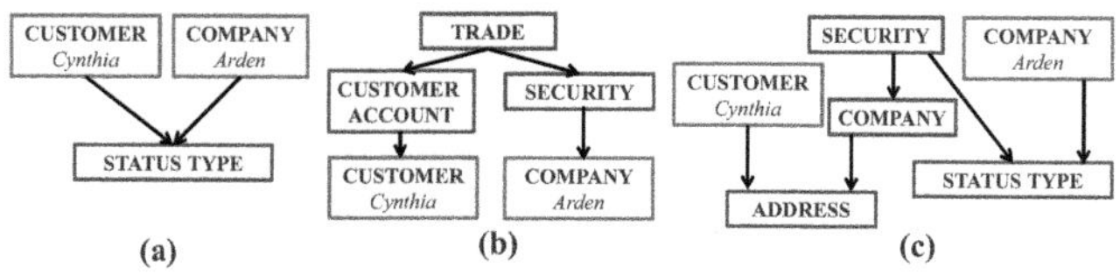

Figure 2: Three possible trees (i.e., MJNSs) for the query *"Arden:company Cynthia:customer"*.

answers when the schema is large and complex. Consider the query {*Arden Cynthia*} over the TPC-E schema. Also, assume that *Arden* refers to a company name and *Cynthia* refers to a customer name. Figure 2 shows three possible join trees of different sizes that could produce answers that connect the company *Arden* and the customer *Cynthia*.

If we rank the trees according to their size (i.e., the number of edges or nodes), the first tree (a) which connects a customer and a company when they have the same status gets the highest rank. However, based on the TPC-E schema description, this is not a strong relationship; *status type* is a dimension table which is connected to six tables in the schema and stores the status value for other entities (such as companies, customers and trades). An answer derived from this tree would say that both *Arden* and *Cynthia* are *active*. Looking at the *customer* and a *company* tables in TPC-E, it turns out that all the customers and companies have the *Active* status. Therefore, any given customer and any given company in the TPC-E database share the same status through the *status type* table. Thus, the first found relationship (a) between *Arden* and *Cynthia* is, in fact, not that interesting or relevant. The second tree (b) states that company *Arden*'s stock is traded by customer *Cynthia*. This is one of the strongest relations between a customer and a company and is related to the purpose of the TPC-E schema. In addition, it usually produces few results since trading the stocks of one specific company by one specific customer is not common. The third tree (c) is the largest and therefore it is not straightforward to interpret. This tree states that the company *Arden* has the same status as a security which is related to a company that has the same address as customer *Cynthia*. Two relations, *address* and *status type*, that are involved in this tree makes it less meaningful and more difficult to interpret for the user.

In [1], the authors take a different tact: they apply information retrieval (IR) measures to the answers to determine an individual measure per answer. We believe that for keyword search in relational databases, the relevance of the tree from which answers derive is paramount. We hypothesize that relevance as measured by adapted IR techniques is much less effective. For example, for the trees in Figure 2, assume that the IR scores of the tuples that contain keywords are the same.[3] Applying the ranking technique of [1], the first tree (a) gets the highest score since it is the smallest one. As we discuss previously, this is not a relevant answer for the given query. In our system, IR scores are used as a secondary sorting key to rank the final answers with the same schema ranking (See Section 3.2 for more details.)

In this demonstration, we showcase a new system for keyword search in relational databases (MeanKS)[4]. The unique features of our system are as follows.

[3]This happens when *Cynthia* is the first name of a customer and the related column contains only "*Cynthia*"

[4]Demo available at http://graph.cse.yorku.ca:8080/meanks

1. The system identifies the database entities that are potentially interesting to the user based on the query keywords the user provides, and allows the user to specify their interests through a user interface.
2. The system returns the top minimal connected tuples that not only contain the query keywords but also cover the user interests (referred to as keyword roles in our system).
3. The system uses schema-based ranking that ranks the answers based on the minimal join trees that cover the keyword roles.
4. The system provides alternative relevance measures for join trees, which consider the importance of nodes, edges or combinations of them.

2. PROBLEM STATEMENT

A relational database schema consists of a set of n relation schemas, denoted as $\{R_1, R_2, \ldots, R_n\}$, where each R_i is described by a set of attributes. Two relation schemas, R_i and R_j, may be related by a *foreign key relationship*, denoted as $R_i \leftarrow R_j$, where the primary key of R_i is referenced by a foreign key of R_j. Thus, a relational database schema can be considered as a graph $G = \langle V, E \rangle$ where nodes are relation schemas and edges represent the foreign key relationships. A relational database is an instance of a relational database schema G. It consists of a set of relations, where each relation $r(R_i)$ is a set of tuples conforming to the relation schema R_i in G. Given a relational database D and a set of l (≥ 2) keywords ($Q = \{k_1, k_2, \ldots, k_l\}$), the problem of keyword search over D is to find a set of tuples that are connected via foreign key relationships and cover all the keywords in Q.

In our framework, the role of a query keyword is identified first. For each query keyword, we first find the list of columns (and relations) that contain the keyword using an inverted index or the built-in support for full-text keyword search in the RDBMS of choice, and then a relation is chosen through interaction with the user from a list as the ***role of the keyword***. With specified keyword roles, our algorithm searches for answers that are defined as follows.

DEFINITION 1. ***Minimal Joining Network of Tuples Covering Roles***. *Given a database D with schema graph G and a query Q containing a set of keywords $\{k_1, k_2, \ldots, k_l\}$ and their respective roles $\{r_1, r_2, \ldots, r_l\}$ (where r_i's are relations in D), a minimal joining network of tuples for query Q is a tree T of tuples that satisfy the following conditions:*

1) Joinable. *For each edge (t_i, t_j) in T, where $t_i \in r(R_i)$ and $t_j \in r(R_j)$, there is an edge $R_i \leftarrow R_j$ or $R_i \rightarrow R_j$ in G and $t_i \bowtie t_j \in r(R_i) \bowtie r(R_j)$.*

2) Role and keyword covering. *For each query keyword role r_i, there exists a node t_j in T such that $t_j \in r_i$ and t_j contains keyword k_i.*

3) Minimal. *If a tuple in T is removed, T is either not joinable or does not cover all the roles or all the keywords.*

For brevity, we refer to the answer defined in Definition 1 as a ***final answer***. A final answer covering roles *customer* and *company* is shown in Figure 1. Given a database, there may be many final answers to a query. Instead of producing all the answers which may overwhelm the user, the goal of our algorithm is to produce the most meaningful final answers. The final answers defined above can be generated

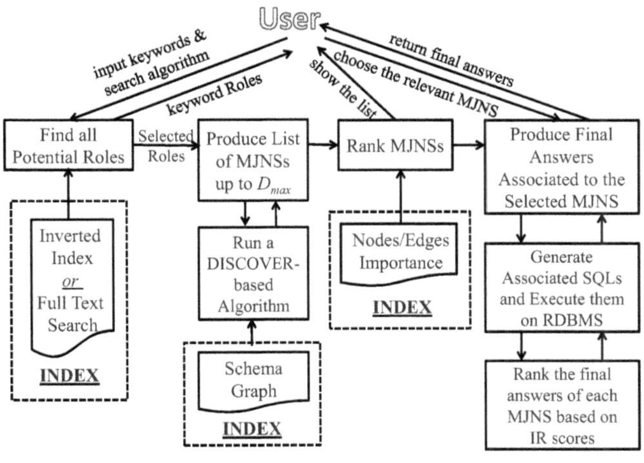

Figure 3: System Architecture.

through a sequence of join operations on the database. To generate such answers, we first generate the *minimal joining networks of schemas (MJNSs)* that represent the join operations for producing the final answers. Next, we define MJNS, and present our method for generating them.

DEFINITION 2. ***Minimal Joining Network of Schemas (MJNS):*** *Given a database D with schema graph G and a set r of query keyword roles $\{r_1, r_2, \ldots, r_l\}$ (where r_i's are relations in D), a minimal joining network of schemas that cover r is a tree T of relation schemas in G that satisfy the following conditions.* ***1) Joinable.*** *Each edge in T is an edge in G.* ***2) Role covering.*** *For each query keyword role r_i, its schema is in T.* ***3) Minimal.*** *If a relation schema in T is removed, T is either not joinable or does not cover all the roles in r.*

Three possible MJNSs for the query *"Arden:company Cynthia:customer"* over TPC-E schema is shown in Figure 2. To generate MJNSs, we use a breadth-first search algorithm similar to the candidate network (CN) generator of DISCOVER [2]. Our algorithm starts with a role schema as an initial tree T and extends T with a relation schema in G that has a foreign key relationship with a node in T. The expansion of T stops once the schemas of all the roles are covered in T. To avoid generating duplicate trees, each generated tree is assigned an ID based on tree isomorphism during the execution of the algorithm. The ID of a tree is checked against the existing IDs that are generated so far and the current tree is accepted if it is not generated previously.

After the MJNSs are generated, final answers can be produced by creating an execution plan to evaluate the MJNSs. Since many final answers can be generated for a query but some answers may not be interesting, we aim at producing the most interesting final answers. To achieve this, we first limit the number of nodes in an MJNS (which is a strategy taken by DISCOVER as well). This limits the size of final answers too.

3. SYSTEM ARCHITECTURE

The architecture of our system for finding meaningful answers is shown in Figure 3. It consists of four functional components and three data components. Below we first describe the data components and then describe the functional components. The search strategy and ranking algorithms are discussed at the end of this section.

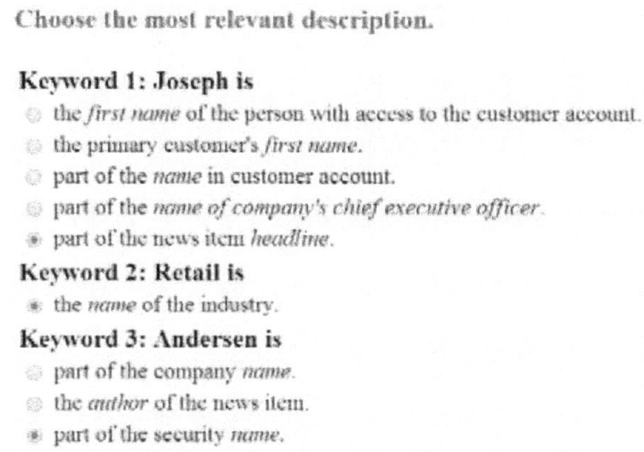

Figure 4: Role selection by the user for query "Joseph Retail Andersen".

3.1 Data Components

For a given relational database and its schema, the following three data structures are pre-built to facilitate the search process.

Inverted Index: For each keyword in the database, the columns with its associated table that contain the keyword are stored in this index, which is maintained and accessed through a table in RDBMS. This index is used to find the roles of each keyword. We can alternatively use the built-in full text search of the RDBMS.

Schema Graph: In order to produce MJNSs, we need to represent the database schema in a graph. In our system, we use the neighbor index to implement the graph. For each node, the neighbors of the node are stored in the index. The relations between the tables (i.e., the foreign key relationships) are stored in this index as well.

Node/Edge Importance: As discussed before, our ranking strategy works based on the importance of nodes and edges of the database schema. In order to improve the performance, the scores of the nodes and edges are calculated offline and is stored in a table in the RDBMS.[5] This information is later used for ranking the list of MJNSs.

3.2 Functional Components

After receiving the query keywords from the user, for each keyword, our system finds the columns that contain one of the keywords using the inverted index. The list of descriptions of these columns for each keyword is shown to the user so s/he may choose the most relevant description. Such descriptions tell the meanings of the attributes, and can be provided by people (such as DBAs) familiar with the database schema.[6] Based on the user selection, the role (i.e., the relevant database entity) of each keyword is identified. The role selection page is shown in Figure 4.

After finding the role of each keyword, these roles are passed to an engine to produce the list of MJNSs (up to the maximum size, D_{max}). The engine uses the schema graph to produce the list of MJNSs. In the next step, this list is sorted according to the chosen MJNS ranking measure. The sorted list is then shown to the user for selecting the appropriate MJNS. Three MJNSs with maximum size of six (among 42 possible MJNSs) for the query *"Arden:company Cynthia:customer"* over TPC-E schema are shown in Figure 2. For example, if the *IF* method (to be described later) is

[5]The scores should be updated periodically if the database content changes.

[6]In our experiments on the TPC-E database, the short attribute descriptions are taken from the TPC-E document.

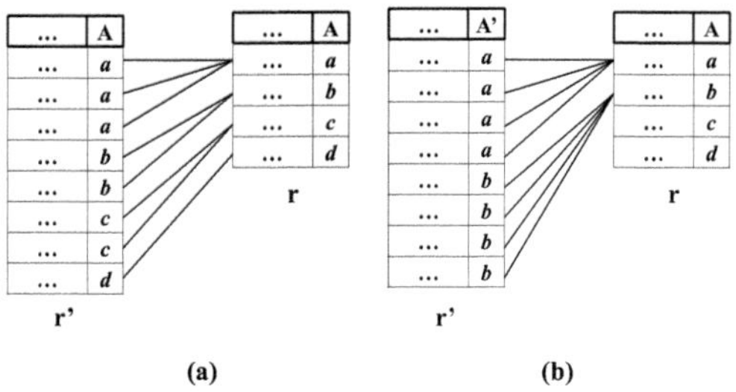

Figure 5: Two different instances of the foreign key connections between tables r and r'

used for ranking, the second MJNS (b), will get the highest rank among the others. For each selected MJNS, the associated SQL statement is generated and executed against the RDBMS. The final answers from this selected MJNS are then ranked by their IR scores. A final answer, associated to the second MJNS in Figure 2 (b), is shown in Figure 1.

3.3 Ranking Strategies

We propose and use several methods for ranking minimal joining networks of schemas (MJNSs). The proposed methods work just based on the database schema and its given instance, assuming that no extra information (e.g., query logs or inheritance relationships among the tables) is available. The methods use information-theoretic measures to evaluate the importance of relations and/or edges in the given database, and rank the MJNSs based on the importance of the relations and/or edges in an MJNS. We classify the proposed methods into three categories: (1) ranking based on the importance of the edges in an MJNS; (2) ranking based on the importance of the nodes in an MJNS; and (3) ranking based on the importance of both nodes and edges in an MJNS (i.e., a hybrid method). We found in [4] that one of the proposed edge based ranking methods (IF) outperforms other methods[7]. (Due to space limit, we only present one ranking method here; however, all are available in the system and for demonstration.) The details of our procedure for ranking MJNSs using other ranking strategies are described in Kargar et al., [4].

We use the average importance score of the tables and edges associated with these non-role relation schemas to compute an importance score for an MJNS. To have a ground truth, we construct a gold standard for relevance of answers from a transaction log of the TPC-E database. This is used to evaluate the effectiveness of our measures which do not require such external information.

Edge-based Ranking, Instantiation Fraction (IF): Intuitively, edge strength can be measured by the fraction of the join key values being instantiated. The more fraction of primary key values are instantiated, the more important the edge is. Unlike methods for summarizing database schema in [5], we do not assume that by increasing the number of connections between two tables, the importance of the edge decreases. Therefore, we propose the following measure, called *instantiation fraction* (IF), to quantify the importance of an edge based on the fractions of instantiated key values.

$$ST_{IF}(r.A, r'.A') = \frac{N_{r.A}^{inst}}{N_r} \times \frac{N_{r'.A'}^{inst}}{N_{r'}}$$

where $N_{r.A}^{inst}$ is the number of tuples in r that instantiates the edge between $r.A$ and $r'.A'$, and N_r is the total number of tuples of table r. $ST_{IF}(r.A, r'.A')$ of the the left and right instances in Figure 5 is equal to 1 and 0.5, respectively. We believe the left instance represents a stronger association between r and r'. This is the reason the first MJNS (a) in Figure 2 gets a lower rank than the second MJNS (b). The *status type* table has five different statuses (i.e., Completed, Active, Submitted, Pending, and Canceled). Neither the *customer* table nor the *company* table instantiate all of the statues of the *status type* table.

[7]We evaluated different methods through a user study and by comparing them to the gold standard.

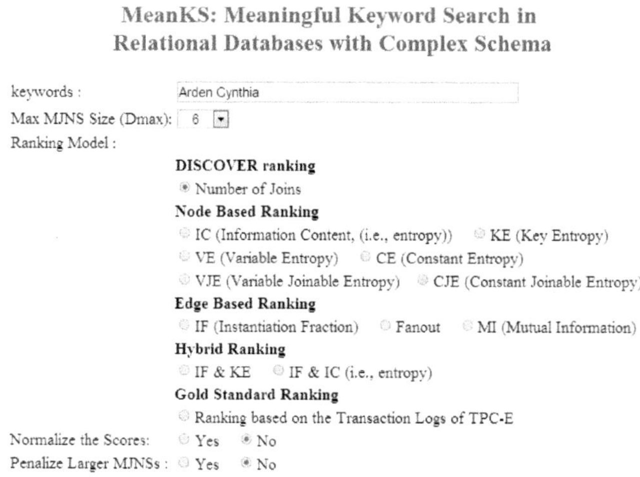

Figure 6: First page of the system with parameters.

4. DEMONSTRATION PLAN

We developed a web-based browsing interface using Java to support interactive keyword search in a relational database (i.e., the TPC-E warehouse). The first page of the interface is shown in Figure 6, where the user can specify query keywords and other parameters of the system (such as the ranking method, whether to penalize larger MJNSs and to normalize the scores) (See [4] for more details.) The second page of the system is for choosing the right roles (Figure 4). Then, the ranked list of MJNSs, based on the selected ranking method, is shown to the user (Figure 2). The last step for the user is to choose the relevant MJNS. The final answers associated to the selected MJNS, which is a list of trees of tuples ranked by their IR scores, are shown in the last page (one final answer is shown in Figure 1). In the demonstration, users are able to try different search methods and compare the accuracies of them against a gold standard.

5. REFERENCES

[1] V. Hristidis, L. Gravano, and Y. Papakonstantinou. Efficient ir-style keyword search over relational databases. In *Proc. of VLDB'03*, 2003.

[2] V. Hristidis and Y. Papakonstantinou. Discover: Keyword search in relational databases. In *Proc. of VLDB'02*, 2002.

[3] M. Kargar and A. An. Keyword search in graphs: Finding r-cliques. In *Proc. of VLDB'11*, 2011.

[4] M. Kargar, A. An, P. Godfrey, J. Szlichta, and X. Yu. Meaningful Keyword Search in RDBMS. Technical report, 2013. www.cse.yorku.ca/techreports/2013.

[5] X. Yang, C. M. Procopiuc, and D. Srivastava. Summarizing relational databases. In *Proc. of VLDB'09*, 2009.

H_2RDF+: An Efficient Data Management System for Big RDF Graphs

Nikolaos Papailiou, Dimitrios Tsoumakos, Ioannis Konstantinou, Panagiotis Karras*, Nectarios Koziris
Computing Systems Laboratory, School of ECE, National Technical University of Athens
{npapa, dtsouma, ikons, nkoziris}@cslab.ece.ntua.gr
*Management Science and Information Systems Rutgers University
karras@business.rutgers.edu

ABSTRACT

The proliferation of data in RDF format has resulted in the emergence of a plethora of specialized management systems. While the ability to adapt to the complexity of a SPARQL query – given their inherent diversity – is crucial, current approaches do not scale well when faced with substantially complex, non-selective joins, resulting in exponential growth of execution times. In this demonstration we present H_2RDF+, an RDF store that efficiently performs distributed Merge and Sort-Merge joins using a multiple-index scheme over HBase indexes. Through a greedy planner that incorporates our cost-model, it adaptively commands for either single or multi-machine query execution based on join complexity. In this paper, we present its key scientific contributions and allow participants to interact with an H_2RDF+ deployment over a Cloud infrastructure. Using a web-based GUI we allow users to load different datasets (both real and synthetic), apply any query (custom or predefined) and monitor its execution. By allowing real-time inspection of cluster status, response times and committed resources the audience will evaluate the validity of H_2RDF+'s claims and perform direct comparisons to two other state-of-the-art RDF stores.

Categories and Subject Descriptors

H.2.4 [**Database Management**]: Distributed Databases

Keywords

RDF, SparQL, Hadoop, MapReduce, HBase, NoSQL, Joins

1. INTRODUCTION

The unprecedented increase in the production of RDF data is greatly attributed to the advent of the Semantic Web in conjunction with the data deluge of modern times. This reality triggered the emergence of specialized RDF (or *triple*) stores, with a goal of achieving small query response times and efficient storage for arbitrarily large datasets. Consequently, schemes that utilize multiple indexing [11, 16], optimized algorithms for RDF joins [3], pure graph data storage[15, 4], etc. have been employed for this purpose. While many research and commercial tools offer centralized RDF data management (e.g., [5, 2]), data growth dictates distributed storage and indexing (e.g., [8, 17]).

Current distributed triple stores decentralize some or all the stages of RDF data management. Yet, they do not flexibly adjust their behavior with respect to the query in hand, either optimizing a single join algorithm or not elastically allocating platform resources. Yet, SPARQL queries require execution adjustment with respect to both query input and its complexity. Specifically, distributed approaches have not yet taken advantage of maintaining all permutations of RDF elements, namely *spo, pso, pos, ops, osp* and *sop* indexes. Such a scheme can offer the following advantages: (1) All SPARQL triple patterns can be answered efficiently using a single index scan on the corresponding index. For example, a triple pattern with bound subject and variable predicate/object can be answered using a range scan on the *spo* or the *sop* index. (2) Merge-joins that exploit the precomputed orderings can be extensively employed. The existence of all six indexes guarantees that every join between triple patterns can be done using efficient merge joins. More expensive join algorithms are needed only when joining unordered intermediate results.

In this work we demonstrate H_2RDF+ [13], a highly efficient, open-source[1] RDF data management system that maintains both of these properties while moving towards a distributed and scalable environment. We summarize the main contributions of the system as follows:

- H_2RDF+ uses HBase for indexing triples. This scheme allows bulk-import jobs to load and index large RDF datasets. The distributed index is optimized by applying aggressive compression and minimizing the storage requirements. The latter is coupled with the use of an intermediate result materialization that maintains groups of bindings.
- Fully scalable, distributed (MapReduce-based) versions of the well-studied multi-way Merge and Sort-Merge join algorithms are implemented.
- A join cost model and a greedy planner are used to decide, on a per-query basis, on the order of joins and the platform resources (central or distributed) of their execution.

Results have shown that H_2RDF+ can be orders of magnitude faster than the state-of-the-art centralized *RDF-3X*

[1] http://h2rdf.googlecode.com

SIGMOD'14, June 22–27, 2014, Snowbird, UT, USA.

http://dx.doi.org/10.1145/2588555.2594535.

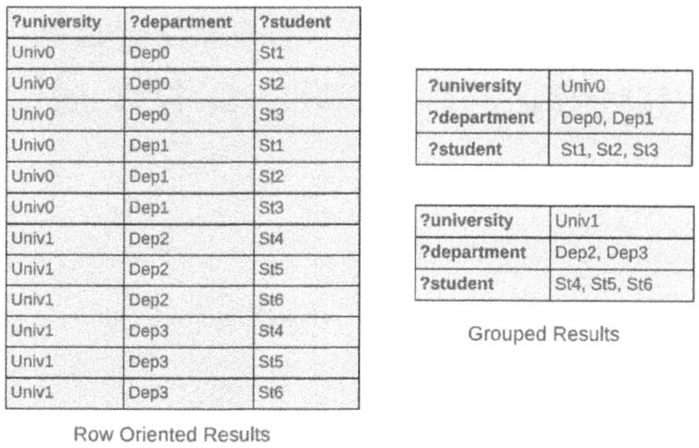

Figure 1: Grouped intermediate results

[11] for complex, non-selective joins, while being only tenths of a second slower in selective ones. Moreover, it proves 6–8 times faster than its previous version [14] and up to orders of magnitude faster than an alternative MapReduce-based scheme [9], scaling easily to 14 billion triples (2.5TB) using a cluster of 35 VMs.

In this demonstration, we will allow participants to interact with a cloud-based deployment of H$_2$RDF+ controlled via a web UI on three levels: (1) Data Indexing: we allow users to choose a dataset to load and index between synthetic with variable size (LUBM [6]) and real ones (Yago2 [7]). Indexing times and resulting index sizes will be available for inspection by the audience. (2) Querying: users may write their own SPARQL query or select a predefined one to execute. During execution, the audience can inspect the produced plan, the progress and size of intermediate results as well as the cluster resources used. (3) Comparison: the same datasets will be accessible from both *H$_2$RDF* [14] and *RDF-3X* [11] systems, allowing their direct comparison.

2. H$_2$RDF+ ARCHITECTURE

H$_2$RDF+[13] materializes six different RDF indexes, one for each possible *permutation* of subject-predicate-object values; these permutations are *spo, pso, pos, ops, osp* and *sop*. These indexes are stored using HBase tables and allow the retrieval of any simple triple pattern at minimal cost. Compared to the three index approach followed in H$_2$RDF, the maintenance of all lexicographic RDF indexes allows for: 1) the replacement of H$_2$RDF's Hash joins with efficient, scalable Merge joins for all joins between indexed triple queries, 2)the use of Sort-Merge joins in cases of joins between both intermediate non-ordered results and RDF index scans. In both cases the network overhead of shuffling data introduced in Hash joins is minimized.

Aggregated index statistics are also materialized and can be used to estimate triple pattern selectivity as well as join output size and join cost. We introduce two categories of aggregated indexes:

- With two out of the three triple elements bound, namely *sp_o, ps_o, po_s, op_s, os_p* and *so_p*. For example, the *sp_o* table contains a set of (subject, predicate, count) records, were the count is the number of triples that contain the respective combination of subject, predicate.
- With one bound element, namely *s_po, p_so, p_os, o_ps, o_sp* and *s_op*. For example, the *p_so* index contains a set of (predicate, count, average) key-values, where count is the number of distinct subjects related to this predicate

Dataset	Raw Size	RDF-3X	H$_2$RDF	H$_2$RDF+
LUBM1k	28 GB	9 GB	25 GB	7 GB
LUBM10k	276 GB	77 GB	214 GB	62 GB
LUBM20k	549 GB	156 GB	529 GB	121 GB
Yago2	26 GB	12 GB	33 GB	10 GB

Table 1: Comparison of storage requirements

and average is the average number of objects related to each subject.

In addition, we implement a bulk, MapReduce, loading process that can handle the indexing of massive RDF datasets. It consists of 4 highly scalable MapReduce jobs that:

- Translate RDF literals to integer IDs with respect to the literal's occurrence frequency in the dataset. For example, a very frequent predicate will get an ID with value close to zero. Both the String-ID and the ID-String dictionaries are stored in separate HBase tables.
- Generate and load HBase tables for all 6 RDF triple indexes along with their respective aggregated statistics.

H$_2$RDF+ utilizes an aggressive compression scheme for storing its indexes using: 1)variable length encoding for writing IDs in conjunction with frequency based String-ID mapping, 2)Google Snappy compression [1], also known as "Zippy" compression to further compress the resulting HBase tables. As depicted in Table 1, although storing 6 rather than 3 indexes and more detailed statistics, H$_2$RDF+ manages to have smaller space requirements than both its previous version and RDF-3X that maintains a similar collection of indexes and aggregated statistics.

Regarding join algorithms, H$_2$RDF+ implements the well known multi-way Merge join and multi-way Sort-Merge join algorithms, utilizing scalable MapReduce jobs executed over our distributed HBase indexes. The major contribution here is the use of the HBase indexes to generate load balanced total ordered partitions for the distributed execution of joins. The notion of *largest* query triple scan is introduced(i.e., the query scan that spans the most HBase regions). We use its HBase partitioning as a total order partition for our join. Furthermore, Merge joins are executed using Map-only job that process locally the HBase regions of the *largest* scan.

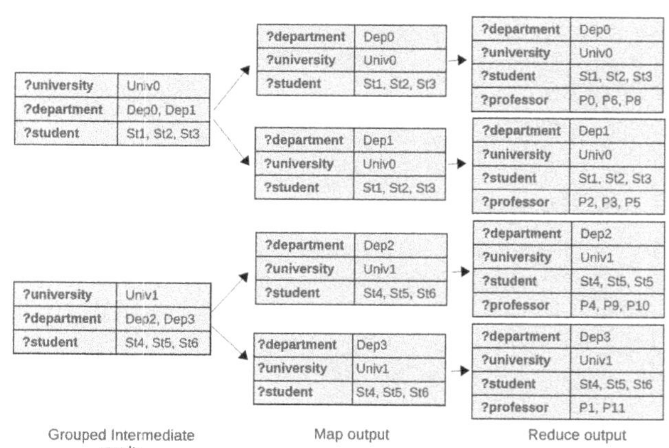

Figure 2: Join on grouped intermediate results

Another, innovative feature of our join algorithms is the use of a lazy materialization of intermediate tuples. By lazy materialization we refer to maintaing groups of intermediate results rather than generating all the combinations of intermediate tuples. Our lazy materialization maintains groups

	Yago2				LUBM10k			LUBM20k			LUBM100k	
	H_2RDF+	H_2RDF	HadoopRDF		H_2RDF+	H_2RDF	HadoopRDF	H_2RDF+	H_2RDF	HadoopRDF	H_2RDF+	H_2RDF
Import(min)	31	26	72	Import(min)	182	168	198	385	312	815	1154	985
YQ1(sec)	0.9	0.9	52	LQ1(sec)	0.6	0.6	152	0.8	0.8	378	0.8	0.9
YQ2(sec)	1.5	1.7	68	LQ3(sec)	0.8	0.8	231	0.9	1	449	1.1	1.1
YQ3(sec)	154	952	1832	LQ4(sec)	2.1	2.4	1289	2.3	2.4	2650	2.4	2.5
YQ4(sec)	87	728	1495	LQ2(sec)	95	635	915	131	880	1367	412	1853
				LQ9(sec)	151	787	1488	292	1034	2933	890	2761

Table 2: Performance comparison of H_2RDF+, H_2RDF and HadoopRDF for LUBM and Yago2 datasets

	Yago2				LUBM10k				LUBM20k			
Resources	8CPU/8GB RAM		64CPU/128GB RAM		8CPU/8GB RAM		64CPU/128GB RAM		8CPU/8GB RAM		64CPU/128GB RAM	
	H_2RDF+	RDF-3X	H_2RDF+	RDF-3X	H_2RDF+	RDF-3X	H_2RDF+	RDF-3X	H_2RDF+	RDF-3X	H_2RDF+	RDF-3X
Import(min)	164	157	26	149	912	605	162	576	2075	1526	349	1398
YQ1/LQ1(sec)	0.9	0.7	0.9	0.7	0.6	0.4	0.6	0.3	0.8	0.4	0.9	0.4
YQ2/LQ4(sec)	1.5	1	1.6	0.9	2.1	0.8	2.1	0.7	2.3	0.8	2.2	0.8
YQ3/LQ2(sec)	241	3037	138	1929	373	2297	89	1277	706	Failed	119	2065
YQ4/LQ9(sec)	123	2973	79	2068	411	68	141	51	753	Failed	264	289

Table 3: Performance comparison of H_2RDF+ and RDF-3X

of bindings that contain: 1) a set of the names of variables contained in the result, 2) for each variable, a list of its bindings. The bindings contained inside a group must satisfy the property of all-to-all connection, i.e., the respective tuples can be materialized by a nested loop over all variables.

As an example, suppose that we execute the following join:

```
?department ub:subOrganizationOf ?university .
?student ub:undergraduateDegreeFrom ?university .
```

Our sorted indexes can retrieve all departments and students grouped per university. We exploit this grouping and instead of generating all row oriented results depicted in Figure 1 we only maintain a group per university. During join execution the groups are split on demand according to the sequence of joins. For example, lets assume that we want to use the above results in the following join:

```
?department ?university ?student .
?professor ub:worksFor ?department .
```

During the map phase of our Sort-Merge join algorithm, the groups are split according to the join variable binding, creating one group for each department. In the reduce phase groups of professors per department are retrieved from the index and are merged with the inputs to form the output groups depicted in Figure 2. We can observe that our lazy materialization process is space efficient avoiding the storage of multiple replicas of bindings.

Finally, H_2RDF+ introduces a greedy planner that decides on both the sequence of joins and their execution utilizing Merge joins, Sort-Merge joins and distributed or centralized adaptive execution. A detailed join cost mode, based on the maintained index statistics and HBase's index scan performance, is also devised in order to allow for accurate join cost estimations. Both centralized and distributed join costs are examined by our greedy planner resulting in plans that can be executed either using MapReduce or a single node of the cluster. This approach provides scalable performance for large joins and interactive responses for selective joins avoiding the MapReduce initialization overhead.

3. EXPERIMENTS

Cluster configuration: The experimental setup consists of an OpenStack private cluster of 6 VM containers. Each container has a 2×6-core Intel Xeon®CPUs at 2.67GHz, 48 GB of RAM and two 2TB disks setup with RAID 0. Worker VMs feature a 2-virtual core processor, 4GB of RAM and 300GB of storage space, allowing the cluster to support a total of 36 VMs. The clusters we use for our evaluation consist of 25 worker VMs plus a single VM in the role of the HDFS, MapReduce and HBase master. Each worker VM runs 2 mappers and 2 reducers, each consuming 512MB of RAM. We utilized Hadoop v1.1.2 and HBase v0.94.5 respectively.

Compared Systems: We compare the performance of H_2RDF+ against three state-of-the-art RDF stores: RDF-3X [11], HadoopRDF [9] as well as the first version of our distributed system H_2RDF [14]. We evaluate the latest version (v0.3.7) of RDF-3X [11, 12]. HadoopRDF was built using the latest SVN rev. 158 from the project repository.

Data Sets Used: We utilize two datasets in our evaluation. The Yago2 dataset [7] consists of real data gathered from various resources such as Wikipedia, WordNet, GeoNames, etc, and contains more than 120 million triples. The LUBM dataset generator [6] creates datasets with academic domain information. By varying LUBM's number of *universities* between 1K to 100K, we create datasets ranging from 140 million (25GB) to 13.8 billion triples (2.5TB).

In order to provide a direct comparison among the different systems, we first test the performance of H_2RDF+ versus the other distributed systems. Table 2 registers the data import times and response times for the selected SPARQL queries using LUBM10k, LUBM20k, LUBM100k and Yago2 datasets. For a fair comparison to the centralized RDF-3X, we run both systems using the same *total* amount of resources: For RDF-3X, we use two single-server configurations (a 2×Quad-Core with 8 GB RAM, 8 GB swap and 1TB disk and a 4×16-Core with 128 GB RAM and 1TB disk); for H_2RDF+, we break the corresponding server in VMs and use them as our cluster infrastructure. These results are reported in Table 3.

We divide SPARQL queries in two categories: 1) selective, small queries and 2) non-selective, complex queries. H_2RDF+ performs noticeably better in large non-selective queries: it proves almost 7× better than H_2RDF and 10× better than HadoopRDF. We also outperform RDF-3X in most of the complex queries both when running on the small and the large server configuration, due to RDF-3X's memory requirements and single threaded execution engine. For small, selective queries H_2RDF+ uses centralized execution and manages to obtain performance comparable to RDF-3X. The difference in performance is mainly attributed to the local disk B+Trees used by RDF-3X that offer better seek and scan performance than our distributed HBase indexes. We also note that HadoopRDF has really poor performance for all selective queries due to the fact that it only executes MapReduce joins that process all input data and cannot take advantage of query selectivity.

To sum up, H$_2$RDF+ manages to correctly identify selective vs. non-selective queries, performing either distributed or centralized joins. It proves almost as efficient as RDF-3X, with a small difference (few tenths of a second), for selective queries. For more data-intensive queries, H$_2$RDF+ proves greatly superior to both central solutions and competitive Hadoop-based schemes due to both our join strategy and lazy intermediate result materialization.

4. DEMONSTRATION DESCRIPTION

For demonstrating our system, we use a comprehensive, real-time GUI that attendees will utilize to interact over dataset, query and comparison levels. The UI controls a cloud-based H$_2$RDF+ deployment over several virtual machines from the ~Okeanos IaaS [10].

Dataset Specification: Participants will be given the choice to index raw triple-sets of various types and sizes. We provide: (i) A set of LUBM synthetic datasets that vary from 140 million to 3 billion RDF triples (sizes ranging from 2.5 GB to 500 GB) and (ii) the Yago2 dataset consisting of real life RDF data. Users will be given an overview of the characteristics of each set before loading it; after this operation finishes, statistics over the duration and resulting index size will be available, allowing commentary on the efficacy of the MapReduce based load job and the size of the indexes versus compression.

Query Specification: Participants will be able to execute different SPARQL queries on the loaded datasets. Regardless the dataset, they can specify their own query using a text-area field. For synthetic datasets, a list of documented LUBM test queries will be available, selected as to provide a good mixture of both simple and complex structures, OWL reasoning, and multiple types of joins. For each of the queries, the exact SPARQL form, description and characteristics of the query (i.e., number of triple patterns, number of variables, number of required joins, selectivity) will be shown. Upon proceeding with the execution, the generated execution plan will be shown to the users; real-time progress will be available through the Hadoop JobTracker's site, which presents all relevant job metrics as well as the committed cloud resources. Participants will be able to observe the intermediate outputs of each join and the final query output from the cluster's HDFS site. After query execution, selected parameters and aggregate metrics such as total execution time and output size will be displayed.

Direct Comparison: Possibly the most interesting part of the demonstration is the direct comparison of different RDF engines that can foster discussion among participants. Our UI will offer interactive querying experience with two directly comparable RDF stores, RDF-3X [11] and H$_2$RDF+'s predecessor [14]. RDF-3X will be deployed over a central, RAM- and storage-rich server and H$_2$RDF over the same cluster as our new system. Allowing users to perform identical queries over three different stores and analyzing (both real time and aggregate) results enables direct comparisons and, most importantly, conclusions on join, indexing and planning algorithm efficiency. We plan to demonstrate the superior performance of 6-ple indexing that allows efficient Merge-Joins as well as the performance gains brought forth by result grouping and data compression. The different query types that best demonstrate these differences will be pointed out to the audience, that can interactively validate these findings.

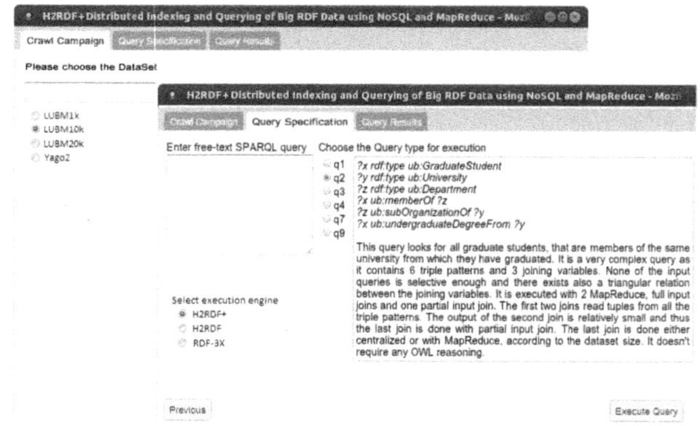

Figure 3: H$_2$RDF+ demo interface.

Acknowledgment

The research leading to these results has received funding from the European Union, Seventh Framework Programme (FP7/2007- 2013) under grant agreement no 619706.

5. REFERENCES

[1] Google Snappy. https://code.google.com/p/snappy.

[2] Sesame. http://www.openrdf.org.

[3] M. Atre, J. Srinivasan, and J. Hendler. BitMat: A Main-memory Bit Matrix of RDF Triples for Conjunctive Triple Pattern Queries. In *ISWC*, 2008.

[4] V. Bonstrom, A. Hinze, and H. Schweppe. Storing rdf as a graph. In *Web Congress, 2003*.

[5] J. J. Carroll, I. Dickinson, C. Dollin, D. Reynolds, A. Seaborne, and K. Wilkinson. Jena: Implementing the Semantic Web Recommendations. In *WWW*, 2004.

[6] Y. Guo, Z. Pan, and J. Heflin. LUBM: A Benchmark for OWL Knowledge Base Systems. *Web Semantics: Science, Services and Agents on the World Wide Web*, 2005.

[7] J. Hoffart, F. M. Suchanek, K. Berberich, E. Lewis-Kelham, G. de Melo, and G. Weikum. YAGO2: Exploring and Querying World Knowledge in Time, Space, Context, and Many Languages. WWW, 2011.

[8] J. Huang, D. J. Abadi, and K. Ren. Scalable SPARQL Querying of Large RDF Graphs. *PVLDB*, 2011.

[9] M. Husain, J. McGlothlin, M. Masud, L. Khan, and B. Thuraisingham. Heuristics-Based Query Processing for Large RDF Graphs Using Cloud Computing. *TKDE*, 2011.

[10] V. Koukis, C. Venetsanopoulos, and N. Koziris. Okeanos: Building a Cloud, Cluster by Cluster. *IEEE Internet Computing*, 17(3):67–71, 2013.

[11] T. Neumann and G. Weikum. The RDF-3X Engine for Scalable Management of RDF Data. *VLDBJ*, 2010.

[12] T. Neumann and G. Weikum. x-RDF-3X: Fast Querying, High Update Rates, and Consistency for RDF Databases. *VLDB*, 2010.

[13] N. Papailiou, I. Konstantinou, D. Tsoumakos, P. Karras, and N. Koziris. H2RDF+: High-performance Distributed Joins over Large-scale RDF Graphs. In *IEEE International Conference on Big Data*, 2013.

[14] N. Papailiou, I. Konstantinou, D. Tsoumakos, and N. Koziris. *H_2RDF*: Adaptive Query Processing on RDF Data in the Cloud. In *WWW*, 2012.

[15] O. Udrea, A. Pugliese, and V. Subrahmanian. GRIN: A graph based RDF index. In *National Conference on Artificial Intelligence*, 2007.

[16] C. Weiss, P. Karras, and A. Bernstein. Hexastore: Sextuple Indexing for Semantic Web Data Management. *PVLDB*, 2008.

[17] K. Zeng, J. Yang, H. Wang, B. Shao, and Z. Wang. A Distributed Graph Engine for Web Scale RDF Data. *PVLDB*, 2013.

DoomDB - Kill the Query

Carsten Binnig, Abdallah Salama, Erfan Zamanian
Baden-Wuerttemberg Cooperative State University
Mannheim, Germany

ABSTRACT

Typically, fault-tolerance in parallel database systems is handled by restarting a query completely when a node failure happens. However, when deploying a parallel database on a cluster of commodity machines or on IaaS offerings such as Amazon's Spot Instances, node failures are a common case. This requires a more fine-granular fault-tolerance scheme. Therefore, most recent parallel data management platforms such as Hadoop or Shark use a fine-grained fault-tolerance scheme, which materializes all intermediate results in order to be able to recover from mid-query faults. While such a fine-grained fault-tolerance scheme is able to efficiently handle node failures for complex and long-running queries, it is not optimal for short-running latency-sensitive queries since the additional costs for materialization often outweigh the costs for actually executing the query.

In this demo, we showcase our novel cost-based fault-tolerance scheme in *XDB*. It selects, which intermediate results to materialize such that the overall query runtime is minimized in the presence of node failures. For the demonstration, we present a computer game called *DoomDB*. *DoomDB* is designed as an ego-shooter game with the goal of killing nodes in an *XDB* database cluster and thus prevent a given query to produce its final result in a given time frame. One interesting use-case of *DoomDB* is to use it for (crowdsourcing) the testing activities of *XDB*.

1. INTRODUCTION

Modern parallel database systems such as SAP HANA [1], Greenplum [6] and Terradata [4] are major platforms for analyzing large amounts of structured data efficiently. Most existing parallel database systems have been designed to run on clusters with highly available hardware components where node failures can be ignored. Thus, fault-tolerance is typically handled in a coarse-grained manner by restarting a query completely when a node failure occurs.

Today, there is a growing trend to build systems for analyzing large amounts of data that run on clusters of commodity machines or on IaaS offerings such as Amazon's Spot Instances where node failures are a common case. Therefore, more recent parallel data management platforms such as Hadoop [7], Impala [3] or Shark [8] use a fine-grained fault-tolerance scheme, which materializes intermediate results to being able to recover from mid-query faults. For example, many of these systems compile queries into MapReduce-based execution plans and typically materialize the output of each map and reduce function (either in memory or on disk).

While such a fine-grained fault-tolerance scheme is able to efficiently handle node failures for complex and long-running queries, such a scheme is not efficient for short-running latency-sensitive queries since the additional costs for materialization often outweigh the costs for actually executing the query. Moreover, adding the materialization costs to the runtime of short-running queries has an additional negative effect since this increases the probability that a node failure occurs during the execution time.

In order to address this problem, we are currently building an open source parallel database system, called *XDB*.[1] *XDB* is implemented using a middleware approach on top of an existing single node database system (MySQL in our case) and offers a cost-based fault-tolerance scheme to restart queries from mid-query faults. Compared to existing systems like Hadoop, *XDB* does not materialize all intermediate results but selects a subset of intermediate results to be materialized (called materialization configuration further on). The main goal of the cost model is to find an optimal materialization configuration for a given query, such that the run-time of a given query is minimized under the presence of node failures.

In this demo, we present our novel cost-based fault-tolerance scheme in *XDB* by showcasing a computer game called *DoomDB*. *DoomDB* is designed as an ego-shooter game and the goal is to kill nodes in an *XDB* database cluster before a given analytical SQL query can produce its complete final result in a given time frame. In the game, database nodes are represented as boxes that need to be destroyed by the user. If a box is destroyed, a node failure is introduced (i.e., the database node is forced to stop working), which triggers *XDB* to redeploy sub-plans executed on that node. The progress of the query execution is displayed in *DoomDB* while the game is running. If *XDB* can not finish the query in a given time frame, the user wins the game. For showcasing different scenarios *DoomDB* takes different input parameters such as a pre-partitioned database and a user-defined SQL query. One interesting use-case of *DoomDB* is to use it for (crowdsourcing) the testing activities of our distributed and parallel database system *XDB*.

2. XDB OVERVIEW

XDB is built using a middleware approach, which leverages an existing single node database for query processing. While the middleware implements our novel concept for the cost-based fault-tolerance scheme (amongst other concepts for data partitioning and parallel query execution), the single node database systems are used

[1] `https://code.google.com/p/xdb/`

SIGMOD'14, June 22–27, 2014, Snowbird, UT, USA.

http://dx.doi.org/10.1145/2588555.2594525

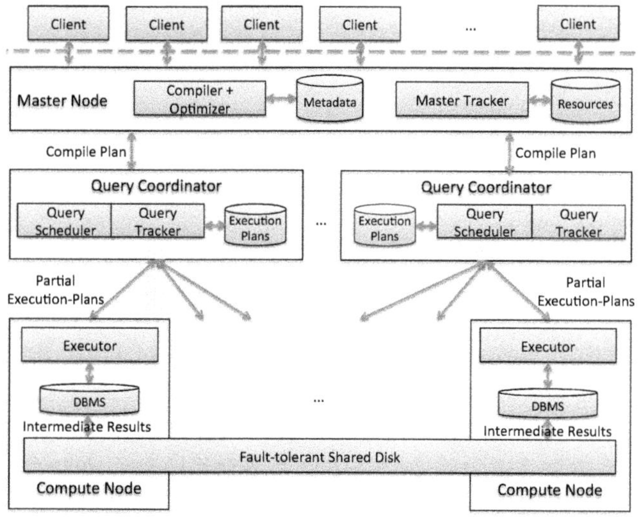

Figure 1: System Architecture of XDB

to efficiently store and query the data.

Figure 1 shows the system architecture of *XDB*. An *XDB* cluster consists of one *Master Node*, which accepts analytical SQL queries from clients, several *Query Coordinators*, which are responsible to coordinate and monitor the query execution and finally a huge number of *Compute Nodes*, which actually execute sub-plans of the given query over the partitioned data. In the following, we briefly discuss the tasks of each node type. Details about *XDB* are given in the technical report [2].

Master Node: The Master Node hosts two components, a *Compiler+Optimizer* and a *Master Tracker*. The *Compiler+Optimizer* component takes a SQL query as input and produces a compile plan using the catalog (which holds the table metadata as well statistics). The compile plan is then optimized using rule-based and cost-based optimizations for join-reordering and predicate push-down. The second component, the *Master Tracker*, has different tasks: First, it monitors the cluster resources (Query Coordinators and Compute Nodes) and restarts them when these nodes fail. Second, the Master Tracker assigns a compile plan to a Query Coordinator, which is responsible for coordinating and monitoring its execution.

Query Coordinator: A Query Coordinator hosts two components: a *Query Scheduler* and a *Query Tracker*. The *Query Scheduler* takes a compile plan from the Master Node and splits it into multiple partial execution plans and sends those plans to different Compute Nodes for parallel execution. The result of each partial execution plan is materialized to a fault-tolerant shared disk. Materialization is thus used for implementing our cost-based fault-tolerance scheme, but also for other reasons such as repartitioning data for parallel query processing. The second component, the *Query Tracker*, is responsible for monitoring and redeploying a partial execution plan in case of a Compute Node failure. We separate the Query Coordinator from the Master Tracker to be able to scale the number of Query Coordinators independently from the load in the system.

Compute Node: As discussed before, a Compute Node receives a partial execution plan (represented as SQL-queries) from the Query Coordinator and the *Executor* component then runs these plans. Moreover, the Executor signals the Query Coordinator once a partial execution plan has finished.

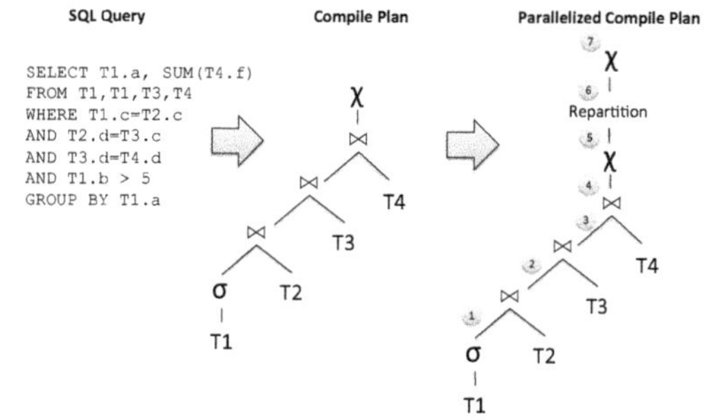

Figure 2: Compilation Process in XDB

3. COST-BASED FAULT-TOLERANCE

In this section, we first present the strategy of how *XDB* enumerates different materialization configurations for a given analytical SQL query. We then present the cost function, which is used to estimate the total runtime resulting for a given query and a materialization configuration.

3.1 Plan Enumeration

XDB uses a two-step approach for enumerating different materialization configurations. It first compiles an optimized parallel compile plan for a given analytical SQL query and then enumerates all possible materialization configurations for the compile plan.

Figure 2 represents an overview of the compilation process: (1) A given analytical SQL query is first compiled and optimized. The result is a left-deep *Compile Plan*, which consists of relational operators. (2) For parallelization, the compile plan is annotated with additional repartition operations that are required when executing the query over a horizontally partitioned database. The result is called a *Parallelized Compile Plan*.

For the resulting *Parallelized Compile Plan*, all the different materialization configurations are enumerated. A materialization configuration defines for each intermediate result whether it should be materialized or not.

For example, in Figure 2 it defines for each of the intermediate results $1-7$ whether it should be materialized. *XDB* currently uses an exhaustive search to enumerate all possible materialization combinations. In general this results in 2^n different combinations for n intermediate results. In its current version, the repartitioning operator of *XDB* always materializes its result. Thus, in our example, we only need to enumerate 2^6 different materialization configurations since the intermediate result 6 is materialized in all cases due to repartitioning.

For each materialization configuration, *XDB* invokes its cost function (described in the next section) to estimate the total runtime under failures and selects the materialization configuration with the minimal estimated total runtime.

3.2 Cost Function

The goal of the cost function is to estimate the runtime for a given *Parallelized Compile Plan* and a given materialization configuration.

Input: For estimating the total runtime under failures, the cost function takes the following parameters as input (1) an *Abstract Execution Plan*, which is derived from the Parallelized Compile Plan, (2) the runtime of each operator for a given materialization configuration (3) the mean-time-between-failures (MTBF) of the Compute Nodes, and (4) the mean-time-to-repair (MTTR).[2]

[2] We assume all Compute Nodes have the same MTBF and MTTR.

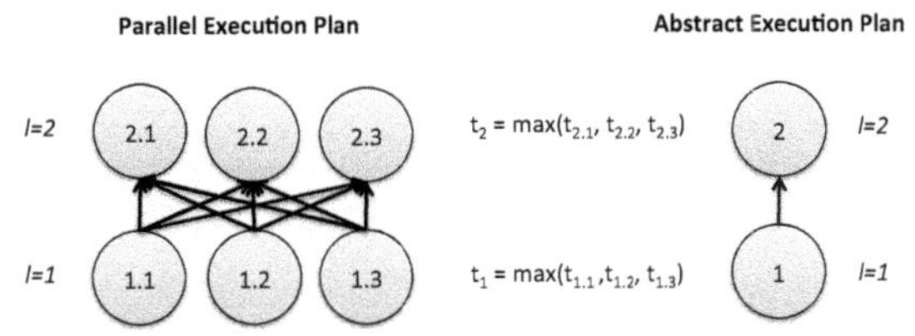

Figure 3: Parallel Execution Plans in XDB

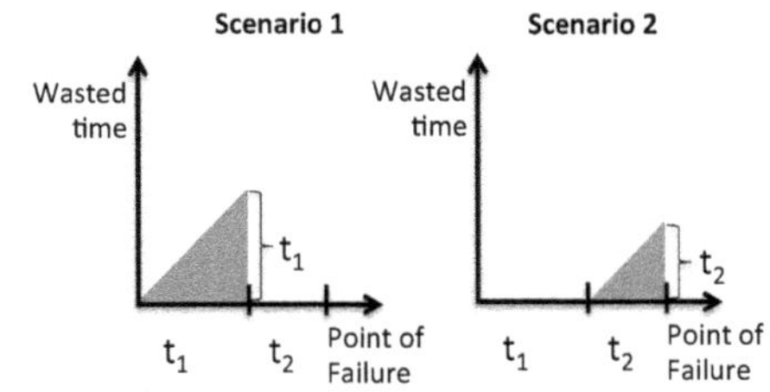

Figure 4: Wasted Time Model in XDB

The first input (1) is an Abstract Execution Plan, which is an abstract version of the actual *Parallel Execution Plan* in *XDB*. The actual Parallel Execution Plan results from the *Parallel Compile Plan* and the selected materialization configuration. Each operator in a Parallel Execution Plan represents a sub-plan of the Parallel Compile Plan that is executed over the horizontally partitioned database (i.e., one node is used to represent the sub-plan over each partition). Figure 3 (left hand side) shows a Parallel Execution Plan for the Parallel Compile Plan in Figure 3. This Parallel Execution Plan has two levels whereas the first level materializes the output of the repartition operator (i.e., intermediate result 6); i.e., the nodes 1.1 to 1.3 of the *Parallel Execution Plan* execute the same sub-plan over different partitions of the database (i.e., 3 partitions in the example), which materialize the intermediate result 6 of the Parallel Compile Plan.

Moreover, a Parallel Execution Plan always executes the same sub-plan in one level l, however, over different partitions. In order to simplify our cost model, we use an Abstract Execution Plan that uses only one operator to represent each level (see right hand side of Figure 3). The idea of an Abstract Execution Plan is that levels are executed sequentially whereas each level materializes its intermediate result. Moreover, we assume that levels are independent from each other (i.e., if one sub-plan in a level fails, it can recover from the materialized result in the level below). In *XDB*, we achieve this independence guarantee by materializing the intermediate results of a sub-plan to a fault-tolerant shared disk (e.g., a shared disk such Amazon EBS when running *XDB* on EC2 instances).

The second input (2) to the cost function is the time required to execute a given sub-plan (which includes its materialization costs). We define the runtime of a level as the maximum runtime of all sub-plans in that level (e.g., the runtime of level $l = 1$ is the maximum runtime of the sub-plans 1.1 to 1.3 in Figure 3). The runtime of an individual sub-plan can be derived by using standard cost models found in databases. It is important to note that we include the materialization costs for each sub-plan into the estimated runtime (e.g., runtime $t_{1.1}$ includes the costs to materialize its intermediate result). Moreover, the network cost for transferring data between Compute Nodes is also included in the consuming sub-plan (e.g., runtime $t_{2.1}$ includes the costs to ship the data over the network).

The last input to the cost function is (3) the MTBF and (4) the MTTR of the Compute Nodes, which can be derived from cluster statistics.

Wasted Time: For the given input, the cost function then enumerates all possible failure scenarios in order to estimate the average wasted time W (i.e., the execution time that is lost due to potential node failures). For a Abstract Execution Plan with L levels, we enumerate L different failure scenarios whereas a individual scenario l represents the case where a node executing a sub-plan in level l fails. For example, Figure 4 shows all possible failure scenarios for the *Abstract Execution Plan* of Figure 3 with two levels: Scenario (1) represents the case where one or more sub-plans in level $l = 1$ fail, and Scenario (2) represents the case where one or more sub-plans in level $l = 2$ fail.

The x-axis in each scenario represents the point in time when the node failure(s) happen during query execution, whereas the y-axis represents the wasted time. Intuitively for Scenario 1, this means the following: if a node in level 1 fails while level 2 is being executed (i.e., a failure happens in the range of $(t_1, t_1 + t_2]$ on the x-axis), we do not waste any time. However, if a node in level 1 fails while level 1 is being executed (i.e., a failure happens somewhere in the range of $[0, t_1]$), we waste the time spend in level 1.

For each scenario l, the average wasted time w_l is thus given by $0.5 \cdot t_l$ whereas t_l is the runtime of level l. In a two-level plan (as in our example), the average wasted time for each three scenarios is thus defined as follows: $w_1 = (0.5 \cdot t_1)$ and $w_2 = (0.5 \cdot t_2)$.

Figure 3 shows that each level consists of one or more sub-plans. The probability that one sub-plan in level l fails is denoted by f_l, and can be derived for a given MTBF as follows: $f_l = (1 - e^{(-t_l/MTBF)})$ where t_l represents the runtime of that level. It is worth noting that probability f_l increases with increasing runtime t_l of that level. Consequently, the probability that one sub-plan in level l succeeds is $s_l = 1 - f_l$.

To this end, the failure scenarios above are not equally likely to happen. For a scenario l, we can calculate its probability p_l as follows. We therefore define $p_l = F_l$, whereas F_l represents the probability that at least one node in level l fails. Moreover, $S_l = 1 - F_l$ is the probability that all nodes in level l succeed, which means that $S_l = (s_l)^n$ where n represents the number of parallel sub-plans in that level (for example, $n = 3$ for both levels in Figure 3).

Finally, based on these findings, we define the average wasted time for a two level plan as $W = \sum_{l=1}^{L} p_l \cdot w_l$, which is $W = p_1 \cdot w_1 + p_2 \cdot w_2$ in the example above.

Estimated Total Runtime: In order to estimate the total runtime T under the presence of node failures for the given input parameters, the idea is to sum up the estimated runtime R of a given query (without a node failure) and the additional runtime resulting from node failures. The additional runtime resulting from node failures is the wasted time W and the mean-time-to-repair multiplied by the number of attempts a needed to achieve a certain success rate for finishing the query (i.e., until the query produces its final result). The runtime R includes the materialization costs for a given materialization configuration.

We first look into the definition of the success rate $S(A \leq a)$ of a query up to attempt a (where $a = 0$ for the first attempt). The success rate of one attempt is $S = S_1 \cdot S_2$ for a two-level plan (remember that S_l is the success rate of a level l) and the failure rate of an attempt is $F = 1 - S$. The success rate up to attempt $a = 0$ is thus defined as $S(A \leq 0) = S$. In general, the success rate up to attempt a (for $a \geq 0$) is: $S(A \leq a) = S + S \cdot F + S \cdot F^2 + ... + S \cdot F^a$. The intuition is that $S(A \leq a)$ defines the cumulative probability that the query finishes in any of the attempts from $A = 0$ to $A = a$.

The formula to calculate $S(A \leq a)$ represents a geometric series. Thus, for $a \to \infty$ the success rate of the query is $S/(1 - F) =$

$S/S = 1$. For a given finite a, the success rate is $S(A \leq a) = S \cdot (1 - F^{(a+1)})/(1-F) = (1 - F^{(a+1)})$. That way, we can derive the number of attempts a needed to achieve a given success rate S (e.g., of 99%), which is a configuration knob in the cost model.

Based on the given number of attempts, we can now estimate the total runtime T of a query (under node failures) as follows: $T = R + W \cdot F + W \cdot F^2 + W \cdot F^3 + ... + W \cdot F^a + a \cdot MTTR = R + (W + W \cdot F + W \cdot F^2 + ... + W \cdot F^a) - W + a \cdot MTTR$. MTTR is the time to repair a sub-plan: i.e., to redeploy it to another node (in case we replicated partitions) or the time until a failed node needs to be restarted (if we do not replicate partitions). The second term of this formula is again a geometric series. Thus, we can easily calculate T as $T = R + W \cdot (1 - F^{(a+1)})/(1-F) - W + a \cdot MTTR$. If we set $F = 0$ and $a = 0$ in this formula (i.e., no node failure happens), then $T = R$ holds.

4. DOOMDB DEMO

In this demo, we showcase our novel cost-based fault-tolerance scheme in *XDB* by presenting a visual computer game called *DoomDB*. *XDB* will be deployed on a Amazon AWS cluster of 10 m1.medium EC2 instances (representing weak commodity machines). The goal of the game is that a user kills database nodes and thus prevents the query from finishing in a given time frame. If *XDB* can not finish the query in a given time, the user wins the game.

When a user starts the game, she can either choose to start a new game or to join an existing game in multi-player mode. When starting a new game, the user can enter the following input parameters:

- **Database:** A pre-partitioned TPC-H database (with 10 partitions per table) of different scaling factors (i.e., $SF = 10$ for short running games and $SF = 100$ for long running games) can be selected.
- **SQL Query:** A SQL query from a subset of the TPC-H benchmark queries can be selected.
- **MTBF:** The mean-time-between-failures of Compute Nodes can be given to influence the materialization configuration.
- **MTTR:** The mean-time-to-repair Compute Nodes can be given.
- **Degree of difficulty ($d \geq 2$):** One of these degrees can be chosen by the player. The higher the degree d is, the more time is given to *XDB* to finish the query (i.e., $d \cdot T$ is given to the player to kill the query where T is the estimated runtime with failures). Thus, for higher degrees the harder it is for players to prevent *XDB* of finishing the query.

After entering the input parameters, the game is started and the user can kill Compute Nodes represented as boxes (see Figure 5). Boxes have guards, which protect the Compute Nodes. Once a Compute Node is killed, its process is stopped. *XDB* then re-deploys the aborted sub-plans of the killed Compute Node and restarts these sub-plans after the Compute Node is repaired (i.e., after the given MTTR). The progress of the query execution is displayed in *DoomDB* while the game is running.

5. RELATED WORK

Two novel approaches, which tackle a similar problem as *XDB* are FTOps [5] and Osprey [9].

FTOps presents a cost-based model for intra-query fault-tolerance without blocking and an optimizer to find the best strategy for an operator (nothing, check-pointing or materializing). Compared to *XDB*, FTOps uses a cost model, which does not define the probability of a node failure based on the runtime of a query. Instead it uses fixed constants for the failure probability.

Osprey is an approach, which is only working for analytical queries over a star schema. It first splits the analytical queries into sub-queries over partitions and then executes a final merge over all intermediate results of sub-queries. If a sub-query fails, it is restarted on a different replica. *XDB* extends the ideas presented in Osprey to arbitrary schemata and queries. Moreover, *XDB* also presents a cost model to find the best deployment under different failure rates.

Figure 5: DoomDB Gaming Screen

6. CONCLUSIONS AND OUTLOOK

In this demo paper we presented our parallel database system called *XDB*, which is implemented using a middleware approach over an existing database system. To showcase the cost-based fault-tolerance scheme in *XDB*, we implemented an ego-shooter computer game called *DoomDB*. The goal of the game is to kill an analytical SQL query running in a fault-tolerant environment on a cluster of database nodes. One important avenue of future work is to extend our current cost model for bushy plans as well as for arbitrary graph-based plans (instead of left-deep plans only).

7. ACKNOWLEDGMENTS

First, we would like to thank the team of students for implementing the DoomDB game: Kai Boernert, Daniel Ingenhaag, Lucas La Salle, Stefano Enzo Leccese of University of Mannheim. Moreover, we also would like to thank Amazon for providing an Amazon AWS in Education Research Grant for the student team.

8. REFERENCES

[1] C. Binnig, N. May, and T. Mindnich. SQLScript: Efficiently Analyzing Big Enterprise Data in SAP HANA. In *BTW*, pages 363–382, 2013.

[2] C. Binnig, A. Salama, E. Zamanian, A. C. Müller, S. Listing, and H. Kornmayer. XDB - A novel Database Architecture for Data Analytics as a Service. Technical report, University of Mannheim, 2013. `http://pi1.informatik.uni-mannheim.de/filepool/publications/XDB/xdb_techreport.pdf`.

[3] Cloudera. Impala. `http://www.cloudera.com/content/cloudera/en/products-and-services/cdh/impala.html`.

[4] M. T. Özsu and P. Valduriez. *Principles of Distributed Database Systems, Third Edition.* Springer, 2011.

[5] P. Upadhyaya, Y. Kwon, and M. Balazinska. A latency and fault-tolerance optimizer for online parallel query plans. In *SIGMOD Conference*, pages 241–252, 2011.

[6] F. M. Waas. Beyond Conventional Data Warehousing - Massively Parallel Data Processing with Greenplum Database. In *BIRTE (Informal Proceedings)*, 2008.

[7] T. White. *Hadoop: The Definitive Guide*. O'Reilly Media, Inc., 1st edition, 2009.

[8] R. S. Xin, J. Rosen, M. Zaharia, M. J. Franklin, S. Shenker, and I. Stoica. Shark: SQL and rich analytics at scale. In *SIGMOD Conference*, pages 13–24, 2013.

[9] C. Yang, C. Yen, C. Tan, and S. Madden. Osprey: Implementing MapReduce-style fault tolerance in a shared-nothing distributed database. In *ICDE*, pages 657–668, 2010.

Should we all be teaching "Intro to Data Science" instead of "Intro to Databases"?

Bill Howe
Computer Science & Engineering
University of Washington
Seattle, WA
billhowe@cs.washington.edu

Michael J. Franklin
Electrical Engineering and Computer Science
University of California, Berkeley
Berkeley, CA
franklin@cs.berkeley.edu

Juliana Freire
Department of Computer Science and Engineering
New York University, New York
juliana.freire@nyu.edu

James Frew
University of California, Santa Barbara
Bren School of Environmental Science and Management
Santa Barbara, CA
frew@bren.ucsb.edu

Tim Kraska
Computer Science Department
Brown University
tim_kraska@brown.edu

Raghu Ramakrishnan
Microsoft Cloud Information Services Laboratory
Microsoft Corporation
raghu@microsoft.com

1. ABSTRACT

The Database Community has a unique perspective on the challenges and solutions of long-term management of data and the value of data as a resource. In current computer science curricula, however, these insights are typically locked up in the context of the traditional Intro to Databases class that was developed years (or in some cases, decades) before the modern concept of Data Science arose and embedded in the discussion of legacy data management systems. We consider how to bring these concepts front and center into the emerging wave of Data Science courses, degree programs and even departments.

Categories and Subject Descriptors

K.3.2.b [**Computer and Education**]: Computer Science Education

2. INTRODUCTION

The term *data science* has recently enjoyed explosive popularity in industry: thousands of data scientist positions are open, and universities are scrambling to train students to fill them. Masters programs, certificate programs, new courses, and workshops and bootcamps have sprung up nationally and internationally, and several new research institutes have also been launched in the last 12 months alone. These programs all tend to involve some combination of topics in data management, visualization, and statistics/ML, with statistics and machine learning topics usually receiving disproportionate attention from students and the popular media. But data science practitioners report that the data management challenges — the forte of the database community — are the real bottlenecks. The acquisition, cleaning, integration, manipulation, and sharing of data — flexibly and scalably — are the issues that "keep them up at night." Moreover, we hear them quip "80% of analytics is just sums and averages" — the implication being that simple statistical methods are more than sufficient for many applications. So while the database community has the potential to take a leadership role in the education and training of the next generation of successful data scientists, we are at risk of allowing other communities to drive the conversation.

The result of these trends is that we are in the process of losing mindshare for data science and big data among upcoming students. Entire courses in data science are taught with R, implicitly conveying to students that datasets larger than main memory aren't all that important to a data scientist. When scale is discussed, NoSQL systems (despite being occasionally softened to mean "Not Only SQL") are positioned as the only viable solution for "web scale" despite the obvious tradeoffs.

Overall, our core strength is about treating data as a resource that is a key part of any information system, one that is not associated with any one particular application or program. This idea is important to teach in any data science curriculum and seize the opportunity to put database techniques and technologies front and center in the data science discussion. For example, we should unapologetically argue that the relational algebra is as important as the linear algebra in the data scientist's toolbox, and that transactions and schemas are important systems-level features that cannot be easily left up to the application programmer.

3. QUESTIONS TO CONSIDER

We consider how the database community can influence data science education nationally and internationally, and how data science should influence how we should teach databases. We ask the following questions:

- Is "Intro to Data Science" the new "Intro to Computer Science"? For instance, the Intro to CS class on Udacity (`https://www.udacity.com/course/cs101`) builds a search engine. Doesn't that say it all?

SIGMOD'14, June 22–27, 2014, Snowbird, UT, USA.
ACM 978-1-4503-2376-5/14/06.
http://dx.doi.org/10.1145/2588555.2600092.

- At what level (junior, senior,...) should Data Science be offered and what are the appropriate pre-requisites? Who are we targeting? Majors, non-majors, working professionals seeking masters degrees, researchers in various fields seeking depth?
- If Intro to Data Science doesn't replace Intro to Computer Science, should it replace our traditional Intro to Database courses?
- Do we all now need to learn about all these statistics and machine learning algorithms in order to teach such a course?
- Is Data Science just another class or two, a reorganization of exsting material, or is it an emerging field on its own?
- What are the core set of skills, tools, theories, etc. that Data Scientists need to know and how should we teach them? Are there "principles of data science" that are distinct from existing material?
- As database researchers, how should we be teaching/positioning our core contributions in the context of data science? What is the role of NoSQL and other not-exactly-database technologies? How much expertise in systems and architectures do data scientists need?
- Which communities in CS (visualization, ML) and other disciplines (stats, sciences, etc) should we engage with on this and in what way?
- How broadly can DB formalisms be applied to data science problems? Can we "jailbreak" the relational algebra from conventional RDBMS systems and used broadly as a reasoning tool?
- How do we better integrate our expertise in other relevant topics — visualization and machine learning in particular?
- What formats should be exploring for the material? Undergrad, masters, PhD programs, certificates, online? What about non-majors? Physicists and biologists are starting successful big data software companies — should we embrace this breadth?
- How do we get industry involvement in the classroom (or should we)?
- Big data resources are important for big data education: How do we partner with industry to provide a shared infrastructure?

Characterizing and Selecting Fresh Data Sources

Theodoros Rekatsinas
University of Maryland
thodrek@cs.umd.edu

Xin Luna Dong
Google Inc.
lunadong@google.com

Divesh Srivastava
AT&T Labs-Research
divesh@research.att.com

ABSTRACT

Data integration is a challenging task due to the large numbers of autonomous *data sources*. This necessitates the development of techniques to reason about the benefits and costs of acquiring and integrating data. Recently the problem of *source selection* (i.e., identifying the subset of sources that maximizes the profit from integration) was introduced as a preprocessing step before the actual integration. The problem was studied for static sources and used the accuracy of data fusion to quantify the integration profit.

In this paper, we study the problem of source selection considering *dynamic* data sources whose content changes over time. We define a set of time-dependent metrics, including *coverage*, *freshness* and *accuracy*, to characterize the quality of integrated data. We show how statistical models for the evolution of sources can be used to estimate these metrics. While source selection is NP-complete, we show that for a large class of practical cases, near-optimal solutions can be found, propose an algorithmic framework with theoretical guarantees for our problem and show its effectiveness with an extensive experimental evaluation on both real-world and synthetic data.

Categories and Subject Descriptors

H.2.m [**Database Management**]: Miscellaneous; G.3 [**Mathematics of Computing**]: [Probability and Statistics]

General Terms

Algorithms, Experimentation, Performance

Keywords

Source Selection; Data Integration; Dynamic Data Sources

1. INTRODUCTION

Integrating data from multiple sources is essential in a growing number of application domains, including large scale enterprises that own many data sources, prediction of societal events, such as disease outbreaks, and targeted data analytics where streams of Web and social media data are heavily used. Analyzing multiple data sources collectively can significantly enhance the value of data; however, acquiring and integrating data comes with a monetary and computational cost. To reason about the *profits* of integration and find the optimal subset of sources to be integrated, Dong et al. [3] introduced the problem of *source selection* focusing on *static sources*, that is, data sources whose content does not change over time. Often, however, data sources are *dynamic* (i.e., their content changes over time) raising several challenges. Next, we use two real-world scenarios to illustrate these challenges.

SIGMOD'14, June 22–27, 2014, Snowbird, UT, USA.

http://dx.doi.org/10.1145/2588555.2610504.

1.1 Challenges

The first scenario is that of *listing aggregation*, such as business, job or rental listings. Typically, aggregators offer a search service to end users by integrating listings from multiple *sources*. Each source provides a set of listings and regular updates as new listings become available, or existing listings get updated or removed. Specifically, we consider aggregating business listings (BL) from 43 data sources providing records for US businesses over 2 years.

A second scenario that is increasingly popular is that of collective analysis of online news media for societal-event monitoring [7, 18]. Here, the analyst integrates events mentioned in a diverse set of news media sources and analyzes them collectively to detect patterns characterizing her domain of interest. In particular, we consider the Global Database of Events, Languages and Tone (GDELT) [10] where news articles from 15,275 sources are aggregated in a single repository over one month for analytic tasks.

The first challenge stems from the fact that sources that update their data more frequently are not always more effective at capturing changes in a timely manner.

EXAMPLE 1. *We focus on BL and the freshness of each source (i.e., the ratio of provided up-to-date listings to the total number of listings in the source) and the update frequency of each source. Figure 1(a) shows the average update frequency and average freshness for each source over the 2 year time window. We observe that there is no clear correspondence between the update frequency and freshness of a source and see that sources with high update frequencies may have low freshness, indicating that sources may add to their content frequently but are ineffective at deleting stale data or capturing value changes of previous data items.* □

Even sources with similar update frequencies exhibit different levels of staleness, as exemplified next in our second domain.

EXAMPLE 2. *We consider the 20 largest sources from GDELT and examine how effective sources are at reporting events in a timely manner. Figure 1(d) shows the average delay with which events are reported and the corresponding fraction of delayed events over the total content of each source over one month. While all sources get updated daily, we see that a significant fraction of events are reported with delays.* □

The second challenge is that the quality of available sources may change over time and often the subset of sources that maximizes the integration quality may also change over time.

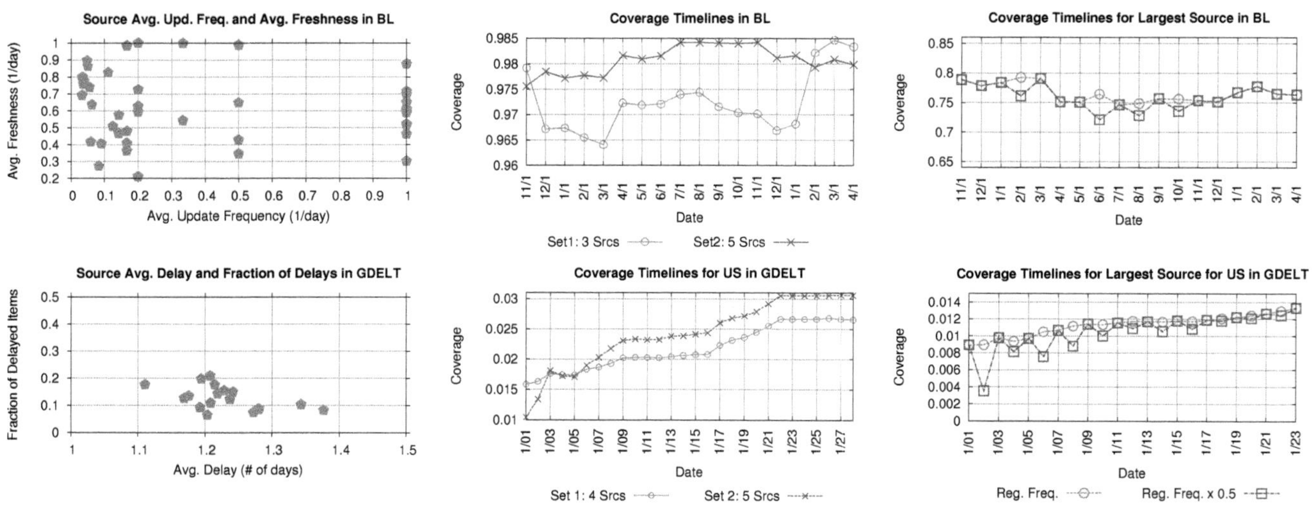

Figure 1: (a) Average update frequencies and average freshness of data sources in BL. (b) Coverage evolution for two sets of sources in BL. (c) Evolution of coverage for the largest source, when incorporating updates with different frequencies for BL. (d) Average delay and fraction of delayed event mentions for the 20 largest sources in GDELT. All sources get updated every day. (e) Coverage evolution for two sets of sources for GDELT corresponding to events in the US. (f) Evolution of coverage for the largest source, when incorporating updates with different frequencies for GDELT.

EXAMPLE 3. *We focus on listings for a single state in BL and consider the coverage (i.e., the ratio of provided instances to total number of instances in the domain) of the integration result for two sets of sources. Both sets contain the two largest sources. Moreover, the first set contains one other source while the second set contains three other sources, with comparable sizes to the source added in the first set. Figure 1(b) shows the evolution of coverage for the two sets. Switching to GDELT, we focus on events for the United States and consider two sets of sources, both containing the two largest sources. The first one contains two extra smaller sources, while the second has three other sources of comparable size. Figure 1(e), shows the coverage evolution for the two sets. In both cases, we observe that the coverage of the two sets differs over time, and the set with the highest quality varies across time.* □

Finally, the third challenge is that choosing to integrate data from a source at a lower frequency than the source update frequency can lead to similar integration quality but reduced cost.

EXAMPLE 4. *For BL, we consider the evolution of coverage for the largest source, when its updates are acquired at half the update frequency. As shown in Figure 1(c), the quality loss is not significant while the cost is reduced significantly since only half of the updates are acquired. We observe the same behavior in GDELT as illustrated in Figure 1(f).*□

1.2 Contributions

Motivated by these examples, we study the problem of *time-aware source selection*, that is, reasoning about the profit of acquiring and integrating dynamic sources to select the optimal subset of sources to be integrated. We build upon the work by Dong et al. [3] that solved this problem for static sources.

We propose a framework that provides the necessary building blocks to derive rigorous time-dependent definitions for data quality metrics, such as coverage and freshness, and statistically models the complex update patterns and data quality changes of different data sources. These models enable us to efficiently and accurately estimate the aforementioned quality metrics at different time points. Our main contributions are as follows:

- We introduce the problem of *time-aware source selection*, where we consider time-dependent data quality metrics to describe the benefit of data integration, and in addition to selecting a subset of sources, we decide the optimal frequency to acquire data from each source (Section 2).
- We introduce a theoretical framework using statistical models to describe the quality and data update patterns of dynamic sources. An overview is presented in Section 2.3 and its components are discussed in detail in Sections 3 and 4.
- While the problem of time-aware source selection is NP-complete [3], we show that many of its instances correspond to well-studied submodular optimization problems for which efficient local-search algorithms with rigorous theoretical guarantees are known (Section 5).
- Finally, we show that our techniques can efficiently find near-optimal solutions on both real-world and synthetic data that contain large numbers of data sources exhibiting various update patterns (Section 6).

2. AN OVERVIEW

In this section we briefly review the source selection problem for static sources. We formally define the problem of *time-aware source selection* and present an overview of our solution.

2.1 Source Selection

Given a set of data sources, we assume two predefined functions that measure the *cost* and *gain* of integration. The cost of integration is a function of the monetary cost to acquire data, and the total resources (including time) needed for integration. The gain quantifies the benefit from the integration and is a function of the integration quality using the same unit as for cost. We define source selection as follows:

DEFINITION 1. (SOURCE SELECTION [3]) *Let* $\bar{\mathbf{S}}$ *be a set of sources,* F *be an integration model,* $G_F(\cdot)$ *be a gain function and* $C_F(\cdot)$ *a cost function using model* F*, and* β_c *be a budget on cost. The Source Selection problem finds a subset* $S_I \subseteq \bar{\mathbf{S}}$ *that maximizes* $G_F(S_I) - C_F(S_I)$ *under constraint* $C_F(S_I) \leq \beta_c$.

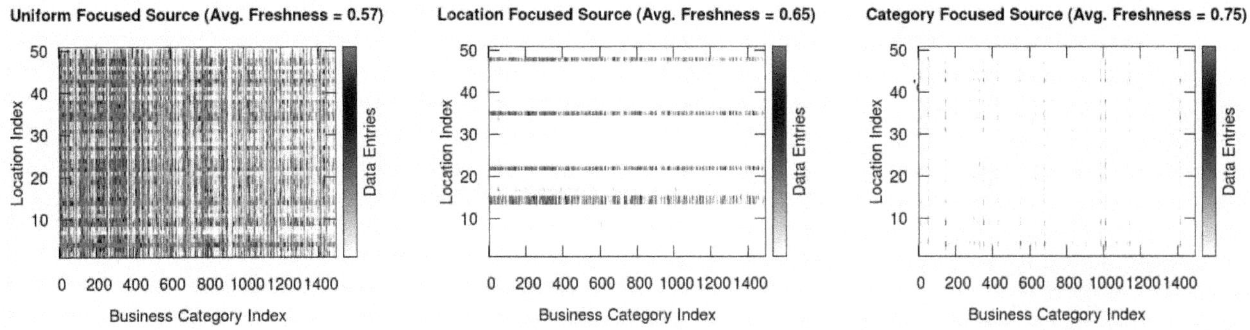

Figure 2: Sources covering different parts of the data domain.

Dong et al. [3] show how $G_F(S_I)$ can be defined in the context of data fusion as the accuracy of the integration result, and use an additive cost function over the costs of the selected sources.

2.2 Selecting Fresh Sources

We consider a data domain Ω where entities change dynamically over time, that is new entities may *appear*, *disappear* or the values of existing entities may change over time. In the remainder of the paper we will refer to this domain as the *world* for convenience. *Dynamic sources* can be viewed as observers of the world that update their content by capturing changes in the world.

DEFINITION 2. *A data source S is dynamic when it is updating its content by capturing entity appearances, disappearances and value changes from a data domain Ω with a frequency f_S.*

We assume knowledge of the data evolution for a past time window T ending at time t_0. We consider a fixed set of future time points, denoted by T_f, and we wish to maximize the profit of integration for Ω and T_f. Let $G_F(S_I, T_f)$ be the overall gain of integrating S_I using model F for T_f, and $C_F(S_I, T_f)$ be the corresponding integration cost. With $G_F(S_I, t)$ denoting the gain of integrating S_I for a single time point $t \in T_f$, and $\mathcal{A}_{t \in T_f}$ denoting an aggregate function (e.g., average or max) over the time points in T_f we define the overall gain as $G_F(S_I, T_f) = \mathcal{A}_{t \in T_f} G_F(S_I, t)$. Similarly to Dong et al. [3] we assume an additive cost model with $C_F(S_I, T_f) = \sum_{S \in S_I} C(S, T_f)$, where $C(S, T_f)$ denotes the cost of source $S \in S_I$ for T_f. We define the problem of time-aware source selection as follows:

DEFINITION 3. (TIME AWARE SOURCE SELECTION) *Let $\bar{\mathbf{S}}$ be a set of sources, F be an integration model, and β_c be a budget on cost. Let T_f be a set of time points of interest. The Time-Aware Source Selection problem finds a subset $S_I \subseteq \bar{\mathbf{S}}$ that maximizes $G_F(S_I, T_f) - C_F(S_I, T_f)$ under the constraint $C_F(S_I, T_f) \leq \beta_c$.*

Generalizing the analysis by Dong et al. [3] one can easily show that time-aware source selection is NP-complete. Next, we introduce two variations of the basic time-aware source selection.

Varying update frequencies: Instead of acquiring every source update, we consider acquiring updates at slower frequencies to reduce cost (Example 4). In this version of the time-aware source selection problem, we wish to select both the subset of sources that maximizes the integration profit and their *optimal frequencies* with which updates should be acquired. Given a set of selected sources S_I and their selected frequencies f_{S_I} let $G_F(S_I, f_{S_I}, T_f)$ denote the integration gain of S_I, under model F, with the frequencies specified in f_{S_I} for T_F, and $C_F(S_I, f_{S_I}, T_f)$ denote the corresponding integration cost. We have the following definition:

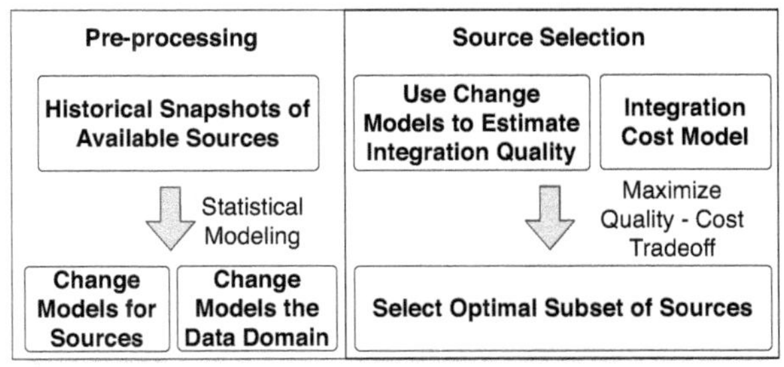

Figure 3: Framework overview.

DEFINITION 4. (VARYING FREQUENCY SOURCE SELECTION) *Let $\bar{\mathbf{S}}$ be a set of sources with variable update frequencies, F be an integration model, and β_c be a budget on cost. Let T_f be a set of time points of interest. The Varying Frequency Source Selection problem finds a subset $S_I \subseteq \bar{\mathbf{S}}$ and their corresponding update frequencies f_{S_I} that maximize $G_F(S_I, f_{S_I}, T_f) - C_F(S_I, f_{S_I}, T_f)$ under the constraint $C_F(S_I, f_{S_I}, T_f) \leq \beta_c$.*

Integrating slices of data: Often the data domain Ω can be high-dimensional, characterized by a set of discrete dimensions $\mathbf{D}_\Omega$, and sources may exhibit significant differences in the types of data they cover. Instead of acquiring all the entities from a source, we consider acquiring only a subset (i.e., *a slice*) to reduce the cost.

To illustrate, we consider the business listings and two dimensions: (a) the location of the listing and (b) the category of business (e.g., restaurants in New York). Figure 2 shows three data sources: (1) one providing entities for most location-category pairs, (2) one providing entities for a specific set of locations but across all categories, and (3) one providing entities for a specific set of categories but across all locations. A user focusing on certain locations may consider acquiring the second source and small parts of the first source to increase the overall coverage at a reduced cost.

In such cases, sources can be viewed as aggregates of multiple micro-sources, i.e., elemental sources focusing on certain slices of the data domain. The basic definition of time-aware source selection can be extended to account for this case as follows:

DEFINITION 5. (SLICE TIME AWARE SOURCE SELECTION) *Let $\bar{\mathbf{S}}_m$ be a set of micro-sources corresponding to slices obtained from a set $\bar{\mathbf{S}}$ of data sources, F be an integration model, and β_c be a budget on cost. Let T_f be a set of time points of interest. The Slice Time-Aware Source Selection problem finds a subset $S_I \subseteq \bar{\mathbf{S}}_m$ that maximizes $G_F(S_I, T_f) - C_F(S_I, T_f)$ under the constraint $C_F(S_I, T_f) \leq \beta_c$.*

The SLICE TIME AWARE SOURCE SELECTION problem can be easily extended to identify optimal update frequencies as well.

2.3 Overview and Scope of Proposed Solution

The different components of our proposed framework for solving time-aware source selection are shown in Figure 3. Assuming knowledge of data changes over a past time window T, we build a collection of statistical models that describe the update patterns in the world and the sources. We also construct a profile for each source summarizing its content at the end of T, and its effectiveness at capturing data changes (Section 4.1). Then, we estimate the quality of integration for an arbitrary set of sources using the aforementioned models and source profiles (Section 4.2), and propose a set of algorithms for solving the problem of time-aware source selection and its variations (Section 5).

We make the following assumptions in the rest of the paper:

- We assume that the majority of inaccuracies occur due to the ineffectiveness of sources at capturing data changes from the world and not erroneous insertions. We found that in both our domains stale data dominates the mistakes. For BL we found that sources exhibit delays in inserting new listings or deleting listings that disappeared from the world, while for GDELT we found that news sources present varying delays at reporting events.
- We assume an integration scheme across sources that follows the union semantics. For example, consider integrating two sources at a time point t and a restaurant listing that is mentioned in the first one but was never mentioned in the second. In this case, the restaurant entry will be present in the integration result of the two sources. On the other hand if the listing was present in the second source for a time point prior to t but deleted by time t then this entry will not be present in the integration result. This integration scheme is used in many practical applications to form the integration result [6, 17].
- We assume that the sources are independent, that is, each source updates its content independently from others. This assumption is used to prove the theoretical guarantees of the proposed algorithms in Section 5. While this assumption is strict and may not fully hold for the BL and GDELT domains, we were still able to obtain solutions of high quality for the different versions of the time-aware source selection problem (Section 6).
- We assume that the content changes *in the world* follow a Poisson random process and that the lifespan of an entity and the time interval between consecutive updates follow an exponential distribution. We observed that both assumptions hold for the BL and GDELT domains (Section 4.1.1). No such assumptions are made for the content changes of sources, for which we use generic statistical models based on empirical distributions capable of capturing complex update patterns that depend on the update frequency of each source (Section 4.1.2).
- Finally, we assume that in our integration scenarios sufficient historical data are available to learn the statistical models described above. Our approach is well suited for highly dynamic sources since they provide us with more training points and hence more accurate models can be learned.

3. QUALITY OF INTEGRATED DATA

As discussed in Section 2.2, the gain of integration $G_F(S_I, t)$ can be quantified using the quality of the integration result. We introduce time dependent versions of *coverage*, *freshness* and *accuracy* to characterize the quality of a set of dynamic sources.

We characterize the entities in a source or the integration result at a time point t using three categories: (a) *up-to-date*, denoted by Up, corresponding to entities mentioned in the source that also exist in the world and their attribute values in the source are in agreement with the world, (b) *out-of-date*, denoted by Out, corresponding to entities mentioned in the source that are present in the world but latest value changes are not captured by the source, and (c) *non-deleted*, denoted by NDel, corresponding to entities mentioned by the source that have disappeared from the world. We next define the quality of the integration result using these categories.

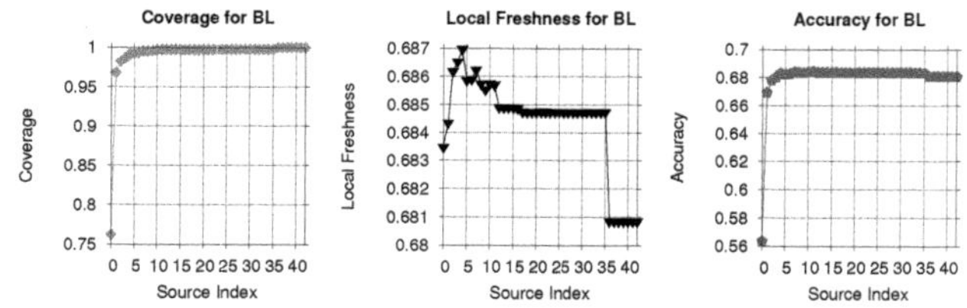

Figure 4: (a) Coverage, (b) freshness and (c) accuracy of integrated data; Sources processed in decreasing order of coverage.

Let S_I be the selected set of sources to be integrated at time t and $F(S_I)$ the integration result using model F. We define the coverage of $F(S_I)$ at time t, denoted by $\mathsf{Cov(F(S_I),t)}$, as the probability that a random entity from the world Ω at time t belongs to $F(S_I)$. We express this probability as:

$$\mathsf{Cov(F(S_I),t)} = \frac{\mathsf{Up(F(S_I),t) + Out(F(S_I),t)}}{|\Omega|_t} \quad (1)$$

where $|\Omega|_t$ denotes the total entities in the world at time t.

Next, we define a localized freshness measure for the integrated data at time t as the probability that a randomly selected entry of $F(S_I)$ is up-to-date. We refer to this metric as *local freshness*, denoted by LF, and express it as:

$$\mathsf{LF(F(S_I),t)} = \frac{\mathsf{Up(F(S_I),t)}}{|\mathsf{F(S_I)}|_t} \quad (2)$$

where $|F(S_I)|_t$ denotes the total number of entities in the integration result at time t. The coverage and local freshness are orthogonal, that is, a source with high-freshness does not necessarily exhibit high coverage. Moreover, while the coverage is expected to increase monotonically as more sources are integrated the same does not hold for freshness. We illustrate this using an example from the business listing domain introduced in Section 1.

EXAMPLE 5. *We consider integrating the available sources in decreasing order of coverage. Figure 4(a) shows the coverage of the integration result. The corresponding local freshness is shown in Figure 4(b). While the coverage increases monotonically, we see that the local freshness of the integration result decreases as more source are integrated.* □

In many cases, we wish to reason about coverage and local freshness collectively. Coverage and local freshness are similar to *recall* and *precision* in information retrieval, and hence, can be combined using an F-type measure. Thus, we introduce the *accuracy* of a source or the integration result as the *match rate accuracy* [14]. Before defining accuracy we need to define a global measure of freshness. We define *global freshness*, as the probability that a randomly selected entity from Ω at time t belongs to $F(S_I)$ and its reference is up-to-date. We have:

$$\mathsf{GF(F(S_I),t)} = \frac{\mathsf{Up(F(S_I),t)}}{|\Omega|_t} \quad (3)$$

We define accuracy as the percentage of correctly matched entities, corresponding to up-to-date entities in $F(S_I)$, to all entiies in $F(S_I)$ together with entities that are present in Ω and not mentioned in $F(S_I)$. We have:

$$\mathsf{Acc}(\mathsf{F}(\mathsf{S_I}),\mathsf{t}) = \frac{\mathsf{Up}(\mathsf{F}(\mathsf{S_I}),\mathsf{t})}{\mid \mathsf{F}(\mathsf{S_I}) \cup \Omega_\mathsf{P} \mid_\mathsf{t}} \quad (4)$$

Using Equations 1, 2 and 3, one can compute accuracy by:

$$\mathsf{Acc}(\mathsf{F}(\mathsf{S_I}),\mathsf{t}) = \frac{\mathsf{GF}(\mathsf{F}(\mathsf{S_I}),\mathsf{t})}{1 - \mathsf{Cov}(\mathsf{F}(\mathsf{S_I}),\mathsf{t}) + \frac{\mathsf{GF}(\mathsf{F}(\mathsf{S_I}),\mathsf{t})}{\mathsf{LF}(\mathsf{F}(\mathsf{S_I}),\mathsf{t})}} \quad (5)$$

Figure 4(c) shows the accuracy corresponding to Example 5.

4. ESTIMATING THE QUALITY METRICS

In this section we first introduce a collection of statistical models that describe the changes in the world and the update patterns in each data source (Section 4.1). Then, we show how these can be used to estimate the quality of integrated data for an arbitrary collection of sources at a future time point (Section 4.2).

4.1 Modeling Data Changes

Estimating the quality of integrated data for future time points requires knowledge of the appearance, disappearance and value update patterns in the world and each source. Extracting the evolution patterns for the world for source-based snapshots requires solving the *history integration* problem [2, 15], that is, unifying the entity streams of the sources into a single stream describing the evolution of the world. The update patterns of sources can then be extracted by comparing the evolution of each source with that of the world.

4.1.1 Modeling Changes in the World

Given a data domain Ω, we assume that (a) entity appearances, disappearances and value changes follow a Poisson random process; and (b) the lifespan of an entity and the time interval for which it does not get updated follow an exponential distribution.

Appearances: We model the number of entity appearances $N_i(\cdot)$ during the time interval $(t, t+\tau]$ as a Poisson distribution with intensity parameter λ_i and have that:

$$\Pr[(N_i(t+\tau) - N_i(t)) = k] = \frac{e^{-\lambda_i \tau}(\lambda_i \tau)^k}{k!} \quad (6)$$

We approximate λ_i as its maximum likelihood estimate (MLE) corresponding to the average rate of data appearances in the world. To compute the latter, we divide the time window T into intervals of fixed length, and calculate the average occurrence rate of entity appearances over these intervals. Finally, we extract the starting point of the Poisson process by calculating the total number of entities in the world by the end of T.

Disappearances: The lifespan of an entity follows an exponential distribution with rate parameter γ_d, that is, the probability that the lifespan of an entity is at most τ is $F_d(\tau) = 1 - e^{-\gamma_d \tau}$. We approximate γ_d by its MLE which is equal to the inverse of the average entity lifespan observed over the time window T. Due to the fixed length of the historical time window we have incomplete observations, that is, there are entities for which we know a lower bound but not their exact lifespan since they did not disappear until the end of T. These observations are called *right censored* and the MLE of γ_d for right censored data is given by:

$$\gamma_d^{-1} = \frac{\text{total lifespan of entities}}{\text{number of disappeared entities}} \quad (7)$$

According to the superposition property of Poisson processes [5], if the appearances of entities occur based on a Poisson process and the lifespan of each entity follows an exponential distribution, the disappearances of entities should also occur based on a Poisson random process with an intensity rate λ_d. Given a time window $(t, t+\tau]$ and with $|\Omega|_x$ denoting the total number of entities in the world at time x we have that $\lambda_d = \frac{1}{\tau}\sum_{x=t}^{t+\tau} \gamma_d \cdot |\Omega|_x$. The intensity parameter λ_d can be estimated using its MLE which corresponds to the average rate of disappearance over the time window T.

Value Updates: We assume that the interval between consecutive value changes of an entity follows an exponential distribution with parameter γ_u. This parameter can be learned similarly to entity disappearance. Moreover, one can easily show that value updates in the world occur based on a Poisson random process with intensity parameter λ_u, following the same process presented above.

Discussion: We presented the aforementioned modeling considering the entire data domain Ω for ease of exposition. However, these techniques are directly generalizable to heterogeneous data domains where different subdomains $\Omega_{<i>} \subseteq \Omega$ exhibit different change patterns, such as the business listing and GDELT domains presented in Section 1. In the case of heterogeneous data domains, we learn a collection of separate models for different homogenous data subdomains. This enables capturing non-uniform update patterns commonly observed in real-world domains. The details are omitted due to space limitations.

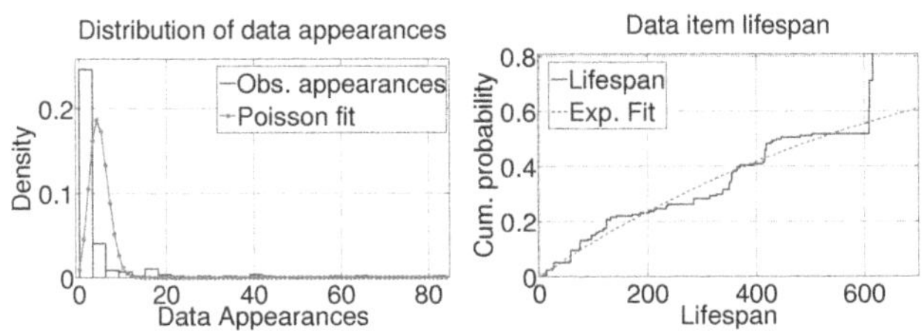

Figure 5: Fitting (a) a poisson distribution to the appearances of data items per time point and (b) an exponential distribution to the lifespan of data items for business listings.

Finally, we show that both BL and GDELT (Section 1) fit these assumptions. We study the distribution of observed appearances per day for various domain points in BL and GDELT and observe that indeed the number of updates per day follows a Poisson distribution. Figures 5(a) and 6 show the fitted and exact distribution for a domain point in BL and GDELT respectively. We next focus on BL, and plot the observed lifespan of data entries for the same domain point as before. Figure 5(b) shows that indeed the lifespan of entities follows an exponential distribution. The observed cumulative distribution for the lifespan presents a peak after 600 days which corresponds to censored data. Similar results were observed for all points in both domains.

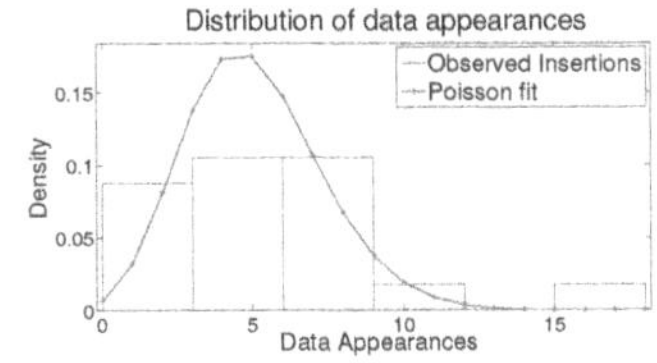

Figure 6: Fitting a poisson distribution to the appearances of data items per time point for GDELT.

4.1.2 Modeling Updates in Data Sources

The update patterns of a data source depend on its effectiveness in capturing changes from the world. We define the effectiveness of a source S in capturing an entity appearance as the probability $G_i(\tau)$ that S will incorporate this entity appearance in its content in a maximum of τ time units. Similarly, we define the probabilities G_d and G_u for entity disappearances and value changes.

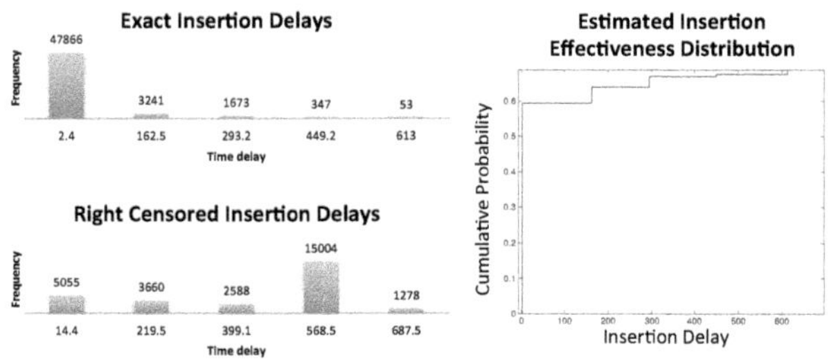

Figure 7: Exact and right censored insertion delay histograms with the effectiveness distribution G_i for a source in BL

Next, we describe how to learn these distributions. For ease of exposition we focus on G_i. The derivations of G_d and G_u are similar. We approximate G_i as the Kaplan-Meier empirical distribution [8] corresponding to the delay between the appearance of an entity in the world and its insertion in a source S. Given the evolution of source S and the world over the time-window T, one can extract two delay histograms characterizing the insertions in S: (a) one corresponding to exact observations, that is, insertions of items that appeared in the world and were also inserted in S before the end of the observed time window T, and (b) one corresponding to right-censored observation, that is, insertions of items that appeared in the world during T but were not inserted in S until the end of T. These two histograms are then combined to extract the empirical distribution G_i. To illustrate this, we consider the business listing domain. Figure 7 shows the two delay histograms corresponding to exact and right-censored observations for a source in BL, together with the learned effectiveness distribution G_i of the source.

The effectiveness distribution G_i assumes as input the duration of the time interval $t - t_c$ between a time point t and the actual occurrence of an entity appearance t_c. However, data sources get updated with a fixed frequency, and hence, the time point t may not be aligned with the latest update point of the source. We extend the effectiveness distributions G_i, G_u and G_d to account for the common case of fixed update frequencies of the sources. Again, we focus on G_i for ease of exposition. Given a source S that gets updated with a frequency f_S, we define $T_S(t)$ to be a function that returns the latest update time point of S until time t inclusive. We define $T_S(t)$ as $T_S(t) = \frac{\lfloor (t-t_0^S) f_S \rfloor}{f_S} + t_0^S$, where t_0^S denotes the last time S was updated during the historical time window T. Using this we update the definition of G_i to be:

$$G_i(t, t_c) = \begin{cases} G_i(T_S(t) - t_c) & \text{if } t \geq T_S(t) \geq t_c \\ 0 & \text{otherwise} \end{cases} \quad (8)$$

Finally, we compute the update frequency of a source S as follows: We consider that $f_S = \frac{1}{u_S}$, where u_S denotes the average update interval of S. Let $M_S = \{t_1, t_2, \ldots, t_m\}$ be the timestamps of different content updates in S ordered by time, and let $I_S = \{t_2 - t_1, t_3 - t_2, \ldots, t_m - t_{m-1}\}$ be the set of observed time intervals for S. We compute u_S by taking the average over the elements of I_S.

Discussion: Similarly to world changes, the aforementioned techniques are directly generalizable to sources that exhibit varying effectiveness on capturing updates for different data subdomains. In this case, we learn a collection of separate models for the different homogenous subdomains to capture the complex update patterns commonly exhibited by real-world sources.

4.2 Quality Estimation

We can now estimate the coverage, freshness and accuracy for integrating a set of data sources S_I at a future time point t. The quality of the integration result for future time points relies on the content changes in the integrated data. We first describe how to estimate the content changes in $F(S_I)$ and we then present how the different quality metrics can be estimated.

4.2.1 Content Changes Under Union Semantics

Given a set of sources S_I we want to estimate the content of the integrated data $F(S_I)$ at a future time point t. For this, we first characterize the content of $F(S_I)$, in terms of up-to-date, out-of-date and non-deleted entities, at the end t_0 of the available historical time window T and then we examine how the content of $F(S_I)$ changes by estimating how effectively the entity appearances, disappearances and value changes occurring in the world up to time $t \succ t_0$ are captured in $F(S_I)$.

To determine the content of $F(S_I)$ for a set S_I at time t_0, we consider the up-to-date, out-of-date and non-deleted entities in each source $S \in S_I$ extracted by comparing the content of S with the actual entities in the world. The set of up-to-date entities in $F(S_I)$ is computed by taking the union of up-to-date entities across all sources in S_I. The set of out-of-date and non-deleted entities are extracted in a similar fashion. Conflicts between entities that are up-to-date in one source and out-of-date in another are resolved by considering only the reference with the most recent time-stamp.

Procedurally, we store three different signatures (bit arrays) for each source $S \in \bar{\mathbf{S}}$: (a) a signature B_S^{up} for the up-to-date items, (b) a signature B_S^{cov} for the up-to-date and out-of-date (i.e., the covered) items, and (c) a signature B_S for all the items in the source. All similar bit arrays have the same size across different sources. Using these signatures the number of entities mentioned in $F(S_I)$ is $|\bigvee_{S \in S_I} B_S|$, the number of up-to-date entities is $|\bigvee_{S \in S_I} B_S^{up}|$, and the number of covered entities is $|\bigvee_{S \in S_I} B_S^{cov}|$.

To estimate the content changes in $F(S_I)$ at time t, we need to estimate the effectiveness of S_I at capturing changes in the world. We focus on insertions of new entities. Let $\Pr(\mathsf{Ins}(F(S_I), t, \tau))$ be the probability that a data appearance at time τ was captured in $F(S_I)$ by time t. Assuming that the sources in S_i are independent, this probability corresponds to the probability of at least one source in S_I capturing the appearance of the new data item and have that:

$$\Pr(\mathsf{Ins}(F(S_I), t, \tau)) = \left(1 - \prod_{S \in S_I} \left(1 - G_i^S(T_S(t), \tau)\right)\right) \quad (9)$$

We continue with deletions in $F(S_I)$ corresponding to disappeared items from the world. Let $\Pr(\mathsf{Del}(F(S_I), t, \tau))$ be the probability that an entity disappearance at time τ was captured by $F(S_I)$ until time t. This probability corresponds to the probability that at least one of the sources in S_I that mentioned this entity at time τ captured the disappearance event until time t. According to Equation (1), the probability of an entity being mentioned in a source at a particular time point is equal to its coverage. We have:

$$\Pr(\mathsf{Del}(F(S_I), t, \tau)) = 1 - \prod_{S \in S_I} (1 - \mathsf{Cov}(\mathsf{S}, \tau) \mathsf{G}_\mathsf{d}^\mathsf{S}(\mathsf{T_S}(\mathsf{t}), \tau)) \quad (10)$$

Following a similar process, we have that the probability of a value update being captured in $F(S_I)$ is given by:

$$\Pr(\mathsf{Upd}(F(S_I), t, \tau)) = 1 - \prod_{S \in S_I} (1 - \mathsf{Cov}(\mathsf{S}, \tau) \mathsf{G}_\mathsf{u}^\mathsf{S}(\mathsf{T_S}(\mathsf{t}), \tau)) \quad (11)$$

4.2.2 Quality Estimation at Future Time Points

We now describe how we estimate the coverage and freshness of the integrated data for a future time point $t \succ t_0$. The accuracy can be derived using Equation (5).

Coverage: Let $\mathbb{E}[|\Omega|_t]$ be the expected number of entities in the world at time t, $\mathbb{E}[\mathsf{Ins}(F(S_I), t)]$ be the expected number of entities of newly appeared entities in the world that have not been deleted until time t and were also insured in $F(S_I)$ up to time t, and $\mathbb{E}[\mathsf{OldCov}(F(S_I), t)]$ the expected number of entities that were already covered by $F(S_I)$ at time t_0 and have not disappeared from the world until time t. We can compute the coverage as follows:

$$\mathsf{Cov}^*(\mathsf{F}(\mathsf{S_I}), \mathsf{t}) = \frac{\mathbb{E}[\mathsf{OldCov}(\mathsf{F}(\mathsf{S_I}), \mathsf{t})] + \mathbb{E}[\mathsf{Ins}(\mathsf{F}(\mathsf{S_I}), \mathsf{t})]}{\mathbb{E}[|\Omega|_\mathsf{t}]} \quad (12)$$

To compute $\mathbb{E}[\mathsf{OldCov}(F(S_I), t)]$ we consider the number of covered entities in $F(S_I)$ at t_0, that is, the sum of up-to-date and out-of-date entities, and multiply that with the probability of an entity not disappearing until time t. Using the memoryless property of the Poisson process for data disappearances we have that:

$$\mathbb{E}[\mathsf{OldCov}(F(S_I), t)] = \mathsf{Cov}(\mathsf{F}(\mathsf{S_I}), \mathsf{t_0}) \cdot |\Omega|_{\mathsf{t_0}} \cdot \mathsf{e}^{-\gamma_d(\mathsf{t}-\mathsf{t_0})} \quad (13)$$

where $\mathsf{Cov}(\mathsf{F}(\mathsf{S_I}), \mathsf{t_0})$ and $|\Omega|_{t_0}$ can be computed by the signatures and extracted statistics described above. Since data appearances and disappearances occur based on a Poisson process we have for $\mathbb{E}[|\Omega_P|_t]$ that:

$$\mathbb{E}[|\Omega|_t] = |\Omega|_{t_0} + \sum_{\tau=t_0}^{t} [\lambda_i - \lambda_d] \quad (14)$$

Finally, we compute $\mathbb{E}[\mathsf{Ins}(F(S_I), t)]$ using Equation (9) and the fact that data appearances follow a Poisson random process and the entity lifespan is exponentially distributed:

$$\mathbb{E}[\mathsf{Ins}(F(S_I), t)] = \sum_{\tau=t_0}^{t} \lambda_i \cdot e^{-\gamma_d(t-\tau)} \cdot \Pr(\mathsf{Ins}(F(S_I), t, \tau)) \quad (15)$$

The coverage estimator corresponds to a non-decreasing submodular function. A set function $G : 2^V \to \mathbb{R}$ mapping subsets $A \subseteq V$ into the real numbers is *submodular* [4] if for all $A \subseteq B \subseteq V$, and $v' \in V \setminus B$, it holds that $G(A \cup \{v'\}) - G(A) \geq G(B \cup \{v'\}) - G(B)$ (i.e., adding v' to a set A increases G no less than adding v' to a superset B of A). Function G is *nondecreasing*, if for every $A \subseteq B \subseteq V$, it holds that $G(A) \leq G(B)$.

THEOREM 1 (SUBMODULAR COVERAGE). *The coverage estimate* $\mathsf{Cov}^*(\cdot)$ *for any set* S_I *and time t is a non-decreasing submodular function.*

PROOF SKETCH. The coverage estimator (Equation (12)) is a non-decreasing submodular function as it is a non-negative linear combination of two monotonic submodular functions. The first function referring to the coverage of $F(S_I)$ at time t_0, can be shown to be non-decreasing submodular as it is derived by the set union function. The second function, corresponding to future time points, is also non-decreasing submodular as it is derived from the probability inclusion exclusion formula for independent events. □

Freshness: Let $\mathbb{E}[\mathsf{Up}(\mathsf{F}(\mathsf{S_I}), \mathsf{t})]$ be the expected number of up-to-date entities in the integration $F(S_I)$ of S_I at time t, $\mathbb{E}[|F(S_I)|_t]$ be the expected number of all entities in $F(S_I)$, and $\mathbb{E}[|\Omega|_t]$ the expected number of entities in the world at time t. We estimate the local and global freshness for S_I as:

$$\mathsf{LF}^*(\mathsf{F}(\mathsf{S_I}), \mathsf{t}) = \frac{\mathbb{E}[\mathsf{Up}(\mathsf{F}(\mathsf{S_I}), \mathsf{t})]}{\mathbb{E}[|F(S_I)|_t]} \quad (16)$$

$$\mathsf{GF}^*(\mathsf{F}(\mathsf{S_I}), \mathsf{t}) = \frac{\mathbb{E}[\mathsf{Up}(\mathsf{F}(\mathsf{S_I}), \mathsf{t})]}{\mathbb{E}[|\Omega_P|_t]} \quad (17)$$

We first show how to compute $\mathbb{E}[|F(S_I)|_t]$. We need to estimate the number of newly inserted and newly deleted entities in $F(S_I)$ until time t. Let $|F(S_I)|_{t_0}$ be the number of entities in $F(S_I)$ at t_0 computed by the signatures in Section 4.2.1. We have:

$$\mathbb{E}[|F(S_I)|_t] = |F(S_I)|_{t_0} + \mathbb{E}[\mathsf{Ins}(F(S_I), t)] - \mathbb{E}[\mathsf{Del}(F(S_I), t)] \quad (18)$$

where $\mathbb{E}[\mathsf{Ins}(F(S_I), t)]$ is as in Equation (15) and $\mathbb{E}[\mathsf{Del}(F(S_I), t)]$ denotes the expected number of deleted items from $F(S_I)$. To compute the expected number of deleted items we multiply the average number of data disappearances per time unit λ_d given by the Poisson occurrence of data disappearances with the probability that an entity disappearance was captured by the sources in S_I. The latter corresponds to $\Pr(\mathsf{Del}(F(S_I), t, \tau))$ computed in Equation (10). We have:

$$\mathbb{E}[\mathsf{Del}(F(S_I), t)] = \sum_{\tau=t_0}^{t} \lambda_d \cdot \Pr(\mathsf{Del}, F(S_I), t, \tau)) \quad (19)$$

Next, we show how to compute $\mathbb{E}[\mathsf{Up}(\mathsf{F}(\mathsf{S_I}), \mathsf{t})]$. The latter can be expressed as the summation of three quantities:

- $\mathbb{E}[\text{OldUp}]$: the expected up-to-date entities already present in $F(S_I)$ that did not change in the world until time t.
- $\mathbb{E}[\text{InsUp}]$: the expected newly inserted entities in $F(S_I)$ that appeared in the world during $[t_0, t]$ and their values were not updated until t.
- $\mathbb{E}[\text{ExUp}]$: the expected entities that were present in both $F(S_I)$ and the world, their latest update was captured in $F(S_I)$, and have not disappeared from the world by t.

We have $\mathbb{E}[\mathsf{Up}(\mathsf{F}(\mathsf{S_I}), \mathsf{t})] = \mathbb{E}[\text{OldUp}] + \mathbb{E}[\text{InsUp}] + \mathbb{E}[\text{ExUp}]$.

To compute the three aforementioned quantities we first need to compute the probability of an entity not disappearing until t, denoted by $\Pr(\text{In } \Omega \text{ at } t)$ and the probability of none of its values getting updated during $[t_0, t]$, denoted by $\Pr(\text{Not Upd.}, t)$. Since the lifespan and update intervals follow exponential distributions, we have that $\Pr(\text{In } \Omega \text{ at } t) = e^{-\gamma_d(t-t_0)}$ and $\Pr(\text{Not Upd.}, t) = e^{-\gamma_u(t-t_0)}$. Finally, recall that the up-to-date entities in $F(S_I)$ are $\mathsf{Up}(\mathsf{F}(\mathsf{S_I}), \mathsf{t_0}) = |\bigvee_{\mathsf{S} \in \mathsf{S_I}} \mathsf{B}_\mathsf{S}^{\mathsf{up}}|$. According to the Poisson arrival of changes, we have:

$$\mathbb{E}[\mathsf{OldUp}] = \mathsf{Up}(\mathsf{F}(\mathsf{S_I}), \mathsf{t_0}) \Pr(\text{In } world \text{ at t}) \Pr(\text{Not upd.}, \mathsf{t})$$

$$\mathbb{E}[\mathsf{InsUp}] = \sum_{\tau=t_0}^{t} \lambda_i \Pr(\text{In } \Omega \text{ at } t) \Pr(\text{Not upd.}, t) \Pr(\mathsf{Ins}(F(S_I), t, \tau))$$

$$\mathbb{E}[\mathsf{ExUp}] = \sum_{\tau=t_0}^{t} \lambda_u \Pr(\text{In } \Omega \text{ at } t) \Pr(\text{Not upd.}, t) \Pr(\mathsf{Upd}(F(S_I), t, \tau))$$

where $\Pr(\mathsf{Ins}(F(S_I), t, \tau))$ and $\Pr(\mathsf{Upd}(F(S_I), t, \tau))$ are as in Equation (9) and Equation (11).

We can prove that the global freshness estimate is also a non-decreasing submodular function. However, the same does not hold for local freshness.

THEOREM 2 (SUBMODULAR GLOBAL FRESHNESS). *The global freshness estimate* $\mathsf{GF}^*(\cdot)$ *for any set* S_I *and time t is a non-decreasing submodular function.*

PROOF SKETCH. Similar to the previous proof sketch. □

Estimator Complexity: Given a set of time points of interest T_f, we need to estimate the quality for each $t \in T_f$ (Section 2.2). The run time complexity is $\mathcal{O}(\sum_{t \in T_f}(t - t_0) \cdot |S_I|)$, since evaluating the estimators presented above requires $\mathcal{O}((t-t_0) \cdot |S_I|)$ operations for each $t \in T_f$.

5. SELECTING FRESH SOURCES

Dong et al. [3] proved that not only source selection in the context of data fusion is NP-complete but also estimating the integration quality is #P-hard. In contrast to static source selection, the quality estimators for time-dependent metrics can be approximated efficiently under an integration model using the union semantics (Section 4.2). Moreover, we identified that the coverage and global freshness estimates are non-decreasing submodular functions. Exploiting submodularity, we next present a set of local-search algorithms for solving the different versions of time-aware source selection (Section 2.2) that come with theoretical guarantees on the quality of the solution.

Next, we focus on integration profit functions that satisfy the submodularity property. We discuss how time-aware source selection can be solved for arbitrary profit functions at the end of this section. Given a set of time points of interest T_f, the necessary conditions for a profit function to be submodular are:

- The integration gain $G_F(S_I, t)$ for each time point $t \in T_f$ has to be a non-negative linear function of either estimated coverage or global freshness of $F(S_I)$.
- The aggregate function A to compute $G_F(S_I, T_f)$ (Section 2.2) should be an average (or non-negative weighted average) since the class of submodular functions is closed under non-negative linear combinations.
- The cost function $C_F(S_I, T_f)$ has to be an additive function, so that the profit function $G_F(S_I, T_f) - C_F(S_I, T_f)$ is also submodular since the difference of a submodular and an additive function is still submodular.

Time-Aware Source Selection: We consider the basic version of time-aware source selection (Definition 3). For simplicity, we consider that no constraint is set on the budget β_c. This version corresponds to the problem of maximizing a monotone submodular function, and can be solved by a local-search algorithm introduced by Feige et al. [4] (Algorithm 1).

Algorithm 1 Submodular Maximization

1: **Input:** $\bar{\mathbf{S}}$: set of sources available; f: value oracle access to submodular function; n: cardinality of $\bar{\mathbf{S}}$;
2: **Output:** S_I: a set of selected sources;
3: Set $v \leftarrow \arg\max\{f(u) | u \in \bar{\mathbf{S}}\}$ and $S_I \leftarrow \{u\}$
4: **while** one of the following local operations applies **do**
5: /* **Addition operation on** S_I. */
6: **if** $e \in \bar{\mathbf{S}} \setminus S_I$ such that $f(S_I \cup \{e\}) > (1 + \frac{\epsilon}{n^2} f(S_I))$ **then**
7: $S_I \leftarrow S_I \cup \{e\}$
8: /* **Deletion operation on** S_I. */
9: **if** $e \in S_I$ such that $f(S_I \setminus \{e\}) > (1 + \frac{\epsilon}{n^2} f(S_I))$ **then**
10: $S_I \leftarrow S_I \setminus \{e\}$
11: **return** $\arg\max_{\bar{S} \in \{S_I, \bar{\mathbf{S}} \setminus S_I\}} (f(\bar{S}))$

This algorithm starts by selecting a single source that maximizes the profit (Ln.3) and then tries to increase the value of the running solution S_I either by *including* a new element in S_I or by *discarding* one of the elements of S_I until a local optimum is reached (Ln. 4 - 10). Once a local optimum is reached, the algorithm checks if the complement of the running selection improves the solution and returns the selected sources (Ln.11). The algorithm is proven to yield a constant-factor approximation of $(1 + \frac{\epsilon}{n^2})$ and is shown to use $\mathcal{O}(\frac{1}{\epsilon} n^3 logn)$ oracle calls [4].

Varying Frequency Source Selection: Selecting the optimal set of sources and their corresponding frequencies can be expressed as an optimization problem with a unified objective function. Let $\bar{\mathbf{S}}$ be the set of available sources. For each source $S_i \in \bar{\mathbf{S}}$ we can select a variable update frequency $f'_{S_i} = \frac{f_{S_i}}{l_i}, l_i \in \{1, 2, \ldots, m_i\}, m_i \in \mathbb{Z}^+$ lower than the original frequency f_{S_i} of the source. We define the *augmented set of available sources* defined as $\mathbf{S_{aug}} = \{S_1^1, S_1^2, \ldots, S_1^{m_1}, \ldots, S_i^1, \ldots, S_i^{m_i}, \ldots S_k^{m_k}\}$ where S_i^j denotes a version of source S_i with an update frequency of $\frac{f_{S_i}}{j}$. We can now select sources from $\mathbf{S_{aug}}$ instead of $\bar{\mathbf{S}}$ - each entry of $\mathbf{S_{aug}}$ can be considered as a different source - under the constraint that only one of the $[l_i]$ versions of an actual source S_i will be selected for integration.

The submodular objective is now defined over the ground set $\mathbf{S_{aug}}$ and the frequency constraints can be expressed as a *uniform matroid constraint*. A uniform matroid U_n^r is defined over a set of n elements, and a subset of the elements is independent if and only if it contains at most r elements. Thus, each of the k constraints corresponds to a uniform matroid constraint of rank 1. Every uniform matroid is also a *partition matroid*. The varying frequency time-aware source selection corresponds to the problem of maximizing a monotone submodular function under a fixed number of partition matroid constraints, and can be solved by an algorithm that yields a constant-factor approximation of $\frac{1}{k+\epsilon}$ [9].

Algorithm 2 Submodular Maximization with Matroid Constraints

1: **Input:** $\mathbf{S_{aug}}$: ground set of sources; k: number of matroid constraints;
2: **Output:** S_{opt}: a set of selected sources;
3: Set $V_1 = \mathbf{S_{aug}}$
4: **for** $i = 1, \cdots, k+1$ **do**
5: Apply the approximate local search procedure A on a ground set V_i to obtain a solution $S_i \subseteq V_i$ corresponding to the problem:
$$max\{f(S) : S \in \cap_{j=1}^{k} \mathcal{I}_j, S \subseteq V_i\}$$
6: Set $V_{i+1} = V_i \setminus S_i$
7: **return** $S_{opt} \leftarrow max\{f(S_1), \cdots, f(S_{k+1})\}$

The algorithm is shown in Algorithm 2. The independent sets defined by the matroid constraints divide the ground set of sources in multiple partitions, each corresponding to the intersection of a combination of independent sets from all constraints. The algorithm identifies $k+1$ disjoint partitions for which the optimization objective is locally maximized and returns the partition with the highest objective value. In fact, the algorithm performs $k+1$ iterations (Ln. 4) and at each iteration i uses a local-search procedure (Ln. 5) similar to the one used in the basic version (Algorithm 3) to select an approximately optimal set of sources over a subset V_i of the available sources. Each of the sets V_i corresponds to the union of a subset of the aforementioned partitions. After each iteration the set of available sources for the next iteration is restricted to sources that were not previously selected (Ln. 6). Finally, the algorithm returns the partition, i.e., a subset of the data sources, with the highest objective value (Ln. 7).

The local search procedure is given a set of available data sources and greedily selects a set of available sources that maximizes the optimization objective under the given constraints. The algorithm detects a single source that yields the highest objective value (Ln. 4) and proceeds by searching the neighborhood of the running solution for solutions that improve the objective. The local neighborhood of the running solution is constructed either by removing a source from the solution (Ln. 5-7) or by exchanging a set of selected sources with a new source such that all the constraints are satisfied (Ln. 8-10). The local search procedure iterates until a local optimum is retrieved. The running time of Algorithm 3 is $\frac{1}{\epsilon} n^{\mathcal{O}(k)}$ with $n = |\mathbf{S_{aug}}|$ and k is the number of matroid constraints, and thus the running time of Algorithm 2 is $\mathcal{O}((k+1)\frac{1}{\epsilon} n^{\mathcal{O}(k)})$ [9].

Algorithm 3 Local Search Procedure

Input: X: ground set of sources; f: value oracle access to submodular function; n: cardinality of $\mathbf{S_{aug}}$;
Output: S_I: a set of selected sources;
Set $v \leftarrow \arg\max\{f(u)|u \in X\}$ and $S_I \leftarrow \{u\}$
while one of the following local operations applies **do**
  /* **Delete operation on S_I.** */
  if $e \in S_I$ such that $f(S_I \setminus \{e\}) > (1 + \frac{\epsilon}{n^4} f(S_I))$ **then**
    $S_I \leftarrow S_I \setminus \{e\}$
  /* **Exchange operation on S_I.** */
  if $d \in X \setminus S_I$ and $e_i \in S_I \cup \{\emptyset\}$ (for $1 \leq i \leq k$) are such that $(S_I \setminus \{e_i\}) \cup \{d\} \in \mathcal{I}_i$ for all $i \in [k]$ and $f((S_I \setminus \{e_1, \cdots e_k\}) \cup \{d\}) \geq (1 + \frac{\epsilon}{n^4}) f(S_I)$ **then**
    $S_I \leftarrow (S_I \setminus \{e_1, \cdots, e_k\}) \cup \{d\}$
return S_I

Slice Time-Aware Source Selection: The basic submodular optimization problem of time-aware source selection can be trivially extended to account for this case by including all the micro-sources in $\bar{\mathbf{S}}$. The set of available sources can also be replaced by its corresponding augmented set to account for variable update frequencies of the micro-sources.

Generic Profit Functions: When the profit function used to quantify the integration profit is not submodular (e.g., when the gain is quantified using the accuracy or local freshness of $F(S_I)$), we use the GRASP heuristic introduced by Dong et al. [3] to solve time-aware source selection. We point out that GRASP needs to be extended only when solving the varying frequency source selection problem to account for the frequency constraints presented above. We refer the reader to Dong et al. [3] for details on the algorithm.

6. EXPERIMENTS

We present an empirical evaluation of the proposed framework. The main questions we seek to address are: (1) how accurately can the proposed models predict the data changes in the world, and how effective they are at estimating the quality of data sources at future time points, (2) how the different source selection algorithms perform under different families of gain and cost functions, and (3) how well do the proposed algorithms scale. We empirically study these questions on both real-world and synthetic datasets.

6.1 Experimental Setup

Data: The first dataset we consider is the business listing (BL) dataset introduced in Section 1 containing daily snapshots from 43 data sources providing business listings over a period of 23 months. Each data entry includes the source-id, a description of the business (i.e., phone, address, category) and the timestamp of the last insertion or update operation performed on it. We assign a deletion timestamp to an entry by considering the timestamp of the latest snapshot mentioning it. If that timestamp corrsponds to the end of the observed time window, we assume the entry was not deleted.

To extract the evolution of the world we first detected duplicates across the source snapshots using standard canonicalization and format standardization techniques together with an exact matching algorithm, and then applied an integration scheme following the union semantics describe earlier. The output was verified against a gold standard provided with BL containing a subset of businesses. The sources provide 84,791,789 listings for 28,094,382 distinct businesses over 51 locations (i.e., states including Washington, DC) corresponding to 1496 business types. Figure 8(a) shows the different types of sources contained in the dataset.

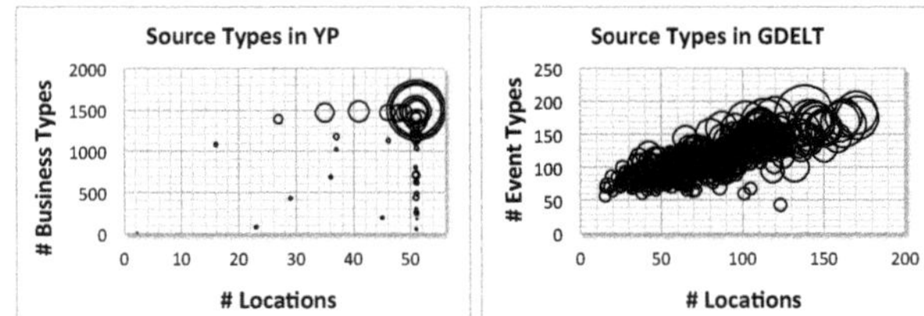

Figure 8: Different source types (a) in BL and (b) GDELT. The radius of each circle is proportional to the size of the source.

The second dataset we use is GDELT (Section 1). GDELT contains daily snapshots of events extracted from articles published in 15,275 news sources over a period of 22 days. All entries contain information about the source reporting the event, and characteristics such as the actors associated with the event, the location and the type of the event. We extract the evolution of the world using similar techniques as for BL. In total the sources provide 2,833,755 entries for 2,219,704 distinct events corresponding to 242 different locations and 236 different event types. Figure 8(b) shows the different types of the 500 largest sources in the dataset.

Finally, we use a collection of synthetically generated datasets BL+ , using BL as a seed, to evaluate the scalability of the proposed algorithms. We decompose the sources in BL into multiple overlapping micro-sources, where each micro-source covers a randomly selected subset of the initial source. If $|L|$ denotes the locations in a source S, we construct each micro-source to contain all the entities from S belonging to a randomly selected subset of locations from the original source. The number of locations in each micro-source is chosen uniformly at random from a uniform distribution $\mathcal{U}(0.2 \cdot |L|, 0.5 \cdot |L|)$. We vary the total number of micro-sources to be in $\{0, 1, 2, 5, 10, 20, 50, 100, 200\}$ obtaining 9 different datasets ranging from 43 to 8643 sources.

Preprocessing: We train the statistical models that describe the changes in BL using the data corresponding to the first 10 months, and evaluate our techniques on the next 13 months. For GDELT, we train the change models using the first 15 days and use the next 7 days for evaluation.

Algorithms: We evaluate the following algorithms:

- Greedy: The same as the greedy algorithm used by Dong et al. [3]. Starting from an empty selection set the algorithm iteratively selects the source that maximizes the integration profit until it reaches a local optimum.
- MaxSub: Depending on the version of time-aware source selection MaxSub corresponds to the submodular optimization algorithms in Section 5.
- GRASP: The GRASP algorithm proposed by Dong et al. [3] for different configurations of (κ, r).

All algorithms are implemented in Java and the evaluation is performed on an Intel(R) Core(TM) i5 2.3 GHz/64bit/8GB machine.

Gain-Cost Models: We consider two families of gain models, i.e., (1) quality driven, and (2) data driven models. For the first, let Q be the quality (i.e., coverage, freshness or accuracy) of the integrated data. We consider: LINEARGAIN assumes that the gain grows linearly with a certain data quality metric Q and sets $G(Q) = 100Q$; QUADGAIN assumes that the gain grows quadratically with Q and sets $G(Q) = 100Q^2$; STEPGAIN assumes that reaching a milestone of quality would significantly increase the gain and sets

$$G(Q) = \begin{cases} 100Q & \text{if } 0 \leq Q < 0.2 \\ 100 + 100(Q - 0.2) & \text{if } 0.2 \leq Q < 0.5 \\ 150 + 100(Q - 0.5) & \text{if } 0.5 \leq Q < 0.7 \\ 200 + 100(Q - 0.7) & \text{if } 0.7 \leq Q < 0.95 \\ 300 + 100(Q - 0.95) & \text{if } 0.95 \leq Q \leq 1.0 \end{cases}$$

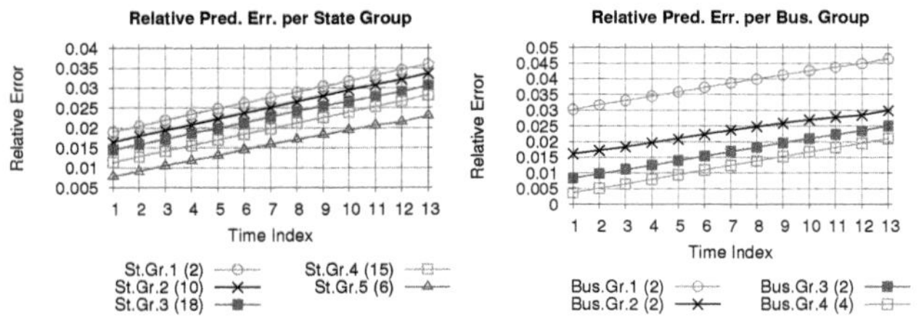

Figure 9: The relative error for predicting the total listings in BL for (a) five state groups and (b) four business category groups over 13 future time points.

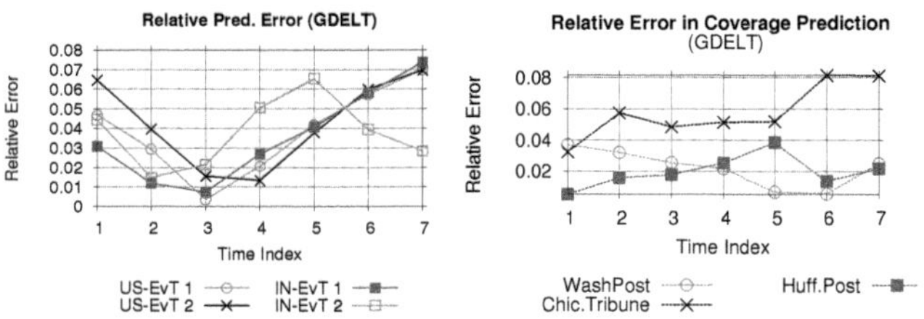

Figure 10: The relative error for predicting (a) the total events for four different event-location pairs in GDELT and (b) the quality of three large US news sources from GDELT for 7 consecutive future time points.

For the second category, denoted by DATAGAIN, we assume a gain of \$10 for each covered item in $F(S_I)$ and for a particular time point t we have $G(F(S_I), t) = 10 \cdot \mathsf{Cov}^*(\mathsf{F(S_I), t})|\Omega|_t$.

Finally, we assume an additive cost function. Similarly to DATAGAIN, we consider that each entity has a basic cost of \$10 and an actual cost of $c = \frac{\$10}{(\#\text{sources mentioning the item})}$. The cost of a source c is the total cost of items contained in it. When considering varying frequencies for sources we assign the source cost to be $c' = c/(1 + m/10)$, where m is the frequency divisor. Finally, we rescale the gain and cost to take values in $[0, 1]$.

6.2 Verifying Model Predictions

We examine how effective our change models are at predicting the world and source changes both in BL and GDELT.

For BL, we predict the number of businesses for the 51 locations, and the ten largest business categories. We compute the relative error between the actual and predicted values. We found that states can be divided in five groups with respect to the absolute value of their prediction error. Figure 9(a) shows the relative error for the representative state of each group. The size of each group is mentioned in the legend. Similarly, the ten largest business categories can be divided in four error groups. Figure 9(b) shows the relative error for the representative business category of each group. Similar behavior was observed for the rest of the business categories. We observe that our models can accurately predict the number of listings as the average relative error is around 2%. Moreover, the increase rate of the error is 0.001.

For GDELT, we predict the number of events for four event-location pairs over 7 days in the future and show the result in Figure 10(a). We observe that the prediction error is relatively small, considering that the amount of training data used in GDELT spanned over a time period of only 15 days. The variation observed is due to the dynamic nature of this domain.

Next, we evaluate our models on predicting the source quality over time. Figure 11 shows the relative error for predicting the coverage, accuracy and local freshness of the two largest sources in BL for 13 months in the future. The maximum relative error is less than 1.5% for the largest source and less than 2.5% for the other source. Figure 10(b) shows the relative error corresponding to the

Table 1: Various algorithms for source selection in BL on the percentage of outputting the best selection and average and worst (reported in parenthesis) profit difference from the best selection. Notation (κ, r) denotes the best performing GRASP algorithm. We consider sources with a fixed update frequency.

			Avg. Selection Quality		
Gain	Metric	Msr.	Greedy	Maxsub	Grasp
Linear	cov.	best	16.7%	50%	100% (5, 20)
		diff.	.005 (.01)%	.001 (.007)%	-
	acc.	best	0%	33.3%	83.3% (2, 100)
		diff.	9.5 (53.7)%	.39 (2.31)%	8.9 (53.7)%
Quad.	cov.	best	33.3%	66.7%	100% (10, 100)
		diff.	.017 (.06)%	.012 (.06)%	-
	acc.	best	100%	100%	100% (1,1)
		diff.	-	-	-
Step	cov.	best	50.0%	66.7%	83.3% (10, 100)
		diff.	7.45 (27.8)%	1.76 (10.6)%	.7 (4.2)%
	acc.	best	50%	66.7%	83.3% (5,100)
		diff.	6 (23.98)%	.8 (4.7)%	3.99 (23.98)%
Data	-	best	16.7%	50%	83.3% (5, 20)
		diff.	.004 (.01)%	.001 (.003)%	.002 (.007)%

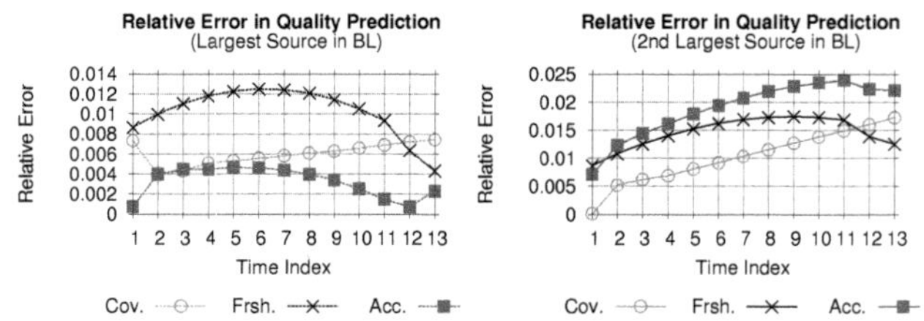

Figure 11: The relative error for predicting the quality of the two largest sources in BL for 13 consecutive future time points.

coverage of the four largest US data sources in GDELT for 7 days in the future. Again, we observe that the relative error is small.

6.3 Source Selection

Next, we evaluate the performance of the proposed source selection algorithms. We focus on two scenarios.

Fixed update frequencies. We assume a fixed update frequency for each data source and consider the basic time-aware source selection problem with a user being interested in ten future time points for six data domain points. We compute the overall gain by taking the average gain across time points. For BL, we select the six largest domain points corresponding to four business types in the states of California and New York. For GDELT, we consider six domain points corresponding to events in the United States. We compare the different algorithms for DATAGAIN, and LINEARGAIN, QUADGAIN, STEPGAIN considering the gain is quantified using coverage and accuracy for BL and coverage for GDELT.

We apply Greedy, MaxSub and GRASP with $\kappa \in \{1, 2, 5, 10\}$ and $r \in \{1, 10, 20, 100\}$ in solving the source selection problem for both datasets. GRASP with $(\kappa = 1, r = 1)$ corresponds to a hill-climbing algorithm. For each gain function, we compare the selections by the various algorithms and choose the one with the highest profit as the best. We report the percentage of times the best selection is returned by each algorithm and for sub-optimal selections we report the average and maximum, reported in parenthesis, profit difference from the best selection. For GRASP we report the (κ, r) configuration that obtained the best selection.

The results for BL are shown in Table 1. MaxSub and GRASP outperform Greedy returning solutions that result in up to 9.5% higher objective values on average and up to 53.7% in the worst case. While GRASP returns the best solution most of the times, the solutions returned by MaxSub are on average comparable to the ones obtained by GRASP with a low average profit difference. This behavior is expected since MaxSub unlike Greedy comes with rigorous theoretical guarantees, and GRASP applies a similar local search procedure to the one used by MaxSub. Nevertheless, we observe that randomization and multiple iterations help GRASP to obtain marginally better solutions. However, if we consider the run time of the algorithms (shown in Table 2), we see that MaxSub is one to two orders of magnitude faster than GRASP. Eventually, depending on the gain function, MaxSub can be a viable alternative compared to GRASP. Although, if the profit requirements are strict one should use GRASP.

Table 2: Average run times of the source selection algorithms for BL. Notation (κ, r) denotes the parameters of GRASP.

		Avg. Run Time (sec)					
Gain	Metric	Greedy	Maxsub	(1,1)	(2,10)	(5,20)	(10,100)
Linear	cov.	0.05	0.16	0.16	2.23	4.35	20.13
	acc.	0.42	1.6	1.5	14.9	39.9	144.2
Quad	cov.	0.03	0.11	0.14	1.6	3.3	17.6
	acc.	0.14	0.35	0.43	5.5	11.9	57.8
Step	cov.	0.03	0.11	0.13	1.6	2.8	15.25
	acc.	0.14	0.46	0.5	6.4	14.16	74.02
Data	-	0.04	0.18	0.17	2.4	4.6	25.7

We observed similar results for GDELT. In Table 3 we report the performance and runtime of the various algorithms. We see that for LINEARGAIN and DATAGAIN both MaxSub and GRASP outperform Greedy. While GRASP never fails to detect the best solution, the profit difference between MaxSub and GRASP is very small and more importantly MaxSub is again one to two orders of magnitude faster. We omit the results for QUADGAIN and STEPGAIN since all algorithms were able to retrieve the same solution.

Table 3: Performance and runtime comparison of the source selection algorithms for GDELT, showing the percentage of outputting the best selection and average and worst (reported in parenthesis) profit difference from the best selection. Notation (κ, r) denotes the best performing GRASP algorithm.

		Avg. Selection Quality		
Gain	Msr.	Greedy	Maxsub	Grasp
Linear Cov.	best	16.7%	50%	100% (10, 100)
	diff.	4.01 (13.7)%	0.5 (2)%	-
	runtime (sec)	8.58 (37)	74.12 (326)	1231.05 (4363)
Data	best	3.3%	0%	100% (10, 100)
	diff.	5.64 (14.9)%	.91 (3)%	-
	runtime (sec)	1.01 (5.03)	8.96 (44)	868.87 (4322)

Next, we report the average quality of the retrieved solution and the average number of sources selected for BL and GDELT. The results for BL are shown in Table 4. As shown, all algorithms tend to choose fewer sources when the gain is measured with respect to accuracy. We observe that all algorithms tend to select fewer large uniform sources and prefer more specialized smaller sources. Figure 12 shows the various source types selected from GRASP when the LINEARGAIN function with coverage and accuracy is used to specify the gain. A similar behavior was observed for all algorithms. Finally, Table 5 shows the results for GDELT. We see that GRASP and MaxSub were able to select significantly more sources and increase the coverage of the retrieved solution by 5% and 8%.

Table 4: Characteristics of the selected sources for various algorithms on BL for fixed source update frequencies.

Alg	Coverage		Accuracy	
	Avg. Qual.	Avg. #Srcs	Avg. Qual	Avg. #Srcs.
Greedy	0.52	10	0.49	8
MaxSub	0.56	11	0.57	7.6
GRASP	0.56	11	0.57	8.6

Variable update frequencies. Next, we consider different versions for each source corresponding to different update frequencies. We focus on BL and take seven different versions $S_i^1 \cdots, S_i^7$ for each original source. As before, we assume that the user is interested in the same ten future time points and the same six data domains.

Table 5: Characteristics of the selected sources for various algorithms on GDELT for fixed source update frequencies.

Alg	Greedy	MaxSub	GRASP
Avg. Coverage	0.57	0.62	0.65
Avg. # Srcs	154	163	167

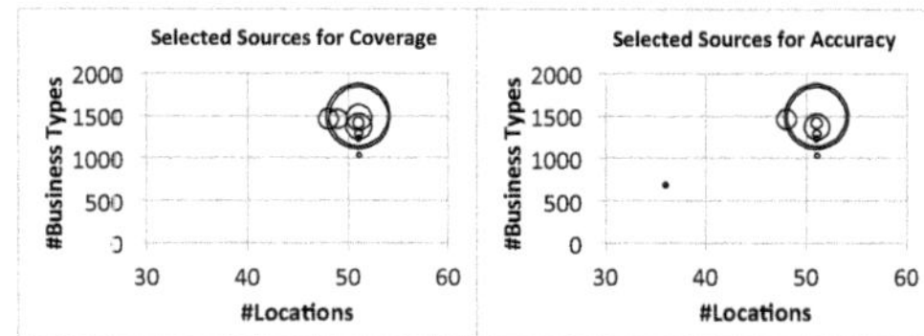

Figure 12: Selected sources when the gain is defined using coverage and accuracy. For accuracy smaller and more specialized sources are preferred.

We observe similar performance for the algorithms, as the one presented above. Namely, GRASP outperforms both Greedy and MaxSub. However, the difference in profit between the retrieved solutions is significantly smaller (less than 0.5% in average) compared to the previous case.

Focusing on the quality of the solutions returned by the various algorithms, we observe that allowing sources to have variable frequencies significantly improves the quality of the retrieved solutions. We observe that the average coverage and accuracy rise to 0.976 and 0.958 respectively, compared to 0.56 and 0.57 for the case of fixed frequencies. The reason is that by reducing the update frequency of a source the corresponding cost is reduced, and hence, the algorithms choose to integrate more sources. We report the corresponding results in Table 6. Finally, we observe that all algorithms preferred selecting large sources with a significantly reduced update frequency. However, for small specialized sources they either select the original update frequency or a small divisor of that. We report the average frequency divisors for uniform and specialized sources in Table 7.

Table 6: Characteristics of the selected sources for various algorithms on BL for sources with variable update frequencies.

Alg	Coverage		Accuracy	
	Avg. Qual.	Avg. #Srcs	Avg. Qual.	Avg. #Srcs.
Greedy	0.96	15.6	0.948	14.6
MaxSub	0.976	15.6	0.958	15
GRASP	0.976	16	0.958	16

6.4 Scalability

First, we evaluate the scalability of the various algorithms as the number of available sources increases. We set the gain function to LINEARGAIN with coverage, and use the synthetically generated datasets BL+ , considering source selection for a single data point for 10 future time points. The corresponding run times are shown in Figure 13(a), where the x-axis corresponds to the number of available data sources and the y-axis (shown in log-scale) to the run time measured in milliseconds. As shown, MaxSub is one to two orders of magnitude faster compared to the best performing alternatives of GRASP, and scales better as the number of sources increases.

Finally, we use BL to examine the scalability of the various algorithms with respect to the size of the input data domain, where the size of the input domain is the number of location-business type pairs specified in a certain user query. We evaluate the performance of Greedy, MaxSub and GRASP with $(\kappa = 5, r = 20)$ for LINEARGAIN with coverage and accuracy. The corresponding run times are shown in Figure 13(b), where the x-axis corresponds to the size of the input domain and the y-axis (shown in log scale) to the run time measured in milliseconds. Again, we observe that MaxSub is an order of magnitude faster than GRASP-(5,20).

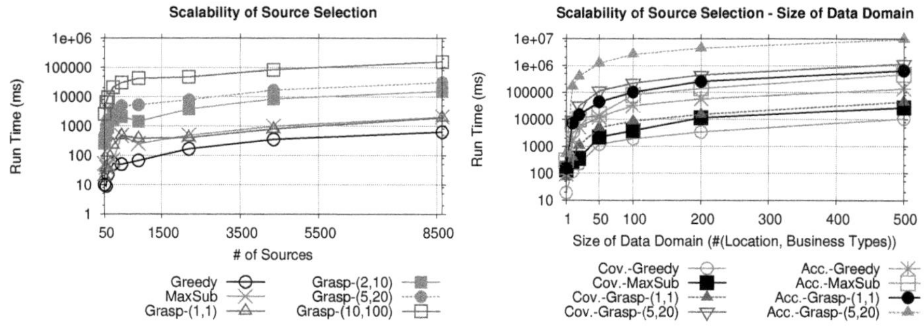

Figure 13: Run time of the various algorithms as (a) the number of sources and (b) the the size of the input domain increases.

Table 7: Average frequency divisor for uniform and specialized sources in the solution of the various algorithms.

Alg	Greedy	MaxSub	GRASP
Uniform Srcs.	4.9	5.2	4.9
Specialized Srcs.	2.6	2.9	3.2

6.5 Discussion

From our experiments we see that the proposed models can accurately estimate the evolution of the world and a source's quality. Also, the quality of the solution returned by MaxSub is comparable to GRASP. However, for large instances of source selection MaxSub is a more appealing option since it is one to two orders of magnitude faster than GRASP and presents better scalability. Finally, selecting the optimal update frequency for the selected set of sources can significantly increase the quality of integrated data.

7. RELATED WORK

Recently, Dong et. al [3] introduced the problem of source selection, and showed how one can maximize the profit of integration by optimizing the gain and cost of integrating sources jointly. However, this work focuses on static sources and is not applicable to sources whose content changes dynamically. Moreover, the proposed algorithms, while effective in practice, do not come with rigorous theoretical guarantees on their performance. In this paper, we considered the problem of source selection for dynamic sources and showed how to select a nearly-optimal set of sources and determine their optimal update frequencies by providing a set of algorithms with rigorous theoretical guarantees.

There has also been a lot of work on source relevance identification [12], but the focus is on finding sources relevant to a given query or domain and not on the quality of sources. A different line of work has considered the problem of online data integration [2, 15], however the cost of acquiring data is not considered. Moreover, a fair amount of work has considered the problem of determining the quality of multiple data sources and leveraging this information during data integration to improve the quality of the outcome [11, 13, 16, 19]. However, this work does not consider dynamic sources. Finally, Cho et al. [1], considered the problem of finding the optimal data extraction frequency from web-pages, but the authors do not reason about their quality and the cost as it is not of high importance in the web-page crawling scenario.

8. CONCLUSIONS AND FUTURE WORK

We studied the problem of source selection for dynamic sources whose content changes over time. We introduced statistical models describing the changes in the data domain and each source, and showed how to estimate the quality of integrated data at future time points. We defined the problem of time-aware source selection where we jointly select the optimal subset of sources to be integrated and their optimal update frequencies. We proposed an efficient local-search algorithm with rigorous theoretical guarantees on the quality of the retrieved solution for a large family of objective functions. Finally, experimental results show the effectiveness and scalability of our proposed framework.

One interesting research direction is to examine scenarios where new sources appear over time. It is of particular interest how sampling or online data integration techniques can be employed to derive meaningful estimates for the quality of newly appeared sources. Finally, we are actively working on relaxing some of the assumptions in the proposed framework such as source independence.

9. REFERENCES

[1] J. Cho and H. Garcia-Molina. Effective page refresh policies for web crawlers. *ACM Trans. Database Syst.*, 28(4), 2003.

[2] X. L. Dong, L. Berti-Equille, and D. Srivastava. Truth discovery and copying detection in a dynamic world. *PVLDB*, 2(1), 2009.

[3] X. L. Dong, B. Saha, and D. Srivastava. Less is more: Selecting sources wisely for integration. *PVLDB*, 6(2), 2012.

[4] U. Feige and V. S. Mirrokni. Maximizing non-monotone submodular functions. In *FOCS*, 2007.

[5] R. G. Gallager. *Discrete Stochastic Processes*. Kluwer Academic Publishers, Boston, 1996.

[6] T. Herzog, F. Scheuren, and W. Winkler. Record linkage. *Wiley Interdisciplinary Reviews: Computational Statistics*, 2010.

[7] T. Hua, C.-T. Lu, N. Ramakrishnan, F. Chen, J. Arredondo, D. Mares, and K. Summers. Analyzing civil unrest through social media. *Computer*, 46(12):80–84, 2013.

[8] E. L. Kaplan and P. Meier. Nonparametric Estimation from Incomplete Observations. *JASA*, 53:457–481, 1958.

[9] J. Lee, V. S. Mirrokni, V. Nagarajan, and M. Sviridenko. Non-monotone submodular maximization under matroid and knapsack constraints. STOC, 2009.

[10] K. Leetaru and P. Schrodt. Gdelt: Global data on events, language, and tone, 1979-2012. *Inter. Studies Association Annual Conf.*, 2013.

[11] X. Li, X. L. Dong, K. Lyons, W. Meng, and D. Srivastava. Truth finding on the deep web: is the problem solved? *PVLDB*, 6(2), 2012.

[12] W. Meng and C. T. Yu. *Advanced Metasearch Engine Technology*. Morgan & Claypool Publishers, 2010.

[13] G. A. Mihaila, L. Raschid, and M.-E. Vidal. Using quality of data metadata for source selection and ranking. In *WebDB*, 2000.

[14] A. C. Morris, V. Maier, and P. Green. From WER and RIL to MER and WIL: improved evaluation measures for connected speech recognition. In *INTERSPEECH*, 2004.

[15] A. Pal, V. Rastogi, A. Machanavajjhala, and P. Bohannon. Information integration over time in unreliable and uncertain environments. In *WWW*, 2012.

[16] G.-J. Qi, C. C. Aggarwal, J. Han, and T. Huang. Mining collective intelligence in diverse groups. WWW, 2013.

[17] M. Stonebraker, D. Bruckner, I. Ilyas, G. Beskales, M. Cherniack, S. Zdonik, A. Pagan, and S. Xu. Data curation at scale: The data tamer system. In *CIDR'13*, 2013.

[18] K. Wilson and J. S. Brownstein. Early detection of disease outbreaks using the internet. *CMAJ*, 180(8):829–831, 2009.

[19] B. Zhao, B. I. P. Rubinstein, J. Gemmell, and J. Han. A bayesian approach to discovering truth from conflicting sources for data integration. *PVLDB*, 5(6), 2012.

Sloth: Being Lazy is a Virtue (When Issuing Database Queries)

Alvin Cheung, Samuel Madden, and Armando Solar-Lezama
MIT CSAIL
{akcheung,madden,asolar}@csail.mit.edu

ABSTRACT

Many web applications store persistent data in databases. During execution, such applications spend a significant amount of time communicating with the database for retrieval and storing of persistent data over the network. These network round trips represent a significant fraction of the overall execution time for many applications and as a result increase their latency. While there has been prior work that aims to eliminate round trips by batching queries, they are limited by 1) a requirement that developers manually identify batching opportunities, or 2) the fact that they employ static program analysis techniques that cannot exploit many opportunities for batching. In this paper, we present Sloth, a new system that extends traditional *lazy evaluation* to expose query batching opportunities during application execution, even across loops, branches, and method boundaries. We evaluated Sloth using over 100 benchmarks from two large-scale open-source applications, and achieved up to a 3× reduction in page load time by delaying computation.

1. INTRODUCTION

Most web applications are backed by database servers that are physically separated from the servers hosting the application. Even though the two machines tend to reside in close proximity, a typical page load spends a significant amount of time issuing queries and waiting for network round trips to complete, with a consequent increase in application latency. The situation is exacerbated by object-relational mapping (ORM) frameworks such as Hibernate and Django, which access the database by manipulating native objects rather than issuing SQL queries. These libraries automatically translate accesses to objects into SQL, often resulting in multiple queries (and round trips) to reconstruct a single object. For example, even with the application and database servers hosted in the same data center, we found that many pages spend 50% or more of their time waiting on network communication.

Latency is important for many reasons. First, even hundreds of milliseconds of additional latency can dramatically increase the dissatisfaction of web application users. For example, a 2010 study by Akamai suggested that 57% of users will abandon a web page that takes more than three seconds to load [9]. As another example, Google reported in 2006 that an extra 0.5 second of latency reduced the overall traffic by 20% [6]. These numbers are likely worse on modern computers where pages load faster and faster, making it increasingly important to reduce the amount of time spent on database queries. Second, ORM frameworks can greatly increase load times by performing additional queries to retrieve objects that are linked to the one that was initially requested, as a result a few 10's of milliseconds per object can turn into seconds of additional latency for an entire web page [12, 2, 7, 10]. Though some techniques (such as Hibernate's "eager fetching") aim to mitigate this, they are far from perfect as we discuss below. Finally, decreasing latency often increases throughput: as each request takes less time to complete, the server can process more requests simultaneously.

There are two general approaches for programs to reduce application latency due to database queries: i) hide this latency by overlapping communication and computation, or ii) reduce the number of round trips by fetching more data in each one. Latency hiding is most commonly achieved by prefetching query results so that the communication time overlaps with computation, and the data is ready when the application really needs it. Both of these techniques have been explored in prior research. Latency hiding, which generally takes the form of asynchronously "prefetching" query results so that they are available when needed by the program, was explored by Ramachandra et al. [24], where they employed static analysis to identify queries that will be executed unconditionally by a piece of code. The compiler can then transform the code so that these queries are issued as soon as their query parameters are computed, and before their results are needed. Unfortunately, for many web applications there is not enough computation to perform between the point when the query parameters are available and the query results are used, which reduces the effectiveness of this technique. Also, if the queries are executed conditionally, prefetching queries requires speculation about program execution and can end up issuing additional useless queries.

In contrast to prefetching, most ORM frameworks allow users to specify "fetching strategies" that describe when an object or members of a collection should be fetched from the database in order to reduce the number of round trips. The default strategy is usually "lazy fetching," where each object is fetched from the database only when it is used by the application. This means that there is a round trip for every object, but the only objects fetched are those that are certainly used by the application. The alternative "eager" strategy causes the all objects related to an object (e.g., that are part of the same collection or referenced by a foreign key) to be fetched as soon as the object is requested. The eager strategy reduces the number of round trips to the database by combining the queries involved in fetching multiple entities (e.g., using joins). Of course, this eager strategy can result in fetching objects that are not needed,

SIGMOD'14, June 22–27, 2014, Snowbird, UT, USA.

http://dx.doi.org/10.1145/2588555.2593672.

and, in some cases, can actually incur *more* round trips than lazy fetching. For this reason, deciding when to label entities as "eager" is a non-trivial task, as evidenced by the number of questions on online forums regarding when to use which strategy, with "it depends" being the most common answer. In addition, for large-scale projects that involve multiple developers, it is difficult for the designer of the data access layer to predict how entities will be accessed in the application and therefore which strategy should be used. Finally, fetching strategies are very specific to ORM frameworks and fail to address the general problem which is also present in non-ORM applications.

This paper describes a new approach for reducing the latency of database-backed applications that combines many features of the two strategies described. The goal is to reduce the number of round trips to the database by *batching* queries issued by the application. The key idea is to collect queries by relying on a new technique which we call *extended lazy evaluation* (or simply "lazy evaluation" in the rest of the paper.) As the application executes, queries are batched into a query store instead of being executed right away. In addition, non-database related computation is delayed until it is absolutely necessary. As the application continues to execute, multiple queries are accumulated in the query store. When a value that is derived from query results is finally needed (say, when it is printed on the console), then all the queries that are registered with the query store are executed by the database in a single batch, and the results are then used to evaluate the outcome of the computation. The technique is conceptually related to the traditional lazy evaluation as supported by functional languages (either as the default evaluation strategy or as program constructs) such as Haskell, Miranda, Scheme and Ocaml [21]. In traditional lazy evaluation, there are two classes of computations; those that can be delayed, and those that force the delayed computation to take place because they must be executed eagerly. In our extended lazy evaluation, queries constitute a third kind of computation because even though their actual execution is delayed, they must eagerly register themselves with the batching mechanism so they can be issued together with other queries in the batch.

Compared to query extraction using static analysis, our approach batches queries dynamically as the program executes, and defers computation as long as possible to maximize the opportunity to overlap query execution with program evaluation. As a result, it is able to batch queries across branches and even method calls, which results in larger batch sizes and fewer database round trips. Unlike fetching strategies, our approach is not fundamentally tied to ORM frameworks. Moreover, we do not require developers to label entities as eager or lazy, as our system only brings in entities from the database as they are originally requested by the application. Note that our approach is orthogonal to other multi-query optimization approaches that optimize batches of queries [17]; we do not merge queries to improve their performance, or depend on many concurrent users issuing queries to collect large batches. Instead, we optimize applications to extract batches from a *single* client, and issue those in a single round trip to the database (which still executes the individual query statements.)

We have implemented this approach in a new system called Sloth. The system is targeted towards applications written in an imperative language that use databases for persistent storage. Sloth consists of two components: a compiler and a number of libraries for runtime execution. Unlike traditional compilers, Sloth compiles the application source code to execute using lazy evaluation. In summary, our paper makes the following contributions:

• We devise a new mechanism to batch queries in database-backed applications based on a combination of a new "lazy-ifying" compiler and dynamic program analysis to generate the queries to be batched. Our transformation preserves the semantics of the original program, including transaction boundaries.

• We propose a number of optimizations to improve the quality of the compiled lazy code.

• We built and evaluated Sloth using real-world web applications totaling over 300k lines of code. Our results show that Sloth achieves a median speedup between 1.3× and 2.2× (depending on network latency), with maximum speedups as high as 3.1×. Reducing latency also improves maximum throughput of our applications by 1.5×.

In the following, we first describe how Sloth works through a motivating example in Sec. 2. Then, we explain our compilation strategy in Sec. 3, followed by optimizations to improve generated code quality in Sec. 4. We describe our prototype implementation in Sec. 5, and report our experimental results using both real-world benchmarks in Sec. 6.

```
1  ModelAndView handleRequest(...) {
2  Map model = new HashMap<String, Object>();
3  Object o = request.getAttribute("patientId");
4  if (o != null) {
5    Integer patientId = (Integer) o;
6    if (!model.containsKey("patient")) {
7      if (hasPrivilege(VIEW_PATIENTS)) {
8        Patient p = getPatientService().getPatient(patientId);
9        model.put("patient", p);
10       ...
11       model.put("patientEncounters",
12         getEncounterService().getEncountersByPatient(p));
13       ...
14       List visits = getVisitService().getVisitsByPatient(p);
15       CollectionUtils.filter(visits, ...);
16       model.put("patientVisits", visits);
17       model.put("activeVisits", getVisitService().
18         getActiveVisitsByPatient(p));
19   ...
20   return new ModelAndView(portletPath, "model", model);
21 }
```

Figure 1: Code fragment abridged from OpenMRS

2. OVERVIEW

In this section we give an overview of Sloth using the code fragment shown in Fig. 1. The fragment is abridged from OpenMRS [8], an open-source patient record web application written in Java. It is hosted using the Spring web framework and uses the Hibernate ORM library to manage persistent data. The application has been deployed in numerous countries worldwide since 2006.

The application is structured using the Model-View-Control (MVC) pattern, and the code fragment is part of a controller that builds a model to be displayed by the view after construction. The controller is invoked by the web framework when a user logs-in to the application to view the dashboard for a particular patient. The controller first creates a model (a `HashMap` object), populates it with appropriate patient data based on the logged-in user's privileges, and returns the populated model to the web framework. The web framework then passes the partially constructed model to other controllers which may add additional data, and finally to the view creator to generate HTML output.

As written, this code fragment can issue up to four queries; the queries are issued by calls of the form `getXXX` on the data access objects, i.e., the `Service` objects, following the web framework's convention. The first query in Line 8 fetches the `Patient` object that the user is interested in displaying and adds it to the model. The code then issues queries on Lines 12 and 14, and Line 18 to fetch various data associated with the patient, and adds this data to the model as well. It is important to observe that of the four round trips that this code can incur, only the first one is essential—without the result of that first query, the other queries cannot be constructed. In fact, the results from the other queries are only stored in the model and not used until the view is actually rendered. This means that in principle, the developer could have collected the last three queries in a single batch and sent it to the database in a single round trip. The developer could have gone even further, collecting in a single batch all the queries involved in building the model until the data from any of the queries in the batch is really needed—either because the model needs to be displayed, or because the data is needed to construct a new query. Manually transforming the code in this way would have a big impact in the number of round trips incurred by the application, but would also impose an unacceptable burden on the developer. In the rest of the section, we describe how Sloth automates such transformation with only minimal changes to the original code, and requires no extra work from the developer.

An important ingredient to automatically transform the code to batch queries is *lazy evaluation*. In most traditional programming languages, the evaluation of a statement causes that statement to execute, so any function calls made by that statement are executed before the program proceeds to evaluating the next statement. In lazy evaluation, by contrast, the evaluation of a statement does not cause the statement to execute; instead, the evaluation produces a *Thunk*: a place-holder that stands for the result of that computation, and it also remembers what the computation was. The only statements that are executed immediately upon evaluation are those that produce output (e.g., printing on the console), or cause an externally visible side effect (e.g., reading from files). When such a statement executes, the thunks corresponding to all the values that flow into that statement will be *forced*, meaning that the delayed computation they represented will finally be executed.

The key idea behind our approach is to modify the basic machinery of lazy evaluation so that when a thunk is created, any queries performed by the statement represented by the thunk are added to a *query store* kept by the runtime to batch queries. Because the computation has been delayed, the results of those queries are not yet needed, so the queries can accumulate in the query store until any thunk that requires the result of such queries is forced; at that point, the entire batch of queries is sent to the database for processing in a single round trip. This process is illustrated in Figure 2; during program execution, Line 8 issues a call to fetch the `Patient` object that corresponds to `patientId` (Q1). Rather than executing the query, Sloth compiles the call to register the query with the query store instead. The query is recorded in the current batch within the store (Batch 1), and a thunk is returned to the program (represented by the gray box in Fig. 2). In Line 12, the program needs to access the patient object `p` to generate the queries to fetch the patient's encounters (Q2) followed by visits in Line 14 (Q3). At this point the thunk `p` is forced, Batch 1 is executed, and its results (`rs1`) are recorded in the query cache in the store. A new non-thunk object `p'` is returned to the program upon deserialization from `rs1`, and `p'` is memoized in order to avoid redundant deserializations. After this query is executed, Q2 and Q3 can be generated using `p'` and are registered with the query store in a new batch (Batch 2). Unlike the patient query, however, Q2 and Q3 are not executed within `handleRequest` since their results are not used (thunks are stored in the model map in Lines 12 and 16). Note that even though Line 15 uses the results of Q3 by filtering it, our analysis determines that the operation does not have externally visible side effects and is thus delayed, allowing Batch 2 to remain unexecuted. This leads to batching another query in Line 18 that fetches the patient's active visits (Q4), and the method returns.

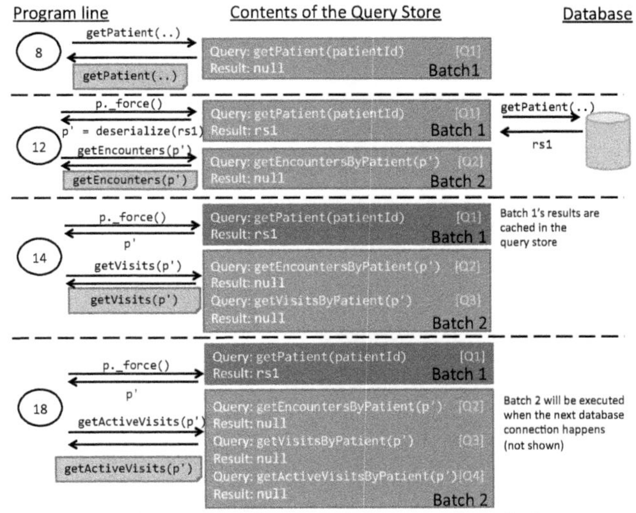

Figure 2: Operational diagram of the example code fragment

Depending on subsequent program path, Batch 2 might be appended with further queries. Q2, Q3, and Q4 may be executed later when the application needs to access the database to get the value from a registered query, or they might not be executed at all if the application has no further need to access the database.

This example shows how Sloth is able to perform much more batching than either the existing "lazy" fetching mode of Hibernate or prior work using static analysis [24]. Hibernate's lazy fetching mode would have to evaluate the results of the database-accessing statements such as `getVisitsByPatient(p)` on Line 14 as its results are needed by the filtering operation, leaving no opportunity to batch. In contrast, Sloth places thunks into the model and delays the filtering operation, which avoid evaluating any of the queries. This enables more queries to be batched and executed together in a subsequent trip to the database. Static analysis also cannot perform any batching for these queries, because it cannot determine what queries need to be evaluated at compile time as the queries are parameterized (such as by the specific patient id that is fetched in Line 8), and also because they are executed conditionally only if the logged-in user has the required privilege.

There are some languages such as Haskell that execute lazily by default, but Java has no such support. Furthermore, we want to tightly control how lazy evaluation takes place so that we can calibrate the tradeoffs between execution overhead and the degree of batching achieved by the system. We would not have such tight control if we were working under an existing lazy evaluation framework. Instead, we rely on our own Sloth compiler to transform the code for lazy evaluation. At runtime, the transformed code relies on the Sloth runtime to maintain the query store. The runtime also includes a custom JDBC driver that allows multiple queries to be issued to the database in a single round trip, as well as extended versions of the application framework, ORM library, and application server that can process thunks (we currently provide extensions to the Spring application framework, the Hibernate ORM library, and the Tomcat application server, to be described in Sec. 5). For monolithic applications that directly use the JDBC driver to interact with the database, developers just need to change such applications to use the Sloth batch JDBC driver instead. For applications hosted on application servers, developers only need to host them on the Sloth extended application server instead after compiling their application with the Sloth compiler.

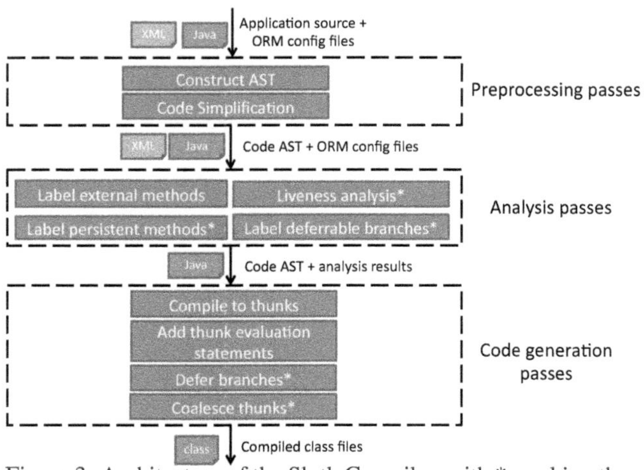

Figure 3: Architecture of the Sloth Compiler, with * marking those components used for optimization

3. COMPILING TO LAZY SEMANTICS

In this section we describe how Sloth compiles the application source code to be evaluated lazily. Figure 3 shows the overall architecture of the Sloth compiler, the details of which are described in this section and next.

3.1 Code Simplification

To ease the implementation, the Sloth compiler first simplifies the input source code. All looping constructs are converted to `while (true)`, where the original loop condition is converted into branches with control flow statements in their bodies, and assignments are broken down to have at most one operation on their right-hand-side. Thus an assignment such as `x = a + b + c` will be translated to `t = a + b; x = t + c;`, with `t` being a temporary variable. Type parameters (generics) are also eliminated, and inner and anonymous classes are extracted into stand-alone ones.

3.2 Thunk Conversion

After simplification, the Sloth compiler converts each statement of the source code into extended lazy semantics. For clarity, in the following we present the compilation through a series of examples using concrete Java syntax. However, beyond recognizing methods that issue queries (such as those in the JDBC API), our compilation is not Java-specific, and we formalize the compilation process in Sec. 3.8 using an abstract kernel language.

In concrete syntax, each statement in the original program is replaced with an allocation of an anonymous class derived from the abstract `Thunk` class after compilation, with the code for the original statement placed inside a new `_force` class method. To "evaluate" the thunk, we invoke this method, which executes the original program statement and returns the result (if any). For example, the following statement:

```
int x = c + d;
```

is compiled into lazy semantics as:

```
Thunk<int> x =
  new Thunk<int>() {
    Integer _force() { return c._force() + d._force(); }
  };
```

There are a few points to note in the example. First, all variables are converted into `Thunk` types after compilation. For instance, `x` has type `Thunk<int>` after compilation, and likewise for `c` and `d`. As a consequence, all variables need to be evaluated before carrying out the actual computation inside the body of `_force`. Secondly, to avoid redundant evaluations, we memoize the return value of `_force` so that subsequent calls to `_force` will return the memoized value instead (the details of which are not shown).

While the compilation is relatively straightforward, the mechanism presented above can incur substantial runtime overhead, as the compiled version of each statement incurs allocation of a `Thunk` object, and all computations are converted to method calls. Sec. 4 describes several optimizations that we have devised to reduce the overhead. Sec. 6.6 quantifies the overhead of lazy semantics, which shows that despite some overhead, it is generally much less than the savings we obtain from reducing round trips.

3.3 Compiling Query Calls

Method calls that issue database queries, such as JDBC `executeQuery` calls, and calls to ORM library APIs that retrieve entities from persistent storage are compiled differently from ordinary method calls. In particular, we want to extract the query that would be executed from such calls and record it in the query store so it can be issued when the next batch is sent to the database. To facilitate this, the query store consists of the following components: a) a buffer that stores the current batch of queries to be executed and associates a unique id with each query, and b) a result store that contains the results returned from batches previously sent to the database; the result store is a map from the unique query identifier to its result set. The query store API consists of two methods:

- `QueryId registerQuery(String sql)`: Add the `sql` query to the current batch of queries and return a unique identifier to the caller. If `sql` is an `INSERT`, `UPDATE`, `ABORT`, `COMMIT`, or `SELECT ... INTO` the current batch will be immediately sent to the database to ensure these updates are not left lingering in the query store. On the other hand, the method avoids introducing redundant queries into the batch, so if `sql` matches another query already in the query buffer, the identifier of the first query will be returned.
- `ResultSet getResultSet(QueryId id)`: check if the result set associated with `id` resides in the result store; if so, return the cached result. Otherwise, issue the current batch of queries in a single round trip, process the result sets by adding them to the result store, and return the result set that corresponds to `id`.

To use the query store, method calls that issue database queries are compiled to a thunk that passes the SQL query to be executed in the constructor. The thunk registers the query to be executed with the query store using `registerQuery` in its constructor and stores the returned `QueryId` as its member field. The `_force` method of the thunk then calls `getResultSet` to get the corresponding result set. For ORM library calls, the result sets are passed to the appropriate deserialization methods in order to convert the result set into heap objects that are returned to the caller.

Note that creating thunks associated with queries require evaluating all other thunks that are needed in order to construct the query itself. For example, consider Line 8 of Fig. 1, which makes a call to the database to retrieve a particular patient's data:

```
Patient p = getPatientService().getPatient(patientId);
```

In the lazy version of this fragment, `patientId` is converted to a thunk that is evaluated before the SQL query can be passed to the query store:

```
Thunk<Patient> p = new Thunk<Patient>(patientId) {
  { this.id = queryStore.regQuery(
          getQuery(patientId._force())); }
  Patient _force() {
    return deserialize(queryStore.getResultSet(id));
  } }
```

Here, `getQuery` calls an ORM library method to generate the SQL string and substitutes the evaluated `patientId` in it, and `deserialize` reconstructs an object from a SQL result set.

3.4 Compiling Method Calls

In the spirit of laziness, it would be ideal to delay executing method calls as long as possible (in the best case, the result from the method call is never needed and therefore we do not need to execute the call). However, method calls might have side effects that change the program heap, for instance changing the values of heap objects that are externally visible outside of the application (such as a global variable). The target of the call might be a class external to the application, such as a method of the standard JDK, where the Sloth compiler does not have access to its source code (we call such methods "internal" otherwise). Because of that, method calls are compiled differently according to the type of the called method as follows. Method labeling is done as one of the analysis passes in the Sloth compiler, and the thunk conversion pass uses the method labels during compilation.

Internal methods without side effects. This is the ideal case where we can delay executing the method. The call is compiled to a thunk with the method call as the body of the `_force` method. Any return value of the method is assigned to the thunk. For example, if `int foo(Object x, Object y)` is an internal method with no side effects, then:

```
int r = foo(x, y);
```

is compiled to:

```
Thunk<int> r = new Thunk<int>(x, y) {
   int _force() { return this.foo(x._force(), y._force()); }
  };
```

Internal methods with externally visible side effects. We cannot defer the execution of such method due to their externally visible side effects. However, we can still defer the evaluation of its arguments until necessary inside the method body. Thus, the Sloth compiler generates a special version of the method where its parameters are thunk values, and the original call site are compiled to calling the special version of the method instead. For example, if `int bar(Object x)` is such a method, then:

```
int r = bar(x);
```

is compiled to:

```
Thunk<int> r = bar_thunk(x);
```

with the declaration of `bar_thunk` as `Thunk<int> bar_thunk(Thunk<Object> x)`.

External methods. We cannot defer the execution of external methods unless we know that they are side-effect free. Since we do not have access to their source code, the Sloth compiler does not change the original method call during compilation, except for forcing the arguments and receiver objects as needed. As an example, Line 3 in Fig. 1:

```
Object o = request.getAttribute("patientId");
```

is compiled to:

```
Thunk<Object> o = new LiteralThunk(
  request._force().getAttribute("patientId"));
```

As discussed earlier, since the types of all variables are converted to thunks, the (non-thunk) return value of external method calls are stored in `LiteralThunk` objects that simply returns the non-thunk value when `_force` is called, as shown in the example above.

3.5 Class Definitions and Heap Operations

For classes that are defined by the application, the Sloth compiler changes the type of each member field to `Thunk` to facilitate accesses to field values under lazy evaluation. For each publicly accessible `final` fields, the compiler adds an extra field with the original type, with its value set to the evaluated result of the corresponding thunk-ified version of the field. These fields are created so that they can be accessed from external methods. Publicly accessible non-final fields cannot be made lazy.

In addition, the Sloth compiler changes the type of each parameter in method declarations to `Thunk` to facilitate method call conventions discussed in Sec. 3.4. Like public fields, since public methods can potentially be invoked by external code (e.g., the web framework that hosts the application, or by JDK methods such as calling `equals` while searching for a key within a `Map` object), the Sloth compiler generates a "dummy" method that has the same declaration (in terms of method name and parameter types) as the original method, The body of such dummy methods simply invokes the thunk-converted version of the corresponding method. If the method has a return value, then it is evaluated on exit. For instance, the following method:

```
public Foo bar (Baz b) { ... }
```

is compiled to two methods by the Sloth compiler:

```
// to be called by internal code
public Thunk<Foo> bar_thunk (Thunk<Baz> b) { ... }
// to be called by external code
public Foo bar (Baz b) {
  return bar_thunk(new LiteralThunk(b))._force(); }
```

With that in mind, the compiler translates object field reads to simply return the thunk fields. However, updates to heap objects are not delayed in order to ensure consistency of subsequent heap reads. In order to carry out the write, however, the receiver object needs to be evaluated if it is a thunk. Thus, the following statement:

```
Foo obj = ...
obj.field = x;
```

is compiled to:

```
Thunk<Foo> obj = ...
obj._force().field = x;
```

Notice that while the *target* of the heap write is evaluated (`obj` in the example), the *value* that is written (`x` in the example) is a thunk object, meaning that it can represent computation that has not been evaluated yet.

3.6 Evaluating Thunks

In previous sections, we discussed the basic compilation of statements into lazy semantics using thunks. In this section we describe when thunks are evaluated, i.e., when the original computation that they represent is actually carried out.

As mentioned in the last section, the target object in field reads and writes are evaluated when encountered. However, the value of the field and the object that is written to the field can still be thunks. The same is applied to array accesses and writes, where the target array and index are evaluated before the operation.

For method calls where the execution of the method body is not delayed, the target object is evaluated prior to the call if the called method is non-static. While our compiler could have deferred the evaluation of the target object by converting all member methods into static class methods, it is likely that the body of such methods (or further methods that are invoked inside the body) accesses some fields of the target object and will end up evaluating the target object. Thus, there is unlikely any significant savings in delaying such evaluation. Finally, when calling external methods all parameters are evaluated as discussed.

In the basic compiler, all branch conditions are evaluated when `if` statements are encountered. Recall that all loops are canonicalized into `while (true)` loops with the loop condition rewritten using branches. We present an optimization to this restriction in Sec. 4.2 below. Similarly, statements that throw exceptions, obtain

$$
\begin{array}{rcl}
c \in \text{constant} & ::= & \text{True} \mid \text{False} \mid \text{literal} \\
e_l \in \text{assignExpr} & ::= & x \mid e.f \\
e \in \text{expr} & ::= & c \mid e_l \mid \{f_i = e_i\} \mid e_1 \; op \; e_2 \mid \neg \, e \mid f(e) \mid e_a[e_i] \mid R(e) \\
c \in \text{command} & ::= & \text{skip} \mid e_l := e \mid \text{if}(e) \text{ then } c_1 \text{ else } c_2 \mid \\
 & & \text{while(True) do } c \mid W(e) \mid c_1 \; ; \; c_2 \\
op \in \text{binary op} & ::= & \wedge \mid \vee \mid > \mid < \mid =
\end{array}
$$

Figure 4: Input language

locks on objects (synchronized), and that spawn new threads of control are not deferred. Finally, thunk evaluations can also happen when compiling statements that issue queries, as discussed in Sec. 3.3.

3.7 Limitations

There are two limitations that we do not currently handle. First, because of delayed execution, exceptions that are thrown by the original program might not occur at the same program point in the Sloth-compiled version. For instance, the original program might throw an exception in a method call, but in the Sloth-compiled version, the call might be deferred until the thunk corresponding to the call is evaluated. While the exception will still be thrown eventually, the Sloth-compiled program might have executed more code than the original program before hitting the exception.

Second, since the Sloth compiler changes the representation of member fields in each internal class, we currently do not support custom deserializers. For instance, one of the applications used in our experiments reads in an XML file that contains the contents of an object before the application source code is compiled by Sloth. As a result, the compiled application fails to re-create the object as its representation has changed. We manually fixed the XML file to match the expected types in our benchmark. In general, we do not expect this to be common practice, given that Java already provides its own object serialization routines.

3.8 Formal Semantics

We now formally define the extended lazy evaluation outlined above. For the sake of presentation, we describe the semantics in terms of the language shown in Fig. 4. The language is simple, but will help us illustrate the main principles behind extended lazy evaluation that can be easily applied not just to Java but to any other object-oriented language. For lack of space, this section provides only an outline of the semantic rules and the main idea behind the soundness proof, the complete semantics are described in [16].

The main constructs to highlight in the language are the expression $R(e)$ which issues a database *read* query derived from the value of expression e, and $W(e)$ a statement that issues a query that can mutate the database, such as INSERT or UPDATE.

We first define the standard execution semantics of the language. Expression evaluation is defined through a set of rules that takes a program state s and an expression e, and produces a new program state along with the value of the expression. The state s of the program is represented by a tuple (D, σ, h), where D is the database that maps queries to their result sets, σ is the environment that maps program variables to expressions, and h is the program heap that maps addresses to expressions.

As an example, the rule to evaluate the binary expression $e_1 \; op \; e_2$ is shown below.

$$\frac{\langle s, e_1\rangle \rightarrow \langle s', v_1\rangle \quad \langle s', e_2\rangle \rightarrow \langle s'', v_2\rangle \quad v_1 \; op \; v_2 \rightarrow v}{\langle s, e_1 \; op \; e_2\rangle \rightarrow \langle s'', v\rangle}$$

The notation above the line describes how the subexpressions e_1 and e_2 are evaluated to values v_1 and v_2 respectively. The result of evaluating the overall expression is shown below the line and it is the result of applying op to v_1 and v_2, together with the state as transformed by the evaluation of the two subexpressions.

As another example, the evaluation of a read query $R(e)$ must first evaluate the query e to a query string v, and then return the result of consulting the database D' with this query string. Note that the evaluation of e might itself modify the database, for example if e involves a function call that internally issues an update query, so the query v must execute on the database as it is left after the evaluation of e:

$$\frac{\langle (D, \sigma, h), e\rangle \rightarrow \langle (D', \sigma, h'), v\rangle}{\langle (D, \sigma, h), R(e)\rangle \rightarrow \langle (D', \sigma, h'), D'[v]\rangle}$$

The rest of the evaluation rules are standard and are included in [16].

To describe lazy evaluation, we augment the state tuple s with the query store Q, which maps a query identifier to a pair (q, rs) that represents the SQL query q and its corresponding result set rs. rs is initially set to null ($\emptyset$) when the pair is created. We model thunks using the pair (σ, e), where σ represents the environment for looking up variables during thunk evaluation, and e the expression to evaluate. In our Java implementation the state is implemented as fields in each generated Thunk class, and e is the expression in the body of the _force method.

As discussed in Sec. 3.2, to evaluate the expression $e_1 \; op \; e_2$ using lazy evaluation, we first create thunk objects v_1 and v_2 for e_1 and e_2 respectively, and then create another thunk object that represents the op. Formally this is described as:

$$\frac{\begin{array}{cc}\langle s, e_1\rangle \rightarrow \langle s', v_1\rangle & \langle s', e_2\rangle \rightarrow \langle s'', v_2\rangle \\ v_1 = (s', e_1') & v_2 = (s'', e_2') \\ \multicolumn{2}{c}{v = (\sigma' \cup \sigma'', e_1' \; op \; e_2')}\end{array}}{\langle s, e_1 \; op \; e_2\rangle \rightarrow \langle s'', v\rangle}$$

Note that the environment for v is the union of the environments from v_1 and v_2 since we might need to look up variables stored in either of them.

On the other hand, as discussed in Sec. 3.3, under lazy evaluation query calls are evaluated by first forcing the evaluation of the thunk that corresponds to the query string, and then registering the query with the query store. This is formalized as:

$$\frac{\begin{array}{cc}\langle (Q, D, \sigma, h), e\rangle \rightarrow \langle (Q', D', \sigma, h'), (\sigma', e)\rangle & id \text{ is a fresh identifier} \\ \text{force}(Q', D', (\sigma', e)) \rightarrow \langle Q'', D'', v\rangle & Q''' = Q''[id \rightarrow (v, \emptyset)]\end{array}}{\langle (Q, D, \sigma, h), R(e)\rangle \rightarrow \langle (Q''', D'', \sigma, h'), ([\,], id)\rangle}$$

The force function above is used to evaluate thunks, similar to that described in the examples above using Java. $\text{force}(Q, D, t)$ takes in the current database D and query store Q and returns the evaluated thunk along with the modified query store and database. When force encounters an id in a thunk, it checks the query store to see if that id already has a result associated with it. If it does not, it issues as a batch all the queries in the query store that do not yet have results associated with them, and then assigns those results once they arrive from the database.

Using the semantics outlined above, we have proven the equivalence of standard and lazy semantics by showing that if evaluating command c on program state $\langle Q, D, \sigma, h\rangle$ results in the new state $\langle D_s, \sigma_s, h_s\rangle$ under standard semantics, and $\langle Q_l, D_l, \sigma_l, h_l\rangle$ under lazy semantics, then after forcing all thunk objects in σ_l and h_l, we have $D_l = D_s, \sigma_l = \sigma_s$, and $h_l = h_s$, regardless of the order in which the thunks are forced. The proof is included in [16].

4. BEING EVEN LAZIER

In the previous section, we described how Sloth compiles source code into lazy semantics. However, as noted in Sec. 3.2, there can be substantial overhead if we follow the compilation procedure naively. In this section, we describe three optimizations. The goal of these optimizations is to generate more efficient code and to further defer computation. As discussed in Sec. 2, deferring computation delays thunk evaluations, which in turn increases the chances of obtaining larger query batches during execution time. Like the previous section, we describe the optimizations using concrete Java syntax for clarity, although they can all be formalized using the language described in Fig. 4.

4.1 Selective Compilation

The goal of compiling to lazy semantics is to enable query batching. Obviously the benefits are observable only for the parts of the application that actually issue queries, and simply adds runtime overhead for the remaining parts of the application. Thus, the Sloth compiler analyzes each method to determine whether it can possibly access the database. The analysis is a conservative one that labels a method as using persistent data if it:

- Issues a query in its method body.
- Calls another method that uses persistent data. Because of dynamic dispatch, if the called method is overridden by any of its subclasses, we check if any of the overridden versions is persistent, and if so we label the call to be persistent.
- Accesses object fields that are stored persistently. This is done by examining the static object types that are used in each method, and checking whether it uses an object whose type is persistently stored. The latter is determined by checking for classes that are populated by query result sets in its constructor (in the case of JDBC), or by examining the object mapping configuration files for ORM frameworks.

The analysis is implemented as an inter-procedural, flow-insensitive dataflow analysis [22]. It first identifies the set of methods m containing statements that perform any of the above. Then, any method that calls m is labeled as persistent. This process continues until all methods that can possibly be persistent are labeled. For methods that are not labeled as persistent, the Sloth compiler does not convert their bodies into lazy semantics—they are compiled as is. For the two applications used in our experiments, our results show about 28% and 17% of the methods do not use persistent data, and those are mainly methods that handle application configuration and output page formatting (see Sec. 6.5 for details).

4.2 Deferring Control Flow Evaluations

In the basic compiler, all branch conditions are evaluated when an `if` statement is encountered, as discussed in Sec. 3.6. The rationale is that the outcome of the branch affects subsequent program path. We can do better, however, based on the intuition that if neither branch of the condition creates any changes to the program state that are externally visible outside of the application, then the entire branch statement can be deferred as a thunk like other simple statements. Formally, if none of the statements within the branch contains: i) calls that issue queries; or ii) thunk evaluations as discussed in Sec. 3.6 (recall that thunks need to be evaluated when their values are needed in operations that cannot be deferred, such as making changes to the program state that are externally visible), then the entire branch statement can be deferred. For instance, in the following code fragment:

```
if (c) a = b; else a = d;
```

The basic compiler would compile the code fragment into:

```
if (c._force())
  a = new Thunk0(b) { ... };
else
  a = new Thunk1(d) { ... };
```

which could result in queries being executed as a result of evaluating `c`. However, since the bodies of the branch statements do not make any externally visible state changes, the whole branch statement can be deferred as:

```
ThunkBlock tb = new ThunkBlock2(b, d) {
  void _force () {
    if (c._force()) a = b._force(); else a = d._force();
  } }
Thunk<int> a = tb.a();
```

where the evaluation of `c` is further delayed. The `ThunkBlock` class is similar to the `Thunk` class except that it defines methods (not shown above) that return thunk variables defined within the block, such as `a` in the example. Calling `_force` on any of the thunk outputs from a thunk block will evaluate the entire block, along with all other output objects that are associated with that thunk block. In sum, this optimization allows us to delay thunk evaluations, which in turn might increase query batches sizes.

To implement this optimization, the Sloth compiler first iterates through the body of the `if` statement to determine if any thunk evaluation takes place, and all branches that are deferrable are labeled. During thunk generation, deferrable branches are translated to thunk objects, with the original statements inside the branches constituting the body of the `_force` methods. Variables defined inside the branch are assigned to output thunks as described above. The same optimization is applied to defer loops as well. Recall that all loops are converted into `while (true)` loops with embedded control flow statements (`break` and `continue`) inside their bodies. Using similar logic, a loop can be deferred if all statements inside the loop body can be deferred.

4.3 Coalescing Thunks

The basic compilation described in Sec. 3.2 results in new `Thunk` objects being created for each computation that is delayed. Due to the temporary variables that are introduced as a result of code simplification, the number of operations (and thus the number of `Thunk` objects) can be much larger than the number of lines of Java code. This can substantially slow down the compiled application. As an optimization, the thunk coalescing pass merges consecutive statements into thunk blocks to avoid allocation of thunks. The idea is that if for two consecutive statements s_1 and s_2, and that s_1 defines a variable `v` that is used in s_2 and not anywhere after in the program, then we can combine s_1 and s_2 into a thunk block with s_1 and s_2 inside its `_force` method (provided that both statements can be deferred as discussed in Sec. 3). This way, we avoid creating the thunk object for `v` that would be created under basic compilation. As an illustrative example, consider the following code fragment:

```
int foo (int a, int b, int c, int d) {
  int e = a + b;
  int f = e + c;
  int g = f + d;
  return g; }
```

Under basic compilation, the code fragment is compiled to:

```
1 Thunk<int> foo (Thunk<int> a, b, c, d) {
2   Thunk<int> e = new Thunk0(a, b) { ... }
3   Thunk<int> f = new Thunk1(e, c) { ... }
4   Thunk<int> g = new Thunk2(f, d) { ... }
5   return g; }
```

Notice that three thunk objects are created, with the additions in the original code performed in the `_force` methods inside the definitions of classes `Thunk0`, `Thunk1` and `Thunk2`, respectively. However, in this case the variables `e` and `f` are not used anywhere, i.e., they are no longer *live*, after Line 4. Thus we can combine the first three statements into a single thunk, resulting in the following:

```
Thunk<int> foo (Thunk<int> a, b, c, d) {
  ThunkBlock tb = new ThunkBlock3(a, b, c, d) { ... }
  Thunk<int> g = tb.g();
  return g; }
```

The optimized version reduces the number of object allocations from 3 to 2: one allocation for `ThunkBlock3` and another one for the `Thunk` object representing `g` that is created within the thunk block. In this case, the `_force` method inside the `ThunkBlock3` class consists of statements that perform the addition in the original code. As described earlier, the thunk block keeps track of all thunk values that need to be output, in this case the variable `g`.

This optimization is implemented in multiple steps in the Sloth compiler. First, we identify variables that are live at each program statement. Live variables are computed using a dataflow analysis that iterates through program statements in a backwards manner to determine the variables that are used at each program statement (and therefore must be live).

After thunks are generated, the compiler iterates through each method to combine consecutive statements into thunk blocks. The process continues until no statements can be further combined within each method. After that, the compiler examines the `_force` method of each thunk block and records the set of variables that are defined. For each such variable `v`, the compiler checks to see if all statements that use of `v` are also included in the same thunk block by making use of the liveness information. If so it does not need to create a thunk object for `v`. This optimization significantly reduces the number of thunk objects that need to be allocated and thus improves the efficiency of the generated code as shown in Sec. 6.5.

5. IMPLEMENTATION

We have implemented a prototype of Sloth. The Sloth compiler is built on top of Polyglot [23]. We have implemented a query store for the thunk objects to register and retrieve query results. To issue the batched queries in a single round trip, we extended the MySQL JDBC driver to allow executing multiple queries in one `executeQuery` call, and the query store uses the batch query driver to issue queries. Once received by the database, our extended driver executes all read queries in parallel. In addition, we have also made the following changes to the application framework to enable them process thunk objects that are returned by the hosted application. Our extensions are not language specific and can be applied to other ORM and app hosting frameworks. Besides the extensions to JDBC driver and JPA layer, the other changes are optional and were done to further increase query batching opportunities.

JPA Extensions. We extended the Java Persistence API (JPA) [5] to allow returning thunk objects from calls that retrieves objects from the database. For example, JPA defines a method `Object find(Class, id)` that fetches the persistently stored object of type `Class` with `id` as its object identifier. We extended the API with a new method `Thunk<Object> find_thunk(Class, id)` that performs the same functionality except that it returns a thunk rather than the requested object. We implemented this method in the Hibernate ORM library. The implementation first generates a SQL query that would be issued to fetch the object from the database, registers the query with the query store, and returns a thunk object to the caller. Invoking the `_force` method on the returned thunk object forces the query to be executed, and Hibernate will then deserialize the result into an object of the requested type before returning to the caller. Similar extensions are made to other JPA methods. Note that our extensions are targeted to the JPA not Hibernate—we implemented them within Hibernate as it is a popular open-source implementation of JPA and is also used by the applications in our experiments, and the extensions were implemented using about 1000 lines of code.

Spring Extensions. We extended the Spring web application framework to allow thunk objects be stored and returned during model construction within the MVC pattern. This is a minor change that consists of about 100 lines of code.

JSP API Extensions. We extended the JavaServer Pages (JSP) API [4] to enable thunk operations. In particular, we allow thunk objects to be returned while evaluating JSP expressions. We also extended the `JspWriter` class from the JSP API that generates the output HTML page when a JSP is requested. The class provides methods to write different types of objects to the output stream. We extended the class with a `writeThunk` method that write thunk objects to the output stream. `writeThunk` stores the thunk to be written in a buffer, and thunks in the buffer are not evaluated until the writer is flushed by the web server (which typically happens when the entire HTML page is generated). We have implemented our JSP API extensions in Tomcat, which is a popular open-source implementation of the JSP API. This is also a minor change that consists of about 200 lines of code.

6. EXPERIMENTS

In this section we report our experiment results. The goals of the experiments are to: i) evaluate the effectiveness of Sloth at batching queries, ii) quantify the change in application load times, and iii) measure the overhead of running applications using lazy evaluation. All experiments were performed using Hibernate 3.6.5, Spring 3.0.7, and Tomcat 6 with the extensions mentioned above. The web server and applications were hosted on a machine with 8GB of RAM and 2.8GHz processor, and data was stored in an unmodified MySQL 5.5 database with 47GB of RAM and 12 2.4GHz processors. Unless stated there was a 0.5ms round trip delay between the two machines (this is the latency of the group cluster machines). We used the following applications for our experiments:

- itracker version 3.1.5 [3]: itracker is an open-source software issue management system. The system consists of a Java web application built on top of the Apache Struts framework and uses Hibernate to manage storage. The project has 10 contributors with 814 Java source files with a total of 99k lines of Java code.
- OpenMRS version 1.9.1 [8]: OpenMRS is an open-source medical record system that has been deployed in numerous countries. The system consists of a Java web application built on top of the Spring web framework and uses Hibernate to manage storage. The project has over 70 contributors. The version used consists of 1326 Java source files with a total of 226k lines of Java code. The system has been in active development since 2004 and the code illustrates various coding styles for interacting with the ORM.

We created benchmarks from the two applications by manually examining the source code to locate all web page files (html and jsp files). Next, we analyzed the application to find the URLs that load each of the web pages. This resulted in 38 benchmarks for itracker, and 112 benchmarks for OpenMRS. Each benchmark was run by loading the extracted URL from the application server via a client that resides on the same machine as the application server.

We also tested with TPC-C and TPC-W coded in Java [11]. Because the implementations display the query results immediately after issuing them, there is no opportunity for batching. We only use them to measure the runtime overhead of lazy evaluation.

6.1 Page Load Experiments

In the first set of experiments, we compared the time taken to load each benchmark from the original and the Sloth-compiled versions of the applications. For each benchmark, we started the web and database servers and measured the time taken to load the entire page. Each measurement was the average of 5 runs. For benchmarks that require user inputs (e.g., patient ID for the patient dashboard, project ID for the list of issues to be displayed), we filled the forms automatically with valid values from the database. We restarted the database and web servers after each measurement to clear all cached objects. For OpenMRS, we used the sample database (2GB in size) provided by the application. For itracker, we created an artificial database (0.7GB in size) consisting of 10 projects and 20 users. Each project has 50 tracked issues, and none of the issues has attachments. We did not define custom scripts or components for the projects that we created. We also created larger versions of these databases (up to 25 GB) and report their performance on selected benchmarks in Section 6.4, showing that our gains continue to be achievable with much larger database sizes.

We loaded all benchmarks with the applications hosted on the unmodified web framework and application server, and repeated with the Sloth-compiled applications hosted on the Sloth extended web framework using the ORM library and web server discussed in Sec. 5. For all benchmarks, we computed the speedup ratios as:

$$\frac{\text{load time of the original application}}{\text{load time of the Sloth compiled application}}$$

Fig. 5(a) and Fig. 6(a) show the CDF of the results (result details are described in [16]), where we sorted the benchmarks according to their speedups for presentation purposes (and similarly for other experiments). The results show that the Sloth compiled applications loaded the benchmarks faster compared to the original applications, achieving up to 2.08× (median 1.27×) faster load times for itracker and 2.1× (median 1.15×) faster load times for OpenMRS. Figure 5(b) and Fig. 6(b) show the ratio of the number of round trips to the database, computed as:

$$\frac{\text{\# of database round trips in original application}}{\text{\# database round trips in Sloth version of application}}$$

For itracker, the minimum number of round trip reductions was 27 (out of 59 round trips) while the maximum reduction was 95 (out of 124 original round trips). For OpenMRS, the minimum number of reductions was 18 (out of 100 round trips) and the maximum number was 1082 (out of 1705 round trips). Although these may seem like large numbers of round trips for a single web page, issues such as the $1+N$ issue in Hibernate [12] make it quite common for developers to write apps that issue hundreds of queries to generate a web page in widely used ORM frameworks.

Finally, Fig. 5(c) and Fig. 6(c) show the CDF of the ratio of the total number of queries issued for the applications. In OpenMRS, the Sloth-compiled application batched as many as 68 queries into a single batch. Sloth was able to batch multiple queries in all benchmarks, even though the original applications already make extensive use of the eager and lazy fetching strategies provided by Hibernate. This illustrates the effectiveness of applying lazy evaluation in improving performance. Examining the generated query batches, we attribute the performance speedup to the following:

Avoiding unnecessary queries. For all benchmarks, the Sloth-compiled applications issued fewer total number of queries as compared to the original (ranging from 5-10% reduction). The reduction is due to the developers' use of eager fetching to load entities in the original applications. Eager fetching incurs extra round trips to the database to fetch the entities and increases query execution time, and is wasteful if the fetched entities are not used by the application. As noted in Sec. 1, it is very difficult for developers to decide when to load objects eagerly during development. Using Sloth, on the other hand, frees the developer from making such decisions while improving application performance.

Batching queries. The Sloth-compiled applications batched a significant number of queries. For example, one of the OpenMRS benchmarks (`encounterDisplay.jsp`) loads observations about a patient's visit. Observations include height, blood pressure, etc, and there were about 50 observations fetched for each patient. Loading is done as follows: i) all observations are first retrieved from the database (Line 3); ii) each observation is iterated over and its corresponding `Concept` object (i.e., the textual explanation of the observed value) is fetched and stored into a `FormField` object (Line 4). The `FormField` object is then put into the model similar to Fig. 1 (Line 8). The model is returned at the end of the method and the fetched concepts are displayed in the view.

```
1 if (Context.isAuthenticated()) {
2   FormService fs = Context.getFormService();
3   for (Obs o : encounter.getObsAtTopLevel(true)) {
4     FormField ff = fs.getFormField(form, o.getConcept(),..);
5     ...
6     obsMapToReturn.put(ff, list);
7   }}
8 map.put("obsMap", obsMapToReturn);
9 return map;
```

In the original application, the concept entities are lazily fetched by the ORM during view generation, and each fetch incurs a round trip to the database. It is difficult to statically analyze the code to extract the queries that would be executed in presence of the authentication check on Line 1, and techniques such as [14] will require a detailed inter-procedural analysis of the loop body to ensure that the methods invoked are side-effect free in order to apply loop fission. On the other hand, since the fetched concepts are not used in the method, the Sloth-compiled application batches all the concept queries and issues them in a single batch along with others. This results in a dramatic reduction in the number of round trips and an overall reduction of 1.17× in page load time.

Finally, there are a few benchmarks where the Sloth-compiled application issued *more* queries than the original, as shown in Fig. 6(c) This is because the Sloth-compiled application registers queries to the query store when they are encountered during execution, and all registered queries are executed when a thunk that requires data to be fetched is subsequently evaluated. However, not all fetched data are used. The original application, with its use of lazy fetching, avoided issuing those queries and that results in fewer queries executed. In sum, while the Sloth-compiled application does not necessarily issue the minimal number of queries required to load each page, our results show that the benefits in reducing network round trips outweigh the costs of executing a few extra queries.

6.2 Throughput Experiments

Next, we compared the throughput of Sloth-compiled application and the original. We fixed the number of browser clients, and each client repeatedly loaded pages from OpenMRS for 10 minutes (clients wait until the previous load completes, and then load a new page.) As no standard workload was available, the pages were chosen at random from the list of benchmarks described earlier. We changed the number of clients in each run, and measured the resulting total throughput across all clients. The results (averaged across 5 runs) are shown in Figure 7.

The results show that the Sloth-compiled application has better throughput than the original, reaching about 1.5× the peak throughput of the original application. This is expected as the Sloth version takes less time to load each page. Interestingly, the Sloth version

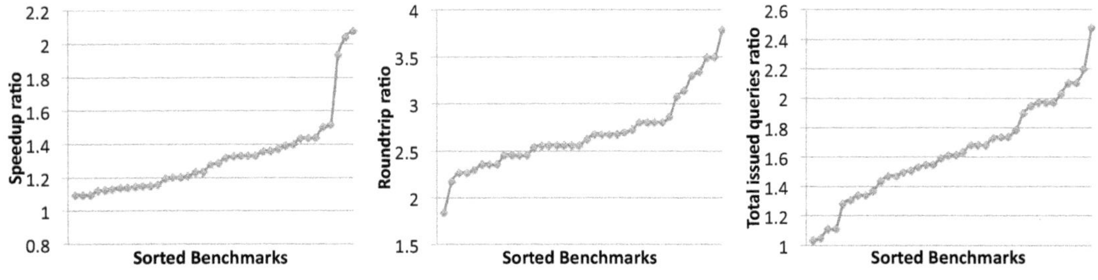

(a) load time ratios CDF (b) round trip ratios CDF (c) queries issued ratios CDF

Figure 5: itracker benchmark experiment results

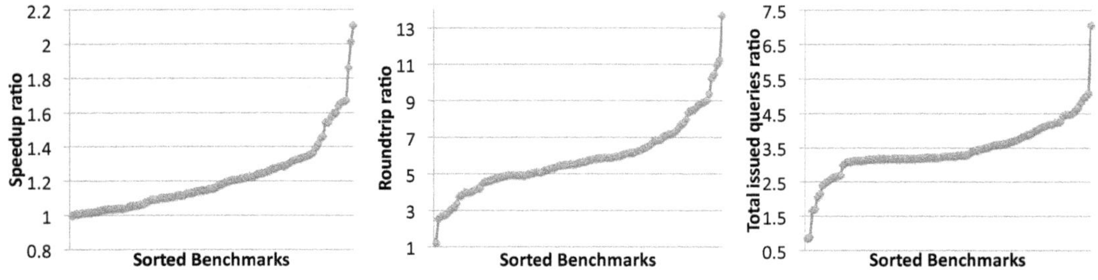

(a) load time ratios CDF (b) round trip ratios CDF (c) queries issued ratios CDF

Figure 6: OpenMRS benchmark experiment results

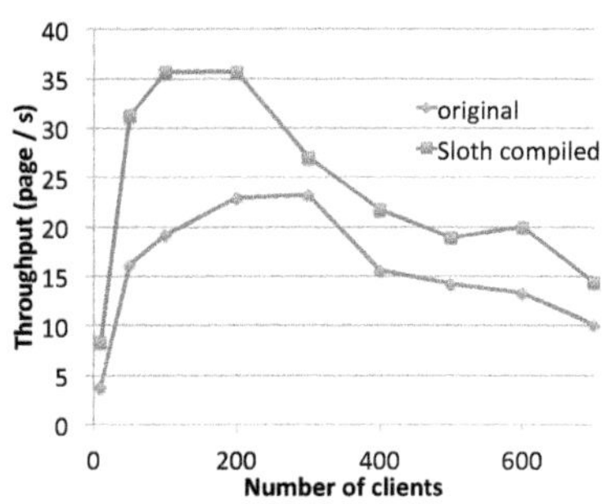

Figure 7: Throughput experiment results

achieves its peak throughput at a lower number of clients compared to the original. This is because given our experiment setup, both the database and the web server were under-utilized when the number of clients is low, and throughput is bounded by network latency. Hence, reducing the number of round trips improves application throughput, despite the overhead incurred on the web server from lazy evaluation. However, as the number of clients increases, the web server becomes CPU-bound and throughput decreases. Since the original application does not incur any CPU overhead, it reaches the throughput at a higher number of clients, although the overall peak is lower due to network round trips.

6.3 Time Breakdown Comparisons

Reducing the total number of queries issued by the application reduces one source of load time. However, there are other of sources of latency. To understand the issues, we measured the amount of time spent in the different processing steps of the benchmarks: application server processing, database query execution, and network communication. We first measured the overall load time for loading the entire page. Then, we instrumented the application server to record the amount of time spent in processing, and modified our batch JDBC driver to measure the amount of time spent in query processing on the database server. We attribute the remaining time as network communication. We ran the experiment across all benchmarks and measured where time was spent while loading each benchmark, and computed the sum of time spent in each phase across all benchmarks. The results for the two applications are shown in Fig. 8.

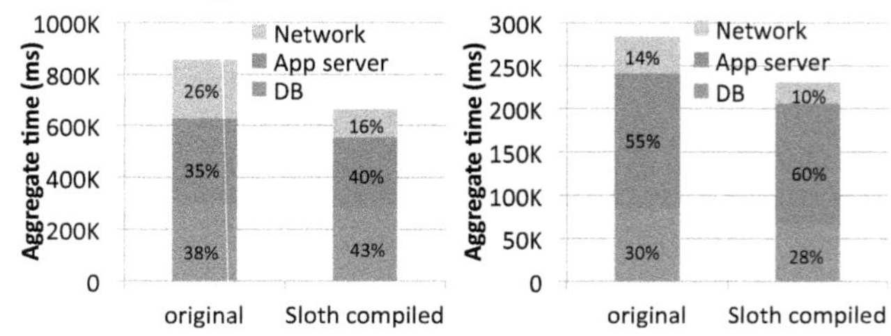

(a) itracker benchmarks (b) OpenMRS benchmarks

Figure 8: Time breakdown of benchmark loading experiments

For the Sloth-compiled applications, the results show that the aggregate amount of time spent in network communication was significantly lower, reducing from 226k to 105k ms for itracker, and 43k to 24k ms for OpenMRS. This is mostly due to the reduction in network round trips. In addition, the amount of time spent in executing queries also decreased. We attribute that to the reduction in the number of queries executed, and to the parallel processing of batched queries on the database by our batch driver. However, the portion of time spent in the application server was higher for the Sloth compiled versions due to the overhead of lazy evaluation.

6.4 Scaling Experiments

In the next set of experiments, we study the effects of round trip reduction on page load times. We ran the same experiments as in Sec. 6.1, but varied the amount network delay from 0.5ms between the application and database servers (typical value for machines within the same data center), to 10ms (typical for machines connected via a wide area network and applications hosted on the cloud). Figure 9 shows the results for the two applications.

While the number of round trips and queries executed remained the same as before, the results show that the amount of speedup dramatically increases as the network round trip time increases (more than 3× for both applications with round trip time of 10ms). This indicates that reducing the number of network round trips is a significant factor in reducing overall load times of the benchmarks, in addition to reducing the number of queries executed.

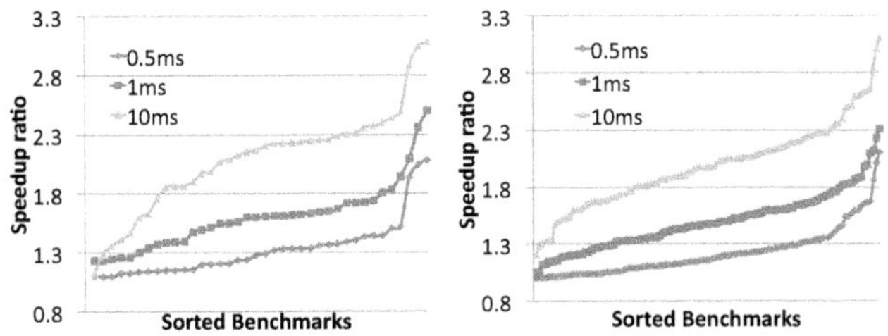

(a) itracker (b) OpenMRS

Figure 9: Network scaling experiment results

Next, we measured the impact of database size on benchmark load times. In this experiment, we varied the database size (up to 25 GB) and measured the benchmark load times. Although the database still fits into the memory of the machine, we believe this is representative of the way that modern transactional systems are actually deployed, since if the database working set does not fit into RAM, system performance drops rapidly as the system becomes I/O bound. We chose two benchmarks that display lists of entities retrieved from the database. For itracker, we chose a benchmark that displays the list of user projects (`list_projects.jsp`) and varied the number of projects stored in the database; for OpenMRS, we chose a benchmark that shows the observations about a patient (`encounterDisplay.jsp`), a fragment of which was discussed in Sec. 6.1, and varied the number of observations stored. The results are shown in Fig. 10(a) and (b) respectively.

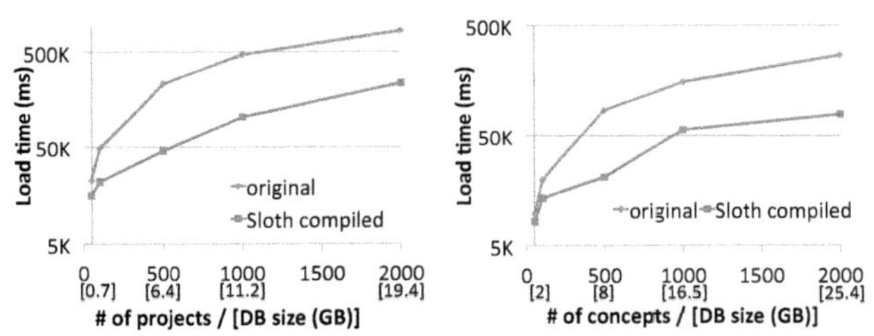

(a) itracker (b) OpenMRS

Figure 10: Database scaling experiment results

The Sloth-compiled applications achieved lower page load times in all cases, and they also scaled better as the number of entities increases. This is mostly due to query batching. For instance, the OpenMRS benchmark batched a maximum of 68, 88, 480, 980, and 1880 queries as the number of database entities increased. Examining the query logs reveals that queries were batched as discussed in Sec. 6.1. While the numbers of queries issued by two versions of the application are the same proportionally as the number of entities increases, the experiment shows that batching reduces the overall load time significantly, both because of the fewer round trips to the database and the parallel processing of the batched queries. The itracker benchmark exhibits similar behavior.

6.5 Optimization Experiments

In this experiment we measured the effects of the optimizations presented in Sec. 4. First, we study the effectiveness of selective compilation. Figure 11 shows the number of methods that are identified as persistent in the two applications. As discussed Sec. 4.1, non-persistent methods are not compiled to lazy semantics.

Application	# persistent methods	# non-persistent methods
OpenMRS	7616	2097
itracker	2031	421

Figure 11: Number of persistent methods identified

Next, we quantify the effects of the optimizations by comparing the amount of time taken to load the benchmarks. We first measured the time taken to load all benchmarks from the Sloth-compiled applications with no optimizations. Next, we turned each of the optimizations on one at a time: selective compilation (SC), thunk coalescing (TC), and branch deferral (BD), in that order. We recompiled each time and Fig. 12 shows the resulting load time for all benchmarks as each optimization was turned on.

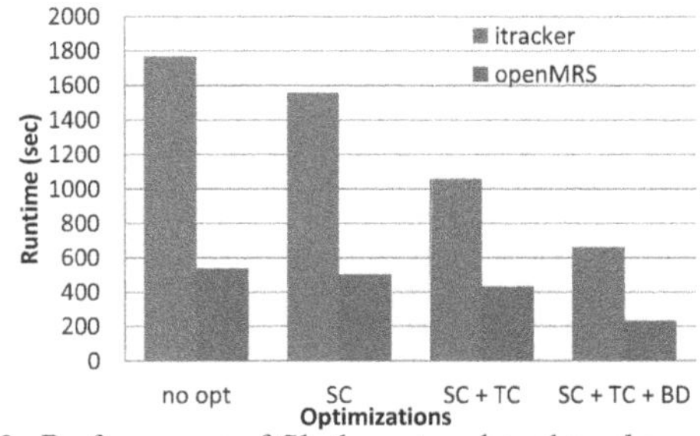

Figure 12: Performance of Sloth on two benchmarks as optimizations are enabled. SC=Selective computation, TC=Thunk Coalescing, BD=Branch Deferral.

Transaction type	Original time (s)	Sloth time (s)	Overhead
TPC-C			
New order	930	955	15.8%
Order status	752	836	11.2%
Stock level	420	459	9.4%
Payment	789	869	10.2%
Delivery	626	665	6.2%
TPC-W			
Browsing mix	1075	1138	5.9%
Shopping mix	1223	1326	8.5%
Ordering mix	1423	1600	12.4%

Figure 13: Overhead experiment results

In both applications, branch deferral is the most effective in improving performance. This makes sense as both applications have few statements with externally visible side-effects, which increases the applicability of the technique. In addition, as discussed in Sec. 4.2, deferring control flow statements further delays the evaluation of thunks, which allows more query batching to take place.

Overall, there was more than a 2× difference in load time between having none and all the optimizations for both applications. Without the optimizations, we would have lost all the benefits from round trip reductions, i.e., the actual load times of the Sloth-compiled applications would have been slower than the original.

6.6 Overhead Experiments

In the final experiment, we measured the overhead of lazy evaluation. We use TPC-C and TPC-W for this purpose. We chose implementations that use JDBC directly for database operations and do not cache query results. The TPC-W implementation is a standalone web application hosted on Tomcat. Since each transaction has very few queries, and the query results are used almost immediately after they are issued (e.g., printed out on the console in the case of TPC-C, and converted to HTML in the case of TPC-W), there are essentially no opportunities for Sloth to improve performance, making these experiments a pure measure of overhead of executing under lazy semantics.

We used 20 warehouses for TPC-C (initial size of the database is 23GB). We used 10 clients, with each client executing 10k transactions, and measured the time taken to finish all transactions. For TPC-W, the database contained 10,000 items (about 1 GB on disk), and the implementation omitted the think time. We used 10 emulated browsers executing 10k transactions each. The experiments were executed on the same machines as in the previous experiments with optimizations turned on. Figure 13 show the results.

As expected, the Sloth compiled versions were 5-15% slower than the original, due to lazy semantics. However, given that the

Java virtual machine is not designed for lazy evaluation, we believe these overheads are reasonable, especially given the significant performance gains observed in real applications.

6.7 Discussion

Our experiments show that Sloth can batch queries and improve performance across different benchmarks. While Sloth does not execute the batched queries until any of their results are needed by the application, other execution strategies are possible. For instance, each batch can be executed asynchronously as it reaches a certain size, or periodically based on current load on the database. Choosing the optimal strategy would be an interesting future work.

7. RELATED WORK

Lazy evaluation was first introduced for lambda calculus [19], with one of the goals to increase the expressiveness of the language by allowing programmers to define infinite data structures and custom control flow constructs. Lazy evaluation is often implemented using thunks in languages that do not readily support it [20, 28]. In contrast, the extended lazy evaluation proposed in this paper is fundamentally different: rather than its traditional uses, Sloth uses lazy evaluation to improve application performance by batching queries, and Sloth is the first system to do so to our knowledge. As our techniques are not specific to Java, they can be implemented in other languages as well, including those that already support lazy evaluation, by extending the language runtime with query batching.

Batching query plans and sharing query results are well-known query optimization techniques [17, 26], and there is also work on re-ordering transactions using developer annotations [25]. However, they aim to combine queries issued by multiple concurrent clients, whereas Sloth batches queries that are issued by the same client over time, although we can make use of such techniques to merge Sloth-generated query batches from multiple clients for further performance improvement. There has been work done on query batching by predicting future queries [13], and using static analysis [18, 14] and remote procedure calls [29]. However, their batching ability is limited due to the imprecision of static analysis. While Sloth does not suffer from precision issues, it incurs some runtime overhead. Thus it would be interesting to combine both techniques to achieve a low-overhead yet high-precision system.

As discussed in Sec. 1, data prefetching is another means to reduce database round trips. Prefetching has been studied theoretically [27] and implemented in open source systems [1], although they all require programmer annotations to indicate what and when to prefetch. Finally, there is work on moving application code to execute in the database as stored procedures to reduce the number of round trips [15], which is similar to our goals. In comparison, Sloth does not require program state to be distributed.

8. ACKNOWLEDGMENT

We thank the anonymous reviewers for the constructive feedback. This research was supported by the Intel Science and Technology Center for Big Data, and NSF grants SHF-1116362 and SHF-1139056.

9. CONCLUSIONS

In this paper we presented Sloth, a new compiler and runtime that speeds up database applications by eliminating round trips between the application and database servers. By delaying computation using lazy semantics, our system reduces round trips to the database substantially by batching multiple queries and issuing them in a single batch. Along with a number of optimization techniques, we evaluated Sloth on different real-world applications. Our results show that Sloth outperforms existing approaches in query batching, and delivers substantial reduction (up to 3×) in application execution time with modest worst-case runtime overheads.

10. REFERENCES

[1] Hibernate fetching strategies. http://docs.jboss.org/hibernate/orm/4.3/manual/en-US/html/ch20.html.
[2] Hibernate performance issue. http://stackoverflow.com/questions/5155718/hibernate-performance.
[3] iTracker issue management system. http://itracker.sourceforge.net.
[4] JSR 152: JavaServer Pages 2.0 specification. http://jcp.org/aboutJava/communityprocess/final/jsr152.
[5] JSR 220: Enterprise JavaBeans 3.0 specification (persistence). http://jcp.org/aboutJava/communityprocess/final/jsr220.
[6] Marissa Mayer at Web 2.0. http://glinden.blogspot.com/2006/11/marissa-mayer-at-web-20.html.
[7] Network latency under Hibernate/c3p0/MySQL. http://stackoverflow.com/questions/3623188/network-latency-under-hibernate-c3p0-mysql.
[8] OpenMRS medical record system. http://www.openmrs.org.
[9] PhoCusWright/Akamai Study on Travel Site Performance. http://connect.phocuswright.com/2010/06/phocuswrightakamai-study-on-travel-site-performance/.
[10] Round trip / network latency issue with the query generated by hibernate. http://stackoverflow.com/questions/13789901/round-trip-network-latency-issue-with-the-query-\generated-by-hibernate.
[11] TPC-C and TPC-W reference implementations. http://sourceforge.net/apps/mediawiki/osdldbt.
[12] What is the n+1 selects issue? http://stackoverflow.com/questions/97197/what-is-the-n1-selects-issue.
[13] I. T. Bowman and K. Salem. Optimization of query streams using semantic prefetching. In *Proc. SIGMOD*, pages 179–190, 2004.
[14] M. Chavan, R. Guravannavar, K. Ramachandra, and S. Sudarshan. Program transformations for asynchronous query submission. In *Proc. ICDE*, pages 375–386, 2011.
[15] A. Cheung, O. Arden, S. Madden, and A. C. Myers. Automatic partitioning of database applications. *PVLDB*, 5(11):1471–1482, 2012.
[16] A. Cheung, S. Madden, and A. Solar-Lezama. Sloth: Being lazy is a virtue (when issuing database queries). *CSAIL Tech Report MIT-CSAIL-TR-2014-006*.
[17] G. Giannikis, G. Alonso, and D. Kossmann. SharedDB: Killing one thousand queries with one stone. *PVLDB*, 5(6):526–537, 2012.
[18] R. Guravannavar and S. Sudarshan. Rewriting procedures for batched bindings. *PVLDB*, 1(1):1107–1123, 2008.
[19] P. Henderson and J. H. Morris, Jr. A lazy evaluator. In *Proc. POPL*, pages 95–103, 1976.
[20] P. Z. Ingerman. Thunks: a way of compiling procedure statements with some comments on procedure declarations. *Comm. ACM*, 4(1):55–58, 1961.
[21] S. L. P. Jones and A. L. M. Santos. A transformation-based optimiser for haskell. *Sci. Comput. Program.*, 32(1-3):3–47, 1998.
[22] G. A. Kildall. A unified approach to global program optimization. In *Proc. POPL*, pages 194–206, 1973.
[23] N. Nystrom, M. R. Clarkson, and A. C. Myers. Polyglot: An extensible compiler framework for Java. In *Proc. CC*, pages 138–152, 2003.
[24] K. Ramachandra and S. Sudarshan. Holistic optimization by prefetching query results. In *Proc. SIGMOD*, pages 133–144, 2012.
[25] S. Roy, L. Kot, and C. Koch. Quantum databases. In *Proc. CIDR*, 2013.
[26] T. K. Sellis. Multiple-query optimization. *ACM Transactions on Database Systems*, 13(1):23–52, 1988.
[27] A. J. Smith. Sequentiality and prefetching in database systems. *ACM Transactions on Database Systems*, 3(3):223–247, 1978.
[28] A. Warth. LazyJ: Seamless lazy evaluation in java. *Proc. FOOL/WOOD Workshop*, 2007.
[29] K. C. Yeung and P. H. J. Kelly. Optimising java RMI programs by communication restructuring. In *Middleware*, volume 2672 of *LNCS*, pages 324–343, 2003.

Dynamically Optimizing Queries over Large Scale Data Platforms

Konstantinos Karanasos
IBM Research - Almaden
kkarana@us.ibm.com

Andrey Balmin*
GraphSQL
andrey@graphsql.com

Marcel Kutsch*
Apple Inc.
kutschm@gmail.com

Fatma Özcan
IBM Research - Almaden
fozcan@us.ibm.com

Vuk Ercegovac*
Google
vuk.ercegovac@gmail.com

Chunyang Xia
IBM Silicon Valley Lab
cxia@us.ibm.com

Jesse Jackson
IBM Silicon Valley Lab
jessejac@us.ibm.com

ABSTRACT

Enterprises are adapting large-scale data processing platforms, such as Hadoop, to gain actionable insights from their "big data". Query optimization is still an open challenge in this environment due to the volume and heterogeneity of data, comprising both structured and un/semi-structured datasets. Moreover, it has become common practice to push business logic close to the data via user-defined functions (UDFs), which are usually opaque to the optimizer, further complicating cost-based optimization. As a result, classical relational query optimization techniques do not fit well in this setting, while at the same time, suboptimal query plans can be disastrous with large datasets.

In this paper, we propose new techniques that take into account UDFs and correlations between relations for optimizing queries running on large scale clusters. We introduce "pilot runs", which execute part of the query over a sample of the data to estimate selectivities, and employ a cost-based optimizer that uses these selectivities to choose an initial query plan. Then, we follow a dynamic optimization approach, in which plans evolve as parts of the queries get executed. Our experimental results show that our techniques produce plans that are at least as good as, and up to 2x (4x) better for Jaql (Hive) than, the best hand-written left-deep query plans.

Categories and Subject Descriptors

H.4 [**Database Management**]: Systems

Keywords

query optimization; large-scale data platforms; adaptive query processing; pilot runs

1. INTRODUCTION

Large scale data processing platforms, such as Hadoop, are being extensively used by enterprises in order to store, manage, analyze and exploit their "big data". These large scale data platforms are popular for various different types of applications, including text analytics on unstructured data or log analysis over semi-structured data, while they are also increasingly used for relational-like processing with many joins over semi-structured and structured data, which is the focus of this paper. In addition to the large data volumes, there are other important characteristics that distinguish this environment from traditional relational query processing. First, nested data structures, such as structs, maps, and arrays, are pervasive as users are commonly storing data in denormalized form. Second, users push more complex business logic closer to the data, resulting in heavy usage of user-defined functions (UDFs) in queries.

High-level declarative languages for large scale data platforms, such as Hive [36], Pig [18] and Jaql [5], gained popularity due to their ease of use, and increased user productivity. As with any declarative query language, query optimization is a key challenge, as the system has to decide in which order to execute various query operators, as well as which implementation method to use for each operator. Join is a particularly important operator with alternative implementations that have very different performance characteristics depending on cardinalities of inputs and output. As a result, many techniques of relational query optimization, such as selectivity and cardinality estimation, join method selection, and join ordering are still applicable to the new large scale data languages.

Obviously, not all aspects of traditional query optimization fit well in these new environments. Traditional query optimizers rely on data statistics to estimate predicate selectivity and result cardinality, and use these estimates to decide on join method and ordering. Even in the relational setting, optimizers are plagued with incorrect cardinality estimates, mainly due to undetected data correlations, existence of UDFs and of external variables (in parameterized queries). Various solutions have been proposed to capture data correlations, such as CORDS [26], but these require very detailed and targeted statistics. Collecting such statistics on all datasets may be prohibitively expensive in large clusters.

In this paper, we address the query optimization problem for large scale data platforms, by continuously collecting statistics during query execution, and feeding these statistics to a cost-based query optimizer to decide the next query sub-expression to execute. We have implemented our techniques in the context of Jaql. When a query is submitted to Jaql, we first identify operations that are local to a table[1], such as selections, projections, and UDFs. We utilize "pilot runs" to execute these local plans over a sample of each base dataset, until enough results are produced to collect meaningful statistics. Then, we present each local sub-plan, along with the collected statistics and the corresponding join graph to a simple

*Work done while the author was at IBM Research.

[1] An operation is local to a table if it only refers to attributes from that table.

SIGMOD'14, June 22–27, 2014, Snowbird, UT, USA.
Copyright 2014 ACM 978-1-4503-2376-5/14/06 ...$15.00.
http://dx.doi.org/10.1145/2588555.2610531.

cost-based optimizer to decide the initial join order. Our optimizer, built on top of the open-source extensible Columbia optimizer [12], estimates join result cardinalities using textbook techniques, however, it operates on very accurate input cardinality estimates for local sub-queries, as these are collected either during pilot runs or previous execution steps. Our optimizer chooses the appropriate join methods and order, as well as marks the joins that can be executed together in the same MapReduce job. We provide this join order as input to the Jaql compiler, which generates the MapReduce jobs to execute the query plan. As the query gets executed, we collect statistics on the intermediate results, which we can use to re-optimize the query, if needed. In our current implementation, we re-optimize after each job, but the infrastructure is rich enough to accommodate more complex conditions. For example, one can decide to re-optimize if the difference between the observed result cardinality and the estimated one exceeds a certain threshold.

There has been a lot of work on adaptive query processing [15, 28, 31, 22] to address the shortcomings of traditional optimizers. These adaptive techniques use various run-time solutions that try to adjust the query plan dynamically, similar to ours. However, these works did not consider pilot runs, which provide the means to accurately estimate the result sizes when there are UDFs, and correlations between different attributes in the query. Although pilot runs introduce overhead, they amortize it by avoiding really bad plan choices. Earlier approaches on adaptive query processing can also benefit from pilot runs, by avoiding mistakes in the first optimization decisions. Further, in a relational setting queries are mostly pipelined and it has been a challenge to identify the correct re-optimization points. On the contrary, in a distributed large scale cluster, checkpoints are typically present, since the system has to account for failure recovery; restarting a long running query may not be a viable option. These checkpoints also enable the system to better utilize resources, as it greatly simplifies load balancing.

In our setting, we exploit the fact that MapReduce jobs always materialize their output and use them as natural re-optimization points, but our techniques are not restricted to MapReduce systems. Pilot runs are applicable to any massively parallel data processing system, provided that the query needs to scan large enough data to amortize its overhead. We believe that intermediate result materialization, which provides us with the opportunity to re-optimize a query, will always be a feature of many large scale data platforms designed for long running queries (e.g., Spark, Tez), not only MapReduce. It is also important to note that although our dynamic techniques are developed within the context of Jaql, they are also applicable to other large-scale query languages, such as Hive.

Our experimental results show that our techniques produce plans that are at least as good as, and often even better than, the best hand-written left-deep query plans. They are also most of the time better than the plans produced by a state-of-the-art relational query optimizer for a shared-nothing DBMS. Pilot runs introduce a small overhead, but provide accurate result size estimation, especially when the query contains UDFs and data correlations. Accurate result size estimation not only leads to better execution plans, but also prevents the optimizer from making fatal mistakes. Re-optimizing the query as it executes proves to be very beneficial as we observed many plan changes in some queries (see Figure 2).

In this paper, we make the following contributions:

- We propose pilot runs, which execute local plans over a sample of the base data, and provide accurate result size estimation, which is essential to choose the right join method and order.
- We utilize a traditional query optimizer to determine the join methods and global join ordering. The optimizer is provided with the statistics of local plans, as if they are base tables, and does not estimate local predicate selectivities.
- We collect result statistics, which can be used to re-optimize the remaining of the query and hence provide a means to adapt the execution plans at runtime.
- Our optimizer produces both left-deep and bushy plans. We exploit bushy plans and explore novel strategies for scheduling multiple jobs in parallel to run in a distributed environment.
- We provide detailed experiments, where we assess the overhead of our techniques, study different execution strategies for bushy plans, and demonstrate that pilot runs and re-optimization can be very beneficial for Jaql, but also for other systems such as Hive.

The paper is organized as follows. Section 2 provides an overview of Jaql, whereas Section 3 describes the architecture of our system. Section 4 presents the pilot runs, and Section 5 details the dynamic re-optimization of execution plans. In Section 6 we present our experimental results, in Section 7 we review related work, then we conclude.

2. JAQL OVERVIEW AND QUERY EXECUTION

In this section we provide a general overview of Jaql [5], and describe its join processing capabilities.

2.1 Jaql Overview

Jaql is a system for analyzing large semistructured datasets in parallel using Hadoop's[2] MapReduce framework [14], and is part of IBM BigInsights[3]. It shares common features with other data processing languages that were also developed for scale-out architectures, such as Hive [36], Pig [18] and DryadLINQ [41]. These common features make the techniques developed in this paper applicable to those systems with slight modifications, as will be discussed in Section 3. Jaql consists of a declarative scripting language, a compiler, and a runtime component for Hadoop, which we briefly present below.

Query language Each Jaql script consists of a set of statements, which are either variable assignments or expressions to be evaluated. Each expression gets an input and produces an output, which can then feed another expression. Jaql supports all relational expressions, such as filter, join, sort, and group by, as well as other expressions, such as split and tee. It also supports a SQL dialect close to SQL-92; SQL queries submitted to Jaql are translated to a Jaql script by the compiler. Finally, users can provide their own UDFs, either as Jaql scripts or in an external language (e.g., Java).

Compiler Jaql's compiler includes a heuristics-based rewrite engine that applies a set of transformation rules in order to optimize the input scripts. Such rules include simplification of the script, translation of declarative expressions (e.g., joins) to low-level operators, various database-style optimizations (e.g., filter push-down), etc. One of the most important rules is the `toMapReduce` rule that, whenever possible, transforms an expression to a `mapReduce` function that can then be evaluated using the MapReduce framework.

Runtime The Jaql interpreter evaluates the script locally on the computer that compiled the script, but spawns interpreters on remote machines using MapReduce, in order to parallelize the execution. Expressions that cannot be parallelized (due to the nature of the script or the limitations of the compiler) are executed locally.

[2]http://hadoop.apache.org

[3]www.ibm.com/software/data/infosphere/biginsights

2.2 Join Processing in Jaql

In this section, we discuss the join algorithms and join optimizations supported by Jaql, as well as their limitations.

2.2.1 *Join Algorithms*

There are three possible join strategies in any distributed query processing system regarding data movement: shuffle none, one or both join tables. Shared-nothing databases implement all three strategies [16, 4], whereas most query processors over large scale data platforms implement only the second and third option (broadcast and repartition join, respectively) [7]. Jaql currently implements a flavor of both the repartition and broadcast joins.

Repartition join This join is implemented in one MapReduce job, comprising a map and a reduce phase. Every map task operates over a split from one of the two input tables, tags each record with the table name, and then outputs the extracted join key value and the tagged record as a (key, value) pair. The outputs are partitioned, merged and sorted by the MapReduce framework, and all records from both tables having the same join key are sent to the same reducer. At every reduce task, for each join key, the corresponding records are separated in two sets according to the table they belong, and then a cartesian product is performed between the two sets.

Broadcast join This join method is implemented in a map-only job and can be used if one of the two input tables fits in memory. Let S be the small table and R be the bigger one. In that case, S is broadcasted to all mappers, and a memory hash join is executed between S and each split of R. Thus, S is the build input and each split of R the probe input of the hash join. In the current Jaql implementation spilling to disk is not supported. Hence, if the build side of the join does not fit in memory (e.g., after the application of a UDF that produces more tuples than its input), the execution of the join, and hence the query fails due to an out of memory error.

As expected, the broadcast join is faster, because it avoids sorting the small relation during the map phase, and, most importantly, avoids reshuffling the big relation over the network.

2.2.2 *Join Optimizations*

The default join algorithm in Jaql is the repartition join. Hence, the compiler translates each join operator to a repartition join, which is executed as a single MapReduce job, that is, an n-way join is translated to n MapReduce jobs. To improve the performance of the join expressions, the user can provide a hint stating a relation is *small*. In this case, the compiler creates a broadcast join having the small relation at the build side of the join. Moreover, Jaql uses a rewrite rule that checks the file size of the two join inputs, and, in case one of them fits in memory, produces a broadcast join plan.

In case of n-way joins, the compiler is capable of producing only left-deep plans. The exact order of the joins depends on the order of the relations in the `FROM` clause of the query. In particular, the relations are picked in the order they appear in the `FROM` clause, as long as this does not lead to cartesian products; in that case, a relation that avoids the creation of cartesian products is picked first.

Finally, when there are more than one consecutive broadcast joins, and the relations that appear in the build side of these joins simultaneously fit in memory, the join expressions can be *chained* in order to be executed in a single map job in a pipelined way.

2.2.3 *Limitations of Current Join Processing*

The current join processing in Jaql has several limitations:

- There is no selectivity estimation for the predicates and UDFs. As a consequence, the application of broadcast joins is limited only to relations that already fit in memory. Thus, we are missing opportunities for broadcast joins in case of relations that could fit in memory after the application of a selective filter. On the other hand, even in cases when relations fit in memory, a UDF could increase the size of the relation, hence we have to be conservative in the application of broadcast joins.
- There is no cost-based join enumeration. Therefore, the performance of a query heavily relies on the way it has been written by the user (order of relations in the `FROM` clause).
- Even if the order of relations in the `FROM` clause is optimal, Jaql only produces left-deep join plans. In the traditional (centralized) relational setting, these plans are usually close to the optimal ones, since they maximize the pipelining of operators. In the MapReduce setting though, where the result of a job is always materialized to disk and pipelining is not useful, the basic optimization goal is to reduce the size of intermediate results. To this regard, bushy plans may be much more efficient, while they also allow executing parts of the plan in parallel. The importance of bushy plans is also pointed out in [39].

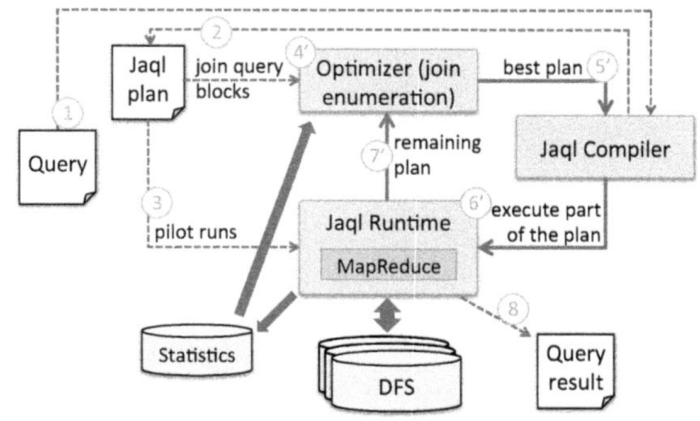

Figure 1: System Architecture.

The above limitations are present in most existing large scale data platforms. Thus, the techniques presented in this work would also be beneficial for those systems. We discuss how our techniques can be extended to other systems in Section 3, while in Section 6.6 we experimentally show how Hive benefits from our techniques.

3. SYSTEM ARCHITECTURE

In this section we introduce DYNO, a system we built for optimizing complex queries over Hadoop data. The architecture of the system is shown in Figure 1. The dashed lines denote actions that are performed only once, whereas the solid lines (associated with primed numbers, 4'-7') refer to repeated actions. When a query arrives in the system (step 1), the Jaql compiler is invoked and some logical heuristic rules, such as filter push-down, are applied [34] (step 2). Once this is done, multiple *join query blocks* are created, which are expressions containing n-way joins, filters and scan operators. Join blocks are separated from each other by aggregates, grouping and ordering operators. Before further optimizing and executing each join block, we first perform the *pilot runs* (step 3) in order to collect statistics that take complex predicates and UDFs into account. Hereafter, we will refer to such predicates/UDFs that are applied right after a scan, simply as *local predicates*, distinguishing them from the non-local ones that are applied on results of joins and cannot be pushed-down to the leaves of the operator tree. For each scan in the join block, along with its local predicates (pushed down by the compiler), we execute the corresponding expression over a sample of the data and collect statistics. More details about this process are given in Section 4.

After the pilot runs, in each join block we consolidate the scans with their local predicates, since the pilot runs statistics capture the

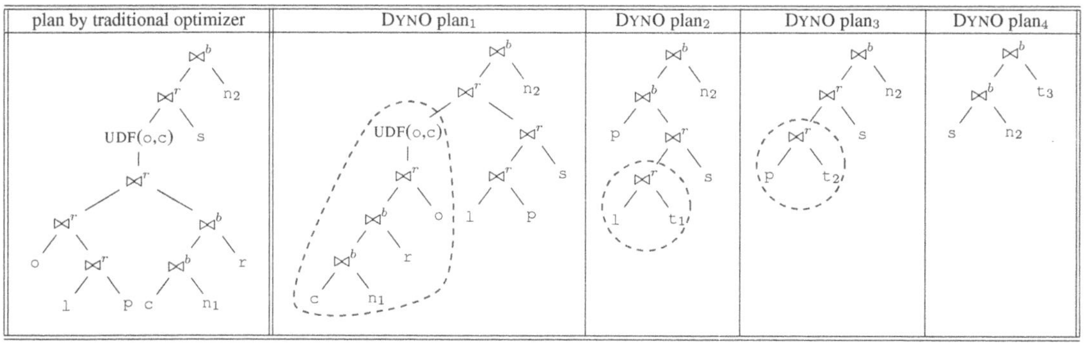

Figure 2: Execution plans for TPC-H query Q8′.

local predicate selectivities. Then, we feed each such join block and the collected statistics to our cost-based optimizer, which now only needs to focus on join enumeration. The best plan output by the optimizer is then passed to the Jaql compiler that translates it to a set of MapReduce jobs (step 5'). Note, however, that instead of executing all the MapReduce jobs at once, we execute only a subset of them (step 6'). The exact subset and the way the jobs will be executed (possibly in parallel) is decided by the compiler. During execution, we collect join column statistics over the output of the jobs and update the existing statistics. Our optimizer is then re-invoked over the part of the join block that was not yet executed (coming back to step 4'). If the statistics of the previous step were not accurate, a new plan, different than the previous one, may be selected by the optimizer. This iterative process is continued until the whole plan gets executed, and is detailed in Section 5. Finally, the result is returned to the client that posed the query (step 8).

As an example, consider TPC-H [37] query Q8, which includes a 7-way join block and to which we added a filtering UDF on the result of the join between `orders` and `customer` tables. On the lefthand side of Figure 2 we depict the plan that we obtained from a state-of-the-art relational optimizer for a shared nothing DBMS[4]. In the same figure, we also give the plans we obtained from our optimizer as the execution of Q8′ proceeds. In particular, $plan_1$ is the plan we got after the pilot runs. Then, during execution, we have three re-optimization points that in turn produce $plan_{2-4}$. Note that the relational optimizer's plan will be executed with one map-only and four map-reduce jobs. On the other hand, $plan_1$ includes four map-reduce jobs, and after re-optimizations Q8′ finally gets executed in three map-reduce and one map-only job.

Applicability to other systems Any query processing system over a large scale data platform that supports the typical join and group-by operators together with UDFs can incorporate our techniques with the following changes:

- Instrument the runtime (e.g., the map and reduce tasks) to collect statistics over attributes.
- Implement the pilot runs by executing the scans together with their local predicates over a sample of the data.
- Our cost-based optimizer for join enumeration can be used as is, since similar join algorithms are supported by most systems, such as Hive and Pig (as discussed in Section 2.2).
- Create a new dynamic join operator that calls the optimizer at runtime to re-optimize the remainder of the query.
- Identify re-optimization points in the plan. If the query already contains checkpoints (e.g., MapReduce job boundaries, Tez stages, explicit checkpoints in Spark), those can be used.

[4]For readability, in both Figures 2 and 3, we use the initials of the TPC-H tables, e.g., `p` denotes `part` and n_x denotes `nation`.

Otherwise, strategies similar to the ones proposed for the relational context [28, 2, 31, 22] can be used to identify the re-optimization points.

4. PILOT RUNS

In this section, we describe the *pilot runs*, which we use to collect the initial statistics for a given query q, taking into account the predicates and UDFs that participate in q.

4.1 The PILR Algorithm

Most traditional relational optimizers rely on statistics for estimating the selectivity of operators, costing alternative execution plans and finally choosing the minimum-cost plan. Some of these optimizers use very detailed data distribution statistics and hence can accurately estimate the selectivity of simple predicates. When multiple predicates are applied on a relation, they usually rely on the independence assumption and simply multiply the selectivities of each simple predicate to compute the final selectivity [35]. However, the independence assumption does not hold when there are correlations between the attributes used in predicates, and simply multiplying the selectivity of individual predicates leads to overly underestimated result sizes. Underestimation can result in extremely poorly performing query plans, as the optimizer will choose operators that will work well when its operands fit in memory, such as sort-merge-join, or broadcast join. Incorrect selectivity estimation is exacerbated in the presence of more complex predicates or UDFs, or when the predicates involve complex data types, such as arrays and structs.

As an example, consider the following query Q_1 that asks for the names of the restaurants in California with zip code 94301, having positive reviews (a UDF is used for the sentiment analysis of the review). Each restaurant can have multiple addresses (thus the `addr` is an array type), but we are interested only in the primary address. The reviews are joined with tweets and a second UDF (`checkid`) is applied to verify the identity of the users:

```
SELECT rs.name
FROM restaurant rs, review rv, tweet t
WHERE rs.id=rv.rsid AND rv.tid=t.id
AND rs.addr[0].zip=94301 AND rs.addr[0].state=CA
AND sentanalysis(rv)=positive AND checkid(rv,t)
```

First, notice the correlation between the two adress predicates: the predicate on the state is redundant, since all restaurants with the given zip code are in CA. In this case, even if the optimizer could deal with the array datatype, the independence assumption would lead to the wrong selectivity estimation. Moreover, the selectivity of the two UDFs cannot be computed by a relational optimizer.

To account for such non-trivial predicates/UDFs in the queries, we employ the *pilot runs*. The basic idea is to apply the predicates/UDFs of each relation R over a sample of R and collect

Algorithm 1: Pilot Runs Algorithm (PILR)

Input : query q, $|\mathcal{R}|$ relations in q, dataset $\mathcal{D}$, number of records k to collect statistics per relation, m map slots in the cluster
Output: Statistics over a sample of the data after applying local predicates and UDFs.

```
1 queryExpr ← jaqlParse(q)
  // Push down predicates/UDFs
2 queryExpr ← filterPushDown(queryExpr)
  // Get table scans with predicates/UDFs
3 leafExprs ← getLeafExprs(queryPlan)
4 foreach lexpR ∈ leafExprs do
5     if lexpR ∉ Statistics then
6         mapJob ← toMapReduce(lexprR)
          // Pick m/|R| random splits for the
             corresponding relation
7         splits ← reservoirSample(input(mapJob), m/|R|)
          // Collect statistics over k records
8         stats ← execute(mapJob, splits, k)
9         addToStatistics(stats)
```

statistics based on the output. The corresponding algorithm (PILR) is given in Algorithm 1. Given a query q, with $\mathcal{R}$ being the set of relations in q, we first use the Jaql compiler to parse the query and perform all the possible predicate/UDF push-downs (lines 1-2). Then, we collect the leaf expressions of q, that is, the scans for each relation in $\mathcal{R}$ together with the predicates/UDFs that appear immediately above the scans (line 2). Clearly, there is one leaf expression for each relation $R \in \mathcal{R}$, denoted $lexp_R$. Subsequently, we transform each $lexp_R$ to a map-only job and execute it over a sample of R until k tuples have been output by the filter or we have finished scanning R (lines 6-8). More details about the sampling process and the execution of the pilot runs (lines 7-8) are provided in Section 4.2. The statistics that are collected during the execution of $lexp_R$ are added to the statistics metastore. In this paper, we store the statistics in a file, but we can employ any persistent storage, including key-value stores, and relational DBMSs.

Coming back to the above query Q_1, three pilot runs need to be executed: one for relation `rs` (applying the two predicates on `addr[0]`), one for `rv` (applying the `sentanalysis` UDF), and one for t (with no predicates). As a second example, consider TPC-H query Q9, which includes a 5-way star join. We have added various UDFs to it, so that all dimensions fit in memory. On the lefthand side of Figure 3 we give the plan that is picked by a state-of-the-art relational optimizer for a shared nothing DBMS. The optimizer cannot estimate the selectivity of predicates involving UDFs and produces a plan where all joins are expensive repartition joins. On the other hand, after performing the pilot runs and feeding our optimizer with the updated statistics, we get a plan having only broadcast joins (righthand side of figure).

Reusability of statistics To avoid performing unnecessary pilot runs in cases when we have already collected statistics for a specific relation R with the same predicates, we associate the statistics in the metastore with an expression signature (corresponding to the leaf expression $lexp_R$). Thus, before executing the pilot runs, we look-up for existing statistics using the corresponding signature and perform the run only in the absence of statistics (line 5). This is useful in cases of recurring queries, or when the same relation and predicates appear in different queries.

Moreover, note that if there are no predicates/UDFs participating in a leaf expression $lexp_R$ and there are already available statistics for relation R, we can avoid executing $lexp_R$ and instead use the existing statistics for R. For instance, in Q_1 above, since no predicates are applied on t, we do not need to execute the third pilot run if we already have statistics for t.

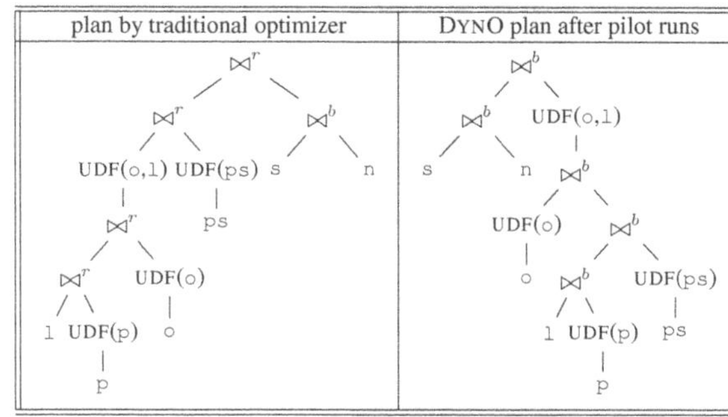

Figure 3: Execution plans for TPC-H query Q9′.

Optimization for selective predicates When the predicates applied on a relation are very selective, the whole input relation may be consumed before outputting k tuples. In this case, we use the output of the corresponding map job (that is in any case written to HDFS) during the actual execution of the query, instead of running it again. This is very beneficial especially for expensive predicates/UDFs that take a considerable amount of time to be executed. Taking this a step further, in such cases, if the job is close to completion when k tuples have been output (e.g., 80% of the base relation is scanned), we can let the job finish in order to be able to reuse the output when the query gets executed.

4.2 Execution of Pilot Runs

We have implemented two different ways of executing the PILR algorithm: PILR_ST and PILR_MT. First, we started by implementing PILR_ST, where we submit the i-th leaf expression $lexp_R$ only after the (i-1)-th leaf expression has finished executing. For each $lexp_R$, all map tasks (or to be precise, at least the first wave of map tasks) are started. Each map task increases a global counter (that is stored in ZooKeeper[5]) as it outputs records. When the global counter becomes bigger than k, the job gets interrupted. This was the simplest approach to implement, since at the time Jaql did not have support for submitting multiple MapReduce jobs in parallel. However, it has various drawbacks. First, by not submitting the leaf jobs simultaneously, we pay the startup cost of the MapReduce jobs (which could be as high as 15-20 seconds) for each relation in the query, and we underutilize the cluster. Moreover, as each job terminates early, its tasks are interrupted before they finish processing their input data blocks. This may lead to a bias in our estimates, due to "inspection paradox", as described in [32]. Essentially, tasks that produce smaller outputs are likely to process records faster and thus skew output statistics. We avoid this "inspection paradox" by finishing processing each data block that we already started.

To address these drawbacks, we implemented the second variant, PILR_MT, where we have modified the input format so that, given a query with $|\mathcal{R}|$ relations, we pick exactly $m/|\mathcal{R}|$ random splits for each relation, where m is the number of map slots in the cluster. We also modified the execution engine of Jaql to submit multiple jobs at a time. To this end, we are now able to start all leaf jobs together, avoiding the job startup cost $|\mathcal{R}|$ times, and better utilizing the resources of the cluster. Note that if the $m/|\mathcal{R}|$ splits are not sufficient for getting our k-record sample, we pick more splits on demand with a technique similar to [38]. Our ability to dynamically add random splits to the sample allows us to solve the main problem of block-sampling, i.e., sample sizing [10]. Note that

[5]http://zookeeper.apache.org

Query	SF100-ST	SF100-MT	SF300-MT	SF1000-MT
Q2	100%	27.7%	26.2%	27.5%
Q8′	100%	16.9%	19.1%	16.0%
Q9′	100%	19.4%	18.9%	20.6%
Q10	100%	24.8%	24.2%	24.4%

Table 1: Relative execution time of PILR for varying queries and scale factors.

requiring k output records is a generic yet imperfect method of assessing the sample quality. However, using a shared data structure in ZooKeeper, we can easily plug in other such methods, such as cross-validation used in [10].

To show the impact of PILR_MT, we have used four TPC-H queries to compare PILR_ST using scale factor 100 with PILR_MT for increasing scale factors (100, 300, 1000). The results are given in Table 1, where the numbers are normalized to the execution time of PILR_ST for SF=100. PILR_MT brings an average performance speedup of 4.6x over PILR_ST. Importantly, the performance of PILR_MT does not depend on the size of the dataset, but only on the size of the sample k.

In the rest of the paper, whenever we refer to PILR, we will be using the PILR_MT variant. As will be shown in Section 6.2, the overhead of PILR on the overall query execution is in most cases about 3%, which is not significant, especially given its advantages.

4.3 Collected Statistics

During the pilot runs we keep global statistics for each table (namely, table cardinality and average tuple size), as well as statistics per attribute (min/max values, and number of distinct values). In order to reduce the overhead of statistics collection, we only collect statistics for the attributes that participate in join predicates.

For each pilot run over a relation R, let R_o be the tuples of R that are output after the application of the predicates, $|R_o|$ be the corresponding number of tuples and $size(R_o)$ the size (in bytes) in disk (these numbers are computed by the counters exposed by Hadoop). Then, the average record size[6] is computed as $rec\_size^{\epsilon}_{avg} = \frac{size(R_o)}{|R_o|}$. Moreover, the table cardinality of R (after the predicates) is estimated as $|R|^{\epsilon} = \frac{size(R)}{rec\_size^{\epsilon}_{avg}}$.

Collecting the minimum and maximum value for each attribute is done by finding for each HDFS split the corresponding values and combining them to find the min and max values for the whole sample. This combination is done in the Jaql client to avoid a reduce phase in the pilot run jobs. Estimating the number of distinct values of an attribute is more involved and is detailed below.

Distinct values estimation via KMV synopsis Let R be one of the relations of the dataset $\mathcal{D}$ and A be one of its attributes for which we want to compute the number of distinct values DV_A. Scanning R and keeping track of all the distinct values of A can incur a prohibitive cost for big relations, especially in terms of memory. Instead, a synopsis for A can be created and then used to estimate DV_A (we denote the estimation by DV^{ϵ}_A). In particular, we opted for the KMV synopsis [6], which allows to create one synopsis for each partition R_p of R and then easily combine the partial synopses to get a global synopsis for the whole relation. Thus, the process can be executed in parallel for each HDFS split.

Let $\mathcal{S}^A_{R_p}$ be the KMV synopsis for partition R_p, and h be a hash function with domain $\{0, 1, \ldots, M\}$. The synopsis $\mathcal{S}^A_{R_p}$ is a set containing the k (with k>0) minimum hash values for the values of A that appear in R_p. For a dataset with D distinct values, the size of the synopsis is $\mathcal{O}(k \log D)$, and the cost of creating it is $\mathcal{O}(|R_p| + \log k \log D)$, where $|R_p|$ the number of tuples in R_p. Creating the global synopsis $\mathcal{S}^A_R$ is equivalent to computing the union $\bigcup_{R_p \in R} \mathcal{S}^A_{R_p}$ of all partial synopses and then keeping the k minimum values of the union. Let h_k be the biggest value in $\mathcal{S}_R$. Then, as shown in [6], we can estimate the number of distinct values $DV^{\epsilon}_{A,R}$ of A in R by using the unbiased estimator via the following formula: $DV^{\epsilon}_{A,R} = \frac{(k-1)M}{h_k}$.

In our setting, we compute the synopsis for each HDFS split that is processed at the map phase of the pilot runs, and then compute the global synopsis out of the partial ones in the Jaql client. Using this estimation, for $k = 1024$, the upper bound on the error of DV^{ϵ}_k is approximately 6%.

Given that during our pilot runs we consume only a sample R^s of each relation R (i.e., $R^s \subseteq R$), we need to extrapolate the distinct value estimation we got over R^s to the whole relation R. Computing the number of distinct values based on a sample of the dataset still remains a challenging task, especially when data is skewed or when there are many distinct values, each having a low frequency [9]. In this work, we used the following simple formula for estimating the number of distinct values for R, given the distinct values for R_s: $DV^{\epsilon}_{A,R} = \frac{|R|}{|R_s|} DV^{\epsilon}_{A,R_s}$. We plan to focus on more precise extrapolations as part of our future work.

Additional statistics Further statistics can be collected, including frequent values, percentile and histograms. This would lead to more accurate cost estimations and possibly better plans, but would increase the overhead of statistics collections. We chose to collect the aforementioned statistics, since these are currently supported by the cost-based optimizer we are using (see Section 5.2).

4.4 Discussion

Shortcomings of pilot runs Despite the significant advantages of the pilot runs that we already discussed in this section, there are still cases for which they may not be sufficient for accurately estimating the costs of the join operators in a plan:

- The joins are not on primary/foreign keys.
- The query contains complex predicates/UDFs that are not local but are applied on results of joins (hence, they cannot be pushed down and are not considered by PILR).
- There are correlations among the join columns.

As we explain in the following section, for these cases it is beneficial not only to perform the pilot runs, but also to adapt the execution plan at runtime, as parts of it get executed.

Placement of predicates in the plan In our approach, in case of multiple predicates per relation, we do not consider an order in their application, although this could have a considerable impact on the execution time. Moreover, the heuristic of pushing selections/UDFs down does not always lead to optimal plans, when expensive predicates are present [24, 11]. Unlike our approach, these works assume that the user provides the selectivity estimation of such predicates, and then focus on finding their optimal place in the execution plan. In practice, such selectivity is difficult to compute, as it also depends on the data, and this is exactly what we try to tackle with the pilot runs. Along the same lines, a recent development in the Stratosphere system [25] focuses on the reordering of expensive predicates, based either on user annotations or static code analysis. We see these works as complimentary to ours. Once we compute the selectivity of a predicate/UDF using the pilot runs, we can use these algorithms to find the right place and order to evaluate those predicates. For instance, if a predicate involving UDFs turns out to be expensive and not selective, we could reverse our decision to push it down, and pull it back up in the query plan.

[6]We use the superscript ϵ to highlight that a value is an estimation.

Algorithm 2: Dynamic Optimization Algorithm (DYNOPT)

```
  Input  : join block expression jb, a set of relations R
  Output: jb(R)
1 while true do
2    bestJoinPlan ← optimize(jb)
3    mapredPlan ← toMapReduce(bestJoinPlan)
4    jobsToRun ← pickLeafJobs(mapredPlan)
5    results ← execute(jobsToRun)
     // If the whole current plan will be
        executed, exit and return result
6    if mapredPlan \ jobsToRun = ∅ then return result
7    updateStatistics()
8    jb ← updatePlan(jb, jobsToRun, results)
```

5. DYNAMIC EXECUTION OF PLANS

As described in Section 3, after performing the pilot runs and gathering the initial statistics, we start the execution of the query's join blocks. In the first iteration, we use the statistics collected in the pilot runs, and find the best join order. After we execute a subset of the joins, we re-optimize the remaining part of the join block using the statistics collected in this execution step, and dynamically adapt the query plan as needed. This corresponds to the loop including steps 4'-7' in Figure 1. In this section we present the corresponding DYNOPT algorithm.

5.1 The DYNOPT Algorithm

Our DYNOPT algorithm (Algorithm 2), takes a join block jb and a set of relations $\mathcal{R}$, and returns $jb(\mathcal{R})$, i.e., the result of evaluating jb on $\mathcal{R}$. It iteratively executes parts of jb, dynamically adapting the query plan as needed, until the whole jb is executed.

At each iteration, we first optimize the current join block using a cost-based optimizer (line 2), which we detail in Section 5.2. Interestingly, when we optimize the current join block, we do not need to consider its local predicates, since local predicates have already been accounted for in its input statistics. The first iteration uses the statistics gathered in the pilot runs, and optimizes the join block where each node is a base relation. In subsequent iterations, the nodes in the join block are the results of previous steps and the statistics are collected during the execution of the jobs that compute the new nodes. Hence, optimizing a join block is tantamount to performing join enumeration, choosing the best join method for each join and picking the join plan with the minimum cost. As an example, the join block corresponding to query Q_1 (introduced in Section 4.1) that gets processed by the cost-based optimizer is the following Q_1':

```
SELECT rs.name
FROM restaurant' rs, review' rv, tweet' t
WHERE rs.id=rv.rsid AND rv.tid=t.id
```

In Q_1' the predicates have been removed, and each relation R is replaced by a new (virtual) relation R' that is the result of applying its local predicates. Although we do not materialize R', the statistics given to the optimizer correspond to R'.

Once the best plan is chosen by the cost-based optimizer, it gets transformed to a workflow of MapReduce jobs (line 3). Then, based on an *execution strategy*, we choose the leaf job(s) of the plan that will be executed in this iteration (lines 4-5). We discuss execution strategies in Section 5.3. During job execution, statistics are collected for specific attributes (details in Section 5.4). If there are no more jobs to execute, we output the result of the last job (line 6). Otherwise, we update the join block by substituting the part of the plan that just got executed with the results of the jobs' execution (line 8), and start the next iteration. For instance, in Figure 2, in the first iteration we execute the job corresponding to the circled part of plan$_1$ and save its results in relation $\mathtt{t}_1$. After re-invoking the optimizer, we get plan$_2$, in which the previously executed partial plan is substituted with $\mathtt{t}_1$.

In our current implementation, we re-optimize in each iteration, since the added overhead is not significant (see Section 6.2). However, the decision to re-optimize could be conditional on a threshold difference between the estimated result size and the observed one.

Executing the whole query For a given query q, DYNOPT gets invoked as many times as the number of join blocks in q. If there are grouping and ordering operators in the query, they get executed after the join that they depend on. Grouping and ordering operators are inserted into the execution plan by the Jaql compiler, hence are not considered by our cost-based optimizer, which focuses on join optimization. When executing the join blocks through DYNOPT, we need to respect the dependencies between blocks: a block can be executed only after all blocks it depends on have already been executed (or when it does not depend on other blocks). As long as dependencies are respected, the exact order of execution of the join blocks does not matter. However, if there are additional available resources in the cluster, there are cases where we can execute join blocks in parallel (by simultaneous invocations of DYNOPT for different blocks). This inter-block parallelism resembles the inter-operator parallelism of a bushy plan that is discussed in Section 5.3.

5.2 Cost-Based Join Optimizer

We built the cost-based optimizer that we use for join enumeration, as discussed in Section 5.1, by extending the Columbia optimizer [12]. Columbia is an open source top-down optimizer, based on the Cascades query optimizer framework [21], focusing on extensibility and efficiency. It takes as input a query, written in the form of a logical operator tree and outputs the minimum-cost physical operator tree, along with the cost of each operator.

For the enumeration of equivalent plans and their translation to executable operators, it relies on two types of rules: transformation and implementation ones. The former transform a logical expression to an equivalent one, whereas the latter replace a logical operator with a physical one. Each rule has a priority, which defines the order of application of the rules. A branch-and-bound algorithm is used to search through the alternative plans for a given query, and the execution cost of each plan is calculated using statistics for the relations, selectivity estimations and cost formulas. The supported statistics are the ones discussed in Section 4.3.

Since we are only interested in join enumeration, we deactivated all other logical operators but the binary join and the scan. The selectivity estimation of a join is computed based on the typical relational formulas [35]. Notice that Columbia is capable of producing bushy plans, whenever those are the cheapest ones. This is a desired feature that enables us to execute parts of the plan in parallel, as will be discussed in Section 5.3. However, the physical join operators that Columbia supports (hash-join, merge-join, etc.) are different from the two join operators that Jaql's runtime supports, namely the repartition ($\bowtie^r$) and broadcast ($\bowtie^b$) joins. Thus, we deactivated the physical joins of Columbia and added two new ones. Given two relations R and S, the cost of the repartition join consists of the cost of reading the relations, reshuffling them to the reducers, doing the join in the reducers, and outputting the results. Hence, the cost of the join is mostly linear in the size of the inputs (plus the cost of outputting the result). The cost formula we use is the following, where c_{rep}, c_{out} are constants, with $c_{rep} > c_{out}$:

$$C(R \bowtie^r S) = c_{rep}(|R| + |S|) + c_{out}|S \bowtie R|$$

As for the broadcast join, assuming S is the small relation, its cost includes loading S and building the corresponding hashtable, reading R and probing each tuple to the hashtable, and finally outputting the results. We use the following cost formula, where $c_{probe}, c_{build}, c_{out}$ are constants, with $c_{probe} > c_{build} > c_{out}$:

$$C(R \bowtie^b S) = c_{probe}|R| + c_{build}|S| + c_{out}|R \bowtie S|$$

Importantly, $c_{rep} >> c_{probe}$, which reflects the fact that $C(R \bowtie^r S) > C(R \bowtie^b S)$, as long as S fits in memory. Note that although the formulas rely only on the size of the relations and not on the characteristics of the cluster or the available resources, they serve the basic purpose of *favouring broadcast joins over repartition joins*. When applicable, broadcast joins are usually preferable, since they get executed in map-only jobs and can also be chained, decreasing the total number of map-reduce jobs needed for a query.

As discussed in Section 2.2.2, Jaql is capable of chaining broadcast joins. To do so, it solely relies on the size of relations in the file system, without taking into account the filters that may be applied prior to the join. To avoid relying on this heuristic rule, we added a new rule to our optimizer that takes as input the maximum memory M_{max} that will be available during execution, and dictates which joins should be chained. Assume we want to join relations $R, S_1, S_2, \ldots, S_k$, and that all $S_i, i = 1, \ldots, k$ fit in memory at the same time. If we chain the k broadcast joins, we avoid the cost of writing to and reading from disk the $k-1$ intermediate results of the joins. The corresponding formula is the following:

$$C((R \bowtie^b S_1) \bowtie^b \ldots) \bowtie^b S_k) = c_{probe}|R| + c_{build}(|S_1| + \ldots + |S_k|) + c_{out}|R \bowtie S_1 \bowtie \ldots \bowtie S_k|$$

Our new rule traverses the operator tree and when it discovers two or more consecutive broadcast joins whose build sides fit in memory, it updates the cost of the first join of the chain using the above formula, setting the costs of the other joins of the chain to zero. Jaql's compiler has also been modified accordingly, in order to use the chain information during the translation to MapReduce jobs.

5.3 Execution Strategies: Choosing Leaf Jobs

Bushy plans provide the opportunity to execute multiple leaf joins in parallel. Various strategies can be used for choosing which joins to execute at the same time. For instance, in plan$_1$ of Figure 2, one could execute first the leftmost (circled) job j_1 or the repartition join j_2 between `l` and `p` or both of them in parallel.

In static optimization where the query plan does not change, the execution order of the (leaf) jobs does not impact query execution time. In this case, we only need to determine which jobs to run in parallel, as these jobs will strive for the same cluster resources [20].

On the contrary, when the execution plan can change at runtime, deciding which leaf job(s) to execute first can have significant impact on execution time, since it determines the way the plan dynamically adapts. For instance, in the aforementioned plan$_1$, executing first j_2 instead of j_1 would lead to a different plan than plan$_2$ of the figure. Even more interestingly, executing more than one job at a time has the additional side effect of changing the number of re-optimization opportunities. For example, if we execute j_1 and j_2 in parallel, we will have one less re-optimization point, since we will only re-optimize at the end of the two jobs. Such an order of application can be determined using an *execution strategy*. To the best of our knowledge, we are the first to consider such strategies, which can also be applicable in the relational setting.

There are two dimensions that an execution strategy has to consider: 1) give a priority to each leaf job (higher priority jobs get executed first), which changes as parts of the plan get executed; 2) decide how many jobs to execute at a time. Different metrics for deciding the priority of the leaf jobs can be devised. Two interesting ones are the following:

Cost The basic idea is to favour the cheapest jobs, so that we reach re-optimization points as soon as possible.

Uncertainty With the notion of uncertainty of a job, we want to reflect the expected error in the result size estimation. Note that we use standard join selectivity formulas, and it has been shown that the estimation error increases exponentially with the number of joins [27]. As a result, we define uncertainty as the number of joins that participate in the job. The idea here is that we want to execute uncertain jobs first to gather actual statistics about them, and fix the remaining plan through re-optimization if needed.

By combining the above dimensions we can get several strategy variants. Our experiments in Section 6.3 include a comparison among different strategies. As future work, we plan to determine the most appropriate strategy for each query based on a cost model.

5.4 Online Statistics Collection

During the execution of a MapReduce job, we collect statistics either at the map phase (if it is a map-only job) or the reduce phase (if it is a map-reduce job). We keep the same statistics as the ones for the pilot runs (see Section 4.3). To minimize the statistics collection overhead, we keep statistics only for the needed attributes for re-optimization, i.e., the ones that participate in join conditions of the still unexecuted part of the join block. Moreover, we do not keep statistics if we know we are not going to re-optimize (e.g., during the last query job) or if statistics for the given job are already in the metastore (see Section 4.1 for reusability of statistics).

For each MapReduce job, we first store in the job configuration the list of attributes we will collect statistics for. Assume we execute a map-only job. During execution, each task collects statistics for its input split. Instead of relying on an extra MapReduce job to combine these partial statistics and get the global ones, every time a task finishes it writes its statistics in a file and publishes the file's URL in ZooKeeper. Once all tasks are finished, the Jaql client that submitted the job finds through ZooKeeper the URLs of all partial statistics files, reads and combines them. The same technique is followed when collecting statistics in the reduce phase.

6. EXPERIMENTAL EVALUATION

In this section, we present our experimental results for DYNO.

6.1 Experimental Setup

Cluster setup We performed our experiments on a cluster of 15 nodes, connected with 10 gigabit Ethernet. Each machine has two 2.2 GHz Intel Xeon E5-2430 6-core CPUs, with 96 GB of RAM and 12 SATA disks of 2 TB each. We deployed Hadoop 1.1.1 with each node having 10 map and 6 reduce slots (leading to a total of 140 map and 84 reduce slots). Each slot was given 2 GB of RAM. HDFS was configured to stripe across all disks of each node (excluding one disk dedicated to the OS), and the HDFS block size was set to 128 MB. For the number of map and reduce tasks per MapReduce job, we used the same values that Hive uses by default. All machines are running Ubuntu Linux 12.04 (with kernel version 3.2.0), Java 6 and ZooKeeper 3.4.5.

Datasets There are not many big data benchmarks, and none is suitable for our study, which requires multiple joins. The Pavlo et al. benchmark [33] has only two relations to be joined, the YCSB benchmark [13] targets NoSQL systems, and the data generators for BigBench [19], which would be a good candidate, were not publicly available at the time of writing this paper. As a result, we settled on TPC-H [37], which provides a data generator that allows us testing at different scales, and contains 8 tables and queries with

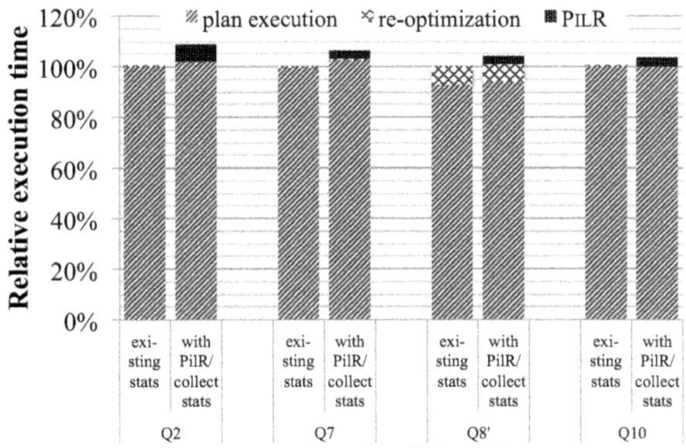

Figure 4: Overhead of pilot runs, re-optimization and statistics collection in DYNOPT.

many joins. We generated datasets of size 100 GB, 300 GB and 1 TB (by using scale factors SF={100,300,1000}, respectively).

Queries From the 22 TPC-H queries, we chose those that include joins between at least 4 relations, namely queries Q2, Q7, Q8, Q9, Q10. We excluded Q5, because it contains cyclic join conditions that are not currently supported by our optimizer. To better assess the performance of DYNO, we used modified versions of Q8 and Q9. In particular, we added a UDF in Q8 that filters the results of the join between `orders` and `customer`. We also added two correlated predicates on `orders` (correlations were identified using the CORDS algorithm [26]). In Q9 we added various filtering UDFs on top of the dimension tables to make them fit in memory. Depending on the experiment, for better readability, we may include only the subset of the above queries that brings interesting insights.

Variants of execution plans We used the following variants of execution plans to evaluate the characteristics of our system:

DYNOPT This is the dynamic execution of a query as dictated by our DYNOPT algorithm (Algorithm 2, described in Section 5). It includes the pilot runs, online statistics collection and re-optimization points.

DYNOPT-SIMPLE This is the plan we get by removing the re-optimization points from DYNOPT, that is, we perform the pilot runs, call our optimizer once and then execute the resulting plan. Apart from the pilot runs, no runtime statistics are collected.

RELOPT Here we employ a state-of-the-art relational optimizer used in a commercial shared-nothing parallel database DBMS-X, which also supports repartition and broadcast joins. DBMS-X is capable of using more detailed statistics (e.g., histograms), and all needed statistics are gathered by the system prior to query execution in this case. The obtained execution plan is then hand-coded to a Jaql script and executed. Note that DBMS-X does not have enough information to estimate selectivity of UDFs during optimization. We used this plan as a representative of the best plan that can be obtained by an existing optimizer.

BESTSTATICJAQL As explained in Section 2, the existing version of Jaql produces only left-deep plans and the join ordering is determined by the order of relations in the `FROM` clause. For each query, we tried all possible orders of relations and picked the best one; BESTSTATICJAQL is the resulting plan. The rewrite rule for using broadcast joins when relations are small is activated.

In our experiments, we used *k=1024* for the KMV synopsis to estimate distinct values (leading to a worst case error bound of 6%). Moreover, we disabled the optimization that avoids executing the

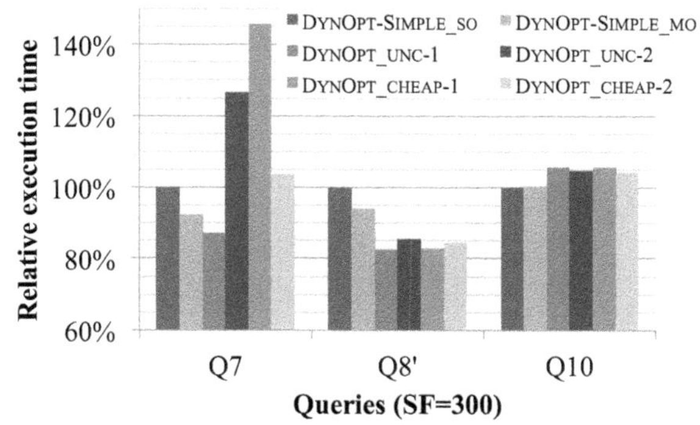

Figure 5: Comparison of execution strategies for DYNOPT.

pilot runs when there are already statistics computed for a given expression. All numbers reported below are averaged over 3 runs.

6.2 Overhead of Dynamic Optimization

In this section we assess the overhead introduced to Jaql execution due to our dynamic optimization techniques, namely the pilot runs, the statistics collection during the execution of the MapReduce jobs, and the calls to the optimizer at each (re-)optimization point. To this end, we report execution times of four TPC-H queries for two different executions. In the first one, we provide upfront all needed statistics to the optimizer, and the only overhead is the (re-)optimization time. To do so, we previously execute the query to add to the metastore all needed statistics, and then re-execute it after enabling the statistics reusability optimization. In the second, all statistics are computed at runtime (through pilot runs and online statistics collection). The overhead of the (re-)optimization and the pilot runs are explicitly measured. The overhead of online statistics collection can be computed by the difference in execution time between the two executions, after the execution time of pilot runs and total (re-)optimization time is deducted. The results are given in Figure 4, where execution times are normalized to the execution time with pre-collected statistics.

As can be seen, total (re-)optimization time is less than 0.25% of the execution time in most cases. It is only for $Q8'$ that it is approximately 7% as this query includes a 7-way join. Note that although $Q8'$ gets (re-)optimized four times, only the initial call to the optimizer (after the pilot runs) is costly, as it includes all 8 relations and is responsible for 90% of the total (re-)optimization time. The subsequent calls are very fast, because, as part of the query has been executed, less relations are included in the optimization.

Furthermore, the overhead of the pilot runs is between 2.5% and 6.7%. Online statistics collection brings a small overhead of 0.1% to 2.8% to the total execution time, depending on the number of attributes for which we need to keep statistics for. For instance, Q10 that has the smallest number of join conditions, also has the smallest statistics collection overhead. Overall, we observe a total of 7-10% overhead. We believe this is acceptable given the benefits brought by our approach, as will be shown in Sections 6.4 and 6.5.

6.3 Comparison of Execution Strategies

In this experiment, we compare various execution strategies both for DYNOPT and DYNOPT-SIMPLE (see Section 5.3 for a related discussion). For DYNOPT-SIMPLE, we use two variants: SO executes only one leaf job at a time, and MO submits all leaf jobs at the same time. For DYNOPT, we use: UNC-1 that executes the single most uncertain leaf job first; UNC-2 that executes the two cheapest most uncertain leaf jobs at the same time (if two leaf jobs exist in the query plan, otherwise one); CHEAP-1 that executes the cheapest leaf job first; CHEAP-2 that executes the two cheapest leaf

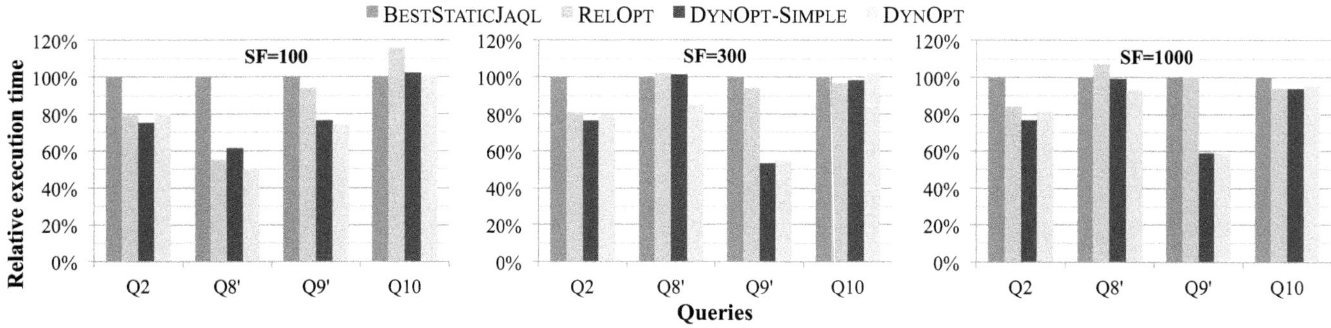

Figure 7: Speedup of execution times for varying queries and scale factors compared to default Jaql execution.

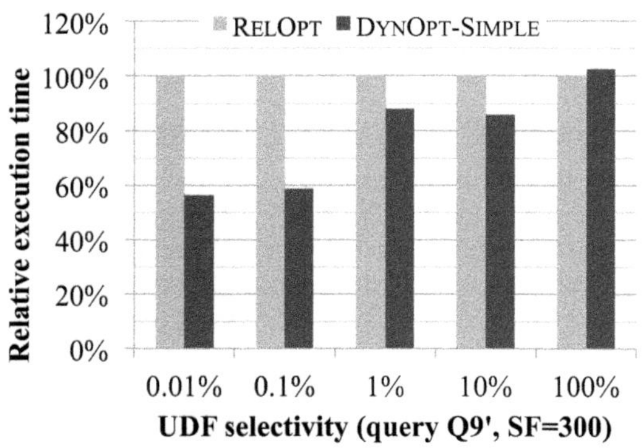

Figure 6: Performance impact of UDF selectivity on Q9′.

jobs first. When executing two jobs j_1 and j_2 in parallel, we use the FIFO scheduler of Hadoop, so as to maximize the utilization of the cluster resources. As future work, we plan to experiment with different schedulers, such as the fair and capacity schedulers. The resulting execution times, normalized to the execution time of DYNOPT-SIMPLE_SO for each query, are given in Figure 6.

As expected, SIMPLE_MO always outperforms SIMPLE_SO, since the former utilizes the cluster better (e.g., when a job is at its reduce phase, another job can start its map phase). The only case the two strategies coincide is for Q10, because a left-deep plan is picked by the optimizer, thus there is no chance for parallelization.

Interestingly, for DYNOPT, parallelization is not always beneficial: executing jobs in parallel increases cluster utilization, but reduces the re-optimization points. For Q10, due to the chosen left-deep plan, all strategies perform the same. However, for Q7 and Q8′, UNC-1 is the winner strategy. For Q7, UNC-1 results in 40% better time over UNC-2 and 13% over SIMPLE_SO. Moreover, executing the most uncertain jobs first is much better than executing the cheapest ones for Q7. In the case of Q8, the cheapest and most uncertain jobs coincide, thus the variants perform the same. Overall, *it is more beneficial for* DYNOPT *to have more re-optimization points than to execute more jobs in parallel.* Due to their better performance, hereafter we will use the MO variant for DYNOPT-SIMPLE, and the UNC-1 variant for DYNOPT.

6.4 Star Join Sensitivity Analysis

In this section we study the performance of DYNOPT-SIMPLE for star join Q9′, as the size of the dimensions changes (by changing the selectivity of the UDFs), in order to see the effectiveness of pilot runs. The results are given in Figure 6, where the execution times are normalized to the execution time of the plan picked each time by RELOPT.

In all but the last case (100% selectivity), all dimensions fit in memory and all joins are broadcast joins. However, not all dimensions fit in memory at the same time, hence the query is executed in multiple jobs. For 0.01% and 0.1% selectivity, all joins are executed in 2 map-only joins (since more joins can be chained), leading to a performance improvement of 1.78x and 1.71x over RELOPT, respectively. For 1% and 10% selectivity, 3 map-only jobs are needed, bringing a (smaller) performance speedup of approx. 1.15x over RELOPT. Finally, when the selectivity is 100%, our optimizer picks the same plan with RELOPT (including 4 jobs), and our execution is slightly worse due to the pilot runs overhead.

The pilot runs enable the optimizer to identify the cases when tables can fit in memory for a broadcast join. Note that if the optimizer's estimate is incorrect and the build table turns out to not fit in memory, the query may not even terminate. As a result, most systems are quite conservative and favour repartition joins to avoid disastrous plans. However, repartition joins lead to worse performance if the table is small enough to fit in memory. Our pilot runs enable making this decision more accurately, avoiding both disastrous cases, as well as not missing good performance opportunities when the build table is indeed small enough to fit in memory. As future work we plan to experiment with more advanced implementations of the broadcast join (e.g., taking advantage of the DistributedCache) to further boost our performance speedup.

6.5 Comparison of Query Execution Times

We now compare the performance of the four execution plans described in Section 6.1 for various queries and scale factors. Figure 7 shows the query execution times normalized to the BESTSTATICJAQL execution time.

First, notice that *both our dynamic techniques (*DYNOPT-SIMPLE *and* DYNOPT*) are at least as good as, and sometimes better than, the best hand-written left-deep plan (*BESTSTATICJAQL*) for all queries and scale factors.* This is not always the case for RELOPT (e.g., Q10 for SF=100, Q8′ for SF=1000). Our techniques produce plans that are also better than the plans generated by the RELOPT in most cases, except Q2 and Q8′ for SF=100, and Q10 for SF=300. Moreover, there are cases for which we are up to 2x faster than BESTSTATICJAQL.

Q2 benefits by considering bushy plans: for all three bushy plans (RELOPT, DYNOPT-SIMPLE, DYNOPT) and all scale factors, there is a performance speedup of approximately 1.2x. This confirms that in a shared-nothing architecture it is crucial to consider bushy plans (to minimize intermediate results) during query optimization. Moreover, given there are no UDFs and joins are on primary/foreign keys, re-optimization does not bring further benefit (in fact, there is a slight degradation due to the added overhead).

Q8′ includes a UDF over the result of a join and in this case re-optimizing proves to be very beneficial: DYNOPT leads to a performance speedup of 2x, 1.17x and 1.07x over BESTSTATICJAQL for the three scale factors. The benefits of re-optimization are not as

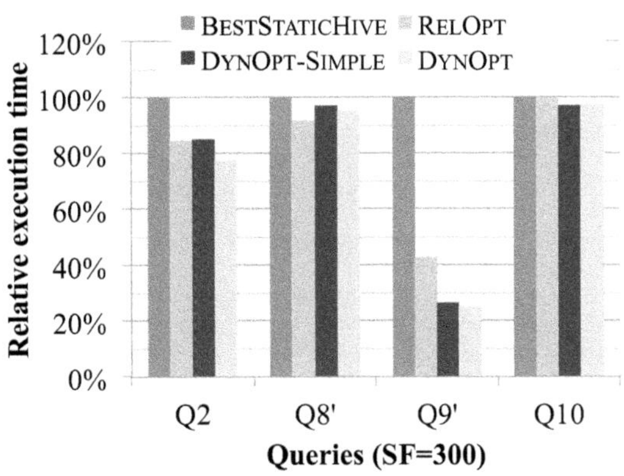

Figure 8: Benefits of applying DYNOPT in Hive.

pronounced for larger scale factors, because as data size increases, there are less opportunities for applying broadcast joins. On the other hand, RELOPT and DYNOPT-SIMPLE manage to speed-up Q8′ only for SF=100. In the case of DYNOPT-SIMPLE, only pilot runs are not sufficient to account for the non-local UDF.

Q9′ is the star join case discussed in Section 6.4. Due to the presence of UDFs, RELOPT does not manage to improve the performance of the query. On the other hand, our techniques manage to make extensive use of broadcast joins, leading to speedups of 1.33-1.88x (depending on the SF). Notice that for larger data sizes, avoiding repartition joins is even more important.

Finally, for Q10, the left-deep BESTSTATICJAQL is very close to the best plan, so performance does not further improve with bushy plans or dynamic optimizations. Notice, however, that even in that case our techniques are as good as the best hand-written plan.

6.6 Benefits of DYNOPT in Hive

As discussed in Section 3, our techniques can be applied to other systems. To show the benefits of using the execution plans produced by our dynamic techniques on a system other than Jaql, we compare the performance of the four execution plans described in Section 6.1 for various TPC-H queries and scale factor SF=300 using Hive. Note that instead of using the BESTSTATICJAQL plan, we use the BESTSTATICHIVE one, that is, the best left-deep for Hive[7]. We chose Hive for this experiment since it is currently one of the most popular systems for SQL queries over HDFS data.

We took the execution plans of DYNOPT and DYNOPT-SIMPLE that were generated by Jaql for the experiment of Section 6.5 (for SF=300) and hand-coded them in Hive. Note that if we had implemented the same sampling and statistics collection and used our join optimizer in Hive, the same plans would have been generated. Figure 8 shows the query execution times for these plans. These numbers do not include the overheads of our techniques, which are typically about 5% of the execution time (see Section 6.2).

We observe similar trends as the ones for Jaql. DYNOPT and DYNOPT-SIMPLE always produce better plans than BESTSTATICHIVE. It is interesting to note that Q9′ has a significantly higher speedup than Jaql (3.98x instead of 1.88x). This is because broadcast joins in Hive 0.12 exploit the Distributed Cache of MapReduce, leading to better performance. This brings an advantage for queries such as Q9′ that include many broadcast joins.

6.7 Discussion

The following are the highlights of our experiments:

- DYNOPT-SIMPLE always produces better plans than the best left-deep plan. Moreover, it is always comparable and most of the times better than the RELOPT plan (with the exception of Q8′ for SF=300). This shows that although it introduces a small overhead, it provides accurate selectivity and result size estimation, especially when the query contains local UDFs and data correlations, as exhibited by Q9′.
- DYNOPT subsumes DYNOPT-SIMPLE. Hence, when further re-optimization is not beneficial, DYNOPT is a bit worse than DYNOPT-SIMPLE due to the increased overhead it introduces. However, it outperforms DYNOPT-SIMPLE when the join result size estimation contains high uncertainty, due to correlations, UDFs on results of joins (this is the case for Q8′), or non primary/foreign key join conditions.
- There are queries for which the left-deep plan is the optimal (see Q10), but there are others that can benefit significantly by considering bushy plans (such as Q2).
- Our Hive experiments show that our techniques are also beneficial for other systems, exhibiting similar performance trends.

Overall, notice that we get the most benefit from pilot runs, which is an interesting remark as most dynamic optimization techniques so far have focused on re-optimizing the query at runtime and not on carefully selecting the first plan before the first re-optimization occurs.

[7]https://issues.apache.org/jira/browse/HIVE-600

7. RELATED WORK

Several higher-level declarative languages have been proposed lately for analyzing large datasets, such as Pig [18], Hive [36], Jaql [5], Stratosphere [3], DryadLINQ [41], SCOPE [8], Spark [42] and Shark [40]. Query optimization in this environment is crucial for translating such higher-level scripts to efficient distributed execution plans. However, most of these systems lack a cost-based optimizer and rely on heuristics, e.g., Hive and Pig [17].

Dynamic techniques are natural in this setting and have already started to be adapted by some of the systems. For instance, Shark can switch from a repartition to a broadcast join at runtime. In RoPE [1] recurring queries get optimized based on observations from their previous executions. The most related work to ours is in the context of SCOPE [8], where statistics are collected at runtime and the execution plan gets re-optimized if needed. One difference is that SCOPE relies on Dryad, which does not provide the natural re-optimization points of Hadoop. Moreover, they do not consider a way of automatically costing UDFs before choosing the initial plan (as we do with the pilot runs). Work has also been done on optimizing directly MapReduce jobs [30], by selecting the correct job configuration based on the characteristics of a job or by merging MapReduce jobs whenever possible. We consider such works as complimentary to ours: after our optimizer has picked an execution plan and our compiler has transformed it to a MapReduce workflow, we can use these works to further optimize the workflow.

Adaptive query processing has been extensively studied in the relational setting [15]. Altering the execution plan at runtime has been considered both in centralized [28, 31, 2] and distributed scenarios [22]. One of the important challenges in these works is deciding when to block query execution and re-optimize the plan (possibly throwing away work). Moreover, the initial plan in these works is obtained from the optimizer using the base table statistics, and as such is subject to potential incorrect result size and cost estimation due to data correlations and UDFs, leading to a possibly suboptimal plan (until re-optimization is invoked).

As far as dealing with complex predicates and UDFs is concerned, most existing works [24, 11] focus on placing such predicates in the right order and position in the plan, given that the selectivity of the predicate is provided. In [25], static code analysis and hints are used to reorder UDFs. Few works have focused on UDF cost models that get adapted based on previous executions [29, 23]. To the best of our knowledge, we are the first to consider calculating the UDF selectivity at runtime through the pilot runs.

8. CONCLUSION AND FUTURE WORK

In this paper, we presented DYNO, which utilizes pilot runs, runtime statistics collection, and re-optimization to optimize complex queries over Hadoop data. We introduced pilot runs, which execute the local filters and UDFs over a small sample of each base relation to collect statistics and estimate result sizes. Pilot runs are especially beneficial when the query contains UDFs and data correlations, because traditional static optimizers fail at estimating result sizes correctly under these conditions. Underestimating result sizes can lead the optimizer to make the wrong decision and use a broadcast join, which can be disastrous with a large data set. We provide the statistics collected via pilot runs to a cost-based optimizer to choose the join order and methods. As the query runs, we collect statistics, and at the completion of each MapReduce job, we can re-optimize the remaining parts of the query. Re-optimization is especially beneficial when 1) there are UDFs that need to be applied on the result of a join, and can impact the intermediate result size, 2) the join condition is not on primary/foreign key relationship, and 3) there is data correlation between the join conditions.

We showed that the plans produced by our system, both DYNOPT and DYNOPT-SIMPLE, are at least as good and often better than the best hand-written left-deep plans, and are most of the times better than the plans produced by a state-of-the-art relational optimizer for a shared nothing DBMS. Finally, we identified interesting strategies for choosing leaf jobs to execute at a given point, and proposed some first heuristic choices. Experimenting with more sophisticated (possibly cost-based) strategies is left as future work.

We are also planning to create a new dynamic join operator that switches between a broadcast and repartition join, without waiting for the current job to finish. Moreover, we consider adapting our techniques to other platforms, such as Tez. Although our optimizer currently focuses on join ordering, we plan to extend it to consider grouping and ordering operators.

9. ACKNOWLEDGMENTS

The authors would like to thank Guy Lohman and Ippokratis Pandis for their useful discussions and insightful feedback.

10. REFERENCES

[1] S. Agarwal, S. Kandula, N. Bruno, M.-C. Wu, I. Stoica, and J. Zhou. Re-optimizing data-parallel computing. In *NSDI*, 2012.

[2] S. Babu, P. Bizarro, and D. J. DeWitt. Proactive re-optimization. In *SIGMOD Conference*, pages 107–118, 2005.

[3] D. Battré, S. Ewen, F. Hueske, O. Kao, V. Markl, and D. Warneke. Nephele/PACTs: a programming model and execution framework for web-scale analytical processing. In *SoCC*, pages 119–130, 2010.

[4] P. A. Bernstein, N. Goodman, E. Wong, C. L. Reeve, and J. B. R. Jr. Query processing in a system for distributed databases (SDD-1). *ACM Trans. Database Syst.*, 6(4):602–625, 1981.

[5] K. S. Beyer, V. Ercegovac, R. Gemulla, A. Balmin, M. Y. Eltabakh, C.-C. Kanne, F. Özcan, and E. J. Shekita. Jaql: A scripting language for large scale semistructured data analysis. *PVLDB*, 4(12), 2011.

[6] K. S. Beyer, P. J. Haas, B. Reinwald, Y. Sismanis, and R. Gemulla. On synopses for distinct-value estimation under multiset operations. In *SIGMOD*, pages 199–210, 2007.

[7] S. Blanas, J. M. Patel, V. Ercegovac, J. Rao, E. J. Shekita, and Y. Tian. A comparison of join algorithms for log processing in MapReduce. In *SIGMOD*, pages 975–986, 2010.

[8] N. Bruno, S. Jain, and J. Zhou. Continuous cloud-scale query optimization and processing. In *VLDB*, 2013.

[9] M. Charikar, S. Chaudhuri, R. Motwani, and V. R. Narasayya. Towards estimation error guarantees for distinct values. In *PODS*, pages 268–279, 2000.

[10] S. Chaudhuri, G. Das, and U. Srivastava. Effective use of block-level sampling in statistics estimation. In *SIGMOD Conference*, 2004.

[11] S. Chaudhuri and K. Shim. Optimization of queries with user-defined predicates. *ACM Trans. Database Syst.*, 24(2):177–228, 1999.

[12] Columbia Query Optimizer. http://web.cecs.pdx.edu/ len/Columbia.

[13] B. F. Cooper, A. Silberstein, E. Tam, R. Ramakrishnan, and R. Sears. Benchmarking cloud serving systems with YCSB. In *SoCC*, pages 143–154, 2010.

[14] J. Dean and S. Ghemawat. MapReduce: Simplified data processing on large clusters. In *OSDI*, pages 137–150, 2004.

[15] A. Deshpande, Z. G. Ives, and V. Raman. Adaptive query processing. *Foundations and Trends in Databases*, 1(1):1–140, 2007.

[16] D. J. DeWitt and J. Gray. Parallel database systems: The future of high performance database systems. *Commun. ACM*, 35(6):85–98, 1992.

[17] A. Gates, J. Dai, and T. Nair. Apache Pig's optimizer. *IEEE Data Eng. Bull.*, 36(1):34–45, 2013.

[18] A. Gates, O. Natkovich, S. Chopra, P. Kamath, S. Narayanam, C. Olston, B. Reed, S. Srinivasan, and U. Srivastava. Building a highlevel dataflow system on top of MapReduce: The Pig experience. *PVLDB*, 2(2):1414–1425, 2009.

[19] A. Ghazal, T. Rabl, M. Hu, F. Raab, M. Poess, A. Crolotte, and H.-A. Jacobsen. BigBench: towards an industry standard benchmark for big data analytics. In *SIGMOD*, pages 1197–1208, 2013.

[20] G. Graefe. Query evaluation techniques for large databases. *ACM Comput. Surv.*, 25(2):73–170, 1993.

[21] G. Graefe. The Cascades framework for query optimization. *IEEE Data Eng. Bull.*, 18(3):19–29, 1995.

[22] W.-S. Han, J. Ng, V. Markl, H. Kache, and M. Kandil. Progressive optimization in a shared-nothing parallel database. In *SIGMOD*, pages 809–820, 2007.

[23] Z. He, B. S. Lee, and R. R. Snapp. Self-tuning cost modeling of user-defined functions in an object-relational dbms. *ACM Trans. Database Syst.*, 30(3):812–853, 2005.

[24] J. M. Hellerstein. Optimization techniques for queries with expensive methods. *ACM TODS*, 23(2):113–157, 1998.

[25] F. Hueske, M. Peters, M. Sax, A. Rheinländer, R. Bergmann, A. Krettek, and K. Tzoumas. Opening the black boxes in data flow optimization. *PVLDB*, 5(11):1256–1267, 2012.

[26] I. F. Ilyas, V. Markl, P. J. Haas, P. Brown, and A. Aboulnaga. CORDS: Automatic discovery of correlations and soft functional dependencies. In *SIGMOD*, pages 647–658, 2004.

[27] Y. E. Ioannidis and S. Christodoulakis. On the propagation of errors in the size of join results. In *SIGMOD Conference*, pages 268–277, 1991.

[28] N. Kabra and D. J. DeWitt. Efficient mid-query re-optimization of sub-optimal query execution plans. In *SIGMOD Conference*, pages 106–117, 1998.

[29] B. S. Lee, L. Chen, J. Buzas, and V. Kannoth. Regression-based self-tuning modeling of smooth user-defined function costs for an object-relational database management system query optimizer. *Comput. J.*, 47(6):673–693, 2004.

[30] H. Lim, H. Herodotou, and S. Babu. Stubby: A transformation-based optimizer for mapreduce workflows. *PVLDB*, 5(11):1196–1207, 2012.

[31] V. Markl, V. Raman, D. E. Simmen, G. M. Lohman, and H. Pirahesh. Robust query processing through progressive optimization. In *SIGMOD*, pages 659–670, 2004.

[32] N. Pansare, V. R. Borkar, C. Jermaine, and T. Condie. Online aggregation for large MapReduce jobs. *PVLDB*, 4(11):1135–1145, 2011.

[33] A. Pavlo, E. Paulson, A. Rasin, D. J. Abadi, D. J. DeWitt, S. Madden, and M. Stonebraker. A comparison of approaches to large-scale data analysis. In *SIGMOD*, pages 165–178, 2009.

[34] H. Pirahesh, J. M. Hellerstein, and W. Hasan. Extensible/rule based query rewrite optimization in Starburst. In *SIGMOD*, pages 39–48, 1992.

[35] P. G. Selinger, M. M. Astrahan, D. D. Chamberlin, R. A. Lorie, and T. G. Price. Access path selection in a relational database management system. In *SIGMOD*, pages 23–34, 1979.

[36] A. Thusoo, J. S. Sarma, N. Jain, Z. Shao, P. Chakka, S. Anthony, H. Liu, P. Wyckoff, and R. Murthy. Hive - a warehousing solution over a Map-Reduce framework. *PVLDB*, 2(2):1626–1629, 2009.

[37] TPC-H Benchmark. http://www.tpc.org/tpch.

[38] R. Vernica, A. Balmin, K. S. Beyer, and V. Ercegovac. Adaptive MapReduce using situation-aware mappers. In *EDBT*, pages 420–431, 2012.

[39] S. Wu, F. Li, S. Mehrotra, and B. C. Ooi. Query optimization for massively parallel data processing. In *SoCC*, page 12, 2011.

[40] R. S. Xin, J. Rosen, M. Zaharia, M. J. Franklin, S. Shenker, and I. Stoica. Shark: SQL and rich analytics at scale. In *SIGMOD*, pages 13–24, 2013.

[41] Y. Yu, M. Isard, D. Fetterly, M. Budiu, Ú. Erlingsson, P. K. Gunda, and J. Currey. DryadLINQ: A system for general-purpose distributed data-parallel computing using a high-level language. In *OSDI*, pages 1–14, 2008.

[42] M. Zaharia, M. Chowdhury, T. Das, A. Dave, J. Ma, M. McCauley, M. J. Franklin, S. Shenker, and I. Stoica. Resilient distributed datasets: a fault-tolerant abstraction for in-memory cluster computing. In *NSDI*, 2012.

A Software-Defined Networking based Approach for Performance Management of Analytical Queries on Distributed Data Stores

Pengcheng Xiong
NEC Laboratories America
Cupertino, CA, USA
pxiong@nec-labs.com

Hakan Hacıgümüş
NEC Laboratories America
Cupertino, CA, USA
hakan@nec-labs.com

Jeffrey F. Naughton
University of Wisconsin
Madison, WI, USA
naughton@cs.wisc.edu

ABSTRACT

Nowadays data analytics applications are accessing more and more data from distributed data stores, creating a large amount of data traffic on the network. Therefore, distributed analytic queries are prone to suffer from poor performance when they encounter network contention, which can be quite common in a shared network. Typical distributed query optimizers do not have a way to solve this problem because they treat the network as a black-box: they are unable to monitor it, let alone control it. With the new era of software-defined networking (SDN), we show how SDN can be effectively exploited for performance management for analytical queries in distributed data store environments. More specifically, we present a group of methods to leverage SDN's visibility into and control of the network's state that enable distributed query processors to achieve performance improvements and differentiation for analytical queries. We demonstrate the effectiveness of the methods through detailed experimental studies on a system running on a software-defined network with commercial switches. To the best of our knowledge, this is the first work to analyze and show the opportunities of SDN for distributed query optimization. It is our hope that this will open up a rich area of research and technology development in distributed data intensive computing.

1. INTRODUCTION

To become more efficient, effective, and competitive, enterprises are expecting ever increasing benefits from data analytics. To meet this demand, data analytics platforms are including more data sources, which may be both internally and externally available. These data sources are often stored in distributed data stores. Data analytics applications or data scientists query the data from these distributed stores and merge and join the data to generate coherent analysis reports [14, 17]. With continuously increasing data sizes, querying and joining data from distributed sources can generate a significant amount of data traffic on the network, an issue that is exacerbated if the network is shared with other applications as well. Therefore, optimizing queries that access the distributed data stores, and specifically optimizing their network utilization, is likely to be an important problem to address in order to deliver improved query performance and query service differentiation.

In this context, we focus on the problem of how a distributed query optimizer can exploit the capabilities offered by software-defined networking (SDN) [13, 15] to improve query performance and provide query service differentiation. For concreteness and simplicity of presentation and implementation, we consider an instance of the problem in which all data stores are relational databases. Although there are significant differences, there are some striking similarities between the problems encountered in modern multi-source distributed data analysis and the traditional distributed database query optimization [12]. In addition to CPU and I/O costs, distributed query optimizers also consider the cost of communication over the network when choosing the best query plan [12].

However, traditionally, the interaction between the query optimizer and the network has been limited in that the optimizer has no direct way to (1) inquire about the current status and performance of the network, or (2) control the network with directives, e.g., making bandwidth reservations, which would improve query performance and query service differentiation.

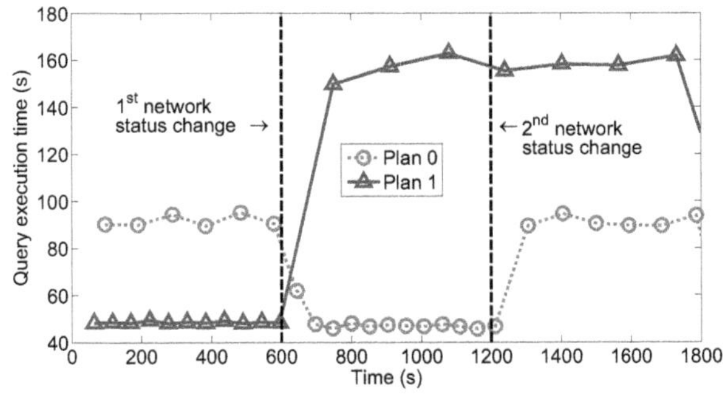

Figure 1: TPC-H Q14 different plans' execution time in a distributed setting

As an illustration, in Figure 1, we show the query execution time (y-axis) of two candidate plans (Plan 0 and 1) for the repeated execution of TPC-H Q14 in a distributed setting, where the join tables are hosted in two separate data store sites. (We will discuss the setup details later in

SIGMOD'14, June 22–27, 2014, Snowbird, UT, USA.

http://dx.doi.org/10.1145/2588555.2593681.

Section 6.) We can see that, as the status of the network between the sites changes (vertical dotted lines) during the experimental period (x-axis), query execution time is significantly affected. If a distributed query optimizer treats the network as a fixed cost, black box resource and sticks to a fixed plan, which is the case for most distributed database query optimizers, it may not be able to choose the plan with the shortest execution time. Although some distributed query optimizers and execution systems try to react in some fashion to unexpected network conditions [3, 19], the decisions they make are either heuristic-driven or potentially inaccurate due to an inability to predict the true costs of remote data access.

It is perhaps reasonable to expect that with greater visibility into the network's state, a distributed query optimizer could make more accurate cost estimates for different query plans and make better informed decisions. Moreover, it is also intuitively clear that if the optimizer could have some control of the network's future state, a distributed query optimizer could request and reserve the network bandwidth for a specific query plan and thereby improve query performance and query service differentiation. The problem is that historically the networks that distributed data management systems rely upon have made both these tasks difficult or impossible.

However, we are currently entering a new era of software-defined networking (SDN) [13, 15]. Networks with SDN enable the distributed query optimizer to achieve such visibility into and control of the network's state. By decoupling the system that makes decisions about where traffic is sent (the control plane) from the underlying systems that forward traffic to the selected destination (the data plane), network services can be managed through an abstraction of lower level functionality. Thus, SDN raises the possibility that it is for the first time feasible and practical for distributed query optimizers to carefully monitor and even control the network. Our goal in this paper is to begin the exploration of this capability, and to try to gain insight into whether it really is a promising new development for distributed query optimization.

Our contributions: In this paper, we give a preliminary answer to the affirmative: SDN can indeed be effectively exploited for the performance management of analytical queries in distributed data store environments. To the best of our knowledge, this is the first work to analyze and show the opportunities SDN provides for distributed query optimization. It is our hope that this will open up a rich area of research and technology development in distributed data intensive computing. Our specific contributions are the following:

(1) We present a method that adaptively selects the optimal query plan based on the information provided by the network before the query execution. This method observes the status of the network and reacts by adapting the query execution plan to one that yields better performance.

(2) We present two methods that allow a distributed query processor to deliver differentiated query service to the users with different priorities. The first method allows for network traffic prioritization and the second method provides the capability of reserving a certain amount of bandwidth for specific queries and making use of that guaranteed bandwidth during query optimization. These methods achieve run-time query service differentiation in shared and highly utilized networks, which was not possible before.

(3) We propose a method to model dynamic communication costs. We integrate the model into a distributed query optimizer along with an existing computational cost model and show its effectiveness.

(4) We report on our implementation of the techniques in a prototype distributed data store environment that is built using multiple instances of open source databases running on a "real" SDN network with commercial OpenFlow enabled switches. Our experimental results confirm our expectations and clearly show the benefits of the SDN technologies.

2. THE SYSTEM

In this section, we describe the system that we have designed and implemented to evaluate the promise of SDN for query optimization and performance differentiation. In this paper, it is not our goal to propose a new system or a complete, general-purpose optimizer. Rather, we capture the essential characteristics of the distributed data store environments we are considering and implement sufficient functionality to allow us to analyze our proposed methods for exploiting SDN in query optimization and evaluation.

2.1 System design considerations

We have the following considerations: (1) Relational and SQL: For concreteness and the simplicity of the presentation, we assume in this paper that the stores are relational databases and that SQL is used to query the databases. (2) Analytical workloads: We consider data intensive analytical workloads as we expect that they are the most likely to benefit from the SDN technologies due to their heavy use of the interconnection network. (Transactional systems are unlikely to consume prolonged, high network bandwidth, as queries are typically very short and involve smaller amounts of data transfer.) Continuing this observation, the queries we consider are mostly read-only, consuming large amounts of network bandwidth. (3) Shared network: We also observe that many data analytics applications run on shared networks along with other applications that use the same network, sometimes competing for the network resources, which is consistent with many real world scenarios [16].

2.2 System architecture

Figure 2 shows the overall system architecture. The evaluation system is mainly composed of a user site, a master site, several data store sites, and an SDN component, which consists of an OpenFlow controller and OpenFlow switches. (The relationship between SDN and OpenFlow will be explained in Section 3.) The unit of distribution in the system is a table and each table is either stored at one data store or can be replicated to more than one data stores. A user or application program submits the query to the master site for compilation. The master site coordinates the optimization of all SQL statements. We assume that only the data store sites store the tables. The master and the data stores run off-the-shelf, modified database servers (PostgreSQL, in our case). A query manager runs on the master site, which consists of a distributed query processor and a network information manager (NIM). The distributed query processor presents an SQL API to users. It also maintains a global view of the meta-data for all the tables in the databases. The query manager communicates with the OpenFlow controller to (1) receive network resource usage information, and update the information in NIM accordingly; and (2) send the control commands to the OpenFlow controller.

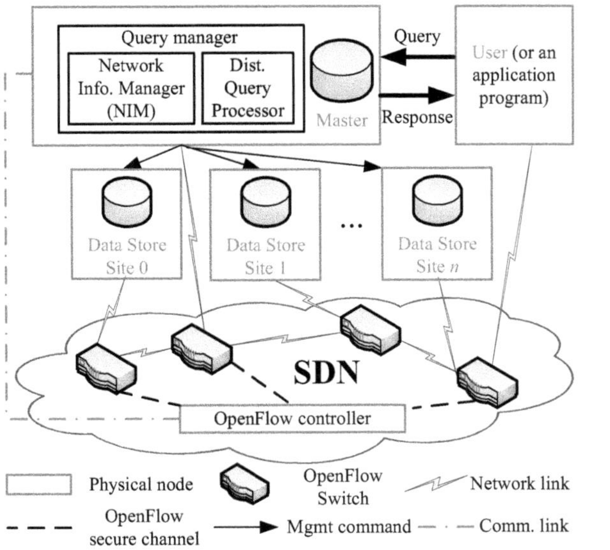

Figure 2: System architecture

The basic operation of the system is as follows: when the query manager receives a query, it parses the query, generates, and optimizes a global query plan. The global query plan is divided into local plans. The local plans are sent to corresponding data store sites for execution via separate threads. The query manager orchestrates the necessary data flows among the data store sites. The query manager also forwards the final results from the master to the user.

Table 1 lists the notations for the rest of the paper.

Table 1: Notations

$T \in \mathcal{T}$	a table
$S \in \mathcal{S}$	a data store site
O_L	a local operator
O_N	a network operator
$P \in \mathcal{P}$	a plan (composed of operators O_L, O_N)
$\mathbb{C}_{O_L,O_N,P}$	cost of O_L, O_N, P, respectively
sc,tc,rc	start_cost, total_cost, run_cost details
U	a user who issues queries
Cap	port capacity (1Gbps in our setting)
D_{O_N}	amount of data transferred by O_N
$\mathbf{A}(U)$	available bandwidth matrix for user U
$C(U)_{O_N}$	real-time bandwidth consumption for O_N
$R(U)_{O_N}$	reserved bandwidth for O_N by user U
UB_{O_N}	upper bound bandwidth consumption for O_N

2.3 Object naming and distributed catalogs

In order to keep the programming simple, how data is stored and accessed via the network should be transparent to users. We map the table names used by the users, which we call the *print names*, to internal System Wide Names, *SWN*. An SWN has the form T^S which denotes that a copy of table T is stored at site S. For convenience, if there is a single copy of table T, we also denote the site that has this copy as S_T. The system uses a distributed catalog. The catalogs at each data store site maintain the information about the tables in the database, including the replicas stored at that site. The catalog at the master site keeps the information indicating where each table is currently stored and this entry is updated if a table is moved.

2.4 Query plans

2.4.1 Name resolution

When an SQL statement is submitted to the system, it is parsed and then undergoes name resolution in which all SQL print names are resolved into SWNs. We take query Q14 from TPC-H benchmark as an example, as shown below. We assume that *lineitem* and *part* tables are located at sites S_l and S_p, respectively. During name resolution, *lineitem* and *part* are resolved to $lineitem^{S_l}$ and $part^{S_p}$, respectively.

```
select
100.00 * sum(case when p_type like 'PROMO%'
then l_extendedprice * (1 -  l_discount)
else 0 end) / sum(l_extendedprice * (1 - l_discount))
as promo_revenue
from lineitem, part
where
   l_partkey = p_partkey and
   l_shipdate >= date '1995-09-01' and
   l_shipdate < date '1995-09-01' + interval '1' month;
```

2.4.2 Plan generation

After name resolution, a set of candidate plans $\mathcal{P}$ are generated. Each plan is a tree such that each node of the tree is a physical operator, such as a sequential scan, sort, or hash join. A physical operator can be either blocking or non-blocking. An operator is blocking if it cannot produce any output tuples without reading all of its input. For instance, the sort operator is a blocking operator.

Three candidate plans, denoted 0, 1, and 2, are generated for Q14 as shown in Figure 3(a). Plan 0 ships the *lineitem* table from S_l to S_p and joins the *part* table at S_p. The aggregation is also done at S_p, and the final result is shipped to the master S_m and displayed there. Figure 3(b) presents the operators in Plan 0. In this plan, scan operators on *lineitem* and *part* take place at site S_l and S_p, respectively. The join and aggregation operators take place at site S_p and *lineitem* and *part* are treated as inner and outer tables of the hash join, respectively.

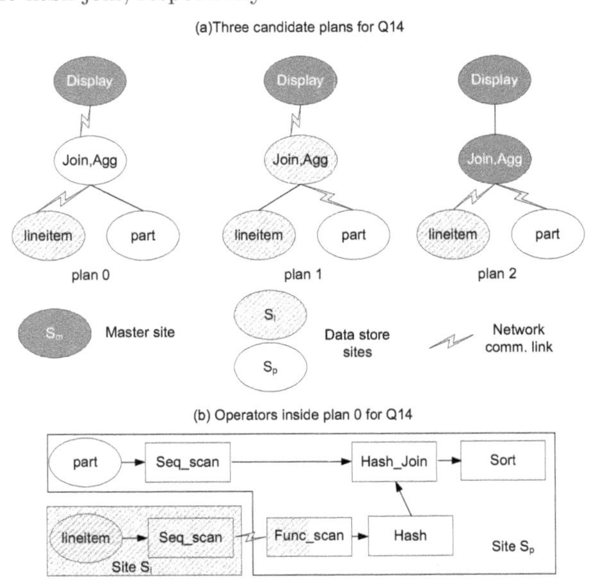

Figure 3: Candidate plans for Q14 and operators inside Plan 0

2.4.3 Cost estimation

There are two cost models that can be used to estimate the cost of a plan [12]. The classic cost model, which estimates the total resource consumption of a query, is useful for maximizing the overall throughput of a system. The response time model, which estimates the total response time of a query, is useful for minimizing query execution time. We use the response time model in this paper.

The optimizer estimates query execution cost by aggregating the cost estimates of the operators in the query plan. To distinguish blocking and non-blocking operators, this cost model considers both the *start_cost* and *total_cost* of each operator: *start_cost* (sc) is the cost before the operator can produce its first output tuple; *total_cost* (tc) is the cost after the operator generates all of its output tuples. Note that the cost of an operator includes the cost of its child operators. The *run_cost* (rc) is defined as $rc = tc - sc$. The total cost of a query plan P, denoted as $\mathbb{C}_P$, is the *total_cost* of the root operator.

There are generally two kinds of operators in a distributed query execution plan, (1) *local operators*, O_L, which do not involve shipping data over the network; and (2) *network operators*, O_N, which do involve data shipping over the network. For example, in Figure 3(b), the scan, hash, and hashjoin operators are local operators, while the function scan (func_scan) operator is a network operator.

Based on the cost models of local and network operators (details are shown in Sections 4 and 5), we summarize how we estimate the cost $\mathbb{C}_P$ for a plan P as follows. Here each brace means a dependency relationship.

$$\mathbb{C}_P \begin{cases} \mathbb{C}_{O_L}(\text{Sec. 5.3}) \\ \mathbb{C}_{O_N} \begin{cases} D_{O_N}(\text{Sec. 5.4.1}) \\ C(U)_{O_N} \begin{cases} UB_{O_N}(\text{Sec. 5.4.2}) \\ A(U)_{O_N} \begin{cases} Flow.rate(\text{Sec. 4.1}) \\ R(U)_{O_N}(\text{Sec. 4.3.2}) \end{cases} \end{cases} \end{cases} \end{cases}$$

The cost $\mathbb{C}_P$ for a plan P depends on the cost of operators O_L and O_N, denoted as $\mathbb{C}_{O_L}$ and $\mathbb{C}_{O_N}$, respectively. $\mathbb{C}_{O_N}$ depends on the amount of data transferred by O_N, denoted as D_{O_N}, and the data transfer rate, i.e., real-time bandwidth consumption for O_N denoted as $C(U)_{O_N}$. $C(U)_{O_N}$ further depends on the upper bound bandwidth consumption for O_N (i.e., UB_{O_N}), the available bandwidth for user U for O_N (i.e., $A(U)_{O_N}$), and the reserved bandwidth for O_N by user U. Generally speaking, we define a network traffic matrix as a $|\mathcal{S}| \times |\mathcal{S}|$ matrix where $|\mathcal{S}|$ is the total number of sites. The rows of the matrix correspond to the source sites while the columns correspond to the destination sites. *Cap* denotes the port capacity, which is a constant 1Gbps in our setting, and all the elements in the matrix should be less than *Cap*. The available bandwidth matrix for user U is a network traffic matrix, denoted as $\mathbf{A}(U)$. If we assume that network operator O_N involves data shipping from S_{src} to S_{dst}, then the available bandwidth for O_N, denoted as $A(U)_{O_N}$ is the value at row S_{src} and column S_{dst} of $\mathbf{A}(U)$.

2.5 Query optimization and execution

Compared with a traditional distributed query optimizer and executor, the query optimizer and executor in our system have the following distinguishing features:

1. A traditional distributed query optimizer generally models the network as a FIFO queue with a constant bandwidth. However, because the total cost $\mathbb{C}_P$ *depends* on $\mathbf{A}(U)$ in our system, our optimizer can adapt to the dynamic network status when choosing the best plan.
2. In traditional distributed query processing, once the best query plan is selected, it will be executed. If many lower priority queries are saturating the network, a traditional distributed query processing can do nothing to expedite an incoming important query. However, our query optimizer can "protect" the important queries by either giving them higher priority to use network bandwidth than the lower priority queries or by reserving and using the reserved network bandwidth.

3. SOFTWARE-DEFINED NETWORKING AND OPENFLOW

In this section we give a brief overview of Software-Defined Networking (SDN) and OpenFlow. In the next section we discuss how we utilize the OpenFlow APIs in our system implementation.

SDN is an approach to networking that decouples the control plane from the data plane. The control plane is responsible for making decisions about where traffic is sent, while the data plane forwards traffic to the selected destination. This separation allows network administrators and application programs to manage network services through abstraction of lower level functionality by using software APIs [15]. From a DBMS point of view, the abstraction and the control APIs allow the DBMS to (1) inquire about the current status and performance of the network, and (2) control the network with directives, for example, with bandwidth reservations.

OpenFlow is a standard communication interface among the layers of an SDN architecture, which can be thought of as an enabler for SDN [13]. An OpenFlow controller communicates with an OpenFlow switch. An OpenFlow switch maintains a flow table, with each entry defining a flow as a certain set of packets by matching on 10 tuple packet information. When a new flow arrives, according to the OpenFlow protocol, a "PacketIn" message is sent from the switch to the controller. The first packet of the flow is delivered to the controller. The controller looks into the 10 tuple packet information, determines the egress (exiting) port and sends a "FlowMod" message to the switch to modify a switch flow table. More specifically, APIs in the OpenFlow switch enable us to attach the new flow to one of the physical transmitter queues behind each port of the switch. When an existing flow times out, according to OpenFlow protocol, a "FlowRemoved" message is delivered from the switch to the controller to indicate that a flow has been removed. There are already OpenFlow controllers and switches that implement the OpenFlow standard from the major vendors in the industry. In our studies we also use actual commercial products from one of those vendors, NEC.

For example, we show a commercial OpenFlow switch NEC PFS5240 and three data store sites $S_{0,1,2}$ connected to the switch at port 0,1,2 in Figure 4. There is a receiver and a transmitter behind each port of the switch and there are 8 transmission queues `q8` to `q1` inside a transmitter. When a new flow $Flow_0$(from S_0 to S_2) under user U's name arrives, a "PacketIn" message is sent from the switch to the controller. The controller looks into the 10 tuple packet information, determines the egress ports (i.e., 2) and one of the transmission queues (e.g., q8) according to the user's priority U_{pri} and sends a "FlowMod" message to the switch to modify a switch flow table. The following packets in the same flow will be sent through the same transmission queue q8 of the egress ports (i.e., 2) to site S_2. If no user information is specified, a default queue (q4) will be used.

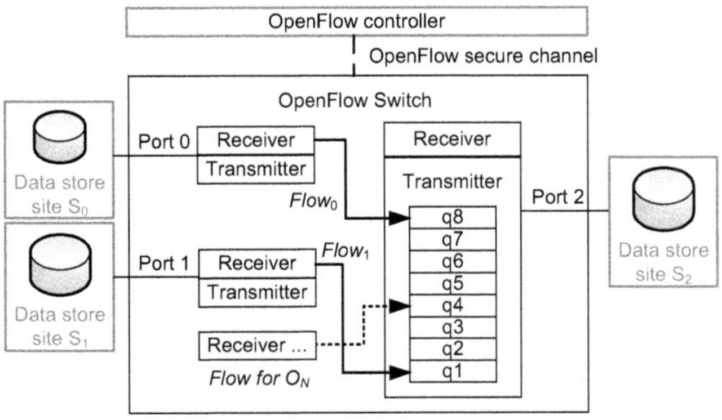

Figure 4: Inside an OpenFlow switch

4. PERFORMANCE MANAGEMENT WITH OPENFLOW APIS

In this section we describe how we utilize the OpenFlow API to implement our performance management methods. Recall that our first contribution in the introduction proposes a method that adaptively selects the optimal query execution plan based on the information provided by the network during query execution. We discuss how we get this information in Section 4.2. For the second contribution, we discuss how to achieve network traffic prioritization and how to reserve network bandwidth in Section 4.3.1 and 4.3.2, respectively.

4.1 Network information manager

The network information manager (NIM) updates and inquires information about the current network state by communicating with the OpenFlow controller. The network information includes the network topology (hosts, switches, ports), queues, and links, and their capabilities. The runtime uses the information to translate the logical actions to a physical configuration, and to host the switch information such as its ports' speeds, configurations, and statistics. It is important to keep this information up-to-date with the current state of the network as an inconsistency could lead to under-utilization of network resources as well as bad query performance. In the NIM, we define a *Flow* as a four tuple:

$$Flow ::= [src, dst, queue, rate]$$

Here *src* and *dst* mean the ingress and egress ports of the switch for the flow, respectively. *queue* means the egress queue of the flow, and *rate* means the traffic rate. For example, we can have two flows, $Flow_0$ = [0, 2, q8, 200Mbps] and $Flow_1$ = [1, 2, q1, 200Mbps] as shown in Figure 4. $Flow_0$ means that the flow is from port 0 (S_0) to q8 of port 2 (S_2) and the rate is 200Mbps.

4.2 Get available network bandwidth

The distributed query processor sends an inquiry to the network information manager to inquire $A(U)_{O_N}$, i.e., the available bandwidth for network operator O_N for user U. More specifically, it is calculated as

$$A(U)_{O_N} = Cap - \sum_{Flow.dst=O_N.dst} Flow.rate \qquad (1)$$

Generally, we are interested in the flows that could compete with O_N at the transmitter. These flows should share the same destination port with O_N, i.e., $Flow.dst = O_N.dst$. We sum up all these flows and the remaining bandwidth is assumed to be the available bandwidth for O_N. Note that $A(U)_{O_N}$ as calculated by the above formula is a very rough estimation of the available bandwidth for O_N as there are various factors that we do not take into consideration, e.g., interaction between different flows with different internet protocols UDP and TCP.

For example, assume that we have two flows, $Flow_0$ and $Flow_1$, and a network operator O_N. O_N's destination port is also port 2 and O_N uses the default queue q4 as shown in Figure 4. Because there is no defined network traffic differentiation at this moment, all the queues q8, q4, q1 have the same priority. Then $A(U)_{O_N}$=1G-(200M+200M)=624Mbps.

4.3 Set network traffic differentiation

Our distributed query processor can communicate with the OpenFlow controller to leverage the OpenFlow APIs to pro-actively notify the switch to give certain priority to or make a reservation for specific flows. The main mechanism in the OpenFlow switch to implement these methods is the transmission queues. We show two examples using a priority queue (PQ) and a weighted fair queue (WFQ) in our system while the other options could also be possible. For example, combining PQ and WFQ could be considered to resolve more difficult network resource contention situations, which could be a future work.

4.3.1 Priority queue (PQ)

In this case, we set the queues within the switch as priority queues (PQ). If more than one queue has queued frames, PQ sends frames in the order of queue priority. During the transmission, this configuration gives higher-priority queues absolute preferential treatment over lower-priority queues. If any port is set as PQ, then the queues from the highest priority to the lowest priority are q8,q7,...,q1. Under this setting, the calculation of the available bandwidth for O_N should be changed accordingly:

$$A(U)_{O_N} = Cap - \sum_{Flow.dst=O_N.dst \wedge Flow.queue.pri \geq U.pri} Flow.rate \qquad (2)$$

Here *Flow.queue.pri* means the priority of *queue* and *U.pri* means the priority of user U (O_N's priority is the same as the user's priority who submits the query). Compared with (1), besides sharing the same destination port with O_N, the competing flows should have equal or higher priority than O_N, i.e., $Flow.queue.pri \geq U.pri$.

For example, assume that we have two flows, $Flow_0$ and $Flow_1$, and a network operator O_N as shown in Figure 4. O_N's destination port is also port 2 and O_N is assigned by OpenFlow controller to use queue q4 according to the user U's priority. Because q4 has higher priority than q1 and lower priority than q8, only $Flow_0$ will compete with O_N. Thus, $A(U)_{O_N}$=1G-200M=824Mbps. We can see that the available bandwidth for O_N is 200Mbps more than the case when no network traffic differentiation is applied (624Mbps). Because the cost of O_N depends on $A(U)_{O_N}$, the distributed query optimizer selects the query plan accordingly.

4.3.2 Weighted fair queue (WFQ)

In this case, we set the port within the switch as weighted fair queues. After setting the weight (minimum guaranteed bandwidth) on every queue, the switch sends the amount of frames equivalent to the minimum guaranteed bandwidth from each queue to begin with. Under this setting, the calculation of the available bandwidth for O_N should be changed accordingly:

$$A(U)_{O_N} = Max(Cap - \sum_{Flow.dst=O_N.dst} Flow.rate, R(U)_{O_N})$$

Here $R(U)_{O_N}$ is the bandwidth reservation for O_N by user U. For example, assume that we have two flows, $Flow_0$ and $Flow_1$, and a network operator O_N as shown in Figure 4. We assume that the user makes an 800Mbps bandwidth reservation for O_N and the other users do not make any bandwidth reservations. By calculation, $A(U)_{O_N}$ is equal to the bandwidth reservation (i.e., 800Mbps). We can see that the available bandwidth for O_N is more than the case when no network traffic differentiation is applied (624Mbps). Similar to the previous cases, this method computes $A(U)_{O_N}$ value, which affects the cost of O_N, and in turn, the plan selection of the distributed query optimizer. Note that WFQ works in a work conserving mode in this switch. That is, although O_N is guaranteed 800Mbps, if O_N does not use 800Mbps, the other flow can use the remaining bandwidth. If O_N indeed uses the capacity and also the other flows also use up the maximum capacity, the system guarantees the reserved capacity for O_N and serves the other flows with the remaining capacity by throttling them as necessary.

5. EXPERIMENTAL SETTINGS AND SYSTEM IMPLEMENTATION

In this section, we describe our experimental settings and system implementation details.

5.1 Experimental settings

Our test bed consists of 10 physical machines. Each of the machines has an Intel Xeon E5-2440 2.4GHz Hexa-Core CPU, 32GB of RAM, 1TB 7200rpm disk running Linux with kernel 2.6.32. Hyper-threading is turned on. Each of the machines has two Gigabit ethernet NICs. There are two networks in our test bed, a management network and an OpenFlow network. The first NIC of each machine is connected by a Gigabit Cisco switch, which forms the management network. The second NIC of each machine is connected by a Gigabit NEC OpenFlow switch (PFS5240), which forms the OpenFlow network. All the traffic related to databases goes through the OpenFlow network. We use an open source OpenFlow controller Beacon [1] as the OpenFlow controller.

There is a single PostgreSQL server running in each physical machine. We modified the source code of PostgreSQL so that a receiver PostgreSQL server can communicate with a remote sender PostgreSQL server to obtain the cardinality of the table being transferred. The buffer pool size is set at 28GB. We use `dblink` [2] for PostgreSQL to implement data shipping, which is a popular choice in the PostgreSQL community. Similar tools exist for other database products.

We test our methods on the TPC-H benchmark database and queries with scaling factors of 5, 10, 20, 50, 100 and 200. We create the workload with 8 TPC-H query templates out of the 22 templates in TPC-H. More specifically, we use the original Q3, Q12, Q14, Q16 templates and we use slightly modified Q4, Q5, Q10, Q19 templates. These templates are chosen because they are fairly complex (involving at least 2 tables and at least one join operation) so they provide significant opportunities for leveraging the OpenFlow-based techniques. We do not include the other 14 templates mainly because they are either too simple (involve only one table) or contain sub-queries, which current version of our system cannot handle. It should be noted that our goal in using TPC-H queries as a starting point is to allow us to examine the approaches using OpenFlow techniques; we do not claim to draw any conclusions about performance on an actual TPC-H benchmark.

There are 8 separate and individual tables in the TPC-H benchmark, i.e., **`customer, orders, lineitem, part, partsupp, supplier, nation, region`**. Three of the tables (**`supplier, nation, region`**) are very small tables so copies of these are replicated to all data store sites. The remaining base tables (**`customer, orders, lineitem, part, partsupp`**) are each placed at a data store site denoted as (S_c,S_o,S_l,S_p,S_s).

5.2 Plan generation and execution

We focus on the implementation of query plan generation and execution in this section.

The query manager's optimizer (at the master site) makes all the inter-site decisions: (1) the order in which tables must be joined; (2) the join site; and (3) if the inner table or the outer table is not stored at the join site chosen, the method for transferring a copy of the table to the join site: (3.a) ship whole: ship a copy of the entire table once to the join site, and store it there as a temporary table; or (3.b) semi-join. A data store's optimizer makes all the intra-site decisions: (4) the local join method; (5) the inner and the outer join table sequence; (6) the access path for each table (e.g., whether to use an index or not).

We apply the following heuristic rules when we enumerate query plans. We use dynamic programming and a query plan is built in a bottom-up way. For the inter-site decisions: (1) We decompose an n-way join as a sequence of $n-1$ two-way joins. (2) We assign the possible join sites for each two-way join. For simplicity, the candidate join sites are limited to S_{master}, S_{outer_table} or S_{inner_table}. (3) We use ship whole for most of the experiments and use semi-join only for comparison purposes in Section 6.3. For the intra-site decisions: (4) We only consider hybrid hash joins. (5) The inner and the outer join table sequence is determined by the PostgreSQL's optimizer at the join site. (6) We ensure that only the columns that are needed in the query processing are actually projected and the predicates are pushed down to the table scan if possible so that the rows can be filtered early in the processing. More specifically, we build a materialized view for each table after the column pruning and the pred-

[1] https://openflow.stanford.edu/display/Beacon/Home

[2] http://www.postgresql.org/docs/9.1/static/dblink.html

icate pushdown. In large scale, distributed analytics report generation settings, it is a common practice in the industry to pre-materialize sub-query results in individual data stores to improve the query execution time [7]. We also follow the same practice by pre-populating the necessary views.

There is a code generation step for each plan. The code is generated at the master site for each data store site involved in the query; each piece is called a subsection. Each subsection contains the code both for calling the local PostgreSQL server, which performs the local data management, and for passing the data and the control to other sites according to the overall plan. A concrete example for Q14 is shown in the Appendix.

5.3 Local operator cost model

We leverage PostgreSQL's optimizer to estimate the execution time of *local* operators. PostgreSQL's optimizer uses a vector of five parameters (referred to as *cost units*) in its cost model: $\mathbf{c} = (c_s, c_r, c_t, c_i, c_o)^\intercal$, defined as follows: (1) c_s: *seq_page_cost*, the I/O cost to sequentially access a page; (2) c_r: *random_page_cost*, the I/O cost to randomly access a page; (3) c_t: *cpu_tuple_cost*, the CPU cost to process a tuple; (4) c_i: *cpu_index_tuple_cost*, the CPU cost to process a tuple via index access; (5) c_o: *cpu_operator_cost*, the CPU cost to perform an operation such as hash or aggregation.

The *run_cost* of an operator O_L in a query plan, denoted as $\mathbb{C}_{O_L}$ is then computed by a linear combination of c_s, c_r, c_t, c_i, and c_o:

$$\mathbb{C}_{O_L} = \mathbf{n}^\intercal \mathbf{c} = n_s \cdot c_s + n_r \cdot c_r + n_t \cdot c_t + n_i \cdot c_i + n_o \cdot c_o.$$

The values $\mathbf{n} = (n_s, n_r, n_t, n_i, n_o)^\intercal$ here represent *the number of pages sequentially scanned, the number of pages randomly accessed*, and so forth, for the execution of an O_L.

Our local operator model needs the $\mathbf{c}$'s and $\mathbf{n}$'s from the query plan as input. Specifying the cost values, $\mathbf{c}$'s, is a difficult, well-known problem in the DBMS community. Meanwhile, the $\mathbf{n}$'s are closely related to cardinality estimation, which is also prone to errors and is another well-known problem in databases. We use the framework proposed in [21] to calibrate the $\mathbf{c}$'s and $\mathbf{n}$'s. We choose this method mainly because (1) it directly works with and leverages the PostgreSQL query optimizer, and (2) it delivers more robust results without requiring expensive training. By following the framework: we use offline profiling to calibrate $\mathbf{c}$ and online sampling to refine $\mathbf{n}$. For the $\mathbf{c}$'s, a set of calibration queries are used to profile the underlying database system. Table 2 presents the calibrated values for the 5 cost units on the machines used in our experiments. For the $\mathbf{n}$'s, a sampling-based approach is used to refine the cardinality estimates.

Table 2: Actual values of PostgreSQL optimizer parameters on data store sites

Optimizer Parameter	Calibrated $\mu \pm \sigma$ (ms)	Default
seq_page_cost	5.03e-2 ± 3.82e-3	1.0
rand_page_cost	4.89e-1 ± 7.44e-2	4.0
cpu_tuple_cost	1.41e-4 ± 1.35e-5	0.01
cpu_index_tuple_cost	3.34e-5 ± 3.85e-5	0.005
cpu_operator_cost	7.10e-5 ± 1.52e-5	0.0025

5.4 Network operator cost model

It is crucial for us to model the cost of the network operators, O_N in a plan P, which is a transfer of a table (possibly a composite table of the result of a join) with size D_{O_N} from site S_{src} to site S_{dst}. If the real-time bandwidth consumption for O_N is $C(U)_{O_N}$, then the *run_cost* of O_N are estimated as follows [3]: $\mathbb{C}_{O_N} = D_{O_N}/C(U)_{O_N}$.

5.4.1 *Estimating* D_{O_N}

The transferred table size, D_{O_N}, can be estimated as the multiplication of the tuple length and the cardinality of the table. We use the similar method in [21] for building the cost model of local operators to obtain the information of the tuple length and the cardinality of the transferred table.

5.4.2 *Estimating* $C(U)_{O_N}$

It is not trivial to estimate $C(U)_{O_N}$ without actually executing the plan. We need to consider two cases when the data transfer happens. (1) Network is saturated. The consumed network bandwidth $C(U)_{O_N}$ is equal to the available network bandwidth $A(U)_{O_N}$. (2) Network is not saturated. This case may happen if the available network bandwidth $A(U)_{O_N}$ is large enough. However, even there is enough available network bandwidth (e.g., in a dedicated network), the real-time bandwidth consumption $C(U)_{O_N}$ may not reach the maximum capacity (e.g., 1Gbps) because other resources, such as CPU, may become saturated at certain point. We define this upper bound consumption of network bandwidth as UB_{O_N} and $C(U)_{O_N}$ is equal to UB_{O_N}. Thus, after considering both cases, we have

$$C(U)_{O_N} = Min(UB_{O_N}, A(U)_{O_N})$$

We observe that UB_{O_N} depends on many factors, e.g., the number of tuples, the length of the tuples, and the schema of the transferred table (or the result of a join). We take all these factors as features and use a machine learning technique (namely Additive Regression) to build a model for UB_{O_N}. For training, we collected 600 samples. We populate TPC-H base tables with a scaling factor 200. For each sample, we create a test table by randomly selecting a table from the base tables with a random number of rows and fields. We then ship the test table from one server to another and measure the upper bound consumption of network bandwidth by using `tcpdump`. For testing, we adopt 10-fold cross validation. The relative absolute error is 20.71% and the root relative squared error is 21.74%. The training process takes 1.8 seconds which can be done off-line. The testing process takes less than 1ms.

Based on the cost models, we summarize the methods used to compute the plan cost as shown in Figure 5.

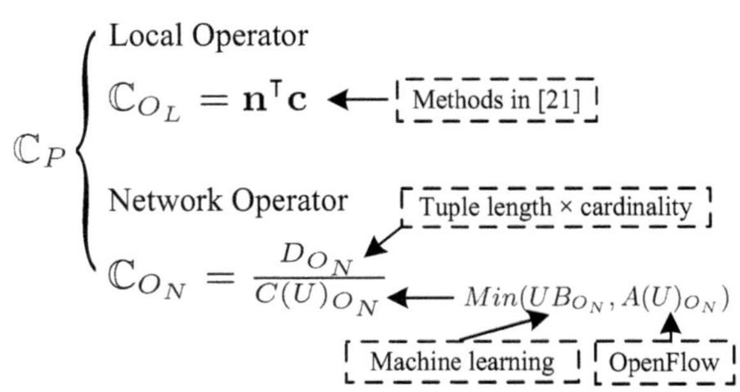

Figure 5: Summary of methods used to compute the plan cost

[3]The *run_cost* should also include the cost of a local scan operator at the destination site. Please see the example in Figure 6 for more details.

6. EVALUATION

In this section, we report our experimental results. Each experiment is run five times and the average (with the standard deviation if applicable) is reported. Due to space limitations, we only report the experimental results for Q14 in TPC-H benchmark with a scaling factor of 100 (except for the plan cost estimation results in Section 6.4). The experimental results of the other queries and the other scaling factors are similar and omitted here. We assume that the materialized views *lineitem_Q*14 and *part_Q*14 for *lineitem* and *part* tables are already created and cached in memory.

6.1 Q14 in TPC-H benchmark

To give more detailed look into the actual execution of a query plan, we report the breakdown of the execution time of individual operators for Q14 Plan 0 in Figure 6 which corresponds to Figure 3(b). Note that the function scan on *dblink* in Figure 6 is comprised of two parts, the data shipping part and the scan part. The data shipping part requires network bandwidth. Only after the data shipping part finishes, i.e., all the data (*lineitem_Q*14) is shipped from S_l to S_p, does the scan part begin. The scan part of the function scan operation overlaps with the hash operation which denotes that they are pipelined. From Figure 6, we also have the following observations. (1) The scanning time of *lineitem_Q*14 and *part_Q*14 is short. This is due to our assumption that *lineitem_Q*14 and *part_Q*14 are materialized and cached in memory. (2) The time spent on data shipping of *lineitem_Q*14 is around 15 seconds, which occupies almost one third of the total query execution time. This indicates that the query execution time would be quite long when network is congested, which is common in a shared network scenario. The time spent on data shipping of the final result is quite short and is negligible.

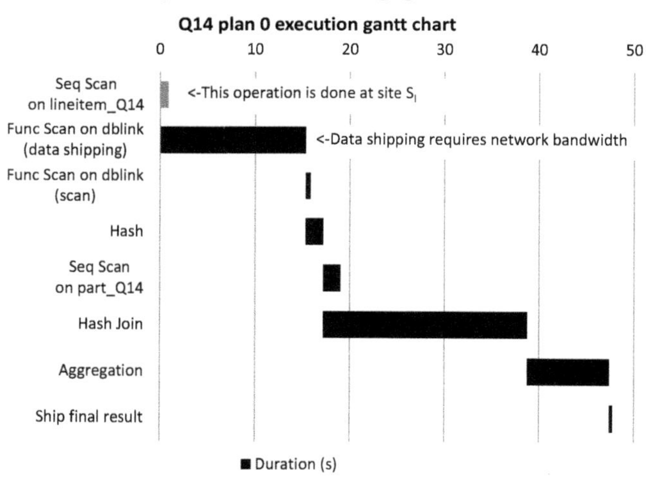

Figure 6: Q14 Plan 0 execution time breakdown

Moreover, we summarize the major data shipping details (omitting the data shipping of final result) and the total execution time for each plan in a dedicated network in Table 3. We can see that Plan 0 is slightly better than Plan 1 while both of them are much better than Plan 2, which is consistent with the results that are predicted by our cost estimator. However, as we will report, when the network is shared, the query execution time for each plan changes dramatically.

Table 3: Alternative query plans for Q14

Plan #	Major Shipping Details	Size (D_{O_N}) (MB)	Speed (UB_{O_N}) (Mbps)	Total time (s)
0	*lineitem_Q*14, $S_l \Rightarrow S_p$	390	206	46
1	*part_Q*14, $S_p \Rightarrow S_l$	1188	486	50
2	*lineitem_Q*14, $S_l \Rightarrow S_p$	390	206	71
	*part_Q*14, $S_p \Rightarrow S_l$	1188	486	

6.2 Case studies

In this section we present the experimental results for a set of situations commonly observed in distributed data stores [16, 6]. More specifically, we consider the following parameters and options as shown in Table 4: **(1) The number of users:** single user versus two users: the premium one (higher priority) and the regular one (lower priority) [6]. **(2) The number of threads:** single thread vs. multiple threads. Each thread will do the following actions in a closed-loop: think for a period of time, issue Q14, obtain the query result. The thinking time follows an exponential distribution with an average of 5 seconds. **(3) The contention network traffic:** no contention traffic (dedicated network) vs. contention traffic emulated by `iperf` [4] (shared network). The objective of each case study is to compare the average query execution time to show the benefits when the SDN is leveraged.

Table 4: Summary of case studies with SDN

Case #	# of Users	# of Threads	Contention traffic	Comparison
1	single	single	iperf	adaptive vs. fix
2	single	multiple	N/A	adaptive vs. fix
3	multiple	multiple	N/A	diff. on vs. off
4	multiple	multiple	iperf	diff. on vs. off
5	single	multiple	iperf	resv. on vs. off

6.2.1 *Case study 1: single user, single-thread, iperf*

In this case we compare the query execution time when the system repeatedly executes a fixed plan (Plan 0 or Plan 1 or Plan 2) with adaptive plan selection method, where the system adaptively selects plans based on the dynamic network status. The network is shared with other applications, which are emulated by iperf as shown in Figure 7. The first two sub-figures show the network traffic contention emulated by iperf to site S_p and S_l while the last sub-figure show the query execution time for fixed plan and adaptive plan. The evaluation lasts for 30 minutes (1800 seconds) for each plan and the figures are aligned along the time line. During this period, a single user uses a single thread to submit Q14 queries.

We divide the whole period into 3 parts (10 minutes each) and analyze them in more detail below. During the first 10 minutes, the inbound traffic to server S_p is high while the inbound traffic to server S_l is low. Due to the high inbound traffic to server S_p, Plan 0 has a longer execution time because the data transfer for *lineitem_Q*14 from S_l to S_p conflicts with the inbound traffic. The other plans, i.e., Plan 1 and 2, are less affected and the best plan should be Plan 1. During the second 10 minutes, the situation changes and the inbound traffic to server S_l is high while the inbound

[4]http://iperf.sourceforge.net/

traffic to server S_p is low. Due to the high inbound traffic to server S_l, Plan 1 has a longer execution time because the data transferring of *part_Q*14 from S_p to S_l conflicts with the inbound traffic. The other plans, i.e., Plans 0 and 2, do not have such a problem and the best plan should be Plan 0. During the third 10 minutes, the inbound traffic to server S_l and the inbound traffic to server S_p are both high. Due to the high inbound traffic, both Plan 0 and 1 have long execution times. For this period, Plan 2 shows the best execution time. In all time intervals, our *adaptive plan selection* method selects the best plan, delivering the best performance. The running overhead for the adaptive algorithm is 8.7ms with a standard deviation of 7.1ms, which is negligible compared with query execution time.

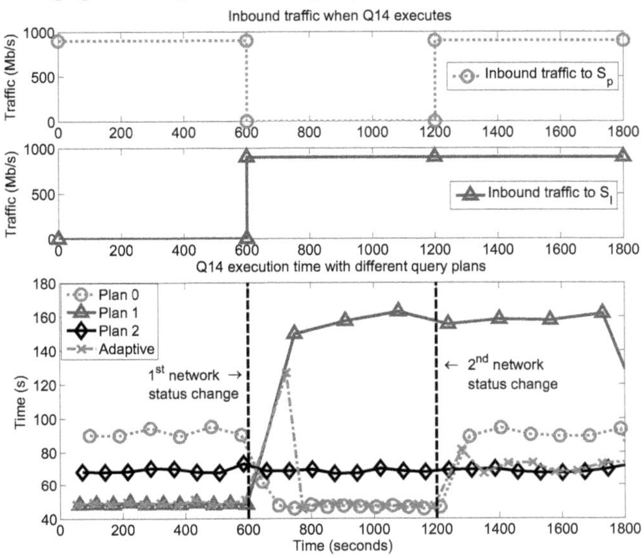

Figure 7: Adaptive plan selection with sharing network traffic

6.2.2 *Case study 2: single user, multiple-thread, no contention traffic*

We evaluate adaptive plan selection when distributed data stores are not sharing the network with others in Figure 8. In this experiment, we have a single user but we increase the number of concurrent threads from 4 to 20. For each number of concurrent threads, the experiment runs for 1800 seconds. The total evaluation time is 9000 seconds. We compare the average query execution time when we fix Plan 0 or Plan 1 with adaptive plan in Figure 8(a) and we compare the throughput in Figure 8(b). We can see that the average query execution time is shorter and throughput is higher when we adaptively select the plan.

More specifically, when the number of concurrent threads is 20, the average query execution time is 20% shorter under adaptive plan than the case when we fix Plan 0. Figure 8(c) shows percentage of the optimizer's selections, which are made dynamically based on the network status, for Plan 0 vs. Plan 1. We can see that, adaptive query optimizer always selects Plan 0 when there are 4 threads. The percentage of Plan 0 decreases as the number of threads increases (all the other plans are Plan 1 and there is no Plan 2). the figure shows that when there is network contention, our system reactively avoids the network traffic by choosing other plans. We have also recorded the CPU and the network utilization during the whole experiment. We find that, besides high inbound network bandwidth utilization of S_p, the CPU utilization of S_p is also high when there are more than 12 concurrent threads with fixed Plan 0. The adaptive action not only avoids the network traffic contention but also shifts the joins, which require CPU cycles from S_p to S_l, further reducing the load on S_p.

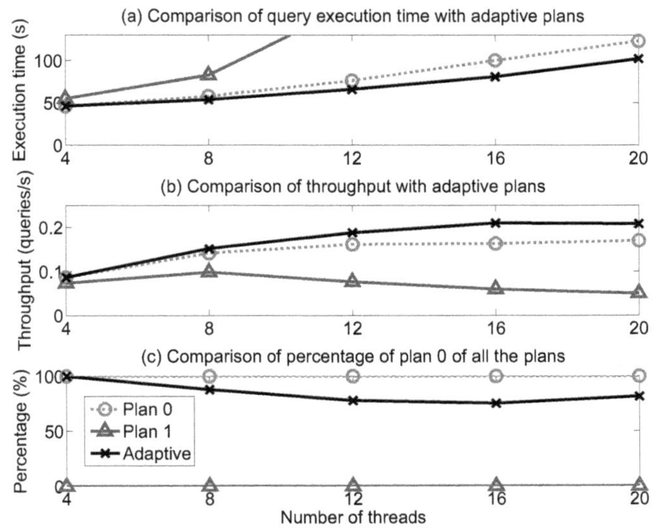

Figure 8: Comparison of query execution time in a dedicated network with a single user

6.2.3 *Case study 3: multiple users, multiple-thread, no contention traffic, priority queue*

This case analyzes the service differentiation method described in Section 4.3.1 when there are multiple users in the system. More specifically, there are two users, a premium user (higher priority) and a regular user (lower priority). This is common in many real life cases [6]. The network traffic issued by the premium user runs on `q8` transmitter while the traffic for the regular user runs on `q1` transmitter in the OpenFlow switch.

In this experiment, we set the OpenFlow switch in priority queue mode. The number of concurrent threads of premium user is fixed at 2 while we increase the number of concurrent threads of regular user from 2 to 18 (x-axis in the figures). We compare the query execution time for both users (premium and regular) when the query service differentiation is turned on and off (no-diff) as shown in Figure 9.

We can see from Figure 9(a) that there is not too much difference in query execution time between premium and regular queries when we fix plan choice as Plan 0. However, the premium queries will have shorter query execution time than the regular ones when we choose Plan 1 (Figure 9(b)). (Note that the y-axis scales are different.) The main reason is that Plan 0 requires much less bandwidth (208Mbps) than Plan 1 (480Mbps). As a result, query service differentiation when we fix Plan 0 is not as obvious as when we fix Plan 1. When adaptive query optimization is used (Figure 9(c)), the premium queries will always choose Plan 0 while the regular queries can choose adaptive plans (Plan 0 or Plan 1) to avoid network contention with premium ones. As a result, the performance of premium and regular queries are close to each other as both of the users are served well.

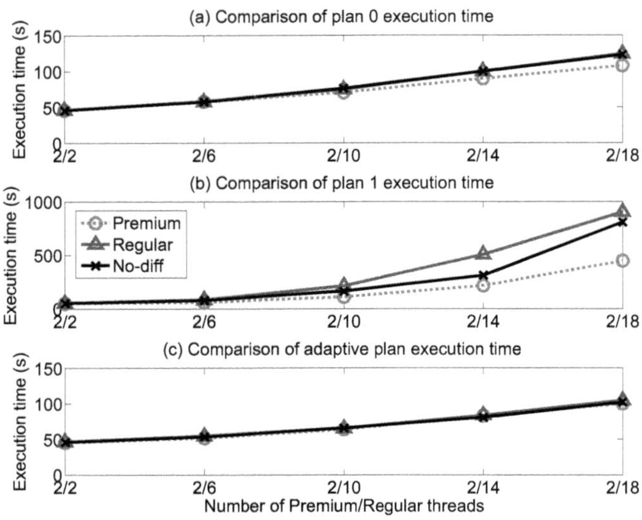

Figure 9: Comparison of query execution time in a dedicated network with multiple users

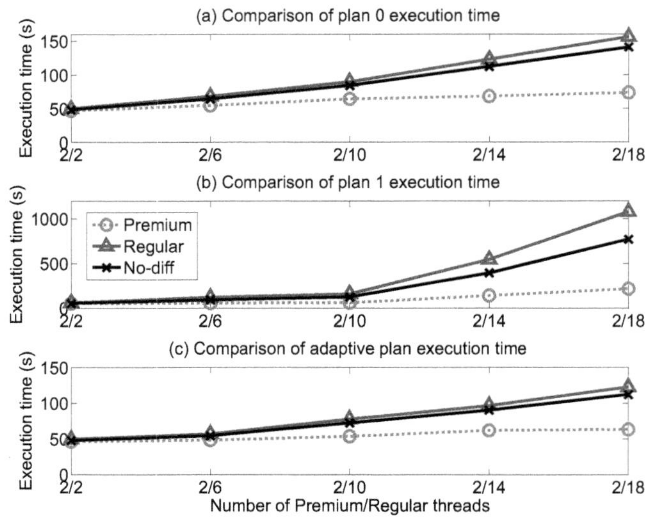

Figure 10: Comparison of query execution time in a shared network with network traffic prioritization

6.2.4 *Case study 4: multiple users, multiple-thread, iperf, priority queue*

Compared with the experimental setting in the previous Section 6.2.3, we use iperf to generate 300Mbps network traffic to S_l, S_p and S_m on q4 transmitter. We compare the query execution time for both users (premium and regular) when the query service differentiation is turned on and off (no-diff) as shown in Figure 10.

We can see that the premium queries have shorter query execution times than the regular ones in all cases when we fix the plan choice as Plan 0, Plan 1 or use adaptive plans. When network is shared with other applications such as iperf, the performance of premium queries is not affected by the network bandwidth shortage because (1) the distributed query optimizer will always choose Plan 0 for the premium queries because of their higher priority and (2) they are actually running on the transmission queues with the highest priority. Another important observation is that, although the system gives higher priority to the premium queries, the adaptive aspect of the method also helps the regular queries by delivering better query execution times for them as well (compare the regular query execution times in Figure 10(a)(b) with (c)).

6.2.5 *Case study 5: single user, multiple-thread, iperf, weighted-fair queue*

This case analyzes the bandwidth reservation method described in Section 4.3.2. We set the OpenFlow switch in weighted-fair queue mode. We use iperf to generate 600Mbps network traffic to S_l, S_p and S_m on q4 transmitter. The user makes the bandwidth reservations. We compare the query execution times in four cases as shown in Figure 11: *(1) Resv off:* The reservation is off, i.e., iperf traffic will compete with non-protected distributed data store traffic. *(2) Resv 500Mbps:* The user makes 500Mbps reservation. *(3) Resv 900Mbps:* The user makes 900Mbps reservation. *(4) Traffic off:* (i.e., "Resv 1Gbps"). There is no iperf traffic.

Based on the results shown in Figure 11(a) and (b), we have the following observations: (1) The query execution time, ranked from the longest to the shortest are *Resv off, Resv 500Mbps, Resv 900Mbps*, and *Traffic off* when we fix Plan 0 or Plan 1, or use adaptive plan. This shows that making bandwidth reservation helps to reduce query execution time no matter what plan is chosen. (2) Even when we use adaptive plan, as shown in Figure 11(c), query execution time is still quite long without any reservation. This shows that the adaptivity is not panacea when network is heavily loaded. (3) When we fix Plan 1, the network bandwidth requirement is high and the reservation can help but not much as shown in Figure 11(b). This shows that it is easy to use up network bandwidth reservation if a plan which requires too much bandwidth is chosen. (4) When we make a large enough reservation, e.g., *Resv 900Mbps*, query execution time is very close to *Traffic off*, i.e., no network sharing.

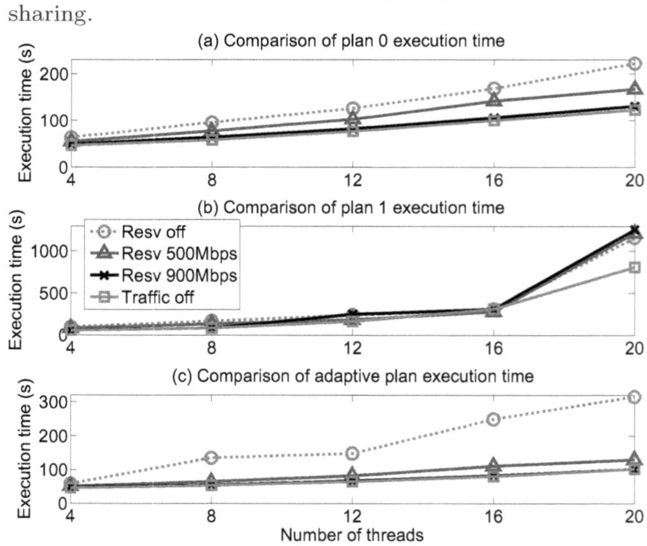

Figure 11: Comparison of query execution time in a shared network with bandwidth reservations

6.3 Semi-join

We have used "ship whole" as the join shipping method in all experiments so far. Semi-join is a known method to improve the performance of distributed joins [5]. A semi-join between two tables returns the rows from the first table where one or more matches are found in the second table. The difference between a semi-join and a join is that the rows in the first table will be returned at most once, even the second table contains more matches for a row in the first table. We compare different query plan execution times with "ship whole" and "semi-join" for Q14 in Figure 12 and Table 5 [5].

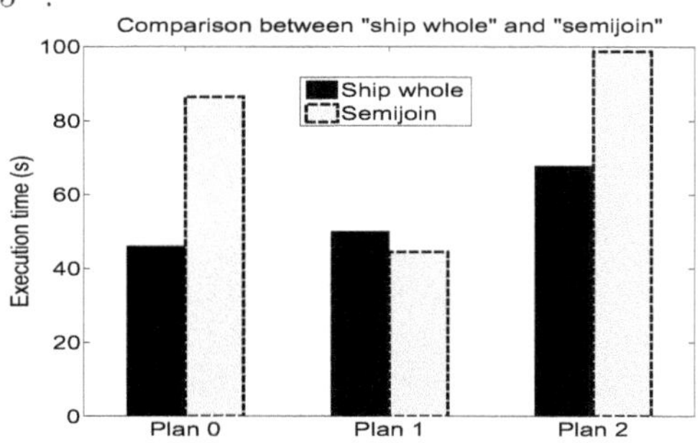

Figure 12: Comparison of query execution time with "ship whole" and "semi-join"

The query execution time when "ship whole" is used is shorter than that when "semi-join" is used for Plan 0 and 2, but it is longer for Plan 1. We decompose the query execution time of plan 0 and 1 into details in Table 5. We can see that, we first ship distinct *p_partkey* from S_p to S_l and then hash semi-join with *lineitem_Q*14 when we apply semi-join for Plan 0. The main motivation is to reduce the shipping size of *lineitem_Q*14. However, the shipping size of *lineitem_Q*14 remains the same because the semi-join selectivity for *lineitem_Q*14 is 1. Thus, applying semi-join for Plan 0 does not have any advantage and delays the query execution by adding an overhead. The situation is different when we apply semi-join for Plan 1. The shipping size of *part_Q*14 is reduced from 1188MB to 268MB (the shipping speed is reduced to 121Mbps as well). Moreover, applying semi-join for Plan 1 not only reduces the shipping size but also reduces the computation time when *part_Q*14 is joined with *lineitem_Q*14.

By decomposing query execution times, we can see that query performance improvement and service differentiation can also be achieved when semi-join is adopted as the distributed join method with SDN.

Table 5: Decomposed query execution time(s) for Q14 when "Ship whole" and "Semi-join" are used

Plan 0				
Methods	Ship *p_partkey* $S_p \Rightarrow S_l$	Ship *lineitem_Q*14 $S_l \Rightarrow S_p$	Other	Total
Ship whole	N/A	15.180	29.847	46.057
Semi-join	15.633	18.538	51.030	86.484
Plan 1				
Methods	Ship *l_partkey* $S_l \Rightarrow S_p$	Ship *part_Q*14 $S_p \Rightarrow S_l$	Other	Total
Ship whole	N/A	19.535	29.234	50.008
Semi-join	4.596	17.655	21.201	44.543

6.4 Cost estimation

We evaluate the accuracy of the cost estimation of a query plan in terms of the *mean relative error* (MRE), a metric used in [1]. MRE is defined as $\frac{1}{N}\sum_{i=1}^{N}\frac{|C_i^{pred}-C_i^{act}|}{C_i^{act}}$, where N is the number of testing query plans, C_i^{pred} and C_i^{act} are the predicted and actual execution cost (in seconds) of the testing query Plan i, respectively.

We show the accuracy of each query's plan cost estimation under all the scaling factors in Figure 13. We can see that each query plan cost estimation has a mean relative error of less than 20%. It should be noted that the cost estimation is one of the hardest problems in query optimization. We are not claiming that our cost estimation is better than any other related work but the method works well enough for our purposes.

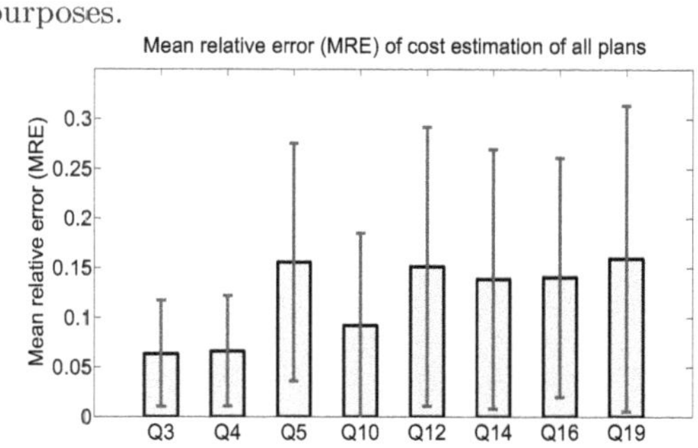

Figure 13: Each query's plan cost estimation under all the scaling factors

7. RELATED WORK

Distributed database query optimizers typically model the network as a FIFO queue with a specified bandwidth, e.g., 12Mb/s was used in [19] and 100Mb/s was used in [10]. A distributed database query optimizer often weights computational cost against communication costs when choosing the best query plan [12]. The best plan is then directly executed albeit the network conditions change over the time [10]. Although Volcano optimizer [8] adapts to changes in the system parameters between compile-time and run-time, it can not modify the resource behavior (e.g., network bandwidth) during runtime. Query scrambling [19] and Xjoin [18] perform optimizations during the query execution. For example, query scrambling [3] materializes remote data while processing is blocked waiting for other sources. The adaptivity in those works is based on the indirect feedback rate of processes while in our work it is based on direct visibility into the network's state. Later work focused on rescheduling runnable sub-plans during initial delays in delivery [19] and attempting to reorder in-flight operators [4]. Compared with those heuristic-driven approaches, our work guarantees the priority or the network bandwidth for a specific schedule or plan. None of the related work proposes defining and using network reservations with the optimizer.

From the networking perspective, Hedera shows that dynamically identifying and placing large flows in a data center can improve throughput up to 113% [2]. Wang *et al.* [20] propose application-aware networking, and argue that distributed applications can benefit from communicating their preferences with the network control-plane. Yap *et al.* have also advocated for an explicit communication channel between applications and software-defined networks, in what they called software-friendly networks [22]. Kim *et al.* [11] describes an OpenFlow controller which configures QoS using application-described requirements and a database of network state. PANE [9] proposes the design, implementation, and evaluation of an API for applications to control an SDN. Our work's major difference is that we show how

[5]Data shipping of the final results is omitted.

DBMS can leverage the communication channel between applications and SDNs, e.g., query performance can be improved with a true database view of network traffic demands and dependencies.

8. CONCLUSION AND FUTURE WORK

In this paper, we proposed and investigated how software-defined networking can be leveraged for the performance management of analytical queries in distributed data stores in a shared networking environment. Specifically, we have showed a way to utilize greater visibility into the network's state and make more informed decisions to adaptively pick the best plan. We have also illustrated how to control the priority of network traffic or make network bandwidth reservations according to different users' priorities, thereby differentiating the query service. In our experiments we have demonstrated that our proposed methods exhibit significant potential for the performance management of analytical queries in distributed data stores. We hope that this work will open up a rich area of research and technology development in distributed data intensive computing by combing SDN and distributed database technologies.

Acknowledgement: We thank Michael J. Carey and Hector Garcia-Molina for their insightful comments on the earlier versions of the work. We thank NEC's business units for their generous support.

9. REFERENCES

[1] M. Akdere, U. Çetintemel, M. Riondato, E. Upfal, and S. Zdonik. Learning-based query performance modeling and prediction. In *Proc. of ICDE*, 2012.

[2] M. Al-Fares, S. Radhakrishnan, B. Raghavan, N. Huang, and A. Vahdat. Hedera: Dynamic flow scheduling for data center networks. In *Proc. of NSDI*, 2010.

[3] L. Amsaleg, M. J. Franklin, A. Tomasic, and T. Urhan. Scrambling query plans to cope with unexpected delays. In *Proc. of PDIS*, 1996.

[4] R. Avnur and J. M. Hellerstein. Eddies: continuously adaptive query processing. In *Proc. of SIGMOD*, 2000.

[5] P. Bernstein and D.-M. Chiu. Using Semi-Joins to Solve Relational Queries. *JACM*, 28:25–40, 1981.

[6] B. Chandramouli, C. Bond, S. Babu, and J. Yang. Query suspend and resume. In *Proc. of SIGMOD*, 2007.

[7] S. Chaudhuri and U. Dayal. An overview of data warehousing and olap technology. *SIGMOD Record*, 26:65–74, 1997.

[8] R. L. Cole and G. Graefe. Optimization of dynamic query evaluation plans. In *Proc. of SIGMOD*, 1994.

[9] A. D. Ferguson, A. Guha, C. Liang, R. Fonseca, and S. Krishnamurthi. Participatory networking: An api for application control of sdns. In *Proc. of SIGCOMM*, 2013.

[10] M. J. Franklin, B. T. Jónsson, and D. Kossmann. Performance tradeoffs for client-server query processing. In *Proc. of SIGMOD*, 1996.

[11] W. Kim, P. Sharma, J. Lee, S. Banerjee, J. Tourrilhes, S.-J. Lee, and P. Yalagandula. Automated and scalable qos control for network convergence. In *Proc. of INM/WREN*, 2010.

[12] D. Kossmann. The state of the art in distributed query processing. *ACM Comput. Surv.*, 32(4), Dec. 2000.

[13] N. McKeown, T. Anderson, H. Balakrishnan, G. Parulkar, L. Peterson, J. Rexford, S. Shenker, and J. Turner. Openflow: enabling innovation in campus networks. *SIGCOMM Comput. Commun. Rev.*, 2008.

[14] K. Morton, R. Bunker, J. D. Mackinlay, R. Morton, and C. Stolte. Dynamic workload driven data integration in tableau. In *Proc. of SIGMOD*, 2012.

[15] Open Networking Foundation. Software-Defined Networking: The New Norm for Networks. 2013.

[16] A. Shieh, S. Kandula, A. Greenberg, C. Kim, and B. Saha. Sharing the data center network. In *Proc. of NSDI*, 2011.

[17] A. Simitsis, K. Wilkinson, M. Castellanos, and U. Dayal. Optimizing analytic data flows for multiple execution engines. In *Proc. of SIGMOD*, 2012.

[18] T. Urhan and M. J. Franklin. Xjoin: A reactively-scheduled pipelined join operator. *IEEE Data Enginerring Bulletin*, 23(2):27–33, 2000.

[19] T. Urhan, M. J. Franklin, and L. Amsaleg. Cost-based query scrambling for initial delays. In *Proc. of SIGMOD*, 1998.

[20] G. Wang, T. E. Ng, and A. Shaikh. Programming your network at run-time for big data applications. In *Proc. of HotSDN*, 2012.

[21] W. Wu, Y. Chi, S. Zhu, J. Tatemura, H. Hacıgümüş, and J. F. Naughton. Predicting query execution time: Are optimizer cost models really unusable? In *Proc. of ICDE*, 2013.

[22] K.-K. Yap, T.-Y. Huang, B. Dodson, M. S. Lam, and N. McKeown. Towards software-friendly networks. In *Proc. of APSys*, 2010.

APPENDIX

In this appendix, we show how to orchestrate PostgreSQL with `dblink` to run a candidate Plan 0 for Q14 in Figure 3(b). After name resolution, we create the materialized view *lineitem_Q*14 at S_l:

```
create table lineitem_Q14 as select l_extendedprice,
l_discount, l_partkey from lineitem where l_shipdate
>= date '1995-09-01' and l_shipdate < date '1995-09
-01' + interval '1' month;
```

We create materialized view *part_Q*14 at S_p:

```
create table part_Q14 as select p_type, p_partkey
from part;
```

We create view *Q14_P0* at S_p for plan 0.

```
create view Q14_P0 as select 100.00 * sum(case when
p_type like 'PROMO%' then l_extendedprice * (1 -
l_discount) else 0 end) / sum(l_extendedprice * (
1 - l_discount)) as promo_revenue from part_Q14,
dblink('host=S_l, dbname','SELECT * From lineitem
_Q14') AS lineitem_Q14(l_partkey integer,l_extended
price decimal(15,2), l_discount decimal(15,2))
where l_partkey=p_partkey;
```

If Plan 0 is selected, then the following command is executed at the master site during the runtime and the time for running the command is recorded as query execution time.

```
psql -h S_p -d dbname -c ''select * from Q14_P0'';
```

The Pursuit of a Good Possible World: Extracting Representative Instances of Uncertain Graphs

Panos Parchas[1] Francesco Gullo[2] Dimitris Papadias[1] Francesco Bonchi[2]

[1]Department of Computer Science and Engineering
Hong Kong University of Science and Technology
{pparchas, dimitris}@cse.ust.hk

[2]Yahoo Labs
Barcelona, Spain
{gullo, bonchi}@yahoo-inc.com

ABSTRACT

Data in several applications can be represented as an uncertain graph, whose edges are labeled with a probability of existence. Exact query processing on uncertain graphs is prohibitive for most applications, as it involves evaluation over an exponential number of instantiations. Even approximate processing based on sampling is usually extremely expensive since it requires a vast number of samples to achieve reasonable quality guarantees. To overcome these problems, we propose algorithms for creating deterministic *representative* instances of uncertain graphs that maintain the underlying graph properties. Specifically, our algorithms aim at preserving the expected vertex degrees because they capture well the graph topology. Conventional processing techniques can then be applied on these instances to closely approximate the result on the uncertain graph. We experimentally demonstrate, with real and synthetic uncertain graphs, that indeed the representative instances can be used to answer, efficiently and accurately, queries based on several properties such as shortest path distance, clustering coefficient and betweenness centrality.

Categories and Subject Descriptors

E.1 [**Data Structures**]: Graphs and Networks; H.2.4 [**Systems**]: Query processing

Keywords

possible world; representative; uncertain graph

1. INTRODUCTION

Graphs constitute an expressive data representation paradigm used to describe entities (vertices) and their relationships (edges) in a wide range of applications. Sometimes the existence of the relationship between two entities is uncertain due to noisy measurements, inference and prediction models, or explicit manipulation. For instance, in biological networks, vertices represent genes and proteins, while edges correspond to *interactions* among them. Since these interactions are observed through noisy and error-prone experiments, each edge is associated with an uncertainty value [4]. In large social networks, uncertainty arises for various reasons [2]; the edge probability may denote the accuracy of a *link prediction* [21], or the influence of one person on another, e.g., in *viral marketing* [17]. Uncertainty can also be injected intentionally for obfuscating the identity of users for privacy reasons [6].

In all these applications the data can be modeled as an *uncertain graph* (also called probabilistic graph), whose edges are labeled with a probability of existence. This probability represents the confidence with which one believes that the relation corresponding to the edge holds in reality. Given the wide spectrum of application domains, querying and mining uncertain graphs has received considerable attention recently.

More formally let $\mathcal{G} = (V, E, p)$ be an uncertain graph, where $p : E \to (0, 1]$ is the function that assigns a probability of existence to each edge. Following the literature, we consider the edge probabilities independent [29, 15, 16] and we assume *possible-world* semantics [1, 9]. Specifically, the possible-world semantics interprets $\mathcal{G}$ as a set $\{G = (V, E_G)\}_{E_G \subseteq E}$ of $2^{|E|}$ possible deterministic graphs (worlds), each defined by a subset of E. The probability of observing any possible world $G = (V, E_G) \sqsubseteq \mathcal{G}$ is:

$$\Pr(G) = \prod_{e \in E_G} p(e) \prod_{e \in E \setminus E_G} (1 - p(e)). \qquad (1)$$

The exponential number of possible worlds usually renders exact query evaluation prohibitive. Indeed, even simple queries on deterministic graphs become #**P**-complete problems on uncertain graphs [32]. To better appreciate this fact, consider a binary predicate $q(G)$ in a deterministic graph G, e.g., q is a *reachability* query, which returns true if two input vertices are reachable from each other. In the context of uncertain graphs, the corresponding *reliability* query would ask for the probability of the vertices being reachable from each other. In general, the probability of predicate q in uncertain graphs is derived by the sum of probabilities of all possible worlds G for which $q(G) = true$:

$$q(\mathcal{G}) = \sum_{\substack{G \sqsubseteq \mathcal{G},\\ q(G)=true}} \Pr(G).$$

As one cannot afford to materialize $2^{|E|}$ possible worlds, a common solution is to apply Monte-Carlo sampling, i.e.,

SIGMOD'14, June 22–27, 2014, Snowbird, UT, USA.
Copyright 2014 ACM 978-1-4503-2376-5/14/06 ...$15.00.
http://dx.doi.org/10.1145/2588555.2593668.

to assess the query on a subset of randomly selected possible worlds. However, sampling is not always a viable option for large graphs because: i) sampling a possible world has a non-negligible cost as it requires generating a random number for each edge $e \in E$ and ii) a large number of samples is necessary to obtain a good approximation. Moreover, when the query output is complex (e.g., a data mining task producing a set of patterns) simple sampling is not sufficient: even if one is able to evaluate the query over a sample, it is not clear how to aggregate different samples.

In these cases the semantics of the analysis must be redefined for uncertain graphs, and new ad-hoc algorithms must be developed. However, designing new methods for data analysis problems is not always feasible. Organizations may have already invested in infrastructure (e.g., graph databases, graph processing software, etc.) for deterministic graphs, which they would wish to utilize, regardless of the uncertainty inherent in the data.

Motivated by the above, we aim at removing the uncertainty by producing representative instances of uncertain graphs. Queries can then be processed efficiently on the deterministic instance using conventional graph algorithms. In order to achieve accuracy, the representative instance should preserve the underlying structure of the uncertain graph. Starting from the observation that the vertex degree is one of the most fundamental properties of the structure of a graph, we conjecture that by preserving the degree of each vertex we capture the essence of the underlying uncertain graph, and thus accurately approximate other properties. The importance of vertex degrees in capturing structural graph properties has been well established in the literature of deterministic graphs, including communication network topologies [22] and complex network modeling [27].

We propose two methods for generating representative instances that capture the vertex degrees: Average Degree Rewiring (ADR) and Approximate B-matching (ABM). ADR involves two phases: first, it generates an instance with the same average vertex degree as the uncertain graph; then, it randomly rewires edges, if they lead to better approximation of the vertex degrees. ABM applies b-matching to obtain an initial instance, which then improves using weighted maximum bipartite matching.

Our extensive experimental evaluation on real and synthetic datasets confirms our conjecture: by preserving the vertex degrees, our representative instances can also capture several structural properties of the graph, including *shortest path distance*, *betweenness centrality* and *clustering coefficient*.

Summarizing, the contributions of the paper are:

1. We introduce the novel problem of extracting representative instances of uncertain graphs.
2. We propose ADR and ABM.
3. We experimentally demonstrate that the extracted representatives can accurately answer a variety of common graph processing tasks.

The rest of the paper is organized as follows. Section 2 overviews the related work. Section 3 defines the problem and presents two benchmark solutions. Sections 4 introduces the ADR algorithm, while Section 5 describes ABM. Section 6 contains an extensive experimental evaluation on real and synthetic datasets, and Section 7 concludes the paper.

2. BACKGROUND AND RELATED WORK

This section starts with an overview of previous work on uncertain graphs. Then, it presents research on node degree distribution due to its relevance to our problem. Finally, it describes *b-matching* because it is used in our ABM method.

2.1 Uncertain graphs

Uncertain relational databases have been well studied from different perspectives, such as SQL query evaluation, mining, ranking and top-k queries [3]. However, in many application domains, such as social, biological, and mobile networks, graphs serve as better models than relational tables. There have been three main directions of research on uncertain graphs: i) queries based on shortest-path distances, ii) pattern mining (frequent, reliable, etc.), and iii) subgraph (similarity) search.

Towards the first direction, Potamias *et al.* [29] study k-nearest neighbors proposing a set of alternative shortest path distance measures. They design methods to compute these distances by combining sampling with Dijkstra's algorithm. Similarly, based on the possible world semantics, Yuan *et al.* [34] return shortest-paths whose probability exceeds an input threshold. Jin *et al.* [16] propose two estimators to boost the accuracy of distance-constrained reachability queries, i.e, given two vertices s and t, return the probability that the distance from s to t is below a user-defined threshold.

In the second line of research, Zou *et al.* investigate mining frequent subgraphs [38] and top-k maximal cliques [37] in uncertain graphs. Jin *et al.* [15] study the problem of finding subgraphs, which are *highly reliable*, i.e., for which the probability of connectivity being maintained under uncertainty is larger than a given threshold.

In the third direction of research, Yuan *et al.* [36] propose a feature-based framework for subgraph search, while in [35] they study subgraph *similarity*. Finally, in a rather different kind of work [6], an uncertain graph is the output, rather than the input of the problem. Specifically, uncertainty is injected intentionally in a social graph for the sake of privacy, with the aim of achieving a form of identity obfuscation for the users.

2.2 Node degree distribution

According to [23], the degree distribution of a graph is the most frequently used topology characteristic. For instance, observations on the Internet's degree distribution had a huge impact on network topology research. Indeed, such studies on the importance of node degrees on the topology of deterministic graphs constitute our main motivation for using vertex degrees to capture the structure of uncertain graphs.

A sequence of non negative integers $d = \{d_1, d_2, \cdots, d_n\}$, with $d_1 \geq d_2 \geq \cdots \geq d_n$ is called *graphic*, if it is the degree sequence of some *simple* graph G. In such case, we say that G *realizes* the sequence d. Erdös and Gallai [10] describe the necessary and sufficient conditions for a sequence to be graphic. The theory on graphic degree sequences finds interesting applications in *complex network modeling* [22]. In order to generate topologies that capture the observed data, a common approach is to construct graphs that realize a predicted degree sequence of the complex network [13]. However, some structural characteristics (e.g. density, connectivity, etc.) depend heavily on the vertex processing order in [13]. Thus, several techniques use the output of [13] as a seed, and take additional steps to *randomize* the graph [5], or induce specific characteristics, such as connectivity. These techniques perform local search by swapping edges in order to reach desired properties. We follow a similar approach in ADR .

Another direction of research studies random processes on networks (the spread of epidemics [28], the evolution of social networks [33] etc.) by constructing *random graphs*. The popular Chung-Lu model [8] predicts the average distance of random graphs constructed with a given *expected* degree sequence, in order to justify facts such as the *small world phenomenon* [18]. Specifically, assuming a weight w_u for each vertex u, *any* edge (u, v) exists with probability $\rho = \frac{w_u w_v}{\sum_i w_i}$. On the other hand, in our uncertain graph model edge probabilities are given explicitly as an input to the problem, instead of being related to vertex weights. Moreover, the concept of *representative graph instance* does not apply to the other graph models. In the experimental section we use the Chung-Lu model to produce synthetic graphs.

2.3 b-Matching

Let an undirected graph $G = (V, E)$, and a set of capacity constraints $b(u)$: $V \to \mathbb{N}$. A subgraph $H = (V, E_H)$ of G is a *b-matching* of G, if the degree of each vertex $u \in V$ in H is at most $b(u)$. The term *b-matching* is used interchangeably to denote the subgraph H, or its edgeset E_H, depending on the context. If $b(u) = 1$ for all vertices of G, then *b-matching* reduces to the well known matching in graph theory. A b-matching is *maximal*, if the addition of any edge violates at least one capacity constraint. A *maximum b-matching* is a maximal b-matching with the largest number of edges.

Figure 1(a) shows an example graph, where the capacity constraint $b(u_i)$ is shown next to u_i. Figure 1(b) illustrates a b-matched graph of Figure 1(a), where the matched edges $((u_2, u_5), (u_3, u_4))$ are shown in bold. Since there is no violation of any capacity constraint, it is a valid b-matching. Figure 1(c) depicts a maximal b-matching: adding any other edge (e.g., (u_1, u_2)) would violate the capacity constraint of at least one vertex (e.g., u_2). Finally, Figure 1(d) illustrates the maximum b-matching.

Numerous exact and approximate solutions have been proposed for finding a maximum *b-matching* (see [14] for a survey). If the capacity constraints are bounded by a constant, the fastest exact algorithm is $O(|E|^{3/2})$ [25]. A greedy 1/2 approximation technique [14] solves the problem in $O(|E|)$. Several methods aim at weighted versions of the problem [24].

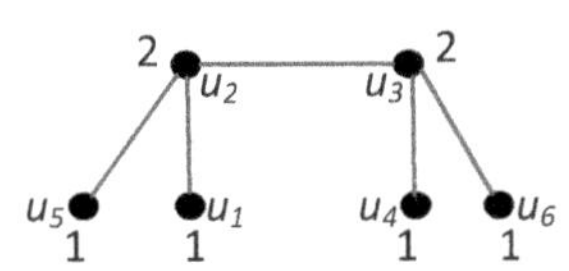

(a) G and constraints

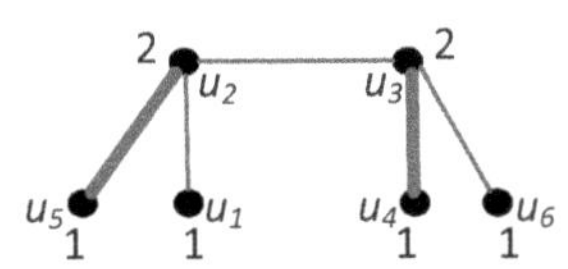

(b) b-matching of G

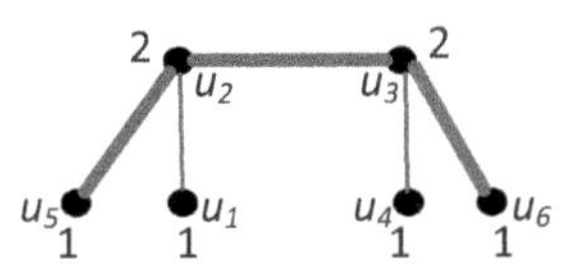

(c) *maximal* b-matching

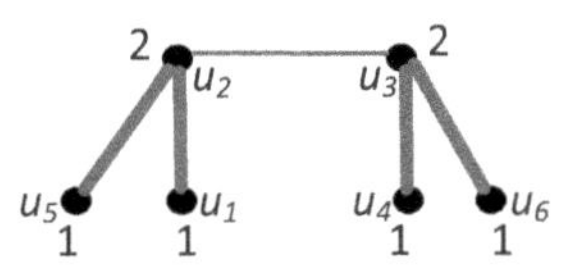

(d) *maximum* b-matching

Figure 1: b-matching example

3. PROBLEM DEFINITION AND BENCHMARK SOLUTIONS

Let $\mathcal{G} = (V, E, p)$ be an undirected uncertain graph, where V is a set of vertices, $E \subseteq V \times V$ is a set of edges, and $p : E \to (0, 1]$ is a function that assigns a probability of existence to each edge. For the sake of brevity, we denote the probability $p(e)$ of any edge $e \in E$ with p_e. We assume independent edge probabilities and possible world semantics, i.e., $\mathcal{G}$ is interpreted as a set $\{G = (V, E_G)\}_{E_G \subseteq E}$ of $2^{|E|}$ possible deterministic graphs (worlds), each defined by a subset of E.

Since most query processing tasks are prohibitively expensive for large uncertain graphs, we propose the extraction of a deterministic *representative instance* $G^* \sqsubseteq \mathcal{G}$ that captures the underlying properties of $\mathcal{G}$. Then, queries on the uncertain $\mathcal{G}$ can be efficiently processed using deterministic algorithms on G^*. In the following, we discuss desired properties of a representative instance, and introduce benchmark solutions for their generation. Table 1 contains the most common symbols throughout the paper.

Table 1: List of frequent symbols used in the paper.

Symbol	Definition
$\mathcal{G}$	uncertain graph
G	instance (possible graph) of $\mathcal{G}$
G^*	representative instance of $\mathcal{G}$
$deg_u(G)$	degree of vertex u in G
$[deg_u(\mathcal{G})]$	expected degree of vertex u in $\mathcal{G}$
$[deg(\mathcal{G})]$	expected average degree of $\mathcal{G}$
$dis_u(G)$	discrepancy of u in G, i.e., $deg_u(G) - [deg_u(\mathcal{G})]$
$\Delta(G)$	discrepancy of an instance G of $\mathcal{G}$
P	sum of probabilities $\sum_{e \in E} p_e$

3.1 Representative instance

The representative instance G^* should conform well with the structural properties of $\mathcal{G}$ in *expectation*. A direct extraction of the "expected graph" from all possible worlds yielded by $\mathcal{G}$ is not easily achievable, as the definition of expected graph is intrinsically ill-posed. Indeed, the notion of expected value of any probability distribution needs i) an ordering among the points/objects of the domain of the distribution, and ii) a way of averaging (aggregating) among such objects. In our context the domain objects are graphs, hence it is not clear how to carry over either i) or ii).

Motivated by the above, we propose a criterion for extracting a representative instance that aims at preserving the *expected degree* of individual vertices. Particularly, our goal is to find a graph $G^* \sqsubseteq \mathcal{G}$ such that the degree of any vertex u in G^* is as close as possible to the *expected degree* of u in $\mathcal{G}$. Formally, given an uncertain graph $\mathcal{G} = (V, E, p)$ and a vertex $u \in V$, the *expected degree* of u in $\mathcal{G}$ is the summation of the probabilities of u's adjacent edges:

$$[deg_u(\mathcal{G})] = \sum_{e=(u,v) \in E} p_e$$

When the uncertain graph is implied, we write for convenience $[deg_u]$. Moreover, we define the *discrepancy* $dis_u(G)$ of a vertex u in an instance $G \sqsubseteq \mathcal{G}$ as the difference of u's degree in G to its expected degree, i.e., $dis_u(G) = deg_u(G) - [deg_u]$. If the graph instance is implied, we equivalently write dis_u. Given the individual vertex discrepancies

dis_u, we define the overall discrepancy Δ of a possible graph G as follows:

DEFINITION 1. *Given an uncertain graph $\mathcal{G} = (V, E, p)$, the* discrepancy *of any possible graph $G \sqsubseteq \mathcal{G}$ is defined as*

$$\Delta(G) = \sum_{u \in V} |dis_u(G)| \tag{2}$$

The problem we tackle in this work is the following:

PROBLEM 1 (REPRESENTATIVE INSTANCE). *Given an uncertain graph $\mathcal{G} = (V, E, p)$, find a possible graph $G^* \sqsubseteq \mathcal{G}$ such that:*

$$G^* = \arg\min_{G \sqsubseteq \mathcal{G}} \Delta(G). \quad \square$$

Characterizing the complexity class of Problem 1 is non-trivial and represents an interesting open question. Our conjecture is that the problem is hard, or at least not solvable exactly in reasonable time for large graphs. To this purpose, note that Problem 1 can alternatively be formulated as an integer linear programming problem. Each edge $e \in E$ is assigned a binary variable $x_e = \{0, 1\}$, where $x_e = 1$ if and only if e is included in the result set. Then, the discrepancy of a vertex u in G can be expressed as $dis_u(G) = \sum_{e=(u,v) \in E}(x_e - p_e)$. Thus, Problem 1 becomes:

$$\begin{aligned} &\min |\mathbf{A}(\mathbf{x} - \mathbf{p})| \\ &\mathbf{x} = \{0, 1\}^{|E|} \end{aligned} \tag{3}$$

where $\mathbf{p} = (0, 1]^{|E|}$ is the vector containing the edge probabilities of the input uncertain graph $\mathcal{G}$ and $\mathbf{A} = \{0, 1\}^{|V| \times |E|}$ is the incidence matrix of $\mathcal{G}$. The formulation in (3) corresponds to a special case of the *closest vector* problem, which is known to be **NP**-hard [26]. Moreover, as discussed in Section 5, when *all* expected degrees are integers, Problem 1 can be solved by *b-matching* algorithms, among which the fastest runs in $O(|E|^{3/2})$ time [25]. Within this view, given that our main goal is to provide solutions that are scalable enough to deal with the large size of today's real-world graphs, we directly aim at approximate, yet efficient algorithms.

Representative instances vastly accelerate query processing on uncertain graphs because: i) they eliminate the overhead of generating a large number of samples and ii) the query is executed once (on the representative) instead of numerous times (for each sample). Consider for example a nearest-neighbor query. State-of-the-art approaches to this query type perform Dijkstra expansions on multiple samples [29]. Depending on the definition of the distance measure, expansion for some samples can be avoided or terminated early, when it cannot improve the current result. Nevertheless, the method has usually very high cost. On the other hand, the same query in our framework can be processed efficiently by applying any deterministic nearest neighbor algorithm on the representative G^*. As shown in our experimental evaluation, the representatives extracted by our algorithms indeed capture well the relevant properties of $\mathcal{G}$, in this case shortest path distances. Thus, the query on G^* is expected to return a good approximation of the nearest neighbor set.

3.2 Benchmark solutions

A straightforward way to generate a representative of an uncertain graph is to consider the instance with the highest probability to incur [29]. According to Equation 1, this *most probable* (MP) instance corresponds to the graph containing all the edges e that have probability $p_e \geq 0.5$. Since MP does not conform with any structural property of $\mathcal{G}$, it is expected to be a poor representative. As an example, if all edges in $\mathcal{G}$ have probability < 0.5, then MP is a graph with no edges.

Algorithm 1 Greedy Probability GP

Input: uncertain graph $\mathcal{G} = (V, E, p)$
Output: approximate representative $G^* = (V, E^*)$
1: $E^* \leftarrow \emptyset$
2: sort E in non-increasing order of their probabilities
3: **for each** $e = (u, v) \in E$ **do**
4:     **if** $|dis_u + 1| + |dis_v + 1| < |dis_u| + |dis_v|$ **then**
5:         $E^* \leftarrow E^* \cup \{e\}$
6: $G^* \leftarrow (V, E^*)$

An alternative benchmark, namely *Greedy Probability* (GP), aims at reducing the overall discrepancy using a greedy approach. Specifically, GP first sorts the edges of the graph in non-increasing order of their probabilities. Then, at each iteration, the algorithm considers an edge $e = (u, v)$ of the sorted list, and includes it to the result set, if $|dis_u + 1| + |dis_v + 1| < |dis_u| + |dis_v|$, i.e., the addition of e decreases the total discrepancy. The complexity of the algorithm is $O(|E| \log |V|)$ because it is dominated by the sorting step.

Algorithm 1 presents the pseudocode of GP. Intuitively, each edge (u, v) affects only the degrees of vertices u, v. Thus, if the condition in line 4 is satisfied, the value of Equation 2 decreases, leading to a better solution. Due to the initial sorting, the most probable edges are considered first. Such edges have large contribution to the expected degrees of the incident vertices, and at the same time they lead to a highly probable representative. However, due to its "blind" search strategy, GP may fail to find a good solution, as shown in the example of Figure 2.

Figure 2(a) illustrates an uncertain graph and the associated edge probabilities. Next to each vertex we include its expected degree, derived from the probabilities of adjacent edges. At the first iteration, GP picks the edge (u_1, u_2) with the highest probability and adds it to the result set E^*. Figure 2(b) shows E^* after the first iteration, where the expected degrees of the vertices have been replaced by their discrepancies. At the second iteration, GP considers edge (u_2, u_3). The inclusion of (u_2, u_3) in E^*, decreases the total discrepancy of u_2 and u_3 from 1.04 to 0.98 (see Figure 2(c); edges of E^* are bold). The final iteration, discards edge (u_3, u_4) since it would increase the discrepancy by 0.99. Thus, the representative returned by GP contains edges $\{(u_1, u_2), (u_2, u_3)\}$ with $\Delta = 0.48 + 0.97 + 0.01 + 0.50 = 1.96$.

The optimal solution shown in Figure 2(d), contains a single edge (u_2, u_3) with $\Delta = 0.52 + 0.03 + 0.01 + 0.50 = 1.06$. Note that for the same example, the representative produced by MP would include *all* edges since their probabilities are at least 0.5. This would yield an even worse solution than that of GP with $\Delta = 2.95$. To overcome the problems of the benchmark solutions, in the following sections we propose more sophisticated algorithms that aim at explicitly improving discrepancy through targeted search.

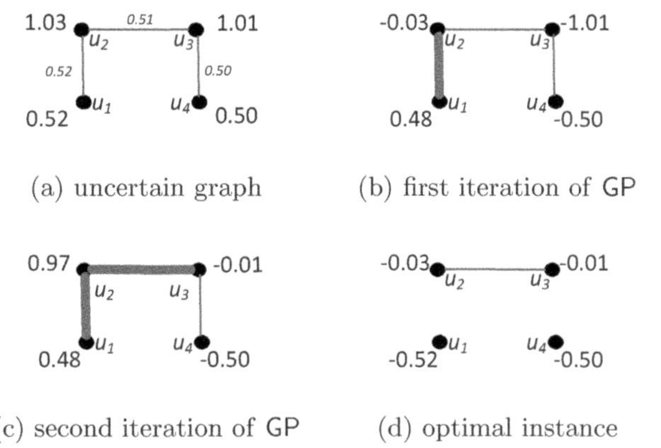

(a) uncertain graph (b) first iteration of GP

(c) second iteration of GP (d) optimal instance

Figure 2: GP example

4. AVERAGE DEGREE REWIRING (ADR)

Average Degree Rewiring (ADR) involves two phases: 1) it creates an instance $G_0 = (V, E_0)$ of the uncertain graph that preserves the average vertex degree and 2) it iteratively improves G_0 by rewiring, i.e., replacing edges in E_0, so that the total discrepancy is reduced.

The following lemma describes the efficient computation of the expected average degree for an uncertain graph.

LEMMA 1. *The expected average degree* $[deg(\mathcal{G})]$ *of an uncertain graph* $\mathcal{G} = (V, E, p)$, *is* $[deg(\mathcal{G})] = \frac{2}{|V|}\mathbf{P}$, *where* $\mathbf{P}$ *is the sum of all the edge probabilities in* $\mathcal{G}$.

PROOF. By definition, the average degree $deg(G)$ of a deterministic graph G is equal to $deg(G) = \frac{1}{|V|}\sum_{u\in V} deg_u$. Due to the linearity of expectation, the expected average degree is:

$$[deg(\mathcal{G})] = \left[\frac{1}{|V|}\cdot\sum_{u\in V} deg_u\right] = \frac{1}{|V|}\cdot\sum_{u\in V}[deg_u] =$$

$$= \frac{2}{|V|}\cdot\sum_{e\in E} p_e = \frac{2}{|V|}\cdot\mathbf{P} \quad \square$$

Given Lemma 1, a representative that preserves $[deg(\mathcal{G})]$ should contain $\mathbf{P}$ edges. Initially, ADR rounds $\mathbf{P}$ to the closest integer $\lfloor\mathbf{P}\rceil$ and sorts the edges on descending order of their probabilities. Consequently, it iterates through the sorted list, and samples each edge e with probability p_e, until it has included $\lfloor\mathbf{P}\rceil$ edges. Algorithm 2 illustrates the pseudocode of ADR, where lines 1-7 correspond to Phase 1.

Phase 2 starts with E_0. At each iteration i, let the current set of edges be E_i. For each node $u \in V$, ADR randomly picks two edges $e_1 = (u, v) \in E_i$ and $e_2 = (x, y) \in E \setminus E_i$ (line 10-11) and computes $d_1 \leftarrow |dis_u - 1| + |dis_v - 1| - (|dis_u| + |dis_v|)$ and $d_2 \leftarrow |dis_x + 1| + |dis_y + 1| - (|dis_x| + |dis_y|)$. Specifically, d_1 is the difference of the absolute discrepancies of u and v, caused by the removal of e_1. Accordingly, d_2 is the difference of the absolute discrepancies of x and y caused by the addition of edge e_2. ADR replaces e_1 with e_2 if $d_1 + d_2 < 0$, i.e., the swapping of edges decreases the overall discrepancy. Since the total number of edges remains $\lfloor\mathbf{P}\rceil$, the expected average degree of $\mathcal{G}$ is preserved throughout the process. The procedure terminates after a user-defined number of iterations *steps*. The value of *steps* depends on the desired trade-off between quality and efficiency. The running time of ADR is $O(|E|\log|V| + steps)$.

Algorithm 2 Average Degree Rewiring (ADR)

Input: uncertain graph $\mathcal{G} = (V, E, p)$, steps
Output: approximate representative $G^* = (V, E^*)$

```
1: E_0 ← ∅, i ← 0
2: P ← Σ_{e∈E} p_e
3: sort E in non increasing order of their probabilities
4: while |E_0| < ⌊P⌉ do
5:     e ← E.next(); r ← random number ∈ [0, 1]
6:     if r ≤ p_e then
7:         E_0 ← E_0 ∪ e
8: for i = 1..steps do
9:     for each u ∈ V do
10:        pick a random edge e_1 = (u, v) from E_i
11:        pick a random edge e_2 = (x, y) from E \ E_i
12:        d_1 ← |dis_u − 1| + |dis_v − 1| − (|dis_u| + |dis_v|)
13:        d_2 ← |dis_x + 1| + |dis_y + 1| − (|dis_x| + |dis_y|)
14:        if d_1 + d_2 < 0 then
15:            E_{i+1} ← (E_i − {e_1}) ∪ {e_2}
16: E* ← E_i
```

We illustrate the application of ADR on the uncertain graph of Figure 3(a), where edge probabilities are denoted with italics, and the expected degree is shown next to each vertex. Initially, ADR computes $\mathbf{P} = 4.4$ and rounds it to the closest integer $\lfloor\mathbf{P}\rceil = 4$. Then, it samples 4 probable edges of the graph and forms the set $E_0 = \{(u_2, u_3), (u_2, u_5), (u_2, u_9), (u_7, u_8)\}$. Figure 3(b) depicts the edges of E_0 with bold lines, and shows the resulting node discrepancies. The value of the total discrepancy at this stage is $\Delta = 3.8$. Next, ADR starts the second phase. Assume that at iteration 0 the algorithm randomly considers the replacement of $e_1 = (u_2, u_5) \in E_0$ with $e_2 = (u_3, u_4) \in E \setminus E_0$. Since $d_1 = 0.6 + 0.45 - (0.40 + 0.55) = 0.1$, $d_2 = 0.1 + 0.7 - (0.9 + 0.3) = -0.4$ and $d_1 + d_2 = -0.3 < 0$, the edges are swapped. Intuitively, the swapping reduces the overall discrepancy by $|d_1 + d_2|$. The discrepancy of the new instance $E_1 = \{(u_2, u_3), (u_2, u_9), (u_3, u_4), (u_7, u_8)\}$ is $\Delta' = \Delta - |d_1 + d_2| = 3.5$.

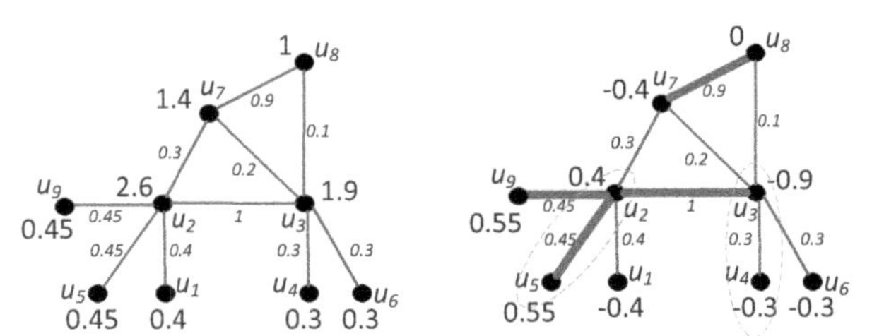

(a) initial graph (b) after Phase 1

Figure 3: ADR example

5. APPROXIMATE B-MATCHING (ABM)

This section presents ABM, which stands for Approximate B-Matching. We first discuss the motivation behind ABM, and then provide the algorithmic framework.

5.1 Motivation

Recall from Section 2.3 that the maximum b-matching problem takes as input a deterministic graph $G = (V, E)$

and a capacity constraint $b(u)$ for every $u \in V$. The output is a set of edges $E_m \subseteq E$, such that each vertex u of V is incident to at most b_u edges of E_m.

We next investigate the relationship of our problem to b-matching, starting with the special case where all the expected degrees of $\mathcal{G}$ are integers, i.e., $[deg_u] \in \mathbb{Z}, \forall u \in V$. As we shall prove shortly, the *optimal instance* (i.e., the one that minimizes the overall discrepancy Δ) is given by a maximum b-matching computed on the uncertain graph $\mathcal{G}$ with capacity constraints $[deg_u]$ for each vertex $u \in V$.

LEMMA 2. *Assume that $[deg_u] \in \mathbb{Z}, \forall u \in V$. Then, there is at least one optimal instance G^* for which $deg_u(G^*) \leq [deg_u]$, for all $u \in V$.*

PROOF. Assume an optimal solution $G^* = (V, E^*)$ that contains *illegal* vertices, i.e., vertices $u \in V$ with $deg_u(G^*) > [deg_u]$. E^* cannot contain an edge (u, v) between two illegal vertices u and v, otherwise G^* is not optimal (i.e., the exclusion of edge (u, v) would decrease the overall discrepancy Δ). Thus, an illegal vertex u can only be adjacent to *legal* vertices, i.e., vertices $x \in V$ for which $deg_x(G^*) \leq [deg_x]$. Assume an edge $e = (u, x) \in E^*$, where u is illegal and x is legal. We first prove that if we remove edge e from E^*, then the remaining graph $G' = (V, E^* - \{e\})$ is also an optimal instance.

Specifically, $dis_u(G^*) > 0$ whereas $dis_x(G^*) \leq 0$, and $dis_u(G') = dis_u(G^*) - 1 \geq 0$ whereas $dis_x(G') = dis_x(G^*) - 1 < 0$. The overall discrepancy of G^* is:
$\Delta(G^*) = |dis_u(G^*)| + |dis_x(G^*)| + \sum_{v \neq u, x \in V} |dis_v(G^*)| = dis_u(G^*) - dis_x(G^*) + \sum_{v \neq u, x \in V} |dis_v(G^*)|$.

Similarly, the discrepancy of G' is:
$\Delta(G') = |dis_u(G')| + |dis_x(G')| + \sum_{v \neq u, x \in V} |dis_v(G')| = (dis_u(G^*) - 1) + (1 - dis_x(G^*)) + \sum_{v \neq u, x \in V} |dis_v(G')|$.

Since graphs G^* and G' only differ by the edge (u, x), $\sum_{v \neq u, x \in V} |dis_v(G^*)| = \sum_{v \neq u, x \in V} |dis_v(G')|$, and thus $\Delta(G^*) = \Delta(G')$. By applying the above argument to all the illegal vertices of G^*, we construct an optimal instance that contains only legal vertices. □

THEOREM 1. *Let $\mathcal{G} = (V, E, p)$ be an uncertain graph where $[deg_u] \in \mathbb{Z}$, $\forall u \in V$. An optimal solution of the* REPRESENTATIVE INSTANCE *problem on input $\mathcal{G}$ is given by solving a maximum b-matching on graph $\mathcal{G}$ using $[deg_u]$ as capacity constraint of vertex u.*

PROOF. Using the previous lemma, there is always an optimal solution $G^* = (V, E^*)$ that ensures that $deg_u(G^*) \leq [deg_u]$, for all $u \in V$. Thus, we can remove the absolute values from the definition of Δ:

$$\Delta(G^*) = \sum_{u \in V} \big| deg_u(G^*) - [deg_u] \big| =$$

$$= \sum_{u \in V} \big([deg_u] - deg_u(G^*) \big) = \sum_{u \in V} [deg_u] - \sum_{u \in V} deg_u(G^*)$$

Since the expected degrees $[deg_u]$ are fixed, this is equivalent to maximizing $\sum_{u \in V} deg_u(G^*)$, which in turn leads to the maximization of $|E^*|$. Therefore, G^* is a maximum b-matching on $\mathcal{G}$ with capacity constraints $[deg_u]$. □

According to the above theorem, a maximum b-matching on graph $\mathcal{G}$ leads to the optimal solution if *all* expected degrees are integers. The fastest algorithm for this computation [25] has time complexity $O(|E|^{3/2})$.

5.2 Algorithm

Since actual uncertain graphs have real valued expected degrees, the b-matching technique of the previous section cannot be applied directly. Moreover, the exact solution to the real-valued problem is expected to be at least as hard as in the case of integers, which is already expensive ($O(|E|^{3/2})$) for large graphs. Thus, we propose a novel approximation technique, based on *matching*.

The main idea is to extract an approximate instance in two phases. In Phase 1, ABM rounds the expected vertex degrees to the closest integers, and computes a maximal b-matching using the rounded values as capacity constraints. In the second phase, ABM partitions the vertices according to their discrepancy. Then, it extracts additional edges that improve the total discrepancy Δ, by performing a bipartite matching. We use approximation techniques for the two phases (i.e., b-matching and bipartite matching) for efficiency reasons.

Algorithm 3 Approximate b-Matching (ABM)

Input: uncertain graph $\mathcal{G} = (V, E, p)$
Output: approximate representative $G^* = (V, E^*)$.
1: calculate the expected degree $[deg_i]$ for all vertices in V.
2: $E_m \leftarrow 0, deg_u \leftarrow 0$
   // Phase 1
3: let $b_i = \text{round}([deg_i])$ to the closest integer
4: **for each** $e = (u, v) \in E$ **do**
5:     **if** $deg_u < b_u$ AND $deg_v < b_v$ **then**
6:         $E_m \leftarrow E_m \cup \{e\}$
7:         $deg_u \leftarrow deg_u + 1; deg_v \leftarrow deg_v + 1$
   // Phase 2
8: $A \leftarrow \emptyset, B \leftarrow \emptyset, C \leftarrow \emptyset$
9: **for each** $u \in V$ **do**
10:     let $dis_u = deg_u - [deg_u]$
11:     **if** $dis_u \leq -0.5$ **then**
12:         $A \leftarrow A \cup \{u\}$
13:     **else if** $-0.5 < dis_u < 0$ **then**
14:         $B \leftarrow B \cup \{u\}$
15:     **else**
16:         $C \leftarrow C \cup \{u\}$
17: $E' \leftarrow E \setminus E_m$
18: **for each** edge $e = (u, v) \in E'$ **do**
19:     weight$= |dis_u| + 2|dis_v| - |1 + dis_u| - 1$
20:     **if** $(u \in A)$ AND $(v \in B)$ AND (weight> 0) **then**
21:         $w(e) \leftarrow$ weight
22:     **else**
23:         discard e
24: Let $G' = ((A \cup B), E', W)$ where $W : w(e) \rightarrow \mathbb{R}$
25: $E_{BP} = \text{bipartite}(G')$
26: $E^* = E_m \cup E_{BP}$

Algorithm 3 contains the pseudocode of ABM. Phase 1 (lines 3-7) corresponds to a greedy approximate maximum b-matching [14] that considers all edges in random order. For each edge $e = (u, v)$, if the capacity constraints of both vertices u and v are not violated, then e is inserted into the result set E_m, and the degrees of u and v are incremented. After all edges have been considered, E_m contains a maximal b-matching of $\mathcal{G}$, whose cardinality is at least half of that of the maximum [14]. Figure 4 applies ABM on the uncertain graph of Figure 3(a). Figure 4(a) shows the vertex degrees after rounding. ABM considers in turn edges $(u_2, u_3), (u_7, u_8)$, which are added to E_m. After that, no other edge can be included in E_m because it would cause a capacity violation. Figure 4(b) includes the node discrepancies after the termination of Phase 1, with respect to their original (i.e., before rounding) degree.

Based on their discrepancies, lines 8-16 partition the vertices into three groups A, B and C. A contains vertices with discrepancy $dis_u \leq -0.5$, B the vertices for which $-0.5 < dis_u < 0$, and C the rest, i.e., vertices with $dis_u \geq 0$. The partitioning is complete (i.e., $A \cup B \cup C = V$) and there is no overlap (i.e., $A \cap B \cap C = \emptyset$). In our running example the groups are $A = \{u_2, u_3\}$, $B = \{u_1, u_4, u_5, u_6, u_7, u_9\}$ and $C = \{u_8\}$.

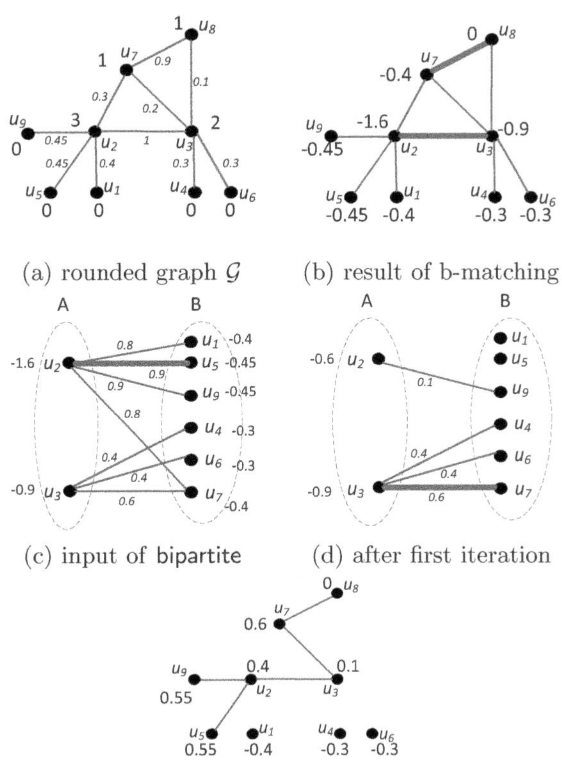

(a) rounded graph $\mathcal{G}$ (b) result of b-matching

(c) input of bipartite (d) after first iteration

(e) G^* of ABM

Figure 4: ABM example

Intuitively, A contains vertices, whose absolute discrepancy will decrease by the addition of an edge. B contains vertices whose absolute discrepancy will increase (after the addition of an edge) by less than 1. C contains vertices that have already reached or exceeded their expected degree[1]; thus, a new adjacent edge will increase their discrepancy by 1. Edges between vertices of A (e.g., (u_2, u_3)) have been added to the result set E_m during Phase 1. The following lemmas discuss the potential for including additional edges, depending on the group of their incident vertices.

LEMMA 3. *Let an edge (u, v) where $u, v \in B$. Including edge (u, v) in the result set cannot improve the overall discrepancy Δ.*

[1]Such vertices are possible because b-matching is performed on the rounded degrees.

PROOF. Since both vertices belong to the set B, it holds that $-0.5 < dis_i < 0$ for $i = \{u, v\}$. Thus, their total discrepancy is $d_1 = |dis_u| + |dis_v| < 1$. The addition of edge (u, v) will change the discrepancies to $dis'_u = dis_u + 1 > 0.5$, and $dis'_v > 0.5$. Thus, the total discrepancy becomes $d_2 = |dis'_u| + |dis'_v| > 1$. Since $d_1 < d_2$, edge (u, v) increases Δ. □

LEMMA 4. *Let an edge (u, v) where $u \in C$. Including edge (u, v) in the result cannot improve the overall discrepancy Δ.*

PROOF. Since u has exceeded its expected degree, adding edge (u, v) will increase dis_u by exactly 1. On the other hand, the absolute discrepancy of v can increase or decrease by at most 1. Thus, Δ can only increase (if $v \in B$ or $v \in C$) or remain the same (if $v \in A$). □

The above lemmas state that the inclusion in the result of an edge that connects i) two vertices in B or ii) a vertex in C with any vertex, cannot improve Δ. Therefore, after Phase 1, the only possible additions are edges that connect vertices in A with vertices in B. Let such an edge $e = (a, b)$ with $a \in A$ and $b \in B$: if the addition of e in the result set decreases the absolute discrepancy of a more than it increases the absolute discrepancy of b, then it improves Δ. The following lemma, quantifies this improvement.

LEMMA 5. *Let $e = (a, b)$ where $a \in A$ and $b \in B$. Including edge e in the result set changes the overall discrepancy Δ by $g_e = |dis_a| + 2|dis_b| - |dis_a + 1| - 1$.*

PROOF. The total discrepancy of vertices a and b *before* (a, b) is, $d_1 = |dis_a| + |dis_b|$. After adding the edge, it becomes $d_2 = |dis_a + 1| + (1 - |dis_b|)$. We define the *gain* g_e of e as the difference between the two discrepancies, i.e., $g_e = d_1 - d_2 = (|dis_a| + |dis_b|) - (|dis_a + 1| + (1 - |dis_b|)) = |dis_a| + 2|dis_b| - |dis_a + 1| - 1$. If g_e is positive, edge e decreases Δ; otherwise it increases it. If $dis_a \leq -1$, then $|dis_a + 1| = |dis_a| - 1$, and the gain becomes $g_e = 2|dis_b|$, i.e., g_e depends only on $|dis_b|$. □

An edge e can improve the overall discrepancy, only if $g_e > 0$. Lines 18-23 of Algorithm 3 consider each edge e in $E' = E - E_m$ connecting vertices in A and B. If $g_e > 0$, e is inserted in a graph $G' = (A \cup B, E', W)$ where $W : E' \to \mathbb{R}$, with $w(e) = g_e$. Figure 4(c) shows the graph G', including the vertex discrepancies and edge weights, which correspond to their gains. The next question is how to efficiently select the subset of edges in E' that minimizes Δ. Towards this, subroutine bipartite(G') (line 25) performs an approximate maximum weight bipartite matching on graph G' with a twist: a vertex of A may be matched with multiple vertices of B, if it has high absolute discrepancy.

Algorithm 4 illustrates bipartite. Initially, the edges of E' are sorted on non-increasing order of their weights/gains. Let Q be a priority queue that contains the sorted list. At each iteration, the head $e = (a, b)$ of Q is inserted into the result set. The inclusion of (a, b) changes the discrepancies of a and b. Specifically, the new discrepancy of b becomes positive; thus, according to Lemma 4, edges adjacent to b cannot reduce Δ, and are removed from Q. Then, bipartite updates the discrepancy of a; let dis_a be the new value. If $dis_a \leq -1$, from Lemma 5, the weights of the other edges (a, x) incident to a do not change since they depend only on $|dis_x|$. If $-1 < dis_a < -0.5$, bipartite updates the weights of these edges using the *gain* definition of Lemma 5 (line 10). If a weight becomes negative, the edge is removed. Finally, if $dis_a > -0.5$, vertex a cannot further improve Δ as it does not belong to group A anymore; thus, it is discarded and all adjacent edges (a, x) are expunged from Q. The function terminates when Q becomes empty.

Continuing the example of Figure 4(c), bipartite first picks the heaviest edge (u_2, u_5) and adds it to the result. Then, it updates the discrepancy of u_2 to $dis_{u2} = -1.6 + 1 = -0.6$; since $-1 < dis_{u2} < -0.5$, the weights of edges adjacent to u_2, (i.e., (u_2, u_1), (u_2, u_7) and (u_2, u_9)) must be updated as well. Edges (u_2, u_1) and (u_2, u_7) yield a negative weight, and are discarded. Figure 4(d) shows the bipartite graph after the first iteration. The next edge (u_3, u_7) in Q is included in the result, updating the discrepancy of vertex u_3 to $dis_{u3} = -0.9 + 1 = 0.1$. Since $dis_{u3} > 0$, all edges adjacent to u_3 are discarded. Finally, bipartite extracts the last edge (u_2, u_9) of Q, adds it to the result and terminates.

Figure 4(e) shows the final output of ABM, which combines the edges added during the two phases. The discrepancy of the extracted graph is 3.2. The total cost of ABM includes the linear-time processing of edges in Phase 1, and the sorting and queuing operations of Phase 2 on E'. Each edge of E' can be processed at most $|B|$ times. Therefore, the complexity of ABM is $O(|E| + |B||E'|\log|E'|)$, where $|E'| \leq |E|$.

Algorithm 4 bipartite

Input: bipartite graph $\mathcal{G} = (A \cup B, E', W)$
Output: the set of edges $E_{BP} \subseteq E'$ with high gain for Δ

1: $E_{BP} \leftarrow \emptyset$
2: sort the edges $e \in E'$ on non-increasing order of their weights $w(e)$ and add them in a priority queue Q.
3: **while** $Q \neq \emptyset$ **do**
4: $\quad e = (a, b) \leftarrow Q.next()$
5: $\quad E_{BP} \leftarrow E_{BP} \cup \{e\}$
6: $\quad$ discard all edges in Q incident to b
7: $\quad dis_a \leftarrow dis_a + 1$
8: $\quad$ **if** $-1 < dis_a < -0.5$ **then**
9: $\quad\quad$ **for each** edge $e' = (a, x) \in E'$ **do**
10: $\quad\quad\quad w(e') \leftarrow |dis_a| + 2|dis_x| - |dis_a + 1| - 1$
11: $\quad\quad\quad$ **if** $w(e') > 0$ **then**
12: $\quad\quad\quad\quad$ update order of e' in Q
13: $\quad\quad\quad$ **else**
14: $\quad\quad\quad\quad$ discard e'
15: $\quad$ **else if** $dis_a > -0.5$ **then**
16: $\quad\quad$ **for each** edge $e' = (a, x) \in E'$ **do**
17: $\quad\quad\quad$ discard e'

6. EXPERIMENTS

In this section, we compare ADR (*Average Degree Rewiring*) and ABM (*Approximate B-Matching*) against the two benchmark approaches MP (*Most Probable*) and GP (*Greedy Probability*). Our goal is to show that in addition to minimizing the node discrepancy, the representatives preserve other important graph properties. To this end, we measure the accuracy of the methods on the following metrics:

- *Vertex degree* corresponds to the percentage of vertices having a certain degree value. It is the property most closely related to the objective function of our algorithms, and its significance to the graph structure has been well established [22].
- *Clustering coefficient* is a measure of how close neighbors of the average k-degree vertex are to forming a clique. Specifically, it is the ratio of the average number of edges between the neighbors of k-degree vertices to the maximum number of such links. It is an important metric for search strategies [11] and social networks [19].
- *Shortest-path distance* is the percentage of pairs at a certain distance, over all pairs of reachable vertices. This metric is crucial for spatial queries [29], routing protocols, and in general, any task involving shortest path computations.
- *Betweenness centrality* is a measure of the node's importance in the graph: it corresponds to the ratio of shortest paths that pass through the node over all pairs of shortest paths. It has been used widely to assess link value of ecological graphs [12], and router utilization of communication networks [31].

The *ground truth* (i.e., the expected value of the measure on the uncertain graph) can be computed exactly only for the *vertex degree*, by summing up the probabilities of the adjacent edges for each vertex. All the other metrics are approximated by Monte Carlo sampling. Specifically, we create a number of random instances of the input uncertain graph, and we approximate the *expected* value of each metric by the weighted average of the sampled graphs. We use 1000 samples since it has been shown [29, 16] that they usually suffice to achieve accuracy convergence. However, *shortest-path distance* and *betweenness centrality* are very expensive because they involve *all-pairs-shortest-path* computations. Their evaluation over 1000 samples of large graphs is prohibitive. To overcome this problem, given an uncertain graph, we use *forest fire* [20] to create a smaller subgraph that has similar properties and we perform the evaluation on that subgraph.

Section 6.1 compares our techniques on *vertex degree* and *clustering coefficient*, using real uncertain graphs. Section 6.2 applies *forest fire* to reduce the size of the real graphs, in order to evaluate *shortest-path distance*, and *betweenness centrality*. Finally, Section 6.3 considers all metrics on synthetic graphs.

6.1 Real graphs

Table 2 summarizes the main characteristics of the uncertain graphs from different real world scenarios, used in our experiments.

Table 2: Characteristics of real datasets

dataset	*vertices*	*edges*	*edge probabilities: mean, SD, quartiles*
BioMine	1 008 201	13 485 878	0.27 ± 0.21, $\{0.12, 0.22, 0.36\}$
DBLP	684 911	4 569 982	0.14 ± 0.11, $\{0.09, 0.09, 0.18\}$
Flickr	78 322	10 171 509	0.09 ± 0.06, $\{0.06, 0.07, 0.09\}$

Flickr [29](`www.flickr.com`): a social network, where the probability of an edge between two users is computed assuming *homophily*, i.e., the principle that similar interests indicate social ties. Homophily is measured by the Jaccard coefficient of the interest groups of the two users.

DBLP [29, 16] (`www.informatik.uni-trier.de/~ley/db/`): a database of scientific publications and their authors. Two

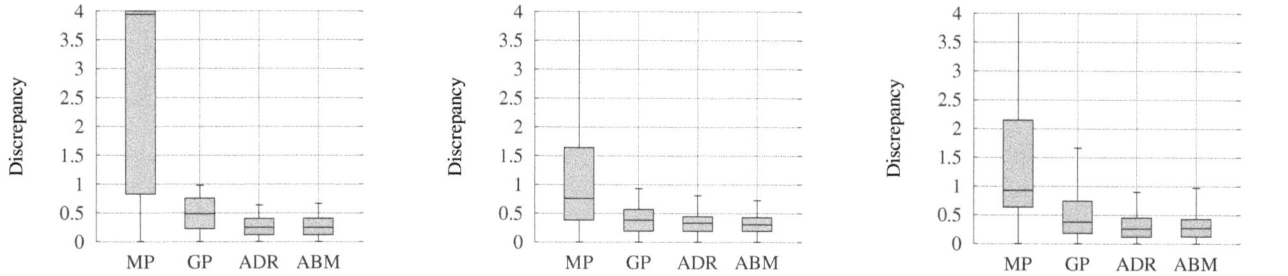

(a) Flickr (b) DBLP (c) BioMine

Figure 5: Box plots of the distribution of discrepancy per node

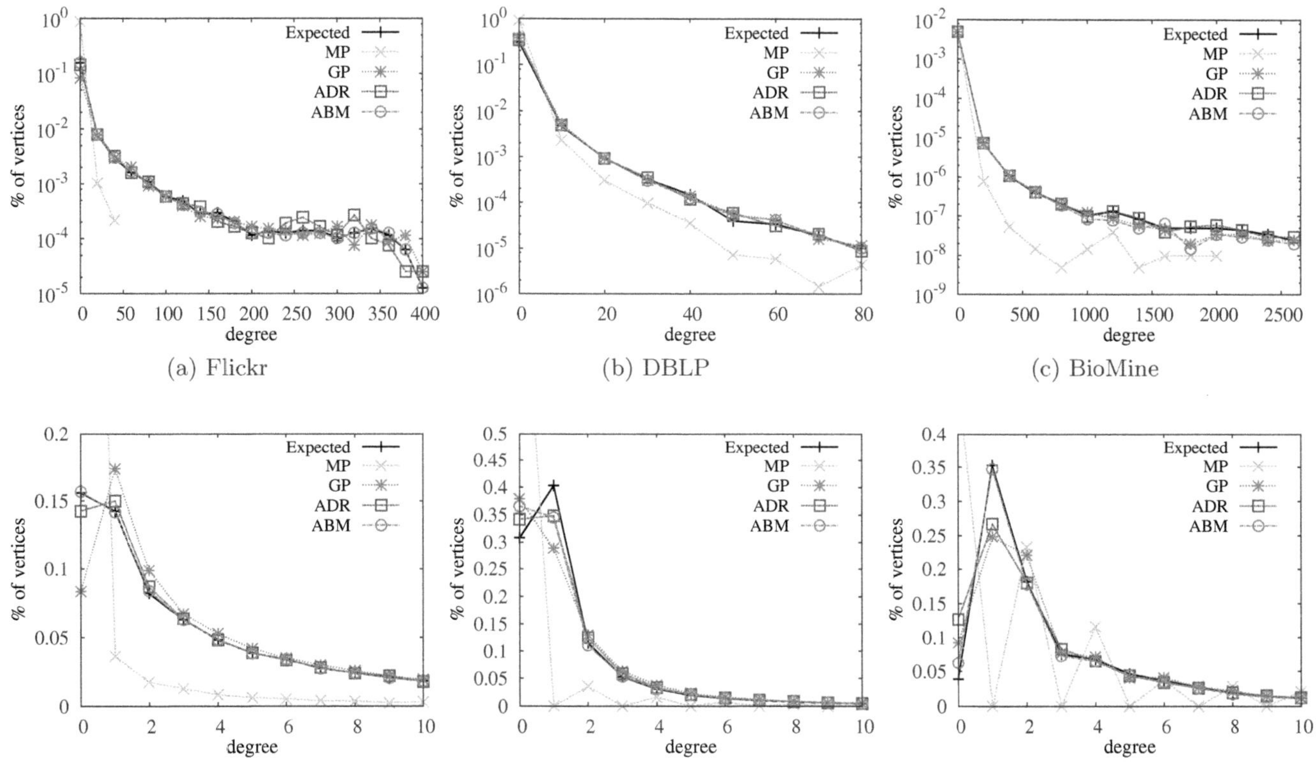

(a) Flickr (b) DBLP (c) BioMine

(d) Flickr (e) DBLP (f) BioMine

Figure 6: Vertex degree (a)-(c) and zoom-in (d)-(f) for most probable degrees (real graphs)

authors are connected, if they have coauthored a publication. The probability of an edge is derived from an exponential function to the number of collaborations.

BioMine [30] (`biomine.org`): a snapshot of the database of the BioMine project containing biological interactions. The probability of any edge corresponds to the confidence that the interaction actually exists.

Figure 5 illustrates the boxplots for the absolute discrepancy distribution. For each method, the vertical line includes 96% of the vertices, the gray rectangle contains 50% of the vertices, and the horizontal line corresponds to the median discrepancy. For instance, in Flickr for the representative produced by GP, 96% of the vertices have absolute discrepancy less than 0.98, 50% of the vertices in the range [0.23, 0.76], and the median discrepancy is 0.48. As expected, the accuracy of MP is very low; the upper bound of the 96% range reaches discrepancy 129 for Flickr and is omitted from Figure 5. GP performs significantly better, but it is clearly outperformed by ADR and ABM, whose median discrepancy is below 0.4, in all datasets.

Table 3: Average discrepancy per vertex

	Flickr	DBLP	BioMine
MP	22.108	1.599	4.260
GP	0.560	0.407	0.678
ADR	0.278	0.352	0.346
ABM	0.280	0.315	0.453

Table 3 shows the average discrepancy per vertex for all datasets. Note that for Flickr the average discrepancy of MP is much higher than the median. This occurs because, as we show in the next experiment, the highest vertex degree of the representative is much lower than the highest expected degree in the uncertain graph. The accuracy of GP is reason-

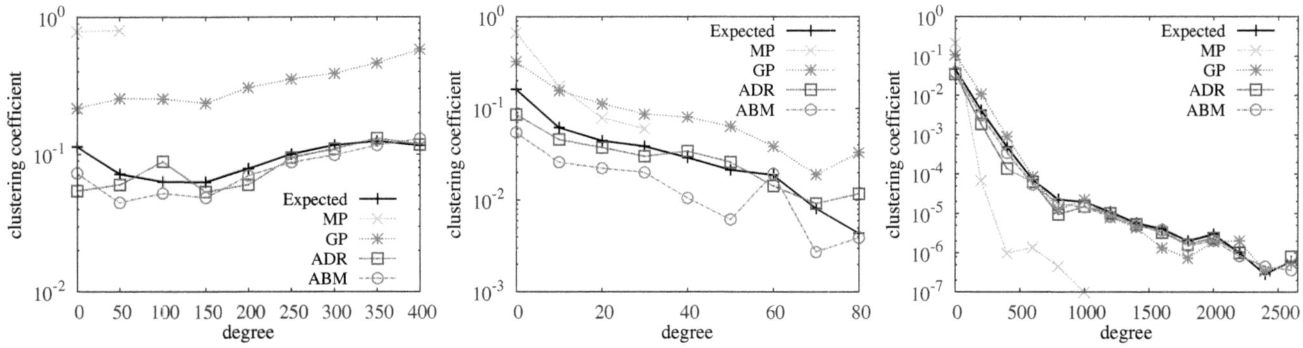

(a) Flickr (b) DBLP (c) BioMine

Figure 7: Clustering coefficient (real graphs)

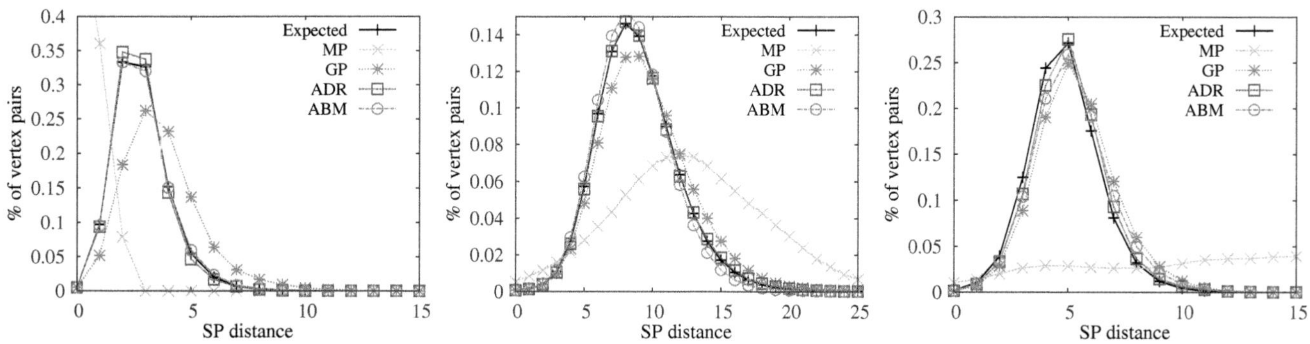

(a) Flickr (b) DBLP (c) BioMine

Figure 8: Shortest path distance (real reduced graphs)

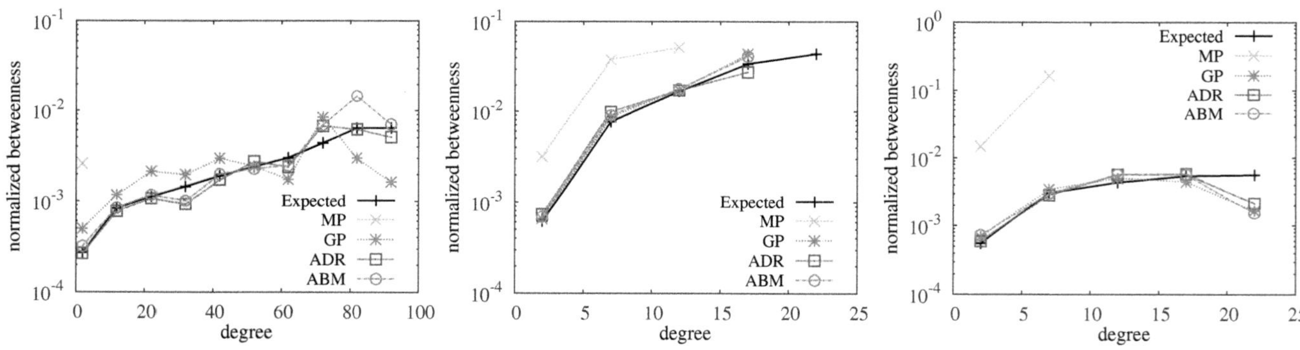

(a) Flickr (b) DBLP (c) BioMine

Figure 9: Betweeness centrality (real reduced graphs)

able, but below that of ADR and ABM for all datasets. ADR and ABM have similar performance for Flickr. For DBLP (BioMine), ABM (ADR) yields better results.

Figure 6 shows the degree distribution, i.e., the percentage of vertices in the representative instance versus the vertex degree. The second row focuses on degrees 0 to 10, which are the most probable. ADR and ABM are very close to the expected distributions in all datasets. Naturally, MP is the worst method; for instance, in Flickr the highest degree of any vertex of its representative is below 50, although there are vertices whose expected degree is up to 400. The inferior performance of GP with respect to ADR and ABM is evident in the zoomed diagrams.

Figure 7 illustrates the clustering coefficient versus the vertex degree. In general, the ranking of the algorithms in terms of accuracy, is the same as that for the node discrepancy. The performance of MP is clearly unacceptable. GP performs well for BioMine but it yields large error for Flickr and DBLP. ADR and ABM achieve the best clustering coefficient approximations, with ADR outperforming ABM for DBLP, which is consistent with the average discrepancy of the algorithms in Table 3.

6.2 Reduced real graphs

In order to evaluate *shortest path (SP) distance* and *betweenness centrality*, we produce subgraphs of the original dataset using *forest fire* [20]. The number of vertices and edges in the resulting subgraphs are: i) Flickr, 5000 and 655275, ii) BioMine, 5000 and 69367, and iii) DBLP, 20000 and 79619. Note that the method used to create reduced

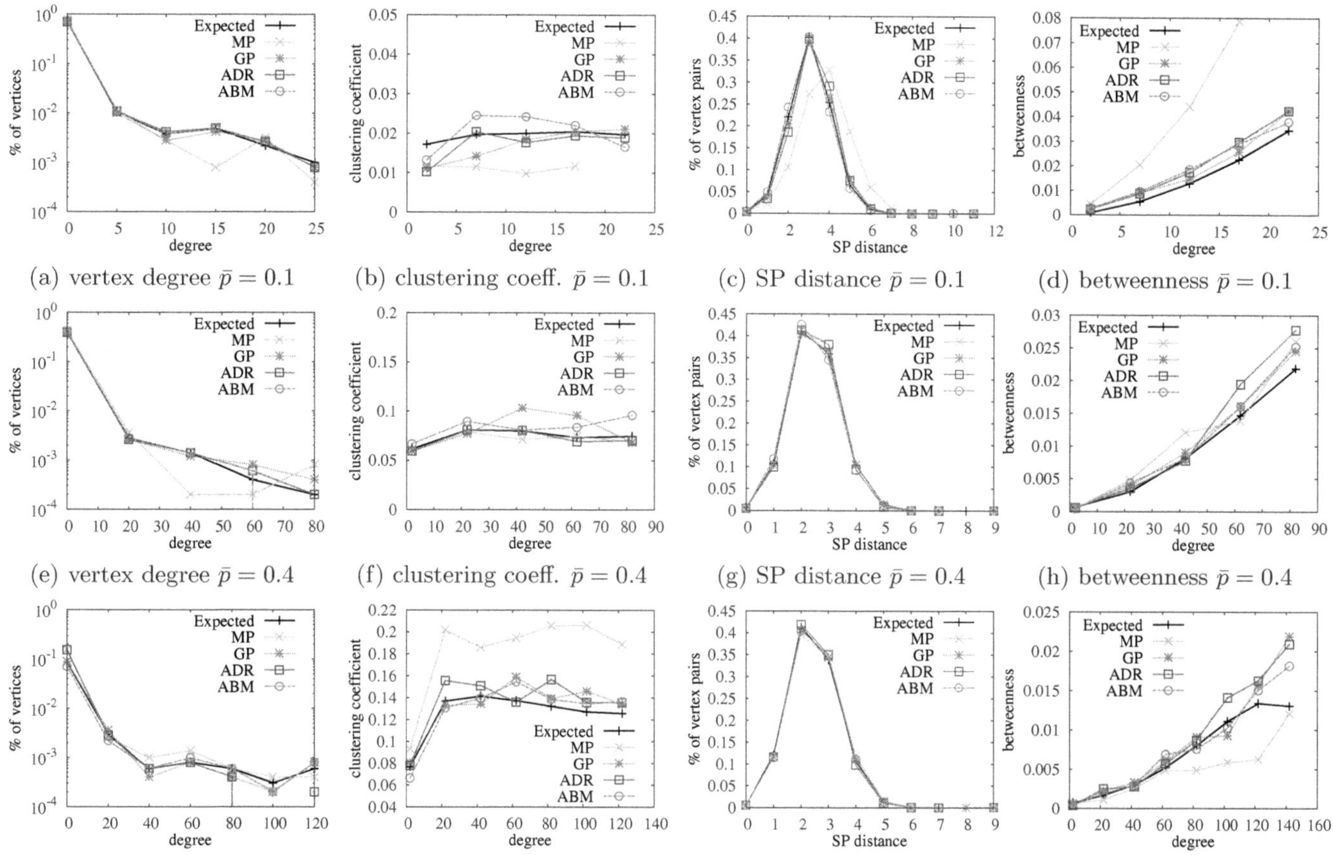

(a) vertex degree $\bar{p} = 0.1$ (b) clustering coeff. $\bar{p} = 0.1$ (c) SP distance $\bar{p} = 0.1$ (d) betweenness $\bar{p} = 0.1$

(e) vertex degree $\bar{p} = 0.4$ (f) clustering coeff. $\bar{p} = 0.4$ (g) SP distance $\bar{p} = 0.4$ (h) betweenness $\bar{p} = 0.4$

(i) vertex degree $\bar{p} = 0.7$ (j) clustering coeff. $\bar{p} = 0.7$ (k) SP distance $\bar{p} = 0.7$ (l) betweenness $\bar{p} = 0.7$

Figure 10: All metrics for different average edge probability (synthetic graphs)

graphs is orthogonal to our work; we expect the proposed techniques to have similar performance with other size reduction methods.

Figure 8 illustrates the shortest path distance distribution, i.e., the percentage of vertices versus the SP distance. Figure 9 shows the betweenness centrality versus the vertex degree. In general, the results are consistent with those of the previous subsection. Specifically, the representatives of ADR and ABM capture very well both metrics in all datasets. Similar to Figure 7, GP performs well for BioMine and poorly for Flickr. However, its accuracy for *SP distance* and *betweeness centrality* in DBLP is rather good, as opposed to the *clustering coefficient* for the same dataset. This indicates that a representative may be suitable for some tasks but not others.

6.3 Synthetic graphs

To create synthetic uncertain graphs, we first generate a degree sequence $d_1, \ldots, d_{|V|}$ by sampling from a power-law distribution. Then, we use the Chung-Lu model [8] to build a graph with the specific degree sequence: for each pair of vertices u and v, we draw the corresponding edge (u, v) with probability proportional to $d_u \cdot d_v$. Finally, for every edge, we assign a probability value from a normalized Zipf distribution because it has been shown that it captures well real-world properties [7].

We experimented with two parameters: i) the density δ defined as the ratio between the number of edges and the number of vertices, and ii) the average edge probability $\bar{p}$. Due to lack of space, we only show the results after fixing density to $\delta = 5$ and varying the average edge probability. In all cases, the node cardinality is fixed to 10000.

Figure 10 measures the accuracy of all algorithms on all metrics for the synthetic data. Specifically, each row corresponds to an average probability value and each column to a metric. Similar to the previous experiments, ADR and ABM produce the best representative. The main difference is that for the synthetic data, GP also performs well in most cases. On the other hand, MP is acceptable only for $\bar{p} = 0.4$ because, if the edge probabilities are close to 0.5, MP is likely to include the expected number of edges in the representative.

Comments on the run-time. The running time of the algorithms is negligible compared to the cost of query processing. A single core of an Intel Xeon server at 2.83GHz CPU and 64GB RAM takes about one minute to generate a representative instance using ADR (the most expensive algorithm[2] on BioMine (the largest dataset with 13M edges). ABM takes around 45 seconds, while the other algorithms are even faster. On the other hand, just the generation of 1000 samples requires several minutes. Moreover, the evaluation of the ground truth on 1000 samples is 1000 times more expensive than the evaluation of the corresponding metric on a representative.

[2]In our implementation we set the *steps* of ADR equal to $10 \cdot \mathbf{P}$

7. CONCLUSION

In this paper, we introduce the problem of extracting representative instances of uncertain graphs. Expensive tasks can then be processed by applying deterministic algorithms on these instances. We propose methods that aim at capturing the expected degree of individual vertices because of its significance in the graph topology. An extensive experimental evaluation with real and synthetic data confirms that the representative instances indeed preserve well a number of important graph metrics.

We intend to investigate the complexity class of the problem as well as approximation bounds for the representatives, which are complicated issues beyond the scope of this work. We will also study additional algorithms that could possibly lead to better results. Finally, an interesting direction for future work concerns specialized algorithms that aim at a specific type of task, e.g., data mining, rather than general graph metrics or properties.

Acknowledgements

Panos Parchas and Dimitris Papadias were supported by grant HKUST 6177/13 from Hong Kong RGC.

8. REFERENCES

[1] S. Abiteboul, P. Kanellakis, and G. Grahne. On the representation and querying of sets of possible worlds. In *SIGMOD*, pages 34–48, 1987.

[2] E. Adar and C. Re. Managing uncertainty in social networks. *IEEE Data Eng. Bull.*, 30(2):15–22, 2007.

[3] C. C. Aggarwal and P. S. Yu. A survey of uncertain data algorithms and applications. *TKDE*, 21(5):609–623, 2009.

[4] S. Asthana, O. D. King, F. D. Gibbons, and F. P. Roth. Predicting protein complex membership using probabilistic network reliability. *Genome Res.*, 14:1170–1175, 2004.

[5] J. Blitzstein and P. Diaconis. A sequential importance sampling algorithm for generating random graphs with prescribed degrees. *Internet Mathematics*, 6(4):489–522, 2011.

[6] P. Boldi, F. Bonchi, A. Gionis, and T. Tassa. Injecting uncertainty in graphs for identity obfuscation. *PVLDB*, 5(11):1376–1387, 2012.

[7] L. Chen and C. Wang. Continuous subgraph pattern search over certain and uncertain graph streams. *TKDE*, 22(8):1093–1109, 2010.

[8] F. R. K. Chung and L. Lu. The average distance in a random graph with given expected degrees. *Internet Mathematics*, 1(1):91–113, 2003.

[9] N. Dalvi and D. Suciu. Efficient query evaluation on probabilistic databases. In *VLDB*, pages 864–875, 2004.

[10] P. Erdös and T. Gallai. Graphs with prescribed degrees of vertices (hungarian). *Mat. Lapok*, 11:264–274, 1960.

[11] P. Fraigniaud. Small worlds as navigable augmented networks: model, analysis, and validation. In *ESA*, pages 2–11, 2007.

[12] A. M. M. Gonzalez, B. Dalsgaard, and J. M. Olesen. Centrality measures and the importance of generalist species in pollination networks. *Ecological Complexity*, 7(1):36–43, 2010.

[13] S. L. Hakimi. On realizability of a set of integers as degrees of the vertices of a linear graph (i). *J. Soc. Indust. Appl. Math.*, 10(3):496–506, 1962.

[14] S. Hougardy. Linear time approximation algorithms for degree constrained subgraph problems. In W. Cook, L. Lovasz, and J. Vygen, editors, *Research Trends in Combinatorial Optimization*, pages 185–200. Springer, 2009.

[15] R. Jin, L. Liu, and C. C. Aggarwal. Discovering highly reliable subgraphs in uncertain graphs. In *KDD*, pages 992–1000, 2011.

[16] R. Jin, L. Liu, B. Ding, and H. Wang. Distance-constraint reachability computation in uncertain graphs. *PVLDB*, 4(9):551–562, 2011.

[17] D. Kempe, J. M. Kleinberg, and É. Tardos. Maximizing the spread of influence through a social network. In *KDD*, pages 137–146, 2003.

[18] J. Kleinberg. Complex networks and decentralized search algorithms. In *Int. Congr. of Mathematicians (ICM)*, 2006.

[19] G. Kossinets and D. J. Watts. Empirical analysis of an evolving social network. *Science*, 311(5757):88–90, 2006.

[20] J. Leskovec and C. Faloutsos. Sampling from large graphs. In *KDD*, pages 631–636, 2006.

[21] D. Liben-Nowell and J. Kleinberg. The link prediction problem for social networks. In *CIKM*, pages 556–559, 2003.

[22] P. Mahadevan, D. Krioukov, K. Fall, and A. Vahdat. Systematic topology analysis and generation using degree correlations. *SIGCOMM Comput. Commun. Rev.*, 36(4):135–146, 2006.

[23] P. Mahadevan, D. Krioukov, M. Fomenkov, X. Dimitropoulos, k. c. claffy, and A. Vahdat. The internet as-level topology: Three data sources and one definitive metric. *SIGCOMM Comput. Commun. Rev.*, 36(1):17–26, Jan. 2006.

[24] J. Mestre. Greedy in approximation algorithms. In *ESA*, pages 528–539, 2006.

[25] S. Micali and V. V. Vazirani. An $O(\sqrt{|V|} \cdot |E|)$ algorithm for finding maximum matching in general graphs. In *FOCS*, pages 17–27, 1980.

[26] D. Micciancio. The hardness of the closest vector problem with preprocessing. *IEEE Trans. on Information Theory*, 47(3):1212–1215, 2001.

[27] M. Mihail and N. K. Vishnoi. On generating graphs with prescribed vertex degrees for complex network modelling. *ARACNE*, pages 1–11, 2002.

[28] M. E. Newman. Spread of epidemic disease on networks. *Phys. Rev. E*, 66(1), 2002.

[29] M. Potamias, F. Bonchi, A. Gionis, and G. Kollios. k-Nearest Neighbors in uncertain graphs. *PVLDB*, 3(1):997–1008, 2010.

[30] P. Sevon, L. Eronen, P. Hintsanen, K. Kulovesi, and H. Toivonen. Link discovery in graphs derived from biological databases. In *DILS*, pages 35–49, 2006.

[31] A. Tizghadam and A. Leon-Garcia. Betweenness centrality and resistance distance in communication networks. *IEEE Network*, 24(6):10–16, 2010.

[32] L. G. Valiant. The complexity of enumeration and reliability problems. *SIAM J. on Computing*, 8(3):410–421, 1979.

[33] D. J. Watts. Collective dynamics of 'small-world' networks. *Nature*, 393:440–442, 1998.

[34] Y. Yuan, L. Chen, and G. Wang. Efficiently answering probability threshold-based shortest path queries over uncertain graphs. In *DASFAA*, pages 155–170, 2010.

[35] Y. Yuan, G. Wang, L. Chen, and H. Wang. Efficient subgraph similarity search on large probabilistic graph databases. *PVLDB*, 5(9):800–811, 2012.

[36] Y. Yuan, G. Wang, H. Wang, and L. Chen. Efficient subgraph search over large uncertain graphs. *PVLDB*, 4(11):876–886, 2011.

[37] Z. Zou, J. Li, H. Gao, and S. Zhang. Finding top-k maximal cliques in an uncertain graph. In *ICDE*, pages 649–652, 2010.

[38] Z. Zou, J. Li, H. Gao, and S. Zhang. Mining frequent subgraph patterns from uncertain graph data. *TKDE*, 22(9):1203–1218, 2010.

Navigating the Maze of Graph Analytics Frameworks using Massive Graph Datasets

Nadathur Satish[†], Narayanan Sundaram[†], Md. Mostofa Ali Patwary[†], Jiwon Seo[⋆], Jongsoo Park[†], M. Amber Hassaan[‡], Shubho Sengupta[†], Zhaoming Yin[§], and Pradeep Dubey[†]

[†]Parallel Computing Lab, Intel Labs | [⋆]Stanford University | [‡]Dept. of Electrical and Computer Engineering, UT Austin | [§]Georgia Tech

ABSTRACT

Graph algorithms are becoming increasingly important for analyzing large datasets in many fields. Real-world graph data follows a pattern of sparsity, that is not uniform but highly skewed towards a few items. Implementing graph traversal, statistics and machine learning algorithms on such data in a scalable manner is quite challenging. As a result, several graph analytics frameworks (GraphLab, CombBLAS, Giraph, SociaLite and Galois among others) have been developed, each offering a solution with different programming models and targeted at different users. Unfortunately, the "Ninja performance gap" between optimized code and most of these frameworks is very large (2-30X for most frameworks and up to 560X for Giraph) for common graph algorithms, and moreover varies widely with algorithms. This makes the end-users' choice of graph framework dependent not only on ease of use but also on performance. In this work, we offer a quantitative roadmap for improving the performance of all these frameworks and bridging the "ninja gap". We first present hand-optimized baselines that get performance close to hardware limits and higher than any published performance figure for these graph algorithms. We characterize the performance of both this native implementation as well as popular graph frameworks on a variety of algorithms. This study helps end-users delineate bottlenecks arising from the algorithms themselves vs. programming model abstractions vs. the framework implementations. Further, by analyzing the system-level behavior of these frameworks, we obtain bottlenecks that are agnostic to specific algorithms. We recommend changes to alleviate these bottlenecks (and implement some of them) and reduce the performance gap with respect to native code. These changes will enable end-users to choose frameworks based mostly on ease of use.

Categories and Subject Descriptors

H.2.4 [**Information Systems**]: Database Management—*Systems*

1. INTRODUCTION

The rise of big data has been predominantly driven by the need to find relationships among large amounts of data. With the increase in large scale datasets from social networks [34, 20], web pages [14], bioinformatics [18] and recommendation systems [9, 7], large scale graph processing has gone mainstream. There has been a lot of interest in creating, storing and processing large graph data [35, 10]. While large scale graph data management is an important problem to solve, this paper is concerned with large scale graph processing (specifically, in-memory processing).

Graph algorithms are typically irregular and difficult to efficiently implement by end-users, often severely under-utilizing system and processor resources – unlike regular compute dominated applications such as Linpack [5]. It is often possible for the "Ninja performance gap" [29] between naively written graph code and well-tuned hand-optimized code to be multiple orders of magnitude. This difficulty has motivated the rise of numerous in-memory frameworks to help improve productivity and performance on graph computations such as GraphLab, Giraph, CombBLAS/KDT, SociaLite and Galois [8, 11, 21, 26, 31]. These frameworks are aimed at computations varying from classical graph traversals to graph statistics calculations such as triangle counting to complex machine learning tasks like collaborative filtering. Currently, there is no consensus on what the "building blocks" of graph processing should be. Different programming frameworks use different bases such as sparse matrix operations [11, 22], vertex programs from the point of view of a single vertex [8, 21], declarative programming [30] or generic task based parallelization [26]. Further, all of the approaches differ in performance, and different frameworks often perform better on different algorithms. This makes it extremely difficult for an end-user to identify which framework would be a good fit for the problem at hand from both performance and productivity angles.

This work proposes to simplify the end-users' choice by creating a roadmap to improve the performance of various graph frameworks in order to bridge the performance gap with respect to native code. Once that gap is bridged, we believe that all frameworks will be feasible to use and the choice of framework then boils down to productivity issues. In order to achieve this, it is essential to first have the right reference point that is only limited by the hardware. This comparison is generally missing from previous work, but it is critical to help set reasonable performance expectations. Moreover, this study has to be done at large scale (several 10's of nodes) since many bottlenecks of graph algorithms do not show up until this point. Consequently, we perform this study on both real-world graph data (typically fitting on 1-16 nodes) e.g. [9, 20], but also on synthetic data scaling up to 64 nodes.

The performance study in this work is intended to help us tease out performance differences between the different frameworks as those due to the fundamental scaling limits in the algorithms, limitations of the programming model or inefficiencies in the implementation of the framework. We follow up this comparison with an analysis of system-level metrics such as CPU utilization, mem-

SIGMOD'14, June 22–27, 2014, Snowbird, UT, USA.

ACM 978-1-4503-2376-5/14/06 ...$15.00.
http://dx.doi.org/10.1145/2588555.2610518.

ory footprint and network characteristics of each framework. This helps identify key strengths and weaknesses of each framework in an algorithm-agnostic way. We use this knowledge to then propose a roadmap for performance improvements of each framework.

We wish to emphasize that this work should not be taken as introducing a new graph benchmark for ranking graph frameworks. Our aim is to analyze the performance of existing graph frameworks and propose changes to improve such performance to an extent where all these frameworks are reasonably close to native code. Our contributions can be summarized as follows:

- Unlike other framework comparisons, we provide native hand-optimized implementations for all the algorithms under consideration (Sec. 5.1). This provides a clear and meaningful reference point that shows the hardware bottlenecks of the algorithms themselves, and exposes the gap in other framework implementations. Our native implementation is only about $2 - 2.5\times$ off the ideal performance; and is faster than other frameworks by $1.1 - 568\times$ on a single node and $1.6 - 494\times$ on multiple nodes (Sec. 5.2 & 5.3).
- We compare different graph frameworks that vary not just in implementations but in fundamental programming models – including vertex programming, sparse matrix operations, declarative programming and task-based programming. We show scaling studies on both real-world and synthetic datasets, ranging in scale from a single node to 64 nodes and graphs of sizes up to 16 billion edges. We do not restrict ourselves only to graph traversals, but also include graph statistics and machine learning algorithms such as collaborative filtering in our study. We believe our workload mix is better representative of data analytics tasks performed on large scale graphs.
- We analyze CPU utilization, memory consumption, achieved network bandwidth and total network transfers in order to characterize the frameworks and algorithms better (Sec. 5.4). This analysis explains much of the performance gap observed between the frameworks and native code.
- We show quantitatively the performance gains from different optimization techniques (use of better communication layers, improved data structures and increased communication efficiency from compression/latency hiding) used in our native code (Sec. 6.1). We provide specific recommendations to bridge the performance gap for all frameworks. We apply some of these ideas to SociaLite and show that it improves performance by about $2\times$ for network bound algorithms.

We believe that our roadmap will help framework developers optimize their frameworks.

2. CHOICE OF ALGORITHMS

We picked 4 different graph algorithms with varying characteristics in terms of functionality (traversal, statistics, machine learning), data per vertex, amount and type of communication, iterative and non-iterative etc. The list is below:

1. PageRank This is an algorithm that is used to rank web pages according to their popularity. This algorithm calculates the probability that a random walk would end in a particular vertex of a graph. This application computes the page rank of every vertex in a directed graph iteratively. At every iteration t, each vertex computes the following:

$$PR^{t+1}(i) = r + (1-r) * \sum_{j|(j,i)\in E} \frac{PR^t(j)}{\text{degree}(j)} \quad (1)$$

where r is the probability of a random jump (we use 0.3), E is the set of directed edges in the graph and $PR^t(i)$ denotes the (unnormalized) page rank of the vertex at iteration t.

2. Breadth First Search (BFS) This is a typical graph traversal algorithm. This algorithm performs the breadth first search of an undirected, unweighted graph from a given start vertex and assigns a "distance" to each vertex. The distance signifies the minimum number of edges that need to be traversed from the starting vertex to a particular vertex. The algorithm is typically implemented iteratively. One can think of the algorithm as performing the following computation once per vertex per iteration:

$$Distance(i) = \min_{j|(j,i)\in E} Distance(j) + 1 \quad (2)$$

with all the distances initialized to infinity (the starting vertex is set to 0). In practice, this computation is only performed for all the neighbors of a vertex after its distance has been updated. This algorithm is part of the Graph500 benchmark [23].

3. Triangle Counting The count of the number of triangles in a graph is part of measuring graph statistics. A triangle is formed when two vertices are both neighbors of a common third vertex. This algorithm counts the number of such triangles and reports them. The algorithm works as follows: Each vertex shares its neighborhood list with each of its neighbors. Each vertex then checks if any of their neighbors overlap with the neighborhood list(s) they received. With directed edges and no cycles, the total number of such overlaps gives the number of triangles in the graph. With undirected edges, the total number of overlaps gives 3 times the number of triangles.

$$N_{triangles} = \sum_{i,j,k,i<j<k} E_{ij} \wedge E_{jk} \wedge E_{ik} \quad (3)$$

where E_{ij} denotes the presence of an (undirected) edge between vertex i and vertex j.

4. Collaborative Filtering This is a machine learning algorithm that estimates how a given user would rate an item given an incomplete set of (user, item) ratings. The matrix-centric and graph-centric views of the problem are shown in Figure 1. Given a ratings matrix $\mathbf{R}$, the goal is to find non-negative factors $\mathbf{P}$ and $\mathbf{Q}$ that are low-dimensional dense matrices. In a graph centric view, $\mathbf{R}$ corresponds to edge weights of a bipartite graph and $\mathbf{P}$ and $\mathbf{Q}$ correspond to vertex properties.

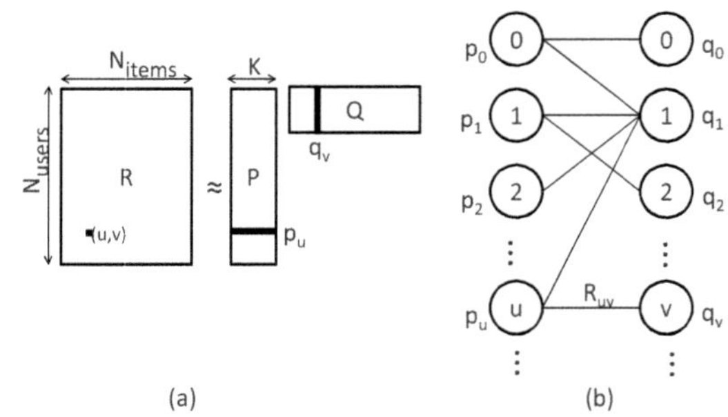

Figure 1: Collaborative filtering (a) Matrix (b) Graph

Collaborative filtering is typically accomplished using incomplete matrix factorization with regularization to avoid overfitting [19]. The problem can be expressed mathematically as follows:

$$\min_{\mathbf{p},\mathbf{q}} \sum_{(u,v)\in R} (\mathbf{R}_{uv} - \mathbf{p}_u^T \mathbf{q}_v)^2 + \lambda_p ||\mathbf{p}_u||^2 + \lambda_q ||\mathbf{q}_v||^2 \quad (4)$$

Algorithm	Graph type	Vertex property	Edge access pattern	Message size (Bytes/edge)	Vertex active?
PageRank	Directed, unweighted edges	Double (pagerank)	Streaming	Constant (8)	All iterations
Breadth First Search	Undirected, unweighted edges	Int (distance)	Random	Constant (4)	Some iterations
Collaborative Filtering	Bipartite graph; Undirected, weighted edges	Array of Doubles ($\mathbf{p_u}$ or $\mathbf{q_v}$)	Streaming	Constant ($8K$)	All iterations
Triangle Counting	Directed, unweighted edges	Long (# triangles)	Streaming	Variable (0-10^6)	Non-iterative

Table 1: Diversity in the characteristics of chosen graph algorithms.

where u & v are indices over users and items respectively, $\mathbf{R}_{uv}$ is the rating of the uth user for the vth item, $\mathbf{p}_u$&$\mathbf{q}_v$ are dense vectors of length K corresponding to each user and item, respectively. This matrix factorization is typically done iteratively using Stochastic Gradient Descent (SGD) or Gradient Descent (GD). For SGD, each iteration consists of performing the following operation for all ratings in a random order:

$$e_{uv} = \mathbf{R}_{uv} - \mathbf{p}_u^T \mathbf{q}_v \quad (5)$$

$$\mathbf{p}_u^* = \mathbf{p}_u + \gamma_t[e_{uv}\mathbf{q}_v - \lambda_p \mathbf{p}_u] \quad (6)$$

$$\mathbf{q}_v^* = \mathbf{q}_v + \gamma_t[e_{uv}\mathbf{p}_u - \lambda_q \mathbf{q}_v] \quad (7)$$

$$(\mathbf{p}_u, \mathbf{q}_v) = (\mathbf{p}_u^*, \mathbf{q}_v^*) \quad (8)$$

where γ_t is the step size for the tth iteration (typically, $\gamma_t = \gamma_0 s^t$ and s is the step size reduction factor $0 < s \leq 1$). GD performs similar operations but updates all the $\mathbf{p}_u$ and $\mathbf{q}_v$ once per iteration instead of once per rating.

We implement all these algorithms on all the graph frameworks that we use for comparison, except for those available publicly (details in Section 3).

2.1 Challenges

The chosen graph algorithms vary widely in their characteristics and correspondingly, their implementations stress different aspects of the hardware system. Table 1 shows the characteristics of the different graph algorithms. The message passing characteristics are based on that of a vertex programming implementation. There are differences from the structure and properties of the graph itself, vertex properties, access patterns, message sizes, and whether vertices are active in all iterations.

The implications of these characteristics are discussed in Section 3 for those algorithms. For example, Triangle counting and Collaborative filtering have total message sizes that are much larger than that of the graph itself, necessitating modifications for Giraph.

We now discuss the graph frameworks considered and how the algorithms map to them.

3. CHOICE OF FRAMEWORKS

The wide variety in graph algorithms that need to be implemented has necessitated the creation of a variety of graph frameworks. There is clearly no consensus on even what programming model gives the best productivity-performance trade-off. In this paper, we consider the following popular graph frameworks - GraphLab, CombBLAS, SociaLite, Galois and Giraph. In addition, we also include hand-optimized code for the algorithms. Each of these frameworks are described below.

GraphLab [21] is a graph framework that provides a sequential, shared memory abstraction for running graph algorithms written as "vertex programs". GraphLab works by letting vertices in a graph read incoming messages, update the values and send messages asynchronously. GraphLab partitions the graph in a 1-D fashion (vertex partitioning). All graph algorithms must be expressed as a program running on a vertex, which can access its own value as well as that of its edges and neighboring vertices. The runtime takes care of scheduling, messaging and synchronization.

The Combinatorial BLAS [11] is an extensible distributed-memory parallel graph library offering a small but powerful set of linear algebra primitives specifically targeting graph analytics. CombBLAS treats graphs as sparse matrices and partitions the non-zeros of the matrix (edges in the graph) across nodes. As such, this is the only framework that supports an edge-based partitioning of the graph (also referred to as 2-D partitioning in the paper). Graph computations are expressed as operations among sparse matrices and vectors using arbitrary user-defined semirings.

SociaLite [30, 31] is based on Datalog, a declarative language that can express various graph algorithms succinctly due to its better support for recursive queries compared to SQL [32]. In SociaLite, the graph and its meta data is stored in tables, and declarative rules are written to implement graph algorithms. SociaLite tables are horizontally partitioned, or sharded, to support parallelism. Users can specify how they want to shard a table at table declaration time, and the runtime partitions and distributes the tables accordingly. SociaLite only supports 1-D partitioning.

Giraph[8] is an iterative graph processing system that runs on top of Hadoop framework. Computation proceeds as a sequence of iterations, called supersteps in a bulk synchronous (BSP) fashion. Initially, every vertex is active. In each superstep each active vertex invokes a Compute method provided by the user. The Compute method: (1) receives messages sent to the vertex in the previous superstep, (2) computes using the messages, and the vertex and outgoing edge values, which may result in modifications to the values, and (3) may send messages to other vertices. The Compute method does not have direct access to the values of other vertices and their outgoing edges. Inter-vertex communication occurs by sending messages. Computation halts if all vertices have voted to halt and there are no messages in flight. Giraph partitions the vertices in a 1-D fashion (vertex partitioning).

Since graph computations can be very irregular (little locality, varying amount of work per iteration etc.), Galois [26], a framework developed for handling irregular computations can also be used for graph processing. Galois is a work-item based parallelization framework that can handle graph computations (and other irregular problems as well). It provides a rich programming model with coordinated and autonomous scheduling, and with and without application-defined priorities. Galois provides its own schedulers and scalable data structures, but does not impose a particular partitioning scheme which may be edge or vertex based depending on how the computation is expressed in the framework.

Other than the explained differences, a major differentiator of the frameworks is the communication layer between different hardware nodes. Our native implementation and CombBLAS use MPI, whereas GraphLab and SociaLite use sockets. Giraph uses a network I/O library (netty), while Galois does not have a multi node implementation as yet.

Table 2 shows a high-level comparison between the different frameworks under consideration in this paper.

3.1 Example - PageRank

We explain the differences in programming model between the frameworks with a small example and see how Pagerank can be implemented in all the frameworks.

Framework	Programming model	Multi node	Lang-usage	Graph Partitioning	Communication layer
Native	N/A	Yes	C/C++	N/A	MPI
GraphLab	Vertex	Yes	C++	1-D	Sockets
CombBLAS	Sparse matrix	Yes	C++	2-D	MPI
SociaLite	Datalog	Yes	Java	1-D	Sockets
Galois	Task-based	No	C/C++	N/A	N/A
Giraph	Vertex	Yes	Java	1-D	Netty

Table 2: High level comparison of the graph frameworks

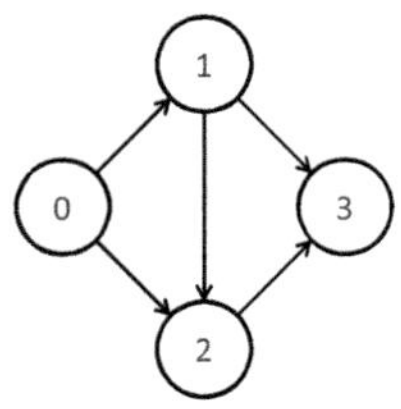

Figure 2: An example directed graph with 4 vertices

Let us begin by finding the most optimal way to execute pagerank. We refer to this hand-optimized version of the algorithm as native implementation. We observe that pagerank computation as given by equation (1) performs one multiply-add operation per edge. Representing the graph in a Compressed-Sparse Row (CSR) format [15], an efficient way of storing sparse matrix (graph) as adjacency list, allows for the edges to be stored as a single, contiguous array. This allows all the accesses to the edge array to be regular and improves the memory bandwidth utilization through hardware prefetching. Since each vertex has to access the pagerank values of all the vertices with incoming edges, we store the incoming edges in CSR format (not outgoing as would generally be the case). For the multi node setup, the graph is partitioned in a 1-D fashion i.e. partitioning the vertices (along with corresponding in-edges) among the nodes so that each node has roughly the same number of edges. Each node calculates the local updates and packages the pagerank values to be sent to the other nodes. These messages are then used to calculate the remote updates. More details on the optimizations in pagerank are given in Section 6.

Let us see how the page rank algorithm maps to vertex programming. In this model, we write a program that executes on a single vertex. This program can only access "local" data i.e. information about the vertices and edges that are directly connected to a given vertex. An example of vertex program (in pseudocode) is provided in Algorithm 1. The exact semantics of how the messages are packed and received, how much local data can be accessed, global reductions etc. vary across different implementations. GraphLab [21] and Giraph [8] are both examples of this approach to graph processing.

Algorithm 1: Vertex program for one iteration of page rank

begin
  $PR \longleftarrow r$
  for $msg \in$ incoming messages **do**
    $PR \longleftarrow PR + (1-r) * msg$
  Send $\frac{PR}{degree}$ to all outgoing edges

Another distinct approach to processing large graphs is to treat them as sparse matrices - an approach embodied in frameworks like CombBLAS[11]. The computations in a single iteration of PageRank can be expressed in matrix form as follows:

$$\mathbf{p}_{t+1} = r\mathbf{1} + (1-r)\mathbf{A}^T\tilde{\mathbf{p}}_t \quad (9)$$

where $\mathbf{A} = \begin{pmatrix} 0 & 1 & 1 & 0 \\ 0 & 0 & 1 & 1 \\ 0 & 0 & 0 & 1 \\ 0 & 0 & 0 & 0 \end{pmatrix}$ (for the graph in Figure 2), $\mathbf{p}_t$ is the vector of all the page rank values at iteration t, $\tilde{\mathbf{p}}_t(i) = \frac{\mathbf{p}_t(i)}{\mathbf{d}(i)}$, $\mathbf{d}$ is the vector of vertex out-degrees and $\mathbf{1}$ is a vector of all 1's.

In SociaLite, pagerank computation is expressed as following:

$$\textsc{Rank}[n](t+1, \$\textsc{Sum}(v)) \text{ :- } v = r$$
$$\text{:- } \textsc{InEdge}[n](s), \textsc{Rank}[s](t, v_0), \textsc{OutDeg}[s](d), v = \frac{(1-r)v_0}{d}.$$

, where the PageRank value of a vertex n at iteration $t+1$ in the rule head ($\textsc{Rank}[n](t+1, \$\textsc{Sum}(v))$) is declared as the summation of the constant term in the first rule, and the normalized PageRank values from neighbor vertices at iteration t in the second rule. The incoming edge table, InEdge, stores vertices in its first column and neighboring vertices in its second column. InEdge is declared as a tail-nested table [30], effectively implementing a CSR format used in the native implementation and CombBLAS. Another version of PageRank is implemented from the perspective of a vertex that distributes its PageRank value to its neighboring vertices, which is expressed as following:

$$\textsc{Rank}[n](t+1, \$\textsc{Sum}(v)) \text{ :- } v = r;$$
$$\text{:- } \textsc{Rank}[s](t, v_0), \textsc{OutEdge}[s](n), \textsc{OutDeg}[s](d), v = \frac{(1-r)v_0}{d}.$$

In this implementation, all join operations in the rule body are locally computed, and there is only a single data transfer for the Rank table update in the rule head. Compared to the previous version, there is one less data transfer, reducing communication overheads. In terms of lock overhead, since we cannot determine which shard of Rank will be updated, locks must be held for every update. Hence, the first version is optimized for a single multi-core machine, while the second is optimized for distributed machines.

The pagerank implementation in Galois is very similar to that of GraphLab or Giraph i.e. the parallelization is over vertices. Each work item in Galois is a vertex program for updating its pagerank. Since Galois runs on only a single node with a shared memory abstraction, each task has access to all of the program's data.

3.2 Mapping Algorithms to Frameworks

As mentioned earlier, the pagerank algorithm can be expressed in a variety of frameworks. In a similar fashion, we also describe the implementations of the other algorithms here:

Breadth First Search: Vertex programs are straight-forward to write for this algorithm. Algorithm 2 shows the pseudocode of BFS implementation. All distances are initialized to infinity (except the starting vertex, which is initialized to 0). The iterations continue until there are no updates to distances.

Algorithm 2: Vertex program for one iteration of BFS.

begin
  for $msg \in$ incoming messages **do**
    $Distance \longleftarrow \min(Distance, msg + 1)$
  Send $Distance$ to all outgoing edges

CombBLAS implementation performs matrix-vector multiplication in every iteration. For example, in order to do traverse the graph from both vertices 0 and 1 in Figure 2, we only have to do the following operation

$$\mathbf{v} = \mathbf{A}^T \mathbf{s} = \begin{pmatrix} 0 & 0 & 0 & 0 \\ 1 & 0 & 0 & 0 \\ 1 & 1 & 0 & 0 \\ 0 & 1 & 1 & 0 \end{pmatrix} \begin{pmatrix} 1 \\ 1 \\ 0 \\ 0 \end{pmatrix} = \begin{pmatrix} 0 \\ 1 \\ 2 \\ 1 \end{pmatrix} \quad (10)$$

where $\mathbf{s}$ is the vector of starting vertices. The positions of non-zeros in $\mathbf{v}$ indicates the next set of vertices to be explored.

Native implementation follows the approach explained in [28]. Optimizations performed are described in Section 6.

SociaLite's BFS is implemented as a recursive rule as following:

$$\text{BFS}(t, \$\text{MIN}(d)) \text{ :- } t = \text{SRC}, d = 0$$
$$\text{ :- } \text{BFS}(s, d_0), \text{EDGE}(s, t), d = d_0 + 1.$$

The first rule handles the source node, and the second rule recursively follows the neighboring vertices. The details of how this rule is evaluated is explained in [31].

A pseudocode of our BFS implementation in Galois is given in Algorithm 3. We used the bulk-synchronous parallel executor provided by Galois, which maintains the work lists for each level behind the scenes, and processes each level in parallel.

Algorithm 3: Galois program for Breadth First Search.

```
begin
    Graph G
    src.level = 0
    worklist[0] = src
    i ⟵ 0
    while NOT worklist[i].empty() do
        foreach ( n : worklist[i] ) in parallel do
            for dst: G.neighbors( n ) do
                if dst.level == ∞ then
                    dst.level ⟵ n.level + 1
                    worklist[i+1].add(dst)
        i ⟵ i+1
```

Triangle counting: In the native implementation, we calculate the neighborhood set of every vertex and send the set to all its neighbors. Then, every vertex computes the intersection of the received sets with their set of neighbors. The sum of all such intersections gives the number of triangles in the graph. Optimizations are possible depending on the data structure used to hold this neighborhood set (details in Section 6).

The implementation is logically straight-forward with vertex programming. GraphLab follows a similar template to that of native code. Giraph, on the other hand, has a memory problem when running on large graphs as the total size of all messages is $O(\sum_{i=1}^{V} d(i)^2)$ where $d(i)$ is the degree of vertex i. To reduce the total size of messages, the neighborhood set distribution is done in phases (Section 6.1.3).

CombBLAS implements triangle counting as the count of the non-zeros that are present in common positions in both $\mathbf{A}$ and $\mathbf{A}^2$. $\mathbf{A}^2$ gives the number of distinct paths of length 2 from vertex i to vertex j. A triangle exists if there is both an edge and a path of length 2 between two vertices. For the example in Figure 2,

$$\mathbf{A}^2 = \begin{pmatrix} 0 & 0 & 1 & 2 \\ 0 & 0 & 0 & 1 \\ 0 & 0 & 0 & 0 \\ 0 & 0 & 0 & 0 \end{pmatrix}, \text{nnz}(\mathbf{A} \cap \mathbf{A}^2) = 2.$$

Triangle counting in SociaLite is a three-way join operation:

$$\text{TRIANGLE}(0, \$\text{INC}(1)) : -\text{EDGE}(x, y), \text{EDGE}(y, z), \text{EDGE}(x, z).$$

Triangle counting is implemented in Galois (Algorithm 4) by computing set-intersection of neighbors of a node with neighbors of neighbors. We sort the adjacency list of each node by node-id, which allows computing set-intersections in linear time.

Algorithm 4: Galois program for Triangle counting.

```
begin
    Graph G
    numTriangles = 0
    foreach (Node n: G) in parallel do
        S1 = { m in G.neighbors(n) | m > n }
        for (m in S1) do
            S2 = { p in G.neighbors(m) | p > m }
            numTriangles ⟵ numTriangles + |S1 ∩ S2|
```

Collaborative Filtering: Native implementation follows the Stochastic Gradient Descent (SGD) parallelization described in [16]. We process edges in a random order and update data corresponding to both vertices ($\mathbf{p}$ and $\mathbf{q}$ in equations (5), (6), and (7)). Partitioning is done so that all updates are local within a single iteration and data sharing happens between iterations. For n processors, the ratings matrix is divided into n^2 2-D chunks. Each iteration involves n sub-steps where a subset of the updates (on n chunks) are applied [16]. SGD is however, hard if not impossible to implement in most of the other frameworks because of the need for data constancy within iterations. Any data written may not be globally visible right away (especially if the writes are to a remote vertex). Hence, we fall back to Gradient Descent, which does away with processing edges in a random order and requires only an aggregate update from all of the edges. In short, instead of updating edges one at a time, we perform the following computation:

$$\mathbf{p}_u^* = \mathbf{p}_u + \gamma_t \sum_{v|(u,v)\in E} [\mathbf{R}_{uv}\mathbf{q}_v - (\mathbf{p}_u^T\mathbf{q}_v)\mathbf{q}_v - \lambda_p \mathbf{p}_u] \quad (11)$$

$$\mathbf{q}_v^* = \mathbf{q}_v + \gamma_t \sum_{u|(u,v)\in E} [\mathbf{R}_{uv}\mathbf{p}_u - (\mathbf{p}_u^T\mathbf{q}_v)\mathbf{p}_u - \lambda_q \mathbf{q}_v] \quad (12)$$

In CombBLAS, a single GD iteration consists of K matrix-vector multiplications where K is the size of the hidden dimension (length of $\mathbf{p}$ or $\mathbf{q}$). The matrix-vector multiplications arise from the terms $\mathbf{R}_{uv}\mathbf{p}_u$ and $\mathbf{R}_{uv}\mathbf{q}_v$. Other operations can be written as data parallel operations on dense vectors. Since CombBLAS does not allow matrices with dimension $<$ number of processors, multiplication with the $\mathbf{p}$ matrix has to be performed in K steps instead of as a single sparse-matrix-dense-matrix multiplication.

With vertex programming, GD involves aggregating information from all neighbors and sending the updated vector at the end of the iteration. The total size of all the messages sent in a single iteration is $O(KE)$ which is quite large for Giraph. Hence, message passing happens in phases so that only $1/s$ vertices have to send messages in a given superstep. Thus, s supersteps correspond to a single gradient descent iteration.

SociaLite stores the length-K vectors for users and items in separate tables. These tables are joined together with the rating table to compute errors and to update user and item vectors. Since this join operation incurs large communication, it is helpful to transfer the tables to target machines in the beginning of each iteration, so that the rest of the computations do not involve any communication.

Galois is the only framework that implements SGD (not just GD) in a fashion similar to that of the native implementation. This is possible because of 2 reasons (1) since partitioning is flexible with Galois, we can apply the n^2 uniform 2D chunk partitioning (2) since Galois is running only on a single node, it can maintain globally consistent state after any update without much performance degradation. Each work-item in Galois performs the SGD update on a single edge (u, v) i.e. it updates both $\mathbf{p}_u$ and $\mathbf{q}_v$.

We note that SGD has much better convergence characteristics than Gradient Descent. For the Netflix dataset, given a fixed convergence criterion, SGD converges in about 40x fewer iterations than GD. Of course, like all machine learning algorithms, both SGD and GD have parameters to choose that affect convergence (learning rate, step size reduction and so forth). We did do a coarse sweep over these parameters to obtain best convergence.

4. EXPERIMENTAL SETUP

We now describe our experimental setup with details about our frameworks, data sets used and our experimental platform.

4.1 Choice of Datasets

We use a mix of both real-world datasets and data generators for synthetic data in our experiments. Both classes of datasets ideally follow a power law (Zipf law) distribution. For the pagerank and triangle counting problems we use directed graphs, whereas for BFS and Collaborating Filtering we use undirected graphs. Collaborative Filtering requires edge-weighted, bipartite graphs that represents the ratings matrix.

4.1.1 Real world Datasets

Dataset	# Vertices	# Edges	Brief Description
Facebook [34]	2,937,612	41,919,708	Facebook user interaction graph
Wikipedia [14]	3,566,908	84,751,827	Wikipedia Link graph
LiveJournal [14]	4,847,571	85,702,475	LiveJournal follower graph
Netflix [9]	480,189 users 17,770 movies	99,072,112 ratings	Netflix Prize
Twitter [20]	61,578,415	1,468,365,182	Twitter follower graph
Yahoo Music [7]	1,000,990 users 624,961 items	252,800,275 ratings	Yahoo! KDDCup 2011 music ratings
Synthetic Graph500 [23]	536,870,912	8,589,926,431	Described in Section 4
Synthetic Collaborative Filtering	63,367,472 users 1,342,176 items	16,742,847,256 ratings	Described in Section 4

Table 3: Real World and largest synthetic datasets

Table 3 provides details on the real-world datasets we used. The Facebook, Wikipedia, Livejournal and Twitter graphs were used to run Pagerank, BFS and Triangle Counting, while the Netflix and Yahoo Music datasets were used to run Collaborative Filtering.

The major issue with the real world datasets is primarily their small size. While these datasets are useful for algorithmic exploration, they are not really scalable to multiple nodes. In particular, the Facebook, Wikipedia, Livejournal and Netflix datasets were small enough to fit on a single machine. We do have two large real-world datasets - Twitter and Yahoo music. These were run on 4 nodes except for Triangle Counting on Twitter, which required 16 nodes to complete in a reasonable amount of time. Even though the twitter graph itself can fit in fewer nodes, as mentioned in Section 3, the total message size is much larger than the graph and needs more resources. To provide a sense of the size of these datasets, the largest dataset, Twitter, is just over 30 GB in size. Although we do have a few large examples, developing data generators that can produce synthetic data that is representative of real world workloads is essential to study scalability.

4.1.2 Synthetic Data Generation

We derive our synthetic data generators from Graph500 RMAT data generators [23]. We generate data to scale the graphs up to 64 nodes. To give a sense on size of the synthetic graphs, a large scale 64 node run for Pagerank and BFS processes over 8 Billion edges. We now describe how we use the Graph500 generator to generate both directed graphs and ratings matrices for our applications.

We use the default RMAT parameters ($A = 0.57$, $B = C = 0.19$) used for Graph500 to generate undirected graphs. The RMAT generator only generates a list of edges (with possible duplicates). For Pagerank, we assign a direction to all the edges generated. For BFS, depending on the framework used we either provide it undirected edges or provide 2 edges in both directions for each generated edge. For triangle counting, we use slightly different RMAT parameters ($A = 0.45$, $B = C = 0.15$) to reduce the number of triangles in the graph. We then assign a direction to edges going from the vertex with smaller id to one with larger id to avoid cycles. This is done to make the implementations efficient on all frameworks.

In order to generate large rating matrices, we wrote a rating matrix generator that follows the power-law distribution of the Netflix data set. In order to achieve this, we start with graphs generated by the Graph500 graph generator. Through experimentation, we found that RMAT parameters of $A = 0.40$ and $B = C = 0.22$ generates degree distributions whose tail is reasonably close to that of the Netflix dataset. Finally, we post-processed the graphs to remove all vertices with degree < 5 from the graph. This yielded graphs that closely follow the degree distributions of the Netflix data set. In order to convert these Graph500 graphs into bipartite graphs of $N_{users} \times N_{movies}$ (items are named movies in case of Netflix data), we first chunk the columns of the Graph500 matrix into chunks of size N_{movies}. We then "fold" the matrix by performing a logical "or" of these chunks.

Given that the power law distribution is what differentiates a real-world dataset, we believe our data generator is much more representative of real collaborative filtering workloads as opposed to other data generators such as that by [16]. [16] generates data by sampling uniformly matching the expected number of non-zeros overall but not as a power law distribution.

For our experiments, we generate synthetic data of up to 16 Billion ratings for 64 million users × 800K movies. For scaling, we generate about 256 million ratings per node, or 16 Billion ratings for 64 nodes.

4.2 Framework versions

We used GraphLab v2.2 [3] for this comparison. We used the CombBLAS v1.3 code from [1]. We obtained the SociaLite code with additional optimizations over the results in [30] from the authors. For Giraph, we used release 1.1.0 from [8]. Finally, we obtained Galois v 2.2.0 from [2].

We implemented all the algorithms on these frameworks wherever a public version did not exist.

4.3 Experimental Platform

We run the benchmarks[1] on an Intel® Xeon®[2] CPU E5-2697 based system. Each node has 64 GB of DRAM, and has 24 cores supporting 2-way Simultaneous Multi-Threading each running at 2.7 GHz. The nodes are connected with an Mellanox Infiniband

[1] Software and workloads used in performance tests may have been optimized for performance only on Intel microprocessors. Performance tests, such as SYSmark and MobileMark, are measured using specific computer systems, components, software, operations and functions. Any change to any of those factors may cause the results to vary. You should consult other information and performance tests to assist you in fully evaluating your contemplated purchases, including the performance of that product when combined with other products. For more information go to http://www.intel.com/performance

[2] Intel, Xeon, and Intel Xeon Phi are trademarks of Intel Corporation in the U.S. and/or other countries.

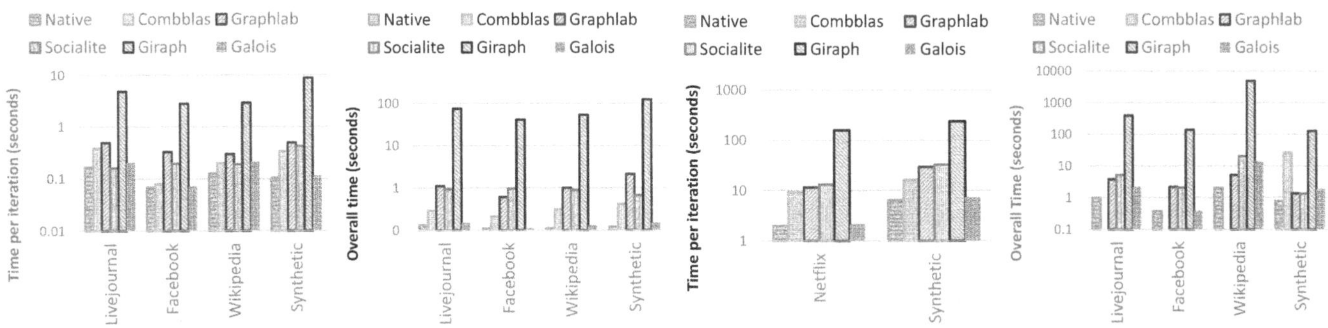

(a) PageRank (b) Breadth-First Search (c) Collaborative Filtering (d) Triangle counting

Figure 3: Performance results for different algorithms on real-world and synthetic graphs that are small enough to run on a single node. The y-axis represents runtime (in log-scale), therefore lower numbers are better.

FDR interconnect. The cluster runs on the Red Hat Enterprise Linux Server OS release 6.4. We use a mix of OpenMP directives to parallelize within the node and MPI code to parallelize across nodes in native code. We use the Intel® C++ Composer XE 2013 SP1 Compiler[3] and the Intel® MPI library to compile the code. GraphLab uses a similar combination of OpenMP and MPI for best performance. CombBLAS runs best as a pure MPI program. We use multiple MPI processes per node to take advantage of the multiple cores within the node. Moreover, CombBLAS requires the total number of processes to be a square (due to their 2D partitioning approach). Hence we use 36 MPI processes per node to run on the 48 hardware threads; and we further run on a square number of nodes (1, 2, 4, 9, 16, 36 and 64 nodes). SociaLite uses Java threads and processes for parallelism. Giraph uses the Hadoop framework for parallelism (we run 4 workers per node). Finally, Galois is a single node framework and uses OpenMP for parallelism.

5. RESULTS

5.1 Native implementation bottlenecks

Since different graph frameworks have their programming models with different implementation trade-offs, it is hard to directly compare these frameworks with respect to each other without a clear reference point. As explained in Section 1, we provide a well-optimized native implementation of these algorithms for both single and multi node systems. Since the native code is optimized, it is easy to see which aspects of the system are stressed by a particular algorithm. Table 4 provides data on the achieved limits of the native implementations on a single node and 4 nodes system.

Algorithm	Single Node		4 Nodes	
	H/W limitation	Efficiency	H/W limitation	Efficiency
PageRank	Memory BW	78 GBps (92%)	Network BW	2.3 GBps (42%)
BFS	Memory BW	64 GBps (74%)	Memory BW	54 GBps (63%)
Coll. Filtering	Memory BW	47 GBps (54%)	Memory BW	35 GBps (41%)
Triangle Count.	Memory BW	45 GBps (52%)	Network BW	2.2 GBps (40%)

Table 4: Efficiency achieved by native implementations of different algorithms on single and 4 nodes.

We find that on both single and multi node implementations, the algorithm performance is dependent on either memory or network bandwidth. The efficiencies are generally within 2-2.5X off the ideal results. Given the diversity of bottlenecks within the 4 algorithms, and also between single and multiple node implementations, we expect that it would be difficult for any one framework to excel at all scales in terms performance and productivity.

5.2 Single node results

We now show the results of running the Pagerank, BFS, Collaborative Filtering and Triangle Counting algorithms on the CombBLAS, GraphLab, SociaLite, Giraph and Galois frameworks.

In the following, we only compare time taken per iteration on various frameworks for Collaborative Filtering and Pagerank. As described in Section 3, the native code for Collaborative Filtering implements Stochastic Gradient Descent which converges much faster than the Gradient Descent implementation in other frameworks. However, we do not see much difference in performance per iteration between Stochastic Gradient Descent and Gradient Descent in native code. Hence we compare time/iteration here to separate out the fact that the frameworks are not expressive enough to express SGD from other potential performance differences. Similarly, some Pagerank implementations differ in whether early convergence is detected for the algorithm, and hence we report time per iteration to normalize for this.

Algorithm	CombBLAS	GraphLab	SociaLite	Giraph	Galois
PageRank	1.9	3.6	2.0	39.0	1.2
BFS	2.5	9.3	7.3	567.8	1.1
Coll. Filtering	3.5	5.1	5.8	54.4	1.1
Triangle Count.	33.9	3.2	4.7	484.3	2.5

Table 5: Summary of performance differences for single node benchmarks on different frameworks for our applications. Each entry is a slowdown factor from native code, hence lower numbers indicate better performance.

Figures 3(a), 3(b) and 3(d) show the results of running Pagerank, BFS, and Triangle Counting respectively on the real-world Livejournal, Facebook and Wikipedia datasets described in Section 4.1 on our frameworks. We also show the results of running a synthetic scale-free RMAT graph (obtained using the Graph500 data generator). Figure 3(c) shows the performance of our frameworks on the Netflix [9] dataset, as well as synthetically generated collaborative filtering dataset. For convenience, we also present the geometric mean of this data across datasets in Table 5. This table shows the slowdowns of each framework w.r.t. native code.

We see the following key inferences: (1) Native code, as expected, delivers best performance as it is optimized for the underlying architecture. (2) Galois performs better than other frameworks,

[3] Intel's compilers may or may not optimize to the same degree for non-Intel microprocessors for optimizations that are not unique to Intel microprocessors. These optimizations include SSE2, SSE3, and SSE3 instruction sets and other optimizations. Intel does not guarantee the availability, functionality, or effectiveness of any optimization on microprocessors not manufactured by Intel. Microprocessor-dependent optimizations in this product are intended for use with Intel microprocessors. Certain optimizations not specific to Intel micro-architecture are reserved for Intel microprocessors. Please refer to the applicable product User and Reference Guides for more information regarding the specific instruction sets covered by this notice. Notice revision #20110804

and is close to native performance (geometric mean of 1.1-1.2X for pagerank, BFS and collaborative filtering, and 2.5X for triangle counting). (3) Giraph, on the other hand, is 2-3 orders of magnitude slower than native code (4) CombBLAS and GraphLab perform well on average. CombBLAS is very good for all algorithms except for Triangle Counting, where it ran out of memory for real-world inputs while computing the $\mathbf{A}^2$ matrix product. This is an expressibility problem in CombBLAS. GraphLab is 3-9X off from native code, but performs reasonably consistently across algorithms. (5) SociaLite performance is typically comparable to GraphLab (sometimes slightly better and sometimes slightly worse).

Finally, note that the trends on the synthetic dataset are in line with real-world data, showing that our synthetic generators are effective in modeling real-world data.

5.3 Multi node results

We first show our scaling results of our frameworks on multiple nodes. A major reason for using multiple nodes to process graph data is to store the data in memory across the nodes. Hence a common use case is *weak-scaling*, where the data per node is kept constant (and hence total data set size increases with number of nodes). If we obtain perfect performance scaling, then the runtime should be constant as we increase node count and data set size. In this study, we include CombBLAS, GraphLab, SociaLite and Giraph frameworks. Galois is currently only a single node framework and we hence do not include results here.

Figures 4(a), 4(b), 4(c) and 4(d) show the results of multi node runs on synthetically generated data sets for our benchmarks. The data sizes are chosen so that all frameworks could complete without running out of memory. Figure 5 shows the corresponding performance results for larger real-world graphs. We run each algorithm using one large dataset – we use the Twitter dataset [20] for Pagerank, BFS and Triangle Counting and the Yahoo Music KDDCup dataset 2011 dataset for Collaborative Filtering [7].

Algorithm	CombBLAS	GraphLab	SociaLite	Giraph
PageRank	2.5	12.1	7.9	74.4
BFS	7.1	29.5	18.9	494.3
Coll. Filtering	3.5	7.1	7.0	87.9
Triangle Count.	13.1	3.6	1.5	54.4

Table 6: Summary of performance differences for multi node benchmarks on different frameworks. Each entry is a slowdown factor from native code, hence lower numbers indicate better performance.

As a convenient summary of performance, Table 6 shows the geometric mean of the performance differences between our frameworks combining real-world and synthetic datasets at different scales. The table shows performance slowdowns of different frameworks for specific algorithms compared to the native code for that algorithm – hence lower numbers are better.

We note the following trends in our multi-node results. (1) There is wide variability in our multi node results; as an example, native code performs anywhere between 2X to more than 560X better than other frameworks on multi node runs (still up to 30X discounting Giraph runtimes). (2) Giraph performs worse by far than other frameworks and is frequently 2-3 orders magnitude off from native performance. (3) CombBLAS is competitive for Pagerank (geomean of 2.5X native performance), BFS (7.1X off native) and Collaborative Filtering (3.5X off native). However, it performs poorly on Triangle Counting due to extra computations performed as a result of framework expressibility issues. CombBLAS also runs out of memory for the Twitter data set and hence this data point is not plotted. (4) GraphLab performs well for Triangle Counting, due to data structure optimizations performed for this case, namely the

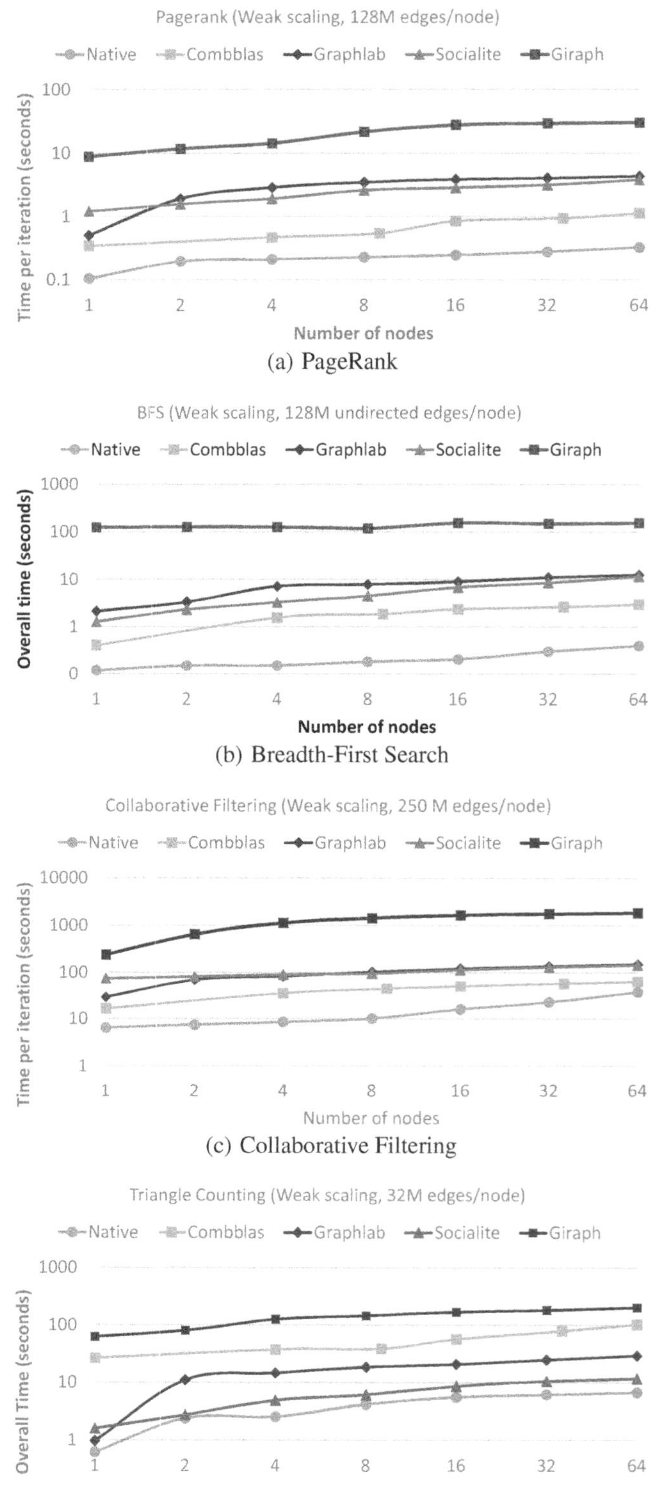

(a) PageRank

(b) Breadth-First Search

(c) Collaborative Filtering

(d) Triangle Counting

Figure 4: Performance results for different algorithms on large scale synthetic graphs. The y-axis represents runtime in log-scale. We perform weak-scaling, where the amount of graph data per node is kept constant, (a) 128 M edges/node for pagerank, (b) 128 M edges/node for BFS, (c) 256M ratings/node for SGD, and (d) 32M edges/node for triangle counting. Horizontal lines represent perfect scaling.

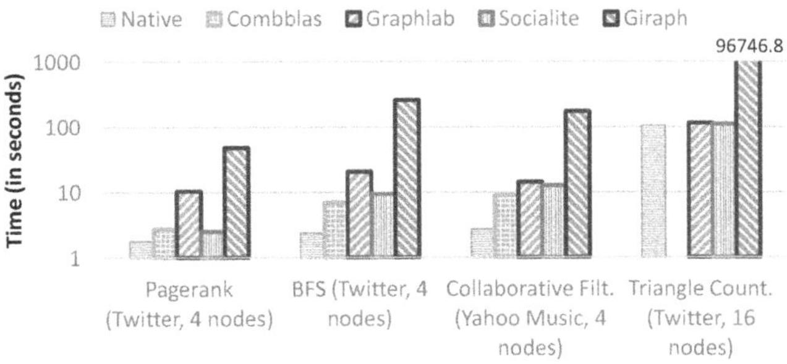

Figure 5: Performance results for large real world graphs run on multiple nodes. We show the results of running (in log-scale) Pagerank, BFS and Triangle Counting on a subset of Twitter [20], and Collaborative Filtering on the Yahoo Music KDDCup dataset [7]

cuckoo hash data structure that allows for a fast union of neighbor lists, which is the primary operation in the algorithm. (5) GraphLab performance drops off significantly for multi node runs (especially for Pagerank) due to network bottlenecks. (6) SociaLite performance is typically between GraphLab and CombBLAS, except for Triangle Counting, where it performs best among our frameworks. It also shows more stable performance for different scales than GraphLab. (7) Native performance is relatively stable on various benchmarks. The performance noticeably drops for Collaborative Filtering where network traffic increases with number of nodes, and the algorithm gradually becomes more network limited. (8) Finally, the trends we see in real-world data are broadly similar to those for synthetic data. In particular, CombBLAS performs best among non-native frameworks for three of the four algorithms - Pagerank, BFS and Collaborative Filtering, while SociaLite performs best for Triangle Counting.

Given the various performance issues we see in the frameworks, we next delve deeper into other metrics beside runtime to gain more insights into the frameworks.

5.4 Framework Analysis

We did further investigation of CPU utilization, memory footprint and network traffic to narrow down the reasons for the observed performance trends. We use the sar/sysstat monitoring tools [4] available in Linux to measure these. These results are summarized in Figure 6. We briefly describe our key findings in this section, and defer a detailed reasoning on what can be done to address these problems to Section 6.

Memory footprint: First, note that our dataset sizes chosen are such that the memory footprint of one or more frameworks (usually Giraph) is more than 50% of total memory – hence we cannot increase dataset sizes per node. The memory footprint is usually not due to just the input graph size, but due to the large intermediate data structures, e.g. message buffers that need to be kept. It is possible to avoid buffering entire messages at once (e.g. GraphLab) and hence improve this behavior of Giraph as discussed in Section 6. Large memory footprints are also seen in CombBLAS (Triangle Counting), where the problem is framework expressibility.

CPU utilization: The CPU utilization of various frameworks is high when it is not I/O or network limited. Giraph has especially low CPU utilization across the board. This is because memory limitations restrict the number of workers that can be assigned to a single node to 4 (even though the number of cores per node is 24). Each worker requires more memory and we cannot add more workers within our memory limit. This limits the utilization to $4/24 \sim 16\%$. Our native code is network limited for Triangle Counting (unlike CombBLAS and GraphLab which are memory bandwidth bound) and has relatively low CPU utilization. Pagerank is limited by network traffic for all the frameworks as well.

Peak Network Transfer Rate: The peak network transfer rate when running different algorithms is relatively stable for a given framework, and is dependent mostly on the communication layer used. Note that Giraph has the lowest peak traffic rate of less than 0.5 GigaBytes per second (GBps), and CombBLAS and Native code the highest of over 5 GBps. Although SociaLite and GraphLab use similar communication layers, SociaLite achieves about twice the peak rate of GraphLab (discussion in Section 6). In fact, the currently available SociaLite code (from the authors) does indeed have low transfer rates, and we were able to improve this behavior substantially using network traffic analysis, which is an important contribution of this paper.

Data volumes: The amount of data transferred varies considerably based on algorithm (as shown in Figure 6), as well as platform (depending on compression schemes and data structures used). We show the latter impact in Section 6.

These measurements are very useful for predicting the slowdowns we see with graph frameworks compared to native implementation. For example, we look at only the measured network parameters for pagerank to estimate performance differences (network bytes sent/peak network bandwidth) from Figure 6. We can estimate that the frameworks would be 1.75, 9.8, 5.6, 32.7$\times$ slower than native code (assuming all network transfers happen at the peak measured rate). Even this rough estimation is within a factor of 2.5 of observed performance differences (Table 6). Similar analysis can be done for other algorithms as well. Bandwidth bound code will need to estimate the number of reads/writes and scale it with the memory footprint.

In the next section, we will discuss optimizations that we perform in native code, show examples of how such optimizations are also useful in other frameworks and describe our key recommendations for other frameworks as well.

6. DISCUSSION

In this section, we discuss the various optimization techniques used to improve the performance of our native code. We then present recommendations on how the frameworks can be optimized to achieve native code level performance.

6.1 Native implementations

6.1.1 Key optimization techniques

The key features for performance and scalability that our native code uses are listed below. Note that not all techniques have been applied or are applicable to every algorithm. However, we maximize the use of these techniques to obtain best possible native code.

Data structures: Careful selection of data structure can benefit performance significantly. For example, algorithms like BFS and Triangle Counting can take advantage of bit-vectors instead of other data structures for constant time lookups while minimizing cache misses. In our native BFS and Triangle Counting code, this results in a benefit of slightly over 2X. GraphLab keeps a cuckoo-hash data structure in Triangle Counting for the same reason, resulting an efficient code that runs at only 2-3X off native performance.

Data Compression: In many cases, the data communicated among nodes is the id's of destination vertices of the edges traversed. Such data has been observed to be compressible using techniques like bit-vectors and delta coding [28]. For BFS and Pagerank, this results in a net benefit of about 3.2 and 2.2X respectively (and a corresponding reduction of bytes transferred in Figure 6). GraphLab and CombBLAS perform a limited form of compression that takes

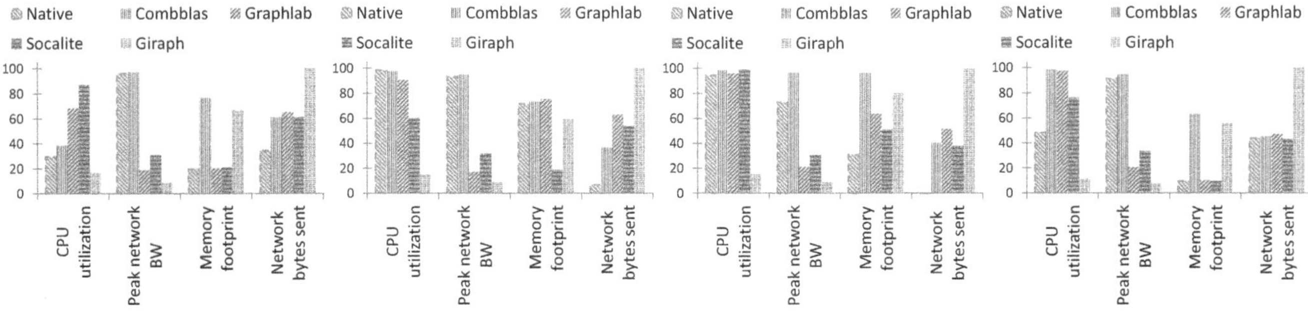

(a) PageRank (b) Breadth-First Search (c) Collaborative Filtering (d) Triangle Counting

Figure 6: Performance metrics including CPU utilization, peak achieved network bandwidth, memory footprint and bytes sent over the network for a 4-node run of our benchmarks. Metrics are normalized so that a value of 100 on the y-axis corresponds to (1) 100% CPU utilization, (2) 5.5 GB/s/node peak network BW (network limit) (3) 64 GB of memory/node (memory capacity) and (4) bytes sent by Giraph/node for each algorithm (1.4 GB/node for pagerank, 0.73 GB/node for BFS, 37.4 GB/node for Collaborative Filtering and 13.0 GB/node for Triangle Counting). Higher numbers are better for CPU utilization and peak network traffic while lower numbers are better for memory footprint and network bytes sent.

advantage of local reductions to avoid repeated communication of the same vertex data to different target vertices in the same node.

Overlap of Computation and Communication: Overlap of computation and communication is possible for many applications where an entire message need not be received before computation can start on the portion of the message that has been received. This allows for hiding the latency of communication with useful computation, and has been shown to improve performance of various optimized implementations [28]. Native code for BFS, pagerank and Triangle Counting all benefit between 1.2-2X. Apart from latency hiding, overlapping communication and computation allows for blocking of a very large message into multiple smaller ones, leading to lower memory footprint for buffer storage. This optimization specifically helps Triangle Counting, and both GraphLab and native codes perform this, leading to low memory footprints.

Message passing mechanisms: Using the right underlying message passing mechanisms can boost performance significantly. The native code uses MPI message passing [6] to drive the underlying fabric (FDR InfiniBand network in our case) for high bandwidth and low latency communication among the nodes. Although it is possible to implement message passing using other techniques such as TCP sockets using IP over IB [33], this suffers from between 2.5-3X lower bandwidth than MPI code, as observed in case of GraphLab. However, if it not possible to use MPI, we observe that multiple sockets between a pair of nodes regains up to 2X of this performance, as in SociaLite.

Partitioning schemes: Most frameworks running on multiple nodes support partitioning the graph among the nodes in such a way that nodes either own a subset of vertices (Giraph, SociaLite) or in a 2D fashion where they store a subset of edges (CombBLAS). GraphLab performs a more advanced partitioning scheme where some nodes with large degree are duplicated in multiple nodes to avoid problems of load imbalance during computation. In line with observations in recent research [25], 2D partitioning as in CombBLAS or advanced 1D partitioning such as GraphLab gives better load balancing, leading to better performance and scalability.

6.1.2 *Impact of the optimization techniques*

We now look at each algorithm and discuss the optimizations having high impact on each (we do not describe all optimizations due to space limits). Figure 7 shows the impact of various performance optimizations on native code for Pagerank and BFS. The main optimizations come from software prefetch instructions that help hide the long latency of irregular memory accesses and mes-

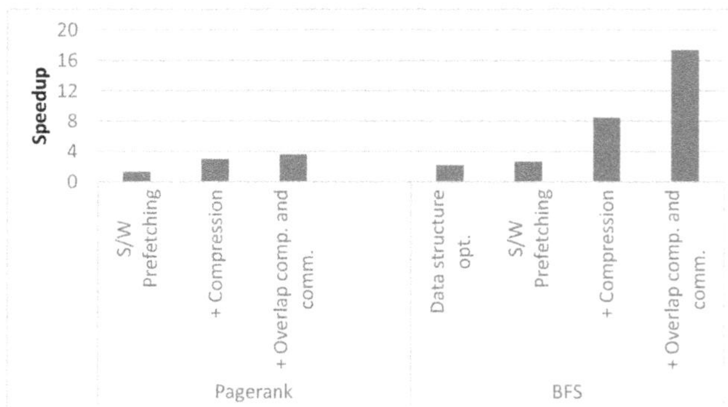

Figure 7: Effect of optimizations performed on native implementations of Pagerank and BFS.

sage optimizations (compressing message containing edges to be sent to other nodes and overlapping computation with communication). For BFS, additional optimization was to use bit-vectors (a data structure optimization) to compactly maintain the list of already visited vertices [12, 28]. For Triangle counting, the same data structure optimization (bit vectors), for quick constant time lookups to identify common neighbors of different vertices, gave a speedup of around 2.2X.

For Collaborative filtering, the key optimizations revolve around efficient parallelization of Stochastic Gradient Descent. We adopt the diagonal parallelization technique used in Gemulla et al. [16] to parallelize SGD both within and across nodes without using locks.

6.1.3 *Testcase: Improving SociaLite and Giraph*

We select SociaLite and Giraph to demonstrate the possible performance improvement of the frameworks using the analysis in Section 5.4 and depth of understanding of the optimization techniques.

SociaLite: We first observed that the code corresponding to published SociaLite results (obtained from the authors) exhibited poor peak network performance of about 0.5 GBps (like Giraph does today) since it uses sockets for communication. Although changing SociaLite to use MPI would have been ideal, it is much difficult due to language and other issues. However, using multiple sockets to communicate between two workers allows for much higher peak bandwidths (of close to 2 GBps). This, along with minor optimizations such as merging communication data for batch processing, and using custom memory allocators to minimize garbage collection time (these had minor impacts on performance), allowed SociaLite results to improve by 1.6-2.4X for network limited algorithms (Pagerank and Triangle Counting). Table 7 presents the old and new SociaLite performance for a 4-node setup for these benchmarks. The results in this paper correspond to the optimized version of SociaLite.

Algorithm	Time Before	Time After	Speedup
PageRank	4.6	1.9	2.4
Triangle Counting	7.6	4.9	1.6

Table 7: Summary of performance speedups for SociaLite on performing network optimizations. Results are for 4 nodes in seconds.

Giraph: One major problem in Giraph is that it tries to buffer all outgoing messages in memory before sending any messages (due to its bulk synchronous model). This leads to high memory consumption especially for Triangle Counting which can run out of memory for the data set sizes we use in this work. The native code deals with this problem by breaking up this large message into multiple smaller messages and using computation-communication overlap as described previously. We perform a conceptually similar optimization at the Giraph code level by breaking up each superstep (iteration) into 100 smaller supersteps, and processing 1% of all vertices at each smaller superstep. This results in much smaller memory footprint (since only 1% messages are created at any time), at the cost of finer grained synchronization. It was only using this optimization that we were able to run Triangle Counting to run on Giraph. A similar optimization was also used in Collaborative Filtering to reduce memory footprint.

6.2 Roadmap for framework improvements

Based on our experience in optimizing native code as well as some frameworks as described in the previous section, we present recommendations for bridging the performance gap of all the frameworks w.r.t. native code. It is however, to be noted that some performance differences between frameworks come from the programming abstractions themselves, and we note these wherever possible.

CombBLAS: CombBLAS incorporates many of our optimizations, and is hence one of the best performing frameworks. For Pagerank and Collaborative Filtering, it is already within $4\times$ of native performance. CombBLAS needs to use data structures such as bitvectors for compression in order to improve BFS performance. Triangle counting performance is limited by CombBLAS' programming abstraction and techniques to perform **inter-operation optimization** (combine $\mathbf{A}^2$ computation with intersection with $\mathbf{A}$, thereby also achieving overlap of computation and communication) can make it more efficient.

GraphLab: GraphLab is mainly limited by network bandwidth. It achieves only 20-25% of what the network hardware provides. We believe this $4 - 5\times$ gap can be minimized by incorporating MPI, or at least by using multiple sockets between pairs of nodes as in SociaLite. Additionally, data compression, prefetching and overlapping computation and communication can also help performance. Incorporating these changes should allow GraphLab to be within $5\times$ of native performance.

Giraph: Giraph does not have most of our optimizations, and hence performs worst among all frameworks. The most serious impediment to performance is poor network utilization ($< 10\%$). Boosting network bandwidth by 10x should make Giraph very competitive with other frameworks. Techniques like data compression (bitvectors) and overlapping computation and communication should also help. Performance will also improve if we can run more workers per node, thereby improving CPU utilization. This would require addressing the high memory consumption of each worker. Techniques to reduce message buffer sizes (e.g. avoiding duplicated communication across nodes if multiple targets are present in the same node) are necessary to achieve this.

SociaLite: SociaLite performs best among all frameworks for multi-node triangle counting (within $2\times$ of native) but its performance for other algorithms is mostly limited by network bandwidth (though it achieves better network BW than Giraph and GraphLab). Even after improvements, the network BW is still about $3 - 4\times$ lower than hardware peak. Fixing this along with the use of data compression (for BFS) will help SociaLite to achieve performance within $5\times$ of native performance.

Galois: The Galois framework, although limited to single-node, does implement optimizations such as prefetching, and as such is one of the best performing single-node frameworks.

Our observations above and in Section 5 should help the end users of the frameworks make informed choices about which frameworks to use. Our analysis should also help framework developers with guidance on what factors limit their performance and are important to optimize for.

7. RELATED WORK

The list of graph frameworks developed in recent years to tackle large scale problems is too long to be listed. Some distributed graph frameworks that we have not studied in this paper include GPS [27], GraphX [35], etc. In addition to these, others have implemented graph workloads on generic distributed frameworks such as Hadoop, YARN, Stratosphere etc. [17]. Our choice was motivated mainly by a need to explore a variety of programming models and not just different implementations of the same programming model. Most common graph programming models are based on vertex-programming and there have been other efforts comparing the differences between various runtime implementations of that model [17, 24]. We briefly distinguish our contributions from these.

Graph Partitioning System (GPS) [27] uses a vertex programming model with Long Adjacency List Partitioning (LALP) i.e. vertex partitioning except for the large degree vertices which are split among multiple nodes. [27] showed that GPS with LALP achieves a 12X performance improvement compared to Giraph, putting it at a performance level comparable to that of the frameworks studied (but much slower than native code).

GraphX [35] is a graph framework built on top of Spark [36] and uses vertex programming. [35] showed that GraphX is about 7X slower than GraphLab for pagerank (including file read). This would put GraphX at the slower end of the spectrum of frameworks considered in this paper.

In addition to above mentioned graph frameworks, there have also been other graph framework comparison efforts in literature. [17] looks at a number of graph algorithms and frameworks. It is quite limited in the types of graph frameworks that are considered (all frameworks are either generic, non-graph specific ones or vertex programming based). While our goal is not to produce a graph benchmark, we do share algorithms with [17] including Pagerank and BFS. Also, we include a hand-optimized native implementation (close to hardware limits) which puts the runtime differences between other frameworks in better perspective, something no other graph comparison effort has done to the best of our knowledge.

[13] shows Pagerank running on a large cluster at about 20 million edges/sec/node with Giraph. In contrast, our Giraph implementation achieves about 9 million edges/sec/node and the difference can be attributed to precision (we use double precision), memory size (they are able to fit much larger graphs in a single node) and improved CPU utilization achieved with more memory and more

workers per node. In contrast, our native implementation processes around 640 million edges/sec/node.

[24] looks at a variety of vertex programming frameworks but at a lower level (Bulk synchronous vs autonomous, scheduling policies etc.). Their work is useful in order to understand and improve the implementations of vertex programming models, whereas our work has different goals. We consider a wider variety of frameworks and our work is more interested in answering the more general productivity-vs-performance question for graph analytics.

In short, our goal is not to come up with a new graph processing benchmark or propose a new graph framework, but to analyze existing approaches better to find out where they fall short especially when used for more general machine learning problems on graphs (such as collaborative filtering) with a native, hand-optimized implementation as a reference point.

8. CONCLUSION

In this paper, we aim at reducing the performance gap between optimized hand-coded implementations and popular graph frameworks for a set of graph algorithms. To this end, we first developed native implementations that are only limited by the hardware and showed that there is a 2-30X performance gap between native code and most frameworks (up to 560X on Giraph). Using a set of performance metrics, we analyzed the behavior of various frameworks and the causes of the performance gap between native and framework code. We use our understanding of optimization techniques from native code and our analysis to propose a set of recommended changes for each framework to bridge the Ninja gap. These recommendations will enable different frameworks to be made competitive with respect to performance, thus simplifying the choice of framework for the end user.

9. REFERENCES

[1] Combinatorial Blas v 1.3. `http://gauss.cs.ucsb.edu/~aydin/CombBLAS/html/`.

[2] Galois v 2.2.0. `http://iss.ices.utexas.edu/?p=projects/galois/download`.

[3] Graphlab v 2.2. `http://graphlab.org`.

[4] sar Manual Page. `http://pagesperso-orange.fr/sebastien.godard/man_sar.html`.

[5] The Linpack Benchmark. `http://www.top500.org/project/linpack/`.

[6] The Message Passing Interface (MPI) standard. `http://www.mcs.anl.gov/research/projects/mpi/`.

[7] Yahoo! - Movie, Music, and Images Ratings Data Sets. http://webscope.sandbox.yahoo.com/catalog.php?datatype=r.

[8] Apache giraph. *http://giraph.apache.org/*, 2013.

[9] J. Bennett and S. Lanning. The Netflix Prize. In *KDD Cup and Workshop at ACM SIGKDD*, 2007.

[10] N. Bronson, Z. Amsden, et al. Tao: Facebooks distributed data store for the social graph. In *USENIX ATC*, 2013.

[11] A. Buluc and J. R. Gilbert. The combinatorial blas: design, implementation, and applications. *HPCA'11*, 25(4):496–509.

[12] J. Chhugani, N. Satish, C. Kim, J. Sewall, and P. Dubey. Fast and efficient graph traversal algorithm for cpus: Maximizing single-node efficiency. In *IPDPS*, pages 378–389, 2012.

[13] A. Ching. Scaling apache giraph to a trillion edges. `www.facebook.com/notes/facebook-engineering/scaling-apache-giraph-to-a-trillion-edges/10151617006153920`, 2013.

[14] T. Davis. The University of Florida Sparse Matrix Collection. http://www.cise.ufl.edu/research/sparse/matrices.

[15] J. Dongarra. Compressed Row Storage. `http://web.eecs.utk.edu/~dongarra/etemplates/node373.html`.

[16] R. Gemulla, E. Nijkamp, P. J. Haas, and Y. Sismanis. Large-scale matrix factorization with distributed stochastic gradient descent. In *ACM SIGKDD*, pages 69–77, 2011.

[17] Y. Guo, M. Biczak, A. L. Varbanescu, A. Iosup, C. Martella, and T. L. Willke. Towards benchmarking graph-processing platforms. In *Poster at Supercomputing*, 2013.

[18] T. Ideker, O. Ozier, B. Schwikowski, and A. F. Siegel. Discovering regulatory and signalling circuits in molecular interaction networks. *Bioinformatics*, 18(1):233–240, 2002.

[19] Y. Koren, R. Bell, and C. Volinsky. Matrix factorization techniques for recommender systems. *Computer*, 42(8):30–37, 2009.

[20] H. Kwak, C. Lee, H. Park, and S. B. Moon. What is twitter, a social network or a news media? In *WWW*, pages 591–600, 2010.

[21] Y. Low, J. Gonzalez, A. Kyrola, D. Bickson, C. Guestrin, and J. M. Hellerstein. GraphLab: A new parallel framework for machine learning. In *UAI*, July 2010.

[22] T. Mattson, D. Bader, et al. Standards for graph algorithm primitives. In *HPEC*, pages 1–2, 2014.

[23] R. C. Murphy, K. B. Wheeler, B. W. Barrett, and J. A. Ang. Introducing the graph 500. *Cray User's Group (CUG)*, 2010.

[24] D. Nguyen, A. Lenharth, and K. Pingali. A lightweight infrastructure for graph analytics. In *Proc. SOSP*, 2013.

[25] M. M. A. Patwary, R. H. Bisseling, and F. Manne. Parallel greedy graph matching using an edge partitioning approach. In *ICFP Workshops at HLPP'10*, pages 45–54. ACM, 2010.

[26] K. Pingali, D. Nguyen, M. Kulkarni, et al. The tao of parallelism in algorithms. In *PLDI*, pages 12–25, New York, NY, USA, 2011. ACM.

[27] S. Salihoglu and J. Widom. Gps: A graph processing system. In *Scientific and Statistical Database Management*. Stanford InfoLab, July 2013.

[28] N. Satish, C. Kim, J. Chhugani, and P. Dubey. Large-scale energy-efficient graph traversal: a path to efficient data-intensive supercomputing. In *SC*, pages 1–11, 2012.

[29] N. Satish, C. Kim, J. Chhugani, P. Dubey, et al. Can Traditional Programming Bridge the Ninja Performance Gap for Parallel Applications? In *ISCA'12*, pages 440–451, 2012.

[30] J. Seo, S. Guo, , and M. S. Lam. SociaLite: Datalog extensions for efficient social network analysis. ICDE'13, pages 278–289, 2013.

[31] J. Seo, J. Park, J. Shin, and M. S. Lam. Distributed SociaLite: A datalog-based language for large-scale graph analysis. *Proceedings of the VLDB Endowment*, 6(14), 2013.

[32] J. D. Ullman. Principles of database and knowledge-base systems, volume ii. 1989.

[33] K. V. IP over InfiniBand (IPoIB) architecture. RFC 4392.

[34] C. Wilson, B. Boe, A. Sala, K. P. N. Puttaswamy, and B. Y. Zhao. User interactions in social networks and their implications. In *EuroSys*, pages 205–218, 2009.

[35] R. S. Xin, J. E. Gonzalez, M. J. Franklin, and I. Stoica. Graphx: a resilient distributed graph system on spark. In *GRADES*, page 2, 2013.

[36] M. Zaharia, M. Chowdhury, M. J. Franklin, S. Shenker, and I. Stoica. Spark: cluster computing with working sets. In *USENIX Hot Cloud*, pages 10–10, 2010.

Local Search of Communities in Large Graphs

Wanyun Cui[§] Yanghua Xiao[§]* Haixun Wang[‡]† Wei Wang[§]
[§]Shanghai Key Laboratory of Data Science, Fudan University, Shanghai, China
[‡]Microsoft Research Asia, Beijing, China
wanyuncui1@gmail.com, shawyh@fudan.edu.cn, haixun@gmail.com, weiwang1@fudan.edu.cn

ABSTRACT

Community search is important in social network analysis. For a given vertex in a graph, the goal is to find the best community the vertex belongs to. Intuitively, the best community for a given vertex should be in the vicinity of the vertex. However, existing solutions use *global search* to find the best community. These algorithms, although straight-forward, are very costly, as all vertices in the graph may need to be visited. In this paper, we propose a *local search* strategy, which searches in the neighborhood of a vertex to find the best community for the vertex. We show that, because the minimum degree measure used to evaluate the goodness of a community is not *monotonic*, designing efficient local search solutions is a very challenging task. We present theories and algorithms of local search to address this challenge. The efficiency of our local search strategy is verified by extensive experiments on both synthetic networks and a variety of real networks with millions of nodes.

Categories and Subject Descriptors

H.2.8 [**Database Management**]: Database Applications—*Data mining*

Keywords

Community search; Social networks; Graph mining

1. INTRODUCTION

Most real-life complex networks, including the Internet, social networks, and biological neural networks, contain *community structures*. That is, the networks can be partitioned into groups within which connections are dense and between which connections are sparse [1]. Finding communities in real networks is an important analytical task, because community structures are imbued with meaning – that is, they are highly correlated with the functionality of the network. For example, on the World Wide Web, communities consist of web sites that share common topics [2]. In protein-protein interaction networks [3] and metabolic networks [4], community structures correspond to functionality modules.

*Correspondence author. This work was supported by the National NSFC (No. 61003001, 61170006, 61171132, 61033010); NSF of Jiangsu Province (No. BK2010280).

†Current affiliation: Google Research, Mountain View, CA.

SIGMOD'14, June 22–27, 2014, Snowbird, UT, USA.

http://dx.doi.org/10.1145/2588555.2612179 .

Due to the significance of community structures, the problem of *community search*, that is, finding the most likely community that a vertex belongs to, is important to many real life networks and applications [5]. Typical applications include:

- *Friend recommendation on Facebook.* Given the friendship network, the system wants to suggest candidate friends to a specific user u. Intuitively, we will only recommend to u those who are in the same community as u are but are not yet u's friends.
- *Advertising on social networks.* People in the same community often share common interests. If we know a user is interested in a particular type of advertisements, we may push the same type of advertisements to other people in his or her community.
- *Infectious disease control.* If a person has come into contact with a highly infectious disease, then who will most likely be affected? Obviously, we may want to monitor people in his or her community.
- *Semantic expansion.* In information retrieval, when a user submits a keyword query, say, "image," he may also be interested in results related to other keywords such as "pictures," "photo," and so on. If a *semantic link network* [6] over keywords is available, then we can expand the query by including keywords in the same "semantic community."

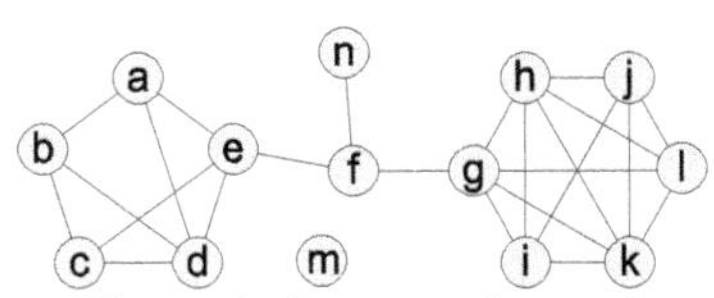

Figure 1: An example graph

To effectively perform community search, we must first determine what a good community is. The goodness of a community is measured by the *closeness* of the vertices in the community. One widely used closeness measure is a community's *minimum degree*, that is, the minimum degree of all the vertices in the subgraph induced by the community. A good community is one that has a large minimum degree. We illustrate this in Example 1.

EXAMPLE 1 (MINIMUM DEGREE). *Suppose we want to find the best community that contains vertex a in Figure 1. Intuitively, $V_1 = \{a, b, c, d, e\}$ forms a community that is highly connected with a. In fact, the subgraph induced by V_1 has a minimal degree of 3. If we include one more vertex f in the community, the minimal degree will drop to 1.*

Another possible measure is *average degree*. Under this measure, the best community for a will also include vertex f and a dense subgraph $V_2 = \{g, h, i, j, k, l\}$, as the average degree of $V_1 \cup \{f\} \cup V_2$ is approximately 3.8, which is larger than the average degree of V_1 (which is 3.2). Intuitively, however, V_1 and V_2

are more likely to be two separate communities, as they are connected only by a weak link through f. Hence, the minimum degree measure captures the intuitive notion of closeness better. In this paper, we adopt the minimum degree measure for community search. Thus, the community search problem will be finding the connected subgraph with the largest minimal degree for a given query vertex.

Besides the above rationale, the following reasons also motivate us to take the minimum degree as the measure of community goodness. First, minimum degree is one of the most fundamental characteristics of a graph. For example, it is used to describe the evolution of random graphs [7], and graph visualization [8]. The properties found in this paper about minimal degree can shed light on other related problems. Second, in social network analysis, minimal degree has been widely used as the measure of the cohesiveness of a group of persons [9, 5, 10]. It can be dated back to the Seidman's research in 1983 [9]. The author compared minimal degree to many other measures of cohesiveness, such as connectedness and diameter, finding that minimum degree is a good measure in social network analysis. In a recent community search study [5], the authors also used the minimum degree as the community measure for organizing a cock tail party. They also found that, in community search problem, minimum degree is better than some other measures, such as average degree and density (measured by $\frac{2|E|}{|V|(|V|-1)}$, where $|V|$ and $|E|$ are the vertex number and edge number, respectively).

A straightforward strategy for community search is known as the *global search* [5]. The search is pessimistic in the sense that it needs to explore the entire graph before deciding the best community for the query vertex. Note that in the worst case, the whole network may be the best community. For example, when the whole network forms a complete graph.

In Example 2, we demonstrate a typical global search procedure on the graph shown in Figure 1. It starts with the whole graph and then it iteratively removes vertices that cannot be part of the answers. The procedure is repeated until no vertex can be removed.

EXAMPLE 2 (GLOBAL SEARCH). *Suppose we want to find the best community for vertex j in the network shown in Figure 1. We repeatedly remove vertices with the minimum degree. Vertices m, n, f, a, b, c, d, e could be removed in turn, and we end up with $V' = \{g, h, i, j, k\}$, wherein j is one of the vertices with the minimum degree. We can show that any subset of V' has a smaller minimal degree. Hence, V' is the best answer.*

Global search is costly as it needs to explore the entire graph. This is unacceptable for large graphs. In this paper, we propose a *local search* strategy. The intuition is that the best community for a given vertex is in the neighborhood of the vertex. Thus, it should not be necessary to involve the entire graph in the search. The local search strategy works as follows: We start at the query vertex. Initially the target community contains the query vertex only. The community expands as we explore in the neighborhood of the query vertex. We stop the search when the current community is the best.

The problem is, how do we know whether the current community we have found is the best? It would be nice if the minimum degree measure is "monotonic," meaning as the community becomes larger, its minimum degree always becomes smaller. Then, we can stop the search when the minimum degree drops below the given threshold. Unfortunately, the minimum degree measure is not monotonic. This is demonstrated by Example 3.

EXAMPLE 3 (LOCAL SEARCH AND NON-MONOTONICITY). *Suppose we want to find the best community for vertex a in Figure 1. Assume the current community includes a's immediate neighbors: b, d, e. The subgraph induced by $S = \{a, b, d, e\}$ has a minimal degree of 2. To enlarge the community, we can add vertex c or f. Adding f will decrease the minimal degree to 1, while adding c will increase it to 3.*

Clearly, as shown by Example 3, the minimum degree measure is not *monotonic*, which means that if S is a partial result containing the query vertex, for a vertex v that is adjacent to S, the subgraph induced by $S \cup \{v\}$ does not necessarily have a smaller or larger minimum degree. This poses a great challenge for us to decide when to terminate the local search procedure.

In this paper, we present theories and algorithms for local search. We investigate sufficient conditions for deciding whether a neighboring vertex should be added to expand the community. If no vertex satisfies the condition, then we terminate the search. We show that such a sufficient condition does exist, but, in the worst case, its evaluation may become as costly as performing a global search. However, a *typical* local search always finds the best community with much less cost than a global search.

The rest of the paper is organized as follows. Section 2 introduces some background information and formulates two community search problems: CST and CSM. Section 3 discusses how to solve the problems using global community search. In Section 4, we give several local search based solutions for the community search with a threshold constraint (CST) problem. In Section 5, we present solutions to the community search with a maximality constraint (CSM) problem. Section 6 reports experimental results. Section 7 reviews related work. We conclude in Section 8.

2. PROBLEM DEFINITION

In this section, we define a "goodness" measure for communities and we define the problems of community search. We then discuss the hardness of the problems. In this work, we are concerned with *simple graphs*, that is, graphs with no self-loops or multi-edges. Also, we focus on *undirected* and *unweighted* graphs only.

$G(V, E)$	A graph with vertex set V and edge set E.
$G[H]$	The subgraph of G induced by a set of vertex H. It contains edges $(H \times H) \cap E$.
$deg_G(v)$	The degree of vertex v in G.
$\delta(G)$	$min\{deg_G(v)\|v \in V\}$
$H^*(G, v)$	Any best communities for vertex v in G.
$m^*(G, v)$	The community goodness of $H^*(G, v)$.
$V_{\geq k}$	$\{v\|deg_G(v) \geq k\}$
$C_{naive}(k)$	Naive set of candidates for CST(k).
$maxcore(G, v_0)$	The maximum core of G w.r.t v_0

Table 1: Notations

2.1 Problem Definition

Let $G(V, E)$ denote an undirected graph with vertex set V and edge set E. For any subset $H \subseteq V$, the *subgraph induced by S*, denoted as $G[H]$, is the graph whose vertex set is H and whose edge set is $(H \times H) \cap E$. Furthermore, we use $deg_G(v)$ to denote the degree of vertex v in graph G. Clearly, we have $deg_{G[H]}(v) \leq deg_G(v)$ since $G[H]$ is a subgraph of G. Table 1 summarizes the notations used in this paper.

DEFINITION 1 (COMMUNITY GOODNESS [5]). *Let $G(V, E)$ be a graph. Let $H \subseteq V$. We consider $G[H]$, the subgraph induced by H, as a community. The community goodness of $G[H]$ is defined by its minimum degree:*

$$\delta(G[H]) = min\{deg_{G[H]}(v)|v \in H\}$$

Minimum degree is one of the most widely used community goodness measures [5]. One important characteristics of $\delta(\cdot)$, which we have illustrated in Example 3, is that it is *non-monotonic*. It means $\delta(G[H \cup \{v\}])$ is not necessarily smaller than $\delta(G[H])$. Because of the non-monotonicity of $\delta(\cdot)$, the problem of finding the best community through local search is nontrivial.

PROBLEM DEFINITION 1 (CSM). *For a graph $G(V, E)$ and an arbitrary vertex $v_0 \in V$, find $H \subseteq V$ such that (1) $v_0 \in H$; (2) $G[H]$ is a connected subgraph; and (3) $\delta(G[H])$ is maximized among all possible choices of H. We denote this problem as CSM, or community search with the maximality constraint.*

For graph G and query vertex v, let $m^*(G, v)$ denote the possible maximum community goodness, and let $H^*(G, v)$ denote any community that has the maximum goodness. We have:

$$0 \leq m^*(G, v) \leq deg_G(v) \quad (1)$$

Note that the optimal solution is not necessarily unique. In general, $m^*(G, v)$ is determined by v and the graph structure of G.

In some applications, instead of finding communities that have the maximum community goodness, we may be interested in finding those that satisfy $\delta(G[H]) \geq k$, where k is a given constraint. Consider the *infectious disease control* problem. Infectious diseases have different risk factors. For a highly contagious disease, we may want to choose a lower k so that people who have little contact with the sick can also be found. For a less contagious disease, we may choose a higher k to focus on people who have very close contact with the sick. By tuning k, we achieve flexibility in controlling the size of the resulting community.

PROBLEM DEFINITION 2 (CST). *For a given graph $G(V, E)$, a query vertex $v_0 \in V$, and a constant k, find $H \subseteq V$ such that (1) $v_0 \in H$; (2) $G[H]$ is a connected graph; and (3) $\delta(G[H]) \geq k$. We denote this problem as CST(k), or community search with threshold constraint.*

EXAMPLE 4. *We use the graph shown in Figure 1 as an example. Suppose the query vertex is a. In CSM, the subgraph induced by $H = \{a, b, c, d, e\}$ is the final solution because $\delta(G[H]) = 3$ and other Hs will have $\delta(G[H]) < 3$. In CST(k), if $k = 3$, then the solution is still H. If $k = 2$, then there are multiple choices for H. For example, $\{a, b, d\}, \{a, d, e\}$ or $\{a, b, c, d, e\}$.*

We illustrate CSM and CST in Example 4. Both CSM and CST may return multiple answers. In fact, as shown in Section 2.2, CST may produce an exponential number of results (with regard to graph size). Hence, we only focus on finding one solution for CST. Alternatively, we may want to find the smallest community. This new problem, which is denoted as mCST, is formally below:

PROBLEM DEFINITION 3 (MCST). *For a graph $G(V, E)$, a query vertex $v_0 \in V$ and a constant k, find $H \subseteq V$ such that (1) $v_0 \in H$; (2) $G[H]$ is a connected graph; (3) $\delta(G[H]) \geq k$; and (4) the size of H is minimized. We denote this problem as mCST(k).*

Unfortunately, the mCST problem is NP-complete as we will prove in Section 2.3. In this paper we focus on CST and CSM.

2.2 Relationship between CSM and CST

CSM is an optimization problem, and it has a corresponding decision problem: deciding whether a subset $H \subseteq V$ exists that satisfies the three conditions specified in CST. Clearly, CST is the *constructive version* of the decision problem of CSM. In other words, we not only need to determine the existence of the valid solution but also need to construct an instance of the solution if the valid solution does exist. Besides these obvious relationships, we further establish some quantitative correlations between CSM and CST that will serve as the foundation for solving these problems.

PROPOSITION 1 (DOWNWARD CLOSURENESS OF CST(k)). *If H is a solution to CST(k), then H is also a solution to CST(k') where $k' < k$.*

PROPOSITION 2. *For a graph $G(V, E)$ and a query vertex v, if H is a solution of CST(k), then $m^*(G, v)$ is no less than k.*

PROPOSITION 3 (PRUNING RULE). *For a vertex v with $deg_G(v) < k$, v will not belong to any solutions to CST(k).*

Proposition 1 and 2 lead to an algorithm of polynomial complexity to solve CSM if we have a polynomial solution for CST. Since $m^*(G, v)$ lies in the interval $[0, deg_G(v)]$, we can employ a binary search procedure starting from $\lceil \frac{N-1}{2} \rceil$ to iteratively visit the median of the interval to check whether the CST instance with the median as the threshold constraint has a valid solution. In this manner, we can solve CSM in $O(\log deg_G(v) f(N))$, where $f(N)$ is the time complexity of CST.

For both CSM and CST, we only look for one solution because there may exist an exponential number of solutions. To see this, consider a graph with N vertices of degree 1 and one vertex of degree N (Figure 2). Suppose the query vertex v_c is the vertex of degree N. Then, obviously we have $m^*(G, v_c) = 1$. But $H^*(G, v_c)$ could be any subset containing v_c. Thus the number of optimal solutions is $\Theta(2^n)$, where n is the number of all vertices of degree 1. To avoid returning an exponential number of solutions, in our problem, we only consider one of them.

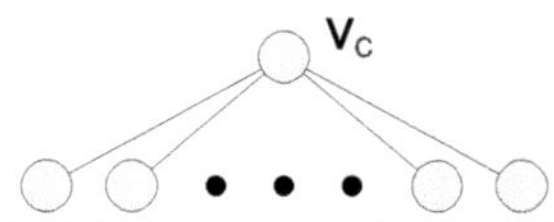

Figure 2: A graph with 1 vertex of degree N and N vertices of degree 1.

2.3 NP-completeness of mCST

Now we show that the mCST problem, which we introduced in Section 2.1, is NP-complete. To do this, we prove a problem related to mCST is NP-Complete, and we reduce that problem to mCST.

LEMMA 1. *For a given graph G, a vertex v_0, and an integer k, if there exists a clique C such that $v_0 \in C$ and $|C| = k + 1$, then C is the smallest solution of CST(k).*

PROBLEM DEFINITION 4 (MCC). *For a graph $G(V, E)$ and $v_0 \in V$, find the maximum clique that contains v_0.*

LEMMA 2. *MCC is NP-Complete.*

PROOF. It is clear that MCC belongs to NP. We prove it by reducing Maximal Clique (MC), a well-known NP-complete problem, to MCC. For any graph $G(V, E)$, we construct a new graph $G'(V', E')$ by adding a vertex v_0 and connecting v_0 to all vertices in G, that is, $V' = V \cup \{v_0\}$ and $E' = E \cup \{(v_i, v_0) | v_i \in V\}$. Thus, an MCC in G' is an MC in G. □

THEOREM 1. *mCST is NP-complete.*

PROOF. It is easy to see that mCST belongs to NP. Now we show that mCST is NP-complete by reducing MCC to it. Let $G(V, E)$ be a graph, and let v_0 be the query vertex. Consider the decision problem that corresponds to the optimization problem of MCC: Determine whether G has a clique of at least size k that contains v_0. We can construct the following decision problem for mCST. Determine whether a solution $H \subseteq V$ exists such that $|H| = k$ and it satisfies the mCST conditions: i) $v_0 \in H$; ii) $G[H]$ is connected; and iii) $\delta(G[H]) \geq k - 1$. If H is the answer, then apparently $G[H]$ is a clique, as any node in H has degree $\geq k - 1$. □

3. GLOBAL SEARCH

In this section, we describe global search based solutions for CST and CSM. The global search approach needs to visit all vertices and edges of the graph, which is costly for big graphs.

3.1 k-core and Maxcore

To understand global search, we first define two concepts: *k-core* and *maxcore*.

DEFINITION 2 (k-CORE). *A subgraph of G is called the k-core of G if it is the biggest subgraph such that each of its vertices has a degree of at least k. Note that the k-core may contain multiple connected components.*

Definition 3 (Maximum Core). *For a vertex v, a* maximum core with regard to v, *denoted as $maxcore(v)$, is the k-core with the maximum k among all the k-cores that contain v.*

Example 5. *Consider graph G in Figure 1. The subgraph induced by $\{a, b, c, d, e, g, h, i, j, k, l\}$ is the 3-core of G; the subgraph induced by $\{g, h, i, j, k, l\}$ is the 4-core of G, which is also the maximum core of G; and the subgraph induced by $\{a, b, c, d, e\}$ is a maximum core with regard to vertex e, that is, $maxcore(G, e)$.*

Example 5 illustrates the concepts of k-core and $maxcore$. We use global search to find the k-core for a given k: We repeatedly remove vertices from G whose degree is less than k until no more vertices can be removed. We need to visit every vertex to find its degree and explore all of the edges in the graph. Hence, the complexity for finding the k-core and $maxcore$ is $O(|V| + |E|)$.

3.2 Solving CST and CSM

For a graph G and a query vertex v_0, we now show that the k-core and the $maxcore(v_0)$ contain the solutions to CST and CSM, respectively. First, consider the problem of $\mathtt{CST}(k)$. If vertex v belongs to any solution of $\mathtt{CST}(k)$, we call v an *admissible vertex*. Let A be the set of all admissible vertices for $\mathtt{CST}(k)$. Similarly, we can define the admissible set A' for the problem of CSM. Example 6 illustrates the admissible sets in Figure 1:

Example 6. *Consider graph G in Figure 1 and query vertex e. For CSM, we have $m^*(G, e) = 3$ and $H^*(G, e) = \{a, b, c, d, e\}$. Since no other $H^*(G, e)$ exists, the admissible set is simply $A = \{a, b, c, d, e\}$. For $\mathtt{CST}(2)$, the solutions include $\{a, b, c, d, e\}$ and $V - \{m, n\}$. Hence, we have $A = V - \{m, n\}$.*

Next, we show that A is a subset of the k-core of G. Similarly, A' is contained in $maxcore(v_0)$. More specifically, we have:

Lemma 3. *For graph G and query vertex v_0, the connected component C_k that contains v_0 in the k-core of graph G is a solution of $\mathtt{CST}(k)$. Furthermore, for any other solution H of $\mathtt{CST}(k)$, we have $H \subset C_k$.*

Lemma 4. *For graph G and query vertex v_0, the connected component that contains v_0 in $maxcore(v_0)$, denoted by $C_{max}(v_0)$, is a solution of CSM. Furthermore, for any other solution H of CSM, we have $H \subset C_{max}(v_0)$.*

Proof. By definition, $C_{max}(v_0)$ is a solution of CSM. If there exists another solution $H \neq C_{max}(v_0)$, then $H \cup C_{max}(v_0)$ will be a connected component in $maxcore(v_0)$, as both H and $C_{max}(v_0)$ contain v_0. This contradicts the definition of $C_{max}(v_0)$. □

Lemma 3 implies that a vertex v is an admissible vertex of $\mathtt{CST}(k)$ if and only if $v \in C_k$; and Lemma 4 implies that v is an admissible vertex of CSM if and only if $v \in C_{max}$. Unfortunately, evaluating these sufficient and necessary conditions is equivalent to global search.

To solve CST, Lemma 3 implies that we can iteratively remove vertices of less than k degree and their incident edges. Then, the connected component that contains the query vertex is certainly a valid solution.

To solve CSM, Lemma 4 implies that we need to find the connected component containing the query vertex in the maximum core with regard to the query vertex. We do this by using a greedy algorithm [5]. Let $G_0 = G$. We delete from G_0 the vertex with the minimum degree as well as its incident edges, and we denote the resulting graph as G_1. We repeat the process and create a sequence of graphs, $G_0, G_1, \cdots, G_t$, until at step t the query vertex v_0 is the next vertex to be deleted. Then, the connected component of G_i $(0 \leq i \leq t)$ with maximum $\delta(G_i)$ that contains the query vertex is an optimum solution [5].

The above two solutions have time complexity $O(|V| + |E|)$[1], which means we need to visit all vertices and edges in the graph.

[1]The linear complexity of a global search based CSM solution is achieved with some special technique. Please refer to [5] for its linear implementation.

4. LOCAL SEARCH FOR CST

In this section, we devise local search algorithms for community search. The biggest challenge is to overcome the non-monotonicity of the minimum degree measure, which enables us to perform community search by exploring only the local neighborhood of the query vertex. In the following, we first present a baseline local search solution, which is of exponential complexity. Then, we present the general framework of our linear solution. Finally, we give optimized realizations of this framework in Section 4.3.1 and Section 4.3.2. As we mentioned, CSM can be solved based on the solutions to the corresponding CST problem. Hence, we focus on CST only.

4.1 The Baseline Solution

We first give an in-depth analysis of the monotonicity of $\delta(\cdot)$, the community goodness function and introduce some notations. Consider the exploration starting from the query vertex. At each step we add a vertex until we get a solution H. Let $v_0, v_1, ..., v_t$ be a sequence of vertices which lead to H (we refer to such a sequence as *a sequence of* H). Let $H_i = \{v_0, \cdots, v_i\}$. We have shown that in general $\delta(\cdot)$ is a non-monotonic function of H. More formally, $\delta(H_i)$ is not necessarily smaller than $\delta(H_{i+1})$. Clearly, the monotonicity of $\delta(H)$ depends on the order in which vertices are added to H. One interesting fact we discovered is that for any vertex $v_0 \in H$, we can always find a vertex sequence (each vertex is in H) starting with v_0 such that $\delta(H_i)$ is a *non-decreasing* function of i.

Theorem 2. *For any vertex $v_0 \in H$ in graph G, there always exists a vertex sequence $v_0, v_1, ..., v_t$ of H starting with v_0 such that $\forall 0 \leq i < t$, $\delta(H_i) \leq \delta(H_{i+1})$.*

Proof. This is equivalent to proving that we can remove vertices one by one from H until v_0 such that the removal of each vertex will not increase the minimal degree of the remaining vertices. Suppose the current set is H'. If $H' = \{v_0\}$, we have already found the vertex sequence. If $H' = \{v_0, v_i\}$, then removing v_i either decreases the minimal degree (if $(v_0, v_i) \in E$) or does not change the minimal degree (if $(v_0, v_i) \notin E$). Next, we consider the case in which there are two or more vertices besides v_0 in H'. In such a case, there must be a vertex $v \in H', v \neq v_0$ and $\delta(G[H']) \geq \delta(G[H' - \{v\}])$. We just need to remove this vertex. If such vertices don't exist, it means that $\forall v \in H', v \neq v_0, \delta(G[H']) < \delta(G[H' - \{v\}])$. This only happens when v is one of the vertices in H' that has the minimal degree because removing a non-minimal degree vertex will only keep the minimal degree or decrease the minimal degree. Thus, there must be two or more such v. Removing each one of these vertices will not produce a larger minimal degree. □

Theorem 2 implies that there is always an order of exploration that monotonically leads to a solution. Theorem 2 also implies any solution H of $\mathtt{CST}(k)$ can be produced by a vertex sequence of H starting from the query vertex v_0 such that $\delta(H_i) \leq \delta(H_{i+1})$ for each i. In general the existence of such a sequence is a necessary but not a sufficient condition to find a valid solution. To see the insufficiency, consider the graph shown in Figure 1 and $\mathtt{CST}(3)$ with query vertex e. Any vertex sequence starting with e, f will not lead to a valid solution, but clearly $\delta(G[e, f])$ is larger than $\delta(G[e])$.

Theorem 2 leads to a straightforward algorithm which is outlined in Algorithm 1. It starts from $H' = \{v_0\}$ and then calls the $search$ function. The $search$ function exhaustively enumerates each vertex v form the neighbors of H' such that $\delta(H' \cup \{v\}) \geq \delta(H')$. If a solution is found, the procedure stops. Otherwise, it calls $search$ recursively. Theorem 2 ensures that such exhaustive enumeration can always find a valid solution to $\mathtt{CST}(k)$. The solution can be directly extended for CSM, but we omit the details here. Clearly, this baseline solution is of exponential complexity. This motivates us to develop a more efficient local search solution. Next, we will present our linear solution.

Algorithm 1 *Search*()

Input: $G(V, E)$, H', k
Output: H
if $\delta(G[H']) = k$ **then**
  $H \leftarrow H'$
  return
end if
for all vertex v in the neighbors of H' **do**
  if $\delta(G[H' \cup \{v\}]) \geq \delta(G[H'])$ **then**
    $Search(H' \cup \{v\})$
    if $H \neq \emptyset$ **then**
      return
    end if
  end if
end for

4.2 A Framework for Solving CST

In this section, we introduce a local search framework for CST. As outlined in Algorithm 2, on the high level, it contains three simple steps. First, we check if the graph meets the necessary condition of containing an answer to CST(k). Second, we perform candidateGeneration(), that is, we explore from the vicinity of the query vertex, and generate candidate set C, which may contain a solution to the problem. In most cases, the second step will find a solution to CST, but if not, in the final step, we perform a global search (see Section 3) in the k-core of the subgraph induced by C to find the solution.

Algorithm 2 A General Framework of CST

Input: $G(V, E)$, v_0, k
Output: solutions to CST(k)
if $k >$upperBound(G) **then**
  return
end if
$C \leftarrow$candidateGeneration(G, v_0, k);
if no solution is found **then**
  perform global search in the k-core of $G[C]$;
end if
return

Algorithm 2 is guaranteed to return a valid solution as long as candidateGeneration() does not remove any admissible vertex. This is summarized by Proposition 4.

PROPOSITION 4. *For graph G and query vertex v_0, if $H \subseteq V$ is a solution of $CST(k)$, then for any $H' \subseteq V$, a k-core of $G[H \cup H']$ that contains v_0 is a valid solution of $CST(k)$.*

In the following, we first introduce the upper bound in Section 4.2.1. We present a naive candidateGeneration() in Section 4.2.2 and we analyze its complexity and effectiveness in depth.

4.2.1 Upper Bound

Before we perform search, can we tell if a graph G has a solution for CST(k) with respect to a query vertex v? Obviously, if the degree of v is less than k, we know immediately that there is no solution to CST(k). In this section, we establish an upper bound of $m^*(G, v)$. If k is larger than the upper bound, then we immediately know there is no solution. The upper bound is given by Theorem 3.

THEOREM 3. *Given a connected simple graph $G(V, E)$, for any $v \in G$, we have*

$$m^*(G, v) \leq \lfloor \frac{1 + \sqrt{9 + 8(|E| - |V|)}}{2} \rfloor$$

PROOF. Since G is a connected graph, we have $|E| \geq |V| - 1$. For simplicity, we use H^* and m^* to denote the optimal community and its minimum degree. Then $G[H^*]$ has at least $\lceil m^*|H^*|/2 \rceil$ edges. For the rest of the vertices in $V - H^*$, there must be at least $|V| - |H^*|$ edges to ensure G is connected. Hence,

$$\lceil \frac{m^*|H^*|}{2} \rceil + |V| - |H^*| \leq |E| \quad (2)$$

It is also easy to see that $|H^*| \geq m^* + 1$. Thus, from Equation 2, we have $\lceil (\frac{m^*}{2} - 1)|H^*| \rceil \leq |E| - |V|$. By simple transformation, we have $(\frac{m^*}{2} - 1)(m^* + 1) \leq |E| - |V|$. Solving the above equation, we get $m^*(G, v) \leq \lfloor \frac{1+\sqrt{9+8(|E|-|V|)}}{2} \rfloor$. □

4.2.2 A Naive Candidate Generation Method

In this section, we present a straightforward implementation of candidateGeneration(). We give a more sophisticated solution in Section 4.3.1.

Algorithm 3 Naive candidateGeneration()

Input: $G(V, E)$, v_0, k
Output: C
$queue.enque(v_0)$; $C \leftarrow \emptyset$;
while $queue$ is not empty **do**
  $v \leftarrow queue.deque()$;
  $C \leftarrow C \cup \{v\}$;
  if $\delta(G[C]) \geq k$ **then**
    A valid solution is found and **Return** C;
  end if
  for $each(v, w) \in E$ **do**
    if w is not visited and $deg_G(w) \geq k$ **then**
      $queue.enque(w)$;
    end if
  end for
end while
return C

We show an example of this pseudo-code in Example 7. In this naive strategy, we generate candidate vertices by BFS starting from the query vertex v_0. As shown in Algorithm 3, we prune vertices of degree less than k as we traverse the graph (Proposition 3 of Section 2.2). Algorithm 3 runs in $\Theta(n' + m')$ time, where n' is the number of vertices and m' is the number of edges in $G[C]$.

4.2.3 Complexity Analysis

Next, we study the time complexity of Algorithm 2 when it implements candidateGeneration() as in Algorithm 3. The last step of the global search has the same complexity as that of candidate generation. Thus, the complexity of Algorithm 2 is $\Theta(n' + m')$. Hence, to reduce the complexity, we need to reduce $n' = |C|$ and m'. Section 4.3 proposes optimization techniques to reduce n' and m'. Before that, we first give the theoretic analysis of n' and m' to evaluate the pruning ability of the naive candidate generation.

Estimation of n'.

First, the value of n' has an obvious upper bound: $|V|$. In the worst case, we have $C = V(G)$. For example, when $k = N - 1$ and the graph is a complete graph with N vertices, for any query vertex, only the entire graph will qualify. Thus, in the worst case, the local search algorithm will not have any advantage over the global search algorithm.

Second, the value of n' has a tighter upper bound: $|V_{\geq k}|$. Let $V_{\geq k} = \{v | deg_G(v) \geq k\}$ be the set of vertices in G with a degree no less than k. Clearly, $G[C]$ belongs to one of the connected components of $G[V_{\geq k}]$. As an example, let G be the graph shown in Figure 1, and let g be the query vertex. Given $k = 4$, we have $C = \{g, h, i, j, k, l\}$, whose induced subgraph is a connected component of the subgraph induced by $V_{\geq 4} = \{d, e, g, h, i, j, k, l\}$.

We show in Figure 3 the simulation of above upper bounds of $|C|$ and the real size of $|C|$ found by the naive candidate generation. We generated scale free graphs of different sizes under the same parameters as that used in Section 6.2. We randomly select 10 vertices as query vertices and record the average metrics of interest. The size of the communities found by the improved local search proposed in Section 4.3.1 is also given (denoted by 'local search'). The simulation results show that $|C|$ and the real community size is quite close to $|V_{\geq k}|$ but far away from $|V|$. This implies that $|V_{\geq k}|$ is a good upper bound of C. In the estimation of m', we will use $|V_{\geq k}|$ as the approximation of $|C|$.

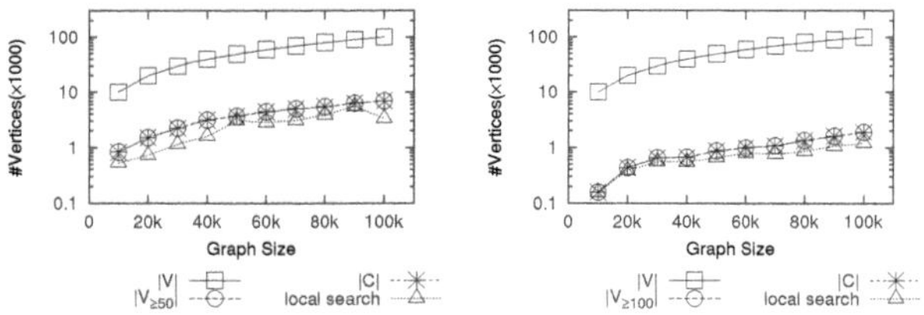

(a) $k = 50$ (b) $k = 100$

Figure 3: Simulation of upper bounds on $|C|$

Estimation of m'.

Clearly, the number of edges in $G[V_{\geq k}]$ is an upper bound of m'. Degree distribution is one of important feature to characterize a real network. We estimate the number of edges in $G[V_{\geq k}]$ based on the degree distribution of G.

Let p_k be the probability that a vertex chosen uniformly at random has degree k. Let $P = \{p_0, p_1, p_2, ..., p_\omega\}$ be the degree distribution of G, where ω is the largest degree of graph G, and $\sum_{0 \leq i \leq \omega} p_i = 1$. In general, it is reasonable to assume that $\omega \in o(|V|)$ for large graphs in real life. Given these assumptions, our major result is: *Given a graph G with degree distribution $P = \{p_0, p_1, p_2, ..., p_\omega\}$ and the maximal degree $\omega \in o(|V|)$, m' can be estimated by*

$$|V_{\geq k}| \sum_{t=1}^{\omega} t \times q_t = n \sum_{i=k}^{\omega} p_i \sum_{t=1}^{\omega} t \times q_t \quad (3)$$

where q_t is defined as Equation 4. This is built upon Theorem 4 and Lemma 5. Theorem 4 gives the degree distribution of $G[V_{\geq k}]$ (in an asymptotic case, that is, when the size of the graph is large enough). Lemma 5 gives the estimation of the largest degree in $G[V_{\geq k}]$. We omit their proofs due to space limitations.

THEOREM 4. *Given a graph G with degree distribution $P = \{p_0, p_1, p_2, ..., p_\omega\}$ and the maximal degree $\omega \in o(|V|)$. Let q_t be the probability that a vertex chosen uniformly at random in $G[V_{\geq k}]$ has degree t. Then we have:*

$$q_t = \sum_{i=t}^{\omega} p_i \binom{i}{t} p^t (1-p)^{(i-t)} \quad (4)$$

where $p = \frac{\zeta(k)}{\zeta(0)}$ and $\zeta(x) = \sum_{i=x}^{\omega} i \times p_i$.

LEMMA 5. *For a graph G with the largest degree ω and degree distribution $P = \{p_0, p_1, p_2, ..., p_\omega\}$. It holds* asymptotically almost surely *that the largest degree of $G[V_{\geq k}]$ is ω as $n \to \infty$, where n is the number of vertices in G.*

4.3 Optimization

In this section, we introduce two optimization techniques that improve the performance of the algorithm by reducing n' and m'.

4.3.1 Intelligent Candidate Selection

Algorithm 3 is naive in the sense that it blindly chooses vertices from the queue. The following example shows that it may take the naive approach more steps to find a solution.

Step1: C={e}	Q={a,c,d,f}	Step1: C={e}	Q={a,c,d,f}
Step2: C={e,a}	Q={b,c,d,f}	Step2: C={e,a}	Q={b,c,d,f}
Step3: C={e,a,f}	Q={b,c,d,g,n}	Step3: C={e,a,d}	Q={b,c,f}
...		Step4: C={e,a,d,b}	Q={c,f}
Step12: C=V-{n,m}	Q={}	Step5: C={e,a,d,b,c}	Q={f}

(a) Naive selection (b) Intelligent selection

Figure 4: Naive vs. intelligent candidate generation

EXAMPLE 7 (CANDIDATE GENERATION). *Consider the graph shown in Figure 1. For query vertex e and $CST(3)$, using the naive candidate generation method, f may be added into C (as shown in the Step 3 of Figure 4(a)), which leads to no valid solution. But the procedure still proceeds until all vertices are exhaustively enumerated (overall 12 steps are needed). On the other hand, if we always choose the vertex with the largest number of connections to C, a valid solution can be found within 5 steps. The procedures for these two selections are illustrated in Figure 4, where Q is the queue from which the vertex is selected.*

To reduce $n' = |C|$, we propose two intelligent candidate selection strategies. The basic idea to refine the candidate generation is using *priority queue* so that we can select the most *promising* vertex that leads to a solution fast. Theoretically, Lemma 3 can be used to compute the "promisingness" of a vertex. However, its computation is too costly. We are interested in lightweight heuristics of constant cost. Next, we will propose two intelligent lightweight heuristics.

Largest increment of goodness (**lg**). Selecting the vertex that leads to the largest increment of the goodness measure is a straight-forward heuristic since the final goal of CST is to find a subset C satisfying $\delta(G[C]) \geq k$. In this strategy the priority of a vertex v, $f(v)$, is defined by

$$f(v) = \delta(G[C \cup \{v\}]) - \delta(G[C]) \quad (5)$$

It is a greedy approach as it only considers the improvement of $\delta(C)$ for the next step. Note that at any time when a vertex is added to C, the increment of the goodness of the current C is at most 1. In other words, for any v, we have $f(v) = 1$ or $f(v) = 0$. Hence, this strategy is equivalent to the random selection from vertices which are adjacent to one of the vertices with the minimal degree in C.

Largest number of incidence (**li**). This is a more intelligent selection strategy. The priority of a vertex v is defined as

$$f(v) = deg_{G[C \cup \{v\}]}(v) \quad (6)$$

In this strategy, we select the vertex with the largest number of connections to the selected vertices. This yields the fastest increase of the mean degree of $G[C]$. In general, the lowest degree of a graph will increase with the growth of its density, and consequently a valid solution C with $\delta(G[C])$ is expected to be found within a limited number of steps if there exists such a solution.

As we have shown in Example 7, these selection strategies generally are quite efficient. However, Example 8 shows that local information generally is not sufficient to construct a valid solution within the WHILE loop. In this case, we need to perform a global search in the k-core of $G[C]$ (line 6) of Algorithm 2. This step ensures a valid solution, as stated in Proposition 4.

EXAMPLE 8 (HARDNESS OF SELECTION). *Continue Example 7, by* **li**, *it is quite possible that f is selected after e. As a result, even after all vertices are visited, no solution can be found.*

Complexity Analysis

Let n' and m' denote the number of vertices and the number of edges in $G[C]$, respectively. In general **lg** and **li** can be implemented in $O(n' + m' \log n')$ time, because each time a new vertex is added into the queue, at most d queue update operations need to be executed (where d is the degree of this vertex). As a result, at most m' update operations will be executed. Each queue operation (insert, delete, or priority update) generally needs $O(\log n')$ time.

By careful design, **li** can be implemented in $O(n' + m')$, achieving $O(1)$ cost of expansion. We maintain a collection of lists each of which, contains vertices of V with the same $f(v)$. Each time a vertex is added to C, the $f(\cdot)$ value of its neighbors (except those already in C) will *increase* 1. For each of these influenced neighbors, we move v from the original $f(v)$'s list to $f(v) + 1$'s list. In this manner, we can always find one vertex with maximal $f(\cdot)$

in $O(1)$ time. We illustrate the above procedure in Figure 5 and Example 9.

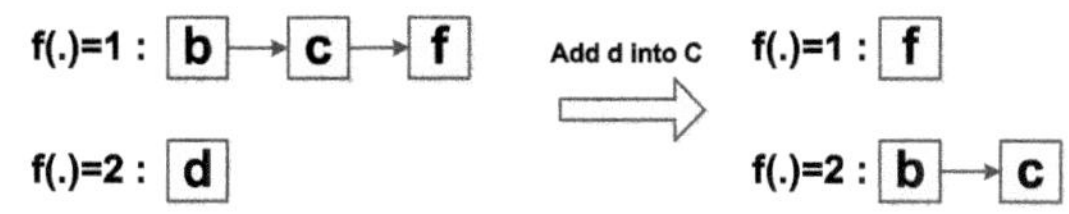

Figure 5: An example of the data structure used in li heuristic.

EXAMPLE 9. *Consider the example graph in Figure 1. Suppose we have added e and a into C (candidate vertices). Then we have $f(b) = f(c) = f(f) = 1, f(d) = 2$. According to the $f()$ function value (i.e. the number of incidence to C), we can organize C's neighbors into two different lists, which are shown in the left part of Figure 5. We also record a pointer to the list with the maximal incidence. The pointer helps find that node d has the most incidences to C (Line 3, Algorithm 3). Then, we move d from its list into C (Line 4, Algorithm 3). And update the two lists by moving b and c from the list $f(.) = 1$ to the list $f(.) = 2$. In this way, we keep the freshness of the lists.*

4.3.2 Intelligent Expansion

We have created a strategy to prune the neighbors we need to visit, i.e. reducing m'. The basic idea is to sort the adjacent list of vertices. We use the adjacent list to represent a graph and sort the adjacent list of each vertex into the descending order of degree. Then, during candidate generation, when we expand a vertex's neighbors (Line 9-11 in Algorithm 3), we stop the expansion immediately when the neighbor has a degree of less than k. Consequently, we can avoid the cost of scanning all neighbors.

For a vertex with d neighbors, we need $O(d \log d)$ time to order its adjacent list. To avoid this cost, we perform the ordering as a pre-computation step before online query processing. In real life applications such as an online social network, numerous community queries may be issued by users. In these cases, precomputation to order the adjacent list is desired. When the graph is dynamically evolving, maintaining the order of adjacent lists is of marginal cost. We can use a binary search tree to represent the ordered adjacency list, costing us only $O(\log(d))$ each time the list changes.

Clearly, this optimization is only effective for local search and cannot be used to speedup global search. Our experiments show that this optimization boosts local search significantly.

5. LOCAL SEARCH FOR CSM

The goal of `CSM` is to find the best community for a given vertex. The challenge is that the goodness measure $\delta(\cdot)$ is not monotonic. In Section 4.1, we have shown an exhaustive enumeration approach. But it is of exponential complexity. In Section 2.2, we introduced a method for solving `CSM` by repeatedly calling `CST`. In this section, we devise a more efficient, bottom-up solution. The algorithm takes 3 steps. First, it expands the search space from the query vertex v_0. Second, it generates a candidate vertex set C in the search space. Third, it invokes the maximum core method to find the final solution in the candidate set.

5.1 Expanding the Search Space

In this step (line 1 to 15 of Algorithm 4), our goal is to expand the search space and find a subset H whose $\delta(G[H])$ is as large as possible while pruning as many invalid vertices as possible under the linear cost. We start with v_0, and at each step we select the vertex that is the local optimal and add it into the current result set. Here, we use the **li** (largest number of incidence) strategy to select the local optimal vertex (line 6 to 7). Then, at the end of each iteration, we know that any vertex whose degree is smaller than $\delta(G[H]) + 1$ cannot appear in any better solution. Thus, in line 14, we expand the set of vertices we need to visit by using H for filtering.

Algorithm 4 A local-search framework to solve `CSM`

Input: a graph $G(V, E)$, v_0 , $-\infty < \gamma < \infty$
Output: H
{Step 1: Iterative searching and filtering.}
1: $H \leftarrow \emptyset$ /* the best solution found so far */
2: $A \leftarrow \{v_0\}$ /* vertices we have visited */
3: $B \leftarrow \{v|(v, v_0) \in E\}$ /* vertices we need to visit */;
4: $s \leftarrow 0$
5: **while** $B \neq \emptyset$ and $s \leq e^{-\gamma}(\lfloor \frac{|E|-|V|}{(\delta(G[H])+1)/2-1} \rfloor - |H|)$ **do**
6: Let v be the vertex with most links to A from B;
7: $s \leftarrow s + 1$; $A \leftarrow A \cup \{v\}$; $B \leftarrow B - \{v\}$;
8: **if** $\delta(A) > \delta(H)$ **then**
9: $H \leftarrow A$;$s \leftarrow 0$;
10: **if** $\delta(H) = \min\{deg_G(v_0), \lfloor \frac{1+\sqrt{9+8(|E|-|V|)}}{2} \rfloor\}$ **then**
11: **Return** H;
12: **end if**
13: **end if**
14: Add v's neighbors with degree larger than $\delta(G[H])$ into B;
15: **end while**
{Step 2: Generating candidates}
16: $C \leftarrow$ Generate candidate vertex set based on H or A;
{Step 3: Finding the solution}
17: $H \leftarrow maxcore(G[C], v_0)$;
18: **return** H;

One critical question is when we can stop expanding the search. Clearly, H is the optimal solution if

$$\delta(H) = \min\{deg_G(v_0), \lfloor \frac{1 + \sqrt{9 + 8(|E| - |V|)}}{2} \rfloor\} \quad (7)$$

However, Equation 7 is a *sufficient but not necessary* condition. For instance, if an invalid vertex is introduced into H in the early stage of expansion, H may never reach the upper bound, even if it already contains the optimal solution. To solve this problem, we introduce another upper bound. We consider the extra number of vertices that need to be added into the current H in order to improve the minimum degree of $G[H]$, given that a better solution that contains the current H exists. This upper bound is given by Corollary 1, which is derived from Theorem 5.

THEOREM 5. *Let $G(V, E)$ be a connected graph, and $v \in V$ be the query vertex. If H is a solution to $\texttt{CST}(k)$, we have*

$$|H| \leq \lfloor \frac{|E| - |V|}{k/2 - 1} \rfloor$$

PROOF. Since G is connected, we have $|E| \geq |V| - 1$. Also, $G[H]$ has at least $k|H|/2$ edges. There exist at least $|V| - |H|$ edges incident with vertices in $V - H$ to maintain the connectivity of graph G. Hence, we have $k \cdot |H|/2 + |V| - |H| \leq |E|$, which leads to $|H| \leq \frac{|E|-|V|}{k/2-1}$. □

COROLLARY 1. *Let $G(V, E)$ be a connected graph, and let H be the current optimal solution found so far in Algorithm 4, if there exists $H' \supset H$ such that $\delta(G[H']) = \delta(G[H]) + 1$, we need to add at most*

$$\lfloor \frac{|E| - |V|}{(\delta(G[H]) + 1)/2 - 1} \rfloor - |H|$$

vertices to find H'.

From Corollary 1, we can see that the larger $\delta(G[H])$, the tighter the upper bound. So this upper bound has better pruning power when the solution has larger m^*.

Given the above upper bound, we use two parameters s and γ (the latter is exposed to users) to control the searching space. The value of s denotes the number of vertices that have been added to H (see line 7 and line 9). In line 5, we use

$$s \leq e^{-\gamma}(\lfloor \frac{|E| - |V|}{(\delta(G[H]) + 1)/2 - 1} \rfloor - |H|) \quad (8)$$

with $-\infty < \gamma < \infty$ to control the search space. We terminate the search when the upper bound is reached. Note that when $\gamma = 0$, Eq 8 degrades into the exact bound given in Corollary 1. When $\gamma > 0$, the number of extra vertices that will be added into H will be less than the exact bound. When $\gamma \to -\infty$, no constraint on s is specified. We will come back to these parameters after the introduction of following steps of the algorithm.

5.2 Generating Candidates

In the second step, we generate a candidate set from H obtained in the first step. Specifically, we propose two solutions to generate C (line 16), and we analyze the tradeoff between their quality and performance. Let $C_{naive}(k)$ be the result of Algorithm 3. That is, $C_{naive}(k)$ is the set of vertices obtained by iteratively removing vertex of degree less than k from the neighborhood of vertex v_0.

Solution 1: $C \leftarrow A$. In this case, we have the following result:

THEOREM 6. *Given graph G and a query vertex v_0, when $\gamma \to -\infty$, Algorithm 4 finds an optimal solution for* CSM.

PROOF. Consider when the WHILE loop exists in Algorithm 4. Let $k = \delta(G[H])$. Clearly, we have $m^*(G, v_0) \geq k$. We have $C_{naive}(k) \subseteq A$. Then, we have $C_{naive}(m^*(G, v_0)) \subseteq C_{naive}(k)$. Thus $C_{naive}(m^*(G, v_0)) \subseteq A$. Thus $maxcore(G[A], v_0)$ is an optimal solution. □

When $C \leftarrow A$, Algorithm 4 also allows us to trade quality for performance by tuning parameter γ. Specifically, when γ is closer to $-\infty$, the solution is of higher quality; when γ is closer to ∞, better performance can be achieved. We will discuss more about this tradeoff in the experiments section.

Solution 2: $C \leftarrow C_{naive}(k)$. Here, $k = \delta(G[H])$.

THEOREM 7. *Given graph G and query vertex v_0, Algorithm 4 always finds an optimal solution: $maxcore(G[C_{naive}(k)], v_0)$, where $k = \delta(G[H])$.*

PROOF. For a graph G and a query vertex v_0, $C_{naive}(k)$ becomes larger when k becomes smaller. Hence, for any k with $\leq m^*(G, v_0)$, $C_{naive}(k)$ contains all valid vertices. Since Algorithm 4 will only return a subset $H \subseteq V$ with $k = \delta(G[H])$ no larger than $m^*(G, v_0)$, $maxcore(C_{naive}(k), v_0)$ is the optimal solution of $\texttt{CSM}(G, v_0)$. □

Note that the choice of γ has no influence on the quality of the solution, but it may influence the running time. In general, when $\gamma \to -\infty$, it is quite possible to find a complete solution or at least a good partial solution before the second step since we have given enough number of tries to find a good H. However, this comes at high cost of run time. If a solution is already found, or a partial solution is found in the first step, the maxcore procedure will be unnecessary or use little time. Hence, it is possible for the existence of an optimal γ leading to the minimal running time. We will show this in the experiment section.

Finally, we highlight that Algorithm 4, under a different implementation strategy, runs in $O(|V| + |E|)$ time in the worst case. However, in general, similar to CST, in CSM a smaller number of vertices are expected to be visited for an optimal solution in our local-search solutions than their global search competitors.

6. EXPERIMENTS

In this section, we use experiments on real life graphs to show the effectiveness and efficiency of our local search method. We also conduct experiments on synthetic graphs to show its scalability. We implemented all of the algorithms in C++ and ran the experiments on a PC with AMD Athlon^{TM}X2 Dual-core QL-62 at 2GHz, 2G memory.

6.1 Experiments on Real Life Graphs

6.1.1 Datasets

We used four real life large graphs in our experiments: DBLP, Berkeley, Youtube, and LiveJournal. DBLP is an author collaboration network, where each vertex represents an author and each edge represents a coauthor relationship. Berkeley is a web graph with nodes representing pages from berkeley.edu and stanford.edu domains and edges representing hyperlinks between them. We ignored the direction of the links. Youtube [11] is a user-to-user link network. LiveJournal is an online social network. For each dataset, we only consider the largest connected component. The statistics of these graphs are reported in Table 2, where the minimal vertex degree of the maximal core of this graph is given as $\delta^*(G)$.

Network	#Vertex	# Edge	$\delta^*(G)$	Opt.(ms)	k=20	40	60
DBLP	481K	1.72M	114	703	0	0	0
Berkeley	654K	6.58M	202	2328	9	0	0
Youtube	1.1M	3M	52	1359	0	0	0
LiveJournal	4.0M	34.7M	360	2381	0	0	0

Table 2: Basic information of real dataset

6.1.2 Case Study

We presented two case studies to justify the minimal degree based community search. The first is on DBLP. We used "Jiawei Han", who is a renowned scientist in Data Mining, as the query vertex. After setting $k = 5$, we got the community shown in Figure 6(a) using $ls - li$. We found that these six authors are all leading scientists in data mining community and their cooperation is very frequent. For example, Jiawei Han and Jian Pei have coauthored over 37 papers, and Haixun Wang has coauthored with Philip S. Yu and Jian Pei over 46 and 15 papers, respectively.

The second case study is on WordNet. WordNet is a semantic network, in which each vertex represents a specific sense, and each edge represents a certain semantic relationship between senses. In this case study, we used the word *pot* as v_0. Using $ls - li$ with $k = 3$, we got the community shown in Figure 6(b). We found that the senses in the community are highly related in semantic: all of them are about the vessel. *pot, bowl, dish* are some vessel entity. *vessel* and *container* are two hypernyms of those entities. And *containerful* is an adjective word related to containers.

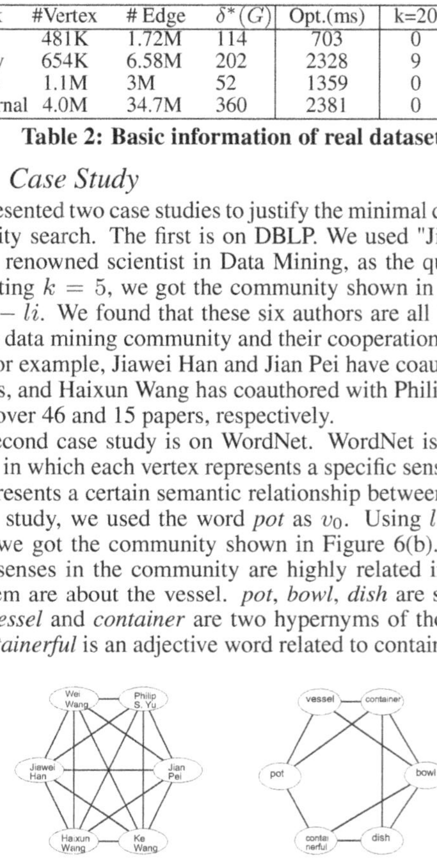

(a) Jiawei's community (b) Community for "Pot"

Figure 6: The effectiveness of community search.

6.1.3 Results for CST

We evaluate the efficiency of our local search solutions for CST by comparing it with the global search solution introduced in Section 2. We denote the global search as **global**, and we denote the three versions of local search, i.e., the local search with naive candidate generation, **li**, and **lg** as **ls-naive**, **ls-li** and **ls-lg** respectively.

Solutions to CST are sensitive to the input parameter k. To evaluate the performance of different solutions, we tested each method with $k = s, 2s, 3s, ..., 8s$, where $s = \delta^*(G)/10$. For each k, we randomly selected 100 vertices as the query vertex from the k-core of the graph so that there was always a meaningful solution containing the query vertex. Then, we averaged the query time of these 100 query vertices.

Baseline solution. We first showed that the baseline solution in general is costly on big graphs. For each real network, we selected $k = 20, 40, 60$. For each k, we randomly selected 100 vertices with a degree of no less than k as the query vertex. We recorded in the last three columns of Table 2 the number of vertices for which the query result can be returned within 1 minute. The results show that in most cases the baseline solution cannot produce result in the given time. Hence, in the following experiments, it will be omitted.

Efficiency of off-line ordering. We first justified the optimization of local search by ordering the adjacency list. We just give the results on DBLP data. Similar results on other real life graphs were obtained and omitted to save space. In Figure 7, we compare local search with optimization (opt) to local search without optimization (non-opt). We can see that, for both **ls-li** and **ls-lg** under most parameter values of k, the optimization technique brings an obvious speedup. The optimization technique has a linear cost as it only requires sorting the adjacent list of each vertex. For example, as reported in Table 2, for DBLP data, it only incurs 703ms. Hence, in all the following experiments, all local search solutions are optimized in this way.

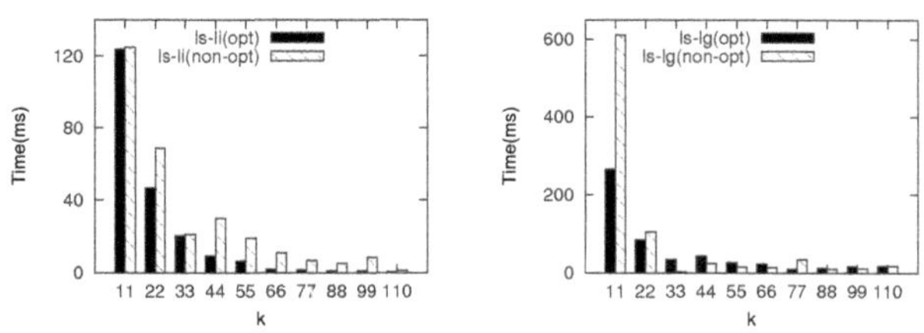

(a) ls-li (b) ls-lg

Figure 7: The effectiveness of the optimization technique.

Performance for CST. We show the performance (mean running time as well as its std) of local search solutions for CST in Figure 8. We can see that, in general, local search performs better than global search in most cases. When k increases, the advantage of local search over global search becomes more obvious. In the best case, for example when k is large on DBLP and Berkeley, ls-li or ls-lg is two orders of magnitudes faster than global search. Only when k is small, global search is comparable to naive local search and the two optimized local search solutions. The reason is that when k is small, most vertices in the graph tend to be involved in the answer, which favors global search. We can also see that among all strategies of local search, in most cases, **ls-li** performs the best. The running time for **ls-li** almost monotonically decreases with the growth of k. This implies **li** is quite effective when k is large.

The stds show that the global approach is the most stable algorithm. This is because the search space of the global algorithm is always the entire graph. In contrast, the local search solutions need to search the entire graph only when the search within the local neighborhoods fails. That is to say, in most cases, local search solution returns results quite fast. Only in some rare cases, its running time is close to global solution (but will not be worse than global search). That is why our solution has larger stds. From the experimental results, we also can see that even considering the worst case, that is *mean running time+ std*, $ls - li$ is better than *global* in most cases.

In some rare cases, for example in Figure 7(c), the global algorithm is better than $ls - lg$ or $ls - naive$. The reason is that $ls - lg$ and $ls - naive$ are not very intelligent. Their search spaces although are less than the global one, in many cases are close to the global one. Furthermore, in general local search solutions need to select the best vertex from candidates, which adds extra computation cost. Consequently, $ls - lg$ or $ls - naive$ may consume more running time. Similar results can be found from Figure 8(b), 8(c) and they can be explained similarly

Influence of small k on local search. To take a close look at the influence of small k (from 1 to 10), we conducted more experiments, the results of which are shown in Figure 9. It is quite interesting to note that when k is extremely small, local search is

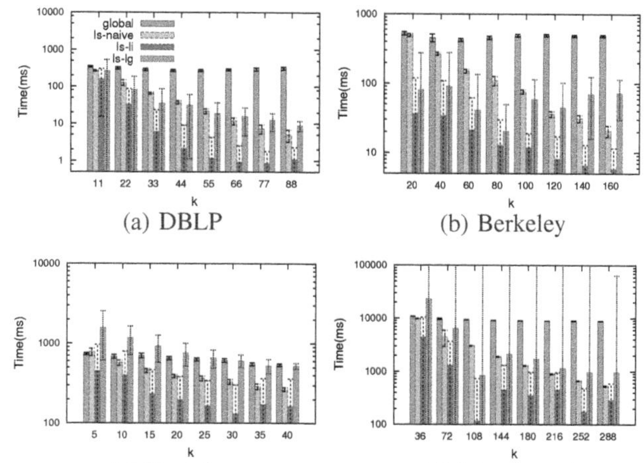

(a) DBLP (b) Berkeley

(c) Youtube (d) LiveJournal

Figure 8: The efficiency of different solutions to CST

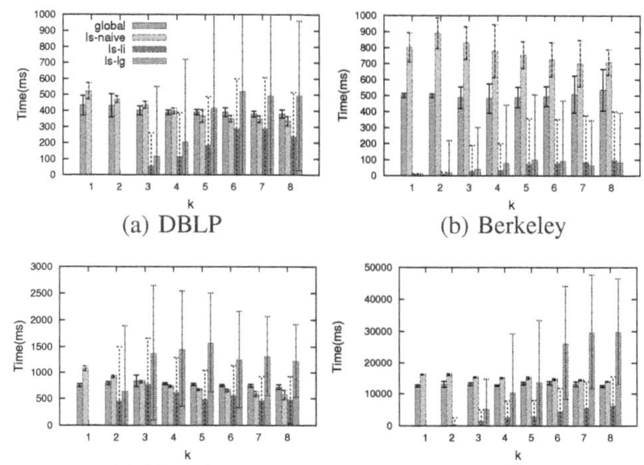

(a) DBLP (b) Berkeley

(c) Youtube (d) LiveJournal

Figure 9: Performance of CST for small k

significantly better than global search (it outperforms global search by two orders of magnitude). This is because when k is extremely small, local search tends to find smaller communities. For example, when $k = 1$, any edge incident with the query vertex will be immediately returned as an answer; when $k = 2$, any cycle containing the query vertex is an answer. In summary, local search is consistently better than global search across a wide range of k.

Performance over arbitrary vertices. In the above experiments, the query vertices come from k-core, which means that a valid community certainly exists. In this experiment, we tested the performance over arbitrary vertices for which a valid community does not necessarily exist. We randomly select 100 query vertices whose degree is no less than k from DBLP (otherwise we can surely find no community for these vertices). We compare the best of local search solutions $ls - li$ to the global search. The result is shown in Figure 10. Similar to previous experiment results, local search is better than global search in almost all the cases. When k grows, the search space of local search becomes smaller. As a result, the mean running time of local search decreases. Instead, the global search is not aware of k and consistently consumes almost the same running time.

Rationale of local search. To understand the rationale of local search, we report the answer size and the number of visited vertices in the search. We show the results for DBLP in Figure 13 (results on other real networks are similar and are omitted to save space). We can see that the local search method tends to produce a small community. In some cases, the community found by **ls-li** or

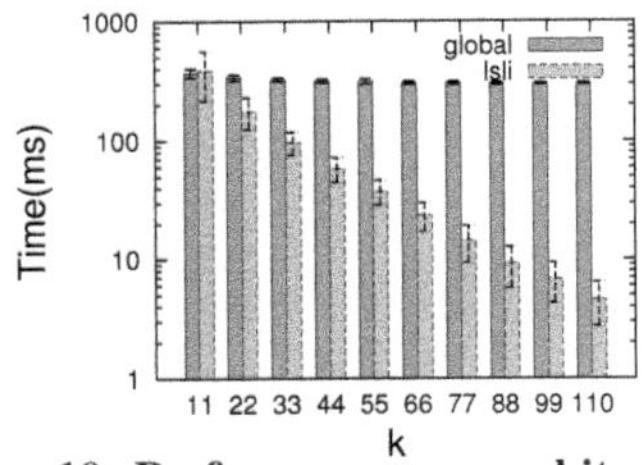

Figure 10: Performance over arbitrary vertices

ls-lg is an order of magnitude smaller than that produced by global search and **ls-naive**. The comparison of the number of visited vertices shows that local search visits a much smaller number of vertices than global search. In many cases, local search outperforms global search by two orders of magnitude. Both smaller answer sizes and a fewer number of visited vertices explain the advantage of local search over global search.

6.1.4 *Results for CSM*

Recall that there are two local search solutions to CSM. We denote the one that generates C by $C \leftarrow A$ as $CSM1$, and the other as $CSM2$. We also compare them with **global**. In local search, we present the results of **li** only, since previous results have already shown its efficiency and effectiveness.

Performance for CSM. For $CSM1$, we can trade the quality of the solution for performance by tuning parameter γ. For the sake of fair comparison, we set $\gamma \rightarrow -\infty$ such that $CSM1$ is not constrained by size s. The result is shown in Figure 11. From the comparisons, we can see that $CSM2$ performs the best. $CSM1$ consumes the most time since we remove the size constraint of s, which means that the search procedure will exhaustively search a huge space. In the next experiment, we will show that by tuning γ, $CSM1$ can run much faster than global search without sacrificing the quality.

Effect of γ on $CSM1$. For $CSM1$, γ controls the tradeoff between quality and performance. We ran $CSM1$ with γ varying from 1 to 15 to observe the change in quality and run time. The quality of $CSM1$ is measured by

$$r_a = \Sigma_{v_0}\delta(H')/\Sigma_{v_0}\delta(H)$$

, where H' is the answer found by $CSM1$, H is one of the optimal answers found by a global search, and the Σ runs over all randomly selected query vertices. We also summarize the time efficiency measured by

$$r_t = \Sigma_{v_0}t_1(v_0)/\Sigma_{v_0}t_2(v_0)$$

, where $t_1(v_0)$ is the run time of $CSM1$ for query vertex v_0, $t_2(v_0)$ is the run time of the global search, and the summarization runs over all sampled query vertices.

The tradeoff between quality and performance is shown in Figure 14. As expected, both performance and quality decrease with the growth of γ. However, performance drops drastically faster than quality. As a result, even running for a short duration, the quality produced by $CSM1$ still remains almost at one hounded of percent, especially for DBLP and Berkeley. For each of the three networks, we can observe a critical point (identified by the dotted line), before which a minor drop of solution quality will bring us a significant improvement of performance. The above results clearly show that the trading of quality for performance in $CSM1$ is quite effective. In real applications, users can specify γ based on their requirement for the tradeoff between performance and accuracy.

Effect of γ on $CSM2$. From Figure 15, we observe that for each graph there is a certain γ that leads to the minimal overall run time of CSM2. The influence of γ on the performance of $CSM2$ generally depends on the network structure. It seems that Berkeley is more sensitive to γ than the other two networks. However, our results show that generally when $4 \leq \gamma \leq 12$, minimal run time of $CSM2$ can be achieved.

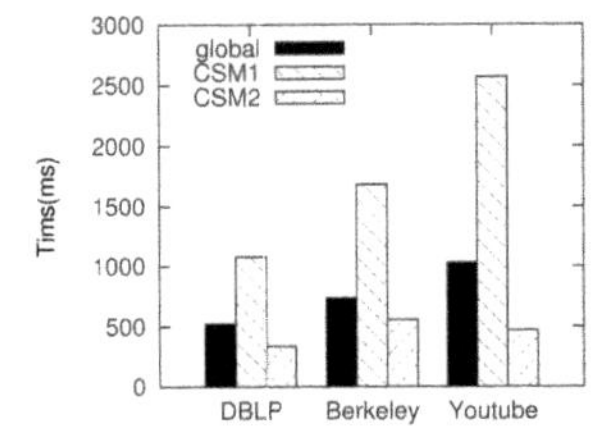

Figure 11: The performance of local search to CSM

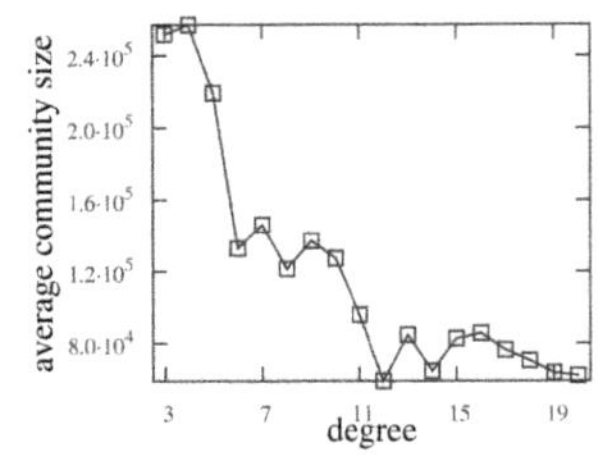

Figure 12: Community size vs vertex degree on DBLP

Selection of γ. Next, we give guidelines for selecting an appropriate γ for a query vertex when solving CSM. In general, the selection of γ depends on the size of the resulting community, which is determined by the local structure near the query vertex. The larger the community size, the larger the search space. Hence, γ should be tuned accordingly. However, it is hard to know the exact community size before a local search is executed. We found that, through the empirical analysis of DBLP data, *the degree of the query vertex is a good hint of the vertex's community size*. We used global search to find a maximal community for a query vertex in DBLP. For each degree, we randomly selected 10 vertices and recorded their average community size. The results are shown in Figure 12. We observe that the community size generally decreases when the degree of the query vertex increases. Hence, we should choose a smaller γ when the query vertex has a large degree (recall that smaller γ leads to larger search space).

6.2 Experiments on Synthetic Networks

To test the scalability and the sensitivity-to-community-structure of our solutions, we generated a collection of synthetic networks. Community search is meaningless on a network without community structures, hence we used a generator [12] that can generate synthetic graphs with a varying degree of "clearness" of community structure. It generates a graph using three parameters α, β, and μ. The degree and the community size follow the power-law distribution with exponent $-\alpha$ and $-\beta$, respectively. Parameter μ indicates the proportion of a vertex's neighbors that reside in other communities. Clearly, by tuning μ, we can vary the clearness of the community structure of the generated synthetic network. Since **ls-li** is the most efficient local search method, in the following experiment, the results of the local search are produced by **ls-li**.

Scalability. Using the above network model, we generated an ensemble of synthetic networks with size varying from $200K$ to $1M$ with $\alpha = 2, \beta = 3, \mu = 0.1$.

The scalability results of the local search are shown in Figure 16. We found that **ls-li**, $CSM1$, and $CSM2$ are consistently more efficient than a global search even on graphs with millions of vertices. Note that the result for $CSM1$ was obtained with 100% accuracy (we omitted the accuracy result). The efficiency of $CSM1$ is quite impressive since it consistently outperforms a global search by about three orders of magnitude without sacrificing the accuracy. We also found that the run time of local search grows more slowly than global search when the graph size increases. In some cases, for example in CST, the advantage of a local search over global search is even more obvious when the graph is larger. These observations verify that a global search needs to visit all vertices. In contrast, a local search only needs to visit the limited neighborhoods around the query vertex. When the neighborhood grows more slowly than the whole graph size, a local search is certainly more efficient than a global search.

Sensitivity to community structure. Local search is sensitive to the clearness of community structures in the network. The more obvious the community structure, the more efficient local search. To verify this conjecture, we generate synthetic networks with μ varying from 0.1 to 0.5. Other parameters were the same as the previous experiment. The larger the value of μ, the clearer the community structure.

We present the result in Figure 17. It is clear that **ls-li** and $CSM1$ are consistently and significantly better than global search for different μ. $CSM2$ exhibits a similar performance as global search, but is still better than global search. The results in Figure 17(c) show that $CSM1$ can help us find a good tradeoff between quality and performance, independent of the community structure of the network.

We can also see that either the local search (both solutions of CST and CSM) or global search consumes more time when the network shows vaguer community structure. When μ is large, the boundary of the communities become vague, thus, for most of k, the result of $CST(k)$ that contains the query vertex will become larger, and the maximal core of the graph tends to become larger. As a result, for both local search and global search, the run time increases with the growth in the answer size.

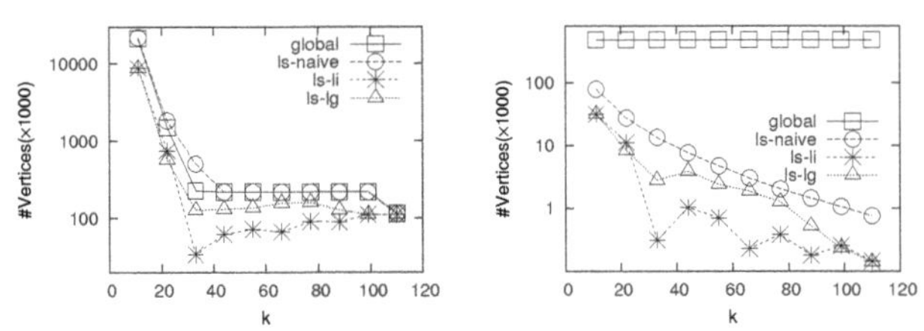

(a) The answer size (b) The number of visited vertices

Figure 13: Answer size and visited vertex size in local search

7. RELATED WORK

The work presented in this paper is closely related to *community detection*, *local search on graphs*, and *k-core decomposition*.

Community detection. Community detection was first modeled as a *modularity* optimization problem. *Modularity* [1] is a well-known measure of the *goodness* of non-overlapping divisions in a network. Unfortunately, finding the division that maximizes the modularity is NP-complete [13]. A typical solution to optimizing modularity is the Newman-Girvan approach [1], which derives good partitions on many real networks but it takes $O(|E|^2|V|)$, or $O(|V|^3)$ time on a sparse graph. It was also shown that modularity optimization may fail in some special networks [14].

Many successors devoted their efforts to improving the quality and performance of community detection. In recent years, label propagation has attracted wide research interest since it in general can produce high-quality communities with almost linear time [15, 16]. In real applications, only top clusters usually interest users. A solution [17] was proposed to mine the top clusters of a network. Sparsification that can preserve the community structure is also used to reduce the size of the graph so that community detection on the sparsified graph is more efficient [18].

Another direction of efforts focuses on extending current solution to support more semantics of communities. The real social networks usually have overlapping communities [19], *i.e.*, vertices are shared among different communities. Some efficient approaches for the identification of overlapping communities in large real network have been proposed, including clique percolation method [20], q-state Potts model based method [21]. Considering the influence of attributes of edges on the semantic of community, SA-Cluster, which utilizes both structure and attribute information, is proposed for graph clustering [22].

All these works do not consider *community search*, which was first proposed in [5]. The community search problem addressed in this paper is a special case of that proposed in [5], where they intend to find a community containing a set of query nodes while

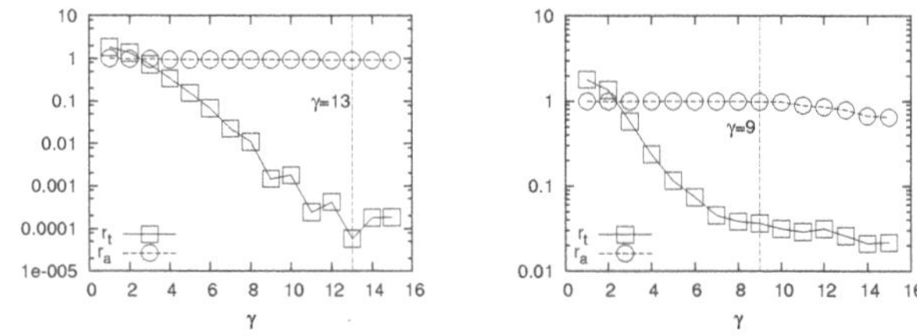

(a) DBLP (b) Berkeley

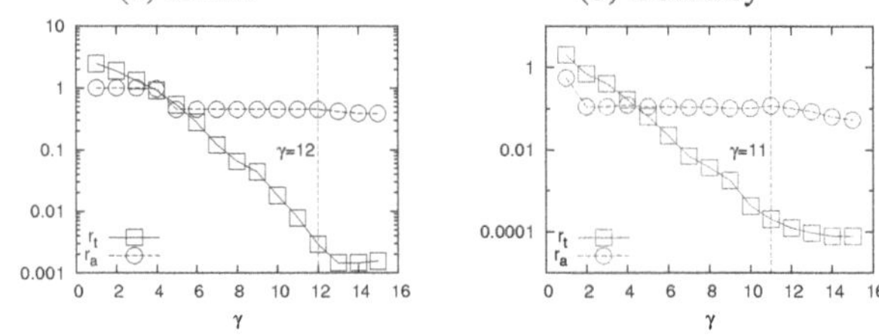

(c) Youtube (d) LiveJournal

Figure 14: γ's affect on $CSM1$

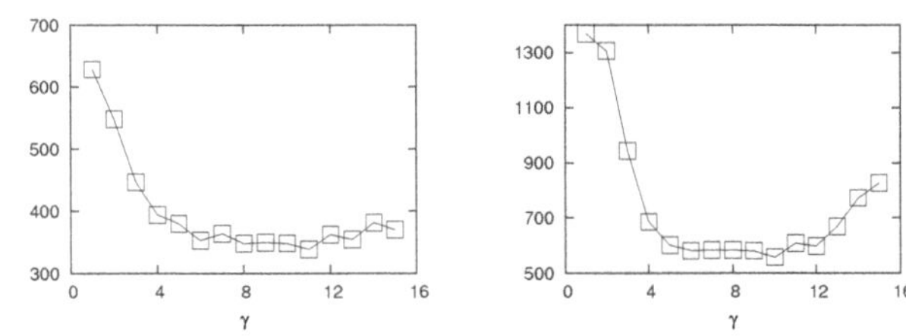

(a) DBLP (b) Berkeley

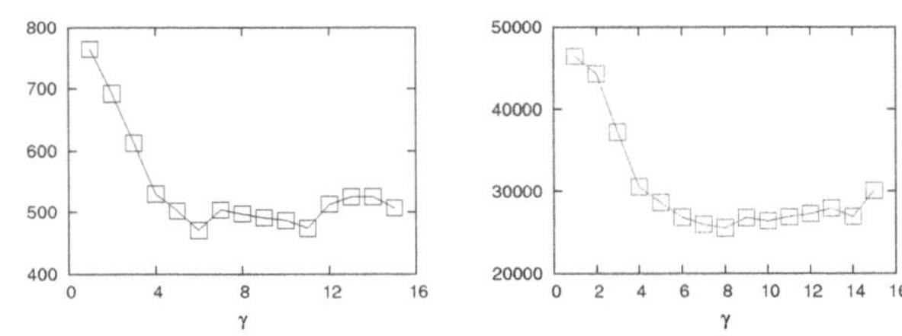

(c) Youtube (d) LiveJournal

Figure 15: γ's affect on $CSM2$

in our problem we are interested in querying the community for a single vertex. However, they solve the community search problem by global search.

Local search for communities. In recent years, local search for communities in real graphs is attracting ever-increasing research interests [29, 30, 31, 32]. Aaron [29] first proposes the problem to find a community with size constraint k for a certain vertex. But he uses "local modularity" as the community goodness measure, which characterizes the relative density within the community to outside of the community. According to the new measure, he proposes a heuristic algorithm with quadratic time complexity regarding to k. Bagrow [30] further improves the performance by selecting the vertex with largest "outwardness", where outwardness of vertex v is the number of v' neighbors outside the community minus the number inside. Local search of community is widely used in existing Sybil defense schemes [31]. Their basic idea is that local community around a trusted node is also trustworthy [31]. And Wanyun [32] studies the overlapping structure of local search.

These local search methods [29, 30] find communities with size constraint to limit the search space. As a result, they cannot ensure to find the best community under corresponding community goodness measure. Another weakness is that the size constraint as

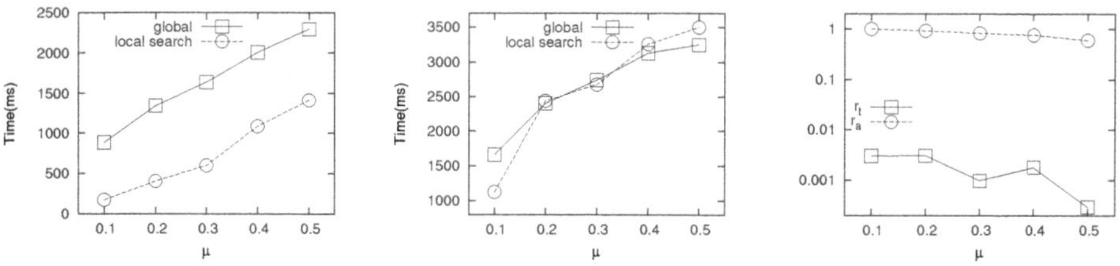

(a) CST (b) CSM2 (c) CSM1

Figure 17: Influence of community structure on efficiency of local search

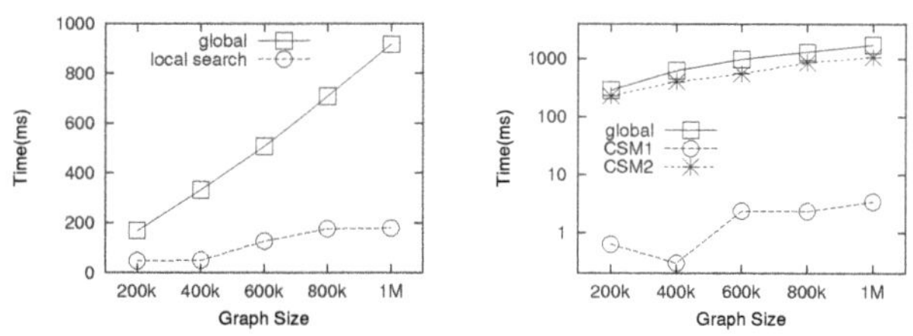

(a) CST (b) CSM

Figure 16: Scalability of local search

an input parameter is hard to select. In general, each vertex has its own the most appropriate community size. Either predefining a global parameter or trying different parameters blindly can hardly find meaningful results.

k-core decomposition. The technique used in this paper is closely related to the estimation of giant component size of random graphs [23, 24] and k-core decomposition [25, 26]. The threshold of sudden emergence of a giant k-core in a random graph is theoretically studied in [25]. Newman *et al.* [24] proposed a novel method to compute the mean component size of random graphs with arbitrary degree distribution using generating function. k-core decomposition is empirically investigated on many real large networks and shown to be a new perspective to characterize the structure and function of real networks [27]. k-core decomposition is also used to visualize large complex networks [26]. An external memory based k-core decomposition solution is developed to handle massive networks [28]. These techniques are rarely used for community search.

8. CONCLUSION

We investigate the problem of finding the best community containing a given query vertex in its neighborhood. We propose a local search method for this purpose. Local search is more efficient than global search since global search needs to visit all vertices in the network for community detection. We address the local search challenge that arises from the non-monotonicity of community goodness measure. In this paper, we propose the CST and the CSM algorithms to solve a variety of community search problems. We conduct extensive experiments on synthetic and a variety of real life, million-node networks. Our future work will consider constraints in community search, so that we can support applications in many emerging social settings, such as micro-blogging and online social networks.

9. REFERENCES

[1] M. E. J. Newman et al., "Finding and evaluating community structure in networks," *Phys. Rev. E*, vol. 69, no. 2, p. 026113.

[2] A. Broder et al., "Graph structure in the web," *Comput. Netw.*, vol. 33, no. 1-6, pp. 309–320, June 2000.

[3] G. Palla et al., "Uncovering the overlapping community structure of complex networks in nature and society," *Nature*, vol. 435, no. 7043, pp. 814–818.

[4] R. Guimera et al., "Functional cartography of complex metabolic networks," *Nature*, vol. 433, no. 7028, pp. 895–900.

[5] M. Sozio et al., "The community-search problem and how to plan a successful cocktail party," in *KDD'10*.

[6] H. Zhuge et al., "Query routing in a peer-to-peer semantic link network," *Computational Intelligience*, vol. 21, no. 2, pp. 197–216.

[7] B. Bollobás, "The evolution of sparse graphs," Graph Theory and Combinatorics, Proc. Cambridge Combinatorial Conf. in honor of Paul Erdos, Academic Press, pp. 35-57.

[8] M. Gaertler et al., "Dynamic analysis of the autonomous system graph," in *IPS 2004*, pp. 13–24

[9] S. B. Seidman., "Network structure and minimum degree," *Social Networks* , Vol. 5, pp. 269–287.

[10] S. N. Dorogovtsev et al., "k-core organization of complex networks," *Phys. Rev. Lett.* Vol.96, pp. 040601.

[11] A. Mislove et al., "Measurement and analysis of online social networks," in *IMC'07*.

[12] A. Lancichinetti et al., "Benchmark graphs for testing community detection algorithms," *Phys. Rev. E*, vol. 78, no. 4, p. 046110.

[13] U. Brandes et al., "On modularity clustering," *TKDE*, vol. 20, no. 2, pp. 172–188.

[14] S. Fortunato et al., "Resolution limit in community detection," *PNAS*, vol. 104, no. 1, p. 36.

[15] U. N. Raghavan et al., "Near linear time algorithm to detect community structures in large-scale networks," *Phys.Rev.E*, vol. 76, p. 036106.

[16] I. X. Y. Leung et al., "Towards real-time community detection in large networks," *Phys.Rev.E*, vol. 79, p. 066107.

[17] K. Macropol et al., "Scalable discovery of best clusters on large graphs," in *VLDB'10*.

[18] V. Satuluri et al., "Local graph sparsification for scalable clustering," in *SIGMOD '11*.

[19] G. Palla et al., "Uncovering the overlapping community structure of complex networks in nature and society," *Nature*, vol. 435, no. 7043, pp. 814–818.

[20] I. Derenyi et al., "Clique percolation in random networks," *Phys. Rev. Letters*, vol. 94, no. 16, p. 160202.

[21] J. Reichardt et al., "Detecting fuzzy community structures in complex x networks with a potts model," *Phys. Rev. Letters*, vol. 93, no. 21, p. 218701.

[22] Y. Zhou et al., "Graph clustering based on structural/attribute similarities," in *VLDB'09*.

[23] B. Bollobas, *Random Graphs*. Cambridge University Press, 2001.

[24] M. E. J. Newman et al., "Random graphs with arbitrary degree distributions and their applications," *Phys. Rev. E*, vol. 64, no. 2, p. 026118.

[25] B. Pittel et al., "Sudden emergence of a giant k-core in a random graph," *J. Comb. Theory Ser. B*, vol. 67, pp. 111–151.

[26] J. I. Alvarez-hamelin et al., "Large scale networks fingerprinting and visualization using the k-core decomposition," in *NIPS'06*.

[27] S. Carmi et al., "From the cover: A model of internet topology using k-shell decomposition," *PNAS*, vol. 104, no. 27, pp. 11 150–11 154, 2007.

[28] J. Cheng et al., "Efficient core decomposition in massive networks," in *ICDE'11*.

[29] A. Clauset., "Finding local community structure in networks," *Phys. Rev. E*, vol. 72, p. 026132. 2005.

[30] J. P. Bagrow, "Evaluating local community methods in networks" *J. Stat. Mech.*, vol. 2008, p. 05001. 2008.

[31] B. Viswanath et al., "An analysis of social network-based sybil defenses," *SIGCOMM Comput. Commun. Rev.*, vol41, pp363–374.

[32] W. Cui et al., "Online Search of Overlapping Communities," in *SIGMOD '13*.

Mining Statistically Significant Connected Subgraphs in Vertex Labeled Graphs

Akhil Arora
aarora@cse.iitk.ac.in

Mayank Sachan
mayasac@cse.iitk.ac.in

Arnab Bhattacharya
arnabb@iitk.ac.in

Dept. of Computer Science and Engineering,
Indian Institute of Technology, Kanpur,
India

ABSTRACT

The steady growth of graph data in various applications has resulted in wide-spread research in finding significant sub-structures in a graph. In this paper, we address the problem of finding statistically significant connected subgraphs where the nodes of the graph are labeled. The labels may be either discrete where they assume values from a pre-defined set, or continuous where they assume values from a real domain and can be multi-dimensional. We motivate the problem citing applications in spatial co-location rule mining and outlier detection. We use the chi-square statistic as a measure for quantifying the statistical significance. Since the number of connected subgraphs in a general graph is exponential, the naïve algorithm is impractical. We introduce the notion of contracting edges that merge vertices together to form a super-graph. We show that if the graph is dense enough to start with, the number of super-vertices is quite low, and therefore, running the naïve algorithm on the super-graph is feasible. If the graph is not dense, we provide an algorithm to reduce the number of super-vertices further, thereby providing a trade-off between accuracy and time. Empirically, the chi-square value obtained by this reduction is always within 96% of the optimal value, while the time spent is only a fraction of that for the optimal. In addition, we also show that our algorithm is scalable and it significantly enhances the ability to analyze real datasets.

Categories and Subject Descriptors

H.2.8 [**Database Management**]: Database Applications—*Data Mining*

Keywords

Graph mining; Statistical significance; Chi-square; Vertex labels; Connected subgraphs; Significant subgraphs

1. MOTIVATION

The significant growth of graph data in a wide range of commercial and scientific applications including bioinformatics, chemoinformatics and social networks has encouraged research in studying various patterns within graphs. Many of these applications rely on extracting significant substructures in the form of paths [26], trees [4], cliques [19], or subgraphs [11, 21, 33].

The problem has been mostly studied with reference to frequent subgraphs [21, 33] where a subgraph is considered to be significant when its frequency exceeds a particular threshold. However, in many applications, this characterization is not always sufficient. Rather, identifying the *statistically significant subgraphs* where the pattern within the subgraph deviates from the expected can potentially unearth interesting properties that merit further thorough analyses. The idea that a frequent subgraph might not be significant was explored in [11] and a new definition of statistical significance was proposed by transforming graphs into feature vectors. In [21], a scalable approach to mine significant patterns was proposed, and in [33], they were searched using dissimilar graph patterns.

There are a broad range of applications where the nature of the graph is such that every vertex of the graph is assigned a label. In biological and chemical networks, vertices are usually labeled from a discrete set of biochemical entities ranging from molecules to genes [35]. The continuous numerical labeling scheme is used in quantifying the amount of traffic at a particular node in communication networks [20] or in assigning scores to nodes in the web networks [32]. Many spatial datasets are represented in the form of such vertex labeled graphs [10, 14, 15, 16, 27].

Depending on the application, the vertex labels can be discrete [14, 27] or continuous [10, 16]. In a spatial dataset pertaining to ecology, the discrete vertex labels can be chosen from a set of boolean features enlisting different vegetation types (an example is the North-East dataset mentioned in Section 5.1) while in a geographical dataset, the vertices may be assigned a continuous numerical attribute such as the density of infected cases in that particular location (the WNV dataset explained in Section 5.2). Moreover, the continuous labels can be multi-dimensional such as rainfall and temperature [15]. Although mapping a continuous range to discrete intervals is sometimes possible, such a reduction may lose significant information and is, therefore, not always desirable.

Consequently, in this paper, we consider the two cases as being inherently different and study them separately for the purpose of mining *statistically significant connected subgraphs*. The condition of connectivity is necessary to guarantee a contiguous region in the space which ensures a meaningful relationship among the nodes. Statistical significance ascertains whether a given outcome is due to some extraneous factors or can be ascribed solely due to chance. It quantifies the deviation of the observed behavior from what is expected according to an underlying *null hypothesis*. The null hypothesis specifies the expected distribution of labels for both discrete and continuous cases. We consider the basic null model in

SIGMOD'14, June 22–27, 2014, Snowbird, UT, USA.

ACM 978-1-4503-2376-5/14/06 ...$15.00.
http://dx.doi.org/10.1145/2588555.2588574.

which the labels of the vertices are assumed to be independently and randomly drawn from a fixed probability distribution. The deviation of the actual labels of the vertices in a subgraph from the expected labels imposed by the null model is used as a measure of statistical significance.

The *p-value* [22] is one of the most widely used metrics for quantifying statistical significance. It denotes the probability of obtaining a test statistic at least as extreme as the one that is actually observed, assuming the underlying null hypothesis to be true. Hence, the lower the p-value, the higher is the statistical significance.

Since p-value computation may require exponential number of steps, we use the *chi-square statistic* [22] to make it practical. The chi-square statistic is the most commonly used estimate [5, 31, 34] of the p-value (the details about this approximation are mentioned in [22]). Higher the chi-square value, lower the p-value, and, thus, more statistically significant is the subgraph.

Our main contribution in this paper is to handle the general problem of identifying such statistically significant connected subgraphs efficiently. To the best of our knowledge, no prior research has been done that uses vertex labels for mining statistically significant connected subgraphs for both discrete and continuous labeled graphs.

Our proposed algorithm finds the most statistically significant connected subgraphs in expected linear time for "dense" graphs (we later formally define what is meant by a dense graph).

The rest of the paper is organized as follows. In Section 2, we explain in detail one application for each of the discrete and continuous labeling cases before the problem statements are presented. Section 3 highlights the related work while Section 4 describes our algorithm and its analysis. In Section 5, experimental results are presented before Section 6 concludes.

2. PROBLEM STATEMENT

Although our problem statement is much more generic and can be applied to a variety of settings, we motivate the discrete case specifically through co-location rule mining and the continuous case through outlier detection problem.

2.1 Discrete Labeling

Mining statistically significant subgraphs is applicable in finding co-location patterns from spatial databases that aim to reveal features that are likely to be closely located with each other in the spatial dimension [14, 27]. Given a set of n locations in a spatial database endowed with a neighborhood relationship $\mathcal{N}$, suppose $F = \{f_1, \ldots, f_l\}$ denotes a set of l boolean spatial features on each node. The objective of the *co-location rule* mining is to find rules of the form $X \Rightarrow Y$, where X and Y are subsets of spatial features. A particular instance of the features is said to be *co-located* if they occur within the neighborhood of each other. For example, a rule *{traffic jam, police}* $\Rightarrow$ *{accident} (80%)* signifies that whenever there are traffic jam and policemen, there is a 80% probability of an accident in the neighborhood. Various algorithms exist for mining such co-location rules [14, 27].

Given any such co-location rule, it may be interesting to find the contiguous regions in the space where this co-location rule is statistically significant. The statistical significance may imply that over that region, instances of X contain an exceptionally large or an exceptionally small ratio of instances of Y in their neighborhood. Once such regions have been identified, it may be useful to study the external forces acting over those regions to establish the causality of such co-location rules.

The space can be modeled as an undirected, un-weighted, labeled graph G where each vertex represents a spatial location. The connectivity of a pair of vertices through an edge is guided by some criterion such as a Euclidean distance threshold or a common border. Each vertex is labeled with a symbol from an alphabet Σ of size l. The boolean set for a co-location rule $X \Rightarrow Y$, therefore, is a set of two symbols c_0 and c_1 where c_0 represents the presence of Y in the neighborhood of X and c_1 represents the absence. The underlying assumption is that these symbols are randomly and independently drawn from a fixed binomial probability distribution $P = \{p_0, p_1\}$ where $p_0 + p_1 = 1$. The choice of p_0 can be either provided by the co-location rule (0.80 in the above example) or can be empirically calculated as the fraction of number of occurrences over the whole space. The null hypothesis states that the co-located patterns are distributed uniformly throughout the space. With respect to the given null hypothesis, the objective is to mine the statistically significant connected subgraphs.

The above analysis can be applied to a general graph as well. Consider a spatially connected graph where the nodes are labeled from a discrete set. Some of the labels can be rare, either due to its semantics, or due to prior empirical expectations. For example, in an ecologically important region where the nodes are marked with biodiversity and disturbance levels, it is intuitive that high disturbance should not allow high biodiversity. Thus, a label that encapsulates the high values together is expected to be rare. Hence, a spatial region that contains a large proportion of such labels will be a statistically significant connected subgraph. Such a finding is extremely important as it highlights an ecologically valuable region under the threat of human disturbance such as poaching.

Statistical significance is quantified by the *chi-square* statistic [22], which measures the deviation of the observed frequencies (O_i) from their expected values (E_i) given by the null model:

$$X^2 = \sum_{\forall \text{labels}} \frac{(O_i - E_i)^2}{E_i}. \quad (1)$$

Consider a subgraph with n vertices and l possible labels having an observed frequency vector $Y = \{Y_1, \ldots, Y_l\}$ where $\sum_{i=1}^{l} Y_i = n$. Since each vertex label is drawn randomly and independently from a fixed probability distribution $P = \{p_1, \ldots, p_l\}$, the expected frequencies are $E_i = n.p_i$. The chi-square, therefore, is

$$X^2 = \sum_{i=1}^{l} \frac{(Y_i - n.p_i)^2}{n.p_i} = \sum_{i=1}^{l} \frac{Y_i^2}{n.p_i} - n. \quad (2)$$

It has been shown that under the assumed null hypothesis, the chi-square statistic follows the chi-square distribution with $l-1$ degrees of freedom, denoted by $\chi^2(l-1)$ [22].

If all the outcomes are independent, the *p-value* can be computed by using the cumulative distribution function (cdf) $F(\cdot)$ of the $\chi^2(l-1)$ distribution. If z is the X^2 value of an observed outcome, then its p-value is $1 - F(z)$.

Although the X^2 statistic for a particular subgraph follows the χ^2 distribution, since the subgraphs share vertices, the individual X^2 values of all the subgraphs are *not* mutually independent. Hence, it is not possible to directly map the X^2_{max} statistic to a *p-value*. Nevertheless, a higher X^2 value will always necessarily point to a smaller p-value. Moreover, as the focus of the paper is not quantifying the degree of statistical significance directly but designing scalable algorithms to find the *most statistically significant connected subgraphs*, i.e, the ones with the *highest* chi-square values, this requirement is not crucial.

DEFINITION 1 (MOST SIGNIFICANT SUBGRAPH). *The* most significant connected subgraph (MSCS) *of a graph is the connected subgraph having the highest chi-square value among all possible connected subgraphs.*

DEFINITION 2 (TOP-t SIGNIFICANT SUBGRAPHS). *The top-t set of significant subgraphs (TSSS) of a graph is the set of t connected subgraphs having the highest chi-square values with the constraint that none of them share any vertex.*

The problem we tackle in this paper is next stated formally.

PROBLEM 1. *Given an undirected un-weighted graph having every vertex of it labeled with one of l possible symbols from Σ, find the MSCS. More generally, find the TSSS.*

One iterative way of obtaining the TSSS set is to first find the MSCS and then delete it from the graph to obtain the MSCS for the next step, and so on.

In order to find these subgraphs, a very useful concept is that of a *local maximally significant connected subgraph.*

DEFINITION 3 (LOCAL MAXIMALLY SIGNIFICANT). *A connected subgraph H of a graph is said to be a* local maximally significant connected subgraph (LMCS) *if it is not possible to increase the chi-square value of H by either adding to or removing from it a vertex such that H still remains connected.*

By definition, a MSCS and all members of TSSS are LMCS.

Several other interesting problems can also be conceived of, e.g., finding the connected subgraphs whose significance is *greater than a threshold* or finding the most significant connected subgraph that *exceeds a particular size*, etc. The TSSS algorithm can be utilized for solving these cases. A sufficiently large t can be chosen such that all subgraphs in the answer set exceed the particular significance threshold. Similarly, a large enough t will allow finding a subgraph whose size is more than the queried threshold size. Thus, although such problems are interesting in their own right, we stick to the more basic MSCS and TSSS problems in this paper.

2.2 Continuous Labeling

Mining statistically significant subgraphs where node labels assume real values can be applied to detecting *spatial outliers*, which are defined as observations that are inconsistent with their neighborhood [10, 16, 28]. Most outlier detection techniques assume that the attribute values (i.e., labels) are dependent on just the neighbors, and accordingly, classify a node as an outlier based only on that.

One standard technique for outlier detection is using *z-scores* [23]. In this technique, first, the value x_i of a node i is scaled according to its neighborhood by subtracting the weighted average of the attribute values of the neighbor set $\mathcal{N}(i)$:[1]

$$y_i = x_i - \sum_{j \in \mathcal{N}(i)} w_j x_j. \tag{3}$$

Scaling helps in eliminating the dependence of x_i on its neighbors, i.e., the y_i values become independent and identically distributed (i.i.d.) under the null hypothesis. The z-score of a node is then calculated using the sample mean $\widehat{\mu}$ and sample standard deviation $\widehat{\sigma}$ of the scaled values (these are representatives of the true values)

$$z_i = (y_i - \widehat{\mu})/\widehat{\sigma}. \tag{4}$$

Since y_i's are i.i.d. random variables, due to the central limit theorem [12], the z-score follows the standard normal distribution $N(0, 1)$. Moreover, similar to y_i's, under the null hypothesis, z_i's are also independent. Hence, the nodes exhibiting large magnitudes of z-scores (either positive or negative) are deemed as outliers.

[1] Some useful weighting schemes have been proposed in [16].

Instead of just finding single outlier nodes, we extend the notion to *outlier spatial regions* as well. The *combined z-score* of a region Z_S containing the set of nodes, S, is defined as the (scaled) sum of the individual z-scores:

$$Z_S = \sum_{i \in S} z_i / \sqrt{|S|}. \tag{5}$$

The sum is scaled by a factor of $1/\sqrt{|S|}$ to ensure that under the null hypothesis the distribution of the combined z-scores remains the same as those of individual nodes. In this way, the statistical significances of regions and single nodes are directly comparable.

The z-score of a set S, composed of a mutually exclusive set of nodes S_1 and S_2 with z-scores Z_1 and Z_2 respectively, is

$$Z_S = \frac{\sqrt{|S_1|}.Z_1 + \sqrt{|S_2|}.Z_2}{\sqrt{|S_1 + S_2|}}. \tag{6}$$

Since all z_i's are i.i.d. $N(0, 1)$ variables, Z_S also follows $N(0, 1)$.

We further extend the notion of z-score to multiple dimensions. Given a set of k independent multiple attributes of a node, the *multi-dimensional z-score* of a set of nodes, S, is a tuple $(Z_S^1, \dots, Z_S^k)$ where Z_S^j represents the z-score of the jth attribute of S. Since the attributes are independent of each other, the z-scores in each dimension are also independent of each other. Further, since each Z_S^j follows $N(0, 1)$, the multi-dimensional z-score $(Z_S^1, \dots, Z_S^k)$ follows a multi-variate standard normal distribution whose *pdf* is

$$f(Z_S^1, \dots, Z_S^k) = \frac{1}{(2\pi)^{k/2}} e^{-\sum_{j=1}^{k} (Z_S^j)^2/2}. \tag{7}$$

The *chi-square* statistic, X^2, of the multi-dimensional z-score is defined as the sum of squares of the z-scores in each dimension:

$$X_S^2 = \sum_{j=1}^{k} (Z_S^j)^2. \tag{8}$$

Since the X^2 statistic appears as a negative power of exponential in the pdf (Eq. (7)), outcomes having higher chi-square statistic values have lesser probability densities and are, therefore, less likely to occur. Since X^2 is the sum of k individual i.i.d. $N(0, 1)$ variables, it follows the $\chi^2(k)$ distribution under the null hypothesis.

The objective, thus, is to find contiguous regions in the space as outliers. These outlier regions are classified as statistically significant with respect to the given null hypothesis.

We reduce this problem to the generic graph problem where the nodes represent the individual locations and edges represent the spatial connectivity or the neighborhood relationships between these locations. A contiguous spatial region corresponds to a connected subgraph of this spatial graph. The problem, therefore, is to find the connected subgraphs exhibiting large chi-square values.

PROBLEM 2. *Given an undirected un-weighted graph with every vertex containing a multi-dimensional z-score value, find the MSCS. More generally, find the TSSS.*

3. RELATED WORK

Randomization tests, also called permutation tests [7], is a common method for testing significance of graphs. Given an input graph, the tests sample data from the class of graphs that share certain structural properties with the input graph. The basic idea in randomization tests is to perturb the original graph by swapping certain edges but still maintaining the structural properties and then carry out experiments with the randomized versions of the graph

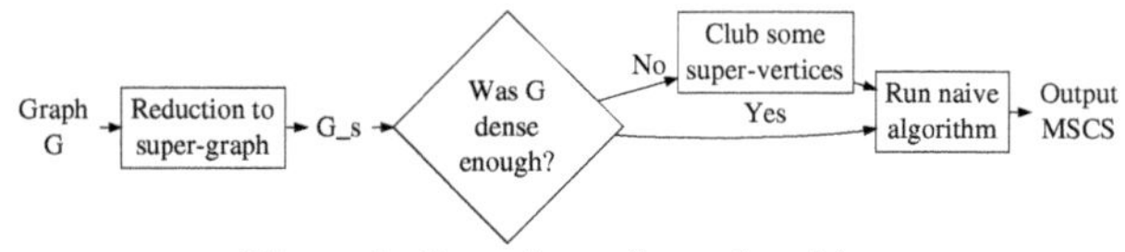

Figure 1: Overview of our algorithm.

thus obtained. Though the objective is similar, our problem is inherently different as the randomization is not in the structure of the graph but in the vertex labels. Moreover, the randomization tests are used to generate the distribution for the test statistic that do not follow any standard distribution, while for us, the null hypothesis assumes the well-known chi-square distribution for vertex labels.

The existing literature has witnessed a host of random graph models, the oldest of which is the Erdős-Rényi (ER) model [9]. Its major drawback is that it does not model real-life phenomena as it assumes independent and equally probable edges. Watts et al. [30] introduced the Watts-Strogatz model with "small-world" properties (high clustering, triadic closures, etc.). This model, however, has unrealistic degree distributions unlike that in standard "scale-free" networks, for which Newman et al. [18] proposed an improvement. Many real world graphs including the world wide web, biological networks, social networks etc. are believed to be scale-free and schemes such as *preferential attachment* have been proposed to explain such networks. The preferential attachment paradigm states that the more popular a node is, the higher is the chance of a new node getting attached to it. The Barabási-Albert (BA) model [1] incorporated this notion with the dynamic growth of a graph as well. Holme et al. [13] extended the BA model by including a triad formation step to improve the clustering coefficient. The importance of triads in real graphs has been highlighted by Durak et al. [6].

Mining statistically significant co-location patterns was studied in [2] where instead of using a threshold, subsets of spatial features that are co-located due to some form of spatial dependency were found. It was extended in [3] where segregation patterns were mined by taking into account the auto-correlation of the co-location rules. Statistical significance techniques were used to locate the most informative set of patterns in [17]. The p-value and z-score computation approaches were used for hotspot detection in [29].

The problem of identifying statistically significant substrings with multinomial distribution as the underlying null hypothesis has been recently studied [25]. The string can be seen as an over-simplified version of a graph with substrings representing the connected subgraphs. Hence, this can be considered a special case of our study.

4. ALGORITHM

4.1 Naïve Algorithm

The naïve algorithm for both the discrete and the continuous case simply examines all the possible connected subgraphs. Since the number of different connected subgraphs for a graph can be exponential in the number of vertices, irrespective of the number of edges, the running time is impractical unless the graph is small.

4.2 Outline of our Algorithm

To solve the problem of finding statistically significant subgraphs efficiently, we propose an algorithm as outlined in Figure 1. We first reduce the input graph $G(V, E)$ to a super-graph $G_s(V_s, E_s)$ by merging together some of the vertices and removing the edges between them. We prove that if the original graph G is dense enough (we will specify exactly what is meant by "dense enough" later), then the size of this super-graph G_s is so small that running the naïve algorithm on it is feasible. The reduction to super-graph for the discrete case has the desirable property that the MSCS and TSSS in the original graph are exactly the same as the MSCS and TSSS in the super-graph. The continuous case, however, may not always exhibit such properties.

Algorithm 1 Construction of Super-graph (Discrete Labels)

Input: Graph $G = (V, E)$
Output: Super-graph $G_s = (V_s, E_s)$
1: Copy $G_c(V_c, E_c) \leftarrow G(V, E)$
2: Delete all non-contracting edges from E
3: $V_s \leftarrow$ Connected components of G_c by performing BFS
4: **for** all edges $e = (u, v) \in E$ **do**
5:   **if** e is not contracting **then**
6:     Super-vertices u_s contains u and v_s contains v
7:     Add super-edge $e_s = (u_s, v_s)$ to G_s
8:   **end if**
9: **end for**
10: **return** $G_s(V_s, E_s)$

If, however, G was not sufficiently dense to start with, the size of G_s is not sufficiently small either. Hence, we need to reduce its size by further clubbing together some of the super-vertices. This step does not guarantee that the final MSCS obtained is the actual MSCS. This, thus, provides a trade-off between running time and accuracy. Through detailed analysis and experiments we show that the obtained solution does not deviate much from the optimal.

Next, we describe the super-graph creation and reduction algorithms in detail. The algorithms are fundamentally similar for discrete and continuous labels.

4.3 Construction of the Super-graph

The *super-graph* $G_s = (V_s, E_s)$ is obtained by clubbing together neighboring vertices of the original graph $G = (V, E)$. The vertices of the super-graph are called *super-vertices*. The set of super-vertices are *mutually exclusive* and *exhaustive*. There exists a *super-edge* between two super-vertices v_{s_1} and v_{s_2} if and only if there exists an edge $(v_1, v_2) \in E$ with $v_1 \in v_{s_1}$ and $v_2 \in v_{s_2}$.

We first explain the notion of a *contracting edge*. An edge is contracting if the two vertices that it joins become part of the same super-vertex; otherwise it is non-contracting. The exact definition of when two vertices can become part of the same super-vertex differs from the discrete to the continuous case, and will be specified when the super-graph construction algorithms are explained.

We start with the discrete labeled graphs and then follow it up with the continuous labeled case.

4.3.1 Discrete Labels

The pseudo-code for the super-graph construction for a discrete labeled graph is shown in Algorithm 1. For discrete labels, an edge $e = (v_1, v_2)$ is *contracting* if and only if the labels of v_1 and v_2 are the same. The algorithm first deletes all non-contracting edges from a copy G_c of the original graph G (lines 1-2). It then finds all the *connected components* in G_c by running a BFS (line 3). Each connected component forms a super-vertex. Two super-vertices are connected if and only if two component vertices of them are connected in the original graph (lines 4-9).

The algorithm requires $O(m + n)$ time for n vertices and m edges. It also leads to the following conclusion.

CONCLUSION 1. *Given any connected subgraph H_s of the super-graph G_s, there exists a corresponding connected subgraph $H \subseteq G$ such that the vertex set of H is the union of the vertices in each super-vertex of H_s.*

The next result is important to understand why a classification of edges into contracting and non-contracting is useful.

LEMMA 1. *For a given connected subgraph H, if addition of one vertex with label c_r to H does not decrease the X^2 value of H, then addition of one more vertex of the same label c_r necessarily increases the X^2 value of H.*

PROOF. Suppose H_1 and H_2 are the subgraphs obtained by adding respectively one and two vertices of label c_r to H. Also, suppose Z_0, Z_1 and Z_2 are the corresponding X^2 values of H, H_1 and H_2 respectively. Further, assume that the sizes of the three subgraphs H, H_1 and H_2 are $t-1$, t and $t+1$ respectively, and their count vectors (i.e., the vectors denoting the number of vertices of each label) are $\{X_1, \dots, X_r - 1, \dots, X_l\}$, $\{X_1, \dots, X_r, \dots, X_l\}$ and $\{X_1, \dots, X_r + 1, \dots, X_l\}$ respectively where $\sum_{i=1}^{l} X_i = t$. Using the definition of X^2 from Eq. (2), we get

$$Z_1 = \sum_{i=1}^{l} \frac{X_i^2}{tp_i} - t. \quad (9)$$

$$\begin{aligned} Z_0 &= \sum_{i=1, i \neq r}^{l} \frac{X_i^2}{(t-1)p_i} + \frac{(X_r - 1)^2}{(t-1)p_r} - (t-1) \\ &= \sum_{i=1}^{l} \frac{X_i^2}{(t-1)p_i} - \frac{2X_r - 1}{(t-1)p_r} - (t-1) \\ &= \frac{1}{t-1}\left[t(Z_1 + t) - \frac{(2x_r - 1)}{p_r} - (t-1)^2\right] \\ &= \frac{1}{t-1}\left[tZ_1 - \frac{(2x_r - 1)}{p_r} + 2t - 1\right]. \quad (10) \end{aligned}$$

$$\begin{aligned} Z_2 &= \sum_{i=1, i \neq r}^{l} \frac{X_i^2}{(t+1)p_i} + \frac{(X_r + 1)^2}{(t+1)p_r} - (t+1) \\ &= \sum_{i=1}^{l} \frac{X_i^2}{(t+1)p_i} + \frac{2X_r + 1}{(t+1)p_r} - (t+1) \\ &= \frac{1}{t+1}\left[t(Z_1 + t) + \frac{(2X_r + 1)}{p_r} - (t+1)^2\right] \\ &= \frac{1}{t+1}\left[tZ_1 + \frac{(2X_r + 1)}{p_r} - 2t - 1\right]. \quad (11) \end{aligned}$$

Since it is given that $Z_1 \geq Z_0$, we have

$$\begin{aligned} Z_1 &\geq \frac{1}{t-1}\left[tZ_1 - \frac{(2X_r - 1)}{p_r} + 2t - 1\right] \\ \Rightarrow (t-1)Z_1 &\geq tZ_1 - \frac{(2X_r - 1)}{p_r} + 2t - 1 \\ \Rightarrow \frac{(2X_r - 1)}{p_r} &\geq Z_1 + 2t - 1 \\ \Rightarrow \frac{(2X_r + 1)}{p_r} &\geq Z_1 + 2t - 1 + \frac{2}{p_r}. \quad (12) \end{aligned}$$

Plugging Eq. (12) in Eq. (11), and using $0 < p_r < 1$, we get

$$\begin{aligned} Z_2 &\geq \frac{1}{t+1}\left[tZ_1 + Z_1 + 2t - 1 + \frac{2}{p_r} - 2t - 1\right] \\ \Rightarrow Z_2 &\geq Z_1 + \frac{1}{t+1}\left(\frac{2}{p_r} - 2\right) > Z_1. \quad (13) \end{aligned}$$

□

Algorithm 2 Construction of Super-graph (Continuous Labels)

Input: Graph $G = (V, E)$
Output: Super-graph $G_s = (V_s, E_s)$

```
V_s ← ∅; E_s ← E
for all vertices v ∈ V do
    v_s ← v; v.super ← v_s
    Add v_s to V_s
end for
for all edges e = (u, v) ∈ E do
    combz ← Combined z-score of u_s and v_s
    if X²_combz > max{X²_{u_s}, X²_{v_s}} then
        Super-vertex w = Merge(u_s, v_s)
        X²_w ← X²_combz
        Add all edges of form (u_s, x) and (v_s, x) as (w_s, x)
        V_s ← (V_s ∪ {w_s}) − {u_s, v_s}; E_s ← E_s − {e}
    end if
end for
return G_s(V_s, E_s)
```

The next result uses Lemma 1 to prove that for all bi-connected LMCS of G (and hence, also the MSCS and the TSSS of G), there exists an equivalent connected subgraph in the super-graph G_s.[2]

LEMMA 2. *Given any bi-connected LMCS $H \subseteq G$, there exists a connected subgraph $H_s \subseteq G_s$ such that every super-vertex of H_s is composed of vertices from H and every vertex of H is also a part of some super-vertex of H_s. Alternatively, $H_s \subseteq G_s$ is equivalent to $H \subseteq G$ as X^2 of H is the same as X^2 of H_s.*

PROOF. We prove this by contradiction. Suppose, the vertices of H_s are chosen as the union of all super-vertices that contain some vertex from H. Now, if the lemma does not hold, then there must exist some super-vertex $v_s \in H_s$ containing vertices v_1 and v_2 with $(v_1, v_2) \in E$ such that $v_1 \in H$ and $v_2 \notin H$. Clearly, as v_1 and v_2 are part of the same super-vertex v_s, they should have the same labels. If H_1 is the subgraph obtained by removing v_1 from H, H_1 is connected since H is bi-connected. Similarly, if H_2 is the subgraph obtained by adding v_2 to H, H_2 is also connected as $(v_1, v_2) \in E$. Further, since H is a LMCS, X^2 value of H_1 or H_2 cannot be more than that of H. Applying Lemma 1 on H_1, H (obtained by adding v_1 to H_1) and H_2 (obtained by adding v_2 to H), we get that X^2 value of H_2 is greater than H, which is a contradiction. □

This leads to the following conclusion.

CONCLUSION 2. *All the bi-connected LMCS of G, and hence, also the MSCS and the TSSS of G have equivalent connected subgraphs H_s in G_s. Thus, they can be extracted by running the naïve algorithm over G_s instead of G.*

The result emphasizes the fact that the super-graph construction technique ensures the *correctness* of the results within the sufficient condition of bi-connectivity. However, the condition is not necessary; a LMCS of G which is not bi-connected can still have an equivalent connected subgraph in G_s.

4.3.2 Continuous Labels

The algorithm for constructing the super-graph for the continuous labels (Algorithm 2) is similar to the discrete case. The main

[2]A connected subgraph is *bi-connected* if it remains connected even after the removal of any vertex from it.

Algorithm 3 Construction of a Erdős-Rényi Random Graph

Input: Number of vertices n of a random graph
Output: Random graph $G = (V, E)$

```
V ← {1, ..., n}; E ← ∅; m ← 0
while G = (V, E) is not connected do
    Choose randomly i, j from {1, ..., n}, i ≠ j
    if (i, j) ∉ E then
        Add edge (i, j) to E
        m ← m + 1
    end if
end while
return G
```

difference is in the way a contracting edge is defined, which depends on the X^2 values of the corresponding vertices. If the X^2 of the combined vertex set is greater than the individual vertices, then the edge is *contracting*. In other words, edge $e = (u, v)$ is contracting if and only if $X^2_{(u,v)} > X^2_u, X^2_v$.

After the two vertices along a contracting edge are clubbed, the algorithm takes into account the changed X^2 value of the merged vertex. The classification of an edge as contracting, being dependent on this updated X^2 value, thus, depends on the order in which the edges are processed. A very simple example is clubbing u with either of its neighbors v or w, where, with both additions, the X^2 value is increased so much that it prevents clubbing of the other neighbor. Thus, only one of the edges of u—the one which is processed before the other—is contracting. Thus, the super-graph constructed may not be unique. Hence, unlike Conclusion 1, there is no strong result for the continuous case. There may be cases where a LMCS of G may not have a corresponding connected subgraph in G_s. Nevertheless, since combining the two vertices always necessarily increases the X^2 value, in general, the X^2 values of super-vertices are likely to be much more than the individual connected components of the original graph.

Next, we analyze the size of super-graphs for both the cases.

4.4 Analysis of the Size of Super-graph

In this section, we analyze how the number of vertices n_s of the super-graph G_s depends on the number of edges m and the number of vertices n of G. We consider two random graph models.

In the Erdős-Rényi (ER) model, each edge is independent and equally likely. Algorithm 3 shows the construction of a random ER graph. It starts with n vertices and no edge, and keeps adding edges randomly to the graph till it becomes connected.

Algorithm 4 outlines how a random graph is constructed for the basic Barabási-Albert (BA) model. Besides the total number of vertices in the graph, it requires another parameter d. Each newly added vertex attaches itself to d old vertices. The initialization step requires d number of disconnected vertices. All the remaining $n-d$ vertices are then added one at a time, thus requiring $n-d$ iterations. Each new vertex prefers attachment to an old vertex that is more heavily connected, i.e., the probability of attaching to an old vertex is proportional to its degree.

The next lemma characterizes the expected number of edges in a *connected* random Erdős-Rényi graph.

LEMMA 3. *The expected number of edges required to make a random ER graph having n vertices connected, is less than $n \ln n$.*

PROOF. At each addition of a random edge, the number of components decrease by at most 1. Suppose the random variable X denotes the total number of edges added and X_c denotes the number of edges added to reduce the number of connected components from $c+1$ to c. Therefore,

$$X = \sum_{c=1}^{n-1} X_c. \tag{14}$$

A random edge $e = (v_1, v_2)$ reduces the number of components by 1 if v_1 and v_2 lie in different connected components. The probability p_c of choosing an edge such that it reduces the number of components from $c+1$ to c is at least $p_c \geq c/(n-1)$ as for any choice of v_1, each of the c other components must contain at least one vertex in them. Thus, at least c out of $n-1$ different possible choices of v_2 will reduce the number of components to c.

We keep drawing edges randomly as part of X_c till one such edge is obtained. Thus, X_c follows a geometric distribution whose expectation is $1/p_c$. Using the linearity of expectations,

$$E[X] = \sum_{c=1}^{n-1} E[X_c] = \sum_{c=1}^{n-1} \frac{1}{p_c} \leq \sum_{c=1}^{n-1} \frac{n-1}{c} < n \ln n. \tag{15}$$

□

A BA random graph, on the other hand, is always connected, as can be seen from its construction.

We next obtain the probability of a random edge being contracting and analyze the two cases of labeling separately.

4.4.1 Discrete Labels

LEMMA 4. *In a random ER graph with discrete labels, the probability of drawing a contracting edge is more than $1/l$ where l is the number of labels.*

PROOF. Suppose the count vector for the random graph is $\{Y_1, \ldots, Y_l\}$ where $\sum_{i=1}^{l} Y_i = n$. A contracting edge between two vertices having label i can be drawn in $\binom{Y_i}{2}$ ways. Therefore, the total number of ways a contracting edge can be drawn is obtained by summing over all possible labels 1 to l. Since the total number of ways of drawing any edge is $\binom{n}{2}$, the probability of drawing a contracting edge is

$$p_c = \sum_{i=1}^{l} \frac{Y_i(Y_i-1)/2}{n(n-1)/2} > \sum_{i=1}^{l} \frac{Y_i(Y_i-1)}{n^2} > \sum_{i=1}^{l} \frac{Y_i^2}{n^2} - \frac{1}{n}. \tag{16}$$

Since Y_i^2 is a convex function with $\sum_{i=1}^{l} Y_i = n$, using Jensen's inequality, we get $\sum_{i=1}^{l} Y_i^2 \geq \frac{n^2}{l}$. Putting it back in Eq. (16),

$$p_c > \frac{1}{l} - \frac{1}{n} \approx \frac{1}{l}. \tag{17}$$

□

The above result states that if the random graph contains more than $l.n \ln n$ edges, the expected number of contracting edges among these will be more than $n \ln n$. Since all these edges can take part in clubbing together of vertices, using Lemma 3, on average these are sufficient to reduce the number of super-vertices to l. Hence, we conclude the following.

CONCLUSION 3. *For graphs with discrete labels, the number of super-vertices obtained from a sufficiently dense graph, i.e., where the number of edges m is greater than $l.n \ln n$ for n vertices and l labels, is very small and is close to l.*

Since l is a small constant in our problem setting, running the naïve algorithm on the obtained super-graph G_s for graphs with

Algorithm 4 Construction of a Barabási-Albert Random Graph

Input: Number of vertices n of the graph and parameter d
Output: Random graph $G = (V, E)$

Initialize $V = \{V_1, \ldots, V_d\}$ with d disconnected vertices
for $i = d + 1$ to n **do**
  $S \leftarrow$ Choose d unique vertices from $\{V_1, \ldots, V_{i-1}\}$ with probability of choosing a vertex proportional to its degree
  for $\forall v$ in S **do**
    Add edge (v, V_i) to E and vertex V_i to V
  end for
end for
return G

$m > l.n \ln n$ is quite feasible. Moreover, as stated in Conclusion 2, all the bi-connected subgraphs of G have a equivalent subgraph in G_s. Further, the following direct result from [8] for ER model states that if $m = \omega(n \log n)$, then the subgraphs are bi-connected.

LEMMA 5. *In a random ER graph G, if $m = \frac{1}{2}n \ln n + n \ln \ln n + \alpha n + o(n)$ where α is a real constant then G is bi-connected with high probability. Hence, if $m = \omega(n \ln n)$, with high probability, any subgraph H of G is bi-connected.*

PROOF. Please see [8]. □

This implies that for graphs dense enough such that $m = \omega(l.n \ln n)$, our algorithm finds all the MSCS and TSSS without any approximation in linear time.

The next lemma shows that a large enough graph generated by the basic BA model is bi-connected with a high probability and, hence, all the previous results on the ER model follow as well.

LEMMA 6. *A random graph G that follows the basic BA model is bi-connected with high probability.*

PROOF. Assume that the parameters of the random BA graph are n and $d > 1$. Initially, the graph contains d disconnected vertices. In the first iteration, when the $(d+1)^{\text{th}}$ vertex is added, the graph assumes a star topology with the new vertex at the center. When the $(d+2)^{\text{th}}$ vertex is added, two cases may occur. In the first, the new vertex attaches itself to the old d vertices. In this case, the graph becomes bi-connected. In the second, one of the original vertices (say v) is not attached to. Then, the center of the star becomes a cut vertex with v on one side and the rest on the other.

Now consider the case after i iterations, i.e., when the $(d+i)^{\text{th}}$ vertex is added. The graph is *not* bi-connected if and only if it was not bi-connected till the previous iteration and the new vertex did not get attached to it, or in other words, none of the previous vertices from $d+1$ to $d+i$ got attached to v. In every iteration, the number of edges increase by $2d$. Thus, the probability that the ith vertex did not get attached to v after d attachments, is

$$P_i = (1 - 1/(2id))^d \tag{18}$$

For any constant α,

$$(1 - 1/(2\alpha d))^d \leq \lim_{d \to +\infty} (1 - 1/(2\alpha d))^d \leq e^{-\frac{1}{2\alpha}} \tag{19}$$

Hence, the probability that the graph is not bi-connected after the ith iteration is

$$P_{\text{not-bi}}(i) = \prod_{j=1}^{i} P_j \leq \prod_{j=1}^{i} e^{-\frac{1}{2j}} = e^{-\sum_{j=1}^{i} \frac{1}{2j}} < e^{-\frac{1}{2} \cdot \ln i} = \frac{1}{\sqrt{i}} \tag{20}$$

Since the iterations run from 1 to $i = n - d$, $P_{\text{not-bi}} = 1/\sqrt{n-d}$. For large n and a constant $d \ll n$, $P_{\text{not-bi}}$ is quite small. □

Algorithm 5 Reducing the Size of Super-graph

Input: Super-graph $G_s = (V_s, E_s)$, threshold N_θ
Output: Reduced super-graph $G_s = (V_s, E_s)$

while G_s.num_vertices$> N_\theta$ **do**
  Choose edge $e = (u, v)$ such that $X_u^2 + X_v^2$ is minimum
  Add vertex w = Merge(u, v) to V_s, and compute X_w^2
  Add all edges of form (u, x) and (v, x) as (w, x) to E_s
  Remove u, v and e from G_s
end while
return $G_s(V_s, E_s)$

4.4.2 Continuous Labels

For continuous labels, we show that the probability of drawing a contracting edge in a random graph is, again, greater than a constant. As the algorithm is similar except for the definition of a contracting edge, the rest of the analysis is exactly the same.

LEMMA 7. *In a random graph with each edge equally likely and the k-dimensional z-scores following the null hypothesis, the probability of drawing a contracting edge is $1/4$.*

PROOF. Please see Appendix A. □

The algorithm for continuous labels is different from the discrete case as the z-scores and X^2 values keep increasing. Thus, the assumption of z-scores being drawn from a normal distribution is not completely valid. However, as shown later in the experimental section, such an increase does not adversely affect the size of the super-graph obtained and the effect is negligibly small for large k. Thus, the following conclusion still approximately holds.

CONCLUSION 4. *For graphs with continuous labels, the number of super-vertices obtained from a sufficiently dense graph, i.e., where the number of edges $m > 4n \ln n$ for n vertices and k-dimensional z-scores, is small.*

Thus, for sufficiently dense graphs, running the naïve algorithm on the obtained super-graph G_s is feasible.

4.5 Reduction of the Super-graph

For sparse graphs, reducing the super-graph size is necessary. We first state a result that provides the central idea for the reduction.

LEMMA 8. *Suppose X_1^2 and X_2^2 represent the X^2 values of super-vertices v_{s_1} and v_{s_2} in G_s. The X^2 value of the new super-vertex X_c^2 formed by clubbing v_{s_1} and v_{s_2} is upper bounded by $X_1^2 + X_2^2$, and trivially lower bounded by 0.*

PROOF. Suppose the sizes of super vertices v_{s_1} and v_{s_2} are n_1 and n_2 respectively and their count vectors are $\{Y_1, \ldots, Y_k\}$ and $\{Z_1, \ldots, Z_k\}$ respectively.

From the definition of X^2 for discrete labels in Eq. (2),

$$X_1^2 + X_2^2 = \left(\sum_{i=1}^{k} \frac{Y_i^2}{n_1 p_i} - n_1\right) + \left(\sum_{i=1}^{k} \frac{Z_i^2}{n_2 p_i} - n_2\right)$$
$$\geq \sum_{i=1}^{k} \frac{(Y_i + Z_i)^2}{(n_1 + n_2) p_i} - (n_1 + n_2) = X_c^2. \tag{21}$$

For continuous labels, suppose $(A_1, \ldots, A_k)$ and $(B_1, \ldots, B_k)$ denote the multi-dimensional z-score values of v_{s_1} and v_{s_2} respectively. The multi-dimensional z-score for the combined vertex

	Low	Moderate	High	Very High
Bio-diversity Richness	A	B	C	D
Disturbance	E	F	G	H
Medicinal	I	J	K	
Economic	L	M	N	

Table 1: Quantization information for the North-East dataset.

along the ith dimension is $\sqrt{\frac{n_1}{n_1+n_2}}A_i + \sqrt{\frac{n_2}{n_1+n_2}}B_i$. From the definition of X^2 for continuous labels in Eq. (8),

$$X_1^2 + X_2^2 = \sum_{i=1}^{k} A_i^2 + \sum_{i=1}^{k} B_i^2$$
$$\geq \sum_{i=1}^{k} \left(\sqrt{\frac{n_1}{n_1+n_2}}A_i + \sqrt{\frac{n_2}{n_1+n_2}}B_i \right)^2 = X_c^2. \tag{22}$$

The lower bound for any X^2 value is trivially 0. □

The algorithm for reducing the size of the super-graph (Algorithm 5) is based on Lemma 8. In each iteration of the algorithm, the edge connecting the two vertices that have the least sum of X^2 values is contracted, thereby reducing the number of super-vertices by 1. The corresponding vertices are merged and all their neighboring vertices become neighbors of this new vertex. As a result, in the final solution, the MSCS or TSSS either contains both these vertices or none of them. This may introduce non-optimality as only one of them may have been part of the optimal solution. However, since the vertices that are merged have low X^2 values to start with, they are unlikely to be part of the optimal solution. Even if they are, Lemma 8 ensures that the maximum error is $X_1^2 + X_2^2$. Hence, if X_1^2 and X_2^2 are small, the solution returned by our algorithm is unlikely to deviate a lot from the optimal. This is confirmed by the experiments as well (Section 5).

The contraction of edges is conducted till the number of super-vertices in the super-graph falls below a threshold N_θ. The naïve algorithm is then run on this reduced super-graph. Thus, the threshold N_θ acts as a trade-off between speed and accuracy. The lower the threshold, the lesser is the size of the reduced graph, and the faster the naïve algorithm finishes, but the farther away from the optimal solution it returns.

4.6 Time Complexity of the Algorithm

The first step of super-graph construction requires an iteration over all the edges. If the edge is non-contracting, the total time spent in that iteration is $O(1)$; otherwise, for contracting edges, every iteration in Algorithm 1 and Algorithm 2 may take $O(deg(v_i))$ time. As the vertex v_i is deleted at the end of such an iteration, the number of contracting edges is at most 1 for every vertex. Thus, the time complexity of this step is $O(m + \sum_i deg(v_i)) = O(m)$. If the graph is dense enough such that the number of super-vertices obtained is effectively a constant, the time complexity of the further steps can be ignored. Thus, the total time complexity of the complete algorithm is linear.

Otherwise, there may be at most n_s iterations in the super-graph reduction algorithm (where n_s is the number of vertices in the super-graph) and every step of it requires extracting the minimum X^2 edge. This can be done in $O(\log m_s)$ time by using heaps, where m_s is the number of edges in the super-graph. Thus, in the worst case, the total time complexity is $O(n_s \log m_s)$. The time complexity of the final step of running the naïve algorithm is exponential on the size of the reduced super-graph, which is a user-controlled parameter.

Co-location Rule	Rule Prob.	MSCS (Top-1) Region		
		Ratio (of 1)	Sizes	Labels
I ⇒ H	0.54	0.00	{98}	{0}
C ⇒ H	0.65	0.00	{92}	{0}
I ⇒ D	0.70	1.00	{75}	{1}
I ⇒ A	0.35	0.03	{48, 3, 42}	{0, 1, 0}
L ⇒ A	0.40	0.01	{50, 1, 29}	{0, 1, 0}
E ⇒ B	0.62	0.90	{15, 2, 4}	{1, 0, 1}

Table 2: Inferences from the North-East dataset.

5. EXPERIMENTS

All the simulations were done using the Boost graph library (http://www.boost.org/) in C++ on an Intel(R) Xeon(R) 24-core machine with 2.4 GHz CPU and 194 GB RAM running Linux Debian 6.0.7. We present results on both real (large) graphs and synthetic datasets (averaged over 10 different runs).

5.1 Real Dataset: Discrete

To test the applicability of our method on a real dataset, we used the North-East Biodiversity data formed as the result of a survey by the Indian Space Research Organisation (ISRO) [24]. The area is one of the most bio-diverse regions of India and the survey was done to understand the trends of depletion of natural reserves and bio-reserves due to poaching or other causes. The dataset comprises of 1202 spatial points along with four types of information: (i) Bio-diversity richness index, (ii) Disturbance index, (iii) Medicinal property, and (iv) Economical property. The first two indices, i.e., bio-diversity richness index and disturbance index, were already quantized by domain experts into four labels each, namely, Low, Moderate, High and Very High. We quantized the medicinal properties to three labels based on the (normalized) ranges $[0, 0.4], (0.4, 0.8], (0.8, 1]$. The economical properties were quantized into three labels $[0, 0.65], (0.65, 0.9], (0.9, 1]$. Thus, finally we have a total of 14 quantized values labeled A to N (Table 1).

This information can be used to infer many hidden characteristics, such as bio-diversity hotspot detection, relationships between a highly bio-diverse region and the type of vegetation found there, etc. We extend these inferences to a deeper level by unraveling certain characteristics that cannot be deciphered by just using co-location rule mining. We incorporate the co-location rule as input and mine the contiguous regions in space where the rule is statistically significant, and not just frequent. We only consider rules of size 2, i.e., co-locations including 2 features $\{X, Y\}$ and the rule $X \Rightarrow Y$, since that provides the most basic understanding.

For a rule $X \Rightarrow Y$, the subgraph inducing only those nodes which has a label X is first extracted. A node in this graph is then given a label of 1 if it exhibits the label Y; otherwise it is labeled as 0. Thus, the number of discrete labels here is $l = 2$ (Y present or absent) and the probability of the 1 event is the same as that of the spatial co-location rule $X \Rightarrow Y$. The probability of the 0 event is, thus, one minus this quantity, i.e., the residual value.

When the rule is quite likely (resp. unlikely), our method finds the largest connected contiguous region of 1 (resp. 0) as the subgraph of interest. This is quite intuitive and equivalent to hot-spot detection. More importantly, the connected subgraphs can display some additional interesting structures such as two large regions of 1 (resp. 0) connected by a bridge of 0 (resp. 1) of a smaller size. Without this bridge, the two 1 (resp. 0) regions would not have been connected. This bigger region can have a larger chi-square than any of the individual 1 (resp. 0) regions, thereby attracting attention to the bridge. A simple hotspot detection method would have failed in this scenario.

Table 2 shows some representative results. For each rule, we mention the probability and the characteristics of the top-1 subgraph mined using it including the ratio of 1 nodes (i.e., proportion of presence), the number of super-vertices along with the number of original nodes and the labels. The first set of results are contiguous regions of either 1 or 0. For example, the first result consisting of 98 nodes ($I \Rightarrow H$) highlights a region (in the Indian state of Manipur) where there is very high disturbance when medicinal plants are low. The second set of results are more interesting as they highlight the bridges mentioned earlier. For example, the top result for the rule $I \Rightarrow A$ is a bridge of 3 label-1 nodes connecting two regions of label-0 nodes of sizes 48 and 42 (in Manipur again). This unearths two regions of low bio-diversity richness connected by a region of higher bio-diversity when all the regions have low medicinal plants. This provides the domain scientists some target areas to try and unravel interesting actions of nature or external factors. We emphasize the fact that a simple co-location rule mining would not have been able to identify such regions.

The total time required to find the top-5 regions for the largest graph (containing 883 nodes and 6066 edges) is only 0.25 s. Since the graph is not dense, the reduced super-graph contains as many as 96 nodes. This is further reduced to 15 nodes. The two reduction steps require only 0.03 s as the original graph is quite small. Consequently, the time to run the naïve algorithm on the 15-vertex super-graph (0.22 s) is the dominating factor.

We also highlight some interesting results from mining the entire spatial graph considering only two labels at a time. A region of 32 nodes was found in Mizoram where even though the bio-diversity is low, the medicinal plants are found in high quantity. The probability of this combined label (low bio-diversity and high medicinal, i.e., AK) is only 5%. Such low probability regions are extremely hard to find using apriori or co-location rule mining as the search space explodes [21]. Interestingly, the almost same region (except one node) was found to be extremely statistically significant when the attributes considered were bio-diversity (low) and economic plants (high). The probability (4%) of this event AN is even lesser. Similarly, another region consisting of 30 nodes was found in Manipur where the bio-diversity is high in spite of high disturbance (label CG). The probability (6%) is again low. These results showcase the importance of our mining algorithm as it reveals spatial regions that can be extremely valuable to domain scientists for unearthing new processes and findings. Discussion with the authors of [24] indeed confirmed the utility of the method; in particular, the last example highlighted an area that requires more ground-level studies on the causes of high disturbance (such as Jhum cultivation) that may cause depletion of bio-diversity in such a highly biodiverse patch. It is extremely important for the government officials to identify such cases at the earliest, and analyze and restrict such harmful practices. Currently, identifying such areas are done by conducting extensive surveys by teams of scientists. Our method can act as a very nice filter to help them.

5.2 Real Dataset: Continuous

The continuously labeled real dataset is the West Nile virus dataset (WNV) provided by the U.S. Center for Disease Control and Prevention (http://www.cdc.gov/ncidod/dvbid/westnile/). The 3109 different counties in USA act as vertices of the graph. Two counties are connected by an edge if they share a border. The label on a vertex is the density of human cases infected by WNV in 2011, i.e., number of cases per unit area. We use the *Weighted Z-value* and *Average Difference* algorithms [16] that take into account the difference in densities between the county and its neighbors to assign the z-score values. The Weighted Z-value approach normalizes the difference of the density of a county from the weighted average of the density of its neighbors while the Avg Diff approach weights sum of differences between the density of a county with its corresponding neighbor to obtain the raw scores which are normalized using the standard technique of Eq. (4) to obtain z-scores. The weights in both the cases are assigned using the inverse centroid distance and the length of common border between a county and its neighbor [16].

	County	Z-score	X^2	Density	Avg. Dens. Neighbors
1	Dist. of Columbia	+47.05	2213.53	0.0776	0.0051
2	Prince George's	-11.47	131.53	0.0007	0.0110
3	St. Louis City	+10.05	100.91	0.0173	0.0007
4	Alexandria	-9.76	95.27	0.0000	0.0232

Table 3: Top counties based on Weighted Z-value approach.

	County	Z-score	X^2	Density	Avg. Dens. Neighbors
1	Dist. of Columbia	+44.43	1974.04	0.0776	0.0051
2	Arlington City	+13.03	169.67	0.0136	0.0132
3	Prince George's	-11.06	122.34	0.0007	0.0110
4	Montgomery	-10.52	110.58	0.0063	0.0132

Table 4: Top counties based on Avg Diff approach.

The top results based on the Weighted Z-value and Avg Diff methods are shown in Table 3 and Table 4 respectively. The District of Columbia (DC) ranks the highest in both. The summary of the corresponding top results for our algorithm are shown in Table 5 and Table 6 respectively. Not very surprisingly, the DC county is the most significant for both the cases. The second results are regions composed of the top counties as well. The third result for Avg Diff is more interesting as it is composed of 7 nodes, none of which is very high ranking by itself, but together form a significant region. We emphasize the fact that without the ability to mine connected subgraphs, this region could never have been found.

The total time required to find the top-10 regions is 66 s. Since there are 3109 nodes and only 8871 edges, the graph is not dense, and the reduced super-graph contains as many as 373 nodes. This is further reduced to 20 nodes. The entire reduction requires only 4 s as the original graph is quite small. Consequently, the time to run the naïve algorithm on the 20-vertex super-graph (62 s) dominates.

5.3 Real Large Datasets

To test the scalability of our algorithm on real graphs that are *not* dense, we used 4 large graphs from the SNAP database at https://snap.stanford.edu/data/. The details are mentioned in Table 7. Continuous labeling was used. The degree of a node was normalized by subtracting the average degree of the graph and scaled by the standard deviation to get the z-score for that node.

The running times are shown in Figure 2. The reduction of the super-graph requires the largest amount of time, especially when the graph is very sparse. The threshold of reduction was kept to 20 nodes for all the datasets. Although the Orkut graph is larger than the LiveJournal one (comparable number of nodes but almost 4 times more number of edges) and, hence, requires a larger time for super-graph conversion (30 minutes against 4 minutes), the overall running time is much better (4 hours against 16 hours) due to its higher density which produces a much smaller super-graph. This shows that our algorithms are able to handle million-scale nodes with close to billion-scale edges.

5.4 Synthetic Datasets

The first set of experiments on synthetic data calibrates the size of the super-graphs after the reduction. The graphs are generated synthetically according to the ER and BA models. For discretely labeled graphs, the labels are drawn uniformly randomly from the total number of possibilities. The multi-dimensional z-scores for

	Counties	Size	Z-score	X^2
1	Dist. of Columbia	1	+47.05	2213.53
2	Prince George's, Alexandria, Montgomery	3	-15.07	226.96
3	St. Louis City	1	+10.05	100.91

Table 5: Significant subgraphs for Weighted Z-value.

	Counties	Size	Z-score	X^2
1	Dist. of Columbia	1	+44.43	1974.04
2	Prince George's, Alexandria, Montgomery, Arlington City	4	-21.84	477.39
3	New York, Hudson, Richmond, Kings, Bronx, Nassau, Queens	7	+10.05	100.91

Table 6: Significant subgraphs for Avg Diff.

continuous labels are drawn from the $N(0,1)$ distribution. The results for synthetic graphs on the two models are very similar. Therefore, only one of them is shown as a representative.

As shown in Figure 3a, the number of super-vertices reduce drastically with the number of edges for discrete labels. When the number of edges is large (around $(l/2)n \ln n$), the number of super-vertices obtained drops to exactly l as predicted by the theory. For graphs that are not sufficiently dense, the number of super-vertices can be large, although in most cases, it falls below 20, thereby making it feasible to run the naïve algorithm.

Figure 3b shows the amount of time required for reduction to the super-graph. For a fixed n, it grows linearly with m. We have omitted showing the time to obtain the significant subgraphs from this reduced super-graph as that is in the order of $2^l (= 32)$ which is a negligible constant (in milliseconds).

The experiments for the continuous case (graph omitted) show the same trend. Around $4n \ln n$ edges, the number of super-vertices decrease and saturate to a small constant. The absolute running times are larger.

Figure 4 profiles the same behavior across different number of discrete labels. The curves tally nicely with the theoretical prediction of the super-graph being reduced to l nodes. The running times grow linearly with m. There is little difference among different l's.

Figure 5 plots the number of super-vertices against different values of k for the continuous case. For values of $k > 1$, there is little difference in the curves. For $k = 1$, the convergence happens when the graph becomes sufficiently dense, i.e., the number of edges goes past $4n \ln n$. This empirically confirms the result to be invariant of k, as shown in Lemma 7. There is little difference in running times for different k's (graph omitted). Once more, we have omitted the times required for running the naïve algorithm on the reduced super-graphs (which for 15 super-vertices is ≈ 2 s).

5.5 Quality Results for Sparse Graphs

The final set of experiments shows the quality of results when the original graph is *not* sufficiently dense, thereby introducing non-optimality in the subsequent reduction.

Figure 6 shows how the chi-square and the time changes when the super-graph is reduced further. The x-axis shows the reduction in the amount of vertices *from* the super-graph. For example, in Figure 6a, the original super-graph starts with 22 super-vertices (indicated by $n_{rg} = 22$), and we reduce it progressively to 2 super-vertices. Thus, the last reduction value is marked by 20 which translates to $n_{rg} = 2$. The y-axis shows the *ratios* of the chi-square and the time obtained as a factor of the optimal values. The optimal values are obtained when no reduction of the super-graph is done, and hence, the ratios start with 1.

Both figures show that the reduction in time is substantial when the number of super-vertices are reduced. This is in tune with the

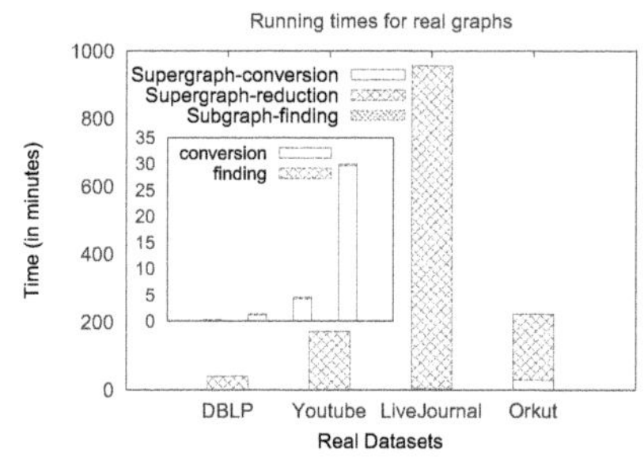

Figure 2: Running time for large real graphs.

Dataset	Nodes	Edges	Avg. Degree
com-DBLP	317,080	1,049,866	3.31
com-Youtube	1,134,890	2,987,624	2.63
com-LiveJournal	3,997,962	34,681,189	8.67
com-Orkut	3,072,441	117,185,083	38.14

Table 7: Large real graphs.

fact that the number of connected subgraphs is exponential with the number of vertices. However, the corresponding decrease in the chi-square value is almost negligible – it is less than 1% for the discrete case and 4% for the continuous case. (In most runs, the chi-square value does not drop at all. We are omitting those results.) This, therefore, justifies our method of reducing the super-graph further without sacrificing much on the accuracy.

6. CONCLUSIONS AND FUTURE WORK

In this paper, we addressed the problem of finding statistically significant connected subgraphs in a vertex-labeled graph where the labels are either discrete or continuous. Since the number of connected subgraphs is exponential in the number of vertices, the naïve algorithm on the entire graph is impractical. Consequently, we designed an efficient algorithm that converts the graph into a super-graph, and if necessary, reduces the size further. We highlighted in detail one real application for each of the cases and showed that our algorithms scale well and are practical for large real graphs as well.

In future, other sub-structures or directed and edge-weighted graphs can be focused upon. Further, our method may also be successfully applied on other important applications including community detection and dense subgraph mining. Finally, the naïve method of exploring all possible subgraphs can be targeted for improvement.

7. REFERENCES

[1] A.-L. Barabási and R. Albert. Emergence of scaling in random networks. *Science*, 286(5439):509–512, 1999.

[2] S. Barua and J. Sander. SSCP: Mining statistically significant co-location patterns. In *STD*, pages 2–20, 2011.

[3] S. Barua and J. Sander. Mining statistically significant co-location and segregation patterns. *TKDE*, 99(pre):1, 2013.

[4] Y. Chi, Y. Yang, and R. Muntz. Indexing and mining free trees. In *ICDM*, pages 509–512, 2003.

[5] A. Denise, M. Régnier, and M. Vandenbogaert. Assessing the statistical significance of overrepresented oligonucleotides. In *WABI*, pages 537–552, 2001.

[6] N. Durak, A. Pinar, T. G. Kolda, and C. Seshadhri. Degree relations of triangles in real-world networks and graph models. In *CIKM*, pages 1712–1716, 2012.

[7] E. Edgington and P. Onghena. *Randomization Tests*. Marcel Dekker, 1995.

[8] P. Erdős and A. Rényi. On the strength of connectedness of a random graph. *Acta Mathematica Scientia Hungary*, 12:261–267, 1961.

[9] P. Erdös and A. Rényi. On random graphs, I. *Publicationes Mathematicae (Debrecen)*, 6:290–297, 1959.

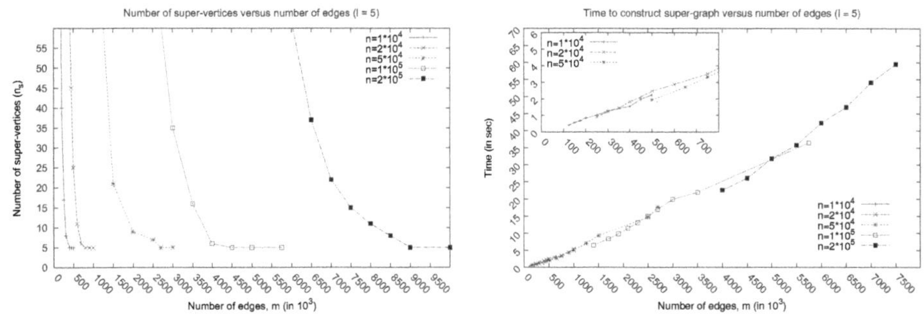

(a) Super-vertices (b) Time

Figure 3: Varying number of edges against number of vertices for discrete labels (Barabási-Albert).

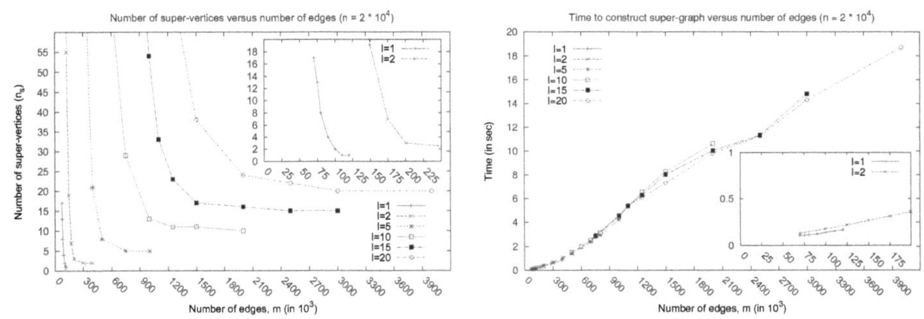

(a) Super-vertices (b) Time

Figure 4: Varying number of edges against number of discrete labels (Erdős-Rényi).

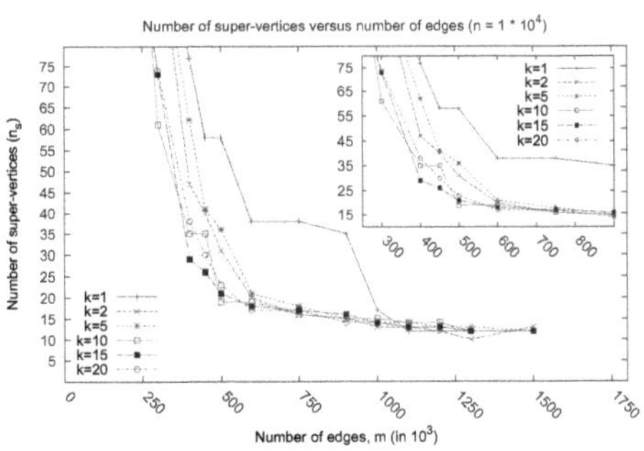

Figure 5: Varying number of edges against dimension of continuous labels (Barabási-Albert).

[10] R. Frank, W. Jin, and M. Ester. Efficiently mining regional outliers in spatial data. In *SSTD*, pages 112–129, 2007.

[11] H. He and A. Singh. Graphrank: Statistical modeling and mining of significant subgraphs in the feature space. In *ICDM*, pages 885–890, 2006.

[12] R. Hogg, A. Craig, and J. McKean. *Introduction to Mathematical Statistics*. Pearson Education, 2004.

[13] P. Holme and B. J. Kim. Growing scale-free networks with tunable clustering. *Physical Review E*, 65(2):026107, 2002.

[14] Y. Huang, J. Pei, and H. Xiong. Mining co-location patterns with rare events from spatial data sets. *GeoInformatica*, 10(3):239–260, 2006.

[15] H. Jiang, J. Cheng, D. Wang, C. Wang, and G. Tan. A general framework for efficient continuous multidimensional top-k query processing in sensor networks. *IEEE Trans. Parallel Distrib. Syst.*, 23(9):1668–1680, 2012.

[16] Y. Kou, C.-T. Lu, and D. Chen. Spatial weighted outlier detection. In *SDM*, pages 613–617, 2006.

[17] J. Lijffijt, P. Papapetrou, and K. Puolamäki. A statistical significance testing approach to mining the most informative set of patterns. In *DMKD*, pages 1–26, 2012.

[18] M. E. J. Newman, S. H. Strogatz, and D. J. Watts. Random graphs with arbitrary degree distributions and their applications. *Physical Review E*, 64(2):026118, 2001.

[19] J. Pei, D. Jiang, and A. Zhang. Mining cross-graph quasi-cliques in gene expression and protein interaction data. In *ICDE*, pages 353–354, 2005.

[20] L. Popa, A. Rostamizadeh, R. Karp, C. Papadimitriou, and I. Stoica. Balancing traffic load in wireless networks with curveball routing. In *MobiHoc*, pages 170–179, 2007.

[21] S. Ranu and A. Singh. Graphsig: A scalable approach to mining significant subgraphs in large graph databases. In *ICDE*, pages 844–855, 2009.

[22] T. Read and N. Cressie. *Goodness-of-Fit Statistics for Discrete Multivariate Data*. Springer, 1988.

[23] M. Régnier and M. Vandenbogaert. Comparison of statistical significance criteria. *J. Bioinf. & Comp. Bio.*, 4:85–97, 2006.

[24] P. Roy and S. Tomar. Biodiversity characterization at landscape level using geospatial modelling technique. *Biological Conservation*, 95(1):95–109, 2000.

[25] M. Sachan and A. Bhattacharya. Mining statistically significant substrings using the chi-square statistic. *PVLDB*, 5(10):1052–1063, 2012.

[26] J. Scott, T. Ideker, R. M. Karp, and R. Sharan. Efficient algorithms for detecting signaling pathways in protein interaction networks. *J. Comp. Bio.*, 13(2):133–144, 2006.

[27] S. Shekhar and Y. Huang. Discovering spatial co-location patterns: A summary of results. In *SSTD*, pages 236–256, 2001.

[28] S. Shekhar, C.-T. Lu, and P. Zhang. Detecting graph-based spatial outliers: algorithms and applications (a summary of results). In *KDD*, pages 371–376, 2001.

[29] D. Wang, W. Ding, H. Z. Lo, T. F. Stepinski, J. Salazar, and M. Morabito. Crime hotspot mapping using the crime related factors – a spatial data mining approach. *Appl. Intell.*, 39(4):772–781, 2013.

[30] D. J. Watts and S. H. Strogatz. Collective dynamics of 'small-world' networks. *Nature*, 393(6684):409–10, 1998.

[31] K. Wongpanya, K. Sripimanwat, and K. Jenjerapongvej. Simplification of frequency test for random number

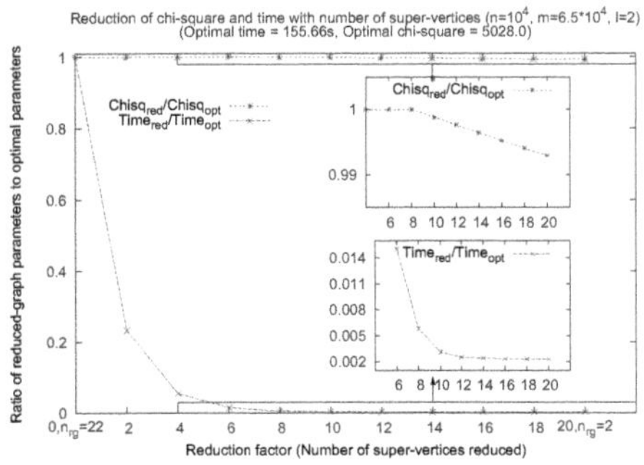

(a) Discrete case

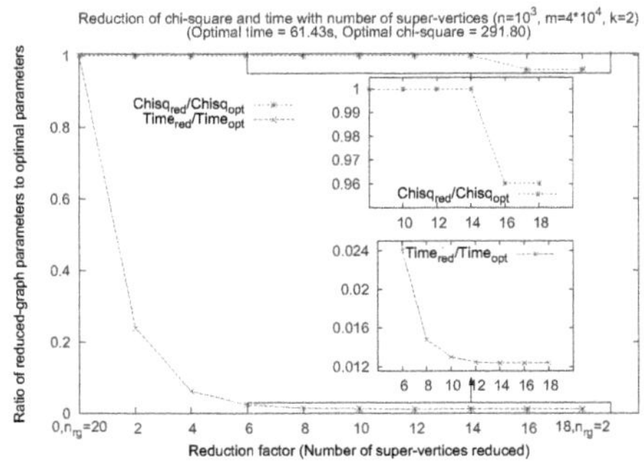

(b) Continuous case

Figure 6: Reduced parameters against number of vertices in reduced super-graph (Erdős-Rényi).

generation based on chi-square. In *AICT*, pages 305–308, 2008.

[32] W. Xing and A. A. Ghorbani. Weighted pagerank algorithm. In *CNSR*, pages 305–314, 2004.

[33] X. Yan, H. Cheng, J. Han, and P. Yu. Mining significant graph patterns by leap search. In *SIGMOD*, pages 433–444, 2008.

[34] N. Ye and Q. Chen. An anomaly detection technique based on a chi-square statistic for detecting intrusions into information systems. *Quality and Reliability Engineering International*, 23, 2001.

[35] C. H. You, L. B. Holder, and D. J. Cook. Temporal and structural analysis of biological networks in combination with microarray data. In *CIBCB*, pages 62–69, 2008.

APPENDIX

A. PROOF OF LEMMA 7

PROOF. We first prove it explicitly for $k = 1$ and then extend the argument for any general k using the principle of symmetry.

Suppose the multi-dimensional z-score values of two adjacent vertices v_1 and v_2 of sizes s_1 and s_2 respectively are $(Z_{11}, \ldots, Z_{1k})$ and $(Z_{21}, \ldots, Z_{2k})$ respectively. Using Eq. (8), the chi-square values of the two vertices, $X^2_{v_1}$ and $X^2_{v_2}$, are

$$X^2_{v_1} = \sum_{i=1}^{k} (Z_{1i})^2 \text{ and } X^2_{v_2} = \sum_{i=1}^{k} (Z_{2i})^2. \quad (23)$$

Using Eq. (6), the combined chi-square value, $X^2_{(v_1,v_2)}$, is

$$X^2_{(v_1,v_2)} = \sum_{i=1}^{k} \frac{(\sqrt{s_1}Z_{1i} + \sqrt{s_2}Z_{2i})^2}{s_1 + s_2}. \quad (24)$$

For an edge to be contracting, this combined z-score value should be greater than the individual z-scores, i.e.,

$$X^2_{(v_1,v_2)} \geq X^2_{v_2} \Rightarrow \sum_{i=1}^{k} \frac{(\sqrt{s_1}Z_{1i} + \sqrt{s_2}Z_{2i})^2}{s_1 + s_2} \geq \sum_{i=1}^{k} (Z_{2i})^2$$

$$\Rightarrow \sum_{i=1}^{k} (s_1 Z_{1i}^2 - s_1 Z_{2i}^2 + 2\sqrt{s_1 s_2} Z_{1i} Z_{2i}) \geq 0 \Rightarrow \sum_{i=1}^{k} A_i \geq 0 \quad (25)$$

$$X^2_{(v_1,v_2)} \geq X^2_{v_1} \Rightarrow \sum_{i=1}^{k} \frac{(\sqrt{s_1}Z_{1i} + \sqrt{s_2}Z_{2i})^2}{s_1 + s_2} \geq \sum_{i=1}^{k} (Z_{1i})^2$$

$$\Rightarrow \sum_{i=1}^{k} (s_2 Z_{2i}^2 - s_2 Z_{1i}^2 + 2\sqrt{s_1 s_2} Z_{1i} Z_{2i}) \geq 0 \Rightarrow \sum_{i=1}^{k} B_i \geq 0 \quad (26)$$

where A_i and B_i stand for the longer expressions. Now, a given edge is contracting if and only if both the conditions $\sum_{i=1}^{k} A_i \geq 0$ and $\sum_{i=1}^{k} B_i \geq 0$ hold simultaneously.

We first show that for $k = 1$, Eq. (25) and Eq. (26) are together satisfied with probability $1/4$. We simplify the conditions further by substituting $R = Z_{11}/Z_{21}$ and $s = \sqrt{s_2/s_1}$. Using these substitutions,

$$A_1 \geq 0 \Rightarrow s_1 Z_{11}^2 - s_1 Z_{21}^2 + 2\sqrt{s_1 s_2} Z_{11} Z_{21} \geq 0$$

$$\Rightarrow s_1 Z_{21}^2 (R^2 - 1 + 2sR) \geq 0 \quad (27)$$

$$B_1 \geq 0 \Rightarrow s_2 Z_{21}^2 - s_2 Z_{11}^2 + 2\sqrt{s_1 s_2} Z_{11} Z_{21} \geq 0$$

$$\Rightarrow s_1 s Z_{21}^2 (s - sR^2 + 2R) \geq 0 \quad (28)$$

Since Z_{11} and Z_{12} follow a continuous distribution, they are non-zero with probability 1. Thus, satisfying $A_1 \geq 0$ and $B_1 \geq 0$ is equivalent to finding the solutions of the quadratic equations $R^2 + 2sR - 1 \geq 0$ and $sR^2 - 2R - s \leq 0$. It can be shown that the range of values of R satisfying both the quadratic equations is

$$(\sqrt{s^2+1} - s) \leq R \leq (\sqrt{s^2+1} + 1)/s. \quad (29)$$

Since both Z_{11} and Z_{21} are i.i.d. random variables and follow $N(0, 1)$, their ratio R follows the Cauchy $(0, 1)$ distribution [12] whose c.d.f. is $F(x) = \frac{1}{\pi}\arctan(x) + \frac{1}{2}$. Hence, the probability of R being in the given range is

$$\frac{1}{\pi}\left[\arctan\left(\frac{\sqrt{s^2+1}+1}{s}\right) - \arctan(\sqrt{s^2+1} - s)\right]. \quad (30)$$

Since $s > 0$, substituting $s = \tan\phi$ with $\phi \in (0, \pi/2)$, we get

$$\begin{aligned} & P(A_1 > 0 \text{ and } B_1 > 0) \\ & = [\arctan((1 + \sec\phi)/\tan\phi) - \arctan(\sec\phi - \tan\phi)]/\pi \\ & = [\arctan(\cot(\phi/2)) - \arctan(\tan(\pi/4 - \phi/2))]/\pi \\ & = [(\pi/2 - \phi/2) - (\pi/4 - \phi/2)]/\pi = \frac{1}{4}. \end{aligned} \quad (31)$$

Thus, for $k = 1$, we have shown that the probability is $1/4$.

For any general k, the problem reduces to finding the probability of $\sum A_i \geq 0$ and $\sum B_i \geq 0$ simultaneously. Given the null hypothesis, since each Z_{1i} and Z_{2i} are i.i.d. standard normal random variables $N(0, 1)$, the random variables A_i and B_i are individually (but not together) i.i.d. as well. Also, we observe that the p.d.f. of each A_i and B_i is an even function as substituting $Z_{1i} \rightarrow -Z_{2i}$ and $Z_{2i} \rightarrow Z_{1i}$ reverses their signs. Further, the probability of the outcomes remains the same due to the p.d.f. of $N(0, 1)$ being an even function as well. Thus, for $k = 1$, we can say that $P(A_i \geq 0)$ and $P(B_i \geq 0)$ are both $1/2$ individually. As the p.d.f. of both A_i and B_i are even functions, given any outcome, the probability of the new outcome by replacing all $A_i \rightarrow -A_i$ and $B_i \rightarrow -B_i$ remains the same. However, this reverses the sign of $\sum A_i$ and $\sum B_i$. So, $P(\sum A_i \geq 0) = P(\sum B_i \geq 0) = 1/2$. Hence, the probability of these two conditions remain the same for any k.

Thus, although we have proved the theorem formally for $k = 1$, for other cases, we have intuitively shown that the probability of an edge being contracting is invariant of k and is, hence, $1/4$. □

The experiments in Section 5.4 show that the cases for $k > 1$ are better than $k = 1$ or are equal. The algorithm remains scalable as long as this is greater than or equal to a constant.

Complete Yet Practical Search for Minimal Query Reformulations Under Constraints

Ioana Ileana
Institut Mines-Télécom; Télécom ParisTech; CNRS LTCI
ileana@telecom-paristech.fr

Bogdan Cautis
Univ. Paris-Sud & Inria Saclay
bogdan.cautis@u-psud.fr

Alin Deutsch
University of California San Diego
deutsch@cs.ucsd.edu

Yannis Katsis
University of California San Diego
ikatsis@cs.ucsd.edu

ABSTRACT

We revisit the Chase&Backchase (*C&B*) algorithm for query reformulation under constraints, which provides a uniform solution to such particular-case problems as view-based rewriting under constraints, semantic query optimization, and physical access path selection in query optimization. For an important class of queries and constraints, *C&B* has been shown to be complete, i.e. guaranteed to find all (join-)minimal reformulations under constraints. *C&B* is based on constructing a canonical rewriting candidate called a universal plan, then inspecting its exponentially many sub-queries in search for minimal reformulations, essentially removing redundant joins in all possible ways. This inspection involves chasing the subquery. Because of the resulting exponentially many chases, the conventional wisdom has held that completeness is a concept of mainly theoretical interest.

We show that completeness can be preserved at practically relevant cost by introducing $Prov_{C\&B}$, a novel reformulation algorithm that instruments the chase to maintain provenance information connecting the joins added during the chase to the universal plan subqueries responsible for adding these joins. This allows it to directly "read off" the minimal reformulations from the result of a single chase of the universal plan, saving exponentially many chases of its subqueries. We exhibit natural scenarios yielding speedups of over two orders of magnitude between the execution of the best view-based rewriting found by a commercial query optimizer and that of the best rewriting found by $Prov_{C\&B}$ (which the optimizer misses because of limited reasoning about constraints).

Categories and Subject Descriptors

H.2 [**Database Management**]: Systems—*Query processing*

Keywords

database views, integrity constraints, query optimization, chase

1. INTRODUCTION

One of the central problems in query processing is that of reformulating a query Q expressed against a source schema S to an equivalent query R against a target schema T, by exploiting the relationship between S and T. In general, there may exist multiple such reformulations and choosing among them may require additional, application-specific criteria, such as a cost model.

Query reformulation includes as particular cases several problems that have occupied database research and practice for decades. Examples are view-based rewriting (both partial and total, in which base tables are allowed, respectively disallowed), physical access path selection in query optimization, and semantic optimization (e.g. redundant join elimination and other instances of rewriting queries under integrity constraints).

Motivated by the fact that these particular case problems had been typically studied in isolation from each other in prior work, publication [10] introduced a uniform solution in the form of the Chase & Backchase (*C&B*) algorithm for query reformulation under constraints. The paper showed how the above problems can be cast as particular query reformulation instances where the relationship between the schemas S and T is expressed by constraints.

The *C&B* algorithm applies to relational conjunctive queries (select - project - join - rename under set semantics), as the language for specifying the original query Q and the reformulation R. The relationship between the schemas S and T is given by a set $\mathcal{C}$ of constraints that are expressed as *tuple-generating dependencies (tgds)* or *equality-generating dependencies (egds)* [4]. Tgds and egds together comprise the embedded implicational dependencies [14], which include essentially all of the naturally-occurring integrity constraints on relational databases (keys, foreign keys, referential integrity, inverse relationships, functional, join, inclusion and multi-valued dependencies, etc.). Furthermore, tgds turn out to be ideally suited for capturing physical access paths typically used in query optimization (materialized views expressed as SPJR queries, indexes, join indexes, access support relations, gmaps, etc.) [10].

In a nutshell, the *C&B* is based on constructing a canonical rewriting called a *universal plan* (because it incorporates redundantly all T-schema elements relevant to the original query), then searching for reformulations among the candidates given by the subqueries of the universal plan. The purpose of the search through the subqueries of the universal plan is to eliminate its redundancy in all possible ways, thus obtaining *minimal* reformulations, i.e. reformulations containing no joins that are redundant under the constraints. The inspected subqueries are checked for equivalence (under the constraints) to the original query. This check is performed using the classical chase procedure [1], which in essence adds to a query redundant joins that are implied by the constraints.

The *C&B* was shown in [10] to discover at least the reformulations found by prior techniques in the particular case problems, and potentially more. More importantly, the *C&B* was shown experimentally to uncover previously missed reformulation opportunities

Supported by INRIA (as OAKSAD associated team) and by the NSF (awards IIS-1117527, -0910820 and CNS-1219220).

SIGMOD'14, June 22–27, 2014, Snowbird, UT, USA.

ACM 978-1-4503-2376-5/14/06 http://dx.doi.org/10.1145/2588555.2593683 $15.00.

stemming from the synergistic combination of opportunities across the settings of the particular case problems. Examples include cases when the integrity constraints are crucial in enabling the use of certain indexes or views, in the sense that the corresponding reformulation that mentions these indexes or views is not equivalent to the original query in the absence of the integrity constraints, but becomes so in their presence [29]. This *C&B* behavior turned out to have a theoretical underpinning: in [13], the *C&B* algorithm was proven to return all equivalent minimal reformulations of a query. The *C&B* is said to be *complete* for finding minimal reformulations.

Completeness is desirable for two reasons. First, there are modern applications (discussed in Section 7) that define a certain measure of a query (e.g. its price or clearance level) as the overall minimum across *all* its reformulations. Second, even in classical optimization the best reformulation among those inspected by an incomplete algorithm can be significantly worse than the optimum one(s), which a complete reformulation algorithm is guaranteed to find. Indeed, our experiments show that even the best reformulation found by a sophisticated commercial relational optimizer in a natural setting involving materialized views can execute orders of magnitude slower than an optimum reformulation.

However, given that the particular case of reformulation corresponding to total view-based rewriting of a query has an NP-hard decision problem even in the absence of constraints [22], conventional wisdom has held so far that completeness of reformulation is likely to remain a concept of mainly theoretical interest. Indeed for the *C&B*, which is the only complete algorithm we are aware of in this context, the search for minimal reformulations does not scale beyond the low end of the spectrum of practically occurring query and constraint set sizes. The reason is that, even when there are few actual minimal reformulations for a query, the *C&B* inspects a number of candidate reformulations that is often exponential in the size of the query and number of views, thus launching exponentially many chases. [29] confirms this fact experimentally, then dedicates the bulk of the results to heuristics that dramatically reduce the search space for minimal reformulations by trading completeness for search speed. Similar trade-offs are adopted by all other existing implementations for query reformulation, even when restricted to reformulating conjunctive queries within the settings of the particular case problems discussed here. This includes the optimizers of relational DBMSs and the follow-up *C&B*-based implementations for XML query reformulation in [12, 27, 32].

Our contributions. In this work, we revisit the *C&B* and we challenge conventional wisdom by showing that the cost of running a complete search for minimal reformulations can be reduced in practice to a small fraction of typical query execution times, while the benefits are potentially huge in certain practically relevant settings. This result is enabled by the following specific contributions.

1. We present $Prov_{C\&B}$, a query reformulation algorithm that constructs the same universal plan as the *C&B*, but employs a novel, much more goal-directed search technique that inspects up to exponentially fewer candidates than the *C&B*. We formally prove that the $Prov_{C\&B}$ is still complete, thus always finding precisely the same minimal reformulations as the *C&B* (namely all existing ones). The $Prov_{C\&B}$'s search is based on a novel *provenance-aware chase*, which tracks provenance information that serves for tracing the added joins back to the universal plan subqueries responsible for the joins being added. This allows $Prov_{C\&B}$ to directly "read off" the minimal reformulations from the result of a single chase of the universal plan, saving the exponentially many chases of its subqueries (which the *C&B* would perform). The reduction in the number of chases is the fundamental reason for the speedup of $Prov_{C\&B}$ over *C&B*. Remarkably, the particular provenance flavor required turns out to coincide with *minimal why-provenance* [6] introduced for a different purpose in the literature.

2. We evaluate $Prov_{C\&B}$ experimentally in a setting involving materialized views and integrity constraints. We confirm experimentally that the savings of $Prov_{C\&B}$ over *C&B* in terms of launched chases can be exponential. The experiments also show that the running time of $Prov_{C\&B}$ is a very small fraction of the query execution time measured for modern commercial database engines. Moreover, they show that running the $Prov_{C\&B}$ is worthwhile: we exhibit scenarios with speedups of over two orders of magnitude between the execution of the best view-based rewriting found by a commercial query optimizer and a rewriting obtained by selecting a minimum-join rewriting among all minimal rewritings enumerated by $Prov_{C\&B}$. The reason is that the optimizer misses the opportunity to exploit available materialized views because it does not realize that they are rendered relevant to the query by the declared key (and sometimes foreign key) constraints. The observed speedups take into account the combined time spent by the $Prov_{C\&B}$ to select a rewriting, and the time to execute it. Finally, in the same materialized view scenario, we evaluate how $Prov_{C\&B}$ scales with the size of the query and combinatoric explosion of available rewritings, showing graceful behavior even in stress-test settings that go significantly beyond what existing commercial optimizers are designed to handle.

3. The provenance-aware chase is interesting in its own right, as a procedure for reasoning about the interaction of provenance and integrity constraints. The design of the provenance-aware chase was technically challenging, as it turns out that the standard chase is not well-suited for instrumentation towards tracking the required provenance. Directly instrumenting the standard chase turns out to compromise soundness of the resulting reformulation algorithm (i.e. it would return non-equivalent reformulations). We were forced to first design a new (provenance-unaware) variation of the standard chase, which we call the *Skolem chase*, showing that its results are equivalent to those of the standard chase. It is this variation that we instrumented to obtain the provenance-aware chase.

Beyond relational conjunctive queries. The original *C&B* algorithm has been extended in follow-up work to apply beyond conjunctive queries (see [11] for a survey of these extensions). The extensions allow disjunction/union [13], nested correlated query blocks, grouping, aggregation, user-defined functions, and show a uniform way to incorporate any additional language primitives by treating them as user-defined functions with black-box semantics [27, 32]. Moreover, extensions support additional data models, such as object-oriented, complex-valued [10] and XML [12, 13, 32]. Not surprisingly, once the supported language features sufficient expressive power even checking equivalence becomes undecidable, so all hope is dashed for a complete reformulation algorithm. However, all existing *C&B* extensions still guarantee soundness, i.e. only equivalent reformulations are reported. They also guarantee to continue finding, within a larger query, all reformulations of the query's fragments that correspond to some language with complete *C&B* (or extension thereof). All *C&B* extensions transfer directly to the $Prov_{C\&B}$ algorithm as they are all reduced to the original *C&B*, relying solely on the input-output behavior of the *C&B* (shared by the $Prov_{C\&B}$) and not on its internal working.

Applications of the $Prov_{C\&B}$. The $Prov_{C\&B}$ algorithm is applicable in a myriad of well-known scenarios involving query reformulation. However, we single out a class of applications that are particularly well-suited for the $Prov_{C\&B}$: they need the optimum among all minimal reformulations, of which there are relatively few, but these are hard to find because the search space for them is large. We discuss this class in Section 7.

Paper organization. We recall the *C&B* in Section 2, then present the $Prov_{C\&B}$ in Section 3, its implementation in Section 4 and its evaluation in Section 5. We discuss related work in Section 6 and conclude in Section 7.

2. OVERVIEW OF *C&B*

We recall the *C&B* algorithm, starting with the problem of query reformulation and continuing with an illustration of the *C&B*. For presentation simplicity, we set the illustration in a very restricted case of query reformulation, namely total rewriting of queries using materialized views in the absence of integrity constraints. Examples including integrity constraints are given in Section 5.

Reformulation. We write $D \models \mathcal{C}$ if a database instance D satisfies all the constraints in a set $\mathcal{C}$. Query Q_1 is contained in query Q_2 under the set $\mathcal{C}$ of constraints (denoted $Q_1 \sqsubseteq_{\mathcal{C}} Q_2$) if and only if $Q_1(D) \subseteq Q_2(D)$ for every database $D \models \mathcal{C}$, where $Q(D)$ denotes the result of Q on D. Q_1 is equivalent to Q_2 under $\mathcal{C}$ (denoted $Q_1 \equiv_{\mathcal{C}} Q_2$) if and only if $Q_1 \sqsubseteq_{\mathcal{C}} Q_2$ and $Q_2 \sqsubseteq_{\mathcal{C}} Q_1$. Let S and T be relational schemas related by set $\mathcal{C}$ of constraints, and Q a query formulated against S. A *T-reformulation* of Q under $\mathcal{C}$ is a query R formulated against T, such that $Q \equiv_{\mathcal{C}} R$.

Minimal reformulation. The *C&B* algorithm applies to queries and reformulations expressed as select-project-join-rename (SPJR) queries with set semantics (a.k.a. conjunctive queries), and constraints expressed as embedded dependencies [1]. In this context, a query is *$\mathcal{C}$-minimal* if it contains no joins that are redundant under the constraints $\mathcal{C}$, i.e. no join can be removed while preserving equivalence (under $\mathcal{C}$) to the original query.

The *C&B* algorithm. We illustrate the *C&B* on the following running example.

EXAMPLE 2.1. *Assume that a software company stores some of its internal information in the following schema:*

R(A,B,C), S(C,D), T(D,E).

The R table shows software engineers' assignment to teams, as tuples engineer id(A), engineer role(B), team id(C). One software engineer can participate in several teams and possibly hold several roles in a given team. The S table represents teams' participation on products, as tuples team id(C), product id(D). A team can of course work on several products, and several teams may collaborate on a given product. Finally, the T table lists the high priority production incidents as tuples product id(D), incident id(E).

To achieve rapid incident resolution, the QA manager needs to email all the engineers that could help fix the incidents. The list of these engineers is determined by issuing the following query[1]

Q : select r.A from R r, S s, T t where r.C=s.C and s.D=t.D,

Now assume that the following views have been materialized:

$V_R(A,C)$:	*select r.A, r.C from R r*
$V_S(C,D)$:	*select s.C, s.D from S s*
$V_{RS}(A,D)$:	*select r.A, s.D from R r, S s where r.C=s.C*
$V_T(D,E)$:	*select t.D, t.E from T t*

V_R shows engineers' participation in teams, regardless of their role. V_{RS} lists every engineer's participation in products. It is easy to see that

R_1: *select* $v_r.A$ *from* $V_R\ v_r,\ V_S\ v_s,\ V_T\ v_t$ *where* $v_r.C=v_s.C$ *and* $v_s.D=v_t.D$

R_2: *select* $v_{rs}.A$ *from* $V_{RS}\ v_{rs},\ V_T\ v_t$ *where* $v_{rs}.D=v_t.D$

are equivalent rewritings of Q using the views (these are total rewritings, as they use no base schema tables). Also, each rewriting is minimal, in the sense that none of their joins can be removed while preserving equivalence to Q.

The C&B *algorithm casts this rewriting problem as the following instance of the reformulation problem. The source schema is the logical schema against which query Q is formulated (tables R, S, and T in this example). The target schema is the schema of the materialized views (tables V_R, V_S, V_{RS} and V_T). The set $\mathcal{C}$ of dependencies relating the schemas is obtained by unioning the set $\mathcal{C}_{\mathcal{I}}$ of integrity constraints (empty in our example) with the set $\mathcal{C}_{\mathcal{V}}$ of embedded dependencies expressing the set $\mathcal{V}$ of view definitions. $\mathcal{C}_{\mathcal{V}}$ is obtained canonically by stating the inclusion (in both directions) between the result of the query defining each view and the view's extent. For the example, $\mathcal{C}_{\mathcal{V}}$ is the following set of constraints (they are all tgds, and thus embedded dependencies):*

$$
\begin{aligned}
c_{V_R}&: \forall r, r \in R \rightarrow \exists v_r, v_r \in V_R \wedge v_r.A = r.A \wedge v_r.C = r.C\\
b_{V_R}&: \forall v_r, v_r \in V_R \rightarrow \exists r, r \in R \wedge r.A = v_r.A \wedge r.C = v_r.C\\
c_{V_S}&: \forall s, s \in S \rightarrow \exists v_s, v_s \in V_S \wedge v_s.C = s.C \wedge v_s.D = s.D\\
b_{V_S}&: \forall v_s, v_s \in V_S \rightarrow \exists s, s \in S \wedge s.C = v_s.C \wedge s.D = v_s.D\\
c_{V_{RS}}&: \forall r, s,\ r \in R \wedge s \in S \wedge r.C = s.C \rightarrow \exists v_{rs}, v_{rs} \in V_{RS} \wedge v_{rs}.A = r.A \wedge v_{rs}.D = s.D\\
b_{V_{RS}}&: \forall v_{rs},\ v_{rs} \in V_{RS} \rightarrow \exists r, s,\ r \in R \wedge s \in S \wedge r.A = v_{rs}.A \wedge s.D = v_{rs}.D \wedge r.C = s.C\\
c_{V_T}&: \forall t, t \in T \rightarrow \exists v_t, v_t \in V_T \wedge v_t.D = t.D \wedge v_t.E = t.E\\
b_{V_T}&: \forall v_t, v_t \in V_T \rightarrow \exists t, t \in T \wedge t.D = v_t.D \wedge t.E = v_t.E
\end{aligned}
$$

The *C&B* algorithm relies on the *chase* procedure, which essentially adds to a query the redundant joins implied by the constraints. This is accomplished by repeatedly applying a syntactic transformation called a *chase step*. To describe it, we introduce some terminology. We call *relational atoms* the membership predicates occurring in the constraints (e.g. $r \in R$ in b_{V_R} in Example 2.1) and use the same name for the variable bindings occurring in the FROM clause of a query (e.g. $R\ r$ in query Q in Example 2.1) because they express the same concept with different syntax. We call *equality atoms* the equalities occurring in constraints or the WHERE clause of a query. The *premise* of a constraint is the set of atoms left of the implication arrow, while the conclusion is the set of atoms to its right. The chase step checks if the premise d_P of a constraint $d \in \mathcal{C}$ matches into the query q, in which case the query is extended with atoms constructed from the conclusion d_C. The match is a function h from the premise variables to the query variables, which maps the premise atoms into query atoms. This function is known as a homomorphism [7]. The extension of q involves adding to the FROM clause the relational atoms from d_C (with fresh variable names to avoid clashes with existing variables in the FROM clause) and to the WHERE clause the equalities from d_C (occurrences of premise variables are replaced by their image under h). If all these atoms already exist in the query, then the chase step is said to *not apply*, and it turns into a no-op.

EXAMPLE 2.2. *We illustrate a chase step of query Q from Example 2.1 with constraint $c_{V_{RS}}$. The identity mapping on the premise variables matches the relational atoms $r \in R$ and $s \in S$ and the*

[1]Since all queries in this paper are interpreted under set semantics, we systematically drop the DISTINCT keyword for conciseness.

equality atom $r.C{=}s.C$ into, respectively, the first and second relational atoms in Q's FROM clause and the first equality atom in its WHERE clause. The chase step adds the conclusion atoms to Q, yielding select r.A from R r, S s, T t, V_{RS} v_{rs} where $r.C{=}s.C$ and $s.D{=}t.D$ and $v_{rs}.A{=}r.A$ and $v_{rs}.D{=}s.D$.

The result of chasing a query Q with a set of constraints $\mathcal{C}$ is obtained by applying a sequence of chase steps until the query can be no longer extended. We denote this result with $Q^{\mathcal{C}}$.[2]

The *C&B* algorithm proceeds in two phases:

Chase: The input query Q is chased with the constraints $\mathcal{C}$, to obtain a chase result $Q^{\mathcal{C}}$. Next, the *universal plan U* is constructed by restricting $Q^{\mathcal{C}}$ to schema T, i.e. by dropping all joins with relations from schema S.

Backchase: This phase checks the subqueries of the universal plan U for equivalence (under $\mathcal{C}$) to Q. Informally, a *subquery* of U is obtained by essentially selecting a subset s of U's tuple variables and keeping only the atoms involving these variables (we say that the subquery is *induced* by s). The minimal equivalent subqueries are returned. Minimal subqueries contain no redundant joins under $\mathcal{C}$, i.e. no joins whose removal would induce a subquery that is itself equivalent to Q under $\mathcal{C}$. The equivalence check is performed according to a classical result [1]: it involves chasing each subquery sq and checking that Q has a containment mapping into $sq^{\mathcal{C}}$.

EXAMPLE 2.3. The chase phase. *When chasing Q with $\mathcal{C} = \mathcal{C}_\mathcal{V}$, the only chase steps that apply involve $c_{V_R}, c_{V_S}, c_{V_T}, c_{V_{RS}}$, yielding the chase result*

$Q^{\mathcal{C}_\mathcal{V}}$: select r.A
from R r, S s, T t, V_R v_r, V_S v_s, V_T v_t, V_{RS} v_{rs}
where r.C=s.C and s.D=t.D and $v_r.A{=}r.A$ and $v_r.C = r.C$
and $v_s.C{=}s.C$ and $v_s.D{=}s.D$ and $v_t.D{=}t.D$
and $v_t.E{=}t.E$ and $v_{rs}.A{=}r.A$ and $v_{rs}.D{=}s.D$

Restricting $Q^{\mathcal{C}_\mathcal{V}}$ to the view schema yields the universal plan[3]

U: select $v_r.A$
from V_R v_r, V_S v_s, V_T v_t, V_{RS} v_{rs}
where $v_r.C{=}v_s.C$ and $v_s.D{=}v_t.D$
and $v_r.A{=}v_{rs}.A$ and $v_s.D{=}v_{rs}.D$

The backchase phase. *In this phase, the subqueries of U are inspected. Notice that R_1, R_2 above are among them, being induced by the sets of tuple variables $\{v_r, v_s, v_t\}$, respectively $\{v_{rs}, v_t\}$.*

We illustrate only for R_2. To show that R_2 is equivalent to Q, the C&B *chases R_2 with $\mathcal{C}_\mathcal{V}$ and searches for a containment mapping from Q into $R_2^{\mathcal{C}_\mathcal{V}}$. The only applicable chase steps involve $b_{V_{RS}}, b_{V_T}$, yielding the result*

$R_2^{\mathcal{C}_\mathcal{V}}$: select $v_{rs}.A$
from V_{RS} v_{rs}, V_T v_t, R r, S s, T t
where $v_{rs}.D{=}v_t.D$ and $r.A{=}v_{rs}.A$ and $s.D{=}v_{rs}.D$
and s.C= r.C and $t.D{=}v_t.D$ and $t.E{=}v_t.E$

Since the identity mapping on variables is a containment mapping from Q to $R_2^{\mathcal{C}_\mathcal{V}}$, R_2 is equivalent to Q, and thus a rewriting. R_2 is moreover minimal, since none of its subqueries is a rewriting of Q (the backchase checks this by trying the subqueries). R_2 is therefore output by the C&B *algorithm. R_1 is discovered analogously. It turns out that there are no other minimal rewritings of Q. The backchase phase determines this by systematically checking the other subqueries of U, but discarding them as not being equivalent to Q, or not being minimal. For instance, the subquery*

sq: select $v_r.A$ from V_R v_r, V_T v_t

is not a rewriting of Q, and the subquery

sq′: select $v_{rs}.A$ from V_{RS} v_{rs}, V_S v_s, V_T v_t
where $v_{rs}.D{=}v_s.D$ and $v_s.D{=}v_t.D$

is a rewriting but is not minimal, since the join with v_s is redundant.

Completeness of the *C&B*. The fact that rewritings R_1 and R_2 in Example 2.1 are discovered among the subqueries of U is not accidental. In [10], it was shown that all minimal rewritings of Q are (isomorphic to) subqueries of U, in the absence of integrity constraints. The result was extended to the presence of integrity constraints expressed as embedded dependencies as long as the chase with them terminates [13].

Chase termination For arbitrary sets $\mathcal{C}$ of constraints, the chase procedure is not guaranteed to terminate. One of the least restrictive (and the most referenced) conditions on $\mathcal{C}$ known to date, that is sufficient to ensure chase termination regardless of the input query Q, is called *weak acyclicity* [15].

Relevant *C&B* implementation details The first *C&B* implementation is described in [29], where the backchase phase is identified as the performance bottleneck. This is expected, since exponentially many subqueries of the universal plan are checked for equivalence with the original query, and each equivalence check involves a chase. While [10] shows that this brute-force search is optimal from a complexity-theoretic point of view, follow-up work concerns itself with practical feasibility and proposes techniques for pruning the search. The only completeness-preserving pruning technique, sketched in [29] and detailed in [28], boils down to enumerating subqueries of the universal plan U in a bottom-up fashion, starting with all single-atom subqueries, next with two-atom subqueries, etc. Since the backchase searches for minimal reformulations, this bottom-up strategy allows pruning the equivalence check for all subqueries *sq* of U that already include as subquery a reformulation, since all such *sq* are non-minimal. In Example 2.3, subquery sq' would be pruned this way.

Even with bottom-up pruning, exponentially many subqueries remain to be chased in the worst case. In practice, this worst case occurs often. For instance, if the minimum number of joins in a reformulation is N, all subqueries of U up to size N are inspected since the pruning never kicks in for them. Their number is exponential in N. In the particular case when we seek total view-based rewritings of a query and none exist, all possible subqueries of U need to be checked. To at least mitigate this case, [29] proposes first checking that Q has a rewriting before even starting the subquery enumeration. This check is performed as follows.

A corollary of the completeness of the *C&B* algorithm states that Q has a reformulation if and only if it has a containment mapping into $U^{\mathcal{C}}$, i.e. into the result of chasing the universal plan U with the dependencies in $\mathcal{C} = \mathcal{C}_\mathcal{V} \cup \mathcal{C}_\mathcal{I}$. In practical implementations (e.g. in [29]), the existence of a containment mapping from Q into $U^{\mathcal{C}}$ is checked by treating $U^{\mathcal{C}}$ as a small symbolic database instance (known as "canonical" instance in the literature [1]), and evaluating Q over it. This amounts to computing the set of *all* containment mappings from Q into $U^{\mathcal{C}}$, and checking its non-emptiness.

[2]While the chase is not guaranteed to terminate in general, we confine ourselves here to terminating chases, which yield a finite result. It is well-known that the resulting query is not necessarily unique, as it depends on the non-deterministic choices made during the chase sequence among simultaneously applicable chase steps. However, the result is unique up to equivalence [1], which suffices for our purposes. We will therefore refer to "the" chase result in the remainder of this paper.

[3]Equalities of terms involving view variables that were implicit in $Q^{\mathcal{C}_\mathcal{V}}$ are made explicit in U.

EXAMPLE 2.4. *Revisiting Example 2.3, a possible chase sequence of U with $\mathcal{C}_\mathcal{V}$ involves, in order, chase steps with $b_{V_{RS}}$, b_{V_R}, b_{V_S} and b_{V_T}, yielding*

$U^{\mathcal{C}_\mathcal{V}}$: *select* $v_r.A$
from $V_R\ v_r,\ V_S\ v_s,\ V_T\ v_t,\ V_{RS},\ v_{rs},$
$R\ r_1,\ S\ s_1,\ R\ r_2,\ S\ s_2,\ T\ t$
where $v_r.C{=}v_s.C$ *and* $v_s.D{=}v_t.D$ *and* $v_r.A{=}v_{rs}.A$
and $v_s.D{=}v_{rs}.D$
and $r_1.A{=}v_{rs}.A$ *and* $s_1.D{=}v_{rs}.D$ *and* $r_1.C{=}s_1.C$
and $r_2.A{=}v_r.A$ *and* $r_2.C{=}v_r.C$
and $s_2.C{=}v_s.C$ *and* $s_2.D{=}v_s.D$
and $t.D = v_t.D$ *and* $t.E = v_t.E$

If we evaluate Q over the canonical instance of $U^{\mathcal{C}_\mathcal{V}}$, we obtain the containment mappings $h_1 = \{r \mapsto r_1, s \mapsto s_1, t \mapsto t\}$ and $h_2 = \{r \mapsto r_2, s \mapsto s_2, t \mapsto t\}$. Therefore, U is a (redundant) rewriting of Q, and it makes sense to start inspecting its subqueries in search of minimal rewritings.

3. A NOVEL ALGORITHM: $Prov_{C\&B}$

The remainder of this paper shows that significantly more can be done to prune the search for minimal reformulations while preserving completeness.

Intuitively, the original backchase enumerates the subqueries of the universal plan U in a bottom-up fashion and chases each of them in isolation from the others, to determine equivalence to the input query Q. This leads to *redundant chasing* of the atoms occurring in common within distinct subqueries of U. It also leads to *fruitless chasing* for subqueries that are not equivalent to Q.

EXAMPLE 3.1. *In our running example, the bottom-up backchase search prunes all strict superqueries of R_1, R_2 except U. This leads to pruning subqueries $v_r \wedge v_{rs} \wedge v_t$ and $v_s \wedge v_{rs} \wedge v_t$.*[4]

In addition, the backchase will prune those subqueries that do not contain the universal plan's head variables, as only safe rewritings are of interest (e.g. it will prune v_s, and $v_s \wedge v_t$).

However, the backchase still carries out fruitless chases of the following 7 subqueries of U, only to determine that none of them are rewritings of Q: v_r, v_{rs}, $v_r \wedge v_s$, $v_r \wedge v_t$, $v_r \wedge v_{rs}$, $v_s \wedge v_{rs}$, $v_r \wedge v_s \wedge v_{rs}$. Notice how the common relational atom $V_T\ v_t$ is chased redundantly multiple times (once when chasing U, then again when chasing R_1, and also when chasing R_2, and in the fruitless chases of the three above-listed subqueries involving v_t).

One might wonder why the backchase won't more aggressively prune away all subqueries whose combined views don't even mention all relations mentioned by Q. In our example, this would immediately dismiss all 7 subqueries listed above. Note that this aggressive pruning is unsafe in general, in the sense of compromising completeness of the backchase. Indeed, if the set of constraints includes tuple-generating dependencies (such as foreign key constraints), the minimal rewritings do not necessarily mention all relations mentioned by the query. It is easy to construct such examples: for instance, assume that $S.D$ is a foreign key referencing $T.D$. Then subqueries $v_r \wedge v_s$ and v_{rs} are minimal rewritings that would be missed by the aggressive pruning.

Our aim is to avoid both fruitless and redundant chasing, by replacing the many isolated subquery chases with a single chase of the universal plan U. To this end, we propose a new backchase strategy that keeps track of the provenance of each atom it creates, where the *provenance* of an atom a gives the set of subqueries of U whose chasing led to the creation of a. This provenance information enables us to run Q over the canonical instance of the result U' of chasing U, identify each image i of Q into U', and trace it back to the subqueries of U that are responsible for the creation of i during the chase of U.

[4]To avoid clutter, in the running example we specify universal plan subqueries by mentioning only their tuple variables.

EXAMPLE 3.2. *We illustrate by revisiting Example 2.4. We show again $U^{\mathcal{C}_\mathcal{V}}$, this time annotating the relational atoms of $U^{\mathcal{C}_\mathcal{V}}$ with their provenance in terms of the view atoms in U. The provenance annotations appear in square brackets.*

$U^{\mathcal{C}_\mathcal{V}}$: *select* $v_r.A$
from $V_R\ v_r[v_r],\ V_S\ v_s[v_s],\ V_T\ v_t[v_t],\ V_{RS}\ v_{rs}[v_{rs}],$
$R\ r_1[v_{rs}],\ S\ s_1[v_{rs}],\ R\ r_2[v_r],\ S\ s_2[v_s],\ T\ t[v_t]$
where $v_r.C{=}v_s.C$ *and* $v_s.D{=}v_t.D$ *and* $v_r.A{=}v_{rs}.A$
and $v_s.D{=}v_{rs}.D$
and $r_1.A{=}v_{rs}.A$ *and* $s_1.D{=}v_{rs}.D$ *and* $r_1.C{=}s_1.C$
and $r_2.A{=}v_r.A$ *and* $r_2.C{=}v_r.C$
and $s_2.C{=}v_s.C$ *and* $s_2.D{=}v_s.D$
and $t.D = v_t.D$ *and* $t.E = v_t.E$

Note that the relational atoms in $U^{\mathcal{C}_\mathcal{V}}$ involving views are annotated with themselves, as they are not introduced by chasing, but instead inherited directly from U. The variable bindings involving R, S, T are introduced by the chase, for instance r_1 by chasing v_{rs} with view dependency $b_{V_{RS}}$ and r_2 by chasing v_r with b_{V_R}.

Recall from Example 2.4 that Q has precisely two containment mapping images into $U^{\mathcal{C}_\mathcal{V}}$: one given by h_1, comprising r_1, s_1 and t, and another given by h_2, comprising r_2, s_2 and t. The provenance of the first image of Q is $v_{rs} \wedge v_t$, which corresponds to rewriting R_2 in Example 2.1, while the provenance of the second image is $v_r \wedge v_s \wedge v_t$, corresponding to rewriting R_1.

Notice how by computing the containment mappings of Q into $U^{\mathcal{C}_\mathcal{V}}$ (a step that is already carried out in the original C&B *algorithm), we immediately identify the two rewritings of Q, saving the fruitless individual chases of the subqueries listed in Example 3.1.*

Also notice how the $V_T\ v_t$ atom is only chased once and for all when chasing U, saving the redundant chasing that would have resulted from chasing R_1 and R_2 in isolation (as prescribed by the original backchase).

Provenance-Aware Chase (pa-chase) Recall from Section 2 that the completeness result of the *C&B* algorithm is based on chasing the subqueries of the universal plan U (U-subqueries for short). The purpose of the pa-chase is to replace all of these chases with a single chase of the universal plan (and thus of all its subqueries simultaneously), capturing during this chase the *C&B*-relevant effect of the isolated chases of the U-subqueries.

Our original motivation in designing the pa-chase was the desire to achieve the following goal:

(†) *The provenance of an atom a constructed during the pa-chase of the universal plan specifies precisely the set of U-subqueries whose standard chases (conducted in isolation from each other) would construct a.*

The benefits of such a design would be that (i) by restricting attention to only those universal plan subqueries identified by the provenance annotations we do not miss any reformulations, thus preserving completeness; and (ii) there is no need to further chase the provenance-identified subqueries to check their equivalence to the original query, thus rendering this single chase of U sufficient.

The technical challenge facing the implementation of this idea is raised by the need to carefully instrument the chase procedure to correctly track provenance according to our initial design goal. As detailed shortly, it turns out that as defined the standard chase is not suited for such instrumentation. We have therefore designed a chase variation we call the Skolem chase. It is provenance-agnostic like the standard chase and equivalent to it in terms of termination behavior and produced result. The Skolem chase is therefore interchangeable with the standard chase within the *C&B* algorithm, and the resulting *C&B*-variation remains complete. The advantage of the Skolem chase is that it lends itself to provenance-tracking instrumentation, yielding the pa-chase which is guaranteed to satisfy the following invariant:

($\diamond$) *The provenance of an atom a constructed during the pa-chase of the universal plan specifies precisely the set of universal plan subqueries whose Skolem chases (conducted in isolation from each other) would construct a.*

The pa-chase tracks provenance by annotating each original relational atom of universal plan U with a unique id called a *provenance term*, and by annotating each (relational or equality) atom a introduced by a pa-chase step with a *provenance formula*. Provenance formulae are constructed from provenance terms using logical conjunction and disjunction. A conjunction c of terms specifies a subquery of U, namely the subquery sq obtained by restricting U's FROM clause to the relational atoms given by the terms in c, and the WHERE clause to the equality atoms involving the corresponding variables. We say that c *induces* sq. Intuitively, a conjunction c of terms is intended to express the fact that the Skolem chase of sq constructs a. Disjunction is intended to express alternative U-subqueries, each of which lead to a's construction when Skolem-chased in isolation.

Before detailing the pa-chase, we show how invariant ($\diamond$) enables the $Prov_{C\&B}$ to replace the *C&B*'s backchase phase.

Search for Reformulations Once the universal plan U is pa-chased into result U', we simply compute the set $\mathcal{H}$ of all containment mappings from Q to U' (as done in the standard *C&B*). For each containment mapping $h \in \mathcal{H}$, invariant ($\diamond$) ensures that the provenance formula $\pi(h(Q))$ attached to Q's image under h gives precisely the (possibly multiple) U-subqueries whose isolated Skolem chases construct this image, thus witnessing equivalence to Q. All of these subqueries are therefore reformulations of Q. The reason we mention multiple U-subqueries is that in general the provenance formula $\pi(h(Q))$ may contain disjunction, signaling alternative U-subqueries each of whose Skolem chases constructs $h(Q)$. These alternative U-subqueries are read off directly from the disjunctive normal form (DNF) of $\pi(h(Q))$: every conjunct c corresponds to the U-subquery induced by the terms of c. The conjuncts of the DNF form of $\bigvee_{h\in\mathcal{H}} \pi(h(Q))$ yield all U-subqueries that are reformulations of Q. Notice how, due to invariant ($\diamond$), there is no need to check these subqueries for equivalence to Q, or to consider any other U-subqueries.

Minimization We still need to minimize the set of reformulations identified by $\Pi = DNF(\bigvee_{h\in\mathcal{H}} \pi(h(Q)))$. In general, given a reformulation R of Q under $\mathcal{C}$, minimizing R would involve searching for its subqueries that are still equivalent to Q (which in turn would be checked by chasing them with $\mathcal{C}$). Once again we employ provenance to avoid chasing. To this end, we observe that conjunct $c_1 \in \Pi$ induces a non-minimal U-subquery if and only if there is a conjunct $c_2 \in \Pi$ that *subsumes* c_1 in the standard Boolean logic sense: c_2's terms are a subset of c_1's. All we need to do therefore is to remove from Π all subsumed conjuncts, obtaining what we call the *reduced form* of Π, $rf(\Pi)$. The conjuncts of $rf(\Pi)$ each induce minimal reformulations. Notice that this minimization not only avoids chasing, but it avoids even the construction of reformulations, involving instead only lightweight manipulations of provenance conjuncts.

EXAMPLE 3.3. *Recall Example 3.2. In its simple setting, the standard chase and the Skolem chase behave identically, so there is no need to know the details of the Skolem chase to understand the provenance annotations resulting from pa-chasing U with $\mathcal{C} = \mathcal{C}_{\mathcal{V}}$ to obtain U'. By Example 3.2, we have $\Pi = \pi(h_1(Q)) \vee \pi(h_2(Q)) = v_{rs} \wedge v_t \vee v_r \wedge v_s \wedge v_t$. Notice that Π is already in reduced form (DNF with no conjuncts subsumed by others). Each of the two conjuncts of Π corresponds to a rewriting of Q: the first to R_2, the second to R_1.*

Putting It All Together We summarize $Prov_{C\&B}$ below.

algorithm $Prov_{C\&B}$
params: source schema S, target schema T
set $\mathcal{C}$ of weakly-acyclic embedded dependencies over $S \cup T$

input: SPJR query Q formulated over S,
output: all minimal SPJR T-reformulations of Q under $\mathcal{C}$

//chase phase:
1. compute universal plan U
by standard-chasing Q with $\mathcal{C}$ and keeping only T-atoms

//provenance-directed reformulation search:
2. compute the result U' of pa-chasing U with $\mathcal{C}$
3. compute the set $\mathcal{H}$ of all containment mappings from Q into U'
4. compute Π as the DNF formula of $\bigvee_{h\in\mathcal{H}} \pi(h(Q))$
5. compute the reduced form $rf(\Pi)$ of Π
6. return the U-subqueries induced by the conjuncts of $rf(\Pi)$.

Formal guarantees Our main result shows that the $Prov_{C\&B}$ algorithm preserves completeness:

THEOREM 3.1. *Let $\mathcal{C}$ be a weakly-acyclic set of dependencies. Then for any SPJR query Q, the $Prov_{C\&B}$ algorithm returns precisely the minimal reformulations of Q under $\mathcal{C}$.*

Details on pa-chase The design of the pa-chase walks a fine line between tracking provenance as desired and ensuring termination of the resulting chase whenever the standard chase terminates.

To detail provenance tracking during the pa-chase, we introduce some notation first. Given atom a, its provenance formula is $\pi(a)$. The provenance of a set of atoms A is the logical conjunction of the provenances of its members: $\pi(A) = \bigwedge_{a\in A} \pi(a)$.

We detail the intuitions that drove the design of the pa-chase step. Recall that, initially, we were attempting to mimic the behavior of the standard chase, which is why the intuitions below initially refer to a *tentative pa-chase step (tpa-step)* modeled after the standard chase step. In due course, we identify the need to substitute the standard chase with the Skolem chase in the actual definition of pa-chase step, and of Goal (†) with Invariant ($\diamond$).

I1: the provenance of the image of the premise is transferred to the atoms introduced by the chase step. Assume that a sequence of pa-chase steps has yielded a result q. Assume that a standard chase step s with dependency d using match h applies on q, adding a set A of atoms to q. By definition of the standard chase step, the premise d_P therefore has an image $h(d_P)$ in q. By Goal (†), the U-subqueries whose chase in isolation creates this image are indicated by $\pi(h(d_P))$. Since each of these chases creates $h(d_P)$ in isolation, they each can be extended with chase step s, so each of the U-subqueries in $\pi(h(d_P))$ when standard-chased in isolation construct the atoms in A. To record this fact, the tpa-step adds the A-atoms and annotates each of them with $\pi(h(d_P))$. For instance, in Example 3.2, the pa-chase step with $b_{V_{RS}}$ matches the premise against the relational atom $V_{RS}\ v_{rs}$, and it introduces the relational and equality atoms involving tuple variables r_1, s_1 (shown in U^{C_V}), annotating relational atoms with provenance v_{rs}.

Towards ensuring termination, the standard chase never applies a step if it attempts to add atoms that are already there (the step turns into a no-op). The notion of being "already there" is formalized in the standard chase to mean that premise's homomorphic match h has an extension to a homomorphic match of the conclusion. Denoting the extended match as h', the atoms in q that are "already there" are the atoms in $h'(d_C)$. In designing the pa-chase step, one would be tempted to parallel the standard chase step, turning the former step into a no-op in this case. It turns out however that the pa-chase step must diverge from its standard counterpart.

I2: when the same atom a can be introduced by chasing several alternative U-subqueries, a's provenance must reflect this. Consider first the case when the atoms that are "already there" are identical copies of the set A of atoms the standard chase step (with d, using premise match h) would attempt to add. Note that when adding relational atoms, the standard chase step invents fresh names for the tuple variables, so when referring to an atom $a \in A$ as a copy of an atom $c \in h'(d_C)$, we mean that all their attributes are pairwise equal. Recall from case *I1* that $\pi(a) = \pi(h(d_P))$. Now if $\pi(a)$ contains at least one U-subquery sq that is not in $\pi(c)$, then the isolated chase of sq would never construct c, hence the standard chase step constructing a would apply. In view of Goal (†), the tpa-step records this behavior by extending the provenance formula of c with a disjunction with $\pi(h(d_P))$. We call such a step *provenance-enriching* because instead of creating new atoms it only enriches the provenance of existing ones.

I3: if the chase step produces atoms that match into q without being identical copies of the match image, these atoms must be added and their provenance recorded. The technically most subtle case for defining the pa-chase step is the one in which the atoms that the standard chase step attempts to add (A) are not identical to those that are "already there" ($h'(d_C)$). We illustrate such a scenario in Example 3.4 below. In this case, we need to record the provenance of the atoms in A. Where can we record this information? The intuition offered by the standard chase would be to add no new atoms to q, because they are "already there" in the form of $h'(d_C)$. If we were to follow this intuition, then the natural way to record the newly discovered provenance would be to enrich the provenance of the atoms in $h'(d_C)$, paralleling intuition *I2*. This would be wrong however, as the U-subqueries in $\pi(h(d_P))$ are only known to cause the construction of the atoms in A and not of the distinct ones in $h'(d_C)$. In fact we can give examples showing that if we defined the pa-chase step in this way, the resulting provenance of the atoms in $h'(d_C)$ would spuriously contain U-subqueries whose standard chase does not actually construct them. As a consequence, such a design would require $Prov_{C\&B}$ to check for equivalence each subquery indicated by a provenance annotation, which would involve launching a chase. To avoid this, the tpa-chase step must behave differently than the standard chase step in case *I3*: it adds the atoms A to q and adorns them with provenance $h(d_P)$, while leaving the atoms in $h'(d_C)$ unaffected.

EXAMPLE 3.4. *Recall the pa-chase of universal plan U from Example 3.2, and assume that this time the first two chase steps applied involve first b_{V_R}, then b_{V_S} (the standard chase selects randomly among the applicable steps, so we can observe a chase sequence distinct from the one in Example 3.2). The intermediate result is U_2 below, in which the tuple variables are named to show correspondence to the tuple variables introduced in Example 3.2.*

U_2: *select* $v_r.A$
from $V_R\ v_r,\ V_S\ v_s,\ V_T\ v_t,\ V_{RS}\ v_{rs},$
$R\ r_2[v_r],\ S\ s_2[v_s]$
where $v_r.C{=}v_s.C$ *and* $v_s.D{=}v_t.D$ *and* $v_r.A{=}v_{rs}.A$
and $v_s.D{=}v_{rs}.D$
and $r_2.A{=}v_r.A$ *and* $r_2.C{=}v_r.C$
and $s_2.C{=}v_s.C$ *and* $s_2.D{=}v_s.D$

Now consider a tpa-chase step with $b_{V_{RS}}$ on U_2 as defined above. The standard chase step would attempt to add the relational atoms $R\ r_1$, $S\ s_1$ as well as all equalities they are involved in (these can be seen in U^{C_V} in Example 3.2). However the standard step would not apply, as there is a match of r_1, s_1 into r_2, s_2, respectively, which matches the equality atoms involving r_1, s_1 into the (explicit or implicit) equality atoms involving r_2, s_2. Notice that r_2 is not *a copy of r_1; indeed the equality $r_1.B{=}r_2.B$ does not follow, because constraint $b_{V_{RS}}$ leaves the B attribute undetermined.*

Still, the provenances of $R\ r_2$ and $R\ r_1$ are distinct (v_r, respectively v_{rs}), so the tpa-chase records the fact that the set A of relational and equality atoms involving r_1, s_1 would have been created by the isolated standard chase of the U-subquery induced by v_{rs} (as illustrated in Example 2.3, when chasing subquery R_2). The tpa-chase step is therefore allowed to add A to U_2, adorning the tuple variables r_1, s_1 with provenance term v_{rs} (see U^{C_V} in Example 3.2).

I4: disallow reapplication of a chase step with same constraint and same premise. As seen in Example 3.4, case *I3* occurs when at least one of the relational atoms in the conclusion of d has some undetermined attribute. *Undetermined attributes* are involved neither directly nor indirectly in equalities with attributes of the relational atoms in the premise d_P, and therefore their value is not determined by the match of d_P. For instance, attribute B of tuple variable r is undetermined in both b_{V_R} and $b_{V_{RS}}$.

While the tentative definition of the pa-chase step according to case *I3* above would keep track of provenance as desired, its divergence from the standard chase step would immediately lead to non-termination because the same chase step now applies infinitely often. Indeed, in Example 3.4 above, the tpa-chase step with $b_{V_{RS}}$ is allowed to introduce tuple variables r_1, s_1 and their atoms A despite their match into r_2, s_2 and their atoms, because for example r_1.B=r_2.B does not hold. But then the same tpa-chase step applies again, introducing fresh tuple variables r_1', s_1' and atoms A', which match into r_1, s_1 and A without being identical copies, because r_1'.B=r_1.B does not hold.

To disallow infinitely many re-applications of a chase step with the same constraint d and premise match h, we normalize d to turn all undetermined attributes in its conclusion into determined attributes. We employ a classical technique from First-Order Logic, namely normalization by equating the undetermined attributes with function calls. Function symbols used in calls must be distinct across constraints (so that the chase step with a constraint is not mistaken for a re-application of a chase step with a distinct constraint). Function calls should intuitively take as arguments all tuple variables of the premise. However, it turns out that to distinguish between non-identical atoms it is sufficient to consider fewer function arguments: namely, those attributes of the premise tuples that also appear in (the equalities of) the conclusion.

EXAMPLE 3.5. *We illustrate only for constraint b_{V_R}, whose normalization involves setting the undetermined attribute r.B equal* *to a function call:* $\forall v_r, v_r \in V_R \rightarrow \exists r, r \in R \wedge r.A = v_r.A \wedge r.C = v_r.C \wedge r.B = f(v_r.A,\ v_r.C)$

Interestingly, these functions correspond to the classical *Skolem functions* one would obtain when eliminating existential quantifiers from the constraints if written in First-Order Logic form. Notice that the attributes that were undetermined in the original form of the dependencies are now determined by the Skolem terms, in short *Skolem-determined*.

Skolem chase. We call the (provenance-unaware) chase flavor using these Skolem functions the *Skolem chase*. When checking whether an atom with a Skolem-determined attribute is "already there", the Skolem chase step requires an identical copy thereof in q (Skolem function calls only match calls with the same function symbol and arguments). We can show that the Skolem chase is essentially equivalent to the standard chase in terms of its termination behavior and its result. Denoting with $Sk(\mathcal{C})$ the skolemized version of set $\mathcal{C}$ of dependencies, we have:

THEOREM 3.2. *(i) If $\mathcal{C}$ is a weakly-acyclic set of dependencies, then the Skolem chase with $Sk(\mathcal{C})$ terminates. (ii) For every SPJR query q, the result of the standard chase of q with $\mathcal{C}$ is equivalent to the result of the Skolem chase of q with $Sk(\mathcal{C})$.*

We can further characterize the comparison between the two chases in terms of their respective number of steps. In the weakly-acyclic case, [15] shows an upper bound on the length of every standard chase sequence. This bound is polynomial in the size of the instance when fixing its schema. While in some cases, as shown in the example, the Skolem chase sequences may be longer than the standard chase ones, we can prove that for weakly-acyclic dependencies the upper bound exhibited in [15] also applies to the Skolem chase.

pa-chase. We now revisit cases *I1* through *I3*, which prescribe the behavior of the tentative tpa-chase step. This was initially modeled on the standard chase step, leading to the non-termination problem described in case *I4*. We adjust this design by making the pa-chase record the provenance of atoms constructed by the Skolem chase instead of the standard chase. More specifically, in the description of the tpa-chase step in cases *I1* through *I3* above, the standard chase step with dependency d is replaced by a Skolem chase step with the skolemized version of d, denoted $Sk(d)$. We can now formally prove that, defined in this way, the pa-chase maintains invariant ($\diamond$):

THEOREM 3.3. *The provenance of an atom a constructed during the pa-chase of the universal plan specifies precisely the set of universal plan subqueries whose Skolem chases (conducted in isolation from each other) would construct a.*

We can show that Invariant ($\diamond$) suffices for our purposes, since Theorems 3.3 and 3.2 imply the completeness of the $Prov_{C\&B}$ algorithm (Theorem 3.1).

4. IMPLEMENTATION

We present some of the key techniques we employed in implementing the $Prov_{C\&B}$ reformulation algorithm.

Standard chase Our chase implementation incorporates several optimizations that are summarized below:

Chase step as query evaluation. A chase step searches for homomorphic matches of the premise and conclusion of constraint d against the query Q. The search for homomorphic matches of the premise can be modeled as running d's premise d_P (viewed as a query) against Q (viewed as a symbolic database known in the literature as the canonical instance of Q [1]). For instance, for constraint $b_{V_{RS}}$ in Example 2.1, matches of the premise are found by the natural join of tables R and S. Extensions of these matches to the conclusion d_C of d are modeled analogously. We implement the search for matches as query evaluation. We compile d_P to a query plan based on relational algebra operators, and we run it over an internal representation of Q using its canonical instance.

Standard query optimizations. Modeling chase steps as query evaluation problems allows us to apply standard query optimization techniques borrowed from the relational query optimization literature. Our implementation includes among others pushing selections and (duplicate-eliminating) projections into the joins.

Efficient in-memory query processing. In contrast to general DBMSs that need to account for large datasets that may not fit in main memory, the chase operates on instances that start from a single query body and are small enough to fit in main memory. This observation allowed us to implement the chase engine as an in-memory query processor. To speed up query processing, we opted for in-memory hash-based implementations of the relational algebra operators (joins and projections).

Bottom-up query evaluation. In a naive chase engine, one would try to apply every constraint each time the instance changes. However, some constraints would not be applicable. To reduce the number of constraints we try to apply, our query processor works in a bottom-up fashion. Whenever a new tuple is added to a relation, it is being pushed up the query trees that scan this relation. Thus, for every change in the underlying instance only those queries that might be affected are evaluated.

Incremental query evaluation. A chase sequence involves evaluating repeatedly the same set of query plans obtained from compiling the constraints. Moreover, these queries are evaluated over evolutions of the *same* instance. The effect of each chase step is to evolve the instance by adding only a few new tuples at a time (these tuples correspond to the atoms constructed by the step). The majority of the instance is unaffected by the step. This creates the opportunity to accelerate chasing by employing incremental query evaluation. Instead of evaluating each query from scratch, we keep its query plan (together with the populated hash tables) in memory and whenever new tuples are added to the evolving instance, we push them to the affected plans.

Efficient maintenance of equalities. Chasing involves introducing equalities between the values present in an instance. Moreover, it involves checking whether two values are equal. To allow efficient querying and updating of equalities, we employ a union-find data structure as in [29].

Pa-chase Our provenance-aware chase implementation reuses the core design choices listed above for the standard chase, adapted of course to account for the Skolem chase and provenance bookkeeping. As a side-effect of our reformulation work, the pa-chase implementation delivers a minimal-why-provenance-tracking processor for conjunctive queries (generalized to support invention of values using Skolem functions).

5. EXPERIMENTS

We evaluated our $Prov_{C\&B}$ implementation in a recreation (and extension) of the setting described in [29] for query rewriting using materialized views and integrity constraints. We chose this setting because we believe it is practically relevant, it allows apples-to-apples comparison with the *C&B*, and because its design was parameterized so as to allow scaling to the point of stress-testing any complete reformulation algorithm by forcing a combinatorial explosion of the existing minimal rewritings.

Chain-of-stars schemas and queries ([29]) The parameterized setting starts from the following basic building block. Consider the query Q given below, which joins relations $R_1(K, A_1, A_2, F)$, $R_2(K, A_1, A_2)$ with $S_{ij}\ (A_i, B)\ (1 \leq i, j \leq 2)$. Figure 1 depicts Q's join graph, in which the nodes represent the query variables and the edges represent equijoins between them.

Q: select $s_{11}.B, s_{12}.B, s_{21}.B, s_{22}.B$
 from $R_1\ r_1, S_{11}\ s_{11}, S_{12}\ s_{12}, R_2\ r_2, S_{21}\ s_{21}, S_{22}\ s_{22}$
 where $r_1.F = r_2.K$ and $r_1.A_1 = s_{11}.A_1$ and $r_1.A_2 = s_{12}.A_2$
 and $r_2.A_1 = s_{21}.A_1$ and $r_2.A_2 = s_{22}.A_2$

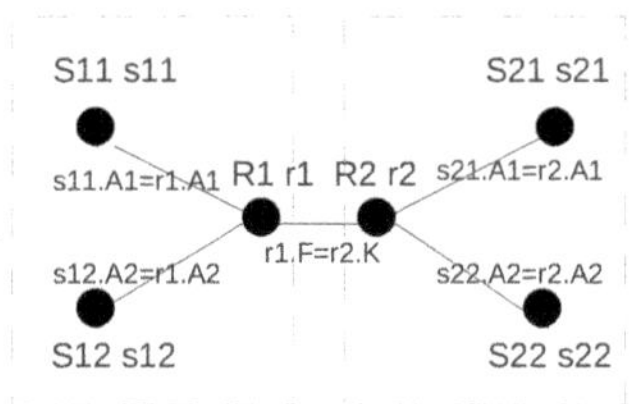

Figure 1: Join graph for a two-star query

One can think of the tables S_{ij} as modeling offered choices in two distinct domains, such as educational and recreational, grouped by several categories. The tables S_{11} and S_{12} could correspond to the lectures and workshops categories, while S_{21} and S_{22} could hold the sports and movies categories respectively. Categories span a range of subcategories (such as action movies), expressed by the A_j attributes, such that in every subcategory there are potentially many offered choices (the B attributes).

On the other hand, the tables R_1 and R_2 correspond to individual "preference profiles" in the respective domains, such that each profile selects, for a given category, either a specific subcategory or no preference (null). The K attributes are unique profile identifiers, thus primary keys. The join of R_1 and R_2 constructs global profiles for a group, with $R_1.F$ being a foreign key referencing K in R_2. Think of R_2 tuples as describing profiles of a "person" entity, while R_1 tuples describe profiles of a "student" entity, with the key-foreign key join implementing the "isA" relationship.

Towards identifying correlations of offered choices across domains, Q finds sets of choices that represent all categories and that co-occur within the global preference profile of some individual.

Assume the existence of materialized views $V_i(K, B_1, B_2)\ (1 \leq i \leq 2)$, where each V_i joins R_i with S_{i1} and S_{i2} and retrieves the B attributes from S_{i1} and S_{i2} together with the key K of R_i :

V_i: select $r.K, s_1.B, s_2.B$
 from $R_i\ r, S_{i1}\ s_1, S_{i2}\ s_2$
 where $r.A_1 = s_1.A_1$ and $r.A_2 = s_2.A_2$

Assuming that only a small fraction of the individuals expresses preferences for all categories, the extent of the materialized views is expected to be relatively small, all the more so when considering that the same offering may appear in several subcategories, for instance action movies and comedies (recall our convention that all queries have an implicit DISTINCT keyword).

Since these views discard, for each domain, the unmatching profiles, we would expect them to be quite useful in speeding up Q's execution. It is easy to see that the join of R_2, S_{21}, and S_{22} can be replaced by a scan over V_2:

Q_1: select $s_{11}.B, s_{12}.B, v_2.B_1, v_2.B_2$
 from $R_1\ r_1, S_{11}\ s_{11}, S_{12}\ s_{12}, V_2\ v_2$
 where $r_1.F = v_2.K$ and $r_1.A_1 = s_{11}.A_1$ and $r_1.A_2 = s_{12}.A_2$

However, the join of R_1, S_{11}, and S_{12} cannot be blindly replaced by a scan over V_1, since Q_2, the obvious candidate for a rewriting of Q using both V_1 and V_2 is not equivalent to Q in the absence of additional semantic information.

Q_2: select $v_1.B_1, v_1.B_2, v_2.B_1, v_2.B_2$
 from $R_1\ r_1, V_1\ v_1, V_2\ v_2$
 where $r_1.K = v_1.K$ and $r_1.F = v_2.K$

The reason is that V_1 does not contain the F attribute of R_1, and there is no guarantee that joining the latter with V_1 will recover the correct values of F. On the other hand, *if we know that K is a key in R_1*, then Q_2 is guaranteed to be equivalent to Q, being therefore an additional (and likely better) plan. V_1 is usable for rewriting Q only by exploiting the key constraint.

Consider now a slightly more complicated version of the above configuration. The query graph is shaped like a chain of 2 stars, star i having R_i for its hub and S_{ij} for its corners ($1 \leq i \leq 2, 1 \leq j \leq 3$). The attributes selected in the output are the B attributes of all corners S_{ij}. Assume the existence of materialized views $V_{il}(K, B_1, B_2)$ ($1 \leq i \leq 2$, $1 \leq l \leq 2$), where each V_{il} joins the hub of star i (R_i) with two of its consecutive corners (S_{il} and $S_{i(l+1)}$). Each V_{il} selects the B attributes of the corner relations it joins, as well as the K attribute of R_i, as depicted in Figure 2.

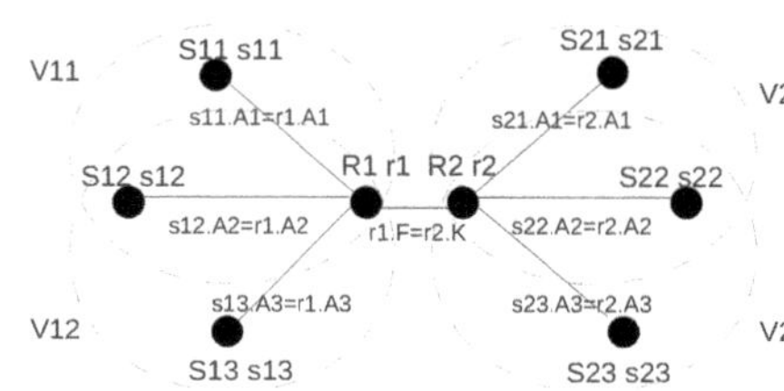

Figure 2: Chain-of stars configuration with 3 corners

Notice that in this setting *all* views require the key constraint to be usable in rewriting.

The chain-of-star configuration generalizes to chains of H stars with C corners each, such that for each star there are $C - 1$ views, each joining the hub with two consecutive corners. As soon as C is greater than 2, the key constraint on the hub table is a prerequisite for the usability of every view involving that hub. Note that the chain-of-star schema shape is inspired by such patterns as star and snowflake schemas, which are well-represented in practice [21].

Platform All experiments were run on an Intel(R) Core(TM) i7-2760QM CPU @ 2.40GHz with 8GB of memory.

Experiment 1: Is complete search worthwhile? We investigated whether the potential overhead induced by running the complete search for rewritings given by $Prov_{C\&B}$ is justified by the speedup achieved over the execution of the original query without using $Prov_{C\&B}$. To assess this speedup, we performed a suite of comparative experiments with a well-known and widely used commercial DBMS. We compared two alternatives: (a) feeding the original query "as is" to the DBMS, versus (b) feeding it the rewriting obtained by running $Prov_{C\&B}$ to enumerate all minimal rewritings using the views and integrity constraints, then picking among these one rewriting with the overall minimum number of joins (randomly selecting one if several exist). Note that we are placing the $Prov_{C\&B}$ on top of the DBMS, which gives a lower bound to the speedup potential achievable by a tighter integration with the DBMS's optimizer.

For the purpose of our experiments, we constructed a chain-of-stars schema, with 5 stars and 5 corners/star, for a total of 30 tables, 20 materialized views, and 5 key constraints. This schema was then extended with an additional 25 tables and 25 foreign key constraints to a total of 55 tables, as described in Experiment 2. The table contents obey the following statistics, which are compatible with the real-life interpretation of our scenario:

- the cardinality of the views V_{ij} is 10% of that of the tables R_i
- we ensure 5% selectivity for the joins between R_i and S_{ij}

Over this schema we ran chain-of-stars queries of various complexity levels, up to a maximum number of 20 joins (the DBMS was timing out too frequently after that), thus leading to the following configurations (our figures refer to them):

#stars	2	3	4	5	2	3	4	5	2	3	4	2	3
#corners	2	2	2	2	3	3	3	3	4	4	4	5	5
#joins	5	8	11	14	7	11	15	19	9	14	19	11	18

For each query, we measured the following elapsed times:

Q_{exec}: the time taken by the DBMS to execute (optimize then run) the original query.

RW_{find}: the time taken by our $Prov_{C\&B}$ implementation to find all minimal rewritings and choose one with the fewest joins.

RW_{exec}: the time taken by the DBMS to execute (optimize then run) this rewriting.

We populated each table in our schema with 5K tuples, generated randomly according to our selectivity parameters (the DBMS automatically created indexes on all key attributes). We enabled the use of materialized views in the optimizer. We set a timeout of 15 minutes (900 seconds) for query execution times. We used the recommended optimization level, which comes preset out of the box[5].

Figure 3 presents the measured values for Q_{exec}, RW_{find} and RW_{exec}, for each of the tested queries. Query (s, c) refers to the configuration with s stars of c corners each. In the graph, s appears above c. Times RW_{find} and RW_{exec} are shown stacked into the same bar, as this is the total time taken when we interpose $Prov_{C\&B}$ before calling the DBMS. Notice that, for all the queries, RW_{find} is a very small fraction of Q_{exec}, which in turn stays larger than the sum of RW_{find} and RW_{exec} even for the smallest query. Also notice that the speedup yielded by $Prov_{C\&B}$ can reach one, and even two orders of magnitude.

The reason we never observe parity between Q_{exec} and RW_{exec} is that the minimum-join rewriting found using $Prov_{C\&B}$ uses views extensively (as explained for query Q_2 above), while the DBMS *fails to detect that views are relevant whenever doing so requires exploiting the key constraint.* The DBMS-provided explanation of the plan choice states that the views were considered but rejected because of the missing foreign key attribute. The only exception when a view is indeed used is for the last star of 2-cornered star queries ((2,2) through (5,2)) because this view is relevant even without the key constraint (recall the discussion for Q_1 above).

The drop in the measured Q_{exec} time from (3,3) to (4,3) is interesting: it is due to the fact that we imposed no restriction on the join between two consecutive stars, other than it being a foreign key join (this is consistent with the targeted real-life scenario interpretation described above). Generally, it may happen that adding a new star to the query actually "filters out" a lot of results. If the filtering join

[5]For fairness we considered all optimization levels. Out of a total of 7, only 4 consider materialized views, and two of these are designed for ultra-specialized queries, spending so much time in optimizing our queries that the optimization time vastly dominates execution time. The remaining two view-aware levels, call L_r the recommended one and L_a the alternative, are similar except that L_a uses a greedy algorithm while L_r uses dynamic programming for join reordering. The speedups for $Prov_{C\&B}$ we observed under L_a are generally even higher than the ones we observed under L_r (we omit them for space reasons).

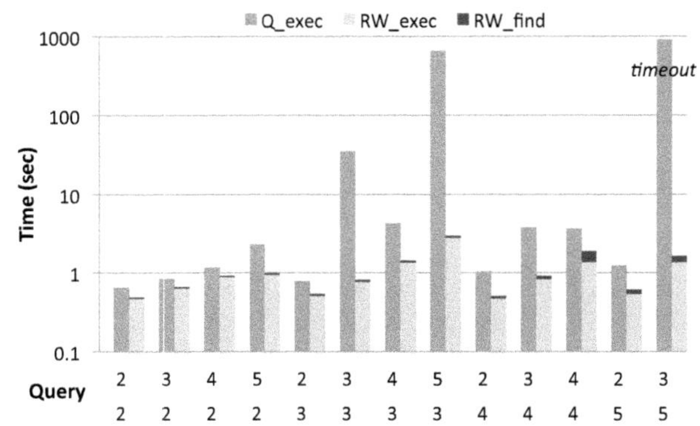

Figure 3: Elapsed times on one database instance

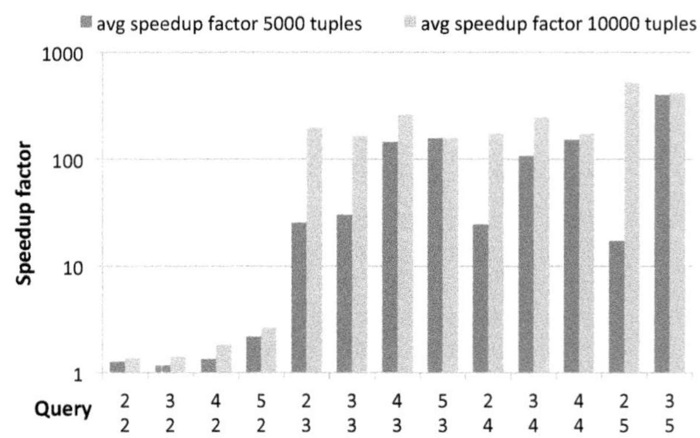

Figure 4: Average speedup factors on 10 database instances

is performed early enough by the DBMS, its small intermediate result can propagate its impact to any cross-star intermediate chain of joins. This is exactly what occurred in this case (as an inspection of the plan explanation confirmed).

This observation called for better accounting of the execution time variations due to the actual data. We therefore repeated the experiment over 10 different randomly populated database instances obeying the same table-size and selectivity criteria. For each database instance and query, we computed the *speedup factor*, defined as *speedup factor* $= \frac{Q_{exec}}{RW_{find}+RW_{exec}}$.

Figure 4 presents, for each query, the speedup factors averaged over the set of 10 database instances, providing a more robust view of the advantage of the rewritings according to the query complexity. Notice that the measurements in Figure 3 were not a lucky fluke, being quite typical (the speedups are in many cases below average). Note that the values for queries (5,3), (4,4) and (3,5) are only lower bounds for the speedup, because these queries time out on several databases.

We remind that, at 5K tuples per table, the database instances are rather small. We repeated the experiments for larger tables of 10K tuples each (timeouts while measuring Q_{exec} prevented us from pushing the experiment any further). Observe that the average speedups increase, a trend we expect to continue with increasing data size. Timeouts are once again responsible for the seemingly marginal increases for queries (5,3), (4,4) and (3,5), since the figure only reports a lower bound for the average speedup.

In conclusion, on small-sized queries the performance of the DBMS's processing engine, coupled with the ability of its optimizer to use views (for the last star of 2-cornered configurations, for which the key constraint is not needed) leads to fast query execution. Although for every database instance and every query we ran, the measured speedup factors are higher than 1 (calling $Prov_{C\&B}$

still results in a speed-up), on the small-sized queries they are less pronounced. On the other hand, as the query complexity increases, the time Q_{exec} dramatically increases, up to the order of minutes even on relatively small instances, and the speedup factors become significantly more substantial as using the views makes increasing difference. As Figure 4 shows, on more complex queries the view-based plans gain an advantage of one and even two orders of magnitude (and often more, but this is masked by the timeouts when measuring Q_{exec}).

Experiment 2: Performance of the $Prov_{C\&B}$ implementation We further analyzed the standalone performance of our implementation. In our evaluation, we also studied the behaviour of our algorithm beyond key constraints. We extended the chain-of-stars schema to also incorporate foreign keys, by adding the tables $T_{ij}(B,C)$ such that (see Figure 5):

- $S_{ij}.B$ is a foreign key referencing $T_{ij}.B$
- the views output the same attributes, but also contain a join with the T tables.

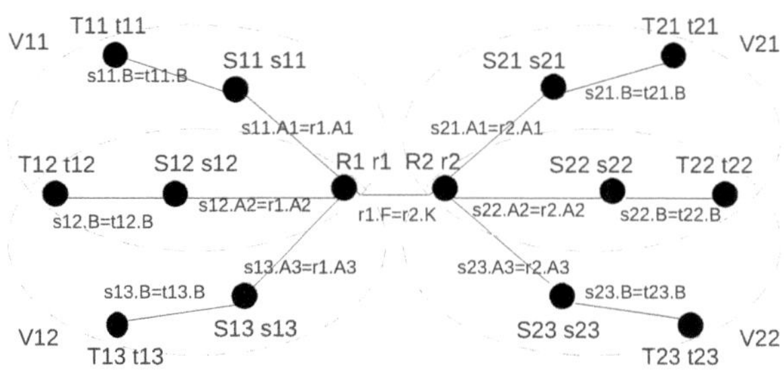

Figure 5: Extended chain-of-stars configuration

The chain-of-stars queries over the new schema, hereafter called the "extended chain-of-stars schema", stay the same. The views however are now recognizable as relevant for rewriting only when exploiting *both keys and foreign keys constraints*. The resulting view-based rewritings are identical to the ones in Experiment 1. The $Prov_{C\&B}$ implementation continues to find them, while the DBMS continues to miss them. This time, the DBMS misses even the views it used to find for the 2-corner case. Their detection now involves reasoning about the foreign keys, which is evidently incomplete in the DBMS. RW_{exec} does not change, while Q_{exec} increases for the 2-corner queries, leading to increased speedups. We omit their values, focusing instead on reporting RW_{find} in Figure 6, which shows average times over the 10 runs (rewriting is unaffected by the database instance, and the measured times are virtually identical). The graph shows rewrite computation times on the two schemas (as expected the foreign keys cause more work, but the difference is not substantial). The two schema types are chosen such that a large number of minimal rewritings is available in the large configurations, to enable a stress-test of our implementation as it pursues all rewritings. In Figure 6, we annotate each query with the number of minimal rewritings it admits (all of whom are found) shown as a bar label. On both schemas, our implementation exhibits sub-second running times. This is true even for configurations with over 2000 minimal rewritings, e.g. (4,4). Note that the rewrite computation times represent a very small fraction of the query execution times reported in Experiment 1.

Experiment 3: Savings over the *C&B* Recall that the original motivation for the design of $Prov_{C\&B}$ was to save the chase sequences launched by the *C&B* algorithm during the backchase phase. We quantify (a lower bound for) these savings here. For both the chain-of-stars schema and its extended version, the *C&B*

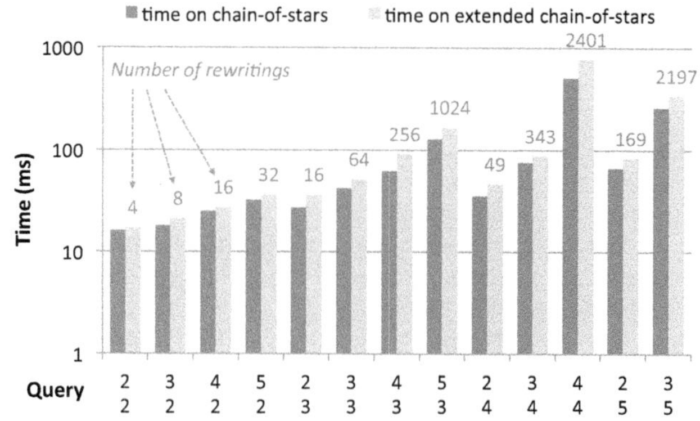

Figure 6: Rewrite computation times (RW_{find})

backchase (called the Full Backchase in [29]) will chase at least each actual minimal rewriting to determine its equivalence to the original query. The $Prov_{C\&B}$ saves at least all these chases, whose number is depicted in Figure 6 as bar labels. We note the exponential trend of savings as the number of hubs or corners increases.

6. RELATED WORK

The problem of query reformulation includes view-based rewriting as particular case. This problem is fundamental to many classic data management tasks, including query optimization using materialized views, data security and integration. It represents a fruitful research area and has been treated in depth for relational databases, for a wide spectrum of model assumptions, from those pertaining to the language of queries and views [22, 3, 2, 8, 31], to going from set semantics to bag or mixed bag-set semantics (see [9] and the references therein), to adding limited access patterns for the views [16, 26], or to using potentially infinite sets of views [23]. In the context of information integration, view-based rewriting has been extended also to finding not-necessarily equivalent (but maximally-contained) rewritings (see [19] and references therein).

The first complete view-based rewriting algorithm for the SQL fragment considered in this paper, in the absence of integrity constraints, was given in [22], where the problem was shown NP-complete. In practice, this leads to either deterministic exponential-time implementations, or to algorithms that rely on view-matching heuristics (e.g., [17, 20, 33, 5]), which are potentially more efficient but may fail to identify some rewriting opportunities. Such heuristic-based approaches may also assume an integrated process within the DBMS's optimizer module, comparing the cost of the found rewritings to that of plans without views. In the presence of constraints, the *C&B*, discussed at length in this paper, is the only complete algorithm we are aware of in this setting.

Our techniques rely on the classic chase procedure [1]. Recently, we have witnessed revived interest in the chase, with studies such as [24] focusing in particular on more permissive conditions that can guarantee termination.

In the pa-chase, the provenance bookkeeping exploits the analogy between chase step application and query evaluation, with the provenance annotations coinciding with the *minimal why-provenance* flavor introduced for query evaluation in [6], and corresponding to a particular case of a provenance semiring [18].

7. DISCUSSION

Chase termination beyond weak acyclicity. We have proven that the pa-chase terminates on weakly-acyclic sets of constraints, as does the standard chase. However, the latter is guaranteed to terminate for a host of more permissive conditions (e.g. see [24]). We are optimistic that the pa-chase terminates for these classes of constraints as well, thus extending the $Prov_{C\&B}$ completeness result to them. We leave this investigation to future work.

Selecting among minimal reformulations. Our experiments have shown that the $Prov_{C\&B}$ can enhance an optimizer's performance even when run on top of the DBMS, using a lightweight cost model to select a rewriting (the number of joins in this case). The advantage of such an approach is to avoid integration within the DBMS (a desirable, but logistically challenging goal). Such integration is avoidable even while using the DBMS's own cost estimator, typically accessible via an API. [29] sketches (and [28] details) a backchase which grows U-subqueries bottom-up from smallest to largest and prunes subqueries as soon as their cost exceeds that of the best reformulation found so far. This strategy returns a cost-optimum reformulation for a large class of cost models, called "monotonic" because they estimate the cost of a query to be at least the cost of its subqueries. This idea carries over to the $Prov_{C\&B}$, only much more efficiently, since the bottom-up cost-based pruning would cost-estimate only the subqueries of the already enumerated minimal reformulations (as opposed to all U-subqueries), memoizing the cost of common subqueries. It turns out that one can do even better by interleaving the enumeration of minimal rewritings with their costing into a cost-based-pruning pa-chase guaranteed to still find all cost-minimum rewritings (the detailed development is beyond the scope of this paper).

Particularly well-suited $Prov_{C\&B}$ applications. Our experiments evaluate the $Prov_{C\&B}$ in a traditional query processing setting. There, partial view-based rewritings are of interest (these are allowed to mention base tables besides the views). Clearly there are exponentially more partial rewritings than total ones (in which only views can be mentioned), so the $Prov_{C\&B}$ can find them even faster (all the more so since often there is no total rewriting: see our own experiments for instance, where the hub tables had to be part of the rewriting). Scenarios that care only for total rewritings and require the overall optimum among them are therefore the ideal $Prov_{C\&B}$ applications (query processing does not fit this bill, even though the $Prov_{C\&B}$ is useful there as we have seen).

One such scenario is access control enforcement via *security views* [25, 30]. Here, a query is considered "safe" only if it has a total rewriting using a set of legal views. In previous work, the existence of such rewriting sufficed for the query to be safe. Let's refine the scenario by having each view require a certain clearance level, and assume that an analyst wishes to establish the minimum clearance level required to answer a query so she can go request it. This involves selecting the minimum-clearance total rewriting(s).

What about NP-hardness? One may wonder how the fast reformulation times we measured square with the NP-hardness of the view-based rewriting problem even in the absence of constraints [22]. The answer is that there is another classical NP-hardness result, namely for evaluating SPJR queries against a database, which commercial DBMSs haven taken in stride since their inception, even for large databases, as it refers to query size only. Our contribution is to reduce reformulation to query evaluation (over toy-sized symbolic databases), opening up the bag of tools of relational query processing. The analogy with query evaluation had been applied in prior *C&B* implementations to speed up standard chase step evaluation and containment mapping search, but it was not clear how the backchase phase could profit from it. The novel pa-chase establishes just such an analogy between the search among universal plan subqueries and (provenance-tracking) query evaluation.

8. REFERENCES

[1] S. Abiteboul, R. Hull, and V. Vianu. *Foundations of Databases*. Addison-Wesley, 1995.

[2] F. N. Afrati, R. Chirkova, M. Gergatsoulis, and V. Pavlaki. Finding equivalent rewritings in the presence of arithmetic comparisons. In *EDBT*, pages 942–960, 2006.

[3] F. N. Afrati, C. Li, and P. Mitra. Answering queries using views with arithmetic comparisons. In *PODS*, 2002.

[4] C. Beeri and M. Y. Vardi. A proof procedure for data dependencies. *J. ACM*, 31(4):718–741, 1984.

[5] R. G. Bello, K. Dias, A. Downing, J. Feenan, J. L. Finnerty, W. D. Norcott, H. Sun, A. Witkowski, and M. Ziauddin. Materialized views in Oracle. In *VLDB*, pages 659–664, 1998.

[6] P. Buneman, S. Khanna, and W. C. Tan. Why and where: A characterization of data provenance. In *ICDT*, pages 316–330, 2001.

[7] A. K. Chandra and P. M. Merlin. Optimal implementation of conjunctive queries in relational data bases. In *STOC*, 1977.

[8] S. Cohen, W. Nutt, and Y. Sagiv. Rewriting queries with arbitrary aggregation functions using views. *ACM TODS*, 31(2), 2006.

[9] D. DeHaan. Equivalence of nested queries with mixed semantics. In *PODS*, pages 207–216, 2009.

[10] A. Deutsch, L. Popa, and V. Tannen. Physical data independence, constraints, and optimization with universal plans. In *VLDB*, 1999.

[11] A. Deutsch, L. Popa, and V. Tannen. Query reformulation with constraints. *SIGMOD Record*, 35(1):65–73, 2006.

[12] A. Deutsch and V. Tannen. Mars: A system for publishing xml from mixed and redundant storage. In *VLDB*, pages 201–212, 2003.

[13] A. Deutsch and V. Tannen. Reformulation of XML queries and constraints. In *ICDT*, 2003.

[14] R. Fagin. Horn clauses and database dependencies. *J. ACM*, 1982.

[15] R. Fagin, P. G. Kolaitis, R. J. Miller, and L. Popa. Data exchange: Semantics and query answering. In *ICDT*, 2003.

[16] D. Florescu, A. Y. Levy, I. Manolescu, and D. Suciu. Query optimization in the presence of limited access patterns. In *SIGMOD*, pages 311–322, 1999.

[17] J. Goldstein and P.-Å. Larson. Optimizing queries using materialized views: A practical, scalable solution. In *SIGMOD*, 2001.

[18] T. J. Green, G. Karvounarakis, and V. Tannen. Provenance semirings. In *PODS*, pages 31–40, 2007.

[19] A. Halevy. Answering queries using views: A survey. *VLDB J.*, 2001.

[20] P.-Å. Larson, J. Goldstein, H. Guo, and J. Zhou. MTCaches: Mid-tier database caching for SQL Server. *IEEE Data Eng. Bull.*, 27(2), 2004.

[21] M. Levene and G. Loizou. Why is the snowflake schema a good data warehouse design? *Information Systems*, 28(3):225 – 240, 2003.

[22] A. Y. Levy, A. O. Mendelzon, Y. Sagiv, and D. Srivastava. Answering queries using views. In *PODS*, pages 95–104, 1995.

[23] A. Y. Levy, A. Rajaraman, and J. D. Ullman. Answering queries using limited external query processors. *J. Comput. Syst. Sci.*, 1999.

[24] M. Meier, M. Schmidt, and G. Lausen. On chase termination beyond stratification. *PVLDB*, 2(1):970–981, 2009.

[25] A. Motro. An access authorization model for relational databases based on algebraic manipulation of view definitions. In *ICDE*, 1989.

[26] A. Nash and B. Ludäscher. Processing first-order queries under limited access patterns. In *PODS*, 2004.

[27] N. Onose, A. Deutsch, Y. Papakonstantinou, and E. Curtmola. Rewriting nested xml queries using nested views. In *SIGMOD*, 2006.

[28] L. Popa. *Object/relational Query Optimization with Chase and Backchase*. PhD thesis, University of Pennsylvania, 2000.

[29] L. Popa, A. Deutsch, A. Sahuguet, and V. Tannen. A chase too far? In *SIGMOD*, pages 273–284, 2000.

[30] S. Rizvi, A. O. Mendelzon, S. Sudarshan, and P. Roy. Extending query rewriting techniques for fine-grained access control. In *SIGMOD*, pages 551–562, 2004.

[31] D. Srivastava, S. Dar, H. V. Jagadish, and A. Y. Levy. Answering queries with aggregation using views. In *VLDB*, 1996.

[32] C. Yu and L. Popa. Constraint-based xml query rewriting for data integration. In *SIGMOD*, pages 371–382, 2004.

[33] M. Zaharioudakis, R. Cochrane, G. Lapis, H. Pirahesh, and M. Urata. Answering complex SQL queries using automatic summary tables. In *SIGMOD*, pages 105–116, 2000.

Query Shredding: Efficient Relational Evaluation of Queries over Nested Multisets

James Cheney
University of Edinburgh
jcheney@inf.ed.ac.uk

Sam Lindley
University of Edinburgh
Sam.Lindley@ed.ac.uk

Philip Wadler
University of Edinburgh
wadler@inf.ed.ac.uk

ABSTRACT

Nested relational query languages have been explored extensively, and underlie industrial language-integrated query systems such as Microsoft's LINQ. However, relational databases do not natively support nested collections in query results. This can lead to major performance problems: if programmers write queries that yield nested results, then such systems typically either fail or generate a large number of queries. We present a new approach to query shredding, which converts a query returning nested data to a fixed number of SQL queries. Our approach, in contrast to prior work, handles multiset semantics, and generates an idiomatic SQL:1999 query directly from a normal form for nested queries. We provide a detailed description of our translation and present experiments showing that it offers comparable or better performance than a recent alternative approach on a range of examples.

Categories and Subject Descriptors

H.2.4 [**Database Management**]: Systems—*Query processing*

Keywords

language-integrated query; querying nested collections

1. INTRODUCTION

Databases are one of the most important applications of declarative programming techniques. However, relational databases only support queries against flat tables, while programming languages typically provide complex data structures that allow arbitrary combinations of types including nesting of collections (e.g. sets of sets). Motivated by this so-called *impedance mismatch*, and inspired by insights into language design based on monadic comprehensions [28], database researchers introduced nested relational query languages [22, 3, 4] as a generalisation of flat relational queries to allow nesting collection types inside records or other types. Several recent language designs, such as XQuery [21] and PigLatin [20], have further extended these ideas, and they have been particularly influential on language-integrated querying systems such as Kleisli [30], Microsoft's LINQ in C# and F# [19, 24, 5], Links [8, 18], and Ferry [10].

This paper considers the problem of translating nested queries over nested data to flat queries over a flat representation of nested data, or *query shredding* for short. Our motivation is to support a free combination of the features of nested relational query languages with those of high-level programming languages, particularly systems such as Links, Ferry, and LINQ. All three of these systems support queries over nested data structures (e.g. records containing nested sets, multisets/bags, or lists) in principle; however, only Ferry supports them in practice. Links and LINQ currently either reject such queries at run-time or execute them inefficiently in-memory by loading unnecessarily large amounts of data or issuing large numbers of queries (sometimes called *query storms* or *avalanches* [11] or the $N + 1$ *query problem*). To construct nested data structures while avoiding this performance penalty, programmers must currently write flat queries (e.g. loading in a superset of the needed source data) and convert the results to nested data structures. Manually reconstructing nested query results is tricky and hard to maintain; it may also mask optimisation opportunities.

In the Ferry system, Grust et al. [10, 11] have implemented shredding for nested list queries by adapting an XQuery-to-SQL translation called *loop-lifting* [14]. Loop-lifting produces queries that make heavy use of advanced On-Line Analytic Processing (OLAP) features of SQL:1999, such as `ROW_NUMBER` and `DENSE_RANK`, and to optimise these queries Ferry relies on a SQL:1999 query optimiser called Pathfinder [13].

Van den Bussche [26] proved expressiveness results showing that it is possible in principle to evaluate nested queries over *sets* via multiple flat queries. To strengthen the result, Van den Bussche's simulation eschews value invention mechanisms such as SQL:1999's `ROW_NUMBER`. The downside, however, is that the flat queries can produce results that are quadratically larger than needed to represent sets and may not preserve bag semantics.

Query shredding is related to the well-studied *query unnesting* problem [16, 9]. However, most prior work on unnesting only considers SQL queries that contain subqueries in WHERE clauses, not queries returning nested results; the main exception is Fegaras and Maier's work on query unnesting in a complex object calculus [9].

In this paper, we introduce a new approach to query shredding for nested multiset queries (a case not handled by prior work). Our work is formulated in terms of the Links language, but should be applicable to other language-integrated query systems, such as Ferry and LINQ, or to other complex-object query languages [9]. Figure 1 illustrates the behaviour of Links, Ferry and our approach.

We decompose the translation from nested to flat queries into a series of simpler translations. We leverage prior work on *normalisation* that translates a higher-order query to a *normal form* in

SIGMOD'14, June 22–27, 2014, Snowbird, UT, USA.

ACM 978-1-4503-2376-5/14/06 ...$15.00.
http://dx.doi.org/10.1145/2588555.2612186.

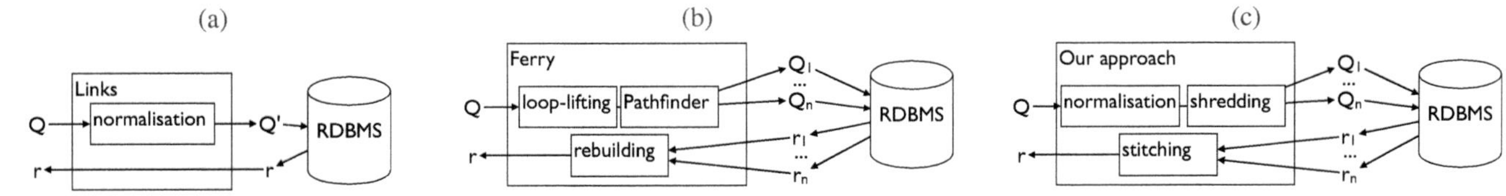

Figure 1: (a) Default Links behaviour (flat queries) (b) Ferry (nested list queries) (c) Our approach (nested bag queries)

which higher-order features have been eliminated [29, 7, 9]. Our algorithm operates on normal forms. We review normalisation in Section 2, and give a running example of our approach in Section 3.

Sections 4–7 present the remaining phases of our approach, which are new. The *shredding* phase translates a single, nested query to a number of flat queries. These queries are organised in a *shredded package*, which is essentially a type expression whose collection type constructors are annotated with queries. The different queries are linked by *indexes*, that is, keys and foreign keys. The shredding translation is presented in Section 4. Shredding leverages the normalisation phase in that we can define translations on types and terms independently. Section 5 shows how to run shredded queries and stitch the results back together to form nested values.

The *let-insertion* phase implements a flat indexing scheme using a let-binding construct and a row-numbering operation. Let-insertion (described in Section 6) is conceptually straightforward, but provides a vital link to proper SQL by providing an implementation of abstract indexes. The final stage is to translate to SQL (Section 7) by flattening records, translating let-binding to SQL's `WITH`, and translating row-numbering to SQL's `ROW_NUMBER`.

We have implemented and experimentally evaluated our approach (Section 8) in comparison with Ulrich's implementation of loop-lifting in Links [25]. Our approach typically performs as well or better than loop-lifting, and can be significantly faster.

Our contribution over prior work can be summarised as follows. Fegaras and Maier [9] show how to unnest complex object queries including lists, sets, and bags, but target a nonstandard nested relational algebra, whereas we target standard SQL. Van den Bussche's simulation [26] translates nested set queries to several relational queries but was used to prove a theoretical result and was not intended as a practical implementation technique, nor has it been implemented and evaluated. Ferry [10, 11] translates nested list queries to several SQL:1999 queries and then tries to simplify the resulting queries using Pathfinder. Sometimes, however, this produces queries with cross-products inside OLAP operations such as `ROW_NUMBER`, which Pathfinder cannot simplify. In contrast, we delay introducing OLAP operations until the last stage, and our experiments show how this leads to much better performance on some queries. Finally, we handle nested multisets, not sets or lists.

Additional details, proofs of correctness, and comparison with related work are available in a companion technical report [6].

2. BACKGROUND

We use metavariables $x, y, \ldots, f, g$ for *variables*, and $c, d, \ldots$ for *constants* and primitive operations. We also use letters $t, t', \ldots$ for *table names*, $\ell, \ell', \ell_i, \ldots$ for *record labels* and $a, b, \ldots$ for *tags*.

We write $M[x := N]$ for capture-avoiding substitution of N for x in M. We write $\vec{x}$ for a vector $x_1, \ldots, x_n$. Moreover, we extend vector notation pointwise to other constructs, writing, for example, $\langle \overrightarrow{\ell = M} \rangle$ for $\langle \ell_1 = M_1, \ldots, \ell_n = M_n \rangle$.

We write: square brackets $[-]$ for the meta level list constructor; $w :: \vec{v}$ for adding the element w onto the front of the list $\vec{v}$; $\vec{v} +\!\!+ \vec{w}$ for the result of appending the list $\vec{w}$ onto the end of the list $\vec{v}$; and

$$
\begin{aligned}
\mathcal{N}[\![x]\!]_\rho &= \rho(x) \\
\mathcal{N}[\![c(X_1, \ldots, X_n)]\!]_\rho &= [\![c]\!](\mathcal{N}[\![X_1]\!]_\rho, \ldots, \mathcal{N}[\![X_n]\!]_\rho) \\
\mathcal{N}[\![\lambda x.M]\!]_\rho &= \lambda v.\mathcal{N}[\![M]\!]_{\rho[x \mapsto v]} \\
\mathcal{N}[\![M\ N]\!]_\rho &= \mathcal{N}[\![M]\!]_\rho(\mathcal{N}[\![N]\!]_\rho) \\
\mathcal{N}[\![\langle \ell_i = M_i \rangle_{i=1}^n]\!]_\rho &= \langle \ell_i = \mathcal{N}[\![M_i]\!]_\rho \rangle_{i=1}^n \\
\mathcal{N}[\![M.\ell]\!]_\rho &= \mathcal{N}[\![M]\!]_\rho.\ell \\
\mathcal{N}[\![\mathsf{if}\ L\ \mathsf{then}\ M\ \mathsf{else}\ N]\!]_\rho &= \begin{cases} \mathcal{N}[\![M]\!]_\rho, & \text{if } \mathcal{N}[\![L]\!]_\rho = \mathsf{true} \\ \mathcal{N}[\![N]\!]_\rho, & \text{if } \mathcal{N}[\![L]\!]_\rho = \mathsf{false} \end{cases} \\
\mathcal{N}[\![\mathsf{return}\ M]\!]_\rho &= [\mathcal{N}[\![M]\!]_\rho] \\
\mathcal{N}[\![\emptyset]\!]_\rho &= [\,] \\
\mathcal{N}[\![M \uplus N]\!]_\rho &= \mathcal{N}[\![M]\!]_\rho +\!\!+ \mathcal{N}[\![N]\!]_\rho \\
\mathcal{N}[\![\mathsf{for}\ (x \leftarrow M)\ N]\!]_\rho &= \mathit{concat}[\mathcal{N}[\![N]\!]_{\rho[x \mapsto v]} \mid v \leftarrow \mathcal{N}[\![M]\!]_\rho] \\
\mathcal{N}[\![\mathsf{empty}\ M]\!]_\rho &= \begin{cases} \mathsf{true}, & \text{if } \mathcal{N}[\![M]\!]_\rho = [\,] \\ \mathsf{false}, & \text{if } \mathcal{N}[\![M]\!]_\rho \neq [\,] \end{cases} \\
\mathcal{N}[\![\mathsf{table}\ t]\!]_\rho &= [\![t]\!]
\end{aligned}
$$

Figure 2: Semantics of λ_{NRC}

concat for the function that concatenates a list of lists. We also make use of the following functions:

$$
\mathit{init}\ [x_i]_{i=1}^n = [x_i]_{i=1}^{n-1} \qquad \mathit{last}\ [x_i]_{i=1}^n = x_n
$$
$$
\mathit{enum}([v_1, \ldots, v_m]) = [\langle 1, v_1 \rangle, \ldots \langle m, v_m \rangle]
$$

In the meta language we make extensive use of comprehensions, primarily list comprehensions. For instance, $[v \mid x \leftarrow xs, y \leftarrow ys, p]$, returns a copy of v for each pair $\langle x, y \rangle$ of elements of xs and ys such that the predicate p holds. We write $[v_i]_{i=1}^n$ as shorthand for $[v_i \mid 1 \leq i \leq n]$ and similarly, e.g., $\langle \ell_i = M_i \rangle_{i=1}^n$ for $\langle \ell_1 = M_1, \ldots, \ell_n = M_n \rangle$.

2.1 Nested relational calculus

We take the higher-order, nested relational calculus (evaluated over bags) as our starting point. We call this λ_{NRC}; this is essentially a core language for the query components of Links, Ferry, and LINQ. The types of λ_{NRC} include base types (integers, strings, booleans), record types $\langle \overrightarrow{\ell : A} \rangle$, bag types $\mathrm{Bag}\,A$, and function types $A \to B$.

$$
\begin{array}{ll}
\text{Types} & A, B ::= O \mid \langle \overrightarrow{\ell : A} \rangle \mid \mathrm{Bag}\,A \mid A \to B \\
\text{Base types} & O ::= \mathit{Int} \mid \mathit{Bool} \mid \mathit{String}
\end{array}
$$

We say that a type is *nested* if it contains no function types and *flat* if it contains only base and record types.

The terms of λ_{NRC} include λ-abstractions, applications, and the standard terms of nested relational calculus.

$$
\begin{array}{lll}
\text{Terms} & M, N ::= & x \mid c(\vec{M}) \mid \mathsf{table}\ t \mid \mathsf{if}\ M\ \mathsf{then}\ N\ \mathsf{else}\ N' \\
& \mid & \lambda x.\,M \mid M\ N \mid \langle \overrightarrow{\ell = M} \rangle \mid M.\ell \mid \mathsf{empty}\ M \\
& \mid & \mathsf{return}\ M \mid \emptyset \mid M \uplus N \mid \mathsf{for}\ (x \leftarrow M)\ N
\end{array}
$$

We assume that the constants and primitive functions include boolean values with negation and conjunction, and integer values with standard arithmetic operations and equality tests. We assume special labels $\#_1, \#_2, \ldots$ and encode tuple types $\langle A_1, \ldots, A_n \rangle$

as record types $\langle \#_1 : A_1, \ldots, \#_n : A_n \rangle$, and similarly tuple terms $\langle M_1, \ldots, M_n \rangle$ as record terms $\langle \#_1 = M_1, \ldots, \#_n = M_n \rangle$. We assume fixed signatures $\Sigma(t)$ and $\Sigma(c)$ for tables and constants. The tables are constrained to have flat relation type (Bag $\langle \ell_1 : O_1, \ldots, \ell_n : O_n \rangle$), and the constants must be of base type or first order n-ary functions ($\langle O_1, \ldots, O_n \rangle \to O$).

Most language constructs are standard. The $\emptyset$ expression builds an empty bag, return M constructs a singleton, and $M \uplus N$ builds the bag union of two collections. The for $(x \leftarrow M)$ N comprehension construct iterates over a bag obtained by evaluating M, binds x to each element, evaluates N to another bag for each such binding, and takes the union of the results. The expression empty M evaluates to true if M evaluates to an empty bag, false otherwise.

λ_{NRC} employs a standard type system similar to that presented in other work [30, 18, 5]. We will also employ several typed intermediate languages and translations mapping λ_{NRC} to SQL. All of these (straightforward) type systems are omitted due to space limits; they will be available in the full version of this paper.

Semantics. We give a denotational semantics in terms of lists. Though we wish to preserve bag semantics, we interpret object-level bags as meta-level lists. For meta-level values v and v', we consider v and v' equivalent as multisets if they are equal up to permutation of list elements. We use lists mainly so that we can talk about order-sensitive operations such as row_number.

We interpret base types as integers, booleans and strings, function types as functions, record types as records, and bag types as lists. For each table $t \in dom(\Sigma)$, we assume a fixed interpretation $[\![t]\!]$ of t as a list of records of type $\Sigma(t)$. In SQL, tables do not have a list semantics by default, but we can impose one by choosing a canonical ordering for the rows of the table. We order by all of the columns arranged in lexicographic order (assuming linear orderings on field names and base types).

We assume fixed interpretations $[\![c]\!]$ for the constants and primitive operations. The semantics of nested relational calculus are shown in Figure 2. We let ρ range over environments mapping variables to values, writing ε for the empty environment and $\rho[x \mapsto v]$ for the extension of ρ with x bound to v.

2.2 Query normalisation

In Links, query normalisation is an important part of the execution model [7, 18]. Links currently supports only queries mapping flat tables to flat results, or *flat–flat* queries. When a subexpression denoting a query is evaluated, the subexpression is first normalised and then converted to SQL, which is sent to the database for evaluation; the tuples received in response are then converted into a Links value and normal execution resumes (see Figure1(a)).

For *flat–nested* queries that read from flat tables and produce a nested result value, our normalisation procedure is similar to the one currently used in Links [18], but we hoist all conditionals into the nearest enclosing comprehension as where clauses. This is a minor change; the modified algorithm is given in the full version of this paper. The resulting normal forms are:

Query terms	$L ::= \biguplus \vec{C}$
Comprehensions	$C ::= \mathsf{for}\ (\vec{G}\ \mathsf{where}\ X)\ \mathsf{return}\ M$
Generators	$G ::= x \leftarrow t$
Normalised terms	$M, N ::= X \mid R \mid L$
Record terms	$R ::= \langle \overrightarrow{\ell = M} \rangle$
Base terms	$X ::= x.\ell \mid c(\vec{X}) \mid \mathsf{empty}\ L$

Any closed flat–nested query can be converted to an equivalent term in the above normal form.

$[\![departments]\!] =$

(id)	name
1	Product
2	Quality
3	Research
4	Sales

$[\![employees]\!] =$

(id)	dept	name	salary
1	Product	Alex	20000
2	Product	Bert	900
3	Research	Cora	50000
4	Research	Drew	60000
5	Sales	Erik	2000000
6	Sales	Fred	700
7	Sales	Gina	100000

$[\![tasks]\!] =$

(id)	employee	task
1	Alex	build
2	Bert	build
3	Cora	abstract
4	Cora	build
5	Cora	call
6	Cora	dissemble
7	Cora	enthuse
8	Drew	abstract
9	Drew	enthuse
10	Erik	call
11	Erik	enthuse
12	Fred	call
13	Gina	call
14	Gina	dissemble

$[\![contacts]\!] =$

(id)	dept	name	client
1	Product	Pam	false
2	Product	Pat	true
3	Research	Rob	false
4	Research	Roy	false
5	Sales	Sam	false
6	Sales	Sid	false
7	Sales	Sue	true

Figure 3: Sample data

THEOREM 1. *Given a closed flat–nested query* $\vdash M :$ Bag A, *there exists a normalisation function* $norm_{\text{Bag}\ A}$, *mapping each* M *to an equivalent normal form* $norm_{\text{Bag}\ A}(M)$.

The normalisation algorithm and correctness proof are similar to those in previous papers [7, 18, 5]. The normal forms above can also be viewed as an SQL-like language allowing relation-valued attributes (similar to the complex-object calculus of Fegaras and Maier [9]). Thus, our results can also be used to support nested query results in an SQL-like query language. In this paper, however, we focus on the functional core language based on comprehensions, as illustrated in the next section.

3. RUNNING EXAMPLE

To motivate and illustrate our work, we present an extended example showing how our shredding translation could be used to provide useful functionality to programmers working in LINQ using F#, Ferry or Links. We first describe the code the programmer would actually write and the results the system produces. Throughout the rest of the paper, we return to this example to illustrate how the shredding translation works.

Consider a flat database schema Σ for an organisation:

$tasks$(employee : $String$, task : $String$)
$employees$(dept : $String$, name : $String$, salary : Int)
$contacts$(dept : $String$, name : $String$, client : $Bool$)
$departments$(name : $String$)

Each department has a name, a collection of employees, and a collection of external contacts. Each employee has a name, salary and a collection of tasks. Some contacts are clients. Figure 3 shows a small instance of this schema. For convenience, we also assume every table has an integer-valued key *id*.

In λ_{NRC}, queries of the form for ... where ... return ... are natively supported. These are *comprehensions* as found in XQuery or functional programming languages, and they generalise idiomatic SQL `SELECT FROM WHERE` queries [3]. Unlike SQL, we can use (nonrecursive) functions to define queries with parameters, or parts of queries, and freely combine them. For example, the following functions define useful query patterns over the above schema:

$$\begin{aligned}
&\mathit{tasksOfEmp}\ e = \mathsf{for}\ (t \leftarrow \mathit{tasks})\\
&\qquad\qquad\qquad \mathsf{where}\ (t.\mathrm{employee} = e.\mathrm{name})\\
&\qquad\qquad\qquad \mathsf{return}\ t.\mathit{tsk}\\
&\mathit{contactsOfDept}\ d = \mathsf{for}\ (c \leftarrow \mathit{contacts})\\
&\qquad\qquad\qquad \mathsf{where}\ (d.\mathrm{dept} = c.\mathrm{dept})\\
&\qquad\qquad\qquad \mathsf{return}\ \langle \mathrm{name} = c.\mathrm{name}, \mathrm{client} = c.\mathrm{client}\rangle\\
&\mathit{employeesByTask}\ t =\\
&\quad \mathsf{for}\ (e \leftarrow \mathit{employees}, d \leftarrow \mathit{departments})\\
&\quad \mathsf{where}\ (e.\mathrm{name} = t.\mathrm{employee} \wedge e.\mathrm{dept} = d.\mathrm{dept})\\
&\quad \mathsf{return}\ \langle b = e.\mathrm{employee}, c = d.\mathrm{dept}\rangle
\end{aligned}$$

Nested queries allow free mixing of collection (bag) types with record or base types. For example, the following query

$$\begin{aligned}
&\mathit{employeesOfDept}\ d = \mathsf{for}\ (e \leftarrow \mathit{employees})\\
&\qquad\qquad \mathsf{where}\ (d.\mathrm{dept} = e.\mathrm{dept})\\
&\qquad\qquad \mathsf{return}\ \langle \mathrm{name} = e.\mathrm{name}, \mathrm{salary} = e.\mathrm{salary},\\
&\qquad\qquad\qquad \mathrm{tasks} = \mathit{tasksOfEmp}\ e\rangle
\end{aligned}$$

returns a nested result: a collection of employees in a department, each with an associated collection of tasks. That is, its return type is Bag $\langle \mathrm{name}{:}\mathit{String}, \mathrm{salary}{:}\mathit{Int}, \mathrm{tasks}{:}\mathrm{Bag}\ \mathit{String}\rangle$

Consider the following nested schema for organisations:

$$\begin{aligned}
\mathit{Task} &= \mathit{String}\\
\mathit{Employee} &= \langle \mathrm{name} : \mathit{String}, \mathrm{salary} : \mathit{Int}, \mathrm{tasks} : \mathrm{Bag}\ \mathit{Task}\rangle\\
\mathit{Contact} &= \langle \mathrm{name} : \mathit{String}, \mathrm{client} : \mathit{Bool}\rangle\\
\mathit{Department} &= \langle \mathrm{name} : \mathit{String}, \mathrm{employees} : \mathrm{Bag}\ \mathit{Employee},\\
&\qquad \mathrm{contacts} : \mathrm{Bag}\ \mathit{Contact}\rangle\\
\mathit{Organisation} &= \mathrm{Bag}\ \mathit{Department}
\end{aligned}$$

Using some of the above functions we can write a query Q_{org} that maps data in the flat schema Σ to the nested type *Organisation*, as follows:

$$\begin{aligned}
Q_{org} = &\ \mathsf{for}\ (d \leftarrow \mathit{departments})\\
&\ \mathsf{return}\ (\langle \mathrm{name} = d.\mathrm{name},\\
&\qquad \mathrm{employees} = \mathit{employeesOfDept}\ d,\\
&\qquad \mathrm{contacts} = \mathit{contactsOfDept}\ d\rangle
\end{aligned}$$

We can also define and use higher-order functions to build queries, such as the following:

$$\begin{aligned}
&\mathit{filter}\ p\ xs = \mathsf{for}\ (x \leftarrow xs)\ \mathsf{where}\ (p(x))\ \mathsf{return}\ x\\
&\mathit{any}\ xs\ p = \neg(\mathsf{empty}(\mathsf{for}\ (x \leftarrow xs)\ \mathsf{where}\ (p(x))\ \mathsf{return}\ \langle\rangle))\\
&\mathit{all}\ xs\ p = \neg(\mathit{any}\ xs\ (\lambda x.\neg(p(x))))\\
&\mathit{contains}\ xs\ u = \mathit{any}\ xs\ (\lambda x.x = u)
\end{aligned}$$

To illustrate the main technical challenges of shredding, we consider a query with two levels of nesting and a union operation.

Suppose we wish to find for each department a collection of people of interest, both employees and contacts, along with a list of the tasks they perform. Specifically, we are interested in those employees that earn less than a thousand euros and those who earn more than a million euros, call them *outliers*, along with those contacts who are clients. The following code defines poor, rich, outliers, and clients:

$$\begin{aligned}
&\mathit{isPoor}\ x = x.\mathrm{salary} < 1000\\
&\mathit{isRich}\ x = x.\mathrm{salary} > 1000000\\
&\mathit{outliers}\ xs = \mathit{filter}\ (\lambda x.\mathit{isRich}\ x \vee \mathit{isPoor}\ x)\ xs\\
&\mathit{clients}\ xs = \mathit{filter}\ (\lambda x.\ x.\mathrm{client})\ xs
\end{aligned}$$

We also introduce a convenient higher-order function that uses its f parameter to initialise the tasks of its elements:

$$\mathit{getTasks}\ xs\ f = \mathsf{for}\ (x \leftarrow xs)\ \mathsf{return}\ \langle \mathrm{name} = x.\mathrm{name}, \mathrm{tasks} = f\ x\rangle$$

Using the above operations, the query Q returns each department, the outliers and clients associated with that department, and their tasks. We assign the special task "buy" to clients.

$$\begin{aligned}
&Q(\mathit{organisation}) =\\
&\quad \mathsf{for}\ (x \leftarrow \mathit{organisation})\\
&\quad \mathsf{return}\ (\langle \mathrm{department} = x.\mathrm{name},\\
&\qquad\quad \mathrm{people} =\\
&\qquad\qquad \mathit{getTasks}(\mathit{outliers}(x.\mathrm{employees}))\ (\lambda y.\ y.\mathrm{tasks})\\
&\qquad\quad \uplus\ \mathit{getTasks}(\mathit{clients}(x.\mathrm{contacts}))\ (\lambda y.\ \mathsf{return}\ \text{"buy"})\rangle)
\end{aligned}$$

The result type of Q is:

$$\begin{aligned}
\mathit{Result} = \mathrm{Bag}\ \langle &\mathrm{department} : \mathit{String},\\
&\mathrm{people} : \mathrm{Bag}\ \langle \mathrm{name} : \mathit{String}, \mathrm{tasks} : \mathrm{Bag}\ \mathit{String}\rangle\rangle
\end{aligned}$$

We can compose Q with Q_{org} to form a query $Q(Q_{org})$ from the flat data stored in Σ to the nested *Result*. The normal form of this composed query, which we call Q_{comp}, is as follows:

$$\begin{aligned}
Q_{comp} = &\ \mathsf{for}\ (x \leftarrow \mathit{departments})\\
&\ \mathsf{return}\ (\\
&\quad \langle \mathrm{department} = x.\mathrm{name},\\
&\quad\ \mathrm{people} =\\
&\qquad (\mathsf{for}\ (y \leftarrow \mathit{employees})\ \mathsf{where}\ (x.\mathrm{name} = y.\mathrm{dept} \wedge\\
&\qquad\qquad (y.\mathrm{salary} < 1000 \vee y.\mathrm{salary} > 1000000))\\
&\qquad\ \mathsf{return}\ (\langle \mathrm{name} = y.\mathrm{name},\\
&\qquad\qquad \mathrm{tasks} = \mathsf{for}\ (z \leftarrow \mathit{tasks})\\
&\qquad\qquad\qquad \mathsf{where}\ (z.\mathrm{employee} = y.\mathrm{name})\\
&\qquad\qquad\qquad \mathsf{return}\ z.\mathrm{task}\rangle))\\
&\quad\ \uplus\ (\mathsf{for}\ (y \leftarrow \mathit{contacts})\\
&\qquad \mathsf{where}\ (x.\mathrm{name} = y.\mathrm{dept} \wedge y.\mathrm{client})\\
&\qquad \mathsf{return}\ (\langle \mathrm{name} = y.\mathrm{name},\\
&\qquad\qquad \mathrm{tasks} = \mathsf{return}\ \text{"buy"}\rangle))\rangle)
\end{aligned}$$

The result of running Q_{comp} on the data in Figure 3 is:

$$\begin{aligned}
&[\langle \mathrm{department} = \text{"Product"},\\
&\quad \mathrm{people} = [\langle \mathrm{name} = \text{"Bert"}, \mathrm{tasks} = [\text{"build"}]\rangle,\\
&\qquad \langle \mathrm{name} = \text{"Pat"}, \mathrm{tasks} = [\text{"buy"}]\rangle]\rangle]\\
&\langle \mathrm{department} = \text{"Research"}, \mathrm{people} = \emptyset\rangle,\\
&\langle \mathrm{department} = \text{"Quality"}, \mathrm{people} = \emptyset\rangle,\\
&\langle \mathrm{department} = \text{"Sales"},\\
&\quad \mathrm{people} = [\langle \mathrm{name} = \text{"Erik"}, \mathrm{tasks} = [\text{"call"}, \text{"enthuse"}]\rangle,\\
&\qquad \langle \mathrm{name} = \text{"Fred"}, \mathrm{tasks} = [\text{"call"}]\rangle,\\
&\qquad \langle \mathrm{name} = \text{"Sue"}, \mathrm{tasks} = [\text{"buy"}]\rangle]\rangle]
\end{aligned}$$

Now, however, we are faced with a problem: SQL databases do not directly support nested multisets (or sets). Our shredding translation, like Van den Bussche's simulation for sets [26] and Grust et al.'s for lists [11], can translate a normalised query such as $Q_{comp} : \mathit{Result}$ that maps flat input Σ to nested output *Result* to a fixed number of flat queries $q_1 : \mathit{Result}_1, \ldots, q_n : \mathit{Result}_n$ whose results can be combined via a *stitching* operation $Q_{stitch} : \mathit{Result}_1 \times \cdots \times \mathit{Result}_n \rightarrow \mathit{Result}$. Thus, we can simulate the query Q_{comp} by running $q_1, \ldots, q_n$ remotely on the database and stitching the results together using Q_{stitch}. The number of intermediate queries n is the *nesting degree* of *Result*, that is, the number of collection type constructors in the result type. For example, the nesting degree of Bag $\langle A : \mathrm{Bag}\ \mathit{Int}, B : \mathrm{Bag}\ \mathit{String}\rangle$ is 3. The nesting degree of the type *Result* is also 3, which means Q can be shredded into three flat queries.

The basic idea is straightforward. Whenever a nested bag appears in the output of a query, we generate an index that uniquely identifies the current context. Then a separate query produces the contents of the nested bag, where each element is paired up with its parent index. Each inner level of nesting requires a further query.

We will illustrate by showing the results of the three queries and how they can be combined to reconstitute the desired nested result.

The outer query q_1 contains one entry for each department, with an index $\langle a, id\rangle$ in place of each nested collection:

$$\begin{aligned}r_1 = [&\langle \text{department} = \text{“Product”}, \text{ people} = \langle a, 1\rangle\rangle,\\ &\langle \text{department} = \text{“Quality”}, \text{ people} = \langle a, 2\rangle\rangle,\\ &\langle \text{department} = \text{“Research”}, \text{people} = \langle a, 3\rangle\rangle,\\ &\langle \text{department} = \text{“Sales”}, \text{ people} = \langle a, 4\rangle\rangle]\end{aligned}$$

The second query q_2 generates the data needed for the people collections:

$$\begin{aligned}r_2 = [&\langle\langle a, 1\rangle, \langle \text{name} = \text{“Bert”}, \text{tasks} = \langle b, 1, 2\rangle\rangle\rangle,\\ &\langle\langle a, 4\rangle, \langle \text{name} = \text{“Erik”}, \text{tasks} = \langle b, 4, 5\rangle\rangle\rangle,\\ &\langle\langle a, 4\rangle, \langle \text{name} = \text{“Fred”}, \text{tasks} = \langle b, 4, 6\rangle\rangle\rangle,\\ &\langle\langle a, 1\rangle, \langle \text{name} = \text{“Pat”}, \text{ tasks} = \langle d, 1, 2\rangle\rangle\rangle,\\ &\langle\langle a, 4\rangle, \langle \text{name} = \text{“Sue”}, \text{ tasks} = \langle d, 4, 7\rangle\rangle\rangle]\end{aligned}$$

The idea is to ensure that we can stitch the results of q_1 together with the results of q_2 by joining the *inner indexes* of q_1 (bound to the people field of each result) with the *outer indexes* of q_2 (bound to the first component of each result). In both cases the static components of these indexes are the same tag a. Joining the people field of q_1 to the outer index of q_2 correctly associates each person with the appropriate department.

Finally, let us consider the results of the innermost query q_3 for generating the bag bound to the tasks field:

$$\begin{aligned}r_3 = [&\langle\langle b, 1, 2\rangle, \text{“build”}\rangle, \langle\langle b, 4, 5\rangle, \text{“call”}\rangle, \langle\langle b, 4, 5\rangle, \text{“enthuse”}\rangle,\\ &\langle\langle b, 4, 6\rangle, \text{“call”}\rangle, \langle\langle d, 1, 2\rangle, \text{“buy”}\rangle, \langle\langle d, 4, 7\rangle, \text{“buy”}\rangle]\end{aligned}$$

Recall that q_2 returns further inner indexes for the tasks associated with each person. The two halves of the union have different static indexes for the tasks b and d, because they arise from different comprehensions in the source term. Furthermore, the dynamic index now consists of two id fields (x.id and y.id) in each half of the union. Thus, joining the tasks field of q_2 to the outer index of q_3 correctly associates each task with the appropriate outlier.

Note that each of the queries q_1, q_2, q_3 produces records that contain other records as fields. This is not strictly allowed by SQL, but it is straightforward to simulate such nested records by rewriting to a query with no nested collections in its result type; this is similar to Van den Bussche's simulation [26]. However, this approach incurs extra storage and query-processing cost. Later in the paper, we explore an alternative approach which collapses the indexes at each level to a pair $\langle a, i\rangle$ of static index and a single "surrogate" integer, similarly to Ferry's approach [11]. For example, using this approach we could represent the results of q_2 and q_3 as follows:

$$\begin{aligned}r'_2 = [&\langle\langle a, 1\rangle, \langle \text{name} = \text{“Bert”}, \text{tasks} = \langle b, 1\rangle\rangle\rangle,\\ &\langle\langle a, 4\rangle, \langle \text{name} = \text{“Erik”}, \text{tasks} = \langle b, 2\rangle\rangle\rangle,\\ &\langle\langle a, 4\rangle, \langle \text{name} = \text{“Fred”}, \text{tasks} = \langle b, 3\rangle\rangle\rangle,\\ &\langle\langle a, 1\rangle, \langle \text{name} = \text{“Pat”}, \text{ tasks} = \langle d, 1\rangle\rangle\rangle,\\ &\langle\langle a, 4\rangle, \langle \text{name} = \text{“Sue”}, \text{ tasks} = \langle d, 2\rangle\rangle\rangle]\end{aligned}$$

$$\begin{aligned}r'_3 = [&\langle\langle b, 1\rangle, \text{“build”}\rangle, \langle\langle b, 2\rangle, \text{“call”}\rangle, \langle\langle b, 2\rangle, \text{“enthuse”}\rangle,\\ &\langle\langle b, 3\rangle, \text{“call”}\rangle, \langle\langle d, 1\rangle, \text{“buy”}\rangle, \langle\langle d, 2\rangle, \text{“buy”}\rangle]\end{aligned}$$

The rest of this paper gives the details of the shredding translation, explains how to stitch the results of shredded queries back together, and shows how to use row_number to avoid the space overhead of indexes. We will return to the above example throughout the paper, and we will use Q_{org}, Q and other queries based on this example in the experimental evaluation.

4. SHREDDING TRANSLATION

As a pre-processing step, we annotate each comprehension body in a normalised term with a unique name a — the static component of an index. We write the annotations as superscripts, for example:

$$\mathsf{for}\,(\vec{G}\,\mathsf{where}\,X)\;\mathsf{return}^a\;M$$

In order to shred nested queries, we introduce an abstract type *Index* of *indexes* for maintaining the correspondence between outer and inner queries. An index $a \diamond d$ has a static component a and a dynamic component d. The static component a links the index to the corresponding return^a in the query. The dynamic component identifies the current bindings of the variables in the comprehension.

Next, we modify types so that bag types have an explicit index component and we use indexes to replace nested occurrences of bags within other bags:

$$\begin{array}{ll}\text{Shredded types} & A, B ::= \mathrm{Bag}\,\langle \mathit{Index}, F\rangle\\ \text{Flat types} & F ::= O \mid \langle \overrightarrow{\ell : F}\rangle \mid \mathit{Index}\end{array}$$

We also adapt the syntax of terms to incorporate indexes. After shredding, terms will have the following forms:

$$\begin{array}{ll}\text{Query terms} & L, M ::= \biguplus \vec{C}\\ \text{Comprehensions} & C ::= \mathsf{return}^a\,\langle I, N\rangle\\ & \quad\mid \mathsf{for}\,(\vec{G}\,\mathsf{where}\,X)\,C\\ \text{Generators} & G ::= x \leftarrow t\\ \text{Inner terms} & N ::= X \mid R \mid I\\ \text{Record terms} & R ::= \langle \overrightarrow{\ell = N}\rangle\\ \text{Base terms} & X ::= x.\ell \mid c(\vec{X}) \mid \mathsf{empty}\,L\\ \text{Indexes} & I, J ::= a \diamond d\\ \text{Dynamic indexes} & d ::= \mathsf{out} \mid \mathsf{in}\end{array}$$

A comprehension is now constructed from a sequence of generator clauses of the form $\mathsf{for}\,(\vec{G}\,\mathsf{where}\,X)$ followed by a body of the form $\mathsf{return}^a\,\langle I, N\rangle$. Each level of nesting gives rise to such a generator clause. The body always returns a pair $\langle I, N\rangle$ of an outer index I, denoting where the result values from the shredded query should be spliced into the final nested result, and a (flat) inner term N. Records are restricted to contain inner terms, which are either base types, records, or indexes, which replace nested multisets. We assume a distinguished top level static index $\top$, which allows us to treat all levels uniformly. Each shredded term is associated with an outer index out and an inner index in. (In fact out only appears in the left component of a comprehension body, and in only appears in the right component of a comprehension body. These properties will become apparent when we specify the shredding transformation on terms.)

4.1 Shredding types and terms

We use *paths* to point to parts of types.

$$\text{Paths}\quad p ::= \epsilon \mid {\downarrow}.p \mid \ell.p$$

The empty path is written ϵ. A path p can be extended by traversing a bag constructor (${\downarrow}.p$) or selecting a label ($\ell.p$). We will sometimes write $p.{\downarrow}$ for the path p with $\downarrow$ appended at the end and similarly for $p.\ell$; likewise, we will write $p.\vec{\ell}$ for the path p with all the labels of $\vec{\ell}$ appended. The function $\mathit{paths}(A)$ defines the set of paths to bag types in a type A:

$$\begin{aligned}\mathit{paths}(O) &= \{\}\\ \mathit{paths}(\langle \ell_i : A_i\rangle_{i=1}^n) &= \textstyle\bigcup_{i=1}^n \{\ell_i.p \mid p \leftarrow \mathit{paths}(A_i)\}\\ \mathit{paths}(\mathrm{Bag}\,A) &= \{\epsilon\} \cup \{{\downarrow}.p \mid p \leftarrow \mathit{paths}(A)\}\end{aligned}$$

We now define a shredding translation on types. This is defined in terms of the *inner shredding* $\llbracket A \rrbracket$, a flat type that represents the contents of a bag.

$$\begin{aligned}\llbracket O \rrbracket &= O\\ \llbracket \langle \ell_i : A_i\rangle_{i=1}^n \rrbracket &= \langle \ell_i : \llbracket A_i \rrbracket\rangle_{i=1}^n\\ \llbracket \mathrm{Bag}\,A \rrbracket &= \mathit{Index}\end{aligned}$$

$$
\begin{aligned}
\lceil\!\lceil L \rceil\!\rceil_p &= \biguplus (\lceil\!\lceil L \rceil\!\rceil^\star_{\top,p}) \\
\lceil\!\lceil \biguplus_{i=1}^n C_i \rceil\!\rceil^\star_{a,p} &= \mathit{concat}([\lceil\!\lceil C_i \rceil\!\rceil^\star_{a,p}]_{i=1}^n) \\
\lceil\!\lceil \langle \ell_i = M_i \rangle_{i=1}^n \rceil\!\rceil^\star_{a,\ell_j.p} &= \lceil\!\lceil M_j \rceil\!\rceil^\star_{a,p} \\
\lceil\!\lceil \mathsf{for}\ (\vec{G}\ \mathsf{where}\ X)\ \mathsf{return}^b\ M \rceil\!\rceil^\star_{a,\epsilon} &= [\mathsf{for}\ (\vec{G}\ \mathsf{where}\ X)\ \mathsf{return}^b\ \langle a \diamond \mathsf{out}, \lfloor\!\lfloor M \rfloor\!\rfloor_b \rangle] \\
\lceil\!\lceil \mathsf{for}\ (\vec{G}\ \mathsf{where}\ X)\ \mathsf{return}^b\ M \rceil\!\rceil^\star_{a,\downarrow.p} &= [\mathsf{for}\ (\vec{G}\ \mathsf{where}\ X)\ C \mid C \leftarrow \lceil\!\lceil M \rceil\!\rceil^\star_{b,p}]
\end{aligned}
\qquad
\begin{aligned}
\lfloor\!\lfloor x.\ell \rfloor\!\rfloor_a &= x.\ell \\
\lfloor\!\lfloor c([X_i]_{i=1}^n) \rfloor\!\rfloor_a &= c([\lfloor\!\lfloor X_i \rfloor\!\rfloor_a]_{i=1}^n) \\
\lfloor\!\lfloor \mathsf{empty}\ L \rfloor\!\rfloor_a &= \mathsf{empty}\ \lceil\!\lceil L \rceil\!\rceil_\epsilon \\
\lfloor\!\lfloor \langle \ell_i = M_i \rangle_{i=1}^n \rfloor\!\rfloor_a &= \langle \ell_i = \lfloor\!\lfloor M_i \rfloor\!\rfloor_a \rangle_{i=1}^n \\
\lfloor\!\lfloor L \rfloor\!\rfloor_a &= a \diamond \mathsf{in}
\end{aligned}
$$

Figure 4: Shredding translation on terms

Given a path $p \in \mathit{paths}(A)$, the type $\lceil\!\lceil A \rceil\!\rceil_p$ is the *outer shredding* of A at p. It corresponds to the bag at path p in A.

$$
\begin{aligned}
\lceil\!\lceil \mathrm{Bag}\ A \rceil\!\rceil_\epsilon &= \mathrm{Bag}\ \langle \mathit{Index}, \lfloor\!\lfloor A \rfloor\!\rfloor \rangle \\
\lceil\!\lceil \mathrm{Bag}\ A \rceil\!\rceil_{\downarrow.p} &= \lceil\!\lceil A \rceil\!\rceil_p \\
\lceil\!\lceil \langle \overrightarrow{\ell : A} \rangle \rceil\!\rceil_{\ell_i.p} &= \lceil\!\lceil A_i \rceil\!\rceil_p
\end{aligned}
$$

For example, consider the result type Result from Section 3. Its nesting degree is 3, and its paths are:

$$\mathit{paths}(\mathit{Result}) = \{\epsilon, \downarrow.\mathrm{people}.\epsilon, \downarrow.\mathrm{people}.\downarrow.\mathrm{tasks}.\epsilon\}$$

We can shred Result in three ways using these three paths, yielding three shredded types:

$$
\begin{aligned}
A_1 &= \lceil\!\lceil \mathit{Result} \rceil\!\rceil_\epsilon \\
A_2 &= \lceil\!\lceil \mathit{Result} \rceil\!\rceil_{\downarrow.\mathrm{people}.\epsilon} \\
A_3 &= \lceil\!\lceil \mathit{Result} \rceil\!\rceil_{\downarrow.\mathrm{people}.\epsilon.\downarrow.\mathrm{tasks}.\epsilon}
\end{aligned}
$$

or equivalently:

$$
\begin{aligned}
A_1 &= \mathrm{Bag}\ \langle \mathit{Index}, \langle \mathrm{department} : \mathit{String}, \mathrm{people} : \mathit{Index} \rangle \rangle \\
A_2 &= \mathrm{Bag}\ \langle \mathit{Index}, \langle \mathrm{name} : \mathit{String}, \mathrm{tasks} : \mathit{Index} \rangle \rangle \\
A_3 &= \mathrm{Bag}\ \langle \mathit{Index}, \mathit{String} \rangle
\end{aligned}
$$

The shredding translation on terms $\lceil\!\lceil L \rceil\!\rceil_p$ is given in Figure 4. This takes a term L and a path p and gives a query $\lceil\!\lceil L \rceil\!\rceil_p$ that computes a result of type $\lceil\!\lceil A \rceil\!\rceil_p$, where A is the type of L. The auxiliary translation $\lceil\!\lceil M \rceil\!\rceil^\star_{a,p}$ returns the shredded comprehensions of M along path p with outer static index a. The auxiliary translation $\lfloor\!\lfloor M \rfloor\!\rfloor_a$ produces a flat representation of M with inner static index a. Note that the shredding translation is linear in time and space. Observe that for emptiness tests we need only the top-level query.

Continuing the example, we can shred Q_{comp} in three ways, yielding shredded queries:

$$
\begin{aligned}
q_1 &= \lceil\!\lceil Q_{comp} \rceil\!\rceil_\epsilon \\
q_2 &= \lceil\!\lceil Q_{comp} \rceil\!\rceil_{\downarrow.\mathrm{people}.\epsilon} \\
q_3 &= \lceil\!\lceil Q_{comp} \rceil\!\rceil_{\downarrow.\mathrm{people}.\epsilon.\downarrow.\mathrm{tasks}.\epsilon}
\end{aligned}
$$

or equivalently:

$$
\begin{aligned}
q_1 = {}& \mathsf{for}\ (x \leftarrow \mathit{departments}) \\
& \mathsf{return}^a\ \langle \top \diamond 1, \langle \mathrm{department} = x.\mathrm{name}, \mathrm{people} = a \diamond \mathsf{in} \rangle \rangle \\
q_2 = {}& (\mathsf{for}\ (x \leftarrow \mathit{departments}) \\
& \mathsf{for}\ (y \leftarrow \mathit{employees})\ \mathsf{where}\ (x.\mathrm{name} = y.\mathrm{dept} \wedge \\
& \qquad (y.\mathrm{salary} < 1000 \vee y.\mathrm{salary} > 1000000)) \\
& \mathsf{return}^b\ (\langle a \diamond \mathsf{out}, \langle \mathrm{name} = y.\mathrm{name}, \mathrm{tasks} = b \diamond \mathsf{in} \rangle \rangle)) \\
& \uplus\ (\mathsf{for}\ (x \leftarrow \mathit{departments}) \\
& \mathsf{for}\ (y \leftarrow \mathit{contacts})\ \mathsf{where}\ (x.\mathrm{name} = y.\mathrm{dept} \wedge y.\mathrm{client}) \\
& \mathsf{return}^d\ (\langle a \diamond \mathsf{out}, \langle \mathrm{name} = y.\mathrm{name}, \mathrm{tasks} = d \diamond \mathsf{in} \rangle \rangle)) \\
q_3 = {}& (\mathsf{for}\ (x \leftarrow \mathit{departments}) \\
& \mathsf{for}\ (y \leftarrow \mathit{employees})\ \mathsf{where}\ (x.\mathrm{name} = y.\mathrm{dept} \wedge \\
& \qquad (y.\mathrm{salary} < 1000 \vee y.\mathrm{salary} > 1000000)) \\
& \mathsf{for}\ (z \leftarrow \mathit{tasks})\ \mathsf{where}\ (z.\mathrm{employee} = y.\mathrm{employee}) \\
& \mathsf{return}^c\ \langle b \diamond \mathsf{out}, z.\mathrm{task} \rangle) \\
& \uplus\ (\mathsf{for}\ (x \leftarrow \mathit{departments}) \\
& \mathsf{for}\ (y \leftarrow \mathit{contacts})\ \mathsf{where}\ (x.\mathrm{name} = y.\mathrm{dept} \wedge y.\mathrm{client}) \\
& \mathsf{return}^e\ \langle d \diamond \mathsf{out}, \text{“buy”} \rangle)
\end{aligned}
$$

As a sanity check, we show that well-formed normalised terms shred to well-formed shredded terms of the appropriate shredded types. We discuss other correctness properties of the shredding translation in Section 5.

THEOREM 2. *Suppose L is a normalised flat-nested query with $\vdash L : A$ and $p \in \mathit{paths}(A)$, then $\vdash \lceil\!\lceil L \rceil\!\rceil_p : \lceil\!\lceil A \rceil\!\rceil_p$.*

4.2 Shredded packages

To maintain the relationship between shredded terms and the structure of the nested result they are meant to construct, we use *shredded packages*. A shredded package $\hat{A}$ is a nested type with annotations, denoted $(-)^\alpha$, attached to each bag constructor.

$$\hat{A} ::= O \mid \langle \overrightarrow{\ell : \hat{A}} \rangle \mid (\mathrm{Bag}\ \hat{A})^\alpha$$

For a given package, the annotations are drawn from the same set. We write $\hat{A}(S)$ to denote a shredded package with annotations drawn from the set S. We sometimes omit the type parameter when it is clear from context.

Given a shredded package $\hat{A}$, we can erase its annotations to obtain its underlying type.

$$
\begin{aligned}
\mathit{erase}(O) &= O \\
\mathit{erase}(\langle \ell_i : \hat{A}_i \rangle_{i=1}^n) &= \langle \ell_i : \mathit{erase}(\hat{A}_i) \rangle_{i=1}^n \\
\mathit{erase}((\mathrm{Bag}\ \hat{A})^\alpha) &= \mathrm{Bag}\ (\mathit{erase}(\hat{A}))
\end{aligned}
$$

We lift the type shredding function $\lceil\!\lceil A \rceil\!\rceil$ to produce a shredded package $\mathit{Shred}(A)$, where each annotation contains the shredded version of the input type or query along the path to the associated bag constructor. We define $\mathit{Shred}(A) = \mathit{Shred}_\epsilon(A)$ as follows:

$$
\begin{aligned}
\mathit{Shred}_p(O) &= O \\
\mathit{Shred}_p(\langle \ell_i : A_i \rangle_{i=1}^n) &= \langle \ell_i : \mathit{Shred}_{p.\ell_i}(A_i) \rangle_{i=1}^n \\
\mathit{Shred}_p(\mathrm{Bag}\ A) &= (\mathrm{Bag}\ (\mathit{Shred}_{p.\downarrow}(A)))^{\lceil\!\lceil B \rceil\!\rceil_p}
\end{aligned}
$$

Similarly, we lift the term shredding function $\lceil\!\lceil L \rceil\!\rceil$ to produce a shredded query package $\mathit{shred}(L) = \mathit{shred}_\epsilon(L)$, where:

$$
\begin{aligned}
\mathit{shred}_p(O) &= O \\
\mathit{shred}_p(\langle \ell_i : A_i \rangle_{i=1}^n) &= \langle \ell_i : \mathit{shred}_{p.\ell_i}(A_i) \rangle_{i=1}^n \\
\mathit{shred}_p(\mathrm{Bag}\ A) &= (\mathrm{Bag}\ (\mathit{shred}_{p.\downarrow}(A)))^{\lceil\!\lceil L \rceil\!\rceil_p}
\end{aligned}
$$

For example, the shredded package for the Result type from Section 3 is:

$$
\begin{aligned}
& \mathit{Shred}_{\mathit{Result}}(\mathit{Result}) = \\
& \quad \mathrm{Bag}\ \langle \mathrm{department} : \mathit{String}, \\
& \qquad \mathrm{people} : \mathrm{Bag}\ \langle \mathrm{name} : \mathit{String}, \\
& \qquad\qquad \mathrm{tasks} : (\mathrm{Bag}\ \mathit{String})^{A_3} \rangle^{A_2} \rangle^{A_1}
\end{aligned}
$$

where A_1, A_2, and A_3 are as shown in Section 4.1. Shredding the normalised query Q' gives the same package, except the type annotations A_1, A_2, A_3 become queries q_1, q_2, q_3.

Again, as a sanity check we show that erasure is the left inverse of type shredding and that term-level shredding operations preserve types.

THEOREM 3. *For any type A, we have $\mathit{erase}(\mathit{shred}_A(A)) = A$. Furthermore, if L is a closed, normalised, flat–nested query such that $\vdash L : A$ then $\vdash \mathit{shred}_L(A) : \mathit{shred}_A(A)$.*

5. QUERY EVALUATION AND STITCHING

Having shredded a normalised nested query, we can then run all of the resulting shredded queries separately. If we stitch the shredded results together to form a nested result, then we obtain the same nested result as we would obtain by running the nested query directly. In this section we describe how to run shredded queries and stitch their results back together to form a nested result.

5.1 Evaluating shredded queries

The semantics of shredded queries $\mathcal{S}[\![-]\!]$ is given in Figure 5. Apart from the handling of indexes, it is much like the semantics for nested queries given in Figure 2. To allow different implementations of indexes, we first define a canonical notion of index, and then parameterise the semantics by the concrete type of indexes X and a function $index : Index \to X$ mapping each canonical index to a distinct concrete index. A canonical index $a \diamond \iota$ comprises static index a and dynamic index ι, where the latter is a list of positive natural numbers. For now we take concrete indexes simply to be canonical indexes, and $index$ to be the identity function. We consider other definitions of $index$ in Section 6.

The current dynamic index ι is threaded through the semantics in tandem with the environment ρ. The former encodes the position of each of the generators in the current comprehension and allows us to invoke $index$ to construct a concrete index. The outer index at dynamic index $\iota.i$ is ι; the inner index is $\iota.i$. In order for a comprehension to generate dynamic indexes we use the function $enum$ (introduced in Section 2) that takes a list of elements and returns the same list with the element number paired up with each source element.

Running a shredded query yields a list of pairs of indexes and shredded values.

$$\begin{array}{ll} \text{Results} & s ::= [\langle I_1, w_1\rangle, \ldots, \langle I_m, w_m\rangle] \\ \text{Flat values} & w ::= c \mid \langle \ell_1 = w_1, \ldots, \ell_n = w_n\rangle \mid I \end{array}$$

Given a shredded package $\hat{A}(S)$ and a function $f : S \to T$, we can map f over the annotations to obtain a new shredded package $\hat{A}'(T)$ such that $erase(\hat{A}) = erase(\hat{A}')$.

$$\begin{aligned} pmap_f(O) &= O \\ pmap_f(\langle \ell_i : \hat{A}_i\rangle_{i=1}^n) &= \langle \ell_i : pmap_f(\hat{A}_i)\rangle_{i=1}^n \\ pmap_f((\mathrm{Bag}\,\hat{A})^\alpha) &= ((\mathrm{Bag}\, pmap_f(\hat{A})))^{f(\alpha)} \end{aligned}$$

The semantics of a shredded query package is a *shredded value package* containing indexed results for each shredded query. For each type A we define $\mathcal{H}[\![A]\!] = shred_A(A)$ and for each flat–nested, closed $\vdash L : A$ we define $\mathcal{H}[\![L]\!]_A : \mathcal{H}[\![A]\!]$ as $pmap_{\mathcal{S}[\![-]\!]}(shred_L(A))$. In other words, we first construct the shredded query package $shred_L(A)$, then apply the shredded semantics $\mathcal{S}[\![q]\!]$ to each query q in the package.

For example, here is the shredded package that we obtain after running the normalised query Q_{comp} from Section 2.2:

$$\begin{aligned} \mathcal{H}[\![Q_{comp}]\!]_A = \mathrm{Bag}\,\langle &\mathrm{department} : String, \\ &\mathrm{people} : \mathrm{Bag}\,\langle \mathrm{name} : String, \\ &\qquad \mathrm{tasks} : (\mathrm{Bag}\, String)^{r_3}\rangle^{r_2}\rangle^{r_1} \end{aligned}$$

where r_1, r_2, and r_3 are as in Section 3 except that indexes are of the form $a \diamond 1.2.3$ instead of $\langle a, 1, 2, 3\rangle$.

5.2 Stitching shredded query results together

A shredded value package can be *stitched* back together into a nested value, preserving annotations, as follows:

$$\begin{aligned} stitch(\hat{A}) &= stitch_{\top \diamond 1}(\hat{A}) \\ stitch_c(O) &= c \\ stitch_r(\langle \ell_i : \hat{A}_i\rangle_{i=1}^n) &= \langle \ell_i = stitch_{r.\ell_i}(\hat{A}_i)\rangle_{i=1}^n \\ stitch_I((\mathrm{Bag}\,\hat{A})^s) &= [(stitch_w(\hat{A})) \mid \langle I, w\rangle \leftarrow s] \end{aligned}$$

The flat value parameter w to the auxiliary function $stitch_w(-)$ specifies which values to stitch along the current path.

Resuming our running example, once the results $r_1 : A_1, r_2 : A_2, r_3 : A_3$ have been evaluated on the database, they are shipped back to the host system where we can run the following code in-memory to stitch the three tables together into a single value: the result of the original nested query. The code for this query Q_{stitch} follows the same idea as the query Q_{org} that constructs the nested $organisation$ from Σ.

$$\begin{array}{l} \mathsf{for}\ (x \leftarrow r_1) \\ \mathsf{return}\ (\langle \mathrm{department} = x.\mathrm{name}, \\ \qquad \mathrm{people} = \mathsf{for}\ (\langle i, y\rangle \leftarrow r_2) \\ \qquad\qquad \mathsf{where}\ (x.\mathrm{people} = i)) \\ \qquad\qquad \mathsf{return}\ (\langle \mathrm{name} = y.\mathrm{name}, \\ \qquad\qquad\quad \mathrm{tasks} = \mathsf{for}\ (\langle j, z\rangle \leftarrow r_3) \\ \qquad\qquad\qquad \mathsf{where}\ (y.\mathrm{tasks} = j) \\ \qquad\qquad\qquad \mathsf{return}\ z\rangle)\rangle) \end{array}$$

We can now state our key correctness property: evaluating shredded queries and stitching the results back together yields the same results as evaluating the original nested query directly.

THEOREM 4. *If* $\vdash L : \mathrm{Bag}\, A$ *then:*

$$stitch(\mathcal{H}[\![L]\!]_{\mathrm{Bag}\,A}) = \mathcal{N}[\![L]\!]$$

PROOF SKETCH. We omit the full proof due to space limits; it is available in the full version of this paper. The proof introduces several intermediate definitions. Specifically, we consider an *annotated semantics* for nested queries in which each collection element is tagged with an index, and we show that this semantics is consistent with the ordinary semantics if the annotations are erased. We then prove the correctness of shredding and stitching with respect to the annotated semantics, and the desired result follows. □

6. INDEXING SCHEMES

So far, we have worked with canonical indexes of the form $a \diamond 1.2.3$. These could be represented in SQL by using multiple columns (padding with NULLs if necessary) since for a given query the length of the dynamic part is bounded by the number of for-comprehensions in the query. This imposes space and running time overhead due to constructing and maintaining the indexes. Instead, in this section we consider alternative, more compact indexing schemes.

We can define alternative indexing schemes by varying the $index$ parameter of the shredded semantics (see Section 5.1). Not all possible instantiations are valid. To identify those that are, we first define a function for computing the canonical indexes of a nested query result.

$$\begin{aligned} \mathcal{I}[\![L]\!] &= \mathcal{I}[\![L]\!]_{\varepsilon,1} \\ \mathcal{I}[\![\textstyle\biguplus_{i=1}^n C_i]\!]_{\rho,\iota} &= concat([\mathcal{I}[\![C_i]\!]_{\rho,\iota}]_{i=1}^n) \\ \mathcal{I}[\![\langle \ell_i = M_i\rangle_{i=1}^n]\!]_{\rho,\iota} &= concat([\mathcal{I}[\![M_i]\!]_{\rho,\iota}]_{i=1}^n) \\ \mathcal{I}[\![X]\!]_{\rho,\iota} &= [\,] \end{aligned}$$

$$\begin{array}{l} \mathcal{I}[\![\mathsf{for}\ ([x_i \leftarrow t_i]_{i=1}^n\ \mathsf{where}\ X)\ \mathsf{return}^a\ M]\!]_{\rho,\iota} = \\ \quad concat([a \diamond \iota.j :: \mathcal{I}[\![M]\!]_{\rho[x_i \mapsto r_i]_{i=1}^n, \iota.j} \\ \quad\mid \langle j, \vec{r}\rangle \leftarrow enum([\vec{r} \mid [r_i \leftarrow [\![t_i]\!]]_{i=1}^n, \mathcal{N}[\![X]\!]_{\rho[x_i \mapsto r_i]_{i=1}^n}])]) \end{array}$$

An indexing function $index : Index \to X$ is *valid* with respect to the closed nested query L if it is injective and defined on every canonical index in $\mathcal{I}[\![L]\!]$. The only requirement on indexes in the proof of Theorem 4 is that $index$ is valid. We consider two alternative valid indexing schemes: *natural* and *flat indexes*.

$$
\mathcal{S}[\![L]\!] = \mathcal{S}[\![L]\!]_{\varepsilon,1} \qquad \begin{aligned} \mathcal{S}[\![\langle \ell = N \rangle_{i=1}^{n}]\!]_{\rho,\iota} &= \langle \ell_i = \mathcal{S}[\![N_i]\!]_{\rho,\iota} \rangle_{i=1}^{n} \\ \mathcal{S}[\![X]\!]_{\rho,\iota} &= \mathcal{N}[\![X]\!]_{\rho} \end{aligned} \qquad \begin{aligned} \mathcal{S}[\![a \diamond \mathsf{out}]\!]_{\rho,\iota.i} &= \mathit{index}(a \diamond \iota) \\ \mathcal{S}[\![a \diamond \mathsf{in}]\!]_{\rho,\iota.i} &= \mathit{index}(a \diamond \iota.i) \end{aligned}
$$

$$
\mathcal{S}[\![\biguplus_{i=1}^{n} C_i]\!]_{\rho,\iota} = \mathit{concat}([\mathcal{S}[\![C_i]\!]_{\rho,\iota}]_{i=1}^{n}) \qquad \mathcal{S}[\![\mathsf{return}^a\, N]\!]_{\rho,\iota} = [\mathcal{S}[\![N]\!]_{\rho,\iota}]
$$

$$
\mathcal{S}[\![\mathsf{for}\ ([x_i \leftarrow t_i]_{i=1}^{n}\ \mathsf{where}\ X)\ C]\!]_{\rho,\iota} = \mathit{concat}([\mathcal{S}[\![C]\!]_{\rho[x_i \mapsto r_i]_{i=1}^{n},\iota.j} \mid \langle j, \vec{r} \rangle \leftarrow \mathit{enum}([\vec{r} \mid [r_i \leftarrow [\![t_i]\!]]_{i=1}^{n}, \mathcal{N}[\![X]\!]_{\rho[x_i \mapsto r_i]_{i=1}^{n}}])])
$$

Figure 5: Semantics of shredded queries

6.1 Natural indexes

Natural indexes are synthesised from row data. In order to generate a natural index for a query every table must have a key, that is, a collection of fields guaranteed to be unique for every row in the table. For sets, this is always possible by using all of the field values as a key; this idea is used in Van den Bussche's simulation for sets [26]. However, for bags this is not always possible, so using natural indexes may require adding extra key fields.

Given a table t, let key_t be the function that given a row r of t returns the key fields of r. We now define a function to compute the list of natural indexes for a query L.

$$
\begin{aligned}
\mathcal{I}^{\natural}[\![L]\!] &= \mathcal{I}^{\natural}[\![L]\!]_{\varepsilon} \\
\mathcal{I}^{\natural}[\![\biguplus_{i=1}^{n} C_i]\!]_{\rho} &= \mathit{concat}([\mathcal{I}^{\natural}[\![C_i]\!]_{\rho}]_{i=1}^{n}) \\
\mathcal{I}^{\natural}[\![\langle \ell_i = M_i \rangle_{i=1}^{n}]\!]_{\rho} &= \mathit{concat}([\mathcal{I}^{\natural}[\![M_i]\!]_{\rho}]_{i=1}^{n}) \\
\mathcal{I}^{\natural}[\![X]\!]_{\rho} &= [\,] \\
\mathcal{I}^{\natural}[\![\mathsf{for}\ ([x_i \leftarrow t_i]_{i=1}^{n}\ \mathsf{where}\ X)\ \mathsf{return}^a\ M]\!]_{\rho} &= \\
&\mathit{concat}([a \diamond \langle \mathit{key}_{t_i}(r_i) \rangle_{i=1}^{n} :: \mathcal{I}^{\natural}[\![M]\!]_{\rho[x_i \mapsto r_i]_{i=1}^{n}} \\
&\quad \mid [r_i \leftarrow [\![t_i]\!]]_{i=1}^{n}, \mathcal{N}[\![X]\!]_{\rho[x_i \mapsto r_i]_{i=1}^{n}}])
\end{aligned}
$$

If $a \diamond \iota$ is the i-th element of $\mathcal{I}[\![L]\!]$, then $\mathit{index}^{\natural}_{L}(a \diamond \iota)$ is defined as the i-th element of $\mathcal{I}^{\natural}[\![L]\!]$. The natural indexing scheme is defined by setting $\mathit{index} = \mathit{index}^{\natural}_{L}$.

An advantage of natural indexes is that they can be implemented in plain SQL, so for a given comprehension all where clauses can be amalgamated (using the $\wedge$ operator) and no auxiliary subqueries are needed. The downside is that the type of a dynamic index may still vary across the component comprehensions of a shredded query, complicating implementation of the query (due to the need to pad some subqueries with null columns) and potentially decreasing performance due to increased data movement. We now consider an alternative, in which row_number is used to generate dynamic indexes.

6.2 Flat indexes and let-insertion

The idea of flat indexes is to enumerate all of the canonical dynamic indexes associated with each static index and use the enumeration as the dynamic index.

Let ι be the i-th element of the list $[\iota' \mid a \diamond \iota' \leftarrow \mathcal{I}[\![L]\!]]$, then $\mathit{index}^{\flat}_{L}(a \diamond \iota) = \langle a, i \rangle$. The flat indexing scheme is defined by setting $\mathit{index} = \mathit{index}^{\flat}_{L}$. Let $\mathcal{I}^{\flat}[\![L]\!] = [\mathit{index}^{\flat}_{L}(I) \mid I \leftarrow \mathcal{I}[\![L]\!]]$ and let $\mathcal{S}^{\flat}[\![L]\!]$ be $\mathcal{S}[\![L]\!]$ where $\mathit{index} = \mathit{index}^{\flat}_{L}$.

In this section, we give a translation called let-insertion that uses let-binding and an index primitive to manage flat indexes. In the next section, we take the final step from this language to SQL.

Our semantics for shredded queries uses canonical indexes. We now specify a target language providing flat indexes. In order to do so, we introduce let-bound sub-queries, and translate each comprehension into the following form:

$$
\begin{aligned}
&\mathsf{let}\ q = \mathsf{for}\ (\overrightarrow{G_{\mathsf{out}}}\ \mathsf{where}\ X_{\mathsf{out}})\ \mathsf{return}\ N_{\mathsf{out}}\ \mathsf{in} \\
&\quad \mathsf{for}\ (\overrightarrow{G_{\mathsf{in}}}\ \mathsf{where}\ X_{\mathsf{in}})\ \mathsf{return}\ N_{\mathsf{in}}
\end{aligned}
$$

The special index expression is available in each loop body, and is bound to the current index value.

Following let-insertion, the types are as before, except indexes are represented as pairs of integers $\langle a, d \rangle$ where a is the static component and d is the dynamic component.

$$
\begin{aligned}
&\text{Types} && A, B ::= \mathrm{Bag}\ \langle \langle \mathit{Int}, \mathit{Int} \rangle, F \rangle \\
&\text{Flat types} && F ::= O \mid \langle \overrightarrow{\ell : F} \rangle \mid \langle \mathit{Int}, \mathit{Int} \rangle
\end{aligned}
$$

The syntax of terms is adapted as follows:

$$
\begin{aligned}
&\text{Query terms} && L, M ::= \biguplus \vec{C} \\
&\text{Comprehensions} && C ::= \mathsf{let}\ q = S\ \mathsf{in}\ S' \\
&\text{Subqueries} && S ::= \mathsf{for}\ (\vec{G}\ \mathsf{where}\ X)\ \mathsf{return}\ N \\
&\text{Data sources} && u ::= t \mid q \\
&\text{Generators} && G ::= x \leftarrow u \\
&\text{Inner terms} && N ::= X \mid R \mid \mathsf{index} \\
&\text{Record terms} && R ::= \langle \overrightarrow{\ell = N} \rangle \\
&\text{Base terms} && X ::= x.\ell \mid c(\vec{X}) \mid \mathsf{empty}\ L
\end{aligned}
$$

The semantics of let-inserted queries is given in Figure 6. Rather than maintaining a canonical index, it generates a flat index for each subquery.

We first give the translation on shredded types as follows:

$$
\begin{aligned}
\mathbf{L}(O) &= O \\
\mathbf{L}(\langle \overrightarrow{\ell : F} \rangle) &= \langle \overrightarrow{\ell : \mathbf{L}(F)} \rangle \\
\mathbf{L}(\mathit{Index}) &= \langle \mathit{Int}, \mathit{Int} \rangle \\
\mathbf{L}(\mathrm{Bag}\ \langle \mathit{Index}, F \rangle) &= \mathrm{Bag}\ \langle \langle \mathit{Int}, \mathit{Int} \rangle, \mathbf{L}(F) \rangle
\end{aligned}
$$

For example:

$$
\mathbf{L}(A_2) = \mathrm{Bag}\ \langle \langle \mathit{Int}, \mathit{Int} \rangle, \langle \mathrm{name} : \mathit{String}, \mathrm{tasks} : \langle \mathit{Int}, \mathit{Int} \rangle \rangle \rangle
$$

Without loss of generality we rename all the bound variables in our source query to ensure that all bound variables have distinct names, and that none coincides with the distinguished name z used for let-bindings. The let-insertion translation $\mathbf{L}$ is defined in Figure 7, where we use the following auxiliary functions:

$$
\begin{aligned}
\mathit{expand}(x, t) &= \langle \ell_i = x.\ell_i \rangle_{i=1}^{n} \\
&\quad \text{where } \Sigma(t) = \mathrm{Bag}\ \langle \overrightarrow{\ell : A} \rangle \\
\mathit{gens}\ (\mathsf{for}\ (\vec{G}\ \mathsf{where}\ X)\ C) &= \vec{G} :: \mathit{gens}\ C \\
\mathit{gens}\ (\mathsf{return}^a\ N) &= [\,] \\
\mathit{conds}\ (\mathsf{for}\ (\vec{G}\ \mathsf{where}\ X)\ C) &= X :: \mathit{conds}\ C \\
\mathit{conds}\ (\mathsf{return}^a\ N) &= [\,] \\
\mathit{body}\ (\mathsf{for}\ (\vec{G}\ \mathsf{where}\ X)\ C) &= \mathit{body}\ C \\
\mathit{body}\ (\mathsf{return}^a\ N) &= N
\end{aligned}
$$

Each comprehension is rearranged into two sub-queries. The first generates the outer indexes. The second computes the results. The translation sometimes produces n-ary projections in order to refer to values bound by the first subquery inside the second.

For example, applying $\mathbf{L}$ to q_1 from Section 4.2 yields:

$$
\begin{aligned}
&\mathsf{for}\ (x \leftarrow \mathit{departments}) \\
&\mathsf{return}\ \langle \langle \top, 1 \rangle, \langle \mathrm{dept} = x.\mathrm{name}, \mathrm{people} = \mathsf{index} \rangle \rangle
\end{aligned}
$$

$$\mathcal{L}[\![L]\!] = \mathcal{L}[\![L]\!]_\varepsilon \qquad \mathcal{L}[\![t]\!]_\rho = [\![t]\!] \qquad \mathcal{L}[\![\langle \ell_j = N_j\rangle_{j=1}^m]\!]_{\rho,i} = \langle \ell_j = \mathcal{L}[\![N_j]\!]_{\rho,i}\rangle_{j=1}^m$$

$$\mathcal{L}[\![\biguplus_{j=1}^m C_j]\!]_\rho = \mathit{concat}([\mathcal{L}[\![C_j]\!]_\rho]_{j=1}^m) \qquad \mathcal{L}[\![q]\!]_\rho = \rho(q) \qquad \mathcal{L}[\![X]\!]_{\rho,i} = \mathcal{N}[\![X]\!]_\rho \qquad \mathcal{L}[\![\mathsf{index}]\!]_{\rho,i} = i$$

$$\mathcal{L}[\![\mathsf{let}\, q = S_{\mathsf{out}}\ \mathsf{in}\ S_{\mathsf{in}}]\!]_\rho = \mathcal{L}[\![S_{\mathsf{in}}]\!]_{\rho[q \mapsto \mathcal{L}[\![S_{\mathsf{out}}]\!]_\rho]}$$

$$\mathcal{L}[\![\mathsf{for}\ ([x_j \leftarrow u_j]_{j=1}^m\ \mathsf{where}\ X)\ \mathsf{return}\ N]\!]_\rho = [\mathcal{L}[\![N]\!]_{\rho[x_j \mapsto r_j]_{j=1}^m, i} \mid \langle i, \vec{r}\rangle \leftarrow \mathit{enum}([\vec{r} \mid [r_j \leftarrow \mathcal{L}[\![u_j]\!]_\rho]_{j=1}^m, \mathcal{N}[\![X]\!]_{\rho[x_j \mapsto r_j]_{j=1}^m}])]$$

Figure 6: Semantics of let-inserted shredded queries

$$\mathbf{L}(\biguplus_{i=1}^n C_i) = \biguplus_{i=1}^n \mathbf{L}(C_i)$$

$$\mathbf{L}(C) = \mathsf{let}\, q = (\mathsf{for}\ (\overrightarrow{G_{\mathsf{out}}}\ \mathsf{where}\ X_{\mathsf{out}})\ \mathsf{return}\ \langle R_{\mathsf{out}}, \mathsf{index}\rangle)\ \mathsf{in}\ \mathsf{for}\ (z \leftarrow q, \overrightarrow{G_{\mathsf{in}}}\ \mathsf{where}\ \mathbf{L}_{\vec{y}}(X_{\mathsf{in}}))\ \mathsf{return}\ \mathbf{L}_{\vec{y}}(N)$$

$$\text{where}\quad \overrightarrow{G_{\mathsf{out}}} = \mathit{concat}\ (\mathit{init}\ (\mathit{gens}\ C)) \qquad \overrightarrow{y = t} = \overrightarrow{G_{\mathsf{out}}} \qquad \overrightarrow{G_{\mathsf{in}}} = \mathit{last}\ (\mathit{gens}\ C) \qquad N = \mathit{body}\ C$$

$$X_{\mathsf{out}} = \bigwedge \mathit{init}\ (\mathit{conds}\ C) \qquad R_{\mathsf{out}} = \langle \mathit{expand}(y_i, t_i)\rangle_{i=1}^n \qquad X_{\mathsf{in}} = \mathit{last}\ (\mathit{conds}\ C) \qquad n = \mathit{length}\ \overrightarrow{G_{\mathsf{out}}}$$

$$\mathbf{L}_{\vec{y}}(x.\ell) = \begin{cases} x.\ell, & \text{if } x \notin \{y_1, \ldots, y_n\} \\ z.1.i.\ell, & \text{if } x = y_i \end{cases}$$

$$\mathbf{L}_{\vec{y}}(c(X_1, \ldots, X_m)) = c(\mathbf{L}_{\vec{y}}(X_1), \ldots, \mathbf{L}_{\vec{y}}(X_m))$$

$$\mathbf{L}_{\vec{y}}(\langle \ell_j = X_j\rangle_{j=1}^m) = \langle \ell_j = \mathbf{L}_{\vec{y}}(X_j)\rangle_{j=1}^m$$

$$\mathbf{L}_{\vec{y}}(a \diamond d) = \langle a, \mathbf{L}(d)\rangle$$

$$\mathbf{L}_{\vec{y}}(\mathsf{empty}\ L) = \mathsf{empty}\ (\mathbf{L}_{\vec{y}}(L))$$

$$\mathbf{L}_{\vec{y}}(\biguplus_{i=1}^n C_i) = \biguplus_{i=1}^n \mathbf{L}_{\vec{y}}(C_i)$$

$$\mathbf{L}_{\vec{y}}(\mathsf{for}\ (\vec{G}\ \mathsf{where}\ X)\ \mathsf{return}^a\ \langle a, N\rangle) = \mathsf{for}\ (\vec{G}\ \mathsf{where}\ \mathbf{L}_{\vec{y}}(X))\ \mathsf{return}\ \langle a, \mathbf{L}_{\vec{y}}(N)\rangle$$

$$\mathbf{L}(\mathsf{out}) = z.2 \qquad \mathbf{L}(\mathsf{in}) = \mathsf{index}$$

Figure 7: The let-insertion translation

and q_2 becomes:

$(\mathsf{let}\, q = \mathsf{for}\ (x \leftarrow \mathit{departments})\ \mathsf{return}\ \langle\langle \text{dept} = x.\text{name}\rangle, \mathsf{index}\rangle\ \mathsf{in}$
$\quad \mathsf{for}\ (z \leftarrow q, y \leftarrow \mathit{employees})\ \mathsf{where}\ (z.1.1.\text{name} = y.\text{dept} \wedge$
$\qquad (y.\text{salary} < 1000 \vee y.\text{salary} > 1000000))$
$\quad \mathsf{return}\ (\langle\langle a, z.2\rangle, \langle \text{name} = y.\text{name}, \text{tasks} = \langle b, \mathsf{index}\rangle\rangle\rangle))$
$\uplus$
$(\mathsf{let}\, q = \mathsf{for}\ (x \leftarrow \mathit{departments})\ \mathsf{return}\ \langle\langle \text{dept} = x.\text{name}\rangle, \mathsf{index}\rangle\ \mathsf{in}$
$\quad \mathsf{for}\ (z \leftarrow q, y \leftarrow \mathit{contacts})\ \mathsf{where}\ (z.1.1.\text{name} = y.\text{dept} \wedge y.\text{client})$
$\quad \mathsf{return}\ (\langle\langle a, z.2\rangle, \langle \text{name} = y.\text{name}, \text{tasks} = \langle d, \mathsf{index}\rangle\rangle\rangle))$

As a sanity check, we show that the translation is type-preserving:

THEOREM 5. *Given shredded query* $\vdash M : \mathrm{Bag}\,\langle \mathit{Index}, F\rangle$, *then* $\vdash \mathbf{L}(M) : \mathbf{L}(\mathrm{Bag}\,\langle \mathit{Index}, F\rangle)$.

To prove the correctness of let-insertion, we need to show that the shredded semantics and let-inserted semantics agree. In the statement of the correctness theorem, recall that $\mathcal{S}^\flat[\![L]\!]$ refers to the version of $\mathcal{S}[\![L]\!]$ using $\mathit{index} = \mathit{index}_L^\flat$.

THEOREM 6. *Suppose* $\vdash L : A$ *and* $\|L\|_p = M$. *Then* $\mathcal{S}^\flat[\![M]\!] = \mathcal{L}[\![\mathbf{L}(M)]\!]$.

PROOF SKETCH. The high-level idea is to separate results into data and indexes and compare each separately. It is straightforward, albeit tedious, to show that the different definitions are equal if we replace all dynamic indexes by a dummy value. It then remains to show that the dynamic indexes agree. The pertinent case is the translation of a comprehension:

$$[\mathsf{for}\ (\vec{G_i} \leftarrow X_i)]_{i=1}^n\ \mathsf{for}\ (\vec{G_{\mathsf{in}}} \leftarrow X_{\mathsf{in}})\ \mathsf{return}^b\ \langle a \diamond \mathsf{out}, N\rangle$$

which becomes $\mathsf{let}\, q = S_{\mathsf{out}}\ \mathsf{in}\ S_{\mathsf{in}}$ for suitable S_{out} and S_{in}. The dynamic indexes computed by S_{out} coincide exactly with those of $\mathcal{I}^\flat[\![L]\!]$ at static index a, and the dynamic indexes computed by S_{in}, if there are any, coincide exactly with those of $\mathcal{I}^\flat[\![L]\!]$. □

7. CONVERSION TO SQL

Earlier translation stages have employed nested records for convenience, but SQL does not support nested records. At this stage, we eliminate nested records from queries. For example, we can represent a nested record $\langle \text{a} = \langle \text{b} = 1, \text{c} = 2\rangle, \text{d} = 3\rangle$ as a flat record $\langle \text{a\_b} = 1, \text{a\_c} = 2, \text{d} = 3\rangle$.

In order to interpret shredded, flattened, let-inserted terms as SQL, we interpret index generators using SQL's OLAP facilities.

Query terms	$L ::= (\mathsf{union\ all})\ \vec{C}$
Comprehensions	$C ::= \mathsf{with}\ q\ \mathsf{as}\ (S)\ C \mid S'$
Subqueries	$S ::= \mathsf{select}\ R\ \mathsf{from}\ \vec{G}\ \mathsf{where}\ X$
Data sources	$u ::= t \mid q$
Generators	$G ::= u\ \mathsf{as}\ x$
Inner terms	$N ::= X \mid \mathsf{row\_number}()\ \mathsf{over}\ (\mathsf{order\ by}\ \vec{X})$
Record terms	$R ::= \overrightarrow{N\ \mathsf{as}\ \ell}$
Base terms	$X ::= x.\ell \mid c(\vec{X}) \mid \mathsf{empty}\ L$

Continuing our example, $\mathbf{L}(q_1)$ and $\mathbf{L}(q_2)$ translate to q_1' and q_2' where:

$q_1' =$ select x.name as i1_name,
$\qquad$ row_number() over (order by x.name) as i1_people
$\quad$ from $\mathit{departments}$ as x
$q_2' =$ (with q as (select x.name as i1_name,
$\qquad$ row_number() over (order by x.name) as i2
$\qquad$ from $\mathit{departments}$ as x)
$\quad$ select a as i1_1, z.i2 as i1_2, y.name as i2_name, b as i2_tasks_1,
$\qquad$ row_number() over (order by z.i1_name, z.i2,
$\qquad\quad$ y.dept, y.employee, y.salary) as i2_tasks_2
$\quad$ from $\mathit{employees}$ as y, q as z
$\quad$ where (z.i1_name $= y$.dept $\wedge$
$\qquad$ (y.salary $< 1000 \vee y$.salary > 1000000)))
union all
(with q as (select x.name as i1_name,
$\qquad$ row_number() over (order by x.name) as i2
$\qquad$ from $\mathit{departments}$ as x)
$\quad$ select a as i1_1, z.i2 as i1_2, y.name as i2_name, d as i2_tasks_1,
$\qquad$ row_number() over (order by z.i1_name, z.i2,
$\qquad\quad$ y.dept, y.name, y.client) as i2_tasks_2
$\quad$ from $\mathit{contacts}$ as y, q as z
$\quad$ where (z.i1_name $= y$.dept $\wedge$ y.client))

Modulo record flattening, the above fragment of SQL is almost isomorphic to the image of the let-insertion translation. The only significant difference is the use of row_number in place of index. Each instance of index in the body R of a subquery of the form $\mathsf{for}\ (\overrightarrow{x \leftarrow t}\ \mathsf{where}\ X)\ \mathsf{return}\ R$ is simulated by a term of the form $\mathsf{row\_number}()\ \mathsf{over}\ (\mathsf{order\ by}\ \overrightarrow{x.\ell})$, where:

$$x_i : \langle \ell_{i,1} : A_{i,1}, \ldots, \ell_{i,m_i} : A_{i,m_i}\rangle$$
$$\overrightarrow{x.\ell} = x_1.\ell_{1,1}, \ldots, x_1.\ell_{1,m_1}, \quad \ldots, \quad x_n.\ell_{n,1}, \ldots, x_n.\ell_{n,m_n}$$

```
QF1: SELECT e.emp FROM employees e
     WHERE e.salary > 10000
QF2: SELECT e.emp, t.tsk
     FROM employees e, tasks t
     WHERE e.emp = t.emp
QF3: SELECT e1.emp, e2.emp
     FROM employees e1, employees e2
     WHERE e1.dpt = e2.dpt
       AND e1.salary = e2.salary
       AND e1.emp <> e2.emp
QF4: (SELECT t.emp FROM tasks t
      WHERE t.tsk = 'abstract')
     UNION ALL (SELECT e.emp FROM employees
                WHERE e.salary > 50000)
QF5: (SELECT t.emp FROM tasks t
      WHERE t.tsk = 'abstract')
     MINUS
     (SELECT e.emp FROM employees e
      WHERE e.salary > 50000)
QF6: ((SELECT t.emp FROM tasks t
       WHERE t.tsk = 'abstract')
      UNION ALL (SELECT e.emp FROM employees e
                 WHERE e.salary > 50000))
     MINUS
     ((SELECT t.emp FROM tasks t
       WHERE t.tsk = 'enthuse')
      UNION ALL (SELECT e.emp FROM employees e
                 WHERE e.salary > 10000))
```

Figure 8: SQL versions of flat queries used in experiments

A possible concern is that row_number is non-deterministic. It computes row numbers ordered by the supplied columns, but if there is a tie, then it is free to order the equivalent rows in any order. However, we always order by *all* columns of all tables referenced from the current subquery, so our use of row_number is always deterministic. (An alternative could be to use nonstandard features such as PostgreSQL's OID or MySQL's ROWNUM, but sorting would still be necessary to ensure consistency across inner and outer queries.)

8. EXPERIMENTAL EVALUATION

Ferry's loop-lifting translation has been implemented in Links previously by Ulrich, a member of the Ferry team [25], following the approach described by Grust et al. [11] to generate SQL:1999 algebra plans, then calling Pathfinder [13] to optimise and evaluating the resulting SQL on a PostgreSQL database. We have also implemented query shredding in Links, running against PostgreSQL; our implementation[1] does not use Pathfinder. We performed initial experiments with a larger ad hoc query benchmark, and developed some optimisations, including inlining certain `WITH` clauses to unblock rewrites, using keys for row numbering, and implementing stitching in one pass to avoid construction of intermediate in-memory data structures that are only used once and then discarded. We report on shredding with all of these optimisations enabled.

Benchmark queries. There is no standard benchmark for queries returning nested results. In particular, the popular TPC-H benchmark is not suitable for comparing shredding and loop-lifting: the TPC-H queries do not return nested results, and can be run directly on any SQL-compliant RDBMS, so neither approach needs to do any work to produce an SQL query.

We selected twelve queries over the organisation schema described in Section 3 to use as a benchmark. The first six queries,

[1] `http://github.com/slindley/links/tree/shredding`

$\mathtt{Q1}$: for $(d \leftarrow \mathit{departments})$
  return $(\langle \text{name} = d.\text{name},$
    $\text{employees} = \mathit{employeesOfDept}\ d,$
    $\text{contacts} = \mathit{contactsOfDept}\ d \rangle$

$\mathtt{Q2}$: for $(d \leftarrow \mathtt{Q1})$
  where $(\mathit{all}\ d.\text{employees}\ (\lambda x.\mathit{contains}\ x.\text{tasks}\ \text{“abstract”}))$
  return $\langle \text{dept} = d.\text{dept} \rangle$

$\mathtt{Q3}$: for $(e \leftarrow \mathit{employees})$
  return $\langle \text{name} = e.\text{name}, \text{task} = \mathit{tasksOfEmp}(e) \rangle$

$\mathtt{Q4}$: for $(d \leftarrow \mathit{departments})$
  return $\langle \text{dept} = d.\text{dept}, \text{employees} = $ for $(e \leftarrow \mathit{employees})$
    where $(d.\text{dept} = e.\text{dept})$
    return $e.\text{employee} \rangle$

$\mathtt{Q5}$: for $(t \leftarrow \mathit{tasks})$ return $\langle a = t.\text{task}, b = \mathit{employeesByTask}\ t \rangle$

$\mathtt{Q6}$: for $(d \leftarrow \mathtt{Q1})$
  return $(\langle \text{department} = d.\text{name},$
    $\text{people} =$
      $\mathit{getTasks}(\mathit{outliers}(d.\text{employees}))\ (\lambda y.\ y.\text{tasks})$
    $\uplus\ \mathit{getTasks}(\mathit{clients}(d.\text{contacts}))\ (\lambda y.$ return “buy”$)\rangle)$

Figure 9: Nested queries used in experiments

named `QF1`–`QF6`, return flat results and can be translated to SQL using existing techniques, without requiring either shredding or loop-lifting. We considered these queries as a sanity check and in order to measure the overhead introduced by loop-lifting and shredding. Figure 8 shows the SQL versions of these queries.

We also selected six queries `Q1`–`Q6` that do involve nesting, either within query results or in intermediate stages. They are shown in Figure 9; they use the auxiliary functions defined in Section 3. `Q1` is the query Q_{org} that builds the nested organisation view from Section 3. `Q2` is a flat query that computes a flat result from `Q1` consisting of all departments in which all employees can do the "abstract" task; it is a typical example of a query that employs higher-order functions. `Q3` returns records containing each employee and the list of tasks they can perform. `Q4` returns records containing departments and the set of employees in each department. `Q5` returns a record of tasks paired up with sets of employees and their departments. `Q6` is the outliers query Q introduced in Section 3.

Experimental results. We measured the query execution time for all queries on randomly generated data, where we vary the number of departments in the organisation from 4 to 4096 (by powers of 2). Each department has on average 100 employees and each employee has 0–2 tasks, and the largest (4096 department) database was approximately 500MB. Although the test datasets are moderate in size, they suffice to illustrate the asymptotic trends in the comparative performance of the different techniques. All tests were performed using PostgreSQL 9.2 running on a MacBook Pro with 4-core 2.6GHz CPU, 8GB RAM and 500GB SSD storage, with the database server running on the same machine (hence, negligible network latency). We measure *total* time to translate a nested query to SQL, evaluate the resulting SQL queries, and stitch the results together to form a nested value, measured from Links.

We evaluated each query using query shredding and loop-lifting, and for the flat queries we also measured the time for Links' default (flat) query evaluation. The experimental results for the flat queries are shown in Figure 10 and for the nested queries in Figure 11. Note that both axes are logarithmic. All times are in milliseconds; the times are medians of 5 runs. The times for small data sizes provide a comparison of the overhead associated with shredding, loop-lifting or Links' default query normalisation algorithm.

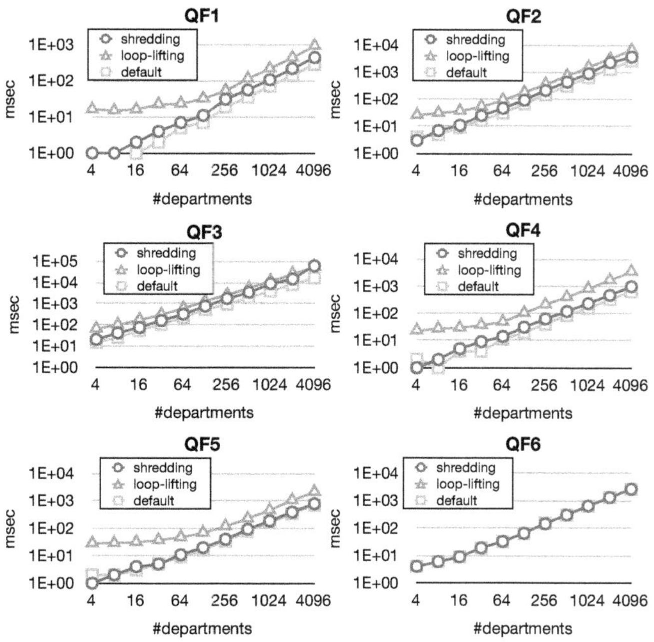

Figure 10: Experimental results (flat queries)

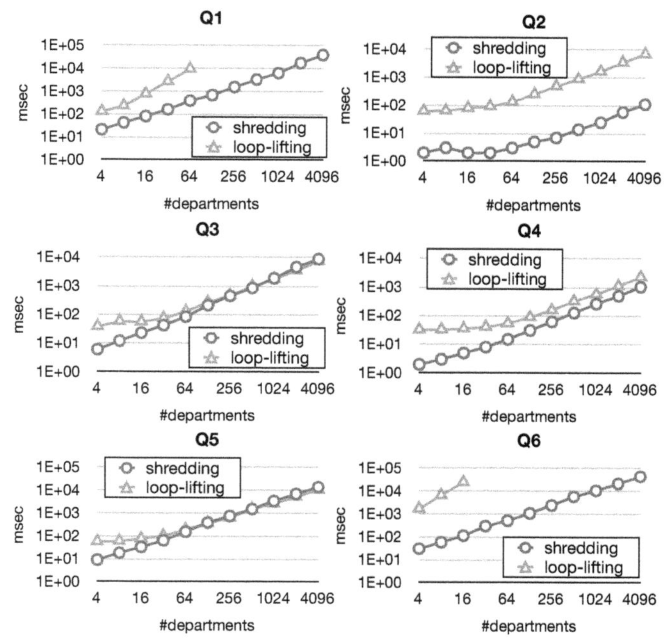

Figure 11: Experimental results (nested queries)

Discussion. We should re-emphasise that Ferry (and Ulrich's loop-lifting implementation for Links) supports grouping and aggregation features that are not handled by our translation. We focused on queries that both systems can handle, but Ferry has a clear advantage for grouping and aggregation queries or when ordering is important (e.g. sorting or top-k queries). Ferry is based on list semantics, while our approach handles multiset semantics. So, some performance differences may be due to our exploitation of multiset-based optimisations that Ferry (by design) does not exploit.

The results for flat queries show that shredding has low per-query overhead in most cases compared to Links' default flat query evaluation, but the queries it generates are slightly slower. Loop-lifting, on the other hand, has a noticeable per-query overhead, likely due to its invocation of Pathfinder and associated serialisation costs. In some cases, such as `QF4` and `QF5`, loop-lifting is noticeably slower asymptotically; this appears to be due to additional sorting needed to maintain list semantics. We encountered a bug that prevented loop-lifting from running on query `QF6`; however, shredding had negligible overhead for this query. In any case, the overhead of either shredding or loop-lifting for flat queries is irrelevant: we can simply evaluate such queries using Links' default flat query evaluator. Nevertheless, these results show that the overhead of shredding for such queries is not large, suggesting that the queries it generates are similar to those currently generated by Links. (Manual inspection of the generated queries confirms this.)

The results for nested queries are more mixed. In most cases, the overhead of loop-lifting is dominant on small data sizes, which again suggests that shredding may be preferable for OLTP or Web workloads involving rapid, small queries. Loop-lifting scales poorly on two queries (`Q1` and `Q6`), and did not finish within 1 minute even for small data sizes. Both `Q1` and `Q6` involve 3 levels of nesting and in the innermost query, loop-lifting generates queries with Cartesian products inside OLAP operators such as `DENSE_RANK` or `ROW_NUMBER` that Pathfinder was not able to remove. The queries generated by shredding in these cases avoid this pathological behaviour. For other queries, such as `Q2` and `Q4`, loop-lifting performs better but is still slower than shredding as data size increases. Comparison of the queries generated by loop-lifting and shredding reveals that loop-lifting encountered similar problems with hard-to-optimise OLAP operations. Finally, for `Q3` and `Q5`, shredding is initially faster (due to the overhead of loop-lifting and calling Pathfinder) but as data size increases, loop-lifting wins out. Inspection of these generated queries reveals that the queries themselves are similar, but the shredded queries involve more data movement. Also, loop-lifting returns sorted results, so it avoids in-memory hashing or sorting while constructing the nested result. It should be possible to incorporate similar optimisations into shredding to obtain comparable performance.

Our experiments show that shredding performs similarly or better than loop-lifting on our (synthetic) benchmark queries on moderate (up to 500MB) databases. Further work may need to be done to investigate scalability to larger databases or consider more realistic query benchmarks.

9. RELATED AND FUTURE WORK

We have discussed related work on nested queries, Links, Ferry and LINQ in the introduction. Besides Cooper [7], several authors have recently considered higher-order query languages. Benedikt et al. [1, 27] study higher-order queries over flat relations. The Links approach was adapted to LINQ in F# by Cheney et al. [5]. Higher-order features are also being added to XQuery 3.0 [21].

Research on shredding XML data into relations and evaluating XML queries over such representations [17] is superficially similar to our work in using various indexing or numbering schemes to handle nested data. Grust et al.'s work on translating XQuery to SQL via Pathfinder [13] is a mature solution to this problem, and Grust et al. [12] discuss optimisations in the presence of unordered data processing in XQuery. However, XQuery's ordered data model and treatment of node identity would block transformations in our algorithm that assume unordered, pure operations.

We can now give a more detailed comparison of our approach with the indexing strategies in Van den Bussche's work and in

Ferry. Van den Bussche's approach uses natural indexes (that is, n-tuples of ids), but does not preserve multiset semantics. Our approach preserves multiplicity and can use natural indexes, we also propose a flat indexing scheme based on row_number. In Ferry's indexing scheme, the surrogate indexes only link adjacent nesting levels, whereas our indexes take information at all higher levels into account. Our flat indexing scheme relies on this property, and Ferry's approach does not seem to be an instance of ours (or vice versa). Ferry can generate multiple SQL:1999 operations and Pathfinder tries to merge them but cannot always do so. Our approach generates row_number operations only at the end, and does not rely on Pathfinder. Finally, our approach uses normalisation and tags parts of the query to disambiguate branches of unions.

Loop-lifting has been implemented in Links by Ulrich [25], and Grust and Ulrich [15] recently presented techniques for supporting higher-order functions as query results. By using Ferry's loop-lifting translation and Pathfinder, Ulrich's system also supports list semantics and aggregation and grouping operations; to our knowledge, it is an open problem to either prove their correctness or adapt these techniques to fit our approach. Ferry's approach supports a list-based semantics for queries, while we assume a bag-based semantics (matching SQL's default behaviour). Either approach can accommodate set-based semantics simply by eliminating duplicates in the final result. In fact, however, we believe the core query shredding translation (Sections 4–6) works just as well for a list semantics. The only parts that rely on unordered semantics are normalisation (Section 2.2) and conversion to SQL (Section 7). We leave these extensions to future work.

Our work is also partly inspired by work on unnesting for nested data parallelism. Blelloch and Sabot [2] give a compilation scheme for NESL, a data-parallel language with nested lists; Suciu and Tannen [23] give an alternative scheme for a nested list calculus. This work may provide an alternative (and parallelisable) implementation strategy for Ferry's list-based semantics [11].

10. CONCLUSION

Combining efficient database access with high-level programming abstractions is challenging in part because of the limitations of flat database queries. Currently, programmers must write flat queries and manually convert the results to a nested form. This damages declarativity and maintainability. Query shredding can help to bridge this gap. Although it is known from prior work that query shredding is possible in principle, and some implementations (such as Ferry) support this, getting the details right is tricky, and can lead to queries that are not optimised well by the relational engine. Our contribution is an alternative shredding translation that handles queries over bags and delays use of OLAP operations until the final stage. Our translation compares favourably to loop-lifting in performance, and should be straightforward to extend and to incorporate into other language-integrated query systems.

Acknowledgements. We thank Ezra Cooper, Torsten Grust, and Jan Van den Bussche for comments. We are very grateful to Alex Ulrich for sharing his implementation of Ferry in Links and for extensive discussions. This work was supported by EPSRC grants EP/J014591/1 and EP/K034413/1 and a Google Research Award.

11. REFERENCES

[1] M. Benedikt, G. Puppis, and H. Vu. Positive higher-order queries. In *PODS*, pages 27–38, 2010.

[2] G. E. Blelloch and G. W. Sabot. Compiling collection-oriented languages onto massively parallel computers. *J. Parallel Distrib. Comput.*, 8:119–134, February 1990.

[3] P. Buneman, L. Libkin, D. Suciu, V. Tannen, and L. Wong. Comprehension syntax. *SIGMOD Record*, 23, 1994.

[4] P. Buneman, S. A. Naqvi, V. Tannen, and L. Wong. Principles of programming with complex objects and collection types. *Theor. Comput. Sci.*, 149(1):3–48, 1995.

[5] J. Cheney, S. Lindley, and P. Wadler. A practical theory of language-integrated query. In *ICFP*, pages 403–416. ACM, 2013.

[6] J. Cheney, S. Lindley, and P. Wadler. Query shredding: efficient relational evaluation of queries over nested multisets (extended version). Technical Report arXiv:1404.7078, arXiv.org, 2014. http://arxiv.org/abs/1404.7078.

[7] E. Cooper. The script-writer's dream: How to write great SQL in your own language, and be sure it will succeed. In *DBPL*, pages 36–51, 2009.

[8] E. Cooper, S. Lindley, P. Wadler, and J. Yallop. Links: web programming without tiers. In *FMCO*, volume 4709 of *LNCS*, 2007.

[9] L. Fegaras and D. Maier. Optimizing object queries using an effective calculus. *ACM Trans. Database Syst.*, 25:457–516, December 2000.

[10] T. Grust, M. Mayr, J. Rittinger, and T. Schreiber. Ferry: Database-supported program execution. In *SIGMOD*, June 2009.

[11] T. Grust, J. Rittinger, and T. Schreiber. Avalanche-safe LINQ compilation. *PVLDB*, 3(1), 2010.

[12] T. Grust, J. Rittinger, and J. Teubner. eXrQuy: Order indifference in XQuery. In *ICDE*, pages 226–235, 2007.

[13] T. Grust, J. Rittinger, and J. Teubner. Pathfinder: XQuery off the relational shelf. *IEEE Data Eng. Bull.*, 31(4):7–14, 2008.

[14] T. Grust, S. Sakr, and J. Teubner. XQuery on SQL hosts. In *VLDB*, pages 252–263, 2004.

[15] T. Grust and A. Ulrich. First-class functions for first-order database engines. In *DBPL*, 2013.

[16] W. Kim. On optimizing an SQL-like nested query. *ACM Trans. Database Syst.*, 7(3):443–469, Sept. 1982.

[17] R. Krishnamurthy, R. Kaushik, and J. F. Naughton. XML-SQL query translation literature: The state of the art and open problems. In *Xsym*, pages 1–18, 2003.

[18] S. Lindley and J. Cheney. Row-based effect types for database integration. In *TLDI*, 2012.

[19] E. Meijer, B. Beckman, and G. M. Bierman. LINQ: reconciling object, relations and XML in the .NET framework. In *SIGMOD*, 2006.

[20] C. Olston, B. Reed, U. Srivastava, R. Kumar, and A. Tomkins. Pig latin: a not-so-foreign language for data processing. In *SIGMOD*, pages 1099–1110, 2008.

[21] J. Robie, D. Chamberlin, M. Dyck, and J. Snelson. XQuery 3.0: An XML query language. W3C Proposed Recommendation, October 2013. http://www.w3.org/TR/xquery-30/.

[22] H. J. Schek and M. H. Scholl. The relational model with relation-valued attributes. *Inf. Syst.*, 11:137–147, April 1986.

[23] D. Suciu and V. Tannen. Efficient compilation of high-level data parallel algorithms. In *SPAA*, pages 57–66. ACM, 1994.

[24] D. Syme, A. Granicz, and A. Cisternino. *Expert F# 3.0.* Apress, 2012.

[25] A. Ulrich. A Ferry-based query backend for the Links programming language. Master's thesis, University of Tübingen, 2011. Code supplement: http://github.com/slindley/links/tree/sand.

[26] J. Van den Bussche. Simulation of the nested relational algebra by the flat relational algebra, with an application to the complexity of evaluating powerset algebra expressions. *Theor. Comput. Sci.*, 254(1-2), 2001.

[27] H. Vu and M. Benedikt. Complexity of higher-order queries. In *ICDT*, pages 208–219. ACM, 2011.

[28] P. Wadler. Comprehending monads. *Math. Struct. in Comp. Sci.*, 2(4), 1992.

[29] L. Wong. Normal forms and conservative extension properties for query languages over collection types. *J. Comput. Syst. Sci.*, 52(3), 1996.

[30] L. Wong. Kleisli, a functional query system. *J. Funct. Programming*, 10(1), 2000.

Plan Bouquets: Query Processing without Selectivity Estimation

Anshuman Dutt
Database Systems Lab, SERC/CSA
Indian Institute of Science, Bangalore, INDIA
anshuman@dsl.serc.iisc.ernet.in

Jayant R. Haritsa
Database Systems Lab, SERC/CSA
Indian Institute of Science, Bangalore, INDIA
haritsa@dsl.serc.iisc.ernet.in

ABSTRACT

Selectivity estimates for optimizing OLAP queries often differ significantly from those actually encountered during query execution, leading to poor plan choices and inflated response times. We propose here a conceptually new approach to address this problem, wherein the compile-time estimation process is completely eschewed for error-prone selectivities. Instead, a small "bouquet" of plans is identified from the set of optimal plans in the query's selectivity error space, such that at least one among this subset is near-optimal at each location in the space. Then, at run time, the actual selectivities of the query are incrementally "discovered" through a sequence of partial executions of bouquet plans, eventually identifying the appropriate bouquet plan to execute. The duration and switching of the partial executions is controlled by a graded progression of isocost surfaces projected onto the optimal performance profile. We prove that this construction results in bounded overheads for the selectivity discovery process and consequently, guaranteed worst-case performance. In addition, it provides repeatable execution strategies across different invocations of a query.

The plan bouquet approach has been empirically evaluated on both PostgreSQL and a commercial DBMS, over the TPC-H and TPC-DS benchmark environments. Our experimental results indicate that, even with conservative assumptions, it delivers substantial improvements in the worst-case behavior, without impairing the average-case performance, as compared to the native optimizers of these systems. Moreover, the bouquet technique can be largely implemented using existing optimizer infrastructure, making it relatively easy to incorporate in current database engines.

Overall, the bouquet approach provides novel guarantees that open up new possibilities for robust query processing.

Categories and Subject Descriptors

H.2.4 [**Database Management Systems**]: Query Processing

Keywords

Selectivity Estimation; Plan Bouquets; Robust Query Processing

SIGMOD'14, June 22–27, 2014, Snowbird, UT, USA.

http://dx.doi.org/10.1145/2588555.2588566.

1. INTRODUCTION

Cost-based database query optimizers estimate a host of *selectivities* while identifying the ideal execution plan for declarative OLAP queries. For example, consider **EQ**, the simple SPJ query shown in Figure 1 for enumerating orders of cheap parts – here, the optimizer estimates the selectivities of a selection predicate ($p\_retailprice$) and two join predicates ($part \bowtie lineitem$, $lineitem \bowtie orders$). In practice, these estimates are often significantly in error with respect to the actual values subsequently encountered during query execution. Such errors, which can even be in *orders of magnitude* in real database environments [18], arise due to a variety of well-documented reasons [23], including outdated statistics, attribute-value independence(AVI) assumptions, coarse summaries, complex user-defined predicates, and error propagation in the query execution operator tree [16]. Moreover, in environments such as ETL workflows, the statistics may actually be *unavailable* due to data source constraints, forcing the optimizer to resort to "magic numbers" for the values (e.g. $1/10$ for equality selections [22]). The net result of these erroneous estimates is that the execution plans recommended by the query optimizer may turn out to be poor choices at run-time, resulting in substantially inflated query response times.

```
select * from lineitem, orders, part
where p_partkey = l_partkey and l_orderkey =
      o_orderkey and p_retailprice < 1000
```

Figure 1: Example Query (EQ)

A considerable body of literature exists on proposals to tackle this classical problem. For instance, techniques for improving the *statistical quality* of the meta-data include improved summary structures [1, 19], feedback-based adjustments [23], and on-the-fly re-optimization of queries [17, 4, 20]. A complementary approach is to identify *robust plans* that are relatively less sensitive to estimation errors [9, 3, 4, 14]. While these prior techniques provide novel and innovative formulations, they are limited in their scope and performance, as explained later in the related work section.

Plan Bouquet Approach

In this paper, we investigate a conceptually new approach, wherein the compile-time estimation process is completely eschewed for error-prone selectivities. Instead, these selectivities are systematically *discovered* at run-time through a calibrated sequence of cost-limited plan executions. In a nutshell, we attempt to side-step the selectivity estimation problem, rather than address it head-on, by adopting a *"seeing is believing"* viewpoint on these values.

1D Example. We introduce the new approach through a restricted 1D version of the EQ example query wherein only the p_retailprice selection predicate is error-prone. First, through repeated invocations of the optimizer, we identify the "parametric optimal set of plans" (POSP) that cover the entire selectivity range of the predicate. A sample outcome of this process is shown in Figure 2, wherein the POSP set is comprised of plans P1 through P5. Further, each plan is annotated with the selectivity range over which it is optimal – for instance, plan P3 is optimal in the (1.0%, 7.5%] interval. (In Figure 2, P = Part, L = Lineitem, O = Order, NL = Nested Loops Join, MJ = Sort Merge Join, and HJ = Hash Join) .

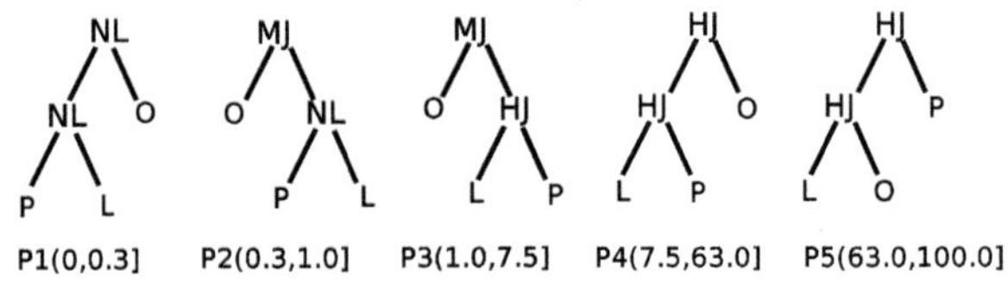

Figure 2: POSP plans on p_retailprice dimension

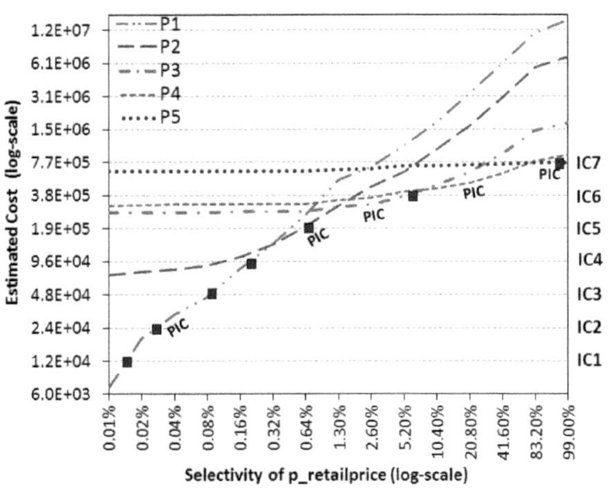

Figure 3: POSP performance (log-log scale)

The optimizer-generated costs of these POSP plans over the selectivity range are shown (on a log-log scale) in Figure 3. On this figure, we first construct the "POSP infimum curve" (**PIC**), defined as the trajectory of the minimum cost from among the POSP plans – this curve represents the ideal performance. The next step, which is a distinctive feature of our approach, is to *discretize* the PIC by projecting a graded progression of *isocost* (IC) steps onto the curve. For example, in Figure 3, the dotted horizontal lines represent a geometric progression of isocost steps, IC1 through IC7, with each step being *double* the preceding value. The intersection of each IC with the PIC (indicated by ■) provides an associated selectivity, along with the identity of the best POSP plan for this selectivity. For example, in Figure 3, the intersection of IC5 with the PIC corresponds to a selectivity of 0.65% with associated POSP plan P2. We term the subset of POSP plans that are associated with the intersections as the "plan bouquet" for the given query – in Figure 3, the bouquet consists of {P1, P2, P3, P5}.

The above exercises are carried out at query compilation time. Subsequently, at run-time, the correct query selectivities are explicitly discovered through a sequence of *cost-limited* executions of bouquet plans. Specifically, beginning with the cheapest isocost step, we iteratively execute the bouquet plan assigned to each step until either:

1. The partial execution overheads exceed the step's cost value – in this case, we know that the actual selectivity location lies beyond the current step, motivating a switch to the next step in the sequence; or
2. The current plan completes execution within the budget – in this case, we know that the actual selectivity location has been reached, and a plan that is at least 2-competitive wrt the ideal choice was used for the final execution.

Example. To make the above process concrete, consider the case where the selectivity of p_retailprice is 5%. Here, we begin by partially executing plan P1 until the execution overheads reach IC1 (1.2E4 | 0.015%). Then, we extend our cost horizon to IC2, and continue executing P1 until the overheads reach IC2 (2.4E4| 0.03%), and so on until the overheads reach IC4 (9.6E4 | 0.2%). At this juncture, there is a change of plan to P2 as we look ahead to IC5 (1.9E5 | 0.65%), and during this switching all the intermediate results (if any) produced thus far by plan P1 are *jettisoned.* The new plan P2 is executed till the associated overhead limit (1.9E5) is reached. The cost horizon is now extended to IC6 (3.8E5 | 6.5%), in the process jettisoning plan P2's intermediate results and executing plan P3 instead. In this case, the execution will complete before the cost limit is reached since the actual location, 5%, is less than the selectivity limit of IC6. Viewed in toto, the net sub-optimality turns out to be 1.78 since the exploratory overheads are 0.78 times the optimal cost, and the optimal plan itself was (coincidentally) used for the final execution.

Extension to Multiple Dimensions. When the above approach is generalized to the multi-dimensional selectivity environment, the IC steps and the PIC curve become surfaces, and their intersections represent selectivity surfaces on which multiple bouquet plans may be present. For example, in the 2-D case, the IC steps are horizontal planes cutting through a hollow 3D PIC surface, typically resulting in hyperbolic intersection contours with different plans associated with disjoint segments of this contour – an instance of this scenario is shown in Figure 6.

Notwithstanding these changes, the basic mechanics of the bouquet algorithm remain virtually identical. The primary difference is that we jump from one IC surface to the next only after it is determined (either explicitly or implicitly) that *none* of the bouquet plans present on the current IC surface can completely execute the given query within the associated cost budget.

Performance Characteristics

At first glance, the plan bouquet approach, as described above, may appear to be utterly absurd and self-defeating because: (a) At compile time, considerable preprocessing may be required to identify the POSP plan set and the associated PIC; and (b) At run-time, the overheads may be hugely expensive since there are multiple plan executions for a single query – in the worst scenario, as many plans as are present in the bouquet!

However, we will attempt to make the case in the remainder of this paper, that it is indeed possible, through careful design, to have *plan bouquets efficiently provide robustness profiles that are markedly superior to the native optimizer's profile.* Specifically, if we define robustness to be the worst-case sub-optimality in plan performance that can occur due to selectivity errors, the bouquet mechanism delivers substantial robustness improvements, while providing comparable or improved average-case performance.

For instance, the runtime performance of the bouquet technique on EQ is profiled in Figure 4 (dark blue curve). We observe that its

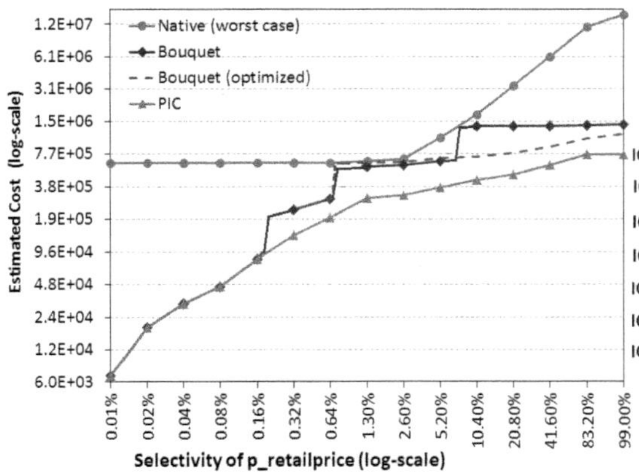

Figure 4: Bouquet Performance (log-log scale)

performance is much closer to the PIC (dark green) as compared to the worst case profile for the native optimizer (dark red), comprised of the supremum of the individual plan profiles. In fact, the worst case sub-optimality for the bouquet is only 3.6 (at 6.5%), whereas the native optimizer suffers a sub-optimality of around 100 when P5 (which is optimal for large selectivities) is mistakenly chosen to execute a query with a low selectivity of 0.01%. The average sub-optimality of the bouquet, computed over all possible errors, is 2.4, somewhat worse than the 1.8 obtained with the native optimizer. However, when the enhancements described later in this paper are incorporated, the optimized bouquet's performance (dashed blue) improves to 3.1 (worst case) and 1.7 (average case), thereby dominating the native optimizer on both metrics.

Our motivation for the cost-based discretization of the PIC is that it leads to *guaranteed* bounds on worst-case performance. For instance, we prove that the cost-doubling strategy used in the 1D example results in an *upper-bound of 4* for the worst-case sub-optimality – this bound is inclusive of all exploratory overheads incurred by the partial executions, and is irrespective of the query's actual selectivity. In fact, we can go further to show that 4 is the best competitive factor achievable by *any* deterministic algorithm. For the multi-dimensional case, the bound becomes 4 times the bouquet cardinality (more accurately, the plan cardinality of the densest contour), and we present techniques to limit this cardinality to a small value. To our knowledge, these robustness bounds are the first such guarantees to be presented in the database literature (although similar characterizations are well established in the algorithms community [8]). Further, we also present a variety of design optimizations that result in a practical performance which is well within the theoretical bounds.

In order to empirically validate its utility, we have evaluated the bouquet approach on PostgreSQL and a popular commercial DBMS. Our experiments utilize a rich set of complex decision support queries sourced from the TPC-H and TPC-DS benchmarks. The query workload includes selectivity spaces with as many as *five* error-prone dimensions, thereby capturing environments that are extremely challenging from a robustness perspective. Our performance results indicate that the bouquet approach typically provides *orders of magnitude* improvements, as compared to the optimizer's native choices. As a case in point, for Query 19 of the TPC-DS benchmark with 5 error prone join selectivities, the worst-case sub-optimality plummeted from about 10^6 to just 10! The potency of the approach is also indicated by the fact that for many queries, the bouquet's average performance is within 4 times of the corresponding PICs.

What is even more gratifying is that the above performance profiles are *conservative* since we assume that at every plan switch, *all* previous intermediate results are completely thrown away – in practice, it is conceivable that some of these prior results could be retained and reused in the execution of a future plan.

Apart from improving robustness, there is another major benefit of the bouquet mechanism: On a given database, the execution strategy for a particular query instance, i.e. the sequence of plan executions, is *repeatable* across different invocations of the query instance – this is in marked contrast to prior approaches wherein plan choices are influenced by the current state of the database statistics and the query construction. Such stability of performance is especially important for industrial applications, where considerable value is attributed to reproducible performance characteristics [3].

Finally, with regard to implementation, the bouquet technique can be largely constructed using techniques (e.g. abstract plan costing) that have already found expression in modern DB engines, as explained later in Section 5.4.

Thus far, we had tacitly assumed the optimizer's *cost model* to be perfect – that is, only *optimizer costs* were used in the evaluations. While this assumption is certainly not valid in practice, improving the model quality is, in principle, an orthogonal problem to that of estimation. Notwithstanding, we also analyze the robustness guarantees in the presence of bounded modeling errors. Moreover, to positively verify robustness improvements, explicit run-time evaluations are also included in our experimental study.

In closing, we wish to highlight that from a deployment perspective, the bouquet technique is intended to *complementarily co-exist* with the classical optimizer setup, leaving it to the user or DBA to make the choice of which system to use for a specific query instance – essential factors that are likely to influence this choice are discussed in the epilogue.

Organization. The remainder of the paper is organized as follows: In Section 2, a precise description of the robust execution problem is provided, along with the associated notations. Theoretical bounds on the robustness provided by the bouquet technique are presented in Section 3. We then discuss its design methodology, the compile-time aspects in Section 4 and the run-time mechanisms in Section 5. The experimental framework and performance results are reported in Section 6. Related work is reviewed in Section 7, while Section 8 presents a critical review of the bouquet approach.

2. PROBLEM FRAMEWORK

In this section, we present our robustness model, the associated performance metrics, and the notations used in the sequel. Robustness can be defined in many different ways and there is no universally accepted metric [13] – here, we use the notion of performance sub-optimality to characterize robustness.

The error-prone selectivity space is denoted as ESS and its dimensionality D is determined by the number of error-prone selectivity predicates in the query. The space is represented by a grid of D-dimensional points with each point $q(s_1, s_2, ..., s_D)$ corresponding to a unique query with selectivity s_j on the jth dimension. The cost of a plan P_i at a query location q in ESS is denoted by $c_i(q)$.

For simplicity, we assume that the estimated query locations and the actual query locations are uniformly and independently distributed over the entire discretized selectivity space – that is, all estimates and errors are equally likely. This definition can easily be extended to the general case where the estimated and actual locations have idiosyncratic probability distributions.

Given a user query Q, denote the optimizer's *estimated* location of this query by q_e and the *actual* location at runtime by q_a. Next, denote the plan chosen by the optimizer at q_e as P_{oe}, and the optimal plan at q_a by P_{oa}. With these definitions, the sub-optimality incurred due to using P_{oe} at q_a is simply defined as the ratio:

$$SubOpt(q_e, q_a) = \frac{c_{oe}(q_a)}{c_{oa}(q_a)} \quad \forall q_e, q_a \in ESS \tag{1}$$

with $SubOpt$ ranging over $[1, \infty)$. The worst-case $SubOpt$ for a given query location q_a is defined to be wrt the q_e that results in the maximum sub-optimality, that is, where selectivity inaccuracies have the maximum adverse performance impact:

$$SubOpt_{worst}(q_a) = \max_{q_e \in ESS}(SubOpt(q_e, q_a)) \quad \forall q_a \in ESS \tag{2}$$

With the above, the global worst-case is simply defined as the (q_e, q_a) combination that results in the maximum value of $SubOpt$ over the entire ESS, that is,

$$\textbf{MSO} = \max_{q_a \in ESS}(SubOpt_{worst}(q_a)) \tag{3}$$

Further, given the uniformity assumption about the distribution of estimated and actual locations, the average sub-optimality over ESS is defined as:

$$\textbf{ASO} = \frac{\sum_{q_e \in ESS} \sum_{q_a \in ESS} SubOpt(q_e, q_a)}{\sum_{q_e \in ESS} \sum_{q_a \in ESS} 1} \tag{4}$$

The above MSO and ASO definitions are appropriate for the way that modern optimizers behave, wherein selectivity estimates are made at compile-time, and a single plan is executed at run-time. However, in the plan bouquet technique, neither of these characteristics is true – error-prone selectivities are not estimated at compile-time, and multiple plans may be invoked at run-time. Notwithstanding, we can still compute the corresponding statistics by: (a) substituting q_e with a "don't care" $*$; (b) replacing P_{oe} with P_b to denote the plan bouquet mechanism; and (c) having the cost of the bouquet, $c_b(q_a)$, include the overheads incurred by the exploratory partial executions. Further, the running selectivity location, as progressively discovered by the bouquet mechanism, is denoted by q_{run}.

Even when the bouquet algorithm performs well on the MSO and ASO metrics, it is possible that for some specific locations $q_a \in$ ESS, it performs poorer than the worst performance of the native optimizer – it is therefore harmful for the queries associated with these locations. This possibility is captured using the following *MaxHarm* metric:

$$\textbf{MH} = \max_{q_a \in ESS}\left(\frac{SubOpt(*, q_a)}{SubOpt_{worst}(q_a)} - 1\right) \tag{5}$$

Note that MH values lie in the range $(-1, MSO_{bouquet} - 1]$ and harm occurs whenever MH is positive.

An assumption that fundamentally underlies the entire bouquet mechanism is that of *Plan Cost Monotonicity* (PCM) – that is, the costs of the POSP plans increase monotonically with increasing selectivity values. This assumption has often been made in the literature [5, 6, 15], and holds for virtually all the plans generated by PostgreSQL on the benchmark queries. The only exception we have found is for queries featuring *existential* operators, where the POSP plans may exhibit *decreasing* monotonicity with selectivity. Even in such scenarios, the basic bouquet technique can be utilized by the simple expedient of plotting the ESS with $(1 - s)$ instead of s on the selectivity axes. Thus, only queries whose optimal cost surfaces have a maxima or minima in the *interior* of the error space, are not amenable to our approach.

3. ROBUSTNESS BOUNDS

We begin our presentation of the plan bouquet approach by characterizing its performance bounds with regard to the MSO metric, initially for the 1D scenario, and then extending it to the general multi-dimensional case.

3.1 1D Selectivity Space

As described in the Introduction, the 1D PIC curve is discretized by projecting a graded progression of isocost steps onto the curve. We assume that the PIC is an increasing function (by virtue of PCM) and continuous throughout ESS; its minimum and maximum costs are denoted by C_{min} and C_{max}, respectively. Now, specifically consider the case wherein the isocost steps are organized in a *geometric* progression with initial value a ($a > 0$) and common ratio r ($r > 1$), such that the PIC is sliced with $m = log_r \lceil \frac{C_{max}}{C_{min}} \rceil$ cuts, $IC_1, IC_2, \ldots IC_m$, satisfying the boundary conditions $a/r < C_{min} \leq IC_1$ and $IC_{m-1} < C_{max} = IC_m$, as shown in Figure 5.

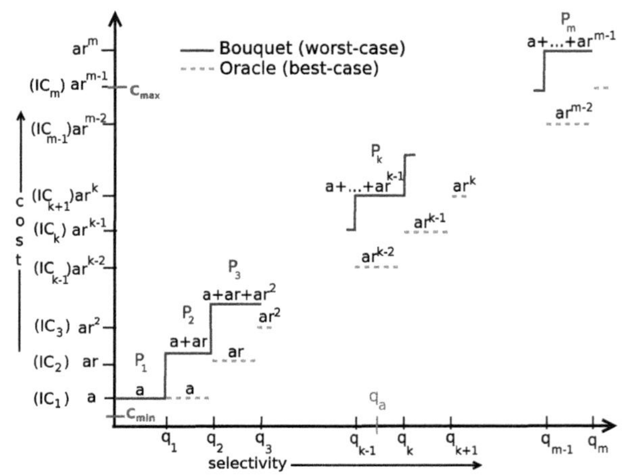

Figure 5: 1D Selectivity Space

For $1 \leq k \leq m$, denote the selectivity location where the kth isocost step (IC_k) intersects the PIC by q_k and the corresponding bouquet plan as P_k. All the q_k locations are unique by definition due to the PCM and continuity requirements on the PIC curve. However, it is possible that some of the P_k plans may be common to multiple intersection points (e.g. in Figure 3, plan P1 was common to steps IC_1 through IC_4). Finally, for mathematical convenience, assign q_0 to be 0.

With this framework, the bouquet execution algorithm operates as follows in the most general case, where a different plan is associated with each step: We start with plan P_1 and budget IC_1, progressively working our way up through the successive bouquet plans $P_2, P_3, \ldots$ until we reach the first plan P_k that is able to fully execute the query within its assigned budget IC_k. It is easy to see that the following lemma holds:

LEMMA 1. *If q_a resides in the range $(q_{k-1}, q_k]$, $1 \leq k \leq m$, then plan P_k executes it to completion in the bouquet algorithm.*

PROOF. We prove by contradiction: If q_a was located in the region $(q_k, q_{k+1}]$, then P_k could not have completed the query due to the PCM restriction. Conversely, if q_a was located in $(q_{k-2}, q_{k-1}]$, P_{k-1} itself would have successfully executed the query to completion. With similar reasoning, we can prove the same for the remaining regions that are beyond q_{k+1} or before q_{k-2}.

Performance Bounds. Consider the generic case where q_a lies in the range $(q_{k-1}, q_k]$. Based on Lemma 1, the associated worst case cost of the bouquet execution algorithm is given by the following expression:

$$C_{bouquet}(q_a) = cost(IC_1) + cost(IC_2) + ... + cost(IC_k)$$

$$= a + ar + ar^2 + ... + ar^{k-1} = \frac{a(r^k - 1)}{r - 1} \tag{6}$$

The corresponding cost for an "oracle" algorithm that magically apriori knows the correct location of q_a is lower bounded by ar^{k-2}, due to the PCM restriction. Therefore, we have

$$SubOpt(*, q_a) \leq \frac{\frac{a(r^k-1)}{r-1}}{ar^{k-2}} = \frac{r^2}{r-1} - \frac{r^{2-k}}{r-1} \leq \frac{r^2}{r-1} \tag{7}$$

Note that the above expression is *independent* of k, and hence of the specific location of q_a. Therefore, we can state for the entire selectivity space, that:

THEOREM 1. *Given a query Q on a 1D error-prone selectivity space, and the associated PIC discretized with a geometric progression having common ratio r, the bouquet execution algorithm ensures that:* $MSO \leq \frac{r^2}{r-1}$

Further, the choice of r can be optimized to minimize this value – the RHS reaches its minima at $r = 2$, at which the value of MSO is **4**. The following theorem shows that this is the *best* performance achievable by any deterministic online algorithm – leading us to conclude that the *doubling* based discretization is the ideal solution.

THEOREM 2. *No deterministic online algorithm can provide an MSO guarantee lower than 4 in the 1D scenario.*

PROOF. We prove by contradiction, assuming there exists an optimal online robust algorithm, R* with a MSO of f, $f < 4$.

Firstly, note that R* must have a monotonically increasing sequence of plan execution costs, $a_1, a_2, \ldots, a_{k^*+1}$ in its quest to find a plan P_{k^*+1} that can execute the query to completion. The proof is simple: If $a_i > a_j$ with $i < j$, then we could construct another algorithm that skips the a_j execution and still execute the query to completion using P_{k^*+1}, and therefore has less cumulative overheads than R*, which is not possible by definition.

Secondly, if R* stops at P_{k^*+1}, then q_a has to necessarily lie in the range $(q_{k^*}, q_{k^*+1}]$ (Lemma 1 holds for any monotonic algorithm). Therefore, the worst-case performance of R* is given by $\frac{\sum_{i=1}^{i=k^*+1} a_i}{a_{k^*}} \leq f$. Since q_a could be chosen to lie in any interval, this inequality should hold true across all intervals, i.e.

$$\forall j \in 1, 2, \ldots, k^*: \quad \frac{\sum_{i=1}^{i=j+1} a_i}{a_j} \leq f$$

Using the notation A_j to represent $\sum_{i=1}^{j} a_i$ and Y_j to represent the ratio $\frac{A_{j+1}}{A_j}$, we can rewrite the above as:

$$\frac{A_{j+1}}{a_j} \leq f \Rightarrow A_{j+1} \leq f(A_j - A_{j-1}) \Rightarrow \frac{A_{j+1}}{A_j} \leq f\frac{(A_j - A_{j-1})}{A_j}$$

that is, $Y_j \leq f(1 - \frac{1}{Y_{j-1}})$.

We can show through elementary algebra that $\forall z > 0$, $(1 - \frac{1}{z}) \leq \frac{z}{4}$. Therefore, we have that $Y_j \leq (\frac{f}{4})Y_{j-1}$, leading to $Y_{k^*} \leq (\frac{f}{4})^{k^*-1} Y_1$. Using the assumption of $f < 4$, we can find a sufficiently large k^* such that $(\frac{f}{4})^{k^*-1} Y_1 < 1$. Hence, $Y_{k^*} < 1$ which implies that $A_{k^*+1} < A_{k^*}$, a contradiction.

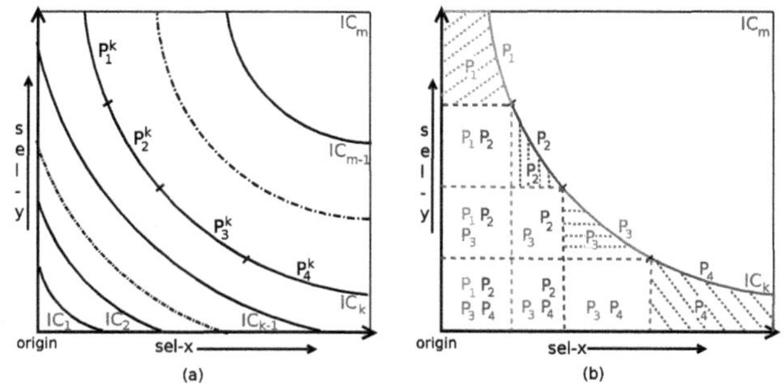

Figure 6: 2D Selectivity Space

3.2 Multi-dimensional Selectivity Space

We now move to the general case of multi-dimensional selectivity error spaces. A sample 2D scenario is shown in Figure 6a, wherein the isocost surfaces IC_k are represented by *contours* that represent a continuous sequence of selectivity locations (in contrast to the single location in the 1D case). Further, multiple bouquet plans may be present on each individual contour as shown for IC_k wherein four plans, P_1^k, P_2^k, P_3^k, P_4^k, are the optimizer's choices over disjoint x, y selectivity ranges on the contour. Now, to decide whether q_a lies below or beyond IC_k, in principle *every* plan on the IC_k contour has to be executed – only if none complete, do we know that the actual location definitely lies beyond the contour.

This need for exhaustive execution is highlighted in Figure 6b, where for the four plans lying on IC_k, the regions in the selectivity space on which each of these plans is guaranteed to complete within the IC_k budget are enumerated (the contour superscripts are omitted in the figure for visual clarity). Note that while several regions are "covered" by multiple plans, each plan also has a region that it alone covers – the hashed regions in Figure 6b. For queries located in such regions, only the execution of the associated unique plan would result in confirming that the query is within the contour.

The basic bouquet algorithm for the multi-dimensional case is shown in Figure 7, using the notation n_k to represent the number of plans on contour k.

```
for cid = 1 to m do                                   ▷ for each cost-contour cid
    for i = 1 to n_cid do                             ▷ for each plan on cid
        start executing P_i^cid
        while running-cost(P_i^cid) ≤ cost-budget(IC_cid) do
            execute plan P_i^cid                      ▷ cost limited execution
            if P_i^cid finishes execution then
                return query result
        stop executing P_i^cid
```

Figure 7: Multi-dimensional Bouquet Algorithm

Performance Bounds. Given a query Q with q_a located in the range $(IC_{k-1}, IC_k]$, the worst-case total execution cost for the multi-D bouquet algorithm is given by

$$C_{bouquet}(q_a) = \sum_{i=1}^{k} [n_i \times cost(IC_i)] \tag{8}$$

Using ρ to denote the number of plans on the *densest* contour, and upper-bounding the values of the n_i with ρ, we get the following performance guarantee:

$$C_{bouquet}(q_a) \leq \rho \times \sum_{i=1}^{k} cost(IC_i) \tag{9}$$

Now, following a similar derivation as for the 1D case, we arrive at the following theorem:

THEOREM 3. *Given a query* Q *with a multidimensional error-prone selectivity space, the associated PIC discretized with a geometric progression having common ratio r and maximum contour plan density ρ, the bouquet execution algorithm ensures that:*

$$MSO \leq \rho \frac{r^2}{r-1}$$

Setting $r = 2$ in this expression ensures that $MSO \leq 4\,\rho$.

3.3 Minimizing IsoCost Surface Plan Density

To the best of our knowledge, the above MSO bounds are the first such guarantees in the literature. While the 1D bounds are inherently strong giving a guarantee of 4 or better, the multi-dimensional bounds, however, depend on ρ, the maximum plan density over the isocost surfaces. Therefore, to have a practically useful bound, we need to ensure that the value of ρ is kept to the minimum.

This can be achieved through the *anorexic reduction* technique described in [15]. Here, POSP plans are allowed to "swallow" other plans, that is, occupy their regions in the ESS space, if the sub-optimality introduced due to these swallowings can be bounded to a user-defined threshold, λ. In [15], it was shown that even for complex OLAP queries, a λ value of 20% was typically sufficient to bring the number of POSP plans down to "anorexic levels", that is, a small absolute number within or around 10.

When we introduce the anorexic notion into the bouquet setup, it has two opposing impacts on the sub-optimality guarantees – on the one hand, the constant multiplication factor is increased by a factor $(1+\lambda)$; on the other, the value of ρ is significantly reduced. Overall, the deterministic guarantee is altered from $4\,\rho_{\text{POSP}}$ to $4\,(1+\lambda)\,\rho_{\text{ANOREXIC}}$.

Empirical evidence that this tradeoff is very beneficial is shown in Table 1, which compares for a variety of multi-dimensional error spaces, the bounds (using Equation 8) under the original POSP configuration and under an anorexic reduction ($\lambda = 20\%$). As a particularly compelling example, consider 5D_DS_Q19, a five-dimensional selectivity error space based on Q19 of TPC-DS – we observe here that the bound plunges by more than an order of magnitude, going down from 379 to 30.4.

Error Space	ρ POSP	MSO Bound	ρ ANOREXIC	MSO Bound
3D_H_Q5	11	**33**	3	**12.0**
3D_H_Q7	13	**34**	3	**9.6**
4D_H_Q8	88	**213**	7	**24.0**
5D_H_Q7	111	**342.5**	9	**37.2**
3D_DS_Q15	7	**23.5**	3	**12.0**
3D_DS_Q96	6	**22.5**	3	**13.0**
4D_DS_Q7	29	**83**	4	**17.8**
4D_DS_Q26	25	**76**	5	**19.8**
4D_DS_Q91	94	**240**	9	**35.3**
5D_DS_Q19	159	**379**	8	**30.4**

Table 1: Performance Guarantees (POSP versus Anorexic)

3.4 Cost Modeling Errors

Thus far, we had catered to arbitrary errors in selectivity estimation, but assumed that the cost model itself was perfect. In practice, this is certainly not the case, but if the modeling errors were to be unbounded, it appears hard to ensure robustness since, in principle, the estimated cost of any plan could be arbitrarily different to the actual cost encountered at run-time. However, we could think of an intermediate situation wherein the modeling errors are non-zero but *bounded* – specifically, the estimated cost of any plan, given correct selectivity inputs, is known to be within a δ error factor of the actual cost. That is, $\frac{c_{estimated}}{c_{actual}} \in [\frac{1}{(1+\delta)}, (1+\delta)]$.

Our construction is lent credence to by the recent work of [24], wherein static cost model tuning was explored in the context of PostgreSQL – they were able to achieve an average δ value of around 0.4 for the TPC-H suite of queries.

This "unbounded estimation errors, bounded modeling errors" framework is amenable to robustness analysis – specifically, it is easy to show that (proof in [12])

$$MSO_{bounded\_modeling\_error} \leq MSO_{perfect\_model} * (1+\delta)^2$$

So, for instance, when $\delta = 0.4$, corresponding to the average in [24], the MSO increases by at most a factor of 2.

4. BOUQUET: COMPILE-TIME

In this section, we describe the compile-time aspects of the bouquet algorithm, whose complete work-flow is shown in Figure 8.

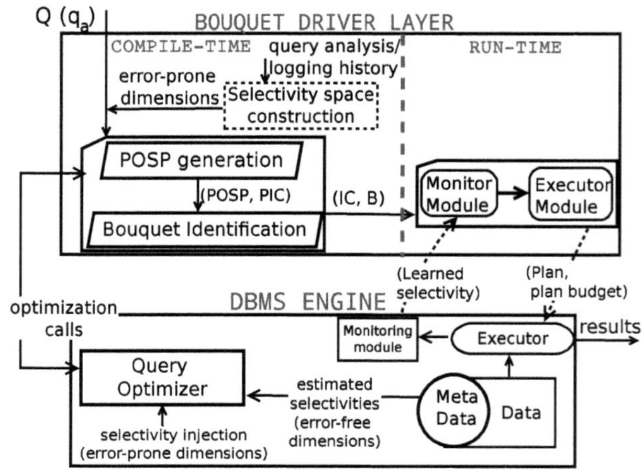

Figure 8: Architecture of Bouquet Mechanism

4.1 Selectivity Space Construction

Given a user query Q, the first step is to identify the error-prone selectivity dimensions in the query. For this purpose, we can leverage the approach proposed in [17], wherein a set of uncertainty modeling rules are outlined to classify selectivity errors into categories ranging from "no uncertainty" to "very high uncertainty". Alternatively, a log could be maintained of the errors encountered by similar queries in the workload history. Finally, there is always the fallback option of making *all* predicates where selectivities are evaluated, to be selectivity dimensions for the query.

The chosen dimensions form the ESS selectivity space. In general, each dimension ranges over the entire [0,100] percentage range – however, due to schematic constraints, the range may be reduced. For instance, the maximum legal value for a PK-FK join is the reciprocal of the PK relation's minimum row cardinality.

4.2 POSP Generation

The next step is to determine the parametric optimal set of plans (POSP) over the entire ESS. Producing the complete POSP set requires repeated invocations of the query optimizer at a high degree of resolution over the space. This process can, in principle, be computationally very expensive, especially for higher-dimensional spaces. However, user queries are often submitted through "canned" form-based interfaces – for such environments it appears feasible to offline *precompute* the entire POSP set.

Further, even when this is not the case, the overheads can be made manageable by leveraging the following observation: The full POSP set is not required, only the subset that lies on the isocost surfaces. Therefore, we begin by optimizing the two locations at the corners of the principal diagonal of the selectivity space, giving us C_{min} and C_{max}. From these values, the costs of all the isocost contours are computed. Then, the ESS is divided into smaller hypercubes, recursively dividing those hypercubes through which one or more isocost contours pass – a contour passes through a hypercube if its cost is within the cost range established by the corners of the hypercube's principal diagonal. The recursion stops when we reach hypercubes whose sizes are small enough that it is cheap to explicitly optimize all points within them. In essence, only a narrow "band" of locations around each contour is optimized.

Finally, note that the POSP generation process is "embarrassingly parallel" since each location in the ESS can be optimized independent of the others. Therefore, hardware resources in the form of multi-processor multi-core platforms can also be leveraged to bring the overheads down to practical levels.

Selectivity Injection. As discussed above, we need to be able to systematically generate queries with the desired ESS selectivities. One option is to, for each new location, suitably modify the query constants and the data distributions, but this is clearly impractically cumbersome and time-consuming. We have therefore taken an alternative approach in our PostgreSQL implementation, wherein the optimizer is instrumented to directly support *injection* of selectivity values in the cost model computations. Interestingly, some commercial optimizer APIs already support such selectivity injections to a limited extent (e.g. IBM DB2 [26]).

4.3 Plan Bouquet Identification

Armed with knowledge of the plans on each of the isocost contour surfaces, which is usually in the several tens or hundreds of plans, the next step is to carry out a cost-based anorexic reduction [15] in order to bring the plan cardinality down to a manageable number. That is, we identify a smaller set of plans, such that each replaced location now has a new plan whose cost is within (1+λ) times the optimal cost. We denote the set of plans on the surface of IC_k with B_k and the union of these sets of plans provides the final plan bouquet i.e. $B = \cup_{k=1}^{m} B_k$. Finally, the isocost surfaces (IC), annotated with their updated costs (the original costs are inflated by $1 + \lambda$ to account for the anorexic reduction), and B, the set of bouquet plans, are passed to the run-time phase.

5. BOUQUET: RUN TIME

In this section, we present the run-time aspects of the bouquet mechanism, as per the work-flow shown in Figure 8.

The basic bouquet algorithm (Figure 7) discovers the location of a query by sequentially executing the set of plans on each contour in a cost-limited manner until either one of them completes, or the plan set is exhausted, forcing a jump to the next contour. Note that in this process, no explicit monitoring of selectivities is required since the execution statuses serve as implicit indicators of whether we have reached q_a or not. However, as we will show next, consciously tracking selectivities can aid in substantively curtailing the discovery overheads. In particular, the tracking can help to (a) reduce the number of plan executions incurred in crossing contours; and (b) develop techniques for increasing the selectivity movement obtained through each cost-limited plan execution.

5.1 Reducing Contour Crossing Executions

In this optimization, during the processing of a contour, the location of q_{run} is *incrementally* updated after each (partial) plan execution to reflect the additional knowledge gained through the execution. An example learning sequence is shown in Figure 9 – here, the q_{run} known at the conclusion of IC_{k-1} is progressively updated via q^1_{run} and q^2_{run} to reach q^3_{run} on IC_k, with the corresponding plan execution sequence being P_1, P_4, P_3 (the contour superscripts are omitted for ease of exposition). The important point to observe here is that the contour crossing was accomplished *without executing* P_2.

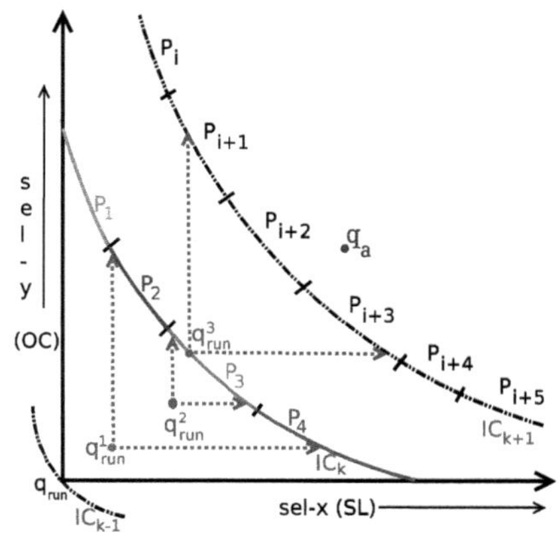

Figure 9: Minimizing Contour Crossing Executions

We now discuss how the plan execution sequence is decided. The strategy used is to ensure that at all times, the actual location is in the *first quadrant* with respect to the current location as origin – this invariant allows us to use the positive axes as a "pincer" movement towards reaching the desired target, in the process eliminating from consideration some plans on the contour. Specifically, at each q_{run} location, we first identify *AxisPlans*, the set of bouquet plans present at the *intersection* of the isocost contour with the dimensional-axes corresponding to q_{run} as origin. For example, in Figure 9, *AxisPlans*(q_{run}) is comprised of P_4 and P_1, corresponding to the x and y dimensions, respectively. Then, from within this set, we heuristically pick, using a combination of structure and cost considerations, the plan that promises to provide the maximum movement towards q_a. The specific heuristic used is the following: The plans in *AxisPlans* are first ordered based on their costs at q_{run}, and then clustered into "equivalence groups" based on the closeness of these costs. From the cheapest equivalence group, the plan with an error-prone node occurring deepest in the plan-tree is chosen for execution. The expectation is that being cheapest at q_{run} provides the maximum spare budget, while having error-prone nodes deep within the plan-tree ensures that this spare budget is not uselessly spent on processing error-free nodes.

In Figure 9, the above heuristic happens to chose P_1 at q_{run} and thereby reach q^1_{run}. The process is repeated with q_{run} set to q^1_{run} – now *AxisPlans* (q^1_{run}) is $\{P_2, P_4\}$, and P_4 is chosen by the heuristic, resulting in a movement to q^2_{run}. Finally, with q_{run} set to q^2_{run}, *AxisPlans* (q^2_{run}) contains only P_3 which is executed to reach q^3_{run}, and hence IC_k. Note, as mentioned before, that P_2 is eliminated from consideration in this incremental process.

There is a further advantage of the incremental updates to q_{run}: When we reach q^3_{run} in Figure 9, we not only learn that q_a lies beyond IC_k but can also ab initio eliminate 3 plans (P_i, P_{i+4}, P_{i+5}) from the list of candidate plans for crossing IC_{k+1}, since these plans lie outside the first quadrant of q^3_{run}.

5.2 Monitoring Selectivity Movement

Having established the utility of incremental updates to q_{run}, we now go into the details of its implementation. Consider the scenario wherein Figure 9 represents the selectivity updation process for a TPC-H based query with error-prone join selectivities s_{SL} and s_{OC} on the x and y dimensions, respectively. Correspondingly, let plans P_1 through P_4 be as shown in Figure 10. Further, each node j of these plans is labeled with the corresponding tuple count, t_j, obtained at the end of the cost-limited execution – these annotations are explicitly shown for P_1 in Figure 10.

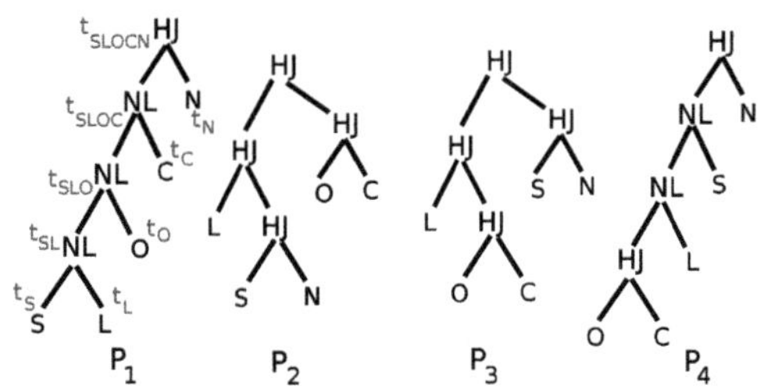

Figure 10: Plans on the kth contour

After P_1's execution, the tuple count on node SL can be utilized to update the running selectivity $\hat{s}_{SL}$ as $\frac{t_{SL}}{|S|_e \times |L|_e}$ where $|S|_e$ and $|L|_e$ denote the cardinalities of the input relations to the SL join. The values in the denominator are clearly known before execution as these nodes are assumed to be error-free. Note that $\hat{s}_{SL}$ is a *lower bound* on s_{SL}, and therefore continues to maintain the "first quadrant" invariant required by the bouquet approach.

The other selectivity s_{OC}, is not present as an independent node in plan P_1. If we directly use $\hat{s}_{OC} = \frac{t_{SLOC}}{t_{SLO} \times |C|_e}$, there is a danger of *overestimation* wrt $q_a(OC)$ since t_{SLO} may not be known completely due to the cost-budgeted execution of P_1. Such overestimations may lead to violation of the "first quadrant" property, and are therefore impermissible. Consequently, we defer the updating of s_{OC} to the subsequent execution of plans P_4 and P_3 where it can be independently computed from fully known inputs.

In general, given any plan-tree, we can learn the lower bound for an error-prone selectivity only after the cardinalities of its inputs are completely known. This is possible when either the inputs are apriori error-free, or any error-prone inputs have been completely learnt through the earlier executions. The latter method of learning allows the bouquet approach to function even in the (unlikely) case where it does not possess plans with independent appearances for all the error-prone selectivities. In the above discussion, an implicit assumption is that all selectivities are *independent* with respect to each other – this is in conformance with the typical modeling framework of current optimizers.

5.3 Maximizing Selectivity Movement

Now we discuss how individual cost-limited plan executions can be modified to yield maximum movement of q_{run} towards q_a in return for the overheads incurred in their partial executions – that is, to "get the maximum selectivity bang for the execution buck".

In executing a budgeted plan to determine error-prone selectivities, we would ideally like the cost budget to be utilized as far as possible by the nodes in the plan operator tree that can provide us *useful* learning. However, there are two hurdles that come in the way: Firstly, the costs incurred by upstream nodes that *precede* the error nodes in the plan evaluation. Secondly, the costs incurred by the downstream nodes in the *pipeline* featuring the error nodes.

The first problem of upstream nodes can be ameliorated by preferentially choosing during the *AxisPlans* routine, as mentioned earlier, plans that feature the error-prone nodes deeper (i.e. earlier) in the plan-tree. The second problem of downstream nodes can be solved by deliberately breaking the pipeline immediately after first error node and *spilling* its output, which ensures that the downstream nodes do not get any data/tuples to process. These changes help to maximize the effort spent on executing the error-prone nodes, and thereby increase the selectivity movement with a given cost budget.

Movement Example. We now illustrate, using the same example scenario as Figure 9, as to how spill-based execution is utilized to achieve increased selectivity movement. In Figure 11, the spilled versions of the plans P_1 through P_4 are shown, denoted using $\tilde{P}$. The modified selectivity discovery process using the spilled partial executions is shown in Figure 12, with the progressive selectivity locations being q^a_{run}, q^b_{run}, q^c_{run} and q^d_{run}.

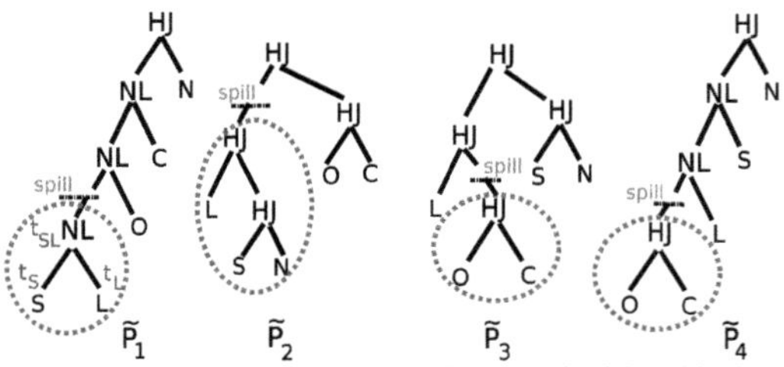

(a) along selectivity-x [S-L] (b) along selectivity-y [O-C]

Figure 11: Plans (spilled version) and their movement direction

The discovery process starts with executing plan $\tilde{P}_1$ until its cost-limit is reached. The tuple count on the error-prone node SL is then used to calculate $\hat{s}_{SL}$, as discussed earlier. Since the budget allotted for the full plan is now solely focused on learning s_{SL}, it is reasonable to expect that there will be materially more movement in s_{SL} as compared to executing generic P_1. In fact, it is easy to prove that, at the minimum, crossing of q_{run} from the third quadrant of the P_1 segment to its fourth quadrant is *guaranteed* – this minimal case is shown in Figure 12 as location q^a_{run}.

After $\tilde{P}_1$ exhausts its cost-budget, the *AxisPlans* routine chooses $\tilde{P}_4$ to take over, which starts learning s_{OC}, and ends up reaching at least q^b_{run} in Figure 12. Continuing in similar vein, $\tilde{P}_2$ is executed to reach q^c_{run}, and finally, $\tilde{P}_3$ is executed to reach q^d_{run} on the next contour. Due to focusing our energies on learning only a single selectivity in each plan execution, the movement of q_{run} follows a *Manhattan* profile from the origin upto q_a, as shown in Figure 12.

A high-level pseudocode of the full bouquet algorithm, incorporating the above optimizations, is presented in Figure 13.

5.4 Implementation Details

For implementing the bouquet mechanism, the database engine needs to support the following functionalities: (1) abstract plan costing; (2) selectivity injection during query optimization; (3) cost-limited partial execution of plans (generic and spilled); and (4) selectivity monitoring on a running basis. Abstract plan costing is supported by quite a few commercial engines including SQL Server [25], while limited selectivity injection is provided in DB2 [26]. The other two features were found to be easy to implement since they leverage pre-existing engine resources. For example, in PostgreSQL, the node-granularity tuple counter required for cost-limited execution, as well as selectivity monitoring, is available through the *instrumentation* data structure [29].

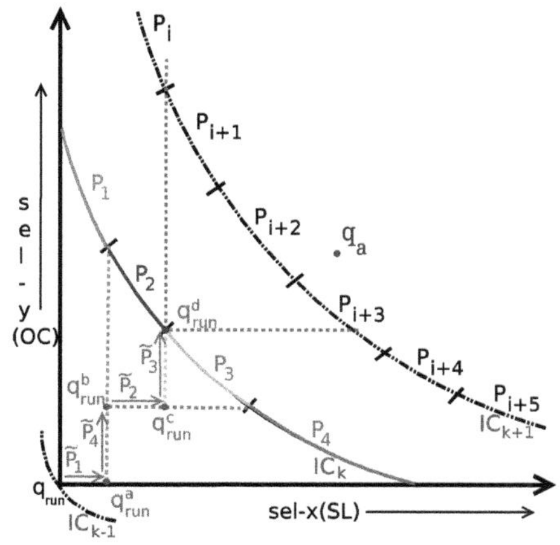

Figure 12: Maximizing Selectivity Movement

```
q_run = (0,0, ...,0);      cid = 1                          ▷ initialization
loop
    P_cur = AxisPlanRoutine(q_run, cid)                     ▷ next plan selection
    while running-cost(P_cur) ≤ cost-budget(IC_cid) do
        execute P_cur                                        ▷ cost limited execution
        if P_cur finishes execution then
            return query result
    update q_run                                             ▷ selectivity updation
    if optimal-cost(q_run) ≥ cost-budget(IC_cid) then
        cid ++                                               ▷ early contour change
```

Figure 13: Optimized Bouquet algorithm

5.5 Summary of Features

We complete this discussion of the mechanics of the bouquet approach with a synopsis of its distinctive features: (a) Compile-time estimation is completely eschewed for error-prone selectivities; (b) Plan switch decisions are triggered by predefined isocost contours (in contrast to dynamic criteria of [17, 18]); (c) Plan switch choices are restricted to an anorexic set of precomputed POSP plans; (d) AVI assumptions on intra-relational predicates are dispensed with since selectivities are explicitly monitored; (e) A first-quadrant invariant between the actual selectivity and the running selectivity is maintained, supporting monotonic progress towards the objective.

6. EXPERIMENTAL EVALUATION

We now turn our attention towards profiling the performance of the bouquet approach on a variety of complex OLAP queries, using the MSO, ASO and MH metrics enumerated in Section 2. As a precursor to these run-time metrics, we also discuss the overheads incurred by the bouquet algorithm in the compile-time phase.

Database Environment. The test queries (full descriptions in [12]) are chosen from the TPC-H and TPC-DS benchmarks to cover a spectrum of join-graph geometries, including *chain*, *star*, *branch*, etc. with the number of base relations ranging from 4 to 8. The number of error-prone selectivities range from 3 to 5 in these queries, all corresponding to join-selectivity errors, for making challenging multi-dimensional ESS spaces. We experiment with the TPC-H and TPC-DS databases at their default sizes of 1GB and 100GB, respectively, as well as larger scaled versions. Finally, the physical schema has indexes on all columns featuring in the queries, thereby maximizing the cost gradient $\frac{C_{max}}{C_{min}}$ and creating "hard-nut" environments for achieving robustness.

The summary query workload specifications are given in Table 2 – the naming nomenclature for the queries is xD_y_Qz, where x specifies the number of dimensions, y the benchmark (H or DS), and z the query number in the benchmark. So, for example, 3D_H_Q5 indicates a three-dimensional error selectivity space on Query 5 of the TPC-H benchmark.

Query	Join-graph (# relations)	$\frac{C_{max}}{C_{min}}$	Query	Join-graph (# relations)	$\frac{C_{max}}{C_{min}}$
3D_H_Q5	chain(6)	16	3D_DS_Q96	star(4)	185
3D_H_Q7	chain(6)	5	4D_DS_Q7	star(5)	283
4D_H_Q8	branch(8)	28	5D_DS_Q19	branch(6)	183
5D_H_Q7	chain(6)	50	4D_DS_Q26	star(5)	341
3D_DS_Q15	chain(4)	668	4D_DS_Q91	branch(7)	149

Table 2: Query workload specifications

System Environment. For the most part, the database engine used in our experiments is a modified version of PostgreSQL 8.4 [28], incorporating the changes outlined in Section 5.4. We also present sample results from a popular commercial optimizer. The hardware platform is a vanilla Sun Ultra 24 workstation with 8 GB memory and 1.2 TB of hard disk.

In the remainder of this section, we compare the bouquet algorithm (with anorexic parameter $\lambda = 20\%$) against the native PostgreSQL optimizer, and the SEER robust plan selection algorithm [14]. SEER uses a mathematical model of plan cost behavior in conjunction with anorexic reduction to provide replacement plans that, at all locations in ESS, either improve on the native optimizer's performance, or are worse by at most the λ factor – it is therefore expected to perform better than the native optimizer on our metrics. It is important to note here that, in the SEER framework, the comparative yardstick is P_{oe}, the optimal plan at the *estimated* location, whereas in our work, the comparison is with P_{oa}, the optimal plan at the *actual* location.[1]

For ease of exposition, we will hereafter refer to the bouquet algorithm, the native optimizer, and the SEER algorithm as **BOU**, **NAT** and **SEER**, respectively, in presenting the results.

6.1 Compile-time Overheads

The computationally expensive aspect of BOU's compile-time phase is the identification of the POSP set of plans in ESS. For this task, we use the contour-focused approach described in Section 4, which ignores most of the space lying between contours. In all of our queries, the number of contours was no more than 10. Therefore, the contour-POSP was generated within a *few hours* even for 5D scenarios on our generic workstation, which appears a feasible investment for canned queries. Moreover, as described in Section 4.2, these overheads could be brought down to a few minutes, thanks to the inherent parallelism in the task.

6.2 Worst-case Performance (MSO)

In Figure 14, the MSO performance is profiled, on a log scale, for a set of 10 representative queries submitted to NAT, SEER and BOU. The first point to note is that NAT is *not* inherently robust – to the contrary, its MSO is huge, ranging from around 10^3 to 10^7. Secondly, SEER also does not provide any material improvement on NAT – this may seem paradoxical at first glance, but is only to be expected once we realize that not *all* the highly sub-optimal (q_e, q_a) combinations in NAT were necessarily helped in

[1]Purely heuristic-based reoptimization techniques, such as POP [18] and Rio [4], are not included in the evaluation suite since their performance could be arbitrarily poor with regard to both P_{oe} and P_{oa}, as explained in [12].

the SEER framework. Finally, and in marked contrast, BOU provides *orders of magnitude* improvements over NAT and SEER – as a case in point, for 5D_DS_Q19, BOU drives MSO down from 10^6 to around just 10. In fact, even in absolute terms, it consistently provides an MSO of *less than ten* across all the queries.

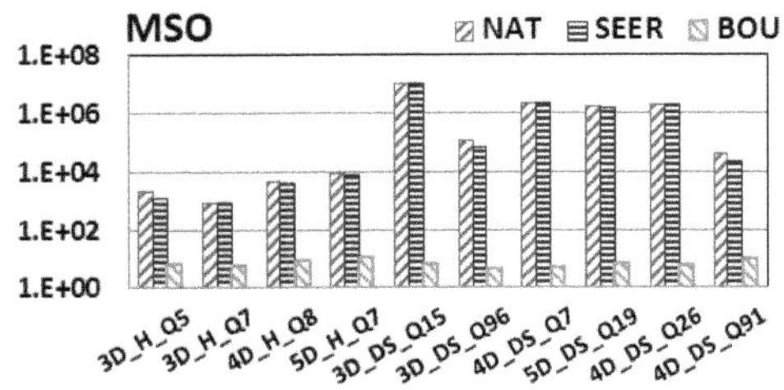

Figure 14: MSO Performance (log-scale)

6.3 Average-case Performance (ASO)

At first glance, it may be surmised that BOU's dramatic improvement in worst-case behavior is purchased through a corresponding deterioration of average-case performance. To quantitatively demonstrate that this is not so, we evaluate ASO for NAT, SEER and BOU in Figure 15, again on a log scale. We see here that for some queries (e.g. 3D_DS_Q15), ASO of BOU is much better than that of NAT, while for the remainder (e.g. 4D_H_Q8) the performance is comparable. Even more gratifyingly, the ASO in absolute terms is typically less than 4 for BOU. On the other hand, SEER's performance is again similar to that of NAT – this is an outcome of the high dimensionality of the error space which makes it extremely difficult to find universally safe replacements that are also substantively beneficial.

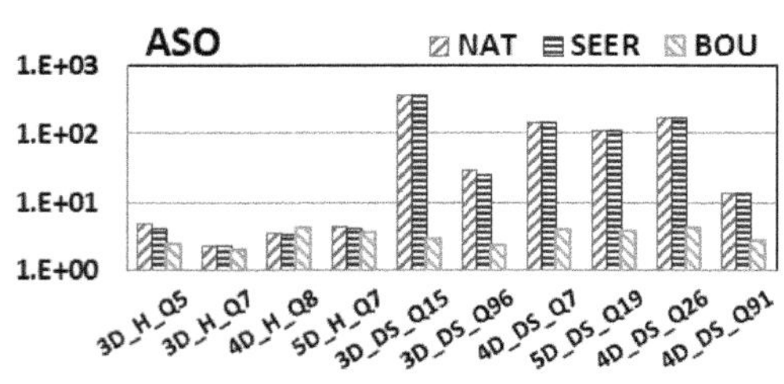

Figure 15: ASO Performance (log-scale)

6.4 Spatial Distribution of Robustness

We now profile for a sample query, namely 5D_DS_Q19, the percentage of locations for which BOU has a specific range of improvement over NAT. That is, the *spatial distribution* of enhanced robustness, $\frac{SubOpt_{worst}(q_a)}{SubOpt(*,q_a)}$. This statistic is shown in Figure 16, where we find that for the vast majority of locations (close to 90%), BOU provides *two or more orders of magnitude improvement* with respect to NAT. SEER, on the other hand, provides significant improvement over NAT for specific (q_e, q_a) combinations, but may not materially help the *worst-case* instance for each q_a. Therefore, we find that its robustness enhancement is less than 10 at all locations in the ESS.

6.5 Adverse Impact of Bouquet (MH)

Thus far, we have presented the improvements due to BOU. However, as highlighted in Section 2, there may be *individual* q_a

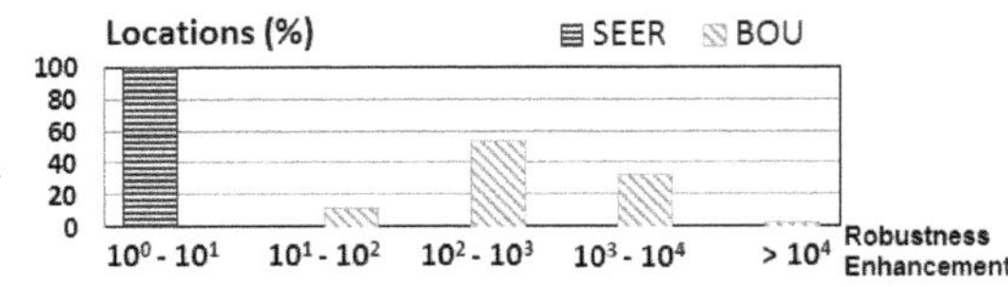

Figure 16: Distribution of enhanced Robustness (5D_DS_Q19)

locations where BOU performs poorer than NAT's worst-case, i.e. $SubOpt(*,q_a) > SubOpt_{worst}(q_a)$. This aspect is quantified in Figure 17 where the maximum harm is shown (on a linear scale) for our query test suite. We observe that BOU may be upto a factor of 4 worse than NAT. Moreover, SEER steals a march over BOU since it *guarantees* that MH never exceeds λ (= 0.2). However, the important point to note is that the percentage of locations for which harm is incurred by BOU is less than 1% of the space. Therefore, from an overall perspective, the likelihood of BOU adversely impacting performance is rare, and even in these few cases the harm is limited ($\leq$ MSO-1), especially when viewed against the order of magnitude improvements achieved in the beneficial scenarios.

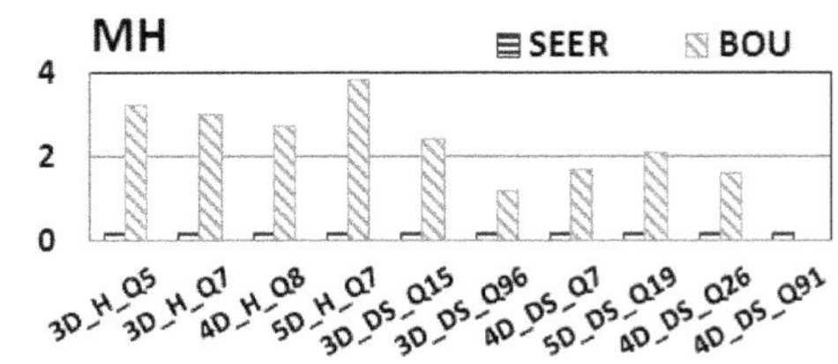

Figure 17: MaxHarm performance

6.6 Plan Cardinalities

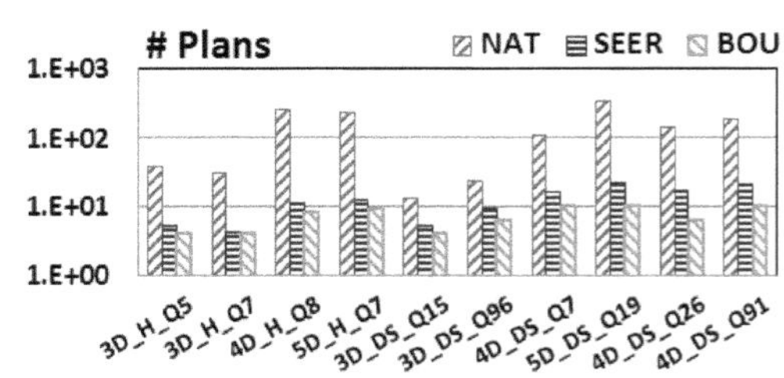

Figure 18: Plan Cardinalities (log-scale)

The plan cardinalities of NAT, SEER and BOU are shown on a log-scale in Figure 18. We observe here that although the original POSP cardinality may be in the several tens or hundreds, the number of plans in SEER is orders of magnitude lower, and those retained in BOU is even smaller – only around 10 or fewer, even for the 5D queries. This is primarily due to the initial anorexic reduction and the subsequent confinement to plan contours. The important implication of these statistics is that the bouquet size is, to the first degree of approximation, effectively *independent of the dimensionality and complexity of the error space.*

6.7 Query Execution Times (TPC-H)

To verify that the promised benefits of BOU are actually delivered at run-time, we also carried out experiments wherein query response times were explicitly measured for NAT and BOU. For this purpose, we crafted query instance 2D_H_Q8a (details in [12]), whose q_a was $(33.7\%, 45.6\%)$, but NAT erroneously estimated the location to be $q_e = (3.8\%, 0.02\%)$ due to incorrect AVI assumptions.[2] As a result, the plan chosen by NAT took almost *580 seconds* to complete, whereas the optimal plan at q_a finished in merely 16 seconds, i.e SubOpt(q_e, q_a) ≈ 36.

When BOU was invoked on the same 2D_H_Q8a query, it identified 6 bouquet plans spread across 7 isocost contours, resulting in an MSO bound of less than 20 (Equation 8). Subsequently, basic BOU produced the query result in about 117 seconds, involving 18 partial executions to cross 5 contours before the final full execution. Moreover, optimized BOU further brought the running time down to less than 70 seconds, using only 11 partial executions.

The isocost-contour-wise breakups of both basic and optimized BOU are given in Table 3, along with a comparative summary of their performance. Overall, the sub-optimality of optimized BOU is ≈ 4, almost an order of magnitude lower than that of NAT (≈ 36). Note that the intended doubling of execution times across contours does not fully hold in Table 3 – this is an artifact of the imperfections in the underlying cost model of the PostgreSQL optimizer, compounded by our not having tuned this default model.

Contour ID	Avg Plan Exec. Time (in sec)	# Exec. (Basic BOU)	Time(sec) (Basic BOU)	# Exec. (Opt. BOU)	Time(sec) (Opt. BOU)
1	0.6	2	1.2	2	1.2
2	3.1	4	12.4	2	6.2
3	4.8	4	19.2	3	14.4
4	6.2	5	31.0	3	18.6
5	12.2	3	36.6	1	12.2
6	16.1	1	16.1	1	16.1
Total		**19**	**116.5**	**12**	**68.7**

Performance Summary (in seconds)	NAT	Basic BOU	Opt. BOU	Optimal
	579.4	116.5	68.7	16.1

Table 3: Bouquet execution for 2D_H_Q8a

6.8 Commercial Database Engine

All the results presented thus far were obtained on our instrumented PostgreSQL engine. We now present sample evaluations on a popular commercial engine, hereafter referred to as COM. Since COM's API does not directly support injection of selectivities, we constructed queries 3D_H_Q5b and 4D_H_Q8b (details in [12]), wherein all error dimensions correspond to selection predicates on the base relations – the selectivities on such dimensions can be indirectly set up through changing only the constants in the query. The database and system environment remained identical to that of the PostgreSQL experiments.

Focusing on the performance aspects, shown in Figure 19, we find that here also large values of MSO and ASO are obtained for NAT and SEER. Further, BOU continues to provide substantial improvements on these metrics with a small sized bouquet. Again, the robustness enhancement is at least an order of magnitude for more than 90% of the query locations, without incurring any harm at the remaining locations (MH < 0). These results imply that our earlier observations are not artifacts of a specific engine.

7. RELATED WORK

A rich body of literature is available pertaining to selectivity estimation issues [11]. We start with the overview of the closely related techniques which can be collectively termed as *plan-switching approaches*, as they involve run-time switching among complete query plans. At first glance, our bouquet approach, with its partial

[2]We explicitly verified that there were no estimation errors in the remaining selectivity dimensions of the query.

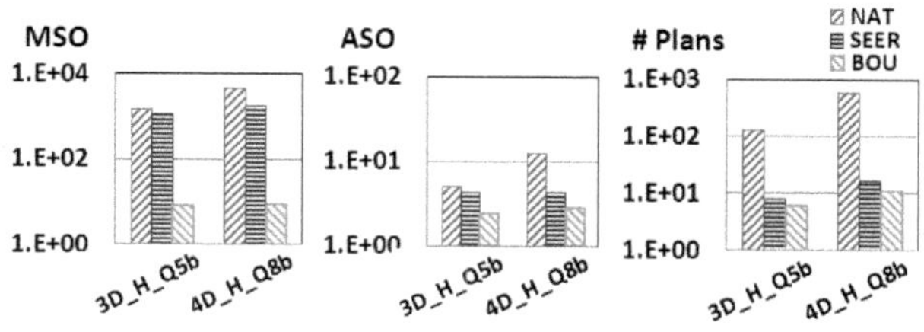

Figure 19: Commercial Engine Performance (log-scale)

execution of multiple plans, may appear very similar to run-time re-optimization techniques such as POP [18] and Rio [4]. However, there are key differences: Firstly, they start with the optimizer's estimate as the initial seed, and then conduct a full-scale re-optimization if the estimate are found to be significantly in error. In contrast, we always start from the origin of the selectivity space, and directly choose plans from the bouquet for execution without invoking the optimizer again. A beneficial and unique side-effect of this start-from-origin approach is that it assures repeatability of the query execution strategy.

Secondly, both POP and Rio are based on heuristics and do not provide any performance bounds. In particular, POP may get stuck with a poor plan since its validity ranges are defined using structure-equivalent plans only. Similarly, Rio's sampling-based heuristics for monitoring selectivities may not work well for join-selectivities and its definition of plan robustness on the basis of performance at corners (principal diagonal) has not been justified.

Recently, a novel interleaved optimization and execution approach was proposed in [20] wherein plan fragments are selectively executed, when recommended by an error propagation framework, to guard against the fallout of estimation errors. The error framework leverages an elegant histogram construction mechanism from [19] that minimizes the multiplicative error. While this technique substantively reduces the execution overheads, it provides no guarantees as it is largely based on heuristics.

Techniques that use a single plan during the entire query execution [9, 3, 14, 19, 6] run into the basic infeasibility of a single plan to be near-optimal across the entire selectivity space. The bouquet mechanism overcomes this problem by identifying a small set of plans that collectively provide the near-optimality property. Further, it does not require any prior knowledge of the query workload or the database contents. On the other hand, the use of only one active plan (at a time) to process the data makes the bouquet algorithm dissimilar from *Routing-based approaches* wherein different data segments may be routed to different simultaneously active plans – for example, plan per tuple [2] and plan per tuple group [21].

Our technique may superficially look similar to PQO techniques, (e.g. PPQO [5]), since a set of plans are identified before execution by exploring the selectivity space. The primary difference is that these techniques are useful for saving on optimization time for query instances with known parameters and selectivities. On the other hand, our goal is to regulate the worst case performance impact when the computed selectivities are likely to be erroneous.

Further, the bouquet technique does not modify plan structures at run-time (modulo spilling directives). This is a major difference from "plan-morphing" approaches, where the execution plan may be substantially modified at run-time using custom-designed operators, e.g. *chooseplan* [10], *switch* [4], *feedback* [7].

Finally, we emphasize that our goal of minimizing the worst case performance in the presence of unbounded selectivity errors, does not coincide with any of the earlier works in this area. Previously considered objectives include (a) improved performance compared to the optimizer generated plan [4, 14, 17, 18, 20]; (b) improved average performance and/or reduced variance [9, 6, 3]; (c) improved accuracy of selectivity estimation structures [1]; and (d) bounded impact of multiplicative estimation errors [19].

8. CRITIQUE OF BOUQUET APPROACH

Having presented the mechanics and performance of the bouquet approach, we now take a step back and critique the technique.

The bouquet approach is intended for use in difficult estimation environments – that is, in database setups where accurate selectivity estimation is hard to achieve. However, when estimation errors are apriori known to be small, re-optimization techniques such as [18, 4], which use the optimizer's estimate as the initial seed, are likely to converge much quicker than the bouquet algorithm, which requires starting at the origin to ensure the first quadrant invariant. But, if the estimates were apriori guaranteed to be *under-estimates*, then the bouquet algorithm can also leverage the initial seed.

Being a *plan-switching* approach, the bouquet technique suffers from the drawbacks generic to such approaches: Firstly, they are poor at serving *latency-sensitive* applications as they have to perforce wait for the final plan execution to return result tuples. Secondly, they are not recommended for update queries since maintaining transactional consistency with multiple executions may incur significant overheads to rollback the effects of the aborted partial executions. Finally, with single-plan optimizers, DBAs use their domain knowledge to fine-tune the plan using "plan-hints". But this is not straightforward in *plan-switching* techniques since the actual plan sequence is determined only at run-time. Notwithstanding the limitations, such techniques are now featured even in commercial products (e.g. [27]).

There are also a few problems that are *specific* to the bouquet approach: Firstly, while it is inherently robust to changes in data *distribution*, since these changes only shift the location of q_a in the existing ESS, the same is not true with regard to database *scale-up*. That is, if the database size increases significantly, then the original ESS no longer covers the entire error space. An obvious solution to handle this problem is to recompute the bouquet from scratch, but most of the processing may turn out to be redundant. Therefore, developing incremental bouquet maintenance strategies is an interesting future research challenge.

Secondly, the bouquet identification overheads increase exponentially with dimensionality. Apart from the obvious amortization over repeated query invocations, we also described some mechanisms for reducing these overheads in Section 6.1. Further, a complex query does not necessarily imply a commensurately large number of error dimensions because: (i) The selectivities of base relation predicates of the form "*column op constant*" can be estimated accurately with current techniques; (ii) The join-selectivities for PK-FK joins can be estimated accurately if the entire PK-relation participates in the join; (iii) The partial derivatives of the POSP plan cost functions along each dimension can be computed on a low resolution mapping of the ESS, and any dimension with a small derivative across all the plans can be eliminated since its cost impact is marginal.

Thirdly, the identification of ESS dimensions may not always be straightforward. For example, in cyclic queries, different plans may combine predicates in different ways. One option to handle this scenario is to first construct the ESS using individual predicates as dimensions. Then, assuming that predicate independence holds, the selectivity of any predicate combination could be *inferred* using the existing values for the individual constituent predicates.

Given the above discussion, the bouquet approach is currently recommended specifically for providing response-time robustness in large archival read-only databases supporting complex decision-support applications that are likely to suffer significant estimation errors. We expect that many of today's OLAP installations may fall into this category.

In closing, we wish to highlight that the bouquet approach provides novel performance guarantees that open up new possibilities for robust query processing.

Acknowledgments. We thank the anonymous reviewers and S. Sudarshan, Prasad Deshpande, Srinivas Karthik, Sumit Neelam and Bruhathi Sundarmurthy for their constructive comments on this work.

9. REFERENCES

[1] A. Aboulnaga and S. Chaudhuri, "Self-tuning Histograms: Building Histograms without Looking at Data", *ACM SIGMOD Conf.*, 1999.

[2] R. Avnur and J. Hellerstein, "Eddies: Continuously Adaptive Query Processing", *ACM SIGMOD Conf.*, 2000.

[3] B. Babcock and S. Chaudhuri, "Towards a Robust Query Optimizer: A Principled and Practical Approach", *ACM SIGMOD Conf.*, 2005.

[4] S. Babu, P. Bizarro and D. DeWitt, "Proactive Re-Optimization", *ACM SIGMOD Conf.*, 2005.

[5] P. Bizarro, N. Bruno, D. Dewitt, "Progressive Parametric Query Optimization", *IEEE TKDE*, 21(4), 2009.

[6] S. Chaudhuri, H. Lee and V. Narasayya, "Variance aware optimization of parameterized queries", *ACM SIGMOD Conf.*, 2010.

[7] S. Chaudhuri, V. Narasayya and R. Ramamurthy, "A Pay-As-You-Go Framework for Query Execution Feedback", *PVLDB*, 1(1), 2008.

[8] M. Chrobak, C. Kenyon, J. Noga and N. Young, "Incremental Medians via Online Bidding", *Algorithmica*, 50(4), 2008.

[9] F. Chu, J. Halpern and J. Gehrke, "Least Expected Cost Query Optimization: What Can We Expect", *ACM PODS Conf.*, 2002.

[10] R. Cole and G. Graefe, "Optimization of Dynamic Query Evaluation Plans", *ACM SIGMOD Conf.*, 1994.

[11] A. Deshpande, Z. Ives and V. Raman, "Adaptive Query Processing", *Foundations and Trends in Databases*, Now Publishers, 2007.

[12] A. Dutt and J. Haritsa, "Query Processing without Selectivity Estimation", *Tech. Report TR-2014-01*, DSL/SERC, IISc, 2014, dsl.serc.iisc.ernet.in/publications/report/TR/TR-2014-01.pdf

[13] G. Graefe et al, "Robust Query Processing (Dagstuhl Seminar 12321)", *Dagstuhl Reports*, 2(8), 2012.

[14] Harish D., P. Darera and J. Haritsa, "Identifying Robust Plans through Plan Diagram Reduction", *PVLDB*, 1(1), 2008.

[15] Harish D., P. Darera and J. Haritsa, "On the Production of Anorexic Plan Diagrams", *VLDB Conf.*, 2007.

[16] Y. Ioannidis and S. Christodoulakis, "On the Propagation of Errors in the Size of Join Results", *ACM SIGMOD Conf.* 1991.

[17] N. Kabra and D. DeWitt, "Efficient Mid-Query Re-Optimization of Sub-Optimal Query Execution Plans", *ACM SIGMOD Conf.* 1998.

[18] V. Markl et al, "Robust Query Processing through Progressive Optimization", *ACM SIGMOD Conf.*, 2004.

[19] G. Moerkotte, T. Neumann and G. Steidl, "Preventing Bad Plans by Bounding the Impact of Cardinality Estimation Errors", *PVLDB*, 2(1), 2009.

[20] T. Neumann and C. Galindo-Legaria, "Taking the Edge off Cardinality Estimation Errors using Incremental Execution", *BTW Conf.*, 2013.

[21] N. Polyzotis, "Selectivity-based partitioning: A Divide and Union Paradigm for Effective Query Optimization", *ACM CIKM Conf.*, 2005.

[22] P. Selinger et al, "Access Path Selection in a Relational Database Management System", *ACM SIGMOD Conf.*, 1979.

[23] M. Stillger, G. Lohman, V. Markl and M. Kandil, "LEO – DB2's LEarning Optimizer", *VLDB Conf.*, 2001.

[24] W. Wu et al, "Predicting Query Execution Times: Are Optimizer Cost Models Really Usable?", *IEEE ICDE Conf.*, 2013.

[25] technet.microsoft.com/en-us/library/ms186954(v=sql.105).aspx

[26] www.ibm.com/developerworks/data/library/tips/dm-0312yip/

[27] www.oracle.com/ocom/groups/public/@otn/documents/webcontent/1963236.pdf

[28] www.postgresql.org/docs/8.4/static/release.html

[29] doxygen.postgresql.org/structInstrumentation.html

Schema-free SQL*

Fei Li
Univ. of Michigan, Ann Arbor
lifei@umich.edu

Tianyin Pan
Univ. of Michigan, Ann Arbor
ptianyin@umich.edu

H. V. Jagadish
Univ. of Michigan, Ann Arbor
jag@umich.edu

ABSTRACT

Querying data in relational databases is often challenging since SQL requires its users to know the exact schema of the database, the roles of various entities in a query, and the precise join paths to be followed. On the other hand, keyword search is unable to express much desired query semantics.

In this paper, we propose a query language, Schema-free SQL, which enables its users to query a relational database using whatever partial schema they know. If they know the full schema, they can write full SQL. But, to the extent they do not know the schema, Schema-free SQL is tolerant of unknown or inaccurately specified relation names and attribute names, and it also does not require information regarding which relations are involved and how they are joined. We present techniques to evaluate Schema-free SQL by first converting it to full SQL. We show experimentally that a small amount of schema information, which one can reasonably expect most users to have, is enough to get queries evaluated as if they had been completely and correctly specified.

Categories and Subject Descriptors

H.2.3 [**Database Management**]: Languages—*Query languages*; H.1.2 [**Information Systems**]: User/Machine Systems—*Human factors*

Keywords

Query Language; Relational Databases; Usability;

1. INTRODUCTION

Querying data in relational databases is often challenging. SQL is the standard method to query relational databases. While expressive and powerful, SQL requires its users to know the exact schema of the database, the roles of various entities in a query, and the precise join paths to be followed. This difficulty is exacerbated by normalization, a process that is central to relational database design, which brings benefits including saved space and avoided update anomalies, at the cost of spreading data across several relations and thus making the database schema more complex. Where queries are predictable, forms-based interfaces and other application-mediated mechanisms can be used. However, these techniques do not support ad hoc queries.

To address these difficulties, there has been a stream of research towards querying information from databases using keywords [6, 4, 8]. In keyword search, the users need to know neither a query language nor the underlying logical structure of the database. All they need to do is to type in some keywords. While very friendly to use, there are intrinsic ambiguities in using an unstructured set of keywords to convey complex information needs. Without properly specified structure information, it is very hard for a system to return prefect query results. Furthermore, keyword search loses many commonly used functions provided by SQL, such as comparison, computation, ordering and aggregation.

Our goal in this paper is to provide means for a user to specify queries without the burden of precise schema knowledge while at the same time not burdening the system with having to guess the desired result of keyword search. Before we describe our approach towards this goal, let us examine a motivating example to appreciate the issues.

Consider a movie database with a simplified schema shown in Figure 1. When trying to use keywords to express the query example, many difficulties arise. First, traditional keyword search is designed to find keywords in database values rather than in metadata. Keywords cannot convey the information that "male" relates to "actor" and that "James Cameron" relates to "director". Fielded keyword queries have been suggested as a means towards addressing this difficulty part-way, but typically require that field names be specified precisely. Moreover, keywords cannot express comparisons and computations such as the clause "from 1995 to 2005". Similarly, "the number of", which is an aggregation function, is not supported in keyword search.

In short, an unstructured set of keywords is not capable of capturing the rich semantics of query intent required to produce good answers. Surely, we can all remember situations where we were frustrated because we couldn't specify some crucial structure in a query (e.g. movies before 2005). Though such distinctions are easy to make in SQL, writing SQL has its own challenges, as we see next.

In Figure 1, the movie information is split into six relations after normalization. As a result, even queries over such

*Supported in part by NSF grants IIS 1250880 and IIS 1017296

SIGMOD'14, June 22–27, 2014, Snowbird, UT, USA.

http://dx.doi.org/10.1145/2588555.2588571.

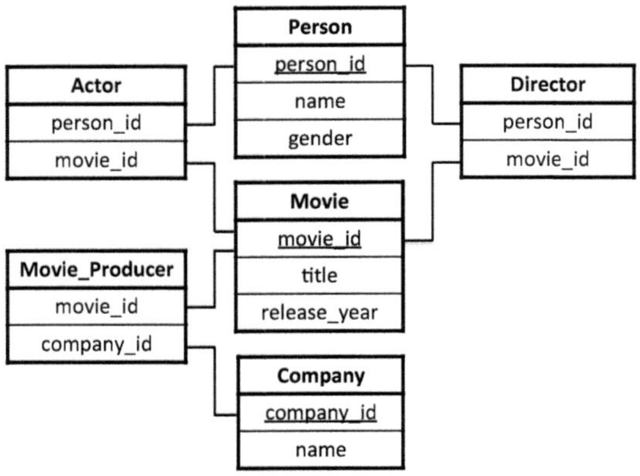

Query Example: Return the number of male actors who have cooperated with director "James Cameron" in a production by "20th Century Fox" from 1995 to 2005.

Figure 1: Running Example.

a tiny schema may be hard to compose in SQL. For example, a simple query for (the name of) the director of "Star Wars" requires a join of three tables (Person, Director, and Movie). The reader can verify that the query example requires joining 7 relations: all 6 relations in the figure and one of them (Person) twice. The corresponding SQL query has over a dozen clauses. Furthermore, it involves tables (such as Person) and columns (such as Person_id) that are not present in the English language statement of the query intent. Only someone knowledgeable about the schema can figure out that these are required. The situation gets much worse in real-world databases when there are large numbers of relations (The Yahoo! Movie database has 43 relations). We have personal experience with scientist collaborators struggling with such schema issues as they attempt to conduct "e-science".

Writing correct SQL is challenging not only for new users, but also for professional DBAs who have to deal with complex enterprise schemas. Even technically competent programmers in MIS shops would appreciate being freed from having to remember large schemas and specify error-prone long sequences of joins. It would be beneficial if users can use SQL structure to express their query logic without spending time to understand the schema in detail.

The basic idea in Schema-free SQL is to reduce the user's burden in writing SQL queries through two important relaxations:

1. *Schema Relaxation*: users do not have to specify schema elements exactly, including relation names and attribute names.
2. *Join Path Relaxation*: users do not need to specify join paths, including which intermediate relations are involved and how they are joined with one another.

If no schema element or join path is specified, observe that the SQL query degrades to a set of attribute values (keywords), but with SQL structure. For example, it is still possible to query for an attribute that is greater than 1995. (In contrast, a pure keyword system could only look for attribute values equal to 1995). However, our relaxation is not that schema information must not be specified, but rather that it *may* not be specified. In other words, to the extent that the user is able to guess (or know) element names and join paths, the user should be able to include it. In the extreme case, the user may even specify a full SQL query, with no relaxation at all. However, in a typical situation, the user will specify as much as they can with ease, and the system should take care of the rest.

EXAMPLE 1. *Figure 2 shows an example of Schema-free SQL for the query example in Figure 1. Observe that many relation names and attribute names are guessed wrong, but are nevertheless intuitively informative. Observe also that the query assumes a database structure different from the actual. For example, it refers to actor.name even though name is not an attribute of the relation Actor: it is the system's responsibility to understand that this refers to Person.name through a join between Person and Actor. Observe, further, that there isn't even a requirement that the user be consistent. For example, the query has in it actor.name and also director_name. Finally, note that the join through Movie remains implicit in this query just as it was in the English language version: while the user may have been able to specify this crucial element, this is exactly the sort of hidden assumption that requires a high level of understanding of the underlying database schema to make it explicit.*

```
SELECT count(actor?.name?)
WHERE actor?.gender? = "male"
    and director_name? = "James Cameron"
    and produce_company? = "20th Century Fox"
    and year? > 1995
    and year? < 2005;
```

Figure 2: Schema-free SQL.

Typically, a schema-free SQL query will be evaluated by an RDBMS after mapping each vague schema element to its similar schema elements in the database, and autocompleting the join path using the strongest join network that connects all the specified schema elements. Specifically, in the mapping process, we first preprocess all schema elements specified in a Schema-free SQL into a set of *relation trees*, in which each relation tree collects user specified schema elements relevant to the same relation. Then, we map relation trees to relations in the database based on a proposed similarity function. In the join path generation, we define the strength for join networks on *view graph*, which is a modification to schema graph. A view graph represents as views all known join path fragments, including those specified by the user and observed from query logs. Intuitively, the join networks constructed from these views are more likely to be "good" join paths than those constructed by connecting each single relation. Based on this intuition, in our system, a join network tends to be evaluated stronger if it contains views. Experimental results show that the strongest join networks generated on view graph are more likely to be the correct join path than those generated on schema graph.

The intellectual contributions of this paper are as follows:

1. *Schema-free SQL Framework.* We present Schema-free SQL in which users can query relational databases with whatever partial knowledge of the schema they have, all the way from full SQL to just keywords.
2. *System Architecture.* In Section 2, we describe a modular architecture that supports Schema-free SQL.

3. *Relation Tree.* In Section 3, we propose relation tree as a data structure to uniformly represent all specified schema elements. We then define an *l-relation trees query* as a generalization of an *l*-keyword search. The result of an *l*-relation trees query is a join network of relations, which contains all the information we need to transform a Schema-free SQL into a full SQL query. However, obtaining a good join network requires some creativity, as we discuss next.
4. *View Graph.* In Section 5, we define view graph as a modification to schema graph, which is widely used in keyword search. Using this concept, we propose algorithms for join networks generation in Section 6.

Other parts of the paper are organized as follows. In Section 4, we provide similarity evaluation functions to map relation trees to relations in the database. In Section 7, the usability and accuracy of our method is tested experimentally. We discuss related work in Section 8. In Section 9, we draw conclusions and point to future work.

2. OVERVIEW

In this section, we define the syntax and semantics of Schema-free SQL and describe the system architecture.

2.1 Syntax and Semantics

Schema-free SQL is an extension of SQL and hence can support all the functions provided by SQL. It follows the syntax of SQL with two relaxations:

1. **Schema Relaxation**: Users do not have to specify the exact schema elements including relation names and attribute names. They can express their uncertainty by means of a question mark in three ways:

   (a) "foo?" indicates that the user guesses the name of the element is foo, but is not sure about this. In the SELECT clause of the query in Figure 2, the user thinks there is a relation called "actor" with an attribute called "name".

   (b) "?x" indicates that the user has no clue about its name. She calls it x as a placeholder. The variable x can be used elsewhere in the query to indicate the same element and distinguish it from other elements, whatever be its name.

   (c) "?" also indicates an element for which the user has no clue of its name. The user doesn't have to bind it to a dummy variable name (such as x in the preceding case). The system generates a unique new dummy variable for each occurrence.

   Users may also choose not to mention the schema element at all. In the WHERE clause of the query in Figure 2, the user mentions an attribute called "year?" without saying which relation it comes from.

2. **Join Path Relaxation**: Users do not need to specify which relations are involved and how they are joined with each other. They can just leave the FROM clause blank (or partially populated), and leave out the foreign-key-primary-key (FK-PK) join path (in the WHERE clause). They can introduce relation names (exact or approximate) in other clauses (such as WHERE and SELECT) without these relations having been mentioned in the FROM clause.

A Schema-free SQL query is an under-specified SQL query, with under-specifications on account of only the two relaxations listed above. In consequence, Schema-free SQL supports all of SQL, including nesting, aggregation, and the many obscure functions provided in any particular vendor-specific implementation.

Once these relaxations are resolved, we obtain a fully specified SQL query, with the usual SQL semantics. Fixing the relaxations in Schema-free SQL is an inherently heuristic task, in which the goal is to infer the user's intent. Specifically, the schema relaxation is resolved by binding each vague schema element to its similar schema elements in the database, while the underspecified join path is completed by the strongest join network that connects all the bound schema elements.

2.2 Architecture

Our system first fixes the two relaxations in a Schema-free SQL query, then translates it into a standard SQL query and finally evaluates it to get accurate query results (it also supports returning top k translations directly to the user before evaluating the best one). A high level representation of the architecture is shown in Figure 3. The Relation Tree Mapper is used to fix the schema relaxation and the Network Builder fixes the join path relaxation. These two main modules are preceded by a Schema-free SQL Parser and succeeded by a Standard SQL Composer. Here we describe these four components of the system intuitively. A more precise and detailed description will have to wait until the following sections.

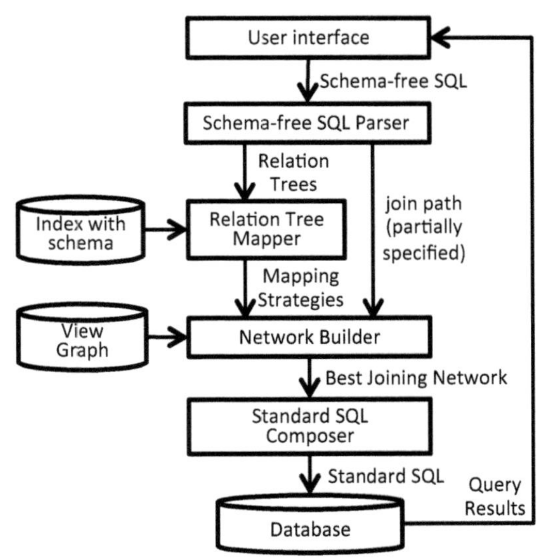

Figure 3: System Architecture.

2.2.1 Schema-free SQL Parser

The schema elements and join paths that users specify in Schema-free SQL can be vague and fragmentary. The Schema-free SQL Parser separates the schema elements and join paths from the rest of the query, which will remain unchanged. The schema elements are merged and uniformly represented as a set of trees called *Relation Trees* while the join paths (if partially specified) are represented by *views* as we will discuss below.

2.2.2 Relation Tree Mapper

For a traditional l-keyword search, it is easy to map a keyword to relations: if one of the tuples in the relation contains the keyword, the keyword can be mapped to that relation. But in the case of mapping relation trees, this is not that obvious since relation trees have a much more complex structure with multiple components to be matched. In the Relation Tree Mapper, we first evaluate the similarity between relation trees and relations in the database, then map them based on their similarity.

2.2.3 Network Builder

To get the full SQL query, we need to generate the correct join network of relations that contains all the relation trees. There is a combinatorial number of possible join networks, only one (or, occasionally, a few) of which is correct. The network builder generates join networks using a view graph, which models all supervised information (e.g. join path fragments specified by the user, query patterns in query logs) as views. Intuitively, join networks composed of these views are more likely to be correct than those constructed by connecting each single relation from scratch. We present ways to rank all join networks and develop algorithms to generate the top k join networks efficiently.

2.2.4 Standard SQL Composer

Each join network obtained from the previous step gives a possible interpretation of the Schema-free SQL query. Based on the join path in this network, and the mapping strategy used, the Standard SQL Composer instantiates exact schema elements in place of user's guesses, introduces appropriate join conditions in the WHERE clause, and fills in the FROM clause. The result is a correctly formed SQL query, which hopefully matches the user's intent. Note that k different SQL queries can be output, one for each join network returned from the preceding step. Typically, we may set k to 1, evaluate the full SQL translated and return the query results to the user. However, the system architecture is capable of returning multiple options when desired.

2.2.5 Nested Query

The sequence of steps described above applies only to a single-block SQL query. Given a nested query, it is processed one block at a time, starting from the outermost block, so that values for any correlated variables and other context is already set when inner blocks are processed.

3. REPRESENTING SCHEMA-FREE CONTENT

Our first task is to instantiate the correct names for all relations and attributes that are insufficiently (or even incorrectly) specified in a given Schema-free SQL query. As a starting point, we have the guesses at names provided by the user in the query itself. Additionally, we may have guesses at structure, relating attribute to table, in the query. Finally, we may have values for some attributes in the query specification, giving us a hint of what those attributes may be. To put all of these constraints together in one framework, we introduce the concept of *relation tree* in this section. Then, in the next section, we consider how to map relation trees to the actual schema of the existing database.

As a first step towards obtaining relation trees, we denote each occurrence of schema-related content by an expression triple, comprising relation name, attribute name, and value condition, some of which may be undefined or inapplicable.

3.1 Expression Triples

There are altogether three kinds of schema-relevant expressions in Schema-free SQL: (a) the relation names in *FROM clause*, both original names and aliases, (b) the attribute names (together with relation names if specified) in all other clauses, and (c) the value constraint conditions (together with relation names and attribute names if specified) in *WHERE clause*. All other information in the query is considered schema-irrelevant, including (a) general keywords like: SELECT, FROM, WHERE, GROUP BY, ORDER BY, ASC, OR, (b) aggregation keywords like SUM, COUNT, MAX, (c) Computation symbols like +, -, *.

EXAMPLE 2. *In the query example in Figure 2, consider the clause "SELECT count(actor?.name?)". We do not need to know what "SELECT" and "count" mean. Instead, the only thing we need to do is to map "actor?.name?" to the attribute "Person.name" in the database. Then the clause is transformed to "SELECT count(Person.name)", which is the SELECT clause in the standard SQL.*

We uniformly represent all expressions as *expression triples* with three entries. The three entries store the relation name, attribute name and condition constraint, respectively. If an expression does not specify the relation name, attribute name or condition constraint, the corresponding entry stores a star mark instead. For convenience, we represent these triples as trees of height three and call the three levels as relation level, attribute level and condition level respectively. The upper part of Figure 4 shows all the expressions in Figure 2. In the next subsection, these expression triples will be merged into relation trees.

3.2 Relation Trees

The expression triples are often not independent of one another. We merge related expression triples according to the following rules:

1. Expression triples with identical relation name (their aliases must also be identical if specified) are merged at the relation level.
2. Expression triples with both identical relation name and identical attribute name are merged at the attribute level.
3. Expression triples that have identical attribute name, but do not specify the relation name, are merged at the attribute level.

The merged results are called **Relation Trees** since each of them collects the schema information related to one relation in the database. Similarly, subtrees at the attribute level are called **Attribute Trees**.

EXAMPLE 3. *The merging process of expression triples in the query example is shown in Figure 4.*

After the preprocessing, all the schema-relevant information are transformed into a set of relation trees, denoted as $RT = \{rt_1, ..., rt_l\}$. We call this an **l-Relation Tree Query**, which can be considered as a generalization of a traditional l-keyword search, with two major differences:

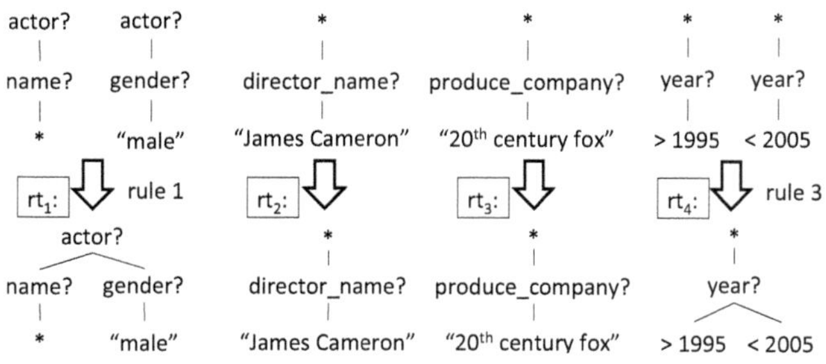

Figure 4: Merging Expression Triples.

- In l-keyword search, it is easy to tell if a keyword should be mapped to a relation using the *contains* function. Since a relation tree often has much more information than a keyword, we cannot use simple containment in an l-relation trees query. In the next section, we provide similarity functions to evaluate the similarity between relation trees and relations, and map them by their similarity.
- In l-keyword search, many join networks of relations which contain all keywords will be evaluated. Their evaluation results are then ranked and the most relevant ones are returned to the user. In contrast, in l-relation trees query, join networks of relations are ranked before evaluation. Only the best join network of relations will be evaluated to return the exact query results to the user. We provide mechanisms to rank join networks in Section 5 and generate the best (or top k) join network efficiently in Section 6.

4. MAPPING RELATION TREES

In this section, we discuss the mapping from relation trees to relations in the database, which is based on their similarity. There are many ways to define similarity based on previous efforts described in the literature. All are heuristic with no clear universal best. The goal of this section is not to find the best similarity evaluation function. Rather, we give a framework for the similarity evaluation function and recommend a "good" one we use in our system.

For each relation tree rt, we call the set of its mapped relations as the *Mapping Set* of r, and denote it by $MAP(rt)$. We define $MAP(rt)$ as follows:

DEFINITION 1 (MAPPING SET OF A RELATION TREE). *Let rt be a relation tree, $V = \{R_1, ..., R_n\}$ be the target database with n relations, $Sim(rt, R_i)$ be a similarity function between rt and relation R_i, and σ be a predefined relative threshold between 0 and 1. The Mapping Set of rt is defined as $\{R_i | Sim(rt, R_i) > \sigma * MAX\{Sim(rt, R_j)|1 \le j \le n\}\}$.*

Note that we do not simply pick the one relation with maximum similarity, since relation tree similarity alone may not give us the right answer. Instead, we would like to keep in play all relations with high similarity. We could define an absolute threshold for this purpose. However, we have preferred to do so in terms of a fraction σ of the maximum, for the following intuitive reason: when the user specifies the name(s) correctly, there is usually one relation with high similarity, and we can ignore all others with low similarity; on the other hand, if the user specifies the name poorly, there is no good match and all similarities are low, and in this case we want to keep around several likely candidates.

4.1 Similarity Evaluation

Let rt be a relation tree with relation name $n(rt)$ and attribute trees $\{at_1, ..., at_m\}$, R be a relation in the database. Intuitively, rt is similar to R if R contains similar information for $n(rt)$ (similar at root level) and each at_i (similar at attribute level). We use $Sim(n(rt), R)$ and $Sim(at_i, R)$ to denote the similarity at root level and attribute level respectively, which will be formally defined later. The similarity between rt and R is defined as follows:

$$Sim(rt, R) = Sim(n(rt), R) \prod_{i=1}^{m} Sim(at_i, R)$$

4.2 Similarity at Root Level

If there is a relation name at the root of a relation tree, similarity with this name is obviously a major indicator of a matching relation in the database. Frequently, the user is off in specifying the relation name because the user has a different schema in mind than the database, with normalization being a common culprit in this regard. To allow for this, we also match the name at the root of a relation tree with names of neighboring relations.

Formally, let $n(rt)$ be the relation name of relation tree rt, $n(R)$ be the relation name of relation R. Suppose that $\{R_{neighbor}\}$ is all the relations that R refers to or is referred by. rt is similar with R at root level if $n(rt)$ is similar to $n(R)$ or there exists a $R_i \in \{R_{neighbor}\}$ with $n(R_i)$ very similar to $n(rt)$. The similarity is formally defined as follows:

$$Sim(n(rt), R) = MAX(Sim(n(rt), n(R)), \{Sim'(n(rt), n(R_i))\})$$

In the equation, R_i iterates over all the relations in $\{R_{neighbor}\}$. $Sim(a, b)$ and $Sim'(a, b)$ are similarity functions between two strings with the constraint that $Sim(a, b)$ is larger than $Sim'(a, b)$. In our implementation, we use the Jaccard Coefficient between the q-gram sets of a and b as $Sim(a, b)$, and multiply it with k_{ref}, a predefined constant between 0 and 1, to compute $Sim'(a, b)$.

EXAMPLE 4. *Take the relation tree rt_1 in Figure 4 and all relations in Figure 1 as an example. The root of rt_1 is actor?. For relation Actor, the similarity at root level, Sim(actor, Actor) is 1. Suppose k_{ref} is 0.7. rt_1's similarity with Person and Movie is 0.7 since they are both referred to by relation Actor.*

Sometimes, $n(rt)$ may not be specified. In this case, we try to find some clues in ats for the mapping. We first set the root similarity to, k_{def}, a small default value, then we use each attribute name in ats instead of $n(rt)$ to compute the similarity at root level. We update the root similarity each time when the computed similarity is higher than the current root similarity.

4.3 Similarity at Attribute Level

Let at be an attribute tree and R be a relation with attributes $\{A_1, ..., A_m\}$. We map at to the attribute A_i that is most similar to at. The similarity between at and R is formally defined as follows:

$$Sim(at, R) = MAX(\{Sim(at, A_i)|1 \le i \le m\})$$

Intuitively, an attribute tree at is similar to an attribute A if (a) their attribute names are similar, (b) the conditions (if specified) under the attribute tree are satisfied by the tuples in the attribute. Let $n(at)$ and $n(A)$ be the attribute name of at and A respectively. The similarity between at and A is defined as follows:

$$Sim(at, A) = Sim(n(at), n(A)) * \frac{m+1}{n+1}$$

In the equation, $Sim(n(at), n(A))$ denotes the string similarity between the attribute names of at and A. $\frac{m+1}{n+1}$ reflects whether the condition constraints are satisfied, in which n denotes the total number of condition constraints under at and m denote the number of conditions constraints which can be satisfied by the tuples in A.

5. VIEW GRAPH

The previous sections mapped relation trees to relations in the database. Our next task is to find a join network that contains these mapped relations, based on which we can specify the equivalent SQL query. A similar problem arises in schema-based keyword search (e.g. DISCOVER [8]). We cannot use their techniques directly for two reasons. First, in Schema-free SQL, the user may specify part of the join path, which should be carefully taken into account in the join path generation. Second, in keyword search, the output of the join path generation is usually all the possible join networks within a length threshold. In contrast, the output in our method is only the (few) best join network(s).

In this section, we introduce the notion of view graph, which captures partially specified join path and the join path fragments in the query log as views, which suggest join networks that are better than others.

5.1 Model

The schema of the database can be represented as an undirected graph $S(V, E)$, where V is the set of relations in the database $\{R_1, ..., R_n\}$, and there exists an edge (R_i, R_j) in E, if a foreign key defined on R_i refers to the primary key defined on R_j (FK-PK relationship). In addition, let $VIEW$ represent the set of predefined views $\{view_1, ..., view_m\}$. A *view* in $VIEW$ is a connected tree of relations with each edge being a join (not necessarily a FK-PK relationship join) in the view definition. We can add these views to the schema, to define an undirected **View Graph**, $G(V, E, VIEW)$.

Views can come from various sources. First, the join path may be partially specified by the user in the schema-free query. If the specified join path is not connected, each of its connected parts will be transformed to a view. Second, query patterns mined from query logs and forms designed by experts may also be suggestive of likely queries, and are therefore transformed into views. More sophisticated techniques, such as those suggested by [13], may also be used beyond this, if desired. Intuitively, join networks constructed from these views are more likely to be reasonable than those constructed by arbitrarily connecting single relations from scratch.

EXAMPLE 5. *Consider the query log along with its corresponding standard SQL shown in Figure 5. We transform it to a view as shown. For simplicity, we take this view as the unique view in the view set. This view set and the schema graph in Figure 1 forms the view graph.*

```
Query log: Return all the directors that "Tom Hanks" has
        cooperated with.

Standard SQL:
  SELECT count(Person_2.name)
  From Person as Person_1, Actor, Movie,
       Director, Person as Person_2
  WHERE Person_1.name = "Tom Hanks",
      and Person_2.person_id = Actor.person_id,
      and Actor.movie_id = Movie.movie_id,
      and Movie.movie_id = Director.movie_id,
      and Director.person_id = Person_2.person_id;
View:
  Person — Actor — Movie — Director — Person
```

Figure 5: View Example.

Given a relation mapping for each relation tree, there are many possible join networks connecting them. In the next section, we will discuss how to score these networks to choose the best. But first we have to deal with the additional complication that there are several candidate mappings for each relational tree. To address this challenge, we introduce the notion of an **Extended View Graph**, denoted as $G_X(V_X, E_X, VIEW_X)$. Given a view graph $G(V, E, VIEW)$ and an l-relation trees query $RT = \{rt_1, ..., rt_l\}$, for each node $R_i \in V$ and each relation tree $rt \in RT$ that maps to R_i, there exists a node in G_X denoted as $R_i^{(rt)}$. There is also a node $R_i^{()}$ in G_X for each node R_i that has no relation tree mapped to it. There exists an edge $(R_1^{(rt1)}, R_2^{(rt2)})$ in E_X if there is an edge (R_1, R_2) in E. Similarly, for each view in G, we have to consider all possible mappings of relation trees to each node in the view. Each of these gives rise to a view in $VIEW_X$.

EXAMPLE 6. *For the four relation trees in Figure 4, we assume that rt_1 and rt_2 map to Person, rt_3 maps to Company and rt_4 maps to Movie. This mapping gives rise to the extended view graph shown in Figure 6. Note that there are two ways to transform the view example in Figure 5, one replaces the leftmost Person by $Person^{(rt1)}$ while the other replaces it by $Person^{(rt2)}$. The values on the edges are their weights, which will be formally defined later.*

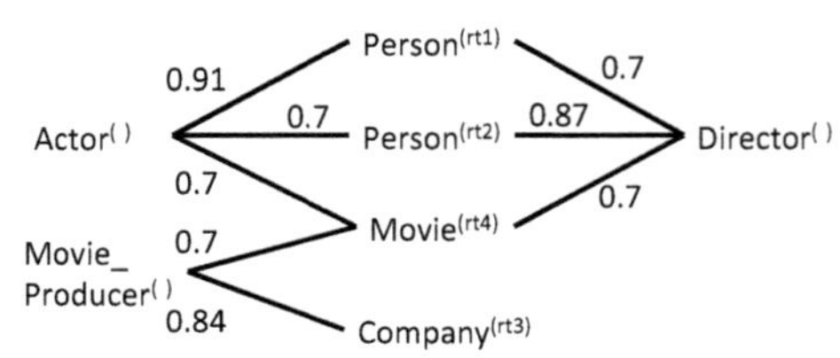

Views:

$view_1$: $Person^{(rt1)}$ — $Actor^{()}$ — $Movie^{(rt4)}$ — $Director^{()}$ — $Person^{(rt2)}$

$view_2$: $Person^{(rt2)}$ — $Actor^{()}$ — $Movie^{(rt4)}$ — $Director^{()}$ — $Person^{(rt1)}$

Figure 6: Extended View Graph.

With the extended view graph in place, we can restrict the join networks we consider to satisfy a given l-relations trees query as follows:

DEFINITION 2 (CANDIDATE JOIN NETWORK). *Given an l-relation trees query $RT = \{rt_1, ..., rt_l\}$ and a relational database with extended view graph $G_X(V_X, E_X, VIEW_X)$, a* *candidate join network is a connected tree of nodes where for every two adjacent nodes $R_1^{(rt1)}$ and $R_2^{(rt2)}$ in the tree, $(R_1^{(rt1)}, R_2^{(rt2)})$ is in E_X or in a view in $VIEW_X$. Note that $(R_1^{(rt1)}, R_2^{(rt2)})$, $(R_1^{(rt1)}, R_2^{(rt3)})$ cannot exist in a join network at the same time if the primary key of R_2 in $R_2^{(rt2)}$ and $R_2^{(rt3)}$ is referred to by the same foreign key in R_1.*

DEFINITION 3 (MINIMAL TOTAL JOIN NETWORK (MTJN)). *An MTJN is a candidate join network that satisfies the following two conditions:*

- *Total: the join network contains all relation trees in RT.*
- *Minimal: the join network is not total if any relation in it is removed.*

5.2 Ranking of Results

Given an l-relational tree query and an extended view graph, the MTJN is not unique. In fact, there will typically be many MTJNs, and only one of them corresponds to the correct interpretation of the query. To be able to tell which MTJN is good, we have to score it, and we do this scoring based on weights we assign to edges in the (extended) view graph. In other words, rather than just considering presence of edges in the view graph, we now weight this presence depending on how likely that edge is.

To each edge e, we assign a weight $w(e)$, with a value between 0 and 1, where a larger weight indicates a stronger connection. While this is *not* formally a probability, it is intuitively useful to think of it as if it were the probability that this edge is in the user-desired query. $w(e)$ initializes all edges to a default constant c. Then for each edge $e = (R_1^{(rt1)}, R_2^{(rt2)})$, its connection is enhanced by the following equation, which follows the standard disjunction of probabilities for independent events: $w(e) = 1 - (1 - c) * (1 - MAX(Sim'(n(rt_1), n(R_2)), Sim'(n(rt_2), n(R_1))))$, where Sim' is defined in Section 4.2. Intuitively, rt_2 contains information specified by the user for R_2. High similarity between rt_2 and R_1 may mean some relationship between $R_1^{(rt1)}$ and $R_2^{(rt2)}$. Thus their connection is enhanced.

EXAMPLE 7. *The edges in Figure 6 are marked with their weights. Let $c = 0.7$. Suppose that $Sim'(n(rt_1), n(Actor))$ equals to 0.7. Then the edge of $(Actor^{()}, Person^{(r1)})$ is weighted $1 - (1 - 0.7)(1 - 0.7) = 0.91$. The weights of other edges are computed similarly.*

The weight of a path is naturally computed as a product of the weights on its edges – intuitively multiplying probabilities of independent events to find the probability of the conjunction.

DEFINITION 4 (BASIC WEIGHT OF JN)). *Let jn be a join network constructed by edges $E' = \{e_i\}$. The basic weight of jn is: $w_{basic}(jn) = \prod_{e_i \in E'} w(e_i)$*

DEFINITION 5 (WEIGHT OF VIEW). *Let v be a view constructed by edges $E' = \{e_i\}$. The weight of v is: $w_{view}(v) = (\prod_{e_i \in E'} w(e_i))^{\frac{1}{2}}$*

In general, the weight assignments on views can be very elaborate. For example, views transformed from partial join path specified by the user should have very high weight. Similarly, query patterns mined from the query log can have different weights according to their frequency and other properties. Such careful tuning is beyond the scope of this paper.

DEFINITION 6 (CONSTRUCTION WEIGHT OF JN). *Let jn be a join network built by views $VIEW' = \{v_i\}$ and edges E' $= \{e_j\}$ (not contained by any v_i). The construction weight of jn is: $w_{con}(jn) = (\prod_{v_i \in VIEW'} w(v_i))(\prod_{e_j \in E'} w(e_j))$*

The above formula gives the weight of a particular construction of a join network. In many cases, the same join network can be constructed in more than one ways, with one constructed only by edges and others containing views. In this case, we take the highest construction weight of the join network as its weight.

DEFINITION 7 (WEIGHT OF JN). *Given a join network jn with all possible construction weights $\{w_{con}^1(jn), ..., w_{con}^n(jn)\}$, the weight of jn is defined as:*

$$w(jn) = MAX(w_{con}^1(jn), ..., w_{con}^n(jn))$$

EXAMPLE 8. *One join network in Figure 6 is shown in Figure 7. If this join network is constructed from scratch, its construction weight is the multiplication of all its edge weights, which is 0.23. Another way to construct the example join network is to use the $view_1$ in Figure 6. $view_1$ itself is weighted $\sqrt{0.91 * 0.7 * 0.7 * 0.87}$, which is 0.62. Thus the construction weight in using $view_1$ is $0.62 * 0.7 * 0.84 = 0.36$. This is the highest construction weight of this join network. So its weight is 0.36.*

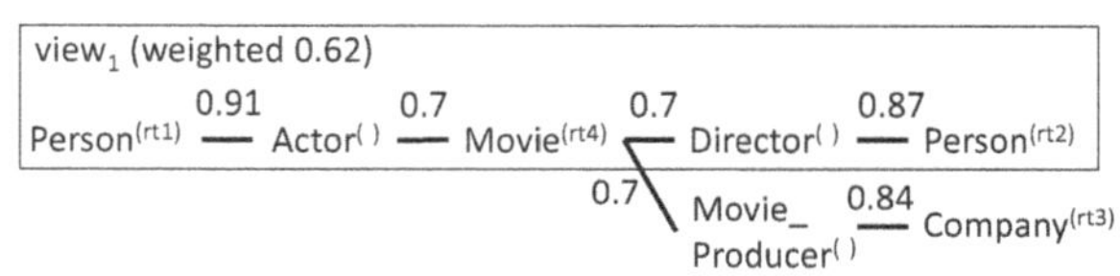

Figure 7: Weight of a Join Network.

6. GENERATING TOP K INTERPRETATIONS OF SCHEMA FREE SQL

The weight functions described above are heuristic, with no guarantee of the top ranked network being the one desired. For this reason, we would like to be able to generate the top several choices. Given the combinatorial number of possible join networks, it is important to develop efficient algorithms to accomplish this. In Section 6.1, we give algorithms to efficiently generate k MTJNs with the highest weights. In Section 6.2, we translate the input Schema-free SQL into a full SQL with the help of an MTJN.

6.1 Top k MTJNs Generation

The basic idea in our algorithm is to first select a set of nodes in the graph as initial JNs and then gradually expand this set until top k minimal total ones are generated. The resulting Algorithm 1 is shown in Figure 8. We choose the nodes that are mapped by the first relation tree as roots to expand. We rank these roots by their potential (line 2) and expand high potential ones first. (How to estimate potential will be discussed at the end of this subsection). KMTJNUpdate, shown in Algorithm 2, is the main workhorse of Algorithm 1. We call it to expand each root and update $kMTJN$

(line 4). To avoid generating isomorphic MTJNs from different roots, we delete each root from the extended view graph after it is expanded (line 5).

The efficiency of the algorithm mainly depends on the total number of JNs expanded. In DISCOVER [8], JNs are expanded arbitrarily. As a result, large numbers of isomorphic JNs are generated since the edges in a JN can be added in different orders. In our algorithm, we use *legality test* to ensure that each JN will be generated only once (line 7). But even without generating isomorphic JNs, the total number of JNs still increases exponentially with the length of JNs. So it is very beneficial if the JNs that do not have the potential to generate a top k MTJN can be pruned out early. In our algorithm, we use *potential estimation* to prune out JNs with no potential early (line 11-12). If a JN cannot expand to an MTJN with weight higher than the current kth MTJN's weight, it will be pruned out. To maximize this pruning benefit, we generate k MTJNs with high weights early by using a priority queue to store all partially expanded JNs ordered by their potential and expanding high potential ones first (line 3-12).

Algorithm 1: InitMTJNGen($G_X(V_X, E_X, VIEW_X)$, RT)

```
1: kMTJN ← Φ
2: rank all R_i mapped by rt_1 by decreasing R_i.potential
3: for all R_i, do
4:    KMTJNupdate(R_i, G_X, kMTJN)
5:    remove R_i from G_X
6: return kMTJN;
```

Figure 8: Top k MTJNs Generation

Algorithm 2: KMTJNupdate(R_i, $G_X(V_X, E_X, VIEW_X)$, $kMTJN$)

```
1: PriorityQueue ← Φ
2: jn = a tree of single node R_i
3: PriorityQueue.push(jn)
4: while PriorityQueue ≠ Φ do
5:    jn = PriorityQueue.pop()
6:    for all e ∈ E_X and view ∈ VIEW_X do
7:       if e (or view) can be legally added to jn then
8:          jn' = a tree expanded from jn by adding e (or view)
9:          if jn' is both minimal and total then
10:            update(kMTJN)
11:         else if jn'.potential ≠ 0 then
12:            PriorityQueue.push(jn)
13: return kMTJN
```

Figure 9: Top k MTJNs Update

Now we discuss the two important functions, legality test and potential estimation, in detail.

Legality Test: We could, by adding edges in different orders, create the same (isomorphic) join network (JN) multiple times from the same root. To avoid that, rightmost path expansion technique has been proposed in [12]. In their method, a unique numeric label is added to each node in the graph and a JN is modeled as a rooted, ordered tree, in which the children of each node are ordered by their numeric label. The intuition is that only the rightmost nodes, at any level, in the tree are allowed to expand and the newly expanded node must be the rightmost node at its level. In the case of extended view graph, the situation is more complex since a JN can be expanded by a view, which means a set of edges will be added to the JN at the same time. We adapt the rightmost path expansion to extended view graph.

Given a join network jn and a view $view$, $view$ can be legally added to jn only if they share exactly one node (the shared node must be a rightmost node in jn). Now, $view$ is also considered as a rooted, ordered tree, which is rooted at the shared node (denoted as $root(view)$) and orders each node's children by their numeric labels. The expansion is considered as the $view$ is added to jn at $root(view)$. $root(view)$ might have children both in $view$ and jn. In this case, the rightmost child of $root(view)$ must be in $view$, not in jn. Otherwise, the expansion will be considered illegal. Also, each view has a numeric label, if jn has already been expanded by some views, the label of the newly added $view$ must be larger than all previously added views. After expanding jn with $view$, all the previous nodes in jn, which are to the left of $view$ (the order of the node is smaller than the biggest order in the view in post-order traversal), are marked non-rightmost. While all newly expanded nodes are marked as rightmost no matter if they are in the rightmost root-to-leaf path. Following these rules, each JN will be generated at most once in the whole process[1].

EXAMPLE 9. *Take the JNs in Figure 10 as an example. We suppose that the numeric label of Movie_Producer is smaller than the numeric label of Actor and the numeric label of Actor is smaller than the numeric label of Director. So if they appear as siblings to each other, Movie_Producer is always to the left of Actor and Actor is always to the left of Director. Look at the JN (e), the nodes of* $Movie^{rt4}$, *Director and* $Person^{rt2}$ *are the rightmost nodes at each level. To distinguish rightmost nodes from others, all the rightmost nodes are marked red. JN (d) can never be expanded from JN (b), since the node Movie_Producer is not rightmost node and cannot be expanded any more. Similarly, the expansion from JN (d) to JN (e) is not an legal expansion, since the newly added node Actor is to the left of an existing child Director. Also, the JN (b) can never be an MTJN since the node Movie_Producer is not rightmost and hasn't been mapped by any relation tree, which will violate the Minimal Condition after it reach the Total Condition. So the expansion from JN (a) to (b) is illegal. JN (c) can be expanded to JN (f) directly by adding the* $view_1$ *in Figure 6, since JN (c) and* $view_1$ *share only one node* $Movie^{rt4}$ *and the rightmost child of* $Movie^{rt4}$ *is Director, which is in* $view_1$*, not in JN (c). Note that all the nodes of the newly added view are marked rightmost.*

Potential Estimation: Our pruning is based on a JN's potential to generate a top k MTJN. Given a JN jn, we approximate the upper bound of the weight of all the MTJNs that can be expanded from jn (denoted as $upper(jn)$) and use it as its potential. We set the potential to 0 if the approximated upper bound is lower than the weight of the current kth MTJN. The benefit of using $upper(jn)$ is two-fold. First, if $upper(jn)$ is lower than the weight of the current kth MTJN, jn can be pruned out almost safely. Second, the higher $upper(jn)$ is, the more likely jn can generate a top k MTJN.

[1]The only exception is when a JN can be constructed in more than one way using different components. For each construction, the JN may be generated once.

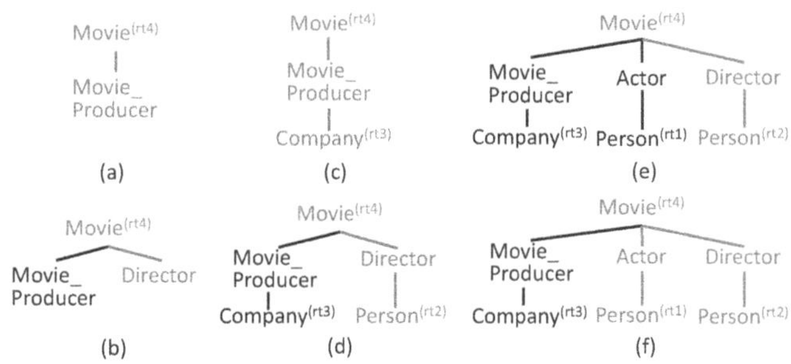

Figure 10: Rightmost Path Expansion

The potential estimation algorithm is shown in Figure 11. We first find all relation trees not contained by jn and then put the nodes mapped by these relation trees into a list L. For each round, we choose the node R^{rtj} that has the shortest (highest weight) path to jn and connect it through the path. After that, we delete all the nodes in L to which rt_j maps. We repeat this process until the jn is total. We use the weight of this jn as its potential. Later, If the potential is lower than the current kth MTJN's weight, it will be set 0. Consider jn may contain views, before we estimate the potential, we set the weight of each edge on the graph as its square root if the edge is contained in a view.

Algorithm 3: PotentialEstimate(*jn*, *G*$_X$(*V*$_X$, *E*$_X$, *VIEW*$_X$), *RT*)

```
jn' = jn; L ; w = jn.weight;
for all rt_i RT
    if jn' does not contain rt_i
        L.addAll(Map(rt_i))
While jn' is not total do
    find R^rtj in L which has shortest path p to jn'
    jn'.add(p)
    w *= weight(p)
    R.removeAll(Map(rt_j))
return w;
```

Figure 11: Potential Estimation

The most computationally complex part in this process is the computation of the shortest paths (highest weight paths) between each pair of nodes in the view graph. Since we can compute all shortest paths once and use them repeatedly, the whole potential estimation process can be efficient.

6.2 Standard SQL Composer

After the generation of the top k MTJNs, k full SQL queries can be generated, one corresponding to each MTJN. This is accomplished as a three-step translation of the given Schema-free SQL query.

1. All the uncertain/unknown relation (attribute) names in the relation tree are replaced by the relation (attribute) names in the corresponding relations in the MTJN.
2. All the relations in the MTJN are included in the *FROM clause*. If a relation appears more than once in the MTJN, the keyword *AS* is used to give an alias to each appearance.
3. All the edges in the MTJN are included in the *WHERE clause* as a join condition to join these relations.

EXAMPLE 10. *Using the MTJN in Figure 7, we transform the Schema-free SQL in Figure 2 into its corresponding full SQL. The transformation process is shown in Figure 12.*

```
SELECT count(actor?.name?)
WHERE actor?.gender? = "male"
    and director?.name? = "James Cameron"
    and produce_company? = "20th Century Fox"
    and year? > 1995
    and year? < 2005;

Step 1:
    actor? → Person^rt1 (name? → name, gender? → gender)
    director_name? → Person^rt2.name
    produce_company → Company^rt3.name
    year? → Movie^rt4.release_year

SELECT count(Person^rt1.name)
WHERE Person^rt1.gender = "male"
    and Person^rt2 .name = "James Cameron"
    and Company^rt3.name = "20th Century Fox"
    and Movie^rt4.release_year > 1995
    and Movie^rt4.release_year < 2005;

Step 2:
    From Person as Person^rt1, Person as Person^rt2, Actor,
        Director, Movie as Movie^rt4, Movie_producer,
        Company as Company^rt3

Step 3:
    Person^rt1.person_id = Actor.person_id
    Actor.movie_id = Movie.movie_id
    Movie.movie_id = Director.movie_id
    Director.person_id = Person^rt2.person_id
    Movie.movie_id = Movie_Producer.movie_id
    Movie_Producer.company_id = Company.company_id

SELECT count(Person^rt1.name)
From Person as Person^rt1, Person as Person^rt2, Actor,
    Director, Movie as Movie^rt4, Movie_producer,
    Company as Company^rt3
WHERE Person^rt1.gender = "male"
    and Person^rt2 .name = "James Cameron"
    and Company^rt3.name = "20th Century Fox"
    and Movie^rt4.release_year > 1995
    and Movie^rt4.release_year < 2005
    and Person^rt1.person_id = Actor.person_id
    and Actor.movie_id = Movie.movie_id
    and Movie.movie_id = Director.movie_id
    and Director.person_id = Person^rt2.person_id
    and Movie.movie_id = Movie_Producer.movie_id
    and Movie_Producer.company_id = Company.company_id;
```

Figure 12: Full SQL Translation Process.

7. EXPERIMENTAL RESULTS

7.1 Evaluation Method

There are two crucial aspects we must evaluate: whether the system can correctly translate Schema-free SQL queries to full SQL queries (effectiveness), and how much work the user has to do in composing Schema-free SQL queries (usability). In addition, we must ensure that the running time of our algorithm is fast enough for interactive use.

Effectiveness: In keyword search systems, researchers often use IR metrics like precision and recall to evaluate the search quality. But these IR metrics would not work very well for Schema-free SQL since they will always be 100% if a Schema-free SQL is correctly translated into full SQL, and will be near 0% in most times when it is not. So, in our system, we evaluate the effectiveness by counting the fraction of Schema-free SQL queries that can be translated correctly in one of the top k translations. In our experiments, we test the cases when k equals 1 and 10.

User Burden: One way to quantify the user's burden in using a query system is to measure the cost (e.g. keystrokes, time) in the query construction. Recently, in [16, 14], researchers quantified the cost by counting the number of schema elements users specified in query construction. Following their lead, we use the concept of **information unit** as an objective metric to quantify the cost. In a query, any schema element, including a relation name and an attribute name, is an information unit. We evaluate the cost of a query by counting the number of information units used. In Schema-free SQL, many schema elements may be specified approximately, or partially. To avoid a complex model involving partial information units, we significantly overestimate the cost of our system by counting each of these as one full information unit.

EXAMPLE 11. *The cost of the example Schema-free SQL in Figure 2 is 6: actor, gender, name, director_name, year and produce_company.*

Many visual SQL query builders [1, 2, 3] interactively help the user to complete the join path when the user drags and drops a relation to the query construction window. As a representative of this class of interfaces, we use Flyspeed SQL Query [2] to conduct experiments for comparison.

For Schema-free SQL, separate evaluation of the effectiveness or usability is meaningless since our system can take in standard SQL, which has a 100% effectiveness but high user burden, or keywords (with SQL structure), which has low user burden but low effectiveness. The point of Schema-free SQL is not to be at either extreme, but rather to be somewhere in between: the user expresses partial schema knowledge they have and the system does the rest. Furthermore, it is reasonable to assume that users can express selections and projections, but may not be able to specify joins. Our experimental assessment focuses on just such a scenario, to assess the degradation in effectiveness and gain in usability compared to fully specified SQL.

There are several tuning parameters in our algorithms. We ran some initial experiments to determine good values for these parameters. Based on these experiments, not reported for lack of space, we set $\sigma = k_{ref} = c = 0.7$ and $k_{def} = 0.3$.

7.2 Movie Database

In this subsection, we evaluate the effectiveness and users' cost in queries over the Yahoo-Movie database, which has 43 relations and 71 FK-PK pairs. The generation of query sets is a challenging task itself. First, Schema-free SQL is supposed to be composed by users who can express query logic in SQL but do not know the exact schema of the database. Second, we would like the queries to cover most of the major functions of SQL to test whether Schema-free SQL can be correctly translated in different cases.

In order to satisfy these conditions, we chose two query sets. The first is composed of 17 example SQL queries[2] in a textbook [15], which are used to illustrate how to compose SQL queries. This query set includes single relation queries, multi-relation queries, queries with multi-level subqueries, and queries with aggregations. These queries were originally written for a mini database composed of 5 relations, not for Yahoo-Movies. We preprocess all these SQL queries in the following steps to remove some misleading information: delete all the FK-PK join paths in WHERE clause and the relation names in the FROM clause, then merge all the column names with their corresponding relation names. When using these queries to query the Yahoo-Movie database through our system, all 17 queries can be correctly translated to full SQLs in the top 1 translation. Note that in this experiment, no view graph is used to enhance effectiveness. The user's burden for these queries is shown in Figure 13. Generally, these Schema-free SQL queries specify only 35 (respectively, 55) percent as many information units as their corresponding full SQL queries (with a visual query builder). In short, a good visual query builder can reduce the query specification cost, compared to full SQL, but Schema-free SQL can reduce it further.

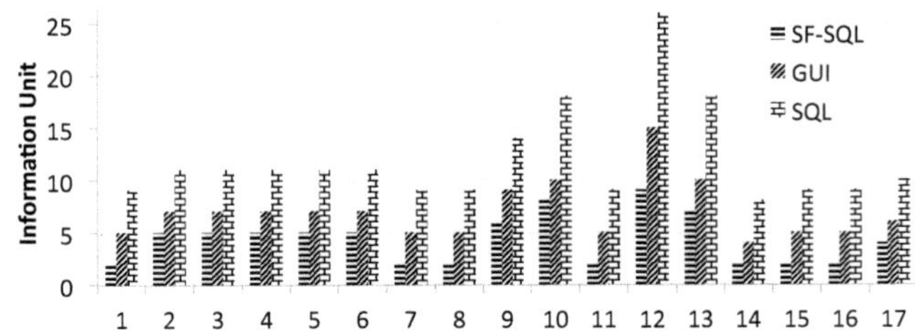

Figure 13: Information Unit Cost for the Queries in the Textbook.

To test the accuracy and usability of our method in sophisticated queries, which refer to many relations and contain complex join paths, we chose six complex queries as our second query set, in which each one has a join path with more than five relations. We recruited five students who are major in information science, all familiar with SQL but not with the schema of Yahoo-Movie, and asked them to specify these six queries, based only on the natural language description shown in Figure 14. The result is that all the users are able to specify all queries in Schema-free SQL and get the correct full SQL queries in the top 1 translation. The average of their information unit cost is only 24 (resp. 45) percent of the full SQL queries (with a visual query builder). Details are shown in Figure 14. Once again, view graphs are not used to enhance effectiveness.

7.3 Course Database

To challenge our system with more sophisticated queries, we obtain a set of 48 complex SQL queries against the course database used in CourseRank [5] comprising 53 relations. We generate Schema-free SQL by deleting all the FK-PK join paths in the WHERE clauses and all the relations in the FROM clauses excepting the relations at the ends of each join path, which are typically used for selection or projection: information which a typical user should be able to specify. We also asked a student with experience in database application development to create his own schema that covers the query intent in all the 48 queries. He designed a schema with only 21 relations, very different from the CourseRank schema. We ran the same Schema-free SQL queries over the two schemas. For each query, we test if it can be translated correctly in the best translation or at least in one of the top 10 translations over the two schemas. In our first test, we use schema graph as the underlying data model abstraction. The result is shown in Figure 15. The

[2]There are altogether 27 complete SQL queries in [15]. We remove 10 of them that contain information outside Yahoo-Movie.

	Queries:	SF-SQL	GUI	SQL
1	Male actors cooperated with director "James Cameron" in the movies produced by company "20th Century Fox" from 1995 to 2010.	6.6	12	22
2	Movies with genre "Drama" and director "Peter Jackson".	3.4	8	15
3	Movies produced by company "Carthago Films", distributed by company "Apollo Films", and directed by director "Fahdel Jaziri".	4.6	11	21
4	The number of movies directed by "Steven Spielberg" and acted by "Tom Hanks".	3.4	8	15
5	Actors acted more than 3 movies with genre "Action Adventure" directed by "Woody Allen".	3.8	10	20
6	Movies with genre "Drama", financed by company "LLC", directed by "Stephen Gaghan".	5	11	21

Figure 14: Sophisticated Queries for Yahoo-Movie Database.

translation quality decreases significantly when the queries become more complex. That is because when a query refers to more relations, the number of possible join paths grows sharply. Unsupervised join path generation cannot accurately tell which join paths are better than others.

In our second test, we use the view graph instead of schema graph as the underlying data model abstraction. We order all the queries by the number of relations they refer to. After each query is tested, we transform it to a view for future use. By doing so, the construction of complex queries can benefit from the previous simple queries by using them as building blocks. The result is shown in Figure 15. The translation quality is improved significantly by using view graph. We see that working with a different schema has virtually little impact on effectiveness, at least for simpler queries. There is a slight effect for complex queries (with 6-10 relations).

Relations referred in Query	Top 1	Top 10	Top 1 with View Graph	Top 10 with View Graph
2 – 4	9/11 (8/11)	11/11 (10/11)	9/11 (8/11)	11/11 (10/11)
5	17/26 (17/26)	22/26 (22/26)	25/26 (25/26)	26/26 (26/26)
6 – 10	5/11 (2/11)	5/11 (2/11)	10/11 (7/11)	11/11 (8/11)

Figure 15: Effectiveness with/without Query Logs (the numbers in parentheses are for the schema with 21 relations)

The information unit costs are shown in Figure 16. In general, Schema-free SQLs only specify 33 (reps. 62) percent as many information units as full SQL queries (with a visual query builder).

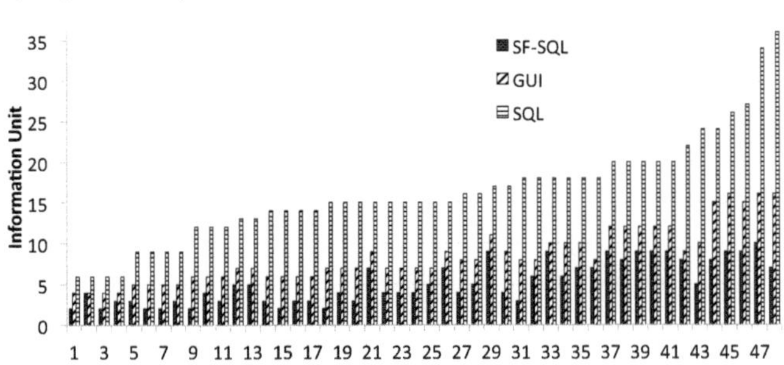

Figure 16: Information Unit Costs in Queries on the Course Database

Finally, we note that the bulk of the execution time is consumed by the Join Network generation. Therefore, we test the efficiency of the algorithms in top k MTJNs generation. We compare the algorithm described in Section 6.1 with the algorithms modified from [8] (Regular) and [12] (Rightmost). The modifications are (a) the expansion stops when the top k MTJNs are generated, and (b) the expansion of a JN can be either adding an edge or adding a view. We test their running time for k equals to 1 and test our algorithms for various k. The results are shown in Figure 17. Note that the time is the average query time for queries with the same number of relations involved (denoted as *size*). The algorithm modified from [8] slows down with *size* quickly since too many isomorphic JNs exist. The algorithm modified from [12] behaves much better since it ensures that each JN will be expanded at most once. For our algorithm, we compute the upper bound of the weight for each partially expanded JN and prune out many JN before their size reach *size*. For these reasons, our algorithm runs substantially faster (notice that the Y-axis is on a log scale). We also see that there is a noticeable, but modest, cost to generating multiple MTJN, and this cost grows with query complexity.

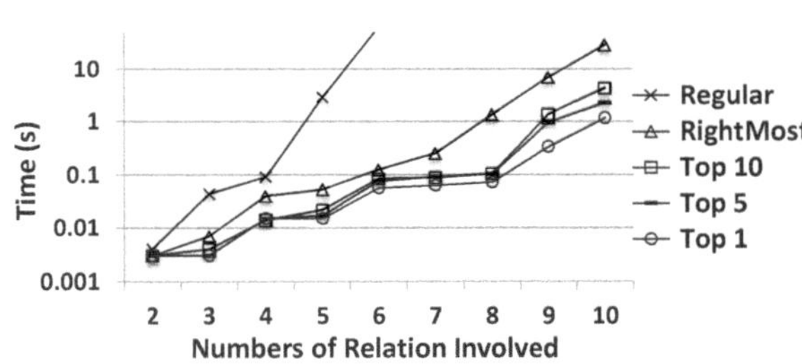

Figure 17: Efficiency Test

8. RELATED WORK

The goal of Schema-free SQL is to make sophisticated queries easier to compose over relational databases. There are various efforts toward making database systems more usable and [9] provides a good review for existing methods.

One strategy towards making relational database usable is using keyword search [17]. Two main families of methods are used: schema-based approaches (e.g. DISCOVER [8]) and graph-based approaches (e.g. BANKS [6]). Schema-based approaches first translate the keywords into a set of minimal total join networks (MTJN) and then evaluate them. Our MTJNs generation follows DISCOVER, but we focus on ranking MTJNs accurately through view graph and design algorithms to generate only the top one or few top k of them efficiently. In graph-based approaches, the database is modeled as a data graph, in which each node is a tuple [6]. Steiner trees of tuples that contain all the keywords are constructed directly on the data graph and outputted as results.

Recently, variations of keyword-based search have been proposed. SQAK [14] supports aggregation functions in keyword search. In [7], keyword search and form-based search are combined. In their system, a set of forms is pre-specified. When a user types in some keywords, the system returns the forms most relevant to the keywords. Qunits [13] represents the database as a collection of independent basic conceptual documents (Qunits), each of which represents the desired results for some queries. Qunits adopts IR-based methods to find the most relevant Qunits as query results.

Visual query builders (e.g. [1, 2, 3]) are widely used to facilitate the building of SQL queries. We view the carefully designed GUI features and our approach as complimentary to each other - while GUI can help to fix the relaxations in Schema-free SQL interactively with the user, Schema-free SQL can provide more powerful functions for metadata exploration and join path auto-completion. Take join path auto-completion as an example. A visual query builder supports creating the join path by dragging and dropping all the relevant relations to a new window. However, this process is not often easy since the meaning of some relations in the join path may be implicit. By merging with our join path generation approach, a user can create a join path by dragging and dropping only the end relations (relations at the end of the join path whose meanings are always explicit for selection or projection), and our system will add the internal ones automatically. A system that performs this merger is left to future work: our experimental evaluation considered the two complementary approaches independently.

SchemaSQL [10] is a principled extension to SQL, which allows its variables to range over relations and attributes in multi-database systems. This paper elegantly supports multi-database heterogeneity, and develops precise semantics to handle concepts that are modeled as attributes in one database but as relations in another and as tuples in a third. In its implementation, all the schema elements are stored in a relation called Federation System Table (FST). By executing SQL on the FST, it resolves the open-ended schema elements of the query into specific ones. In this resolution of schema element variables, Schema-free SQL bears some superficial resemblance to SchemaSQL. However, the problem being addressed is fundamentally different. SchemaSQL gives users the tools to manage semantic heterogeneity, but does not relieve them of the burden of knowing the target schema, and of writing a precise query. Given a SchemaSQL query, there is only one correct interpretation of the query against any given schema (at most). In contrast, our focus is not directly on heterogeneity, but rather on the user's lack of schema knowledge, to which heterogeneity is likely to be an important contributing factor. Schema-free SQL queries are under-specified, and do not have unique interpretations. Our task is to infer user intent.

To facilitate users in querying XML database, Schema-free XQuery [11] integrates keyword search functionality into XQuery as built-in functions. By doing this, it enables users to query XML documents based on whatever partial knowledge they have. Our work is directly inspired by this.

9. CONCLUSION AND FUTURE WORK

In this paper, we proposed Schema-free SQL, which enables its users to compose complex queries over relational databases without requiring full knowledge of the database schema. To support Schema-free SQL, we provide a modular architecture and specific techniques in each module: representing the partial schema information in relation trees, mapping relation trees to relations in the database based on the similarity evaluation, generating "good" minimal total join networks of relations on the view graph, and finally translating the Schema-free SQL into full SQL. Our experiments suggest that Schema-free SQL can greatly decrease users' burden, particularly for complex queries, with hardly any loss in effectiveness compared to standard SQL.

Substantial scope for further work remains. First, to take the most advantage of view graph, we will develop techniques to manage the views: mining frequently appearing query patterns in the query log and setting a proper weight for each view. Second, we will merge Schema-free SQL with visual query builders to both resolve relaxations in Schema-free SQL interactively and provide more powerful functions for visual query builder in metadata exploration and join path auto-completion. Third, we want to take a step further in usability by developing a natural language query system over Schema-free SQL, which can enable naive users to compose complex queries over relational databases.

10. REFERENCES

[1] Active query builder: www.activequerybuilder.com.

[2] Flyspeed sql query: www.activedbsoft.com.

[3] Sqleo visual query builder: sqleo.sourceforge.net.

[4] S. Agrawal, S. Chaudhuri, and G. Das. Dbxplorer: A system for keyword-based search over relational databases. In *ICDE*, pages 5–16, 2002.

[5] B. Bercovitz, F. Kaliszan, G. Koutrika, H. Liou, Z. M. Zadeh, and H. Garcia-Molina. Courserank: a social system for course planning. In *SIGMOD Conference*, pages 1107–1110, 2009.

[6] G. Bhalotia, A. Hulgeri, C. Nakhe, S. Chakrabarti, and S. Sudarshan. Keyword searching and browsing in databases using banks. In *ICDE*, pages 431–440, 2002.

[7] E. Chu, A. Baid, X. Chai, A. Doan, and J. F. Naughton. Combining keyword search and forms for ad hoc querying of databases. In *SIGMOD Conference*, pages 349–360, 2009.

[8] V. Hristidis and Y. Papakonstantinou. Discover: Keyword search in relational databases. In *VLDB*, pages 670–681, 2002.

[9] H. V. Jagadish, A. Chapman, A. Elkiss, M. Jayapandian, Y. Li, A. Nandi, and C. Yu. Making database systems usable. In *SIGMOD Conference*, pages 13–24, 2007.

[10] L. V. S. Lakshmanan, F. Sadri, and S. N. Subramanian. Schemasql: An extension to sql for multidatabase interoperability. *ACM Trans. Database Syst.*, 26(4):476–519, 2001.

[11] Y. Li, C. Yu, and H. V. Jagadish. Schema-free xquery. In *VLDB*, pages 72–83, 2004.

[12] A. Markowetz, Y. Yang, and D. Papadias. Keyword search on relational data streams. In *SIGMOD Conference*, pages 605–616, 2007.

[13] A. Nandi and H. V. Jagadish. Qunits: queried units in database search. In *CIDR*, 2009.

[14] S. Tata and G. M. Lohman. Sqak: doing more with keywords. In *SIGMOD Conference*, pages 889–902, 2008.

[15] J. D. Ullman and J. Widom. *A first course in database systems (2. ed.).* Prentice Hall, 2002.

[16] C. Yu and H. V. Jagadish. Querying complex structured databases. In *VLDB*, pages 1010–1021, 2007.

[17] J. X. Yu, L. Qin, and L. Chang. Keyword search in relational databases: A survey. *IEEE Data Eng. Bull.*, 33(1):67–78, 2010.

iCheck: Computationally Combating "Lies, D—ned Lies, and Statistics"

You Wu† Brett Walenz† Peggy Li† Andrew Shim† Emre Sonmez†
Pankaj K. Agarwal† Chengkai Li‡ Jun Yang† Cong Yu§
†Duke University, ‡University of Texas at Arlington, §Google Research

ABSTRACT

Are you fed up with "lies, d—ned lies, and statistics" made up from data in our media? For claims based on structured data, we present a system to automatically assess the quality of claims (beyond their correctness) and counter misleading claims that cherry-pick data to advance their conclusions. The key insight is to model such claims as parameterized queries and consider how parameter perturbations affect their results. We demonstrate our system on claims drawn from U.S. congressional voting records, sports statistics, and publication records of database researchers.

1 Introduction

Claims of "fact" are made from data constantly—by journalists, politicians, lobbyists, public relations specialists, sports fans, etc. Wherever numbers and data are involved, they can be laden with so-called "lies, d—ed lies, and statistics." Consider the following.

Example 1 (drawn from [5, 6]). ***Giuliani's adoption claim*** *(from* factcheck.org*). During a Republican presidential candidates' debate in 2007, Giuliani claimed that "adoptions went up 65 to 70 percent" in the New York City "when he was the mayor." More precisely, the comparison is between the total number of adoptions during 1996-2001 and that during 1990-1995 (he was in office 1994-2001). The claim "checks out" according to data, but why does it compare these two particular periods? As it turns out, the underlying data actually show that adoption began to slow down in 1998, a trend that continued through 2006. Lumping data into the two six-year periods masks this trend. Comparing the beginning and the end of his tenure would have yielded only a 17% increase.*

One-of-the-few NBA players claim*. "Only 10 players in NBA history had more points, more rebounds, and more assists per game than Sam Lacey in their career." There are nearly 4000 players in NBA history, so "one of the 11" sounds impressive. However, we can claim the exact same or stronger for 112 other players (that no more than 10 players dominate them in these three stats).*

Vote correlation claim *(from* factcheck.org*). A TV ad in the 2010 elections claimed that Jim Marshall, a Democratic incumbent from Georgia, "is a long way from Nancy Pelosi," as he "voted the same as Republican leaders 65 percent of the time." This comparison was made with Republican Leader John Boehner over the votes in 2010. If we start the comparison from 2007, however, the number would have been only 56 percent, which is not very high considering that even the Democratic Whip, Jim Clyburn, voted 44 percent of the time with Boehner during that period.*

SIGMOD'14, June 22–27, 2014, Snowbird, UT, USA.

ACM 978-1-4503-2376-5/14/06 ...$15.00.
http://dx.doi.org/10.1145/2588555.2594522.

Today's highly connected world has made it ever easier to perpetuate lies; at the same time, the movement of "democratizing data" has also made it possible to counter these lies with an increasing array of publicly available data. Thus, there is pressing demand for data-driven fact-checking today. But checking claims—even those based on clean, structured data—is challenging. For example, all claims above are actually "correct," but they present rather misleading views of data. Thus, we must go beyond correctness to find better measures of claim quality to catch lies. Even before we can check a claim, however, we may have to clarify it: many claims, such as Giuliani's and Marshall's above, are stated vaguely (often intentionally). Finally, to help explain to the public why a claim has a low quality, we need "counterarguments": e.g., for Giuliani's claim, we highlighted that "*Comparing the beginning and the end of his tenure would have yielded only a 17% increase*."

Organizations such as *factcheck.org* and *PolitiFact.com* rely on their expert editorial staff to check claims. However, manual approaches are difficult to scale because of the demand on human expertise and effort. *FactMinder* [4] is a tool that assists fact-checkers in annotating text, extracting entities, linking sources, and collaboratively building a knowledge base. *Truth Goggles* (*truthgoggl.es/demo.html*) and *Dispute Finder* [3] detect claims on the Web that have already been checked or refuted by authoritative sources. However, computational tools for checking claims directly using data are still sorely lacking.

To fill this void, we present a system called *iCheck*, which demonstrates that we can, in fact, cast the problem of checking claims based structured data as a computational one. With a general modeling framework and an extensible system, iCheck rates claims of various kinds using quality measures that capture the intuition behind the type of analysis seen in Example 1. iCheck can also automatically "reverse-engineer" a vague claim to recover missing details, and come up with counterarguments to low-quality claims. Interestingly, the same machinery that allows iCheck to combat lies can also be used to generate "interesting" claims including lies. In the demonstration, we will pit iCheck against itself over U.S. congressional voting records, sports statistics, and publication records of database researchers, letting users generate claims in these domains, and then offering a healthy dose of reality check.

2 Modeling Overview

The key intuition behind our approach is remarkably simple. Think of a claim as a parameterized query—we can learn a lot about it by

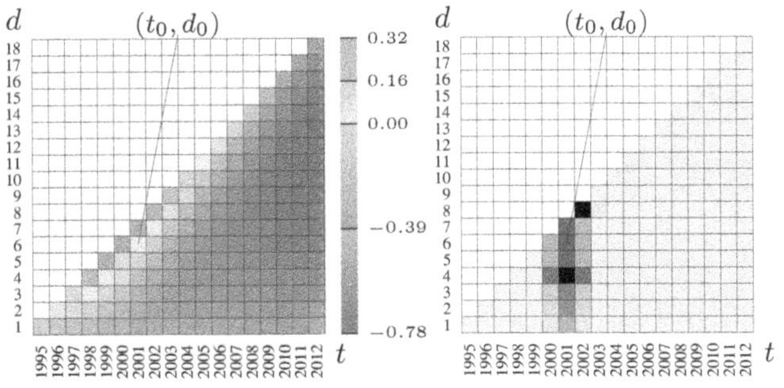

(a) Relative result strength (b) Parameter sensibility

Figure 1: (From [6].) Perturbing t and d in Giuliani's claim while fixing $w = 6$. The data became available in 1989, so $t - d - w \geq 1988$.

"perturbing" its parameters.[1] To illustrate, Giuliani's claim in Example 1 is parameterized by (w, t, d), where $w = 6$ is the length of the aggregation window (in years), $t = 2001$ is the end of the second window, and $d = 6$ is the distance between the two windows being compared. Perturbing the parameter setting to $(1, 2001, 8)$, for example, changes the increase to merely 17%. As another example, the one-of-the-few claim in Example 1 is parameterized by the player (Sam Lacey for the original claim). Perturbing this parameter to other players reveals how unique Sam Lacey is. Finally, the vote correlation claim in Example 1 is parameterized by both the period of comparison and the legislators being compared.

The QRS Framework We proposed this framework in [6] to formalize various claim quality measures and formulate problems in finding and checking claims. Briefly, we model a *claim template* with m parameters as a function $q : \mathcal{P} \to \mathcal{R}$ (given a fixed database instance). Here, $\mathcal{P} \subseteq P_1 \times \cdots \times P_m$ is the *parameter space*, where P_i is the domain of the i-th parameter. Given a parameter setting $\vec{p} = (p_1, \ldots, p_m)$, $q(\vec{p})$ denotes the result of the query instantiated with $\vec{p}$. $\mathcal{R}$ is the domain of results. The points $\{(\vec{p}, q(\vec{p})) \mid \vec{p} \in \mathcal{P}\}$ in $\mathcal{P} \times \mathcal{R}$ form q's *query response surface* (*QRS*).

Intuitively, a fact-checker explores the QRS by trying various perturbations to see how they weaken or strengthen the original claim. Not all perturbations are equally useful to investigation—useful perturbations should be "relevant" (i.e., they stay within the context of the claim) and "natural" (e.g., changing "58 months" to "5 years" makes the claim more concise), and should significantly "weaken" the original claim. With this intuition, we introduce two scoring functions as helpers (see [6] for additional details):

- A *(relative) result strength function* $\mathsf{SR} : \mathcal{R} \times \mathcal{R} \to \mathfrak{R}$. $\mathsf{SR}(r; r_O)$ captures how much $r \in \mathcal{R}$ (result for a perturbed claim) deviates from a *reference* result $r_O \in \mathcal{R}$ (usually the result of the original claim). Negative $\mathsf{SR}(r; r_O)$ means the claim is weakened.
- A *(relative) parameter sensibility function* $\mathsf{SP} : \mathcal{P} \times \mathcal{P} \to \mathfrak{R}$. $\mathsf{SP}(\vec{p}; \vec{p}_O)$ captures how "sensible" a parameter setting $\vec{p} \in \mathcal{P}$ is with respect to a *reference* setting $\vec{p}_O \in \mathcal{P}$. High $\mathsf{SP}(\vec{p}; \vec{p}_O)$ means $\vec{p}$ is natural and relevant to the original claim context.

As an example, consider again Giuliani's claim. Since the full space of (w, t, d) is difficult to visualize, Figure 1a fixes $w = 6$ and plots the result strength function over (t, d) relative to the original claim at (t_O, d_O). While some perturbations (near the diagonal, shown in greener colors) strengthen the original claim, most perturbations (shown in redder colors) weaken it. However, not all perturbations are equally sensible. Figure 1b plots the relative parameter sensibility function; a darker color indicates higher sensibility. Sensibility scores generally drop around the original parameter setting (they become less relevant), but bumps occur at $d = 4$ and 8 (they are more natural because a mayor's term is four years). High-sensibility regions of $\mathcal{P}$ are more useful in checking the claim.

Measures of Claim Quality With the QRS framework, we can now define claim quality measures formally. As examples, we present the two measures used in our demonstration scenarios. We assume a finite and discrete $\mathcal{P}$ (generalization to the infinite and continuous case is straightforward).

- *Robustness* is defined as
$$\exp(-\textstyle\sum_{\vec{p} \in \mathcal{P}} \mathsf{SP}(\vec{p}; \vec{p}_O) \cdot (\min(0, \mathsf{SR}(q(\vec{p}); r_O)))^2).$$
Intuitively, it is based on the mean squared deviation of randomly perturbed claims (we consider the deviation to be 0 if the perturbed claim is stronger than the original). Robustness of 1 means all perturbations result in claims that are at least equally strong; robustness close to 0 means the original claim can be easily weakened. Giuliani's claim has low robustness.
- *Uniqueness* is defined as $\sum_{\vec{p} \in \mathcal{P}} \frac{1}{|\mathcal{P}|} \cdot \mathbf{1}(\mathsf{SR}(q(\vec{p}); r_O) < 0)$, where $\mathbf{1}(\cdot)$ is the indicator function. Intuitively, uniqueness is the fraction of parameter settings that yield results weaker than the original claim. Low uniqueness means it is easy to find perturbed claims at least as strong as the original. The one-of-the-few claim in Example 1 about Sam Lacey has low uniqueness.

Finding Counterarguments Besides quantifying claim quality, we can, with the help of QRS, cast the task of *finding best counterarguments* also as a computational problem. To counter a low-uniqueness claim, we show a (large enough) sample of the parameter settings that yield claims at least as strong as the original. To counter a low-robustness claim, we find the best counterarguments by bi-criteria optimization over the QRS: given a bound $-\delta$ on the deviation from the original claim result r_O, find the perturbed parameter setting $\vec{p}$ from the original setting $\vec{p}_O$ such that $\mathsf{SR}(q(\vec{p}); r_O) \leq -\delta$ and $\mathsf{SP}(\vec{p}; \vec{p}_O)$ is maximized. The dual and Pareto-optimal formulations are also plausible.

Reverse-Engineering Vague Claims With QRS, we can also cast the problem of reverse-engineering vague claims as finding the "isoline" of the QRS that contains the original claim result. With the help of parameter sensibility function SP, we can find the recovered claim that is the most sensible. More precisely, suppose the original claim has result r_O, and let $\vec{p}_O$ be a reasonable parameter setting capturing the claim context (without worrying about whether $q(\vec{p}_O) = r_O$). For example, Giuliani's adoption claim specifies none of the three parameter values; we simply pick $\vec{p}_O = (w_O, t_O, d_O) = (1, 2001, 8)$, reflecting that Giuliani was in office 1994–2001. Then, the most sensible recovered parameter setting $\vec{p}$ is the one that maximizes $\mathsf{SP}(\vec{p}; \vec{p}_O)$ while satisfying $\mathsf{SR}(q(\vec{p}); r_O) \approx 0$ (with an error bound allowing for the case when the original claim states its result vaguely).

Making Claims The QRS framework also allows us to formulate the task of making claims as computational problems. Given a claim template and a dataset, we can find all claims with high quality measures (such as uniqueness); we tackled this problem for one-of-the-few claims in [5]. Alternatively, further given an object of interest, we can find all parameter settings involving this object with high parameter sensibility and high result strength. This latter problem is the same as finding counterarguments to low-robustness claims discussed earlier, except it reverses the sign of the objective function for result strength. Note that the optimization criteria in this case do not include any quality measures, so we can generate "lies," which are useful to our demo (see Section 4 for details).

[1] In fact, we can also consider perturbing the data over which the query is evaluated, or even consider parameter and data perturbations jointly. Our current system, however, focuses only on perturbing parameters. Therefore, we will present our framework only in terms of parameter perturbations.

3 System Overview

Having seen how to model fact-checking tasks as computational problems, we now discuss how to implement this computational approach. A main challenge is the diversity of claims and domains. Such diversity manifests itself in both computation and modeling—different claim templates may require different algorithms to process efficiently, and knowledge about different domains needs to be captured by domain-specific scoring functions. Implementing each new claim template or applying it to each new domain completely from scratch will be too labor-intensive. Thus, our overarching design goal is to make the iCheck architecture general and extensible.

iCheck offers "pay-as-you-go" extensibility. The idea is that new claim templates and domains can be added with little effort to enable basic support, but if needed, better modeling and algorithms can be achieved with extra effort. We implement this idea by factoring out common domain properties, model components, and algorithmic ideas, and providing reasonable "defaults" that can be overridden by more sophisticated "plugins." In the following, we highlight how various aspects of iCheck implement this idea.

Algorithmic Framework In [6], we developed an algorithmic framework consisting of a suite of "meta" algorithms with pluggable low-level building blocks. The baseline meta algorithms are the most general and assume no special building blocks. More efficient meta algorithms assume building blocks that enable enumeration of points in the parameter space $\mathcal{P}$ in the order of sensibility. The most efficient meta algorithms use building blocks that enable a divide-and-conquer approach over $\mathcal{P}$. Thus, new templates are supported by the baseline algorithms with little effort upfront; higher efficiency can be achieved with more sophisticated building blocks, without re-implementing the high-level algorithms.

As an example, for Giuliani's claim in Example 1, consider the problem of finding the strongest counterarguments given a sensibility threshold. The *baseline* algorithm simply examines the 3-d parameter space $\mathcal{P}$ and tries every (w, t, d) setting. This algorithm is acceptable for this particular claim, because the time series of adoption numbers is small and the number of parameter settings is limited. In general, however, faster algorithms may be needed.

The algorithm based on *ordered enumeration* enumerates parameter settings in decreasing order of sensibility, and stops as soon as it reaches the sensibility threshold. For Giuliani's claim, the parameter sensibility function is a monotone combination of three per-dimension scores (for w, t, and d). Therefore, we only need to provide a building block for each dimension that enumerates the parameter values in this dimension in decreasing order of per-dimension score. The meta algorithm combines these building blocks to enable ordered enumeration in $\mathcal{P}$.

Finally, the *divide-and-conquer* meta algorithm works by dividing the parameter space into a number of *zones*, and solving the optimization problem in each zone. To enable this approach for Giuliani's claim, we provide a building block that divides the subset of $\mathcal{P}$ above the sensibility threshold into a series of zones, where each zone is a 2-d eclipse of possible (t, d) values (further bounded by linear constraints) with a given w value. Within each such zone, we can find the strongest counterargument (the parameter setting minimizing the relative strength with respect to the original claim) efficiently by reducing this problem to the well-studied range-maximum query over a static sequence; see [6] for details.

In sum, faster algorithms can be enabled by more sophisticated building blocks that are increasingly specialized for the claim template and domain. For the example above, if we assume that all parameter settings meeting the sensibility threshold fall within a sphere of radius $\tilde{r}$, then ordered enumeration takes $O(\tilde{r}^3 \log \tilde{r})$ time; divide-and-conquer only takes $O(\tilde{r}^2)$ time. In comparison, baseline always takes $O(|\mathcal{P}|)$ time, regardless of how small $\tilde{r}$ is.

Domain Knowledge Toolbox Various functions in our modeling and algorithmic frameworks capture domain knowledge needed to assess claim quality and enable efficient computation. As an example, for Giuliani's claim, the parameter sensibility function SP is the product of three scores, one for each of (w, t, d). The score for d, the distance between the two windows begin compared, further consists of two components: 1) *relevance*, which measures how relevant a perturbed d is to the context of the original claim; and 2) *naturalness*, which captures how intrinsically natural the perturbed d value is. We model relevance of d by $\exp(-(\frac{d-d_0}{\sigma_d})^2)$, where d_0 is the setting used in the original claim, and σ_d is used to control the weight of d's relevance relative to its naturalness and to the scores of other parameters. Intuitively, this relevance function penalizes big perturbations in d to favor counterarguments that are "close" to the original claim in their parameter settings. As for d's naturalness, because the New York City mayor has four-year terms, it is more natural to compare with windows that are multiples of 4 years apart; therefore, we assign higher naturalness to d values that are divisible by 4. For details, see [6].

Setting up such functions is not trivial, and we cannot afford to repeat this process for every parameter of every claim template for every dataset. Fortunately, for most of claims that we have examined, a handful of functional forms work well. For example, most parameters can be scored by a relative relevance term and an absolute naturalness term, like the parameter d discussed above. As another example, most numeric parameters have periodic naturalness scores, though their periods vary (e.g., quantities that are multiples of thousands, hundreds, or tens appear more natural in claims than those are not; numbers of months in the multiples of 12 are more natural). Therefore, iCheck implements a toolbox of such function forms, which user can choose and instantiate for the problem at hand. For the supported forms of sensibility functions, the toolbox also provides the enumeration functions required to enable meta algorithms based on ordered enumeration.

To simplify the task of encoding domain knowledge, iCheck provides a learning-based tool, which presents the user with a series of questions, such as asking the user to judge an alternative claim's strength and sensibility relative to the original claim. The tool then uses the answers to select appropriate function forms for SP and SR, and to train their parameters automatically.

Claim Template Library The same claim template are often applicable to many different scenarios. To avoid re-implementing the same template for different datasets and domains, iCheck maintains an extensible library of *generic* claim templates, which allow different datasets and SP/SR functions to be plugged in.

A generic claim template assumes that essential data are available through a *canonical schema*, which includes relational tables, and, in some cases, user-defined functions. The canonical schema hides the complexities of the actual datasets to which this template may be applied. For example, the vote correlation claim in Example 1 is an instance of the generic *TSS* (*time series similarity*) claim template. The TSS template assumes a table `series(id, t, v)`, where `id` identifies an object of interest (e.g., a legislator), `t` is a timestamp, and `v` is the value associated the object at `t`. The template also assumes a user-defined function `match(v1, v2)` that tests whether two values match. A TSS claim states that two objects' values match for some fraction of the time over a period.

Applying a generic claim template to a particular dataset requires us to define the mapping of actual data to tables defined by the canonical schema, and to supply the required user-defined functions. For example, given a database of the U.S. congressional voting records, to check claims about Representatives, we would define `series` as a view returning all relevant votes in the House; we would also define $\texttt{match}(v_1, v_2)$ to compare recorded votes appropriately (with attention to special values such as "present" or "not voting"). In addition, we need to provide functions to convert a TSS query with parameter values and result to a more human-readable form tailored toward the domain. For example, instead of making generic TSS counterarguments showing raw `t`'s and `id`'s, iCheck will invoke the conversion functions to show sentences talking about vote correlations over periods of dates, with full names of Representatives and URLs for additional information about them.

Generic claim template code specifies default choices of functions used by our modeling and algorithmic frameworks. It can also implement optimizations and algorithmic building blocks specific to this claim template. When applying the claim template to a specific scenario, we may find the defaults supplied by the template code already adequate; if so, this new application takes minimal effort. Otherwise, we need to override the defaults, with help from the domain knowledge toolbox described earlier, including the learning-based tool for setting up SP and SR. In any case, based on the functions available, the template code will invoke the most efficient meta algorithm that is enabled.

4 Demo Scenarios and User Interface

We will demonstrate most functionalities of iCheck through a website. This website has been customized for several domains (described further at the end of this section), but the underlying machinery for finding and checking facts remains the same.

The website provides an *object-centric view* that consolidates information about an object of interest, e.g., a U.S. legislator. On this view, a user can browse the list of claims known to iCheck about this object. These claims can be sorted by template, quality (using the measures defined in Section 2), and popularity (based on the level of user activities), allowing the user to spot interesting claims easily. From the object-centric view, the user can manually enter a claim about the object (e.g., from an attack ad against an incumbent) by selecting the claim template and filling out a form. Alternatively, the user can ask the system to come up some claims about this object that are correct, though possibly misleading. For example, the user can ask for claims implying that a legislator is too liberal (by citing vote correlation with well-known liberals).

The *claim-centric view* is where iCheck scrutinizes a claim. This view shows applicable quality measures, the list of counterarguments, as well as a list of "related" claims (whose definition depends on the domain). For vague claims, e.g., the vote correlation claim in Example 1, this view shows the list of possible reversed-engineered claims, each with its own view. Users can comment on the claim-centric views and share claims via social media. We will set up a Twitter hash tag so that conference followers not present at our demo will also be able to get a taste of it.

Besides comments, users can provide feedback in a number of ways. They can vote for the best counterarguments and reversed-engineered claims. We randomly challenge user to gauge the quality of a claim before showing our verdict and evidence; they will then be asked to judge the effectiveness of our fact-checking. User feedbacks will be summarized and shown on relevant views together with measures computed automatically by iCheck.

For those interested in the inner workings of iCheck, we will demonstrate, on a command-line interface, the process of making a new claim template, and applying an existing template to a new dataset (including using the tool that learns appropriate SP and SR through user feedbacks discussed in Section 3).

Domains We have prepared three domains: U.S. congressional voting records, sports statistics, and publication records of database researchers. The congressional voting records from *govtrack.us* contain more than 22 millions votes cast since May 1789 and are updated daily. We focus on vote correlation claims such as the one in Example 1, but additionally consider perturbing the subset of bills on which comparison is made. One useful subset is that of "controversial" bills, on which votes are largely divided between party lines. We also define subsets by legislative topics (e.g., gun control and health care), allowing users to explore "related" claims that zoom in on issues they care about.

For sports, we use NBA and MLB player statistics. From a popular EPSN blog (*espn.go.com/espn/elias*) by Elias Sports Bureau, we have chosen a few frequently used claim templates about players, including the "one-of-the-few" template in Example 1.

Interested in neither politics nor sports? We have a domain just for the SIGMOD audience. Using the DBLP (*dblp.uni-trier.de*) dataset, we allow a user to find impressive-sounding snippets to include in c.v. or tenure and promotion letters, and, if so desired, have a reality check on these snippets. For example, iCheck finds that one of the authors of this paper had a great year of publications—only 8 other researchers have ever managed to publish as much as (or more than) him in one year in all three venues: SIGMOD, VLDB, and ICDE. Of course, iCheck then readily points out that the same claim can be made for 89 other researchers!

5 Conclusion

This work falls under the general theme of *computational journalism* [2, 1], a nascent discipline that harnesses computing to help journalism cope with the challenges and opportunities of the digital age. iCheck is only a first step toward a computational approach to fact-checking. We have not addressed a number of related issues, such as continuously monitoring media for checkable claims, and automatically mapping natural-language claims to known templates. Furthermore, not all lies can be detected automatically by inspecting data and numbers alone; fact-checking in general needs to leverage collective human intelligence. Nonetheless, our demonstration illustrates the potential of computational techniques—in reducing cost and increasing effectiveness—for certain types of investigation tasks with growing importance today, as more structured datasets become available either directly or by information extraction. There has been some work already on computer-aided fact-checking (e.g., [3, 4]) complementing ours; we hope more will join us in tackling this problem of significant societal importance.

Acknowledgments The authors are supported by NSF grants IIS-09-16027, CCF-09-40671, IIS-10-18865, CCF-10-12254, CCF-11-17369, CCF-11-61359, and IIS-13-20357. Addition support comes from ERDC Contract W9132V-11-C-0003, ARO Contract W911NF-13-P-0018, Grant 2012/229 from the U.S.-Israel Binational Science Foundation, HP Labs Innovation Research Awards, and a Google Faculty Research Award. Any opinions, findings, and conclusions in this publication are those of the author(s) and do not necessarily reflect the views of the funding agencies.

References

[1] Sarah Cohen, James T. Hamilton, and Fred Turner. Computational journalism. *Communications of the ACM*, 54(10):66–71, 2011.

[2] Sarah Cohen, Chengkai Li, Jun Yang, and Cong Yu. Computational journalism: A call to arms to database researchers. In *CIDR* 2011.

[3] Rob Ennals, Beth Trushkowsky, and John Mark Agosta. Highlighting disputed claims on the Web. In *WWW* 2010.

[4] François Goasdoué, Konstantinos Karanasos, Yannis Katsis, Julien Leblay, Ioana Manolescu, and Stamatis Zampetakis. Fact checking and analyzing the Web. In *SIGMOD* 2013.

[5] You Wu, Pankaj K. Agarwal, Chengkai Li, Jun Yang, and Cong Yu. On "one of the few" objects. In *KDD* 2012.

[6] You Wu, Pankaj K. Agarwal, Chengkai Li, Jun Yang, and Cong Yu. Toward computational fact-checking. *PVLDB*, 7(7), 2014.

ABS: a System for Scalable Approximate Queries with Accuracy Guarantees

Kai Zeng[†] Shi Gao[†] Jiaqi Gu[†] Barzan Mozafari[‡] Carlo Zaniolo[†]
[†]University of California, Los Angeles [‡]University of Michigan
[†]{kzeng, gaoshi, gujiaqi, zaniolo}@cs.ucla.edu [‡]mozafari@umich.edu

ABSTRACT

Approximate Query Processing (AQP) based on sampling is critical for supporting timely and cost-effective analytics over big data. To be applied successfully, AQP must be accompanied by reliable estimates on the quality of sample-produced approximate answers; the two main techniques used in the past for this purpose are (i) closed-form analytic error estimation, and (ii) the bootstrap method. Approach (i) is extremely efficient but lacks generality, whereas (ii) is general but suffers from high computational overhead. Our recently introduced *Analytical Bootstrap* method combines the strengths of both approaches and provides the basis for our *ABS* system, which will be demonstrated at the conference. The *ABS* system models bootstrap by a probabilistic relational model, and extends relational algebra with operations on probabilistic relations to predict the distributions of the AQP results. Thus, *ABS* entails a very fast computation of bootstrap-based quality measures for a general class of SQL queries, which is several orders of magnitude faster than the standard simulation-based bootstrap. In this demo, we will demonstrate the generality, automaticity, and ease of use of the *ABS* system, and its superior performance over the traditional approaches described above.

Categories and Subject Descriptors

H.2.4 [**Systems**]: Query processing

Keywords

Approximate Query Processing; Error Estimation; Bootstrap

1. INTRODUCTION

Today's business, science and engineering disciplines are predominantly data-driven. The ever-growing size of data calls for timely and cost-effective analysis. This situation has brought even more attention to the already-active area of Approximate Query Processing (AQP). As a critical and general approach for coping with massive datasets, sampling is widely used in databases [4, 6, 9, 11, 12, 13, 18], Map-Reduce systems [5, 16], and data stream management systems [7, 17].

Sampling refers to the commonly used technique of evaluating the queries froma small random *sample* of the original database. The quality of the obtained approximate query answers plays an important role to their utility. As an example, during exploratory analysis, the analyst will seek assurance that the answer derived from the small sample is of "good quality", e.g., within $\pm 1\%$ of the correct answer with probability $\geq 95\%$. Thus, assessing the quality (i.e. error estimation) is a fundamental aspect of AQP.

The past two decades have seen much work on error estimation, which can be categorized into two main approaches. The first approach [5, 8, 9, 11, 19, 22] analytically derives closed-form error estimates. Although computationally appealing, analytic error quantification is restricted to a very limited set of queries (simple group-by-aggregate queries) [20].

To address this problem, a second approach, named *bootstrap*, has emerged as a more general method for error estimation [15, 16, 20], and is becoming increasingly popular due to its wide applicability and automaticity [15, 16, 20]. Bootstrap [10, 21] is a Monte-Carlo procedure, which given an initial sample (i) repeatedly forms simulated datasets by resampling tuples i.i.d. (identically and independently) from the given sample, (ii) recomputes the query on each of the simulated datasets, and (iii) assesses the quality of answer on the basis of the empirical distribution of the produced query answers. However, bootstrap is highly computation-demanding, since it requires hundreds or even thousands of trials to obtain a reliable estimate [15, 20].

In this demonstration, we introduce the *ABS* system, a fast error estimation system for AQP. The *ABS* system is designed and developed to bridge the gap between the two aforementioned approaches by dovetailing their merits while avoiding their limitations: *ABS* inherits the general and automatic nature of bootstrap, and thus can be applied to a much more general class of SQL queries, but does not require the Monte-Carlo simulation, and thus is highly computationally efficient. These merits of *ABS* enable complex exploratory data analysis on large volumes of data.

ABS achieves these merits by exploiting a new technique, called the *analytical bootstrap*. Analytical boostrap succinctly models the set of all possible simulated datasets generated by bootstrap trials as a single *probabilistic multiset database* (PMDB for short), by annotating each tuple in the database with an integer-valued random variable. The random variable represents the possible multiplicity with which the tuple would appear in the simulated datasets. Then, *ABS* extends relational operators to manipulate these random variables during query evaluation, which produces an annotated relation where the annotations encode the distribution of all possible answers that could be generated by bootstrap. In particular, *ABS* evaluates the query only once, but can accurately estimate the empirical distribution of the query answers that would be produced by hundreds or thousands of bootstrap trials. Furthermore, analyti-

SIGMOD'14, June 22–27, 2014, Snowbird, UT, USA.

http://dx.doi.org/10.1145/2588555.2594532.

cal bootstrap can be easily integrated into existing database engines through user-defined types and user-defined functions.

During the demonstration, users will experience, through hands-on experience on real-life databases and queries, the convenience and efficiency of using *ABS* for error estimation in approximate query answering. The user interacts with *ABS* by simply providing the target query and specifying the desired error measure. The *ABS* will transparently rewrite the query to add quality quantification support, execute the rewritten query and deliver the query result as well as the quality measure in an interactive manner. The user can also compare analytical bootstrap against the closed-form approach and the standard simulation-based bootstrap to experience the generality and efficiency of the *ABS* system.

The rest of the paper is organized as follows: Section 2 provides a summary of the theoretical background. We present the system architecture in Section 3. Section 4 briefly describes the demonstration we are proposing. We conclude in Section 5.

2. ANALYTICAL BOOTSTRAP

We briefly review the background on bootstrap, and exemplify the analytical bootstrap method which is the key technique of the *ABS* system. Interested readers are referred to [23] for more details on analytical bootstrap.

Sampling and Bootstrap Sampling is widely used in approximate query processing, which consists in (i) taking a random sample D from the original database, (ii) evaluating a potentially modified query q on D, and (iii) using $q(D)$ as an approximation for the original query. However, the obtained approximate results are of little use if they are not accompanied with accuracy estimation.

Bootstrap [10, 21] is powerful tool for estimating the quality of $q(D)$, which consists in a simple Monte-Carlo procedure: it repeatedly carries out a sub-routine, called a *trial*. Each trial generates a simulated database, say $\hat{D}_i$, which is of the same size as D (by sampling $|D|$ tuples i.i.d. from D *with* replacement), and then computes query q on $\hat{D}_i$. Consider a simplified version of the *lineitem* relation and the "Small-quantity-order Revenue" query q (see Example 1) from the TPC-H benchmark [3]. A sample D of *lineitem* is shown in shown in Figure 1(a).[1] Figure 1(b) and 1(c) show one possible resample from a bootstrap trial and the corresponding query result, respectively. The collection $\{q(\hat{D}_i)\}$ from all the bootstrap trials forms an empirical distribution, based on which various accuracy measures, e.g., variance and confidence intervals, can be computed.

EXAMPLE 1 (SMALL-QUANTITY-ORDER REVENUE).

```
SELECT l_partkey, SUM(l_extendedprice) as revenue
FROM   lineitem as outer
WHERE  l_quantity < (
       SELECT SUM(l_quantity) / 3
       FROM   lineitem as inner
       WHERE  inner.l_partkey = outer.l_partkey)
GROUP BY l_partkey
```

Bootstrap is effective and robust over a wide range of practical situations [15, 20, 16]. However, as mentioned above, bootstrap suffers from high computational overhead, as it requires hundreds or even thousands of bootstrap trials in order to obtain an accurate quality estimate. Next, we introduce analytical bootstrap, which has been proven equivalent to the simulation-based bootstrap, but avoids the computational overhead [23].

Probabilistic Multiset Database Each bootstrap resample generates a multiset relation. E.g., in the resample shown in Figure 1(b), tuple t_2 is drawn twice, while tuple t_3 is not selected. These multiset relations can be represented in a functional way, where each tuple t is annotated with an integer $\pi(t)$, representing its multiplicity in the resample. Figure 3(a) shows the functional representation of Figure 1(b).

lineitem, $D =$

	l_pk	l_q	l_ep
t_1	p01	4	20
t_2	p01	5	25
t_3	p01	3	15
t_4	p02	1	10
t_5	p02	8	80

(a)

lineitem, $\hat{D} =$

tuple
t_1
t_2
t_2
t_4
t_5

(b)

l_pk	revenue
p01	20
p02	10

(c)

Figure 1: (a) An example database sample D, (b) a resample of D, and (c) the corresponding query result

The key idea of analytical bootstrap is to model all possible bootstrap resamples as a single relation, where tuples are annotated with nondeterministic multiplicities, and thus a query can be evaluated once on this relation, instead of on many different resamples. Since the annotations are probabilistic, the obtained database is called a *probabilistic multiset database* (PMDB). For instance, Figure 3(f) is the PMDB modeling all possible bootstrap resamples of Figure 1(a), where the nondeterministic multiplicities $(\pi_1, \pi_2, \pi_3, \pi_4, \pi_5)$ jointly follow a multinomial distribution $Multinomial(5, [0.2, 0.2, 0.2, 0.2, 0.2])$. Figure 1(b) is an instantiation of Figure 3(f) by assigning $\pi_1 = 1$, $\pi_2 = 2$ and so on.

Extending Relational Algebra Evaluating queries on bootstrap resamples simply follows relational algebra with multiset semantics. Green et al. [14] showed that one can query a multiset database by extending the relational algebra with the $+$ and $\cdot$ operators, which manipulate the annotated multiplicities: for projection, we add the multiplicities of all input tuples that are projected to the same result tuple, while for join, we multiply the multiplicities of joined tuples. I.e., inductively:

- **Selection** $\sigma_c(R)$. $\pi_{\sigma_c(R)}(t) = \pi_R(t) \cdot \mathbb{1}(c(t))$, where $\mathbb{1}(c(t))$ returns 1 if $c(t)$ is true and 0 otherwise.
- **Projection** $\Pi_A(R)$. $\pi_{\Pi_A(R)}(t) = \sum_{t'[A]=t} \pi_R(t')$ where $t'[A]$ is the projection of t' on A.
- **Join** $R_1 \bowtie R_2$. $\pi_{R_1 \bowtie R_2}(t) = \pi_{R_1}(t_1) \cdot \pi_{R_2}(t_2)$, where t_i is t on U_i.

Consider the query plan for Example 1 as shown in Figure 2.[2] Figure 3(b) to 3(e) demonstrate the evaluation steps using the extended relational algebra.

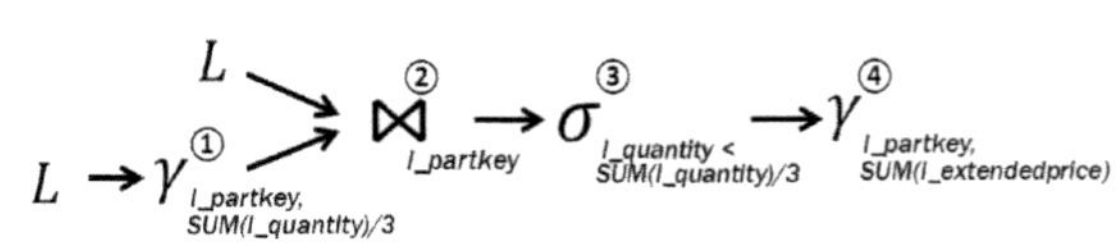

Figure 2: Query plan for the running example

Even with the extended relational algebra, the simulation-based bootstrap still needs to evaluate the query many times on different resample instances. In contrast, the analytical bootstrap extends relational algebra with operators that directly manipulate the annotations in the PMDB, i.e., random variables representing the nondeterministic multiplicities. Specifically, the analytical bootstrap introduces two operators on the annotated random variables, namely $+$ *convolution* ($\oplus$) and $\cdot$ *convolution* ($\odot$), defined as: for any two random variables r_1 and r_2, $r_1 \oplus r_2$ ($r_1 \odot r_2$) is a new random variable, where

$$\Pr(r_1 \oplus r_2 = s) = \sum\{\Pr(r_1 = x \wedge r_2 = y) \mid \forall x, y, x + y = s\}$$

$$\Pr(r_1 \odot r_2 = s) = \sum\{\Pr(r_1 = x \wedge r_2 = y) \mid \forall x, y, x \cdot y = s\}$$

[1] We use *l_pk*, *l_q* and *l_ep* as short for *l_partkey*, *l_quantity* and *l_extendedprice*, respectively.

[2] $\gamma_{A,\alpha(B)}$ denotes applying aggregate α on B group by A.

lineitem

t	π
t_1	1
t_2	2
t_3	0
t_4	1
t_5	1

(a)

l_pk	ϖ_{sum}	π
p01	$4 \times 1 + 5 \times 2 + 3 \times 0 = 14$	$\mathbb{1}(1 + 2 + 0) = 1$
p02	$1 \times 1 + 8 \times 1 = 9$	$\mathbb{1}(1 + 1) = 1$

(b) Step ① in Figure 2

t	ϖ_{sum}	π
t_1	14	$1 \times 1 = 1$
t_2	14	$2 \times 1 = 2$
t_3	14	$0 \times 1 = 0$
t_4	9	$1 \times 1 = 1$
t_5	9	$1 \times 1 = 1$

(c) Step ② in Figure 2

t	π
t_1	$\mathbb{1}(14 > 12) \times 1 = 1$
t_2	$\mathbb{1}(14 > 15) \times 1 = 0$
t_3	$\mathbb{1}(14 > 9) \times 0 = 0$
t_4	$\mathbb{1}(9 > 3) \times 1 = 1$
t_5	$\mathbb{1}(9 > 24) \times 1 = 1$

(d) Step ③ in Figure 2

l_pk	ϖ_{SUM}
p01	$1 \times 20 + 0 \times 25 + 0 \times 15 = 20$
p02	$10 \times 1 + 80 \times 0 = 10$

(e) Step ④ in Figure 2

lineitem

t	π
t_1	π_1
t_2	π_2
t_3	π_3
t_4	π_4
t_5	π_5

(f)

l_pk	ϖ_{sum}	π
p01	$\varpi_1 = 4\pi_1 \oplus 5\pi_2 \oplus 3\pi_3$	$\pi_1' = \mathbb{1}(\pi_1 \oplus \pi_2 \oplus \pi_3)$
p02	$\varpi_2 = 1\pi_4 \oplus 8\pi_5$	$\pi_2' = \mathbb{1}(\pi_4 \oplus \pi_5)$

(g) Step ① in Figure 2

t	ϖ_{sum}	π
t_1	ϖ_1	$\pi_1 \odot \pi_1'$
t_2	ϖ_1	$\pi_2 \odot \pi_1'$
t_3	ϖ_1	$\pi_3 \odot \pi_1'$
t_4	ϖ_2	$\pi_4 \odot \pi_2'$
t_5	ϖ_2	$\pi_5 \odot \pi_2'$

(h) Step ② in Figure 2

t	π
t_1	$\pi_1'' = \mathbb{1}(\varpi_1 > 12) \odot \pi_1 \odot \pi_1'$
t_2	$\pi_2'' = \mathbb{1}(\varpi_1 > 15) \odot \pi_2 \odot \pi_1'$
t_3	$\pi_3'' = \mathbb{1}(\varpi_1 > 9) \odot \pi_3 \odot \pi_1'$
t_4	$\pi_4'' = \mathbb{1}(\varpi_2 > 3) \odot \pi_4 \odot \pi_2'$
t_5	$\pi_5'' = \mathbb{1}(\varpi_2 > 24) \odot \pi_5 \odot \pi_2'$

(i) Step ③ in Figure 2

l_pk	ϖ_{sum}
p01	$20\pi_1'' \oplus 25\pi_2'' \oplus 15\pi_3''$
p02	$10\pi_4'' \oplus 80\pi_5''$

(j) Step ④ in Figure 2

Figure 3: (a) One resample instance with annotations, (b)-(e) evaluation steps in multiset semantics, (f) the PMDB for Figure 1(a), and (g)-(j) evaluation steps of analytical bootstrap

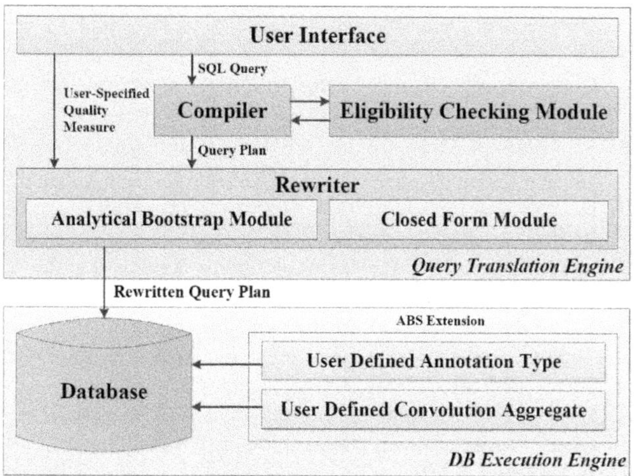

Figure 4: *ABS* Architecture

Similar to the extended relational algebra for multiset semantics, analytical bootstrap applies $\oplus$ operator whenever summing the annotations, and applies $\odot$ operator whenever multiplying the annotations. Figure 3(g) to 3(j) show the corresponding evaluation steps of analytical bootstrap for Figure 2.

Efficient Evaluation It is both space and time consuming to manipulate random variables symbolically. Thus, at query time, analytical bootstrap represents and manipulates the random variables by their marginal distributions. Specifically, analytical bootstrap represents each annotation π by a pair $(n, \mathbf{p})$, namely the *multinomial representation*, where (i) n is the number of multinomial trials in a bootstrap trial, which is the size of the relation being resampled, and (ii) $\mathbf{p}$ is the probability vector of a single multinomial trial, i.e., probability of this tuple being picked ($\mathbf{p}[1]$) or not picked ($\mathbf{p}[0]$). E.g., π_1 is represented by $(5, [\mathbf{p}[1] = 0.2, \mathbf{p}[0] = 0.8])$.

In contrast to symbolic manipulation, this evaluation technique can only be applied to the cases where tuples in any intermediate results are generated from disjoint set of tuples from the base relation. Fortunately, query plans that satisfy the requirement, called *eligible plans* [23], can be detected at compile time.

3. SYSTEM ARCHITECTURE

Figure 4 shows the high-level architecture of the *ABS* system, which can be divided into two main components: (1) *Query Translation Engine*: transparently compiling, checking and rewriting the query to support error estimation. (2) *DB Execution Engine*: evaluating the query augmented with error estimation operations, and delivering the accuracy measures in user-specified metrics. The two components are decoupled by the rewritten query plans:

Query Translation Engine Taking a SQL query, the compiler generates a query plan expressed in relational algebra. Then, the compiler passes the execution plan along with the basic settings of the input database to the eligibility checking module. Based on the eligibility rules defined in [11, 23], the eligibility checking module verifies if the input query plan is suitable to perform analytical bootstrap and/or the closed-form method.

If an eligible plan is found, the compiler passes the plan to the rewriter. The rewriter takes into consideration the user-specified quality measures, and rewrites the plan into a new query plan with annotation enhanced operations in order to support error estimation, i.e., with additional annotations, and functions that propagate the annotations according to the methods discussed in Section 2. The rewritten query plan preserves the result of the original query, and adds the desired error measures specified by the user.

DB Execution Engine The rewritten query plan is then submitted to the execution engine. Through user-defined type and user-defined aggregates/functions, the execution techniques of the *ABS* system, i.e., extended relational algebra in Section 2, can be easily integrated into common database engines as an extension module (*ABS* extension as shown in Figure 4). Specifically, the *ABS* system expresses the annotations in the form of user-defined types, and the convolution operations of the annotations as user-defined aggregates/functions. Currently, we implement the *ABS* system on top of Hive [1], an open source distributed data warehouse that supports efficient query evaluation on massive data sets. Furthermore, since our implementation is built as an extension module of Hive, it is easy to deploy *ABS* on other query engines (e.g., Shark [2]).

4. DEMONSTRATION DESCRIPTION

The demonstration is organized into three phases: (1) a brief introduction to the main system functionalities, in which we will exhibit the key components and features of our system; (2) a "hands-on" phase in which the public is invited to directly interact with the system and test its capabilities; and (3) a performance comparison, in which we demonstrate the superior performance of *ABS* by comparing it against the closed-form approach and the standard simulation-based bootstrap.

In the demonstration of the system functionalities, we will show how the system interface (e.g., figure 5) guides the user through the steps of query processing:

(i) *Query Eligibility Verification.* In this step, the *ABS* system first loads the database and the corresponding database sample speci-

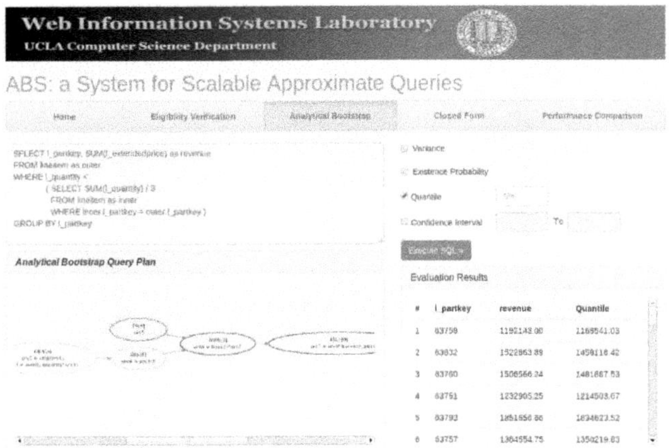

Figure 5: *ABS* Web Interface: analytical bootstrap evaluation

fied by user. Then the user can submit the query of interest to be evaluated on the loaded database. The system compiles the input query to a query plan explained in relational algebra, and provides users a visualization of the query plan. Based on this query plan, the system checks whether it is eligible for applying efficient analytical bootstrap method and/or closed-form method to estimate the approximation error of the query. Non-eligible operators will be marked out with detailed information indicating which eligible rule is violated.

In addition, the system will also provide a list of applicable error estimation methods, which could include one or more of (i) closed-form evaluation, (ii) analytical bootstrap method, and (iii) the standard bootstrap. If neither analytical bootstrap nor closed form evaluation is not applicable, the system will choose the standard bootstrap as default. At this point, the user can determine the evaluation method for the submitted query.

(ii) *Query Rewriting*. In this step, the *ABS* system presents how a query is rewritten into a new query that can provide error measures alongside the approximate answers. For analytical bootstrap evaluation, *ABS* extends the query plan by augmenting the query plan with annotation manipulation operations; while for closed form evaluation, the query plan will be augmented with functions to collect the statistics required in the prediction formulas, such as mean and variance of target columns in the query. The new query plan is then passed to our database engine.

(iii) *Query Evaluation and Error Measurement*. Once the rewritten query plan is ready, our database engine evaluates it on the chosen database sample. To demonstrate the result of query evaluation, the *ABS* system provides different kinds of error measures (e.g., variance, quantiles and confidence intervals) for the user to choose from based on the application purpose. Figure 5 shows the web interface of analytical bootstrap in *ABS*.

(iv) *Performance Comparison*. To better explore the various error estimation methods supported, the user can compare the methods in terms of the result accuracy and the evaluation efficiency. We have prepared several TPC-H datasets in different scales for comparison purposes. Since the standard bootstrap requires hundreds of iterations to reach reliable estimation, we have also prepared the bootstrap results for a few queries in advance.

5. CONCLUSION

The *ABS* system represents a major step forward for error estimation in AQP, achieving a level of generality, automaticity and superior efficiency that have not been obtained by previous approaches. The demonstration highlights the main functionalities of the system, and exhibits how this important error estimation technique can be easily integrated into existing database systems.

6. REFERENCES

[1] Apache Hive Project. https://hive.apache.org/.

[2] Shark Project. http://shark.cs.berkeley.edu/.

[3] TPC-H Benchmark. http://www.tpc.org/tpch/.

[4] S. Acharya, P. B. Gibbons, et al. The Aqua Approximate Query Answering System. In *SIGMOD*, pages 574–576, 1999.

[5] S. Agarwal, B. Mozafari, et al. BlinkDB: Queries with Bounded Errors and Bounded Response Times on Very Large Data. In *EuroSys*, pages 29–42, 2013.

[6] B. Babcock, S. Chaudhuri, et al. Dynamic Sample Selection for Approximate Query Processing. In *SIGMOD*, pages 539–550, 2003.

[7] B. Babcock, M. Datar, et al. Load Shedding for Aggregation Queries over Data Streams. In *ICDE*, page 350, 2004.

[8] M. Charikar, S. Chaudhuri, et al. Towards Estimation Error Guarantees for Distinct Values. In *PODS*, pages 268–279, 2000.

[9] S. Chaudhuri, G. Das, et al. Optimized stratified sampling for approximate query processing. *TODS*, 32(2):9, 2007.

[10] B. Efron and R. J. Tibshirani. *An Introduction to the Bootstrap*. Chapman & Hall, New York, 1993.

[11] J. M. Hellerstein, P. J. Haas, et al. Online Aggregation. In *SIGMOD*, pages 171–182, 1997.

[12] Y. Hu, S. Sundara, et al. Estimating Aggregates in Time-Constrained Approximate Queries in Oracle. In *EDBT*, pages 1104–1107, 2009.

[13] C. Jermaine, S. Arumugam, et al. Scalable Approximate Query Processing with DBO Engine. In *SIGMOD*, pages 1–54, 2007.

[14] G. Karvounarakis and T. J. Green. Semiring-Annotated Data: Queries and Provenance? *SIGMOD Record*, 41(3):5–14, 2012.

[15] A. Kleiner, A. Talwalkar, et al. A General Bootstrap Performance Diagnostic. In *KDD*, pages 419–427, 2013.

[16] N. Laptev, K. Zeng, et al. Early Accurate Results for Advanced Analytics on MapReduce. *PVLDB*, 5(10):1028–1039, 2012.

[17] B. Mozafari and C. Zaniolo. Optimal Load Shedding with Aggregates and Mining Queries. In *ICDE*, pages 76–88, 2010.

[18] C. Olston, E. Bortnikov, et al. Interactive Analysis of Web-Scale Data. In *CIDR*, 2009.

[19] N. Pansare, V. R. Borkar, et al. Online Aggregation for Large MapReduce Jobs. *PVLDB*, 4(11):1135–1145, 2011.

[20] A. Pol and C. Jermaine. Relational Confidence Bounds Are Easy With The Bootstrap. In *SIGMOD*, pages 587–598, 2005.

[21] A. van der Vaart and J. Wellner. *Weak Convergence and Empirical Processes*. Springer, corrected edition, Nov. 2000.

[22] S. Wu, B. C. Ooi, et al. Continuous Sampling for Online Aggregation over Multiple Queries. In *SIGMOD*, pages 651–662, 2010.

[23] K. Zeng, S. Gao, et al. The Analytical Bootstrap: a New Method for Fast Error Estimation in Approximate Query Processing. In *SIGMOD*, 2014.

NADEEF/ER: Generic and Interactive Entity Resolution

Ahmed Elmagarmid[1] Ihab F. Ilyas[2] Mourad Ouzzani[1]
Jorge-Arnulfo Quiané-Ruiz[1] Nan Tang[1] Si Yin[1]

[1]Qatar Computing Research Institute [2]University of Waterloo
{aelmagarmid, mouzzani, jquianeruiz, ntang, siyin}@qf.org.qa ilyas@uwaterloo.ca

ABSTRACT

Entity resolution (ER), the process of identifying and eventually merging records that refer to the same real-world entities, is an important and long-standing problem. We present NADEEF/ER, a generic and interactive entity resolution system, which is built as an extension over our open-source generalized data cleaning system NADEEF. NADEEF/ER provides a rich programming interface for manipulating entities, which allows generic, efficient and extensible ER. In this demo, users will have the opportunity to experience the following features: (1) *Easy specification* – Users can easily define ER rules with a browser-based specification, which will then be automatically transformed to various functions, treated as *black-boxes* by NADEEF; (2) *Generality and extensibility* – Users can customize their ER rules by refining and fine-tuning the above functions to achieve both effective and efficient ER solutions; (3) *Interactivity* – We also extended the existing NADEEF dashboard with summarization and clustering techniques to facilitate understanding problems faced by the ER process as well as to allow users to influence resolution decisions.

Categories and Subject Descriptors

H.2.m [**Database Management**]: Miscellaneous - Data cleaning

Keywords

NADEEF, Entity resolution, Generic, Interactive

1. INTRODUCTION

Entity resolution (ER) (*a.k.a.* record linkage and deduplication) is a well known problem that arises in many applications. The goal is to identify and link different representations (*e.g.,* records in a relational database) of the same real world entity. A large chunk of research has been dedicated to tackle different issues related to ER such as using entity features and relational features for matching, leveraging machine learning techniques, combining crowd sourcing and active learning, taking into different constraints on the data during ER, and so on (see [8] for a tutorial).

ER is usually computationally expensive, since it may require comparing all possible pairs of entities. Multiple techniques such as blocking, sorted neighborhood, clustering, and canopies (see [6] for a survey) have been proposed. In addition, parallelization and Hadoop-based solutions have also been studied to further improve efficiency, *e.g.,* Dedoop [9]. Crowd has been used to improve effectiveness [12]. There have been also some efforts in supporting generality for ER. For example, Swoosh [1] proposes a generic approach where the users implement two user defined functions (UDFs): match() and merge(). Swoosh would then take care of how to invoke these two UDFs.

Despite all of these rich contributions, allowing easy *user-tunable* parameters as well as providing *generic* interfaces for users to implement application specific functions remain hard to achieve in one single system.

We recently presented NADEEF, an open-source[1] data cleaning system [3]. NADEEF distinguishes between a programming interface and a core to achieve generality and extensibility for data cleaning. We demonstrated these two features in [4]. This work inspired us in our solution to the above stated ER issues: *How to allow both easy user-tunable parameters and generic interfaces for ER?* In this demo, we present NADEEF/ER, a generic and interactive ER system. NADEEF/ER, which is built on top of NADEEF, supports a large variety of ER applications by providing a rich programming interface and an interactive dashboard. The demo will demonstrate the following three key features:

(1) *Easy specification.* NADEEF/ER provides a succinct GUI that allows users to declare advanced ER rules. NADEEF/ER, in turn, automatically transforms these rules into various UDFs, following NADEEF model, for execution.

(2) *Generality and extensibility.* Users can modify or override any NADEEF/ER interface functions in order to manipulate entities more effectively and efficiently. For example, users might provide their own matching, merging, blocking, and clustering functionalities. This offers freedom to fully customize NADEEF/ER for specific ER applications. Users can perform any of these code editing/checking via the GUI provided by NADEEF/ER.

(3) *Interactivity.* NADEEF/ER provides a dashboard where users can better visualize duplicated entities. This will not

SIGMOD'14, June 22–27, 2014, Snowbird, UT, USA.
Copyright 2014 ACM 978-1-4503-2376-5/14/06 ...$15.00.
http://dx.doi.org/10.1145/2588555.2594511.

[1]https://github.com/Qatar-Computing-Research-Institute/NADEEF

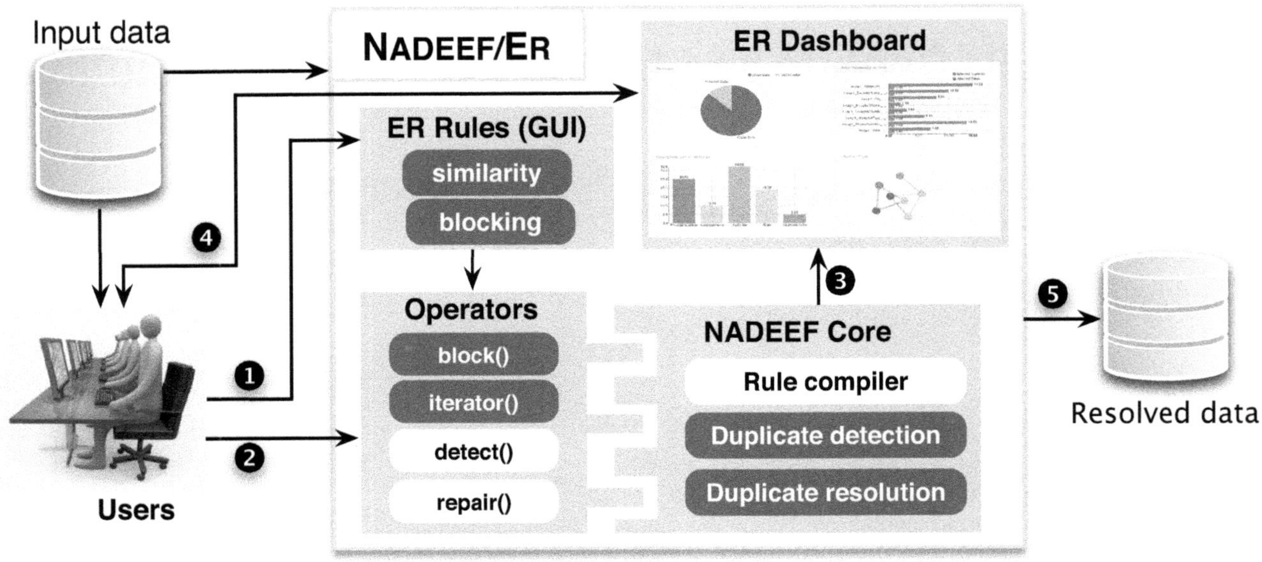

Figure 1: Architecture of NADEEF/ER

only help users to understand resolution problems, but also permit users to influence resolution decisions.

Related work. Matching techniques (see [6] for a more comprehensive survey) are a crucial tool for ER. These techniques range from character-based similarity metrics (*e.g.,* edit distance, Jaro distance, *Q*-gram distance) and token-based similarity metrics (*e.g., tf.idf*) to phonetic similarity metrics (*e.g.,* Soundex). In NADEEF/ER, we use the SimMetrics library[2] that supports many of these techniques. Moreover, using NADEEF/ER generic interface, users can implement other functions for numeric metrics and probabilistic matching models (*e.g.,* Bayes decision rules).

Achieving efficiency in ER aims to reduce the number of entity comparisons and has been tackled with techniques such as blocking, sorted neighborhood, clustering and canopies. NADEEF/ER supports these techniques through two functions, block() and iterator(). The former partitions entities into blocks, while the latter specifies how entities are actually compared within a block. Other researchers have also studied different indexing techniques for improving efficiency (*e.g.,* inverted indices, suffix arrays, see [2] for a comprehensive study). Supporting these indices is not the focus of NADEEF/ER.

There have also been many ER systems in the past. Some provide a declarative language (*e.g.,* AJAX [7]) or a GUI for rich user-tunable parameters (*e.g.,* TAILOR [5], Febrl and FRIL). Others target generic ER solutions *e.g.,* Swoosh [1]. In contrast, NADEEF/ER aims at a generic yet efficient system, by providing various functions to customize the system, to achieve both effective (as match() and merge() in Swoosh) and efficient (via block() and iterator()) ER solutions.

Another line of work is to learn ER rules with training datasets (*e.g.,* ALIAS [11]). These are essentially orthogonal, but complementary, to NADEEF/ER.

2. NADEEF/ER ARCHITECTURE

In this section, we discuss the architecture of NADEEF/ER (Fig. 1), an ER system built on top of NADEEF [3]. NADEEF/ER consists of the following components: a GUI for defining ER rules, a programming interface for defining data quality rules, NADEEF core for duplicate detection and resolution, and an ER dashboard for user interaction.

NADEEF/ER works as follows. (1) Users specify ER rules via a GUI. (2) User-specified ER rules via the GUI will be automatically transformed into data quality rules, expressed in a set of basic functions: block(), iterator(), detect(), and repair(). Users can also customize these rules by refining any of these four functions. (3) NADEEF core then compiles these rules and uses them to detect duplicated entities and eventually merge them. NADEEF treats these four functions as black-boxes. (4) Users can interact with the dashboard to explore and visualize information for duplicated entities. This allows users to refine ER rules as in steps (1) and (2), or to influence resolution decisions (by confirming duplicates/non-duplicates). (5) After iterations of the above process, NADEEF returns all detected duplicates, or produces a duplicate-free dataset if a repair() function for merging duplicates is provided by the users.

ER rules. This component collects user-specified ER rules via a GUI, as shown in Fig. 2. Given two tables (which might be the same table), users can drag lines to define attributes to be compared and define the similarity functions as well as corresponding thresholds. For each ER rule, the users can also specify the blocking strategy along with the generation function for its blocking key. NADEEF/ER will then automatically transform rules into four basic functions (or operators), as we explain below.

Operators. The unified programming interface for a data quality rule in NADEEF is as follows:

```
class Rule {
  Collection⟨Table⟩ block(Collection⟨Table⟩ tb);
  void iterator(Collection⟨Table⟩ tbs, IteratorStream⟨TuplePair⟩ is);
  Collection⟨Violation⟩ detect(TuplePair tp);
  Collection⟨Fix⟩ repair(Violation v);
}
```

While one can use these four functions for generalized data cleaning tasks, in the following, we explain them in the context of entity resolution only.

(1) block() takes a set of tables as input and returns partitions for each table. One can use this function to implement

[2]https://github.com/Simmetrics/simmetrics

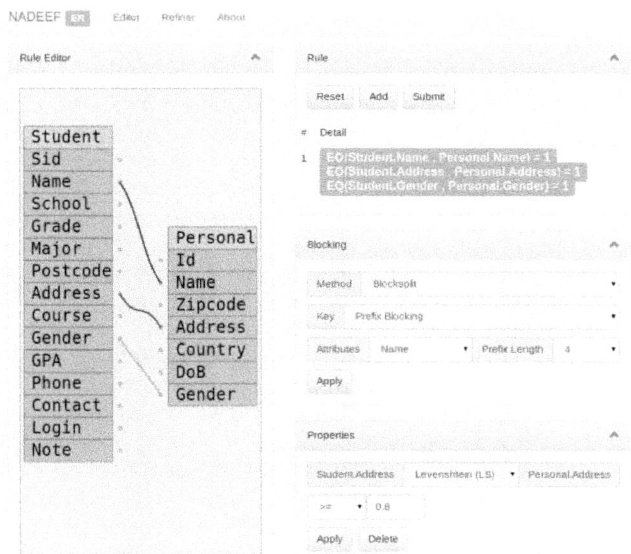

Figure 2: ER rule specification

most blocking/clustering algorithms, allowing a more generalized blocking strategy beyond key-based blocking.

(2) iterator() takes a set of tables which could be base tables or blocks from the function block() as input and outputs pairs of tuples. Intuitively, this function allows users to implement smart ways to populate pairs of entities to be compared, *e.g.,* sorted neighborhood, in contrast to enumerating all pairs of entities within a given block.

(3) detect() takes a pair of tuples as input. If they are duplicates, it will return both tuples, referred to as a *Violation*. Otherwise, it returns an empty result, indicating that the two input tuples are not duplicates.

(4) repair() takes a pair of duplicated tuples (*i.e.,* a *Violation*) as input and specifies how to merge them.

When users specify ER rules via GUI, NADEEF/ER will transform them to the above four functions as follows. The similarity metrics on how to decide whether two entities are duplicates will be transformed into the detect() function. The blocking strategy will be transformed into the block() function. The other two functions, repair() (for merging entities) and iterator() (for smartly populating entity pairs), will have to be implemented by users. In Section 3, we show how these can be easily done.

NADEEF core. This module takes all user provided rules as input and treats all UDFs as *black-boxes*. NADEEF is responsible for efficiently invoking these black-boxes to identify and resolve duplicates.

ER dashboard. The ER dashboard (by extending NADEEF dashboard [4]) helps users understand the results of the ER process, by showing summarized, sampled, ranked and clustered duplicates. This facilitates the solicitation of user feedback for refining ER rules.

Implementation details. We have developed NADEEF/ER as a single-page application (SPA) with modern web application stack. The HTML5 client provides GUI and visualization to help users build ER rules, set a blocking strategy, and view the output matrix. Client requests for rule execution are processed asynchronously by a thin Java based server layer. The server wraps the requests and sends them to the NADEEF service for execution. NADEEF/ER's architecture

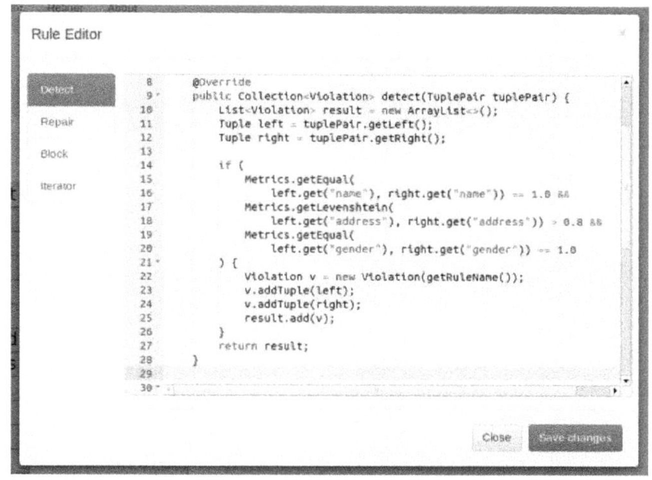

Figure 3: ER rule editor

is designed to be scalable to process multiple requests and multiple users at the same time. The communication among different services is built using Apache Thrift infrastructure, which is able to make requests execution scalable to many compute nodes.

3. DEMONSTRATION OVERVIEW

In this demonstration, we will use real-life datasets to give users the opportunity to experience the features provided by NADEEF/ER. Notice that this demonstration significantly differs from the one presented in [4] in two main aspects: (1) we will show the audience how easily they can specify ER rules via the NADEEF/ER GUI; and (2) we will also show the audience how to modify the four provided functions for customized ER rules via a web-browser. Additionally, we will show: (3) how the data quality dashboard can help users understand duplicate data, and how users can interact with NADEEF/ER to further refine ER rules; and (4) how existing ER algorithms can be easily implemented in NADEEF/ER.

(1) ER rule specification. Figure 2 displays the NADEEF/ER GUI for specifying ER rules. For each ER rule, the audience will be able to specify, by dragging lines between two attributes, the attributes to compare and the similarity (or equality) metrics to employ. Moreover, the audience can select pre-defined blocking functions for each ER rule. After specifying the parameters of one ER rule, the audience can press the "Add" button (on the top-right of Fig. 2) to register this rule in NADEEF/ER. Similarly, the audience will be able to specify more ER rules. Each ER rule will be automatically transformed into the four functions provided by NADEEF/ER.

(2) ER rule customization editor. We will demonstrate how to customize an ER rule by modifying any of the four functions provided by NADEEF/ER. For each ER rule, we will invite the audience to select one of these functions to revise, as shown in Fig. 3. After revision, NADEEF/ER check and highlight syntactic errors in the audience's provided code. If the code is syntactically correct, the audience can submit their changes by pressing the "Save changes" button.

Notice that in the context of ER, one can consider NADEEF detect() (resp. repair ()) having the same functionality as Swoosh match() (resp. merge()) function. In general, how-

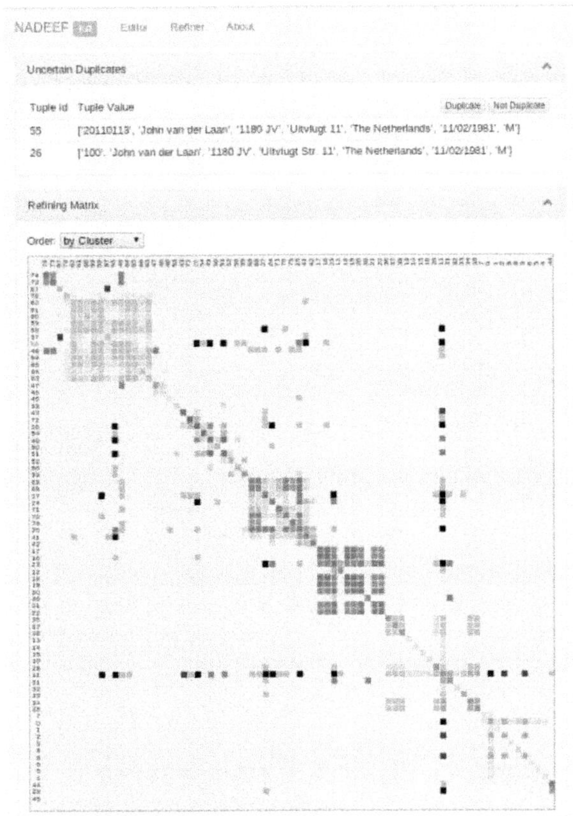

Figure 4: Co-occurrence matrix of duplicates

ever, the detect() (resp. repair ()) function is more general than their Swoosh counterparts (see [3] for more details).

Moreover, we will demonstrate two functions that are not present, neither in NADEEF [3,4] nor Swoosh [1]: the block() and iterator() functions.

- block() function: besides standard blocking functions, we will show how users can implement clustering-based method *canopies* [10].
- iterator() function: we will show how users can implement a sorted neighborhood approach, assuming duplicated records will be close at a certain sorted order. Beyond this, we also want to show that for a specific application and under certain assumptions, users can write a better iterator() function that would help reduce the number of entity pairs to be examined.

(3) Dashboard and user interaction. NADEEF/ER comes with a dashboard to allows user to better understand ER results. This dashboard differs from the dashboard presented in [4] as it provides a new graph that is especially designed for entity resolution: the *co-occurrence matrix of duplicates*. But also, NADEEF/ER dashboard inherits the existing visualization tools from NADEEF: a pie chart to show the overall number of tuples that have duplicates (*overview*); a bar chart to show the number of duplicates for each ER rule (*duplicate distribution*); a bar chart to show, for each attribute, the number of different values involved in duplicate entities (*duplicate distribution on attributes*); and a graph to visualize tuples with duplicates, where each node is a tuple and an edge between two tuples means that they are duplicates (*violation graph*).

Figure 4 depicts the *co-occurrence matrix of duplicates*. Each coloured cell in the matrix diagram represents two entities that have been detected as duplicates; darker cells indicate duplicates that co-occurred more frequently, *i.e.*, detected as duplicates by more ER rules. Clustering algorithms are used to group these cells. Cells with the same color indicate that they belong to the same cluster, *e.g.*, all yellow cells. A grey cell means that this cell is an island, *i.e.*, not in any cluster. By clicking a cell, NADEEF/ER provides its details, shown on top of Fig. 4. The users can investigate and decide to include/exclude them as duplicates. Based on user decisions, NADEEF/ER automatically adds special conditions to refine corresponding functions (operators). With the drop-down menu, users can select how to re-order the matrix, by *e.g.*, sorting on Name attribute to further explore the data. It is worth noting that this matrix only shows tuples that are detected as duplicates. When the number of (possible) duplicated tuples is large, partitioning techniques are used to show this matrix. It is also worth noting that the result about including/excluding uncertain duplicates can be used as training datasets for learning-based algorithms.

(4) Extensibility. Besides showing that NADEEF/ER can support generic entity matching and various optimization techniques, we will also show how various algorithms can be easily implemented in NADEEF/ER.

Summary. This demonstration aims at exhibiting the features of NADEEF/ER. We focus on: (*i*) A GUI that provides a rich set of user-tunable parameters for defining ER rules ((1) above); (*ii*) The NADEEF programming interfaces that helps users specify highly customized rules ((2) above); (*iii*) The data quality dashboard that can help users effectively interact with the system to refine ER rules((3) above); (*iv*) NADEEF/ER is generic and extensible ((4) above); (*v*) A real application exploiting all features of NADEEF/ER.

4. REFERENCES

[1] O. Benjelloun, H. Garcia-Molina, D. Menestrina, Q. Su, S. E. Whang, and J. Widom. Swoosh: a generic approach to entity resolution. *VLDB J.*, 18(1), 2009.

[2] P. Christen. A survey of indexing techniques for scalable record linkage and deduplication. *IEEE Trans. Knowl. Data Eng.*, 24(9), 2012.

[3] M. Dallachiesa, A. Ebaid, A. Eldawy, A. K. Elmagarmid, I. F. Ilyas, M. Ouzzani, and N. Tang. NADEEF: a commodity data cleaning system. In *SIGMOD*, 2013.

[4] A. Ebaid, A. K. Elmagarmid, I. F. Ilyas, M. Ouzzani, J.-A. Quiané-Ruiz, N. Tang, and S. Yin. NADEEF: A generalized data cleaning system. *PVLDB*, 2013.

[5] M. G. Elfeky, A. K. Elmagarmid, and V. S. Verykios. Tailor: A record linkage tool box. In *ICDE*, 2002.

[6] A. K. Elmagarmid, P. G. Ipeirotis, and V. S. Verykios. Duplicate record detection: A survey. *TKDE*, 2007.

[7] H. Galhardas, D. Florescu, D. Shasha, and E. Simon. Ajax: An extensible data cleaning tool. In *SIGMOD*, 2000.

[8] L. Getoor and A. Machanavajjhala. Entity resolution for big data. In *KDD*, 2013.

[9] L. Kolb, A. Thor, and E. Rahm. Dedoop: Efficient deduplication with hadoop. *PVLDB*, 2012.

[10] A. McCallum, K. Nigam, and L. H. Ungar. Efficient clustering of high-dimensional data sets with application to reference matching. In *KDD*, 2000.

[11] S. Sarawagi and A. Bhamidipaty. Interactive deduplication using active learning. In *KDD*, 2002.

[12] J. Wang, T. Kraska, M. J. Franklin, and J. Feng. Crowder: Crowdsourcing entity resolution. *PVLDB*, 2012.

SerpentTI: Flexible Analytics of Users, Boards and Domains for Pinterest

Alex Cheng
Computer Science
University of Toronto
hyc@cs.toronto.edu

Mary Malit
Computer Science
University of Toronto

Chuanxi Zhang
Computer Science
University of Toronto

Nick Koudas
Computer Science
University of Toronto
koudas@cs.toronto.edu

ABSTRACT

Pinterest is a pinboard style photo sharing web service that allows its users to manage, share and express their interests via a collection of theme based photos. A few design choices of Pinterest makes it highly desirable to social media practitioners and marketers as a new, high quality data source for deep analysis, or as a complimentary data stream to existing social data such as Twitter and Facebook. The analysis capabilities at the current Pinterest site are minimal however as the focus is currently on user experience. We provide a description of SerpentTI, a system that currently crawls, indexes and aggregates more than 31 million users, 96 million boards and 3.1 billion pins from Pinterest to enable flexible and deep analytics.

Categories and Subject Descriptors

H.0 [**Information Systems**]: General; H.3.3 [**Information Systems**]: Information Search and Retrieval

Keywords

Pinterest, social media, analytics

1. INTRODUCTION

Social media web services are mainstream with billions of people participating, generating massive quantities of both labelled and unlabelled data. Popular services such has Twitter have over 200 million users generating more than 350 million tweets per day. Novel analytical services based on content from popular services such as Twitter and Facebook have surfaced. However, analytical services for new sites such as Pinterest are lacking. This may be due to a multitude of reasons, such as lack of accesible APIs and limited data availability.

SIGMOD'14, June 22–27, 2014, Snowbird, UT, USA.

ACM 978-1-4503-2376-5/14/06 ...$15.00.
http://dx.doi.org/10.1145/2588555.2594518.

Pinterest[2] is a social media web service that allows its users to express their interests by sharing photos of their liking via a pinboard style interface to group related photos by themes. Pinterest is notable for having acquired many active users in a short period of time [3]. As of July of 2013, Pinterest has 70 million users, with 30% of the users having actively engaged with the site (either pinned, repinned or liked and image). More specifically, Pinterest encourages its users to share pins. A pin is usually composed of an image, a descriptive text about the image, with the URL that the pin was retrieved from, when applicable. Pinterest allows domain owners to embed a *Pin It* button on their website in order to facilitate the process of pinning from other domains, similar to Twitter and Facebook website integrations for sharing content. Pinterest requires that the pins be grouped into *boards*. Users routinely create boards containing pins of similar theme, and assign the boards textual descriptions as they see fit. (e.g. A user can pin an image of a fruit punch bowl from target.com, share it on Pinterest in a board that he/she creates, and assign the board title *For Fridayś party*). Users also have the option to assign each board one of 33 categories (e.g. Food & Drink, Weddings, Gardening, Technology ...) predefined by Pinterest. Once the set of boards and pins are in place, Pinterest encourages its users to stay up to date with each other by following other users. Users of Pinterest can also interact with each other by liking others' pins, and commenting on others' pins. If they so find a particular pin really interesting, they may wish to *repin* that pin onto a board of their own, in effect, sharing that pin with their own followers.

Several design choices of Pinterest make it attractive for high quality data mining and analytics. First, Pinterest positions the users' primary action around pin/repin onto boards. This is a direct indication of users' interest. (hence the name, *pin-interest*). Both the pins and the boards often have user assigned descriptive titles, and the user usually assigns one of the predefined categories to the boards. From our collection of 96 million boards, 51% of the boards have a user assigned category. As a consequence, Pinterest enables its users to build a massive *interest graph.* Second, board titles often contains highly actionable data about a user as often one indicates strongly, the kind of goods and services one desires and annotates them with a descriptive board title. (e.g. the board *"For My Wedding"* may contain pins about wedding gowns, flowers, cakes or the type of

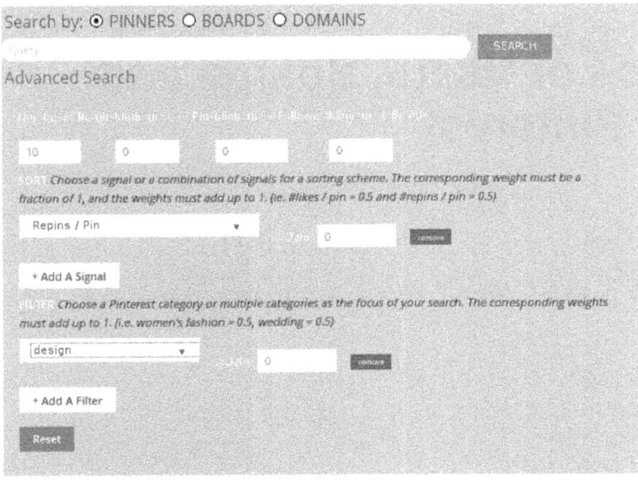

Figure 1: The SerpentTI Search Interface

chapel that a user desires). In terms of user management, Pinterest requires its users to login with their email, Twitter or Facebook account. This makes Pinterest a central hub that implicitly links existing social media profiles. Using our repository of Pinterest user database, 80% of the users have logged in through their Facebook account, while 20% have logged in using their Twitter account. Furthermore, due to the lack of a publishing API, Pinterest is less prone to the effect of massive spamming content. Despite these good qualities, Pinterest offers only a rudimentary, content based search functionality over pins and boards on its website with a static, fixed result ranking function.

We present SerpentTI [1] [1], a system that crawls, aggregates and indexes Pinterest with the goal to enable flexible and rich analytics of users, boards and domains. As can be seen in Figure 1, SerpentTI presents a familiar search box, with the option to toggle user, board or domain analytics with advanced filtering and scoring customizations. SerpentTI enhances its users' ability to extract value from the Pinterest interest graph in several practical ways:

Granular indexed fields Users perform full textual boolean search over the titles/descriptions of boards and pins, domain URLs or the contents of the pins. One particularly interesting aspect of this is that queries can be formed to capture users' desire for products or services, restricted to certain criteria. (e.g. "places I want to go" for users in California that have pinned information about yachts).

Flexible ranking functions If required, the result ranking can also be altered by selecting a combination of various statistics and filtering attributes. For example, a user may wish to re-rank the list of Pinterest users from Toronto that are into real estate, ranked by the average followers per pin, as a measure of influence. SerpentTI renormalized all supported ranking attributes to the range of 0 to 100 and it supplies an interface to specify arbitrary weighted combinations of attributes. This allows the scoring function to be very flexible in practice (e.g. a user might want to weight comments / pin twice more important than the fraction of the boards that are in mens fashion).

Deep user/board insight a "More Info" button is available with each user and board result on SerpentTI to deliver further insights including hourly posting activity, related keywords, followers of various authority and activity statistics.

Similar user/board suggestions For search results returning boards and users, SerpentTI provides an efficient and high quality user and board suggestion based on an analysis of the pin content signature of users and boards.

Domain analytics Domain analysis is possible with SerpentTI by aggregating and indexing the domain of origin of pins. This tool is useful for domain owners in order to measure engagement of their domain on Pinterest. Domain analytics provides a dashboard to quickly visualize popular pins, top pinners with authority, gender breakdown, with a word cloud summarizing the biography of repinners and the contents of their pins (to aid better understanding of those engaging with the domain). The domain analytics tab also makes it possible to visualize the volume of repins from the domain as a function of time.


```
{/*pin*/
    'domain':'...',
    'like_count':'...',
    'images':'...',
    'id':'...',
    'price_currency':'...',
    'pinner':'...',
    'comments':'...',
    'access':'...',
    'comment_count':'...',
    'board':'...',
    'method':'...',
    'attribution':'...',
    'description':'...',
    'price_value':'...',
    'is_playable':'...',
    'link':'...',
    'is_repin':'...',
    'is_uploaded':'...',
    'description_html':'...',
    'repin_count':'...',
    'created_at':'...',
    'dominant_color':'...',
    'embed':'...',
    'rich_summary':'...',
    'is_video':'...'
}

{/*user*/
    'last_name':'...',
    'domain_verified':'...',
    'following_count':'...',
    'image_medium_url':'...',
    'like_count':'...',
    'full_name':'...',
    'image_small_url':'...',
    'id':'...',
    'first_name':'...',
    'secret_board_count':'...',
    'location':'...',
    'indexed':'...',
    'is_partner':'...',
    'website_url':'...',
    'board_count':'...',
    'username':'...',
    'repins_from':'...',
    'twitter_url':'...',
    'facebook_url':'...',
    'follower_count':'...',
    'pin_count':'...',
    'about':'...',
    'has_board':'...',
    'image_large_url':'...',
}

{/*board*/
    'description':'...',
    'pin_thumbnail_urls':'...',
    'collaborator_count':'...',
    'owner':'...',
    'pin_count':'...',
    'id':'...',
    'category':'...',
    'name':'...',
    'privacy':'...',
    'url':'...',
    'follower_count':'...',
}
```


Figure 2: Pinterest JSON schemata

2. TECHNOLOGY

Our hardware is from Dell with 72GB of RAM, 12TB of mechanical disks and 16 physical processors. Since there is no publically available content API for Pinterest, we have wrote several specialized crawlers to consume content from Pinterest. Pinterest continuously updates each of the 33 category pages (refered to as **C** in what follows) with the newest activities. Our crawler continuously extracts the set of pins, user and boards from **C**. Another set of crawlers then performs bread first search outwards from this seed set to further collect pins, boards, followers of boards and users. We also materialize different versions of the user, and board profile in order to display the follower growth history of boards and users on SerpentTI. In order to expediate the crawling process, we have deployed more than 200 processes across a cluster of 16 machines to handle each of the different crawling tasks. The crawlers materialize the

[1] "SerpentTI" is an anagram of "Pinterest"

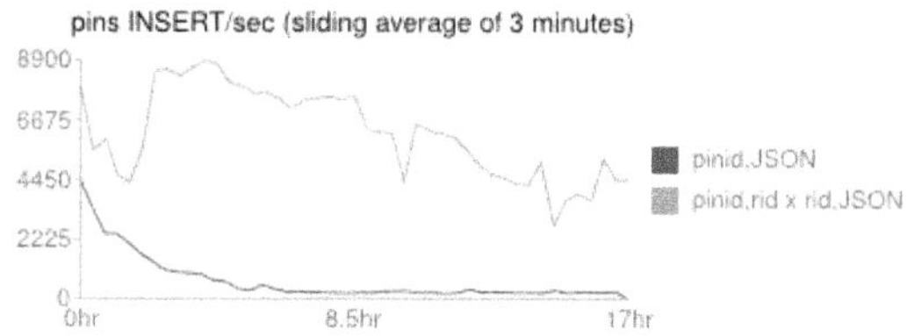

Figure 3: Update throughput for Pin storage: update throughput VS hours into benchmark

pins, users and boards data as JSON and commits them into a MySQL database for easy retrieval. A subsequent set of consumers then derives secondary statistics (e.g. number of pin per day for a specific domain) that is also used by SerpentTI. As materializing all these data from various JSON sources can be painful to manage, we have developed a small but general extract, transform and load (ETL) framework in Java that is capable of loading streamed JSON and perform database related business logic in a batched setting, which expediates database write throughput. The set of JSON consumers on ETL is also distributed across the same cluster of 16 machines to allow parallel data loading. One interesting statistic that we are able to materialize using this crawler architecture, is the growth over time for the number of likes, comments and repin counts for every pin that shows up in **C**. Since Pinterest pushes pins with new comments, repins to the top of **C**, our crawler will periodically observe these activities, and will be able to infer the state of the pin from the JSON metadata. Apache Lucene is used to support searching for users and boards. Due of the amount of data involved, our indexing process is also pipelined into three stages to minimize database stalls. In terms of the database write throughput, we observed the update throughput for pins gets worse very quickly as the database gets bigger. This is due to page misses on the pins table. As the pins get updated to the databases in random pin ID order, the page miss rate increases as the database gets physically larger. We can make much better use of the page cache by partitioning these types of updates into two tables. Effectively, the first table is an append only table where the payload for pins is appended to the table with an auto increment row ID. A second table then establishes the link between the auto increment row ID with the pin ID. As we can see in figure 3, the steady state performance of this second strategy is at least 20 times better than the original, straight forward strategy for storing pins. We make one further optimization to compact multiple pin payloads into one row to achieve better compression. Another secondary optimization SerpentTI uses is to place a part of the data on solid state drives to minimize the read/write latency. At this time, our crawlers have crawled more than 3.1 billion pins, and can update profiles for 30 million users in about 12 days and the board profiles for the 96 million boards in roughly 45 days. After each iteration of crawling, the set of newly discovered users and boards will be shuffled with the existing set of users and boards, before proceeding with next round of distributed crawling on the cluster.

3. DEMO EXPERIENCE

SerpentTI is online at *santiago3.cs.toronto.edu/pinterest/*. A search box that supports the full boolean semantics is shown to the user. On the top of the search box is a list of toggle buttons for the user to indicate the types of analytics desired. SerpentTI currently supports analysis for *boards,users*, and *domains*. As usual, a few predefined fields are indexed and can be queried using the regular boolean syntax. For example, a user can find all the boards owned by a Toronto user with regards to jewelry by writing: *jewelry AND location:toronto*. The list of fields that indexed include: *location*, *about*, *boardNameDesc*, *pinDesc*, *domains*, *hasFacebookUrl*, *hasTwitterUrl*, and *hasWebsiteUrl*. With these fields indexed and ready to go, users can write queries such as *domains:homedepot.com AND ("for the" OR "for my")* to search for the users that are interested in products from homedepot.com, effectively performing a search by *need*. As the search results are returned, users will be presented with a *More Info* button per result item for further drill down. For the case of a board result, *More Info* shows the user a few thumbnails of the pins from the board, followed by basic board statistics including the number of pins, followers and collaborators. After that, a series of normalized signal values follow. These include followers per pin, average boards per pin, unique domains per pin, repins per pin, likes per pin and comments per pin. A list of followers for the board is also returned and partitioned by their own follower count into three buckets, corresponding to high, medium and low follower counts. Lastly, a set of similar boards (utilizing our own algorithms) is presented with a snapshot of the pin descriptions at the bottom. Similar drill down capability is also presented for Users allowing deeper analytics. SerpentTI also offers a unique domain analytics tool. Users select the *domains* toggle button to analyze pins shared from a particular domain on Pinterest. By entering *target.com* as the query, the user will now obtain analytics for pins shared from target.com. On the top of the domain result page, a list of highly repinned pins is presented, followed by the daily volume graph, showing the number of pins from the domain as a function of time. After that, a gender breakdown, authority break down of the pinners followed by the familiar summary word cloud of the pinner's contents and their profile biography. As can be seen in Figure 1, SerpentTI provides the possibility of a customized ranking function per search. For the case of a *user* search, one can control the result ranking as a combination of normalized authority measures such as repins per pin, likes per pin, comments per pin or average followers per pin. The user can also further combine these scoring metrics with board category weights. Similar advanced scoring manipulation is also present for *board* search. With these constructs available, one can express fairly sophisticated result semantics such as "people showing pinning activity in the technology category who have pinned jewelry images, ranked by repins per pin". SerpentTI is online and fully functional. All functionalities outlined are available today. During the demo users will have the opportunity to interact with the system in real time. Users will be able to issue queries and perform all analysis outlined above.

4. REFERENCES

[1] `http://santiago3.cs.toronto.edu/pinterest/`.

[2] `http://www.pinterest.com/`.

[3] J. Slegg. Pinterest tops 70 million users; 30% pinned, repinned, or liked in June. `http://bit.ly/13rl0h0`, July 2013.

Figure 4: Screenshot of Domain Analytics on SerpentTI

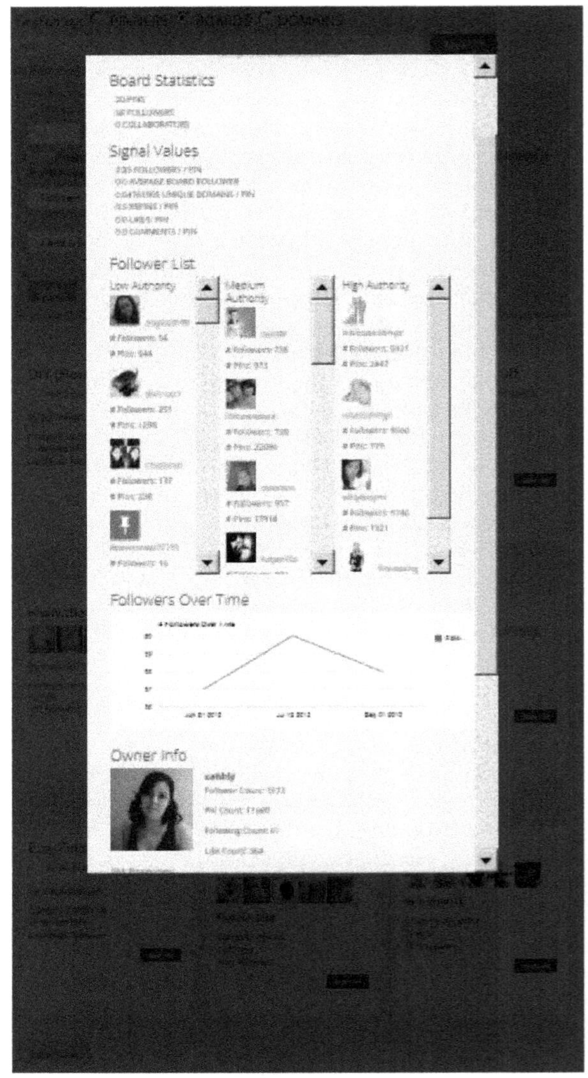

Figure 5: Screenshot of Board Analytics,More Info on SerpentTI

Interactive Redescription Mining

Esther Galbrun*
Department of Computer Science
Boston University
Boston, MA, USA
galbrun@cs.bu.edu

Pauli Miettinen
Max Planck Institute for Informatics
Saarbrücken, Germany
pmiettin@mpi-inf.mpg.de

ABSTRACT

Exploratory data analysis consists of multiple iterated steps: a data mining method is run on the data, the results are interpreted, new insights are formed, and the resulting knowledge is utilized when executing the method in a next round, and so on until satisfactory results are obtained.

We focus on redescription mining, a powerful data analysis method that aims at finding alternative descriptions of the same entities, for example, ways to characterize geographical regions in terms of both the fauna that inhabits them and their bioclimatic conditions, so-called *bioclimatic niches.*

We present SIREN, a tool for interactive redescription mining. It is designed to facilitate the exploratory analysis of data by providing a seamless environment for mining, visualizing and editing redescriptions in an interactive fashion, supporting the analysis process in all its stages. We demonstrate its use for exploratory data mining.

Simultaneously, SIREN exemplifies the power of the various visualizations and means of interaction integrated into it; Techniques that reach beyond the task of redescription mining considered here, to other analysis methods.

Categories and Subject Descriptors

H.2.8 [**Information Systems**]: Database Applications—*Data Mining*; H.5.2 [**Information Interfaces and Presentation**]: User Interfaces—*Data Visualization Methods*

Keywords

Redescription Mining; Interactive Data Mining; Visualization; Brush-and-Link; Parallel Coordinates

1. INTRODUCTION

The goal of data mining is to find surprising but useful new patterns and relations from the data. This process involves multiple steps such as preparing the data, selecting and applying the data mining methods, and interpreting the results. Furthermore, it is generally iterative, with the results of the first round used to inform the decisions made in the second round, *et cetera.*

The analysis is — or at least should be — done by a domain expert, as only a domain expert can judge what kind of results are surprising or useful. But to allow the domain expert to perform the data analysis as effectively as possible, the process should be as seamless as possible. Typically, it is unreasonable to assume that the domain experts are proficient on using half a dozen different programs, often with arcane command-line interfaces, to deploy the full analysis process. There are two common ways to achieve the desired consistency: either via a workflow integrated into a well-known general-purpose analysis framework, such as R or Matlab, or via a special-purpose tool specifically designed for the task at hand.

SIREN takes the latter approach: it is a tool for interactively mining and visualizing redescriptions. *Redescription mining* [9] is a data analysis method that aims to find different ways of characterizing the same things and, vice versa, to find things that admit the same alternative characterizations. For instance, consider the task of bioclimatic niche finding [10]: we are given a set of geographical regions (e.g. 50 km squares) with information about the species inhabiting these regions, on one hand, and the bioclimatic conditions (e.g. temperature and precipitation) encountered in each of them, on the other hand. The task is then to find a set of species and a set of bioclimatic conditions such that the bioclimatic conditions explain exactly (or as well as possible) the areas where the species live, and vice versa. Such a pair forms a redescription since it characterizes (approximately) the same area in two different ways.

An example redescription from bioclimatic niche finding characterizes Scandinavia and the Baltic as the habitat of the Moose, on one hand, and in term of its specific cold climate, on the other hand. A map plot of this redescription can be seen in the foreground of Figure 1. We will use niche finding as our example application throughout this paper, although we emphasize that redescription mining is not limited to any single application, or to any specific domain. Examples of other applications and redescription mining in general are discussed further in [9, 1], for instance.

SIREN can also be seen as a case study of the combination of various visualizations and interaction techniques into a powerful data analysis tool. Such integration could potentially also benefit methods other than redescription mining.

*The work was done while the author was a doctoral student at the University of Helsinki, with support from the Academy of Finland, Grant 255675.

SIGMOD'14, June 22–27, 2014, Snowbird, UT, USA.

ACM 978-1-4503-2376-5/14/06 ...$15.00.
http://dx.doi.org/10.1145/2588555.2594520.

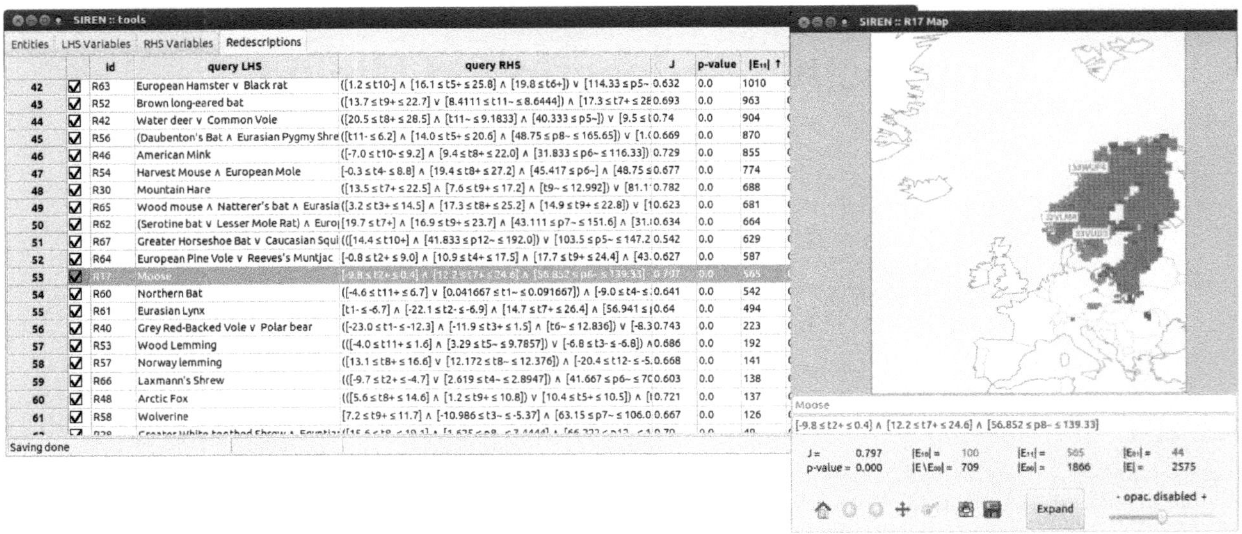

Figure 1: The Siren interactive mining and visualization tool. The panel in the background contains a list of redescriptions while the foreground panel displays the map plot of a selected redescription.

In the next section we provide a very brief introduction to redescription mining and cover some related work. Section 3 explains the main features of SIREN and why we think they are important. Section 4 outlines techniques used for implementing this tool, and Section 5 is a brief walk-through of the demonstration.

We presented a preliminary version of SIREN in [3]. That version introduced the GUI and preliminary connections to the mining algorithm. However, it lacked visualizations other than plotting results on a map and did not have the more sophisticated interactive features of the current version. Furthermore, the underlying architecture has been significantly improved. In this paper we focus on the new features, except when necessary to understand the broader functionality. In other words, features discussed here are new compared to [3], unless otherwise mentioned.

More details about SIREN, including videos, a user guide and further references on redescription mining are available on the associated webpage.[1]

2. REDESCRIPTION MINING

Redescription mining is a descriptive data analysis task. It aims at simultaneously finding multiple descriptions of a subset of entities which is not previously specified [9]. This is in contrast with other methods like *emerging pattern mining*, *contrast set mining*, or *subgroup discovery* (see [7] for a unifying survey) or general classification methods, where target subsets of entities are specified via labels.

We consider data that contains entities with two sets of characterizing variables, such as the fauna and bioclimatic conditions. In this setting, the redescription mining task consists in finding a pair of queries, one query for each set of variables, such that both queries describe (almost) the same set of entities. We refer to the two sets of variables as left and right hand side data, and the queries over them, respectively, as left and right hand side queries. A redescription is simply a pair of queries over variables from the two sets. The support of a query is the subset of entities for which the query holds true. The *accuracy* of a redescription is measured by the *Jaccard coefficient* (denoted as J) of the supports of its two queries; p-values indicating how likely it is to observe such an overlap for independent queries can be used to reject uninteresting redescriptions.

Several algorithms for redescription mining have been proposed over the years and in principle SIREN can use any of them as the method to mine the redescriptions. To the best of our knowledge, however, only the REREMI algorithm [2] can handle numerical or categorical data and missing values. It is therefore our algorithm of choice.

Our example application here is *bioclimatic niche-finding*. The aim is to determine the bioclimatic constraints that must be met for a certain species to survive, called the species' bioclimatic envelope, or niche [4]. Finding such envelopes could help, for instance, to predict the results of global warming [8]. Unlike other tools developed over the past ten years to model the bioclimatic envelope, such as BIOMOD [11], redescription mining allows automatically finding both the set of species and their envelope.

While we cannot cover other applications in this demonstration proposal due to space constraints, we refer the interested user to the aforementioned web page where we give three other example applications from different domains.

3. THE FEATURES OF SIREN

SIREN provides a complete environment for redescription mining, from loading the data to finally exporting the results into various formats, through mining, visualizing, and editing the redescriptions. SIREN allows for a seamless interaction with both the mining and visualization, enabling the user to interactively edit the redescriptions in the visualizations and to call the mining algorithm, e.g. to extend the current results. In what follows, we cover some of the main features of SIREN and argue why they are important.

Mining. Obviously, the core of SIREN is mining the redescriptions. Having just a GUI atop the mining algorithm is not enough, however, in particular because mining all the redescriptions from a dataset can be a time-consuming task.

[1] `http://www.cs.helsinki.fi/u/galbrun/redescriptors/siren/`

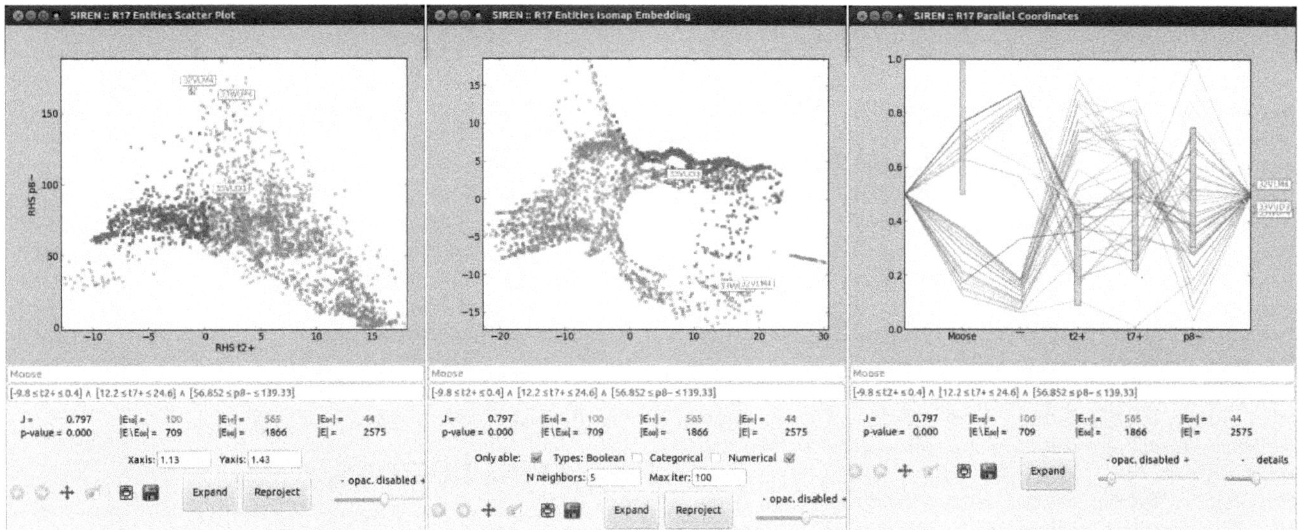

(a) (b) (c)

Figure 2: Alternative visualizations of the redescription shown in the foreground panel of Figure 1. Three selected entities are highlighted across the different visualizations.

To avoid extensive waiting times, mining redescriptions in SIREN is an asynchronous any-time process, meaning that the user will start seeing results from the mining algorithm as soon as the first (partial) results are ready. The user can start working with and editing these redescriptions while the mining algorithm continues in the background. While SIREN was capable of doing this already in [3], we have improved the implementation of the asynchronous computations to take full benefit from the multiple cores in modern CPUs. Furthermore, the new asynchronous model allows SIREN to off-load heavy computational tasks to an external server.

When exploring the data, the user often wants to extend existing redescriptions, either those returned by the algorithm or else some queries she has constructed herself, e.g. to test a hypothesis about the data. SIREN allows to use an existing redescription as a starting point for the mining process. The user can also select only one side of the redescription to be extended. In bioclimatic niche finding, for example, this can be used to see how good a bioclimatic envelope the algorithm can find for a specific combination of species.

Furthermore, the user may specify a subset of entities that she wants to be emphasized during the mining process. For example, if the user wants to add some entities (in this case, geographic areas) to the support of the redescription shown in Figure 1, she can ask SIREN to extend the given redescription with emphasis on including them in the support. In other words, the user can manipulate a redescription both through its queries and through its support.

The user can also disable variables and/or entities so that they will not be used in the mining process. For example, there can be known anomalous areas (e.g. coastal regions or valleys in mountain ranges) that the user might want to exclude, to prevent them from affecting the algorithm. The user can also disable the entities after the mining is done, in which case SIREN will automatically update the support and accuracy of all redescriptions.

Visualizing. Visualization is the key to understanding the results of the mining process. As, for example, Heer and Shneiderman [5] argued, having multiple concurrent visualizations of the same data reinforces their explanatory power. While the preliminary version of SIREN was only capable of plotting redescriptions on a map, multiple different visualizations of the entities are now available. They are also applicable to data without spatial coordinates, thereby lifting the restriction to geospatial data.

The simplest of these visualizations are the various projections of the data into the 2D space. Different types of projections have been studied intensively, and SIREN provides a number of them, including Karhunen–Loève transform (i.e. PCA), multi-dimensional scaling and various scatter plots. Figure 2 (a) and (b) are two alternative projections for the same example redescription, namely a scatter plot and an isomap embedding. In all visualizations, colors encode whether an entity belongs to the support of the left hand side query (denoted as E_{10}), the right hand side query (E_{01}), or both (E_{11}). Here, we use red, blue, and purple respectively. Adding new projections is straightforward due to the modular nature of SIREN. Computing these projections for larger datasets can be computationally intensive, but that too can be off-loaded to an external server.

Parallel coordinates plots [6] are particularly suited for visualizing redescriptions. In such a plot, the entities are represented by lines going through a series of parallel vertical axes, one for each literal appearing in the queries. The position where a line crosses an axis indicates the value of the associated variable for the corresponding entity. For each literal, the range of values that make the truth assigment hold is represented by a grey interval box. An extra axis separates the two sides and registers the support of the queries. Figure 2 (c) shows an example of a parallel coordinates plot. The same color code is used for the entities as with other visualizations. In addition, grey lines represent entities that do not support either query (E_{00}).

An example use case for the multiple visualizations is to study why some entities are not included in the support of both queries. To facilitate the analysis of such situations,

SIREN provides brush-and-link capabilities. The user can select (brush) an entity or a set of entities by clicking them or by drawing a polygon around them on any of the visualizations and the corresponding entities are highlighted in all associated visualizations. This way, the user can use the map to select areas of interest then use the 2D projections to quickly see whether these areas behave anomalously compared to other areas. In our example redescription, some areas where the Moose lives do not appear in the support of the climate query (drawn in red). We select three of them and notice from the two projections that the coastal areas of Norway (32VLM4 and 33WUP4) have a climatic profile which is clearly distinct from most covered areas, unlike the area in southern Sweden (33VUD3). From the parallel coordinates plot we then determine that raising the upper bound on February maximum temperature would allow to cover the latter area.

Editing. A redescription can be edited from any visualization by using the text fields under the plot. Thus, the user might adjust the conditions in the queries, add or remove variables, as well as build entirely new redescriptions by hand. Upon editing a query, the plot and the statistics of the redescriptions are recomputed to account for the modifications. This behavior was already implemented in the preliminary version of SIREN.

Now, it is also possible to edit the queries directly from the parallel coordinates plot by dragging the interval boxes to modify the bounds or categories for the variables. Continuing with our example, we can simply drag the top of the second grey box up to the highlighted line to include the area in the support (and some other areas as well). This will trigger the update of all the associated visualizations and re-computation of the statistics of the redescription.

4. IMPLEMENTATION DETAILS

SIREN is available as a desktop program. Both SIREN and REREMI are implemented in Python to ensure cross-platform compatibility. The interface is built with the `wxPython` Open Source cross-platform GUI toolkit and relies on the `matplotlib` library for the visualizations. The 2D projections are implemented as modular functions that take a `numpy` matrix as an input and output a list of 2D points. Most of the projections call the corresponding routines from the `scikit-learn` package.

In SIREN, all mining and projection tasks are handled in separate processes, using Python's standard `multiprocessing` library. Multiple independent computations can thus be run simultaneously, fully exploiting modern multi-core CPU architectures. The tasks can either be run locally or be off-loaded to an external server. The communication between SIREN and the computational server are also handled with `multiprocessing` and we use a server-client architecture, so that a single server can serve multiple SIREN clients by spawning a new worker for each job request.

5. DEMONSTRATION SCENARIO

In the demonstration we will present SIREN following a usage scenario of finding bioclimatic niche with redescription mining, unless the audience prefers some other application.

After a brief explanation of the concepts underlying redescription mining and the chosen application scenario, we will demonstrate the features of SIREN. In particular, we will highlight how the multiple visualizations together with the brush-and-link workflow support a better understanding and interpretation of the redescriptions and how the interface intuitively allows to impart domain knowledge to the mining process, so as to improve the results in subsequent iterations.

For the interest of time, we will start with few pre-mined redescriptions, but will then invite the audience to edit these redescriptions and to use the mining algorithm to extend them. Since SIREN is a fully functional program that anyone can download from the web page, the demonstration can be fully interactive, with the users directly trying out the tool, possibly on their own datasets.

We have prepared a short video showing a sample walk-through of the demonstration. It can be seen in the aforementioned accompanying web page.

6. CONCLUSIONS

SIREN provides a seamless environment for interactively mining, visualizing, and editing redescriptions. Its multiple visualizations, coordinated plots, brush-and-link workflow, and tight integration to the mining algorithm make it a very effective exploratory data analysis tool.

This tool also provides a case study on the power of various means of visualization and interaction which are potentially relevant in the context of other exploratory data analysis methods as well.

7. REFERENCES

[1] E. Galbrun. *Methods for Redescription Mining.* PhD thesis, University of Helsinki, Helsinki, Dec. 2013.

[2] E. Galbrun and P. Miettinen. From Black and White to Full Colour: Extending Redescription Mining Outside the Boolean World. *Stat. Anal. and Data Min.*, 5(4):284–303, 2012.

[3] E. Galbrun and P. Miettinen. Siren: An interactive tool for mining and visualizing geospatial redescriptions – Demo. In *KDD*, pages 1544–1547, 2012.

[4] J. Grinnell. The niche-relationships of the California Thrasher. *The Auk*, 34(4):427–433, 1917.

[5] J. Heer and B. Shneiderman. Interactive dynamics for visual analysis. *Comm. ACM*, 55(4):45–54, Apr. 2012.

[6] A. Inselberg. *Parallel coordinates: Visual multidimensional geometry and its applications.* Springer, 2009.

[7] P. K. Novak, N. Lavrac, and G. I. Webb. Supervised descriptive rule discovery: A unifying survey of contrast set, emerging pattern and subgroup mining. *J. Mach. Learn. Res.*, 10:377–403, 2009.

[8] R. G. Pearson and T. P. Dawson. Predicting the impacts of climate change on the distribution of species: Are bioclimate envelope models useful? *Global Ecol. Biogeogr.*, 12:361–371, 2003.

[9] N. Ramakrishnan, D. Kumar, B. Mishra, M. Potts, and R. F. Helm. Turning CARTwheels: An alternating algorithm for mining redescriptions. In *KDD*, pages 266–275, 2004.

[10] J. Soberón and M. Nakamura. Niches and distributional areas: Concepts, methods, and assumptions. *PNAS*, 106(Supplement 2):19644, 2009.

[11] W. Thuiller, B. Lafourcade, R. Engler, and M. B. Araújo. Biomod – a platform for ensemble forecasting of species distributions. *Ecography*, 32(3):369–373, 2009.

ONTOCUBO: Cube-based Ontology Construction and Exploration

Carlos Garcia-Alvarado
Pivotal Inc.
Palo Alto, CA 94304, USA

Carlos Ordonez
University of Houston
Dept. of Computer Science
Houston, TX 77204, USA

ABSTRACT

One of the major challenges of big data analytics is the diverse information content, which has no pre-defined structure or classification. This is in contrast to the well-designed structure of a database specified on an ER model. A standard mechanism for understanding interrelationships and the structure of documents is using ontologies. With such motivation in mind, we present a system that enables data management and querying of documents based on ontologies by leveraging the functionality of the DBMS. In this paper, we present ONTOCUBO, a novel system based on our research for text summarization using ontologies and automatic extraction of concepts for building ontologies using Online Analytical Processing (OLAP) cubes. ONTOCUBO is a database-centric approach that excels in its performance, due to an SQL-based single pass summarization phase through the original data set that computes values such as keyword frequency, standard deviation, and lift. This approach is complemented with a set of User-Defined-Function-based algorithms that analyze the summarization results for concepts and their interrelationships. Finally, we show in detail our application that extracts and builds an ontology, but also allows concept summarizations and allows domain experts to explore and modify the resulting ontology.

Categories and Subject Descriptors

H.2.4 [**Database Management**]: Systems—
Relational databases

Keywords

Ontologies; OLAP; DBMS

1. INTRODUCTION

Several artificial intelligence, information retrieval, and natural language processing systems that are used across semantic web applications have relied on a declarative representation of knowledge (ontologies) for effective querying and exploration of a corpus [5]. Despite the need of these systems to have an ontology, this labor-intensive task is normally tailored for a specific domain of knowledge and a set of domain experts, making it cost-prohibitive to build a new ontology every time that the domain is extended or modified. Automatic ontology building arises as an alternative for easing this difficult task. However, automatically finding the concepts and their relationships is especially challenging in text corpora without a known structure or classification. Concept extraction has been approached through natural language processing [6], clustering [2], singular value decomposition (SVD), and statistical techniques. While normal applications of Online Analytical Processing (OLAP) include business reports and financial analysis [1], in this work, we show that OLAP can also be useful in concept extraction for building ontologies and computing summarizations. More specifically, we show that cuboids of an OLAP cube can be used to efficiently obtain concepts (classes) and their relationships. In this case, the data is represented by the collection of keywords and documents, while the level of aggregation allows us to obtain various combinations of these keywords to generate concepts. These concepts are now filtered and pruned to compute ontologies. ONTOCUBO is a novel system inside database management systems (DBMS), extended from our research shown in [3, 4], in which we integrated both works and refined the resulting ontologies. A DBMS is used due to the support for computing efficient aggregations with SQL queries and the ability to adapt, in an efficient manner, the cube operator.

SIGMOD'14, June 22–27, 2014, Snowbird, UT, USA.

http://dx.doi.org/10.1145/2588555.2594521.

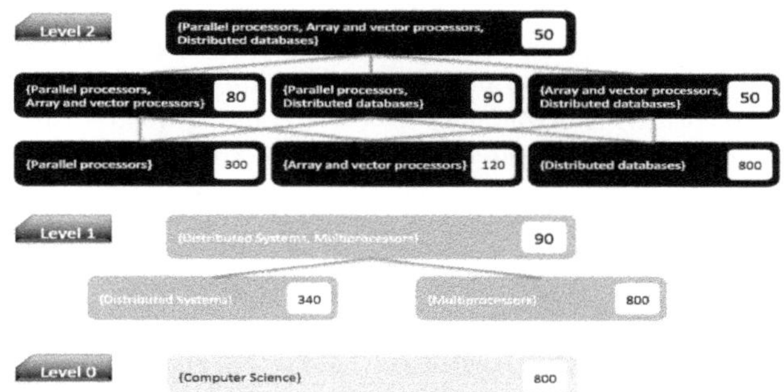

Figure 1: OLAP Cube with Concepts.

2. DEFINITIONS

Let C be a collection, or corpus, of n documents $C = \{d_1, d_2, \ldots, d_n\}$, where each document d_i is composed of a

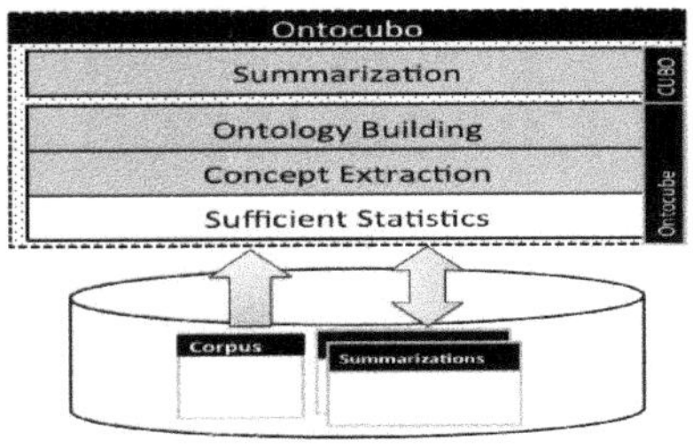

Figure 2: ONTOCUBO Architecture.

set of keywords $\{k_1, k_2, \dots\}$. In addition, let x_i be a frequency vector of all the different keywords in C for each document d_i. Every concept that is part of an ontology is defined as a class, and the relationship between classes is modeled as a taxonomy of "is a" or "has a" relationship. An ontology $\mathcal{O}$, on the other hand, is a tree-like structure where the nodes represent dimensions (sets of concepts) and the branches model the relationships between them.

Inside the DBMS, C is stored in a vertical list format. This list is stored in a distance table $D(i, k, p)$ that contains the document id, keyword, and position of a keyword in the d_i document. A summarization table stores the x_i vector of every document in a vertical format, too. The summarization table is defined as table $S(i, k, f)$, where S contains the document id, the keyword, and the keyword frequency f. The size of the OLAP data cubes that generates the classes (concepts of different keyword lengths) is $2^{\hat{k}} - 1$ cuboids, where $\hat{k}$ is the number of most frequent keywords selected from $\sum_i^n x_i$. A cuboid (or depth) l of the lattice is denoted by $\binom{\hat{k}}{l}$, such that $l \leq \hat{k}$. Finally, these classes are validated with the computation of correlation and lift using sufficient statistics (represented by n , L, Q). Let L be an additional set containing the total sum of all the different keywords in the collection ($L = \sum_{i=1}^n x_i$). In addition, let Q be a lower triangular matrix containing the squared measures between the keywords ($Q = \sum_{i=1}^n x_i x_i^t$). Moreover, lift λ is computed as $\lambda = \frac{n_{k,k'}}{Max(n_k, n_{k'})}$, where n_k and $n_{k'}$ are the number of documents containing keywords k and k', respectively. The final step of the computation is the aggregation of measurements by exploiting the ontology generated. The array of OLAP cubes is exemplified in Figure 1.

3. ONTOCUBO

ONTOCUBO, which builds on our previous work on ONTOCUBE and CUBO, is the result of three phases as shown in Figure 2: concept extraction, ontology building, and ontology summarization. The first phase extracts the most important concepts by computing the sufficient statistics from table S, and computing the frequency of the concepts of size l from table D. The second phase takes the computed concepts from the previous phase and generates the final ontology based on the measurements obtained with the sufficient statistics, the frequencies computed with OLAP, and the hypernyms (semantic relation of the type-of form) given by an existing conceptualization [8]. The third phase takes the extracted concepts and generates OLAP cubes with the computed measurements. In the following subsections, we present the basic steps for achieving concept extraction, ontology building, and the final OLAP cube summarization of measurements.

3.1 Document Corpus Preprocessing

The concept extraction, which is a one-time preprocessing step, focuses on computing the frequency of the keywords and generates combinations between the most frequent ones. In order to find valid concepts, the following questions must be answered: (1) Do $k_1, k_2, \dots$ appear in the same documents frequently? (2) Are $k_1, k_2, \dots$ close to each other? (3) How often do $k_1, k_2, \dots$ appear together within the corpus? (4) How often is a k found in a d_i but not in d_j?

These questions are answered by computing statistical measurements (in a single pass through S) such as the correlation between a pair of keywords, the distance between a pair of keywords, and the ratio between the number of documents containing a pair of keywords and the maximum of their frequency (lift). The algorithm for obtaining such classes is as follows in a single scan on D: (1) Obtain all available classes by pairing all keywords $\hat{k}$ within each document. (2) For each class, determine the frequency of occurrence and average position gap within the corpus. (3) Filter out all classes whose keywords have a position gap greater than a user-defined threshold, T. (4) Filter out all classes whose frequency, correlation, or lift does not meet user-defined thresholds for all the pairs of keywords in a class.

3.2 Ontology Building

The second phase is ontology building (see [3]), which takes a set of rules based on the correlation, lift and frequencies computed in the previous step and decides the relation between the concept in the form of a "is a" or "has a" relation.

Initially, there is a need to determine if there is a relationship of any type between two classes. In order to do so, each class is paired with all the other classes within the class pool. Let each set of two classes be a relationship if for every possible pair between all the keywords of the concept there is a high correlation and lift. For example, suppose we are looking for a relationship between the classes $\{k_1, k_2\}$, $\{k_3, k_4\}$. In order to find out if there is a relationship, we need to obtain the correlation and lift for the following set of keywords: $\{k_1, k_3\}$, $\{k_1, k_4\}$, $\{k_2, k_3\}$, and $\{k_2, k_4\}$. Pairing them would allow us to observe how closely related these two classes are to one another. A high correlation and a high lift from any one of these four subsets would confirm that this is a valid relationship. Otherwise, if these four subsets do not show a connection, we discard this relationship.

The parent of a class is determined with a heuristic based on the frequency of appearance of a pair of classes. We consider a class A be the parent of a class B if the following criteria is satisfied: (1) The number of documents containing class A minus the number of documents containing class B is less than a user threshold θ (e.g. 10%) of total documents. (2) The number of classes containing keywords in class A is greater than the number of classes containing keywords in class B.

If a hypernym is a available for any of the classes, the class is substituted by the corresponding hypernym. Moreover, during the pairing, all the classes substituted for the same hypernym are pruned. The rationale behind this step is to limit the number of instances that are identified as

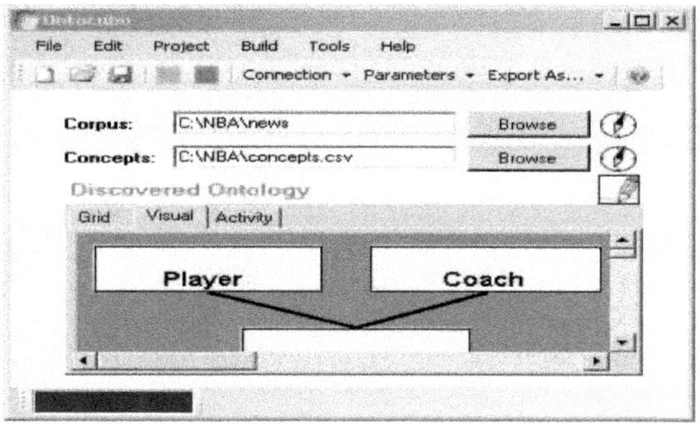

Figure 3: ONTOCUBO Building.

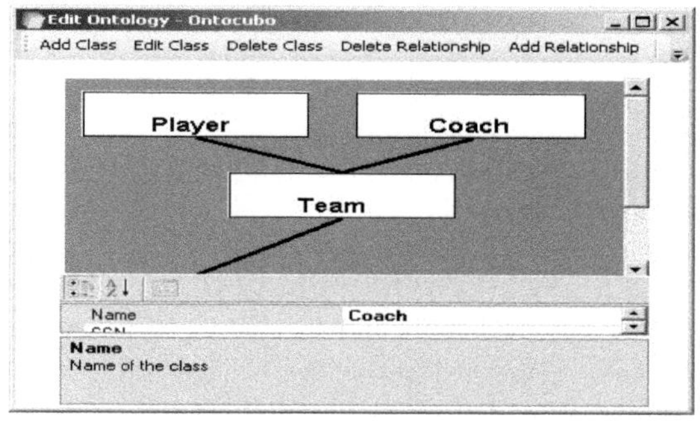

Figure 4: ONTOCUBO Exploration.

valid classes. In addition to this, if we discover that several classes that contain the same hypernyms have been assigned differently, we select the relationship with more incidences. If there is a tie, we select one of the relationships arbitrarily.

3.3 Ontology Exploration

CUBO is an array of data cubes, given a set of dimensions, that summarizes a set of measurements from a fact table D. These dimensions are the classes obtained by ONTOCUBE. The notion of CUBO is based on the premise that a set of documents does not contain all of the dimensions in every document. Thus, only a set of "on-demand" computations of the dimensions are required for every document. Our algorithm takes advantage of this property when computing the aggregation on superior levels in the ontology hierarchy. In other words, CUBO has a lazy policy that waits to perform computations until it is absolutely necessary. Furthermore, the algorithm avoids redundant computations by focusing only on storing those dimensions that contain attributes to aggregate. If the entire data cube is desired, a post-processing phase can be executed to compute all the missing combinations.

The algorithm for obtaining the CUBO given an ontology $\mathcal{O}$, input corpus D, dimensions, and a maximum ontology depth is shown in [4]. The result is temporarily stored in R that contains a level, combination of classes (combo) and the aggregation measurements. Furthermore, the entire computation of all the data cubes is computed through a single scan over the filtered data set. This additional scan can be avoided if the desired measurement is already contained from the original ontology generation. CUBO is composed of three major steps: load ontology (which is computer as part of ONTOCUBE), computation of on-demand combinations and the data cube aggregation. The final step of our algorithm stores the resulting data cubes into a relational table.

4. SYSTEM OVERVIEW

ONTOCUBO is a standalone system developed entirely in C# as two modules: a thin client that uses ODBC to connect to the DBMS and call plain SQL queries, and User-defined functions (UDFs) deployed inside the DBMS. This is also shown in Figure 2, in which the tasks performed with SQL queries are represented in white boxes, while the tasks performed in user-defined functions are shown in shaded boxes. The computation of sufficient statistics (stored for later use in a new table) is executed with an efficient SQL query of the form:

```
SELECT S1.kid as k1, S2.kid as k2
 , sum(S1.f) as L1, sum(S2.f) as L2
 , sum(S1.f*S1.f) as Q1, sum(S2.f*S2.f) as Q2
 , sum(S1.f*S2.f) as Q12
FROM S as S1, S as S2
WHERE S1.kid<=S2.kid AND S1.i=S2.i
GROUP BY S1.kid, S2.kid
```

Notice that the keyword was encoded as numbers to allow an efficient computation. In addition to this, indexes were added in the surrogate keys in order to obtain an efficient join. Also notice that this query would compute the sufficient statistics for the whole collection C, and this should be limited for the most frequent keywords $\hat{k}$.

The computation of the OLAP cuboids and resulting ontologies are then obtained inside a table-valued function (which is a type of UDF that allows returning a table) by calling: "SELECT * FROM ONTOCUBE('D_table', 2, 10, 2, 0.10)", where the first parameter represents the distance table, the second parameter has the cuboid(s) l, the third parameter contains the top-k keywords for exploring $\hat{k}$, the fourth parameter represents the maximum gap between keywords T, and the last parameter is the parent class validation criterion θ.

In Figure 3, the main screen of ONTOCUBO is shown. Our system allows the user to select a location in the file system containing the corpus to import. In addition to this, the application takes as possible input a file containing an existing conceptualization; otherwise WordNet 2.1 is used for hypernyms [7]. Another setting needs to be provided to the program, such as the connection details for the DBMS and the tuning parameters l (a full data cube is also possible but the system is constrained by the memory allocated to the DBMS), T, and θ during the ontology building. Once all the parameters have been set, the user can start the automatic concept extraction and ontology building. Progress of the execution is shown in the status bar of ONTOCUBO, and the current ontology is shown to the user "on-the-fly". In Figure 4, the domain expert has the option of exploring and modifying the resulting ontology directly in our application, which includes adding, removing, or modifying an existing class; as well as adding and removing an existing relationship. Our system also allows exporting the resulting ontology as RDF or OWL files. The last step of our system allows building with the resulting ontology an OLAP cube with the desired measurements. As such, a CUBO is built through a single pass on the original data set, via a TVF, unless the required summarizations were previously computed. Our application has been tested, as shown in [3], by using data sets of sports news. The main advantage of ONTOCUBO is that the minimum number of parameters that are required to be tuned allows our system to be used in a variety of data sets. Furthermore, our single pass sufficient statistics computations, in-main memory OLAP computation, and rules allow the building of an ontology in an efficient manner.

5. SYSTEM DEMONSTRATION

Our demonstration will show how it is possible to obtain automatically generated ontologies from medium size document collections, including digital libraries, with OLAP cubes and show the resulting CUBO. A local computer will show how a large data set, remotely available, is explored efficiently and generates ontologies without human intervention. All the algorithms (sufficient statistics, summarizations, measurements, and generated pairs) will be available as UDFs. In addition, the user will have the opportunity to explore every partial result of the entire ontology generation. The data set and the algorithms will be loaded in a remote machine running an instance of a commercial relational database system on a computer with 32 bit CPU, 4 GB RAM and 1 TB of storage. Resulting tables will be transferred to a local computer using ODBC. The user will analyze text data sets of different sizes, such as abstracts from dbpedia ($\sim$ 70 GBs), Reuters 21578 ($\sim$ 20 MBs), and a data set of sports news articles ($\sim$ 1 GB). These articles are already preprocessed and stored in the format defined in Section 2.

5.1 Demonstration Goals

Our demonstration aims to spur the discussion of automatic ontology generators, the research challenges (e.g. OLAP), and the possibility of using the SQL language and User-Defined Functions for ontology extraction and OLAP cube summarizations. The main contribution of our work is that we bring together the exploration power of OLAP to extract ontologies in a new manner. In this paper, we have proposed an extension to ONTOCUBE and CUBO, two novel proposals that exploit OLAP techniques for building ontologies and compute summarizations inside a relational database management system. The core of the proposal is a system that relies on obtaining in an efficient manner the sufficient statistics with a one-pass SQL query for computing the correlation and lift from pairs of keywords from a corpus. Moreover, an efficient in-main-memory user-defined function OLAP algorithm is exploited to efficiently generate cuboids (or the entire cube if desired) of sets of keywords and verify if they are valid classes. Later, an ontology is then built and refined by using hypernyms support, which proved to be important for avoiding returning ontologies with a large number of instances. We found that OLAP cubes are suitable candidates for this type of application. This is due to the fact that the dimensionality limitation that accompanies OLAP when generating the data cube is never met, because we rarely need to generate the entire cube (we mostly have concepts with less than 4 keywords which are represented by cuboids with a depth of less than 3).

Thus in this demonstration we will emphasize the following points: (1) It is possible to analyze efficiently large text data sets within a relational database management system. (2) OLAP cubes can be used to gather the required summarizations. (3) Understanding how multiple heuristics can be applied for generating an ontology in an automated fashion. (4) Understanding the in-memory processing for OLAP cubes using User-Defined Functions. Finally, our demonstration will motivate the discussion on the quality of the automatically generated ontology which is part of our ongoing work.

5.2 Demonstration Scenarios

The user will have the opportunity to navigate the original data sets through a graphical user interface. After selecting the desired text data set, the user will have the opportunity of choosing if the ontology is going to be generated in an automated fashion from the entire data set, or from a sample of keywords. In addition, the user has the capability of assigning a value to several parameters for the automatic generation, such as: the number of keywords to pair, position gap between keywords, keyword frequency, correlation value, lift and the parent class threshold. The user will also have the capability of adding new hypernyms for any of the classes.

Once the desired parameters have been set, the user will observe how the ontology is generated online and explore the early results in the GUI. It is also possible to explore the intermediate and final results by querying the resulting tables stored in the server. With the final result, the user will have the opportunity to resolve conflicts or export the results as RDF or OWL files. Additionally, the user will be capable of querying the resulting ontology and performing additional analysis of the results stored in tables. Finally, the user will be able to compute the CUBO with the desired measurements, for example, the frequency of classes in a document, frequency average of the classes in document, or average correlation among the involved classes, among many others.

6. REFERENCES

[1] Z. Chen, C. Ordonez, and C. Garcia-Alvarado. Fast and dynamic OLAP exploration using UDFs. In *ACM SIGMOD*, pages 1087–1090, 2009.

[2] N. Choi, I.Y. Song, and H. Han. A survey on ontology mapping. *ACM SIGMOD Record*, 35(3):34–41, 2006.

[3] C. Garcia-Alvarado, Z. Chen, and C. Ordonez. ONTOCUBE: efficient ontology extraction using OLAP cubes. In *Proc. of ACM CIKM*, pages 2429–2432, 2011.

[4] C. Garcia-Alvarado and C. Ordonez. Query Processing on Cubes Mapped from Ontologies to Dimension Hierarchies. In *Proc. ACM DOLAP Workshop*, pages 57–64, 2012.

[5] A.Y. Halevy and J. Madhavan. Corpus-based knowledge representation. In *Proc. of Joint Conference on Artificial Intelligence*, volume 18, pages 1567–1572, 2003.

[6] A. Maedche and R. Volz. The ontology extraction and maintenance framework text-to-onto. In *Proc. of ICDM Workshop on Integrating Data Mining and Knowledge Management*, 2001.

[7] G.A. Miller. Wordnet: A lexical database for english. *Communications of the ACM*, 13(11):39–41, 1995.

[8] S. Scott and S. Matwin. Text classification using WordNet hypernyms. In *Proc. of the Conference Use of WordNet in Natural Language Processing Systems*, pages 38–44, 1998.

An Extendable Framework for Managing Uncertain Spatio-Temporal Data

Tobias Emrich, Maximilian Franzke, Hans-Peter Kriegel, Johannes Niedermayer, Matthias Renz, Andreas Züfle
Institute for Informatics, Ludwig-Maximilians-Universität München
{emrich,franzke,kriegel,niedermayer,renz,zuefle}@dbs.ifi.lmu.de

ABSTRACT

This demonstration presents our Uncertain-Spatio-Temporal (UST) framework that we have developed in recent years. The framework allows not only to visualize and explore spatio-temporal data consisting of (location, time, object)-triples but also provides an extensive codebase easily extensible and customizable by developers and researchers. The main research focus of this UST-framework is the explicit consideration of uncertainty, an aspect that is inherent in spatio-temporal data, due to infrequent position updates, due to physical limitations and due to power constraints. The UST-framework can be used to obtain a deeper intuition of the quality of spatio-temporal data models. Such models aim at estimating the position of a spatio-temporal object at a time where the object's position is not explicitly known, for example by using both historic (traffic-) pattern information, and by using explicit observations of objects. The UST-framework illustrates the resulting distributions by allowing a user to move forward and backward in time. Additionally the framework allows users to specify simple spatio-temporal queries, such as spatio-temporal window queries and spatio-temporal nearest neighbor (NN) queries. Based on recently published theoretic concepts, the UST-framework allows to visually explore the impact of different models and parameters on spatio-temporal data. The main result showcased by the UST-framework is a minimization of uncertainty by employing stochastic processes, leading to small expected distances between ground truth trajectories and modelled positions.

Categories and Subject Descriptors

H.3.3 [**INFORMATION STORAGE AND RETRIEVAL**]: Information Search and Retrieval—*Query Processing*

Keywords

Uncertain Trajectories, Uncertain Spatio-Temporal, Framework

1. INTRODUCTION

Both the current trends in technology such as smartphones, general mobile devices, stationary sensors and satellites as well as a new user mentality of utilizing this technology to voluntarily share information produce a huge flood of geo-spatio-temporal data. The main goal of this demonstration is to provide an intuitive yet powerful framework to evaluate and explore techniques for managing and querying historical spatio-temporal data in explicit consideration of the inherent uncertainty. By *historical spatio-temporal data* ([5]), we refer to a collection of data triples having the form (location, time, object). In a plethora of research fields and industrial applications, these techniques can substantially improve decision making, minimize risk and unearth valuable insights that would otherwise remain hidden. In practice, such triples correspond to observations (e.g. GPS positions, RFID signals, or visual observations) of *moving objects* in the past. Thus, each triple corresponds to an observation of the *trajectory* of a moving object.

In many applications, the position of an object is observed at discrete times only, leading to an inherent uncertainty between these discrete times and creating the notion of *uncertain spatio-temporal data* – an aspect raising an imminent need for scalable and flexible data management. In practice, moving objects for which the position at any time cannot be determined deterministically, are denoted as *uncertain moving objects*. The indeterministic trajectory of an uncertain moving object is an *uncertain trajectory*. Existing works to model, manage and query uncertain spatio-temporal data, including interpolation models ([8, 9, 10, 12, 11]) and geometric approximation models ([14, 15, 16, 6, 4, 13]), identify trajectories that may possibly satisfy a user-specified query predicate. These approaches cannot return to the user an indication of the likelihood of these trajectories to satisfy the query predicate, i.e., these approaches cannot give the user any information about the quality and significance of the returned result. First approaches to alleviate this problem have been proposed in [6, 18, 1, 17]. These approaches return uncertain moving objects associated with a probability estimating the likelihood of the corresponding object to satisfy the query predicate. They treat realizations of uncertain moving objects at different points of time as mutually independent random variables. However, the location of objects at subsequent discrete points of time are highly correlated, as commanded for example by laws of physics and speed limits. Ignoring this positive correlation leads to systematic and significant errors as shown in [7].

The shortcomings of these models have been addressed in previous work ([3, 2, 7]), by applying models from statistics, namely stochastic processes and Bayesian inference, to treat uncertain moving objects in a probabilistic way. In the following Section 2, the theoretic base of these works is sketched. Section 3 describes the system architecture, functionality and the main purpose of the UST-framework. Finally, Section 4 describes the demonstrator, by describing the impact on the field of managing spatio-temporal data, and explaining how the framework's visualization tools will be used to convince the audience of this impact.

SIGMOD'14, June 22–27, 2014, Snowbird, UT, USA.

http://dx.doi.org/10.1145/2588555.2594523.

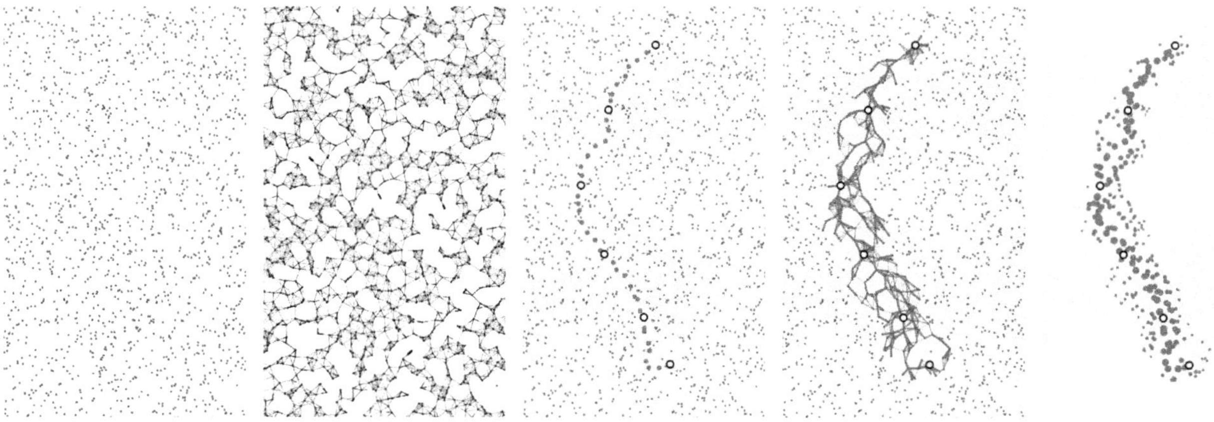

(a) State space (b) A-priori transitions (c) Single trajectory (d) Transition probabil. (e) State probabilities

Figure 1: Data Visualization

2. PRELIMINARIES

A main challenge of uncertain spatio-temporal data is to infer the position of an uncertain object o at time t when the exact position has not been observed. The quality of this inference depends on our ability to effectively use the wealth of information stored in a spatio-temporal database. Firstly, we need to consider information about movement patterns, such as turn probabilities at a road intersection, learned empirically from historical data. Secondly, observations of o that may temporally precede or succeed t need to be considered to predict the position of o at time t.

The key idea of the demonstrated approach to model uncertain spatio-temporal data is to model possible object trajectories by a stochastic process, more precisely a Markov chain. Employing the Markov chain model for representing spatio-temporal data has three major advantages over previous work:

1. It allows answering queries such that results are associated with their corresponding probabilities.
2. Dependencies between object locations at consecutive points in time are taken into account.
3. It is often possible to express queries using simple matrix operations only, thus allowing to utilize highly efficient existing solutions for interactive query processing.

The Markov model is estimated empirically. The resulting model is called *a-priori model* and contains general transition probabilities; i.e., probabilities of any object moving from one node to an adjacent node in the network. However, using the a-priori model, i.e., the usage of a Markov random-walk model yields unacceptable inference quality in applications such as traffic monitoring, where objects aim at moving on a more-or-less shortest path, rather than randomly selecting a new direction at each intersection of a road network.

To solve this problem, the main challenge that we approached in our most recent publication ([7]) is to enrich these general movement patterns given by the Markov model by knowledge of individual observations of an uncertain moving object. We pre-compute the probabilities that, at a given time, a given object performs a transition between two nodes of the network, given all observations of an object, at past, present and future times. These adapted transition probabilities define an *a-posteriori* model, which combines all sources of information given by a spatio-temporal database. A main experimental result of this work shows that the adapted a-posteriori model, i.e., the fusion between empirical trajectory data and observation data of objects, allows to accurately estimate the position of an uncertain moving object at times between observations. In particular, the expected error in terms of distance between the real trajectory and the modelled position (which is a random variable) was shown to be vastly reduced by this data integration. For a detailt evaluation of the runtime of queries under the Markov model we refer to the corresponding papers [3, 2, 7].

Figure 1(a) visualizes the set of spatial states used for the Markov model. During a preprocessing phase, these states have to be extracted from a spatio-temporal data set. Furthermore it is necessary to build an a-priori Markov model as described in our initial work ([3]). The resulting data is then imported into the database. The model is visualized in Figure 1(b), where line segments indicate possible transitions, and the thickness of a line indicates the probability of making a transition between the pair of connected nodes.[1] The ground-truth object trajectories are visualized in Figure 1(c). This figure shows the full trajectory of an object, independent of time. In the above picture, observations are highlighted by larger black circles. Based on such observations, the a-posteriori model can be derived using our techniques of [7]. Figure 1(d) illustrates the a-posteriori model, analogous to Figure 1(b). Given the adapted model, the probability to visit each node of the network is visualized in Figure 1(e).

In our recent work we have used distance metrics, especially the expected distance between the ground truth data and the model based on observations, to numerically prove the vast improvement over other approaches. Yet, the intention of this demonstration is *not* to re-run existing experiments on modeling and querying uncertain spatio-temportal data. Rather, the main goal is to present to a broad audience the practical impact of this data integration of combining historical trajectory data and concrete observations of an object to reduce uncertainty in spatio-temporal data. The main modules of the UST-framework, which show this impact and which we wish to present to the SIGMOD audience, will be described in the following two sections.

[1]The image shows the maximum transition probabilities of both directions. On the other hand, it would also be possible to split line segment into two equi-distant parts, each having individual thickness.

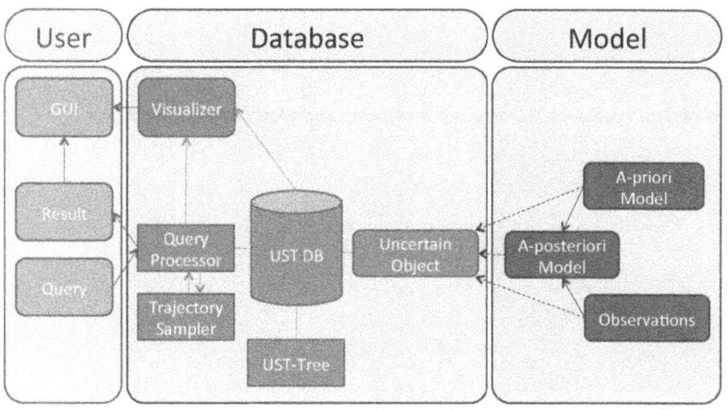

Figure 2: UST-framework: System Architecture

3. FRAMEWORK DESCRIPTION

For the purpose of exploring data models for uncertain spatio-temporal data, a first aspect of our demonstrator allows visualization of various aspect of such data. For this purpose, a data set consisting of (location, time, object)-triples can be imported into the framework. The data sets that we want to demonstrate include – in addition to a number of artificial spatio-temporal data sets – the T-Drive data set ([19]) pertaining to GPS-traces of taxis in the city of Beijing. In addition to simple data visualization, the framework can also be used to evaluate the model accuracy of uncertainty models, such as interpolation (which has been used previously in [8, 9, 10, 12, 11]), geometric models (that have been investigated in [14, 15, 16, 6, 4, 13]) and stochastic processes, especially under the Markov chain model ([3, 7]). Beside the Markov chain model we have implemented two exemplary approaches, an interpolation approach based on the shortest paths between observations, and a geometric approach representing the uncertainty area between observations by diamonds. While the accuracy of our approach has already been evaluated in [7], this numeric evaluation gives little insights on the impact this research can have on concrete systems. This demonstration shows how the fusion of both data sources, historic traffic data and current object observations, can very accurately describe the motion of an uncertain spatio-temporal object. The main features of the UST-framework are:

- Integration of the latest techniques for managing and querying uncertain spatio-temporal data.
- A powerful visualization toolbox used for spatio-temporal data sets and query results.
- An intuitive framework which can easily be extended by new query types, visualization techniques, and index structures.

The general structure of the framework is sketched in Figure 2: The database consists of a set of uncertain objects, each represented by a set of (location, time) pairs called observations. Uncertain objects are stored in a database (UST DB) that stores all uncertain objects and contains one or more index structures (for example a UST-Tree) to efficiently access them. The database stores an a-priori Markov model ([3]), i.e. a (global) transition matrix. This model is usually learned from the full historical data set stored in the database. Using observations of individual objects, the transition matrix can be adapted using the approach from [7]. The resulting a-posteriori Markov model accounts for these observartions by adapting transition probabilities such that all possible trajectories match all observations. While these models could be computed during query time, they are stored in the database to improve the runtime performance of the system.

The implemented interpolation and geometric models are stored in the system as well, together with their corresponding index structures. Queries are posed on a query processor that forwards the query to the database and underlying index structure. Depending on the hardness of the query, the query process either computes exact result probabilities, or employs a sampling approach to approximate result probabilities. The visualizer module is used to visualize both the database contents and query results.

4. DEMONSTRATION SCENARIOS

Per default, the spatio-temporal T-Drive [19] data set will be showcased, using the street network of Beijing, China. During the presentation, the presenter will browse the data set by moving the current focus to different parts of the city, moving forward and back in time and switching between data models. A snapshot of the framework is shown in Figure 3. In our demonstration we will present several application scenarios to the audience with the goal of providing visual insights to the practical impact resulting from our previous theoretical work. For this purpose we will address three different scenarios, which we will present using real-world as well as synthetic data sets:

4.1 Database Visualization

The framework visualizes a database of uncertain spatio-temporal objects. After opening the database connection, the user has access to a map showing the uncertain objects in the database at a given point in time, and a timeline visualizing the distribution of uncertain objects over the database time horizon. To illustrate the underlying road network (of Beijing in Figure 3), the demonstrator uses Open-Street-Map data. The map view provides bounding boxes of the uncertain objects approximating the position of each object at the given point of time. The visualized boxes correspond to spatial approximations of our spatio-temporal index structure ([2]) for the Markov model. The implemented geometric model is described by these bounding boxes as well. Certain and interpolated trajectories are visualized by their discrete positions. For a selected object (Markov model) the map shows non-zero probabilities of staying at the corresponding position as circles, while non-zero transition probabilities of moving from a given state to a neighboring state are visualized as lines between states.

4.2 Spatio-Temporal Query Processing

We further provide an easy-to-use interface for performing window queries to the user. The user interface for this feature is also depicted in Figure 3. To pose a window query on the database, the user has to first select a time-horizon on the timeline located in the bottom part of the user interface. Furthermore, the user is required to specify a spatial query window in the map view located at the upper-left part of the user interface. After defining the spatio-temporal window query, results are shown in a result view on the right-hand side. The type of result depends on the selected uncertainty model. In the case of interpolation models, a set of objects, corresponding to a raw guess (which might indeed not even be possible) is returned. In the case of geometric models, a set of possible results (which may indeed have a zero probability) are returned. If the Markov model ([3]) is selected, objects are returned together with their probabilities of being results. Furthermore, result objects can be highlighted in the map visualization. In the case of nearest neighbor queries, the user defines a query point on the map and a time interval on the timeline. After query processing, the user can highlight the objects with a nearest neighbor probability greater than zero for the given time interval on the map.

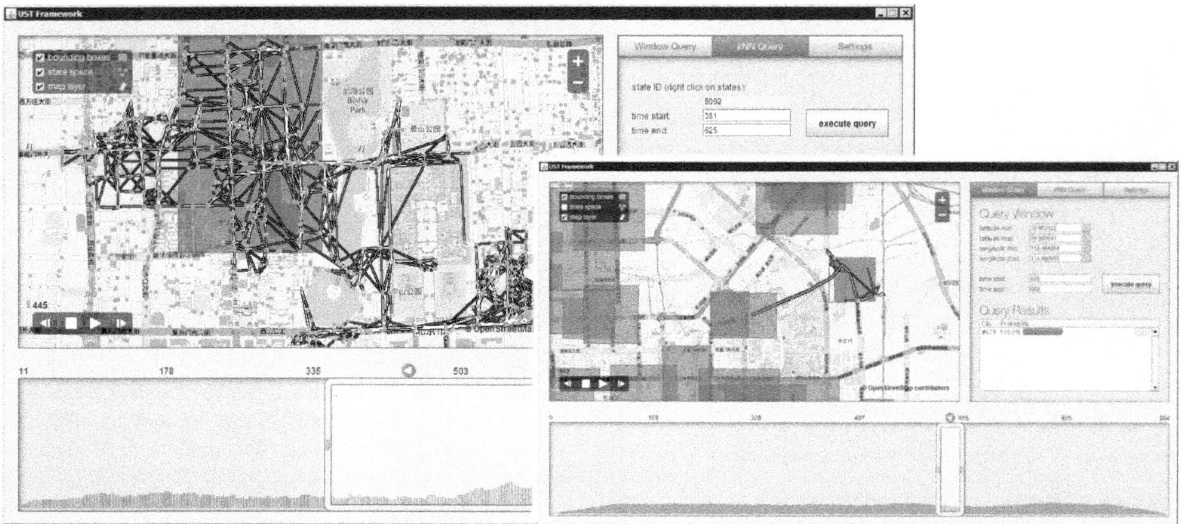

Figure 3: Graphical user interfaces for window queries (left) and NN queries (right).

4.3 Data Modification

Last but not least we will show how the user is able to insert new observations to uncertain trajectories. This is particularly of interest since the integration of new observations into the model yields new uncertainty regions of the corresponding object leading to a smaller degree of uncertainty. The uncertainty regions of all models are adapted to the new observation after insertion.

The demonstration will be side-kicked by a poster, to introduce the audience to the field of modeling uncertainty in spatio-temporal data. The main purpose of the poster is to present theoretic foundations of our recent publications ([3, 2, 7]) which are too complex (and thus time consuming) to be presented orally. Thus, the poster will provide the basics of our Markov model and the approach used to perform a data integration between historic movement patterns and individual object observations. Our UST-framework has been implemented in C++ and Java. For further information regarding the model and framework we refer to the UST project page.

Acknowledgements

This work is partially suppported by Deutsche Forschungsgemeinschaft (DFG), under grant RE 2667/5änd by German Accademic Exchange Service (DAAD), under grant "56048240".

5. REFERENCES

[1] J. Aßfalg, H.-P. Kriegel, P. Kröger, and M. Renz. Probabilistic similarity search for uncertain time series. In *Proc. SSDBM*, pages 435–443, 2009.

[2] T. Emrich, H.-P. Kriegel, N. Mamoulis, M. Renz, and A. Züfle. Indexing uncertain spatio-temporal data. In *CIKM*, pages 395–404, 2012.

[3] T. Emrich, H.-P. Kriegel, N. Mamoulis, M. Renz, and A. Züfle. Querying uncertain spatio-temporal data. In *Proc. ICDE*, pages 354–365, 2012.

[4] B. Kuijpers and W. Othman. Trajectory databases: Data models, uncertainty and complete query languages. In *JCSS*, pages 538–560, 2010.

[5] N. Mamoulis, H. Cao, G. Kollios, M. Hadjieleftheriou, Y. Tao, and D. W. Cheung. Mining, indexing, and querying historical spatiotemporal data. In *Proc. KDD*, pages 236–245, 2004.

[6] H. Mokhtar and J. Su. Universal trajectory queries for moving object databases. In *Mobile Data Management (MDM)*, pages 133–144, 2004.

[7] J. Niedermayer, A. Züfle, T. Emrich, M. Renz, N. Mamoulis, L. Chen, and H.-P. Kriegel. Probabilistic nearest neighbor queries on uncertain moving object trajectories. In *VLDB*, 2014.

[8] D. Pfoser, C. S. Jensen, and Y. Theodoridis. Novel approaches to the indexing of moving object trajectories. In *Proc. VLDB*, pages 396–406, 2000.

[9] S. Saltenis, C. S. Jensen, S. T. Leutenegger, and M. A. Lopez. Indexing the positions of continuously moving objects. In *Proc. SIGMOD*, pages 331–342, 2000.

[10] Y. Tao and D. Papadias. Time-parameterized queries in spatio-temporal databases. In *Proc. SIGMOD*, pages 334–345, 2002.

[11] Y. Tao, D. Papadias, and Q. Shen. Continuous nearest neighbor search. In *Proc. VLDB*, pages 287–298, 2002.

[12] Y. Tao, D. Papadias, and J. Sun. The tpr*tree: An optimized spatio-temporal access method for predictive queries. In *Proc. VLDB*, pages 790–801, 2003.

[13] G. Trajcevski, A. N. Choudhary, O. Wolfson, L. Ye, and G. Li. Uncertain range queries for necklaces. In *11th International Conference on Mobile Data Management (MDM 2010), Kansas City, Missouri*, pages 199–208, 2010.

[14] G. Trajcevski, R. Tamassia, H. Ding, P. Scheuermann, and I. F. Cruz. Continuous probabilistic nearest-neighbor queries for uncertain trajectories. In *Proc. EDBT*, pages 874–885, 2009.

[15] G. Trajcevski, O. Wolfson, K. Hinrichs, and S. Chamberlain. Managing uncertainty in moving objects databases. *ACM Trans. Database Syst.*, 29(3):463–507, 2004.

[16] G. Trajcevski, O. Wolfson, F. Zhang, and S. Chamberlain. The geometry of uncertainty in moving objects databases. In *Proc. EDBT*, pages 233–250, 2002.

[17] C. Xu, Y. Gu, L. Chen, J. Qiao, and G. Yu. Interval reverse nearest neighbor queries on uncertain data with markov correlations. In *Proc. ICDE*, 2013.

[18] M.-Y. Yeh, K.-L. Wu, P. S. Yu, and M. Chen. Proud: A probabilistic approach to processing similarity queries over uncertain data streams. In *Proc. EDBT*, pages 684–695, 2009.

[19] J. Yuan, Y. Zheng, C. Zhang, W. Xie, X. Xie, and Y. Huang. T-drive: Driving directions based on taxi trajectories. In *Proc. ACM GIS*, 2010.

NewsNetExplorer: Automatic Construction and Exploration of News Information Networks

Fangbo Tao[†], George Brova[†], Jiawei Han[†], Heng Ji[‡], Chi Wang[†], Brandon Norick[†], Ahmed El-Kishky[†], Jialu Liu[†], Xiang Ren[†], Yizhou Sun[◇]

[†] Department of Computer Science, University of Illinois at Urbana-Champaign
[‡] Department of Computer Science, Rensselaer Polytechnic Institute
[◇] College of Computer and Information Science, Northeastern University

ABSTRACT

News data is one of the most abundant and familiar data sources. News data can be systematically utilized and explored by database, data mining, NLP and information retrieval researchers to demonstrate to the general public the power of advanced information technology. In our view, news data contains rich, inter-related and multi-typed data objects, forming one or a set of gigantic, interconnected, heterogeneous information networks. Much knowledge can be derived and explored with such an information network if we systematically develop effective and scalable data-intensive information network analysis technologies.

By further developing a set of information extraction, information network construction, and information network mining methods, we extract types, topical hierarchies and other semantic structures from news data, construct a semi-structured news information network NewsNet. Further, we develop a set of news information network exploration and mining mechanisms that explore news in multi-dimensional space, which include (i) OLAP-based operations on the hierarchical dimensional and topical structures and rich-text, such as cell summary, single dimension analysis, and promotion analysis, (ii) a set of network-based operations, such as similarity search and ranking-based clustering, and (iii) a set of hybrid operations or network-OLAP operations, such as entity ranking at different granularity levels. These form the basis of our proposed NewsNetExplorer system. Although some of these functions have been studied in recent research, effective and scalable realization of such functions in large networks still poses multiple challenging research problems. Moreover, some functions are our on-going research tasks. By integrating these functions, NewsNetExplorer not only provides with us insightful recommendations in NewsNet exploration system but also helps us gain insight on how to perform effective information extraction, integration and mining in large unstructured datasets.

SIGMOD'14, June 22–27, 2014, Snowbird, UT, USA.

http://dx.doi.org/10.1145/2588555.2594537.

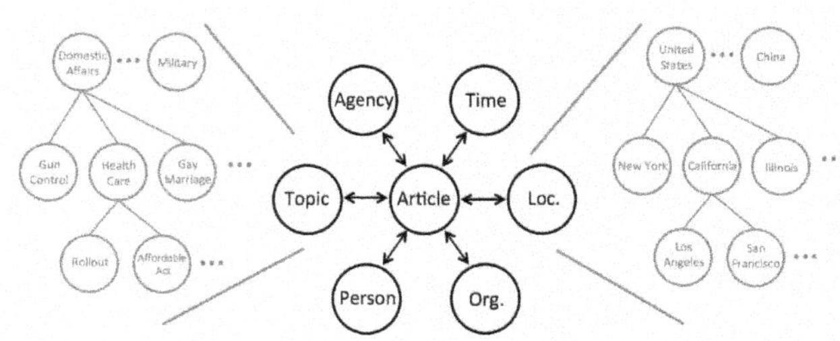

Figure 1: News Network Schema: The hierarchies of "*Topic*" and "*Location*" are illustrated in the graph, the hierarchies of "*Person*", "*Time*" and "*Organization*" are not shown for simplicity.

Categories and Subject Descriptors

H.2.8 [**Information Systems Applications**]: Database Applications—*Data Mining*

Keywords

Information Network Construction, Network-OLAP

1. INTRODUCTION

We are living in the dawn of big data era. Massive amount of data has been generated in fast pace from every corner of our society. It is important for database and data mining researchers to demonstrate the promise of our technology using massive real datasets. News data is one of the most abundant and well-understood data sources. It is ideal to explore news data thoroughly and use it to systematically demonstrate the power of information technology. Unfortunately, unlike research publication data sets (*e.g.*, DBLP) or most relational database data, news data is largely unstructured. It is a big challenge to turn such unstructured news data to semi-structured data automatically.

In our recent research, we have made progress in two frontiers. First, we have systematically studied methods for data mining in heterogeneous information networks [4] and developed a set of methods for mining heterogeneous information networks. Taking computer science bibliographic networks extracted from DBLP as an example, one can (i) cluster and rank venues, authors and terms in computer science by RankClus and NetClus [4], (ii) derive quality classification models for multi-typed entities and present their ranking as by-product by GNetMine and RankClass [3], (iii) conduct effective similarity search across networks by PathSim [5], and *etc.*Clearly, modeling heterogeneous datasets as structured heterogeneous information networks often captures richer node/link semantics and generates better mining and search results than their underlying relational databases. Such mechanisms can be transferred to news data analysis if the multi-dimensional structured information can be extracted from news data and a heterogeneous, semi-structured news information network can be constructed automatically.

Second, we have been developing effective methods for constructing heterogeneous information networks from unstructured text data. We have studied how to extract typed data from news data with advanced NLP technology, which forms the base for construction of a preliminary heterogeneous information network. Moreover, we have recently developed a phrase mining framework for recursive construction of topical hierarchies from text data [10] and from heterogeneous information networks [11]. By further refinement of the above processes, a quality NewsNet will be able to be generated systematically.

In this demo, we will show how a quality NewsNet can be constructed by integration of NLP, phrase mining, and information network analysis methods, and how OLAP and heterogenous network mining can be successfully performed on NewsNet. NewsNetExplorer is our new project based on our recent research and based on experience on the development of the two previous demo systems: Research-Insight on the DBLP data [9] and EvenCube on NASA's Aviation Safety Report data [8].

2. NETWORK CONSTRUCTION

The news corpora released through Linguistic Data Consortium (**LDC**) to research communities is a rich news collection to build a comprehensive news network. It includes 10 million news articles from 7 different major news agencies in the Gigaword Corpus[1]. For such an enormous collection of plain text articles, the very first process we apply is extracting typed entities from text and construct an interconnected network with sophisticated hierarchies associated to these typed entities. As shown in Figure 1, we build a network, generated by taking *Article* as a center type, linking to multiple typed nodes including *Person, Organization, Agency, Time, Location* and *Topic*. Moreover, except the center type *Article* and *Agency*, other typed nodes are organized in a hierarchical way as illustrated in Figure 1.

2.1 Entity extraction using NLP

From the free text or the text segments of the textual attributes in the integrated structured and text news data, natural language processing (**NLP**) (especially Information Extraction) tools are used to extract essential entities such as time, location, person, organization. Moreover, concept hierarchies (*i.e.*, higher-level entities) are associated with extracted entities (*e.g.*, Chicago is associated with state: Illinois) based on a user- or expert-provided dictionary.

2.2 Entity extraction using hierarchical topic ontology finding

For *Topic* extraction of NewsNetExplorer we have developed a method[10] that construct a topical hierarchy from a collection of text. The framework called **CATHY** (Construct A Topical HierarchY) is a recursive clustering and ranking approach for topical hierarchy generation. In the news collection, many pieces can describe the same topic; meanwhile, different topics may reflect the same fact at different levels of granularity. The aim of [10] is to construct a hierarchy where each topic is represented by a ranked list of phrases, such that a child topic is a subset of its parent topic. This strategy also works well specifically for news data since news articles tend to use different phrases to report the same topics.

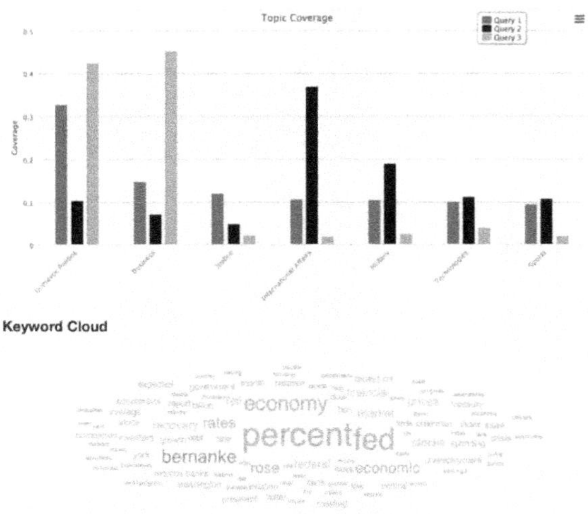

Figure 2: A comparison of topic distributions between "Barack Obama", "Hillary Clinton" and "Ben Bernanke". The tag cloud is a summary for Ben Bernanke's news articles.

3. MAJOR FUNCTIONAL MODULES

By extracting the entities from millions of news articles and building highly sophisticated hierarchies for those typed entities, we can view the structured information from two different perspectives: (1) Heterogeneous Information Network with Rich Text, and (2) Multi-dimensional Hierarchical Data Cube with Rich Text. Clearly, modeling a heterogeneous network as Figure 1 captures richer node/link semantics and generate better mining result than a homogeneous network or unstructured text collection. Meanwhile, a multi-dimensional data cube enables us to carry out advanced online analytical processing (**OLAP**) operations at different levels of granularity. We also explore a new direction of leveraging both information network and multi-dimensional data cube structures, conducting network-based mining algorithms at different levels of granularity of the network. The major functional modules are described in this section.

3.1 OLAP Operations on News Data

3.1.1 Hierarchical Cell Summary

OLAP techniques are efficient and effective for mining and analyzing structured data like data cubes. With rich text gained from millions of news articles, it also becomes possible to mine the text data and analyze latent topics in an OLAP fashion. By combining OLAP and probabilistic topic modeling together, we treat topic distribution of a set of news articles as an aggregation function. By exploring at different granularity levels and comparing topic distributions for different cells, we can reveal deeper insights in the huge news collection. The algorithm implemented here is proposed by our TopicCube model [13] that constructs

Rank	Cell	#Document	Avg-Relevance
1	Time:Nov-2009, Organization:House of Rep.	93	2.1201770279997136
2	Time:2010, Organization:White House	51	1.9302240668558608
3	Time:2013, Topic:Healthcare.gov rollout	20	1.9351981639862061

Figure 3: Top-ranked cells for the query "Healthcare", the top results indicate 1). House of Representatives passed the bill, 2). The President signed the bill. 3). The website rollout.

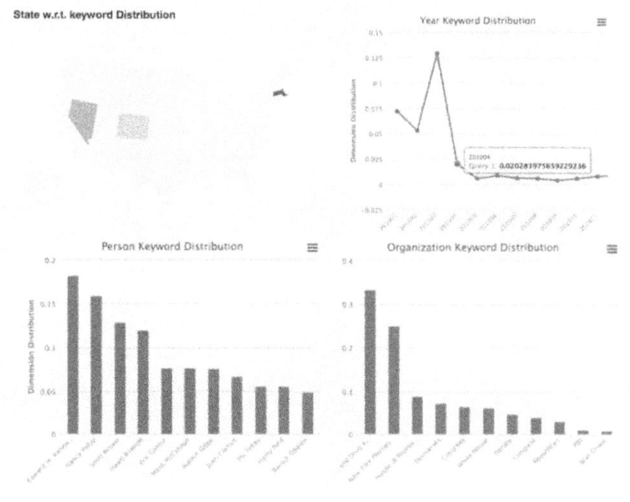

Figure 4: Single dimension distribution for query "healthcare bill". We find top related *Location, Time, Person and Organization.*

a hierarchical topic tree on a data cube to define a topic dimension for exploring text information. An example on news data is shown in Figure 2.

3.1.2 Promotion Analysis in News Cube

A cell in the text cube aggregates a set of documents with matching dimension values on a subset of dimensions. Given a keyword query on the news, we want to enable people to find most relevant cells in the data cube. A most relevant cell needs to be generated from two aspects: (1). It is a combination of relevant dimensions. (2). It needs to find the best level of granularity of each dimension to describe the cell. For a query like "Healthcare bill", we may need to find a cell as "{Organization: Congress, Time:2009}", while for a query like "Nelson Mandela", a "{Time:Dec/2013, Topic:Death}" cell is better. The top-ranked cells should not only be highly relevant, but also be significant for the query. A relevance scoring model and efficient ranking algorithm has been proposed in [2] and [12]. It optimizes the search order and prunes the search space by estimating the upper bounds of relevance scores in the corresponding subspaces, so as to explore as few cells as possible for finding top-k answers. An example on the News dataset to generate top-k cells is shown in Figure 3.

3.1.3 Hierarchical Single Dimension Distributions

For each news search query, it is desirable to provide many insights for analysts if the data distribution can be provided on each dimension. For instance, if people want to know more about the *healthcare bill*, other than providing a list of relevant documents for them to read, it's helpful to show top relevant entities on *Person, Organization, Time* and *Topic* dimensions. This structured summary can also be hierarchical, which will enable users to explore along different levels of the *Time, Topic* or *Location* hierarchies. In NewsNetExplorer we aggregate the relevant documents on every dimension to show the heatmap of the keywords for *Location* dimension, time series of the keywords for *Time* dimension and the ranked list for other dimensions. An example on query "Healthcare Bill" can be found in Figure 4. To achieve both efficiency and effectiveness, we propose a framework that combines offline and online computation together to generate real-time single dimension distribution results for every query.

3.2 Information Network Mining Operations

3.2.1 Similarity Search

Similarity search often plays an important role in the analysis of networks. For a news collection we use, which contains millions of articles covering several decades of various news stories, it's critical and challenging to find the connections between entities in the network. By considering different linkage paths in a network, one can derive various semantics on similarity. A meta-path based similarity measure is introduced [5], where a meta-path is a structural path defined at the meta level (*i.e.*, relationships among object types). It turns out to be more meaningful in many scenarios compared with random-walk based similarity measures and is also efficient for top-k similarity search in heterogeneous networks. In NewsNetExplorer we implemented this similarity algorithm in a brand new scenario of news network.

Example 1: Similarity Search in NewsNetExplorer. Given a person (*e.g.*, Barack Obama), find his/her top-k similar people and explain why (by summarizing their connections and the corresponding similarity measure). We expect to find other presidents by meta-path *P(erson) - O(organization) - P(erson)* and to find most relevant contemporary politicians by meta-path *P(erson) - T(opic) - P(erson)*. Do the same for an organization (*e.g.*, Senate), a state (*e.g.*, Illinois) and a topic(*e.g.*, Iran nuclear crisis). Potential extensions include finding top-k most related heterogeneous typed objects (*e.g.*, given a person (*e.g.*, Lady Gaga), find his/her top-k most related organizations and topics). ■

3.2.2 Ranking-based Clustering

Suffering from the complexity of news articles, it has always been important to apply clustering based on news content. More than traditional approaches, we apply a link-based clustering algorithm to utilize the structured network, which explores links across heterogeneous types of data. Our recent studies develop a ranking-based clustering approach, represented by RankClus [6] and NetClus [7], that generates interesting results for both clustering and ranking efficiently. A significant difference from traditional text clustering is that we also cluster typed entities like *Person, Topic and Organization.* This approach is based on the observation that ranking and clustering can mutually enhance each other because objects highly ranked in each cluster may contribute more towards unambiguous clustering, and objects more dedicated to a cluster will be more likely to be highly ranked in the same cluster.

Example 2: Rank-based clustering in NewsNetExplorer. Given a subnetwork (*e.g.*, network formed under specific conditions, *e.g.*, years 2005-2008) and a desired number of clusters (*e.g.*, 4), perform rank-based clustering and show top-k objects of each type (*i.e.*, *Person, Topic, Organization*) in each cluster. ■

3.3 Network-OLAP Operations

3.3.1 Entity Ranking on Different Granularity Levels

Entity Ranking is an important feature to help readers understand different news lines better without going through the related articles. People are interested in questions like "*who are the most important people in 2013*", "*what are the most relevant organizations about 911 attack?*" and "*what's the major topics of China during 2000 to 2010?*". To be expressed in our framework, given a cell of the data cube, find the top-ranked entities under the cell condition. We applied a linkage-based ranking algorithm here, in which we first build the subnetwork according to the cell, then apply the ranking function for different kinds of entities in the sub-network. We introduced a two-step approach to combine both global ranking and local ranking together into the ranking function. We treat a graph algorithm as our aggregation function, that traditional OLAP algorithms cannot be applied to improve the efficiency.

Example 3: Entity Ranking in NewsNetExplorer. Given a cell (*e.g.*, *2013 and Iran Nuclear Crisis*), perform and show top-k objects of each type (*i.e.*, *Person, Topic, Organization, Time and Location*). Drill down to {*2013-Nov, Iran Nuclear Crisis*} or roll up to {*2013, International Affairs*} to see the new ranking result for each type. ■

4. ABOUT THE DEMO

In this demo, we build a complete automatic workflow to analyze a collection of news articles. We build a text-rich news information network by extracting the typed entities and their hierarchical structure from the *Gigaword* news collection [1], implement three different kinds of mining or search operations based on myriad research work. Users can interactively make their structured queries or text queries to explore the news world in an efficient and effective way.

5. REFERENCES

[1] http://catalog.ldc.upenn.edu/LDC2011T07.

[2] B. Ding, B. Zhao, C. X. Lin, J. Han, C. Zhai, A. Srivastava, and N. C. Oza. Efficient keyword-based search for top-k cells in text cube. *IEEE Trans. on Knowledge and Data Engineering (TKDE)*, 23:1795–1810, 2011.

[3] M. Ji, J. Han, and M. Danilevsky. Ranking-based classification of heterogeneous information networks. In *Proc. 2011 ACM SIGKDD Int. Conf. on Knowledge Discovery and Data Mining (KDD'11)*, San Diego, CA, Aug. 2011.

[4] Y. Sun and J. Han. *Mining Heterogeneous Information Networks: Principles and Methodologies*. Morgan & Claypool Publishers, 2012.

[5] Y. Sun, J. Han, X. Yan, P. S. Yu, and T. Wu. PathSim: Meta path-based top-k similarity search in heterogeneous information networks. In *Proc. 2011 Int. Conf. Very Large Data Bases (VLDB'11)*, Seattle, WA, Aug. 2011.

[6] Y. Sun, J. Han, P. Zhao, Z. Yin, H. Cheng, and T. Wu. RankClus: Integrating clustering with ranking for heterogeneous information network analysis. In *Proc. 2009 Int. Conf. Extending Data Base Technology (EDBT'09)*, Saint-Petersburg, Russia, Mar. 2009.

[7] Y. Sun, Y. Yu, and J. Han. Ranking-based clustering of heterogeneous information networks with star network schema. In *Proc. 2009 ACM SIGKDD Int. Conf. Knowledge Discovery and Data Mining (KDD'09)*, Paris, France, June 2009.

[8] F. Tao, K. H. Lei, J. Han, C. Zhai, X. Cheng, M. Danilevsky, N. Desai, B. Ding, J. Ge, H. Ji, R. Kanade, A. Kao, Q. Li, Y. Li, C. X. Lin, J. liu, N. Oza, A. Srivastava, R. Tjoelker, C. Wang, D. Zhang, and B. Zhao. Eventcube: Multi-dimensional search and mining of structured and text data. In *Proc. 2013 ACM SIGKDD Int. Conf. on Knowledge Discovery and Data Mining (KDD'13)*, Chicago, IL, Aug. 2013.

[9] F. Tao, X. Yu, K. H. Lei, G. Brova, X. Cheng, J. Han, R. Kanade, Y. Sun, C. Wang, L. Wang, and T. Weninger. Research-insight: Providing insight on research by publication network analysis. In *Proc. of 2013 ACM SIGMOD Int. Conf. on Management of Data (SIGMOD'13)*, New York, NY, June 2013.

[10] C. Wang, M. Danilevsky, N. Desai, Y. Zhang, P. Nguyen, T. Taula, and J. Han. A phrase mining framework for recursive construction of a topical hierarchy. In *Proc. 2013 ACM SIGKDD Int. Conf. on Knowledge Discovery and Data Mining (KDD'13)*, Chicago, IL, Aug. 2013.

[11] C. Wang, X. Yu, Y. Li, C. Zhai, and J. Han. Content coverage maximization on word networks for hierarchical topic summarization. In *Proc. of 2013 Int. Conf. on Information and Knowledge Management (CIKM'13)*, San Francisco, CA, Oct. 2013.

[12] T. Wu, Y. Sun, C. Li, and J. Han. Region-based online promotion analysis. In *Proc. 2010 Int. Conf. on Extending Data Base Technology (EDBT'10)*, Lausanne, Switzerland, March 2010.

[13] D. Zhang, C. Zhai, J. Han, A. Srivastava, and N. Oza. Topic modeling for OLAP on multidimensional text databases: Topic cube and its applications. *Statistical Analysis and Data Mining*, 2:378–395, 2009.

Acknowledgments. This work was supported by the U.S. Army Research Laboratory under Cooperative Agreement No. W911NF-09-2-0053 (NS-CTA), the U.S. Army Research Office under Cooperative Agreement No. W911NF-13-1-0193, U.S. NSF CAREER Award under Grant IIS-0953149, U.S.DARPA Award No. FA8750-13-2-0041 in the Deep Exploration and Filtering of Text (DEFT) Program, U.S. National Science Foundation grants CNS-0931975, IIS-1017362, IIS-1320617, IIS-1354329, DTRA, MIAS, a DHS-IDS Center for Multimodal Information Access and Synthesis at UIUC, a Microsoft Research Gift, and an NSF Graduate Fellowship, IBM Faculty award and RPI faculty start-up grant.

IQR: An Interactive Query Relaxation System for the Empty-Answer Problem

Davide Mottin
University of Trento
mottin@disi.unitn.eu

Alice Marascu
IBM Research-Ireland
alice.marascu@ie.ibm.com

Senjuti Basu Roy
U of Washington Tacoma
senjutib@uw.edu

Gautam Das
UT Arlington & QCRI
gdas@{uta.edu,qf.org.qa}

Themis Palpanas
Paris Descartes University
themis@mi.parisdescartes.fr

Yannis Velegrakis
University of Trento
velgias@disi.unitn.eu

ABSTRACT

We present IQR, a system that demonstrates optimization based interactive relaxations for queries that return an empty answer. Given an empty answer, IQR dynamically suggests one relaxation of the original query conditions at a time to the user, based on certain optimization objectives, and the user responds by either accepting or declining the relaxation, until the user arrives at a non-empty answer, or a non-empty answer is impossible to achieve with any further relaxations. The relaxation suggestions hinge on a probabilistic framework that takes into account the probability of the user accepting a suggested relaxation, as well as how much that relaxation serves towards the optimization objective. IQR accepts a wide variety of optimization objectives - user centric objectives, such as, minimizing the number of user interactions (i.e., effort) or returning relevant results, as well as seller centric objectives, such as, maximizing profit. IQR offers principled *exact* and *approximate* solutions for generating relaxations that are demonstrated using multiple, large real datasets.

Categories and Subject Descriptors

H.3.3 [**Information Storage and Retrieval**]: Information Search and Retrieval—*Search process*

Keywords

Empty-answer problem; Query Relaxation; Optimization framework

1. INTRODUCTION

Numerous web applications allow users to search for items of interest like homes, cars, apparel, etc., by specifying their desired attribute values that are later on turned into conjunctive query predicates and the query gets executed over the underlying data source. *Information under-load* or the *empty-answer* is a frequently encountered problem for such queries, where the user over-specifies the query conditions and consequently the system finds no item in the source satisfying them all. To circumvent the *empty-answer problem*, *query relaxation* has been proposed as an effective strategy that reformulates the original query into a new query by removing or relaxing conditions and is considered as a novel alternative to the top-k ranked retrieval model [5]. Existing query relaxation strategies are mostly non-interactive, i.e., they suggest multiple relaxations to the user at a time, and are not designed to offer relaxations that guarantee the optimization of certain objectives in the returned results.

In this demonstration paper, we showcase IQR[1]- an interactive query relaxation system that not only proposes step-by-step relaxation suggestions to the users, but the suggestions are designed to optimize certain objective functions in the returned non-empty results.[2] As such, IQR is meaningful for scenarios in which the user interacts with the data source via a small device (e.g., mobile phone), or for applications where customer-agent interactions unfold step-by-step over the phone (e.g., purchase of travel insurance, reservation of a holiday house, etc.).

IQR accepts a wide range of optimization objectives: *user-centric* objectives, such as, suggesting relaxations that will return the user *most relevant* products, or the *cheapest* products, or *minimize user's navigational effort* by minimizing the number of relaxation steps, as well as, *seller-centric* objectives, such as, suggesting relaxations that will return *the most expensive* products. In order to decide what should be the next proposed relaxation, IQR first computes the *likelihood* that the user will respond positively to a proposal, as well as quantify the effectiveness of the proposal with respect to the optimization objective. Since IQR does not know the exact user intent before she makes the choice, it resorts to a *probabilistic framework* for reasoning about this question.

The IQR Approach: Given a user query that returns an empty-answer, IQR suggests one relaxation at a time. The user responds to it with a "yes"/"no". Based on the response, the next relaxation is suggested and this iterative process continues until one of the two conditions are satisfied: (a) the user has arrived at a non-empty result set; (b) non-empty result set is impossible to achieve with any further relaxations. We describe a running example next.

[1] `http://youtu.be/v9CXnQyZ9jw`

[2] Full description of the IQR theory can be found in [6].

SIGMOD'14, June 22–27, 2014, Snowbird, UT, USA.

http://dx.doi.org/10.1145/2588555.2594512.

	Make	Model	Price	ABS	MP3	Alarm	4WD	DSL	Manual	HiFi	ESP	Turbo
t_1	VW	Touareg	$62K	1	0	0	0	0	1	0	1	0
t_2	Askari	A10	$206K	0	1	0	0	1	1	1	1	0
t_3	Honda	Civic	$32K	1	0	0	0	0	0	0	0	0
t_4	Porsche	911	$126K	0	0	0	0	1	0	1	1	0

Figure 1: An instance of a car database.

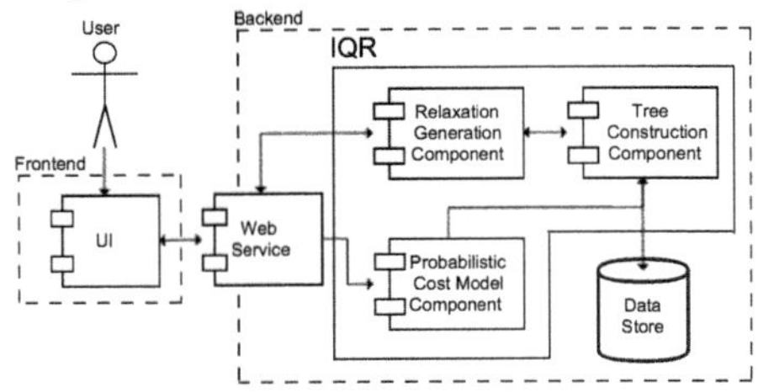

Figure 2: Architecture of the system IQR

Running Example: Imagine that a user is interested in a car that has anti-lock braking system (ABS), dusk-sensing light (DSL), and manual transmission. The data instance of Figure 1 reveals that no car satisfies these requirements.

User-centric Optimization: Consider the optimization objective is to return the *most relevant result.* Imagine that the most relevant tuples to the user query are the VW and the Askari (both satisfy two out of the three query constraints). However, if IQR knows that the most users prefer cars with ABS (i.e., the user has a very high likelihood of responding "no" to the suggestion), then it would instead suggest her to relax DSL to return the VW to her.

Seller-centric Optimization: Conversely, if the seller wants to sell the *most expensive* car (i.e., Askari) to the user, IQR would instead propose cars with no ABS.

IQR is designed to take all of these issues into account while proposing relaxation suggestions based on a certain optimization objective. The effectiveness of a relaxation suggestion is quantified by its *expected cost* by capturing *how well* it serves towards the optimization objective and *how likely* the user will accept it. Given the initial query, the underlying solution then relies on constructing a query relaxation tree [6] that captures the space of possible relaxations as well as user responses and computing the *expected cost* (probabilistic) for each of them. After that, this tree needs to be traversed in a top down fashion to suggest a relaxation that optimizes the expected cost.

A big challenge is raised by the fact that the relaxation suggestions must be generated in real-time, given that the size of the query relaxation tree is exponential to the number of query constraints. IQR offers novel algorithms to ensure scalability by proposing efficient exact solutions, as well as principled approximate solutions.

2. THE IQR SYSTEM

IQR is a web-application (the architecture and flow of information of the system is shown in Figure 2), which can be invoked from the computers or from the mobile devices. The *Query Builder* tab allows the user to select a data source and build a conjunctive query from a drop-down list. The *Search* tab enables searching. If the initial query returns an empty-answer, then the interface allows the user to perform interactive step-by-step relaxation by appropriately selecting the optimization objective. The user can also select the

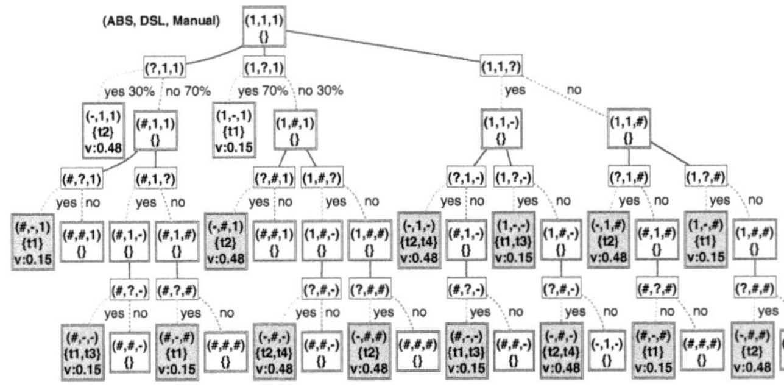

Figure 3: Query Relaxation tree of the running example.

relaxation strategy (i.e., exact or approximate) from the interface. Finally, the *Results* tab shows the returned results along with additional statistics. The back-end consists of the following three components: (a) *Relaxation tree construction*, (b) *Probabilistic cost model*, and (c) *Relaxations generation*. The tree construction component interacts with the database. To enable faster database retrieval, IQR first converts the database to a Boolean type and then designs bitmap indexes for fast retrieval. The probabilistic cost model is abstracted as a framework which could be easily instantiated for different objective functions, or different implementations for computing probabilities. We describe these components next.

2.1 Relaxation Tree Construction

To encode the different relaxation suggestions and user choices that may occur for a given empty-query Q, we employ a special tree structure called the *query relaxation tree* (Figure 3 represents the running example query). The tree contains two types of nodes: the *relaxation* nodes (marked with double-line rectangles in Figure 3) and the *choice* nodes (marked with single-line rectangles in Figure 3). Note that the children of relaxation nodes are choice nodes, and the children of choice nodes are relaxation nodes.

A *relaxation node* represents a relaxed query Q'. The root node represents the original query Q. A relaxation node does not have any children when the respective query returns a non-empty answer, or returns an empty-answer but cannot be relaxed further.

Conversely, a *choice node* models an interaction with the user and always has two children: one that corresponds to a positive ("yes") response, and one that corresponds to a negative ("no") response. A choice node can never be a leaf. Thus, any root-to-leaf path in the tree starts with a relaxation node, ends with a relaxation node, and consists of an alternating sequence of relaxation and choice nodes.

$\mathfrak{Constrs}(Q)$ denotes the set of query constraints some of which may be fundamental; these are referred to as *hard constraints* and all the others as *soft constraints.* We use the "#" symbol to indicate a hard constraint in a query, and "?" to indicate a question to the user for the relaxation of the respective constraint. With every "no" response associated with a suggested relaxation, it becomes a *hard constraint.*

2.2 Probabilistic Cost Model

Once the tree is constructed, IQR needs to probabilistically compute the "cost" associated with each possible relaxation suggestion. Intuitively, the probability that a user responds positively to a proposed relaxation depends on the (a) *prior* function, *prior*(Q, Q', t) - which measures the user belief that a certain tuple t satisfying the relaxed query Q' exists

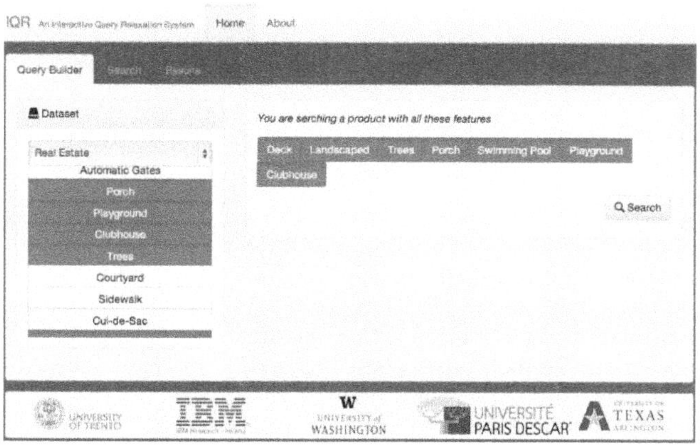

(a) Query building and search.

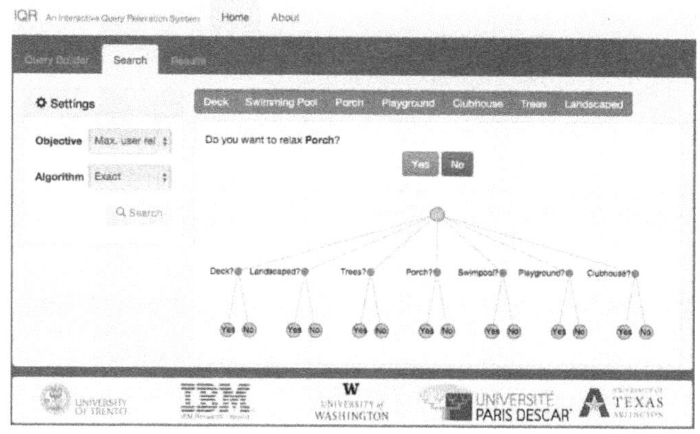

(b) Exact algorithm for max. relevance suggests "Porch" first.

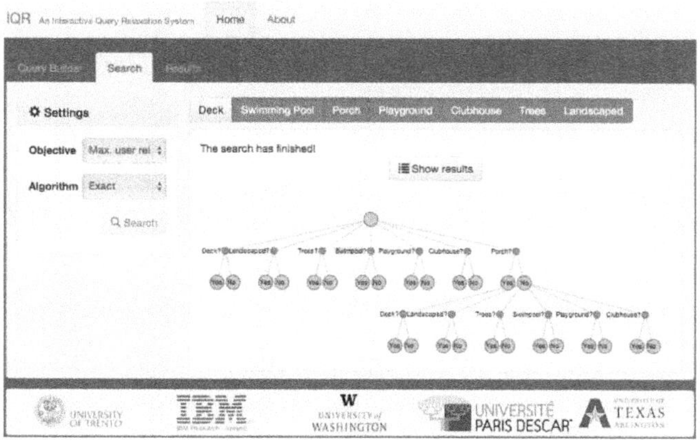

(c) Interaction ends with "no" to "Porch","yes" to "Deck".

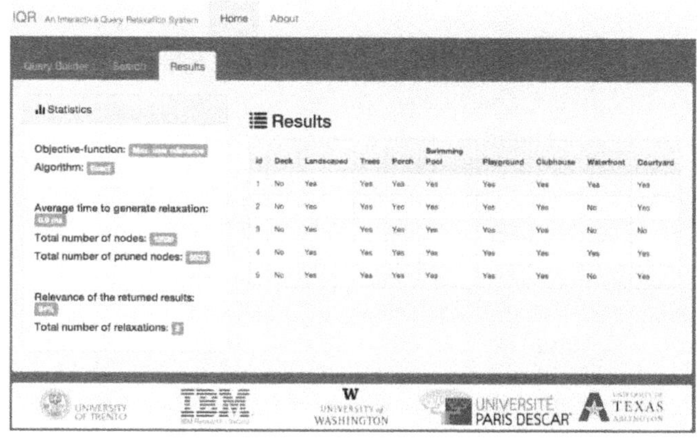

(d) Final page enlists results and additional statistics.

Figure 4: The interactive query relaxation system **IQR**.

in the database, and the (b) *preference* function, $pref(t, Q)$ - which estimates the probability that a user will like a tuple t (even though it only partially satisfy the initial query).

Even though any prior function or preference function (i.e, ranking/scoring) [3, 1] could be adapted in **IQR**, in our implementation, we use the Iterative Proportional Fitting (IPF) [4] technique on the instance data to compute the prior and the Normalized Inverse Document Frequency [1] to calculate the preference.[6] contains further details.

Therefore, the probability to reject a relaxation Q' is:

$$relPref_{no}(Q, Q') = \sum_{t \in Q'} (1 - pref(t, Q')) * prior(t, Q, Q')$$

which represents the probability of not liking any of the tuples associated to the relaxation. Thus, the probability of accepting the relaxation is the probability that the user likes at least one tuple, namely,

$$relPref_{yes}(Q, Q') = 1 - relPref_{no}(Q, Q')$$

A *probabilistic cost* value is associated to every node of the relaxation tree that quantifies how suitable a certain relaxation is towards a specific optimization objective.

The *expected cost* of a choice node n can be expressed as:

$$Cost(n) = relPref_{yes}(Q, Q') * (C_1 + Cost(n_{yes})) + relPref_{no}(Q, Q') * (C_1 + Cost(n_{no})) \quad (1)$$

where the n_{yes} and n_{no} are the two children (relaxation) nodes of n, Q is the query corresponding to the parent of n, and Q' corresponds to the suggested relaxation of Q at node n and the variable C_1 is a constant, that is used to quantify any additional cost incurred for answering the current relaxation proposal.

Since the cost of a node depends on the below subtree, to produce the optimal solution, we select that relaxation node which optimizes (maximizes or minimizes) the cost, such as:

$$Cost(n) = optimize_{c \in S} Cost(n_c) \quad (2)$$

where S is the set of soft constraints in $\mathfrak{Constrs}(Q)$, and n_c is the choice child node of n that corresponds to an attempt to relax the soft constraint c. These equations capture a generic cost and have to be appropriately instantiated for a specific application as described in Section 2.2.1.

Finally, the *cost* of a leaf node depends on the "value" of the tuples in that leaf which quantifies the effectiveness of those tuples towards the specific objective, which is potentially different from the value of the *preference* function.

2.2.1 *Application Specific Cost Computation*

Next we describe how to instantiate the above cost model under different application scenarios by appropriately modifying the *preference, value, and the cost* computation.

The preference for a tuple (1) could be independent of the query Q and static; or, (2) it could be query dependent, but only depends on the initial query and does not change after that; or, (3) it could depend on the latest relaxed query the user has accepted - this is a very dynamic scenario where after each step of the interactive session the preference can change. These different preference computation approaches are referred to as Static, Semi-Dynamic, and Dynamic respectively. An astute reader may notice that Static is applicable to optimization objectives that are agnostic to query constraints (such as minimize cost, maximize profit), Semi-

Dynamic is for applications that require the preference to be proportional to the original query Q (e.g., maximizing relevance), and Dynamic is designed for applications where the preference changes with every accepted relaxation (e.g., minimizing user effort). The *value* calculation of a tuple t is similar, except that it needs to quantify the contribution of t towards a specific objective.

Similarly, when the objective is *maximize* (*minimize*), the cost of a relaxation node is the *maximum* (*minimum*) cost of its children. The cost of a choice node is calculated using Equation 1 by setting $C_1 = 0$ to all optimization objectives except effort minimization ($C_1 = 1$ in this case), since the latter case incurs a cost of 1 with every additional relaxation suggestions. We refer to [6] for further details.

2.3 Relaxations Generation

IQR proposes an *exact algorithm* and an *approximate algorithm* to efficiently generate the relaxation suggestions.

2.3.1 Exact Query Relaxation Algorithm

To avoid computing the entire query relaxation tree, IQR constructs the tree partially only up to a certain level $L < |\mathfrak{Constrs}(Q)|$, and try to assign the cost of all the nodes in level L and higher by calculating the *upper and lower bound* of cost. From the ranges of the costs that the computation provides, it identifies those branches that cannot lead to optimal cost. For example, when the specific optimization minimizes (maximizes) cost, these are the branches starting with a node that has as a *lower bound (upper bound) for its cost that is higher (lower) than the upper bound (lower bound) of the cost of another sibling node.* By pruning these branches the required computations are significantly reduced. This way, the computation proceeds level by level until all query $|\mathfrak{Constrs}(Q)|$ constraints are relaxed.

The challenge here is to *tightly* estimate the upper bound and lower bound of cost of the tree nodes for different optimization objectives without compromising the correctness. As discussed in [6], IQR indeed offers this efficient alternative under a variety of optimization objectives.

2.3.2 Approximate Query Relaxation Algorithm

Although the strategy discussed in Section 2.3.1 generates optimum-cost relaxations and builds the relaxation tree on demand, it may still have to construct the entire tree first in the worst case, even before suggesting any relaxation to the user. Applications that demand fast response time but allow slight imprecision (such as, online air-ticket or rental-car reservation systems) may not be able to tolerate such latency. IQR proposes a *novel approximate solution* that takes L (# levels) as an input parameter and constructs the tree only upto level L leading to a *significantly smaller* tree.

This strategy computes first the exact structure of the relaxation tree up to level L. Next, it approximates the cost of each L-th level choice nodes by considering the cost distributions of its children and proceeds with a bottom-up computation of the remaining nodes until the root. At the root node, the best relaxation child node is selected, and the remaining ones are pruned. Upon suggesting this new relaxation, the algorithm continues further based on the user response. Essentially, the task is to probabilistically compute the *cost distribution* (or pdf of cost in short) of the relaxation and choice nodes at level L and higher by computing the *Sum, Min, or Max convolutions* [2] of the respective pdfs. Efficiency is guaranteed by approximating the convolutions using histograms. We omit the details for brevity and refer to the main IQR article [6].

3. SYSTEM DEMONSTRATION

In this demonstration, the users will experience IQR's domain independent approach for efficient interactive relaxation suggestions under different optimization objectives using both exact and approximate solutions. The users will be able to select the US Homes or the Yahoo Autos as the underlying data source. The former database has 18 attributes and over 250,000 tuples, while the latter has 31 attributes and about 500,000 tuples. The demo will first show the scalability of the system with empty-queries of increasing size. The users will then select the dataset and build their own query (Figure 4a), with the guidance of the system. If it results in an empty-answer, then they will select a specific optimization objective and an algorithm type (exact or approximate), as shown in Figure 4b. After that the users will be suggested interactive relaxations (Figure 4b, 4c) at end of which the results and additional statistics will be returned (Figure 4d). Based on users' interactions, the statistics page presents interesting information, such as, the effectiveness of the returned results towards the optimization objective, the average relaxation time, the total number of suggested relaxations, the total number of pruned nodes in the relaxation tree by the underlying algorithm, etc. Additional statistical information will be provided, such as the typical response times and the mean number of interactions computed during the demo session. In particular, the users will experience IQR under three different optimization objectives.

1. **Relevance Maximization** - This is an instantiation of Semi-Dynamic preference computation as shown in Figure 4b. The process ends when the users arrive at a non-empty results (Figure 4d), or no further relaxation could generate non-empty answer. The final results maximize relevance and the exact solution may return different relaxations or tuples than the approximate one to the users, while the latter will appear more interactive. The users will be presented interesting statistics about her interactive relaxation session at the end of the relaxation process (Figure 4d).
2. **Profit Maximization** - This is an instantiation of Static preference computation and the attendees will experience that IQR will attempt to return the most expensive homes or cars to them based on their respective interactions.
3. **Effort Minimization** - This is an instantiation of Dynamic preference computation and the users will experience that IQR will attempt to return non-empty results by suggesting minimum number of relaxations .

4. REFERENCES

[1] S. Agrawal, S. Chaudhuri, G. Das, and A. Gionis. Automated ranking of database query results. In *CIDR*, 2003.

[2] B. Arai, G. Das, D. Gunopulos, and N. Koudas. Anytime measures for top-k algorithms on exact and fuzzy data sets. *VLDB J.*, 18(2):407–427, 2009.

[3] R. A. Baeza-Yates and B. A. Ribeiro-Neto. *Modern Information Retrieval.* Addison-Wesley New York, 2011.

[4] Y. Bishop, S. Fienberg, and P. Holland. *Discr. Multivariate Analysis: Theory and Practice.* MIT Press, 1975.

[5] S. Chaudhuri, G. Das, V. Hristidis, and G. Weikum. Probabilistic information retrieval approach for ranking of database query results. *TODS*, 2006.

[6] D. Mottin, A. Marascu, S. B. Roy, G. Das, T. Palpanas, and Y. Velegrakis. A probabilistic optimization framework for the empty-answer problem. *PVLDB*, 6(14):1762–1773, 2013.

OceanRT: Real-Time Analytics over Large Temporal Data

Shiming Zhang* Yin Yang# Wei Fan* Liang Lan* Mingxuan Yuan*
*Noah's Ark Lab, Huawei, Science Park, Shatin, Hong Kong
{simon.zhangsm, david.fanwei, lan.liang, yuan.mingxuan}@huawei.com
Advanced Digital Sciences Center, Singapore
yin.yang@adsc.com.sg

ABSTRACT

We demonstrate OceanRT, a novel cloud-based infrastructure that performs online analytics in real time, over large-scale temporal data such as call logs from a telecommunication company. Apart from proprietary systems for which few details have been revealed, most existing big-data analytics systems are built on top of an offline, MapReduce-style infrastructure, which inherently limits their efficiency. In contrast, OceanRT employs a novel computing architecture consisting of interconnected Access Query Engines (AQEs), as well as a new storage scheme that ensures data locality and fast access for temporal data. Our preliminary evaluation shows that OceanRT can be up to 10x faster than Impala [10], 12x faster than Shark [5], and 200x faster than Hive [13]. The demo will show how OceanRT manages a real call log dataset (around 5TB per day) from a large mobile network operator in China. Besides presenting the processing of a few preset queries, we also allow the audience to issue ad hoc HiveQL [13] queries, watch how OceanRT answers them, and compare the speed of OceanRT with its competitors.

Categories and Subject Descriptors

H.2 [**Database Management**]: Systems

General Terms

Design, Management, Performance

1. INTRODUCTION

We have entered the big data era, in which organizations routinely collect terabytes or even petabytes of data. For instance, one of Huawei's client, a large mobile network operator in China, accumulates over 5 TB of call logs each day. The capability to gain useful knowledge from such big data is thus crucial to the success of today's organizations. In the past much work has been done to develop the capabilities to perform offline analytics, which involve complex tasks that take hours or days to finish, even on a modern cloud platform. For example, MapReduce [3] harnesses the computing power of interconnected commodity servers, provides strong fault tolerance and high parallelism for job processing, while hiding the complexity of the system and exposing a simple interface to users. Recently, considerable attention has been shifted to answering analytics queries online (also referred to as *interactive* or *real-time* analytics), which outputs results within seconds once the user issues a query. Such capabilities are an important complement to offline analytics; in particular, they enable users to quickly explore and obtain initial insights of the big data. Since the user often waits online for the results, speed is key in online analytics. Meanwhile, in such applications a simple programming language such SQL is often preferred, since it lets the user focus on the logic of the analytics, rather than implementation details in, e.g., a MapReduce program.

Early attempts build analytics capabilities on top of a MapReduce system, e.g., Hadoop [14]. Notably, Hive [13] translates SQL queries into MapReduce jobs, and subsequently executes them using Hadoop. YSmart [7], another SQL-to-MapReduce translator, provides sophisticated optimizations for complex queries. This approach, however, is not suitable for online analytics, since MapReduce is designed for offline tasks, and, thus, involves high overhead for starting and executing each job. Another methodology is to build MapReduce/RDBMS hybrids. For instance, HadoopDB [1] (commercialized as Hadapt [2]) uses relational databases to perform MapReduce tasks. PolyBase [4] improves the scalability of SQL Server using a novel "split query processing" method that transforms queries into MapReduce jobs. Finally, Sailfish [9] improves MapReduce performance by batching disk I/Os. These systems tend to inherit the offline processing designs of MapReduce, and, thus, are not ideal for real-time query processing.

Recently, following Google's publication of Dremel [8] and F1 [12, 11], there has been increasing interests in building real-time query processing tools that answer queries directly, without invoking MapReduce. For example, Cloudera Impala [10] processes SQL queries over data stored in HDFS, the file system of Hadoop, and/or in HBase[1], a "NoSQL" data management system that features a high level of schema flexibility at the expense of limited query processing capabilities compared to an RDBMS. Shark [5] is the online query processing module built on top of Spark[15], a novel in-memory big data processing platform. Proprietary systems include Amazon Redshift[2], which, like Google's Dremel and F1, has few technical details revealed.

Our goal is to perform online, real-time analytics over big temporal data, such as call logs from a large mobile network operator. Queries on such data often contain temporal operations. We observe that existing systems have two major limitations that render them unsuitable for our cause. First, as we show in Section 2,

[1]http://hbase.apache.org
[2]http://aws.amzaon.com/redshift

SIGMOD'14, June 22–27, 2014, Snowbird, UT, USA.
Copyright 2014 ACM 978-1-4503-2376-5/14/06 ...$15.00.
http://dx.doi.org/10.1145/2588555.2594513.

the current generation of existing systems cannot fully utilize the parallel computing capabilities of modern servers, which typically have multiple CPU cores and hard drives. While it is possible to subdivide each server into virtual machines, doing so incurs high overhead, e.g., communications between virtual machines has to go through network sockets. Second and more importantly, existing systems are not optimized for temporal data. Hence, we have been building OceanRT (pronounced "ocean art"), a novel online analytics engine for large temporal data. Instead of reusing components from a MapReduce-like system, OceanRT redesigns the computing architecture and storage scheme to obtain a higher level of parallelism and improved data locality, and to manage temporal data more efficiently. We have implemented a prototype of OceanRT, and evaluated it using large real data and queries. The results indicate that OceanRT can obtain up to 10x speedup compared to the current state-of-the-art, especially for complex queries involving joins and subqueries. We thus plan to demonstrate OceanRT to SIGMOD attendees with real data and use cases.

In the following, Section 2 describes the OceanRT system. Section 3 presents preliminary evaluation results comparing OceanRT with existing systems on real data. Section 4 describes our plan for the demo. Section 5 contains concluding remarks.

2. SYSTEM OVERVIEW

OceanRT includes both a novel computing architecture and a new storage scheme for performing analytics in real time over temporal data. Sections 2.1 and 2.2 present the computing architecture and the storage scheme of OceanRT, respectively.

2.1 Computing Architecture

An OceanRT cluster consists of multiple interconnected commodity servers. We employ Zookeeper[3] to manage the states of the nodes. Similar to Impala, the user can submit a HiveQL query (a dialect of SQL used in Hive [13]) to any node in OceanRT; the node receiving the query is responsible for parsing the query, dispatching (parts of) the query to relevant nodes for execution, collecting (partial) query results, and returning the results to the user. To do this, each node runs a Parsing Engine (PE), shown in Figure 1(a). The PE contains (i) a parser, which parses incoming SQL queries into execution plans, (ii) an optimizer, which optimizes the plans, e.g., by re-ordering joins and (iii) a dispatcher, which routes the query to nodes that stores relevant data. OceanRT employs PostgreSQL[4] parser and optimizer modules in its PE, which leverages the time-proven query optimization techniques in PostgreSQL.

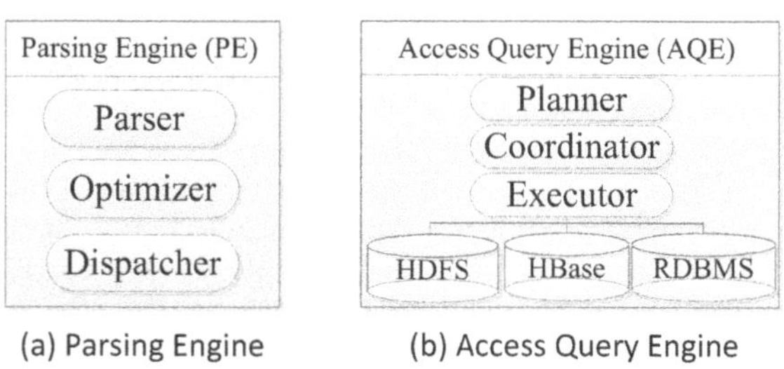

Figure 1: PE and AQE in OceanRT

After generating the query execution plan, the dispatcher module of the PE assigns each logical operator to an Access Query Engine (AQE), which executes the operator and generates (intermediate) results. The dispatching is performed according to the AQE state information (e.g., busy/idle) maintained by Zookeeper, as well as the network distance between an AQE and the data required by the logical operator (e.g., AQEs with local data are preferred). As we detail soon, each node runs multiple AQEs, depending on its hardware configuration. As illustrated in Figure 1(b), an AQE contains a planner, a coordinator, and an executor. It can read/write data stored in HDFS, HBase, or a relational database such as PostgreSQL. As their respective names suggest, the planner determines the appropriate algorithm for executing the assigned task; the coordinator coordinates with other AQEs to retrieve data (e.g., when processing a join) or partial/subquery results; the executor performs the action specified in the logical operator.

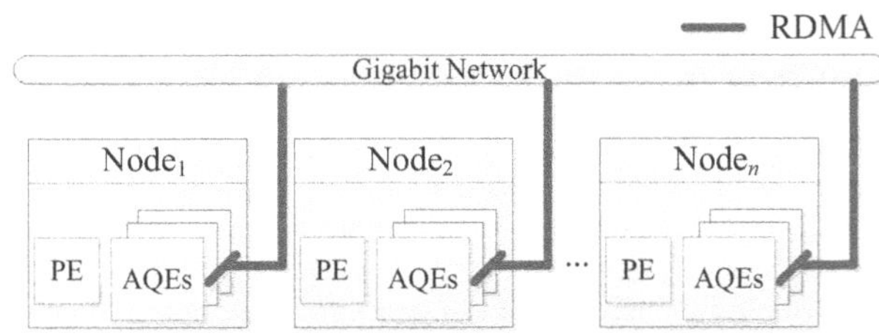

Figure 2: Architecture of OceanRT

So far, our designs for the PE and AQE are fairly standard for an online analytics engine, e.g., they resemble the design of the Impala daemon, albeit more refined with the help of PostgreSQL. The main novelty in the architectural design of OceanRT lies in two aspects: (i) each physical nodes runs multiple AQEs, according to its hardware configuration, and (ii) all AQEs are connected through Remote Direct Memory Access (RDMA) [6]. Figure 2 shows the architecture of OceanRT. Having multiple AQEs inside each node enables OceanRT to achieve a higher degree of parallelism, compared to existing real-time analytics systems in which every node is a single processing unit. For instance, consider a node with two hard drives and two CPU cores. By dividing the computation resources into two AQEs, each with a hard drive and a CPU core, the node is able to perform two independent data retrieval and/or processing tasks simultaneously. In practice, a higher number of AQEs may improve overall performance, e.g., when one AQE is busy reading data from disk, another may perform CPU-intensive computations, and yet another retrieving data from the network. Determining the appropriate number of AQEs per node, and scheduling them properly to maximize performance are interesting research topics of their own.

All AQEs are connected through an RDMA link, which performs data transmission directly between two memory buffers, without consuming CPU cycles or copying data to/from kernel memory. This implies (i) that data transfer between different AQEs within the same node incurs negligible overhead, as the data are simply copied from one memory location to another, and (ii) data exchange between AQEs in different nodes are also faster than existing systems. Our current prototype of OceanRT applies a software implementation of RDMA contained in Hadoop-RDMA [6]. Hardware RDMA promises even better performance. Note that effective use of RDMA is non-trivial as it complicates the memory management of an AQE, such as a page that is currently being transferred to another AQE under RDMA must not be swapped to disk.

2.2 Storage Scheme

As described in Section 2.1, OceanRT can process data stored in HDFS, HBase, and/or a relational DBMS. In order to provide high fault-tolerance, HBase uses HDFS as the underlying file system. For the same reason, in our current implementation of OceanRT,

[3]http://zookeeper.apache.org
[4]http://www.postgresql.org

the RDBMS (in particular, PostgreSQL) also employs HDFS to store data files. Hence, data storage in OceanRT ultimately relies on HDFS. To further improve the performance of OceanRT, we modified HDFS to better fit the computing architecture of OceanRT as well as temporal data management, leading to a novel storage scheme. It is worth mentioning that our modifications to HDFS do not compromise the functionalities of stock HDFS; in other words, OceanRT-optimized HDFS can be directly used in place of HDFS whenever the latter is applicable.

In a nutshell, HDFS achieves fault tolerance as follows. Each data file is partitioned into blocks of fixed size, e.g., 128MBytes. Each block is replicated on multiple servers (3 by default). Specifically, when appending a new block to a file, stock HDFS stores one copy of the block at the node performing the write operation, another copy at a random node at the same rack as the first copy, and yet another copy at a random node not in the same rack [14]. Accordingly, after writing the entire file to HDFS, the node performing the write operation stores a complete copy of the file; the other two copies of the same file, however, are fragmented, among nodes within the same rack and nodes not in the same rack, respectively. Such file fragmentation adversely affects the performance of OceanRT. For instance, consider the situation that the query requires scanning multiple blocks of a file, and the node storing the complete file is busy. The PE then dispatches the scan to an AQE that only stores parts of the file, which must request for blocks from other nodes, leading to high latency due to network transmissions.

To alleviate file fragmentation, OceanRT organizes blocks of a file into larger partitions. Each partition contains M blocks; meanwhile, each partition is stored completely in at least N nodes. For instance, when $M = 10$ and $N = 2$, each partition contains 10 blocks; these 10 blocks are stored together in at least 2 nodes, each of which is able to scan the entire partition locally without network transmissions. M and N are system parameters whose best values depend upon the application. Higher values of M and/or N lead to a lower level of fragmentation, but also increased risk for workload imbalance, and vice versa. Hence, a larger M and/or N is more suitable for applications that involve the scanning of large portions of files. Note that organizing blocks into larger partitions is different from having large block sizes; the latter approach leads to increased network transmissions as a block is a basic unit of reading, as well as limited parallelism. Meanwhile, since the smallest unit of storage is still a block, introducing partitions does not compromise existing functionalities of HDFS. Hence, OceanRT-optimized-HDFS is backward compatible with stock HDFS.

Finally, using the new partition-block file organization, we optimize OceanRT storage for temporal data and queries, as follows. Each block of a temporal data file is assigned a hash value computed based on the temporal attributes of the records contained in the block. Then, blocks are assigned to partitions according to their hash values. Thus, each partition stores data with similar temporal attributes, achieving the effect of a primary index on the temporal attributes. When processing a query with a temporal range selection, instead of scanning an entire relation, OceanRT only scans the partitions that contain records whose temporal attributes fall within the range. Note that building a traditional primary index is not feasible, as such an index requires sorting the entire file, which is costly for big data; further, since updates are not ordered by time, they may cause frequent re-organizations, which is prohibitively expensive. The hashing scheme in OceanRT does not incur these costs; as a tradeoff, it also retrieves a larger portion of the data compared to a traditional primary index. We omit further details for brevity, and our demo will show the data storage of OceanRT using a real example.

3. PERFORMANCE OF OCEANRT

We use a real mobile call log dataset to evaluate OceanRT. Due to data confidentiality issues, we are not allowed to publish details of the data or its schema. Hence, for the sake of the evaluation, we extracted a random sample from the real data, and transformed the sample to fit an artificial schema. Figure 3 illustrates this schema, which contains 5 tables: Users, Services, Locations, CallLogs, and Apps. Among these, Services, CallLogs and Users contain temporal data.

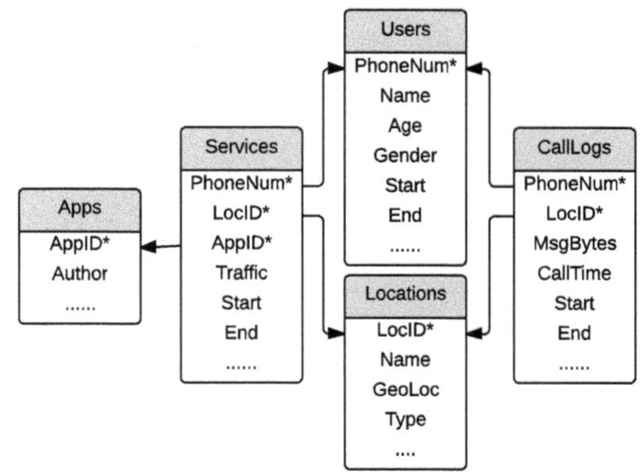

Figure 3: Schema of the dataset used in the evaluations

Figure 4 lists the three queries used in our evaluations, which were composed based on real analytics tasks and the schema shown in Figure 3. Queries Q1 and Q2 represent single-table selections and GROUPBY aggregations, respectively. Q3 is a complex join query involving multiple subqueries, GROUPBY aggregation, sorting and top-k selection. All three queries involve temporal selections, which are common in analytics tasks on the call log dataset.

Q1: Single-table selection
```
SELECT PhoneNum, AppID, LocID
FROM Services
WHERE Traffic > 100M AND Start ≥ DATE('20131001')
AND End ≤ DATE('20131003')
```
Q2: Single-table aggregation
```
SELECT PhoneNum, LocID, SUM(MsgBytes), SUM(CallTime)
FROM CallLogs
WHERE Start ≥ DATE('20131001') AND End ≤ DATE('20131003')
GROUP BY PhoneNum, LocID
```
Q3: Complex join with subqueries
```
SELECT Name, SUM(MsgBytes) SumMB, SUM(CallTime) SumCT,
   SUM(Traffic) SumTR
FROM Users U
   INNER JOIN CallLogs C ON U.PhoneNum = C.PhoneNum
   INNER JOIN Services S ON C.PhoneNum = S.PhoneNum AND
   C.LogID = S.LocID
WHERE LocID IN
   (SELECT LocID FROM Locations
    WHERE GeoLoc in ('GUANGZHOU', 'SHENZHEN'))
AND AppID IN
   (SELECT AppID FROM Apps WHERE Author='YOUTUBE')
AND S.Start ≥ DATE('20131001') AND S.End ≤ DATE('20131003')
AND U.Age ≥ 18
GROUP BY U.name ORDER BY SumMB, SumCT, SumTF
LIMIT 1000
```

Figure 4: Queries used in the evaluation

We performed preliminary evaluations on a small cluster of 10 commodity servers connected through a Gigabit Ethernet. Each node is equipped with two Intel i7-3770 CPUs, 16 GB RAM, and two 1TB hard drives. OceanRT assigns 2 AQEs per node. The HDFS block size is fixed to 64MB. Figure 5 summarizes the evaluation results, comparing OceanRT with Hive 0.10, Shark 0.80 and

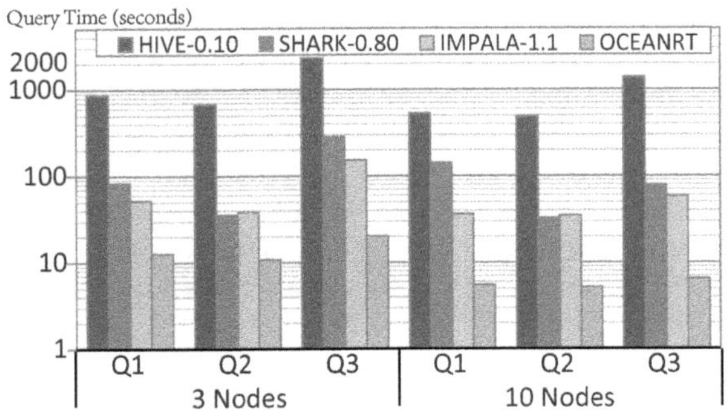

Figure 5: Evaluation results

Impala 1.1. For all three queries, OceanRT is significantly faster than its competitors. The performance advantage of OceanRT is more pronounced with more nodes in the cluster, and for complex queries such as Q3. The performance of Shark and Impala are comparable, with Impala slightly faster than Shark. OceanRT is between 3x (Q2 with 3 nodes) to 10x (Q3 with 10 nodes) faster than Impala, and between 60x to 200x faster than Hive.

4. DEMONSTRATION SCENARIO

The demo will show the system architecture and storage scheme of OceanRT. It will also compare the performance of OceanRT with its competitors using the real call log dataset from a large Chinese mobile network operator, which contains roughly 5 TB (about 4 billion records) per day. A random sample of the data is used in our performance evaluations in Section 3.

Setup. Since the dataset is confidential, we will host it in a private cloud with 100 nodes, and connect to the cloud remotely during the demo. Meanwhile, the demo will only show the performance (in terms of total running time and a breakdown into CPU, I/O, networking costs, etc.) of different systems, not the data records or query answers. OceanRT and its competitors, e.g., Hive, Impala, Shark and possibly others, will be deployed to the private cloud. Besides showing a performance comparison with a set of preset queries, SIGMOD attendees can also issue ad hoc queries to any of the deployed systems, using a command line interface.

Visualization. We will visualize the computing architecture and storage scheme of OceanRT during the demo. Specifically, we will show how the data is stored in the cloud, including statistics on blocks, partitions, and temporal information. Using a number of pre-selected queries, including Q1-Q3 described in Section 3, we will demonstrate how these queries are parsed into logical execution plans, and dispatched to AQEs for execution. We will also show the internals of an AQE when executing a task, such as table scan, join, and GROUPBY/aggregation.

Story line. Consider that a mobile network operator wants to investigate the behaviors of its subscribers in order to launch a new promotion campaign. To do this, it first finds heavy users of the mobile network, and analyzes their phone call patterns (e.g., whether they make calls during the day or at night), web browsing history (e.g., frequently visited websites), usage of value-add services (e.g., customized ringtones), and geo-locations. Using this information, the mobile network operator decides on the selected customers of the campaign, as well as the service package, e.g., browsing a news website will be free of charge at night for customers in an area who subscribe to a value-add service. Since there are numerous possible designs of the campaign, the mobile network operator may issue many queries, and expect each to return results within seconds. Hence, low-latency query processing is key in this application.

5. CONCLUSION

We have been building OceanRT, a real-time data analytics tool for large temporal data. Compared to existing systems, OceanRT employs a novel computing architecture with enhanced parallelism, and a new storage scheme optimized for the new system architecture as well as temporal data and queries. Evaluations using real data and workload show that OceanRT can achieve 10x speedup compared to state-of-the-art systems such as Impala and Shark. The demo will show the performance and internal workings of OceanRT, using real data on a private cloud. Regarding future work, and interesting direction is to incorporate elastic resource provisioning into OceanRT, so that each query only consumes cloud resources (e.g., AQEs) sufficient to meet its quality-of-service requirements [16].

6. REFERENCES

[1] A. Abouzeid, K. Bajda-Pawlikowski, D. Abadi, A. Silberschatz, and A. Rasin. HadoopDB: An architectural hybrid of MapReduce and DBMS technologies for analytical workloads. *PVLDB*, 2(1), 2009.

[2] K. Bajda-Pawlikowski, D. J. Abadi, A. Silberschatz, and E. Paulson. Efficient processing of data warehousing queries in a split execution environment. In *ACM SIGMOD*, 2011.

[3] J. Dean and S. Ghemawat. MapReduce: Simplified data processing on large clusters. In *USENIX OSDI*, 2004.

[4] D. J. DeWitt, A. Halverson, R. Nehme, S. Shankar, J. Aguilar-Saborit, A. Avanes, M. Flasza, and J. Gramling. Split query processing in polybase. In *ACM SIGMOD*, 2013.

[5] C. Engle, A. Lupher, R. Xin, M. Zaharia, M. J. Franklin, S. Shenker, and I. Stoica. Shark: Fast data analysis using coarse-grained distributed memory. In *ACM SIGMOD*, 2012.

[6] N. S. Islam, M. W. ur Rahman, J. Jose, R. Rajachandrasekar, H. Wang, H. Subramoni, C. Murthy, and D. K. Panda. High performance RDMA-based design of hdfs over infiniband. In *IEEE/ACM SC*, 2012.

[7] R. Lee, T. Luo, Y. Huai, F. Wang, Y. He, and X. Zhang. YSmart: Yet another SQL-to-MapReduce translator. In *IEEE ICDCS*, 2011.

[8] S. Melnik, A. Gubarev, J. J. Long, G. Romer, S. Shivakumar, M. Tolton, and T. Vassilakis. Dremel: Interactive analysis of web-scale datasets. *PVLDB*, 3(1-2), 2010.

[9] S. Rao, R. Ramakrishnan, A. Silberstein, M. Ovsiannikov, and D. Reeves. Sailfish: A framework for large scale data processing. In *ACM SOCC*, 2012.

[10] J. Russell. Cloudera impala: Real-time queries in apache hadoop. In *OŔeilly Strata Conference*, 2013.

[11] J. Shute, M. Oancea, S. Ellner, B. Handy, E. Rollins, B. Samwel, R. Vingralek, C. Whipkey, X. Chen, B. Jegerlehner, K. Littlefield, and P. Tong. F1: The fault-tolerant distributed RDBMS supporting Google's ad business. In *ACM SIGMOD*, 2012.

[12] J. Shute, R. Vingralek, B. Samwel, B. Handy, C. Whipkey, E. Rollins, M. Oancea, K. LittleïňAeld, D. Menestrina, S. Ellner, J. Cieslewicz, I. Rae, T. Stancescu, and H. Apte. F1: A distributed SQL database that scales. In *VLDB*, 2013.

[13] A. Thusoo, J. S. Sarma, N. Jain, Z. Shao, P. Chakka, S. Anthony, H. Liu, P. Wyckoff, and R. Murthy. Hive: A warehousing solution over a map-reduce framework. *PVLDB*, 2(2), 2009.

[14] T. White. *Hadoop: The Definitive Guide, MapReduce for the Cloud*. O'Reilly Media, 2nd edition, 2009.

[15] M. Zaharia, M. Chowdhury, T. Das, A. Dave, J. Ma, M. McCauley, M. J. Franklin, S. Shenker, and I. Stoica. Resilient distributed datasets: A fault-tolerant abstraction for in-memory cluster computing. In *USENIX NSDI*, 2012.

[16] Z. Zhang, R. Ma, J. Ding, and Y. Yang. Abacus: An auction-based approach to cloud service differentiation. In *IEEE IC2E*, 2013.

H_2O: A Hands-free Adaptive Store

Ioannis Alagiannis[*] Stratos Idreos[‡] Anastasia Ailamaki[*]

[*]Ecole Polytechnique Fédérale de Lausanne
{ioannis.alagiannis, anastasia.ailamaki}@epfl.ch

[‡]Harvard University
stratos@seas.harvard.edu

ABSTRACT

Modern state-of-the-art database systems are designed around a single data storage layout. This is a fixed decision that drives the whole architectural design of a database system, i.e., row-stores, column-stores. However, none of those choices is a universally good solution; different workloads require different storage layouts and data access methods in order to achieve good performance.

In this paper, we present the H_2O system which introduces two novel concepts. First, it is flexible to support multiple storage layouts and data access patterns in a single engine. Second, and most importantly, it decides on-the-fly, i.e., during query processing, which design is best for classes of queries and the respective data parts. At any given point in time, parts of the data might be materialized in various patterns purely depending on the query workload; as the workload changes and with every single query, the storage and access patterns continuously adapt. In this way, H_2O makes no a priori and fixed decisions on how data should be stored, allowing each single query to enjoy a storage and access pattern which is tailored to its specific properties.

We present a detailed analysis of H_2O using both synthetic benchmarks and realistic scientific workloads. We demonstrate that while existing systems cannot achieve maximum performance across all workloads, H_2O can always match the best case performance without requiring any tuning or workload knowledge.

Categories and Subject Descriptors

H.2.2 [**Database Management**]: Physical Design - Access methods; H.2.4 [**Database Management**]: Systems - Query Processing

General Terms

Algorithms, Design, Performance

Keywords

Adaptive storage; adaptive hybrids; dynamic operators

1. INTRODUCTION

Big Data. Nowadays, modern business and scientific applications accumulate data at an increasingly rapid pace. This data explosion gives birth to new usage scenarios and data analysis opportunities but it also significantly stresses the capabilities of current data management engines. More complex scenarios lead to the need for more complex queries which in turn makes it increasingly more difficult to tune and set-up database systems for modern applications or to maintain systems at a well-tuned state as an application evolves.

SIGMOD'14, June 22–27, 2014, Snowbird, UT, USA.

http://dx.doi.org/10.1145/2588555.2610502.

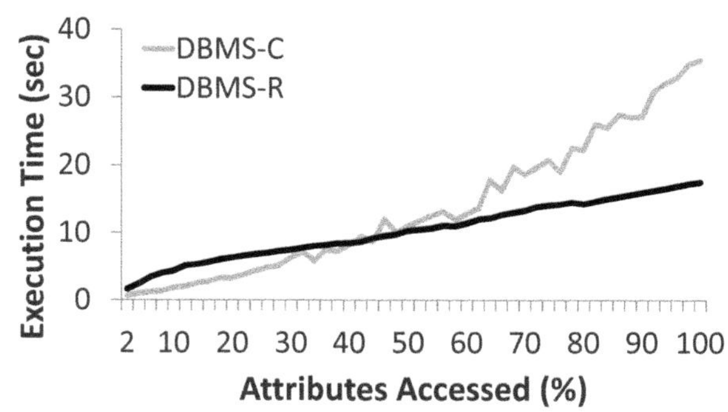

Figure 1: Inability of state-of-the-art database systems to maintain optimal behavior across different workload patterns.

The Fixed Storage Layout Problem. The way data is stored defines how data should be accessed for a given query pattern and thus it defines the maximum performance we may get from a database system. Modern state-of-the-art database systems are designed around a single data storage layout. This is a fixed decision that drives the whole design of the architecture of a database system. For example, traditional row-store systems store data one row at a time [20] while modern column-store systems store data one column at a time [1]. However, none of those choices is a universally good solution; different workloads require different storage layouts and data access methods in order to achieve good performance. Database systems vendors provide different storage engines under the same software suite to efficiently support workloads with different characteristics. For example, MySQL supports multiple storage engines (e.g., MyISAM, InnoDB); however, communication between the different data formats on the storage layer is not possible. More importantly, each storage engine requires a special execution engine, i.e., an engine that knows how to best access the data stored on each particular format.

Example. Figure 1 illustrates an example of how even a well-tuned high-performance DBMS cannot efficiently cope with various workloads. In this example, we test 2 state-of-the-art commercial systems, a row-store DBMS (DBMS-R) and a column-store DBMS (DBMS-C). We report the time needed to run a single analytical select-project-aggregate query in a modern machine. Figure 1 shows that none of those 2 state-of-the-art systems is a universally good solution; for different classes of queries (in this case depending on the number of attributes accessed), a different system is more appropriate and by a big margin (we discuss the example of Figure 1 and its exact set-up in more detail later on).

The root cause for the observed behavior is the fixed *data layout* and the fixed *execution strategies* used internally by each DBMS. These are closely interconnected and define the properties of the query engine and, as a result, the final performance. Intuitively, column stores perform better when columns are processed independently, while row-stores are more suited for queries touching many attributes. In both systems, the data layout is a static input parameter leading to compromised designs. Thus, it restricts these systems from adapting when the workload changes. Contrary to common belief that column-stores always outperform row-stores for analytical queries, we observe that row-stores can show superior performance in a class of workloads which becomes increasingly important. Such workloads appear both in business (e.g., network performance and management applications) and scientific domains (e.g., neuro-science, chemical and biological applications) and the common characteristic is that queries access an increased number of attributes from wide tables. For example, neuro-imaging datasets used to study the structure of human brain consist of more than 7000 attributes. In this direction, commercial vendors are continuously increasing the support for wide tables e.g., SQL Server today allows a total of 30K columns per table while the maximum number of columns per SELECT statement is now at 4096, aiming at serving the requirements of new research fields and applications.

Ad-hoc Workloads. If one knows the workload a priori for a given application, then a specialized hybrid system may be used which may be perfectly tuned for the given workload [16, 29]. However, if the workload changes a new design is needed to achieve good performance. As more and more applications, businesses and scientific domains become data-centric, more systems are confronted with ad-hoc and exploratory workloads where a single design choice cannot cover optimally the whole workload or may even become a bottleneck. As a result modern businesses often need to employ several different systems in order to accommodate workloads with different properties [52].

H_2O: An Adaptive Hybrid System. An ideal system should be able to combine the benefits of all possible storage layouts and execution strategies. If the workload changes, then the storage layout must also change in real time since optimal performance requires workload-specific storage layouts and execution strategies.

In this paper, we present the H_2O system that does not make any fixed decisions regarding storage layouts and execution strategies. Instead, H_2O continuously adapts based on the workload. Every single query is a trigger to decide (or to rethink) how the respective data should be stored and how it should be accessed. New layouts are created or old layouts are refined on-the-fly as we process incoming queries. At any given point in time, there may be several different storage formats (e.g., rows, columns, groups of attributes) co-existing and several execution strategies used. In addition, the same piece of data may be stored in more than one formats if different parts of the query workload need to access it in different ways. The result is a query execution engine DBMS that combines Hybrid storage layouts, Hybrid query plans and dynamic Operators (H_2O).

Contributions. Our contributions are as follows:

- We show that fixed data layout approaches can be sub-optimal for the challenges of dynamic workloads.
- We show that adaptive data layouts along with hybrid query execution strategies can provide an always tuned system even when the workload changes.
- We discuss in detail lightweight techniques for making on-the-fly decisions regarding a good storage layout based on query patterns, for refining the actual data layouts and for compiling on-the-fly the necessary operators to provide good access patterns and plans.
- We show that for dynamic workloads H_2O can outperform solutions based on static data layouts.

2. BACKGROUND AND MOTIVATION

In this section, we provide the necessary background regarding the basics of column store and row store layouts and query plans. Then we motivate the need for a system that always adapts its storage and execution strategies. We show that different storage layouts require completely different execution strategies and lead to drastically different behavior.

2.1 Storage Layout and Query Execution

Row-stores. Traditional DBMS (e.g., Oracle, DB2, SQL Server) are mainly designed for OLTP-style applications. They follow the N-ary storage model (NSM) in which data is organized as tuples (rows) and is stored sequentially in slotted pages. The row-store data layout is optimized for write-intensive workloads and thus inserting new or updating old records is an efficient action. On the other hand, it may impose an unnecessary overhead both in terms of disk and memory bandwidth if only a small subset of the total attributes of a table is needed for a specific query. Regarding query processing, most NSM systems implement the volcano-style processing model in which data is processed one tuple (or block) at a time. The tuple at a time model comes with nearly negligible materialization overhead in memory; however, it leads to increased instruction misses and a high function call overhead [7, 40].

Column-stores. In contrast, modern column-store DBMS (e.g., SybaseIQ [35], Vertica [32], Vectorwise [54], MonetDB [7]) have been proven the proper match for analytical queries (OLAP applications) since they can efficiently execute queries with specific characteristics such as low projectivity and aggregates. Column-stores are inspired by the decomposition storage model (DSM) in which data is organized as columns and is processed one column at a time. The column-store data layout allows for loading in main memory only the relevant attributes for a query and thus significantly reducing I/O cost. Additionally, it can be efficiently combined with low-level architecture-conscious optimizations and late materialization techniques to further improve performance. On the other hand, reconstructing tuples from multiple columns and updates might become quite expensive.

Query Processing. Lets assume the following query.

$$\text{Q1: } \textit{select } a+b+c \textit{ from } R \textit{ where } d<v_1 \textit{ and } e>v_2$$

In a typical row-store query execution, the system reads the data pages of relation R and processes single tuples one-by-one according to the operators in the query plan. For $Q1$, firstly, the query engine performs predicate evaluation for the two conditional statements. Then, if both predicates qualify, it computes the expression in the select clause. The aforementioned steps will be repeated until all the tuples of the table have been processed.

For the same query, a column-store follows a different evaluation procedure. The attributes processed in the query are accessed independently. Initially, the system reads column d (assuming d is the highly selective one) and evaluates the predicate $d < X$ for all the values of column d. The output of this step is a list of tuple IDs of the qualifying tuples which is used to fetch all the qualifying tuples of e and materialize them in a new intermediate column. Then, the intermediate column is accessed and the predicate $e > Y$ is evaluated. Finally, a new intermediate list of IDs is created for the qualifying tuples considering both predicates in the where clause. The

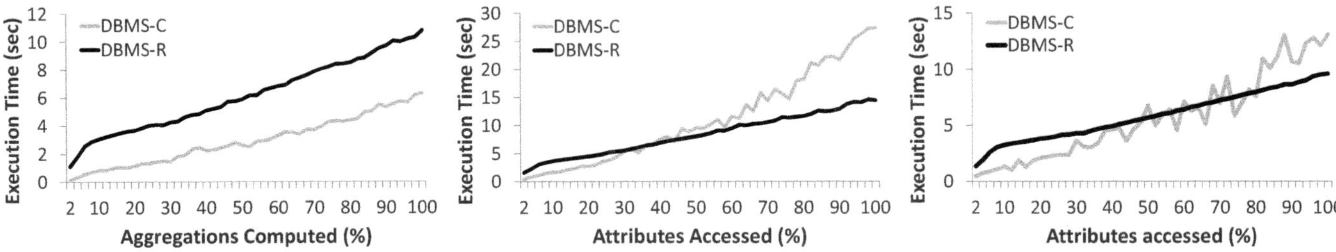

(a) Selectivity 100% (no *where* clause) (b) Selectivity 40% (c) Selectivity 1%

Figure 2: DBMS-C vs. DBMS-R: the "optimal" DBMS changes with the workload.

latter list of tuple IDs is used to filter columns *a*, *b* and *c* processed in the select clause before applying the sum operator to compute the final aggregation result. The above query processing algorithm is based on a late tuple re-construction policy. There are more possible implementations and optimizations for the same query plan (e.g., using early materialization, bit-vectors instead of list of IDs, considering the vectorized execution paradigm). Nevertheless, the common characteristic is the materialization overhead of intermediate results which becomes significant when many attributes are accessed in the same query.

Overall, a column-store DBMS exploits different execution strategies than a row-store DBMS to fully benefit from the column-oriented data layout [2]. To identify the optimal way for executing a query not only the storage layout but the execution model should be considered. Each choice of data layout and execution strategy comes with pros and cons, and the right combination depends on the target application and workload.

2.2 One Size Does Not Fit All

We now revisit our motivating experiment from Section 1 to discuss in more detail the fact that even well-tuned systems cannot provide optimal performance when the workload changes.

Software and Methodology. We use two state-of-the-art disk-based commercial DBMS, a row-store and a columns-store. To preserve anonymity we refer to the column-store DBMS as "DBMS-C" and to the row-store DBMS as "DBMS-R". The data fits in main memory and we report execution time from hot runs to focus on the in-memory processing part of the query engine and avoid any interference with disk I/O operations and especially compression that can hide storage layout specific characteristics. Additionally, indexes are not used. Both systems compute query results over uncompressed data in memory and are tuned to use all the available CPUs on our server. Comparing full systems is not trivial as these systems are very complex and full of rich features that may affect performance. To the best of our knowledge the above comparison isolates as best as possible the performance relevant to the storage layout and execution patterns in these commercial systems.

Database Workload. The input relation consists of 50 million tuples and each tuple contains 250 attributes with integers randomly distributed in the range $[-10^9, 10^9]$. We examine two different types of queries: a) project and b) select-project. In both cases the queries compute aggregations on a set of attributes and the projectivity progressively increases from 2% to 100%. We use aggregations to minimize the number of tuples returned from the DBMS and thus we avoid any overhead that might affect the execution times. The second set of queries has an extra *where* clause consisting of multiple filter conditions. The attributes accessed in the *where* clause and in the *select* clause are the same. We generate the filter conditions so as the selectivity remains the same for all queries. The purpose of these sets of queries is to study the behavior of the two different DBMS when gradually the number of attributes involved in the query increases. For this input relation, we report a 13% larger memory footprint for DBMS-R. This is due to the overhead that comes with traditional organization of attributes into tuples and pages. Accessing more data is translated into an additional performance penalty for the above read-only workloads.

Results. Figure 2 complements the graph in Figure 1. Figure 2(a) illustrates the difference in terms of performance between DBMS-C and DBMS-R when the queries compute only aggregations. DBMS-C is always faster from 6*x* when only 5 attributes are accessed up to 65% when all attributes are accessed. In Figures 2(b) and 2(c), we observe the same behavior as in Figure 1 even though the selectivity is lower, 40% and 1% respectively. When few attributes are accessed DBMS-C is faster; however, as the number of attributes accessed both in the select and the where clause increases, we find that there is a crossover point where query processing with DBMS-C is no longer the optimal for the given queries.

Discussion. We observe that none of the two systems attains optimal performance for the whole experiment. On the contrary, which is the "best" DBMS changes as we modify the query characteristics. Row-stores expected to perform poorly when analytical queries are executed on wide tables without index support. However, we show that even with such a setup row-stores can actually be faster for certain queries demonstrating the need to have the option to move from one layout to another. Overall, selecting the underlying data layout (row-store or column-store) is a critical first tuning decision which is hard to change if the workload evolves. In this work we focus on full-table scans and we do not investigate index-accesses. Deciding which index to build, especially if there is no a priori workload knowledge is a problem orthogonal to the techniques we present.

3. THE H_2O SYSTEM

Column-stores and row-stores are extremes of the design space. If we knew the workload exactly, we could prepare the perfect hybrid design, i.e., store the frequently accessed columns together and we could also create execution strategies that perfectly exploit these layouts. However, workload knowledge is not always available while preparing all possible layouts and execution strategies up front is not possible due the vast number of choices. There is not enough space to store these alternatives and there is not enough time to prepare them. Furthermore, a system would need an equal number of specialized operators/code to properly access these layouts in order to extract all possible benefits.

In this section, we discuss the design of H_2O an adaptive hybrid query execution engine which identifies workload changes and evolves both the data organization and the execution strategy according to the workload needs. Additionally, we show how different storage data layouts can coexist in the same query engine and be combined with different execution strategies, how H_2O creates access operators on-the-fly and finally, we discuss the adaptation mechanism used by H_2O to change the data layouts.

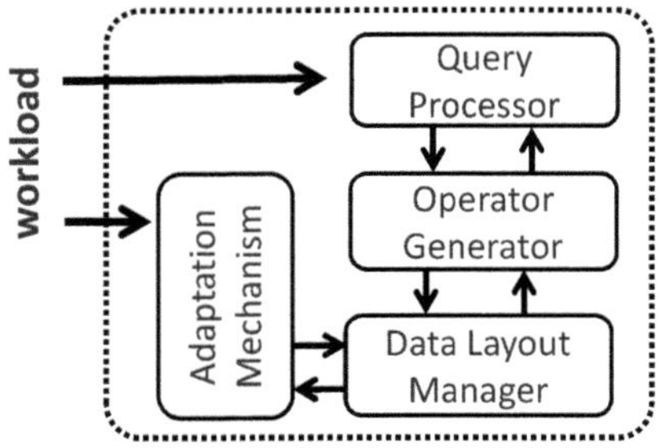

Figure 3: H_2O architecture.

Architecture. Figure 3 shows the architecture of H_2O . H_2O supports several data layouts and the Data Layout Manager is responsible for creating and maintaining the different data layouts. When a new query arrives, the Query Processor examines the query and decides how the data will be accessed. It evaluates the alternative access plans considering the available data layouts and when the data layout and the execution strategy have been chosen the Operator Generator creates on-the-fly the proper code for the access operators. The adaptation mechanism of H_2O is periodically activated to evaluate the current data layouts and propose alternative layouts to the Layout Manager.

3.1 Data Storage Layouts

H_2O supports three types of data layouts:

Row-major. The row-major layout in H_2O follows the typical way of organizing attributes into tuples and storing tuples sequentially into pages (Figure 4b). Attributes are densely-packed and no additional space is left for updates.

Column-major. In the column-store layout data is organized into individual columns (Figure 4a). Each column maintains only the attribute values and we do not store any tuple IDs.

Groups of Columns. The column-major and row-major layouts are the two extremes of the physical data layout design space but not the only options. Groups of columns are hybrid layouts with characteristics derived from those extremes. The hybrid layouts are integral part and the driving force of the adaptive design we have adopted in H_2O. A group of columns is a vertical partition containing a subset of the attributes of the original relation (Figure 4c).

In H_2O groups of columns are workload-aware vertical partitions used to store together attributes that are frequently accessed together. Attributes *d* and *e* in Figure 4c can be such an example. The width of a group of columns depends on the workload characteristics and can significantly affect the behavior of the system. Wide groups of columns in which only few attributes are accessed decrease memory bandwidth utilization, similarly with a row-major layout while a narrow group of columns might come with increased space requirements due to padding. For all the above data layouts, we consider fixed length attributes.

3.2 Continuous Layout Adaptation

H_2O targets dynamic workloads in which data access patterns change and so it needs to continuously adapt. One extreme approach is to adapt for every query. In this context, every single query can be a potential trigger to change how the respective data is stored and how it should be accessed. However, this is feasible in practice only if the cost of generating a new data layout can be amortized over a number of future queries. Covering more than one query with a new data layout can help to amortize the cost faster. H_2O gathers statistics regarding the incoming queries. The recent query history is used as a trigger to react in changes of the workload. H_2O decides a candidate layout pool by estimating the expected benefit and selecting the most fitting solution.

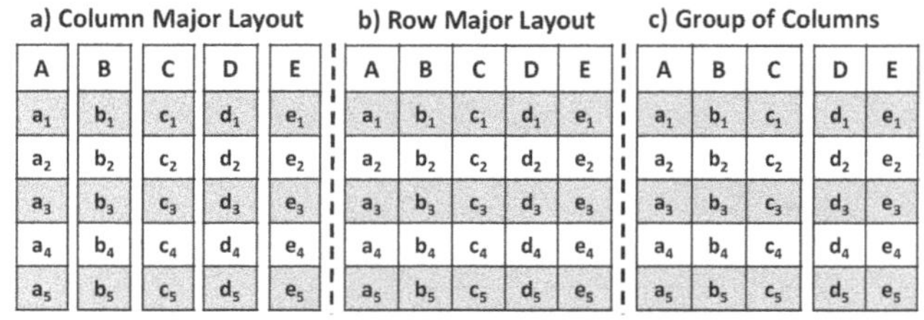

Figure 4: Data Layouts.

Monitoring. H_2O uses a dynamic window of *N* queries to monitor the access patterns of the incoming queries. The window size defines how aggressive or conservative H_2O is and the number of queries from the query history that H_2O considers when evaluating the current schema. For a given set of input queries H_2O focuses on statistics about attribute usage and frequency of attributes accessed together. The monitoring window is not static but it adapts when significant changes in the statistics happen. H_2O uses the statistics as an indication of the expected queries and to prune the search space of candidate data layouts. The access patterns are stored in the form of two affinity attribute matrices [38] (one for the *where* and one for the *select* clause). Affinity among attributes expresses the extent to which they are accessed together during processing. The basic premise is that attributes accessed together and have similar frequencies should be grouped together. Differentiating between attributes in the *select* and the *where* clause allows H_2O to consider appropriate data layouts according to the query access patterns. For example, H_2O can create a data layout for predicates that are often evaluated together.

Alternative Data Layouts. Determining the optimal data layout for a given workload is equivalent to the well-known problem of vertical partitioning which is NP-hard [48]. Enumerating through all the possible data layouts is infeasible in practice especially for tables with many attributes (e.g., a table with 10 attributes can be vertically partitioned into 115975 different partitions). Thus, proper heuristic techniques should be applied to prune the immense search space without putting at risk the quality of the solution.

H_2O starts with the attributes accessed by the queries to generate potential data layouts. The initial configuration contains the narrowest possible groups of columns. When a narrow group of columns is accessed by a query, all the attributes in the group are referenced. Then, the algorithm progressively improves the proposed solution by considering new groups of columns. The new groups are generated by merging narrow groups with groups generated in previous iterations. The generation and selection phases are repeated multiple times until no further improvement is possible for the input workload.

For a given workload $W = \{q_1, q_2, ..., q_n\}$ and a configuration C, H_2O evaluates the workload and transformation cost T using the following formula.

$$cost(W, C_i) = \sum_{j=1}^{n} q_j(C_i) + T(C_{i-1}, C_i) \quad (1)$$

Intuitively, the initial solution consists of attributes accessed together within a query and by merging them together H_2O reduces the joining overhead of groups. The size of the initial solution is in the worst case quadratic to the number of narrow partitions and allows to effectively prune the search space without putting at risk the quality of the proposed solution. H_2O considers attributes accessed together in the *select* and the *where* clause as different potential groups which allows H_2O to examine more executions strategies (e.g., to exploit a group of columns in the *where* clause to generate a vector of tuple IDs for the qualifying tuples). H_2O also considers the transformation cost from one data layout to another in the evaluation method. This is critical, since the benefit of a new data layout depends on the cost of generating it and on how many times H_2O is going to use it in order to amortize the creation cost.

Data Reorganization. H_2O combines data reorganization with query processing in order to reduce the time a query has to wait for a new data layout to be available. Assuming Q1 from Section 2 and two data layouts $R1(a,b,c)$ and $R2(d,e)$. The selected data layout from the adaptation mechanism requires to merge those two data layouts into $R(a,b,c,d,e)$. In this case, blocks from $R1$ and $R2$ are read and stitched together into blocks with tuples (a,b,c,d,e). Then, for each new tuple, the predicates in the *where* clause are evaluated and if the tuple qualifies the arithmetic expression in the *select* is computed. The early materialization strategy allows H_2O to generate the data layout and compute the query result without scanning the relation twice. The same strategy is also applied when the new data layout is a subset of a group of columns.

H_2O follows a lazy approach to generate new data layouts. It does not apply the selected data layout immediately but it waits until the first query requests a new layout. Then, H_2O creates the new data layout as part of the query execution. The source code for the physical operator that generates the new data layout while computing the result of the input query is created by applying code generation techniques described in Section 3.4.

Oscillating Workloads. An adaptation algorithm should be able to detect changes to the workload and act quickly while avoiding overreacting for temporary changes. Actually, such a trade-off is part of any adaptation algorithm and it is not specific to H_2O. In the case of H_2O, adapting too fast might create additional overhead during query processing while slow adaptation might lead to suboptimal performance. H_2O minimizes the effect of false-positives due to oscillating workloads by applying the lazy data layouts generation approach described in this subsection. To completely eliminate the effect of oscillating workloads requires predicting future queries with high probability; however this is not trivial. H_2O detects workload shifts by comparing new queries with queries observed in the previous query window. It examines whether the input query access pattern is new or if it has been observed with low frequency. New access patterns are an indication that there might be a shift in the workload. In this case, the adaptation window decreases to progressively orchestrate a new adaptation phase while when the workload is stable, H_2O increases the adaptation window.

3.3 Execution Strategies

Traditional query processing architectures assume not only a fixed data layout but predetermined query execution strategies as well. For example, in a column-store query plan a predicate in the *where* clause is evaluated using vectors of tuple IDs to extract the qualifying tuples while a query plan for a row-store examines which tuples qualify one-by-one and then forwards them in the next query operator. In this paper, we show that a data layout should be combined with the proper execution strategy in a query plan. To maximize the potential of the selected query plan, tailored code should be created for the query operators in the plan (e.g., in filters it enhances predicate evaluation). Having multiple data layouts in H_2O also requires to support the proper execution strategies. Having different execution strategies means providing different implementations integrated in the H_2O query engine.

H_2O provides multiple execution strategies and adaptively selects the best combination of data layout and execution strategy according to the requirements of the input query. Execution strategies in H_2O are designed according to the vectorized query processing model [7] in which data is represented as small arrays (vectors). Vectors fit in the L1 cache for better cache locality.

Row-major. The execution strategies for a row-major layout follow the volcano execution model. Additionally, predicate evaluation is pushed-down to the scan operator for early tuple filtering.

Column-major. For a column-major layout the execution strategy of H_2O materializes intermediate results from filter evaluations into vectors of matching positions. Similarly, it handles the output of complex arithmetic expressions. For example, in Q1 of Section 2 computing the expression $a+b+c$ results into the materialization of two intermediate columns, one for $a+b$ and one for the result of the addition of the previous intermediate result with c.

Groups of columns. Regarding group of columns, there is no unique execution strategy. Data layouts can apply any of the strategies used for columns-major or row-major layouts. For example, predicate evaluation can be pushed-down or it can be computed using vectors of matching positions as in the case of a column-major layout. During query processing, H_2O evaluates the alternative execution strategies and selects the most appropriate one.

All executions strategies materialize the output results in memory using contiguous memory blocks in a row-major layout.

3.4 Creating Operators On-the-fly

The data independence abstraction in databases provides significant flexibility by hiding many low-level details (e.g., how the data is stored). However, it comes with a hit in performance due to the considerable interpretation overhead [46]. For example, computing the qualifying tuples for Q1 from Section 2 using volcano-style processing requires evaluating a conjunctive boolean expression ($d<v_1$ and $e>v_2$) for each one of the tuples. In the generic case, the engine needs to be able to compute predicates for all the supported SQL data types (e.g., integer, double) and additionally complicated sub-expressions of arbitrary operators. Thus, a generic operator interface leads to spending more time executing function calls and interpreting code of complex expressions than computing the query result [7]. Column-stores suffer less from the interpretation overhead but this comes with the cost of expensive intermediate results (e.g., need to materialize lists of IDs) and larger source code base (e.g., maintain a different operator implementation per data type).

H_2O maintains data into various data layouts and thus to obtain the best performance needs to include the implementation of numerous execution strategies.

For example, having a system that has all the possible code upfront is not possible especially when workload-aware layouts should be combined in the same query plans. The potential combinations of data layouts and access methods are numerous. To compute $a > X$ and $(a+b) > X$ requires different physical operators. A generic operator can cover both cases. However, the performance will not be optimal due to the interpretation overhead; the overhead of dynamically interpreting complex logic (e.g., expressions of predicates) to low level code. Thus, H_2O creates dynamic operators for accessing on-the-fly the data referenced from the query regardless of the way it is internally stored in the system (pure columnar or group of columns format). H_2O generates dynamic operators not only to reduce the interpretation overhead but also in order to combine workload-specific data layouts and execution strategies in the same access operator.

To generate layout-aware access operators, H_2O uses source code templates. Each template provides a high-level structure for different query plans (e.g., filter tuples with or without list of tuple IDs). Internally, a template invokes functions that generate the specialized code for specific basic operations; for example, accessing specific attributes in a tuple, evaluate boolean expressions, express

```
1   // Compiled equivalent of vectorized primitive
2   // Input: Column group R(a,b,c,d,e)
3   // For each tuple evaluate both predicates in one step
4   // Compute arithmetic expression for qualifying tuples
5   long q1_single_column_group(const int n,
6                       const T* res, T* R, T* val1, T* val2) {
7       int i, j = 0;
8       const T *ptr = R;
9       for ( i = 0 ; i < n; i++) {
10          if ( ptr[3] < *val1 && ptr[4] > *val2)
11              res[j++] = ptr[0] + ptr[1] + ptr[2];
12          ptr = getNextTuple(i);
13      }
14      return j;
15  }
```

Figure 5: Generated code for Q1 when all the data is stored in a single column group.

```
// Compiled equivalent of vectorized primitives
// Input: Column groups R1(a,b,c) and R2(d,e)
// For each batch of tuples call
nsel = q1_sel_vector(n, sel, R2, val1, val2);
q1_compute_expression(nsel, res, R1, sel);

// Compute arithmetic expression using the positions from sel
void q1_compute_expression(const int n,
        const T* res, T* R1, int* sel) {
    int i = 0;
    const T *ptr = R1;
    if (sel == NULL) {
        for ( i = 0 ; i < n; i++) {
            res[i] = ptr[0] + ptr[1] + ptr[2];
            ptr = getNextTuple(i); }
    } else {
        for ( i = 0 ; i < n; i++) {
            ptr = getNextTuple(sel, i);
            res[sel[i]] = ptr[0] + ptr[1] + ptr[2]; }
    }
}

// Compute selection vector sel for both predicates in R2(d,e)
int q1_sel_vector(const int n,
                const T* sel, T* R2, T* val1, T* val2) {
    int i, j = 0;
    const T *ptr = R2;
    for ( i = 0 ; i < n; i++) {
        if ( ptr[0] < *val1 && ptr[1] > *val2)
            sel[j++] = i;
        ptr = getNextTuple(i);
    }
    return j;
}
```

Figure 6: Generated code for Q1 when the needed attributes are stored into two different column groups.

complex arithmetic expressions, perform type casting, etc. The code generation procedure takes as input the needed data layouts from the data layout manager and the set of attributes required by the query, selects the proper template and generates as an output the source code of the access operator. The source code is compiled using an external compiler into a library and then, the new library is dynamically linked and injected in the query execution plan. To minimize the overhead of code generation, H_2O stores newly generated operators into a cache. If the same operator is requested by a future query, H_2O accesses it directly from the cache. The available query templates in H_2O support select-project-join queries and can be extended by writing new query operators.

Example. Figures 5 and 6 show two dynamically compiled equivalents of vectorized primitives for access operators for two different data layouts.

Figure 5 shows the generated code when all the accessed attributes for Q1 (a,b,c,d,e) are stored in the same column group. The on-the-fly code takes as input the group of columns, the constant values $val1$ and $val2$ used for the predicate evaluation and an output buffer for storing the result of the expression $a+b+c$ for the qualifying tuples. For each tuple H_2O evaluates in one step the two predicates for the conditional statement (Line 9) pushing down the selection to the scan operator. If both predicates are true then the arithmetic expression in the *select* clause is computed. The code is tailored for the characteristics of the available data layout and query. It fully utilizes the attributes in the data layout and thus avoids unnecessary memory accesses. Additionally, it is CPU efficient (the filter and the arithmetic expression are computed without any overhead) while it does not require any intermediate results. This code can be part of a more complex query plan.

The second on-the-fly code in Figure 6 is generated assuming two available groups of columns $R1(a,b,c)$ and $R2(d,e)$ storing the attributes in the *select* and *where* clause respectively. Since there are two groups of columns we can adopt a different execution strategy to optimize performance. In this case, the generated code exploits the two column groups by initiating a column-store like execution strategy. The query is computed using two functions; one for tuple selection and one for computing the expression. Initially, a selection vector containing the IDs of the qualifying tuples is computed. The selection vector is again computed in one step by evaluating the predicates together. The code that computes the arithmetic expression takes as parameter the selection vector, additionally to the group of columns and the values $val1$ and $val2$. Then, it evaluates the expression only for the tuple with these IDs and thus, avoiding unnecessary computation. On the other hand, the materialization of the selection vector is required.

3.5 Query Cost Model

To select the optimal combination of data layout and execution strategy, H_2O evaluates different access methods for the available data layouts and estimates the expected execution cost. The query cost estimation is computed using the following formula:

$$q(L) = \sum_{i=1}^{|L|} max(cost_i^{IO}, cost_i^{CPU}) \tag{2}$$

For a given query q and a set of data layouts L, H_2O considers the I/O and CPU cost for accessing the layouts during query processing. The cost model assumes that disk I/O and CPU operations overlap. In practice, when data is read from disk, disk accesses dominate the overall query cost since disk access latency is orders of magnitude higher than main-memory latency.

H_2O distinguishes between row-major and column-major layouts. Groups of columns are modeled similarly to the row-major layouts. The cost of sequential I/O is calculated as the amount of data accessed (e.g., number of tuples multiplied by the average tuple width for a row) divided by the bandwidth of the hard disk while the cost of random I/O additionally considers block accesses and read buffers (e..g, through a buffer pool).

H_2O estimates the CPU cost based on the number of cache misses incurred when a data layout is processed. Data cache misses have significant impact (due to cache misses cause CPU-stalls) on query processing [5] and thus, they can provide a good indication regarding the expected execution cost of query plans. A data cache miss occurs when a cache line has to be fetched from a higher level in the memory hierarchy, stalling the current instruction until needed data is available. For a given query Q and a given data layout L the cost model computes the number of data cache misses based on the data layout width, the number of tuples and the number of data words accessed for an access pattern following an approach similar to [16]. The cost of accessing intermediate results is also considered. This is important since not all execution strategies in H_2O generate intermediate results.

4. EXPERIMENTAL ANALYSIS

In this section, we present a detailed experimental analysis of *H_2O*. We show that *H_2O* can gracefully adapt to changing workloads by automatically adjusting the physical data layout and automatically producing the appropriate query processing strategies and access code. In addition, we present a sensitivity analysis on the basic parameters that affect the behavior of H_2O such as which physical layout is best for different types of queries. We examine how *H_2O* performs in comparison with approaches that use a static data layout advisor. We use both fine tuned micro-benchmarks and the real-life workload SDSS from the SkyServer project.[1]

The main benefit of hybrid data layouts comes during scan operations which are responsible for touching the majority of the data. In our analysis, we focus on scan based queries and we do not consider joins. In an efficient modern design a join implemented as in memory cache conscious join, e.g., radix join [36], would typically compute the join using only the join keys with positions (row ids) being the payload. Thus, the actual data layout of the data will have little effect during the join. On the other hand, post join projection will be affected positively (compared to using full rows) as we can fetch the payload columns from hybrid layouts.

System Implementation. We have designed and implemented a *H_2O* prototype from scratch using C++ with all the functionality of adaptively generating data layouts and the supporting code. Our code-generation techniques use a layer of C++ macros to generate tailored code. The compilation overhead in our experiments varies from 10 to 150 ms and depends on the query complexity. Orthogonally to this work, the compilation overhead can be further reduced by using the LLVM framework [34]. In all experiments, the compilation overhead is included in the query execution time.

Experimental Setup. All experiments are conducted in a Sandy Bridge server with a dual socket Intel(R) Xeon(R) CPU E5-2660 (8 cores per socket @ 2.20 GHz), equipped with 64 KB L1 cache and 256 KB L2 cache per core, 20 MB L3 cache shared, and 128 GB RAMrunning Red Hat Enterprise Linux 6.3 (Santiago - 64bit) with kernel version 2.6.32. The server is equipped with a RAID-0 of 7 250 GB 7500 RPM SATA disks. The compiler used is icc 13.0.0.

4.1 Adapting to Workload Changes

In this experiment, we demonstrate how H_2O automatically adapts to changes in the workload and how it manages to always stay close to the optimal performance (as if we had perfectly tuned the system a priori assuming enough workload knowledge).

Micro-benchmark. Here we compare H_2O against a column-store implementation and a row-store implementation. In both cases, we use our own engines which share the same design principles and much of the code base with H_2O; thus these comparisons purely reflect the differences in data layouts and access patterns.

For this experiment we use a relation R of 100 million tuples. Each tuple consists of 150 attributes with integer values randomly generated in $[-10^9, 10^9)$. We execute a sequence of 100 queries. The queries are select-project-aggregation queries and each query refers to z randomly selected attributes of R, where $z = [10, 30]$.

Figure 7 plots the response time for each query in the workload, i.e., we see the query processing performance as the workload evolves. In addition to H_2O, column-store and row-store, we plot a fourth curve in Figure 7 which represents the optimal performance; that is, the performance we would get for each single query if we had a perfectly tailored data layout as well as the most appropriate code to access the data (without including the cost of creating the data layout). We did this manually assuming for the sake of comparison against the theoretical case of having perfect workload knowledge and ample time to prepare the layout for each query.

Row-store	Column-store	H_2O
538.2 sec	283.7 sec	204.7 sec

Table 1: Cumulative Execution Time of the Queries in Figure 7.

For this experiment, relation R is initially stored in a column-major format. This is the more desirable starting point as it is easier to morph to other layouts. However, H_2O can adapt regardless of the initial data layout. The initial data layout affects the query performance of the first few queries only. We discuss such an experiment in detail later on.

Initially, H_2O executes queries using the available data layout. In this way, we see in Figure 7 that H_2O matches the behavior of the column-store system. Periodically, though, H_2O activates the adaptation mechanism and evaluates the current status of the system (set initially at a window size of 20 queries here but this window size also adaptively adjusts as the workload stabilizes or changes more rapidly). H_2O identifies groups of columns that are being accessed together in queries (e.g., 5 out of the 20 queries refer to attributes $a_1, a_5, a_8, a_9, a_{10}$). Then, H_2O evaluates alternative data layouts and execution strategies and creates a candidate list of 4 new groups of columns. H_2O does not create the new layout immediately. This happens only if a query refers to the attributes in this group of columns and can benefit from the creation of the new data layout. These estimations are performed using the cost model.

Following Query 20, and having the new candidate layouts as possible future layouts, in the next 10 queries, 2 out of the 4 candidate groups of columns are created. This happens for queries 23 and 29 and these queries pay the overhead of creating the new data layout. Query 23 pays a significant part of the creation overhead; however, 4 queries use the new data layouts and enjoy optimal performance. From query 29 up to query 68 no data reorganization is required. Another data reorganization takes place after 80 and a new data layout is added to H_2O .

There are queries for which H_2O cannot match the optimal performance. For example a group of columns is better for queries 2 to 8; however, there is no query that triggers the adaptation mechanism. In the end of the first evaluation it recognizes the change in the workload and proposes the needed data layouts. For 80% of the queries H_2O executes queries using a column group data layout while for the rest of the queries it uses a column-major layout. For the given workload a row-major data layout is suboptimal.

Overall, we observe that H_2O outperforms both the static column-store and row-store alternative approaches by 38% and 1.6x respectively, as shown in Table 1. More importantly it can adapt to workload changes, meaning that it can be used in scenarios where otherwise more than one systems would be necessary. Query performance in H_2O gets closer to the optimal case without requiring a priori workload knowledge.

H_2O using Real Workload. In this experiment, we evaluate H_2O using the SkyServer workload. We test against a scenario where we use AutoPart [41], an offline physical, design tool for vertical partitioning, in order to get the best possible physical design recommendation. For the experiment, we use a subset of the "PhotoObjAll" table which is the most commonly used and 250 of the SkyServer queries. Figure 8 shows that H_2O manages to outperform the choices of the offline tool. By being able to adapt to individual queries as opposed to the whole workload we can optimize performance even more than an offline tool.

Dynamic window. In this experiment, we show how H_2O benefits from a dynamic adaptation window when the workload changes. We use as input the same relation R as in the previous experiment

[1] `http://skyserver.sdss.org`

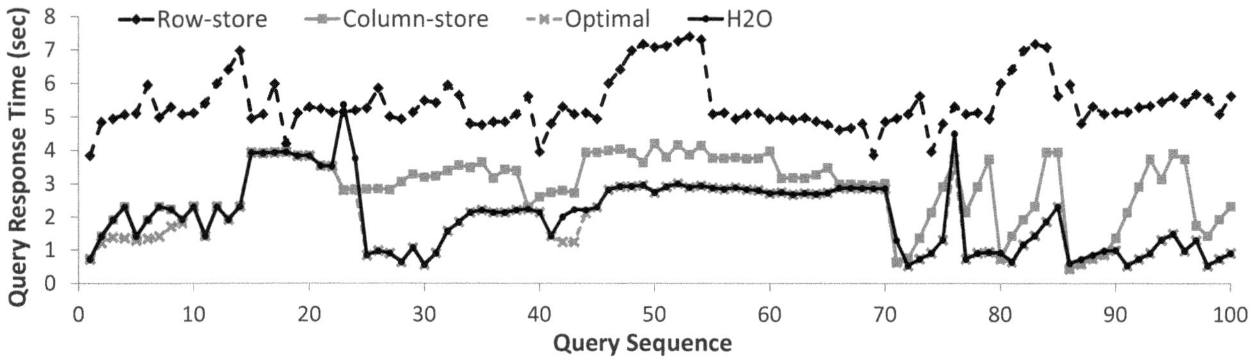

Figure 7: H_2O vs. Row-store vs. Column-store.

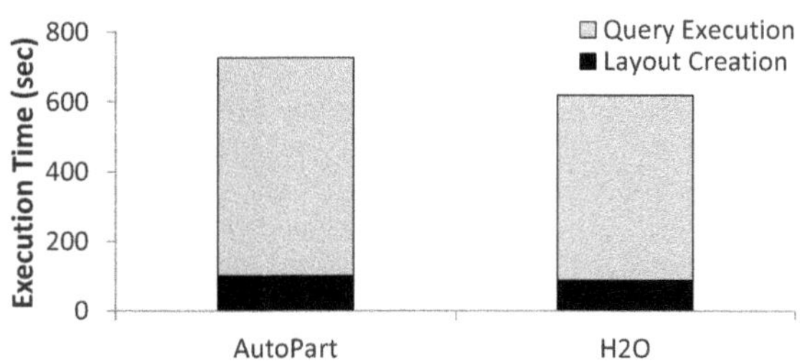

Figure 8: H_2O vs. AutoPart on the SkyServer workload.

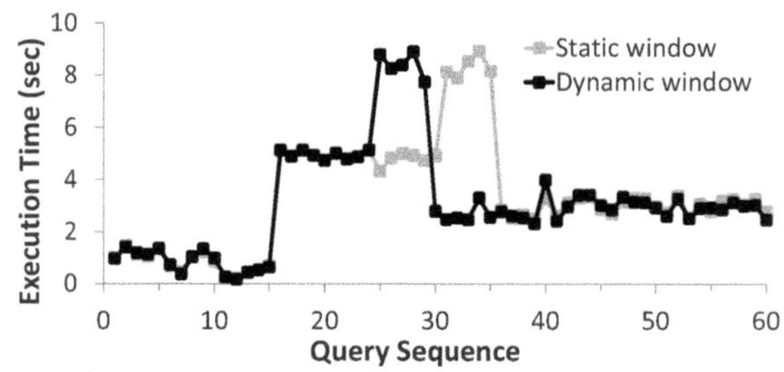

Figure 9: Static vs. dynamic adaptation window.

in which data this time is organized in a row-major format and a query sequence of 60 queries. Each query refers 5 to 20 attributes. The queries compute arithmetic expressions. The first 15 queries focus on a set of 20 specific attributes while the other 45 queries to a different one. We compare two variations of H_2O, with static and with dynamic window. The size of the window is 30 queries.

Figure 9 depicts the benefit of the dynamic window. H_2O with dynamic window detects the shift in the workload after the 15th query and progressively decreases the window size to force a new adaptation phase. The adaptation algorithm is finally triggered in the 25th query generating new groups of columns layouts that can efficiently serve the rest of the workload. On the other hand, when using a static window we cannot adapt and we have to wait until the 30th query before generating new layouts and thus fails to adapt quickly to the new workload. Overall, H_2O with dynamic windows manages to adapt to changes in the workload following even if they do not happen in a periodic way.

4.2 H2O: Sensitivity Analysis

Next, we discuss a sensitivity analysis of various parameters that affect the design and behavior of H_2O . For the experiments in this section, we use a relation *R* containing 100 million tuples. Each tuple contains 150 attributes with integer values randomly generated in the range $[-10^9, 10^9)$.

4.2.1 Effect of Data Layouts

In this experiment, we present the behavior of the different data layouts integrated in H_2O using queries with different characteristics. Queries are executed using column-major, row-major and group of columns layouts. Each group of columns contains only the attributes accessed by the query. All queries are executed using the H_2O custom operators. We use as input a wide table (100 million tuples, 150 attributes) to stress test H_2O and examine how some representative query types behave as we increased the number of attributes accessed. We consider simple select project queries and queries which compute aggregations and arithmetic expressions. Queries are based on variations of the following templates:

i. "*select* a, b, ..., *from* R *where* <predicates>" for projections

ii. "*select* max(a), max(b),..., *from* R *where* <predicates>" for aggregations

iii. "*select* a + b + ... *from* R *where* <predicates>" for arithmetic expressions

The accessed attributes are randomly generated. The cost of creating each group of columns layout is not considered in the measurements. We examine queries with and without *where* clause. In Figures 10(a-c) we vary the number of attributes accessed from 5 to 150 while there is no *where* clause. In Figures 10(d-f) each query accesses 20 attributes randomly selected from *R* while one of these attributes is the predicate in the *where* clause. We progressively vary selectivity from 0.1% to 100%. Figure 10 depicts the results (in all graphs the *y*-axis is in log scale). We report numbers from hot runs and each data point we report is the average of 5 executions. We discuss each case in detail below.

Projections. Figure 10(a) plots the query execution time for the three alternative data layouts as we increase the projected attributes while there is no *where* clause in the queries. The group of columns layout outperforms the row-major and column-major layouts regardless of the number of projected attributes. For projections of less than 30 attributes a column-major layout is faster than the row-major layout; however, when more than 20% of the attributes are referenced, performance falls up to 15X due to the high tuple reconstruction cost. As expected performance of the row-major layout and of groups of columns matches when all attributes are accessed.

For the same query template (i), in Figure 10(d) we additionally consider the effect of predicates in the *where* clause. We keep the number of projected attributes the same (20 attributes) while we vary selectivity from 0.1% to 100%. Regardless of the selectivity working with groups of columns is faster than using the other two data layouts.

Aggregations. Figure 10(b) shows the response time as we increase the number of aggregations in the queries. Using a column-major layout outperforms the other two data layouts. The biggest performance difference is when 5 aggregations are computed 1.5X and 15X from the group of columns layout and the row-major layout respectively. The gap between groups of columns and column-

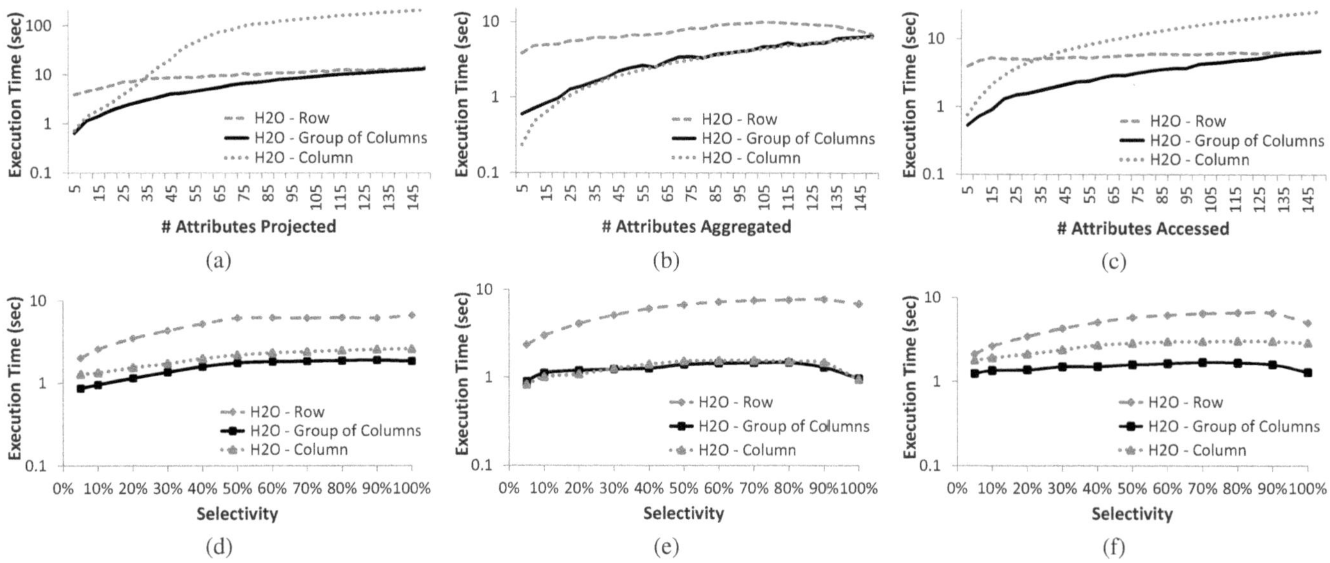

Figure 10: Basic operators of H_2O.

major layout gets smaller as more aggregations are computed. The group of columns layout improves the performance in comparison to the row-major layout by reducing cache misses.

In Figure 10(e) we vary the selectivity of a query that computes 20 aggregations. The column-major layout and the group of columns layout clearly outperform the row-major layout. The column-major layout is slightly faster than the row-major layout for low selectivities but as selectivity increases the group of columns layout is marginally faster.

Arithmetic Expressions. Figure 10(c) plots the execution time for each one of the data layouts as we vary the number of attributes accessed to compute an arithmetic expression. Group of columns surpasses the column-major layout from 42% when few attributes are accessed up to 3X when more accesses required. The difference in performance is due to the cost of having to materialize intermediate results in case of the column-major layout. On the other hand, combining a group of columns with volcano-style executions allows for avoiding this overhead.

Figure 10(f) plots execution time for queries based on the third template with *where* clause. The results show that the group of columns layout has superior performance for the whole selectivity range since does not require the usage of intermediate results.

Discussion. All the above data layouts are part of H_2O. H_2O combines them with the proper execution strategies to always achieve the best performance. H_2O explores this design space to generate cache friendly operators without intermediate results if possible.

4.2.2 Effect of Groups of Columns

At any given point in time, H_2O maintains multiple layouts. Typically these are multiple column groups since plain column-major or row-major extreme cases. In this way, one reasonable question is how does performance vary depending on which column group we access. It might be that we do not always have available the optimal column group or we have to fetch the data needed for a single query from multiple column groups or we have to access a given column group containing more columns than the ones we need.

We first test the case where queries need to access only a subset of the attributes stored in a column group. Here, we use a group of 30 randomly selected attributes from *R*. The queries compute aggregations with filter following the template presented in the previous subsection, accessing 5, 10, 15, 20 and 25 randomly selected out of the 30 attributes of the column group. We examine the difference in performance for queries with 1%, 10%, 50% and 100% selectivity using the same attribute in the *where* clause. For each query, we compare the execution time with the optimal case in which a tailored data layout has been created containing only the needed attributes to answer this particular query.

Figure 11 depicts the results. It shows the performance penalty to access the whole column group as opposed to accessing the perfect column group as a ratio. The graph plots the results for each query grouped according to the selectivity. We observe that as less useful attributes are accessed the higher the performance penalty. This penalty varies with the number of useful attributes accessed. For example, when only 5 out of the 30 attributes of the group of columns are accessed, we observe the most significant drop in performance, up to 142%. This drop is due to the unnecessary memory accesses in comparison with the optimal group of columns. On the other hand, when a query accesses 25 out of the 30 attributes the overhead is almost negligible (3% in the worse case).

Other than queries having to access only a subset of a column group, another important case is when a single query needs to access multiple column groups. The question for an adaptive system in this case is whether we should build a new column group to fit the query or fetch the data from existing column groups. To study this problem, we use an aggregation with filter query *Q* that refers 25 attributes from *R*. We vary the number of groups of columns the query has to access from 2 to 5. In each case, the union of groups of columns contains all the needed attributes. For example, when 2 column groups are accessed, the first column group contains 10 of the needed attributes and the second column group the remaining 15 attributes. We experiment with selectivity 1%, 10%, 50% and 100%. We compare the response time of *Q* using the optimal column group with the cases we have to increase the number of accessed groups of columns. Figure 12 plots the response of each query normalized by the response time of queries accessing all the attributes in a single group of columns. Accessing more than one group of columns in the same query does not necessarily impose an additional overhead. On the contrary, combining two groups of columns might even be beneficial for highly selective queries.

Discussion. Accessing only a subset of the attributes of a column group, accessing multiple column groups or accessing multiple groups each one containing a subset of the columns needed

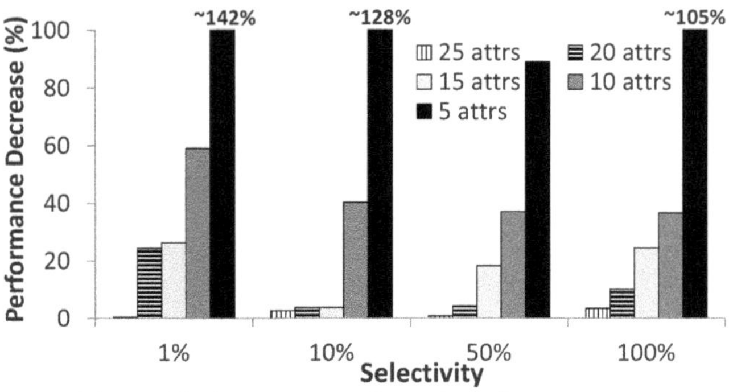

Figure 11: Accessing a subset of a column group.

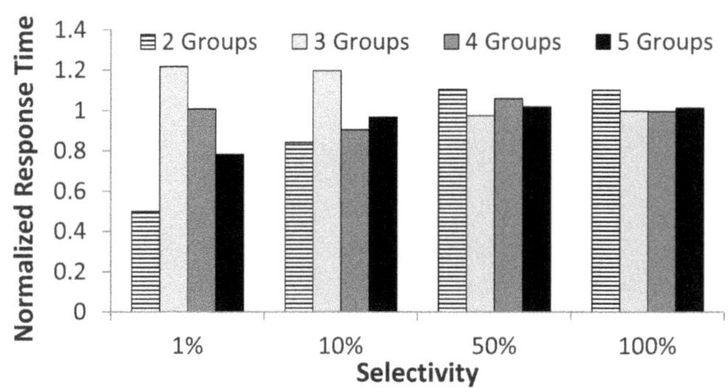

Figure 12: Accessing more than one group of columns.

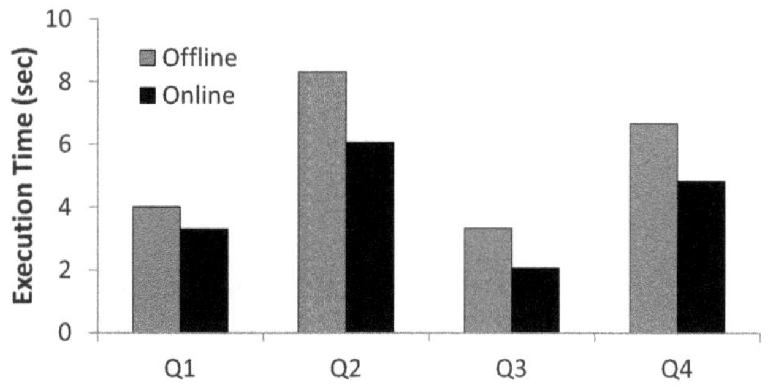

Figure 13: Online vs. Offline reorganization.

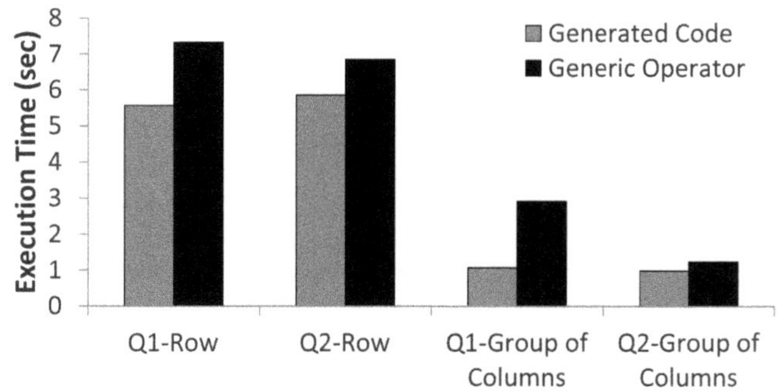

Figure 14: Generic Operator vs. Generated Code.

are few of the important scenarios when multiple column groups co-exist. The previous experiments show that groups of columns can be effective even if not the optimal group of columns is available and thus it is ok to extend monitoring periods and not to react instantly to changes in the workload in this case. Additionally, narrow groups of columns can be gracefully combined in the same query operator without imposing significant overhead.

4.2.3 Data Reorganization

H_2O adapts continuously to the workload. One approach would be to separate the preparation of data layouts from query processing. Instead H_2O answers an incoming query while adapting the physical layout for this queries. This is achieved by generating an operator that integrates the creation of a new data layout and the code needed to answer the query in one physical operator

In this experiment we show that online adaptation brings significant benefits. The set up is as follows. We assume that two new groups of columns are created from relation *R* (100 million tuples, 100 attributes with integer values). The first one contains 10 and the second 25 attributes. In the offline case, the column groups are created and then queries are executed while in the online case the column group creation and the query execution overlap. We test two scenarios. In the first scenario the initial layout is row-major (Q1 and Q2) while in the second scenario the initial layout is column-major (Q3 and Q4). In both cases, we test the cost to transform those initial layouts into the optimal set of column groups for a set of queries. We use two queries in each scenario. *Q*1 and *Q*3 trigger the generation of a new group of columns which contains 10 attributes, while *Q*2 and *Q*4 create a group of 20 columns. The queries compute 10 and 20 aggregations (without *where* clause) respectively on the attributes of the new layouts.

Figure 13 shows the results. The offline bars depict the cumulative response time for creating the column group and executing the query as two separate steps, i.e., first the data layout is created separately and only then we can process the queries. The specialized operator generated by H_2O performs the same tasks but in one step. The online case is faster regardless of the storage of the initial relation and the width of the new column group. The improvement varies from 22% to 37% when the initial relation is stored in a columnar layout and from 38% to 61% when the initial data is in a row-oriented layout. For all cases online reorganization is significantly faster than performing the same operation offline. By overlapping execution and data organization H_2O manages to improve significantly the overall execution time of the two tasks.

4.2.4 Importance of Dynamic Operators

In this experiment, we showcase the benefit of creating tailored code on-the-fly to match the available data layouts. The set-up is as follows. *Q*1 is an aggregation and *Q*2 is an arithmetic expression query following the templates presented in Section 4.2.1 and accessing 20 out of the 150 attributes of *R*. We test the execution time achieved by a generic database operator versus an operator that uses tailored code created on the fly to match the underlying layout. We examine the effect both for row-major layout and groups of columns. The code generation time is included in the overall query execution time of the dynamically generated operator and varies from 63 ms to 84 ms. Figure 14 shows the results. We observe from 16% up to 1.7x performance improvement by creating tailored code which is due to removing the interpretation overhead. This justifies the choices in H_2O in creating fully adaptive layouts and code on the fly.

5. RELATED WORK

A large body of recent work both in industry and academia propose different flavors of *hybrid* solutions to cope with the recent data deluge, complex workloads and hardware changes. The need for hybrid approaches is especially amplified when trying to provide a unified solution for workloads with different characteristics. In this section, we review this body of related work and we highlight how our work pushes the state-of-the-art even further.

A Case for Hybrid Systems. Recent research ideas have recognized the potential of exploring different physical data representations under a unified processing system [43, 11]. Fractured mirrors [43] exploit the benefits of both NSM and DSM layouts in the same system. Data is duplicated in both storage layouts and queries are executed using the appropriate mirror. This path has been recently adopted in industry, by the main-memory DBMS SAP HANA [12] which combines OLTP and OLAP workloads in the same system. Similarly, SQL Server which provides a row-store memory-optimized database engine for OLTP applications and an in-memory data warehouse using ColumnStore Index for OLAP applications [33]. The hybrid approach of mixing of columnar and row-oriented representations in the same tablespace provided by DB2 with BLU Acceleration [45] is the most related with H_2O. In addition, HyPer [29], a main-memory hybrid workload system, combines the benefits of OLTP and OLAP database by executing mixed workloads of analytical and transactional queries in parallel on the same database. Furthermore, recent vision works highlight the importance of hybrid designs. RodentStore [10] envisions a hybrid system which can be tuned through a declarative storage algebra interface while Idreos et al. [22] presents the idea of a fully adaptive system that directly reads raw files and stores data in a query driven way.

The above hybrid approaches expand the capabilities of conventional systems to support mixed workloads assuming, however, static (pre-configured) data layouts and thus cannot cope with dynamic workloads.

Our work here is focused on dynamic environments to enable quick reactions and exploration when the workload is not known up front and with limited time to invest in initialization costs. It focuses on hybrid data layouts for analytical workloads providing a fully adaptive approach both at the storage and the execution level to efficiently support dynamic workloads. In that respect, we also share common ground with other early works in exploration based techniques, e.g., [6, 10, 22, 26, 30, 37].

Layout and Workload-aware Optimizations. When considering hybrid architectures, most existing approaches are centered around storage aspects, i.e., they optimize the way tuples are stored inside a database page and the proper way of exploiting them during query processing. Harizopoulos et al. [19] explore performance trade-offs between column- and row-oriented architectures in the context of read-optimized systems showing that the DSM layout performs better when only few attributes are accessed. Zukowski et al. [55] present a comprehensive analysis of the overheads of DSM and NSM models and show that combining the two layouts in the same plan can be highly beneficial for complex queries.

Organizing attributes into groups either inside the data blocks or the data pages extends the traditional space of NSM and DSM layouts with cache-friendly layouts allowing for workload specific optimizations. To improve cache locality of traditional NSM, Ailamaki et al. [4] introduce a page layout called PAX. In PAX, data is globally organized in NSM pages, while inside the page attributes are organized into vertical partitions optimizing for reducing the number of cache misses. A generalization of PAX layout is proposed in data morphing [18], where the tuples in a page can be stored in an even more flexible form combining vertical decomposition and arbitrary groups of attributes and increasing spatial locality. Multi-resolution Block Storage Model [53] stores attributes columnwise as PAX maintaining cache efficiency and groups disk blocks into "super-blocks" with tuples stored among the blocks of a super-block improving I/O performance of scan operations. In a similar fashion, Blink [44] vertically partitions columns in byte-aligned column groups called banks, allowing for efficient ALU operations. Blink assigns particular columns into banks trying to minimize padding overhead and wasted space.

All approaches above provide valuable design alternatives. However, one still needs to know the workload before deciding which system to use and needs multiple of those systems to accommodate varying workloads. H_2O pushes the state-of-the-art further by providing a design which continuously adapts to the workload.

Auto-tuning Techniques. In the past years, there has been considerable work on automated physical design tuning. These techniques facilitate the process of automatically selecting auxiliary data structures (e.g., indices, materialize views) for a given workload to improve performance. Offline approaches [3, 8, 41] assume a priori knowledge of the workload and cannot cope with dynamic scenarios while online approaches [49] try to overcome this limitation by monitoring and periodically tuning the system. Online partitioning [28] adapts the database partitions to fit the observed workload. However, the above approaches are designed assuming a static data layout while the execution strategies remain fixed.

Adapting Storage to Queries with Adaptive Indexing. Adaptive indexing [13, 14, 15, 17, 23, 24, 25, 27, 50] tackles the problem of evolving workloads in the context of column-stores by building and refining partial indexes during query processing. The moto of adaptive indexing is that the "queries define how the data should be stored". We share this motivation here as we also adapt the storage layout on-the-fly based on queries. However, adaptive indexing research has focused on refining the physical order of data within a single column at a time without considering co-locating values across columns. The work on partial sideways cracking considers multiple columns [25] but what it does is to physically reorganize more than one columns in the same way as opposed to enforcing co-location of values from multiple columns as we do here.

In addition, the interest in systems with hybrid storage layouts has given rise to layout-aware workload analysis tools. Data morphing [18] uses a cache miss cost model to select the proper attribute grouping within an individual page that maximizes performance for a given workload. The hybrid engine HYRISE [16] applies the same idea and presents an offline physical deign tool that uses a cache misses cost model to evaluate the expected performance of different data partitions and proposes the proper vertical partitioning for a given workload. A storage advisor for SAP HANA database is presented by Rösch et al. [47] considering both, queries and data characteristics, to propose horizontal and vertical partitioning schemas. H_2O extends AutoPart [41], an offline vertical partitioning algorithm to work for dynamic scenarios. The above approaches use a static storage layout that is determined when the relation is created, are optimized assuming a known workload and cannot adapt to dynamic changes in the workload. In this paper, we highlight that no static layout can be optimal for every query and we design a system that can autonomously refine its storage layouts and execution strategies as the workload evolves.

Just-In-Time Compilation. Compilation of SQL queries into native code goes back to System R [9]. Recently, there have been many efforts to take advantage of dynamic translation techniques, such as Just-In-Time (JiT) compilation in the context of DBMS to alleviate the interpretation overhead of generic expressions, improve data locality, generate architecture specific source code and thus, significantly enhance performance. JiT techniques have been applied to main-memory DBMS using the LLVM framework [39, 34], column-stores [51], group of column systems [42] and stream processing systems [21] to generate code for the whole query execution plan [31], to revise specific code segments or to generate building primitives for higher-order composite operators. H_2O applies similar techniques to generate layout-aware access operators.

6. CONCLUSIONS

Traditional systems use a static and fixed design regarding data layouts. However, as applications become more and more data-driven and with ad-hoc workloads it becomes increasingly hard for a single traditional system, i.e., with a fixed layout, to be able to efficiently cover a multitude of scenarios. In this way, today it is not uncommon for businesses to employ more than one systems.

In this paper, we showcase the problem that for analytical queries multiple layouts can be beneficial depending on the query workload. To get the optimal performance, we not only need the optimal layout but also query processing strategies and access operator code that are tailored for a given layout. All these together reduce cache misses, instruction misses and interpretation overhead during query execution. We propose H_2O, a system that adaptively and continuously adjusts all three of these elements. It generates on-the-fly the appropriate layouts, execution strategies and code to match the workload, as the workload evolves. Using both synthetic benchmarks and real life experiments, we demonstrate that H_2O gracefully adapts as workloads change and stays close to the optimal performance without requiring any workload knowledge.

Adaptive systems in which new data layouts are created or old layouts are refined on-the-fly as incoming queries are processed can create new exciting research paths. For example, one challenging area with potential high impact is to study (adaptive) indexing together with adaptive data layouts and execution strategies.

Acknowledgments. The authors would like to thank the anonymous reviewers for their valuable comments and suggestions on how to improve the paper. This work has been supported by the EU FP7, project No. 317858 "BigFoot - Big Data Analytics of Digital Footprints" and Swiss National Science Foundation, project No. CRSII2 136318/1, "Trustworthy Cloud Storage".

7. REFERENCES

[1] D. Abadi, P. Boncz, S. Harizopoulos, S. Idreos, and S. Madden. The design and implementation of modern column-oriented database systems. *Foundations and Trends in Databases*, 5(3):197–280, 2013.

[2] D. Abadi, S. Madden, and N. Hachem. Column-stores vs. row-stores: how different are they really? In *SIGMOD*, 2008.

[3] S. Agrawal, V. Narasayya, and B. Yang. Integrating vertical and horizontal partitioning into automated physical database design. In *SIGMOD*, 2004.

[4] A. Ailamaki, D. DeWitt, M. Hill, and M. Skounakis. Weaving relations for cache performance. In *VLDB*, 2001.

[5] A. Ailamaki, D. DeWitt, M. Hill, and D. Wood. DBMSs on a modern processor: Where does time go? In *VLDB*, 1999.

[6] I. Alagiannis, R. Borovica, M. Branco, S. Idreos, and A. Ailamaki. NoDB: efficient query execution on raw data files. In *SIGMOD*, 2012.

[7] P. Boncz, M. Zukowski, and N. Nes. MonetDB/X100: Hyper-pipelining query execution. In *CIDR*, 2005.

[8] N. Bruno and S. Chaudhuri. Automatic physical database tuning: A relaxation-based approach. In *SIGMOD*, 2005.

[9] D. Chamberlin et al. A history and evaluation of System R. *Commun. ACM*, 24(10):632–646, 1981.

[10] P. Cudré-Mauroux, E. Wu, and S. Madden. The case for RodentStore: An adaptive, declarative storage system. In *CIDR*, 2009.

[11] J. Dittrich and A. Jindal. Towards a one size fits all database architecture. In *CIDR*, 2011.

[12] F. Färber et al. SAP HANA database: data management for modern business applications. *SIGMOD Record*, 40(4):45–51, 2011.

[13] G. Graefe, F. Halim, S. Idreos, H. A. Kuno, and S. Manegold. Concurrency control for adaptive indexing. *PVLDB*, 5(7):656–667, 2012.

[14] G. Graefe, F. Halim, S. Idreos, H. A. Kuno, S. Manegold, and B. Seeger. Transactional support for adaptive indexing. *VLDB J.*, 23(2):303–328, 2014.

[15] G. Graefe and H. Kuno. Self-selecting, self-tuning, incrementally optimized indexes. In *EDBT*, 2010.

[16] M. Grund, J. Krüger, H. Plattner, A. Zeier, P. Cudré-Mauroux, and S. Madden. HYRISE - a main memory hybrid storage engine. *PVLDB*, 4(2):105–116, 2010.

[17] F. Halim, S. Idreos, P. Karras, and R. Yap. Stochastic database cracking: Towards robust adaptive indexing in main-memory column-stores. *PVLDB*, 5(6):502–513, 2012.

[18] R. Hankins and J. Patel. Data morphing: An adaptive, cache-conscious storage technique. In *VLDB*, 2003.

[19] S. Harizopoulos, V. Liang, D. Abadi, and S. Madden. Performance tradeoffs in read-optimized databases. In *VLDB*, 2006.

[20] J. Hellerstein, M. Stonebraker, and J. R. Hamilton. Architecture of a database system. *Foundations and Trends in Databases*, 1(2):141–259, 2007.

[21] M. Hirzel et al. IBM streams processing language: Analyzing big data in motion. *IBM Journal of Research and Development*, 57(3/4):7, 2013.

[22] S. Idreos, I. Alagiannis, R. Johnson, and A. Ailamaki. Here are my data files. Here are my queries. Where are my results? In *CIDR*, 2011.

[23] S. Idreos, M. L. Kersten, and S. Manegold. Database cracking. In *CIDR*, 2007.

[24] S. Idreos, M. L. Kersten, and S. Manegold. Updating a cracked database. In *SIGMOD*, 2007.

[25] S. Idreos, M. L. Kersten, and S. Manegold. Self-organizing tuple reconstruction in column-stores. In *SIGMOD*, 2009.

[26] S. Idreos and E. Liarou. dbTouch: Analytics at your fingertips. In *CIDR*, 2013.

[27] S. Idreos, S. Manegold, H. Kuno, and G. Graefe. Merging what's cracked, cracking what's merged: adaptive indexing in main-memory column-stores. *PVLDB*, 4(9), 2011.

[28] A. Jindal and J. Dittrich. Relax and let the database do the partitioning online. In *BIRTE*, 2011.

[29] A. Kemper and T. Neumann. Hyper: A hybrid OLTP&OLAP main memory database system based on virtual memory snapshots. In *ICDE*, 2011.

[30] M. L. Kersten, S. Idreos, S. Manegold, and E. Liarou. The researcher's guide to the data deluge: Querying a scientific database in just a few seconds. *PVLDB*, 4(12):1474–1477, 2011.

[31] K. Krikellas, S. Viglas, and M. Cintra. Generating code for holistic query evaluation. In *ICDE*, 2010.

[32] A. Lamb et al. The Vertica analytic database: C-Store 7 years later. *PVLDB*, 5(12):1790–1801, 2012.

[33] P.-Å. Larson et al. Enhancements to SQL Server column stores. In *SIGMOD*, 2013.

[34] C. Lattner and V. Adve. LLVM: A compilation framework for lifelong program analysis & transformation. In *CGO*, 2004.

[35] R. MacNicol and B. French. Sybase IQ Multiplex - designed for analytics. In *VLDB*, 2004.

[36] S. Manegold, P. Boncz, and M. Kersten. Optimizing database architecture for the new bottleneck: memory access. *VLDB J.*, 9(3):231–246, 2000.

[37] A. Nandi and H. V.Jagadish. Guided interaction: Rethinking the query-result paradigm. In *VLDB*, 2011.

[38] S. Navathe, S. Ceri, G. Wiederhold, and J. Dou. Vertical partitioning algorithms for database design. *ACM Trans. Database Syst.*, 9(4):680–710, 1984.

[39] T. Neumann. Efficiently compiling efficient query plans for modern hardware. *PVLDB*, 4(9):539–550, 2011.

[40] S. Padmanabhan, T. Malkemus, R. Agarwal, and A. Jhingran. Block oriented processing of relational database operations in modern computer architectures. In *ICDE*, 2001.

[41] S. Papadomanolakis and A. Ailamaki. AutoPart: Automating schema design for large scientific databases using data partitioning. In *SSDBM*, 2004.

[42] H. Pirk et al. CPU and cache efficient management of memory-resident databases. In *ICDE*, 2013.

[43] R. Ramamurthy, D. DeWitt, and Q. Su. A case for fractured mirrors. *VLDB J.*, 12(2):89–101, 2003.

[44] V. Raman et al. Constant-time query processing. In *ICDE*, 2008.

[45] V. Raman et al. DB2 with BLU acceleration: So much more than just a column store. *PVLDB*, 6(11):1080–1091, 2013.

[46] J. Rao, H. Pirahesh, C. Mohan, and G. M. Lohman. Compiled query execution engine using JVM. In *ICDE*, 2006.

[47] P. Rösch, L. Dannecker, G. Hackenbroich, and F. Faerber. A storage advisor for hybrid-store databases. *PVLDB*, 5(12):1748–1758, 2012.

[48] D. Saccà and G. Wiederhold. Database partitioning in a cluster of processors. *ACM Trans. Database Syst.*, 10(1):29–56, 1985.

[49] K. Schnaitter, S. Abiteboul, T. Milo, and N. Polyzotis. COLT: continuous on-line tuning. In *SIGMOD*, 2006.

[50] F. M. Schuhknecht, A. Jindal, and J. Dittrich. The Uncracked Pieces in Database Cracking. *PVLDB*, 7(2), 2013.

[51] J. Sompolski, M. Zukowski, and P. Boncz. Vectorization vs. compilation in query execution. In *DaMoN*, 2011.

[52] M. Stonebraker and U. Çetintemel. "One size fits all": An idea whose time has come and gone. In *ICDE*, 2005.

[53] J. Zhou and K. Ross. A multi-resolution block storage model for database design. In *IDEAS*, 2003.

[54] M. Zukowski and P. Boncz. Vectorwise: Beyond column stores. *IEEE Data Eng. Bull.*, 35(1):21–27, 2012.

[55] M. Zukowski, N. Nes, and P. Boncz. DSM vs. NSM: CPU performance tradeoffs in block-oriented query processing. In *DaMoN*, pages 47–54, 2008.

Fine-grained Partitioning for Aggressive Data Skipping

Liwen Sun, Michael J. Franklin, Sanjay Krishnan, Reynold S. Xin[†]
AMPLab, UC Berkeley and [†]Databricks Inc.
{liwen, franklin, sanjay, rxin}@cs.berkeley.edu

ABSTRACT

Modern query engines are increasingly being required to process enormous datasets in near real-time. While much can be done to speed up the data access, a promising technique is to reduce the need to access data through *data skipping*. By maintaining some metadata for each block of tuples, a query may skip a data block if the metadata indicates that the block does not contain relevant data. The effectiveness of data skipping, however, depends on how well the blocking scheme matches the query filters.

In this paper, we propose a fine-grained blocking technique that reorganizes the data tuples into blocks with a goal of enabling queries to skip blocks aggressively. We first extract representative filters in a workload as *features* using frequent itemset mining. Based on these features, each data tuple can be represented as a feature vector. We then formulate the blocking problem as a optimization problem on the feature vectors, called *Balanced MaxSkip Partitioning*, which we prove is NP-hard. To find an approximate solution efficiently, we adopt the bottom-up clustering framework. We prototyped our blocking techniques on Shark, an open-source data warehouse system. Our experiments on TPC-H and a real-world workload show that our blocking technique leads to 2-5x improvement in query response time over traditional range-based blocking techniques.

Categories and Subject Descriptors

H.2.2 [**Database Management**]: Physical Design

Keywords

Data warehouse; Partitioning; Query processing; Algorithms

1. INTRODUCTION

Data analytics has been proven critical in many applications, ranging from business decision making to scientific discovery. Many of these applications require *interactively* unlocking insights from enormous data. To meet this need, designs of modern query engines (e.g., [8, 37, 32, 2, 35]) are

SIGMOD'14, June 22–27, 2014, Snowbird, UT, USA.

ACM 978-1-4503-2376-5/14/06 ...$15.00.
http://dx.doi.org/10.1145/2588555.2610515.

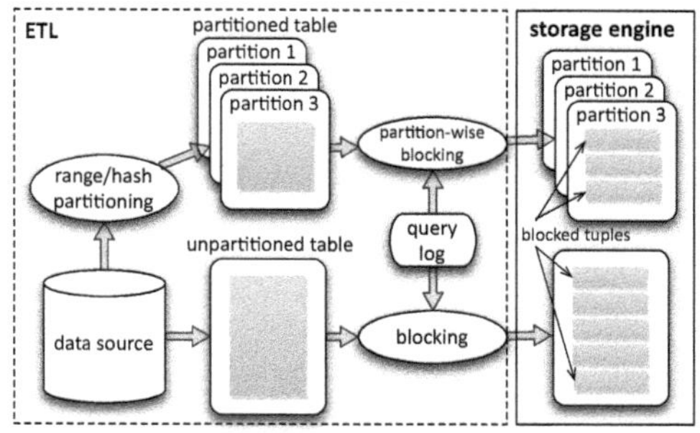

Figure 1: Blocking at Data Loading

striving to identify opportunities to shorten query response time. One dimension of this effort focuses on improving the data scan *throughput*, such as memory caching, parallelization, and data compression. Another dimension is to *reduce* the data access. For example, columnar-oriented data layout prevents the queries from accessing irrelevant columns, and sampling provides approximate answers by scanning only a small subset of data. Along these lines, there has recently been an increasing interest in reducing data access through *data skipping* [1, 6, 35, 37]. Intelligently skipping *blocks* of tuples can significantly speed up the query processing.

1.1 Background

Traditionally, data skipping has long been implemented via partition pruning. In a data warehouse environment, many tables are partitioned by time and most queries have a time range filter. A query can check the time ranges of the partitions and decide which partitions to scan and which to skip. While this is an effective way to prune data, the remaining partitions can still contain a lot of tuples.

Recent systems [28, 1, 34, 7, 6, 37, 35] support skipping data *blocks*. A block in these systems is a horizontal partition that is fairly small (e.g., 1000's or 10,000's of tuples). Each block is associated with some metadata such as min and max values. Before scanning a block, data skipping first evaluates the query filter against this metadata and then decides if the block can be skipped, i.e., the block does not need to be accessed. The salient features of data skipping include avoiding random disk access and incurring minimal storage and maintenance overhead [28, 34, 6, 35]. Block skipping speeds up table scans by accessing less data, which is beneficial to both disk- and memory-resident tables.

1.2 Goals

The effectiveness of block skipping depends on how the data tuples are partitioned into blocks. We refer to this

	time	id	event	category	publisher	revenue
t1	08:01:01	102	click	jeans	groupon	0.0
t2	08:01:01	103	click	shirts	google	-0.5
t3	08:01:01	104	click	shirts	groupon	0.0
t4	08:01:02	105	buy	jeans	google	12.0
t5	08:01:03	106	click	jeans	google	-0.5
t6	08:01:04	107	buy	shoes	shoedeal	30.0

(a) tuples

	features	weight
F1	event='buy'	50
F2	product='jeans'	20
F3	publisher='google' revenue < 0	10

(b) features

	vector (F_1, F_2, F_3)
t1	(0,1,0)
t2	(0,0,1)
t3	(0,0,0)
t4	(1,1,0)
t5	(0,1,1)
t6	(1,0,0)

(c) vectors

	blocking
P1 (1,1,0)	t1 (0,1,0) t4 (1,1,0)
P2 (0,1,1)	t2 (0,0,1) t5 (0,1,1)
P3 (1,0,0)	t3 (0,0,0) t6 (1,0,0)

(d) blocks

Figure 2: Example of Blocking

process as *blocking*. Current systems adopt very small block sizes for data skipping. For example, IBM DB2 BLU [35] uses 1,000-tuple blocks; Google's PowerDrill [6] suggests 50,000 tuples; Shark [37] skips data on HDFS blocks, each of which is 128MB by default. These systems rely on range partitioning to generate such blocks. While range partitioning has been useful for many purposes, it may not be ideal for generating fine-grained blocks for skipping. Specifically, range partitioning lacks of a principled way of: (1) setting the fine-grained ranges on each column that matches the data skew and workload skew, (2) allocating the number of partitions for different columns and (3) capturing inter-column data correlation and filter correlation.

In this paper, we propose a workload-driven blocking technique, with a goal of (horizontally) partitioning the data into *fine-grained, balance-sized* blocks in a way that queries can maximally skip the blocks. This is an offline process that executes at data loading time and may be re-executed later to account for a more recent workload. Figure 1 depicts the use of blocking in an ETL process. Note that our blocking techniques can co-exist with traditional horizontal partitioning techniques, as these techniques may be used for a different purpose, such as load balancing and roll-in/roll-out operations. Specifically, our techniques can be applied to further segment each individual partition. As shown in Figure 1, we take as input the data tuples and a query log, and write the blocked tuples to the storage engine; if the incoming tuples are partitioned, we can block each partition individually (in parallel). A newly-inserted partition can be blocked on its own and will not affect existing partitions.

First, we extract some filter predicates as *features* from a past query workload using frequent itemset mining. We then generate feature vectors by precomputing these filter predicates on the data and solve an optimization problem to guide the data blocking. In many real-world workloads, especially the reporting and scheduled workloads, similar queries are repeatedly run on different time-ranged data. We also analyze real-world workloads in Section 2, which show that (1) a small set of representative filters are commonly used by many queries and (2) many queries use recurring filters. These findings suggest that our workload-driven approach can be effective for real query workloads.

Some previous work also utilizes workloads for physical database design, e.g., [17, 21, 12, 10]. Specifically, our work is related to materialized view selection (MVS) [16, 10]. Like MVS, we exploit precomputation. However, our partitioning techniques are at the physical-record level and are complementary to materialized views. In fact, our techniques can be applied to partition large materialized views, e.g., data cubes. As we will show shortly, we maintain concise feature-based metadata derived from precomputation. Another proposed data skipping technique involves the use of small materialized aggregates (SMAs) associated with partitions [28, 34]. These SMAs have been shown to improve query performance in range-partitioned systems. In contrast, our work is focused on constructing fine-grained partitions that more closely capture the access patterns of complex analytics workloads. Like materialized views, SMAs are also complementary to our approach and in fact could be implemented on our partitions as well. We defer the detailed discussion of related work to Section 8.

1.3 Example

Suppose we are given a table as shown in Figure 2(a), an example log of online events. We first look at the log of queries that were posed on this table and extract a set of features, each of which is a representative filter with possibly multiple conjunctive predicates. Suppose the features extracted are as shown in Figure 2(b). Given these features, we then transform the data tuples into feature vectors. This process can be done by scanning the table once and batch-evaluating the features on each tuple. As shown in Figure 2(c), each feature vector is (in this case) a 3-dimensional bit vector, whose i-th bit indicates whether this tuple satisfies filter F_i. In practice, the number of features can be kept small, e.g., < 50. We then partition the tuples according to these vectors. Intuitively, tuples that do not satisfy the same features should be placed in the same block such that, when a query uses one of these features as filter, this block of tuples can be skipped altogether. An example of the resulting blocked tuples is shown in Figure 2(d). For each block, we compute a *union vector* by taking a bitwise `OR` of all the feature vectors in it. If the i-th bit of the union vector is 0, then we know that no tuple in this block satisfies feature i. In this case, any query whose filter is F_i can skip this block. For example, a query on F_3 can skip the blocks P_1 and P_3. More generally, a query can skip blocks if its filter *is subsumed by* (i.e., is stricter than) some features. For example, a query with filter $event$ = *'buy'* $\wedge$ $product$ = *'jeans'* is subsumed by both features F_1 and F_2, which lead to the skipping of P_2 and P_3 respectively.

1.4 Contributions

To realize this design, we address a few technical challenges as outlined below.

Feature Selection. Indeed, selecting the right features to guide partitioning is critical. We develop a *workload analyzer* to identify representative filters as features from a query log. We consider a feature representative if it could be used to help many queries. If some filter predicates are frequently used together, we should combine these predicates as one feature to skip data more effectively, e.g., feature F_3 in Figure 2. To capture both *frequency* and *co-occurrence* of filters, we model the feature selection as a frequent itemset mining problem. Due to their subsumption relations, some features can be redundant. For example, *revenue* > 0 could be redundant if there is already a feature *revenue* > 100. We develop a principled way to eliminate redundancy.

Optimal Partitioning. Given a set of features, we compute a feature bit-vector for each tuple. The problem then is to find an optimal partitioning over these vectors. This is clearly a hard problem, as different features may be conflicting, may be correlated, and may have different selectivities. We formulate the *Balanced MaxSkip* partitioning problem: given a desired number of tuples per block, find a partitioning over a collection of tuples (represented as bit vectors) that maximizes the number of tuples that can be skipped. This objective is fundamentally different from other well-known partitioning objectives, such as k-means and distance-based clustering [29]. We prove that *Balanced MaxSkip* is NP-hard, by a reduction from the hypergraph bisection problem [24]. We conjecture that *k-MaxSkip*, a variant without the balance constraint, is also NP-hard. To find an approximate solution efficiently, we adopt the classic bottom-up clustering framework, as it naturally incorporates our objective function and is a widely-understood framework with scalable implementations, e.g., [38, 5].

Scalability. It is prohibitively expensive to run a clustering algorithm on large datasets. Fortunately, we observe that the input size can be reduced from the number of tuples to the number of distinct feature vectors. The latter mostly depends on the number of features and can be small (e.g., $<10k$) in practice. As shown in Section 7, although we run a sophisticated partitioning algorithm on the vectors, the cost bottleneck of the entire blocking process is still the actual data movement instead of the partitioning algorithm.

We prototype our blocking techniques on Shark [37], an open-source data warehouse system. We conduct experiments on TPC-H benchmark and a real-world ad-hoc workload from a video streaming company. The results show that our techniques reduce the data access by a factor of 4-7 over existing skipping techniques on top of range partitioning. We also demonstrate that this reduction can directly translate to a reduction in query response time, on both disk and memory resident data. Specifically, we improve the query response time by 5-14x over full table scans without skipping and by 2-5x over existing skipping techniques.

The remainder of paper is organized as follows. Section 2 gives an overview of our blocking approach. Section 3 presents the workload analyzer. We discuss the partitioner in Section 4. We show how skipping works during query execution in Section 5. Section 6 discusses the practical issues. We report our experimental results in Section 7. Section 8 reviews the related work and Section 9 concludes the paper.

2. OVERVIEW

In this section, we first discuss the assumptions for our techniques and then give an overview of the workflow.

2.1 Workload Assumptions

We extract representative filters as features from the workload to guide the blocking. In order for our approach to work well, we expect two properties of the workload:

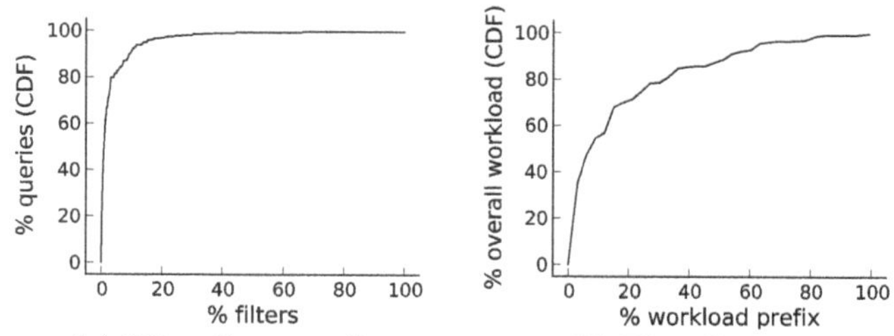

(a) Filter Commonality (b) Filter Stability

Figure 3: Filter Analysis on Real Ad-hoc Workloads

Filter Commonality. We expect that there is a small set of filters that are commonly used by many queries. If each query uses a distinct filter, then it would be difficult to find representative filters.

Filter Stability. Since we base our blocking decision on a past workload, it is important that most of the filters in future queries have occurred before. In other words, we expect that most of filters are *recurring* and only a small portion are entirely new over time.

Obviously, the commonality and stability of filters can be observed in recurring scheduled or reporting queries. Such queries are usually generated from templates and the same set of filters would be repeatedly used on the data of different time ranges. The effectiveness of using past queries to guide database design was also evidenced in many previous works, e.g., [10, 21, 17, 12].

We conducted empirical analysis on a real-world production SQL workload from a video streaming company called Conviva. These 8664 ad-hoc queries, spanning the period from 06/2010 to 01/2012, were used for problem diagnosis and data analytics over an access log of video streams. Note that each query uses possibly multiple filter predicates. For each predicate, e.g., *event* = *'click'*, we count its frequency, i.e., how many queries use it. In Figure 3(a), we sort the filters by descending frequency and plot the cumulative percentage of the queries that use the filters. A point (x, y) indicates that the most frequent $x\%$ filters are used by $y\%$ of queries. We can see that the filter usage is highly skewed, e.g., 10% of the unique filters were used by 90% of the queries. This implies that using only 10% of filters as features can benefit 90% of the queries.

We then examine the queries in the order as they arrive. To prevent our analysis from being biased towards a particular starting point, we divided the 8664 queries into 5 disjoint time windows and plotted five curves. Figure 3(b) shows an average over these five curves. A point (x, y) means that, as we have seen $x\%$ of the queries (or $x\%$ workload prefix), the filters in these $x\%$ are used by $y\%$ of all the queries in the workload. If every query used completely new filters, i.e., there is no recurring filter, this curve would be a function of $y = x$. The plot, however, shows that many queries use recurring filters. In particular, 80% of the entire workload uses the filters that already occur in the 30% prefix. Since the filters are recurring, we can infer that most of the future filters are predictable based on a past workload.

2.2 The Blocking Workflow

Having described our workload assumptions, we now overview the blocking overflow, as depicted in Figure 4. This workflow consists of three standard data marshaling steps (shaded arrows) and two important modules named the workload analyzer and the partitioner.

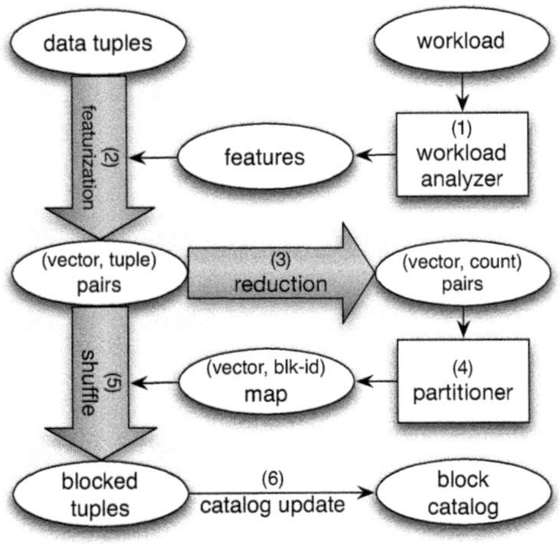

Figure 4: The Blocking Workflow

The input is a table and a workload represented as a collection of queries on this table. The query workload can be obtained by collecting query logs of the system. We now walk through the individual steps in the workflow:

(1) Workload Analyzer. The workload analyzer (Section 3) extracts a set of features from the query workload. A feature is a representative filter with possibly multiple predicates.

(2) Featurization. Given the features, i.e., filters, from Step 1, we scan the table once and batch evaluate these filters for each tuple. This step transforms each tuple to a (vector, tuple)-pair.

(3) Reduction. Since our blocking only depends on the feature vectors, not the actual tuples, we *group-by* the (vector, tuple)-pairs into (vector, count)-pairs. This is an important step to reduce the input size for the partitioner.

(4) Partitioner. The partitioner (Section 4) runs a partitioning algorithm on the (vector, count)-pairs. This generates a *blocking map* (from a feature vector to a block id).

(5) Shuffle. In this step, each of the augmented tuples (output of Step 3) finds its destination block by consulting the blocking map (output of Step 4).

(6) Catalog Update. We add the features and one union vector (e.g., Figure 2(d)) for each block to the *block catalog* (Section 5). After this step, we can drop the feature vectors, and the blocked tuples are ready to serve queries.

The above workflow can be executed as an offline process at data loading time and may be re-executed later to account for workload changes. In the event that the data arrival rate is high or that the new data needs to be queried immediately, the blocking process can be postponed. As stated in Section 1, in many data warehouse applications, tables are partitioned by time ranges, and new tuples are typically batch-inserted as a new partition. We can consider our blocking as a "secondary" partitioning scheme under each such coarse-grained partition. For example, when a new partition `dt='1994-11-03'` is added to the table `logs`:

```
ALTER TABLE logs ADD PARTITION (dt='1994-11-03') ...
```

we can invoke our blocking process on this newly inserted partition without affecting existing data. To re-block a horizontally partitioned table, we can block each partition individually in parallel.

Having outlined the workflow, in the following sections, we will discuss the different components in detail.

3. WORKLOAD ANALYSIS

The goal of workload analysis is to extract features from the query trace. We follow two intuitions. First, we should use representative filters as features to guide the blocking. A feature is representative if it can potentially help a large number of queries skip data. Second, the filter predicates that are frequently used together should be considered as one single feature, e.g., F_3 in Figure 2, as these predicates will likely be used together in the future queries and combining them can greatly maximize block skipping. To take into account the counting and co-occurrence of predicates, we model the workload analysis as a *frequent itemset mining* problem [22]. In this section, we first formulate the problem and then present a principled approach for feature selection.

3.1 Workload Model

A workload is a collection of queries. Each query is associated with a filter, which evaluates a data tuple and returns a boolean value. Without loss of generality, we assume each query uses a conjunction of *predicates*, where a predicate is a disjunction of filter literals. A filter literal can be an equality or range condition, a string matching operation, or a boolean user defined function. Since we are only concerned with the filter part of the queries, we represent the workload by $\mathcal{Q} = \{Q_1, Q_2, \ldots, Q_m\}$, where each Q_i is a set of (conjunctive) predicates. An example workload is given in Example 1.

EXAMPLE 1. *An example workload, each of which is represented as a set of conjunctive predicates:*
Q_1: *product* = *'shoes'*
Q_2: *product in ('shoes', 'shirts'), revenue* > 32
Q_3: *product* = *'shirts'* $\wedge$ *revenue* > 21

The workload is thus modeled as a transactional database [9], where a predicate is an item and a query is a transaction. For example, Q_1 can be viewed as a transaction of only one item *product='shoes'*. Let F be the set of all predicates that occurred in $\mathcal{Q}$. We call any set of conjunctive predicates $F_i \subseteq F$ a *predicate set* (analogous to *itemset*). By definition, each Q_i is a predicate set.

Two predicates are equal if all their components are equal, including the columns, the constants and the filtering condition. Given two predicates f_i and f_j, we use $f_i \sqsubseteq f_j$ to denote that f_i *is subsumed by* f_j or f_j *subsumes* f_i, i.e., f_i is equal to or stricter than f_j. For example, the predicate *product* = *'shoes'* is subsumed by *product* in (*'shoes'*, *'shirts'*). Given two predicate sets F_i and F_j, we say F_i *is subsumed by* F_j, or F_j subsumes F_i, denoted by $F_i \sqsubseteq F_j$, if for any $f_u \in F_j$, there exists f_v in F_i such that $f_v \sqsubseteq f_u$. Clearly, $F_i \sqsubseteq F_j$ if $F_j \subseteq F_i$.

3.2 Predicate Augmentation

We want to select representative predicate sets as features. As discussed in Section 1 and Section 5, a feature can be used to skip data blocks, but only for the queries it subsumes. Let us show this using Example 1. Suppose we use {*product* in (*'shoes'*, *'shirts'*)} as a feature. We can see that this feature subsumes both Q_1 and Q_2. If there is a block that does not contain any tuple that satisfies {*product* in (*'shoes'*, *'shirts'*)} (indicated by the union vector, as discussed), we can then infer that no tuple in this block satisfies Q_1 or Q_2, because these queries are subsumed by (i.e., even stricter than) this feature. In this case, Q_1 and Q_2 can safely skip this block.

Since a predicate set, if selected as a feature, is only helpful to the queries it subsumes, we should select the predicate sets that subsume a lot of queries. This problem can be modeled as frequent itemset mining. There is a difference, however, between the number of queries a predicate set subsumes and the number of occurrences this predicate set has. Directly applying a frequent itemset mining algorithm on the queries would miss important features. For example, $\{revenue > 21\}$ subsumes both Q_2 and Q_3, and $\{product$ in ('*shoes*','*shirts*')$\}$ subsumes both Q_1 and Q_2; each of these two predicate sets has only 1 occurrence but subsumes 2 queries. To adjust this difference, we perform a filter augmentation step as follows. For each query $Q_i \in \mathcal{Q}$, we augment Q_i with all the predicates in F that subsumes Q_i, using the following procedure.

```
for each Q_i ∈ 𝒬:
    for each f_j ∈ F:
        if ∃f_k ∈ Q_i s.t. f_k ⊑ f_j:
            Q_i ← Q_i ∪ {f_j}
```

After this augmentation step, the number of occurrences of a predicate set equals to the number of queries it subsumes. For example, the workload in Example 1 becomes:

Q_1: *prod.*='*shoes*', *prod.* in ('*shoes*', '*shirts*')

Q_2: *prod.* in ('*shoes*', '*shirts*'), *revenue*>32, *revenue*> 21

Q_3: *prod.*='*shirts*', *revenue*>21, *prod.* in ('*shoes*', '*shirts*')

By setting a minimum frequency threshold T, we can now use an off-the-shelf frequent itemset mining algorithm to compute the predicate sets that subsume at least T queries.

3.3 Redundant Predicate Set Elimination

We now have obtained a set of predicate sets that subsume at least T queries. Unfortunately, some of these predicate sets may be redundant. For example, if there is a predicate set $\{$*publisher*='*google*', *revenue*<0$\}$ in the result, both its subsets $\{$*revenue*<0$\}$ and $\{$*publisher*= '*google*'$\}$ would also be present, due to the apriori property [9]; but the predicate set $\{$*publisher*='*google*', *revenue*<0$\}$ is only useful for the queries that cannot be subsumed by either of the subsets. In addition, the filter augmentation step may also introduce redundant results. For example, if $\{revenue > 32\}$ is present, then $\{revenue > 21\}$ is also present due to the augmentation. Again, $\{revenue > 21\}$ is only helpful for the queries that cannot be subsumed by $\{revenue > 32\}$. Existing approaches that keep only *maximal* or *closed* frequent itemsets [22] do not capture the subsumption relations in our specific problem.

We develop a principled way to remove redundancy from the frequent predicate sets. Notice that the frequency threshold T used in Section 3.2 indicates that we are only interested in the predicate sets that subsume at least T queries. We will use the same principle for redundancy removal. Specifically, let $\mathcal{F}$ be the frequent predicate sets, we consider a predicate set F_i in $\mathcal{F}$ to be redundant and remove it, if the number of queries F_i *additionally* subsumes, given the predicate sets that are already in $\mathcal{F}$, is less than the threshold T. We denote by $subsume(F_i, \mathcal{Q}) \subseteq \mathcal{Q}$ the set of queries in $\mathcal{Q}$ that are subsumed by F_i. We use the following procedure to eliminate the redundant predicate sets:

```
sort 𝓕 by the (partial) order of ⊑, i.e., F_i ⊑ F_j for i < j
𝒬_c ← ∅, 𝓡 ← ∅
for each F_i in 𝓕:
    I(F_i) ← |subsume(F_i, 𝒬) − 𝒬_c|
    if I(F_i) < T:
        remove F_i
    else:
        𝓡 ← 𝓡 ∪ {(I(F_i), F_i)}
        𝒬_c ← subsume(F_i, 𝒬) ∪ 𝒬_c
```

We examine the predicate sets in $\mathcal{F}$ in the (partial) order of increasing generality, such that the eliminating decision of the current predicate set does not affect that of the previous predicate sets. For each F_i, we calculate $I(F_i)$, the number of queries that F_i additionally subsumes. If $I(F_i)$ is smaller than T, F_i is removed; otherwise, we add the pair $(I(F_i), F_i)$ to $\mathcal{R}$ and update $\mathcal{Q}_c$, the cumulative set of queries subsumed by all the predicate sets in $\mathcal{R}$. At the end, we sort $\mathcal{R}$. Given a parameter $numFeat$, the workload analyzer returns $numFeat$ predicate sets from $\mathcal{R}$ with the highest $I(\cdot)$ values.

The cost of workload analysis is dominated by the frequent itemset mining phase. In practice, we expect this process to be very efficient, since most queries would not have many predicates. Next, we discuss the partitioner, which incorporates the data-related aspects such as correlation and selectivity, by solving a optimization problem on the feature vectors.

4. THE PARTITIONING PROBLEM

In this section, we first formulate the optimization problem and prove its hardness. We then discuss the reduction step which is critical to scaling. Finally, we present the bottom-up framework.

4.1 Problem Definition

Suppose we have a set of m features obtained from the workload analysis, denoted by $\mathcal{F} = \{F_1, F_2, \ldots, F_m\}$. We denote by w_j the weight of the features F_j, i.e., the number of queries it subsumes. Based on these features, the data tuples are augmented with binary vectors (Step (1) in Figure 4). We now formulate the partitioning problem on the m-dimensional bit vectors.

Let $V = \{v_1, v_2, \ldots, v_n\}$ be a collection of m-dimensional bit vectors, where each vector corresponds to a tuple. We will focus on our discussion on the vectors, finding as a partitioning on the vectors is equivalent to finding a blocking on the tuples. The *j-th* bit of v_i, denoted by v_{ij}, indicates whether v_i satisfies feature F_j. Let $\mathcal{P} = \{P_1, P_2, \ldots, P_k\}$ be a *partitioning* over V, i.e., $\mathcal{P}$ is a set of disjoint subsets of V whose union is V. Let $\overline{v}(P_i)$ be the union vector of all vectors in P_i, i.e., $\overline{v}(P_i) = \bigvee_{v_j \in P_i} v_j$. We say a feature F_j *prunes* a partition P_i if none of the vectors in P_i satisfies F_j, i.e., the j-th bit of $\overline{v}(P_i)$ is 0, denoted by $\overline{v}(P_i)_j = 0$. If F_j prunes P_i, then F_j prunes $|P_i|$ tuples, as each vector corresponds to a tuple. Note that the weight w_j of F_j is the number of queries F_j subsumes in the workload. If F_j prunes P_i, when we run all the queries in the workload, the sum of tuples that can be skipped would be $w_j \cdot |P_i|$. Given a partition P_i, we define the cost function $C(P_i)$ as the sum of tuples in P_i that can be skipped when we execute all the queries in the workload, we have:

$$C(P_i) = |P_i| \sum_{1 \le j \le m} w_j (1 - \overline{v}(P_i)_j) \tag{1}$$

Consider the example blocking scheme P_1 in Figure 2(d). The union vector $\overline{v}(P_1)$ is $(1, 1, 0)$, so only feature F_3 prunes P_1. We also know that $|P_1| = 2$ and the weight of F_3, w_3, is 10 as given in Figure 2(b). Therefore, we have: $C(P_1) = 2 \times 10 = 20$ using Equation 1. We then define the cost function $\mathbb{C}(\mathcal{P})$ over a partitioning, which is the sum of $C(P_i)$ over all P_i in $\mathcal{P}$:

$$\mathbb{C}(\mathcal{P}) = \sum_{P_i \in \mathcal{P}} C(P_i) \tag{2}$$

Intuitively, the objective function $\mathbb{C}(\mathcal{P})$ is the sum of tuples that can be skipped if we run all the queries in the workload. From the perspective of a real system, we also have to constrain that the block sizes are almost balanced. If some block is too small, it incurs significant overhead to process the block and maintain block-level metadata; if some block is much bigger than others, it may become a straggler in parallel executions. We now define the *Balanced MaxSkip* partitioning problem:

PROBLEM 1 (BALANCED MAXSKIP PARTITIONING). *Given a set V of binary vectors, where $|V|$ is a multiple of p, find a partitioning $\mathcal{P}$ over V such that $\mathbb{C}(\mathcal{P})$ is maximized, i.e.,*

$$\arg\max_{\mathcal{P}} \mathbb{C}(\mathcal{P})$$
$$\textit{subject to} \quad |P_i| = p \quad \forall P_i \in \mathcal{P}$$

The balance constraint is important from the perspective of a large-scale system, such as parallel processing of data blocks, but not necessary for data skipping purposes. For theoretical interests, we also formulate a *k-MaxSkip partitioning* problem without the balance constraint:

PROBLEM 2 (k-MAXSKIP PARTITIONING). *Given a set V of binary vectors, find a k-partitioning $\mathcal{P}$ over V such that $\mathbb{C}(\mathcal{P})$ is maximized.*

In this paper, we will focus on Problem 1.

4.2 NP-Hardness

We now prove that Problem 1 is NP-hard even in the special case where $p = |V|/2$, by reduction from hypergraph bisection [18]. Given a hypergraph instance $H = (V, E)$, where V is a set of vectices and E is a set of hyper edges. Since each hyper edge connects a set of vertices, we denote by $v_i \in E_j$ if v_i is in E_j. The hypergraph bisection problem finds a balanced 2-partitioning on the vectices such that the number of hyperedges across the two partitions is minimum.

We construct an input to our problem from this instance as follows. We construct a bit vector v_i for each vertex. Each vector has $|E|$ dimensions, where the j-th dimension corresponds to an edge e_j in E. Specifically, the value v_{ij} is 1 if $v_i \in e_j$ and 0 otherwise. By setting the partition size to be $|V|/2$, a solution $\mathcal{P} = \{P_1, P_2\}$ to our problem is a balanced partitioning over V. Let n_1 and n_2 be the number of vectors in P_1 and P_2, respectively, and let m_1, m_2 and m_c be the number of hyperedges in P_1, in P_2 and across both, respectively. The value of our objective function for this solution is:

$$\mathbb{C}(\mathcal{P}) = n_1 m_1 + n_2 m_2 + n m_c \tag{3}$$

Now that the partitions are balanced, i.e., $n_1 = n_2$, we have:

$$\mathbb{C}(\mathcal{P}) = \frac{1}{2} n m_1 + \frac{1}{2} n m_2 + n m_c = nm + n m_c \tag{4}$$

Since n and m are constant, minimizing Equation 4 is equivalent to minimizing m_c. Hence, an optimal solution to our problem solves the hypergraph bisection problem on H.

From Equation 3, we can see that our objective function involves the product of number of vertex and number of edges for each vertex partition. We conjecture that Problem 2, the variant that does not have the balance constraint, is also NP-hard.

4.3 Reduction Step

The partitioning problem defined in Section 4.1 is solely based on the vectors, not the actual tuples. As an optimization step, we *group-by* the vectors into (vector, count)-pairs. This step does not affect the quality of partitioning, since the same vectors should go to the same partition anyway. Each vector now is associated with a weight, denoting the number of tuples it represents. To compute Equation 1, we simply replace $|P_i|$ with the weighted sum of all the vectors in P_i.

Note that this step is the key to scale our partitioning techniques to large datasets. Theoretically, the number of distinct vectors is upper-bounded by $min(2^m, n)$. In practice, however, this number is usually very small, e.g., $<10k$, as many tuples may have the same feature vectors. We will empirically examine this number in Section 7.

4.4 The Bottom Up Framework

Since Problem 1 is NP-hard, we will turn to Ward's method as a heuristic algorithm to find an approximate solution efficiently. Ward's method [36], originally proposed for minimizing the error sum of squares, is a general bottom-up clustering framework and has been used for various objective functions [29].

Base on Ward's method, every data point is a partition by itself initially. At each iteration, we select two partitions to merge that maximizes $\mathbb{C}(\mathcal{P})$. Recall that $\mathbb{C}(\mathcal{P})$ is a sum of $C(P_i)$ for all $P_i \in \mathcal{P}$. We denote by $\delta(P_i, P_j)$ the change of $\mathbb{C}(\mathcal{P})$ caused by merging partitions P_i and P_j, i.e.,

$$\delta(P_i, P_j) = \mathbb{C}(\mathcal{P} \cup \{P_i \cup P_j\} - \{P_i, P_j\}) - \mathbb{C}(\mathcal{P}) \tag{5}$$

When we merge P_i and P_j, their union vectors are `OR`ed, i.e.,

$$\overline{v}(P_i \cup P_j) = \overline{v}(P_i) \vee \overline{v}(P_j) \tag{6}$$

Since the merging of P_i and P_j does not affect the costs of other partitions, we have:

$$\begin{aligned} \delta(P_i, P_j) &= C(P_i \cup P_j) - C(P_i) - C(P_j) \\ &= |P_i| \sum_{1 \le k \le m} w_k(\overline{v}(P_i)_k - \overline{v}(P_i)_k \vee \overline{v}(P_j)_k) \\ &\quad + |P_j| \sum_{1 \le k \le m} w_k(\overline{v}(P_j)_k - \overline{v}(P_i)_k \vee \overline{v}(P_j)_k) \end{aligned}$$

In the bottom up algorithm, we represent each partition as P_i as a $(\overline{v}(P_i), |P_i|)$-pair. Thus, $\delta(P_i, P_j)$ can be evaluated efficiently (constant time to the size of partitions). We also have the following lemma.

LEMMA 1 (MONOTONICITY). *The objective function $\mathbb{C}(\mathcal{P})$ is non-increasing through a partition merge, i.e., $\delta(P_i, P_j) \le 0$ for any $P_i, P_j \in \mathcal{P}$.*

Lemma 1 guarantees that our objective function can fit in Ward's method correctly. The objective $\mathbb{C}(\mathcal{P})$ has the maximal value when every vector is a partition by itself.

We iteratively find a pair of points whose merge hurts $\mathbb{C}(\mathcal{P})$ the least.

In practice, we set a parameter $minSize$. A partition is removed from being further merged if its size reaches $minSize$. Thus, a merge of two blocks of size less than $minSize$ would be smaller than $2 \cdot minSize$. We simply accept the blocks of size in $[minSize, 2 \cdot minSize)$. The bottom-up procedure is shown as follows:

$\mathcal{P} \leftarrow \{\{v_1\}, \{v_2\}, \ldots, \{v_n\}\}$, $\mathcal{R} \leftarrow \emptyset$
while $\mathcal{P}$ *is not empty*:
  · *merge the pair* $P_i, P_j \in \mathcal{P}$ *with the largest* $\delta(P_i, P_j)$
  · *if* $|P_i \cup P_j| > minSize$ *or* $P_i \cup P_j$ *is the last one in* $\mathcal{P}$:
    · *remove* $P_i \cup P_j$ *from* $\mathcal{P}$ *and add it to* $\mathcal{R}$
return R

A straightforward implementation of this algorithm has a complexity of $O(n^2 \log n)$ [29]. As bottom-up clustering is a classic algorithmic framework, scalable implementations have been proposed, e.g., [38, 5]. Due to the reduction step, the input size becomes much smaller than the number of tuples. Our results in Section 7 indicate that the partitioning algorithm can run efficiently even with a naïve implementation, and the cost bottleneck of the entire blocking process is still on the actual data movement, not on the partitioning algorithm.

Constructing the blocking map. The output of the algorithm is a partitioning of the vectors. We use this output to construct a *blocking map* which returns a block id for a given feature vector. A data tuple can be routed to the right block by consulting the blocking map with its corresponding feature vector.

5. FEATURE-BASED DATA SKIPPING

In order to enhance the data skipping, we now introduce the block catalog, which maintains the metadata for skipping. We also discuss how a query optimizer might use it.

As mentioned earlier, many query engines support data skipping using the value ranges or bloom filters. We could import our block data to these systems and rely on the built-in skipping mechanism. This, however, may miss some data skipping opportunities. For example, the features we used to guide partitioning can involve multiple columns (e.g.,F_3 in Figure 2); checking the aggregates of the two columns individually may not be able to prune the block, while maintaining multi-dimensional statistics is expensive. In addition, it is unclear how the aggregates can be used to prune string matching and general user-define functions. To fully exploit our blocking scheme for data skipping, we propose a feature-based skipping mechanism, which can be used in conjunction with existing data skipping mechanisms based on the aggregates.

Block Catalog. After the blocking, we obtain a union vector for each block. If the i-th bit of the union vector is 0, then we know that no tuple in this block satisfies feature i. Therefore, the queries that are subsumed by feature i can safely skip this partition. To realize this, we store the features used and one union vector for each block in a *block catalog*, which can be part of the system catalog in a database system. Figure 5 shows the partition catalog for the example blocking in Figure 2. Note that the block catalog is very compact: we store the features once and then one bit vector for each block.

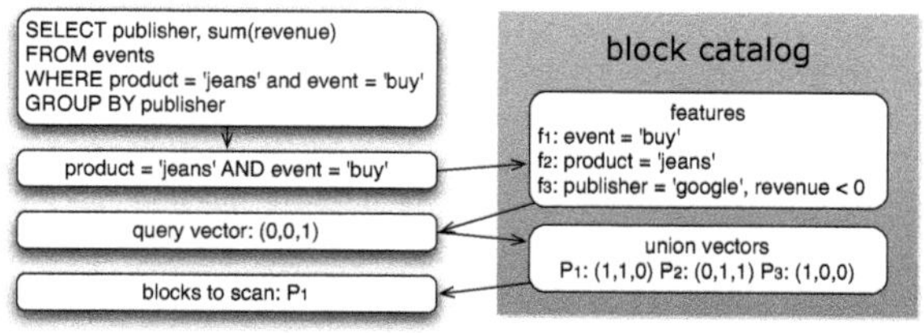

Figure 5: Data Skipping in Query Execution

Query Execution. Let us see how a query interacts with the block catalog in Figure 5. When a query comes, we first extract the filter operator from the query. We check which features in the block catalog can subsume this query. The subsumption check can be implemented as hard-coded rules. We find that F_1 and F_2 can subsume the query. We represent this information by a *query vector* $(0, 0, 1)$, the i-th bit of which is 0 if i-th feature subsumes the query. We then compute, for each block, a bitwise `OR` between the query vector and the union vector. For any block, if the resulting vector of the `OR` operation has at least one 0 bit, then this block can be skipped. In Figure 5, the `OR`ed vectors for P_1, P_2 and P_3 are $(1, 1, 1)$, $(0, 1, 1)$ and $(1, 0, 1)$ respectively. Thus, we know that we only need to scan P_1. This information is then passed to table scan operator.

The above procedure happens before the table scan operator and is independent of the rest of query execution. As we can see, we only need to maintain minimal metadata and add an simple module between query compilation and the start of the query execution. We have implemented this functionality in less than 100 lines of code in Shark [37].

6. DISCUSSION

In this section, we discuss the practical issues of using our techniques.

Data Update. Our blocking techniques were designed for a data warehouse setting, where there are infrequent ad-hoc updates and data are batch-inserted and batch-deleted as partitions. We can apply our fine-grained blocking on each partition separately. Therefore, the insertion or deletion of partitions will not affect other parts of data. Nevertheless, we now discuss how ad-hoc updates can be handled for our blocked data.

Since our techniques produce small balanced-sized data blocks, ad-hoc insertions should be put into new blocks instead of modifying existing blocks. These new blocks are ready to serve queries. Once we have accumulated enough new data, e.g., 50 blocks' worth of data, we can use our techniques to re-organize these data. An ad-hoc deletion can be handled trivially, as a tuple can be removed from a block without modifying the block metadata. When there is an ad-hoc update in a block, we check if we need to update the block metadata, i.e., the union vector. To allow for high-throughput updates, we can simply *invalidate* the union vector by setting all of its bits to 1's to eliminate the checking overhead. After many updates, the blocking scheme may become ineffective, then we can re-partition the data.

Parameter Selection. Two key parameters were used in our blocking process, namely, $numFeat$, the number of features, and $minSize$, the minimum number of tuples per block. For a real-world workload, we expect $numFeat$ to be small. We can use cross validations to choose an appropriate number of features that prevents under- and over-fitting.

The choice of $minSize$ can depend on the underlying system. In our prototype on Shark, we set $minSize$ to be 50,000, which results in 64-128MB blocks. Each block nicely fits with a Spark/HDFS block. Intuitively, if a block is bigger than 128MB, the system will break it down into many HDFS blocks anyway. If the blocks are too small, the metadata storage and skip checking overhead may become significant.

Overhead of Skip Checking. In many large-scale query engines, the query optimizer runs in a single node. We can easily perform the skip checking (Section 5) in a single-node optimizer. This might seem counter-intuitive, as a large table can have many blocks. To see if this makes sense, we can do some back-of-the-envelope analysis. Assuming an average block size of 128MB, 100TB of data would have less than 1 million blocks. It only takes 13MB to store the bit vectors for all these partitions if each vector is 128-bit, i.e., 128 features used. The block catalog can easily fit in the memory of a single machine. In a modern CPU, a bitwise operation of two 128-bit vectors can be computed using only a single instruction. The block checking incurs minimal overhead even for interactive queries.

Objective Function. Our objective function for partitioning (Equation 2) is defined as the sum of query costs in the workload, where the cost of a query is quantified as the number of tuples scanned. We chose the current objective function as it is simple, commonly used in database designs (e.g., [20]) and works reasonably well in practice. In some applications, we may want to define the objective differently, e.g., we can maximize the number of queries in the workload that can finish in 30 seconds. In this case, we may need to estimate the query costs and weight the queries based on their costs. Incorporating these in our framework would be an interesting avenue of future work.

7. EXPERIMENTAL EVALUATION

In this section, we report the experiment results. All experiments were conducted on an Amazon Spark EC2 cluster of 25 m2.4xlarge instances, each with 8 × 2.66 GHz CPU cores, 64.8 GB of RAM and 2 × 840 GB disk storage. The datasets are stored in HDFS.

7.1 System Prototype

We prototype our blocking techniques on Shark [37], a fully Apache Hive [8]-compatible data warehousing system using Apache Spark [25] as runtime. Shark parses and compiles HiveQL (SQL-like) queries to a query plan, which are then translated to Spark tasks. A Shark table is stored as a Spark data abstraction called Resilient Distributed Dataset (RDD), which is physically stored as a list of data blocks, each of which can be either memory- or disk-resident. Each block in Spark is a data processing unit and has a default size of 128MB. Shark supports data skipping over such data blocks. At data import time, Shark collects the data statistics for each block. These statistics are maintained in the system catalog. Before a table scan, the query filter is applied on these statistics, and then the block ids to be scanned are passed to the table scan operator.

We now briefly discuss how our techniques were implemented on Shark.

Workload Analyzer. We can collect a query trace from the query logging system of Shark or from an external source. We used Shark's query parser to convert each query string into a set of conjunctive filter operators. We implemented a `isSubsume`(f_1, f_2) function using a set of rules to check if filter f_1 subsumes filter f_2. A module was added in Shark to implement the techniques in Section 3.

Featurization, Reduce. We wrote a map function for featurization and a reduce function to group by the vectors.

Partition, Shuffle. We implemented a bottom-up clustering algorithm as a module in Shark. Note that this module is independent of the other parts of the blocking workflow, and thus external libraries could be used here. We then constructed a Spark Partitioner, which returns the destination block id for an (vector, tuple) pair. The table (an RDD) are then shuffled using this Partitioner.

Catalog Update. We added the metadata described in Section 5 to the Shark system catalog. A table scan now can utilize two tiers of skipping mechanisms: our feature-based skipping (Section 5) and the existing skipping.

7.2 Datasets

TPC-H. We use the TPC-H benchmark with a scale factor of 100. To focus on the effect of reduced table scan, we denormalize all the tables against the *lineitem* table, which results in a single table of roughly 600 million rows and 700 GB in size. We select eight query templates (q_3, q_5, q_6, q_8, q_{10}, q_{12}, q_{14}, q_{19}) from the TPC-H workload, as these templates involve the *lineitem* table and have selective filters. The FROM clauses in these templates were all changed to be the denormalized table. In a query template, some filters are fixed while the others are parametric. For example, the return item reporting query (q_{10}) has a fixed filter *l_returnflag = 'R'*, which will appear in every query generated from this template, and a parametric filter *o_orderdate >= date '[DATE]'*, where *[DATE]* is replaced with a constant at each run. Using the TPC-H query generator, we generate 800 queries as the training workload, 100 from each template. We then independently generate 80 queries for testing, 10 from each template. TPC-H represents a workload of template-generated queries, which is very common in real-world applications. Note that our approach can greatly take advantage of the fixed filters in a template (e.g., *l_returnflag = 'R'*), as they are perfectly predictable.

TPC-H Skewed. The TPC-H query generator assumes a uniform distribution for the predicate constants. In many real-world workloads, the constant distributions are skewed. For example, *region='North America'* may be queried much more often than the other regions for a U.S. company. To test a skewed distribution, we modified the TPC-H query generator to follow a Zipf distribution. As most parameters in the query templates have a small number of possible values, we chose a high skew factor of 3. For example, `REGION` only has 5 possible values, and by using a skew factor of 3, the most frequent 20% values occur in 84.3% of the generated queries. Note that we only added the skewness to the non-date filters, while [DATE] is still uniformly distributed. We similarly generate 800 train queries and 80 test queries under this Zipf distribution.

Conviva. The Conviva data is an anonymized user access log of video streams. The data consists of a single large fact table with 104 columns, such as customer ID, city, media URL, genre, date, time, browser type and request response time. We also obtained an in-production SQL query trace from Conviva, which has 735 queries for problem diagnosis and data analytics issued on the log data. The queries were between 08/01/2012 and 11/30/2012. We split the query

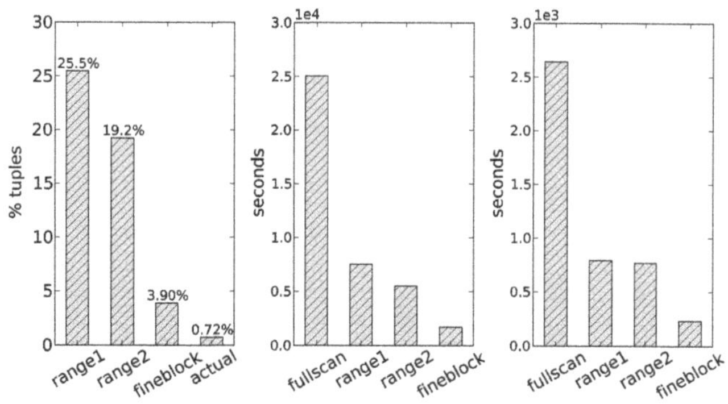

(a) % tuples scanned (b) on-disk query (c) in-memory query

Figure 6: Query Performance on TPC-H

trace at the date of 11/24/2012, which results in 674 training queries (before 11/24/2012) and 61 testing queries (on and after 11/24/2012). Based on the training queries, we partition the log data from 11/24/2012 to 11/30/2012. This snapshot of the log has 680 million tuples and is roughly 1 TB in size when stored as text. We evaluate the performance of running the test queries on the blocked data.

7.3 TPC-H Results

7.3.1 Query Performance

We evaluate the effect of our blocking techniques on query performance. We measure the number of tuples scanned and end-to-end query response time for different blocking and skipping schemes in Figure 6. Specifically, we compare the following alternatives:

`fullscan`: We disable the data skipping and do a full scan for each query. The blocking scheme is immaterial here.

`range1`: We perform a workload-oblivious partitioning on *o_orderdate* and each date is a partition. This leads to roughly 2300 partitions. Shark's data skipping is used.

`range2`: We manually devise a composite range partitioning scheme on multiple columns. By identifying the frequently queried columns from the workload, we perform a range partitioning on {*o_orderdate* (by month, 78 partitions), *r_name* (customer region name, 5 partitions), *c_mktsegment* (5 partitions), *quantity* (5 partitions)}. This results in roughly 9000 partitions. Shark's data skipping is used.

`fineblock`: This is our approach. We first partition by month on *o_orderdate*. We use the workload analyzer to extract 15 features from the 800 training queries (by setting $numFeat$=15). Note that we do not consider any date filters as features and will rely on the month partitions to prune data. Using these features, we run a partitioner instance on each month partition in parallel. An average month partition has 7.7 million tuples. By setting $minSize$= $50k$, a month partition has around 100 blocks. The total number of blocks is roughly 8000. We used both our feature-based skipping (Section 5) and Shark's existing skipping.

We evaluate the performance of running 80 test queries (as mentioned in Section 7.2) using the above alternatives. Figure 6(a) shows the percentage of tuples scanned for the 80 queries relative to `fullscan`. As we can see, the existing data skipping with `range1` and `range2` only scan 25% and 19% of the tuples scanned by `fullscan` respectively. The tuples scanned by `fineblock` is only 3.9% of `fullscan`, a 5x improvement over the manual range partitioning scheme `range2`. As a reference, the bar `actual` shows the percentage of tuples that must be scanned, i.e., the tuples that actually satisfy the filters, which is 0.7% of `fullscan`.

To test the end-to-end query response time, we consider two scenarios: when the table is entirely on disk and when the data is entirely in memory. Figure 6(b) shows the query response times for on-disk data. We run the 80 test queries in a sequence and record the sum of their response time. We cleared the OS cache before running each query. As shown, the query response time for `range1` and `range2` are 30% and 21% of that for `fullscan`. `fineblock` only took 7% of the time for *fullscan*, 23% for `range1` and 30% for `range2`. This is an 3-4x improvement over the range partitioning schemes. Figure 6 shows the query response time for memory-resident data. In Shark, we can simply cache a table in memory by executing:

```
create table tpch_cached as select * from tpch;
```

We configured our distributed RAM cache to be large enough to hold the entire table. As we can see, `fineblock` only took 30% and 32% of the time taken for `range1` and `range2`, respectively. This is roughly a 3x improvement. It is interesting to note that the end-to-end improvement for in-memory data is slightly smaller than that for on-disk data. As scanning in-memory data is much faster, the effect of skipping in-memory blocks is less significant.

We also tested the end-to-end performance for TPC-H Skewed. The amount of tuples scanned by `fineblock` is only 8% and 10% of that by `range1` and `range2` respectively. For the on-disk data, `fineblock` took 20% and 23% of the time for `range1` and `range2` respectively; for the in-memory data, `fineblock` took 22% and 29% of the time for `range1` and `range2` respectively. Note that our improvement for TPC-H Skewed is better than for TPC-H. The skewness in the filter distribution allows a small number of features to subsume even more queries, and thus makes our techniques even more effective for TPC-H Skewed.

On both TPC-H and TPC-H Skewed, we observe that our approaches significantly reduce the data scanned, which effectively translate to an improvement in end-to-end query response time for both disk- and memory-resident data.

7.3.2 Effect of minSize

Intuitively, the smaller the block size is, the more chance we can skip data. In Figure 7, we plot the total number of tuples scanned using our approach for answering the 80 test queries in TPC-H and TPC-H Skewed by varing $minSize$, with $numFeat$=15. Since the two curves represent two different workloads, for fair comparison, we plot the ratio of the number of tuples scanned to the number of tuples that have to be scanned. Thus, a y-value of 5 in the curve means we scanned 5 times as many tuples as necessary.

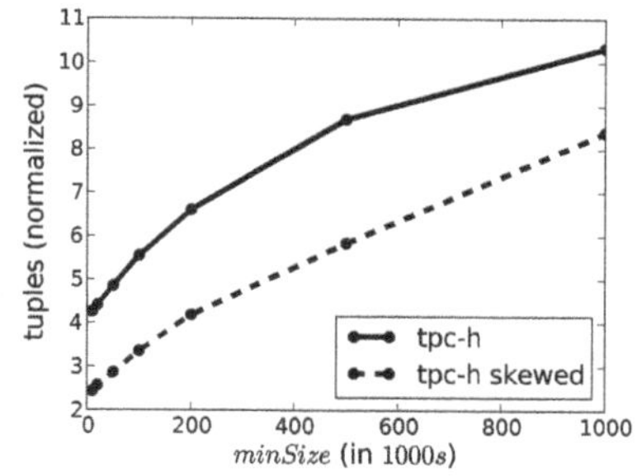

Figure 7: Effect of *minSize* on TPC-H

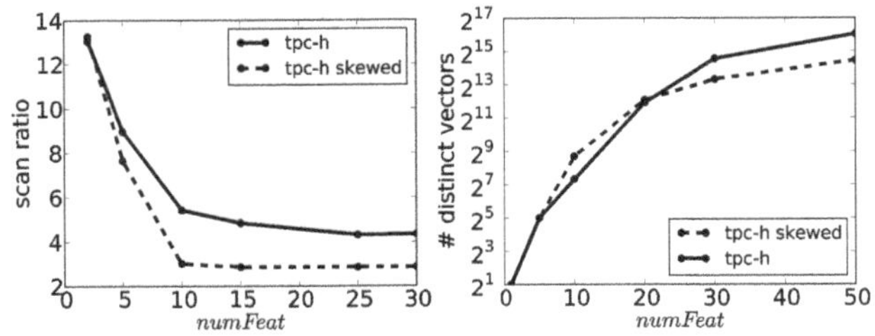

(a) % tuples vs. *numFeat* (b) # vectors vs. *numFeat*

Figure 8: Effect of *numFeat* on TPC-H

We make several observations. First, for both curves, we scan more data as the block size increases. Second, data skipping is even more effective on TPC-H skewed. Recall our workload assumptions in Section 2, many real workloads tend to have skewed predicate distribution. If the filter predicates are skewed, a small set of features can cover more queries. Third, the number of tuples scanned is not sensitive to the block size. In particular, increasing *minSize* from $5k$ to $200k$ only make the scan twice as much for both workloads. This gives us a wide range of choosing *minSize*. For example, in our experiment on Shark, we set *minSize*=$50k$, which make each block nicely fit in a Spark/HDFS block file (128MB by default).

7.3.3 Effect of *numFeat*

Figure 8 plots the number of tuples scanned by varying *numFeat*. The numbers are also normalized as in Figure 7. As we can see, when using too few features, e.g., < 5, we have to scan a lot of more tuples, as these features are not representative enough for the workload. As we add more features, the effectiveness of skipping quickly stabilizes and TPC-H Skewed consistently benefits more from our blocking. We can see that, for both TPC-H and TPC-H Skewed, a small set of features is sufficient. Even though the predicates in TPC-H are uniformly distributed, the fixed filters play an important role as features. For example, the feature *l_returnflag = 'R'* in template q_{10} can subsume 100 out of 800 training queries (and also 10 out of 80 testing queries), since all the queries generated from template q_{10} have this filter. TPC-H Skewed performs even better due to the skewness in the parametric predicates. This curve also suggests that adding more features will not significantly hurt the effectiveness of skipping, though this may hurt the blocking efficiency. This is because the highly weighted features will dominate and adding more features with small weights will not dramatically change the blocking solution.

As discussed, one important effect of *numFeat* is on the number of distinct feature vectors. We cannot afford to run a bottom-up clustering algorithm if the number of distinct vectors is too large, e.g., close to the number of tuples. Theoretically, with m features and n tuples, the number of distinct vectors is upper-bounded $min(2^m, n)$. In Figure 8, we plot the actual number of distinct vectors by varying *numFeat* in base-2 log scale. The plot shows that the number of distinct vectors is much smaller than either 2^m or n. This is because these features have low selectivities and can be correlated.

7.3.4 Blocking Time

Figure 9 shows the breakdown cost of blocking a month partition in TPC-H. An average month partition has 7.7 million tuples and 8G in size and can be divided into roughly

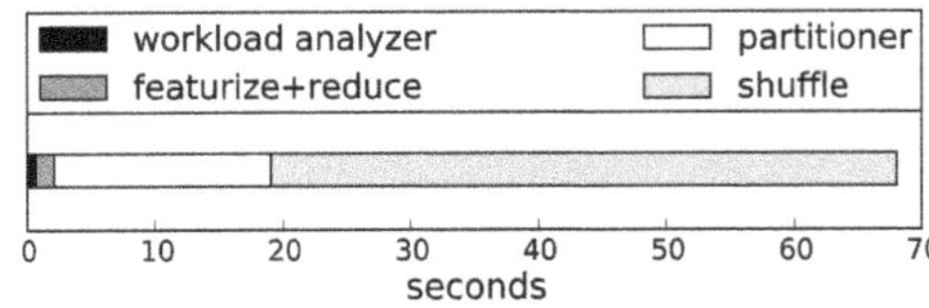

Figure 9: Breakdown of blocking time

100 blocks. We set *numFeat* = 15 and *minSize* = 50. It took about 1 minute for the entire workflow. When loading multiple partitions simultaneously, we can run multiple blocking processes in parallel. As we can see, the shuffling is still the bottleneck, although we run sophisticated algorithms in the workload analyzer and the partitioner. The workload analyzer runs a frequent itemset-based algorithm from 800 queries. The partitioner runs a bottom-up clustering algorithm on 1315 feature vectors. In our experiments, we only used our own vanilla implementations for these algorithms running on a single thread, which were sufficiently efficient. Notice that both components can be further optimized, e.g., using an off-the-shelf library. We combined the cost of featurization and reduce, as they were implemented as Spark map and reduce functions which can pipelined.

7.4 Conviva Results

7.4.1 Query Performance

For evaluating the query performance, we compare the following alternatives:

`fullscan`: We perform a full scan for each query.

`range`: We perform a range partitioning on date and a frequently queried column. We use Shark's data skipping.

`fineblock`: We first partition by date. After extracting 40 features from the training queries (*numFeat*=40), we block each date partition with *minSize* =$50k$. We use both our feature-based and Shark's existing skipping mechanisms.

Figure 10(a) shows the percentage of tuples scanned for evaluating the test queries, relative to `fullscan`. As we can see, `range` already reduced the scan to be 1.81% of `fullscan`, `fineblock` only scans 0.23% of the data. The average selectivity of these queries (i.e., `actual` is 0.03% of `fullscan`. Figure 10(b) shows the query response times for on-disk data. We can find that `range` spent 13% the time as `fullscan`, and `fineblock` further reduced the time to be 2.6% of `fullscan`. This is a 5x improvement over `range`. Figure 10(c) shows the query time for in memory data. We find that `range` and `fineblock` used 16% and 8.1% of the time taken by `fullscan`. The improvement of `fineblock` over the range partitioning schemes is 2x.

As scanning in-memory data is fast, the effect of data scan reduction is diminished by the cost from other parts of the query evaluation such as aggregations. Specifically, we observed that some Conviva queries computed many aggregated values in the SELECT statement, which can be CPU-intensive after the data scan. Incorporating techniques that speed up these aggregations (e.g., materializations) may make our end-to-end improvement more significant.

7.4.2 Effect of *numFeat*

We now study the effect of *numFeat* on the Conviva workload. Figure 11(a) plots the scan ratio by varying *numFeat*. The number of tuples scanned is dramatically reduced as *numFeat* is increased from 2 to 20. As we continue to add more features, however, the curve is relative flat. This is

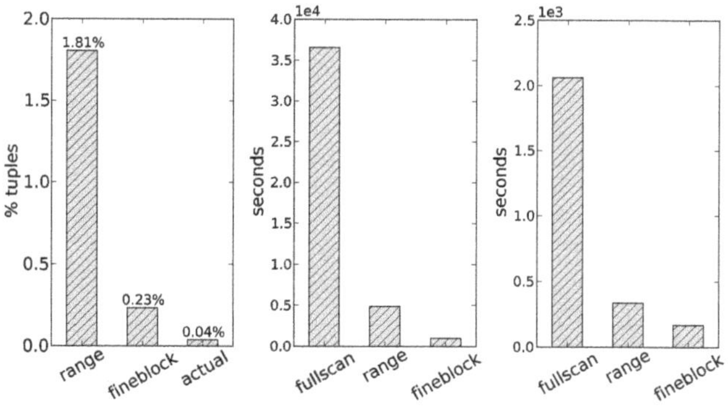

(a) % tuples scanned (b) on-disk query (c) in-memory query

Figure 10: Query Performance on Conviva

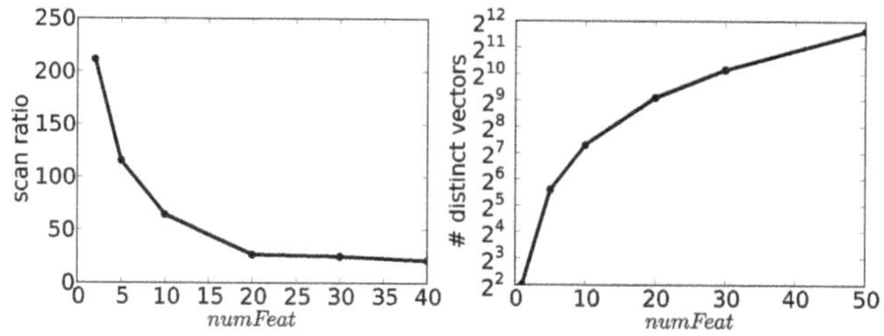

(a) % tuples vs. *numFeat* (b) # vectors vs. *numFeat*

Figure 11: Effect of *numFeat* on Conviva

inline with the results on TPC-H (Figure 8), except that this curves starts to stabilize at 20 instead of 10. This result confirms that a small number of features is sufficient for a real workload. In Figure 11(b), we can see that the number of distinct vectors is small.

We can conclude that, in a real-world workload, (1) our blocking can effectively help queries skip data and in turn reduce the query response time significantly for both on-disk and in-memory data, and (2) the blocking can be done effectively and efficiently with a small number of features.

8. RELATED WORK

In this section, we review the related work.

Horizontal Partitioning. Range and hash partitioning are the most widely used horizontal partitioning techniques and serve for many purposes, such as load balancing. Advanced and automated partitioning techniques have also been extensively studied [15, 39, 30, 11], but they were built on top of range or hash partitioning. Although the blocking problem we study is a form of horizontal partitioning, we generate a tuple-level partitioning map by solving an optimization problem instead of using explicit range constraints. Our techniques can be used to further segment a date-range partition into finer blocks for skipping purposes. While Schism [17] also used fine-grained tuple-level partitioning, they had a different objective, which is reducing cross-machine transactions for OLTP workloads.

Materialized Aggregates and Skipping. Many databases utilize range partitions to enhance query performance. Partition pruning (e.g., Oracle [3] and Postgres [4]) allows queries to skip partitions based on partition key ranges (e.g., date). Extending this idea, other works [28, 34] have proposed maintaining small materialized aggregates (SMAs) for each range-partitioned block, such as min, max, count, sum and histograms for each column. For a given query, these SMAs can be used to classify the data blocks into three categories: (C1) *irrelevant* blocks, the ones in which no tuple satisfies the query, (C2) *relevant* blocks, the ones in which all the tuples satisfy the query, and (C3) *suspect* blocks, the ones in which some tuples may satisfy the query.

Obviously, the blocks in C1 can be safely skipped. The C3 blocks can also be skipped when the requested aggregates can be answered by SMAs. We note that the opportunity of identifying and skipping C3 blocks can be rather limited in practice, as it requires that 1) all the (conjunctive) filters of the query subsume the block's min and max ranges and 2) all the requested aggregates can be answerable by the chosen SMAs and if the query contains a group-by, the SMAs must be stored for all of the potentially relevant groups. A number of systems, e.g., [7, 37, 6, 35], use a simplified version of SMAs, which only skip C1 blocks and do not distinguish C2 from C3 blocks. Similar to these systems, our techniques only consider skipping C1 blocks. While these previous approaches are built on top of range partitioning, our main contribution is to develop a novel fine-grained partitioning technique based on workload analysis, which can turn more blocks into C1 blocks than a range partitioning. Nevertheless, the idea of using SMAs to skip C3 blocks can also be implemented on top of our partitioning scheme.

Materialized View Selection. Our work is related to the well studied problem of materialized view selection (MVS), since both exploit pre-computations for query performance improvement. These two problems, however, differ fundamentally in several ways. First, our partitioning is at the file-organization level, while MVS is at the application level; in fact, our techniques can be used to partition large materialized views. Second, we utilize pre-computation to guide the tuple re-arrangement and only need to maintain minimal metadata (i.e., a bit vector per block), while MVS does not change the original data but store the precomputed results, which can incur significant space overhead, e.g., data cubes. Third, MVS is an optimization problem constrained on space [20, 10] or maintenance cost [19], while ours is constrained on the number of partitions.

Similar to our approach, some MVS approaches also exploit workload information. Most of these focus on the group-by columns of the queries (e.g., [16, 14]) for deciding which columns to pre-aggregate. Others (e.g., [10]) also consider which columns are filtered on for selecting indexes and materialized views in an integrated manner. Different from this work, our workload analysis aims to identify representative filters, including both filter columns and constants, and their subsumption relations for skipping purposes. We consider all kinds of filters, such as equality/range conditions, string matching and user defined functions.

Workload-driven Physical Design. Many research efforts have been devoted to utilizing workload information for automating database design. For example, the AutoAdmin project [10, 11] integrates many physical design problems, such as selecting indexes and materialized views; Database Cracking [21] reorders the data columns as a byproduct of query processing to benefit future queries; ARF [12] tunes a range-based filter for skipping cold data; BlinkDB [31] prepares samples offline based on the workload.

Optimization Problems for Partitioning. Finding an optimal partitioning over a set of data points is an important problem in many applications, such as data mining, computer vision [33], gene expression analysis [23] and VLSI design [24]. The partitioning problem is NP-hard for many objective functions, e.g., [13]. To the best of our knowledge, no existing work has formulated the k-MaxSkip problem before, although we found k-MaxSkip and $BalancedMaxSkip$ are closely related to several partitioning problems, such as hypergraph cut [24], discrete basis partitioning problem [27] and row-exclusive biclustering [26].

9. CONCLUSION

We presented fine-grained data blocking techniques, which partition the data tuples into blocks in a way that could help queries skip data. The key components were: (1) a workload analyzer, which generates a set of features from a query log, (2) a partitioner, which computes a blocking scheme by solving a optimization problem, (3) a feature-based block skipping framework used in query execution. We prototyped our techniques on Shark, which showed that our blocking modules can be easily added to an existing query engine and the data flow can be executed using standard data marshalling steps, such as map and reduce.

We evaluated the effectiveness of our techniques using TPC-H workload and a real-world ad-hoc workload, which showed that our blocking scheme made the queries scan 5-7x less data than traditional range-based blocking schemes. The results also indicated that the reduction on data scan can directly translate to the reduction on query response time, for both memory- and disk-resident data.

Acknowledgements. We thank Ion Stoica for providing the Conviva dataset. We also thank Sameer Agarwal, Ameet Talwalkar, Di Wang, Jiannan Wang and the reviewers for their insightful feedback. This research is supported in part by NSF CISE Expeditions Award CCF-1139158, LBNL Award 7076018, and DARPA XData Award FA8750-12-2-0331, and gifts from Amazon Web Services, Google, SAP, The Thomas and Stacey Siebel Foundation, Apple, Inc., Cisco, Cloudera, EMC, Ericsson, Facebook, GameOnTalis, Guavus, Hortonworks, Huawei, Intel, Microsoft, NetApp, Pivotal, Samsung, Splunk, Virdata, VMware, WANdisco and Yahoo!.

10. REFERENCES

[1] IBM Netezza. http://www.netezza.com.
[2] Impala. https://github.com/cloudera/impala.
[3] Oracle. http://docs.oracle.com/.
[4] Postgres. http://www.postgresql.org/docs/.
[5] H. Koga *et al.* Fast agglomerative hierarchical clustering algorithm using locality-sensitive hashing. *Knowledge and Information Systems*, 12(1), 2007.
[6] A. Hall *et al.* Processing a trillion cells per mouse click. *PVLDB*, 5(11):1436–1446, 2012.
[7] A. Lamb *et al.* The Vertica analytic database: C-Store 7 years later. *VLDB*, 5(12):1790–1801, 2012.
[8] A. Thusoo *et al.* Hive: a warehousing solution over a map-reduce framework. *PVLDB*, 2(2):1626–1629, 2009.
[9] R. Agrawal and R. Srikant. Fast algorithms for mining association rules in large databases. In *VLDB*, pages 487–499, 1994.
[10] S. Agrawal, S. Chaudhuri, and V. R. Narasayya. Automated selection of materialized views and indexes in SQL databases. In *VLDB*, pages 496–505, 2000.
[11] S. Agrawal, V. Narasayya, and B. Yang. Integrating vertical and horizontal partitioning into automated physical database design. In *SIGMOD*, pages 359–370, 2004.
[12] K. Alexiou, D. Kossmann, and P.-A. Larson. Adaptive range filters for cold data: Avoiding trips to Siberia. *PVLDB*, 6(14):1714–1725, 2013.
[13] D. Aloise, A. Deshpande, P. Hansen, and P. Popat. NP-hardness of euclidean sum-of-squares clustering. *Machine Learning*, 75(2):245–248, 2009.
[14] K. Aouiche, P.-E. Jouve, and J. Darmont. Clustering-based materialized view selection in data warehouses. In *Advances in Databases and Information Systems*, pages 81–95, 2006.
[15] B. Bhattacharjee *et al.* Efficient query processing for multi-dimensionally clustered tables in DB2. In *VLDB*, pages 963–974, 2003.
[16] E. Baralis, S. Paraboschi, and E. Teniente. Materialized views selection in a multidimensional database. In *VLDB*, volume 97, pages 156–165, 1997.
[17] C. Curino, E. Jones, Y. Zhang, and S. Madden. Schism: a workload-driven approach to database replication and partitioning. *PVLDB*, 3:48–57, 2010.
[18] M. R. Garey and D. S. Johnson. *Computers and Intractability*. 1990.
[19] H. Gupta and I. Mumick. Selection of views to materialize under a maintenance cost constraint. In *ICDT*, pages 453–470, 1999.
[20] V. Harinarayan, A. Rajaraman, and J. D. Ullman. Implementing data cubes efficiently. In *SIGMOD Record*, volume 25, pages 205–216, 1996.
[21] S. Idreos, M. L. Kersten, and S. Manegold. Database cracking. In *CIDR*, pages 68–78, 2007.
[22] J. Han *et al.* Frequent pattern mining: current status and future directions. *DMKD*, 15(1):55–86, 2007.
[23] D. Jiang, C. Tang, and A. Zhang. Cluster analysis for gene expression data: a survey. *IEEE TKDE*, 16(11), 2004.
[24] G. Karypis, R. Aggarwal, V. Kumar, and S. Shekhar. Multilevel hypergraph partitioning: applications in VLSI domain. *IEEE Trans. on VLSI*, 7(1):69–79, 1999.
[25] M. Zaharia *et al.* Resilient distributed datasets: a fault-tolerant abstraction for in-memory cluster computing. In *NSDI*, pages 2–2, 2012.
[26] S. C. Madeira and A. L. Oliveira. Biclustering algorithms for biological data analysis: A survey. *IEEE Trans. on Computational Biology and Bioinformatics*, 1(1):24–45, 2004.
[27] P. Miettinen, T. Mielikainen, A. Gionis, G. Das, and H. Mannila. The discrete basis problem. *IEEE TKDE*, 20(10):1348–1362, 2008.
[28] G. Moerkotte. Small materialized aggregates: A light weight index structure for data warehousing. In *VLDB*, pages 476–487, 1998.
[29] A. Rajaraman and J. D. Ullman. *Mining of massive datasets*. Cambridge, 2012.
[30] J. Rao, C. Zhang, N. Megiddo, and G. Lohman. Automating physical database design in a parallel database. In *SIGMOD*, pages 558–569, 2002.
[31] S. Agarwal *et al.* BlinkDB: queries with bounded errors and bounded response times on very large data. In *EuroSys*, pages 29–42, 2013.
[32] S. Melnik *et al.* Dremel: interactive analysis of webale datasets. *PVLDB*, 3(1-2):330–339, 2010.
[33] J. Shi and J. Malik. Normalized cuts and image segmentation. *IEEE TPAMI*, 22:888–905, 1997.
[34] D. Ślęzak, J. Wróblewski, V. Eastwood, and P. Synak. Brighthouse: An analytic data warehouse for ad-hoc queries. *PVLDB*, 1(2):1337–1345, 2008.
[35] V. Raman *et al.* DB2 with BLU acceleration: So much more than just a column store. *PVLDB*, 6(11):1080–1091, 2013.
[36] J. Ward. Hierarchical grouping to optimize an objective function. *J. American statistical association*, (301):236–244.
[37] R. S. Xin, J. Rosen, M. Zaharia, M. J. Franklin, S. Shenker, and I. Stoica. Shark: SQL and Rich Analytics at Scale. In *SIGMOD*, pages 13–24, 2013.
[38] T. Zhang, R. Ramakrishnan, and M. Livny. Birch: An efficient data clustering method for very large databases. In *SIGMOD*, pages 103–114, 1996.
[39] J. Zhou, N. Bruno, and W. Lin. Advanced partitioning techniques for massively distributed computation. In *SIGMOD*, pages 13–24, 2012.

DSH: Data Sensitive Hashing for High-Dimensional k-NN Search

Jinyang Gao[‡] H. V. Jagadish[§] Wei Lu[‡] Beng Chin Ooi[‡]

[‡]School of Computing
National University of Singapore
{jinyang.gao, luwei1, ooibc}@comp.nus.edu.sg

[§]Department of EECS
University of Michigan
jag@umich.edu

ABSTRACT

The need to locate the k-nearest data points with respect to a given query point in a multi- and high-dimensional space is common in many applications. Therefore, it is essential to provide efficient support for such a search. Locality Sensitive Hashing (LSH) has been widely accepted as an effective hash method for high-dimensional similarity search. However, data sets are typically not distributed uniformly over the space, and as a result, the buckets of LSH are unbalanced, causing the performance of LSH to degrade.

In this paper, we propose a new and efficient method called *Data Sensitive Hashing* (DSH) to address this drawback. DSH improves the hashing functions and hashing family, and is orthogonal to most of the recent state-of-the-art approaches which mainly focus on indexing and querying strategies. DSH leverages data distributions and is capable of directly preserving the nearest neighbor relations. We show the theoretical guarantee of DSH, and demonstrate its efficiency experimentally.

Keywords

High Dimensions, Similarity Search, Hashing, LSH

1. INTRODUCTION

In a wide range of applications, data can be represented as points in a multi-dimensional space. For example, feature vectors are often used to represent multi-media data such as images and music. Similarly, a company may use a number of attributes for profiling each customer, or for each product. Each attribute, or each element of a feature vector, can be considered as a dimension in a multi-dimensional space in which each object is a point. Similarity search consequently is transformed to finding points in this multi-dimensional space that are close to a given query point. In many applications, we may be interested in data points that are within some distance of a query point. However, we may not have a meaningful way of setting a distance threshold, and instead we seek the k-nearest points (e.g. the results displayed in the first page of search engine). Therefore, it is essential to support efficient k-nearest neighbor (k-NN) search.

SIGMOD'14, June 22–27, 2014, Snowbird, UT, USA.

http://dx.doi.org/10.1145/2588555.2588565.

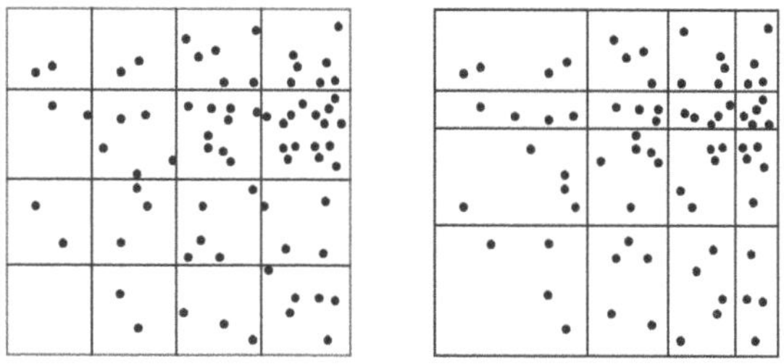

(a) LSH (b) DSH

Figure 1: Motivation

Access methods in the multi-dimensional space, including the k-NN problem, have been studied extensively. However, most of them suffer from the so-called curse of dimensionality and demonstrate poor performance when the number of dimensions is high [21]. One technique that shows promise in high-dimensional spaces is locality sensitive hashing (LSH) [10]. LSH relaxes the k-NN problem to a *c-approximate k-NN problem* that aims to find k points within distance $c \times R$ where R is the maximum distance between the query point and its k-nearest neighbors. In essence, LSH solves k-NN problem by first obtaining a set of *similar points* to q and then extracting the k-nearest points from these similar points. For this purpose, LSH designs a novel scheme to hash the points so that the possibility of collision is much higher for similar points than for dissimilar points. Similar objects are then identified by examining a certain number of points that collide with the query point. However, defining similar points is challenging, and as such LSH simply adopts a constant value r to define two points as similar if their distance is no greater than r. In essence, LSH searches for near neighbors within a radius r. For k-NN search, LSH performs well in a uniform data distribution setting in which a good-quality r can be derived. When the data are skewed, the distance between k-NN pairs can vary greatly, using a consistent r to define all similar points is inadequate. It is for this reason that LSH performance suffers. Figure 1a shows an example of the hashing results of LSH. On the indexing level, we see that the hashing is unbalanced, where some buckets are empty while a few buckets contain too many points. From the k-NN perspective, as the distance between k-nearest neighbor pairs can vary greatly, LSH solutions either have to maintain a huge set of indexes for different values r, or use one (or a few fixed) r which may lead to arbitrary bad results. More discussion will be given in Section 2.

Recently, there has been increasing attention focused on designing new indexes [20] or query strategies [13, 9] to alleviate the limitations of LSH. However, to the best of our knowledge, all of them are still based on locality-sensitive hashing families, i.e. random projections, which cannot adapt based on data distributions. Real data distributions are often non-uniform and frequently very skewed. Consequently, these methods still suffer from poor hashing effectiveness. In this paper, instead of trying to enhance LSH with the use of more efficient structures or processing strategies, we seek to address a more fundamental question: are there methods that can provide consistently effective hashing results regardless of the data distribution. To this end, we propose the concept of data-sensitive hashing (DSH) as an efficient mechanism for addressing the k-NN problem.

DSH directly deals with the k-NN problem instead of finding neighbors within a distance r. Hence, DSH avoids the issue of selecting the distance r that is required in LSH. DSH designs a novel scheme to facilitate the retrieval of a set of k-nearest neighbors with respect to a query point. Figure 1b shows the intuition of DSH. Since each bucket has a similar number of objects, its radius is adapted to the distance of k-NN. The basic idea of DSH is to hash the points such that the possibility of collision is much higher for k-NN pairs(unidirectional or bidirectional) than for non-k-NN pairs. It follows the same procedure as LSH for similarity search, the key difference being within the corresponding hashing families. Compared with random projections which have a large probability to hash the objects within a distance r together, our hashing family needs to have a large probability to hash the k-NN pairs together.

To find such hashing families, we learn from the data. Since we expect each k-NN pair to collide in most of the hashing functions, the requirement for hashing family can be represented as a strong classifier. Obviously, a single hashing function cannot protect all the k-NN pairs while separating all the non-k-NN pairs. Using spectral techniques, we can do an optimization on preserving the k-NN pairs while cutting the others. It is well known that adaptive boosting [8] is an efficient algorithm to generate a strong classifier using a set of weak classifiers. Therefore, we treat the hashing family as the strong classifier, and each hashing function in the family as a weak classifier. We adopt the adaptive boosting technique to ensure that the k-NN relations are theoretically protected by most of the hashing functions.

We summarize the contributions of the paper as follows.

- We propose a novel access method called Data Sensitive Hashing (DSH) to answer the k-nearest neighbor queries. Compared with LSH, DSH is able to capture the data distribution more effectively. Equipped with the distribution knowledge, DSH is able to deal with the k-NN problem in a more direct and efficient manner. DSH focuses on the hashing family, and thus most LSH extensions designed to enhance LSH are orthogonal to our proposal, and can be applied to DSH easily. (Sec. 3).

- We design an efficient algorithm to generate the data-sensitive hashing family – the key challenge for DSH. The algorithm combines adaptive boosting and spectral techniques, resulting in a good theoretical guarantee. The indexing time is also comparable with LSH. (Sec. 4).

- We experimentally verify the effectiveness and efficiency of our proposed DSH using three real datasets. Compared with LSH, our hashing results are much more balanced. Consequently, DSH is three times more efficient than LSH in query response time and index size in order to achieve the same quality of search results. (Sec. 5).

2. PRELIMINARIES

In this section, we provide the problem definition followed by a brief introduction and analysis of LSH. In the end, we review related work.

2.1 Problem Definition

In this paper, we consider data objects represented as points in a d-dimensional vector space R^d. Let $\|p,q\|$ be the distance measure between two points p and q in R^d. The k-nearest neighbor(k-NN) problem is defined as follows:

DEFINITION 1. **(k-nearest neighbor problem)** *Given a set O of n data points, a point $q \in R^d$ and an integer k, we aim to find the k data points that are nearest to q in O. We denote this answer set by $NN(q,k)$. Formally, $|NN(q,k)| = k$, $\forall o \in NN(q,k)$, $o' \in O \backslash NN(q,k)$, $\|q,o\| \le \|q,o'\|$.*

Typically, finding exact k-NN potentially results in a sequential scan of the entire dataset O, and its cost grows linearly with the cardinality of O. For this reason, approximate k-nearest neighbor problem is accepted as a compromise since the cost of the solution grows sub-linearly with the cardinality of O while the quality is within an acceptable level. We define the approximate k-nearest neighbor problem as follows:

DEFINITION 2. **(δ-recall k-NN problem)** *Given a set O of n data points, a point $q \in R^d$ and an integer k, the δ-recall k-NN problem aims to find a set of k points $\delta NN(q,k)$, such that $|\delta NN(q,k)| = k$, $|\delta NN(q,k) \cap NN(q,k)| \ge \delta \times k$.*

The definition provides a lower bound of the recall that at least $k \times \delta$ points of exact k-NN are returned. δ-recall k-NN problem is indeed compatible with c-approximate k-NN problem discussed in Section 1. In c-approximate k-NN problem, it provides the upper bound of the distance for the points to be returned. To achieve a similar upper bound in the δ-recall k-NN problem, we can relax k to a larger k' ($k' = k/\delta$), and select k points from $\delta NN(q,k')$ with the smallest distances. As a result, we can guarantee that the farthest distance of these k points to q is within R' where R' is the maximum distance between q and the k'th-NN.

2.2 Locality Sensitive Hashing

Locality Sensitive Hashing is an efficient approximate algorithm for high dimensional similarity search. It is efficient and provides a rigorous quality guarantee for finding similar points within a distance r, i.e. the r-NN problem.

DEFINITION 3. **(r-NN problem)** *Given a set O of n data points, a point $q \in R^d$ and a distance r, we aim to find the data points that are within a distance r to q in O. We denote the sphere centered at point q by $B(q,r)$. Formally, $B(q,r) = \{p | p \in R^d, \|p,q\| \le r\}$. The r-NN problem aims to find $\{o | o \in O \text{ and } o \in B(q,r)\}$.*

LSH leverages a family of functions where each function hashes the points in such a way that the possibility of collision is higher for similar points than for dissimilar points. Formally, an LSH family can be defined as follows [1]:

DEFINITION 4. **(LSH Family, $\mathcal{H}$)** *A family $\mathcal{H} = \{h : R^d \rightarrow U\}$ of functions is called (r, cr, p_1, p_2)-sensitive if for any $p, q \in R^d$*

- *if $p \in B(q,r)$, then $Pr_{\mathcal{H}}(h(p) = h(q)) \geq p_1$;*
- *if $p \notin B(q,cr)$, then $Pr_{\mathcal{H}}(h(p) = h(q)) \leq p_2$;*

The family of hash functions are generated through the use of random projections – the intuition is that points that are nearby in the space will also be nearby in all projections. While two distance points can also be close in all projections, the possibility is extremely small if enough number of projections is taken. Usually, the difference between p_1 and p_2 is not enough to be used directly. To enlarge the difference, a concatenation of LSH functions is applied to generate a hash key for each point in R^d.

DEFINITION 5. **(Concatenation LSH Functions, $\mathcal{G}$)** *A set of concatenation LSH functions $\mathcal{G} = \{g : R^d \rightarrow U^m\}$. Each $g_i \in \mathcal{G}$ consists of a sequence of m hash functions randomly extracted from $\mathcal{H}$. Formally,*

$$g_i(p) = (h_{i_1}(p), ..., h_{i_m}(p)),$$

where m is the number of hash functions in each concatenation and $h_{i_1}, ..., h_{i_m}$ are randomly selected from the LSH Family $\mathcal{H}$.

LSH applies these concatenation LSH functions to construct the hash tables. As a result,

- $\forall p \in B(q,r)$, $Pr(g(p) = g(q)) \geq p_1^m$
- $\forall p \in R^d \backslash B(q,cr)$, $Pr(g(p) = g(q)) \leq p_2^m$

Further, the expected number of points in O that collide with q but are outside the ball $B(q, cr)$ is less than $p_2^m * |O|$. However, the recall for one hash table, p_1^m, is not large. To raise the overall recall, LSH typically applies l concatenation LSH functions and constructs l hash tables. Each concatenation LSH function randomly chooses m functions in $\mathcal{H}$. When the number of functions in $\mathcal{H}$ is large enough, the hash results of different concatenation functions can be regarded as independent. Thus, for any $o \in B(q,r)$, the possibility that o collides with q in at least one hash table is at least $1 - (1 - p_1^m)^l$, which is very close to 1. To summarize, LSH answers c-approximate r-NN problem as follows:

1. **Pre-processing:** LSH maintains l hash tables, and each hash table is attached with a concatenation hash function. Each hash table applies its concatenation hash function to hash the points in O, where each concatenation hash function consists of m hash functions randomly selected from the hashing family $\mathcal{H}$;
2. **Query processing:** Given a query object q, LSH finds c-approximate r-NN by examining points that collide with q in each of the l hash tables. In particular, the expected number of objects outside the $B(q, cr)$ is limited by $l * p_2^m * |O|$. This property guarantees its query efficiency.

While LSH has been shown to be very effective in finding nearby points in high-dimensional space, we should note that this is accomplished with respect to a specified radius r, and an approximation allowance factor c. For a k-NN problem, the corresponding radius for different query points may vary by orders of magnitude. In such a case, LSH has to either (i) be run repeatedly with different values of r, cr,c^2r ... which leads to substantial increase in the query time and index storage cost, or (ii) use an ad-hoc r which leads to low quality guarantee.

Further, LSH implicitly splits the whole space into lattices so that points in the same lattice cells are hashed into the same bucket. As a result, for real data distributions that are non-uniform, the hashing results are often unbalanced. We find that an unbalanced hashing leads to performance degradation of LSH. The reasons are two-fold. First, for the case that the number of points in one bucket is too small, LSH cannot find c-approximate r-NN and a further examination on a larger r is required; second, for the case that too many points collide in one bucket, LSH needs to examine each of these and so its performance suffers.

2.3 Related Work

There is extensive work on high-dimensional indexes for k-NN queries, and there are surveys [7, 11] that provide good literature on the indexes. In this paper, since we are concerned with a specific well known indexing mechanism, namely LSH, we shall focus on work related to it (the comparison among LSH-based indexes and other indexes, such as iDistance [23], can be found in [20]).

Approximate k-NN provides approximate answers with acceptable error while constraining the growth of the cost sub-linearly with respect to the cardinality of the dataset. Locality sensitive hashing (LSH) methods [10, 1] are the best known approaches for approximate nearest neighbor search. The LSB-tree [20], entropy-LSH [15], multi-probe LSH [13] and Bayesian LSH [17] improve the performance of LSH by using some novel indexes or query strategies. Data Sensitive Hashing is orthogonal to these state-of-the-art methods, and can be regarded as a replacement of the LSH family. In the design of hashing families, query-sensitive embeddings(QSE)[4] and distance-based hashing(DBH)[5] have been proposed as the hash family for embedding and non-metric space, and [19, 12] were proposed for distance measure in the manifold. These works illustrate the potential for hashing family improvement. However, unlike existing work, DSH is the first hashing family leveraging the data distribution to directly improve the k-NN search.

There are also some spectral hashing [22] and data representation [16, 6, 14, 4, 3] methods that focus on optimizing the hashing function based on the data distribution. They significantly outperform LSH-based methods on precision. However, for the similarity search problem, we place much more emphasis on recall. This is because the recall affects the quality of the final result, while precision only affects performance by determining how many points have to be checked. DSH is designed to optimize both the recall and query efficiency.

3. DATA SENSITIVE HASHING

In this section, we introduce the basic concepts and principles of Data Sensitive Hashing (DSH), and propose two variants of DSH hashing families, DSH-basic and DSH-relaxed. The associated algorithms are presented in Section 4.

Intuitively, the problem we wish to solve is to directly search for the k-NN, whereas LSH is designed to find the r-NN. Therefore, we seek to define a new hashing family DSH. We begin with a DSH hashing family definition that migrates all the properties from LSH hashing family, called the DSH-utopia family. Here, the basic binary hashing $R^d \to \{0,1\}$ is employed for DSH.

DEFINITION 6. **(DSH-utopia Family)** *A family $\mathcal{H} = \{h : R^d \to \{0,1\}\}$ is called (k, ck, p_1, p_2)-sensitive if for any $q \in R^d$ and $o \in O$*

- *if $o \in NN(q,k)$, then $Pr_{\mathcal{H}}(h(o) = h(q)) \geq p_1$;*
- *if $o \notin NN(q,ck)$, then $Pr_{\mathcal{H}}(h(o) = h(q)) \leq p_2$;*

Unfortunately, while the above definition allows us to express what we desire, it has no known efficient implementation. Therefore, we fall back on the intrinsic properties that affect the effectiveness of a hashing-based approach. We define the following properties that should be satisfied in our DSH concatenation functions.

DEFINITION 7. **(Effectiveness for k-NN)** *For two probability values P_a and P_b, s.t. $P_a \gg P_b$,*

- **(Recall)** *for any query point $q \in R^d$, and $o \in NN(q,k)$, $\forall g_i \in \mathcal{G}$, $Pr(g_i(q) = g_i(o)) \geq P_a$;*
- **(Efficiency)** *for any query point $q \in R^d$, $\forall g_i \in \mathcal{G}$, $|\{o | o \in O \backslash NN(q,ck), g_i(q) = g_i(o)\}| \leq P_b \times |O|$.*

This definition provides two conditions to qualify a DSH concatenation function. The first condition provides a lower bound of recall and the second condition gives an upper bound (i.e., $ck + P_b \times |O|$) of the number of points in each bucket. By applying multiple hash tables to raise the recall, high quality results can be achieved, and the algorithm is still efficient. In addition, the results of different hash tables should be independent. If each concatenation function randomly chooses some functions from a large enough hashing family $\mathcal{H}$, this condition is always satisfied. The following theorem shows the relation between the quality and efficiency under such concatenation functions.

THEOREM 1. *If the concatenation functions satisfy the properties in Definition 7, to achieve an expected recall δ, the number of points to be checked is at most :*

$$\left\lceil \frac{\log(1-\delta)}{\log(1-P_a)} \right\rceil \times (ck + P_b \times |O|)$$

PROOF. Considering that l hash tables are used, we have:

$$(1-\delta) = (1-P_a)^l$$

To achieve an expected recall δ, the number of hash tables required is:

$$l = \left\lceil \frac{\log(1-\delta)}{\log(1-P_a)} \right\rceil$$

On the other hand, the number of points in each bucket is at most $ck + P_b \times |O|$. Thus, the number of points to be checked is at most:

$$\left\lceil \frac{\log(1-\delta)}{\log(1-P_a)} \right\rceil \times (ck + P_b \times |O|) \qquad \square$$

The quality of results is decided by δ, while c is only an efficiency factor. c and P_b decide the total number of points to be checked, and there is a trade-off between them. Obviously, the pairs with a longer distance are easier to be hashed to different values, and choosing a higher c often results in a smaller P_b.

To devise an effective hashing-based approach, according to the above guiding principles in Definition 7, there is no need that each **individual hash function** $h \in \mathcal{H}$ has a large probability to hash a pair correctly. Instead, we only need to design a **hash family** $\mathcal{H}$ such that most of the hash functions hash data correctly. As a concatenation LSH function is obtained by randomly picking m hash functions from $\mathcal{H}$, such a family can produce a good set of effective $g_i \in \mathcal{G}$ that satisfies the properties of recall and efficiency. Intuitively, based on following definition, we may design a set of hash functions each of which complements the others.

DEFINITION 8. **(DSH-basic Family)** *A family $\mathcal{H} = \{h : R^d \to \{0,1\}\}$ is called (k, ck, p_1, p_2)-sensitive if for any query point $q \in R^d$ and $o \in O$*

- *if $o \in NN(q,k)$, then $\frac{|\{h | h(o)=h(q), h \in \mathcal{H}\}|}{|\mathcal{H}|} \geq p_1$;*
- *if $o \notin NN(q,ck)$, then $\frac{|\{h | h(o)=h(q), h \in \mathcal{H}\}|}{|\mathcal{H}|} \leq p_2$;*

THEOREM 2. *The concatenation functions generated using DSH-basic family are effective, i.e. they have the properties given in Definition 7.*

PROOF. Using m randomly chosen hash functions in the DSH-basic family, setting $P_a = {p_1}^m$ and $P_b = {p_2}^m$, we have: **Recall:** $\forall q \in R^d, o \in NN(q,k), g_i \in \mathcal{G}$,

$$\begin{aligned} &Pr(g_i(q) = g_i(o)) \\ &= \prod_{j=1}^{m} Pr(h_{i_j}(q) = h_{i_j}(o)) \\ &= \{\frac{|\{h | h(o) = h(q), h \in \mathcal{H}\}|}{|\mathcal{H}|}\}^m \\ &\geq {p_1}^m \end{aligned}$$

Efficiency: Likewise, $\forall q \in R^d, o \in O \backslash NN(q,ck), g_i \in \mathcal{G}$, $Pr(g_i(q) = g_i(o)) \leq {p_2}^m$. Thus,

$\sum_{o \in O \backslash NN(q,ck)} Pr(g_i(q) = g_i(o)) \leq |O| \times {p_2}^m$ $\square$

We further note that the purpose of the second condition in the **Effectiveness** is to prevent too many false hits. In the DSH-basic family, this is accomplished by keeping the probability of inclusion low for each non-ck-NN. However, we do not really care what the probability of inclusion is for any **individual non-answer point**: all we wish to do is to limit the **total number of false positives**. Accordingly, we can relax the second condition:

DEFINITION 9. **(DSH-relaxed Family)** *A family $\mathcal{H} = \{h : R^d \to \{0,1\}\}$ is called (k, ck, p_1, p_2)-sensitive if for any query point $q \in R^d$*

- *for all $o \in NN(q,k)$, $\frac{|\{h | h(o)=h(q), h \in \mathcal{H}\}|}{|\mathcal{H}|} \geq p_1$;*
- *$\sum_{o \notin NN(q,ck)} (\frac{|\{h | h(o)=h(q), h \in \mathcal{H}\}|}{|\mathcal{H}|})^m \leq {p_2}^m * |O|$;*

Similar to Theorem 2, the concatenation functions generated using the DSH-relaxed family still have the **Effectiveness** properties given in Definition 7.

4. DSH FAMILY GENERATION

After having specified the properties of data sensitive hash functions, we now show how we can find such functions. For LSH, there is a straightforward geometric interpretation, so random projection turns out to work well. For DSH, there is no such easy geometric interpretation. Instead, the hash function must adapt based on the data distribution. We borrow and adapt machine learning techniques for this purpose. In particular, we first learn good atomic hash functions, and then use boosting to get even better results with an ensemble of hash functions, as we describe in this section.

4.1 Overview

Given an query-object pair $\langle q_i, o_j \rangle$, let

$$\varphi_h(\langle q_i, o_j \rangle) = (h(q_i) - h(o_j))^2. \tag{1}$$

In particular, if q_i collides with o_j according to hash function h, then $\varphi_h(\langle q_i, o_j \rangle)$ equals to 0; otherwise, it becomes 1. For DSH-basic family, based on Definition 8, the requirements for each hash function can be rewritten as:
For every pair q_i and o_j,

$$\begin{cases} \sum_{h\in\mathcal{H}} \varphi_h(\langle q_i, o_j \rangle) \le (1-p_1)|\mathcal{H}|, \text{if } o_j \text{ is a } k\text{-NN of } q_i; \\ \sum_{h\in\mathcal{H}} \varphi_h(\langle q_i, o_j \rangle) \ge (1-p_2)|\mathcal{H}|, \text{if } o_j \text{ is a non-}ck\text{-NN of } q_i; \end{cases} \tag{2}$$

Through this expression, we observe that the hashing family is actually required to be a strong classifier for the pairs, i.e. if we combine all the hash function in $\mathcal{H}$ together and use Equation 2 to classify the pairs, every k-NN pair and non-ck-NN pair can be well classified. [We can also obtain similar requirements for DSH-relaxed family. The difference here is that DSH-relaxed only requires all the k-NN pairs to be well classified. For those non-ck-NN pairs, DSH-relaxed limits the total number of false-positives for each query q.]

Adaptive boosting [8] is an efficient meta-algorithm to generate a strong classifier. Given an algorithm that can generate a weak classifier, adaptive boosting can generate a set of weak classifiers by tweaking the weight of training instances, such that their combination constitutes a strong classifier. In our problem, we do not really combine them to generate a strong classifier. Instead, each weak classifier is used as a hash function h in the family $\mathcal{H}$, while the family $\mathcal{H}$ has the above desirable properties. Therefore, we have to adapt standard adaptive boosting.

We divide the problem into two parts: (1) computing the optimal weak classifier, and (2) applying appropriate adaptive boosting algorithm to tune the input weights of the weak classifier. In both parts, we use a weight matrix W to represent the k-NN and non-ck-NN relations. For the reason that non-ck-NN relations are much more than k-NN relations, we only sample parts of them to reduce the computation cost, and make the number of samples comparable with the number of k-NN relations. Thus, W is a sparse matrix, as it only contains some sampled query-object pairs ($O(k)$ non-zero elements per query, and $O(qk)$ non-zero elements in total). Using $i \in [1, m]$ to denote those queries, and $j \in [1, n]$ to denote those data points, we have:

$$W_{ij} = \begin{cases} 1, \text{if } o_j \text{ is a } k\text{-NN of } q_i \ ; \\ -1, \text{if } o_j \text{ is a sampled non-}ck\text{-NN of } q_i \ ; \\ 0, \text{else.} \end{cases} \tag{3}$$

Each hash function h hashes the points. On the other hand, we regard it as a weak classifier φ_h for the pairs. Therefore, we expect it to optimize the resultant pairs based on the weight matrix. The weight of the matrix will be tuned by the adaptive boosting procedure. And the optimization for each function is defined as follows.

Figure 2 outlines how we generate DSH family. Given some sampled queries based on the query distribution, we get a series of query-object pairs. The k-NN pairs are expected to collide more in DSH family and vice versa. We represent this optimization target in a weight matrix form. And based on the weight matrix, we compute the optimal hash function and put it into hashing family. We then hash the points based on the hash function and check if it performs well on each pair. After that, we run the adaptive boosting procedure: for the pairs that are hashed correctly (k-NN pairs collide and vice versa), we reduce their weight in the matrix; for the pairs that are hashed mistakenly, we increase their weight in the matrix. Then we get a new weight matrix and compute a new optimal hash function. As shown in [8], after repeating this procedure multiple times, the weight of every pair becomes smaller than the original one, and a smaller weight means the pair has a larger probability to be hashed correctly.

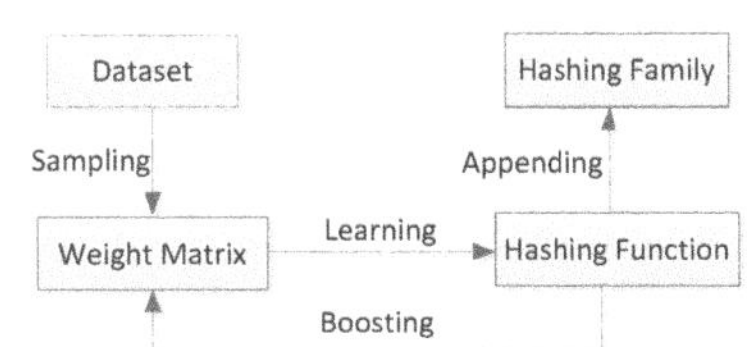

Figure 2: Overview of DSH Family Generation

The formal optimization problem set up requires specification of the data points, the query points, and the parameter k for k-NN. However, the principle of DSH is to leverage the distribution knowledge, but not tune the hash function based on specific points. We only seek to obtain the properties of DSH family for sampled queries based on the query distributions. Every sampled query should achieve high recall and be efficient. When the query distribution is hard to estimate, we can still use the uniform query distribution to cover all the potential queries. In the experimental section we show that the results obtained are not very sensitive to the query distribution or to the value of k. However, they do depend strongly on the data distribution.

DEFINITION 10. **(Hash Function Optimization)** Given the dataset O, the sampled queries Q and the weight matrix W, we aim to find the best hash function such that

$$\arg\min_h \sum_{ij} \varphi_h(\langle q_i, o_j \rangle) W_{ij} \tag{4}$$

$s.t.\ q_i \in Q, o_j \in O, \forall p \in R^d, h(p) \in \{0, 1\}.$

4.2 Single Hash Function Optimization

We would like to solve the optimization problem defined in Definition 10. However, finding the exact optimal hash function is an NP-hard problem.

THEOREM 3. *Hash Function Optimization (HFO) is an NP-hard problem.*

Algorithm 1: Hash Function Optimization

Input: Weight matrix $W_{q\times n}$, data point matrix $X_{d\times n}$, query point matrix $Q_{d\times q}$.
Output: Hash Function h.

Compute the eigenvector $\mathbf{a}$ with the minimal eigenvalue in Theorem 4 ;
$h \leftarrow \mathbf{a}^T X$;
Generate h' based on Equation 10;
return h'

PROOF. We can reduce a well-known NP-hard problem, Minimum Graph Bisection (MGB) [2] to the hash function optimization (HFO) problem. To make this reduction, we construct a mapping in the following way: let the $n \times n$ weight matrix in MGB be W and the largest weight in W be w_{max}. For each vertex v_i in MGB, we create o_i and q_i in HFO. We begin with the initial weight matrix W in MGB. Then, we ensure that o_i and q_i must be assigned to the same value by setting $W'_{ii} = n^4 \times w_{max}$. Finally, we set $W'_{ij} = W_{ij} - n^2 \times w_{max}$. The intuition here is that if a large penalty is added for every pair that is not separated, then HFO will absolutely choose a balanced partition(the minimal penalty) while doing the optimization in MGB.

□

To tackle this problem efficiently, we consider the hash function in a linear form, i.e. separating the space by a hyperplane. This has been widely adopted, and shown to be effective [14]. Moreover, it has been shown in [18] that linear classifiers fit well with boosting algorithms.

That is, $h(o_j)$,$h(q_i)$ can be represented as $\mathbf{a}^T X_j$,$\mathbf{a}^T Q_i$, where $\mathbf{a}$ is the projection vector and X_j,Q_i is the d dimension vector presentation of o_j, q_i(suppose it has been regularized to $\overline{X_j} = \mathbf{0}$).

However, the range of $\mathbf{a}^T X_j$ is R instead of $\{0,1\}$. The mean of $h(o_j)$ is always 0, as $\overline{h(o_j)} = \overline{\mathbf{a}^T X_j} = \mathbf{a}^T \overline{X_j} = 0$. To protect the result from being affected by the scaling of $\mathbf{a}$, we give a constraint $\mathbf{a}^T X X^T \mathbf{a} = 1$ to fix the variance of $h(o_j)$. We transform the problem of hash function generation as follows:

$$\arg\min_{\mathbf{a}} \sum_{ij} (\mathbf{a}^T Q_i - \mathbf{a}^T X_j)^2 W_{ij} \tag{5}$$

subject to $\mathbf{a}^T X X^T \mathbf{a} = 1$.

THEOREM 4. *The vector in Equation 5 is equal to the minimal general eigenvector of*

$$((XD - QW)X^T + (QD' - XW^T)Q^T)\mathbf{a} = \lambda X X^T \mathbf{a} \tag{6}$$

where $D_{n\times n}$ and $D'_{q\times q}$ are two diagonal matrices defined as follows:

$$D_{jj} = \sum_i W_{ij} \qquad D'_{ii} = \sum_j W_{ij} \tag{7}$$

PROOF.

$$\sum_{ij} (\mathbf{a}^T Q_i - \mathbf{a}^T X_j)^2 W_{ij}$$
$$= \sum_j \mathbf{a}^T X_j D_{jj} X_j^T \mathbf{a} - 2\sum_{ij} \mathbf{a}^T Q_i W_{ij} X_j^T \mathbf{a} + \sum_i \mathbf{a}^T Q_i D'_{ii} Q_i^T \mathbf{a}$$
$$= \mathbf{a}^T ((XD - QW)X^T + (QD' - XW^T)Q^T)\mathbf{a}$$

Therefore, the vector in Equation 5 is equal to

$$\arg\min_{\mathbf{a}} \mathbf{a}^T ((XD - QW)X^T + (QD' - XW^T)Q^T)\mathbf{a} \tag{8}$$

subject to $\mathbf{a}^T X X^T \mathbf{a} = 1$. All the two matrices are symmetric. Therefore, $\mathbf{a}$ is equal to the eigenvector with the minimal eigenvalue in the following generalized eigenvector problem:

$$((XD - QW)X^T + (QD' - XW^T)Q^T)\mathbf{a} = \lambda X X^T \mathbf{a} \tag{9}$$

□

The computational complexity of solving the eigenvector problem is $O(nd^2 + qkd + d^3)$, where n is the number of objects plus sampled queries, d is the number of dimensions and q is the number of sampled queries. The main cost here is to compute $((XD-QW)X^T+(QD'-XW^T)Q^T)$. Here D only has n non-zero values, D' has q non-zero values, and W has $O(qk)$ non-zero values. And for the general eigenvector problem, the computation cost is $O(d^3)$. Noted that the size of dataset is nd, our algorithm runs in time that is at most **linear** with the size of dataset.

After computing the hashing function $h : R^d \rightarrow R$, we convert it to the desired binary hash function $h' : R^d \rightarrow \{0,1\}$ as:

$$h'(o) = \begin{cases} 0, \text{if } h(o) \le 0 \\ 1, \text{else} \end{cases} \tag{10}$$

4.3 Adaptive Boosting for DSH-basic

Adaptive boosting [8] is a meta-algorithm for building a strong classifier using a set of weak classifiers, and can be used in conjunction with many other learning algorithms. Theoretical results that adaptive boosting always obtains a strong classifier can be found in [8]. Here we only show the intuitions. The weight for each instance depends on its results (well classified or not) on the weak classifiers, and thus represents if it is well classified using their combination. If its weight is smaller than the original, then it is well classified using the linear combination. On the other hand, in each step, the weak classifier performs better than random so that the weight of well classified instances is larger than the weight of misclassified instances. Therefore, the total weight of all instances is always reduced by the weak classifier. As the weight is tuned exponentially, the total weight also reduces exponentially. After logarithmic number of steps, the total weight is reduced to be less than the original weight for a single instance, and by then, every instance has a weight less than its initial weight and is therefore well classified.

For our specific problem, not only a strong classifier is needed, but also the difference between p_1 and p_2 is expected to be large. Obviously we cannot expect the boosting algorithm to achieve $p_1 = 1$ and $p_2 = 0$. However, the boosting algorithm optimizes to enlarge the difference [18]. Therefore, we choose some appropriate p_1 and p_2 and iterate based on the following weight updating function in which α is a weight tuning parameter of boosting:
For k-NN pairs, we have:

$$W_{ij}^{(t+1)} = W_{ij}^{(t)} * \alpha^{(p_1 - 1 + \varphi_{h_t}(\langle q_i, o_j\rangle))} \tag{11}$$

For non-ck-NN pairs, we have:

$$W_{ij}^{(t+1)} = W_{ij}^{(t)} * \alpha^{-(p_2 - 1 + \varphi_{h_t}(\langle q_i, o_j \rangle))} \quad (12)$$

Algorithm 2 describes our boosting procedure in which *itrCounter* is the number of hash functions that we aim to obtain. We next prove that if every instance has a weight smaller than its initial, then $\mathcal{H}$ conforms to DSH-basic family defined in Definition 8 for the sampled data when the updating function is based on Equation 11 and 12.

THEOREM 5. *$\forall \langle q_i, o_j \rangle$, if $|w_{ij}^{(t)}| \leq |w_{ij}^{(0)}|$, $\mathcal{H}$ conforms to Definition 8 for all sampled pairs.*

PROOF. Let T_{ij} be $|\{h | h(q_i) = h(o_j), h \in \mathcal{H}\}|$, and S_{ij} be $|\{h | h(q_i) \neq h(o_j), h \in \mathcal{H}\}|$. Obviously, $S_{ij} = |\mathcal{H}| - T_{ij}$. Hence, for every k-NN pair $\langle q_i, o_j \rangle$,

$$
\begin{aligned}
& w_{ij}^{(0)} \geq w_{ij}^{(t)} \\
\Longrightarrow & w_{ij}^{(0)} \geq w_{ij}^{(0)} \times \alpha^{(p_1-1)|\mathcal{H}| + S_{ij}} \\
\Longrightarrow & \alpha^{(p_1-1)|\mathcal{H}| + S_{ij}} \leq 1 \\
\Longrightarrow & (p_1 - 1)|\mathcal{H}| + S_{ij} \leq 0 \\
\Longrightarrow & p_1 |\mathcal{H}| - T_{ij} \leq 0 \\
\Longrightarrow & \frac{|\{h | h(o_i) = h(o_j), h \in \mathcal{H}\}|}{|\mathcal{H}|} \geq p_1
\end{aligned}
$$

For every non-ck-NN pair $\langle q_i, o_j \rangle$, it is analogous to prove that $\frac{|\{h|h(q_i)=h(o_j), h \in \mathcal{H}\}|}{|\mathcal{H}|} \leq p_2$. □

4.4 Adaptive Boosting for DSH-relaxed

Now we give the adaptive boosting solution for DSH-relaxed. The procedure is similar to that for DSH-basic except one major difference, i.e., we only limit the total number of points in each bucket. Therefore, for every query, the non-ck-NN relations now construct one big instance. For ease of presentation, we assume that all the pairs are sampled and the size of the current H is large enough. However, as only a small number of pairs are sampled and the algorithm begins with empty H, some trivial regularization should be applied in the implementation. We use the expected number of points that collide with q_i to measure the efficiency of query q_i, which is defined as:

$$Collision_i = \sum_j \left(1 - \frac{\sum_{h \in \mathcal{H}} (\varphi_h(\langle q_i, o_j \rangle))}{|\mathcal{H}|}\right)^m \quad (13)$$

Note that if the collision rate bound is p_2, then the upper bound of the false-positives is $n * {p_2}^m$. Thus, $(\frac{Collision_i}{|O|})^{\frac{1}{m}}$ is the equivalent collision rate to get the same upper bound of the false positives. After being regularized, the weight for each query is:

$$weight_i^{(t)} = \alpha^{t * (p_2 - (\frac{Collision_i}{|O|})^{\frac{1}{m}})} \quad (14)$$

For k-NN pairs, we tune their weight as usual. On the other hand, we tune the weight for each query q_i based on $Collision_i$. However, our hash function optimization algorithm is based on the weight for every query-object pair. For this reason, we have to assign the weight of each query q_i to its related pairs. Here, we still expect the hash function to minimize the total weight of training instances. Thus,

Algorithm 2: Adaptive Boosting Procedure

initialize$t \leftarrow 0$; $\mathcal{H} \leftarrow \emptyset$;
initialize $W^{(0)} = W$ given in Equation 3;
while $t < itrCounter \,||\, \exists w_{ij}^{(t)}, w_{ij}^{(0)}, |w_{ij}^{(t)}| > |w_{ij}^{(0)}|$ **do**
  compute $h^{(t)}$ based on Algorithm 1 using $W^{(t)}$ as input;
  $\mathcal{H} \leftarrow \mathcal{H} \cup \{h^{(t)}\}$;
  updating $W^{(t+1)}$;
return $\mathcal{H}$;

we study the "gradient" vector of $Collision_i$, i.e. how much it will be changed when a new hash function hashes each point $o_1 ... o_n$ together with q_i or not. We then adjust the weight for each related pair based on its "partial derivative". Formally, the "partial derivative" is defined as:

$$\Delta Collision_{ij} = \frac{m}{|\mathcal{H}|} \times \left(1 - \frac{\sum_{h \in \mathcal{H}} (\varphi_h(\langle q_i, o_j \rangle))}{|\mathcal{H}|}\right)^{m-1} \quad (15)$$

Intuitively, if an object has a larger probability to collide with the query, it will have a larger weight. For those objects that are almost impossible to collide, there is little benefit to separate them with the query in the new hash function, and the weight for them is close to zero.

Now we define the weight updating function for those non-ck-NN pairs:

$$W_{ij}^{(t)} = weight_i^{(t)} \Delta Collision_{ij} \quad (16)$$

The weight updating function for k-NN pairs remains the same.

4.5 Difference with other learning based methods

So far, all the discussion is based on the similarity search prospective. There are many other learning based hashing or embedding methods such as [22, 4, 3, 16, 6, 14]. Now we will discuss our difference with them. Compared with these methods, DSH is distinctive in the optimization target. Traditional learning based methods mostly focus on the high precision end, and evaluate their performance using PR-value, F_1-measure or MAP. However, this may not be appropriate for our similarity search problem. As we have a validation step, the precision itself is not a crucial measure. We aim to achieve a high recall with acceptable candidate size. For example, to solve a 20-NN search problem in 1M points, we expect the algorithm to return 2000 points that contain all the positives, but not to return 20 points that contain 12 of them. We can validate those 2000 points one by one and obtain the exact answer. However, for the 20 points set, we cannot expand it to obtain a higher recall. Although the algorithm that outputs 2000 points has a 1% precision, the check rate is only 0.2%. For this reason, we focus on the relatively lower precision area, and optimize our algorithm to yield a higher recall. Distinguished with traditional methods, DSH does not pay much to filter every false positive, but to ensure every true answer is in the result, while most other methods pay equal emphasis to these two targets.

Table 1: Overall comparative study: DSH-relaxed is the most efficient in terms of query time and space usage

	(a) Forest				(b) Flickr				(c) DBPedia			
method	recall	query time	error ratio	# hash tables	recall	query time	error ratio	# hash tables	recall	query time	error ratio	# hash tables
LSH		18.6	1.012	100		40.8	1.004	90		/	/	/
DSH-basic	0.94	12.8	1.012	80	0.96	28.6	1.004	72	0.95	25.6	1.002	64
DSH-relaxed		6.2	1.013	30		16.0	1.004	36		15.6	1.002	32
LSH		12.1	1.024	50		26.0	1.008	40		38.8	1.006	75
DSH-basic	0.9	6.8	1.027	32	0.92	17.2	1.009	36	0.91	14.4	1.006	28
DSH-relaxed		3.8	1.025	14		9.8	1.010	16		9.4	1.006	16
LSH		8.2	1.036	25		19.2	1.013	25		24.8	1.018	35
DSH-basic	0.86	4.4	1.036	16	0.88	12.0	1.014	20	0.87	11.6	1.017	20
DSH-relaxed		2.4	1.038	8		8.0	1.014	10		7.6	1.021	10

Following this guideline, in the design of DSH-relaxed, we provide zero tolerance to the false negatives, and a much higher tolerance to the false positives. For the false negatives, we use boosting techniques to ensure all the positives are well classified. And for the false positives, we only give a very weak limitation on the total numbers, and do our best for each individual. By using this heterogeneous solution, our optimization target is realized.

4.6 Incremental Maintenance

DSH is sensitive to data distribution, unlike LSH. Indeed, that is the whole point. This raises the question of what to do if the data distribution changes over time in a dynamic setting. Fortunately, incremental update of DSH hashing family is straightforward: simply replace any hash function that has a negative effect on the weight of boosting by a newly computed one since the boosting procedure aims at reducing the total weight of the weight matrix. The cost of such updates can be limited by changing at most one hash function each time. In practice, it turns out to be enough to make one such incremental update after 1-5% of the data has changed.

5. EXPERIMENTS

5.1 Experimental Setup

We evaluate the performance using three real datasets: scientific data, images and text. Properties of these three datasets are summarized in Table 2 and described in detail below:

- **Forest**[1] dataset is provided by the US Forest Service. We observe that some attributes are strongly correlated since they describe related information. For example, there are some attributes describing Hillshade Index at different times of a day. For this reason, Forest dataset is ideal to study the performance of indexing methods with respect to **data skew**;

- **Flickr**[2] is an image hosting website in which members can upload their images. Over this dataset, we do similarity search based on the feature space of images instead of pixel space. Following common practice, we use the PCA technique to pre-process the images and keep 80 feature dimensions. In contrast to the Forest dataset, the PCA feature space is **orthogonal**;

- **DBPedia**[3] is a project aiming to extract structured content from the Wikipedia database. We utilize LDA to pre-process the dataset, and keep 150 topic dimensions. The data points after employing LDA topic model transformation lie in the probability distribution space, and hence we use KL-divergence as the distance measure since it is widely used in this space. We use DBPedia dataset to study the effectiveness of DSH when a **non-Euclidean distance** measure is used.

Table 2: Dataset properties

Dataset	# Objects	# Dimension	Property
Forest	580K	54	skewness
Flickr	1M	80	orthogonal
DBPedia	1M	150	non-Euclidean

We evaluate the following methods in the experiments:

- **LSH.** E2LSH[1] is a recent state-of-the-art implementation for LSH.

- **DSH-basic.** Our method proposed in Section 4.3.

- **DSH-relaxed.** Our method proposed in Section 4.4.

- **Query-Sensitive Embedding**[4] is one efficient embedding hashing method that also applies boosting to guarantee the performance of similarity search.

- **Spectral Hashing**[22] is a state-of-the-art learning based hashing methods.

We randomly remove 1000 points from each dataset and use them as query points in our performance study. The ground-truth for each query point is obtained by a linear scan of the entire dataset. The sampled queries used in DSH are generated via random selection that is independent of the query set. Unless otherwise specified, the sample rate is 0.5%, k is set to 20 and c is set to 5 throughout the experiments. For all algorithms, each hash table contains 2000 buckets(i.e. m is set to 11). To avoid duplicating the

[1] http://archive.ics.uci.edu/ml/datasets/Covertype

[2] http://www.flickr.com/

[3] http://wiki.dbpedia.org

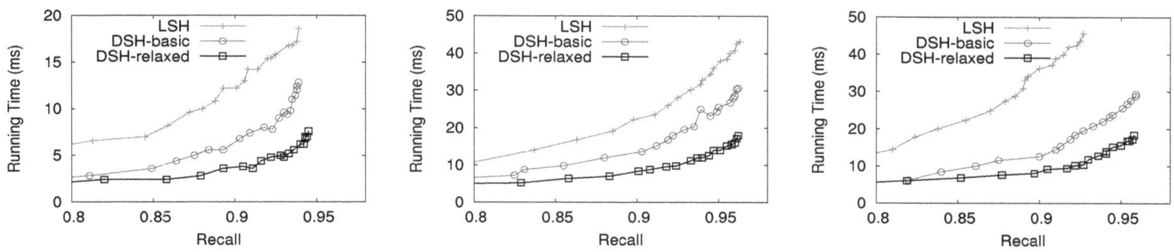

(a) Forest (b) Flickr (c) DBPedia

Figure 3: Average running time executed using different access methods to achieve a certain query quality: DSH-relaxed achieves the highest recall in the same running time, followed by DSH-basic and LSH.

points, entries in the table are in form of point IDs instead of the points. For this reason, the storage cost can be reduced by about 100 times. Besides, all these methods keep the entire indexes as well as the original dataset in main memory.

We evaluate the performance in terms of the following three aspects:

- **Query Quality** is measured by *recall* and *error ratio*. Let $\widehat{NN(q,k)}[i]$ (resp. $NN(q,k)[i]$) be the point in $\widehat{NN(q,k)}$ (resp. $NN(q,k)$) with the ith smallest distance to q. The *error ratio* [13] is to measure how close are the distances between points in $\widehat{NN(q,k)}$ and points in $NN(q,k)$:

$$error\ ratio = \frac{1}{|Q| \times k} \sum_{q \in Q} \sum_{i=1}^{k} \frac{|\widehat{NN(q,k)}[i], q|}{|NN(q,k)[i], q|} \quad (17)$$

- **Query Efficiency** is measured by the *running time* to answer k-NN queries. The *precision* in those learning based methods can also be viewed as a measurement of efficiency, since $\frac{recall \times k}{precision}$ is the number of points to be checked.

- **Space Requirement** is measured by the *number of hash tables being used*. The space cost for one hash table is about the same for each method, and is a good surrogate for index size.

5.2 Comparison with LSH

In this study, we compare our proposed methods, namely DSH-basic and DSH-relaxed, with LSH. We choose the best width parameter W for LSH, and the parameters for DSH tuned as discussed in Section 5.5.

Table 1 summarizes the average results over all the datasets. In each table, we report the query time, the error ratio and the number of hash tables required per query to achieve three different query quality levels (in terms of recall). First, we observe that DSH-relaxed is significantly more space and time efficient than DSH-basic and LSH. It is worth mentioning that for the DBPedia dataset, LSH cannot find approximate k-nearest neighbors to achieve recall 0.94 within acceptable time. Further, we note that all three methods provide almost the same error ratio across all the datasets and each error ratio is close to 1, in which the exact k-NN are identified.

Typically, a larger δ will result in a higher query cost. We therefore study the relationship between recall δ and query performance in detail for all three access methods. Figure 3 summarizes the results. First, we observe that the query time increases super-linearly to achieve a higher recall. Second, both DSH-relaxed and DSH-basic perform better than LSH by a wide margin and there is an obvious trend of increasing time to achieve a higher recall. Finally, we observe that DSH-relaxed and DSH-basic outperform LSH by a wider margin over the DBPedia dataset than the other two datasets. The reason will be provided when we discuss the relationship between the recall and the space usage.

Regarding the comparative methods, the query performance basically depends on the number of candidates to be probed in the same buckets that collide with the query points. Hence, we report the distribution of bucket size of hash tables and discuss how this affects the query performance. Figure 4 shows the distribution of bucket size of hash tables. The points are distributed more unevenly in hash tables of LSH than those of DSH-basic and DSH-relaxed. In particular, for hash tables in LSH, the top 1% buckets take 21%, 13%, 13% points of the Forest, Flickr and DBPedia datasets, respectively. Obviously, the query performance suffers when the query points are hashed to these buckets. Typically, the query distribution follows the data distribution, and in this case, the query points are often hashed to the buckets with a large number of points. Consequently, the number of candidates in LSH is larger on average than that in DSH methods, and incurs a higher query cost.

We proceed to study the relationship between the recall and the space usage, and report the results in Figure 5. To achieve a higher recall, a larger number of hash tables is typically required. In particular, DSH-relaxed outperforms DSH-basic and LSH by a wide margin. The trends are fairly similar to Figure 3. However, there exists a slight difference between them. We note that using similar number of hash tables, LSH incurs about 25% longer query time than DSH methods. The reasons are two-fold. First, due to the unbalanced hashing in LSH, the number of points to be checked in each table is about 3 times larger than that in DSH. Second, there exist many more duplicates from different tables in LSH than those in DSH where each point will be checked at most once. As a result, DSH methods still benefit from its balanced hash tables.

In addition, DSH-relaxed and DSH-basic outperform LSH by a wider margin on the DBPedia dataset than the other two datasets. Due to the difference between Euclidean distance and KL-divergence, the recall of LSH is limited at 94%. Although DSH methods are not specially designed for

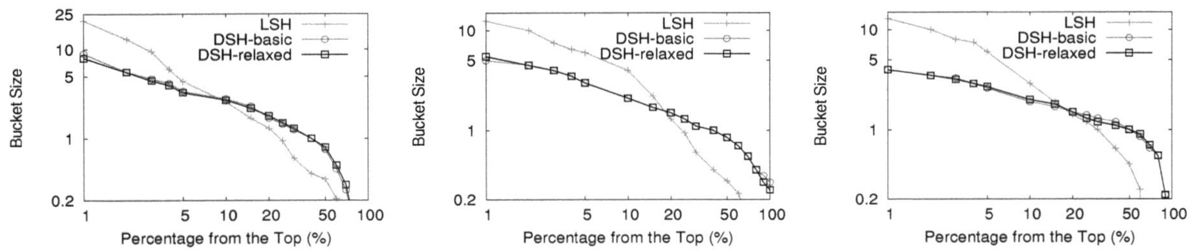

(a) Forest (b) Flickr (c) DBPedia

Figure 4: Distribution of Bucket Size

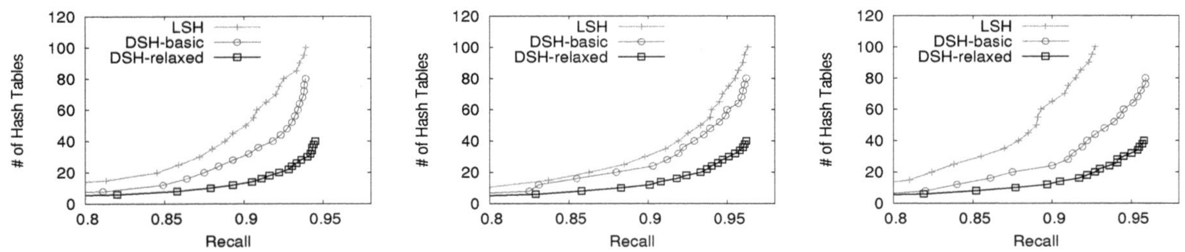

(a) Forest (b) Flickr (c) DBPedia

Figure 5: Number of hash tables that are required by different access methods to achieve a certain query quality: DSH-relaxed achieves the highest recall by using the same number of hash tables, followed by DSH-basic and LSH.

Table 3: Query time and recall for various distributions

Query		Dense	Sparse	Original
LSH	query time	581	42	130
	recall	0.99	0.803	0.916
DSH-basic	query time	161	58	98
	recall	0.978	0.893	0.932
DSH-relaxed	query time	150	59	90
	recall	0.984	0.922	0.962

KL-divergence measurement, they achieve a recall of 96%, which can be improved further by using a larger number of hash tables.

We also investigate the performance of each method under different query distributions. Besides the *original* queries that are randomly extracted from each dataset, we generate two additional query sets for each dataset and each set consists of 100 queries. Queries in the first set (labeled as *dense*) are randomly selected and the distances between each query and its k-NNs are small. Queries in the second set (labeled as *sparse*) are randomly selected as well and the distances between each query and its k-NNs are large. The results (dense, sparse and the original) of using $l = 40$ on Flickr dataset are shown in Table 3. Due to the space constraint, in what follows, we only report the results on the Flickr dataset whenever the results on the other two datasets exhibit similar trend. From the result we can see that the performance for DSH is generally consistent in all cases. However, the recall of LSH drops greatly in the sparse area, and the query time increases significantly in the dense area.

5.3 Scalability

Table 4 summarizes the indexing time for the comparative methods. To test the scalability of our indexing method, we

Table 4: Indexing time (s)

Dataset	Forest		Flickr		DBPedia	
Size	1×	10×	1×	10×	1×	10×
LSH	57	502	92	875	105	1001
DSH-basic	37	331	148	1350	84	798
DSH-relaxed	32	286	109	980	77	719

also conduct an experiment where all the data points are duplicated for 10 times. Notice that both DSH and LSH treat those duplicated points as new points, thus indicating the expected performance with a larger data set. First we can see that both LSH and DSH take 9-10 times longer in the 10 times larger dataset, suggesting that the indexing time grows linearly with size of data set for all methods.

We also note that neither DSH methods nor LSH takes the minimum indexing time across all three datasets, and the indexing time over different datasets for all methods varies slightly. Specifically, DSH-relaxed and DSH-basic are more efficient than LSH on Forest and DBPedia datasets while we get a reverse result on Flickr dataset. Note that in all comparative methods, the indexing time consists two components: (1) the time to obtain the hash functions; (2) the cost of hashing points to the hash tables. LSH uses the random projection to generate hash functions and hence it performs much better than DSH-relaxed and DSH-basic in obtaining the hash functions. However, DSH-relaxed and DSH-basic require fewer hash tables, and incur less cost to hash points. By considering both factors, the overall indexing time for DSH is comparable with LSH.

5.4 Comparison with Learning Based Methods

We now compare DSH with other learning based methods. As discussed in Section 4.5, the optimization target of DSH

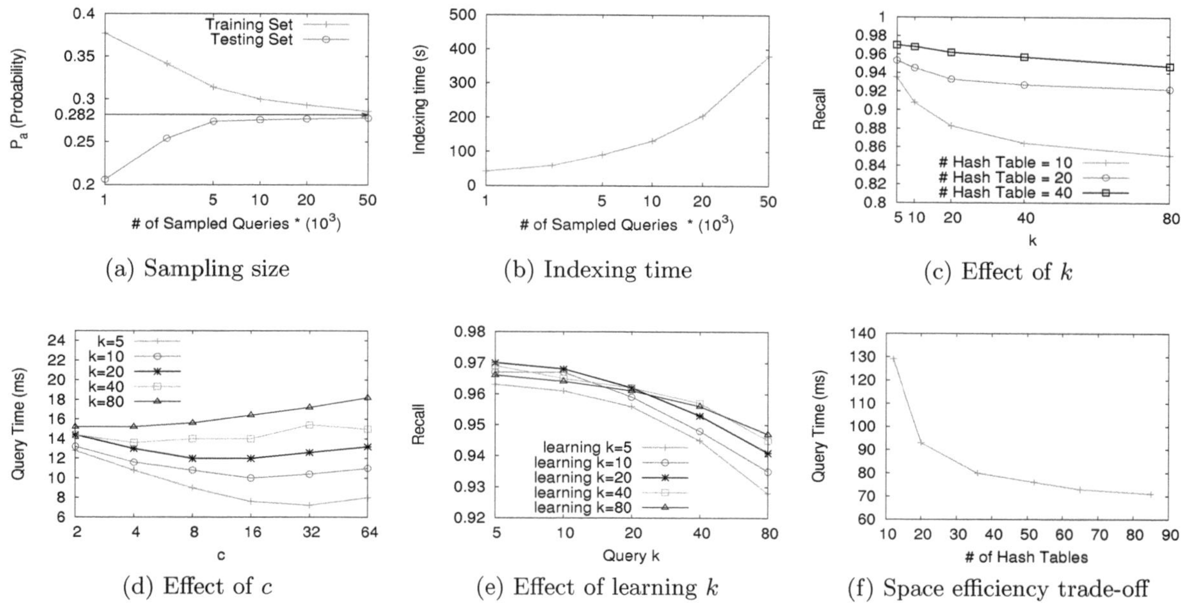

(a) Sampling size (b) Indexing time (c) Effect of k

(d) Effect of c (e) Effect of learning k (f) Space efficiency trade-off

Figure 6: Effect of parameters in DSH

Table 5: Precision-recall comparison with learning methods

Precision	0.1	0.03	0.01	0.003	0.001
C/N(%)	0.01	0.03	0.1	0.3	1
LSH	0.551	0.704	0.8	0.852	0.916
DSH-basic	0.684	**0.816**	0.869	0.904	0.932
DSH-relaxed	0.652	0.812	**0.894**	**0.936**	**0.962**
[22]	**0.738**	0.808	0.864	0.888	0.919
[4]	0.677	0.794	0.864	0.897	0.925

is different from that of other learning based methods. Table 5 gives the comparison with query-sensitive embedding and spectral hashing. In this table, we use the precision-recall trade-off to show the basic difference illustrated in Section 4.5. We give each method equal space limitation $l = 40$, and evaluate their precision and recall when m is varied.

DSH-relaxed performs worse than the others in the high precision end, as it allows too many false positives into the results. But as a payback, it wins the highest recall in the relative lower precision area. On the other hand, spectral hashing performs the best in the high precision area. However, in the low precision area, its performance is the worst (similar with the performance of LSH) since it does not make any guarantee for each individual and some positive objects are totally lost. DSH-basic and Query Sensitive Hashing lie in the middle, as they both enforce a strict constraint on both false positives and false negatives. And DSH-basic outperforms query-sensitive hashing about 1% for the reason that it preserves the collision probability for each k-NN point, while query-sensitive hashing only guarantees that the probability is larger than those non-k-NNs. When the precision is 1%, the check rate(candidate size/datasize) is only 0.1%. Thus, we focus more on the performance in the relatively lower precision area and DSH-relaxed outperforms other algorithms.

For embedding or data representation applications, there is a need to compute the similarity in the transformation space. Thus, the precision itself is very important. However, to answer the similarity search, the validation is conducted in the original space. For this reason, all those false-positives can be pruned. From this experiment we see that the most suitable algorithms for these two scenarios are different.

5.5 Parameter Studies

In this study, we investigate the parameters that potentially affect the performance of DSH, and suggest guidelines for parameter setting.

We first study the effect of sample rate by varying from 0.1%(1K queries) to 5%(50K). We evaluate the recall property P_a DSH can achieve when the efficiency property is guaranteed by is $P_b = 0.005$. Figure 6a shows the results. By enlarging the sample size, a more accurate model can be trained to capture the distribution of the whole dataset. The value in the training set shows that the upper bond of P_a is less than 0.282. On the other hand, the real performance becomes very close to that value when sample rate is larger than 0.5%(5K). Therefore, we set the sample rate to 0.5%. Also, for each query, we only acquire 10 k-NN relations and 10 non-ck-NN relations. The recall needed here is only 50%. Thus, we can process the sampling process efficiently by some approximate search algorithm. Figure 6b shows the indexing time when different sample size are used.

We next study the effect of k by varying k from 5 to 80. Figure 6c shows the results. In general, the recall drops slightly when k increases. It turns out to be increasingly insensitive to k by using a larger number of hash tables.

We also study the relationship between c and query efficiency, and report the query time in Figure 6d using different k. In general, the optimal c that achieves the minimal query time differs when k varies. However, we can see that for every k, the value ck that achieves the minimal query time always falls in the range from 100 to 200. As shown in

Table 6: Augmentation with multi-probe proposed for LSH

Method	# table		Query time	
	original	multi-probe	original	multi-probe
LSH	90	9	40.8	44.2
DSH-basic	72	7	28.6	29.4
DSH-relaxed	36	4	16	17.2

Theorem 1, the efficiency is decided by both $P_b \times N$ and ck. Thus, the best ck value depends on the bucket size. In our experiments, the bucket size is about 500 points, and the ck that achieves the best query performance lies in the range from 100 to 200.

Besides, there is a need to generate a DSH family for various k. Thus, we study the performance using different k in both the learning and query phase. Using $l = 40$, the result in Figure 6e shows a larger k in the learning phase performs well over various query k in the query phase. For DSH, using $k = 80$ only introduces a cost of checking 80 points for each bucket at most. Meanwhile, when a larger k is applied in the learning phase, the query quality performance for those smaller k will also be guaranteed. Thus, we can use a larger k to learn DSH in the various query k scenario.

Finally, we study the space-efficiency trade-off of DSH. Typically, to achieve the same level of recall, using larger m and l will reduce the query time, while leading to additional storage cost. Thus, we study the relationship between query time and storage cost when the recall requirement is fixed to 0.96, and the results are shown in Figure 6f. We can observe that by increasing the number of hash tables, the query time drops and the performance gain becomes smaller.

5.6 Extensibility

DSH is orthogonal to most of the research works that use LSH family as a foundation and improve on LSH. Therefore, the results from most of these works can be applied to DSH as an alternative to LSH. As an example, we adapt Multi-probe LSH [13] into DSH. The results to obtain 0.96 recall are given in Table 6. We can see that the combination further reduces the number of tables needed while requiring almost the same query time.

6. CONCLUSION

In this paper, we propose an efficient indexing method called *Data Sensitive Hashing* (DSH) for high-dimensional approximate k-NN search problem. The hashing family is directly designed for k-NN search. By leveraging knowledge from the sampled data, DSH balances its buckets even in non-uniform data distributions, and aims to preserve most k-NN relations in its hashing. We conducted extensive experiments using three real datasets, and the results confirm the efficiency and robustness of the DSH. The DSH-relaxed variant is the most efficient, which requires only 1/3 of the hash tables and query time of the LSH. Furthermore, existing LSH extensions can easily be applied to the DSH.

Acknowledgments

This work was in part supported by the National Research Foundation, Prime Minister's Office, Singapore under its Competitive Research Programme (CRP Award No. NRF-CRP8-2011-08) and Singapore Ministry of Education Grant No. R-252-000-454-112. Jagadish was partially supported by NSF grant IIS 1250880.

7. REFERENCES

[1] A. Andoni and P. Indyk. Near-optimal hashing algorithms for approximate nearest neighbor in high dimensions. In *FOCS*, pages 459–468, 2006.

[2] K. Andreev and H. Racke. Balanced graph partitioning. *Theory of Computing Systems*, pages 929–939, 2006.

[3] V. Athitsos, J. Alon, S. Sclaroff, and G. Kollios. Boostmap: A method for efficient approximate similarity rankings. In *CVPR*, pages II–268, 2004.

[4] V. Athitsos, M. Hadjieleftheriou, G. Kollios, and S. Sclaroff. Query-sensitive embeddings. In *SIGMOD*, pages 706–717, 2005.

[5] V. Athitsos, M. Potamias, P. Papapetrou, and G. Kollios. Nearest neighbor retrieval using distance-based hashing. In *ICDE*, pages 327–336, 2008.

[6] M. Belkin and P. Niyogi. Laplacian eigenmaps for dimensionality reduction and data representation. *Neural computation*, pages 1373–1396, 2003.

[7] E. Chávez, G. Navarro, R. Baeza-Yates, and J. L. Marroquín. Searching in metric spaces. *ACM Computing Surveys*, pages 273–321, 2001.

[8] Y. Freund and R. E. Schapire. A desicion-theoretic generalization of on-line learning and an application to boosting. In *Computational Learning Theory*, pages 23–37, 1995.

[9] J. Gan, J. Feng, Q. Fang, and W. Ng. Locality-sensitive hashing scheme based on dynamic collision counting. In *SIGMOD*, pages 541–552, 2012.

[10] A. Gionis, P. Indyk, and R. Motwani. Similarity search in high dimensions via hashing. In *VLDB*, pages 518–529, 1999.

[11] G. R. Hjaltason and H. Samet. Index-driven similarity search in metric spaces (survey article). *TODS*, pages 517–580, 2003.

[12] B. Kulis and K. Grauman. Kernelized locality-sensitive hashing for scalable image search. In *ICCV*, pages 2130–2137, 2009.

[13] Q. Lv, W. Josephson, Z. Wang, M. Charikar, and K. Li. Multi-probe lsh: efficient indexing for high-dimensional similarity search. In *VLDB*, pages 950–961, 2007.

[14] X. Niyogi. Locality preserving projections. In *NIPS*, pages 153–160, 2004.

[15] R. Panigrahy. Entropy based nearest neighbor search in high dimensions. In *SODA*, pages 1186–1195, 2006.

[16] R. Salakhutdinov and G. E. Hinton. Learning a nonlinear embedding by preserving class neighbourhood structure. In *AI and Statistics*, pages 412–419, 2007.

[17] V. Satuluri and S. Parthasarathy. Bayesian locality sensitive hashing for fast similarity search. *VLDB*, pages 430–441, 2012.

[18] R. E. Schapire. The boosting approach to machine learning: An overview. *LECTURE NOTES IN STATISTICS*, pages 149–172, 2003.

[19] G. Shakhnarovich, P. Viola, and T. Darrell. Fast pose estimation with parameter-sensitive hashing. In *ICCV*, pages 750–757, 2003.

[20] Y. Tao, K. Yi, C. Sheng, and P. Kalnis. Quality and efficiency in high dimensional nearest neighbor search. In *SIGMOD*, pages 563–576, 2009.

[21] R. Weber, H.-J. Schek, and S. Blott. A quantitative analysis and performance study for similarity-search methods in high-dimensional spaces. In *VLDB*, pages 194–205, 1998.

[22] Y. Weiss, A. Torralba, and R. Fergus. Spectral hashing. In *NIPS*, pages 1753–1760, 2008.

[23] C. Yu, B. C. Ooi, K.-L. Tan, and H. V. Jagadish. Indexing the distance: An efficient method to knn processing. In *VLDB*, pages 421–430, 2001.

Fast and Unified Local Search for Random Walk Based K-Nearest-Neighbor Query in Large Graphs

Yubao Wu †, Ruoming Jin ‡, Xiang Zhang †
†Department of Electrical Engineering and Computer Science, Case Western Reserve University
‡Department of Computer Science, Kent State University
yubao.wu@case.edu, jin@cs.kent.edu, xiang.zhang@case.edu

ABSTRACT

Given a large graph and a query node, finding its k-nearest-neighbor (kNN) is a fundamental problem. Various random walk based measures have been developed to measure the proximity (similarity) between nodes. Existing algorithms for the random walk based top-k proximity search can be categorized as *global* and *local* methods based on their search strategies. Global methods usually require an expensive precomputing step. By only searching the nodes near the query node, local methods have the potential to support more efficient query. However, most existing local search methods cannot guarantee the exactness of the solution. Moreover, they are usually designed for specific proximity measures.

Can we devise an efficient local search method that applies to different measures and also guarantees result exactness? In this paper, we present FLoS (Fast Local Search), a unified local search method for efficient and exact top-k proximity query in large graphs. FLoS is based on the *no local optimum* property of proximity measures. We show that many measures have no local optimum. Utilizing this property, we introduce several simple operations on transition probabilities, which allow developing lower and upper bounds on the proximity. The bounds monotonically converge to the exact proximity when more nodes are visited. We further show that FLoS can also be applied to measures having local optimum by utilizing relationship among different measures. We perform comprehensive experiments to evaluate the efficiency and applicability of the proposed method.

Categories and Subject Descriptors

H.2.8 [**Database Management**]: Database Applications—*Data mining*; G.2.2 [**Discrete Mathematics**]: Graph Theory—*Graph algorithms*

Keywords

Local search; nearest neighbors; top-k search; random walk; proximity search

http://dx.doi.org/10.1145/2588555.2610500.

1. INTRODUCTION

Given a large graph and a query node, finding its k-nearest-neighbor (kNN) is a primitive operation that has recently attracted intensive research interests in the database research community [18, 5, 13, 9]. In general, there are two challenges in this problem. One is to design proximity measures that can effectively capture the similarity between nodes. Another is to devise efficient algorithms to compute the top-k nodes for a given measure.

Designing effective proximity (similarity) measures is a difficult task. Random walk based measures have been shown to be effective in many applications. Some examples include discounted/truncated hitting time [17, 18], penalized hitting probability [11, 21], and random walk with restart [1, 20, 3].

Although various proximity measures have been developed, how to efficiently compute them remains a challenging problem. For most random walk based measures, the naive method requires matrix inversion, which is prohibitive for large graphs. Two *global* approaches have been developed. One applies the power iteration method over the entire graph [16, 9]. Another approach precomputes and stores the inversion of a matrix [20, 8, 10]. The precomputing step is usually expensive and needs to be repeated whenever the graph changes.

To improve efficiency, local methods dynamically expand the search range to visit nodes near the query node [17, 19, 18, 21]. Node proximities are estimated based on local information only. Without using the global information, however, most of the existing local search methods cannot guarantee to find the exact solution. Moreover, they are designed for specific measures and cannot be generalized to other measures.

In this paper, we propose FLoS (Fast Local Search), a simple and unified local search method for efficient and exact top-k proximity query in large graphs. FLoS has several desirable properties.

- It guarantees to find the exact top-k nodes.
- It is a general method that can be applied to a variety of random walk based proximity measures.
- It uses a simple local search strategy that needs neither preprocessing nor iterating over the entire graph.

The key idea behind FLoS is that we can develop upper and lower bounds on the proximity of the nodes near the query node. These bounds can be dynamically updated when a larger portion of the graph is explored and will finally converge to the exact proximity value. The top-k nodes can be identified once the differences between their upper and lower bounds are small enough to distinguish them from the remaining nodes.

The theoretical basis of FLoS relies on the no local optimum property of proximity measures. That is, given a query node q, for any node i ($i \neq q$) in the graph, i always has a neighbor that is closer to q than i is. We show that many measures have no local optimum. This property ensures that the proximity of unvisited nodes is bounded by the maximum proximity (or minimum proximity for some measures) in the boundary of the visited nodes. It can be utilized to find the top-k nodes without exploring the entire graph under the assumption that the exact proximity can be computed based on local information. However, for most measures, the exact proximity cannot be computed without searching the entire graph. To tackle this challenge, we introduce several simple operations to modify transition probabilities, which enable developing upper and lower bounds on the proximity of visited nodes. The developed upper (lower) bounds monotonically decrease (increase) when more nodes are visited. We further study the relationship among different measures and show that FLoS can also be applied to measures having local optimum. Extensive experimental results show that, for a variety of measures, FLoS can dramatically improve the efficiency compared to the state-of-the-art methods.

2. RELATED WORK

Various random walk based proximity measures have been proposed recently [6]. Examples include truncated or discounted hitting time [17, 19, 18], penalized hitting probability [11, 21], and random walk with restart [1, 20, 18] and its variants such as effective importance (degree normalized random walk with restart) [3].

The basic approach for proximity query is to use the power iteration method [16]. An improved iteration method designed for random walk with restart decomposes the proximity into random walk probabilities of different length [9]. It tries to reduce the number of iterations by estimating the proximity based on the information collected so far. Another approach precomputes the information needed for proximity estimation during the query process [20, 8, 10]. However, this step is time consuming and becomes infeasible when the graph is large or constantly changing. Graph embedding method embeds nodes into geometric space so that node proximities can be preserved as much as possible [22]. The embedding step is also time-consuming. Moreover, the proximities in the new space are not exactly the same as the ones in the original graph.

Based on the intuition that nodes near the query node tend to have high proximity, local search methods try to visit a small number of nodes to approximate the proximities. Best-first [21] and depth-first [14] search strategies simply extract a fixed number of nodes near the query node. An approximate local search algorithm is proposed for truncated hitting time [17]. The key idea is to develop upper and lower bounds that can be used to approximate the proximities of local nodes. Methods in [18, 3] apply a similar idea on the effective importance proximity measure. Most of the existing local search methods cannot guarantee the exactness. Moreover, all of them are designed for specific proximity measures. It is unclear whether the local search methods can be generalized to other measures.

Table 1: Main symbols

Symbol	Definition
$G(V,E)$	undirected graph G with node set V and edge set E
N_i	neighbors of node i
w_{ij}	weight of edge (i,j)
w_i	weighted node degree $w_i = \sum_{j \in N_i} w_{ij}$
q	query node
k	number of returned nodes
S	a set of nodes
$\bar{S}$	complement of S: $\bar{S} = V \setminus S$
δS	boundary of S: $\{i \in S \mid \exists j \in N_i \cap \bar{S}\}$
$\delta\bar{S}$	boundary of $\bar{S}$: $\{i \in \bar{S} \mid \exists j \in N_i \cap S\}$
$\mathbf{r}$	$n \times 1$ vector, $\mathbf{r}_i$ is the proximity of node i w.r.t. query q
$\bar{\mathbf{r}}$	upper bound of $\mathbf{r}$: $\bar{\mathbf{r}}_i \geq \mathbf{r}_i$ ($\forall i \in S$)
$\underline{\mathbf{r}}$	lower bound of $\mathbf{r}$: $\underline{\mathbf{r}}_i \leq \mathbf{r}_i$ ($\forall i \in S$)
$p_{i,j}$	transition probability from node i to j; $p_{i,j} = w_{ij}/w_i$
$\mathbf{P}$	transition probability matrix with $\mathbf{P}_{i,j} = p_{i,j}$
$\mathbf{T}$	modified $\mathbf{P}$: $\mathbf{T}_{i,j} = 0$, if $i = q$; $\mathbf{T}_{i,j} = \mathbf{P}_{i,j}$, if $i \neq q$
d, $\mathbf{r}_{\mathrm{d}}$	a dummy node d with constant proximity value $\mathbf{r}_{\mathrm{d}}$
c	decay factor (PHP or DHT); restart probability (RWR)

3. NO LOCAL OPTIMUM PROPERTY

In this section, we first introduce the basic concept of no local optimum property of proximity measures and discuss how it can be used to bound the proximity of the unvisited nodes. Then we study whether commonly used measures have no local optimum and discuss the relationship between them. Table 1 lists the main symbols and their definitions.

3.1 Theoretical Basis

Note that for some measures, such as penalized hitting probability, random walk with restart and effective importance, the larger the proximity the closer the nodes. In this case, no local optimum means no local maximum. For other measures, such as discounted/truncated hitting time, the smaller the proximity the closer the nodes. In this case, no local optimum means no local minimum.

Given an undirected and edge weighted graph $G = (V, E)$ and a query node $q \in V$, let $\mathbf{r}$ be the proximity vector with $\mathbf{r}_i$ representing the proximity of node $i \in V$ with respect to the query node q.

DEFINITION 1. [No Local Maximum] *A proximity measure has no local maximum if for any node $i \neq q$, there exists a neighbor node j of i (i.e., $j \in N_i$), such that $\mathbf{r}_j > \mathbf{r}_i$.*

DEFINITION 2. [No Local Minimum] *A proximity measure has no local minimum if for any node $i \neq q$, there exists a neighbor node j of i (i.e., $j \in N_i$), such that $\mathbf{r}_j < \mathbf{r}_i$.*

We say that a proximity measure has no local optimum if it has no local maximum or minimum. In Section 3.2, we will examine whether the commonly used proximity measures have no local optimum. Unless otherwise mentioned, in the next, we assume that the larger the proximity the closer the nodes, and focus on the no local maximum property. All conclusions can also be applied to the proximity measures with no local minimum.

Let S be a set of nodes, and $\bar{S} = V \setminus S$ be the remaining nodes. We use $\delta S = \{i \in S \mid \exists j \in N_i \cap \bar{S}\}$ to denote the *boundary* of S, and $\delta\bar{S} = \{i \in \bar{S} \mid \exists j \in N_i \cap S\}$ to denote the boundary of $\bar{S}$.

Algorithm 1: Basic top-k local search

Input: $G(V, E)$, q, $\mathbf{r}$, k
Output: Top-k nodes set K

$S \leftarrow \{q\}$; $\delta\bar{S} \leftarrow N_q$;
while $|S| < k+1$ **do**
  $u = \arg\max_{i \in \delta\bar{S}} \mathbf{r}_i$;
  $S = S \cup \{u\}$; $\delta\bar{S} = \delta\bar{S} \setminus \{u\} \cup (N_u \setminus S)$;
return $S \setminus \{q\}$;

Figure 1(a) shows an undirected graph with 8 nodes. Suppose that the node set $S = \{1, 2, 3, 4\}$, then we have $\bar{S} = \{5, 6, 7, 8\}$, $\delta S = \{3, 4\}$, and $\delta\bar{S} = \{5, 6, 7\}$.

THEOREM 1. *Let S be a node set containing the query node, and u be the node with the largest proximity in δS. If a proximity has no local maximum, we have that $\mathbf{r}_u > \mathbf{r}_j$ ($\forall j \in \bar{S}$).*

PROOF. Suppose otherwise. We have that $\exists j \in \bar{S}$, such that $\mathbf{r}_u \leq \mathbf{r}_j$. Now suppose that node v is the node with the largest proximity in $\bar{S}$. We have that $\forall i \in \bar{S} \cup \delta S$, $\mathbf{r}_v \geq \mathbf{r}_i$. The neighbors of node v must exist in $\bar{S} \cup \delta S$, i.e., $N_v \subseteq \bar{S} \cup \delta S$. Therefore, we have $\mathbf{r}_v \geq \mathbf{r}_i$ ($\forall i \in N_v$), which means node v is a local maximum. This contradicts the assumption. $\square$

Theorem 1 can also be generalized to $\delta\bar{S}$.

COROLLARY 1. *Let S be a node set containing the query node, and u be the node with the largest proximity in $\delta\bar{S}$. If a proximity has no local maximum, we have that $\mathbf{r}_u \geq \mathbf{r}_j$ ($\forall j \in \bar{S}$).*

PROOF. Let $S' = S \cup \delta\bar{S}$. We have $\delta S' \subseteq \delta\bar{S}$. Suppose that node $b \in \delta S'$ has the largest value in $\delta S'$. We have $\mathbf{r}_u \geq \mathbf{r}_b$. From Theorem 1, we have $\mathbf{r}_b > \mathbf{r}_i$ ($\forall i \in \bar{S}'$). Then, we have $\mathbf{r}_u \geq \mathbf{r}_j$ ($\forall j \in \bar{S} = \bar{S}' \cup \delta\bar{S}$). $\square$

Based on Corollary 1, assuming that we already have the exact proximity vector $\mathbf{r}$, we can design a simple local search strategy as shown in Algorithm 1 to find the top-k nodes. It begins from the query node q and uses S to store the top-k nodes. In each iteration, the algorithm finds the node u that has the largest proximity in $\delta\bar{S}$ and put it in S. $\delta\bar{S}$ is then updated accordingly. The algorithm continues until $|S| = k + 1$.

Let h be the average number of neighbors of a node. In each iteration i, on average h nodes are added to $\delta\bar{S}$. This takes $O(h \log hi)$ time for a sorted list. The overall complexity of Algorithm 1 is thus $O(\sum_{i=1}^{k} h \log hi) = O(hk \log hk)$.

3.2 Measures with and without local optimum

Table 2 summarizes whether the commonly used proximity measures have no local optimum property. Next, we use penalized hitting probability (PHP) [11, 21] as an example to illustrate that it has no local maximum. We use w_i to denote the weighted degree of node i, and w_{ij} to denote the edge weight between i and j. The transition probability from i to j is thus $p_{i,j} = w_{ij}/w_i$.

Suppose the undirected graph in Figure 1(a) has unit edge weight. Node 3 has weighted degree 3, thus its transition probability to node 4 is $p_{3,4} = 1/3$. Based on these transition probabilities, we can construct the corresponding transition graph as shown in Figure 1(b). In the transition graph, each directed edge and the number on the edge represent the transition probability from one node to the other.

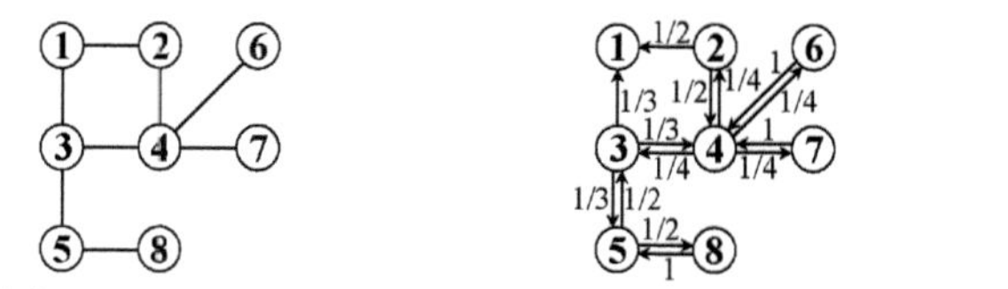

(a) Original graph (b) Transition graph (PHP, $q = 1$)

Figure 1: An example graph and its transition graph

Table 2: No local optimum property of some measures

Proximity measures	Abbr.	Ref.	Property
Penalized hitting probability	PHP	[11, 21]	No local maximum
Effective importance	EI	[3]	No local maximum
Discounted hitting time	DHT	[18]	No local minimum
Truncated hitting time	THT	[17]	No local minimum (within L hops)
Random walk with restart	RWR	[20]	Local maximum

PHP penalizes the random walk for each additional step. It can be defined as the following recursive function:

$$\mathbf{r}_i = \begin{cases} 1 & \text{if } i = q; \\ c\sum_{j \in N_i} p_{i,j}\mathbf{r}_j & \text{if } i \neq q. \end{cases}$$

where c ($0 < c < 1$) is the decay factor in the random walk process. In [11], $c = e^{-1}$ is used as the decay factor. The query node q in PHP has constant proximity value 1, and there is no transition probability going out of the query node. For example, there is no outgoing edges from the query node 1 in the transition graph in Figure 1(b).

Let $\mathbf{P}$ be the transition probability matrix with $\mathbf{P}_{i,j} = p_{i,j}$, and $\mathbf{T}$ be the modified transition probability matrix with

$$\mathbf{T}_{i,j} = \begin{cases} 0 & \text{if } i = q; \\ \mathbf{P}_{i,j} & \text{if } i \neq q. \end{cases}$$

Then the proximity $\mathbf{r}$ based on PHP can be written in the following matrix form

$$\mathbf{r} = c\mathbf{T}\mathbf{r} + \mathbf{e}_q,$$

where $\mathbf{e}_q(i) = 1$ if $i = q$, and $\mathbf{e}_q(i) = 0$ if $i \neq q$.

LEMMA 1. *PHP has no local maximum.*

PROOF. Suppose that node i is a local maximum. We have $\mathbf{r}_i = c\sum_{j \in N_i} p_{i,j}\mathbf{r}_j \leq c\sum_{j \in N_i} p_{i,j}\mathbf{r}_i = c\mathbf{r}_i < \mathbf{r}_i$. We get a contradiction that $\mathbf{r}_i < \mathbf{r}_i$. $\square$

The proofs of other proximity measures in Table 2 can be derived in a similar way. The detailed proofs can be found in the Appendix.

Some proximity measures have inherent relationship. The following theorem says that PHP, EI, and DHT are equivalent in terms of ranking.

THEOREM 2. *PHP, EI, and DHT give the same ranking results.*

PROOF. The proof is in the Appendix. $\square$

From the discussion in this section, we know that if a proximity measure has no local optimum, we can apply local search described in Algorithm 1 to find the top-k nodes under the assumption that the proximity values of all the nodes

(a) Deletion and restoration (b) Destination change

Figure 2: Basic operations on transition probability

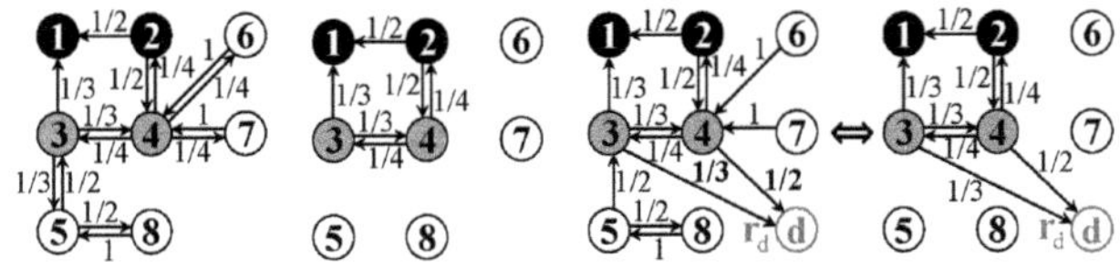

(a) Original $\mathbf{r}$ (b) LB $\underline{\mathbf{r}}$ (c) UB $\bar{\mathbf{r}}$

Figure 3: Lower and upper bounds based on basic operations

are given. However, without exploring the entire graph, the exact values of all the nodes are unknown. To tackle this challenge, we can develop lower and upper bounds on the proximity values of the visited nodes. When more nodes are visited, the lower and upper bounds become tighter and eventually converge to the exact proximity value.

Next, we will use PHP, which has no local optimum, as a concrete example to explain how to derive the lower and upper bounds. The strategy can be applied to other proximity measures with no local optimum, and their bounds are shown in the Appendix. How to apply the local search strategy to the measure having local optimum will be discussed in Section 5.6.

4. BOUNDING THE PROXIMITY

To develop the lower and upper bounds, we introduce three basic operations, i.e., deletion, restoration, and destination change of transition probability. We show how proximities change if we modify transition probabilities according to these operations. Then we discuss how to derive lower and upper bounds based on them.

4.1 Modifying Transition Probability

We first introduce the operation of deleting a transition probability. Figure 2(a) shows an example, in which the original graph is on the top, with node 1 being the query node and transition probabilities $p_{2,1} = p_{2,3} = 0.5$ and $p_{3,2} = 1$. After deleting $p_{2,3}$, the resulting graph is shown at the bottom. Note that deleting a transition probability is different from deleting an edge. Deleting an edge will change the transition probabilities on the remaining graph, while deleting a transition probability will not.

THEOREM 3. *Deleting a transition probability will not increase the proximity of any node.*

PROOF. Let $\mathbf{T}$ be the original transition probability matrix of PHP. Deleting $\mathbf{T}_{i,j}$ from $\mathbf{T}$ is the same as setting $\mathbf{T}_{i,j}$ to 0. Let $\mathbf{T}'$ represent the resulting matrix. PHP proximity $\mathbf{r}$ is computed based on $\mathbf{T}$, and $\mathbf{r}'$ is based on $\mathbf{T}'$.

Let $\Delta\mathbf{r} = \mathbf{r} - \mathbf{r}'$, and $\Delta\mathbf{T} = \mathbf{T} - \mathbf{T}'$. Note that $\Delta\mathbf{T}$ has only one non-zero element $\Delta\mathbf{T}_{i,j} = \mathbf{T}_{i,j}$. We have that $\Delta\mathbf{r} = c(\mathbf{T}' + \Delta\mathbf{T})\mathbf{r} - c\mathbf{T}'\mathbf{r}' = c\mathbf{T}'\Delta\mathbf{r} + c\Delta\mathbf{T}\mathbf{r} = c\mathbf{T}'\Delta\mathbf{r} + \mathbf{e}_i$, where $\mathbf{e}_i$ is a vector with the only non-zero element $\mathbf{e}_i(i) = c\mathbf{T}_{i,j}\mathbf{r}_j$. The solution of the previous equation is $\Delta\mathbf{r} = (\mathbf{I} - c\mathbf{T}')^{-1}\mathbf{e}_i$. The elements of $c\mathbf{T}'$ are non-negative and $||c\mathbf{T}'||_\infty < 1$. It can be expanded by Neumann series [15] as $(\mathbf{I} - c\mathbf{T}')^{-1} = \sum_{l=0}^{\infty}(c\mathbf{T}')^l > 0$. Thus the solution $\Delta\mathbf{r}$ must be non-negative. This completes the proof. □

Continue with the example in Figure 2(a). Suppose that the decay factor $c = 0.5$. The original PHP proximity vector is $\mathbf{r} = [1, 2/7, 1/7]$. After deleting $p_{2,3}$, the new proximity vector is $\mathbf{r}' = [1, 1/4, 1/8]$.

It can be shown in a similar way that if we restore the transition probability as shown in Figure 2(a), the proximities will not decrease.

THEOREM 4. *Restoring a deleted transition probability will not decrease the proximity of any node.*

PROOF. Omitted. □

Figure 2(b) shows an example in which we change the destination of the original transition probability $p_{3,2}$ from node 2 to 1. Thus $p_{3,1}$ is set to $p_{3,2}$, and $p_{3,2}$ is set to 0.

THEOREM 5. *Changing the destination of transition probability $p_{i,j}$ from node j to node l with $\mathbf{r}_l \geq \mathbf{r}_j$ ($\mathbf{r}_l \leq \mathbf{r}_j$) will not decrease (increase) the proximity of any node.*

PROOF. The proof is in the Appendix. □

Let us continue with the example in Figure 2(b), where node 1 is the query node. After we change the destination of $p_{3,2}$ from node 2 to 1, the proximity values should be non-decreasing. With a decay factor $c = 0.5$, the proximity vectors before and after the destination change are $\mathbf{r} = [1, 2/7, 1/7]$ and $\mathbf{r}' = [1, 3/8, 1/2]$ respectively.

The proofs for other measures having no local optimum are similar and omitted here.

4.2 Lower Bound

Recall that in Algorithm 1, S, $\bar{S}$, δS and $\delta\bar{S}$ represent the set of visited nodes, the set of unvisited nodes, the boundary of S, and the boundary of $\bar{S}$, respectively. From Theorem 3, if we delete all transition probabilities $\{p_{i,j} : i \text{ or } j \in \bar{S}\}$ in the original graph, the proximity value of any node u computed using the resulting graph, $\underline{\mathbf{r}}_u$, will be less than or equal to its original value $\mathbf{r}_u$, i.e., $\underline{\mathbf{r}}_u \leq \mathbf{r}_u$. Therefore, $\underline{\mathbf{r}}$ can be used as the lower bound of $\mathbf{r}$.

Let us take the undirected graph in Figure 1(a) for example. Its transition graph is shown in Figure 3(a), with node 1 being the query node and transition probabilities shown on the edges. Suppose that the current set of visited nodes $S = \{1, 2, 3, 4\}$. Thus $\bar{S} = \{5, 6, 7, 8\}$, $\delta S = \{3, 4\}$, and $\delta\bar{S} = \{5, 6, 7\}$. The nodes in S but not in δS are black. The nodes in δS are gray. The nodes in $\bar{S}$ are white.

Figure 3(b) shows the resulting graph after deleting all transition probabilities $\{p_{i,j} : i \text{ or } j \in \bar{S}\}$. The proximity values $\underline{\mathbf{r}}$ computed based on Figure 3(b) will lower bound the original proximity values $\mathbf{r}$ for the nodes in S.

4.3 Upper Bound

From Theorem 5, if we change the destination of the transition probabilities $\{p_{i,j} : i \in \delta S, j \in \delta\bar{S}\}$ to a newly added dummy node d with a constant proximity value $\mathbf{r}_\mathrm{d}$ and $\mathbf{r}_\mathrm{d} > \mathbf{r}_v$ ($\forall v \in \bar{S}$), the proximity value of any node u computed using the resulting graph, $\bar{\mathbf{r}}_u$, will be greater than or equal to its original value $\mathbf{r}_u$, i.e., $\bar{\mathbf{r}}_u \geq \mathbf{r}_u$. Therefore, $\bar{\mathbf{r}}$ can be used as the upper bound of $\mathbf{r}$.

Continue with the example in Figure 3(a). In the original graph, $\delta S = \{3, 4\}$, $\delta\bar{S} = \{5, 6, 7\}$, $p_{3,5} = 1/3$, $p_{4,6} = p_{4,7} = 1/4$. The left figure in Figure 3(c) shows the resulting graph

Algorithm 2: Fast top-k local search (FLoS)

```
Input: G(V, E), q, k, c, τ
Output: Top-k nodes set K
S^0 ← {q}; δS^0 ← {q}; r̲_q^0 = 1; r̄_q^0 = 1; T^0_{q,q} = 0;
bStop = false; t = 0;
while bStop == false do
    t++;
    LocalExpansion();
    UpdateLowerBound();
    UpdateUpperBound();
    CheckTerminationCriteria();
return K;
```

Algorithm 3: LocalExpansion()

```
u = arg max_{i∈δS^{t-1}} 1/2 (r̲_i^{t-1} + r̄_i^{t-1});
S^t = S^{t-1} ∪ N_u;
Update δS^t;
```

after we change all the transition probabilities going from δS to $\delta\bar{S}$ to the newly added dummy node d. Specifically, $p_{3,\mathrm{d}} = 1/3$ and $p_{4,\mathrm{d}} = p_{4,6} + p_{4,7} = 1/2$. Note that after changing the destination to d, there will be no transition probability from any node in S to any node in $\bar{S}$. Therefore, for the nodes in S, the upper bounds can be computed by the subgraph induced by the nodes in S and the dummy node d, as shown on the right in Figure 3(c).

Note that to get the upper bound, we need to add a dummy node d with constant proximity value $\mathbf{r}_\mathrm{d} \geq \mathbf{r}_v$ ($\forall v \in \bar{S}$). In the next section, we will present the fast local search algorithm, FLoS, and discuss how to choose $\mathbf{r}_\mathrm{d}$.

5. FAST LOCAL SEARCH

In this section, we present the FLoS algorithm, which utilizes the bounds developed in Section 4 to enable local search. We show that the bounds can only change monotonically when more nodes are visited. A theoretical analysis on the number of visited nodes is also provided.

5.1 The FLoS Algorithm

Algorithm 2 describes the FLoS algorithm. It has four main steps. In the first step, the algorithm expands locally to the neighbors of a selected visited node. In the second and third steps, it updates the lower and upper bounds of the visited nodes. Finally, it checks whether the top-k nodes are identified.

The local expansion step is shown in Algorithm 3. It picks the node in δS having the largest average lower and upper bound values, and expands to the neighbors of this node. S and δS are then updated accordingly. We take the average of the lower and upper bound value as an approximation of the exact proximity value. Expanding the node with the largest value is the best-first search strategy.

Algorithm 4 shows how to update the lower bound by using PHP as an example. It can also be applied to other measures with no local optimum. To update the bounds, we first construct the modified transition matrix $\mathbf{T}$. Note that the size of $\mathbf{T}$ is $|S| \times |S|$ instead of $|V| \times |V|$. We do not allocate memory for the full matrix $\mathbf{T}$, and only use adjacent list to represent it. The lower bound vector $\underline{\mathbf{r}}$ is initiated the same as in the previous iteration or 0 for the newly added nodes. We then use the standard iterative method (as shown

Algorithm 4: UpdateLowerBound()

```
T^t_{i,j} = w_ij / Σ_{l∈N_i} w_il, if node i or j are newly added;
T^t_{i,j} = T^{t-1}_{i,j}, if nodes i and j exist in the last iteration;
r̲_i^t = 0, if node i is newly added;
r̲_i^t = r̲_i^{t-1}, if node i exists in the last iteration;
e(i) = 1, if i = q; e(i) = 0, otherwise;
r̲^t = IterativeMethod(T^t, r̲^t, e, c, τ);
```

Algorithm 5: UpdateUpperBound()

```
1: Extend T^t with 1 column and 1 row for the dummy node d;
2: T^t_{i,d} = 1 − Σ_{j∈N_i} T^t_{i,j}, if node i ∈ δS^t;
3: T^t_{i,d} = 0, if i ∈ S^t \ δS^t;
4: T^t_{d,i} = 0, for any node i;
5: r̄_i^t = 1, if node i is newly added;
6: r̄_i^t = r̄_i^{t-1}, if node i exists in the last iteration;
7: r̄_d^t = r_d^t = max_{i∈δS^{t-1}} r̄_i^{t-1};          // dummy node value
8: Extend e with 1 new element e(d) = r_d^t for the node d;
9: r̄^t = IterativeMethod(T^t, r̄^t, e, c, τ);
```

Algorithm 6: CheckTerminationCriteria()

```
if |S^t \ δS^t \ {q}| ≥ k then
    K ← k nodes in S^t \ δS^t \ {q} with largest r̲^t;
    if min_{i∈K} r̲_i^t ≥ max_{i∈S^t\K\{q}} r̄_i^t then bStop = true;
```

Algorithm 7: IterativeMethod()

```
Input: T, r_in, e, c, τ
Output: r_out
r^0 = r_in; n = 0;
repeat n++; r^n = cTr^{n-1} + e; until ||r^n − r^{n-1}|| < τ;
return r^n;
```

in Algorithm 7) to solve the linear equation $\underline{\mathbf{r}} = c\mathbf{T}\underline{\mathbf{r}} + \mathbf{e}$ to update $\underline{\mathbf{r}}$.

Algorithm 5 shows how to update the upper bound. The transition matrix $\mathbf{T}$ has one additional dummy node d and its related transition probabilities $\{p_{i,\mathrm{d}} : i \in \delta S\}$. The values in $\bar{\mathbf{r}}$ are initiated the same as the values in the previous iteration or 1 for the newly added nodes. The smaller the value of $\mathbf{r}_\mathrm{d}$, the tighter the upper bounds. On the other hand, we also need to make sure that the value $\mathbf{r}_\mathrm{d}$ is larger than the exact proximity value of any unvisited node. Therefore in line 7, we use the largest upper bound value in the boundary of the last iteration as $\mathbf{r}_\mathrm{d}^t$. We have $\mathbf{r}_\mathrm{d}^t = \max_{i\in\delta S^{t-1}} \bar{\mathbf{r}}_i^{t-1} \geq \max_{i\in\delta S^{t-1}} \mathbf{r}_i > \mathbf{r}_j (\forall j \in \bar{S}^{t-1})$, where the last inequality is based on Theorem 1. Thus $\mathbf{r}_\mathrm{d}^t > \mathbf{r}_j (\forall j \in \bar{S}^t)$, since $\bar{S}^t \subseteq \bar{S}^{t-1}$. This guarantees the correctness of the upper bound according to Theorem 5. Finally, we solve the linear equation $\bar{\mathbf{r}} = c\mathbf{T}\bar{\mathbf{r}} + \mathbf{e}$ to update $\bar{\mathbf{r}}$ by using Algorithm 7. Algorithm 7 is very efficient in practice. This is because when the initial values of the iterative method is close to the exact solution, the algorithm will converge very fast. In our method, between two adjacent iterations, the proximity values of the visited nodes are very close. Therefore, updating the proximity is very efficient.

Algorithm 6 shows the termination criteria. We select the k nodes in $S \setminus \delta S \setminus \{q\}$ with largest $\underline{\mathbf{r}}$ values. If the minimum lower bound of the selected nodes is greater than the maximum upper bound of the remaining visited nodes, the selected nodes will be the top-k nodes in the entire graph.

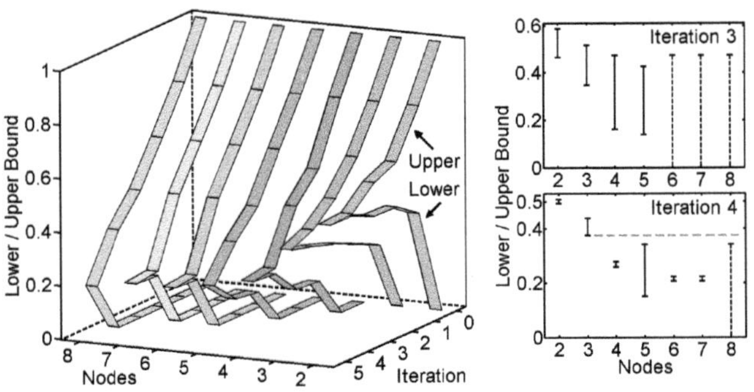

Figure 4: Lower and upper bounds in different iterations (PHP: $q = 1$, $c = 0.8$)

Table 3: Newly visited nodes in each iteration

Iteration	1	2	3	4	5
Newly visited nodes	{2, 3}	{4}	{5}	{6, 7}	{8}

This is because the maximum proximity of unvisited nodes is bounded by the maximum proximity in δS, which is in turn bounded by the maximum upper bound in δS.

Figure 4 shows the lower and upper bounds at different iterations using the example graph in Figure 1(a). One iteration represents one local expansion process. The newly visited nodes in each iteration are listed in Table 3.

The left figure in Figure 4 shows how the lower and upper bounds change through local expansions. Query node 1 has constant proximity value 1.0 thus is not shown. It can be seen that the bounds monotonically change and eventually converge to the exact proximity value when all the nodes are visited. The monotonicity of the bounds is proved theoretically in next section.

The right figure in Figure 4 shows the lower and upper bounds in iteration 3 (at the top) and 4 (at the bottom). The interval from the lower to upper bounds is indicated by the vertical line segment. The interval of the unvisited node is indicated by the dashed line segment. In iteration 3, nodes $\{6, 7, 8\}$ are unvisited, and their upper bound is the upper bound for node 4, which is the maximum upper bound for the boundary nodes $\{4, 5\}$. In iteration 4, the bounds become tighter, and the minimum lower bound of nodes $\{2, 3\}$ is larger than the maximum upper bound of the remaining nodes $\{4, 5, 6, 7, 8\}$, which is indicated by the horizontal red dashed line. Therefore, nodes $\{2, 3\}$ are guaranteed to be the top-2 nodes after iteration 4, even though node 8 is still unvisited.

5.2 Monotonicity of the Bounds

We first consider the monotonicity of the lower bound. Let S^{t-1} and S^t represent the set of visited nodes in iterations $(t-1)$ and t respectively. From iteration $(t-1)$ to t, we only restore some transition probabilities in $\{p_{i,j} : i \text{ or } j \in S^t \setminus S^{t-1}, i \neq q\}$. From Theorem 4, we have $\underline{\mathbf{r}}_i^t \geq \underline{\mathbf{r}}_i^{t-1} (\forall i \in S^{t-1})$. Therefore, the lower bound will monotonically non-decrease when more nodes are visited.

Next we examine the monotonicity of the upper bound. From iteration $(t-1)$ to t, we add new nodes in $S^t \setminus S^{t-1}$ and decrease $\mathbf{r}_\mathrm{d}$. After adding new nodes, the transition probabilities need to be updated accordingly. Specifically, we need to (1) add transition probabilities $\{p_{i,j}\}$ from the newly added nodes $i (\in S^t \setminus S^{t-1})$ to nodes $j (\in \delta S^{t-1})$, and

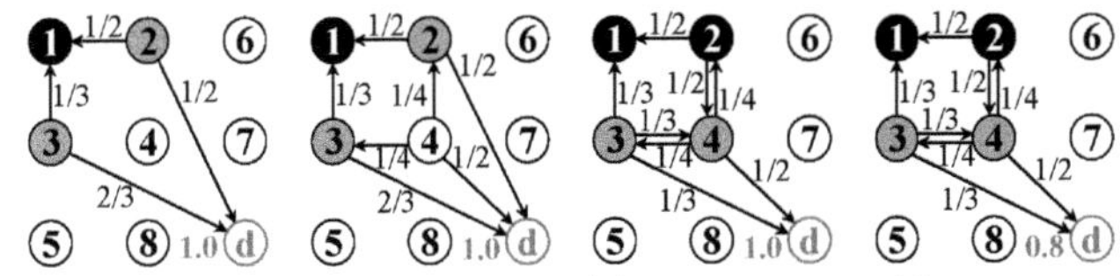

Figure 5: Transition graphs between two adjacent iterations

$\{p_{i,\mathrm{d}}\}$ from i to the dummy node d; (2) add the transition probabilities $\{p_{j,i}\}$ from nodes $j (\in \delta S^{t-1})$ to the newly added nodes $i (\in S^t \setminus S^{t-1})$, and remove their correspondences in $\{p_{j,\mathrm{d}}\}$.

An example is shown in Figure 5. Figure 5(a) shows the transition graph for the first iteration. Figure 5(b) shows the resulting graph after applying step 1. Figure 5(c) shows the resulting graph after applying step 2. Reducing $\mathbf{r}_\mathrm{d}$ in Figure 5(c) will result in the final transition graph for the next iteration as shown in Figure 5(d).

Note that applying step 1 will not change the upper bound values for the nodes in S^{t-1}, since all the newly added transition probabilities begin from nodes $i (\in S^t \setminus S^{t-1})$. Step 2 resets the transition probabilities from nodes $j (\in \delta S^{t-1})$ to the newly added nodes $i (\in S^t \setminus S^{t-1})$. This is equivalent to destination change, i.e., changing $\{p_{j,\mathrm{d}}\}$ to $\{p_{j,i}\}$. Moreover, we have $\mathbf{r}_\mathrm{d} \geq \mathbf{r}_\mathrm{i}$. Thus, step 2 will not increase the upper bound values according to Theorem 5. From Theorem 5, reducing the value of $\mathbf{r}_\mathrm{d}$ will not increase the upper bound values. Therefore, the upper bound will be monotonically non-increase from iteration $(t-1)$ to t.

5.3 Tightening the Bounds

The bounds used in FLoS can be further tightened by adding self-loop transition probabilities to the nodes in δS. We will still use PHP as an example to illustrate the process. We first define the star-to-mesh transformation on the transition graph, which is inspired by the star-mesh transformation in circuit theory [12].

DEFINITION 3. [Star-to-mesh transformation] *(1) Delete a node $u \in V \setminus \{q\}$ and its incident transition probabilities; (2) For any pair of nodes $i, j \in N_u$, add transition probabilities $p'_{i,j} = c p_{i,u} p_{u,j}$.*

Note that if $i = j$, it becomes the self-loop transition probability $p'_{i,i} = c p_{i,u} p_{u,i}$. Applying the star-to-mesh transformation for a node will not change the PHP proximity values of the remaining nodes.

LEMMA 2. *Applying the star-to-mesh transformation of node u will not change the PHP proximity values of nodes $V \setminus \{q, u\}$.*

PROOF. This can be proved by plugging the equation $\mathbf{r}_u = c \sum_{i \in N_u} p_{u,i} \mathbf{r}_i$ into the recursive equations of neighbor nodes $i \in N_u$ in the original transition graph. □

The self-loop transition probabilities generated in the star-to-mesh transformation can be used to further tighten the lower and upper bounds.

LEMMA 3. *Adding self-loop transition probability $p_{i,i} = c \sum_{j \in N_i \cap \delta \bar{S}} p_{i,j} p_{j,i}$ $(\forall i \in \delta S)$ will tighten the lower bound.*

(a) Adding self-loop for LB $\underline{\mathbf{r}}$ (b) Adding self-loop for UB $\overline{\mathbf{r}}$

Figure 6: Transition graphs with self-loops

PROOF. Adding a self-loop transition probability is equivalent to changing the destination of the transition probability $p_{i,i}$ from a dummy node with proximity value 0 to node i. Therefore, the lower bound values of all the nodes will be non-decreasing.

Next we show the new bound values are still lower bounds. For the nodes in $\delta\bar{S}$, we apply star-to-mesh transformation sequentially in any order. After the star-to-mesh transformation of one node $j \in \delta\bar{S}$, we delete all the newly added transition probabilities except the self-loop transition probabilities of nodes in δS. After all the nodes in $\delta\bar{S}$ have been deleted, the self-loop transition probability of a node $i \in \delta S$ is $p_{i,i} = c\sum_{j \in N_i \cap \delta\bar{S}} p_{i,j}p_{j,i}$. During this process, we only apply star-to-mesh transformation and transition probability deletion. Therefore, the new bound values are still lower bounds. □

LEMMA 4. *Adding self-loop transition probability* $p_{i,i} = c\sum_{j \in N_i \cap \delta\bar{S}} p_{i,j}p_{j,i}$ *and set* $p_{i,\mathrm{d}} = c\sum_{j \in N_i \cap \delta\bar{S}} p_{i,j}(1 - p_{j,i})$ *(*$\forall i \in \delta S$*) will tighten the upper bound.*

PROOF. Note that the sum is $p_{i,i} + p_{i,\mathrm{d}} = c\sum_{j \in N_i \cap \delta\bar{S}} p_{i,j} < \sum_{j \in N_i \cap \delta\bar{S}} p_{i,j}$, which is the transition probability to dummy node d in the original transition graph. This means that we change the destination of transition probability $p_{i,i}$ from node d to node i. Since the proximity of d is no less than that of i, the upper bound of all nodes will be non-increasing. We can prove that the proximity values are still upper bounds through the star-to-mesh transformation. □

Figure 6 shows the transition graphs with self-loop probabilities for computing the lower and upper bounds. The original ones are shown in Figure 3.

5.4 Analysis on the Number of Visited Nodes

In this subsection, we analyze the number of visited nodes. Let h be the average number of neighbors of a node. Suppose that the nodes in the boundary of visited nodes are ρ hops away from the query node q. We assume that the number of visited nodes equals h^ρ. Note that this is an upper bound of the number of visited nodes. In Section 6, we show the actual number of visited nodes in real graphs.

The proximity of one node will decrease by a factor of c when it is one hop farther away from the query node. The nodes in the boundary of the visited nodes have proximity less than c^ρ because they are ρ hops away from the query.

What is the distribution of the gaps between the upper and lower bounds? The upper bound $\overline{\mathbf{r}}$ is computed based on the recursive equation $\overline{\mathbf{r}} = c\mathbf{T}\overline{\mathbf{r}} + \mathbf{e}_{q,\mathrm{d}}$, where vector $\mathbf{e}_{q,\mathrm{d}}$ has only two non-zero elements $\mathbf{e}_{q,\mathrm{d}}(q) = 1$ and $\mathbf{e}_{q,\mathrm{d}}(\mathrm{d}) = \mathbf{r}_\mathrm{d}$. When we set the proximity value of dummy node to 0, i.e., $\mathbf{e}_{q,\mathrm{d}}(\mathrm{d}) = 0$, we will get the recursive equation $\underline{\mathbf{r}} = c\mathbf{T}\underline{\mathbf{r}} + \mathbf{e}_q$ for the lower bound $\underline{\mathbf{r}}$. Let $\mathbf{r}' = \overline{\mathbf{r}} - \underline{\mathbf{r}}$ be the gaps between the upper and lower bounds. We have that $\mathbf{r}' = c\mathbf{T}\mathbf{r}' + \mathbf{e}_\mathrm{d}$, where vector $\mathbf{e}_\mathrm{d}$ has only one non-zero element $\mathbf{e}_\mathrm{d}(\mathrm{d}) = \mathbf{r}_\mathrm{d}$. Thus the gaps $\mathbf{r}'$ can be interpreted as the PHP proximity values when the query node is the dummy node d with constant proximity value $\mathbf{r}_\mathrm{d}$.

Based on this observation, the gap $\mathbf{r}'_u$ of one node u will decrease by a factor of c when it is one hop farther away from the boundary. Let ρ_u denote the number of hops that u is away from the query node. Node u is $\rho - \rho_u$ hops away from the boundary. So, the gap $\mathbf{r}'_u$ is less than $c^{\rho-\rho_u} \cdot c^\rho$, i.e., $\mathbf{r}'_u < c^{2\rho-\rho_u}$.

For any two nodes u and v, we can distinguish their rankings if $\mathbf{r}'_u + \mathbf{r}'_v < \epsilon$, where ϵ is the difference of the exact proximity values of nodes u and v. We already derive that $\mathbf{r}'_u < c^{2\rho-\rho_u}$ and $\mathbf{r}'_v < c^{2\rho-\rho_v}$. Thus if we have that $\rho > \frac{1}{2}\log_c \epsilon - \frac{1}{2}\log_c(c^{-\rho_u} + c^{-\rho_v})$, then the pair of nodes u and v can be distinguished.

Now we consider the case when u and v are the kth and $(k+1)$th nodes in the exact ranking list respectively. We have $h^{\rho_u} \geq k$ and $h^{\rho_v} \geq k+1$. Thus, the number of visited hops should satisfy $\rho > \frac{1}{2}\log_c \frac{\epsilon}{2} + \frac{1}{2}\log_h k$. Therefore, we need to visit $h^\rho = O((kh^{\log_c \frac{\epsilon}{2}})^{\frac{1}{2}})$ nodes to distinguish the kth and $(k+1)$th nodes.

5.5 Complexity

Assume Algorithm 2 executes in β iterations, which is proportional to $(kh^{\log_c \frac{\epsilon}{2}})^{\frac{1}{2}}$. Let h be the average number of neighbors of a node. The LocalExpansion step takes $O(hi)$ time to find the node to expand. To update the lower bound, updating $\mathbf{T}$ needs $O(h^2)$ operations, and updating $\underline{\mathbf{r}}$ and $\mathbf{e}$ needs $O(h)$ operations. Subgraph induced by S has $O(h^2 i)$ edges, so matrix $\mathbf{T}$ has $O(h^2 i)$ non-zero entries. Therefore using the iterative method to solve linear equations takes $O(\alpha h^2 i)$ time, where α is the number of iterations. Thus the overall complexity of UpdateLowerBound in the ith iteration is $O(\alpha h^2 i)$. The complexity of UpdateUpperBound function is the same as that of UpdateLowerBound. In CheckTerminationCriteria step, finding the nodes with largest lower bounds takes $O(hi)$ time. Therefore, the overall complexity of FLoS is $O(\sum_{i=1}^{\beta}(\alpha h^2 i + hi)) = O(\alpha h^2 \beta^2)$.

Note that so far, we have used PHP to illustrate the key principles underlying the fast local search method. All results are applicable to other measures with no local optimum such as DHT, THT, and EI. The derivations are similar to those of PHP and omitted here.

5.6 Extension to RWR

In this section, we discuss how to apply local search to RWR which has local optimum. The key idea is to utilize the relationship between RWR and PHP. Utilizing such relationship, we can easily derive the lower and upper bounds for RWR based on the lower and upper bounds for PHP.

Random walk with restart (also known as personalized PageRank) [20] is a widely used proximity measure. RWR can be described as follows. From a node i, the random walker can walk to its neighbors with probabilities proportional to the edge weights. In each step, it has a probability of c to return to i, where c is a constant. The proximity of node i w.r.t. q is defined as the stationary probability that the walker will finally stay at q. RWR can be defined recursively as $\mathbf{r}_i = (1-c)\sum_{j \in N_i} p_{j,i}\mathbf{r}_j$, if $i \neq q$, and $\mathbf{r}_q = (1-c)\sum_{j \in N_q} p_{j,q}\mathbf{r}_j + c$, where c $(0 < c < 1)$ is the constant restart probability.

Let RWR(i) and PHP(i) represent the proximity of node i based on RWR and PHP respectively. We first show that RWR and PHP have the following relationship.

THEOREM 6. $\mathrm{RWR}(i) = \frac{\mathrm{RWR}(q)}{w_q} \cdot w_i \cdot \mathrm{PHP}(i)$

PROOF. Based on the recursive definition of RWR, we have $\frac{\mathrm{RWR}(i)}{w_i} = (1-c)\sum_{j \in N_i} \frac{w_{ij}}{w_j} \cdot \frac{\mathrm{RWR}(j)}{w_i} = (1-c)\sum_{j \in N_i} \frac{w_{ij}}{w_i} \cdot \frac{\mathrm{RWR}(j)}{w_j}$, for $\forall i \neq q$. So, we have $\frac{\mathrm{RWR}(i)}{w_i} = (1-c)\sum_{j \in N_i} p_{i,j} \cdot \frac{\mathrm{RWR}(j)}{w_j}$, for $\forall i \neq q$. This degree normalized RWR, $\frac{\mathrm{RWR}(i)}{w_i}$, has the same recursive equation as PHP with decay factor $(1-c)$. So we have $\frac{\mathrm{RWR}(i)}{w_i \cdot \mathrm{PHP}(i)} = \frac{\mathrm{RWR}(q)}{w_q \cdot \mathrm{PHP}(q)}$. □

Based on Theorem 6, we have that $\mathrm{RWR}(i) \propto w_i \cdot \mathrm{PHP}(i)$ when the query node q is fixed. Suppose node $b \in \delta S$ has the largest PHP proximity value. Based on Theorem 1, we have $\mathrm{PHP}(i) \leq \mathrm{PHP}(b), \forall i \in \bar{S}$. Let $w(\bar{S})$ denote the maximum degree of unvisited nodes in $\bar{S}$. We have $w_i \cdot \mathrm{PHP}(i) \leq w(\bar{S}) \cdot \mathrm{PHP}(i) \leq w(\bar{S}) \cdot \mathrm{PHP}(b)$. Therefore, if we maintain the maximum degree of the unvisited nodes, we can develop upper bound for the proximity values of unvisited nodes.

Specifically, we can apply FLoS to RWR as follows. In Algorithm 3, change line 1 to $u = \arg\max_{i \in \delta S^{t-1}} \frac{w_i}{2}(\underline{\mathbf{r}}_i^{t-1} + \overline{\mathbf{r}}_i^{t-1})$. In Algorithm 6, we select k nodes in $S^t \setminus \delta S^t \setminus \{q\}$ with largest $w_i \cdot \underline{\mathbf{r}}_i^t$ values, and change the termination criteria to $(\min_{i \in K} w_i \cdot \underline{\mathbf{r}}_i^t \geq \max_{i \in S^t \setminus K \setminus \{q\}} w_i \cdot \overline{\mathbf{r}}_i^t)$ and $(\min_{i \in K} w_i \cdot \underline{\mathbf{r}}_i^t \geq w(\bar{S}) \cdot \max_{i \in \delta S^t} \overline{\mathbf{r}}_i^t)$. All other processes remain the same.

6. EXPERIMENTAL RESULTS

In this section, we present extensive experimental results on evaluating the performance of the FLoS algorithm. The datasets are shown in Table 4. The real datasets are publicly available from the website *http://snap.stanford.edu/data/*. The synthetic datasets are generated using the Erdös-Rényi random graph (RAND) model [7] and R-MAT model [4] with different parameters. All programs are written in C++. All experiments are performed on a server with 32G memory, Intel Xeon 3.2GHz CPU, and Redhat 4.1.2 OS.

6.1 State-of-the-art Methods

The measures we use include PHP, EI, THT, and RWR. We compare FLoS with the state-of-the-art methods for each measure as summarized in Table 5. These methods are categorized into global and local methods.

The global iteration (GI) method directly applies the iterative method on the entire graph [16]. It guarantees to find the exact top-k nodes. The graph embedding (GE) method can answer the query in constant time after embedding [22]. It can only be applied to RWR. However, the embedding process is very time consuming. Moreover, it only returns approximate results. The Castanet algorithm is specifically designed for RWR. It improves the GI method and guarantees the exactness of the results [9]. K-dash is the state-of-the-art matrix-based method for RWR which guarantees result exactness [8]. Note that K-dash and GE can only be applied on two medium-sized real graphs because of the expensive preprocessing step.

Dynamic neighborhood expansion (DNE) method applies a best-first expansion strategy to find the top-k nodes using PHP [21]. This strategy is heuristic and does not guarantee to find the exact solution. The number of visited nodes is fixed to 4,000 in the experiments. NN_EI applies the push style method [2, 5] in local search, and guarantees the exactness of the top-k results [3]. Since PHP and EI are equivalent in terms of ranking, we can compare the methods for PHP and EI directly. LS_RWR also applies the push style method [2, 5] in local search [18]. It returns approximate results. LS_EI is based on LS_RWR and has similar performance [18]. LS_THT is a local search method for THT [17]. In the experiments, we set the truncated length to 10. The decay factor in PHP and the restart probability in RWR and EI are set to 0.5.

Table 4: Datasets used in the experiments

Datasets		Abbr.	Nodes	Edges
Real	Amazon	AZ	334,863	925,872
	DBLP	DP	317,080	1,049,866
	Youtube	YT	1,134,890	2,987,624
	LiveJournal	LJ	3,997,962	34,681,189
Synthetic	In-memory	–	Varying size	
		–	Varying density	
	Disk-resident	–	Varying size	

Table 5: State-of-the-art methods used for comparison

Our methods (Exact)	State-of-the-art methods			
	Abbr.	Key idea	Ref.	Exactness
FLoS_PHP	GI_PHP	Global iteration	[16]	Exact
	DNE	Local search	[21]	Approx.
	NN_EI	Local search	[3]	Exact
	LS_EI	Local search	[18]	Approx.
FLoS_RWR	GI_RWR	Global iteration	[16]	Exact
	GE_RWR	Graph embedding	[22]	Approx.
	Castanet	Improved GI	[9]	Exact
	K-dash	Matrix inversion	[8]	Exact
	LS_RWR	Local search	[18]	Approx.
FLoS_THT	GI_THT	Global iteration	[16]	Exact
	LS_THT	Local search	[17]	Approx.

6.2 Evaluation on Real Graphs

We study the efficiency of the selected methods on real graphs when varying the number of returned nodes k. For each k, we repeat the experiments 10^3 times, each with a randomly picked query node. The average running time is reported. For methods using the iteration procedure in Algorithm 7, the termination threshold is set to $\tau = 10^{-5}$. We also perform experiments using a fixed number of 10 iterations. The results are similar and omitted here due to the space limit.

6.2.1 Evaluation of FLoS_PHP

Figure 7 shows the running time of different methods for PHP. The running time of DNE is almost a constant for different k, because it visits a fixed number of nodes. The running time of NN_EI increases when k increases. FLoS_PHP is more efficient than NN_EI, which demonstrates that the bounds of FLoS are tighter. LS_EI has a constant running time. This is because it extracts the cluster containing the query node. Note that LS_EI takes tens of hours in the preprocessing step to cluster the graphs.

Figure 9(a) shows the ratio between the number of visited nodes using FLoS_PHP and total number of nodes in the graph. The value indicated by the bar is the average ratio of 10^3 queries. The minimum and maximum ratios are also shown in the figure. As can be seen from the figure, only a very small part of the graph is needed for FLoS to find the exact solution. Moreover, the ratio decreases when the graph size increases. This indicates that FLoS is more effective for larger graphs.

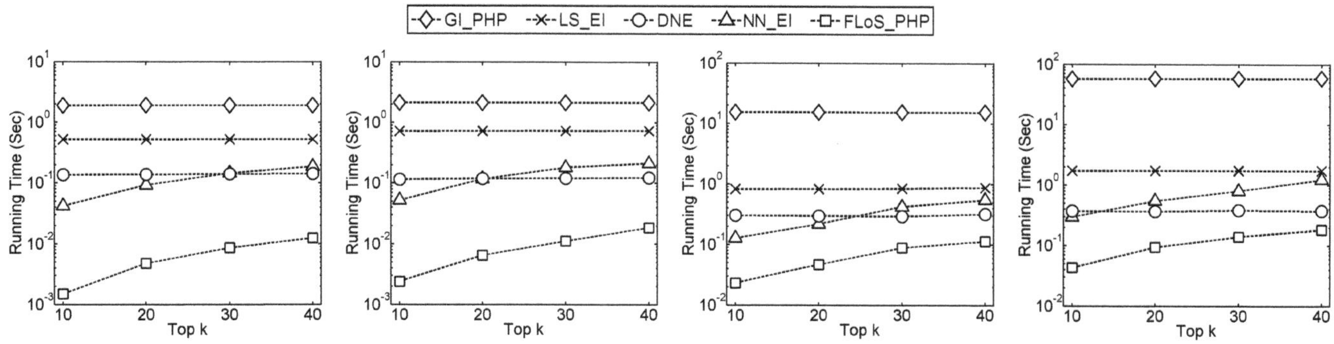

(a) AZ (b) DP (c) YT (d) LJ

Figure 7: Running time of different methods for PHP on real graphs

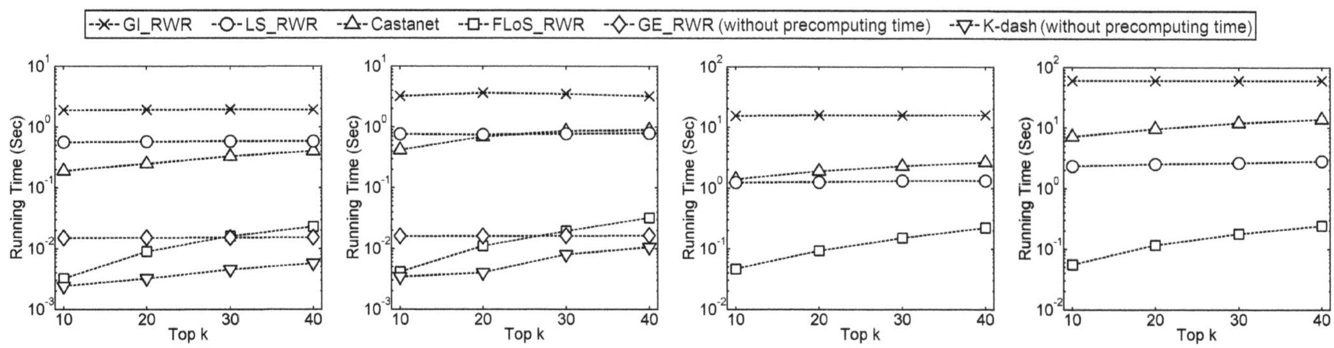

(a) AZ (b) DP (c) YT (d) LJ

Figure 8: Running time of different methods for RWR on real graphs

6.2.2 *Evaluation of FLoS_RWR*

Figure 8 shows the running time for RWR. K-dash has the best performance after precomputing the matrix inversion as shown in Figures 8(a) and 8(b). The precomputing step of K-dash takes tens of hours for the medium-sized AZ and DP graphs and cannot be applied to the other two larger graphs. GE_RWR also has fast response time. However, as discussed before, its embedding step is time consuming and not applicable to larger graphs. Moreover, it does not find the exact solution. Castanet method cuts the running time from the GI method by 72% to 91%. LS_RWR method has constant running time, and it needs tens of hours in the precomputing step to cluster the graphs.

Figure 9(b) shows the ratio of the number of visited nodes of the FLoS_RWR method. The results are similar to that of Figure 9(a).

6.2.3 *Evaluation of FLoS_THT*

Figure 10 shows the running time for THT. FLoS_THT runs faster than LS_THT, which is specifically designed to speed up the computation for THT. This is because the lower and upper bounds of FLoS_THT are tighter than those of LS_THT. Both of the two local search methods are 2 to 3 orders of magnitude faster than GI_THT.

6.3 Evaluation on In-Memory Synthetic Graphs

We use synthetic graphs with different parameters to evaluate the selected methods. Specifically, we study two types of graphs: Erdös-Rényi random graph (RAND) [7]

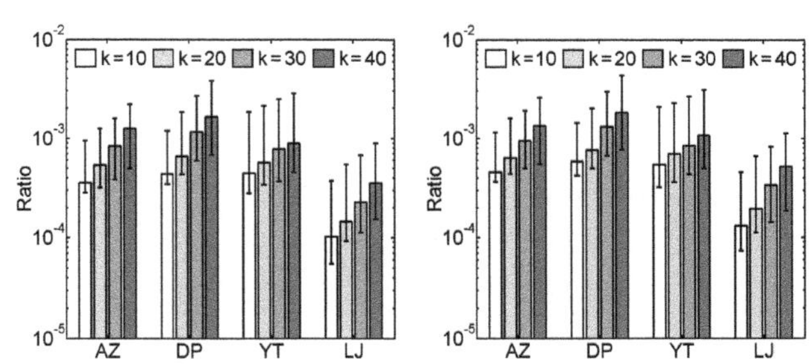

(a) FLoS_PHP (b) FLoS_RWR

Figure 9: Ratio between the number of visited nodes and the total number of nodes on real graphs

and scale-free graph based on R-MAT model [4]. There are two parameters, the size and density of the graphs. We study how these two parameters affect the running time of different methods for PHP and RWR.

We download the graph generator available from the website *http://www.cse.psu.edu/~madduri/software/GTgraph/* and use the default parameters to generate two series of graphs with varying size and varying density, using RAND and R-MAT respectively. The graphs with varying size have the same density but different number of nodes. The graphs with varying density have the same number of nodes but different densities. The statistics are shown in Table 6.

We apply the selected methods for PHP and RWR on these graphs with $k = 20$. For each graph, we repeat the query 10^3 times with randomly picked query nodes, and report the average running time.

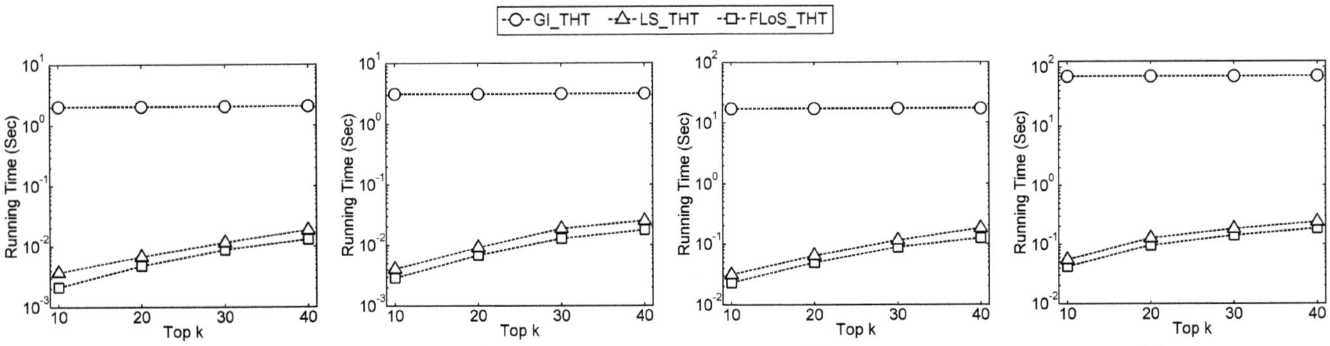

(a) AZ (b) DP (c) YT (d) LJ

Figure 10: Running time of different methods for THT on real graphs

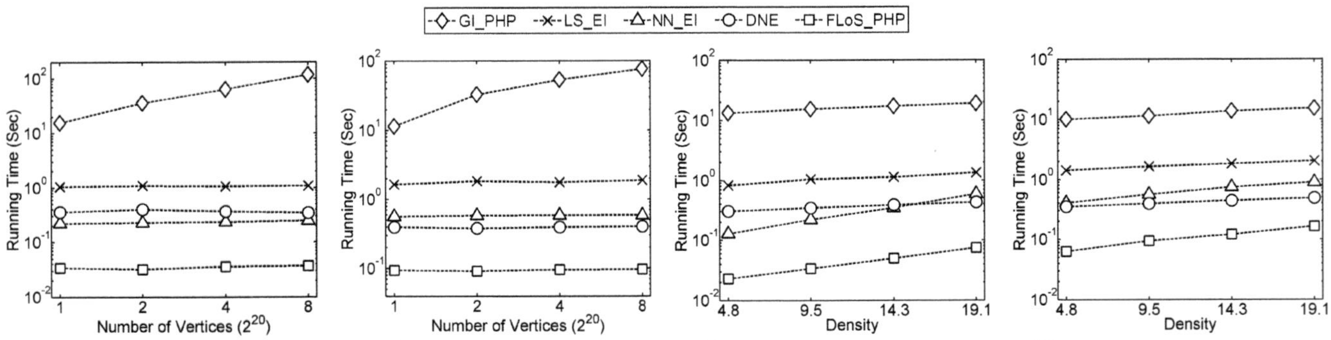

(a) Varying size, RAND (b) Varying size, R-MAT (c) Varying density, RAND (d) Varying density, R-MAT

Figure 11: Running time of different methods for PHP on in-memory synthetic graphs ($k = 20$)

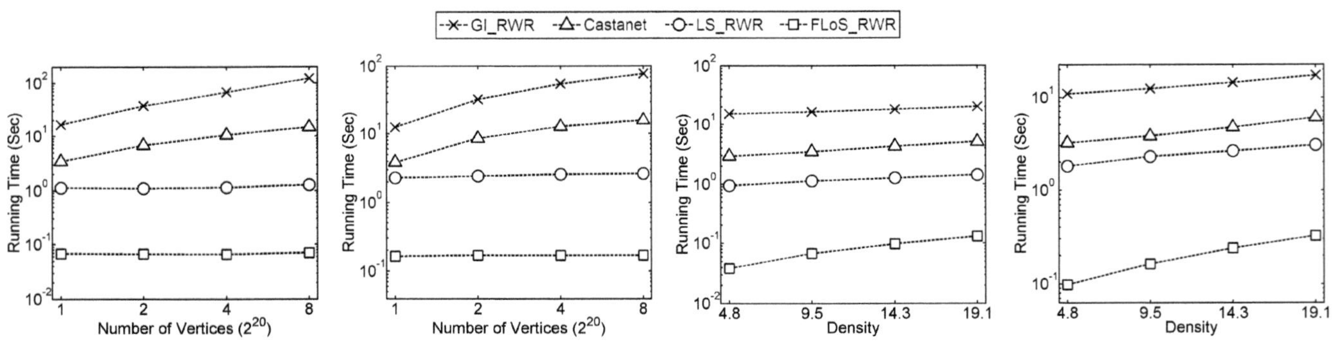

(a) Varying size, RAND (b) Varying size, R-MAT (c) Varying density, RAND (d) Varying density, R-MAT

Figure 12: Running time of different methods for RWR on in-memory synthetic graphs ($k = 20$)

Table 6: Statistics of in-memory synthetic graphs

Varying size	$\|V\|$	1×2^{20}	2×2^{20}	4×2^{20}	8×2^{20}
	$\|E\|$	1×10^7	2×10^7	4×10^7	8×10^7
	Density	9.5	9.5	9.5	9.5
Varying density	$\|V\|$	1×2^{20}	1×2^{20}	1×2^{20}	1×2^{20}
	$\|E\|$	5×10^6	10×10^6	15×10^6	20×10^6
	Density	4.8	9.5	14.3	19.1

6.3.1 Evaluation of FLoS_PHP

Figure 11(a) shows the running time of the selected methods for PHP on the series of RAND graphs with varying size. The running time of GI_PHP increases as the number of nodes increases. FLoS_PHP, DNE, NN_EI and LS_EI all have almost constant running time when the number of nodes increases. This is because these methods only search locally. When the density of the graph is fixed, adding more nodes to the graph will not change the size of the search space of these methods. Figure 11(b) shows the running time on the series of R-MAT graphs with varying size. Similar trends are observed. Comparing Figure 11(a) and 11(b), GI_PHP has less running time on R-MAT than on RAND graphs, while other methods have more. The reason is that R-MAT graphs have the power-law distribution, thus it is easier for FLoS_PHP, DNE, NN_EI and LS_EI to encounter hub nodes with larger degree when expanding subgraph. The faster performance of GI_PHP on R-MAT may be because of the greater data locality due to the hub node.

Figure 11(c) shows the running time of the selected methods for PHP on the series of RAND graphs with varying density. The running time of all the methods increases as the density increases. FLoS_PHP and NN_EI have increasing running time because the number of visited nodes in these two methods increases when the density becomes larger. LS_EI has increasing running time because the number of nodes and edges increases in local clusters. Figure 11(d) shows the running time on the series of R-MAT graphs with varying density. Similar trends are observed.

6.3.2 *Evaluation of FLoS_RWR*

Figure 12(a) shows the running time of the selected methods for RWR on the series of RAND graphs with varying size. The running time of GI_RWR and Castanet increases as the number of nodes increases. Castanet method cuts the running time from the GI method by 69% to 88%. FLoS_RWR and LS_RWR both have almost constant running time when the number of nodes increases. This is because FLoS_RWR and LS_RWR only search locally. Figure 12(b) shows the running time on the series of R-MAT graphs with varying size. Similar trends are observed. Comparing Figure 12(a) and 12(b), GI_RWR has less running time on the R-MAT graphs than on the RAND graphs, while other methods have more. The reason is similar as what discussed previously.

Figure 12(c) shows the running time on the series of RAND graphs with varying density. The running time of all the methods increases as the density increases. Figure 12(d) shows the running time on the series of R-MAT graphs with varying density. Similar trends are observed.

6.4 Evaluation on Disk-Resident Synthetic Graphs

What if the graphs are too large to fit into memory? To test the performance of FLoS on disk-resident graphs, we generate disk-resident R-MAT graphs, whose statistics are in Table 7. We use the open source Neo4j (available from *http://www.neo4j.org*) version 2.0 graph database. The FLoS method for disk-resident graphs only calls some basic query functions provided by Neo4j, such as, querying the neighbors of one node. And the remaining work is the same as that for in-memory graphs. We apply the FLoS_PHP and FLoS_RWR methods on the disk-resident graphs with $k = 20$. We repeat the query 10^3 times with randomly picked query nodes and report the average running time. In the experiments, we restrict the memory usage to 2 GB.

Figure 13(a) shows the running time of the FLoS_PHP and FLoS_RWR methods. From the figure, we can see that FLoS can process disk-resident graphs in tens of seconds. The reason is that FLoS only needs to find the neighbors of visited nodes and the transition probabilities on the edges. These results also verify that FLoS has almost constant running time when the number of nodes increases. Figure 13(b) shows the ratio of the number of visited nodes to the total number of nodes in the graph. FLoS only needs to explore a small portion of the whole graph to return the top-k nodes. When the graph size becomes larger, the portion of visited nodes becomes smaller.

Table 7: Statistics of disk-resident synthetic graphs

$\|V\|$	16×2^{20}	32×2^{20}	48×2^{20}	64×2^{20}
$\|E\|$	16×10^7	32×10^7	48×10^7	64×10^7
disk size	3.1 G	6.5 G	9.9 G	13.2 G

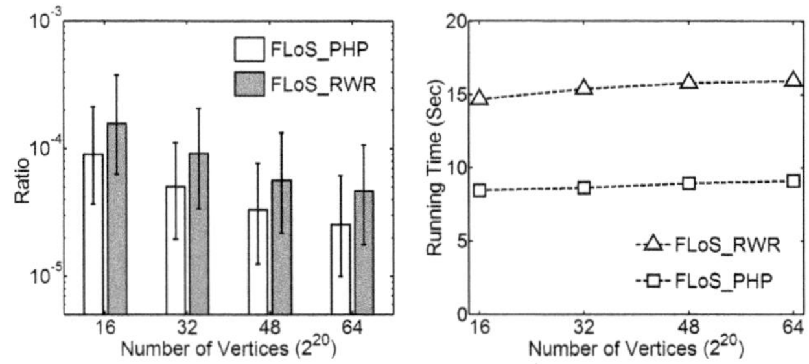

(a) Running time (b) Visited nodes

Figure 13: Results of FLoS_PHP and FLoS_RWR on disk-resident synthetic graphs ($k = 20$)

7. CONCLUSION

Top-k nodes query in large graphs is a fundamental problem that has attracted intensive research interests. Existing methods need expensive preprocessing steps or are designed for specific proximity measures. In this paper, we propose a unified method, FLoS, which adopts a local search strategy to find the exact top-k nodes efficiently. FLoS is based on the no local optimum property of proximity measures. By exploiting the relationship among different proximity measures, we can also extend FLoS to the proximity measures having local optimum. Extensive experimental results demonstrate that FLoS enables efficient and exact query for a variety of random walk based proximity measures.

8. ACKNOWLEDGEMENTS

This work was partially supported by the National Science Foundation grants IIS-1162374, IIS-1218036, IIS-0953950, the NIH/NIGMS grant R01GM103309, and the OSC (Ohio Supercomputer Center) grant PGS0218. We would like to thank anonymous reviewers for their valuable comments.

9. REFERENCES

[1] D. Aldous and J. Fill. Reversible markov chains and random walks on graphs, 2002.

[2] P. Berkhin. Bookmark-coloring algorithm for personalized PageRank computing. *Internet Mathematics*, 3(1):41–62, 2006.

[3] P. Bogdanov and A. Singh. Accurate and scalable nearest neighbors in large networks based on effective importance. In *CIKM*, pages 523–528, 2013.

[4] D. Chakrabarti, Y. Zhan, and C. Faloutsos. R-MAT: A recursive model for graph mining. In *SDM*, pages 442–446, 2004.

[5] S. Chakrabarti, A. Pathak, and M. Gupta. Index design and query processing for graph conductance search. *VLDB*, 20(3):445–470, 2011.

[6] S. Cohen, B. Kimelfeld, and G. Koutrika. A survey on proximity measures for social networks. In *Search Computing*, pages 191–206, 2012.

[7] P. Erdős and A. Rényi. On the evolution of random graphs. *Magyar Tud. Akad. Mat. Kutató Int. Közl*, 5:17–61, 1960.

[8] Y. Fujiwara, M. Nakatsuji, M. Onizuka, and M. Kitsuregawa. Fast and exact top-k search for random walk with restart. *VLDB*, 5(5):442–453, 2012.

[9] Y. Fujiwara, M. Nakatsuji, H. Shiokawa, T. Mishima, and M. Onizuka. Efficient ad-hoc search for personalized PageRank. In *SIGMOD*, pages 445–456, 2013.

[10] Y. Fujiwara, M. Nakatsuji, T. Yamamuro, H. Shiokawa, and M. Onizuka. Efficient personalized PageRank with accuracy assurance. In *KDD*, pages 15–23, 2012.
[11] Z. Guan, J. Wu, Q. Zhang, A. Singh, and X. Yan. Assessing and ranking structural correlations in graphs. In *SIGMOD*, pages 937–948, 2011.
[12] E. A. Guillemin. *Introductory circuit theory.* John Wiley & Sons, 1953.
[13] P. Lee, L. V. Lakshmanan, and J. X. Yu. On top-k structural similarity search. In *ICDE*, pages 774–785, 2012.
[14] Q. Mei, D. Zhou, and K. Church. Query suggestion using hitting time. In *CIKM*, pages 469–478, 2008.
[15] C. Meyer. *Matrix analysis and applied linear algebra.* SIAM, 2000.
[16] Y. Saad. *Iterative methods for sparse linear systems.* SIAM, 2003.
[17] P. Sarkar and A. W. Moore. A tractable approach to finding closet truncated communicate time nieghbors in large graphs. In *UAI*, pages 335–343, 2007.
[18] P. Sarkar and A. W. Moore. Fast nearest-neighbor search in disk-resident graphs. In *KDD*, pages 513–522, 2010.
[19] P. Sarkar, A. W. Moore, and A. Prakash. Fast incremental proximity search in large graphs. In *ICML*, pages 896–903, 2008.
[20] H. Tong, C. Faloutsos, and J.-Y. Pan. Fast random walk with restart and its applications. In *ICDM*, pages 613–622, 2006.
[21] C. Zhang, L. Shou, K. Chen, G. Chen, and Y. Bei. Evaluating geo-social influence in location-based social networks. In *CIKM*, pages 1442–1451, 2012.
[22] X. Zhao, A. Chang, A. D. Sarma, H. Zheng, and B. Y. Zhao. On the embeddability of random walk distances. *VLDB*, 6(14), 2013.

10. APPENDIX

10.1 Proofs of No Local Optimum Property for Other Proximity Measures

Effective importance (EI) [3] is the degree normalized version of RWR, which can be defined as $\mathbf{r}_i = (1-c)\sum_{j\in N_i} p_{i,j}\mathbf{r}_j$, if $i \neq q$, and $\mathbf{r}_q = (1-c)\sum_{j\in N_q} p_{q,j}\mathbf{r}_j + \frac{c}{w_q}$, where c $(0 < c < 1)$ is a constant restart probability.

LEMMA 5. *EI has no local maximum.*

PROOF. Suppose that node i is a local maximum. We have $\mathbf{r}_i = (1-c)\sum_{j\in N_i} p_{i,j}\mathbf{r}_j \leq (1-c)\sum_{j\in N_i} p_{i,j}\mathbf{r}_i = (1-c)\mathbf{r}_i < \mathbf{r}_i$. Thus we get a contradiction that $\mathbf{r}_i < \mathbf{r}_i$. □

Discounted hitting time (DHT) [18] is a variant of HT which can be defined as $\mathbf{r}_i = 1 + (1-c)\sum_{j\in N_i} p_{i,j}\mathbf{r}_j$, if $i \neq q$, and $\mathbf{r}_q = 0$, where c $(0 < c < 1)$ is a constant used to penalize the transition probability in each step.

LEMMA 6. *DHT has no local minimum.*

PROOF. The maximum discounted hitting time that a node could have is $\frac{1}{c}$, when it can never reach q. For connected graph, we have $\mathbf{r}_i < \frac{1}{c}$. Now suppose that node i is a local minimum. We have $\mathbf{r}_i = 1 + (1-c)\sum_{j\in N_i} p_{i,j}\mathbf{r}_j \geq 1 + (1-c)\sum_{j\in N_i} p_{i,j}\mathbf{r}_i = 1 + (1-c)\mathbf{r}_i$. Thus $\mathbf{r}_i \geq \frac{1}{c}$, which contradicts that $\mathbf{r}_i < \frac{1}{c}$. □

Truncated hitting time (THT) [17] is another variant of HT. The L-truncated hitting time only considers paths of length less than L, which can be defined as $\mathbf{r}_q = 0$ and $\mathbf{r}_i^L = 1 + \sum_{j\in N_i} p_{i,j}\mathbf{r}_j^{L-1}$, if $i \neq q$. If a node is more than L hops away from the query node, its proximity is set to be L.

LEMMA 7. *THT has no local minimum for the nodes within L hops from the query node.*

PROOF. For any node i within L hops from q, we have $\mathbf{r}_i^L < L$. Now suppose i is a local minimum, i.e., $\mathbf{r}_j^L \geq \mathbf{r}_i^L$ $(\forall j \in N_i)$. We have $\mathbf{r}_i^L = 1+\sum_{j\in N_i} p_{i,j}\mathbf{r}_j^{L-1} = \sum_{j\in N_i} p_{i,j}(1 + \mathbf{r}_j^{L-1}) > \sum_{j\in N_i} p_{i,j}\mathbf{r}_j^L \geq \sum_{j\in N_i} p_{i,j}\mathbf{r}_i^L = \mathbf{r}_i^L$. We get a contradiction that $\mathbf{r}_i^L > \mathbf{r}_i^L$. □

LEMMA 8. *RWR has local maximum.*

PROOF. Counter examples can be used to show that RWR has local maximum, which are omitted. □

10.2 The Proof of Theorem 2

PROOF. First, we show that PHP and EI are equivalent. Suppose the decay factor in PHP is set to be $(1-c)$, and the restart probability in EI is c. Then PHP and EI have the same recursive definition for any node $i \neq q$, and we have $\frac{\mathrm{EI}(i)}{\mathrm{PHP}(i)} = \frac{\mathrm{EI}(q)}{\mathrm{PHP}(q)}$, which is a constant when q is fixed. Thus PHP(i) is a linear function of EI(i).

Next, we show that PHP and DHT are equivalent. Suppose the decay factors in PHP and DHT are set to be $(1-c)$ and c respectively. The relationship between PHP and DHT is $\mathrm{PHP}(i) = 1 - c \cdot \mathrm{DHT}(i)$, which can be proved by substituting it in the recursive definition of PHP. Thus PHP(i) is a linear function of DHT(i). □

10.3 The Proof of Theorem 5

PROOF. Let $\mathbf{T}$ be the original transition probability matrix of PHP. Changing the destination of transition probability $p_{i,j}$ from node j to node l is the same as adding $\mathbf{T}_{i,j}$ to $\mathbf{T}_{i,l}$ and setting $\mathbf{T}_{i,j}$ to 0. Let $\mathbf{T}'$ represent the resulting matrix. PHP proximity $\mathbf{r}$ is computed based on $\mathbf{T}$, and $\mathbf{r}'$ is based on $\mathbf{T}'$.

Let $\Delta\mathbf{r} = \mathbf{r}'-\mathbf{r}$, and $\Delta\mathbf{T} = \mathbf{T}-\mathbf{T}'$. Note that $\Delta\mathbf{T}$ has only two non-zero elements $\Delta\mathbf{T}_{i,j} = \mathbf{T}_{i,j}$ and $\Delta\mathbf{T}_{i,l} = -\mathbf{T}_{i,j}$. We have that $\Delta\mathbf{r} = c\mathbf{T}'\mathbf{r}' - c(\mathbf{T}' + \Delta\mathbf{T})\mathbf{r} = c\mathbf{T}'\Delta\mathbf{r} - c\Delta\mathbf{T}\mathbf{r} = c\mathbf{T}'\Delta\mathbf{r} + \mathbf{e}_i$, where $\mathbf{e}_i$ is a vector with the only non-zero element $\mathbf{e}_i(i) = c\mathbf{T}_{i,j}(\mathbf{r}_l - \mathbf{r}_j)$. If $\mathbf{r}_l \geq \mathbf{r}_j$, $\Delta\mathbf{r}$ must be non-negative. Otherwise, it is non-positive. This completes the proof. □

10.4 Lower and Upper Bounds of Other Proximity Measures

For THT, deleting a transition probability will not increase the proximity of any node. Therefore, when we delete all the transition probabilities $\{p_{i,j} : i \text{ or } j \in \bar{S}\}$ in the original transition graph, the proximity value of any node computed based on the modified transition graph will be the lower bound. For the upper bound, we add a dummy node with value L, which is the largest possible proximity value of THT.

EI and DHT are equivalent with PHP thus there is no need to discuss the bounds.

Global Immutable Region Computation

Jilian Zhang Kyriakos Mouratidis HweeHwa Pang
School of Information Systems
Singapore Management University
80 Stamford Road, Singapore 178902
{jilian.z.2007, kyriakos, hhpang}@smu.edu.sg

ABSTRACT

A top-k query shortlists the k records in a dataset that best match the user's preferences. To indicate her preferences, the user typically determines a numeric weight for each data dimension (i.e., attribute). We refer to these weights collectively as the *query vector*. Based on this vector, each data record is implicitly mapped to a score value (via a weighted sum function). The records with the k largest scores are reported as the result. In this paper we propose an auxiliary feature to standard top-k query processing. Specifically, we compute the maximal locus within which the query vector incurs no change in the current top-k result. In other words, we compute all possible query weight settings that produce exactly the same top-k result as the user's original query. We call this locus the *global immutable region* (GIR). The GIR can be used as a guide to query vector readjustments, as a sensitivity measure for the top-k result, as well as to enable effective result caching. We develop efficient algorithms for GIR computation, and verify their robustness using a variety of real and synthetic datasets.

Categories and Subject Descriptors

H.2.8 [**Information Systems**]: Database Management - Database applications

Keywords

Top-k Search; Sensitivity Analysis

1. INTRODUCTION

Consider a service like HungryGoWhere.com or Yelp.com, where users rate and search for restaurants. The former, for instance, maintains for each registered restaurant the average user ratings in terms of *food quality*, *ambience*, *value for money*, and *service*. Users looking for restaurants base their decisions on these four factors, yet different users weigh each factor differently.

A user interested in dining options can provide a numeric weight for each decision factor and request for a personalized recommendation of, say, the top-10 restaurants according to her preferences. Through those weights, which we collectively refer to as the *query vector*, each restaurant is implicitly associated with a score value, computed as the weighted sum of its four average ratings. The online service may employ an off-the-shelf top-k processing algorithm to report the 10 restaurants with the largest scores.

SIGMOD'14, June 22–27, 2014, Snowbird, UT, USA.

http://dx.doi.org/10.1145/2588555.2610508.

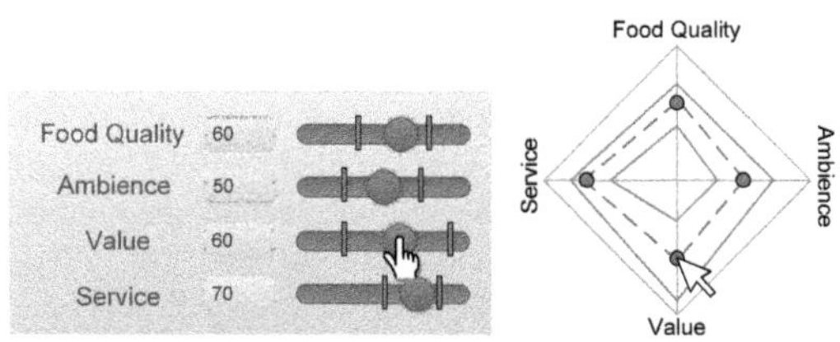

(a) Text input and slide-bars (b) Radar chart

Figure 1: Weight input and GIR-induced bounds

In this work we propose to supplement the top-k result with a *global immutable region* (GIR). The GIR indicates all the possible weight settings for which the current top-k recommendation holds. For the common case of linear scoring functions, the GIR is a convex polytope in query space, wherein the query vector may freely shift without inducing any changes in the result. In our restaurant example, the query space involves four dimensions, each corresponding to the weight for a factor, e.g., the first axis refers to the weight w_1 for food quality, the second to the weight w_2 for ambience, etc; the GIR is a 4-dimensional polytope in that space. The GIR can be used to guide weight readjustment, for the purpose of sensitivity analysis, as well as for effective top-k result caching.

Suppose that the user in our restaurant example requests for a top-10 recommendation, using an interface like the text-boxes/slide-bars in Figure 1(a) or the radar chart in Figure 1(b), which captures preferences in the form of movable locations on each of the four axes. Assuming weights in the range from 0 to 100, the user requests for a top-10 recommendation by specifying query vector $q = (60, 50, 60, 70)$ – this implies a weight $w_1 = 60$ for food quality, $w_2 = 50$ for ambience, etc. Should the user decide to explore alternative recommendations, she may change the weights and reissue the query. Primarily, she would want to avoid a blind readjustment that induces no change in the top-10 result. At the same time, she would need a sense of how drastically each weight affects the recommendation, so as to avoid overly radical changes. Using the GIR, we may derive a lower and an upper bound mark on each slide-bar (like those shown in Figure 1(a)) in between which the corresponding weight value induces no change in the result. Furthermore, we can inform the user what the new result will be at each of these bounds. Figure 1(b) represents the same bounds in the form of an inner and an outer solid polygon that connect the "tipping points" on the four axes.

GIR computation finds application in sensitivity analysis as well. Effective decision support involves providing the user with both a recommendation, and a measure of its robustness [13, 28]. For example, a robust top-k result would offer the user higher confidence in her decision, while a sensitive one would trigger deeper deliberation. An intuitive robustness measure for a top-k result is the ratio of the GIR volume to the volume of the entire query space. This ratio determines the probability that a randomly and uniformly generated query vector would have the same top-k result as the user's query. The higher this probability, the more robust the result. This measure of robustness was proposed in [30], without however considering efficient approaches to compute it.

Another application of GIR computation is result caching. Suppose that previous top-k results are maintained, along with their GIRs. If the query vector of a new request falls within the GIR of a cached result, the latter can be directly reported. Even if k in the new query is larger than that of the cached result, it is still desirable to report the available (highest-scoring) recommendations immediately [31], before producing the rest of the top-k list. Note that this is orthogonal to top-k view materialization [15, 36], since the requested result either matches exactly a cached one or not.

In this paper we develop scalable algorithms for GIR computation. We determine the conditions under which changes in the query vector invalidate the result, represent them in computational geometric terms, and make crucial observations that enable fast processing. Along the way, our GIR algorithms also compute the new top-k result should the query vector shift to any point on the GIR boundary. We verify the generality and efficiency of our methods using real and synthetic data with different characteristics.

2. RELATED WORK

As the notion of GIR builds on the top-k query, we first review top-k processing. Next, we survey safe regions for spatial queries, per-dimension (local) immutable regions for top-k queries, and sensitivity analysis in operations research. We also briefly cover convex hull computation, a foundation for our algorithms.

Given a database D and a scoring function, a top-k query retrieves the k records from D that achieve the highest scores. Top-k queries have been studied in various domains, including relational databases [21], middle-ware information systems [17], joins [33], and dynamic databases [1, 22]. Suiting our problem setting, BRS [32] is a top-k algorithm for low-dimensional data indexed by a spatial access method (e.g., an R-tree [19]). Designed for the broad class of monotone scoring functions, BRS applies the *branch-and-bound* methodology. Specifically, it uses a max-heap to organize the entries of visited R-tree nodes so as to access them in decreasing order of their *maxscore*. The *maxscore* of an R-tree node is the largest among the scores of its MBB corners (MBB stands for the node's minimum bounding box) and serves as an upper bound for the score of any record under the node. When a leaf node is accessed, the score of records inside is computed and the interim top-k result is updated accordingly. BRS terminates when the record with the k-th largest score in the interim result has a score no smaller than the *maxscore* of the last R-tree entry popped from the search heap. BRS is I/O optimal, meaning that it reads the minimum possible number of pages (R-tree nodes) from the disk.

Another related problem is the reverse top-k query [35, 34], which involves a database D and a collection of user preference functions represented as query vectors. A reverse top-k query returns those query vectors from the collection that include a given record $p \in D$ in their top-k result.

The most relevant existing study is [24], which determines immutable regions on individual decision factors. An immutable region there takes the form of a validity interval for an isolated query weight, *assuming that all the other weights are kept constant.* One interval is defined for each decision factor. We term those *local immutable regions* (LIRs) to distinguish from the GIR. In the context of Figure 1, [24] produces the same original marks and inner/outer polygons. However, due to the local nature of the LIRs, it cannot support simultaneous readjustments to multiple weights. More importantly, if a weight w_i is updated, the immutable regions for all the other factors are invalidated, *even if the new value of w_i remains within its LIR.* Referring to Figure 1 again, if w_3 shifts to 40 (which is still inside its permissible range) the technique in [24] needs to compute from scratch new LIRs for all the remaining factors. At the heart of LIR computation lie a pruning and a thresholding technique, both of which are tailored to LIRs and are inapplicable to GIR formation. Note that we may trivially derive LIRs from the GIR (as we discuss in Section 7.3), but the reverse does not hold.

Another related work is [30] which considers uncertain scoring functions and proposes methods to compute representative top-k results. It also introduces two sensitivity measures, STB and LIK. Given a top-k query with a linear scoring function, STB computes the largest ball around the query vector (in query space) where the top-k result remains the same. This ball is enclosed in (i.e., a subset of) our GIR, the latter being the *maximal* locus that preserves the result. Moreover, STB requires a scan of the dataset, which is prohibitive for large disk-resident data.

LIK defines a sensitivity measure that is equivalent to the ratio of the GIR volume to the volume of the query space. Other than the definition, however, [30] is not concerned with efficiency. It sketches an approach based on half-space[1] intersection that scans the entire dataset. With a time complexity of $O(n^{2^{d-2}})$, it is impractical for sizable databases. In Section 3.3 we sketch a straightforward approach to compute the GIR which, although it has a superior complexity of $O(n^{d/2})$ (compared to LIK), it is still hugely impractical, thus motivating the elaborate techniques in this paper.

In location-based services, while processing spatial queries such as nearest neighbors and window queries, servers face the problem of frequent index maintenance and result re-computation as data objects move around and update their locations. Safe region techniques are designed to alleviate this problem by assigning to each mobile object an area, known as *safe region*, within which it is guaranteed not to alter the result of any spatial query in the system [27, 25]. Safe region techniques are inapplicable to our problem, since they consider the notion of spatial proximity, as opposed to the score-based ranking involved in top-k processing.

Another topic that is related to GIR is sensitivity analysis in operations research, which addresses how changes in the input parameters affect the output of a model [29, 20]. This includes studying to what extent the input is allowed to change, so that the output continues to be optimal. There are two approaches. The first, one-factor-at-a-time (OFAT), varies one input factor while fixing the rest. Although simple to use, OFAT is known to miss out optimal combinations, as it cannot capture the interaction among multiple input parameters. This motivates the second approach, named multi-parameter sensitivity analysis (MPSA). MPSA varies multiple input factors simultaneously and observes the changes (in terms of variance) in the model output under the combined influence of the inputs. OFAT is also known as local sensitivity analysis, and MPSA as global sensitivity analysis. In a sense, the LIRs in [24] are analogous to OFAT, while our GIR to MSPA. Both the OFAT and MPSA techniques, however, consider the effect of different inputs to the variance of a value (i.e., the model's output). In our

[1] A half-space is either of the two parts into which a hyperplane divides a coordinate space. In two dimensions, it is a half-plane.

problem, instead, the output changes refer to updates in the order or composition of a top-k result.

Our solutions touch upon and employ convex hull computation algorithms. The convex hull of a dataset D in a d-dimensional space is the smallest convex set that encloses all the records in D. In two dimensions, the hull is a convex polygon, whereas in higher dimensions it is a convex polytope [6]. The boundary of the hull is represented by vertices (i.e., data records) and facets. Algorithms for efficient convex hull computation in two and three dimensions include gift-wrapping [10], Graham's scan [18], and Chan's algorithm [9]. For higher dimensions, Quickhull [3] and Clarkson's algorithm [14] are the most common, with a time complexity of $O(n^{d/2})$. Our solutions share some of the key operations in Clarkson's algorithm. Its crux is to incrementally build the hull by processing the data records one by one. If the current record lies above one or more facets of the hull (i.e., it is not enclosed by the hull), these facets are replaced by new ones that include the new record.

3. PRELIMINARIES

3.1 Definition of Global Immutable Region

We consider top-k processing in a low-dimensional space. The dataset D consists of n records. Each record $p \in D$ has an identifier and d numeric attributes $x_1, x_2, ..., x_d$ (also referred to as *dimensions*). The top-k query is defined by a vector of weights $q = (w_1, w_2, ..., w_d)$, called the *query vector*, which can be seen as a d-dimensional point. For ease of presentation, we assume that the data space and query space are normalized, i.e., data attributes and query weights have values in the range $[0, 1]$. The score of a data record p with respect to q is given by the dot product $\mathcal{S}(p, q) = q \cdot p = \sum_{i=1}^{d} w_i x_i$. This definition of $\mathcal{S}(p, q)$ is equivalent to what is also commonly referred to as a linear scoring function. The result R of the query is a list of k records with the highest scores in D, sorted in decreasing score order. In other words, $R = \{p_1, p_2, ..., p_k\}$ where p_i is the record with the i-th highest score ($1 \leq i \leq k$).

When the query vector q changes, we say that R is *preserved* if both its composition and the score order among its members are unaltered. The problem we address in this paper is the computation of the maximal locus in the query space where R is preserved. We call this locus the *global immutable region* (GIR) of q.

DEFINITION 1. ***Global immutable region (GIR)***. *Given a dataset D and a top-k query q with result $R = \{p_1, p_2, ..., p_k\}$, the GIR is the locus of all vectors q' in query space where*

1. *$\mathcal{S}(p_i, q') \geq \mathcal{S}(p_{i+1}, q')$ for each $i \in [1, k)$, and*
2. *$\mathcal{S}(p_k, q') \geq \mathcal{S}(p, q')$ for every record $p \in D \backslash R$.*

3.2 Nature of Global Immutable Region

A first step to understanding the problem is to determine the shape of the GIR. For the score order within result R to be preserved, $k - 1$ conditions must hold, each of the form $\mathcal{S}(p_i, q') \geq \mathcal{S}(p_{i+1}, q')$ (for $i \in [1, k)$). For the k-th result record p_k to remain ahead of all the non-result records p, another $n - k$ conditions must hold, each of the form $\mathcal{S}(p_k, q') \geq \mathcal{S}(p, q')$. Due to the form of the scoring function, each of these $n - 1$ conditions corresponds to a half-space in query space, whose defining hyperplane passes through the origin[2]. The top-k result is preserved if and only if the query vector remains within the intersection of these $n - 1$ half-spaces. This intersection constitutes the GIR of the query. Any intersection of half-spaces (and therefore the GIR too) is by definition a convex polytope.

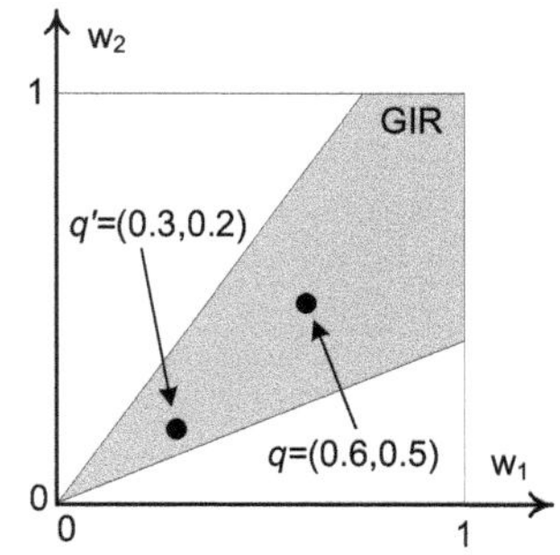

Figure 2: GIR example in 2-dimensional (query) space

Figure 2 shows how the GIR looks in 2-dimensional space (i.e., $d = 2$). Query vector $q = (0.6, 0.5)$ represents the user's original weight setting. In two dimensions, each of the $n - 1$ conditions derived from Definition 1 corresponds to a half-plane (instead of a half-space), whose defining line (instead of defining hyperplane) passes through the origin. Their intersection (i.e., the GIR) is a wedge like the one shown shaded in the figure. Any query vector lying inside this area (like the depicted $q' = (0.3, 0.2)$) is guaranteed to preserve the top-k result. Furthermore, this is the maximal locus in the query space where result R is preserved.

Without loss of generality, each line that bounds the GIR corresponds to one of the original $n - 1$ conditions. This implicitly determines what the new top-k result will be if the query shifts to a particular line. For instance, assume that the upper bounding line of the GIR corresponds to condition $\mathcal{S}(p_k, q') \geq \mathcal{S}(p, q')$, where p is a non-result record. If the query is adjusted to fall on this line, the new result will be the same as the current one, except that p will replace the k-th record in R. If the bounding line corresponds to condition $\mathcal{S}(p_i, q') \geq \mathcal{S}(p_{i+1}, q')$, the resulting update in R is that p_{i+1} overtakes record p_i in score, i.e., the perturbation is a reordering between p_i and p_{i+1} in the result.

In the following we focus on the GIR computation. *Determining the exact result perturbation when the query moves to the boundary of the GIR happens along the way, by identifying the record responsible for each of the half-spaces that bound the GIR.*

3.3 Challenges, Assumptions and Setting

Our goal is to develop efficient GIR computation algorithms that are scalable to large datasets. The discussion in the previous session hints at a possible GIR computation approach, based on half-space intersection. However, deriving the $n - 1$ half-spaces stated in Definition 1 requires scanning the entire dataset, and incurs a large data access cost. Furthermore, performing the intersection of $n - 1$ half-spaces requires an excessive amount of computations, specifically, $\Omega(n^{d/2})$ which explodes for large datasets. The main challenge we address is how to reduce the number of records/half-spaces considered so as to minimize (i) the data access cost to retrieve those records, and (ii) the processing time for half-space intersection, while still guaranteeing correct/exact GIR computation.

Targeted at large scale, low-dimensional datasets, we assume that D is indexed by a spatial access method. Our implementation

[2]Consider for example condition $\mathcal{S}(p_k, q') \geq \mathcal{S}(p, q')$, which in dot product notation is $p_k \cdot q' \geq p \cdot q' \Rightarrow (p_k - p) \cdot q' \geq 0$. Since vector $(p_k - p)$ is fixed (with attribute values in both records being constant), the inequality implies that q' lies on a half-space that is bounded by hyperplane $(p_k - p) \cdot q' = 0$. The latter passes through the origin of the query space.

Symbol	Description
d	Data dimensionality
D	Dataset in $[0,1]^d$
n	Number of records in D
p	A data record in D
q	User query (vector in $[0,1]^d$)
$\mathcal{S}(p,q)$	Score of p w.r.t. q
R	Top-k result
p_i	The i-th record in R ($1 \le i \le k$)
$\mathcal{SL}$	Skyline of $D \backslash R$
$\mathcal{CH}$	Convex hull of non-result records
$\mathcal{CH}'$	Convex hull of set $\{p_k\} \cup D \backslash R$

Table 1: Notation

	x_1	x_2	$p \cdot q$
p_1	.54	.5	.516
p_2	.5	.48	.488
p_3	.52	.35	.418
p_4	.4	.4	.4

(a) Top-k records

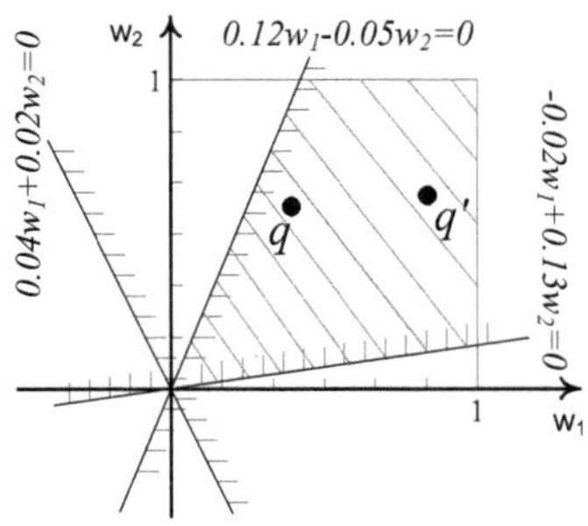

(b) Half-planes in query space

Figure 3: Phase 1 example ($k = 4$, $d = 2$)

employs the ubiquitous R*-tree [4], though our techniques apply directly to other space- or data-partitioning indices. The index and data could reside in memory or on disk, the latter being our default setting (although we evaluate our techniques in both scenarios).

When a query q is posed, prior to GIR computation, its top-k result R must be retrieved. For this we employ the state-of-the-art BRS technique [32], yet our work is not directly dependent on the choice of top-k algorithm. To facilitate subsequent GIR-related processing, we maintain all the data records encountered by BRS (but not included in the top-k result), as well as its search heap.

After the top-k result is produced, GIR computation commences. That comprises two phases. The first derives an interim GIR based on the first set of conditions in Definition 1 (considering only records in R). The second phase shrinks the interim GIR according to the second set of conditions (imposed by non-result records). In Table 1 we summarize the notation used in the paper.

4. PROCESSING IN PHASE 1

Given the original top-k result R, the first phase derives an interim GIR from the first set of conditions in Definition 1. There are $k-1$ conditions, each defining a half-space in query space. The interim GIR in Phase 1 is obtained by intersecting these half-spaces. Formally, the interim GIR is the following polytope in query space:

$$\bigcap_{i=1}^{i=k-1} \{q' | q' \in [0,1]^d \text{ such that } (p_i - p_{i+1}) \cdot q' \ge 0\} \qquad (1)$$

Consider a query with $q = (0.4, 0.6)$ and $k = 4$. Suppose that a top-k algorithm (BRS in our implementation) reports in the result records p_1, p_2, p_3, and p_4, whose attributes and scores are shown in Figure 3(a). Phase 1 commences by deriving the half-plane that preserves the order between p_1 and p_2, i.e., half-plane $(p_1 - p_2) \cdot q' \ge 0 \Rightarrow 0.04w_1 + 0.02w_2 \ge 0$. Figure 3(b) represents the half-plane by its bounding line ($0.04w_1 + 0.02w_2 = 0$) in the query space. Similarly, preserving the order between p_2 and p_3 defines the half-plane $(p_2 - p_3) \cdot q' \ge 0 \Rightarrow -0.02w_1 + 0.13w_2 \ge 0$. In turn, p_3 and p_4 define $(p_3 - p_4) \cdot q' \ge 0 \Rightarrow 0.12w_1 - 0.05w_2 \ge 0$. The interim GIR is the striped area at the intersection of the three half-planes. Any query vector in this area is guaranteed to uphold the score order among the four result records. We use a 2-dimensional example here for ease of presentation. The process is very similar in higher dimensions.

Phase 1 is fast because the number of result records k is typically much smaller than the number of non-result records that need to be considered. It is also uniform across all methods in our framework. The distinction among them lies entirely in Phase 2, the bottleneck in GIR computation.

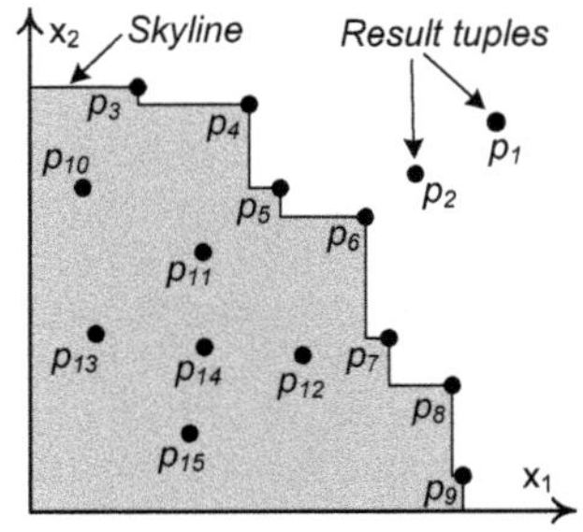

Figure 4: SP example ($k = 2, d = 2$, data space)

5. BASIC METHODS FOR PHASE 2

Phase 2 further shrinks the GIR to ensure that no non-result record can overtake the k-th result record p_k in score. As explained in Section 3, the efficiency of this phase hinges on the ability to reduce the number of non-result records examined. In this section, we present two basic methods for pruning the set $D \backslash R$ to safely discard records that could not affect the GIR.

5.1 Skyline Pruning Method

The first method relies on the *skyline* operator [8]. The skyline of a set includes only those members that are not *dominated* by any other member. In our context, we say that record p dominates another record p' if the value of p in every dimension is no smaller than the corresponding value of p', and the two records differ on at least one dimension. Due to the definition of dominance, record p could have a score no smaller than p' under any monotone scoring function [21] (which is a superclass of the linear scoring functions we assume). Since the score of p' never exceeds that of p regardless of the query vector, record p' cannot overtake the current p_k before p overtakes p_k. In other words, $\mathcal{S}(p, q') \ge \mathcal{S}(p', q')$ for any $q' \in [0,1]^d$ so, by satisfying the condition $\mathcal{S}(p_k, q') \ge \mathcal{S}(p, q')$, our GIR automatically also upholds $\mathcal{S}(p_k, q') \ge \mathcal{S}(p', q')$. Hence, it is safe to ignore p' in GIR computation.

To generalize, we may safely prune the set $D \backslash R$ by retaining only the records in its skyline $\mathcal{SL}$. The final GIR can be derived by intersecting the interim GIR from Phase 1 with the half-spaces formed from inequalities $(p_k - p) \cdot q' \ge 0$ for each record $p \in \mathcal{SL}$. We term this approach *Skyline Pruning* (SP). Figure 4 shows a 2-dimensional example where $k = 2$, the dataset comprises records $p_1, p_2, ..., p_{15}$, and the result includes p_1 and p_2. The skyline $\mathcal{SL}$ of the non-result records includes $p_3, p_4, ..., p_9$, which are the only records considered by SP in Phase 2. Records that fall in the shaded area are dominated by at least one member of the skyline.

Although SP can potentially disqualify many records from $D \backslash R$, the cardinality of the skyline may still be large. As an indication, the number of records in $\mathcal{SL}$ is in the order of $O((\log n)^{d-1})$ [5]

for independent data, while there are common (e.g., anti-correlated) distributions where the cardinality is even higher.

In terms of implementation, the state-of-the-art algorithm for skyline computation on spatial access methods is BBS [26], which follows the *branch-and-bound* paradigm. It utilizes an R-tree on the dataset to incrementally retrieve nearest neighbors (NNs) to the top corner of the data space, i.e., to point $(1, 1, ..., 1)$. The first NN is guaranteed to be in the skyline, and is used to prune the part of the space it dominates. Then, the next NN is retrieved in the remaining part of the space; it is also included in the skyline and used to further prune the search space. The process continues until no more NNs can be found in the non-dominated part of the space.

To see how BBS applies in our situation, recall that (before GIR computation) the top-k result was produced by BRS, and that we have retained its search heap and all the non-result records that were encountered during its execution. We initialize $\mathcal{SL}$ by computing the skyline of the encountered non-result records (using any main memory algorithm [8]), and then invoke BBS on the retained search heap to consider records that may belong to $\mathcal{SL}$ but were not accessed during BRS execution. Recall that the search heap of BRS is organized on *maxscore*. That is, in our BBS execution, instead of incrementally retrieving NNs to the top corner of the data space, we retrieve records in decreasing $\mathcal{S}(p, q)$ order. This does not affect the correctness of BBS, since the distance from the top corner of the data space (in vanilla BBS) can be replaced by any monotone scoring function to determine the retrieval order [26]. Another modification is that any record p retrieved by BBS is inserted into $\mathcal{SL}$ only if it is not dominated by any of its members, while if p dominates any existing members, the latter are removed from $\mathcal{SL}$.

5.2 Convex Hull Pruning Method

Our second basic solution for Phase 2 prunes non-result records based on the concept of the convex hull. If we treat the records of a dataset as points in d-dimensional space and compute their convex hull, the geometric properties of the hull guarantee that the top-1 record under any linear scoring function (defined over the same d dimensions) lies on the hull[3] [23, 11].

Let $\mathcal{CH}$ be the convex hull of the non-result records. The above property guarantees that for any query vector $q' \in [0, 1]^d$ and any record p' that is strictly enclosed by $\mathcal{CH}$ (as opposed to lying on it), there is at least one record p on the hull (i.e., $p \in \mathcal{CH}$) such that $\mathcal{S}(p, q') \geq \mathcal{S}(p', q')$. This implies that p' cannot overtake the current k-th result record p_k until some record on the hull has overtaken p_k. Hence, only records on $\mathcal{CH}$ could affect the GIR.

Utilizing the above observation directly would prune $D \backslash R$ by retaining only those records that fall on its convex hull. Nevertheless, we can do better. To exemplify, Figure 5 illustrates the convex hull of the non-result records, assuming the same setting/dataset as Figure 4. The records that lie on (as opposed to inside) $\mathcal{CH}$ are $p_3, p_4, p_6, p_8, p_9, p_{15}, p_{13}, p_{10}$. However, we observe that p_{15}, p_{13}, p_{10} are dominated by p_4, and could therefore not affect the GIR (by the same reasoning as in SP). This observation gives rise to our second baseline algorithm, *Convex Hull Pruning* (CP), which considers in Phase 2 only those non-result records that belong to the skyline and at the same time fall on the convex hull of $D \backslash R$, i.e., records $p \in \mathcal{SL} \cap \mathcal{CH}$. Referring to the example in Figure 5, CP considers only records p_3, p_4, p_6, p_8, p_9.

In implementing CP, we first retrieve the skyline of $D \backslash R$, using the same BBS-based approach as SP. Following that, we compute the convex hull *of the skyline records only* (using Clarkson's algorithm [14]). This hull is shown shaded in the example of Figure 5.

[3]When we say that a record "lies on" or "belongs to" the hull, we mean that it lies *on the boundary* of the hull.

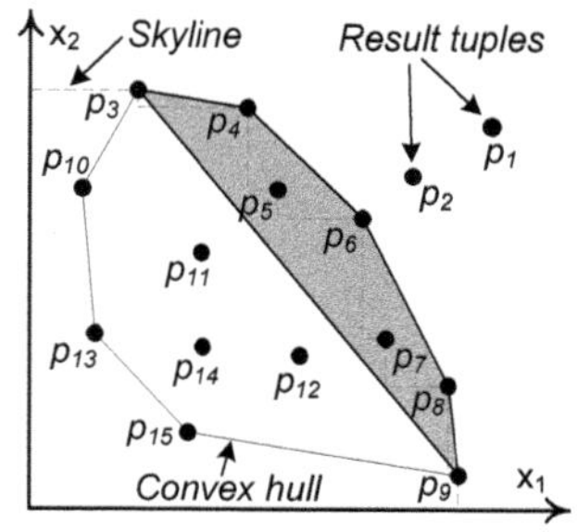

Figure 5: CP example ($k = 2, d = 2$, data space)

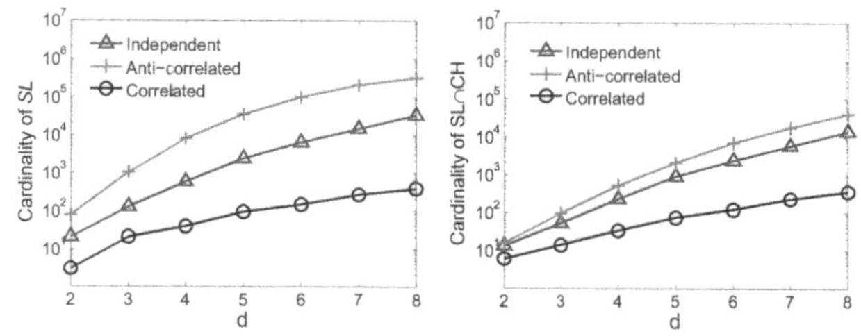

(a) Cardinality of $\mathcal{SL}$ (b) Cardinality of $\mathcal{SL} \cap \mathcal{CH}$

Figure 6: SP and CP effectiveness (n = 1M, k = 20)

The records that lie on the hull are used for half-space intersection with the interim GIR from Phase 1 to derive the final GIR. An alternative approach would be to compute the convex hull before disqualifying the dominated among its records. This would be inefficient, because it would access parts of the space that are too far (and irrelevant) from the GIR, like the vicinity of p_{15}, p_{13}, p_{10} in Figure 5. Moreover, the only existing convex hull algorithm that utilizes a spatial index [7] applies only to 2-dimensional space.

5.3 Performance Indications

We now provide preliminary indications of the performance (and shortcomings) of SP and CP. We use three types of synthetic datasets (independent, anti-correlated, and correlated) with cardinality 1M each. We defer the description of these data, but note that they are standard benchmarks for preference-based queries.

Figure 6(a) plots, for different dimensionalities, the number of records that belong to the skyline of $D \backslash R$, i.e., the non-result records that SP needs to process in Phase 2. As anticipated, although SP prunes a large fraction of $D \backslash R$, it still needs to consider numerous records. The problem is exacerbated with growing d.

CP retains only the records in $\mathcal{SL} \cap \mathcal{CH}$, i.e., a subset of those examined in SP. In Figure 6(b) we present the number of records remaining after CP pruning in the same setting as Figure 6(a). CP aggressively reduces the number of non-result records in Phase 2. However, its effective pruning comes at the price of a convex hull computation over $\mathcal{SL}$, which entails substantial processing time.

6. ADVANCED SOLUTION FOR PHASE 2

The shortcomings of SP and CP motivate the development of an efficient and scalable Phase 2 algorithm that also copes better with dimensionality. We call this method *Facet Pruning* (FP). To provide the intuition behind it, we explore the nature of top-k query.

6.1 Rationale of Facet Pruning Method

In Figure 7(a) we assume the same dataset and top-k query as in Figures 4 and 5. Computing the top-k result can be seen as scanning the data space from its top corner (i.e., point $(1, 1)$) towards

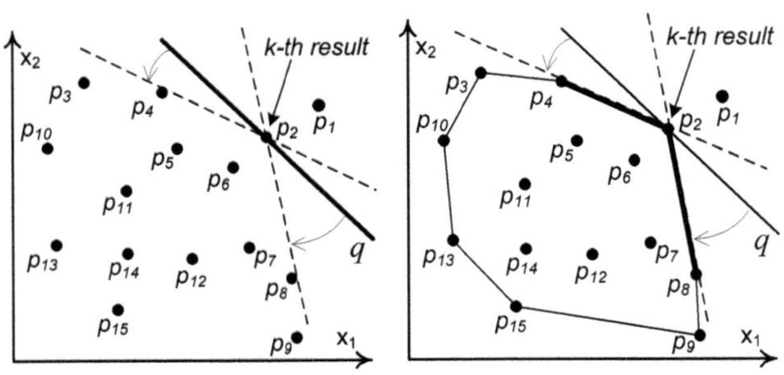

(a) Tilting around p_k (b) Determining facets

Figure 7: Intuition behind FP ($k = 2, d = 2$, data space)

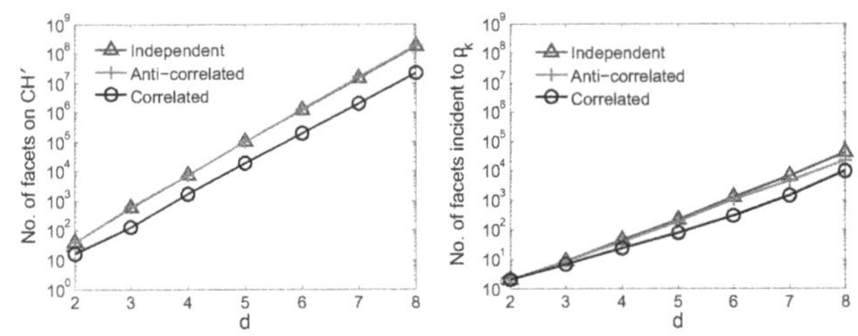

(a) Facets on $\mathcal{CH}'$ (b) Facets incident to p_k

Figure 8: FP effectiveness (n = 1M, k = 20)

the origin, with a line (or hyperplane, in higher dimensions). The orientation of the line is fixed, and it is determined by the query vector[4]. The first encountered record has the highest score, the second encountered record has the next highest score, and so on. The search stops after finding k data records, which form the result R.

In our example, the sweeping line would first encounter p_1 and stop when it hits p_2 (recall that $k = 2$). The line position when it hits $p_k \equiv p_2$ is defined by equation $w_1x_1 + w_2x_2 = \mathcal{S}(p_k, q)$ and is drawn in bold in Figure 7(a). It partitions the data space into two regions – all records above the line have higher scores than p_k and belong to R, whereas records below the line have lower scores (than p_k) and are not among the top-k. Any records on the line have the same score as p_k (yet, without loss of generality, we assume that there are no ties).

For now, let us ignore reorderings within R, and focus on the second set of conditions in Definition 1, which ensure that no non-result record overtakes p_k in score. Returning to Figure 7(a) and the nature of top-k processing, a tilt in the orientation of the sweeping line is equivalent to a shift in the query vector. Assume that we pin the sweeping line at p_k but allow it to rotate. A rotated position of the line is *permissible* if it keeps all non-result records below it. This implies that p_k still scores higher than them, and the query vector q' that corresponds to the new line orientation preserves R.

Consider a clockwise rotation in Figure 7(a). The first record hit by the line (i.e., p_8) bounds the permissible clockwise rotations, because any further tilting would perturb the result (p_8 would score higher than the current $p_k \equiv p_2$). Similarly, the permissible anticlockwise rotations are bounded by p_4. Any other non-result record cannot provide a stricter rotation bound than p_4 and p_8.

We make a crucial observation that hints at a general methodology to identify records like p_4 and p_8. In Figure 7(b) we show the convex hull of set $\{p_k\} \cup D \backslash R$ (i.e., the set of non-result records extended by p_k). The two facets that are incident[5] to p_k on the hull (i.e., facets $\overline{p_4, p_2}$ and $\overline{p_2, p_8}$) correspond to the records of interest (p_4 and p_8, respectively).

This is aligned with the property of the convex hull that each of its facets keeps all the records on one of its sides (specifically, the one toward the interior of the hull), which holds for any dimensionality [6]. Since the sweeping line (or the sweeping hyperplane, in higher dimensions) is pinned at p_k, its permissible orientations are determined only by *the facets of the convex hull that are incident to* p_k. We call the records that are incident to those facets *critical.* They are the only non-result records that could affect the GIR.

[4]Vector q is a *normal vector* to the sweeping line (or hyperplane, for $d > 2$), meaning that it is perpendicular to the line (or hyperplane, respectively).

[5]A record and a facet are incident to each other if the record lies at a corner of the facet. In two dimensions, for example, a facet is a line segment, and it is incident to the two records at its endpoints.

Intuitive as this fact may sound, translating it into an efficient Phase 2 algorithm is challenging. Let $\mathcal{CH}'$ denote the convex hull of set $\{p_k\} \cup D \backslash R$. A naïve implementation would compute $\mathcal{CH}'$, get the hull facets that are incident to p_k, collect their incident records (i.e., the critical records), and derive the GIR using only these records for half-space intersection. Convex hull computation, however, has a time complexity of $\Omega(n^{d/2})$, which is equivalent to the complexity of the exhaustive half-space intersection described in Section 3.3 (actually, convex hull computation and half-space intersection are dual to each other [6]). The situation becomes worse if one considers that there is no off-the-shelf convex hull algorithm for disk-resident data in more than two dimensions.

To alleviate the problem, our FP approach computes *only the relevant part of the convex hull*, i.e., only the hull facets that are incident to p_k. This approach provides scalability with respect to both dataset cardinality and dimensionality. We thoroughly demonstrate this fact in Section 8, yet here we provide some preliminary empirical evidence that substantiates the FP rationale. In Figures 8(a) and 8(b) we plot the total number of facets in $\mathcal{CH}'$ and the number of facets that are incident to p_k, for the same setting as Figure 6. The charts suggest that FP needs to compute/consider only a very small fraction of the hull facets. We remark that a critical record may be incident to more than one facet, i.e., the number of critical records may be smaller than the number of facets shown in Figure 8(b). For example, for independent data and $d = 4$, there are 45 facets incident to p_k and 16 critical records, while for $d = 6$ the number of incident facets is 1258 and that of critical records is 98.

Next, we present the detailed FP algorithm. We distinguish between the FP versions for $d = 2$ (discussed in Section 6.2) and $d > 2$ (covered in Section 6.3), because the nature of 2-dimensional space allows for special-purpose enhancements.

6.2 Facet Pruning in Two Dimensions

The convex hull/incident facet observation exemplified in Figure 7(b) is general and particularly useful for $d > 2$. In the special case of 2-dimensional space, however, the visualization in Figure 7(a) already suggests an effective processing methodology. That is, FP needs to simply identify the two records that constrain the rotation of the sweeping line around p_k in the clockwise and anticlockwise directions. Recall that some of the records in $D \backslash R$ have already been fetched from the disk by BRS during the initial top-k computation, and kept in memory, as explained in Section 3.3. Let T denote this set of records. The remaining non-result records are on the disk and are accessible via the R-tree on D.

FP consists of two steps. The first considers T and identifies two *candidate* critical records or, equivalently, *interim* facets incident to p_k. The second refines those facets by exploring data from the disk (using the index), until it identifies the two actual critical records.

The first step starts by removing from T the records that are dominated by p_k, as they cannot overtake it in score under any query vector $q' \in [0, 1]^2$. Then, it angularly sorts the remaining records

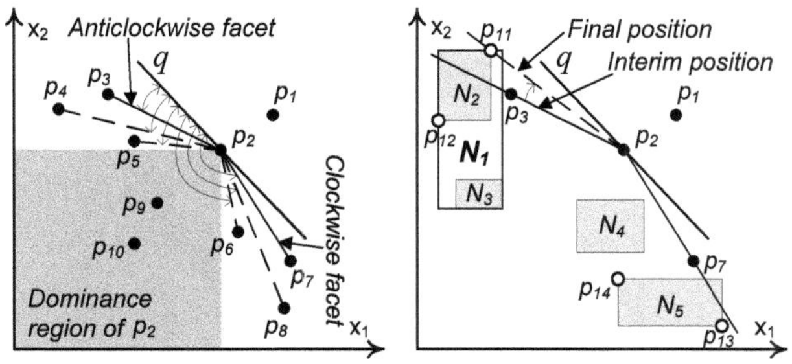

(a) First step (b) Second step

Figure 9: FP example ($k = 2, d = 2$, data space)

in T. That is, for every record $p \in T$, it computes the angle by which the sweeping line must rotate (in the anticlockwise direction) in order to hit p. It then picks as candidate critical records the two with the minimum and maximum angles. The minimum-angle record corresponds to the anticlockwise interim facet, and the maximum-angle record to the clockwise interim facet.

We demonstrate the first step of FP in Figure 9(a), where T includes records $p_3, p_4, ..., p_{10}$. We first remove p_9 and p_{10} from T because they are dominated by $p_k \equiv p_2$. The angle for each of the remaining records in T is illustrated by a curved two-headed arrow. The minimum-angle record is p_3, while p_7 is the maximum-angle one. These records define the interim facets $\overline{p_3, p_2}$ and $\overline{p_2, p_7}$. Note that if the area above the dominance region of p_2 was empty (i.e., if p_3, p_4, p_5 were not there), the anticlockwise interim facet would be the line segment between p_2 and its projection on the vertical axis. Similarly, if p_6, p_7, p_8 were not there, the clockwise interim facet would connect p_2 with its projection on the horizontal axis.

In the second step of FP we consider non-result records that were not encountered during top-k computation (i.e., records not fetched from the disk as yet), utilizing the R-tree on D and the retained search heap of BRS. We iteratively pop the heap, using its *maxscore* key as is. If the popped entry corresponds to an R-tree node, and the minimum bounding box (MBB) of the node lies completely below the interim facets, we prune/ignore it. Alternatively (i.e., if at least a part of the MBB is above an interim facet), we fetch the node from the disk. If it contains index entries (i.e., it is an internal node of the R-tree), we push its children into the heap, with key equal to their *maxscore* according to q. On the other hand, if it contains data records (i.e., it is a leaf of the R-tree), we consider each of these records p as follows. If p lies above an interim facet, we update the facet to connect p_k with p; otherwise, we ignore p. The process terminates when the heap becomes empty, reporting the interim facets as the final ones. Our implementation uses the beneath-and-beyond technique in [3] to check whether an MBB or record lies below the interim facets.

In Figure 9(b) we demonstrate the second step of FP, continuing the example of Figure 9(a). The interim facets $\overline{p_3, p_2}$ and $\overline{p_2, p_7}$ from the first step are shown as solid lines. Records p_1, p_2, p_3, and p_7 that are already known to the algorithm, are represented as solid points. Records shown as hollow points are on the disk and have not been encountered yet. In the beginning of the process, the search heap of BRS is assumed to include index entries that correspond to R-tree nodes N_5, N_4, N_1 (stated here in decreasing order of *maxscore*). The first entry popped from the heap corresponds to N_5. A part of its MBB lies above the clockwise facet $\overline{p_2, p_7}$. Hence, node N_5 is fetched from the disk. It includes two records, p_{13} and p_{14}, none of which lies above $\overline{p_2, p_7}$. Therefore, the clockwise facet remains as is. The second popped entry corresponds to N_4, which lies completely below both interim facets and is thus ignored.

The next popped entry corresponds to N_1. The node is read from the disk, since part of its MBB is above the anticlockwise interim facet $\overline{p_3, p_2}$. The two child entries in N_1 point at N_2 and N_3, which are pushed into the heap (with key equal to their *maxscore* according to q). The heap is popped again, producing the entry of N_2. Node N_2 is fetched from the disk, because it is not completely below facet $\overline{p_3, p_2}$. Between records p_{11}, p_{12} contained in the node, p_{11} lies above the anticlockwise facet. The facet is therefore updated to $\overline{p_{11}, p_2}$, shown as a dashed line in the figure. The last entry popped from the heap corresponds to N_3, which is below both the current facets and hence ignored. The heap is now empty and the final facets derived are $\overline{p_{11}, p_2}$ and $\overline{p_2, p_7}$. The correctness of the second step relies on the fact that (i) any pruned index entry or data record lies below both interim facets and therefore is unable to update either of them, and (ii) the process terminates only when the search heap becomes empty.

The facets derived by FP indicate the critical records, e.g., in Figure 9 the critical records are p_{11} and p_7. From these records, we derive half-planes $(p_2 - p_{11}) \cdot q' \geq 0$ and $(p_2 - p_7) \cdot q' \geq 0$, respectively, that embody the second set of conditions in Definition 1. The GIR from Phase 1 is intersected with those two half-planes to produce the final GIR. We summarize FP in Algorithm 1. Lines 1-2 implement the first step of FP to compute the interim anticlockwise and clockwise facets f_a and f_c, respectively. Lines 3-16 correspond to the second step of FP, while Lines 17-19 intersect the interim GIR from Phase 1 with the half-planes derived from critical records p_a, p_c to produce the final GIR.

Algorithm 1: Facet Pruning

Input: heap H of BRS, query vector q, k-th result p_k
Output: Final GIR
1 $T \leftarrow$ set of non-result records encountered by BRS;
2 $f_a, f_c \leftarrow InterimFacets(T, q, p_k)$;
3 **while** *H is not empty* **do**
4   Pop the top entry e from H;
5   **if** *e is below both facets f_a, f_c* **then**
6   Continue;
7   **if** *e corresponds to a leaf node* **then**
8   Fetch the node from the disk;
9   **for** *each record p in the node* **do**
10   **if** *p is above f_a* **then**
11   Update f_a to $\overline{p, p_k}$;
12   **if** *p is above f_c* **then**
13   Update f_c to $\overline{p_k, p}$;
14   **if** *e corresponds to an internal node* **then**
15   Fetch the node from the disk;
16   Push all the child entries of the node into H;
17 $p_a, p_c \leftarrow$ records incident to f_a and f_c, respectively;
18 Intersect GIR from Phase 1 with half-planes $(p_k - p_a) \cdot q' \geq 0$ and $(p_k - p_c) \cdot q' \geq 0$;
19 Return GIR;

6.3 Facet Pruning in Higher Dimensions

In more than two dimensions, a top-k query q can be seen as a sweeping hyperplane (to which the query vector is perpendicular). Following the FP paradigm, if we pin the sweeping hyperplane at p_k and allow it to rotate freely in any direction, the critical records are those (among the non-result records) that bound its movement, so as to keep all non-result records under the hyperplane. To vi-

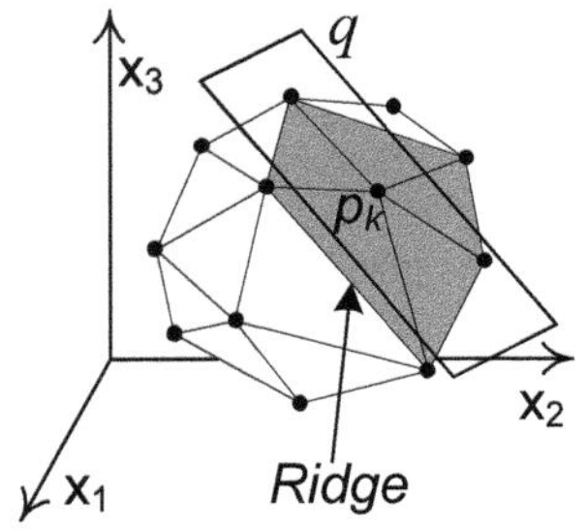

Figure 10: Facets incident to p_k ($d = 3$, data space)

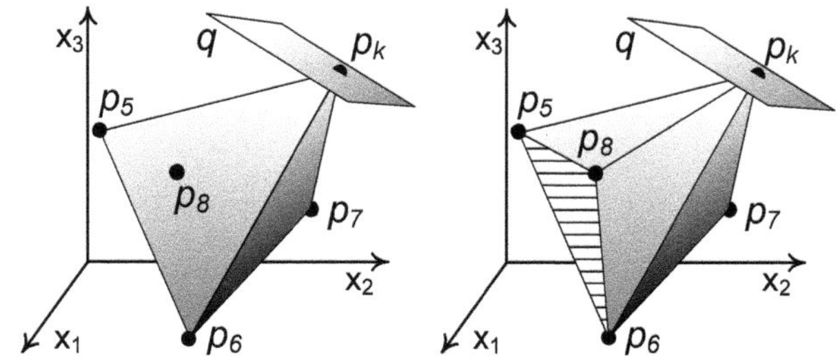

(a) Processing record p_8 (b) Updated set of facets $\mathcal{F}$

Figure 11: FP example ($d = 3$, data space)

sualize, we use a 3-dimensional example in Figure 10. The figure illustrates the convex hull $\mathcal{CH}'$ of set $\{p_k\} \cup D \backslash R$ and the sweeping plane that is pinned at p_k. The goal in FP is to compute the hull facets that are incident to p_k so as to collect the critical records. In our example, there are five such facets (shown shaded) that lead to five incident/critical records, excluding p_k.

Before we present algorithmic details, we note that a facet is a $(d-1)$-dimensional object that is generally defined by d records. A *ridge* is a $(d-2)$-dimensional object representing the intersection of two neighboring facets. For $d = 3$, the ridge is a line segment where two facets meet, and it is defined by the two records at its endpoints. In Figure 10 we point out a ridge at the intersection of a shaded and a normal facet.

The main idea in FP is to avoid computing the entire hull by maintaining only the facets that are incident to p_k. This is carried out in two steps, at the heart of which lies a strategy that incrementally updates the set of incident facets as new records are considered. The first considers the set T of non-result records encountered by BRS, and the second those still on the disk.

6.3.1 First Step of FP

The first step starts by discarding/removing from T those records that are dominated by p_k. Then, it draws d records[6] from T and computes a convex hull on these records and p_k (note that the cost to compute the convex hull of $d + 1$ records is trivial). The hull facets that are incident to p_k are maintained in set $\mathcal{F}$, while the rest are discarded. Consider the 3-dimensional example in Figure 11(a) where p_5, p_6, p_7 are drawn from T. From the convex hull of p_5, p_6, p_7, p_k, we keep in $\mathcal{F}$ the three facets incident to p_k, i.e., $(p_k, p_5, p_6), (p_k, p_6, p_7)$, and (p_k, p_7, p_5). The bottom facet (p_5, p_6, p_7) is not incident to p_k and is discarded.

Next, we process each record p in T and incrementally update $\mathcal{F}$. If p lies below all the facets in $\mathcal{F}$, it is discarded. Otherwise, we update $\mathcal{F}$ following a process reminiscent of Clarkson's algorithm, yet focused on facets incident to p_k only.

Specifically, we initialize a set $\mathcal{F}_v$ and place in it all the facets from $\mathcal{F}$ that p lies above of. In Figure 11(a) the only facet that is below p_8 is (p_k, p_5, p_6). Then, we collect all the ridges that are shared between a facet in $\mathcal{F}_v$ and a facet in $\mathcal{F} \backslash \mathcal{F}_v$. In the literature these are called *horizon ridges*. In our example the horizon ridges are $\overline{p_5, p_k}, \overline{p_6, p_k}$ and $\overline{p_5, p_6}$. Among them, we keep only those incident to p_k (i.e., the former two). We update $\mathcal{F}$ by (i) removing the facets that belong to $\mathcal{F}_v$, and (ii) inserting one new facet for each of the retained horizon ridges (the new facets are formed by connecting p with the respective ridge). Figure 11(b) shows the updated $\mathcal{F}$ after processing p_8. Observe that facet (p_k, p_5, p_6) is removed and is replaced by two new facets. The first is defined by p_8 and horizon ridge $\overline{p_5, p_k}$, and the second by p_8 and $\overline{p_6, p_k}$. Note that the striped facet was never created nor inserted in the updated $\mathcal{F}$. That facet would not be incident to p_k, and we avoided its unnecessary formation through our strategy to discard those horizon ridges that were not incident to p_k (i.e., ridge $\overline{p_5, p_6}$).

We optimize the first step with a heuristic. Recall that in the beginning of this step, we draw d records from T to (build a convex hull and) form the initial set $\mathcal{F}$. Instead of a random choice, we pick the d records from T with the maximum values along each of the d dimensions. The rationale is that many non-result points are likely to lie below the formed facets, and thus be pruned directly later on.

6.3.2 Second Step of FP

In the second step we refine $\mathcal{F}$ by considering non-result records that have not been encountered (not fetched into memory) before. $\mathcal{F}$ is updated gradually as we pop entries from the search heap of BRS. The exploration of the R-tree is similar to the 2-dimensional case. Index nodes are pruned (ignored) if they lie completely below each facet in $\mathcal{F}$; otherwise, they are read from disk. When an internal node is read, its child entries are pushed into the heap with key set to their *maxscore* according to q. When a leaf node is read, each of its records is checked against $\mathcal{F}$, the latter being updated if the record lies above some of its facets. The update process is identical to the description in Section 6.3.1. The process terminates when the heap becomes empty, and the critical records are collected from the final set $\mathcal{F}$. Every critical record p is mapped into a half-space of the form $(p_k - p) \cdot q' \geq 0$ and intersected with the interim GIR from Phase 1 in order to produce the final GIR[7].

Although the visual examples used in Section 6.3 are for $d = 3$, both steps of the FP methodology apply to higher dimensions without modification, by simply using the conventional notions of facets and ridges in the respective space.

We conclude the discussion about FP with a note on its complexity. According to [12], the number of facets on $\mathcal{CH}'$ is $O(n^{d/2})$, while the number of facets incident to a record on the hull (e.g., to p_k) is $O(n^{\frac{d}{2}-1})$. Computing these facets is the bottleneck in FP. FP uses a process based on Clarkson's algorithm, whose complexity for the entire hull is $O(n^{d/2})$. Following a similar reduction to [12], the cost to compute only the facets incident to p_k is $O(n^{\frac{d}{2}-1})$.

7. EXTENSIONS AND VISUALIZATION

In this section we extend our methodology to order-insensitive GIR, discuss the handling of non-linear scoring functions, and describe possible GIR visualization techniques.

[6] If T contains fewer than d records, we may use instead the projections of p_k on each of the d axes. This is equivalent to our strategy in Section 6.2 when the first step of FP encountered empty areas around the dominance region of p_k.

[7] An optimization is possible where the interim GIR from Phase 1 is mapped into facets and can be incorporated into the first step of Phase 2 to further "tighten" the criteria for fetching nodes from the disk in the second step of Phase 2.

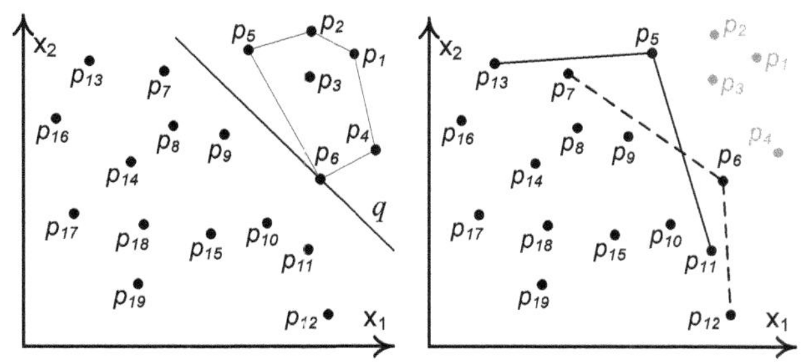

(a) Result pruning (b) Facet sets $\mathcal{F}_5$ and $\mathcal{F}_6$

Figure 12: GIR* computation ($k = 6, d = 2$, data space)

7.1 Order-Insensitive GIR

A variant of the GIR problem arises when the user or application is concerned only about the composition of the top-k result (but not the order of records in it). The *order-insensitive* GIR is the maximal locus in query space where the composition of R is preserved. We denote it as GIR*.

DEFINITION 2. ***Order-insensitive GIR (GIR*).*** *Given a dataset D and a top-k query q with result $R = \{p_1, p_2, ..., p_k\}$, the GIR* is the locus of all vectors q' in query space where*

$$\mathcal{S}(p_i, q') \geq \mathcal{S}(p, q')$$

for each $i \in [1, k]$ and every record $p \in D \backslash R$.

The GIR* is defined by looser conditions than the (order-sensitive) GIR, and hence it fully encloses the latter. Definition 2 suggests a straightforward processing approach. Consider a result record $p_i \in R$. Let GIR$_i$ be the GIR derived if we (skip Phase 1 and) apply Phase 2 by having p_i play the role of p_k, using any of the methods in Sections 5 or 6. GIR$_i$ is the maximal region in query space where $\mathcal{S}(p_i, q') \geq \mathcal{S}(p, q')$ for every record $p \in D \backslash R$. By Definition 2, the GIR* is the intersection of the GIR$_i$ regions for each $i \in [1, k]$, i.e., GIR* $= \bigcap_{i=1}^{i=k}$ GIR$_i$.

To optimize this process, we observe that not every record in R could affect the GIR*. In Figure 12(a), where $k = 6$ and $R = \{p_1, ..., p_6\}$, we consider the convex hull of R. Any record p_j inside the hull (e.g., p_3) can be ignored. The rationale is similar to CP in Section 5.2. For every query vector q' there is at least one result record p_i that lies on the hull, such that $\mathcal{S}(p_i, q') \leq \mathcal{S}(p_j, q')$. Thus, for any non-result record p to overtake p_j in score, p would first have to overtake a result record that lies on the hull.

Further result pruning is possible. Observe that p_2 dominates p_5, i.e., for every query vector $q' \in [0, 1]^d$, p_5 scores lower than p_2. Hence, any non-result record would have to overtake p_5 before it can reach p_2 in score. That is, we can safely disregard all result records that dominate at least another record in R. This strategy prunes p_2, p_1, p_4 (the first dominates p_5 and the other two p_6).

In summary, we disregard result records that (i) lie inside the convex hull of R or (ii) dominate at least one other record in R. We denote by R^- the remaining result records. In our example, $R^- = \{p_5, p_6\}$. Subsequent processing follows SP, CP or FP.

SP and CP produce the GIR$_i$ region for each $p_i \in R^-$ in the same way as in Section 5, and report $\bigcap_{i=1}^{i=|R^-|}$ GIR$_i$ as GIR*. Note that $\mathcal{SL}$ and $\mathcal{SL} \cap \mathcal{CH}$ over the non-result records (in SP and CP, respectively) are computed once and used for all GIR$_i$ derivations.

FP, in its first step, considers the set T of non-result records encountered during top-k computation. For every $p_i \in R^-$, it computes the set $\mathcal{F}_i$ of facets that are incident to p_i (on the convex hull of set $\{p_i\} \cup T$). This is done in the same fashion as in Sections 6.2 or 6.3.1, depending on dimensionality.

In the second step, FP maintains the $\mathcal{F}_i$ sets concurrently as it fetches new non-result records from the disk. The process is similar to Section 6. The main difference is that index nodes (that are popped from the search heap) are only pruned if they lie below all the facets in every $\mathcal{F}_i$ set. Also, each record p fetched from disk is checked against all the $\mathcal{F}_i$ sets and used to update those that include at least one facet below p. When the search heap becomes empty, each $\mathcal{F}_i$ set is used to derive the respective GIR$_i$ region. Finally, FP reports GIR* $= \bigcap_{i=1}^{i=|R^-|}$ GIR$_i$.

Continuing our example, Figure 12(b) illustrates facet sets $\mathcal{F}_5$ and $\mathcal{F}_6$. Each facet in $\mathcal{F}_5$ determines a half-space of the form $(p_5 - p) \cdot q' \geq 0$. The intersection of these half-spaces is GIR$_5$. Region GIR$_6$ is derived similarly, and FP reports GIR* $=$ GIR$_5 \cap$ GIR$_6$.

7.2 Non-Linear Scoring Functions

Our main focus in this paper is on linear scoring functions. While CP and FP (rely on convex hull properties that) may not extend to more general function types, SP can handle a broader class of functions. The following discussion considers the original (order-sensitive) GIR, but it translates easily to the GIR* context too.

There are two components in SP, namely, (i) pruning non-result records, and (ii) using the remaining non-result records to form the GIR. SP pruning applies to any monotone[8] scoring function. In other words, the only non-result records that could overtake the k-th record in R, under any such function, are guaranteed to belong to the skyline of $D \backslash R$ [21].

Identifying the non-result records that could affect the GIR helps to limit the number of conditions in Definition 1. Forming the GIR, however, requires translating these conditions to a locus in query space. If the scoring function is of the form $\mathcal{S}(p, q) = \sum_{i=1}^{d} w_i g_i(p)$, where each $g_i(p)$ is a function over the attributes of p, the GIR is derived using half-space intersection as per normal. To see this, the GIR is defined by conditions of the form $\mathcal{S}(p, q') \geq \mathcal{S}(p', q')$ for various pairs of records p, p'. Condition $\mathcal{S}(p, q') \geq \mathcal{S}(p', q')$ can be rewritten as $\sum_{i=1}^{d} w_i g_i(p) \geq \sum_{i=1}^{d} w_i g_i(p') \Rightarrow \sum_{i=1}^{d} w_i (g_i(p) - g_i(p')) \geq 0$. Since we are comparing specific records p and p', the factors $(g_i(p) - g_i(p'))$ are constants, and thus the condition corresponds to a half-space in query space. That is, Phase 1 and Phase 2 may employ plain half-space intersection to produce the GIR.

For scoring functions that do not belong to the above category, conditions of the form $\mathcal{S}(p, q') \geq \mathcal{S}(p', q')$ no longer correspond to half-spaces. This implies that the GIR is no longer a convex polytope but a general convex set. Exact representation of the GIR in such cases is computationally expensive or not possible at all, which would call for approximate GIR representation techniques, such as polytope approximation, Monte Carlo simulation, etc [30].

7.3 GIR Visualization

One of the GIR applications in Introduction is to give the user a sense of the weight shift required to induce a change in the top-k result. Being a d-dimensional polytope, GIR is challenging to visualize for $d > 2$. We describe two possible visualization options.

Assuming that the GIR is already derived using any of our methods, the first visualization technique computes the maximum-volume axis-parallel hyper-rectangle (MAH) that (i) contains the

[8]We follow the convention that the larger a record's attributes the higher its score. A scoring function $\mathcal{S}(p, q)$ is monotone iff for any dimension $i \in [1, d]$ and for any pair of records p, p' with $p.x_i \geq p'.x_i$ and $p.x_j = p'.x_j \; \forall j \neq i$, it holds that $\mathcal{S}(p, q) \geq \mathcal{S}(p', q)$.

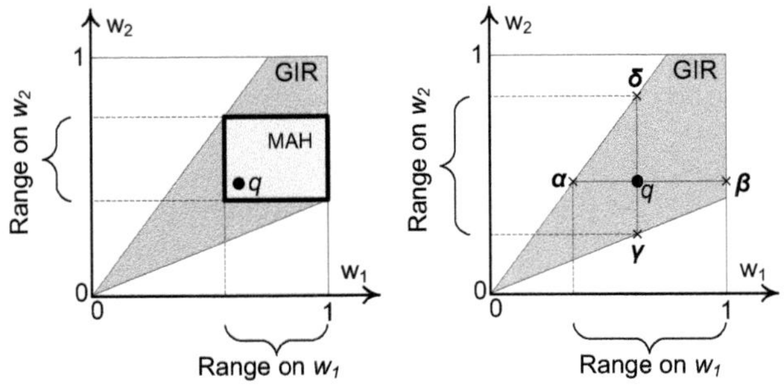

(a) MAH (b) Interactive projection

Figure 13: GIR visualization ($d = 2$, query space)

query vector q and (ii) lies completely inside the GIR. This is an instance of the *bichromatic rectangle problem*, for which several algorithms are available [2, 16]. Figure 13(a) shows the MAH in a 2-dimensional query space. The MAH can be visualized easily by projecting its sides on the different axes, producing for example bounds like those in Figure 1. The advantage of this approach is that the bounds are fixed as long as the query vector remains inside the MAH. The disadvantage is that the MAH is a subset of the GIR.

An alternative is the interactive projection approach, which does not sacrifice maximality (i.e., it allows exploration of the full extent of the GIR) but requires on-the-fly readjustment of the bounds plotted on the interface. Consider the query vector in Figure 13(b). We first find the horizontal projections of q on the GIR, i.e., points α and β, and map them on the w_1 axis to derive an upper and lower bound for w_1 like those in Figure 1. Similarly, we project q vertically on the GIR (getting points γ and δ) and produce the bounds for w_2. Note that the derived ranges are equivalent to the LIRs in [24]. Should the user shift the query vector (by varying one or multiple weights), we may interactively re-project the new location of q on the GIR, and redraw on-the-fly the new permissible ranges for each factor. That is, as the user shifts q (within the GIR), she sees the bounds for each factor being adjusted in real time.

8. EXPERIMENTS

In this section we evaluate the efficiency of the SP, CP, and FP algorithms, using synthetic and real datasets. The synthetic datasets include *Independent* (IND), *Correlated* (COR), and *Anti-correlated* (ANTI), which are standard benchmarks for preference-based queries [8]. IND is uniformly and independently distributed. In COR, records that have a large value in one dimension tend to have large values in the other dimensions too. In ANTI, a record with a large value in one dimension tends to have small values in the rest. We also use real datasets HOUSE and HOTEL (from *ipums.org* and *hotelsbase.org*, respectively). HOUSE contains 315,265 records, each with six attributes representing an American family's expenditure in gas, electricity, water, heating, insurance, and property tax. HOTEL contains 418,843 hotel records with four attributes, namely stars, price, number of rooms, and number of facilities. All attributes are normalized to $[0, 1]$. The datasets are indexed by an R*-tree using 4KByte disk pages.

In the default setting, we place data and indices on the disk and evaluate performance in terms of CPU and I/O time[9]. However, the CPU charts in isolation indirectly also evaluate the scenario where data and indices are kept in memory. Unless otherwise specified, we compute the order-sensitive GIR. We present total CPU and I/O times, accounting for Phases 1 and 2. A buffer for disk pages can-

[9]Note that SP and CP have identical I/O cost, because they access the disk through the same BBS process.

Parameter	Range of values
Dimensionality, d	2, 3, **4**, 5, 6, 7, 8
Dataset cardinality, n	0.5M, **1M**, 5M, 10M, 20M
Top-k result size, k	5, 10, **20**, 50, 100

Table 2: Experiment Parameters

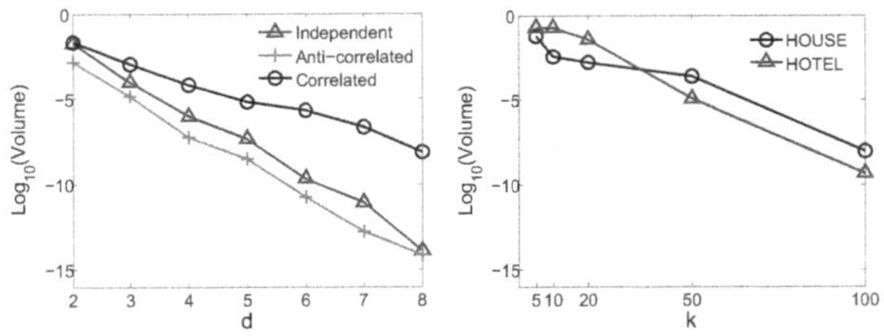

(a) Varying d (Synthetic) (b) Varying k (Real data)

Figure 14: Ratio of GIR volume to query space volume

not improve I/O time, since none of the methods fetches the same index or data page twice. Thus, we do not use one. All methods are implemented in C++ and use the Qhull library (*qhull.org*) for half-space intersection. Experiments are run on a PC with Intel Core2Duo 3GHz CPU. Table 2 summarizes the investigated parameters, along with their tested values and defaults (in bold). With the real datasets we control only the last parameter (i.e., k). Each reported measurement is the average over 100 random queries.

We first provide insight into the nature of the GIR. In Figure 14 we present the ratio of GIR volume to the volume of the query space, which coincides with the sensitivity measure discussed in the Introduction and the LIK probability in [30]. In Figure 14(a) we use synthetic data and vary d. The GIR volume drops exponentially with d, and Figure 8(b) provides the reason. As d increases, so does the number of facets incident to p_k, which implies that more conditions (half-spaces) bound the GIR. The GIR is the largest in COR and the smallest in ANTI, because COR has the fewest incident facets among our synthetic data, while ANTI has the most (as shown in Figure 8(b)). The trends in Figure 14(a) also reveal an interesting fact about the nature of the top-k query itself; the alternative top-k results become dramatically less distinguishable as d grows. In Figure 14(b) we plot the volume ratio versus k for the real data. A larger k implies more half-spaces induced from the first set of conditions in Definition 1, leading to a smaller GIR.

In Figure 15 we study the effect of dimensionality d on the performance of SP, CP, and FP, using synthetic data. All the charts for this experiment are in logarithmic scale. FP outperforms SP and CP in all cases, with SP being the runner-up. The largest differences are observed for ANTI, where FP takes 53 to 2700 times shorter I/O time than SP, and 1.3 to 47 times shorter CPU time. The difference is smaller in COR (because there are fewer skyline records than in IND and ANTI), with FP, however, still performing 9.6 to 224 times fewer I/Os and 1.8 to 24 times fewer computations. Interestingly, the CPU time of CP is longer than SP. Although CP prunes more records, its expensive convex hull computation outweighs the benefits of pruning (an issue discussed at the end of Section 5.3).

In Figure 16 we use IND and investigate the effect of dataset cardinality n, varying it from 0.5M to 20M tuples. CPU and I/O times naturally increase with n in all methods. The important finding is that FP scales much better with cardinality, as a result of focusing only on the (relatively few) convex hull facets that are incident to p_k. In terms of I/O cost, it outperforms the runner-up (SP) by 460 to 1748 times, and by 2.8 to 16.5 times in terms of CPU cost.

In Figure 17 we assess the effect of k using the real datasets. A larger k implies more records in T, i.e., more non-result records encountered during top-k computation by BRS. The larger T leads

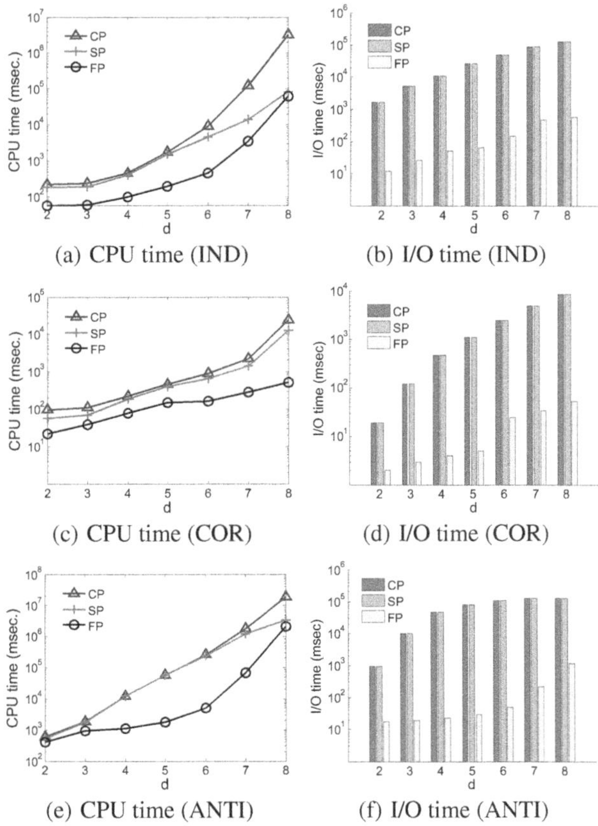

(a) CPU time (IND) (b) I/O time (IND)

(c) CPU time (COR) (d) I/O time (COR)

(e) CPU time (ANTI) (f) I/O time (ANTI)

Figure 15: Effect of dimensionality d for synthetic data

to an increase in CPU time. On the other hand, the effect of k on I/O cost involves two conflicting factors. A larger T implies that most critical records (in FP) and skyline records (in SP/CP) have already been fetched from disk (by BRS). This leads to a slight decrease in I/O cost for all methods in HOTEL. In HOUSE, however, due to its higher dimensionality (six instead of four) and different distribution, the inclusion of more records in the top-k result (and thus their exclusion from $D\backslash R$) deprives the skyline computation module (BBS) of records with high dominating/pruning power and "widens" the skyline, thus raising the I/O cost for SP and CP. In contrast, FP is independent of the skyline, and its I/O cost slightly decreases with k in this dataset as well.

In Figure 18 we evaluate our algorithms for the computation of *order-insensitive* GIR. We set all parameters to their defaults and vary n (for IND data). The trends are similar to Figure 16; however, the cost of all methods increases. The reason is that, as explained

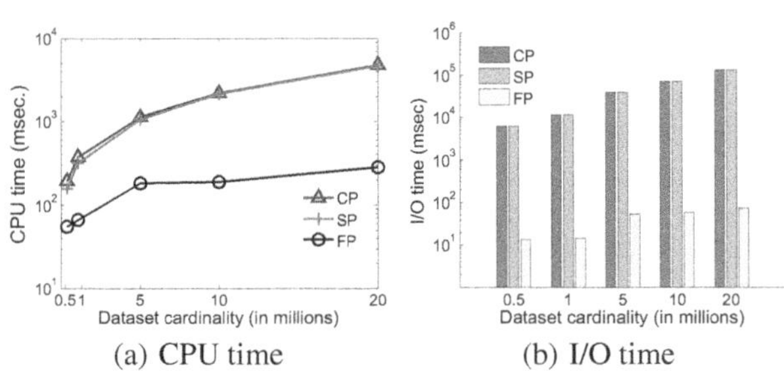

(a) CPU time (b) I/O time

Figure 16: Effect of dataset cardinality n (IND)

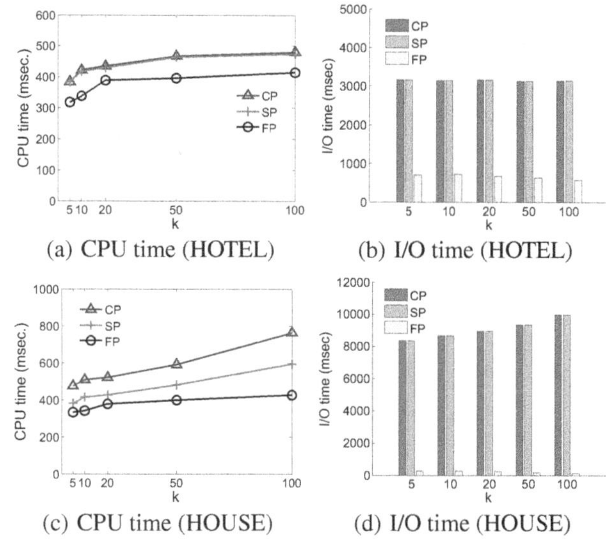

(a) CPU time (HOTEL) (b) I/O time (HOTEL)

(c) CPU time (HOUSE) (d) I/O time (HOUSE)

Figure 17: Effect of k for real data

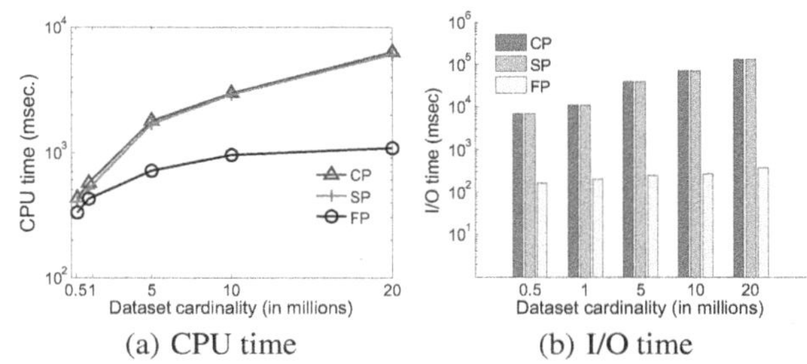

(a) CPU time (b) I/O time

Figure 18: Order-insensitive GIR, effect of n (IND)

in Section 7.1, multiple result records need to be considered against the non-results (as opposed to just considering p_k against them).

Returning to the default, order-sensitive GIR, in Figure 19 we consider *non-linear* scoring functions. Using HOTEL and varying k, we investigate the performance of SP for (monotone) functions $\mathcal{S}(p,q) = w_1x_1^4 + w_2x_2^3 + w_3x_3^2 + w_4x_4^1$ and $\mathcal{S}(p,q) = w_1x_1^2 + w_2e^{x_2} + w_3\log x_3 + w_4\sqrt{x_4}$ (recall that HOTEL is 4-dimensional). We label these functions as "Polynomial" and "Mixed", respectively. For comparison, we also include "Linear".

SP performance is similar for all functions. That is because skyline computation by BBS is independent of the function type (thus the comparable I/O cost), which in turn leads to a similar number of half-spaces to intersect for GIR derivation (thus the comparable CPU time). Results with other monotone functions are similar and omitted in order not to clutter the charts.

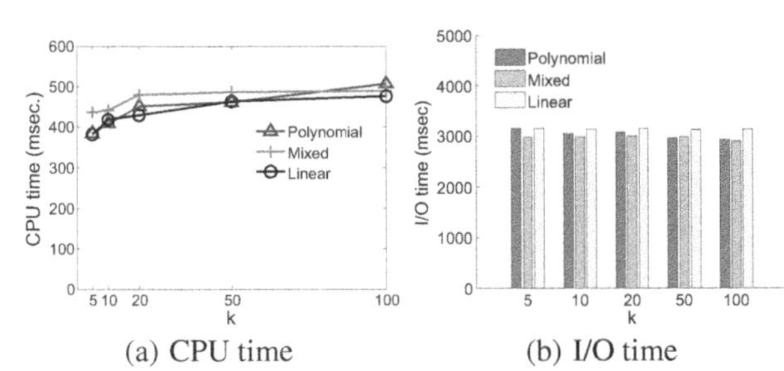

(a) CPU time (b) I/O time

Figure 19: Non-linear scoring functions, effect of k (HOTEL)

9. CONCLUSIONS

In this paper we study the problem of global immutable region (GIR) computation. Assuming a top-k query with a linear scoring function, the GIR indicates all the possible weight settings that produce exactly the same result as the original query. The GIR can be used as a guide for query weight refinement, as a sensitivity measure, and as a means for result caching. We propose a suite of scalable algorithms that exploit the geometric properties of the problem to achieve efficient GIR computation. A direction for future work is to extend the GIR notion to other query types and complex scoring functions.

10. ACKNOWLEDGMENTS

This work was supported by the Singapore National Research Foundation under its International Research Centre @ Singapore Funding Initiative and administered by the IDM Programme Office. Jilian Zhang was also supported by travel grant 61363009 from China NSF.

11. REFERENCES

[1] B. Babcock and C. Olston. Distributed top-k monitoring. In *SIGMOD Conference*, pages 28–39, 2003.

[2] J. Backer and J. M. Keil. The bichromatic rectangle problem in high dimensions. In *CCCG*, pages 157–160, 2009.

[3] C. B. Barber, D. P. Dobkin, and H. Huhdanpaa. The quickhull algorithm for convex hulls. *ACM Transactions on Mathematical Software*, 22(4):469–483, 1996.

[4] N. Beckmann, H.-P. Kriegel, R. Schneider, and B. Seeger. The r*-tree: An efficient and robust access method for points and rectangles. In *SIGMOD Conference*, pages 322–331, 1990.

[5] J. L. Bentley, H. T. Kung, M. Schkolnick, and C. D. Thompson. On the average number of maxima in a set of vectors and applications. *JACM*, 25(4):536–543, 1978.

[6] M. D. Berg, O. Cheong, M. V. Kreveld, and M. Overmars. *Computational geometry: algorithms and applications*. Springer, 2008.

[7] C. Böhm and H.-P. Kriegel. Determining the convex hull in large multidimensional databases. In *DaWaK*, pages 294–306, 2001.

[8] S. Börzsönyi, D. Kossmann, and K. Stocker. The skyline operator. In *ICDE*, pages 421–430, 2001.

[9] T. M. Chan. Optimal output-sensitive convex hull algorithms in two and three dimensions. *Discrete and Computational Geometry*, 16(4):361–368, 1996.

[10] D. R. Chand and S. S. Kapur. An algorithm for convex polytopes. *JACM*, 17(1):78–86, 1970.

[11] Y.-C. Chang, L. Bergman, V. Castelli, C.-S. Li, M.-L. Lo, and J. R. Smith. The onion technique: Indexing for linear optimization queries. In *SIGMOD*, pages 391–402, 2000.

[12] B. Chazelle. An optimal convex hull algorithm and new results on cuttings. In *FOCS*, pages 29–38, 1991.

[13] H. Christopher Frey and S. R. Patil. Identification and Review of Sensitivity Analysis Methods. *Risk Analysis*, 22(3):553–578, 2002.

[14] K. Clarkson, K. Mehlhorn, and R. Seidel. Four results on randomized incremental constructions. *Computational Geometry*, 3(4):185–212, 1993.

[15] G. Das, D. Gunopulos, N. Koudas, and D. Tsirogiannis. Answering top-k queries using views. In *VLDB*, pages 451–462, 2006.

[16] J. Eckstein, P. L. Hammer, Y. Liu, M. Nediak, and B. Simeone. The maximum box problem and its application to data analysis. *Computational Optimization and Applications*, 23(3):285–298, 2002.

[17] R. Fagin, A. Lotem, and M. Naor. Optimal aggregation algorithms for middleware. *JCSS*, 66(4):614–656, 2003.

[18] R. L. Graham. An efficient algorithm for determining the convex hull of a finite planar set. *Information processing letters*, 1(4):132–133, 1972.

[19] A. Guttman. R-trees: A dynamic index structure for spatial searching. In *SIGMOD Conference*, pages 47–57, 1984.

[20] D. M. Hamby. A review of techniques for parameter sensitivity analysis of environment models. *Environmental Monitoring and Assessment*, 32(2):135–154, 1994.

[21] I. F. Ilyas, G. Beskales, and M. A. Soliman. A survey of top-k query processing techniques in relational database systems. *ACM Comp. Surveys*, 40(4), 2008.

[22] C. Jin, K. Yi, L. Chen, J. X. Yu, and X. Lin. Sliding-window top-k queries on uncertain streams. In *PVLDB*, pages 301–312, 2008.

[23] J. Matousek and O. Schwarzkopf. Linear optimization queries. In *ACM Symposium on Computational Geometry*, pages 16–25, 1992.

[24] K. Mouratidis and H. Pang. Computing immutable regions for subspace top-k queries. In *PVLDB*, pages 73–84, 2013.

[25] S. Nutanong, R. Zhang, E. Tanin, and L. Kulik. The v*-diagram: a query-dependent approach to moving knn queries. In *PVLDB*, pages 1095–1106, 2008.

[26] D. Papadias, Y. Tao, G. Fu, and B. Seeger. Progressive skyline computation in database systems. *ACM Transactions on Database Systems*, 30(1):41–82, 2005.

[27] S. Prabhakar, Y. Xia, D. V. Kalashnikov, W. G. Aref, and S. E. Hambrusch. Query indexing and velocity constrained indexing: Scalable techniques for continuous queries on moving objects. *IEEE Trans. Computers*, 51(10):1124–1140, 2002.

[28] A. Saltelli, K. Chan, E. M. Scott, et al. *Sensitivity analysis*. Wiley New York, 2000.

[29] A. Saltelli, S. Tarantola, and K.-S. Chan. A quantitative model-independent method for global sensitivity analysis of model output. *Technometrics*, 41(1):39–56, 1999.

[30] M. A. Soliman, I. F. Ilyas, D. Martinenghi, and M. Tagliasacchi. Ranking with uncertain scoring functions: semantics and sensitivity measures. In *SIGMOD Conference*, pages 805–816, 2011.

[31] K.-L. Tan, P.-K. Eng, and B. C. Ooi. Efficient progressive skyline computation. In *VLDB*, pages 301–310, 2001.

[32] Y. Tao, V. Hristidis, D. Papadias, and Y. Papakonstantinou. Branch-and-bound processing of ranked queries. *Inf. Syst.*, 32(3):424–445, 2007.

[33] P. Tsaparas, T. Palpanas, Y. Kotidis, N. Koudas, and D. Srivastava. Ranked join indices. In *ICDE*, pages 277–288, 2003.

[34] A. Vlachou, C. Doulkeridis, Y. Kotidis, and K. Nørvåg. Monochromatic and bichromatic reverse top-k queries. *IEEE Trans. Knowl. Data Eng.*, 23(8):1215–1229, 2011.

[35] A. Vlachou, C. Doulkeridis, K. Norvag, and Y. Kotidis. Branch-and-bound algorithm for reverse top-k queries. In *SIGMOD*, pages 481–492, 2013.

[36] M. Xie, L. V. S. Lakshmanan, and P. T. Wood. Efficient top-k query answering using cached views. In *EDBT*, pages 489–500, 2013.

Answering Top-*k* Representative Queries on Graph Databases

Sayan Ranu
Dept. of CSE
IIT Madras
Chennai, India.
sayan@cse.iitm.ac.in

Minh Hoang
Dept. of Computer Science
University of California
Santa Barbara, CA, USA.
mhoang@cs.ucsb.edu

Ambuj Singh
Dept. of Computer Science
University of California
Santa Barbara, CA, USA.
ambuj@cs.ucsb.edu

ABSTRACT

Given a function that classifies a data object as relevant or irrelevant, we consider the task of selecting k objects that best represent all relevant objects in the underlying database. This problem occurs naturally when analysts want to familiarize themselves with the relevant objects in a database using a small set of k exemplars. In this paper, we solve the problem of *top-k representative queries* on graph databases. While graph databases model a wide range of scientific data, solving the problem in the context of graphs presents us with unique challenges due to the inherent complexity of matching structures. Furthermore, top-k representative queries map to the classic Set Cover problem, making it NP-hard. To overcome these challenges, we develop a greedy approximation with theoretical guarantees on the quality of the answer set, noting that a better approximation is not feasible in polynomial time. To further optimize the quadratic computational cost of the greedy algorithm, we propose an index structure called *NB-Index* to index the θ-neighborhoods of the database graphs by employing a novel combination of Lipschitz embedding and agglomerative clustering. Extensive experiments on real graph datasets validate the efficiency and effectiveness of the proposed techniques that achieve up to two orders of magnitude speed-up over state-of-the-art algorithms.

Categories and Subject Descriptors

H.3.3 [**Information Search and Retrieval**]: Search process

General Terms

Algorithms, Performance

Keywords

Graph Search, Representative power, top-k

1. INTRODUCTION

Top-k queries play a critical role in various domains such as e-commerce, social networks, and multimedia and scientific databases. In traditional top-k formulations [22], given a function to quantify object relevance, the goal is to identify the k most relevant objects. However, if multiple objects in the answer set are highly similar to each other, the information content embedded in these objects is significantly diminished. For example, in drug design, chemists often want to extract from a molecular database only a small subset of molecules that exhibit high binding affinity toward certain protein targets while preserving other desirable properties such as low toxicity. More importantly, this subset should be compact and informationally dense to be manageable for a human-centric analysis and inexpensive assay. Traditional top-k framework would return the k best molecules according to a scoring function on the desired properties of the molecules. A hypothetical answer set under this framework is shown in Fig. 1(a), which contains two molecules: chloro-benzene and bromo-benzene. Even if both molecules are scored high by the top-k query function, a chemist is likely aware of the fact that replacing the chlorine with any other halogen would result in a molecule with similar properties. Therefore, to maximize the utility of the answer set, it is desirable to identify molecules that are high-scoring, structurally diverse, and representative of the different structural groupings in the database.

The possibility of information redundancy in traditional top-k formulations has ignited much interest in diversification of search results [2,3,6,9,15,24,25,27]. While different models of diversity exist, at their core, all models penalize the relevance of an object if it is not diverse enough with regard to the objects that have already been added to the answer set. Focusing on diversity however, is not enough to maximize the information content. Consider the metric space in Fig. 1(b), where red-filled objects denote those that are relevant. Assume g_1 has already been added to the answer set and g_3 and g_4 are equi-distant to g_1. In a diversity-aware model, both g_3 and g_4 have the same score since they are equally relevant and diverse. However, it is clear that g_3 is representative of a cluster of other relevant objects, whereas g_4 is a relevant outlier. In other words, a diverse cluster center such as g_3 encodes more information than a diverse outlier like g_4 and should therefore be preferred. Thus, to combat information redundancy, we address the following

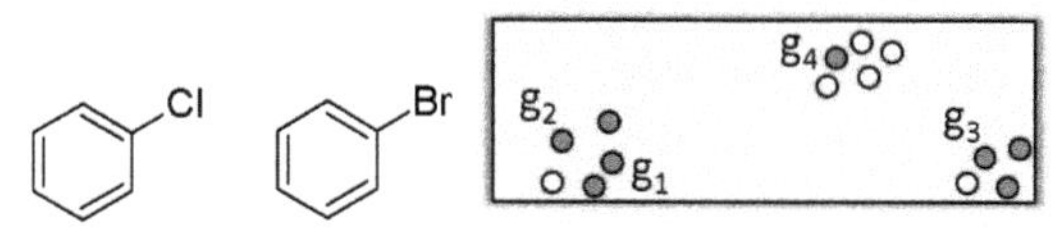

(a) (b)

Figure 1: (a) An example of redundant information in traditional top-k answer sets. (b) A sample metric space where two objects are similar if they are located close to each other. Red objects denote those that are relevant.

SIGMOD'14, June 22–27, 2014, Snowbird, UT, USA.

ACM 978-1-4503-2376-5/14/06 ... $15.00.
http://dx.doi.org/10.1145/2588555.2610524.

Table 1: Example applications with the combination of feature vectors and graphs. The properties of each graph g_i in the database is characterized by a feature vector $\overrightarrow{g_i}$. A graph is relevant if $q(\overrightarrow{g_i})$ is higher than some relevance threshold.

Property	Example 1: Molecular Library	Example 2: Information Cascades	Example 3: Bug Analysis	Example 4: Social Networks
Graph object g_i	A molecule in the database	An information cascade structure	A function call graph	d-hop neighborhood of an expert in a social network
Feature vector $\vec{g_i} = (v_{i,1}, v_{i,2}, \cdots, v_{i,m})$	Binding compatibility against m different proteins	Set of topics covered in the cascade	Count frequency over m days	Expertise areas of the social or collaboration group g_i
Target	Molecules with the most desirable properties	Most relevant cascades on a given topic set T	Frequently occurring bugs	Most knowledgeable groups of users on expertise areas E
Query function $q(\vec{g_i})$	$q(\vec{g_i}) = \sum_{j=1}^{m} v_{i,j}$	$q(g_i, T) = \frac{\lvert\vec{g_i} \cap T\rvert}{\lvert\vec{g_i} \cup T\rvert}$	$q(\vec{g_i}) = w^T \vec{g_i}$,	$q(\vec{g_i}, E) = \lvert\vec{g_i} \cap E\rvert$

problem: *Given a budget k, which are the k relevant objects that best represent the underlying database?* More specifically, let $\mathbb{D}$ be a database, and each object $o \in \mathbb{D}$ is tagged with a feature vector $\overrightarrow{o}$. Users provide a query function $q : \overrightarrow{o} \rightarrow \{-1, 1\}$ to categorize o as relevant (1) or non-relevant (-1). In addition, an object o is *representative* of another object $o' \in \mathbb{D}$ if $d(o, o') \leq \theta$, for some distance function d and a user-provided distance threshold θ. Our goal is now to identify the k objects that are relevant and most representative of the remaining relevant objects in the database.

In this paper, we focus on the setting where each object is a graph. Such graphs can be used to model a wide range of scientific data such as chemical compounds [20,23], system call graphs [8], communication graphs [17], social networks [7] and gene interaction networks [21], as demonstrated in Table 1. Example 1 in Table 1 formalizes the problem for molecular libraries discussed earlier. Example 2 identifies the spectrum of information cascade patterns under a set of user-provided topics. A traditional top-k query is prone to identifying cascades from a single community of highly active users. For example, cascades arising out of populous countries such as USA, China or India are likely to eclipse remaining communities. This effect can be negated by being aware of the representative power of each cascade and favor those that are active and remain to be represented. Example 3 computes a summary of the most diverse set of bugs that occurred recently in software bug analysis. A traditional top-k query here is likely to identify function call graphs that share the same core bug-inducing subgraph. By rewarding representativeness and diversity, we can identify the entire spectrum of subgraphs that induce bugs. Finally, in social or collaboration networks such as DBLP [1] (example 4), each node (or user) can be described by a collection of tags to represent his/her interests or expertise areas. Given a set of expertise areas as query, we can identify the most knowledgeable groups, where each group is based on the neighborhood of a node. A traditional top-k query in this case is likely to return groups with large overlaps among them. In contrast, a top-k representative query finds neighborhoods that are relevant as well as non-overlapping. In a nutshell, the combination of feature vectors with graphs, as well as the need to maximize information content within a budget k, positions the proposed problem in a unique space, which has not been studied before. Our main contributions are as follows:

- We propose a flexible and intuitive model for diversity to reward the representative power of the answer set. The flexibility is achieved by allowing users to define relevance at query-time and controlling the answer set size through a budget. While we focus on graphs, the proposed algorithm is generalizable to all metric spaces.
- We prove that top-k representative query is NP-hard and propose a technique to compute a constant factor approximation of the optimal answer set. We also show that no other polynomial time algorithm can provide a better approximation unless $P = NP$.
- We develop an index structure called *NB-Index* to index the θ-neighborhoods of graphs. Our proposed index structure employs a novel combination of Lipschitz embedding [5] and agglomerative clustering to expedite the answer set computation. In addition to fast answering of top-k representative queries, NB-Index also allows *interactive refinement* of θ to reach the optimal zoom level, while incurring minimal overhead cost.
- Empirical results on real graph datasets demonstrate higher information density in answer sets and a superior performance by up to 2 orders of magnitude speedup over state-of-the-art techniques.

2. PROBLEM FORMULATION

We assume a graph database $\mathbb{D} = \{g_1, \cdots, g_n\}$, where each graph g_i is tagged with a feature vector $\overrightarrow{g_i} = [g_{i,1}, \cdots, g_{i,m}]$ to characterize its properties. Based on a user-provided query function $q : \overrightarrow{g} \rightarrow \{-1, 1\}$, which operates on the feature vector $\overrightarrow{g}$, g is classified as either relevant (1) or irrelevant (-1). Our goal is to maximize the *representative power* of the answer set within a budget k.

DEFINITION 1. TOP-k REPRESENTATIVE QUERIES: *Given a query function $q(\overrightarrow{g})$, distance threshold θ and a budget k, compute the set of graphs $\mathbb{A}$, such that*

$$\mathbb{A} = \arg\max_{\mathbb{S}} \{\pi_\theta(\mathbb{S}) \mid \mathbb{S} \subseteq \mathbb{L}_q,\ |\mathbb{S}| = k\} \quad (1)$$

where $\mathbb{L}_q = \{g \in \mathbb{D} \mid q(\overrightarrow{g}) = 1\}$ is the set of relevant graphs with respect to q, and $\pi_\theta(\mathbb{S})$ is the representative power of $\mathbb{S}$.

To quantify the representative power of a graph or a set of graphs, we first define the *θ-neighborhood* of a graph.

DEFINITION 2. θ-NEIGHBORHOOD. *The θ-neighborhood of a graph g, denoted as $N_\theta(g)$, contains all relevant database graphs within a distance threshold θ from g.*

$$N_\theta(g) = \{g' \in \mathbb{L}_q \mid d(g, g') \leq \theta\} \quad (2)$$

where $d(g, g')$ is the classical graph edit distance [12,28] and θ is a user provided threshold. In other words, g is a structural representative of all graphs in its θ-neighborhood $N_\theta(g)$. Consequently, it is not desirable to have two graphs with a large overlap between their θ-neighborhoods in the answer set. By combining these intuitions, the representative power $\pi_\theta(\mathbb{S})$ of a set of graphs $\mathbb{S}$ is defined as the proportion of relevant graphs represented by $\mathbb{S}$.

$$\pi_\theta(\mathbb{S}) = \frac{\left|\bigcup_{g \in \mathbb{S}} N_\theta(g)\right|}{|\mathbb{L}_q|} \quad (3)$$

The proposed model captures as much of the various relevant structural groupings as possible within the provided budget. As a natural consequence of maximizing the representative power, the

Table 2: Summary of the notations used.

Notation	Explanation
$q(\cdot)$	User-provided relevance function that maps each object to {-1,1}.
$\mathbb{L}_q$	The set of relevant graphs with respect to relevance function $q(\cdot)$.
θ	User-provided distance threshold to quantify if two graphs are similar.
$N(g)$	All graphs that are within distance θ of g, and therefore *represented* by g.
$\pi(\mathbb{S})$	The representative power of a set of graphs as defined in Eq. 3.
$d(g, g')$	The edit distance between graphs g and g'.
$d_v(g, g')$	The vantage distance between graphs g and g' as defined in Def. 4.

answer set also favors structural diversity. For brevity's sake, hereon, we denote the representative power $\pi_\theta(\{g\})$ of a graph g as $\pi_\theta(g)$. Additionally, the notations $\pi(g)$ and $N(g)$ are used to denote the representative power and θ-neighborhood, respectively, for arbitrary θ's. Our notation is summarized in Table 2.

3. EXISTING DIVERSITY MODELS

As discussed in Sec. 1, a number of models exist to favor diversity in the top-k answer set. In this section, we discuss two recent models that are closest to ours.

3.1 DisC

DisC [9] recognized the need to go beyond diversity and focus on the representative power of the answer set. Given the set of relevant objects $\mathbb{S}$, DisC attempts to find the smallest set of objects that represent all relevant objects. Mathematically, DisC computes an answer set $\mathbb{A}$, such that $\forall o_1 \in \mathbb{S}, \exists o_2 \in \mathbb{A}$, where $d(o_1, o_2) \leq \theta$ and $\forall o_2, o_3 \in \mathbb{A}, o_2 \neq o_3, d(o_2, o_3) > \theta$. There are two main differences between our approach and DisC.

1. Static set of relevant objects: DisC assumes that the set of relevant objects in a given database is static. At times, the set of relevant objects are query-dependent even though the underlying database may be static. For example, in a database of information cascade graphs, one might be interested in only those that discuss a certain topic, such as sports. Owing to this assumption, the index structure proposed in DisC needs to be rebuilt whenever the relevant objects change. In this paper, we focus on a dynamic setting where the relevant objects are defined at query time by the user through a query function $q(\cdot)$.

2. Coverage of answer set: DisC requires the coverage of all relevant objects while we quantify the coverage of an answer set and seek to maximize it. DisC's requirement to represent all relevant objects can make the answer set too large. Such scenarios occur when a dataset contains some objects that are relevant but not clustered together with other relevant objects. Graph g_4 in Fig. 1(b) is an example of such objects. These relevant outliers have low representative power. Consequently, their presence in the answer set dilutes the *compression ratio* $\frac{|\mathbb{S}|}{|\mathbb{A}|}$, which is the average number of relevant objects represented by each object in the answer set.

To study this phenomenon empirically, we examined the answer set produced by DisC in a graph database representing the DUD molecular repository [10]. We use the classical graph edit distance [12, 28] for this experiment under a distance threshold $\theta = 10$ to define if a graph g_1 represents graph g_2. First, we identify the set of relevant molecules that are active against the enzyme Acetylcholine ezterase (AChE), a key component for curing Alzheimer's disease [4]. Next, we plot the growth rate in the answer set size as the number of relevant objects is varied. Fig. 2(a) presents the results. The growth rate is almost linear and on average, the answer set is one third of the number of relevant molecules. Clearly, a higher compression ratio is desirable and this is compromised due to the presence of relevant outliers. More critically however, there is no control over the answer set size.

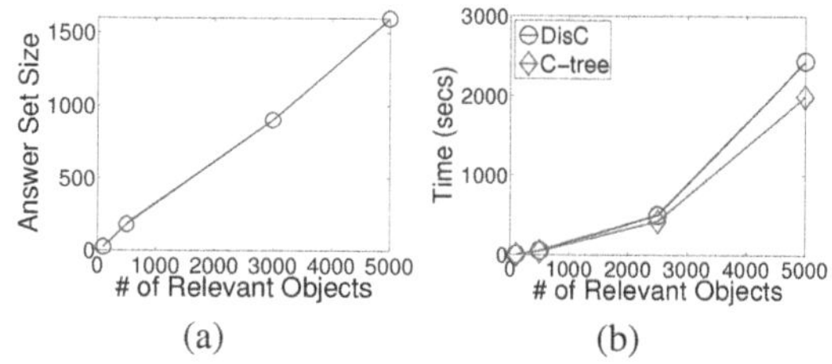

Figure 2: (a) The growth rate of DisC answer set size against the number of relevant objects. (b) The growth rate in the running time of the DisC model in the presence of graphs.

3.2 Tuning diversity models to reward representativeness

One of the most generic diversity models is proposed in [19]. Let us refer to this technique as *DIV*. Given a database of objects $\mathbb{D}$, the goal is to identify the subset $\mathbb{S} \subseteq \mathbb{D}$ of k objects, such that $\sum_{g \in \mathbb{S}} score(g)$ is maximized and $\forall g_1, g_2 \in \mathbb{S}, d(g_1, g_2) > \theta$. $score(g)$ denotes the value of an object (or graph) g. In our problem, the goal is to maximize representativeness. Thus, by assigning $\pi(g)$ as the score of graph g, we can attempt to maximize the representativeness of the answer set. However, in this model, $score(g)$ of a graph g is assumed to be static and independent of other objects in the answer set. In contrast, in our model, $\pi(g)$ is dependent on other graphs that are already in the answer set. More formally, for DIV, when $\pi(g)$ is used as the score, even in the presence of the constraint $\forall g_1, g_2 \in \mathbb{S}, d(g_1, g_2) > \theta$, the maximization function $score(\mathbb{S}) = \sum_{\forall g \in \mathbb{S}} score(g) = \sum_{\forall g \in \mathbb{S}} \pi(g) \neq \pi(\mathbb{S})$. Consequently, the model cannot be used to solve our problem. To ensure score independence, we need to enforce the stricter constraint of $\forall g_1, g_2 \in \mathbb{S}, d(g_1, g_2) > 2\theta$. This constraint, however, poses the risk of ruling out highly representative graphs from inclusion in the answer set and therefore will not maximize $\pi(\mathbb{S})$.

From the indexing perspective, three different schemes are proposed in DIV. However, all of them rely on an upper bound, which assumes scores of graphs in the answer set to be mutually independent. As a result, the proposed indexing techniques cannot be used in our problem. Beyond the independence assumption, DIV constructs a *diversity-graph* where each node is a graph in the database and two nodes are connected if $d(g_1, g_2) \leq \theta$. Since θ is provided at query-time in our model, the diversity-graphs need to be computed online, which is a computational bottleneck.

4. PROPERTIES OF TOP-k REPRESENTATIVE QUERIES

In this section, we analyze the complexity of the proposed problem and investigate the theoretical guarantees that can be achieved.

4.1 NP-hardness

THEOREM 1. *Top-k representative query is NP-hard.*

PROOF: We reduce the *Set Cover problem* to the problem of answering top-k representative queries. The Set Cover problem is defined as follows: Given a universe of elements $U = \{e_1, e_2, \cdots, e_n\}$ and a collection of subsets $S = \{S_1, S_2, \cdots, S_m\}$, the Set Cover problem seeks to determine whether there exists a collection $S' \subseteq S$ of k subsets, such that $\bigcup_{S_i \in S'} S_i = U$.

Given an arbitrary instance of the Set Cover problem, we construct a graph database containing three sets of graphs: D_1, D_2, and D_3 all of which are relevant. D_1 contains graph s_i corresponding to each set $S_i \in S$, and D_2 contains graph u_j corresponding to each element $e_j \in U$. Graph $u_j \in N(s_i)$ if and only if $e_j \in S_i$. From symmetry of graph edit distance, the θ-neighborhoods of all graphs in D_2 can be computed analogously. Now, let $x = max\{\pi(u)|u \in D_2\}$. D_3 contains $|S|$ disjoint groups of graphs, such that each group G_i contains x graphs and all graphs in G_i are in the θ-neighborhood of graph $s_i \in D_1$. In other words, D_3 contains $x|S|$ graphs and it ensures that any graph in D_1 has a higher representative power than graphs in D_2 or D_3. We now perform top-k representative query on this database.

It is easy to see that there is a set cover of size k if and only if there exists an answer set $\mathbb{A}$ where $\pi(\mathbb{A}) = \frac{|D_2|+k(x+1)}{|D_1|+|D_2|+|D_3|}$. From our construction, no graph from either D_2 or D_3 will be selected in $\mathbb{A}$. Additionally, the number of graphs added to $\pi(\mathbb{A})$ from D_3 is a constant number kx. As a result, $\pi(\mathbb{A})$ is maximized when, in addition to the k answer set graphs and their corresponding kx neighbors from D_3, all graphs in D_2 are in $\pi(\mathbb{A})$. On the other hand, if subsets $S_{i_1}, S_{i_2}, \cdots, S_{i_k}$ form a set cover, then including the corresponding graphs in answer set $\mathbb{A}$ results in $\pi(\mathbb{A}) = \frac{|D_2|+k(x+1)}{|D_1|+|D_2|+|D_3|}$. □

4.2 Submodularity

A function $f(.)$ is submodular if the marginal gain from adding an element to a set S is at least as high as the marginal gain from adding it to a superset of S. Mathematically, it satisfies:

$$f(S \cup \{o\}) - f(S) \geq f(T \cup \{o\}) - f(T) \quad (4)$$

for all elements o and all pairs of sets $S \subseteq T$. For submodular and monotone functions, the greedy algorithm of iteratively adding the element with the maximum marginal gain approximates the optimal solution within a factor of $(1 - \frac{1}{e})$ [18]. We omit the proof of monotonicity for Eqn. 3 due to space limitations.

THEOREM 2. *Eqn. 3 is submodular.*

PROOF BY CONTRADICTION: Assume,

$$\pi(T \cup \{g\}) - \pi(T) > \pi(S \cup \{g\}) - \pi(S) \quad (5)$$

where S and T are sets of graphs, such that $S \subseteq T$, and $g \in \mathbb{D}$ is the graph being added. From Eqn. 5, we can say:

$$N(g) \backslash N(T) > N(g) \backslash N(S)$$
$$\text{or, } S \not\subseteq T \quad (6)$$

which contradicts the assumption that $S \subseteq T$. □
Thus,

$$\pi(\mathbb{A}_{greedy}) \geq (1 - \frac{1}{e}) \pi(\mathbb{A}^*) \quad (7)$$

where $\mathbb{A}_{greedy}$ is the answer set computed using a greedy algorithm and $\mathbb{A}^*$ is the optimal answer set. Since the scoring function is normalized, i.e., $\pi(\emptyset) = 0$, no other polynomial time algorithm can provide a better approximation guarantee than $(1 - \frac{1}{e})$ unless $P = NP$, as proved in [11].

5. THE SIMPLE GREEDY APPROACH

Alg. 1 presents the pseudocode for the baseline greedy approach. From Theorem 2, Alg. 1 guarantees an approximation of $(1 - \frac{1}{e})$ or better. Unfortunately, in the presence of graphs, this approach is not scalable. The bottleneck lies in the neighborhood update step

Algorithm 1 Baseline-greedy($q(\cdot), \theta, k$)

1: Compute $\mathbb{L}_q$
2: $\mathbb{A} \leftarrow \emptyset$
3: **while** $|\mathbb{A}| < k$ **do**
4: $\quad g^* \leftarrow \arg\max_g \{\pi(\mathbb{A} \cup g) - \pi(\mathbb{A}) \mid g \in \mathbb{L}_q\}$
5: $\quad \mathbb{A} \leftarrow \mathbb{A} \cup g$
6: $\quad$ **for** $\forall g \in \mathbb{L}_q \backslash \mathbb{A}$ **do**
7: $\quad\quad N(g) \leftarrow N(g) \backslash N(g^*)$
8: **return** $\mathbb{A}$

(lines 6-7), which is performed at each iteration and requires $O(n^2)$ edit distance computations in the worst case. Computing the edit distance between two graphs is NP-hard [28]. As a result, Alg. 1 is not scalable to large databases. To mitigate this bottleneck, we need to index the neighborhood update step. More precisely, given the θ-neighborhoods of two graphs, we need to compute their overlap without incurring a quadratic computation cost with respect to the neighborhood sizes.

Indexing graph edit distance has been studied in the context of top-k nearest neighbor queries [12, 28]. The demands of indexing θ-neighborhoods, however, are different.

1. Overlap quantification: Instead of identifying the k nearest neighbors to a query graph, our goal is to compute the extent of the overlap between θ-neighborhoods of two graphs without incurring a quadratic computational cost. This ensures an efficient update of their representative power at each iteration.

2. Order independence: In our problem, ordering neighbors based on distance is not necessary; just detecting containment within the θ-neighborhood is sufficient. In top-k similarity queries, the ordering is central to solving the problem.

To establish the scalability challenge in the presence of graphs, we study the running time growth rate of Alg. 1 against database size. Furthermore, we also investigate the impact of two index structures that are both built for indexing nearest neighbor queries: the state-of-the-art graph indexing technique C-tree [12] and the index structure proposed by DisC, which is an adaptation of M-tree [29]. Fig. 2(b) shows the results. Regardless of the underlying indexing technique, it takes more than 35 minutes to compute the answer even on a small dataset containing only 5000 objects. This result highlights the need to go beyond traditional graph indexing techniques, which optimize nearest neighbor queries. To scale our problem, we need to index θ-neighborhoods.

6. INDEXING θ-NEIGHBORHOODS

Equipped with the insights derived from Sec. 5, we proceed toward analyzing the properties of graph edit distance, and then design an index structure called *NB-Index*.

6.1 Triangular inequality based pruning

The graph edit distance satisfies triangular inequality when the individual vertex and edge distances are metric. Mathematically, $d(g_1, g_2) + d(g_2, g_3) \geq d(g_1, g_3)$ for any three graphs g_1, g_2, g_3. Based on this property, we can easily derive the following theorem.

THEOREM 3. *For any two graphs g_1 and g_2, if $d(g_1, g_2) > 2\theta$, $N(g_1) \cap N(g_2) = \emptyset$.*

Theorem 3 highlights the property that, once the graph providing the highest marginal gain is added to the answer set, only the θ-neighborhoods of those relevant graphs within a distance of 2θ from that new graph will need to be updated. While this property does reduce the computational cost, scalability cannot be guaranteed. First, its efficiency depends on the value of θ. The smaller the value of θ is, the more efficient this property becomes. More importantly, to have a significant impact on the scalability, a technique must be designed to efficiently update the θ-neighborhoods of graphs which are within the 2θ boundary. Thus, to further improve scalability, we employ a Lipschitz embedding [5] of the metric space and design the concept of *Vantage Ordering*.

6.2 Vantage Ordering

Vantage Orderings (VO) perform a Lipschitz embedding of the metric space to speed up the indexing of the θ-neighborhoods.

DEFINITION 3. VANTAGE POINT AND VANTAGE ORDERING: *Given a metric space* $\mathcal{M} : \{\mathbb{D}, d : (\mathbb{D}, \mathbb{D}) \rightarrow \mathbb{R}_{+}\}$*, let* $v \in \mathbb{D}$ *be a randomly selected graph.* $\forall g \in \mathbb{D}$*,* $\mathcal{M}$ *is embedded into a 1-dimensional feature space* $\mathcal{F}_v$*, where the feature vector of a graph* g *is* $[d(v, g)]$*. The 1-dimensional ordering of graphs in* $\mathcal{F}_v$ *is termed the Vantage Ordering of* $\mathcal{M}$ *with respect to the vantage point* v*.*

As defined above, VO captures a feature space representation of $\mathcal{M}$ from the viewpoint of the vantage point (VP) v. To disambiguate the resultant feature space of Lipschitz embedding from the feature vector representation of a graph on which the query function operates, hereon, we use the term vantage space to denote $\mathcal{F}_v$. Now, to quantify the distance between two graphs from a VP's viewpoint in $\mathcal{F}_v$, we introduce the concept of *Vantage Distance*.

DEFINITION 4. VANTAGE DISTANCE $d_v(g, g')$: *Given a vantage point* v*, the vantage distance* $d_v(g, g')$ *between any two graphs* $g,\ g' \in \mathbb{D}$ *is* $|d(v, g) - d(v, g')|$*.*

Now, we observe the following.

THEOREM 4. *Given a VP* v*, if* $d_v(g, g') > \theta$*,* $g' \notin N(g)$*.*

PROOF: From triangular inequality, $d(g, g') \geq |d(v, g) - d(v, g')| = d_v(g, g') > \theta$. Thus, $g' \notin N(g)$. □

Theorem 4 provides a mechanism to bound the maximum vantage distance between any two graphs g, g', where $g' \in N(g)$. It is straightforward to see that the information retained in the vantage space can be boosted by employing a set of VPs $\mathbb{V}$ rather than a single one. We denote this vantage space as $\mathcal{F}_{\mathbb{V}}$. In $\mathcal{F}_{\mathbb{V}}$, we can deduce the following theorem.

THEOREM 5. *Let* $\hat{N}(g) = \{g' | d_v(g, g') \leq \theta\ \forall v \in \mathbb{V}\}$*.* $\hat{N}(g) \supseteq N(g)$*.*

Theorem 5 allows us to compute an upper bound on the actual θ-neighborhoods based on the VOs. The VOs can be pre-computed as part of indexing procedure, and thus, computing $\hat{N}(g)$ only requires $|\mathbb{V}|$ linear scans. Furthermore, since the entire computation is performed on the vantage space, the expensive NP-hard computations of edit distances are required only on graphs $g' \in \hat{N}(g)$.

6.2.1 Choosing VPs

The performance gain achieved due to VPs is directly proportional to the *False Positive Rate (FPR)*, which is the probability of a graph being in $\hat{N}(g)$ but not in $N(g)$. FPR is quantified as follows under the simplifying assumption that the distances $d(g, g')$ and $d(g, g'')$ are independent.

$$\begin{aligned} FPR &= P(g' \in \hat{N}(g) \backslash N(g)) \\ &= P(d(g, g') > \theta) \prod_{v \in \mathbb{V}} P(d_v(g, g') \leq \theta) \end{aligned} \tag{8}$$

It is clear from Theorem 5 that the higher the number of VPs, the better the tightness of $\hat{N}(g)$. On the other hand, both the computational cost of $\hat{N}(g)$ and the storage footprint of the VOs increase with $|\mathbb{V}|$. It is therefore critical to have a deep understanding of the relationship between the FPR and $|\mathbb{V}|$. Towards that goal, given the number of VPs $|\mathbb{V}|$, we derive theoretical bounds on the FPR. The FPR is dependent on the underlying distribution of the graph distances. We thus choose the two most commonly encountered distributions, *Gaussian* and *Uniform*, and derive the bounds below.

1. Normally distributed metric space: Let us assume that the distance between any two randomly chosen graphs is distributed normally where $d(g, g') \in \mathcal{N}(\mu, \sigma^2)$ and $m\theta$ is the diameter of the metric space $\mathcal{M}$. Under this assumption,

$$\begin{aligned} P(d(g, g') > \theta) &= P\left(\frac{d(g, g') - \mu}{\sigma} > \frac{\theta - \mu}{\sigma}\right) \\ &= P\left(Z > \frac{\theta - \mu}{\sigma}\right) \\ &= 1 - \phi\left(\frac{\theta - \mu}{\sigma}\right) \end{aligned} \tag{9}$$

where $Z = \mathcal{N}(0, 1)$ is the standard normal variable and $\phi(x)$ is the cumulative distribution function of Z.

The next step in computing the FPR is to compute $P(d_v(g, g') \leq \theta)\ \forall v \in \mathbb{V}$. With respect to a vantage point v, if $d(g, v) = x$, then $P(d_v(g, g') \leq \theta) = P(x - \theta \leq d(g', v) \leq x + \theta)$. Therefore,

$$\begin{aligned} &P(d_v(g, g') \leq \theta) \\ &= \int_0^{m\theta} P\left(d(g, v) = x\right) P\left(x - \theta \leq d(g', v) \leq x + \theta\right) \mathrm{d}x \\ &= \int_0^{m\theta} P\left(d(g, v) = x\right) P\left(\frac{x - \theta - \mu}{\sigma} \leq Z \leq \frac{x + \theta - \mu}{\sigma}\right) \mathrm{d}x \\ &\leq \int_0^{m\theta} P\left(d(g, v) = x\right) P\left(\frac{\mu - \theta - \mu}{\sigma} \leq Z \leq \frac{\mu + \theta - \mu}{\sigma}\right) \mathrm{d}x \\ &= \left(\phi\left(\frac{\theta}{\sigma}\right) - \phi\left(\frac{-\theta}{\sigma}\right)\right) \int_0^{m\theta} P\left(d(g, v) = x\right) \mathrm{d}x \\ &= 2\phi\left(\frac{\theta}{\sigma}\right) - 1 \end{aligned} \tag{10}$$

Combining Eq. 9 and Eq. 10, the FPR for $|\mathbb{V}|$ vantage points can be expressed as:

$$FPR \leq \left(1 - \phi\left(\frac{\theta - \mu}{\sigma}\right)\right)\left(2\phi\left(\frac{\theta}{\sigma}\right) - 1\right)^{|\mathbb{V}|} \tag{11}$$

2. Uniformly distributed metric space: Let us assume that $d(g, g') \in \mathcal{U}(0, m\theta)$ where m is the diameter of the metric space. Now, since the VPs are selected randomly, for any graph g, each dimension $d(v, g)$ is distributed uniformly. The FPR can therefore be quantified as:

$$\begin{aligned} FPR &= \frac{m\theta - \theta}{m\theta} \prod_{v \in \mathbb{V}} \frac{\theta}{m\theta} \\ &= \frac{m - 1}{m} \frac{1}{m^{|\mathbb{V}|}} \end{aligned} \tag{12}$$

6.3 Updating representative power based on clusters

Sec. 6.2 provides an upper bound on the θ-neighborhood of a graph based on a vantage space analysis. In this section, we analyze the structural space directly and develop techniques to update the representative power of a graph in the presence of clusters. The technique developed in this section allows *batch updates*: a single calculation to compute upper bounds on the representative power of a cluster of similar graphs. Here, a cluster is a set of structurally

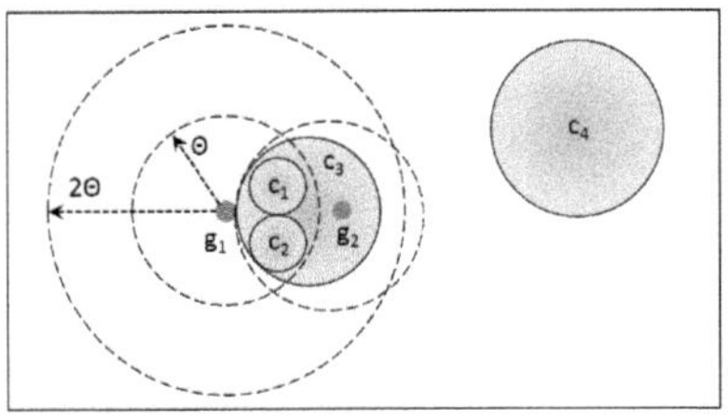

Figure 3: A representation of the structural space in the presence of clusters.

similar graphs. Fig. 3 shows a sample structural space of graphs with four clusters, c_1-c_4, depicted as shaded circles. Clusters c_1 and c_2 are contained within c_3. Consider two relevant graphs g_1 and g_2, where g_2 is contained within cluster c_3. The two dashed rings centered on g_1 with radii of θ and 2θ represent $N(g_1)$ and the space of graphs whose θ-neighborhoods overlap with $N(g_1)$. g_2 represents one such graph.

Now, assume that g_1 has been added to the answer set in the last iteration, and the θ-neighborhoods of the rest of the relevant graphs need to be updated. Since c_4 is more than 2θ away from g_1, neighborhoods of all graphs in c_4 are unaffected and do not need to be updated. In contrast, the neighborhoods of all graphs in clusters c_1, c_2 and c_3 are affected and need updating. Moreover, both c_1 and c_2 are fully contained within the θ-neighborhood of g_1. Thus, for any graph in c_1, their updated θ-neighborhoods must not contain any of the graphs in c_1. The same rule applies for c_2 as well. Whereas, this rule does not work for c_3 because it is not fully contained within the θ-neighborhood of g_1. However, graphs in c_3, such as g_2, could be affected. More specifically, $N(g_2)$, depicted using the dashed ring centered on g_2, needs to be reduced by its overlap with $N(g_1)$, depicted as the ring of radius θ centered on g_1. Furthermore, since c_1 and c_2 are completely contained within this overlap region, $N(g_2)$ must at least be reduced by the combined "area" of c_1 and c_2.

To formalize the above insights, we first introduce the definitions of *cluster radius* and *cluster diameter* with respect to a metric space. Since a cluster is essentially a set of graphs, we use set notations in the following definitions and proofs. Let $centroid(c)$ denote the centroid graph of a cluster c.

DEFINITION 5. CLUSTER RADIUS AND DIAMETER: *The radius of a cluster is the maximum of all the pairwise distances between the centroid and other constituent graphs in the cluster. Similarly, the diameter is the largest of all the pairwise distances.*

$$radius(c) = max\,\{d(centroid(c), g)\ \forall g \in c\}$$
$$diameter(c) = max\,\{d(g, g')\ \forall g,\ g' \in c\} \leq 2 \times radius(c)$$

Now, given a cluster c, we can derive the upper bound $d_{ub}(g, c)$ and lower bound $d_{lb}(g, c)$ for the distance between a graph g and $\forall g' \in c$ using triangular inequality.

$$d_{ub}(g, c) = d(g, centroid(c)) + radius(c)$$
$$d_{lb}(g, c) = max\,\{0, d(g, centroid(c)) - radius(c)\}$$

Now, let g represent the latest graph added to the answer set, c be a cluster, and $\pi(g')^*$ and $\pi(g')$ be the representative power of graph g' after and before g is added to the answer set respectively. Additionally, let $c_q = c \cap \mathbb{L}_q$ be the subset of relevant graphs in c. Using the distance bounds stated above, we have the following theorems:

THEOREM 6. *If $d_{lb}(g, c) > 2\theta$, then $\forall g' \in c$, $\pi(g')^* = \pi(g')$.*

PROOF: We omit the proof for its simplicity. □

THEOREM 7. *If $d_{ub}(g, c) \leq \theta$ and $diameter(c) \leq \theta$, then $\forall g' \in c$, $\pi(g')^* \leq \pi(g') - \frac{|c_q|}{|\mathbb{L}_q|}$.*

PROOF: Since $diameter(c) \leq \theta$, for any graph $g' \in c$,

$$N(g') \supseteq c.$$

Since $d_{ub}(g, c) \leq \theta$, $N(g) \supseteq c$. Thus,

$$N(g) \cap N(g') \supseteq c.$$
$$\text{or, } \pi(g')^* \leq \pi(g') - \frac{|c_q|}{|\mathbb{L}_q|}$$ □

THEOREM 8. *Let c be a cluster and $\mathbb{C} = \{c' \mid c' \subseteq c, c'$ satisfies Theorem 7$\}$ be the set of sub-clusters of c that satisfy Theorem 7. Additionally, all clusters in $\mathbb{C}$ are disjoint, i.e., $\forall c_i,\ c_j \in \mathbb{C}, c_i \cap c_j = \emptyset$. If $\theta \leq d_{ub}(g, c) \leq 2\theta$ and $diameter(c) \leq \theta$, then $\forall g' \in c$, $\pi(g')^* \leq \pi(g') - \sum_{c' \in \mathbb{C}} \frac{|c'_q|}{|\mathbb{L}_q|}$*

PROOF: Since $diameter(c) \leq \theta$, for any graph $g' \in c$,

$$N(g') \supseteq c.$$

Now, $N(g) \supseteq \bigcup_{c' \in \mathbb{C}} N(c')$. Thus,

$$N(g) \cap N(g') \supseteq \bigcup_{c' \in \mathbb{C}} N(c').$$

Since clusters in $\mathbb{C}$ are disjoint,

$$\pi(g')^* \leq \pi(g') - \sum_{c' \in \mathbb{C}} \frac{|c'_q|}{|\mathbb{L}_q|}$$ □

The three theorems above allow us to obtain tight upper bounds on the representative power of a graph by performing a small number of distance computations. An important constraint that drives the efficiencies of Theorems 7 and 8 are the diameters of clusters. If the diameter of any cluster is above θ, then it cannot be used to estimate the overlap between the θ-neighborhoods of two graphs. Therefore, the lower the value of θ, the less effective Theorems 7 and 8 become. Fortunately, the efficiency of Theorem 6 is inversely proportional to θ. As a result, the combined efficiency is *elastic* in nature; for a small θ, Theorem 6 is effective, whereas for a large θ, Theorems 7 and 8 are effective.

6.4 NB-Index

In this section, we develop the index structure called *NB-Index*, which unifies VO and the cluster based bounds into one coherent framework. NB-Index contains two components:

1. Vantage Points: A set of VPs, $\mathbb{V}$, is chosen to capture a feature space representation of database graphs. For each VP, NB-Index maintains the VO of the entire database.

2. NB-Tree: A hierarchical clustering is performed on the database to group structurally similar graphs into disjoint sub-spaces. In our clustering procedure, disjoint clusters are formed in a top-down, recursive manner to form a tree. In this tree, each leaf node is a graph and non-leaf nodes are clusters of its children. As a result, two clusters can overlap only if one is a descendant of the other. Each non-leaf node stores the centroid, radius, and diameter of the corresponding cluster. At leaf nodes, only the feature vectors of the corresponding graphs are stored. While building the tree, we ensure that each non-leaf node contains at most b children. The fan-out controls the desired depth of the tree. For an on-disk implementation, b should be chosen based on the disk-page size for optimizing the cost of node look-ups. On the other hand, in a memory-resident implementation, a small b yields better performance.

The clustering procedure starts at the root node, which contains the entire database. First, b graphs are chosen as pivots to partition the dataset. The first of the b pivots is chosen randomly. For the second pivot, we choose the graph that is farthest from first one. Continuing in the same manner, in each iteration, the pivot is the graph whose minimum distance to the already chosen pivots is the highest. The process is repeated through b iterations. Next, the pivots are assigned as cluster centroids, and all remaining graphs in the database are assigned to the cluster with the closest centroid. Finally, the process is repeated recursively on each of the clusters till the size of a cluster drops below b.

Since computing edit distance is NP-hard, and the indexing procedure requires a large number of pairwise edit distance computation, we use VPs to expedite NB-Tree construction. More specifically, to determine if pivot p is the closest pivot to a graph g, we first compute the VP-based distance $\forall v \in \mathbb{V}$, $\max\{d_v(g,p)\}$, which is a lower bound on the actual edit distance $d(g,p)$. If the lower bound is larger than the currently closest edit distance between g and any of the already evaluated pivots, then p is discarded from consideration. Similarly, to compute the radius of a cluster from the centroid p, if the upper bound $\forall v \in \mathbb{V}$, $\min\{d(v,p)+d(v,g)\}$ is smaller than the current radius, then g is ignored. As a result, expensive edit distances are computed on a small minority of pairs. The diameter of a cluster is set to the summation of the two largest distances from the centroid.

EXAMPLE 1. *Fig. 4 demonstrates the NB-Tree built on the corresponding graph database at $b = 2$. For simplicity, we use a 1D feature vector, denoted as $\vec{g_i}$, to characterize each graph, and these are chosen arbitrarily. The explanation of $\hat{\pi}$-vectors (highlighted in red), which are computed during query time, is discussed in the next section.*

Storage Cost: The storage cost for maintaining the VO of the entire database is $O(|\mathbb{V}||\mathbb{D}|)$, where $\mathbb{V}$ is the set of VPs, and $\mathbb{D}$ is the graph database. The second component of the index is the NB-Tree. Assuming a balanced branching factor of b, the height of NB-Tree is bounded within $\log_b |\mathbb{D}|$. Since the number of nodes at each level of NB-Tree follows a geometric progression, the storage cost is bounded by $O(\frac{b|\mathbb{D}|-1}{b-1})$. The total storage cost is therefore $O(\frac{b|\mathbb{D}|-1}{b-1}) + |\mathbb{V}||\mathbb{D}|)$.

Index Construction Time: For each VP, we need to compute its distance to all graphs in the database. Thus, the cost of constructing the VO is $O(|\mathbb{V}||\mathbb{D}|)$. For NB-Tree, at each level, each graph is compared to b pivots to identify the closest one. Since the height of the tree is bounded by $O(\log_b |\mathbb{D}|)$, a graph is compared to b pivots $\log_b |\mathbb{D}|$ times. Thus, the computation cost is $O(|\mathbb{D}| \times b \log_b |\mathbb{D}|)$. Combining the costs of both VPs and the NB-Tree, the total index construction time is $O\left(|\mathbb{D}| \times (|\mathbb{V}| + b \log_b |\mathbb{D}|)\right)$.

7. QUERY PROCESSING

The goals of the query processing algorithm are two-fold:

1. Flexibility: Maximize flexibility by allowing query time definitions of the relevance function $q(\cdot)$ and the distance threshold θ.

2: Interactive Refinement: While domain scientists have a crude idea on the appropriate θ for the task at hand, the optimal one might often be reached through a series of trials. This operation is similar in nature to finding the optimal "zoom" level in Google Maps. In

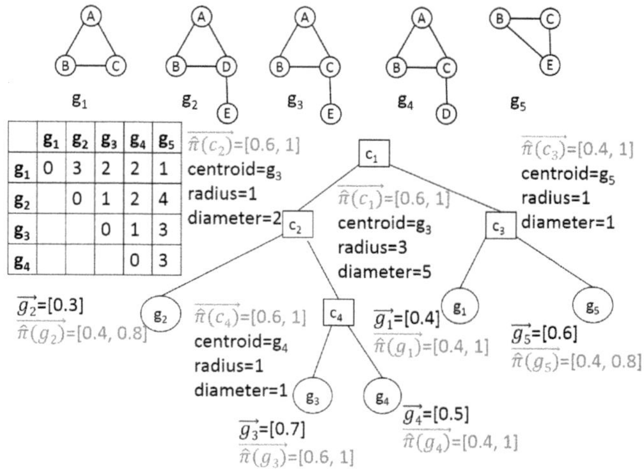

Figure 4: The NB-Tree built on the shown 5 graphs at $b = 2$. The $\hat{\pi}$-vectors, highlighted in red, are maintained only during query time. For simplicity, we assume all graphs are relevant.

other words, fine-tuning θ is an interactive procedure and a good index structure should adapt to those needs by performing refinements faster than a brand new query with a new relevance function.

To achieve the above outlined goals, the query processing algorithm runs in two phases: the *initialization* phase and the *search-and-update* phase. The initialization phase is performed only once as long as $q(\cdot)$ remains unchanged. For any subsequent refinements of θ, only the search-and-update phase needs to be repeated.

1. Initialization phase: VPs drive the initialization phase. First, VOs are used to compute a $\hat{\pi}$*-vector* for each relevant graph.

DEFINITION 6. $\hat{\pi}$-VECTOR. *The $\hat{\pi}$-vector of a graph g is a vector of $\hat{\pi}_{\theta_i}(g)$ computed at multiple distance thresholds θ_i, where $\hat{\pi}_{\theta_i}(g) \geq \pi_{\theta_i}(g)$ is an upper bound on the representative power of g computed using Theorem 5. Mathematically,*

$$\overrightarrow{\hat{\pi}(g)} = [\hat{\pi}_{\theta_1}(g), \cdots, \hat{\pi}_{\theta_n}(g)] \tag{13}$$

where $\theta_1 < \theta_2 < \cdots < \theta_{n-1} < \theta_n$ are n different thresholds.

The $\hat{\pi}$-vector allows us to compute an upper bound on the representative power for any given distance threshold θ. More specifically, a binary search can be performed on the indexed thresholds in the $\hat{\pi}$-vector to find the smallest $\theta_i \geq \theta$ and an upper bound $\hat{\pi}_{\theta_i}(g)$ can be derived to guide the searching process. We discuss which θs to index in Sec. 7.1.

Once the $\hat{\pi}$-vector is computed for all leaf-nodes (or graphs), the information is propagated upwards on NB-Tree by recursively computing and storing the ceiling of the $\hat{\pi}$-vectors of all children of a non-leaf node. Owing to this initialization procedure, an upper bound on the marginal gain in representative power of any graph g can be computed from any of its ancestor nodes. More specifically, for any non-leaf node n, and any set of graphs $\mathbb{S}$, the following property can be guaranteed.

$$\pi(\mathbb{S} \cup \{n\}) \geq \pi(\mathbb{S} \cup \{c\}) \text{ for any child } c \text{ of } n \tag{14}$$

Note that in the absence of interactive refinement, the $\hat{\pi}$-vector is not required since the input θ is already known; $\hat{\pi}_\theta(g)$ can be computed directly. However, if the threshold is refined to θ', then $\pi_{\theta'}(g)$ needs to be recomputed. More importantly, the information contained in any of the previously used θs cannot be leveraged. Thus, we pre-compute the representative powers at a series of distance thresholds in the initialization phase and use them as required

Algorithm 2 nextGraph($q(\cdot), \theta, k$)

1: PQ $\leftarrow$ priority queue containing $NB\text{-}tree.root$
2: lb $\leftarrow$ 0
3: best $\leftarrow$ **null**
4: **while** PQ is not empty **do**
5:     entry $\leftarrow$ PQ.dequeue()
6:     **if** entry.gain$<$lb **then**
7:         **return** best
8:     **if** entry is a graph **then**
9:         Compute $\hat{N}_\theta(entry)$ using VOs
10:         $N_\theta(entry) \leftarrow \{g \mid g \in \hat{N}_\theta(entry),\ d(entry, g) \le \theta\}$
11:         gain$\leftarrow$ $\pi(\mathbb{A} \cup entry) - \pi(\mathbb{A})$
12:         **if** gain$>$ lb **then**
13:             best$\leftarrow$ entry
14:             lb$\leftarrow$ gain
15:     **else**
16:         **for** each child c $\in$ entry **and** $q(entry) \ge \eta$ **do**
17:             gain$\leftarrow$ $\pi(\mathbb{A} \cup c) - \pi(\mathbb{A})$
18:             **if** gain$>$ lb **then**
19:                 PQ.insert(gain,c)
20: **return** best

for refinements. In other words, the initialization phase is insulated from refinements of θ.

EXAMPLE 2. *Fig. 4 demonstrates how $\hat{\pi}$-vectors are constructed and propagated upwards in the tree through the ceiling operation. For simplicity, we assume all graphs are relevant. The $\hat{\pi}$-vector is computed on $\theta_1 = 1$ and $\theta_2 = 3$.*

2. Search and Update: The second phase can be divided into two subcomponents: search and update, which are performed iteratively k times.

2a. Search: Alg. 2 presents the pseudocode. First, a search is performed to identify the graph providing the highest marginal gain in representative power. The search starts from the root node (line 1). When a node is explored (line 5), each of its children is added to a priority queue where the nodes are ordered based on their marginal gains in representative power (lines 15-18). Since the marginal gain at any non-leaf node provides an upper bound on the marginal gains of all graphs in its subtree, they are used to prioritize the exploration of the unexplored nodes. The process is repeated iteratively till a graph is found whose actual marginal gain is higher than all candidates in the priority queue (lines 6-7). Only for such a graph, its θ-neighborhood is computed using graph edit distance to compute the exact marginal gain in the representative power (lines 8-14). As a result, expensive edit distance computations are reserved for only strong candidates and the computational cost is drastically reduced.

2b. Update: The cluster based bounds identified in Sec. 6.3 drive the update step. At the addition of a graph g to the answer set, the $\hat{\pi}$-vectors of nodes in NB-Tree are impacted. Now, instead of accurate re-computations of $\hat{\pi}$-vectors, a search is initiated from the root to identify clusters (or non-leaf nodes) that are within a distance of 2θ from g and consequently, affected (Theorem 6). For such clusters, using Theorems 7-8, the $\hat{\pi}$-vectors are updated. To identify the relevant graphs in a cluster, only graphs in its subtree need to be scanned. As noted earlier, Theorems 6-8 provide the benefit of computing a single upper bound for a group of structurally similar graphs that are located in the same cluster. Finally, the ceilings of the changed $\hat{\pi}$-vectors are propagated upwards, as in the initialization step, to reflect the "current state" of the search.

7.1 Choosing thresholds to index in the $\hat{\pi}$-vector

A bad choice of thresholds in the $\hat{\pi}$-vector would produce loose upper bounds which in turn would reduce the efficiency of the search-and-update procedure. Therefore, to make a more informed selection, the following factors need to be considered: domain knowledge, the history of previous queries, and the memory budget. Note that the selection of thresholds to index is an offline procedure and is decided by the index designer. The user who issues the query needs no prior information.

The number of thresholds to index can easily be decided based on the memory budget. For example, in an index with 1 million nodes, a $\hat{\pi}$-vector of size 10 would consume $\frac{4 \times 10 \times 10^6}{10^6}$ =40MB. For the more critical decision of choosing the thresholds, depending on the information and resources available, one of the following schemes can be adopted.

1. Query log: If the distribution of distance thresholds on previous top-k queries is available, then the thresholds to index can be sampled (without replacement) from that distribution.

2. No information is available: When no prior information is available, the distribution of $\pi(g)$ across θ can be computed from a small sample of graphs in the database. Next, the thresholds to index can be chosen proportional to the slopes in the distribution. More specifically, a higher number of thresholds should be indexed for the θ intervals where the slope is high since such intervals indicate regions where the upper bounds vary steeply even for a small difference in θ's.

Table 3: Graph datasets used for evaluation

Dataset	Avg. # of nodes	Avg. # of edges	# of graphs
DUD	26	28	128332
DBLP	55	263	11362
Amazon	29	189	9120

8. EXPERIMENTS

This section summarizes experimental results that examine the quality and the scalability of our approach:
1. Information Density: The proposed model has a higher information density than DisC [9] and a diversity-based model [19].
2: Scalability: By indexing θ-neighborhoods of graphs instead of their nearest neighbors, NB-Index ensures scalability in answering top-k representative queries on graph databases.

8.1 Datasets

We use three different graph datasets to benchmark our techniques. Table. 3 summarizes the various properties of the datasets.

1. DUD: The DUD [10] dataset contains 128,332 molecules that were assayed against 10 different protein targets. Consequently, each molecule is tagged with a 10-dimensional feature vector that represents its binding affinity to each of the targets. In the graph representation of a molecule, each vertex corresponds to an atom, and the edges represent atom-atom bonds. Our goal is to identify molecular structures that are compatible with the structure of the protein targets. The DUD dataset allows us to assess the natural correlations that exist between the feature and the structural space, and their resultant effects on top-k queries.

2. DBLP: In the DBLP network [1], each node corresponds to an author, and two authors are connected if they have at least one paper together. Furthermore, each author is tagged with the community he/she belongs too. For our evaluation, the goal is to understand if the most active groups collaborate within the community or span across multiple communities. For that purpose, we replace the author in each node label with the person's community. Next, we extract the complete 2-hop neighborhood subgraph around each node to construct our graph database. Finally, the combined activity level of each graph, denoting a collaboration group, is characterized with a one-dimensional feature vector.

Table 4: Compression ratios (CR) $|N_\theta(\mathbb{A})|/|\mathbb{A}|$ and $\pi(\mathbb{A})$ achieved by REP and DIV [19] at various ks. The last row indicates the compression ratio of DisC along with its answer set size in parentheses.

Property	DUD						DBLP						Amazon					
	REP		DIV(θ)		DIV(2θ)		REP		DIV(θ)		DIV(2θ)		REP		DIV(θ)		DIV(2θ)	
	CR	$\pi(\mathbb{A})$	CR	$\pi(\mathbb{A})$	CR	$\pi(\mathbb{A})$	CR	$\pi(\mathbb{A})$	CR	$\pi(\mathbb{A})$	CR	$\pi(\mathbb{A})$	CR	$\pi(\mathbb{A})$	CR	$\pi(\mathbb{A})$	CR	$\pi(\mathbb{A})$
$k = 10$	115	0.23	31	0.06	28.8	0.06	45.4	0.16	23.1	0.08	19.1	0.07	84.3	0.17	37.8	0.21	27	0.12
$k = 25$	80	0.40	22.9	0.11	16.4	0.08	25	0.22	12	0.11	10.7	0.09	41.9	0.46	19.6	0.22	15.9	0.17
$k = 50$	58	0.58	17	0.17	9.9	0.09	15.3	0.27	7.5	0.13	6.4	0.11	23.7	0.52	12	0.26	9.3	0.2
$k = 100$	35	0.70	10.1	0.2	4.7	0.09	11.6	0.41	4.7	0.17	4	0.14	15	0.66	6.9	0.3	5.4	0.24
DisC	2.77 (1782)						1.78 (1590)						2.5(912)					

3. Amazon: The Amazon network [1] is structured in a manner similar to DBLP. Each node corresponds to an item, and two items are connected if they are frequently co-purchased. In addition, each item is classified under a category. Our goal is to understand if cross-category coupling exists among items that are popular. Thus, similar to the processing in the DBLP dataset, we replace the node labels with the category of the item and then extract its 2-hop neighborhood subgraph. As in the DBLP dataset, a feature vector is used to characterize the popularity of each co-purchase graph.

8.2 Experimental setup

Our algorithms are implemented in Java 1.6.0 and benchmarked on an Intel i7 2.67GHz quad core processor PC with 12GB of main memory running Ubuntu 12.10. We refer to our proposed model as *REP*, and the diversity model in [19] is termed *DIV*.

1. Quality Evaluation: To evaluate the quality of the answer set produced REP, we compare its representative power with the full DisC answer set, and the top-k answer sets of DIV.

2. Scalability Evaluation: We benchmark the performance of NB-Index against the 'Grey-Greedy-DisC(Pruned)' algorithm of DisC [9], the 'div-cut' approach in DIV [19] and C-tree [12]. For DisC, we stop the computation as soon as it attains a size of k. For DIV, we use C-Tree to compute the 'diversity-graph', which is subsequently used by the 'div-cut' algorithm, to speed up processing.

Due to the extremely slow running times of DisC, DIV and C-tree on the entire DUD database, we select a random sample of $25,000$ graphs. Nonetheless, for scalability experiments against dataset size, we use the entire DUD database. For DBLP and Amazon, we use the entire dataset for all experiments.

8.2.1 Query Arguments

1. $q(\cdot)$**:** One primary goal in REP is to support query time definition of relevant graphs. To model this requirement, in DUD, we select a random subset of d dimensions where $1 \leq d \leq 10$, and the feature-space score is quantified as $\sum_1^d \frac{g_i}{d}$. Both the DBLP and Amazon datasets are characterized using 1D feature vectors, which act as their feature space scores. A graph is considered relevant if its feature-space score falls within the first quartile.

2. θ**:** Our goal is to select a θ that is realistic and yet poses a significant scalability challenge in answering top-k representative queries. Towards that goal, we study the cumulative distribution of the graph distances in each dataset (Figs. 5(a)-5(b)). While the distributions are similar for DUD and DBLP, distances between graphs in the Amazon dataset are much farther apart. Based on these observations, for DUD and DBLP we set $\theta = 10$ and for Amazon, $\theta = 75$. For DBLP and DUD, addition of a graph to the answer set impacts the $\pi(g)$ of any graph g within a distance of $2\theta = 20$; for Amazon, graphs within a distance of 150 are affected.

3. k**:** The default k is set to 10.

8.2.2 Parameters

1. $\hat{\pi}$**-vector:** The $\hat{\pi}$-vector is chosen based on the cumulative distance distributions in Figs. 5(a)-5(b). Given the high slope between $\theta = 10$ and $\theta = 40$ for both DUD and DBLP, we index 10 different distance thresholds at 5, 12, 16, 20, 25, 30, 35, 40, 75, 100. We index at θs beyond 40 just for the sake of completeness so that a query on any θ can be supported. For amazon, we adapt $\hat{\pi}$-vector using the same strategy. Owing to the high slope between $\theta = 50$ and $\theta = 200$, we index at 20, 60, 90, 120, 150, 180, 200, 300, 400, 500.

2. Number of VPs: The number of VPs is chosen based on Eqn. 11. The distance distributions in the three datasets (Figs. 5(c)-5(e)) are approximated as a Gaussian of their means and standard deviations. To limit the FPR below 5% at the realistic zone of $5 \leq \theta \leq 20$ for DUD and DBLP, and at $50 \leq \theta \leq 200$ for Amazon, we choose 100 VPs.

3. Branching Factor: The maximum branching factor in NB-Index is set to 40.

8.3 Quantitative analysis

In this section, we quantify the performance of the proposed techniques over the current state of the art.

8.3.1 Efficacy

One of our primary motivations in this work is to allow users to control the size of the answer set, so that a smaller set of exemplars can be identified and investigated in further detail. Towards that goal, we compare the *compression ratios (CR)* of REP, with the ones achieved by DisC and DIV. The CR of an answer set $\mathbb{A}$ is defined as $\frac{|N_\theta(\mathbb{A})|}{|\mathbb{A}|}$, which is simply the ratio of the number of relevant objects represented to the answer set size. In this experiment, for DUD, we consistently use the same subset of feature vector dimensions since it is essential to capture the natural correlations between the feature and structural space, which in turn affects the CR.

Table 4 presents the results. The CRs in REP are significantly higher than both DisC and DIV. This result establishes the utility of operating in a budgeted setting as well as the advantage of a representative-aware model over a diversity-aware model. For DIV, we compute the result at two different settings. In the first setting, DIV(θ), we use the original model in [19], which ensures all answer set objects are at least θ apart. However, this model assumes that the scores of graphs are mutually independent. In reality, the representative powers of the graphs are dependent on each other. Therefore, to also study the performance when the independence assumption is followed, we enforce the stricter condition of $\forall g_1, g_2,\ d(g_1, g_2) > 2\theta$. The produced answer set is denoted as DIV(2θ). As can be seen, DIV(2θ) further lowers the CRs since the stricter condition to guarantee score independence rules out many representative graphs from inclusion in the answer set.

To further analyze the representation of relevant objects, we also compute the growth of $\pi(\mathbb{A})$ with k. As shown in Table 4, REP covers close to a quarter of the relevant objects using just 10 exemplars. As k increases beyond 100, it is futile to try to represent relevant objects using exemplars, since either the remaining non-

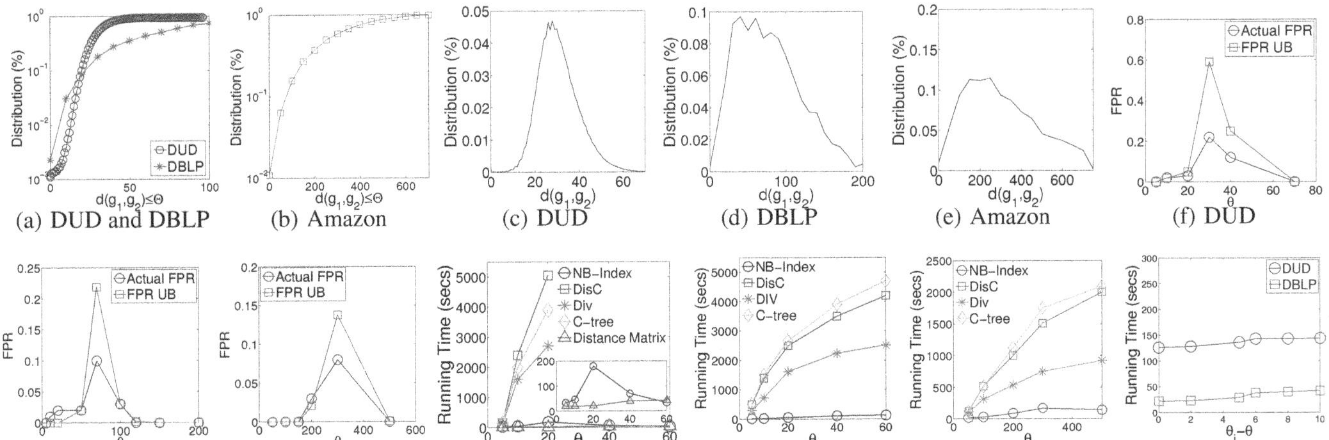

(a) DUD and DBLP (b) Amazon (c) DUD (d) DBLP (e) Amazon (f) DUD
(g) DBLP (h) Amazon (i) DUD (j) DBLP (k) Amazon (l) DUD and DBLP

Figure 5: (a-b). The cumulative distance distributions. (c-e) The distance distributions. (f-h) Observed FPRs, and FPR Upper Bounds (FPR UB) with θ. (i-k) Growth rates of query times against θ and (l) distance to the closest indexed threshold θ_i.

represented objects are outliers or their θ-neighborhoods have large overlaps with already represented objects. Consistent with the results observed while analyzing the CRs, DIV(θ) and DIV(2θ) have up to 6 times lower representative powers due to relying on an indirect maximization approach. Overall, DIV is unable to model the semantics of representativeness, and consequently, the quality of the answer set is compromised.

A detailed theoretical analysis on the optimal number of VPs is performed in Sec 6.2.1 to predict an upper bound on the False Positive Rate (FPR). We now verify how well the empirical results conform to the theoretical analysis. Figs 5(f)-5(h) present the results. The FPR is highest in the DUD dataset, due to the low standard deviation of the distances. Intuitively, if all graphs are similar to each other and clustered together, the performance of VPs deteriorates. For this reason, on DBLP and Amazon, which are not as densely clustered, the FPR is much lower. At low θs in DBLP and DUD, the FPR Upper Bound (≈ 0.01) is slightly lower than the observed FPR. This results from the fact that the distance distribution in DBLP and Amazon slightly deviates from a normal distribution.

8.3.2 Scalability

First, we evaluate the performance of NB-Index against the distance threshold θ. Figs. 5(i)-5(k) show the growth rates of query times as θ is varied. NB-Index is up to two orders of magnitude faster than existing techniques. Due to the enormous running times of DisC, C-tree and DIV on DUD, we do not show their results beyond $\theta > 20$. The growth rates of existing techniques are similar since they all index nearest neighbor queries through triangular inequality; while DisC and C-tree propose their own index structures, in DIV, we use C-tree as the underlying graph indexing technique to construct the 'diversity-graph', on which DIV performs further processing. A bulk of the computation time is spent in initializing the θ-neighborhoods of relevant graphs. This operation needs to be performed online since both θ and the relevance function are query parameters. DIV assumes the representative powers of graphs to be mutually independent, and thus does not re-compute them after each answer set update. Consequently, at the cost of quality, it is faster than both DisC and C-tree. In NB-Index, majority of the computations happen in the feature space through VPs. As already shown in Figs. 5(f)-5(h), the FPRs in VPs are low. Furthermore, beyond VPs, the cluster based bounds outlined in Theorems 6-8 index the θ-neighborhoods in structural space itself and allows batch updates of representative power.

To further evaluate our performance, we also compare its running time to the scenario where the distance matrix of the entire graph database is pre-computed. Due to the fast running times of both the approaches, the inset in Fig. 5(i) presents a zoomed-in view to better compare the two approaches. Practically, storing the entire distance matrix is not feasible in large databases since it incurs a huge storage cost. Nonetheless, we benchmark our performance against the best-case scenario from the running time perspective. Except at $\theta = 20$, the performance of NB-Index is 1.5 to 2 times higher than storing the distance matrix. Another important property that is emphasized in the inset of Fig. 5(i) is that NB-Index is most efficient at the two extreme ends of the θ range. When θ is large, Theorems 7 and 8 are more effective in pruning the search space. On the other hand, Theorem 6 is more efficient at low θs. Thus, mid-range θs present the most challenging scenario, which results in a bell shaped growth rate of the query time.

Next, we analyze the performance deterioration as the difference between the user-provided distance threshold θ and the closest higher indexed threshold θ_i in NB-Tree increases. This analysis shows how sparsity in the $\hat{\pi}$-vector affects the performance of NB-Index. Note that a non-indexed θ only affects the performance of the structural bounds. The performance of VOs remain unaffected. Figs. 5(l), 6(a) show the growth rates of running times. Even when the difference is as high as 10 for DUD and DBLP, and 300 for Amazon, NB-Index consumes less than 25 seconds of additional time. As evident from Figs. 5(a)-5(b), the slopes are extremely steep between $10 \leq \theta \leq 20$ for DUD and DBLP and $50 \leq \theta \leq 200$ for Amazon. Thus, upper bounding π_{10} with π_{20} (in DUD and DBLP) provides a particularly tough setting. However, even in such cases, the performance of NB-Index is significantly better thanks to the efficiency of the VOs and the fast upper bounds derived using Theorems 7 and 8.

Figs. 6(b)-6(d) demonstrate the growth rate of running time against dataset size. NB-Index scales significantly better than all three existing techniques and achieves a performance that is more than an order of magnitude faster. This result stems from indexing the θ-neighborhoods of graphs, which negates the need to perform $O(n^2)$ nearest neighbor queries. Figs. 6(e)-6(g) further establish the superiority of NB-Index as k is varied from 5 to 100. The growth rate of

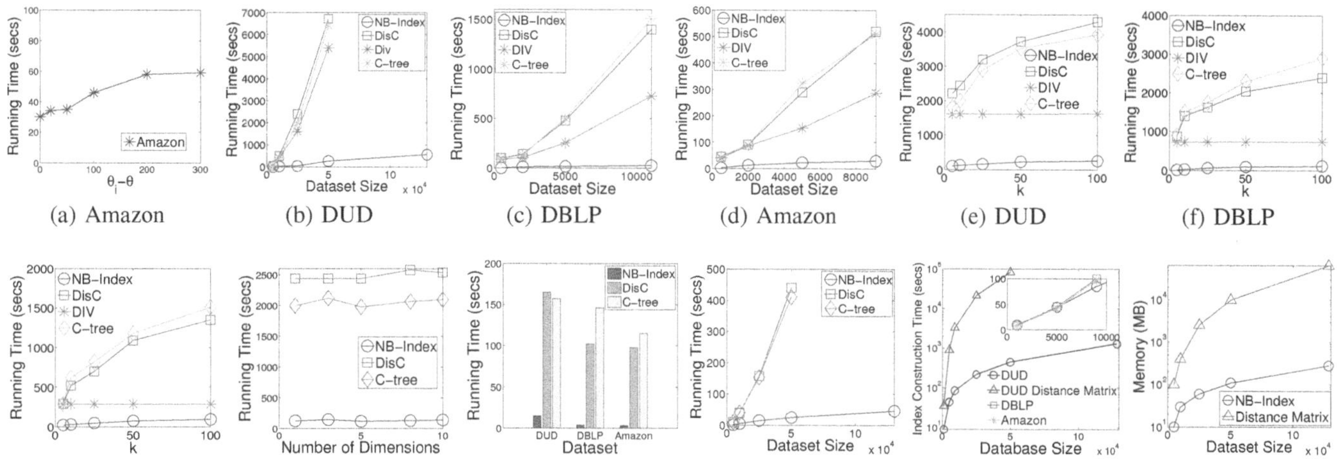

(a) Amazon (b) DUD (c) DBLP (d) Amazon (e) DUD (f) DBLP

(g) Amazon (h) DUD (i) Incremental query (j) Incremental query (k) Index construction (l) Index size

Figure 6: Growth rate of query times with (a) difference between user-provided distance threshold θ and closest indexed threshold θ_i, (b-d) dataset size, (e-g) k and (h) number of dimensions. (i) Running times for incremental zoom-in and zoom-out. (j) Growth rate of incremental zoom-in and zoom-out query time with dataset size. Growth rate of (k) index construction time and (l) indexing memory footprint against dataset size.

query time with k is much lower for NB-Index due to the same reason of indexing the θ-neighborhoods of graphs. The running time of DIV is almost constant across k since it assumes the representative powers of graphs to be mutually independent. Thus, after the diversity-graph is constructed, all remaining computations occur in the feature space, which is minuscule when compared to the cost of constructing the diversity-graph.

Fig. 6(h) investigates the performance as the number of dimensions in feature vectors is varied between 1 and 10 in the DUD dataset. A feature vector of dimension d is constructed by randomly choosing a subset of d dimensions from the overall 10. The query time is almost identical across different numbers of dimensions for all three techniques since the cost of operating in the feature space is negligible compared to the cost of computing graph edit distances while updating θ-neighborhoods. The minor variation in running times results from the correlations between feature and structural space where a higher correlation results in faster query times.

Fig. 6(i) compares query times in the interactive θ refinement scenario. In this experiment, first, a query is performed on the default θ outlined in Sec. 8.2.1. Next, a new θ is selected, which is either 10% smaller or larger, and the answer set is re-computed. This process is repeated 20 times and the average computation time is reported. NB-Index tackles refinements of θs within 10 seconds across all three datasets. On the other hand, DisC and C-tree takes up to 160 seconds to adapt to a new θ. To further study the response times in an interactive setting, we analyze its growth rate against dataset size in Fig. 6(j). Similar to the previous results, NB-Index is more than an order of magnitude faster.

Finally, we analyze the computation and storage costs of the proposed index structure. Fig. 6(k) presents the growth rate of the index construction time against dataset size. While the main plot compares the construction time of NB-Index with that of computing the entire distance matrix in the DUD database, the inset shows the construction times across all three datasets. In DUD, which contains a total of $\approx 130,000$ graphs, the index construction completes within 20 minutes. Compared to the cost of computing the entire distance matrix, we are more than two orders of magnitude faster. This efficiency is achieved through VP-based pruning in pivot and radius computations where actual edit distances are computed for less than 1% of the candidate pairs. The scalability of NB-Index also extends to its storage cost. As expected from the theoretical analysis, a linear growth rate is observed in Fig. 6(l) and less than 300MB is required to store the index for the entire DUD dataset. The reported result includes the memory consumption from storing the $\tilde{\pi}$-vectors, which are computed at query-time.

8.4 Qualitative analysis

In this section, we highlight the utility of a representative model over the traditional top-k framework. Towards that goal, we perform a top-k query and a top-k representative query using the same scoring function and compare the two answer sets. To construct the database, we extract molecules from the DUD repository that are active against the enzyme Acetylcholine ezterase (AChE). Extracted molecules are characterized based on their binding affinity to AChE, which is one of the primary targets for drugs treating Alzheimer's disease [4]. A molecule is considered relevant, if its binding affinity, denoted as BA, is within the top quartile.

Fig. 8.4 shows the two top-5 answer sets. As illustrated in Fig. 8.4 using color coding, all molecules in the traditional answer set are structurally similar to each other. Although they exhibit high binding affinity toward AChE, the traditional answer set represents just one structural family of high scoring molecules. On the other hand, the representative answer set contains molecules that are all structurally diverse, high scoring, and representative of other high-scoring molecules in the dataset. The efficacy of the proposed model is well highlighted in the shown result where the entire class of molecules in the traditional answer set is summarized by the top molecule in the representative answer set. In the context of drug discovery, the traditional answer set provides only one class of molecules that can be further optimized to develop drugs. Whereas, the representative answer set provides five different classes of molecules, each of which can be studied further for drug discovery.

9. RELATED WORK

A detailed comparison with DisC [9] and [19] has already been performed. A closely related query, called top-k typicality queries

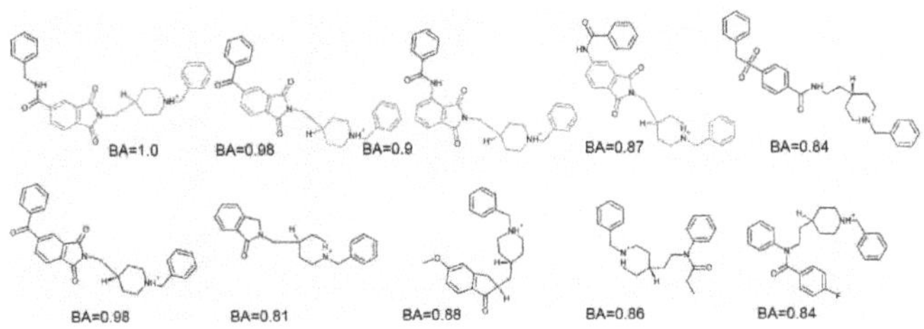

Figure 7: Answer sets computed using traditional top-k query (first row) and top-k representative query (second row). In the top row, the subgraph in red occurs in four of the five molecules, indicating the core structure of a single class of molecules.

is formulated in [13, 14]. An object o is considered "typical" if its distances to other objects in the database are small. While the typicality score is conceptually similar to the proposed idea of representative power, the paper does not explore the coverage maximization aspect. Consequently, the typicality scores of two objects are independent and there is no penalty when highly typical objects from the same cluster are included in the answer set. As a result, the problem in [14] is not NP-hard, whereas ours is. In addition, instead of high-dimensional objects, we focus on graphs where computing the distance itself is NP-hard. Consequently, the scalability challenges faced are unique to our problem.

The idea of representativeness has been explored in the context of skyline queries [16]. An object in a database is a skyline point if it is not *dominated* by any of the database objects. The representativeness of a skyline point is the number of point it dominates. The goal in this work is to identify the k skyline points that dominates the maximum number of database points. Thus, while in our work, an object represents another object if their distance is within a threshold, in [16], an object o_1 represents object o_2 if o_1 dominates o_2. Consequently, the modeling requirements and the proposed indexing techniques are different. In addition, we focus on graphs whereas [16] focuses on high-dimensional points.

Beyond diversification of results, indexing graphs for similarity queries [12, 26, 28, 30] is related to our problem. As shown in our experimental results, indexing graphs for nearest neighbor queries is not enough to scale top-k representative queries. Consequently, our work takes a more direct approach by indexing the θ-neighborhoods of graphs, which lies at the core of updating graph representative powers. Embedding graphs into a feature space has been explored by Zou et. al. [31]. Their goal is to index shortest part queries between nodes by embedding nodes in a feature space. In our work, instead of a single large graph, we have multiple graphs each of which is embedded in a feature space. Additionally, instead of indexing shortest paths, our goal is to index their θ-neighborhoods, which is a function of graph edit distance. Due to this basic difference in the entities being embedded and their associated indexing goals, the technique, the bounds derived from the techniques, and the error guarantees do not transfer.

10. CONCLUSION

In this work, we formulated the problem of top-k representative queries on graph databases. By allowing online definitions of object relevance and answer set budget, the proposed formulation provides a higher degree of flexibility to users. We showed that the problem is NP-hard and submodular. Based on this result, we designed a greedy constant factor approximation of the optimal answer set. To achieve scalability, we designed an index structure called NB-Index that indexes the θ-neighborhoods of database graphs by employing a novel combination of Lipschitz embedding and agglomerative clustering. NB-Index not only facilitates fast answering of queries, but also allows interactive refinement of θ to reach the optimal zoom level. Empirical evaluations on real graph datasets demonstrate significantly higher information density and a performance improvement of up to two orders of magnitude over the state of the art.

Acknowledgements: The work was supported by NSF grant IIS-1219254. We also thank Google for travel grant PO 55022251.

11. REFERENCES

[1] SNAP, http://snap.stanford.edu/.
[2] R. Agrawal, S. Gollapudi, A. Halverson, and S. Ieong. Diversifying search results. In *WSDM*, 2009.
[3] A. Angel and N. Koudas. Efficient diversity-aware search. In *SIGMOD Conference*, pages 781–792, 2011.
[4] C. G. Ballard. Advances in the treatment of alzheimer's disease: benefits of dual cholinesterase inhibition. *Eur Neurol*, 47(1):64–70, 2002.
[5] J. Bourgain. On lipschitz embedding of finite metric spaces in hilbert space. *Israel Journal of Mathematics*, 52:46–52, 1985.
[6] G. Capannini, F. M. Nardini, R. Perego, and F. Silvestri. Efficient diversification of web search results. *PVLDB*, 4, 2011.
[7] V. Chaoji, S. Ranu, R. Rastogi, and R. Bhatt. Recommendations to boost content spread in social networks. In *WWW*, pages 529–538, 2012.
[8] H. Cheng, D. Lo, Y. Zhou, X. Wang, and X. Yan. Identifying bug signatures using discriminative graph mining. In *Symposium on software testing and analysis*, 2009.
[9] M. Drosou and E. Pitoura. Disc diversity: result diversification based on dissimilarity and coverage. *PVLDB*, 6(1):13–24, 2012.
[10] DUD. http://dud.docking.org/r2/.
[11] U. Feige. A threshold of ln n for approximating set cover. *J. ACM*, 45:634–652, July 1998.
[12] H. He and A. K. Singh. Closure-tree: An index structure for graph queries. In *ICDE*, 2006.
[13] M. Hua, J. Pei, A. Fu, X. Lin, and H.-F. Leung. Top-k typicality queries and efficient query answering methods on large databases. *The VLDB Journal*, 18(3):809–835, 2009.
[14] M. Hua, J. Pei, A. W. C. Fu, X. Lin, and H. fung Leung. Efficiently answering top-k typicality queries on large databases. In *VLDB*, pages 890–901, 2007.
[15] R. Li and J. X. Yu. Scalable diversified ranking on graphs. In *ICDM*, 2011.
[16] X. Lin, Y. Yuan, Q. Zhang, and Y. Zhang. Selecting stars: The k most representative skyline operator. In *ICDE*, pages 86–95, 2007.
[17] K. Macropol and A. Singh. Content-based modeling and prediction of information dissemination. In *ASONAM*, 2011.
[18] G. L. Nemhauser, L. A. Wolsey, and M. L. Fisher. An analysis of approximations for maximizing submodular set functions-i. *Mathematical Programming*, 14(1):265–294, 1978.
[19] L. Qin, J. X. Yu, and L. Chang. Diversifying top-k results. *PVLDB*, 5(11):1124–1135, 2012.
[20] S. Ranu, B. T. Calhoun, A. K. Singh, and S. J. Swamidass. Probabilistic substructure mining from small-molecule screens. *Molecular Informatics*, 30(9):809–815, 2011.
[21] S. Ranu, M. Hoang, and A. Singh. Mining discriminative subgraphs from global-state networks. In *SIGKDD*, pages 509–517, 2013.
[22] S. Ranu and A. K. Singh. Answering top-k queries over a mixture of attractive and repulsive dimensions. *PVLDB*, 5(3):169–180, 2011.
[23] S. Ranu and A. K. Singh. Indexing and mining topological patterns for drug discovery. In *EDBT*, pages 562–565, 2012.
[24] H. Tong, J. He, Z. Wen, R. Konuru, and C.-Y. Lin. Diversified ranking on large graphs: an optimization viewpoint. In *SIGKDD*, 2011.
[25] E. Vee, U. Srivastava, J. Shanmugasundaram, P. Bhat, and S. Amer-Yahia. Efficient computation of diverse query results. In *ICDE*, 2008.
[26] X. Yan, P. S. Yu, and J. Han. Substructure similarity search in graph databases. In *SIGMOD*, 2005.
[27] C. Yu, L. Lakshmanan, and S. A. Yahia. It takes variety to make a world: diversification in recommender systems. In *EDBT*, 2009.
[28] Z. Zeng, A. K. H. Tung, J. Wang, J. Feng, and L. Zhou. Comparing stars: On approximating graph edit distance. *PVLDB*, 2(1), 2009.
[29] P. Zezula, G. Amato, V. Dohnal, and M. Batko. *Similarity Search - The Metric Space Approach*. Springer-Verlag, 2006.
[30] Y. Zhu, L. Qin, J. X. Yu, and H. Cheng. Finding top-k similar graphs in graph databases. In *EDBT*, pages 456–467, 2012.
[31] L. Zou, L. Chen, and M. T. Özsu. Distance-join: Pattern match query in a large graph database. *PVLDB*, 2(1):886–897, 2009.

Modeling Entity Evolution for Temporal Record Matching

Yueh-Hsuan Chiang
University of Wisconsin
Madison
1210 W Dayton Street
Madison, WI 53706, USA
yhchiang@cs.wisc.edu

AnHai Doan
University of Wisconsin
Madison
1210 W Dayton Street
Madison, WI 53706, USA
anhai@cs.wisc.edu

Jeffrey F. Naughton
University of Wisconsin
Madison
1210 W Dayton Street
Madison, WI 53706, USA
naughton@cs.wisc.edu

ABSTRACT

Temporal record matching recognizes that if the entities represented by the records change over time, approaches that use temporal information may do better than approaches that do not. Any such temporal matching method relies at its heart on a temporal model that captures information about how entities evolve. In their pioneering work, Li *et al.* used an efficiently computable model that simply tries to predict if an attribute is expected to change over a given time interval. In our work, we propose and evaluate a more detailed model that focuses on the probability that a given attribute value reappears over time. The intuition here is that an entity might change its attribute value in the way that is dependent on its past values. In addition, our model considers sets of records (rather than simply pairs of records) to improve robustness and accuracy. Experimental results show that the resulting approach improves both accuracy and resistance to noise while incurring a minimal overhead.

1. INTRODUCTION

Record matching takes a collection of records and determines which records belong to the same real world entity (see [8, 12] for recent surveys). The vast majority of work in record matching has assumed that the records come with no temporal information. In practice, however, we often have temporal information in the form of time stamps associated with records. Examples include author records in DBLP [2], donor records in federal campaign finance data sets [3], and time stamps in tweets [4].

It has been shown that approaches that use temporal information can do better than approaches that do not, especially when the entities described by a data set may change or evolve their attribute values over time [14]. Any such temporal matching method relies at its heart on a temporal model that captures information about how entities evolve. This immediately gives rise to the question: "what kind of model should one use?" It should be simple enough to be easy to construct, yet powerful enough to be effective and robust in the presence of noise.

In their pioneering work, Li *et al.* used an efficiently computable model that simply tries to predict if an attribute is expected to change over a given time interval [14]. Because it only models "change" and "no change" it, for example, cannot tell the difference between an attribute that changes from one value to another chosen at random, and an attribute that changes only between values drawn from a small, entity-dependent set. Their model is also a "point to point" model that considers pairs of records rather than sets of records.

Table 1: Records of the same author from DBLP.

rid	eid	name	affiliation	co-authors	year
r_1	e_1	Lei Wang	Xidian University	Licheng Jiao	1999
r_2	e_1	Lei Wang	Xidian University	Licheng Jiao	2000
r_3	e_1	Lei Wang	Xidian University	Licheng Jiao	2001
r_4	e_1	Lei Wang	Xi'an Univ. of Tech.	Yinling Nie, Weike Nie, Licheng Jiao	2005
r_5	e_1	Lei Wang	Xi'an Univ. of Tech.	Yinling Nie, Weike Nie, Licheng Jiao	2006
r_6	e_1	Lei Wang	Xi'an Univ. of Tech.	Liya Wang, Yinling Nie	2006
r_7	e_1	Lei Wang	Xidian University	Jiaji Wu, Licheng Jiao, Li Zhang, Guangming Shi	2007
r_8	e_1	Lei Wang	Beijing U. of A&A	Zheng Wang, Chen Yang, Li Zhang, Qiang Ye	2009
r_9	e_1	Lei Wang	Xidian University	Licheng Jiao, Jiaji Wu, Guangming Shi	2009
r_{10}	e_1	Lei Wang	Xidian University	Licheng Jiao, Jiaji Wu, Guangming Shi, Yanjun Gong	2010

We present and evaluate a more complex model. It is not "point to point"; rather, when processing records in increasing temporal order, and deciding whether or not to add a new record to a growing cluster, it uses all the records in the cluster to answer the question. That is, rather than saying "given record r_1, does record r_2 refer to the same entity?", it says "given a cluster C of records already determined to refer to a single entity, does a new record r refer to the same entity?"

Furthermore, our model is able to learn patterns more detailed than just "change/no change." In particular, our model focuses on the probability of a value re-appearing over time. The intuition here is that an entity might change its attribute values in a way that is dependent on or predicted by its past values. One possibility is that some of an entity's attributes might change over time yet have an affinity for a small set of values that are associated with the entity. For example, if a person's location attribute has taken on the values {Madison, Silicon Valley, Taiwan} in the past, then these values may be more likely to appear in this person's records in the future than, say, "France." In other cases, it is also possible that an evolving attribute never changes its value back to a previously seen value. As we will show, by learning probabilities of recurrence, our model is able to make better predictions than those made by simply predicting "change/no change".

EXAMPLE 1.1. *Consider a real world example from DBLP shown in Table 1, which contains several publication records associated with the same author — Lei Wang. From his publication records, we observe that Lei Wang changed both his affiliation and co-authors over time, but in both attributes there exist underlying affinities: Lei Wang returned to Xidian University in 2007 after leaving there in 2001, and over time he also had certain reappearing co-authors*

SIGMOD'14, June 22–27, 2014, Snowbird, UT, USA.

http://dx.doi.org/10.1145/2588555.2588560.

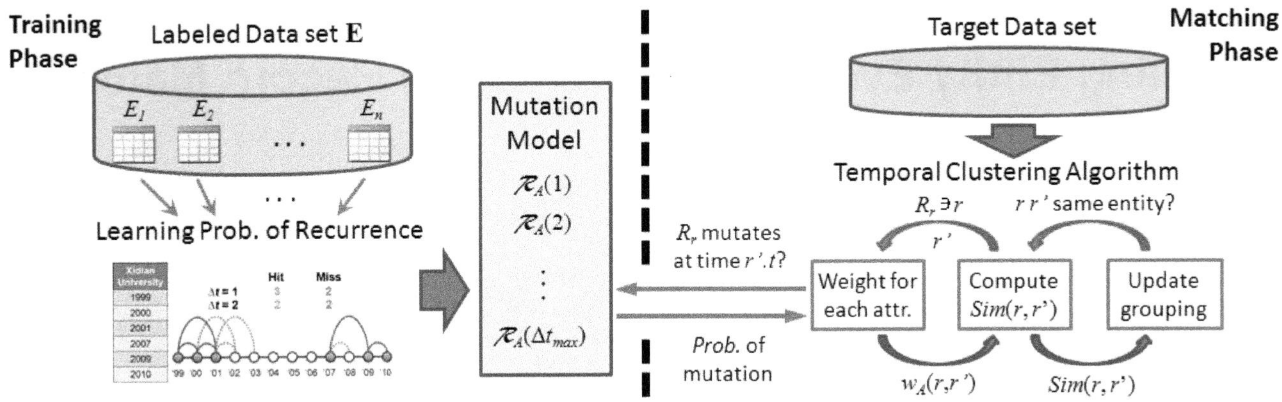

Figure 1: How the proposed model works in the training and matching phases of a temporal matching framework.

even though the coauthor set itself evolved over time. Thus there is potential for a model that considers the recurrence of values to provide better insight than one that does not. □

At a high level, shown in Figure 1, our approach to record matching is the following. We begin with a training data set, which consists of a set of records and their associated entities. We train a temporal model with this data set, attempting to capture useful information about how the entities in the data set evolve. Later, when we are solving the target record matching problem over an unlabeled data set, we use this temporal model as input to the similarity computations performed in the course of this matching. Intuitively speaking, the temporal model tells us how to weight similarities on various attributes. For example, if the temporal model suggests that similarity on a given attribute is not very reliable due to entity evolution, then the result of the similarity computation will be given a low weight. In this paper we focus on the definition of a new temporal model and use it along with previously proposed temporal clustering techniques.

Returning to the training phase of our model, there are many different things we could try to learn. A simple approach would be to merely learn how frequently values change in each attribute of the record set under consideration (this is the approach in [14]). More complicated approaches could focus on either evolution within entities, or global evolution among entities, or both. We consider evolution within entities, because, as we will see in our experiments, if one has good predictions about intra-entity evolution, one can draw useful conclusions about inter-entity evolution.

Our approach for intra-entity evolution is to look at the entire sequence of records corresponding to each entity in the labeled data set and to calculate the probability for each time period that the entity corresponding to the records is likely to change its value to one not seen previously. We call this a "mutation model," and it allows us to answer the question "given that two records with time stamps disagree on some attribute A, how likely is that they refer to the same entity that has evolved to change its A-value?" (If the answer is "it is likely" then we would view this disagreement on attribute A as unconvincing and give it low weight in the similarity computation.)

Perhaps surprisingly, this mutation model can also help answer the question "given two records with different time stamps from two different entities, how likely is it that they will evolve to share a value on some attribute?" As a partial intuition for this, note that for every pair of entities that evolve to share attribute values, at least one of them must have evolved to change attribute values — which is captured by the mutation model.

The precise definition and computation of this mutation model is somewhat complex. However, our experiments show that the greater insight provided by the mutation model is useful, leading to substantially better precision and recall, along with lower sensitivity to noisy or missing data, than the previously proposed frequency of change model.

Of course, such a model does not come for free, so a reasonable question is: is this more detailed model worth it? Does it take a long time to compute? Does it lead to better clustering decisions? Does it have any other good properties? In the rest of this paper, we will show (a) how to compute the proposed model in a way that is not expensive, and (b) how it can be used to make better matching decisions, and (c) that it is more robust to noise.

In more detail, we make the following contributions:

- We introduce the notion of *mutation*, which describes the situation when an entity changes an attribute to a value that has not appeared in that attribute in the history of that entity.
- We describe an algorithm that learns and uses statistics about attribute value recurrence to model entity evolution based on the notion of mutation. Our model is able to handle both single-valued and multi-valued attributes.
- We demonstrate how to utilize entity-dependent information to improve matching accuracy when records are processed in increasing temporal order.
- We propose an effective approximation of our model that reduces computational overhead while producing equivalent matching quality.
- We analyze the matching accuracy and robustness to noise of our model by a set of experiments on several real world temporal matching tasks. The results show that our model improves both matching accuracy (up to 40% in F-1 score) and robustness to noisy data over the state-of-the-art temporal model, while producing minimum computational overhead (less than 5%).

The paper is organized as follows. The next section defines the problem of temporal record matching and reviews necessary background. Section 3 describes our temporal model and its learning process. Section 4 introduces how to apply our temporal model in similarity computation. Section 5 presents our experiments. Section 6 reviews related work, and Section 7 discusses future work and draws conclusions.

2. PRELIMINARIES

This section gives the problem definition and briefly reviews the state of the art technique for temporal record matching proposed in [14].

2.1 Definitions

We now define the problem of temporal record matching.

DEFINITION 2.1. (TEMPORAL RECORD MATCHING) *Consider a domain $\mathcal{D}$ of entities (not known a-priori) and a set* R *of records. Each record $r \in$ R is of the form of $\langle x_1, ..., x_n, t\rangle$, where t is the time stamp of the record r, and each x_i, $1 \leq i \leq n$, is the value of attribute A_i at time t for the associated entity in domain $\mathcal{D}$. The goal of* temporal record matching *is to find a clustering of the records in* R *that satisfies the following properties: 1) records in the same cluster refer to the same entity in domain $\mathcal{D}$, and 2) records in different clusters refer to different entities in domain $\mathcal{D}$.* □

As the entities described by a temporal data set may change or evolve their attribute values over time, a temporal matching technique must deal with ambiguity caused by this evolution. One of such ambiguity is *within-entity temporal disagreement*, or *temporal disagreement* for short:

DEFINITION 2.2. (WITHIN-ENTITY TEMPORAL DISAGREEMENT). *Within-entity temporal disagreement arises when two records referring to the same entity have dissimilar values on one attribute because over time their associated entity evolves its state on that attribute.* □

For example, a person may change his or her address and phone number, so two records referring to the same person at different times may disagree on those attributes.

A second kind of ambiguity is *between-entity temporal agreement*, or *temporal agreement* for short:

DEFINITION 2.3. (BETWEEN-ENTITY TEMPORAL AGREEMENT). *Between-entity temporal agreement arises when two records referring to two different entities have identical or highly similar values on one attribute because over time one of the entities evolved to have the same value in some attribute as that previously held by the other.* □

Returning to our example, it is possible that one person might get the phone number of a second person when the first person takes over the second person's office.

As a result, a temporal matching algorithm must handle how entities might evolve over time to resolve temporal disagreement and agreement.

2.2 Notation

We will use the following terms. For attribute values, we use the term "A-value" to describe a value for attribute A, $r.A$ and $r.t$ to denote the A-value and the time stamp of record r respectively, and $v \in A$ to denote v is an A-value.

To describe the attributes and the time stamps of an entity or a list of records, we use the following notation. Let E be an entity and $\langle r_1, ..., r_n\rangle$ be a list of records associated with E. We use $E.A$ to denote the set of A-values of E, which is the union of A-values of its associated records:

$$E.A = \{r_1.A, r_2.A, ..., r_n.A\}. \tag{1}$$

If A is a set-valued attribute, then $E.A$ is defined as the union of elements of the A-values of E's associated records:

$$E.A = \{v|v \in r.A \wedge r \in E\}. \tag{2}$$

We use $E.t$ to denote the ordered list of time stamps of E given records $r_1, ..., r_n$, sorted in increasing temporal order:

$$E.t = \langle r_1.t, r_2.t, ..., r_n.t\rangle. \tag{3}$$

2.3 Review of Temporal Record Matching

Existing techniques for non-temporal record matching typically consist of two main components: a similarity measure to determine how likely it is that two records refer to the same real world entity, and a clustering algorithm that groups records based on their similarity. Li *et al.* [14] proposed the first solution for temporal record matching. It consists of three main components — a similarity measure, a *temporal model*, and a *temporal clustering algorithm*. Here we review the two temporal components in more detail:

Temporal model: Typically, the similarity between two records is computed based on attribute value similarities. However, if entities evolve over time, attributes that change become less reliable indicators for record matching. In view of this, Li *et al.* proposed building a temporal model that learns how entities evolve in a labeled data set and use it to determine the importance of each attribute in record similarity computations as follows:

$$sim(r, r') = \frac{\sum_{A \in \mathbf{A}} w_A(r, r') \cdot sim_A(r.A, r'.A)}{\sum_{A \in \mathbf{A}} w_A(r, r')} \tag{4}$$

where sim_A is the similarity metric for attribute A and w_A is the weighting function derived from a temporal model. Intuitively, attributes that are less "stable" are less trusted as indicators in matching.

Temporal clustering: In [14], the term *temporal clustering* was presented to describe clustering algorithms that process records in increasing temporal order. One can view a cluster of records all with time stamp previous to time t as representing the history of its associated entity up to time t.

As the main focus of this paper is on temporal modeling, we will omit reviewing temporal clustering algorithms, focusing instead on the temporal modeling approach — the time decay model — proposed in [14].

2.3.1 The Time Decay Model

The time decay model [14] attempts to capture the effect of time elapsing on value evolution. It consists of two components. The first is *disagreement decay*, which handles the ambiguity caused by within-entity temporal disagreement:

DEFINITION 2.4. (DISAGREEMENT DECAY). *Let Δt be a time interval and $A \in \mathbf{A}$ be a single-valued attribute. The disagreement decay of A over time Δt, denoted by $d^{\neq}(A, \Delta t)$, is the probability that an entity changes its A-value within time Δt.* □

The second component is *agreement decay*, which handles the ambiguity caused by between-entity temporal agreement:

DEFINITION 2.5. (AGREEMENT DECAY). *Let Δt be a time interval and $A \in \mathbf{A}$ be an attribute. The agreement decay of A over time Δt, denoted by $d^{=}(A, \Delta t)$, is the probability that two different entities share the same A-value within time Δt.* □

When computing the similarity between two records, the weight of each attribute value is determined by the complement of the agreement- and disagreement-decay on that attribute. Specifically, consider two records r and r'. The weight w_A of their similarity on attribute A is computed as follows:

$$w_A(r,r') = \begin{cases} 1 - d^{=}(A,\Delta t) & sim_A(r,r') > \theta_h \\ 1 - d^{\neq}(A,\Delta t) & sim_A(r,r') < \theta_l \\ 1 - sim_A(r,r') \cdot d^{=}(A,\Delta t) & \text{otherwise} \\ \quad -(1 - sim_A(r,r')) \cdot d^{\neq}(A,\Delta t) & \end{cases} \quad (5)$$

where $sim_A(r,r')$ denotes the A-value similarity between r and r', Δt is the time difference between r and r', and θ_l and θ_h are thresholds indicating low and high similarity respectively.

3. OUR TEMPORAL MODEL

This section describes our temporal model — the mutation model. During the discussion, we will assume that, as proposed in [14], a clustering algorithm that processes records in increasing temporal order will be used.

3.1 Approach Overview

At the most basic level, our mutation model answers the following question: consider a cluster C of records that have been determined to correspond to the same entity, and a record r with time stamp $r.t$ greater than that of any record in C. Suppose that r also corresponds to the entity associated with C. For a given attribute A of r, what is the probability that the value in $r.A$, say v, does not appear in attribute A in any record in C? As a bit of terminology, if v does not appear in A in any record of C, then we call r a "mutant record," attempting to capture the notion that the entity in question has changed substantially. Hence our goal can be restated as computing the probability that r is a mutant record.

We will explain later how this is used in temporal matching, but the intuition is that if it is likely that r is a mutant record, then the fact that v does not match any A value in C should not be construed to suggest that r and C do not refer to the same entity. In addition, if we are expecting a mutation based C, then we are not expecting to see a C record with a matching A-value, so if we see a matching A-value it is possibly from temporal agreement.

Our main idea is to calculate, for each attribute, the probability that the value appearing in that attribute will recur after one, two, three, ... time units. So if C has only one record in it, say r_1, with time stamp $r_1.t$, and $r.t - r_1.t = \Delta t$, then the probability p that the value $r_1.A$ will reappear in Δt time units is the complement of the probability that r is a mutant record, and $1 - p$ is our desired probability.

Extending this to multiple records in C requires combining the "predictions" of each of the records in C (since they are all at different temporal distances from r). We use a heuristic, described below, to do so.

3.2 Entity Mutation

This section introduces our concept of entity mutation. We say that an entity has had a mutation if an attribute changes to a value that has not been seen in the last Δt time units, where Δt is a tunable parameter.

DEFINITION 3.1. (ENTITY MUTATION). *Let E be an entity and A be an attribute. We say that E has a* mutation *on attribute A at time t if E changes its A-value at time t to a value v such that none of the records associated with E in the past Δt time units from time t has v as its A-value.* □

If A is a set-valued attribute, then the mutation condition is defined as E changing its A-value to v such that none of the elements in v appears in any A-values in E in the past Δt time units from time t.

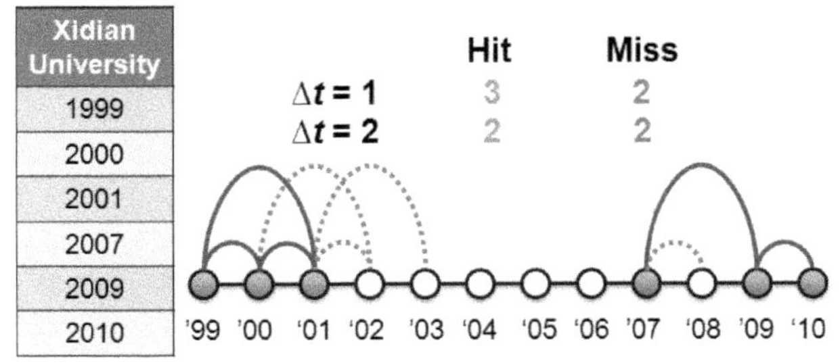

Figure 2: Example of learning attribute value recurrence where each solid / dashed line represents a recurrence his / miss respectively.

Based on the concept of mutation, we further define the notions of *mutant record* and *mutation point* of an entity as follows.

DEFINITION 3.2. (MUTATION POINT / MUTANT RECORD). *Let Δt be a time interval and $A \in \mathbf{A}$ be an attribute, which can be either single-valued or multi-valued. Let r be a record associated with a real world entity E with time stamp $r.t$ and value $r.A = \{r.a_1, ..., r.a_n\}$ on attribute A. We call r a* mutant record *of entity E on attribute A within time Δt if none of the records in E Δt time units ago share a common value with r on attribute A, and we call $r.t$ a* mutation point *of entity E.* □

As a special case, if Δt is set to infinity, then mutant records of one entity on a single-valued attribute are those records containing a value on that attribute that has not appeared in any record associated with the same entity previously.

EXAMPLE 3.1. *Consider an example from DBLP shown in Table 1. If we look at the affiliation attribute and set the time interval Δt to be less than 7 years, then r_1, r_4, r_7, r_8 are mutant records of entity e_1 on the affiliation attribute, and time points 2005, 2007, and 2009 are the mutation points of entity e_1 respectively. However, if we set Δt to be greater than or equal to 7 years, then only r_1, r_4 and r_8 are mutant records of entity e_1. If we look at the co-authors attribute, then r_1 and r_4 would be the only mutant records on the co-author attribute if Δt is between 2 to 4 years. In addition, if Δt is greater than 4 years, then only the first record r_1 would be the mutant record on the co-author attribute.* □

We now introduce the mutation function $\mathcal{M}_A(R, t)$:

DEFINITION 3.3. (MUTATION FUNCTION). *Let A be an attribute, $R = \{r_1, ..., r_n\}$ be a list of records associated with an entity E, and t a specified time. The mutation function $\mathcal{M}_A(R, t)$ returns the probability of entity E having a mutant record on attribute A at time t given the record history R of entity E.* □

While an upper-bound time interval Δt could be included in the mutation function, here we omit this parameter and set it to infinity for simplicity. This makes the mutation function $\mathcal{M}_A(R, t)$ return the probability that the entity associated with the input list R of records has an A-value at time t that is different from all the A-values in R.

In the rest of this section, we will introduce how we learn the mutation function from a training data set based on statistics about attribute value recurrence. How to apply the mutation function in similarity computation will be described in the next section (Section 4).

3.3 Attribute Value Recurrence

To learn the mutation function, we collect the statistics of attribute value recurrence from the given training data set. Here we first introduce the notion of *recurrence hit* and *miss*:

DEFINITION 3.4. (Δt RECURRENCE HIT). *We say that a value v has a Δt* recurrence hit, *or Δt* recurrence *for short, if v satisfies following conditions: 1) value v occurs in some entity E on attribute A, and 2) v recurs Δt time units later in the same entity E.* □

DEFINITION 3.5. (Δt RECURRENCE MISS) *We say that a value v has a Δt* recurrence miss *on attribute A if v satisfies following conditions: 1) value v occurs in some entity E on attribute A, and 2) v does not recur in E over the next Δt time units.* □

EXAMPLE 3.2. *Consider an example from DBLP shown in Table 1 and look at the value 'Licheng Jiao' on the co-authors attribute. We can see that value 'Licheng Jiao' appears in year 1999, 2000, 2001, 2005, 2006, 2007, 2009, and 2010. By the definition of recurrence, 'Licheng Jiao' has five 1-year recurrences, three 2-year recurrences (1999 to 2001, 2005 to 2007 and 2007 to 2009), and several other recurrences.* □

Now we describe how we learn the statistics of attribute value recurrence. Without loss of generality, we may assume all attributes are set-valued attributes by viewing each single-valued attribute as a set-valued attribute having a single element, and we will use the notation described in Section 2.2.

Given a training data set $\mathbf{E}$, where records are grouped according to their associated entities, we learn the statistics of value recurrence on attribute A as follows:

Step 1: For each entity $E = \langle r_1, r_2, ...\rangle$ with its records sorted in increasing temporal order, maintain the *occurrence history* $E.t_{v\in A} \subseteq E.t$ for each value $v \in E.A$ that appears in E on attribute A. Each occurrence history $E.t_{v\in A} = \langle t_1, t_2, ...\rangle$ is an ordered list of time stamps sorted in increasing temporal order, where each time stamp describes a time point when entity E has value v on attribute A. For example, consider the entity shown in Table 1. Its occurrence history of value 'Licheng Jiao' on the co-authors attribute would be $\langle$1999, 2000, 2001, 2005, 2006, 2007, 2009, 2010$\rangle$.

Step 2: For each occurrence history $E.t_{v\in A}$, identify and fill in possible missing occurrences. For each consecutive pair of time stamps t_i, t_{i+1} in $E.t_{v\in A}$, if entity E does not have any records with time stamp within (t_i, t_{i+1}), then we assume that entity E has its A-value equal to v from time t_i to t_{i+1} and insert all possible time stamps $t_i < t < t_{i+1}$ into $E.t_{v\in A}$. For example, consider the example in Table 1. Since 'Licheng Jiao' is listed in the co-author attribute of entity e_1 in 2001 and 2005, and e_1 has no records from 2002 to 2004, we shall not exclude the possibility that e_1 in fact worked with 'Licheng Jiao' from 2001 to 2005. Therefore, the missing occurrences of 'Licheng Jiao' between 2002 and 2004 should be filled in.

Step 3: Count and aggregate the numbers of hits $h^A_{\Delta t}$ and misses $m^A_{\Delta t}$ of Δt-recurrences on attribute A from the updated occurrence histories of all attribute values for each $0 < \Delta t \leq t_{max}$. This can be done by using a sliding window that iterates through each occurrence history.

Step 4: For each Δt, smooth the hit and miss counts of its recurrence by applying a Gaussian filter with variance in proportional to Δt.

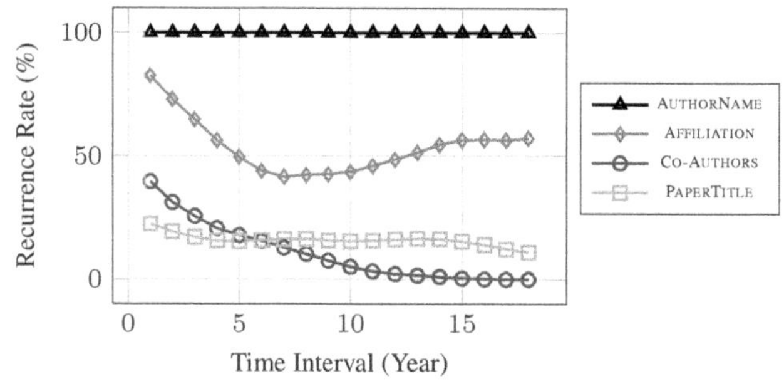

Figure 3: The results of learning the probability of Δt recurrence from the DBLP-Ambiguous data set on different attributes. Note that both paper title and co-authors attributes are processed as set-valued attributes.

Step 5: Construct the recurrence function $\mathcal{R}_A(\Delta t)$ based on the following equation:

$$\mathcal{R}_A(\Delta t) = \begin{cases} 1 & \Delta t = 0 \\ \dfrac{h^A_{\Delta t}}{(h^A_{\Delta t} + m^A_{\Delta t})} & 1 \leq \Delta t \leq t_{max} \\ \dfrac{h^A_{\Delta t_{max}}}{(h^A_{\Delta t_{max}} + m^A_{\Delta t_{max}})} & \Delta t \geq t_{max} \\ 0 & \text{otherwise} \end{cases} \tag{6}$$

We set $\mathcal{R}_A(\Delta t) = \mathcal{R}_A(\Delta t_{max})$ for all $\Delta t > \Delta t_{max}$ for simplicity.

EXAMPLE 3.3. *Consider Table 1 again, where we would like to learn the recurrence function of the affiliation attribute. Suppose we are currently processing value "Xidian University" and would like to count the recurrence hits and misses for one- and two-year time intervals. Then we will learn* $(3, 2)$ *and* $(2, 2)$ *recurrence hits and misses for one- and two-year time intervals respectively. Figure 2 shows the occurrence history of value "Xidian University" and its recurrence hits and misses for one- and two-year time intervals.* □

Figure 3 shows the curves of recurrence rates on four different attributes: author's name, author's affiliation, paper title (segmented into terms) and co-authors, learned from the DBLP-Ambiguous data set (described in detail in Section 5). We observe that 1) the proposed model is able to learn different evolution types; 2) authors in this data set never change their names; 3) authors are more likely to move back to their previous affiliations after publishing papers for many years; 4) the probabilities of working with the same scholar and working on similar topics decays over time, but their speed of these decays differ.

We give the algorithm for learning attribute value recurrence in Algorithm 1.

3.4 Capturing Entity Mutation

We now discuss how to construct the mutation function $\mathcal{M}_A(R, t)$. We start by considering single values and then extend the idea to consider multiple values.

Consider the case where we compute part of the mutation function by looking at only one value v on attribute A given a list R of records associated with the same real world entity. We use $\mathcal{M}_{v\in A}(R, t)$ to denote the simplified mutation function that only returns the probability of the entity described by R *not* having its A-value equal or contain v at time t. To compute such an entity-dependent probability, we first consider all records in R that have

Algorithm 1 LEARNVALUERECURRENCE($\mathbf{E}, A, \Delta t_{max}$)

Input:

- $\mathbf{E}$, a set of entities, where each entity $E = \langle r_1, ..., r_{|E|} \rangle$ consists of a list of records sorted in increasing temporal order.
- A, the attribute of interest.
- Δt_{max}, the maximum time interval considered.

Output:

- $\mathcal{R}_A(\Delta t)$, the recurrence function.

// Initialize the counters for Δt recurrence hit / miss.
for $\Delta t = 1$ to t_{max} **do**
  $h^A_{\Delta t} \leftarrow 0, m^A_{\Delta t} \leftarrow 0$
end for
$C^A \leftarrow \{\langle h^A_1, m^A_1 \rangle ..., \langle h^A_{\Delta t_{max}}, m^A_{\Delta t_{max}} \rangle\}$
for all $E \in \mathbf{E}$ **do**
  $E.A \leftarrow \{\}$ // The set of ever-occurred A-values in E.
  $E.t \leftarrow \langle\rangle$ // The list of ever-occurred time stamps in E.
  for all $r_i \in E$ **do**
    $E.t = E.t \cup r_i.t$
    for all $v \in r_i.A$ **do**
      if $v \notin E.A$ **then**
        $E.A \leftarrow E.A \cup v$
        $E.t_{v \in A} \leftarrow \langle\rangle$ // Init the occurrence history for v.
      end if
      // Update the occurrence history.
      $E.t_{v \in A} \leftarrow E.t_{v \in A} \cup r_i.t$
    end for
  end for
  for all $v \in E.A$ **do**
    // Functions are defined in Algorithm 2. and 3.
    $E.t_{v \in A} \leftarrow$ UPDATEHISTORY($E.t_{v \in A}, E.t$)
    // Update the recurrence counts ($h^A_{\Delta t}$ and $m^A_{\Delta t}$) in C^A.
    $C^A \leftarrow$ UPDATECOUNTS($E.t_{v \in A}, C^A, \Delta t_{max}$, max($E.t$))
  end for
end for
// Construct the recurrence function $\mathcal{R}_A(\Delta t)$.
$\mathcal{R}_A \leftarrow \{\langle 0, 1 \rangle\}$
$\mathcal{R}_A \leftarrow \mathcal{R}_A \cup \{ \langle \Delta t, \frac{h^A_{\Delta t}}{(h^A_{\Delta t} + m^A_{\Delta t})} \rangle | \ 1 \leq \Delta t \leq \Delta t_{max}\}$
$\mathcal{R}_A \leftarrow \mathcal{R}_A \cup \{ \langle \Delta t, \frac{h^A_{\Delta t_{max}}}{(h^A_{\Delta t_{max}} + m^A_{\Delta t_{max}})} \rangle | \ \Delta t > \Delta t_{max}\}$
$\mathcal{R}_A \leftarrow \mathcal{R}_A \cup \{\langle \Delta t, 0 \rangle | \ \Delta t < 0\}$
return $\mathcal{R}_A$

Algorithm 2 UPDATEHISTORY($E.t_{v \in A}, E.t$)

Input:

- $E.t_{v \in A}$, time stamps of v's occurrence of E in increasing temporal order.
- $E.t$, time stamps of entity E in increasing temporal order.

Output:

- $E.t_{v \in A}$, the updated time stamps of v's occurrence.

for all $t_i \in E.t_{v \in A}$ **do**
  // If true, then E has no records with
  // its time stamp between t_{i-1} and t_i.
  if $i > 1$ and $\neg \exists t \in E.t$ s.t. $t_{i-1} < t < t_i$ **then**
    // Insert the missing time stamps of occurrence.
    for $t = t_{i-1} + 1 \rightarrow t_i - 1$ **do**
      $E.t_{v \in A} \leftarrow E.t_{v \in A} \cup t$
    end for
  end if
end for
return $E.t_{v \in A}$

Algorithm 3 UPDATECOUNTS($E.t_{v \in A}, C^A, \Delta t_{max}, t_{E_{latest}}$)

Input:

- $E.t_{v \in A}$, time stamps of v's occurrence of entity E in increasing order.
- $C^A = \{\langle h^A_1, m^A_1 \rangle ..., \langle h^A_{\Delta t_{max}}, m^A_{\Delta t_{max}} \rangle\}$, $h^A_{\Delta t}$ and $m^A_{\Delta t}$ are the Δt-recurrence hit and miss counters respectively.
- Δt_{max}, the maximum time difference considered.
- $t_{E_{latest}}$, the latest time stamp of entity E.

Output:

- C^A, the updated C^A.

// update the recurrence hits $h^A_{\Delta t}$ and misses $m^A_{\Delta t}$
// stored in C_A for all possible Δt.
for all $t \in E.t_{v \in A}$ **do**
  for $\Delta t = 1$ to Δt_{max} **do**
    if $t + \Delta t \leq t_{E_{latest}}$ **then**
      if $t + \Delta t \in E.t_{v \in A}$ **then**
        $h^A_{\Delta t} \leftarrow h^A_{\Delta t} + 1$
      else
        $m^A_{\Delta t} \leftarrow m^A_{\Delta t} + 1$
      end if
    end if
  end for
end for
return C^A

their A-value equal to v and time stamps earlier than t. Then, we view each such record r as a "predictor" and invoke the recurrence function with time interval $t - r.t$ to obtain the probability that value v reappears at time t given that v appears at time $r.t$. Finally, we combine all the probabilities estimated by each predictor record.

How to best combine the predictions from the predictor records is an interesting question. The combination should be a probability (between zero and one); also, the combination probability that a value appears plus the combination probability that a value does not appear should equal one. A possible approach that satisfies this would be to average the probabilities from all the predictors. But this is somehow unsatisfying; for one thing, a sum tends to lessen the impact of variations in small probabilities (for example, if most of the probabilities are close to one, the impact of an outlier small probability changing from say 0.01 to 0.02 is negligible.)

Accordingly, instead we use the product of the probability that all of the predictors will say "no" (the value will not recur) normalized by the sum of the probability that all predictors will say "yes" and the sum of the probability that all predictors will say "no." We express this more precisely below.

$$\mathcal{M}_{v\in A}(R,t) = \frac{\prod_{r\in R_{v,t}} (1-\mathcal{R}_A(t-r.t))}{\prod_{r\in R_{v,t}} \mathcal{R}_A(t-r.t) + \prod_{r\in R_{v,t}} (1-\mathcal{R}_A(t-r.t))} \quad (7)$$

$$R_{v,t} = \{r | r \in R \wedge r.t < t \wedge v \in r.A\} \quad (8)$$

The denominator of the above equation contains two products: the left product computes the probability of all observer records in $R_{v,t}$ saying that value v will reappear at time t, while the other product on the right computes the probability of all observer records in $R_{v,t}$ saying that value v will not reappear at time t.

Note that the overall goal is to improve matching by deciding weights for attributes. The important thing here is the relative weights of the attributes, not the absolute values of the weights.

Intuitively, the general form of the mutation probability $\mathcal{R}_A(R,t)$ can be computed by considering all possible values $v \in R.A$ (using the notation defined in Equation 2) that have appeared in at least one of the records in R:

$$\mathcal{M}_A(R,t) = \prod_{v\in R.A} \mathcal{M}_{v\in A}(R,t) \quad (9)$$

The computation of mutation function could be expensive. This can be somewhat amortized by caching the result and reusing it for each R during the clustering process. When R is updated by including one additional record, the result can be incrementally updated by further maintaining the occurrence history of different values for each cluster.

3.5 An Approximation of Mutation Function

While caching improves the computational cost of our algorithm, in some cases it may still be too high. Therefore, we propose the following approximation, which essentially treats all different values in $R.A$ as the same value instead. This relaxes the need for maintaining and iterating through the occurrence history of each attribute value. Again, without loss of generality, we assume each attribute is a set-valued attribute by treating each single-valued attribute as a set-valued attribute with one value.

$$\mathcal{M}_A(R,t) = \frac{\prod_{r\in R_t} (1-\mathcal{R}_A(t-r.t))^{|r.A|}}{\prod_{r\in R_t} \mathcal{R}_A(t-r.t)^{|r.A|} + \prod_{r\in R_t} (1-\mathcal{R}_A(t-r.t))^{|r.A|}} \quad (10)$$

$$R_t = \{r | r \in R \wedge r.t < t\} \quad (11)$$

where $|r.A|$ is the number of values on attribute A in r.

The above approximation looks very similar to the single-valued mutation function (Equation 7) as it treats different values of $R.A$ as the same value. In addition, the iterating of each individual value $v \in R.A$ is replaced by simply counting the number of elements in $R.A$. Note that as we will later discuss in this section, the full version (Equation 9 and 7) and the approximated version (Equation 10) have identical numerators. The difference is in the denominator, where the approximated version has a value no greater than that of the full version. In addition, when the target attribute is a single-valued attribute, the two versions will be identical. Our experiments (described in Section 5.5) show that the two versions of mutation functions do not have noticeable differences in result quality, but the approximated version can substantially improve running time.

Here we further discuss the difference between the full version and the approximated version of the mutation function.

We first look at the numerators of the two versions. In the original mutation function, the numerator is the product of the numerators of $\mathcal{M}_{v\in A}(R,t)$ of all different values in $R.A$, which can be rewritten as follows:

$$\prod_{v\in R.A} \prod_{r\in R_{v,t}} (1-\mathcal{R}_A(t-r.t)) = \prod_{r\in R_t} \prod_{v\in r.A} (1-\mathcal{R}_A(t-r.t)) \quad (12)$$

where both sides of the above equation enumerate all possible values on attribute A in R which time stamp is greater than t. Since the values of any record r on attribute A will have the same time stamp, the above equation can be simplified further:

$$\prod_{r\in R_t} \prod_{v\in r.A} (1-\mathcal{R}_A(t-r.t)) = \prod_{r\in R_t} (1-\mathcal{R}_A(t-r.t))^{|r.A|} \quad (13)$$

where the right hand side of the equation gives the numerator of the approximated mutation function (Equation 10), which further shows that both the full version and the approximated version of the mutation function have identical numerator.

Now we turn our focus on their denominators. In the full version of the mutation function, its denominator is the product of the denominators of the $\mathcal{M}_{v\in A}(R,t)$, which can be expended and rewritten as follows:

$$\prod_{v\in R.A} \left(\prod_{r\in R_{v,t}} \mathcal{R}_A(t-r.t) + \prod_{r\in R_{v,t}} (1-\mathcal{R}_A(t-r.t)) \right) = \prod_{v\in R.A} \prod_{r\in R_{v,t}} \mathcal{R}_A(t-r.t) + \prod_{v\in R.A} \prod_{r\in R_{v,t}} (1-\mathcal{R}_A(t-r.t))) + \text{remaining terms.} \quad (14)$$

where on the right hand side, the first term is the product of all possible recurrence rates $\mathcal{R}_A(t-r.t)$ reported by the observer records in R and the second term is the product of the complements of all possible recurrence rates $(1-\mathcal{R}_A(t-r.t))$ reported by the observer records in R. These two terms forms the denominator of the approximated mutation function.

3.6 Application to Fuzzy Clustering

In fuzzy clustering algorithms, the probability $p(r \in R)$ of each record belonging to a cluster is "fuzzy" (between 1 to 0) in the same sense as fuzzy logic. This probability is determined at run time by a fuzzy clustering algorithm, and a record could be put into multiple clusters with differing probabilities for each. To extend our model to work for fuzzy clustering algorithms, we further weight the importance of each observer record based on the probability $p(r \in R)$ of each record belonging to its cluster. Below is the modified version of the mutation function that works for fuzzy clustering techniques:

$$\mathcal{M}_{v\in A}(R,t) = \frac{\prod_{r\in R_{v,t}} p(r\in R)(1-\mathcal{R}_A(t-r.t))}{\prod_{r\in R_{v,t}} p(r\in R)\mathcal{R}_A(t-r.t) + \prod_{r\in R_{v,t}} p(r\in R)(1-\mathcal{R}_A(t-r.t))} \quad (15)$$

$$\mathcal{M}_A(R,t) = \prod_{v\in R.A} \mathcal{M}_{v\in A}(R,t) \quad (16)$$

where we reuse the previous notation $R_{v,t}$ defined in Equation 8.

Similarly, we extend the approximated version of the mutation function as follows:

$$\mathcal{M}_A(R,t) = \frac{\prod_{r\in R_t} p(r\in R)(1-\mathcal{R}_A(t-r.t))^{|r.A|}}{\prod_{r\in R_t} p(r\in R)\mathcal{R}_A(t-r.t)^{|r.A|} + \prod_{r\in R_t} p(r\in R)(1-\mathcal{R}_A(t-r.t))^{|r.A|}} \tag{17}$$

and again, the definition of R_t can be found in Equation 11.

4. APPLYING OUR TEMPORAL MODEL

We now describe how we utilize the proposed mutation model to weight the importance of each attribute in similarity computations. The weight is computed based on the entity-dependent probability of temporal agreement and disagreement. Then, we will introduce how we compute the similarity between two records.

We will use the following example task during the discussion.

EXAMPLE 4.1. *Consider a pair of records r and r'. We would like to compute their similarity based on attribute value similarities. We use $sim_A(r.A, r'.A)$ to denote their value similarity on attribute A. Without loss of generality, we assume that r' has a time stamp no later than the time stamp of r, and let $\Delta t = r'.t - r.t$ be the time difference between r and r'. In addition, we assume that record r is currently grouped into cluster C_r that consists of a list $R_r = \{r_1, ..., r_n\}$ of n records.* □

Given two records r and r', we ask the following two questions: 1) if r and r' have dissimilar values on attribute A, what is the probability that the value $r.A$ in the entity described in cluster C_r does not recur at time $r'.t$? 2) if r and r' have similar values on attribute A, what is the probability that the value $r.A$ does not recur in the entity described by cluster C_r at time $r'.t$? To answer the above questions, we utilize the value-based mutation function $\mathcal{M}_{v\in A}$ defined in Equation 7 to determine the probability of all values in $r.A$ *not* reappearing at time $r'.t$:

$$\mathcal{M}_{v\in r.A}(R_r, r'.t) = \prod_{v\in r.A} \mathcal{M}_{v\in A}(R_r, r'.t) \tag{18}$$

If the approximate version is used, then we use Equation 10 to approximate $\mathcal{M}_{v\in r.A}(R_r, r'.t)$.

To answer the first question, if the value in $r.A$ is not likely to reappear at time $r'.t$, the fact that $r.A$ and $r'.A$ do not have similar values should not be construed as suggesting that r and r' do not refer to the same entity. As a result, a lower weight will be assigned to attribute A.

On the other hand, in the second question, if we are expecting that the values in $r.A$ will not reappear at time $r'.t$, then we are not expecting to see a record belonging to C_r having its A-value similar to $r.A$ at time $r'.t$. So, if $r.A$ and $r'.A$ match in this case, it is likely from between-entity temporal agreement, and thus we should still assign a lower weight to A.

Putting it all together, we use the following equation to determine the weight of each attribute:

$$w_A(r,r') = \begin{cases} 1 + \vartheta_{\mathcal{M}} \cdot (1 - \mathcal{M}_{v\in r.A}(R_r, r'.t)) & sim(r.A, r'.A) \geq \theta_A \\ 1 - \vartheta_{\mathcal{M}} \cdot \mathcal{M}_{v\in r.A}(R_r, r'.t) & \text{otherwise} \end{cases} \tag{19}$$

where $\vartheta_{\mathcal{M}}$ is a parameter that controls the importance of the mutation function, and θ_A again is a learned threshold indicating high similarity on attribute A.

Here we have used the heuristic that the weights given to the attributes where the two records agree on their values are always higher than the weights given to the attributes where the two records disagree. This heuristic ensures that the final record similarity will never be dominated by several low similarity attributes if at least one high similarity attribute is observed.

Finally, the temporal similarity between two records r and r' is defined to be the weighted average of their attribute value similarities based on the weights derived from our mutation model:

$$sim(r,r') = \frac{\sum_{A\in\mathbf{A}} w_A(r,r') \cdot sim(r.A, r'.A)}{\sum_{A\in\mathbf{A}} w_A(r,r')} \tag{20}$$

5. EXPERIMENTAL EVALUATION

This section describes our experimental setup and results.

5.1 Experiment Settings

5.1.1 Data Sets

To evaluate the matching quality of different approaches, we consider three subsets from two real world data sets: a benchmark of European patent data [1] and the DBLP data set [2]. Two of the tasks, Euro-Patent and DBLP-WW, are the tasks used in Li's work [14].

DBLP-Ambi matching task: We created a labeled subset from DBLP by selecting 21 different groups of records which contain 2664 records in total. Each group contains multiple authors sharing the same name. Examples are "Ajy Gupta", "Li Zhang", "Rajesh Kumar", "Min-Soo Kim", "Arnab Roy", and so forth. Again, in this matching task, the author's affiliation information is manually filled in for each record.

Euro-Patent matching task: From the patent data, which is also used in [14], we extracted inventor records with attributes name and address; the time stamp of each record is the patent filing date. The benchmark involves 359 inventors of French patents. For purpose of comparison, we also followed the practice in [14] of using only last name initial and first name for each inventor.

DBLP-WW matching task: From the DBLP data, we used the labeled "Wei Wang" subset also used in [14] containing 738 records. The data provider has manually identified 18 authors for ground truth and filled in the author affiliation attribute for each record. One important property of this matching task is that all authors have the same name, *Wei Wang*.

Table 2 briefly summarizes the matching tasks used in our experiment.

5.1.2 Implementation

We consider the following approaches for handling temporal agreement and disagreement:

- -NONE: This approach does not use any strategy to handle temporal agreement and disagreement.
- -DECAY: This is the time decay model proposed in [14].
- -MUTA^{A}: This is the approximate version of our proposed model (Eq. 10, described in Section 3).
- -MUTA^{F}: This is the full version of -MUTA^{A} (Eq. 7 and Eq. 18, described in Section 3 and Section 4). This model is only used for analyzing the effectiveness of our proposed approximation.

Recall that in general a temporal matching approach requires both a temporal model and a clustering algorithm. In our experiments we tried three different clustering algorithms, testing each with all four temporal models. The clustering algorithms used were:

- PART: The partition algorithm proposed in [10], a single-stage approach that does not cluster in any temporal order.

Table 2: Temporal matching tasks

Name	Total # Records	# Pairwise Record Relations	Attributes	Years	Note
DBLP-Ambi	2664	3.5 million	author's name, affiliation (manually filled), paper title, co-authors	1987 - 2012	258 authors share only 21 names; most entities evolve.
DBLP-WW	738	0.3 million	author's name, affiliation (manually filled), co-authors	1991 - 2010	All authors share the same name; most entities evolve. also used in [14]
Euro-Patent	1871	1.7 million	author first name initial, author last name, affiliation	1978 - 2003	Fewer entities evolve; also used in [14].

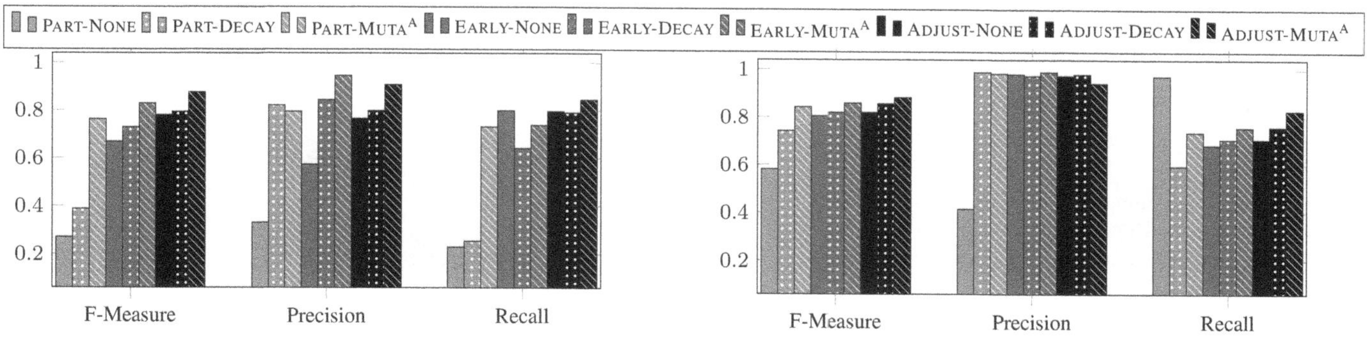

(a) Results on DBLP-Ambiguous.

(b) Results on DBLP-WW.

Figure 4: Result quality on DBLP matching tasks.

- EARLY: The early binding algorithm [14], a single-stage temporal clustering approach that considers records in increasing temporal order and uses a single pair of records when making cluster merging decisions.
- ADJUST: The adjusted binding algorithm [14], the leading clustering approach in that paper, a multi-stage temporal clustering approach which uses an EM-style fuzzy clustering to iteratively refine the temporal clustering results.

All the techniques were implemented as single-threaded Java programs, and we ran the experiments on a Linux machine with a 2.40 GHz Intel CPU and 1GB of RAM.

Similarity measure: We applied edit distance similarity [13] for all scalar attributes. For multi-valued attributes, we did not use the regular Jaccard similarity [11] because the records in our matching tasks rarely share more than one or two elements on the multi-valued attributes we considered (e.g., co-authors). As a result, the regular Jaccard similarity usually reports a low similarity score even when two records show substantial match on the multi-valued attributes in our matching tasks. Instead, we use the following variation on Jaccard similarity, where the denominator is the size of the smaller set:

$$sim_A(r.A, r'A) = \frac{|r.A \cap r'.A|}{min(|r.A|, |r'.A|)} \quad (21)$$

This variation returns the percentage of the smaller set covered by the larger.

Models and thresholds learning: We used a cross-validation process to learn the temporal models and the thresholds for each matching task. We used a three-fold cross-validation, which divides the data set into three disjoint partitions with nearly equal size. We learned temporal models and thresholds from one partition at a time and used them to test with the rest of the data set.

Parameter settings: For the time decay model and the temporal clustering algorithms proposed in [14], we followed the parameter settings that were used in their experiment. For the parameters that used in our model, we set $\theta_{\mathcal{M}} = 0.5$ (used in Eq. 19) in our experiments.

5.1.3 *Metrics*

We compared pairwise matching decisions with the ground truth and measured the quality of the result by *precision* (P), *recall* (R), and *F-measure* (F). We denote the set of false positive pairs by F_N, the set of false negative pairs by F_N, and the set of true positive pairs by T. Then, $\mathrm{P} = \frac{|T|}{|T|+|F_P|}$, $\mathrm{R} = \frac{|T|}{|T|+|F_N|}$, and $\mathrm{F} = \frac{2\mathrm{PR}}{\mathrm{P+R}}$.

5.2 Matching Accuracy

Here we explore and discuss the matching accuracy of different approaches on the three matching tasks.

5.2.1 *DBLP-Ambiguous Matching Task*

In this matching task, 258 entities share only 21 different names, and most author entities evolve on all other attributes: affiliations, paper titles, and co-authors. As a result, the key to high matching accuracy is to resolve the ambiguity on name by handling evolution on all other attributes. Figure 4a shows the matching accuracy of different clustering algorithms paired with different temporal models. Note that since we do not profile MUTA^{F}, three clustering algorithms with three temporal models gives nine approaches. Higher is better in this graph.

From the results, we first observe the pure non-temporal technique PART-NONE only produces 27.01% in F-1 score. However, when being paired with a temporal model, PART can produce a higher matching accuracy: a 38.68% in F-1 score when paired with the time decay model and a 76.28% in F-1 score when paired with our proposed model — MUTA^{A}. Second, applying a temporal model to a clustering algorithm in general improves F-1 score: our model MUTA^{A} improves 10% to 50% in F-1 score compared with no temporal model while the time decay mode — DECAY improves from 2% to 12% in F-1 score as compared with no temporal model.

The readers might wonder at this point why a non-temporal matching technique might produce a lower precision than a temporal matching technique. It is because without considering temporal

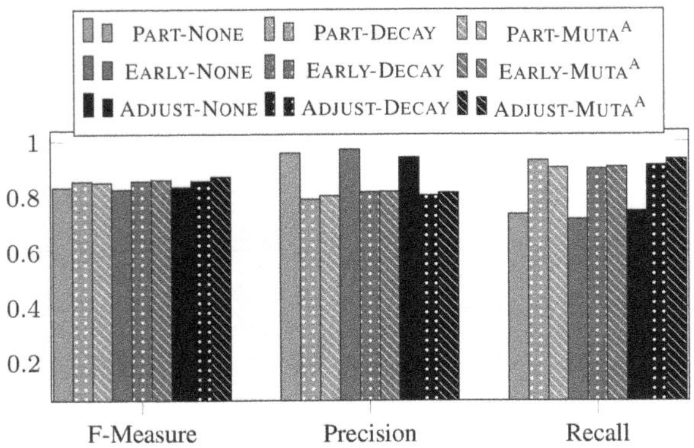

Figure 5: Result quality on the Euro-Patent matching task.

information, a non-temporal matching technique might incorrectly merge two records which in fact refer to two different entities caused by between-entity temporal agreement. This contributes to its low precision.

In addition to the case where authors might move back to their "home affiliations", we also observed the following cases where our mutation model does better than the time decay model: 1) an author might have out-of-date affiliation associated with his / her publications for one or two years when he / she moves from one affiliation to another; 2) publications of the same author are usually associated with different co-authors over time while many of his / her co-authors re-appear in that author's publication history over time.

Comparing our mutation model with the time decay model, our approach improves 40% in matching accuracy over the time decay model when a non-temporal clustering technique is used and improves 8% to 10% in matching accuracy over the time decay model when temporal clustering approaches are used.

5.2.2 DBLP-WW Matching Task

The DBLP-WW matching task evaluates how each approach handles the special case when all author entities in the same data set share the same name. In addition, author entities also evolve on all other attributes. Figure 4b compares the result qualities of different clustering techniques paired with different models for handling evolution and ambiguity.

Similar to what we have seen in the DBLP-Ambiguous matching task, applying a temporal model will improve matching accuracy over applying no temporal model: The proposed MUTA^A improves 5% to 25% in F-1 score over using no temporal model, while the state-of-the-art model — DECAY — improves 2% to 15% in F-1 score over using no temporal model.

Compared with the state-of-the-art temporal model — DECAY, our model MUTA^A improves up to 10% in F-1 score in the DBLP-WW matching task.

5.2.3 Euro-Patent Matching Task

Unlike the previous two matching tasks, there are relatively few entities described in the Euro-Patent matching set whose attributes evolve over time. This situation has two implications. First, as this matching task has fewer evolving entities, all approaches have less trouble separating records belonging to the same entity. Second, because fewer entities evolve over time, there are relatively fewer temporal clues that any temporal model can utilize. Figure 5 shows the matching accuracy of different approaches.

First, as we have discussed, since there are fewer evolving entities, the non-temporal solution — PART-NONE — performs relatively better than it did in the previous two matching tasks: 83.17% in F-1 score with 95.65% precision and 73.58% recall. Second, temporal cluster approaches alone without using a temporal model do not bring noticeable improvement on accuracy ($\leq$ 1% improvement). Third, we observe that while not many temporal clues are available in this matching task, using a temporal model still brings some improvement in matching accuracy: our model MUTA^A improves 2% to 4% in F-1 score over using no temporal model while the decay model improves 2% to 3% in F-1 score over using no temporal model.

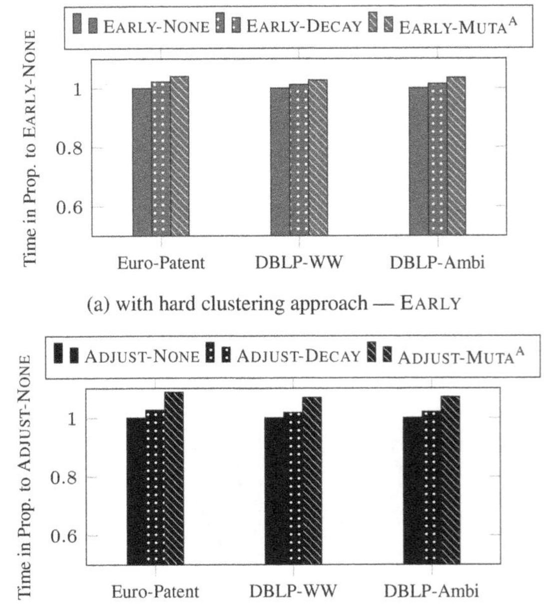

(a) with hard clustering approach — EARLY

(b) with fuzzy clustering approach — ADJUST

Figure 6: Running time comparison.

5.2.4 Summary

When most entities described in the data set evolve over time, our proposed model improves 10% to 50% in matching accuracy over using no temporal model while the state-of-the-art temporal model improves 2% to 15% over using no temporal model. When only a few of the entities described in the data set evolve over time, the temporal models provide a limited improvement (2% to 4%) in accuracy over using no temporal model.

Compared with the state-of-the-art temporal model, our model improves up to 40% in F-1 score when a non-temporal clustering algorithm is used, and up to 10% in F-1 score when a temporal clustering algorithm is used.

5.3 Results on Running Time Efficiency

We analyzed the running time efficiency of different temporal models by running them with different clustering approaches. As different clustering techniques spend different amounts of time finishing different matching tasks, we treat the running time of using no temporal model as 1.0 and report the running time of using temporal models in proportion to that.

The results in Figure 6 show that both DECAY and MUTA^A introduce acceptable running time overhead compared to a solution without using any temporal model. Compared with DECAY, our model MUTA^A introduces 2% running time overhead when running with a hard clustering algorithm (EARLY) and 5% running time overhead when running with a fuzzy clustering algorithm (ADJUST). The difference between hard- and fuzzy- clusterings is due to the

Table 3: Attributes and the types of their simulated noise.

Attribute	Considered types of simulated noise
Name	typo
Affiliation	typo, missing value, incorrect reference
Co-authors	typo, missing value
Publication Year	numerical error

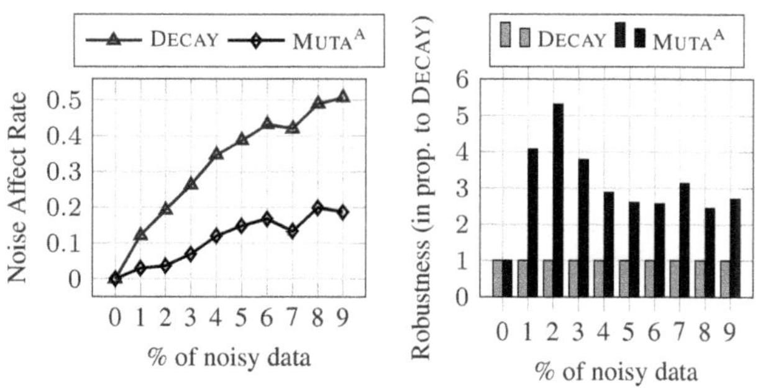

(a) Noise affect rate.

(b) Robustness to noise.

Figure 7: Results on robustness to noise.

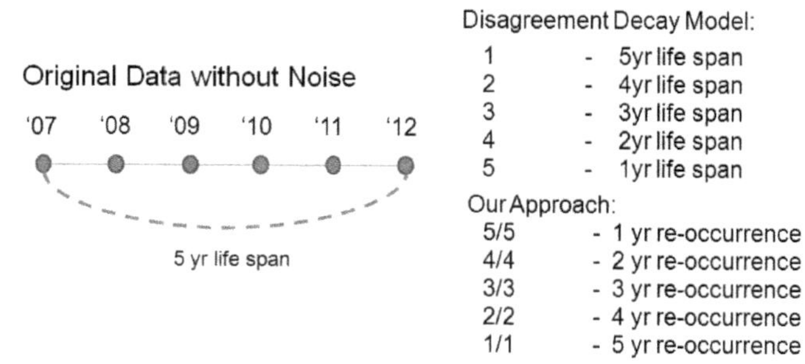

(a) Example statistics learned from clean data.

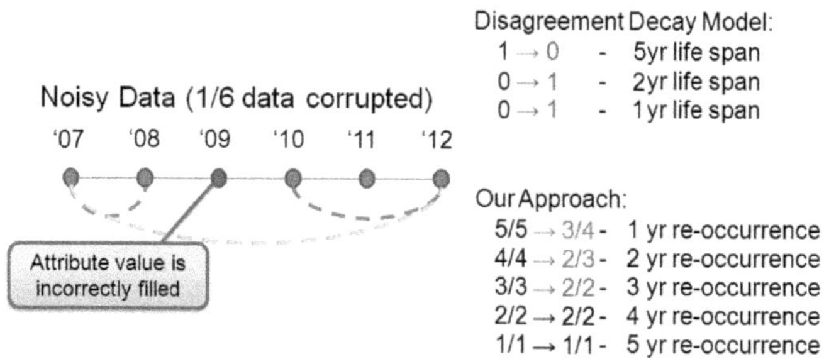

(b) Example statistics learned from noisy data.

Figure 8: Learning from clean and noisy data.

fact that clusters in the fuzzy clustering tend to have more frequent updates. As a result, the caching strategy used in our model will become less effective.

5.4 Results on Noise Tolerance

To test the impact of noise on different temporal models, we simulated the following and added them to the original data sets:

- **typo**: simulated by randomly replacing a small number of characters by their keyboard neighbors. Characters include numbers.
- **missing value**: simulated by deleting the whole value.
- **incorrect reference**: simulated by replacing the original value by a completed random value.
- **numerical error**: simulated by adding or subtracting a small number in proportion to the original value.

Table 3 lists the types of noise we added to different attributes in our matching tasks.

We analyze the noise tolerance of different temporal modeling approaches by comparing their learned model, which essentially can be described as a sequence of numeric values, from the clean data set and the one from the noisy data set and measuring the difference. We here define the noise affect rate as the difference in proportion to the original value sequence. Let $V_c = \langle v_{c,1}, ..., v_{c,t} \rangle$ and $V_n = \langle v_{n,1}, ..., v_{n,t} \rangle$ be two sequences of values learned by the same temporal model from the original clean data set and the noisy data set respectively, where t is the maximum time interval we considered. We define the noise affect rate as the sum of absolute difference between each pair of values over the sum of the values of the clean value sequence V_c:

$$\text{NOISEAFFECTRATE}(V_c, V_n) = \frac{\sum_{i=1}^{t} |v_{c,i} - v_{n,i}|}{\sum_{i=1}^{t} v_{c,i}} \quad (22)$$

Figure 7 compares the noise affect rates and the robustness against noise of the time decay model [14] (DECAY) and the proposed mutation model (MUTA^A). The robustness against noise is defined as the inverse of the noise affect rate, and the figure shows the normalized result where we treat the robustness of DECAY as 1.00.

From the results shown in Figure 7, we observe that our proposed model has better noise resistance than the previously proposed model. Here are reasons that might contribute to this result. First, our model does not impose a continuous life span segmented by change points. This improves robustness to noise as any continuous life span could be easily corrupted by noise into multiple shorter life spans. Second, since our mutation model looks at multiple records when making its predictions, it is more robust than the decay model, which only looks at a single record.

Overall, our mutation model is 2X to 5X more robust against noise than the existing time decay model.

EXAMPLE 5.1. *Consider an example shown in Figure 8a where we have a value with 5-year life span in the original data. In this data, the disagreement decay model will simply learn one sample of a 5-year life span. However, suppose the attribute value of one record is incorrectly represented as shown in Figure 8b. Then the observed life span pattern will be corrupted and thus the disagreement decay model learns one sample of 2-years and one sample of 1-year life spans instead: $1/6$ records corrupted introduces significant differences in the learned result. In contrast, since our approach learns the mutation function based on the statistics about each individual value recurrence, such incorrect data only introduces a limited effect. In the clean data, our approach learns a $\{5/5, 4/4, 3/3, 2/2, 1/1\}$ of 1- to 5-year recurrence rates, while in the noisy data, our model learns a $\{3/4, 2/3, 2/2, 2/2, 1/1\}$ of 1- to 5-years recurrence rate: $1/6$ records corrupted introduce a 11.67% (less than 1/6) bias in the recurrence rate learned from surrounding records of the corrupted one.* □

5.5 Effectiveness of Approximation

Here we compare the result quality and running time between the full version of the mutation function and the approximated version of mutation function discussed in Section 3.4 by applying them to different temporal matching tasks and measuring the resulting quality and running time. Since the running time varies with the size of matching tasks, we treat the running time of the full version

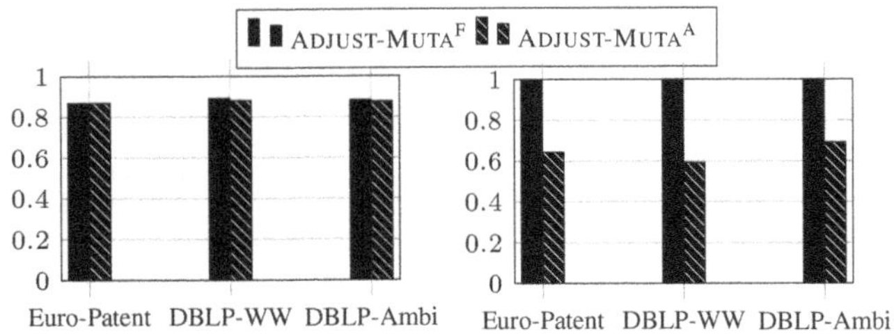

(a) Result quality comparison (in F-1 score).

(b) Running time comparison (in prop. to ADJUST-MUTA^F).

Figure 9: Full vs. approximate versions of our model.

ADJUST-MUTA^F as 1.0 and report the running time of the approximated version in proportion to ADJUST-MUTA^F. The results are shown in Figure 9.

Our experimental results show that when using the approximated version of the mutation function, we can save around 30% to 40% in running time without losing noticeable level of result quality: the approximated version finishes 2664 records in 1320 seconds while the full version finishes in 1905 seconds.

6. RELATED WORK

[7, 9, 18] proposed different record matching / deduplication techniques, but their techniques all assume value difference are due to different representations of the same value and record values do not change over time. Several temporal data models [15] and temporal knowledge discovery paradigms [16] have been proposed in the past. However, their main focus are not on record matching. Yakout *et al.* proposed behavior based linkage [19] based on periodical behavior patterns of each entity. While our approach is based on the statistics about event recurrences, it does not try to find periodic entity evolution patterns. [17] proposed a recurrence based approach to learn and recognize complex temporal sequence, but their model is based on neural networks and Hebbian learning rules. Both [5], [6], and [14] proposed the notion of time decays, but their definition and application of time decay are different. [5] and [6] use time decay to reduce the effect of older tuples on data analysis. Li *et al.* [14] is the work closest to our work here, and we have discussed it in detail inline where appropriate.

7. CONCLUSION

We have proposed a new temporal model for handling entity evolution. Unlike existing models, our model focuses on the probability of a value re-appearing over time. Our experimental results on various real world temporal matching tasks show that our model improves both matching accuracy (up to 10% to 40%) and noise resistance (2X to 5X) over the state-of-the-art model while introducing minimal running time overhead ($\leq 2\%$).

Substantial room for future work remains. For example, entity evolution breaks the assumptions of blocking techniques [8]. An evolution aware blocking operator is needed for matching temporal records at large scale. Also, our model is of course only one point in a spectrum of models that seek to be more sophisticated in modeling evolution — it would be interesting to explore whether more complex models can yield better matching quality with acceptable overhead. Finally, in some sense temporal matching works by recognizing that the temporal dimension in a matching problem has special properties. It would be interesting to see if other dimensions can also be exploited — in particular, a special treatment of spatial information might be useful.

8. ACKNOWLEDGEMENT

This material is based upon work supported by the National Science Foundation under grant no. IIS-1018792.

9. REFERENCES

[1] Academic patenting in Europe (APE-INV). http://www.esf-ape-inv.eu/.

[2] The DBLP computer science bibliography. http://www.informatik.uni-trier.de/ ley/db/.

[3] Fec-standardizer - an experiment to standardize individual donor names in campaign finance data. https://github.com/cjdd3b/fec-standardizer.

[4] Twitter - an online social networking and microblogging service. https://twitter.com/.

[5] E. Cohen and M. Strauss. Maintaining time-decaying stream aggregates. *Journal of Algorithms*, 59(1):19–36, 2006.

[6] G. Cormode, V. Shkapenyuk, D. Srivastava, and B. Xu. Forward decay: A practical time decay model for streaming systems. In *IEEE 25th International Conference on Data Engineering (ICDE)*, pages 138–149. IEEE, 2009.

[7] P. Domingos. Multi-relational record linkage. In *Proc. of the KDD-2004 Workshop on Multi-Relational Data Mining*. KDD, 2004.

[8] A. Elmagarmid, P. Ipeirotis, and V. Verykios. Duplicate record detection: A survey. *IEEE Transactions on Knowledge and Data Engineering*, 19(1):1–16, 2007.

[9] I. Fellegi and A. Sunter. A theory for record linkage. *Journal of the American Statistical Association*, pages 1183–1210, 1969.

[10] O. Hassanzadeh, F. Chiang, H. Lee, and R. Miller. Framework for evaluating clustering algorithms in duplicate detection. *Proceedings of the VLDB Endowment*, 2(1):1282–1293, 2009.

[11] P. Jaccard. *Distribution de la Flore Alpine: dans le Bassin des dranses et dans quelques régions voisines*. Rouge, 1901.

[12] N. Koudas, S. Sarawagi, and D. Srivastava. Record linkage: similarity measures and algorithms. In *Proceedings of the 2006 ACM SIGMOD international conference on Management of data*, pages 802–803. ACM, 2006.

[13] V. Levenshtein. Binary codes capable of correcting deletions, insertions, and reversals. In *Soviet physics doklady*, volume 10, pages 707–710, 1966.

[14] P. Li, X. Dong, A. Maurino, and D. Srivastava. Linking temporal records. *Proceedings of the VLDB Endowment*, 4(11):956–967, 2011.

[15] G. Ozsoyoglu and R. Snodgrass. Temporal and real-time databases: A survey. *IEEE Transactions on Knowledge and Data Engineering*, 7(4):513–532, 1995.

[16] J. Roddick and M. Spiliopoulou. A survey of temporal knowledge discovery paradigms and methods. *IEEE Transactions on Knowledge and Data Engineering*, 14(4):750–767, 2002.

[17] D. Wang and M. A. Arbib. Complex temporal sequence learning based on short-term memory. *Proceedings of the IEEE*, 78(9):1536–1543, 1990.

[18] W. Winkler. Methods for record linkage and bayesian networks. Technical report, Statistical Research Division, US Census Bureau, Washington, DC, 2002.

[19] M. Yakout, A. Elmagarmid, H. Elmeleegy, M. Ouzzani, and A. Qi. Behavior based record linkage. *Proceedings of the VLDB Endowment*, 3(1-2):439–448, 2010.

Resolving Conflicts in Heterogeneous Data by Truth Discovery and Source Reliability Estimation*

Qi Li[1], Yaliang Li[1], Jing Gao[1], Bo Zhao[2], Wei Fan[3], and Jiawei Han[4]
[1]SUNY Buffalo, Buffalo, NY USA
[2]Microsoft Research, Mountain View, CA USA
[3]Huawei Noah's Ark Lab, Hong Kong
[4]Univesrity of Illinois, Urbana, IL USA
[1]{qli22,yaliangl,jing}@buffalo.edu, [2]bozha@microsoft.com,
[3]david.fanwei@huawei.com, [4]hanj@illinois.edu

ABSTRACT

In many applications, one can obtain descriptions about the same objects or events from a variety of sources. As a result, this will inevitably lead to data or information conflicts. One important problem is to identify the true information (i.e., the *truths*) among conflicting sources of data. It is intuitive to trust reliable sources more when deriving the truths, but it is usually unknown which one is more reliable *a priori*. Moreover, each source possesses a variety of properties with different data types. An accurate estimation of source reliability has to be made by modeling multiple properties in a unified model. Existing conflict resolution work either does not conduct source reliability estimation, or models multiple properties separately. In this paper, we propose to resolve conflicts among multiple sources of heterogeneous data types. We model the problem using an optimization framework where truths and source reliability are defined as two sets of unknown variables. The objective is to minimize the overall weighted deviation between the truths and the multi-source observations where each source is weighted by its reliability. Different loss functions can be incorporated into this framework to recognize the characteristics of various data types, and efficient computation approaches are developed. Experiments on real-world weather, stock and flight data as well as simulated multi-source data demonstrate the necessity of jointly modeling different data types in the proposed framework[1].

1. INTRODUCTION

Recently, the Big Data challenge is motivated by a dramatic increase in our ability to extract and collect data from the physical world. One important property of Big Data is its wide *variety*, i.e., data about the same object can be obtained from various sources. For example, customer information can be found from multiple databases in a company, a patient's medical records may be scattered in different hospitals, and a natural event may be observed and recorded by multiple laboratories.

Due to recording or transmission errors, device malfunction, or malicious intent to manipulate the data, data sources usually contain noisy, outdated, missing or erroneous records, and thus multiple sources may provide conflicting information. In almost every industry, decisions based on untrustworthy information can cause serious damage. For example, erroneous account information in a company database may cause financial losses; wrong diagnosis based on incorrect measurements of a patient may lead to serious consequences; and scientific discoveries may be guided to the wrong direction if they are derived from incorrect data. Therefore, it is critical to *identify the most trustworthy answers from multiple sources of conflicting information*. This is a non-trivial problem due to the following two major challenges.

Source Reliability

Resolving conflicts from multiple sources have been studied in the database community for years [4, 5, 10, 13] resulting in multiple ways to handle conflicts in data integration. Among them, one commonly used approach to eliminate conflicts for categorical data is to conduct majority voting so that information with the highest number of occurrences is regarded as the correct answer; and for continuous values, we can simply take the mean or median as the answer. The issue of such Voting/Averaging approaches is that they assume all the sources are equally reliable, and thus the votes from different sources are uniformly weighted. In the complicated world that we have today, it is crucial to **estimate source reliability** to find out the correct information from conflicting data, especially when there exist sources providing low quality information, such as faulty sensors that keep emanating wrong data, and spam users who propagate false information on the Internet. However, there is no oracle telling us which source is more reliable and which piece of information is correct.

Heterogeneous Data

Motivated by the importance but lack of knowledge in source reliability, many truth discovery approaches have been proposed to estimate it and infer true facts without any supervision [3, 8, 9, 11, 12, 14–16, 18, 19, 21–24]. However, these approaches are mainly designed for single-type data and they do not take advantage of a joint inference on **data with heterogeneous types**.

In real data integration tasks, heterogeneous data is ubiquitous. An object usually possesses multiple types of data. For example, in the integration of multiple health record databases, a patient's record includes age, height, weight, address, measurements, etc; we may want to infer correct information for a city's population, area, mayor, and founding year among conflicting information presented

*The first two authors contributed equally to this work and should be considered as joint first authors.

[1]Codes and data sets can be downloaded from http://www.cse.buffalo.edu/~jing/crh.htm

SIGMOD'14, June 22–27, 2014, Snowbird, UT, USA.

http://dx.doi.org/10.1145/2588555.2610509 .

on the Internet; and when we combine the predictions from multiple weather forecast tools, we need to resolve conflicts in weather conditions, temperature, humidity, wind speed, wind direction, etc. In all these cases, the data to be integrated involve categorical, continuous or even more complicated data types.

Due to the wide existence of missing values, we usually do not have sufficient amount of data to estimate source reliability correctly purely from one type of data. When source reliability is consistent on the entire data set, which is often valid in reality, a model that infers from various data types together will generate accurate estimates of source reliability, which will in turn help infer accurate information. Therefore, instead of separately inferring trustworthy information for individual data types, we should develop a unified model that conducts a joint estimation on all types of data simultaneously.

However, it is non-trivial to unify different types of data in one model. During source reliability estimation, we need to estimate how close a source input is to the correct answer, but different data types should be treated differently in this process because the concept of closeness varies among different data types. For categorical data, each observation will be either correct or wrong (i.e., whether the observation is the same as or different from the true fact). It is very different when a property has continuous values. For example, if the true temperature is 80F, then an observation of 79F is closer to the true value than 70F. If such differences are not taken into account and we regard each continuous input as a fact, we will inevitably make wrong estimates of source reliability and derive incorrect results. Therefore, we need a framework that can seamlessly integrate data of heterogeneous data types by estimating information trustworthiness.

Summary of Proposed CRH Framework

These observations motivate us to develop a ***C**onflict **R**esolution on **H**eterogeneous Data* (CRH) framework to infer the truths (also referred to as the true information or correct answers) from multiple conflicting sources each of which involves a variety of data types. We formulate the problem as an optimization problem to minimize the overall weighted deviation between the identified truths and the input. The weights in the objective function correspond to source reliability degrees. We propose to leverage heterogeneous data types by allowing any loss function for any type of data, and find out both truths and source reliability by solving the joint optimization problem. In the experiments (Section 3), we show that the proposed CRH framework outperforms existing conflict resolution approaches applied separately or jointly on heterogeneous data because each baseline approach either does not conduct source reliability estimation, or takes incomplete single-type data, or ignores the unique characteristics of each data type.

In summary, we make the following contributions:

- We design a general optimization framework to model the conflict resolution problem on heterogeneous data by incorporating source reliability estimation. The proposed objective function characterizes the overall difference between unknown truths and input data while modeling source reliability as unknown source weights in the framework.
- Under this framework, weight assignment schemes are introduced to capture source reliability distributions. Various loss functions can be plugged into the framework to characterize different types of data. In particular, we discuss several common choices and illustrate their effectiveness in modeling conflict resolution on heterogeneous data.
- We propose an algorithm to solve the optimization problem by iteratively updating truths and source weights. We derive effective solutions for commonly used loss functions and weight assignment schemes, and show the convergence of the algorithm. The running time is linear in the number of observations. Also, the proposed approach can be adapted to MapReduce model, so it can scale to very large data sets.
- We validate the proposed algorithm on both real-world and simulated data sets, and the results demonstrate the advantages of the proposed approach in resolving conflicts from multi-source heterogeneous data. The CRH framework can improve the performance of existing approaches due to its ability of tightly coupling various data types in the conflict resolution and source reliability estimation process. Running time on both single and Hadoop cluster machines demonstrates its efficiency.

2. METHODOLOGY

In this section, we describe our design of the CRH model, which computes truths and source weights from multi-source heterogeneous data. We formulate the conflict resolution problem as an optimization problem which models the truths as the weighted combination of the observations from multiple sources and incorporates a variety of loss functions for heterogeneous data types. An iterative weight and truth computation procedure is introduced to solve this optimization problem. Under this general framework, we present several loss functions and constraints, discuss other possible choices and analyze the time complexity.

2.1 Problem Formulation

We start by introducing important terms and defining the conflict resolution problem. We use an example on demographic database (Table 1) to illustrate these concepts.

DEFINITION 1. *An* object *is a person or thing of interest; a* property *is a feature used to describe the object; and a* source *describes the place where information about objects' properties can be collected.*

EXAMPLE 1. *"Bob" is an object; height is a property; and a database that provides the information is a source.*

DEFINITION 2. *An* observation *is the data describing a property of an object from a source.*

EXAMPLE 2. *The observation on Bob's height from Source 1 is 1.74m.*

DEFINITION 3. *An* entry *is a property of an object, and the* truth *of an entry is defined as its accurate information, which is unique.*

EXAMPLE 3. *Bob's height is an entry. The real height of Bob is the truth of the entry.*

The mathematical notation is as follows. Suppose there are N objects, each of which has M properties whose data types can be different, and these objects are observed by K sources.

Input

DEFINITION 4. *The observation of the m-th property for the i-th object made by the k-th source is $v_{im}^{(k)}$.*

DEFINITION 5 (SOURCE OBSERVATION TABLES). *The k-th source $\mathcal{X}^{(k)}$ is the collection of observations made on all the objects by the k-th source. It is denoted as a matrix whose im-th entry is $v_{im}^{(k)}$. $\{\mathcal{X}^{(1)}, \mathcal{X}^{(2)}, \ldots, \mathcal{X}^{(K)}\}$ are the K source observation tables.*

Table 1: Observation Tables

	$\mathcal{X}^{(1)}$		$\mathcal{X}^{(2)}$		$\mathcal{X}^{(3)}$	
Object	City	Height	City	Height	City	Height
Bob	NYC	1.72	NYC	1.70	NYC	1.90
Mary	LA	1.62	LA	1.61	LA	1.85
Kate	NYC	1.74	NYC	1.72	LA	1.65
Mike	NYC	1.72	LA	1.70	DC	1.85
Joe	DC	1.72	NYC	1.71	NYC	1.85

Table 2: Ground Truth and Conflict Resolution Results

	Ground Truth		Voting/Averaging		CRH	
Object	City	Height	City	Height	City	Height
Bob	NYC	1.72	NYC	1.77	NYC	1.72
Mary	LA	1.62	LA	1.69	LA	1.62
Kate	NYC	1.75	NYC	1.70	NYC	1.74
Mike	NYC	1.71	DC	1.76	NYC	1.72
Joe	DC	1.73	NYC	1.76	DC	1.72

EXAMPLE 4. *Suppose we have three databases (sources) that provide the information on a group of people. Table 1 shows the observation tables of $\mathcal{X}^{(1)}$, $\mathcal{X}^{(2)}$, and $\mathcal{X}^{(3)}$, which store all observations made by Sources 1, 2 and 3 respectively. Source 1 states that the citizenship for Bob (row 1 and column 1 in $\mathcal{X}^{(1)}$) is "NYC", so $v_{11}^{(1)}$ is "NYC".*

Remark. To simplify the notations, we assume that the observations of all the sources about all the objects are available in the formulation. However, the proposed framework is general enough to cover the cases with missing observations. More discussion can be found in Section 2.5.

Output of CRH Framework

DEFINITION 6 (TRUTH TABLE).
$v_{im}^{(*)}$ denotes the truth of the m-th property for the i-th object. The truths of all the objects on all the properties are stored in a truth table $\mathcal{X}^{(*)}$ whose im-th entry is $v_{im}^{(*)}$.

EXAMPLE 5. *Table 2 shows the ground truth, the results obtained by Voting/Averaging, and the results obtained by the proposed framework CRH from the input tables. CRH resolves conflicts from different sources for each entry. It provides more accurate results comparing with Voting/Averaging.*

Remark. Comparing with the ground truths, it is clear that Source 1 provides accurate information more often (more reliable) while Source 2 and 3 are not very reliable. Due to the various reliability degrees, voting cannot work well. For example, voting fails on Joe's citizenship because the majority answer is stated by the unreliable sources and majority voting gives a wrong answer – "NYC". Although only Source 1 states that Joe's citizenship is "DC", as it is a reliable source, we should take this observation as the truth.

However, ground truths and source reliability are usually unknown *a priori*. Existing truth discovery approaches [3,8,9,11,12, 14–16, 18,21–24] and the proposed method try to estimate source reliability in an unsupervised manner. The difference from existing approaches is that the proposed approach estimates source reliability jointly with heterogeneous data, which is discussed as follows.

DEFINITION 7 (SOURCE WEIGHTS).
Source weights are denoted as $\mathcal{W} = \{w_1, w_2, \ldots, w_K\}$ in which w_k is the reliability degree of the k-th source. A higher w_k indicates that the k-th source is more reliable and observations from this source is more likely to be accurate.

Remark. As for the approaches that incorporate source reliability estimation, if this estimation is only conducted on individual properties separately, the estimated reliability result is not accurate enough due to insufficient observations. In the example shown in Table 1, if we only consider citizenship, the reliability degrees of Sources 1 and 3 cannot be easily distinguished. In contrast, if we consider all the properties in the source reliability estimation, we can find that Source 1 is better than Source 3 in terms of the ability of providing accurate information. To characterize this phenomenon, the proposed framework unifies heterogeneous properties in the source reliability estimation. It will output both source weights and a truth table which are computed simultaneously by estimating source reliability from all the properties.

2.2 CRH Framework

The basic idea behind the proposed framework is that reliable sources provide trustworthy observations, so the truths should be close to the observations from reliable sources, and thus we should minimize the weighted deviation from the truths to the multi-source input where the weight reflects the reliability degree of sources. Based on this principle, we propose the following optimization framework that can unify heterogeneous properties in this process:

$$\min_{\mathcal{X}^{(*)},\mathcal{W}} \quad f(\mathcal{X}^{(*)},\mathcal{W}) = \sum_{k=1}^{K} w_k \sum_{i=1}^{N}\sum_{m=1}^{M} d_m(v_{im}^{(*)}, v_{im}^{(k)})$$
$$\text{s.t.} \quad \delta(\mathcal{W}) = 1, \quad \mathcal{W} \in \mathcal{S}. \qquad (1)$$

We are trying to search for the values for two sets of unknown variables $\mathcal{X}^{(*)}$ and $\mathcal{W}$, which correspond to the collection of truths and source weights respectively, by minimizing the objective function $f(\mathcal{X}^{(*)}, \mathcal{W})$. There are two types of functions that need to be plugged into this framework:

- *Loss function.* d_m refers to a loss function defined based on the data type of the m-th property. This function measures the distance between the truth $v_{im}^{(*)}$ and the observation $v_{im}^{(k)}$. This loss function should output a high value when the observation deviates from the truth and a low value when the observation is close to the truth.
- *Regularization function.* $\delta(\mathcal{W})$ reflects the distributions of source weights. It is also required mathematically. If each source weight w_k is unconstrained, then the optimization problem is unbounded because we can simply take w_k to be $-\infty$. To constrain the source weights $\mathcal{W}$ into a certain range, we need to specify the regularization function $\delta(\mathcal{W})$ and the domain $\mathcal{S}$. Note that we set the value of $\delta(\mathcal{W})$ to be 1 for the sake of simplicity. Different constants for $\delta(\mathcal{W})$ do not affect the results, as we can divide $\delta(\mathcal{W})$ by the constant.

These two types of functions should be chosen based on our knowledge on the characteristics of heterogeneous data and the source reliability distributions, and more details about these functions will be discussed later. Intuitively, if a source is more reliable (i.e., w_k is high), high penalty will be received if this source's observation is quite different from the truth (i.e., difference between $v_{im}^{(*)}$ and $v_{im}^{(k)}$ is big). In contrast, the observation made by an unreliable source with a low w_k is allowed to be different from the truth. In order to minimize the objective function, the truths $\mathcal{X}^{(*)}$ will rely more on the sources with high weights.

The truths $\mathcal{X}^{(*)}$ and source weights $\mathcal{W}$ should be learned together by optimizing the objective function through a joint procedure. In an optimization problem that involves two sets of variables, it is natural to iteratively update the values of one set to minimize the objective function while maintaining the values of another set

Algorithm 1 CRH Framework

Input: Data from K sources: $\{\mathcal{X}^{(1)}, \ldots, \mathcal{X}^{(K)}\}$.
Output: Truths $\mathcal{X}^{(*)} = \{v_{im}^{(*)}\}_{i=1,m=1}^{N,M}$, source weights $\mathcal{W} = \{w_1, \ldots, w_K\}$.

```
Initialize the truths X^(*);
repeat
    Update source weights W according to Eq(2) to reflect sources' reliability
    based on the estimated truths;
    for i ← 1 to N do
        for m ← 1 to M do
            Update the truth of the i-th object on the m-th property v_im^(*) according
            to Eq(3) based on the current estimation of source weights;
        end for
    end for
until Convergence criterion is satisfied;
return X^(*) and W.
```

until convergence. This iterative two-step procedure, referred to as block coordinate descent approach [2], will keep reducing the value of the objective function. To minimize the objective function in Eq(1), we iteratively conduct the following two steps.

Step I: Source Weights Update. With an initial estimate of the truths $\mathcal{X}^{(*)}$, we first weight each source based on the difference between the truths and the observations made by the source:

$$\mathcal{W} \leftarrow \arg\min_{\mathcal{W}} f(\mathcal{X}^{(*)}, \mathcal{W}) \quad \text{s.t.} \quad \delta(\mathcal{W}) = 1, \quad \mathcal{W} \in \mathcal{S}. \quad (2)$$

At this step, we fix the values for the truths and compute the source weights that jointly minimize the objective function subject to the regularization constraints.

Step II: Truths Update. At this step, the weight of each source w_k is fixed, and we update the truth for each entry to minimize the difference between the truth and the sources' observations where sources are weighted by their reliability degrees:

$$v_{im}^{(*)} \leftarrow \arg\min_{v} \sum_{k=1}^{K} w_k \cdot d_m(v, v_{im}^{(k)}). \quad (3)$$

By deriving the truth using this equation for every entry, we can obtain the collection of truths $\mathcal{X}^{(*)}$ which minimizes $f(\mathcal{X}^{(*)}, \mathcal{W})$ with fixed $\mathcal{W}$.

The pseudo code of this framework is summarized in Algorithm 1. We start with an initial estimate of truths and then iteratively conduct the source weight update and truth update steps until convergence. In the following, we explain the two steps in detail using example functions, and discuss the convergence and other practical issues of the proposed approach.

2.3 Source Weight Assignment

We propose the following regularization function:

$$\delta(\mathcal{W}) = \sum_{k=1}^{K} \exp(-w_k). \quad (4)$$

This function regularizes the value of w_k by constraining the sum of $\exp(-w_k)$.

THEOREM 1. *Suppose that the truths are fixed, the optimization problem Eq(1) with constraint Eq(4) is convex. Furthermore, the global optimal solution is given by*

$$w_k = -\log\left(\frac{\sum_{i=1}^{N}\sum_{m=1}^{M} d_m(v_{im}^{(*)}, v_{im}^{(k)})}{\sum_{k'=1}^{K}\sum_{i=1}^{N}\sum_{m=1}^{M} d_m(v_{im}^{(*)}, v_{im}^{(k')})}\right). \quad (5)$$

PROOF. Since the truths are fixed, the optimization problem Eq(1) has only one set of variables $\mathcal{W}$. To prove the convexity of Eq(1), we introduce another variable t_k so that $t_k = \exp(-w_k)$. Now we express the optimization problem in terms of t_k:

$$\min_{\{t_k\}_{k=1}^{K}} \quad f(t_k) = \sum_{k=1}^{K} -\log(t_k) \sum_{i=1}^{N}\sum_{m=1}^{M} d_m(v_{im}^{(*)}, v_{im}^{(k)})$$
$$\text{s.t.} \quad \sum_{k=1}^{K} t_k = 1. \quad (6)$$

The constraint in Eq(6) is linear in t_k, which is affine. The objective function is a linear combination of negative logarithm functions and thus it is convex. Therefore, the optimization problem Eq(1) with Eq(4) is convex, and any local optimum is also global optimum [6].

We use the method of Lagrange multipliers to solve this optimization problem. The Lagrangian of Eq(6) is given as:

$$L(\{t_k\}_{k=1}^{K}, \lambda) = \sum_{k=1}^{K} -\log(t_k) \sum_{i=1}^{N}\sum_{m=1}^{M} d_m(v_{im}^{(*)}, v_{im}^{(k)}) + \lambda(\sum_{k=1}^{K} t_k - 1), \quad (7)$$

where λ is a Lagrange multiplier. Let the partial derivative of Lagrangian with respect to t_k be 0, and we can get:

$$\sum_{i=1}^{N}\sum_{m=1}^{M} d_m(v_{im}^{(*)}, v_{im}^{(k)}) = \lambda t_k. \quad (8)$$

From the constraint that $\sum_{k=1}^{K} t_k = 1$, we can derive that

$$\lambda = \sum_{k'=1}^{K}\sum_{i=1}^{N}\sum_{m=1}^{M} d_m(v_{im}^{(*)}, v_{im}^{(k')}). \quad (9)$$

Plugging Eq(9) and $w_k = -\log(t_k)$ into Eq(8), we obtain Eq(5). □

This weight computation equation indicates that a source's weight is inversely proportional to the difference between its observations and the truths at the log scale. The negative log function maps a number in the range of 0 and 1 to a range of 0 and ∞, so it helps to enlarge the difference in the source weights. A source whose observations are more often close to the truths will have a higher weight. Therefore, Eq(4) is a reasonable constraint function which leads to the meaningful and intuitive weight update formula.

In order to distinguish the source weights even better so that reliable sources can play a more important role in deriving the truths, we use the maximum rather than the sum of the deviations as the normalization factor when computing the weights. It still ensures that a source's weight is inversely proportional to the difference between its observations and the truths at the log scale.

EXAMPLE 6. *Considering the databases given in Table 1, if* Voting/Averaging *results are adopted as the initial truths, we can get weights 0.67, 0.41, and 0.01 for Sources 1, 2, and 3 respectively using the proposed weight computation equation (Eq(5)). As the proposed method is iterative, we show the converged source weights here (more details are given in Table 3 after we discuss all the steps in the iterative framework). Source 1 is the most reliable one and Source 3 is the least reliable one, as Source 1 makes the fewest errors while Source 3 makes the most errors.*

The aforementioned weight assignment scheme considers a combination of sources. By setting different regularization functions, we can conduct source selection under the framework. For example, the following function defined based on L^p-norm can be used to select sources:

$$\delta(\mathcal{W}) = \sqrt[p]{w_1^p + w_2^p + \ldots + w_K^p} = 1,$$
$$w_k \in \mathbb{R}^+ \ (k = 1, \ldots, K), \qquad (10)$$

where p is a positive integer. When p equals to 1 or 2, it corresponds to the most widely used L^1-norm or L^2-norm. If L^p-norm regularization is employed, the optimal value of the problem in Eq(1) will be 0, which is achieved when we select one of the sources and set its weight to be 1, set all the other source weights to be 0, and simply regard the chosen source's observations as the truths. Different from the regularization function shown in Eq(4), this regularization function does not combine multiple sources but rather assumes that there only exists one reliable source.

We can also incorporate integer constraints to conduct source selection with more than one source, i.e., choose j sources out of all K sources:

$$\delta(\mathcal{W}) = \frac{1}{j}(w_1 + w_2 + \ldots + w_K) = 1,$$
$$w_k \in \{0, 1\} \ (k = 1, \ldots, K). \qquad (11)$$

If $w_k = 1$, the k-th source is selected in truth computation, otherwise its observations will be ignored when updating the truths in the next step. Due to the integer constraints defined in Eq(11), Eq(1) becomes an NP-hard problem. Approximation algorithms can be developed to solve this problem, the details of which are omitted.

In many problems, we will benefit from integrating the observations from multiple sources, but there is a variation in the overall reliability degrees. Therefore, in this paper, we focus on the weight assignment scheme with max normalization factor where sources are integrated and variation is emphasized.

2.4 Truth Computation

The truth computation step (Eq(3)) depends on the data type and loss function. We respect the characteristics of each data type and utilize different loss functions to describe different notions of deviation from the truths for different data types. Accordingly, truth computation will differ among various data types. Below we discuss truth computation in detail based on several loss functions for categorical and continuous data, the two most common data types.

On categorical data, the most commonly used loss function is 0-1 loss in which an error is incurred if the observation is different from the truth. Formally, if the m-th property is categorical, the deviation from the truth $v_{im}^{(*)}$ to the observation $v_{im}^{(k)}$ is defined as:

$$d_m(v_{im}^{(*)}, v_{im}^{(k)}) = \begin{cases} 1 & \text{if } v_{im}^{(k)} \neq v_{im}^{(*)}, \\ 0 & \text{otherwise}. \end{cases} \qquad (12)$$

THEOREM 2. *Suppose that the weights are fixed, based on 0-1 loss function, to minimize the objective function at this step (Eq(3)), the truth on the m-th property of the i-th object should be the value that receives the highest weighted votes among all possible values:*

$$v_{im}^{(*)} \leftarrow \arg\max_{v} \sum_{k=1}^{K} w_k \cdot \mathbb{1}(v, v_{im}^{(k)}), \qquad (13)$$

where $\mathbb{1}(x, y) = 1$ if $x = y$, and 0 otherwise.

PROOF. We plug Eq(12) into the objective function in Eq(1):

$$v_{im}^{(*)} \leftarrow \arg\min_{v} \sum_{k=1}^{K} w_k \cdot d_m(v, v_{im}^{(k)}), \qquad (14)$$

which is equivalent to Eq(13). □

This computation follows the principle that an observation stated by reliable sources will be regarded as the truth.

EXAMPLE 7. *If we use the weights 0.67, 0.41, and 0.01 for Sources 1, 2, and 3 from Example 6, the proposed approach will output the citizenship for Joe as "DC" (different from "NYC" output by voting), because Source 1's weight is higher than the sum of Source 2 and 3's weights. With an accurate source weight estimation, we correct the mistake given by Voting/Averaging.*

For the scenarios where multiple values of $v_{im}^{(*)}$ are probable, we introduce a strategy to incorporate probability into truth computation. This strategy is probabilistic-based and we assume that observations from reliable sources should have higher probability to be true. We represent categorical data by binary index vectors, which characterize the probability distributions of observations over all possible values. Formally, if the m-th property has L_m possible values and $v_{im}^{(k)}$ is the l-th value, then the index vector $I_{im}^{(k)}$ for $v_{im}^{(k)}$ is defined as:

$$I_{im}^{(k)} = (0, \ldots, \overset{l}{1}, 0, \ldots, 0)^T. \qquad (15)$$

We can use squared loss function to describe the distance between the observation index vector $I_{im}^{(k)}$ and the truth vector $I_{im}^{(*)}$:

$$\begin{aligned} d_m(v_{im}^{(*)}, v_{im}^{(k)}) &= d_m(I_{im}^{(*)}, I_{im}^{(k)}) \\ &= (I_{im}^{(*)} - I_{im}^{(k)})^T (I_{im}^{(*)} - I_{im}^{(k)}). \end{aligned} \qquad (16)$$

THEOREM 3. *Suppose that the weights are fixed, the optimization problem Eq(1) with Eq(16) is convex. The optimal $I_{im}^{(*)}$ should be the weighted mean of the probability vectors of all the sources:*

$$I_{im}^{(*)} \leftarrow \frac{\sum_{k=1}^{K} w_k \cdot I_{im}^{(k)}}{\sum_{k=1}^{K} w_k}. \qquad (17)$$

PROOF. Since the weights are fixed, the optimization problem Eq(1) has only one set of variables $\mathcal{X}$ and the optimization problem is unconstrained. As $d_m(I_{im}^{(*)}, I_{im}^{(k)})$ is convex, Eq(1) is a linear combination of convex functions, and thus it is convex.

We plug Eq(16) into the objective function in Eq(1) and then let the partial derivative with respect to $I_{im}^{(*)}$ be 0:

$$\sum_{k=1}^{K} w_k \sum_{i=1}^{N} \sum_{m=1}^{M} 2(I_{im}^{(*)} - I_{im}^{(k)})^T = 0, \qquad (18)$$

which leads to Eq(17). □

Here, $I_{im}^{(*)}$ denotes the probability distribution of the truths, in which $v_{im}^{(*)}$ is the corresponding value with the largest probability in $I_{im}^{(*)}$, i.e., the most possible value.

EXAMPLE 8. *We use the same scenario as in Example 7. Source weights are 0.67, 0.41, and 0.01; the observations are "DC", "NYC", and "NYC" from the corresponding sources. If "DC" is coded as (1,0) and "NYC" as (0,1), we can calculate the truth vector for that entry as $I_{im}^{(*)} = \frac{(1,0)\times 0.67 + (0,1)\times 0.41 + (0,1)\times 0.01}{0.67+0.41+0.01} = (0.61, 0.39)$. Therefore, the truth is "DC" with a probability of 0.61.*

Comparing with the 0-1 loss strategy, this strategy gives a soft decision instead of a hard decision. However, this method has relatively high space complexity due to the representation of categories for input data.

As for the continuous data, the loss function should characterize the distance from the input to the truth with respect to the variance of entries across sources. One common loss function is the normalized squared loss, which is defined as:

$$d_m(v_{im}^{(*)}, v_{im}^{(k)}) = \frac{(v_{im}^{(*)} - v_{im}^{(k)})^2}{std(v_{im}^{(1)}, \ldots, v_{im}^{(K)})}. \quad (19)$$

THEOREM 4. *Suppose that the weights are fixed, the optimization problem Eq(1) with Eq(19) is convex. The truth that minimizes the overall weighted distance should be the weighted average of the observations:*

$$v_{im}^{(*)} \leftarrow \frac{\sum_{k=1}^{K} w_k \cdot v_{im}^{(k)}}{\sum_{k=1}^{K} w_k}. \quad (20)$$

PROOF. The proof of convexity is similar to the proof in Theorem 3. We plug Eq(19) into the objective function Eq(1) and then let the partial derivative with respect to $v_{im}^{(*)}$ be 0:

$$\sum_{k=1}^{K} w_k \sum_{i=1}^{N} \sum_{m=1}^{M} 2(v_{im}^{(*)} - v_{im}^{(k)})/std(v_{im}^{(1)}, \ldots, v_{im}^{(K)}) = 0. \quad (21)$$

Therefore, we can get the optimal truth shown in Eq(20). □

EXAMPLE 9. *Consider Bob's height from Table 1. The observations from Sources 1, 2, and 3 are 1.72, 1.70, and 1.90 respectively. Suppose the weights are 0.67, 0.41, and 0.01 for Sources 1, 2, and 3 respectively. Then Bob's height can be calculated as:* $\frac{1.72\times0.67+1.70\times0.41+1.90\times0.01}{0.67+0.41+0.01} = 1.71$. *It is obvious that the result is closer towards the observation from Source 1 because it is more reliable.*

This truth computation strategy simulates the idea that observations from a reliable source should contribute more to the computation of the truth. However, this method is sensitive to the existence of outliers, as an outlier will receive a huge loss because of the square term, and thus can only work well in the data set in which outliers are removed.

To mitigate the effect of outliers, we can use the normalized absolute deviation as the loss function on continuous data:

$$d_m(v_{im}^{(*)}, v_{im}^{(k)}) = \frac{|v_{im}^{(*)} - v_{im}^{(k)}|}{std(v_{im}^{(1)}, \ldots, v_{im}^{(K)})}. \quad (22)$$

THEOREM 5. *Based on Eq(22), the truth that minimizes the overall weighted absolute deviation should be the weighted median.*

Proof is omitted as the derivation is similar to the previous cases. Specifically, we use the following definition of weighted median[2]. Given a set of numbers $\{v^1, ..., v^K\}$ with weights $\{w_1, ...w_K\}$, the weighted median of this set is the number v^j, such that

$$\sum_{k:v^k<v^j} w_k < \frac{1}{2}\sum_{k=1}^{K} w_k \quad \& \quad \sum_{k:v^k>v^j} w_k \leqslant \frac{1}{2}\sum_{k=1}^{K} w_k. \quad (23)$$

The sum of weights on the numbers that are smaller than the weighted median, and the sum of weights on the numbers that are greater than the weighted median should both be roughly half of the total weights on the whole set. To find the weighted median, we compare the cumulative sum computed on numbers smaller than v^j or greater than v^j. Note that conventional median can be regarded as a special case where we give the same weight to all the numbers so that median becomes the number separating the higher half from the lower half. It is known that median is less sensitive to the existence of outliers, and thus the weighted median approach for truth computation is more desirable in noisy environments.

[2]http://www.mathworks.com/matlabcentral/fileexchange /23077-weighted-median/content/weightedMedian.m

EXAMPLE 10. *Using the same example as in Example 9, we first sort all observations in ascending order: (1.70, 1.72, 1.90), and the corresponding source weight is (0.41, 0.67, 0.01). Then Bob's height by weighted median using Eq(23) is 1.72.*

Besides the aforementioned loss functions, the proposed general framework can take any loss function that is selected based on data types and distributions. Some other examples include Mahalanobis distance for continuous data, edit distance or KL divergence for text data, etc. To deal with complex data types, we can either use loss functions defined on raw data or on abstraction of raw data, such as motifs in time series, frequent sub-graphs in graphs, and segments in images. The framework can even be adapted to take the ensemble of multiple loss functions for a more robust loss computation. We can also convert a similarity function into a loss function, which allows the usage of numerous techniques in similarity computation developed in the data integration community.

2.5 Discussions & Practical Issues

Here we first discuss several important issues to make the framework practical including *initialization, convergence, normalization,* and *missing values.* Then we show the algorithm flow using a running example. Finally, we analyze the time complexity of the proposed CRH framework.

Initialization. The initialization of the truths can be obtained using existing conflict resolution approaches. In our experiments, we find that the result from Voting/Averaging approaches is typically a good start. In fact, initialization will not affect the final results if the optimization problem is convex.

Convexity and Convergence. The convexity depends on the loss functions and regularization function. An example of a family of convex loss functions is *Bregman divergence* [1], which includes a variety of loss functions such as squared loss, logistic loss, Itakura-Saito distance, squared Euclidean distance, Mahalanobis distance, KL-divergence and generalized I-divergence. Using several loss functions discussed in this paper, we prove the convergence of the CRH framework as follows. Note that the proof on the convergence can be derived in the same way if other convex functions are used.

THEOREM 6. *When Eq(4) is used as constraint, Eq(16) or/and Eq(19) is/are used as loss functions, the convergence of CRH framework is guaranteed.*

PROOF. For the optimization problem of Eq(1), we proved earlier in Theorem 1 that the unique minimum with respect to weights $\mathcal{W}$ can be achieved when truths $\mathcal{X}^{(*)}$ are fixed; we proved in Theorem 3 and Theorem 4 that the unique minimum with respect to truths $\mathcal{X}^{(*)}$ can be achieved when weights $\mathcal{W}$ are fixed. According to the proposition on the convergence of block coordinate descent [2], we can derive that the proposed iterative procedure will converge to a stationary point of the optimization problem. □

In Algorithm 1, the convergence criterion is that the decrease in the objective function is small enough compared with the previous iterations. In the experiments we find that the convergence of this approach is easy to judge because the first several iterations incur a huge decrease in the objective function, and once it converges, the results become stable. Experimental results on convergence are shown in Section 3.2.3.

Although the analysis on non-convex or non-differentiable functions need to be conducted differently [17,20], we find that some of these approaches work well in practice, such as the absolute deviation for continuous data.

Normalization. Another important issue is the normalization of deviations on each property. As illustrated in the weight computation equation (Eq(5)), we need to sum up the deviations to the truths across different properties. If various loss functions applied on different properties have significantly different scales, the weight computation will be biased towards the property that has bigger range in the deviation. To solve this issue, we normalize the output of each loss function on each property so that the deviation computed on all the properties fall into the same range.

Missing Values. Note that for the sake of simplicity, we assume that all the sources observe all the objects on all the properties in the proposed optimization framework (Eq(1)), but it can be easily modified to handle missing values when different sources observe different subsets of the objects on different subsets of properties. When the number of observations made by different sources is quite different, we can normalize the overall distance of each source by the number of observations.

Running Example. Using the same databases in Table 1, we display both the truth tables and the source weights for the first three iterations using Voting/Averaging as initialization. We use weighted vote for categorical data and weighted median for continuous data to update truths. The algorithm updates source weights and truths repeatedly until the convergence criterion is satisfied. The results are shown in Table 3 and 4. Comparing with the ground truths in Table 2, the truth table gets more and more accurate with more iterations. The algorithm converges after three iterations.

Table 3: Source Weights for the First Three Iterations

	Iteration 1	Iteration 2	Iteration 3
Source 1	0.2729	0.5552	0.6734
Source 2	0.2521	0.4539	0.4077
Source 3	0.1349	0.0149	0.0141

Table 4: Truth Tables for the First Three Iterations

	Iteration 1		Iteration 2		Iteration 3	
Object	City	Height	City	Height	City	Height
Bob	NYC	1.72	NYC	1.72	NYC	1.72
Mary	LA	1.62	LA	1.62	LA	1.62
Kate	NYC	1.72	NYC	1.74	NYC	1.74
Mike	NYC	1.72	NYC	1.72	NYC	1.72
Joe	NYC	1.72	DC	1.72	DC	1.72

Time Complexity. When we utilize the aforementioned functions Eq(5), Eq(13) and Eq(23), the running time is linear with respect to the total number of observations, i.e., $O(KNM)$, where K is the number of sources, N is the number of objects, and M is the number of properties. In addition, the algorithm can be adapted to run on the MapReduce platform to further speed up the process on large-scale data sets. It is obvious that the truth computation step (Eq(3)) can be executed independently for each object and thus this step is easy to parallelize. If we use Eq(5) to compute source weights, this step can be expressed using summation form [7], and thus it can be parallelized by aggregating partial sums. The time complexity is experimentally validated in the following section, in which we show the running time of the proposed approach on both single machine and Hadoop cluster.

2.6 Summary

Our major contribution is that we unify data of various types in truth discovery to resolve conflicts on heterogeneous data. The proposed optimization framework (Eq(1)), which targets at minimizing overall weighted difference between truths and input data, provides a nice way to combine data of various types when deriving source weights and truths. Under this general framework, we discussed several common data types and loss functions, derived effective solutions, and analyzed its convergence. Different from existing truth discovery approaches that focus on facts [9, 12, 18, 22] or continuous data [23], the proposed CRH model learns source reliability degrees jointly from various properties with different data types. Unique characteristics of each data type is considered, and all types contribute to source reliability estimation together. This joint inference improves source reliability estimation and leads to better truth discovery on heterogeneous data.

3. EXPERIMENTS

In this section, we report the experimental results on both real-world and simulated data sets, which show that the proposed CRH method is efficient and outperforms state-of-the-art conflict resolution methods when integrating multiple sources of heterogeneous data. We first discuss the experiment setup in Section 3.1, and then present experimental results in Section 3.2.

3.1 Experiment Setup

In this part, we present the performance measures and discuss the baseline methods.

3.1.1 Performance Measures

The problem setting is that we have multi-source input and the ground truths. All the conflict resolution methods are conducted in an unsupervised manner in the sense that the ground truths will only be used in evaluation. In this experiment, we focus on two types of data: categorical and continuous. To evaluate the performance of various conflict resolution methods, we adopt the following measures for these two data types:

- Error Rate: For categorical data, we use *Error Rate* as the performance measure of an approach, which is computed as the percentage of the approach's output that are different from the ground truths.
- MNAD: For continuous data, we can measure the overall absolute distance from each method's output to the ground truths, which indicates how close the output are to the ground truths. As different entries may have different scales, we normalize the distance on each entry by its own variance, and then calculate their mean. This leads to the measure *Mean Normalized Absolute Distance (MNAD)*.

For both measures, the **lower** the value, the closer the method's estimation is to the ground truths and thus the **better** the performance.

3.1.2 Baseline Methods

For the proposed CRH method, we use weighted voting (Eq(13)) for categorical data due to its time and space efficiency. On continuous data, we use weighted median (Eq(23)), which is efficient and robust in noisy environment with outliers. Weight assignment is computed by the inverse logarithm of the ratio between the deviation to the truth and the maximum distance so that the difference in source reliability is emphasized. We compare the proposed approach with the following baseline methods that cover a wide variety of ways to resolve conflicts. These approaches can be partitioned into three categories.

Conflict Resolution Methods Applied on Continuous Data Only. The following approaches can only be applied on continuous data, and thus they will ignore the input from categorical properties.

- Mean: Mean simply takes the mean of all observations on each property of each object as the final output.
- Median: Median calculates the median of all observations on each property of each object as the final output.

- GTM [23]: Gaussian Truth Model (GTM) is a Bayesian probabilistic approach especially designed for solving conflict resolution problem on continuous data. Note that this approach only uses partial data (continuous) while other truth discovery methods use all the data (categorical and continuous), and thus insufficient data may lead to performance degrade in GTM compared with others. However, we still include GTM in the comparison as it is an important truth discovery method applied on continuous data.

Among them, Mean and Median are traditional conflict resolution approaches, and GTM is a truth discovery approach which considers source reliability estimation.

Conflict Resolution Methods Applied on Categorical Data Only. We apply majority voting approach on categorical properties only. This is the traditional way of resolving conflicts in categorical data without source reliability estimation.

- Voting: The value which has the highest number of occurrences is regarded as the fused output.

Conflict Resolution Methods by Truth Discovery. Many of the existing conflict resolution approaches that consider source reliability (often referred to as "truth discovery" approaches) are developed to find true "facts" for categorical properties. However, we can enforce them to handle data of heterogeneous types by regarding continuous observations as "facts" too.

- Investment [18]: In this approach, a source "invests" its reliability uniformly on the observations it provides, and collects credits back from the confidence of those observations. In turn, the confidence of an observation grows according to a non-linear function defined based on the sum of invested reliability from its providers.
- PooledInvestment [18]: PooledInvestment is similar to Investment. The only difference is that the confidence of an observation is linearly scaled instead of non-linearly scaled.
- 2-Estimates [12]: This approach is proposed based on the assumption that "there is one and only one true value for each entry". If a source provides an observation for an entry, 2-Estimates assumes that this source votes against different observations on this entry.
- 3-Estimates [12]: 3-Estimates improves 2-Estimates by considering the difficulty of getting the truth for each entry, the estimation of which will affect the source's weight.
- TruthFinder [22]: TruthFinder adopts Bayesian analysis, in which for each observation, its confidence is calculated as the product of its providers' reliability degrees. Similarity function is used to adjust the vote of a value by considering the influences between facts.
- AccuSim [9]: AccuSim also applies Bayesian analysis and it also adopts the usage of the similarity function. Meanwhile, it considers complement vote which is adopted by 2-Estimates and 3-Estimates. Note that in [9], other algorithms have been proposed to tackle source dependency issues in resolving conflicts, which are not compared here because we do not consider source dependency in this paper but leave it for future work.

The comparison between the proposed framework with these baseline approaches on heterogeneous data can show that 1) using both types of data jointly gives better source reliability estimation than using individual data types separately, but 2) an accurate weight can only be obtained by taking unique characteristics of each data type into consideration.

We implement all the baselines and set the parameters according to their authors' suggestions. All the experimental results in this section except for MapReduce experiments are conducted on a Windows machine with 8G RAM, Intel Core i7 processor.

3.2 Experimental Results

In this section, by comparing the proposed CRH approach with the baseline methods, we show the power of simultaneously modeling various data types in a joint framework on both real-world and simulated data sets. We also show the efficiency of the proposed approach on single machine and Hadoop cluster.

3.2.1 Real-world Data Sets

We use three real-world data sets to demonstrate the effectiveness of the proposed method.

Weather Forecast Data Set. Weather forecast integration task is a good test bed because the data contains heterogeneous types of properties. Specifically, we integrate weather forecasting data collected from three platforms: Wunderground[3], HAM weather[4], and World Weather Online[5]. On each of them, we crawl the forecasts of three different days as three different sources, so altogether there are nine sources. For each source, we collected data of three properties: high temperature, low temperature and weather condition, among which the first two are continuous and the last is categorical. To get ground truths, we crawl the true weather information for each day. We collected the data for twenty US cities over a month.

Stock Data Set. The stock data [15], crawled on every work day in July 2011, consists of 1000 stock symbols and 16 properties from 55 sources, and the ground truths are also provided. Here, we treat the data set as heterogeneous. More specifically, property *volume*, *Shares outstanding* and *Market cap* are considered as continuous type, and the rest ones are considered as categorical type.

Flight Data Set. The flight data [15], crawled over one-month period starting from December 2011, consists of 1200 flights and 6 properties from 38 sources. We conduct pre-processing on the data to convert the gate information into the same format and the time information into minutes. The ground truths are also available. In this work, we show results on the flight data by treating gate information as categorical type and time information as continuous type. Note that we have a different task setting compared with [15] for Stock and Flight data when we treat them as heterogeneous types.

Table 5 shows the statistics of these three data sets. Note that the number of entries does not equal to the number of ground truths because we only have a subset of entries labeled with ground truths. The ground truths are not used by any of the approaches, but only used in the evaluation.

Table 5: Statistics of Real-world Data Sets

	Weather Data	Stock Data	Flight Data
# Observations	16038	11748734	2790734
# Entries	1920	326423	204422
# Ground Truths	1740	29198	16572

In Table 6, we summarize the performance of all the methods in terms of *Error Rate* on categorical data and *MNAD* on continuous data for three real-wold data sets. Although our approach outputs truths on both data types simultaneously, we evaluate the

[3]http://www.wunderground.com
[4]http://www.hamweather.com
[5]http://www.worldweatheronline.com

Table 6: Performance Comparison on Real-world Data Sets

Method	Weather Data		Stock Data		Flight Data	
	Error Rate	MNAD	Error Rate	MNAD	Error Rate	MNAD
CRH	**0.3759**	**4.6947**	**0.0700**	**2.6445**	**0.0823**	**4.8613**
Mean	NA	4.7840	NA	7.1858	NA	8.2894
Median	NA	4.9878	NA	3.9334	NA	7.8471
GTM	NA	4.7914	NA	3.4253	NA	7.6703
Voting	0.4844	NA	0.0817	NA	0.0859	NA
Investment	0.4913	5.2361	0.0983	2.8081	0.0919	6.4153
PooledInvestment	0.4948	5.5788	0.0990	2.7940	0.0925	5.8562
2-Estimates	0.5327	5.5258	0.0726	2.8509	0.0885	7.4347
3-Estimates	0.4810	5.1943	0.0818	2.7749	0.0881	7.1983
TruthFinder	0.4586	5.1293	0.1194	2.7140	0.0950	8.1351
AccuSim	0.4672	5.0862	0.0726	2.8503	0.0881	7.3204

performance separately on these two data types due to the different measures for different data types. It can be seen that the proposed CRH approach achieves better performance on both types of data compared with all the baselines. For example, on weather data, the number of mismatches from ground truths drops from 266 (the best baseline) to 218 out of 580 entries by using CRH (on categorical data). On Stock and Flight data sets where baselines have already achieved good performance, we still can see the performance improvement of CRH over the best baseline (1719 ->1657 out of 23677, and 427 ->414 out of 4971). Similarly, the gain on continuous data can be consistently observed on all three data sets.

By outperforming various conflict resolution approaches applied separately on categorical data and continuous data, the proposed CRH approach demonstrates its advantage in modeling source reliability more accurately by jointly inferring from both types of data. GTM can not estimate source reliability accurately merely by continuous data which may not have sufficient information. This also justifies our assumption that each source's reliability on continuous and categorical data is consistent so the estimation over different data types complements each other.

The reason that the proposed CRH approach beats the other conflict resolution approaches that are applied on both types of data is that these approaches cannot capture the unique characteristics of each data type. This is further supported by the fact that the performance of those approaches is relatively better on categorical data, but deviates more from the truths on the continuous data. In contrast to existing approaches, the proposed CRH framework can take data type into consideration, which will provide a better estimation of source reliability, and thus result in more accurate truth estimation.

As source reliability is the key to obtain correct truths, we further show the source reliability degrees estimated for the 9 sources by various approaches on the weather forecast data set. We choose this data set because it consists of nine sources only, which is more practical to demonstrate. We first compute the true source reliability by comparing the observations made by each source with the ground truths. Reliability of a source is defined as the probability that the source makes correct statements on categorical data, and the chance that the source makes statements close to the truth on continuous data. To simplify the presentation, we combine the reliability scores of continuous and categorical data into one score for each source. To make it clear, we show the source reliability degrees in three plots presented in Figure 1, each of which shows the comparison between the ground truths and some of the approaches.

Figure 1(a) shows that the source reliability degree estimated by CRH method is in general consistent with that obtained from the ground truths. By effectively characterizing different data types in a joint model, the proposed approach can successfully distinguish good sources from bad ones, and accordingly derive the truth based on good sources. In Figures 1(b) and 1(c), we show the reliability degrees of 9 sources estimated by GTM, AccuSim, 3-Estimates and PooledInvestment compared with the ground truth reliability. We particularly show the results on these approaches because 3-Estimates and PooledInvestment are improved solutions compared with 2-Estimates and Investment respectively claimed in the corresponding papers, and TruthFinder has similar performance with AccuSim on this data set. As different methods adopt various functions to estimate the source reliability scores, to make them comparable, we normalize all the scores into the range $[0, 1]$. Among these approaches, 3-Estimates and GTM calculate the unreliability degrees, so we convert their scores to reliability degrees to show the comparison. The plots show that the baseline methods can capture the difference among sources in making accurate claims to a certain extent, but the patterns in source reliability detected by them are not very consistent with the ground truths, which can thus explain the increased error in truth detection in Table 6.

Note that the improved performance of the proposed approach is achieved when each individual data type's characteristics are fully taken into account in the joint modeling of heterogeneous data. To demonstrate this point, we show that using heterogeneous data without distinguishing data types cannot help improve the performance. As shown in Table 7, the baseline approaches, which regard all data types the same, have similar performance when they are applied on heterogeneous data and on categorical data only. This indicates that the incorporation of continuous data does not make difference for these approaches. To further investigate this behavior, we plot the source weights obtained by AccuSim, 3-Estimates, and PooledInvestment on categorical data and heterogeneous data respectively in Figure 2. From the plots, we can see that for any of these approaches, these two groups of source reliability scores are close to each other. The reason behind this phenomenon is that unlike categorical data, continuous data are noisier and wider distributed, and sources disagree much more on the values. When these approaches ignore the characteristics of different data types, they cannot find meaningful truths. Thus, the deviations are rather random and uniform across different sources. When summing up the deviations on both categorical and continuous data to compute source weights, the inputs from the continuous side do not significantly affect the source weight distribution because it is quite similar across sources. In other words, the incorporation of continuous data without considering their characteristics can hardly benefit or even harm the weight estimation. Therefore, these approaches get similar source weight distributions with and without continuous data and the results are not improved. This phenomenon further proves that only utilizing heterogeneous data by considering the characteristics of different data types in source reliability estimation can obtain a good result. That is the reason why the proposed approach performs better than baseline approaches.

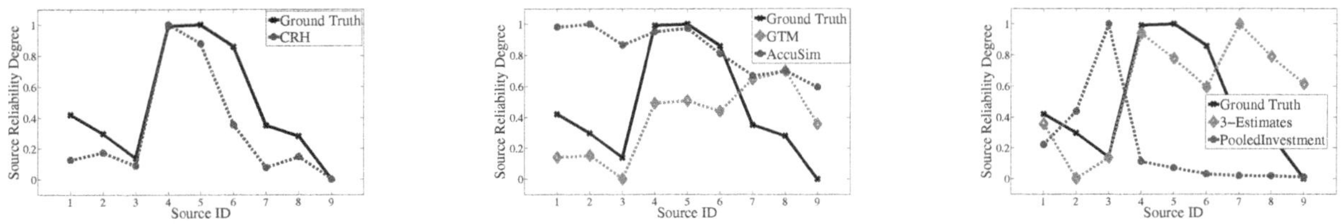

(a) CRH (b) Baselines (c) Baselines

Figure 1: Comparison of Source Reliability Degrees with Ground Truths

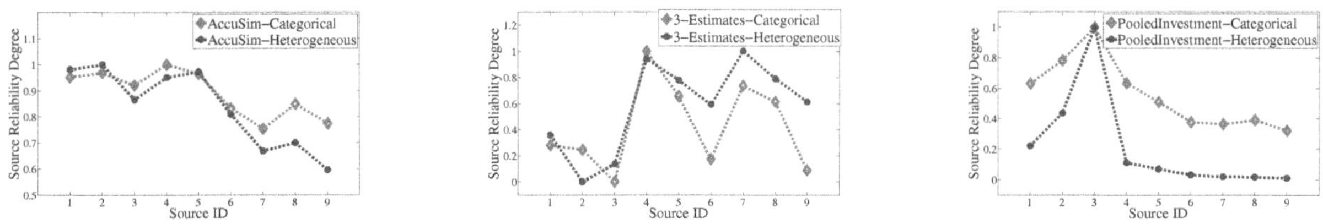

(a) AccuSim (b) 3-Estimates (c) PooledInvestment

Figure 2: Comparison of Source Reliability Degrees between Methods Applied on Categorical and Heterogeneous Data

Table 7: Comparison for Baselines on Weather Data

	Heterogeneous Data		Categorical Data	
Method	Error Rate	MNAD	Error Rate	MNAD
Investment	0.4913	5.2361	0.4776	NA
PooledInvestment	0.4948	5.5788	0.4914	NA
2-Estimates	0.5327	5.5258	0.5121	NA
3-Estimates	0.4810	5.1943	0.4638	NA
TruthFinder	0.4586	5.1293	0.4603	NA
AccuSim	0.4672	5.0862	0.4620	NA

3.2.2 *Noisy Multi-source Simulations*

To further demonstrate the advantages of the proposed framework in the environment involving various reliability degrees and different loss functions, we conduct experiments on simulated data sets generated from UCI machine learning data sets. We choose two data sets: UCI Adult[6] and Bank[7] data sets, each of which has both continuous and categorical properties. The original data sets are regarded as the ground truths, and based on each of them, we generate a data set consisting of multiple conflicting sources by injecting different levels of noise into the ground truths as the input to our approach and baseline methods. Gaussian noise is added to each continuous property, and values in categorical properties are randomly flipped to generate facts that deviate from the ground truths. To better simulate the real-world data, we round the continuous type data based on their physical meaning. A parameter α is used to control the reliability degree of each source (a lower α indicates a lower chance that the ground truths are altered to generate observations). In this way, we generate data sets which contain 8 sources with various degrees of reliability ($\alpha = \{0.1, 0.4, 0.7, 1, 1.3, 1.6, 1.9, 2\}$). Table 8 shows the statistics of these two data sets.

Table 8: Statistics of Simulated Data Sets

	Adult Data	Bank Data
# Observations	3646832	5787008
# Entries	455854	723376
# Ground Truths	455854	723376

Tables 9 summarizes the results of all the approaches on these two data sets. It can be seen that CRH can fully recover all the truths on categorical data, and find the true value for continuous data with very small distance by inferring accurate source reliability degrees. Similar to the experiments on the weather data set, we can still observe the great improvement in truth detection performance compared with baseline approaches due to the proposed method's advantage in source reliability estimation. Existing approaches cannot provide accurate estimate of source reliability because they either take incomplete data (only categorical or continuous), or do not model the characteristics of both data types jointly.

Table 9: Performance Comparison on Simulated Data Set

	Adult Data		Bank Data	
Method	Error Rate	MNAD	Error Rate	MNAD
CRH	**0.0000**	**0.0637**	**0.0000**	**0.0789**
Mean	NA	0.3673	NA	0.3671
Median	NA	0.2470	NA	0.2491
GTM	NA	0.0810	NA	0.0948
Voting	0.1029	NA	0.2314	NA
Investment	0.0530	0.1391	0.1197	0.1588
PooledInvestment	0.0215	0.1008	0.0241	0.0866
2-Estimates	0.0497	0.1355	0.1152	0.1583
3-Estimates	0.0497	0.1355	0.1152	0.1583
TruthFinder	0.0346	0.1272	0.1097	0.1589
AccuSim	0.0288	0.1145	0.0681	0.1571

On these simulated data sets, we also investigate how the performance of the proposed CRH approach varies with respect to different distributions of source reliability degrees. To illustrate the effect more clearly, we choose two reliability degrees: $\alpha = 0.1$ and $\alpha = 2$, which correspond to reliable and unreliable sources respectively. We now fix the total number of sources as 8, and change the number of reliable sources to conduct a series of experiments. Figures 3 and 4 show the performance of the proposed approach and baseline methods on Adult and Bank data sets respectively. In each of them, we show the performance on categorical and continuous data respectively when we vary the number of reliable sources from 0 to 8 (out of 8 sources in total).

The following observations can be made from the results: 1) The plots support our previous findings that the CRH framework outperforms existing conflict resolution techniques, which ignore the unique characteristics of each data type. When sources are equally reliable or unreliable (number of reliable sources equals to 0 or 8), the CRH model achieves similar performance as that of vot-

[6]http://archive.ics.uci.edu/ml/datasets/Adult

[7]http://archive.ics.uci.edu/ml/datasets/Bank+Marketing

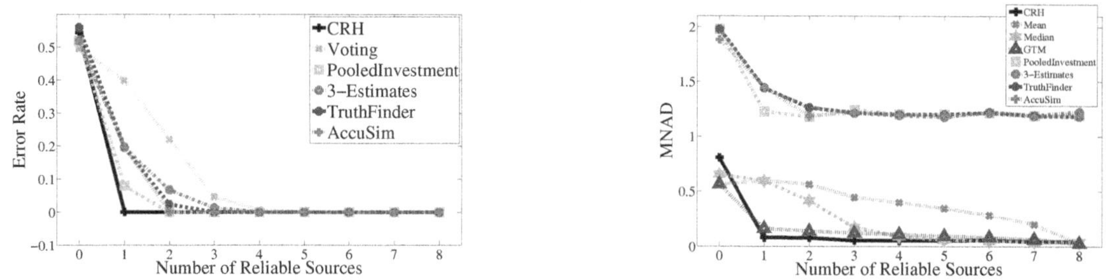

(a) Categorical Data (b) Continuous Data

Figure 3: Performance w.r.t. # Reliable Sources on Adult Data Set

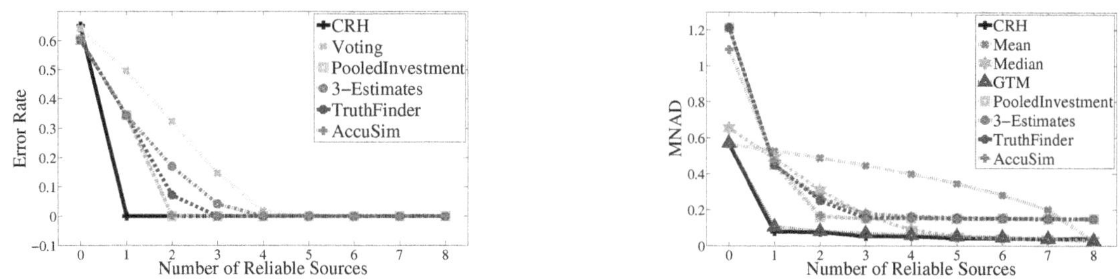

(a) Categorical Data (b) Continuous Data

Figure 4: Performance w.r.t. # Reliable Sources on Bank Data Set

Table 10: Comparison for Different Loss Functions

	Method	Error Rate	MNAD
Scenario 1	Eq(13) + Eq(20)	0.0125	0.1533
	Eq(13) + Eq(23)	0.0125	0.1938
	Eq(17) + Eq(20)	0.0375	0.1628
	Eq(17) + Eq(23)	0.0125	0.1938
Scenario 2	Eq(13) + Eq(20)	0.0375	0.3030
	Eq(13) + Eq(23)	0.0250	0.2052
	Eq(17) + Eq(20)	0.0375	0.2899
	Eq(17) + Eq(23)	0.0250	0.2052

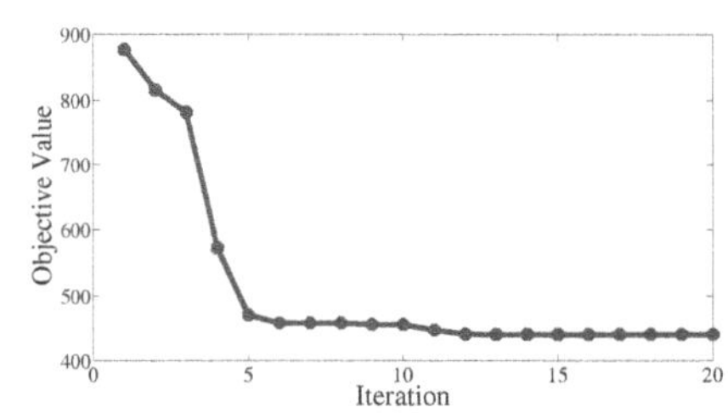

Figure 5: Convergence Rate

ing/averaging approaches. However, when the reliability degree varies across sources, CRH performs much better. 2) In general, it is easier to detect truths when we have a bigger number of reliable sources. However, on categorical data, even when only 1 out of 8 sources is reliable, CRH can still discover most of the truths. Clearly, the proposed approach can successfully infer source reliability and thus detect the truths that are stated by the minority. 3) On continuous data, we can see that the convergence rate is slower than that on categorical data. Conflict resolution on continuous data is in general more difficult due to the higher complexity of the truth space and more complicated definition of closeness to the truths.

Next we discuss the effect of loss functions and give some guidelines on how to choose appropriate loss functions under different scenarios (Table 10).

Under Scenario 1, we generate five sources with different levels of noise and the levels of noise are relatively low on all sources ($\alpha = \{0.5, 0.5, 0.5, 1, 1\}$), which means that sources have low variance on continuous data and tend to agree with each other on categorical data. The combination of Eq(13) and Eq(20) achieves the best performance (using traditional 0-1 and squared loss). Under Scenario 2, we add more noise on two out of the five sources ($\alpha = \{0.5, 0.5, 1, 3.5, 4.5\}$). These two sources contain outliers on continuous data, and many mistakes on categorical data. We find that Eq(13) + Eq(23) and Eq(17) + Eq(23) work better than the others. This is because that normalized absolute deviation gives a smaller penalty on outliers than normalized squared loss does, and thus is more tolerant of outliers.

3.2.3 Efficiency

In this section, we study the efficiency of the proposed CRH framework. We first explore its convergence rate in practice, and then show its running time on both single machine and Hadoop cluster.

Convergence Rate. As we proved in Theorem 6, the convergence of CRH framework is guaranteed when Eq(4) is used as constraint, Eq(16) or/and Eq(19) is/are used as loss functions. We further demonstrate the convergence rate using weather data set. Figure 5 shows the change of the objective value with respect to each iteration. We can see that the objective value decreases fast at the first five iterations and then reaches a stable stage, showing that the proposed method converges quickly in practice.

Running Time. We sample different number of observations and entries from weather data set to show the running time of the CRH framework on single machine. As shown in Table 11, the proposed approach has linear complexity in the number of observations. To further demonstrate this, we compute Pearson's correlation coefficient, which is a commonly used method to test linear relationship between variables. It ranges from 1 to -1. The closer it is to 1 (or -1), the stronger positive (or negative) linear relationship the variables have. In our experiment, the Pearson's correlation coefficient for running time and the number of observations is higher than 0.99, which indicates that they are highly linearly correlated.

As mentioned in the discussions of the CRH framework, it can be easily adapted to MapReduce programming model. As the number of observations can be easily varied in a large range, we use the simulated data sets to evaluate the running time of CRH on Hadoop cluster. Based on the Adult data set, we generate large-scale data sets by adding different noise levels on the original data set as we discussed. The number of observations vary from 10^4 to 10^8. The proposed CRH framework is implemented using MapReduce model. The experiments are conducted on a 4-node Dell Hadoop cluster with Intel Xeon E5-2403 processor (4x 1.80 GHz, 48 GB RAM). As shown in Table 11, the fusion process using the MapReduce version of the proposed approach can finish in a short time. The running time mainly comes from the setup overhead when the number of observations is not very large, but the speed-up in the execution time is more obvious when the number of observations increases. For example, on a data set with size 10^8, the whole process only took 669s.

Table 11: Running Time

Single Machine		Hadoop Cluster	
# Observations	Time (s)	# Observations	Time (s)
5×10^4	1.5575	1×10^4	94
7×10^4	2.3265	1×10^5	96
9×10^4	2.9505	1×10^6	100
1.2×10^5	3.4133	1×10^7	193
1.4×10^5	4.3827	1×10^8	669
1.6×10^5	4.6724	4×10^8	1384
Pearson Correlation	0.9903	Pearson Correlation	0.9811

4. CONCLUSIONS

To extract insightful knowledge from an overwhelming amount of information generated by numerous industries, it is crucial to automatically identify trustworthy information and sources from multiple conflicting data sources. As heterogeneous data is ubiquitous, a joint estimation on various data types can lead to better estimation of truths and source reliability. However, existing conflict resolution work either regards all the sources equally reliable, or models different data types individually. Therefore, we propose to model the conflict resolution problem on data of heterogeneous types using a general optimization framework called CRH that integrates the truth finding process on various data types seamlessly. In this model, truth is defined as the value that incurs the smallest weighted deviation from multi-source input in which weights represent source reliability degrees. We derive a two-step iterative procedure including the computation of truths and source weights as a solution to the optimization problem. The advantage of this framework is its ability of taking various loss and regularization functions to characterize different data types and weight distributions effectively. We derive efficient computation approach that is linear with respect to the number of observations and the approach can be easily implemented in MapReduce model. We conduct experiments on weather, stock and flight data sets collected from multiple platforms as well as simulated multi-source data generated from UCI machine learning data sets. Results demonstrate the efficiency and the advantage of the proposed CRH approach over existing conflict resolution approaches in finding truths from heterogeneous data. In the future, we plan to adapt the framework to more complicated conflict resolution scenarios, such as the cases involving multiple truths and source dependency.

5. ACKNOWLEDGMENTS

We would like to thank the anonymous reviewers for their valuable comments and suggestions, which help us tremendously in improving the quality of the paper. We also thank Lu Su for his discussions and suggestions. The work was supported in part by National Key Basic Research Program of China (973 Program) under Grant No. 2014CB340304, the National Science Foundation under Grant NSF IIS-1319973, the U.S. Army Research Laboratory under Cooperative Agreement No. W911NF-09-2-0053 (NS-CTA), and the U.S. Army Research Office under Cooperative Agreement No. W911NF-13-1-0193.

6. REFERENCES

[1] A. Banerjee, S. Merugu, I. S. Dhillon, and J. Ghosh. Clustering with bregman divergences. *JMLR*, 6:1705–1749, 2005.
[2] D. P. Bertsekas. *Non-linear programming*. Athena Scientific, 1999.
[3] L. Blanco, V. Crescenzi, P. Merialdo, and P. Papotti. Probabilistic models to reconcile complex data from inaccurate data sources. In *Proc. of CAiSE*, pages 83–97, 2010.
[4] J. Bleiholder and F. Naumann. Conflict handling strategies in an integrated information system. In *Proc. of IIWeb*, 2006.
[5] J. Bleiholder and F. Naumann. Data fusion. *ACM Computing Surveys*, 41(1):1:1–1:41, 2009.
[6] S. Boyd and L. Vandenberghe. *Convex optimization*. Cambridge University Press, 2004.
[7] C.-T. Chu, S. K. Kim, Y.-A. Lin, Y. Yu, G. Bradski, A. Y. Ng, and K. Olukotun. Map-reduce for machine learning on multicore. In *NIPS*, pages 281–288, 2006.
[8] C. Dai, D. Lin, E. Bertino, and M. Kantarcioglu. An approach to evaluate data trustworthiness based on data provenance. In *Proc. of SDM*, pages 82–98, 2008.
[9] X. L. Dong, L. Berti-Equille, and D. Srivastava. Integrating conflicting data: The role of source dependence. *PVLDB*, 2(1):550–561, 2009.
[10] X. L. Dong and F. Naumann. Data fusion: Resolving data conflicts for integration. *PVLDB*, 2(2):1654–1655, 2009.
[11] X. L. Dong and D. Srivastava. Big data integration. In *Proc. of ICDE*, pages 1245–1248, 2013.
[12] A. Galland, S. Abiteboul, A. Marian, and P. Senellart. Corroborating information from disagreeing views. In *Proc. of WSDM*, pages 131–140, 2010.
[13] Z. Jiang. A decision-theoretic framework for numerical attribute value reconciliation. *TKDE*, 24(7):1153–1169, 2012.
[14] G. Kasneci, J. V. Gael, D. H. Stern, and T. Graepel. Cobayes: Bayesian knowledge corroboration with assessors of unknown areas of expertise. In *Proc. of WSDM*, pages 465–474, 2011.
[15] X. Li, X. L. Dong, K. B. Lyons, W. Meng, and D. Srivastava. Truth finding on the deep web: Is the problem solved? *PVLDB*, 2013.
[16] A. Marian and M. Wu. Corroborating information from web sources. *IEEE Data Engineering Bulletin*, 34(3):11–17, 2011.
[17] J. Nocedal and S. Wright. *Numerical optimization*. Springer, 2006.
[18] J. Pasternack and D. Roth. Making better informed trust decisions with generalized fact-finding. In *Proc. of IJCAI*, pages 2324–2329, 2011.
[19] G.-J. Qi, C. C. Aggarwal, J. Han, and T. Huang. Mining collective intelligence in diverse groups. In *Proc. of WWW*, pages 1041–1052, 2013.
[20] P. Tseng. Convergence of a block coordinate descent method for nondifferentiable minimization. *JOTA*, 109(3):475–494, 2001.
[21] V. Vydiswaran, C. Zhai, and D. Roth. Content-driven trust propagation framework. In *Proc. of KDD*, pages 974–982, 2011.
[22] X. Yin, J. Han, and P. S. Yu. Truth discovery with multiple conflicting information providers on the web. In *Proc. of KDD*, pages 1048–1052, 2007.
[23] B. Zhao and J. Han. A probabilistic model for estimating real-valued truth from conflicting sources. In *Proc. of QDB*, 2012.
[24] B. Zhao, B. I. P. Rubinstein, J. Gemmell, and J. Han. A bayesian approach to discovering truth from conflicting sources for data integration. *PVLDB*, 5(6):550–561, 2012.

A Probabilistic Model for Linking Named Entities in Web Text with Heterogeneous Information Networks

Wei Shen†, Jiawei Han‡, Jianyong Wang†

†Tsinghua National Laboratory for Information Science and Technology (TNList), Department of Computer Science and Technology, Tsinghua University, Beijing, China

‡Department of Computer Science, University of Illinois at Urbana-Champaign, Urbana, IL

†chen-wei09@mails.tsinghua.edu.cn, jianyong@tsinghua.edu.cn

‡hanj@cs.uiuc.edu

ABSTRACT

Heterogeneous information networks that consist of multi-type, interconnected objects are becoming ubiquitous and increasingly popular, such as social media networks and bibliographic networks. The task to link named entity mentions detected from the unstructured Web text with their corresponding entities existing in a heterogeneous information network is of practical importance for the problem of information network population and enrichment. This task is challenging due to name ambiguity and limited knowledge existing in the information network. Most existing entity linking methods focus on linking entities with Wikipedia or Wikipedia-derived knowledge bases (e.g., YAGO), and are largely dependent on the special features associated with Wikipedia (e.g., Wikipedia articles or Wikipedia-based relatedness measures). Since heterogeneous information networks do not have such features, these previous methods cannot be applied to our task. In this paper, we propose SHINE, the first probabilistic model to link the named entitieS in Web text with a Heterogeneous Information NEtwork to the best of our knowledge. Our model consists of two components: the *entity popularity model* that captures the popularity of an entity, and the *entity object model* that captures the distribution of multi-type objects appearing in the textual context of an entity, which is generated using *meta-path constrained random walks* over networks. As different meta-paths express diverse semantic meanings and lead to various distributions over objects, different paths have different weights in entity linking. We propose an effective iterative approach to automatically learning the weights for each meta-path based on the expectation-maximization (EM) algorithm without requiring any training data. Experimental results on a real world data set demonstrate the effectiveness and efficiency of our proposed model in comparison with the baselines.

SIGMOD'14, June 22–27, 2014, Snowbird, UT, USA.

http://dx.doi.org/10.1145/2588555.2593676.

Categories and Subject Descriptors

H.3.3 [**Information Systems**]: Information Storage and Retrieval—*Information Search and Retrieval*

Keywords

Entity linking; Heterogeneous information networks; Domain-specific entity linking

1. INTRODUCTION

Heterogeneous information networks (HIN) that involve a large number of multi-type objects are becoming ubiquitous and prevalent, since real world physical and abstract data objects are all connected via different relations, forming diverse heterogeneous information networks [28]. For example, in a bibliographic dataset, objects of multiple types, such as papers (P), authors (A), publication venues (V), and title terms (T), and relations of multiple types, such as *write*, *publish*, and *contain* are interconnected together, providing rich information and forming a heterogeneous information network. However, object names in a heterogeneous network are potentially ambiguous: the same textual name may refer to several different entities. As the example shown in Figure 1, in the DBLP network, the object name "Wei Wang" may refer to 45 different authors, including "Wei Wang" at University at Albany, SUNY, "Wei Wang" at Fudan Univ., China, "Wei Wang" at UCLA, and "Wei Wang" at UNSW, Australia.

Despite there exist many large-scale heterogeneous information networks, information contained in them is limited. For example, there does not exist the *advisor* relation between authors in the DBLP network. Furthermore, as the world evolves, new facts come into existence and are digitally expressed on the Web. Therefore, populating and enriching the existing heterogeneous information networks with the newly extracted facts (such as relations and descriptive paragraphs for entities) become increasingly important. However, integrating the newly extracted facts derived from the information extraction systems into an existing heterogeneous information network inevitably needs a system to map the entity mentions associated with the extracted facts to their corresponding entities in the heterogeneous information network. For instance, we could extract the *graduateFrom* relation between the author name "Wei Wang" and the organization name "UCLA" from the Web document in Figure 1. Before populating this relation into the DBLP network, we need to map the author name "Wei Wang" in

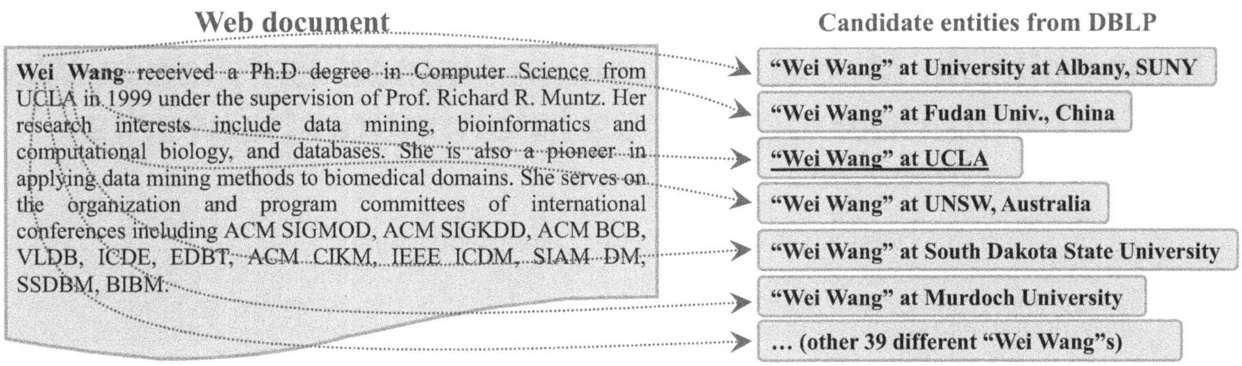

Figure 1: An illustration for the task of linking an entity mention in the Web document with the DBLP bibliographic network. Named entity mention detected from the Web document is in bold face; candidate entities from the DBLP network for this entity mention are shown on the right; true mapping entity is underlined.

this relation to its true mapping author (i.e., "Wei Wang" at UCLA) as there are 45 different authors having the same name "Wei Wang" in the DBLP network.

On the other hand, to some extent, some heterogeneous information networks could be regarded as domain-specific knowledge bases [6]. For example, the DBLP network (or the IMDb network) contains more interesting and diverse knowledge than Wikipedia with respect to the domain of computer science (or entertainment). In this case, we could regard this task as one type of *domain-specific entity linking*. In our task, we focus on linking entity mentions appearing in the domain-specific unstructured Web text, which pertains to the same domain as the heterogeneous information network. Therefore, this task is beneficial for bridging the unstructured documents and the semi-structured heterogeneous information networks, which can facilitate many tasks such as information integration and information retrieval. Meanwhile, this task can be used to automatically annotate the domain-specific Web text with the related knowledge mined from a heterogeneous information network, which could significantly improve user experience. For instance, when a user is reading the Web document in Figure 1, we could show some related knowledge about the author "Wei Wang" mined from the DBLP network (e.g., publication records, similar authors, research areas, etc.) after linking it with "Wei Wang" at UCLA in the DBLP network.

Traditional entity linking methods mainly focus on linking entities with Wikipedia or Wikipedia-derived knowledge bases (e.g., YAGO[26]) [3, 4, 14, 11, 23, 10, 22, 21, 24]. They mainly rely on the context knowledge embedded in the Wikipedia article [3, 4, 14, 10, 21, 22, 24], Wikipedia-based semantic relatedness measures [14, 21, 11, 23, 24] (e.g., Wikipedia Link-based Measure [19]), and some special structures in Wikipedia [3, 4, 14, 10, 21, 23, 22, 24] (e.g., disambiguation page and hyperlink in the Wikipedia article). While in this paper, we study the problem of linking entities in Web text with a heterogeneous information network. Heterogeneous information networks do not have these specific features associated with Wikipedia. Thus, these traditional entity linking methods cannot be applied to our task. For example, an essential step in these previous approaches [3, 4, 14, 10, 11, 21, 24] is to define a context similarity measure between the Wikipedia article associated with the candidate entity and the text around the entity mention, while for each author entity in the DBLP network, we do not have her descriptive article and cannot calculate the context similarity measure. In addition, the Wikipedia Link-based Measure [19] has been utilized to calculate the topical coherence between mapping entities in many existing entity linking methods [14, 21, 11, 23, 24]. However, this measure is based on the hyperlink structure among Wikipedia articles and cannot be used to calculate the topical coherence between entities in the DBLP network.

To deal with this problem, we propose a probabilistic model, which combines the *entity popularity model* and the *entity object model.* The entity popularity model is context-independent and captures the popularity of an entity. For example, a famous professor named "Wei Wang" who has published many papers is usually considered more popular than a student who is also named "Wei Wang" and has published very few papers.

The entity object model captures the probability of multi-type objects appearing in the textual context of an entity. In a heterogeneous information network, multi-type objects are connected via different types of relations or sequences of relations, forming a set of *meta-paths* [27]. Meta-path is a path consisting of a sequence of relations between different object types (i.e., structural path at the meta level). Different meta-paths imply distinct semantic meanings, which may lead to diverse distributions over objects. For example, in a bibliographic network, A-P-A is a meta-path denoting a relation between an author and her coauthor, whereas A-P-V denotes a relation between an author and a venue where her paper is published. Random walks starting from one author along the meta-path A-P-A may generate the distribution of coauthors for that author, while the meta-path A-P-V may lead to the distribution of venues for that author. A question then arises: *which meta-paths are more important for the entity linking task?* The remaining problem of our model is to determine which meta-paths (or their weighted combination) are used for the specific entity linking task. It is difficult to ask a user to explicitly specify the weights for such sophisticated meta-paths. To address this problem, an effective iterative approach is proposed to automatically learn the most appropriate weights of meta-paths based on the expectation-maximization (EM) algorithm without requiring any training data. With regard to different meta-path sets for arbitrary heterogeneous in-

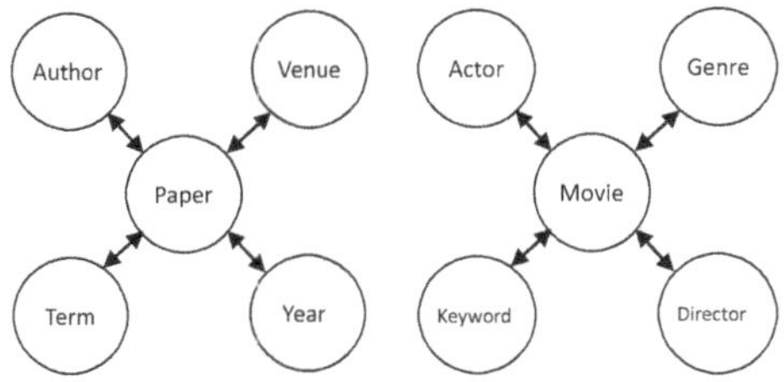

(a) DBLP (b) IMDb

Figure 2: DBLP and IMDb network schema

formation networks, our model can automatically learn the proper meta-path weights, which makes our model general and flexible enough to accommodate various types of heterogeneous networks.

Contributions. The main contributions of this paper are summarized as follows.

- We are among the first to explore the problem of linking entities with a heterogeneous information network, a new and increasingly important issue due to the proliferation of network data and its broad applications.
- We propose an effective probabilistic model called SHINE to deal with this task, which unifies the entity popularity model with the entity object model.
- An effective iterative approach is proposed to automatically learn the weights of meta-paths based on the EM algorithm without requiring any training data, which makes our model unsupervised.
- To verify the effectiveness and efficiency of SHINE, we conducted experiments over a real heterogeneous information network and manually annotated Web document collection. The experimental results show that SHINE significantly outperforms the baselines in terms of accuracy, and scales very well.

The remainder of this paper is organized as follows. Section 2 introduces some preliminaries and notations. We present the probabilistic model in Section 3, and introduce the model learning algorithm in Section 4. Section 5 presents the experimental results and Section 6 discusses the related work. Finally, we conclude this paper in Section 7.

2. PRELIMINARIES AND NOTATIONS

In this section, we begin by introducing some concepts in heterogeneous information networks. Next, we define the task of linking entities in Web text with a heterogeneous information network (entity linking with a HIN for short).

2.1 Heterogeneous information network

A heterogeneous information network G is an information network with multiple types of objects and multiple types of links [28, 27].

DEFINITION 1 (**Heterogeneous information network**). *A heterogeneous information network is defined as a directed graph $G = (V, Z)$, where V is the object set and Z is the link set. Each object $v \in V$ belongs to a particular object type T, and each link $z \in Z$ belongs to a particular relation type R. Moreover, the number of object types $|\{T\}| > 1$ and the number of relation types $|\{R\}| > 1$.*

The DBLP bibliographic network[1] is a typical heterogeneous information network, containing five types of objects: papers (P), authors (A), publication venues (V), title terms (T), and publication years (Y). Links exist between authors and papers by the relations *write* and *write*$^{-1}$, between publication venues and papers by *publish* and *publish*$^{-1}$, between papers and title terms by *contain* and *contain*$^{-1}$, and between papers and publication years by *publishedIn* and *publishedIn*$^{-1}$. Network schema (i.e., meta-level description for the network) for the DBLP network is shown in Figure 2(a). The IMDb network[2] (see schema in Figure 2(b)) is also a heterogeneous information network, containing five types of objects: movies (M), actors (Ac), genres (G), description keywords (K), and directors (D). Links exist between actors and movies by the relations *perform* and *perform*$^{-1}$, between movies and genres by *belongTo* and *belongTo*$^{-1}$, between movies and description keywords by *contain* and *contain*$^{-1}$, and between directors and movies by *direct* and *direct*$^{-1}$. In a heterogeneous information network, two objects can be connected via different types of relations or sequences of relations, forming a set of meta-paths, which are defined as follows.

DEFINITION 2 (**Meta-path**). *A meta-path p is a path defined over the network schema of a given network G, and is denoted in the form of $T_1 \xrightarrow{R_1} T_2 \xrightarrow{R_2} \ldots \xrightarrow{R_l} T_{l+1} (l \geq 1)$, which defines a composite relation $R_1 \circ R_2 \circ \ldots \circ R_l$ between object types T_1 and T_{l+1}, where $\circ$ denotes the composition operator on relations.*

Meta-path p can be also described as a sequence of relations (denoted by $R_1 - R_2 - \ldots - R_l$), or a sequence of object types (denoted by $T_1 - T_2 - \ldots - T_{l+1}$) if there exist no multiple relations between the same pair of object types for simplicity. The length of meta-path p is the number of relations in p. For example, in the DBLP network, A-P-V is a length-2 meta-path denoting a relation between an author and a venue where her paper is published, and A-P-A-P-V is a length-4 meta-path denoting a relation between an author and a venue where the paper of her coauthor is published. In the IMDb network, Ac-M-D is a length-2 meta-path denoting a relation between an actor and a director who directs the movie she performs, Ac-M-K is a length-2 meta-path denoting a relation between an actor and a description keyword her movie contains, Ac-M-G-M-Ac is a length-4 meta-path denoting a relation between actors who perform the same genre of movies, and Ac-M-Ac-M-G is a length-4 meta-path denoting a relation between an actor and a genre to which the movie of her co-actor belongs.

2.2 Entity linking with a HIN

According to the task setting, we take (1) a collection of unstructured Web documents (denoted by D), (2) named entity mentions recognized in the given documents D (denoted by M), and (3) a heterogeneous information network G as input. Each Web document $d \in D$ should pertain to the same domain as the heterogeneous information network G; otherwise, the document d does not have any common knowledge with the information network, which makes entity linking meaningless. For example, if we link with the DBLP network, the Web document $d \in D$ should pertain

[1]http://www.informatik.uni-trier.de/~ley/db/
[2]http://www.imdb.com/

Table 1: Notations

G	A heterogeneous information network
V	The object set in G
$v \in V$	An object in the object set V
Z	The link set in G
$z \in Z$	A link in the link set Z
T	An object type
R	A relation type
p	A meta-path
D	A Web document collection
$d \in D$	A document in the document collection D
M	Named entity mentions recognized in D
$m \in M$	A named entity mention recognized in a document d
E	The set of entities in G having the same type as M
$e \in E$	An entity in the entity set E

to the domain of computer science (CS), such as CS researcher's homepage, news article in CS department website, CS talk/seminar introduction page, etc. Each entity mention $m \in M$ detected from document d is a token sequence (or surface form) of a named entity that is potentially linked with an entity in the heterogeneous information network G. E is the set of entities in the heterogeneous information network G which have the same object type as the type of entity mentions M. Each entity in E is denoted by e. Generally, the entity set E is a subset of the object set V in the network G (i.e., $E \subset V$). For example, if we want to link author name mentions in Web text with the DBLP network, the entity set E should be the object set of author type in the DBLP network. Here, we formally state the task of entity linking with a HIN as follows.

DEFINITION 3 (**Entity linking with a HIN**). *Given a named entity mention set M detected from a Web document collection D and a heterogeneous information network G, the goal is to identify the mapping entity $e \in E$ in the heterogeneous information network G for each entity mention $m \in M$ in a document $d \in D$.*

For illustration, we show a running example of the task of entity linking with a HIN.

Example 1: (Entity linking with a HIN). In this example, we consider the task of entity linking with a HIN shown in Figure 1. Named entity mention "Wei Wang" in the Web document of Figure 1 needs to be linked with its referring author in the DBLP bibliographic network. There are totally 45 different candidate author entities in the DBLP network according to Figure 1. For the named entity mention "Wei Wang" in this example, we should output its true mapping author entity (i.e., "Wei Wang" at UCLA), which is underlined in Figure 1.

In this paper, due to limited scope we assume that the heterogeneous information network G contains all the mapping entities for all the named entity mentions M. The method for predicting entity mentions that do not have their corresponding entity records in the heterogeneous information network is left for future research. Some notations used in this paper are summarized in Table 1.

3. THE PROBABILISTIC MODEL

In this section, we propose a probabilistic model to deal with the task of entity linking with a HIN. Given a named entity mention $m \in M$ detected from a document $d \in D$, we want to find its most likely mapping entity $e \in E$ in the heterogeneous information network G. This leads to the following inference problem.

PROBLEM 1 (**Inference**). *Given a named entity mention m appearing in a document d, compute*

$$\arg\max_{e \in E} \mathbf{P}(e|m, d) \tag{1}$$

i.e., the most likely mapping entity e given an entity mention m in a document d.

According to Formula 1, given a named entity mention m appearing in a document d, we could find its mapping entity e as follows:

$$\arg\max_{e \in E} \mathbf{P}(e|m, d) = \arg\max_{e \in E} \frac{\mathbf{P}(m, d, e)}{\mathbf{P}(m, d)} = \arg\max_{e \in E} \mathbf{P}(m, d, e) \tag{2}$$

We assume that there is an underlying distribution $\mathbf{P}$ over the set $M \times D \times E$. Therefore, our goal is to model $\mathbf{P}(m, d, e)$. The probability of an entity mention m whose context is the document d referring to a specific entity e could be expressed as the following formula (here we assume that m and d are independent given e):

$$\mathbf{P}(m, d, e) = \mathbf{P}(e)\mathbf{P}(m|e)\mathbf{P}(d|e) \tag{3}$$

The mapping entity e should have the name of surface form m and we denote entities that could be referred by the name of surface form m as the candidate entities for entity mention m. For simplicity, we assume that the probability $\mathbf{P}(m|e)$ of observing the name of surface form m given each candidate entity e for mention m is the same and defined as a constant η where $0 < \eta \leq 1$. For example, given each of the 45 author entities named "Wei Wang" shown in Figure 1, we assume that the likelihood of observing "Wei Wang" as her name is the same. Under this reasonable assumption, the complete model can be expressed as

$$\mathbf{P}(m, d, e) = \eta \cdot \mathbf{P}(e)\mathbf{P}(d|e) \tag{4}$$

where e is a candidate entity for entity mention m. This probabilistic model as shown in Formula 4 mainly consists of two components.

(1) The entity popularity model $\mathbf{P}(e)$ captures the popularity of an entity e, which is the likelihood of observing an entity e appearing in a document without knowing any context information.

(2) The entity object model $\mathbf{P}(d|e)$ denotes the probability of observing document d as the textual context for entity e.

In the following subsections, we discuss the entity popularity model (Section 3.1) and the entity object model (Section 3.2) in more detail.

3.1 Entity popularity model

Given a heterogeneous information network G, to model the entity popularity $\mathbf{P}(e)$, in the simplest way we could assume that each entity e in the entity set E has the uniform popularity. We call it the uniform popularity model and estimate it as:

$$\mathbf{P}(e) = \frac{1}{|E|} \tag{5}$$

where $|E|$ is the number of entities in the entity set E. However, this uniform popularity model does not reflect well the real situation. We have the observation that each entity in the heterogeneous information network has different popularity. Some entities in the heterogeneous information network are obviously more prevalent than other entities. For example, a professor named "Rakesh Kumar" who has published many papers is usually regarded more popular than a Ph.D student who has published very few papers and has the same name "Rakesh Kumar".

Most previous entity linking systems estimate the popularity of an entity using the entity frequency in the Wikipedia article corpus [14, 10, 11, 21, 23, 22, 24]. However, this approach cannot be applied to our task of entity linking with a HIN. Entities in the heterogeneous information network are connected via different relations, and the popularity of an entity in the network relies on the visibility of other connected entities. For example, in the DBLP bibliographic network, the popularity of an author depends on some features, such as her coauthors' popularity, her publication quantity, and the authoritativeness of the venues where her papers are published.

As we know, PageRank [2] is a general-purpose network node importance measure which is fairly successful for many tasks. The basic idea of PageRank is that if object v_1 has a link to object v_2, then object v_1 implicitly confers some importance to object v_2. For simplicity, we ignore the object types in the information network G, and let $|V|$ be the number of objects in the information network G. We use $1 \leq k \leq |V|$ to index the object in V, and the object with index k is denoted by v_k.

Suppose that we want to compute the PageRank score vector $\overrightarrow{\mathbf{pr}} = (pr_1, ..., pr_k, ..., pr_{|V|})$ where pr_k is the PageRank score for object v_k to indicate the popularity of object v_k. The PageRank score pr_k of each object v_k is decided by the combination of its initial PageRank score and the propagated score of other connected objects, and the final PageRank score vector $\overrightarrow{\mathbf{pr}}$ can be computed efficiently by matrix multiplication. Let $\overrightarrow{\mathbf{ip}}$ be the initial PageRank score vector and $\overrightarrow{\mathbf{ip}} = (ip_1, ..., ip_k, ..., ip_{|V|})$, where ip_k is the initial PageRank score for object v_k. In this paper, we assume each object v_k has the same initial PageRank score (i.e., $\frac{1}{|V|}$) and assign a uniform vector to $\overrightarrow{\mathbf{ip}}$. Let B be the $|V| \times |V|$ matrix corresponding to the link structure of network G, assuming each object in G has at least one outgoing link. If there is a link from object v_k to object $v_{k'}$, we let the matrix entry $b_{k',k}$ have the value $\frac{1}{N_k}$, where N_k is the outdegree of object v_k. Thus, the matrix B is a column-normalized matrix. Formally, we define the computation of the PageRank score vector $\overrightarrow{\mathbf{pr}}$ as:

$$\overrightarrow{\mathbf{pr}} = \lambda \overrightarrow{\mathbf{ip}} + (1 - \lambda) B \cdot \overrightarrow{\mathbf{pr}} \tag{6}$$

where $\lambda \in [0, 1]$ is a parameter that balances the relative importance of the two parts (i.e., the initial PageRank score $\overrightarrow{\mathbf{ip}}$ and the propagated score of other connected objects $B \cdot \overrightarrow{\mathbf{pr}}$). As Formula 6 is in a recursive form, in order to calculate the final PageRank score vector $\overrightarrow{\mathbf{pr}}$, we firstly initialize the final PageRank score vector $\overrightarrow{\mathbf{pr}}$ by setting $\overrightarrow{\mathbf{pr}} = \overrightarrow{\mathbf{ip}}$ and then apply Formula 6 iteratively until $\overrightarrow{\mathbf{pr}}$ stabilizes within some threshold. Since the PageRank score is context-independent, we could compute their PageRank scores pr_k's for each object v_k offline.

For each entity $e \in E \subset V$, let $pr(e)$ be its PageRank score calculated via Formula 6. Then our entity popularity model uses the PageRank score to estimate the popularity $\mathbf{P}(e)$ of entity e as follows.

$$\mathbf{P}(e) = \frac{pr(e)}{\sum_{e' \in E} pr(e')} \tag{7}$$

Table 2: Entity popularity in Example 1

Candidate entity	Entity popularity
"Wei Wang" at University at Albany, SUNY	$4.441*10^{-6}$
"Wei Wang" at Fudan Univ., China	$7.373*10^{-6}$
"Wei Wang" at UCLA	$1.08*10^{-5}$
"Wei Wang" at UNSW, Australia	$6.202*10^{-6}$
"Wei Wang" at South Dakota State University	$3.868*10^{-6}$
"Wei Wang" at Murdoch University	$4.180*10^{-7}$

For illustration, we show in Table 2 the entity popularity $\mathbf{P}(e)$ for each candidate entity e in Example 1. From the results in Table 2, we can see that the popularity of the author entity "Wei Wang" at UCLA (i.e., $1.08*10^{-5}$) is the highest among all the candidates, which demonstrates that the author "Wei Wang" at UCLA is the most popular entity in the candidate entity set with respect to the entity mention "Wei Wang" that is consistent with our intuition, while the author "Wei Wang" at Murdoch University who has just published one paper in DBLP has the lowest entity popularity (i.e., $4.180*10^{-7}$). It can be seen that the entity popularity model suitably expresses the popularity of the candidate entity. Moreover, the experimental results in Section 5.2 also demonstrate that our entity popularity model (Formula 7) is more effective than the simple uniform popularity model (Formula 5) in the entity linking task.

3.2 Entity object model

The entity object model $\mathbf{P}(d|e)$ captures the probability of observing document d as the textual context for entity e. That is to say, it will assign a high probability $\mathbf{P}(d|e)$ if the entity e frequently appears in the context of document d, and will assign a low probability $\mathbf{P}(d|e)$ if the entity e rarely appears in the context of document d.

Since we are dealing with heterogeneous information networks which involve a large number of multi-type objects, we assume the document d consists of various multi-type objects v's from the heterogeneous information network and the observation of these different objects given the entity is independent. In Example 1, the Web document where the entity mention "Wei Wang" appears as shown in Figure 1 consists of an object of author type (i.e., *Richard R. Muntz*), some objects of venue type (such as *SIGMOD*, *SIGKDD*, *BCB*, *VLDB*, *ICDE*, *EDBT*, *CIKM*, etc.), some objects of term type (such as *computer*, *data*, *mining*, *bioinformatics*, *computational*, *biology*, *database*, etc.), and an object of year type (i.e., *1999*).

Then the entity object model $\mathbf{P}(d|e)$ can be expressed as the product of the probabilities $\mathbf{P}(v|e)$ under the assumption that the document d is composed of various multi-type objects v's from the heterogeneous information network and the observation of these different objects v's given the entity e is independent, which is similar to unigram language modeling [18]. Thus we have:

$$\mathbf{P}(d|e) = \prod_{v \in d} \mathbf{P}(v|e) \tag{8}$$

From Formula 8, we can see that the entity object model captures the probability of multi-type objects v's appearing in the textual context of entity e. The distribution $\mathbf{P}(v|e)$ encodes the probability of observing object v given entity e, which can be estimated from the associated network about entity e in the heterogeneous information network. For example, with respect to the entity "Wei Wang" at UCLA,

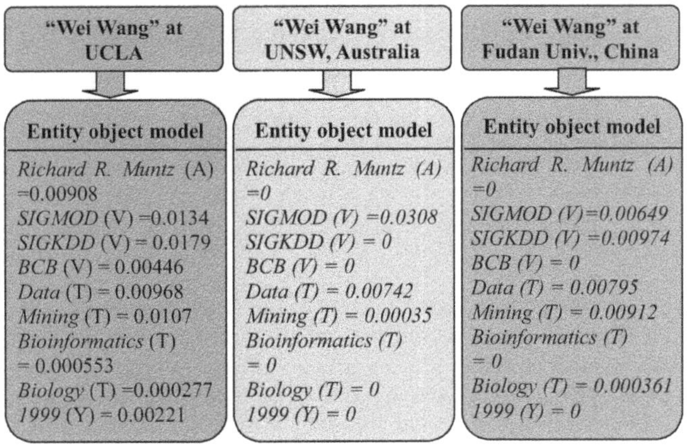

Figure 3: Entity object model for three candidate entities in Example 1. The letter in the parentheses after each object represents its object type.

the probability of observing venue object *SIGMOD* should be higher than the probability of observing venue object *VLDB*, because the author "Wei Wang" at UCLA has published much more papers in the *SIGMOD* conference (i.e., six papers) than the *VLDB* conference (i.e., one paper) in DBLP.

Figure 3 shows parts of the entity object model for three candidate entities with the highest entity popularity in Example 1 (i.e., "Wei Wang" at UCLA, "Wei Wang" at UNSW, Australia, and "Wei Wang" at Fudan Univ., China), which is generated using *meta-path constrained random walks* (its definition is given in Formula 11). From Figure 3, we can see that the probability $\mathbf{P}(d|$"Wei Wang" at UCLA$)$ of observing the Web document d in Figure 1 given the entity "Wei Wang" at UCLA is likely to be significantly higher than the probability $\mathbf{P}(d|$"Wei Wang" at Fudan Univ., China$)$ and the probability $\mathbf{P}(d|$"Wei Wang" at UNSW, Australia$)$, because the probabilities of observing most of the representative objects appearing in the document d (e.g., author object *Richard R. Muntz*, venue objects *SIGKDD* and *BCB*, term objects *Data*, *Mining*, *Bioinformatics*, and year object *1999*) given the entity "Wei Wang" at UCLA are higher than the probabilities of observing these objects given each of the other two candidate entities.

From Figure 3, we can also see that the probability of observing some object given an entity is equal to 0 (e.g., the probability of observing author object *Richard R. Muntz* given the entity "Wei Wang" at Fudan Univ., China, $\mathbf{P}($Richard R. Muntz$|$"Wei Wang" at Fudan Univ., China$))$ due to the sparse data problem. This leads to that the product of probabilities in Formula 8 equals zero. To avoid this problem, we further smooth $\mathbf{P}(v|e)$ using a generic object model for the domain.

Formally, given a document d that is the textual context for entity e, each object $v \in d$ is drawn randomly from a mixture of two object models: an entity-specific object model $\mathbf{P_e}(v)$ which is a distribution over objects with respect to entity e and can be generated using *meta-path constrained random walks* (its definition is given in Formula 11), and a generic object model for the domain $\mathbf{P_g}(v)$ which is independent of entity e and can be estimated from the whole collection. Thus, we could further define the entity object model $\mathbf{P}(d|e)$ as:

$$\mathbf{P}(d|e) = \prod_{v \in d} (\theta \cdot \mathbf{P_e}(v) + (1-\theta) \cdot \mathbf{P_g}(v)) \tag{9}$$

where $\theta \in (0,1)$ is a parameter that balances the two parts (i.e., the entity-specific object model $\mathbf{P_e}(v)$ and the generic object model for the domain $\mathbf{P_g}(v)$). The generic object model for the domain $\mathbf{P_g}(v)$ can be learned by counting the frequencies of multi-type objects appearing in the document collection D. The remaining problem is to estimate the entity-specific object model $\mathbf{P_e}(v)$ for each entity $e \in E$.

To estimate the entity-specific object model $\mathbf{P_e}(v)$, an intuitive way is to apply random walks starting from entity e in the heterogeneous information network G, which may generate the distribution of different objects for entity e. This random walker can follow any type of relation with uniform probability at each step. However, this intuitive way does not distinguish the different semantic meanings embedded in various relation types and regards various relation types as the same.

In a heterogeneous information network, an object could link to many different types of objects by multiple meta-paths. Different meta-paths imply different semantic meanings, which may lead to rather diverse distributions over objects. For example, in a bibliographic network, A-P-A is a meta-path denoting a relation between an author and her coauthor, whereas A-P-T denotes a relation between an author and a title term that her paper contains.

Thus, we explore meta-paths to guide the random walks over the heterogeneous information network G. In this paper, we propose to use *meta-path constrained random walks* [15] to estimate the entity-specific object model $\mathbf{P_e}(v)$. Formally, let meta-path $p = R_1 - R_2 - \ldots - R_l$, and each relation R_k be a binary relation. We define $R_k(v', v) = 1$ if object v' and object v are linked by relation R_k, and $R_k(v', v) = 0$ otherwise. We also define $R_k(v') = \{v | R_k(v', v)\}$, which is the set of objects that are linked with object v' via the relation R_k. Given the meta-path $p = R_1 - R_2 - \ldots - R_l$ which starts with the same object type as entity e, we define $\mathbf{P_e}(v|p)$, i.e., the distribution of observing object v given entity e and meta-path p, as follows. Firstly, if meta-path p is an empty path, we define

$$\mathbf{P_e}(v|p) = \begin{cases} 1 & \text{if object } v \text{ is entity } e, \\ 0 & \text{otherwise.} \end{cases} \tag{10}$$

If $p = R_1 - R_2 - \ldots - R_l$ is a nonempty path, then let $p' = R_1 - R_2 - \ldots - R_{l-1}$, and define

$$\mathbf{P_e}(v|p) = \sum_{v' \in V} \mathbf{P_e}(v'|p') \cdot \frac{R_l(v', v)}{|R_l(v')|} \tag{11}$$

where $|R_l(v')|$ is the number of objects that are linked with the object v' via the relation R_l. This definition (Formula 11) is in a recursive form and is called *meta-path constrained random walks*, i.e., random walks starting from entity e along meta-path p. Given each meta-path, we could calculate the distribution of observing objects for each entity using Formula 11.

For example, given the meta-path A-P-V, with respect to the entity "Wei Wang" at UCLA, the probability of observing venue object *SIGMOD* is 0.0536, while the probability of observing venue object *VLDB* or venue object *SIGMETRICS* is the same (i.e., 0.00893) in the DBLP network, because the author "Wei Wang" at UCLA has published 6 papers in

Table 3: Meta-paths in the DBLP network used in our experiments

Meta-path	Semantic meaning of the realtion
A-P-A	Authors who coauthor with author e
A-P-A-P-A	Authors who coauthor with the coauthors of author e
A-P-V-P-A	Authors who publish papers in the same venues as author e's papers
A-P-V	Venues where author e publishes papers
A-P-A-P-V	Venues where the coauthors of author e publish papers
A-P-T-P-V	Venues that publish papers containing the same title terms as author e's papers
A-P-T	Terms that author e's papers contain
A-P-A-P-T	Terms that the papers of author e's coauthors contain
A-P-V-P-T	Terms that are contained in the papers that are published in the same venues as author e's papers
A-P-Y	Years when author e's papers are published

the *SIGMOD* conference, and has published just one paper in the *VLDB* conference and the *SIGMETRICS* conference respectively, from the DBLP network. Additionally, given the meta-path A-P-A-P-V, with respect to the entity "Wei Wang" at UCLA, the probability of observing venue object *VLDB* (i.e., 0.00863) is much higher than the probability of observing venue object *SIGMETRICS* (i.e., 0.00471) in the DBLP network, since the coauthors of author "Wei Wang" at UCLA have published much more papers in the *VLDB* conference than the *SIGMETRICS* conference. It can be seen that different meta-paths may imply different semantic meanings, which may lead to rather diverse distributions over objects and further lead to different entity linking results.

Therefore it is desirable to learn the relative importance for each meta-path for the specific entity linking task. In order to quantify the importance for each meta-path p, we give a meta-path weight w_p for each meta-path p. Given a set of meta-paths, the entity-specific object model $\mathbf{P_e}(v)$ could be the weighted sum of the probabilities of observing object v given entity e along each meta-path p. We define the entity-specific object model $\mathbf{P_e}(v)$ as follows.

$$\mathbf{P_e}(v) = \sum_p w_p \mathbf{P_e}(v|p) \tag{12}$$

where $\sum_p w_p = 1$. A larger w_p indicates a higher importance for the meta-path p with respect to the entity linking task. We define the meta-path weight vector as $\overrightarrow{W}$, in which each item w_p is the weight for meta-path p. Note that, we do not consider negative w_p in this model, which means relationships with a negative impact to the entity linking process are not considered, and the extreme case of $w_p = 0$ means the relationships in this meta-path are totally irrelevant to the entity linking process.

A set of meta-paths starting from the same object type as entity e, which might be useful for the entity linking task, should be provided as the input of this model. The set of meta-paths used in our experiments are shown in Table 3, where the semantic meanings of each relation denoted by each meta-path are given in the second column. These meta-paths could be determined either according to users' expert knowledge, or by traversing the network schema starting from the same object type as entity e with a length constraint using standard traversal methods such as the BFS (breadth-first search) algorithm. A very long meta path that will propagate relationships to remote neighborhoods may not carry much meaningful semantic meaning [27] and is not very useful in entity linking.

Note that the meta-path weights w_p's for each meta-path p are the only parameters which need to be learned in our model. The estimation problem of our model could be solved as follows.

PROBLEM 2 (**Estimation**). *Given a heterogeneous information network G and a set of named entity mentions M recognized in the given document collection D, determine parameters (i.e., meta-path weights w_p's for each meta-path p) that maximize the likelihood of observing named entity mentions M in the document collection D.*

Once we learn the model, we could use it to link entities with a heterogeneous information network G. In the following, we introduce how to solve the estimation problem of our model, which is inspired by the model estimation method in [5].

4. THE LEARNING ALGORITHM

Given a set of named entity mentions M recognized in the given document collection D, we want to estimate parameters (i.e., meta-path weights w_p's for each meta-path p) that maximize the likelihood of observing these named entity mentions M in the document collection D. Thus, we want

$$\arg\max_{w_p} \prod_{(m,d)} \mathbf{P}(m,d) \tag{13}$$

We have

$$\mathbf{P}(m,d) = \sum_{e \in E} \mathbf{P}(m,d,e) \tag{14}$$

where $\mathbf{P}(m,d,e)$ is given in Formula 4. Then, we have

$$\arg\max_{w_p} \prod_{(m,d)} \sum_e \eta \cdot \mathbf{P}(e)\mathbf{P}(d|e) = \arg\max_{w_p} \prod_{(m,d)} \sum_e \mathbf{P}(e)\mathbf{P}(d|e) \tag{15}$$

Since this objective function is in a product of sum form that is difficult to optimize directly, we define a hidden random variable $\pi(m,d,e)$ for each triple (m,d,e) to simplify its form as follows.

$$\pi(m,d,e) = \begin{cases} 1 & \text{if mention } m \text{ in } d \text{ refers to } e, \\ 0 & \text{otherwise.} \end{cases} \tag{16}$$

Then our optimization function could be written as

$$\arg\max_{w_p} \prod_{(m,d)} \prod_e (\mathbf{P}(e)\mathbf{P}(d|e))^{\pi(m,d,e)} \tag{17}$$

Now we can apply the expectation-maximization (EM) method iteratively to optimize this objective function. In the initialization step, we assume some initial values of the parameters (i.e., give some initial values to the meta-path weight vector $\overrightarrow{W}$).

E-step. In the expectation step, using the current values of the parameters, we could find the expected values of the hidden variables using the following formula.

$$\mathbf{E}(\pi(m,d,e)) = \mathbf{P}(e|m,d) = \frac{\mathbf{P}(m,d,e)}{\mathbf{P}(m,d)} = \frac{\mathbf{P}(m,d,e)}{\sum_{e'} \mathbf{P}(m,d,e')} \tag{18}$$

As in Formula 4, entity e is defined as the candidate entity for entity mention m. Therefore, for each entity mention m

in a document d, we maintain a candidate entity set, and assume the probability of linking with other entities to be 0. Thus, this expression can be calculated by iterating over each candidate entity in the candidate entity set for each given mention-document tuple.

M-step. In the maximization step, we use the value $f(m,d,e) = \mathbf{E}(\pi(m,d,e))$ calculated in the E-step, and find the parameters w_p's that maximize the following function:

$$\prod_{(m,d),e} (\mathbf{P}(e)\mathbf{P}(d|e))^{f(m,d,e)} = \prod_{(m,d),e} (\mathbf{P}(e))^{f(m,d,e)} \cdot \prod_{(m,d),e} (\mathbf{P}(d|e))^{f(m,d,e)} \tag{19}$$

We can see that the first product $\prod_{(m,d),e}(\mathbf{P}(e))^{f(m,d,e)}$ does not involve the parameters w_p's and does not depend on these parameters. Therefore, we just need to find the optimal parameters w_p's that maximize the following function:

$$\prod_{(m,d),e} (\mathbf{P}(d|e))^{f(m,d,e)} \tag{20}$$

By obtaining the logarithm of the above objective function, we get the objective function:

$$J = \sum_{(m,d),e} f(m,d,e) ln \mathbf{P}(d|e) \tag{21}$$

By substituting Formula 9 and Formula 12, the objective function of Formula 21 can be derived as:

$$J = \sum_{(m,d),e} f(m,d,e) \sum_{v} ln(\theta \cdot \sum_{p} w_p \mathbf{P_e}(v|p) + (1-\theta) \cdot \mathbf{P_g}(v)) \tag{22}$$

We use gradient descent approach to solve this optimization problem. The basic idea of gradient descent is to find the direction (gradient) so that the objective function climbs up and makes a small step towards the direction via iteratively updating the meta-path weights w_p's in the vector $\overrightarrow{W}$. Specifically, it is an iterative algorithm with the updating formula as:

$$w_p^{(t)} = w_p^{(t-1)} + \alpha \cdot \frac{\partial J}{\partial w_p}|_{w_p = w_p^{(t-1)}} \tag{23}$$

where α is the learning rate, which decides the step size towards the increasing direction and is usually set to a small enough number to guarantee the increase of the objective function J. The partial derivative of w_p can be derived as:

$$\frac{\partial J}{\partial w_p} = \sum_{(m,d),e} f(m,d,e) \sum_{v} \frac{\theta * \mathbf{P_e}(v|p)}{\mathbf{P}(v|e)} \tag{24}$$

After each iteration of updating the weights for meta-paths using Formula 23, we normalize the meta-path weights to satisfy the constraint $\sum_p w_p = 1$.

The learning algorithm proposed in our model SHINE is summarized in Algorithm 1. Overall, it is an iterative algorithm based on the expectation-maximization (EM) method. The optimization of meta-path weights w_p's contains an inner loop of gradient descent algorithm (line 9-line 15). This learning algorithm can automatically learn the weights of meta-paths by maximizing the likelihood of observing named entity mentions M in the given document collection D without requiring any training data, which makes SHINE unsupervised.

Algorithm 1 *The Learning Algorithm*

Input: Heterogeneous information network G, named entity mentions M, document collection D, and entity set E.

Output: The meta-path weight vector $\overrightarrow{W}$.

1: **for** each meta-path p **do**
2:   Initialize the weight $w_p = 0$
3: **end for**
4: **repeat**
5:   **E-step:** update $\mathbf{E}(\pi(m,d,e))$ by Formula 18
6:   **M-step:**
7:   $\overrightarrow{W}^0 = \overrightarrow{W}$
8:   $t = 1$
9:   **repeat**
10:     **for** each meta-path p **do**
11:       Update $w_p^{(t)}$ by Formula 23
12:     **end for**
13:     Normalize $w_p^{(t)}$ to satisfy $\sum_p w_p^{(t)} = 1$
14:     $t = t + 1$
15:   **until** objective function J (Formula 22) converges
16:   $\overrightarrow{W} = \overrightarrow{W}^{(t-1)}$
17: **until** meta-path weight vector $\overrightarrow{W}$ stabilizes within some threshold

We analyze the time complexity for this learning algorithm. Formally, for the inner gradient descent algorithm, the time complexity is $O(t_1|M| \cdot |E_m| \cdot |V_d| \cdot |\overrightarrow{W}|)$, where t_1 is the number of iterations, $|M|$ is the number of entity mentions in M, $|E_m|$ is the number of candidate entities for entity mention m, $|V_d|$ is the number of objects involved in the document d where mention m appears, and $|\overrightarrow{W}|$ is the number of meta-paths. The time complexity for the whole learning algorithm is $O(t(t_1|M| \cdot |E_m| \cdot |V_d| \cdot |\overrightarrow{W}| + |M| \cdot |E_m| \cdot |V_d| \cdot |\overrightarrow{W}|)) = O(t(t_1|M| \cdot |E_m| \cdot |V_d| \cdot |\overrightarrow{W}|))$ where t is the number of iterations for the EM algorithm. Therefore, we can see that the inner gradient descent algorithm consumes most of running time of the whole learning algorithm. Though we do not know the upper bound on the number of iterations this EM learning algorithm may run until it terminates, in our experiments, we observe that it converges quickly and typically takes only a few iterations. Moreover, as $|E_m|$, $|V_d|$, and $|\overrightarrow{W}|$ are usually small constants, the running time of this learning algorithm and the inner gradient descent algorithm is linear to the number of entity mentions in M, which has been confirmed by our experiments shown in Section 5.3. When the number of entity mentions in M is enormous, our learning algorithm becomes a little expensive. At that time, we could use stochastic gradient descent method that is very effective for large-scale learning problem, which samples a subset of entity mentions at each iteration and updates the parameters w_p's on the basis of these sampled entity mentions only [1]. Then, the running time of our learning algorithm is linear to the number of sampled entity mentions.

We state that our probabilistic model is flexible and can be applied to arbitrary heterogeneous information networks directly. For example, given another bibliographic network, we have a new object type (e.g., organizations (ORG)) and links existing between authors and organizations by the relations *isAffiliatedWith* and *isAffiliatedWith*$^{-1}$. To leverage this affiliation information to link entities with this new bibliographic network, we could simply add some new meta-paths (such as A-ORG and A-P-A-ORG) into the meta-path set used in our model. Then, our model can automatically learn the relative importance for these new meta-paths. For linking entities with other types of heterogeneous information networks, we just need to change the meta-path set used in our model. For example, if we want to link actor name mentions in Web text with the IMDb network, a set of meta-paths starting from the actor type in the IMDb network could be provided as the input of this model, such as Ac-M-Ac, Ac-M-Ac-M-Ac, Ac-M-G-M-Ac, Ac-M-D-M-Ac, Ac-M-G, Ac-M-Ac-M-G, Ac-M-D-M-G, Ac-M-K, Ac-M-Ac-M-K, Ac-M-G-M-K, Ac-M-D-M-K, Ac-M-D, Ac-M-Ac-M-D, Ac-M-G-M-D. Subsequently, we could leverage our learning algorithm to learn the weights for these meta-paths for this new entity linking task.

5. EXPERIMENTAL STUDY

To evaluate the effectiveness and efficiency of our model SHINE, we present a thorough experimental study in this section. We firstly describe the experimental setting in Section 5.1 and then study the effectiveness of SHINE in Section 5.2. In Section 5.3, we evaluate the efficiency and scalability of SHINE. In Section 5.4, we study the impact of parameters to the performance of SHINE. Lastly, we investigate the meta-path weights learned by our learning algorithm. All the programs were implemented in JAVA and all the experiments were conducted on a server (four 2.67GHz CPU cores, 48GB memory) with 64-bit Windows. In this paper, we do not utilize the parallel computing technique and just consider single machine implementation.

5.1 Experimental setting

To the best of our knowledge, there is no publicly available benchmark data set for the task of entity linking with a HIN. Thus, we create a gold standard data set for this task. Since the annotation task for entity linking with a HIN consists of disambiguating entities that would be linked with in the heterogeneous information network, generating the test Web documents that pertain to the same domain as the information network, detecting named entity mentions in them, and identifying their corresponding mapping entities existing in the network, the annotation task is difficult and very time consuming. Therefore, we just create one data set for evaluation.

In our experiments, we adopt the DBLP bibliographic network, which has been introduced in Section 2.1, as the underlying heterogeneous information network. We downloaded the March 2013 version of DBLP data set and built the DBLP network according to the network schema introduced in Figure 2(a). This DBLP network contains over 1.2M authors, 2.1M papers, and 7K venues (conferences/journals). The terms in the paper titles are filtered by a stop word list of size 667 and stemmed by Porter Stemmer[3], which converts the morphological variation of each word to its root form. We finally got around 408K terms. According to our task setting, the entities in the network which would be linked with should be disambiguated. The DBLP network has some highly ambiguous author names (such as "Wei Wang", "Eric Martin", etc.) that have been disambiguated (i.e., determine which author names in publication records refer to the same author entity), and these ambiguous names are followed by a space character and a four digit number (e.g., "Wei Wang 0010" and "Eric Martin 0001") to uniquely represent each distinct author [16]. In addition, we combined the DBLP network with the author disambiguation results from the publicly available data set used in [29], which contains 110 author names and their gold standard disambiguation results, to create a partially disambiguated DBLP network.

To illustrate the ability of our model, we focus on Web documents that pertain to the domain of computer science. Given any Web document, we could develop a highly accurate classifier to predict whether it pertains to the domain of computer science. Since the main focus of this paper is to investigate the effectiveness of our model for entity linking, we consider developing such classifiers as an orthogonal effort to our task, and opted for querying Web search engine (i.e., Google) to generate the test document collection D. We formed the Web search queries by including the ambiguous author names, as well as some domain representative phrases (such as "computer science", "database", "data mining", etc.). Each returned Web document, along with all candidate author entities with respect to the ambiguous author name in this document, is presented to annotators, and the documents which contain ambiguous author names referring to the entities existing in the DBLP network are collected. This yields a collection of 709 Web documents, each of which has one author name mention that needs to be linked.

To generate the candidate author entities for each author name mention, we use a method based on string comparison between names of the author mention and the author entity. All author entities in the DBLP network that satisfy the predefined rules are extracted as the candidate entities. The rules used in this paper include: (1) two author names exactly match; (2) two author names have the same first name and last name, and one of them has no middle name (e.g., Richard Muntz and Richard R. Muntz) or one middle name is another middle name's initial (e.g., Michael J. Jordan and Michael Jeffrey Jordan). For each test HTML Web document, we firstly extracted the full text of the article and removed the author name mention itself. As we assume that each Web document d consists of various multi-type objects v's from the heterogeneous information network, we recognized objects of author type and objects of venue type from DBLP in it using dictionary-based exact matching method. We identified objects of year type using regular expression. All remaining terms in the document (removing all punctuation symbols) are filtered by a stop word list and stemmed by Porter Stemmer. Lastly, we regarded these stemmed terms as the object set of term type.

In Section 5.4, we evaluate how accuracy changes by varying θ from 0.1 to 0.9 in our data set. The parameter θ is set to 0.2 in the other experiments. The learning rate α in Formula 23 decides the step size towards the increasing direction. When α gets too big, the gradient descent algorithm would fail to converge. α is set to 0.000003 in all experiments. The parameter λ in Formula 6 is set to 0.2 in all experiments. To evaluate the performance of SHINE, in this paper we adopt the evaluation measure *accuracy*, which is used in most work about entity linking [3, 4, 7, 21, 10, 23, 22, 24]. The accuracy is calculated as the number of correctly linked entity mentions divided by the total num-

[3]http://tartarus.org/martin/PorterStemmer/

Table 4: Experimental results of baseline VSim with different object type set

Object type set	# correctly linked	Accuracy
Coauthor	547	0.772
Venue	430	0.606
Term	576	0.812
Year	256	0.361
Coauthor+Venue	574	0.810
Coauthor+Term	598	0.843
Venue+Term	578	0.815
Coauthor+Venue+Term	602	0.849
Coauthor+Venue+Term+Year	**604**	**0.852**

ber of all mentions. All the operations introduced in this subsection are regarded as preprocessing.

5.2 Effectiveness study

In this subsection, we study the effectiveness of our model SHINE under different configurations, and compare them with some baselines.

5.2.1 *Baselines*

Since no previous work deals with the task of entity linking with a HIN, we created two baselines in this paper. The first one is entity popularity-based method (POP). The feature of entity popularity has been found to be very useful in previous entity linking systems [12, 11, 21, 22, 23, 24]. In this POP baseline method, we used our entity popularity model (Formula 7) introduced in Section 3.1 to estimate the popularity for each candidate entity. The entity with the highest popularity among all the candidate entities for each entity mention is considered as the mapping entity for this entity mention.

The second baseline is vector similarity-based method (VSim). In this VSim method, we constructed a context vector for each author mention and a profile vector for each candidate author entity. Specifically, for each author mention, we firstly got object sets of different types which compose the document where this author mention appears. To compute the bag of words context vector, we added each object in these object sets of different types, together with its frequency into the vector. For each candidate author entity, we obtained all her publication records from our partially disambiguated DBLP network. To compute the bag of words profile vector, we added objects of different types (i.e., her coauthors, venues, title terms, and publication years) in her publications, together with their frequencies into the vector. Then we measure the cosine similarity of these two vectors for each pair of author mention and candidate entity. Finally, the entity with the highest similarity is considered as the mapping entity for the author mention. To analyze the effectiveness of different object types for the baseline VSim, we show the accuracy and the number of correctly linked author mentions obtained by VSim with different object type sets in Table 4. It can be seen from Table 4 that every object type has a positive impact to the performance of VSim, and with the combination of all object types VSim can obtain the best result.

5.2.2 *Our model SHINE*

The set of meta-paths used in our experiments have been shown in Table 3. Among them, there are four length-2 meta-paths and six length-4 meta-paths. To analyze the effectiveness of different meta-path sets, we refer to our model that just utilizes the four length-2 meta-paths as SHINE_4, and refer to our model that utilizes all ten meta-paths as $\text{SHINE}_{\text{all}}$. To analyze the effectiveness of our entity object model (Formula 9) alone to our SHINE's performance, we substitute the uniform popularity model (Formula 5) for the entity popularity model (Formula 7) in the methods SHINE_4 and $\text{SHINE}_{\text{all}}$, and refer to these models as $\text{SHINE}_{\text{4-eom}}$ and $\text{SHINE}_{\text{all-eom}}$, respectively.

Table 5: Experimental results of all approaches

Approach	# correctly linked	Accuracy
POP	345	0.487
VSim	604	0.852
$\text{SHINE}_{\text{4-eom}}$	651	0.918
SHINE_4	655	0.924
$\text{SHINE}_{\text{all-eom}}$	660	0.931
$\text{SHINE}_{\text{all}}$	**668**	**0.942**

The experimental results of all approaches over our data set are shown in Table 5. From the results, we can see that different configurations of our proposed probabilistic model all significantly outperform the two baseline methods (i.e., POP and VSim), which demonstrates the effectiveness of our model. Also, we can see that the methods $\text{SHINE}_{\text{all-eom}}$ and $\text{SHINE}_{\text{4-eom}}$ that just leverage the entity object model achieve high accuracy (i.e., 0.931 and 0.918, respectively) over our data set, which shows that our entity object model alone is very effective for this linking task. Additionally, we can see that $\text{SHINE}_{\text{all}}$ and SHINE_4 outperform the models $\text{SHINE}_{\text{all-eom}}$ and $\text{SHINE}_{\text{4-eom}}$, respectively. This means, our entity popularity model is more effective compared with the uniform popularity model when combined with our entity object model in dealing with the task of entity linking with a HIN. Moreover, it can be also seen from Table 5 that the methods $\text{SHINE}_{\text{all}}$ and $\text{SHINE}_{\text{all-eom}}$ that leverage all ten meta-paths outperform SHINE_4 and $\text{SHINE}_{\text{4-eom}}$ respectively, which just utilize the four length-2 meta-paths. The more useful meta-paths, the better the entity linking accuracy, which is consistent with our intuition, since our entity object model can obtain more related knowledge about the candidate entity from the information network by leveraging more useful meta-paths.

5.3 Efficiency and scalability study

In this subsection, we study the scalability of SHINE using different subsets of our entity mention set. Figure 4(a) plots the average running time for one iteration of the EM algorithm and one iteration of the inner gradient descent algorithm with varied size of the entity mention set. From the results, we can see that the average running time for one iteration of both the EM algorithm and the inner gradient descent algorithm is about linear to the number of entity mentions in the data set, which is consistent with the time complexity analysis of Algorithm 1 described in Section 4. This evaluation demonstrates the scalability of SHINE. Figure 4(b) depicts the accuracy performance of $\text{SHINE}_{\text{all}}$ with varied size of the entity mention set. We can see that our proposed model $\text{SHINE}_{\text{all}}$ can achieve relatively stable and high accuracy with different size of data set, which demonstrates the robustness of our model. SHINE can automatically learn the meta-path weights by maximizing the likelihood of observing named entity mentions in the given document collection. Over various entity mention sets, despite the learned meta-path weights are different, the final en-

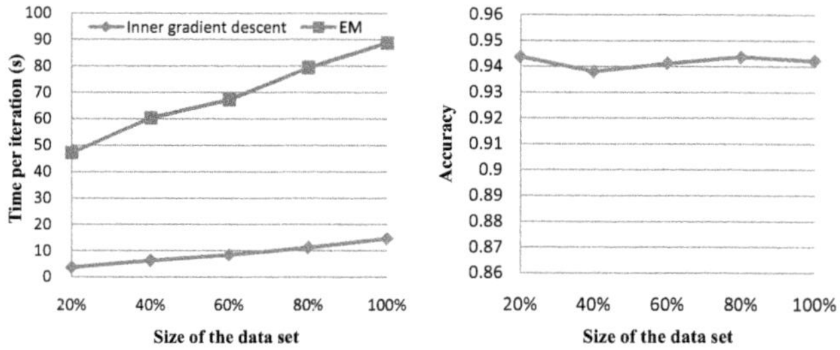

(a) Running time (b) Accuracy performance

Figure 4: Scalability evaluation on our data set

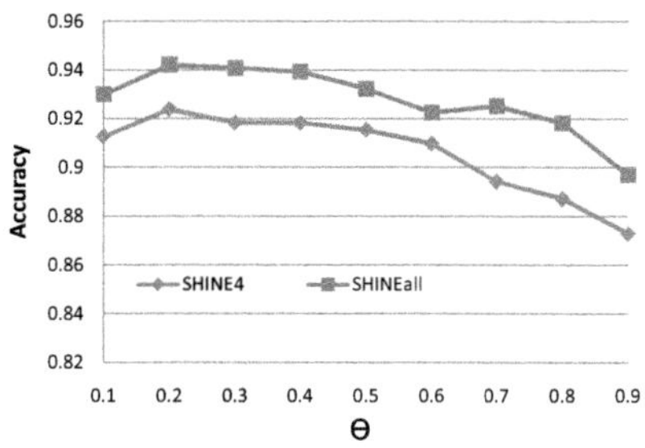

Figure 5: Parameter study of θ

tity linking accuracy of our model is stable and high, which means SHINE can select the most appropriate meta-paths according to different entity linking tasks.

5.4 Sensitivity analysis

To better understand the performance characteristics of our proposed model, we conducted sensitivity analysis to understand the impact of the parameter θ to the SHINE's performance. θ in Formula 9 balances the two parts (i.e., the entity-specific object model and the generic object model for the domain). Figure 5 shows the performance of $SHINE_{all}$ and $SHINE_4$ with varied parameter θ from 0.1 to 0.9 in our data set. From the trend plotted in Figure 5, it can be seen that $SHINE_{all}$ and $SHINE_4$ obtain similar trend with varied θ. We can also see that when $\theta \in [0.1, 0.5]$, the accuracy achieved by $SHINE_{all}$ is all greater than 0.93. Thus, we can say that when θ is varied from 0.1 to 0.5, the performance of SHINE is not very sensitive to parameter θ.

5.5 Case study on meta-path weights

One of the major contributions of SHINE is that it can learn the right meta-path weights for a given entity linking task. We now show the learned weights for all the ten meta-paths by $SHINE_{all}$ over the whole data set in Table 6. From the results, we can see that for our data set, the meta-paths connecting author object with term object (i.e., A-P-T, A-P-A-P-T, and A-P-V-P-T) obtain the highest weights learned by our model. This means, terms play significant roles in the task of entity linking with a HIN, and provide much more knowledge for this linking process than other types of objects, which is consistent with our intuition since Web documents consist of much more terms than the other types of objects.

In order to demonstrate the effectiveness of our learned weights, we evaluated the accuracy performance of our model SHINE with different meta-path sets, and at each time, we

Table 6: The learned weights for meta-paths by $SHINE_{all}$

Meta-path	Weight	Meta-path	Weight
A-P-V-P-T	0.198	A-P-A	0.0702
A-P-A-P-T	0.187	A-P-A-P-V	0.0527
A-P-T	0.183	A-P-V	0.0481
A-P-A-P-A	0.0958	A-P-V-P-A	0.0475
A-P-Y	0.0746	A-P-T-P-V	0.0431

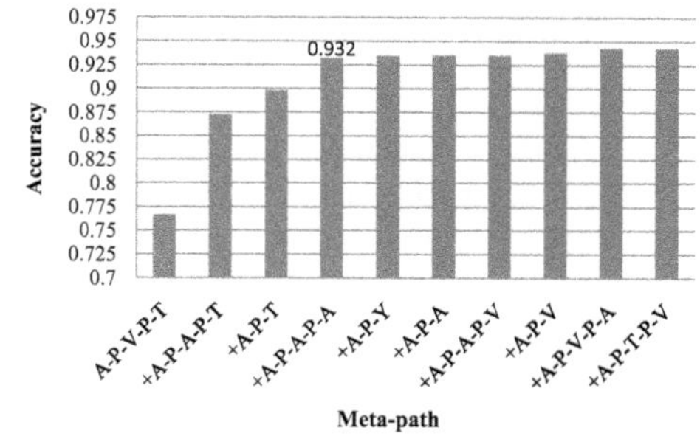

Figure 6: Performance of SHINE with different meta-path sets

added one meta-path in decreasing order of their learned weights into the meta-path set SHINE leverages. The experimental results are shown in Figure 6. From Figure 6, we can see that each meta-path has a nonnegative impact to the SHINE's performance, and with all meta-paths SHINE can obtain the best result. Moreover, the accuracy (i.e., 0.932) achieved by our model that leverages the four meta-paths with the highest weights (i.e., A-P-V-P-T, A-P-A-P-T, A-P-T, and A-P-A-P-A) is higher than the accuracy (i.e., 0.924) obtained by $SHINE_4$ that utilizes the same size of four length-2 meta-paths over the data set. This means, the meta-paths with higher weights are more important and effective for the linking process, which demonstrates the effectiveness of our learned weights.

6. RELATED WORK AND DISCUSSION

As object (or entity) names in information networks (such as bibliographic networks) are inherently ambiguous, considerable progresses have been made in the task of name disambiguation for these networks [30, 13, 25, 29, 17], which make completely disambiguated heterogeneous information networks possible. Given a set of entity names appearing in a network, the task is to determine which entity names refer to the same underlying entity. In [30], Yin et al. proposed DISTINCT, which combines two types of relational similarity (i.e., set resemblance of neighbor tuples and random walk probability) for name disambiguation in DBLP, and achieved 0.883 F_1-*measure* on a DBLP data set. Kanani et al. [13] formulated the author name disambiguation problem as graph partitioning with trained edge weights, and incorporated additional Web information to increase disambiguation accuracy. On their test DBLP data set, they obtained 0.903 F_1-*measure*. Shu et al. [25] proposed a generative latent topic model that involves both author names and words by extending the Latent Dirichlet Allocation model[9], and achieved over 0.9 F_1-*measure* on the data set from DBLP. Wang et al. [29] proposed an active name disambiguation algorithm, aiming to improve the disambiguation performance by integrating feedbacks of correction from users. Finally, their system reaches 0.969 F_1-*measure* over a publication data set with several active user interactions. In addition, Li et al. [17] leveraged the temporal information associated with each publication record to improve author name disambiguation, and achieved about 0.97 F_1-*measure* over a data set from DBLP. For a comprehensive survey of the approaches for author name disambiguation, you could refer to the survey paper [8]. There are also many online scholarly literature search systems, such as Google scholar[4] and Microsoft Academic Search[5]. For most of scholars, these systems have their profile pages containing all their publications, created through users and automatic approaches. These disambiguated information networks make our task of entity linking with a HIN very meaningful.

Another thread of related work is about entity linking. Most existing entity linking methods focus on linking entities with Wikipedia or Wikipedia-derived knowledge bases (e.g., YAGO) [3, 4, 14, 11, 23, 10, 22, 21, 24], and are largely dependent on the special features associated with Wikipedia (e.g., Wikipedia articles or Wikipedia-based relatedness measures), which have been introduced in Section 1. Recently, some work has been proposed to deal with the domain-specific entity linking problem. Pantel and Fuxman [20] associated search engine queries with entities from a large product catalog, and Dalvi et al. [5] exploited the geographic aspects of tweets to infer the matches between tweets and restaurants. Both systems link search engine queries or tweets (rather than entity mentions) with an entity list instead of a heterogeneous information network. Therefore, our task is different from these existing entity linking problems, and no previous methods can be applied to address it.

7. CONCLUSION

In this paper, we have studied a new problem on entity linking with a heterogeneous information network. We propose a probabilistic model called SHINE to deal with this new task. SHINE combines the entity popularity model that captures the popularity of an entity with the entity object model that captures the distribution of multi-type objects appearing in the textual context of an entity. An effective learning algorithm is proposed to automatically learn the best weights of meta-paths without requiring any training data. The experimental results have shown that SHINE can output more accurate linking results compared with the baselines, and is efficient and scalable.

8. ACKNOWLEDGMENTS

This work was supported in part by National Natural Science Foundation of China under Grant No. 61272088, National Key Basic Research Program of China (973 Program) under Grant No. 2014CB340505, a Samsung Research Grant, Tsinghua University Initiative Scientific Research Program, the U.S. ARL W911NF-09-2-0053 (NS-CTA), the U.S. ARO W911NF-13-1-0193, U.S. NSF grants CNS-0931975, IIS-1017362, IIS-1320617, IIS-1354329, DTRA, and DHS.

9. REFERENCES

[1] L. Bottou and O. Bousquet. The tradeoffs of large scale learning. In *NIPS*, pages 161–168, 2008.

[2] S. Brin and L. Page. The anatomy of a large-scale hypertextual web search engine. In *WWW*, pages 107–117, 1998.

[3] R. Bunescu and M. Pasca. Using Encyclopedic Knowledge for Named Entity Disambiguation. In *EACL*, pages 9–16, 2006.

[4] S. Cucerzan. Large-Scale Named Entity Disambiguation Based on Wikipedia Data. In *EMNLP-CoNLL*, pages 708–716.

[5] N. Dalvi, R. Kumar, and B. Pang. Object matching in tweets with spatial models. In *WSDM*, pages 43–52, 2012.

[6] O. Deshpande, D. S. Lamba, M. Tourn, S. Das, S. Subramaniam, A. Rajaraman, V. Harinarayan, and A. Doan. Building, maintaining, and using knowledge bases: A report from the trenches. In *SIGMOD*, pages 1209–1220, 2013.

[7] M. Dredze, P. McNamee, D. Rao, A. Gerber, and T. Finin. Entity disambiguation for knowledge base population. In *Proceedings of the 23rd International Conference on Computational Linguistics*, pages 277–285, 2010.

[8] A. A. Ferreira, M. A. Gonçalves, and A. H. Laender. A brief survey of automatic methods for author name disambiguation. *SIGMOD Rec.*, 41(2):15–26, 2012.

[9] T. L. Griffiths and M. Steyvers. Finding scientific topics. *National Academy of Sciences*, 101, 2004.

[10] X. Han and L. Sun. A generative entity-mention model for linking entities with knowledge base. In *ACL*, 2011.

[11] J. Hoffart, M. A. Yosef, I. Bordino, H. Fürstenau, M. Pinkal, M. Spaniol, B. Taneva, S. Thater, and G. Weikum. Robust disambiguation of named entities in text. In *EMNLP*, 2011.

[12] H. Ji and R. Grishman. Knowledge base population: successful approaches and challenges. In *ACL*, pages 1148–1158, 2011.

[13] P. Kanani, A. McCallum, and C. Pal. Improving author coreference by resource-bounded information gathering from the web. In *IJCAI*, pages 429–434, 2007.

[14] S. Kulkarni, A. Singh, G. Ramakrishnan, and S. Chakrabarti. Collective annotation of wikipedia entities in web text. In *SIGKDD*, pages 457–466, 2009.

[15] N. Lao and W. W. Cohen. Relational retrieval using a combination of path-constrained random walks. *Mach. Learn.*, 81(1):53–67, Oct. 2010.

[16] M. Ley. Dblp: some lessons learned. *Proc. VLDB Endow.*, 2(2):1493–1500, Aug. 2009.

[17] P. Li, X. L. Dong, A. Maurino, and D. Srivastava. Linking temporal records. *Proceedings of the VLDB Endowment*, 4(11):956–967, Aug. 2011.

[18] C. D. Manning, P. Raghavan, and H. Schütze, editors. *An Introduction to Information Retrieval*. Cambridge University Press, 2009.

[19] D. Milne and I. H. Witten. An effective, low-cost measure of semantic relatedness obtained from Wikipedia links. In *WIKIAI*, 2008.

[20] P. Pantel and A. Fuxman. Jigs and lures: associating web queries with structured entities. In *ACL*, pages 83–92, 2011.

[21] L. Ratinov, D. Roth, D. Downey, and M. Anderson. Local and global algorithms for disambiguation to wikipedia. In *ACL*, 2011.

[22] W. Shen, J. Wang, P. Luo, and M. Wang. Liege: Link entities in web lists with knowledge base. In *SIGKDD*, pages 1424–1432, 2012.

[23] W. Shen, J. Wang, P. Luo, and M. Wang. Linden: linking named entities with knowledge base via semantic knowledge. In *WWW*, pages 449–458, 2012.

[24] W. Shen, J. Wang, P. Luo, and M. Wang. Linking named entities in tweets with knowledge base via user interest modeling. In *SIGKDD*, pages 68–76, 2013.

[25] L. Shu, B. Long, and W. Meng. A latent topic model for complete entity resolution. In *ICDE*, pages 880–891, 2009.

[26] F. Suchanek, G. Kasneci, and G. Weikum. Yago: A core of semantic knowledge unifying wordnet and wikipedia. In *WWW*, pages 697–706, 2007.

[27] Y. Sun, J. Han, X. Yan, P. S. Yu, and T. Wu. Pathsim: Meta path-based top-k similarity search in heterogeneous information networks. In *VLDB'11*.

[28] Y. Sun, B. Norick, J. Han, X. Yan, P. S. Yu, and X. Yu. Integrating meta-path selection with user-guided object clustering in heterogeneous information networks. In *SIGKDD*, 2012.

[29] X. Wang, J. Tang, H. Cheng, and P. S. Yu. Adana: Active name disambiguation. In *ICDM*, pages 794–803, 2011.

[30] X. Yin, J. Han, and P. S. Yu. Object distinction: Distinguishing objects with identical names. In *ICDE*, 2007.

[4] http://scholar.google.com/

[5] http://academic.research.microsoft.com/

Matching Heterogeneous Event Data

Xiaochen Zhu[§] Shaoxu Song[§] Xiang Lian[†] Jianmin Wang[§] Lei Zou[‡]

[§]KLiss, MoE; TNList; School of Software, Tsinghua University, China
zhu-xc10@mails.tsinghua.edu.cn {sxsong, jimwang}@tsinghua.edu.cn
[†]University of Texas - Pan American, USA lianx@utpa.edu
[‡]Peking University, China zoulei@pku.edu.cn

ABSTRACT

Identifying duplicate events are essential to various business process applications such as provenance querying or process mining. Distinct features of heterogeneous events including opaque names, dislocated traces and composite events, prevent existing data integration from techniques performing well. To address these issues, in this paper, we propose an event similarity function by iteratively evaluating similar neighbors. We prove the convergence of iterative similarity computation, and propose several pruning and estimation methods. To efficiently support matching composite events, we devise upper bounds of event similarities. Experiments on real and synthetic datasets demonstrate that the proposed event matching approaches can achieve significantly higher accuracy than the state-of-the-art matching methods.

Categories and Subject Descriptors

H.2.5 [**Database Management**]: Heterogeneous Databases

Keywords

Schema matching; event matching

1. INTRODUCTION

Owing to various mergers and acquisitions, information systems (e.g., Enterprise Resource Planning (ERP) and Office Automation (OA) systems), probably developed independently in different branches or subsidiaries in large-scale corporations, keep on generating heterogeneous event logs. We surveyed a major bus manufacturer who recently started a project on integrating their event data in the OA systems of 31 subsidiaries. These OA systems have been built independently on 5 distinct middleware products in the past 20 years. More than 8190 business processes are implemented in these systems, among which 68.8% are indeed different implementations of the same business activities in different subsidiaries. For instance, in the following Example 1, we illustrate two versions of turbine order processing processes in 31 subsidiaries. Duplicate events commonly exist in these heterogeneous processes for the same business activities.

The company has started to integrate these heterogeneous event data into a unified business process data warehouse [3, 4], where different types of analyses can be performed, e.g., querying similar complex procedures or discovering interesting event patterns in different subsidiaries (complex event processing, CEP [6]), comparing business processes in different subsidiaries to find common parts for process simplification and reuse [19], or obtaining a more abstract global picture of business processes (workflow views [2]) in the company. Without exploring the correspondence among heterogeneous events, applications such as query and analysis over the event data may not yield any meaningful results.

The event matching problem is to construct the similarity and matching relationship of events from heterogeneous sources. Although there are 49 system integrators (subject-matter experts) employed by the bus manufacturer in the project of OA system integration, given the large number of more than 100,000 event activities, manually checking the correspondences of all possible event pairs is highly impractical for two reasons: 1) manual checking is obviously inefficient, and 2) manual checking results could be inaccurate and contradictory. An automatic approach is highly demanded for matching these heterogeneous event data.

Different from conventional schema matching on attributes in relational databases [7], there are strong relationships of consecutive occurrence among events. The event data integration is challenging due to the following features commonly observed in the general event data.

(1) Event names could be *opaque*, due to various encoding, syntax or language conventions in heterogeneous systems.

(2) Event traces might be *dislocated*. Only a part (e.g., the beginning) of a trace 1 corresponds to a distinct part (e.g., the end) of another trace 2.

(3) *Composite* event may exist. That is, one event in a source corresponds to several decomposed ones in another source, known as composite event in CEP [6].

Example 1. *Figure 1 illustrates two fragments of event logs $\mathcal{L}_1$ and $\mathcal{L}_2$ for turbine order processing in two different subsidiaries of the bus manufacturer, respectively. Two example traces are shown in each fragment, and each trace denotes a sequence of events (steps) for processing one order. An event log consists of many traces, among which the sequences of events may be different, since some of the events can be executed concurrently (e.g.* Ship Goods(E) *and* Email

SIGMOD'14, June 22–27, 2014, Snowbird, UT, USA.

http://dx.doi.org/10.1145/2588555.2588570.

ID	Trace
t1	Paid by Cash (A) → Check Inventory (C) → Validate (D) → Ship Goods (E) → Email Customer (F)
t2	Paid by Credit Card (B) → Check Inventory (C) → Validate (D) → Email Customer (F) → Ship Goods (E)
...	......

(a) Event log $\mathcal{L}_1$

ID	Trace
s1	Order Accepted (1) → Paid by Cash (2) → Inventory Checking & Validation (4) → ????????? (5) → Send Notification (6)
s2	Order Accepted (1) → Paid by Credit Card (3) → Inventory Checking & Validation (4) → Send Notification (6) → ???????? (5)
...	......

(b) Event log $\mathcal{L}_2$

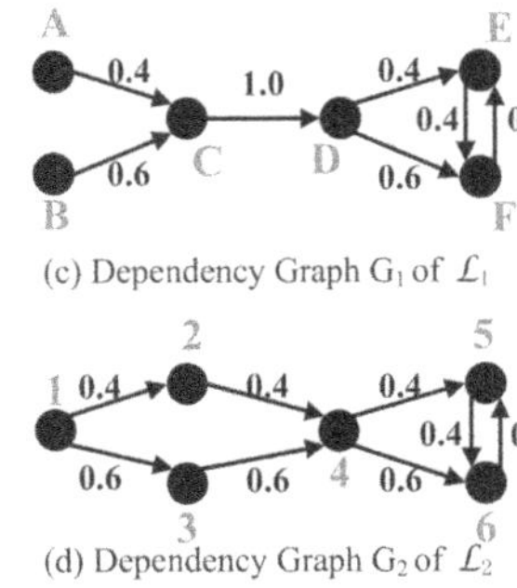

Figure 1: Fragments of two event logs and their dependency graphs

Customer(F) in $\mathcal{L}_1$), or exclusively (e.g., Paid by Cash(2) or Paid by Credit Card(3) in $\mathcal{L}_2$).

Note that opaque names exist in $\mathcal{L}_2$ as shown in Figure 1(b). The event "????????(5)" is collected from a database whose encoding is distinct from others, which makes the event name garbled. According to expert investigation, the original name of "????????(5)" should be "Delivery(5)", and the true event corresponding relation between $\mathcal{L}_1$ and $\mathcal{L}_2$ is highlighted by red dashed lines in Figures 1(a) and (b).

Dislocated matching exists between the first traces in $\mathcal{L}_1$ and $\mathcal{L}_2$. Event Paid by Cash(A) that appears at the beginning of traces in $\mathcal{L}_1$ corresponds to event Paid by Cash(2), which appears in the middle of traces in $\mathcal{L}_2$, having another event Order Accepted(1) before it.

Moreover, two events Check Inventory(C) and Validate(D) in $\mathcal{L}_1$ correspond to one composite event Inventory Checking & Validation(4). For simplicity, we use $ABCDEF$ to denote event names in $\mathcal{L}_1$, while 123456 are events in $\mathcal{L}_2$.

Unfortunately, existing techniques cannot effectively address the aforesaid three challenges in event matching. A straightforward idea of matching events is to compare their names (a.k.a. event labels). String edit distance (syntactic similarity) [13] as well as word stemming and the synonym relation (semantic similarity) [20] are widely used in the label similarity based approaches [14, 19, 5, 23]. As shown in Example 1, such a *typographical similarity* cannot address the identified Challenge 1, i.e., opaque event labels.

Structural similarity may be considered besides the typographical similarity. The idea is to construct a graph for describing the relationships among events, e.g., the frequency of appearing consecutively in an event log [8]. Once the graphical structure is obtained, graph matching techniques can be employed to identify the event (behavioral/structural) similarities. Unfortunately, existing graph matching techniques cannot handle well the dislocated matching of events[1], i.e., the aforesaid Challenge 2. Graph edit distance (GED) [5] for general graph data and normal distance for matching with opaque names (OPQ) [11] concern a local evaluation of similar neighbors. However, as illustrated in Example 1, dislocated matching events may have distinct neighbors (see more details below). Rather than local neighbors, another type of Simrank [10] like behavioral similarity (BHV) [19] considers a global evaluation via propagating similarities in the entire graph in multiple iterations. Unfortunately, directly applying the global propagation does not help in matching dislocated events that do not have any predecessor, e.g., Paid by Cash(A) in Figure 1.

Example 2. *Figures 1(c) and 1(d) capture the statistical and structural information of $\mathcal{L}_1$ and $\mathcal{L}_2$, respectively (see Definition 1 for constructing G_1 and G_2). Each vertex in the directed graph denotes an event, while an edge between two events (say AC in Figure 1(c) for instance) indicates that they appear consecutively in at least one trace (e.g., trace 1 in Figure 1(a)). The numbers attached to edges represent the normalized frequencies of consecutive event pairs. For instance, 0.4 of AC means that A, C appear consecutively in 40% of the traces of the event log.*

Since GED and OPQ concern more about the local similarity, e.g., the high similarity of (A, C) and $(1, 2)$, an event mapping $M = \{A \to 1, B \to 3, C \to 2, D \to 4, E \to 5, F \to 6\}$ will be returned by GED with distance 0.16 and OPQ with score 10.7. The true mapping $M' = \{A \to 2, B \to 3, C/D \to 4, E \to 5, F \to 6\}$ in ground truth shows a higher GED distance 0.233 (lower is better) and lower OPQ score 10 (higher is better) instead. BHV does not help in capturing dislocated mapping, e.g., between A and 2 with BHV similarity 0. Instead, A and 1 with no input neighbors have higher similarity 1, i.e., unable to find the dislocated matching.

When matching composite events, i.e., Challenge (3), computing efficiency becomes a major issue. For instance, one may be interested in composite events $\{C, D\}$, $\{D, E\}$ and $\{E, F\}$ in Figure 1(c). Given a candidate set of n composite events, there may exist 2^n possible combinations, for each of which we need to evaluate the corresponding event similarities. Unfortunately, structural similarities such as GED are already costly to compute for one combination.

Contributions. In this paper, we propose a similarity function that supports dislocated matching and opaque events, by iteratively computing neighbor similarities. Our major contributions in this paper are summarized as follows.

(1) We formally define the similarity function, which is iteratively computed by incorporating other similarity criteria in the iteration. Intuitively, as discussed in Example 2, directly applying OPQ that concerns a local evaluation of similar neighbors is ineffective in matching dislocated events with possibly distinct neighbors. In contrast, the proposed iteration based similarity function concerns the global evaluation via propagating similarities, and thus overcomes the impact of local neighbor distinctness.

(2) We prove the convergence of the proposed iteration based similarity function and devise a pruning technique

[1]According to our survey on 5642 processes with redundancy (68.8% of 8190) of the bus manufacturer, more than 44% of them involve dislocated event traces.

Table 1: Frequently used notations

Symbol	Description
$v \in V$	an event v in event set V
$G(V, E, f)$	an event dependency graph
v^X	an artificial event
$\bullet v, v\bullet$	the pre/post set of an event
$\mathcal{S}^n(v_1, v_2)$	the similarity between events v_1 and v_2 after the nth iteration
$l(v_1)$	the longest distance from v^X to v_1
U	a composite event
$\mathcal{U}$	a collection of composite event candidates

for efficient computations. Moreover, we introduce a fast estimation with a constant number of iterations. In particular, by varying the number of maximum iterations from 0 to larger, it provides a trade-off between matching accuracy and computing time.

(3) We study the complexity bound of the composite event matching problem. The problem of finding the optimal composite event matching is proved to be NP-hard. Owing to the large number of possible composite event matching candidates, applying existing OPQ is inefficient (as discussed in related work in Section 6 and observed in the experiments in Section 5). Therefore, we propose greedy heuristics for efficiently matching composite events, identify event pairs that can avoid updating similarities between greedy steps, and design upper bounds of similarities for efficient pruning.

(4) We report an extensive experimental evaluation on both real and synthetic datasets. The results demonstrate that our proposed matching methods can achieve higher accuracy than the state-of-the-art methods.

The remainder of this paper is organized as follows. Section 2 gives an overview of the event matching framework. Section 3 illustrates the computation of event similarity between two event logs. Section 4 extends the matching approach to capture composite event similarities. Section 5 reports the experimental evaluation. Finally, Section 6 discusses related work and Section 7 concludes this paper.

2. OVERVIEW OF EVENT MATCHING

We formalize syntax and definitions for the event matching problem. Table 1 lists the frequently used notation in this paper. Let V be a set of events, i.e., events that can be recorded in a log. A trace is a finite sequence of events from V. An event log $\mathcal{L}$ is a multi-set of traces from V^*.

Capturing structural information. Detecting correspondences on raw logs is difficult, since the event names could be "opaque". Other than typographic similarity, we can exploit the structural information for matching events.

Following the same line of [11], we employ a simple graph model, namely *dependency graph*, which consists of both dependency relations and frequencies.

Definition 1 (Event Dependency Graph). *An event dependency graph G is a labeled directed graph (V, E, f), where each vertex in V corresponds to an event, E is an edge set, and f is a labeling function of normalized frequencies that*

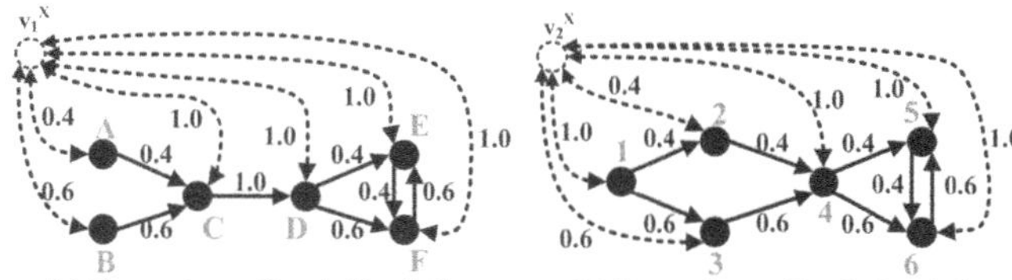

(a) Dependency Graph G_1 of $\mathcal{L}_1$ (b) Dependency Graph G_2 of $\mathcal{L}_2$

Figure 2: Dependency graphs with artificial events

(1) for each $v \in V$, $f(v, v)$ is the normalized frequency of event v, i.e., the fraction of traces in $\mathcal{L}$ that contain v, and (2) for each edge $(v_1, v_2) \in E$, $f(v_1, v_2)$ is the normalized frequency of two consecutive events $v_1 v_2$, i.e., the fraction of traces in which $v_1 v_2$ occur consecutively at least once.
For any $v \in V$, the pre-set of v is defined as $\bullet v = \{v' | (v', v) \in E\}$ and the post-set of v is defined as $v\bullet = \{v' | (v, v') \in E\}$.

With the presence of dislocated matching, any event in an event log can be a starting/ending event. That is, a trace can start/end with any event v within it by ignoring those events before/after v. Based on this intuition, we extend the dependency graph G by adding an artificial event v^X and several artificial edges as follows.

(1) An artificial event v^X is added into V, which denotes the virtual beginning/end of all traces in an event log.

(2) For each event $v \in V$ except v^X, we add two artificial edges (v, v^X) and (v^X, v), i.e., each event can be a virtual starting event (edge (v^X, v)) and a virtual ending event (edge (v, v^X)). Moreover, we associate $f(v^X, v) = f(v, v^X) = f(v)$ based on the intuition that a trace can start/end with event v at all the locations where v occurs.

Example 3. *In order to support dislocated matching, we add an artificial events and edges into dependency graphs, denoted by vertices and edges in dashed lines in Figures 2(a) and 2(b). As the virtual beginning/end of all traces, v_1^X and v_2^X connect to all the events in V_1 and V_2, respectively. The weight on each artificial edge is assigned by the normalized frequency of the occurrence of each event. For instance, since event C appears in all the traces of $\mathcal{L}_1$, we have $f(v_1^X, C) = 1.0$. Event A only appears in 40% traces of $\mathcal{L}_1$, which indicates $f(v_1^X, A) = 0.4$.*

Filtering with minimum frequency control. Intuitively, edges in the dependency graph with low frequencies may not help much in matching events since they have few statistical information. We can filter out those edges whose frequencies are lower than a predefined threshold. The average degree of a dependency graph may decrease after filtering out those edges, which can accelerate the computation of similarity. Hence, the minimum edge frequency control could be interpreted as a trade-off between accuracy and efficiency.

Computing pair-wise similarities. Based on the dependency graphs of statistical information in two event logs, the similarity between each event pair, denoted $\mathcal{S}(v_1, v_2)$, can be computed. Motivated by the unique features of heterogeneous events as indicated in the introduction, we propose a similarity measure by iteratively utilizing structural information in Section 3. In particular, the proposed measure is extensible by integrating with other similarities such as typographic or linguistic similarities [20].

Selecting matching correspondences. Once all the pair-wise similarities are gained, there are various existing approaches to capture the corresponding events. It is worth noting that the event pairs containing either v_1^X or v_2^X should be omitted since these two events are introduced artificially and do not actually exist in event logs. As it is not the focus of this study, we briefly outline the approaches of selecting correspondences from pair-wise similarities in Section 6.

Matching composite events. Most existing graph matching approaches are restricted to finding 1:1 correspondences [14], i.e., one event should be mapped exactly to another. Such a strong restriction fails to detect the matching of composite events. Owing to heterogeneous settings, a single event in one process could be divided into several events in another process. Therefore, the m:n correspondences, which are called complex matches in [23], should also be addressed.

When matching composite events with various candidate combinations, it needs to frequently compute the (composite) event similarities. We devise upper bounds of the proposed similarity function for efficient pruning in Section 4.

3. EVENT MATCHING SIMILARITY

Three categories of techniques may be considered for evaluating event similarities: 1) content-based such as typographic similarities [20], 2) structure-based similarities which concern local structures such as GED [5] and OPQ [11], and 3) structure-based similarities with a global view of the entire graph like Simrank [10]. Unfortunately, as illustrated in the introduction, content based similarities often fail to perform owing to opaque event names, while GED and OPQ cannot handle dislocated matching well. On the other hand, the widely used Simrank [10] is not directly applicable to event data for two reasons: 1) Simrank concerns only the pure structural similarity, while the utilization of other criteria such as typographic similarities is not supported, even when they are available; 2) Simrank does not take edge similarities into consideration, which are the key properties of consecutive occurrence between events.

In this section, we present an adaption of Simrank like structural similarity function for matching events, and discuss its convergence. Efficient pruning of unnecessary similarity updates based on early convergence and fast (one iteration) estimation of similarities are devised.

3.1 Structural Similarity Function

Intuitively, following the same line of Simrank, an event, say $v_1 \in V_1$, is similar to event $v_2 \in V_2$, if they frequently share similar predecessors (in-neighbors). We use $s(v_1, v_2)$ to denote how often a predecessor v_1' of $v_1, v_1' \in \bullet v_1$, can find a similar $v_2' \in \bullet v_2$, predecessor of v_2. Note that this s measure is asymmetric, i.e., $s(v_1, v_2) \neq s(v_2, v_1)$.

Next, to adapt Simrank like evaluation for event similarity, we further take edge similarities into consideration. Although the predecessors v_1' and v_2' of v_1 and v_2, respectively, have high similarity, if the frequency of (v_1', v_1) deviates far from the frequency of (v_2', v_2), the similarity of v_1' and v_2' will have less effect on the similarity of v_1 and v_2.

Finally, although it supports matching events with opaque names, we take label similarities (typographic similarities of event names) into account, in case they are available.

Following these intuitions, we define a forward similarity.

Definition 2. *The* forward similarity *of two events is*

$$\mathcal{S}(v_1, v_2) = \alpha(s(v_1, v_2) + s(v_2, v_1))/2 + (1-\alpha)\mathcal{S}^L(v_1, v_2),$$

where $\mathcal{S}^L(v_1, v_2)$ is the label similarity of v_1 and v_2, $\alpha \in [0, 1]$ is a weight, $s(v_1, v_2)$ and $s(v_2, v_1)$ are one-side similarities

$$s(v_1, v_2) = \frac{1}{|\bullet v_1|} \sum_{v_1' \in \bullet v_1} \max_{v_2' \in \bullet v_2} C(v_1, v_1', v_2, v_2')\mathcal{S}(v_1', v_2'),$$

given that $C(v_1, v_1', v_2, v_2') = c*(1 - \frac{|f(v_1, v_1') - f(v_2, v_2')|}{f(v_1, v_1') + f(v_2, v_2')})$, where c is a constant that has $0 < c < 1$.

We now explain how these formulas implement our intuition. In the formula of $s(v_1, v_2)$, for each in-neighbor v_1' of v_1, we find an event v_2' with the highest similarity to v_1' among all the in-neighbors of v_2. Besides the node similarity $S(v_1', v_2')$ which evaluates how similar v_1' and v_2' are, we also consider the similarity of the edges (v_1', v_1) and (v_2', v_2) which denote the consecutive occurring relationships of events, by $C(v_1, v_1', v_2, v_2')$. Obviously, if (v_1', v_1) and (v_2', v_2) have similar normalized frequencies, $C(v_1, v_1', v_2, v_2')$ is close to c; otherwise close to 0, where c gives the rate of similarity decay across edges. To support label similarity, we use a weighted aggregation of the structural similarity $\frac{1}{2}(s(v_1, v_2) + s(v_2, v_1))$ and the label similarity $\mathcal{S}^L(v_1, v_2)$.

3.2 Iterative Computation

To compute $\mathcal{S}(v_1, v_2)$ from predecessors, we present an iteration method by iteratively applying the formulas in Definition 2. Let $\mathcal{S}^n(v_1, v_2)$ denote the forward similarity of (v_1, v_2) after the nth iteration. The computation has two steps: the initialization step which assigns $\mathcal{S}^0(v_1, v_2)$ for every event pair (v_1, v_2), and the iteration step which computes the value of $\mathcal{S}^n(v_1, v_2)$ by using $\mathcal{S}^{n-1}(v_1, v_2)$ according to Definition 2, when $n \geq 1$.

1) Initialization. For the artificial events v_1^X and v_2^X, the initial similarities $\mathcal{S}^0(v_1^X, v_2^X)$ is set to 1.0 since both of them are defined as the virtual beginning and ending of traces. $\mathcal{S}^0(v_1^X, v_2)$ (and $\mathcal{S}^0(v_1, v_2^X)$) is set to 0 if one event is real but the other is artificial. For any other real event pair (v_1, v_2), $\mathcal{S}^0(v_1, v_2)$ is set to 0, since there is no priori knowledge for assigning nonzero values as initial similarities.

2) Iteration. In each iteration, we refresh $\mathcal{S}$ for each event pair (v_1, v_2) using the similarities of their neighbors in the previous iteration. For instance, according to Definition 2, $\mathcal{S}^n$ which denotes the forward similarity of (v_1, v_2) after the nth iteration can be computed by:

$$\mathcal{S}^n(v_1, v_2) = \alpha(s^n(v_1, v_2) + s^n(v_2, v_1))/2 + (1-\alpha)\mathcal{S}^L(v_1, v_2),$$
$$s^n(v_1, v_2) = \frac{1}{|\bullet v_1|} \sum_{v_1' \in \bullet v_1} \max_{v_2' \in \bullet v_2} C(v_1, v_1', v_2, v_2')\mathcal{S}^{n-1}(v_1', v_2'). \quad (1)$$

The similarities between artificial events and real events (e.g. $\mathcal{S}(v_1^X, v_2)$, $\mathcal{S}(v_1, v_2^X)$ and $\mathcal{S}(v_1^X, v_2^X)$) are not updated during the iteration. The algorithm stops when the difference between $\mathcal{S}^n(v_1, v_2)$ and $\mathcal{S}^{n-1}(v_1, v_2)$ for all event pairs (v_1, v_2) is less than a predefined threshold.

Example 4 (Example 2 continued). *At the beginning of the iteration, $\mathcal{S}^0(v_1^X, v_2^X)$ is assigned with 1.0, and $\mathcal{S}^0(v_1, v_2)$ is* *assigned with 0 for any other event pairs where $v_1 \neq v_1^X$ and $v_2 \neq v_2^X$. Consider the event pair $(A, 1)$. Let $\alpha = 1$, on the 1st iteration, we have $s^1(A,1) = \frac{1}{|\bullet A|}C(v_1^X, A, v_2^X, 1)\mathcal{S}^0(v_1^X, v_2^X) = 0.457$ and $s^1(1,A) = \frac{1}{|\bullet 1|}C(v_1^X, 1, v_2^X, A)\mathcal{S}^0(v_1^X, v_2^X) = 0.457$, so that $\mathcal{S}^1(A,1) = 0.5 * (s^1(A,1) + s^1(1,A)) = 0.457$. For the event pair $(A, 2)$, we have $s^1(A,2) = \frac{1}{|\bullet A|}\max(C(v_1^X, A, v_2^X, 2)\mathcal{S}^0(v_1^X, v_2^X), C(v_1^X, A, 1, 2)\mathcal{S}^0(v_1^X, 1)) = 0.8$ and $s^1(2, A) = \frac{1}{|\bullet 2|}(C(v_2^X, 2, v_1^X, A)\mathcal{S}^0(v_2^X, v_1^X) + C(1, 2, v_1^X, A)\mathcal{S}^0(1, v_1^X)) = 0.4$, so that $\mathcal{S}^1(A,2) = 0.5 \times (0.8 + 0.4) = 0.6$. It is notable that A and 2 have higher similarity than A and 1, which solves the problem of dislocated matching. Consequently, we can compute an average similarity of all the event pairs in the true mapping M' in Example 2, i.e., 0.551, which is higher than the average similarity 0.506 of M.*

The time complexity of computing forward similarity is $O(k|V_1||V_2|d_{avg})$, where k is the number of iterations and d_{avg} is the average degree of all the events in the dependency graph. When the density of the dependency graph as well as the numbers of iterations is high (i.e., d_{avg} and k are high), the iterative computation is time-consuming.

3.3 Convergence

We show that the iterative computation converges to limits satisfying the similarity function in Definition 2.

Theorem 1. *For all $v_1 \in V_1, v_2 \in V_2, \lim_{n\to\infty} \mathcal{S}^n(v_1, v_2) = \mathcal{S}(v_1, v_2)$.*

Proof. **Existence**. Firstly, the monotonicity of $\mathcal{S}^n(v_1, v_2)$ can be simply proved by induction.

Monotonicity: $0 \leq \mathcal{S}^{n-1}(v_1, v_2) \leq \mathcal{S}^n(v_1, v_2) \leq 1$, for all $v_1 \in V_1, v_2 \in V_2, n \geq 1$.

Basis: Let $n = 1$. According to formula (1), there is $s^1(v_1, v_2) = \frac{1}{|\bullet v_1|}\sum_{v_1' \in \bullet v_1} \max_{v_2' \in \bullet v_2} C(v_1, v_1', v_2, v_2')\mathcal{S}^0(v_1', v_2')$. That is, $s^1(v_1, v_2) \in (0, 1]$ *iff* $v_1^X \in \bullet v_1$ and $v_2^X \in \bullet v_2$; otherwise, $s^1(v_1, v_2)$ must be 0. Similarly, we have $s^1(v_2, v_1) \in [0, 1]$, and thus $\mathcal{S}^1(v_1, v_2) \in [0, 1]$. Since the similarity $\mathcal{S}^n(v_1, v_2)$ will be updated only if both v_1 and v_2 are real events, we have $\mathcal{S}^0(v_1, v_2) = 0$ and $\mathcal{S}^1(v_1, v_2) \in [0, 1]$, that is, $0 \leq \mathcal{S}^0(v_1, v_2) \leq \mathcal{S}^1(v_1, v_2) \leq 1$. Therefore, the monotonicity holds for $n = 1$.

Induction: Assume that the monotonicity holds for $n = k$, i.e., $0 \leq \mathcal{S}^{k-1}(v_1, v_2) \leq \mathcal{S}^k(v_1, v_2) \leq 1$. According to formula (1), we have $s^{k+1}(v_1, v_2) = \frac{1}{|\bullet v_1|}\sum_{v_1' \in \bullet v_1} \max_{v_2' \in \bullet v_2} C(v_1, v_1', v_2, v_2') \times \mathcal{S}^k(v_1', v_2') \geq \frac{1}{|\bullet v_1|}\sum_{v_1' \in \bullet v_1} \max_{v_2' \in \bullet v_2} C(v_1, v_1', v_2, v_2') \times \mathcal{S}^{k-1}(v_1', v_2') = s^k(v_1, v_2)$. It thus follows $\mathcal{S}^{k+1}(v_1, v_2) \geq \mathcal{S}^k(v_1, v_2)$, and implies that $0 \leq \mathcal{S}^{n-1}(v_1, v_2) \leq \mathcal{S}^n(v_1, v_2) \leq 1$ also holds for $n = k + 1$.

As both basis and induction have been performed, by mathematical induction, the monotonicity holds for all $n \geq 1$.

Therefore, for any event pair (v_1, v_2), the sequence $\mathcal{S}^n(v_1, v_2)$ is bounded and non-decreasing along with the increase of n. According to the Completeness Axiom of calculus, each sequence $\mathcal{S}^n(v_1, v_2)$ has a limit $\mathcal{S}(v_1, v_2) \in [0, 1]$.

Uniqueness. We prove the uniqueness of the limit of $\mathcal{S}(v_1, v_2)$ by contradiction. Suppose that there are two distinct limits of forward similarity, denoted by $\mathcal{S}_1$ and $\mathcal{S}_2$. For each event pair (v_1, v_2), let $\Delta(v_1, v_2) = \mathcal{S}_1(v_1, v_2) - \mathcal{S}_2(v_1, v_2)$ be the difference of two limits, and $\Delta_M = \max_{v_1 \in V_1, v_2 \in V_2} |\Delta(v_1, v_2)|$ be the maximum absolute value of any $\Delta(v_1, v_2)$. For artificial events v_1^X and v_2^X, we have $\Delta(v_1^X, v_2) = \Delta(v_1, v_2^X) = 0$ because their similarity is never updated during an iteration. Otherwise, for two real events v_1 and v_2, we have:

$$
\begin{aligned}
\Delta_M =& \mathcal{S}_1(v_1, v_2) - \mathcal{S}_2(v_1, v_2) \\
=& \frac{\alpha}{2}\Big(\frac{1}{|\bullet v_1|}\sum_{v_1' \in \bullet v_1}(\max_{v_2' \in \bullet v_2} C(v_1, v_1', v_2, v_2')\mathcal{S}_1(v_1', v_2') \\
&- \max_{v_2' \in \bullet v_2} C(v_1, v_1', v_2, v_2')\mathcal{S}_2(v_1', v_2')) \\
&+ \frac{1}{|\bullet v_2|}\sum_{v_2' \in \bullet v_2}(\max_{v_1' \in \bullet v_1} C(v_1, v_1', v_2, v_2')\mathcal{S}_1(v_1', v_2') \\
&- \max_{v_1' \in \bullet v_1} C(v_1, v_1', v_2, v_2')\mathcal{S}_2(v_1', v_2'))\Big) \\
\leq& \frac{\alpha}{2}\Big(\frac{1}{|\bullet v_1|}\sum_{v_1' \in \bullet v_1}(\max_{v_2' \in \bullet v_2}(C(v_1, v_1', v_2, v_2')\mathcal{S}_1(v_1', v_2') \\
&- C(v_1, v_1', v_2, v_2')\mathcal{S}_2(v_1', v_2'))) \\
&+ \frac{1}{|\bullet v_2|}\sum_{v_2' \in \bullet v_2}(\max_{v_1' \in \bullet v_1}(C(v_1, v_1', v_2, v_2')\mathcal{S}_1(v_1', v_2') \\
&- C(v_1, v_1', v_2, v_2')\mathcal{S}_2(v_1', v_2')))\Big) \\
\leq& \frac{\alpha}{2}c(\frac{1}{|\bullet v_1|}|\bullet v_1|\Delta_M + \frac{1}{|\bullet v_2|}|\bullet v_2|\Delta_M) = c\alpha\Delta_M
\end{aligned}
$$

Note that, $\Delta_M \leq c\alpha\Delta_M$ and Δ_M is an absolute number. If it holds $\Delta_M > 0$, we have $1 \leq c\alpha$, which is in contradiction with $0 \leq c\alpha \leq 1$. It concludes $\Delta_M = 0$, and thus, $\mathcal{S}_1(v_1, v_2) = \mathcal{S}_2(v_1, v_2)$.[2] □

3.4 Pruning

Next, we identify that the similarities of some node pairs are guaranteed to converge in a certain number (say h) of iterations. These similarities do not need to be updated in the nth iterations, where $n > h$.

Intuitively, for a node v_1 (often the source node) with only one predecessor, artificial v_1^X, we can show that the similarity of v_1 to any node will be fixed (converged) after one iteration according to the similarity definition. Consequently, in the next iteration, a node whose predecessors are all converged (like v_1) is guaranteed to converge too.

Let $l(v)$ denote the longest distance from v^X to v (could be ∞ if loops exist from v^X to v).

Proposition 2. *For any two events $v_1 \in V_1$ and $v_2 \in V_2$, $\mathcal{S}^{h+1}(v_1, v_2) - \mathcal{S}^h(v_1, v_2) = 0$, for all $h \geq \min(l(v_1), l(v_2))$.*

Proof. This proposition can be proved by induction.

Basis: Obviously, when $\min(l(v_1), l(v_2)) = 1$, $\mathcal{S}^h(v_1, v_2)$ will never change after the first iteration.

Induction: Assume that the proposition holds for all v_1 and v_2 satisfying $\min(l(v_1), l(v_2)) = k$. For all v_1 and v_2 satisfying $\min(l(v_1), l(v_2)) = k + 1$, the similarity $\mathcal{S}^h(v_1', v_2')$ of their input neighbors will never change after the kth iteration due to the assumption. Therefore, $\mathcal{S}^h(v_1, v_2)$ will never change after the $(k + 1)^{th}$ iteration.

By mathematical induction, the proposition holds for all $\min(l(v_1), l(v_2)) \geq 1$. □

Based on this proposition, we first compute $l(v_1)$ and $l(v_2)$ for all the events, so that there is no need to compute those similarities for event pairs (v_1, v_2) with $\min(l(v_1), l(v_2)) < k$

[2] Due to the limit of space, we include the complete proof in http://ise.thss.tsinghua.edu.cn/sxsong/doc/ematch.pdf

at the kth iteration. In addition, we can say for sure that the iterative computation will stop after the nth iteration, where $n = \min(\max_{v_1 \in V_1} l(v_1), \max_{v_2 \in V_2} l(v_2))$. It is worth noting that if G_1 and G_2 have loops, the early convergence property still holds for those node pairs (v_1, v_2) where all the ancestors of v_1 and v_2 are not involved in loops.

Example 5. *Considering the event pair* $(A, 1)$ *where* $h = \min(l(A), l(1)) = 1$. *According to formula (1), the value of* $\mathcal{S}^n(A, 1)$ *will only be affected by the value of* $\mathcal{S}^{n-1}(v_1^X, v_2^X)$. *Since* $\mathcal{S}^n(v_1^X, v_2^X)$ *never changes, the value of* $\mathcal{S}^n(A, 1)$ *will not change after the* 1st *iteration. Likewise, the value of* $\mathcal{S}^n(C, 2)$ *will not change after the* 2nd *iteration, since* $\mathcal{S}(A, 1)$ *and* $\mathcal{S}(A, 2)$ *converged at the* 1st *iteration. Therefore, we prune the computation of* $\mathcal{S}^n(A, 1)$ *and* $\mathcal{S}^n(B, 1)$ *where* $n \geq 1$, *the computation of* $\mathcal{S}^n(C, 2)$ *and* $\mathcal{S}^n(C, 3)$ *where* $n \geq 2$ *and the computation of* $\mathcal{S}^n(D, 4)$ *where* $n \geq 3$.

3.5 Estimation

We further improve the efficiency by introducing an estimation of each $\mathcal{S}(v_1, v_2)$ with fewer iterations, e.g., even with only one iteration. Thereby, the estimation has an $O(|V_1||V_2|)$ time complexity in an extreme case that only one iteration is conducted, or conduct more iterations to make the estimated similarity closer to the exact similarity, which can be interpreted as trading the accuracy for efficiency.

First, we rewrite the formula of $\mathcal{S}^n(v_1, v_2)$ as follows:

$$\begin{aligned}\mathcal{S}^n(v_1, v_2) =& \frac{\alpha}{2}\Big[\frac{1}{|\bullet v_1|}\Big(C(v_1^X, v_1, v_2^X, v_2)\mathcal{S}(v_1^X, v_2^X) + \\ & \sum_{v_1' \in \{\bullet v_1\} \backslash \{v_1^X\}} \max_{v_2' \in \bullet v_2} C(v_1, v_1', v_2, v_2')\mathcal{S}^{n-1}(v_1', v_2')\Big) \\ & + \frac{1}{|\bullet v_2|}\Big(C(v_1^X, v_1, v_2^X, v_2)\mathcal{S}(v_1^X, v_2^X) + \\ & \sum_{v_2' \in \{\bullet v_2\} \backslash \{v_2^X\}} \max_{v_1' \in \bullet v_1} C(v_1, v_1', v_2, v_2')\mathcal{S}^{n-1}(v_1', v_2')\Big)\Big].\end{aligned}$$

In the formula above, we assume that each $C(v_1, v_1', v_2, v_2')$ achieves the maximum value c, and we replace the similarity of v_1' and v_2' by the similarity of v_1 and v_2. For simplicity, we denote C as $C(v_1, v_1', v_2, v_2')$, A as $|\bullet v_1|$, and B as $|\bullet v_2|$. The formula is further derived.

$$\begin{aligned}\mathcal{S}^n(v_1, v_2) \approx \mathcal{S}_{\text{es}}^n(v_1, v_2) =& \frac{\alpha c(2AB - A - B)}{2AB}\mathcal{S}_{\text{es}}^{n-1}(v_1, v_2) \\ & + \frac{\alpha(A + B)}{2AB}C + (1 - \alpha)\mathcal{S}^L(v_1, v_2).\end{aligned}$$

Let $q = \frac{\alpha c(2AB - A - B)}{2AB}$ and $a = \frac{\alpha(A+B)}{2AB}C + (1 - \alpha)\mathcal{S}^L(v_1, v_2)$. It follows

$$\begin{aligned}\mathcal{S}_{\text{es}}^n(v_1, v_2) =& q\mathcal{S}_{\text{es}}^{n-1}(v_1, v_2) + a \\ q\mathcal{S}_{\text{es}}^{n-1}(v_1, v_2) =& q^2\mathcal{S}_{\text{es}}^{n-2}(v_1, v_2) + aq \\ & \vdots \\ q^{n-I-1}\mathcal{S}_{\text{es}}^{I+1}(v_1, v_2) =& q^{n-I}\mathcal{S}_{\text{es}}^{I}(v_1, v_2) + aq^{n-I-1},\end{aligned}$$

where $0 \leq I \leq n - 1, I \in \mathbb{N}$. By eliminating the corresponding items on the left and the right sides, it implies

$$\mathcal{S}_{\text{es}}^n(v_1, v_2) = q^{n-I}\mathcal{S}_{\text{es}}^I(v_1, v_2) + a(1 + q + q^2 + \cdots + q^{n-I-1}).$$

By summing the geometric sequence, $\mathcal{S}_{\text{es}}^n(v_1, v_2)$ is given by

$$\mathcal{S}_{\text{es}}^n(v_1, v_2) = q^{n-I}\mathcal{S}_{\text{es}}^I(v_1, v_2) + \frac{a(1 - q^{n-I})}{1 - q}. \quad (2)$$

According to the early convergence proposed in Section 3.4, n should not be greater than $h = \min(l(v_1), l(v_2))$ (or n could be ∞, if $l(v_1)$ or $l(v_2)$ is ∞). Thereby, the estimation of $\mathcal{S}(v_1, v_2)$ is $\mathcal{S}_{\text{es}}^h(v_1, v_2)$. Noting that I is a constant number of iterations of exact computation before estimation, $\mathcal{S}_{\text{es}}^I(v_1, v_2)$ can be replaced by the exact value $\mathcal{S}^I(v_1, v_2)$. It provides a trade-off between accuracy and time. The larger I is, the closer the estimation values and the exact values are, which costs more time to do the iterations (see the experiments in Section 5 for the effect of varying I). In addition, I should be no greater than h according to early convergence.

Example 6. *Referring to the estimation formula, given* $I = 0$ *and* $\alpha = 1$. *The value of* $S(A, 1)$ *can be estimated by* $\mathcal{S}_{\text{es}}^1(A, 1) = C(v_1^X, A, v_2^X, 1)c = 0.6$, *which is equal to the exact value of* $\mathcal{S}(A, 1)$. *However, for the event pair* $(C, 4)$, *the estimated value is* 0.409 *while the exact value is* 0.587. *This is because the estimation formula treats the similarity of event* C *and* 4 *as the similarity of their ancestors. However, if we set* $I = 10$, *the estimated similarity of event pair* $(C, 4)$ *is* 0.557, *which is closer to the exact value.*

3.6 Algorithm

Finally, Algorithm 1 summarizes the procedure of iterative computation and estimation of forward similarity. All the similarities are initialized in Line 1. From Line 2 to Line 5, we first conduct I rounds of iterations according to formula (1). We consider the early convergence in Line 4, by skipping the iterative computations for those similarities that are early converged. Then, the estimation is conducted from Line 6 to Line 8 based on formula (2). Algorithm 1 has the lowest time complexity $O(|V_1||V_2|)$ when $I = 0$, and is equivalent to the exact algorithm if we set $I > \min(l(v_1), l(v_2))$, for all $v_1 \in V_1$ and $v_2 \in V_2$.

Algorithm 1 EXACTESTIMATIONTRADEOFF(G_1, G_2, I)

Input: two dependency graphs G_1 and G_2, and a constant I of iterations
Output: the 1:1 matching similarity $\mathcal{S}$
1: $\mathcal{S}^0(v_1, v_2) := 1$ for v_1^X and v_2^X, otherwise $\mathcal{S}^0(v_1, v_2) := 0$
2: **for** each i from 1 to I **do**
3:   **for** each $v_1 \in V_1 \setminus \{v_1^X\}$, $v_2 \in V_2 \setminus \{v_2^X\}$ **do**
4:     **if** $i \leq \min(l(v_1), l(v_2))$ and $\mathcal{S}^i(v_1, v_2)$ is not converged **then**
5:       $\mathcal{S}^i(v_1, v_2) := \alpha(s^{i-1}(v_1, v_2) + s^{i-1}(v_2, v_1))/2 + (1 - \alpha)\mathcal{S}^L(v_1, v_2)$
6: **for** each $v_1 \in V_1 \setminus \{v_1^X\}$, $v_2 \in V_2 \setminus \{v_2^X\}$ **do**
7:   **if** $I < h = \min(l(v_1), l(v_2))$ **then**
8:     $\mathcal{S}_{\text{es}}(v_1, v_2) := q^{h-I}\mathcal{S}^I(v_1, v_2) + \frac{a(1-q^{h-I})}{1-q}$
9: **return** $\mathcal{S}_{\text{es}}$

Similarities in two directions

The similarity function in Definition 2 considers only the predecessors (in-neighbors, e.g., events A and B of event C in Figure 1), known as *forward similarity*. Symmetrically, we may also investigate successors (out-neighbors, e.g., events 2 and 3 are out-neighbors of event 1), namely *backward simi-*

larity. As shown in the experiments, by aggregating the forward and backward similarities together (e.g., by average), we can successfully address the matching with dislocations.

4. MATCHING COMPOSITE EVENTS

As mentioned earlier, an event in one source could possibly correspond to multiple events in another source, known as composite events [6]. For the set V of events appearing in an event log $\mathcal{L}$, let $U \subseteq V$ denote a composite event that consists of a subset of singleton events from V. We consider a collection of composite event candidates $\mathcal{U} = \{U \subseteq V\}$, where different candidates may overlap.[3] We call $\mathcal{W} \subseteq \mathcal{U}$ a *subset of non-overlapping composite events*, i.e., $\forall U_1, U_2 \in \mathcal{W}, U_1 \cap U_2 = \emptyset$.

Let $\mathcal{W}_1, \mathcal{W}_2$ be two sets of composites from the candidate sets $\mathcal{U}_1, \mathcal{U}_2$ for $\mathcal{L}_1$ and $\mathcal{L}_2$, respectively. To evaluate the similarities with composite events, i.e., $\mathcal{S}(\mathcal{W}_1, \mathcal{W}_2)$, we can simply treat each composite event as one node (in constructing the dependency graph) and thus directly apply the similarity function in Definition 2.

It is easy to see the large number of possible combinations of non-overlapping composite events in each event log. Different combinations may yield distinct similarity results. Intuitively, the higher the similarities in $\mathcal{S}(\mathcal{W}_1, \mathcal{W}_2)$, the better the composite events are matched. We denote $avg(\mathcal{S}(\mathcal{W}_1, \mathcal{W}_2)) = \frac{\sum_{W_1 \in \mathcal{W}_1, W_2 \in \mathcal{W}_2} \mathcal{S}(W_1, W_2)}{|\mathcal{W}_1| \cdot |\mathcal{W}_2|}$ the average of all the pair-wise similarities between composite events in $\mathcal{W}_1, \mathcal{W}_2$.

Problem 1 (Composite event matching). *Given two sets of candidate composite events $\mathcal{U}_1$ and $\mathcal{U}_2$ for two event logs $\mathcal{L}_1$ and $\mathcal{L}_2$, respectively, the optimal composite event matching problem is to find two subsets of non-overlapping composite events $\mathcal{W}_1 \subseteq \mathcal{U}_1$ and $\mathcal{W}_2 \subseteq \mathcal{U}_2$ such that the average composite event similarity $avg(\mathcal{S}(\mathcal{W}_1, \mathcal{W}_2))$ is maximized.*

Unfortunately, the problem is highly non-trivial.

Theorem 3. *The problem of finding the optimal composite event matching is* NP*-hard.*

Proof idea. To show the NP-hardness, we build a reduction from the maximum set packing problem, which is one of Karp's 21 NP-complete problems [12]. Given a universe V and a family $\mathcal{U}$ of subsets of V, a packing is a subfamily $\mathcal{W} \subseteq \mathcal{U}$ of sets such that all sets in $\mathcal{W}$ are pairwise disjoint. The maximum set packing problem asks for the maximum weighted aggregation of pairwise disjoint sets, which is analogous to a set of composite events with the maximum similarity in the matching problem. □

Hence, in the following, we focus on greedy heuristics that iteratively select one composite event in a step to form the results. Note that in each step of selecting one composite event, similarities of some node pairs may not be affected and thus have no need to be recomputed. Moreover, to enable pruning among possible combinations, we devise the upper bounds of similarities.

4.1 Heuristics

Consider all the remaining candidate composite events that can be further selected $\mathcal{C}_1 = \{U \in \mathcal{U}_1 \mid U \cap W = \emptyset, W \in \mathcal{W}_1\}$, i.e., those U not overlapping with any composite event W in $\mathcal{W}_1$. As mentioned above, for a $U \in \mathcal{C}_1$, we can directly obtain the dependency graph w.r.t. $\mathcal{W}_1 \cup \{U\}$ by updating the graph of $\mathcal{W}_1$.

[3]Candidates of composite events can either be manually identified or automatically discovered [6].

In each step, we greedily select a composite event $U_1 \in \mathcal{C}_1$ of $\mathcal{L}_1$ that can maximize the average similarity, i.e.,

$$U_1 = \arg\max_{U \in \mathcal{C}_1} avg(\mathcal{S}(\mathcal{W}_1 \cup \{U\}, \mathcal{W}_2)) - avg(\mathcal{S}(\mathcal{W}_1, \mathcal{W}_2)).$$

Similarly, we obtain a $U_2 \in \mathcal{C}_2$ of $\mathcal{L}_2$. The one, either $U_1 \in \mathcal{C}_1$ or $U_2 \in \mathcal{C}_2$, with higher average similarity improvement will be confirmed to add to the corresponding $\mathcal{W}_1$ or $\mathcal{W}_2$.

Since the similarity improvement could be negative, a threshold δ of minimum similarity improvement can be specified, e.g. $\delta = 0$ with the requirement of similarity increase $avg(\mathcal{S}(\mathcal{W}_1 \cup \{U_1\}, \mathcal{W}_2)) - avg(\mathcal{S}(\mathcal{W}_1, \mathcal{W}_2)) > 0$ or $avg(\mathcal{S}(\mathcal{W}_1, \mathcal{W}_2) \cup \{U_2\}) - avg(\mathcal{S}(\mathcal{W}_1, \mathcal{W}_2)) > 0$.

Example 7. *Suppose that composite event candidates are $\mathcal{U}_1 = \{\{A\}, \{B\}, \{C\}, \{D\}, \{E\}, \{F\}, \{C, D\}, \{E, F\}\}$ for $\mathcal{L}_1$ on the dependency graph shown in Figure 1(c) and δ is* 0.005. *We first compute the pairwise similarities of singleton events of G_1 and G_2, $\mathcal{S} = \mathcal{S}(\{A, B, C, D, E, F\}, \{1, 2, 3, 4, 5, 6\})$, having $avg(\mathcal{S}) = 0.502$ (let $\alpha = 1$). Then, we construct two new dependency graphs $G_1^{\{C,D\}}$ and $G_1^{\{E,F\}}$ by merging events CD and EF in G_1, respectively. The pairwise event similarities of each candidate $\mathcal{S}^{\{C,D\}} = \mathcal{S}(\{A, B, CD, E, F\}, \{1, 2, 3, 4, 5, 6\})$ and $\mathcal{S}^{\{E,F\}} = \mathcal{S}(\{A, B, C, D, EF\}, \{1, 2, 3, 4, 5, 6\})$ are computed, with average similarities $avg(\mathcal{S}^{\{C,D\}}) =$* 0.508 *and $avg(\mathcal{S}^{\{E,F\}}) = 0.478$. The composite event candidate $\{C, D\}$ with higher $avg(\mathcal{S}^{\{C,D\}}) - avg(\mathcal{S}) > \delta$ is accepted. Since $\{C, D\}$ and $\{E, F\}$ do not overlap, we further test merging both CD and EF in G_1 by computing $\mathcal{S}^{\{C,D\},\{E,F\}} = \mathcal{S}(\{A, B, CD, EF\}, \{1, 2, 3, 4, 5, 6\})$. However, the average similarity $avg(\mathcal{S}^{\{C,D\},\{E,F\}}) = 0.478 < avg(\mathcal{S}^{\{C,D\}})$ decreases. $\{C, D\}$ is returned in composite event matching.*

4.2 Identifying Unchanged Similarities

Since introducing a new composite event U changes the structure of the dependency graph, the similarity of existing events (not involved in U) may change. A straightforward idea is to recompute all the similarities from scratch. We note, however, if there does not exist a path from U to v, the similarities on v will not change in this iteration.

Let U be the currently selected composite event in a greedy step. We denote $AN(v)$ all the ancestors of a node v w.r.t. prerequisites.

Proposition 4. *If $AN(v) \cap U = \emptyset$, all the similarities $\mathcal{S}(v, u)$ will be unchanged after integrating U.*

Proof. According to formula (1), the similarity of $\mathcal{S}(v, u)$ will only be affected by the similarities of $AN(v)$ and $AN(u)$. Obviously, if $AN(v) \cap U = \emptyset$, the pairwise similarities of the ancestors of v and u remain unchanged, thus $\mathcal{S}(v, u)$ will not change after integrating U. □

Therefore, we only need to update the similarities whose ancestors are changed w.r.t. the composite event U.

4.3 Pruning via Similarity Upper Bounds

Although a greedy heuristic is employed, it is still costly in each greedy step to compute the similarity for selecting each possible composite event candidate. In the following, we show that we can compute an upper bound of similarity for any pair of events between two dependency graphs. Such an upper bound enables pruning of composite event candidates, whose similarity upper bound is lower than some currently computed results.

The idea is that the similarity is not only increasing (Theorem 1) between two iterations, but also increases within a certain bound w.r.t. the iteration number. For those event pairs that converge in a constant number of iterations (Proposition 2), we can develop a certain bound of similarity. A general upper bound for any event pair is also derived.

Lemma 5. *Let $v_1 \in V_1$ and $v_2 \in V_2$ be two events, c the upper bound of function C. The difference of similarity between the nth and $(n-1)^{th}$ iterations ($n \geq 1$) holds:*

$$0 \leq \mathcal{S}^n(v_1, v_2) - \mathcal{S}^{n-1}(v_1, v_2) \leq (\alpha c)^n$$

Proof. $0 \leq \mathcal{S}^n(v_1, v_2) - \mathcal{S}^{n-1}(v_1, v_2)$ has been proved by the monotonicity, and we only need to prove $\mathcal{S}^n(v_1, v_2) - \mathcal{S}^{n-1}(v_1, v_2) \leq c^n$. It can be proved by induction.
Basis: Let $n = 1$. $\mathcal{S}^1(v_1, v_2) - \mathcal{S}^0(v_1, v_2)$

$$= \frac{\alpha}{2}\Big(\frac{1}{|\bullet v_1|}\sum_{v_1' \in \bullet v_1} \max_{v_2' \in \bullet v_2} C(v_1', v_1, v_2', v_2)\mathcal{S}^0(v_1', v_2') + \frac{1}{|\bullet v_2|}\sum_{v_2' \in \bullet v_2} \max_{v_1' \in \bullet v_1} C(v_1', v_1, v_2', v_2)\mathcal{S}^0(v_1', v_2')\Big).$$

Since $0 \leq \mathcal{S}^0(v_1', v_2') \leq 1$, we have

$$\mathcal{S}^1(v_1, v_2) - \mathcal{S}^0(v_1, v_2) \leq \frac{\alpha}{2}\Big(\frac{1}{|\bullet v_1|}|\bullet v_1|c + \frac{1}{|\bullet v_2|}|\bullet v_2|c\Big) = \alpha c.$$

The lemma holds for $n = 1$.
Induction: Assume that the lemma holds for $n = k$, i.e., $\mathcal{S}^k(v_1, v_2) - \mathcal{S}^{k-1}(v_1, v_2) \leq (\alpha c)^k$. When $n = k+1$, according to Definition 2, we have

$$\begin{aligned}
&\mathcal{S}^{k+1}(v_1, v_2) - \mathcal{S}^k(v_1, v_2) \\
\leq &\frac{\alpha}{2}\Big(\frac{c}{|\bullet v_1|}\sum_{v_1' \in \bullet v_1} \max_{v_2' \in \bullet v_2} (\mathcal{S}^k(v_1', v_2') - \mathcal{S}^{k-1}(v_1', v_2')) \\
&+ \frac{c}{|\bullet v_2|}\sum_{v_2' \in \bullet v_2} \max_{v_1' \in \bullet v_1} (\mathcal{S}^k(v_1', v_2') - \mathcal{S}^{k-1}(v_1', v_2'))\Big) \\
\leq &\frac{\alpha}{2}\Big(\frac{c}{|\bullet v_1|}|\bullet v_1|(\alpha c)^k + \frac{c}{|\bullet v_2|}|\bullet v_2|(\alpha c)^k\Big) = (\alpha c)^{k+1}.
\end{aligned}$$

Thus, the conclusion also holds for $n = k+1$.

By mathematical induction, Lemma 5 holds for $n \geq 1$. □

We are now ready to compute an upper bound of similarity between any two events.

Proposition 6. *Let v_1, v_2 be two events, c be the upper bound of function C, and $\mathcal{S}^k(v_1, v_2)$ be the similarity after k^{th} iteration. The upper bound of similarity $\mathcal{S}(v_1, v_2)$ is:*

$$\mathcal{S}_U(v_1, v_2) = \mathcal{S}^k(v_1, v_2) + \frac{(\alpha c)^k}{1 - \alpha c}.$$

Proof. According to Lemma 5, we have

$$\begin{aligned}
\mathcal{S}^n(v_1, v_2) =&\mathcal{S}^k(v_1, v_2) + (\mathcal{S}^{k+1}(v_1, v_2) - \mathcal{S}^k(v_1, v_2)) \\
&+ (\mathcal{S}^{k+2}(v_1, v_2) - \mathcal{S}^{k+1}(v_1, v_2)) + \cdots \\
&+ (\mathcal{S}^n(v_1, v_2) - \mathcal{S}^{n-1}(v_1, v_2)) \\
\leq&\mathcal{S}^k(v_1, v_2) + (\alpha c)^{k+1} + (\alpha c)^{k+2} + \cdots + (\alpha c)^n \\
=&\mathcal{S}^k(v_1, v_2) + \frac{(\alpha c)^k - (\alpha c)^n}{1 - \alpha c}.
\end{aligned}$$

When $n \to \infty$, $(\alpha c)^n \to 0$, we have $\mathcal{S}(v_1, v_2) \leq \mathcal{S}^k(v_1, v_2) + \frac{(\alpha c)^k}{1-\alpha c}$. □

According to Proposition 2, if there exists a longest path with finite length h from the artificial node v^X to v, the similarity on v will always converge in h steps. Rather than the general bound in Proposition 6, we can develop an upper bound of such events as follows.

Corollary 7. *For any two events $v_1 \in V_1$ and $v_2 \in V_2$, let $h \geq \min(l(v_1), l(v_2))$. The upper bound of similarity $\mathcal{S}(v_1, v_2)$ is:*

$$\mathcal{S}_U(v_1, v_2) = \mathcal{S}^k(v_1, v_2) + \frac{(\alpha c)^k - (\alpha c)^h}{1 - \alpha c}.$$

Finally, Algorithm 2 presents the procedure of greedy merge. At the beginning, the event similarity $\mathcal{S}$ of original dependency graph G_1 and G_2 is computed. From Line 2 to Line 12, we use the greedy strategy to determine the best solution of node aggregation. We first gain all the possible candidates $\mathcal{U}$. For each candidate, we reconstruct the dependency graphs by merging events (or composite events). Then, we compute $\mathcal{S}'$ for reconstructed G_1' and G_2' in Line 6. It is worth noting that the pruning methods proposed in Sections 4.2 and 4.3 can be utilized in this step. After all the candidates are processed, we compare the maximum average similarity $avg(\mathcal{S}^{max})$ among all the $\mathcal{S}'$ in this iteration with the maximum average similarity $avg(\mathcal{S})$ of last iteration. If the increment is higher than a predefined threshold δ, the candidate that produces $\mathcal{S}^{max}$ is confirmed as a proper merging candidate, and the iteration will go on. Otherwise, we return $\mathcal{S}$ as the best similarity since the average similarity cannot be improved significantly.

Algorithm 2 COMPOSITEPRUNE(G_1, G_2)

Input: two dependency graph G_1 and G_2
Output: the m:n matching similarity $\mathcal{S}$

1: $\mathcal{S}$:= compute event similarity of G_1 and G_2
2: **for** i from 1 to infinite **do**
3:    $\mathcal{U}$:=all possible candidate pairs
4:    **for** each candidate $\mathcal{W}$ in $\mathcal{U}$ **do**
5:       G_1', G_2' := reconstructed G_1 and G_2 by merging events
6:       $\mathcal{S}'$:= compute event similarity of G_1' and G_2'
7:       **if** $avg(\mathcal{S}') > avg(\mathcal{S}^{max})$ **then**
8:          $\mathcal{S}^{max}$:=$\mathcal{S}'$,G_1^{max} := G_1',G_2^{max} := G_2'
9:    **if** $avg(\mathcal{S}^{max}) - avg(\mathcal{S}) < \delta$ **then**
10:       break
11:    **else**
12:       $\mathcal{S}$:= $\mathcal{S}^{max}$,G_1 := G_1^{max},G_2 := G_2^{max}
13: **return** $\mathcal{S}$

Example 8 (Example 7 continued). *Suppose that we now consider the composite event candidate $U = \{E, F\}$ in Figure 1 (c). For those events in V_1, we have $AN(A) \cap U = AN(B) \cap U = AN(C) \cap U = AN(D) \cap U = \emptyset$. Hence, for event $v_1 \in \{A, B, C, D\}$, we have $\mathcal{S}^{\{C,D\}}(v_1, v_2) = \mathcal{S}(v_1, v_2)$ according to Proposition 4.*

Now suppose that we are computing $\mathcal{S}^{\{E,F\}}$ after $avg(\mathcal{S}^{\{C,D\}})$ = 0.508 is gained. When the 15th iteration is done, the upper bound of average similarity $avg(\mathcal{S}_U^{\{E,F\}})$ is lower than 0.504, which satisfies $avg(\mathcal{S}_U^{\{E,F\}}) < avg(\mathcal{S}^{\{E,F\}})$. Therefore, we can immediately stop the computation of $\mathcal{S}^{\{E,F\}}$.

5. EVALUATION

In this section, we report an experimental evaluation on comparing our method with the state-of-the-art event matching approaches, *graph edit distance* (GED) [5], *opaque name matching* (OPQ) [11] and *behavioral similarity* (BHV) [19].

5.1 Implementation and Settings

Data sets. We employ a real data set of 149 event log pairs, which are extracted from 10 different functional areas in the OA systems of two subsidiaries of a bus manufacturer. Each event log pair denotes two event logs doing the same or similar works in two subsidiaries, respectively. The matching relationships in event log pairs are manually identified.

The data set is divided into two groups, where the first group with 103 event log pairs does not contain composite events, while the remaining 46 event logs in the second group have composite events.

To study the performance on dislocations, we categorize the dataset into 3 testbeds w.r.t. matching positions. The first one, namely DS-F, consists of 23 event log pairs where the dislocated events appear at the end of traces between two logs. In the second testbed, namely DS-B with 22 event log pairs, those dislocated events locate in the beginning of traces between two logs. Finally, DS-FB may involve dislocated events at both the beginning and the end of traces.

A state-of-the-art string similarity measure, cosine similarity with q-grams [9], is employed to compute the label similarity. Candidates of composite events are obtained by grouping singleton events that always appear consecutively, following the convention of SEQ pattern in CEP [6].

Besides real data sets, we also generate a synthetic data set to evaluate the scalability of our approaches. Firstly, we generate 10 groups of random process specifications by varying event sizes ranging from 10 to 100. Each event size contains 20 distinct process specifications. For each process specification, we randomly generate 2 event logs, which form an event log pair. Therefore, we have 20 event log pairs on each distinct event size. Obviously, the events in two logs with the same name correspond to each other. All these models and logs are generated by an open source toolkit BeehiveZ[4] using existing generating approaches [18, 15].

Criteria. After pair-wise similarities of events are computed, we use the maximum total similarity selection method [17] to select event correspondences. The ground truth, i.e., the true mapping of events among 149 event log pairs, is supplied by 49 subject-matter experts in MIS (Management Information Systems) departments of each subsidiaries of the bus manufacturer during a long-period deliberation. Let found denote the matching correspondences produced by event matching approaches. We use the f-measure of precision and recall to evaluate the accuracy of event matching, given by $precision = \frac{|\text{truth} \cap \text{found}|}{|\text{found}|}$, $recall = \frac{|\text{truth} \cap \text{found}|}{|\text{truth}|}$, and $f\text{-}measure = 2 \cdot \frac{precision \cdot recall}{precision + recall}$. A larger f-measure indicates a higher matching accuracy.

Besides the accuracy performance, we also evaluate time costs of matching approaches.

[4]http://code.google.com/p/beehivez/

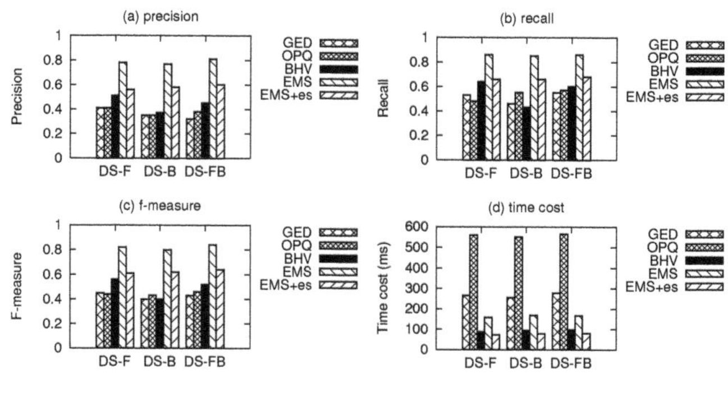

Figure 3: Performance on matching singleton events

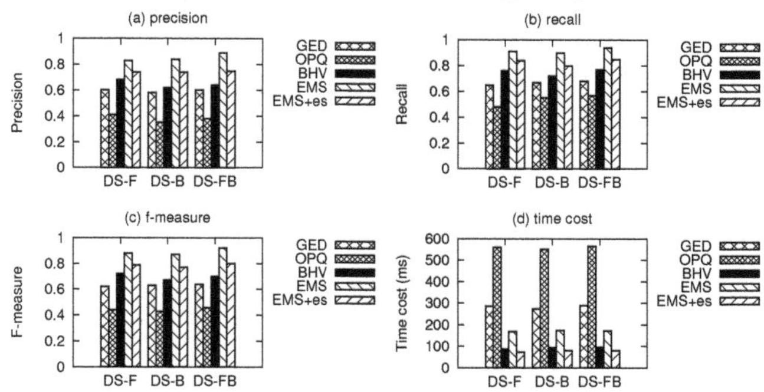

Figure 4: Integrating with typographic similarity

Our programs are implemented in Java and all experiments were performed on a PC with Intel(R) Core(TM) i7-2600 3.40GHz CPU and 8 GB memory.

5.2 Evaluating Event Similarity

We first report the experimental results on computing singleton event similarity. The compared approaches include our proposed event matching similarity (EMS) and the estimation EMS+es with $I = 5$, as well as existing approaches GED, OPQ and BHV.

Figure 3 presents the average accuracy and time costs of event matching. In order to observe the performance in the scenario of opaque events, we do not employ other similarities such as typographic similarities on event names, and rely on the structural similarity of dependency graphs only. First, the accuracy of our proposed EMS is higher than all the existing methods in all the testbeds. The rationale is that GED and OPQ concern local similarity, while dislocated events often have distinct neighbors and prevent these two approaches performing well as explained in Example 2. Moreover, BHV performs better than GED and OPQ on testbed DS-F, where the correspondences of events at the beginning of traces can be addressed by the forward similarity of BHV. However, BHV's accuracy is much lower on testbed DS-B compared with DS-F, since it only considers one-direction similarity and cannot handle well the dislocated events at the beginning of traces (in DS-B as well as DS-FB) as indicated in Example 1. Our EMS considers similarities in both directions (as indicated in Section 3.6) and employs the artificial event to reduce the impact of distinct neighbors of dislocated events. Consequently, EMS outperforms BHV on all the testbeds.

The corresponding time cost of EMS is no more than the double of BHV's and significantly lower than that of GED

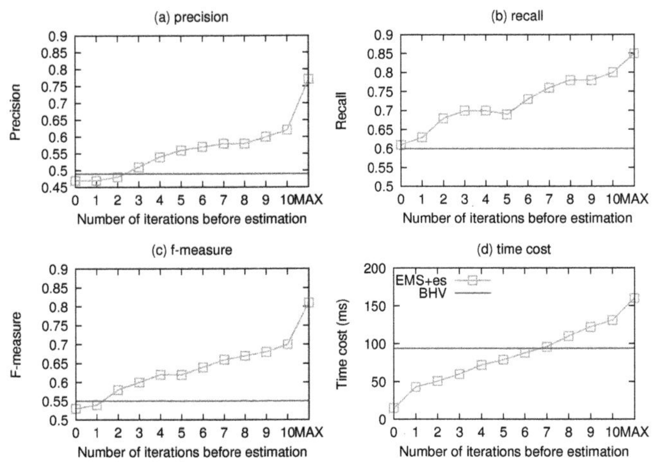

Figure 5: Trade-off in estimation

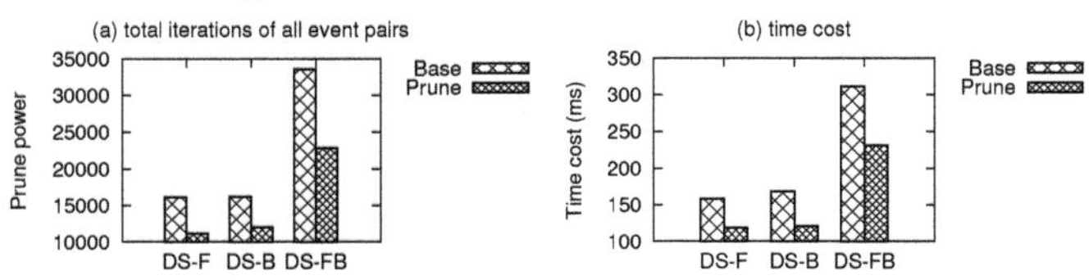

Figure 6: Prune power of early convergence

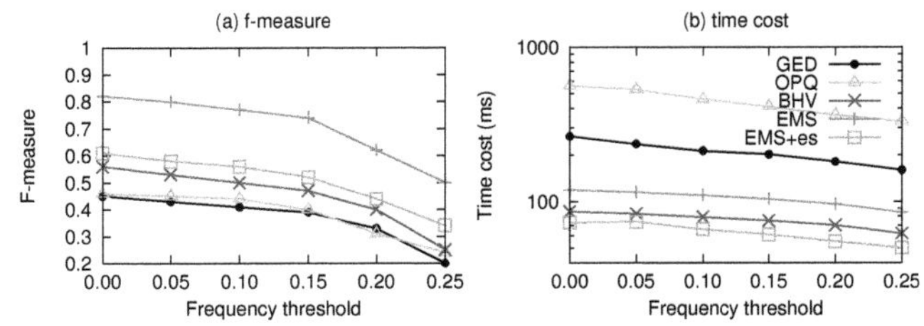

Figure 7: Trade-off by frequency filtering

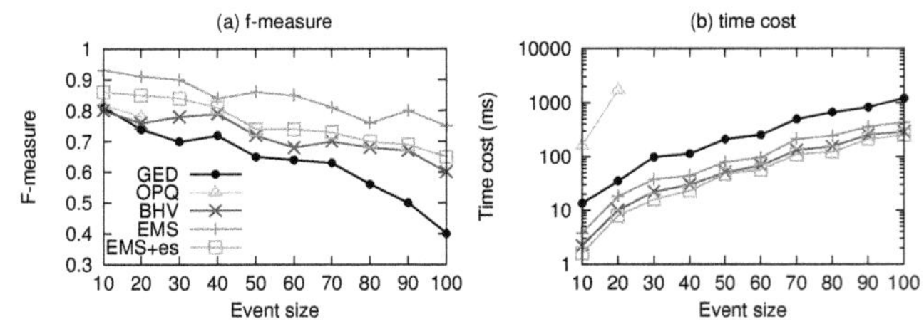

Figure 8: Scalability on the number of events

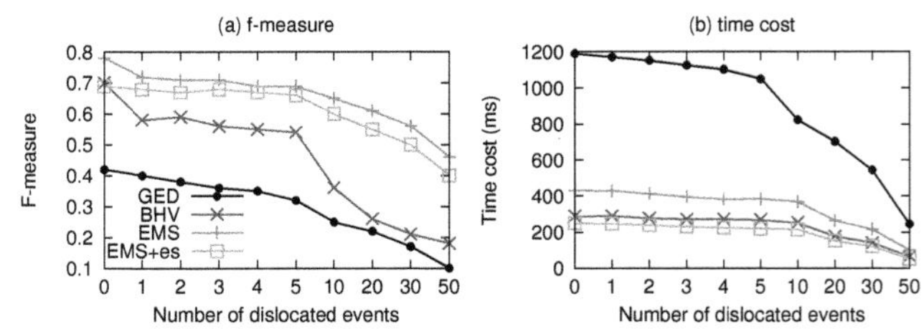

Figure 9: Performance on handling dislocated events

and OPQ. It is not surprising owing to the high complexity of computing graph edit distance or normal distance. Most importantly, the similarity estimation approach (EMS+es, with 5 iterations) shows the lowest time cost among all the evaluated approaches. Although the improvement in terms of time by EMS+es is not great compared with BHV, the accuracy of EMS+es outperforms BHV significantly (especially in DS-B and DS-FB), which is also observed in the following experiments such as Figure 4.

Figure 4 illustrates the results by integrating structural similarities with typographic similarities (cosine similarity of event names). In general, the results are very similar to Figure 3 without considering the typographic similarity. The major difference is that the accuracies of all approaches are improved except OPQ, since OPQ does not benefit from label similarity. The results demonstrate that our proposed similarity measure can improve the matching accuracy, no matter with or without typographic similarities.

Figure 5 evaluates the trade-off in performance by estimation. As shown in the figure, when the number of fixed iterations is small, e.g., 0, the estimation f-measure is comparable with the state-of-the-art BHV and shows about an order of magnitude improvement in time costs. On the other hand, for a large number of iterations, such as 10 or MAX (precise measure without estimation), the improvement of f-measure is up to 0.25, i.e., from 0.55 to 0.8.

Figure 6 evaluates the performance of the pruning method proposed in Section 3.4. Note that when pruning is applied, each pair of events may need a different number of iterations (each iteration performs a computation of formula (1)). Thereby, we observe the total number of iterations w.r.t. all event pairs, i.e., the total times of calculating formula (1). As illustrated in Figure 6(a), the total number of iterations for all event pairs can be significantly reduced by pruning, and the corresponding time costs are reduced in Figure 6(b).

To evaluate the minimum frequency control proposed in Section 2, we gradually remove the edges with frequency lower than a threshold (varying from 0.05 to 0.25) from dependency graphs. According to the result reported in Figure 7(a), the accuracy decreases along with the increase of pruning ratio, due to the absence of more statistic and structural information. Nevertheless, the time cost also decreases as shown in Figure 7(b), since the average degree of dependency graph is decreasing, which makes the computation faster. Hence, we can utilize the minimum frequency control to trade the accuracy for computation efficiency.

Figure 8 reports the results of scalability on the number of events (up to 100 events).[5] As shown in Figure 8(a), the accuracy of all the approaches decreases along with the increase of event size. It is not surprising since more choices of events lead to a higher chance of mismatching. Remarkably, the falling speed of our EMS is slower than other approaches, which means the EMS method is more reliable in event logs with a large number of distinct events. The time cost of all approaches increases heavily in Figure 8(b). OPQ cannot even finish the matching of events more than 30, due to the highest time complexity $O(n!)$. Nevertheless, EMS+es always achieves the lowest time cost when the number of events is increasing from 10 to 100.

Figure 9 evaluates the performance over various sizes of dislocated events (in the synthetic dataset of 100 events). To

[5] Real event logs, however, often have the number of events bounded by about 60, according to the recent survey [22]. Indeed, referring to the process modeling guidelines [16], workflows should be decomposed if they have more than 50 events, so that they are easier to read and understand.

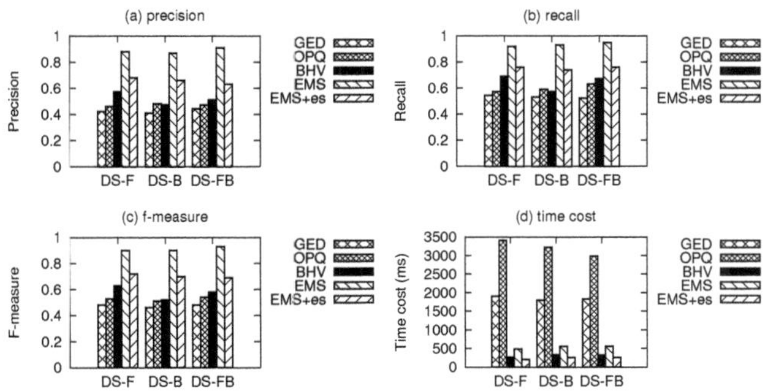

Figure 10: Matching composite events

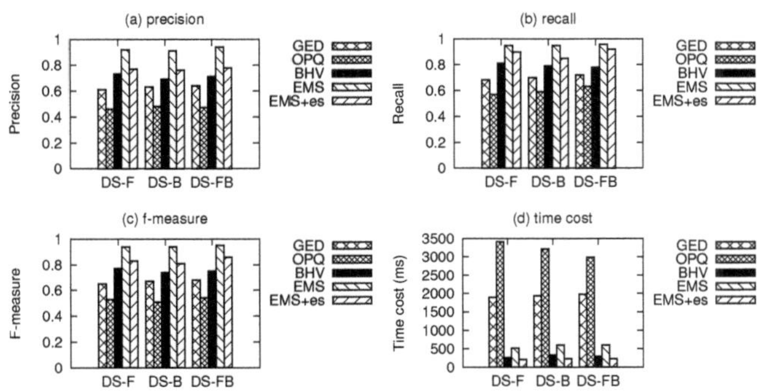

Figure 11: Performance on matching composite events by integrating with typographic similarity

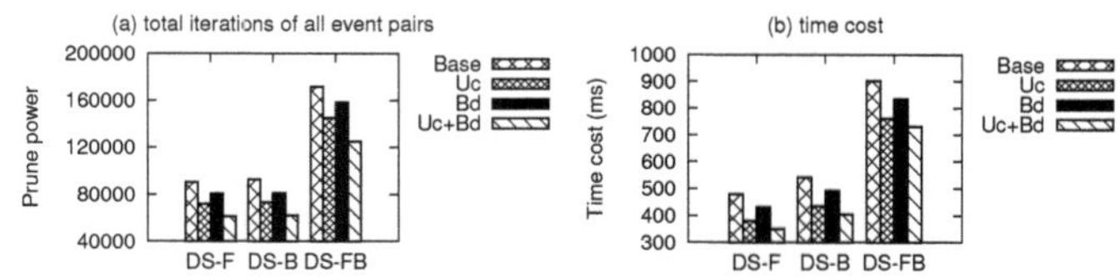

Figure 12: Prune power of unchanged similarities and upper bounds of similarities

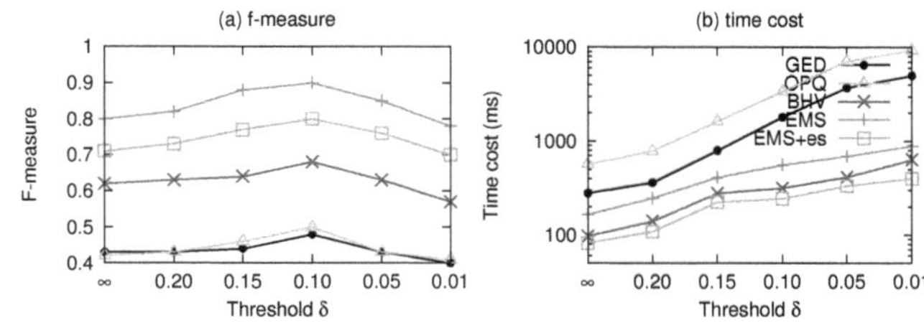

Figure 13: Performance on varying threshold δ

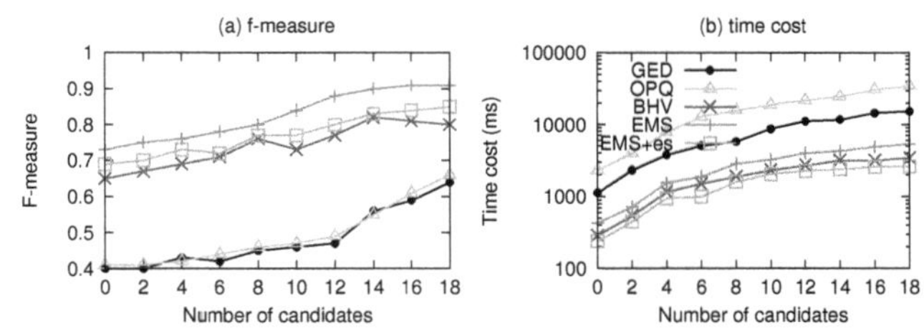

Figure 14: Performance on varying candidate sizes

simulate the different sizes of dislocated events presented in Example 1, we synthetically remove the first m events of each trace in one event log for every event log pair. By increasing m, i.e., the number of dislocated events, the accuracy of all the approaches drops. In particular, BHV's accuracy drops fast, with performance as poor as GED when the dislocated event size is large. Our proposed EMS shows the highest and relatively steady accuracy. These results verify again the superiority and demonstrate scalability of EMS in handling a larger number of dislocated events.

5.3 Matching Composite Events

In Figures 10 and 11, we report the results on matching composite events, without and with typographic similarity, respectively. In general, the results are very similar to Figures 3 and 4 of matching singleton events. That is, our similarity such as EMS can achieve higher accuracy, while the time cost of computation with estimation is much lower. A major difference observed in matching composite events is the significantly higher time costs of GED and OPQ. As mentioned in the introduction, we need to frequently compute the similarities of events for various combinations of candidate composite events, which is not affordable for similarity measures with high computational costs (such as GED and OPQ). Nevertheless, our proposed similarity measures can keep time costs low. Especially, EMS+es shows 1-2 orders of magnitude time cost improvement while the accuracy still outperforms GED.

Figure 12 reports the effectiveness of pruning methods, i.e., identifying unchanged similarities (Uc) in Section 4.2 and pruning with similarity upper bounds (Bd) in Section 4.3. Again, we first observe the total number of iterations (times of computing formula (1)) for all event pairs. As illustrated, both these approaches show an improvement of time performance, and the combination of two pruning methods can further reduce the time cost.

Figure 13 evaluates the effect of δ in Algorithm 2. According to Algorithm 2, a lower δ prefers more composite events. As illustrated in Figure 13(a), the f-measure first grows up along with the decrease of δ, since the algorithm does discover some true matching of composite events. However, the f-measure starts to drop when δ decreases lower than 0.10, since many false positive composite events are involved. That is, a moderately large threshold δ is preferred, in order to achieve a high matching accuracy. It is not surprising that the time cost significantly grows along with the decrease of δ in Figure 13(b), since Algorithm 2 needs to conduct the iterative computation of similarity for all the composite events discovered.

Finally, as shown in Figure 14, by considering more candidates, we can identify the matching of more composite events and thus increase the matching accuracy. The corresponding time costs, however, increase significantly fast.

6. RELATED WORK

A graph is often employed to represent the structural information among events. While vertices usually denote events, the edges in the graph are associated with various semantics exploited from event logs in different perspectives. Ferreira et al. [8] used a graphical form of Markov transition matrix whose edges are weighted by the conditional probability of one event directly followed by another. However, the conditional probability cannot tell the significance of the edge. In this paper, we employ the dependency graph proposed in [11] by weighting vertices and edges with normalized frequencies, since it distinguishes the significance of distinct edges, and is easy to interpret. An important difference from [11] is the novel artificial node v^X introduced in the dependency graph for matching dislocated events.

Schema matching techniques [21], as a fundamental problem in many database application domains, can be employed to evaluate event similarities. Kang et al. [11] studied the matching on opaque data. However, as discussed in Example 2, OPQ concerns a local evaluation of similar neighbors, while dislocated matching events may have distinct neighbors which prevents OPQ performing well. In contrast, our proposed iterative similarity function concerns the global evaluation via propagating similarities and thus overcome the effect of local neighbor distinctness. Moreover, [11] needs to enumerate all the possible matching correspondences and select the one with the highest normal distance, which is extremely time-consuming. Consequently, the performance of [11] is poor in the experimental evaluation in Section 5.

A SimRank [10] like behavioral similarity [19] is employed by iteratively considering the predecessor similarities of two events. Unfortunately, this behavioral similarity fails to consider the distinct feature of dislocated events. Therefore, as illustrated in the experimental evaluation in Section 5, our proposed similarity measure with the consideration of dislocation shows higher matching accuracy. Weidlich et al. [23] studies matching composite events due to the different levels of granularity of business process [1]. However, it uses label similarity of events to judge m:n matching, which is non-effective on opaque event names. Another graph based similarity is graph edit distance [5] which falls short in matching dislocated events. Moreover, another defeat of graph edit distance is its high computation cost. When matching composite events with various combinations of candidates, the large matching time costs become a major issue, which is also observed in the experimental evaluation in Section 5.

7. CONCLUSIONS

In this paper, we first identify the unique features that often exist in heterogeneous event logs, such as **opaque, dislocated** and **composite** events. Since possibly opaque event names prevent most existing typographic or linguistic similarities from performing well, we focus on the structural information for matching. In particular, an iterative similarity function is introduced with the consideration of dislocation issues. We prove that the iterative computation of the proposed similarity function converges. Efficient pruning with the identification of early convergence is developed. We also propose a fast estimation of similarities with only a constant number (including 0) of iterations. To efficiently match composite events, we devise upper bounds of similarities for pruning. Experimental results demonstrate that our event similarity shows significantly higher accuracy than state-of-the-art matching approaches. Moreover, the similarity estimation can significantly reduce time costs while keeping matching accuracy higher/comparable with existing approaches. Since it is not clear about the difference of substituting $\mathcal{S}(v_1, v_2)$ and $\mathcal{S}(v_1', v_2')$, thus far, we do not get any theoretical bound of estimation. It is interesting to investigate the bound of estimation as a future study.

Acknowledgment. This work is supported in part by China NSFC under Grants 61325008, 61202008, 61370055, and National Grand Fundamental Research 973 Program of China under Grant 2012-CB316200.

8. REFERENCES

[1] Z. Bao, S. B. Davidson, and T. Milo. Labeling workflow views with fine-grained dependencies. *PVLDB*, 5(11):1208–1219, 2012.

[2] O. Biton, S. C. Boulakia, S. B. Davidson, and C. S. Hara. Querying and managing provenance through user views in scientific workflows. In *ICDE*, pages 1072–1081, 2008.

[3] F. Casati, M. Castellanos, U. Dayal, and N. Salazar. A generic solution for warehousing business process data. In *VLDB*, pages 1128–1137, 2007.

[4] F. Casati, M. Castellanos, N. Salazar, and U. Dayal. Abstract process data warehousing. In *ICDE*, pages 1387–1389, 2007.

[5] R. M. Dijkman, M. Dumas, and L. García-Bañuelos. Graph matching algorithms for business process model similarity search. In *BPM*, pages 48–63, 2009.

[6] L. Ding, S. Chen, E. A. Rundensteiner, J. Tatemura, W.-P. Hsiung, and K. S. Candan. Runtime semantic query optimization for event stream processing. In *ICDE*, pages 676–685, 2008.

[7] A. Doan, A. Halevy, and Z. Ives. *Principles of data integration*. Morgan Kaufmann, 2012.

[8] D. R. Ferreira, D. Gillblad, and D. Gillblad. Discovering process models from unlabelled event logs. In *BPM*, pages 143–158, 2009.

[9] L. Gravano, P. G. Ipeirotis, N. Koudas, and D. Srivastava. Text joins in an rdbms for web data integration. In *WWW*, pages 90–101, 2003.

[10] G. Jeh and J. Widom. Simrank: a measure of structural-context similarity. In *KDD*, pages 538–543, 2002.

[11] J. Kang and J. F. Naughton. On schema matching with opaque column names and data values. In *SIGMOD Conference*, pages 205–216, 2003.

[12] R. M. Karp. Reducibility among combinatorial problems. In R. E. Miller and J. W. Thatcher, editors, *Complexity of Computer Computations*, pages 85–103. Plenum Press, 1972.

[13] V. I. Levenshtein. Binary codes capable of correcting deletions, insertions, and reversals. *Soviet Physics Doklady*, 10(8):707–710, 1966.

[14] S. Melnik, H. Garcia-Molina, E. Rahm, and E. Rahm. Similarity flooding: A versatile graph matching algorithm and its application to schema matching. In *ICDE*, pages 117–128, 2002.

[15] J. Mendling, J. Recker, M. Rosemann, and W. M. P. van der Aalst. Generating correct epcs from configured c-epcs. In *SAC*, pages 1505–1510, 2006.

[16] J. Mendling, H. A. Reijers, and W. M. P. van der Aalst. Seven process modeling guidelines (7pmg). *Information & Software Technology*, 52(2):127–136, 2010.

[17] J. Munkres. Algorithms for the assignment and transportation problems. *Journal of the Society for Industrial & Applied Mathematics*, 5(1):32–38, 1957.

[18] J. Nakatumba, M. Westergaard, and W. M. P. van der Aalst. Generating event logs with workload-dependent speeds from simulation models. In *CAiSE Workshops*, pages 383–397, 2012.

[19] S. Nejati, M. Sabetzadeh, M. Chechik, S. M. Easterbrook, and P. Zave. Matching and merging of statecharts specifications. In *ICSE*, pages 54–64, 2007.

[20] T. Pedersen, S. Patwardhan, and J. Michelizzi. Wordnet: : Similarity - measuring the relatedness of concepts. In *AAAI*, pages 1024–1025, 2004.

[21] E. Rahm and P. A. Bernstein. A survey of approaches to automatic schema matching. *VLDB J.*, 10(4):334–350, 2001.

[22] J. Wang, T. Jin, R. Wong, and L. Wen. Querying business process model repositories - a survey of current approaches and issues. *World Wide Web*, 17(3):427–454, 2014.

[23] M. Weidlich, R. M. Dijkman, and J. Mendling. The icop framework: Identification of correspondences between process models. In *CAiSE*, pages 483–498, 2010.

HAWQ: A Massively Parallel Processing SQL Engine in Hadoop

Lei Chang, Zhanwei Wang, Tao Ma, Lirong Jian, Lili Ma, Alon Goldshuv
Luke Lonergan, Jeffrey Cohen, Caleb Welton, Gavin Sherry, Milind Bhandarkar
Pivotal Inc
{lchang, zwang, tma, ljian, lma, agoldshuv,
llonergan, jcohen, cwelton, gsherry, mbhandarkar}@gopivotal.com

ABSTRACT

HAWQ, developed at Pivotal, is a massively parallel processing SQL engine sitting on top of HDFS. As a hybrid of MPP database and Hadoop, it inherits the merits from both parties. It adopts a layered architecture and relies on the distributed file system for data replication and fault tolerance. In addition, it is standard SQL compliant, and unlike other SQL engines on Hadoop, it is fully transactional. This paper presents the novel design of HAWQ, including query processing, the scalable software interconnect based on UDP protocol, transaction management, fault tolerance, read optimized storage, the extensible framework for supporting various popular Hadoop based data stores and formats, and various optimization choices we considered to enhance the query performance. The extensive performance study shows that HAWQ is about 40x faster than Stinger, which is reported 35x-45x faster than the original Hive.

Categories and Subject Descriptors

H.2.4 [**Database Management**]: System—*parallel databases*

General Terms

Database, Hadoop, Query Processing

1. INTRODUCTION

The decreasing cost of storing data in Hadoop [1] is continuously changing how enterprises address data storage and processing needs. More and more Pivotal Hadoop customers are using HDFS as a central repository (aka, data lake) for all their history data from diverse data sources, for example, operational systems, web, sensors and smart devices. And unlike traditional enterprise data warehouses, data can be both structured and unstructured. To take maximum advantage of big data, the customers are favoring a new way of capturing, organizing and analyzing data. In the new way, instead of carefully filtering and transforming the source data through a heavy ETL process to data warehouses designed specifically for predefined analysis applications, the original data from data sources with few or no transformation is directly ingested into the central repository. The new paradigm increases the agility of new analytical application development. For example, when in need of some new data in new applications, analytic users do not need to go back to the data sources, change the ETL process or develop new ETL processes to get what they need but missed or filtered in the rigid design that is optimized for existing known analytical applications. And obviously, the new paradigm also gives data scientists more flexibility at ad-hoc analysis and exploration of the data.

SIGMOD'14, June 22–27, 2014, Snowbird, UT, USA.

http://dx.doi.org/10.1145/2588555.2595636

The following are the typical requirements from customers who are willing to use Hadoop for their daily analytical work.

- **Interactive queries**: Interactive query response time is the key to promote data exploration, rapid prototyping and other tasks.
- **Scalability**: Linear scalability is necessary for the explosive growth of data size.
- **Consistency**: Transaction makes sense and it takes the consistency responsibility away from application developers.
- **Extensibility**: The system should support common popular data formats, such as plain text, SequenceFile, and new formats.
- **Standard compliance**: Keeping the investment in existing BI and visualization tools requires standard compliance, for example, SQL and various other BI standards.
- **Productivity**: It is favorable to make use of existing skill sets in the organization without losing productivity.

Currently, Hadoop software stack is still hardly satisfying all of the above requirements. MapReduce [19, 20] is the basic working horse behind the processing of both structured and unstructured data. It runs on commodity hardware, and it is scalable and fault tolerant. However, it has many known limitations, for example, not being suitable for interactive analytics due to its poor performance [27, 29, 32], and low-level programming model makes it not friendly for business analysts. Although some systems such as Hive [36, 37] and Pig [30] are developed to alleviate these issues, the performance is still not satisfactory for real-time data exploration. In addition, data consistency is a nightmare from application developer side. Without the transaction capability provided by infrastructure software, application programming is quite error prone and often leads to ugly and unmaintainable code [18, 34].

In database community, one of the major recent trends is the wide adoption of Massively Parallel Processing (MPP) systems [4, 6, 11], which are distributed systems consisting of a cluster of independent nodes. MPP database shares many good features with Hadoop, such as scalable shared-nothing architecture. And it is particularly excellent at structured data processing, fast query processing capability (orders of magnitude faster than MapReduce and

Hive [27, 32]), embedded automatic query optimization and industry SQL standard compatible interfaces with BI tools, and it is particularly easy to use for data analysts.

Motivated by the limitations of current Hadoop and performance advantages of MPP databases, we developed HAWQ, which is a SQL query engine that combines the merits of Greenplum Database [4], and Hadoop distributed storage. The HAWQ architecture is different from Greenplum Database because of the underlying distribution storage characteristics and tight integration requirements with Hadoop stack. HAWQ was alpha released in 2012, in production in early 2013, and is now being used by hundreds of Pivotal Hadoop customers. It is SQL compliant and designed to support the large-scale analytics processing for big data [17, 25]. And it has excellent query performance and can also interactively query various data sources in different Hadoop formats.

This paper gives a detailed introduction about the HAWQ architecture and the novel design of various internal components. HAWQ runs side by side with HDFS. A typical HAWQ cluster consists of one master host, one standby master host, two HDFS NameNode hosts with HA configuration, and multiple compute hosts that run both HDFS DataNodes and stateless segments (the basic compute units of HAWQ). User data is stored on HDFS. The master accepts queries through JDBC, ODBC or libpq connections. Queries are parsed, analyzed and optimized into physical query plans. And the dispatcher dispatches plans to segments for execution. The executor executes plans in a pipeline manner and the final results are sent back to the master and presented to clients. On the master, there is a fault detector. When a node fails, segments on the node are marked as "down", and future queries will not be dispatched to these segments anymore. Specifically, we make the following contributions in this paper:

- A stateless segment based database architecture is proposed, which is supported with metadata dispatch and self-described plan execution.
- A UDP based interconnect is designed to eliminate the limitation of TCP for the tuple communication between execution slices.
- A swimming lane based transaction model is proposed to support concurrent update operations. And HDFS is enhanced with truncate operation for transaction rollback.
- Extensive experiments on industry benchmark show that HAWQ is about 40x faster than Stinger, which is reported orders of magnitude faster than the original Hive.

The rest of the paper is organized as follows. We first give an overview of the HAWQ architecture in Section 2. A brief description of query processing is provided in Section 3. In Section 4, the interconnect design is discussed and transaction management is presented in Section 5. The extension framework is discussed in Section 6. Section 7 gives related work. Experimental results on industry benchmark are presented in Section 8. Finally, we conclude the work in Section 9.

2. THE ARCHITECTURE

A HAWQ cluster is built from commodity hardware components, i.e., no proprietary hardware is used. One design choice is to avoid the explicit software customization on special hardware characteristics. This leads to an easy-to-maintain code base, better portability across different platforms and makes the system less sensitive to variations in hardware configurations.

As shown in Figure 1, HAWQ has a layered architecture. An MPP shared-nothing compute layer sits on top of a distributed stor-

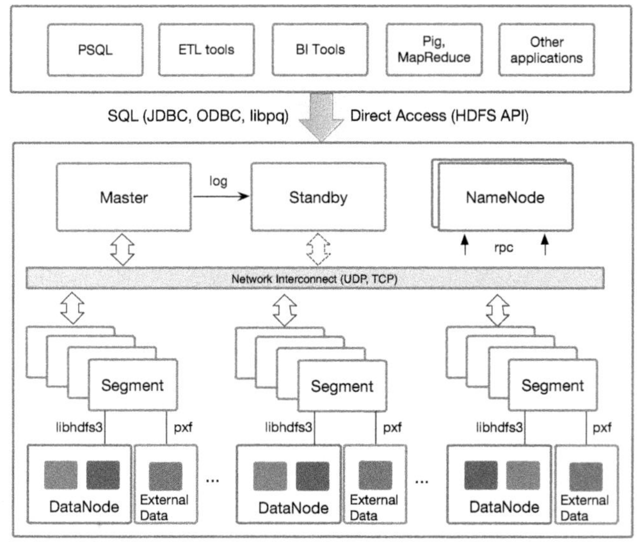

Figure 1: HAWQ architecture

age layer. A minimal HAWQ production configuration[1] has three kinds of nodes: HAWQ masters, HDFS NameNodes, and segment hosts running both HAWQ segments and HDFS DataNodes. The master node provides an external interface for the HAWQ cluster. All user interactions go through the master node, which is responsible for authentication and authorization, query parsing, generating query plans, starting query executors and dispatching plans. The master node also tracks the query execution status and gathers the individual results into a final result. The master has a corresponding warm standby master. The standby synchronizes with the master via log shipping. A segment host often has a HDFS DataNode and multiple segments configured to increases the resource utilization of underlying multi-core architecture. HDFS DataNodes are collocated with segments for better data locality. Segments access HDFS through libhdfs3, which is a protobuf based C++ HDFS client. Pivotal Extension Framework (PXF) is an extensible framework, which enables SQL access to a variety of external data sources such as HBase and Accumulo.

2.1 Interfaces

Like classical relational databases, applications and external tools interact with HAWQ via standard protocols, such as JDBC, ODBC, and libpq that is used by PostgreSQL and Greenplum database. To further simplify the interaction between HAWQ and external systems, especially, new applications developed in Hadoop ecosystem, the design choice here is to enhance standard interfaces with open data format support. External systems can bypass HAWQ, and access directly the HAWQ table files on HDFS. HDFS file system API can be used for this purpose. In addition, open MapReduce InputFormats and OutputFormats for the underlying storage file formats are developed. The feature is quite useful for data loading and data exchange between HAWQ and external applications. For example, MapReduce can directly access table files on HDFS instead of reading HAWQ data through SQL.

2.2 Catalog service

There are two kinds of data: catalog and user data. Catalog is the brain of the system. It describes the system and all of the user

[1]In real deployments, HAWQ can be installed side by side with other components too, for example Hadoop MapReduce.

objects in the system. The catalog is critical to almost all operational processes, such as creating databases and tables, starting and stopping the system, and planning and executing queries. The following are the categories of HAWQ catalog.

- **Database objects**: Description about filespaces, tablespaces, schemas, databases, tables, partitions, columns, indexes, constraints, types, statistics, resource queues, operators, functions and object dependencies.
- **System information**: Information about the segments and segment status.
- **Security**: Users, roles and privileges.
- **Language and encoding**: Languages and encoding supported.

The catalog is stored in the unified catalog service (UCS[2]). External applications can query the catalog using standard SQL. All internal catalog access within HAWQ is provided via a catalog query language, CaQL, which is a subset of SQL. CaQL replaces a more tedious and error-prone process where developers had to manually code catalog queries using C primitives on a combination of internal caches, heaps, indexes, and locking structures, specifying low-level key comparison functions and type conversions. The decision to implement CaQL, instead of using a full functional SQL, was made after a thorough catalog access behavior analysis. Most internal operations are simple OLTP-style lookups using a fixed set of indexes, so sophisticated planning, join optimization, and DDL are unnecessary. A simplified catalog language is faster, and it is much easier to implement and scale from an engineering perspective. In current HAWQ, CaQL only supports basic single-table SELECT, COUNT(), multi-row DELETE, and single row INSERT/UPDATE. More details about the syntax are omitted due to space limitations.

2.3 Data distribution

Besides catalog tables, which are located in UCS, all data is distributed across the cluster, similar to the horizontal partitioning used in Gamma database machine [21]. Several modes are offered to assign data to segments. Each segment has a separate directory on HDFS. Assigning data to segments means storing the data in the segment data directories. The most frequently used policy is hash distribution that distributes rows by hashing of the designated distribution columns. Hash distribution policy gives users the ability to align tables to improve the processing of some important query patterns. For example, if two tables are frequently joined together in queries, and if they are hash distributed with the join key, the equi-join on the two tables can be executed without any data redistribution or shuffling. This improves query performance and saves a lot of network bandwidth. The following syntax is used to designate a set of columns as distribution columns. In this example, the rows of TPC-H *orders* table are distributed based on hash function against the column *o_orderkey*. The rows with the same hash value will be distributed to the same segment.

```
CREATE TABLE orders (
  o_orderkey INT8 NOT NULL,
  o_custkey INTEGER NOT NULL
  o_orderstatus CHAR(1) NOT NULL,
  o_totalprice DECIMAL(15,2) NOT NULL,
  o_orderdate DATE NOT NULL,
  o_orderpriority CHAR(15) NOT NULL,
  o_clerk CHAR(15) NOT NULL,
  o_shippriority INTEGER NOT NULL,
  o_comment VARCHAR(79) NOT NULL
) DISTRIBUTED BY (o_orderkey);
```

[2]In current HAWQ release, UCS is located on master only. Future plan is to externalize UCS as a service, which is quite useful for the tight integration and interaction with other Hadoop components.

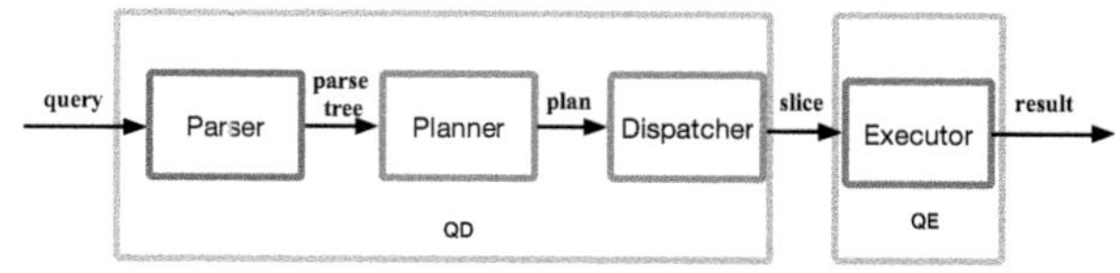

Figure 2: Query execution workflow

HAWQ also provides another distribution policy named RANDOMLY. In random distribution, rows are distributed across segments in a round-robin fashion. Rows with columns having the same values will not necessarily be located on the same segment. A random distribution ensures even data distribution, and it is quite useful for tables with only a very small number of distinct rows. Hashing will assign the data to a small number of segments, thus introduce skew in the data distribution. Random distribution solves this issue quite elegantly.

Table partitioning: Table partitioning is used by HAWQ to support large tables and can also be used to facilitate database maintenance tasks, such as rolling out some old data. Tables are partitioned at CREATE TABLE time using the PARTITION BY clause. Both range partitioning and list partitioning are supported. When you partition a table, you are actually creating a top-level parent table with one or more levels of child tables. Internally, HAWQ creates an inheritance relationship between the top-level table and its underlying partitions. The following example creates a table *sales* with a date range partition. Each partition of a partitioned table is distributed like a separate table by using the distribution columns.

```
CREATE TABLE sales(
  id INT, date DATE, amt DECIMAL(10,2))
DISTRIBUTED BY (id)
PARTITION BY RANGE (date)(
  START (date '2008-01-01') INCLUSIVE
  END (date '2009-01-01') EXCLUSIVE
  EVERY (INTERVAL '1 month'));
```

Table partitioning is quite helpful for improving query performance, especially for queries that only touch some partitions. Planner considers partition elimination automatically when generating a plan, which saves disk IOs and is faster compared with a full table scan.

2.4 Query execution workflow

The overall query execution workflow is shown in Figure 2. When a user connects to the master, the postmaster forks a query dispatcher (QD) process. The QD, responsible for the user session, interacts with the user and is the controller of the whole query execution process. After receiving a query, it first parses the query into a raw parse tree, and semantic analysis is run against the tree to validate the tree references. Semantic analysis phase accesses the catalog and checks the correctness of tables, columns, and types involved in the query. After semantic analysis, the query parse tree is rewritten according to rewrite rules (for example view definitions).

The planner takes a query parse tree, and generates a parallel execution plan that encodes how the query should be executed. The query plan is then sliced into plan slices at the data movement (motion) boundary. A slice is an execution unit that does not cross motion boundary. To execute a slice, the QD starts a gang of QEs and dispatches the plan to them. The QEs in the gang execute the same slice against different parts of data, and finally results are assembled and returned to the user through QD.

2.5 Storage

Traditionally, relational data for OLTP systems is stored in rows, i.e., all columns of each tuple are stored together on disk. However, analytical databases tend to have different access patterns than OLTP systems. Instead of having many small transactions with single-row reads and writes, analytical databases often deal with larger and more complex queries that touch much larger volumes of data, i.e., read-mostly with big scanning reads (frequently on selected columns), and infrequent batch appends of data.

HAWQ has built-in flexibility supporting a variety of storage models on HDFS. For each table (or a partition of a table), the user can select the storage and compression settings that suit the way in which the table is accessed. The transformation among different storage models is currently done at the user layer. Automatic storage model transformation is in product roadmap.

- **Row-oriented/Read optimized AO**: Optimized for read-mostly full table scans and bulk append loads. DDL allows optional compression ranging from fast/light to deep/archival schemas such as gzip and quicklz.
- **Column-oriented/Read optimized CO**: Data is vertically partitioned [24], and each column is stored in a series of large, densely packed blocks that can be efficiently compressed (gzip, quicklz and RLE), and it tends to see notably higher compression ratios than row-oriented tables. The implementation scans only those columns required by the query which is good for those workloads suited to column-store. It stores columns in separate segment files.
- **Column-oriented/Parquet**: Similar to CO, data is vertically partitioned. The difference is that Parquet is a PAX [13] like storage format and it stores columns vertically in a row group instead of separate files. Furthermore, it natively supports nested data.

2.6 Fault tolerance

For the high availability of the master node, a standby master instance can be optionally deployed on a separate host. The standby master host serves as a warm standby when the primary master host becomes unavailable. The standby master is kept synchronized by a transaction log replication process, which runs on the standby master host. Since the master does not contain any user data, only the system catalog tables need to be synchronized between the primary and standby. These tables are not updated frequently, but when they are, changes are automatically copied over to the standby master so that it is always kept current with the primary.

From segment side, fault tolerance is different from master mirroring mechanism. HAWQ segments are stateless, which simplifies segment recovery process and provides better availability. A stateless segment means it does not contain private persistent data that should be recovered if it fails. Any alive segment can act as a replacement for a failed segment.

The master has a fault detector that checks the health of all segments periodically. If a failure happens, in-flight queries will fail and the transaction mechanism will keep the consistency of the system. This design is based on the observation that, most of the time, heavy materialization based query recovery is slower than simple query restart. After the failure is detected, the segments on the failed host are marked as "down" in the system catalog. Different user sessions will randomly failover failed segments to the remaining active segments. In a system running concurrent queries, this mechanism provides good load balance across the cluster. After the failed segment host is fixed, a recovery utility can be used to recover the segments on the host, and future queries will be scheduled to the recovered segments. And other utilities are also provided to move failed segments to a new host.

HAWQ supports two level disk failure fault tolerance. User data is stored on HDFS, so disk failures for user data access are masked by HDFS. When one disk failure is identified, HDFS will remove the disk volume from the list of valid disk volumes. There is another kind of disk failures when reading or writing intermediate data for large queries. HAWQ spills intermediate data to local disks for performance reason. For example, when no enough memory is available for a sort operator on a large table, an external sort is used and intermediate data is spilled to local disks. If a failure is encountered during intermediate data access, HAWQ will mark the failed disk as "down" and will not use the failed disk for future queries anymore.

3. QUERY PROCESSING

In this section, we discuss some details about how query processing works. Two critical components in query processing are query planner and executor. The planner accepts a query parse tree and outputs an optimized parallel query plan. A plan describes the execution steps the executor should follow to execute the query. The planner obtains a plan by using a cost-based optimization algorithm to evaluate a vast number of potential plans and selects the one that leads to the most efficient query execution. Based on the data queries access, we classify them into three categories.

- **Master-only queries**: These queries access only catalog tables on master or execute expressions that can be evaluated without dispatching query slices to segments. Master-only queries are handled like queries executed on a single node database.
- **Symmetrically dispatched queries**: Physical query plans are dispatched to all segments, which execute them in parallel against different portions of data. These are the most common queries involving user data distributed on the underlying storage system. According to the complexity of a query, the query plan can be as simple as a scan with a gather motion, and can also contain a lot of intermediate data redistribution operators in order to get a final correct result.
- **Directly dispatched queries**: Whenever the planner can guarantee that a slice accesses data from a single segment directory, the plan is only dispatched to that segment. A typical directly dispatched query is a single value lookup or single row insert query. Direct dispatch saves network bandwidth and improves concurrency of small queries.

In the following sections, we focus on symmetrically dispatched queries which often involve data movement. A query plan contains well-known relational operators, scans, joins, sorts, aggregations, and so on, as well as parallel "motion" operators that describe when and how data should be transferred between nodes. The distribution of each table is tracked in catalog known to query planner at compile time. Based on the knowledge, query planner gets a query plan that takes into account where the data is located. Join and aggregation operations require specific distribution to guarantee correct results. Redistribution often introduces both CPU and network overhead, thus the planner often generates a plan either considering the colocation of data and existing distribution or redistributing correctly the data before other operators. Three kinds of parallel motion operators are utilized to transfer data among query executors.

- **Broadcast Motion (N:N)**: Every segment sends the input tuples to all other segments. The common usage of broadcast motion is for joins with non equal predicates. One big relation is distributed and the other small relation is broadcasted and thus replicated on each segment.
- **Redistribute Motion (N:N)**: Every segment rehashes the input tuples according to the values of a set of columns and redistributes each tuple to the appropriate segment. It is often used in equi-joins to redistribute non-colocated relations according to the join columns, and aggregation operators to group tuples according to aggregation columns.
- **Gather Motion (N:1)**: Every segment sends the input tuples to a single segment (usually the master). Gather motion is often used by QD to gather final results. It can also be used in the middle of plan before executing an operation that cannot be executed in parallel on different segments.

Encapsulating the distribution logic into self-contained operators enables concise reasoning over query plans [23]. Like other operators, the motion operators are also pipelined, i.e., data is exchanged whenever available. Internally, a software UDP based interconnect is used to implement motion operators, which is described in more details in Section 4.

3.1 Metadata dispatch

As described in Section 2, HAWQ has a rich set of catalog tables. Different sets of metadata are used by different components at different query execution phases. For instance, object definition related catalog tables, like table schemas, database and tablespace information, are used by the parser to do semantic analysis. Statistics are used by the planner to optimize queries, and table, column and function definitions are necessary for query execution.

Catalog exists only on master, and segments are stateless. While executing the slices received from QD, QEs on segments need to access catalog tables. An example usage is: it accesses table schema and column type information to decode the storage format while doing table scan. In order to access catalog, one straightforward method is for QEs to set up connections to the master and query metadata. When the cluster scale is large, there are a large number of QEs querying the master concurrently. The master will become a bottleneck. Thus, "*metadata dispatch*" is proposed to tackle this issue. After a parallel plan is generated, we decorate the plan with the metadata needed in the execution phase. A plan with needed metadata included is called a *self-described plan*. The self-described plan contains all information needed for query execution, so QEs do not need to consult unified catalog service anymore. For some queries, such as insert, some metadata is changed by QEs. To record the changes, we piggyback the changes in the master-to-segment connections. And the changes are updated on master in a batch manner. Typically, metadata change is small, so it does not introduce much overhead to master.

A practical issue for metadata dispatch is the plan size. For a very complex query, the plan size can be multiple megabytes. Here, two optimizations are used to solve the issue. For query execution, a lot of native metadata, such as natively supported types and functions, is read only, and is not changed during the life of the HAWQ. So we bootstrapped a readonly catalog store on each segment that contains all constant metadata. The metadata in the readonly store is excluded from a self-described plan. After the plan is generated, a compression algorithm is run against the plan to further reduce the plan size.

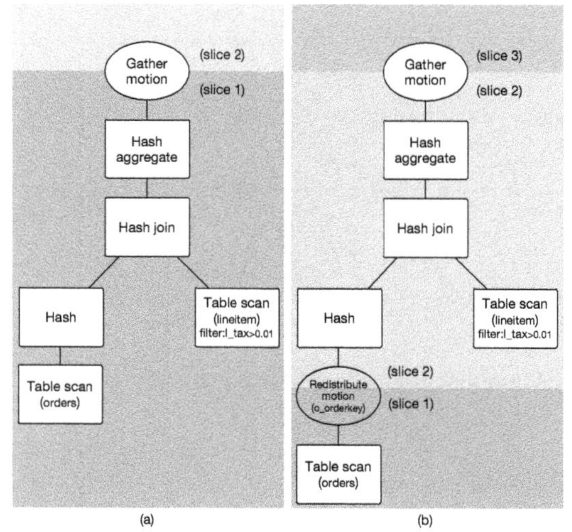

Figure 3: Sliced query plans

3.2 A query processing example

Figure 3 shows the query plans of the following query over standard TPC-H schema with different distributions.

```
SELECT l_orderkey, count(l_quantity)
FROM lineitem, orders
WHERE l_orderkey=o_orderkey AND l_tax>0.01
GROUP BY l_orderkey;
```

In Figure 3(a), *lineitem* and *orders* are both distributed by *l_orderkey*. Since the distribution key and the join key are the same for the two tables, they can be joined locally on each segment without any data movement. It saves both CPU time and network bandwidth. The aggregation in this example is against the same key *l_orderkey*, so it can be done locally too. Finally, the local segment results are assembled at QD side through a gather motion, and returned to the end user.

From the figure, we can see that there are two slices which is obtained by cutting at the gather motion boundary. The function of a motion is implemented as two parts: a "send" motion and a "receive" motion in the two adjacent slices respectively. The lower slice sends tuples while the upper one receives tuples. During execution, two gangs are created to execute the plan. One gang has the QD that executes the receive part of the gather motion (1-Gang), and the other gang (N-Gang) has one QE for each segment that executes the operators in the bottom slice and sends tuples to QD.

Figure 3(b) shows a different plan, where the *orders* table is randomly distributed. In order to execute the join, *orders* is redistributed by hashing the *o_orderkey* column. Thus, one more slice is created compared with the plan in Figure 3(a). Query planner makes the decision in a cost based manner. In this example, there are three gangs created to execute the three slices, of which two are N-Gangs and one is 1-Gang. Two N-Gangs communicate to each other by executing the send and receive parts of the redistribution motion respectively.

4. INTERCONNECT

The interconnect is responsible for tuple communication between execution slices (see Figure 4), and it provides communication atomics for motion nodes. Each motion node has many "streams" over which it communicates with its peers. HAWQ has two intercon-

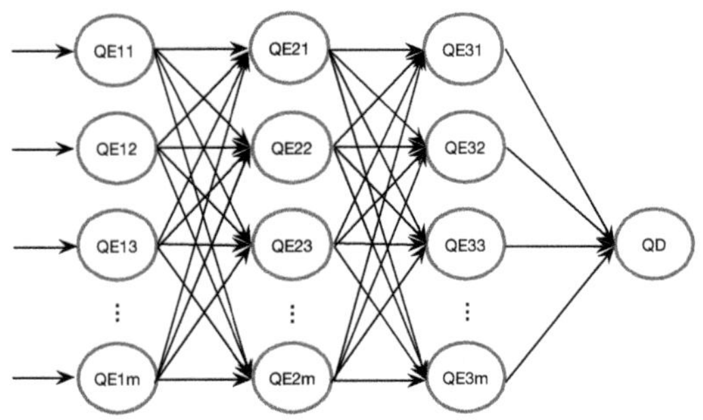

Figure 4: Interconnect for pipelined execution

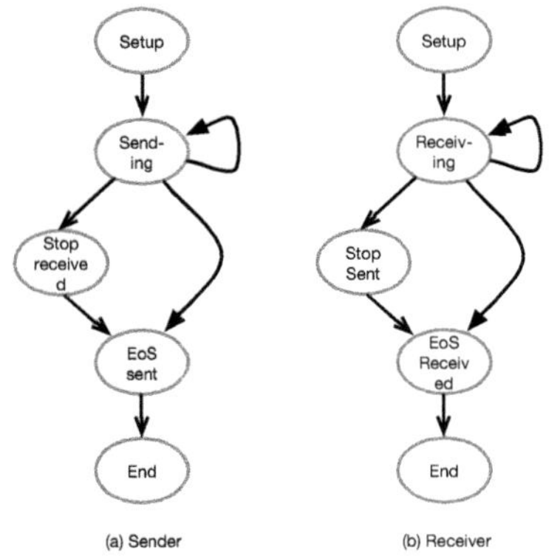

Figure 5: Interconnect sender and receiver state machines

nect implementations based on TCP and UDP respectively. TCP interconnect is limited by the number of slices it can support due to the port number limitation of TCP (about 60k per IP address) and time consuming connection setup step for a large number of concurrent connections. For example, with 1,000 segments, a typical 5-slice query needs to set up about 3 million connections, and on each node, there are thousands of connections. The connectionless UDP based interconnect solves the two issues elegantly by multiplexing multiple tuple-streams over a single UDP socket on each segment and thus provides a better scalability. In this section, we will show the design of the UDP based interconnect, which should achieve the following goals.

- **Reliability**: Network hardware elements and operating system are free to throw out packets, and the operating system UDP protocol does not guarantee reliable packet delivery. The interconnect must be capable of recovering from any packet losses.
- **Ordering**: Operating system UDP protocol does not have packet ordering assurance, so it is the interconnect's responsibility to deliver the packets in order.
- **Flow control**: Receiver processes, operating system and network elements may not match the speed of sender processes, flow control is necessary for UDP based interconnect.
- **Performance and scalability**: The implementation should have high performance and scales without hitting limitation from underlying operating system.
- **Portability**: It should be portable through various platforms and avoid using private features from some hardware and operating systems.

4.1 The protocol

In the interconnect, a packet contains a self-describing header specifying the complete motion node and peer identity along with the session and command-id. Header fields are evenly aligned for performance and portability.

Figure 5 (a) and (b) illustrate the state machines for data sending and data receiving respectively. "EoS" means "End of Stream" which is sent by senders when it has finished tuple sending for the stream, and "Stop" message is used by receivers to stop senders, which is typical for queries with "limit" subclauses when senders have received enough data.

4.2 The implementation

Each sender has a separate "virtual" connection to each receiver. Here we call a connection "virtual" since there is no physical connection for each sender and receiver pair. All the connections in a sender share a common socket. Multiplexing tuple streams from multiple peers over a single UDP socket requires that the kernel socket buffers be emptied rapidly (to avoid packet losses). To facilitate emptying the kernel socket buffers quickly, the communication is multithreaded such that receive, verification, acknowledgment, and receive buffer management execute concurrently with the rest of the executor.

Each connection on sender side has a send queue and an expiration queue ring that is used to store unacknowledged packets and facilitate fast packet expiration check. The expiration queue ring is shared by all sender connections in a sender process. When a sender fills up a packet, it adds the packet to the send queue, and tries to send it if there is capacity for the packet in the receiver side and the current flow control window *cwnd* is not full. The *flow control window* defines the maximal number of packets that have not received acknowledgements from the receiver. When the sender gets an acknowledgement from the receiver, it will free buffers and keep sending packets in the send queue. If the timer for an unacknowledged packet expires, the packet is resent.

At the receiver side, the receiving thread listens on a port and continuously accepts packets from all other senders. For each sender, the receiver has a separate channel to cache the packets from the sender (a separate channel is required to avoid potential deadlock for some types of queries). When the thread gets a packet from a sender, it places it into the corresponding queue and sends an acknowledgement to the sender. The executor thread continuously picks up packets from the receive queues and assembles tuples. Two important fields are contained in an acknowledgement packet: SC (the sequence number of the packet the receiver has already consumed) and SR (the largest packet sequence number it has already received and queued). SC is used to compute the capacity left on the receiver side and SR is used to identify the packets the receiver has already received. The packets that are queued by receiver can be removed from the expiration queue ring in the sender side.

4.3 Flow control

Flow control is used to avoid overwhelming receivers, operating system and intermediate network elements including NICs and switches from sender side. Retransmission timeouts (RTO) are dynamically computed based on round trip time (RTT) which is obtained from the time between the packet is sent and the acknowledgement for the packet is received. A loss based flow control method is implemented to dynamically tune the sending speed. Specifically, a flow control window is used to control the sending speed. Whenever the sender gets an expired packet (which indicates some potential losses that occurred in the operating system and network hardware), it decreases the flow control window to a minimal predefined value. Then a slow start process is used to increase the window to a suitable size.

4.4 Packet losses and out-of-order packets

The interconnect keeps the incoming packets sorted. A naive implementation requires a sort of the incoming packets, and it is obviously not efficient. Here we use a ring buffer to held the packets without any overhead introduced to sort the packets. When a packet loss or out-of-order packet is detected, the receiver immediately sends an OUT-OF-ORDER message to the sender, which contains the packets that were possibly lost. When the sender gets the feedback, it resends the packets. When a duplicate packet is detected in the receiver side, the background thread immediately sends a DUPLICATE message with accumulative acknowledgement information to the sender. When the sender gets the message, it removes any received packets from the expiration queue ring to avoid future duplicated retransmissions.

4.5 Deadlock elimination

One possible deadlock case occurs when there are a lot of lost acknowledgements. It can be explained by an example. Assume a connection has two sender buffers and two receive buffers. Firstly, the sender sends two packets p_1 and p_2 to the receiver. The receiver buffers now are all occupied. If the receiver is very slow at processing packets. It is possible that sender will resend a packet (say p_1), and after receiver gets the packet, it gives sender an acknowledgement that says p_1 and p_2 have been received and buffered. Then the sender removes p_1 and p_2 from expiration queue ring. After the receiver consumes p_1 and p_2, the acknowledgement says that the two packets have been consumed. If the acknowledgement is lost, then sender and receiver will deadlock. The sender does not know the receiver has consumed the packets and will not send or resend packets anymore, and the receiver is waiting for packets. The solution is to introduce a deadlock elimination mechanism. It works as follows. When there is a long period that the sender does not receive any acknowledgement from its peer, and it knows that there is no capacity left on receiver side, the unacknowledged queue is empty and it has some packets to send, it will send a status query message to the receiver. The receiver will respond with an acknowledgement about SC and SR.

5. TRANSACTION MANAGEMENT

HAWQ is fully transactional, which makes it much easier for developers to develop analytic applications. It is because it is very error prone to keep consistency from application side. In this section, we discuss the transaction management and concurrency control in HAWQ. As described earlier, HAWQ distinguishes two kinds of data in HAWQ: catalog and user data. For catalog, write ahead log (WAL) and multi-version concurrency control (MVCC) are used to implement transaction and concurrency control. But for user data, it can be appended, but can not be updated. And HAWQ does not write log and use multiple versions. Visibility is controlled by recording the logical length of data files in system catalog. This works since the HDFS files are append-only. The logical length of a file is the length of useful data in the file. Sometimes, the physical length is not the same as the logical length when an insert transaction fails. And the garbage data needs to be truncated before next write to the file.

Different from many other distributed systems like Greenplum database, HAWQ does not use distributed commit protocol such as two phase commit (2PC). Transaction is only noticeable on master node and segments do not keep transaction states. Self-described plans contain the snapshot information which controls the visibility of each tables. On each segment, dispatched catalog can be modified during the execution, and these modifications are sent back to the master when the query finishes, and finally the master updates all changes in the UCS. Transaction commits only occur on the master node. If a transaction is aborted, the data which has been written into the segment files on HDFS needs to be truncated.

5.1 Isolation levels

Technically, HAWQ uses multi-version concurrency control and supports snapshot isolation [14]. Users can request any one of the four SQL standard isolation levels, but internally, like PostgreSQL, HAWQ only supports: read committed and serializable. Read uncommitted is treated as read committed, while repeatable read is treated as serializable. For serializable isolation level in HAWQ, it does not allow the three phenomena in SQL standard: dirty read, non-repeatable read and phantom read. But the definition is not the same to true mathematical serializability, which does not prevent "write skew" and other phenomena [33] that are in snapshot isolation.

- **Read committed**: A statement can only see rows committed before it began. When you request read uncommitted, actually, you get read committed.
- **Serializable**: All statements of the current transaction can only see rows committed before the first query or data changed in this transaction.

By default, HAWQ sets transactions under "read committed" isolation level. Each query in the transaction gets a snapshot of the database as of the instant the query is started. While the queries in the transaction use the same snapshot at the start of the transaction if the isolation level is set to serializable.

5.2 Locking

HAWQ uses locking techniques to control the conflicts between concurrent DDL and DML statements. For example, the transaction gets an access shared lock before selecting a table, and a concurrent alter table statement will pend on acquirement of an access exclusive lock. The alter table query will continue to execute after the select query is committed or aborted.

HAWQ has its own deadlock checking mechanism. Master node and segments run deadlock checking routine periodically. The transaction is aborted if a deadlock is detected.

5.3 HDFS truncate

Systems with transaction support often need to undo changes made to the underlying storage when a transaction is aborted. Currently HDFS does not support truncate, a standard Posix operation, which is a reverse operation of append. It makes upper layer applications use ugly workarounds, such as keeping track of the discarded byte range per file in a separate metadata store, and periodically running a vacuum process to rewrite compacted files. In Pivotal Hadoop HDFS, we added truncate to support transaction. The signature of the truncate is as follows.

void **truncate**(Path src, long length) throws IOException;

The truncate() function truncates the file to the size which is less or equal to the file length. If the size of the file is smaller than the target length, an IOException is thrown. This is different from Posix truncate semantics. The rationale behind is HDFS does not support overwriting at any position.

For concurrent operations, only single writer/appender/truncater is allowed. Users can only call truncate on closed files. The atomicity of a truncate operation is guaranteed. That is, it succeeds or fails, and it does not leave the file in an undefined state. Concurrent readers may read content of a file that is truncated by a concurrent truncate operation. But they must be able to read all the data that are not affected by the concurrent truncate operation.

The implementation of truncate is straightforward. At first, a lease is obtained for the to-be-truncated file F. If the truncate operation is at block boundary, the NameNode only needs to delete the to-be-truncated blocks. If the operation is not at block boundary, let the result file be R after truncation, the HDFS client copies the last block B of R to a temporary file T, then the tail blocks of file F including block B, $B+1$ to the end of F are dropped. Then R is obtained by contacting F and T. Finally, the lease for the file is released.

5.4 Concurrent updates

For catalog tables, multi-version concurrency control and locking are used to support concurrent updates. For user data tables, they are append only and stored on HDFS. A light-weight *swimming lane* based method is used to support concurrent inserts. Simply speaking, different inserts change different files, which is quite like different writers are in different *swimming lanes* and do not interfere with each other. For typical OLAP workload, tables are often batch loaded at night time, or continuously updated by a small number of concurrent writers. And files can be appended by another transaction after one transaction is completed. Thus, allocating a separate file for a concurrent writer is reasonable and does not lead to unlimited number of small files. Internally, to support concurrent writers, a catalog table for each user table is created to record the information about all the data files of the table. Each tuple in the catalog table records the logic length, uncompressed length and other useful information of a segment file. The logic length is the most important information to support transaction. The physical file length might differ from the logic length due to failed transactions. Queries use logic length in the transaction snapshot when scanning a file.

6. EXTENSION FRAMEWORK

In this section we describe the PXF, which is a fast and extensible framework that connects HAWQ to any data store of choice. The main idea behind PXF is to provide the ability to use HAWQ's extensive SQL language support, smart query planner, and fast executor to access any kind of data that is external, in the form of a HAWQ external table. Existing PXF connectors include transparent and parallel connectivity to HBase, Accumulo, GemFireXD, Cassandra and Hive tables, various common HDFS file types such as Sequence file, Avro file, RCFile, plain text (delimited, csv, JSON), and various record serialization techniques as well. The framework is highly extensible, and exposes a parallel connector API. It is possible for any user to implement this API in order to create a connector for any kind of data stores, or for a proprietary data format that is used internally as a part of the business process. The result is the ability to use HAWQ to run any type of SQL directly on data sets from such external data stores. This also transparently enables running complex joins between internal HAWQ tables and external PXF tables (e.g, an Avro file on HDFS). And, PXF can export internal HAWQ data into files on HDFS. From transaction support perspective, PXF is not transaction aware.

6.1 Usage

HAWQ and Pivotal Hadoop come with a set of built-in PXF connectors. To connect to a data store that has a built-in connector, we need to specify the connector name and the data source. If a built-in connector does not exist, then PXF can be made to support it as described later on in the Section 6.4. As an example, let us assume we want to access data from an HBase table in parallel, and the HBase table name is 'sales'. And assume that we are interested in column family 'details' and qualifiers 'store', 'price' only. A corresponding HAWQ table with a PXF protocol looks as follows:

```
  CREATE EXTERNAL TABLE my_hbase_sales (
    recordkey BYTEA,
    "details:storeid" INT,
    "details:price" DOUBLE)
  LOCATION('pxf://<pxf service location>/sales?
profile=HBase')
  FORMAT 'CUSTOM' (formatter='pxfwritable_import
');
```

We can then perform all kinds of SQL on these HBase table attributes and HBase row keys. For example,

```
  SELECT sum("details:price")
  FROM my_hbase_sales
  WHERE recordkey < 20130101000000;
```

or even join with an internal HAWQ table

```
  SELECT <attrs>
  FROM stores s, my_hbase_sales h
  WHERE s.name = h."details:storeid";
```

6.2 Benefits

The PXF functionality opens the door to rethinking about restrictive decisions that had to be made previously with respect to placing and processing various data sets. New possibilities are now created as a real connection between various data stores, which can be very easily made on demand, and data can be truly shared. If specific data sets are to be used for various purposes (e.g, operational and analytical), it is now a valid choice to choose to store the data in an in-memory transactional database such as GemFireXD, and directly analyze that same data using HAWQ on demand. Additionally, since interesting joins are made possible, big data designs can be made more flexible. There is also the possibility to insert the data of interests into a local HAWQ table if there is an intention to use this data in many future analytics jobs. Lastly, since HAWQ's planner and executor are highly efficient and proven to be extremely fast, it is the case that many external jobs (such as MapReduce) that can be translated into SQL queries, will run much faster with HAWQ/PXF.

6.3 Advanced functionality

PXF is performance aware, and therefore multiple enhancements are built into the core of the framework. Data locality awareness is implemented in order to assign parallel units of work in a way that will reduce network traffic to a minimum. Each splittable data source, whether an HBase table, an HDFS file, or anything else, consists of one or more "data fragments". For example, in an HDFS file or Hive table, a data fragment can be represented by a file block, and in HBase it can be a table region. The HAWQ query planner uses this information along with the location (host name/ip) of each fragment, and allocates the job of reading that fragment to a segment database that is local to it.

PXF also exposes a filter push down API, which can be used to do record filtering at where the data is stored, instead of reading all the data records and filtering them in HAWQ later on. Also related is the existing support for excluding data partitions that do not match the query filter. This is a classic case for the PXF Hive connector, and it knows which nested data directories to ignore when processing the query. In both of these cases, HAWQ pushes out the query scan qualifiers and makes it available for the PXF to use as it sees fit.

PXF also supports planner statistics collection. Since the query planner's decisions highly depend on knowledge of the underlying data, PXF has an API to make that happen. It is therefore possible to run an ANALYZE command on a PXF table and store statistics about that table's external data in the HAWQ's catalog, making it available to the query planner when planning a query that involves that PXF table. The statistics collected includes number of tuples, number of pages and some other advanced statistics.

6.4 Building connectors

The connector API includes three plugins that need to be implemented, with another optional one. Once these plugins are implemented they need to be compiled and placed across the system nodes in a way that is accessible by PXF in runtime. The plugin API includes:

- **Fragmenter**: Given a data source location and name, return a list of data fragments and their locations.
- **Accessor**: Given a data fragment, read all the records that belong to that fragment.
- **Resolver**: Given a record from the accessor, deserialize it (if needed) and parse it into attributes. The output of the resolver gets translated into a HAWQ record that can be processed by HAWQ normally.
- **Analyzer** (optional): Given a data source location and name, return a good estimate of the number of records and other statistics of interest.

7. RELATED WORK

A large amount of work has been done in recent years on the distributed data processing area. It can be classified into the following four categories.

- **Data processing framework**: MapReduce [19, 20] and its open source implementation Hadoop [1] become very popular. MapReduce is designed for batch data processing, and delivers a highly-available service on top of a highly-scalable distributed storage. Dryad [26] is a general-purpose distributed data flow execution engine for coarse-grain data-parallel applications. RDDs [40], implemented in Spark [8], is a distributed memory abstraction that lets programmers perform in-memory computations on large clusters in a fault-tolerant manner.
- **Framework extension**: Pig [30], Hive [36, 37], Tenzing [16] and FlumeJava [15], based on MapReduce, and Dryad-LINQ [39], based on Dryad, are the examples of framework extensions. They provide procedural or declarative query languages to end users. Based on Spark, Shark [38] is a data analysis system running SQL queries and sophisticated analytics functions.
- **Native SQL engines on HDFS**: Like HAWQ, Impala [5], Presto [7] and Drill [3], which is an open source implementation of Dremel [29], adopt database technologies to improve query performance to meet the requirements of ad-hoc queries and provide interactive response time. They all use pipelined execution models. And the major architecture level differences between HAWQ and these systems are at the transaction support (none of them support transactions), the stateless segments and the unique UDP based interconnect.
- **Database and Hadoop mix**: Traditional parallel DBMS vendors such as DB2 [31], Oracle [35], Greenplum database [4], Asterdata [2], Netezza [6], Vertica [11] and Polybase [22] on the other hand, integrate Hadoop with their own database systems to enable their system to access Hadoop data or run MapReduce jobs. HadoopDB [12], which is commercialized in Hadapt [28], builds on MapReduce framework and DBMS technology and provides a hybrid approach to data analysis.

8. EXPERIMENTS

In this section, a thorough experimental study on TPCH benchmark datasets and queries is conducted to evaluate the performance of HAWQ. All the tested systems are deployed on a 20-node cluster connected by a 48-port 10 GigE switch, of which 16 nodes are used for segments and DataNodes, and 4 nodes are used for masters and NameNodes. Each node has two 2.93GHz Intel Xeon 6-core processors, and runs 64-bits CentOS 6.3 with 2.6.23 kernel. And it has 48GB memory, 12×300GB hard disks and one Intel X520 Dual-Port 10 GigE NIC.

8.1 Tested Systems

Stinger[3]: Stinger [9] is a community-based effort to optimize Apache Hive. Stinger phase two (available in Hive 0.12) makes several significant improvements, including ORCFile, basic and advanced optimizations, VARCHAR and DATE support, and is reported 35x-45x faster than the original Hive [9]. For the experiments in this paper, MapReduce jobs from Stinger are managed by YARN with data stored on HDFS. A DataNode and a NodeManager are started on each node. We assign 36GB RAM for YARN to use on each node, thus totally 576GB memory on the cluster. The minimum unit of memory to allocate for a container is set to 4GB. To make the performance comparison fair, we tuned the YARN/Stinger default parameters, adapt the test queries, schemas and data formats to leverage the Stinger improvements. Since Stinger cannot run standard TPC-H queries directly, the transformed queries at [10] are used.

HAWQ: On each node, 6 HAWQ segments are configured, which makes 96 segments in total on the cluster. 6GB memory is allocated to each segment. For all other configurations, default parameters are used.

8.2 TPC-H Results

The performance of the two systems are evaluated against TPC-H datasets. The datasets are first generated by the dbgen program as plain text files stored on HDFS, and then loaded into the systems using system-specific storage formats. HAWQ supports three native storage formats: AO, CO and Parquet. And by default, the tables are hash partitioned. For Stinger, ORCFile, the latest and most efficient format in Hive, is used with default configuration. To ensure exclusive access to the cluster's resources, each system executes the benchmark tasks separately.

TPC-H queries are run against datasets of two scales: 160GB (10GB/node) and 1.6TB (100GB/node). Since the 160GB dataset can be loaded into memory completely, this is a CPU-bound case; while the 1.6TB case is IO-bound. We first present the overall query execution time, and then focus on some specific queries to explain how and why HAWQ outperforms Stinger.

8.2.1 Overall Results

Figure 6 outlines the overall execution time of all 22 TPC-H queries against the 160GB datasets. In this task, HAWQ with Parquet storage format run fastest, taking only 172 seconds, followed by CO, 211 seconds, and AO, 239 seconds. Stinger is the slowest

[3] We planned to compare Impala and Presto, but stopped since TPCH queries on large datasets failed frequently on our system due to out of memory issues in the two systems.

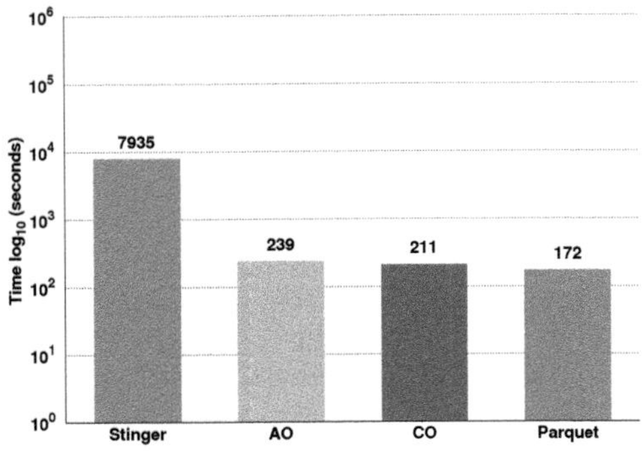

Figure 6: Overall execution time with 160GB

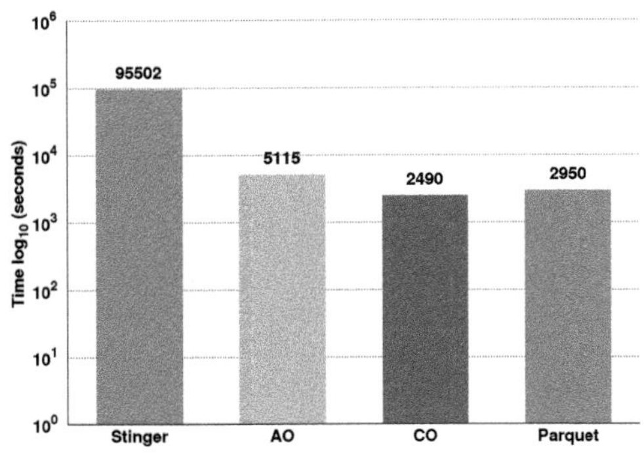

Figure 7: Overall execution time with 1.6TB

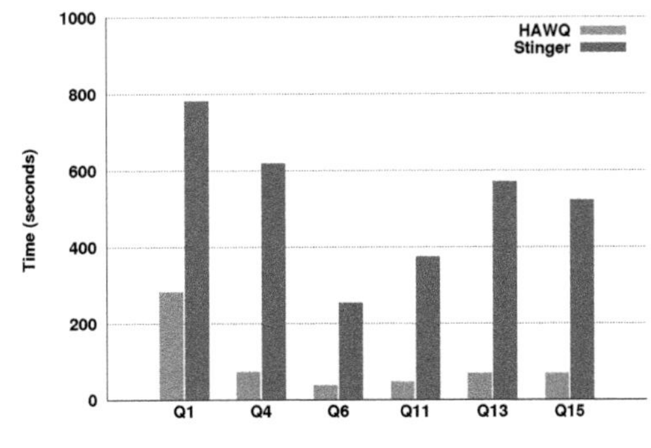

Figure 8: Simple selection queries

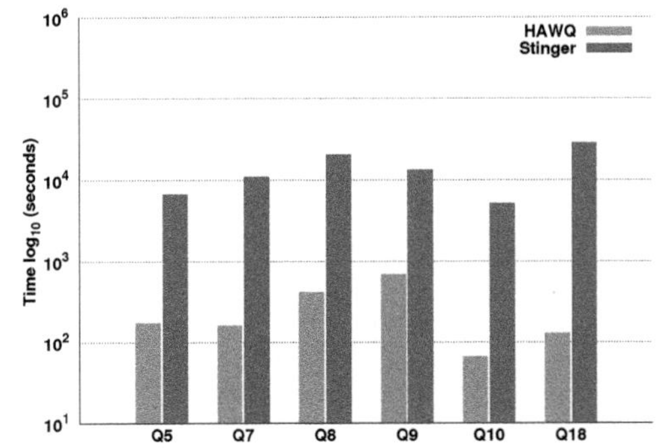

Figure 9: Complex join queries

one, taking more than 7,900 seconds. Thus, no matter with which storage format, HAWQ is about 45x faster than Stinger for this CPU-bound test case.

We only present the overall execution time of 19 out of 22 TPC-H queries on the 1.6TB dataset in Figure 7, since the 3 queries left failed with Stinger (Reducer out of memory). In this task, HAWQ with CO storage format is the fastest one, taking only 2,490 seconds, followed by HAWQ with Parquet, 2,950 seconds, and HAWQ with AO, 5,115 seconds. Hive takes about 96,000 seconds, which is about 40x slower than HAWQ.

The above results are consistent with each other. Both demonstrate that HAWQ is significantly faster than Stinger in either CPU-bound or IO-bound scenarios.

8.2.2 Specific Query Results

Based on the complexity of their execution plans, we categorize 12 out of 22 TPC-H queries into two groups: simple selection queries and complex join queries. Due to space limitation, we only consider the 1.6TB dataset here.

Simple selection queries: Six queries fall into this category. All these queries either perform simple selection and aggregation against one single table (Query 1 and 6), or straightforward join of two or three tables (Query 4, 11, 13 and 15). Here we take Query 6 as an example. This query quantities the amount of revenue increase that would have resulted from eliminating certain company-wide discounts in a given percentage range in a given year. Only the table $lineitem$ is involved. The execution plan of this query is simple: first a sequential scan, and then a two-phase aggregation. Figure 8 shows that, for such simple queries, HAWQ is 10x faster than Stinger. There are several factors contributing to this performance gap. Firstly, the task start-up and coordination of HAWQ is much more efficient than YARN. Secondly, data movement in HAWQ is pipelining, while MapReuce jobs materialize the output of each stage, either locally or remotely on HDFS.

Complex join queries: This category contains Query 5, 7, 8, 9, 10, and 18. The common characteristics of these queries are that the selection and aggregation operations are run against several tables of various sizes, involving a join on 3 or more tables (include the two largest tables $orders$ and $lineitem$). These queries are too complex to be optimized manually. For example, Query 5 lists the revenue volume done through local suppliers. Tables $customer$ (240M rows), $orders$ (2.4B rows), $lineitem$ (9.6B rows), $supplier$ (16M rows), $nation$ (25 rows) and $region$ (5 rows) are involved and joined together. In such case, the join order and data movement efficiency have significant impacts on query execution performance. As illustrated in Figure 9, HAWQ is 40x faster than Stinger for complex join queries. Besides the factors discussed previously for simple selection queries, this huge performance gain is also closely related to planning algorithms. Given the table statistics, HAWQ employs a cost-based query optimizing algorithm, which makes it capable to figure out an optimal plan. Stinger uses a simple rule-based algorithm and makes little use of such hints. Thus, most of the time, Stinger can only give a sub-optimal query plan. Furthermore, multiple table join introduces large volume data movement. The HAWQ interconnect can provide much higher data transfer throughput than the HTTP-based one of MapReduce.

8.3 Data Distribution

As we discussed in Section 2.3, HAWQ supports two distribution policies: one is RANDOMLY, and the other one is HASH distribution based on customized distribution columns. The following

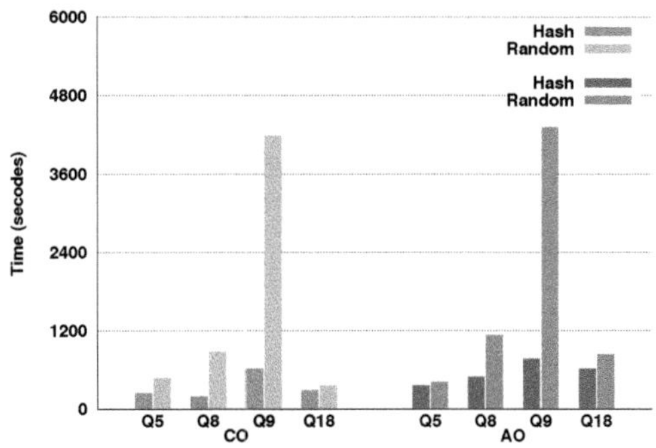

Figure 10: Data Distribution

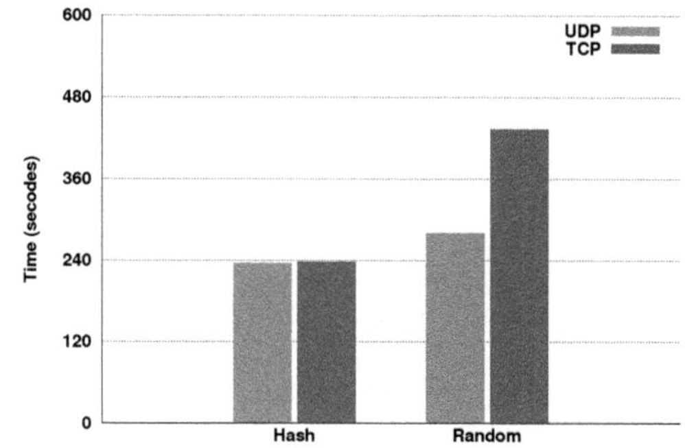

Figure 12: TCP vs. UDP

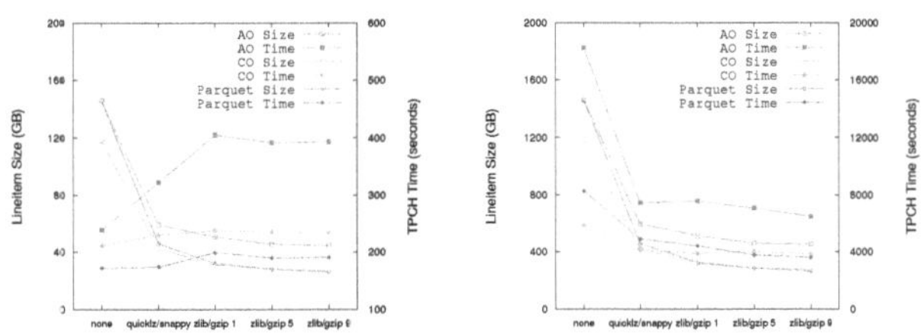

(a) 160GB dataset. (b) 1.6TB dataset

Figure 11: Compression

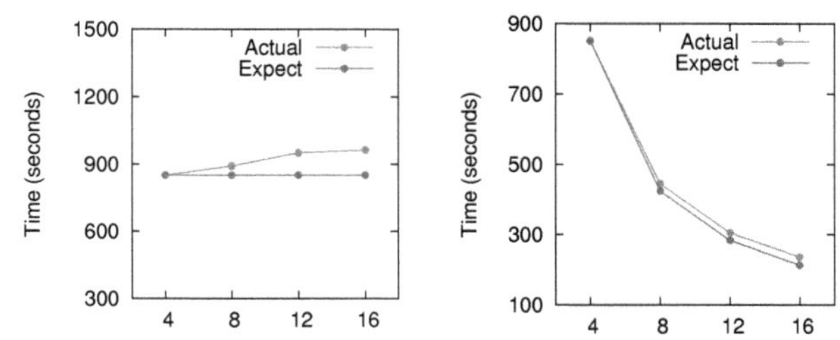

(a) 40GB per node (b) 160GB per cluster

Figure 13: Scalability

experiment shows how a good designated distribution key can improve query performance.

The results of Query 5, 8, 9 and 18 are presented in Figure 10. Overall, distribution keys bring 2x performance improvement for these queries. Here we take Query 9 as an example to illustrate how this works. Query 9 determines how much profit is made on a given line of parts, broken out by supplier nation and year. This query involves equi-join of tables $part$, $supplier$, $lineitem$, $partsupp$, $orders$, and $nation$, with the join key as the primary key of $part$, $supplier$, $partsupp$ and $nation$ respectively. Designating the primary key as its distribution key for each table saves a lot of data redistribution cost when performing the equi-join, compared to random distribution.

8.4 Compression

We evaluate how different compression algorithms affect the storage usage and query execution time. For AO and CO storage formats, no compression, quicklz, and zlib with level 1, 5, 9 are considered; while for Parquet, we tested no compression, snappy, and gzip with level 1, 5, 9. The compressed data size of the *lineitem* table and TPC-H query execution time under different compression algorithms are shown in Figure 11.

For both datasets, 160GB and 1.6TB, from the perspective of compressed data size, quicklz brings a roughly 3x compression ratio, and zlib with level 1 outperforms quicklz a little, and gets better as its compression level increases, but very slightly. This result suggests that for datasets like TPC-H, zlib with level 1 can bring good enough compression results, and very little benefit is gained by increasing its level. In addition, because CO and Parquet are column-oriented storage formats, better compression results are achieved from them, comparing to AO format, which is row-oriented.

On the other hand, from the execution time view, the two datasets are telling different stories. For the 160GB one, execution time increases as having higher compression ratio, for all three storage formats. This is because doing CPU-intensive compression introduce more extra CPU cost but little IO benefit. The 160GB dataset can be loaded into memory completely with or without compression. For comparison among AO, CO and Parquet, the performance downgrade of AO is more serious than CO and Parquet with compress ratio increased. The reason is column-oriented formats only fetch and decompress columns the queries need, while AO needs to fetch and decompress all the columns. For 1.6TB dataset, the result is opposite. Queries run faster as compression ratio improves. This is because data compression brings some IO benefit, which makes the CPU cost of decompression negligible.

8.5 Interconnect

As discussed in Section 4, HAWQ has two interconnect implementations based on TCP and UDP respectively. In this section, we evaluated the performance of these two interconnect implementations against the 160GB dataset.

Figure 12 shows the overall TPC-H query execution time of two cases: hash distribution and random distribution. UDP and TCP have similar performances for hash distribution. For random distribution, UDP outperforms TCP by 54%. This is because, compared with hash distribution, random distribution leads to deeper plans with more data movements and thus more interconnect connections, and UDP interconnect has less connection setup cost and higher data transfer rate at high concurrency than TCP interconnect.

8.6 Scalability

To evaluate the scalability of HAWQ, two tests are designed. The first one fixes data size per node to 40GB, while the other one fixes the total data size to 160GB and distributes the data to a variable number of nodes by the distribution columns. We run this task on the cluster size of 4, 8, 12 and 16 nodes. It measures how well HAWQ scales as the cluster size is increased.

The result of the first test is shown in Figure 13(a), where the red ones are the actual test results, while the green ones are the ideal linear expectations. When the cluster size scales from 4 nodes to 16 nodes, the dataset being processed increases from 160GB to 640GB, and the execution time increases slightly, approximately about 13%. This result implies that the size of dataset which HAWQ can process is near-linearly increased as the size of the cluster increases.

Figure 13(b) illustrates the result of the second test. The execution time decreases from 850 seconds to 236 seconds, about 28% of the former one, as the cluster size scales from 4 nodes to 16 nodes. This result suggests that for a fixed dataset, the execution time is near-linearly decreased as the cluster size increases.

9. CONCLUSION

This work presented HAWQ, a massively parallel processing SQL engine that combines the merits of MPP database and Hadoop into a single runtime. On the one hand, employing HDFS as the underlying storage layer, HAWQ provides novel data replication and fault tolerance mechanisms. On the other hand, HAWQ is standard SQL compliant, highly efficient and fully transactional, which are from its inherence of MPP database. The architecture design and implementation are discussed, including query processing, UDP-based interconnect, transaction management, fault tolerance, read optimized storage, and extensible framework for supporting various popular data stores and formats. The experimental study shows that HAWQ outperforms Stinger by a large margin.

10. REFERENCES

[1] Apache hadoop, http://hadoop.apache.org/.

[2] Asterdata, http://www.asterdata.com/sqlh/.

[3] Drill, http://incubator.apache.org/drill/.

[4] Greenplum database, http://www.gopivotal.com.

[5] Impala, https://github.com/cloudera/impala.

[6] Netezza, http://www-01.ibm.com/software/data/netezza/.

[7] Presto, http://prestodb.io.

[8] Spark, http://spark.incubator.apache.org/.

[9] Stinger, http://hortonworks.com/labs/stinger/.

[10] TPC-H on hive, https://github.com/rxin/TPC-H-Hive.

[11] Vertica, http://www.vertica.com.

[12] A. Abouzeid, K. Bajda-Pawlikowski, D. Abadi, A. Silberschatz, and A. Rasin. HadoopDB: An architectural hybrid of MapReduce and DBMS technologies for analytical workloads. In *VLDB*, 2009.

[13] A. Ailamaki, D. J. Dewitt, M. D. Hill, and M. Skounakis. Weaving relations for cache performance. In *VLDB*, 2001.

[14] H. Berenson, P. Bernstein, J. Gray, J. Melton, E. O'Neil, and P. O'Neil. A critique of ANSI SQL isolation levels. In *SIGMOD*, 1995.

[15] C. Chambers, A. Raniwala, F. Perry, S. Adams, R. R. Henry, R. Bradshaw, and N. Weizenbaum. FlumeJava: Easy, efficient data-parallel pipelines. In *PLDI*, 2010.

[16] B. Chattopadhyay, L. Lin, W. Liu, S. Mittal, and et al. Tenzing: A SQL implementation on the MapReduce framework. In *VLDB*, 2011.

[17] J. Cohen, B. Dolan, M. Dunlap, J. M. Hellerstein, and C. Welton. MAD skills: New analysis practices for big data. In *VLDB*, 2009.

[18] J. C. Corbett, J. Dean, M. Epstein, and et al. Spanner: Google's globally-distributed database. In *OSDI*, 2012.

[19] J. Dean and S. Ghemawat. MapReduce: Simplified data processing on large clusters. In *OSDI*, 2004.

[20] J. Dean and S. Ghemawat. MapReduce: simplified data processing on large clusters. *Communications of the ACM*, 51(1):107–113, 2008.

[21] D. J. DeWitt, S. Ghandeharizadeh, D. Schneider, A. Bricker, H. Hsiao, and R. Rasmussen. The Gamma database machine project. *IEEE Trans. Knowl. Data Eng.*, 2(1):44–62, 1990.

[22] D. J. DeWitt, A. Halverson, R. V. Nehme, S. Shankar, J. Aguilar-Saborit, A. Avanes, M. Flasza, and J. Gramling. Split query processing in Polybase. In *SIGMOD*, 2013.

[23] G. Graefe. Encapsulation of parallelism in the Volcano query processing system. In *SIGMOD*, 1990.

[24] S. Harizopoulos, P. A. Boncz, and S. Harizopoulos. Column-oriented database systems. In *VLDB*, 2009.

[25] J. Hellerstein, C. Ré, F. Schoppmann, D. Z. Wang, E. Fratkin, A. Gorajek, K. S. Ng, C. Welton, and et al. The MADlib analytics library or MAD skills, the SQL. In *VLDB*, 2012.

[26] M. Isard, M. Budiu, Y. Yu, A. Birrell, and D. Fetterly. Dryad: Distributed data-parallel programs from sequential building blocks. In *EuroSys*, 2007.

[27] D. Jiang, B. C. Ooi, L. Shi, and S. Wu. The performance of MapReduce: An in-depth study. In *VLDB*, 2010.

[28] D. J. A. Kamil Bajda-Pawlikowski and, A. Silberschatz, and E. Paulson. Efficient processing of data warehousing queries in a split execution environment. In *SIGMOD*, 2011.

[29] S. Melnik, A. Gubarev, J. J. Long, G. Romer, S. Shivakumar, M. Tolton, and T. Vassilakis. Dremel: Interactive analysis of web-scale datasets. In *VLDB*, 2010.

[30] C. Olston, B. Reed, U. Srivastava, R. Kumar, and A. Tomkins. Pig Latin: a not-so-foreign language for data processing. In *SIGMOD*, 2008.

[31] F. özcan, D. Hoa, K. S. Beyer, A. Balmin, C. J. Liu, and Y. Li. Emerging trends in the enterprise data analytics: connecting Hadoop and DB2 warehouse. In *SIGMOD*, 2011.

[32] A. Pavlo, E. Paulson, A. Rasin, D. J. Abadi, D. J. DeWitt, S. Madden, and M. Stonebraker. A comparison of approaches to large-scale data analysis. In *SIGMOD*, 2009.

[33] D. R. K. Ports and K. Grittner. Serializable snapshot isolation in PostgreSQL. In *VLDB*, 2012.

[34] J. Shute, R. Vingralek, B. Samwel, and et al. F1: A distributed SQL database that scales. In *VLDB*, 2013.

[35] X. Su and G. Swart. Oracle in-database Hadoop: When MapReduce meets RDBMS. In *SIGMOD*, 2012.

[36] A. Thusoo, J. S. Sarma, N. Jain, and et al. Hive - a warehousing solution over a MapReduce framework. In *VLDB*, 2009.

[37] A. Thusoo, J. S. Sarma, N. Jain, and et al. Hive - a petabyte scale data warehouse using Hadoop. In *ICDE*, 2010.

[38] R. S. Xin, J. Rosen, M. Zaharia, M. J. Franklin, S. Shenker, and I. Stoica. Shark: SQL and rich analytics at scale. In *SIGMOD*, 2013.

[39] Y. Yu, M. Isard, D. Fetterly, and et al. DryadLINQ: a system for general-purpose distributed data-parallel computing using a high-level language. In *OSDI*, 2008.

[40] M. Zaharia, M. Chowdhury, T. Das, and et al. Resilient distributed datasets: A fault-tolerant abstraction for in-memory cluster computing. In *NSDI*, 2012.

Major Technical Advancements in Apache Hive

Yin Huai[1] Ashutosh Chauhan[2] Alan Gates[2] Gunther Hagleitner[2] Eric N. Hanson[3]
Owen O'Malley[2] Jitendra Pandey[2] Yuan Yuan[1] Rubao Lee[1] Xiaodong Zhang[1]

[1]The Ohio State University [2]Hortonworks Inc. [3]Microsoft

[1]{huai, yuanyu, liru, zhang}@cse.ohio-state.edu
[2]{ashutosh, gates, ghagleitner, owen, jitendra}@hortonworks.com
[3]ehans@microsoft.com

ABSTRACT

Apache Hive is a widely used data warehouse system for Apache Hadoop, and has been adopted by many organizations for various big data analytics applications. Closely working with many users and organizations, we have identified several shortcomings of Hive in its file formats, query planning, and query execution, which are key factors determining the performance of Hive. In order to make Hive continuously satisfy the requests and requirements of processing increasingly high volumes data in a scalable and efficient way, we have set two goals related to storage and runtime performance in our efforts on advancing Hive. First, we aim to maximize the effective storage capacity and to accelerate data accesses to the data warehouse by updating the existing file formats. Second, we aim to significantly improve cluster resource utilization and runtime performance of Hive by developing a highly optimized query planner and a highly efficient query execution engine. In this paper, we present a community-based effort on technical advancements in Hive. Our performance evaluation shows that these advancements provide significant improvements on storage efficiency and query execution performance. This paper also shows how academic research lays a foundation for Hive to improve its daily operations.

Categories and Subject Descriptors

H.2 [**Database Management**]: Systems

Keywords

Databases; Data Warehouse; Hadoop; Hive; MapReduce

1. INTRODUCTION

Apache Hive is a data warehouse system for Apache Hadoop [1]. It has been widely used in organizations to manage and process large volumes of data, such as eBay, Facebook, LinkedIn, Spotify, Taobao, Tencent, and Yahoo!. As an open source project, Hive has a strong technical development community working with widely located and diverse users and organizations. In recent years, more than 100 developers have made technical efforts to improve Hive on more than 3000 issues. With its rapid development pace, Hive has been significantly updated by new innovations and research since the original Hive paper [45] was published four years ago. We will present its major technical advancements in this paper.

Hive was originally designed as a translation layer on top of Hadoop MapReduce. It exposes its own dialect of SQL to users and translates data manipulation statements (queries) to a directed acyclic graph (DAG) of MapReduce jobs. With an SQL interface, users do not need to write tedious and sometimes difficult MapReduce programs to manipulate data stored in Hadoop Distributed Filesystem (HDFS).

This highly abstracted SQL interface significantly improves the productivity of data management in Hadoop and accelerates the adoption of Hive. The efficiency and productivity of Hive are largely affected by how its data warehouse layer is designed, implemented, and optimized to best utilize the underlying data processing engine (e.g. Hadoop MapReduce) and HDFS. In order to make Hive continuously satisfy requirements of processing increasingly high volumes of data in a scalable and efficient way, we must improve both data storage as well as query execution aspect of Hive. First, Hive should be able to store datasets managed by it in an efficient way which guarantees both storage efficiency as well as fast data access. Second, Hive should be able to generate highly optimized query plans and execute them using a query execution model that utilizes hardware resources well.

Closely working with many users and organizations, the Hive development community has identified several shortcomings in its file formats, query planning, and query execution, which largely determine performance of queries submitted to Hive. In this paper, we present a community-based effort on addressing these several shortcomings with strong support and scientific basis from several academic research results. The main contributions of this paper are:

1. A new file format, Optimized Record Columnar File (ORC File), has been added to Hive which provides high storage and data access efficiency with low overhead.
2. The query planning component has been updated with insightful analyses in complex queries, significantly reducing unnecessary operations in query plans.
3. A vectorized query execution model has been introduced to Hive, which significantly improves the efficiency of query execution at runtime by better utilizing Modern CPUs.

The rest of this paper is organized as follows. Section 2 provides an overview of Hive's Architecture. Section 3 presents shortcomings we have identified and the rationale of the related advancements. Section 4 introduces the advancement on the file format component. Section 5 introduces the advancement on the query

SIGMOD'14, June 22–27, 2014, Snowbird, UT, USA.

http://dx.doi.org/10.1145/2588555.2595630.

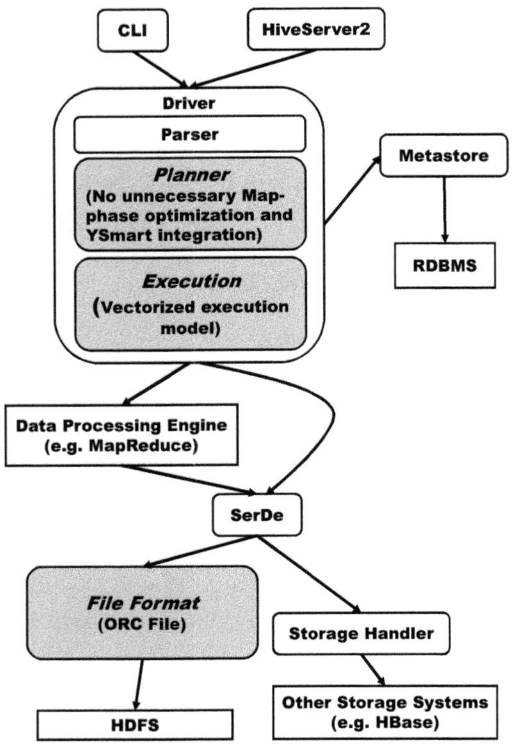

Figure 1: The architecture of Hive. Rounded rectangles are components in Hive. Shaded rounded rectangles are advanced components, and they also show major advancements that will be introduced in this paper.

planning component. Section 6 introduces the advancement on the query execution component. Section 7 reports results of our evaluation on these advancements. Section 8 surveys related work. Section 9 is the conclusion.

2. HIVE ARCHITECTURE

Figure 1 shows the architecture of Hive. Hive exposes two interfaces to users to submit their statements. These interfaces are *Command Line Interface (CLI)* and *HiveServer2* [2]. Through these two interfaces, a statement will be submitted to the *Driver*. The Driver first parses the statement and then passes the Abstract Syntax Tree (AST) corresponding to this statement to the *Planner*. The Planner then chooses a specific planner implementation to analyze different types of statements. During the process of analyzing a submitted statement, the Driver needs to contact the *Metastore* to retrieve needed metadata from a Relational Database Management System (RDBMS), e.g. PostgreSQL.

Queries used for data retrieval and processing are analyzed by the *Query Planner*. Hive translates queries to executable jobs for an underlying data processing engine that is currently Hadoop MapReduce [1]. For a submitted query, the query planner walks the AST of this query and assembles the operator tree to represent data operations of this query. An operator in Hive represents a specific data operation. For example, a `FilterOperator` is used to evaluate predicates on its input records. Because a query submitted to Hive will be evaluated in a distributed environment, the query planner will also figure out if an operator requires its input records to be partitioned in a certain way. If so, it then inserts a boundary represented by one or multiple `ReduceSinkOperators` (`RSOps`) before this operator to indicate that the child operator of these `RSOps` need rows from a re-partitioned dataset. For example, for a group-by clause `GROUP BY key`, a `RSOp` will be used to tell the underlying MapReduce engine to group rows having the same value of `key`. After an operator tree is generated, the query planner applies a set of optimizations to the operator tree. Then, the entire operator tree will be passed to the task compiler, which breaks the operator tree to multiple stages represented by executable tasks. For example, the MapReduce task compiler generates a DAG of Map/Reduce tasks assembled in MapReduce jobs based on an operator tree. In the end of query planning, another phase of optimizations are applied to generated tasks.

After the query planner has generated MapReduce jobs, the Driver will submit those jobs to the underlying MapReduce engine to evaluate the submitted query. In the execution of a Map/Reduce task, operators inside this task are first initialized and then they will process rows fetched by the MapReduce engine in a pipelined fashion. To read/write a table with a specific file format, Hive assigns the corresponding file reader/writer to tasks reading/writing this table. For a file format, a serialization-deserialization library (called SerDe in the rest of this paper) is used to serialize and deserialize data. After all MapReduce jobs have finished, the Driver will fetch the results of the query to the user who submitted the query.

Besides processing data directly stored in HDFS, Hive can also process data stored in other storage systems, e.g. HBase [4]. For those systems, a corresponding *Storage Handler* is needed. For example, the HBase storage handler is used when a query needs to read or write data from or to HBase.

3. IDENTIFIED SHORTCOMINGS

For increasingly diverse organizations, Hadoop has become the de facto place for data storage and processing [46]. Meanwhile, Hive has become one of primary gateways to manipulate, retrieve, and process data stored and managed in Hadoop and its supported systems. With increasing adoption of Hive in production systems, the data volume managed by Hive has increased many folds. At the same time, query workloads on Hive have become much more diverse. From the storage perspective, users expect Hive to efficiently store high volumes of data in a given storage space. This helps users achieve a cost-effective deployment of HDFS. From the query execution perspective, Hive already delivers a high throughput by utilizing Hadoop MapReduce at runtime. However, with new users coming on board, there is an increasing expectation for Hive to provide faster response time. Another motivating factor to deliver a low latency response is a better integration of Hive with business intelligence tools. Users of such tools expect an interactive response time. To meet these two demands, the storage efficiency and query execution performance of Hive must be further improved. In the rest of this section, we will revisit those critical components determining the storage efficiency and query execution performance, and identify shortcomings in these components.

In Hive, the storage efficiency is determined by SerDes and file formats. Hive originally used two simple file formats provided by Hadoop, which are `TextFile` and `SequenceFile`. A file stored with `TextFile` contains plain text data. While, a file stored with `SequenceFile` is a flat file consisting of binary key/value pairs. Because these two formats are data-type-agnostic, Hive uses SerDes to serialize every row into plain text or binary sequences when writing data to HDFS, and to deserialize files in these two formats back to rows with their original schema when reading data from HDFS. Because these two formats store rows in a row-by-

[1]Starting from Hive 0.13, a query can also be translated to a job that is executable in Apache Tez [3]. Without loss of generality, we will mainly use MapReduce in our paper since it is the original data processing engine used by Hive.

row manner, rows have more entropy, which make them hard to be densely compressed. In Hive 0.4, Record Columnar File (RCFile) [27] was introduced. Because RCFile is a columnar file format, it achieved certain improvement on storage efficiency. However, RCFile is still data-type-agnostic and its corresponding SerDe serializes a single row at a time. Under this structure, data-type specific compression schemes cannot be effectively used. Thus, **the first key shortcoming of Hive on storage efficiency is that data-type-agnostic file formats and one-row-at-a-time serialization prevent data values being efficiently compressed**.

The query execution performance is largely determined by the file format component, the query planning component (the query planner), and the query execution component containing implementation of operators. Although RCFile is a columnar file format, its SerDe does not decompose a complex data type (e.g. `Map`). Thus, when a query needs to access a field of a complex data type, all fields of this type have to be read, which introduces inefficiency on data reading. Also, RCFile was mainly designed for sequential data scan. It does not have any index and it does not take advantages of semantic information provided by queries to skip unnecessary data. Thus, **the second key shortcoming of the file format component is that data reading efficiency is limited by the lack of indexes and non-decomposed columns with complex data types**.

The query planner in the original Hive translates every operation specified in this query to an operator. When an operation requires its input datasets to be partitioned in a certain way [2], Hive will insert `RSOps` as the boundary between a Map phase and a Reduce phase. Then, the query planner will break the entire operator tree to MapReduce jobs based on these boundaries. During query planning and optimization, the planner only focuses on a single data operation or a single MapReduce job at a time. This query planning approach can significantly degrade the query execution performance by introducing unnecessary and time consuming operations. For example, the original query planner was not aware of correlations between major operations in a query [31]. Thus, **the third key shortcoming of the query planner is that the query translation approach ignores relationships between data operations, and thus introduces unnecessary operations hurting the performance of query execution**.

The query execution component of Hive was heavily influenced by the working model of Hadoop MapReduce. In a Map or a Reduce task, the MapReduce engine fetches a key/value pair and then forwards it to the Map or Reduce function at a time. For example, in the case of word count, every Map task processes a line of a text file at a time. Hive inherited this working model and it processes rows with a one-row-at-a-time way. However, this working model does not fit the architecture of modern CPUs and introduces high interpretation overhead, under-utilized parallelism, low cache performance, and high function call overhead [19] [35] [50]. Thus, **the fourth key shortcoming of the query execution component is that the runtime execution efficiency is limited by the one-row-at-a-time execution model**.

4. FILE FORMAT

To address the shortcoming of the storage and data access efficiency, we have designed and implemented an improved file format called Optimized Record Columnar File (ORC File) [3] which

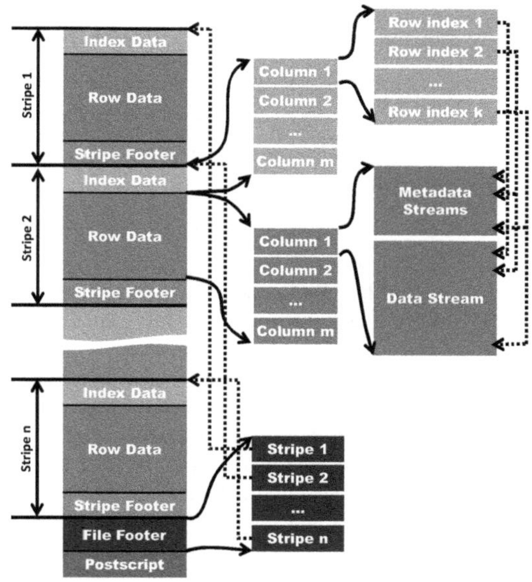

Figure 2: The structure of an ORC file. Round-dotted lines represent position pointers.

has several significant improvements over RCFile. In ORC File, we have de-emphasized its SerDe and made the ORC file writer data type aware. With this change, we are able to add various type-specific data encoding schemes to store data efficiently. To efficiently access data stored with ORC File, we have introduced different kinds of indexes that do not exist in RCFile. Those indexes are critical to help the ORC reader find needed data and skip unnecessary data. Also, because the ORC writer is aware of the data type of a value, it can decompose a column with a complex data type (e.g. `Map`) to multiple child columns, which cannot be done by RCFile. Besides these three major improvements, we also have introduced several practical improvements in ORC File, e.g. a larger default stripe size and a memory manager to bound the memory footprint of an ORC writer, aiming to overcome inconvenience and inefficiency we have observed through years' operation of RCFile.

In this section, we give an overview of ORC File and its improvements over RCFile. First, we introduce the way that ORC File organizes and stores data values of a table (table placement method). Then, we introduce indexes and compression schemes in ORC File. Finally, we introduce the memory manager in ORC File, which is a critical and yet often ignored component. This memory manager bounds the total memory footprint of a task writing ORC files. It can prevent the task from failing caused by running out of memory. Figure 2 shows the structure of an ORC file. We will use it to explain the design of ORC File.

4.1 The Table Placement Method

When a table is stored by a file format, the table placement method of this file format describes the way that data values of this table are organized and stored in underlying filesystems. Based on the definition in [28], the table placement method of ORC File shares the basic structure with that of RCFile. For a table stored in an ORC file, it is first horizontally partitioned to multiple *stripes*. Then, in a stripe, data values are stored in a column by column way. All columns in a stripe are stored in the same file. Also, to be adaptive to different query patterns, especially ad hoc queries, ORC File does not put columns into column groups.

From the perspective of the table placement method, ORC File has three improvements over RCFile. First, it provides a larger de-

[2] In the rest of this paper, this kind of data operations are called major operations and an operator evaluating a major operation is called a major operator.

[3] In the rest of this paper, we use *ORC File* to refer to the file format we introduced and we use *an ORC file* or *ORC files* to refer to one or multiple files stored in HDFS with the format of ORC File.

Table 1: The approach to decomposing a column with a complex data type.

Data type	Child columns
`Array`	A single child column containing array elements.
`Map`	Two child columns, the key field and the value field.
`Struct`	Every field is a child column.
`Union`	Every field is a child column.

fault stripe size (256 MB). While, the default stripe size in RCFile size is 4 MB [4]. With a larger stripe, ORC File can achieve more efficient data reading operations than RCFile because the reader of ORC File can better utilize the sequential bandwidth of hard disks and read less unnecessary data from its underlying filesystem.

The second improvement is that for a column with a complex data type (e.g. `Map`), unlike RCFile, the writer of ORC File decomposes this column to multiple child columns. Table 1 summarizes complex data types in Hive and how they are decomposed. After the process of column decomposition, columns in a table form a tree structure and only leaf nodes (leaf columns) are storing data values of this table. Actual data of a leaf column are stored in a data stream. To facilitate the reader of an ORC file, the metadata of a column are also stored in metadata streams. In the column tree, internal columns (represented by internal nodes in the tree structure) are used to record metadata, e.g. the length of an array. So, those internal columns will not have data streams. Figure 3 shows an example table (defined in Figure 3(a)) and the column tree of it. The schema of the table defines a row with a `Struct` type which is the root column (Column id is 0). Because `col1`, `col2`, `col4`, and `col9` are four fields of a row, they appear as child columns of the root columns. With the decomposition shown in Table 1, this table is decomposed to six leaf columns. When reading a stripe, those leaf columns are read in a column by column way. With the help from those internal columns, we can reconstruct a row from those leaf columns. Also, for a column with a complex data type, the ORC reader is able to only read needed child columns [5].

The last improvement of ORC File over RCFile from the perspective of a table placement method is that users of ORC File can have the choice to align stripe boundaries in an ORC file with the HDFS block boundaries. For an ORC file, the stripe is usually smaller than the HDFS block size used for this ORC file. Without this alignment, it is possible that a stripe is stored in two HDFS blocks, which means this stripe may be stored in different machines. So, reading a stripe stored in two HDFS blocks likely involves remote data reading operations. When this alignment is enabled and the remaining space of a HDFS block cannot fit a stripe, the writer of an ORC file will pad data to the end of this HDFS block. The next stripe will start at the beginning of next HDFS block. With this alignment, a stripe will be always stored in a single HDFS block.

4.2 Indexes

To efficiently read data from HDFS, we have added indexes to ORC File. Because the speed of loading data into Hive and storage efficiency are important to a file format in Hive, in the design of ORC File, we decided to only use sparse indexes. There are two kinds of sparse indexes that are data statistics and position pointers.

[4]To be consistent with ORC File, we use the term stripe at here. Actually, a stripe in RCFile is called a row group.

[5]As of Hive 0.13, Hive has not taken advantage of this ORC File feature. Future releases of Hive will be able to only read needed child columns of a column with a complex data type.

```
CREATE TABLE tbl (
  col1 Int,
  col2 Array<Int>,
  col4 Map<String,
           Struct<col7:String,
                  col8:Int>>,
  col9 String
)
```

(a) The schema of the table

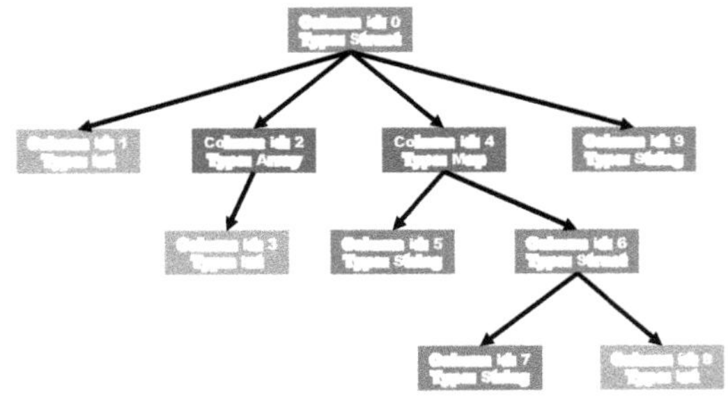

(b) The column tree after column decomposition.

Figure 3: An example table and how columns in it are decomposed.

Data Statistics.

Data statistics are used by the ORC reader to not read unnecessary data from the HDFS. These statistics are created when the ORC writer is creating an ORC file. Representative statistics are the number of values, the minimum value, the maximum value, the sum, and the length (for text types and binary type). For complex data types, `Array`, `Map`, `Struct` and `Union`, their child columns also record data statistics.

In ORC File, data statistics have three levels. First, columns in an ORC file have file level statistics which are recorded at the end of this file. These statistics are used in query optimizations, and they are also used to answer simple aggregation queries. Second, ORC File stores stripe level statistics for every column. ORC readers use these statistics to analyze which stripes are needed to evaluate a query. Those unneeded stripes will not be read from HDFS. Third, to further reduce the amount of unnecessary data read from HDFS, besides stripe level statistics, we have fine-grained statistics inside a stripe, which are called index group level statistics. We logically break data values of a column to multiple index groups with a fixed number of values. The default number of values in an index group is 10000. Data statistics are recorded for every index group. With data statistics for every index group, the query processing engine of Hive can push certain predicates to the reader of an ORC file and an ORC reader will not read unnecessary index groups from HDFS. The number of values in an index group is configurable. An index group containing a small number of values can provide more fine-grained statistics about a column. However, the size of data statistics will increase. Thus, users should tradeoff the size and the granularity of data statistic when determining the number of values in an index group.

Position Pointers.

When reading an ORC file, the reader needs to know two kinds of positions to perform efficient data reading operations. First, because a column in a stripe has multiple logical index groups, the reader of an ORC file needs to know the starting points of every index group in metadata streams and data streams. In Figure 2, round-dotted lines pointing to the metadata stream and data stream represent this kind of position pointers. Second, an ORC file can contain multiple stripes and a HDFS block of this ORC file can contain multiple stripes. To efficiently locate the starting point of a stripe, position pointers of stripes are needed. Those pointers are stored in the file footer of an ORC file (round-dotted lines pointing to starting points of stripes in Figure 2).

4.3 Compression

ORC File uses a two-level compression scheme. A stream is first encoded by a stream type specific data encoding scheme. Then, an optional general-purpose data compression scheme can be used to further compress this stream.

For a column, it is stored in one or multiple streams. Based on the type of a stream, we can divide streams to four primitive types. Based on its type, a stream has its own data encoding scheme. These four types of primitive streams are introduced as follows.

- **Byte Stream**: A byte stream basically stores a sequence of bytes and it does not encode data.
- **Run Length Byte Stream**: A run length byte stream stores a sequence of bytes. For a sequence of identical bytes, it stores the repeated byte and the occurrences.
- **Integer Stream**: An integer stream stores a sequence of integers. It can encode these integers with run length encoding and delta encoding. The specific encoding schemes used for a sub-sequence of integers are determined based on the pattern of it.
- **Bit Field Stream**: A bit field stream is used to store a sequence of boolean values. In this stream, a bit represents a boolean value. Under the cover, a bit field stream is backed by a run length byte stream.

Due to the page limit, we are unable to explain what streams are used for every column type. We will present how an `Int` column and a `String` column are stored as two examples. Interested readers may refer to [5] for details. For an `Int` column, one bit field stream and one integer stream are used. The bit field stream is used to record if a value is null. The integer stream is used to record integer values of this `Int` column. For a `String` column, the ORC writer will first check if using dictionary encoding can store data efficiently by evaluating if the ratio of the number of distinct entries in the dictionary to the number of encoded values is not greater than a configurable threshold (the default threshold is 0.8). If so, the ORC writer will use dictionary encoding scheme, and this column will be stored in one bit field stream, one byte stream, and two integer streams. Like an `Int` column, the bit field stream is used to record if a value is null. The byte stream is used to store the dictionary. One integer stream is used to store the length of each entry in the dictionary. The second integer stream is used to store values of this column. If the ratio of the number of distinct entries in the dictionary to the number of encoded values is greater than the threshold, the ORC writer will know that there are many distinct values and using dictionary encoding cannot efficiently store the data. Thus, it will automatically store this column without the dictionary encoding. Instead of storing the dictionary and storing values as indexes to the dictionary, the ORC writer will use a byte stream to store values of this `String` column and use an integer stream to store the length of each value.

In ORC File, besides those stream type specific schemes, users can further ask the writer of an ORC file to compress streams with a general-purpose codec among ZLIB, Snappy and LZO. For a stream, the general-purpose codec will compress this stream to multiple small compression units. In the current implementation, the default size of a compression unit is 256 KB.

4.4 Memory Manager

When the writer of an ORC file writes data, it buffers the entire stripe in memory. Thus, the memory footprint of an ORC writer is the size of a stripe. Because the default size of a stripe is large, when there are lots of writers concurrently writing to multiple ORC files in a single Map or Reduce task (for example, when a user uses dynamic partitioning, and partitioning columns have lots of distinct values), this task can run out of memory. To bound the memory consumption of those concurrent writers, we add a memory manager in ORC File. In a Map or Reduce task, the memory manager sets a threshold which bounds the maximum amount of memory that can be used by writers in this task [6]. Then, every new writer registers to this memory manager with its stripe size (registered stripe size). When the total amount of memory used by writers (the total registered stripe sizes) exceeds the memory threshold, the memory manager will scale down the actual stripe sizes used in those writers with a ratio of the memory threshold to the total registered stripe sizes. When a writer is closed, the memory manager will subtract the registered stripe size of this writer from the total registered stripe size. If the total registered stripe size is under the threshold, the actual stripe sizes of all writers will be set back to their original stripe sizes. With this control mechanism, the memory footprint of active writers of ORC files in a Map or Reduce task is bounded.

5. QUERY PLANNING

To address the shortcoming of the query planner, we first have identified three major issues caused by the the original query translation approach of Hive, introducing unnecessary operations and data movements, and significantly degrading the performance of a query. These issues are summarized as follows.

- **Unecessary Map phases.** Because a MapReduce job can only shuffle data once, it is common that a query will be executed by multiple MapReduce jobs. In this case, the Map phase loading intermediate results is used merely to load data back from HDFS for data shuffling. Thus, if a MapReduce job generating intermediate results does not have a Reduce phase, it introduces an unnecessary Map phase to load its outputs back from HDFS.
- **Unnecessary data loading.** For a query, a table can be used by multiple operations. If these operations are executed in the same Map phase, Hive can load the table once. However, if these operations are in different MapReduce jobs, this table will be loaded multiple times, which introduce extra I/O operations to the query evaluation.
- **Unnecessary data re-partitioning.** Originally, Hive generates a MapReduce job for every major operation (a data operation requiring its input datasets to be partitioned in a certain way). In a complex query, the input datasets of a major operation may be already partitioned in a proper way by its previous major operations. For this case, we call these two operations are correlated. The original Hive ignores correlations between major operations and thus, can introduce unnecessary data re-partitioning, which results in unnecessary MapReduce jobs and poor query evaluation performance.

For unnecessary Map phases, we have analyzed when Hive will generate Map-only jobs and added an optimization to merge a Map-only job to its child job (Section 5.1). For unnecessary data loading and re-partitioning, we have introduced a Correlation Optimizer to eliminate unnecessary MapReduce jobs (Section 5.1). In this sec-

[6] The default threshold is half of the total memory allocated to this task.

```
SELECT big1.key, small1.value1, small2.value1,
       big2.value1, sq1.total
FROM big1
JOIN small1 ON (big1.sKey1 = small1.key)
JOIN small2 ON (big1.sKey2 = small2.key)
JOIN (SELECT key,
             avg(big3.value1) AS avg,
             sum(big3.value2) AS total
      FROM big2 JOIN big3 ON (big2.key = big3.key)
      GROUP BY big2.key) sq1 ON (big1.key = sq1.key)
JOIN big2 ON (sq1.key = big2.key)
WHERE big2.value1 > sq1.avg;
```

(a) Query

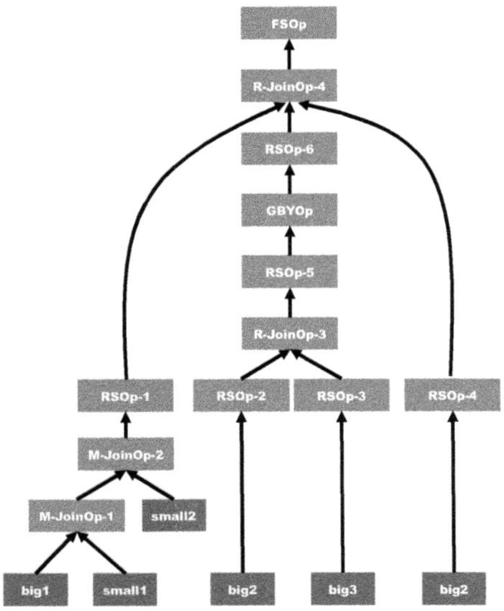

(b) Operator tree

Figure 4: The running example used in Section 5. For an arrow connecting two operators, it starts from the parent operator and ends at the child operator.

tion, we use a running example shown in Figure 4(a) to illustrate optimizations that we will introduce in the rest of this section.

5.1 Eliminating Unnecessary Map phases

In Hive, a Map-only job is generated when the query planner converts a MapReduce job for a Reduce Join to a Map Join. In a Reduce Join, input tables are shuffled and they are joined in Reduce tasks. On the other hand, in a Map Join, two tables are joined in Map tasks. There are several join schemes for a Map Join. One representative example is, for a two way join, to build a hashtable for the smaller table and load it in every Map task reading the larger table for a hash join.

Because we convert a Reduce Join to a Map Join after MapReduce jobs have been assembled, we have a Map-only job for every Map Join at first. Consequently, we would introduce unnecessary operations and elapsed time to the evaluation of the submitted query. To eliminate those unnecessary Map phases, every time when we convert a Reduce Join to a Map Join, we try to merge the generated Map-only job to its child job if the total size of small tables used to build hash tables in the merged job is under a configurable threshold. This threshold is used to prevent a Map task loading a partition of the big table running out of memory.

In our example shown in Figure 4, `small1` and `small2` are two small tables, and `big1` is a large table. At first, Hive generates regular Reduce Joins for Joins involving `small1` and `small2`. Then, Hive automatically converts these two Reduce Joins to Map Joins, which are shown as `M-JoinOp-1` and `M-JoinOp-2` in Figure 4(b). With the optimization introduced in this subsection, these two Map Joins are merged into the same Map phase and will be executed in a pipelined fashion. The results of these two Map Joins will be emitted to the shuffling phase for the Reduce Join `R-JoinOp-4`.

5.2 Correlation Optimizer

To eliminate unnecessary data loading and re-partitioning, we have introduced a Correlation Optimizer into Hive. This optimizer is based on the idea of correlation-aware query optimizations proposed in YSmart [31]. The main idea of this optimizer is to analyze if a major operation really needs to re-partition its input datasets and then to eliminate unnecessary MapReduce jobs through removing boundaries between a Map phase and a Reduce phase. The optimized plan will have less number of shuffling phases. Also, in the optimized plan, a table originally used in those MapReduce jobs are used in the same MapReduce job and Hive can automatically load the common table once instead of multiple times in the original plan.

In this section, we first introduce correlations exploited by this optimizer. Then, we introduce how we have implemented this optimizer. We will also cover new challenges we have overcome and how the design of the Correlation Optimizer is different from the original YSmart.

5.2.1 *Correlations*

In the implementation of the Correlation Optimizer, we consider two kinds of correlations in a query, input correlation and job flow correlation. An input correlation means that a table is used by multiple operations originally executed in different MapReduce jobs. A job flow correlation means that when a major operator depends on another major operator, these two major operators require their input datasets to be partitioned in the same way. Interested readers may refer to the original paper of YSmart [31] for details about correlations.

5.2.2 *Implementation*

During the development of the Correlation Optimizer, we found that the biggest challenge was not to identify optimization opportunities in a query, but to make the optimized plan executable. Except for scanning a table once for operations appearing in the same Map phase, we found that Hive did not have any support for multi-query optimizations. Moreover, the push-based model inside a Reduce task requires an intrinsic coordination mechanism between major operators executed in the same Reduce task to make those major operations work in the same pace. To make the optimized plan work, we needed to extend the query execution layer with the development of the optimizer.

Correlation Detection.

In Hive, every query has one or multiple terminal operators which are the last operators in the operator tree. Those terminal operators are called `FileSinkOperators` (`FSops`). To give an easy explanation, if an operator `A` is on another operator `B`'s path to a `FSOp`, `A` is the downstream of `B` and `B` is the upstream of `A`.

For a given operator tree like the one shown in Figure 4(b), the Correlation Optimizer starts to visit operators in the tree from those `FSOps` in a depth-first way. The tree walker stops at every `RSOp`. Then, a correlation detector starts to find a correlation from this `RSOp` and its siblings by finding the furthest correlated upstream `RSOps` in a recursive way. If we can find any correlated upstream `RSOp`, we find a correlation. Currently, there are three conditions to determine if an upstream `RSOp` and a downstream `RSOp` are correlated, which are (1) emitted rows from these two `RSOps` are

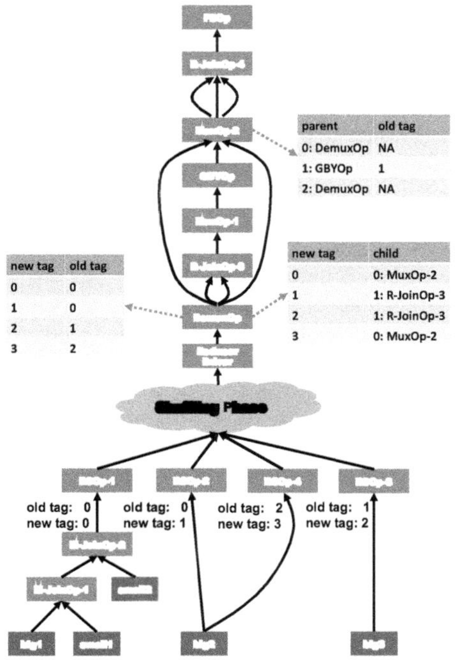

Figure 5: The optimized operator tree of the running example shown in Figure 4.

sorted in the same way; (2) emitted rows from these two `RSOps` are partitioned in the same way; and (3) these `RSOps` do not have any conflict on the number reducers. Interested readers may refer to our implementation [6] and design document [7] for details.

For the example shown in Figure 4(b), the Correlation Optimizer can find one correlation containing six `RSOps`, which are `RSOp-1` to `RSOp-6`.

Operator Tree Transformation.

After the Correlation Optimizer finds all correlations in an operator tree, it starts to transform the operator tree.

There are two kinds of `RSOps` in a correlation. First, we have a list of bottom layer `RSOps` which are necessary ones used to emit rows to the shuffling phase. Originally, because the MapReduce engine considers the input data of the Reduce phase as a single data stream, each bottom layer `RSOp` was assigned a tag which is used to identify the source of a row at the Reduce phase. For a correlation, we reassign tags to those bottom layer `RSOps` and keep the mapping from new tags to old tags. For example, in Figure 5, `RS1`, `RS2`, `RS3` and `RS4` are bottom layer `RSOps` and their old tags are 0, 0, 1, and 2, respectively. After the transformation, their new tags are 0, 1, 2, and 3, respectively.

Second, we have a set of unnecessary `RSOps` which can be removed from the operator tree. Because the Reduce phase of the optimized plan can have multiple major operators consuming input rows from the shuffling phase, we added `DemuxOperator` (`DemuxOp`) in the beginning of the Reduce phase (after the Reducer Driver, which is the entry point of a Reduce phase) to reassign rows to their original tags and dispatch rows to different major operators based on new tags. For example, two mappings tables of the `DemuxOp` in Figure 5 show how `DemuxOp` reassigns tags and dispatches rows. Then, we remove all unnecessary `RSOps` in this correlation inside the Reduce phase. Finally, for every `GroupByOperator` (`GBYOp`) and `JoinOp`, we add a `MuxOperator` (`MuxOp`) as the single parent. For a `GBYOp`, its parent `MuxOp` is used to inform when this `GBYOp` should buffer input rows and emit output rows. For a parent `MuxOp` of a `JoinOp`, besides what a `MuxOp` does for a `GBYOp`, its also needs to assign original tags to rows passed to this `JoinOp`. For example, the `MuxOp-2` shown in Figure 5 basically forwards rows from the `DemuxOp` and it needs to assign tags for rows from the `GBYOp`.

Operator Coordination.

Hive inherits the push-based data processing model in a Map and a Reduce task from the MapReduce engine. Because of this execution model, simply removing unnecessary `RSOps` does not make the plan executable. For example, an operator in a Reduce phase generated by the Correlation Optimizer can have two `JoinOps` and one is at the upstream of another one. By simply removing the downstream `RSOp`, this `JoinOp` will not know when to start buffer its input rows and when to generate output rows. To make the optimized plan work, an operator coordination mechanism is needed.

Currently, this coordination mechanism is implemented in the `DemuxOp` and `MuxOp`. When a new row is sent to the Reducer Driver, it checks if it needs to start a new group of rows by checking values of those key columns. If a new group of rows is coming, it first sends the signal of ending the existing row group to the `DemuxOp`. Then, the `DemuxOp` will propagate this signal to the operator tree. When a `MuxOp` gets this ending group signal, it will check if all of its parent operators have sent this signal to it. If so, it will ask its child to generate results and send this signal to its child. After the signal of ending group has been propagated through the entire operator tree in the Reduce phase, the Reducer Driver then will send a signal of starting a new row group to the `DemuxOp`. This signal will also be propagated through the entire operator tree. Finally, the Reducer Driver will forward the new row to `DemuxOp`. Interested readers may refer to our design document [7] for more details.

6. QUERY EXECUTION

To address the shortcoming of the runtime execution efficiency, we need to design a new execution model that takes advantage of characteristics of modern CPUs. The original Hive heavily relies on using lazy deserialization to reduce the amount of data being deserialized. The data is read as byte arrays and the column values are deserialized only when being accessed. Lazy deserialization does help in saving some deserialization costs, but introduces virtualized calls to deserialization routines in the inner loop of execution, which slows down the execution pipelines.

As demonstrated in [19], the effective execution speed of modern CPUs greatly depends on parallelism. Modern CPUs have multi-staged pipelines with large number of stages, and superscalar architectures contain more than one such pipelines. To fully utilize the parallelism in such a pipelined architecture, it is important to avoid unnecessary branches in the instructions. Also, the higher the data independence among the instructions being executed at different stages of a pipeline, the more parallelism can be achieved. Moreover, processing rows in a one-row-at-a-time model also causes poor cache performance [35] [50]. To address all of these issues, we have designed and implemented the vectorized execution model in Hive. In this section, we provide an overview of the vectorized query execution model in Hive. Interested readers can also refer to [8] [9] for details.

6.1 Vectorized Query Execution

In the vectorized execution model, a dataset is represented as batches of rows. In a row batch, data values of a column are represented as a column vector. The number of rows in the batch is configurable and should be chosen to fit the entire batch in the pro-

```
class VectorizedRowBatch {
    boolean selecetedInUse;
    int[] selected;
    int size;
    ColumnVector[] columns;
}
```

Figure 6: A snippet of a row batch.

```
class LongColumnVector extends ColumnVector {
   long[] vector
}
```

Figure 7: A column vector for `long` encapsulates an array of `long`s. `LongColumnVector` is used to represent all varieties of integers, boolean and timestamp data types..

```
class LongColumnAddLongScalarExpression {
  int inputColumn;
  int outputColumn;
  long scalar;
  void evaluate(VectorizedRowBatch batch) {
    long [] inVector = ((LongColumnVector)
      batch.columns[inputColumn]).vector;
    long [] outVector = ((LongColumnVector)
      batch.columns[outputColumn]).vector;
    if (batch.selectedInUse) {
      for (int j = 0; j < batch.size; j++) {
        int i = batch.selected[j];
        outVector[i] = inVector[i] + scalar;
      }
    } else {
      for (int i = 0; i < batch.size; i++) {
        outVector[i] = inVector[i] + scalar;
      }
    }
  }
}
```

Figure 8: Expression to add a long column with a constant. The array `selected[]` in the batch is used to keep track of valid rows without a branch instruction.

cessor cache. By default, this number is set to 1024, which was carefully chosen to minimize overhead and typically allows one row batch to fit in the processor cache. The query execution progresses by applying each expression on the entire column vector. Figure 6 shows a snippet of a row batch and Figure 7 shows a snippet of a column vector.

In row mode of execution (one-row-at-a-time), each row traverses the whole operator tree before the next row is processed. While, in vectorized execution, a whole row batch is processed through the operator tree. The expressions have been re-implemented as vectorized expressions that work directly on column vectors and produce output in column vectors.

Vectorized query execution doesn't support lazy deserialization and assumes that data reader will provide deserialized data. This will not introduce much overhead that lazy deserialization wanted to avoid because filters and projections are pushed down to the data reader, which will read only relevant data.

6.2 Vectorized Expressions

The biggest chunk of this work has been to implement vectorized expressions for each row mode expression. Vectorized expressions process column vectors in a tight loop and minimize branching and method calls from within the loop. Specialized expressions are implemented for each data type. For example, there are different expressions for adding two long columns or a long column plus a double column. Similarly, different expressions have been implemented that add a column to a constant. Figure 8 shows the snippet of a vector expression that adds a long column to a constant.

The inner loop in Figure 8 is a very tight loop with no branches or method calls. The iterations are completely independent of each other and can be parallelized in the superscalar instruction pipelines of modern CPUs. If the batch fits into the L1 cache, cache misses will be minimal. Additionally, there is a strong locality of reference in the instruction cache.

There are more optimizations that have been implemented into the expressions. The column vectors contain a no-null flag that is set, by the data reader, to true if it is known that the column doesn't contain any null in the batch. The expressions avoid a null check in the inner loop if the no-null flag is set. If this flag is not set, a null check is necessary. There is also an is-repeating flag to indicate if all values of the column are the same. The expressions further optimize for this case by doing computation in constant time if possible for the whole column vector, rather than time proportional to the vector size. This can allow the benefits of run-length encoding to extend to faster query execution.

Vectorized expressions for `AND`, `OR` and comparison expressions have two sets of implementations, one that produces a boolean output column, and other that does not produce an output but achieves in-place filtering by manipulating the `selected` array. The array of `selected` is populated with the index of the rows that are passed by the expression. Subsequent expressions only work on rows that are selected by the previous expressions.

6.3 Vectorized Expression Templates

Many vectorized expressions have similar code for different data types. These expressions are generated from pre-defined templates by variable substitution. For example, there is a template for all comparison operations among numeric types that generate a boolean output column. The expressions are generated at build time and compiled into the Hive jar. There is no dynamic code generation. Dynamic code generation can achieve more optimized code but that work has been left for the future.

6.4 Vectorization Optimizer

Vectorization has been added as a rule based optimization in the query planner. The planner first generates a non-vectorized plan and then vectorization optimization is invoked if configured. The vectorization optimization first validates the plan to ensure vectorization is applicable to the operators and expressions used in the plan. If validation succeeds, the optimizer iterates through all the operators and expressions, and replaces each expression tree with corresponding vectorized expressions, as applicable.

6.5 Vectorized Reader

Vectorized query execution works with any file format that can provide data input as vectorized row batch (Figure 6). The columnar file formats fit more naturally with vectorized query execution because column vectors in the row batch can be more efficiently read from the underlying data layout. The reader must deserialize the data and should also populate various flags (e.g. no-null flag) to enable optimizations as mentioned in Section 6.2.

7. PERFORMANCE EVALUATION

To show the effectiveness of those advancements introduced in Section 4, Section 5, and Section 6, we report results of our experiments in this section. Our experiments were designed to show benefits from each advancement separately. We will first introduce the setup of our experiments and then report results.

7.1 Setup

We conducted our experiments in a cluster with 11 nodes launched in Amazon EC2 . The instance type was `m1.xlarge` which has 4 cores, 15 GB memory, and 4 disks. The operating system used for these nodes was Ubuntu Server 12.04.3 LTS 64-bit. The Hadoop version was 1.2.1. The Hive version was 0.13-SNAPSHOT built on

Table 2: **Sizes of datasets (GB) stored by Text, RCFile, RCFile with Snappy compression, ORC File, and ORC File with Snappy compression.**

	SS-DB	TPC-H	TPC-DS
Text	248.35	323.84	279.87
RCFile	128.23	269.00	159.69
RCFile Snappy	55.15	118.33	105.28
ORC File	53.51	168.96	102.24
ORC File Snappy	39.20	86.67	94.05

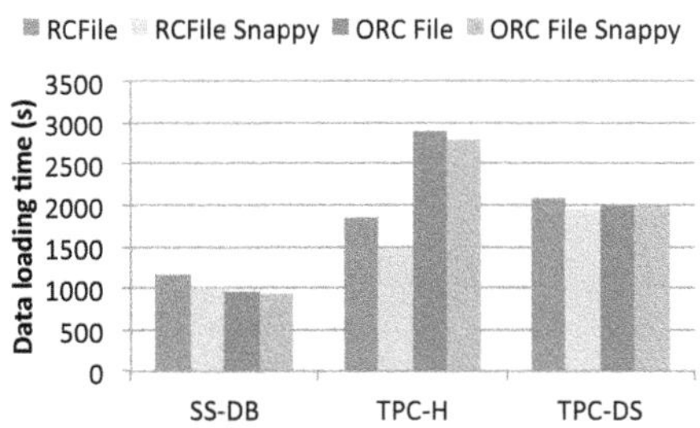

Figure 9: Elapsed times of loading datasets to file formats of RCFile, RCFile with Snappy compression, ORC File, and ORC File with Snappy compression.

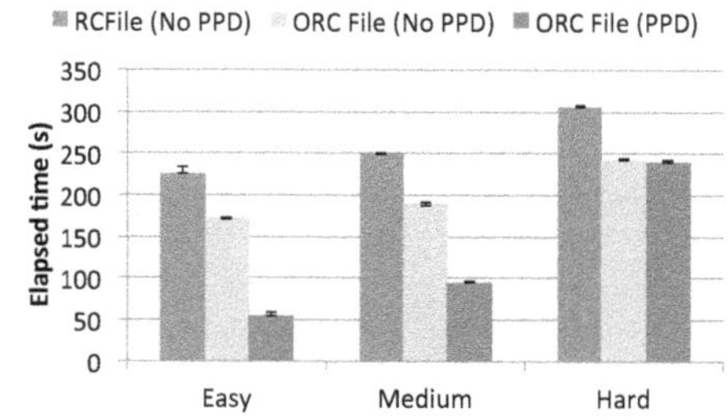

(a) Elapsed times

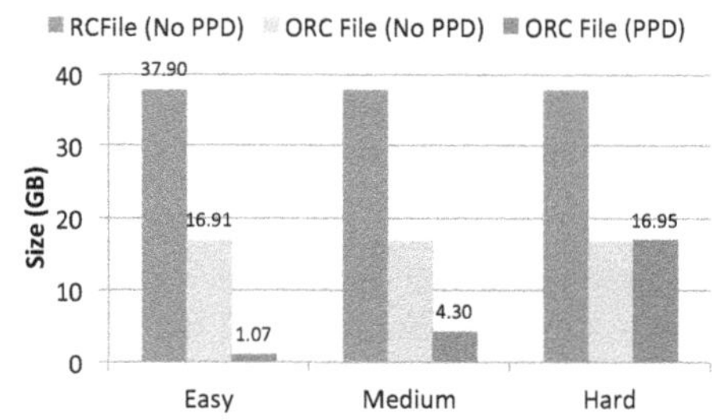

(b) Amounts of data read from HDFS

Figure 10: Elapsed times and sizes of data read from HDFS of SS-DB query 1.easy, 1.medium, and 1.hard. `No PPD` **means that predicates were not pushed down to the ORC reader level. While,** `PPD` **means that predicates were pushed down to the ORC reader level and ORC File used indexes to determine what data to read.**

Nov. 28th, 2013 for experiments of file formats and query execution and Hive 0.14-SNAPSHOT built on Mar. 7th, 2014 for experiments of query planning. This Hadoop cluster had 1 master node running NameNode and JobTracker, and 10 slave nodes running DataNode and TaskTracker.

In our experiments, we used queries from three benchmarks, which are SS-DB [22], TPC-H [10], and TPC-DS [11]. SS-DB is a standard science DBMS benchmark and it is used to simulate applications that manipulate array-oriented data. We used a `large` scale factor to generate the SS-DB dataset. This dataset contains 1000 images which are divided to 50 cycles (20 images in each cycle). In our experiments, we only used one cycle of images. TPC-H and TPC-DS are two standard decision support benchmarks. We used the scale factor of 300 for both of them. In our experiments, all tables in TPC-H and TPC-DS were loaded into Hive. For every query used in our experiments, we tested it five times. For elapsed times, we will report medians, and 25% and 50% percentiles will be reported as error bars. To eliminate the impact from OS buffer caches, before every run of a query, we freed all cached objects, and then freed OS page cache, dentries and inodes.

For Hadoop, we set that the Reduce phase starts after the entire Map phase has finished. For a slave node, it can run three concurrent Map tasks or Reduce tasks. The HDFS block size was set to 512 MB. Due to the page limit, we cannot introduce all configuration properties used in Hadoop and Hive, and show queries used in our experiments. Interested readers may refer to https://github.com/yhuai/hive-benchmarks for details.

7.2 File Format

In this section, we show the storage efficiency and data reading efficiency of ORC File. To show the storage efficiency, we compared the sizes of datasets of SS-DB, TPC-H and TPC-DS stored by RCFile and ORC. For each file format, we also stored datasets with and without using Snappy compression (referred to as RCFile Snappy and ORC File Snappy). Table 2 shows the sizes of those datasets stored with RCFile, RCFile Snappy, ORC File, and ORC File Snappy. The sizes of datasets stored in plain text are also provided in Table 2 (referred to as Text) as references. As we can seen, without Snappy compression, datasets of SS-DB and TPC-DS have already had smaller sizes than RCFile with Snappy, which shows the effectiveness of data type specific encoding schemes in ORC File. With Snappy compression, sizes of datasets stored with ORC File were further reduced. For datasets of SS-DB and TPC-DS, this further reduction on sizes is not as significant as that shown in the dataset of TPC-H. It is because every table in TPC-H has a column of `comment`, which contains random strings. The cardinality of such a column is high and the dictionary encoding scheme is not effective. Thus, the size of the dataset of TPC-H can be significantly reduced by using a general-purpose data compression technique, such as Snappy.

Besides sizes of datasets, we also report data loading times at here. Figure 9 shows the times taken to load the plain text datasets to RCFile, RCFile Snappy, ORC File, and ORC File Snappy. For datasets of SS-DB and TPC-DS, the time taken to load a dataset to ORC File was about the same with RCFile. However, the data loading time taken to store the TPC-H dataset in ORC File was around two times as long as that taken to store the dataset in RCFile. We believe that it was caused by those columns with random strings mentioned above. Because the dictionary encoding scheme was not effective for those columns, operations for the dictionary encoding scheme were basically useless work which contributed to the longer time on loading the TPC-H dataset.

To show the data reading efficiency of ORC File, we used three variations of SS-DB query 1. The query template is shown below.

```
SELECT SUM(v1), COUNT(*) FROM cycle
WHERE x BETWEEN 0 and var AND
      y BETWEEN 0 and var;
```

These variations are referred to as query 1.easy, query 1.medium, and query 1.hard. The value of `var` corresponds to these queries are 3750, 7500, and 15000, respectively. With the increase of the difficulty (e.g. from easy to medium), the number of rows satisfying predicates in the query increases, and all rows will satisfy

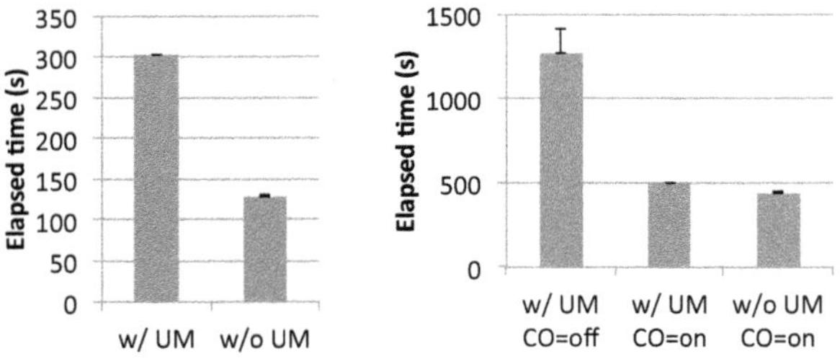

(a) TPC-DS query 27 (b) TPC-DS query 95

Figure 11: Elapsed times of TPC-DS query 27 and query 95. `w/ UM` **means that the plan had all unnecessary map phases.** `w/o UM` **means that the plan did not have any unnecessary map phase.** `CO=off` **and** `CO=on` **means that the Correlation Optimizer was disabled and enabled, respectively.**

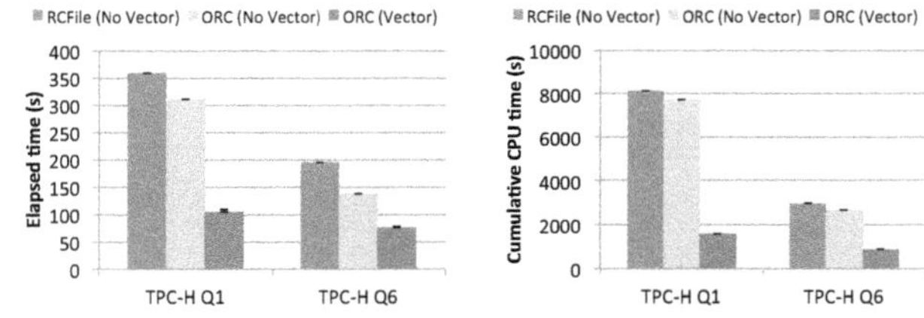

(a) Total elapsed times (b) Cumulative CPU times

Figure 12: Elapsed times and cumulative CPU times of TPC-H query 1 and TPC-H query 6. `No Vector` **and** `Vector` **means that the vectorized query execution engine was disabled and enabled, respectively.**

predicates in query 1.hard. This three queries are suitable for evaluating the data reading efficiency of ORC File and the effectiveness of indexes provided by ORC File. Figure 10 shows elapsed times of these queries and the amounts of data read from HDFS. For ORC File, it can use its indexes to evaluate predicates at the ORC reader level. If there is no row in a stripe satisfying predicates, the ORC reader does not read this stripe. If an index group does not satisfy predicates, ORC File does not read rows in it from HDFS. From Figure 10, we have three observations. First, without using indexes, ORC File's large default stripe size (i.e. 256 MB) can provide better data reading efficiency which is shown by a less query elapsed time and a less amount of data read from HDFS than a smaller default stripe size provided in RCFile (i.e. 4 MB). This observation confirms the study in [28]. Second, with indexes, ORC File is able to significantly further reduce the amount of unnecessary data read from HDFS. For query 1.easy, with the help from indexes, the amount of data read from HDFS was 1.07 GB comparing to 16.91 GB data without using indexes. Third, the overhead of using indexes is low. For query 1.hard, because all rows satisfy predicates, indexes are useless for this query. In this case, with using indexes, ORC File read around 40 MB extra data (storing indexes) and introduced around 2 extra seconds than without using indexes.

7.3 Query Planning

To show the effectiveness of optimizations introduced in Section 5, we show performance of TPC-DS query 27 and query 95. The TPC-DS query 27 first has a five-table star join. Then, the result of this star join is aggregated and sorted. For the star join in this query, it involves a large fact table and four small dimension tables. Without the optimization introduced in Section 5.1, the plan of this query has four Map-only jobs and one MapReduce job. Each Map-only job corresponds to a join between the large table and a small dimension table. The last MapReduce job is used to generate the final result. This plan yields poor query evaluation performance because it has four unnecessary Map phases. After eliminating these unnecessary Map phases, the optimized plan has a single MapReduce job. Those Map Joins are executed in the Map phase. Figure 11(a) shows the performance of these two plans. The speedup of the optimized plan is around 2.34x.

The TPC-DS query 95 is a very complex query. Because the limitation of Hive on supporting sub-queries in the `WHERE` clause, we flatten sub-queries in this query for this experiment. This query can be optimized by eliminating unnecessary Map phases and exploiting correlations. Without these two optimizations, the plan of this query has three Map-only jobs and five MapReduce jobs. By exploiting correlations with the Correlation Optimizer, the plan has three Map-only jobs and two MapReduce jobs. By further eliminating unnecessary Map phases, the optimized plan has only two MapReduce jobs. Figure 11(b) shows the performance of these three plans. With the Correlation Optimizer, we can achieve a speedup of 2.57x. Then, after further eliminating unnecessary Map phases, we can achieve a combined speedup of 2.92x.

7.4 Query Execution

To show the effectiveness of the vectorized query execution engine in Hive, we conducted experiments with TPC-H query 1 and TPC-H query 6. These two queries use the largest table in the TPC-H benchmark, i.e. `lineitem`. The TPC-H query 1 has one predicate and eight aggregations. The TPC-H query 6 has four predicates and one aggregation. Both of these two queries were executed in a single MapReduce job. Figure 12(a) shows the elapsed times of these two queries with and without the vectorized query execution engine. The elapsed times based on RCFile with the original Hive execution engine are also reported at here as references. As we can seen, with the vectorized query execution engine, the elapsed times of these query were significantly reduced. We also report cumulative CPU times in Figure 12(b). For the TPC-H query 1, the cumulative CPU time of the original Hive execution engine is around five times as long as that with the vectorized execution engine. For the TPC-H query 6, the cumulative CPU time of the original Hive execution engine is around three times as long as that with the vectorized execution engine.

8. RELATED WORK

The advancements we introduced in this paper come from a combined result of years' operating experience on Hive, and the foundation of both traditional database research and recent research efforts on Hadoop-based data management systems. In this section, we summarize related work to file formats, query planning, and query execution.

8.1 File Formats

File formats (or storage models in traditional database research) are one of the most important and long-lasting topics. There were several research projects on this topic, e.g. [21] [18] [49]. As shown in [44] and [30], columnar file formats are most suitable for data warehouse workloads. In the ecosystem of Hadoop, there has been several work on file formats. RCFile [27] was the first widely used columnar file format. It has triggered several projects targeting on this topic, including [23] [24] [33] [29] [12].

To introduce columnar file formats into Hive, characteristics of Hive, HDFS and MapReduce need to be considered. First, every HDFS block of every file takes a certain space in the memory of a HDFS master node, which requires that a file format should occupy as less space as possible in the HDFS master node. Thus, in the design of ORC File, we store all columns of a stripe in a single file instead of storing columns of a stripe to multiple files. This design also significantly simplifies the integration with Hive. Moreover, based on [28], it is not necessary to store a stripe to multiple files when the stripe size is large (e.g. 256 MB default stripe size used in ORC File). Second, the task scheduler in MapReduce tries to co-locate a task with its input data. Thus, ORC File stores metadata and indexes with their corresponding data. Third, because ad hoc queries are an important workload of Hive, the adaptivity of a columnar file format to different query patterns is critical. Thus, in ORC File, columns will not be grouped. Also, a recent study has shown that grouping columns has insignificant performance benefits on I/O when the stripe size is large enough [28].

Another related work is Parquet [13]. Based on the definition of table placement methods provided in [28], ORC File and Parquet share the same basic structure. They both first partition a table to multiple stripes [7] and then store columns in a stripe in a column-by-column fashion. The main difference between them is that they store values of a column in different ways. Parquet stores values of a column in a way based on the nested columnar storage introduced in Dremel [34].

8.2 Query Planning

Planning a query based on its semantics and data properties can be traced back to System R which cooperates ordering information of intermediate results in a query when choosing the join method [40]. There are several projects that aim to infer and exploit intermediate data properties for optimizing the plan of a query. Representatives are [42] on sorting operations; [26] on partitioning operations; [36] on both sorting and grouping operations; and [48] on partitioning, sorting and grouping operations. To increase effective disk bandwidth and reduce unnecessary operations, both data sharing and work sharing are also exploited in [41] [25] [51] [20].

In the ecosystem of Hadoop, there have been several recent research projects exploiting sharing opportunities and eliminating unnecessary data movements, e.g. [31] [37] [47] [32]. The Correlation Optimizer in Hive is a YSmart-based design. YSmart [31] looks at a single query. It exploits shared data scan opportunities and eliminates unnecessary data shuffling operations by merging multiple MapReduce jobs into a single one. The main difference between Correlation Optimizer and other related work (including YSmart) is that Correlation Optimizer is specifically designed for the push-based data processing model used by Hive. Existing work mainly focuses on generating optimized query plans. While, Correlation Optimizer also considers how to execute optimized plans under the push-based model.

8.3 Query Execution

Early work discussed processing a block of rows organized with the N-ary Storage Model in memory [38] and using a special buffer operator to create blocks without modifying regular operators to offer a better instruction cache locality [50]. The vectorized execution design for Hive was motivated by the work on MonetDB/X100 [19]. This work shows the inefficiency of the one-row-at-a-time execution model and shares their experience on building a vectorized query execution system. A recent paper proposed to dynamically generate code to further improve query processing performance [35]. Other recent work argues that for highest query execution performance, vectorization is essential, and it must be judiciously combined with compilation techniques [43].

[7] A stripe in Parquet is called a row group, which is the same term used in RCFile.

In the ecosystem of Hadoop, Apache Drill [14] and Impala [15] also attempt to improve runtime query execution efficiency. Drill uses a vectorized execution model [16] and Impala processes a row batch at a time instead of a single row at a time.

9. CONCLUSION

In this paper, we have presented major advancements in Hive. Specifically, we introduced (1) a highly efficient file format, ORC File; (2) an updated query planner that effectively reduces unnecessary data operations and movements by eliminating unnecessary Map phases and exploiting correlations in a query; and (3) a new vectorized query execution engine that significantly improves the performance of query execution through better utilizing modern CPUs. The performance and resource utilization efficiency of the updated Hive have been demonstrated by our experiments. We have also received positive feedbacks from the Hive-based data processing community. For example, the storage efficiency in Facebook's Hive production system has been significantly improved after adopting ORC File [39].

These major technical advancements come from strong collaborative efforts from both research and development communities. Some academic research projects have directly influenced the new developments of Hive with strong technical and analytical basis. On the other hand, the engineering efforts in systems implementation have addressed several challenges in order to make Hive gain substantial benefits in practice.

Recently, several new features have been added into Hive or under development. Interested readers may refer to [17] for details. From the perspective of functionalities, we have been working on expending Hive's SQL capabilities, such as advanced analytic functions, new data types, extending the sub-queries support, common table expressions, and improved support for join syntax. Hive has introduced limited form of support for transactions. Language level support for transaction is under development and is expected to be released later this year. Also, Hive now supports SQL standard based authorization model. HiveServer2 has been enhanced to support different protocols and Kerberos authentication. From the perspective of performance, we have been integrating Hive with Apache Tez [3] for its support on more general query execution plans and better performance. Except eliminating unnecessary Map phases (it is a MapReduce-specific issue), all of advancements introduced in this paper are still applicable and important to Hive running on Tez. Hive has introduced cost based optimizer. Currently, its used to do join ordering. Work is in progress to use cost based optimizer for wider range of queries.

10. ACKNOWLEDGMENTS

We would like to thank the Hive development community. In recent years, more than 100 developers have made technical efforts to improve Hive on more than 3000 issues. We thank those individuals who have operated, tested, supported and documented Hive in various platforms and applications. We are grateful to the Hive user community who has provided us with numerous valuable feedbacks that drive the development and advancements of Hive. We thank anonymous reviewers for their constructive comments. This work has been partially supported by the National Science Foundation under grants CCF-0913050, OCI-1147522, and CNS-1162165.

11. REFERENCES

[1] https://hadoop.apache.org/.
[2] https://cwiki.apache.org/confluence/display/Hive/Setting+up+HiveServer2.

[3] https://tez.incubator.apache.org/.
[4] https://hbase.apache.org/.
[5] https://svn.apache.org/viewvc/hive/trunk/ql/src/java/org/apache/hadoop/hive/ql/io/orc/WriterImpl.java?view=log.
[6] https://svn.apache.org/viewvc/hive/trunk/ql/src/java/org/apache/hadoop/hive/ql/optimizer/correlation/CorrelationOptimizer.java?view=log.
[7] https://cwiki.apache.org/confluence/display/Hive/Correlation+Optimizer.
[8] https://issues.apache.org/jira/browse/HIVE-4160.
[9] https://issues.apache.org/jira/secure/attachment/12603710/Hive-Vectorized-Query-Execution-Design-rev11.pdf.
[10] http://www.tpc.org/tpch/.
[11] http://www.tpc.org/tpcds/.
[12] http://avro.apache.org/docs/current/trevni/spec.html.
[13] https://github.com/Parquet/parquet-format.
[14] https://incubator.apache.org/drill/.
[15] https://github.com/cloudera/impala.
[16] http://www.slideshare.net/ApacheDrill/oscon-2013-apache-drill-workshop-part-2.
[17] https://hive.apache.org/.
[18] A. Ailamaki, D. J. DeWitt, M. D. Hill, and M. Skounakis. Weaving Relations for Cache Performance. In *VLDB*, 2001.
[19] P. A. Boncz, M. Zukowski, and N. Nes. MonetDB/X100: Hyper-Pipelining Query Execution. In *CIDR*, 2005.
[20] Y. Cao, G. C. Das, C.-Y. Chan, and K.-L. Tan. Optimizing Complex Queries with Multiple Relation Instances. In *SIGMOD*, 2008.
[21] G. P. Copeland and S. N. Khoshafian. A Decomposition Storage Model. In *SIGMOD*, 1985.
[22] P. Cudre-Mauroux, H. Kimura, K.-T. Lim, J. Rogers, S. Madden, M. Stonebraker, S. B. Zdonik, and P. G. Brown. SS-DB: A Standard Science DBMS Benchmark. http://www-conf.slac.stanford.edu/xldb10/docs/ssdb_benchmark.pdf.
[23] A. Floratou, J. M. Patel, E. J. Shekita, and S. Tata. Column-Oriented Storage Techniques for MapReduce. In *VLDB*, 2011.
[24] S. Guo, J. Xiong, W. Wang, and R. Lee. Mastiff: A Mapreduce-based System for Time-Based Big Data Analytics. In *CLUSTER*, 2012.
[25] S. Harizopoulos, V. Shkapenyuk, and A. Ailamaki. QPipe: A Simultaneously Pipelined Relational Query Engine. In *SIGMOD*, 2005.
[26] W. Hasan and R. Motwani. Coloring Away Communication in Parallel Query Optimization. In *VLDB*, 1995.
[27] Y. He, R. Lee, Y. Huai, Z. Shao, N. Jain, X. Zhang, and Z. Xu. RCFile: A Fast and Space-efficient Data Placement Structure in MapReduce-based Warehouse Systems. In *ICDE*, 2011.
[28] Y. Huai, S. Ma, R. Lee, O. O'Malley, and X. Zhang. Understanding Insights into the Basic Structure and Essential Issues of Table Placement Methods in Clusters. In *VLDB*, 2013.
[29] A. Jindal, J.-A. Quiané-Ruiz, and J. Dittrich. Trojan Data Layouts: Right Shoes for a Running Elephant. In *SOCC*, 2011.
[30] A. Lamb, M. Fuller, R. Varadarajan, N. Tran, B. Vandier, L. Doshi, and C. Bear. The Vertica Analytic Database: C-Store 7 Years Later. In *VLDB*, 2012.
[31] R. Lee, T. Luo, Y. Huai, F. Wang, Y. He, and X. Zhang. YSmart: Yet Another SQL-to-MapReduce Translator. In *ICDCS*, 2011.
[32] H. Lim, H. Herodotou, and S. Babu. Stubby: A Transformation-based Optimizer for Mapreduce Workflows. In *VLDB*, 2012.
[33] Y. Lin, D. Agrawal, C. Chen, B. C. Ooi, and S. Wu. Llama: Leveraging Columnar Storage for Scalable Join Processing in the Mapreduce Framework. In *SIGMOD*, 2011.
[34] S. Melnik, A. Gubarev, J. J. Long, G. Romer, S. Shivakumar, M. Tolton, and T. Vassilakis. Dremel: Interactive Analysis of Web-Scale Datasets. In *VLDB*, 2010.
[35] T. Neumann. Efficiently Compiling Efficient Query Plans for Modern Hardware. In *VLDB*, 2011.
[36] T. Neumann and G. Moerkotte. A Combined Framework for Grouping and Order Optimization. In *VLDB*, 2004.
[37] T. Nykiel, M. Potamias, C. Mishra, G. Kollios, and N. Koudas. MRShare: Sharing Across Multiple Queries in Mapreduce. In *VLDB*, 2010.
[38] S. Padmanabhan, T. Malkemus, R. C. Agarwal, and A. Jhingran. Block Oriented Processing of Relational Database Operations in Modern Computer Architectures. In *ICDE*, 2001.
[39] J. Parikh. Data Infrastructure at Web Scale. http://www.vldb.org/2013/video/keynote1.flv.
[40] P. G. Selinger, M. M. Astrahan, D. D. Chamberlin, R. A. Lorie, and T. G. Price. Access Path Selection in a Relational Database Management System. In *SIGMOD*, 1979.
[41] T. K. Sellis. Multiple-Query Optimization. *ACM Trans. Database Syst.*, 13(1):23–52, Mar. 1988.
[42] D. Simmen, E. Shekita, and T. Malkemus. Fundamental Techniques for Order Optimization. In *SIGMOD*, 1996.
[43] J. Sompolski, M. Zukowski, and P. A. Boncz. Vectorization vs. Compilation in Query Execution. In *DaMoN*, 2011.
[44] M. Stonebraker, D. J. Abadi, A. Batkin, X. Chen, M. Cherniack, M. Ferreira, E. Lau, A. Lin, S. Madden, E. O'Neil, P. O'Neil, A. Rasin, N. Tran, and S. Zdonik. C-Store: A Column-oriented DBMS. In *VLDB*, 2005.
[45] A. Thusoo, J. S. Sarma, N. Jain, Z. Shao, P. Chakka, N. Zhang, S. Anthony, H. Liu, and R. Murthy. Hive - A Petabyte Scale Data Warehouse Using Hadoop. In *ICDE*, 2010.
[46] V. K. Vavilapalli, A. C. Murthy, C. Douglas, S. Agarwal, M. Konar, R. Evans, T. Graves, J. Lowe, H. Shah, S. Seth, B. Saha, C. Curino, O. O'Malley, S. Radia, B. Reed, and E. Baldeschwieler. Apache Hadoop YARN: Yet Another Resource Negotiator. In *SoCC*, 2013.
[47] X. Wang, C. Olston, A. D. Sarma, and R. Burns. CoScan: Cooperative Scan Sharing in the Cloud. In *SoCC*, 2011.
[48] J. Zhou, P.-Å. Larson, and R. Chaiken. Incorporating Partitioning and Parallel Plans into the SCOPE Optimizer. In *ICDE*, 2010.
[49] J. Zhou and K. A. Ross. A Multi-resolution Block Storage Model for Database Design. In *IDEAS*, 2003.
[50] J. Zhou and K. A. Ross. Buffering Database Operations for Enhanced Instruction Cache Performance. In *SIGMOD*, 2004.
[51] M. Zukowski, S. Héman, N. Nes, and P. Boncz. Cooperative Scans: Dynamic Bandwidth Sharing in a DBMS. In *VLDB*, 2007.

JSON Data Management – Supporting Schema-less Development in RDBMS

Zhen Hua Liu, Beda Hammerschmidt, Doug McMahon

Oracle Corporation

500 Oracle Parkway

Redwood Shores, CA 94065, USA

{zhen.liu, beda.hammerschmidt, doug.mcmahon}@oracle.com

ABSTRACT

Relational Database Management Systems (RDBMS) have been very successful at managing structured data with well-defined schemas. Despite this, relational systems are generally not the first choice for management of data where schemas are not pre-defined or must be flexible in the face of variations and changes. Instead, No-SQL database systems supporting JSON are often selected to provide persistence to such applications. JSON is a light-weight and flexible semi-structured data format supporting constructs common in most programming languages. In this paper, we analyze the way in which requirements differ between management of relational data and management of JSON data. We present three architectural principles that facilitate a *schema-less development style* within an RDBMS so that RDBMS users can store, query, and index JSON data without requiring schemas. We show how these three principles can be applied to industry-leading RDBMS platforms, such as the Oracle RDBMS Server, with relatively little effort. Consequently, an RDBMS can unify the management of both relational data and JSON data in one platform and use SQL with an embedded JSON path language as a single declarative language to query both relational data and JSON data. This SQL/JSON approach offers significant benefits to application developers as they can use one product to manage both relational data and semi-structured flexible schema data.

Categories and Subject Descriptors

H.2.4 [**Database Management**]: Systems – *Relational databases, transaction processing.*

General Terms

Algorithms, Management, Performance, Design, Standardization, Languages.

Keywords

JSON, SQL/JSON, Schema-less, No-SQL,XML, SQL/XML.

SIGMOD/PODS'14, June 22–27, 2014, Snowbird, Utah, USA.

http://dx.doi.org/10.1145/2588555.2595628

1. INTRODUCTION

RDBMS platforms are based on the relational data model [8] which uses the 'schema first, data later' approach. Before users can load and store any data, they must first design a schema. Not all data fit naturally into the relational model. There are significant amounts of semi-structured data, such as documents, emails, and spreadsheets that do not have a fixed schema or do not have structures that can be effectively modelled as relational schemas. Moreover, skipping the schema design provides productivity gains in today's agile development environments. No SQL systems which support the 'data first, schema later or never' paradigm have rapidly evolved and have a growing customer base.

Semi-structured data management within the RDBMS is available with SQL/XML [5, 14, 23, 25]. However, the XML data format originates from the document processing world and has many rules to represent document-oriented semi-structured data. This complexity makes XML a less than ideal format for representing data-oriented semi-structured data. For data-oriented use cases, JSON [15] has become a popular format because the format is simple and compact and comparatively efficient to process. Native support in languages such as JavaScript has contributed to its popularity. JSON is increasingly the focus of the NoSQL community [3, 6] with products like MongoDB [24] providing native JSON stores.

As JavaScript is heavily used in mobile and web application development (on both clients and servers), the volume of JSON data grows and the trend towards use of NoSQL systems for data persistence accelerates. This trend leads to increased complexity of the management of data with polyglot persistence [11]. Users cannot manage all of their data in one platform; they have to work with different data platforms and deal with the integration of data from these platforms in their application programs. The burden of joining data from different data platforms falls on the shoulders of application developers. Furthermore, developers cannot query all of their data using a single high level declarative query language. Finally, each of the different data management systems has its own operating tasks requiring coordination among administrators.

Our goal is to enable the RDBMS platform to support management of JSON data along with relational data and thereby provide the same advanced and mature data management capabilities to both relational and JSON data. To accomplish this, we need to overcome the challenge that classical RDBMS platform requires data to have full schema to be storable, queryable, and indexable. This schema-oriented development style needs to be relaxed to support **schema-less development style where data can be stored, queried, and indexed without a schema.** The introduction of SQL/XML for RDBMS took on this challenge but has not been embraced by application developers seeking a schema-less development style. Reasons include the existence of XML schema, the complexity of XML as a data format, and the need to use an alternative query language (XQuery [31]) as an alternative to SQL. SQL/JSON overcomes these problems.

Recall that RDBMS extensibility technologies support user defined types (UDT) [29,21] by storing UDTs in native form without attempting to shred them relationally, by extending SQL with user defined functions (UDF) to query UDTs declaratively, and by indexing UDT with user defined indices to provide efficient access to UDF. Inspired by the extensibility approach, we propose the following three architectural principles for management of JSON data in RDBMS platforms:

- **Storage Principle for JSON**: Leverage the document-object-store model by storing JSON data natively without attempting to shred it into relational form. In this way, JSON data can be stored without schemas and a JSON object collection can contain a variety of JSON object instances without a common schema. Common attributes, if available as a partial schema, can be projected out as a relational view over the JSON object collection.

- **Query Principle for JSON**: Leverage SQL as a declarative **S**et-oriented **Q**uery **L**anguage instead of a specialized **S**tructured **Q**uery **L**anguage just for relational data. Extend SQL with SQL/JSON operators that embed a simple JSON path language to navigate and query JSON object instances.

- **Index Principle for JSON**: Index JSON using partial-schema-aware index methods and schema agnostic index methods. Although functional indexes and materialized relational views can boost query performance based on a partial schema for a JSON object collection, the JSON inverted index can support efficient ad-hoc query access patterns over a JSON object collection without any knowledge of schema information for the collection.

These principles are formulated based on our decades of experience supporting object, XML and full-text indexing using database extensibility technology. Although database extensibility technology [29,21] is well-known as RDBMS engineering practice, we found that abstracting these practices and experiences into the three basic principles helped us to address the challenges of supporting JSON data management to host schema-less development style in RDBMS. To minimize development effort and time to market, it is possible to implement these principles without introducing a new JSON SQL data type. This is in contrast with the SQL/XML standard [14] that requires adding XML as SQL data type in RDBMS. Our SQL/JSON approach is comparatively light weight so that we can support the storage principle, query principle and index principle for JSON data in Oracle RDBMS with minimal effort.

The main **contribution** of this paper is the formulation of the above three JSON data management principles and the design and implementation strategies of these principles in the industry-strength Oracle RDBMS. In addition, the paper also articulates the requirement difference between schema-less JSON data management and schema-oriented relational data management. The requirement clearly justifies why RDBMS needs to apply the three principles to manage JSON data. Supporting SQL/JSON provides a quick yet natural evolutionary path for extending RDBMS to support the schema-less development style that is a de-facto standard in the No-SQL community. Once the RDBMS overcomes the schema-less challenge, the power of SQL as a mature declarative language will be fully unleashed. To the best our knowledge, this is the first industrial paper that articulates the three principles for addressing the challenges of schema-less development in RDBMS via supporting native JSON data management.

Outline: Section 2 compares our work to related work. Section 3 analyzes use case requirement differences between the management of relational data and JSON data to identify what is lacking in the RDBMS platforms to support JSON data management. Sections 4, 5, and 6 present the three principles for JSON support in detail with the design and implementation strategies to support these principles in the Oracle RDBMS. Section 7 presents the results of performance experiments. Section 8 discusses future work. Section 9 concludes the paper with acknowledgements.

2. RELATED WORK

Although XML and JSON are different data formats, at a high level both of them are hierarchical semi-structured data models. Many principles of past work on XML can be applied to JSON. There is a lot of work on XML storage, index and query processing in both academia and industry with major RDBMS vendors supporting the SQL/XML standard in their products during last decade [5, 23, 25]. For XML storage, there are shredded relational mappings with or without the help of XML schema and aggregated native binary XML storage [5, 25, 26]. For indexing XML, there are XPath or XMLTABLE expression based methods which require at least a partial schema of the XML document collection [5, 19]. There is also the path-value based method which avoids any requirement to specify schema information for the XML document collection [23, 33]. For processing of XQuery over XML, there is a query rewrite technique to transform XML query into equivalent SQL with XML extension operators to leverage the underlying physical XML storage and index methods [20].

More recently, there is published work on storing and querying JSON data. Enabling JSON store in Relational System [9] is an approach where JSON objects are decomposed using a schema-less shredding approach into a path-value vertical relational table recording the paths and values of the original JSON object. It proposes Argo/SQL, a SQL like query language for querying JSON objects. Argo/SQL is transformed into equivalent SQL that queries the underlying vertical table. Conceptually, the vertical shredding approach is similar to the path-value based XML Index [23,33] and to the use of a vertical storage table to store flexible schema data [2]. The Argo/SQL to SQL transformation is in principle the same as that of transforming XQuery/XPath into equivalent SQL queries over the path-value XML index table [20]. Paper [9] also defines a NOBENCH benchmark to run a set of queries over a JSON object collection.

The JSON object collection defined by the NOBENCH benchmark models the characteristics of semi-structured data collections very well.

Google F1 database [28] stores protocol buffer format [36], a binary form similar to JSON, and extends SQL with path expressions and a PROTO JOIN construct to query protocol buffers stored in a table. Protocol buffer storage is in principle the same as that of native aggregated binary XML storage without shredding [5, 25]. MongoDB [24] stores JSON in a binary format BSON [38] and provides an API to JSON object collections that can find BSON objects using filter criteria and produce projections of components of BSON objects. MongoDB supports JSON index by projecting out commonly queried fields from the JSON object collection. This is in principle the same as that of XML indexing that requires knowing a partial schema of XML collection [5,19]. Vertica [40] flexible table approach can let user obtain values of common fields from JSON object collection and load them into a relational table. This is basically materializing JSON_TABLE() results declaratively. However, the flexible table does not seem to provide mechanism to load each element of a JSON array into a separate detail table. Like XMLTABLE(), JSON_TABLE() has mechanism to chain the result of array into separate detail table.

Our JSON storage principle is aligned with the approach in MongoDB [24], Google F1 DB [28] and LinkedIn Espresso [39]. We store JSON objects natively, without shredding, avoiding the cost of reconstructing the original JSON object during queries. Our JSON query principle is to extend SQL with SQL/JSON operators that embed a JSON path language in the same way that SQL/XML operators embedded the XQuery language. However, the SQL/JSON path language is a simple path navigation language, not a complex standalone language such as Jaql [4], JSONiq[17] or XQuery[31]. We choose a simple JSON path language because in RDBMS, SQL and PL/SQL (SQL/PSM) have already provided rich set query language constructs and procedural control flow constructs respectively. Our SQL/JSON approach is aligned with the Google F1 DB [28] approach of extending SQL to query JSON. The PROTO JOIN construct in Google F1 DB is essentially equivalent to the XMLTABLE() construct in SQL/XML standard [14] and the JSONTABLE() construct discussed in section 5.2. The JSON object path access is directly inlined in Google F1 DB SQL. Semantically it is a syntactic sugar to SQL/JSON JSON_VALUE() operator to be discussed in section 5.2. Similar to MongoDB [24], SQL/JSON path language has a lax mode to accommodate querying of heterogeneous JSON object collections. This is in contrast with JSONiq [17] that does strict mode only. We will discuss this in section 5.2.

Our JSON index principle supports both schema-aware and schema agnostic indexing. The schema-aware indexing method is conceptually the same as that of functional indexing [29] and XMLTABLE indexing [19] method. The schema agnostic indexing method is functionality the same as XML path-value indexing [23,33] and the Argo-SQL vertical shredding approach [9]. However, we will show that the underlying design of schema agnostic indexing method should be based on inverted index architecture originated in the information retrieval community [27]. LinkedIn Espresso [39] uses Lucene inverted index. However, our approach generalizes the idea of inverted index to not only index keywords but also to index JSON paths and values in JSON object. We will discuss this in section 6.2. Furthermore, unlike index over distributed data service platform [39], our JSON inverted index is a domain index that is consistent with base data just as any other index in RDBMS. Each RDBMS replication site maintains its own index over its data replica.

3. Requirements of JSON data management in RDBMS

There are significant differences between managing relational data and semi-structured data represented as JSON. We analyze these differences from the perspective of JSON data storage, data query, and data index.

3.1 Data Modeling Difference: Schema First Versus Schema Later/Never

RDBMS is originally designed to manage structured data whose structures can be cleanly separated from the content. Structures are defined as schema that is managed as system meta-data by the RDBMS. Entity/Relationship (E/R) modelling [7] is very effective at breaking down structures into tables linked with primary and foreign keys to support typical master-detail join pattern. Structural changes require DDL statements to alter the system meta-data before new data with the changed shape can be loaded. If a schema is not available, data cannot even be loaded. Such 'schema-first, data later' requirements have caused a 'birth-pain' problem in RDBMS [12].

However, not all data fits naturally into the relational model. For a collection of semi-structured data objects, the structure of data is not easily separable from the content because the structure of data varies from instance to instance. A collection of JSON objects may have a small number of common attributes complemented by a large variety of varying attributes resulting in a large number of *sparsely populated columns* [2] when stored relationally. In NOBENCH benchmark [9], *sparse_XXX* is a series of sparsely-populated attributes from *sparse_000* to *sparese_999*. Storing all of them using an E/R model requires a table with over 1000 columns. This may exceed design limits of and RDBMS, and will have large numbers of NULL values on every row. We call this the sparse-attribute issue. A second problem is that an attribute may have a different datatype in different data instances. In NOBENCH benchmark[9], *dyn1* is a dynamically typed value that is either a number or a string. RDBMS does not support multi-typed column natively. We call this the polymorphic typing issue. A third problem is that the cardinality of an attribute may vary from one instance to another, or over time. An attribute may be a singleton value at first and later become a JSON array. For example, a *person* object may initially have one *contact phone number* but is later altered to have an array of *contact phone numbers*. Such singleton to array schema evolution causes data migration issues if we use an E/R design [7] and must storing array data in a separate detail table joined with the master table. We call this the singleton-to-collection issue. Lastly, it is not uncommon for JSON objects to possess recursive structures. This is common in XML constructs as well. Modelling recursive structures in E/R model is feasible but SQL doesn't widely support such constructs as first class operations. We call this the recursive structure issue. In summary, it is often hard to define one relational schema to capture all of the JSON data in a collection using the classical E/R model - at best, developers may derive some partial schema. In the NOBENCH benchmark [9], the *str1*, *str2*, *num*, *bool*, *nested_obj.str*, *nested_obj.num* can be considered partial schemas as they are common in all JSON object instances and thus their values can be extracted out of JSON objects. Partial schema is not sufficient to decompose all data into relational schema. Instead they can be modelled as virtual columns or relational views on top of JSON object collections. This is the idea of *partial shredding that leverages the relational model as an auxiliary structure on top of a native object collection.*

3.2 Querying Difference: Querying Flattened Data with Static Schema Versus Querying Hierarchical Object with Dynamic Schema

First, using an E/R model, data structures are decomposed relationally by first registering object structural schema as meta-data. Consequently, the structure of the data is known ahead of query execution time so that only data is examined during query execution time. Therefore, SQL does not need constructs that can query the structure of data during query execution. For JSON data whose schema is not registered as system meta-data, the query language needs to have constructs that can query both the structure and data together during query execution. SQL alone is not sufficient - SQL needs to be enhanced to have language constructs that can query both structures and data of JSON objects at run time.

Second, the E-R approach models hierarchies of data using the master-detail pattern, so querying hierarchical data decomposed into a relational model requires the use of explicit joins of primary key and foreign key columns when traversing a hierarchy. However, for JSON objects which are not stored in decomposed manner, it is more natural to express hierarchical traversal using a path navigation language. SQL needs to embrace path navigation constructs for querying JSON objects natively. Although SQL99 supports object type with a path navigation construct, SQL99 still requires the schema of object type to be registered with RDBMS as meta-data. Therefore, SQL99 object type support is still based on a static schema model. JSON object support requires dynamic schemas. Furthermore, when a path language is applied to semi-structured data, it needs to support wildcard steps in the path as well as traversal of hierarchical structures without knowing the exact number levels of descent needed. All of these constructs are supported in XPath 1.0.

Third, while relational queries result in columns values that are always scalar values, path navigation results represent projections of both scalars and sub-structures from underlying JSON objects. SQL needs to support JSON operators that are able to extract or update components of JSON data and are able to construct new JSON data.

Finally, JSON data may contain text content that is useful to index for full text search. However, unlike pure textual documents, the content is embedded inside JSON object members and array elements. JSON full text search needs to incorporate path navigation. Such a keyword search operation is shown as Q8 in NOBENCH benchmark [9].

3.3 Indexing Difference: Partial-Schema-aware Indexing Method Versus Schema agnostic Indexing Method

Index and materialized view are auxiliary structures that are built on top of relational store to speed up queries in RDBMS. However, defining B+ tree index, bitmap index, and materialized views all require relational schema; e.g., their creation is based on the '*schema first, index definition later*' approach.

Partial schema discussed in section 3.1 can be used to define virtual columns and relational views on top of the collection. Virtual columns can be used to construct B+ tree or bitmap indexes, - all of these techniques serve to boost the performance of queries whose patterns are known. Supporting partial schema-ware indexing is a natural consequence of adopting the '*data first, schema later*' approach in RDBMS. However, since a JSON object in a row may have array consisting of multiple values to be indexed, therefore, classical B+ tree index that assumes one indexed value per row is not sufficient to index multiple values within an array of a JSON object. This is known as index cardinality issue.

Ad-hoc queries for exploratory and search purposes must be supported by a JSON indexing method that does not rely on knowing any partial schema for the target collection. Such an indexing method requires both JSON member and array names to be indexed together with the data. Supporting schema-less indexing method is a natural consequence of supporting the '*data first, schema never*' approach in RDBMS.

4. JSON Storage Principle: Support for Document-Object Store Model without Relational Shredding

No shredding of JSON object: To host schema-less development with a collection of heterogeneous JSON objects, we store each JSON object instance as one aggregated object in a column without any relational decomposition. A JSON object collection is modelled as a table having one column storing JSON objects. Each row in the table holds a JSON object instance in the collection. This design embraces the document-object model in No-SQL DB systems [6]. We don't perform the vertical shredding as presented in paper [9]. We will justify this decision from a performance perspective in section 7.

No JSON SQL datatype: We do not introduce JSON as a new distinct SQL datatype. Supporting a new native SQL datatype would require changes throughout the RDBMS kernel and require enhancements to all client APIs, as well as development tools and frameworks. Given widely distributed RDBMS client installations, it would require a client upgrade to use the new JSON functionality. Another issue is that there are already many different JSON-like representations: besides the JSON textual format, there is the BSON binary format [38], the Protocol Buffer binary format [36], and the AVRO binary format [37]. It is not clear which format(s) will be widely adopted. In the future, new formats may be introduced. Finally, JSON data can be stored in file systems external to the RDBMS (such as HDFS) and then mapped as an external table to support SQL queries. In such cases the RDBMS must have the ability to consume JSON data **as is**.

Storing JSON using existing SQL datatypes with Check Constraint: We have chosen to give developers the flexibility of storing JSON data in SQL VARCHAR, CLOB, RAW, or BLOB columns, rather than adding JSON as an abstract SQL datatype as what we have done to support XMLType in the Oracle RDBMS [25]. In lieu of this, we provide an *IS JSON* SQL built-in operator to verify whether the input text or binary is a valid JSON object. Developers can use the *IS JSON* predicate as column check constraint to enforce table column values storing only valid JSON data. T1 of Table 1 shows a DDL statement to define a table storing JSON text capturing shopping cart information with the *IS JSON* check constraint. INS1 and INS2 of Table 1 are two SQL insertion statements to load JSON objects into the JSON object collection table. Oracle VARCHAR and RAW data types can support up to 32K size. Beyond that, the CLOB and BLOB data types can be used to hold large JSON object instances. Oracle LOB column infrastructure can provide compression, de-duplication, and encryption features for LOB data[18] - all of which are available for use with JSON objects to reduce storage size and improve query performance. Small size data improves I/O performance because I/O is still the main performance bottleneck in DBMS [10]. Column level encryption provides additional security access control for JSON objects stored in RDBMS. In short, using existing SQL data types to store JSON ensures full operational completeness for JSON data with minimal effort. This includes features as partitioning, replication, import/export, and bi-temporal features, all of which are critical to support the full data operational life cycle for any data including JSON data. If JSON data were shredded relationally, supporting all of these features on shredded JSON objects would require significant development effort.

Virtual Relational Columns over JSON object collection: For partial schema use cases, data in a JSON object collection can be projected out as virtual columns attaching to the collection table using the JSON_VALUE() operator. See *sessionId* and *creationTime* as virtual columns listed in T1 of Table1. Composite B+ tree indexes can be created on virtual columns to facilitate range queries over projected scalar values.

T1	*CREATE TABLE shoppingCart_tab (shoppingCart VARCHAR2(4000) check (shoppingCart is JSON), sessionId NUMBER AS (JSON_VALUE(shoppingCar ,'$.sessionId' RETURNING NUMBER)) VIRTUAL, userlogin varchar2(30) AS (CAST(JSON_VALUE(shoppingCart,,'$.userLoginId') AS varchar2(30))) VIRTUAL)*
INS1	*INSERT INTO shoppingCart_tab(shoppingCart) VALUES(' {"sessionId" : 12345, "creationTime": "12-JAN-09 05.23.30.600000 AM", "userLoginId" : "johnSmith3@yahoo.com", "Items" : [{"name": "iPhone5", "price" :99.98, "quantity" :2, "used": true, "comment" : "minor screen damage"}, {"name": "refrigerator", "price" :359.27, "quantity" :1, "weight": 210, "Height" : 4.5, "Length" : 3, "manufacter": "Kenmore", "color" : "Gray"}]} ')*
INS2	*INSERT INTO shoppingCart_tab(shoppingCart) VALUES(' {"sessionId" : 37891, "creationTime": "13-MAR-13 15.33.40.800000 PM", "userLoginId" : "lonelystar@gmail.com", "Items" : {"name": "Machine Learning", "price" :35.24, "quantity" :3, "used" : false, "category" :"Math Computer", "weight":"150gram"}} ')*
IDX	*CREATE INDEX shoppingCart_Idx ON shoppingCart_tab(userlogin, sessionId)*

Table 1 – JSON object collection DDL

In summary, the **storage principle of JSON** avoids shredding objects into relational forms. Instead, each JSON instance is stored in an aggregated form with everything stored together so that it is **self-contained without relying on a central schema dictionary**. This facilitates import/export of JSON data and distributed operation among Oracle RDBMS servers and clients. Aggregated storage also eliminates the cost of reassembling the original data from multiple relational tables via joins.

5. JSON Query Principle: Embedding JSON object query language in SQL

5.1 Leverage SQL as inter-JSON object Set-oriented Query Language to query JSON object collection

Instead of 'Structured Query Language', we call SQL as 'Set oriented Query Language'. Being a *set-at-a-time* query language, SQL can be used as an *inter-object query language* to query objects stored in the object collection table. Therefore, there is no theoretical reason to construct yet another set-at-a-time query language, such as JSONiq [17], having equivalent set algebra specifically targeted at JSON collections. However, classical SQL assumes the element of a set is one relational row with relational columns where as JSON collection is a set of JSON object instances. To provide declarative navigational access of JSON object instance, we need a JSON path language. The JSON path language is used as an intra-object query language in conjunction with SQL as the overall Set Query Language and Oracle PL/SQL or SQL/PSM as the overall procedural language.

5.2 SQL/JSON Standard

Based on industrial research and development experiences for SQL/XML[14], Zhen Hua Liu originates SQL/JSON standard that defines a set of SQL/JSON query operators that embed a simple JSON path language to provide declarative query language over a collection of JSON objects and a set of SQL/JSON construction functions from pure relational data. The working group of SQL/JSON standard consists of SQL standard representatives and research engineering architects from IBM and Oracle: Beda Hammerschmidt, Krishna Kulkarni, Zhen Hua Liu, Doug McMahon, Jim Melton, Jan-Eike Michels, Hamid Pirahesh, Fatma Ozcan, Fred Zemke. The working group defines a SQL/JSON path language as an intra-object query language over a JSON object instance and exact semantics of SQL/JSON query operators and construction functions.

5.2.1 SQL/JSON query operators

Similar to SQL/XML [14] query operators, SQL/JSON query operators are used in strategic places in SQL as shown in Figure 1. The SQL/JSON operators can query JSON objects stored in VARCHAR, CLOB, RAW, or BLOB columns with proper JSON format clauses. If the input data type is VARCHAR or CLOB, the input is assumed to contain textual JSON. If the input data type is RAW or BLOB, input may contain JSON text in standard utf-8 character encoding, or, using an optional format clause to indicate the input data is in one of the binary formats: BSON, Avro, or Protocol buffer [36,37,38].

SQL WHERE clause for JSON object Search: JSON_EXISTS(), JSON_VALUE() are used in a SQL WHERE clause to search and filter JSON object instances stored in a

JSON object collection. See Table 6 Q3, Q4, Q5, Q6, Q7, Q9, Q10, and Q11 for examples of using these operators. In addition, to support full text search within JSON path navigation as described in section 3.2, **Oracle RDBMS also supports JSON_TEXTCONTAINS(), which is not part of SQL/JSON standard, in the WHERE clause.** See Table 6 Q8 for keyword search within JSON array.

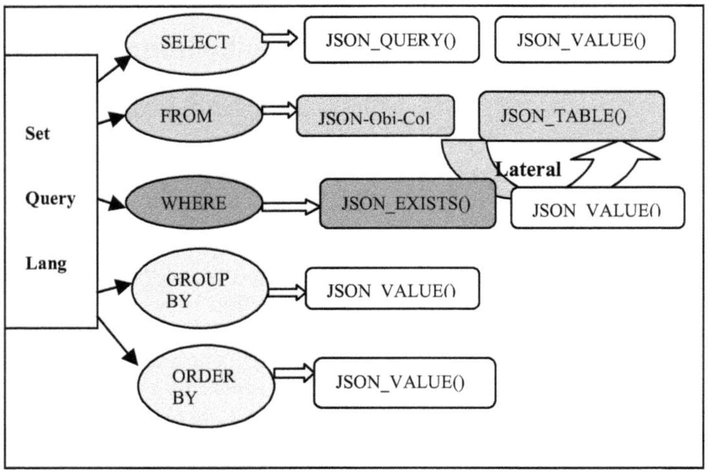

Figure 1 – SQL/JSON operators usage in SQL

SQL FROM Clause to iterate JSON object component: JSON_TABLE() is used in the SQL FROM clause to convert arrays within JSON object instances into a virtual relational table. It is defined as a lateral join with the JSON object collection table. The JSON path language can be used in both row and column expressions of JSON_TABLE(). Table 2 Q2 shows an example. The typical use case of JSON_TABLE() is to expand a JSON array within a JSON object into a set of relational rows, each of which corresponds to an element within the array. JSON_TABLE() acts as a bridge between relational data and JSON data so that islands of structural data within JSON object can be projected out. Effectively, *JSON_TABLE() enables RDBMS users to capture partial schema in a JSON object collection as a set of relational views.*

SQL SELECT, GROUP BY, ORDER BY Clauses to retrieve SQL scalar value from JSON: JSON_VALUE() is used to extract scalar values within the JSON object and cast them into values corresponding to standard SQL built-in types such as VARCHAR, NUMBER, DATE. Extracted values can be used in scalar value expressions in SELECT, GROUP BY, and ORDER BY clauses where scalar values are expected. See Table 6 Q10 GROUP BY clause. In case that extracted scalar value is not castable to the desired datatype, error handling options, such as NULL ON ERROR, DEFAULT value ON ERROR, ERROR ON ERROR, are provided. By default, it is NULL ON ERROR option which makes JSON_VALUE() to return SQL NULL value in case of error so as to gracefully handle polymorphic typing issue discussed in section 3.1.

SQL SELECT Clauses to project JSON object component from JSON object: JSON_QUERY() is used to extract complex sub-components from within JSON objects or to construct new JSON objects so that they can be used in a SELECT clause. See Table 2 Q1. Unlike JSON_VALUE(), whose return value is always a SQL scalar, JSON_QUERY() returns a JSON object or JSON array. However, since we don't introduce a SQL JSON data type, JSON_QUERY() supports a return clause to specify the SQL data type, such as VARCHAR or LOB to hold the JSON_QUERY() result.

SQL UPDATE clause of JSON Object Collection: JSON object collections can be updated using regular SQL Delete, Insert and Update statements. JSON_EXISTS() is typically used in the WHERE clause to qualify documents or objects to be deleted or updated. The right hand side of assignment in UPDATE clauses can be any SQL expression that constructs a new JSON object instance to replace an existing JSON object. See Table 2 Q3 for an example of an update. Future work in SQL/JSON standard will allow JSON_QUERY() used as the right side expression of a SQL UPDATE statement to replace an existing JSON object with a new object by applying updating transformation expressions on the existing JSON object. This is conceptually the same as the XQuery Update Facility in SQL/XML that can update XML documents stored in an XML document collection [22]. All of these enhancements will be part of the process for the evolving SQL/JSON standard.

SQL JOIN among Object Collections: In No-SQL system, join operations are typically not supported. Because the document storage model does NOT shred and normalize objects into nested tables linked by primary and foreign key, intra-object joins are not needed. However, there is still need to do inter-object join across multiple JSON object collections. No-SQL system seems to lack of such join capabilities and require application programmers to perform any needed joins in their application code. In SQL, joins can be performed directly, leveraging the full power of the RDBMS to optimize the query, and ensuring that unselective parts of joins are not needlessly transported to the client application. See Table 6 Q11 for an example of a self-join on a JSON object collection. See Table 2 Q4 for an example of a join across different JSON object collections. In this case, *customerTab* is a table with a *customer* column storing JSON object instances representing customers. Moreover, joins are not restricted to JSON object collections - users can freely join against XML document collections or traditional relational tables.

5.2.2 SQL/JSON Path Language

The SQL/JSON path language is structurally similar to XPath 1.0 and JsonPath [16]. Currently, SQL/JSON path language has only path step expressions with filter expressions used as predicates for path steps. Each path step expression is either the JSON object member accessor or the JSON array element accessor. In the near future, SQL/JSON standard may extend the language to have constructor expressions and update expressions to do component-wise updates of JSON objects. Here, we present some subtle issues in designing the SQL/JSON path language.

Q1	*SELECT p.sessionId, **JSON_QUERY**(p.shoppingCar, '$.items[1]' RETURN AS VARCHAR(2000))* *FROM shoppingCart_tab p* *WHERE **JSON_EXISTS**(p.shoppingCar , '$.item?(name="iPhone"))')* *ORDER BY p.userlogin*
Q2	*SELECT p.sessionId, p.userlogin, v.Name, v.price, v.Quantity* *FROM shoppingCart_tab p,* ***JSON_TABLE**(p.shoppingCart , '$.items[*]'* *COLUMNS* *Name VARCHAR(20) PATH '$.name',* *price number PATH '$.price',* *Quantity integer PATH '$.Quantity') v*

Q3	**UPDATE** shoppingCart_tab p SET p.shoppingCart_tab = <SQL-Expr constructing JSON> WHERE **JSON_EXISTS**(p.shoppingCart , '$.item?(name="iPhone"))')
Q4	SELECT COUNT(*) FROM customerTab p, shoppingCart_Tab p2 WHERE JSON_VALUE(p.customer, '$p.contact-info.email-address') = JSON_VALUE(p2.shoppingCart, '$."userLoginId"')

Table 2 – SQL/JSON Query Example

Sequence Data Model: XML documents are not a complete data model for query processing. Likewise, JSON objects and arrays are also incomplete as a foundation for processing. A path language requires expression results to form a closure under the chosen data model. Therefore, the SQL/JSON path language defines a JSON data model which is a sequence of items, each of which is a JSON data model item. Each item can be either a JSON object, JSON array, JSON atomic value. The JSON atomic value can be of string, number, or boolean type. In addition, the atomic value can be of date, time, timestamp, or interval values using the semantics of the equivalent SQL built-in types. Note that JSON array is not used to represent the sequence data model because a JSON array may be an item in the sequence data model, and arrays can be nested whereas sequences cannot. JSON sequence data model follows the same algebraic property as that of the sequence data model in XQuery [31] and JSONiq [17]. That is, it does not support nested sequences. A singleton item is equivalent to a sequence of that singleton item.

Predicate Filter expression: Unlike XQuery that introduces cumbersome rules on effective boolean value for any sequence, SQL/JSON path language differentiates filter expressions from path expression so that filter expressions can be used only as predicates of path expressions. *'$.items?(exists(weight) && exists(height))'* is the SQL/JSON path expression to test if an *item* has both *weight* and *height* member. The exists() function is explicitly used to convert a set into a boolean value by testing the emptiness of the set. This design is similar to that of SQL which uses EXISTS() subquery to test the emptiness of a set.

Lax Mode for object and array accessor: An important difference between XML and JSON is the treatment of collection-valued items. In XML, there is no special construct to differentiate a singleton element node and a collection of element nodes having the same name - elements can simply be repeated. Therefore, to query either a single element node with element name '*item*' or a collection of element nodes with the same element name '*item*', the same XPath step '*/item*' is sufficient. In contrast, JSON has an explicit array construct to hold multi-valued properties. A singleton item is therefore distinguished from an array with a single value. Because of this, querying singleton items and array items from a JSON collection require different path expressions. Consider the two JSON objects inserted as INS1 and INS2 of Table1. To access the first item in the *shoppingCart* of JSON object in Tabel1.INS1, the JSON path language expression is *'$.items[1]'* because *items* is an array. To access the first item in the *shoppingCart* for JSON object in Tabel1.INS2, the JSON path language expression is *'$.items'* because items is not an array. This makes writing JSON path language to handle singleton-to-collection issue discussed in section 3.1 for JSON object collection quite complicated. It also poses a challenge for schema-less development in that the author of a query may not know which construct to use. To solve this, the SQL/JSON path language uses lax mode. In lax mode, there is an implicit wrapping and unwrapping operation applied at each step in the path. When an array element accessor is applied to a JSON object item, a singleton item is implicitly wrapped as an array of that item. When an object member accessor is applied on a JSON array item, the array is implicitly unwrapped so that the object member accessor is applied to each item of the JSON array. This is in contrast with JSONiq [17] which does not provide such lax mode flexibility.

Lax Error Handling: The SQL/JSON path language is more forgiving of errors by returning false in filter expressions instead of raising error. Such forgiving behaviour is important to handle the polymorphic typing issue discussed in section 3.1. Consider applying the JSON path expression *'$.items?(weight > 200)'* to the JSON object in INS2 of Table 1 - the value of "*weight*" is '*150gram*' which is not a number comparable with 200. Rather than raising a type error, this results in false. Such lax mode of error handling is in contrast with JSONiq [17] that does not provide such flexibility for error handling.

5.3 Design and Implementation Strategies of SQL/JSON in Oracle RDBMS

To ensure that the SQL/JSON path language can be evaluated efficiently, we support streaming processing without materializing entire JSON objects in memory. Figure 4 shows the JSON event stream flow diagram for SQL/JSON Path language processor.

Our JSON text parser and JSON binary decoders generate a JSON event stream. The JSON event stream is conceptually similar to that of an XML SAX event stream. It is composed of BEGIN-OBJ, END-OBJ, BEGIN-ARRAY, END-ARRAY, BEGIN-PAIR, END-PAIR, and ITEM events. The BEGIN-PAIR and END-PAIR event wraps a JSON member name and its content pair. The name of the member can be obtained from the BEGIN-PAIR event. The ITEM event represents a typed scalar value that is within the BEGIN-PAIR and END-PAIR event, or within an array. Each JSON path expression is compiled into a state machine to listen and process the JSON event stream. The SQL/JSON path language processor can process multiple JSON path expressions as the same JSON event stream from the source JSON object can be consumed by multiple JSON state machines. This situation is typical of the multiple path expressions found in the JSON_TABLE() operator. For efficiency, we implemented JSON_VALUE(), JSON_EXISTS(), JSON_QUERY() as RDBMS server built-in kernel operators, rather than as user defined functions. JSON_TABLE() is built as a RDBMS server kernel row source that is processed iteratively and corresponding to the overall SQL iterator row source design [13]. The streaming evaluation model of SQL/JSON path language processor fits with the SQL iterator row source design very well. We use a lazy evaluation strategy for SQL/JSON operators by pulling items from the JSON path processor in a streaming fashion. For JSON_EXISTS(), as soon as there is one item returned from the JSON path processor, it can return TRUE and the evaluation stops. For JSON_TABLE(), it pulls the item from the JSON path processor as the parent row source demands it. For JSON_VALUE(), it is an error if there is more than one item. Only JSON_QUERY() needs to aggregate items flowing from the JSON path processor .

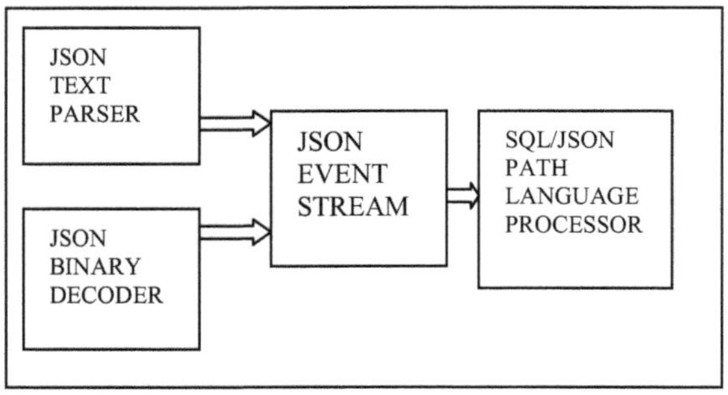

Figure 4 – SQL/JSON PATH PROCESSOR

Both the row and column JSON path expressions of JSON_TABLE() are all passed to the JSON path processor so that all of them can be evaluated simultaneously from a common JSON event stream. Furthermore, if JSON_TABLE() is not outer joined with the JSON object collection, then no row is returned for the JSON object in the JSON object collection if the row expression returns no item. This is equivalent to attaching a JSON_EXISTS() operator using the row expression of JSON_TABLE() to the WHERE clause of the JSON object collection. This can improve performance significantly if an index can be used to evaluate the JSON_EXISTS() operator. See T1 transformation rule in Table 3. Multiple JSON_VALUE() operators applied on the same JSON object input can be transformed into one JSON_TABLE() construct during compile time. See transformation rule T2 in Table 3. Multiple JSON_EXISTS() operators on the same JSON object input column can be combined into one JSON_EXISTS() operator. See transformation rule T3 in Table 3. Both T2 and T3 transformation is done so that we can share the evaluations of multiple JSON path expressions by streaming the JSON object once during run time.

Qry#	Original Query	Transformed Query for optimization
T1	SELECT p.sessionId, p.creationTime, v.Name, v.price, v.Quantity FROM shoppingCart_tab p, **JSON_TABLE**(p.shoppingCart , '$.items[*]' COLUMNS Name VARCHAR(20) PATH '$.name', price number PATH '$.price', Quantity integer PATH '$.Quantity') v	SELECT p.sessionId, p.creationTime, v.Name, v.price, v.Quantity FROM shoppingCart_tab p, **JSON_TABLE**(p.shoppingCart , '$.items[*]' COLUMNS Name VARCHAR(20) PATH '$.name', price number PATH '$.price', Quantity integer PATH '$.Quantity') v **WHERE** **JSON_EXISTS(p.shoppingCart, '$.items[*]')**
T2	SELECT JSON_VALUE(p.shoppingCart ,'$.items[1].name), JSON_VALUE(p.shoppingCart , '$.items[1].price RETURNING NUMBER), JSON_VALUE(p.shoppingCart , '$.items[2].name), JSON_VALUE(p.shoppingCart , '$.items[2].price RETURNING NUMBER), FROM shoppingCart_tab p	SELECT v.item1_nm, v.item1_price, v.item2_nm, v2.item2_price FROM shoppingCart_tab p, **JSON_TABLE**(p.shoppingCart , '$.items' COLUMNS vitem1_nm VARCHAR(20) PATH '$[1].name', vitem1_price NUMBER PATH '$[1].price', vitem2_nm VARCHAR(20) PATH '$[2].name', vitem2_price NUMBER PATH '$[2].price')
T3	SELECT count(*) FROM shoppingCart_tab p WHERE JSON_EXISTS(p.shoppingCart , '$.item?(name="iPhone"))) AND JSON_EXISTS(p.shoppingCart , '$.item?(price > 100)')	SELECT count(*) FROM shoppingCart_tab p WHERE **JSON_EXISTS**(p.shoppingCart, **'$?(item? (name="iPhone") and item?(price > 100))')**

Table 3 – SQL/JSON Transformation Rule for Optimization

6. JSON Index Principle: Partial Schema-Aware Index Method & Schema-Argnostic Index Method

6.1 Partial Schema-Aware Index Method

Situations where common path expressions or members can be identified for a collection are referred to as partial schemas. Such partial schemas can be projected out as auxiliary structures on top of the original JSON object collection in the form of functional indexes, virtual columns to speed query performance. The simplest indexing method is functional indexing using JSON_VALUE() to facilitate range searches on the result of JSON_VALUE(). If multiple members from a JSON object collection need to be range queried together, we can create a composite B+ tree index over multiple virtual columns, each of which is a projection of a member. IDX of Table 1 illustrates this approach.

Recall index cardinality issue in section 3.3, JSON objects commonly include arrays representing master-detail relationships. For example, a *shoppingCart* item stores a collection of items. To index all values in a JSON array, we use JSON_TABLE() that projects out master-detail relationship as shown in Table 2 Q2. To avoid storing repeated master records for each detailed item, we support a construct similar to the widely used XML Table index [19]. The table index internally creates master-detail relational tables to hold the relational results computed by evaluation of JSON_TABLE(). The master-detail table is linked by internally generated keys so that the column values in the master table are NOT repeatedly stored in detail tables. Indeed, the table index layout is the same as if certain parts of JSON objects were decomposed and stored relationally using E-R design [7]. The significance of table index is that it speeds up relational projection over a JSON object collection significantly. Unlike materialized view, table index is maintained synchronized with DML, multiple JSON_TABLE() expressions can be captured in one table index and maintained optimally by processing the input document once.

In summary, partial schema-aware indexing is very flexible because it builds secondary structures on top of the primary JSON object collection. Such secondary structures can be dropped and re-created without affecting the base JSON object collection. Users have the flexibility to drop and recreate index based on query workload and to accommodate schema evolution. **Therefore, it is more flexible to use partial schema to define index structures instead of using schema to define base table storage structures.**

6.2 Schema Agnostic Index Method

When there does not exist any partial schema in a JSON object collection, or when users can not anticipate query search patterns for a collection, we refer to this as the ad-hoc query use case. In such use case, JSON_EXISTS() is applied to a JSON object collection to search for existence of a certain JSON path with a member value satisfying range criteria. See Q1 of Table 2. One approach to index a JSON object collection in a schema agnostic way is to leverage the same idea as that of the XML path-value Index [23, 33]. A path-value XML Index provides the same index functionality as that of the vertical shredding approach proposed in [9]. Although a vertical shredding approach can leverage SQL query over path-index relational tables directly to answer ad-hoc queries over XML or JSON object collections, it is inefficient to run the multiple self-join queries. Moreover, the resulting path-value index table size is much larger than the original document collection. It is typically at least 2 times of the original data size. This size problem gets worse if secondary indexes are included on the path-value index table. We propose to leverage inverted index layout [27,35] originated in the information retrieval community to build a schema agnostic JSON-aware inverted index to support ad-hoc queries. The advantage of an inverted index is that even though it indexes all keywords of all documents in a collection, the posting list for each keyword in the inverted index is highly compressed so that the total size of the inverted index is smaller than the size of original document collection [35]. A smaller index size improves I/O performance, generally the primary performance bottleneck in a DBMS. Each document in a document collection indexed by the inverted index is identified by an ordinal number as a DOCID. The DOCIDs of all documents containing the keyword are stored in a sorted manner with delta-compression as a posting list. Multi-predicate pre-sorted merge join (MPPSMJ) can be performed on the posting list in order to handle multi-keywords searches conjunctive query predicates [35, 41, 42] efficiently. We have leveraged and extended Oracle's built-in text index, an inverted index built inside RDBMS, which is similar to what is presented in [41] to not only index plain text documents but also index XML documents and JSON objects. By indexing XML tags and their hierarchical relationships, inverted index can be extended to support efficient processing of *containment queries* [34] which search for keywords within hierarchical paths in XML documents. Oracle builds XML full text index [42] by extending Oracle's text index to answer full text path containment queries for XQuery Full Text [32] expressions.

In the same way, we build a **JSON inverted index** by extending Oracle's text index to index JSON object member names, their hierarchical relationships and their content leaf data. JSON array elements are indexed with the parent array name containing them. Since we store JSON in ordinary SQL columns, we inherent the text index's ability to index textual content stored in VARCHAR, CLOB, RAW, or BLOB columns. Table 4 shows a DDL statement to create a JSON inverted index. Oracle text index internally assigns an ordinal number DOCID to each row of the table and maintains a bi-directional mapping between DOCID and ROWID of the table so that DOCIDs returned from inverted index lookup can return to the SQL engine as their corresponding ROWIDs and be subject to normal SQL processing.

Create index jidx on shoppingCart_tab (shoppingCart) index type context index (parameters ***'JSON enable'****)*

Table 4 – JSON inverted index

Unlike a standard text indexing tokenizer, the JSON inverted indexer operates on a JSON event stream derived from the underlying VARCHAR, RAW, CLOB, or BLOB column containing the JSON data. This event stream is generated by the JSON parser or one of the binary format decoders, as described in section 5.3. Concurrently, the JSON event stream consumer in the JSON indexer assigns each JSON object member name fetched from the event stream with an interval of starting and ending offset position. The interval of starting and ending offset position of an object member name is always contained by the interval of its parent object member name so that a hierarchical containment relationship between member names can be determined via testing the interval bounds. Leaf scalar data of a member is tokenized as keywords to facilitate full text search. Each keyword is assigned an offset position that is contained by the interval of the parent JSON object member name.

Each JSON object member name is indexed with a posting list consisting of the DOCIDs of JSON objects that contain the object member name and their list of intervals. Each keyword in the leaf data of a JSON object member content is indexed with a posting list consisting of the DOCIDs of JSON objects that contain the keyword and their list of offset positions. By performing an MPPSMJ join of the posting lists for both keywords and JSON object member names, we can facilitate full text query with JSON path navigation. The containment test between two path steps is done by testing containment of their intervals. The containment test between the keyword and the leaf path step is done by testing containment of the keyword offset position contained within the interval of the leaf path step.

By indexing both structures and data found in JSON objects, the JSON inverted index can be used to efficiently evaluate JSON_EXISTS() and JSON_TEXTCONTAINS() predicate used in SQL WHERE clause.

7. Performance Experiment

7.1 Experiment Setup

We use NOBENCH benchmark [9] data and run all queries Q1 to Q11 to evaluate query performance so as to evaluate the performance of our JSON native store and indexing strategy and how the strategy comparing with vertical JSON object shredding strategy used in paper [9]. We run performance experiments using Oracle RDBMS server that supports SQL/JSON that described in this paper. We create a table *NOBENCH_main* with a VARCHAR(4000) column *jobj* and load the table with JSON object instances generated using the criteria described in paper [9]. We create 3 functional indices and a JSON inverted index on the column *jobj* as shown in Table 5 with Q1-Q11 SQL/JSON queries shown in Table 6. We refer this as the 'Aggregated Native JSON Store' approach (**ANJS**) in this section. We have also implemented the vertical shredding approach of Argo/SQL for JSON objects as described in [9] using path-value relational table. We refer it as the 'Vertical Shredding JSON Store' (**VSJS**) in this section. All experiments are conducted on a PC running Linux kernel 2.6.18 with a 2.53 GHz Intel Xeon CPU and 6GB of main memory.

JSON OBJECT COLLECTION	*CREATE TABLE NOBENCH_MAIN(JOBJ VARCHAR2(4000))*
Functional Index	*create index j_get_str1 on NOBENCH_main(JSON_VALUE(jobj, '$.str1'));* *create index j_get_num on NOBENCH_main(JSON_VALUE(jobj, '$.num' RETURNING NUMBER));* *create index j_get_dyn1 on NOBENCH_main(JSON_VALUE(jobj, '$.dyn1' RETURNING NUMBER));*
JSON Inverted Index	*create index NOBENCH_idx on NOBENCH_main(jobj) indextype is ctxsys.context parameters('json enable ')*

Table 5 – NOBENCH Table and Index SetUp using Oracle RDBMS supporting SQL/JSON

Qry#	SQL/JSON Query
Q1	*SELECT JSON_VALUE(jobj, '$.str1') as str,* *JSON_VALUE(jobj, '$.num' \ RETURNING NUMBER) as num* *FROM nobench_main*
Q2	*SELECT JSON_VALUE(jobj, '$.nested_obj.str') as nested_str,* *JSON_VALUE(jobj, '$.nested_obj.num' RETURNING NUMBER) as nested_num* *FROM nobench_main*
Q3	*SELECT JSON_VALUE(jobj, '$.sparse_000') as sparse_xx0,* *JSON_VALUE(jobj, '$.sparse_009') as sparse_yy0* *FROM nobench_main* *WHERE* *JSON_EXISTS(jobj, '$.sparse_000') AND JSON_EXISTS(jobj, '$.sparse_009' j)*
Q4	*SELECT JSON_VALUE(jobj, '$.sparse_800') as sparse_800,* *JSON_VALUE(jobj, '$.sparse_999') as sparse_999* *FROM nobench_main* *WHERE* *JSON_EXISTS(jobj, '$.sparse_800')* *OR* *JSON_EXISTS(jobj, '$.sparse_999' j)*
Q5	*SELECT jobj* *FROM nobench_main* *WHERE JSON_VALUE(jobj, '$.str1') = :1*
Q6	*SELECT jobj* *FROM nobench_main* *WHERE JSON_VALUE(jobj, '$.num' RETURNING NUMBER) BETWEEN :1 AND :2*
Q7	*SELECT jobj* *FROM nobench_main* *WHERE JSON_VALUE(jobj, '$.dyn1' RETURNING NUMBER) BETWEEN :1 AND :2*
Q8	*SELECT jobj* *FROM nobench_main* *WHERE JSON_TEXTCONTAINS(jobj, '$.nested_arr', :1)*
Q9	*SELECT jobj* *FROM nobench_main* *WHERE JSON_VALUE(jobj, '$.sparse_367') = :1*
Q10	*SELECT count(*)* *FROM nobench_main* *WHERE JSON_VALUE(jobj, '$.num' RETURNING NUMBER) BETWEEN 1 AND 4000* *GROUP BY JSON_VALUE(jobj, '$.thousandth')*
Q11	*SELECT left.jobj* *FROM nobench_main left* *INNER JOIN* *nobench_main right* *ON* *(JSON_VALUE(left_jobj, '$.nested_obj.str') =* *JSON_VALUE(right_jobj, '$.str1'))* *WHERE JSON_VALUE(left_jobj, '$.num' RETURNING NUMBER) BETWEEN :1 AND :2*

Table 6 –NOBENCH Queries using Oracle RDBMS supporting SQL/JSON

7.2 Performance Comparison of JSON query performance with and without JSON index

In this experiment, we use ANJS and compare Q1-Q11 performance with and without any JSON indices. Figure 5 shows the execution time ratio of running Q1-Q11 without having any indices and with indices. It represents the speed up due to using an index. Functional indices are used to speed up Q5, Q6, Q7, Q10, Q11 queries for dense static schema. A JSON inverted index is used to speed up Q3, Q4, Q8, Q9 queries for sparse dynamic schema. Other than Q1 and Q2, a JSON index speeds up queries significantly. Q1 and Q2 are queries to project out scalar values from JSON object without any predicates used in the WHERE clause so an index can't improve their performance.

7.3 Performance Comparison of JSON native store approach Versus vertical shredding store approach

We have implemented the Argo/3 approach of vertically shredding JSON objects and storing the resulting vertical relational table in the Oracle RDBMS. In this approach, there is a main path-value relational table similar to the table *argo_people_data* described in [9], holding objid, keystr and valstr. The valstr is indexed by a B+ tree index representing the *argo_people_str* table in [9]. An additional numeric B+ tree index is created on the valstr column for those string values that are valid numbers. This is the same as the Argo/3 table *argo_people_num* in [9]. Figure 6 shows the execution time ratio of running Q1-Q11 using VSJS with ANJS. It shows that ANJS with functional and inverted JSON indexes is faster than the VSJS approach.

The storage size of VSJS is much more than that of ANJS. For 50,000 JSON object instances, its total text size is 39MB. In ANJS, the *NOBENCH_main* table size is 39MB, the space for functional indices is 3.7MB and the JSON inverted index is 31MB. However, in VSJS, the base *argo_people_data* table size is 59MB. To facilitate string value search and number value range search, a B+ tree index to index *valstr* column of the *argo_people_data* table is created with an index size of 26MB. A B+ tree index to index valid numbers from valstr column of the *argo_people_data* table is created with an index size of 5MB. To facilitate keystr search, a B+ tree index on keystr column of the *argo_people_data* table is created with an index size of 39MB. Therefore, for VSJS, the total space consumption of *argo_people_data* with all of its secondary indices is 129.6MB which is 2.3 times more than the size of the base object collection of 34MB. In contrast with ANJS, the total space consumption of functional indices and inverted index is 34.7MB, which is 89% of the size of the base object collection size of 39MB. Figure 7 shows the size ratio comparison. A columnar store [1,30] of *argo_people_data* should be able to compress the storage size because all rows shredded from the same JSON object have the same object id column value, which can be compressed. A columnar store can also compress numeric and Boolean value columns that having many NULL values in Argo/1. Indeed the Argo/3 layout logically implements the column store and columnar store is known to be able to handle efficient storage and query of vertically shredded table. However, even if a columnar store is used, the reconstruction of full objects by assembling all the pieces stored in the vertical table is still expensive as demonstrated below.

Because any JSON store based on vertical shredding does **not** store the JSON object as a whole, it is costly to respond to common queries that retrieve the whole JSON object as their results. The store needs to run queries over the *argo_people_data* table to group all rows belonging to the same object id and then aggregate all columns of these rows to construct the full JSON object. This is mentioned in [9]: "Argo on the relational systems also suffers from more difficult object reconstruction as scale increases because it must access many (sometimes un-contiguous) rows when reconstructing matching objects". However, for ANJS, there is no need to construct the JSON object. Figure 8 shows the execution time ratio of VSJS versus ANJS for full JSON object retrieval query. The ANJS approach is 35 times faster than VSJS approach.

Therefore, VSJS is not a viable approach for storing JSON objects. Extending an inverted index to add JSON path support appears to be a more straightforward approach. Indeed, the inverted index architecture has much in common with columnar storage [1,30] for optimizing data layout to maximize query efficiency and has embraced all the index functionality of VSJS approach.

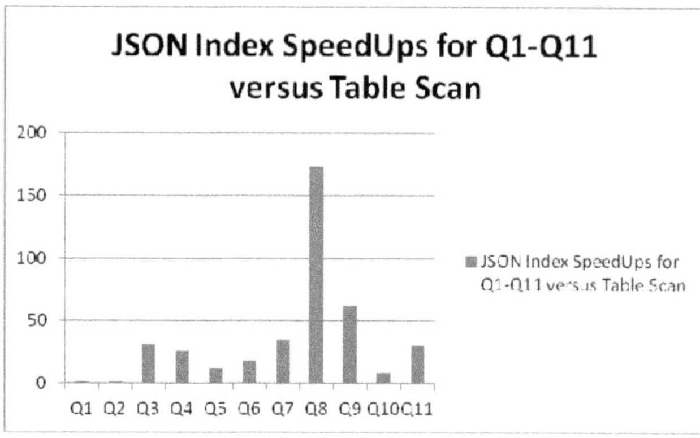

Figure 5 – JSON Index SpeedUps versus Table Scan

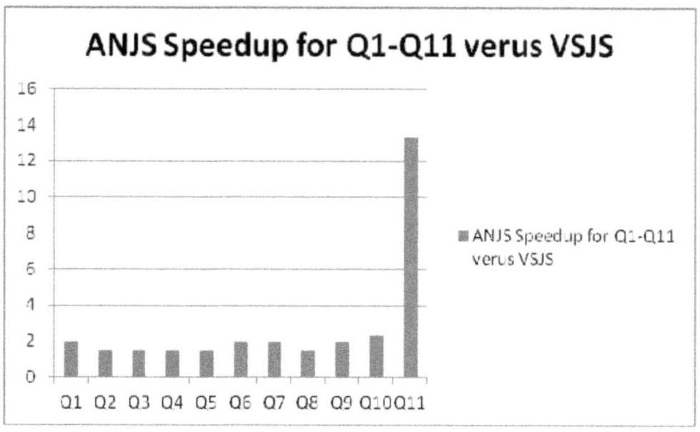

Figure 6 – ANJS SpeedUps for Q1-Q11 versus VSJS

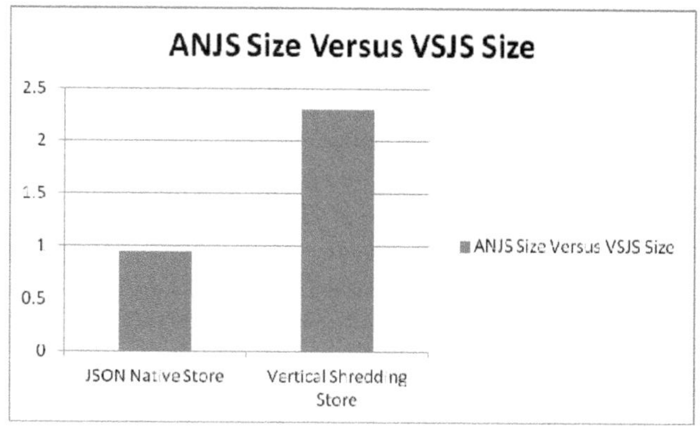

Figure 7 – ANJS Size versus VSJS Size

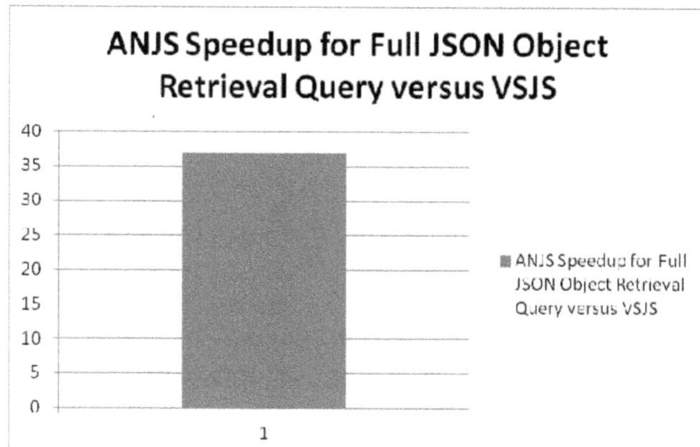

Figure 8 – ANJS Speedups for full JSON object retrieval Query versus VSJS

8. Future Work

JSON Rest API Access: A JSON object collection style of REST API can be supported to provide a simple API to access JSON persistence service in the RDBMS from a variety of imperative programming language environments that need to manipulate JSON data. A REST API will provide a No-SQL user experience to application developers; the underlying implementation can use the SQL/JSON operators described in this paper.

JSON inverted index supporting range value search: Compared with textual oriented documents, JSON objects are more data centric. Many JSON object members can be of data types such as numbers and dates where non-textual domain semantics are required for correct range semantics. Processing range expressions requires extending the JSON inverted index to index numbers, dates embedded in JSON objects.

JSON benchmark: NoBENCH [9] models the characteristics of JSON collection very well. However, to support OLTP and OLAP decision support workload for JSON object collections: we will work on benchmark that models multi-user CRUD operations on JSON object collections in high transaction context; we will also work on benchmark that models ad-hoc query and search over JSON object collection.

9. Conclusion

We are living in an interesting time where E.F Codd's relational model that relies on the existence of static data schema to store, query and index data is being challenged. This paper starts to address this challenge by extending the RDBMS to support schema-less development styles in conjunction with the classical schema-oriented development styles. The storage, query and indexing principles proposed in this paper are applicable not only to JSON and XML but to other semi-structured data management. In particular, the query principle positions SQL as a **S**et oriented **Q**uery **L**anguage so that the declarative power of SQL can be applied beyond plain relational data. Yet, the schema-less advantage of No-SQL is fully embraced in RDBMS with the three principles. The relational model has bought us tremendous success in structured data management. We hope that following the three principles of schema-less storage, query and indexing will help us build on this success continuously.

10. Acknowledgements

The authors like to express their thanks to following colleagues who have been in the working group to formulate SQL/JSON standard: Krishna Kulkarni, Fatma Ozcan, Jim Melton, Jan-Eike Michels, Hamid Pirahesh, and Fred Zemke along with authors of this paper. We thank Vikas Arora, Andrew Witkowski for management efforts of SQL/JSON development at Oracle.

11. REFERENCES

[1] D. J. Abadi, S. Madden, M. Ferreira: Integrating compression and execution in column-oriented database systems. SIGMOD Conference 2006: 671-682

[2] R. AgRAWal, A. Somani, Y. Xu: Storage and Querying of E-Commerce Data. VLDB 2001

[3] P. Atzeni, C.S. Jensen, G. Orsi, S. Ram, L. Tanca, R. Torlone: The relational model is dead, SQL is dead, and I don't feel so good myself. SIGMOD Record, 42(2):64-68, 2013

[4] Beyer, K; Ercegovac, V; Gemulla, R; Balmin, A; Eltabakh, M; Kanne, C; Ozcan, F; Shekita, E: *Jaql: A Scripting Language for Large Scale Semistructured Data Analysis*

[5] K. Beyer, R. Cochrane, V. Josifovski, J. Kleewein, G. Lapis, G.M.Lohman, R.Lyle, F. Özcan, H. Pirahesh, N. Seemann, T. C. Truong, B.V. Linden, B. Vickery, C. Zhang: System RX: One Part Relational, One Part XML. SIGMOD Conference 2005: 347-358

[6] R. Cattell: Scalable SQL and NoSQL data stores. SIGMOD Record, 39(4):12-27, 2010.

[7] Chen P.: The Enity-Relationship Model: Toward a Unified View of Data. VLDB 1975: 173

[8] Codd, E. A Relational Model of Data for Large Shared Data Banks. Commun. ACM 13(6): 377-387 (1970)

[9] Chasseur, C; Li Y; Patel, J: *Enabling JSON Document Stores in Relational Systems* . WebDB 2013

[10] D.J. DeWitt: From 1 to1000 MIPS cs.wisc.edu/~dewitt/includes/passtalks/pass2009.pptx

[11] Fowler, M; Pramod Sadalage, P: *NoSQL databases and Polyglot Persistence:* http://martinfowler.com/articles/nosql-intro

[12] Jagadish, H: *Making Database Systems Usable*. SIGMOD 2007 Keynotes

[13] G. Grafe, Query Evaluation Techniques for Large Databases, in ACM Computing Surveys, 25(2):73–170, 1993.

[14] I.O. for Standardization (ISO). Information Technology-Database Language SQL-Part 14: XML-Related Specifications (SQL/XML)

[15] JSON: http://www.json.org/

[16] http://goessner.net/articles/JsonPath/

[17] JSONiq: http://www.jsoniq.org/

[18] K. Kunchithapadam, W. Zhang, A. Ganesh, N. Mukherjee: Oracle database filesystem. SIGMOD Conference 2011: 1149-1160

[19] Z. H. Liu, M. Krishnaprasad, H. J. Chang, V. Arora: XMLTABLE Index - An Efficient Way of Indexing and Querying XML Property Data, ICDE 2007

[20] Z. H. Liu, Chandrasekar,S; Baby T; Chang, H: Towards a physical XML independent XQuery/SQL/XML engine. PVLDB: 1356-1367 (2008)

[21] Z. H. Liu. "Object-Relational Features in Informix Internet Foundation."Informix technical notes. 9.4(Q4 1999):77-95.

[22] Z.H.Liu, H.J.Chang, B. Sthanikam: Efficient Support of XQuery Update Facility in XML Enabled RDBMS. ICDE 2012: 1394-1404

[23] Pal, S; Cseri, G; Schaller, O; Seeliger, L; Giakoumakis, V; Zolotov, V: *Indexing XML Data Stored in a Relational Database*. VLDB 2004: 1134-1145

[24] MongoDB : http://www.mongodb.org/

[25] R. Murthy, Z. H. Liu, M. Krishnaprasad, S. Chandrasekar, A. Tran, E. Sedlar, D. Florescu, S. Kotsovolos, N. Agarwal, V. Arora, V. Krishnamurthy: Towards an enterprise XML architecture. SIGMOD Conference 2005: 953-957

[26] R. Murthy, S. Banerjee: XML Schemas in Oracle XML DB. VLDB 2003 1009-1018

[27] G. Salton and M. McGill. Introduction to Modern Information Retrieval. McGRAW-Hill, New York, 1983.

[28] Shute, J; Vingralek, R; Samwel, B; Handy Ben; Menestrina, D; ellner, Stephan; Cieslewicz; J, Rae I; Stancescu, T; Apte, H: F1: A Distributed SQL Database That Scales. VLDB Conference 2013.

[29] Stonebraker,M;, Brown,P; Moore, D. *Object-Relational DBMSs*, Second Edition Morgan Kaufmann 1998

[30] Stonebraker, M.; Abadi, D; Batkin, A.;Chen,X.;Cherniack, M;Ferreira,M.;Lau, E.;Lin,A.;Madden,S; O'Neil, E.;O'Neil,P.;Rasin,A.;Tran,N.;Zdonik,S. *C-Store: A Column-oriented DBMS*. VLDB 2005: 553-564

[31] XQuery: http://www.w3.org/TR/xquery/

[32] XQuery Full Text: http://www.w3.org/TR/xpath-full-text-10/

[33] Yoshikawa, M; Amagasa, T; Shimura, T; Uemura, S: Xrel: A Path-Based Approach to Storage and Retreival of XML documents using Relational Databases

[34] C. Zhang, J.Naughton, D. DeWitt.J, Luo. Q, G.Lohman. On Supporting Containment Queries in Relational Database Management Systems. SIGMOD Conference 2001: 425-436

[35] J. Zobel, A. Moffat: Inverted files for text search engines. ACM Computing. Surveys. 38(2): (2006).

[36] Protocol Buffers: http://code.google.com/p/protobuf/

[37] Avro http://avro.apache.org/docs/1.7.5/spec.html

[38] BSON http://bsonspec.org/

[39] Qiao, L. etc: On Brewing Fresh Expresso: Linkedin's Distributed Data Serving Platform. SIGMOD 2013

[40] Vertica Flex Table https://my.vertica.com/docs/7.0.x/PDF/HP_Vertica_7.0.x_Flex_Tables.pdf

[41] I. Rae, A. Halverson, J. Naughton: In-RDBMS Inverted Indexes revisited. ICDE 2014: 352-363

[42] Z.H.Liu, Y. Lu, H.Chang: Efficient Support of XQuery Full Text in SQL/XML Enabled RDBMS. ICDE 2014: 1132-1143

Querying Encrypted Data

Arvind Arasu, Ken Eguro, Raghav Kaushik, Ravi Ramamurthy
Microsoft Research
{arvinda,eguro,skaushi,ravirama}@microsoft.com

ABSTRACT

Data security is a serious concern when we migrate data to a cloud DBMS. Database encryption, where sensitive columns are encrypted before they are stored in the cloud, has been proposed as a mechanism to address such data security concerns. The intuitive expectation is that an adversary cannot "learn" anything about the encrypted columns, since she does not have access to the encryption key. However, query processing becomes a challenge since it needs to "look inside" the data. This tutorial explores the space of designs studied in prior work on processing queries over encrypted data. We cover approaches based on both classic client-server and involving the use of a trusted hardware module where data can be securely decrypted. We discuss the privacy challenges that arise in both approaches and how they may be addressed. Briefly, supporting the full complexity of a modern DBMS including complex queries, transactions and stored procedures leads to significant challenges that we survey and open problems which we highlight.

1. INTRODUCTION

There is an increasing interest in *database-as-a-service* in the cloud (*cloud DBMS*) [3, 8, 18]. While cloud DBMSes offer well-documented cost and manageability advantages [8], they come with known data security risks. Data stored in the cloud is potentially accessible to snooping administrators and other untrusted entities that have or gain access to the cloud servers. Such data risks and associated privacy concerns have been in the limelight recently from revelations of extensive surveillance by NSA and other government entities [21]. Several surveys indicate that data security concerns is a significant barrier to adoption of cloud technologies [10].

A natural mechanism to improve cloud data security is encryption. By encrypting data before storing it in the cloud we can ensure an adversary such as a snooping administrator does not learn anything about the data. In the context of cloud DBMSes, encryption, however, makes query processing challenging. Encryption is designed to "hide" the underlying data while query processing needs to the "see" the data to perform required computations. Addressing the query processing challenges introduced by encryption has been the subject of a lot of research and industry effort [15, 19, 22, 2, 6, 14, 24] beginning with the seminal work of Hacigümüs et al. [13], which recently was awarded the SIGMOD test of time award.

The goal of this (90 minute) tutorial is an in-depth coverage of architectural and technical ideas of query processing over encrypted data. Briefly, we motivate and introduce the problem of query processing over encrypted data, present relevant background material from security, cryptography, and *secure* hardware to make the tutorial self-contained and accessible to a database audience. While covering the proposed solution approaches, we introduce interesting "dimensions" to structure the space of solutions that helps us better understand each approach and compare and contrast different approaches. One such dimension that does not get sufficient attention in previous work and tutorials is security: How do different solutions for query processing over encrypted data compare in terms of the security that they provide? We highlight limitations of current approaches and discuss new hardware trends and other technical developments that might influence future ones. Throughout, we strive to present a systems perspective of the area and focus less on algorithmic and mathematical details.

This tutorial proposal reflects our belief that now is an interesting time to be working on the problem of query processing over encrypted data. Apart from the emerging motivation provided by the cloud, many technologies relevant to this area are in a state of flux compelling us to revisit existing solutions and question their underlying assumptions. For example, there are several emerging hardware-based alternatives such as Intel Software Guard Extensions (SGX) [16, 17] and secure FPGAs [9] for performing secure computations in an untrusted environment. These hardware trends, along with recent developments in cryptography (e.g., homomorphic encryption) and databases (main memory databases, column stores, Hadoop) have the potential to fundamentally alter the landscape of query processing over encrypted data and represent a tremendous opportunity for database research.

2. PREVIOUS RELATED TUTORIALS

In VLDB 2007, Radu Sion presented a related tutorial on secure data outsourcing [25]. Compared to [25], our tutorial represents a more focused and more detailed survey of query processing issues over encrypted data. For example, we do

SIGMOD'14, June 22–27, 2014, Snowbird, UT, USA.

http://dx.doi.org/10.1145/2588555.2588893 .

not cover topics such as cryptographically proving correctness of outsourced query answers; on the other hand, we cover in greater detail how secure hardware can be leveraged for query processing over encrypted data. Further, a lot of new research work and industry developments have happened since 2007 when [25] was presented. Another related tutorial was presented by Divyakant Agrawal et al [1] in VLDB 2012 and ICDE 2013. Again, the main difference is our focused and detailed coverage on query processing issues. For example, we do not cover privacy topics such as k-anonymity. Also, we focus more on end-to-end system issues (e.g., indexes over encrypted data) and less on algorithmic building blocks, so our tutorials nicely complement each other. An earlier version of this tutorial was presented in ICDE 2013 [5] (in the same venue as [1]). For the version proposed for SIGMOD we plan to incorporate newer results and hardware trends (e.g., Intel SGX technology [16]).

3. TUTORIAL OUTLINE

The outline of the tutorial is as follows:

1. Building Blocks of Encryption: Homomorphic encryption is a specially designed encryption scheme that allows computation directly over encrypted data. A *full* homomorphic encryption can in principle be used to implement query processing over encrypted data. We present state-of-the-art homomorphic encryption schemes and argue why they are not practical. There exist many *partial* homomorphic encryption schemes that allow specific (not arbitrary) computation. These include *order-preserving* [7] encryption that allows comparisons over encrypted data, *deterministic* encryption that allows equality predicates, and *Paillier system* [23] that allows sum operation. Such partial homomorphic encryption schemes are exploited by the recent CryptDB system [24]. We present technical underpinnings of these schemes, their security guarantees, computations they allow, and their performance implications.

2. Trusted Client based Approaches: Here, query processing over part of data in plaintext or encrypted using (partially) homomorphic encryption is performed at the server and the remainder, at the client, which is assumed to be trusted. The initial, seminal work on query processing over encrypted data by Hacigumus et al [13] belongs to this category. We discuss query processing ideas and the interaction between communication costs and the completeness of SQL supported.

3. Trusted Hardware based Approaches: These approaches use a secure, tamper-proof hardware at the server to securely decrypt data and perform computations [4, 6]. We present various alternatives for secure hardware including secure co-processors, FPGAs, and Hardware Security Modules, and discuss their advantages and disadvantages [9]. We present novel query processing challenges that arise due to distributed computation between trusted and commodity hardware [20]. The data movement between trusted and commodity hardware potentially leaks information, so the end-to-end data security provided by these approaches differs from data-at-rest security provided by encryption. This has interesting connections to oblivious computations [12], access-pattern hiding [11], and private information retrieval [26], which we discuss in the tutorial. We also present recent hardware trends including Intel SGX technology [16] and discuss the challenges and opportunities it introduces.

4. End-to-End Security: The tutorial talks about combining encryption building blocks in different ways including the trusted client and trusted hardware approaches. Independent of the approach chosen, it is important to understand the end-to-end security offered by the system. An important fact that we highlight is encryption in itself does not ensure end-to-end security. Even with strong encryption, the very act of query processing can potentially reveal information about the underlying data. We survey techniques for preventing such information leakage such as Oblivious RAM (ORAM) simulations [11]. Again, we focus on systems issues such as implications of ORAM simulations for locality of reference and performance of memory hierarchy and less on theoretical performance characteristics.

5. Challenges and open issues: Although the area of query processing over encrypted data has been active for more than ten years, there exist significant challenges and open issues that we cover extensively in the tutorial. As discussed in Section 1, some of these challenges are introduced by new hardware trends and developments in cryptography. Other challenges are more fundamental: Every system that has been proposed represents a tradeoff between functionality, security, and performance, and many aspects of this tradeoff remain poorly understood. For example, can we get acceptable security and performance if we need to support functionality such as stored procedures going beyond standard SQL queries; What is the performance cost of "higher" end-to-end security that goes beyond basic encryption? The open issues also range from low-level technical challenges such as making Paillier schemes update friendly to grand challenges such as tackling application security since a database is just one of the tiers of an application two- or three-tier architecture.

4. TARGET AUDIENCE

While the primary audience is likely to be researchers and practitioners interested in data security and privacy, the tutorial should be of interest and would be specifically structured to be accessible to the broader database community. We believe that while there has been a lot of prior work in this space [15, 19, 22, 6, 14, 24, 4], the problem of designing a fully functional DBMS that securely and efficiently processes queries over encrypted data remains open. One of the main goals of this tutorial is to highlight the open issues and challenges and get the broader database community interested in encrypted databases.

5. BIOGRAPHY

Arvind Arasu, Ken Eguro, Raghav Kaushik and Ravi Ramamurthy are researchers at Microsoft. They are currently working on the Cipherbase [4] project whose goal is to design a functionally rich, industrial strength DBMS that supports encryption. Arvind, Raghav and Ravi have previously worked on a variety of problems related to data security including data masking and data auditing and Ken has worked extensively on applications of reconfigurable computing platforms, with a focus on security and cryptography.

6. BIOGRAPHY

Arvind Arasu, Ken Eguro, Raghav Kaushik and Ravi Ramamurthy are researchers at Microsoft. They are currently working on the Cipherbase [4] project whose goal is to design a functionally rich, industrial strength DBMS that supports encryption. Arvind, Raghav and Ravi have previously worked on a variety of problems related to data security including data masking and data auditing and Ken has worked extensively on applications of reconfigurable computing platforms, with a focus on security and cryptography.

7. REFERENCES

[1] Divyakant Agrawal, Amr El Abbadi, and Shiyuan Wang. Secure and privacy-preserving database services in the cloud. In *ICDE*, 2013. (To appear).

[2] Rakesh Agrawal, Jerry Kiernan, Ramakrishnan Srikant, and Yirong Xu. Order-preserving encryption for numeric data. In *SIGMOD Conference*, pages 563–574, 2004.

[3] Amazon Corporation. Amazon Relational Database Service. http://aws.amazon.com/rds/.

[4] Arvind Arasu, Spyros Blanas, Ken Eguro, et al. Orthogonal security with cipherbase. In *CIDR*, 2013.

[5] Arvind Arasu, Ken Eguro, Raghav Kaushik, and Ravi Ramamurthy. Querying encrypted data. In *ICDE*, pages 1262–1263, 2013.

[6] Sumeet Bajaj and Radu Sion. TrustedDB: a trusted hardware based database with privacy and data confidentiality. In *SIGMOD Conference*, pages 205–216, 2011.

[7] Alexandra Boldyreva, Nathan Chenette, and Adam O'Neill. Order-preserving encryption revisited: Improved security analysis and alternative solutions. In *CRYPTO*, pages 578–595, 2011.

[8] Carlo Curino, Evan P. C. Jones, Raluca A. Popa, Nirmesh Malviya, Eugene Wu, Samuel Madden, Hari Balakrishnan, and Nickolai Zeldovich. Relational cloud: a database service for the cloud. In *CIDR*, pages 235–240, 2011.

[9] K. Eguro and R. Venkatesan. FPGAs for trusted cloud computing. In *FPL*, 2012.

[10] An sme perspective on cloud computing (survey). European Network and Information Security Agency, 2009.

[11] Oded Goldreich and Rafail Ostrovsky. Software protection and simulation on oblivious rams. *J. ACM*, 43(3):431–473, 1996.

[12] Michael T. Goodrich. Data-oblivious external-memory algorithms for the compaction, selection, and sorting of outsourced data. In *SPAA*, pages 379–388, 2011.

[13] Hakan Hacigümüs, Balakrishna R. Iyer, Chen Li, and Sharad Mehrotra. Executing sql over encrypted data in the database-service-provider model. In *SIGMOD Conference*, pages 216–227, 2002.

[14] Bijit Hore, Sharad Mehrotra, and Hakan Hacigümüs. Managing and querying encrypted data. In *Handbook of Database Security*, pages 163–190. 2008.

[15] IBM Corporation. IBM InfoSphere Guardium Data Encryption for DB2 and IMS Databases. `http://www-01.ibm.com/software/data/db2imstools/db2tools/ibmencrypt/`.

[16] Intel software guard extensions (intel SGX). `http://software.intel.com/en-us/intel-isa-extensions#pid-19539-1495`.

[17] Frank Mckeen, Ilya Alexandrovich, et al. Innovative instructions and software model for isolated execution. In *Workshop on Hardware and Architectural Support for Security and Privacy (HASP)*, 2013.

[18] Microsoft Corporation. SQL Azure. http://www.windowsazure.com/en-us/home/features/sql-azure/.

[19] Microsoft Corporation. SQL Server Encryption. `http://technet.microsoft.com/en-us/library/bb510663.aspx`.

[20] R. Müller, J. Teubner, and G. Alonso. Data processing on fpgas. *PVLDB*, 2(1), 2009.

[21] Global surveillance disclosure. `http://en.wikipedia.org/wiki/Global_surveillance_disclosure`.

[22] Oracle Corporation. Transparent Data Encryption. `http://www.oracle.com/technetwork/database/options/advanced-security/index-099011.html`.

[23] Pascal Paillier. Public-key cryptosystems based on composite degree residuosity classes. In *EUROCRYPT*, pages 223–238, 1999.

[24] R. A. Popa, C. M. S. Redfield, N. Zeldovich, et al. Cryptdb: protecting confidentiality with encrypted query processing. In *SOSP*, pages 85–100, 2011.

[25] Radu Sion. Secure data outsourcing. In *VLDB*, pages 1431–1432, 2007.

[26] Peter Williams and Radu Sion. Usable pir. In *NDSS*, 2008.

Towards Unified Ad-hoc Data Processing

Xiaogang Shi[♯] Bin Cui[♯] Gillian Dobbie[§] Beng Chin Ooi[†]
[♯]Key Lab of High Confidence Software Technologies (MOE), School of EECS, Peking University
[§]Department of Computer Science, University of Auckland
[†]School of Computing, National University of Singapore
[♯]{sxg, bin.cui}@pku.edu.cn, [§]gill@cs.auckland.ac.nz, [†]ooibc@comp.nus.edu.sg

ABSTRACT

It is important to provide efficient execution for ad-hoc data processing programs. In contrast to constructing complex declarative queries, many users prefer to write their programs using procedural code with simple queries. As many users are not expert programmers, their programs usually exhibit poor performance in practice and it is a challenge to automatically optimize these programs and efficiently execute the programs.

In this paper, we present UniAD, a system designed to simplify the programming of data processing tasks and provide efficient execution for user programs. We propose a novel intermediate representation named UniQL which utilizes HOQs to describe the operations performed in programs. By combining both procedural and declarative logics, we can perform various optimizations across the boundary between procedural and declarative codes. We describe optimizations and conduct extensive empirical studies using UniAD. The experimental results on four benchmarks demonstrate that our techniques can significantly improve the performance of a wide range of data processing programs.

Categories and Subject Descriptors

H.2.4 [**Database Management**]: Systems—*Query Processing*; F.3.2 [**Logics and Meanings of Programs**]: Semantics of Programming Languages—*Program Analysis*

Keywords

ad-hoc data processing, unified optimization, program analysis

1. INTRODUCTION

Ad-hoc data processing has proven to be a critical component for a variety of applications such as business intelligence, data mining and scientific computing. In a typical scenario, a user collects a set of data and has a list of questions about the data. As many ideas are hit on by accident, the lack of standard tools forces the user to write customized program himself to answer his questions.

Since many users are non-experts in programming, a simple but efficient method is needed for them to describe their tasks. Declarative languages are attractive tools as they can abstract away implementation details. Experienced users can write their programs with little effort and let optimizers choose efficient execution plans. Many existing data processing systems, such as relational databases, Pig [22] and Hive [28], provide declarative languages to users. But to achieve the benefits brought by these systems, programmers have to formulate their problems to specialized paradigms provided by the systems. These paradigms are usually limited in expressiveness and functionality. As many problems targeted by ad-hoc data processing are very complex, problem formulation in these systems is not a trivial task [35, 11]. Very often, users feel more comfortable writing their programs in procedural languages with embedded declarative primitives.

SIGMOD'14, June 22–27, 2014, Snowbird, UT, USA.

ACM 978-1-4503-2376-5/14/06 ...$15.00.
http://dx.doi.org/10.1145/2588555.2610492.

```
LOOP @d_id FROM 0 TO N
    SELECT o_id INTO @o_id_list[@d_id]
    FROM order
    WHERE d_id = @d_id;
```

Figure 1: An example for optimizing

Though many systems offer general purpose programming languages integrated with declarative queries such as PL/SQL and LINQ [34], we observe that the optimization and execution for the procedural and declarative parts are still separated in these systems. For example, many modern databases allow users to write stored procedures with procedural extensions to SQL. But the procedural and declarative parts are executed in different execution engines. The procedural execution engine treats SQL queries as black boxes and calls database interfaces to execute the queries.

This separation makes it difficult to optimize programs. Consider the code fragment in Figure 1. If there is an index built on the attribute *d_id*, it performs well when executed. But if the index does not exist, unfortunately the executor will have to sequentially scan the entire table in each iteration of the loop. The performance would be significantly degraded due to the redundant table scans. Neither the program compiler nor the query optimizer can perform any optimization on the program — the program compiler does not have the knowledge of indexes while the query optimizer is unaware of the existence of the loop.

The performance is further hampered in the context of parallel processing due to the separate execution of procedural and declarative code. With the exponential growth in data size in many applications, there is an increasing need to process data in parallel. Although declarative queries can be easily executed in parallel, procedural code is usually executed sequentially. The benefit brought about by the parallelism of declarative queries is significantly limited by the interaction between the procedural code and the declarative queries. After submitting a query, the program has to wait until the results are returned. Then the program consumes the results by iterating over the results in sequence and performing computation on the results. It becomes a bottleneck if the amount of data is big or the application logic is complex.

To improve the performance of these data processing programs, programmers have to examine both the procedural code and declarative queries in programs manually. Existing techniques in program compilation and query optimization cannot be directly applied to these programs. Attempts were made to allow automatic optimizations of such programs. D. Lieuwen et al. developed a rule-based optimizer to transform loops into joins [19] while R. Guravannavar et al. proposed to automatically rewrite iteratively invoked queries [13]. Some other studies focus on identifying the procedural code which can be translated into SQL queries [32, 33, 4]. The idea behind these attempts is to extract relational conditions from procedural code and construct equivalent SQL queries. Program performance might benefit from the query optimization in database systems. But as the relational algebra is unable to match the expressiveness of procedural languages, much procedural code cannot be translated into SQL queries and thus the benefits they gain are limited.

In this paper, we present a new system targeted for ad-hoc data processing, called UniAD, which stands for *Uni*fied execution for *A*d-hoc *D*ata processing. UniAD simplifies the programming of data processing tasks. Rather than constructing complex queries for their problems, users can write their programs in a procedural language with simple queries. User programs can be automatically optimized by UniAD and achieve good performance even if they are written poorly.

Unlike existing systems, UniAD takes both the procedural and declarative logics into consideration and can perform optimizations across the boundary between procedural code and SQL queries. These optimizations were hard to perform before due to the lack of a uniform representation suitable for the optimization of data processing programs. UniAD addresses the problem by translating user programs into a novel intermediate representation called Unified Query Language (UniQL).

UniQL deploys a simple and expressive mechanism, named High Order Query (HOQ), to describe used persistent data and performed operations in programs. HOQs provide a high level description of how persistent data is processed. SQL queries in programs can be easily translated into HOQs. Benefits gained from query optimization, including the utility of indexes, can be carried out in UniAD. Moreover, realizing that HOQs are logically equivalent to loops in procedural code, we can apply loop optimization techniques to HOQs. As operations described by SQL queries and procedural code are unified in HOQ, UniAD can find optimization opportunities previously ignored because of the separate optimization of procedural and declarative code.

UniAD also enables parallel execution of user programs even when programs are written assuming the sequential execution model. By combining computation logic with corresponding data in HOQs, UniAD can execute the computation logic in parallel in the place where its data resides.

To summarize, the main contributions of our work include:

- We design a new architecture to unify the optimization and execution of user programs, which are written in procedural languages with embedded declarative queries.
- We propose a novel intermediate representation that provides a uniform mechanism to describe data processing tasks in programs.
- We propose a transformation-based optimizer to automatically optimize programs. We show that the proposed intermediate representation allows concise and efficient implementation of many optimizations.
- We implement a prototype system and conduct extensive empirical studies on four different benchmarks including TPC-C [29] and SEATS [27]. We validate that we can achieve significant speed-ups for a variety of data processing programs.

The rest of the paper is organized as follows. We first introduce UniAD's intermediate representation in Section 2. Then we give an overview of UniAD and describe how UniAD executes user programs in Section 3. Details of program translation and optimization are presented in Section 4 and Section 5 respectively. Some practical issues in the implementation are discussed in Section 6. We evaluate our system in Section 7 and discuss related work in Section 8. Finally, we conclude the paper in Section 9.

2. HIGHER ORDER QUERY

It's challenging to optimize programs written in procedural languages with embedded SQL queries. Procedural code describes the exact operations performed in a program, whereas SQL queries provide a high level execution semantics and encapsulate detailed implementation methods. The encapsulation enables query optimizers to devise optimal execution plans for SQL queries. But meanwhile, the encapsulation creates a boundary between SQL queries and procedural code. This boundary makes it challenging to provide unified optimization and execution for procedural programs with embedded SQL queries. The problem is another form of the well-known *impedance mismatch* problem [20].

To address the problem, a uniform representation is needed to describe the operations in programs. The representation must satisfy the following requirements:

- First, the representation must be expressive and bridge the gap between procedural code and SQL queries. Relational algebra is beautiful yet powerful in representing queries on relations, but it is not capable of describing operations performed in procedural code such as loops and branches.
- Second, the representation must provide enough information for optimization and execution at a high level. Procedural code and other low level languages can express operations in SQL queries. However, because they eliminate the execution semantics, it is difficult to optimize the programs.
- Third, transformations on the representation must be available. The availability of transformations allows opportunities for program optimization.
- Finally, the representation must be as simple as possible. Unlike the operators provided to users, the representation is used for program optimization and execution in the system. A simple representation can reduce the complexity of optimization as the optimizer can further simplify various cases.

Some representations were proposed to solve the mismatch between declarative queries and procedural code [30, 1, 10], but they are not suitable for optimizing data processing programs. These representations have their roots in functional languages. Side effects such as I/O and shared states are eliminated, which makes it difficult to optimize the procedural code where side effects are frequently used.

Data-centric programming models have received considerable attention over the past few years. As one of the most well-known data-centric programming models, MapReduce was proposed by Google to simplify parallel data processing. A programmer can easily build their applications by specifying two relatively simple basic functions: *map* and *reduce*. Despite the simplicity of the paradigm, many useful computations can be efficiently abstracted.

```
/* selector */
ACCESS order WHERE o_w_id = @w_id
{
  /* processor */
  @total_amount += o_amount;
  if(o_status == 'ready')
    o_delivery_d = current_time;
}
```

Figure 2: An example of HOQ

These data-centric programming models share common characteristics in the manner in which they attach computation to corresponding data. Although these models resemble higher order functions in functional languages [18], user-defined functions are written in procedural languages. It provides a simple but expressive method to describe operations in the programs. By partitioning the data, application computation can also be executed simultaneously in the place where the data resides.

Inspired by the simplicity and expressiveness provided by data-centric programming models, UniAD uses HOQs to describe operations in the programs. An example of HOQ is given in Figure 2. Each HOQ consists of a selector and a processor. The selector uses a WHERE clause to indicate the tuples selected. The statements below the selector comprise the HOQ's processor, which describe the operations performed on each selected tuple. When viewed in this form, a processor acts as an anonymous function and is bounded to each selected tuple in the HOQ. So a HOQ can be viewed as a higher-order version of a SQL query, hence its name.

Algorithm 1 HOQ Execution Semantics

```
for each tuple t in table do
    if t satisfies HOQ's selector then
        perform HOQ's processor on t
    end if
end for
```

HOQ's execution semantics is illustrated in Algorithm 1 and is easy to understand. Once a qualified tuple is selected, the operations defined in the HOQ's processor are performed on the tuple.

Using the HOQs, UniQL is an efficient intermediate representation for programs in UniAD. First, by breaking the encapsulation of SQL queries and translating SQL queries into HOQs, we can have a clear and uniform picture about the data used in the programs and operations performed on the data. Such information can be used to guide our optimizations.

Second, HOQ is capable of describing a wide variety of execution plans. It allows us to find efficient execution plans which cannot be expressed in relational algebra. Consider the operations performed in Figure 2. The code fragment calculates the sum of field *o_amount* and for those tuples whose field *o_status* is *'ready'*, updates their field *o_delivery_d* to current time. The HOQ in Figure 2 provides an efficient execution plan to perform these operations. These operations can be performed by scanning the table *order* in one pass. Although many features, such as MERGE and window functions, have been added into the SQL standard to support efficient execution plans, it is still impossible to use relational algebra to express the query described in Figure 2.

Finally, HOQ can facilitate concise and efficient implementation of many program optimizations. As the selected data is described in a declarative manner, the executor is free to choose different methods to fetch data. With the knowledge of physical storage and available indexes, the executor can fetch data efficiently. Moreover, note that the HOQ's execution sequentially iterates over retrieved data, we can conceptually treat HOQs as loops. Hence, many well-studied loop optimization techniques can be applied to HOQs.

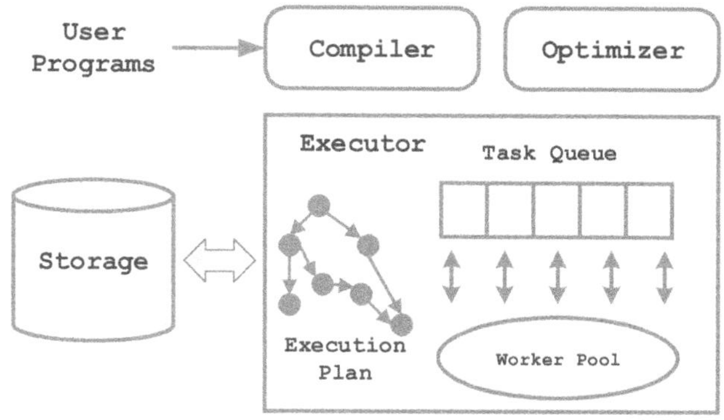

Figure 3: System architecture

3. SYSTEM OVERVIEW

In this section, we will introduce the UniAD system and describe how a program is compiled, optimized and executed in UniAD.

The high-level architecture of UniAD is illustrated in Figure 3. UniAD deploys a relational data model. User data is structured as a collection of tables and stored in the underlying storage. UniAD also allows users to create indexes if needed, and stores the information about tables and indexes in the catalog.

The language provided by UniAD is similar to those procedural languages in modern databases which are extensions to the SQL language. But UniAD differs from these databases which only provide execution for SQL queries, in that UniAD provides unified execution of user programs.

When a user program is passed to UniAD, it is parsed by the compiler. To enable further optimizations, the compiler translates the SQL queries in the program into HOQs. For example, the code fragment in Figure 1 is translated into the following UniQL code:

```
LOOP @d_id FROM 0 TO N
  ACCESS order WHERE d_id = @d_id
    @o_id_list[@d_id].append(o_id);
```

Details of program translation will be described in Section 4.

Program analysis is also applied to the translated program and the output of the compilation is a directed cyclic graph. An example of the graph is illustrated in Figure 4. Nodes in the graph are statements to be executed and edges show the dependency between these nodes. There are three types of nodes in the graph, namely basic blocks, HOQs and loops. They are represented by B, Q and L in the graph respectively. Branches are translated into conditions in the edges.

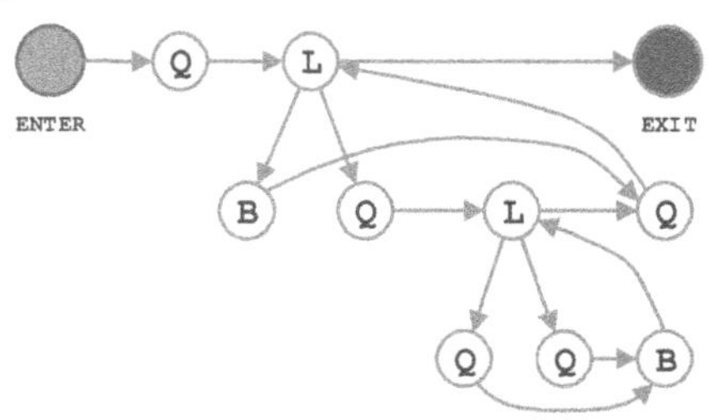

Figure 4: An execution plan graph

The graph represents an execution plan for the program. It is different from a control flow graph as we allow more than one node to be executed simultaneously. A node can not be executed until all nodes directed to it have completed their execution. Loop nodes are handled as a special case since they lead to cyclic dependencies in the graph. The nodes directing to a loop node can be divided into two categories according to whether they are inside the loop's body or not. If a node is outside the loop's body, the loop node cannot be executed until the node finishes its execution. But once the loop node has started its execution, it will not depend on the node any more. It will be re-executed when all the nodes inside its loop body have finished their execution.

The optimizer in UniAD is invoked to find a better execution plan for the program. The optimizer consists of a set of transformation rules. UniAD deploys a greedy heuristic optimization algorithm, which examines the execution plan graph iteratively and performs a transformation on the graph if the transformation rule's condition is satisfied. The optimizer stops when it cannot find any further optimization opportunities. For example, realizing that the above code fragment has to scan the table repeatedly, the optimizer will interchange the HOQ and loop, and generate the following HOQ:

```
ACCESS order
  LOOP @d_id FROM 0 TO N
    IF(d_id == @d_id)
      @o_id_list[@d_id].append(o_id);
```

Since the HOQ can be executed by scanning the table once, the performance of the original code fragment is improved. We will introduce the transformation rules used in UniAD in Section 5.

After the execution plan for the program is generated, an executor responsible for the program's execution will be created. Each executor consists of a set of worker threads and operations in the execution plan will be executed by these workers. The executor maintains a task queue which contains all nodes that can be executed. At the beginning, only the program's enter node is put in the task queue. Each idle worker picks a task from the task queue and executes the task. To utilize the data parallelism, data is partitioned and assigned to different workers. HOQs will be decomposed into a set of instances and executed by corresponding workers.

When a task is completed, the worker examines all the nodes directly connected to the task. A node will be put in the task queue if all the nodes connected to it have completed their execution. The execution of the program is completed when the program's exit node is executed.

4. PROGRAM TRANSLATION

When a user program is passed to the compiler, SQL queries in the program are translated into HOQs. We mainly focus on SQL queries with standard SQL features such as selection, projection, join, aggregation, sorting and from clause subqueries. To preserve the efficiency brought by query optimization, UniAD uses an embedded query optimizer to generate an optimal execution plan for each SQL query in the program and translates queries into HOQs according to their execution plans.

The execution plan for an SQL query is usually expressed as a query plan tree (QPT). Each node in the QPT represents an operator needed to execute the query along with the method to implement the operator. Each SQL query can be translated into HOQs by traversing its QPT in post order and converting each visited operator according to the operator's implementation method.

```
SELECT SUM(l_extendedprice)/7.0 INTO @sum_price
FROM lineitem, part,
    (SELECT l_pkey AS aq_pkey,
            0.2*AVG(l_quan) AS aq_quan
    FROM lineitem
    GROUP BY l_pkey) AS avgquantity
WHERE p_brand = 'BRAND#1'
AND p_container = 'LG CASE'
AND p_pkey = l_pkey
AND p_pkey = aq_pkey
AND l_quan < aq_quan;
```

The above SQL query is a variation of TPC-H Q17 which contains rich SQL features, and we use it as an example to illustrate the translation. The QPT for the query is illustrated in Figure 5 while the generated code fragment is illustrated in Figure 6.

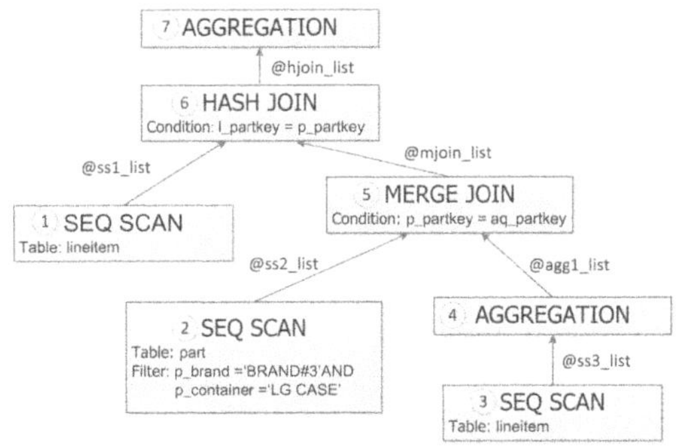

Figure 5: A query plan tree

```
/*NODE 1: Generated HOQ to scan the table*/
ACCESS lineitem
  @ss1_list.append(MAKE_TUPLE(l_pkey, l_quan, ...));

/*NODE 2: Generated HOQ to scan the table*/
ACCESS part
WHERE p_brand = 'BRAND#1'
  AND p_container = 'LG CASE' {
  @ss2_list.append(p_pkey);
}

/*NODE 3: Generated HOQ to scan the table*/
ACCESS lineitem
  @ss3_list.append(MAKE_TUPLE(l_pkey, l_quan));

/*NODE 4: Generated code to perform aggregation*/
@agg1_list = ... @ss3_list ... ;

/*NODE 5: Generated code to perform merge join*/
@mjoin_list = ...@ss2_list...@agg1_list...;

/*NODE 6: Generated code to perform hash join*/
@hjoin_list = ...@ss1_list...@mjoin_list...;

/*NODE 7: Generated code to perform aggregation*/
@sum_price = ...@hjoin_list...;
```

Figure 6: Generated code fragment

Each node in the QPT is labeled with the sequence number of the visit in post order iteration. Except for the root node, all other nodes in the QPT have a parent node. Each node's output is fed as input to the parent node. We format both input and output of each node as lists of tuples and use local variables to store these intermediate results. For example, we store the tuples selected by Node 1 into $@ss1\_list$, which is then used by Node 6 to produce $@hjoin\_list$.

There are three leaf nodes in the QPT and they are all scan nodes. A HOQ will be constructed for each of them by putting the scan node's predicate in the selector and creating necessary statements in the processor. Other nodes in the QPT are internal nodes and necessary procedural code will be generated to implement these nodes' functionality. UniAD maintains a set of code templates and each operator will be translated into procedural code according to the method selected by the query optimizer.

A code template for merge join operators is illustrated in Figure 7, which contains five parameters. #ListA and #ListB are two tuple lists to perform join; #ExprA and #ExprB are expressions in the join condition, and #OutputList is the result list. To translate the operator defined in Node 5, we will pass necessary arguments to the template and generate code.

The translation is in essence similar to query rewriting in databases. Our method resembles the ones proposed in [17, 21], but we focus on high-level execution semantics. We attempt to keep the translation process as simple as possible and do not take the data and instruction locality into consideration. The complexity of the

```
MergeJoin<#ListA, #ExprA, #ListB, #ExprB, #OutputList>
  SORT #ListA ON #ExprA
  SORT #ListB ON #ExprB
  LOOP @i FROM 0 TO #ListA.size()
    LOOP @j FROM 0 TO #ListB.size()
      IF(#ExprA < #ExprB)
        @i++;
      ELSE IF(#ExprA > #ExprB)
        @j++;
      ELSE {
         #OutputList.append(MAKE_TUPLE(...));
         @i++;
         @j++;
      }
```

Figure 7: A code template for merge join operator

translation is $O(N)$ where N is the number of relational operators in the program. As the number of relational operators is limited in a given program, the translation overhead is considered proportional to the code size. The code size is generally orders of magnitude less than the data size, and hence the translation overhead is negligible. Some intermediate variables and inefficient code will be introduced by the translation, but they will not degrade the overall performance as the optimizer can eliminate this inefficient code at a later stage in our system.

5. OPTIMIZATION

In this section, we present the details of the optimizations performed in UniAD. We focus on those optimizations across the boundary between the procedural and declarative parts. These optimizations share similar ideas to some techniques in program compilation and query optimization, which however cannot be directly applied to user programs in UniAD.

We begin with the introduction of our optimizations, using an example to illustrate the transformation and its benefits. We then discuss the prerequisites for the rules that are necessary to ensure that a program's results are consistent. To ensure the correctness, we reduce our transformations to other transformations that are well-studied in the program analysis field. By applying data dependency analysis [16] to programs, we check each transformation's validity before it is performed. Finally, a formal specification of the optimization rule and required preconditions are given.

5.1 Preliminary Notation

Before we introduce our transformation rules, we shall first describe the symbols we use in the rules.

An ordered list $\mathcal{B} = [\mathtt{s}_1, \mathtt{s}_2, ..., \mathtt{s}_n]$ is used to express a list of statements in sequence. The operator $\odot$ is used to concatenate two statement lists. Suppose $\mathcal{B}_1 = [\mathtt{s}_1, \mathtt{s}_2, ..., \mathtt{s}_n], \mathcal{B}_2 = [\mathtt{t}_1, \mathtt{t}_2, ..., \mathtt{t}_m]$, then $\mathcal{B}_1 \odot \mathcal{B}_2 = [\mathtt{s}_1, \mathtt{s}_2, ..., \mathtt{s}_n, \mathtt{t}_1, \mathtt{t}_2, ..., \mathtt{t}_m]$.

$\mathtt{s}_{[a/b]}$ is used to express the statement produced by replacing all variables named a in statement s by b.

There are four types of statements in translated programs, namely assignments, loops, branches and HOQs.

Assignments are statements assigning expressions to variables. We use *Assign(*v*,* E*)* to express the statement of the form $v = \mathsf{E}$.

Branches are statements with conditions. We use *Branch(*C*,* $\mathcal{B}$*)* to express a statement of the form ***if*** C ***do*** $\mathcal{B}$, where C is the condition expression and $\mathcal{B}$ contains the statements to be executed when the condition holds.

Loops are statements executed repeatedly. We use *Loop(*I*,* $\mathcal{B}$*)* to express a loop of the form ***foreach*** i ***in*** I ***do*** $\mathcal{B}$, where I is the iterator space and $\mathcal{B}$ contains the statements executed in each iteration.

HOQs of the form ***access*** S ***do*** $\mathcal{P}$ are expressed by *HOQ(*S*,* $\mathcal{P}$*)* where S is the selector to filter tuples and $\mathcal{P}$ contains the statements in the HOQ's processor.

5.2 Extracting Conditions

Predicates in a HOQ's selector indicate the tuples to be processed by the HOQ. If only on a subset of selected tuples are processed by the HOQ, it is, of course, inefficient to fetch unused tuples.

Consider the following code fragment:

```
ACCESS order
  IF(w_id == 30)
    @cost += price;
```

As no predicate is given in the HOQ's selector, the selector has to scan the entire table sequentially and select all tuples in the table. Note that the statement '$@cost+=price$' is executed only when the accessed tuple's attribute w_id is 30. If there is an index built on the attribute w_id, redundant tuple accesses can be eliminated by fetching tuples from the index with the condition in the branch statement. Therefore, the following HOQ is more efficient than the above one:

```
ACCESS order WHERE w_id = 30
    @cost += price;
```

The condition '$w\_id == 30$' is now put in the selector and it is extracted from the common condition of branch statements in the processor. The transformation is analogous to *predicate pushdown* in query optimization while viewed in the program optimization, it is another form of *loop-invariant code motion*. To preserve the semantics, the extracted common condition should be loop-invariant in the HOQ.

The transformation rule can be formalized as follows:

RULE 1 (EXTRACT CONDITIONS). *Suppose* q *=* *HOQ(*S*,* $\mathcal{P}$*)* *is a HOQ,* $\mathcal{P} = [Branch(\mathsf{C}_i, \mathcal{B}_i)]$ *and* $\mathsf{CC} = \bigcup \mathsf{C}_i$*.* q *can be transformed to* q' *=* *HOQ(*S'*,* $\mathcal{P}'$*), where* $\mathsf{S}' = \mathsf{S} \cap \mathsf{CC}$ *and* $\mathcal{P}' = [Branch(\mathsf{C}_i, \mathcal{B}_i)]$ *if* CC *is loop-invariant in the HOQ.*

The condition of the branch statement can be eliminated if it's a subset of the condition in the selector.

5.3 Fusing HOQs and Loops

Many programs use sequential loops to examine the tuples produced by declarative queries and perform computation on these tuples one tuple at a time. We can combine the computation performed in the loop with the HOQ and replace the loop and the HOQ with a new HOQ.

The transformation is a very useful optimization in UniAD. In combination with *dead code elimination*, the transformation can help us remove useless intermediate variables which are introduced in the translation. Another benefit brought about by the transformation is that by attaching the computation to selected tuples, it is possible for us to perform more computation in situ and in parallel. Besides, the transformation binds the computation with the corresponding data and shields the processing details performed on the data. As we will see in the later section, the transformation can help us focus on the selected data and find more opportunities for optimization.

As each HOQ can be viewed as a loop, the transformation is essentially loop fusion or function composition. It is not always safe to fuse a HOQ and a loop, dependencies in both the HOQ and loop have to be examined. Note that the order in which a HOQ is iterated is not preserved, we enhance the requirement by prohibiting any loop fusion which will lead to loop-carried dependencies in the combined HOQ. With such a requirement, no loop-carried dependencies will exist in the HOQ then the HOQ can be executed in parallel safely.

The requirement that no loop-carried dependencies are allowed in the HOQ is too rigid and as a consequence we will miss many opportunities for transformation. The requirement can be relaxed if loop-carried dependencies are caused by commutative operators.

Commutative operators can produce identical results regardless of the order they are executed. We notice that commutative operators are common in programs, so it is necessary to provide parallel execution for these operators. UniAD predefines a set of commutative operators, such as append and addequal. We can execute these operators in parallel to get partial results and merge partial results to get a final result.

The transformation rule can be formally specified as follows:

RULE 2 (FUSE HOQS AND LOOPS). *Suppose* q = *HOQ*(S, $\mathcal{P}$) *is a HOQ,* l = *Loop*(I, $\mathcal{B}$) *is a loop.* $[\,q, l\,]$ *can be transformed to* $[q'] = [\,HOQ(\mathsf{S}, \mathcal{P}')\,]$, *where* $\mathcal{P}' = \mathcal{P} \odot \mathcal{B}$, *if the following conditions are satisfied:*

- *There exists a one-to-one producer-consumer relationship between q and l.*
- *All dependencies in q' are caused by commutative operators.*

A special case of the transformation is that the output of a HOQ is only one tuple. In such a case, we can also put all statements consuming the output into the HOQ.

5.4 Merging HOQs

Multiple Query Optimization (MQO) [26] is an efficient method to improve program performance by sharing common intermediate results and eliminating redundant tuple accesses. However, we observe that opportunities to perform MQO are often limited in practice.

Consider the following code fragment. It is selected from a transaction in TPC-C named $NewOrder$.

```
SELECT s_quantity INTO @s_quantity
FROM Stock
WHERE s_i_id = @ol_i_id
AND s_w_id = @ol_supply_w_id;

IF(@s_quantity > @ol_quantity)
  @s_quantity = @s_quantity - @ol_quantity;
ELSE
  @s_quantity = @s_quantity - @ol_quantity + 91;

UPDATE Stock
SET s_quantity TO @s_quantity
WHERE s_i_id = @ol_i_id
AND s_w_id = @ol_supply_w_id;
```

The program first retrieves the item's quantity from table $stock$ and stores the value into $@s\_quantity$. After $@s\_quantity$'s value is computed in the branch statement, $@s\_quantity$'s value is written back to the tuple's field $s\_quantity$ by the update statement. Both the SELECT and UPDATE statements have to probe the table to fetch selected tuples. Given that they actually access the same tuples, it's inefficient to select the tuples twice. MQO can't be directly used to merge these queries and reduce the redundant table access because MQO cannot deal with the procedural code.

By translating SQL queries into HOQs, it is easier for us to merge the queries. We find that the branch statement can be fused with the first HOQ as it is a consumer of the HOQ. After applying Rule 2, we get the following code fragment:

```
ACCESS Stock
WHERE s_i_id = @ol_i_id
AND s_w_id = @ol_supply_w_id {
  @s_quantity = s_quantity;
  IF(@s_quantity > @ol_quantity)
    @s_quantity = @s_quantity - @ol_quantity;
  ELSE
    @s_quantity = @s_quantity - @ol_quantity + 91;
}
ACCESS Stock
WHERE s_i_id = @ol_i_id
AND s_w_id = @ol_supply_w_id {
  s_quantity = @s_quantity;
}
```

As the two HOQs have the same selector, it is clear that the two HOQs operate on the same set of tuples. We can combine them by simply putting statements in their processors together. We get the following code fragment:

```
ACCESS Stock
WHERE s_i_id = @ol_i_id
AND s_w_id = @ol_supply_w_id {
  @s_quantity = s_quantity;
  IF(@s_quantity > @ol_quantity)
    @s_quantity = @s_quantity - @ol_quantity;
  ELSE
    @s_quantity = @s_quantity - @ol_quantity + 91;
  s_quantity = @s_quantity;
}
```

Compared with the original code fragment which has to fetch the tuples twice, the above HOQ can be executed by fetching the tuples only once.

We can generalize the transformation by allowing the merging of any two HOQs that access a common subset of tuples. Branches should be added to make the combined HOQ perform properly. Given that merging two HOQs is another form of loop fusion, examinations needed for loop fusion are also required here. The transformation rule can be formulated as follows:

RULE 3 (MERGE HOQS). *Given two HOQs* q_1 = *HOQ*(S_1, $\mathcal{P}_1$) *and* q_2 = *HOQ*(S_2, $\mathcal{P}_2$), $[\,q_1, q_2\,]$ *can be transformed to* $[q = HOQ(\mathsf{S}, \mathcal{P})]$ *where* $\mathsf{S} = \mathsf{S}_1 \cup \mathsf{S}_2$ *and P* = [*Branch*(S_1, $\mathcal{P}_1$), *Branch*(S_2, $\mathcal{P}_2$)] *if the following conditions are satisfied:*

- S *is loop-invariant in both* q_1 *and* q_2.
- *All loop-carried dependencies in q are caused by commutative operators.*

5.5 Prefetching Results

Prefetching is an efficient method to reduce program latency. UniAD's optimizer utilizes prefetching to reduce unnecessary waits in programs when two HOQs can be executed simultaneously.

Consider the following code fragment:

```
Q1: ACCESS customer WHERE c_name = @c_name
      @c_id = c_id;
    IF(@c_id == 0)
Q2:   ACCESS frequentflyer WHERE ff_name = @c_name
        @c_id = ff_c_id;
```

The code fragment retrieves a customer's id by its name. It first probes the table $customer$ to find the customer's id. If the customer's id is not found in the table $customer$, it then proceeds to probe the table $frequentflyer$.

In the above code fragment, Q2 cannot be executed until Q1's result is returned. When the condition in the branch statement is satisfied, we have to scan table $customer$ and $frequentflyer$ in sequence. The program latency is $t_1 + t_2$, where t_1 and t_2 are the time to execute Q1 and Q2 respectively.

As the execution of Q2 does not depend on Q1's result, we can execute Q2 speculatively and use an variable to prefetch Q2's result. If the condition in the branch statement is satisfied, we will use the prefetched result, without probing the table $frequentflyer$ again.

The following is the transformed code fragment:

```
ACCESS customer WHERE c_name = @c_name
  @c_id = c_id;
ACCESS frequentflyer WHERE ff_name = @c_name
  @prefetch_c_id = ff_c_id;
IF(@c_id == 0)
  @c_id = @prefetch_c_id;
```

Since the two HOQs can be executed simultaneously, the program latency of the above code fragment is $\max(t_1, t_2)$, which is less than the original one.

We use $def(\mathcal{B})$ to refer to the variables defined in the statement list $\mathcal{B}$. Then the formal transformation rule is given as follows:

RULE 4 (PREFETCH RESULT). *Given two HOQs* $q_1 = HOQ(\mathsf{S}_1, \mathcal{P}_1)$ *and* $q_2 = HOQ(\mathsf{S}_2, \mathcal{P}_2)$*, a branch* $b = Branch(\mathsf{C}, [\, q_2 \,])$. $[q_1, b]$ *can be transformed to* $[q_1] \odot \mathcal{B}_1 \odot [q_2'] \odot \mathcal{B}_2$*, where* $\mathcal{B}_1 = [Assign(v', v)]$, $q_2' = HOQ(\mathsf{S}_2, [\, \mathsf{s}_{[v/v']} \mid \mathsf{s} \in \mathcal{P}_2 \wedge v \in def(\mathcal{P}_2) \,])$, $\mathcal{B}_2 = [\, Branch\,(\, \mathsf{C}, [\, Assign(v, v') \mid v \in def(\mathcal{P}_2) \,]\,)\,]$ *if* q_2 *can be executed simultaneously with* q_1.

The transformation may lead to unnecessary execution when the branch statement's condition is not satisfied. In practice, we only choose to apply the transformation when the speculatively executed HOQ can be merged with previous HOQs.

5.6 Interchanging Loop and HOQ

Recall the code fragment in Figure 1. By translating the SQL query into a HOQ, we get the following code fragment:

```
LOOP @d_id FROM 0 TO N
  ACCESS order WHERE d_id = @d_id
    @order_list[@d_id].append(o_id);
```

If there is no index built on the attribute *d_id*, the executor will sequentially scan the table at each iteration of the loop. The redundant table scans will degrade the performance significantly. Given that the HOQ is logically also a loop, we can interchange the HOQ and the loop and get the following code fragment:

```
ACCESS order
  LOOP @d_id FROM 0 TO N
    IF(d_id == @d_id)
      @order_list[@d_id].append(o_id);
```

The loop now is nested in the HOQ. Though the complexity of the code fragment is unchanged, the above code fragment eliminates the redundant table scans and can be executed with only one table scan.

As in the case of program optimization, loop interchange may reorder the endpoints of a dependency, which will lead to an invalid transformation. We should check the dependencies in the loop and ensure the safety of the transformation.

The transformation can be specified as follows:

RULE 5 (INTERCHANGE HOQS AND LOOPS). *Suppose* $l = Loop(\mathsf{l}, [q])$ *is a loop and* $q = HOQ(\mathsf{S}, \mathcal{P})$ *is a HOQ.* l *can be transformed into* $q' = HOQ(\emptyset, [l'])$*, where* $l' = Loop(\mathsf{l}, Branch(\mathsf{S}, \mathcal{P}))$ *if the following conditions are satisfied:*

- *No indexes are available for* S.
- *Endpoints of all dependencies in* q *are not reordered in* l'.

5.7 Flattening Nested Loops

Though Rule 5 provides a transformation to optimize the code fragment in Figure 1, we can execute the code fragment more efficiently.

We begin with the code fragment in Figure 1. Due to the logical equivalence of HOQs and loops, we can express the HOQ nested in the loop in the loop format:

```
LOOP @d_id FROM 0 TO N
  FOREACH t IN order
    IF(t.d_id == @d_id)
S:    @order_list<@d_id>.append(t.o_id);
```

The value of field *o_id* is fetched in S if the branch statement's condition is satisfied. Using the idea described in Section 5.5, we can speculatively prefetch the field's value into a hash map and assign the value in the map to $@order\_list[@d\_id]$. Then we get:

```
LOOP @d_id FROM 0 TO N
  FOREACH t IN order
    @o_id_map<t.d_id>.append(t.o_id);
    IF(t.d_id == @d_id)
      @order_list[@d_id] = @o_id_map<@d_id>;
```

Note that we store the value in $@o\_id\_map < t.d\_id >$ but access the value by $@o\_id\_map < @d\_id >$. It is allowed as we only access the value when $t.d\_id == @d\_id$.

As there does not exist any cycle of dependencies in the loop on table *order*, we can split the loop and get the following code fragment:

```
    LOOP @d_id FROM 0 TO N
L1:   FOREACH t IN order
        @o_id_map<t.d_id>.append(t.o_id);
L2:   FOREACH t IN order
        IF(t.d_id == @d_id)
          @order_list[@d_id] = @o_id_map<@d_id>;
```

The loop on table *order* now splits into two loops inside the outer loop, namely L1 and L2. The variables inside L1 are all invariant in the outer loop, hence we can put L1 outside the outer loop. The branch statement inside L2 is also invariant in L2, we can directly remove L2. Finally, we get the following code fragment:

```
ACCESS order
  @o_id_map<d_id>.append(o_id);
LOOP @d_id FROM 0 TO N
  @order_list[@d_id] = @o_id_map<@d_id>;
```

Both the original code fragment and the code fragment optimized by Rule 5 contain nested loops and their complexity is $O(N*M)$ if the table's size is M. If $@o\_id\_map$ is a hash map, both insert and search operations on the map are performed in $O(1)$ generally. The complexity of the code fragment above is $O(max(M, N))$, which is much better than both of its counterparts.

This transformation rule provides a more efficient optimization on programs than Rule 5, but it is limited as it can only deal with HOQs with equality predicates. It can be easily understood when explained in the context of joins. The original code fragment actually implements an *equi-join* between a temporary table $\{@d\_id\}$ and the table *order* using *nested loop join*. The intuition behind the transformation is that we choose to implement the equi-join using *hash join* instead.

Both loop fission and loop-invariant code motion are used in the transformation. Their safety will be taken into consideration when the transformation is applied. To split the loop on table *order*, the statements in the HOQ should not contain any cycles of dependencies. Besides, both the variable $@order\_list[@d\_id]$ and the expression $@d\_id$ should also be invariant in the loop on table *order*. Otherwise, we cannot delete the loop L2.

The transformation can be described as follows:

RULE 6 (FLATTEN NESTED LOOPS). *Suppose* $l = Loop(\mathsf{l}, [q])$ *is a loop and* $q = HOQ(c\text{=}\mathsf{e}, \mathcal{P})$ *is a HOQ,* v *is a variable defined in* $\mathcal{P}$ *and* c *is a column .* $[l]$ *can be transformed into* $[\, q', l' \,]$ *where* $q' = HOQ(\emptyset, \{\mathsf{s}_{[v/map<c>]} | \mathsf{s} \in \mathcal{P}\})$ *and* $l' = Loop(\mathsf{l}, [Assign(v, map<\mathsf{e}>)])$*, if the following conditions are satisfied:*

- *No indexes are available for* $c = \mathsf{e}$.
- *There is no cycle of dependencies in* $\mathcal{P}$.
- v *and* e *are loop-invariant in* q.

6. IMPLEMENTATION DETAILS

In this section, we will discuss some practical issues in the system implementation and introduce our methods for addressing these issues.

6.1 Heap Synchronization

When a HOQ is executed in parallel, the HOQ will be sent to all corresponding worker threads and an instance of the HOQ will be executed in each worker thread.

In UniAD, each program's heap is shared among all worker threads executing the program. As a HOQ can access free variables that are defined outside their lexical scope, worker threads might access shared data simultaneously when executing the HOQ. Though data dependency analysis ensures that the operations performed on the data do not conflict with each other, contention is still possible in practice. The contention may arise from the explicit updates on a loop iterator or implicitly when an element is inserted into a map.

One method to address the problem is to use a fine-grained locking mechanism to ensure strictly exclusive access to shared data. But this method is too costly and performance might be harmed. It also reduces the parallelism as threads might be queued when performing updates on shared data.

Another method to solve the problem, which is borrowed from many programming languages that support closures, is to create a referencing environment for each executing instance of the HOQ and copy all variables into the environment which the HOQ instance will use in the execution. By doing this, the execution of each instance is completely independent as their heaps are separated. This method requires an accurate analysis of the free variables used in the execution to avoid unnecessary data copies. It is not trivial as the data that an instance will access cannot be easily known before it is executed.

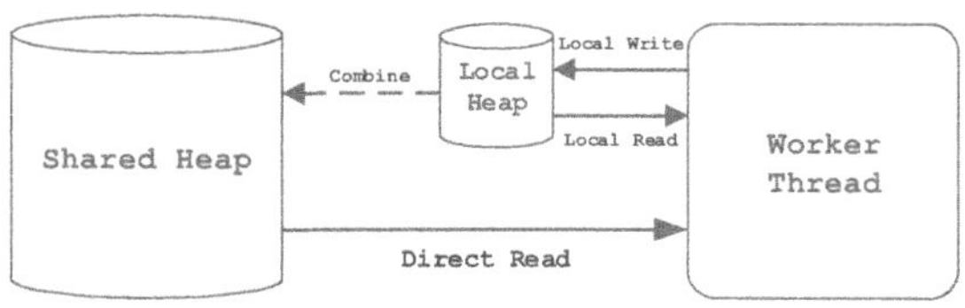

Figure 8: Heap synchronization

UniAD adopts the idea of contention detection proposed in [5], and modifies it to avoid contention between different threads in our implementation. The method is illustrated in Figure 8.

We create a local heap for each worker thread. When the worker thread needs to read a variable's value, it first probes the value in its local heap. If the variable does not reside in the local heap, then the worker proceeds to probe it from the shared heap. Recall that each instance of the same HOQ does not rely on the outputs of other instances, outputs of the worker thread will be buffered in its local heap. After all instances of the HOQ are completed, their outputs will be pulled out from local heaps and merged into the shared heap. Additional computation will be needed for those variables whose values are produced by commutative operators.

6.2 Consistent Execution

UniAD allows different programs executing concurrently by deploying the two-phase locking (2PL) protocol. Each program performs as a transaction in a database. Before accessing a tuple, the program must hold the locks associated with it and held locks are released when the program completes its execution. The locking protocol can solve the problem of synchronizing access to shared data, but inconsistent execution may still happen in UniAD.

Consider the following HOQ:

```
ACCESS item WHERE quantity < @threshold
  quantity -= @delta;
```

For each tuple whose $quantity$ is less than $@threshold$, its value of $quantity$ is subtracted by $@delta$. Suppose tuples are fetched using a B^+-Tree index built on the attribute $quantity$. As the tuple's entry in the index will also be updated when its value of $quantity$ is updated, a tuple might be revisited and be fetched more than once, which will lead to incorrect results.

Concurrency control mechanisms, including the locking protocol, do not help solve the problem as the problem is not caused by concurrent accesses of different programs. The problem is due to the inconsistent snapshots seen at each iteration of the HOQ. During the execution of a HOQ, the HOQ's processor will be invoked each time a qualified tuple is selected. Each qualified tuple should be selected only once in the execution. But the updates performed in the processor may violate the requirement.

The problem is similar to the problem caused by performing updates within a *sensitive cursor* in stored procedures. Most databases solve it by materializing the set of data used for the cursor and storing the entire set in a temporary table. It is not efficient if a large number of tuples are fetched.

UniAD solves the problem by storing multiple versions of the same tuple. In UniAD, each tuple has a version number TV. UniAD maintains a number CV to record the number of writes which have been processed. When an update is performed on a tuple, a new version of the tuple will be created. The value of CV is incremented and its value will be used as the new tuple's TV. When a HOQ is to be executed, it first gets the current value of CV and stores it into QV. Only those tuples whose TV is less than the HOQ's QV are visible to the HOQ. Since those tuples produced during the HOQ's execution must have a larger TV than the HOQ's QV, they will not be processed by the HOQ.

The mechanism is similar to a timestamp-based implementation of Multi-version Concurrency Control (MVCC), except in the standard implementation of MVCC, a new tuple produced by a HOQ would be visible to the program immediately. However in UniAD, the tuple cannot be seen by the program until the HOQ's execution is completed.

7. EVALUATION

In this section, we present the experimental evaluation of our UniAD system. The evaluation consists of two parts. We first evaluate the benefits brought by the optimization techniques in Section 7.1, followed by the capability of UniAD to execute the programs in parallel in Section 7.2. All the experiments are performed on a CentOS-5.5 server with 48GB RAM and two Intel E7-4807 processors, each of which contains six cores clocked at 1.86GHz.

7.1 Evaluation on Program Optimization

We first evaluate how effectively UniAD can optimize the user programs. The programs from four different benchmarks are adopted in the experiments: TPC-C [29], SEATS [27], PageRank and TF-IDF. They together represent a variety of programs for data processing, e.g., online transaction processing and data analytic applications.

For the tables in the experiments, only a unique hash index is created on the primary key by default. Accesses by the primary keys can be performed in constant time on average while other accesses have to scan the entire table. Also, to eliminate the influence of lock conflicts, only one worker thread is used to execute the programs in this set of experiments.

7.1.1 Effect on TPC-C

TPC-C models an order processing system and consists of five short-running transactions. We implement these transactions according to the sample programs in [29] and use them in our experiments. We compare the performance of the original and the optimized execution plans for each transaction by measuring the transaction's average latency at different scale factors. Note that, the execution time of an optimized program includes the code translation cost which is negligible compared with overall latency. The total size of tables on disk is about 70MB per scale factor.

The latency of each transaction while varying the number of warehouses is shown in Figure 9. The results illustrate that three of the five transactions, namely New Order, Payment and Delivery, benefit from the optimization of UniAD significantly. Not surprisingly, the performances of transactions Stock Level and Order Sta-

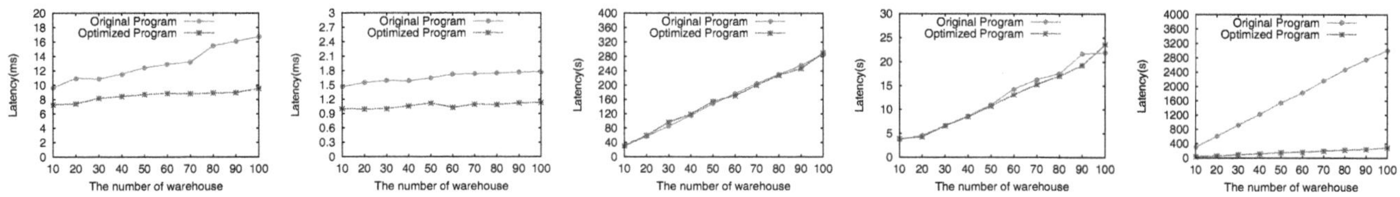

(a) New Order (b) Payment (c) Stock Level (d) Order Status (e) Delivery

Figure 9: Performance of transactions in TPC-C

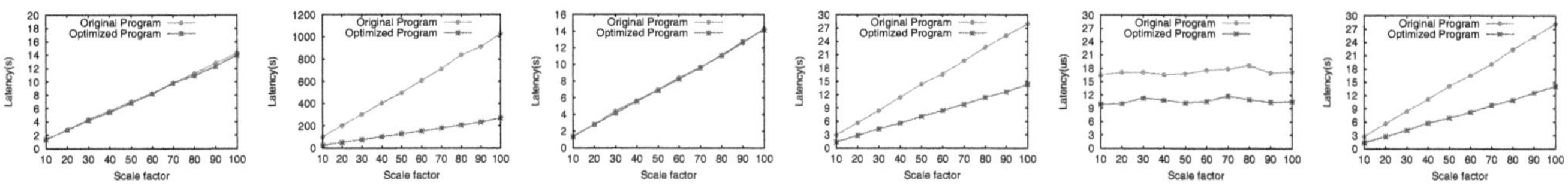

(a) Delete Reservation (b) Find Flight (c) Find Open Seat (d) New Reservation (e) Update Customer (f) Update Reservation

Figure 10: Performance of transactions in SEATS

tus are comparable, because these two transactions are quite simple without much optimization space, e.g., Order Status transactions include table scans nested in the loop but they access the table *orderline* by primary keys.

The performances of New Order and Payment transactions are improved by the reduction of tuple accesses. Both of them include updates to a small number of keys in the system. To update a tuple, the transaction first extracts the tuple's value from the table, computes its new value and updates the tuple with the new value. As the select and update statements are executed separately, two index accesses are needed to perform an update. By applying Rule 3, UniAD can merge the operations performed on the same tuple and the number of I/O operations is reduced.

The performance of Delivery transactions is significantly improved by avoiding the table scan nested in a loop. The Delivery transactions use a loop to process a batch of orders and some statements inside the loop access the table using partial keys. As only a hash index is built for each table in the experiment and the hash index does not support searches by the partial keys, sequential table scans are needed to execute these statements. By applying Rule 5, UniAD can share common table scans and Figure 9(e) shows that the optimized program yields remarkable improvement.

The results are quite interesting as TPC-C transactions are written by database experts. However, Delivery transactions exhibit poor performance when no indexes are available. It implies that even for those experts in data processing, without knowledge of the underlying storage, may also write programs which exhibit poor performance in practice. It is impractical for the programmers to write different programs for different data sets, and hence an automatic program optimization method is highly preferred.

7.1.2 *Effect on SEATS*

SEATS is an open source workload from the well-known H-Store project. It models an airline ticketing system and has been widely applied recently [9]. There are six transactions in the workload, namely Delete Reservation, Find Flight, Find Open Seat, New Reservation, Update Customer and Update Reservation. A data set generated by the standard utility is used in the experiments and the size of tables on disk is about 130MB per scale factor.

Figure 10 shows the effect on the performance of unoptimized and optimized programs by varying the scale factor. The result shows that UniAD is able to find optimization opportunities for five of the six transactions and significantly improve the performance of four transactions.

To update a customer's information, the Update Customer transaction has to probe the table customer first. The unoptimized transaction has to read two tuples and update one tuple. By merging the two table scans on the table *customer*, the optimized program is able to perform the update without another table scan. As a result, only two tuple fetches are needed and the latency of Update Customer transactions is reduced to about 2/3 of the original latency.

For New Reservation and Update Reservation transactions, UniAD achieves a 2x speedup over the unoptimized programs. A New Reservation transaction reserves an empty seat for a customer while an Update Reservation transaction updates a customer's seat to a new one. To ensure correctness, both transactions have to check whether (1) the required seat is available and (2) the customer does not have another seat on the flight. These conditions are checked in sequence — the second condition is checked only if the first condition is satisfied. The unoptimized programs hence have to scan the table *reservation* twice. UniAD observes that the second condition can be checked together with the first one. By applying Rule 4 and Rule 3, UniAD can check the conditions simultaneously and thus eliminate the redundant table scan.

The Find Flight transaction finds available flights between two cities. The transaction first gets the nearby airports for the departure and arrival cities and then iterates over the nearby airports to find available flights. Given a nearby airport, a sequential table scan on the table *flight* is needed to find available flights. Similar to Delivery transactions, the performance of Find Flight transactions is degraded by the nested table scan. UniAD can eliminate the nested table scan and hence improve the performance.

UniAD can also find optimization opportunities in Delete Reservation transactions. Table scans on the table *customer* can be merged and the number of tuples a transaction accesses is reduced. But the benefit gained from the optimization is limited. It is because Delete Reservation transactions access the table *customer* by primary keys while they have to sequentially scan the table *reservation*. In comparison with all the tuple accesses in the transactions, the tuple access we reduced is negligible.

7.1.3 *Effect on PageRank*

PageRank is a link analysis algorithm, which is used in many Web applications, and we use it as a representative of data mining programs to evaluate the effectiveness of UniAD. As PageRank cannot be easily expressed in SQL, many programmers choose to implement it in a procedural language with SQL queries. In [25], the author gave an implementation of PageRank (shown in Figure 11), which is used in our experiments.

In addition to the original program and the program optimized by the UniAD optimizer, a hand-optimized program is also used in the experiment. The hand-optimized program retrieves each node's

```
SELECT url INTO @url_list,
       score INTO @score_list
FROM page;
LOOP @i FROM 0 TO @url_list.size()
{
    SELECT from_url INTO @from_url_list
    FROM link
    WHERE to_url = @url_list[@i];

    @score = 0.15*@score_list[@i];
    LOOP @j FROM 0 to @from_url_list.size()
    {
        SELECT score INTO @from_score
        FROM page
        WHERE url = @from_url_list[@j];

        SELECT COUNT(to_url) INTO @from_cnt
        FROM link
        WHERE from_url = @from_url_list[@j];

        @score += @from_score / @from_cnt * 0.85;
    }
    UPDATE page
    SET score = @score
    WHERE url = @url_list[@i];
}
```

Figure 11: The PageRank program used in the experiment

score and outdegree at the beginning of the program, and hence the program can get each node's score and outdegree without scanning tables, which is the most optimal implementation.

Data Set	Nodes	Edges
wiki-Talk	2,394,385	5,021,410
soc-pokec	1,632,803	30,622,564
cit-Patents	3,774,768	16,518,978
web-Google	875,713	5,105,039
LiveJournal	4,847,570	68,993,773

(a) Data sets

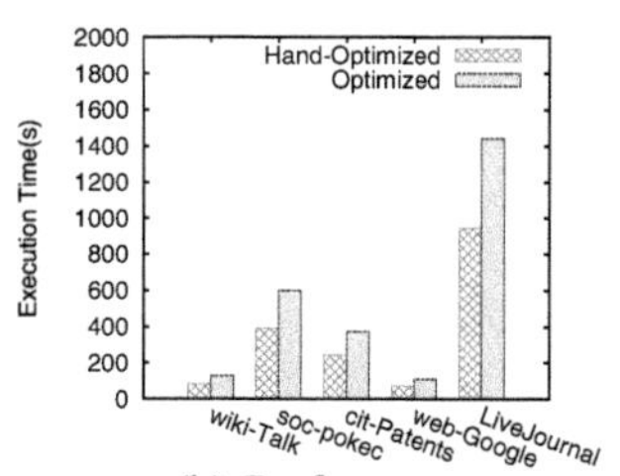

(b) Performance

Figure 12: PageRank Performance

We evaluate the performance of UniAD on the pagerank programs with various datasets, the details of which are illustrated in Figure 12(a). These data sets are downloaded from the SNAP project [1]. The results are shown in Figure 12(b). Since the execution of the original program cannot be completed in six hours on the data sets which is much slower than the other two competitors, the results of the original program are omitted in Figure 12(b) for clarity.

The main cause of the original program's poor performance is the table scans nested in the loops. For each node in the graph, the program first retrieves the nodes pointing to it using the select statement. Then for each retrieved node, the program gets its score and outdegree using the statements. The procedure is repeated for each node. As a node may point to more than one node, its score and outdegree will be retrieved repeatedly.

Rule 6, Rule 2 and Rule 3 are used to optimize the original program in UniAD. By applying Rule 6, the statements in the nested loops are moved out of the loops. After that, shared table scans and corresponding loops are combined according to Rule 2 and Rule 3. To apply Rule 6, hashing maps along with the insert and search operations are introduced in the programs. Each node's score and outdegree are stored in the maps and values in the maps are used in the following statements. It resembles the method used in the hand-optimized program to improve the performance, but it is automatically constructed by the optimizer in UniAD. Because the insert and search operations performed in maps are also introduced in UniAD, which is the cost overhead, the hand-optimized program outperforms the optimized program.

Nevertheless, although the user program is not properly written, it can be efficiently executed in UniAD, yielding a comparative performance to the hand-optimized program.

[1] http://snap.stanford.edu

```
SELECT COUNT(DISTINCT(doc_id)) INTO @doc_cnt
FROM corpus;

SELECT DISTINCT(word_id) INTO @word_list
FROM corpus;

SELECT doc_id, SUM(frequency) INTO @doc_term_freqs
FROM corpus;

LOOP @i FROM 0 TO @word_list.size() {
  @word_id = @word_list[@i];

  SELECT COUNT(doc_id) INTO @doc_freq
  FROM corpus WHERE word_id = @word_id;

  @idf = @doc_freq / @doc_cnt;

  SELECT doc_id INTO @doc_inc_word_list
  FROM corpus WHERE word_id = @word_id;

  LOOP @j FROM 0 TO @doc_inc_word_list.size() {
    @doc_id = @doc_inc_word_list[@j];

    SELECT SUM(frequency) INTO @term_freq
    FROM corpus
    WHERE doc_id = @doc_id and word_id = @word_id;

    @tf = @term_freq / @doc_term_freqs[@doc_id];
    @tfidf = @tf * @idf;
  }
}
```

Figure 13: The TF-IDF program used in the experiment

7.1.4 *Effects on TF-IDF*

Term Frequency-Inverse Document Frequency (TF-IDF) is a classic method to measure a term's relevance to a document, which is popularly used in many information retrieval systems.

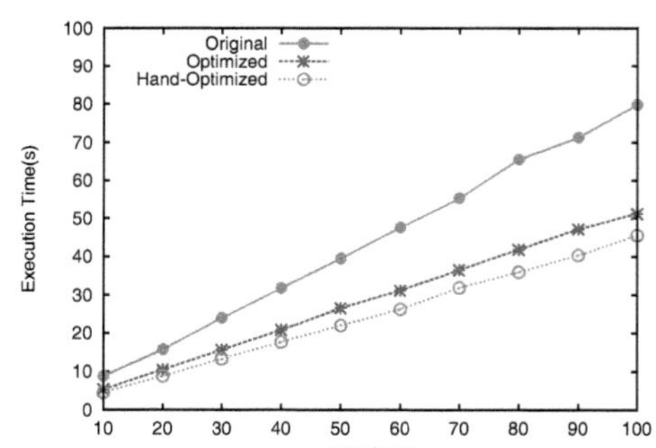

Figure 14: TF-IDF performance

In the experiment, we implement the program shown in Figure 13 to calculate the TF-IDF value of each term-document pair in the corpus. The input corpus used is randomly generated and stored in the table whose schema is $(word\_id, doc\_id, frequency)$. The number of words is fixed to 1,000 and the number of documents is 10,000 per scale factor. We also build a B^+-Tree index on the attribute *word_id*. We again measure the performances of the original program, the program optimized by UniAD and the hand-optimized program, and the results are presented in Figure 14.

Due to the existence of the index on *word_id*, the program in Figure 13 is a good implementation of the TF-IDF algorithm. But we still observe that the optimized program can achieve up to 40% performance promotion against the original one. By examining the execution plan generated by the UniAD optimizer, we find that the select statements in line 13 and line 18 are merged, which eliminates the redundant tuple accesses.

The hand-optimized program exhibits a better performance as it scans the *corpus* table to calculate each term's document frequency. As all words are listed in the *@word_list*, index accesses are thus eliminated. Our optimizer is not able to perform such optimizations as it does not know the number of words in the *@word_list*.

7.2 Evaluation on Parallelism

By analyzing the user programs, UniAD is able to extract logic computation that can be combined with data manipulation. The extracted logic computation might be executed in different worker threads simultaneously and the performance is improved by parallel processing. In this set of experiments, we evaluate the benefits gained from parallel program execution in UniAD. We vary the number of worker threads in the executor and measure the performance of PageRank and K-Means respectively.

We first run the PageRank program on the LiveJournal graph. To exploit data parallelism, the graph is partitioned into different partitions by hash partitioning. The number of partitions is equal to the number of worker threads and each partition is assigned to a worker thread. We measure the performance of PageRank with different numbers of worker threads and the results are plotted in Figure 15(a).

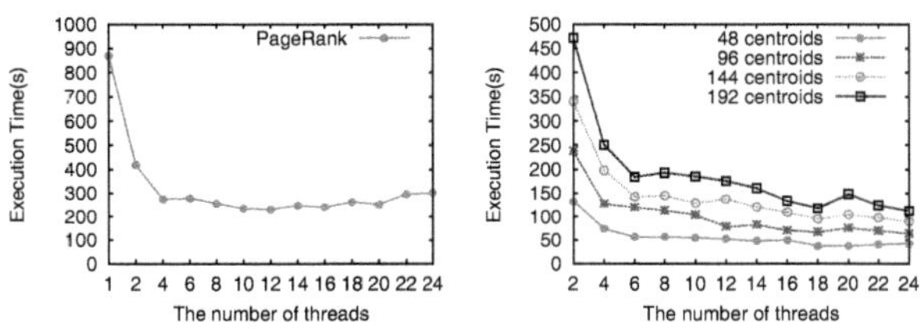

(a) PageRank (b) K-Means

Figure 15: Parallel performance

At the beginning, with the increased number of worker threads, the execution time for PageRank improves sharply. As the number of threads continues to increase, the performance remains steady and the execution time is reduced from 871s to 231s, achieving a speedup of 278%.

We evaluate K-Mean's performance with various numbers of centroids. In each step of K-Means, each node has to calculate its distance with all the centroids. The computation can be combined with the node and be executed in parallel. Thus, the amount of computation that is executed in parallel is proportional to the number of centroids. The performances of these configurations while varying the numbers of centroids are illustrated in Figure 15(b). We notice that the performance with more centroids benefits more from parallel execution. The execution time with 48 centroids can be reduced to approximate 1/3 of its original execution time while the execution time with 192 centroids is reduced to approximate 1/4.

The results exhibit that the benefits gained by parallel execution is limited by the synchronization overhead. For example, when executing a HOQ in PageRank, each node's information is gathered and written to each thread worker's local heap. When the HOQ's execution is completed, the data stored in the local heap will be flushed into the shared heap. The procedure is similar to the shuffling phase in MapReduce. As the number of worker threads increases, the amount of computation performed in each worker thread is reduced as well. However, the synchronization overhead remains the same and it finally overwhelms the benefits brought by the parallelism.

8. RELATED WORK

UniAD is closely related to many research areas including parallel data processing, programming languages, and compiler optimization. We briefly review the related work in this section.

Data processing systems. How to improve programming productivity is one of the most critical issues in computer science. Many data processing systems have been constructed to enable programmers to efficiently process data with little effort.

Relational databases have been massively successful over the past decades. Their success lies in the usage of SQL and query optimization. Users can write their tasks using SQL queries and the database can find an efficient method to execute the task. But one problem with SQL is that it is too limited to support various applications [34]. Many users have to construct very complex queries for their tasks. Object-oriented databases attempt to overcome the limitations of the relational databases by providing flexible data models and powerful development facilities, but they usually lack a suitable framework for query optimization [12, 6].

MapReduce [7] has emerged as a popular programming model for parallel data processing recently. It simplifies the development of distributed parallel applications. However, it is also criticized for its reduced functionality, considerable amount of programming efforts and lack of automatic optimization. To make MapReduce easier to use, a number of high-level languages have been developed, including Hive [28] and Pig [22].

These data processing systems all separate the execution of procedural and declarative parts in programs, which makes them fall somewhere between expressiveness brought by procedural languages and efficiency brought by declarative languages. By performing automatic optimizations across different abstractions and unifying the execution, UniAD benefits from both features of procedural and declarative programming.

Optimizations by program analysis. Some researchers proposed to apply program analysis to improve performance of data processing programs. Extracting declarative queries from imperative code has been thought to be an efficient method to improve the performance as transformed programs might benefit from the query optimization based on the relational algebra. The method is applicable for both database [19, 32, 33, 4] and MapReduce programs [14, 15]. Though these attempts try to minimize the gap between the procedural and declarative logic, the benefits they gain are limited as relational algebra is unable to match the expressiveness of procedural languages.

Other works target the applications executed in multi-tier architectures. Guravannavar et al. [13] and Cheung et al. [3] proposed different methods to reduce the overhead incurred by the communication between the applications and databases, i.e., rewrite the iteratively invoked queries into a batch form [13], and partition database programs into separate parts and execute some parts in the databases [3]. Chavan et al. [2] and Ramachandra et al. [23] studied the transformation methods to reduce the program latency by prefetching the query results.

Uniform program representation. There exist many prior studies in providing uniform intermediate representations for database programs. Some of them, such as structural recursion [1] and monoid comprehension [10], have their roots in functional programming languages. They obtain many nice properties from functional programming, e.g., they are able to abstract away detailed computation logic while retaining expressive power. But they are not suited for optimizing data processing programs as they eliminate side effects caused by I/O and shared states in programs, which makes it hard to capture the I/O efficiency of programs and limits the expression of flexible execution plans.

The other approaches include translating SQL queries into imperative code or machine code [24, 17, 21, 31, 8]. Program performance can be improved due to better data and instruction locality and the reduction of unpredictable branches. Compared with their studies, we focus on higher level optimizations and consequently we can find optimization opportunities which are ignored when programs are translated into low level code.

9. CONCLUSION

In this paper, we have presented a new system for ad-hoc data processing called UniAD. UniAD was specifically designed to simplify the programming of ad-hoc data processing tasks. Users can write their programs in procedural languages with simple queries, without the need to construct complex queries. UniAD benefits from both procedural and declarative programming by unifying the optimization and execution of user programs. We proposed a novel intermediate representation named UniQL to describe user programs. By translating user programs into HOQs, UniAD can efficiently optimize and execute user programs. We also proposed a set of optimization rules and demonstrated their efficiency through a comprehensive experimental study.

Note that, UniAD is not aimed to replace the existing data processing systems, such as Hadoop and Pregel. UniAD targets ad-hoc data processing, where the users have a relatively small set of data at hand and want to conduct a set of tests on the data immediately. UniAD frees the users from formulating their problems and thinking about the efficiency of their programs, by providing *efficient* execution for their programs even when they are *poorly* written. Once users decide to deploy a program as a standard tool, they can carefully optimize the program and run the program in a more efficient data processing system such as Hadoop.

There are several directions for future development of UniAD to provide better performance and user experience. Currently, UniAD deploys a rule-based optimizer and we would like to design a cost-based optimizer to provide more efficient optimizations. Other ongoing research involves extending the functionality of UniAD to facilitate a distributed environment.

ACKNOWLEDGEMENTS

The research is supported by the National Natural Science Foundation of China under Grant No. 61272155 and 973 program under No. 2014CB340405. Beng Chin's research is partially funded by the Singapore National Research Foundation and the publication is supported under the Campus for Research Excellence And Technological Enterprise (CREATE) programme.

10. REFERENCES

[1] V. Breazu-Tannen, P. Buneman, and S. Naqvi. Structural recursion as a query language. In *DBPL-3*, pages 9–19, 1992.

[2] M. Chavan, R. Guravannavar, K. Ramachandra, and S. Sudarshan. Program transformations for asynchronous query submission. In *ICDE '11*, pages 375–386, 2011.

[3] A. Cheung, S. Madden, O. Arden, and A. C. Myers. Automatic partitioning of database applications. *Proc. VLDB Endow.*, 5(11):1471–1482, July 2012.

[4] A. Cheung, A. Solar-Lezama, and S. Madden. Optimizing database-backed applications with query synthesis. In *PLDI '13*, pages 3–14, 2013.

[5] J. Cieslewicz, K. A. Ross, K. Satsumi, and Y. Ye. Automatic contention detection and amelioration for data-intensive operations. In *SIGMOD '10*, pages 483–494, 2010.

[6] S. Cluet and C. Delobel. A general framework for the optimization of object-oriented queries. In *SIGMOD '92*, pages 383–392, 1992.

[7] J. Dean and S. Ghemawat. MapReduce: Simplified data processing on large clusters. *Commun. ACM*, 51(1):107–113, Jan. 2008.

[8] C. Diaconu, C. Freedman, E. Ismert, P.-A. Larson, P. Mittal, R. Stonecipher, N. Verma, and M. Zwilling. Hekaton: SQL Server's memory-optimized OLTP engine. In *SIGMOD '13*, pages 1243–1254, 2013.

[9] D. E. Difallah, A. Pavlo, and P. Curino, C.and Cudré-Mauroux. Oltp-bench: An extensible testbed for benchmarking relational databases. *Proc. VLDB Endow.*, 7(4):277–288, 2013.

[10] L. Fegaras and D. Maier. Optimizing object queries using an effective calculus. *ACM Trans. Database Syst.*, 25(4):457–516, Dec. 2000.

[11] J. Gao, R. Jin, J. Zhou, J. X. Yu, X. Jiang, and T. Wang. Relational approach for shortest path discovery over large graphs. *Proc. VLDB Endow.*, 5(4):358–369, 2011.

[12] G. Graefe and D. Maier. Query optimization in object-oriented database systems: A prospectus. In *LNCS on Advances in Object-oriented Database Systems*, pages 358–363, 1988.

[13] R. Guravannavar and S. Sudarshan. Rewriting procedures for batched bindings. *Proc. VLDB Endow.*, 1(1):1107–1123, Aug. 2008.

[14] M.-Y. Iu and W. Zwaenepoel. HadoopToSQL: A MapReduce query optimizer. In *EuroSys '10*, pages 251–264, 2010.

[15] E. Jahani, M. J. Cafarella, and C. Ré. Automatic optimization for mapreduce programs. *Proc. VLDB Endow.*, 4(6):385–396, Mar. 2011.

[16] K. Kennedy and J. R. Allen. *Optimizing Compilers for Modern Architectures: A Dependence-based Approach.* Morgan Kaufmann Publishers Inc., 2002.

[17] K. Krikellas, S. Viglas, and M. Cintra. Generating code for holistic query evaluation. In *ICDE '10*, pages 613–624, 2010.

[18] R. Lämmel. Google's mapreduce programming model: Revisited. *Sci. Comput. Program.*, 68(3):208–237, 2007.

[19] D. F. Lieuwen and D. J. DeWitt. Optimizing loops in database programming languages. In *DBPL3*, pages 287–305, 1992.

[20] D. Maier. Representing database programs as objects. In *DBPL*, pages 377–386, 1987.

[21] T. Neumann. Efficiently compiling efficient query plans for modern hardware. *Proc. VLDB Endow.*, 4(9):539–550, June 2011.

[22] C. Olston, B. Reed, U. Srivastava, R. Kumar, and A. Tomkins. Pig Latin: A not-so-foreign language for data processing. In *SIGMOD '08*, pages 1099–1110, 2008.

[23] K. Ramachandra and S. Sudarshan. Holistic optimization by prefetching query results. In *SIGMOD '12*, pages 133–144, 2012.

[24] J. Rao, H. Pirahesh, C. Mohan, and G. Lohman. Compiled query execution engine using JVM. In *ICDE '06*, pages 23–23, 2006.

[25] T. Segaran. *Programming Collective Intelligence.* O'Reilly, first edition, 2007.

[26] T. K. Sellis. Multiple-query optimization. *ACM Trans. Database Syst.*, 13(1):23–52, Mar. 1988.

[27] Stonebraker, M. and Pavlo, A. SEATS benchmark. `http://hstore.cs.brown.edu/projects/seats/`.

[28] A. Thusoo, J. S. Sarma, N. Jain, Z. Shao, P. Chakka, S. Anthony, H. Liu, P. Wyckoff, and R. Murthy. Hive: A warehousing solution over a map-reduce framework. *Proc. VLDB Endow.*, 2(2):1626–1629, Aug. 2009.

[29] TPC. TPC-C benchmark. `http://www.tpc.org/tpcc/`.

[30] P. W. Trinder. Comprehensions, a query notation for dbpls. In *DBPL-3*, pages 55–68, 1992.

[31] S. D. Viglas. Just-in-time compilation for SQL query processing. *Proc. VLDB Endow.*, 6(11):1190–1191, Aug. 2013.

[32] B. Wiedermann and W. R. Cook. Extracting queries by static analysis of transparent persistence. In *POPL '07*, pages 199–210, 2007.

[33] B. Wiedermann, A. Ibrahim, and W. R. Cook. Interprocedural query extraction for transparent persistence. In *OOPSLA '08*, pages 19–36, 2008.

[34] Y. Yu, M. Isard, D. Fetterly, M. Budiu, U. Erlingsson, P. K. Gunda, and J. Currey. Dryadlinq: A system for general-purpose distributed data-parallel computing using a high-level language. In *OSDI'08*, pages 1–14, 2008.

[35] B. Zou, X. Ma, B. Kemme, G. Newton, and D. Precup. Data mining using relational database management systems. In *PAKDD'06*, pages 657–667, 2006.

Partial Results in Database Systems

Willis Lang, Rimma V. Nehme, Eric Robinson, Jeffrey F. Naughton*
Microsoft Gray Systems Lab, *University of Wisconsin
{wilang,rimman,errobins}@microsoft.com, *naughton@cs.wisc.edu

ABSTRACT

As the size and complexity of analytic data processing systems continue to grow, the effort required to mitigate faults and performance skew has also risen. However, in some environments we have encountered, users prefer to continue query execution even in the presence of failures (e.g., the unavailability of certain data sources), and receive a "partial" answer to their query. We explore ways to characterize and classify these partial results, and describe an analytical framework that allows the system to perform coarse to fine-grained analysis to determine the semantics of a partial result. We propose that if the system is equipped with such a framework, in some cases it is better to return and explain partial results than to attempt to avoid them.

1. INTRODUCTION

In this paper we consider evaluating relational queries over multiple information sources, some of which might return incomplete tuple sets. This situation could arise in a wide variety of scenarios. For example, it could arise with queries spanning a collection of loosely coupled cloud databases, if one or more of them is temporarily down or unusable (say due to network congestion or misconfigurations); we may also see it with queries in a traditional parallel RDBMS, if a node fails during query evaluation and its data becomes unavailable; or it could even appear with queries in a single node system, if some base tables or views are known to be incomplete.

Consider a specific example the authors have encountered: today, with public clouds (e.g., AzureDB), users can sign up for multiple independent instances of relational databases. A significant number of these users choose to "self-shard" (or horizontally partition) their tables across hundreds to thousands of these databases. A critical point is that in such a scenario, each of the sharded relational database systems is an independent entity, and there is no unifying system collectively managing the collection of relational systems. These customers often wish to query over the totality of these systems, but unfortunately, poor latency, connection failures, misconfigurations, or system crashes are all quite possible in any of the loosely coupled databases. At this point the law of large numbers becomes fatal — even with 99.9% uptime, a query over a 1000-shard table will likely have at least one inaccessible shard, and if executing the distributed query requires all of the 1000 systems to be accessible during execution, the query may literally never complete.

SIGMOD'14, June 22–27, 2014, Snowbird, UT, USA.

http://dx.doi.org/10.1145/2588555.2612176 .

In every instance of an incomplete input, our traditional database instincts tell us that the solution is to fix the problem: we should either replicate the data sources comprising the distributed system or make them more reliable; we should add replication and failover to the nodes of our parallel DBMS; or we should embark on data cleaning and repairing efforts to fix the incomplete tables and views in the single node system [4, 5, 7, 10, 14, 16, 20, 30, 33–36]. However, these solutions can be either financially costly, performance hindering, or both. Furthermore, in certain cases, such as querying over loosely coupled cloud sources, an error external to the database or misconfigurations may be impossible to fix. Finally, consistent querying techniques that rely on functional dependencies and integrity constraints currently become inapplicable in this environment. That is why, in this paper we consider a different approach: letting the query run to "completion" despite the incomplete input(s).

In some cases, of course, this is a very bad idea. When reporting numbers to the SEC, or billing a customer, or the like, incomplete answers are not acceptable. However, there are use cases in which the user may be willing to accept an answer computed with incomplete inputs. For example, the user may be doing exploratory work to gain some insight, or may be interested in answering a query like "find me 1000 customers satisfying the following condition..." In such cases, it may be preferable to return imperfect answers rather than to have the query fail, or to incur a delay, or incur the cost and effort of ensuring that such failures happen very rarely.

The astute reader may be wondering "haven't I seen something like this approximate result stuff before?" Undoubtedly the answer is "yes," but here we are working in a very different setting. Rather than viewing query processing as an incremental process in which the query processor systematically explores more and more of the input to yield successively closer approximations to the true result [23, 28, 31], we are interested in query processing in which, due to forces out of the control of the query processor, part of the input is simply not available and will not become available during the query's lifetime.

Of course, merely returning such an answer to an unsuspecting user would be very poor form; the system needs to tell the user that this result is computed based upon incomplete data. Furthermore, the more the system can guarantee about the partial result, or explain to the user about the result, the better. This raises the following intriguing question: is there anything we can say about a computed answer based upon incomplete data other than "be careful, this is based on incomplete data?" For example, can we make any guarantees (about what the user may or may not receive)? Can we classify the types of anomalies that might result and develop sound mechanisms for determining when they can and cannot occur?

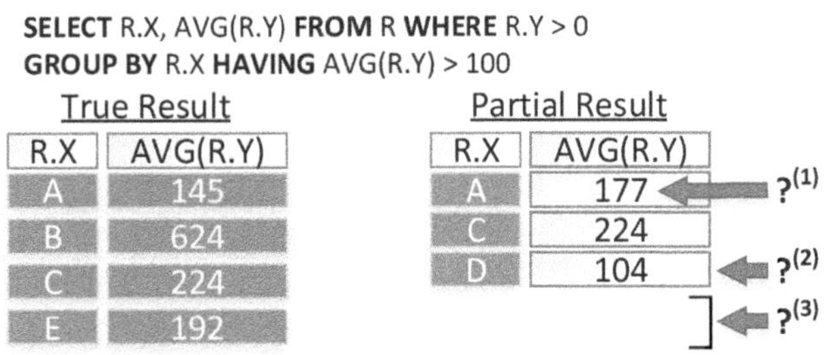

Figure 1: Example: a *True result* versus a *Partial result*.

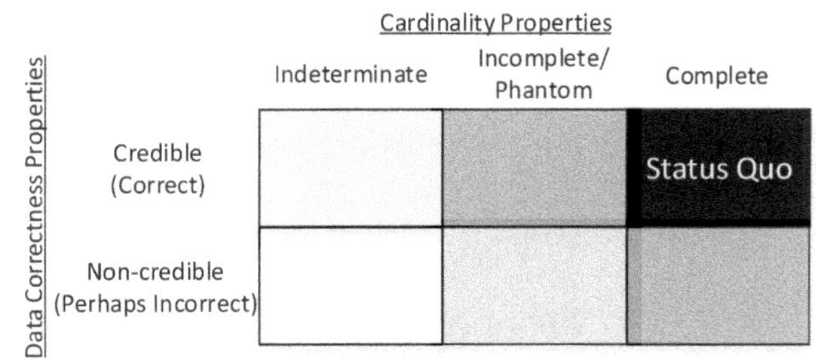

Figure 2: Characterizing partial results.

This brings us to the heart of this work: we present a broad classification of what can "go wrong" when evaluating queries over incomplete data, and show how to detect the various anomalies that arise by analyzing how they are created and propagated through the operators in a query plan. This classification can be used either proactively, where the user specifies "I will only tolerate the following kind of anomalies;" or after the fact, where the system returns "here is what I can tell you about the anomalies that might exist in this result." We present our initial approach to interactively displaying such information to the user in Section 6.

Note that although the root cause of incomplete information may be straightforward, its impact on a query plan is less obvious. The nature of a query result over incomplete inputs is not simply that we receive fewer tuples. Figure 1 shows a simple query that concisely illustrates "all that can go wrong" when a system produces a partial result. In the figure, we consider the result of a simple aggregation query over table R. Suppose that the scan of R is incomplete (perhaps R itself is incomplete, or perhaps R is partitioned and some partition of R resides on a currently inaccessible node.)

In our example, the result for group 'C' is correct, but every other row is problematic. The three main differences between the true result and the result over incomplete data are: (1) the average value calculated for group 'A' is incorrect; (2) a tuple for group 'D' is produced even though it is not found in the true result; and (3) the partial result does not have a tuple for either group 'B' or group 'E'. Each of these anomalies occurred because the scan of table R was not complete, but these anomalies surface at different times and for different reasons during query execution. For anomaly (1), if we are missing any tuples from R that contribute to the group for 'A', it is not hard to see that the average calculation may be wrong. For anomaly (3), the result tuple for group 'B' is perhaps missing, because all of the tuples in R that contribute to group 'B' are missing, while the result tuple for group 'E' may be absent because tuples missing from the scan of R caused the computation of an incorrect average for group 'E', which in turn failed the HAVING clause. Finally, anomaly (2) arose because an incorrect value for the aggregate for group 'D' caused the group to mistakenly satisfy the HAVING clause. Anomaly (2) is unique because it demonstrates that results over incorrect inputs may have "extra" tuples in their output (not in the True result); we call such tuples "phantom" tuples.

This example provides the intuition behind our classification of the errors that can arise when evaluating relational queries over incomplete inputs. Our classification can be viewed as expanding the space of answers produced by database systems as shown in Figure 2. The status quo, of course, is to return only complete and correct tuple sets. But in addition to these complete and correct results, Figure 2 characterizes additional kinds of results with two orthogonal axes: cardinality and correctness. For cardinality we consider four possible categories: complete, missing tuples but no phantom tuples, phantom tuples but no missing tuples, or indeterminate (both missing tuples and phantom tuples). Correctness refers to the values in the tuples that are returned, and is simpler: either the values are credible (correct) or not credible (possibly incorrect). Figure 3 displays this same taxonomy in a different format, representing the options in the cardinality dimension as a partial order.

The challenge, of course, is to determine, for a particular query with a given incomplete input, where in this classification the result set lies. This is the key to returning only the result sets that satisfy user requirements if they impose them. For example, if the user specifies that she wants no phantom tuples, we should analyze the query execution and only return result tuples if we can guarantee phantom tuples are not present, or refuse to return any answer at all if we cannot. It is also the key to providing a user with after the fact information about the result if that is their desire. For example, telling the user that both phantoms and missing tuples could have occurred and letting them decide whether to accept the answer or not. Due to the dynamic nature of failure detection, the classification of a partial result is plan dependent. The precision of our classification depends on the depth to which we are willing to analyze all the information about the missing data and the query. Finally, the last challenge is to communicate our partial result semantics back to the user in a meaningful yet intuitive way.

In this work, we present partial result production as a first-class approach to deal with data access failures in database systems. Existing work that is similar to ours focuses on the basic tenet of producing the true result, albeit through the analysis of iterations of partial answers and through certain operating assumptions [9,37]. Our work is complementary to existing research in the areas such as online aggregation [23,28,31], data provenance and lineage [8,13,19,26,39], and approximate query processing [2,11,15,18,32] in that we are providing certainties for an uncertain result *produced due to failures*.

The contributions of this paper are as follows:

- We identify the tuple set properties that can be used to classify partial results. (Section 2)
- We present a partial result analysis framework with four models that determine the degree of our partial result classification precision. (Section 3)
- We describe how relational operators propagate partial result semantics in our framework. (Section 4)
- We describe the relationship between query optimization, failure models, and our partial result classification. (Section 5)
- We implemented a prototype system and discuss how a user may use and tune a partial result-aware system. (Section 6)

Related work follows in Section 7 along with our conclusions and future work in Section 8.

2. PARTIAL RESULTS TAXONOMY

We provide a way to classify results by the guarantees that can be made on different partial result properties. We define a "partial result" as a tuple set that is produced from some query execution where some data needed by the query is unavailable. The system

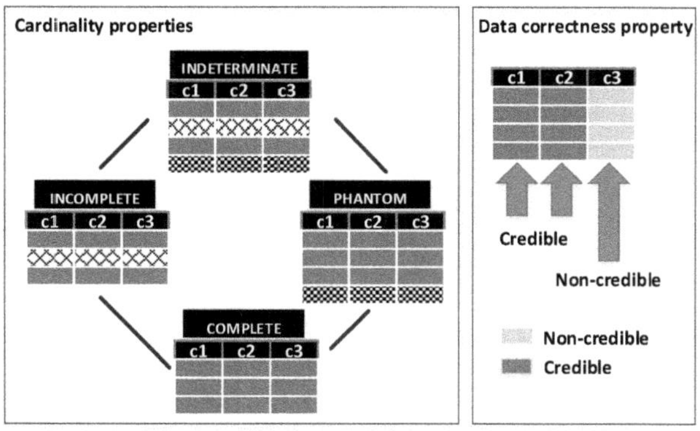

Figure 3: Cardinality and correctness partial results.

has registered the failure and continues query execution using only the available data. Thus, a partial result may not be the same as the result that would have been produced had the query read the base tables completely (the **True result**).

Our partial result semantics are based on a combination of two basic properties of a tuple set. As we show in Figure 3, these two properties are used to describe how a particular partial result tuple set differs from the True result. These two properties are the **cardinality** and the **correctness** of a partial result.

2.1 Cardinality of Partial Results

There are two basic aspects that characterize the **cardinality** of a result set relative to the corresponding True result. The partial result may be missing some tuples, which we call the **Incomplete** aspect; Or, the partial result may have some extra tuples, which we call the **Phantom** aspect.

While it may be obvious how we may classify a result as *Incomplete*, the *Phantom* aspect may not be as straightforward. We have already seen one way that we may encounter the *Phantom* aspect: they can be generated by a predicate over values that are incorrect. This was the case in the "HAVING" clause in Figure 1. Another way Phantom tuples can be produced is by **non-monotone** relational operations such as SET DIFFERENCE. To see this, note that for the SET DIFFERENCE $A - B$, if B is Incomplete, then the result of $A - B$ may have more tuples than if B were complete.

If we cannot rule out the *Incomplete* aspect of the cardinality of a result, and simultaneously cannot rule out the *Phantom* aspect, then we call partial result **Indeterminate**. Conversely, if we can simultaneously rule out both the *Incomplete* and *Phantom* aspects, then we say that the cardinality of the result is **Complete**.

Therefore, given the presence or absence of these two cardinality aspects, a result set's cardinality can be labeled as either *Complete*, *Incomplete*, *Phantom*, or *Indeterminate*. These four labels are placed in a partial order lattice in Figure 3. At the bottom of the lattice, a partial result is **Complete** if we are able to *guarantee* that each of the tuples that are returned correspond to a tuple of the True result. When we *lose cardinality guarantees*, we may "**escalate**" the state of the tuple set to another state. **Escalation** of a partial result (and its properties) means that we have lost the ability to make guarantees that we could make lower in the lattice. As we will see in Section 4, many operators exhibit this escalation behavior under different circumstances.

2.2 Correctness of Partial Results

The other partial result property we consider is the **correctness** of the data values in the result. The cardinality property is separate from the correctness property because *Completeness* does not imply data correctness and vice versa. For example, we can have a partial result tuple set that is guaranteed to be *Complete* even though none of the data values can be guaranteed to be correct. (As a simple example, consider a COUNT aggregation without a GROUP BY clause: we will always get the correct cardinality of exactly one tuple.)

We classify data that cannot be guaranteed to be correct as **Non-credible**, while correct data is classified as **Credible**. For simplicity, in this paper, we assume that the input data read off of persistent (potentially remote) data storage is *Credible* (although this need not be the case in general). This means that data can only lose the *Credible* guarantee when it is calculated (produced by an expression) during query processing. For example, calculating a COUNT over a partial result that is *Indeterminate* means that the result value may be wrong, so we have to classify it as *Non-credible*. We can describe a data set with respect to credibility at different granularities. At the coarsest granularity, we can say the entire result set is *Non-credible*, but sometimes we can do better. For instance, if we know which column was created by an expression evaluation, then we may be able to distinguish some parts of the partial result as *Credible* and other parts as *Non-credible*.

The **correctness** property of a result is not the only property where we can classify a tuple set at different granularities. The **cardinality** property can be further refined for horizontal partitions of the data. Next, we will discuss different analysis levels and data granularities at which we can classify partial results.

3. PARTIAL RESULT ANALYSIS MODELS

We will start by providing an overview of how we can analyze queries to provide partial result semantics. Consider the distributed querying example from Section 1, where we have a "table" defined over a set of remote databases. Suppose a data access failure occurs while querying these databases and the user has elected to accept partial results. Our goal is to provide information to help the user understand the quality of this partial result. Depending on how much we know about what has failed, and how deep we are willing to drill into the semantics of the query, we can provide the user with different partial result guarantees.

Initially, suppose that we know nothing about how the tables are partitioned or the query being executed, and only know that some node that the system tried to access for data was unavailable. In this situation we cannot guarantee any nontrivial partial result properties on the output. This translates to *Indeterminate* and *Non-credible* semantics. However, if we know which query was executed, and which tables were *Incomplete* due to failures, we can make more meaningful guarantees.

Furthermore, if we look into the detailed semantics of the operators applied in the query (e.g., which columns a PROJECT eliminates), we can be even more precise and provide semantics on the vertical partitions of the tuple set. Finally, if we can identify which specific data nodes were unavailable, and we know the horizontal partitioning strategy of the tables, we can classify subsets of tuples (horizontal partitions of the result).

In this section, we will discuss these four models with different analysis "granularities" (see Figure 4). A finer granularity model requires an increased understanding of the data failure that occurred and the operator tree executed. We present four models because this emphasizes that many levels of result quality guarantees are possible. The four models we discuss in this section are representative of a reasonable spectrum of models, and illustrate that there is a tradeoff between the precision and implementation effort required and the guarantees that are possible.

3.1 From Query to Partition Level Analysis

For concreteness, we will use an example based on a TPC-H benchmark Query 15. The view creation query is over a single

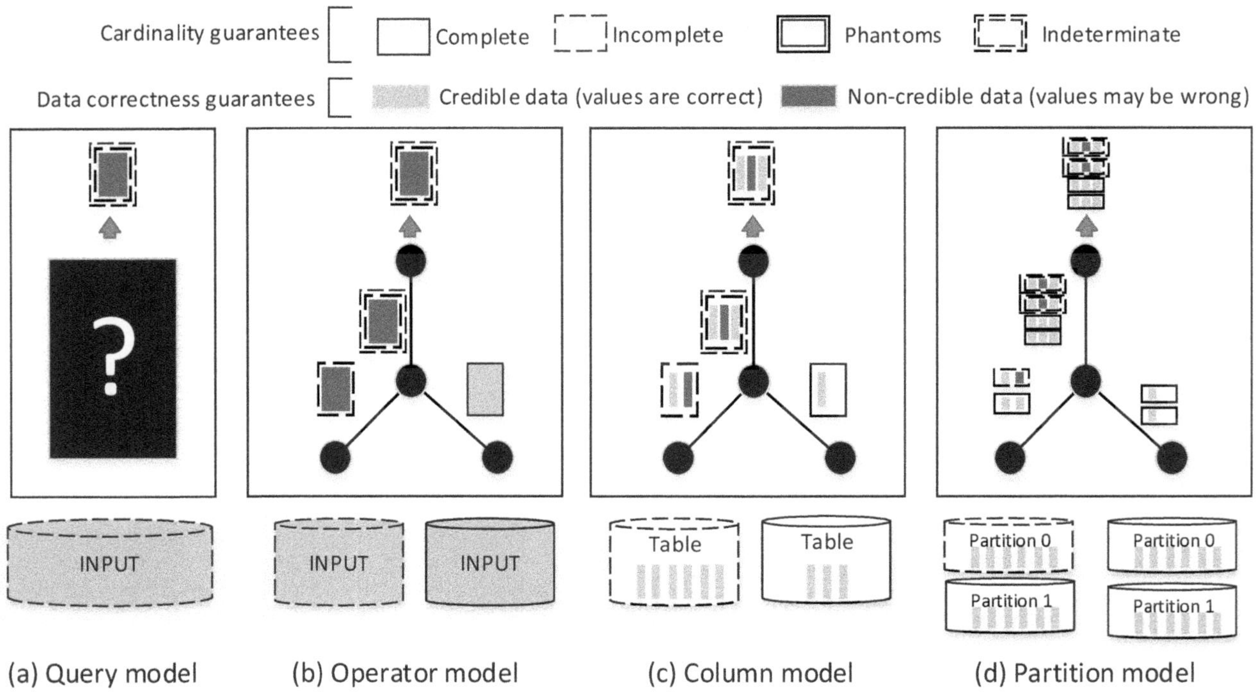

Figure 4: Partial result analysis models.

column name	data type	column name	data type
L_ORDERKEY	identifier	L_RETURNFLAG	fixed text, size 1
L_PARTKEY	identifier	L_LINESTATUS	fixed text, size 1
L_SUPPKEY	identifier	L_SHIPDATE	date
L_LINENUMBER	integer	L_COMMITDATE	date
L_QUANTITY	decimal	L_RECEIPTDATE	date
L_EXTENDEDPRICE	decimal	L_SHIPINSTRUCT	fixed text, size 25
L_DISCOUNT	decimal	L_SHIPMODE	fixed text, size 10
L_TAX	decimal	L_COMMENT	var text, size 44

Table 1: TPC-H LINEITEM table

LINEITEM table (whose schema is shown in Table 1) and the view definition is as follows:

View Definition For TPC-H Q15

```
CREATE VIEW REVENUE (SUPPLIER_NO, TOTAL_REVENUE) AS
SELECT L_SUPPKEY, SUM(L_EXTENDEDPRICE x (1-L_DISCOUNT))
FROM LINEITEM
WHERE L_SHIPDATE >= DATE '[DATE]' AND
L_SHIPDATE < DATE '[DATE]' + INTERVAL '3' MONTH
GROUP BY L_SUPPKEY
```

Consider a few queries over this view. In addition to simply scanning the view, we will consider a query variant that essentially adds a `HAVING` clause to the SUM AGGREGATE:

Q1 – `SELECT * FROM REVENUE`

Q2 – `SELECT * FROM REVENUE WHERE TOTAL_REVENUE > 100000`

Figure 4 describes the four different models of analysis that one can do to determine the partial result semantics when we have a table access failure. We will discuss each of the four models next, starting with the coarsest analysis.

3.1.1 Query Model

At the Query Model granularity, we treat a query as a black box that has produced a partial result (Figure 4(a)) given that the input data to it is *Incomplete*. We do not know what is "wrong" with the partial result (i.e., how it deviates from the True result), so we cannot provide any guarantees about it. Therefore, for both queries Q1 and Q2, the partial results that are produced are classified as *Indeterminate* and *Non-credible*:

Query Model:
Q1 – *Indeterminate, Non-credible*; Q2 – *Indeterminate, Non-credible*

3.1.2 Operator Model

Now suppose we are willing to look into a query and analyze its logical operator tree. Furthermore, suppose that for multi-table queries, we can distinguish between *Incomplete* and *Complete* tables based on the failures (as we show in Figure 4(b)). With this information, we can now provide stronger guarantees. At this granularity, for each operator in the tree, we need to know the input's partial result semantics (i.e., whether it is *Incomplete*; *Phantom*; or *Credible*). Then, for each operator, we need to determine the semantics of the output tuple set that it returns.

For query **Q1**, we may have the following query plan:

```
PROJECT -> SELECT -> SUM
```

The input to the PROJECT operator is *Incomplete* (but fully *Credible*) because we were unable to read the LINEITEM table in its entirety.[1] We need to figure out if and how it will change the partial result guarantees of the query's output. Given a tuple set that may be *Incomplete*, but is *Credible*, a PROJECT operator does not change the partial result semantics of the tuple set and simply produces a result labeled with the same semantics as its input.

Moving up the operator tree, the input to the SELECT is still *Incomplete* but *Credible*. Here, the SELECT doesn't change the partial result semantics since all the data is *Credible*, so the output from the SELECT is still *Incomplete* and *Credible*.

Finally, the SUM aggregate takes as input *Incomplete* and *Credible* results and computes a SUM using a single column for the GROUP BY. Given that the input tuple set may be missing some tuples, we cannot guarantee that the SUM produces the correct value. Furthermore, we don't know if we captured all the groups of

[1] In our paper, we consider the SQL version of PROJECT instead of the duplicate-eliminating relational PROJECT operator. Duplicate eliminating PROJECT can be thought of as a composition of PROJECT – AGGREGATE – PROJECT where the AGGREGATE is a simple COUNT with a GROUP BY over all the columns.

Partial Result Credibility Semantics

	→ Query plan operator order →				
Q1 query plan	scan	π	σ	sum	
Q3 query plan	scan	π	σ	sum	σ
L_ORDERKEY	T				
L_PARTKEY	T				
L_SUPPKEY	T	T	T	T	T
L_LINENUMBER	T				
L_QUANTITY	T				
L_EXTENDEDPRICE	T	T	T		
L_DISCOUNT	T	T	T		
L_TAX	T				
L_RETURNFLAG	T				
L_LINESTATUS	T				
L_SHIPDATE	T	T	T		
L_COMMITDATE	T				
L_RECEIPTDATE	T				
L_SHIPINSTRUCT	T				
L_SHIPMODE	T				
L_COMMENT	T				
Σ -TOTAL_REVENUE				F	F

Partial Result Cardinality Semantics

Incomplete	T	T	T	T	T
Phantom	F	F	F	F	T

Table 2: Column-model semantics for Q1 and Q2.

the GROUP BY. Thus the output of the SUM will be labeled with *Incomplete* and *Non-credible* partial result semantics.

Query **Q2** performs a SELECT filter on the aggregated column of the (unmaterialized) view, which essentially can be treated as a `GROUP BY ... HAVING`. Given *Incomplete* and *Non-credible* input, the SELECT "escalates" the partial result semantics to *Indeterminate*. This is because the input values are *Non-credible*, and we don't know if we are correctly allowing tuples to pass the filter or not.

Therefore, the output of these two queries will have the following partial result semantics:

Operator Model:
Q1 – *Incomplete, Non-credible*; Q2 – *Indeterminate, Non-credible*

While the operator tree analysis model allows us to distinguish different partial result semantics, it still produces overly conservative guarantees. This is because, while it no longer treats the entire query as a black box, the Operator model still treats the inputs and outputs as black boxes. If we tease apart the columns of a tuple set, it will allow us to be more precise about the partial result semantics, which leads us to the Column model of analysis.

3.1.3 Column Model

At the operator level of analysis, we treat the input and output data as a homogeneous group of data and set the partial result semantics for *all* of the tuples and columns without distinction. If we study partial result semantics at the column-level, then *we are able to discern and track the credibility of different parts of a tuple.* To do this, we must identify the parameters of the operators to know which columns of the tuple they are processing. We now revisit the view definition query from TPC-H Query 15 and show the differences between the Column model of analysis and the prior Operator model analysis.

The operators in the query plan for the view are of course the same PROJECT, SELECT, and AGGREGATE operators considered in the Operator-model analysis. However, each operator is now aware of the credibility of individual columns. In Table 2, we show the column credibility semantics produced by each operator. We can see in Table 2 that for query **Q1**, the columns read off of storage, through the PROJECT, and the SELECT are all *Credible*. The tuple set is also *Incomplete*. However, when we calculate the SUM aggregate over the *Incomplete* tuple set, the resulting TOTAL_REVENUE column is determined to be*Non-credible*. For query **Q2**, the SELECT predicate evaluating a *Non-credible* column (TOTAL_REVENUE) results in an escalation to *Indeterminate* (both *Incomplete* and *Phantom* aspects cannot be ruled out).

LINEITEM partitioning		
	Node 1	Node 2
Column-level	1 <L_SUPPKEY< 10000	
Partition-level	LO: 1 <L_SUPPKEY< 5000	HI: 5001 <L_SUPPKEY < 10000

Table 3: Partition model analysis exploits the systems knowledge of how the table data is partitioned across the data nodes.

The Column model of analyzing partial result semantics provides finer granularity precision for making partial result guarantees:

Column Model:
Q1 – *Incomplete, Credible*(L_SUPPKEY) *Non-credible*(TOTAL_REVENUE)
Q2 – *Indeterminate, Credible*(L_SUPPKEY) *Non-credible*(TOTAL_REVENUE)

Compared to the partial result semantics produced when using the Operator model, we now know that certain columns of the output have correct values. For the two queries, we now have a mix of *Credible* and *Non-credible* columns, which can be considered the hallmark of the Column model of analysis (as shown in Figure 4(c)).

3.1.4 Partition Model

So far we have only considered what happens when the entire input data is classified as *Incomplete* or *Complete*. In the Partition model, by contrast, we consider the input table to be a collection of partitions, and use properties of partitions in our analysis. In large-scale parallel data processing systems typically data is partitioned according to appropriate partitioning schemes [40].

Recall our example working environment of querying over loosely coupled remote databases, where a table is "sharded" across the individual shards. If we know which nodes were unavailable or returned incomplete data, then we can classify the other partitions of the table as *Complete* and *Credible*. This means that, if the partition properties can be propagated through the analysis of the query, we can determine that certain partitions of the result match the corresponding partitions in the True result. This is depicted in Figure 4(d), where Partition-level analysis breaks all of the tuple sets (input, intermediate, and final) horizontally into partitions. If we revisit our running example of querying over TPC-H Q15's view, then we will find that the partition-model analysis gives us an even more precise classification than column-model analysis.

Assume that the LINEITEM table was partitioned across two nodes using the L_SUPPKEY column. Call one partition 'HI' and the other 'LO', where the HI partition has the half of the tuples with the larger L_SUPPKEY values (see Table 3). The input to our queries **Q1** and **Q2** are now the two partitions of LINEITEM where one is *Complete* (e.g., HI) and the other is *Incomplete* (LO).

When the initial PROJECT operator takes the tuples from the *Complete* partition (HI) as input, it produces a *Complete* (and still fully *Credible*) output. On the other hand, when it processes the *Incomplete* partition, the output analysis is the same as the Column-level analysis: *Incomplete* and all columns are *Credible*. Here, the PROJECT processes these two partitions and the output can be divided into two partitions because the partitioning column, L_SUPPKEY, was retained. Next, the SELECT operator processes the two partitions in the same manner as the PROJECT. Its output can also be thought of as two separate partitions: the HI tuples and the LO tuples. Again, it is key that the SELECT operator does not remove columns, so we retain the partitioning knowledge in L_SUPPKEY. Finally, since the SUM operator performs a GROUP

Partial result semantics	Query model		Operator model		Column model			Partition model			
	card.	cred.	card.	cred.	card.	cred.		part	card.	cred.	
						L_SUPPKEY	TOTAL_REVENUE			L_SUPPKEY	TOTAL_REVENUE
Q1: SELECT L_SUPPKEY, TOTAL_REVENUE FROM REVENUE	Indet.	F	Incomp.	F	Incomp.	T	F	HI LO	Complete Incomp.	T T	T F
Q2: SELECT L_SUPPKEY, TOTAL_REVENUE FROM REVENUE WHERE TOTAL_REVENUE > 100000	Indet.	F	Indet.	F	Indet.	T	F	HI LO	Complete Indet.	T T	T F

Table 4: Side-by-side comparison of partial result semantics determined using four different analysis models for Q1 and Q2.

BY on L_SUPPKEY, its output tuples are also partitioned into the HI and LO partitions. Here we see the advantages of Partition-level analysis. Since the HI partition was *Complete* and all the columns were *Credible*, the SUM on any of the HI groups is correct and can be classified *Credible*. This means the partial results of query **Q1** will have semantics as follows:

Partition Model:
Q1:
HI – {*Complete*, *Credible* (L_SUPPKEY, TOTAL_REVENUE)}
LO – {*Incomplete*, *Credible* (L_SUPPKEY) *Non-credible* (TOTAL_REVENUE)}

Since query **Q2** essentially adds a SELECT operator to process the results of the AGGREGATE, it will also take the HI and LO partitions as input. The partial result semantics of **Q2** is:

Q2:
HI – {*Complete*, *Credible* (L_SUPPKEY, TOTAL_REVENUE)}
LO – {*Indeterminate*, *Credible*(L_SUPPKEY) *Non-credible*(TOTAL_REVENUE)}

We can see that with partition-level analysis, for all partial results, we are able to identify and return some tuples that are exactly the same as in the True result. The partition model for analysis provides the most precise guarantees in its partial result semantics by providing the finest granularity in its data classification. However, it is also the most complex.

Summary: In Table 4, we summarize our analysis for two queries based on the TPC-H Q15 view as we draw tighter boxes around the data. The partial result semantics for each query using the four levels of analysis are shown with the coarsest Query-level granularity on the left and the finest-granularity Partition-level analysis on the right. As we move from left to right, we see that we are able to classify more and more of the result set as *Complete* and *Credible* which provides better value for the user.

4. PROPAGATION OF PARTIAL RESULT SEMANTICS

In the previous section we illustrated by examples how the relational operators of a query may change the partial result semantics of a tuple set as it processes the data. In this section, we will select a few common relational operators (four unary operators and three binary operators), and describe in detail their behavior with respect to partial result semantics.

Here we discuss the way operators propagate partial result semantics using the Partition model of analysis. Since the other three models are essentially "roll-ups" of the Partition model in terms of precision, the operators' behavior in those models can all be derived from our description of the Partition model.

4.1 Unary Operators

The four unary operators we study are SELECT, PROJECT, EXTENDED PROJECT, and AGGREGATION. For the SELECT operator, we will limit our scope to "simple" predicate types that involve expressions (using $<, \leq, =, \geq, >, <>$) on the columns of the tuples being processed. We differentiate projection into two categories: those that simply remove columns (PROJECT), and those

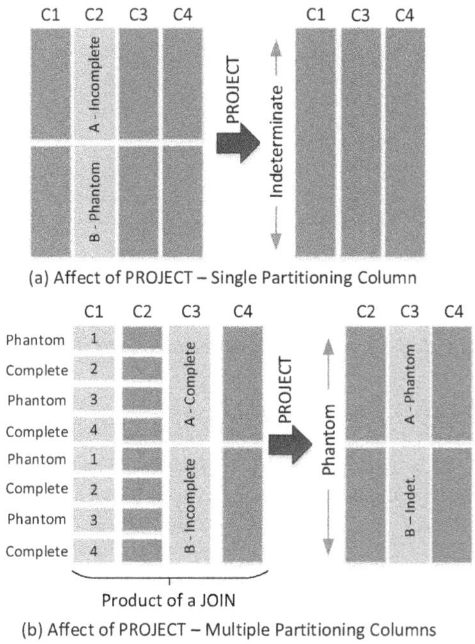

Figure 5: (a) Removing the sole partitioning column. (b) Removing a partitioning column from a tuple set that has multiple partitioning columns.

that can define a new column through an expression (EXTENDED PROJECT). For the AGGREGATE operators, we only consider the basic types: COUNT, SUM, AVG, MIN, and MAX.

For each operator we will describe how it is affected by the input with certain partial result semantics and how it defines the partial result semantics of the result set.

4.1.1 SELECT

As we discussed in Section 3, the SELECT operator affects partial result semantics if it has a predicate expression that operates over columns that are *Non-credible*. In that case, since we don't trust the data values that we are evaluating expressions over, then we can't be confident of the elimination of tuples and the retention of tuples. In this case we must set the cardinality property of the result to *Indeterminate*. If the predicate is defined over all-*Credible* data, it simply propagates the partial result semantics from input to output.

4.1.2 PROJECT

The PROJECT operator only affects the partial result cardinality property of a tuple set. The only way it can do this is when the tuple set is partitioned. Figure 5 illustrates how the PROJECT operator can "**taint**" the semantics of a tuple set if it eliminates the partitioning column. Figure 5(a) shows a simple partitioned tuple set where partition 'A' is *Incomplete* and partition 'B' is *Phantom*. If the PROJECT operator eliminates the partitioning column C2, then the tuple set becomes a single "partition" and we can no longer know if tuples are missing or if *Phantom* tuples exist (thus making

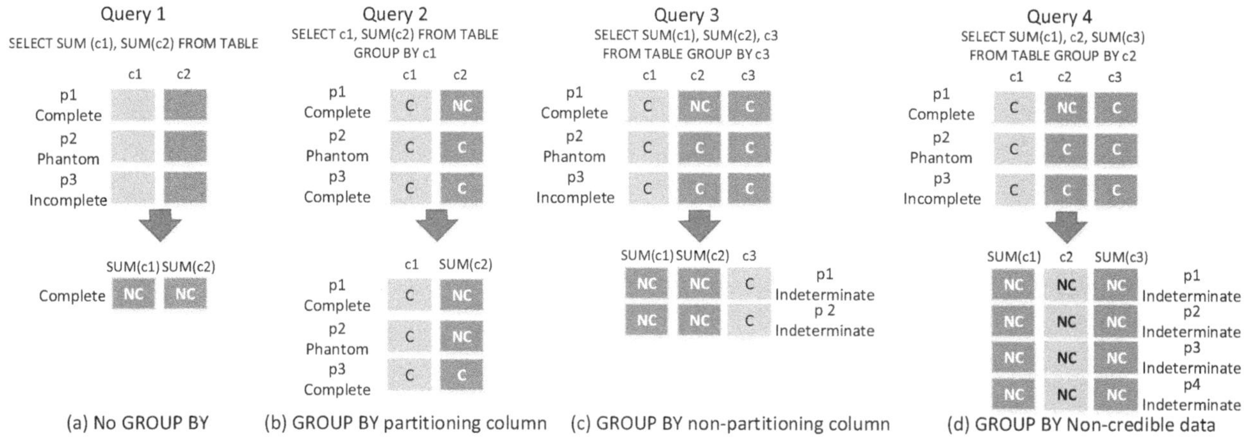

Figure 6: Aggregation operators behave very differently depending on which columns are used in the GROUP BY clause. C – *Credible*, NC – *Non-credible*, the partitioning column is shaded lighter.

it *Indeterminate*). Hence the resulting "merge" of the two partitions taints the result set.

In Figure 5(b) we look at a more complicated example, where the input to the PROJECT operator is the product of a CARTESIAN PRODUCT/JOIN (see Section 4.2.2). Column C1 is 4-way partitioned while column C3 is 2-way partitioned. Column C1 has two partitions (partitions 1 and 3) that have *Phantom* semantics while the other two are *Complete*. Column C3's partitions are *Complete* and *Incomplete*. If we remove C1 through PROJECT, we can no longer identify sets of tuples that may harbor *Phantoms*. Therefore, both partitions defined by C3 are now tainted by the partitions of C1 and thus are escalated to *Phantom* and *Indeterminate*.

On the other hand, if the PROJECT operator removes a non-partitioning column, then PROJECT simply propagates the remaining rows' partial result semantics. Intuitively, in this case the PROJECT operator is not affected by, nor does it affect, the credibility of columns.

4.1.3 EXTENDED PROJECT

The EXTENDED PROJECT operator can create a new column using an expression that may rely on the other columns of the tuple set, and so it is affected by input data with Non-credible columns. Intuitively, if an expression computes a value using *Non-credible* values as input, then the output is also *Non-credible*. If the expression parameters are all *Credible*, then this operator produces a column that we can guarantee as *Credible*. The EXTENDED PROJECT operator does not affect the cardinality semantics (i.e., *Incomplete* and *Phantom*) of a partial result.

4.1.4 AGGREGATE

We consider five types of AGGREGATE functions in this operator: COUNT, SUM, AVG, MIN and MAX. To simplify our discussion, we only consider instances where we apply the functions over one column of the input tuple set.[2] We also assume that there is no implicit PROJECT operation happening over the input that is eliminating columns (i.e., if five columns are provided as input, the output will also have five columns).

The four queries we use to describe AGGREGATE behavior are shown in Figure 6. In the figure, C means the data is *Credible*, NC means the data is *Non-credible*, and the partitioning column is lightly shaded. First, Figure 6(a) (Query 1) shows that an AGGREGATE without any GROUP BY clause always creates a single tuple, so it will always be *Complete*. AGGREGATE is the only operator with this ability to take a non-Complete (Phantom, Incomplete, or Indeterminate) input and produce a *Complete* output. However, we show that if any of the input partitions are not *Complete*, the results will always be *Non-credible*.

In Figure 6(b) (Query 2), if the GROUP BY clause is over partition columns, then the output rows will take the partial result semantics of the source partitions. For example, if a partition has *Phantom* semantics, then the resulting tuple is also classified as *Phantom*. Furthermore, similar to Query 1, computing over Non-complete data results in *Non-credible* results. (Query 4 shows what happens if we GROUP BY a column that is *Non-credible*.)

Figure 6(c) (Query 3) shows a GROUP BY over a non-partitioning column that is *Credible*. In this case, since the input had *Phantom* and *Incomplete* partitions, the output tuples are tainted by these partitions and are escalated to *Indeterminate* (see Figure 3).

Finally, in Figure 6(d) (Query 4), we show that if the GROUP BY clause includes any columns that have *Non-credible* values, then all the output is escalated to *Indeterminate* and all data is deemed *Non-credible*. This is the only way a partitioning column becomes *Non-credible*, since by our assumption, partitioning columns read from the base tables are deemed *Credible*.

4.2 Binary Operators

The binary operators we consider are UNION ALL, CARTESIAN PRODUCT, and SET DIFFERENCE. Using Figure 7, we will describe examples that illustrate the key partial result behavior of these three operators.

4.2.1 UNION ALL

The UNION ALL operator takes two tuple sets and creates a new one by combining all of the tuples. UNION ALL's partial result behavior is to escalate the cardinality property of the output based on the combination of the two input's cardinality properties. For data correctness, an output column is escalated to *Non-credible* if either of the corresponding input columns are *Non-credible*.

In Figure 7, we show two examples that illustrate this behavior. In Figure 7(a), two tuple sets with identical partitioning strategies are given as input. The output will maintain this partitioning strategy, and thus the semantics of partition 1 becomes *Indeterminate* because the two inputs were *Phantom* and *Incomplete*. Furthermore, the credibility of column 2 is lost because one of the inputs for column 2 was *Non-credible*. Similarly, for partition 2, the escalation (based on the lattice "join" in Figure 3) of *Incomplete* and *Complete* results in an *Incomplete* result.

[2] Any scenario where we want to compute an aggregate over an expression can be broken down into an EXTENDED PROJECT followed by an AGGREGATE.

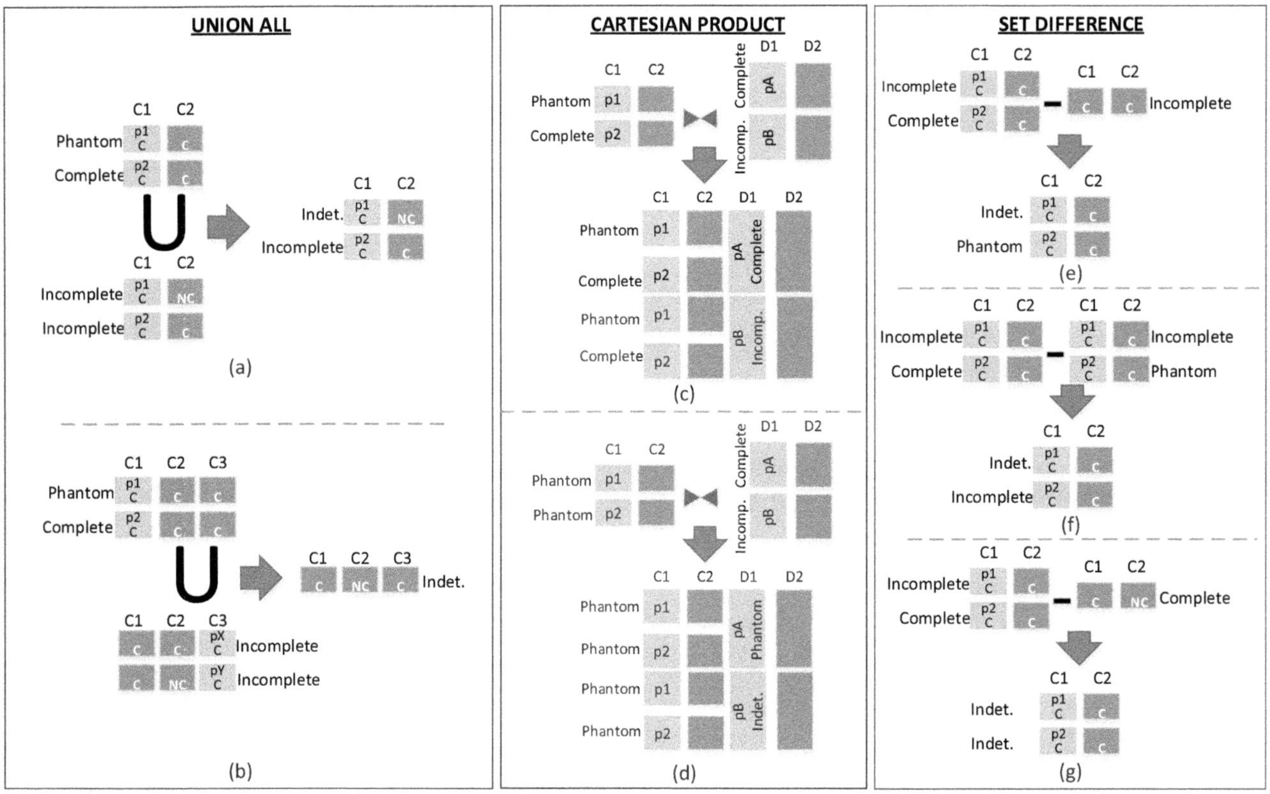

Figure 7: Examples of how UNION ALL, CARTESIAN PRODUCT, and SET DIFFERENCE behave when given partial result input. C – *Credible*, NC – *Non-credible*, the partitioning column is shaded lighter and partitions are identified by "p<ID>".

In the second example in Figure 7(b), we show that if we don't have partition alignment for the two inputs to UNION ALL, we lose all the partitions. The result is then considered a single "partition," where all of the cardinality semantics of the input partitions escalate the output. In this case, the result is *Indeterminate*. The column credibility is also escalated to *Indeterminate* for column C2.

4.2.2 CARTESIAN PRODUCT

The CARTESIAN PRODUCT is relatively straightforward in its behavior. It performs a cross of the two sets of partitions to create the output. It is not affected by, nor does it change the credibility of the data values. However, the CARTESIAN PRODUCT may or may not simply propagate the input semantics to the output. In Figure 7(c), we show a case where the semantics of the input partitions are all retained.

In contrast, in Figure 7(d), we show how the CARTESIAN PRODUCT operator can cause partial result semantic tainting. In Figure 7(d), all of the partitions of C1 were (homogeneously) *Phantom*, the CARTESIAN PRODUCT taints the cardinality semantics of partition A (column D1) to *Phantom* and partition B to *Indeterminate*.

4.2.3 SET DIFFERENCE

In Figure 7(e)-(g), we depict three scenarios for the SET DIFFERENCE operator. As we have mentioned, SET DIFFERENCE is a non-monotone operator so it can create *Phantom* results. In the first example in Figure 7(e), we see that *Phantom* semantics are set if the second input is *Incomplete*. Here, the second input is not partitioned, thus both input partitions get tainted by the *Phantom* aspect.

The second example (Figure 7(f)) shows what happens if the second input is partitioned. In this case, the corresponding partitions are processed together: p1 with p1 and p2 with p2. We also show that if the second input has *Phantom* semantics, the output is tainted by the *Incomplete* aspect since we may have removed tuples we shouldn't have.

Finally, in Figure 7(g), we show that if the second input has *Non-credible* data, all partitions of the result are escalated to *Indeterminate* since we cannot trust the presence (or the absence) of any tuples in the output. If the first input has any *Non-credible* data, then we would also escalate the partial result to *Indeterminate*.

5. DEPENDENCE ON QUERY PLAN

At an abstract level, we envision our classification system being applied as follows. The optimizer chooses a plan to be run; the system then begins running the plan, which consists of a tree of operators. The data accessed by these operators is stored in multiple shards. If at any point during execution an input to an operator "fails" (perhaps the site is or becomes unavailable), then we use the techniques from Section 4 to determine and propagate the effect of these errors up the query plan. Each operator in turn passes the result of this analysis to operators further up in the tree, until at the root, the answer set is classified.

5.1 Dynamically Detecting Failures

Since errors are determined dynamically and by the specific plan executed, it is reasonable to ask how the result classification depends upon the plan chosen. After all, a foundational principle of query evaluation in traditional settings is that the same result is computed independent of the plan; it would be nice if this carried over to partial results analysis so that here, the result classification was independent of the plan. Unfortunately, this is not the case when we consider failures during execution, for at least two main reasons, neither of which are due to our analysis or propagation models.

First, consider two plans (L1) $R \bowtie S$ and (L2) $S \bowtie R$ where the join is computed by a hash-join operator. Here L1 and L2 differ in that they reverse the build and probe relations of the hashjoin. Now suppose that it turns out that some shard storing a partition of R fails during the execution. The question is when. If the shard fails during the later part of the execution, it is possible that plan L1 may not even "see" this, since it may have completed its read of R before the failure, whereas plan L2 might see the failure, if it occurred during the scan of R at the end of the query plan.

Here we have a remarkable result that the query result itself differs depending upon which plan is chosen. We emphasize that this is not the "fault" of any design decision; we think it is actually reasonable in the world of unplanned failures in large distributed computations. However, it definitely means that our result classification is not independent of the plan chosen; it would seem unreasonable to expect it to be.

This does raise another question: what about scenarios where the failures do not impact the final result? Is it possible that, whenever two plans give the same result in an execution possibly containing failures, our classification scheme always yields the same classification? Unfortunately, the answer is again "no." Consider two physical plans P1 and P2 for a simple selection query on a relation sharded across multiple loosely coupled data sources. Plan P1 scans all of the data sources in parallel applying the selection. Plan P2 is more clever, using a global index that matches the selection predicate, and thus it is able to execute the query by only consulting the subset of shards that actually contain results to the query. The alert reader will likely see what is coming: suppose that some node(s) that contains no results has failed. Plan P1 will see the failure, but Plan P2 will not, because it does not even access the failed node(s).

Of course, this dependency on plan choice occurs even in traditional centralized systems — as a contrived example, one can imagine a situation where a table has a corrupted index, so the plans that use the index will fail while the plans that don't will succeed. What is new here is that we are now accepting partial query results and trying to classify their properties — this exposes the interaction between plans and failures.

At this point the reader might wonder if there are any guarantees we can make whatsoever. It turns out that this is tied to the class of plans and failures considered. To illustrate this, the rest of this section will focus on the following: first, we consider the case where all failures occur *before* the query begins executing and persist throughout the entire execution (we call this the "**persistent failure model**"); second, we consider plans that are equivalent modulo transformations enabled by exploiting the relational algebraic property commutativity. As the following section shows, under these assumptions, we can say that equivalent plans yield identical partial results classification.

5.2 Partial Results Consistency with Operator Re-orderings

In this section we will show the following: *under the persistent failure model, for different orderings (plans) of commutative operators, we will have identical classifications of the partial result outputs.*

Problem Statement: For two commutative operators α and β, we wish to show that for the sequences (α -> β) and (β -> α), under the persistent failure model, the partial result guarantees produced by our analysis are identical for any (partial) inputs.

The persistent failure assumption means that for any set of reorderings, the (partial result) input to the operator plans will be the same, and also, no failures occur in the middle of the plans. Due to space limitations, we do not provide a formal proof. However, we will thoroughly illustrate how all pairs of commutative operators

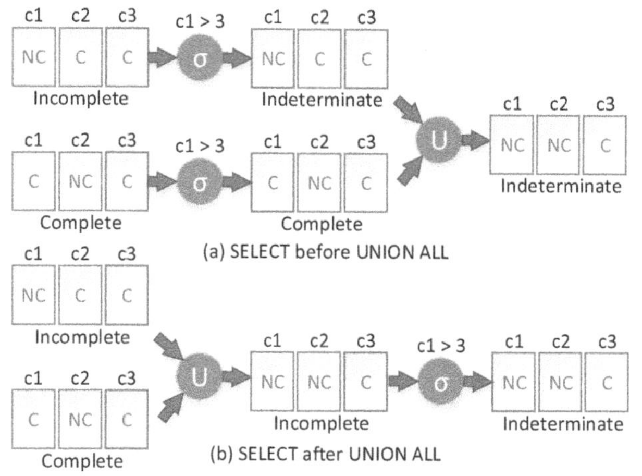

Figure 8: Commutative pairs of SELECT and UNION ALL.

from our operator set maintain partial result consistency when reordered.

5.2.1 Commutative Pairs of Unary Operators

Commutative pairs of unary operators are two operators α and β, such that given an input tuple set R, if we execute either α-> β or β->α, then the output will always be S . This restricts the pairs we need to examine because of the conditions under which two operators are commutative. For example, a PROJECT cannot eliminate the column that a SELECT requires for its predicate.

Below we will discuss commutative pairs where one of the operators is a SELECT; and a commutative pair of PROJECT and EXTENDED PROJECT. AGGREGATE is not commutative with PROJECT or EXTENDED PROJECT (recall we define AGGREGATE to use all of the tuple's columns for either GROUP BY or the aggregate function.)

Pairs involving SELECT: We want to show that for any pair involving a SELECT, given any ordering, the classification of the output will be the same. The key behavior of SELECT is that it only affects partial result properties if the predicate is on a *Non-credible* column. The propagation behavior of SELECT (when the predicate is defined on all-*Credible* columns) means: *if the SELECT predicate is defined over solely Credible columns, then any commutative pairing with any operator will have consistent partial result semantics.*

Now we only need to discuss when the SELECT predicate is defined over *Non-credible* columns. In this case, the SELECT operator doesn't change any of the credibility properties, but escalates the output cardinality to *Indeterminate*. Therefore, it suffices to show that if we pair the SELECT (with a *Non-credible* predicate) with any of the other three unary operators, the output will always be *Indeterminate* and the credibility of the partial result will be consistent. We can reason about this by "proof by contradiction" reasoning. Suppose we paired a SELECT (with a *Non-credible* predicate) with either PROJECT, EXTENDED PROJECT, or AGGREGATE whereby (a) the result was not classified as *Indeterminate* in the ordering where the SELECT operator is first, and/or (b) different operator orderings result in data being classified as *Credible* and *Non-credible*. Then case (a) is not possible because the only operator that can "de-escalate" the *cardinality* property is AGGREGATE (when there is no GROUP BY) and here, GROUP BY columns must exist for SELECT to be commutative with AGGREGATE. Case (b) is not possible because under the commutative conditions and the *Non-credible* SELECT predicate, the AGGREGATE will only produce *Non-credible* data, and EXTENDED PROJECT is unaffected by the cardinality property.

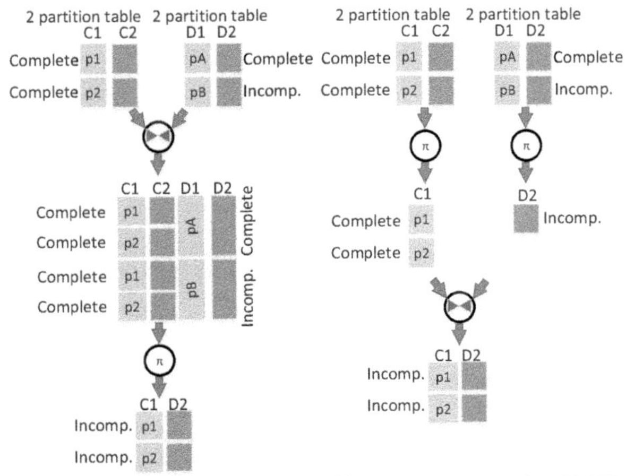

(a) CARTESIAN PRODUCT before PROJECT (b) CARTESIAN PRODUCT after PROJECT

Figure 9: Commutative pairs of PROJECT and CARTESIAN PRODUCT (light shade – partitioning columns).

Commutative PROJECT and EXTENDED PROJECT: Since the PROJECT operator's behavior is only concerned with the partial result cardinality property while the EXTENDED PROJECT operator's behavior is only concerned with the partial result data correctness property, we will always classify the result the same way regardless of the ordering of this pair.

5.2.2 *Commutative Unary/Binary Pairs*

We will break up this discussion into three parts for three different unary operators. The AGGREGATE operator is not generally commutative with our binary operators so we omit it.

Pairs involving SELECT: If the SELECT predicate is defined over all-*Credible* data, the operator simply propagates the partial result semantics of its input to its output. Therefore, similar to the argument for unary operator pairs with SELECT, for any unary/binary pair where the SELECT predicate is defined over all-*Credible* data, partial result semantics are consistent in the presence of re-ordering.

If the SELECT predicate is defined over a column that is *Non-credible*, the SELECT always escalates the result's cardinality property to *Indeterminate*. Furthermore, we know that the SELECT operator does not affect the column's credibility. The UNION ALL operator is commutative with the SELECT operator. UNION ALL "taints" (see Section 4.1.2) its output's partial result semantics with the semantics of its inputs. As we show in Figure 8, the SELECT, UNION ALL commutative pair maintains partial result consistency because the SELECT will always receive the *Non-credible* column for its predicate.

Pairing SELECT with either the CARTESIAN PRODUCT or the SET DIFFERENCE operator does not result in an inconsistent partial result classification. Using the similar reasoning by counter example that we used above, there is no condition under which an operator re-ordering leads to different partial result semantics.

PROJECT: The PROJECT operator is only commutative with the UNION ALL and CARTESIAN PRODUCT operators. For PROJECT and CARTESIAN PRODUCT, we show in Figure 9 that regardless of how we order the two operators, the PROJECT operator will always taint the output of the pair in the same way. This is because the CARTESIAN PRODUCT "crosses" all of the partitions from each input and combines the inputs' columns together. In Figure 9(a), the CARTESIAN PRODUCT operator propagates the input partitions' semantics to its output and then the PROJECT operator "taints" its output when it removes the partitioning column D1. In Figure 9(b), the PROJECT removes the partitioning column D1, creating a single *Incomplete* partition. Then, the CARTESIAN

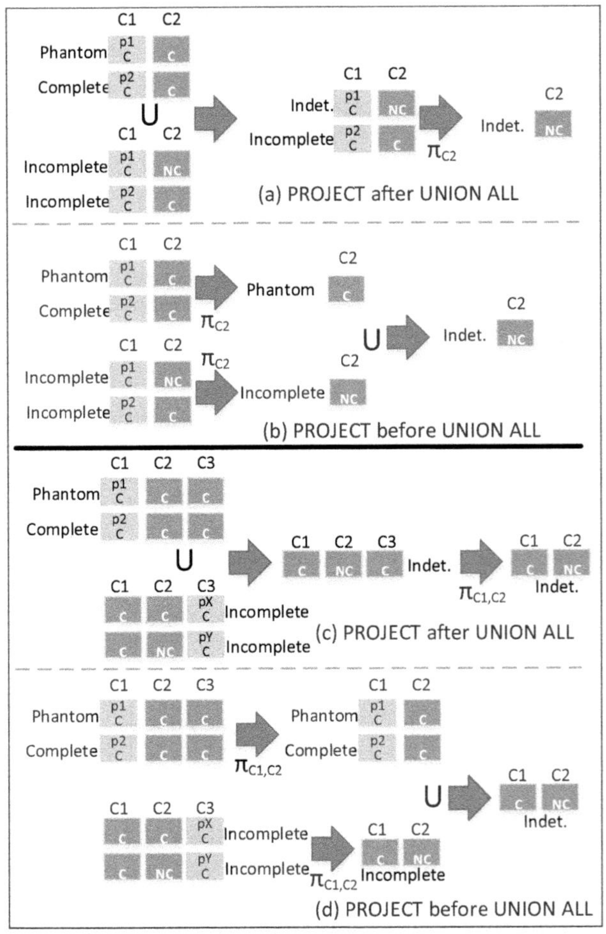

Figure 10: Commutative pairs of PROJECT and UNION ALL (light shade – partitioning columns).

PRODUCT operator taints its output partitions' semantics, since one of its inputs is homogeneously *Incomplete*. As a result, both orderings result in two partitions classified as *Incomplete*. Neither of these operators are affected by or can affect the data credibility property. Thus, PROJECT and CARTESIAN PRODUCT commutative pair have consistent partial result semantics.

For the PROJECT and UNION ALL pair, we only need to consider the case where PROJECT removes a partitioning column (since removal of a non-partitioning column is straightforward). Furthermore, we only need to consider the partial result cardinality classification since the PROJECT operator's behavior does not affect credibility. In Figure 10, two examples illustrate that this pair of operators will be classified consistently regardless of the order. In Figures 10(a) and (b) we show the case when the two inputs have partition alignment (C1), while Figures 10(c) and (d) show the case where the two inputs don't have partition alignment (C1 and C3).

EXTENDED PROJECT: Commutative pairs of EXTENDED PROJECT – UNION ALL operators or EXTENDED PROJECT – CARTESIAN PRODUCT operators have consistent partial result semantics. Since EXTENDED PROJECT's (XPROJ) behavior only involves data credibility and CARTESIAN PRODUCT is concerned with partial result cardinality, it is straightforward to see that we will always classify the result consistently.

Similarly, since XPROJ does not affect the cardinality semantics of a result, for pairs with the UNION ALL operator, we only need to show that a new column produced by the XPROJ operator that is *Credible* in one ordering cannot be *Non-credible* in the opposite operator ordering. The reason this is true is straightforward to understand: if the new column were ever *Non-credible* in one ordering, then this would mean that one of the inputs to the pair of operators had a *Non-credible* column necessary for the XPROJ expression. Therefore, since the UNION ALL operator taints the output's credibility with both of its input's credibility, we will always classify the result consistently.

5.2.3 *Pairs of Binary Operators*

Binary operators are only commutative (and associative) with themselves (i.e., we cannot have a heterogeneous set of binary operators that is commutative.) Thus, we only need to show that pairs of homogeneous binary operators will be consistently classified. Due to space limitations we will omit this discussion in this paper.

6. EXPERIENCE & IMPLEMENTATION

So far, we have discussed the way a database system can analyze queries to produce partial result guarantees in the presence of input failures. Of course, another important aspect of partial results is how users can control and use a partial result-aware system along with the impact of implementing such a framework into a system.

First, we will discuss how users may interact with partial result-aware database systems. We consider two aspects of user interaction: user input to the system, and presentation of the partial result output to users. Both aspects are key to increasing the value of partial results to a user. We will briefly describe our initial approach to how users may interact with a partial result-aware system. Clearly other approaches could be considered as well, and we present the ideas in this section as a high-level example of what could be done, rather than as a definitive proposal for the best way to interact with partial result-aware systems.

A user that elects to receive partial results from a database can control how the database behaves to ultimately increase the value of a potential partial result output. For example, depending on whether or not the consumer of the result is a human or an application, the user may wish to receive *any partial result* or may chose to *set constraints* that limit the types of anomalies that are acceptable. In the former case, perhaps a human is doing exploratory, ad-hoc data analysis and is willing to accept any result anomaly. In the latter case, an application may accept only certain partial result classifications such as *Incomplete* and *Credible* results, otherwise return an error. In all of these cases, we may wish to provide the user with a way to signal her intentions to the system; perhaps in the form of session controls, DDLs, or query (or table) hints.

On the output side of the problem, there may be many different ways that a partial result can be presented to the user. If we consider the ad-hoc, exploratory user who accepts all partial results, perhaps an operator-by-operator style presentation of how the partial result guarantees are made would be useful. In Figure 11, we show a prototype interface that we have built and connected to our real, partial result-aware database system. Here a user can zoom in on any operator of a query plan and examine the partial result guarantees made about the data at that point. In the figure, the focus is on the PROJECT operator before a CARTESIAN PRODUCT. With this style of interface, the user may wish to receive the partial result output from any operator in the plan to maximize the value of the query's execution. Alternatively, one can imagine an interface that presents the actual raw data output to the user with appropriate meta-data tags. Perhaps with these interfaces, a user may even wish to "bless" the result at a given point in the plan to manipulate the meta-data tags directly and gauge the effects. While our paper has focused on how a database system can internalize the notion of partial results, ultimately, the way users can interact with the system is key to providing value through partial results.

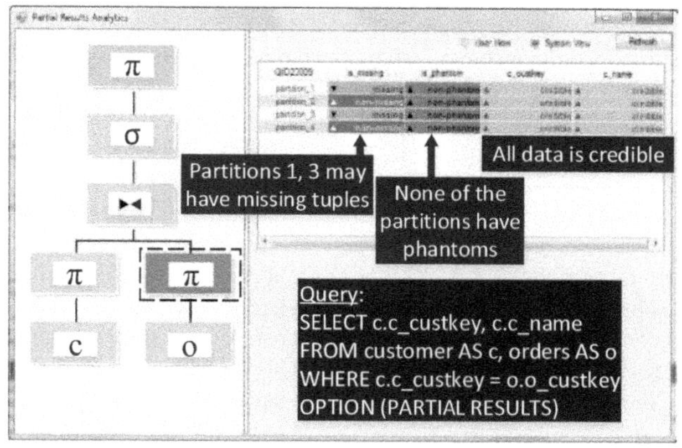

Figure 11: An interface example for partial results exploration.

Incorporating partial results analysis into an existing DBMS requires minimal changes to the codebase, and has almost no impact on the performance of the system. When failures occur, they must be detected, which most systems already do today. Instead of returning an error message when some base data is unavailable, the engine continues the query execution (as if it had 100% of the data), and just before the final answers are returned back to the user, the partial results analyzer (a stand-alone component) would take the detected runtime failures and the query plan used as its inputs and produce the partial results guarantees. This implementation whereby failures are simply passed to the stand-alone analyzer at the end also allow us to manage intermediate data access errors. We would simply retag the inputs or outputs of certain operators if some failure happened between any two operators. Our framework does not impose anything that precludes intermediate failures from being detected and applied. These guarantees along with the result tuples are returned back to the user as the final answer.

7. RELATED WORK

Our paper is related to many research areas, including fault tolerance in big-data systems, data provenance and lineage, online aggregation, approximate query processing, and data quality. Perhaps the most closely related works to ours include the "partial answers" work by Bonnet et al. [9], the view lineage paper by Cui et al., the Trio project [17, 39], and the semantic analysis of approximate answers by Vrbsky et. al., with their APPROXIMATE system [37]. While Bonnet et al. focused on combining partial answers into a complete answer (using "parachute" queries), their work does not focus on classifying and analyzing partial answers and how the operators in the query pipelines may propagate the partial results semantics [9].

The Trio project focuses on a data model, query language, and execution strategies for a system that allows the querying of either inexact data or lineage data [3, 17, 39]. Our work here is different because we are describing how to identify and derive characterizations for partial results when failures occur while querying traditional relational data. The semantic tags produced by our framework along with the partial results could be stored within the Trio system.

The APPROXIMATE system focused on monotone query processing and did not study aggregations or data credibility (correctness of values) issues [37]. Other related works includes characterizing errors in cardinality estimates [25, 27] and identification of phantoms through non-monotone operators [38], which cover only certain aspects of the entire "partial result" space that we study here.

In the theoretical database research community, "naïve querying" over incomplete databases discussed query evaluation and "certain answers" over relations that have null values due to causes such as incomplete data integrations [21]. Other theoretical work includes the seminal work that characterizes consistent data in an inconsistent database for the purposes of database repair [5]. Such work relies on the knowledge provided by the semantics of integrity constraints and functional dependencies whereas in our target environment of loosely coupled, independent cloud databases, these logical semantics are generally not available. If future cloud services are able to capture user-provided (or even machine-learned) constraints and dependencies (and monitor and enforce them) across 100s to 1000s of cloud databases, then we may be able to leverage the complex reasoning techniques of these prior works to identify tuples that we may have lost or tuples that could never have been present. This is the focus of our future work.

Computing partial results in the absence of complete table data is also similar in spirit to producing results via online aggregation [23, 28, 31], continuous querying of data streams [6, 12], and querying over sampled data [2, 22, 24]. These systems heavily rely on random sampling to provide an "early returns" approximation of a correct answer that may otherwise take much longer to compute. We, on the other hand, attempt to provide guarantees with respect to which parts of the returned results are identical to those in the true result, and which ones are not, and how they may differ if they do indeed differ. Ultimately, our approach provides a taxonomy of partial results that could be utilized by all of these other systems to further subdivide results produced based on their types and provide even tighter guarantees.

The research problem of data lineage and data provenance that provide the capability to see and track back where the data came from has been well studied in many contexts including data exploration, privacy and security, and uncertain database systems [1, 8, 11, 13, 15, 18, 19, 26, 29, 32, 39, 41]. While those approaches focused on developing logical data models, query languages, and physical execution methods for querying uncertain data, our work focuses on the process in which relational queries can produce partial results when failures occur during query processing. In other words, one can see a partial result-aware system that we have described here as populating the kinds of databases that these prior state-of-the-art works have described.

8. CONCLUSIONS AND FUTURE WORK

In this paper we deal with the problem of partial results, whereby query execution continues and results are produced even when some data may be unavailable. We identify partial result classes and present a classification framework equipped with four different models for analyzing partial results semantics at various granularities. The contributions of this paper can be utilized in large scale systems as either a mitigation mechanism for frequent failures or unexpected unavailability of data sources, as well as for exploratory, time-constrained query processing.

Substantial room for future work exists. For example, it would be interesting to explore partial results-aware query optimization, including the development of cost functions and plan selection algorithms that take into account user preferences regarding partial results semantics and the likelihood/impact of particular data access failures. Another direction to explore is a deeper investigation of the interaction between the schema, partitioning functions (including columnar storage and vectorized execution), queries, and specifics of incomplete inputs that may yield finer granularity reports on the quality of results. As discussed in the related work section, if our knowledge of the loosely coupled cloud databases is enhanced with constraints and dependencies, then we can provide even more precise guarantees. Finally, exploring alternatives for presenting partial result information to users is fertile ground for further research.

9. REFERENCES

[1] S. Acharya, P. B. Gibbons, V. Poosala, and S. Ramaswamy. Join Synopses for Approximate Query Answering. In *SIGMOD*, 1999.

[2] S. Agarwal, B. Mozafari, A. Panda, et al. BlinkDB: Queries with Bounded Errors and Bounded Response Times on Very Large Data. In *EuroSys*, 2013.

[3] P. Agrawal, O. Benjelloun, A. D. Sarma, et al. Trio: A system for data, uncertainty, and lineage. In *PVLDB*, 2006.

[4] T. Akidau, A. Balikov, K. Bekiroğlu, S. Chernyak, J. Haberman, et al. MillWheel: Fault-tolerant Stream Processing at Internet Scale. In *VLDB*, 2013.

[5] M. Arenas, L. Bertossi, and J. Chomicki. Consistent Query Answers in Inconsistent Databases. In *PODS*, 1999.

[6] S. Babu and J. Widom. Continuous Queries over Data Streams. *SIGMOD Record*, 2001.

[7] J. Barr, A. Narin, and J. Varia. Building Fault-Tolerant Applications on AWS. 2011. `http://bit.ly/1cD6k4w`.

[8] O. Benjelloun, A. Das Sarma, A. Halevy, M. Theobald, and J. Widom. Databases with Uncertainty and Lineage. *VLDB Journal*, 2008.

[9] P. Bonnet and A. Tomasic. Partial Answers for Unavailable Data Sources. *INRIA Technical Report*, 1997.

[10] Y. Cao, W. Fan, and W. Yu. Determining the Relative Accuracy of Attributes. In *SIGMOD*, 2013.

[11] K. Chakrabarti, M. Garofalakis, R. Rastogi, and K. Shim. Approximate Query Processing Using Wavelets. *VLDB Journal*, 2001.

[12] S. Chandrasekaran, O. Cooper, A. Deshpande, M. J. Franklin, J. M. Hellerstein, et al. TelegraphCQ: Continuous Dataflow Processing. In *SIGMOD*, 2003.

[13] A. Chapman and H. V. Jagadish. Why Not? In *SIGMOD*, 2009.

[14] R. Cheng, J. Chen, and X. Xie. Cleaning Uncertain Data with Quality Guarantees. In *VLDB*, 2008.

[15] R. Cheng, D. V. Kalashnikov, and S. Prabhakar. Evaluating Probabilistic Queries over Imprecise Data. In *SIGMOD*, 2003.

[16] J. C. Corbett, J. Dean, M. Epstein, A. Fikes, C. Frost, et al. Spanner: Google's Globally-distributed Database. In *OSDI*, 2012.

[17] Y. Cui, J. Widom, and J. L. Wiener. Tracing the Lineage of View Data in a Warehousing Environment. *TODS*, 2000.

[18] N. Dalvi and D. Suciu. Management of Probabilistic Data: Foundations and Challenges. In *PODS*, 2007.

[19] D. Fabbri and K. LeFevre. Explanation-based Auditing. In *VLDB*, 2011.

[20] F. Geerts, G. Mecca, P. Papotti, and D. Santoro. The LLUNATIC Data-Cleaning Framework. In *PVLDB*, 2013.

[21] A. Gheerbrant, L. Libkin, and C. Sirangelo. When is Naive Evaluation Possible? In *PODS*, 2013.

[22] P. B. Gibbons and Y. Matias. New Sampling-Based Summary Statistics for Improving Approximate Query Answers. In *SIGMOD*, 1998.

[23] J. M. Hellerstein, P. J. Haas, and H. J. Wang. Online Aggregation. In *SIGMOD*, 1997.

[24] Y. Hu, S. Sundara, and J. Srinivasan. Supporting Time-constrained SQL Queries in Oracle. In *VLDB*, 2007.

[25] Y. E. Ioannidis and S. Christodoulakis. On the Propagation of Errors in the Size of Join Results. In *SIGMOD*, 1991.

[26] A. Meliou, W. Gatterbauer, et al. The Complexity of Causality and Responsibility for Query Answers and non-Answers. In *PVLDB*, 2010.

[27] S. Nirkhiwale, A. Dobra, and C. M. Jermaine. A Sampling Algebra for Aggregate Estimation. In *PVLDB*, 2013.

[28] N. Pansare, V. R. Borkar, C. Jermaine, and T. Condie. Online Aggregation for Large MapReduce Jobs. In *PVLDB*, 2011.

[29] H. Park, R. Ikeda, and J. Widom. RAMP: A System for Capturing and Tracing Provenance in MapReduce Workflows. In *PVLDB*, 2011.

[30] V. Raman and J. M. Hellerstein. Potter's Wheel: An Interactive Data Cleaning System. In *VLDB*, 2001.

[31] V. Raman and J. M. Hellerstein. Partial Results for Online Query Processing. In *SIGMOD*, 2002.

[32] C. Ré and D. Suciu. Approximate Lineage for Probabilistic Databases. In *VLDB*, 2008.

[33] J. Shanmugasundaram, K. Tufte, et al. Architecting a Network Query Engine for Producing Partial Results. In *WebDB*, 2000.

[34] J. Shute, R. Vingralek, B. Samwel, B. Handy, C. Whipkey, et al. F1: A Distributed SQL Database That Scales. In *VLDB*, 2013.

[35] H. Singh. Fault-tolerance in Windows Azure SQL Database. 2012. `http://bit.ly/1bUS3V5`.

[36] M. A. Soliman, I. F. Ilyas, and S. Ben-David. Supporting Ranking Queries on Uncertain and Incomplete Data. *VLDB Journal*, 2010.

[37] S. V. Vrbsky and J. W. S. Liu. APPROXIMATE – A Query Processor That Produces Monotonically Improving Approximate Answers. *TKDE*, 1993.

[38] T.-Y. Wang, C. Ré, and D. Suciu. Implementing NOT EXISTS Predicates over a Probabilstic Database. In *MUD*, 2008.

[39] J. Widom. Trio: A System for Integrated Management of Data, Accuracy, and Lineage. Technical report, Stanford InfoLab, 2004.

[40] J. Zhou, P. A. Larson, and R. Chaiken. Incorporating Partitioning and Parallel Plans into the SCOPE Optimizer. In *ICDE*, 2010.

[41] W. Zhou, S. Mapara, Y. Ren, Y. Li, A. Haeberlen, Z. Ives, B. T. Loo, and M. Sherr. Distributed time-aware provenance. In *PVLDB*, 2013.

Parallel In-Situ Data Processing with Speculative Loading

Yu Cheng
UC Merced
5200 N Lake Road
Merced, CA 95343
ycheng4@ucmerced.edu

Florin Rusu
UC Merced
5200 N Lake Road
Merced, CA 95343
frusu@ucmerced.edu

ABSTRACT

Traditional databases incur a significant *data-to-query* delay due to the requirement to *load data* inside the system before querying. Since this is not acceptable in many domains generating massive amounts of raw data, e.g., genomics, databases are entirely discarded. *External tables*, on the other hand, provide instant SQL querying over raw files. Their performance across a query workload is limited though by the speed of repeated full scans, tokenizing, and parsing of the entire file.

In this paper, we propose SCANRAW, a novel database physical operator for in-situ processing over raw files that integrates data loading and external tables seamlessly while preserving their advantages: optimal performance across a query workload and zero time-to-query. Our major contribution is a *parallel super-scalar pipeline implementation* that allows SCANRAW to take advantage of the current many- and multi-core processors by overlapping the execution of independent stages. Moreover, SCANRAW overlaps query processing with loading by *speculatively* using the additional I/O bandwidth arising during the conversion process for storing data into the database such that subsequent queries execute faster. As a result, SCANRAW makes optimal use of the available system resources – CPU cycles and I/O bandwidth – by switching *dynamically* between tasks to ensure that optimal performance is achieved.

We implement SCANRAW in a state-of-the-art database system and evaluate its performance across a variety of synthetic and real-world datasets. Our results show that SCANRAW with speculative loading achieves optimal performance for a query sequence at any point in the processing. Moreover, SCANRAW maximizes resource utilization for the entire workload execution while speculatively loading data and without interfering with normal query processing.

Categories and Subject Descriptors

H.2.2 [**Database Management**]: Physical Design—*access methods*; H.2.4 [**Database Management**]: Systems—*query processing*

1. INTRODUCTION

In the era of data deluge, massive amounts of data are generated at an unprecedented scale by applications ranging from social networks to scientific experiments and personalized medicine. The vast majority of these read-only data are stored as application-specific files containing hundreds of millions of records. Due to the upfront loading cost and the proprietary file format, *databases* are rarely considered as a storage solution even though they provide enhanced querying functionality and performance [10, 5]. Instead, the standard practice is to write dedicated applications encapsulating the query logic on top of *generic file access libraries* that provide instant access to data through a well-defined API. While a series of applications for a limited set of parametrized queries are provided with the library, new queries typically require the implementation of a completely new application even when there is significant logic that can be reused. Relational databases avoid this problem altogether by implementing a declarative querying mechanism based on SQL. This requires though data representation independence—achieved through loading and storing data in a proprietary format.

External tables [25, 17] combine the advantages of file access libraries and the declarative query execution mechanism provided by SQL—data can be queried in the original format using SQL. Thus, there is no loading penalty and querying does not require the implementation of a complete application. There is a price though. When compared to standard database query optimization and processing, external tables use linear scan as the single file access strategy since no storage optimizations are possible—data are external to the database. Every time data are accessed, they have to be converted from the raw format into the internal database representation. As a result, query performance is both constant and poor. Databases, on the other hand, trade query performance for a lengthy loading process. Although time-consuming, data loading is a one-time process amortized over the execution of a large number of queries. The more queries are executed, the more likely is that the database outperforms external tables in response time.

Motivating example. To make our point, let us consider a representative example from genomics. SAM/BAM files [9] – SAM are text, BAM are binary – are the standard result of the next-generation genomic sequence aligners. These files consist of a series of tuples – known as reads – encoding how fragments of the sequenced genome align relative to a reference genome. There are hundreds of millions of reads in a standard SAM/BAM file from the *1000 Genomes* project [2]. Each read contains 11 mandatory fields and a variable number of optional fields. There is one such read on every line in the SAM file—the fields are tab-delimited.

A representative type of processing executed over SAM/BAM files is variant, i.e., genome mutation responsible for causing hereditary diseases, identification [1]. It requires computing the distribution of the CIGAR field [9] across all the reads overlapping a position in the genome where certain patterns occur in at least one read. This can be expressed in SQL as a standard group-by aggregate

SIGMOD'14, June 22–27, 2014, Snowbird, UT, USA.

http://dx.doi.org/10.1145/2588555.2593673.

query and executed inside a database using the optimal execution plan selected by the query optimizer based on data statistics. Geneticists do not use databases though. Their solution to answer this query – and any other query for that matter – is to write application programs on top of generic file access libraries such as SAMtools [9] and BAMTools [7] that provide instant access to the reads in the file through a well-defined API. Overall, a considerably more intricate procedure than writing a SQL query.

Problem statement. We consider the general problem of *executing SQL-like queries in-situ over raw files*, e.g., SAM/BAM, with a database engine. Data converted to the database processing representation at query time can be loaded into the database. Our objective is to design a solution that provides instant access to data and also achieves optimal performance when the workload consists of a sequence of queries. There are two aspects to this problem. First, methods that provide single-query optimal execution over raw files have to be developed. These can be applied both to external table processing as well as standard data loading. And second, a mechanism for query-driven gradual data loading has to be devised. This mechanism interferes minimally – if at all – with normal query processing and guarantees that converted data are loaded inside the database for every query. If sufficient queries are executed, all data get loaded into the database. We assume the existence of a procedure to extract tuples with a specified schema from the raw file and to convert the tuples into the database processing format.

Contributions. The major contribution we propose in this paper is SCANRAW—a novel database physical operator for in-situ processing over raw files that integrates data loading and external tables seamlessly while preserving their advantages—optimal performance across a query workload and zero time-to-query. SCANRAW has a *parallel super-scalar pipeline architecture* that overlaps data reading, conversion into the database representation, and query processing. SCANRAW implements *speculative loading* as a gradual loading mechanism to store converted data inside the database. The main idea in speculative loading is to find those time intervals during raw file query processing when there is no disk reading going on and use them for database writing. The intuition is that query processing speed is not affected since the execution is CPU-bound and the disk is idle.

Our specific contributions can be summarized as follows:

- Design SCANRAW, the first parallel super-scalar pipeline operator for in-situ processing over raw data. The stages in the SCANRAW pipeline are identified following a detailed analysis of data loading and external table processing.
- Design speculative loading as a gradual data loading mechanism that takes advantage dynamically of the disk idle intervals arising during data conversion and query processing.
- Implement SCANRAW in the DataPath [6] database system and evaluate its performance across a variety of synthetic and real-world datasets. Our results show that SCANRAW with speculative loading achieves optimal performance for a query sequence at any point in the processing.

Overview. In Section 2 we provide a formal characterization for in-situ data processing over raw files. The SCANRAW architecture and operation are introduced in Section 3 while speculative loading is presented in Section 4. Experimental results are shown in Section 5. We conclude with a detailed look at related work (Section 6) and plans for future work (Section 7).

2. RAW FILE QUERY PROCESSING

Figure 1 depicts the generic process that has to be followed in order to make querying over raw files possible. The input to the process is a raw file – SAM/BAM in our running example – a schema, and a procedure to extract tuples with the given schema from the raw file. The output is a tuple representation that can be processed by the execution engine. For each stage, we introduce trade-offs involved and possible optimizations. Before discussing in detail the stages of the conversion process though, we emphasize the generality of the procedure. Stand-alone applications and databases alike have to read data stored in files and convert them to an in-memory representation suitable for processing. They all follow some or all of the stages depicted in Figure 1.

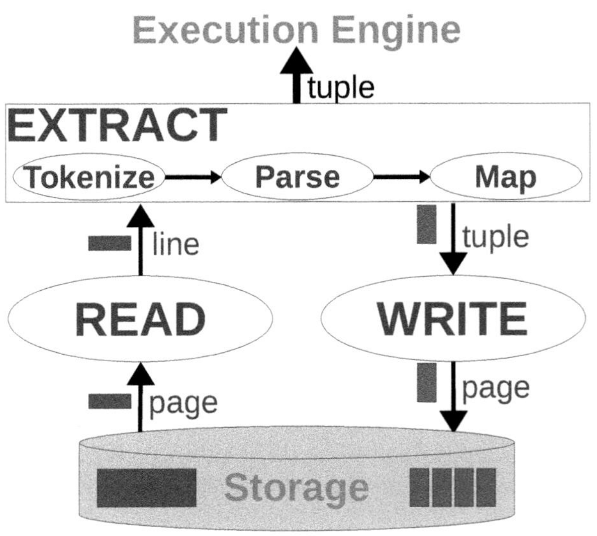

Figure 1: Query processing over raw files.

READ. The first stage of the process requires reading data from the original flat file. Without additional information about the structure or the content – stored inside the file or in some external structure – the entire file has to be read the first time it is accessed. This involves reading the lines of the file one-by-one and passing them to EXTRACT. As an optimization – already implemented by the *file system* – multiple lines co-located on the same page are read together. An additional optimization – also implemented by the file system – is the caching of pages in memory buffers such that future requests to the same page can be served directly from memory without accessing the disk. Thus, while the first access is limited by the disk throughput, subsequent accesses can be much faster as long as data are already cached.

Further reading optimizations beyond the ones supported by default by the file system aim at reducing the amount of data – the number of lines – retrieved from disk and typically require the creation of auxiliary data structures, i.e., *indexes*. For example, if the tuples are sorted on a particular attribute range queries over that attribute can be answered by reading only those tuples that satisfy the predicate and a few additional ones used in the binary search to identify the range. Essentially, any type of index built inside a database can be also applied to flat files by incurring the same or higher construction and maintenance costs. In the case of our genomic example, BAI files [7] are indexes built on top of BAM files. Columnar storage and compression are other strategies to minimize the amount of data read from disk—orthogonal to our discussion.

TOKENIZE. Abstractly, EXTRACT transforms a tuple from text format into the processing representation based on the schema provided and using the extraction procedure given as input to the process. We decompose EXTRACT into three stages – TOKENIZE, PARSE, and MAP – with independent functionality. Taking a text line corresponding to a tuple as input, TOKENIZE is responsible for identifying the attributes of the tuple. To be precise, the output of TOKENIZE is a vector containing the starting position for every attribute in the tuple. This vector is passed along with the text into PARSE. The implementation of TOKENIZE is quite simple. Iterate over the text line character-by-character, identify the delimiter character that separates the attributes, and store the corresponding position in the output vector. To avoid copying, the delimiter can be replaced with the end-of-string character. Overall, a *linear scan* over the text line with little opportunities for optimization.

A first optimization is aimed at *reducing the size of the linear scan* and is applicable only when a subset of attributes have to be converted in the processing representation, i.e., selective tokenizing and parsing [5]. The idea is to stop the linear scan over the text as soon as the end of the last attribute to be converted is identified. Maximum reductions are obtained when the length of the text is large and the attributes are located at the edges—we can go for a backward scan if the length is shorter. A second optimization is targeted at *saving the work done*, i.e., the vector of positions or positional map [5], from one conversion to another. Essentially, when the vector is passed to PARSE, it is also cached in memory. The positional map can be complete or partially filled—when combined with adaptive tokenizing. While a complete map allows for immediate identification of the attributes, a partial map can provide significant reductions even for the attributes whose positions are not stored. The idea is to find the position of the closest attribute already in the map and scan forward or backward from there.

PARSE. In PARSE, attributes are converted from text format into the binary representation corresponding to their type. This typically involves the invocation of a function that takes as input a string parameter and returns the attribute type, e.g., atoi. The input string is part of the text line. Its starting position is determined in TOKENIZE and passed along in the positional map. Intuitively, the higher the number of function invocations, the higher the cost of parsing. Since the only direct optimization – implement faster conversion functions – is a well-studied problem with clear solutions, alternative optimizations target other aspects of parsing. Selective parsing [5] is an immediate extension of selective tokenizing aimed at *reducing the number of conversion function invocations*. Only the attributes required by the current processing are converted. If processing involves selections, the number of conversions can be reduced further by first parsing the attributes which are part of selection predicates, evaluating the condition, and, only if satisfied, parsing the remaining attributes. In the case of highly selective predicates and queries over a large number of attributes, this push-down selection technique [5] can provide significant reductions in parsing time. The other possible optimization is to *cache the converted attributes in memory* such that subsequent processing does not require parsing anymore since data are already in memory in binary format.

MAP. The last stage of extraction is MAP. It takes the binary attributes converted in PARSE and organizes them in a data structure suitable for processing. In the case of a row-store execution engine, the attributes are organized in a record. For column-oriented processing, an array of the corresponding type is created for each attribute. Although not a source of significant processing, this reorganization can become expensive if not implemented properly. Copying data around has to be avoided and replaced with memory mapping whenever possible.

At the end of EXTRACT, data are loaded in memory and ready for processing. Multiple paths can be taken at this point. In external tables, data are passed to the execution engine for query processing and discarded afterwards. In NoDB [5] and in-memory databases, data are kept in memory for subsequent processing. READ and EXTRACT do not have to be executed anymore as long as data are already cached. In standard database loading, data are first written to disk and only then query processing can begin. This typically requires reading data again—from the database though. It is important to notice that these stages have to be executed for any type of processing and for any type of raw data, not only text. In the case of binary raw data though the bulk of processing is very likely to be concentrated in MAP instead of TOKENIZE and PARSE.

WRITE. WRITE is present only in database loading. Data converted in the processing representation is stored in this format such that subsequent accesses do not incur the tokenization and parsing cost. The price is the storage space and the time to write data to disk. Since READ and WRITE contend for I/O throughput, their disk access has to be carefully synchronized in order to minimize the interference. The typical sequential solution is to read a page, convert the tuples from text to binary, write them as a page, and then repeat the entire process for all the pages in the input raw file. This READ-EXTRACT-WRITE pattern guarantees non-overlapping access to disk. An optimization that is often used in practice is to buffer as many pages with converted tuples as possible in memory and to flush them at once when the memory is full.

The interaction between WRITE and the various optimizations implemented in TOKENIZE and PARSE raises some complicated trade-offs. If query-driven partial loading is supported, the database has to provide mechanisms to store incomplete tuples inside a table. A simple solution – the only available in the majority of database servers – is to implement loading with INSERT and UPDATE SQL statements. The effect on performance is very negative though. The situation gets less complicated in column-oriented databases, e.g., MonetDB [21], which allow for efficient schema expansion by adding new columns. Loading new attributes reduces to writing the pages with their binary representation in this case. Push-down selection in PARSE complicates everything further since only the tuples passing the selection predicate end-up in the database. To enforce that a tuple is processed only once – either from the raw file or from the database – detailed bookkeeping has to be set in place. While the effect on a single query might be positive, it is very likely that the overhead incurred across multiple queries is too high to consider push-down selection in PARSE as a viable optimization. This is true even without loading data into the database.

3. THE SCANRAW OPERATOR

In this section, we consider *single query execution* over raw data. Given a set of raw files and a SQL-like query, the objective is to minimize query execution time. The fundamental research question we ask is how to design a parallel in-situ data processing operator targeted at the current many- and multi-core processors? What architectural choices to make in order to take full advantage of the available parallelism? How to integrate the operator with a database server? We propose SCANRAW, a novel physical operator implementing query processing over raw data based on the decomposition presented in Section 2. Our major contribution is a *parallel super-scalar pipeline architecture* that allows SCANRAW to overlap the execution of independent stages. SCANRAW overlaps reading, tokenizing, and parsing with the actual processing across data partitions in a pipelined fashion, thus allowing for multiple partitions to be processed in parallel both across stages and inside a conversion stage. Each stage can itself be sequential or parallel.

To the best of our knowledge, SCANRAW is the first operator that provides generic query processing over raw files using a fully parallel super-scalar pipeline implementation. The other solutions proposed in the literature are sequential or, at best, use data partition-

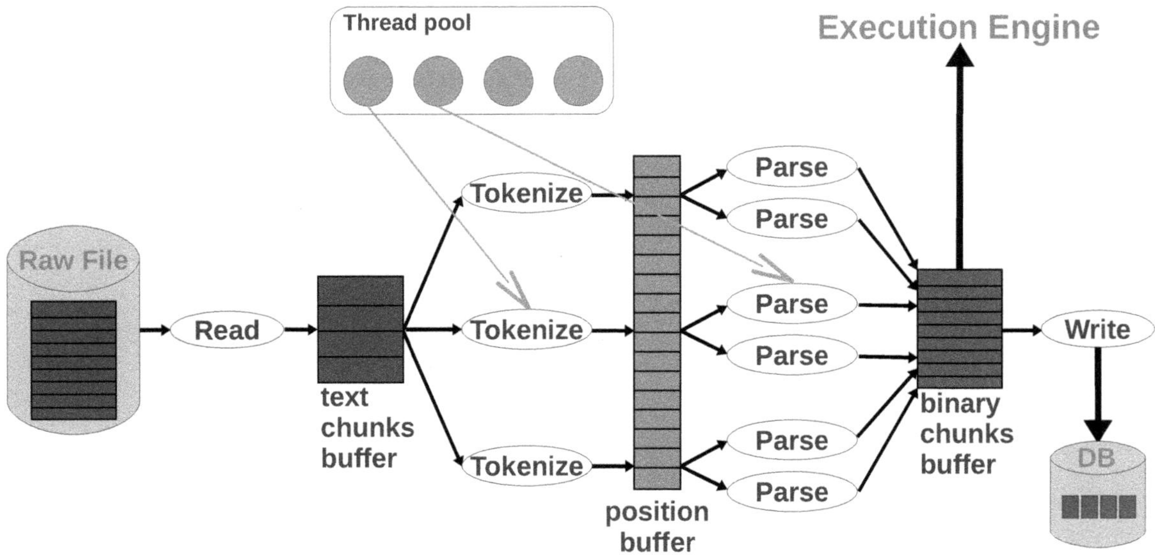

Figure 2: SCANRAW architecture.

ing parallelism [8]—also implemented in SCANRAW. Some solutions follow the principle READ-EXTRACT-PROCESS, e.g, external tables and NoDB [10, 5], while others [4] operate on a READ-EXTRACT-LOAD-PROCESS pattern. In SCANRAW, the processing pattern is dynamic and is determined at runtime based on the available system resources. By default, SCANRAW operates as a parallel external table operator. Whenever I/O bandwidth becomes available during processing – due to query execution or to conversion into the processing representation – SCANRAW switches automatically to partial data loading by overlapping conversion, processing, and loading. In the extreme case, all data accessed by the query are loaded into the database, i.e., SCANRAW acts as a query-driven data loading operator.

3.1 Architecture

The super-scalar pipeline architecture of SCANRAW is depicted in Figure 2. Although based on the abstract process representation given in Figure 1, there are significant structural differences. Multiple TOKENIZE and PARSE stages are present. They operate on different portions of the data in parallel, i.e., data partitioning parallelism [8]. MAP is not an independent stage anymore. In order to simplify the presentation, we consider it is contained in PARSE. The scheduling of these stages is managed by a scheduler controlling a pool of worker threads. The scheduler assigns worker threads to stages dynamically at runtime. READ and WRITE are also controlled by the scheduler thread in order to coordinate disk access optimally and avoid interference. The scheduling policy for WRITE dictates the SCANRAW behavior. If the scheduler never invokes WRITE, SCANRAW becomes a parallel external table operator. If the scheduler invokes WRITE for every tuple – or group of tuples, to be precise – SCANRAW degenerates into a parallel Extract-Transform-Load (ETL) operator. While both these scheduling policies are supported in SCANRAW, we propose a completely different WRITE behavior—*speculative loading* (Section 4). The main idea is to trigger WRITE only when READ is blocked due to the text chunks buffer being full. Remember that our objective is to minimize execution time not to maximize the amount of loaded data.

Dynamic structure. The structure of the super-scalar pipeline can be static – the case in CPU design – or dynamic. In a static structure, the number of stages and their interconnections are set ahead of operation and they do not change. Since the optimal pipeline structure is different across datasets, each SCANRAW instance has to be configured accordingly. For example, a file with 200 numeric attributes per tuple requires considerably more PARSE stages than a file with 200 string attributes per tuple. SCANRAW avoids this problem altogether since it has a dynamic pipeline structure [20] that configures itself according to the input data. Whenever data become available in one of the buffers, a thread is extracted from the thread pool and is assigned the corresponding operation and the data for execution. The maximum degree of parallelism that can be achieved is equal to the number of threads in the pool. The number of threads in the pool is configured dynamically at runtime for each SCANRAW instance. Data that cannot find an available thread are stored in the corresponding buffer until a thread becomes available. This effect is back-propagated through the pipeline structure downto READ which stops producing data when no empty slots are available in the text chunk buffer.

Buffers. Buffers are characteristic to any pipeline implementation and operate using the standard producer-consumer paradigm. The stages in the SCANRAW pipeline act as producers and consumers that move chunks of data between buffers. The entire process is regulated by the size of the buffers which is determined based on memory availability. The *text chunk buffer* contains text fragments read from the raw file. The file is logically split into horizontal portions containing a sequence of lines, i.e., chunks. Chunks represent the reading and processing unit. The *position buffer* between TOKENIZE and PARSE contains the text chunks read from the file and their corresponding positional map computed in TOKENIZE. Finally, *binary chunks buffer* contains the binary representation of the chunks. This is the processing representation used in the execution engine as well as the format in which data are stored inside the database. In binary format, tuples are vertically partitioned along columns represented as arrays in memory. When written to disk, each column is assigned an independent set of pages which can be directly mapped into the in-memory array representation. It is important to emphasize that not all the columns in a table have to be present in a binary chunk.

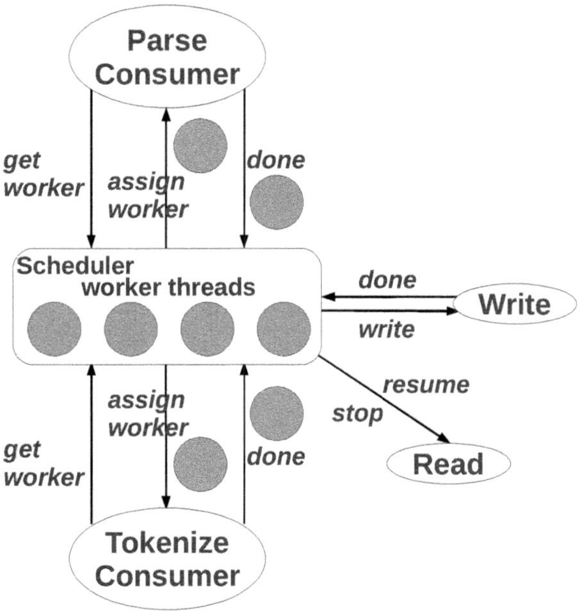

Figure 3: SCANRAW threads and control messages.

Caching. While each of the buffers present in the SCANRAW architecture can act as a cache if the same instance of the operator is employed across multiple query plans, the only buffer that makes sense to operate as a cache is the binary chunks buffer. There are two reasons for this. First, caching raw file chunks takes memory space from the binary chunks cache. Why do not cache more binary chunks, if possible? Moreover, the file system buffers act as an automatic caching mechanism for the raw file. Second, the other entity that can be cached is the positional map generated by TOKENIZE and stored in the position buffer. While this also takes space from the binary chunks cache, the main reason it has little impact for SCANRAW is that it cannot avoid reading the raw file and parsing. These two stages are more likely to be the bottleneck than TOKENIZE which requires only an adequate degree of parallelism to be fully optimized.

The binary chunks buffer provides caching for the converted chunks. Essentially, all the chunks in the raw file end up in the binary chunks cache—not necessarily at the same time. From there, the chunks are passed into the execution engine – external tables processing – or to WRITE for storing inside the database—data loading. What makes SCANRAW special is that in addition to executing any of these tasks in isolation, it can also combine their functionality. The binary chunks cache plays a central role in configuring the SCANRAW functionality. By default, all the converted binary chunks are cached, i.e., they are not eliminated from the cache once passed into the execution engine or WRITE. If all the chunks in the raw file can be cached, SCANRAW simply delivers the chunks to the execution engine and the database becomes an in-memory database. Chunks are expelled from the cache using the standard LRU cache replacement policy biased toward chunks loaded inside the database, i.e., chunks stored in binary format are more likely to be replaced.

Pre-fetching. SCANRAW functions as a self-driven asynchronous process with the objective to produce chunks for the execution engine as fast as possible. It is not a pull-based operator that strictly satisfies requests. Essentially, SCANRAW pre-fetches chunks continuously and caches them in the binary chunks buffer. This process stops only when the buffer is full with chunks not already processed by the execution engine. Processed chunks are replaced using the cache replacement policy. They can be either dropped altogether or stored in the database—if the necessary I/O throughput is available. Notice that pre-fetching works both for raw chunks as well as for chunks already loaded in the database and it is regulated by the operation of the binary chunks cache, i.e., SCANRAW and the execution engine synchronize through the binary chunks cache.

3.2 Operation

Given the architectural components introduced previously, in this section we present how they interact with each other. At a high level, SCANRAW consists of a series of asynchronous stand-alone threads corresponding to the stages in Figure 2. The stand-alone threads – depicted in Figure 3 – communicate through control messages while data are passed through the architectural buffers. Notice that these threads – READ, WRITE, TOKENIZE, PARSE, and SCHEDULER – are separate from the thread pool which contains worker threads that are configured dynamically with the task to execute. In the following, we first present each of the stand-alone threads and their operation. Then we discuss the types of work performed by the thread-pool workers.

3.2.1 Stand-Alone Threads

READ thread. The READ thread reads chunks asynchronously from the raw file and deposits them in the text chunks buffer. READ stops producing chunks when the buffer is full and restarts when there is at least an empty slot. The scheduler can force READ to stop/resume in order to avoid disk interference with WRITE. If the raw file is read for the first time, sequential scan is the only alternative. If the file was read before, a series of optimizations can be applied. First, chunks can be read in other order than sequential or they can be ignored altogether if the selection predicate cannot be satisfied by any tuple in the chunk. This can be checked from the minimum/maximum values stored in the metadata. Second, cached chunks can be processed immediately from memory. And third, chunks loaded inside the database can be read directly in the binary chunks buffer without any tokenizing and parsing. When all the optimizations can be applied, SCANRAW delivers the chunks to the execution engine in the following order. First, the cached chunks, followed by the chunks loaded in the database, and finally the chunks read from the raw file.

An interesting situation arises when only some of the columns required for query processing are loaded either in cache or in the database. Since raw file access is required in this case to read the remaining columns, SCANRAW has to decide what is optimal: use extra CPU cycles to tokenize and parse all the required columns? or read the already loaded columns from the database and convert only the additional columns? While the second alternative is more likely to be optimal when the chunk is cached or when a large part of the required columns are loaded in the database, it imposes severe restrictions on cache operation since that is where chunks are assembled. If the execution is I/O-bound converting all the columns from the raw file is the optimal choice since it avoids additional reading. This is the implementation used throughout our experiments which are I/O-bound when sufficient threads are available.

WRITE thread. The WRITE thread is responsible for storing binary chunks inside the database. Essentially, WRITE extracts chunks from the binary chunks buffer and materializes them to disk in the database representation. It also updates the catalog metadata accordingly. SCANRAW has to enforce that only one of READ or WRITE accesses the disk at any particular instant in time. This is necessary in order to reduce disk interference and maximize I/O throughput.

Consumer threads. A consumer thread monitors each of the internal buffers in the SCANRAW architecture. TOKENIZE consumer monitors the text chunks buffer while PARSE consumer monitors the position buffer, respectively. Whenever a chunk becomes available in any of these buffers, work has to be executed by one of the workers in the thread pool. The consumer thread is responsible for acquiring the worker thread, scheduling its execution on a chunk, and moving the result data in the subsequent buffer. It is important to emphasize that chunk processing is executed by the worker thread not the consumer thread. For example, the TOKENIZE consumer makes a request to the thread pool whenever a chunk is ready for tokenizing. Multiple such requests can be pending at the same time. Once a worker thread is allocated, the requesting chunk is extracted from the buffer and sent for processing. This triggers READ to produce a new chunk if the buffer is not full. When the processing is done, the TOKENIZE consumer receives back the worker thread and the chunk and its corresponding positional map. It releases the worker thread and inserts the result data into the position buffer. PARSE consumer follows similar logic.

Scheduler thread. The scheduler thread is in charge of managing the thread pool and satisfying the requests made by the consumer threads monitoring the buffers. Whenever a request can be satisfied, the scheduler extracts a thread from the pool and returns it to the requesting consumer thread. Notice that even if a thread is available, it can only be allocated if there is empty space in the destination buffer. Otherwise, the result chunk cannot move forward. For example, a request from the PARSE consumer can be accomplished only if there is empty space in the binary chunks buffer. The scheduler requires access to all the buffers in the architecture in order to take the optimal decision in assigning worker threads. The objective is to have all the threads in the pool running while moving chunks fast enough through the pipeline such that the execution engine is always busy. At the same time, the scheduler has to make sure that progress is always possible and the pipeline does not block. While designing a scheduling algorithm that guarantees progress is an achievable task, designing an optimal algorithm is considerably more complicated. For this reason, it is common in practice to develop heuristics that guarantee correctness while providing some kind of optimality in certain conditions. This is exactly the approach we take in SCANRAW. In our implementation, the scheduler uses a best-effort heuristic and satisfies requests in the order in which they are received while guaranteeing progress.

3.2.2 *Worker Threads*

Stand-alone threads are static. The task they perform is fixed at implementation. Worker threads, on the other hand, are dynamically configured at runtime with the task they perform. As a general rule, stand-alone threads perform management tasks that control the data flow through the pipeline while worker threads perform the actual data processing. Since the entire process of assigning threads incurs overhead, it has to be the case that the time taken by data processing offsets the overhead. This is realized by making tasks operating over chunks or vectors of tuples rather than individual tuples. As depicted in Figure 2, two types of tasks can be assigned to worker threads—TOKENIZE and PARSE. The operations that are executed by each of them and possible optimizations are discussed in Section 2. The scheduler selects the task to assign to each worker from a set of requests made by the corresponding consumer threads.

3.3 Integration with a Database

Query processing. At a high level, SCANRAW is similar to the database *heap scan* operator. Heap scan reads the pages corresponding to a table from disk, extracts the tuples, and maps them in the internal processing representation. Relative to the process depicted in Figure 1, the extract phase in heap scan consists of MAP only. There is no TOKENIZE and PARSE. It is natural then for the database engine to treat SCANRAW similar to the heap scan operator and place it in the leaves of query execution plans. Moreover, SCANRAW morphs into heap scan as data are loaded in the database. The main difference between SCANRAW and heap scan though – and any other standard database operator for that matter – is that SCANRAW is not destroyed once a query finishes execution. This is because SCANRAW is not attached to a query but rather to the raw file it extracts data from. As such, the state of the internal buffers is preserved across queries in order to guarantee improved performance—not the case for the standard heap scan. When a new query arrives, the execution engine first checks the existence of a corresponding SCANRAW operator. If such an operator exists, it is connected to the query execution plan. Only otherwise it is created. When is a SCANRAW instance completely deleted then? Whenever it loaded the entire raw file into the database.

Query optimization. To effectively use SCANRAW in query optimization, additional data, i.e., statistics, have to be gathered. This is typically done as a stand-alone process executed at certain time intervals. In the case of SCANRAW, statistics are collected while data are converted in the database representation which is triggered in turn by query processing. Statistics are stored in the metadata catalog. The types of statistics collected by SCANRAW include the position in the raw file where each chunk starts and the minimum/maximum value corresponding to each attribute in every chunk. More advanced statistics such as the number of distinct elements and the skew of an attribute – or even samples – can be also extracted during the conversion stage. The collected statistics are later used for two purposes. First, the number of chunks read from disk can be reduced in the case of selection predicates. For this to be effective though, data inside the chunk have to be clustered. While WRITE can sort data in each chunk prior to loading, SCANRAW does not address the problem of completely sorting and reorganizing data based on queries, i.e., database cracking [22]. The second use case for statistics is cardinality estimation for traditional query optimization.

Resource management. SCANRAW resources are allocated dynamically at runtime by the database resource manager in order to better control the operation and to optimize system utilization. For this to be possible though, measurements accounting for CPU usage and memory utilization have to be taken and integrated in the resource allocation procedure. The scheduler is in the best position to monitor resource utilization since it manages the allocation of worker threads from the pool and inspects buffer utilization. These data are relayed to the database resource manager as requests for additional resources or are used to determine when to release resources. For example, if the scheduler assigns all the worker threads in the pool for task execution but the text chunks buffer is still full – SCANRAW is CPU-bound – additional CPUs are needed in order to cope with the I/O throughput. With respect to memory utilization, it makes sense to allocate more memory to SCANRAW instances that are used more often since this increases the rate of data reuse across queries.

4. SPECULATIVE LOADING

By default, SCANRAW operates as a parallel external table operator. It provides instant access to data without pre-loading. This results in optimal performance for the first query accessing the raw data. What about a workload consisting of a sequence of queries? What is the SCANRAW behavior in that case? The default external table regime is sub-optimal since tokenizing and parsing have to be executed again and again. Ideally, only useful work, i.e., reading and processing, should be performed starting with the second data access. Traditional databases achieve this by pre-loading the data in their processing format. They give up instant data access though.

Is it possible to achieve both optimal execution time for all the queries in a sequential workload and instant data access for the first query? This is the research question we ask in this section. Our solution is *speculative loading*. In speculative loading, instant access to data is guaranteed. It is also guaranteed that subsequent queries accessing the same data execute faster and faster, achieving database performance at some point—the entire data accessed by the query are read from the database at that time. Moreover, speculative loading achieves database performance the earliest possible while preserving optimal execution time for all the queries in-between. In some cases this is realized from the second query. The main idea in speculative loading is to find those time intervals during raw file query processing when there is no disk reading going on and use them for database writing. The intuition is that query processing speed is not affected since the execution is CPU-bound and the disk is idle. Notice though that a highly-parallel architecture consisting of asynchronous threads capable to detect free I/O bandwidth and overlap processing with disk operations is required in order to implement speculative loading. SCANRAW accomplishes these requirements.

There are two solutions in the literature that are related to speculative loading. In invisible loading [4], a fixed amount of data – specified as a number of chunks – are loaded for every query even if that slows down the processing. In fact, invisible loading increases execution time for all the queries accessing raw data. NoDB [5] achieves optimal execution time for all the queries in a workload only when all the accessed data fit in memory. Loading is not considered in NoDB. Only in-memory caching. A possible extension to NoDB – explored in [10] – is to flush data into the database when the memory is full. This results in oscillating query performance, i.e., whenever flushing is triggered query execution time increases.

How does speculative loading work? The central idea in speculative loading is to let SCANRAW decide adaptively at runtime what data to load, how much, and when while maintaining optimal query execution performance. These decisions are taken dynamically by the scheduler, in charge of coordinating disk access between READ and WRITE. Since the scheduler monitors the utilization of the buffers and assigns worker threads for task execution, it can identify when READ is blocked. This can happen for two reasons. First, conversion from raw format to database representation – tokenizing and parsing – is too time-consuming. Second, query execution is the bottleneck. In both cases, processing is CPU-bound. At that time, the scheduler signals WRITE to load chunks in the database. While the maximum number of chunks to be loaded is determined by the scheduler based on the pipeline utilization, the actual chunks are strictly determined by WRITE based on the catalog metadata. In order to minimize the impact on query execution performance, only the "oldest" chunk in the binary cache that was not previously loaded into the database is written at a time. This increases the chance to load more chunks before they are eliminated from the cache. It is important for the scheduler not to allow reading start before writing finishes in order to avoid disk interference. This is realized with the resume control message (Figure 3) whenever worker threads become available and WRITE returns.

Why does speculative loading not interfere with query execution? Speculative loading is triggered only when there is no disk utilization. Rather than let the disk idle, this "dead" time is used for loading—a task with minimal CPU usage that has little to no impact on the overall CPU utilization. Especially for the modern multi-core processors with a high degree of parallelism. What about memory interference in the binary chunks cache? Something like this can happen only when the chunk being written to disk has to be expelled from the cache. As long as there is at least one other chunk already processed, that chunk can be eliminated instead. The larger the cache size, the higher the chance to find such a chunk.

How do we guarantee that new chunks are loaded for every query? Since speculative loading is entirely driven by resource utilization in the system, there is no guarantee that new chunks will get loaded for every query. For example, if I/O is the bottleneck in query processing, no loading is possible whatsoever. Thus, we have to develop a *safeguard mechanism* that enforces a minimum amount of loading but without decreasing query processing performance. Our solution is based on the following observation. At the end of a scan over the raw file, the binary chunks cache contains a set of converted chunks that are kept there until the next query starts scanning the file. These chunks are the perfect candidates to load in the database. Writing can start as soon as the last chunk was read from the raw file—not necessarily after query processing finishes. Moreover, the next query can be admitted immediately since it can start processing the cached chunks first. Only the reading of new chunks from disk has to be delayed until flushing the cache to disk. This is very unlikely to affect query performance though. If it does, an alternative solution is to delay the admission of the next query until flushing the cache is over—a standard procedure in multi-query processing. It is important to emphasize that the safeguard mechanism is the norm for invisible loading [4] while in speculative loading it is invoked only in rare circumstances. There is nothing stopping us to invoke it for every query though.

How does speculative loading improve performance for a sequence of queries? The chunks written to the database do not require tokenization and parsing. This guarantees improved query performance as long as new data are loaded for every query. The safeguard mechanism enforces chunk loading independent of the system resource utilization. In order to show how speculative loading improves query execution, we provide an illustrative example. Since the amount of data loaded due to resource utilization is non-deterministic – thus hard to illustrate – we focus on the safeguard mechanism. For the purpose of this example, we assume that the safeguard is invoked after every query. Consider a raw file consisting of 8 chunks. The binary cache can contain 2 chunks. The first query that accesses the file reads all the data and converts them to binary representation. For simplicity, assume that chunks are read and processed in sequential order. At the end of the first query, chunk 7 and 8 reside in the cache. Thus, the safeguard mechanism flushes them to the database. Query 2 processes the chunks in the order $\{7, 8, 1, 2, 3, 4, 5, 6\}$, with chunk 7 and 8 delivered from the cache. Since fewer chunks are converted from raw format, query 2 runs faster than query 1. At the end of query 2, chunk 5 and 6 reside in the cache and they are flushed to the database. Query 3 processes the chunks in the order $\{5, 6, 7, 8, 1, 2, 3, 4\}$. The first two chunks are in the cache, the next two are read from the database without tokenizing and parsing while only the remaining 4 are converted from the raw file. This makes query 3 execute faster than query 2. Repeating the same process, chunk 3 and 4 are loaded in the database at the end of query 3 and by the end of query 4 all data are loaded.

5. EXPERIMENTAL EVALUATION

The objective of the experimental evaluation is to investigate the SCANRAW performance across a variety of datasets – synthetic and real – and workloads—including a single query as well as a se-

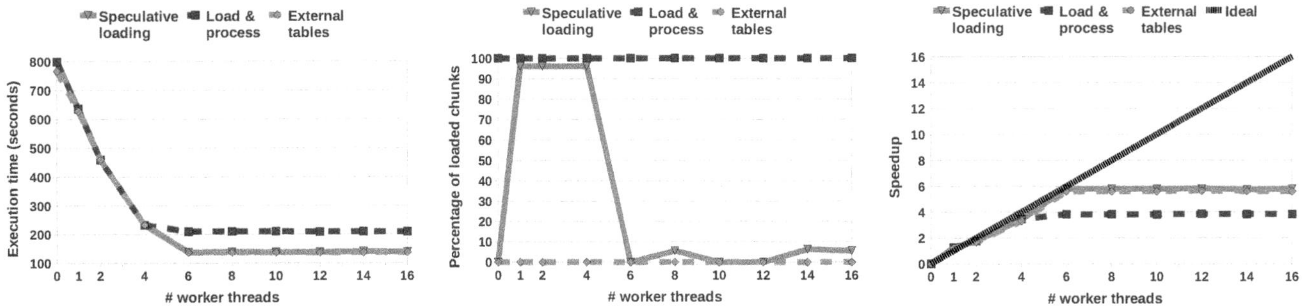

(a) (b) (c)

Figure 4: Execution time (a), percentage of loaded data (b), and speedup (c) as a function of the number of worker threads.

quence of queries. Additionally, the sensitivity of the operator is quantified with respect to many configuration parameters. Specifically, the experiments we design are targeted to answer the following questions:

- How is parallelism improving SCANRAW performance and what speedup does SCANRAW achieve?
- What is the performance of speculative loading compared to external tables and database loading & processing, respectively, for a single query? For a sequence of queries?
- Where is the time spent in the pipeline? How does the dynamic SCANRAW architecture adapt to data characteristics? Query characteristics?
- What resource utilization does SCANRAW achieve?
- How does SCANRAW performance compare to other file access libraries?

Implementation. SCANRAW is implemented as a C++ prototype. Each stand-alone thread as well as the workers are implemented as pthread instances. The code contains special function calls to harness detailed profiling data. In the experiments, we use SCANRAW implementations for CSV and tab-delimited flat files, as well as BAM [7] binary files. Adding support for other file formats requires only the implementation of specific TOKENIZE and PARSE workers without changing the basic architecture. We integrate SCANRAW with a state-of-the-art multi-thread database system [6] shown to be I/O-bound for a large class of queries. This guarantees that query processing is not the bottleneck except in rare situations and allows us to isolate the SCANRAW behavior for detailed and accurate measurements. Notice though that integration with a different database requires mapping to a different processing representation without changes to SCANRAW architecture.

System. We execute the experiments on a standard server with 2 AMD Opteron 6128 series 8-core processors (64 bit) – 16 cores – 40 GB of memory, and four 2 TB 7200 RPM SAS hard-drives configured RAID-0 in software. Each processor has 12 MB L3 cache while each core has 128 KB L1 and 512 KB L2 local caches. The storage system supports 240, 436 and 1600 MB/second minimum, average, and maximum read rates, respectively—based on the Ubuntu disk utility. The cached and buffered read rates are 3 GB/second and 565 MB/second, respectively. Ubuntu 12.04.3 SMP 64-bit with Linux kernel 3.2.0-56 is the operating system.

Methodology. We perform all experiments at least 3 times and report the average value as the result. If the experiment consists of a single query, we always enforce data to be read from disk by cleaning the file system buffers before execution. In experiments over a sequence of queries, the buffers are cleaned only before the first query. Thus, the second and subsequent queries can access cached data.

5.1 Micro-Benchmarks

Data. We generate a suite of synthetic CSV files in order to study SCANRAW sensitivity in a controlled setting. There are between 2^{20} and 2^{28} lines in a file in powers of 4 increments. Each line corresponds to a database tuple. The number of columns in a tuple ranges from 2 to 256 in powers of two. Overall, there are 40 files in the suite, i.e., 5 numbers of tuples times 8 numbers of columns. The smallest file contains 2^{20} rows and 2 columns – 20 MB – while the largest is 638 GB in size—2^{28} rows with 256 columns each. The value in each column is a randomly-generated unsigned integer smaller than 2^{31}. The dataset is modeled based on [5, 4]. While we execute the experiments for every file, unless otherwise specified, we report results only for the configuration $2^{26} \times 64$—40 GB in text format.

Query. The query used throughout experiments has the form SELECT SUM($\sum_{j=1}^{K} C_{i_j}$) FROM FILE where K columns C_{i_j} are projected out. By default, K is set to the number of columns in the raw file, e.g., 64 for the majority of the reported results. This simple processing interferes minimally with SCANRAW thus allowing for exact measurements to be taken.

Parallelism. Figure 4 depicts the effect the number of workers in the thread pool has on the execution of speculative loading, query-driven loading and execution – load all data into the database only when queried – and external tables. Notice that all these three regimes are directly supported in SCANRAW with simple modifications to the scheduler writing policy. Zero worker threads correspond to sequential execution, i.e., the chunks go through the conversion stages one at a time. With one or more worker threads, READ and WRITE are separated from conversion—TOKENIZE and PARSE. Moreover, their execution is overlapped. While the general trend is standard – increasing the degree of parallelism results in better performance – there are multiple findings that require clarification. The execution time (Figure 4a) – and the speedup (Figure 4c) – level-off beyond 6 workers. The reason for this is that processing becomes I/O-bound. Increasing the number of worker threads does not improve performance anymore. As expected, loading all data during query processing increases the execution time. What is not expected though is that this is not the case when the number of worker threads is 1, 2, and 4. In these cases, full loading, speculative loading, and external tables have identical execution time. The reason for this behavior is that processing is CPU-bound and – due to parallelism – SCANRAW manages to overlap conver-

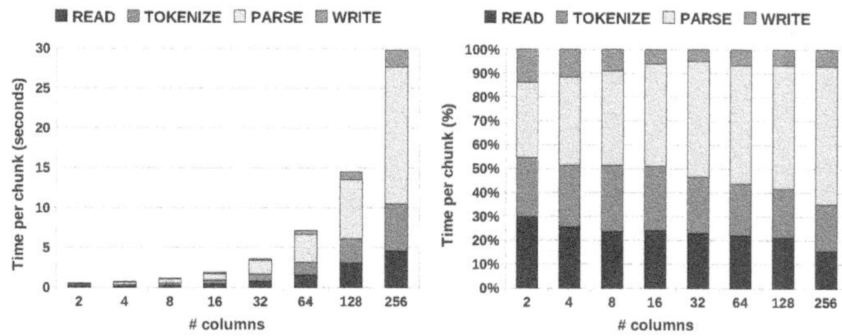

(a) (b)

Figure 5: Pipeline execution time: (a) absolute, (b) relative.

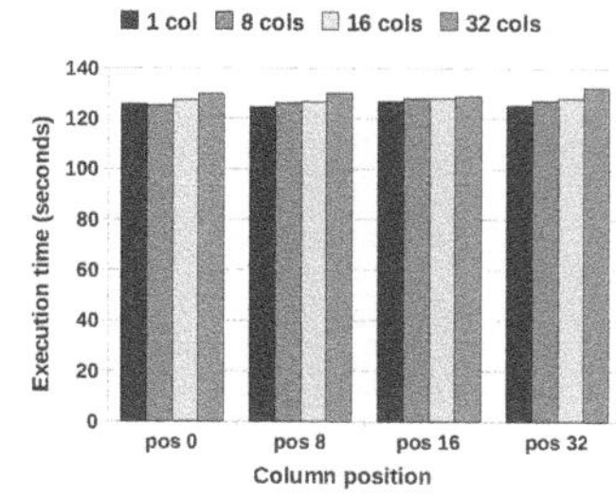

Figure 6: Position and number of columns.

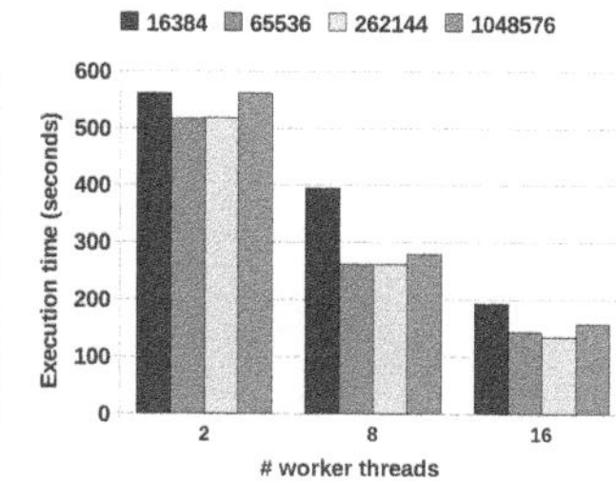

Figure 7: Chunk size.

sion to binary and loading into the database completely. Essentially, loading comes for free since the disk is idle. All the unique SCANRAW features – super-scalar pipeline, asynchronous threads, dynamic scheduling – combine together to make loading and processing as efficient as external tables. We are not aware of any other raw file processing operator capable to achieve this performance. The effect of parallel processing on speculative loading is illustrated in Figure 4b. As long as the execution is CPU-bound, speculative loading operates as full loading, writing almost all the converted chunks into the database. This happens for a small number of worker threads, i.e., less than 6. As soon as there are enough workers (6 or more) to handle all data read from disk – the execution becomes I/O-bound – SCANRAW switches to external tables and does not load any chunks at all, i.e., there is no speculative loading. In Figure 4a, the curves for external tables and speculative loading are always overlapped for more than one thread. Independent of the number of workers, SCANRAW minimizes query execution time.

Pipeline analysis. Figure 5 depicts the duration of each stage in the SCANRAW pipeline for all the column sizes considered in the experimental dataset, i.e., 2 to 256 in powers of 2. The number of lines in all the files is 2^{26}. WRITE time is included in these measurements since the experiment is executed with full data loading. We report the average time per chunk in each stage over all the chunks in the file. The absolute time to process a chunk is shown in Figure 5a. As expected, when the number of columns increases, so does the chunk processing time. More exactly, the time doubles with the doubling in the number of columns. For more than 16 columns, PARSE is by far the most time-consuming stage. This is where database processing over binary data outperforms standard external tables. This is also the operation point targeted by SCANRAW with massive parallelism supported by the modern many- and multi-core processors. Essentially, SCANRAW transforms this CPU-bound task into typical database I/O-bound processing (Figure 4a) over raw files, thus making data loading obsolete. Figure 5b gives the relative distribution of the data in Figure 5a. The relative significance of I/O operations – READ and WRITE – drops from 45% for 2 columns to approximately 20% for 256 columns. PARSE doubles from 30% to 60%. This proves that PARSE is the stage to optimize in order to make raw file processing efficient. SCANRAW achieves this through parallelization. The other alternative is saving (caching) the binary conversion.

Position and number of columns. Figure 6 depicts the effect of two parameters on SCANRAW performance—the number of columns projected by the query and the starting position of the first column. In this experiment, we consider that only a continuous subset of the 64 columns are required in the query. The starting position of the subset – the first column – is also a parameter. The purpose is to measure the effect of selective tokenizing and parsing on SCANRAW performance. SCANRAW is configured with 8 worker threads. Increasing the number of columns required in the query results in a slight increase in the conversion time—less than 5%. This is expected since the number of function calls in PARSE increases. The position of the first column in the subset does not impact performance. The reason for this is that the minimal increase in tokenization time is completely hidden by parallel execution. These results confirm once more that PARSE is the stage to optimize in raw file processing.

Chunk size. The chunk size – number of lines in the file processed as a unit – has a dramatic impact on the pipeline efficiency—depicted in Figure 7. The chunk size has to be large enough to hide the overhead introduced by the dynamic allocation of tasks to worker threads. If too large, it takes longer to fill and free the pipeline since the amount of overlap is limited. While the actual chunk size is dependent on the data, we found that between 2^{17} and 2^{19} tuples per chunk are optimal for our datasets. The chunk size used throughout the experiments is $2^{19} \approx 500K$.

Speculative loading for a query sequence. Figure 8 depicts SCANRAW performance for a query sequence consisting of 6 standard queries, i.e., SELECT SUM($\sum_{i=1}^{64} C_i$) FROM $2^{26}\times 64$. Executing instances of the same query guarantees that the same data are accessed in every query. This allows us to detect and quantify the effect the data source has on query performance. The methods we compare are database loading, buffered loading, i.e., data are written to the database only when the binary cache buffer is full, external tables, and speculative loading. The size of the binary cache used in buffered and speculative loading, respectively, is 32 chunks. Since SCANRAW is configured with 16 worker threads, speculative loading behaves similar to external tables. This allows us to verify the effectiveness of the safeguard mechanism. Since the number of chunks loaded during query processing is non-deterministic, it is more difficult to observe. Figure 8a shows the execution time for every query in the sequence. As expected, this is (almost) constant for external tables. Data are always read from the raw file, tokenized, and parsed before being passed to the execution engine. The same is true for database execution starting from the second query—the first query incurs the entire loading time, thus it takes significantly longer. The difference is that database execution is considerably faster than external tables—a factor of 2.5. In SCANRAW, this is entirely due to the difference in size between text and binary format—40 GB and 16 GB, respectively. Buffered loading distributes the loading time over the first two queries since not all data fit in memory. Every chunk expelled from the cache is automatically written to the database. As a result, there is a decrease in

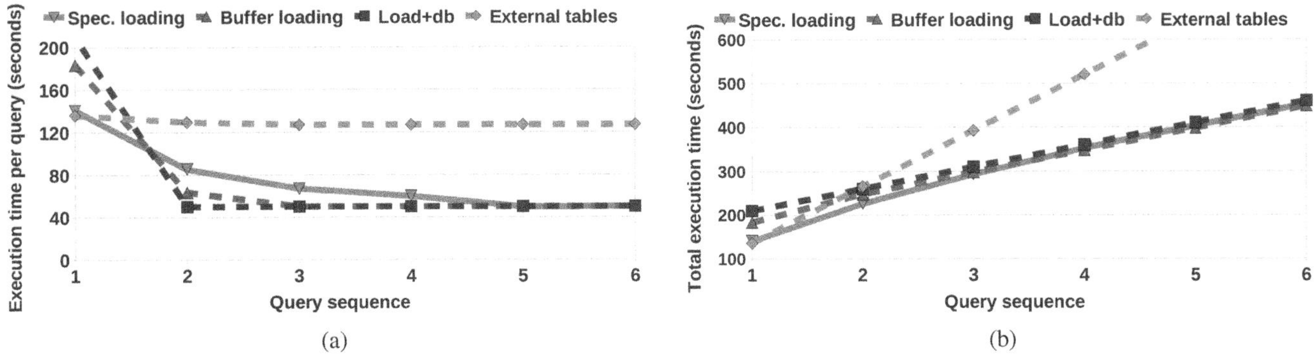

Figure 8: Execution time for a sequence of queries. (a) Execution time for query i. (b) Overall execution time up to query i.

runtime for the first query when compared to standard loading. For the second query though, execution time is larger. Speculative loading exhibits a considerably more interesting behavior. It has exactly the same execution time as external tables for the first query – this is the absolute minimum that can be achieved – and then converges to the database execution time after a number of queries. According to Figure 8a, it takes only 5 queries. This is expected since the size of the cache is $1/4^{\text{th}}$ of the number of chunks accessed by the query. Even though speculative loading operates in external tables mode, it manages to load additional chunks – 2-4 chunks, to be precise – into the database in the interval between reading finishes and query execution completes. This is possible only because of the asynchronous multi-thread SCANRAW architecture.

Figure 8b shows the overall execution time after i queries in the sequence, where i goes from 1 to 6. At least two important observations can be drawn. First, after only two queries data loading already pays off since the database performance is equal to external tables. This proves that SCANRAW loading is optimal. Second, speculative loading is always more efficient than database processing. This is somehow unexpected since database processing is supposed to be optimal when a large enough number of queries are executed. The reason this is happening is because even though speculative loading goes multiple times to the raw file, it only reads data not cached or loaded. The difference becomes even larger when the text file has a size comparable to the binary format. Moreover, speculative loading achieves optimal performance at any point in the query sequence—including the first query. This is not true for buffered loading even though not all data are loaded into the database. It is important to notice that speculative loading has similar behavior as buffered loading when all data fit in memory. The only difference is that speculative loading materializes cached data into the database proactively, when resources are available.

Resource utilization. In Figure 9, we display the SCANRAW CPU and I/O utilization for processing a 256 column raw file with speculative loading. In this situation, the execution is CPU-bound even for 8 worker threads—the reason why CPU utilization goes to 800. The interesting aspect to observe here is how the SCANRAW scheduler alternates between READ and WRITE in order to utilize resources optimally. Whenever the CPU is fully-utilized and no reading is executed, WRITE is triggered to load data into the database. This results in a temporary decrease in disk utilization since writing is done one chunk at a time. As soon as worker threads become available, the scheduler resumes reading and disk utilization goes back to 100% since a sequence of chunks are typically read at a time.

5.2 Real Data

Method	Execution time (sec)
External tables (SAM)	370
External tables (BAM + BAMTools)	2714
Data loading (SAM)	945
Database processing	122
Speculative loading (SAM)	370

Table 1: SCANRAW performance on SAM/BAM data.

In order to evaluate SCANRAW on a real dataset, we use genomic sequence alignment data from the *1000 Genomes* project [2]. These data come in two formats—SAM is text while BAM is compressed binary. We use the file corresponding to individual NA12878 containing more than 400 million reads. SAM is 145 GB in size while BAM is 26 GB. As for processing, we compute the distribution of the CIGAR field at positions in the genome where reads exhibit a certain pattern. The SQL equivalent is a group-by aggregate query with a pattern matching predicate. Table 1 shows the results we obtain for different SCANRAW configurations. In all the queries over SAM files, we use a SCANRAW implementation for processing tab-delimited text files. The tokenizing and parsing are handled inside SCANRAW. For BAM file processing, we use BAMTools [7] to extract the tuples from binary and implement only MAP in SCANRAW. There is a single operation executed in MAP—convert the BAMTools internal representation to SCANRAW. While the results are standard – database processing is fastest, followed by external tables, and data loading – the comparison between SAM and BAM processing is surprising. SCANRAW takes more than 7 times less to process a file more than 5 times larger. After careful investigation, we found the problem to be BAMTools. The SAM implementation in SCANRAW parallelizes tokenizing and parsing such that processing becomes I/O-bound. For BAM, file data access and decompression are sequential and handled inside BAMTools. The process is heavily CPU-bound. While we did not modify the BAMTools code, we parallelized MAP—without any performance gains.

5.3 Discussion

The experimental results confirm the benefits of the SCANRAW super-scalar pipeline architecture for in-situ data processing. Parallel execution at chunk granularity results in linear speedup for CPU-bound tasks. SCANRAW with speculative loading achieves optimal performance across a sequence of queries at any point in the execution. It is similar to external tables for the first query and more efficient than database processing in the long run. Moreover, SCANRAW makes full data loading efficient to the point where database processing – with pre-loading – achieves better overall execution time than external tables even for a two-query sequence. While the time distribution is split almost equally between I/O and CPU-intensive pipeline stages when the number of columns in the file is small, CPU-intensive stages – TOKENIZE and PARSE – account for more than 80% of the time to process a chunk when the raw file contains a large number of numeric attributes. By overlapping processing across multiple chunks and between stages, SCANRAW makes even this type of execution I/O-bound. This guarantees optimal resource utilization in the system. Due to parallel conversion from text to binary, SCANRAW outperforms BAMTools by a factor of 7 while processing a file 5 times larger.

6. RELATED WORK

Several researchers [13, 3, 23, 16, 15] have recently identified the need to reduce the analysis time for processing tasks operating over massive repositories of raw data. In-situ processing [14] has been confirmed as one promising approach. At a high level, we can group in-situ data processing into two categories. In the first category, we have extensions to traditional database systems that allow raw file processing inside the execution engine. Examples include external tables [25, 18, 17] and various optimizations that eliminate the requirement for scanning the entire file to answer the query [10, 5, 11]. The second category is organized around the MapReduce programming paradigm [12] and its implementation in Hadoop. While some of the data extraction is implemented by adapters that convert data from various representations into the Hadoop internal format [19], the application is still responsible for a significant part of the conversion, i.e., the Map and Reduce functions contain large amounts of tokenizing and parsing code. The work in this category focuses on eliminating the conversion code by caching the already converted data in memory or storing it in binary format inside a database [4].

External tables. Modern database engines, e.g., Oracle [25] and MySQL [17], provide external tables as a feature to directly query flat files using SQL without paying the upfront cost of loading the data into the system. External tables work by linking a database table with a specified schema to a flat file. Whenever a tuple is required during query processing, it is read from the flat file, parsed into the internal database representation, and passed to the execution engine. Our work can be viewed as a parallel pipelined implementation of external tables that takes advantage of the current multi-core processors for improving performance significantly when mapping data into the processing representation is expensive. As far as we know, SCANRAW is the first parallel pipelined solution for external tables in the literature. Moreover, SCANRAW goes well beyond the external tables functionality and supports speculative loading, tokenizing, and parsing.

Adaptive partial loading [10]. The main idea in adaptive partial loading is to avoid the upfront cost of loading the entire data into the database. Instead, data are loaded only at query time and only the attributes required by the query, i.e., push-down projection. An additional optimization aimed at further reducing the amount of loaded data is to push the selection predicates into the loading operator, i.e., push-down selection, such that only the tuples participating in the other query operators are loaded. The proposed adaptive loading operator is invoked whenever columns or tuples required in the current query are not stored yet in the database. It is important to notice that the operator executes a partial data loading before query execution can proceed. While SCANRAW supports adaptive partial loading, it avoids loading all the data into the database the first time they are accessed. Query processing has higher priority. Data are loaded only if sufficient I/O bandwidth is available.

NoDB [5]. NoDB never loads data into the database. It always reads data from the raw file thus incurring the inherent overhead associated with tokenizing and parsing. Efficiency is achieved by a series of techniques that address these sources of overhead. Caching is used extensively to store data converted in the database representation in memory. If all data fit in memory NoDB operates as an in-memory database, without accessing the disk. Whenever data have to be read from the raw file, tokenizing and parsing have to be executed. This is done adaptively though. A positional map with the starting position of all the attributes in all the tuples completely eliminates tokenizing. The positional map is built incrementally, from the executed queries. Moreover, only the attributes required in the current query are parsed. When the positional map, selective parsing, and caching are put together, NoDB achieves performance comparable – if not better – to executing queries over data stored in the database. This happens though only when NoDB operates over cached data, as an in-memory database. The main difference between SCANRAW and NoDB is that SCANRAW still loads data into the databases—without paying any cost for it though. Additionally, SCANRAW implements a parallel pipeline for data conversion. This is not the case in NoDB which is implemented as a PostgreSQL extension.

Data vaults [11]. Data vaults apply the same idea of query-driven just-in-time caching of raw data in memory. They are used in conjunction with scientific repositories though and the cache stores multi-dimensional arrays extracted from various scientific file formats. Similar to NoDB, the cached arrays are never written to the database. The ability to execute queries over relations stored in the database, cached arrays, and scientific file repositories using SciQL as a common query language is the main contribution brought by data vaults.

Invisible loading [4]. Invisible loading extends adaptive partial loading and caching to MapReduce applications which operate natively over raw files stored in a distributed file system. The database is used as a disk-based cache that stores the content of the raw file in binary format. This eliminates the inherent cost of tokenizing and parsing data for every query. Notice though that processing is still executed by the MapReduce framework, not the database. Thus, the database acts only as a more efficient storage layer. In invisible loading, data converted into the MapReduce internal representation are first stored in the database and only then are passed for processing. While this is similar to adaptive partial loading [10], an additional optimization is aimed at reducing the storing time. Instead of saving all the data into the database, only a pre-determined fraction of a file is stored for every query. The intuition is to spread the cost of loading across multiple queries and to make sure that loaded data are indeed used by more than a single query. The result is a smooth decrease in query time instead of a steep drop after the first query—responsible for loading all the required data. The proposed speculative loading implemented in SCANRAW brings two novel contributions with respect to invisible loading. First, the amount of data loaded for every query changes dynamically based on the available system resources. Speculative loading degenerates to invisible loading only in the case when no I/O bandwidth is available. And second, speculative loading overlaps entirely with query processing without having any negative effects on query performance. This is the result of the SCANRAW pipelined architecture.

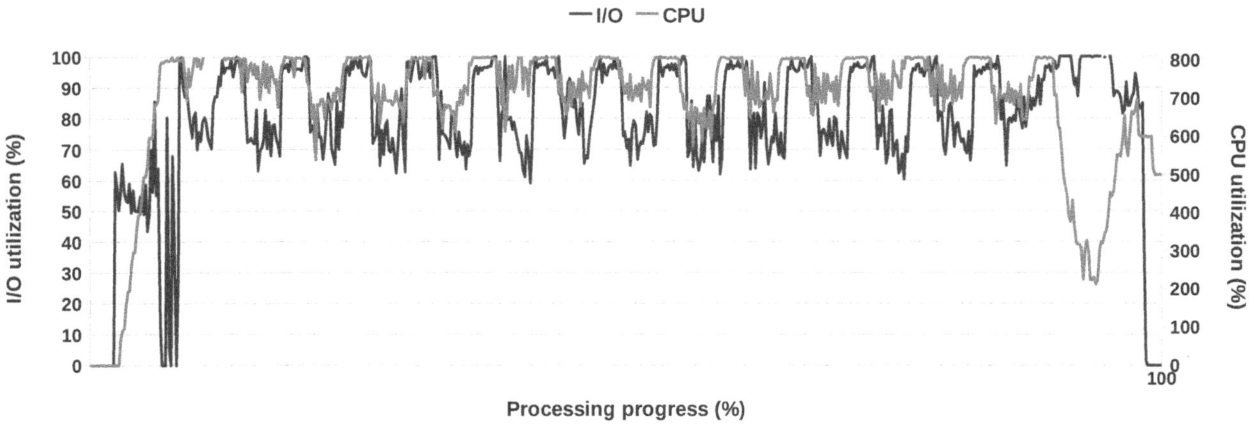

Figure 9: Resource utilization in SCANRAW.

Instant loading [24]. Instant loading proposes scalable bulk loading methods that take full advantage of the modern super-scalar multi-core CPUs. Specifically, vectorized implementations using SSE 4.2 SIMD instructions are proposed for tokenizing and parsing. These stages are still executed sequentially though for every data partition—there is no pipeline parallelism. Moreover, instant loading does not support raw file query processing. SCANRAW on the other hand overlaps the execution of tokenizing and parsing both across data partitions and for each partition individually. And with the actual query processing and/or loading. Overall, instant loading introduces faster algorithms for tokenizing and parsing that can be immediately integrated in SCANRAW. We plan to do so in the future and investigate the performance of SCANRAW with tokenizing and parsing implemented using the vectorized techniques proposed in [24].

7. CONCLUSIONS AND FUTURE WORK

In this paper, we propose SCANRAW—a novel database physical operator for in-situ processing over raw files that integrates data loading and external tables seamlessly while preserving their advantages. SCANRAW supports single-query optimal execution with a *parallel super-scalar pipeline implementation* that overlaps data reading, conversion into the database representation, and query processing. SCANRAW implements *speculative loading* as a gradual loading mechanism to store converted data inside the database. We implement SCANRAW in a state-of-the-art database system and evaluate its performance across a variety of synthetic and real-world datasets. Our results show that SCANRAW with speculative loading achieves optimal performance for a query sequence at any point in the processing. In future work, we plan to focus on extending SCANRAW with support for multi-query processing over raw files.

8. REFERENCES

[1] New NIH-Funded Resource Focuses on Use of Genomic Variants in Medical Care, 2013. http://www.nih.gov/news/health/sep2013/nhgri-25.htm.

[2] 1000 Genomes. http://www.1000genomes.org/data.

[3] A. Ailamaki, V. Kantere, and D. Dash. Managing Scientific Data. *Commun. ACM*, 53, 2010.

[4] A. Abouzied, D. Abadi, and A. Silberschatz. Invisible Loading: Access-Driven Data Transfer from Raw Files into Database Systems. In *EDBT/ICDT 2013*.

[5] I. Alagiannis, R. Borovica, M. Branco, S. Idreos, and A. Ailamaki. NoDB: Efficient Query Execution on Raw Data Files. In *SIGMOD 2012*.

[6] S. Arumugam, A. Dobra, C. Jermaine, N. Pansare, and L. Perez. The DataPath System: A Data-Centric Analytic Processing Engine for Large Data Warehouses. In *SIGMOD 2010*.

[7] BAMTools. http://sourceforge.net/bamtools/.

[8] D. J. DeWitt and J. Gray. Parallel Database Systems: The Future of Database Processing or a Passing Fad? *SIGMOD Rec.*, 19, 1991.

[9] H. Li et al. The Sequence Alignment/Map Format and SAMtools. *Bioinformatics*, 25(16), 2009.

[10] S. Idreos, I. Alagiannis, R. Johnson, and A. Ailamaki. Here Are My Data Files. Here Are My Queries. Where Are My Results? In *CIDR 2011*.

[11] M. Ivanova, M. L. Kersten, and S. Manegold. Data Vaults: A Symbiosis between Database Technology and Scientific File Repositories. In *SSDBM 2012*.

[12] J. Dean and S. Ghemawat. MapReduce: Simplified Data Processing on Large Clusters. *Commun. ACM*, 51(1), 2008.

[13] J. Gray et al. Scientific Data Management in the Coming Decade. *SIGMOD Rec.*, 34, 2005.

[14] K. Lorincz et al. Grep versus FlatSQL versus MySQL: Queries using UNIX tools vs. a DBMS, 2003. Harvard University.

[15] M. Kersten, S. Idreos, S. Manegold, and E. Liarou. The Researcher's Guide to the Data Deluge: Querying a Scientific Database in Just a Few Seconds. *PVLDB*, 4, 2011.

[16] M. Stonebraker et al. Requirements for Science Data Bases and SciDB. In *CIDR 2009*.

[17] MySQL CSV Storage Engine. http://dev.mysql.com/doc/refman/5.0/en/csv-storage-engine.html.

[18] N. Alur et al. *IBM DataStage Data Flow and Job Design*. 2008.

[19] Optiq. https://github.com/julianhyde/optiq.

[20] R. Avnur and J. Hellerstein. Eddies: Continuously Adaptive Query Processing. In *SIGMOD 2000*.

[21] S. Idreos et al. MonetDB: Two Decades of Research in Column-Oriented Database Architectures. *IEEE Data Eng. Bull.*, 35(1), 2012.

[22] S. Idreos, S. Manegold, H. Kuno, and G. Graefe. Merging What's Cracked, Cracking What's Merged: Adaptive Indexing in Main-Memory Column-Stores. *PVLDB*, 4, 2011.

[23] T. Hey, S. Tansley, and K. Tolle. The Fourth Paradigm: Data-Intensive Scientific Discovery, 2009. Microsoft Research.

[24] T. Muhlbauer et al. Instant Loading for Main Memory Databases. *PVLDB*, 6(14), 2013.

[25] A. Witkowski, M. Colgan, A. Brumm, T. Cruanes, and H. Baer. Performant and Scalable Data Loading with Oracle Database 11g, 2011.

Approximation Schemes for Many-Objective Query Optimization*

Immanuel Trummer and Christoph Koch
École Polytechnique Fédérale de Lausanne
{firstname}.{lastname}@epfl.ch

ABSTRACT

The goal of multi-objective query optimization (MOQO) is to find query plans that realize a good compromise between conflicting objectives such as minimizing execution time and minimizing monetary fees in a Cloud scenario. A previously proposed exhaustive MOQO algorithm needs hours to optimize even simple TPC-H queries. This is why we propose several approximation schemes for MOQO that generate guaranteed near-optimal plans in seconds where exhaustive optimization takes hours.

We integrated all MOQO algorithms into the Postgres optimizer and present experimental results for TPC-H queries; we extended the Postgres cost model and optimize for up to nine conflicting objectives in our experiments. The proposed algorithms are based on a formal analysis of typical cost functions that occur in the context of MOQO. We identify properties that hold for a broad range of objectives and can be exploited for the design of future MOQO algorithms.

Categories and Subject Descriptors

H.2.4 [**Database Management**]: Systems—*Query processing*

Keywords

Query optimization; multi-objective optimization

1. INTRODUCTION

Minimizing execution time is the only objective in classical query optimization [23]. Nowadays, there are however many scenarios in which additional objectives are of interest that should be considered during query optimization. This leads to the problem of multi-objective query optimization (MOQO) in which the goal is to find a query plan that realizes the best compromise between conflicting objectives. Consider the following example scenarios.

*This work was supported by ERC grant 279804.

SIGMOD'14, June 22–27, 2014, Snowbird, UT, USA.
Copyright 2014 ACM 978-1-4503-2376-5/14/06 ...$15.00.
http://dx.doi.org/10.1145/2588555.2610527.

Scenario 1. A Cloud provider lets users submit queries on data that resides in the Cloud. Queries are processed in the Cloud and users are billed according to the accumulated processing time over all nodes that participated in processing a certain query. The processing time of aggregation queries can be reduced by using sampling but this has a negative impact on result quality. From the perspective of the users, this leads to the three conflicting objectives of minimizing execution time, minimizing monetary costs, and minimizing the loss in result quality. Users specify preferences in their profiles by setting weights on different objectives, representing relative importance, and by optionally specifying constraints (e.g., an upper bound on execution time). Upon reception of a query, the Cloud provider needs to find a query plan that meets all constraints while minimizing the weighted sum over different cost metrics.

Scenario 2. A powerful server processes queries of multiple users concurrently. Minimizing the amount of system resources (such as buffer space, hard disk space, I/O bandwidth, and number of cores) that are dedicated for processing one specific query and minimizing that query's execution time are conflicting objectives (each specific system resource would correspond to an objective on its own). Upon reception of a query, the system must find a query plan that represents the best compromise between all conflicting objectives, considering weights and bounds defined by an administrator.

The main contribution in this paper are several MOQO algorithms that are generic enough to be applicable in a variety of scenarios (including the two scenarios outlined above) and are much more efficient than prior approaches while they formally guarantee to generate near-optimal query plans.

1.1 State of the Art

The goal of MOQO, according to our problem model, is to find query plans that minimize a weighted sum over different cost metrics while respecting all cost bounds. This means that multiple cost metrics are finally combined into a single metric (the weighted sum); it is still not possible to reduce MOQO to single-objective query optimization and use classic optimization algorithms such as the one by Selinger [23]. Ganguly et al. have thoroughly justified why this is not possible [11]; we quickly outline the reasons in the following. Algorithms that prune plans based on a single cost metric must rely on the single-objective principle of optimality: replacing subplans (e.g., plans generating join operands) within a query plan by subplans that are better according to that cost metric cannot worsen the entire query plan according to that metric. This principle breaks when the cost metric of interest is a weighted sum over multiple metrics that are calculated according to diverse cost formulas.

EXAMPLE 1. *Assume that each query plan is associated with a two-dimensional cost vector of the form* (t, e) *where* t *represents execution time in seconds and* e *represents energy consumption in Joule. Assume one wants to minimize the weighted sum over time and energy with weight 1 for time and weight 2 for energy, i.e. the sum* $t + 2e$*. Let* p *be a plan that executes two subplans* p_1 *with cost vector* $(7, 1)$ *and* p_2 *with cost vector* $(6, 2)$ *in parallel. The cost vector of* p *is* $(7, 3)$ *since its execution time is the maximum over the execution times of its subplans (*$7 = \max(7, 6)$*) while its energy consumption is the sum of the energy consumptions of its subplans (*$3 = 1+2$*). Replacing* p_1 *within* p *by another plan* p_1' *with cost vector* $(1, 3)$ *changes the cost vector of* p *from* $(7, 3)$ *to* $(6, 5)$*. This means that the weighted cost of* p *becomes worse (it increases from 13 to 16) even if the weighted cost of* p_1' *(7) is better than the one of* p_1 *(9).*

The example shows that the single-objective principle of optimality can break when optimizing a weighted sum of multiple cost metrics. Based on that insight, Ganguly et al. proposed a MOQO algorithm that uses a multi-objective version of the principle of optimality [11]. This algorithm guarantees to generate optimal query plans; it is however too computationally expensive for practical use as we will show in our experiments. The algorithm by Ganguly et al. is the only MOQO algorithm that we are aware of which is generic enough to handle all objectives that were mentioned in the example scenarios before. Most existing MOQO algorithms are specific to certain combinations of objectives where the single-objective principle of optimality holds [2, 28, 16].

1.2 Contributions and Outline

We summarize our contributions before we provide details:

- Our primary contribution are **two approximation schemes** for MOQO that scale to many objectives. They formally guarantee to return near-optimal query plans while speeding up optimization by several orders of magnitude in comparison with exact algorithms.
- We **formally analyze cost formulas** of many relevant objectives in query optimization and derive several common properties. We exploit these properties to design efficient approximation schemes and believe that our observations can serve as starting point for the design of future MOQO algorithms.
- We integrated the exact MOQO algorithm by Ganguly et al. [11] and our own MOQO approximation algorithms into the Postgres optimizer and **experimentally compare** their performance on TPC-H queries.

Our approximation schemes formally guarantee to generate query plans whose cost is within a multiplicative factor α of the optimum in each objective. Parameter α can be tuned seamlessly to trade near-optimality guarantees for lower computational optimization cost. The near-optimality guarantees distinguish our approximation schemes from pure *heuristics*, since heuristics can produce arbitrarily poor plans in the worst case. We show in our experimental evaluation that our approximation schemes reduce query optimization time from hours to seconds, comparing with an existing exact MOQO algorithm proposed by Ganguly et al. that is referred to as EXA in the following.

We discuss related work in Section 2 and introduce the formal model in Section 3. Our experimental evaluation is based on an extended version of Postgres that we describe in Section 4. Note that our algorithms for MOQO are not specific to Postgres and can be used within any database system. We present the first experimental evaluation of the formerly proposed EXA in Section 5. Our experiments relate the poor scalability of EXA to the high number of Pareto plans (i.e., plans representing an optimal tradeoff between different cost objectives) that it needs to generate. The representative-tradeoffs algorithm (RTA), that we present in Section 6, generates only one representative for multiple Pareto plans with similar cost tradeoffs and is therefore much more efficient than EXA. We show that most common objectives in MOQO allow to construct near-optimal plans for joining a set of tables out of near-optimal plans for joining subsets. Due to that property, RTA formally guarantees to generate near-optimal query plans if user preferences are expressed by associating objectives with weights (representing relative importance). If users can specify cost bounds in addition to weights (representing for instance a monetary budget or a deadline), RTA cannot guarantee to generate near-optimal plans anymore and needs to be extended. We present the iterative-refinement algorithm (IRA) in Section 7. IRA uses RTA to generate a representative plan set in every iteration. The approximation precision is refined from one iteration to the next such that the representative plan set resembles more and more the Pareto plan set. IRA stops once it can guarantee that the generated plan set contains a near-optimal plan. A carefully selected precision refinement policy guarantees that the amount of redundant work (by repeatedly generating the same plans in different iterations) is negligible. We analyze the complexity of all presented algorithms and experimentally compare our two approximation schemes (RTA and IRA) against EXA in Section 8.

2. RELATED WORK

Algorithms for **Single-Objective Query Optimization (SOQO)** are not applicable to MOQO or cannot offer any guarantees on result quality. Selinger et al. [23] presented one of the first exact algorithms for SOQO which is based on dynamic programming. **Multi-Objective Query Optimization** is the focus of this paper. The algorithm by Ganguly et al. [11] is a generalization of the SOQO algorithm by Selinger et al. This algorithm is able to generate optimal query plans considering a multitude of objectives with diverse cost formulas. We describe it in more detail later, as we use it as baseline for our experiments.

Algorithms for MOQO have not been experimentally evaluated for more than three objectives. They are usually tailored to very specific combinations of objectives. Neither the proposed algorithms nor the underlying algorithmic ideas can be used for many-objective QO with diverse cost formulas. Allowing only additive cost formulas (and user preference functions) [28, 16] excludes for instance run time as objective in parallel execution scenarios (where time is calculated as maximum over parallel branches). The approach by Aggarwal et al. [2] is specific to the two objectives run time and confidence. Multiple objectives are only considered by selecting an optimal set of table samples prior to join ordering which does not generalize to different objectives. Optimizing different objectives separately misses optimal tradeoffs between conflicting objectives [1]. Separating join ordering and multi-objective optimization (e.g., by generating a time-optimal join tree first, and mapping join operators to sites considering multiple objectives later [12, 21]) assumes that the same join tree is optimal for all objectives. This is only valid in special cases. Papadimitriou and Yannakakis [21] present multi-objective approximation algorithms for mapping operators to sites. Their algorithms do not optimize join order and the underlying approach does not generalize to more than one bounded objective. Algorithms for multi-objective optimization of data processing workflows [24, 25, 17] are not directly applicable to MOQO. Furthermore, the proposed approaches can be classified into heuristics that do not offer near-optimality guarantees [25, 17], and exact algorithms that do not scale [24].

Parametric Query Optimization (PQO) assumes that cost formulas depend on parameters with uncertain values. The goal is for instance to find robust plans [4, 3] or plans that optimize expected cost [7]. PQO and MOQO share certain problem properties while subtle differences prevent us from applying PQO algorithms to MOQO problems in general. Several approaches to PQO split for instance the PQO problem into several SOQO problems [10, 15, 5] by fixing parameter values. This is not possible for MOQO since cost values, unlike parameter values, are only known once a query plan is complete and cannot be fixed in advance. Other PQO algorithms [15] directly work with cost functions instead of scalar values during bottom-up plan construction. This assumes that all parameter values can be selected out of a connected interval which is typically not the case for cost objectives such as time or disc footprint. Our work connects to **Iterative Query Optimization** since we propose iterative algorithms. Kossmann and Stocker [19] propose several iterative algorithms that break the optimization of a large table set into multiple optimization runs for smaller table sets, thereby increasing efficiency. Their algorithm is only applicable to SOQO and does not offer formal guarantees on result quality. Work on **Skyline Queries** [18] and **Optimization Queries** [13] focuses on *query processing* while we focus on *query optimization*. Our work is situated in the broader area of **Approximation Algorithms**. We use generic techniques such as *coarsening* that have been applied to other optimization problems [8, 20]; the corresponding algorithms are however not applicable to query optimization and the specific coarsening methods differ.

3. FORMAL MODEL

We represent **queries** as set of tables Q that need to be joined. This model abstracts away details such as join predicates (that are however considered in the implementations of the presented algorithms). **Query plans** are characterized by the join order and the applied join and scan operators, chosen out of a set $\mathbb{J}$ of available operators. The two plans generating the inputs for the final join in a query plan p are the **sub-plans** of p. The set $\mathbb{O}$ contains all **cost objectives** (e.g., $\mathbb{O} = \{\text{buffer space, execution time}\}$); we assume that a cost model is available for every objective that allows to estimate the cost of a plan. The function $\mathbf{c}(p)$ denotes the multi-dimensional cost of a plan p (bold font distinguishes vectors from scalar values). Cost values are real-valued and non-negative. Let $o \in \mathbb{O}$ an objective, then $\mathbf{c}^o$ denotes the

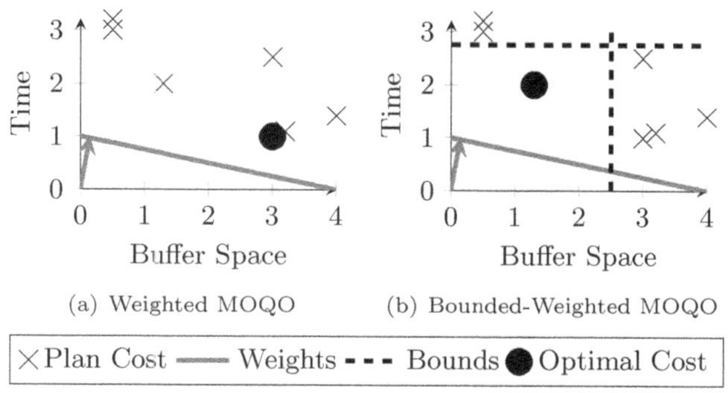

Figure 1: The two MOQO problem variants

cost for o within vector $\mathbf{c}$. Let $\mathbf{W}$ a vector of non-negative weights, then the function $C_{\mathbf{W}}(\mathbf{c}) = \sum_{o\in\mathbb{O}} \mathbf{c}^o\mathbf{W}^o$ denotes the **weighted cost** of $\mathbf{c}$. Let $\mathbf{B}$ a vector of non-negative bounds (setting $\mathbf{B}^o = \infty$ means no bounds), then cost vector $\mathbf{c}$ **exceeds** the bounds if there is at least one objective o with $\mathbf{c}^o > \mathbf{B}^o$. Vector $\mathbf{c}$ **respects** the bounds otherwise. The following two variants of the MOQO problem differ by the expressiveness of the user preference model.

Definition 1. **Weighted MOQO Problem.** A weighted MOQO problem instance is defined by a tuple $I = \langle Q, \mathbf{W}\rangle$ where Q is a query and $\mathbf{W}$ a weight vector. A solution is a query plan for Q. An optimal plan minimizes the weighted cost $C_{\mathbf{W}}$ over all plans for Q.

Definition 2. **Bounded-Weighted MOQO Problem.** A bounded-weighted MOQO problem instance is defined by a tuple $I = \langle Q, \mathbf{W}, \mathbf{B}\rangle$ and extends the weighted MOQO problem by a bounds vector $\mathbf{B}$. Let P the set of plans for Q and $P_{\mathbf{B}} \subseteq P$ the set of plans that respect $\mathbf{B}$. If $P_{\mathbf{B}}$ is non-empty, an optimal plan minimizes $C_{\mathbf{W}}$ among the plans in $P_{\mathbf{B}}$. If $P_{\mathbf{B}}$ is empty, an optimal plan minimizes $C_{\mathbf{W}}$ among the plans in P.

Figure 1(a) illustrates weighted MOQO. It shows cost vectors of possible query plans (considering time and buffer space as objectives) and the user-specified weights (as vector from the origin). The line orthogonal to the weight vector represents cost vectors of equal weighted cost. The optimal plan is found by shifting this line to the top until it touches the first plan cost vector. Figure 1(b) illustrates bounded-weighted MOQO. Additional cost bounds are specified and a different plan is optimal since the formerly optimal plan exceeds the bounds. We will use the set of cost vectors depicted in Figure 1 as **running example** throughout the paper. The relative cost function ρ measures the cost of a plan relative to an optimal plan.

Definition 3. **Relative Cost.** The relative cost function ρ_I of a weighted MOQO instance $I = \langle Q, \mathbf{W}\rangle$ judges a query plan p by comparing its weighted cost to the one of an optimal plan p^*: $\rho_I(p) = C_{\mathbf{W}}(\mathbf{c}(p))/C_{\mathbf{W}}(\mathbf{c}(p^*))$. The relative cost function of a bounded-weighted MOQO instance $I = \langle Q, \mathbf{W}, \mathbf{B}\rangle$ is defined in the same way if no plan exists that respects $\mathbf{B}$. Otherwise, set $\rho_I(p) = \infty$ for any plan p that does not respect $\mathbf{B}$ and $\rho_I(p) = C_{\mathbf{W}}(\mathbf{c}(p))/C_{\mathbf{W}}(\mathbf{c}(p^*))$ if p respects $\mathbf{B}$.

Let $\alpha \geq 1$, then an α**-approximate solution** to a weighted MOQO or bounded-weighted MOQO instance I is a plan p

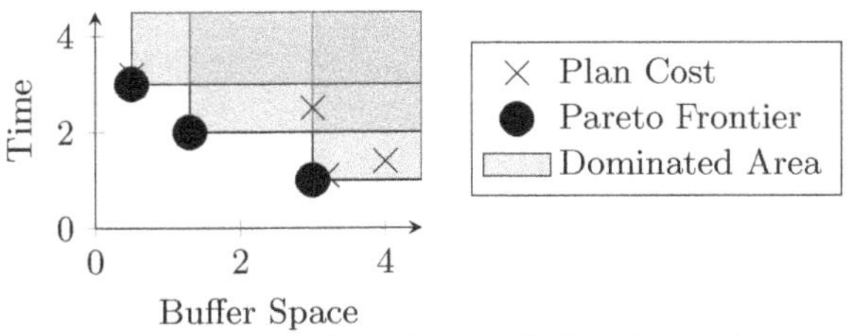

Figure 2: Pareto frontier and dominated area

whose relative cost is bounded by α: $\rho_I(p) \leq \alpha$. The following classification of MOQO algorithms is based on the formal near-optimality guarantees that they offer.

Definition 4. **MOQO Approximation Scheme.** An approximation scheme for MOQO is tuned via a user-specified precision parameter α_U and guarantees to generate an α_U-approximate solution for any MOQO problem instance.

Definition 5. **Exact MOQO Algorithm.** An exact algorithm for MOQO guarantees to generate a 1-approximate (hence optimal) solution for any MOQO problem instance.

The following definitions express relationships between cost vectors. A vector $\mathbf{c}_1$ **dominates** vector $\mathbf{c}_2$, denoted by $\mathbf{c}_1 \preceq \mathbf{c}_2$, if $\mathbf{c}_1$ has lower or equivalent cost than $\mathbf{c}_2$ in every objective. Vector $\mathbf{c}_1$ **strictly dominates** $\mathbf{c}_2$, denoted by $\mathbf{c}_1 \prec \mathbf{c}_2$, if $\mathbf{c}_1 \preceq \mathbf{c}_2$ and the vectors are not equivalent ($\mathbf{c}_1 \neq \mathbf{c}_2$). Vector $\mathbf{c}_1$ **approximately dominates** $\mathbf{c}_2$ with precision α, denoted by $\mathbf{c}_1 \preceq_\alpha \mathbf{c}_2$, if the cost of $\mathbf{c}_1$ is higher at most by factor α in every objective, i.e. $\forall o : \mathbf{c}_1^o \leq \mathbf{c}_2^o \cdot \alpha$. A plan p and its cost vector are **Pareto-optimal** for query Q (short: **Pareto plan** and **Pareto vector**) if no alternative plan for Q strictly dominates p. A **Pareto set** for Q contains at least one cost-equivalent plan for each Pareto plan. The **Pareto frontier** is the set of all Pareto vectors. Figure 2 shows the Pareto frontier of the running example and the area that each Pareto vector dominates. An **α-approximate Pareto set** for Q contains for every Pareto plan p^* a plan p such that $\mathbf{c}(p) \preceq_\alpha \mathbf{c}(p^*)$. An **$\alpha$-approximate Pareto frontier** contains the cost vectors of all plans in an α-approximate Pareto set. During complexity analysis, $j = |\mathbb{J}|$ denotes the number of operators, $l = |\mathbb{O}|$ the number of objectives, $n = |Q|$ the number of tables to join, and m the maximal cardinality over all base tables in the database. Users formulate queries and have direct influence on table cardinalities. Therefore, n and m (and also j) are treated as variables during asymptotic analysis. Introducing new objectives (that cannot be derived from existing ones) requires changes to the code base and detailed experimental analysis to provide realistic cost formulas. This is typically not done by users, therefore l is treated as a constant (the number of objectives is often treated as a constant when analyzing multi-objective approximation schemes [21, 8]).

4. PROTOTYPICAL IMPLEMENTATION

We extended the Postgres system (version 9.2.4) to obtain an experimental platform for comparing MOQO algorithms. We extended the cost model, the query optimizer, and the user interface. The extended cost model supports nine objectives. The cost formulas used in the cost model are taken from prior work and are not part of our contribution. Evaluating their accuracy is beyond the scope of this

L=Lineitem; O=Orders; C=Customers; HashJ=Hash Join; SMJ=Sort-Merge Join; IdxNL=Index-Nested-Loop Join

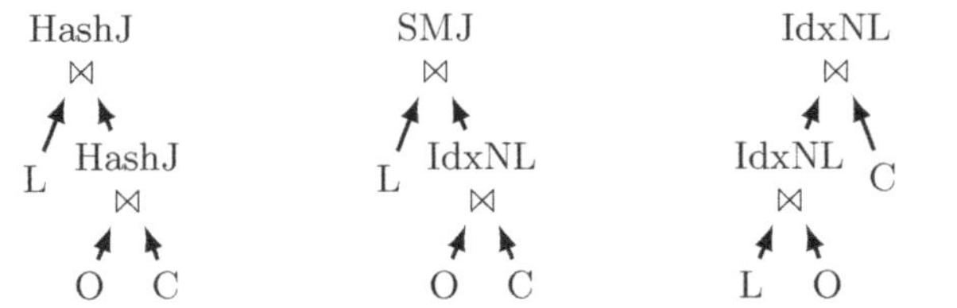

(a) Time-Optimal Plan for Bounded Tuple Loss (= 0)	(b) Additional Weight on Buffer Space Leads to Plan Without Hash Joins	(c) Additional Bound on Startup Time Requires Using Nested-Loop Joins

Figure 3: Evolution of optimal plan for TPC-H Query 3 when changing user preferences

paper. We quickly describe the nine implemented cost objectives. **Total execution time** (i.e., time until all result tuples have been produced) and **startup time** (i.e., time until first result tuple is produced) are estimated according to the cost formulas already included in Postgres. Minimizing **IO load**, **CPU load**, **number of used cores**, **hard disc footprint**, and **buffer footprint** is important since it allows to increase the number of concurrent users. The five aforementioned objectives often conflict with run time since using more system resources can often speed up query processing. **Energy consumption** is not always correlated with time [28, 9]. Dedicating more cores to a query plan can for instance decrease execution time by parallelization while it introduces coordination overhead that results in higher total energy consumption. Energy consumption is calculated according to the cost formulas by Flach [9]. Sampling allows to trade result completeness for efficiency [14]. The **tuple loss** ratio is the expected fraction of lost result tuples due to sampling and serves as ninth objective. Joining two operands with tuple loss $a, b \in [0, 1]$, the tuple loss of the result is estimated by the formula $1 - (1 - a)(1 - b)$.

We extended the plan space of the Postgres optimizer by introducing new operators and parameterizing existing ones (we did not implement those operators in the execution engine). The extended plan space includes a parameterized sampling operator that scans between 1% and 5% of a base table. Join and sort operators are parameterized by the degree of parallelism (DOP). The DOP represents the number of cores that process the corresponding operation (up to 4 cores can be used per operation). The Postgres optimizer uses several heuristics to restrict the search space: in particular, *i)* it considers Cartesian products only in situations in which no other join is applicable, and *ii)* it optimizes different subqueries of the same query separately. We left both heuristics in place since removing them might have significant impact on performance. Not using those heuristics would make it difficult to decide whether high computational costs observed during MOQO are due to the use of multiple objectives or to the removal of the heuristics.

The original Postgres optimizer is single-objective and optimizes total execution time. We implemented all three MOQO algorithms that are discussed in this paper: EXA, RTA, and IRA. The implementation uses the original Postgres data structures and routines wherever possible. Users can switch between the optimization algorithms and can choose the approximation precision α for the two approx-

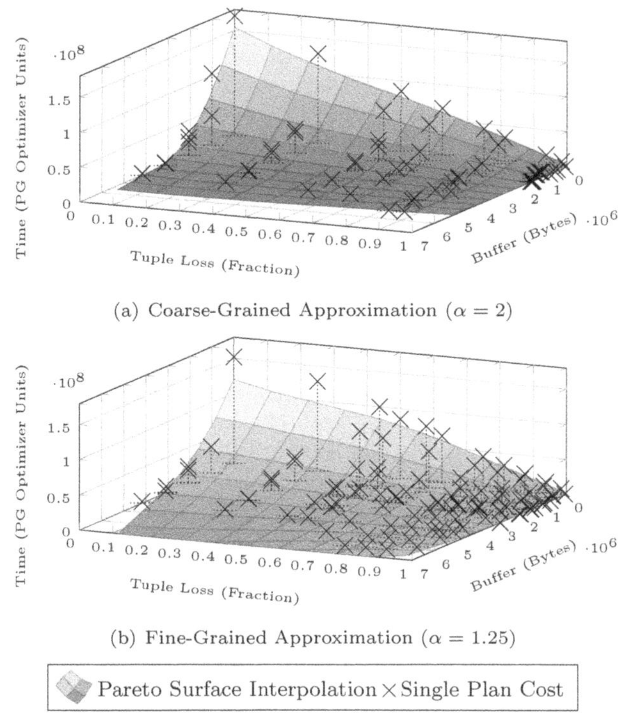

(a) Coarse-Grained Approximation ($\alpha = 2$)

(b) Fine-Grained Approximation ($\alpha = 1.25$)

Figure 4: Three-dimensional Pareto frontier approximations for TPC-H Query 5

imation schemes. Users can specify weights and bounds on the different objectives. The higher the weight on some objective, the higher its relative importance. Bounds allow to specify cost limits for specific objectives (e.g., time limits or energy budgets). When optimizing a query, the optimizer tries to find a plan that minimizes the weighted cost among all plans that respect the bounds. Figure 3 shows how the optimal query plan for TPC-H query 3 changes when user preferences vary. Initially, the tuple loss is upper-bounded by zero (i.e., all result tuples must be retrieved) and all weights except the one for total execution time are set to zero. So the optimizer searches for the plan with minimal execution time among all plans that do not use sampling. Figure 3(a) shows the resulting plan. Increasing the weight on buffer footprint leads to a plan that replaces the memory-intensive Hash joins by Sort-Merge and Index-Nested-Loop (IdxNL) joins (see Figure 3(b)). Setting an additional upper bound on startup time leads to a plan that only uses IdxNL joins (see Figure 3(c)).

Users cannot make optimal choices for bounds and weights if they are not aware of the possible tradeoffs between different objectives. A user might for instance want to relax the bound on one objective, knowing that this allows significant savings in another objective. All implemented MOQO algorithms produce an (approximate) Pareto frontier as byproduct of optimization. Our prototype allows to visualize two and three dimensional projections of the Pareto frontier. Figure 4 shows the cost vectors of the approximate Pareto frontier for TPC-H query 5 (and an interpolation of the surface defined by those vectors), considering objectives tuple loss, buffer footprint, and total execution time. Figure 4(a) shows a coarse-grained approximation of the real Pareto frontier (with $\alpha = 2$) and Figure 4(b) a more fine-grained approximation for the same query ($\alpha = 1.25$).

```
// Find best plan for query Q, weights W, bounds B
function ExactMOQO(Q, W, B)
    // Find Pareto plan set for Q
    P ← FindParetoPlans(Q)
    // Return best plan out of Pareto plans
    return SelectBest(P, W, B)

// Find Pareto plan set for query Q
function FindParetoPlans(Q)
    // Calculate plans for singleton sets
    for all q ∈ Q do
        P^q ← ∅
        for all p_N access path for q do
            Prune(P^q, p_N)
    // Consider table sets of increasing cardinality
    for all k ∈ 2..|Q| do
        for all q ⊆ Q : |q| = k do
            P^q ← ∅
            // For all possible splits of set q
            for all q1, q2 ⊂ q : q1 ∪̇ q2 = q do
                // For all sub-plans and operators
                for all p1 ∈ P^q1, p2 ∈ P^q2, j ∈ J do
                    // Construct new plan out of sub-plans
                    p_N ← Combine(j, p1, p2)
                    // Prune with new plan
                    Prune(P^q, p_N)
    return P^Q

// Prune plan set P with new plan p_N
procedure Prune(P, p_N)
    // Check whether new plan useful
    if ¬∃p ∈ P : c(p) ⪯ c(p_N) then
        // Delete dominated plans
        P ← {p ∈ P | ¬(c(p_N) ⪯ c(p))}
        // Insert new plan
        P ← P ∪ {p_N}

// Select best plan in P for weights W and bounds B
function SelectBest(P, W, B)
    P_B ← {p ∈ P | c(p) ⪯ B}
    if P_B ≠ ∅ then
        return arg min[p ∈ P_B] C_W(c(p))
    else
        return arg min[p ∈ P] C_W(c(p))
```

Algorithm 1: Exact algorithm for MOQO

5. ANALYSIS OF EXACT ALGORITHM

Ganguly et al. [11] proposed an exact algorithm (EXA) for MOQO. This algorithm is not part of our contribution but we provide a first experimental evaluation in a many-objective scenario and a formal analysis under less optimistic assumptions than in the original publication. Algorithm 1 shows the pseudo-code of EXA (compared with the original publication, the code was slightly extended to generate bushy plans in addition to left-deep plans). EXA first calculates a Pareto plan set for query Q and finally selects the optimal plan out of that set (considering weights and bounds). EXA uses dynamic programming and constructs Pareto plans for a table set out of the Pareto plans of its subsets. It is a generalization of the seminal algorithm by Selinger et al. [23], generalizing the pruning metric from one to multiple cost objectives. EXA starts by calculating Pareto plans for single tables. Plans generating the same result are compared and *pruned*, meaning that dominated plans are discarded. EXA constructs Pareto plans for table sets of increasing cardinality. To generate plans for a specific table set, EXA considers *i)* all possible splits of that set into two non-empty subsets (every split corresponds to one choice of

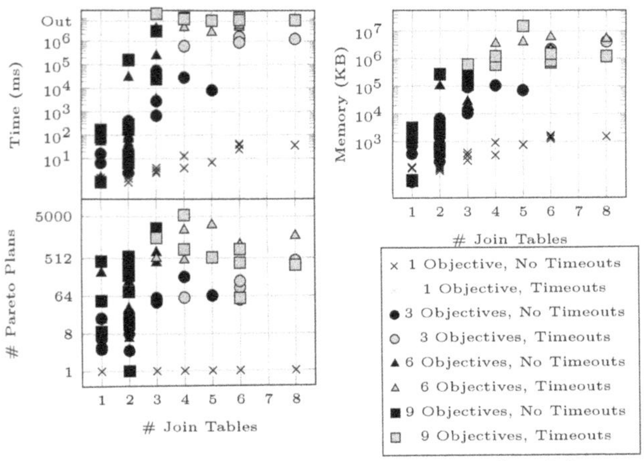

Figure 5: Performance of exact algorithm on TPC-H: Prohibitive computational cost due to high number of Pareto plans (timeout at 2 hours)

operands for the last join), *ii)* all available join operators, and *iii)* all combinations of Pareto plans for generating the two inputs to the last join.

5.1 Experimental Analysis

We implemented EXA within the system described in Section 4. The implementation allows to specify timeouts (the corresponding code is not shown in Algorithm 1). If the optimization time exceeds two hours, the modified EXA finishes quickly by only generating one plan for all table sets that have not been treated so far. We experimentally evaluated EXA using the TPC-H [26] benchmark. We generated several test cases for each TPC-H query by randomly selecting subsets of objectives with a fixed cardinality out of the total set of nine objectives. All experiments were executed on a server equipped with two six core Intel Xeon processors with 2 GHz and 128 GB of DDR3 RAM running Linux 2.6 (64 bit version). We ran five optimizer threads in parallel.

The goal of the evaluation was to answer three questions: *i)* Is the performance of EXA good enough for use in practice? *ii)* If not, how can the performance be improved? *iii)* What assumptions are realistic for the formal complexity analysis of MOQO algorithms? Figure 5 shows experimental results for the three metrics optimization time, allocated memory during optimization, and number of Pareto plans for the last table set that was treated completely (before a timeout occurred or before the optimization was completed). Every marker represents the arithmetic average value over 20 test cases for one specific TPC-H query and a specific number of objectives. The TPC-H queries are ordered according to the maximal number of tables that appears in any of their from-clauses. This number correlates (with several caveats[1]) with the search space size. Gray markers indicate that some test cases incurred a timeout. If a timeout occurred, then the reported values are lower bounds on the values of a completed computation.

Optimizing for one objective never requires more than 100 milliseconds per query and never consumes more than 1.7 MB of main memory. For multiple objectives, the computational cost of EXA becomes however quickly prohibitive with growing number of tables (referring to Question *i)*). EXA often reaches the timeout of two hours and allocates gigabytes of main memory during optimization. This happens already for queries joining only three tables; while the number of possible join orders is small in this case, the total search space size is already significant as over 10 different configurations are considered for the scan and for the join operator respectively (considering for instance different sample densities and different degrees of parallelism).

Figure 5 explains the significant difference in time and space requirements between SOQO and MOQO: The number of Pareto plans per table set is always one for SOQO but grows quickly in the number of tables (and objectives) for MOQO. The space consumption of EXA directly relates to the number of Pareto plans. The run time relates to the total number of considered plans which is much higher than the number of Pareto plans but directly correlated with it[2]. Discarding Pareto plans seems therefore the most natural way to increase efficiency (referring to Question *ii)*).

Ganguly et al. [11] used an upper bound of 2^l (l designates the number of objectives) on the number of Pareto plans per table set for their complexity analysis of EXA. This bound derives from the optimistic assumption that different objectives are not correlated. Figure 5 shows that this bound is unrealistic (8, 64, and 512 are the theoretical bounds for 3, 6, and 9 objectives). The bound is a mismatch from the *quantitative* perspective (as the bound is exceeded by orders of magnitude[3]) and from the *qualitative* perspective (as the number of Pareto plans seems to correlate with the search space size while the postulated bound only depends on the number of objectives). Therefore, this bound is not used in the following complexity analysis (referring to Question *iii)*).

5.2 Formal Complexity Analysis

All query plans can be Pareto-optimal in the worst case (when considering at least two objectives). The following analysis remains unchanged under the assumption that a constant fraction of all possible plans is Pareto-optimal. If only one join operator is available, then the number of bushy plans for joining n tables is given by $(2(n-1))!/(n-1)!$ [11]. If j scan and join operators are available, then the number of possible plans is given by

$$\mathcal{N}_{bushy}(j,n) = j^{2n-1}(2(n-1))!/(n-1)!.$$

THEOREM 1. *EXA has space complexity*

$$O(\mathcal{N}_{bushy}(j,n)).$$

PROOF. Plan sets are the variables with dominant space requirements. A scan plan is represented by an operator ID and a table ID. All other plans are represented by the operator ID of the last join and pointers to the two sub-plans generating its operands. Therefore, each stored plan needs only $O(1)$ space. Each stored cost vector needs $O(1)$ space as well, since l is a constant (see Section 3).

Let Q the set of tables to join. EXA stores a set of Pareto plans for each non-empty subset of Q. The total number of stored plans is the sum of Pareto plans over all subsets.

[1]The Postgres optimizer may for instance convert EXISTS predicates into joins which leads to many alternative plans even for queries with only one table in the from-clause.

[2]All plans considered for joining a set of tables are combinations of two Pareto plans; the number of considered plans therefore grows quadratically in the number of Pareto plans.

[3]We generate up to 443 Pareto plans on average when considering three objectives and up to 3157 plans when considering six objectives.

Let $k \in \{1, \ldots, |Q|\}$ and denote by x_k the total number of Pareto plans, summing over all subsets of Q with cardinality k. Each plan is Pareto-optimal in the worst case, therefore $x_k = \binom{n}{k}\mathcal{N}_{bushy}(j,k)$. It is $x_k \leq 2x_{k+1}$ for $k > 1$. Therefore, the term $x_n = \mathcal{N}_{bushy}(j,n)$ dominates. The analysis is tight since all possible plans are stored in the worst case. □

THEOREM 2. *EXA has time complexity*

$$O(\mathcal{N}^2_{bushy}(j,n)).$$

PROOF. Every plan is compared with all other plans that generate the same result. So the time complexity grows quadratically in the number of Pareto plans and a similar reasoning as in the proof of Theorem 1 can be applied. □

The main advantage of the single-objective Selinger algorithm [23] over a naive plan enumeration approach is that its complexity only depends on the number of table sets but not on the number of possible query plans. The preceding analysis shows that this advantage vanishes when generalizing the Selinger algorithm to multiple cost objectives (leading to EXA). The complexity of EXA is even worse than that of an approach that successively generates all possible plans while keeping only the best plan generated so far.

6. APPROXIMATING WEIGHTED MOQO

EXA is computationally expensive since it generates all Pareto plans for each table set. We present a more efficient algorithm: the representative-tradeoffs algorithm (RTA). The new algorithm generates an approximate Pareto plan set for each table set. The cardinality of the approximate Pareto set is much smaller than the cardinality of the Pareto set. Therefore, RTA has lower computational cost than EXA while it formally guarantees to return a near-optimal plan. RTA exploits a property of the cost objectives that we call the *principle of near-optimality.* We provide a formal definition in Section 6.1 and show that most relevant objectives in query optimization possess that property. We describe RTA in Section 6.2 and prove that it produces near-optimal plans. In Section 6.3, we analyze its time and space complexity. We prove that its complexity is more similar to the complexity of SOQO algorithms than to the one of EXA.

6.1 Principle of Near-Optimality

The *principle of optimality* states the following in the context of MOQO [11]: If the cost of the sub-plans within a query plan decreases, then the cost of the query plan cannot increase. A formal definition follows.

Definition 6. **Principle of Optimality (POO).** Let P a query plan with sub-plans p_L and p_R. Derive P^* from P by replacing p_L by p_L^* and p_R by p_R^*. Then $\mathbf{c}(p_L^*) \preceq \mathbf{c}(p_L)$ and $\mathbf{c}(p_R^*) \preceq \mathbf{c}(p_R)$ together imply $\mathbf{c}(P^*) \preceq \mathbf{c}(P)$.

The POO holds for all common cost objectives. EXA generates optimal plans as long as the POO holds. We introduce a new property in analogy to the POO. The *principle of near-optimality* intuitively states the following: If the cost of the sub-plans within a query plan increases by a certain percentage, then the cost of the query plan cannot increase by more than that percentage.

Definition 7. **Principle of Near-Optimality (PONO).** Let P a query plan with sub-plans p_L and p_R and pick an arbitrary $\alpha \geq 1$. Derive P^* from P by replacing p_L by p_L^* and p_R by p_R^*. Then $\mathbf{c}(p_L^*) \preceq_\alpha \mathbf{c}(p_L)$ and $\mathbf{c}(p_R^*) \preceq_\alpha \mathbf{c}(p_R)$ together imply $\mathbf{c}(P^*) \preceq_\alpha \mathbf{c}(P)$.

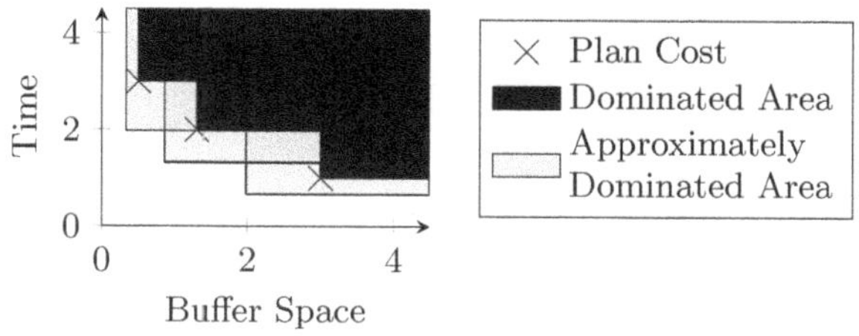

Figure 6: Dominated versus approximately dominated area (with $\alpha = 1.5$) in cost space

We will see that the PONO holds for the nine objectives described in Section 4 as well as for other common objectives. Cost formulas in query optimization are usually recursive and calculate the (estimated) cost of a plan out of the cost of its sub-plans. Different formulas apply for different objectives and for different operators. Most cost formulas only use the functions sum, maximum, minimum, and multiplication by a constant. The formula $\max(t_L, t_R) + t_M$ estimates for instance execution time of a plan whose final operation is a Sort-Merge join whose inputs are generated in parallel; the terms t_L and t_R represent the time for generating and sorting the left and right input operand and t_M is the time for the final merge. Let F any of the three binary functions sum, maximum, and minimum. Then $F(\alpha a, \alpha b) \leq \alpha F(a,b)$ for arbitrary positive operands a, b and $\alpha \geq 1$. Let $F(a)$ the function that multiplies its input by a constant. Then trivially $F(\alpha a) \leq \alpha F(a)$. Therefore, the PONO holds as long as cost formulas are combined out of the four aforementioned functions (this can be proven via structural induction). The formula for tuple loss is an exception since it multiplies two factors that depend on the tuple loss in the sub-plans: The tuple loss of a plan is estimated out of the tuple loss values a and b of its sub plans according to the formula $F(a,b) = 1 - (1-a)(1-b)$. It is $F(\alpha a, \alpha b) = \alpha(a+b) - \alpha^2 ab$. This term is upper-bounded by $\alpha(a+b-ab) = \alpha F(a,b)$ since $0 \leq a, b \leq 1$ and $\alpha \geq 1$. Note that **failure probability** is calculated according to the same formula as tuple loss (if the probabilities that single operations fail are modeled as independent Bernoulli variables). Objectives such as **monetary cost** are calculated according to similar formulas as energy consumption.

6.2 Pseudo-Code and Near-Optimality Proof

We exploit the PONO to transform EXA into an approximation scheme for weighted MOQO. Algorithm 2 shows the parts of Algorithm 1 that need to be changed. RTA is the resulting approximation scheme. RTA takes a user-defined precision parameter α_U as input. It generates a plan whose weighted cost is not higher than the optimum by more than factor α_U. We formally prove this statement later. RTA uses a different pruning function than EXA: New plans are still compared with all plans that generate the same result. But new plans are only inserted if no other plan *approximately* dominates the new one. This means that RTA tends to insert less plans than EXA. Figure 6 helps to illustrate this statement: EXA inserts new plans if their cost vector does not fall within the dominated area, RTA inserts new plans if their cost vector does neither fall into the dominated nor

```
// Find α_U-approximate plan for query Q, weights W
function RTA(Q, W, α_U)
    // Find α_U-approximate Pareto plan set
    P ← FindParetoPlans(Q, α_U)
    // Return best plan in P for infinite bounds
    return SelectBest(P, W, ∞)

// Find α_U-approximate Pareto plan set
function FindParetoPlans(Q, α_U)
    // Derive internal precision from α_U
    α_i ← |Q|√α_U
    ...
    // Prune access paths for single tables
    Prune(P^q, p_N, α_i)
    ...
    // Prune plans for non-singleton table sets
    Prune(P^q, p_N, α_i)
    ...
// Prune set P with plan p_N using precision α_i
procedure Prune(P, p_N, α_i)
    // Check whether new plan useful
    if ¬∃p ∈ P : c(p) ⪯_{α_i} c(p_N) then
    ...
```

Algorithm 2: The Representative-Tradeoffs Algorithm: An approximation scheme for Weighted MOQO. The code shows only the differences to Algorithm 1.

into the approximately dominated area. The following theorems exploit the PONO to show that RTA guarantees to generate near-optimal plans. They will implicitly justify the choice of the internal precision that is used during pruning.

THEOREM 3. *RTA generates an $\alpha_i^{|Q|}$-approximate Pareto set.*

PROOF. The proof uses induction over the number of tables $n = |Q|$. RTA examines all available access paths for single tables and generates an α_i-approximate Pareto set. Assume RTA generates α_i^n-approximate Pareto sets for joining $n < N$ tables (inductional assumption). Let p^* an arbitrary plan for joining $n = N$ tables and p_L^*, p_R^* the two sub-plans generating the operands for the final join in p^*. Due to the inductional assumption, RTA generates a plan p_L producing the same result as p_L^* with $\mathbf{c}(p_L) \preceq_{\alpha_i^{N-1}} \mathbf{c}(p_L^*)$, and a plan p_R producing the same result as p_R^* with $\mathbf{c}(p_R) \preceq_{\alpha_i^{N-1}} \mathbf{c}(p_R^*)$. The plans p_L and p_R can be combined into a plan p that generates the same result as p^* and with $\mathbf{c}(p) \preceq_{\alpha_i^{N-1}} \mathbf{c}(p^*)$, due to the PONO. RTA might discard p during the final pruning step but it keeps a plan $\widetilde{p}$ with $\mathbf{c}(\widetilde{p}) \preceq_{\alpha_i} \mathbf{c}(p)$, therefore $\mathbf{c}(\widetilde{p}) \preceq_{\alpha_i^N} \mathbf{c}(p^*)$ and RTA produces an α_i^N-approximate Pareto set. □

COROLLARY 1. *RTA is an approximation scheme for weighted MOQO.*

PROOF. RTA generates an α_U-approximate Pareto set according to Theorem 3 (since $\alpha_i^{|Q|} = \alpha_U$). This set contains a plan p with $\mathbf{c}(p) \preceq_{\alpha_U} \mathbf{c}(p^*)$ for any optimal plan p^*. It is $C_{\mathbf{W}}(\mathbf{c}(p)) \leq \alpha_U \cdot C_{\mathbf{W}}(\mathbf{c}(p^*))$ for arbitrary weights $\mathbf{W}$ and p is therefore an α_U-approximate solution. □

The pruning procedure is sensitive to changes. It seems for instance tempting to reduce the number of stored plans further by discarding all plans that a newly inserted plan approximately dominates. Then the cost vectors of the stored plans can however depart more and more from the real Pareto frontier with every inserted plan. Therefore, the additional change would destroy near-optimality guarantees.

6.3 Complexity Analysis

We analyze space and time complexity. The analysis is based on the following observations.

OBSERVATION 1. *The cost of a plan that operates on a single table with t tuples grows at most quadratically in t.*

OBSERVATION 2. *Let $F(t_L, t_R, c_L, c_L)$ the recursive formula calculating—for a specific objective and operator—the cost of a plan whose final join has inputs with cardinalities t_L and t_R and generation costs c_L and c_R. Then F is in*

$$O(t_L c_R + c_L + (t_L t_R)^2).$$

OBSERVATION 3. *There is an intrinsic constant for every objective such that the cost of all query plans for that objective is either zero or lower-bounded by that constant.*

Observations 1 and 2 trivially hold for objectives whose cost values are taken from an a-priori bounded domain such as reliability, coverage, or tuple loss (domain $[0, 1]$). They clearly hold for objectives whose cost are proportional to input and output sizes[4] such as buffer or disc footprint (the maximal output cardinality of a join is $t_L t_R$ which is dominated by the term $(t_L t_R)^2$). Quicksort has quadratic worst-case complexity in the number of input tuples. It is the most expensive unary operation in our scenario, according to objectives such as time, energy, number of CPU cycles, and number of I/O operations. The (startup and total) time of a plan containing join operations can be decomposed into *i)* the time for generating the inputs to the final join, *ii)* the time for the join itself, *iii)* and the time for post-processing of the join result (e.g., sorting, hashing, materialization). The upper bound in Observation 2 contains corresponding terms, taking into account that the right (inner) operand might have to be generated several times. It does not include terms representing costs for pre-processing join inputs (e.g., hashing) as this is counted as post-processing cost of the plan generating the corresponding operand. Observation 2 can be justified similarly for objectives such as energy, number of CPU cycles, and number of I/O operations.

Observation 3 clearly holds for objectives with integer cost domains such as buffer and disc footprint (bytes), CPU cycles, time (in milliseconds), and number of used cores. It also covers objectives with non-discrete value domains such as tuple loss. Tuple loss has a non-discrete value domain since—given enough tables in which we can vary the sampling rate—the tuple loss values of different plans can get arbitrarily close to each other (e.g., compare tuple loss ratio of one plan sampling 1% of every table with one that samples 2% in one table and 1% of the others, the values get closer the more tables we have). Assuming that the scan operators are parameterized by a discrete sampling rate (e.g., a percentage), there is still a gap between 0 and the minimal

[4]Using size and cardinality as synonyms is a simplification since tuple (byte) size may vary. It is however realistic to assume a constant upper bound for tuple sizes (e.g., the buffer page size). Also, the analysis can be generalized.

tuple loss ratio greater than zero. This gap does not depend on the number of tables (sampling at least one table with 99% creates a tuple loss of at least 1%). We derive a non-recursive upper bound on plan costs from our observations.

LEMMA 1. *The cost of a plan joining n tables of cardinality m is bounded by $O(m^{2n})$ for every objective.*

PROOF. Use induction over n. The lemma holds for $n = 1$ due to Observation 1. Assume the lemma has been proven for $n < N$ (inductional assumption). Consider a join of N tables. Cost is monotone in the number of processed tuples for any objective with non-bounded domain (not for tuple loss). So every join is a Cartesian product in the worst case and that implies $(t_L t_R)^2 = m^{2N}$. The inductional assumption implies $c_L + t_L c_R \in O(m^{2N-1})$ so $(t_L t_R)^2$ remains the dominant term. □

The cost bounds allow to define an upper bound on the number of plans that RTA stores per table set.

LEMMA 2. *RTA stores $O((n \log_{\alpha_i} m)^{l-1})$ plans per table set.*

PROOF. Function δ maps continuous cost vectors to discrete vectors such that $\delta^o(\mathbf{c}) = \llcorner \log_{\alpha_i}(\mathbf{c}^o) \lrcorner$ for each objective o and internal precision α_i. If $\delta(\mathbf{c}_1) = \delta(\mathbf{c}_2)$ for two cost vectors $\mathbf{c}_1$ and $\mathbf{c}_2$, then $\mathbf{c}_1 \preceq_{\alpha_i} \mathbf{c}_2$ and also $\mathbf{c}_2 \preceq_{\alpha_i} \mathbf{c}_1$. This means that the cost vectors mutually approximately dominate each other. Therefore, RTA can never store two plans whose cost vectors are mapped to the same vector by δ. The number of plans that have cost value zero for at least one objective is (asymptotically) dominated by the number of plans with non-zero cost values for every objective. Considering only the latter plans, their cost is lower-bounded by a constant (assume 1 without restriction of generality) and upper-bounded by a function in $O(m^{2n})$. The cardinality of the image of δ is therefore upper-bounded by $O((n \log_{\alpha_i} m)^l)$. As RTA discards strictly dominated plans, the bound tightens to $O(l(n \log_{\alpha_i} m)^{l-1})$ which equals $O((n \log_{\alpha_i} m)^{l-1})$ since l is constant (see Section 3). □

The function $\mathcal{N}_{stored}(m, n) = (n \log_{\alpha_i} m)^{l-1}$ denotes in the following the asymptotic bound on plan set cardinalities.

THEOREM 4. *RTA has space complexity*

$$O(2^n \mathcal{N}_{stored}(m, n)).$$

PROOF. Plan sets are the variables with dominant space consumption. Each stored plan needs only $O(1)$ space as justified in the proof of Theorem 1. Summing over all subsets of Q yields the total complexity. □

THEOREM 5. *RTA has time complexity*

$$O(j3^n \mathcal{N}^3_{stored}(m, n)).$$

PROOF. There are $O(2^k)$ possibilities of splitting a set of k tables into two subsets. Every split allows to construct $O(j\mathcal{N}^2_{stored}(m, k-1))$ plans. Each newly generated plan is compared against all $O(\mathcal{N}_{stored}(m, k-1))$ plans in the set[5]. Summing time complexity over all table sets yields $\sum_{k=1..n} \binom{n}{k} 2^k j \mathcal{N}^3_{stored}(m, k) \leq j3^n \mathcal{N}^3_{stored}(m, n)$. □

[5]This analysis assumes that plans are compared pairwise to identify Pareto plans. Alternatively, spatial data structures [22] can be used to verify quickly if a plan's cost lie within an approximately dominated cost space area.

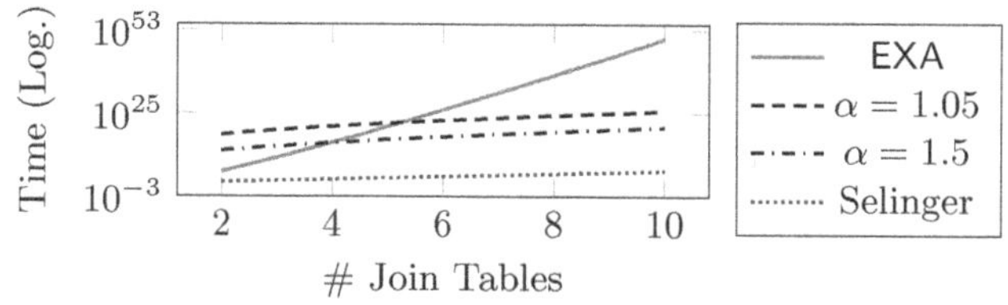

Figure 7: Comparing time complexity of the exact MOQO algorithm (EXA), the MOQO approximation scheme with $\alpha = 1.05$ and $\alpha = 1.5$, and Selinger's SOQO algorithm (Setting $j = 6$, $l = 3$, and $m = 10^5$)

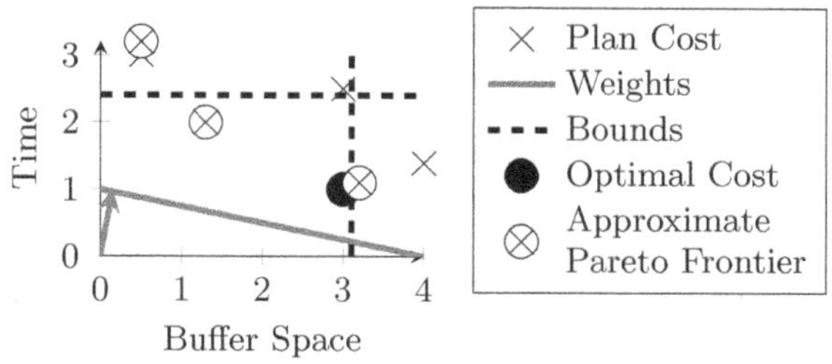

Figure 8: An approximate Pareto set does not necessarily contain a near-optimal plan if bounds are considered

The time complexity is exponential in the number of tables n. This cannot be avoided unless $P = NP$ since finding near-optimal query plans is already NP-hard for the single-objective case [6]. The time complexity of RTA differs however only by factor $\mathcal{N}^3_{stored}(m, n)$ from the single-objective Selinger algorithm for bushy plans [27] (which has complexity $O(j3^n)$). This factor is a polynomial in number of join tables and table cardinalities. Unlike EXA, the complexity of RTA does not depend on the total number of possible plans. This lets expect significantly better scalability (see Figure 7 for a visual comparison).

7. APPROXIMATING BOUNDED MOQO

RTA finally selects an α_U-approximate plan out of an α_U-approximate Pareto set. This is always possible since similar cost vectors have similar weighted cost. This principle breaks when considering bounds in addition to weights. Even if two cost vectors are extremely similar, one of them can exceed the bounds while the other one does not. Figure 8 illustrates this problem. There is no $\alpha \leq \alpha_U$ except $\alpha = 1$ that guarantees a-priori that an α-approximate Pareto set contains an α_U-approximate plan. Choosing $\alpha = 1$ leads however to high computational cost and should be avoided (RTA corresponds to EXA if $\alpha = 1$).

Assuming that the pathological case depicted in Figure 8 occurs always for $\alpha > 1$ is however overly pessimistic. An α_U-approximate Pareto set *may* very well contain an α_U-approximate solution. We present an iterative algorithm that exploits this fact: The iterative-refinement algorithm (IRA) generates an approximate Pareto set in every iteration, starting optimistically with a coarse-grained approximation precision and refining the precision until a near-optimal plan is generated. This requires a stopping condition that detects whether an approximate Pareto set contains a near-optimal plan (without knowing the optimal plan or its cost). We present IRA and a corresponding stopping condition in Section 7.1. A potential drawback of an iterative approach is redundant work in different iterations. We

// Find α_U-approximate plan for query Q,
// weights $\mathbf{W}$, bounds $\mathbf{B}$
function IRA($Q, \mathbf{W}, \mathbf{B}, \alpha_U$)
  $i \leftarrow 0$ // Initialize iteration counter
  repeat
    $i \leftarrow i + 1$
    // Choose precision for this iteration
    $\alpha \leftarrow \alpha_U^{2^{-i/(3l-3)}}$
    // Find α-approximate Pareto plan set
    $\mathcal{P} \leftarrow$ FindParetoPlans(Q, α)
    // Select best plan in $\mathcal{P}$
    $p_{opt} \leftarrow$SelectBest($\mathcal{P}, \mathbf{W}, \mathbf{B}$)
  until $\nexists p \in \mathcal{P} : \mathbf{c}(p) \preceq \alpha\mathbf{B} \wedge \frac{C_{\mathbf{W}}(\mathbf{c}(p))}{\alpha} < \frac{C_{\mathbf{W}}(\mathbf{c}(p_{opt}))}{\alpha_U}$
  return p_{opt}

Algorithm 3: The Iterative-Refinement Algorithm: An Approximation Scheme for Bounded-Weighted MOQO. The Code Uses Sub-Functions From Algorithm 2.

analyze the complexity of IRA in Section 7.2 and show how a carefully selected precision refinement policy makes sure that the amount of redundant work is negligible. We also prove that IRA always terminates.

7.1 Pseudo-Code and Near-Optimality Proof

Algorithm 3 shows pseudo-code of IRA. IRA uses the functions FindParetoPlans and SelectBest which were already defined in Algorithm 2. IRA chooses in every iteration an approximation precision α and calculates an α-approximate Pareto set. The precision gets refined from one iteration to the next. We will discuss the particular choice of precision formula in the next subsection. At the end of every iteration, IRA selects the best plan p_{opt} in the current approximate Pareto set. It terminates, once that plan is guaranteed to be α_U-optimal. The stopping condition of IRA compares p_{opt} with the best plan that can be found if the bounds are slightly relaxed (i.e., multiplied by a factor). This termination condition makes sure that IRA does not terminate before it finds an α_U-approximate plan. This implies that IRA is an approximation scheme.

THEOREM 6. *IRA is an approximation scheme for bounded-weighted MOQO.*

PROOF. Denote by $\mathcal{P}$ the set of plans generated in the last iteration, by α the precision used in the last iteration, and by p_{opt} the best plan in $\mathcal{P}$. The termination condition was met in the last iteration so there is no plan $p \in \mathcal{P}$ respecting the relaxed bounds $\alpha\mathbf{B}$ with $C_{\mathbf{W}}(\mathbf{c}(p))/\alpha < C_{\mathbf{W}}(\mathbf{c}(p_{opt}))/\alpha_U$. Let p^* be an optimal plan for the input query (not necessarily contained in $\mathcal{P}$). Assume first that p^* respects the bounds $\mathbf{B}$. Plan set $\mathcal{P}$ contains a plan p_R whose cost vector is similar to the one of p^*: $\mathbf{c}(p_R) \preceq_\alpha \mathbf{c}(p^*)$. The weighted cost of p_R is near-optimal: $C_{\mathbf{W}}(\mathbf{c}(p_R)) \leq \alpha C_{\mathbf{W}}(\mathbf{c}(p^*))$. Plan p_R can violate the bounds $\mathbf{B}$ by factor α but respects the relaxed bounds: $\mathbf{c}(p_R) \preceq \alpha\mathbf{B}$. Let p be the best plan in $\mathcal{P}$ that respects the relaxed bounds $\alpha\mathbf{B}$, the weighted cost of p is smaller or equal to the one of p_R. Therefore, $C_{\mathbf{W}}(\mathbf{c}(p))/\alpha$ is a lower bound on $C_{\mathbf{W}}(p^*)$. If the weighted cost of p_{opt} is not higher than that by more than factor α_U, then p_{opt} is an α_U-approximate solution. Assume now that p^* does not respect the bounds $\mathbf{B}$. Then no possible plan respects the bounds and weighted cost is the only criterion. Since $\alpha \leq \alpha_U$, the set $\mathcal{P}$ must contain an α_U-approximate solution (p_{opt}). □

7.2 Analysis of Refinement Policy

The formula for calculating the approximation precision α should satisfy several requirements. First, the formula needs to be strictly monotonically decreasing in i (the number of iterations) since IRA otherwise executes unnecessary iterations that do not generate new plans. Second, it should decrease quickly enough in i such that the time required by the new iteration is higher or at least comparable to the time required in all previous iterations[6]. This ensures that the amount of redundant work is small compared with the total amount of work, as IRA can generate the same plans in several iterations. Third, it should decrease as slowly as the other requirements allow; choosing a lower α than necessary should be avoided, since the complexity of the Pareto set approximation grows quickly in the inverse of α. The formula $\alpha = \alpha_U^{2^{-i/(3l-3)}}$ is strictly monotonically decreasing in i. It also satisfies the second and third requirement as we see next. The following theorem concerns space and time complexity of the i-th iteration of IRA. The proof is analogous to the proofs in Section 6.3.

THEOREM 7. *The i-th iteration of IRA has*
space complexity $O(2^n 2^{i/3}(n^2 \log m/\log \alpha_U)^{l-1})$,
and time complexity $O(j3^n 2^i (n^2 \log m/\log \alpha_U)^{3l-3})$.

Assume that the time per iteration is *proportional* to the worst-case complexity, or within a factor that does not depend on i (but possibly on n, m, or l). Then the required time doubles from one iteration to the next, so the time of the last iteration is dominant. So the precision formula satisfies the second requirement and (approximately) the third, since decreasing iteration precision significantly slower would violate the second requirement.

THEOREM 8. *IRA always terminates.*

PROOF. For a fixed bounded-weighted MOQO instance $I = \langle Q, \mathbf{W}, \mathbf{B}\rangle$ and plan space, there is only a finite number of possible query plans. Therefore, there is an $\alpha > 1$ such that no plan p exists which satisfies $\mathbf{c}(p) \preceq \alpha\mathbf{B}$ but not $\mathbf{c}(p) \preceq \mathbf{B}$. The precision refinement formula is strictly monotonically decreasing in i (iteration counter). So the aforementioned α is reached after a finite number of iterations. Then the best plan that respects the strict bounds is equivalent to the best plan that respects the relaxed bounds, so the termination condition is satisfied. □

8. EXPERIMENTAL EVALUATION

We experimentally compare the approximation schemes against EXA. The algorithms were implemented within the system described in Section 4. A timeout of two hours was specified, using the technique outlined in Section 5.1. The experiments were executed on the hardware platform described in Section 5.1. We generated 20 test cases for each TPC-H query and three, six, and nine objectives respectively. Every test case is characterized by a set of considered objectives (selected randomly out of the nine implemented objectives), by weights on the selected objectives (chosen randomly from $[0, 1]$ with uniform distribution), and (only for bounded MOQO) by bounds on a subset of the selected objectives. Bounds for objectives with a-priori bounded

[6]Memory space can be reused in the new iteration so we only consider run time in the choice of α.

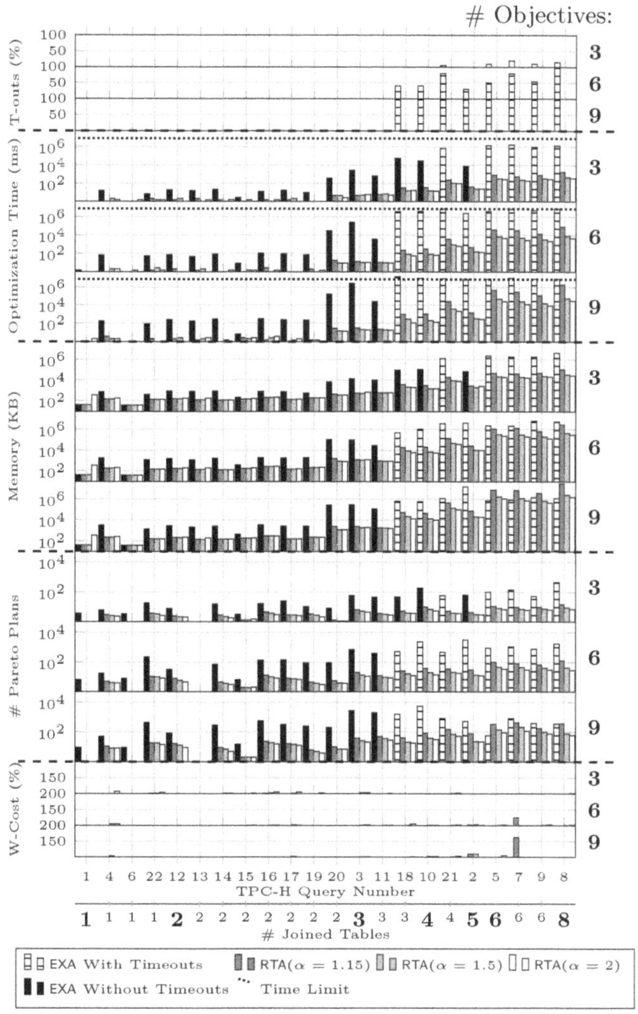

Figure 9: Optimizer performance comparison for weighted MOQO using timeout of two hours

value domain (e.g., tuple loss) are chosen with uniform distribution from that domain. Bounds for other objectives are chosen by multiplying the minimal possible value for a given objective and query by a factor chosen uniformly from [1, 2].

Figure 9 compares the performance of EXA and RTA with $\alpha \in \{1.15, 1.5, 2\}$. Figure 9 shows for each TPC-H query and each number of objectives *i)* the percentage of test cases that resulted in a timeout, and arithmetic average values for the metrics *ii)* optimization time (in milliseconds), *iii)* allocated memory during optimization (in kilobytes), *iv)* number of Pareto plans for the last table set that was treated completely (before a timeout or before optimization finished), and *v)* weighted cost of the generated plan (as percentage of the optimal value over the plans generated by all algorithms for the same test case). Queries are ordered on the x-axis according to the maximal number of tables joined in any of their from-clauses as this relates to the search space size (with the caveats mentioned in Section 5.1). The time limit is marked by a dotted line in the subfigure showing optimization times. The fill pattern of the bars representing results for EXA varies depending on whether EXA had at least one timeout for the corresponding query and the corresponding number of objectives (RTA did not incur any timeouts). If EXA had timeouts, then the reported values for time and memory consumption are lower bounds on the corresponding values for a completed optimizer run.

The search space size correlates with the number of tables to join, and the number of objectives influences how many plans can be pruned during optimization. Therefore, the percentage of timeouts (for EXA), the optimization time, and the memory consumption all tend to increase in the number of objectives and the number of joined tables, as long as no timeouts distort the results. EXA occasionally has timeouts already when considering only three objectives. For nine objectives, EXA is not able to solve a single test case within the limit of two hours for queries that join more than three tables. Choices related to join order, operator selection, table sample density, and parallelization create a search space of considerable size, even for only four join tables. We have seen in Section 5 that exact optimization takes less than 0.1 seconds despite the size of the search space, as long as only one objective is considered. Considering multiple objectives makes exact pruning however ineffective and leads to the high computational overhead of EXA. RTA is orders of magnitude faster than EXA; increasing α reduces optimization time and memory footprint. For nine objectives, RTA with $\alpha = 1.15$ generates for instance near-optimal plans for TPC-H query 2 within less than 1.5 seconds average time. EXA reaches the timeout of two hours for all 20 test cases.

The average quality of the plans produced by RTA is often significantly better than the worst case guarantees. Even for $\alpha = 2$, RTA generates plans with an average cost overhead of below 1% (100 times better than the theoretical bound) for 19 out of the 22 TPC-H queries. The Postgres optimizer selects locally optimal plans for the subqueries within a query. We left this mechanism in place as justified in Section 4, even if it weakens the formal approximation guarantees for queries that contain subqueries (TPC-H queries 2, 4, 7, 8, 9, 11, 13, 15, 16, 17, 18, 20, 21, 22). In practice, the approximation guarantees were only violated in one case (TPC-H query 7) and only for specific choices of α ($\alpha = 1.15$).

Figure 10 shows the results for bounded MOQO. EXA is compared against IRA (instead of RTA) since only IRA guarantees to generate query plans that respect all hard bounds if such plans exist. Optimization always considers all nine objectives while the number of bounds varies between three and nine. Figure 10 reports the number of iterations (instead of the number of Pareto plans), the reported numbers for memory consumption refer to the memory reserved in the last iteration (memory that was allocated before can be reused). The performance of EXA is insensitive to the number of bounds. The performance of IRA varies with the number of bounds: Time and memory consumption tend to be higher when hard bounds are specified. This can be seen by comparing Figure 10 with Figure 9, as IRA behaves exactly like RTA if no bounds are specified. The reason is that IRA may have to choose a much smaller internal approximation factor than RTA, in order to verify if the best generated query plan is near-optimal among all plans respecting the bounds. The performance gap between approximate and exact MOQO is still significant: Summing over all test cases for bounded MOQO, EXA had 464 timeouts while each IRA instance had at most 4 timeouts. The total optimization time was more than 1200 hours for EXA and less than 15 hours for IRA with $\alpha = 1.15$. The number of iterations of IRA increases sometimes with the user-defined approximation factor. If hard

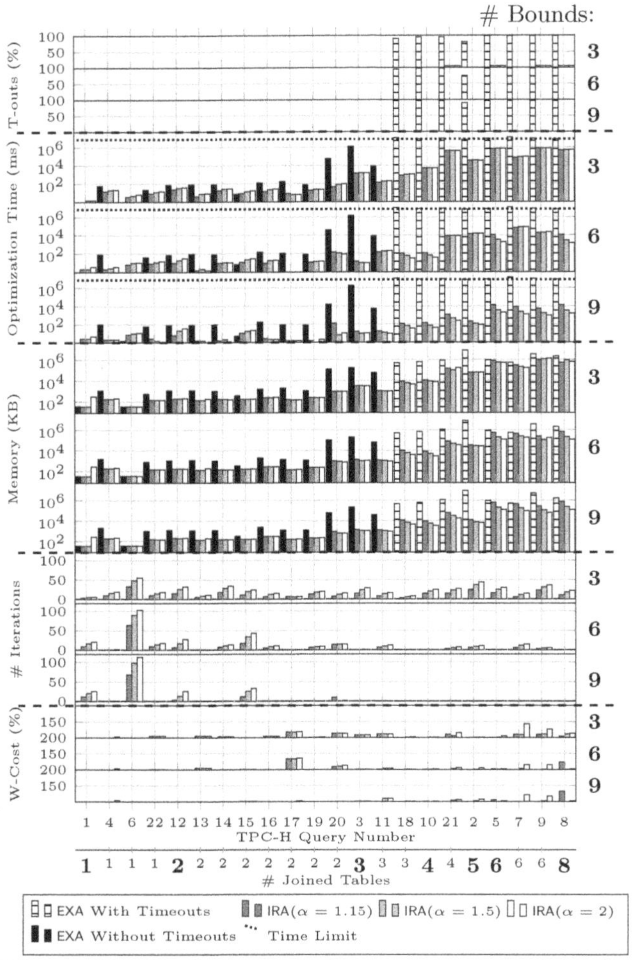

Figure 10: Optimizer performance comparison for bounded MOQO using timeout of two hours

bounds are set then the internal approximation precision required to guarantee a near-optimal plan does not necessarily correlate with the user-defined precision. However, even if the number of iterations increases, the total optimization time is not influenced significantly (except for queries with very low total optimization time where overhead by repeated query preprocessing is non-negligible). This was the goal of our precision refinement policy.

9. CONCLUSION

Our MOQO approximation schemes find guaranteed near-optimal plans within seconds where exhaustive optimization takes hours. We analyzed the cost formulas of typical cost metrics in MOQO and identified common properties. We believe that our findings can be exploited for design and analysis of future MOQO algorithms.

10. REFERENCES

[1] Z. Abul-Basher, Y. Feng, and P. Godfrey. Alternative Query Optimization for Workload Management. In *Database and Expert Systems Applications*, 2012.

[2] S. Agarwal, A. Iyer, and A. Panda. Blink and It's Done: Interactive Queries on Very Large Data. *PVLDB*, 5(12), 2012.

[3] B. Babcock and S. Chaudhuri. Towards a Robust Query Optimizer: a Principled and Practical Approach. *SIGMOD Conf.*, 2005.

[4] S. Babu, P. Bizarro, and D. DeWitt. Proactive Re-Optimization. *SIGMOD Conf.*, 2005.

[5] P. Bizarro, N. Bruno, and D. DeWitt. Progressive Parametric Query Optimization. *Trans. on KDE*, 21(4), Apr. 2009.

[6] S. Chatterji and S. Evani. On the Complexity of Approximate Query Optimization. *PODS*, 2002.

[7] F. Chu, J. Halpern, and J. Gehrke. Least Expected Cost Query Optimization: What can we Expect? *SIGMOD Conf.*, 2002.

[8] T. Erlebach, H. Kellerer, and U. Pferschy. Approximating multiobjective knapsack problems. *Management Science*, 48(12), 2002.

[9] T. Flach. Optimizing Query Execution to Improve the Energy Efficiency of Database Management Systems. Technical report, 2010.

[10] S. Ganguly. Design and Analysis of Parametric Query Optimization Algorithms. *VLDB*, 1998.

[11] S. Ganguly, W. Hasan, and R. Krishnamurthy. Query Optimization for Parallel Execution. In *SIGMOD Conf.*, 1992.

[12] M. Garofalakis and Y. Ioannidis. Multi-Dimensional Resource Scheduling for Parallel Queries. In *SIGMOD Conf.*, 1996.

[13] S. Guha, D. Gunopoulos, N. Koudas, D. Srivastava, and M. Vlachos. Efficient approximation of optimization queries under parametric aggregation constraints. In *VLDB*, 2003.

[14] P. Haas. Speeding Up DB2 UDB Using Sampling. *The IDUG Solutions Journal*, pages 1–10, 2003.

[15] A. Hulgeri. *Parametric Query Optimization.* PhD thesis, 2004.

[16] S. Kambhampati, U. Nambiar, Z. Nie, and S. Vaddi. Havasu: A Multi-Objective, Adaptive Query Processing Framework for Web Data Integration. *ASU CSE*, 2002.

[17] H. Kllapi, E. Sitaridi, M. M. Tsangaris, and Y. E. Ioannidis. Schedule Optimization for Data Processing Flows on the Cloud. In *SIGMOD Conf.*, 2011.

[18] D. Kossmann, F. Ramsak, S. Rost, and Others. Shooting Stars in the Sky: an Online Algorithm for Skyline Queries. In *VLDB*, 2002.

[19] D. Kossmann and K. Stocker. Iterative Dynamic Programming: a New Class of Query Optimization Algorithms. *Trans. on Database Systems*, 1(212), 2000.

[20] R. Marinescu. Efficient approximation algorithms for multi-objective constraint optimization. *Algorithmic Decision Theory*, 2011.

[21] C. Papadimitriou and M. Yannakakis. Multiobjective Query Optimization. *PODS*, 2001.

[22] H. Samet. *The Design And Analysis Of Spatial Data Structures.* 1990.

[23] P. G. Selinger, M. M. Astrahan, D. D. Chamberlin, R. A. Lorie, and T. G. Price. Access Path Selection in a Relational Database Management System. In *SIGMOD Conf.*, 1979.

[24] A. Simitsis, P. Vassiliadis, and T. Sellis. State-Space Optimization of ETL Workflows. *Trans. on KDE*, 17(10), 2005.

[25] A. Simitsis, K. Wilkinson, M. Castellanos, and U. Dayal. Optimizing Analytic Data Flows for Multiple Execution Engines. *SIGMOD Conf.*, 2012.

[26] TPC. TPC-H Benchmark, 2013.

[27] B. Vance and D. Maier. Rapid Bushy Join-Order Optimization with Cartesian Products. *SIGMOD Conf.*, 1996.

[28] Z. Xu, Y. C. Tu, and X. Wang. PET: Reducing Database Energy Cost via Query Optimization. *PVLDB*, 5(12), 2012.

Querying K-Truss Community in Large and Dynamic Graphs

Xin Huang†, Hong Cheng†, Lu Qin‡, Wentao Tian†, Jeffrey Xu Yu†
†The Chinese University of Hong Kong, China
‡Centre for Quantum Computation and Intelligent Systems, University of Technology, Sydney, Australia
†{xhuang,hcheng,wttian,yu}@se.cuhk.edu.hk, ‡lu.qin@uts.edu.au

ABSTRACT

Community detection which discovers densely connected structures in a network has been studied a lot. In this paper, we study *online community search* which is practically useful but less studied in the literature. Given a query vertex in a graph, the problem is to find meaningful communities that the vertex belongs to in an online manner. We propose a novel community model based on the k-truss concept, which brings nice structural and computational properties. We design a compact and elegant index structure which supports the efficient search of k-truss communities with a linear cost with respect to the community size. In addition, we investigate the k-truss community search problem in a dynamic graph setting with frequent insertions and deletions of graph vertices and edges. Extensive experiments on large real-world networks demonstrate the effectiveness and efficiency of our community model and search algorithms.

Categories and Subject Descriptors

H.2.8 [**DATABASE MANAGEMENT**]: Database Applications—*Data mining*; G.2.2 [**DISCRETE MATHEMATICS**]: Graph Theory—*Graph algorithms*

Keywords

k-truss; community search; dynamic graph

1. INTRODUCTION

Community structure exists in many real-world networks, for example, social networks and biological networks. Community detection, which is to find communities in a network, has been studied a lot in the literature [15, 16, 17, 1, 25]. A different but related problem is *online community search*, which finds communities containing a query vertex in an online manner. These two tasks have different goals: community detection targets all communities in the entire network and usually applies a global criterion to find qualified communities. In contrast, online community search provides *personalized community detection* for a query vertex. As the communities for different vertices in a network may have very different characteristics, this user-centered personalized search is more meaningful. Furthermore, as the communities a user participates in represent the social contexts of the user, online community search provides a useful tool for other analytical tasks, such as social circle discovery [14] and social contagion modeling [20]. In this paper, we study the modeling and querying of the communities of a query vertex.

SIGMOD'14, June 22–27, 2014, Snowbird, UT, USA.

http://dx.doi.org/10.1145/2588555.2610495.

A recent study by Cui et al. [9] has proposed a novel approach for online overlapping community search. A new community model was defined as an α-adjacency-γ-quasi-k-clique. A γ-quasi-k-clique is a k-node graph with at least $\lfloor \gamma \frac{k(k-1)}{2} \rfloor$ edges. Another parameter α is imposed to union two γ-quasi-k-cliques if they share at least α vertices. Given a query vertex q, the problem is to find all α-adjacency-γ-quasi-k-cliques containing q. However, there are several limitations in this community model.

1. γ as an average density measure, may not necessarily guarantee a cohesive community structure. Consider the graph in Figure 1 which is a 0.8-quasi-7-clique containing query vertex q. However, q is only connected with one vertex in the community, thus it is not a cohesive community for q obviously.
2. There are three parameters α, γ, k in this model, the setting of which may vary significantly for different query vertices. For example, in a research collaboration network, the communities of a famous scholar and a junior scholar can be dramatically different in terms of the community size and density. Thus it is difficult to choose proper values for the three parameters given a query vertex.
3. Finding α-adjacency-γ-quasi-k-clique has been proven to be NP-hard [9], which imposes a severe computational bottleneck. The approximate algorithms for clique enumeration and expansion [9] reduce the complexity, but cannot give a theoretic guarantee of the approximation quality.

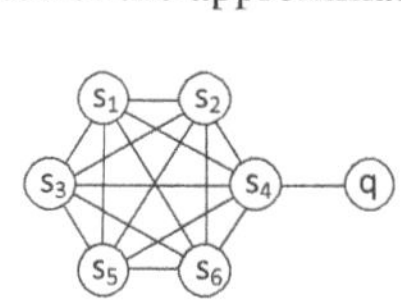

Figure 1: A 0.8-quasi-7-clique containing q

Considering these limitations, we propose a novel community model based on the k-truss concept. Given a graph G, the k-truss of G is the largest subgraph in which every edge is contained in at least $(k-2)$ triangles within the subgraph [7]. The k-truss is a type of cohesive subgraph defined based on triangle which models the stable relationship among three nodes. However, the k-truss subgraph may be disconnected, for example, the two shaded regions form the 4-truss subgraph in Figure 2(a) which is obviously disconnected.

So the k-truss subgraph may not correspond to a meaningful community. On top of the k-truss, we impose an *edge connectivity* constraint, that is, any two edges in a community either belong to the same triangle, or are reachable from each other through a series of adjacent triangles. Here two triangles are defined as *adjacent* if they share a common edge. The edge connectivity requirement ensures that a discovered community is connected and cohesive. This defines our novel ***k-truss community model***. To the best of our knowledge, this is the first work that proposes the k-truss community. Compared with the α-adjacency-γ-quasi-k-clique model, our community model has the following advantages.

1. **Cohesive community**. The k-truss community has cohesive structure according to our analysis in Section 2. For example, the graph in Figure 1 is not a valid k-truss community containing q for $k \geq 3$, as the edge (q, s_4) is not in any of the triangles.
2. **Fewer parameter**. Our community model only needs to specify the trussness value k. In addition, a $(k+1)$-truss community is contained in a k-truss community. Thus by using different k values for community query, we can get a hierarchical community structure of a query vertex.
3. **Polynomial time algorithm**. There exist polynomial time algorithms for computing the k-truss subgraphs [7, 21], which make the k-truss community model computationally tractable and efficient.

Simply searching k-truss community by its definition may incur a large number of wasteful edge accesses as shown in Section 3.2. Thus the key to efficient k-truss community query processing is to design an effective index. Towards this goal, we first apply an efficient truss decomposition algorithm [21] on a graph G which computes the k-truss subgraphs for all k values. Then we design a novel and elegant index structure, called TCP-Index, to index the pre-computed k-truss subgraphs. The TCP-Index preserves the trussness value and the triangle adjacency relationship in a compact tree-shape index, and supports the query of k-truss community in *linear time* with respect to the community size, which is optimal.

We further study k-truss community search in dynamic graphs, where graph vertices and edges can be frequently inserted or deleted. We present a theoretical analysis to identify the scope in a graph that is affected by edge insertion/deletion. Specifically, we derive a tight upper bound of the trussness for a newly inserted edge, which allows us to precisely identify the affected region with a light cost. Then we design efficient algorithms to update the trussness value and the TCP-Index in the affected region. The incremental update algorithms effectively support querying k-truss community in highly dynamic graphs.

We conduct extensive experimental studies on large real-world networks and have the following findings. First, the k-truss community search using the TCP-Index is highly efficient in all networks. The query time is from one millisecond for the low degree query vertex to a few seconds for the high degree query vertex which has large and dense communities. The TCP-Index is very compact and can be constructed very efficiently. Second, the TCP-Index can be updated in milliseconds given an edge insertion/deletion. Thus it is highly efficient to support the k-truss community search in dynamic graphs. Last, we evaluate the quality of the discovered communities on two social networks with ground-truth communities and a scientific collaboration network. The results show that our community model can find cohesive and meaningful communities of a query vertex.

The rest of this paper is organized as follows. We formulate the k-truss community search problem in Section 2. We design a novel TCP-Index and an efficient k-truss community search algorithm

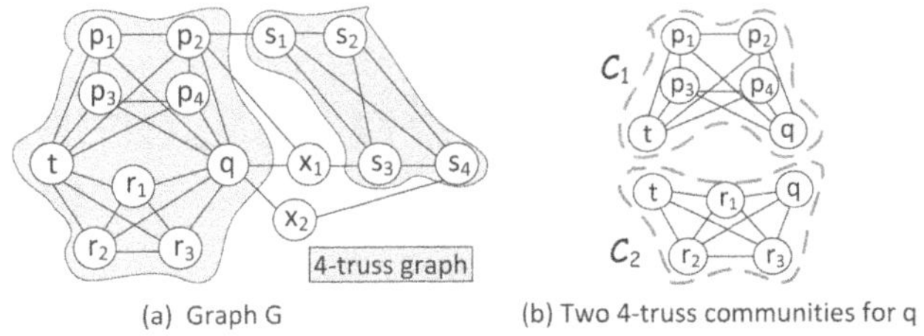

(a) Graph G (b) Two 4-truss communities for q

Figure 2: K-truss community example

in a static graph in Section 3. We further study how to maintain the TCP-Index for query processing in a dynamic graph in Section 4. Extensive experimental results on large real-world networks are reported in Section 5. We discuss related work in Section 6 and conclude this paper in Section 7.

2. K-TRUSS COMMUNITY

2.1 Problem Definition

We consider an undirected, unweighted simple graph $G = (V, E)$ with $n = |V|$ vertices and $m = |E|$ edges. We denote the set of neighbors of a vertex v by $N(v)$, i.e., $N(v) = \{u \in V : (v, u) \in E\}$, and the degree of v by $d(v) = |N(v)|$. We use d_{max} to denote the maximum vertex degree in G.

A triangle in G is a cycle of length 3. Let $u, v, w \in V$ be the three vertices on the cycle, and we denote this triangle by $\triangle_{uvw}$. Then the *support* of an edge is defined as follows.

DEFINITION 1 (SUPPORT). *The support of an edge $e(u, v) \in E$ in G, denoted by sup(e, G), is defined as $|\{\triangle_{uvw} : w \in V\}|$. When the context is obvious, we replace sup(e, G) by sup(e).*

If an edge e is contained in a triangle $\triangle$, we denote it by $e \in \triangle$. Now we give the definitions of *triangle adjacency* and *triangle connectivity* below.

DEFINITION 2 (TRIANGLE ADJACENCY). *Given two triangles $\triangle_1, \triangle_2$ in G, they are adjacent if $\triangle_1$ and $\triangle_2$ share a common edge, which is denoted by $\triangle_1 \cap \triangle_2 \neq \emptyset$.*

DEFINITION 3 (TRIANGLE CONNECTIVITY). *Given two triangles $\triangle_s, \triangle_t$ in G, $\triangle_s$ and $\triangle_t$ are triangle connected, if there exist a series of triangles $\triangle_1, \ldots, \triangle_n$ in G, where $n \geq 2$, such that $\triangle_1 = \triangle_s$, $\triangle_n = \triangle_t$ and for $1 \leq i < n$, $\triangle_i \cap \triangle_{i+1} \neq \emptyset$.*

For the graph G in Figure 2(a), $e(q, p_4)$ is contained in $\triangle_{qp_3p_4}$ and $\triangle_{qp_2p_4}$, thus its support $sup(e(q, p_4)) = 2$. $\triangle_{qp_3p_4}$ and $\triangle_{qp_2p_4}$ are triangle adjacent as they share a common edge $e(q, p_4)$. $\triangle_{tp_3p_4}$ and $\triangle_{qp_2p_4}$ are triangle connected through $\triangle_{qp_3p_4}$ in G.

On the basis of the definitions of support and triangle connectivity, we define the *k-truss community* as follows.

DEFINITION 4 (K-TRUSS COMMUNITY). *Given a graph G and an integer $k \geq 2$, G' is a k-truss community, if G' satisfies the following three conditions:*

(1) K-Truss. *G' is a subgraph of G, denoted as $G' \subseteq G$, such that $\forall e \in E(G')$, sup$(e, G') \geq (k-2)$;*

(2) Edge Connectivity. *$\forall e_1, e_2 \in E(G')$, $\exists \triangle_1, \triangle_2$ in G' such that $e_1 \in \triangle_1$, $e_2 \in \triangle_2$, then either $\triangle_1 = \triangle_2$, or $\triangle_1$ is triangle connected with $\triangle_2$ in G';*

(3) Maximal Subgraph. *G' is a maximal subgraph satisfying conditions (1) and (2). That is, $\nexists G'' \subseteq G$, such that $G' \subset G''$, and G'' satisfies conditions (1) and (2).*

Actually the largest subgraph that satisfies condition (1) is exactly the k-truss definition used in the literature [7, 21]. However, the k-truss condition itself is insufficient to define a cohesive and meaningful community due to the following two reasons. First, a k-truss subgraph can be disconnected, thus does not represent a cohesive community. For example, the two shaded regions in Figure 2(a) form the 4-truss subgraph of G, which is obviously disconnected. So this 4-truss subgraph does not correspond to a meaningful community. Second, for a fixed k value, any vertex can belong to at most one k-truss subgraph. This cannot deal with a common scenario that a user can participate in multiple communities.

With these considerations, we impose the edge connectivity requirement in condition (2) to ensure the discovered communities are connected and cohesive. The rationale is that, a triangle represents the strong and stable relationship among three vertices. If any two edges in a subgraph are reachable from each other through a series of adjacent triangles, the subgraph must be connected, and have a cohesive structure among all involved vertices. This definition also allows a vertex to participate in multiple communities.

Example 1: Two 4-truss communities containing vertex q are shown in Figure 2(b) as C_1 and C_2, respectively. We can verify that every edge in C_1 is contained in at least two triangles in C_1, any two edges in C_1 are reachable through adjacent triangles, and C_1 is maximal. Thus C_1 is a 4-truss community. These properties also hold for another 4-truss community C_2. As the edges in C_1 cannot reach the edges in C_2 through adjacent triangles, C_1 and C_2 cannot merge as one large community. This is very reasonable, as there is no connection between the two vertex sets $\{p_1, p_2, p_3, p_4\}$ and $\{r_1, r_2, r_3\}$. In addition, we can see that vertices q and t participate in both communities. □

Problem Definition. The problem of **k-truss community search** studied in this paper is defined as follows. Given a graph $G(V, E)$, a query vertex $v_q \in V$ and an integer $k \geq 2$, find all k-truss communities containing v_q. In addition, we study k-truss community search in dynamic graphs, where vertices and edges are frequently inserted or deleted.

2.2 Why K-Truss Community?

Compared with the latest α-adjacency-γ-quasi-k-clique [9] community model, the k-truss community model has three significant advantages: stronger guarantee on cohesive structure, fewer parameters and lower computational cost. These nice properties, which are inherited from the k-truss subgraph [7], not only lead to the discovery of more cohesive and meaningful communities, but also enable the design of more efficient, scalable and easier-to-use algorithms for community search. We present these properties in the following.

Bounded Diameter in K-Truss Community. The diameter of a k-truss community C with $|C|$ vertices is no larger than $\lfloor \frac{2|C|-2}{k} \rfloor$ [7]. This property guarantees that the shortest distance between any two vertices in a community is bounded, which has been considered as an important feature of a good community in [10].

Consider the 4-truss community C_1 in Figure 2(b) as an example. The diameter of C_1 is 2, which is the same as the diameter upper bound $\lfloor \frac{2\times 6-2}{4} \rfloor = 2$.

(K-1)-Edge-Connected Graph. A graph is $(k-1)$-edge-connected if it remains connected whenever fewer than $k-1$ edges are removed [11]. A k-truss community is $(k-1)$-edge-connected [7]. This property ensures the high connectivity of a community, which has been proposed as a criterion of a good community in [13].

In contrast, the γ-quasi-k-clique is not $(k-1)$-edge-connected for $\gamma < 1$. The 0.8-quasi-7-clique in Figure 1 becomes disconnected when one edge is removed.

Fewer Parameter. In the k-truss community model, we only need to specify the trussness value k, which controls or affects the diameter, the edge connectivity, and the edge support in a community. In contrast, the α-adjacency-γ-quasi-k-clique model uses three parameters, the adjacency parameter α, the density γ and the clique size k. Although having more parameters may give more leverage on the properties of the community, it is much more difficult to choose proper values for different parameters.

Polynomial Time Complexity. There exist polynomial time algorithms [7, 21] for computing k-truss subgraphs. By applying such algorithm, we can compute the k-truss subgraphs for all k. The pre-computed results enable us to design compact index structures and efficient algorithms for querying k-truss communities. In contrast, finding γ-quasi-k-cliques has been proven to be NP-hard [9], which imposes a severe computational bottleneck.

2.3 Variations of K-Truss Community

The k-truss community can be extended to several interesting variants.

Densest K-Truss Community. It is interesting to discover the densest k-truss community containing a user q, that is, a k-truss community containing q that maximizes the trussness value k.

Most Diverse Communities. It is interesting to know how diverse the social contexts of a user q are, where a community represents a distinct social context. For a set of k-truss communities containing q as $\{C_1, \ldots, C_l\}$, the community diversity is measured by the entropy of the community vertex size distribution: $Div(q, k) = -\sum_{1 \leq i \leq l} \frac{|C_i|}{\sum_{1 \leq j \leq l} |C_j|} \log \frac{|C_i|}{\sum_{1 \leq j \leq l} |C_j|}$. By choosing k which maximizes the diversity, i.e., $k = \arg\max_k Div(q, k)$, we can find the most diverse communities.

Other Community Models. The community model can be generalized using other dense subgraph definitions, such as the k-core community, and k-edge-connected component community.

The proposed techniques for k-truss community search in this paper can be extended to solve the above variant forms.

3. QUERYING K-TRUSS COMMUNITY

In this section, we study how to process a k-truss community query on a graph. We first design a simple k-truss index which is then proven to incur unnecessary computational overhead for query processing. Then we design a compact and elegant structure, called *Triangle Connectivity Preserved Index* (TCP-Index), and a highly efficient algorithm to process a k-truss community query.

3.1 Subgraph and Edge Trussness

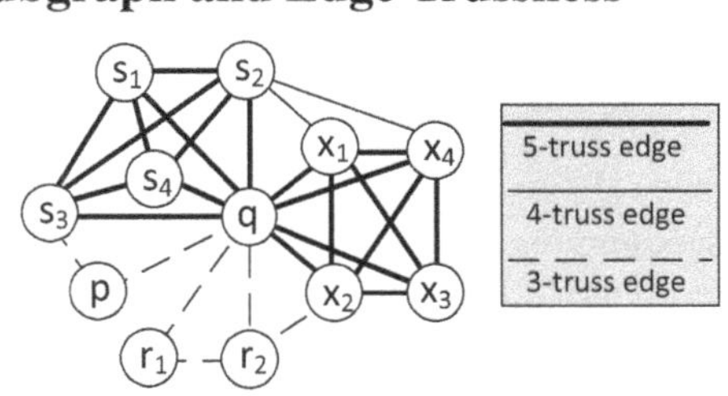

Figure 3: An example graph for k-truss community search

We define the trussness of a subgraph and an edge as follows.

DEFINITION 5 (SUBGRAPH TRUSSNESS). *The trussness of a subgraph $H \subseteq G$ is the minimum support of an edge in H, denoted by $\tau(H) = \min\{sup(e, H) : e \in E(H)\}$.*

DEFINITION 6 (EDGE TRUSSNESS). *The trussness of an edge $e \in E(G)$ is defined as $\tau(e) = \max_{H \subseteq G}\{\tau(H) : e \in E(H)\}$.*

Algorithm 1 Truss Decomposition

Input: $G = (V, E)$
Output: $\tau(e)$ for each $e \in E$

1: $k \leftarrow 2$;
2: compute $sup(e)$ for each edge $e \in E$;
3: sort all the edges in ascending order of their support;
4: **while**($\exists e$ such that $sup(e) \leq (k-2)$)
5: let $e = (u, v)$ be the edge with the lowest support;
6: assume, w.l.o.g, $deg(u) \leq deg(v)$;
7: **for** each $w \in N(u)$ **and** $(v, w) \in E$ **do**
8: $sup((u, w)) \leftarrow sup((u, w)) - 1$;
$sup((v, w)) \leftarrow sup((v, w)) - 1$;
9: reorder (u, w) and (v, w) according to their new support;
10: $\tau(e) \leftarrow k$, remove e from G;
11: **if**(*not* all edges in G are removed)
12: $k \leftarrow k + 1$;
13: **goto** Step 4;
14: **return** $\{\tau(e) | e \in E\}$;

Such a subgraph H which defines $\tau(e)$ is denoted as H^e. It follows that $\tau(H^e) = \tau(e)$. For an edge e and $2 \leq k \leq \tau(e)$, we denote the k-truss community containing e as H_k^e, which is unique in the sense that no other k-truss community contains e. We use k_{gmax} to denote the maximum trussness of any edge in G.

Consider the graph in Figure 3 as an example. The trussness of the edge $e(s_1, s_2)$ is $\tau(e) = 5$, and the subgraph H^e is the 5-clique on the vertex set $\{q, s_1, s_2, s_3, s_4\}$.

3.2 A Simple K-Truss Index

We first design a simple k-truss index and propose an algorithm for k-truss community search based on the index.

K-Truss Index Construction. We first apply a truss decomposition algorithm [21] on the graph G, which computes the trussness of each edge. For the self-completeness of this paper, the truss decomposition algorithm [21] is outlined in Algorithm 1. After the initialization, for each k starting from $k = 2$, the algorithm iteratively removes a lowest support edge $e(u, v)$ if $sup(e) \leq k - 2$. We assign the trussness of the removed edge as $\tau(e) = k$. Upon the removal of e, we also decrement the support of all other edges that form a triangle with e, and reorder them according to their new support. This process continues until all edges with support less than or equal to $(k - 2)$ are removed. In this way, we compute the trussness of all edges in G.

For each vertex $v \in V$, we sort its neighbors $N(v)$ in descending order of the edge trussness $\tau(e(u, v))$ for $u \in N(v)$. For each distinct trussness value $k \geq 2$, we mark the position of the first vertex u in the sorted adjacency list where $\tau(e(u, v)) = k$. This supports efficient retrieval of v's incident edges with a certain trussness value. We also use a hashtable to keep all the edges and their trussness values. This is the simple k-truss index.

Query Processing. Algorithm 2 outlines the procedure to process a k-truss community query based on the simple index. Given an integer k and a query vertex v_q, the algorithm checks every incident edge on v_q to search k-truss communities. If there exists an unvisited edge (v_q, u) with $\tau((v_q, u)) \geq k$, (v_q, u) is the seed edge to form a new community C_l. By definition, all the other edges in C_l can be reached from (v_q, u) through adjacent triangles. So we push (v_q, u) into a queue Q and perform a BFS traversal to search for other edges for expanding C_l, i.e., edges which have trussness no less than k and form triangles with edges already in C_l (line 6-13). When Q becomes empty, all edges in C_l have been found. Then the algorithm checks the next unvisited incident edge of v_q for forming a new community C_{l+1}. This process iterates until all incident edges of v_q have been processed. Finally a set of k-truss communities containing v_q are returned.

Algorithm 2 Query Processing Using K-Truss Index

Input: $G = (V, E)$, an integer k, query vertex v_q
Output: k-truss communities containing v_q

1: $visited \leftarrow \emptyset$; $l \leftarrow 0$;
2: **for** $u \in N(v_q)$ **do**
3: **if** $\tau((v_q, u)) \geq k$ **and** $(v_q, u) \notin visited$
4: $l \leftarrow l + 1$; $C_l \leftarrow \emptyset$; $Q \leftarrow \emptyset$;
5: $Q.push((v_q, u))$; $visited \leftarrow visited \cup \{(v_q, u)\}$;
6: **while** $Q \neq \emptyset$
7: $(x, y) \leftarrow Q.pop()$; $C_l \leftarrow C_l \cup \{(x, y)\}$;
8: **for** $z \in N(x) \cap N(y)$ **do**
9: **if** $\tau((x, z)) \geq k$ **and** $\tau((y, z)) \geq k$
10: **if** $(x, z) \notin visited$
11: $Q.push((x, z))$; $visited \leftarrow visited \cup \{(x, z)\}$;
12: **if** $(y, z) \notin visited$
13: $Q.push((y, z))$; $visited \leftarrow visited \cup \{(y, z)\}$;
14: **return** $\{C_1, \ldots, C_l\}$;

The correctness of Algorithm 2 is apparent since the algorithm essentially computes k-truss communities by definition, that is, exploring triangle connected edges with trussness no less than k in a BFS manner. We show the complexity of the simple k-truss index construction and query processing by Algorithm 2 as follows.

THEOREM 1. *The construction of the simple k-truss index takes $O(\sum_{(u,v)\in E} \min\{d(u), d(v)\})$ time and $O(m)$ space. The index size is $O(m)$. Algorithm 2 takes $O(d_{Amax}|Ans|)$ time to process one query, where $Ans = C_1 \cup \ldots \cup C_l$ is the union of the produced k-truss communities, $|Ans|$ is the edge number in Ans and d_{Amax} is the maximum vertex degree in Ans.*

PROOF. The truss decomposition algorithm (Algorithm 1) takes $O(\sum_{(u,v)\in E} \min\{d(u), d(v)\})$ time and $O(m)$ space for computing the trussness of all edges. Sorting the adjacency lists of all vertices in G takes $O(m)$ time and $O(m)$ space. Building an edge hashtable costs $O(m)$ time and $O(m)$ space. Thus, the construction of the k-truss index takes $O(\sum_{(u,v)\in E} \min\{d(u), d(v)\})$ time and $O(m)$ space. The index size is $O(m)$.

In k-truss community search, for each edge (u, v) in the generated communities, Algorithm 2 accesses the common neighbors of u and v, i.e., $N(u) \cap N(v)$ (line 7-9), whose size is bounded by d_{Amax}. Thus the query time complexity is $O(d_{Amax}|Ans|)$. □

Example 2: Suppose we want to query the 4-truss communities containing vertex q in the graph in Figure 3. Algorithm 2 first visits edge (q, s_1) with $\tau((q, s_1)) = 5 \geq 4$, and adds it into Q. The algorithm pops (q, s_1) from Q and inserts it into a new community C_1. Then the algorithm checks the common neighbors of q and s_1 and the edges between them. Consider a common neighbor s_2 as an example. As $\tau((q, s_2)) \geq 4$ and $\tau((s_1, s_2)) \geq 4$, both edges (q, s_2) and (s_1, s_2) are then inserted into C_1 and also pushed into Q for further expansion. This BFS expansion process continues until Q is empty and the 4-truss community C_1 is the induced subgraph by the vertex set $\{q, s_1, s_2, s_3, s_4, x_1, x_2, x_3, x_4\}$. □

3.3 A Novel TCP-Index

3.3.1 Limitations of Simple K-Truss Index

Algorithm 2 has two drawbacks in its query processing mechanism by using the simple k-truss index. Specifically, in line 8-13, for any edge (x, y) that has already been included in C_l, the algorithm needs to access adjacent edges (x, z) and (y, z) for each common neighbor z of x and y. The following two cases lead to unnecessary and excessive computational overhead.

1. **Unnecessary access of disqualified edges**: If $\tau((x,z)) < k$ or $\tau((y,z)) < k$, $(x,z),(y,z)$ will not be included in C_l, thus accessing and checking such disqualified edges *become a waste*.
2. **Repeated access of qualified edges**: For each edge (u,v) in C_l, it is accessed at least $2(k-2)$ times in the BFS traversal, which is a huge waste. This is because $\tau((u,v)) \geq k$, (u,v) is contained in at least $(k-2)$ triangles by definition. For each such triangle denoted as $\triangle_{uvw}$, (u,v) will be accessed twice when we do BFS expansion from the other two edges $(u,w),(v,w)$. It follows that the query time of Algorithm 2 is lower bounded by $\Omega(k|Ans|)$.

Considering these two drawbacks, we design a novel Triangle Connectivity Preserved Index, or TCP-Index in short, which avoids the computational problems in Algorithm 2. Remarkably, the TCP-Index supports the k-truss community query in $O(|Ans|)$ time, which is essentially optimal. Meanwhile, the TCP-Index can be constructed in $O(\sum_{(u,v)\in E}\min\{d(u),d(v)\})$ time and stored in $O(m)$ space, which has exactly the same complexity as the simple k-truss index.

3.3.2 TCP-Index Construction

We first make some observations from the example in Figure 3.

Observation 1: *Consider $\triangle_{pqs_3}$ in which the three edge trussness values are 5, 3, and 3. Then $\triangle_{pqs_3}$ can appear in a 3-truss community, but not in 4- or 5-truss communities, due to the two 3-truss edges. To generalize, a triangle $\triangle_{xyz}$ can appear only in k-truss communities where $k \leq \min\{\tau((x,y)),\tau((x,z)),\tau((y,z))\}$.*

Observation 2: *Consider a subgraph in Figure 4(a) which is extracted from Figure 3. By definition, vertices x_1,x_2,x_3 belong to the same 5-truss community containing q, as each involved edge is 5-truss, and $\triangle_{qx_1x_2}$ and $\triangle_{qx_1x_3}$ are adjacent via edge (q,x_1). Thus we can use a compact representation for vertex q as depicted in solid line in Figure 4(b), which preserves the trussness and adjacency information for community search. Note that there is no need to include edge (x_2,x_3), as the tree-shape structure clearly indicates that x_2,x_3 belong to the same 5-truss community by triangle adjacency.*

(a) Subgraph extracted from Fig. 3 (b) Compact representation

Figure 4: Compact representation of a community with q

Observation 3: *From Figure 3, we can see the two 5-truss communities $\{q,x_1,x_2,x_3,x_4\}$, $\{q,s_1,s_2,s_3,s_4\}$ involving vertex q are contained in the 4-truss community $\{q,x_1,x_2,x_3,x_4,s_1,s_2,s_3,s_4\}$, which is in turn contained in the 3-truss community, which is the whole graph.*

Based on the above observations, we are ready to construct the TCP-Index using Algorithm 3. For each vertex $x \in V$, we build a graph G_x, where $V(G_x) = N(x)$, and $E(G_x) = \{(y,z)|(y,z) \in E(G), y,z \in N(x)\}$. For each edge $(y,z) \in E(G_x)$, we assign a weight $w(y,z) = \min\{\tau((x,y)),\tau((x,z)),\tau((y,z))\}$, which indicates that $\triangle_{xyz}$ can appear only in k-truss community where $k \leq w(y,z)$ based on Observation 1. The TCP-Index for vertex x is a tree structure, denoted as $\mathcal{T}_x$, which is initialized to be the node set $N(x)$. Then in line 8-12, for each k from the largest weight k_{max} to 2, we iteratively collect the set of edges $S_k \subseteq E(G_k)$

Algorithm 3 TCP-Index Construction

Input: $G = (V,E)$
Output: TCP-Index $\mathcal{T}_x$ for each $x \in V$

```
1:  Perform truss decomposition for G;
2:  for x ∈ V do
3:      G_x ← {(y,z)|y,z ∈ N(x),(y,z) ∈ E};
4:      for (y,z) ∈ E(G_x) do
5:          w(y,z) ← min{τ((x,y)),τ((x,z)),τ((y,z))};
6:      T_x ← N(x);
7:      k_max ← max{w(y,z)|(y,z) ∈ E(G_x)} ;
8:      for k ← k_max to 2 do
9:          S_k ← {(y,z)|(y,z) ∈ E(G_x), w(y,z) = k};
10:         for (y,z) ∈ S_k do
11:             if y and z are in different connected components in T_x
12:                 add (y,z) with weight w(y,z) in T_x;
13: return {T_x|x ∈ V};
```

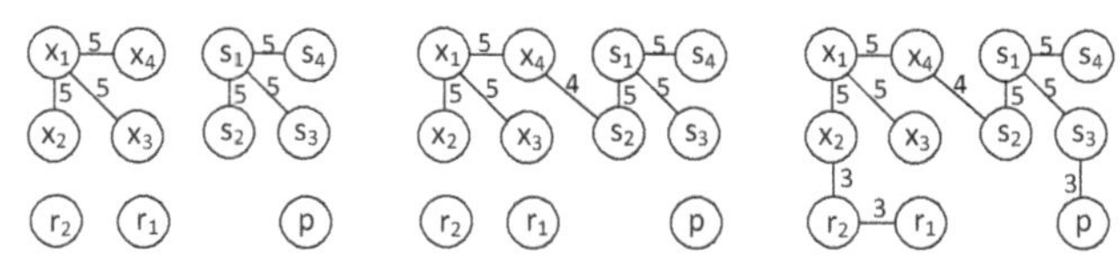

(a) 5-truss level (b) 4-truss level (c) 3-truss level

Figure 5: TCP-Index construction of vertex q

whose weight is k. For each $(y,z) \in S_k$, if y,z are still in different components of $\mathcal{T}_x$, we add (y,z) with a weight $w(y,z)$ into $\mathcal{T}_x$. Essentially, $\mathcal{T}_x$ is the maximum spanning forest of G_x. The trees $\mathcal{T}_x$ for all $x \in V$ form the TCP-Index of graph G.

Example 3: Figure 5 shows the TCP-Index for vertex q in the graph in Figure 3. $\mathcal{T}_q$ is initialized to be $N(q)$. Figure 5(a) shows the tree structure when we add edges whose weights are 5. According to Observation 2, when the edges (x_1,x_2) and (x_1,x_3) are added into $\mathcal{T}_q$, the edge (x_2,x_3) will not be added into $\mathcal{T}_q$, as x_2,x_3 are already connected in $\mathcal{T}_q$ and we know that x_2,x_3 belong to the same 5-truss community by triangle adjacency. This is essential to keep $\mathcal{T}_q$ as a compact forest. The complete TCP-Index for q is shown in Figure 5(c). According to the community containment relationship in Observation 3, it is sufficient to use a single structure $\mathcal{T}_q$ for all trussness levels from k_{max} to 2. □

THEOREM 2. *The TCP-Index of graph G can be constructed in $O(\sum_{(u,v)\in E}\min\{d(u),d(v)\})$ time and $O(m)$ space by Algorithm 3. The index size is $O(m)$.*

PROOF. The first step costs $O(\sum_{(u,v)\in E}\min\{d(u),d(v)\})$ time. For a vertex $x \in V$, it takes $O(\sum_{y\in N(x)}\min\{d(x),d(y)\})$ time to list all triangles containing x to obtain G_x in line 3. The edge number $|E(G_x)|$ is bounded by $O(\sum_{y\in N(x)}\min\{d(x),d(y)\})$, thus $\mathcal{T}_x$ can be computed in $O(\sum_{y\in N(x)}\min\{d(x),d(y)\})$ time by Kruskal's algorithm. For all vertices in V, it takes $O(\sum_{x\in V}\sum_{y\in N(x)}\min\{d(x),d(y)\})$ time in total to build the TCP-Index. Thus the time cost of Algorithm 3 is $O(\sum_{(u,v)\in E}\min\{d(u),d(v)\})$.

For a vertex $x \in V$, G_x, as a subgraph of G, takes $O(m)$ space, which can be released after obtaining $\mathcal{T}_x$. $\mathcal{T}_x$, as a spanning forest on the vertex set $N(x)$, takes $O(|N(x)|)$ space. Thus the TCP-Index size for all vertices is $O(\sum_{x\in V}|N(x)|) = O(m)$. □

REMARK 1. *According to [6], $O(\sum_{(u,v)\in E}\min\{d(u),d(v)\}) \subseteq O(\rho m)$ where ρ is the arboricity of a graph G. $\rho \leq \min\{\lceil\sqrt{m}\rceil, d_{max}\}$ holds for any graph. Thus the TCP-Index construction time is $O(\sum_{(u,v)\in E}\min\{d(u),d(v)\}) \subseteq O(\rho m) \subseteq O(m^{1.5})$.*

3.3.3 *Query Processing Using TCP-Index*

We first illustrate query processing through an example, before we formally present the algorithm. According to the design of the TCP-Index, if two vertices are connected through a series of edges with weight $\geq k$ in $\mathcal{T}_x$ for $x \in V$, these two vertices belong to the same k-truss community via adjacent triangles. Consider $\mathcal{T}_q$ in Figure 5(c). As x_2, x_3 are connected through two edges with weight 5, they belong to the same 5-truss community. Thus we first define the *k-level connected vertex set* on a tree $\mathcal{T}_x$ to find all such vertices that belong to a k-truss community.

DEFINITION 7 (K-LEVEL CONNECTED VERTEX SET). *For $x \in V$ and $y \in N(x)$, we use $V_k(x, y)$ to denote the set of vertices which are connected with y through edges of weight $\geq k$ in $\mathcal{T}_x$. We regard y also belongs to this set, i.e., $y \in V_k(x, y)$.*

Example 4: If we want to query 5-truss communities containing q, we first visit an incident edge on q, (q, x_1) where $\tau((q, x_1)) = 5$. From $\mathcal{T}_q$ we retrieve the vertex set $V_5(q, x_1) = \{x_1, x_2, x_3, x_4\}$ as they are connected through edges with weight 5. According to Observation 2, these four vertices belong to the same 5-truss community with q. As $V_5(q, x_1) \subset N(q)$, we can construct part of the community as shown in Figure 6(a).

At this stage, we still miss the edges between the four vertices, for example, $(x_2, x_3), (x_3, x_4)$, etc. This is because $\mathcal{T}_q$ which is a spanning forest does not keep all the edges between the vertices. To fully recover all the edges in the 5-truss community, for each vertex $x_i \in V_5(q, x_1)$, we "reverse" the edge (q, x_i) to (x_i, q), then further expand the community in x_i's neighborhood. Take vertex x_2 as an example. We reverse (q, x_2) to (x_2, q) and then query x_2's index $\mathcal{T}_{x_2}$ to get the vertex set $V_5(x_2, q) = \{q, x_1, x_3, x_4\}$, as x_1, x_3, x_4 are connected with q in $\mathcal{T}_{x_2}$. Then we can obtain the edges between x_2 and every vertex in $V_5(x_2, q)$. After this, the community is shown in Figure 6(b). Similarly, we perform the reverse operation for each vertex x_1, x_3, x_4 and get the complete 5-truss community in Figure 6(c). We can observe that in this search process, each edge in a community is accessed exactly twice, for example, accessing (q, x_2) from $\mathcal{T}_q$ and (x_2, q) from $\mathcal{T}_{x_2}$. □

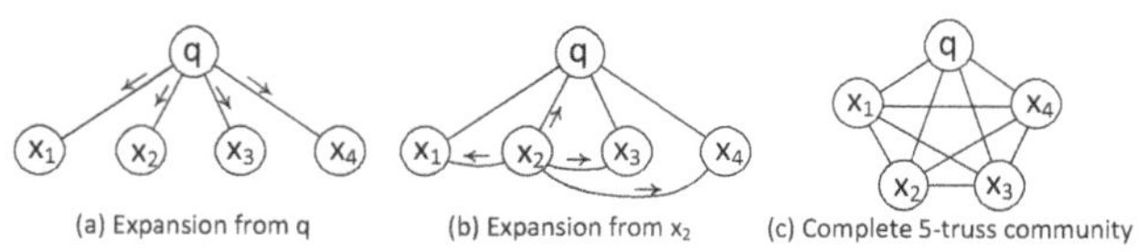

Figure 6: 5-truss community query on q using TCP-Index

Algorithm 4 outlines the procedure of query processing using the TCP-Index. Similar to Algorithm 2, Algorithm 4 computes the k-truss communities for a query vertex v_q by expanding from each incident edge on v_q in a BFS manner. If there exists an unvisited edge (v_q, u) with $\tau((v_q, u)) \geq k$, (v_q, u) is the seed edge to form a new community C_l (line 2-4). Then the algorithm performs a BFS traversal using a queue Q in line 5-13. For an unvisited edge (x, y), it searches the vertex set $V_k(x, y)$ from $\mathcal{T}_x$. The procedure of computing $V_k(x, y)$ is listed in line 15-16. For each $z \in V_k(x, y)$, the edge (x, z) is added into C_l. Then we perform the reverse operation, i.e., if (z, x) is not visited yet, it is pushed into Q for z-centered community expansion using $\mathcal{T}_z$. Note that (z, x) and (x, z) are considered different here. When Q becomes empty, all edges in C_l have been found. The process iterates until all incident edges of v_q have been processed. Finally a set of k-truss communities containing v_q are returned.

We prove the correctness of Algorithm 4 as follows.

Algorithm 4 Query Processing Using TCP-Index

Input: $G = (V, E)$, an integer k, query vertex v_q
Output: k-truss communities containing v_q

1: $visited \leftarrow \emptyset$; $l \leftarrow 0$;
2: **for** $u \in N(v_q)$ **do**
3:   **if** $\tau((v_q, u)) \geq k$ **and** $(v_q, u) \notin visited$
4:     $l \leftarrow l + 1$; $C_l \leftarrow \emptyset$; $Q \leftarrow \emptyset$;
5:     $Q.push((v_q, u))$;
6:     **while** $Q \neq \emptyset$
7:       $(x, y) \leftarrow Q.pop()$;
8:       **if** $(x, y) \notin visited$
9:         compute $V_k(x, y)$;
10:         **for** $z \in V_k(x, y)$ **do**
11:           $visited \leftarrow visited \cup \{(x, z)\}$; $C_l \leftarrow C_l \cup \{(x, z)\}$;
12:           **if** the reversed edge $(z, x) \notin visited$
13:             $Q.push((z, x))$;
14: **return** $\{C_1, \cdots, C_l\}$;

15: **Procedure** compute $V_k(x, y)$
16: **return** $\{z | z$ is connected with y in $\mathcal{T}_x$ through edges of weight $\geq k\}$;

LEMMA 1. *Given a query vertex $x \in V$ and an integer k, Algorithm 4 correctly computes all k-truss communities containing x.*

PROOF. First, for an edge (y, z) in $\mathcal{T}_x$, according to the definition $w(y, z) = \min\{\tau((x, y)), \tau((x, z)), \tau((y, z))\}$, if $w(y, z) \geq k$, $\triangle_{xyz}$ is included in a k-truss community of x.

Second, for two adjacent edges $(y, z_1), (y, z_2)$ in $\mathcal{T}_x$, it means $\triangle_{xyz_1}, \triangle_{xyz_2}$ are adjacent via edge (x, y).

Third, $V_k(x, y)$ contains the set of vertices which are connected with y through edges of weight $\geq k$ in $\mathcal{T}_x$. Based on the above two points, it leads to the discovery of all the triangles with weight $\geq k$ that can reach edge (x, y) in x's neighborhood. These connected triangles appear in the same k-truss community containing x.

Last, for an edge (x, z) where $z \in V_k(x, y)$, the same operation on its reverse edge (z, x) will further expand the k-truss community in z's neighborhood via $\mathcal{T}_z$. Thus the k-truss community is expanded via adjacent triangles in a BFS manner.

Based on the above points, we have established the correctness of Algorithm 4. □

THEOREM 3. *The time complexity of Algorithm 4 is $O(|Ans|)$, where $Ans = C_1 \cup \ldots \cup C_l$ is the union of the produced k-truss communities and $|Ans|$ is the number of edges in Ans.*

PROOF. Each edge (x, y) in the generated communities is accessed exactly twice: accessing (x, y) from $\mathcal{T}_x$ and (y, x) from $\mathcal{T}_y$. Thus the time complexity of Algorithm 4 is $O(|Ans|)$. □

Complexity Comparison. By using the TCP-Index and the simple k-truss index, each edge in a k-truss community is accessed *exactly twice versus at least $2(k-2)$ times*. In addition, the TCP-Index successfully avoids the unnecessary access of disqualified edges whose trussness is less than k. These are the key reasons to explain the query time difference between Algorithms 4 and 2, i.e., $O(|Ans|)$ versus $O(d_{Amax}|Ans|)$. Meanwhile, the TCP-Index construction has exactly the same time and space complexity as the simple k-truss index.

4. QUERYING K-TRUSS COMMUNITY IN DYNAMIC GRAPHS

In this section, we study k-truss community search in dynamic graphs where vertices and edges are inserted or deleted. We mainly focus on edge insertion and deletion, because vertex insertion/deletion can be regarded as a sequence of edge insertions/deletions preceded/followed by the insertion/deletion of an isolated vertex.

Consider the insertion of edge $e_0(x, y)$ into G which leads to a set of new triangles $\{\triangle_{xyz} : z \in N(x) \cap N(y)\}$. Due to a new $\triangle_{xyz}$, the support of both edges $(x, z), (y, z)$ increases by 1. This may increase the subgraph trussness, $\tau(H)$, for $H \subseteq G$ which contains $\triangle_{xyz}$ since $\tau(H) = \min\{sup(e, H) : e \in E(H)\}$. It may in turn increase the trussness of those edges contained in H, as $\tau(e) = \max_{H \subseteq G}\{\tau(H) : e \in E(H)\}$, however, such edges may not necessarily be incident on vertices x or y. Edge deletion has a similar effect on decreasing edge trussness. To handle the edge trussness update efficiently, the key is to identify the affected region in the graph precisely. Thus, in Section 4.1 we present a theoretical analysis to define the scope that an edge insertion/deletion may affect. We design algorithms for updating the edge trussness and the TCP-Index in Sections 4.2 and 4.3, respectively.

4.1 Scope of Affected Edges

We use $\tau(e)$ and $\hat{\tau}(e)$ to represent the trussness of an edge e before and after an edge insertion/deletion respectively. We have the following three properties.

Rule 1: If e_0 is inserted into G with $\hat{\tau}(e_0) = l$, then $\forall e \in E(G)$ with $\tau(e) \geq l$, $\hat{\tau}(e) = \tau(e)$ holds.

Rule 2: If e_0 is deleted from G with $\tau(e_0) = l$, then $\forall e \in E(G) \setminus \{e_0\}$ with $\tau(e) > l$, $\hat{\tau}(e) = \tau(e)$ holds.

Rule 3: $\forall e \in E(G) \setminus \{e_0\}$, $|\hat{\tau}(e) - \tau(e)| \leq 1$ holds.

The rationale of Rules 1 and 2 is that e_0 is not included in a $(l + 1)$-truss subgraph. Rule 3 holds since the support of any edge changes by at most 1 with an edge insertion/deletion. These three properties can be rigorously proved, but the proof is omitted due to the space limit. In order to apply Rule 1, we need to obtain $\hat{\tau}(e_0)$ first. However, computing $\hat{\tau}(e_0)$ itself is costly. So we resort to an alternative, that is, we estimate an upper bound of $\hat{\tau}(e_0)$, denoted as $\overline{\hat{\tau}(e_0)}$, with a light cost, and apply Rule 1' instead of Rule 1.

Rule 1': If e_0 is inserted into G, then $\forall e \in E(G)$ with $\tau(e) \geq \overline{\hat{\tau}(e_0)} \geq \hat{\tau}(e_0)$, $\hat{\tau}(e) = \tau(e)$ holds.

To estimate $\overline{\hat{\tau}(e_0)}$, we define the *k-level triangles* of an edge.

DEFINITION 8 (K-LEVEL TRIANGLES). *For an edge $e(u, v)$ and $k \geq 2$, we denote the k-level triangles containing e by $\triangle^k_{(u,v)} = \{\triangle_{uvw} : \min\{\tau((u, w)), \tau((v, w))\} \geq k\}$. The number of triangles in $\triangle^k_{(u,v)}$ is denoted by $|\triangle^k_{(u,v)}|$.*

Lemma 2 gives the lower and upper bound of $\hat{\tau}(e_0)$.

LEMMA 2. *If an edge $e_0(u, v)$ is inserted into a graph, then $\hat{\tau}(e_0)$ satisfies $k_1 \leq \hat{\tau}(e_0) \leq k_2$ and $k_2 - k_1 \leq 1$, where $k_1 = \max_k\{k : |\triangle^k_{e_0}| \geq k - 2\}$, $k_2 = \max_k\{k : |\triangle^{k-1}_{e_0}| \geq k - 2\}$.*

PROOF. We first prove $\hat{\tau}(e_0) \geq k_1$. Since $k_1 = \max_k\{k : |\triangle^k_{e_0}| \geq k - 2\}$, we can find triangles $\triangle_{uvw_1}, \ldots, \triangle_{uvw_{k_1-2}}$ in which all edges have trussness no less than k_1 except for e_0. Each of such edges $(u, w_1), (v, w_1), \ldots, (u, w_{k_1-2}), (v, w_{k_1-2})$ corresponds to a unique k_1-truss community as $H^{(u,w_1)}_{k_1}$, $H^{(v,w_1)}_{k_1}, \ldots,$ $H^{(u,w_{k_1-2})}_{k_1}$, $H^{(v,w_{k_1-2})}_{k_1}$. Then we union all these k_1-truss communities with edge e_0 to form a connected subgraph H which becomes a seed of k_1-truss community by definition. Thus, for $e_0 \in H$, $\hat{\tau}(e_0) \geq k_1$ is true.

Next we prove $\hat{\tau}(e_0) \leq k_2$ by contradiction. Suppose to the contrary that $\hat{\tau}(e_0) = l > k_2$, then there exists an l-truss community $H^{e_0}_l$ in which edges have trussness no less than l, and have $l - 2$ triangles containing e_0 by definition. Since the trussness of all edges except e_0 increases by at most 1 after insertion by Rule 3, we have $|\triangle^{l-1}_{e_0}| \geq l - 2$ before insertion and then derive $k_2 \geq l$ by the definition of k_2, which is a contradiction.

Finally, we prove $k_2 - k_1 \leq 1$. By the definition of k_2, we have $|\triangle^{k_2-1}_{e_0}| \geq k_2 - 2 \geq k_2 - 3$, and derive $k_1 \geq k_2 - 1$ by the definition of k_1. Thus $k_2 - k_1 \leq 1$ is true. $\square$

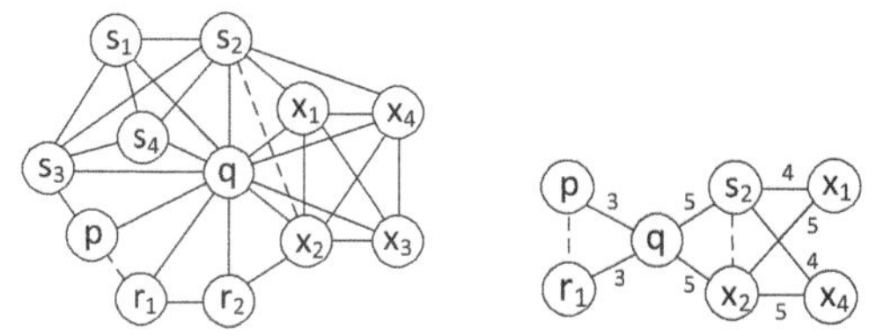

(a) G with Edge Insertion (b) Trussness Update

Figure 7: An example graph with edge insertion

COROLLARY 1. $\overline{\hat{\tau}(e_0)} = \max_k\{k : |\triangle^{k-1}_{e_0}| \geq k - 2\}$ *is an upper bound of* $\hat{\tau}(e_0)$.

The upper bound in Corollary 1 is extremely tight, as it may be larger than the real trussness by at most 1. For example, if we insert edge (p, r_1) into the graph in Figure 7(a), we have $\triangle^3_{(p,r_1)} = \{\triangle_{qpr_1}\}$ and $k_1 = k_2 = 3$ by Lemma 2. So we get $\hat{\tau}((p, r_1)) = 3$. If we insert another edge (s_2, x_2), we have $\triangle^4_{(s_2,x_2)} = \{\triangle_{s_2x_2q}, \triangle_{s_2x_2x_1}, \triangle_{s_2x_2x_4}\}$, $k_1 = 4$, $k_2 = 5$ by Lemma 2.

Due to the insertion/deletion of edge e_0, there are two reasons for edge $e \in E(G) \setminus \{e_0\}$ to change trussness, i.e., $\hat{\tau}(e) \neq \tau(e)$: (1) e forms/breaks a triangle with e_0 when e_0 is inserted/deleted; or (2) the edges of the triangles in which e lies have changed their trussness. We study the insertion case in Lemma 3.

LEMMA 3. *If an edge e_0 is inserted into a graph, we first assign $\tau(e_0) = \max_k\{k : |\triangle^k_{e_0}| \geq k - 2\}$. Then for $e(x, y) \in E(G) \cup \{e_0\}$ with $\tau(e) = l < \overline{\hat{\tau}(e_0)}$, e may have $\hat{\tau}(e) = l + 1$* ***only in two cases:***

(1) A new triangle with edges e, e_0 and another e' is formed, and $\min\{\tau(e_0), \tau(e')\} \geq l$ holds; or

(2) For $e(x, y)$, $\exists z \in N(x) \cap N(y)$, $\min\{\tau((x, z)), \tau((y, z))\} = l$ holds.

PROOF. An edge may increase the trussness by at most 1 with an insertion by Rule 3. For $e(x, y)$, assume $\tau(e) = l$, $\hat{\tau}(e) = l + 1$. This implies $|\triangle^{l+1}_{(x,y)}| < l + 1$ before insertion, and $|\hat{\triangle}^{l+1}_{(x,y)}| \geq l + 1$ after insertion, where $\hat{\triangle}^{l+1}_{(x,y)} = \{\triangle_{xyz} : \min\{\hat{\tau}((x, z)), \hat{\tau}((y, z))\} \geq l + 1\}$. Then we prove cases (1) and (2) may lead to the increased trussness of e.

For case (1), the trussness of e_0 or e' may increase due to the edge insertion, thus it is possible to have $\min\{\hat{\tau}(e_0), \hat{\tau}(e')\} \geq l + 1$, and $|\hat{\triangle}^{l+1}_{(x,y)}| \geq l + 1$.

For case (2), as $\min\{\tau((x, z)), \tau((y, z))\} = l$, we know $\triangle_{xyz} \notin \triangle^{l+1}_{(x,y)}$. With an edge insertion, it is possible to have $\min\{\hat{\tau}((x, z)), \hat{\tau}((y, z))\} \geq l + 1$, and $|\hat{\triangle}^{l+1}_{(x,y)}| \geq l + 1$.

Next consider any edge $e(x, y) \in E(G) \cup \{e_0\}$ with $\tau(e) = l$, if it does not satisfy case (1), there is no new triangle containing e formed to account for trussness increase. Thus it is impossible to have $\hat{\tau}(e) = l + 1$. If it does not satisfy case (2), then the existing triangle $\triangle_{xyz}$ is with either $\min\{\tau((x, z)), \tau((y, z))\} < l$ or $\min\{\tau((x, z)), \tau((y, z))\} \geq l + 1$. After insertion we respectively have $\min\{\hat{\tau}((x, z)), \hat{\tau}((y, z))\} < l + 1$ or $\min\{\hat{\tau}((x, z)), \hat{\tau}((y, z))\} \geq l + 1$. For either situation, we can derive $|\hat{\triangle}^{l+1}_{(x,y)}| = |\triangle^{l+1}_{(x,y)}| < l + 1$. Thus if e satisfies neither case (1) nor (2), it is impossible to have the trussness increase as $\hat{\tau}(e) = l + 1$. $\square$

According to Lemma 3, we summarize the affected edge trussness due to edge insertion/deletion.

Scope of Affected Edges. We define the weight of a triangle by the minimum edge trussness in the triangle. Then the insertion/deletion of an edge e_0 may lead to the following trussness update.

(1) **Insertion case.** For $e \in E(G) \cup \{e_0\}$ with $\tau(e) < \overline{\hat{\tau}(e_0)}$, if e, e_0 and another e' form a new triangle with weight $\tau(e)$, or e is connected with e_0 through a series of adjacent triangles each with weight $\tau(e)$, then e may have $\hat{\tau}(e) = \tau(e) + 1$.

(2) **Deletion case.** For $e \in E(G) \setminus \{e_0\}$ with $\tau(e) \leq \tau(e_0)$, if e, e_0 belong to a triangle with weight $\tau(e)$, or e is connected with e_0 through a series of adjacent triangles each with weight $\tau(e)$ before deletion, then e may have $\hat{\tau}(e) = \tau(e) - 1$.

4.2 Updating Edge Trussness

In this section, we propose an algorithm to update the edge trussness when an edge e_0 is inserted. The algorithm to handle edge deletion is similar and thus omitted. From Section 4.1 we know that only edges which have $\tau(e) < \overline{\hat{\tau}(e_0)}$, and are either in the same triangle with e_0 or connected to e_0 through adjacent triangles at the same trussness level may increase their trussness. Thus we first collect all edges in case (1) of Lemma 3 as candidates, then expand the candidate edges and examine their edge trussness level by level according to case (2). Finally, we use a variant of truss decomposition algorithm to finalize the trussness update.

The procedure to update edge trussness given an inserted edge e_0 is outlined in Algorithm 5. We first insert the edge e_0 and compute the range of $\hat{\tau}(e_0)$ as $[k_1, k_2]$ by Lemma 2. Then the algorithm sets $\tau(e_0) = k_1$ and the maximum edge trussness $k_{max} = k_2 - 1$ by Rule 1'. In line 4-9, by case (1) of Lemma 3, we collect every edge which forms a triangle with e_0, and has the minimum trussness in the triangle with $\tau(e) = k \leq k_{max}$. These edges are inserted into L_k. Then in line 10-30, for each k from k_{max} to 2, the algorithm updates the trussness of edges with $\tau(e) = k$ using three steps, namely, edge expansion (line 11-20), edge eviction (line 21-28), and trussness update (line 29-30). In the edge expansion step, the algorithm expands L_k by finding all edges with trussness k using breadth-first search through adjacent triangles with weight k by case (2) of Lemma 3 (line 14-20). Meanwhile, it computes the number of k-level triangles $|\triangle_e^k|$ as $s[e]$ (line 16). In the edge eviction step, the algorithm iteratively evicts edges with $s[e] \leq k - 2$ from L_k (line 22) until no such edges exist. After evicting an edge e, for each edge $e' \in L_k$ that forms a triangle of weight k with e, $s[e']$ is decreased by 1 (line 24-28). In the trussness update step, each edge $e \in L_k$ has $s[e] \geq k - 1$ and gets trussness update $\hat{\tau}(e) = k + 1$ (line 29-30). The three steps can be further optimized by pushing the edge eviction operation (line 21-28) into the edge expansion step (line 11-20) after each $s[(x, y)]$ is calculated, in order to avoid expanding useless edges in an early stage. The technique is similar to the early node eviction technique proposed in [18] for k-core update. Thus, we omit the detailed discussion on this heuristic due to space limitation.

Example 5: We update the edge trussness with the insertion of $e_0(s_2, x_2)$ in the graph shown in Figure 7(a). We first compute $k_1 = 4$, $k_2 = 5$, and assign $\tau(e_0) = 4$ and $k_{max} = 4$. Since $\tau(e_0) = k_{max}$ which indicates that e_0 may increase its trussness, we add (s_2, x_2) into L_4. Then the algorithm checks the edges forming new triangles with e_0 as shown in Figure 7(b), and adds (s_2, x_1) and (s_2, x_4) into L_4. Next the algorithm uses BFS to find the edges connected with those in L_4 through adjacent triangles with weight 4. As there is no such edge satisfying this condition, L_4 remains unchanged. Meanwhile, for each $e \in L_4$, it computes $|\triangle_e^4|$ as $s[e]$, that is, $s[(s_2, x_2)] = s[(s_2, x_1)] = s[(s_2, x_4)] = 3$ (shown in Figure 7(a)). As the three edges have $s[e] > 2$, the algorithm updates $\hat{\tau}(s_2, x_2) = \hat{\tau}(s_2, x_1) = \hat{\tau}(s_2, x_4) = 5$. □

Algorithm 5 Trussness Update with Edge Insertion

Input: $G = (V, E)$, the inserted edge $e_0 = (u, v)$
Output: Updated trussness $\hat{\tau}(e)$ for $e \in E(G) \cup \{e_0\}$

1: $G.insert(e_0)$;
2: compute $[k_1, k_2]$ for $\hat{\tau}(e_0)$ by Lemma 2;
3: $\tau(e_0) \leftarrow k_1$; $k_{max} \leftarrow k_2 - 1$;
4: **for** $k \leftarrow 2$ to k_{max} **do** $L_k \leftarrow \emptyset$;
5: **for** $w \in N(u) \cap N(v)$ **do**
6: $\quad k \leftarrow \min\{\tau((w, u)), \tau((w, v))\}$;
7: $\quad$**if** $k \leq k_{max}$ **then**
8: $\quad\quad$**if** $\tau((w, u)) = k$ **then** $L_k \leftarrow L_k \cup \{(w, u)\}$;
9: $\quad\quad$**if** $\tau((w, v)) = k$ **then** $L_k \leftarrow L_k \cup \{(w, v)\}$;
10: **for** $k \leftarrow k_{max}$ to 2 **do**
11: $\quad Q \leftarrow \emptyset$; $Q.push(L_k)$;
12: $\quad$**while** $Q \neq \emptyset$
13: $\quad\quad (x, y) \leftarrow Q.pop()$; $s[(x, y)] \leftarrow 0$;
14: $\quad\quad$**for** $z \in N(x) \cap N(y)$ **do**
15: $\quad\quad\quad$**if** $\tau((z, x)) < k$ **or** $\tau((z, y)) < k$ **then continue**;
16: $\quad\quad\quad s[(x, y)] \leftarrow s[(x, y)] + 1$;
17: $\quad\quad\quad$**if** $\tau((z, x)) = k$ **and** $(z, x) \notin L_k$ **then**
18: $\quad\quad\quad\quad Q.push((z, x))$; $L_k \leftarrow L_k \cup \{(z, x)\}$;
19: $\quad\quad\quad$**if** $\tau((z, y)) = k$ **and** $(z, y) \notin L_k$ **then**
20: $\quad\quad\quad\quad Q.push((z, y))$; $L_k \leftarrow L_k \cup \{(z, y)\}$;
21: $\quad$**while** $\exists s[(x, y)] \leq k - 2$ in L_k
22: $\quad\quad L_k \leftarrow L_k \setminus \{(x, y)\}$;
23: $\quad\quad$**for** $z \in N(x) \cap N(y)$ **do**
24: $\quad\quad\quad$**if** $\tau((x, z)) < k$ **or** $\tau((y, z)) < k$ **then continue**;
25: $\quad\quad\quad$**if** $\tau((x, z)) = k$ **and** $(x, z) \notin L_k$ **then continue**;
26: $\quad\quad\quad$**if** $\tau((y, z)) = k$ **and** $(y, z) \notin L_k$ **then continue**;
27: $\quad\quad\quad$**if** $(x, z) \in L_k$ **then** $s[(x, z)] \leftarrow s[(x, z)] - 1$;
28: $\quad\quad\quad$**if** $(y, z) \in L_k$ **then** $s[(y, z)] \leftarrow s[(y, z)] - 1$;
29: $\quad$**for** $(x, y) \in L_k$ **do**
30: $\quad\quad \hat{\tau}((x, y)) \leftarrow k + 1$;

4.3 Updating TCP-Index

We study updating the TCP-Index. Recall that, for $x \in V$, the index $\mathcal{T}_x$ is the maximum spanning forest of x's neighborhood graph G_x, where $V(G_x) = N(x)$, and $E(G_x) = \{(y, z) | (y, z) \in E(G), y, z \in N(x)\}$. Thus the key problem is how to update the maximum spanning forest of G_x given an edge insertion/deletion and the consequent edge trussness update.

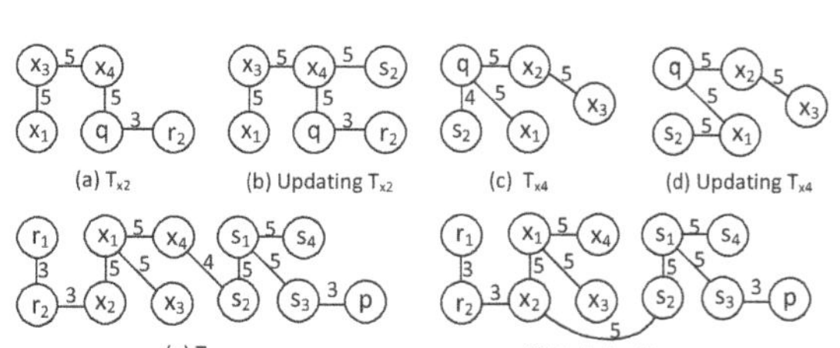

Figure 8: Updating TCP-Index

4.3.1 *Updating TCP-Index With Edge Insertion*

Index Update with Edge Insertion. With an inserted edge $e_0(u, v)$, we first consider how to update $\mathcal{T}_u$ and $\mathcal{T}_v$. Take vertex u as an example. G_u now includes a new vertex v and a set of new edges $\{(v, w) | w \in N(u) \cap N(v)\}$. Then we update the maximum spanning forest $\mathcal{T}_u$ with the new vertex and edges in G_u. The time cost is $O(|N(u)| + |N(u) \cap N(v)|) \subseteq O(|N(u)|)$.

For example, consider the insertion of (s_2, x_2) in Figure 7(a). The index $\mathcal{T}_{x_2}$ before insertion is shown in Figure 8(a). Now vertex

s_2 and three edges $(s_2, q), (s_2, x_1), (s_2, x_4)$ all with weight 5 are inserted into G_{x_2}. So the updated $\mathcal{T}_{x_2}$ is shown in Figure 8(b).

Now we consider how to update $\mathcal{T}_w$ for $w \in N(u) \cap N(v)$. G_w includes a new edge (u, v). We first compute the weight $w(u, v) = \min\{\hat{\tau}((u, v)), \hat{\tau}((u, w)), \hat{\tau}((v, w))\}$. If u, v are in different components of $\mathcal{T}_w$, we add the edge (u, v) with weight $w(u, v)$ into $\mathcal{T}_w$; otherwise, we can find a unique path P between u and v in $\mathcal{T}_w$. Then we compute the minimum weight on P as $w^* = \min_{e \in P} w(e)$. If $w^* \geq w(u, v)$, $\mathcal{T}_w$ remains unchanged; if $w^* < w(u, v)$, the corresponding edge is replaced by (u, v) in $\mathcal{T}_w$. The time cost is $O(|N(w)|)$.

Continue with the above example. With the insertion of (s_2, x_2), their common neighbor q's index before insertion is shown in Figure 8(e). There is a path (s_2, x_4, x_1, x_2) with a minimum weight 4. So we replace (s_2, x_4) by (s_2, x_2) with weight 5 in Figure 8(f).

Index Update with Trussness Increase. Besides the above cases, we also need to consider the index maintenance for an existing edge $e(x, y)$ which has trussness update $\hat{\tau}(e) = \tau(e) + 1$ due to the insertion of e_0. We discuss the update of $\mathcal{T}_x$ (and similarly $\mathcal{T}_y$). For every triangle $\triangle_{xyz}$, we denote $w_{xyz} = \min\{\tau((x, y)), \tau((x, z)), \tau((y, z))\}$, and $\hat{w}_{xyz} = \min\{\hat{\tau}((x, y)), \hat{\tau}((x, z)), \hat{\tau}((y, z))\}$. If $\hat{w}_{xyz} = w_{xyz}$, $\mathcal{T}_x$ remains unchanged. Otherwise, for $\hat{w}_{xyz} = w_{xyz} + 1$, if $(y, z) \in \mathcal{T}_x$, we update the edge weight $w(y, z) = \hat{w}_{xyz}$ in $\mathcal{T}_x$; if $(y, z) \notin \mathcal{T}_x$, we find the unique path P between y and z in $\mathcal{T}_x$ and update P with the new weight $w(y, z)$ in a similar process as described above for updating $\mathcal{T}_w$. For the neighbor vertex $z \in N(x) \cap N(y)$, the index $\mathcal{T}_z$ can be updated similarly.

Continue with the above example. With the insertion of (s_2, x_2), we have $\hat{\tau}((s_2, x_4)) = \tau((s_2, x_4)) + 1$, and $\hat{w}_{s_2 x_4 x_1} = 5$. The index $\mathcal{T}_{x_4}$ before insertion is shown in Figure 8(c). We use (s_2, x_1) with weight 5 to replace (s_2, q) with weight 4 in Figure 8(d).

4.3.2 Updating TCP-Index With Edge Deletion

Index Update with Edge Deletion. With a deleted edge $e_0(u, v)$, we first consider how to update $\mathcal{T}_u$ and $\mathcal{T}_v$. Take vertex u as an example. We first delete vertex v and edges $\{(v, w) | (v, w) \in \mathcal{T}_u\}$ from $\mathcal{T}_u$. Then we update the maximum spanning forest $\mathcal{T}_u$ with the available edges in $E(G_u)$.

Now we consider how to update $\mathcal{T}_w$ for $w \in N(u) \cap N(v)$. If $(u, v) \in \mathcal{T}_w$, we try to find an edge $(u', v') \in E(G_w)$ where $u' \in V_2(w, u), v' \in V_2(w, v)$ with the maximum weight to replace (u, v) in $\mathcal{T}_w$. If no such replacement edge exists, we simply remove (u, v). On the other hand, if $(u, v) \notin \mathcal{T}_w$, $\mathcal{T}_w$ remains unchanged.

Index Update with Trussness Decrease. Besides the above cases, we also need to consider the index maintenance for an existing edge $e(x, y)$ which has trussness update $\hat{\tau}(e) = \tau(e) - 1$ due to the edge deletion. We discuss the update of $\mathcal{T}_x$ (and similarly $\mathcal{T}_y$). For every $\triangle_{xyz}$, we denote $w_{xyz} = \min\{\tau((x, y)), \tau((x, z)), \tau((y, z))\}$, and $\hat{w}_{xyz} = \min\{\hat{\tau}((x, y)), \hat{\tau}((x, z)), \hat{\tau}((y, z))\}$. If $\hat{w}_{xyz} = w_{xyz}$, $\mathcal{T}_x$ remains unchanged. Otherwise, for $\hat{w}_{xyz} = w_{xyz} - 1$, if $(y, z) \notin \mathcal{T}_x$, $\mathcal{T}_x$ remains unchanged; if $(y, z) \in \mathcal{T}_x$, we try to find an edge $(y', z') \in E(G_x)$ where $y' \in V_{w_{xyz}}(x, y), z' \in V_{w_{xyz}}(x, z)$ and $w(y', z') = w_{xyz}$ to replace (y, z) in $\mathcal{T}_x$. If no such replacement edge exists, we just update $w(y, z) = \hat{w}_{xyz}$. For the neighbor vertex $z \in N(x) \cap N(y)$, the index $\mathcal{T}_z$ can be updated in a similar way.

5. EXPERIMENTS

We evaluate the efficiency and effectiveness of our proposed algorithms on real-world networks. All algorithms are implemented in C++ and all the experiments are conducted on Windows Server with 2.67GHz six-core CPU and 100GB main memory.

Datasets. We use 6 publicly available real-world networks to evaluate the algorithms. The network statistics are shown in Table 1. Except for Wise[1] (a micro-blogging network from WISE 2012 Challenge) and UK2002[2] (a web graph from a 2002 crawl of the .uk domain), all the other datasets are downloaded from the Stanford Network Analysis Project[3]. All networks are treated as undirected in the experiments.

Table 1: Network statistics (K $= 10^3$ and M $= 10^6$)

Network	$\lvert V_G \rvert$	$\lvert E_G \rvert$	d_{max}	k_{gmax}
WikiTalk	2.4M	5M	100029	53
Flickr	80K	11.8M	5706	308
LiveJournal	4.8M	69M	20333	362
Orkut	3.1M	117.2M	33313	78
Wise	58.6M	265.1M	278489	80
UK2002	18.6M	298.1M	194955	944

5.1 Query Processing

We evaluate and compare the performance of the two k-truss community query algorithms: Algorithm 2 that uses the simple k-truss index and Algorithm 4 that uses the TCP-Index.

In the first experiment, we select query vertices with different degrees to test the query processing time. For each network, we sort the vertices in descending order of their degrees and partition them into 10 equal-sized buckets. We randomly select 100 vertices from each bucket for query. The average query processing time for each degree group is reported in Figure 9. We fix $k = 10$ for all networks except for WikiTalk and Wise which use $k = 4$, because the edges in these two networks have smaller trussness. As we can see, for the high degree query vertices which usually have larger and denser k-truss communities, the TCP-Index based method is two orders of magnitude faster than the k-truss index based method; whereas for the low degree query vertices which have smaller and sparser k-truss communities for the same k, the query time of the two methods is very close and is around a few milliseconds. This shows the superiority of the TCP-Index based query processing, especially for high degree query vertices.

In the second experiment, we vary the parameter k to test the query time for k-truss community search. For each network, we randomly generate two test sets: a set of 100 high degree query vertices (degree in top 30%) and another set of 100 low degree query vertices (degree in the remaining 70%). We denote the two query methods on the high/low degree test sets as Truss-H/Truss-L and TCP-H/TCP-L, respectively. Figure 10 shows the average query processing time of each method when we vary the parameter k. As we can see, for the high degree query vertices, the TCP-Index based method is two to three orders of magnitude faster than the k-truss based method for all k values; while for the low degree query vertices, the TCP-Index based method is still one to two orders of magnitude faster in most networks especially when k is small. Finally we can see that the query processing time decreases when k increases, because the discovered communities become smaller when k increases. This experiment again demonstrates the advantage of the TCP-Index based query processing and conforms with the time complexity analysis of the two query methods.

5.2 Index Construction

In this experiment, we compare the two indexing schemes: the simple k-truss index and the TCP-Index in terms of index size and index construction time in Table 2. Note that the index is main-

[1] `http://www.wise2012.cs.ucy.ac.cy/challenge.html`

[2] `http://law.di.unimi.it/datasets.php`

[3] `snap.stanford.edu`

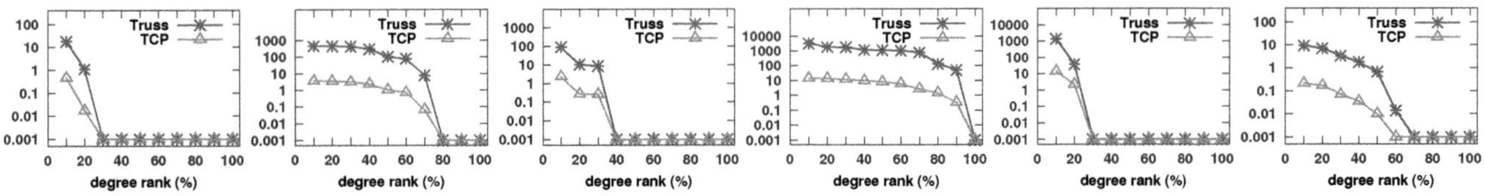

(a) WikiTalk (b) Flickr (c) LiveJournal (d) Orkut (e) Wise (f) UK2002

Figure 9: Query time (in seconds) of different algorithms for query vertices in different degree percentile groups

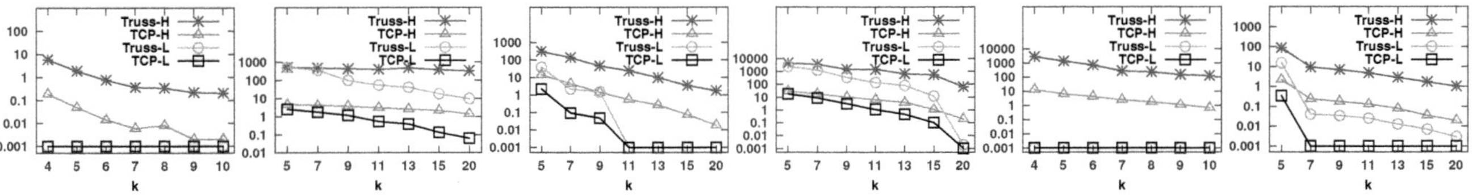

(a) WikiTalk (b) Flickr (c) LiveJournal (d) Orkut (e) Wise (f) UK2002

Figure 10: Query time (in seconds) of different algorithms for different k

tained in memory for both schemes. The reported index time includes the truss decomposition time and index construction time.

We can observe that the size of the TCP-Index is about 3 times that of the k-truss index, and 4.3 times of the original graph size. This confirms that both indexing schemes have $O(m)$ space complexity and are very compact. In addition, the index construction is very efficient for both schemes. The index time of the TCP-Index is around 1.4–3.4 times that of the k-truss index. The longest TCP-Index time is 1.9 hours on Wise. The TCP-Index costs more time and space than the k-truss index for building the maximum spanning forest structure.

Table 2: Comparison of index size (in Megabytes) and index construction time (wall-clock time in seconds)

Network	Graph Size	Index Size		Index Time	
		K-Truss	TCP-Index	K-Truss	TCP-Index
WikiTalk	80	118	296	41	138
Flickr	90	135	485	690	1326
LiveJournal	672	1003	3174	1176	1686
Orkut	1792	2662	8714	2291	3342
Wise	4209	5960	11049	3078	6997
UK2002	4055	5980	21238	1374	2860

5.3 Updating TCP-Index in Dynamic Graphs

In this experiment, we evaluate the performance of incremental update of the TCP-Index when the input network is updated. For each network, we randomly insert/delete 1K edges, and update the edge trussness and the TCP-Index after each edge insertion/deletion. The average update time, including the edge trussness update time and the index update time, is reported in Table 3. In addition, we report the batch update time for the 1K edge insertions/deletions. All the experiments are repeated for 20 times, and the average performance is reported. For comparison, we also report the time for constructing the TCP-Index from scratch when the network is updated with an edge insertion/deletion.

Table 3: TCP-Index update time (wall-clock time in milliseconds)

Network	Insertion Per Edge	Insertion 1K Edges	Deletion Per Edge	Deletion 1K Edges	Computing from scratch
WikiTalk	0.2	125	3.9	2509	138000
Flickr	10.2	6344	58	33763	1326000
LiveJournal	0.7	693	3.9	1891	1686000
Orkut	16.1	17190	29.6	21351	3342000
Wise	7.8	3902	38.8	31282	6997000
UK2002	3.9	4065	12.2	12326	2860000

The results in Table 3 show that the update time per edge insertion ranges from 0.2 to 16.1 milliseconds. The batch update for 1K edge insertions can achieve further performance improvement, compared with the instant update which handles the inserted edges one by one. Thus, handling edge insertion is highly efficient.

For the deletion case, the update time per edge deletion ranges from 3.9 to 38.8 milliseconds. The batch update for 1K edge deletions also achieves further performance improvement. Compared with the insertion case, handling edge deletion is a little more costly, as it has a larger search space for finding a replacement edge in the TCP-Index.

We can see that the incremental update approach is several orders of magnitude faster than constructing the TCP-Index from scratch when a network is updated. This demonstrates the superiority of our proposed incremental update algorithms.

In addition, we also compare our edge trussness update method (Algorithm 5) with the update method for triangle k-core [26], which has the same definition with k-truss. The average update time upon an edge insertion/deletion is reported in Table 4. Our method takes 15 milliseconds or less for updating trussness in all networks. It is two to three orders of magnitude faster than the update method in [26]. The poor efficiency of [26] is due to its mechanism which updates the trussness by inserting/deleting triangles one by one for an edge insertion/deletion. Processing k-core triangles is very costly especially in dense graphs such as Flickr and Orkut.

Table 4: Edge trussness update time (wall-clock time in milliseconds)

Network	Insertion Per Edge		Deletion Per Edge	
	Triangle k-core	Our method	Triangle k-core	Our method
WikiTalk	0.21	0.07	40.43	0.19
Flickr	16700	5.99	17224	6.11
LiveJournal	1.75	0.54	60.45	0.63
Orkut	2453	15.13	179.2	1.67
Wise	5.59	3.21	18.33	1.32
UK2002	68.2	3.14	1445	2.76

5.4 Quality Evaluation

5.4.1 *Social Networks with Ground-truth Communities*

To evaluate the effectiveness of the k-truss community model, we use two social networks: Facebook and Twitter from the Stan-

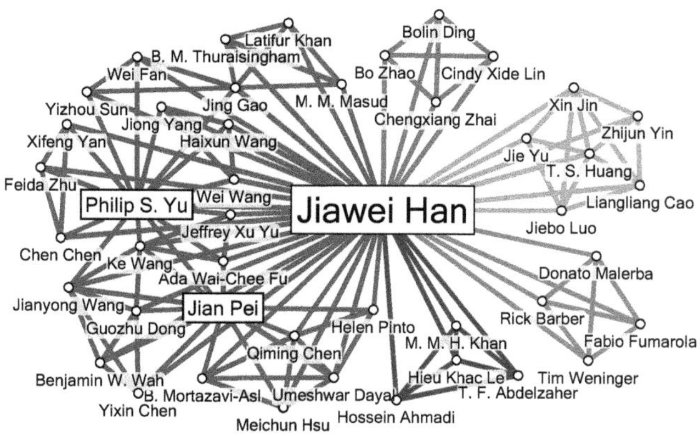

Figure 12: Five 5-truss communities containing Jiawei Han

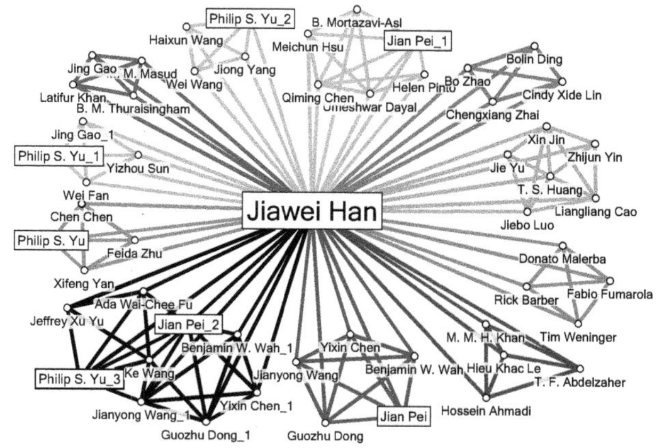

Figure 13: Eleven 4-adjacency-1.0-quasi-5-clique communities containing Jiawei Han

ford Network Analysis Project[3], both of which contain ground-truth communities for individual nodes. The Facebook network contains 4,039 vertices, 88,234 edges, and 10 query vertices with ground-truth communities in their neighborhood. The Twitter network contains 81,306 vertices, 1,768,149 edges, and 973 query vertices with ground-truth communities in their neighborhood. For a query, we denote the discovered communities as $\mathcal{C} = \{C_1, \ldots, C_i\}$, and the ground-truth communities as $\overline{\mathcal{C}} = \{\overline{C}_1, \ldots, \overline{C}_j\}$. We use the F_1 score to measure the alignment between a discovered community C and a ground-truth community $\overline{C}$. Since we do not know the correspondence between communities in $\mathcal{C}$ and $\overline{\mathcal{C}}$, we compute the optimal match via linear assignment [14] by maximizing

$$\max_{f:\mathcal{C}\to\overline{\mathcal{C}}} \frac{1}{|f|} \sum_{C\in dom(f)} F_1(C, f(C)), \tag{1}$$

where f is a (partial) correspondence between $\mathcal{C}$ and $\overline{\mathcal{C}}$.

We compare the F_1 score of our k-truss community model and the α-adjacency-γ-quasi-k-clique model [9] using the executable program provided by the authors with a time limit of 60 seconds for a query. For our model, we vary the trussness parameter k; for the quasi-clique model, we follow the experimental setting in [9] to use the $(k-1, 1)$-OCS model ($\alpha = k-1$, $\gamma = 1$) and vary the clique size k. Figure 11(a) and (c) show the F_1 score of the detected communities by both methods versus their respective parameter k on Facebook and Twitter. Although the parameter k has different meanings in the two models, the results still show a comprehensive performance comparison of our model and [9] over a broad range of parameter values. On both networks, we observe that our k-truss model has a very stable performance when we vary the trussness k. The $(k-1, 1)$-OCS model is consistently worse than our method. For the quasi-clique model, we also tried other α and γ values. However, when we set $\alpha < k-1$ or $\gamma < 1$, the program cannot output all communities within the time limit set in the executable program due to the expensive quasi-clique enumeration.

Figure 11(b) and (d) report the average query time of our method and [9]. Our method is clearly more efficient than the $(k-1, 1)$-OCS model.

5.4.2 *Case Study on DBLP*

We build a collaboration network from the DBLP data set[4] for case study. A vertex represents an author and an edge is added between two authors if they have co-authored 3 times or more. The network contains 234,879 vertices and 541,814 edges.

We query the 5-truss community containing 'Jiawei Han' which is shown in Figure 12. For comparison, we follow the case study in [9] which uses the $(k-1, 1)$-OCS model to query 'Jiawei Han' by setting $k = 5, \alpha = 4, \gamma = 1$, which produces communities at a similar scale as shown in Figure 13. Note that we duplicate some authors who participate in more than one community in Figure 13, e.g., 'Jian Pei', 'Jian Pei_1' and 'Jian Pei_2', for a better visualization effect. We have the following observations.

(1) Our model generates 5 communities containing 'Jiawei Han', among which the 4 smaller ones are also found by the $(k-1, 1)$-OCS model and depicted using the same color in Figure 13.

(2) The largest 5-truss community depicted in blue in Figure 12, however, is decomposed into 7 smaller communities by the $(k-1, 1)$-OCS model in Figure 13. This phenomenon can be explained by the different mechanisms of the two community models. The $(k-1, 1)$-OCS model tends to find the small, clique-based "*paper communities*", in which all the involved scholars appear in the same paper. For example, a paper community is formed by 'Jiawei Han', 'Philip S. Yu', 'Chen Chen', 'Xifeng Yan', and 'Feida Zhu'. In contrast, such small paper communities can be merged into a larger dense one by the triangle adjacency condition in our k-truss model. For example, two small paper communities can be merged if they share a common edge as ('Jiawei Han', 'Philip S. Yu') and form a 5-truss graph after being merged.

(3) A less restrictive community criterion can be realized by tuning α and γ in [9]. But in our experiment, if we set $\alpha < k-1$ or $\gamma < 1$, it cannot output all communities within the time limit set in the executable program due to the expensive quasi-clique enumeration.

(4) Finally, we observe a community containing 'Guozhu Dong' and 5 other authors (depicted in purple) in Figure 13 is completely subsumed by another bigger community (depicted in black) in the same figure. Such duplicate output, which is not desired, may be explained by the approximate heuristics for clique enumeration and expansion in [9].

6. RELATED WORK

The related work to our study include community search and detection, and dense subgraph mining.

Community Search and Detection. Cui et al. [9] have recently studied the problem of online search of overlapping communities for a query vertex by designing a new α-adjacency γ-quasi-k-clique model. It is the most related work to ours and has been discussed in detail in Section 2 and compared empirically in Section 5. A different but related problem is community detection, which identifies communities in the entire network. There are two major cat-

[4] http://dblp.uni-trier.de/xml/

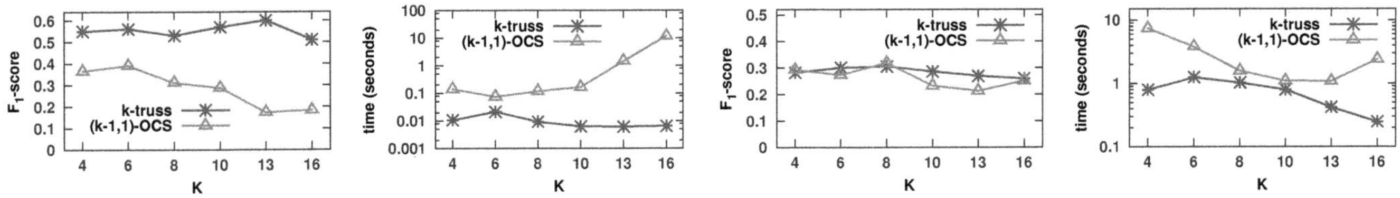

(a) Facebook F_1 score (b) Facebook query time (c) Twitter F_1 score (d) Twitter query time

Figure 11: Quality evaluation on social networks

egories: non-overlapping community detection [15, 17] and overlapping community detection [16, 1, 25].

Dense Subgraph Mining. There are different definitions of dense subgraph patterns, including clique [3, 5, 22, 24], quasi-clique [19], k-core [2, 4], k-truss [7, 21, 26], dense neighborhood graph [23], dense bipartite subgraph [12], etc.

Clique and quasi-clique enumeration methods include the classical algorithm [3], the external-memory H^*-graph algorithm [5], redundancy-aware clique enumeration [22], maximum clique computation in MapReduce [24], and optimal quasi-clique mining [19].

Core decomposition and truss decomposition have been studied in various settings, including in-memory algorithms [2, 7, 26], external-memory algorithms [4, 21], and MapReduce algorithm [8]. Sarıyüce et al. [18] proposed the first incremental k-core decomposition algorithms for graph stream. Zhang and Parthasarathy [26] designed an incremental algorithm for updating triangle k-core (equivalent to k-truss) with edge insertions/deletions. In our work, our focus is to update the TCP-Index in a dynamic setting, which relies on the incremental update of the edge trussness. We have also compared with [26] experimentally in updating edge trussness, and our updating method is two to three orders of magnitude faster.

Wang et al. [23] defined a dense neighborhood graph based on the common neighbors. Gibson et al. [12] studied mining dense bipartite subgraphs.

7. CONCLUSIONS

In this paper, we study the online community search problem in a network. We propose a novel k-truss community model based on the k-truss concept which is shown to have cohesive and hierarchical community structure. To support the efficient search of k-truss community, we design a novel and compact tree-shape index, called the TCP-Index, which preserves the edge trussness and the triangle adjacency relationship, and supports community search in linear time with respect to the community size. We further study the k-truss community search in dynamic graphs and propose efficient incremental algorithms to update the index. We conduct extensive experiments on large real-world networks, and the results demonstrate the effectiveness and efficiency of the proposed algorithms.

8. ACKNOWLEDGMENTS

The work is supported by the Hong Kong Research Grants Council (RGC) General Research Fund (GRF) Project No. CUHK 411211, 411310, 418512. Lu Qin is supported by ARC DE140100999.

9. REFERENCES

[1] Y.-Y. Ahn, J. P. Bagrow, and S. Lehmann. Link communities reveal multiscale complexity in networks. *Nature*, 466(7307):761–764, 2010.

[2] V. Batagelj and M. Zaversnik. An o (m) algorithm for cores decomposition of networks. *arXiv preprint cs/0310049*, 2003.

[3] C. Bron and J. Kerbosch. Finding all cliques of an undirected graph (algorithm 457). *Commun. ACM*, 16(9):575–576, 1973.

[4] J. Cheng, Y. Ke, S. Chu, and M. T. Özsu. Efficient core decomposition in massive networks. In *ICDE*, pages 51–62, 2011.

[5] J. Cheng, Y. Ke, A. W.-C. Fu, J. X. Yu, and L. Zhu. Finding maximal cliques in massive networks by h*-graph. In *SIGMOD*, pages 447–458, 2010.

[6] N. Chiba and T. Nishizeki. Arboricity and subgraph listing algorithms. *SIAM J. Comput.*, 14(1):210–223, 1985.

[7] J. Cohen. Trusses: Cohesive subgraphs for social network analysis. Technical report, National Security Agency, 2008.

[8] J. Cohen. Graph twiddling in a mapreduce world. *Computing in Science and Engineering*, 11(4):29–41, 2009.

[9] W. Cui, Y. Xiao, H. Wang, Y. Lu, and W. Wang. Online search of overlapping communities. In *SIGMOD*, pages 277–288, 2013.

[10] J. Edachery, A. Sen, and F. J. Brandenburg. Graph clustering using distance-k cliques. In *Proceedings of the 7th International Symposium on Graph Drawing*, pages 98–106, 1999.

[11] M. R. Garey and D. S. Johnson. *Computers and Intractability: A Guide to the Theory of NP-Completeness*. W. H. Freeman, 1979.

[12] D. Gibson, R. Kumar, and A. Tomkins. Discovering large dense subgraphs in massive graphs. In *VLDB*, pages 721–732, 2005.

[13] E. Hartuv and R. Shamir. A clustering algorithm based on graph connectivity. *Information Processing Letters*, 76(4–6):175–181, 2000.

[14] J. J. McAuley and J. Leskovec. Learning to discover social circles in ego networks. In *NIPS*, pages 548–556, 2012.

[15] M. E. Newman and M. Girvan. Finding and evaluating community structure in networks. *Physical review E*, 69(2):026113, 2004.

[16] G. Palla, I. Derényi, I. Farkas, and T. Vicsek. Uncovering the overlapping community structure of complex networks in nature and society. *Nature*, 435(7043):814–818, 2005.

[17] M. Rosvall and C. T. Bergstrom. Maps of random walks on complex networks reveal community structure. *Proceedings of the National Academy of Sciences*, 105(4):1118–1123, 2008.

[18] A. E. Sarıyüce, B. Gedik, G. Jacques-Silva, K.-L. Wu, and Ü. V. Çatalyürek. Streaming algorithms for k-core decomposition. *PVLDB*, 6(6):433–444, 2013.

[19] C. E. Tsourakakis, F. Bonchi, A. Gionis, F. Gullo, and M. A. Tsiarli. Denser than the densest subgraph: Extracting optimal quasi-cliques with quality guarantees. In *KDD*, pages 104–112, 2013.

[20] J. Ugander, L. Backstrom, C. Marlow, and J. Kleinberg. Structural diversity in social contagion. *Proceedings of the National Academy of Sciences*, 109(16):5962–5966, 2012.

[21] J. Wang and J. Cheng. Truss decomposition in massive networks. *PVLDB*, 5(9):812–823, 2012.

[22] J. Wang, J. Cheng, and A. W.-C. Fu. Redundancy-aware maximal cliques. In *KDD*, pages 122–130, 2013.

[23] N. Wang, J. Zhang, K.-L. Tan, and A. K. H. Tung. On triangulation-based dense neighborhood graphs discovery. *PVLDB*, 4(2):58–68, 2010.

[24] J. Xiang, C. Guo, and A. Aboulnaga. Scalable maximum clique computation using mapreduce. In *ICDE*, pages 74–85, 2013.

[25] J. Xie, S. Kelley, and B. K. Szymanski. Overlapping community detection in networks: The state-of-the-art and comparative study. *ACM Comput. Surv.*, 45(4):43, 2013.

[26] Y. Zhang and S. Parthasarathy. Extracting analyzing and visualizing triangle k-core motifs within networks. In *ICDE*, pages 1049–1060, 2012.

Reachability Queries on Large Dynamic Graphs: A Total Order Approach

Andy Diwen Zhu[†] Wenqing Lin[†] Sibo Wang[†] Xiaokui Xiao[‡]
School of Computer Engineering
Nanyang Technological University
Singapore
[†]{diwen.zhu, keamoulin, wangsibo.victor}@gmail.com [‡]xkxiao@ntu.edu.sg

ABSTRACT

Reachability queries are a fundamental type of queries on graphs that find important applications in numerous domains. Although a plethora of techniques have been proposed for reachability queries, most of them require that the input graph is *static*, i.e., they are inapplicable to the *dynamic* graphs (e.g., social networks and the Semantic Web) commonly encountered in practice. There exist a few techniques that can handle dynamic graphs, but none of them can scale to sizable graphs without significant loss of efficiency. To address this deficiency, this paper presents a novel study on reachability indices for *large dynamic graphs*. We first introduce a general indexing framework that summarizes a family of reachability indices with the best performance among the existing techniques for static graphs. Then, we propose general and efficient algorithms for handling vertex insertions and deletions under the proposed framework. In addition, we show that our update algorithms can be used to improve the existing reachability techniques on static graphs, and we also propose a new approach for constructing a reachability index from scratch under our framework. We experimentally evaluate our solution on a large set of benchmark datasets, and we demonstrate that our solution not only supports efficient updates on dynamic graphs, but also provides even better query performance than the state-of-the-art techniques for *static* graphs.

Categories and Subject Descriptors

G.2.2 [**Graph Theory**]: Graph Algorithms

General Terms

Algorithms, Experimentation

1. INTRODUCTION

Given a directed graph G and two vertices s and t in G, a reachability query asks whether there exists a path from s to t in G. Reachability queries are a fundamental operation on graphs and have numerous important applications, such as query processing on social networks, the Semantic Web, XML documents, road networks, and program workflows. Devising index structures for reachability queries is non-trivial, as it requires a careful balancing act between pre-computation cost, index size, and query processing overhead. In particular, if we pre-compute and store the reachability results for all pairs of vertices, then we can process any reachability query in $O(1)$ time but suffer prohibitive costs of preprocessing and space. On the other hand, if we omit indexing and process reachability queries directly on G using depth-first search (DFS) or breadth-first search (BFS), then we minimize space and pre-computation overhead, but fail to ensure query efficiency on large graphs.

Previous work [3–14, 16, 19, 22–25, 27–32] has proposed numerous indexing techniques to efficiently support reachability queries without significant space and pre-computation overheads. Most techniques, however, assume that the input graph G is *static*, which makes them inapplicable for the *dynamic* graphs commonly encountered in practice. For example, the social graph of Twitter is constantly changing, with thousands of new users added per day; the Semantic Web is frequently updated with new concepts and relations; even road networks are subject to changes due to road closures and constructions. There exist a few techniques [4, 12, 13, 16, 22, 24, 32] that are designed for dynamic graphs, but as we discuss in Sections 3 and 8, none of those techniques can scale to sizable graphs without significant loss of efficiency. Specifically, the methods in [4, 12, 13, 16, 22, 24] incur prohibitive preprocessing costs on graphs with more than one million vertices. Meanwhile, the approach in [32] can handle million-vertex graphs, but it offers a query performance that is *generally not much better than a simple BFS approach*, as shown in our experiments.

In summary, no existing method is able to effectively handle reachability queries on *large dynamic graphs*. Motivated by this, we present a comprehensive study on scalable reachability indices that support updates. We first introduce a *total order labeling (TOL)* framework, which summarizes three most advanced methods [8, 17, 30] for reachability queries on static graphs. TOL has two important properties: (i) every reachability index under TOL uniquely corresponds to a *total order* of vertices in the input graph, and (ii) the total order *solely* decides the index's performances in terms of preprocessing, space, and queries. Given these properties, we investigate algorithms that enable us to insert or delete a vertex in a TOL index without changing the order of the other vertices, i.e., without significantly degrading the performance of the index. This results in general algorithms for handling insertions and deletions on indices under TOL. In particular, our insertion algorithm is *optimal* in that it leads to the minimum index size after insertion.

Interestingly, we observe that our update algorithms can be utilized to reduce the space consumptions and query costs of a TOL index, by adjusting the total order pertinent to the index. This leads to a general approach for improving any index under TOL, includ-

SIGMOD'14, June 22–27, 2014, Snowbird, UT, USA.

ACM 978-1-4503-2376-5/14/06 ...$15.00.
http://dx.doi.org/10.1145/2588555.2612181.

ing the state-of-the-art techniques [8, 17, 30]. The effectiveness of our adjusting approach shows that the total orders of the techniques in [8, 17, 30] leave much room for enhancement, which motivates us to devise new methods for deriving improved total orders for TOL indices. As a result, we present a new reachability index, *Butterfly*, which offers reduced preprocessing, space, and query costs than any existing indices under TOL [8, 17, 30]. We experimentally evaluate TOL using a large variety of benchmark datasets with up to twenty million vertices, and we demonstrate the superiority of TOL against alternative solutions for static and dynamic graphs.

In summary, this paper makes the following contributions:

- We propose general and efficient algorithms that enable *any* index under the TOL framework to support *large dynamic graphs* (Section 5).
- We develop a technique that can postprocess the state-of-the-art reachability indices [8, 17, 30] to significantly enhance their performances in terms of space overheads and query efficiency (Section 6).
- We devise algorithms to derive improved vertex ordering under TOL, based on which we propose Butterfly, a new reachability index that dominates the states of the art (Section 7).
- We evaluate our solution on a large set of real and synthetic graphs, and we demonstrate that our solution not only supports efficient updates on large dynamic graphs, but also provides even better query performance than the state-of-the-art techniques for *static* graphs (Section 8).

2. PRELIMINARIES

Let $G = (V, E)$ be a directed graph with a set V of vertices and a set E of edges. For any two vertices s and t in V, we say that s can *reach* t (denoted as $s \to t$), iff there exists a directed path in G that starts from s and ends at t. Given s and t, a reachability query returns TRUE if $s \to t$, and FALSE otherwise. We refer to s and t as the *source vertex* and *terminal vertex* of the query, respectively.

If $s \to t$ and $t \to s$ both holds, then s and t are *strongly connected*. Accordingly, a *strongly connected component (SCC)* of G is defined as a maximal subset of V where any two vertices are strongly connected. Observe that a vertex u can reach another vertex v, iff either of the following conditions holds: (i) u and v belong to the same SCC, or (ii) there is a path that starts from the SCC containing u to the SCC containing v. Given this observation, there exists a simple method that reduces G into a smaller graph G^* to improve the efficiency of reachability queries:

1. Compute all SCCs of G. (This can be done in $O(|V| + |E|)$ time [26].
2. Map each SCC C to a vertex $f(C)$. For any two SCCs C and C', if G contains an edge that starts at a vertex in C and ends at a vertex in C', then construct an directed edge from $f(C)$ to $f(C')$. Denote the resulting graph as G^*.
3. Given a reachability query from s to t on G, we first retrieve the SSC S (resp. T) of G that contains s (resp. t). Then, we return TRUE for the query, if and only if (i) S and T are the same or (ii) $f(S)$ can reach $f(T)$ in G^*.

In the remainder of the paper, we assume that G has been preprocessed with the above reduction method, i.e., G does not contain any strongly connected component with more than one vertex. (The same assumption is made in existing work [].) Under this assumption, G should be a *directed acyclic graph (DAG)*. In addition,

Notation	Description
$G = (V, E)$	a DAG with a vertex set V and an edge set E
$o(v)$	the topological rank of a vertex v (see Section 2)
$N_{in}(v)$	the set of v's in-neighbors
$N_{out}(v)$	the set of v's out-neighbors
$l(v)$	the level of v (see Section 4)
$\mathcal{L}$	a total order labeling of G
$L_{in}(v)$	the in-label set of vertex v (see Definition 1)
$L_{out}(v)$	the out-label set of vertex v (see Definition 1)
$I_{in}(v)$	the inverted index for v's in-labels (see Equation 3)
$I_{out}(v)$	the inverted index for v's out-labels (see Equation 4)

Table 1: Table of notations.

there exists a total order o on V, such that for any two vertices u and v in G, if $u \to v$ then $o(u) < o(v)$ (but not necessarily vice versa). Such a total order can be derived in linear time using a DFS on G [8]. We refer to o as a *topological order*, and $o(u)$ as the *topological rank* of u. For ease of reference, Table 1 lists the notations that will be frequently used in this paper.

3. RELATED WORK

The existing work on reachability queries can be roughly divided into three categories (based on their query processing schemes): *pruned depth-first search*, *transitive closure retrieval*, and *two-hop label matching*. In the following, we survey the techniques in each category for static graphs, and then discuss the existing methods on dynamic graphs.

Pruned Depth-first Search. Techniques [6, 27, 31] in this category process each reachabilty query using DFS on G, but they pre-compute certain auxiliary information on G to prune the search space of DFS, which helps improve query efficiency. The state-of-the-art algorithm in this category is GRAIL [31]. It preprocesses G by assigning an interval to each vertex, such that, for any two vertices u and v, if the interval of u does not fully contain the interval of v, then $u \not\to v$ must hold. Given such intervals, GRAIL answers any reachability query using a DFS from the source vertex, and it avoids visiting any vertex whose interval does not cover the terminal vertex's interval. GRAIL is shown to incur small overheads of preprocessing and space, but its query efficiency is generally much worse than methods in the other two categories.

Transitive Closure Retrieval. The *transitive closure* of a vertex u is defined as the set of all vertices that u can reach in G. Methods based on transitive closure retrieval [3, 7, 8, 10, 14, 19, 25, 28, 29] pre-compute and compress the transitive closures of each vertex in G. Given any reachability query, they first retrieve the transitive closure of the source vertex, decompress it, and then check whether the terminal vertex is contained in the transitive closure. Such methods are generally efficient for query processing, but they cannot scale to large graphs due to the significant pre-computation and space overheads in deriving and storing transitive closures.

2-Hop Label Matching. Techniques in this category [5, 8–11, 23, 30] preprocess G by constructing two sets of *labels* for each vertex v, namely, an *out-label set* $L_{out}(v)$ and an *in-label set* $L_{in}(v)$. Specifically, each label in $L_{out}(v)$ is a vertex in G that v can reach, while $L_{in}(v)$ contains a subset of the vertices in G that can reach v. The label sets are created in a way such that, for any two vertices s and t, we have $s \to t$ if and only if $L_{out}(s) \cap L_{in}(t) \neq \emptyset$. In other words, any reachability query can be simply answered by taking the intersection of the source vertex's out-label set and the terminal vertex's in-label set. This leads to high query efficiency, *when the label sets are small.*

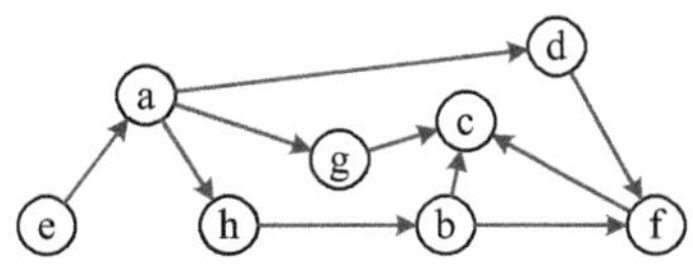

Figure 1: DAG G.

Cohen et al. [11] present the first study on 2-hop labelling techniques. They prove that it is generally NP-hard to minimize the total size of label sets, and they propose a $(\log|V|)$-approximate solution to the problem. However, the approximate solution requires $O(|V| \cdot |E| \log(|V|^2/|E|))$ preprocessing time, which renders it inapplicable for sizable graphs. Motivated by this, numerous heuristic techniques [2, 5, 8–10, 15, 18, 23, 30] have been proposed to improve the practical efficiency of 2-hop labelling, albeit discarding the approximation guarantee of Cohen et al.'s method). Among those techniques, the most advanced ones are *TF-Label* [8], *Distribution Labeling (DL)* [17], and *Pruned Landmark Labeling (PLL)* [30], as they are shown to provide better overall performance than other existing methods (including the ones based on pruned DFS or transitive closure retrieval). In Section 4, we will present a framework that summarizes TF-Label, DL, and PLL.

Methods for Dynamic Graphs. While the aforementioned techniques all focus on static graphs, there also exist a few studies [4, 12, 13, 16, 21, 22, 24] on reachability indices for dynamic graphs. In particular, [12, 13, 21, 22] propose algorithms for incrementally maintaining transitive closures on dynamic graphs. Those algorithms, however, cannot scale to graphs with more than a few thousand vertices, as shown by Krommidias et al. [20]. There also exist two methods [4, 24] that extend Cohen et al.'s 2-hop labeling approach [11] to handle updates. Nevertheless, the method in [24] is restricted to XML graphs, while [4] is unable to handle any of the million-node graphs used in our experiments. In addition, [16] presents an algorithm for performing updates on a reachability index, but the index itself incurs tremendous preprocessing costs on large graphs. Very recently, Yildirim et al. propose *Dagger* [32], an extension of GRAIL [31] that supports dynamic graphs. As we show in Section 8, however, Dagger's query performance is up to 10^7 times worse than the solution in this paper, and is generally not much better than a simple BFS approach.

4. TOTAL ORDER LABELING

This section presents *total order labeling (TOL)*, a reachability indexing framework that can be instantiated into various 2-hop labeling indices. The instantiation of TOL requires two input parameters, namely, a DAG $G = (V, E)$ and a *strict* total order l on V. We refer to l as a *level order*. For any vertex v, we define $l(v) \in [1, |V|]$ as the rank of v in l, and refer to $l(v)$ as the *level* of v. In addition, we say that v has a *higher* (resp. lower) level than another vertex u, if $l(v) < l(u)$ (resp. $l(v) > l(u)$).

Definition of TOL Indices. Given G and l, TOL uniquely defines a 2-hop labeling index $\mathcal{L}$ on G as follows:

DEFINITION 1 (TOTAL ORDER LABELING $\mathcal{L}$). *Given a DAG $G = (V, E)$ and a level order l, a TOL index $\mathcal{L}$ is a 2-hop labeling index where each vertex is associated with an in-label set $L_{in}(v)$ and an out-label set $L_{out}(v)$, such that $L_{in}(v)$ (resp. $L_{out}(v)$) contains every vertex u satisfying all of the following constraints:*

- *Reachability Constraint: $u \rightarrow v$ (resp. $v \rightarrow u$);*
- *Level Constraint: $l(u) < l(v)$;*
- *Path Constraint: No simple path from u to v (resp. from v to u) in G contains a vertex w with $l(w) < l(u)$.*

	TOL index $\mathcal{L}_1$			TOL index $\mathcal{L}_2$		
v	$l_1(v)$	$L_{in}(v)$	$L_{out}(v)$	$l_2(v)$	$L_{in}(v)$	$L_{out}(v)$
a	1	$\emptyset$	$\emptyset$	7	$\emptyset$	{b,c,d,f,g,h}
b	2	{a}	$\emptyset$	4	$\emptyset$	{c,f}
c	3	{a,b}	$\emptyset$	2	{g}	$\emptyset$
d	4	{a}	{c}	5	$\emptyset$	{c,f}
e	5	$\emptyset$	{a}	8	$\emptyset$	{a,b,c,d,f,g,h}
f	6	{a,b,d}	{c}	3	$\emptyset$	{c}
g	7	{a}	{c}	1	$\emptyset$	$\emptyset$
h	8	{a}	{b}	6	$\emptyset$	{b,c,f}

Table 2: Two TOL indices for the DAG G in Figure 1.

We illustrate Definition 1 with the following example.

EXAMPLE 1. Given the DAG G shown in Figure 1, Table 2 shows two TOL indices on G (i.e., $\mathcal{L}_1$ and $\mathcal{L}_2$) with level orders l_1 and l_2, respectively. Consider vertex g in G. Its in-label set in $\mathcal{L}_1$ contains a since (i) a can reach g, (ii) a has a higher level than g, and (iii) G contains only one simple path from a to g, and the path does not contain any vertex with a higher level than a. In addition, g's in-label set does not contain any vertex other than a, since the path from any other vertex to g must pass through a, whereas a has the smallest level in l_1, i.e., adding any other vertex to $L_{in}(g)$ violates the Path Constraint in Definition 1.

In contrast, g's in-label set in $\mathcal{L}_2$ is $\emptyset$. This is because g has the smallest level in l_2, due to which we cannot add any vertex into g's in-label set without violating the Level Constraint in Definition 1. In general, the label sets in $\mathcal{L}_1$ are drastically different from their counterparts in $\mathcal{L}_2$, due to the differences between l_1 and l_2. □

As demonstrated in Example 1, the level order l used to instantiate TOL has a profound effect on resulting reachability index. Therefore, if we are to obtain a TOL index with high efficiency, it is essential that we choose an appropriate level order l. In Sections 5 and 7, we will discuss how a good level order can be derived and incrementally maintained for dynamic graphs. For convenience, we define the size of a TOL index $\mathcal{L}$ as the total size of the label sets in $\mathcal{L}$, i.e.,

$$|\mathcal{L}| = \sum_{v \in V} \left(|L_{in}(v)| + |L_{out}(v)| \right).$$

Query Algorithm. Given a reachability query from a vertex s to another vertex t, a TOL index $\mathcal{L}$ processes the query in the same way as other 2-hop labeling methods do. In particular, $\mathcal{L}$ first retrieves the out-label sets of s and the in-label set of t, and then computes a *witness set* as follows:

$$W(s,t) = \left(L_{out}(s) \cup \{s\}\right) \cap \left(L_{in}(t) \cup \{t\}\right). \quad (1)$$

If the witness set is empty, then $\mathcal{L}$ returns FALSE for the query; otherwise, $\mathcal{L}$ returns TRUE. The following lemma shows the correctness of the above query processing approach.

LEMMA 1. *Given any two vertices s and t, we have $W(s,t) \neq \emptyset$ iff $s \rightarrow t$ in G.*

PROOF. We first prove that $W(s,t) \neq \emptyset$ implies $s \rightarrow t$. Observe that, when $W(s,t) \neq \emptyset$, at least one of the following three cases must hold: (i) $t \in L_{out}(s)$, (ii) $s \in L_{in}(t)$, and (iii) $L_{in}(t) \cap L_{out}(s) \neq \emptyset$. By Definition 1, both $t \in L_{out}(s)$ and $s \in L_{in}(t)$ indicate that $s \rightarrow t$. Meanwhile, if $L_{out}(s) \cap L_{in}(t) \neq$

$\emptyset$, then for any $u \in L_{out}(s) \cap L_{in}(t)$, we have $s \rightarrow u$ and $u \rightarrow t$, which leads to $s \rightarrow t$.

Next, we show that if $s \rightarrow t$, then $W(s,t) \neq \emptyset$. Consider the set of all simple paths from s to t in G. Let v be the vertex with the highest level among all vertices on those paths. We differentiate three cases: (i) $v = t$, (ii) $v = s$, and (iii) $v \neq s$ and $v \neq t$. If $v = t$, then by Definition 1, we have $t \in L_{out}(s)$, in which case $W(s,t)$ contains t, i.e., $W(s,t) \neq \emptyset$. Meanwhile, if $v = s$, then $s \in L_{in}(t)$ holds, which leads to $W(s,t) \supseteq \{s\} \neq \emptyset$. Finally, if $v \neq s$ and $v \neq t$, then v must appear in both $L_{out}(s)$ and $L_{in}(t)$, in which case $W(s,t) \supseteq \{v\} \neq \emptyset$. □

Interestingly, the label sets in any TOL index $\mathcal{L}$ are *minimal*, in the sense that no label can be removed without affecting the correctness of TOL's query processing algorithm:

LEMMA 2. *Let $\mathcal{L}$ be a TOL index on G with a level ordering l. For any vertex u, if we remove a vertex v_1 from $L_{out}(u)$, then $W(u, v_1) = \emptyset$ but $u \rightarrow v_1$. Meanwhile, if we remove a vertex v_2 from $L_{in}(u)$, then $W(v_2, u) = \emptyset$ but $v_2 \rightarrow u$.*

PROOF. Consider vertex v_1. Given that $v_1 \in L_{out}(u)$, we have $u \rightarrow v_1$ and $l(u) > l(v_1)$ by Definition 1. Since $l(u) > l(v_1)$, we have $u \notin L_{in}(v_1)$ by the Level Constraint in Definition 1.

Assume on the contrary that, after v_1 is removed from $L_{out}(u)$, $W(u, v_1) \neq \emptyset$. Then, by Equation 1 and $u \notin L_{in}(v_1)$, there must exist a vertex $w \in L_{out}(u) \cap L_{in}(v_1)$. In that case, G must contain a simple path from u to v_1 via w, and w must have a higher level than both u and v_1. This contradicts the Path Constraint in Definition 1 since $v_1 \in L_{out}(u)$ initially holds. The case for vertex v_2 can be established in a similar manner. □

Existing Instantiations of TOL. By Definition 1, TOL defines a family of 2-hop labeling approaches that satisfy the Reachability, Level, and Path Constraints. This index family does not include all existing 2-hop labeling methods (as many of them violate the aforementioned constraints), but it captures the three most advanced 2-hop labeling techniques, i.e., TF-Label [8], DL [17], and PLL [30]. In particular, TF-Label utilizes a topological order o of the vertices in G (see Section 2 for the definition of o). It constructs indices in way such that (i) a label set of a vertex v only contains vertices u with $o(v) < o(u)$, and (ii) the label sets are minimal. It can be shown the TF-Label corresponds to a TOL index that uses o as the level order (with ties broken arbitrarily when multiple vertices have the same rank in o).

Meanwhile, DL sorts the vertices in G in descending order of their degrees, and it follows the sorted order to inspect vertices in G and constructs label sets accordingly. Specifically, each time it examines a vertex v, it uses two constrained BFSs on G to identify a number of vertices that (i) are connected to v and (ii) rank lower than v in the sorted order; then, it adds v into the label sets of those vertices. It can be proved that DL is equivalent to a TOL index where the level order ranks vertices in descending order of their degrees. Finally, as PPL is shown to be equivalent to DL [17], it is also an instantiation of TOL.

It is noteworthy that, if we modified the vertex order in DL, and use the modified order to construct a reachability index based on DL's preprocessing algorithm, then the resulting index is equivalent to a TOL index adopting the same modified order. In other words, any TOL index can be obtained using a modified version of DL's pre-computation algorithm. Nevertheless, the paper that describes DL [17] does not summarize the Reachability, Level, and Path Constraints (see Definition 1) that underpin TOL. The summarization of those constraints is crucial in the context of our paper, as they are imperative in our analysis on how TOL indices can be incrementally updated (see Section 5).

5. INCREMENTAL UPDATES

In this section, we study how a TOL index $\mathcal{L}$ can be incrementally updated when a vertex is inserted into or deleted from G. Our objective is twofold:

1. *$\mathcal{L}$ should remain a TOL index after any update*, i.e., it should always satisfy the constraints in Definition 1. This is to ensure the correctness of $\mathcal{L}$'s query algorithm and the minimality of $\mathcal{L}$'s label sets
2. *Inserting or deleting a vertex should not change the level order l on the other vertices.* Intuitively, this reduces the amount of changes required in the label sets of $\mathcal{L}$, and helps retain the performance of $\mathcal{L}$ after the update, since a TOL index's label sets (and thus, its performance) are solely decided by its level order.

5.1 Insertion Algorithm

Consider that we insert a new vertex v into G and connect v with some existing vertices in G. Let $G' = (V', E')$ be the graph obtained after the insertion. Following previous work [4, 32], we assume that G' is also a DAG. The case when G' is not a DAG can be handled by incrementally maintaining the strongly connected components in G, as discussed in [32]. Let $\mathcal{L}$ be a TOL index on G with a level order l. As mentioned, our objective is to update $\mathcal{L}$ into a TOL index $\mathcal{L}'$ on G' with a level order l', such that for any two vertices $u_1, u_2 \in V$, $l(u_1) < l(u_2)$ iff $l'(u_1) < l'(u_2)$.

In a nutshell, our insertion algorithm runs in two steps: In Step 1, it decides the value of $l'(v)$, and then sets $l'(u)$ for any vertex u in G as follows:

$$l'(u) = \begin{cases} l(u) & \text{if } l(u) < l'(v) \\ l(u) + 1 & \text{otherwise} \end{cases} \tag{2}$$

Then, in Step 2, it updates the label sets in $\mathcal{L}$ according to l', which transforms $\mathcal{L}$ into $\mathcal{L}'$. For ease of exposition, we will first elaborate Step 2, assuming that l' has been constructed.

5.1.1 Step 2: Updating Label Sets

Given G', $\mathcal{L}$, and l', the second step of our insertion algorithm is further divided into two sub-steps. In Step 2.1, we create the label sets $L'_{in}(v)$ and $L'_{out}(v)$ for the new vertex v, and insert v into the label sets of other vertices. Then, in Step 2.2, we further refine the label sets of the vertices in V, so as to convert $\mathcal{L}$ into $\mathcal{L}'$. Throughout the algorithm, for each vertex u, we maintain two *inverted lists* $I_{in}(u)$ and $I_{out}(u)$, such that

$$I_{in}(u) = \{w \mid u \in L_{in}(w)\}, \tag{3}$$

$$I_{out}(u) = \{w \mid u \in L_{out}(w)\}. \tag{4}$$

In other words, if u appears in the in-label (resp. out-label) set of a vertex w, then w is recorded in the inverted list $I_{in}(u)$ (resp. $I_{out}(u)$). These inverted lists enable us to efficiently identify the label sets that are affected by any vertex u. In addition, they can be easily maintained with respect to changes in the label sets.

Step 2.1. Algorithm 1 shows the pseudo-code for the first sub-step. The algorithm first creates a *candidate set* $C_{in}(v)$ (Lines 1-4), and then refines it into the in-label set $L'_{in}(v)$ of v (Lines 5-10). In particular, the candidate set $C_{in}(v)$ contains all in-neighbors of v (i.e., the starting vertices of the edges pointing to v), as well as the in-label sets of those in-neighbors (Line 3-4).

By Definition 1, $C_{in}(v)$ is a superset of v's in-labels in $\mathcal{L}'$. To explain, consider a vertex u that is an in-label of v in $\mathcal{L}'$. By the Reachability Constraint, there exists a path P from u to v in G'. Let w be the in-neighbor of v on P. Then, u can reach w. In addition,

Algorithm 1: INSERT-STEP-2.1

input : G', $\mathcal{L}$, l', and v
output: $L'_{in}(v)$, $L'_{out}(v)$, and a modified version of $\mathcal{L}$

1 create two candidate label sets $C_{in}(v)$ and $C_{out}(v)$;
2 set $L'_{in}(v) = L'_{out}(v) = C_{in}(v) = C_{out}(v) = \emptyset$;
3 **for** *each of v's in-neighbors* u **do**
4   $C_{in}(v) = C_{in}(v) \cup L_{in}(u) \cup \{u\}$;
5 **for** *each* $u \in C_{in}(v)$ *in ascending order of* $l'(u)$ **do**
6   **if** $L_{out}(u) \cap L'_{in}(v) = \emptyset$ **then**
7   **if** $l'(u) < l'(v)$ **then**
8   add u into $L'_{in}(v)$;
9   **else**
10   add v into $L_{out}(u)$;
11 **for** *each of v's out-neighbors* u **do**
12   $C_{out}(v) = C_{out}(v) \cup L_{out}(u) \cup \{u\}$;
13 Repeat Lines 5-10 with subscripts "in" and "out" exchanged ;
14 **return** $L'_{in}(v)$, $L'_{out}(v)$, and the label sets in $\mathcal{L}$;

Algorithm 2: INSERT-STEP-2.2

input : G', l', v, and the output of Algorithm 1
output: A TOL index $\mathcal{L}'$ for G' with a level order l'

1 **for** *each vertex* $u \in L'_{in}(v)$ *in ascending order of* $l'(u)$ **do**
2   **for** *each vertex* $w \in L'_{out}(v) \cup \{v\}$ *with* $l'(w) > l'(u)$ **do**
3   **if** $L_{out}(u) \cap L_{in}(w) = \emptyset$ **then**
4       $L_{in}(w) = L_{in}(w) \cup \{u\}$;
5   **for** *each vertex* $x \in I_{in}(w)$ **do**
6   **if** $L_{out}(u) \cap L_{in}(x) = \emptyset$ **then**
7         $L_{in}(x) = L_{in}(x) \cup \{u\}$;
8   **for** *each vertex* $x' \in I_{in}(u)$ **do**
9   **for** *each vertex* $y' \in I_{out}(u)$ **do**
10   **if** $y' \in L_{in}(x')$ **then**
11   remove y' from $L_{in}(x')$;
12   **if** $x' \in L_{out}(y')$ **then**
13   remove x' from $L_{out}(y')$;
14 Repeat Lines 1-14 with subscripts "in" and "out" exchanged ;
15 **return** the revised label sets ;

$l(u) < l(w)$; otherwise, w is a vertex on P with a higher level than u, which violates the Path Constraint. Finally, all paths from u to w should contain only vertices with levels lower than u; otherwise, u should not be an in-label of v in the first place. All of the above indicates that u is an in-label of w, as it fulfills the three constraints in Definition 1. Therefore, $C_{in}(v)$ is superset of v's in-labels in $\mathcal{L}'$.

To refine $C_{in}(v)$ into $L'_{in}(v)$, Algorithm 1 removes the vertices in $C_{in}(v)$ that violate any of the Level and Path Constraints in Definition 1 (Lines 5-10). (The Reachability Constraint is ignored as all vertices in $C_{in}(v)$ can reach v.) Specifically, the algorithm examines the vertices in $C_{in}(v)$ in ascending order of their level values. For each vertex u with $l'(u) < l'(v)$ (i.e., u satisfies the Level Constraint), the algorithm adds u into $L'_{in}(v)$ if $L_{out}(u) \cap L'_{in}(v) = \emptyset$. The rationale is that, if $L_{out}(u) \cap L'_{in}(v) = \emptyset$, then no vertex with a higher level than $l(u)$ can connect u to v, in which case u fulfills the Path Constraint. Meanwhile, if $L_{out}(u) \cap L'_{in}(v) = \emptyset$ but $l'(u) > l'(v)$, then we add v into u's out-label set $L_{out}(u)$ instead.

After $L'_{in}(v)$ is created, Algorithm 1 constructs $L'_{out}(v)$ (Lines 11-13) and then terminates. We omit the discussion on $L'_{out}(v)$ as it is similar to the case of $L'_{in}(v)$.

Step 2.2. Given Step 2.1's output, Step 2.2 of our algorithm proceeds to refine the label sets in $\mathcal{L}$, as shown in Algorithm 2. The rationale is that, since the insertion of v creates new paths among the vertices in V, we may need to adjust the label sets in $\mathcal{L}$ to ensure that $\mathcal{L}$ remains a TOL index. Specifically, Algorithm 2 first inspects the vertices in $L'_{in}(v)$ in ascending order of their level values (Line 1). For each vertex u, the algorithm examines each vertex w in $L'_{out}(v) \cup \{v\}$ with lower levels than u (Line 2). Notice that, for every such pair of vertices u and w, the insertion of v creates a new path from u to w via v. Accordingly, the algorithm adds u into w's in-label set $L_{in}(w)$ if $L_{out}(u) \cap L_{in}(w) = \emptyset$, i.e., if inserting u into $L_{in}(w)$ does not violate the Path Constraint in Definition 1 (Lines 3-4). Similarly, the algorithm also inserts u into $L_{in}(x)$ for any vertex $x \in I_{in}(w)$, i.e., any vertex x that has w as an in-label (Line 5-7).

After that, the algorithm proceeds to check whether the operations in Lines 2-7 have resulted in unnecessary labels (Lines 8-13). In particular, it examines each pair of vertices $x' \in I_{out}(u)$ and $y' \in I_{in}(u)$, i.e., x' has u as an out-label and y' has u as an in-label. For each pair of x' and y', the algorithm checks whether y' appears in the out-label of x'; if so, it removes y' from $L_{out}(x')$, since (i) u has higher level than both x' and y' and (ii) u connects x' to y', which leads to a violation of the Path Constraint. Similarly, if x' is in the out-label set of y', and it is removed.

Once the above nested loop is finished, Algorithm 2 enters another nested-loop, where (i) the outer loop linearly scans each vertex u in $L'_{out}(v)$ in ascending order of level values, and (ii) the inner loop examines each vertex w in $L'_{in}(v) \cup \{v\}$ with $l'(u) < l'(w)$. This nested loop complements the previous nested loop, in that the former processes vertex pairs in $L'_{in}(v)$ and $L'_{out}(v)$ that are ignored by the latter. Finally, Algorithm 2 terminates and returns the revised label sets, which constitute $\mathcal{L}'$.

5.1.2 Step 1: Deciding Vertex Level

Our algorithms in Section 5.1.1 require that the level $l'(v)$ of the new vertex v is decided. A straightforward approach is to set $l'(v) = |V| + 1$, i.e., give v the lowest possible level. This leads to relatively small update overheads because, when $l'(v)$ is maximized, we do not need to insert v into the label sets of any other vertex (due to the Level Constraint in Definition 1). In terms of space overhead and query efficiency, however, setting $l'(v) = |V| + 1$ could be highly sub-optimal than other choices $l'(v)$. To address this issue, we present an alternative solution that sets $l'(v)$ to a value that minimizes the total size of the label sets. Such a $l'(v)$ is also likely to improve query efficiency, since the cost of a reachability query on a TOL index is linear to the sizes of the source and terminal vertices' label sets.

Let $\mathcal{L}_k$ be the TOL index obtained by inserting v into $\mathcal{L}$ with $l'(v) = k$. To identify the value of k that minimizes $\mathcal{L}$, we examine all possible $k \in [1, |V|+1]$, but avoid repeatedly using Algorithms 1 and 2 to construct all $\mathcal{L}_k$. Instead, we propose a lightweight approach for deriving

$$\Delta_k = |\mathcal{L}_k| - |\mathcal{L}_{k+1}| \tag{5}$$

for any $k \in [1, |V|]$. Once Δ_k is computed, we can easily determine the optimal value of $l'(v)$.

The key observation behind our approach is as follows. When we change $l'(v)$ from k to $k-1$, the level order of all vertices remain unchanged, except for v and the vertex u with $l(u) = k-1$ (since the order between u and v would be reversed). As a consequence, the size difference between $\mathcal{L}_k$ and $\mathcal{L}_{k-1}$ only depends on the label sets that concern u and v. Intuitively, tracking the changes in those label sets is much simpler than creating a TOL index from

Algorithm 3: INSERT-STEP-1

input : $G = (V, E)$, $\mathcal{L}$, l, and v
output: the value for $l'(v)$ that minimizes $|\mathcal{L}'|$

1 set $l'(v) = |V| + 1$;
2 construct $L'_{in}(v)$, $L'_{out}(v)$, $I'_{in}(v)$, and $I'_{out}(v)$ as in Algorithm 1 (without materializing any changes to $\mathcal{L}$) ;
3 **for** $k = |V|, |V| - 1, \cdots, 1$ **do**
4 $\quad \Delta_k = 0$;
5 $\quad$ let u be the vertex with $l(u) = k$;
6 $\quad$ **if** $u \in L'_{in}(v)$ **then**
7 $\quad\quad$ remove u from $L'_{in}(v)$ and add it into $I'_{out}(v)$;
8 $\quad\quad$ **for** *each vertex* $w \in I'_{in}(v)$ *such that* $u \in L_{in}(w)$ **do**
9 $\quad\quad\quad \Delta_k = \Delta_k - 1$;
10 $\quad\quad$ **for** *each vertex* $w' \in I_{out}(u)$ *such that* $v \notin L_{out}(w)$ **do**
11 $\quad\quad\quad \Delta_k = \Delta_k + 1$;
12 $\quad\quad\quad$ add w' into $I'_{out}(v)$;
13 $\quad$ repeat Lines 6-12 with subscripts "in" and "out" exchanged ;
14 initialize variables $\theta_1, \theta_2, \ldots, \theta_{|V|+1}$;
15 $\theta_{|V|+1} = 0$;
16 **for** $k = |V|, |V| - 1, \cdots, 1$ **do**
17 $\quad \theta_k = \theta_{k+1} + \Delta_k$;
18 **return** $\arg\min_k\{\theta_k\}$;

scratch, and hence, deriving Δ_k can be much more efficient than constructing $\mathcal{L}_k$.

Algorithm 3 shows the pseudo-code of our approach. It first sets $l'(v) = |V| + 1$, and applies Algorithm 1 to compute, for v, two label sets $L'_{in}(v)$ and $L'_{out}(v)$ and two inverted lists $I'_{in}(v)$ and $I'_{out}(v)$ (Lines 1-2). The subsequent part of the algorithm consists of $|V|$ iterations (Lines 3-14). In the $(|V| - k + 1)$-th iteration, the algorithm considers the case when $l'(v)$ changes from $k + 1$ to k, and evaluates the corresponding changes in the label sets, based on which it derives Δ_k.

Specifically, the algorithm first sets $\Delta_k = 0$ and inspects the vertex u with $l(u) = k$, i.e., the vertex whose level is to be exchanged with v when $l'(v)$ is decreased from $k + 1$ to k. Observe that, if the exchange between u and v leads to changes in some label sets, then $u \in L'_{in}(v) \cup L'_{out}(v)$ should hold. The reason is that, when $u \notin L'_{in}(v) \cup L'_{out}(v)$, either (i) there is no path between u and v or (ii) all paths between u and v contain at least one vertex with higher level than u and v. In either case, switching levels between u and v would not lead to violations of the Reachability, Level, or Path Constraint in any label sets. Therefore, if $u \notin L'_{in}(v) \cup L'_{out}(v)$, then no label set would be affected by swapping u and v's levels. Based on this analysis, Algorithm 3 sets the final value of Δ_k to 0, whenever $u \notin L'_{in}(v) \cup L'_{out}(v)$ (Lines 4-13).

Now consider that $u \in L'_{in}(v)$. After we exchange u and v's levels, u should be removed from $L'_{in}(v)$, and v should become an out-label of u. This explains Line 7 in Algorithm 3. Meanwhile, for any vertex $w \in I'_{in}(v)$ (i.e., w has v as an in-label), we check if u is an in-label of w (Line 8). If $u \in L_{in}(w)$, then after the levels of u and v are swapped, u should be removed from $L_{in}(w)$ due to the Path Constraint, which reduces the size of $L_{in}(w)$ by one. Accordingly, Algorithm 3 decreases Δ_k by 1 for each such vertex w (Line 9). In addition, for any vertex $w' \in I_{out}(u)$ (i.e., u is an out-label for w'), we examine if v is not out-label of w' (Line 10). If $v \notin L_{out}(w')$, then after we swap u and v's levels, v will become an out-label of w', i.e., the size of $L_{out}(w')$ is increased by one. Therefore, for each such vertex w', Algorithm 3 increases Δ_k by 1 and inserts w' into $I'_{out}(v)$ (Lines 11 and 12). It can be verified that, apart from the label sets mentioned above, no other label sets would be affected by the exchange between u and v.

Although the above discussion assumes $u \in L'_{in}(v)$, it can be easily extended to the case when $u \in L'_{out}(v)$ (Line 13). Once all Δ_k are obtained, Algorithm 3 derives $|V| + 1$ variables $\theta_1, \theta_2, \ldots, \theta_{|V|+1}$, such that $\theta_{|V|+1} = 0$ and $\theta_k = \theta_{k+1} + \Delta_k$ ($k \in [1, |V|]$). By the definition of Δ_k, the value of k that minimizes θ_k should also minimize $|\mathcal{L}_k|$. Accordingly, Algorithm 3 terminates by returning $\arg\min_k\{\theta_k\}$ (Line 18).

5.1.3 Correctness and Complexity

We first show the correctness of our insertion algorithm in Lemma 3, and then analyze its complexity.

LEMMA 3. *Given G and a new vertex v, Algorithms 1 and 2 produces a TOL index on G', and Algorithm 3 computes a level for v that minimizes the label size of $\mathcal{L}'$.*

PROOF. We start by proving that the index $\mathcal{L}'$ produced by Algorithm 1 and 2 is a TOL index on G'. In particular, we first show that Algorithm 1 and Lines 1-7 in Algorithm 2 create label sets that are supersets of corresponding label sets in the TOL on G', and then show that Lines 8-13 in Algorithm 2 remove all redundant labels.

Recall that we have shown the correctness of $L'_{in}(v)$ and $L'_{out}(v)$ created by Algorithm 1 in Section 5.1.1. In the following, we prove that, for any vertex u other than v, Lines 1-7 in Algorithm 2 create an in-label set that is a superset of u's in-label set in the TOL on G'. Given two vertices u and x, according to Definition 1, the insertion of v causes u to become an in-label of x, only if all of the following conditions hold: (i) $l'(u) < l'(x)$; (ii) u can reach v in G' and v can reach x in G'; (iii) no simple path from u to x contains a vertex that has a higher level than u. Accordingly, in Line 1, we omit any vertex u that is not in $L'_{in}(v)$. This is because if u is not in $L'_{in}(v)$, then for the vertex z with the highest level among all the paths from u to v, we have $z \neq u$. In addition, z is also on the path from u to any x that can be reached by v. In that case, condition (iii) is violated, and hence, u will never become an in-label of any vertex in G'.

Next, consider any vertex x eliminated by Line 2. If x has a higher level than u, then it should be eliminated as it violates condition (i). On the other hand, if x has lower level than u, then x is not in $L'_{out}(v) \cup \{v\}$. In that case, for the vertex z with the highest level in all the paths from v to x be z, we have $z \in L'_{out}(v)$. If $l'(z) > l'(u)$, then x is examined in the loop when $w = z$. If $l'(z) < l'(u)$, then there is a path from u to x that contains a vertex (i.e, z) that has higher level than u, violating condition (iii). In addition, Line 3 and Line 6 also guarantee that the newly created labels do not violate condition (iii). In summary, Lines 1-7 only omits vertices that will never lead to a label creation, and hence, the set of in-label sets created in Lines 1-7 are supersets of the corresponding in-label sets in the TOL on G'.

After adding u into $L_{in}(x)$, some existing labels related to x may become redundant. By Definition 1, neither the Level Constraint nor the Reachability Constraint would be affected for an existing label, i.e., the only possible violation is on the Path Constraint. In particular, u may be an out-label of a vertex y, such that y is an in-label of x or x is an out-label of y, either of which leads to a violation of the Path Constraint since (i) there is a path from y to x with u on it, and (ii) u has higher level than both y and x. To address this issue, Algorithm 2 enumerates all relevant x and y in Lines 8 and 9, and remove redundant labels in Lines 10-13.

After that, we repeat the above procedure (Line 14) with "in" and "out" exchanged to update the in-label sets of the vertices that can reach v, as well as the out-label sets of the vertices that v can reach. Summarizing the above discussion, Algorithms 1 and 2 result in a TOL on G'.

Finally, as Algorithm 3 precisely evaluates the size differences between consecutive levels for v, i.e., $\Delta_i, i = 1, ..., |V|$ (as shown in Section 5.1.2), it identifies a level k for v, such that the size of the resulting index is minimized. □

Complexity Analysis. To analyze our algorithm, we consider the complexity step by step. In Step 1, given a vertex v for insertion, Algorithm 3 inspects all the vertices $u \in L'_{in}(v) \cup L'_{out}(v)$, and derives Δ_k by computing all vertices $w \in I_{in}(u) \cup I_{out}(u)$, each with one set operation, i.e., Lines 8 and 10. Let β be the cost of one set operation, then the complexity of Step 1 is bounded by $O(|V|^2\beta)$. In Step 2.1, Algorithm 1 incurs $|C_{in}(v)| + |C_{out}(v)|$ number of set operation in Line 6, therefore, its cost is bounded by $C_2 = O((|C_{in}(v)| + |C_{out}(v)|)\beta)$. In Step 2.2, Algorithm 2 performs the set operations for each pair of vertices in the worse case, resulting a complexity of $O(|V|^2\beta)$. Note that, Lines 9-14 inspects the vertices in $I_{in}(u) \cap L_{in}(x')$ and $I_{out}(u) \cap L_{out}(y')$, which can be implemented in set operations as well. Hence, the complexity for our entire insertion algorithm is $O(|V|^2\beta)$.

5.2 Deletion Algorithm

Next, we discuss our algorithm handling deletion in G. Let $G' = (V', E')$ be the graph obtained by removing a vertex v from G. As with the case of insertion, we assume that G' is a DAG, and we aim to transform $\mathcal{L}$ into a TOL index $\mathcal{L}'$ on G', such that the level orders of $\mathcal{L}$ and $\mathcal{L}'$ sort the vertices in V' in the same order.

Algorithm 4 presents the pseudo-code of our deletion method. It first removes v from every label set that it appears (Lines 1-4). Then, it refines the label sets in $\mathcal{L}$ to convert it into $\mathcal{L}'$ (Lines 5-22). In particular, it first retrieves the set $B^+(v)$ of all vertices that v can reach, using a BFS from v that follows the outgoing edges of each vertex. Then, it inspects the vertices in $B^+(v)$ in ascending order of their topological ranks (see Section 2), and reconstructs the in-label set of each vertex. (Note that the out-label sets of those vertices are not affected by the deletion of v.)

For each vertex $u \in B^+(v)$, the algorithm first creates a candidate set $C_{in}(u)$ (Line 8). Then, for each of u's in-neighbors z such that $z \neq v$, the algorithm inserts the in-labels of z into $C_{in}(u)$ (Lines 9-10). It can be proved that $C_{in}(u)$ is a superset of the in-labels of u in $\mathcal{L}'$. To refine $C_{in}(u)$ into u's in-label set, the algorithm examines each vertex w in $C_{in}(u)$ in ascending order of $l(w)$ (Line 12). If $l(w) < l(u)$ and $L_{out}(w) \cap L_{in}(u) = \emptyset$, then we identify w as an in-label of u in $\mathcal{L}'$ (Line 14). Subsequently, we remove the labels that become redundant due to the insertion of w into $L_{in}(u)$ (Lines 15-17). In particular, for each vertex s having w as an out-label, if u is also in the out-label set of s, then we remove u from the out-label of s.

Once all vertices in $B^+(v)$ are processed, the algorithm derives the set $B^-(v)$ of vertices that can reach v, by applying a BFS from v that follows the incoming edges of each vertex. After that, it reconstructs the out-label set of each vertex in $B^-(v)$, in a way similar to the case of $B^+(v)$ (Lines 18-21). Finally, it returns the modified label sets for all vertices expect v, i.e., the label sets that form $\mathcal{L}'$.

Correctness Proof. Lemma 4 proves the correctness of our deletion algorithm.

LEMMA 4. *Given G and a vertex v to be deleted, the updated labeling $\mathcal{L}'$ produced by Algorithm 4 is a TOL on G'.*

PROOF. We first prove that the candidate set $C_{in}(u)$ generated in Lines 8-10 is a superset of $L'_{in}(u)$. Then, we show that redundant labels in $L'_{in}(u)$ are removed in Lines 12-19.

Algorithm 4: DELETE

input : $G = (V, E)$, $\mathcal{L}$, and $v \in V$
output: $\mathcal{L}'$

1 **for** *each* $x \in I_{out}(v)$ **do**
2   remove v from $L_{out}(x)$;
3 **for** *each* $y \in I_{in}(v)$ **do**
4   remove v from $L_{in}(y)$;
5 identify the set $B^+(v)$ of vertices that v can reach, using a BFS from v that follows the outgoing edges of each vertex ;
6 **for** *each* $u \in B^+(v)$ *in ascending order of* $o(u)$ **do**
7   let $N_{in}(u)$ be the set of in-neighbors of u ;
8   create a candidate set $C_{in}(u) = \emptyset$;
9   **for** *each* $z \in N_{in}(u)$ *such that* $z \neq v$ **do**
10         $C_{in}(u) = C_{in}(u) \cup L_{in}(z) \cup \{z\}$;
11     $L_{in}(u) = \emptyset$;
12   **for** *each* $w \in C_{in}(u)$ *in ascending order of* $l(w)$ **do**
13   **if** $l(w) < l(u)$ *and* $L_{out}(w) \cap L_{in}(u) = \emptyset$ **then**
14   add w into $L_{in}(u)$;
15   **for** *each* $s \in I_{out}(w)$ **do**
16   **if** $u \in L_{out}(s)$ **then**
17   remove u from $L_{out}(s)$;
18 identify the set $B^-(v)$ of vertices that can reach v, using a BFS from v that follows the incoming edges of each vertex ;
19 **for** *each* $u \in B^-(v)$ *in descending order of* $o(u)$ **do**
20   let $N_{out}(u)$ be the set of out-neighbors of u ;
21   repeat Lines 8-17 with subscripts "in" and "out" exchanged ;
22 **return** the label sets of all vertices except v ;

Consider each vertex x that is an updated in-label of u (i.e. $x \in L'_{in}(u)$). By the Reachability Constraint and the Path Constraint in Definition 1, we know that there is a path from x to u in G', and x is the highest-level vertex on the path. Let z be the in-label of u on the path. Then, either $x = z$ or x is an updated in-label of z (i.e., $x \in L'_{in}(z)$). To understand this, assume on the contrary that $x \neq z$ and $x \notin L'_{in}(z)$. Then, there must be a path P from x to z that contains a vertex with a higher level than both x and z. Consider a path P' that goes from x to z via P, and then from z to u. Observe that P' connects x to u and contains a vertex with a level higher than x. This contradicts the Path Constraint since $x \in L'_{in}(u)$. In summary, for any vertex x in $L'_{in}(u)$, it is either an in-neighbor of u or an in-label of an in-neighbor of u. Accordingly, Lines 8-10 constructs the candidate set $C_{in}(u)$ by combining all the in-neighbors of u as well as the in-labels of those in-neighbors. In addition, since we construct $L'_{in}(u)$ in the ascending order of $o(u)$, we ensure that the in-label sets of the in-neighbors of u are updated before the construction of $C_{in}(u)$, which guarantees that $C_{in}(u)$ is a superset of $L'_{in}(u)$.

Next, for each vertex w in $C_{in}(u)$, we add it into $L'_{in}(u)$ if $l(w) < l(u)$ and $L_{out}(w) \cap L'_{in}(u) = \emptyset$. This guarantees the Level and Path Constraints. Since the Reachability Constraint is already ensured in the construction of the candidate sets, we know that adding w to $L'_{in}(u)$ does not affect the TOL properties. However, some existing labels related to w and u may become redundant. By Definition 1, neither the Level Constraint nor the Reachability Constraint will be affected, and the only possible violation is on the Path Constraint. In particular, if w is also an out-label of a vertex s and if u is in the out-label of s, then u violates the Path Constraint, since there is a path from s to u that contains w, and w has higher level than u. On the other hand, the case that s is an in-label of u never occurs, since we add w into $L'_{in}(u)$ in ascending order of $l(w)$.

Summarizing the above discussion, for each vertex u, we first generate a superset of $L'_{in}(u)$, and then construct the $L'_{in}(u)$ by adding vertices from the superset. In addition, for each w that is added into $L'_{in}(u)$, we remove, on the fly, all redundant labels caused by w. As such, Algorithm 4 results in a TOL on G'. □

Complexity Analysis. The complexity of computing $B^+(v)$ and $B^-(v)$ is equivalent to the complexity of BFS in G, which is $O(|E|)$. Next, consider the computation cost for a vertex u in $B^+(v)$. In Lines 9-10, as we merge the updated in-label sets of the in-neighbors of u to form the candidate set for u, the complexity is bounded by $|V|\beta$, where β is the complexity of a set operation. Then, for each vertex x in the candidate set $C_{in}(u)$, it takes a constant number of set operations to add x to $L_{in}(u)$ and remove redundant labels. Thus, the total computation cost on u is bounded by $O(|V|\beta)$. As such, the complexity of the deletion algorithm is $O(|V|^2\beta)$.

6. ITERATIVE LABEL REDUCTION

The update algorithms in Section 5 retains the level order on the vertices in G, which, as mentioned, helps ensure that the performance of $\mathcal{L}$ does not significantly degrade after updates. As the initial level order l is retained during updates, however, it is essential that l is chosen carefully. Otherwise, if l renders $\mathcal{L}$ inefficient, then this inefficiency is likely to persist even after updates.

A straightforward solution to choose the initial l is to enumerate all possible level orders (i.e., all permutations of vertices in V), then construct a TOL index based on each order, and finally select the one that optimizes performance. However, this approach is far from practical due to the enormous number of possible level orders. As an alternative solution, one may select an initial level order l using some heuristic approach (e.g., using the existing TOL instantiations [8, 17, 30]), and then adjusts the level order l to improve $\mathcal{L}$. Interestingly, our update algorithms can be utilized for such adjustments of l.

Specifically, given $\mathcal{L}$, we can first remove a vertex v using Algorithm 4, and then insert v back using the insertion algorithm in Section 5.1. By the properties of the insertion algorithm, when v is re-inserted, its level $l(v)$ is set to a value that minimizes $|\mathcal{L}|$, i.e., the total size of the label sets in $\mathcal{L}$. Therefore, $|\mathcal{L}|$ is likely to decrease (and will never increase) after the *deletion and re-insertion* of v. By repeating this process for each vertex v, we can obtain an improved version of $\mathcal{L}$ with a (much) reduced total size. This decrease in $|\mathcal{L}|$ not only reduces space consumption, but also improves query efficiency (as $\mathcal{L}$ process queries by scanning label sets). In Section 8, we experimentally show that this label reduction approach can significantly enhance the performance of existing TOL instantiations [8, 17, 30].

7. CONSTRUCTION OF INITIAL $\mathcal{L}$

Although the label reduction algorithm improves the performance of $\mathcal{L}$, we observe from our experiments that it incurs substantial computation costs on large graphs. This motivates us to investigate more efficient methods for choosing a good initial level order l. In the following, we first present a new algorithm for construct an initial l (Section 7.1), and then discuss the construction of $\mathcal{L}$ given l (Section 7.2).

7.1 Deciding Vertex Level

Given a G and a vertex $v \in V$, let $S_{in}(v, G)$ be the set of vertices that can reach v in G, and $S_{out}(v, G)$ be the set of vertices that v can reach in G. Suppose that we set the level of v higher than the level of any vertex in $S_{in}(v, G) \cup S_{out}(v, G)$. Then, in the corresponding TOL index, we need to add v to the in-label sets of the vertices in $S_{in}(v, G)$, as well as the out-label set of the vertices in $S_{out}(v, G)$. In that case, v contributes $|S_{in}(v, G)| + |S_{out}(v, G)|$ labels in $\mathcal{L}$.

On the other hand, if we set the level of v to a lower level than all vertices in $S_{in}(v, G) \cup S_{out}(v, G)$, then we need to (i) add each vertex in $S_{in}(v, G)$ into $L_{in}(v)$, and (ii) add each vertex in $S_{out}(v, G)$ into $L_{out}(v)$. Furthermore, if v happens to be the only vertex that connects vertices in $S_{in}(v, G)$ to those in $S_{out}(v, G)$, then in the worst case, we have to add every vertex in $S_{out}(v, G)$ to the out-label set of every vertex in $S_{in}(v, G)$. In that scenario, v contributes $|S_{in}(v, G)| \cdot |S_{out}(v, G)| + |S_{in}(v, G)| + |S_{out}(v, G)|$ labels in $\mathcal{L}$.

We define $|S_{in}(v, G)|$ and $|S_{out}(v, G)|$ as the *in-score* and *out-score* of v, respectively. In addition, we define a *score function* f as follows:

$$f(v, G) = \frac{|S_{in}(v, G)| \cdot |S_{out}(v, G)| + |S_{in}(v, G)| + |S_{out}(v, G)|}{|S_{in}(v, G)| + |S_{out}(v, G)|}.$$

In the pathological case when $|S_{in}(v, G)| + |S_{out}(v, G)| = 0$, we define $f(v, G) = 0$. Intuitively, if $f(v, G)$ is large, then v should be given a higher order than the vertices in $S_{in}(v, G) \cup S_{out}(v, G)$, so as to avoid the worst-case space cost of $|S_{in}(v, G)| \cdot |S_{out}(v, G)| + |S_{in}(v, G)| + |S_{out}(v, G)|$.

Based on the above intuition, we can design an algorithm to derive a good level order l as follows. Given G, we first identify the vertex v_1 that maximizes $f(v_1, G)$, and then set $l(v_1) = 1$, i.e., we assign v_1 to the highest level. After that, we remove v_1 from G, and proceed to identify the vertex v_2 that maximizes $f(v_2, G)$ in the modified G, then set $l(v_2) = 2$. We repeat this process until all vertices are removed from G, i.e., until each vertex is given a level.

Although the above algorithm is intuitively, it is difficult to implement efficiently, as (i) the computation of $f(v, G)$ requires us to derive the in-score and out-score of v using BFS (or DFS) on G, and (ii) the in-score and out-score of a vertex need to be recomputed whenever another vertex is removed from G. To address this deficiency, we propose to *approximate* the in-scores and out-scores of the vertices in G.

Let $S^{\top}_{in}(v)$ and $S^{\top}_{out}(v)$ be the approximate in-score and out-score of a vertex v, respectively. For each vertex w in G with no in-neighbor (resp. out-neighbor), we set $S^{\top}_{in}(w) = 0$ (resp. $S^{\top}_{out}(w) = 0$) to zero; note that this is also the exact in-score (resp. out-score) of w. After that, based on those vertices w, we recursively compute the approximate in-score and out-score of each remaining vertex v as follows:

$$S^{\top}_{in}(v) = \begin{cases} \sum_{u \in N_{in}(v)} \left(S^{\top}_{in}(u) + 1\right), & \text{if } N_{in}(v) \neq \emptyset; \\ 0, & \text{otherwise.} \end{cases}$$

$$S^{\top}_{out}(v) = \begin{cases} \sum_{u \in N_{out}(v)} \left(S^{\top}_{out}(u) + 1\right), & \text{if } N_{out}(v) \neq \emptyset; \\ 0, & \text{otherwise.} \end{cases}$$

where $N_{in}(v)$ and $N_{out}(v)$ denote the sets of in-neighbors and out-neighbors of v, respectively. It can be verified that $S^{\top}_{in}(v)$ and $S^{\top}_{out}(v)$ are upperbounds of v's in-score and out-score, respectively. As an alternative solution, we also consider using a lower-bound of v's in-score (resp. out-score), denoted as $S^{\perp}_{in}(v)$ (resp. $S^{\perp}_{out}(v)$), for approximation. In particular, $S^{\perp}_{in}(v) = 0$ if v has no in-neighbor, and $S^{\perp}_{out}(v) = 0$ if v has no out-neighbor. For any other vertex, we have:

$$S^{\perp}_{in}(v) = \begin{cases} \sum_{u \in N_{in}(v)} \frac{S^{\perp}_{in}(u)+1}{|N_{out}(u)|}, & \text{if } N_{in}(v) \neq \emptyset; \\ 0, & \text{otherwise.} \end{cases}$$

$$S^{\perp}_{out}(v) = \begin{cases} \sum_{u \in N_{out}(v)} \frac{S^{\perp}_{out}(u)+1}{|N_{out}(u)|}, & \text{if } N_{out}(v) \neq \emptyset; \\ 0, & \text{otherwise.} \end{cases}$$

Note that we can compute $S^{\top}_{in}(v)$ for all vertices v in G, using a linear scan of the vertices. Specifically, we inspect the vertices v in ascending order of their topological ranks $o(v)$ (see Section 2). As G is a DAG, the vertices with the smallest ranks must have no in-neighbors, and hence, we have $S^{\top}_{in}(u) = 0$ for any of those vertices. By the definition of topological ranks, when we inspect any other vertex w, the $S^{\top}_{in}$ values of w's in-neighbor must have been computed. Therefore, $S^{\top}_{in}(w)$ can be easily derived. In summary, we can compute $S^{\top}_{in}(v)$ for all vertices v in $O(|V|+|E|)$ time. The same algorithm can be easily extended to compute $S^{\perp}_{in}(v)$. Meanwhile, we can derive $S^{\top}_{out}(v)$ and $S^{\perp}_{out}(v)$ for all vertices v, using a linear scan of the vertices in G in descending order of their topological ranks.

7.2 Labeling Algorithm

As discussed in Section 4, a level order l uniquely decides a TOL index $\mathcal{L}$. In this section, we introduce an algorithm for constructing $\mathcal{L}$ given a level order l computed using the methods in Section 7.1. Similar approaches have been proposed in [2, 17] for specific instantiations of TOL (with specific level orderings), but the correctness analysis therein is not immediately applicable under the general TOL framework. Therefore, we present our algorithm and analysis for the sake of completeness.

Algorithm. Algorithm 5 presents our method (referred to as *Butterfly* for constructing $\mathcal{L}$ given a level order l on G. The algorithm first creates a copy of G (referred to as G_1), and then it runs in $|V|$ iterations. In the k-th iteration, it removes from G_k the vertex v with $l(v) = k$, and inserts v into the label sets of other vertices. In particular, we first obtain the set $B^{+}(v)$ of vertices in G_k that v can reach, using a BFS from v that follows the outgoing edges of each vertex. Then, for each vertex $w \in B^{+}(v)$, if $L_{out}(v) \cap L_{in}(w) = \emptyset$, then we add v into $L_{in}(w)$. After that, we perform a BFS on G_k from v following the incoming edges of each vertex, to identify the set $B^{-}(v)$ of vertices that can reach v in G_k. For each $u \in B^{-}(v)$, we insert v into $L_{out}(u)$ if $L_{out}(u) \cap L_{in}(v) = \emptyset$. At the end of the iteration, we remove v from G_k, and denote the resulting graph as G_{k+1}. After that, we proceed to the $(k+1)$-th iteration. Once all iterations are finished, Algorithm 5 returns the label sets constructed, which form a TOL index $\mathcal{L}$ on G.

Correctness and Complexity. We prove the correctness of Algorithm 5 by the following lemma.

LEMMA 5. *Given a DAG $G = (V, E)$ and a vertex level, Algorithm 5 outputs a TOL index of G.*

PROOF. Observe that, for any two vertices u and v, Algorithm 5 inserts u into the in-label (resp. out-label) set of v, only when $l(u) < l(v)$ and u can reach v (v can reach u). Therefore, the index constructed by Algorithm 5 never violates the Rechability or Level Constraint in Definition 1.

By contradiction, assume that the output of Algorithm 5 is not a TOL index. Then, there exist two vertices u and v such that (i) u is in the in-label or out-label of v, and (ii) u violates the Path Constraint. We first discuss the case when u is in the in-label of v, i.e., $u \rightarrow v$, and the same discussion can be extended to the alternative case.

Since u does not fulfill the Path Constraint, there exists a vertex w in the path from u to v, such that the level of w is higher than the levels of u and v. In case that there exist several such paths, we let w be the vertex with highest level in all those paths. Since the level of w is higher than the levels of u and v, w is removed before the removals of u and v. Then, when Algorithm 5 removes w, it must add w into the out-label set of u and the in-label set of v. Now observe that, when Algorithm 5 removes u, it adds u into the in-label set of v, only if $L_{out}(u) \cap L_{in}(v) = \emptyset$. However, since w has been inserted into both $L_{out}(u)$ and $L_{in}(v)$, $L_{out}(u) \cap L_{in}(v) \neq \emptyset$. This indicates that u should not be in $L_{in}(v)$, leading to a contradiction. □

Algorithm 5: BUTTERFLY

```
input : G and a level order l
output: a TOL index 𝓛
let G_1 = G ;
for k = 1, ··· , |V| do
    let v be the vertex whose level is k ;
    identify the set B+(v) of vertices that v can reach in G_k, using a
      BFS from v that follows the outgoing edges of each vertex ;
    identify the set B−(v) of vertices that can reach v in G_k, using a
      BFS from v that follows the incoming edges of each vertex ;
    for each vertex u in B+(v) do
        if L_out(v) ∩ L_in(u) = ∅ then
            add v to L_in(u) ;
    for each vertex u in B−(v) do
        if L_out(u) ∩ L_in(v) = ∅ then
            add v to L_out(u) ;
    remove v and G_k and denote the resulting graph as G_{k+1} ;
return the label sets of all vertices in G ;
```

We now discuss the complexity of Algorithm 5. Let $G_k = (V_k, E_k)$ be the input graph to the k-th iteration, and denote the vertex with highest vertex level in G_k by v. The complexity of forward and backward BFS is bounded by $|E_k|$, and total size of $B^{-}(v)$ and $B^{+}(v)$ is bounded by $|V_k|$. Besides, the size of in-label or out-label of any vertex at k-th iteration is at most k since only the vertices whose levels are higher than v are added the current labels. As such, the complexity of each operation, intersection or addition, can be bounded by $O(k)$. In sum, we bound the complexity at k-iteration as $O(|E_k| + k|V_k|)$. Note that, as we remove a vertex from G_k at the end of the k-th iteration, the graph for computing becomes smaller and smaller, that is, the complexity at the k-th iteration decreases significantly when k increases.

8. EXPERIMENTS

This section experimentally evaluates our solution against the state of the art. We implement our algorithms in C++, and we adopt the C++ implementations of all competitors provided by their authors. All of our experiments are conducted on a machine with an Intel Xeon 2.4GHz CPU and 48GB RAM, running Ubuntu 12.4. In each experiment, we measure the performance of each method for 5 times, and we report the average measurement. If a method requires more than 24 hours or more than 48GB RAM to preprocess a dataset D, we omit the method from the experiments on D.

Datasets and Queries. Table 3 shows the datasets used in our experiments. Among them, RG5, RG10, RG20, and RG40 are synthetic DAGs generated using the method in experiments in [8], varying the average degree of vertices from 5 to 40, setting the *topological level* to 8 (see [8] for details). The other 11 datasets are the largest DAGs that have been adopted in the literature. In particular, *uni-22m*, *uni-100m*, *uni-150m*, *wiki*, *citeseerx*, *go-uniprot*,

dataset	$\|V\|$	$\|E\|$	avg. deg.
RG5	1.0M	5.0M	5.00
RG10	1.0M	10.0M	10.00
RG20	1.0M	20.0M	20.00
RG40	1.0M	40.0M	40.00
uniprot22m (uni-22m)	1.6M	1.6M	1.00
uniprot100m (uni-100m)	16.1M	16.1M	1.00
uniprot150m (uni-150m)	25.0M	25.0M	1.00
wiki	2.3M	2.3M	1.01
Twitter	16.6M	18.4M	1.10
Yago2	16.1M	25.7M	1.59
Web-UK	20.4M	37.8M	1.85
citeseerx	6.3M	14.8M	2.36
GovWild	8.0M	23.7M	2.95
patent	3.7M	15.7M	4.27
go-uniprot	7.0M	34.8M	4.99

Table 3: Datasets (M = 10^6).

and *patents* are from [8, 17], while *GovWild*, *Yago2*, *Twitter*, and *Web-UK* are used in [25].

On each dataset G, we generate a set of 10^6 reachability queries. In particular, we first derive a topological order on the vertices in G. Then, for each query q, we randomly select two vertices from G, and we choose the vertex with lower (resp. higher) topological rank as the source (resp. terminal) vertex s (resp. t). This method of query generation ensures that none of the queries can be answered by trivially checking whether the terminal vertex has a lower topological rank than the source vertex[1].

For each experiment on updates on G, we randomly remove 10^4 vertices one by one from G, and measure the average deletion time of each method. After that, we insert the deleted vertices back into G, in reverse order of their removal. During this process, we evaluate the average insertion time of each algorithm.

Experiments on Dynamic Graphs. Our first set of experiments evaluates our solution against existing techniques for dynamic graphs. As mentioned in Section 3, there exist a few methods [4, 12, 13, 16, 22, 24, 32] for handling updates on reachability indices. Among them, [12,13,22] are shown to be restricted to small graphs with at most a few thousand vertices [20], while [24] only handles XML graphs. We test the remaining methods, and find that only Dagger [32] is able to run on more than one datasets in our experiments. Therefore, we choose Dagger as our competitor. In addition, we evaluate two versions of our solution, namely, *Butterfly-U (BU)* and *Butterfly-L (BL)*, such that BU adopts $S_{in}^{\top}$ and $S_{out}^{\top}$ as its score functions, and BL adopts $S_{in}^{\perp}$ and $S_{out}^{\perp}$ (see Section 7).

Figure 2 shows the average insertion time of BU, BL, and Dagger. Observe that BU is more efficient than Dagger in most cases. In particular, on Twitter, BU's insertion time is lower than that of Dagger by four orders of magnitude. Meanwhile, BL is evidently less efficient than BU, although it still outperforms Dagger on half of the datasets. (Note that we omit BL on RG40, as it incurs excessive memory consumption on the graph.) The performance gap between BU and BL indicates that the vertex ordering adopted by BU is superior to that by BL. Meanwhile, Dagger considerably outperforms BU and BL on uni-22m, uni-100m, and uni-150m, since (i) each of those three graphs is a tree, and (ii) Dagger is particularly efficient on trees [32].

Figure 3 illustrates the total query time (for processing 10^6 queries) of BU, BL, Dagger, as well as a simple baseline approach. In particular, given a reachability query q on a graph G, the baseline approach performs a BFS from the source vertex of q (following the outgoing edges of each vertex), as well as a BFS from the terminal vertex of q (following the incoming edges of each vertex). The two BFSs take turns to traverse the vertices in G, until a common vertex is visited by both BFSs (i.e., when a path from the source vertex to the terminal vertex is found). As shown in Figure 3, BU consistently outperforms Dagger and the BFS approach, and BL's query time is slightly worse than BU's in general. On the other hand, Dagger is only slightly better than the BFS approach on most datasets, and is more than 900 (resp. 700) times slower than the latter on Wiki (resp. Twitter). This shows that Dagger is *not* a favorable approach for handling updates on dynamic graphs, as it incurs significantly higher update overheads than the BFS approach without providing substantially better query performance. (Note that the BFS approach entails zero update costs as it does not maintain any index.)

Finally, Figure 4 shows the average deletion time of each method. BU and BL's performance is generally comparable to Dagger's, except on RG40 and wiki. The slightly inferior performance of BU on deletion is justified by its superior efficiency on insertions and queries.

Experiments on Static Graphs. Our second set of experiments compares BU and BL with three state-of-the-art methods for static graphs, namely, *TF-label (TF)* [8], *hierarchical labeling (HL)* [17], *distribution labeling (DL)* [17]. For completeness, we also include Dagger in the experiments. Figure 5 illustrates the space consumption of each method. Observe that BU and BL generally outperform both TF and DL. To explain, recall that BU, BL, TF, and DL are all instantiations of the TOL framework. As such, their performance are *solely* decided by the vertex orderings that they adopt. The vertex ordering in DL (resp. TF), however, simply ranks vertices based on their degrees (topological ranks). In contrast, both BU and BL rank vertices based on advanced score functions that take into account the characteristics of the input graphs. As such, the vertex orderings employed by BU and BL are superior to those by TF and DL, and hence, lead to smaller index sizes. In particular, on RG10, the space overhead of BU is 5 times smaller than that of DL. Meanwhile, the space cost of HL is always higher than that of DL, which is consistent with the experimental results in [17].

Figure 6 illustrates the preprocessing time of each method. The relative performance of BU, BL, TF, HL, and DL are similar to the case of Figure 5, since a smaller index size indicates fewer labels in the label sets, and hence, the construction cost for the label sets is generally smaller. We omit HL and DL on RG20 and RG40, since their memory consumptions on those graphs exceed 48GB. On RG10, the preprocessing costs of HL, DL, and TF are at least an order of magnitude higher than that of BU, which indicates that the former are more sensitive to the average degree of the input graph. Figure 7 plots each algorithm's total query time for 10^6 random queries. Again, BU and BL consistently outperform TF and DL, due to their improved vertex orderings. In particular, on RG10, the query time of BU is 4 (resp. 7) times less than that of TF (resp. DL). Meanwhile, the query cost of HL is comparable to that of DL.

Experiments on Label Reduction. Our last set of experiments evaluates the label reduction approach presented in Section 6. Specifically, we first use DL and TF to construct reachability in-

[1]We have also experimented with alternative query sets that disregard the topological ranks of vertices; the experimental results are qualitatively similar to those reported in this paper, and are included in our online technical report [1].

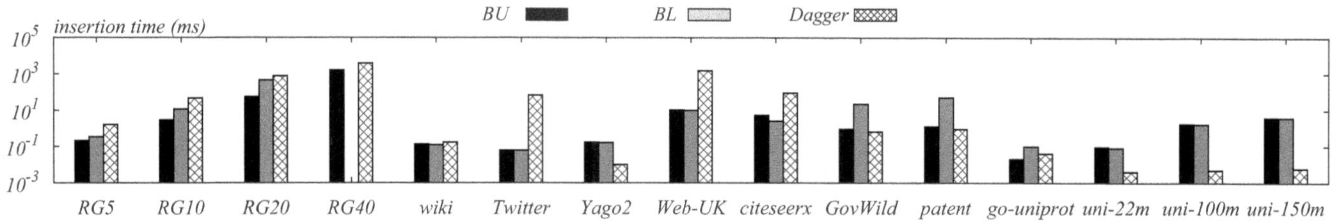

Figure 2: Average insertion time on dynamic graphs.

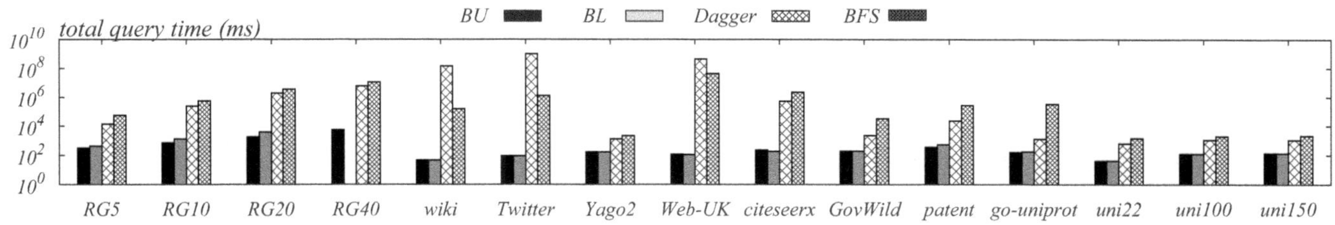

Figure 3: Total query time on dynamic graphs.

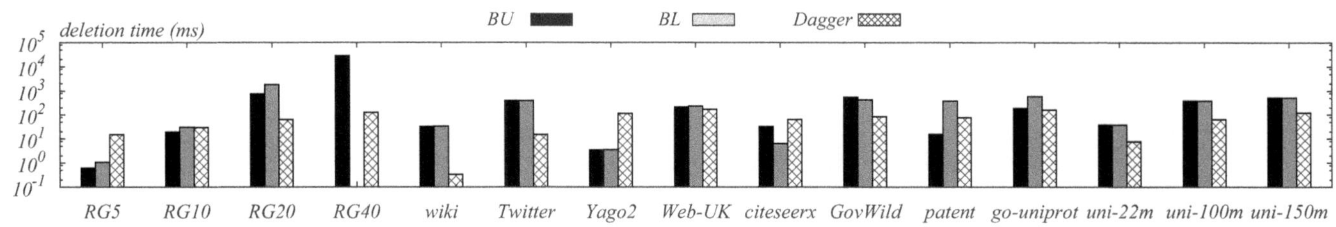

Figure 4: Average deletion time on dynamic graphs.

	DL			TF		
	$\Delta_{\mathcal{L}}$(MB)	$\Delta_{\mathcal{L}}/\lvert\mathcal{L}\rvert$	time (s)	$\Delta_{\mathcal{L}}$(MB)	$\Delta_{\mathcal{L}}/\lvert\mathcal{L}\rvert$	time (s)
RG5	98.91	51.94%	986.3	877.22	82.79%	2.9K
RG10	1.63K	81.61%	98.9K	—	—	—
uni-22m	0.00	0.00%	0.1	0.00	0.01%	0.3
uni-100m	0.71	0.96%	3.6	2.26	3.89%	5.5
uni-150m	3.14	2.46%	201.1	4.77	10.59%	324.2
wiki	0.00	0.00%	0.1	0.01	0.74%	0.3
Twitter	0.00	0.00%	3.7	0.02	8.41%	6.5
Yago2	0.00	0.00%	18.9	0.00	0.00%	18.8
Web-UK	38.69	21.80%	456.3	820.17	47.02%	12.7K
citeseerx	9.14	13.95%	773.2	192.71	96.23%	1.5K
GovWild	20.69	16.24%	844.1	2.40K	94.62%	59.3K
patent	255.09	48.92%	3.0K	3.69K	93.27%	186.5K
go-uniprot	53.24	26.91%	2.9K	104.61	66.38%	5.4K

Table 4: Performance of label reduction ($K = 10^3$).

dices $\mathcal{L}$ on each graph, and then apply our label reduction algorithm on $\mathcal{L}$ to obtain an improved index $\mathcal{L}^*$. Then, we measure the difference $\Delta_{\mathcal{L}}$ between the sizes of $\mathcal{L}^*$ and $\mathcal{L}$, and we divide $\Delta_{\mathcal{L}}$ by the size of $\mathcal{L}$ to derive the ratio of space reduction. Observe that the ratio of space reduction is up to 81.61% and 96.23% for DL and TF, respectively. This demonstrates the effectiveness of our label reduction approach. Nevertheless, the label reduction process incurs significant computation overheads on some of the graphs (e.g., patent). This indicates that one should not overly rely on the label reduction approach to improve the performance of a TOL index, but should adopt a good initial vertex order (e.g., the ones adopted by BU and BL). Note that no result is presented for TF on RG10, since the label reduction process takes excessive time on the graph. In addition, we omit RG20 and RG40 from the experiments, since both DL and TF incur prohibitive memory consumption on those two datasets.

9. CONCLUSIONS

This paper presents a novel study on reachability queries on *large dynamic graphs*. We propose general and efficient algorithms for processing vertex insertions and deletions on reachability indices, and we show that our algorithms can also be used to improve the performance of existing techniques for static graphs. In addition, we devise a new algorithm for constructing an efficient reachability index on an input graph from scratch. We evaluate our solution on a large set of real and synthetic graphs, and we demonstrate that our solution not only supports efficient updates on large dynamic graphs, but also provides even better query performance than the state-of-the-art techniques for *static* graphs. To our knowledge, we are the first in the literature to present a reachability index that can efficiently handle updates while offering superior query performance. For future work, we plan to investigate how our solutions can be extended to massive graphs that do not fit in main memory.

10. ACKNOWLEDGMENTS

This work was supported by the Nanyang Technological University under SUG Grant M4080094.020, by the Microsoft Research Asia under a gift grant, and by the Ministry of Education (Singapore) under AcRF Tier-2 Grant ARC19/14.

11. REFERENCES

[1] https://sites.google.com/site/totalorderlabelling.

[2] I. Abraham, D. Delling, A. V. Goldberg, and R. F. F. Werneck. Hierarchical hub labelings for shortest paths. In *ESA*, pages 24–35, 2012.

[3] R. Agrawal, A. Borgida, and H. V. Jagadish. Efficient management of transitive relationships in large data and knowledge bases. In *SIGMOD*, pages 253–262, 1989.

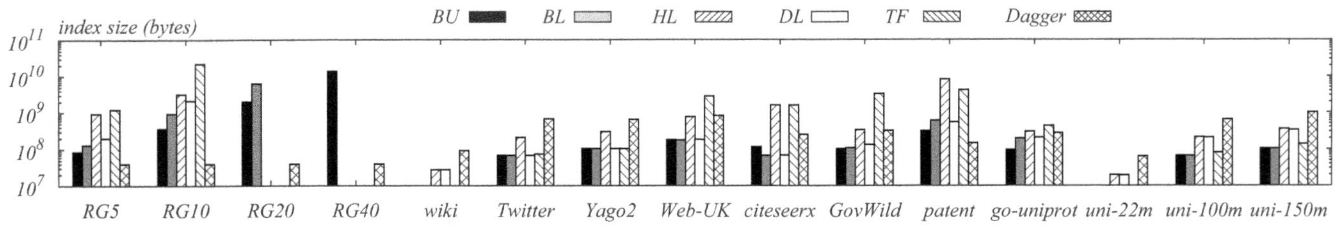

Figure 5: Index sizes on static graphs.

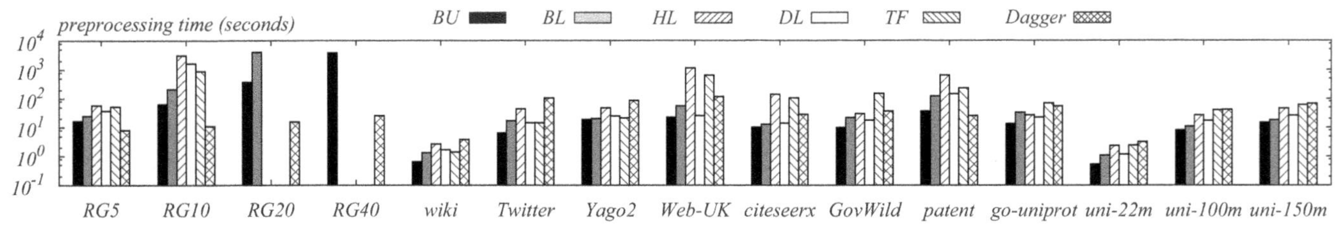

Figure 6: Preprocessing time on static graphs.

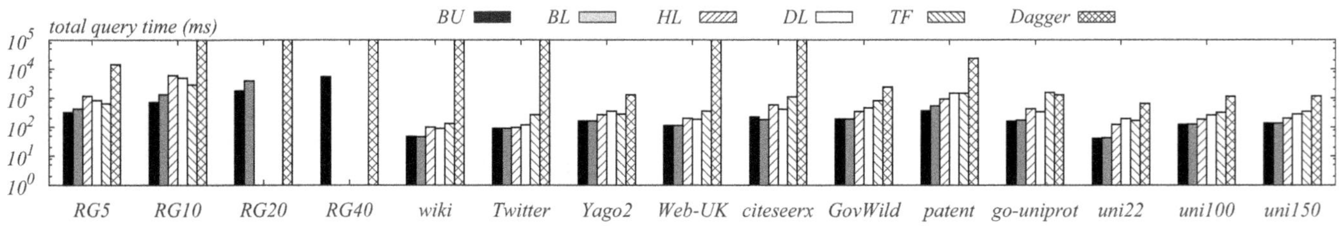

Figure 7: Total query time on static graphs.

[4] R. Bramandia, B. Choi, and W. K. Ng. Incremental maintenance of 2-hop labeling of large graphs. *IEEE Trans. Knowl. Data Eng.*, 22(5):682–698, 2010.

[5] J. Cai and C. K. Poon. Path-hop: efficiently indexing large graphs for reachability queries. In *CIKM*, pages 119–128, 2010.

[6] L. Chen, A. Gupta, and M. E. Kurul. Stack-based algorithms for pattern matching on dags. In *VLDB*, pages 493–504, 2005.

[7] Y. Chen and Y. Chen. An efficient algorithm for answering graph reachability queries. In *ICDE*, pages 893–902, 2008.

[8] J. Cheng, S. Huang, H. Wu, and A. W.-C. Fu. Tf-label: a topological-folding labeling scheme for reachability querying in a large graph. In *SIGMOD*, pages 193–204, 2013.

[9] J. Cheng, Z. Shang, H. Cheng, H. Wang, and J. X. Yu. K-reach: Who is in your small world. *PVLDB*, 5(11):1292–1303, 2012.

[10] J. Cheng, J. X. Yu, X. Lin, H. Wang, and P. S. Yu. Fast computing reachability labelings for large graphs with high compression rate. In *EDBT*, pages 193–204, 2008.

[11] E. Cohen, E. Halperin, H. Kaplan, and U. Zwick. Reachability and distance queries via 2-hop labels. In *SODA*, pages 937–946, 2002.

[12] C. Demetrescu and G. F. Italiano. Fully dynamic all pairs shortest paths with real edge weights. *J. Comput. Syst. Sci.*, 72(5):813–837, 2006.

[13] M. R. Henzinger and V. King. Fully dynamic biconnectivity and transitive closure. In *FOCS*, pages 664–672, 1995.

[14] H. V. Jagadish. A compression technique to materialize transitive closure. *ACM Trans. Database Syst.*, 15(4):558–598, 1990.

[15] R. Jin, N. Ruan, S. Dey, and J. X. Yu. Scarab: scaling reachability computation on large graphs. In *SIGMOD*, pages 169–180, 2012.

[16] R. Jin, N. Ruan, Y. Xiang, and H. Wang. Path-tree: An efficient reachability indexing scheme for large directed graphs. *ACM Trans. Database Syst.*, 36(1):7, 2011.

[17] R. Jin and G. Wang. Simple, fast, and scalable reachability oracle. *PVLDB*, 6(14):1978–1989, 2013.

[18] R. Jin, Y. Xiang, N. Ruan, and D. Fuhry. 3-hop: a high-compression indexing scheme for reachability query. In *SIGMOD*, pages 813–826, 2009.

[19] R. Jin, Y. Xiang, N. Ruan, and H. Wang. Efficiently answering reachability queries on very large directed graphs. In *SIGMOD*, pages 595–608, 2008.

[20] I. Krommidas and C. D. Zaroliagis. An experimental study of algorithms for fully dynamic transitive closure. *ACM Journal of Experimental Algorithmics*, 12, 2008.

[21] L. Roditty. Decremental maintenance of strongly connected components. In *SODA*, pages 1143–1150, 2013.

[22] L. Roditty and U. Zwick. A fully dynamic reachability algorithm for directed graphs with an almost linear update time. In *STOC*, pages 184–191, 2004.

[23] R. Schenkel, A. Theobald, and G. Weikum. Hopi: An efficient connection index for complex xml document collections. In *EDBT*, pages 237–255, 2004.

[24] R. Schenkel, A. Theobald, and G. Weikum. Efficient creation and incremental maintenance of the hopi index for complex xml document collections. In *ICDE*, pages 360–371, 2005.

[25] S. Seufert, A. Anand, S. J. Bedathur, and G. Weikum. Ferrari: Flexible and efficient reachability range assignment for graph indexing. In *ICDE*, pages 1009–1020, 2013.

[26] R. E. Tarjan. Depth-first search and linear graph algorithms. *SIAM J. Comput.*, 1(2):146–160, 1972.

[27] S. Trißl and U. Leser. Fast and practical indexing and querying of very large graphs. In *SIGMOD*, pages 845–856, 2007.

[28] S. J. van Schaik and O. de Moor. A memory efficient reachability data structure through bit vector compression. In *SIGMOD*, pages 913–924, 2011.

[29] H. Wang, H. He, J. Yang, P. S. Yu, and J. X. Yu. Dual labeling: Answering graph reachability queries in constant time. In *ICDE*, page 75, 2006.

[30] Y. Yano, T. Akiba, Y. Iwata, and Y. Yoshida. Fast and scalable reachability queries on graphs by pruned labeling with landmarks and paths. In *CIKM*, pages 1601–1606, 2013.

[31] H. Yildirim, V. Chaoji, and M. J. Zaki. Grail: Scalable reachability index for large graphs. *PVLDB*, 3(1):276–284, 2010.

[32] H. Yildirim, V. Chaoji, and M. J. Zaki. Dagger: A scalable index for reachability queries in large dynamic graphs. *CoRR*, abs/1301.0977, 2013.

EAGr: Supporting Continuous Ego-centric Aggregate Queries over Large Dynamic Graphs

Jayanta Mondal Amol Deshpande

Dept. of Computer Science, University of Maryland, College Park, MD 20742
{jayanta, amol}@cs.umd.edu

ABSTRACT

In this paper, we present EAGr, a system for supporting large numbers of continuous neighborhood-based ("ego-centric") aggregate queries over large, highly dynamic, rapidly evolving graphs. Examples of such queries include computation of *personalized, tailored trends* in social networks, *anomaly or event detection* in communication or financial transaction networks, *local search* and *alerts* in spatio-temporal networks, to name a few. Key challenges in supporting such continuous queries include very high update rates typically seen in these situations, large numbers of queries that need to be executed simultaneously, and stringent low latency requirements. We propose a flexible, general, extensible in-memory framework for executing different types of ego-centric aggregate queries over large dynamic graphs with low latencies. Our framework is built around the notion of an *aggregation overlay graph*, a pre-compiled data structure that encodes the computations to be performed when an update or a query is received. The overlay graph enables *sharing of partial aggregates* across different ego-centric queries (corresponding to different nodes in the graph), and also allows *partial pre-computation* of the aggregates to minimize the query latencies. We present several highly scalable techniques for constructing an overlay graph given an aggregation function, and also design incremental algorithms for handling changes to the structure of the underlying graph itself. We also present an optimal, polynomial-time algorithm for making the pre-computation decisions given an overlay graph. Although our approach is naturally parallelizable, we focus on a single-machine deployment and show that our techniques can easily handle graphs of size up to 320 million nodes and edges, and achieve update and query throughputs of over 500,000/s using a single, powerful machine.

Categories and Subject Descriptors

H.2.4 [**Database Management**]: Systems—*Query Processing*

Keywords

Graph databases; Continuous queries; Aggregates; Data streams; Ego-centric analysis; Graph compression; Social networks

SIGMOD '14, June 22-27, 2014, Snowbird, Utah, USA.

1. INTRODUCTION

Graph-structured data arises naturally in a variety of application domains, including social networks, communication networks, phone call networks, email networks, financial transaction networks, to name a few. There is an increasing need to support graph structure-aware queries and analysis tasks over such graphs, leading to much work in this area over the last few years. In many of these domains, the datasets are not only large in terms of the sheer number of nodes and edges in the graph, but they also produce a large amount of data at a very high rate, generating a *data stream* that must be ingested and queried in real time. The graph data can be seen as comprising of two major components: (a) a graph (*network*) component that captures the underlying interconnection structure among the nodes in the graph, and (b) *content* data associated with the nodes and the edges. The graph data stream contains updates to both these components. The structure of the graph may itself change rapidly in many cases, especially when things like webpages, user tags (e.g., Twitter *hashtags*), financial trades, etc., are treated as nodes of the graph. However, most of the data stream consists of updates to the content data associated with the nodes and edges, e.g., status updates or photos uploaded by social network users, phone calls or messages among users, transactions in a financial network, etc. Real-time, continuous query processing over such dynamic graph-structured data has become a critical need in the recent years.

In this paper, we focus on a prevalent class of queries over dynamic graphs, called *neighborhood-based or ego-centric aggregate queries*. In an ego-centric aggregate query, the querier (called *user* henceforth) corresponds to a node in the graph, and is interested in an aggregate over the current state or the recent history of a local neighborhood of the node in the graph; such local neighborhoods are often called *ego networks* of the nodes [25, 15]. An example of such a query is *ego-centric trend analysis in social networks* where the goal is to find, for each user, the trends (e.g., popular topics of discussion, news items) in his or her local neighborhood [1, 17]. The neighborhood here could be 1-hop neighborhood, or could extend beyond that. Similarly, in a phone-call network or an analogous communication network, we may be interested in identifying interesting events or anomalies (e.g., higher than normal communication activity among a group of nodes); that often boils down to continuously computing ego-centric aggregates over recent activity in a large number of local neighborhoods simultaneously (with an anomaly defined by a predicate on the aggregate) [2, 29]. In spatio-temporal social networks, users are often interested in events happening in their social networks, but also physically close to them.

We make a distinction between between *continuous* queries and what we call *quasi-continuous* queries (somewhat surprisingly, we have not seen this distinction made in prior work). In the latter case, the query result only needs to produced or updated when the user requests it (we call such user requests *reads*); whereas in the former case, the query result must be kept up-to-date whenever the inputs change. The first query above (trend analysis) is an example of a quasi-continuous query since there is no need to produce the result unless the user asks for it (for reducing latency, full or partial pre-computation may be performed). However, anomaly detection queries must be executed continuously as new updates arrive.

The high update rates typically seen in these application domains make it a challenge to execute a large number of such queries with sufficiently low latencies. A naive *on-demand* approach, where the neighborhood is traversed in response to a read, is unlikely to scale to the large graph sizes, and further, would have unacceptably high query latencies. On the other hand, a *pre-computation-based approach*, where the required query answers are always pre-computed and kept up-to-date will likely lead to much wasted computation effort for most queries. Furthermore, both these approaches ignore many potential optimization opportunities, in particular, the possibility of *sharing* the aggregate computation across different queries (corresponding to different ego networks).

In this paper, we propose an approach that maintains a special directed graph (called an *aggregation overlay graph* or simply an *overlay*) that is constructed given an ego-centric aggregate query and a subset of nodes in the data graph for which it needs to be evaluated continuously (or quasi-continuously). The overlay graph exposes sharing opportunities by explicitly utilizing *partial aggregation* nodes, whose outputs can be shared across queries. The nodes in the overlay are labeled with *dataflow decisions* that encode whether data should be *pushed* to that node in response to an update, or it should be *pulled* when a query result needs to be computed. During execution, the overlay simply reacts to the events (i.e., reads and writes) based on the encoded decisions, and is thus able to avoid unnecessary computation, leading to very high throughputs across a spectrum of workloads. Constructing the optimal overlay graph is NP-Hard for arbitrary graph topologies. Further, given the large network sizes that are typically seen in practice, it is infeasible to use some of the natural heuristics for solving this problem. We present a series of highly efficient overlay construction algorithms and show how they can be scaled to very large graphs. Surprisingly, the problem of making the dataflow decisions for a given overlay is solvable in polynomial time, and we present a *max-flow*-based algorithm for that purpose. Our framework can support different neighborhood functions (i.e., 1-hop, 2-hop neighborhoods), and also allows filtering neighborhoods (i.e., only aggregating over subsets of neighborhoods). The framework also supports a variety of aggregation functions (e.g., *sum, count, min, max, top-k*, etc.), exposes an aggregation API for specifying and executing arbitrary user-defined aggregates. We conduct a comprehensive experimental evaluation over a collection of real-world networks, our results show that overlay-based execution of aggregation queries saves redundant computation and significantly boosts the end-to-end throughput of the system.

Outline: We begin with a brief overview of the problem by discussing the data and the query model (Section 2). Then we present the details of our proposed aggregation framework. Next we analyze the optimization problem of constructing an *overlay graph* (Section 3), and propose several scalable heuristics. Following that, we discuss how we make the dataflow (push/pull) decisions to minimize data movement in the overlay (Section 4). Then we describe our experimental setup and present a comprehensive experimental evaluation (Section 5), and discuss some of the most related work (Section 6).

Notation	Description
$\mathcal{G}(V, E)$	Underlying data graph
$\mathcal{N}()$	Neighborhood selection function
$\mathcal{F}()$	Aggregate function
write on v	An update to node v's content
read on v	A read to query result at v, i.e., $\mathcal{F}(\mathcal{N}(v))$
$A_{\mathcal{G}}(V', E')$	Bipartite directed writer/reader graph: for each node $v \in \mathcal{G}(V, E)$, it contains two nodes v_w (writer) and v_r (reader), with edges going from writers to readers
$O_{\mathcal{G}}(V'', E'')$	Overlay Graph
$\mathcal{I}(ovl)$	Set of writers aggregated by overlay node ovl
$w(v)$	write frequency of node v
$r(v)$	read (query) frequency of node v
$f_h(v)$	push frequency of node v in an overlay
$f_l(v)$	pull frequency of node v in an overlay

Table 1: Notation

2. OVERVIEW

We start with describing the underlying data and query model, followed by an overview of our proposed aggregation framework.

2.1 Data and Query Model

Data Model: Let $\mathcal{G}(V, E)$ denote the underlying connection graph, with V and E denoting the sets of nodes and edges respectively. In general, $\mathcal{G}$ is a heterogeneous, multi-relational graph that may contain many different types of nodes and may contain both directed and undirected edges. For example, for a social network, we may have nodes representing the users of the network as well as nodes representing communities, groups, user tags, webpages, and so on. Similarly, E may include not only symmetric *friendship* (or analogous) edges but also asymmetric *follows* edges, *membership* edges, and other types of semi-permanent edges that are usually in existence from the time they are formed till the time they are deleted (or till the current time). The *content* associated with the nodes and edges is captured through a set of *attribute-value* pairs.

We capture the structure updates (i.e., node or edge additions or deletions) as a time-stamped data stream $S_{\mathcal{G}}$ (called *structure data stream*). For simplicity, we assume that all the content is associated with nodes, and for a node v, we capture the content updates associated with it as a time-stamped data stream, S_v (called *content data streams*). We further assume that all the content streams are homogeneous, i.e., all updates are of the same type or refer to the same attribute. It is straightforward to relax both these assumptions. A content update on node v is also called a *write on v*.

Unlike most prior work in data streams or publish-subscriber networks where the producers of data (i.e., writers) and the consumers of data (i.e., readers) are distinct from each other, in our case, a node acts both as a writer and a reader. Hence, for clarity of description, when referring to a node v in the rest of the paper, we often denote its role in the context using a subscript – v_w (similarly, v_r) denoting the node as a writer (reader).

Query Model: An ego-centric aggregate query is specified by four parameters: $\langle \mathcal{F}, w, \mathcal{N}, pred \rangle$, where $\mathcal{F}$ denotes the aggregate function to be computed, w denotes a sliding window over the content data streams, $\mathcal{N}$ denotes the neighborhood selection function (i.e., $\mathcal{N}(v)$ forms the input list to be aggregated for each v), and *pred* selects a subset of V for which the aggregate must be computed (i.e., $\mathcal{F}$ would be computed for all nodes for which $pred(v)$ is *true*). Following the data streams literature, w may be a time-based sliding window or a tuple-based sliding window; in the former case, we are given a time interval T, and the updates that arrive within the last T time are of interest, whereas in the latter case, we are given a number c, and the last c updates are of interest. The query may be specified to be a *continuous* query or a *quasi-continuous* query. For a continuous query, the query results must be kept up-to-date as

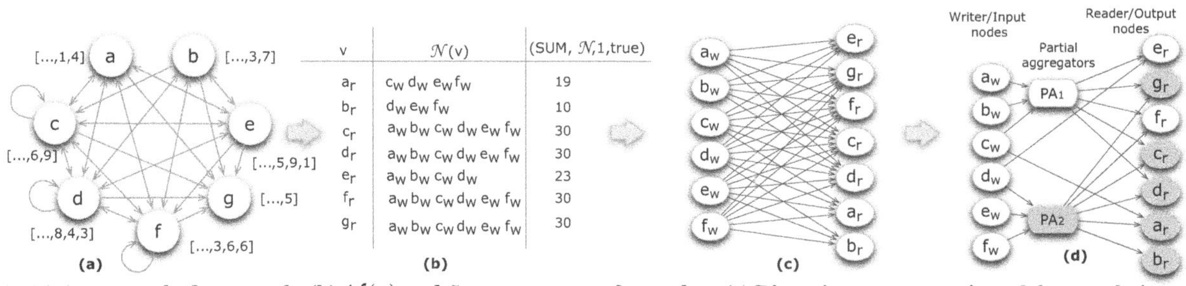

Figure 1: (a) An example data graph, (b) $\mathcal{N}(v)$ and SUM aggregates for each v, (c) Bipartite representation of the graph, i.e, $A_{\mathcal{G}}$ (note, g does not form input to any reader), (d) An overlay graph (shaded nodes indicate *pull* decisions, unshaded ones indicate *push*).

new updates arrive, whereas for a quasi-continuous query, the query result for a node v is only needed when a user requests it (we call this a *read on* v); in the latter case, pre-computation may be done to reduce not only user latencies but also total computational effort.

Since our approach is based on pre-computation and maintenance of partial aggregates, we assume that the aggregate function (and $\mathcal{N}$) are pre-specified. In some cases, it is possible to share the intermediate data structures and partial aggregates for simultaneous evaluation of different aggregates; we do not consider that option further in this paper. Our system supports a set of built-in aggregate functions like *sum, max, min, top-k, etc.*, and we allow the user to define arbitrary aggregation functions (Section 2.2.3). Our system treats $\mathcal{F}$ as a blackbox, but the user may optionally specify whether the aggregation function is *duplicate-insensitive* or supports efficient *subtraction* (Section 3.1), and that information will be used to further optimize the computation.

Example: Figure 1 shows an example instance of this problem. Figure 1(a) depicts the data graph. $\mathcal{N}(x)$ is defined to be $\{y|y \rightarrow x\}$ (note that, all edges are not bidirectional). The numbers in the square brackets denote individual content streams. For example, there have been two *recent writes* on node a with values 1 and 4. The query is $\langle \text{SUM}, c = 1, \mathcal{N}, v \in V\rangle$, which states that for each node $v \in V$, the most recent values written by nodes in $\mathcal{N}(v)$ need to be aggregated using SUM. Figure 1(b) enumerates $\mathcal{N}(v)$ for each v. The last column of Figure 1(b) shows the results of the *read* queries on each node. For example, here $\mathcal{N}(a)$ evaluates to $\{c, d, e, f\}$, and a *read* query on a returns: $(9) + (3) + (1) + (6) = 19$. Figure 1(c) represents the corresponding directed bipartite graph $A_{\mathcal{G}}$ where nodes are duplicated and divided based on their roles; a node might or might not play both the roles.

Scope of the Approach: Here, we briefly summarize the key assumptions that we make and the limitations of our approach. Our compilation-based approach requires upfront knowledge of the query to be executed, including the specific aggregate function, the neighborhood to aggregate over, and the sliding window parameters (the last of which only impacts dataflow decisions). Further, given the high overlay construction cost, the query needs to be evaluated continuously for a period of time to justify the cost. Thus our approach would not be suitable for ad hoc ego-centric aggregate queries over graphs. We also note that, although our framework can handle arbitrary aggregation functions, the benefits of our approach, especially of sharing partial aggregates, are higher for *distributive* and *algebraic* aggregates than for *holistic* aggregates like *median, mode*, or *quantile* (however, approximate versions of holistic aggregates can still benefit from our optimizations). Our approach to making dataflow decisions based on expected read/write frequencies also requires the ability to estimate or predict those frequencies. As with most workload-aware approaches, our approach will likely not work well in face of highly unpredictable and volatile workloads. Finally, we also assume that the data graph itself changes relatively slowly; although we have developed incremental techniques to modify the overlay in such cases, our approach is not intended for scenarios where the structure of the data graph changes rapidly.

2.2 Proposed Aggregation Framework

In this section, we describe our proposed framework to support different types of ego-centric aggregate queries. We begin with explaining the notion of an *aggregation overlay graph* and key rationale behind it. We then discuss the execution model and some of the key implementation issues.

2.2.1 Aggregation Overlay Graph

Aggregation overlay graph is a pre-compiled data structure built for a given ego-centric aggregate query, that enables sharing of partial aggregates, selective pre-computation, partial pre-computation, and low-overhead query execution. Given a data graph $\mathcal{G}(V, E)$ and a query $\langle \mathcal{F}, w, \mathcal{N}, pred\rangle$, we denote an aggregation overlay graph for them by $O_{\mathcal{G}}(V'', E'')$.

There are three types of nodes in an overlay graph: (1) the *writer* nodes, denoted by subscript $\_w$, one for each node in the underlying graph that is *generating* data, (2) the *reader* nodes, denoted by subscript $\_r$, one for each node in V that satisfies *pred*, and (3) the *partial aggregation* nodes (also called *intermediate* nodes). We use the term *aggregation* node to refer to either a reader node or a partial aggregation node, since both of those may perform aggregation. In Figure 1(d), PA_1 and PA_2 are two partial aggregation nodes that are introduced after analyzing the structure of the network and the query. PA_1 corresponds to a partial aggregator that aggregates the inputs a_w, b_w, c_w, and serves e_r, g_r, f_r, c_r, d_r.

For correctness, there can only be one (directed) path from a writer to a reader in an overlay graph (to avoid duplicate contributions from that writer to the aggregate computed for that reader). However, there are two exceptions to this. First, this is not an issue with the so-called *duplicate-insensitive* aggregates like MAX, MIN, UNIQUE. We exploit this by constructing overlays that allow such multiple paths for those aggregates, if it leads to smaller overlays (in most cases, we observed that to be the case).

Second, we allow an overlay to contain what we call *negative* edges to "subtract" such duplicate contributions. A negative edge from a node u to an aggregation node v indicates that the input from u should be "subtracted" (i.e., its contribution removed) from the aggregate result computed by v. Such edges should only be used when the "subtraction" operation is efficiently computable. Although negative edges may appear to lead to wasted work, in practice, adding negative edges (where permissible) can actually lead to significant improvements in the total throughput. We discuss this issue further in Section 3.1.

The overlay graph also encodes pre-computation decisions (also called *dataflow decisions*). Each node in the overlay graph is annotated either *pull* or *push*. If a node is annotated *push*, the partial aggregate that it computes is always kept up-to-date as new updates arrive. The writer nodes are always annotated *push*. For an aggregation node to be annotated *push*, all its input nodes must also be annotated *push*. Analogously, if a node is annotated *pull*, all the nodes downstream of it must also be annotated *pull*. In Figure 1(d), the push and pull decisions are shown with unshaded and shaded nodes respectively. This overlay graph fully pre-computes the query results for nodes e_r and f_r (thus leading to low latencies for those queries); on the other hand, a read on node g_r will incur a high latency since the computation will be done fully on demand.

Note that, we require that the decisions be made for each node in the overlay graph, rather than for each edge. Thus, all the inputs to an aggregation node are either pushed to it, or all the inputs are pulled by it. This simplifies the bookkeeping significantly, without limiting the choices of partial pre-computation. If we desire to pre-compute a partial aggregate over a subset of a node's inputs, a separate partial aggregation node can be created instead. We discuss more details about this in Section 4.

Finally, we note that the aggregation overlay graph can be seen as a pre-compiled query plan where no unnecessary computation or reasoning is performed when an update arrives or a read query is posed. This enables us to handle much higher data rates than would be possible otherwise. We discuss the resulting execution model and related architectural decisions in the following sections.

2.2.2 Execution Model

We begin with describing how new updates and queries are processed using the overlay graph, and briefly discuss some of the implementation issues surrounding multi-threaded execution.

Execution Flow: We describe the basic execution flow in terms of the *partial aggregate objects (PAOs)* that are maintained at various nodes in the overlay graph. A PAO corresponds to a partial aggregate that has been computed after aggregating over a subset of the inputs. The PAO corresponding to a node labeled *push* is always kept up-to-date as new updates arrive in any of the streams it is defined over, or if the sliding windows shift and values drop out of the window. Specifically, the updates originate at the writer nodes, and propagate through the overlay graph as far as indicated by the dataflow decisions on the nodes. The nodes labeled *push* maintain partial state and perform incremental computation to keep their corresponding PAOs up-to-date. On the other hand, no partial state is maintained at the nodes labeled *pull*. When an overlay node u makes a *read* request from another node v upstream of it, if v is labeled *push*, the partial aggregate is returned immediately without delay. On the other hand, if v is labeled *pull*, it issues *read* requests on all its upstream overlay nodes, merges all the PAOs it receives, and returns the result PAO to the requesting node.

Single-threaded vs Multi-threaded Execution: A naive implementation of the above execution model is using a single thread, that processes the *writes* and *reads* in the order in which they are received, finishing each one fully (i.e., pushing the writes as far as required, and computing the results for *reads*) before handling the next one. Although it leads to well-defined and consistent execution, this approach cannot exploit parallelism in the system, and is unlikely to scale. On the other hand, a multi-threaded version requires careful implementation to guarantee correctness. First, the computations on the overlay graph must be made thread-safe to avoid potential state corruption due to race conditions. We can do this either by using thread-safe data structures to store the PAOs or through explicit synchronization. We use the latter approach in our implementation of the aggregates; however, user-defined aggregates may choose either of the two options. A more subtle issue is that of consistency. Consider a read on node a_r in Figure 1(d). It is possible that the result generated contains a more recent update on node f_w, but does not see a relatively older update on node c_w (as f_w is read later than c_w). We ignore the potential for such inconsistencies in this work and plan to address this in future.

We use two thread pools, one for servicing the read requests and one for servicing the write requests. The relative sizes of the two thread pools can be set based on the expected number of reads vs writes; assigning more threads to processing reads may reduce latency, but increases the possibility of stale results.

Further, there are two ways to process a read or a write using multiple threads: (1) a *uni-thread* model, where a thread that picks up a request (read or write) executes it fully before processing a new request, or (2) a *queueing* model, where the tasks are subdivided into micro-tasks at the granularity of the overlay nodes, each of which is responsible for a single PAO operation at an overlay node (update for writes, and computation for reads). Queueing model is likely to be more scalable and result in better throughputs, but the latencies for reads are substantially higher. We follow a hybrid approach, and use uni-thread model for reads and queueing for writes.

2.2.3 User-defined Aggregate API

One of the key features of our system is the ability for the users to define their own aggregate functions. We build upon the standard API for user-defined aggregates for this purpose [19, 36, 24], and briefly describe it here for completeness. The user must implement the following functions.

- INITIALIZE(*PAO*): Initialize the requisite data structures to maintain the partial aggregate state (i.e., PAOs).
- UPDATE(*PAO, PAO_old, PAO_new*): This is the key function that updates the partial aggregate at an overlay node (PAO) given that one of its inputs was updated from *PAO_old* to *PAO_new*.
- FINALIZE(*PAO*): Compute the final answer from the PAO.

Note that, we require the ability to *merge* two PAOs in order to fully exploit the potential for sharing through overlay graphs – this functionality is typically optional in user-defined aggregate APIs.

3. CONSTRUCTING THE OVERLAY

Our overall optimization goal is to construct an overlay graph annotated with pre-computation (dataflow) decisions that maximize the overall throughput, given a data graph and an ego-centric aggregate query. To make the dataflow decisions optimally, we also need information about the expected read (query) and write (update) frequencies for the nodes in the graph. However, these two sets of inputs have inherently different dynamics – the data graph is expected to change relatively slowly, whereas the read/write frequencies are expected to show high variability over time. Hence, we decouple the overall problem into two phases: (1) we construct a compact overlay that maximizes the sharing opportunities given a data graph and a query, and (2) then make the dataflow decisions for the overlay nodes (as we discuss in the next section, we allow the second phase to make restricted local modifications to the overlay). The overlay construction is a computationally expensive process, and we expect that an overlay, once constructed, will be used for a long period of time (with incremental local changes to handle new nodes or edges). On the other hand, we envision re-evaluating the dataflow decisions on a more frequent basis by continuously monitoring the read/write frequencies to identify significant variations.

In this section, we focus on the overlay construction problem. We begin with defining the optimization goal, and present several

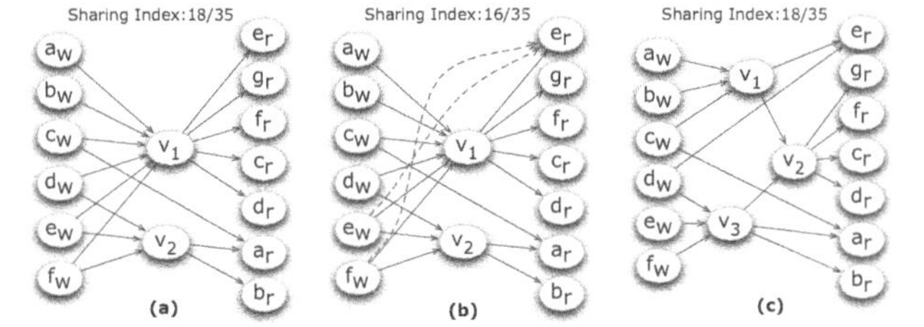

Figure 2: (a) A duplicate-insensitive overlay; (b) An overlay with two negative edges; (c) A multi-level overlay.

scalable algorithms to construct an overlay. We then briefly discuss our approach to handling structural changes to the data graph.

3.1 Preliminaries

As a first step, we convert the given data graph $\mathcal{G}(V, E)$ into an equivalent bipartite graph $A_{\mathcal{G}}(V', E')$, by identifying the query nodes, and the input nodes for each of the query nodes, given the user-provided query (as discussed in Section 2.1). We use the total number of edges in the overlay as our optimization metric, the intuition being that, each edge in the overlay corresponds to a distinct data movement and computation. We justify the use of this somewhat abstract metric by noting that the runtime cost of an overlay is highly dependent on the distribution of the read/write frequencies; for the same query and data graph, the optimal overlays could be wildly different for different distributions of read/write frequencies (which are not available at the overlay construction phase). We believe that the use of an abstract metric that rewards sharing is likely to prove more robust in highly dynamic environments. In future work, we plan to further validate our choice by comparing it against other optimization metrics.

More formally, we define the *sharing index* of an overlay to be:

$$1 - \frac{\textit{\# of edges in the overlay}}{\textit{\# of edges in } A_{\mathcal{G}}}$$

Figure 2 shows three overlays for our running example, and their sharing indexes. Figure 2(a) shows an overlay where there are multiple paths between some reader-writer pairs. As we discussed earlier, such an overlay cannot be used for a duplicate-sensitive aggregate function (like SUM, COUNT, etc.), but for duplicate-insensitive aggregate functions like MAX, it typically leads to better sharing index as well as better overall throughput. The second overlay uses *negative edges* to bring down sharing index. This should only be done for aggregate functions where the subtraction operation is incrementally computable (e.g., SUM, or COUNT). Finally, third overlay is an example of a *multi-level* overlay, and has the lowest sharing index for our running example (without use of negative edges or duplicate paths). In most cases, such multi-level overlays exhibit the best sharing index. Note that multi-level overlays can also be duplicate insensitive or contain negative edges.

The problem of maximizing the sharing index is closely related to the *minimum order bi-clique partition* problem [16], where the goal is to cover all the edges in a bipartite graph using fewest edge-disjoint bicliques. In essence, a biclique in the bipartite graph $A_{\mathcal{G}}$ corresponds to a set of readers that all share a common set of writers. Such a biclique can thus be replaced by a partial aggregation node that aggregates the values from the common set of writers, and feeds them to the readers. In Figure 1(d), node PA_1 corresponds to such a biclique (between writers a_w, b_w, c_w and readers c_r, d_r, e_r, f_r, g_r). Finding bicliques is known to be NP-Hard. Sharing index (SI) is also closely related to the *compression ratio* (CR) metric used in many of the works in *representational graph compression* [10] ; specifically, $CR = 1/(1 - SI)$. However, given the context of aggregation and the possibility of having *negative* and *duplicate-insensitive* edges in the overlay, we differentiate it from compression ratio. The problem of finding a good overlay is also closely related to the problem of *frequent pattern mining* [20, 18] as we discuss in the next section.

3.2 Overlay Construction Algorithms

In this section, we present our algorithms for constructing different types of overlays as outlined in the previous section. Given the NP-Hardness of the basic problem, and further the requirement to scale the algorithms to graphs containing tens of millions of nodes, we develop a set of efficient heuristics to achieve our goal. Our first set of proposed algorithms (called VNM$_A$, VNM$_N$, and VNM$_D$) builds upon a prior algorithm (called VNM) for bipartite graph compression by Buehrer et al. [10], which itself is a adaptation of the well-known FP-Tree algorithm for frequent pattern mining [20, 18]. In our exploratory evaluation, we found that algorithm to offer the best blend of scalability and adaptability for our purposes. Our second algorithm (called IOB) is an incremental algorithm that builds the overlay one reader at a time.

3.2.1 Background: FP-Tree and VNM Algorithms

We begin with a brief recap of the *FP-Tree* algorithm for frequent pattern mining, considered to be one of the most efficient and scalable algorithms for finding frequent patterns. We briefly outline the algorithm using the terminology of readers and writers rather than transactions and items. First, the writers are sorted in the increasing order by their overall frequency of occurrence in the reader input sets, i.e., their out-degree in $A_{\mathcal{G}}$. In our running example, the sort order (breaking ties arbitrarily) would be $\{d_w, c_w, e_w, f_w, a_w, b_w\}$. Then all the reader input lists are rewritten according to that sort order; e.g., we would write the input list of a_r as $\{d_w, c_w, e_w, f_w\}$. Next, the FP-Tree is built incrementally by adding one reader at a time, starting with an empty tree. For the reader under consideration, the goal is to find its longest prefix that matches with a path from the root in the FP-Tree constructed so far. As an example, Figure 3 shows the FP-Tree built after addition of readers a_r, b_r, and e_r. A node in the FP-Tree is represented by: $x_w\{S(x_w)\}$ where x_w is a writer and $S(x_w)$ is a list of readers that contain x_w in their input lists (called *support set*). Now, for reader c_r, the longest prefix of it that matches a path from root is d_w, c_w, e_w, f_w. That reader would then be added to the tree nodes in that path (i.e., to the support sets along that path). If the reader input list contains any additional writers, then a new branch is created in the tree (for e_r a new branch will be created with nodes $a_w\{e_r\}$ and $b_w\{e_r\}$).

Once the tree is built, in the *mining phase*, the tree is searched to find bicliques. A path P in the tree from the root to the node $x_w\{S(x_w)\}$ corresponds to a biclique between the writers corresponding to the nodes in P and the readers in $S(x_w)$. Since our goal is to maximize the number of edges removed from the overlay graph, we search for the biclique that maximizes:

$$benefit(P) = L(P) * |S(P)| - L(P) - |S(P)|,$$

where $L(P)$ denotes the length of the path P and $S(P)$ denotes the support for the last node in the path. Such a biclique can be found in time linear to the size of the FP-Tree. After finding each such biclique, ideally we should remove the corresponding edges (called the *mined edges*) and reconstruct the FP-Tree to find the next biclique with best benefit. Mining the same FP-Tree would still find bicliques but with lower benefit (since the next biclique we find cannot use any of the edges in the previously-output biclique).

We now briefly describe the VNM algorithm [10], which is a highly scalable adaptation of the basic FP-Tree mining approach

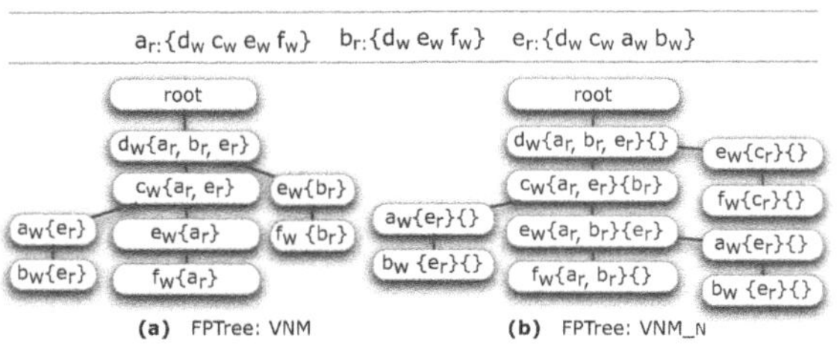

Figure 3: An example of FP-Tree construction for VNM and VNM$_N$: (a) Basic version, (b) FP-Tree with negative edges.

described above; VNM was developed for compressing very large (web-scale) graphs, and in essence, replaces each biclique with a virtual node to reduce the total number of edges. The main optimization of VNM relies on limiting the search space by creating small groups of readers, and looking for bicliques that only involve the readers in one of the groups. This approach is much more scalable than building an FP-Tree on the entire data graph. VNM uses a heuristic based on *shingles* [13, 14] to group the readers. Shingle of a reader is effectively a signature of its input *writers*. If two *readers* have very similar *adjacency lists*, then with high probability, their shingle values will also be the same. In a sense, grouping readers by shingles increases the chance of finding big bicliques (with higher benefit) within the groups. The algorithm starts by computing multiple shingles for each reader, and then doing a lexicographical sort of the readers based on the shingles. The sorted list is then chunked into equal-sized groups of readers, each of which is passed to the FP-Tree algorithm separately. Mining all the reader groups once completes one iteration of the algorithm. The process is then repeated with the modified bipartite graph (where each biclique is replaced with a virtual node) to further compress the graph. Since the virtual nodes are treated as normal nodes in such subsequent iterations, a biclique containing virtual nodes may be replaced with another virtual node, resulting in connections between virtual nodes; in our context, this gives rise to *multi-level overlays* where partial aggregation nodes feed into other partial aggregators.

3.2.2 *VNM$_A$: VNM Adaptive*

Our first adaptation of the basic VNM algorithm is aimed at addressing a major deficiency of that algorithm, namely lack of a systematic way to choose the chunk size. Our initial experiments with VNM suggested that the effect of the chunk size on the final compression achieved is highly non-uniform across various graphs like web graphs and social graphs. We noticed that a bigger chunk size typically finds bigger bicliques, but it can't find all big bicliques, especially when there is big overlap in the reader sets of two potential bicliques. This is because the reader sets of two subsequent mining phases in VNM are mutually exclusive. Second, a bigger chunk size makes it harder to find small bicliques, which is especially a problem with later iterations; since many of the original edges have been deleted in the first few iterations, only small bicliques remain in the graph. On the other hand, using a small chunk size from the beginning ignores large bicliques that can deliver huge savings.

To address this problem, we develop an adaptive variation of VNM that uses different chunk sizes for different iterations. For the first iteration, we use a large chunk size (100 in our experiments) and dynamically reduce it for future iterations. For the ith iteration, let c_i denote the chunk size, and let B_i^s denote the sum total of the *benefits* (defined in Section 3.2.1) for all the bicliques found in that iteration with reader set size $= s$ (note that, $s \leq c_i$). We choose $c_{i+1} \leq c_i$ to be the smallest c such that: $\sum_{s \leq c} B_i^s > 0.9 \sum_{s \leq c_i} B_i^s$. Although our algorithm also requires setting two parameter values, our extensive experimental evaluation on many real-world graphs showed that the algorithm is not sensitive to the initial chunk size to within an order of magnitude, and to the second parameter between 0.8 and 1.

3.2.3 *VNM$_N$: VNM with Negative Edges*

Next, we present our adaptation to VNM that considers adding negative edges to reduce the overlay size. In essence, we look for *quasi-bicliques* that may be a few edges short of being complete bicliques (this problem is also known to be NP-Hard [23]). For scalability, our algorithm employs the same basic structure as the VNM$_A$ algorithm discussed above (with grouping of readers using shingles); however, we modify the FP-Tree construction and mining algorithms to support negative edges.

Recall that a node in an FP-Tree is represented by $x_w\{S(x_w)\}$ where x_w is a writer and $S(x_w)$ contains the readers that contain x_w in their input lists. To accommodate negative edges, we now represent a node by $x_w\{S(x_w)\}\{S'(x_w)\}$, where $S'(x_w)$ contains readers that do not contain x_w in their input list, but may contain the writers corresponding to the nodes below this node in the FP-Tree. Benefit of a path P in the FP-Tree is now given by:

$$benefit(P) = L(P) * |S(P)| - L(P) - |S(P)| - \sum_P |S'(x_w)|,$$

where the last term captures the number of negative edges along P.

In our proposed algorithm, when an FP-Tree is augmented to include a new reader r, we add r along up to k_1 paths in the FP-Tree that maximize the benefit given the FP-Tree constructed so far. More specifically, we exhaustively explore the FP-Tree in a breadth-first manner, and for each node visited, we compute the benefit of adding r along the path. We then choose up to k_1 paths with the highest benefit and add the reader along those paths. As with the original FP-Tree algorithm, additional branches may have to be created for the remaining writer nodes in r. Figure 3(b) shows an example where both b_r and e_r create two paths in the overlay, one of which uses a negative edge.

Although our algorithm finds the best paths to add the reader along, it runs in time linear to the size of the FP-Tree constructed so far. However, since the FP-Tree, in essence, now encodes information about k_1 times as many readers as it did before, the size of the FP-Tree itself is expected to be larger by about the same factor. To improve efficiency, we stop the breadth-first exploration down a path if more than k_2 negative edges are needed to add r along that path (we set $k_2 = 5$ in our experiments). This optimization has little impact on performance since it is unlikely that quasi-bicliques requiring a large number of negative edges will be beneficial.

3.2.4 *VNM$_D$: Duplicate-insensitive VNM*

Next, we discuss our proposed algorithm for finding overlays that exploit the duplicate-insensitive nature of some aggregates and allow for multiple paths between a writer and a reader. There are two natural ways to extend the VNM algorithm for reusing edges in this fashion. First, we can keep the basic structure of the VNM algorithm and modify the FP-Tree algorithm itself to find multiple bicliques in each mining phase, while ignoring the overlap between bicliques. However, by construction, the bicliques mined from a single FP-Tree tend to have very high overlap, and the benefits for additional bicliques found can be very low. It is also not clear how many aggregate nodes to add in a single mining phase; adding all bicliques for which the benefit is non-zero is likely to lead to many partial aggregate nodes, each providing low benefit.

Instead, in our proposed algorithm VNM$_D$, we modify the reader grouping phase itself. In VNM, in each iteration, the readers are grouped into disjoint groups before passing to the FP-Tree construction and mining phase. Instead, we allow the groups of readers to overlap. Specifically, given an overlap percentage p (an algorithm parameter), we allow two consecutive groups of readers to have $p\%$ readers in common. The FP-Tree construction and mining phases themselves are unchanged with the following exceptions. First, instead of representing an FP-Tree node as $x_w\{S(x_w)\}$, we represent it as $x_w\{S^{notmined}(x_w)\}\{S^{mined}(x_w)\}$, where $S^{mined}(x_w)$ contains the readers r such that the edge from x_w to r was present in a previously used biclique. Second, we modify the formula for computing the benefit of a path as follows:

$benefit(P) = L(P) * |S(P)| - L(P) - |S(P)| - \sum_P |S^{mined}(x_w)|$; the last term captures the number of *reused* edges in the biclique.

3.2.5 *IOB: Incremental Overlay Building*

The overlay constructions algorithms that we have developed so far are all based on identifying sharing opportunities by looking for bicliques in $A_\mathcal{G}$. However, to make those algorithms scalable, two heuristics have to be used: one to partition the readers into small groups, and one to mine the bicliques themselves. In essence, both of these focus the search for sharing opportunities to small groups of readers and writers, and never consider the entire $A_\mathcal{G}$ at once. Next, we present an incremental algorithm for building the overlay that starts with an empty overlay, and adds one reader at a time to the overlay. For each reader, we examine the entire overlay constructed till that point which, as our experimental evaluation demonstrates, leads to more compact overlays.

We begin with ordering the readers using the shingle order as before, and add the readers one at a time in that order. In the beginning, the overlay graph simply contains the (singleton) writer nodes. Let $\langle r, \mathcal{N}(r)\rangle$ denote the next reader to be added. Let $\langle ovl_n, \mathcal{I}(ovl_n)\rangle$ denote a node in the overlay constructed so far, where $\mathcal{I}(ovl_n)$ is the set of writers whose partial aggregate ovl_n is computing. For reader r, our goal is to reuse as much of the partial aggregation as possible in the overlay constructed so far. In other words, we would like to find the smallest set of overlay nodes whose aggregates can be used to compute the aggregate for r. This problem is essentially the *minimum exact set cover problem*, which is known to be NP-Complete.

We use a standard greedy heuristic commonly used for solving the set cover problem. We start by finding the overlay node that has maximum overlap with $\mathcal{N}(r)$, and restructure the overlay to make use of that overlap. We keep on repeating the same process until all nodes in $\mathcal{N}(r)$ are covered (since the singleton writer nodes are also considered part of the overlay, we can always cover all the nodes in $\mathcal{N}(r)$). Let $\langle v_1, B\rangle$ denote the overlay node that was found to have the highest overlap with the uncovered part, denoted A, of $\mathcal{N}(r)$. If $B \subseteq A$, then we add an edge from v_1 to r, and repeat the process with $A - B$. Otherwise, we restructure the overlay to add a new node $\langle v_1', A \cap B\rangle$, reroute the appropriate incoming edges (i.e., the incoming edges corresponding to the writers in $A \cap B$) from v_1 to v_1', and add a directed edge from v_1' to v_1. We then also add an edge from v_1' to r. If $A - A \cap B$ is non-empty, then we repeat the process to cover the remaining inputs to r.

As with the VNM-based algorithms, we use multiple iterations to improve the overlay. In each iteration (except the 1st iteration), we revisit the decisions made for each of the partial aggregator nodes, and do local restructuring of the overlay if better decisions are found for any of the partial aggregator nodes (using the same set cover-based algorithm as above).

For efficient execution of the algorithm we maintain both a *reverse index* and a *forward index*. For a writer node w, the reverse index tells us which overlay nodes are aggregating w. For example, a_w's reverse index entry will have both v_1 and v_2. Note that even though there is no direct edge from a_w to v_2, a_w's reverse index entry has v_2 because v_2 is effectively aggregating a_w. This index helps us to find the overlay node that provides maximum cover to a set of input nodes using one single scan of the input list. Similarly, for any node n in the overlay, the forward index tells us the input list of n; e.g., v_2's forward index entry will have v_1 and v_3 in it.

Although the above algorithm could be extended to allow for negative edges and/or duplicate paths, we do not discuss those extensions here. This is because, although IOB finds significantly smaller overlays, the overlays tend to be deep (with many levels) and in our experimental evaluation, the end-to-end throughput for the overlays was lower than for the overlays found with the VNM$_A$ algorithm. Thus, although the IOB algorithm is a better algorithm for finding compact overlays and for compressing bipartite graphs, VNM-based algorithms are better suited for our purpose.

3.3 Handling Dynamic Changes

We adapt the basic ideas underlying the IOB algorithm to incrementally update the overlay in response to structural changes (i.e., addition/deletion of nodes/edges) to the data graph. More details can be found in the extended version of the paper [26].

4. MAKING DATAFLOW DECISIONS

Next, we discuss how to make the dataflow (i.e., precomputation) decisions to maximize the total throughput given an overlay network, and the expected read/write frequencies for the nodes. Surprisingly, the problem can be solved optimally in polynomial time. We begin with the preliminaries related to the cost of a dataflow decisions and then provide the formal problem definition and present the analysis along with the algorithms that we propose.

Preliminaries: For each node $v \in V$ in the data graph, let $r(v)$ denote its read frequency (i.e., the number of times a query is issued at node v), let $w(v)$ denote its write frequency (i.e., the number of times v is updated)[1]. Given these, with each node $u \in V''$ in the overlay graph $O_\mathcal{G}(V'', E'')$, we associate two numbers, $f_l(u)$ and $f_h(u)$, called *pull frequency* and *push frequency*, respectively. $f_h(u)$ captures the number of times data values would be *pushed* to u if all nodes in the overlay are assigned *push* decisions. Similarly, $f_l(u)$ indicates the number of times data values would be *pulled* from u if all nodes in the overlay are assigned *pull* decisions.

The push and pull frequencies are computed as follows. For computing push frequencies, we start by assigning $f_h(a_w) = w(a_w)$ for all writer nodes a_w, and then propagate the push frequencies from left to right (downstream). For an aggregation node or a reader node u, $f_h(u)$ is computed by summing up the push frequencies for all nodes that are immediately upstream of u. Similarly, the pull frequencies are computed by starting with the reader nodes, then recursively computing the pull frequencies for the rest of the nodes. Figure 4(i)-(iii) illustrates this with an example that we also use to show how our algorithm makes the dataflow decisions.

Push and Pull Costs: As discussed before, a *push* decision on a node implies that the aggregate corresponding to that node will be (incrementally) precomputed and will be available for immediate consumption. On the other hand, a *pull* decision on a node implies that the aggregate will be computed on demand when the node is read. To reason about the tradeoff between push and pull, we need to be able to compute the cost of a push or a pull. This cost typically depends on the nature of the aggregate, and the type and the size of the sliding window [6]. We capture these costs as two functions:

[1] See Table 1 for a summary of notation.

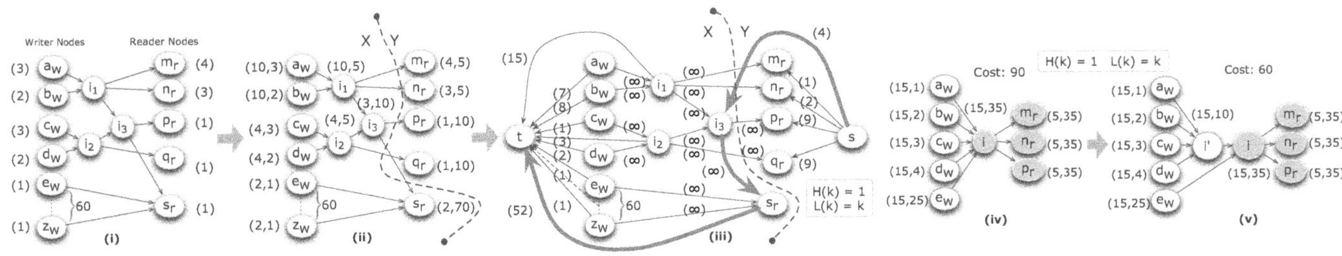

Figure 4: (i) An example overlay annotated with read/write frequencies; (ii) Computing (*pull, push*) frequencies; (iii) Construction of the *s-t* augmented graph (with the annotations denoting the edge weights); (iv-v) Splitting a node based on push-pull frequencies.

$H(k)$ denotes the average cost of one push for an aggregation node with k inputs, and $L(k)$ denotes the average cost of one pull for that node. For example, for a SUM aggregate node, we expect $H(k) \propto 1$ and $L(k) \propto k$, whereas for a MAX aggregate node, if we use a priority queue for handling incremental updates, then $H(k) \propto \log_2(k)$ and $L(k) \propto k$. To handle sliding windows, we implicitly assign w inputs to each writer where w is the average number of values in the sliding window at a writer – thus if the sliding window is of size 10, then $PUSH$ and $PULL$ costs of the writer node will be $H(10)$ and $L(10)$ respectively. We assume $H()$ and $L()$ are either provided, or are computed through a calibration process where we invoke the aggregation function for a range of different inputs and learn the $H()$ and $L()$ functions.

Problem Definition: The dataflow decisions made by a solution induce a *node partition*, denoted $(X, Y), X \cap Y = \phi$, on the overlay graph, where X contains nodes that are designated *push*, Y contains nodes designated *pull* (Figure 4(ii)). Since all nodes upstream of a *push* node must also be designated *push* (and similarly all nodes downstream of a *pull* node must also be *pull*), the partition induced by any consistent set of dataflow decisions must satisfy the constraint that there is no edge from a node in Y to a node in X.

For an overlay node v, let $PUSH(v) = f_h(v) * H(deg(v))$ denote the cost incurred if it is designated a *push* node, let $PULL(v) = f_l(v) * L(deg(v))$ denote the cost if it is a *pull* node. Although the push/pull decisions cannot be made for the nodes independently (because of the aforementioned constraint), $PUSH()$ and $PULL()$ costs can be computed independently; this is because the computations that happen at a node when it is invoked, do not depend on the dataflow decisions at its input or output nodes. Thus, to minimize the total computational cost, our goal reduces to finding an (X, Y) partition of the overlay (with no edges going from Y to X) that minimizes: $\sum_{v\in X} PUSH(v) + \sum_{v\in Y} PULL(v)$.

Query Latencies: Another consideration in making dataflow decision is the impact on query *latencies*. Throughput maximization may lead to higher use of *pull* decisions, especially if reads are less frequent than writes, that may result in high query latencies. As we show in Section 5, because our system is entirely in-memory and does not need to do distributed network traversals, the query latencies are quite low even in the worst-case. In future work, we plan to investigate latency-constrained optimization as well as understand the interplay between throughput and latency better.

Algorithm: We design an algorithm for a slightly more general problem, that we describe first. We are given a directed acyclic graph $H(H_V, H_E)$, where each vertex $v \in H_V$ is associated with a weight $w(v)$; $w(v)$ may be negative. For ease of exposition, we assume that $\forall v, w(v) \neq 0$. We are asked to find a graph partition (X, Y), such that there are no edges from Y to X, that maximizes: $\sum_{v\in X} w(v) - \sum_{v\in Y} w(v)$. Note that, the solution is trivially $(X = H_V, Y = \phi)$ if all node weights are positive. We also note that, the metric has the maximum possible value if all nodes with $w(v) < 0$ are assigned to Y, all nodes with $w(v) > 0$ to X. However, that particular assignment may not guarantee that there are no edges from Y to X.

To reduce our problem to this problem, we set:

$$w(v) = f_l(v)L(deg(v)) - f_h(v)H(deg(v)) = PULL(v) - PUSH(v)$$

That is, the weight of node v is the *"benefit"* of assigning it a *push* decision (which is negative if $PULL(v) < PUSH(v)$). Then:

$$\sum_{v\in X} w(v) - \sum_{v\in Y} w(v)$$
$$= \sum_{v\in X} (PULL(V) - PUSH(v)) - \sum_{v\in Y} (PULL(V) - PUSH(v))$$
$$= \underline{\sum_{v\in H_V} (PULL(v) + PUSH(v))} - 2(\sum_{v\in X} PUSH(v) + \sum_{v\in Y} PULL(v))$$

Since the underlined term is a constant, maximizing this is equivalent to minimizing $\sum_{v\in X} PUSH(v) + \sum_{v\in Y} PULL(v)$.

To solve this more general problem, we construct an edge-weighted graph $H'(H'_V, H'_E)$ from $H(H_V, H_E)$ (in practice, we do not make a copy but rather augment H in place). H'_V contains all the vertices in H_V and in addition, it contains a *source* node s and a *sink* node t (nodes in H' are unweighted). Similarly, H'_E contains all the edges in H_E, with edge weights set to ∞. Further, for each $v \in H_V$ such that $w(v) < 0$, we add a directed edge in H' from s to v with weight $w'(s, v) = -w(v)$. Similarly for $v \in H_V, s.t.\ w(v) > 0$, we add a directed edge in H' from v to t with weight $w'(v, t) = w(v)$ (see Figure 4(iii) for an example).

We note that, this construction may seem highly counter-intuitive, since a lot of nodes in H' have either no outgoing or no incoming edges and there are few, if any, directed paths from s to t. In fact, the best case scenario for the algorithm is that: *there is no directed path from s to t*. This is because, a path from s to t indicates a *conflict* between two or more nodes. The highlighted path form s to t in Figure 4(iii) provides an example. The best decision for node i_3 in isolation would be *pull* ($PULL(i_3) = 6, PUSH(i_3) = 10$), but that for s_r is *push* because of its high in-degree and because $L(k) = k$ ($PULL(s_r) = 2 * 60 = 120, PUSH(s_r) = 70$). However, a *pull* on i_3 would force a *pull* on s_r, hence both of them cannot be assigned the optimal decision in isolation.

After constructing H', we find an s-t directed min-cut in this directed graph, i.e., a set of edges $C \in H'_E$ with minimum total edge-weight, such that removing those edges leaves no directed path from s to t. Let Y denote the set of nodes in H' reachable from s after removing the edges in C (excluding s), let X denote the set of remaining nodes in H' (excluding t).

THEOREM 4.1. *(X, Y) is a node partition of H s.t. there are no edges from Y to X, $\sum_{v\in X} w(v) - \sum_{v\in Y} w(v)$ is maximized.*[2]

We use the Ford-Fulkerson algorithm to construct an s-t max-flow in H', and use it to find the optimal (X, Y) partition of H.

[2]Proofs can be found in the extended version of the paper [26].

Pre-processing: Although the above algorithm runs in polynomial time, it is not feasible to run max-flow computations on the graphs we expect to see in practice. However, a simple pre-processing pruning step, run on H before augmenting it, typically results in massive reduction in the size of the graph on which the max-flow computation must be run.

Consider node a_w in the example graph in Figure 4(ii). The best decision for that node by itself is a *push* decision (since $PUSH(a_w) = 3 < PULL(a_w) = 10$). Since there is no node upstream of a_w (which is a writer node), we can assign this node a *push* decision without affecting decisions at any other node (any node downstream of a_w can still be assigned either decision), and remove it from the graph. Similarly we can assign push decision to node b_w and remove it from H. After that, we can see that node i_1 can also now be assigned a *push* decision (optimal for it in isolation) without affecting any other node. Similarly, we can assign *pull* decisions to nodes m_r, n_r, p_r, q_r and remove them by an analogous reasoning.

We now state the pruning rules, which are applied directly to H (i.e., before constructing the augmented graph): (P1) recursively remove all nodes v such that $w(v) > 0$ and v has no incoming edges, and assign them *push* decisions, (P2) recursively remove all nodes v such that $w(v) < 0$ and v has no outgoing edges, and assign them *pull* decisions. This pruning step can be applied in linear time over the overlay graph. We apply the above max-flow-based algorithm to each of the connected components separately.

THEOREM 4.2. *Use of pruning rules P1 and P2 does not compromise optimality.*

Greedy Alternative to the Max-flow-based Algorithm: We also sketch a simpler greedy algorithm for making dataflow decisions (we did not encounter a need for this algorithm in our extensive experimental evaluation). We traverse the overlay graph starting from the writers in a breadth-first manner, assigning each node v the optimal decision (i.e., a *push* decision if $PUSH(v) < PULL(v)$, and *pull* otherwise), with one exception: if a node should be assigned a *push* decision, but some of its input nodes are assigned *pull* decisions, we make a greedy cost-based decision among the two choices (this is only done if no nodes further upstream from v are assigned a *pull* decision). A detailed exposition can be found in [26]. This greedy algorithm runs in time linear in the number of edges (each edge is processed at most twice), and is thus highly efficient.

Partial Precomputations by Splitting Nodes: Making decisions on a per-node basis can lose out on a significant optimization opportunity – based on the push and pull frequencies, it may be beneficial to partially aggregate a subset of the inputs to an aggregate node. Figure 4(iv)-(v) shows an example. Here, because of the low write frequencies for inputs a_w, b_w, c_w, and d_w for aggregator node i, it is better to compute a partial aggregate over them, but compute the full aggregate (including e_w) only when needed (i.e., on a read).

One option is to make pre-computation decisions on a per-edge basis. However, that optimization problem is much more challenging because the cost of an incremental update for an aggregate node depends on how many of the inputs are being incrementally aggregated and how many on demand; thus the decisions for different edges are not independent of each other. Next we sketch an algorithm that achieves the same goal, but in a more scalable manner.

For every node v in the overlay graph, we consider splitting its inputs into two groups. Let f denote the pull frequency for v, and let $f_1, ..., f_k$ denote the push frequencies of its input nodes, sorted in the increasing order. For every prefix $f_1, ..., f_l$, of this sequence, we compute: $\sum_{i \le l} f_i H(l) + f \times L(l)$. We find the value of l that minimizes this cost; if $l \neq 0$ and $l \neq k$, we construct a new node v' that aggregates the inputs corresponding to frequencies $f_1, ..., f_l$, remove all those inputs from v, add v' as an input to v. As we show in our experimental evaluation, this optimization results in significant savings in practice.

Adapting the Dataflow Decisions: Most real-world data streams, including graph data streams, show significant variations in read/write frequencies over time. We propose and empirically evaluate, a simple adaptive scheme to handle such variations. For a subset of the overlay nodes (specified below), we monitor the observed push/pull frequencies over recent past (the window size being a system parameter). If the observed push/pull frequencies at a node are significantly different than the estimated frequencies, then we reconsider the dataflow decision just for that node and change it if deemed beneficial. Dataflow decisions can be unilaterally changed in such a manner only for: *pull* nodes all of whose upstream nodes are designated *push*, and *push* nodes all of whose downstream nodes are designated *pull* (we call this the *push/pull frontier*). Hence, these are the only nodes for which we monitor push/pull frequencies (it is also easier to maintain the push/pull frequencies at these nodes compared to other nodes). Techniques for more sophisticated adaptive schemes is a rich area which we plan to pursue in future.

5. EVALUATION

In this section, we present a extensive experimental evaluation using several real-world information networks. Our results show that our approach results in orders of magnitude improvements in the end-to-end throughputs over baselines, and that our overlay construction algorithms are effective at finding compact overlays.

5.1 Experimental Setup

We ran our experiments on a 2.2GHz, 24-core Intel Xeon server with 64GB of memory, running 64-bit Linux. Our prototype system is implemented in Java. We use a set of dedicated threads to play back the write and read traces (i.e., to send updates and queries to the system), and a thread pool to serve the read and write queries.

Datasets and Query Workload: We evaluated our approach on several real-world information networks, and here we report results for 4 of them[3]: (1) LiveJournal (*soc-LiveJournal1*: 4.8M nodes/69M edges), (2) Google+ social circles (*ego-Gplus*:107k/13M), (3) *EU2005* Web Graph (862k /19M), and (4) *UK2002* Web Graph (18.5M /298M).

We report results for three ego-centric aggregate queries: SUM, MAX, and TOP-K, all specified over 1-hop neighborhoods. SUM and MAX queries ask us to compute the total sum and the max over the input values respectively. TOP-K asks for the k most *frequent* values among the input values, and is a holistic aggregate [24].[4]

Since the user activity patterns (i.e., read/write frequencies) are not available for any real-world network that we are aware of, we generate those synthetically using a Zipfian distribution; event rates in many applications like tweets in Twitter, page views in Yahoo!'s social platform have been shown to follow a Zipfian distribution [30, 9]. Further, we assume that the read frequency of a node is linearly related to its write frequency; we vary the write-to-read ratio itself to understand its impact on the overall performance. For some of the experiments, we used real network packet traces to simulate user activity [5]: (1) EPA-HTTP, and (2) UCB Home IP Web Traces.

[3] First two are available at http://snap.stanford.edu/data/index.html, and the latter two at http://law.di.unimi.it/.

[4] In other words, TOP-K is a generalization of *mode*, not *max*.

[5] Available at http://ita.ee.lbl.gov/html/traces.html.

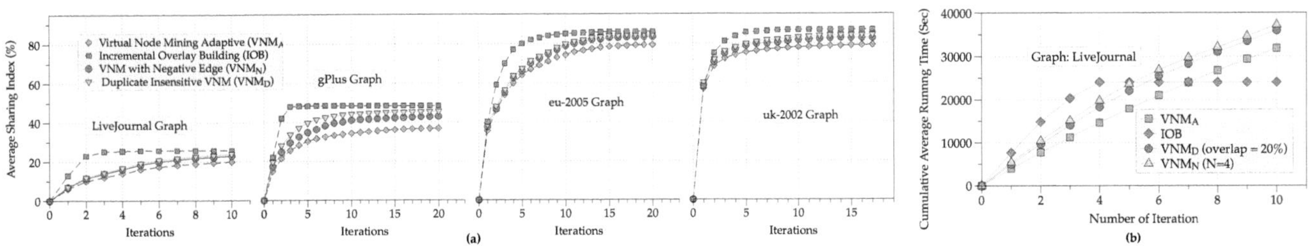

Figure 5: (a) Comparing overlay construction algorithms on real networks; (IOB should not be directly compared against VNM$_N$ or VNM$_D$ since it doesn't use negative edges or duplicate paths); (b) Running time comparison of the overlay construction algorithms.

Evaluation Metric: Our main evaluation metric is the *end-to-end throughput of the system*, i.e., the total number of read and write queries served per second. This metric accounts for the side effects of all potentially unknown system parameters whose impact might not show up for a specifically designed metric, and thereby reveals the overall efficacy of the system. When comparing the overlay construction algorithms, we also use the following metrics: sharing index (SI), memory consumption, and running time.

Comparison Systems or Algorithms: For overlay construction, we compare five algorithms: VNM, VNM$_A$, VNM$_N$, VNM$_D$, and IOB. For overall throughput comparison, we compare three approaches: (1) *all-pull*, where all queries are evaluated on demand (i.e., no sharing of aggregates and no pre-computation), (2) *all-push*, where all aggregates are pre-computed, but there is no sharing of partial aggregates, and (3) *dataflow-based overlay*, i.e., our approach with sharing of aggregates and selective pre-computation. We chose the baselines based on industry standards: *all pull* is typically seen in social networks, whereas *all push* is more prevalent in data streams and complex event processing (CEP) systems.

5.2 Overlay Construction

Sharing Index: First we compare the overlay construction algorithms with respect to the *average sharing index* achieved per iteration, over 5 runs (Figure 5(a)). As we can see, IOB finds more compact overlays (we observed this consistently for all graphs that we tried). The key reason is that: IOB considers the entire graph when looking for sharing opportunities, whereas the VNM variations consider small groups of readers and writers based on heuristical ordering of readers and writers. Note that, IOB should only be compared against VNM$_A$, and not VNM$_N$ or VNM$_D$, since it doesn't use negative edges or duplicate paths. We also note that, for IOB, most of the benefit is obtained in first few iterations, whereas the VNM-based algorithms require many iterations before converging. Further, the overlays found by VNM$_N$ and VNM$_D$ are significantly better than those found by VNM$_A$. This validates our hypothesis that using

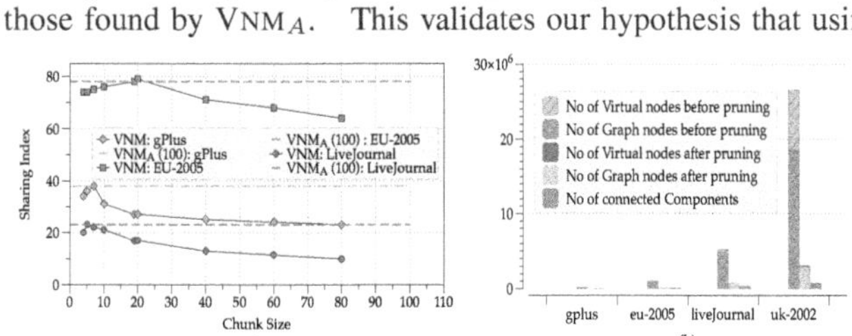

Figure 6: (a) Effect of chunk size on VNM; (b) Benefits of pruning before running maxflow.

negative edges and reusing mined edges, if possible, results in better overlays. Another important trend that we see here is that the sharing indexes for web graphs are typically much higher those for the social graphs. Kumar et al. also notice similar difficulties in achieving good structural compression in social networks [13].

Comparing VNM and VNM$_A$: Figure 6(a) shows SI achieved by our adaptive VNM$_A$ algorithm and by VNM$_A$ as the chunk size is varied. As we can see, VNM is highly sensitive to this parameter, whose optimal value is quite different for different data graphs. On the other hand, VNM$_A$ is able to achieve as compact an overlay (in some cases, slightly better) as the best obtained by VNM.

Running time and Memory Consumption: Figure 5(b) shows the running time for the different construction algorithms with the increasing number of iterations for the LiveJournal graph. As we can see IOB takes more time for first few iterations, but is overall faster than the VNM$_A$ and its variations since it converges faster. As expected, both VNM$_N$ and VNM$_D$ take more time per iteration than VNM$_A$. We also compared the total memory consumption of the overlay construction algorithms (not plotted). For LiveJournal, VNM$_A$ and its variations used approximated 4GB of memory, whereas IOB used 8GB at its peak; this is not surprising considering that IOB needs to maintain additional global data structures.

Additional experiments [26]: We found that IOB creates a deeper overlay with average depth of 4.66 (vs 3.44 for VNM$_A$), where overlay depth for a reader is defined to be the length of the longest path from one of its inputs to itself. We also found that for VNM$_N$ the number of negative edges has a significant impact on the sharing index, however the benefit diminishes beyond 3-4 negative edges.

5.3 Dataflow Decisions

Effectiveness of Pruning: Figure 6(b) shows the effectiveness of our pruning strategy to reduce the input to the max-flow algorithm. We have plotted the result for a read/write ratio of 1:1, as intuitively pruning is expected to be least effective in this case. Results for other read/write ratios show similar trend and can be found in the extended version [26]. Each vertical bar in the figure has been divided to show the composition of intermediate overlay nodes and original graph nodes, before and after pruning the overlays that we got using VNM$_A$. We get similar results for other overlay construction algorithms as well. The pruning step not only reduces the size of the graphs (to below 14% in all cases), but the resulting graphs are also highly disconnected with many small connected components, leading to low running times for the max-flow computations.

Baseline for Dataflow Decisions: Figure 8(b) shows the effectiveness of the dataflow decisions on the overlay. In this experiment we kept the number of threads (12) and read/write ratio (1:1) of the queries fixed and computed the average throughput for: (a) overlay with all push, (b) overlay with dataflow decisions, and (c) overlay with all pull. As we can see, for all aggregate functions, overlay with optimal dataflow performs much better than overlay with all pull and all push thereby justifying our hypothesis. We observed similar results for other read/write ratios as well.

Adaptive Dataflow Decisions on a Real Trace: Figure 8(a) shows the ability of our proposed adaptive scheme to adapt to varying read/write frequencies. We used the EPA-HTTP network packet

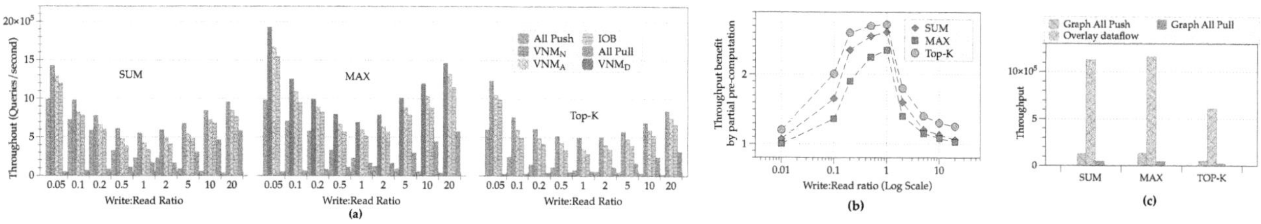

Figure 7: (a) End-to-end throughput comparison for different aggregate functions for the LiveJournal graph, with 24 threads; (b) Benefits of partial pre-computation through node splitting; (c) Throughput comparison for 2-hop aggregates.

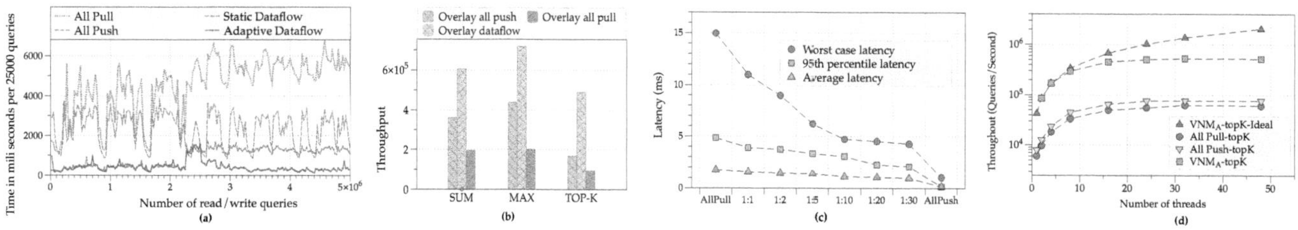

Figure 8: (a) Effect of workload variations on different approaches; (b) Baseline to motivate dataflow decisions; (c) Read latency for different push:pull cost; (d) Effect of increasing parallelism on throughput.

trace to simulate read/write activity for nodes. We used average read/write frequencies of the nodes to make static dataflow decisions. At a half-way point, we modified the read/write frequencies by increasing the read frequencies of a set of nodes with the highest read latencies till that point. As we can see, the static dataflow decisions turn out to be significantly suboptimal once this change is introduced. However, our simple adaptive approach is able to quickly adapt to the new set of read/write frequencies.

5.4 Throughput Comparison

Varying Read-Write Ratio: Figure 7(a) shows the results of our main end-to-end throughput comparison experiments for the three ego-centric aggregate queries. We plot the throughputs for the two baselines as well as for the overlays constructed by the different algorithms, as the write/read ratio changes from 0.05 (i.e., the workload contains mostly reads) to 20. As we can see, the overlay-based approaches consistently outperform the baselines in all scenarios. For the more realistic write/read ratios (i.e., around 1), the throughput improvement over the best of the two baselines is about a factor of 5 or 6. For read-heavy workloads, the overlay-based approach is multiple orders of magnitude better than the *all-pull* approach, and about a factor of 2 better than the *all-push* approach, whereas the reverse is true for the write-heavy workloads.

Comparing different aggregate functions, the performance improvements are much higher for the computationally expensive TOP-K aggregate. In some sense, simple aggregates like SUM and MAX represent a worst case for our approach; the total time spent in aggregate computation (which our approach aims to reduce through sharing) forms a smaller fraction of the overall running time.

Comparing the different overlay construction algorithms, we note that VNM_N shows significant performance improvements over the rest of the overlay construction algorithms, whereas IOB is typically the worst; the higher depth of the overlay increases the total amount of work that needs to be done for both writes and reads.

Effect of Splitting Aggregate Nodes: Figure 7(b) shows the effect of our optimization of splitting an overlay aggregate node based on the push frequencies of its inputs (Section 4) on the LiveJournal graph. As we can see, for all the aggregate functions, this optimization increases the throughput by more than a factor of 2 when write-to-read ratio is around 1. In the two extreme cases (i.e., very low or very high write-to-read ratios) where the decisions are either all push or all pull, this optimization has less impact.

Latency: Figure 8(c) shows the *worst case*, *95th percentile*, and *average* latency for the read queries for TOP-K as the push cost to pull cost ratio is varied. Here we used the network packet trace EPA-HTTP to simulate read/write activity. Since the number of distinct IP addresses in the trace is much smaller than the number of nodes in the (LiveJournal) graph, we randomly split the trace for each IP address among a set of nodes in the graph. We eliminated contention by ensuring that each query or update runs in isolation. As we can see, increasing the *pull cost* bring down the read latencies, as *pushes* get favored while making dataflow decision. We also note that the worst-case latencies in our system are quite low.

Two-hop Aggregates: Figure 7(c) shows the throughput comparison for different aggregates specified over 2-hop neighborhoods for VNM_A overlay compared to all pull and all push; we used the write-to-read ratio of 1 over the LiveJournal graph. The relative performance of the overlay approach compared to all push or all pull is better for 2-hop aggregates than 1-hop aggregate, which can be attributed to better sharing opportunities in such queries.

Parallelism: Figure 8(d) shows how the throughput varies as we increase the number of threads serving the read and write requests for the three approaches; we use the TOP-K query over the LiveJournal graph, with write-to-read ratio of 1. Because of the synchronization overheads, we don't see perfect scaleup (note that the y-axis is in log-scale); for all three approaches, the throughput increases steadily till about 24 threads, and then plateaus out (our machine has 24 cores with hyperthreading enabled).

6. RELATED WORK

Of the prior work on data stream management, the work on evaluating continuous aggregate queries over data streams is most closely related to our work [5, 3, 22, 7]. However, the sharing opportunities in ego-centric aggregate computation over graphs are fundamentally different and have not been studied in that prior work. Further, most of the prior work on evaluating continuous aggregates has only considered the *all-push* model of query evaluation. There has also been much work on aggregate computation in sensor networks and distributed databases, some of which has considered sharing of partial aggregates (e.g., [32, 31, 24]). However the primary optimization goal in that work has been minimizing communication cost during distributed execution, and hence the techniques developed are quite different. Several lines of work have considered the problems in deciding when to push vs pull based on monitoring read/write frequencies, in the context of replication in distributed data management systems (e.g., [34, 27]), and publish-subscribe systems (e.g., [30]). That work has typically focused on minimizing communication cost in distributed settings rather that the CPU cost of computation. Recently, several researchers have looked at the problem of executing subgraph pattern matching queries over streaming graph data (e.g., [33]). Two extensions to SPARQL have also been proposed in recent work for specifying continuous queries over streaming RDF data [8, 4]. There is also much work on streaming algorithms for specific problems like *counting triangles*, PageRank computation, sketching, etc. Two very recent works, Kineograph [12] and GraphInc [11], also address continuous analytics over graphs. Ego-centric analysis of information networks has been getting increasing attention in recent years in *network science* community; here the main focus is on structural analysis of a node's neighborhood [21] as well as on answering specialized pattern matching queries [28]. In a recent work, Yan et al. [35] investigate neighborhood aggregation queries aimed at finding top-k nodes (w.r.t. aggregates over their h-hop neighborhood) in the entire graph. They develop pruning techniques by noting that the aggregate values of two adjacent nodes are similar. However, none of that prior work considers execution of a large number of ego-centric aggregate queries, or exploit many of the optimization opportunities (e.g., aggressive sharing, pre-computations, adaptivity, etc.) that are crucial to handle very high data-rate streams.

7. CONCLUSIONS

In this paper, we presented the design of a continuous query processing system to efficiently process large numbers of ego-centric aggregation queries over highly dynamic, large-scale graphs. Our definition of an ego-centric aggregation query is very general, and captures a range of querying and analytics tasks including personalized trend detection, anomaly or event detection, even complex real-time analytics over neighborhoods in the graph. We proposed a general framework that supports user-defined aggregate queries and enables efficient evaluation of such queries over highly dynamic graphs; we also developed novel scalable algorithms for exploiting sharing opportunities and for making dataflow decisions based on expected activity patterns. Our system is able to handle graphs containing 320M nodes and edges on a single machine with 64GB of memory, achieving update and query throughputs over 500k/s. With the large-memory, many-core machines that are available today, we expect such a centralized approach to be sufficient in most application domains. However, our approach is also naturally parallelizable through use of standard graph partitioning-based techniques. The *readers* can be partitioned in a disjoint fashion over a set of machines, and for each machine, an overlay can be constructed for the readers assigned to that machine; the writes for each *writer* would be sent to all the machines where they are needed.

Acknowledgments: This work was supported by NSF under grant IIS-1319432, by Air Force Research Lab (AFRL) under contract FA8750-10-C-0191 and by an IBM Faculty Award.

8. REFERENCES

[1] F. Abel, Q. Gao, G.-J. Houben, and K. Tao. Analyzing user modeling on twitter for personalized news recommendations. In *UMAP*. 2011.

[2] L. Akoglu, M. McGlohon, and C. Faloutsos. Oddball: Spotting anomalies in weighted graphs. In *KDD*. Springer, 2010.

[3] L. Al Moakar. *Class-Based Continuous Query Scheduling in Data Stream Management Systems*. PhD thesis, Univ. of Pittsburgh, 2013.

[4] D. Anicic, P. Fodor, S. Rudolph, N. Stojanovic. EP-SPARQL: a unified language for event processing and stream reasoning. *WWW*, 2011.

[5] A. Arasu, S. Babu, and J. Widom. The CQL continuous query language: semantic foundations and query execution. *VLDB*, 2006.

[6] A. Arasu and J. Widom. Resource sharing in continuous sliding-window aggregates. In *VLDB*, 2004.

[7] B. Babcock, M. Datar, and R. Motwani. Load Shedding for Aggregation Queries over Data Streams. In *ICDE*, 2004.

[8] D. F. Barbieri, D. Braga, S. Ceri, and M. Grossniklaus. An execution environment for C-SPARQL queries. In *EDBT*, 2010.

[9] L. Breslau, P. Cao, L. Fan, G. Phillips, S. Shenker. Web caching and Zipf-like distributions: Evidence and implications. *INFOCOM*, 1999.

[10] G. Buehrer and K. Chellapilla. A scalable pattern mining approach to web graph compression with communities. In *WSDM*, 2008.

[11] Z. Cai, D. Logothetis, and G. Siganos. Facilitating real-time graph mining. In *CloudDB*, 2012.

[12] R. Cheng et al. Kineograph: taking the pulse of a fast-changing and connected world. In *EUROSYS*, 2012.

[13] F. Chierichetti, R. Kumar, S. Lattanzi, M. Mitzenmacher, A. Panconesi, P. Raghavan. On compressing social networks. *SIGKDD*, 2009.

[14] E. Cohen et al. Finding Interesting Associations without Support Pruning. In *ICDE*, 2000.

[15] M. Everett and S. Borgatti. Ego network betweenness. *Social networks*, 2005.

[16] T. Feder and R. Motwani. Clique partitions, graph compression and speeding-up algorithms. In *STOC*, 1991.

[17] I. Guy, N. Zwerdling, I. Ronen, D. Carmel, and E. Uziel. Social media recommendation based on people and tags. In *SIGIR*, 2010.

[18] J. Han, J. Pei, and Y. Yin. Mining frequent patterns without candidate generation. In *SIGMOD*, 2000.

[19] J. M. Hellerstein et al. The MADlib analytics library: or MAD skills, the SQL. *VLDB*, 2012.

[20] A. Inokuchi, T. Washio, and H. Motoda. An Apriori-Based Algorithm for Mining Frequent Substructures from Graph Data. In *PKDD*, 2000.

[21] J. M. Kleinberg, S. Suri, E. Tardos, and T. Wexler. Strategic network formation with structural holes. *SIGecom*, 2008.

[22] S. Krishnamurthy, C. Wu, and M. J. Franklin. On-the-fly sharing for streamed aggregation. In *SIGMOD*, 2006.

[23] X. Liu, J. Li, and L. Wang. Quasi-bicliques: Complexity and binding pairs. In *Computing and Combinatorics*. Springer, 2008.

[24] S. Madden, M. J. Franklin, J. M. Hellerstein, W. Hong. TAG: a Tiny Aggregation service for Ad-Hoc sensor networks. In *OSDI*, 2002.

[25] J. J. McAuley and J. Leskovec. Learning to discover social circles in ego networks. In *NIPS*, 2012.

[26] J. Mondal and A. Deshapnde. EAGr: Supporting Continuous Ego-centric Aggregate Queries over Large Dynamic Graphs. *arXiv preprint arXiv:1404.6570*, 2014.

[27] J. Mondal and A. Deshpande. Managing large dynamic graphs efficiently. In *SIGMOD*, 2012.

[28] W. E. Moustafa, A. Deshpande, and L. Getoor. Ego-centric graph pattern census. In *ICDE*, 2012.

[29] B. A. Prakash et al. BGP-Lens: Patterns and anomalies in internet routing updates. In *SIGKDD*, 2009.

[30] A. Silberstein, J. Terrace, B. F. Cooper, R. Ramakrishnan. Feeding frenzy: selectively materializing users' event feeds. *SIGMOD*, 2010.

[31] A. Silberstein and J. Yang. Many-to-Many Aggregation for Sensor Networks. In *ICDE*, 2007.

[32] N. Trigoni, Y. Yao, A. J. Demers, J. Gehrke, and R. Rajaraman. Multi-query Optimization for Sensor Networks. In *DCOSS*, 2005.

[33] C. Wang and L. Chen. Continuous subgraph pattern search over graph streams. In *ICDE*, 2009.

[34] O. Wolfson, S. Jajodia, and Y. Huang. An adaptive data replication algorithm. *TODS*, 1997.

[35] X. Yan, B. He, F. Zhu, and J. Han. Top-K aggregation queries over large networks. In *ICDE*, 2010.

[36] Y. Yu, P. K. Gunda, and M. Isard. Distributed aggregation for data-parallel computing: interfaces and implementations. In *SIGOPS*, 2009.

Localizing Anomalous Changes in Time-evolving Graphs

Kumar Sricharan
Palo Alto Research Center
sricharan.kumar@parc.com

Kamalika Das
UARC, NASA Ames Research Center
kamalika.das@nasa.gov

ABSTRACT

Given a time-evolving sequence of undirected, weighted graphs, we address the problem of localizing anomalous changes in graph structure over time. In this paper, we use the term 'localization' to refer to the problem of identifying abnormal changes in node relationships (edges) that cause anomalous changes in graph structure. While there already exist several methods that can detect whether a graph transition is anomalous or not, these methods are not well suited for localizing the edges which are responsible for a transition being marked as an anomaly. This is a limitation in applications such as insider threat detection, where identifying the anomalous graph transitions is not sufficient, but rather, identifying the anomalous node relationships and associated nodes is key. To this end, we propose a novel, fast method based on commute time distance [23] called **CAD** (Commute-time based Anomaly detection in Dynamic graphs) that detects node relationships responsible for abnormal changes in graph structure. In particular, CAD localizes anomalous edges by tracking a measure that combines information regarding changes in graph structure (in terms of commute time distance) as well as changes in edge weights. For large, sparse graphs, CAD returns a list of these anomalous edges and associated nodes in $O(n \log n)$ time per graph instance in the sequence, where n is the number of nodes. We analyze the performance of CAD on several synthetic and real-world data sets such as the Enron email network, the DBLP co-authorship network and a worldwide precipitation network data. Based on experiments conducted, we conclude that CAD consistently and efficiently identifies anomalous changes in relationships between nodes over time.

Categories and Subject Descriptors

H.2.8 [**Database Management**]: Database applications—*Data Mining*

SIGMOD'14, June 22–27, 2014, Snowbird, UT, USA.
Copyright 2014 ACM 978-1-4503-2376-5/14/06 ...$15.00.
http://dx.doi.org/10.1145/2588555.2612184.

Keywords

graph analysis; temporal graphs; anomaly localization; anomaly detection; commute time distance; random walks

1. INTRODUCTION

Mining for anomalies in data sets is an important problem [7], with diverse areas of application including security, finance, health care and several other industries. While this problem has been studied extensively for unstructured data sets, it is only recently that methods have been developed for detecting outliers for structured forms of data such as graph data. Graph structured data has become ubiquitous as a powerful representation framework for relational data such as social interactions, communication networks, web graphs, citation networks, gene interaction networks etc. Detecting anomalies in graphs is necessary to address several problems such as network intrusion, spam filtering, gene network analysis, and churn analysis in social networks.

Detection of anomalous nodes in *static* graphs has been well studied [10, 17, 2, 14]. Recently, several papers have addressed the problem of anomaly detection in *dynamic* graphs. These include methods based on temporal clustering [20], node-based features extraction [1], matrix decomposition [21], graph distance based time series analysis methods [18], and spectral methods [12]. All of these methods for dynamic graphs, however, are designed for event detection, *i.e.* to detect when anomalous changes in graph structure occur, and do not address the problem of localization, *i.e.* identifying changing node relationships that contribute to such anomalous changes in graph structure. In a subset of these methods ([1, 12]), it is possible to identify a set of anomalous nodes by computing their contribution to the overall anomaly score at each temporal transition. While this set of nodes that contribute to the anomaly score may include nodes that exhibit anomalous changes in relationships, they also include other non-anomalous nodes that are either affected by such structural changes or exhibit benign changes in relationships, resulting in a large number of false alarms. This point is further elaborated in Section 3.4.

In this paper, we are interested in identifying anomalous changes in node relationships that are responsible for abnormal changes in graph structure, and the corresponding anomalous nodes associated with these edges. The motivation for our work comes from the problem of identifying malicious individuals in an organization by detecting abnormal or unexpected changes in their social interactions (email, instant messenger etc.) with other employees in the organization [16]. Graph based insider threat detection has been previously studied, but only for static graphs [10].

To this end, we propose a novel method based on commute time distance [23] called **CAD** (Commute-time based Anomaly detection in Dynamic graphs) to localize anomalous changes in graph structure. The commute time distance between any pair of nodes is the average time needed to traverse the distance between these two nodes via random walks [23]. CAD localizes anomalous edges by tracking a measure that combines information regarding changes in graph structure (in terms of commute time distance) as well as change in edge weights. The anomalous edge information is subsequently summarized to identify the anomalous nodes associated with these edges. For large, sparse graphs with n nodes, CAD has a run-time of $O(n \log n)$ per graph instance in the sequence.

Finally, we note that while our motivation comes from the specific problem of insider threat detection, CAD can be applied to several other problems where detecting edges and associated nodes responsible for changes in structure is of interest. Examples include scientific collaboration networks where CAD can be used to identify changes in collaboration patterns, and in networks of geographic locations where CAD can be used to identify abnormal climate patterns over time. In this paper, we verify using ground truth information or external anecdotal evidence that CAD consistently finds anomalous changes in node relationships over time for several synthetic and real-world data sets including the Enron data, the DBLP data and world-wide precipitation data.

The rest of this paper is organized as follows. In Section 2, the problem framework is described. In Section 3, CAD is discussed as a solution to the problem. Section 4 describes the results obtained when CAD is applied to synthetic and real-world data sets. Conclusions are given in Section 5.

2. PROBLEM FRAMEWORK

Let G_t, $t = 1, \ldots, T$ be a temporal sequence of graphs. Each G_t is a weighted undirected graph with a fixed vertex (node) set $V = \{v_1, .., v_n\}$. Define the edge set $E = \{e_{(1,1)}, .., e_{(n,n)}\}$ of size n^2, with $e_{(i,j)}$ denoting the edge between nodes v_i and v_j. For each graph G_t, denote the corresponding symmetric adjacency matrix by $A_t \in \mathbb{R}^{n \times n}$, *i.e.* the edge weight of edge $e_{(i,j)}$ in graph G_t is given by $A_t(i,j)$.

Note that our definition of the edge set E includes the set of all n^2 edges in a complete graph. This does not imply that the graphs G_t, $t = 1, \ldots, T$ are complete. Rather, the absence of an edge between nodes i and j in graph G_t is reflected by $A_t(i,j) = 0$. Let the average number of edges with non-zero edge weight in the graphs G_t, $t = 1, \ldots, T$ per time instance be given by m. In our experiments in Section 4, we find that the large, real world graphs we analyze are sparse graphs [3], where $m = O(n) \ll n^2$.

2.1 Problem Statement

For each transition between graph instances G_t and G_{t+1}, our goal is to detect the set of anomalous edges $E_t \subseteq E$ whose change in weights are responsible for structural differences between G_t and G_{t+1}. We are interested in the following three different cases involving changes in edge weight. They can be categorized as:

i. Case 1: high magnitude change (increase or decrease) in edge weight from time t to $t+1$.

ii. Case 2: new edges that bring distant nodes closer.

iii. Case 3: decrease in edge weight (or deletion of edges) between central or bridge nodes in the graph that push proximal nodes far apart.

We illustrate the reason for choosing these three specific cases in Section 2.2 using a toy example. We note that there exist other possible cases involving changes in edge weights such as small changes in edge weights including addition or deletion of edges between tightly-coupled node pairs (node pairs $i, j \in V$ which are well-connected via neighboring nodes even if the edge between i, j is deleted) which are not significant enough for the overall graph structure to change substantially. Such cases are not of interest in this paper. A node $v_i \in V$ is deemed to be anomalous with respect to the transition from t to $t+1$ if $e_{(i,j)} \in E_t$ for some $j \in \{1, .., n\}$. Denote the set of anomalous nodes with respect to the transition from t to $t+1$ as V_t. Note that the anomaly sets E_t and V_t can be an empty sets in the absence of any anomalous structural differences in the transition from time t to $t+1$.

2.2 Illustrative example

Let us consider a dynamic undirected weighted graph of 17 nodes that are loosely partitioned into two sets: blue(b) and red(r). The nodes are labeled $b_1, .., b_8, r_1 .., r_9$. In Figure 1, two instances of this graph at time slices t and $t+1$ are shown. In time slice t, the edge weight (indicating say, the number of communications) is indicated by the width of the black lines. In time slice $t+1$, black lines are used to indicate edges which remain unchanged in the transition from t to $t+1$, while green lines indicate modified edges. Bold green lines indicate edges whose weights have increased, while dotted green lines indicate edges whose weights have decreased.

Change in edge weights: We enumerate the set of changes in edge weights from time slice t to $t+1$ with respect to Figure 1. We stress that the 5 different scenarios (S1:S5) considered here are only example instances of the cases described in Section 2.1

- *S1: New edge between* b_1, r_1 (refers to Case 2)
- *S2: Small decrease in edge weight between* r_7, r_8 (refers to Case 3)
- *S3: Large increase in edge weight between* b_4, b_5 (refers to Case 1)
- *S4: Small decrease in edge weight between* b_1, b_3
- *S5: Small increase in edge weight between* b_2, b_7

Real-world scenarios: Anomalies in dynamic graphs mean different things in different application contexts. For example, in an insider threat detection application, anomalies are people who might have malicious intentions that get reflected in some of their social interactions with colleagues. In an organizational event detection setting, the anomalous communication patterns among top corporate, finance, and legal executives are indicative of a major event involving the organization. On the other hand, for a scientific collaboration network, anomalies are simply interesting observations indicating change in research interests, unexpected collaborations, and so on. In the interest of space, we map our toy example to two such real-world dynamic network settings.

Insider threat detection setting: In an insider threat detection setting, these nodes can be thought of as 17 employees in an organization, who are loosely partitioned into two

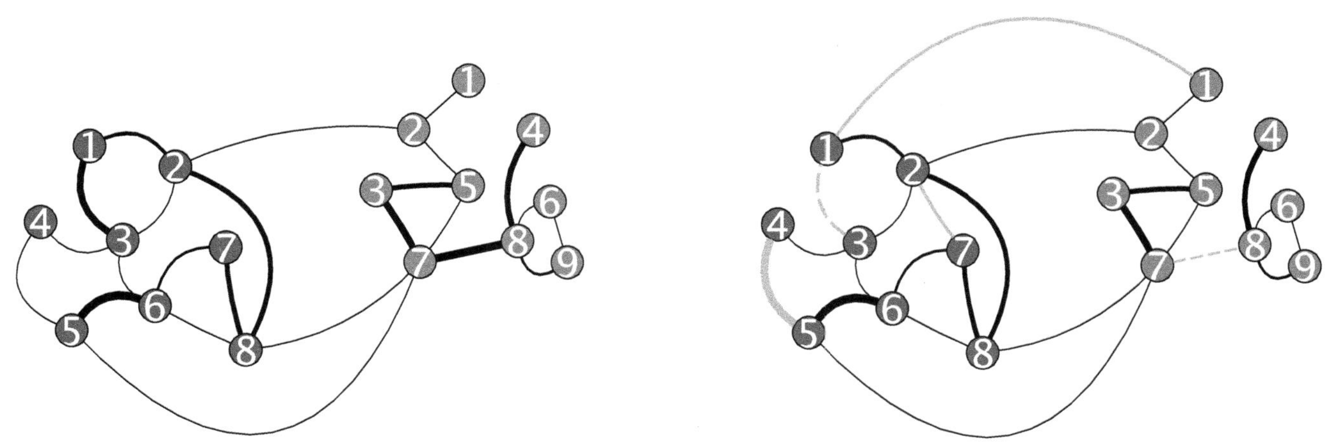

Figure 1: Time slices t (left) and $t+1$ (right) of the dynamic graph in the toy example with 17 nodes labeled $b_1, .., b_8, r_1 .., r_9$. In time slice t, the edge weight is indicated by the width of the black lines. In time slice $t+1$, black lines are used to indicate edges which remained unchanged, while green lines indicate modified edges. Bold green lines indicate new edges, while dotted green lines indicate existing edges whose weights have decreased. The two sets of node colors, blue and red, indicate two loosely connected sets of nodes with limited interactions among them in time slice t.

sets of users based on their communication patterns, perhaps indicative of different groups within the organization. In this case, S1 is suspicious because it involves contact between two employees who are fairly unrelated in terms of their job roles and can be indicative of collusion. S2 can reveal employee actions responsible for creating inter-group factions with possibly malicious motivation. Likewise, S3 is suspicious because the large increase in communication can be indicative of an organized collusion effort. On the other hand, S4 and S5 reflect the dynamic nature of the graph and are benign from the perspective of threat detection.

Scientific collaboration network setting: In a author collaboration network setting, these nodes can be thought of as 17 different authors, who are loosely partitioned into two sets of authors based on their research areas. In this case, S1 is interesting because it can indicate collaboration between two authors who are fairly unrelated in terms of their research areas. Likewise, S3 is interesting because it suggests much stronger and probably a more expanded research collaboration, even possibly the presence of a new funding mechanism. The nodes connected to these edges can be considered the seeds for discovering a new micro-community within the research area. The weakening of strong ties within a community, as described in S2, can probably indicate the splitting of a big research area into distinct groups.

In summary, the first three edge weight changes would imply significant change in relationship between nodes in the graph, either due to a increase (decrease) in the amount of communication between two nodes that are weakly (strongly) connected, or due to sharp change in volume of such communication. Such changes are therefore examples of anomalous changes. The last two changes reflect the dynamic nature of the graph and should be treated as benign from the perspective of threat detection. Based on this setup, the nodes $r_1, r_7, r_8, b_1, b_4, b_5$ connected through the anomalous edges should be considered as anomalous nodes.

In the subsequent sections, we solve the problem defined in Section 2.1 by casting it as an optimization problem.

2.3 Graph distance metrics

For any subset of edges $S \subset E$, let $\bar{d}_S(G,H)$ be a generic notion of distance between any two graphs G, H that captures structural differences (of the form highlighted in Section 2.1 (listed as Cases (i), (ii) and (iii))) that arise due to abnormal changes in the edges in the complimentary set $E - S$ when transitioning between G and H. This notion is formalized via the following definition:

DEFINITION 2.1. *Given a distance function $\bar{d}_S(G,H)$ between any two graphs G, H that captures structural differences due to changes in edges in $E-S$ and a dissimilarity threshold δ, two graphs G and H are considered similar with respect to the edge set $E-S$ at level δ if $\bar{d}_S(G,H) < \delta$, and considered dissimilar if $\bar{d}_S(G,H) \geq \delta$.*

Given a graph G_t at time instance t, and its instantiation G_{t+1} at time instance $t+1$, a significant structural change is then said to occur between graphs G_t and G_{t+1} with respect to the edges in $E-S$ when one or more edge weights in $E-S$ change in magnitude such that $\bar{d}_S(G_t, G_{t+1}) \geq \delta$.

If $\bar{d}_S(G_t, G_{t+1}) < \delta$ for some subset S, then by Definition 2.1, $E-S$ excludes the anomalous set E_t with respect to $\bar{d}_S(.,.)$ at level δ, *i.e.*, $E_t \subseteq S$. On the other hand, if $\bar{d}_S(G_t, G_{t+1}) > \delta$, then $S - E_t \neq \phi$. The quantity $\bar{d}_S(G_t, G_{t+1})$ can therefore be minimized over S in order to identify the anomalous set E_t with respect to $\bar{d}_S(.,.)$ at level δ during the transition from t to $t+1$. Based on this, we define the problem of structural change identification in temporal graphs using an optimization framework.

2.4 Optimization framework

We define the set of anomalous edges E_t with respect to $\bar{d}_S(.,.)$ at level δ as solution to the optimization problem:

$$E_t \quad := \quad \arg\min_S \quad |S| \qquad \text{subject to} \quad \bar{d}_S(G_t, G_{t+1}) < \delta. \tag{1}$$

The goal of this optimization problem is to identify anomalous edges as the minimal set of edges, which when left unchanged during the transition from t to $t+1$, would result in the graphs $G_t(S)$ and $G_{t+1}(S)$ being structurally similar at level δ with respect to $\bar{d}_S(.,.)$, *i.e.* $\bar{d}_S(G_t, G_{t+1}) < \delta$.

2.4.1 Polynomial-time solution

Observe that the above formulation defined in (1) is a combinatorial optimization problem that is intractable in practice for any reasonably large sized graphs. The solution to this problem, however, can be reduced to polynomial time if $\bar{d}_S(.,.)$ has the following structure: for any $S \subseteq E$,

$$\bar{d}_S(G_t, G_{t+1}) = \sum_{e \in E-S} \Delta E_t(e), \tag{2}$$

where $\Delta E_t(e)$ is a non-negative functional of the graphs G_t and G_{t+1} independent of the set S. If the distance metric satisfies the structure in (2), the optimization problem in (1) is equivalent to simply sorting the set of values

$$\{\Delta E_t(e); \forall e \in E\}$$

and choosing E_t to be the smallest set of edges S (in terms of the cardinality $|S|$ of S) such that $\sum_{e \in E-S} \Delta E_t(e) < \delta$, which can be solved in polynomial time.

2.4.2 Existing distance measures

Several distance functions between graphs have been proposed previously, including (i) Maximum Common Subgraph [19], (ii) Graph edit distance [11], (iii) Modality distance [6] and (iv) Spectral distance [13]. However, none of these distance measures satisfy (2), which means it would require exhaustive search on the candidate edges for solving the combinatorial optimization problem in (1). To address this, we propose a new distance measure that satisfies (2).

2.5 Proposed distance metric

Let $d_t(i,j)$ represent some suitable notion of distance between two nodes v_i and v_j with respect to graph G_t. Then, a possible measure for capturing the structural distance between the graphs G_t and G_{t+1} due to any changes corresponding to scenarios (i), (ii) or (iii) would be: For any subset $S \subseteq E$, define

$$\bar{d}_S^{(1)}(G_t, G_{t+1}) = \sum_{e(i,j) \in E-S} |d_t(i,j) - d_{t+1}(i,j)|.$$

However, this distance measure $\bar{d}_S^{(1)}(G_t, G_{t+1})$ is a poor choice for identifying anomalous edges for the following reason. The use of $\bar{d}_S^{(1)}(G_t, G_{t+1})$ in (1) would result in E_t being the set of edges $e_{(i,j)}$ with large values for $|d_t(i,j) - d_{t+1}(i,j)|$. However, structural changes induced by an anomalous edge $e(i,j)$, not only causes the distance between nodes v_i and v_j to change sharply (*i.e.*, $|d_t(i,j) - d_{t+1}(i,j)| \gg 0$), but also causes the distance between nodes connected to node v_i and nodes connected to node v_j to change significantly. This is illustrated in detail in Section 3.4 (please see discussion on COM method) via the illustrative example described earlier. As a result, employing $\bar{d}_S^{(1)}(G_t, G_{t+1})$ in (1) would result in E_t consisting of several benign or non-anomalous edges.

To address this issue with $\bar{d}_S^{(1)}(G_t, G_{t+1})$, we propose the following modified distance function. For any $S \subseteq E$, define

$$\bar{d}_S^{(0)}(G_t, G_{t+1}) = \sum_{e \in E-S} \Delta E_t(e),$$

where $\Delta E_t(e)$ for $e = e_{i,j}$is given by

$$\Delta E_t(e_{i,j}) = |A_{t+1}(i,j) - A_t(i,j)| \times |d_{t+1}(i,j) - d_t(i,j)|.$$

For anomalous edges corresponding to large changes in magnitude (Case 1), $|A_{t+1}(i,j) - A_t(i,j)|$ will be large, which will result in $|c_{t+1}(i,j) - c_t(i,j)|$ being large and as a result, $\Delta E_t(e_{i,j})$ will be large. For edges corresponding to Case 2 involving new edges that bring distant nodes together, $|d_{t+1}(i,j) - d_t(i,j)|$ will be large while $A_{t+1}(i,j) - A_t(i,j)$ will be non-zero and positive and as a result $\Delta E_t(e_{i,j})$ will be large. Finally, in Case 3, once again $|d_{t+1}(i,j) - d_t(i,j)|$ will be large while $A_{t+1}(i,j) - A_t(i,j)$ will be non-zero and negative, and once again $\Delta E_t(e_{i,j})$ will be large. Thus, edges corresponding to all the three different cases will be marked with a high anomaly score.

For non-anomalous edges $e(i,j)$ involving small magnitude changes $|A_{t+1}(i,j) - A_t(i,j)|$ between node-pairs i,j that are tightly coupled, $|d_{t+1}(i,j) - d_t(i,j)|$ will also be small due to the coupling and therefore the product $\Delta E_t(e_{i,j})$ will also be small. The other scenario involving non-anomalous edges is as follows: let $e(i,j)$ be an anomalous edge corresponding to Cases 2 or 3. In this case, for some neighboring node of i (say n_i) and j (say n_j), the distance $|d_{t+1}(n_i,n_j) - d_t(n_i,n_j)|$ will be large because $|d_{t+1}(i,j) - d_t(i,j)|$ will be large. But because the edge between n_i and n_j is non-anomalous, and therefore does not belong to Cases 2 or 3, it follows that $|A_{t+1}(i,j) - A_t(i,j)|$ will be 0, and as a result $\Delta E_t(e_{i,j})$ will be 0. In either case, the score $\Delta E_t(e_{(i,j)})$ will be small for non-anomalous edges.

As a result, employing $\bar{d}_S^{(0)}(G_t, G_{t+1})$ in (1) would result in E_t primarily consisting of edges with abnormal changes corresponding to Cases (i), (ii) and (iii) that are of interest in this paper. Furthermore, observe that condition (2) is trivially satisfied by $\bar{d}_S^{(0)}(G_t, G_{t+1})$. Because of these desirable properties, we use $\bar{d}_S^{(0)}(G_t, G_{t+1})$ in the CAD algorithm (described next) for localizing anomalous edges and nodes.

3. COMMUTE TIME BASED ANOMALY DETECTION

In this section, we review the commute time distance measure, and subsequently describe the CAD algorithm based on the distance metric $\bar{d}_S^{(0)}(G_t, G_{t+1})$ proposed in Section 2.5.

3.1 Commute time distance

Given an arbitrary adjacency matrix A, a random walk on the corresponding graph is a sequence of nodes described by a finite Markov chain which is time-reversible [11]. The commute time is the expected number of steps that a random walk starting at i will take to reach j once and go back to i for the first time [14]. The commute time can be computed from the Moore-Penrose pseudoinverse of the graph Laplacian matrix. Denote the degree matrix corresponding to the weighted adjacency matrix A by D. Further denote $L = D - A$ and L^+ as the graph Laplacian matrix and its pseudoinverse respectively. The commute time is:

$$c(i,j) = V_G(l_{ii}^+ + l_{jj}^+ - 2l_{ij}^+), \tag{3}$$

where $V_G = \sum_{i=1}^n D(i,i)$ is the volume of the graph, and l_{ij}^+ is the (i,j) element of L^+. The commute time $c(i,j)$ has been shown to be a valid distance metric between any pair of nodes i,j. In particular, the commute time between the nodes on a graph is the Euclidean distance in the space spanned by the eigenvectors of the graph Laplacian L corresponding to A. Commute time distance has been used previously to capture structure in graphs in clustering [23] and for anomaly detection in static graphs [14].

Denote the commute time distance with respect to each of the adjacency matrices $A_t, t = \{1, .., T\}$ by $c_t(.,.)$. In this paper, we choose $d_t(.,.) := c_t(.,.)$. We note that there exist several other ways to determine distances between nodes in a graph, including shortest path, alternative distance measures based on random walks and others [8, 9]. While any of these distance measures can be used as an alternative to commute time distance, we chose to use commute time distance for the following two reasons. (i) Robustness - the fact that commute time is averaged over all paths (and not just the shortest path) makes it more robust to data perturbations, and (ii) scalability - there have been recent breakthroughs [15] in approximately computing the commute time with high accuracy using methods that scale to very large graphs, which we discuss next.

Computation of commute time distance for a single graph instance having n nodes using (3) is $O(n^3)$. Clearly, this is prohibitively expensive to use on large graphs with several thousands of nodes. In order to address this issue, Khoa and Chawla [15] have proposed an approximate commute time embedding method to compute the commute time with high accuracy in $O(kn)$ time, where k (referred to as k_{RP} in [15]) is the dimension of the approximate embedding, using near-linear time solvers for diagonally dominant systems of equations. Furthermore, they show that for the choice of $k = O(\log n/\epsilon^2)$, their method computes commute time distances accurately within error of the order of ϵ^2 (please refer to equation (5.2) in [15]). For this choice of $k = O(\log n/\epsilon^2)$, the run-time complexity of [15] is $O(n \log n)$.

3.2 CAD algorithm

The CAD algorithm is formally defined next. First, the commute time distances $c_t(i,j)$ are calculated for every pair of nodes $v_i, v_j \in V$ and every time instance $t = 1, .., T$ with embedding dimension k using [15]. Subsequently, the scores $\Delta E_t(.)$ are given by

$$\Delta E_t(e_{i,j}) = |A_{t+1}(i,j) - A_t(i,j)| \times |c_{t+1}(i,j) - c_t(i,j)|.$$

are computed for each $t = 1, \ldots, T$ and $i, j \in \{1, \ldots, n\}$. Anomalous edges E_t at each transition t to $t+1$ are detected using the scores $\Delta E_t(.)$ as described in Section 2.4.1, by simply sorting the set of values

$$\{\Delta E_t(e); \forall e \in E\}$$

and choosing E_t to be the smallest set of edges S (in terms of the cardinality $|S|$ of S) such that $\sum_{e \in E-S} \Delta E_t(e) < \delta$ for a threshold δ. Once the anomalous edges have been determined, the nodes V_t associated with these edges are declared as anomalous nodes. The pseudocode for the resulting CAD algorithm is formally stated in Algorithm 1.

CAD has two input parameters: approximation parameter k and threshold δ. The process for choosing k and δ in practice is described in Section 4.1.1.

3.3 Runtime of CAD

The computation of the commute time distance per graph instance is given by $O(n \log n)$ [15]. The number of non-zero entries in $\{\Delta E_t(e); \forall e \in E\}$ will be of the same order as the number of non-zero entries in $A_t, A_t + 1$, *i.e.* $O(m)$. This implies that the runtime for sorting the set of values $\{\Delta E_t(e); \forall e \in E\}$ and subsequently determining the smallest set of edges S such that $\sum_{e \in E-S} \Delta E_t(e) < \delta$ will require runtime of order $O(m \log m)$. The total runtime of CAD is clearly dominated by these two operations and is therefore given by $O(n \log n + m \log m)$.

For all large, sparse, real world graphs $m = O(n) \ll n^2$ [3]. Therefore, the overall running time for CAD is given by $O(n \log n + n \log n) = O(n \log n)$.

3.4 Comparison with related methods

We now describe the existing methods [20, 1, 21, 18, 12] in the context of the illustrative example and contrast them with CAD. Of these, all but [1] are designed only to detect whether a graph transition is anomalous or not, and do not address the problem of localizing anomalous edges and nodes.

The activity vector method (henceforth referred to as ACT) proposed by Ide and Kashima [12], is based on eigenvectors of adjacency matrices. ACT identifies anomalies by comparing the activity vectors (first eigenvector of adjacency matrices) at successive graph instances. Akoglu and Faloutsos' [1] method (henceforth referred to as AFM) extend this work by first constructing dependency matrices based on correlations between local node features, and then applying ACT to these derived dependency matrices. As mentioned in the introduction section, AFM [1] identifies anomalous nodes by determining which nodes contribute the most to the anomaly score during that transition. The same strategy can be used to find anomalous nodes using ACT as well.

The drawback with using ACT to identify anomalous nodes is that all nodes which are affected by changes in structure contribute to the anomaly score and will be classified as anomalies, resulting in false alarms. On the other hand, AFM uses *local* features (average edge weight, degree etc.) based on the egonets (1-step neighborhoods) of each node, which do not necessarily differentiate between significant changes in graph structure with benign changes.

For example, consider the change in edge weight between nodes r_7 and r_8. When using AFM, the local features for r_7 and r_8 only change marginally, more or less to the same extent as the change in local features of nodes b_1, b_3 (due to decrease in edge weight between b_1 and b_3). As a result, when using AFM, several non-anomalous nodes (for *e.g.*, b_1, b_3) will be detected along with anomalous nodes (for *e.g.*, r_7, r_8), resulting in a large number of false alarms. Also, as a consequence of the change in edge weight between nodes r_7 and r_8, nodes r_4, r_6, r_8, r_9 become a loosely connected component with respect to the rest of the graph. As a result, when using ACT, all the nodes r_4, r_6, r_8, r_9 will contribute to the anomaly score during the transition from t to $t+1$ and will be classified as anomalies, once again resulting in false alarms. This is verified experimentally in the AFM paper [1] (in Section III.D and Section IV).

We note that the edges associated with nodes r_4, r_6, r_9 *remain the same*, and that the edge responsible for this change in graph structure is associated only with node r_8. In other words node r_8 is responsible for the significant structural change in the graph during this transition. A similar argument holds true for node r_7. The objective of CAD is to only identify anomalous nodes such as r_8, as opposed to identifying non-anomalous nodes that exhibit superficial changes

Algorithm 1 CAD

Input: Vertex set V, edge set E, adjacency matrix sequence $A_t, t = 1, .., T$, threshold δ, embedding dimension k
Output: Anomalous edge sets E_t, node sets V_t
for t in {1, .., T-1} **do**
    Compute commute time distance $c_t(i, j)$ for every pair of nodes $v_i, v_j \in V$ with embedding dimension k using [15]
end for
for t in {1, .., T-1} **do**
    Compute $\Delta E_t(e_{(i,j)}) = |A_{t+1}(i, j) - A_t(i, j)| \times |c_{t+1}(i, j) - c_t(i, j)|$ for every pair of nodes $v_i, v_j \in V$
    Choose anomaly edge set E_t as the set of edges S with smallest cardinality $|S|$ such that $\sum_{e \in E-S} \Delta E_t(e) < \delta$
    for Edge $e_{(i,j)}$ in E_t **do**
        $v_i \cup v_j \rightarrow V_t$
    end for
    Output anomalous edges E_t, anomalous nodes V_t
end for

in relationships (such as b_1, b_3) or are affected by change in structure (such as r_4, r_6, r_9).

There are two other related methods to CAD: (i) ADJ, where $\Delta E_t(e_{(i,j)})$ is set to be $|A_{t+1}(i, j) - A_t(i, j)|$, and (ii) COM, where $\Delta E_t(e_{(i,j)})$ is set to be $|c_{t+1}(i, j) - c_t(i, j)|$. ADJ therefore only looks at difference in adjacency matrices, and COM only looks at differences in commute times. Observe that both ADJ and COM satisfy condition (2).

However, both of them will result in detection of benign edges as anomalies. This can be seen in the case of the toy example as follows. In the case of ADJ, the change in relationship between nodes b_2 and b_7 is benign, but will be classified as anomalous to the same extent as the edge between b_1, r_1 due to similar changes in edge weight. On the other hand, in the case of COM, while $\Delta E_t(r_7, r_8)$ will be large, $\Delta E_t(r_i, r_j)$ will also be large for all pairs of i, j : $i \in \{1, 2, 3, 5, 7\}, j \in \{4, 6, 8, 9\}$ because of the decreased edge strength between r_7 and r_8.

Unlike ADJ and COM, $\Delta E_t(b_2, b_7)$ will be smaller than $\Delta E_t(b_1, r_1)$ in the case of CAD because $|c_{t+1}(b_2, b_7) - c_t(b_2, b_7)|$ will be smaller relative to $|c_{t+1}(b_1, r_1) - c_t(b_1, r_i)|$ due to the tight coupling between b_2, b_7. Also, $\Delta E_t(r_i, r_j)$ will be small for all pairs of i, j : $i \in \{1, 2, 3, 5, 7\}, j \in \{4, 6, 8, 9\}$ except $i = 7, j = 8$ because $|A_{t+1}(i, j) - A_t(i, j)| = 0$ in these cases. CAD therefore should perform favorably compared to ADJ and COM. This is corroborated in Section 4.1 via experimental results.

3.5 Quantitative performance of CAD on toy example

Using the toy example in Figure 1, we describe how CAD determines anomalous nodes during the transition from time slice t to $t + 1$. Because of the small number of nodes ($n = 17$), we determine the exact commute time distance using (3), and subsequently calculate the anomaly scores $\Delta E_t(.)$.

Recall that the commute time distance $c_t(i, j)$ is equal [14] to the Euclidean distance in an embedded space given by the eigenvectors [4] of the Laplacian matrix L_t. Ignoring the trivial first eigenvector of all 1's, we plot the second (Fiedler vector) and third eigenvectors corresponding to the Laplacians of A_t and A_{t+1} in Figure 2. From equation (5) in [14], the commute time distance is approximately equal to the Euclidean distance in the 2-dimensional embedding in Figure 2. This implies that pairs of nodes with smaller commute time distances should be closer to each other in Figure 2, and pairs of nodes with larger commute time distances should be farther apart. In Figure 2(a), in agreement with our intuition, all the red nodes are close together, all the blue nodes are close together, and the blue and red nodes are reasonably well separated. In Figure 2(b), we observe that the nodes r_4, r_6, r_8, r_9 become distant from the rest of the nodes - this is in agreement with the structure change in the graph due to the weakening of the edge between r_7 and r_8. Also, nodes r_1 and b_1 are a lot closer in 2(b) compared to 2(a), due to the new edge between r_1 and b_1. Finally, nodes b_4 and b_5 are a lot closer due to the strengthening of the edge between them.

It follows from these observations that the anomaly scores $\Delta E_t(.)$ corresponding to (b_1, r_1) (b_4, b_5) and (r_7, r_8) should be large, and the rest of the anomaly scores should be small. This is indeed the case, as seen from Table 1 where the anomaly scores $\Delta E_t(.)$ for all the edges with non-zero scores are listed. For some suitable threshold δ, edges between nodes (b_1, r_1) (b_4, b_5) and (r_7, r_8) and corresponding nodes $b_1, b_4, b_5, r_1, r_7, r_8$ will be identified as anomalies.

Edge	b_1, r_1	b_4, b_5	r_7, r_8
$\Delta E_i(.)$	10.6	9.56	8.99
Edge	b_1, b_3	b_2, b_7	Rest
$\Delta E_i(.)$	0.1	0.22	0

Table 1: Table listing the values of $\Delta E_t(.)$ for edges in the illustrative example.

3.5.1 *Comparison with ACT*

Since the ACT method by Ide *et al.* [12] is closest to CAD in terms of being an eigenvector based anomaly detection technique, we use this method as a baseline for comparing our results. We point out that ACT takes graph sequences as inputs, computes the leading eigenvector (called activity vector) $a_t \in \mathbb{R}^n$ of the adjacency matrices A_t, and returns a decision as to whether the t to $t+1$ graph transition is anomalous based on an anomaly measure computed using the activity vectors. Although the anomaly detection method of Akoglu and Faloutsos (AFM) [1] is an extension of ACT, we do not use this method as a baseline. This is because, AFM, unlike ACT and CAD, does not base its analysis on the graph adjacency matrix, but on dependency matrices constructed from *local* features based on egonets of nodes in the graph. Also, depending on which local features

Node	b_1	b_2	b_3	b_4	b_5	b_6	b_7	b_8	r_1	r_2	r_3	r_4	r_5	r_6	r_7	r_8	r_9
ΔN_t	10.5	0.30	0.20	9.56	9.56	0.00	0.30	0.00	10.29	0.00	0.00	0.00	0.00	0.00	8.99	8.99	0.00

Table 2: Table listing values of $\Delta N_t(.)$ for nodes in the illustrative example.

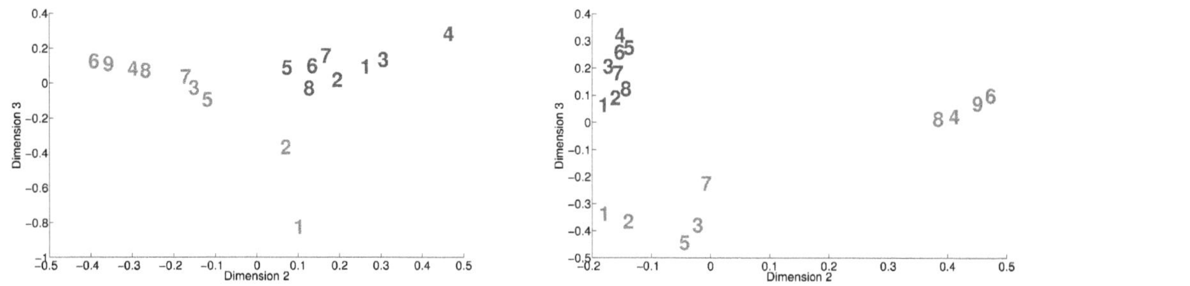

(a) Time t (b) Time $t+1$

Figure 2: Illustrative example: 2 dimensional Laplacian eigenmap embeddings corresponding to graph instances at time t, $t+1$. The colored numbers indicate the node locations for $r_1, .., r_9$ (labeled in red) and $b_1, .., b_8$ (labeled in blue).

are being used, AFM can return different sets of anomalies, making comparison of results difficult.

We apply the ACT algorithm to this data set, and compare the results of CAD and ACT in Figure 3. Using the procedure described in [1], ACT can be used to identify anomalous nodes with respect to the transition by comparing the summary r_t of the activity vector from $t-w+1$-th (w being the window size) to the tth transition to the activity vector a_{t+1} of the $(t+1)^{th}$ instance. The anomaly scores being reported for ACT for each node v_i are given by the absolute difference $|a_{t+1}(i) - r_t(i)|$, with $w = 1$. For the purposes of comparing with ACT, we define anomaly scores with respect to CAD for nodes as follows: The anomaly score for each node $v_i \in V$ for a transition from t to $t+1$ is given by

$$\Delta N_t(i) \quad = \quad \sum_{j \in \{1,\ldots,n\}} \Delta E_t(e_{(i,j)}).$$

Anomaly scores $\Delta N_t(.)$ for all nodes are listed in Table 2.

For fair comparison, we normalize the anomaly scores from CAD and ACT by the respective maximum anomaly score. From Figure 3, it is clear that the anomaly scores $\Delta N_t(i)$ generated by CAD are significantly higher for the responsible nodes b_1, b_4, b_5, r_1, r_7, r_8 compared to the rest of the nodes. On the other hand, while the anomaly scores generated using ACT for the 4 nodes b_4, b_5, r_7, r_8 is higher compared to the rest, the scores for b_1, r_1 are small. Furthermore, the difference between the scores corresponding to these 4 nodes b_4, b_5, r_7, r_8 and the rest of the nodes is not as large as is the case with CAD. This comparison reiterates the observation in Section 3.4 that CAD only identifies responsible nodes, whereas ACT can also potentially identify nodes which are affected by the change in graph structure.

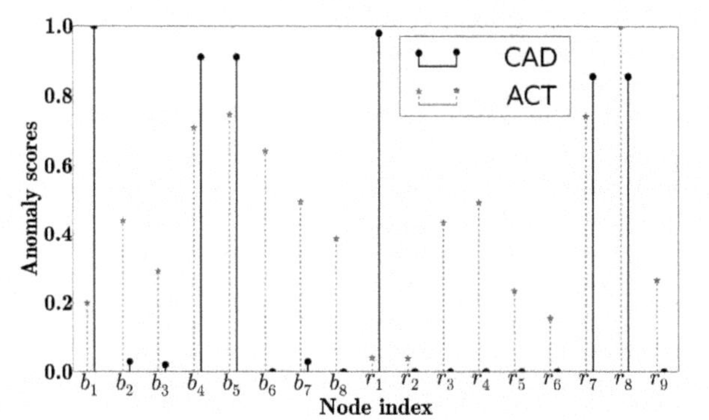

Figure 3: Normalized anomaly scores for CAD and ACT on toy data set. CAD identifies only responsible nodes, whereas ACT also assigns significant scores to nodes affected by change in graph structure.

4. EXPERIMENTS

CAD is applied to several synthetic and real world data sets in order to localize anomalous edges and nodes responsible for significant changes in graph structure over time. Since the real data sets only provide anecdotal evidence of anomalies, we create a synthetic data set from Gaussian mixtures to quantitatively analyze the performance of CAD, and to compare against ACT. The three real world data sets on which we run CAD are (i) the Enron email network data[1], (ii) the DBLP co-authorship network data[2], and (iii) a world-wide precipitation network data[3]. The results on these data sets are presented as a proxy for our results on a proprietary organizational email network data, collected from a corporation for experimental purposes for insider threat detection.

We compare the performance of CAD against several different algorithms. In addition to ACT, we also compare the performance of two variants of ACT - the ADJ and COM methods discussed in Section 3.4. Recall that ADJ only looks at difference in adjacency matrices, and COM only looks at differences in commute times. Finally, given

[1] `http://www.isi.edu/~adibi/Enron/Enron.htm`
[2] `http://dblp.org/xml/`
[3] `thttp://www.cdc.noaa.gov/data/gridded/data.ncep.reanalysis.html`

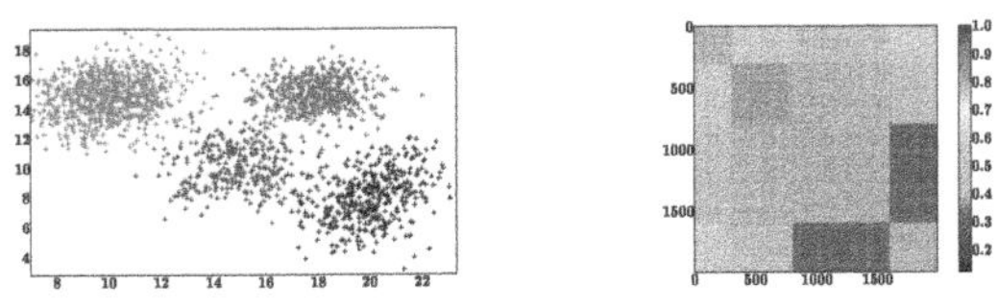

(a) (b)

Figure 4: Random realizations from 4-component Gaussian mixture, and the corresponding adjacency matrix.

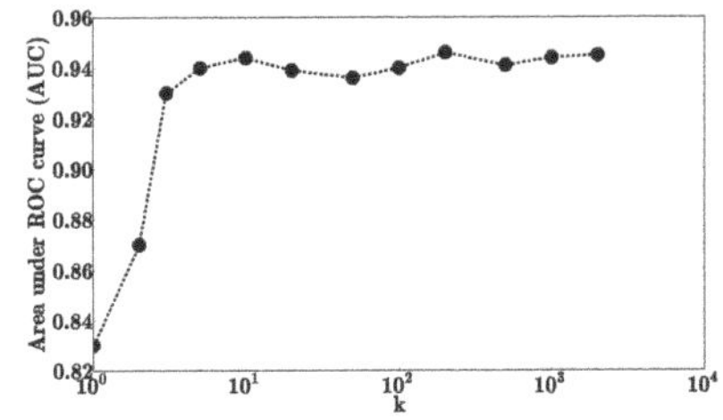

Figure 5: Variation of AUC against k. From the figure, it is clear that the performance of CAD is invariant to the choice of k for values of $k > 10$.

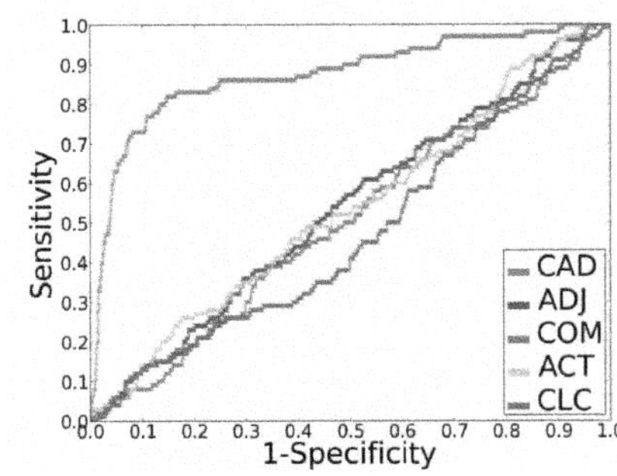

Figure 6: ROC curves comparing the 4 methods: CAD, ACT, COM and ADJ. The performance of COM and ADJ are close to the random baseline, and the performance of ACT is marginally better. CAD outperforms the other methods by a significant margin.

the commonplace nature of node centrality measures [5], we also evaluate the performance of centrality for the purpose of determining anomalous nodes. In particular, let $cc_t(i)$ denote the closeness centrality measure of nodes v_i with respect to graphs G_t. The anomaly scores for the closeness centrality (CLC) method for each node v_i are given by $|cc_{t+1}(i) - cc_t(i)|$. The measures $|cc_2(i) - cc_1(i)|$ are then thresholded to identify anomalous nodes.

Experimental setup: CAD, as well as all algorithms compared as baselines, have been implemented in python and run on a 64-bit 2.327 GHz dual quad core Dell Precision T7500 desktop running Red Hat Enterprise Linux version 6.0 having 32 GB of physical memory.

4.1 Quantitative analysis: synthetic data

We perform experiments to evaluate the following characteristics of CAD: (i) robustness to parameter selection, (ii) accuracy, and (iii)scalability using synthetic data generated as follows. We draw 2000 random samples from a 2-dimensional Gaussian mixture distribution with 4 components. Figure 4a shows this data set with data from each component represented by a different color. For any pair of points i, j in this sample, we compute the Euclidean distance $d(i, j)$ between them. We then construct an adjacency matrix P where $P(i, j) = \exp(-d(i, j))$. The adjacency matrix corresponding to the set of realizations in Figure 4a is shown in Figure 4b. The graph corresponding to this adjacency matrix constitutes nodes belonging to 4 different clusters, with strong intracluster edges and weaker inter-cluster edges. We perturb this adjacency matrix P by adding a small amount of random noise to the data, and compute the adjacency matrix Q in an identical manner to P. We also construct a random matrix $R \in \mathbb{R}^{2000\times2000}$, where each entry $R(i, j)$ in this random matrix is given by

$$R(i,j) = \begin{cases} 0 & \text{with probability } p = 0.95 \\ \text{u(i,j)} & \text{with probability } p = 0.05, \end{cases}$$

where $u(i, j)$ is a random number drawn uniformly between 0 and 1. We then consider a dynamic graph sequence with two temporal instances $\{A_t, t = 1, 2\}$, with $A_1 = P$ and $A_2 = Q + (R + R')/2$.

In the transition from A_1 to A_2, we keep track of all edges for which $R(i, j) \neq 0$ such that i, j belong to different clusters. We consider these edges and the associated nodes to be anomalous because these edges establish ties between nodes belonging to different clusters, thereby contributing to anomalous change in graph structure.

4.1.1 Parameter selection

There are 2 user-given parameters for CAD: δ and k. Clearly, the anomaly scores $\Delta E_t(.)$ returned by CAD are independent of the choice of δ and do not affect the ROC performance of CAD. The approximation parameter k for commute time distance computation, however, affects the accuracy of the anomaly scores. For the synthetic data, we run CAD with various different choices of k, compute the area under the ROC curve (AUC) as before, and plot the variation of AUC against k in Figure 5. It is clear from the figure that the performance of CAD is invariant to the choice of k for values of $k > 10$, for the synthetic data.

4.1.2 Accuracy

We generate 100 sets of realizations of this synthetic data. For each instance, we run CAD (with $k = 50$) and determine the anomaly scores $\Delta E_1(.)$ for all pairs of nodes. We then determine the anomalous node and edge sets E_1 and V_1 for a range of different values δ using Algorithm 1. The accuracy of CAD can be evaluated either by contrasting E_1 against the ground truth set of anomalous edges, or by contrasting V_1 against the ground truth set of anomalous nodes. Qualitatively, the performance in terms of either edges or nodes should be fairly similar and therefore either can be chosen for the sake of evaluation. Because we intend to compare the performance of CAD against ACT, we chose to evaluate accuracy in terms of nodes instead of edges.

In order to compare the performance of the five methods - CAD, COM, ADJ, ACT and CLC, ROC curves are generated for each of these methods by sweeping over different values of the threshold δ and comparing the resulting anomalous node sets against ground truth. The ROC curves for these five algorithms averaged over the 100 sets of realizations of synthetic data is shown in Figure 6. From this figure, we note that performance of ADJ, COM, ACT and CLC is close to the random baseline. This is in sharp contrast to the performance of CAD, which is significantly better. The area under the ROC curves for CAD, ADJ, COM, ACT and CLC are respectively given by 0.88, 0.53, 0.51, 0.53 and 0.49. It is interesting to note that suitably combining the adjacency matrix information in ADJ and commute time information in COM together in CAD results in significant increase in anomaly detection performance.

4.1.3 *Scalability*

We generate symmetric random graphs of varying sizes to study the scalability of CAD and the different alternatives. Based on our observation in Section 4.1.1, we select with $k = 10$ wherever relevant. Since most real-world graphs are sparse with $m = O(n)$ [3], we fix the sparsity level at $1/n$ for this study. The results indicate that CAD is able to process synthetically generated random graphs having $n = O(10^7)$ nodes and $m = O(10^7)$ edges in 5 minutes on average over 10 trials. Since COM relies on the similar computations, the running time of COM is comparable with CAD. ACT only has to compute the largest eigen vector and has a significantly low computation time of close to 1 minute for graphs having $n = O(10^7)$ nodes and $m = O(10^7)$. Since ADJ computes the differences in sparse adjacency matrices, the running time of ADJ is the lowest at an average of 10 seconds. For the different graph size, the CLC method takes approximately one third the time taken by CAD. However, the running time of CLC is highest affected by the graph sparsity, and even for modestly higher sparsity such as $m = 10n$, it performs worse than all the alternatives. In summary, CAD can comfortably operate on very large graphs with runtimes comparable to its alternatives, while providing the highest accuracy for detecting anomalous changes.

4.2 Qualitative analysis: real data

We run CAD on 3 real-world data sets and verify the identified anomalies based on anecdotal evidence.

Choice of approximation parameter k: During analysis on real-world data sets, similar to our observations with the synthetic data, we observed that we get a very consistent set of anomalies using CAD for any choice of $k > 10$. Based on these observations and also those presented in [15], we conclude that the results are largely robust to the choice of k and we use $k = 50$ in all our experiments.

Threshold (δ) *selection*: We automate the selection of the threshold δ as follows. Let $l > 0$ be the average number of anomalies the user is interested in per graph instance. Then, δ is chosen such that the total number of anomalous nodes given by $\sum_{t=1}^{T-1} |V_t| = l(T-1)$. This selection of the threshold δ ensures that l anomalous nodes are selected on average for each transition t to $t+1$. By selecting a single threshold for all $t = 1, .., T-1$ rather than selecting the top l anomalies for each transition t to $t+1$, we ensure that no anomalies are reported for transitions when there is no anomalous activity, and similarly ensure that more than l anomalies are selected for transitions where anomalies are present. We note that while this procedure for threshold selection needs to be done offline, the procedure can be suitably modified in an online setting by aggregating scores up to the current graph instance and updating the threshold.

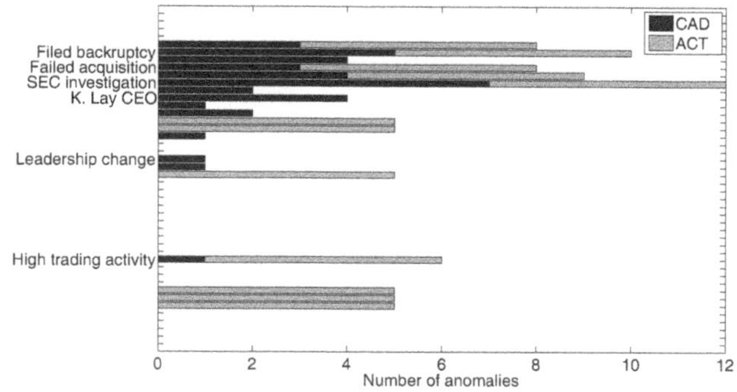

Figure 7: Bar plot of anomalous graph instances detected by CAD (blue) and ACT(green) against the Enron scandal timeline.

ACT results: We determine anomalies using ACT in the following manner. We use ACT to determine which of the transitions are anomalous. For each such anomalous transition, we declare the top 5 nodes with the highest, non-zero anomaly scores $|a_{t+1}(i) - r_t(i)|$ to be anomalous. This is identical to the presentation of results in [1] (Figure 7).

4.2.1 *Enron email network data*

The Enron email network data is a sparse graph constructed based on emails exchanged among the 151 employees of Enron Corporation between the months of December 1998 and November 2002. This graph data set containing 151 nodes and approximately 300 edges for the most dense graph instances, has been used in the past for evaluating anomaly detection algorithms [22]. We aggregate the data on a monthly basis leading to 48 monthly graph instances represented as 151×151 symmetric adjacency matrices, where the edge weights in each matrix indicate the number of times emails are exchanged between any two employees in the corresponding month. We run CAD and ACT on this data, with threshold δ corresponding to $l = 5$ for CAD and $w = 3$ for ACT. For ACT, we report the top 5 anomalies. Since the Enron data set only has 151 nodes, we did not need the approximation in commute distance calculation. The algorithm finished processing each graph instance in a few seconds even using the exact calculation given by (3) for commute distance. With the hypothesis that emailing pattern within the organization was influenced by the scandal, we verify whether the anomalous edges and nodes detected during the different times overlap with the list of key players and correspond to the scandal timeline.

Figure 7 shows a timeline of the Enron scandal and the anomalous graph transitions found by CAD (in blue) and ACT(in green) as a stacked bar plot. Presence of bars indicate that those graph transitions have been marked anomalous by the respective algorithms due to the presence of anomalous relationship changes. The length of the bars indicate the number of identified anomalous nodes, dependent on the choice of δ. It can be seen that both ACT and CAD find graph transitions corresponding to important scandal events to be anomalous. The first 23 months in the data set from Dec 1998 to Sept 2000, is a period of calm in the organizational email network, with ACT reporting 4 and

CAD reporting 1 graph transition as anomalous. The common anomalous graph transition (transition number 12, Oct 1999 - Nov 1999) is when one of the traders, Chris Germany[4] starts interacting with a lot of other traders within the company, probably indicating a sudden increase in trading activity within the organization. The portion of data corresponding to Mar 2002 to Nov 2002 is also a calm period corresponding to the end of the scandal. The period of turmoil for Enron was from Feb 2001 to Feb 2002 (graph instances 27-39), with Jeff Skilling being hired as CEO in Feb 2001, followed by questionable reporting of earnings in the next quarter, leading to unstable stock prices. CAD has identified 10 transitions to be anomalous during the 12 month of the scandal, whereas ACT has identified 6, all of which overlap with CAD.

We found that Kenneth Lay is involved in the highest number of anomalous edges in the anomalous edge set E_{32}, which corresponds to the transition from Jul to Aug 2001 (transition between graph instances 32 and 33). This coincides with the time when Kenneth Lay was reappointed as CEO of Enron and the scandal was starting to get press attention. Figure 8a shows the histogram of email communication to and from Kenneth Lay over the entire 44 month period. The histogram shows a huge spike in his volume of emails in the 33rd month. Figure 8b is the subgraph for Kenneth Lay (the red node in the center) for months 32 and 33. It is observed that he started interacting with many people belonging to different job roles within the company during graph instance 33. Therefore, it is justifiable that Kenneth Lay is picked up as an anomaly during that transition. For the top 5 anomalies we have reported for ACT, Kenneth Lay has never been identified as an anomaly in any transition. During the same transition (32 - 33), the top anomaly found by ACT is James Steffes, VP of government affairs. However, on careful examination of his connections during this transition, it is observed that there is more than 50% overlap in his connections. Also, the new connections are similar to the existing ones in terms of job roles. Steffes was sending few emails to these people in July 2001, whereas in Aug the volume of emails multiplied by many folds. The biggest change in his network is therefore in terms of volume. This change is therefore not as important in terms of anomalous behavior causing structural change in the network, as the Kenneth Lay example.

Additionally, CAD has successfully found Rosalie Fleming (assistant to Kenneth Lay) as an anomaly just before Jeff Skilling took over as CEO from Kenneth Lay during Dec 2000. David Delainey, CEO of Enron Energy, has also been tagged as an anomaly by CAD during the Oct 2001-Nov 2001 transition. On further investigation, we found that this was due to his involvement in the Dynergy acquisition that was being planned in Oct 2001. During the period of Nov 2001 to Feb 2002, most anomalous edges found in E_t belong to Enron employees having job roles of legal specialists, president and vice presidents, and traders. This is expected, since it was during this time that the acquisition failed and Enron declared bankruptcy. In summary, CAD not only identifies the transition periods that are most tumultuous in the Enron scandal timeline, but, unlike ACT, also localizes the key players of the scandal with high level of accuracy.

[4] `http://www.ids.cs.columbia.edu/sites/default/files/hierarchyv3.pdf`

the anomalies identified by CAD, unlike ACT, correlate strongly with the timeline of the Enron scandal and the key players involved in it.

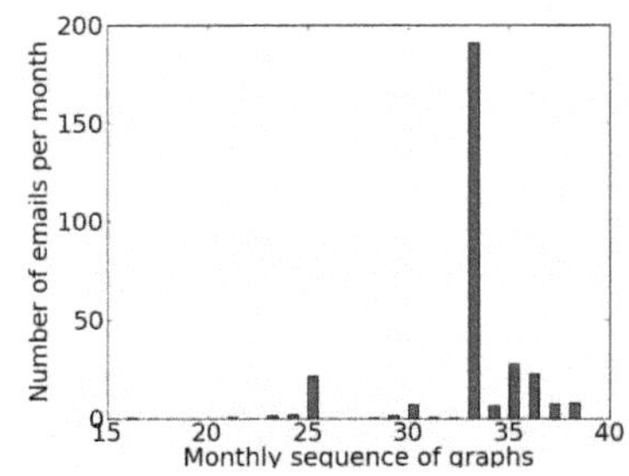

(a) Histogram of emails sent/received by Kenneth Lay during the 44 months.

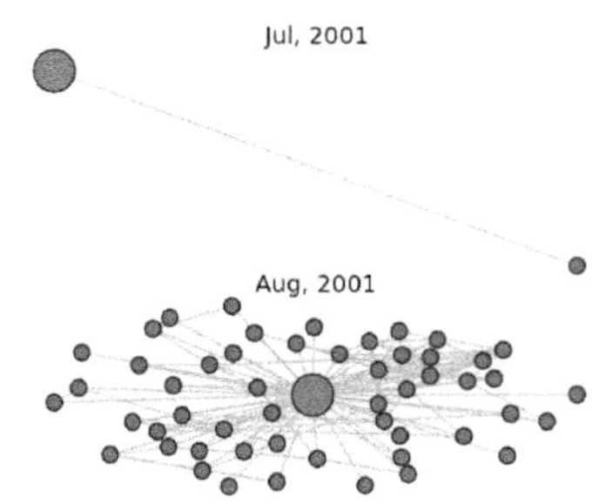

(b) Subgraph showing K. Lay during July and Aug 2001.

Figure 8: Email pattern of ex-CEO Kenneth Lay of Enron.

4.2.2 DBLP data

The DBLP data set is a collaboration network from the scientific community in which each node represents an author and the edge weight between two authors indicates how many papers they have coauthored every year. We filter the data to consider 6574 authors who published at least two papers every year from 2005 to 2010. The sparse graphs constructed for each of the time instances had approximately 30K edges. We ran CAD on this data set (with threshold δ corresponding to $l = 20$) in order to discover authors who established collaborations in new research areas. On average, CAD processed each graph instance in 40 seconds for $k = 50$. We uncovered several interesting anomalies, but for sake of brevity, we report three specific examples:

(i) During the 2005-06 transition, author Atanas Rountev was involved in the most number of anomalous edges returned in E_t. Among these, the edge with the largest score $\Delta E_t(.)$ was between Atanas Rountev and P. Sadayappan. On further investigation it turns out that Atanas Rountev's research focus till 2005 was software engineering, but in 2006 he started collaborating with P. Sadayappan, whose focus is high performance computing, and published multiple papers in several high performance computing conferences.

(ii) During the same 2005-06 transition, the anomalous edge set E_t returned edges connecting Salvatore Orlando with the authors Francesco Bonchi and Fosca Giannotti. On further examination, we found that prior to 2006, Salvatore Orlando researched performance aspects of databases. In 2006, he started collaborating with Francesco Bonchi and Fosca Giannotti, and started publishing in core database conferences. We note that anomaly scores $\Delta E_t(.)$ in this case are lower compared to the scores for Atanas Rountev, which agrees with the fact that the switch from performance aspects of databases to core databases is less severe compared to the switch from software engineering to high performance computing.

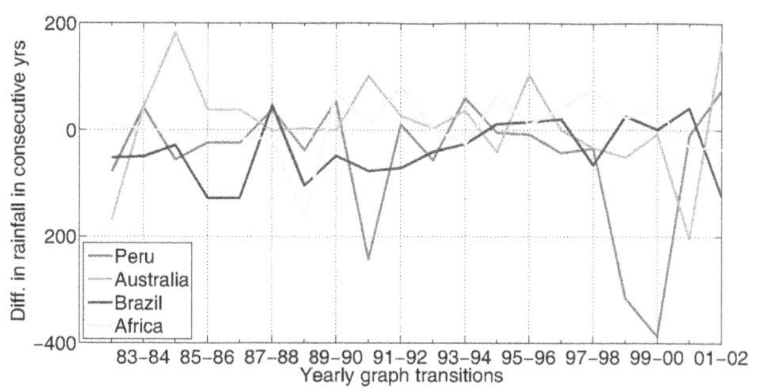

Figure 10: Difference in consecutive years' rainfall in January from 1982-02.

(iii) The third example concerns the severed relationship between Oliver Brdiczka and Max Mühlhäuser during the transition 2008-09. It can be explained by the fact that Oliver and Max published several papers in 2008 as colleagues at Technische Universität Darmstadt. However, in 2009, Oliver switched to publishing in human computer interaction conferences which coincided with his move to the Palo Alto Research Center.

4.2.3 World-wide precipitation data

The world-wide precipitation (rainfall) data consists of monthly averages of observations between 1982 and 2002 recorded at $0.5°$ resolution on the entire earth's grid. Precipitation recordings are only available on land surface and there are 67,420 such data locations for every month. Precipitation has a seasonal and spatial variation that is reasonably stable over time. Abnormal weather patterns can therefore be uncovered by detecting abnormal variations in precipitation data. In order to determine such abnormal variations, we construct 10-nearest neighbor graphs for each month over the 67,420 locations, where the edge strength between a node i and one of its 10 neighbors j is given by $\exp\left(-\|p_i - p_j\|^2/2\sigma^2\right)$ with p_i and p_j corresponding to precipitation levels recorded at i and j for that month and σ is the kernel bandwidth. In order to account for seasonal trends, we at a time restrict our attention to the 21 graphs corresponding to one particular month of the year, and apply CAD to each of the 12 sequences of 21 graphs each. To run CAD with $k = 50$ on each graph instance (with threshold δ corresponding to $l = 30$), the average running time was bounded by 2 minutes.

We discovered several interesting anomalies upon running CAD on this data set. In the interest of space, we present one set of interesting anomalies discovered by CAD for the month of January during the transition from 1994 to 1995. The top anomalous edges reported by CAD during the transition from January, 1994 to January, 1995 were those between southern Africa and eastern equatorial Africa, Brazil and eastern equatorial Africa, Peru and the Amazon basin, Peru and the southeast Asian island of Malaysia, and between Australian inland and equatorial Africa. Figure 9 shows these location pairs connected by these anomalous edges (in blue) using red squares and yellow circles. Analyzing the data it can be observed that locations in southern Africa and Brazil received much higher rainfall during that year compared to the past year, whereas Peru and Australia received less rain than the year before. During the same transition, rainfall in equatorial Africa as well as the Amazon basin did not change. Therefore, the edge strength (similarity value computed using the exponential function described above) between these location pairs changed compared to the previous year. On verification using external evidence, we found that the La Niña[5] weather pattern occurred in 1995, which is characterized by wetter winters in southern Africa and Brazil, very high rainfall in southeast Asian islands, and drought-like conditions in Peru, Chile, and eastern equatorial Africa. Therefore, we can easily verify that the top anomalies found by CAD except Australia can be explained by the La Niña phenomenon. During the same time, the Australian plains suffered one of the worst droughts since 1900[6] and therefore, experienced much lower rainfall than normal, which is why it became closer to drier regions like the African plains. These evidences corroborate the fact that the anomalous relationships identified by CAD are indeed valid anomalies.

The *difference* in average precipitation experienced by southern Africa, Brazil, Peru and Australia between successive years from 1981 to 2012 during the month of January is shown in Figure 10. From this figure, we note that locations in southern Africa and Brazil were found to have received higher rainfall during 1995 as compared to 1994, whereas Peru and Australia received less rain than usual. However, observe that increase and decrease in rainfall in these locations, as shown in Figure 10, is very subtle relative to some of the other variations seen in the figure. It is therefore unlikely that these anomalies would have been detected using time series analysis on the average precipitation data. The reason CAD was able to detect this anomalous weather pattern was because it resulted in simultaneous, albeit subtle changes in precipitation across several locations, which in turn resulted in significant changes in the structure of the nearest neighbor graphs. This ability of CAD in picking up subtle but simultaneous changes in precipitation across several locations therefore makes CAD useful for identifying teleconnections[7], *i.e.* climate anomalies related to each other at long distances.

5. CONCLUSION

A novel method called CAD is proposed for localizing abnormal changes in nodes relationships (edges) that are responsible for anomalous change in structure in weighted dynamic graphs. Existing anomaly detection methods for dynamic graphs such as ACT are primarily designed only to detect whether a graph structure change is anomalous or not, and are not well suited for identifying the responsible edges and nodes. This makes CAD, to the best of our knowledge, the first of its kind for localizing anomalies in *time-evolving* graphs. CAD tracks changes in edge strength and structure (via commute time distance) in order to determine these anomalies. CAD has an $O(n \log n)$ run-time

[5]https://en.wikipedia.org/wiki/El_Nino

[6]http://en.wikipedia.org/wiki/2000s_Australian_drought

[7]http://en.wikipedia.org/wiki/Teleconnection

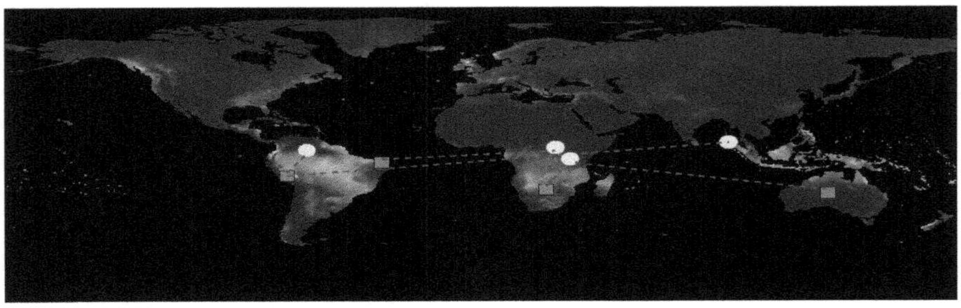

Figure 9: Heat map of rainfall for January 1995. Red squares and yellow circles are nodes associated with anomalous edges (indicated by blue dotted lines) found by CAD.

complexity per graph instance for large, sparse graphs, making it scalable. Our experimental studies on synthetic and large real world datasets showed that CAD consistently and efficiently localizes anomalous edges and associated nodes responsible for anomalous changes in graph structure.

6. ACKNOWLEDGEMENT

This research has been funded by the DARPA/ADAMS program under contract W911NF-11-C-0216. The authors would like to thank Prof. Stephen Boyd at Stanford University for initial discussions on this work and Prof. Sanjay Chawla and Nguyen Lu Dang Khoa at University of Sydney for providing code for the spielman-teng solver. Finally, the authors would like to thank the reviewers for their very detailed reviews and comments.

7. REFERENCES

[1] L. Akoglu and C. Faloutsos. Event detection in time series of mobile communication graphs. In *Army Science Conference*, 2010.

[2] L. Akoglu, M. McGlohon, and C. Faloutsos. Oddball: Spotting anomalies in weighted graphs. *Advances in Knowledge Discovery and Data Mining*, pages 410–421, 2010.

[3] J. Batson, D. Spielman, N. Srivastava, and S. Teng. Spectral sparsification of graphs: theory and algorithms. *Comm. of the ACM*, 56(8):87–94, 2013.

[4] M. Belkin and P. Niyogi. Laplacian eigenmaps and spectral techniques for embedding and clustering. *Advances in NIPS*, 14:585–591, 2001.

[5] S. P. Borgatti. Centrality and network flow. *Social Networks*, 27(1):55–71, 2005.

[6] H. Bunke, P. Dickinson, A. Humm, C. Irniger, and M. Kraetzl. Computer network monitoring and abnormal event detection using graph matching and multidimensional scaling. In *Advances in Data Mining Applications in Medicine, Web Mining, Marketing, Image and Signal Mining*, pages 576–590. 2006.

[7] V. Chandola, A. Banerjee, and V. Kumar. Anomaly detection: A survey. *ACM Computing Surveys*, 41(3):1–58, 2009.

[8] P. Chebotarev and E. Shamis. On proximity measures for graph vertices. *arXiv preprint math/0602073*, 2006.

[9] J. Chen and I. Safro. A measure of the local connectivity between graph vertices. In *Proc. of Int. Conf. on Computational Science*, pages 196–205, 2011.

[10] W. Eberle and L. Holder. Discovering structural anomalies in graph-based data. In *ICDM Workshops*, pages 393–398, 2007.

[11] X. Gao, B. Xiao, D. Tao, and X. Li. A survey of graph edit distance. *Pattern Analysis and Applications.*, 13(1):113–129, 2010.

[12] T. Ide and H. Kashima. Eigenspace-based anomaly detection in computer systems. In *ACM SIGKDD*, pages 440–449, 2004.

[13] I. Jovanović and Z. Stanić. Spectral distances of graphs. *Linear Algebra and its Applications*, 436(5):1425–1435, 2012.

[14] N. Khoa and S. Chawla. Robust outlier detection using commute time and eigenspace embedding. In *Advances in Knowledge Discovery and Data Mining*, pages 422–434. 2010.

[15] N. Khoa and S. Chawla. Large scale spectral clustering using resistance distance and spielman-teng solvers. In *Discovery Science*, pages 7–21, 2012.

[16] M. Maybury, P. Chase, B. Cheikes, D. Brackney, S. Matzner, B. Wood, T. Longstaff, T. Hetherington, C. Sibley, J. Marin, L. Spitzner, J. Copeland, S. Lewandowski, and J. Haile. Analysis and detection of malicious insiders. In *Conference on Intelligent Analysis.*, 2005.

[17] C. Noble and D. Cook. Graph-based anomaly detection. In *ACM SIGKDD*, pages 631–636, 2003.

[18] B. Pincombe. Anomaly detection in time series of graphs using arma processes. *ASOR Bulletin*, 24, 2005.

[19] P. Shoubridge, M. Kraetzl, W. Wallis, and H. Bunke. Detection of abnormal change in a time series of graphs. *Journal of Interconnection Networks*, 3:85–101, 2002.

[20] J. Sun, C. Faloutsos, S. Papadimitriou, and P. Yu. Graphscope: parameter-free mining of large time-evolving graphs. In *ACM SIGKDD*, pages 687–696, 2007.

[21] J. Sun, Y. Xie, H. Zhang, and C. Faloutsos. Less is more: Compact matrix decomposition for large sparse graphs. Technical report, CS Dept., CMU, 2007.

[22] B. Thompson and T. Eliassi-rad. Dapa-v10: Discovery and analysis of patterns and anomalies in volatile time-evolving networks. In *Workshop on Information in Networks*, 2009.

[23] L. Yen, D. Vanvyve, F. Wouters, F. Fouss, M. Verleysen, and M. Saerens. Clustering using a random walk based distance measure. In *Proceedings of ESANN*, pages 317–324, 2005.

Online Optimization and Fair Costing for Dynamic Data Sharing in a Cloud Data Market

Ziyang Liu
NEC Laboratories America
Cupertino CA, USA
ziyang@nec-labs.com

Hakan Hacıgümüş
NEC Laboratories America
Cupertino CA, USA
hakan@nec-labs.com

ABSTRACT

The data markets are emerging to address many organizations' need to find more useful external data sets for deeper insights. Existing data markets have two main limitations. First, they either sell a whole data set or some fixed views, but do not allow arbitrary ad-hoc queries. Second, they only sell static data, but not data that are frequently updated. While there exist proposed solutions for selling ad-hoc queries, it is an open question what mechanism should be used to sell ad-hoc queries on dynamic data. In this paper, we study a data market framework that enables the sale or sharing of dynamic data, where each sharing is specified by an ad-hoc query. To keep the shared data up-to-date, the service provider should create a view of the shared data and maintain the view for the data buyer. We provide solutions to two important problems in this framework: how to efficiently maintain the views, and how to fairly determine the cost each sharing incurs for its view to be created and maintained by the service provider. Both problems are challenging since in the first problem, different sharings with the same operations in their plans may reuse these operations, and each sharing plan must be generated online. In the second problem, there are several factors that impact the fairness of a costing function and a straightforward mechanism won't work. We propose an intuitive online algorithm for sharing plan selection, as well as a set of fair costing criteria and an algorithm that maximizes the fairness.

1. INTRODUCTION

In the big data era, data has become an integral part of decision making and user experience enhancement. An important observation is that organizations not only use internal data but also find compelling ways of integrating external data (such as publicly available data sets, surveys, curated data from other organizations, etc.) into their decision making and planning processes. As a result, several data markets have emerged, where the data can be sold and bought (e.g., Microsoft Azure Marketplace [3], Infochimps [2], Xignite [5], Gnip [1], etc,), or in some cases data are freely shared with the public in the cloud [4].[1]

[1]Since data can be shared freely or at a price, which could also be called a sale, we use *sharing* and *sale* interchangeably.

SIGMOD'14, June 22–27, 2014, Snowbird, UT, USA.

http://dx.doi.org/10.1145/2588555.2593679.

These recently emerged data markets are limited in functionality in two aspects. First, they either sell a whole data set or some fixed views of a data set, but do not allow arbitrary ad-hoc queries. This limitation leads to buyers needing to browse a large set of pre-defined views and possibly buying more data than what they need [19, 20]. Second, current data markets only sell static data sets[2], e.g., the GDP of a country from 1997 to 2011. This limits the sale of many useful data sets that receive frequent updates. For example, a food retailer may be interested in purchasing users' check-ins at restaurants, tweets, etc., in order to infer a user's food preference and recommend corresponding products; a hotel booking service may be interested in purchasing users' flight booking data and calendar data in order to recommend hotels and design targeted promotions; a deal service may find helpful to purchase users' location data in order to alert the users of good deals near them. The data to be purchased in all these scenarios are dynamic and frequently updated. There are proposed solutions for the first limitation [19, 20], where the authors developed a mechanism that automatically prices ad-hoc queries, which is proved to achieve certain desirable properties such as arbitrage-free.

In this paper, we focus on the second limitation, and propose *a way to sell dynamic data in a data market*. The data market has three roles: *data owner*, *data buyer*, and *data market service provider*. An individual or an organization may be both an owner and a buyer. The data owner is willing to sell/share the data at a price. Although the data owner may choose to sell the data directly to the data buyer, this direct sell would require significant amount of automation, as well as infrastructure efforts. Hence, data sellers typically prefer to go through the data market and leverage the services it offers, which is a common practice in cloud computing. As the data owners benefit from the services provided by the data market, the provider also benefits from serving a multitude of data owners and data buyers by consolidating them to achieve economies of scale.

When a buyer specifies the data sets she's willing to buy, the service provider has two tasks: (1) deliver and maintain the data in a way that minimizes the operational cost (analogous to finding a query plan with minimum cost), and (2) calculate the price of the data, which should be a function of the monetary value of the data specified by the owner, and the operational cost. In this paper we discuss how to deal with these two problems. For problem (2), we only focus on calculating the operational cost. The monetary value of the data is assumed to be determined by the data owner. The function that maps the cost to the price is an economics problem that is out of scope of this work and interested readers can refer to [23, 35] for pricing strategies.

[2]Certain data sets in the markets may be updated, however, the buyers need to buy the updated data set again.

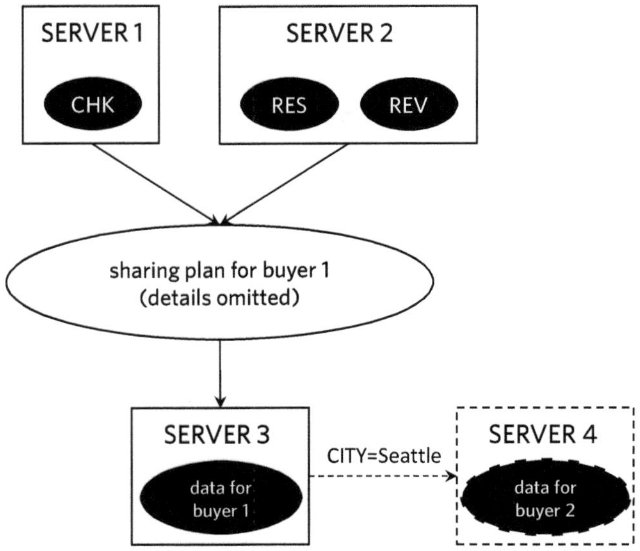

Figure 1: Sharing plans for two buyers. Source data are located on servers 1-2, and the purchased data (view) are located on server 3 (for buyer 1) and server 4 (for buyer 2).

The following example illustrates the problems studied in this paper. Following the terminology in [9], we use the term *dynamic data sharing* to refer to the sale or sharing of such dynamic data sets. A *sharing plan* specifies the set of operations/subexpressions to prepare the data for the buyer (such as the order of joins among the requested tables, time to apply predicates, time to move data between servers, etc.), which is analogous to a query plan for a SQL query.

EXAMPLE 1.1. ***[Selecting Sharing Plans]****: Consider three data sets in the data market in the form of relational tables: check-in at restaurants (CHK), restaurant information (RES), and restaurant reviews (REV). A data buyer (buyer 1) is interested in a dynamic data sharing that joins these three tables. These tables may be owned by different data owners and reside in different physical servers in the cloud infrastructure. It is not trivial to design a plan with minimum cost that delivers and maintains the data requested by buyer 1, which involves the order of join, the way to move data between the servers, etc.; each of these operations may incur a dollar cost for the service provider, especially if the service provider rents infrastructures from an IaaS provider. Furthermore, if there's an existing data sharing that maintains the join of CHK and RES, it should be taken into account when choosing the plan for the new sharing, since the data of the existing sharing (CHK ⋈ RES) may be reused.*

[Costing Sharing Plans]*: Suppose we've selected a plan for this data sharing, as shown in solid lines in Figure 1 with details omitted. Later another buyer (buyer 2) is also interested in a dynamic data sharing that joins CHK, RES and REV, but she is only interested in restaurants in Seattle. The service provider decides that the best plan for this buyer is to reuse the previous plan, and add a filter "city = Seattle" in the end, as shown in the dotted part in Figure 1. Now suppose that the operational cost of maintaining these two sharings is \$200/month. Then, what is the operational cost of each sharing? If we use a trivial approach that evenly divides the cost of each operation/subexpression among the sharings using the subexpression, the second sharing will be considered more costly than the first, since the second sharing plan has an additional step, "city = Seattle". Consequently, buyer 2 may pay a higher price than buyer 1. However, this is not fair to buyer 2 because if buyer 1 did not exist, the second sharing plan may apply the predicate "city = Seattle" earlier, which may make the RES table much smaller and the sharing plan much cheaper.*

There are similarities between the problem of selecting sharing plans and some classic problems such as distributed query processing, multiple query optimization, view maintenance, and index/view selection. These problems are indeed related but are also fundamentally different. More detailed related work discussion is presented in Section 2.

For selecting sharing plans, we propose an online algorithm. The algorithm should be online since it needs to service a sharing request as soon as it is received without knowing future requests. Our algorithm makes a significant improvement upon an existing work [9], which uses a greedy online algorithm (referred to as algorithm GREEDY in this paper). Algorithm GREEDY enumerates the plans for the new sharing and chooses the plan that incurs the smallest additional dollar cost after integrating into the plans for existing sharings (referred to as *global plan*). We show that algorithm GREEDY can perform arbitrarily badly even for very simple instances of the problem. We also analyze another baseline algorithm named algorithm NORMALIZE, which normalizes the cost of a subexpression using the number of prior occurrences of the subexpression, and show that it can also perform arbitrarily badly. In contrast, our proposed algorithm, named algorithm MANAGEDRISK, judiciously chooses the plan for each sharing such that it neither avoids taking risks nor takes too much risks, which avoids making arbitrarily bad decisions for those instances where the baseline algorithms fail.

For costing sharing plans, we propose a set of *fairness criteria* for costing data sharings that consists of five conditions (details will be given in Section 5) . These five conditions capture the degree of fairness, which is represented as a value between 0 and 1. The five conditions are non-redundant since it is possible to meet any four conditions but not the remaining one. We further present the necessary and sufficient condition of their satisfiability, and present an algorithm, named algorithm FAIRCOST, that maximizes the degree of fairness.

Our contributions are summarized as:

- We propose an online algorithm, algorithm MANAGEDRISK, that selects sharing plans for dynamic data sharings in a cloud data market. Algorithm MANAGEDRISK avoids the pitfalls in the baseline algorithms and avoids making bad decisions observed on the baseline algorithms.
- This is the first study on fair costing of data sharing in a data market. We propose fairness criteria which represent fairness as a value between 0 and 1, and design an algorithm to find the costing function that maximizes the fairness.
- Our experiments verified the effectiveness and efficiency of the proposed approaches.

The rest of the paper is organized as follows. Section 2 discusses related work. Section 3 presents backgrounds, including the data market model, dynamic data sharings, sharing plans and cost of a sharing plan. Section 4 discusses several online algorithms for sharing plan selection, including two baseline algorithms GREEDY and NORMALIZE, as well as the proposed algorithm MANAGEDRISK. Section 5 introduces fairness criteria for costing data sharings, and explains an algorithm that maximizes fairness. Results of evaluations are reported in Section 6. Section 7 makes conclusions and discusses future works.

2. RELATED WORK

2.1 Selecting Sharing Plans

The problem of selecting sharing plans is related to but different from several classic problems such as distributed query processing, multiple query optimization, view maintenance and index/view selection.

Distributed Query Processing aims to quickly find a good plan for a query whose data are distributed in multiple machines [18, 25, 27]. In our problem the algorithm for selecting sharing plans doesn't need to have a very short response time, and thus for each sharing, we can often afford to explore a much larger space of possible plans or even enumerate all possible plans. The challenge in our problem is that, since there are multiple sharings and we process them in an online fashion, it is difficult to choose the right plan for each query that will optimize the total cost of the global plan, which is the focus of our proposed algorithm MANAGEDRISK. As to be shown later, if we simply use the cheapest plan for each query (i.e., algorithm GREEDY), the result can be arbitrarily bad even for simple instances of the problem.

The studies on *Multiple Query Optimization* have different focuses. Earlier works such as [32, 33, 34] focus on choosing the right plan for each query such that common subexpressions in multiple queries can be reused. It is related to our problem, however, it is an offline problem where all queries are known in advance and it starts to process all queries at the same time. Algorithms for this problem are based on heuristics such as A* search. Later works mainly focus on how to synchronize a single operation (such as table scan) among multiple query plans that use this operation, which is a hard problem if different queries are submitted at different times [10, 11, 15, 16]. By contrast, in our problem the shared data need to be constantly maintained, and our focus is which plan should be used for each sharing, which is an orthogonal problem.

View maintenance is complementary to the problem of selecting sharing plans. In view maintenance, the views to be maintained are given and the optimization goal is to decide when to propagate updates, reduce the number of queries to bring a view to a consistent state, decide whether to maintain views in incremental or recomputation fashion, etc. [6, 22, 28, 29]. In our problem, the main focus is to determine a plan for each sharing, and after a plan is selected, view maintenance techniques can be applied to maintain the views for the selected plan.

Index/view selection is the problem of selecting indexes to build or views to materialize in relational databases based on the workload [7, 8, 13, 14, 30, 31, 37]. The idea is to select indexes/views which benefit a window of recent queries, with the assumption that queries in the near future will be similar as recent queries. There are mainly three types of algorithms: hill climbing approaches([7, 8, 13, 14]) which enumerate small subsets of indexes/views, select subsets with large benefits and small costs, and greedily increase the size of the subsets until a target is reached; Knapsack approaches([37]), which alter the benefits/costs of indexes/views in a way that accounts for the interactions among indexes/views, and use the knapsack algorithm for index/view selection; and feedback-based approaches([30]) that involve elicitation from DBAs. Many aspects of the index/view selection problem differ from those of our problem, for example: (1) we focus on dynamic data and the views in our problem are constantly maintained; (2) in our problem we cannot choose each view independently, since each sharing plan is composed of multiple views which must be materialized together if this plan is selected; (3) the goal of index/view selection is to maximize the benefit of the selected indexes/views given a storage budget, whereas the goal of our problem is minimizing the cost of the global sharing plan where sharings are received online; (4) in our problem it is much more difficult to determine how selecting a particular plan for one sharing affects (positively or negatively) the cost of another sharing, since the cost may be collectively affected by the plans selected for many other sharings.

A knapsack-based algorithm is not suitable for our problem since there are a large number of interactions among different sharings as well as different plans for the same sharing, and it is infeasible to assign an independent benefit and cost for each individual view or sharing plan. A feedback-based approach is also ineffective since a sharing may have a large number of possible plans that involve an even larger number of views, and they heavily interact with one another. It is difficult for a human being to come up with a feedback for each view or plan. The hill climbing idea is applicable to our problem: given a new sharing, we can generate a subset of plans and select the most desirable one, using the hill climbing philosophy. The two baseline algorithms to be introduced in Section 4, algorithm Greedy and algorithm Normalize, are based on similar ideas. However, their solutions may have an unbounded cost for simple instances of the problem.

2.2 Costing Sharing Plans

Pricing data has been studied in several publications in the database community [17, 19, 20, 21, 36]. [17] aims to help database service providers determine the prices of structures (indexes, materialized views, cached columns) built by the service provider that benefit future queries. [36] has a similar setting as [17] where an optimization can be built that benefits future users. It takes a bidding approach where each user tells the service provider how much she's willing to pay for an optimization. An optimization is built if a set of users can be found such that, by charging each users the same amount, the cost of the optimization can be recovered, and this amount does not exceed each user's budget.

Both [17] and [36] study how to determine the price of a product assuming the cost of the product can be easily obtained. On the other hand, we focus on the problem of determining the *cost* of a product (i.e., sharing), since different sharings interact in the global sharing plan, and it is challenging to calculate the cost of each sharing in a fair way. In our case, given the cost, determining the price is an independent problem, where methodologies in the economics field can be applied. Besides, although the pricing strategies in [17, 36] are also fair, it is much more challenging to achieve fairness in costing sharing plans. In [17, 36], since different users/queries are independent, fairness is simply achieved by charging each user/query the same price to use the same optimization/structure. However, in our costing problem many sharing plans interact in the global plan by reusing subexpressions. It is further complicated by the fact that each sharing has multiple possible plans, and a plan may need to be considered even if it is not used, as shown in Example 1.1. A simple approach that equally distributes the cost of each subexpression to the sharing plans that use this subexpression is *not* fair.

[19] studies the problem of pricing a query that returns a set of tuples, given the price of the whole data set and the prices of some views of the data. The main idea is to find the cheapest data-dependent rewriting of the query using views, and price the query as the sum of the prices of these views (the price of computation is neglected, which is fair for static data since the monetary value of the data may far exceed the cost of computation). If a rewriting cannot be found, the query will have the same price as the whole data set. In this way, the price of the query satisfies two desirable properties: arbitrage-free and discount-free. [20] extends [19] by formulating the rewriting problem for a wide range of queries, most

of which makes the rewriting NP-hard, as ILP. It further discusses how to avoid double-charging when the user buys similar queries, how to price data updates, and how to fairly share the revenue if the query involves data from multiple data sellers.

The problems studied in [19, 20] are orthogonal to ours. They study the price of *data*, rather than the operational cost, i.e., cost of *delivering and maintaining the data*. Our problem, on the other hand, focuses on the latter, as explained in Section 1.

3. PRELIMINARIES

3.1 Data Market and Dynamic Data Sharing

We use the data market model proposed in [9]. A data market is a cloud computing infrastructure where tenants pay to use computing resources to run their applications and have the opportunity to sell data to one another through data sharings. Since tenants' applications keep collecting new data (e.g., the CHK table in Figure 1 keeps collecting new check-in information), the data sold in the data market are dynamic. This is in contrast to the type of data markets like Microsoft Azure Marketplace, Infochimps, etc., where static data sets are sold.

A data owner willing to sell a data set makes the data set accessible to the service provider. In this paper we follow [9, 19, 20] in considering data in the form of relational tables, but other forms can also be used. A buyer willing to purchase data may submit a data sharing request to the service provider in the form of a query, such as the example in Section 1 where a buyer wants to purchase the join of CHK, RES and REV. To service the request, the service provider is responsible for creating and maintaining the view specified in the query, which incurs dollar costs for using resources such as storage, CPU, network, etc., if the service provider rents resources from an IaaS provider such as AWS. As explained before, the price of a data sharing is a function of the data price specified by the data owner, as well as the operational cost incurred to deliver and maintain the data for the buyer.

3.2 Sharing Plan

A sharing plan determines how data should be moved among the servers, in which order the joins and predicates should be applied, etc., in order to maintain the shared data. Each join in the sharing plan can be specified as

$$(A, s_1) \bowtie (B, s_2) \rightarrow s_3$$

where s_1, s_2 are the servers that have a copy of A and B, respectively, which may be frequently updated, and s_3 is where the result should be placed. A possible plan for this join where s_1 = server 1 and s_2, s_3 = server 2 is shown in Figure 2, where an ellipse denotes a base relation and a rounded rectangle denotes a *delta relation*, which receives updates to the corresponding base relation. Note that this plan avoids copying base relations across servers, and only copies delta relations.

For multiple sharings with common subexpressions, such as the two sharings in Example 1.1, the computation of a common subexpression can be reused so that the subexpression is only computed once. A plan involving multiple sharings is called a *global plan*. Next we introduce the costing of sharing plans in the global plan.

3.3 Costing of Sharing Plans

We assume that the data market service provider has a cost model for estimating the dollar cost of each subexpression, e.g., copy, merge, join, etc. To obtain the cost model, there exist analytical models to estimate resource usages for various operations in the cloud [24], and the resource usages can be directly mapped to dollar cost in cloud services such as AWS. Thus the service provider

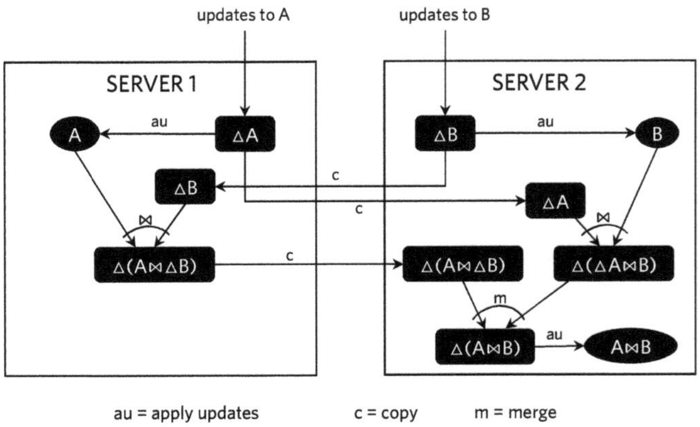

Figure 2: A possible plan for joining relation A on server 1 and relation B on server 2 such that the resulting view $A \bowtie B$ is placed on server 2

can calculate the cost per time unit of an individual sharing plan, which is the sum of the cost of each subexpression in the plan, multiplied by the number of times they are executed per time unit. However, this is not sufficient, as the service provider needs to determine the cost incurred by each sharing plan in the global plan in order to calculate the price of each sharing. This is complicated since different sharing plans in the global plan may reuse common subexpressions, and as said before, simply dividing the cost of each subexpression by the number of sharing plans that use it isn't fair.

Suppose the cost of the global plan is $cost(GP)$ and there are n sharing plans $P_1, \cdots, P_n$ where the cost attributed to P_i (referred to as "attributed cost") is $AC(P_i)$, then the total cost of these sharing plans should equal the cost of the global plan, i.e.,

$$\sum_{i=1}^{n} AC(P_i) = cost(GP)$$

and $cost(GP)$ should be distributed to each $AC(P_i)$ in a fair way. Section 5 will further discuss the criteria of fairness and how to achieve maximum fairness.

4. ONLINE SHARING PLAN SELECTION

4.1 Problem Definition

As discussed before, the service provider needs to select a sharing plan for each new sharing without knowing future sharings. Thus the algorithm needs to be online. We define the following online sharing plan selection problem.

DEFINITION 4.1 (ONLINE SHARING PLAN SELECTION). *The input contains a sequence of dynamic data sharings, a cost model and the initial state of the system. The service provider should select a sharing plan for each sharing without the knowledge of future sharings. The goal of the service provider is to minimize the total cost of servicing the sequence of sharings.*

The cost model is used to calculate the cost of each subexpression in a sharing plan, and the initial state of the system refers to the initial placement of data, i.e., which table is on which servers, and the server capacity constraint, which can be expressed in multiple ways such as how many tuples the server can handle per second.

For ease of illustration and explanation, we first consider a special case of the problem, where servers have unlimited capacity, and each sharing is a join-only query with no predicates or projections.

We will discuss the general case in Section 4.5. Note that servers having unlimited capacity doesn't mean that all sharings are processed on a single server, since different source data may be stored on different servers.

In the following, we denote a sharing as a set of source tables. For example, let a, b, c be three tables. A sharing that joins these three tables is denoted as (a, b, c).[3] A subexpression (i.e., join) is denoted by two sets of tables, e.g., ab is the join of a and b, and $a(bc)$ is the join of a with $b \bowtie c$. A sharing plan is represented by a sequence of joins, e.g., $a(bc)$ is the plan where we first join b with c, and then join the result with a. Note that notation $a(bc)$ may represent either a subexpression or a sharing plan, but it is not a problem when the context is clear.

We use $C[\cdot]$ to represent the cost of a sharing plan and $c[\cdot]$ to represent the cost of a subexpression. For example, $C[a(bc)]$ is the cost of the aforementioned sharing plan, and $c[a(bc)]$ denotes the cost of joining a with $b \bowtie c$. Thus $C[a(bc)] = c[bc] + c[a(bc)]$. Let $\#join(S)$ be the number of joins in a plan of sharing S. For example, the value of $\#join$ for sharing (a, b, c) is 2, and all plans for this sharing have 2 joins.

Next, we discuss two baseline algorithms, namely algorithm GREEDY and algorithm NORMALIZE, before presenting our proposed algorithm MANAGEDRISK. Both baseline algorithms adopt the idea of hill-climbing, which is seen in the algorithms of many classic problems including index/view selection [13]. It refers to the attempt to add a good plan of the new sharing to the global plan. Algorithm GREEDY prefers a plan that adds the smallest cost to the global plan, while Algorithm NORMALIZE considers the subexpressions occurred in the existing sharings and assumes that they will occur again in future, and thus it chooses a plan with this assumption in mind. At a high level, for each sharing, all three algorithms enumerate all possible plans, but use different criteria to decide which plan to select.

Note that in most cases we can afford to enumerate all possible plans, since choosing sharing plans is not an interactive or time-critical task. In case the sharing involves a complex query for which enumerating all plans is infeasible, we can use various heuristics, such as hill climbing and beam search, to generate a manageable subset of all possible plans [12].

4.2 Algorithm Greedy

Algorithm GREEDY is adopted in an existing work [9]. As its name suggests, it enumerates all possible plans for a sharing, and chooses the one with the minimum additional cost after adding it to the global plan. The following example shows how algorithm GREEDY works and why it may perform poorly, even if each sharing has at most two joins.

EXAMPLE 4.1. *Suppose there is a single server, and all sharings are processed within this server. Consider a sequence of sharings* $(a, b, c_1), (a, b, c_2), \cdots$. *Suppose there are two possible plans for each sharing:* $(ab)c_x$ *and* $a(bc_x)$, *such that* $c[ab] = 100$, $c[(ab)c_x] = \epsilon$ *where* ϵ *is a negligibly small positive number, and* $C[a(bc_x)] = 10$. *If there are sufficiently many such sharings (more than 10), an optimal algorithm will use plan* $(ab)c_1$ *for the first sharing, so that all other sharings can reuse the result of* ab *and will only cost* ϵ *each. Suppose there are* n *sharings, the total optimal cost is* $100 + n\epsilon$. *Algorithm* GREEDY, *on the other hand, will always use plan* $a(bc_x)$ *for each sharing, and has a total cost of* $10n$, *which is unbounded compared to the optimal cost.*

[3]We focus on natural joins, so no further specification is needed for a sharing. Our approach supports other types of joins but they will make the notations in this paper unnecessarily more complicated.

As we can see, algorithm GREEDY does not take any risk (here "risk" refers to using plan $(ab)c_x$, since we do not know whether there will be future sharings to amortize the cost of ab, $c[ab]$). At the first glance, this seems what an algorithm should do, since it does not know the future and there is no incentive to take the risk and use plan $(ab)c_x$. However, we will show in Section 4.4 that this is not necessarily true.

4.3 Algorithm Normalize

An attempt to solve the weakness of algorithm GREEDY can lead to another baseline algorithm, which we name algorithm NORMALIZE. To explain it, we introduce the following definition.

DEFINITION 4.2. *A sharing* S *is said to* contain *a subexpression* s, *denoted as* $s \lessdot S$, *if the subexpression occurs in one of the possible plans for the sharing.*

For example, a sharing (a, b, c, d) may contain subexpressions ab, bc, cd, ac, $(ab)c$, $a(bcd)$, $(ab)(cd)$, etc. (depending on joinability between tables), each of which denotes a join.

Algorithm NORMALIZE normalizes the cost of each subexpression in the current sharing by the number of sharings seen so far that contain this subexpression. Let C_n and c_n denote the normalized cost of a sharing plan and a subexpression, respectively. Algorithm NORMALIZE selects the plan with the smallest normalized cost. For the sharing sequence in Example 4.1, when NORMALIZE processes the xth sharing, if the first $x - 1$ sharings all use plan $a(bc_x)$, then $c_n[ab]$ in the xth sharing is considered to be its original cost (100) divided by x, because ab is contained in all x sharings seen so far.

In this way, NORMALIZE will use $a(bc_x)$ for the first 10 sharings, and for the 11th sharing, $c_n[ab]$ is 100/11, so $C_n[(ab)c_{11}] < C_n[a(bc_{11})]$ and NORMALIZE will select plan $(ab)c_{11}$. In other words, although NORMALIZE makes the wrong choices for the first 10 sharings, it eventually realizes that subexpression ab has occurred many times and decides to use ab even though it adds more cost to the global plan than the other option. Although it doesn't give the optimal solution, its cost is bounded in this particular example compared with the optimal solution.

Although NORMALIZE works better than GREEDY for Example 4.1, it may still have an unbounded cost even if each sharing has at most two joins, as shown in the following example.

EXAMPLE 4.2. *Consider a sequence of* n *sharings* (a, b, c_1), $(a, b, c_2), \cdots, (a, b, c_n)$. *Again, suppose there are two possible plans for each sharing:* $(ab)c_x$ *and* $a(bc_x)$. $c[ab] = n$. *For* $1 \le x \le n - 1$, $C[a(bc_x)] = \epsilon$ *and* $c[(ab)c_x] = \epsilon$. *For the nth sharing,* $C[a(bc_n)] = 1 + 2\epsilon$ *and* $c[(ab)c_n] = \epsilon$.

For this sharing sequence, NORMALIZE *will choose* $a(bc_x)$ *for the first* $n - 1$ *sharings, incurring a cost of* $(n - 1)\epsilon$. *For the last sharing,* $c_n[ab] = 1$ *(since it is contained in all n sharings), thus* $C_n[(ab)c_n] = 1 + \epsilon < C_n[a(bc_n)] = 1 + 2\epsilon$, *and* NORMALIZE *chooses plan* $(ab)c_n$. *The total cost of* NORMALIZE *is* $n + n\epsilon$. *An optimal algorithm would choose plan* $a(bc_x)$ *for all sharings for a total cost of* $1 + (n + 1)\epsilon$. *Since* n *can be arbitrarily large and* ϵ *can be arbitrarily small, algorithm* NORMALIZE *has an unbounded cost compared with the optimal cost.*

As we can see, NORMALIZE takes a big risk for the last sharing by using plan $(ab)c_n$, for which it gets no reward since it is the last sharing. To address the problem in both algorithms discussed so far, next we propose algorithm MANAGEDRISK.

4.4 Algorithm ManagedRisk

We can see from the previous two examples that we need to take some risk, since an algorithm that takes no risk, such as GREEDY, has a poor performance; however, the risk we take needs to be somehow controlled to avoid the situation in Example 4.2. The idea of algorithm ManagedRisk, at a high level, is that we should take risks, but we should only take a risk on a sharing if the cost of previous sharings are sufficiently high, so that even if the risk we take turns out to be a bad one, the additional cost incurred can be "absorbed" by previous sharings. We introduce the concept of *regret* to capture this idea.

Definition 4.3. *Let $S_1, S_2, \cdots$ be a sequence of sharings, and let P_i denote the sharing plan for S_i. For each sharing S_i and each subexpression $s \lhd S_i$, the regret of s wrt S_i, denoted by $rg_i(s)$, is recursively defined as: if the result of s is not produced in any $P_j (1 \le j < i)$,*

$$rg_i(s) = \sum_{S_j | j<i, s \lhd S_j} \frac{C[P_j] - \sum_{s' \in P_j} rg_j(s')}{m-1} \quad (1)$$

where $m = \#join(S_i)$. Otherwise, $rg_i(s) = 0$.

"The result of s is not produced in any $P_j(1 \le j < i)$" means that the result of s is not available when we process sharing S_i, i.e., if we wish to use s in the plan of S_i, we need to pay a cost of $c[s]$. For example, if $s = (ab)c$, then this means that no sharing prior to S_i uses subexpression $(ab)c$ or $a(bc)$ in its sharing plan.

Algorithm ManagedRisk is shown in Algorithm 1. For each sharing S_i in the sequence and each plan P_{ij} for S_i, it uses a scoring function $score(P_{ij})$ defined as

$$score[P_{ij}] = \sum_{s \in P_{ij}} rg_i(s) - C[P_{ij}] \quad (2)$$

A sharing plan with large regret and small cost gets a high score. ManagedRisk chooses the plan for sharing S_i with the maximum score among all possible plans for S_i.

The intuition of algorithm ManagedRisk is as follows. When we process a sharing S_i, if there exists a subexpression $s \lhd S_i$ which is contained in some of the previous sharings but is never used before, then we give algorithm ManagedRisk an incentive to use s equivalent to $rg_i(s)$. $rg_i(s)$ is large if there are many sharings prior to S_i that contain subexpression s. By giving such an incentive, we can avoid the problem in Example 4.1 where a subexpression is never used, because the incentive keeps increasing if we don't use it, and at some point the incentive will be big enough that the subexpression will be used. Even if this is a bad choice, e.g., future sharings will never utilize this subexpression (like the situation in Example 4.2: after algorithm Normalize uses *ab*, there is no more sharing to benefit from it), the "damage" it causes will likely be controlled, because the incentive to use this subexpression won't be too large (otherwise it should have been used earlier). These are of course intuitions rather than strict statements, but we will show in Example 4.3 that algorithm ManagedRisk does avoid the pitfalls in both previous examples.

Note that the regrets of subexpressions used in each P_j (i.e., $rg_j(s')$ in Eq. (1)) are subtracted from $rg_i(s)$, because $rg_j(s')$ has already made an impact on choosing plan P_j for sharing S_j, and it should not make another impact on choosing the plan for S_i. Otherwise, the selected plans may have an unbounded cost compared with the optimal cost even if each sharing has at most two joins. The factor of $1/(m-1)$ in Eq. (1) is to avoid the total regret of a sharing plan with many subexpressions being too large.

Example 4.3. *Consider the sharing sequence in Example 4.1. For the first 10 sharings,* ManagedRisk *uses plan $a(bc_x)$, and pays a cost of 10 for each plan. When it processes the 11th sharing, we have $rg_{11}(ab) = 100$, and the regrets of all other subexpressions are 0. Since*

$$rg_{11}(ab) - C[(ab)c_{11}] = -\epsilon > -C[a(bc_{11})] = -10,$$

algorithm ManagedRisk *chooses plan $(ab)c_{11}$ for this sharing. Note that even if the 11th sharing is the last sharing, which means using $(ab)c_{11}$ at this point is a bad choice, the cost of* ManagedRisk *won't be arbitrarily bad because the incentive given to* ManagedRisk *to use ab is no more than the total cost of the first 10 sharing plans. In this example the cost of* ManagedRisk *is no more than twice the optimal cost.*

Now consider the sharing sequence in Example 4.2. For $1 \le x \le n-1$, ManagedRisk *uses plan $a(bc_x)$, incurring a cost of $(n-1)\epsilon$, and thus $rg_n(ab) = (n-1)\epsilon$. For the nth sharing, since the regrets of all other subexpression are 0, we have*

$$rg_n(ab) - C[(ab)c_n] < -C[a(bc_n)]$$

thus ManagedRisk *will choose $a(bc_n)$. In this case, even though subexpression ab is contained in many sharings seen before,* ManagedRisk *still doesn't use ab for the nth sharing, since the total cost of all previous sharings that contain ab (i.e., $rg_n(ab)$) is too small and thus the incentive to use ab is not big enough.* ManagedRisk *finds the optimal plans for this sharing sequence.*

Algorithm 1: Algorithm ManagedRisk for the Special Case

Input : a sequence of sharings $S_1, \cdots, S_n$. The algorithm processes each sharing S_i without the information of sharings after S_i.

```
foreach sharing S_i do
    foreach subexpression p ◁ S_i do
        compute rg_i(p) using Eq. 1
    end
    enumerate all plans for S_i
    foreach possible plan P_ij of S_i do
        compute C(P_ij) using the cost model
        score(P_ij) = Σ_{s∈P_ij} rg_i(s) − C(P_ij)
    end
    j = arg max score(P_ij)
    use plan P_ij for sharing S_i
end
```

There is a similar notion of regret (also called opportunity loss) in decision theory [26], which is defined as the additional payoff if a different action is chosen. Although the idea is somewhat similar, there are some key differences. First, decision theory aims to make a choice (such as determining the inventory level of a product) that minimizes the future regret if something goes wrong in future; whereas we do not analyze what can possibly happen in the future (because we don't know or make assumptions on how many sharings we will receive in the future, and what they are). Instead, regret is computed from previous sharings. Second, regret in decision theory is simply the difference in payoff, whereas in our problem the "difference in payoff" cannot be easily computed, because using a different plan for one sharing may affect the "difference in payoff" of many other sharings.

After explaining how algorithm ManagedRisk works in a special setting, in the next subsection we discuss how to apply algorithm ManagedRisk in the general case.

Algorithm 2: Algorithm ManagedRisk for the General Case

Input : a sequence of sharings $S_1, \cdots, S_n$. The algorithm processes each sharing S_i without the information of sharings after S_i.

foreach *sharing* S_i **do**
  foreach *subexpression* $p \triangleleft S_i$ **do**
    compute $rg_i(p)$ using Eq. 1
  end
  enumerate all plans for S_i
  foreach *possible plan* P_{ij} *of* S_i **do**
    compute $C(P_{ij})$ using the cost model
    $score(P_{ij}) = \sum_{s \in P_{ij}} rg_i(s) \cdot perc_s(P_{ij}) - C(P_{ij})$
  end
  foreach *possible plan* P_{ij} *of* S_i *in descending order of score* **do**
    if P_{ij} *does not violate server capacity* **then**
      use plan P_{ij} for sharing S_i
      break
    end
  end
  if *no feasible plan exists* **then**
    reject S_i
  end
end

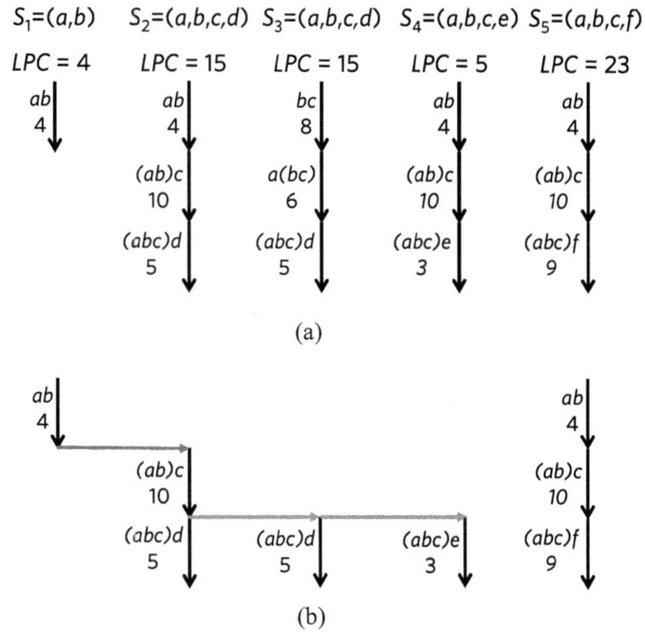

Figure 3: Individual Plans (a) and Global Plan (b) for Five Sharings

4.5 Extension of Algorithm ManagedRisk for the General Case

We previously made two simplifications: (1) server capacity is considered unlimited; (2) sharings are join-only with no projections or predicates. To cope with the general case, we propose the following extensions of Algorithm ManagedRisk.

When a server has limited capacity such that the desired plan violates the capacity of some servers, we will use the best plan that does not violate any server capacity. If no such plan exists, the sharing is rejected.

When sharings have predicates and projections, we modify the way we compute the score of a sharing plan (Eq. 2). Intuitively, even if the regret of a subexpression s (e.g., $a \bowtie b$) is high, if a sharing plan P for the current sharing only computes a small subset of the result of s (e.g., $s' = a_{a.x<10} \bowtie b$), then it is not very helpful to use plan P, since it only has a small chance to be helpful for future sharings that contain $a \bowtie b$. Consequently, the incentive to use s' should be smaller than the regret of s. We use $perc_s(P)$ to denote the percentage of tuples computed by subexpression s (possibly with predicates) in plan P, compared with the tuples computed by the same subexpression with no predicate. For a plan P with no predicate, $perc_s(P) = 100\%$ for all $s \in P$. Otherwise, $perc_s(P)$ may be smaller than 100%, which can be estimated using various existing techniques for selectivity estimation. We modify Eq. 2 as follows:

$$score(P_{ij}) = \sum_{s \in P_{ij}} rg_i(s) \cdot perc_s(P_{ij}) - C(P_{ij}) \tag{3}$$

The extension of Algorithm 1 for the general case is shown in Algorithm 2.

5. FAIR COSTING FOR SHARINGS

Calculating the operational cost incurred for the service provider to provide and maintain the view of a sharing is necessary in pricing the sharing. We have shown in Example 1.1 that a fair costing mechanism is not trivial to obtain. To better motivate our proposed fairness criteria, we use a more sophisticated example as follows.

Example 5.1. *Consider five sharings shown in Figure 3. Figure 3(a) shows the plans for the sharings generated by an algorithm, where each edge represents a subexpression, and is annotated by the subexpression it represents, along with its cost. It also shows the minimum cost of a plan for this sharing alone, denoted by LPC(·) (lowest possible cost). Figure 3(b) shows the global plan where some common subexpressions in the plans are reused. The red arrow denotes reusing the result of ab and the green arrows denote reusing the result of (ab)c.*

Next we introduce and explain the fair costing criteria. We use AC (attributed cost) to denote the cost attributed to each sharing, and our goal is to compute a fair AC for each sharing.

(1) For any two identical sharings $S_1 = S_2$, $AC(S_1)$ should be identical with $AC(S_2)$ regardless of the plans chosen for them. Buyers only request data sharings. They do not know or care about what plans the service provider decides to use for their sharings. The service provider may use different plans for the same sharings for several reasons, e.g., server capacity limit, reuse of subexpressions, etc. From the buyers' points of view, in order to be fair, neither should get a lower or higher attributed cost than the other. In Example 5.1, sharings S_2 and S_3 are identical. Although they use different plans, i.e., $((ab)c)d$ for S_2 and $(a(bc))d$ for S_3, they should have the same AC.

(2) For any sharing S, $AC(S)$ should be no more than $LPC(S)$. Since $LPC(S)$ is the lowest cost of S if no other sharing exists (thus there's no reuse of subexpressions), it represents the actual complexity of S. A sharing with a high LPC is inherently expensive in terms of operational cost, and conversely, a sharing with a low LPC is inherently cheap. For global optimization purpose, the service provider may not use the cheapest plan for a sharing, such as the one with predicate "city = Seattle" in Example 1.1, as well as S_4 in Example 5.1. Both of them use plans that have an additional step after some expensive operations. However, from the fairness

perspective, buyers of such inherently cheap sharings should not be penalized by the optimization, and thus we propose that *AC* cannot be more than *LPC* for a sharing.

(3) For two sharings S_1 and S_2, if S_1's query is contained in S_2's query (i.e., the tuples retrieved by S_1 are a subset of those retrieved by S_2), and $LPC(S_1) \leq LPC(S_2)$, then $AC(S_1)$ should be no more than $AC(S_2)$. Because otherwise, even if a buyer only needs the data of S_1, she can purchase S_2 for a lower price. This is undesirable for the service provider since the service provider pays more but gets a lower revenue.

(4) A sharing plan that has common subexpressions with other sharings, which gives the service provider the opportunity to save cost by reusing subexpressions, should be compensated. In Example 5.1, sharing plans for S_1, S_2, S_4 and S_5 all compute $a \bowtie b$ (denoted by *ab*), and sharing plans for S_2, S_3, S_4 and S_5 all compute $a \bowtie b \bowtie c$. These common intermediate results enable the service provider to reuse them in different sharing plans and reduce the cost. Although an intermediate result may not be reused by all sharing plans that contain this intermediate result (e.g., $a \bowtie b$ in S_1's plan is only reused by S_2), all sharings whose plans contain the intermediate result should be equally rewarded. To capture this idea we introduce the concept of *saving* of an intermediate result in a sharing plan.

DEFINITION 5.1 (SAVING OF AN INTERMEDIATE RESULT). *The saving of an intermediate result r, denoted as saving(r), is the increase of the cost of the global plan if r is no longer reused in the global plan, i.e., all sharings whose plans include r need to compute r and pay the cost of the corresponding subexpressions.*

In Example 5.1, there are two intermediate results that are reused, shown in red (*ab*) and green (*abc*). If we remove the red arrow, sharing S_2 will need to use a separate subexpression *ab*, thus the cost of the global plan increases by 4. If we remove the two green arrows, sharing S_3 will need to use subexpressions *bc* and *a(bc)*, and sharing S_4 will need to use subexpressions *ab* and *(ab)c*, and the cost of the global plan increases by 28.

We require that part of the saving of an intermediate result should be equally awarded to the sharings whose plans include this intermediate result. Let α be a parameter that indicates at least how much percentage of the saving is awarded to the sharings. Let *num(r)* denote the number of sharings in the global plan whose plans include *r* as an intermediate result. We require that

$$AC(S) \leq GPC(S) - \alpha \cdot \sum_{r \in S} \frac{saving(r)}{num(r)} \quad (4)$$

where $GPC(S)$ is the cost of S's plan in the global plan. It is calculated by summing up the cost of all edges in S's plan, even if an edge is used by other sharing plans. In Example 5.1, the *GPC* for the five sharings are 4, 19, 19, 17, 23, respectively.

Parameter α reflects the degree of fairness. $\alpha = 0$ means the savings of the intermediate results are not awarded to the relevant sharings, which is the least fair since a sharing with much commonality with other sharings is treated in the same way as a sharing with no commonality with others. $\alpha = 1$ means that the savings are maximally awarded to the sharings. $\alpha = 1$ is not always achievable because of other fairness requirements, and thus we want to find the maximum possible value of α.

(5) Finally, the sum of AC of all sharings in the global plan should equal the cost of the global plan, i.e., the cost of the global plan should be recovered. This is not directly related to fairness per se, but it is a necessary requirement for a costing function.

The five criteria above are collectively referred to as the *fairness criteria*. The following lemmas show that these requirements are non-redundant, as well as the condition under which they are achievable. We omit the proofs due to space limitation.

LEMMA 5.1. *The five fairness conditions are non-redundant: it is possible to satisfy any four not the fifth.*

LEMMA 5.2. *All five fairness conditions are satisfiable on a global plan GP for a set $\mathcal{S}$ of sharings if and only if $\sum_{S \in \mathcal{S}} LPC(S) \geq cost(GP)$.*

Given a specific value of α, we can use the fairness criteria to compute an upper bound cost for each sharing. Note that conditions (1) and (3) make the set of sharings in the global plan a partially ordered set, which means the cost upper bound of a sharing depends on other sharings. Thus we should calculate the upper bound cost of the sharings according to the partial order, i.e., the cost upper bound of a sharing can be determined only after the cost upper bounds of all its predecessors have been determined. If the sum of all cost upper bounds are higher than the cost of the global plan, it means this value of α is feasible.

The algorithm for computing the maximum value of α, named algorithm FAIRCOST, is shown in Algorithm 3. Note that its input is the global plan and the output is the attributed cost (*AC*) for each sharing, and thus when a new sharing arrives, the costs of existing sharings may change. This is because if the costs of existing sharings cannot be changed, it is impossible to satisfy the above fairness criteria in a non-trivial way (i.e., $\alpha > 0$). However, the price of each sharing S won't change arbitrarily as it will never exceed $LPC(S)$.

Algorithm 3: Algorithm FAIRCOST

```
Input  : global plan GP, sharings S_1, ..., S_n
if Σ_{S_i} LPC(S_i) < cost(GP) then
  | return IMPOSSIBLE
end
build a DAG: each node is a sharing (or multiple identical
sharings); each arc (S_i, S_j) indicates that S_i is contained in S_j
and LPC(S_i) ≤ LPC(S_j)
foreach intermediate result r in GP do
  | calculate saving(r) according to definition 5.1
end
lowα = 0, highα = 1, α = 0.5
while true do
    foreach sharing S in increasing order of LPC do
        let P_S be the predecessors of S in DAG
        costUB(S) =
        min{LPC(S), min_{S'∈P_S} costUB(S'), GPC(S) − α ·
            Σ_{r∈S} saving(r)/num(r)}
    end
    if Σ_{S_i} costUB(S_i) = cost(GP) then
      | break
    end
    else if Σ_{S_i} costUB(S_i) < cost(GP) then
      | highα = α − ε
    end
    else
      | lowα = α + ε
    end
    α = (lowα + highα)/2
end
foreach sharing S_i do
  | AC(S_i) = costUB(S_i)
end
```

Algorithm FAIRCOST first builds a DAG to reflect the partial order between sharings. Multiple identical sharings can be represented by a single node in the DAG. We then do a binary search on α. For a specific value of α, we compute the cost upper bounds for the sharings in the order of *LPC*, which ensures that a sharing is processed after all its predecessors in the DAG have been processed. If the total cost upper bound is more than *cost(GP)* we search for a higher α value, and if the total cost upper bound is less than *cost(GP)* we search for a lower α value.

If we run Algorithm FAIRCOST on Example 5.1, it first computes the savings of the intermediate results: $savings(ab) = 4$ and $saving(abc) = 28$. There are 4 sharings whose plans include *ab*: S_1, S_2, S_4 and S_5, and there are 4 sharings whose plans include *abc*: S_2, S_3, S_4 and S_5. The maximum possible value of α in this case is 0.8, and the attributed cost of the sharings are: $AC(S_1) = 3.2$, $AC(S_2) = 12.6$, $AC(S_3) = 12.6$, $AC(S_4) = 5$, $AC(S_5) = 16.6$. Their sum is 50, which is exactly the cost of the global plan in Figure 3(b). A higher value of α would mean that the attributed costs of S_1, S_2, S_3 and S_5 all need to be reduced, which is not possible, because the attributed cost of S_4 cannot be increased as it is the same as its *LPC*.

6. EVALUATION

6.1 Setup

6.1.1 Algorithms Evaluated

The evaluation has two parts. The first part (Section 6.2) evaluates online sharing plan selection, and the second part (Section 6.3) evaluates the fair costing of sharings. In the first part we test four algorithms: algorithms GREEDY, NORMALIZE, MANAGEDRISK presented in Section 4, as well as algorithm EXHAUSTIVE, which is an offline algorithm that knows all sharings in the sequence in advance, and searches for the optimal global plan exhaustively. Algorithm EXHAUSTIVE is not feasible in practice, since we do not know all sharings in advance, and even if we do, the search space is much too large. We only test Algorithm EXHAUSTIVE for small sharing sequences.

In the second part we compare Algorithm FAIRCOST with a baseline algorithm that evenly distributes the cost of each subexpression in the global plan to the sharings whose plans use the subexpression. This is a commonly adopted criterion for fairness, e.g., in [17, 36], all users/queries that use the same structure built by the service provider pay the same price for it. As an example, for the global plan in Figure 3(b), the baseline algorithm distributes the cost of *ab* to S_1, S_2, S_3 and S_4, and distributes the cost of *(ab)c* to S_2, S_3 and S_4. The two algorithms are compared based on whether they satisfy the fairness criteria discussed in Section 5.

6.1.2 Environment

The experiments were performed on a machine with two Intel Xeon 2.40GHz cores, 12GB memory, running Windows 7 Ultimate. We collected tweets on twitter from a gardenhose stream, which is composed of a 10% sampling of tweets in a 6-month period starting from September 2010. The tweets are stored in 9 base relations: USERS, TWEETS, CURLOC, LOC, SOCNET, URLS, FOURSQ, HASHTAGS, PHOTOS. These base tables are distributed in a round-robin fashion among a number of machines that varies from 5 to 9 machines (6 by default).

We specified 25 base sharings, each of which is a join of two or more tables. These sharings were derived from real mobile applications that join the mentioned tables. The base sharings are shown in Table 1. For each base sharing, we give an existing real application that may benefit from such a sharing (e.g., twitaholic may benefit from USERS $\bowtie$ SOCNET). Predicates are randomly generated and added to the base sharings; each predicate has the form of "Table.Attribute [>, <, =] Constant".

In order to test the scalabilities of the algorithms, we also generated a set of synthetic tables/sharings, which are used in Section 6.2.2. The synthetic data has a star schema with up to 5 fact tables and 30 dimension tables distributed among 1-20 machines, and the sharing sequence contains up to 2500 sharings, each of which is a star-join with no predicates. The cost of each join is a random number between 1 and 10^5.

In a prior work [9] we developed a cost model used to calculate the cost of each subexpression in a sharing plan, which is proved fairly accurate. Thus in this paper we use the cost model in [9] for sharing plan cost calculation instead of setting up and running the sharings in the system.

The algorithm for costing sharings are invoked on the output of Algorithm MANAGEDRISK on the Twitter data.

6.2 Online Sharing Plan Selection

6.2.1 Effectiveness of Plan Selection

We run the three online algorithms, GREEDY, NORMALIZE and MANAGEDRISK, on the 25 base sharings in Table 1. We vary the number of sharings in the sequence (10 to 60), number of predicates in each sharing (0 to 3) and number of machines (5 to 9). On average, the global plans generated by the three algorithms have similar costs. However, there exists certain sharing sequences where each algorithm performs much better (up to 3 times) than the other two. In general, GREEDY tends to use a subexpression *too late* as shown in Example 4.1; NORMALIZE tends to use a subexpression *too early* as shown in Example 4.2. Algorithm MANAGEDRISK generally avoids using a subexpression too late or too early, although it sometimes can still be a bit earlier or later than the optimal solution, which makes it occasionally have a higher cost than either GREEDY or NORMALIZE. However, by taking managed risks, algorithm MANAGEDRISK does not make choices that cause unbounded damages, as shown below.

To further illustrate the worst case scenario, we generate sequences of synthetic sharings, each of which consists of a three-way join without predicates. The synthetic sharings consists of cases similar as Example 4.1 where there exists a subexpression contained in many sharings and used by the optimal solution, and cases similar as Example 4.2 where there exists a subexpression contained in many sharings but not used by the optimal solution, among others. Figure 4 shows the worst case scenario in this test for each algorithm, e.g., "Greedy/MR" is the largest cost ratio between GREEDY and MANAGEDRISK on a sharing sequence in the test. As

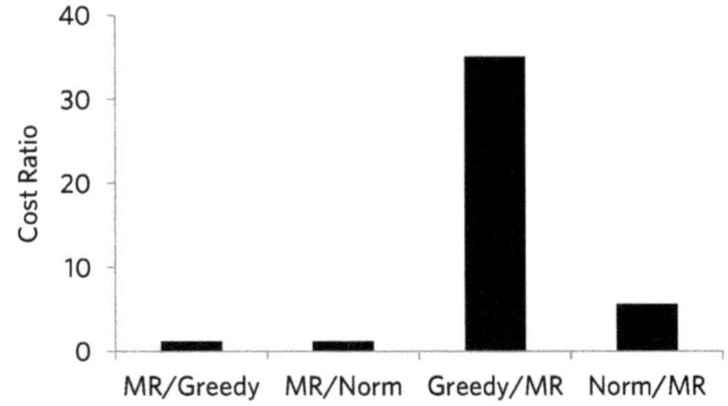

Figure 4: Worst Case Performance for Online Sharing Plan Selection

Table 1: Sharings Used in the Evaluations

S_1	USERS ⋈ SOCNET (twitaholic)	S_9	FOURSQ ⋈ TWEETS (checkoutcheckins)	S_{17}	USERS ⋈ LOC (twittermap)
S_2	USERS ⋈ TWEETS ⋈ CURLOC (twellow)	S_{10}	HASHTAGS ⋈ TWEETS (monitter)	S_{18}	USERS ⋈ TWEETS ⋈ PHOTOS ⋈ CURLOC (twittermap)
S_3	USERS ⋈ TWEETS ⋈ URLS (tweetmeme)	S_{11}	FOURSQ ⋈ USERS ⋈ TWEETS ⋈ CURLOC (arrivaltracker)	S_{19}	USERS ⋈ TWEETS ⋈ HASHTAGS ⋈ CURLOC (hashtags.org)
S_4	USERS ⋈ TWEETS ⋈ URLS ⋈ CURLOC (twitdom)	S_{12}	FOURSQ ⋈ USER ⋈ TWEETS (route)	S_{20}	USERS ⋈ TWEETS ⋈ HASHTAGS ⋈ PHOTOS ⋈ CURLOC (nearbytweets)
S_5	USERS ⋈ TWEETS (tweetstats)	S_{13}	FOURSQ ⋈ USER ⋈ TWEETS ⋈ LOC (locc.us)	S_{21}	USERS ⋈ TWEETS ⋈ FOURSQ ⋈ PHOTOS ⋈ CURLOC (nearbytweets)
S_6	TWEETS ⋈ CURLOC (nearbytweets)	S_{14}	TWEETS ⋈ LOC (locafollow)	S_{22}	FOURSQ ⋈ CURLOC (nearbytweets)
S_7	URLS ⋈ CURLOC (nearbyurls)	S_{15}	USERS ⋈ LOC ⋈ TWEETS ⋈ CURLOC (twittervision)	S_{23}	PHOTOS ⋈ CURLOC (twitxr)
S_8	TWEETS ⋈ PHOTOS (twitpic)	S_{16}	FOURSQ ⋈ USERS ⋈ TWEETS ⋈ SOCNET (yelp)	S_{24}	HASHTAGS ⋈ CURLOC (nearbytweets)
				S_{25}	HASHTAGS ⋈ USERS ⋈ TWEETS (twistori)

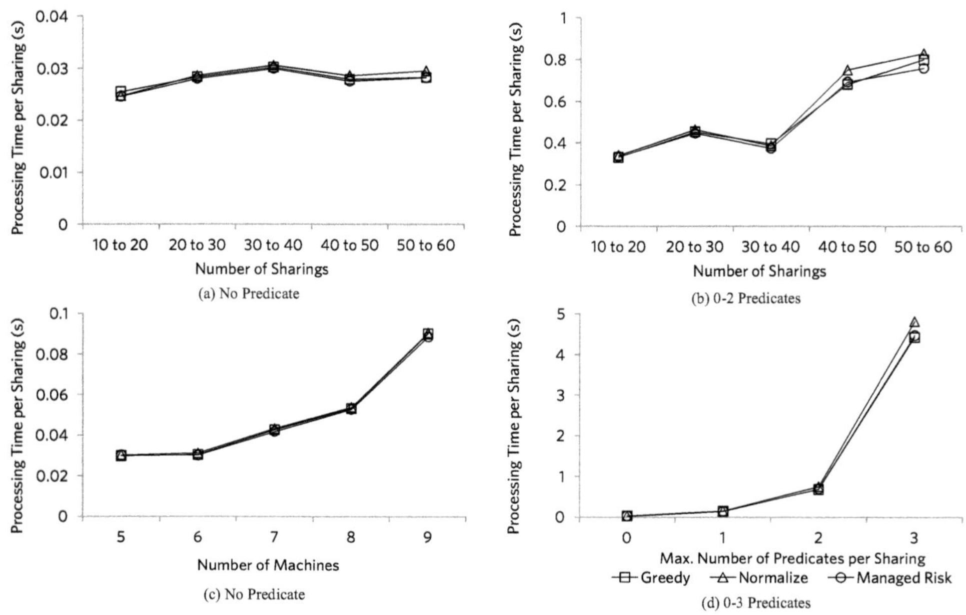

Figure 5: Running Time on Twitter Data

we can see, the sharing plans generated by MANAGEDRISK have much more stable qualities than those generated by the baselines, which validates the effectiveness of our strategy to take managed risks when selecting sharing plans.

6.2.2 Efficiency and Scalability

Figure 5 shows the running time of the sharings on Twitter data. In (a), sharings have no predicates and we vary the number of sharings in the sequence from 10 to 60. In (b), sharings in the sequence have 0-2 predicates. Half of the sharings in a sequence have no predicate, and the other half have 1 or 2 randomly generated predicates. In (c), the number of available machines varies from 5 to 9. In (d), the maximum number of predicates per sharing increases from 0 to 3. When the maximum number of predicates is 1, 2 or 3, half of the sharings have no predicates and the other half have random predicates. For example, when the maximum number of predicates is 3, 1/6 of the sharings in the sequence have 1 predicate, 1/6 have 2 predicates, 1/6 have 3 predicates, and the other 1/2 have no predicate.

The running time of the three algorithms are similar. Compared with Algorithm GREEDY, Algorithm NORMALIZE and Algorithm MANAGEDRISK need to maintain the counts and the regrets, respectively, of subexpressions that are contained in previous sharings but not used in existing sharing plans, but they do not add much overhead. The running time grows exponentially with number of predicates (Figure 5(d)) since the number of possible sharing plans grows exponentially. However, the processing time for 3 predicates is under 5 seconds, and as mentioned before, if the sharings are more complicated, heuristics can be applied to filter sharing plans [12].

To test Algorithm EXHAUSTIVE, we use a smaller sharing sequence that consists of 3-5 sharings, each of which has at most 1 predicate. The result is shown in Table 2, which is the average of 50 sharing sequences. The cost of MANAGEDRISK is never 3 times higher than that of EXHAUSTIVE for any sharing sequence. When each sharing sequence contains up to 10 sharings, EXHAUSTIVE cannot finish processing a test case of 50 sharing sequences within 48 hours, and thus we do not further test EXHAUSTIVE for scalability.

Figure 6 is the result of scalability test on synthetic data and randomly generated sharings, in order to test the scalability of the system at larger input scales. By default there's one fact table, 20 dimension tables, and the sequence contains 1000 sharings, each of which consists of a fact table and up to 7 dimension tables. (a)

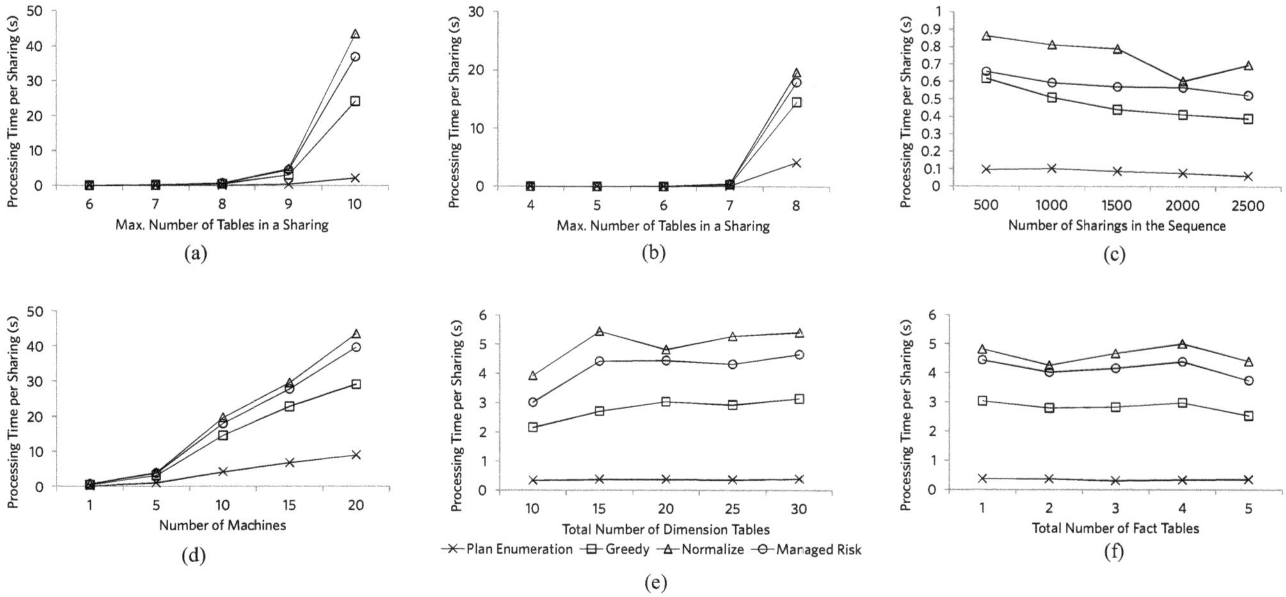

Figure 6: Running Time on Synthetic Data

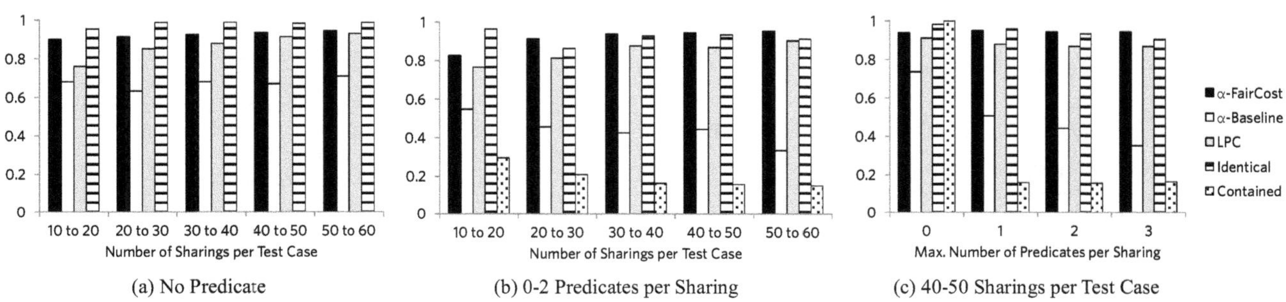

Figure 7: Fair Costing Results

Table 2: Performance of Algorithm EXHAUSTIVE

	MANAGEDRISK	EXHAUSTIVE
cost	1	0.84
time	1	2.18

shows the running time with increasing sharing size on a single machine (where, for example, sharing size of 10 means 1 fact table and 9 dimension tables). (b) shows the running time with increasing sharing size on 10 machines. The running time increases exponentially because the algorithms enumerates all plans, whose numbers increase exponentially wrt the sharing size. But it can be observed that the running time is reasonable for sharings of up to 10 tables on a single machine and sharings of up to 8 tables on multiple machines. And as said before, if the sharings are so big that exhaustive plan enumeration is not feasible, we can use heuristics to explore a manageable subset of plans.

(c) shows the running time wrt the number of sharings in the sequence on a single machine. The running time slightly declines with more sharings since sharings that come later in the sequence have higher probabilities of having occurred before and these sharings don't need to be processed. In (d) we increase the number of machines used from 1 to 20. More machines leads to more possible plans and thus longer processing times. In (e) and (f) we vary the total number of dimension tables and fact tables used in all sharings. These two paramters have little effect on the average processing time per sharing.

6.3 Fair Costing

Figure 7 shows the qualities of the two costing algorithms measured by the fairness criteria proposed in Section 5. *LPC*, *Identical* and *Contained* are for the baseline algorithm (for algorithm FAIRCOST their values are always 1). *LPC* is the percentage of sharings in the sequence whose costs assigned by the baseline algorithm are no more than their LPCs. *Identical* is the percentage of pairs of identical sharings whose costs assigned by the baseline algorithm are the same. *Contained* is the percentage of pairs of sharings such that the first sharing is contained in the second sharing and has a lower LPC than the second sharing, and the cost assigned to the first sharing is no more than that assigned to the second sharing. α is the minimum percentage of the saving of a sharing plan that is awarded to the corresponding sharing, as introduced in Section 5. Higher α, *LPC*, *Identical* and *Contained* values indicate a higher degree of fairness. Note that Figure 7(a) doesn't have "Contained" bars since those sharings have no predicate, and thus the value of "Contained" is always 1.

The results indicate that Algorithm FAIRCOST achieves much better fairness compared with the baseline algorithm.

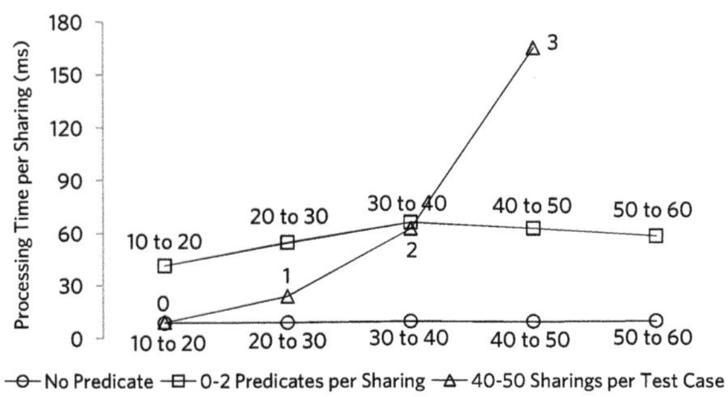

Figure 8: Running Time for Algorithm FairCosting

Figure 8 shows the average processing time of algorithm FAIRCOST for each sharing. ○ and □ test various numbers of sharings per test case, with no predicate (○) or up to 2 predicates per sharing (□); △ tests various numbers of predicates per sharing (from 0 to 3), with 40-50 sharings per test case. The results indicate that the processing time has no noticeable increase for later sharings in the sequence compared to earlier sharings, and that algorithm FAIRCOST is very efficient in calculating the cost of sharings, although the processing time increases fast with the number of predicates, because more predicates leads to a larger number of possible plans, hence more expensive computation of LPC. Heuristics can be applied to prune the search space if necessary.

7. CONCLUSIONS AND FUTURE WORK

This paper studies two problems in building a data market that enables the sharing of dynamic data specified by ad-hoc queries: how to design an online algorithm for selecting sharing plans, and how to fairly calculate the cost of each sharing plan. There are a few interesting future works, for example, whether it is feasible to change the plan of an existing sharing when a new sharing arrives, and how it effects the strategies for selecting sharing plans and costing the sharings; whether it is beneficial to create and maintain views that do not belong to any existing sharing plan (so that future sharings may reuse them), rather than reusing only those views created by existing sharing plans, and how to determine which views to create.

Acknowledgement: We thank Magdalena Balazinska and Dan Suciu for their insightful comments on the earlier versions of the work.

8. REFERENCES

[1] Gnip. http://gnip.com/.
[2] Infochimps. http://infochimps.com/.
[3] Microsoft Azure Marketplace. https://datamarket.azure.com.
[4] Public Data Sets on AWS. http://aws.amazon.com/publicdatasets/.
[5] Xignite. http://xignite.com/.
[6] D. Agrawal, A. El Abbadi, A. K. Singh, and T. Yurek. Efficient View Maintenance at Data Warehouses. In *SIGMOD Conference*, pages 417–427, 1997.
[7] S. Agrawal, S. Chaudhuri, and V. R. Narasayya. Automated Selection of Materialized Views and Indexes in SQL Databases. In *VLDB*, pages 496–505, 2000.
[8] S. Agrawal, S. Chaudhuri, and V. R. Narasayya. Materialized View and Index Selection Tool for Microsoft SQL Server 2000. In *SIGMOD Conference*, page 608, 2001.
[9] S. Al-Kiswany, H. Hacıgümüş, Z. Liu, and J. Sankaranarayanan. Cost Exploration of Data Sharings in the Cloud. In *EDBT*, pages 601–612, 2013.
[10] S. Arumugam, A. Dobra, C. M. Jermaine, N. Pansare, and L. L. Perez. The DataPath System: A Data-Centric Analytic Processing Engine for Large Data Warehouses. In *SIGMOD Conference*, pages 519–530, 2010.
[11] G. Candea, N. Polyzotis, and R. Vingralek. A Scalable, Predictable Join Operator for Highly Concurrent Data Warehouses. *PVLDB*, 2(1):277–288, 2009.
[12] S. Chaudhuri. An Overview of Query Optimization in Relational Systems. In *PODS*, pages 34–43, 1998.
[13] S. Chaudhuri, M. Datar, and V. R. Narasayya. Index Selection for Databases: A Hardness Study and a Principled Heuristic Solution. *IEEE Trans. Knowl. Data Eng.*, 16(11):1313–1323, 2004.
[14] S. Chaudhuri and V. R. Narasayya. An Efficient Cost-Driven Index Selection Tool for Microsoft SQL Server. In *VLDB*, pages 146–155, 1997.
[15] G. Giannikis, G. Alonso, and D. Kossmann. SharedDB: Killing One Thousand Queries With One Stone. *PVLDB*, 5(6):526–537, 2012.
[16] S. Harizopoulos, V. Shkapenyuk, and A. Ailamaki. QPipe: A Simultaneously Pipelined Relational Query Engine. In *SIGMOD Conference*, pages 383–394, 2005.
[17] V. Kantere, D. Dash, G. Gratsias, and A. Ailamaki. Predicting Cost Amortization for Query Services. In *SIGMOD Conference*, pages 325–336, 2011.
[18] D. Kossmann. The State of the Art in Distributed Query Processing. *ACM Comput. Surv.*, 32(4):422–469, 2000.
[19] P. Koutris, P. Upadhyaya, M. Balazinska, B. Howe, and D. Suciu. Query-Based Data Pricing. In *PODS*, pages 167–178, 2012.
[20] P. Koutris, P. Upadhyaya, M. Balazinska, B. Howe, and D. Suciu. Toward Practical Query Pricing with QueryMarket. In *SIGMOD Conference*, pages 613–624, 2013.
[21] C. Li, D. Y. Li, G. Miklau, and D. Suciu. A Theory of Pricing Private Data. In *ICDT*, pages 33–44, 2013.
[22] H. Mistry, P. Roy, S. Sudarshan, and K. Ramamritham. Materialized View Selection and Maintenance Using Multi-Query Optimization. In *SIGMOD Conference*, pages 307–318, 2001.
[23] T. Nagle, J. Hogan, and J. Zale. *The Strategy and Tactics of Pricing: A Guide to Growing More Profitably*. Prentice Hall, 2010.
[24] T.-V.-A. Nguyen, S. Bimonte, L. d'Orazio, and J. Darmont. Cost Models for View Materialization in the Cloud. In *EDBT/ICDT Workshops*, pages 47–54, 2012.
[25] M. T. Ozsu and P. Valduriez. *Principles of Distributed Database Systems*. Springer, 2011.
[26] M. Peterson. *An Introduction to Decision Theory*. Cambridge University Press, 2009.
[27] S. K. Rahimi and F. S. Haug. *Distributed Database Management Systems: A Practical Approach*. Wiley-IEEE Computer Society Pr, 2010.
[28] K. A. Ross, D. Srivastava, and S. Sudarshan. Materialized View Maintenance and Integrity Constraint Checking: Trading Space for Time. In *SIGMOD Conference*, pages 447–458, 1996.
[29] K. Salem, K. S. Beyer, R. Cochrane, and B. G. Lindsay. How To Roll a Join: Asynchronous Incremental View Maintenance. In *SIGMOD Conference*, pages 129–140, 2000.
[30] K. Schnaitter and N. Polyzotis. Semi-Automatic Index Tuning: Keeping DBAs in the Loop. *PVLDB*, 5(5):478–489, 2012.
[31] K. Schnaitter, N. Polyzotis, and L. Getoor. Index Interactions in Physical Design Tuning: Modeling, Analysis, and Applications. *PVLDB*, 2(1):1234–1245, 2009.
[32] T. K. Sellis. Multiple-Query Optimization. *ACM Trans. Database Syst.*, 13(1):23–52, 1988.
[33] T. K. Sellis and S. Ghosh. On the Multiple-Query Optimization Problem. *IEEE Trans. Knowl. Data Eng.*, 2(2):262–266, 1990.
[34] K. Shim, T. K. Sellis, and D. S. Nau. Improvements on a Heuristic Algorithm for Multiple-Query Optimization. *Data Knowl. Eng.*, 12(2):197–222, 1994.
[35] T. J. Smith. *Pricing Strategy: Setting Price Levels, Managing Price Discounts and Establishing Price Structures*. Cengage Learning, 2011.
[36] P. Upadhyaya, M. Balazinska, and D. Suciu. How to Price Shared Optimizations in the Cloud. *PVLDB*, 5(6):562–573, 2012.
[37] G. Valentin, M. Zuliani, D. C. Zilio, G. M. Lohman, and A. Skelley. DB2 Advisor: An Optimizer Smart Enough to Recommend Its Own Indexes. In *ICDE*, pages 101–110, 2000.

A Comparison of Platforms for Implementing and Running Very Large Scale Machine Learning Algorithms

Zhuhua Cai
Rice University
Houston, TX, 77251
caizhua@gmail.com

Zekai J. Gao
Rice University
Houston, TX, 77251
jacobgao@rice.edu

Shangyu Luo
Rice University
Houston, TX, 77251
lsyurd@gmail.com

Luis L. Perez
Rice University
Houston, TX, 77251
lp6@rice.edu

Zografoula Vagena
LogicBlox, Inc.
Atlanta, GA, 30309
foula@acm.org

Christopher Jermaine
Rice University
Houston, TX, 77251
cmj4@rice.edu

ABSTRACT

We describe an extensive benchmark of platforms available to a user who wants to run a machine learning (ML) inference algorithm over a very large data set, but cannot find an existing implementation and thus must "roll her own" ML code. We have carefully chosen a set of five ML implementation tasks that involve learning relatively complex, hierarchical models. We completed those tasks on four different computational platforms, and using 70,000 hours of Amazon EC2 compute time, we carefully compared running times, tuning requirements, and ease-of-programming of each.

1. INTRODUCTION

Many platforms have been proposed to provide programming and runtime support for distributed/parallel machine learning (ML) codes, including OptiML [19], GraphLab [11, 8], SystemML [6], and SimSQL [4]. MLBase [10] and ScalOps [21] also address the problem, though the most recent published descriptions indicate that these systems are more immature. Other systems such as Pregel [12], Giraph [2], Spark [24], Ricardo [5], Nyad [14], and DryadLinq [22] may not have been developed only for ML, but count it as an important application.

We describe an objective benchmark of some of the platforms available to a user who wants to run a specific ML inference algorithm over a large data set, but cannot find an existing implementation and thus must "roll her own" ML code. Given the wide variety of ML models, this will not be an uncommon occurrence.[1] We draw a distinction between a user who wants to implement and apply a brand new ML code, and someone who just wants to use a code, and focus on the former. The implementor will want to balance ease of implementation with performance, whereas an end user has little concern for the effort required to engineer the code and will be happy with an intricately constructed C and MPI code as long as it is fast and easy to use.[2]

Our contributions. Our specific contributions are:

(1) We shed some light on the relative merits of some (quite different) platforms for implementing large-scale ML algorithms. Our results will surprise many readers.

(2) Second, we demonstrate (through example) what a scientific study of a platform for writing large-scale ML codes might look like. We have carefully chosen a set of tasks that involve learning relatively complex, hierarchical statistical models. We have purposely avoided simple, convex models whose parameters can be optimized using easily-implemented techniques such as gradient descent. Their simplicity means they benefit relatively little from the abstractions provided by the platforms we consider.

(3) Finally, we hope that our efforts will grow into a widely used, standard benchmark for this sort of platform. In the future, a implementor of a new or existing platform need only implement these codes and compare with our numbers.

2. STATISTICAL ML: A PRIMER

In statistical ML, one first postulates a generative, statistical model for a data set, characterized by a distribution function $f(X|\theta)$. Here, X is the data set, and θ is the unseen model parameters and hidden variables. *Learning* is the process of choosing a value $\hat{\theta}$ for θ so that $\hat{\theta}$ does a good job of describing how the model could have produced X. Learning is typically quite expensive computationally, especially if the data set is very large. Hence platforms that can support parallel and/or distributed ML are attractive.

We focus on learning relatively complex, hierarchical models. Such models are often characterized by the fact that the Bayesian approach to ML. In the Bayesian approach, the user expresses his or her prior belief about the model by supplying a *prior distribution* $f(\theta)$ over θ. The goal learning is to understand something about the *posterior distribution* for θ, written as $f(\theta|X)$. The posterior relates to the prior via *Bayes' Rule*:

$$f(\theta|X) \propto f(\theta)f(X|\theta).$$

[1]For example, it is telling that of the five standard Bayesian ML inference algorithms we consider in this study, it appears that only the collapsed LDA inference algorithm [3] is available as part of an existing package, and even then we are aware of no "non-collapsed" Gibbs sampler implementation (See Section 8 of the paper).

[2]Our focus on giving an implementor an idea of what platform to use means that we do not consider the task of benchmarking ML libraries that are not meant as a platform for writing new codes, such as Mahout [17], MADLib [9] and Vowpal Wabbit [1].

SIGMOD'14, June 22–27, 2014, Snowbird, UT, USA.

http://dx.doi.org/10.1145/2588555.2593680.

The simplest, most universal, and the most common way to analyze the posterior is to draw a set of samples from it via Markov chain Monte Carlo (MCMC) [7]. To apply MCMC to the problem, a Markov chain is defined over all possible values for θ. This Markov chain is a random walk over a graph, where each vertex in the graph is a possible value for θ, and an edge between two possible values $\hat{\theta}_1$ and $\hat{\theta}_2$ for θ is labeled with a weight describing the likelihood of transitioning from $\hat{\theta}_1$ to $\hat{\theta}_2$ during the walk. The graph is defined so that observing the current state after an infinite-length walk is equivalent to drawing a sample $\hat{\theta}$ from the target $f(\theta|X)$. In practice a simulation that traverses only a few dozen to a few thousand possible values for θ will suffice to "mix" the chain.

3. EXPERIMENTAL OVERVIEW

3.1 Platforms Tested

The platforms we evaluate in the paper are:

Spark [24], which embodies the MapReduce/data-flow approach. We choose Spark because it purports to be both higher performance and easier to program than Hadoop MapReduce.

SimSQL [4], which is a parallel, relational database that supports an SQL-based approach to running large-scale MCMC simulations.

GraphLab [11], which supports a graph-based abstraction for writing distributed machine learning codes. For large-scale MCMC, one can map the various components of θ to nodes in a graph, with edges representing statistical dependencies.

Giraph [2] which is a graph-based platform that exemplifies the BSP approach, widely known to be used extensively by Facebook.

These four were chosen as representative of various approaches. Spark exemplifies the dataflow/MapReduce approach, SimSQL the database approach, GraphLab the graph-based approach, and Giraph the BSP approach. Our choices to a certain extent were motivated with our pre-existing familiarity with the platform. For example, one of our team members has extensive Giraph experience, and several of our team members designed and implemented SimSQL. However, other options certainly exist. For example, we could have used a commercial parallel database system; these have been used for statistical ML for a long time [16], and we could have even borrowed some of MADLib's existing infrastructure. Or, instead of Spark, we could have used something like Pig [15].

3.2 ML Models Considered

We use each of these platforms to implement MCMC codes for learning the following five models. We chose them as being representative complex, hierarchical, statistical model that one might want to learn over a large data set:

(1) A Gaussian mixture model (GMM) for data clustering.

(2) The Bayesian Lasso [18], a Bayesian regression model.

(3) A hidden Markov model (HMM) for text.

(4) Latent Dirichlet allocation (LDA), a model for text mining.

(5) A Gaussian model for missing data imputation.

3.3 Balancing Performance and Ease-Of-Use

Since we focus on evaluating the platforms from the point-of-view of a user-implementor, our study focuses both on performance and on programmability. These are frequently at odds—since these platforms can all execute arbitrary Java/C++/Python code, there is always a temptation to bypass the platform to gain high performance. Thus, we adopted a simple guideline when considering the question of how to implement the MCMC simulations we study in this paper. We first attempt to implement each code in the "purest" way possible; that is, the way in which was most in-keeping with the conceptual design of the platform being evaluated. For example, in a graph, this means mapping each variable or data point to a vertex, and using the graph to manage the computation, avoiding the use of mechanisms such as synchronized global variables.

Unfortunately, there were cases where such a "clean" implementation would not work. In such situations, we made things work by writing code that takes some of the burden of managing the data and computation away from the platform.

3.4 Experimental Platform

All of the experiments reported in this paper were performed using Amazon EC2 m2.4xlarge machines, running Ubuntu (each machine had eight virtual cores, two disks, and 68 GB of RAM). In all, we used approximately 70,000 hours of compute time, considering debugging, tuning and testing.

We were initially concerned about variability in EC2 performance from day-to-day and machine-to-machine. When we tested the same MCMC simulation on five different days using five different compute clusters, we found that the standard deviation in per-iteration running time was only 32 seconds (out of 27 minutes on average) and so we decided that such variations were insignificant.

4. PLATFORMS EVALUATED

4.1 Spark

Spark [24] is an open source cluster computing system designed for large scale data analytics. Spark utilizes Resilient Distributed Datasets (RDDs) [23], which provide a fault-tolerant, distributed memory abstraction. RDDs are built by running coarse-grained transformations over either a data set or other existing RDDs. Spark provides fault tolerance by tracking data lineage, so it can rebuild lost data partitions. The designers of Spark argue that since RDDs allow for in-memory computations without concern for lost data, they can facilitate very fast performance.

To us, one of the most attractive aspects of Spark is that it provides a Python-based programming interface. Python is now one of the most popular languages for ML-oriented programming (along with other high-level languages such as R and Matlab), and we were eager to evaluate a Python-based platform.

4.2 SimSQL

SimSQL [4] is a distributed, relational database system, whose design has been augmented to support stochastic analytics. Specifically, SimSQL has native support for a special type of user-defined function known as a *variable generation* (VG) *function*. VG functions are randomized, table-valued functions. Using SimSQL's dialect of SQL, it is possible to define a random database table whose contents are constructed from one or more VG function invocations, as well as from deterministic data stored within the database. Random table definitions in SimSQL's SQL dialect can be mutually recursive. Hence one can define, in SQL, MCMC simulations.

SimSQL is written mostly in Java, with a Prolog query optimizer. SimSQL VG functions are written in C++. SimSQL compiles SQL into Java classes that are executed as Hadoop MapReduce jobs.

4.3 GraphLab

GraphLab [11] is a graph-based distributed computing platform written in C++. The so-called "graph-parallel" abstraction used by

GraphLab is a useful abstraction for ML, since many ML inference algorithms are naturally centered around variables/data (which map to vertices in a graph) and the statistical relationships between them (which map to edges). GraphLab is unique in that its computational model is pull-based and asynchronous. Each vertex in the graph constantly requests data from its neighbors in order to update its own state. Asynchronicity is the single most defining (and unique) characteristic of the GraphLab approach, and allows for a very appealing computational model, since when writing the code associated with a vertex, one need only consider the computation required to update the state of that vertex; one can more or less ignore the remainder of the computation.

4.4 Giraph

Giraph [2] is also a graph-based, distributed computing platform. It is written in Java and runs on top of Hadoop. It is often viewed as an open-source version of Pregel [12]. Giraph differs fundamentally from GraphLab in that its model is push-based and synchronous, using the so-called bulk synchronous parallel (BSP) model [20]. Giraph divides a graph algorithm into a sequence of *super-steps*. In each super-step, every vertex executes the same user-defined compute function in parallel, where the vertex receives messages from other vertices in super-step $i-1$, accesses and updates its local state, and then sends its messages to the other vertices for super-step $i+1$. Vertices can work together to perform tasks such as aggregation in a tree-based fashion using combiners to speed the computation.

4.5 Versions Tested

We tested version 0.1 of SimSQL, version 2.2 of GraphLab, version 1.0.0 of Giraph. GMM/Bayesian Lasso was implemented using Spark 0.7.3 and the other models using Spark 0.8.0.

5. GAUSSIAN MIXTURE MODEL

We begin our experimental evaluation by considering a classical data clustering model: the Gaussian mixture model (GMM). A GMM views a data set as being produced by a set of K Gaussian (multi-dimensional normal) distributions; the kth Gaussian is parameterized by a mean vector μ_k and a covariance matrix Σ_k, and has an associated probability π_k. To produce the jth point in the data set, the model first selects a Gaussian by generating a sampled vector $\mathbf{c}_j$ vector from a Multinomial$(\pi, 1)$ distribution ($c_{j,k}$ is then a 1 if and only if the k Gaussian was used to produce the data point x_j, and zero otherwise). The data point itself is then sampled from the Gaussian indicated by $\mathbf{c}_j$. We put a Dirichlet(α) prior on π, a Normal(μ_0, Λ_0^{-1}) prior on each μ_k, and an InvWishart(v, Ψ) prior on each Σ_k. The goal during learning is then to discover all of the unseen c_j values, as well as all of the Gaussian parameters.

Let $\mathbf{p}_j^{(i)}$ denote the unit-length vector whose kth entry is proportional to $\pi_k^{(i)} \times$ Normal $\left(\mathbf{x}_j | \mu_k^{(i)}, \Sigma_k^{(i)}\right)$. That is, it gives the posterior probability that point k came from the jth cluster, given the parameters at the ith MCMC iteration. A Markov chain to learn the desired, posterior distribution can be derived as:

$$\mu_k^{(i)} \sim \text{Normal}\Bigg(\left(\Lambda_0 + n\left(\Sigma_k^{(i-1)}\right)^{-1}\right)^{-1} \times \left(\Lambda_0\mu_0 + \left(\Sigma_k^{(i-1)}\right)^{-1} \sum_j c_{j,k}^{(i-1)} \mathbf{x}_j\right), \left(\Lambda_0 + n\left(\Sigma_k^{(i-1)}\right)^{-1}\right)^{-1}\Bigg)$$

$$\Sigma_k^{(i)} \sim \text{InvWish}\left(n + v, \Psi + \sum_j c_{j,k}^{(i-1)} (\mathbf{x}_j - \mu_k^{(i)})(\mathbf{x}_j - \mu_k^{(i)})^T\right)$$

$$\pi_k^{(i)} \sim \text{Dirichlet}\left(\alpha + \sum_j c_j^{(i-1)}\right) \quad c_j^{(i)} \sim \text{Multinom}\left(\mathbf{p}_j^{(i)}, 1\right)$$

The task is to write a distributed code that simulates this chain.

5.1 Spark Implementation

We begin by creating a RDD named `data`, which is read and parsed from data in permanent storage (HDFS in our example):

```
lines = sc.textFile("hdfs://master:54310/data.txt")
data = lines.map(parseLine).cache()
```

The `cache()` function asks the system to store RDD in the memory, which can accelerate subsequent visits and operations on `data`.

Next, we compute the hyper-parameters μ and Λ_0^{-1} as the observed mean and dimensional variance of the data:

```
num = data.count()
hyper_mean = data.reduce(add)/num
hyper_cov_diagonal = data.map(lambda x: square(x -
            hyper_mean)).reduce(add)/num
numpy.fill_diagonal(hyper_cov, hyper_cov_diagonal)
```

Based on those parameters, we initialize the model (π_i, μ_i and Σ_i) for each Gaussian component:

```
c_model = sc.parallelize(range(0, K)).map(lambda x:
          (x, (mvnrnd(hyper_mean, hyper_cov),
          invWishart(hyper_cov, len(hyper_mean)+2))))
          .collectAsMap()
pi = np.zeros(K, float)
pi.fill(1.0/K)
```

Here, `mvnrnd(.)` and `invWishart(.)` are user-defined functions that call PyGSL library functions. `collectAsMap()` is a built-in function that transforms the RDD to a Python dictionary.

Finally, we come to the main loop of the program, which consists of three MapReduce jobs. The first dominates the overall runtime:

```
c_agg = data.map(lambda x:
        sample_mem(x, pi, c_model))
        .reduceByKey(lambda (x1, y1, z1),
        (x2, y2, z2):(x1+x2, y1+y2, z1+z2))
```

On the Map side, the output of the function `sample_mem(x, pi, c_model)` is a tuple `(k, (1, x, sq_x))`, where `k` is the membership of data point `x` and `sq_x` is the matrix $\hat{\Sigma} = (x - \mu_k)(x - \mu_k)^T$, μ_k is the mean of kth Gaussian component. On the Reduce side, tuples with the same membership are aggregated into a single tuple.

The second job is Map-only. This job samples μ_k and Σ_k for each Gaussian component in parallel:

```
c_model = c_agg.mapValues(lambda (c_num, x_sum,
          sq_sum): updateModel(c_num, x_sum, sq_sum,
          len(hyper_mean)+2, hyper_mean, hyper_cov)
          ).collectAsMap()
```

The third job collects the number of data points assigned to each cluster, which is then used to update π:

```
c_num = c_agg.mapValues(lambda (c_num, x_sum,
                        sq_sum): c_num).collectAsMap()
pi = sample_dirichlet(c_num)
```

5.2 SimSQL Implementation

The simulation is implemented in SimSQL using a database schema with four random tables that correspond to the four classes of variables listed above:

```
clus_means[i](clus_id,dim_id, dim_value)
clus_covas[i](clus_id, dim_id1, dim_id2,dim_value)
clus_prob[i](clus_id, prob)
membership[i](data_id, clus_id)
```

The data to be processed are stored in a database table:

```
data(data_id, dim_id, data_val)
```

as are the various entries in the α vector (the hyperparameter for the Dirichlet prior on π):

```
cluster(dim_id, alpha)
```

In addition, several views are used to store the other hyperparameters, which are computed empirically from the data. For example, the vector μ_o is computed as the mean of the entire data set:

```
create view mean_prior(dim_id, dim_val) as
  select dim_id, avg(data_val)
  from data
  group by dim_id;
```

Aside from this, the entire SimSQL code consists of (1) initialization codes for the first three random tables, (2) recursive definitions for all four random tables, and (3) a C++ implementation of the `multinomial_membership` VG function, which is used to update `membership[i]` (the other VG functions are all library functions).

As an example, consider the following initialization:

```
create table clus_prob[0] (clus_id, prob) as
  with diri_res as Dirichlet
    (select clus_id, pi_prior
     from cluster)
  select diri_res.out_id, diri_res.prob
  from diri_res;
```

This code uses the hyperparameters stored in the `cluster` table to parameterize the Dirichlet VG function, which then outputs the value of $\pi^{(0)}$ as a set of $(k, \pi_k^{(0)})$ pairs, that are then stored in the `clus_prob[0]` table.

Here is an example of a recursive definition:

```
create table clus_prob[i](clus_id, prob) as
  with diri_res as Dirichlet
    (select cmem.clus_id,
       cmem.count_num+clus.pi_prior as diri_para
     from (select cm.clus_id as clus_id,
                  count(cm.data_id) as count_num
           from membership[i-1] as cm
           group by clus_id) as cmem, clus
     where cmem.clus_id = clus.clus_id)
  select diri_res.out_id, diri_res.prob
  from diri_res;
```

This code parameterizes the Dirichlet distribution by performing the required $\alpha + \sum_j c_j^{(i-1)}$ computation, in order to re-sample the selection probability for each of the clusters. This computation requires that we compute the number of times that each data point is assigned to each cluster, which is done via SQL aggregation.

5.3 GraphLab Implementation

We define three types of vertices: data vertices, cluster vertices, and the mixture-proportion vertex. There is a one-to-one mapping between data points and data vertices. The clusters are put into a separate cluster vertex, and the vector of mixing proportions π is maintained by the mixture-proportion vertex. The cluster vertices and data vertices define a complete, bipartite graph and the mixture-proportion vertex is connected to each of the data vertices.

Each Gibbs sampler iteration is implemented using GraphLab's *gather-apply-scatter* abstraction. In the gather phase, each node "gathers" the state of all of its neighbors. In our implementation, the jth data vertex exports a view of itself that contains three values: the data point $\mathbf{x}_j$, the vector $\mathbf{c}_j$ identifying the cluster that produced the jth data point; and the matrix $\hat{\Sigma}_j = (\mathbf{x}_j - \mu_{1(\mathbf{c}_j)})(\mathbf{x}_j - \mu_{1(\mathbf{c}_j)})^T$. Here, $1(\mathbf{c}_j)$ returns the identity of the entry in $\mathbf{c}_j$ having the value "1". This is stored as a triple $\langle \mathbf{c}_j, \mathbf{x}_j, \hat{\Sigma}_j \rangle$. This triple is "gathered" by all of the nodes attached to the data vertex. The mixture-proportion vertex sums up all of the $\mathbf{c}_j$ vectors as it examines the triples associated with each data vertex, and the kth cluster vertex sums up all of the $\mathbf{x}_j$ values (and all of the Σ_j values) for those data vertices having a 1 in the kth position in $\mathbf{c}_j$.

Likewise, each data vertex "gathers" the state of the model from the mixture-proportion vertex (where it receives the vector π) and from each of the cluster vertices (where it receives the cluster mean vector μ_k and cluster covariance matrix Σ_k).

Next comes the apply phase, where each one of the vertices re-samples its own state. Each data vertex re-samples $\mathbf{c}_j$, the mixing-proportion vertex re-samples π, and the cluster vertices re-sample the cluster mean and covariance matrix.

In the scatter phase, each vertex signals all of its adjacent vertices, letting them know that the apply phase has completed.

5.4 Giraph Implementation

The graph we use for Giraph is identical to the GraphLab graph. However, as we will describe, the Giraph programming model is more oriented towards message-passing, as opposed to computation over a predefined set of edges. These messages can be constructed case-by-case, whereas in GraphLab a vertex must simple export a single view of its internals to the rest of the world.

The actual learning computation begins with an initialization of the cluster-related parameters $\langle \mu_k^{(0)}, \Sigma_k^{(0)}, \pi_k^{(0)} \rangle$ stored in the each cluster vertex followed by an initialization of the membership of each data point $\mathbf{c}_j^{(0)}$ stored in each data vertex.

After initialization, the cluster-membership vertex sends the current value of π_k to the kth cluster vertex, so K messages are sent in all. Each cluster vertex receives this mixing-proportion message and broadcasts the triple $\langle \mu_k, \Sigma_k, \pi_k \rangle$ to the whole system. The jth data vertex receives these K messages, and samples its membership $\mathbf{c}_j$. It computes the matrix $\hat{\Sigma}_j = (\mathbf{x}_j - \mu_{1(\mathbf{c}_j)})(\mathbf{x}_j - \mu_{1(\mathbf{c}_j)})^T$. (Again, $1(\mathbf{c}_j)$ returns the identity of the entry in $\mathbf{c}_j$ having the value "1".) It then sends the double $\langle \mathbf{x}_j, \hat{\Sigma}_j \rangle$ to the cluster vertex indicated by $\mathbf{c}_j$. Each cluster aggregate those messages, and resamples its posterior covariance Σ_k and mean μ_k. Each cluster counts the number of points assigned to it, and sends this count in a message to the cluster-membership vertex, which updates π.

We attempted to optimize the computation as much as possible. To save the memory, we do not record the edges between the data vertices and the cluster vertices explicitly; we instead use broadcast to communicate from the cluster vertices to data vertices, and we use a naming scheme allowing each data vertex to send a message to the appropriate cluster vertex without the system recording the edge. Giraph's combiner functionality is used to reduce communication and increase load balancing during aggregation.

Numerical Computing in Java. One significant issue is the difficulty of finding an appropriate Java-language statistical/numerical software package. We went with the Mallet library [13] due to its completeness. We found Mallet to be slow for problems requiring high-dimensional linear algebra. A library such as JBLAS that wraps a high-performance C linear algebra package might be faster, but passing the Java/C barrier can be expensive, and such solutions are generally not "plug and play."

5.5 Experiments and Results

We tuned each code and platform in order to obtain the fastest per-iteration running time possible. We then created a synthetic data set having ten dimensions, generated using a mixture of ten Gaussians, and used each platform to learn these Gaussians. For each platform, we ran the GMM inference code on three compute clusters of different sizes: five machines, 20 machines, and 100 machines. The amount of data per machine was kept constant at ten million data points, so (for example) the 100 machine cluster was used to perform GMM inference over one billion data points.

In addition, we created a second data set with 100 dimensions. We then ran an experiment where we kept the amount of data constant at one million data points per machine. We performed inference for this data set only on the five-machine compute cluster.

Note that each platform is running exactly the same MCMC simulation (with only minor differences in the initialization and order of the updates in each iteration). Thus, it is not informative to examine the actual models learned.

The results are shown in Figure 1 (a). In this figure we show, for each experiment, the average per-iteration running time, computed over the first five iterations of the MCMC simulation. In parens, we give the time required to initialize the simulation (this typically includes choosing the initial cluster parameters and perhaps doing the initial assignment of data points to clusters). This is a one-time cost. "Fail" means that while the code could be executed on a small problem size, it could not be made to run at the scale required by the experiment via any reasonable amount of tuning.

5.6 Discussion

SimSQL, Spark and Giraph: No Significant Differences. Putting aside for a moment the failure of Giraph to scale to 100 machines or handle the 100-dimensional problem, there is not a significant difference in the non-GraphLab runtimes depicted in Figure 1 (a). The exception is SimSQL at 100 dimensions, which has a per-iteration time that is twice that of Spark. The reason for this is that the GMM simulation must aggregate one $(\mathbf{x}_j-\mu)(\mathbf{x}_j-\mu)^T$ matrix (which is a 10,000 entry matrix for 100-dimensional data) for each data point. In SimSQL, this is performed using a costly `GROUP BY`, which is slower than the Spark matrix/vector operations.

Java vs. Python. We were curious as to whether there was a performance hit using Python with Spark as opposed to Java with Spark. We chose Python because the Spark + Python interface is very nice, leading to beautiful codes, and Python is now commonly used for statistical/numerical computing (NumPy and PyGSL, which we used, are quite popular, for example). However, Spark + Python uses Py4J, which uses sockets to send data back and forth between a Python interpreter and the JVM. This may be slow.

Thus, we re-implemented the Spark GMM MCMC code in Java with Mallet, and ran the experiments once again. The results are shown in Figure 1 (b). For the ten-dimensional inference problem, Java takes around 50% of the Python time. But for the 100-dimensional problem, it is more than eight times slower, presumably due to the cost of 100-dimensional Java linear algebra.

We re-visit this in Section 10 of the paper, where we compare Spark Java vs. Spark Python on the LDA learning task.

GraphLab, Giraph and Super Vertex Codes. Our GraphLab implementation failed every attempt to run it at the scale required by the experiments. Why? In a typical "hand-coded" implementation of the GMM inference algorithm, a program would store the current model in RAM, and then cycle through all of the data points in sequence, updating the cluster membership for each. In GraphLab, there is no notion of pinning a single copy of the model in RAM and cycling through the data points. Instead, the data vertex associated with each node must gather a copy of the model via the links in the graph, and the user cannot control this process. In practice, GraphLab seems to simultaneously materialize one 50KB copy of the model for each data point, which quickly exhausts the available memory and the computation fails.

How can one get around this problem? One method we considered was to move the model out of the graph, eschew the gather-apply-scatter mechanism, and perform the aggregation needed to update the model with one of GraphLab's distributed aggregation facilities. The issue is that such an implementation would not use GraphLab's graph abstraction in any meaningful way.

In the end, we settled on the idea of combining a large numbers (hundreds of thousands) of data points together to form "super vertices" (we use 8000 super vertices on our 100 machine cluster). The gather phase in this implementation changes in that there is only *one* copy of the model obtained for the *entire* super vertex. Further, the view of the super vertex exported to its neighbors becomes an array of $\langle k, n_k, \mu_k, \Sigma_k \rangle$ tuples, with one tuple for each value of k in $1...K$. Here, n_k is the number of points in the super vertex assigned to cluster k, μ_k is the sum over $\mathbf{x}_j$ where $\mathbf{x}_j$ has been assigned to cluster k, and Σ_k is computed similarly from a sum over $(\mathbf{x}_j - \mu_k^{(i)})(\mathbf{x}_j - \mu_k^{(i)})^T$ for those points assigned to cluster k. A cluster vertex in the gather phase collects only the one triple assigned to it by each super vertex. In the apply phase, the super vertex then runs through each of its data points, in sequence.

In addition to radically reducing the memory requirements, this has the additional benefit of distributing most of the heavy-duty aggregation to the super vertices, instead of at the cluster vertices.

The result is a very fast GMM implementation, as shown in Figure 1 (b). A similar "super vertex" construction was a necessary part of each one of the GraphLab implementations described in the paper; without it, none of our GraphLab codes would run.

Super Vertex Codes on Other Platforms. Naturally, GraphLab is not the only platform that can benefit from the super vertex construction. By grouping data points together and handling them as a single unit in "hand-coded" C++ (SimSQL/GraphLab), Java (in Giraph), or Python (Spark) we can often realize significant speedups. In Figure 1 (c) which shows the running times obtained through GMM super vertex codes on each of the platforms. SimSQL in particular can be made to run extremely fast using a super vertex construction; the 100-dimensional GMM implementation ran in a time that was only 20% of its nearest competitor (GraphLab).

6. THE BAYESIAN LASSO

The Bayesian Lasso [18] is a well-known regularized Bayesian linear regression formulation and associated MCMC sampler. Let the data set D consist of a set of n $\langle \mathbf{x}, y \rangle$ pairs. The model consists of a p-dimensional vector of regression coefficients β, where the (centered) response $\tilde{y}$ associated with the data point $\mathbf{x}$ is assumed to be generated as $\tilde{y} \sim \text{Normal}(\beta \cdot \mathbf{x}, \sigma^2)$, and σ^2 has an inverse-gamma prior.

To simplify the MCMC simulation used to learn the model, a set of p auxiliary variables $\tau_1^2, \tau_2^2, ...$ are introduced that control the variance of the various regression coefficients as they are updated.

(a) GMM: Initial Implementations					
		10 dimensions			100 dimensions
	lines of code	5 machines	20 machines	100 machines	5 machines
SimSQL	197	27:55 (13:55)	28:55 (14:38)	35:54 (18:58)	1:51:12 (36:08)
GraphLab	661	Fail	Fail	Fail	Fail
Spark (Python)	236	26:04 (4:10)	37:34 (2:27)	38:09 (2:00)	47:40 (0:52)
Giraph	2131	25:21 (0:18)	30:26 (0:15)	Fail	Fail

(b) GMM: Alternative Implementations					
		10 dimensions			100 dimensions
	lines of code	5 machines	20 machines	100 machines	5 machines
Spark (Java)	737	12:30 (2:01)	12:25 (2:03)	18:11 (2:26)	6:25:04 (36:08)
GraphLab (Super Vertex)	681	6:13 (1:13)	4:36 (2:47)	6:09 (1:21)*	33:32 (0:42)

(c) GMM: Super Vertex Implementations				
	10 dimensions, 5 machines		100 dimensions, 5 machines	
	w/o super vertex	with super vertex	w/o super vertex	with super vertex
SimSQL	27:55 (13:55)	6:20 (12:33)	1:51:12 (36:08)	7:22 (14:07)
GraphLab	Fail	6:13 (1:13)	Fail	33:32 (0:42)
Spark (Python)	26:04 (4:10)	29:12 (4:01)	47:40 (0:52)	47:03 (2:17)
Giraph	25:21 (0:18)	13:48 (0:03)	Fail	6:17:32 (0:03)

Figure 1: GMM MCMC implementation; lines of code (excluding libraries) and average time per iteration. Time in parens is for the initialization/setup. Format is HH:MM:SS or MM:SS. *We were actually unable to run GraphLab at 100 machines. Past 40 machines, GraphLab would not boot up at many cluster sizes. The closest to 100 machines that we were able to get was 96 machines.

Let $\tilde{\mathbf{y}}$ be the centered response vector and $\mathbf{X}$ denote the matrix of regressors constructed from D. Then the MCMC simulation for learning the model is as follows:

$$1/(\tau_j^{(i)})^2 \sim \text{InvGaussian}\left(\sqrt{\frac{\lambda^2(\sigma^{(i-1)})^2}{(\beta_j^{(i-1)})^2}}, \lambda^2\right)$$

$$\beta^{(i)} \sim \text{Normal}\left((\mathbf{A}^{(i)})^{-1}\mathbf{X}^T\tilde{\mathbf{y}}, \sigma^2(\mathbf{A}^{(i)})^{-1}\right), \text{ where}$$

$$\mathbf{A}^{(i)} = \mathbf{X}^T\mathbf{X} + (\mathbf{D}_\tau^{(i)})^{-1} \text{ and}$$

$$\mathbf{D}_\tau^{(i)} = diag\left((\tau_1^{(i)})^2, (\tau_2^{(i)})^2, \ldots\right)$$

$$(\sigma^{(i)})^2 \sim \text{InvGamma}\left(\frac{1+n+p}{2}, \frac{2+\sum_{\langle \mathbf{x},y\rangle\in D}(\tilde{y}-\beta^{(i)}\cdot\mathbf{x})^2 + \sum_j(\beta_j^{(i)})^2/(\tau_j^{(i)})^2}{2}\right)$$

6.1 Spark Implementation

In the Spark implementation, we first create a RDD `data` by reading the input files from HDFS, and use the RDD to compute the centered response $\tilde{\mathbf{y}}$:

```
data = lines.map(parseData).cache()
y_sum = data.map(lambda (id, (x, y)): y).sum()
y_avg = y_sum/data.count()
data = data.map(lambda (id,(x, y)): (id, (x, y-y_avg)))
```

Next, the Gram matrix and the quantity vector are computed:

```
XX = data.flatMap(lambda (id, (x, y)):
      computePairSum(x, y)).reduceByKey(add)
XY = data.flatMap(lambda (id, (x, y)):
      computeXYSum(x, y)).reduceByKey(add)
```

Most of the code of the main loop of the Gibbs sampler is run locally, since most of the computation required by the loop is quite modest for data of low to medium dimensionality (up to a few thousand dimensions). Only one actual MapReduce job is needed per iteration. Specifically, we must compute $\sum_{\langle \mathbf{x},y\rangle\in D}(\tilde{y}-\beta\cdot\mathbf{x})^2$ in a distributed fashion in order to parameterize the inverse-gamma distribution needed to compute $(\sigma^{(i)})^2$. The code is:

```
remain_sum1 = data.map(lambda (id,(x, y)):
       computeRemainSquare(x, y, beta)).sum()
```

6.2 SimSQL Implementation

The SimSQL implementation begins by creating three materialized views that will be used repeatedly, in each iteration of the MCMC simulation. The three materialized views include (1) the Gram matrix computed over $\mathbf{X}$, (2) the centered response vector $\tilde{\mathbf{y}}$, and (3) the quantity $||y_i \times \mathbf{x}_i||_1$. The most expensive of these views to actually compute is the Gram matrix $\mathbf{X}^T\mathbf{X}$.

Aside from those three materialized views, the SimSQL implementation of the Bayesian Lasso utilizes three random tables: (1) the `beta[i]` table which stores the $\beta^{(i)}$ vector as a set of tuples, (2) the `sigma[i]` table (with one tuple) that stores the ith value of $(\sigma^{(i)})^2$, and (3) the `tau[i]` that stores one tuple for each $1/(\tau_j^{(i)})^2$ value. These `CREATE TABLE` statements for these three tables have a very close correspondence with the three different MCMC update steps described above. Consider `tau[i]`:

```
CREATE TABLE tau[i](rigid, tau Value) AS
  FOR EACH r IN regressor IDs
    WITH IG AS InvGaussian(
      (SELECT sqrt((pr1.lambda * pr1.lambda * s.sigma)
                  / (b.bet * b.bet))
       FROM prior pr1, sigma[i] s, beta[i-1] b
       WHERE b.rigid = r.grid),
      (SELECT (pr2.lambda * pr2.lambda)
       FROM prior pr2))
  SELECT r.grid, (1.0 / IG.out) FROM IG;
```

Here, the table `prior` has a single tuple that gives all of the prior hyperparameters.

6.3 GraphLab Implementation

Again, we use a super vertex-based implementation. The ith data vertex in the graph is made up of a large number of data points, forming a matrix $\mathbf{X}_i$ and vector $\mathbf{y}_i$. The jth model vertex consists of the inverse of the auxiliary variable $1/\tau_j^2$. We use one more vertex to store the regression coefficient vector β and the variance σ^2. This vertex sits in the center of the graph structure.

We begin using GraphLab's `map_reduce_vertices` method to obtain a couple of invariant statistics. While using an operation that measures the (non-existent!) global state of an asynchronous system might be problematic during the actual Markov chain simulation, it is a nice way to collect statistics before the simulation begins. We use one MapReduce to calculate the Gram matrix $\mathbf{X}^T\mathbf{X}$ and to center the response. Based on $\overline{y}$, the second MapReduce calculates $\mathbf{X}^T\tilde{\mathbf{y}}$ and stores it as a global variable.

Next we use GraphLab's gather-apply-scatter abstraction to simulate the required Markov Chain. The gather phase collects $\langle\beta_j, \sigma^2\rangle$ for the j-th model vertex from the center vertex. The center vertex collects the vector of auxiliary variables $1/\tau^2$ from the model vertices, as well as $\sum_{\langle \mathbf{x},y\rangle \in D} (\tilde{y} - \beta \cdot \mathbf{x})^2$ from the data vertices.

The apply phase then updates the center vertex by sampling new β and σ^2 values, and updates each model vertex by sampling $1/(\tau_j)^2$ from the inverse Gaussian distribution based on σ^2 and β_j.

6.4 Giraph Implementation

Our implementation uses three types of graph vertices: data vertices, dimensional vertices and a model vertex, which are used to store the dataset, collect required statistics such as the Gram matrix $\mathbf{X}^T\mathbf{X}$, and update the model (β, σ^2 and each τ_j^2), respectively. A dimensional vertex is associated with each data dimension.

The actual learning computation begins with the computation of $\mathbf{X}^T\mathbf{X}$ and $\mathbf{X}^T\tilde{\mathbf{y}}$. First, each data vertex computes $\mathbf{x}^T\mathbf{x}$ and sends this quantity along with $\mathbf{y}$ these to the other two types of vertices. The jth dimensional vertex collects the statistics for the jth row of the Gram matrix, while the model vertex computes $\tilde{\mathbf{y}}$. The Gram matrix is saved to the model vertex based on the messages passed from the dimensional vertices, while each data vertex computes $\mathbf{x}^T\tilde{\mathbf{y}}$, and sends it to the model vertex. The model vertex first initializes each $1/\tau_j^2$, σ^2, and β. The model vertex then broadcasts β to the data vertices so that they can compute $(\tilde{y} - \beta \cdot \mathbf{x})^2$. The model vertex obtains the sum of these values over all data vertices, and then updates each $1/\tau_j^2$, σ^2, and β. The updated β is then re-broadcast to all of the data vertices and the process is repeated. We make use of Giraph's combiner and aggregator facilities wherever possible to speed the computation and reduce communication.

6.5 Experiments and Results

To test these four implementations, we created a synthetic data set having 10^3 regressor dimensions and a one-dimensional response. As in GMM experiments, we held the number of data points per machine constant at 10^5 and tested compute clusters consisting of five, 20, and 100 machines. The results are shown in Figure 2. Giraph was unable to run without implementing the simulation using the super vertex construction.

6.6 Discussion

SimSQL, Spark, and Long Initialization Times. Note the substantial performance gap between SimSQL and Spark on one hand and GraphLab and Giraph on the other, considering the time to run the initialization code. Both of the former systems require between one and three hours for initialization/startup, while GraphLab takes under one minute. Normally, MCMC initialization time is not particularly important, since initialization is run only once. But in the case of the Bayesian Lasso, the simulation converges very quickly, magnifying the importance of the initialization.

SimSQL's relatively slow performance can be explained by its lack of support for vector and matrix operations. Consider the initialization phase of the simulation, which requires computing the Gram matrix $\mathbf{X}^T\mathbf{X}$ over the data set. In SimSQL, the computation is performed as an aggregate-`GROUP BY` query, with one group for every one of the one million entries in the Gram matrix.

In contrast, consider GraphLab's super vertex code. The ith super vertex in the GraphLab implementation has several thousand data points, which are stored in C++ as a matrix $\mathbf{X}_i$. This super vertex locally computes $\mathbf{X}_i^T\mathbf{X}_i$ using a fast matrix multiplication. At the same time, a similar computation is taking place all over the compute cluster. The resulting few thousand, million-entry matrices are then sent to a central location and added together.

In the latter case, most of the computational work is done in a high-performance linear algebra library. In the former, it is done using the relational engine. This accounts for the huge difference.

SimSQL's Relatively High Per-Iteration Times. SimSQL is also slow on a per-iteration bases. SimSQL takes about ten times as long as Spark, 20 times as long as GraphLab, and five times as long as Giraph, per iteration. This means that SimSQL would spend around five hours to initialize and run twelve iterations, as opposed to two hours 15 minutes for Spark. Here again, SimSQL seems to suffer greatly from the fact that each $\mathbf{x}_i$ is stored as one thousand tuples rather than a single vector, and $\mathbf{A}^{-1}\mathbf{X}^T\tilde{\mathbf{y}}$ must be computed using set-oriented aggregates.

7. HIDDEN MARKOV MODEL

The next model we consider is a hidden Markov model (HMM) for text. This model and the associated MCMC simulation are somewhat more intricate than the previous two.

Assume that $\mathbf{x}_j$ is the ordered list or vector of words that make up the jth document. Each word $x_{j,k}$ in $\mathbf{x}_j$ is assumed to be produced by one of K hidden states. Hidden state s has an associated probability vector Ψ_s, where $\Psi_{s,w}$ is the probability that state s would produce word w. Since the model is sequential, there is also a state-to-state transition probability vector δ_s associated with state s. Thus, $\delta_{s,s'}$ is the probability of transitioning from state s to state s' when one moves to the next word in the document.

Let $\mathbf{y}_j$ be the vector of n state assignments associated with the jth document. To generate $\mathbf{y}_j$ using the HMM, we imagine that the start state $y_{j,1}$ for document j is first selected by sampling from a Categorical(δ_0) distribution (since there does not exist a zeroth state, δ_0 is used to control the start state of each document). Then, for each k in $2...n$, $\Pr[y_{j,k+1}|y_{j,k}] = \delta_{y_{j,k},y_{j,k+1}}$. Finally, we generate the ith document by sampling each $x_{j,k}$ from a Categorical($\Psi_{y_{j,k}}$) distribution. We put a Dirichlet(α) prior on each δ_s, and a Dirichlet(β) prior on each Ψ_s.

To learn this model, we utilize a simulation that updates every other state assignment in a given step. Specifically, if the current step i of the simulation is even and k is even, or if the current step ith is odd and k is odd, we have:

$$\begin{aligned}\Pr[y_{j,k}^{(i)} = s] &\propto \delta_{0,s}^{(i-1)} \times \Psi_{s,x_{j,k}}^{(i-1)} \times \delta_{s,y_{j,k+1}^{(i-1)}}^{(i-1)} \text{ if } k = 1\\ &\propto \delta_{y_{j,k-1}^{(i-1)},s}^{(i-1)} \times \Psi_{s,x_{j,k}}^{(i-1)} \text{ if } k \text{ ends the document}\\ &\propto \delta_{y_{j,k-1}^{(i-1)},s}^{(i-1)} \times \Psi_{s,x_{j,k}}^{(i-1)} \times \delta_{s,y_{j,k+1}^{(i-1)}}^{(i-1)} \text{ otherwise.}\end{aligned}$$

Otherwise, the state assignment does not change in iteration i:

$$y_{j,k}^{(i)} = y_{j,k}^{(i-i)}$$

Bayesian Lasso				
	lines of code	5 machines	20 machines	100 machines
SimSQL	100	7:09 (2:40:06)	8:04 (2:45:28)	12:24 (2:54:45)
GraphLab (Super Vertex)	572	0:36 (0:37)	0:26 (0:35)	0:31 (0:50)
Spark (Python)	168	0:55 (1:26:59)	0:59 (1:33:13)	1:12 (2:06:30)
Giraph	1871	Fail	Fail	Fail
Giraph (Super Vertex)	1953	0:58 (1:14)	1:03 (1:14)	2:08 (6:31)

Figure 2: Bayesian Lasso MCMC implementation; lines of code and average time per iteration. Format is HH:MM:SS or MM:SS.

The other updates are as follows. Let $f(w, s) = \sum_{j,k} one(x_{j,k} = w \text{ and } y^{(i)}_{j,k} = s)$, where $one()$ returns 1 if the Boolean argument is true and 0 otherwise. Similarly, $g(s) = \sum_j one(y^{(i)}_{j,0} = s)$ and $h(s, s') = \sum_{j,k} one(y^{(i)}_{j,k} = s \text{ and } y^{(i)}_{j,k+1} = s')$. Then:

$$\Psi^{(i)}_s \sim \text{Dirichlet}(\beta + \langle f(1, s), f(2, s), f(3, s)...\rangle)$$
$$\delta^{(i)}_0 \sim \text{Dirichlet}(\alpha + \langle g(1), g(2), g(3)...\rangle)$$
$$\delta^{(i)}_s \sim \text{Dirichlet}(\alpha + \langle h(s, 1), h(s, 2), h(s, 3)...\rangle)$$

7.1 Spark Implementation

We describe our document-based Spark implementation, where Spark is asked to manage and aggregate data at the document, rather than the word level. This Spark implementation begins by creating a RDD called d_w_seq. This RDD stores, for each document, the document identifier and its associated list of words. Then, a transformation is applied to randomly initialize the states, so the list of words in each document in d_w_seq is replaced by a list of (word, state) pairs. In the following code snippets, we use d_id and s_id to refer to the the document identifier and state identifier, and state_size to store the total number of states:

```
d_w_seq = lines.map(parseDoc).cache()
d_w_s_seq = d_w_seq.mapValues(lambda w_seq:
          init_state(w_seq, state_size))
```

Now it comes the main sampler. In each iteration, we first sample the state transition matrix δ by using two jobs. The first job computes, for each state s (used as the key), the total number of state transitions (s, s') for each target state s' that occurred in the previous iteration. These aggregates are then used to parameterize a MapReduce job that updates the δ values:

```
h = d_w_s_seq.flatMap(lambda (d_id, w_s_seq):
     comp_h(w_s_seq, state_size)).reduceByKey
     lambda p1,p2: addStateCount(p1, p2, state_size))
delta = h.mapValues(lambda h_s: sample_delta(h_s,
     state_size)).collectAsMap()
```

Similarly, we use two jobs to sample Ψ. One more MapReduce job applies a self-transformation of d_w_s_seq to the states:

```
d_w_s_seq = d_w_s_seq.mapValues(lambda w_s_seq:
               update_state(w_s_seq, delta, psi))
```

Note that update_state(.) is a user-defined function, that alternatively updates the states for the even words and the odd words.

7.2 SimSQL Implementation

The word-based SimSQL HMM relies on four random tables: states[i], starts[i], trans[i], and emits[i]. These four tables store all of the $\mathbf{y}^{(i)}_j$ vectors, the δ_0 vector, all of the $\delta^{(i)}_s$ vectors, and all of the $\Psi^{(i)}_s$ vectors, respectively.

At the heart of the SimSQL implementation is the states[i] table, with schema (docID, prevPos, curPos, nextPos, prevStateID, curStateID). This table stores the current set of state assignments. If i is even, then for each (j, k) pair where k is even, there will be one tuple in this table that stores:

$$(j, k-1, k, k+1, y^{(i)}_{j,k}, y^{(i)}_{j,k+1})$$

If i is odd, then there will be one such tuple for each odd k.

To update each tuple to create the $(i+1)$th version of the states table, we would update the above tuple to produce:

$$(j, k-2, k-1, k, y^{(i+1)}_{j,k-1}, y^{(i+1)}_{j,k})$$

All of the new tuples produced in this way from states[i] then constitute the new contents of states[i+1].

Performing this update requires (a) setting $y^{(i+1)}_{j,k}$ in the new tuple to be equal to $y^{(i)}_{j,k}$ in the old tuple, and (b) sampling a new value of $y^{(i+1)}_{j,k-1}$ using the Categorical() VG function. Performing this sampling in turn requires having access to three types of data, in addition to the tuple being updated: (1) the value for $y^{(i)}_{j,k-2}$, (2) all of transition probabilities out of state $y^{(i)}_{j,k-2}$, and (3) the probability that each and every possible state would emit word $x_{j,k-1}$. Gathering all of these values together actually requires a six-table join to parameterize the Categorical VG function.

The reader may wonder why we included all three of prevPos, curPos, and nextPos in each tuple in states[i]. Why not simply include curPos? The reason is a quirk in the SimSQL implementation. The six-table join required to parameterize the Categorical VG function requires join predicates of the form t1.curPos = t2.curPos + 1. The SimSQL optimizer has problems with this sort of equality predicate, implementing it inefficiently as a cross-product. Our way around this was to explicitly store nextPos, so the join could be written as t1.curPos = t2.nextPos, which is handled efficiently as an equi-join.

7.3 GraphLab Implementation

The graph we use for the HMM simulation contains only two types of vertices. Each data (super) vertex contains the $\mathbf{x}_j$ vectors for a large number of documents as well as the corresponding state assignment vectors. In addition, there is one state vertex associated with each of the K hidden states. The state vertex for state s stores the word emission probability vector Ψ_s and the state-to-state transition probability vector δ_s. This graph is complete and bipartite.

The GraphLab computation begins by initializing the state assignment for each word by performing a transform_vertices operation over all the data vertices. Then the gather-apply-scatter computation begins. In the gather phase, the data vertices collect Ψ_s and δ_s from all the state vertices, while each state vertex s computes $f(w, s)$, $g(s)$, $h(s, s')$ based on the words whose state assignments are also s from the data vertices. The *apply* phase simply updates $\mathbf{y}$, Ψ_s and δ_s according to the rules described above.

7.4 Giraph Implementation

Similarly, two types of vertices are used in the Giraph implementation. Since (unlike for GraphLab) we did not implement only a super vertex version of the Giraph simulation, depending upon the level of granularity, a data vertex could correspond to a word, a document, or a set of documents. Just as in the GraphLab implementation, a state vertex maintains Ψ_s and δ_s.

Consider the simple, word-based Giraph implementation, where each data vertex stores only a word. In this case, there is an edge between the vertex associated with each $x_{j,k}$ and the vertices associated with both $x_{j,k-1}$ and $x_{j,k+1}$. To begin the computation, the data vertices randomly initialize each $y_{j,k}$, and then send $y_{j,k}$ to their neighbors. All the data vertices then record their neighbor's states $y_{j,k-1}$ and $y_{j,k+1}$, and then send a word-count pair $\langle x_{j,k}, 1\rangle$ and a state-count pair $\langle y_{j,k+1}, 1\rangle$ to the $(y_{j,k})$th state vertex, where they are aggregated. To facilitate fast aggregation, we use the Giraph combiner mechanism. Next, the state vertices update their emission and transition probability vectors based on the collected statistics. Both probability vectors are broadcast back to the data vertices for updating their states.

7.5 Experiments and Results

To test the four implementations, we created a synthetic document database. To create each "document", we choose two newsgroup postings from the ubiquitous 20 newsgroups data set and concatenate the postings end-on-end. Since there are 20,000 posts in this data set, it was possible to create up to 400 million different synthetic documents in this way. We used a dictionary size of 10 thousand words and used $K = 20$ different states. The average document in the database was 210 words in length. As before, we tested the ability of each implementation to run on various compute cluster sizes, and we kept the amount of data on each machine constant. We used 2.5 million documents on each machine.

In our first experiment, we tested "word-based" HMM implementations built on top of Giraph, SimSQL, and Spark. Here "word-based" corresponds to the simulation where each word (with its associated hidden state) is individually pushed through the system. Since only SimSQL was able to handle this simulation (and SimSQL took more than eight hours per iteration), we only ran this simulation on five machines. The results are shown at the left in Figure 3 (a). Note the "NA" for the number of lines of code for Spark. We could not get Spark to perform the required self-join of the the set state assignments with itself without failing. Since this join is a prerequisite for running a"word-based" HMM, we did not implement the rest of the algorithm.

We also tested a "document-based" HMM implementation built on Giraph, SimSQL, and Spark; the experiment was run using five machines. In this implementation, the re-sampling of all of the hidden states for an entire document is handled as a group, and hand-coded in Java (Giraph), Python (Spark), or C++ (SimSQL). For all of the platforms, this has three main benefits. First, the state of the model (all of the $\Psi_s^{(i)}$ and $\delta_s^{(i)}$ vectors) need only be associated with each *document*, and not with each word individually. Second, the platform itself need not link up all of the adjacent words and states in order to re-sample each $y_{j,k}^{(i)}$. This linking can be done internally, within the user-supplied code. On all platforms except for SimSQL, the statistics necessary to update all of the $\Psi_s^{(i)}$ and $\delta_s^{(i)}$ vectors can be output at once on a per-document basis. The results are shown at the right in Figure 3 (a).

Finally, we wrote a "super vertex" HMM implementation for all four platforms where a large number of documents are grouped together, and the hidden states associated with all of the words for all of the documents are updated together. The results obtained by running the HMM super vertex implementation for each of the four platforms is shown in Figure 3 (b).

7.6 Discussion

The Giraph HMM Simulation Is Really Fast. This much is obvious; we consider some of the reasons now.

Giraph's Speed Relative to SimSQL. Even though the SimSQL super vertex implementation groups a large number of documents together, and then generates all of the $y_{j,k}^{(i)}$ vales associated with each word in each document in the group via a single C++ VG function invocation, all of those generated values must be output by the VG function as tuples. SimSQL must then aggregate all of the output tuples to compute the $f(.)$, $g(.)$, and $h(.)$ functions required by the simulation. This is very time-consuming. True, the process could likely be sped up considerably by doing pre-aggregation within the VG function (a similar tactic was used to make the SimSQL GMM super vertex simulation the fastest of all of the platforms) but this is a bit awkward because it requires encoding all of the output $y_{j,k}^{(i)}$ values plus all of the aggregates as a single output table. Giraph, on the other hand, need not output all of the $y_{j,k}^{(i)}$ values; they are stored internally, within the super vertex.

Comparing GraphLab and Giraph. Why was Giraph so much faster than GraphLab, and why does it scale better?

We tackle the second question first. All failures were memory-related. It is not that the data set itself is too large for GraphLab to handle. Our compute cluster has 7× the RAM needed to store the corpus. In practice, however, we were constantly struggling to overcome memory problems with GraphLab. It appears that this is related to the lack of control that a GraphLab programmer has over the way that data are materialized and moved around. Consider the problem of aggregating all of the data required to compute $f(w, s)$, $g(s)$, and $h(s, s')$ for a particular s—this aggregation is going to happen at each of the 20 graph vertices that correspond to the 20 hidden HMM states. Each super vertex will produce around 10MB of data that counts the number of times that each particular state-to-state transition happens as well as the number of times that each word is associated to each state. If this set of counts arrives at a state vertex from each of the 10,000 super vertices, we could easily end up having to materialize 100GB of data, killing the computation.

Giraph provides a richer programming interface that allowed us to sidestep some of the more serious computational and memory-related problems that are associated with mapping the simulation to a graph. For example, consider the aggregate computation described above. Giraph features graph-based aggregation functionality (with combiners) that offers a far faster (and safer) mechanism for gathering the required statistics.

8. LATENT DIRICHLET ALLOCATION

Latent Dirichlet Allocation (LDA) is a model for text mining. It views each word in a document as being produced by a latent *topic*, so that if a topic t produces the kth word in document j (denoted as $w_{j,k}$), then $\Pr[w_{j,k} = \omega] = \phi_{t,\omega}$, where ϕ_t represents the word distribution for topic t. Further, each document has a topic distribution, where the distribution for document j is a vector θ_j. Let $z_{j,k}$ indicate which topic produced word k in document j; then $\Pr[z_{j,k} = t] = \theta_{j,t}$. A Dirichlet$(\alpha)$ prior is put on each θ_j vector, and a Dirichlet(β) parameter is put on each ϕ_t vector.

Gibbs sampling is the typical way that an LDA model is learned. The "collapsed" LDA Gibbs sampler is standard. Here "collapsed" means that one or more variables have been integrated out in the

(a) HMM: Word-based and document-based implementations				
	Word-based, 5 machines		Document-based, 5 machines	
	lines of code	running time	lines of code	running time
SimSQL	131	8:17:07 (10:51:32)	123	3:42:40 (20:44)
Spark (Python)	NA	Fail	214	4:21:36 (27:36)
Giraph	1717	Fail	1470	11:02 (7:03)

(b) HMM: Super Vertex Implementations				
	lines of code	5 machines	20 machines	100 machines
Giraph	1735	2:27 (1:12)	2:44 (1:52)	3:12 (2:56)
GraphLab	681	20:39 (16:28)	Fail	Fail
Spark (Python)	215	3:45:58 (11:02)	4:01:02 (13:04)	Fail
SimSQL	136	2:05:12 (1:44:45)	2:05:31 (1:44:36)	2:19:10 (2:04:40)

Figure 3: HMM results. Time in parens is for the initialization/setup. Format is HH:MM:SS or MM:SS.

derivation of the Gibbs sampler. We choose, however, to include the non-collapsed sampler in our benchmark for two reasons. First, it is more interesting as a benchmark because it is a bit more complicated, including more parameters that must be computed. Second, there is the issue of correctness. It is very challenging to parallelize the collapsed LDA Gibbs sampler correctly because of the complex correlation structure that the collapsing induces among the updates to the various $\mathbf{z}_j$ vectors. Most parallel/distributed LDA Gibbs samplers ignore these correlations and update the vectors in parallel, disregarding the effect of the concurrent updates of the $\mathbf{z}_j$ vectors. We are uncomfortable with benchmarking an aggressive (and somewhat questionable) computational trick.

This simulation corresponding to the non-collapsed sampler is then defined as follows. Let $f(j,t) = \sum_k one(z_{j,k}^{(i)} = t)$ and let $g(t,\omega) = \sum_{j,k} one(w_{j,k} = \omega \text{ and } z_{j,k}^{(i)} = t)$. Then:

$$\Pr[z_{j,k}^{(i)} = t] \propto \theta_{j,t}^{(i-1)} \times \phi_{t,w_{j,k}}^{(i-1)}$$

$$\theta_j^{(i)} \sim \text{Dirichlet}(\alpha + \langle f(j,1), f(j,2), f(j,3), ...\rangle)$$

$$\phi_t^{(i)} \sim \text{Dirichlet}(\beta + \langle g(t,1), g(t,2), g(t,3), ...\rangle)$$

8.1 Experiments and Results

We used the document database used in the HMM experiments, a dictionary size of 10,000 words, and a model size of 100 topics.

The first thing that we wanted to do was to implement a "pure", word-based LDA. In this implementation, the $w_{j,k}$ and $z_{j,k}^{(i)}$ values are managed as individual elements by the underlying compute platform. However, since neither Spark nor Giraph were able to handle the word-based HMM simulation (and GraphLab was unable to handle a similar simulation for the relatively simple GMM inference problem), it seemed unlikely that we would be able to develop a word-based LDA for any of those platforms. Thus, we only implemented this version of the LDA simulation for SimSQL. The result of running this simulation on five machines (again with 2.5 million documents per machine) is shown in Figure 4 (a).

We next implemented a document-based LDA, where all of the $z_{j,k}^{(i)}$ values are re-sampled on a per-document basis. In SimSQL, these values still need to be output (and aggregated) as individual tuples, but the VG function for re-sampling all of the $z_{j,k}^{(i)}$ values for a single document need be parameterized only once. In Spark, we output only a single $\mathbf{z}_j^{(i)}$ vector for a document, which should result in an even more efficient sampler than the one written in SimSQL. Giraph should be more efficient still, since they never need to output any $z_{j,k}^{(i)}$ values; these an be maintained internally, in memory, within a graph vertex. Results are shown in Figure 4 (a).

Finally we implemented a super vertex version of the code four each of the four platforms. The results are shown in Figure 4 (b).

8.2 Discussion

Everyone Fails Except for SimSQL. The LDA simulation is quite similar to the HMM simulation, particularly the document-based and super vertex versions. The big difference is that since there are 100 topics, the size of the model that must be learned (and the size of the set of statistics computed) is around five times as large as in the case of the HMM. This appears to makes the task a bit more difficult, especially for Giraph. Our Giraph LDA implementation ran about ten times longer than the HMM implementation, and, perhaps most significantly, failed to run at all on 100 machines. SimSQL was the only platform that was able to run the LDA simulation on 100 machines and 250 million documents.

9. GAUSSIAN IMPUTATION

The last model we consider is the most complicated of the five models, though not the most difficult model to handle computationally: a GMM modified to impute missing values in the data. The MCMC simulation to learn the GMM and simultaneously use it to impute the missing null values is similar to the GMM simulation, but with one additional step where we must estimate the censored values. For the jth data point, let $\mathbf{x}_j^1$ denote the vector of censored values from $\mathbf{x}_j$ and let $\mathbf{x}_j^2$ denote the vector of un-censored values. Then $\mathbf{x}_j^1 \bullet \mathbf{x}_j^2$ is equivalent to $\mathbf{x}_j$, with the dimensions "scrambled" so that the first few dimensions were the ones that were censored. Let μ_j denote mean vector of the cluster that (according to $\mathbf{c}_j^{(i-1)}$) produced the jth data point, and let Σ_j denote the corresponding covariance matrix. Re-arrange and partition the dimensions of μ_j and Σ_j so that it is the case that:

$$\mathbf{x}_j^1 \bullet \mathbf{x}_j^2 \sim \text{Normal}\left(\begin{bmatrix} \mu_j^1 \\ \mu_j^2 \end{bmatrix}, \begin{bmatrix} \Sigma_j^{11}\Sigma_j^{12} \\ \Sigma_j^{21}\Sigma_j^{22} \end{bmatrix}\right)$$

We add an additional step to the GMM simulation. For each $\mathbf{x}_j^1$:

$$(\mathbf{x}_j^1)^{(i)} \sim \text{Normal}\left(\mu_j^1 + \Sigma_j^{12}(\Sigma_j^{22})^{-1}(\mathbf{x}_j^2 - \mu_j^2), \Sigma_j^{11} - \Sigma_j^{12}(\Sigma_j^{22})^{-1}\Sigma_j^{21}\right)$$

As was the case with LDA, space precludes us from describing each of our Gaussian imputation implementations in detail.

9.1 Experiments and Results

We used the ten-dimensional data from the GMM experiments, but performed a bit of additional post-processing. For each data

(a) LDA: Word-based and document-based implementations				
	Word-based, 5 machines		Document-based, 5 machines	
	lines of code	running time	lines of code	running time
SimSQL	126	16:34:39 (11:23:22)	129	4:52:06 (4:34:27)
Spark (Python)	NA	NA	188	≈15:45:00 (≈2:30:00)
Giraph	NA	NA	1358	22:22 (5:46)

(b) LDA: Super Vertex Implementations				
	lines of code	5 machines	20 machines	100 machines
Giraph	1406	18:49 (2:35)	20:02 (2:46)	Fail
GraphLab	517	39:27 (32:14)	Fail	Fail
Spark (Python)	220	≈3:56:00 (≈2:15:00)	≈3:57:00 (≈2:15:00)	Fail
SimSQL	117	1:00:17 (3:09)	1:06:59 (3:34)	1:13:58 (4:28)

Figure 4: LDA results. Time in parens is for the initialization/setup. Format is HH:MM:SS or MM:SS.

point, we took a sample $p \sim \text{Beta}(1, 1)$, which gave us a probability p of between 0 and 1, with a 0.5 average. Each of the ten attribute values within the data point was then censored by flipping a synthesized coin which came up heads with probability p. If a heads was observed, the value was replaced with a $\varnothing$. In this way, 50% of the attribute values in the data set were censored.

As before, we kept the amount of data constant at 10 million data points per machine, and tested the per-iteration running times at five, 20, and 100 machines. The results are shown in Figure 5.

9.2 Discussion

Spark's Increase in Running Time. What struck us as remarkable here was how these results look almost exactly the same to the GMM results, with the exception of a very significant running time increase for Spark. The reason may be that in the case of the GMM, we can store all of the data in memory using the `cache()` function. However, in the imputation model, the actual data set changes constantly as imputation is being performed.

10. SUMMARY OF FINDINGS

Giraph and GraphLab. We begin by discussing the two graph-based platforms: Giraph and GraphLab.

On the positive side, they are both quite fast—typically faster than Spark and SimSQL. However, both Giraph and GraphLab suffer greatly from memory-related difficulties, and for that reason could not be made to run on the largest, most complicated problems. The data sets were not too large to fit into RAM. Our largest data set was around 1TB in size, which fits comfortably in the 7TB of aggregate RAM of our 100 machine compute cluster. In fact, our experiments demonstrate how the constant mantra that "memory is the new disk" must be applied carefully. True, there are few problems (even "big data" problems) where the raw data cannot fit into RAM, but ML inference problems typically require the computation of large sets of complicated statistics, and the computation can temporarily blow up the size of the data by orders of magnitude.

Giraph scaled better than GraphLab, seemingly because Giraph's BSP-based model maps nicely to the bipartite structure of the models tested. Had we tested models with a sparser dependency graph which more closely matched GraphLab's targeted applications, results may have been different. Moreover, Giraph's synchronous programming model includes mechanisms (such as combiners for performing distributed, in-graph aggregation) that can be used to overcome some of the memory-related problems that plagued the graph-based platforms. The downside is that Giraph had large and complex codes. GraphLab codes were small and elegant, especially considering the language is C++.

LDA Spark Java Implementation			
lines of code	5 machines	20 machines	100 machines
377	9:47 (0:53)	19:36 (1:15)	Fail

Figure 6: Average time per iteration (and start-up time).

SimSQL. SimSQL was often—though not always—slower than Giraph and GraphLab. SimSQL's purely tuple-oriented approach can hurt its performance, because (for example) a 1,000 by 1,000 matrix is pushed through the system as a set of one million tuples. This can result in some very long compute times—see the section on the Bayesian Lasso (though, interestingly, SimSQL's Gram matrix computation times were only a bit slower than Spark's). It seems that this is an issue that needs to be addressed.

On the positive side, SimSQL was consistently able to perform computations that none of the other three platforms could run, and was the only platform that never failed to run any of the computations tested. All of the other platforms were clearly at or beyond their limit on the largest problems, whereas SimSQL appeared ready to scale up further. This robustness is due to the fact that under the hood, SimSQL looks a lot like a parallel database system—it is well-understood how to scale such a system.

Spark. On the positive side, Spark codes (particularly those written in Python) are incredibly short and beautiful. Spark's succinctness rivals that of SimSQL's SQL codes, though many users will find Spark codes to be preferable, since they are imperative/functional.

On the negative side, Spark was slower than the two graph-based platforms. We were a bit worried these results were related to our choice of Python instead of Scala or Java. We had already tested both Python and Java GMM implementations, but just to be sure, we tested a Java Spark LDA implementation as well. The results are shown in Figure 6. The speed is much better than the Python implementation, but we could still not get Spark to run the LDA inference algorithm on 100 machines. The implementation failed on 20 machines after 18 iterations as well.

Spark in general required a lot of tuning and experimentation to get things to work on large and/or complicated problems. There was some disagreement among the authors of this paper as to why. One explanation is that Spark relies greatly upon techniques such as "lazy evaluation" for speed and job scheduling, which looks a lot like pipelining in a database system. However, database systems often use statistical information to decide when and how to pipeline. Without this, it is easy to make bad decisions, and in general, we spent a lot of time tuning Spark, doing things such as forcing RDDs to disk. Perhaps the ultimate solution is to make

Gaussian Imputation				
	lines of code	5 machines	20 machines	100 machines
Giraph	2274	28:43 (0:19)	31:23 (0:18)	Fail
GraphLab (Super vertex)	1197	6:59 (3:41)	6:12 (8:40)	6:08 (3:03)
Spark (Python)	294	1:22:48 (3:52)	1:27:39 (4:03)	1:29:27 (4:27)
SimSQL	182	28:53 (14:29)	30:41 (15:30)	39:33 (22:15)

Figure 5: Gaussian imputation results. Time in parens is for the initialization/setup. Format is HH:MM:SS or MM:SS.

Spark—and other dataflow systems—work more like a database system, carefully planning computational choices such as RDD materialization and pipelining using cost models.

Final Thoughts. In the end, the "correct" platform choice is highly problem- and user-dependent, depending on whether ease of implementation, ease of use, or performance are most important. Spark + Python was (in our opinion) the most attractive platform simply in terms of ease-of-coding, though it was challenging to get it to work on the larger and more complicated problems. GraphLab was fast on smaller problems, but it did not scale well. This might be because none of the models we considered naturally map to a graph. Giraph, on the other hand, which is really more of a BSP platform than a graph platform, did very well, though memory was an issue on the largest problems. SimSQL was most attractive on the largest and most complicated problems.

Finally, the problems we studied (by design) tended to skew to the more complicated end of the spectrum: hierarchical Bayesian models considered are more complex than least-squares linear regression or k-means, which are the ML methods used most widely in practice. The models we considered require a lot of CPU and data movement/communication. Had we considered simpler problems, or those that map naturally to a graph (for example, labeling the nodes in a Markov random field where the model parameters are already known), the results might have been different.

Acknowledgments. Material in this paper was supported by the National Science Foundation under grant number 0915315, and the Department of Energy under grant number DE-SC0001779. We are indebted to the many people (including the anonymous reviewers) who gave helpful feedback on the paper.

11. REFERENCES

[1] A. Agarwal, O. Chapelle, M. Dudík, and J. Langford. A reliable effective terascale linear learning system. *arXiv preprint arXiv:1110.4198*, 2011.

[2] C. Avery. Giraph: Large-scale graph processing infrastructure on hadoop. *Proceedings of the Hadoop Summit. Santa Clara*, 2011.

[3] D. M. Blei. Probabilistic topic models. *Communications of the ACM*, 55(4):77–84, 2012.

[4] Z. Cai, Z. Vagena, L. Perez, S. Arumugam, P. J. Haas, and C. Jermaine. Simulation of database-valued markov chains using simsql. In *SIGMOD*, pages 637–648, 2013.

[5] S. Das, Y. Sismanis, K. S. Beyer, R. Gemulla, P. J. Haas, and J. McPherson. Ricardo: integrating r and hadoop. In *SIGMOD*, pages 987–998, 2010.

[6] A. Ghoting, R. Krishnamurthy, E. Pednault, B. Reinwald, V. Sindhwani, S. Tatikonda, Y. Tian, and S. Vaithyanathan. Systemml: Declarative machine learning on mapreduce. In *ICDE*, pages 231–242, 2011.

[7] W. R. Gilks, S. Richardson, and D. J. Spiegelhalter. *Markov chain Monte Carlo in practice*, volume 2. CRC press, 1996.

[8] J. E. Gonzalez, Y. Low, H. Gu, D. Bickson, and C. Guestrin. Powergraph: Distributed graph-parallel computation on natural graphs. In *OSDI*, pages 17–30, 2012.

[9] J. M. Hellerstein, C. Ré, F. Schoppmann, D. Z. Wang, E. Fratkin, A. Gorajek, K. S. Ng, C. Welton, X. Feng, K. Li, et al. The madlib analytics library: or mad skills, the sql. *PVLDB*, 5(12):1700–1711, 2012.

[10] T. Kraska, A. Talwalkar, J. C. Duchi, R. Griffith, M. J. Franklin, and M. I. Jordan. Mlbase: A distributed machine-learning system. In *CIDR*, 2013.

[11] Y. Low, J. Gonzalez, A. Kyrola, D. Bickson, C. Guestrin, and J. M. Hellerstein. Graphlab: A new framework for parallel machine learning. *arXiv preprint arXiv:1006.4990*, 2010.

[12] G. Malewicz, M. H. Austern, A. J. Bik, J. C. Dehnert, I. Horn, N. Leiser, and G. Czajkowski. Pregel: a system for large-scale graph processing. In *SIGMOD*, pages 135–146, 2010.

[13] A. McCallum. Mallet: A machine learning for language toolkit. *http://mallet.cs.umass.edu/*, 2002.

[14] D. G. Murray, F. McSherry, R. Isaacs, M. Isard, P. Barham, and M. Abadi. Naiad: a timely dataflow system. In *SOSP*, pages 439–455, 2013.

[15] C. Olston, B. Reed, U. Srivastava, R. Kumar, and A. Tomkins. Pig latin: a not-so-foreign language for data processing. In *SIGMOD*, pages 1099–1110. ACM, 2008.

[16] C. Ordonez and P. Cereghini. Sqlem: Fast clustering in sql using the em algorithm. In *SIGMOD*, pages 559–570, 2000.

[17] S. Owen, R. Anil, T. Dunning, and E. Friedman. *Mahout in action*. Manning, 2011.

[18] T. Park and G. Casella. The bayesian lasso. *JASA*, 103(482):681–686, 2008.

[19] A. Sujeeth, H. Lee, K. Brown, T. Rompf, H. Chafi, M. Wu, A. Atreya, M. Odersky, and K. Olukotun. Optiml: an implicitly parallel domain-specific language for machine learning. In *ICML*, pages 609–616, 2011.

[20] L. G. Valiant. A bridging model for parallel computation. *Communications of the ACM*, 33(8):103–111, 1990.

[21] M. Weimer, T. Condie, R. Ramakrishnan, et al. Machine learning in scalops, a higher order cloud computing language. In *BigLearn*, volume 9, pages 389–396, 2011.

[22] Y. Yu, M. Isard, D. Fetterly, M. Budiu, Ú. Erlingsson, P. K. Gunda, and J. Currey. Dryadlinq: A system for general-purpose distributed data-parallel computing using a high-level language. In *OSDI*, volume 8, pages 1–14, 2008.

[23] M. Zaharia, M. Chowdhury, T. Das, A. Dave, J. Ma, M. McCauley, M. Franklin, S. Shenker, and I. Stoica. Resilient distributed datasets: A fault-tolerant abstraction for in-memory cluster computing. In *USENIX*, pages 2–2, 2012.

[24] M. Zaharia, M. Chowdhury, M. J. Franklin, S. Shenker, and I. Stoica. Spark: cluster computing with working sets. In *USENIX*, pages 10–10, 2010.

Re-evaluating Designs for Multi-Tenant OLTP Workloads on SSD-based I/O Subsystems

Ning Zhang #1, Junichi Tatemura *2, Jignesh M. Patel #3, Hakan Hacıgümüş *4
#University of Wisconsin-Madison
1nzhang@cs.wisc.edu, 3jignesh@cs.wisc.edu
*NEC Laboratories America
2tatemura@nec-labs.com, 4hakan@nec-labs.com

ABSTRACT

Multi-tenancy is a common practice that is employed to maximize server resources and reduce the total cloud operation costs. The focus of this work is on multi-tenancy for OLTP workloads. Several designs for OLTP multi-tenancy have been proposed that vary the trade-offs made between performance and isolation. However, existing studies have not considered the impact of OLTP multi-tenancy designs when using an SSD-based I/O subsystem. In this paper, we compare three designs using both open-source and proprietary DBMSs on SSD-based I/O subsystems. Our study reveals that in contrast to the case of an HDD-based I/O subsystem, *VM-based designs* have fairly competitive performance compared to the non-virtualized designs (generally within 1.3–2X of the best performing case) on SSD-based I/O subsystems. Whereas previous studies were based on traditional hard disk-based environments, our results indicate that switching to a pure SSD-based I/O subsystem requires rethinking the trade-offs for multi-tenant OLTP workloads.

Categories and Subject Descriptors

H.2.4 [**Information Systems**]: Database Management—*systems*

Keywords

Database Virtualization, Flash-optimized, Multi-Tenancy, NVRAM storage

1. INTRODUCTION

Today, it is common to consolidate multiple database workloads onto a single server to reduce the total cloud operating cost. This practice is called "multi-tenancy." Several multi-tenancy designs are available for online transaction processing (OLTP) workloads, such as, the "share-everything" design [10,16], where a *single* database management system (DBMS) instance is used to process the requests on behalf of multiple database workloads. In this paper, we call this design as the **Non-Virtualized Single DBMS** design, or simply the **NVSD** design. Another design is to install multiple DBMS instances on the same machine, with each DBMS instance dedicated to serving requests from one database client. We call this design as the **Non-Virtualized Multiple DBMS** design, or the **NVMD** design. The third design employs a virtual machine monitor (VMM) to create multiple virtual machine (VM) instances, and an independent DBMS instance is run in each VM [18].

As a motivating scenario, consider the provisioning of private clouds for multi-tenant OLTP applications. The cloud designers usually face a critical design choice: Although they tend to prefer the VM-based design for better management and isolation, they are concerned about potential performance penalties associated with running a database service in a VM, especially since previous work has indicated that the VM-based design leads to a severe performance penalty [10], since the disk device is now multiplexed across different VMs for log and data write operations, as well as the frequent and expensive processor context switches. Our key motivation for this paper is to help designers make well-informed decisions regarding multi-tenancy DBMS designs with SSD-based I/O subsystems.

Our work aims to fill two research needs in this area. First, while there is existing work studying various multi-tenancy OLTP designs (e.g. [10,16,18]), a comprehensive direct comparison of these designs is missing. Second, there is a critical move in the industry towards servers with pure SSD-based storage [5], and most previous works have examined multi-tenant OLTP designs using I/O subsystems with hard disk drives (HDDs). Hence, it is not clear if these previous results hold with I/O subsystems that use SSDs.

In this paper, we identify key factors that are crucial to the performance of three multi-tenant OLTP designs (NVSD, NVMD, and VM-based designs) on a modern SSD-based I/O subsystem. We also compare these designs with each other on both HDD and SSD-based I/O configurations, and show that switching to a pure SSD-based I/O subsystem produces different results than what previous studies have found when using an HDD-based I/O subsystem.

To the best of our knowledge, this is the first paper that presents results from an evaluation of three dominant multi-tenant OLTP designs on a modern SSD-based I/O subsystem. In this work, we use both open-source and proprietary VMMs and DBMSs.

The key contributions of this paper are as follows: First, we observe that in our settings, the VM-based designs are about 1.3–2X slower than the fastest alternative on a modern SSD-based I/O subsystem, showing far lower degradation than the 6–12X that was observed for traditional HDD-based I/O subsystems [10].

Second, our experiments show that the NVSD design still maintains a performance advantage over the VM-based designs on an SSD-based I/O subsystem, as long as it can minimize the con-

SIGMOD'14, June 22–27, 2014, Snowbird, UT, USA.
Copyright 2014 ACM 978-1-4503-2376-5/14/06 ...$15.00.
http://dx.doi.org/10.1145/2588555.2588567.

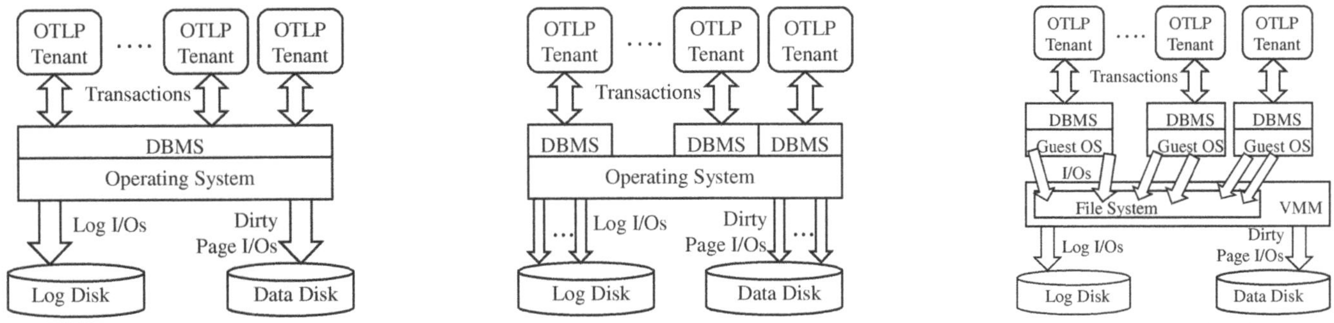

(a) Non-Virtualized Single DBMS (NVSD) Design

(b) Non-Virtualized Multiple DBMS (NVMD) Design

(c) VM-based Design

Figure 1: Overview of the different multi-tenant OLTP designs

tention on shared resources, such as locks on internal DBMS data structures.

Finally, in our pure SSD-based configuration, the NVMD design generally presents the best performance, since it avoids the traditional resource contention problem that is associated with the NVSD designs [13, 16], and the performance penalties that are associated with the VM-based designs [10].

The remainder of this paper is organized as follows: Section 2 describes the multi-tenant OLTP designs that we consider in this paper. The experimental setup and results are reported in Section 3. Related work is presented in Section 4, and Section 5 contains our concluding remarks.

2. MULTI-TENANT OLTP SOLUTIONS

In this section, we describe the multi-tenant OLTP designs that we consider in this paper.

2.1 Non-Virtualized Single DBMS Design

In the Non-Virtualized Single DBMS (**NVSD**) design, a single DBMS instance is installed on a physical server to process the transactions on behalf of all the tenants. Figure 1(a) illustrates this design. Most internal DBMS structures are shared across the tenants; for example, one Write-Ahead-Logging (WAL) writer process and one background writer process are shared across all the tenants when writing the transaction logs, and when dirty pages are flushed from the buffer pool.

2.2 Non-Virtualized Multiple DBMS Design

The Non-Virtualized Multiple DBMS (**NVMD**) design, installs multiple DBMS instances on a single physical server, and each tenant only interacts with its own DBMS instance. Figure 1(b) shows this design. The internal structures for each instance are not shared across the tenants. For example, there is a dedicated WAL writer process, and a dedicated background writer process for each DBMS instance. Notice, however, that in this design, the log and the data I/O devices need to handle multiple concurrent log and dirty page I/Os, respectively.

2.3 Virtual Machine Design

The Virtual Machine (VM) based design, as shown in Figure 1(c), shares the underlying hardware resources by creating multiple VMs. Here, each tenant is associated with a DBMS instance that is installed in an independent VM. Different VMMs employ different techniques to virtualize the resources (CPU, memory, network and IO resources), and here we consider the two leading VMMs: namely, Xen [1] and VMWare [2].

IOPS	H-SSD	SSD RAID
Sequential Read	20,863	6,062
Random Read	13,692	3,084
Sequential Write	17,085	6,118
Random Write	12,623	2,701

Table 1: IOPS for the H-SSD and the SSD RAID devices for four different I/O patterns. These numbers were obtained by using a single-process benchmark program (run on CentOS 6.3) that sends synchronous 8KB direct I/O calls to a 20GB file. The observed disk capacity utilization when running this benchmark was around 27% for the H-SSD device, and 6% for the SSD RAID device.

3. EXPERIMENTAL RESULTS

In this section, we present results from running an open-source implementation of the TPC-C benchmark [6] on the three multi-tenant OLTP designs that were presented above. We note that this benchmark has also been used before in a number of studies in this area, including [14, 15].

3.1 Hardware and Software Specifications

3.1.1 Hardware Configuration

We ran our experiments on a server with dual quad-core 2.26GHz Intel(R) Xeon CPU E5520, with 64 GB of ECC memory, a SATA 7200 RPM hard disk drive (HDD) to hold the OS, an SSD RAID 0 system (**SSD RAID**), and a high-end (**H-SSD**). The SSD RAID subsystem consists of three Intel Series 320 SSD 120 GB in a RAID 0 configuration, and the H-SSD subsystem consists of one 80GB Fusion IO ioDrive. The raw performance of these devices is shown in Table 1. We ran the system with hyper-threading turned on.

In keeping with the key theme of this paper – i.e. focusing on the impact of SSDs for OLTP multi-tenancy – all the results presented in this paper, except for those in Section 3.7, place both the data and the log files on the SSD devices. To connect with previous work [10] that used only HDDs, in Section 3.7 we also consider the case when both the data and the log files are placed on HDDs.

3.1.2 Multi-tenancy Design Settings

The server described above is used as the hardware for each design. For the DBMS software, we use an open-source DBMS and a popular commercial DBMS. The open-source DBMS is PostgreSQL 9.2.4 (referred to as PostgreSQL). The proprietary DBMS is called DBX. (The proprietary DBMS name has been anonymized to respect the licensing terms.)

The software setting for each design is discussed below.

The **NVMD design** is implemented on a CentOS 6.3 server with multiple independent DBMS instances running concurrently. Each tenant stores its data and runs its queries within a dedicated DBMS instance.

The **NVSD design** runs on a CentOS 6.3 server with only one DBMS instance. All tenants run their queries and store their data within this shared DBMS instance.

The **VMware Multiple DBMS (VMMD)** design uses VMware ESXi 5.1.0 as the VMM. We set up this VM by following the standard best practices guideline [7]. Each guest OS (CentOS 6.3) has three virtual disks: one HDD holds the OS and the DBMS binaries, one for the SSD RAID, and the last one for the H-SSD. Each VM runs one dedicated DBMS instance.

The **Xen Multiple DBMS (XenMD)** design runs Xen 4.1.2, and is set up by following its best practices [4]. Each guest OS[1] is installed with para-virtualization and runs one dedicated DBMS instance. We note that para-virtualization has been used in a similar context before to consolidate and run database workloads [11]. In the same way as in the VMMD design, each guest OS has three attached virtual disks: one HDD to hold the OS and the DBMS binaries, one SSD RAID, and one H-SSD.

3.1.3 Data and Workload Settings

Each tenant generates TPC-C workload exclusively against one TPC-C database with no think time. The actual size of the TPC-C database varies depending on the specific experiment. Each tenant runs on a separate server, which is connected to the experimental platform via a 1Gbps network. All tenants run simultaneously, and the first 10 minutes are used to ramp up their database caches. Then, we collect and report the average aggregate performance over the next 60-minute measurement window.

Note that in OLTP environments (and in other database environments [17]), tenants are often consolidated so that their working sets mostly fit in the main memory, so that the extra data-related I/O does not degrade performance significantly. For example, one of the key contributions of [10] is a profiling method to identify the effective size of the working sets (hence the optimal degree of multi-tenancy). In this paper, we largely focus on the case when the working sets of all tenants reside in the main memory, but we also conduct additional experiments (see Section 3.6) to consider the case when the working set is larger than the main memory size. We recognize that dealing with workload fluctuations is an important and related aspect, but it is also an active and independent research area. To keep this paper focused, we only consider the scenario described above.

Finally, we note that even when the working sets fit in main memory, there is still significant write I/O traffic because of the continual checkpointing process(es) and log writes.

We place the log files and the data files for the tenant databases on separate disks (or virtual disks), using either the SSD RAID to save the log files and the H-SSD to save the data files, or vice versa, in order to find the highest-performing disk assignment for each design. Note that for different designs, the highest-performing disk assignment may be different. For simplicity, we call the disk on which the log files are stored as the *log disk*, and the disk on which the data files are stored as the *data disk*.

[1] In this case we use CentOS 5.9. At the time of writing this paper, this OS has more mature support for para-virtualization.

Design	Log Disk	Data Disk
NVMD design with PostgreSQL	H-SSD	SSD RAID
NVSD design with DBX	SSD RAID	H-SSD
NVSD with PostgreSQL	SSD RAID	H-SSD
XenMD with PostgreSQL	H-SSD	SSD RAID
XenMD with DBX	H-SSD	SSD RAID
VMMD design with PostgreSQL	H-SSD	SSD RAID
VMMD design with DBX	H-SSD	SSD RAID

Table 2: Highest-performing disk assignment for each design

3.1.4 Database Parameter Settings

In our experiments, we use the published optimized configuration parameters for PostgreSQL [3], and the default parameters for DBX.

3.2 Key Result: Overview of the Evaluation

Based on the three multi-tenancy designs introduced in Section 2, we compare the seven designs listed in the first column of Table 2. Note that we could not get the "Non-Virtualized Multiple DBX" to work reliably as it involves deploying multiple DBX instances in the same server. This configuration is not supported by the vendor, and there are various stability issues with running this configuration. Licensing costs further complicate this scenario. Hence, we do not report any results for this configuration.

Before we analyze each design, we first present a comparison of these designs based on the configuration (the location of the data and the log files) that produce their individual best performance. Table 2 shows the best (highest-performing) allocation of the log and data disks (to H-SSD or SSD RAID) for each design. In Figure 2, we present a direct comparison of the seven designs. The comparison is based on the aggregate throughput performance metric, i.e. the New-Order transactions per minute (**tpmC**), over 1, 2, 4, 8, 16 or 32 homogeneous tenants. These tenants all share the same physical machine based on the specific multi-tenancy design. Each tenant has 15 warehouses (1.5 GB database) and creates 15 concurrent threads to generate the TPC-C workload.

From Figure 2, we observe that the NVMD design with PostgreSQL (black bars in the figure) outperforms all other designs, and in all cases. The reason for this behavior is as follows: (1) The ability of the SSD devices to deal with multiple independent I/O streams effectively fits well with the NVMD design. The NVMD design benefits most from the SSD-based I/O subsystem, significantly speeding up the transaction log I/O and checkpointing (dirty page) I/O processing, which in turn pushes up its transaction commit rates. (2) Compared to the VM-based designs, the NVMD design has no virtualization-related overheads (CPU, memory, I/O). Thus, it can utilize all the hardware resources in the server more effectively. (3) The NVMD design isolates the tenants at the DBMS-level by using multiple PostgreSQL instances, so it can eliminate potential contentions that are incurred when sharing the same DBMS instance across different tenants. Note that in this experiment, each

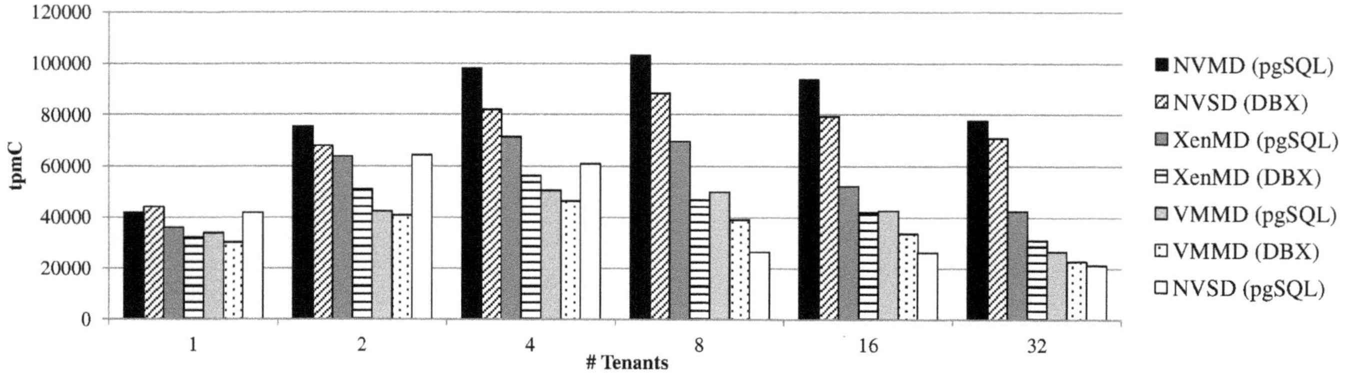

Figure 2: Varying the number of tenants: Comparison of all designs, each at their best performance configuration

tenant has 15 clients for a 15-warehouse TPC-C database. Consequently, each client works exclusively on the data in a single warehouse. In other words, there is no competition between two clients for the data in the same warehouse.

Surprisingly, the four VM-based designs (XenMD with PostgreSQL, XenMD with DBX, VMMD with PostgreSQL, VMMD with DBX) are not significantly slower than the NVMD design. For example, Xen with PostgreSQL is only 1.3X slower than the NVMD design at their best performance point (i.e., when the number of tenants is 8). This is an interesting result as it shows that an SSD-based system has different tradeoffs (for multi-tenant OLTP workloads) compared to an HDD-based I/O subsystem. In [10], the authors showed that the NVSD design has 6X-12X better (tpmC) performance than the VMware design, mostly because the VMs generate multiple independent and random write I/Os for the log and the data file (on the HDD), while the NVSD design sequentially writes to one log file and coordinates data writes on the HDD. However, SSDs have far better I/O performance (than HDDs) for random I/Os, and as a result, using a VM-based design with SSDs is fairly competitive.

In addition, as seen in Figure 2, the NVSD design generates significantly different results when using the open-source DBMS versus using the proprietary DBMS. With (the proprietary) DBX, the NVSD design outperforms all other designs except the NVMD design. However, when using PostgreSQL in the NVSD design, we observed the worst performance (as seen in Figure 2) when more than 4 tenants (e.g. 8, 16, 32) are consolidated. This is because when all the tenants run on one shared PostgreSQL instance, lightweight locks are needed to serialize the accesses to the shared PostgreSQL resources (e.g. WAL buffer pool). When the I/O subsystem is fast (because of SSDs), the contention for these lightweight locks becomes very prominent. However, with DBX, we observed that the lock contention problem is not significant, so the NVSD design yields better performance. In other words, the internal locking overhead has been better optimized in DBX compared to PostgreSQL, making DBX a better candidate to exploit (in the NVSD design) the higher I/O performance that is associated with SSD-based I/O subsystems.

Having presented the key results, we now describe the configuration for each design that results in its best performance.

3.3 Non-Virtualized Multiple DBMS Design

In this section, we first describe how we achieved the best performance on the NVMD design with PostgreSQL.

Recall that the NVMD design isolates the tenants at the DBMS-level by using multiple PostgreSQL instances. Now, since the performance of the TPC-C workload is mainly determined by the speed of log I/O processing, having multiple PostgreSQL instances inevitably leads to multiple log files co-existing on the same log disk. Logically, each log file is written in a sequential manner. But, from the log disk's point of view, in this case, the physical I/O pattern is close to a "concurrent sequential writes" pattern – a pseudo-random I/O pattern, which can potentially degrade the overall performance. As was also observed in [9], this access pattern has good performance on SSDs if the number of concurrent streams is a low number (in our measurement using the uFlip benchmark [9], this number was around 16 with our SSDs).

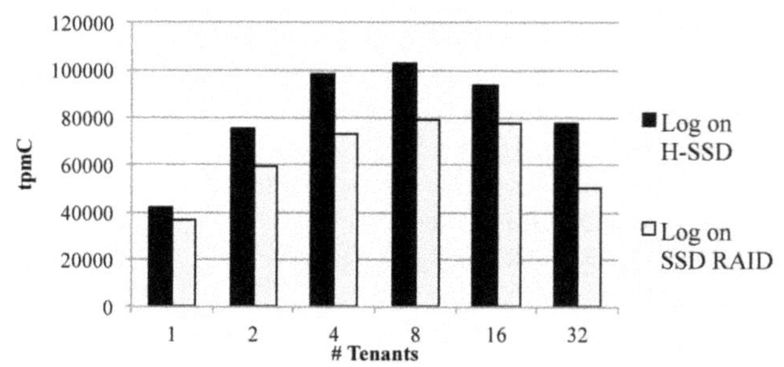

Figure 3: NVMD Design with PostgreSQL: Comparing the two different disk assignments

Next, we consider the impact of assigning the log file to either the SSD RAID or the H-SSD devices, and vice versa for the data file(s).[2]

As can be seen in Figure 3, the performance is higher when using the H-SSD device as the log disk, across all the multi-tenancy levels. The reason for this behavior is that the log I/O speed is an important factor that impacts the performance of the TPC-C workload, and the H-SSD is far more efficient than the SSD RAID in handling the log I/O requests.

To better understand this behavior, we collect the disk I/O statistics (by using the "sar" command in Linux) to compare these two disk assignments.

[2]We acknowledge that another interesting setup for measuring the impact of log disk is to keep the data disk unchanged, and to simply swap the log disk. But our experimental server only supports four SATA-based and one PCIe-based disks. Since our H-SSD is PCIe-based, and we use one SATA-based HDD for the OS disk and the remaining three SATA slots for an SSD RAID, there is no additional slots for another SSD.

	Log disk (H-SSD)						Data disk (SSD RAID)					
# tenants	1	2	4	8	16	32	1	2	4	8	16	32
await	0.35	0.36	0.53	2.3	11.3	15.4	6.6	7.4	11.4	13.1	13.7	38.7
util%	29.6	39.4	47.8	75.6	90.9	95.9	2.7	6.4	8.5	14.2	18.8	88.5

(a) Disk I/O statistics when using H-SSD as the log disk

	Log disk (SSD RAID)						Data disk (H-SSD)					
# tenants	1	2	4	8	16	32	1	2	4	8	16	32
await	0.58	1.13	1.67	3.75	16.4	24.1	3.6	3.3	3.7	5.2	11.7	34.5
util%	57.2	85.3	95.9	99.5	99.7	100	1.1	1.9	3.4	7.9	15.2	70.5

(b) Disk I/O statistics when using SSD RAID as the log disk

Table 3: NVMD Design with PostgreSQL: Disk I/O statistics observed from the Linux OS

Components	**Definition**
CPU run time	The time spent when a server process is executing code on a CPU core.
CPU wait time	The time spent when a server process waits in some CPU wait queue.
I/O time	The time spent when a server process waits for an I/O to complete.
`WAL InsertLock` **wait**	The time spent when a server process wants to acquire a `WAL InsertLock` to insert a WAL record into the WAL buffer, but needs to wait for another process to release the `WAL InsertLock` first.
`WAL WriteLock` **wait**	The time spent when a server process wants to acquire a `WAL WriteLock` to dump the WAL records in the WAL buffer to the log disk when a transaction commits (or the WAL buffer is full), but needs to wait for another process to release the `WAL WriteLock` first.
Other	The time spent when a server process is in a state other than the above states.

Table 4: Components measured in the time-breakdown of a PostgreSQL server process

We present two representative disk I/O statistics: average wait time (in milliseconds) of I/O requests to be served (`await`), and the average disk utilization (`util%`). In Table 3, we notice that when the SSD RAID device is used as the log disk (shown in Table 3 (b)), both the average disk utilization and I/O wait time are higher than the case when the H-SSD device is used as the log disk (shown in Table 3 (a)). For example, when there are four tenants, the average log I/O time and disk utilization for the H-SSD device are 0.53 and 47% respectively, compared to 1.67 and 96% when using the SSD RAID device as the log disk. Essentially, using the H-SSD device as the log disk results in better performance, as in this case, the log disk performance is the dominant factor in determining the overall performance. Notice that as shown in Table 3, the data disk utilization is low, so the data disk is not the bottleneck in this design.

As can be observed in Figure 2, the performance of the NVMD design is relatively stable from 4 to 16 tenants, and decreases when the number of tenants is 32. To explain this behavior, we choose to analyze the PostgreSQL server processes, which are created to serve the tenant requests. We broke down the execution time of each process into the components that are listed in Table 4.

The two crucial variables in Table 4 are the lightweight locks in PostgreSQL, namely the `WAL InsertLock` and the `WAL WriteLock`. For the `WAL InsertLock`, its wait time depends on the number of active server processes that are concurrently inserting WAL records into the WAL buffer. On the other hand, for the `WAL WriteLock`, its wait time is dependent on the time it takes to flush/write the WAL records from the WAL buffer to the log disk.

The time-breakdown analysis of NVMD design is shown in Figure 4, across all the multi-tenancy levels. Since all tenants are homogeneous, we randomly select a server process for the analysis.

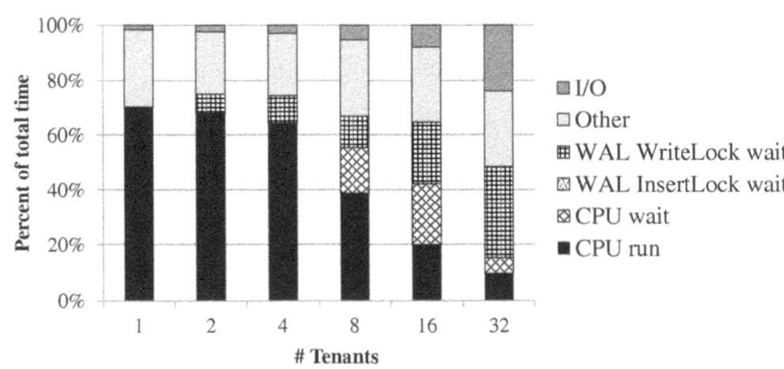

Figure 4: NVMD Design with PostgreSQL: Time-breakdown

In Figure 4, we notice that when there are 8 and 16 concurrent tenants, the `CPU wait` time component appears in the time-breakdown, which means the workload is largely CPU-bound. This is because in this case, the I/O device has sufficient resources to "keep up" with the workload that is generated. As can be seen in Table 3(a) the disk utilization for both the log and the data disk is below 90%. Thus, with 8 and 16 concurrent tenants, the overall throughput is largely determined by the speed with which the CPU can process the workload.

Then, in Figure 4, we notice that at 32 concurrent tenants, the `CPU wait` time component of the breakdown is now no longer the dominant portion (the `CPU run` and the `CPU wait` times are less than 30% of the total time). At this point, the system is slowed down by the log and data disk. As can be seen in Table 3 (a), at 32 tenants, the data disk utilization is 88.5%. However, it is only 18.8% when there are 16 tenants.

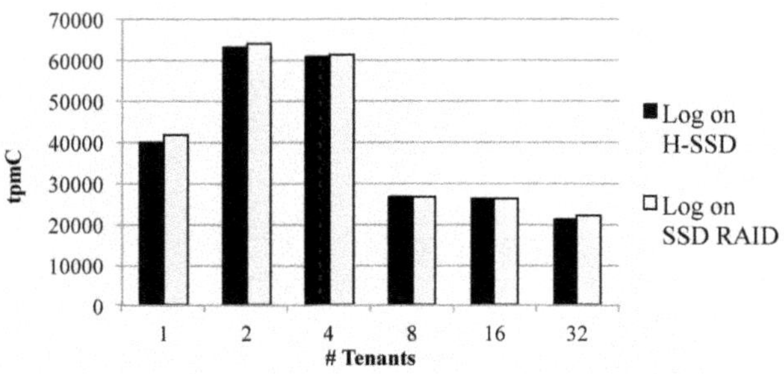

Figure 5: NVSD Design with PostgreSQL: Comparing the two different disk assignments

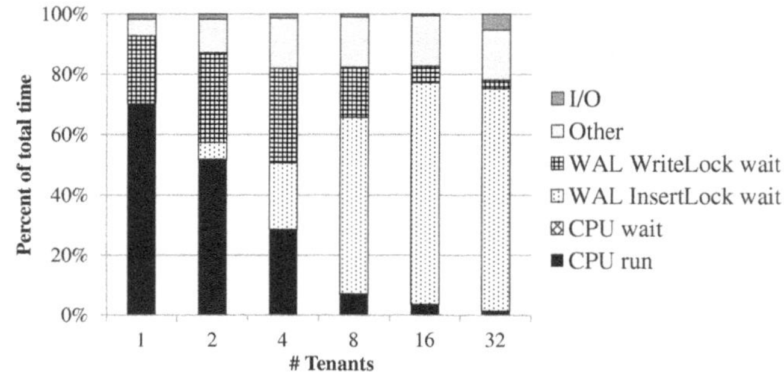

Figure 6: NVSD Design with PostgreSQL: Time-breakdown

Finally, in Figure 4, we note that the `WAL WriteLock` wait time component is not significant (compared to the other components). This is because when the log is on the H-SSD device, it can mostly handle the random-like concurrent log writes to the log disk. This behavior can be observed in Table 3 (a) that shows the log disk utilization is always below 90% when the degree of concurrency increases from 1 to 8. Thus, when the log is on the H-SSD device, the `WAL WriteLock` wait time component is not a large fraction of the total runtime. In other words, the log disk is not a significant bottleneck in most cases.

To summarize, for this design: (1) Because concurrent log I/O requests can generate large amounts of *random-like* and *synchronous* writes to the log disk, choosing the H-SSD as the log disk produces a higher performance configuration. (2) The checkpointing (dirty page) I/Os (sent to the data disk) are *asynchronous*, which means that the dirty page write requests are not as critical as the log writes. Consequently, using SSD RAID as the data disk and H-SSD as the log disk results in the best performing configuration.

3.4 Non-Virtualized Single DBMS Design

For the NVSD design, we first analyze the case when it is deployed with PostgreSQL.

3.4.1 *Non-Virtualized Single DBMS Design with PostgreSQL*

First, we compare the performance when assigning the log file to either the SSD RAID or the H-SSD devices, and vice versa for the data file(s). These results are shown in Figure 5. As can be seen from this figure, the performance of these two configurations is close to each other, which indicates that the disk I/O devices are not the key performance factors. To support this hypothesis, we show the disk I/O statistics for these two disk assignments in Table 5. As can be seen in Table 5, both the log and the data disks are far below 100% utilization – and in fact are always under 65%.

More importantly, as seen in Figure 2, the NVSD design performs poorly when the number of tenants is larger than 4. To explain this behavior, we conducted a time-breakdown analysis of the execution time for this design, which is shown in Figure 6. From this figure, we observe that when the number of tenants is larger than 4, the `WAL InsertLock` wait time component, as shown by the *dotted white bar*, starts to dominate the total runtime. The reason for this behavior is as follows: the NVSD design has only one PostgreSQL instance and all the tenants concurrently try to insert the WAL records into the shared WAL buffer pool. Now, the `WAL InsertLock`, which protects shared access to the WAL buffer pool, becomes a key source of contention and a bottleneck. When the

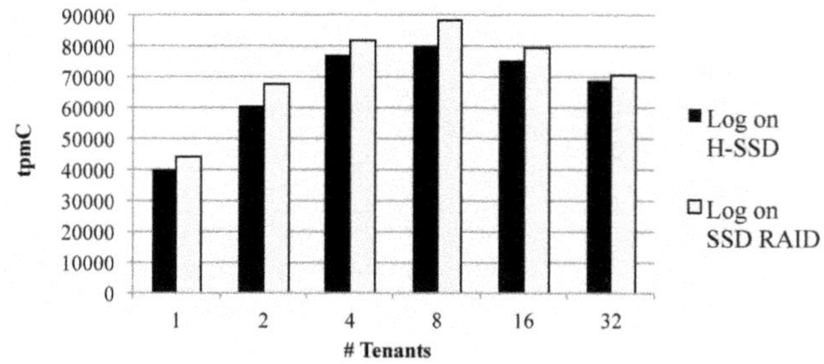

Figure 7: NVSD Design with DBX: Comparing the two different disk assignments

number of tenant is 8 or more, performance starts to decline (as can be seen in Figure 2), as the contention for the `WAL InsertLock` is very high. The above analysis also explains why the log and data disks are under utilized (as shown in Table 5).

3.4.2 *Non-Virtualized Single DBMS Design with DBX*

Compared to the result generated by the NVSD design with PostgreSQL, the NVSD design with DBX is the overall second highest-performing design (recall Figure 2).

First, we study the impact of assigning the log file to either the SSD RAID device or the H-SSD device, and vice versa for the data file(s).

The performance with these two disk assignments is shown in Figure 7. Notice that using the SSD RAID device as the log disk slightly outperforms the case when using the H-SSD device as the log disk. (This is the opposite of the best disk assignment in the NVMD PostgreSQL design.) The NVSD design generates relatively sequential log I/O pattern, allowing the SSD RAID device to keep up with the log I/O traffic. In addition, in this configuration, using the H-SSD device as the data disk is more efficient (than using the SSD RAID device as the data disk) in handling the checkpointing (dirty page) I/Os. To validate this hypothesis, we show the disk I/O statistics for these two disk assignments in Table 6.

From Table 6(a), we note that when the H-SSD device is used as the log disk, the H-SSD device is not fully utilized as its maximum utilization is only 70% (shown in Table 6(a)). But for the data disk (which is SSD RAID device), its utilization and I/O wait time are already over 90% and 2.5ms with 8 concurrent tenants. On the other side, when the SSD RAID device is used to handle the log I/Os, although the log disk gets close to 100% busy with 32 concur-

	Log disk (H-SSD)						Data disk (SSD RAID)					
# tenants	1	2	4	8	16	32	1	2	4	8	16	32
await	0.35	0.32	0.29	0.32	0.46	1.33	6.6	10.6	10.7	11.5	13.6	20.5
util%	29.6	29.1	30.5	28.3	24.9	19.9	2.7	8.4	10.7	10.8	25.9	65.1

(a) Disk I/O statistics when using H-SSD as the log disk

	Log disk (SSD RAID)						Data disk (H-SSD)					
# tenants	1	2	4	8	16	32	1	2	4	8	16	32
await	0.58	0.79	0.68	0.71	0.76	1.1	3.6	4.3	3.4	3.6	6.7	8.0
util%	57.2	65.8	62.2	48.9	42.3	37.2	1.1	2.4	4.8	4.6	15.8	39.6

(b) Disk I/O statistics when using SSD RAID as the log disk

Table 5: NVSD Design with PostgreSQL: Disk I/O statistics as observed from the Linux OS

	Log disk (H-SSD)						Data disk (SSD RAID)					
# tenants	1	2	4	8	16	32	1	2	4	8	16	32
await	0.06	0.07	0.12	0.17	0.45	0.94	0.31	0.47	0.99	2.5	5.8	8.1
util%	27.4	42.8	55.8	62.1	68.7	70.2	39.1	63.8	85.2	94.5	98.6	100

(a) Disk I/O statistics when using H-SSD as the log disk

	Log disk (SSD RAID)						Data disk (H-SSD)					
# tenants	1	2	4	8	16	32	1	2	4	8	16	32
await	0.32	0.55	0.68	0.98	1.1	1.3	0.13	0.18	0.26	0.45	1.7	2.9
util%	59.1	75.8	84.2	88.9	91.3	99.2	10.7	18.5	25.7	41.9	80.1	95.6

(b) Disk I/O statistics when using SSD RAID as the log disk

Table 6: NVSD Design with DBX: Disk I/O statistics as observed from the Linux OS

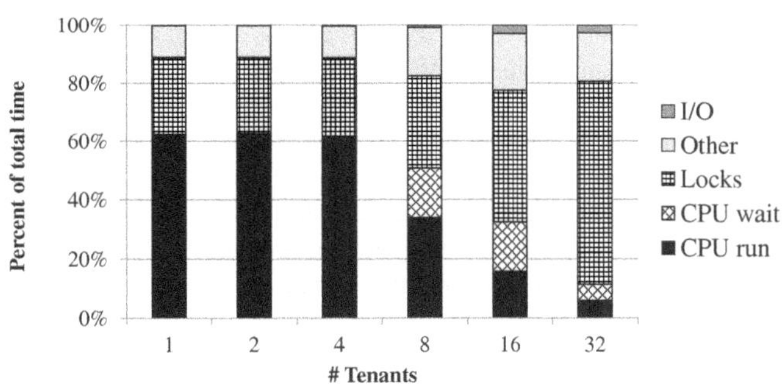

Figure 8: NVSD Design with DBX: Time-breakdown

rent tenants (shown in Table 6(b)), it has enough capacity to keep up with the log I/O traffic in most cases, because the average log I/O time increases very smoothly from 1 to 32 tenants. Moreover, in this disk assignment, using the H-SSD device as the data disk is more efficient in handling the checkpointing I/O traffic because of its lower disk utilization and shorter I/O wait time than using the SSD RAID device as the data disk.

As one might imagine, it was harder to carry out a detailed time-breakdown analysis of the lock waits in this case (since DBX is a closed-source product). Instead, in Figure 8, we use "Locks" to denote the time that is spent waiting for all types of locks. Comparing Figure 8 to Figure 6, the lock time shown in Figure 8 is much smaller than the NVSD design with PostgreSQL. For example, when the number of tenants is 16, the NVSD design with PostgreSQL spends 70% of the total time waiting for the `WAL InsertLock` (shown in Figure 6), while the NVSD design with DBX spends 40% of the total time waiting for locks (shown in Figure 8). Thus, the lock contention for the NVSD design with DBX is much smaller than that for the NVSD design with PostgreSQL.

Another observation indicating that the lock contention is smaller within DBX than PostgreSQL in the NVSD design is to compare Table 6 with Table 5. When using PostgreSQL in the NVSD design, both the log and the data disks are under utilized because the lock contention is the bottleneck. However, when using the NVSD design with DBX, the disks have much higher utilizations (see Table 6).

Note that both the NVSD designs (with PostgreSQL and DBX), experience performance drops as the number of tenants increases to 8, and beyond. This is partially related to the I/O performance degradation as more tenants are consolidated (shown in Tables 5 and 6). In addition, both these NVSD designs see a sharp increase in the lock time for 8 or more tenants, as shown in Figures 6 and 8. In Section 3.4.1, we noted that the high lock time in the NVSD design with PostgreSQL is due to the contention for the WAL buffer pool. The contention for the WAL buffer lock is high in this scenario since there is a single PostgreSQL instance, and each tenant tries to write logs to the single buffer pool.

3.5 Virtual Machine Design

For all the designs based on virtual machines, the highest performing configuration was always the case when the H-SSD device

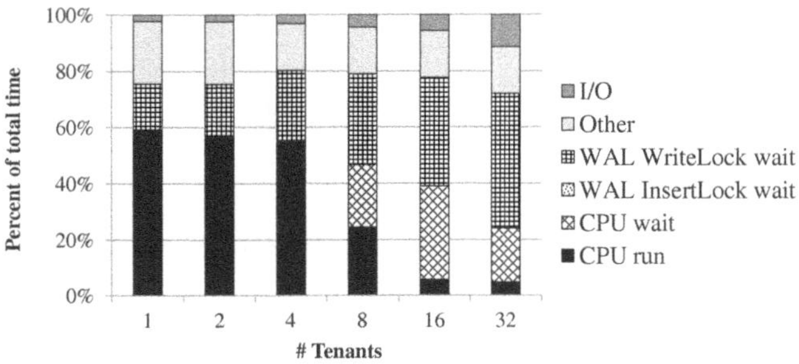

Figure 9: VMMD Design with PostgreSQL: Time-Breakdown

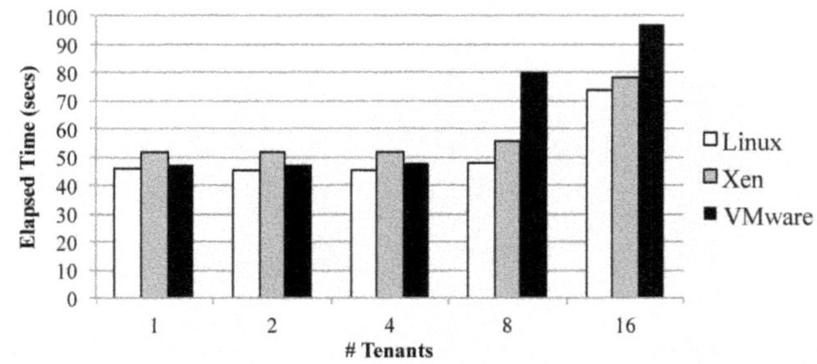

Figure 10: The CPU prime numbers benchmark runs on standard Linux, VMware, and Xen

# tenants	1	2	4	8	16	32
await	0.46	0.82	2.3	5.8	7.35	9.69
util%	29.7	46.2	67.7	83.3	97.6	99.4

Table 7: VMMD Design with PostgreSQL: Log disk I/O statistics as observed from the guest OS

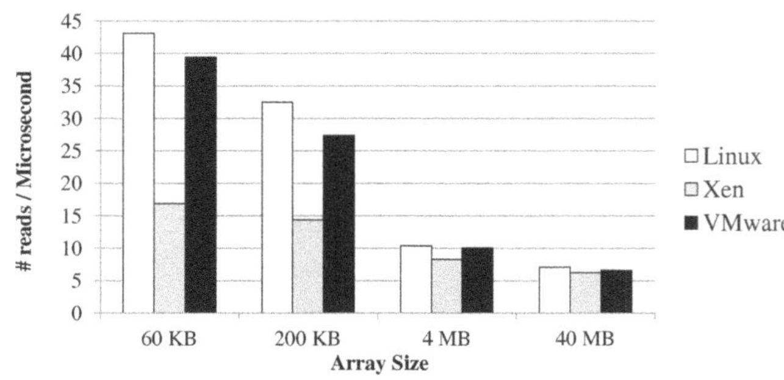

Figure 11: The cache benchmark on standard Linux, VMware, and Xen

was used as the log disk and the SSD RAID device was used as the data disk, as shown in Table 2. The reason for this behavior is similar to the NVMD design – since the physical log I/O traffic that is produced by the multiple VMs is synchronous and not sequential, using the H-SSD device is more effective in handling the log writes, which improves the overall transaction commit rates.

First, we analyze the VMware Multiple DBMS (VMMD) with PostgreSQL in Section 3.5.1, followed by analyzing the VMMD design with DBX in Section 3.5.2. The Xen Multiple DBMS design (XenMD) with PostgreSQL is described in Section 3.5.3, and finally we discuss the XenMD design with DBX in Section 3.5.4.

3.5.1 VMware Multiple DBMS Design with PostgreSQL

The VMMD design with PostgreSQL is similar to the one used in [10], in which one DBMS instance was installed in each VM that was running VMware ESXi.

As before, we start with a time-breakdown analysis, which is shown in Figure 9. As the number of tenants increases, the sum of the `WAL WriteLock` wait time and the `CPU wait` time constitute a bulk of the total runtime. In our previous analysis (in Section 3.3), we explained that the length of the `WAL WriteLock` wait time is related to the log disk performance. Here, we present statistics about the log disk I/O, as observed from the guest OS, to explain the relationship between the `WAL WriteLock` wait time and the log disk performance. Table 7 shows the log disk I/O statistics and we notice that both the average log I/O time and the log disk utilization keeps increasing as the degree of multi-tenancy increases from 1 to 32. This mostly explains why the `WAL WriteLock` wait time component grows as a fraction of the total runtime (as seen in Figure 9).

Meanwhile, starting from a degree of multi-tenancy of 8, the `CPU wait` time component in Figure 9 starts becoming significant. We speculate that the increase in the `CPU wait` time component is partially due to the performance penalty associated with virtualizing the CPU resources. To quantify this penalty, we conducted: (1) a CPU benchmark, and (2) a CPU cache and main memory benchmark, which we describe next.

First, we benchmark the CPU by executing the prime numbers test from SysBench [8]. This test is a single-threaded workload that computes prime numbers up to 30,000. In this test, we vary the degree of multi-tenancy by concurrently running 1, 2, 4, 8 or 16 instances of this benchmark in the following three configurations: (1) a standard Linux OS with no virtualization, (2) each benchmark instance runs in a VM that is supported by VMware, and (3) each benchmark instance runs in a VM that is supported by Xen.

To quantify the performance penalty associated with this CPU computation, we measured the average time to run this benchmark for each configuration described above (the variance was close to zero, so using the average is a good measure for this test). The results for this experiment are presented in Figure 10. We note that when the number of benchmark instances is larger than 4, the VMware setup is the slowest, and is about 25% slower than the native Linux implementation. In contrast, the Xen setup has very low overhead (less than 5%) over the native Linux implementation, likely due to the use of *para-virtualization*, which is designed to reduce the CPU overhead that is associated with virtualization.

Next, we run another benchmark to examine the impact of virtualization on the CPU cache and main memory. This test is a single-threaded random array lookup test. It first creates an integer array, and then randomly reads one integer from the array at a time. We repeat the "random read" 20,000 times. Since our CPU has a 64 KB L1 cache, a 256 KB L2 cache, and a 8 MB L3 cache, we want to test the "cache" hierarchies (L1 $\rightarrow$ L2 $\rightarrow$ L3 $\rightarrow$ memory) level by level. This benchmark uses 4 different array sizes – 60 KB (less than the L1 cache size), 200 KB (bigger than the L1 cache size, but less than the L2 cache size), 4MB (bigger than the L2 cache size, but less than the L3 cache size), and 40MB (bigger than the L3 cache size). To fully load all the 8 CPU cores in the server, we concurrently run 8 instances of this benchmark in the following three configurations: (1) a standard Linux OS with no virtualization, (2) each benchmark instance runs in a VM that is supported

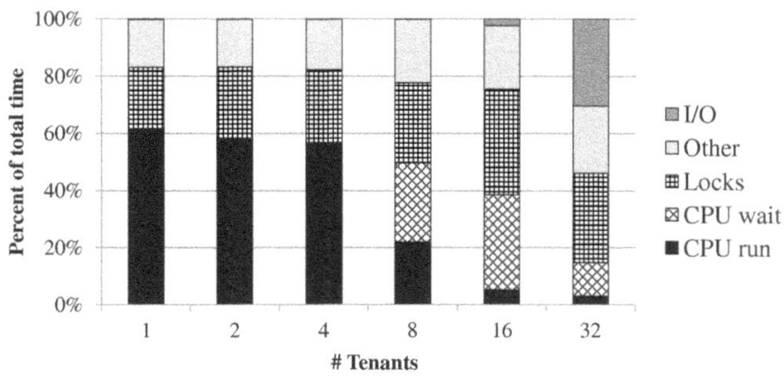

Figure 12: VMMD Design with DBX: Time-breakdown

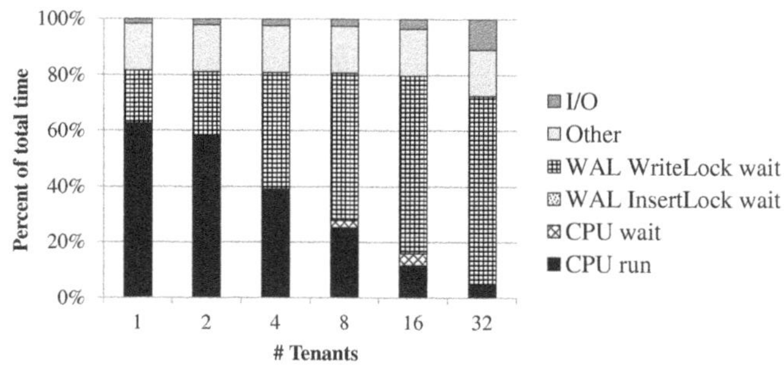

Figure 13: XenMD Design with PostgreSQL: Time-breakdown

by VMware, and (3) each benchmark instance runs in a VM that is supported by Xen.

In this experiment, we use the average number of reads per microsecond as the performance metric. The results for this benchmark are shown in Figure 11. Compared to the VMware and the native Linux cases, Xen has a large overhead when accessing the L1 and L2 caches. However, for the L3 cache and the main memory access scenarios, Xen is only marginally slower than the VMware and the native Linux configurations.

Moreover, from Figure 10, we notice that as more VMs are consolidated, the CPU virtualization overhead in VMware increases. For example, when the number of VMs is 8 or more, VMware has a larger CPU overhead compared to the case with 4 or fewer VMs.

Furthermore, starting at 16 tenants (16 VMs), we observed that a small amount of read I/O requests are being sent to the data disk in all the VM-based designs, which indicates that the TPC-C working sets now no longer fit in main memory. For example, when we consolidate 16 tenants, the read IOPS observed in one VM is about 5.5. While with 32 tenants, the read IOPS observed in one VM is about 286 – a 52X increase.

Note that in this experiment, the VMMD design with PostgreSQL is at most 2X worse than the NVMD design (shown in Figure 2). This may be an interesting finding for cloud operators who prefer using virtualization because of its nice isolation and manageability properties, but are concerned about the huge virtualization penalty (e.g. this overhead was reported to be 6X-12X in previous studies for non-SSD based I/O subsystems).

3.5.2 VMware Multiple DBMS Design with DBX

The VMMD design with DBX is a popular deployment with operators who want to use proprietary VMM and DBMS for their advanced features, better manageability, and higher reliability.

The time-breakdown analysis for this design is shown in Figure 12. Similar to the behavior seen in Figure 9, with 8 or more tenants, the CPU wait time and the lock time contribute a large portion to the total runtime. The appearance of the CPU wait time shown in Figure 12 is primarily because of the CPU virtualization overhead that is associated with the VMM, which has been described in Section 3.5.1. As can be also be seen in Figure 12, when there are 32 tenants, the bottleneck starts to shift from the CPU to the I/O.

When considering the performance penalty associated with this design, Figure 2 shows that the VMware design with DBX is within a range of 2X (slower) compared to the NVSD design with DBX, mostly because of the virtualization penalties. Furthermore, when we move beyond 16 tenants, the data disk sees additional read I/Os as the working set is much larger than the available main memory.

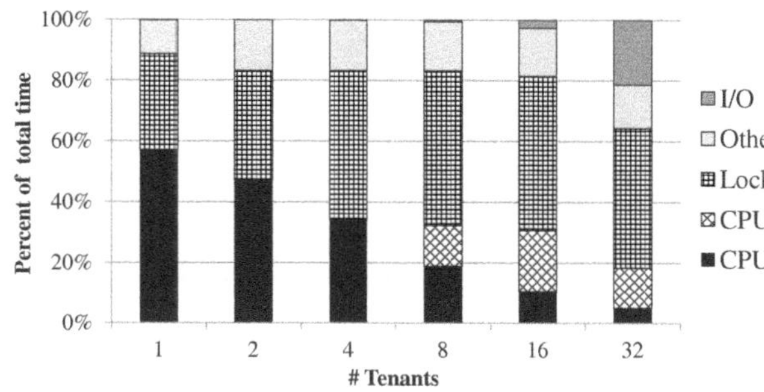

Figure 14: XenMD Design with DBX: Time-breakdown

3.5.3 Xen Multiple DBMS Design with PostgreSQL

Contrasting to the VMware design with DBX, the XenMD design with PostgreSQL uses a (free) open-source VMM and a (free) open-source DBMS.

As seen in Figure 2, the XenMD design with PostgreSQL is the best VM-based design, and is only about 1.3X slower than the NVMD design when the number of tenants is less than 16. To explain this result, we look at the time-breakdown of a PostgreSQL server process, as shown in Figure 13. In this figure, we notice that the CPU wait time is much smaller than the case when using the VMware as the VMM (as seen in Figure 9). In Figure 10, we compared the CPU virtualization overhead of Xen and VMware, and our conclusion is that Xen has a very low CPU overhead, primarily since Xen uses para-virtualization.

As the CPU virtualization overhead is relatively smaller (compared to the VMMD designs), the workload stresses the log disk (H-SSD), which becomes critical to the overall performance. As seen in Figure 13, when there are more than 4 tenants, the `WAL WriteLock` consumes a large fraction of the total execution time. To better understand the disk performance in the XenMD design, we show the disk I/O statistics from the host OS level in Table 8. This disk performance behaviors are comparable to the ones observed from the NVMD design (shown in Table 3(a)). As seen in Table 8, the log disk I/O statistics of the XenMD design with PostgreSQL are close to the NVMD design.

To summarize, since the XenMD design with PostgreSQL has low virtualization-related penalties, it shows very competitive performance (1.3X overhead) to the NVMD design up to 8 tenants, as seen in Figure 2. However, this design is 2X slower at 8 or more tenants since the TPC-C working sets are larger than the main memory size, and now the working sets spill onto the disk.

	Log disk (H-SSD)						Data disk (SSD RAID)					
# tenants	1	2	4	8	16	32	1	2	4	8	16	32
await	0.32	0.45	0.65	2.7	10.4	19.1	2.1	3.2	3.9	7.2	14.7	31.2
util%	30.2	42.3	57.9	81.5	90.7	98.4	1.3	5.1	10.8	20.9	42.4	98.5

Table 8: XenMD design: disk I/O statistics

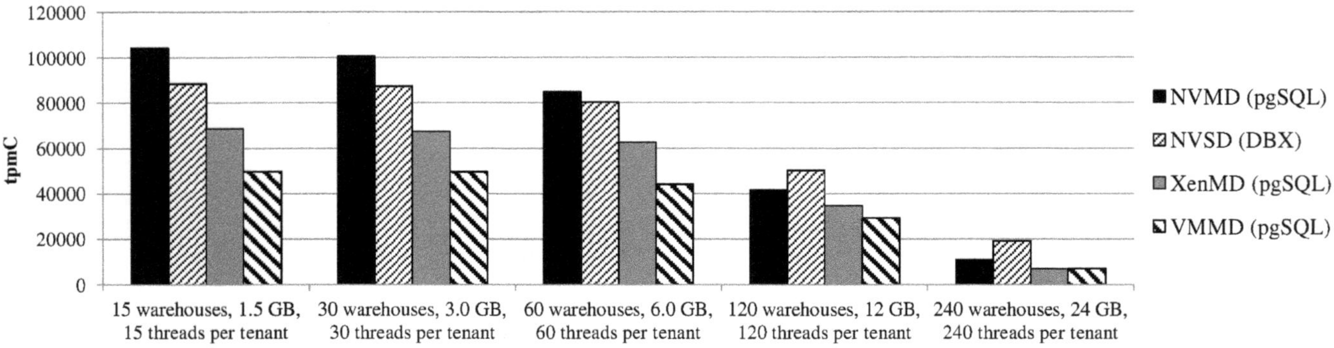

Figure 15: Effect of varying the tenant database size (8 tenants): Comparison of the four designs, each at their best performance configuration. Starting from 30 warehouses, the VM-based designs (VMware and Xen) start to run out of main memory space for the working sets. However, for the NVMD and the NVSD designs, their working sets are always memory resident at 30 warehouses. For 60 or more warehouses, the working sets for all designs are larger than the available main memory.

3.5.4 Xen Multiple DBMS Design with DBX

We also carried out performance analysis for the XenMD design with DBX. The time-breakdown analysis for this design is shown in Figure 14. Comparing to the behavior shown in Figure 12, the CPU wait time incurred when running DBX on Xen is lower than the case when running DBX on VMware, at 8 ,16 and 32 tenants. The reason for this behavior is because Xen can better virtualize the CPU computation than VMware, as shown in Figure 10. However, as shown in Figure 2, the XenMD design with DBX does not perform as well as the XenMD design with PostgreSQL since the DBX is more CPU-intensive than PostgreSQL.

3.6 Increasing the Database Size

In this section, we increase the size of the database so that the working set if far larger than than the server memory.

We consolidate 8 tenants on the same server (because most designs show their best performance with 8 tenants, as shown in Figure 2), and the data size for each tenant is varied from 1.5 GB with 15 threads to 24 GB with 240 threads. The size of each warehouse remains the same at 100MB (as in the experiments above).

Here we use four best-performing designs as example, and show their performance in Figure 15. These four designs are: the NVMD design with PostgreSQL, the NVSD design with DBX, the XenMD design with PostgreSQL, and the VMMD design with PostgreSQL.

In Figure 15, we show the performance of the four designs with different tenant database sizes. When the database grows from 15 to 30 warehouses, the main memory can still hold the working set in the NVMD and the NVSD designs. However at 30 warehouses, the VM-based designs (VMMD and XenMD) run out of memory for the working sets, but the amount of additional read I/O traffic is very small, so we observe that the performance of each design is not strongly affected by this data size growth.

As the data size (i.e. # warehouses) continues to grow beyond 60 warehouses, the working set size becomes larger than the memory size for all designs, and query execution now needs to read data from the disks. As can be seen in Figure 15, the performance of each design starts to drop. At 120 and 240 warehouses, the data disk I/O becomes the bottleneck in each design. In Table 9, we present both the log and the data disk I/O statistics for the NVMD design with PostgreSQL and the XenMD design with PostgreSQL (as representative results).

As seen in Table 9 (a), for the NVMD design at 120 and 240 warehouses, the data disk utilization is close to 100% and the average I/O time is large, indicating that the data disk is the bottleneck. Since the data disk is now the bottleneck, the pressure on the log disk is lower. For example, as can be seen in Table 9 (a), the log disk utilization decreases from 99% to 41% when the number of warehouses increases from 60 to 240. The above observations also hold true for the XenMD design, as seen in Table 9 (b).

Additionally, when the number of warehouses is 120 or 240, as seen in Figure 15, the NVSD design with DBX outperforms all other designs. We infer that this is because when the (checkpointing and read) I/O traffic to the data disk becomes the dominant performance factor, the DBMS buffer management becomes very important for overall performance. The NVSD design with DBX manages a single uniform buffer pool, so that it can better utilize it to cache the most important data to minimize the I/O traffic, and to generate a better pattern of write to the I/O device. While for the other designs (e.g. NVMD and VM-based), each DBMS manages its own buffer pool and potentially loses this global view.

3.7 Hybrid and HDD-based I/O subsystem

To connect with previous work [10], and to shed some lights on hybrid I/O subsystems, we compare the NVSD, the NVMD, and the XenMD designs with PostgreSQL on two disk configurations: (1) an HDD-based I/O subsystem and (2) an hybrid I/O subsystem.

Specifically, the HDD-based I/O subsystem uses two identical SATA HDDs (2TB 7200 RPM WD Caliver Blue); one HDD is used

	Log disk (H-SSD)					Data disk (SSD RAID)				
# warehouses	15	30	60	120	240	15	30	60	120	240
await	2.3	4.1	11.8	10.8	2.7	7.4	11.6	12.7	13.3	15.7
util%	75.6	91.8	98.8	83.6	40.9	14.2	31.3	69.1	95.5	99.7

(a) NVMD design: disk I/O statistics

	Log disk (H-SSD)					Data disk (SSD RAID)				
# warehouses	15	30	60	120	240	15	30	60	120	240
await	2.7	2.5	2.2	1.8	2.0	3.9	4.6	23.9	58.3	56.5
util%	81.5	64.9	47.9	40.2	20.1	20.9	51.3	89.1	98.5	99.4

(b) Xen design: disk I/O statistics

Table 9: Increasing the database size: disk I/O statistics in the NVMD and the XenMD designs

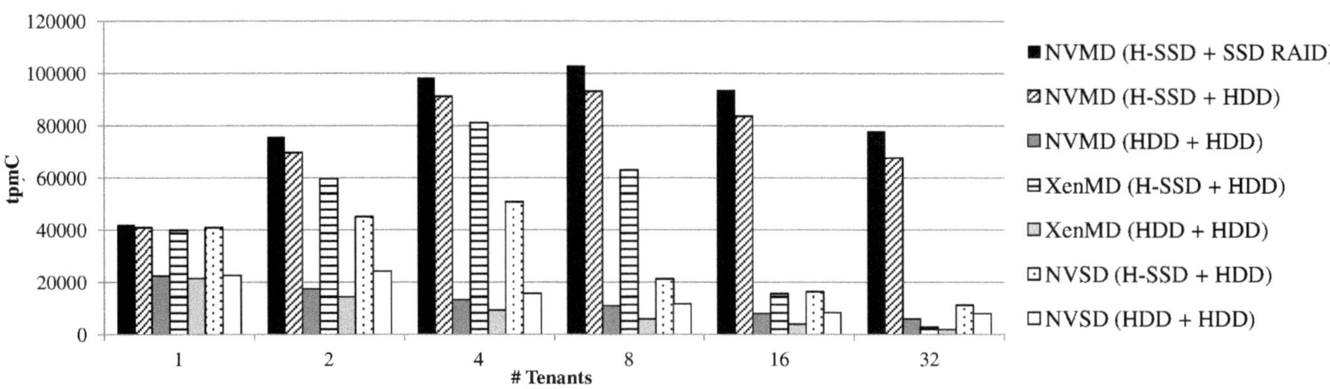

Figure 16: Comparing the NVSD, NVMD and XenMD designs on the Hybrid and HDD-based I/O subsystems

as the log disk and the other as the data disk. For the hybrid I/O subsystem, we use the H-SSD as the log disk and the above HDD as the data disk, since (cf. Section 3.3) the NVMD design achieves better performance when the log is placed on the faster device.

For this experiment, each tenant has 15 warehouses (1.5 GB database) and we create 15 concurrent client threads to generate the TPC-C workload.

Figure 16 shows the results for this experiment. In this figure, we also show the best-performing SSD-based design (i.e. the NVMD design) from the previous experiments. There are several observations that we can make from the results shown in Figure 16.

First, the NVMD design with the hybrid I/O subsystem has comparable performance to the NVMD design with only SSDs. This is because in the NVMD design, the data disk was not a bottleneck (see Table 3), and the traffic to the data disk was largely asynchronous page I/Os. Consequently, switching to a faster device for the data disk has a small impact on the overall performance.

Second, the NVMD design running on the hybrid I/O subsystem shows significant performance improvement over the NVMD design running on the pure HDD-based I/O subsystem. In the NVMD design, the log I/O component is a key factor in determining the overall performance, and the ability of the SSDs to better deal with random I/Os is crucial in improving the performance of the log component.

Third, when we compare the XenMD design and the NVMD design with the hybrid I/O subsystem, we notice that as the number of tenants increases, the relative performance of the NVMD design over the XenMD design increases, and the performance gap rises quite sharply as we move to 16 and 32 tenants. As discussed in Section 3.5.1, the working set size increases beyond the available main memory in the XenMD design, and spilling to HDDs degrades the performance rapidly.

Fourth, when considering all the designs and using a pure HDD-based I/O subsystem, the NVSD design always performs better than the other designs (i.e. the NVMD and the XenMD designs). At 32 tenants, the NVSD design is about 6X better than the XenMD design, which matches the observation in [10].

Recall that when analyzing the NVSD design in Section 3.4.1, we found that the lock contention is a significant problem when the I/O subsystem is not the bottleneck (because of the SSDs). However, for the pure HDD-based I/O subsystem, we did not observe serious lock contention because the "new" performance bottleneck is now the I/O subsystem.

4. RELATED WORK

There has been a flurry of recent work examining various aspects of multi-tenancy for database workloads, driven in a large part by the move towards cloud database services. For example, Soror et al. [18] proposed using VMs to consolidate mixed workloads and provided a virtualization design advisor to split the physical computing resources, and provision each VM in order to achieve the best aggregate performance. However, that work does not consider the performance overheads associated with using VMs, or compare the performance of their VM-based solution to the solutions that do not use a VM.

Curino et al. [10] propose consolidating multiple DB workloads using a "share-everything" solution (a single DBMS instance) without virtualization. They proposed a consolidation technique, called Kairos, to measure the hardware requirements of the workloads and predict the combined resource utilization of all the workloads. The authors compared Kairos with a VMware-based solution, and concluded that Kairos has a factor of 6X-12X higher throughput than the VMware-based solution when using traditional HDDs. Our results largely match their conclusion when the I/O subsystem uses traditional HDDs. However, a big motivation of our work is to revisit this issue when considering pure SSD-based I/O subsystems.

Another work [16] performed a detailed performance analysis of OLTP deployments in servers with multiple cores per CPU (multicore) and multiple CPUs per server (multisocket). They compared different database deployment strategies and varied the number and size of independent database instances that are run on a single server. Similar to their work, we systematically compare and evaluate OLTP deployments on a single server. However, their work focused on optimizing OLTP deployments on different CPU architectures, while our work focuses on comparing multi-tenant OLTP designs on different I/O subsystems.

Recently, Narasayya et al. proposed a method to support multi-tenant relational Database-as-a-Service (Daas) scenarios [12]. Their method, called SQLVM, provides performance isolation by reserving key database server resources (such as the CPU, the I/O and the memory resources) for each tenant. For data analytic workload, Wong et al. [19] proposed Thrifty, which uses tenant placement strategies and query routing to consolidate thousands of parallel database tenants onto a shared hardware infrastructure, while guaranteeing that the tenant workload meets a target performance SLAs. Collectively these methods point to potential techniques that could be used to improve the effectiveness of VMs when supporting database workloads.

To our best knowledge, this paper presents the first comprehensive study evaluating multi-tenant OLTP designs on SSD-based I/O subsystems.

5. CONCLUSIONS AND FUTURE WORK

In this paper, we have examined various multi-tenancy designs for OLTP workloads on a modern SSD-based I/O subsystem. We make the following key observations: (1) The VM-based design shows fairly competitive performance to the non-virtualization based design (from 1.3X to 2X performance degradation) on a modern SSD-based I/O subsystem, which is far lower than what was shown in previous studies that only considered traditional HDD-based I/O subsystems. Thus, when switching to an pure SSD-based I/O system, the performance penalty that holds for traditional HDD-based I/O systems does not hold. (2) The Non-Virtualized Single DMBS design has a performance advantage over the VM-based designs on an SSD-based I/O subsystem, as long as it can minimize the contention on the internal DBMS shared resources. (3) The Non-Virtualized Multiple DMBS design with PostgreSQL presents the best performance compared to all other designs, for the TPC-C like workload that we considered in this paper. This is mostly because it can avoid the resources contention problem in the Non-Virtualized Single DMBS design [13, 16], and the performance penalties associated with the VM-based design [10].

There are a number of directions for future work, including dealing with dynamic workloads, expanding to more complex (e.g. OLAP workloads) and mixed workloads, examining mixed devices (HDDs and SSDs), and extending this study to conduct a full price v/s performance analysis of various solutions that includes aspects such as amortized hardware costs and software licensing costs.

6. ACKNOWLEDGEMENTS

This research was supported in part by the National Science Foundation under grants IIS-0963993 and IIS-1250886. Part of the work by Ning Zhang was done when he was at the NEC Laboratories of America and at RocketFuel. We also thank the reviewers of this paper for their valuable feedback on an earlier draft of this paper, and for what appears to have been a spirited conversation in the discussion phase.

7. REFERENCES

[1] http://www.xen.org/.
[2] http://www.vmware.com/.
[3] http://oltpbenchmark.com/experiments/dbms_config/postgresql.conf.
[4] Best practices for xen. http://wiki.xensource.com/xenwiki/XenBestPractices.
[5] Flash drives replace disks at Amazon, Facebook, Dropbox. http://www.wired.com/wiredenterprise/2012/06/flash-data-centers/.
[6] OLTPBenchmark. http://oltpbenchmark.com/wiki/index.php?title=Main_Page.
[7] Performance best practices for VMware vSphere 4.0, VMware ESX 4.0 and ESXi 4.0, vCenter Server 4.0. http://www.vmware.com/pdf/Perf_Best_Practices_vSphere4.0.pdf.
[8] SysBench: a system performance benchmark. http://sysbench.sourceforge.net/.
[9] L. Bouganim, B. T. Jónsson, and P. Bonnet. uFLIP: Understanding flash io patterns. In *CIDR*, 2009.
[10] C. Curino, E. P. C. Jones, S. Madden, and H. Balakrishnan. Workload-aware database monitoring and consolidation. In *SIGMOD Conference*, pages 313–324, 2011.
[11] U. F. Minhas, J. Yadav, A. Aboulnaga, and K. Salem. Database systems on virtual machines: How much do you lose? In *ICDE Workshops*, pages 35–41, 2008.
[12] V. R. Narasayya, S. Das, M. Syamala, B. Chandramouli, and S. Chaudhuri. SQLVM: Performance isolation in multi-tenant relational database-as-a-service. In *CIDR*, 2013.
[13] I. Pandis, P. Tözün, R. Johnson, and A. Ailamaki. Plp: Page latch-free shared-everything oltp. *PVLDB*, 4(10):610–621, 2011.
[14] A. Pavlo, C. Curino, and S. Zdonik. Skew-aware automatic database partitioning in shared-nothing, parallel OLTP systems. In *SIGMOD*, pages 61–72, 2012.
[15] A. Pavlo, E. P. Jones, and S. Zdonik. On predictive modeling for optimizing transaction execution in parallel OLTP systems. *Proc. VLDB Endow.*, 5:85–96, 2011.
[16] D. Porobic, I. Pandis, M. Branco, P. Tözün, and A. Ailamaki. OLTP on hardware islands. *PVLDB*, 5(11):1447–1458, 2012.
[17] J. Schaffner, T. Januschowski, M. Kercher, T. Kraska, H. Plattner, M. J. Franklin, and D. Jacobs. RTP: robust tenant placement for elastic in-memory database clusters. In *SIGMOD Conference*, pages 773–784, 2013.
[18] A. A. Soror, U. F. Minhas, A. Aboulnaga, K. Salem, P. Kokosielis, and S. Kamath. Automatic virtual machine configuration for database workloads. In *SIGMOD Conference*, pages 953–966, 2008.
[19] P. Wong, Z. He, and E. Lo. Parallel analytics as a service. In *SIGMOD Conference*, pages 25–36, 2013.

Secure Query Processing with Data Interoperability in a Cloud Database Environment

Wai Kit Wong* Ben Kao† David Wai Lok Cheung† Rongbin Li† Siu Ming Yiu†
wongwk@hsmc.edu.hk, {kao, dcheung, rbli, smyiu}@cs.hku.hk
*Department of Computing, Hang Seng Management College
†Department of Computer Science, University of Hong Kong

ABSTRACT

We address security issues in a cloud database system which employs the DBaaS model. In such a model, a data owner (DO) exports its data to a cloud database service provider (SP). To provide data security, sensitive data is encrypted by the DO before it is uploaded to the SP. Existing encryption schemes, however, are only partially homomorphic in the sense that each of them was designed to allow one specific type of computation to be done on encrypted data. These existing schemes cannot be integrated to answer real practical queries that involve operations of different kinds. We propose and analyze a secure query processing system (SDB) on relational tables and a set of elementary operators on encrypted data that allow *data interoperability*, which allows a wide range of SQL queries to be processed by the SP on encrypted information. We prove that our encryption scheme is secure against two types of threats and that it is practically efficient.

1. INTRODUCTION

Advances in cloud computing has recently led to much research work on the technological development of cloud database systems that deploy the *Database-as-a-service model* (DBaaS). Commercial cloud database services, such as Amazon's RDS[1] and Microsoft's SQL Azure[2], are also available. Under the DBaaS model, a *data owner* (DO) uploads its database to a *service provider* (SP), which hosts high-performance machines and sophisticated database software to process queries on behalf of the DO. The SP thus provides *storage*, *computation* and *administration* services. There are numerous advantages of outsourcing database services, such as highly scalable and elastic computation to handle bursty workloads. Also, with multi-tenancy, cloud databases can greatly reduce the total cost of ownership.

Most of existing works on cloud databases focus on performance issues, such as live migration [10], workload and resource management [28, 9], virtualization [24].

However, *data security* has not been satisfactorily addressed so far. The goal of this paper is to design a secure query processing system in a cloud database environment under the DBaaS model. In particular, we propose a secret-sharing scheme between a DO and an SP such that a wide range of database queries can be executed on the SP without revealing sensitive information.

The common practice to protect sensitive data in database outsourcing is to encrypt the data before storing it at the SP. For instance, Oracle database 11g provides Transparent Data Encryption (TDE), which encrypts disk-resident data using conventional encryption algorithms. The SP thus provides a reliable repository with storage and administration services (such as backup and recovery). To process queries, the encrypted data has to be shipped back to the DO, which has to process the sensitive data by itself. The powerful computation services given by the SP is mostly lost.

In order to leverage the computation resources of the SP in query processing, we need *homomorphic encryption*. A *fully homomorphic encryption* (FHE) scheme is one that allows any computation to be done on ciphertext [12]. Although FHE is of great theoretical significance, existing schemes are very computationally expensive [13]. It is not practical to apply FHE to even very small-scale computations, let alone database query processing which are highly data intensive.

As a compromise, there have been many previous works [1, 23, 20, 6] on designing *partially homomorphic encryption* (PHE) such that certain restricted kinds of computation can be done on ciphertext. For example, OPES [1] is an order-preserving encryption scheme which allows the order of plaintext to be deduced by comparing encrypted values and so it supports range queries. Other examples include RSA [23] (for multiplication), Paillier's cryptosystem [20] (for addition), and PEKS [6] (for keyword search on encrypted strings). A problem with these PHE schemes is that each of them was designed to process one particular type of operation. Since they employ different encryption functions, they are naturally not data interoperable. In other words, one cannot compose complex operations by piecing together the various simple operations these PHE schemes support. For example, one cannot express a simple selection clause such as "*quantity* $\times$ *unit-price* $>$ \$10,000," which requires both multiplication and comparison.

Considering the limitations of FHE and PHE schemes, we take another approach to design a secure query processing system. Our approach is based on the secret sharing idea

[1]http://aws.amazon.com/rds/
[2]https://sql.azure.com/

SIGMOD/PODS'14, June 22 - 27 2014, Snowbird, UT, USA

http://dx.doi.org/10.1145/2588555.2588572

of the Secure Multiparty Computation (SMC) model [30]. In secret sharing, each plain value is decomposed into several *shares* and each share is kept by one of multiple parties. While no party can recover the plain values by its own shares, a protocol executed by the parties can be defined to compute a deterministic function of the values. It has been shown that any computation that can be expressed as a circuit can be done under the SMC model [14].

One can consider applying SMC in a cloud database environment by decomposing sensitive data into multiple shares, each being kept by an independent SP. For example, ShareMind [4] provides secure storage based on SMC. It also provides a set of protocols for executing various elementary operations such as addition and multiplication. Although theoretically one can execute ShareMind's protocols to answer SQL queries on sensitive data, there are two issues: First, ShareMind requires at least three non-colluding parties (SP's). This incurs significant costs in outsourcing the database. Second, the protocols for computing general functions are expensive, both in terms of the computations at SP's and the communication among them.

In this paper we propose a secure query processing system, SDB, which shares similar flavors with SMC/ShareMind in that sensitive data is decomposed into shares. Here we summarize the distinctive features of SDB:

[Two Parties] Unlike ShareMind, SDB requires only two parties — the DO and one SP.

[Asymmetry] SDB is asymmetric — the DO is trusted and the SP is untrusted. As we will see later, the asymmetric property of SDB allows us to design computation protocols that require the DO to perform minimal works with minimal storage, while the bulk of computations and data storage for query processing is taken up by the SP. This characteristic fits perfectly to the DBaaS model.

[Efficient Operators with Data Interoperability] SDB provides a set of elementary operators that operate on secret shares. These operators operate on data that is encrypted using the *same* encryption scheme. The output of an operator can therefore be taken as input of another. We call the feature that different operators sharing the same encryption scheme and thus an operator can be applied on the results of another operator "*data interoperability*". With data interoperability, a wide range of SQL queries can be expressed and processed in SDB. Moreover, our protocols for executing the various operators are practically efficient.

[Plain and Encrypted Data Handling] In practice, much of the DO's data is not sensitive and needs not be encrypted. In SDB, the protocols for implementing the various operators can be applied to both encrypted data and plain data, or a mixture of them.

[Database System Integration] SDB can be implemented as a software layer on top of any off-the-shelf DBMSs. As our prototype illustrates, SDB can be integrated seamlessly with existing DBMSs and utilize many of their functionality.

The rest of the paper is organized as follows. Section 2 discusses some related works. In Section 3 we describe our system architecture, the data and query model, and the security model. Section 4 gives the basic idea of our secret sharing scheme. Section 5 explains in details the protocols for implementing the various data interoperable operators. In Section 6 we present our experimental results. Finally, Section 7 concludes the paper.

2. RELATED WORK

The DBaaS model in a cloud database environment has attracted much research attention lately. Most of these works focus on performance issues such as query processing efficiency and scalability. For example, techniques like database partitioning and workload assignments for processing queries over an array of distributed servers are investigated in [8]. Our encryption system is orthogonal to those techniques and can be integrated into existing systems.

Security in cloud databases has been studied in [15, 16, 3, 22, 25]. In [15, 16], an outsourced database is encrypted by a deterministic encryption scheme (e.g., RSA), which supports equality testing. However, other operations such as ordering comparisons are not naturally supported. CryptDB [22] is a well-known system for processing queries on encrypted data. It employs multiple encryption functions and encrypts each data item under various sequences of encryption functions in an *onion approach*. For example, CryptDB uses a non-deterministic encryption (e.g., RSA with padding) E_1, a deterministic encryption (e.g., RSA) E_2, and an order-preserving encryption (e.g., OPES [1]) E_3 for encrypting numeric data. These encryptions provide different levels of security strength and different levels of computational support — E_1 does not support encrypted data computation but provides the strongest security; E_2 allows equality checks on encrypted data; E_3 allows both equality check and ordering comparison but is not secure against chosen plaintext (CPA) attack [19]. A data item x can be encrypted as $E_1(E_2(E_3(x)))$ before it is stored at the SP. To perform computation on x at SP, the encrypted value has to be decrypted to an appropriate level. For example, to perform equality checking, the data owner has to send the decryption key of E_1 to the SP for it to obtain $E_2(E_3(x))$. Under CryptDB, data security is gradually relaxed to a level that is appropriate for the required computation on the data.

MONOMI [25] is based on CryptDB with a special focus on efficient analytical query processing. It employs a split client/server execution approach. The idea is to intelligently analyze a query plan to identify the computation that can be carried out by the SP over encrypted data and the computation that needs to be performed by the client over decrypted plaintext. A number of optimization techniques are proposed in [25] to improve query performance.

Both CryptDB and MONOMI employ different encryption functions to support different operators. The supported operators are thus not data interoperable. As a result, complex queries that require *piping* the output of one operator to another may not be carried out completely at the SP. For example, the selection clause "*quantity* $\times$ *unit-price* > \$10,000" cannot be evaluated by the SP on encrypted data. Instead, the encrypted data has to be shipped back to the owner who will evaluate the selection clause itself. MONOMI avoids the data interoperability issue by pre-computation. For example, if it is known that *quantity* $\times$ *unit-price* is frequently evaluated, one can precompute the columns' product and store that as an encrypted materialized column (say C) at the SP. In this case, MONOMI can evaluate the selection clause ($C > \$10,000$) by applying the ordering comparison operator over encrypted data.

Our approach differs from that of CryptDB and MONOMI in that we focus on designing an encryption method that supports data interoperable operators. This allows a wider range of computation on encrypted data to be carried out

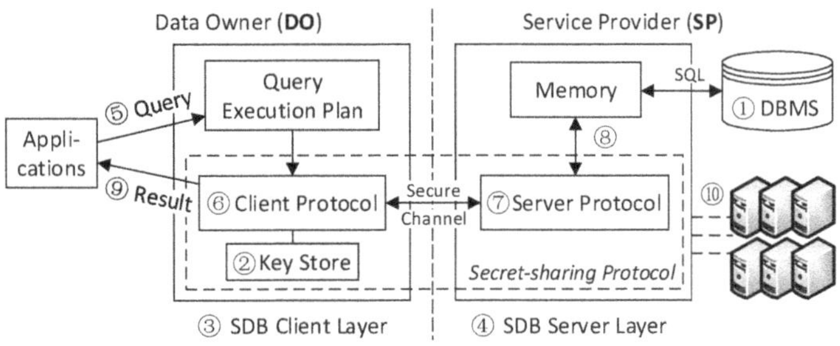

Figure 1: SDB's architecture

directly at the SP, and reduces the work at the client/owner.

In [7] and [27], each tuple in the database is encrypted as a whole. Additional encrypted indices are proposed to support simple point and range queries. In [11], a secure database system based on the SMC protocols is proposed. The difference between their approach and ours is that their system requires three non-colluding SPs to answer general queries while SDB requires only one SP.

Trusted DB [3] and Cipherbase [2] take a hardware approach to provide data security. The SP installs secure coprocessors (SCPUs), e.g., the IBM 4764 Cryptographic Coprocessor to its machines. SCPUs are tamper-resistant and attackers cannot inspect data stored in an SCPU's memory. Sensitive data is encrypted by the DO, who then distributes the decryption key to the SCPUs via secure channels and sends the encrypted data to the SP. To answer queries, the SP passes the encrypted data to the SCPUs for processing and receives encrypted results. The advantages of the hardware approach are (1) it provides strong security protection as long as the SCPUs are not compromised, and (2) it does not limit query expressiveness. However, SCPUs are expensive (e.g., the IBM 4764 costs about USD $10,000 in 2009). In this paper we focus on an algorithmic approach to solving the secure database problem. Since our solution does not rely on special hardware, it can be implemented using inexpensive off-the-shelf machines.

3. MODELS

In this section we describe our data model, the architecture of SDB, two attack models, and the query model.

[Data] First, we briefly mention how data is encrypted. We employ a secret sharing scheme between the DO and the SP. Each sensitive data item v is split into two shares, one kept at the DO and another at the SP. We use $[\![v]\!]$ to denote a sensitive value (the $[\![\,]\!]$ symbolize that the value is secret and should be kept in a safe). We call the share of $[\![v]\!]$ to be kept at the DO, denoted by v_k, the *item key* of $[\![v]\!]$. The share of $[\![v]\!]$ kept at the SP is denoted by v_e, which is regarded as the *encrypted value* of $[\![v]\!]$. Our objective is to prevent attackers from recovering the set of sensitive data $[\![v]\!]$'s given their encrypted values v_e's. Our solution is built on the relational model and so the database consists of a set of tables. We assume that each table column is categorized as either sensitive or non-sensitive. So, for each column A, either all values in A are encrypted or none is.

[Architecture] Figure 1 shows the architecture. The SP employs a DBMS (①) to store two types of data: (1) the plaintext of non-sensitive data and (2) the encrypted values v_e's of sensitive data. The DO holds the item keys v_k's. As we will explain later in Section 4, the DO does not need to physically maintain and store all the item keys. Instead, for each sensitive column A, the DO stores a *column key* ck_A from which all the item keys of the items in column A are derived. In this way, only a small number of column keys need to be kept at the DO's key store (②).

SDB is implemented as two software layers: a *client layer* (③) which resides at the DO and a *server layer* (④) which resides at the SP. The client layer receives queries from applications and translates each query into a query execution plan (⑤). A plan derives a sequence of operations on data. If an operation involves only non-sensitive data, it is passed directly to the SP, otherwise, the operation is carried out by a secret-sharing protocol. Each such protocol consists of a light-weight *client protocol* (⑥) and a *server protocol* (⑦). The client protocol prepares a message which includes an identification of the data involved, the operation to be executed, and a *hint*. As we will explain in Section 4, a *hint* is derived from relevant column keys and is needed for the SP to carry out the computation on encrypted data properly. The client layer sends the instruction message to the SP's server layer via a secure channel. At the SP, when the server layer receives an instruction message, it first identifies the relevant data. If the data is already residing in memory (e.g., the data required is an intermediate result obtained from previous operations), the server layer executes the server protocol of the operation on the memory-resident data (⑧); Otherwise, the required data is first retrieved from the DBMS before the the server protocol is executed. If the executed operation is the last one of the execution plan, the computed result is shipped back to the client layer, which decrypts it to recover the result's original plaintext values (⑨). In our current implementation, data is stored on a DBMS running MySQL. The server layer executes on a distributed PC cluster (⑩), which is a typical setup of cloud databases.

[Security threats] We consider three kinds of knowledge that an attacker may obtain by hacking the SP. We explain our security levels against those attackers' knowledge.

Database (DB) Knowledge — The attacker sees the encrypted values v_e's stored in the DBMS of the SP. This happens when the attacker hacks into the DBMS and gains accesses to the disk-resident data.

Chosen Plaintext Attack (CPA) Knowledge — The attacker is able to select a set of plaintext values $[\![v]\!]$'s and observe their associated encrypted values v_e's. For example, an attacker may open a few new accounts at a bank (the DO) with different opening balances and observe the new encrypted values inserted into the SP's DB. We remark that while CPA knowledge is easy to obtain for public key cryptosystems, it is much harder to get under the cloud database environment. This is because the attacker typically does not have control on the number, order, and kinds of operations that are submitted by other users of the system and so it is difficult for it to associate events on plain values with the events on the encrypted ones.

Query Result (QR) Knowledge — The attacker is able to see the queries submitted to the SP and all the intermediate (encrypted) results of each operator involved in the query. QR Knowledge may be obtained in a few ways. For example, the attacker could have compromised the SP to inspect the instructions the client sends to the SP and the memory-based computations carried out by the SP. Or the attacker could intercept messages passed between the client and the server over the communication channel. We remark that it is typically more difficult to obtain QR Knowledge than

DB Knowledge. This is because memory-based computation is of transient existence while data on disk persists. The window of opportunity for an attacker to observe desired queries and their (encrypted) results is thus limited. Moreover, there are sophisticated industrial standards to make a communication channel highly secure.

Our security goal is to prevent an attacker from recovering plaintext values $[\![v]\!]$'s given that the attacker has acquired certain combinations of knowledge listed above. First, we argue that DB knowledge is typically easier to obtain than the others and so we assume that the attacker has DB knowledge. Second, it has been proven that no schemes are secure against an attacker that has both CPA knowledge and QR knowledge [5]. Therefore, we assume that the attacker does not have both of these knowledges. Fortunately, as we have explained, CPA and QR knowledges are typically difficult to obtain in a cloud database environment and so the chances of an attacker having both is small. Our system, SDB, is designed to be secure against the following threats:

- **DB+CPA Threat**: The attacker has both DB knowledge and CPA knowledge.
- **DB+QR Threat**: The attacker has both DB knowledge and QR knowledge.

Besides the three types of knowledge we mentioned above, there could be scenarios in which the attacker has acquired other knowledge. As an example, an attacker might know the domain of a certain column and the frequency distribution of the values in the domain. Combining this frequency knowledge with, e.g., the results of a group-by operation might allow an attacker to launch a frequency counting attack. Additional measures need to be taken to guard against such attacks. For example, fake tuples with carefully chosen values could be added to tables to disturb the frequency distribution of a column's values. In this paper we focus on DB, CPA, and QR knowledge because these knowledges are relatively easier to obtain by a malicious SP. We will prove that SDB is secure against the two threats derived from these knowledges. Readers are referred to [22] for a discussion on other knowledge and how the functionality of a secure outsourced database could be lowered to guard against attackers with such additional knowledge.

[Query] We describe the range of queries that SDB supports. First, any queries that involve only non-sensitive data are processed by the DBMS at the SP directly. In this case, any SQL queries can be answered. SDB provides a set of secure operators that operate on encrypted data. These operators are data interoperable and so they can be combined to formulate complex queries. Since our data encryption scheme (see Section 4) is based on modular arithmetic, our operators are applicable only to data values of integer domains. Data values of other domains such as strings and real numbers can be encoded as integers with limited precisions. However, certain specific operators on such domains are not natively supported by SDB and have to be implemented indirectly via other means. We will elaborate on this issue and briefly explain how to provide restricted support on non-integer values at the end of this section. For the moment, we assume that data values are all integers and operators take integers input and produce integers output. Table 1 lists the secure operators provided in SDB.

The first 5 operators ($\times$, $+$, $-$, $=$, $>$) are arithmetic and comparison operators. Although they are defined on column operands, a constant operand can also be used by interpreting it as a *constant column*. These operators can be used to formulate selection clauses, such as "*quantity* $\times$ *unit-price* $>$ \$10,000". More complex selection clauses such as conjunction and disjunction of boolean expressions are also supported by SDB. Projection (π), which does not involve encrypted value manipulation, is trivially supported. By combining Cartesian product and selection, theta-join is supported. SDB also supports group-by, sum, average and count and so it provides some aggregation functionality.

operator	expression	description
$\times$	$A \times B$	vector dot product of two columns of the same table
$+$ $-$	$A + B$ $A - B$	vector addition/subtraction of two columns of the same table
$=$	$A = B$	equality comparison on two columns of the same table and output a binary column of '0' and '1'
$>$	$A > B$	ordering comparison on two columns of the same table and output a binary column of '0' and '1'
π	$\pi_S(R)$	project table R on attributes specified in an attribute set S
$\otimes$	$R_1 \otimes R_2$	Cartesian product of two relations
$\bowtie_S$	$R_1 \bowtie_S R_2$	equijoin of two relations on a set of join keys S
$\bowtie$	$R_1 \bowtie R_2$	natural join between two relations
GroupBy	GroupBy(R, A)	group rows in relation R by column A's values
Sum/Avg	Sum/Avg(R, A)	sum or average the values of column A in relation R
Count	Count(R)	count the number of rows in a relation

Table 1: List of secure primitive operators

[Limitations] With data interoperability, SDB is able to support a wide range of SQL queries. Comparing to existing systems, such as CryptDB and MONOMI, which implement various operators using different encryption functions (and thus are not data interoperable), SDB allows much more complex queries to be processed fully at the SP. There are, however, certain limitations on the operators SDB supports. In particular, SDB does not natively support operators that output non-integer values, such as square-root ($\sqrt{A}$). Here, we briefly discuss a few approaches to handle these non-integer operators.

(1) *Table lookup*: If a sensitive data column A of a table R that requires $\sqrt{\ }$ is known to have values from a small integer domain, say D, we can compute $\sqrt{A}$ by the following trick. We precompute a relation $T(D, \sqrt{D})$ with two columns, D (which is the domain of A) and $\sqrt{D}$. $\sqrt{A}$ is computed by evaluating $\pi_{\sqrt{D}}(R \bowtie_{A=D} T)$, which can be done with our secure operators. (2) *Query rewriting*: If $\sqrt{\ }$ is used in a selection clause, the selection condition can be rewritten to remove $\sqrt{\ }$. For example, the selection clause "$\sqrt{X+Y} > Z$" is equivalent to "$X+Y > Z \times Z$", which can be evaluated by our operators. (3) *Split client/server execution*: A third option is to adopt MONOMI's split client/server execution approach. The idea is to compute as much as possible at the SP. The execution of non-integer operators are delayed and finally carried out at the DO. For example, if a query requests the values of "$\sqrt{X+Y}$", the SP computes a column $C = X+Y$, returns C to the DO, which then computes $\sqrt{C}$ after decrypting C. With the last option, query plan analysis techniques studied in MONOMI [25] will be very useful.

SDB can also be extended to answer queries that involve conjunctions or disjunctions of selection clauses that involve numerical data and string data separately. For example, we can use PEKS [6] to encrypt strings, which allows keyword search on encrypted strings. Queries such as 'SELECT * WHERE Name LIKE "%John%" AND Salary $> 10,000$' can be evaluated by combining the Boolean results obtainable through PEKS and our secret-sharing scheme.

We remark that although there are limitations on SDB's operators, our design of data interoperable operators is the first of its kind. Our goal is to support the processing of a wide range of SQL queries on encrypted data. In particular, we evaluated SDB over the TPC-H benchmark (Section 6) and all queries in the benchmark are natively supported by SDB. We leave the study of non-integer operators as future work and focus on integer operators in this paper.

4. SECRET SHARING

In this section we describe how SDB encrypts sensitive data using a secret-sharing method. The DO maintains two secret numbers, g and n. The number n is generated according to the RSA method, i.e., n is the product of two big random prime numbers ρ_1, ρ_2. The number g is a positive number that is co-prime with n.[3] Define,

$$\phi(n) = (\rho_1 - 1)(\rho_2 - 1). \quad (1)$$

We have, based on the property of RSA,

$$(a^{ed} \bmod n = a) \quad \forall a, e, d \text{ such that } ed \bmod \phi(n) = 1.$$

Consider a sensitive column A of a relational table T of N rows $t_1, \ldots, t_N$. The DO assigns to each row t_i in T a distinct random row id r_i. Moreover, the DO randomly generates a *column key* $ck_A = \langle m, x \rangle$, which consists of a pair of random numbers. We require $0 < r_i, m, x < n$.

To simplify our discussion, let us assume that the schema of T is (row-id, A). (Additional columns of T, if any, can be handled similarly.) The idea is to store table T encrypted on the SP. This consists of two parts: (1) Sensitive values in column A are encrypted using secret sharing based on the column key $ck_A = \langle m, x \rangle$ and the row ids. (2) Since the row ids are used in encrypting column A's values, the row ids have to be encrypted themselves. In our implementation, row ids are encrypted using an additive homomorphic encryption $E()$, e.g., SIES [21].

The reason why row-id and A are encrypted differently is that row ids are never operated on by our secure operators (i.e., we assume row ids are not part of user queries). Hence, a simpler encryption method suffices. As we will see later, in order to correctly implement the secure operators, the encryption function, $E()$, applied on row ids needs only be additive homomorphic. On the other hand, sensitive data is encrypted using secret sharing so that computational protocols can be defined to implement our secure operators. The secret sharing encryption process consists of two steps:

Step 1 (item key generation). Consider a row with row id r and a sensitive value (of A) $[\![v]\!]$. Under secret sharing, our objective is to split $[\![v]\!]$ into an item key v_k and an encrypted value v_e. Conceptually, v_e is kept at the SP and v_k is kept at the DO. Since we want to minimize the storage requirement of the DO, the item key v_k is materialized on demand and is generated from the column key ck_A (which is stored at the DO's key store) and the row id r, which is stored encrypted at the SP. Specifically,

DEFINITION 1. *(Item key generation) Given a row id r and a column key $ck_A = \langle m, x \rangle$, the item key v_k is given by,*

$$v_k = gen(r, \langle m, x \rangle) = mg^{(rx \bmod \phi(n))} \bmod n.$$

For simplicity, in the following discussion, we sometimes omit "mod $\phi(n)$" in various expressions with an understanding that the exponent of the above formula is computed in modular $\phi(n)$. So, we write,

$$v_k = gen(r, \langle m, x \rangle) = mg^{rx} \bmod n. \quad (2)$$

Step 2 (Share computation). Shares of $[\![v]\!]$ are determined by a *multiplicative secret sharing* scheme. While v_k is one of the share, the other share v_e, which is considered the encrypted value of $[\![v]\!]$, is computed by the following encryption function $\mathcal{E}$.

DEFINITION 2. *(Encrypted value) Given a sensitive value $[\![v]\!]$ and its item key v_k, the encrypted value v_e is given by,*

$$v_e = \mathcal{E}([\![v]\!], v_k) = [\![v]\!] v_k^{-1} \bmod n, \quad (3)$$

where v_k^{-1} denotes the modular multiplicative inverse of v_k, i.e., $v_k v_k^{-1} \bmod n = 1$.

To recover $[\![v]\!]$, one needs both shares v_k and v_e and compute

$$[\![v]\!] = \mathcal{D}(v_e, v_k) = v_e v_k \bmod n. \quad (4)$$

It has been proven in [19] that $[\![v]\!]$ cannot be determined with only v_e. Therefore, our scheme is secure against attackers with DB knowledge. Also, we outline the proof in Appendix A that our scheme is secure against CPA attacks. That is, if an attacker is given a set S of $\langle [\![v]\!], v_e \rangle$ pairs, it cannot deduce other sensitive data $[\![v']\!]$ that are not mentioned in S from their encrypted values v'_e. Hence, our scheme is secure against attackers with DB+CPA knowledge.

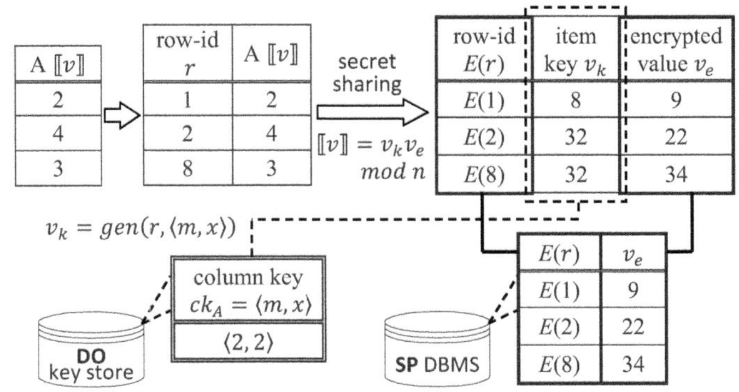

Figure 2: Encryption procedure ($g = 2$, $n = 35$).

Figure 2 summarizes the whole encryption procedure and illustrates how sensitive data (e.g., a column A) is transformed into encrypted values v_e's. It also shows that the DO only needs to maintain a column key in its key store, while the SP stores the bulk of the data.

Finally, after the SP has computed a query's results, the (encrypted) results are shipped back to the DO, which decrypts them to obtain plaintext results. In this process, the SP might have to send the (encrypted) row ids back to the DO for decryption. We will explain the result decryption procedure in the next section, when we discuss how each secure operator is implemented.

5. OPERATORS

In this section we discuss how the secure operators listed in Table 1 are implemented in SDB. First a few notes.

[Protocols] Each operator is executed by a protocol, which consists of a client protocol and a server protocol. Recall that our data model is column-based. Each sensitive column A is transformed by our secret sharing scheme into a column of item keys v_k's and a column of encrypted values

[3]In our implementation, ρ_1 and ρ_2 are 512-bit numbers and so n is 1024-bit.

v_e's. Moreover, the item keys are generated by a column key $ck_A = \langle m_A, x_A \rangle$[4], which is physically maintained by the DO, while the encrypted values are stored at the SP. Since an operator takes one or more columns as input and produces one or more columns as output[5], the client protocol takes column key(s) as input and produces column key(s) as output, while the server protocol's input and output are column(s) of encrypted values.

[Notations] We use capital letters, e.g., A, B to represent table columns and we use their lower case counterparts to denote values in columns. For example, we use "a" to denote a value (of a certain row) in column A. We use other lower case letters, e.g., p, q to represent other scalar values. For a sensitive value, say a, we use $[\![a]\!]$, a_k, a_e to represent the plaintext value, the item key, and the encrypted value of a, respectively. Moreover, we use A_e to represent the column of encrypted values a_e's stored at the SP.

[Operator Modes] A column operand of an operator is not necessarily sensitive. For example, the "+" operator could add a sensitive (encrypted) column A with a plain column B. Moreover, for the arithmetic and comparison operators, one of the operands could be a scalar (constant) value. For example, we could multiple a column with a constant as in the selection clause "$2 \times A > B$". We thus consider three modes for the operators, namely, EE mode (both operands are encrypted), EP mode (one operand is encrypted, the other is plain), and EC mode (one operand is encrypted, the other is a constant). We will first discuss EE mode and EC mode implementation. EP mode will be covered at the end of this section.

[Security] We show that the implementation of the operators are secure against DB+QR Threat. Specifically, we show that in the execution of an operator, even an attacker sees the message given to the SP and the results of the operator, the attacker cannot deduce the column keys kept by the DO based on the encrypted values stored at the SP. Without the column keys, the attacker cannot deduce the item keys and thus it cannot recover sensitive values $[\![v]\!]$'s. An outline of the proof that SDB is secure against DB+QR threat is given in Appendix B.

[Operator Output] The output of an operator in many cases is an intermediate result of a query and thus it is of transient existence and may not be physically stored in the database. For example, to evaluate the expression "$A \times 2 > B$", the query processor computes a column $C = A \times 2$ first, which is the output of "$\times$" in EC mode. Note that the output column C is also represented using secret sharing, i.e., it is represented by a column key ck_C (at DO) and an encrypted column C_e (at SP). As we will see later, for the EC mode of "$\times$", the output column (e.g., C) and the input column (e.g., A) share the same column of encrypted values. For efficiency, the SP does not physically duplicate A_e to obtain C_e. Instead, a reference is made to associate C_e to A_e. Figure 3 illustrates this idea. For simplicity, in the following discussion, we will only focus on how to compute an operator's output, which includes some column key(s) and some encrypted column(s). We will omit the details of how this data is physically stored.

[Additional Columns] To properly implement the various secure operators, we add two columns: S and R to each table T. Each value in S is the constant 1. Each value in R is a positive random number. The columns S and R are encrypted using secret sharing. In particular, their column keys (ck_S, ck_R) are stored at the DO and their encrypted columns (S_e, R_e) are stored at the SP.

[4]We use the subscript A here to denote that the key is associated with the column A.

[5]We consider a single numeric value output by an aggregate operator as a column of one single row.

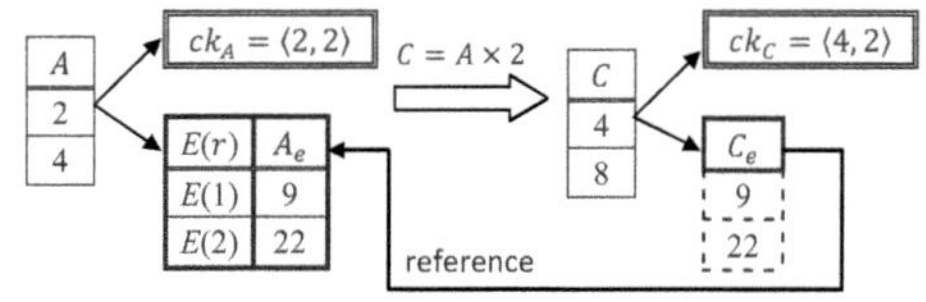

Figure 3: A_e as a reference of C_e.

Before we give the details of our protocols, we first list two simple properties of our secure sharing scheme. Consider a sensitive column A encrypted with column key $ck_A = \langle m, x \rangle$. If $x = 0$, from Equation 2, we have

$$v_k = gen(r, \langle m, 0 \rangle) = mg^{(r \cdot 0)} \bmod n = m. \quad (5)$$

It follows that

$$(ck_A = \langle 1, 0 \rangle) \Rightarrow (v_k = 1). \quad (6)$$

Also, from Equation 3, we have

$$(v_k = 1) \Rightarrow \left(v_e = \mathcal{E}([\![v]\!], 1) = [\![v]\!] 1^{-1} \bmod n = [\![v]\!]\right). \quad (7)$$

PROPERTY 1. *If $ck_A = \langle m, 0 \rangle$, then all values in column A has the same item key m.*

PROPERTY 2. *If $ck_A = \langle 1, 0 \rangle$, then all encrypted values v_e's of column A are equal to their corresponding plaintext values $[\![v]\!]$.*

Note that any column key $\langle m, x \rangle$ the DO generates to encrypt a column should have $x > 0$. However, we will show that for some operators, our protocols will purposely convert a column key to $\langle m, 0 \rangle$ or even $\langle 1, 0 \rangle$. The latter case is typically done to reveal the plaintext of an operator's result, such as the result of a comparison operator specified in a selection clause. We will show that no sensitive information is leaked through this conversion. Next we discuss the client/server protocols of the various operators.

5.1 Multiplication ($\times$)

We first discuss the EE and the EC modes of "$\times$".

[EE Mode] Consider two sensitive columns A and B of a table T whose column keys are $ck_A = \langle m_A, x_A \rangle$ and $ck_B = \langle m_B, x_B \rangle$, respectively. Let $C = A \times B$ be the output column with column key $ck_C = \langle m_C, x_C \rangle$. For a row t, let r be its row-id and let a, b and c be the values of A, B, C in row t, respectively. Our objective is to derive (1) the column key ck_C and (2) the encrypted value c_e of c such that $[\![c]\!] = [\![a]\!] \cdot [\![b]\!]$.

To achieve that, the client protocol sets $ck_C = \langle m_C, x_C \rangle = \langle m_A m_B, x_A + x_B \rangle$ and the server protocol computes $c_e = a_e \cdot b_e$ for each row. By Equation (2),

$$c_k = m_C \cdot g^{r x_C} = m_A \cdot m_B \cdot g^{r(x_A + x_B)} = a_k b_k \pmod{n}. \quad (8)$$

By Equations (3), (4), (8) we have, in modular n,

$$[\![c]\!] = c_e c_k = a_e b_e c_k = [\![a]\!] a_k^{-1} [\![b]\!] b_k^{-1} a_k b_k = [\![a]\!][\![b]\!].$$

The protocol is thus correct. Note that the client layer sends a message to the server layer instructing it to compute $c_e =$

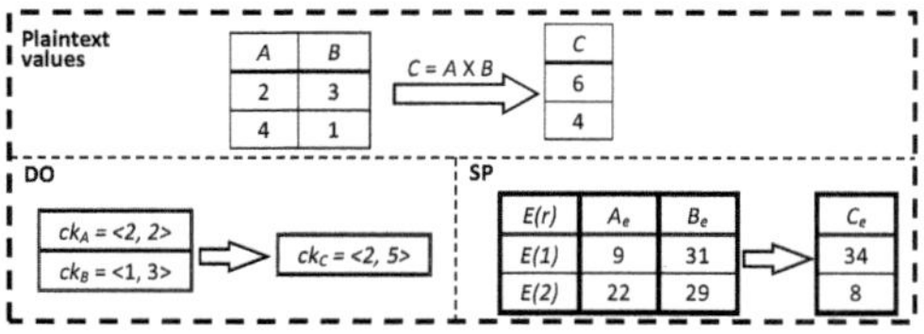

Figure 4: $C = A \times B$ ($g = 2$, $n = 35$).

$a_e \cdot b_e$ for each row in table T. The message contains no information of any keys. The protocol is thus secure. Figure 4 illustrates the protocol: Given $ck_A = \langle 2, 2\rangle$, $ck_B = \langle 1, 3\rangle$, the client protocol computes $ck_C = \langle 2 \times 1, 2 + 3\rangle = \langle 2, 5\rangle$. The server protocol computes $a_e \times b_e \bmod n$ for each row, e.g., the second row gives $22 \times 29 \bmod 35 = 8$.

[EC Mode] We compute $C = A \times p$ for a column A and a constant p. In this case, the client protocol sets $ck_C = \langle pm_A, x_A\rangle$ and the server protocol sets $c_e = a_e$ for each row in the table. In fact, those c_e's need not be materialized. Instead, a reference indicating that $C_e = A_e$ suffices. (See Figure 3.) Note that $c_k = p \cdot m_A g^{rx_A} = p \cdot a_k$. Hence,

$$[\![c]\!] = c_e c_k = a_e c_k = [\![a]\!] a_k^{-1} c_k = [\![a]\!] a_k^{-1} \cdot p \cdot a_k = p[\![a]\!].$$

The protocol is thus correct. Also, no messages with any key information are sent to the server layer. The protocol is thus secure.

5.2 Key Update

Before we continue with other secure operators, let us first discuss a helper operator called *key update*, denoted by κ. The operator, written as, $\kappa(A, \langle m_C, x_C\rangle)$ takes two operands: a column A and a *target column key* $\langle m_C, x_C\rangle$. The output of κ is a column C such that:

(1) C and A have the same plaintext values. That is, for each row-id r, $[\![c]\!] = [\![a]\!]$ where c and a are the values of C and A in row r, respectively.

(2) The column key of C is given by the specified target, i.e, $ck_C = \langle m_C, x_C\rangle$.

Recall that a column S (of plaintext $[\![s]\!] = 1$) is added to each table. By Equation 3, we have $s_e = s_k^{-1}$. Given the column key of S ($ck_S = \langle m_S, x_S\rangle$), to execute key update, the client protocol computes two numbers p, q:

$$p = x_S^{-1}(x_C - x_A) \bmod \phi(n); \quad q = m_A m_S^p m_C^{-1} \bmod n \qquad (9)$$

and sends them to the server layer. The server protocol then computes, for each row (of row-id) r, the encrypted value of C by

$$c_e = q \cdot a_e \cdot s_e^p. \qquad (10)$$

To prove the correctness of the protocols, we need to show that $[\![c]\!] = [\![a]\!]$ given the column key $ck_C = \langle m_C, x_C\rangle$. In modular arithmetic, we have,

$$\begin{aligned}
[\![c]\!] = c_e c_k &= m_A \cdot m_S^p \cdot m_C^{-1} \cdot a_e \cdot s_e^p \cdot m_C \cdot g^{rx_C} && \text{by (2, 4, 9, 10)}\\
&= m_A \cdot m_S^p \cdot a_e \cdot (s_k^{-1})^p \cdot g^{rx_C} && \because s_e = s_k^{-1}\\
&= m_A \cdot m_S^p \cdot a_e \cdot ((m_S \cdot g^{rx_S})^{-1})^p \cdot g^{rx_C} && \text{by (2)}\\
&= m_A \cdot a_e \cdot (g^{r \cdot x_S \cdot x_S^{-1} \cdot (x_C - x_A)})^{-1} \cdot g^{rx_C} && \text{by (9)}\\
&= a_e \cdot (m_A \cdot g^{rx_A}) = [\![a]\!] && \text{by (2), (4).}
\end{aligned}$$

Note that the client layer sends a message with the values of p and q to the server layer. Since the two numbers are derived from A, C, and S's column keys, we need to ensure that an attacker knowing p and q cannot deduce any key information. In particular, we prove the following properties:

PROPERTY 3. *An attacker with DB knowledge cannot recover ck_A or ck_S even if he observes p, q and knows ck_C.*

PROPERTY 4. *An attacker with DB knowledge cannot recover ck_C or ck_S even if he observes p, q and knows ck_A.*

Due to space limitation, readers are referred to [29] for the proofs. Properties 3 and 4 will be used to prove the security of other operators to be discussed next.

5.3 Addition/Subtraction (+/−)

We describe the protocol for "+". The protocol for "−" is very similar so it is omitted.

[EE Mode] Given two sensitive columns A and B, we compute a column $C = A + B$. Consider a row for which the (plaintext value, item key) of A, B, C are ($[\![a]\!]$, a_k), ($[\![b]\!]$, b_k), ($[\![c]\!]$, c_k), respectively. Our objective is to encrypt $[\![c]\!] = [\![a]\!] + [\![b]\!]$ without revealing $[\![a]\!]$ or $[\![b]\!]$. We observe that if $a_k = b_k = c_k = k$ (i.e., if all the values are associated with the same item key k), then our encryption function is *additive isomorphic*, i.e.,

$$\begin{aligned}
a_e + b_e &= \mathcal{E}([\![a]\!], k) + \mathcal{E}([\![b]\!], k) = [\![a]\!]k^{-1} + [\![b]\!]k^{-1}\\
&= ([\![a]\!] + [\![b]\!])k^{-1} = \mathcal{E}([\![a]\!] + [\![b]\!], k) \pmod n.
\end{aligned}$$

Hence to implement "+", the server protocol only needs to set $c_e = a_e + b_e$ for each row in the table because then $c_e = \mathcal{E}([\![a]\!] + [\![b]\!], k)$, which is the desired encrypted value of $[\![c]\!]$. By giving A, B, C the same column key, their item keys in the same row will be the same. This can be achieved by applying key update on the columns.

Specifically, to compute $C = A + B$, the client protocol first generates a column key $ck_C = \langle m_C, x_C\rangle$. Then it executes the protocol of key update to get $A' = \kappa(A, \langle m_C, x_C\rangle)$ and $B' = \kappa(B, \langle m_C, x_C\rangle)$. This gives $A' = A$, $B' = B$, and the columns keys of A', B', C are all ck_C. After that, the client layer sends a message to the server layer instructing it to add the encrypted values of A' and B' to get the encrypted values of C, i.e., $c_e = a'_e + b'_e$.

In executing the protocol, two key updates are done. Although each execution of key update is secure, two related key updates may reveal more information than two independent ones. Here, we show that even an attacker relates the key updates, he cannot obtain any information of the keys.

First, an attacker may observe the (p, q) pair (see Equation 9) submitted to the server layer in a key update operation. Let (p_A, q_A) and (p_B, q_B) be the pairs for executing κ on A and on B, respectively. From Equation 9 we have,

$$\begin{aligned}
& x_A + p_A x_S = x_C; \quad x_B + p_B x_S = x_C && \pmod{\phi(n)},\\
\Rightarrow\ & x_A = x_B + (p_B - p_A) x_S && \pmod{\phi(n)},\\
\Rightarrow\ & x_A = x_B + p_{AB} \cdot x_S && \pmod{\phi(n)},
\end{aligned}$$

where $p_{AB} = p_B - p_A$. The attacker can thus relate x_A, x_B and x_S, which are parts of A, B, S's column keys. Suppose there are h columns $A_1, \ldots, A_h$ of a table on which we may apply the addition operator. Let $x_1, \ldots, x_h$ be the "x parts" of these columns' column keys (as in $ck_{A_i} = \langle m_i, x_i\rangle$). Over time, an attacker may collect equations of the form $x_i = x_j + p_{ij} \cdot x_S \pmod{\phi(n)}$, for which p_{ij}'s are known. The following theorem says that it is infeasible to recover the keys (x_i's, x_S) from the system of linear equations.

THEOREM 1. *Given a set of $h{+}1$ variables $\{x_1, x_2, \ldots, x_h\}$ and x_S, and a system of equations of the form $x_i = x_j + p_{ij} \cdot x_S \pmod{\phi(n)}$ with known $p'_{ij}s$, there are at least $\phi(n)$*

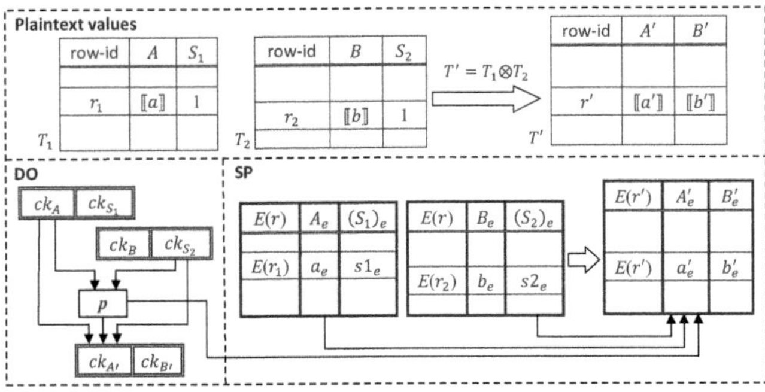

Figure 5: $T' = T_1 \otimes T_2$

solutions of the variables that satisfy the system of equations.

Since $\phi(n)$ is a 1024-bit number, the solution space is huge. The attacker therefore cannot recover the "x parts" of the column keys. We can also prove that relating q_A and q_B does not allow the attacker to recover the "m parts" of the column keys either. Our protocol is thus safe. Due to space limitation, readers are referred to [29] for the proofs.

[EC Mode] Computing $C = A+u$, where u is a constant, can be done by computing $A + (S \times u)$, where S is the constant column (of 1's) of the table. This is done by first executing an EC multiplication followed by an EE addition.

5.4 Comparison ($=$ / $>$)

We consider two comparison operators, namely, equality ($=$) and ordering ($>$). Given two columns A and B, the objective is to compute a *plaintext* column C such that, for each row, $c = 1$ if the comparison is "true" and $c = 0$ otherwise. Note that we do not encrypt the output column C because the comparison operators are mostly used in selection clauses and the server layer needs to know the truth value of each selection in processing queries.

To compute C, our protocol first computes $Z = R \times (A - B)$, where R is the random column of the table Next, we perform a key update to obtain $Z' = \kappa(Z, \langle 1, 0\rangle)$. Hence, Z' is equal to Z but with the column key $ck_{Z'} = \langle 1, 0\rangle$. By Property 2, the plaintext values of Z' are all revealed to the server. Hence, the server observes the plain values of $R \times (A - B)$. Note that the values of $A - B$ are randomized by the column R, the server therefore cannot observe $A - B$. On the other hand, the server protocol can deduce, for each row, (1) if $z' = 0$, then $[\![a]\!] = [\![b]\!]$, and (2) if z' is positive, then $[\![a]\!] > [\![b]\!]$. With these observations, the server protocol can construct the plain output column C accordingly.

5.5 Projection (π)

The projection operator does not manipulate values in a table. It is supported by instructing the server protocol to return the desired encrypted columns. The client protocol then decrypts the values with its column keys using Eq. 4.

5.6 Cartesian Product ($\otimes$) and Joins ($\bowtie$)

We compute the Cartesian product $T' = T_1 \otimes T_2$ of two tables T_1 and T_2. Readers are referred to Figure 5, which illustrates Cartesian product and the various symbols we use in the following discussion. For simplicity, let us assume that T_1 has only one column A and T_2 has only one column B. (Additional columns can be handled similarly.) Recall that a constant column S is added to each table. Let S_1 and S_2 be the constant columns of T_1 and T_2, respectively. Consider a row in Table T_1 with row-id r_1 and a row in Table T_2 with row-id r_2. Let the values of A and B in these rows be $[\![a]\!]$ and $[\![b]\!]$, respectively. Furthermore, let (plaintext, item key, encrypted value) of S_1 in row r_1 and those of S_2 in row r_2 be $([\![s1]\!], s1_k, s1_e)$ and $([\![s2]\!], s2_k, s2_e)$, respectively. Finally, recall that S_1 and S_2 are columns of 1's. So,

$$[\![s1]\!] = [\![s2]\!] = 1. \tag{11}$$

The output of "$\otimes$" is a table T' with two columns A' and B'. For each pair of rows ($r_1 \in T_1$, $r_2 \in T_2$), a row r' in T' is created. Let the values of A' and B' in row r' be $[\![a']\!]$ and $[\![b']\!]$. We want $[\![a']\!] = [\![a]\!]$ and $[\![b']\!] = [\![b]\!]$.

Recall that tables are encrypted using secret sharing, our protocol needs to compute T' in our secret-sharing format based on the column keys, the (encrypted) row-ids, and the encrypted column values of T_1 and T_2. We illustrate the computation by describing the client and server protocols for computing the followings:

(1) **[The column key of A']**. Given the column keys $ck_A = \langle m_A, x_A\rangle$ and $ck_{S_2} = \langle m_{S_2}, x_{S_2}\rangle$, the client protocol first computes $p = x_{S_2}^{-1} x_A \bmod \phi(n)$. It then sets

$$ck_{A'} = \langle m_{A'}, x_{A'}\rangle = \langle m_A (m_{S_2})^p, x_A\rangle. \tag{12}$$

(2) **[The encrypted row-id of r']**. The server protocol sets $E(r') = E(r_1) + E(r_2)$. Recall that row-ids are encrypted using SIES (see Section 4), which is additive homomorphic:

$$E(r') = E(r_1) + E(r_2) = E(r_1 + r_2). \quad \text{So,} \quad r' = r_1 + r_2. \tag{13}$$

(3) **[The encrypted value a'_e of $[\![a']\!]$]**. The client protocol sends p to the server protocol, which sets

$$a'_e = a_e \cdot (s2_e)^p. \tag{14}$$

By symmetry, other computations, such as the column key of B' and the encrypted values of B' can be similarly done.

To prove that the protocol is correct, we need to show that $[\![a']\!] = [\![a]\!]$. Let a'_k be the item key of a'. We have, in modular arithmetic,

$$\begin{aligned}
a'_k &= gen(r', ck_{A'}) = gen(r', \langle m_A (m_{S_2})^p, x_A\rangle) && \text{(by (12))}\\
&= m_A (m_{S_2})^p g^{r' \cdot x_A} && \text{(by (2))}\\
[\![a']\!] = a'_e a'_k &= (a_e (s2_e)^p) \left(m_A (m_{S_2})^p g^{(r_1+r_2)x_A}\right) && \text{(by (4, 13, 14))}\\
&= (a_e (s2_e)^p) \left(m_A (m_{S_2})^p g^{r_1 x_A + r_2 p x_{S_2}}\right) && (\because p = x_{S_2}^{-1} x_A)\\
&= (m_A g^{r_1 x_A} a_e) \left((m_{S_2})^p g^{r_2 p x_{S_2}} (s2_e)^p\right) &&\\
&= (a_k a_e)(s2_k s2_e)^p && \text{(by (2))}\\
&= [\![a]\!][\![s2]\!]^p = [\![a]\!] 1^p = [\![a]\!]. && \text{(by (11))}
\end{aligned}$$

Note that the client protocol sends $p = (x_{S_2})^{-1} x_A$ to the server protocol. This information is similar to that sent in the key update operation (see Equation 9). Readers are referred to [29] for the proof that the protocol for $\otimes$ is safe. Joins are basically Cartesian product with selection. Therefore, joins with selection clauses that are expressible with our arithmetic and comparison operators are supported.

5.7 Sum, Count, Average and Group-By

Consider a column A of N values a_1, ..., a_N. We want to compute the sum, $\sigma_A = \sum_{i=1}^{N} [\![a_i]\!]$ from encrypted values.

To do so, we generate a random number m_Z and transform A into a column Z by a key update: $Z = \kappa(A, \langle m_Z, 0\rangle)$.

We have the plain values of Z equal to those of A and the column key of Z is $ck_Z = \langle m_Z, 0\rangle$. Let the values in Z be $z_1, \ldots, z_N$. By Property 1, all z_i's share the same item key m_Z. Let σ_Z be the sum of the encrypted values of column Z, we have,

$$\sigma_Z = \sum_{i=1}^{N}(z_i)_e = \sum_{i=1}^{N}(\mathcal{E}([\![z_i]\!], m_Z) = \sum_{i=1}^{N}([\![z_i]\!](m_Z)^{-1})$$
$$= (m_Z)^{-1}\sum_{i=1}^{N}[\![z_i]\!] = (m_Z)^{-1}\sum_{i=1}^{N}[\![a_i]\!] = (m_Z)^{-1}\sigma_A. \quad (15)$$

Hence, $\sigma_A = m_Z \cdot \sigma_Z$. In other words, to compute the sum, the server protocol adds all encrypted values of column Z and returns that sum (σ_Z) to the client protocol, which "decrypts" the value by multiplying it with the secretly generated m_Z.

The COUNT operator can be implemented by having a server protocol that counts the number of rows of a column. With SUM and COUNT, Average can be trivially done.

Group-By can be done by using the column Z. Since values in Z share the same item keys, two values $[\![z_i]\!]$, $[\![z_j]\!]$ are the same if their encrypted values are the same (i.e., if $(z_i)_e = (z_j)_e$). By inspecting the encrypted values of Z, the server can partition the rows of A into groups such that the rows in each group share the same value. Due to space limitation, we leave the proof that attackers cannot recover m_Z (and thus the aggregate operators are secure) in [29].

5.8 EP Mode of operations

Our secure operators can be applied to a mix of sensitive and non-sensitive columns. This is because, by Property 2, we can treat a plain column A as a sensitive one with the column key $\langle 1, 0\rangle$. However, in our proofs of operators' security, we assumed that the server does not know the column keys of the operands. Having the secure operator operates on a column with known column key ($\langle 1, 0\rangle$) could invalidate our security proofs. To avoid this problem, whenever a plain column A is involved in any secure operation, we first apply a key update on A and transform it into a column $C = \kappa(A, ck_C)$, where $ck_C = \langle m_C, x_C\rangle$ is a secret column key that the client layer picks. Any subsequent operations on A will be applied on C instead. Note that by Property 4, even if an attacker knows $ck_A = \langle 1, 0\rangle$, he cannot deduce ck_C or any other column keys by observing the key update messagesl. Hence, subsequent operators on C are secure.

5.9 Optimization

We end this section with a brief note on performance optimization. First, we note that our encrypt/decrypt functions involve computing modular exponentials, which are typically expensive. There are various methods to speed up such computation, e.g., by using Garner's algorithm [19]. Second, there are studies on secure indexing techniques, e.g., [17]. The general idea is to partition the range of a column's values into coarse ranges. Tuples whose values fall into the same range are grouped together. Such an index helps filter away irrelevant rows (those whose values do not fall in the desired ranges) of a query. Our study is orthogonal to secure indexing. In particular, index filtering can be applied before we process a query using our secure operators.

6. EXPERIMENT

We evaluate the performance of SDB by conducting experiments on our prototype. The prototype was built based on the architecture shown in Figure 1. We use MySQL 5.6.10 as the underlying DBMS. The client layer is running on one machine while the server layer is running on a cluster of 8 machines. So, the server has 8 times more computing power than the client. Each machine has an Intel Core i7-3770 CPU@3.4GHz with 16GB RAM and is running Ubuntu. Both layers are written in C++ using the GMP library[6].

Our experiment is designed to address two questions. First, a focus of SDB is data interoperability. So, $\mathcal{Q}1$: *"Just how important it is for the secure database operators to be data interoperable in a cloud database environment?"* Second, protecting sensitive data by means of encryption always incurs overheads, e.g., ciphertext is typically larger than plaintext. Also, as we mentioned in the introduction, processing data using a fully homomorphic encryption scheme (to achieve data interoperability) is many orders of magnitude slower than plaintext processing, which makes it infeasible for data-intensive applications. So, $\mathcal{Q}2$: *"Is our SDB approach practical in terms of query-processing efficiency?"*

We answer $\mathcal{Q}1$ by comparing the performance of SDB with the *Decrypt-Before-Query* (DBQ) model and MONOMI [25] (Section 6.1). Both DBQ and MONOMI are implemented on the same platform as that of SDB. In particular, they use the same machine configurations for the client and the server as those of SDB, as well as the same DBMS for storing data. For DBQ, since no computation on encrypted data is carried out by the SP, sensitive data is encrypted using RSA encryption. For MONOMI, data is encrypted using various encryption schemes to support different types of operations (see [25]). For DBQ, the server only serves to retrieve relevant (encrypted) columns from the DBMS and to ship them back to the client, which decrypts the data and processes the query to obtain results by itself. CryptDB [22] and ODB [15, 16], for example, have to resort to the DBQ model to process complex queries unless some extensive precomputation is done (see Section 2). MONOMI adopts a split client/server execution approach. The SP computes as much as possible of the query. For the parts that can't be computed by the SP, they will be passed to the DO. In this case, the DO decrypts all the intermediate results and continue the query computation on plain values. We implemented MONOMI's protocols as detailed in [25].

To answer $\mathcal{Q}2$, we evaluate SDB using the TPC-H benchmark and compare SDB's performance against pure plaintext processing as a reference (Section 6.2). The TPC-H benchmark queries are mostly aggregation queries. They thus amplify the issue of data-intensive query processing. The benchmark is therefore a good stress test of our approach.

6.1 Comparing SDB, DBQ and MONOMI

We compare SDB with an implementation of the DBQ model (or simply DBQ) and MONOMI database (denoted as MDB) using a simple synthetic dataset on which a range of queries are executed. The dataset is a table T with three sensitive columns A, B, C. The values in each column are integers randomly generated with a uniform distribution over

[6]The GNU Multiple Precision Arithmetic Library. http://gmplib.org

the range [0, 1M]. We execute 4 queries which cover the various secure operators of SDB:
[Range]: SELECT A, B, C from T WHERE $A + B < q$.
[Count]: SELECT COUNT(*) from T WHERE $A+B < q$.
[Sum]: SELECT SUM($A * B$) from T WHERE $A + B < q$.
[Join]: SELECT SUM($t_1.B * t_2.A$) FROM T as t_1, T as t_2 WHERE $t1.A = t2.B$.

The parameter q controls the queries' *selectivity*. A smaller q gives a more selective query and a smaller query result. In our baseline setting, we have q set to a value such that the selection clauses of the range, count, sum queries return 1% of the table's rows. All the implemented methods employ the domain partitioning indexing technique [17] mentioned in Section 5.9. Specifically, each domain is divided into 50 equal-sized partitions. The index helps us reduce the amount of data retrieved from the DBMS. For example, for the range query, the index filters away any rows in T whose A or B values are larger than q because these rows are guaranteed to fail the selection criterion.

We compare the execution times of SDB, DBQ and MDB. The cost of each is divided into three components: (1) DB Access: the time taken by the DBMS in processing queries and retrieving data for the server layer. (2) Server cost: the time taken by the server layer in executing server protocols. (3) Client cost: the time taken by the client layer in executing client protocols, result decryption and any post-decryption processing. Note that under the DBQ model, there are no secret-sharing protocols and the client computes query results by itself. So, for DBQ, the server cost is null and the client cost includes those for data decryption and query execution on plain data. With encrypted data processing, the server cost and the client cost are mostly dominated by modular arithmetic computation.

Figure 6 shows the results for the four queries as the table size increases from 100K to 500K rows. Execution times are shown as stacked bars, each with three components (although in most cases, one component dominates all others in the figures shown).

From Figure 6, we make a few observations. (1) DB access times are very small (almost unnoticeable in the figures). This is because with a 1% selectivity, the secure index is quite effective in filtering away many irrelevant rows. Data accesses by the DBMS are thus efficient. (2) The server cost of MDB is much lower than that of SDB. There are two reasons for that: (a) For MDB, the server is only computing parts of a query. For example, consider the range query '$A + B < q$'. The SP can only perform the addition. To complete the query, the encrypted results of the addition operation have to be transferred to the client, which will decrypt the results and evaluate the comparison operation. On the other hand, for SDB, the SP evaluates the query completely. (b) MDB employs various homomorphic encryption schemes that allow computation on encrypted data to be done more efficiently. On the other hand, SDB uses secret sharing to encrypt data. Computation based on secret sharing encryption is generally slower than other homomorphic schemes. (3) The client cost of MDB is much higher than that of SDB for the first three queries. This is because much of the computation involved in evaluating a query has to be carried out by the client under MDB. We observe that the client cost of MDB is even higher than that of DBQ. This is because some of the homomorphic encryption functions, e.g., Paillier cryptosystem employed by MDB are more expensive to decrypt than the simple RSA encryption we used for DBQ. (4) For SDB, the cost is predominately server cost (about 93% of total execution time). This is because queries are computed by the server protocols, which deal with the bulk of the data. The client, on the other hand, only has to decrypt the result. (5) For the join query, MDB and SDB show comparable total costs. Moreover, MDB's client cost is lower than that of DBQ, which is in contrast to the results of the first three queries. This is because the join query requires only a single operation (equality comparison), which can be handled efficiently by the server under MDB. The client only has to decrypt the join result. While most of that cost for MDB is on the client side, for SDB, it is the server that bears most of the cost. In a cloud database environment, however, our objective is to minimize the client cost. So, based on the experimental results, we see that SDB compares very favorably against DBQ and MDB.

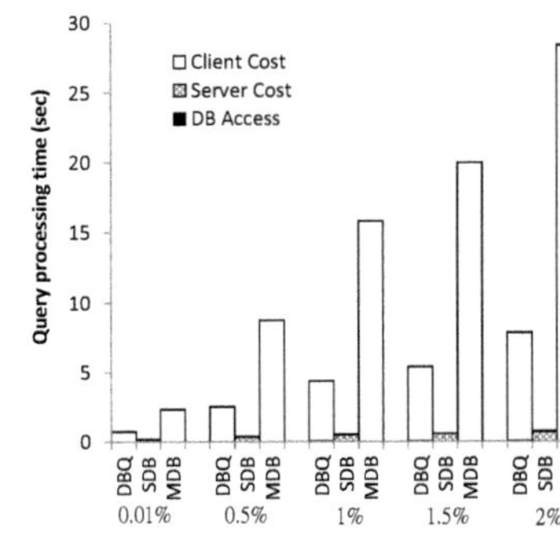

Figure 7: Execution times vs. selectivity

Figure 7 shows the execution times of SDB, DBQ and MDB for the range query as we change the selectivity of the query (by adjusting the parameter q) from 0.01% (very selective) to 2% (less selective). The relative costs of the three components remain similar to those we have observed in Figure 6. In particular, SDB gives much smaller query execution times and that most of the costs under SDB are borne by the server.

6.2 Benchmark

Data processing on encrypted data in intrinsically slower than plaintext processing. After all, ciphertext is generally bigger than plain values. Fully homomorphic encryption (FHE), which supports full-fledged data interoperability, is of theoretical interest only because there are no practically efficient implementations of it. With SDB, we aim at designing a data interoperable system that is practically efficient. The tradeoff is that we have to impose certain restrictions on the data model (SDB is limited to values of integral domains) and on the operators (SDB is limited to operators with integral outputs). In this section, we look at how SDB performs in practice.

We apply the TPC-H benchmark[7] on SDB. We use the sample database of the benchmark at scale 1, which contains 8 tables. The database size is around 1GB, which contains details of suppliers, customers, and orders. There are 22 decision-support queries named Q1 to Q22. Most of these queries involve multiple operators and these queries can be answered completely by the server only if those operators

[7]http://www.tpc.org/tpch/

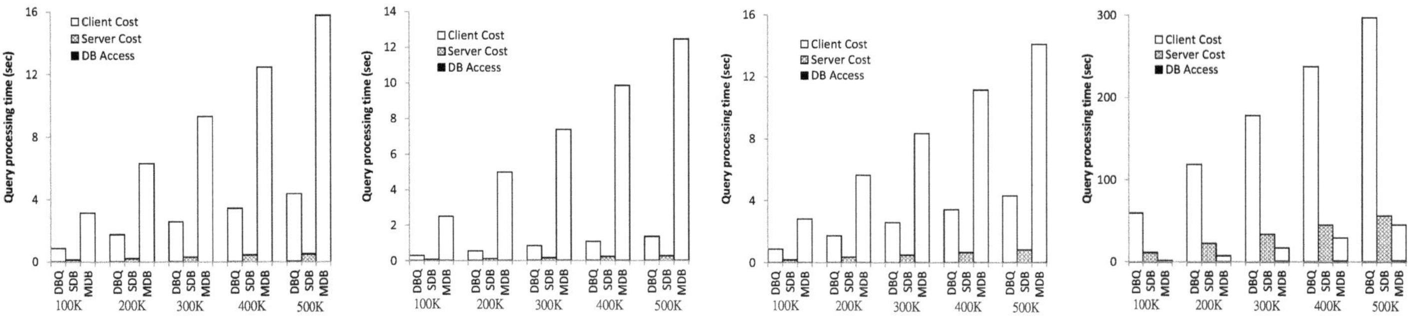

(a) Range (b) Count (c) Sum (d) Join

Figure 6: Execution times of SDB and DBQ for the 4 sample queries

are data interoperable. For example, one query requires the evaluation of an expression $A \times (1 - B)$ on columns A, B. This requires multiplication be done on the output of a subtraction. Note that many of the TPC-H queries are aggregate queries. They are thus highly data-intensive. In this experiment, secure index is not applied. We remark that all queries in the benchmark can be implemented by SDB's secure operators.

In practice, not all data is sensitive. We inspected the benchmark data and identified 7 columns as sensitive information. These columns contain information on account balances, pricings, or orders[8]. The 7 columns are encrypted using our secret-sharing scheme while other columns are stored as plaintext. Among the 22 queries, 6 of them (Q4, Q11, Q12, Q13, Q16, Q21) do not involve any sensitive columns. These 6 queries can be handled directly by the DBMS (running MySQL) on plaintext. So, we omit them in the experiment.

We evaluate SDB by executing the other 16 queries on our prototype. SDB analyzes a query and "pushes" as much work as possible to the DBMS, as long as the work does not involve sensitive data. For example, consider the query Q: "SELECT $A \times B$ ... WHERE $C > D$". If columns C and D are not sensitive, then the selection can be done by the DBMS. The server protocol has to compute $A \times B$ only for those rows that satisfy the selection clause.

The execution time of SDB (T_{SDB}) for each query is noted. We then execute the queries on the DBMS directly with all columns stored as plaintext data, bypassing all the secure operator protocols. The execution time under this scenario (T_{DBMS}) for each query is also noted. The ratio $\alpha = T_{SDB}/T_{DBMS}$ captures the *slow-down* of SDB compared with plaintext processing if that were performed by the client itself. The larger α is, the higher is the price we pay for providing data security on a cloud database.

Table 2 shows T_{DBMS} for all 16 queries tested. Figure 8 shows the α ratios of the queries. Again the bars are shown as stacked bars with the three components of execution times displayed.

From Figure 8, we see that α is below 5 for 11 out of the 16 queries. The worst slow-down is observed in Q18, which is about 23. Furthermore, we observe that: (1) For some queries (e.g., Q5, Q19), the execution times are dominated by DB Access times, and these queries generally have small slow-downs. We find that the selection clauses of these queries are mostly on non-sensitive columns. As we have discussed, SDB pushes these (non-sensitive) selections to the DBMS. In these cases, the DBMS returns a small set of relevant rows, which are further processed by the secure server protocols (e.g., to compute a SUM over a sensitive column). Since the sets of rows processed by secure protocols in these queries are small, the server costs are relatively small. (2) For some queries (e.g. Q1, Q18), the server costs are very significant. These cases are opposite to those discussed in observation (1). They tend to have selection clauses that involve mostly sensitive columns. In these cases, the DBMS cannot perform effective filtering. Instead, all rows of relevant columns have to be retrieved and submitted to the server layer by which the secure protocols are executed. This leads to a high server cost. (3) For all 16 queries, the client costs are minimal. This is because the SP takes care of most of the query processing. The client protocols only need to manipulate column keys and to decrypt small summarized results computed by the server.

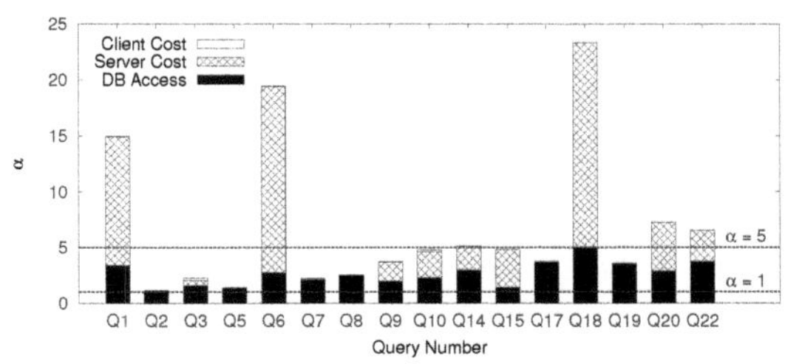

Figure 8: α of 16 TPC-H queries

7. CONCLUSIONS

In this paper we gave a comprehensive description and analysis of SDB, which supports secure query processing on cloud databases with a set of secure, data-interoperable operators. By employing an asymmetric secret-sharing scheme, SDB allows complex SQL queries to be processed entirely by the server (SP). Client's (DO's) computation is mostly limited to result decryption. By experiment, we showed that SDB is applicable to many real-life queries and applications (e.g., the whole TPC-H benchmark can be executed on it). SDB is also practically efficient. This is in sharp contrast to existing FHE schemes, which are many orders of magnitude

[8]The seven columns are S_ACCTBAL, C_ACCTBAL, O_TOTALPRICE, L_QUANTITY, L_EXTENDEDPRICE, L_DISCOUNT, L_TAX.

Q1	Q2	Q3	Q5	Q6	Q7	Q8	Q9	Q10	Q14	Q15	Q17	Q18	Q19	Q20	Q22
5.38	1643.18	10.82	23.58	5.19	9.20	25.18	41.66	7.63	5.51	10.86	13.77	35.71	10.00	11.28	0.27

Table 2: T_{DBMS}. Execution times of 16 TPC-H queries processed on plaintext data (in sec.)

slower than plaintext processing. We believe that the ability of SDB in offloading secure computation to servers represents a significant advancement in secure cloud database systems.

8. REFERENCES

[1] R. Agrawal and J. Kiernan et al. Order-preserving encryption for numeric data. In *SIGMOD*, 2004.

[2] A. Arasu et al. Secure database-as-a-service with cipherbase. In *SIGMOD*, 2013.

[3] S. Bajaj et al. Trusteddb: a trusted hardware based database with privacy and data confidentiality. In *SIGMOD*, 2011.

[4] D. Bogdanov et al. A universal toolkit for cryptographically secure privacy-preserving data mining. In *PAISI*, 2012.

[5] A. Boldyreva et al. Order-preserving encryption revisited: Improved security analysis and alternative solutions. In *CRYPTO*, 2011.

[6] D. Boneh et al. Public key encryption with keyword search. In *EUROCRYPT*, 2004.

[7] E. Damiani et al. Balancing confidentiality and efficiency in untrusted relational dbmss. In *CCS*, 2003.

[8] S. Das and D. Agrawal et al. Elastras: An elastic transactional data store in the cloud. *CoRR*, 2010.

[9] S. Das, V. Narasayya, and F. Li et al. CPU sharing techniques for performance isolation in multi-tenant relational database-as-a-service. *PVLDB*, 2014.

[10] A. J. Elmore, S. Das, D. Agrawal, and A. El Abbadi. Zephyr: live migration in shared nothing databases for elastic cloud platforms. In *SIGMOD*, 2011.

[11] F. Emekçi, D. Agrawal, and A. El Abbadi. Privacy preserving query processing using third parties. In *ICDE*, 2006.

[12] C. Gentry. Fully homomorphic encryption using ideal lattices. In *STOC*, 2009.

[13] C. Gentry et al. Fully homomorphic encryption with polylog overhead. In *EUROCRYPT*, 2012.

[14] O. Goldreich, S. Micali, and A. Wigderson. How to play any mental game. In *STOC*, 1987.

[15] H. Hacigümüs, S. Mehrotra, and B. R. Iyer. Providing database as a service. In *ICDE*, 2002.

[16] H. Hacigümüs et al.and B. R. Iyer, C. Li, and S. Mehrotra. Executing sql over encrypted data in the database-service-provider model. In *SIGMOD*, 2002.

[17] B. Hore, S. Mehrotra, and G. Tsudik. A privacy preserving index for range queries. In *VLDB*, 2004.

[18] M. Kantarcioglu and C. Chris. Privacy-preserving distributed mining of association rules on horizontally partitioned data. *TKDE*, 2004.

[19] A. J. Menezes, P. C. Oorschot, and S. A. Vanstone. *Handbook of Applied Cryptography*. CRC Press, 1996.

[20] P. Paillier. Public-key cryptosystems based on composite degree residuosity classes. In *EUROCRYPT*, 1999.

[21] S. Papadopoulos et al. Secure and efficient in-network processing of exact sum queries. In *ICDE*, 2011.

[22] R. A. Popa et al. Cryptdb: processing queries on an encrypted database. *CACM*, 2012.

[23] R. L. Rivest et al.and A. Shamir and L. M. Adleman. A method for obtaining digital signatures and public-key cryptosystems. *CACM*, 1978.

[24] A. Soror et al. Automatic virtual machine configuration for database workloads. In *SIGMOD*, 2008.

[25] S. Tu and M. F. Kaashoek et al. Processing analytical queries over encrypted data. In *PVLDB*, 2013.

[26] J. Vaidya et al. Secure set intersection cardinality with application to association rule mining. *JCS*, 2005.

[27] S. Wang, D. Agrawal, and A. El Abbadi. A comprehensive framework for secure query processing on relational data in the cloud. In *SDM*, 2011.

[28] P. Wong, Z. He, and E. Lo. Parallel analytics as a service. In *SIGMOD*, 2013.

[29] W. K. Wong et al. Secure query processing with data interoperability in a cloud database environment. Technical Report TR-2014-03, Department of Computer Science, University of Hong Kong, 2014.

[30] A. C. Yao. Protocols for secure computations (extended abstract). In *FOCS*, 1982.

APPENDIX

We give outlines of proofs that SDB is secure against both DB+CPA and DB+QR threats. A complete formal mathematical proof that SDB is secure is given in [29].

A. DB+CPA THREAT

We show that our encryption scheme can be reduced to RSA. Specifically, we show that if an attacker can recover the keys in the DO's keystore, the attacker can break RSA to recover RSA's keys. Since RSA has been proven secure against DB+CPA attacks, so is SDB.

B. DB+QR THREAT

To show that our system is secure against DB+QR threat, we need to show that any composition of operators is secure. This is done in two steps. First, we show that the information revealed by each operator can be bounded using the simulation technique employed in secure multiparty computation [26, 18]. Then, we show that the union of all the information revealed by the operators cannot help the attacker to recover the column keys stored at the DO. In particular, the attacker can use the above revealed information to set up a system of linear equations with the column keys being the variables. However, we show that there are at least $\phi(\phi(n))$ solutions, i.e., column keys, satisfying the system of equations, where ϕ is Euler's totient function[9]. In our system, $\phi(\phi(n))$ is at least 680-bits. The solution space is too big for an attacker to recover the true column keys.

[9]Euler's totient function $\phi(x)$ is the number of positive integers $\leq x$ that are co-prime with x.

Are We Experiencing a Big Data Bubble?

Fatma Özcan
IBM Almaden Research Center
San Jose, CA
fozcan@us.ibm.com

Nesime Tatbul
Intel Labs and MIT
Cambridge, MA
tatbul@csail.mit.edu

Daniel J. Abadi
Yale University
New Haven, CT
dna@cs.yale.edu

Marcel Kornacker
Cloudera
San Francisco, CA
marcel@cloudera.com

C Mohan
IBM Almaden Research Center
San Jose, CA
cmohan@us.ibm.com

Karthik Ramasamy
Twitter, Inc.
San Francisco, CA
karthik@twitter.com

Janet Wiener
Facebook, Inc.
Menlo Park, CA
jlw@fb.com

Categories and Subject Descriptors

H.4 [**Database Management**]: Systems

1. INTRODUCTION

Over the last decade, the database field has seen resurgence with the big data wave. Accelerated increase in data volumes, and modern hardware have been two major factors that brought in significant investment in new database technologies. Our field has benefited from this increased interest and focus. There is now an abundance of NoSQL, NewSQL, and SQL-on-Hadoop systems.

According to nosql-database.org, the list of NoSQL databases [6] has reached 150. Many of these systems claim horizontal scalability, and support for non-relational data. However, this high scalability usually comes at the cost of strong support for ACID transactions. Most of them only provide eventual consistency, or even worse, defer managing transactional semantics to the application layer.

Another important aspect of these NoSQL systems is the lack of declarative query interfaces. Most only support programmable APIs and do not have a query language. While this allows them to support flexible schemas and nested data types easily, it comes at the cost of physical independence and query optimization. Application programmers now have the responsibility to write their own optimized data access plans.

Yet another aspect is their restrictive feature set and specialized domain focus. Most only support object-level put and get interfaces, and have trouble providing even simple grouping and aggregation support. As these systems evolve, the need for more functionality is pushing them to consider providing more traditional database-like features. However, their ad-hoc designs prevent their wider adaptability and extensibility.

It is important to note that NoSQL systems are very popular with application programmers, despite the above-mentioned issues. Because they offer simple to use programmable APIs, flexible schemas, and high scalability. Application programmers can implement, deploy, and scale out their applications very easily and quickly.

NewSQL systems [2, 5] have emerged as a new class of relational database management systems to match the scalable performance of NoSQL systems without giving up ACID guarantees and a SQL-based declarative query interface. They achieve high performance and scalability by offering clean-slate architectural redesigns that take better advantage of modern hardware platforms such as shared-nothing clusters of many-core machines with large or non-volatile in-memory storage.

On the analytics side, MapReduce emerged as the platform for all analytics needs of the enterprise. It even fueled a major controversy about parallel databases. Hive [9] was the first SQL-on-Hadoop solution which provided an SQL-like interface, and used the underlying MapReduce infrastructure for scheduling and data movement. Hadapt [1] tried to take the best of MapReduce and databases for efficient SQL processing over Hadoop data. Over the last year, there was a major shift in SQL-on-Hadoop systems to more database-like architectures, such as Impala [4], Presto [7], and Tajo [8]. There are now even solutions that use existing parallel database technology, such as HAWQ [3].

All these advances prove the importance of the basic principles of database systems, which is the result of several decades of database research. Most of these systems seem to be coming full circle back to core database techniques. Yet, it is also important to note that traditional databases failed to provide the needed features, such as high horizontal scalability and flexible schemas, which fueled the development of these new technologies in the first place.

In this panel, we would like to explore the implications of these systems and the role of database researchers in shaping the next decade of data management solutions.

2. PANEL QUESTIONS

- Are all these systems addressing many niche markets, or is there too much overlap and redundancy?
- Without standard APIs or languages, is it chaos out there? Do we need new standards?
- Did we all give up on declarative languages, query processing and optimization?

SIGMOD'14, June 22–27, 2014, Snowbird, UT, USA.
Copyright 2014 ACM 978-1-4503-2376-5/14/06 ...$15.00.
http://dx.doi.org/10.1145/2588555.2610531.

- Why are so many application developers willing to give up on ACID transactions? Is there something different about modern applications?
- There is a renewed interest in SQL, especially in the enterprise. Is it a sufficiently rich language to support the big data ecosystem, or do we need specialized languages?
- Is there something fundamentally new in these systems, or are we reinventing the wheel?
- What can we learn from NoSQL, NewSQL, and SQL-on-Hadoop systems?
- How will the data management market look like in 5 years? How many of these systems will survive?
- What is the opportunity and the responsibility of database researchers to shape this future?

3. REFERENCES

[1] A. Abouzeid, K. Bajda-Pawlikowski, D. J. Abadi, A. Rasin, and A. Silberschatz. HadoopDB: An Architectural Hybrid of MapReduce and DBMS Technologies for Analytical Workloads. *PVLDB*, 2(1):922–933, 2009.

[2] M. Aslett. How Will the Database Incumbents Respond to NoSQL and NewSQL? The 451 Group, 2011.

[3] Pivotal HAWQ. `http://pivotalhd.docs.gopivotal.com/getting-started/hawq.html`.

[4] Impala. `github.com/cloudera/impala`.

[5] Michael Stonebraker and Samuel Madden and Daniel J. Abadi and Stavros Harizopoulos and Nabil Hachem and Pat Helland. The End of an Architectural Era (It's Time for a Complete Rewrite). In *VLDB*, pages 1150–1160, 2007.

[6] C. Mohan. History Repeats Itself: Sensible and NonsenSQL Aspects of the NoSQL Hoopla. In *EDBT*, 2013.

[7] Presto. `http://prestodb.io/`.

[8] Tajo. `http://tajo.incubator.apache.org/`.

[9] A. Thusoo, J. S. Sarma, N. Jain, Z. Shao, P. Chakka, N. Zhang, S. Anthony, H. Liu, and R. Murthy. Hive - A Petabyte Scale Data Warehouse Using Hadoop. In *ICDE*, pages 996–1005, 2010.

Mining Latent Entity Structures from Massive Unstructured and Interconnected Data

Jiawei Han
Department of Computer Science
University of Illinois at Urbana-Champaign
Urbana, IL, USA
hanj@illinois.edu

Chi Wang
Department of Computer Science
University of Illinois at Urbana-Champaign
Urbana, IL, USA
chiwang1@illinois.edu

ABSTRACT

The "big data" era is characterized by an explosion of information in the form of digital data collections, ranging from scientific knowledge, to social media, news, and everyone's daily life. Examples of such collections include scientific publications, enterprise logs, news articles, social media and general Web pages. Valuable knowledge about multi-typed entities is often hidden in the unstructured or loosely structured but interconnected data. Mining latent structured information around entities uncovers sematic structures from massive unstructured data and hence enables many high-impact applications.

In this tutorial, we summarize the closely related literature in database systems, data mining, Web, information extraction, information retrieval, and natural language processing, overview a spectrum of data-driven methods that extract and infer such latent structures, from an interdisciplinary point of view, and demonstrate how these structures support entity discovery and management, data understanding, and some new database applications. We present three categories of studies: mining conceptual, topical and relational structures. Moreover, we present case studies on real datasets, including research papers, news articles and social networks, and show how interesting and organized knowledge can be discovered by mining latent entity structures from these datasets.

Categories and Subject Descriptors

H.4.0 [**Information Systems**]: General

Keywords

Latent structure; Entity Knowledge Engineering

1. INTRODUCTION

The success of database technology is largely attributed to the efficient and effective management of *structured data*. The construction of a well-structured database is often the premise of subsequent applications. However, the explosion of "big data" poses great challenges on this practice since the real world data are largely unstructured. Thus, it is crucial to uncover latent structures of real-world entities, such as people, locations and organizations, and bring massive unstructured data into better semantic structures. By mining massive unstructured or loosely structured data where the entities occur, one can construct semantically rich structures which reveal the relationships among entities and provide conceptual or topical grouping of them. The uncovered entity relationships and groupings facilitate browsing information and retrieving knowledge from data that are otherwise hard to handle due to the lack of structures.

Example: Latent entity structures in scientific literature and news media. In a bibliographic database like DBLP[1] and PubMed[2], research papers are explicitly linked with authors, venues and terms. Many interesting semantic relationships such as advisor-advisee between authors are hidden in the publication records; moreover, the research topics of authors, venues and terms are also hidden or unorganized, preventing insightful organization of the entities. In news articles, multiple types of entities like people, locations and organizations are involved in many events of different topics. The topics, as well as the entity concepts and relations are buried in the text rather than in the form of relational tuples. In the web scale, it is crucial to mine the entity structures hidden in web pages and tables since they are extensive resources to enrich open-domain knowledge-bases; also, mining the entity structures hihdden in social media will help reorganize scattered information and improve the service for individuals.

This tutorial presents a comprehensive overview of the principles and methods developed for latent entity structure discovery in recent years. The following key issues will be covered: (i) mining latent entity structures for construction of structured databases; (ii) typing entities; (iii) topic modeling with entities; (iv) discovery of hidden relationships among entities; (v) case studies: research publications, news articles and social networks; and (vi) research frontiers on mining latent entity structures.

2. A PRELIMINARY OUTLINE OF THE TUTORIAL

1. Preliminaries on mining latent entity structures

[1] `http://www.informatik.uni-trier.de/`
[2] `http://www.ncbi.nlm.nih.gov/pubmed/`

SIGMOD'14, June 22–27, 2014, Snowbird, UT, USA.
Copyright 2014 ACM 978-1-4503-2376-5/14/06 ...$15.00.
http://dx.doi.org/10.1145/2588555.2588890.

(a) Entity-related services as database applications

(b) Entities in documentary data collections

(c) Latent structures: concepts, topics and relations

2. Mining entity concepts for typing

   (a) Generation of taxonomies in large scale

      i. Taxonomies built from human-curated knowledge-bases: DBpedia, YAGO, WikiTaxonomy

      ii. Taxonomies constructed from free text: Know-ItAll, TextRunner, Probase

   (b) Type entities in text: Wikifier, AIDA, Mention-Rank, MENED

   (c) Type entities in web tables and lists

3. Discovery of topical grouping of entities

   (a) PLSA and LDA: Bag-of-words topic modeling

   (b) CATHY and CATHYHIN: Phrase and entity based topical hierarchy construction

4. Discovery of hidden entity relations

   (a) Patterns, rules and constraints for reasoning

      i. Text and linkage patterns

      ii. Dependency rules and constraints

   (b) Representative mining paradigms

      i. Measuring similarities of relationships

      ii. Classifying or clustering entity relationships

      iii. Slot filling

   (c) Methodologies for dependency modeling

5. Case studies: Mining latent entity structures from research publications, news articles, web pages and online social networks

6. Recent research progress and open problems on mining latent entity structures

   (a) Mining relations and concepts from multiple sources

   (b) Integration of NLP and data mining approaches

Acknowledgments

The work was supported in part by the U.S. Army Research Laboratory under Cooperative Agreement No. W911NF-09-2-0053 (NS-CTA) and the U.S. Army Research Office under Cooperative Agreement No. W911NF-13-1-0193, DTRA, DHS, and U.S. National Science Foundation grants CNS-0931975, IIS-1017362, IIS-1320617, IIS-1354329.

3. REFERENCES

[1] N. Bach and S. Badaskar. A review of relation extraction. *Literature review for Language and Statistics II*, 2007.

[2] K. Bollacker, C. Evans, P. Paritosh, T. Sturge, and J. Taylor. Freebase: A collaboratively created graph database for structuring human knowledge. In *SIGMOD*, 2008.

[3] O. Etzioni, M. Banko, S. Soderland, and D. S. Weld. Open information extraction from the web. *Commun. ACM*, 51(12), Dec. 2008.

[4] J. Hoffart, M. Yosef, I. Bordino, H. Fürstenau, M. Pinkal, M. Spaniol, B. Taneva, S. Thater, and G. Weikum. Robust disambiguation of named entities in text. In *EMNLP*, 2011.

[5] H. Ji and R. Grishman. Knowledge base population: Successful approaches and challenges. In *ACL*, 2011.

[6] H. Kim, X. Ren, Y. Sun, C. Wang, and J. Han. Semantic frame-based document representation for comparable corpora. In *ICDM*, 2013.

[7] R. Li, C. Wang, and K. Chang. User profiling in ego network: An attribute and relationship type co-profiling approach. In *WWW*, 2014.

[8] Y. Li, C. Wang, F. Han, J. Han, D. Roth, and X. Yan. Mining evidences for named entity disambiguation. In *KDD*, 2013.

[9] G. Limaye, S. Sarawagi, and S. Chakrabarti. Annotating and searching web tables using entities, types and relationships. *Proceedings of the VLDB Endowment*, 3(1-2):1338–1347, 2010.

[10] S. P. Ponzetto and M. Strube. Deriving a large scale taxonomy from wikipedia. In *AAAI*, 2007.

[11] L. Ratinov, D. Roth, D. Downey, and M. Anderson. Local and global algorithms for disambiguation to wikipedia. In *ACL*, 2011.

[12] R. Socher, D. Chen, C. D. Manning, and A. Ng. Reasoning with neural tensor network s for knowledge base completion. In *NIPS*, 2013.

[13] F. M. Suchanek, G. Kasneci, and G. Weikum. Yago: A core of semantic knowledge unifying wordnet and wikipedia. In *WWW*, 2007.

[14] P. Venetis, A. Halevy, J. Madhavan, M. Paşca, W. Shen, F. Wu, G. Miao, and C. Wu. Recovering semantics of tables on the web. *Proceedings of the VLDB Endowment*, 4(9):528–538, 2011.

[15] C. Wang, K. Chakrabarti, T. Cheng, and S. Chaudhuri. Targeted disambiguation of ad-hoc, homogeneous sets of named entities. In *WWW*, 2012.

[16] C. Wang, M. Danilevsky, N. Desai, Y. Zhang, P. Nguyen, T. Taula, and J. Han. A phrase mining framework for recursive construction of a topical hierarchy. In *KDD*, 2013.

[17] C. Wang, M. Danilevsky, J. Liu, N. Desai, H. Ji, and J. Han. Constructing topical hierarchies in heterogeneous information networks. In *ICDM*, 2013.

[18] C. Wang, J. Han, Y. Jia, J. Tang, D. Zhang, Y. Yu, and J. Guo. Mining advisor-advisee relationships from research publication networks. In *KDD*, 2010.

[19] C. Wang, J. Han, Q. Li, X. Li, W.-P. Lin, and H. Ji. Learning hierarchical relationships among partially ordered objects with heterogeneous attributes and links. In *SDM*, 2012.

[20] W. Wong, W. Liu, and M. Bennamoun. Ontology learning from text: A look back and into the future. *ACM Computing Surveys (CSUR)*, 44(4):20, 2012.

[21] W. Wu, H. Li, H. Wang, and K. Q. Zhu. Probase: A probabilistic taxonomy for text understanding. In *SIGMOD*, 2012.

[22] M. Yakout, K. Ganjam, K. Chakrabarti, and S. Chaudhuri. Infogather: entity augmentation and attribute discovery by holistic matching with web tables. In *SIGMOD*, 2012.

Explainable Security for Relational Databases

Gabriel Bender*
Cornell University
Ithaca, NY 14853, USA
gbender@cs.cornell.edu

Łucja Kot
Cornell University
Ithaca, NY 14853, USA
lucja@cs.cornell.edu

Johannes Gehrke
Cornell University
Ithaca, NY 14853, USA
johannes@cs.cornell.edu

ABSTRACT

Companies and organizations collect and use vast troves of sensitive user data whose release must be carefully controlled. In practice, the access policies that govern this data are often fine-grained, complex, poorly documented, and difficult to reason about. As a result, principals frequently request and are granted access to data they never use.

To encourage developers and administrators to use security mechanisms more effectively, we propose a novel security model in which all security decisions are formally *explainable*. Whether a query is accepted or denied, the system returns a concise yet formal explanation which can allow the issuer to reformulate a rejected query or adjust his/her security credentials. Our approach has a strong formal foundation based on previously unexplored connections between *disclosure lattices* and *policy algebras*. We build on this foundation and implement a disclosure control system that handles a wide variety of real SQL queries and can accommodate complex policy constraints.

> *"Smelling isn't everything" said the Elephant. "Why," said the Bulldog, "if a fellow can't trust his nose, what is he to trust?" "Well, his brains perhaps," she replied mildly.*
>
> – C.S. Lewis, *The Magician's Nephew*

Categories and Subject Descriptors

H.2 [**Information Systems**]: Database Management

Keywords

database security; view rewriting; access control

1. INTRODUCTION

Over the past few decades we have seen the emergence of companies like Google and Facebook that collect and store large amounts of personal user information. This data can be used to deliver highly relevant content to end users. It can also be used to match advertisements with users' interests, thereby creating significant value for advertisers.

However, companies risk serious damage to their reputations if they lose control over this data. Fine-grained permissions provide better control over who can access what resources, and as a result, platforms such as Google Android and Facebook Apps have dozens of distinct permissions, each regulating access to a different resource or type of user data. Similarly, commercial solutions such as IBM LBAC [5] and Oracle VPD [6] give database administrators precise control over which principals can see which parts of a database. Such control is largely motivated by the Principle of Least Privilege [23], which states that principals should be granted the least permissions needed to do their jobs.

Unfortunately, this flexibility comes with a high cost: fine-grained permissions structures are inherently complex and difficult to reason about. To make matters worse, the documentation for these permissions structures is often inaccurate or buggy. [8, 16] If a query fails due to insufficient permissions, the path of least resistance is to blindly request more permissions until the problem goes away. As a result, principals frequently violate the Principle of Least Privilege by acquiring permissions that they never use. [16]

In order to address this problem, we propose a new security model that is designed to ensure that all policy decisions are *explainable*. Instead of simply rejecting unauthorized queries, our system provides the issuer with concise *explanation* of why the queries were rejected and what additional permissions would need to be granted for a successful execution. The principal can then refine the queries or request additional permissions based on the explanation. In addition to its ability to generate explanations, our approach provides *strong formal security guarantees*, yet is able to *handle real SQL queries and security policies.*

Before presenting our work in more depth, we introduce our system model, overview existing disclosure control approaches, and justify why a new solution is needed.

1.1 Enforcing Security Policies

We begin with a generic architecture for access control that is applicable to many modern DBMSs. We clarify how our *explainable* model compares to traditional database security models and identify concrete properties that should be satisfied by explanations for policy decisions.

The example database shown in Figure 1 is based on the schema that Facebook exposes to third party app developers through the Facebook Query Language (FQL) [3]. The

*Work done while at the University of Washington

SIGMOD'14, June 22–27, 2014, Snowbird, UT, USA.

User

UID	Name	Hobby
1	Babbage, Charles	math
2	Church, Alonzo	math
3	Lovelace, Ada	music
4	Turing, Alan	chess
5	von Neumann, John	history

Friend

UID1	UID2
1	3
3	1
2	4
4	2
4	5
5	4

```
CREATE VIEW V1 AS
  (SELECT name, hobby FROM User WHERE uid = 1);

CREATE VIEW V2 AS
  (SELECT name FROM User WHERE uid = 1);

CREATE VIEW V3 AS
  (SELECT U.uid, U.name FROM User U, Friend F
    WHERE U.uid = F.uid2 AND F.uid1 = 1);
```

Figure 1: Database and security views.

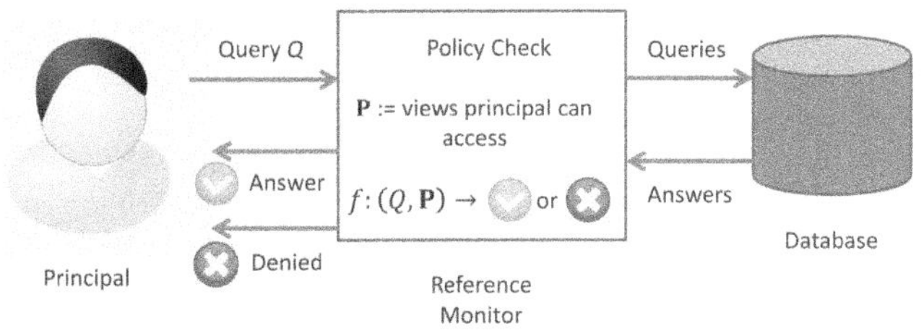

Figure 2: Disclosure control system model

schema contains two tables: `User`, which has a User ID (UID), Name, and Hobby for each user in the dataset, and `Friend`, which tracks friendship relations between users.

The system controls disclosure of this data using a *reference monitor* (RM) that enforces a *security policy*. At the time that the database schema is designed, a trusted system administrator defines a set of *security views* that reveal known types of information about the dataset. All subsequent policy decisions are made with the help of these security views. In Figure 1, `V1` reveals the UID, Name, and Hobby of User 1 (Charles Babbage) while `V2` reveals his UID and Name but not his Hobby and `V3` reveals the UIDs and Names of his friends. In a real system, an analogous set of security views would be generated for each end user; appropriate security views can easily be generated from templates defined by a human administrator. Many permissions used by Facebook [4] and Android [2] are essentially simple security views, though they are not formally defined in SQL.

The RM sits between the query evaluation engine and the principals who issue queries (Figure 2). When a principal issues a database query Q, the RM performs a policy check in order to determine whether the query should be accepted or rejected. This policy check is divided into two steps.

In the first step, the RM computes the subset $\mathbf{P}$ of the security views to which the principal has been granted access. An untrusted third-party app running on Charles Babbage's behalf might be permitted to see the contents of `V2` but not of `V1` or `V3`. In practice, this computation might be based on an *Access Control List* (ACL), a set of *Credentials* supplied by the issuer, or a *Role-Based* security mechanism.

In the second step, the RM checks whether the views in $\mathbf{P}$ contain enough information to answer the principal's original query. The determination is made by a *policy function* f that takes Q and $\mathbf{P}$ as inputs and returns 0 or 1. If f returns 1 then the principal receives the query results; otherwise, the query is denied. The function f is said to be *database-dependent* if its output can depend on the current state of the database, or *database-independent* otherwise. Our focus in this work is on *database-independent* policies; this ensures that neither policy decisions nor the corresponding explanations can leak potentially sensitive information about the current state of the database.

Ideally, f would be based on a simple mathematical criterion: it would determine whether the security views that the principal had access to contained enough information to answer Q. If so, f would output 1. Otherwise, it would output 0. In practice, however, f is typically a very crude and conservative algorithm.

In traditional implementations of view-based security, the onus is on the principal to write the query in terms of the views he or she can access. Let us return to Figure 1; suppose an app that has been granted access to `V2` but not `V1` issues the following query:

```
SELECT name FROM V1;
```

This query will be rejected even though it only reveals information that the app is allowed to access – specifically, it reveals the name of User 1, which can be computed from `V2`. The function f is not *data-derived* [8]: it checks whether the principal is allowed to access all the views in the `FROM` clause, but it does not account for the information that the query and the views reveal about the underlying database.

When the query is rejected it would be helpful for the RM to point out that the query can be rewritten using `V2` – which the principal has access to – in the following manner:

```
SELECT name FROM V2;
```

Better yet, the reference monitor should be able to search for rewritings automatically, and use them – if found – whenever it enforces a policy or generates an explanation.

It is not that we are lacking a formal theory of disclosure or the ability to compute rewritings; in previous work [8] we introduced a formal framework for reasoning about information disclosure in view-based security. However, this research is theoretical and does not deal with expressive real-world query languages and policies. In practice, explanations for rejected queries are often insufficient or nonexistent [20]. Even worse, systems such as Oracle's Virtual Private Database [6] accept unauthorized queries and modify their execution semantics without users' knowledge [22].

In summary, there is a fundamental connection between using a *data-derived* policy function f and the ability to provide explanations. Theoretical work shows how to compute data-derived functions f but does not extend to real-world systems; policy functions used in practice are not data-derived, which leads to poor explainability.

1.2 Our Contributions

In this paper, we introduce a novel instance of view-based security in which every policy decision made by the RM comes with a *concise*, *data-derived*, and *mathematically rigorous explanation*. Our work bridges the gap between existing theoretical work on disclosure lattices [8] and the needs of practical systems which must deal with complex SQL queries and sophisticated security policies.

In our system, both policy decisions and explanations are based on Boolean formulas in a *policy algebra*. Given a query Q we can generate a formula φ such that $\mathbf{P} \vdash \varphi$ if and only if $f(Q, \mathbf{P}) = 1$. For example, the query above would be associated with the policy formula $\texttt{V1} \vee \texttt{V2}$, indicating that a principal who is granted access to at least one of V1 and V2 should be authorized to execute the query. If the principal has access to V2 but not V1 then we can easily verify that $\texttt{V2} \vdash \texttt{V1} \vee \texttt{V2}$, which means the query is allowed. The RM uses such formulas, which we refer to as *policy formulas*, to make policy decisions as well as to generate explanations.

The contributions of this paper are as follows. First (Sections 3.1, 3.2) we provide a formal foundation for data-derived policies that connects disclosure lattices and policy algebras. Each query is associated with a policy formula which is automatically computed to reflect the true information disclosure by Q. To the best of our knowledge, our work is the first to discover and exploit the connection between policy algebras and disclosure lattices.

Second (Section 3.3), we introduce *explanations*, which are mathematical objects that the RM can return to the principal together with its decision. The explanation, which concisely represents the permissions that contributed to the RM's decision, gives principals whose queries were denied accurate guidance for reformulating their queries or requesting additional permissions.

Third, we show how our foundation can be used to build a security solution for real SQL (Section 4). We define a core language of *filter-project queries* that is simple enough to reason about in a mathematically sound manner but is expressive enough to capture a wide variety of real-world security policies. Next, we show how arbitrary SQL queries can be compiled to our core language. Due to the complexity of the SQL query language, the compilation process is necessarily conservative and may lead to unnecessary query denials. However, we can help developers address such denials by automatically identifying the parts of a query that were responsible for its rejection. We have fully implemented our solution; we explain the architecture and functionality of our prototype system.

Fourth, we present experimental results from an evaluation of our system on realistic workloads (Section 5).

2. THEORETICAL BACKGROUND

This section presents the necessary theoretical background for our work, including in particular disclosure lattices [8].

2.1 Query Languages

The results in Section 3 are independent of any specific database query language. However, it is useful to show examples in a concrete language to facilitate presentation. We therefore illustrate our results with conjunctive queries under bag semantics. We stress, however, that the same theoretical framework is applicable to other query languages as well, including conjunctive queries under set semantics [8] and *filter-project* queries (formally defined in Section 4.2), which combine elements of both set and bag semantics.

A conjunctive query (or view) has the form

$$H :- B$$

where H is a relational atom and B a conjunction of relational atoms over database relations. H and B are the *head* and *body* of the query, respectively. Each atom may contain constants and variables. Any variables that appear in H must also appear in B. A *distinguished* variable is one that appears in the head of the query and an *existential* variable is one that appears only in the body. We say that two queries are *equivalent* if they return the same answer on every dataset. Classically, conjunctive queries are evaluated under *set semantics*, which means that relations do not contain duplicates and duplicates are removed from the result of each query. However, we instead focus on conjunctive queries under *bag semantics*, where both relations and query answers can contain duplicates; bag semantics more accurately model the execution of real SQL queries. [13]

For the database schema from Figure 1, define

$$\begin{aligned} V_1(n,h) &:- \texttt{U}(1,n,h) \\ V_2(n) &:- \texttt{U}(1,n,h) \\ V_3(u,n) &:- \texttt{U}(u,n,h), \texttt{F}(1,u) \end{aligned}$$

where U and F refer to the **User** and **Friend** relations respectively. Under bag semantics, the views V_1, V_2, and V_3 correspond exactly to the views V1, V2, and V3 in Figure 1. If the views were instead evaluated under set semantics then duplicate tuples would automatically be removed from the outputs of V_1, V_2, and V_3.

Just as in SQL, the output of a set of views $\mathbf{V}$ can be used as the input to a query Q. If every predicate referenced in the body of Q is a view in $\mathbf{V}$ then we say that Q is a *rewriting using* $\mathbf{V}$. The following is a rewriting using $\{V_1, V_3\}$:

$$Q_4(u) :- V_1(n,h), V_3(u,n)$$

The following queries are *not* rewritings using $\{V_1, V_3\}$. The first body atom of each query directly references the User relation rather than V_1 or V_3.

$$\begin{aligned} Q_5(u) &:- \texttt{U}(1,n,h), V_3(u,n) \\ Q_6(u) &:- \texttt{U}(1,n,h), \texttt{U}(u,n,h'), \texttt{F}(1,u) \end{aligned}$$

However, we can show that Q_4 and Q_6 return the same answer on every possible dataset. Since the body of Q_4 just references views in $\{V_1, V_3\}$ and the body of Q_6 just references relations in the base schema, we say that Q_4 is an *equivalent rewriting of* Q_6 *using* $\{V_1, V_3\}$. The existence of such a rewriting implies that the answers to V_1 and V_3 uniquely determine the answer to Q_6 on any possible dataset.

2.2 Disclosure Orders

We now present *disclosure orders* [8], which formalize the intuition that some views (or sets of views) reveal more information about the dataset than others. We treat views as formal objects drawn from some finite universe $\mathcal{U}$. The relative amounts of information revealed by different sets of views can be compared using a binary relation $\preceq$ that operates on subsets of $\mathcal{U}$. Intuitively, if $\mathbf{V}$ and $\mathbf{V}'$ are sets of views, $\mathbf{V} \preceq \mathbf{V}'$ means that the answers to all the views in $\mathbf{V}$ are uniquely determined by the views in $\mathbf{V}'$.

DEFINITION 1. *A* ***disclosure order*** *is a binary relation on subsets of* $\mathcal{U}$ *such that*

(i) If $\mathbf{V} \subseteq \mathbf{V}'$ *then* $\mathbf{V} \preceq \mathbf{V}'$.

(ii) If $\mathbf{V} \preceq \mathbf{V}'$ *and* $\mathbf{V}' \preceq \mathbf{V}''$ *then* $\mathbf{V} \preceq \mathbf{V}''$.

(iii) If $\mathbf{V} \preceq \mathbf{V}''$ *and* $\mathbf{V}' \preceq \mathbf{V}''$ *then* $\mathbf{V} \cup \mathbf{V}' \preceq \mathbf{V}'$.

The first axiom ensures that adding new elements to a set of views can only increase the amount of information it reveals about the dataset. The second axiom is a standard transitivity condition. The third axiom ensures that upper bounds on information disclosure remain meaningful even when information is combined across multiple queries.

We next present three different examples of disclosure orders. In each case, we assume that $\mathcal{U}$ is the set of conjunctive queries under bag semantics.[1]

(i) **Set containment**: $\mathbf{V} \preceq \mathbf{V}'$ if and only if $\mathbf{V} \subseteq \mathbf{V}'$.

(ii) **View determinacy**: $\mathbf{V} \preceq \mathbf{V}'$ if and only if the answers to the views in $\mathbf{V}'$ uniquely determine the answers to the views in $\mathbf{V}$ on every possible dataset.

(iii) **View rewriting**: $\mathbf{V} \preceq \mathbf{V}'$ if and only if every view in $\mathbf{V}$ has a rewriting using $\mathbf{V}'$.

Although every disclosure order is a *preorder* (i.e., it is reflexive and transitive), disclosure orders are not generally partial orders. The reason is that two different views can reveal the same information. For instance, define

$$V_7(u_1, u_2) :- \mathtt{F}(u_1, u_2)$$
$$V_8(u_2, u_1) :- \mathtt{F}(u_1, u_2)$$

Intuitively, the views should reveal the same information about the dataset despite being unequal because the answer to each view can be computed from the other.

We are not aware of any efficient solution for checking dataset-independent view determinacy; under slightly different assumptions, it is an open question whether the problem is even decidable. [19] In contrast, checking set containment is trivial and checking whether an equivalent rewriting exists is NP-complete in the size of the input. [13] Since queries are typically quite small, this check is fast in practice.

2.3 Disclosure Lattices

Disclosure orders can be extended to *disclosure lattices*, which allow us to answer two basic questions. First, given two sets of views $\mathbf{V}$ and $\mathbf{V}'$, what *common* information is revealed both by $\mathbf{V}$ alone and by $\mathbf{V}'$ alone? And second, what *combined* information can be learned from looking at the answers to the views in $\mathbf{V}$ and $\mathbf{V}'$ together? By combining two sets of views, it is often possible to obtain information that cannot be learned by looking at either set on its own; this is the classic problem of *information combination* [18].

We would like sets of views to form a lattice where the *greatest lower bound* (GLB) of $\mathbf{V}$ and $\mathbf{V}'$ (denoted $\mathbf{V} \sqcap \mathbf{V}'$) represents the information that is common to the two sets and the *least upper bound* (LUB) of $\mathbf{V}$ and $\mathbf{V}'$ (denoted $\mathbf{V} \sqcup \mathbf{V}'$) represents the combined information from the two sets. However, this is not quite right: if $\preceq$ was a lattice order then it would need to be antisymmetric, so that $\mathbf{V} \preceq \mathbf{V}'$ and $\mathbf{V}' \preceq \mathbf{V}$ would together imply $\mathbf{V} = \mathbf{V}'$. We have seen that disclosure orders need not satisfy this property.

To fix the problem, we define a new unary operator $(\Downarrow \mathbf{V})$:

$$(\Downarrow \mathbf{V}) = \{V \in \mathcal{U} : \{V\} \preceq \mathbf{V}\}$$

Intuitively, $(\Downarrow \mathbf{V})$ contains every view in $\mathcal{U}$ whose answer is uniquely determined by $\mathbf{V}$. We can use this new operator to obtain a *disclosure lattice* with the desired properties. [8]

[1] To ensure that $\mathcal{U}$ is finite, we assume that queries are expressed in a language with finitely many distinct symbols and that the size of every query is bounded above by a very large but arbitrarily selected constant.

$$V_9(u, n, h) :- \mathtt{U}(u, n, h)$$
$$V_{10}(u, n) :- \mathtt{U}(u, n, h)$$
$$V_{11}(1, n, h) :- \mathtt{U}(1, n, h)$$
$$V_{12}(h) :- \mathtt{U}(u, n, h)$$
$$V_{13}(u_1, u_2) :- \mathtt{F}(u_1, u_2)$$
$$V_{14}(1, u_2) :- \mathtt{F}(1, u_2)$$

Figure 3: A set of security views

THEOREM 1. *Let $\mathcal{U}$ be a set of views, and let $\preceq$ be a disclosure order for $\mathcal{U}$. Define $\mathcal{I} = \{\Downarrow \mathbf{V} : \mathbf{V} \subseteq \mathcal{U}\}$. Then $(\mathcal{I}, \preceq)$ is a lattice; details are as follows:*

- *LUB:* $(\Downarrow \mathbf{V}) \sqcup (\Downarrow \mathbf{V}') = \Downarrow (\mathbf{V} \cup \mathbf{V}')$.
- *GLB:* $(\Downarrow \mathbf{V}) \sqcap (\Downarrow \mathbf{V}') = (\Downarrow \mathbf{V}) \cap (\Downarrow \mathbf{V}')$.
- *Top element* $\top = (\Downarrow \mathcal{U}) = \mathcal{U}$, *bottom element* $\bot = (\Downarrow \emptyset)$.

Data-derived policy functions can be expressed in terms of disclosure lattices. Suppose a principal who is authorized to see the contents of a set of security views $\mathbf{P}$ tries to execute a query Q. The query is permitted only when the views in $\mathbf{P}$ contain enough information to answer Q, which is true precisely when $\{Q\} \preceq \mathbf{P}$. Translated into the lattice above, the check is equivalent to one that requires Q to be answerable using the combined information from all the views in $\mathbf{P}$. Equivalently, we require that $\Downarrow \{Q\} \preceq \Downarrow \mathbf{P}$.

3. POLICIES AND EXPLANATIONS

Now that we have introduced disclosure lattices, we can move to the first two major contributions of our paper. First, we introduce *policy formulas* that explicitly represent which combinations of views a principal must have access to before executing a given query. We explain how to compute policy formulas that are *data-derived*. Next, we show how to use policy formulas to generate data-derived *explanations* for system decisions to allow or deny queries.

3.1 Policy Formulas

We start with a set of *security views* $\mathbf{V}$ defined by a human administrator. Each view in $\mathbf{V}$ roughly corresponds to a single *permission* that a principal may or may not be granted. A policy formula is a Boolean formula in which every security view is treated as a variable. *Policy formulas over* $\mathbf{V}$ are formally defined using the BNF grammar

$$\tau \quad ::= \quad 0 \quad | \quad 1 \quad | \quad V \quad | \quad (\tau \vee \tau) \quad | \quad (\tau \wedge \tau)$$

where each V is a security view in $\mathbf{V}$. The constant 0 corresponds to a policy in which a query's execution is never permitted, while the constant 1 corresponds to a policy in which a query's execution is always permitted.

Consider the set of security views in Figure 3. The policy formula V_9 indicates that a principal must be granted access to the view V_9 in order to execute a given query. The formula $(V_9 \vee V_{11})$ indicates that the principal must be granted access to *either* the view V_9 *or* the view V_{11}. The formula $(V_9 \wedge V_{14})$ indicates that the principal must be granted access to *both* the view V_9 *and* the view V_{14}.

In general, a policy formula φ can be attached to any query Q (or more generally, any *set* of queries) over the dataset; the formula is then used by the reference monitor to decide whether a given principal can execute Q. Given the set of security views $\mathbf{P}$ that the principal is granted access to, the reference monitor (RM) checks whether $\mathbf{P} \vdash \varphi$. If so, the RM will allow the principal to execute Q; otherwise, the RM will deny the request. This check can be performed in linear time by recursively applying the following rules:

$$\mathbf{P} \vdash 1 \text{ and } \mathbf{P} \nvdash 0$$

$$\mathbf{P} \vdash V \text{ if and only if } V \in \mathbf{P}$$

$$\mathbf{P} \vdash (\varphi \vee \psi) \text{ if and only if } \mathbf{P} \vdash \varphi \text{ or } \mathbf{P} \vdash \psi$$

$$\mathbf{P} \vdash (\varphi \wedge \psi) \text{ if and only if } \mathbf{P} \vdash \varphi \text{ and } \mathbf{P} \vdash \psi$$

It is important to realize that the check described above is agnostic to the question of how the views in $\mathbf{P}$ are computed. Consequently, the model is relevant even for systems that rely on role-based access control or similar schemes where the process of computing $\mathbf{P}$ can be arbitrarily complicated.

3.2 Generating Data-Derived Formulas

We now show how to generate data-derived policy formulas for database queries. Recall that a data-derived policy specifies that a principal with access to views in $\mathbf{P}$ can receive the answer to query Q if and only if $\{Q\} \preceq \mathbf{P}$. As explained in the Introduction, most policies used in practice are not data-derived; we believe this is because checking directly whether $\{Q\} \preceq \mathbf{P}$ makes policy decisions computationally expensive and tricky for humans to understand.

On the other hand, given a policy formula φ, checking whether $\mathbf{P} \vdash \varphi$ is straightforward and can be performed quickly even for large formulas. We therefore propose to encode data-derived policy functions using policy formulas. That is, we want a system that can take a query Q and compute a policy formula φ such that, for any subset $\mathbf{P}$ of the security views, $\mathbf{P} \vdash \varphi$ if and only if $\{Q\} \preceq \mathbf{P}$. Intuitively, φ tells us precisely which combinations of the security views contain enough information to uniquely determine the answer to Q. For example, consider the query

$$Q_{15}(h) :- \mathtt{U}(1, n, h)$$

Given the security views defined in Figure 3, Q_{15} can be answered if the principal is granted access to at least one of the views V_9 or V_{11}. This is both a necessary and a sufficient condition. No other view except V_{12} reveals the Hobby field of the `User` relation, and V_{12} does not contain enough information to determine which hobby is associated with User 1. The policy formula for Q_{15} is therefore

$$(V_9 \vee V_{11})$$

The question arises whether it is always possible to compute the formula φ we desire. The answer is *yes*; there is a very deep connection between disclosure lattices and policy formulas. Given any set of queries $\mathbf{Q}$ over the dataset there is a policy formula φ such that $\mathbf{P} \vdash \varphi$ if and only if $\mathbf{Q} \preceq \mathbf{P}$ for every subset $\mathbf{P}$ of the security views. Furthermore, it is possible to compute φ in a completely automated fashion.

Efficiency, however, is another matter entirely. The number of security views can be quite large, and the size of a policy formula can be exponential in the number of security views. We must limit policy formulas to a manageable size if they are to be used in practice. We can ensure that this is the case by requiring the universe $\mathcal{U}$ of possible views to be *decomposable*.

```
1: procedure POLICY(Q, V)
2:     φ ← 1
3:     for Q ∈ Q do
4:         ψ ← 0
5:         for V ∈ V do
6:             if {Q} ⪯ {V} then
7:                 ψ ← (ψ ∨ V)
8:             end if
9:         end for
10:        φ ← (φ ∧ ψ)
11:    end for
12:    return φ
13: end procedure
```

Figure 4: Algorithm for computing data-derived policy formulas (decomposable case)

Formally, $\mathcal{U}$ is said to be *decomposable* if for every query Q and all sets of views $\mathbf{V}$ and $\mathbf{V}'$, $\{Q\} \preceq \mathbf{V} \cup \mathbf{V}'$ implies $\{Q\} \preceq \mathbf{V}$ or $\{Q\} \preceq \mathbf{V}'$. Put another way, if neither $\mathbf{V}$ alone nor $\mathbf{V}'$ alone contains enough information to answer Q then the union of the two sets still will not contain enough information to answer Q.

Decomposability holds when we restrict our attention to the universe $\mathcal{U}_{single}$ of single-atom conjunctive queries and views; it does not generally hold when applied to multi-atom queries and views in the obvious way. We restrict our attention to single-atom queries and views for now and explain how to handle a more general class of queries and views in Section 4.2.

When decomposability holds, it is possible to compute concise policy formulas for arbitrary queries. Given a set of queries $\mathbf{Q}$ and a set of security views $\mathbf{V}$, the following formula allows us to compute the formula governing $\mathbf{Q}$:

$$\text{policy}(\mathbf{Q}) = \bigwedge_{Q \in \mathbf{Q}} \left(\bigvee_{V \in \mathbf{V}:\ \{Q\} \preceq \{V\}} V \right)$$

For any subset $\mathbf{P}$ of the security views, $\mathbf{P} \vdash \text{policy}(\mathbf{Q})$ if and only if $\mathbf{Q} \preceq \mathbf{P}$. Consequently, policy($\mathbf{Q}$) tells us exactly which combinations of the security views reveal enough information to answer all the queries in $\mathbf{Q}$. Furthermore, its size is polynomial in both the number of queries and the number of security views.

The algorithm in Figure 4 computes the policy formula for a set of queries $\mathbf{Q}$ with respect to a collection of security views $\mathbf{V}$. It begins by setting the policy formula to 1 (Line 2) – an empty set of queries should always be permitted. It then loops through the list of queries in $\mathbf{Q}$ (Lines 3-11), computes a separate policy formula for each query (Line 4-9), and returns the conjunction of all the resulting formulas (Line 12); the result is a policy formula over the views in $\mathbf{V}$.

The inner loop (Lines 4-9) computes the policy formula for a single query Q. It starts by setting the formula to 0 (Line 4) – if no security view contains enough information to answer Q then the query's execution should be disallowed. It then loops through all the security views in $\mathbf{V}$ and takes the disjunction of all the views that contain enough information to answer Q (Lines 5-9).

For example, let $\mathbf{Q}$ contain the queries

$$Q_{16}(1,n) :- \mathtt{U}(1,n,h)$$
$$Q_{17}(h) :- \mathtt{U}(u,n,h)$$

and let $\mathbf{V}$ consist of the views from Figure 3. Then

$$\text{policy}(\{Q_{16}\}) = V_9 \vee V_{10} \vee V_{11}$$
$$\text{policy}(\{Q_{17}\}) = V_9 \vee V_{12}$$

and therefore

$$\text{policy}(\{Q_{16}, Q_{17}\}) = (V_9 \vee V_{10} \vee V_{11}) \wedge (V_9 \vee V_{12})$$

For the other direction, given a policy formula φ, the recursive function disc(φ) defined below allows us to determine precisely what information about the dataset (represented as a point in the disclosure lattice $\mathcal{I}$) can be obtained by executing only queries that are permitted by φ:

$$\begin{aligned} \text{disc}(\varphi \vee \psi) &= \text{disc}(\varphi) \sqcap \text{disc}(\psi) \\ \text{disc}(\varphi \wedge \psi) &= \text{disc}(\varphi) \sqcup \text{disc}(\psi) \\ \text{disc}(V) &= \Downarrow V \end{aligned}$$

In the example above,

$$\begin{aligned} &\text{disc}((V_9 \vee V_{10} \vee V_{11}) \wedge (V_9 \vee V_{12})) \\ &= (\Downarrow V_9 \sqcap \Downarrow V_{10} \sqcap \Downarrow V_{11}) \sqcup (\Downarrow V_9 \sqcap \Downarrow V_{12}) \end{aligned}$$

$\mathbf{P} \vdash \varphi$ implies disc(φ) $\preceq \mathbf{P}$, but the converse does not always hold because $\mathbf{P}$ can be inconsistent. For instance, it is possible to grant a principal access to V_9 but not V_{10} even though the former reveals strictly more information about the dataset than the latter. If we disallow such inconsistencies, the reverse implication holds as expected.

In summary, we have shown how to represent the security policy governing any query over the dataset as a data-derived policy formula. We do this by exploiting a deep connection between disclosure lattices that precisely quantify information disclosure and policy formulas that are easy for a reference monitor to evaluate. For every query Q we compute a formula φ; the reference monitor makes policy decisions by evaluating φ against the list of permissions $\mathbf{P}$ that were granted to the principal. If the universe of queries is decomposable then policy formulas are guaranteed to be small and easy to reason about. However, it is possible to compute policy formulas for queries even when decomposability does not hold.

3.3 Explanations

Policy formulas are not just useful for enforcement; they can be used to generate *explanations*, which are mathematical objects that justify the RM's policy decisions.

Explanations come in two varieties: *why-so explanations* and *why-not explanations*. If the execution of a query Q is authorized, a why-so explanation indicates which of the principal's permissions were responsible for the positive authorization decision. If the execution of Q is not authorized, a why-not explanation indicates which additional permissions need to be granted before the query can be successfully executed. Both types of explanations can be efficiently computed from policy(Q).

As before, let $\mathbf{Q}$ denote a set of queries, $\mathbf{V}$ denote a set of security views, and let $\mathbf{P} \subseteq \mathbf{V}$ be the subset of the security views that a principal has been granted access to. A why-so explanation for Q characterizes exactly which subsets of $\mathbf{P}$ contain enough information to answer $\mathbf{Q}$. It can be obtained by replacing every view V in policy($\mathbf{Q}$) that the principal has not been granted access to with the constant 0. For example, suppose $\mathbf{Q} = \{Q_{16}, Q_{17}\}$, so that

$$\text{policy}(\mathbf{Q}) = (V_9 \vee V_{10} \vee V_{11}) \wedge (V_9 \vee V_{12})$$

If the principal is granted access to V_9 and V_{10} then the why-so explanation for $\mathbf{Q}$ w.r.t. $\{V_9, V_{10}\}$ is

$$(V_9 \vee V_{10} \vee 0) \wedge (V_9 \vee 0) = (V_9 \vee V_{10}) \wedge (V_9) = V_9$$

indicating that V_9 was solely responsible for the positive authorization decision. If the principal is instead granted access to $\{V_{10}, V_{11}, V_{12}\}$, the why-so explanation for $\mathbf{Q}$ is

$$(0 \vee V_{10} \vee V_{11}) \wedge (0 \vee V_{12}) = (V_{10} \vee V_{11}) \wedge (V_{12})$$

indicating that in order to answer the query, the principal would need access to V_{12} and at least one of V_{10} and V_{11}.

If the RM's authorization decision is negative, a why-not explanation identifies the additional permissions that would need to be granted in order to reverse the decision. A why-not explanation is obtained by replacing every view V in policy($\mathbf{Q}$) that the principal *has* been granted access to with the constant 1. If

$$\text{policy}(\mathbf{Q}) = (V_9 \vee V_{10} \vee V_{11}) \wedge (V_9 \vee V_{12})$$

then the why-not explanation for $\mathbf{Q}$ w.r.t. $\{V_{10}, V_{11}\}$ is

$$(V_9 \vee 1 \vee 1) \wedge (V_9 \vee V_{12}) = 1 \wedge (V_9 \vee V_{12}) = (V_9 \vee V_{12})$$

indicating that in order to execute the queries in $\mathbf{Q}$, the principal would need to be granted additional access to at least one of the permissions V_9 and V_{12}. Similarly, the why-not explanation for $\mathbf{Q}$ w.r.t. $\{V_{12}\}$ is

$$\begin{aligned} &(V_9 \vee V_{10} \vee V_{11}) \wedge (V_9 \vee 1) \\ =\ &(V_9 \vee V_{10} \vee V_{11}) \wedge 1 \\ =\ &(V_9 \vee V_{10} \vee V_{11}) \end{aligned}$$

indicating that the principal would need to be granted access to at least one of the views V_9, V_{10}, and V_{11} before all the queries in $\mathbf{Q}$ could be answered.

Why-so and why-not explanations are helpful to both the principal and the system administrator. From the administrator's perspective, if the principal holds some permissions that never show up in why-so explanations for his or her queries, this may be an indication that the principal is *over-privileged* and that those unused permissions should be revoked. On the other hand, from the principal's perspective, if a query is denied, the why-not explanation provides clear guidance on which additional permissions to request from the appropriate granting entity. With our data-derived policy formulas, both kinds of explanations are straightforward to compute at query time.

4. DISCLOSURE CONTROL IN PRACTICE

At this point we have given a theoretical foundation for computing data-derived policy formulas and explanations. We now introduce our system, which generates policy formulas and explanations for real SQL queries. In addition, our system can handle realistic security policies that are *reflective*, which means that the policies governing tuples in one part of the database can depend on a different part of the same database. Such policies arise frequently in practice. For instance, Facebook's security policies distinguish

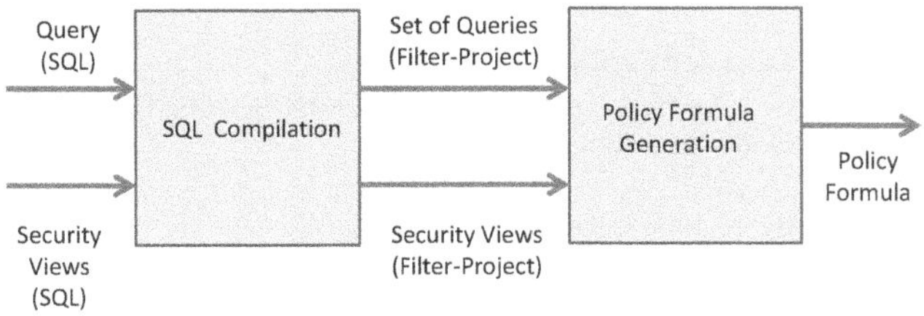

Figure 5: Computing policy formulas – System Architecture

between queries that reveal information about friends of the current user and queries that reveal information about arbitrary users; the former may be permitted when the latter are disallowed. To express and enforce such a policy, the following security view is required:

```
SELECT U1.uid, U1.name FROM User U1 WHERE U1.uid IN
  (SELECT F1.uid2 FROM Friend F1 WHERE F1.uid1 = 1)
```

This security view contains a semijoin and as such cannot be handled efficiently by algorithms in previous work [8].

4.1 Overview

Our prototype system can handle a wide variety of features that arise in real SQL queries, including:

- Aggregate operators such as `SUM` and `COUNT`.
- Algebraic expressions, equalities, and inequalities.
- Logical boolean connectives, including `AND`, `OR`, and `NOT`.
- Nested subqueries including the `EXISTS` and `IN` keyword and set-comparisons operators such as `X >= ANY (...)`. We also support correlated subqueries.
- `JOIN ON` and `WHERE` clauses.
- `GROUP BY` and `HAVING` clauses.
- Left, right, and full outer joins.
- Null values, `IS NULL`, and `IS NOT NULL`.
- The `UNION`, `INTERSECT`, and `EXCEPT` set operators.
- Temporary tables.

If additional SQL features are desired, it is possible to extend our implementation to support them.

Security views can also be defined using standard SQL syntax, but not all SQL features are supported. Every security view must be expressible as a *filter-project* query. Roughly speaking, this means that each security view must be a `SELECT-FROM-WHERE` query with semijoins but not inner or outer joins. While this is a nontrivial restriction, it is sufficient to capture many security constraints that arise in practice, including the Facebook friends query above.

Filter-project queries represent a sweet spot, as they are simple enough to reason about in a mathematically rigorous way but sophisticated enough to capture a wide range of real-world security policies.

The high-level architecture of our system is shown in Figure 5. Computing policy formulas is a two-stage process. First, queries issued by a principal are fed to a SQL processor that compiles them into filter-project queries. Compilation is conservative: the compiled versions of the queries disclose at least as much information as the original SQL queries, and may reveal strictly more information in some cases. This may cause the reference monitor to overestimate the information disclosed by and consequently reject certain legal queries. It will, however, ensure that illegal queries are never accepted. A policy formula therefore represents an upper bound on the information needed to answer a query.

Security views are similarly compiled into filter-project queries at initialization time; the compilation process for security views is lossless due to the restriction we imposed above. Once the compilation is complete, the system computes a policy formula for the compiled query using the algorithm from Figure 4. The entire pipeline is database-independent; policy formulas and explanations can reveal information about the database schema but cannot leak information about the contents of the underlying database.

The remainder of this Section describes the architecture of our system in more detail. In Section 4.2 we formally introduce filter-project queries and describe how to compute policy formulas and explanations for these queries. In Section 4.3 we discuss the early stages of our compilation pipeline, which output a collection of single-atom projection queries without equality constraints. In Section 4.4 we discuss the later stages of our compilation pipeline, which convert the single-atom projection queries to filter-project queries.

4.2 Filter-Project Queries

We now motivate and formalize filter-project queries, which serve as an intermediate representation within our system.

We begin by introducing some terminology, namely *tables* and *table instances*. *Tables* are query-independent and belong to the underlying database. *Table instances*, on the other hand, originate in the `FROM` clauses of SQL queries. Thus, a query containing a self-join has two table instances yet references just one table. The query

```
SELECT U1.uid, U1.name FROM User U1, Friend F1
 WHERE F1.uid1 = 1 AND F1.uid2 = U1.uid
```

has two table instances: `U1` and `F1`.

The reference monitor's job is determine whether the execution of a specified query should be permitted or denied. In our system, the RM ends up performing a separate policy check for each table instance in the query. This policy check takes into account two different types of information. First, which *columns* in each table instance can affect the query's output? And second, which *rows* in each table instance can affect the query's output?

The first question can be answered relatively easily. In the query above, the columns `uid` and `name` of the table instance `U1` can affect the query's output, and the columns `uid1` and `uid2` of the table instance `F1` can affect the query's output.

The answer to the second question is more subtle. A row in `F1` can affect the query's output if (i) `F1.uid1` is equal to 1 and (ii) there is a row in the `User` relation whose `uid` is equal to `F1.uid2`. Similarly, a row in `U1` can affect the query's output if there is a corresponding row in `Friend` whose `uid1` is equal to 1 and whose `uid2` is equal to `U1.uid`.

In order to encode the types of constraints described above, we define a class of queries called *filter-project queries*. These are related to the familiar select-project and select-project-join queries, but they are distinct from both.

A filter-project query contains a *head atom* H, a *main body atom* B (or just a *body atom* for short), and zero or more *filter atoms* $F_1, F_2, \ldots$, and is written as

$$H :- B \ltimes F_1 \wedge F_2 \wedge \ldots$$

When the set of filter atoms is empty, this is shortened to

$$H :- B$$

As the latter syntax implies, filter-project queries generalize single-atom conjunctive queries under bag semantics.

In our running example, the filter-project query for U1 is

$$Q_{18}(u, n) :- \mathtt{U}(u, n, h) \ltimes \mathtt{F}(1, u)$$

This encodes both the row-based constraints and the column-based constraints mentioned above. The distinguished variables in the query's head are bound to the columns `uid` and `name` of the `User` relation. And the tuples that appear in the query's output are precisely those for which U1 is joined with a tuple of the `Friend` relation that satisfies `uid1 = 1`.

Similarly, the filter-project query associated with F1 is

$$Q_{19}(u) :- \mathtt{F}(1, u) \ltimes \mathtt{U}(u, n, h)$$

Notice that the answers to Q_{18} and Q_{19} jointly contain enough information to uniquely determine the answer to the original SQL query on any possible dataset.

The main atom of a filter-project query is evaluated under bag semantics, whereas the remaining atoms are evaluated under set semantics. The filter atoms of a query act as selection predicates in the sense that they can remove tuples from the query answer but cannot add new tuples. Furthermore, only variables that appear in the query's main body atom can be referenced in the query head.

In our running example, Q_{18} is equivalent to the following SQL query:

```
SELECT U1.uid, U1.name FROM User U1 WHERE U1.uid IN
  (SELECT uid2 FROM Friend WHERE uid1 = 1)
```

and Q_{19} is equivalent to

```
SELECT F1.uid2 FROM Friend F1 WHERE F1.uid1 = 1
   AND F1.uid2 IN (SELECT uid FROM User)
```

More generally, filter atoms in our query language correspond to semijoins in standard SQL.

We can now define a *disclosure order* (Section 2.2) that allows us to compare the information revealed by different filter-project queries. In contrast with the disclosure orders seen earlier, we order filter-project queries according to the amount of information that they disclose about their *main body atoms*. According to our criterion, the following query reveals strictly more information than Q_{18} above:

$$Q_{20}(u, n) :- \mathtt{U}(u, n, h)$$

The reason is that Q_{18} just reveals information about `Users` who are friends of User 1, whereas Q_{20} reveals information about every tuple in the `User` relation. The analysis depends only on the query definitions and is independent of the contents of the underlying dataset.

Restricting our attention to the information disclosed by queries' main body atoms serves two purposes. First, it ensures that the RM will perform exactly one policy check for each table instance in the original SQL query. For the SQL query above, the RM will perform one check to determine whether the execution of Q_{18} is authorized and another to determine whether Q_{19} is authorized. If both are authorized then the SQL query will be accepted. Otherwise, the RM will be able to point to a specific table instance that was responsible for the failed authorization decision: U1 if the check for Q_{18} fails and F1 if the check for Q_{19} fails.

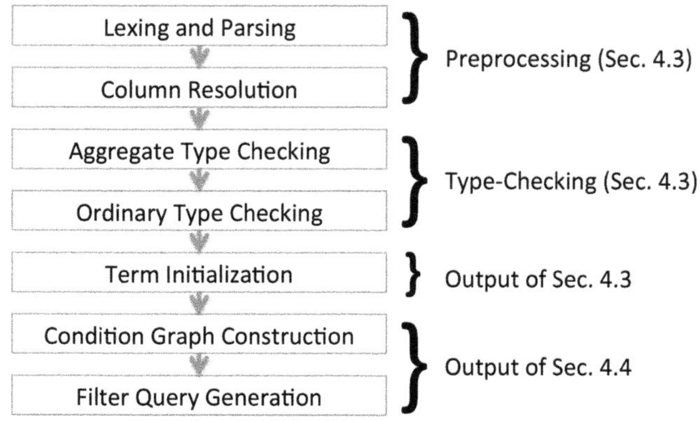

Figure 6: Query compilation pipeline

A second advantage of this disclosure order is that it ensures that the universe of filter-project queries is decomposable even if the queries contain multiple filter atoms. Consequently, filter-project queries are compatible with the efficient policy formula generation and explanation algorithms from Section 3.

We can formalize our desired disclosure order using *query homomorphisms* [11, 13, 14]. In our disclosure order, it is the case that $\{Q_{18}\} \preceq \{Q_{20}\}$. Given filter-project queries Q and Q', the problem of determining whether $\{Q\} \preceq \{Q'\}$ is NP-hard; however, queries are typically small in practice. Given sets of queries $\mathbf{Q}$ and $\mathbf{Q}'$, we can check whether $\mathbf{Q} \preceq \mathbf{Q}'$ using $O(|\mathbf{Q}| \cdot |\mathbf{Q}'|)$ comparisons between pairs of singleton queries; details are omitted due to space restrictions.

4.3 Preprocessing and Term Initialization

We now explain the early passes of our compiler, which transform an arbitrary SQL query into a set of *projection queries*, or single-atom conjunctive queries without constants or equality constraints. Although not particularly useful on its own, the pipeline will be extended in Section 4.4 in order to generate a collection of *filter-project* queries in the language described in Section 4.2

Our compiler begins by lexing and parsing the raw SQL queries using JSqlParser [1], an open-source query parsing library written in Java. We then execute a series of passes on the resulting *abstract syntax tree* (AST). Each pass corresponds to a complete traversal of the AST. A complete depiction of the passes is seen in Figure 6.

Our running example focuses on the query

```
SELECT name FROM User U1, Friend F1
 WHERE uid1 = 1 AND uid2 = uid
```

Preprocessing and column resolution: Parsing the raw SQL queries yields an AST representation as mentioned earlier. Once the AST is available, we identify table instances and perform column resolution. In our example, we identify U1 as a table instance associated with the `User` table and F1 as a table instance associated with the `Friend` table. Using information about the database schema, we infer that the columns `uid` and `name` belong to U1 whereas the columns `uid1` and `uid2` belong to F1. (See Figure 7a.) When applicable, column resolution also takes into account information about the query's nested structure.

```
(a) SELECT U1.name FROM User U1, Friend F1
     WHERE F1.uid1 = 1 AND F1.uid2 = U1.uid

(b) SELECT U1.name
      FROM User U1 LEFT OUTER JOIN Friend F1
        ON (F1.uid1 = 1 AND F1.uid2 = U1.uid)

(c) SELECT U1.name
      FROM User U1 FULL OUTER JOIN Friend F1
        ON (F1.uid1 = 1 AND F1.uid2 = U1.uid)

(d) SELECT U1.name
      FROM User U1, Friend F1, Friend F2
     WHERE F1.uid1 = 1 AND F1.uid2 = F2.uid1
       AND F2.uid2 = U.uid

(e) SELECT U1.name FROM User U1 WHERE U1.uid IN
      (SELECT F1.uid2 FROM Friend F1
        WHERE F1.uid1 = 1)
```

Figure 7: SQL queries handled by our system

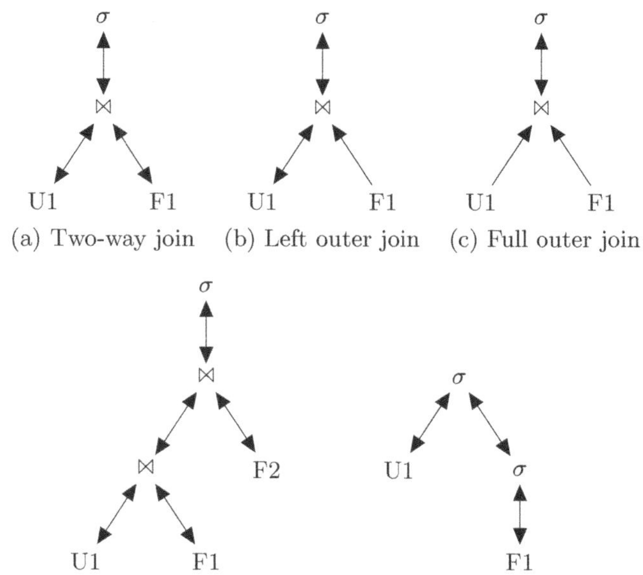

(a) Two-way join (b) Left outer join (c) Full outer join

(d) Three-way join (e) Nested subquery

Figure 8: Condition graphs for queries from Fig. 7

Type-checking: We perform aggressive type-checking on the AST in order to ensure that it corresponds to a semantically well-defined query. The motivation for performing type-checking is simple: we can't reason about the disclosure of a query unless we understand its semantics. Our system performs two different kinds of type-checking. *Aggregate type-checking* detects bad queries such as

```
SELECT SUM(SUM(U1.uid)) FROM User U1
```

that mix aggregate and non-aggregate expressions in illegal ways. *Ordinary type-checking* detects bad queries such as

```
SELECT * FROM User U1 WHERE U1.uid IN
  (SELECT F1.uid1, F1.uid2 FROM Friend F1)
```

that provide invalid inputs to built-in functions, operators, and predicates.

Term initialization: The next step is to convert the AST for a SQL query Q into a collection of projection queries $Q_1, Q_2, \ldots, Q_n$ that together reveal enough information to uniquely determine the answer to Q on any possible dataset. In Section 4.4 we will describe an extension to this process that converts the resulting projection queries into filter-project queries of the form described in Section 4.2.

The extraction proceeds as follows. First, we generate one query for each table instance in Q. For example, given any of the SQL queries from Figure 7a, Figure 7b, or Figure 7c, we generate two queries: $Q_{\mathtt{U1}}$ and $Q_{\mathtt{F1}}$. The sole body atom of $Q_{\mathtt{U1}}$ references the `User` relation whereas the body atom of $Q_{\mathtt{F1}}$ references the `Friend` relation.

We now determine which variables in our queries should be existential and which should be distinguished. A variable is marked as existential if the corresponding column is never referenced in the definition of Q, and is marked as distinguished in all other cases. This ensures that the output queries reveal all the columns needed to evaluate any arithmetic expression or inequality or logical predicate that appears in Q. We obtain the same values for $Q_{\mathtt{U1}}$ and $Q_{\mathtt{F1}}$ for all of the queries in Figures 7a, 7b, and 7c:

$$Q_{\mathtt{U1}}(u, n) :- \mathtt{U}(u, n, h)$$
$$Q_{\mathtt{F1}}(u_1, u_2) :- \mathtt{F}(u_1, u_2)$$

4.4 Generating Filter-Project Queries

The output of the compilation process described in Section 4.3 is a conservative upper bound on the information revealed by Q. However, it is missing information that is essential for driving policy decisions in practice. For instance, there is no way to know just by looking at $Q_{\mathtt{F1}}$ that the query in Figure 7a only needs a list of friends of User 1 (Charles Babbage) rather than information about arbitrary tuples in the `Friend` relation. Similarly, there is no way to tell just by looking at $Q_{\mathtt{U1}}$ that the query only needs to access tuples in the `User` relation that correspond to friends of User 1. In order to address these shortcomings, we build a *condition graph* that allows us to determine which equality constraints and filter atoms should be added to $Q_{\mathtt{U1}}$ and $Q_{\mathtt{F1}}$.

The condition graph for a query Q contains one node (labeled σ) for each `SELECT` statement in the query, one node (labeled $\bowtie$) for each two-way join in the query's logical evaluation plan, and one node for each table instance defined by the query. Figures 8a through 8e show the condition graphs for the SQL queries from Figures 7a through 7e respectively.

In many cases, condition graphs bear a deceptive resemblance to expression trees in the Relational Algebra. However, there are a number of important differences between the two. Edges in condition graphs can be unidirectional or bidirectional, and every condition graph must contain a `SELECT` node at its root. Furthermore, the same nodes appear in the graph regardless of whether we perform an inner join or an outer join. However, the directions of edges between those nodes can change depending on the type of join we are dealing with (Figures 8a, 8b, and 8c). And finally, `SELECT` nodes can have multiple children (Figure 8e). One child represents the `FROM` clause of the corresponding `SELECT` statement, while the remaining children represent correlated subqueries that appear in the statement's `WHERE` and `HAVING` clauses. Temporary tables (not shown here) are handled in a similar manner to nested subqueries.

Once we have constructed the condition graph, we can determine which semijoin filter atoms should appear in each of the output queries. Our criterion is based on reachability in the condition graph: a directed path from table instance R to table instance S indicates that a tuple in R can only affect the query's output if it can be joined with a tuple from S. In our running example, $Q_{\mathtt{U1}}$ should contain a filter atom for `F1` precisely when the node associated with `F1` is reachable from the node associated with `U1` in the condition graph. For the query in Figure 7a we obtain

$$Q_{\mathtt{U1}}(u,n) \;:-\; \mathtt{U}(u,n,h) \ltimes \mathtt{F}(u_1,u_2)$$
$$Q_{\mathtt{F1}}(u_1,u_2) \;:-\; \mathtt{F}(u_1,u_2) \ltimes \mathtt{U}(u,n,h)$$

The situation will be similar for the left outer join query in Figure 8b except that $Q_{\mathtt{U1}}$ will not contain any filter atoms. For the full outer join query in Figure 8c neither $Q_{\mathtt{U1}}$ nor $Q_{\mathtt{F1}}$ will contain any filter atoms. An analogous criterion can be used for other types of queries, including those in Figures 8d and 8e from our running example.

The next step is to find equality constraints that should be added to $Q_{\mathtt{U1}}$ and $Q_{\mathtt{F1}}$. We begin by finding all `SELECT` nodes that are reachable from the condition graph node associated with `U1`. We then check the `WHERE` and `HAVING` clauses of the corresponding `SELECT` statements for equality constraints that must hold for all tuples in the statements' outputs. In the query from Figure 7a, we obtain two constraints: `(F1.uid1 = 1)` and `(F1.uid2 = U1.uid)`. When we integrate both constraints into $Q_{\mathtt{U1}}$ we obtain the query

$$Q_{\mathtt{U1}}(u,n) \;:-\; \mathtt{U}(u,n,h) \ltimes \mathtt{F}(1,u)$$

An analogous process can be performed with $Q_{\mathtt{F1}}$ to obtain

$$Q_{\mathtt{F1}}(1,u_2) \;:-\; \mathtt{F}(1,u_2) \ltimes \mathtt{U}(u_2,n,h)$$

The filter-project queries $Q_{\mathtt{U1}}$ and $Q_{\mathtt{F1}}$ comprise the output of our extraction algorithm.

4.5 Summary and Extensions

Our system takes as input queries and security views expressed in SQL, with the restriction that security views must be expressible as filter-project queries. It then compiles each input SQL query to a set of filter-project queries. Because the universe of filter-project queries is decomposable, the system can generate policy formulas and explanations using the efficient algorithms from Section 3.

The number of SQL features that our system is able to handle has gradually increased throughout the course of its development and can be further increased as needed. By default, our system errs on the side of overestimating information disclosure when new language features are added. For example, an earlier version of our system required a principal who wished to execute the query

```
SELECT uid FROM User U1
 WHERE EXISTS (SELECT * FROM Friend F1)
```

to obtain permissions to access all of the columns in the `Friend` relation. The term initialization stage of our pipeline was subsequently extended with rules for handling selected columns in `WHERE EXISTS` subclauses more precisely.

5. EXPERIMENTAL EVALUATION

The goal of our experimental evaluation was three-fold. First, we wanted to verify that SQL queries containing a wide range of commonly used features could be correctly handled by the compiler discussed in Section 4. Second, we wanted to determine whether the language of filter-project queries described in Section 4.2 was powerful enough to represent a variety of practical security constraints. And third, we wanted to determine whether policy formulas could be generated quickly enough to be used in practical systems.

We implemented a prototype system in Java. Our system consisted of three main components: (i) a compiler for translating SQL queries into filter-project queries, (ii) a module for representing and reasoning about filter-project queries, and (iii) a module for representing and evaluating policy formulas and generating why-so and why-not explanations. The implementation of our compiler consisted of just over 5,500 lines of Java code, while filter-project queries were implemented in about 1,000 lines, and policy formulas were implemented in 250.

For the first goal, we began by writing end-to-end tests for our compiler based on several dozen SQL queries taken from a standard undergraduate database textbook. (See Chapter 5 of [21].) We gradually added more tests over time to keep track of the border cases we encountered. At the time of publication, we had 110 of our 115 end-to-end tests running successfully, and the remaining five were rejected as being semantically invalid. Of these, three were rejected due to limitations of JSqlParser. The last two were valid according to the SQL standard, but were considered to be invalid by both MySQL and PostgreSQL. The results gave us confidence that our compilation-based approach to disclosure control could be successfully applied to a broad range of real-world SQL features.

For the second and third goals, we ran experiments on a database inspired by the one used by the Facebook Query Language (FQL). [3] The schema has a rich and diverse set of security requirements. For example, albums containing media such as photos and videos can be made visible to friends of the current user, to friends of friends, or to the public at large. The membership of a group can be made world-visible, can be restricted to members of that group, or can be completely hidden. Lists of attendees for events can similarly be made world-visible can be restricted to other attendees. All of these contingencies were accounted for using filter-project security views.

Our test database schema contained 18 relations with a grand total of 269 distinct columns – or an average of 15 columns per relation. We deliberately selected relations that had nontrivial security policies. The number of columns per relation ranged from two for the `Friend` relation (which stores information about friendship relations between users) to 62 for the `Application` table (which stores information about third-party Facebook Apps). We ended up defining a total of 75 security views. Equality constraints appeared in all but one of our security views; the exception was a view over the `Application` table that listed certain types of publicly available information about Facebook Apps. Filter atoms appeared in 59 security views. Column projections were used in just four of the security views.

In addition to the qualitative experiments above, we also evaluated the performance of our prototype system. Our experiments were run on a workstation with two 4-core 2.13 GHz Intel Xeon processors and 50 GB of RAM. Our code was run on the OpenJDK 1.7 VM on Ubuntu 12.04.

Our experiments made use of a synthetic query generator that worked by recursively stringing together predefined templates. Our use of templates allowed us to gener-

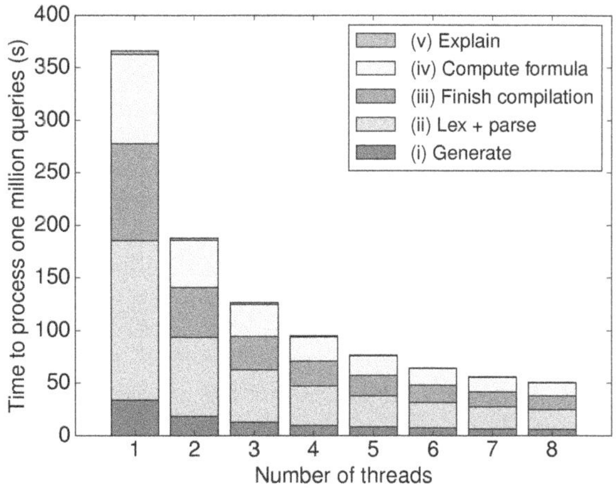

Figure 9: Performance for ordinary queries

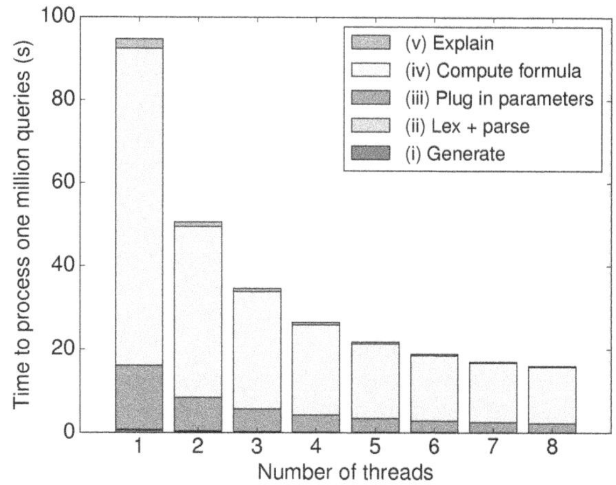

Figure 10: Performance for prepared statements

ate realistic-looking queries whose joins and equality predicates encoded meaningful security-related constraints. Each of the queries we generated contained between one and six table instances; the median 2 and the mean was 2.5. The experiment focused exclusively on filter-project queries with equality constraints. Such queries are especially challenging for our pipeline because they tend to yield filter-project queries with many filter atoms; experiments on other types of queries are available in a digital appendix.[2]

We measured the wall time needed to (i) randomly generate queries, (ii) lex and parse them, (iii) extract filter-project queries from the parsed output, (iv) compute policy formulas from the resulting filter-project queries, and (v) generate a policy decision for each query, a why-so explanation for each permitted query, and a why-not explanation for each denied query. Since each stage depended on the output of the previous stage, these measurements were cumulative: we measured the time for (i) alone, the time for (i) + (ii), and so on. We also varied the number of execution threads between 1 and 8. All of our algorithms are trivially parallelizable, and the threads operated completely independently of each other. In each case, we measured the time needed to process 1,000,000 queries. All numbers are averaged across five runs; the variation across runs was less than one second in almost all cases.

The results are shown in Figure 9. As expected, throughput scaled nearly linearly with the number of cores. The analysis pipeline took a total of 366 seconds on a single core or 50 seconds on 8 cores. If we exclude the time needed to randomly generate queries, these numbers change to 333 and 44 seconds respectively. If we focus on the last three stages (which are where we claim algorithmic contributions), the numbers fall to 181 and 26 seconds respectively. All computation was CPU-bound, and memory consumption ranged from 60 MB to 220 MB per thread. The time needed to perform policy checks and generate explanations was negligible compared to the rest of the system – about 3.5 seconds on a single core or 0.5 seconds on eight cores – and is barely visible in Figure 9.

[2]`http://www.cs.cornell.edu/~lucja/Publications/sigmod2014appendix.pdf`

Since query compilation time dominated the benchmark numbers in Figure 9, we speculated that throughput could be significantly improved by using prepared statements. The filter-project queries associated with prepared statements only needed to be calculated once (as a preprocessing step), and could retrieved on demand when the prepared statements were executed. Parameters passed to prepared statements at execution time could be substituted directly into the compiled filter-project queries, bypassing the need for a heavy-weight compilation step.

Results are shown in Figure 10. Our use of prepared statements yielded around a 3x improvement in overall throughput. The time spent on query generation, lexing and parsing was negligible, and the time needed to retrieve filter-project queries and plug in parameter values paled in comparison with the time needed to perform end-to-end query compilation. As a result, computation of policy formulas dominated the running time.

6. RELATED WORK

Disclosure lattices, which we originally proposed in [8], generalize the *lattice of information* [18]. Our current work is geared towards real-world SQL queries and complex security policies, while previous work focuses on conjunctive queries under set semantics and restricts security views to single-atom conjunctive queries.

Although there is a large body of work on enforcing access control policies through *view rewriting*, we are not aware of any previous work in the database security literature on generating human-readable explanations for policy decisions.

Access control mechanisms based on view rewriting can be classified as *Truman* or *non-Truman*. Non-Truman mechanisms (e.g., [22]) analyze queries to determine whether they should be accepted or rejected; the principal who issues a query receives either an answer (if the query is accepted) or a denial (if the query is refused). *Truman* mechanisms modify queries' execution semantics in order to ensure that they are consistent with an administrator-defined security policy; commercial Truman mechanisms include IBM LBAC [5] and Oracle VPD [6]. Our approach is non-Truman, but the use of filter-project security views is more commonly associated with Truman mechanisms (e.g., [12, 20]).

Our work has a strong connection to the problem of *query pricing* [17] proposed by Koutris et al. In the framework of query pricing, we are given a set of administrator-provided views (similar to our *security views*), and a monetary price is assigned to each view. Given a query Q, the goal of [17] is to find a subset of the views that contain enough information to answer Q and whose total cost is minimal subject to that constraint. Their model of information disclosure is database-dependent, whereas ours is database-independent. The policy formulas computed by our system can be used to derive linear programs that solve a *database-independent* variant of the query pricing problem. Details are omitted here due to space limitations.

Dwork's Differential Privacy [15] provides a formal basis for privacy-preserving data publishing. Differential privacy assigns a numeric privacy cost to any possible query over the dataset, but does not provide meaningful feedback about *whose* information is disclosed or *what types* of information are disclosed by a given query. In contrast, the policy formulas and explanations generated by our system are specifically designed to answer these types of questions.

In [10], Brodsky et al. propose an algorithm for enumerating the facts that could be learned from a collection of database queries. Their work provides a *lower bound* (expressed as a set of facts) on the information disclosed by a set of queries. Our techniques place an *upper bound* on the permissions needed to answer a set of queries.

Our *policy algebras* are related to formalisms proposed for composable security policies (e.g., [9]) and general-purpose authorization logics (e.g., NAL [24] and SecPal [7]). Compared to these systems, our model is simpler, easier to reason about, and can be used to produce data-derived policy formulas. Constructive authorization logics such as NAL ensure that all positive authorization decisions are accompanied by formal proofs that are in some sense analogous to our *why-so explanations*. We are not aware of any direct analogues to our *why-not explanations*.

7. FUTURE WORK

In the future, we plan to extend our system to make it even more broadly useful. Notably, we plan to explore the problem of generating *database-dependent* explanations that make use of information about the current state of the database. We also plan to improve the usefulness of the explanations by suggesting concrete possible courses of action for the principal and ranking them according to an appropriate metric.

7.1 Acknowledgments

This research was supported by the National Science Foundation under Grants IIS-1012593 and IIS-0911036, by the iAd Project funded by the Research Council of Norway, and by a Google Research Award. Any opinions, findings, conclusions or recommendations expressed in this paper are those of the authors and do not necessarily reflect the views of the sponsors.

8. REFERENCES

[1] `https://github.com/JSQLParser/JSqlParser`.

[2] Android permissions. `http://developer.android.com/guide/topics/security/permissions.html`.

[3] Facebook query language. `https://developers.facebook.com/docs/reference/fql/`.

[4] Facebook query language (fql) reference. https://developers.facebook.com/docs/reference/fql/.

[5] Label-based access control (lbac) overview. `http://publib.boulder.ibm.com/infocenter/db2luw/v9/index.jsp?topic=%2Fcom.ibm.db2.udb.admin.doc%2Fdoc%2Fc0021114.htm`.

[6] Virtual private database. `http://www.oracle.com/technetwork/database/security/index-088277.html`.

[7] Moritz Y Becker, Cédric Fournet, and Andrew D Gordon. Secpal: Design and semantics of a decentralized authorization language. *CSF*, 2006.

[8] Gabriel M Bender, Lucja Kot, Johannes Gehrke, and Christoph Koch. Fine-grained disclosure control for app ecosystems. *SIGMOD*, 2013.

[9] Piero Bonatti, Sabrina De Capitani di Vimercati, and Pierangela Samarati. An algebra for composing access control policies. *TISSEC*, 2002.

[10] Alexander Brodsky, Csilla Farkas, and Sushil Jajodia. Secure databases: Constraints, inference channels, and monitoring disclosures. *TKDE*, 12(6):900–919, 2000.

[11] Ashok K Chandra and Philip M Merlin. Optimal implementation of conjunctive queries in relational data bases. *STOC*, 1977.

[12] Surajit Chaudhuri, Tanmoy Dutta, and S Sudarshan. Fine grained authorization through predicated grants. *ICDE*, 2007.

[13] Surajit Chaudhuri and Moshe Y Vardi. Optimization of real conjunctive queries. *SIGMOD*, 1993.

[14] Sara Cohen. Equivalence of queries that are sensitive to multiplicities. *VLDB*, 2009.

[15] Cynthia Dwork. Differential privacy. In *Automata, languages and programming*, pages 1–12. Springer, 2006.

[16] Adrienne Porter Felt, Erika Chin, Steve Hanna, Dawn Song, and David Wagner. Android permissions demystified. *CCS*, 2011.

[17] Paraschos Koutris, Prasang Upadhyaya, Magdalena Balazinska, Bill Howe, and Dan Suciu. Query-based data pricing. *PODS*, 2012.

[18] Jaisook Landauer and Timothy Redmond. A lattice of information. *CSFW*, 1993.

[19] Alan Nash, Luc Segoufin, and Victor Vianu. Views and queries: Determinacy and rewriting. *TODS*, 2010.

[20] Lars E Olson, Carl A Gunter, and P Madhusudan. A formal framework for reflective database access control policies. *CCS*, 2008.

[21] Raghu Ramakrishnan and Johannes Gehrke. *Database Management Systems*. McGraw-Hill, Inc., New York, NY, USA, 3 edition, 2003.

[22] Shariq Rizvi, Alberto Mendelzon, Sundararajarao Sudarshan, and Prasan Roy. Extending query rewriting techniques for fine-grained access control. *SIGMOD*, 2004.

[23] Jerome H Saltzer and Michael D Schroeder. The protection of information in computer systems. *Proceedings of the IEEE*, 63(9):1278–1308, 1975.

[24] Fred B Schneider, Kevin Walsh, and Emin Gün Sirer. Nexus authorization logic (nal): Design rationale and applications. *TISSEC*, 14(1), 2011.

PrivBayes: Private Data Release via Bayesian Networks

Jun Zhang[1] Graham Cormode[2] Cecilia M. Procopiuc[3] Divesh Srivastava[3] Xiaokui Xiao[1]

[1]Nanyang Technological University
{jzhang027, xkxiao}@ntu.edu.sg

[2]University of Warwick
g.cormode@warwick.ac.uk

[3]AT&T Labs – Research
{magda, divesh}@research.att.com

ABSTRACT

Privacy-preserving data publishing is an important problem that has been the focus of extensive study. The state-of-the-art goal for this problem is differential privacy, which offers a strong degree of privacy protection without making restrictive assumptions about the adversary. Existing techniques using differential privacy, however, cannot effectively handle the publication of high-dimensional data. In particular, when the input dataset contains a large number of attributes, existing methods require injecting a prohibitive amount of noise compared to the signal in the data, which renders the published data next to useless.

To address the deficiency of the existing methods, this paper presents PRIVBAYES, a differentially private method for releasing high-dimensional data. Given a dataset D, PRIVBAYES first constructs a Bayesian network $\mathcal{N}$, which (i) provides a succinct model of the correlations among the attributes in D and (ii) allows us to approximate the distribution of data in D using a set $\mathcal{P}$ of low-dimensional marginals of D. After that, PRIVBAYES injects noise into each marginal in $\mathcal{P}$ to ensure differential privacy, and then uses the noisy marginals and the Bayesian network to construct an approximation of the data distribution in D. Finally, PRIVBAYES samples tuples from the approximate distribution to construct a synthetic dataset, and then releases the synthetic data. Intuitively, PRIVBAYES circumvents the curse of dimensionality, as it injects noise into the low-dimensional marginals in $\mathcal{P}$ instead of the high-dimensional dataset D. Private construction of Bayesian networks turns out to be significantly challenging, and we introduce a novel approach that uses a surrogate function for mutual information to build the model more accurately. We experimentally evaluate PRIVBAYES on real data, and demonstrate that it significantly outperforms existing solutions in terms of accuracy.

Categories and Subject Descriptors

H.2.7 [**Database Administration**]: Security, integrity & protection

Keywords

Differential privacy; synthetic data generation; Bayesian network

SIGMOD'14, June 22–27, 2014, Snowbird, UT, USA.
Copyright 2014 ACM 978-1-4503-2376-5/14/06 ...$15.00.

1. INTRODUCTION

The problem of privacy-preserving data publishing (PPDP) has become increasingly important in recent years. Often, we encounter situations where a data owner wishes to make available a data set without revealing private, sensitive information. For example, this arises in the case of revealing detailed demographic information about citizens (census), patients (health data), investors (financial data), and so on. In each example, there are many potential uses and users for the data: for social analysis, for medical research, for freedom-of-information and other legal disclosure reasons. The canonical case in PPDP is when the database can be modeled as a table, where each row may contain information about an individual (say, details of their medical status, or employment information). Then, the aim is to release some manipulated version of this information so that this can still be used for the intended purpose, but the privacy of individuals in the database is preserved.

Following many attempts to formally define the requirements of privacy, the current state-of-the-art solution is to seek the differential privacy guarantee [16]. Informally, this model requires that what can be learned from the released data is (approximately) the same, whether or not any particular individual was included in the input database. This model offers strong privacy protection, and does not make any limiting assumptions about the power of the notional adversary: it remains a strong model even in the face of an adversary with much background knowledge and reasoning power.

Putting differential privacy into practice remains a challenging problem. Since its proposal, there have been many efforts to develop mechanisms and processes for data release for different kinds of input database, and for different objectives for the end use. However, it seems that all existing techniques encounter difficulties when trying to release even moderately high-dimensional data – that is, an input table with half a dozen columns or more. The reasons for these problems are two-fold:

- *Output Scalability:* Most algorithms (see, e.g., [37]) either explicitly or implicitly represent the database as a vector x of size equal to the *domain size*, that is, the product of cardinalities of the attributes. For many natural data sets, the domain size m is orders of magnitude larger than the data size n [13]. Hence, these algorithms become inapplicable for any realistic dataset with a moderate-to-high number of attributes. For example, a million row table with ten attributes, each of which has 20 possible values, results in a domain size (and hence an output size) of $m = 20^{10} \approx 10TB$, which is very unwieldy and slow to use compared to the input which can be measured in megabytes.

- *Signal-to-noise ratio:* When the high dimensional database is represented as a vector x, the average count in each entry, given by n/m, is typically very small. Once noise is added to x (or some transformation of it) to obtain another vector x^*, the noise completely dominates the original signal, making the published vector x^* next to useless. For example, if the table above has size $n = 1M$, the average entry count is $n/m = 10^{-7}$. By contrast, the average noise injected to achieve, e.g., differential privacy with parameter $\varepsilon = 0.1$ has expected magnitude around 10. Even if the data is skewed in the domain space, i.e., there are some entries $x[i]$ with high counts, such peaks are infrequent and so the vast majority of published values $x^*[i]$ are useless.

1.1 Related Work

A full survey of methods to realize differential privacy is beyond the scope of this work. Here, we identify the most related efforts, and discuss why they cannot fully solve the problems above.

Initial efforts released projections of the data on subsets of dimensions, via Fourier decompositions [5]. This reduces the impact of higher dimensionality, but requires the data owner to determine (somehow) which set of dimensions are of interest, and for the data to be mapped into a space where a Fourier decomposition can be computed. Subsequent work followed this template, for example by searching for meaningful "subcubes" of the datacube representation to release privately [15]. These can be aggregated to answer lower-dimensional cube queries, where the signal-to-noise ratio in each cell is significantly higher than in the original domain. A major limitation is that the running time is exponential in the dimensionality of the domain, making it inapplicable for all but small sets. Accuracy is improved by additional post-processing of the output to restore "consistency" of the counts mandated by the structure (e.g. using the fact that counts in a hierarchy should sum to the count of an ancestor) [5, 15, 21]; however, this improvement does not overcome the inherent error incurred in high dimensions.

Another approach is to use data reduction techniques to avoid dimensionality issues. For example, [13] proposes various sampling mechanisms to reduce the size of (and time to produce) the output x^*, while approximately preserving the accuracy of subset-sum queries. However, the accuracy guarantee is with respect to the accuracy of using the entire vector x^*, rather than the original vector x, which degrades rapidly with data dimensionality. The approach in [12] tries to keep the domain size of the output small, and the density of data within the new domain high, by adaptively grouping some of the attribute values. In the example above, suppose that on each of the ten attributes, we grouped the 20 values into two groups. Thus, we reduce the output size from 20^{10} to $2^{10} \approx 1MB$. This coarser grid representation of the data loses precision, and in this example still leads to small average counts of the order of 1. Cormode et al. [12] address the latter problem by using spatial decompositions to define irregular grids over the domain of x, such that the count $x[i]$ in each grid cell is sufficiently large. This makes sense only for range queries, and requires all attributes to have an ordering.

Other approaches find other ways to recast the input data and release it, so that the noise from the privacy transformation has less impact on certain statistics. In particular, Xiao et al. [37] make use of the wavelet transformation of data. This addresses range queries, and means that the noise incurred by a range query scales proportionately to the logarithm of its length, rather than to its length directly. The value of this is confined primarily to low-dimensional databases where range queries are anticipated. More generally, the matrix mechanism of Li and Miklau [25, 26] and subsequent related approaches [20, 38, 39] take in a query workload (expressed in terms of a weighted set of inner-product queries), and seek to release a version of the database that minimizes the noise for these queries. The cost of this optimization can be high, and critically assumes the foreknowledge of the query distribution.

The above discussion focuses on methods that produce an output in a general form that can be used flexibly for a variety of subsequent analyses. There is also a large class of results that instead generate a description of the output of a specific algorithm computed under privacy, for example the result of building a classifier for the data. Prominent examples include the work of McSherry and Mironov [30] to mask the preferences of individual raters in recommendation systems; Rastogi and Nath [34] to release time-series data based on leading Fourier coefficients; and McSherry and Mahajan [29] for addressing common queries over network trace data. Differential privacy has also been applied to other sophisticated data analysis tasks, e.g., coresets for summarizing geometric data [18], building classifiers in the form of decision trees [19], and support vector machines [35], and mining the occurrence of frequent patterns [6, 27].

Some frameworks have been proposed to solve a class of optimization problems. For example, Chaudhuri et al. [8, 9] and Kifer et al. [22] consider differentially private convex empirical risk minimization, which can be applied to a wide range of optimization problems (e.g., logistic regression and support vector machines). Zhang et al. [40] propose the *PrivGene* framework, which is a combination of genetic algorithms and an enhanced version of the *exponential mechanism* for differentially private model fitting. Smith et al. [33, 36] and Mohan et al. [32] respectively present and implement the *sample and aggregate* framework that can be used for any analysis task whose results are not affected by the number of records in the database. While this class of methods obtains generally good results for the target problem, it requires fixing this objective at the time of data release, and limits the applicability of the output for other uses.

1.2 Our Contributions

In this paper, we propose a powerful solution to the problem of publishing differentially private high-dimensional data. Unlike the bulk of prior work, which focuses on optimizing the output for specific workloads (e.g., range queries, cube queries), we aim to approximate the high-dimensional distribution of the original data with a data-dependent set of well-chosen low-dimensional distributions, in the belief that, for a sufficiently accurate approximation, the resulting data will maintain high accuracy for almost any type of (linear or non-linear) query. Since our approach is query-independent, many different queries can be evaluated (accurately) on the same set of released data. Query-independence means that our approach may be weaker than approaches that target a particular query set; however, we show empirically that the gap is small or non-existent in many natural cases. By working in low-dimensional spaces, we avoid the signal-to-noise problem. Although we compare to the full-dimensional distribution for evaluation purposes, our approach never needs to compute this explicitly, thus avoiding the scalability problem.

To achieve this goal, we start from the well-known *Bayesian network* model, which is widely studied in the statistical and machine learning communities [23]. Bayesian networks combine low-dimensional distributions to approximate the full-dimensional distribution of a data set, and are a simple but powerful example of a graphical model. Our algorithm, dubbed PRIVBAYES, consists of the following steps:

1. (*Network learning*) We describe how to compute a differentially private Bayesian network that approximates the full-dimensional distribution via the Exponential Mechanism (EM). This step requires new theoretical insights, which are described in Section 3. We improve on this basic approach by defining a new quality function for use in EM, which results in significantly better networks

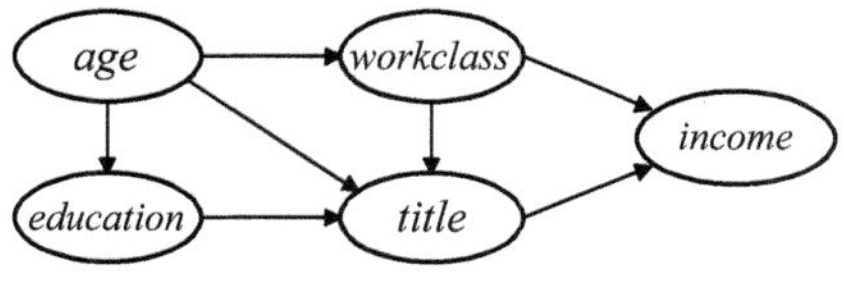

Figure 1: A Bayesian network $\mathcal{N}_1$ over five attributes

being found. The definition and computation of this function are one of our main technical contributions; see Section 4.

2. (*Distribution learning*) We explain how to compute the necessary differentially private distributions of the data in the subspaces of the Bayesian network, via the Laplace Mechanism.

3. (*Data synthesis*) We show how to generate synthetic data from the differentially private Bayesian network, without explicitly materializing the global distribution.

In Section 5, we provide an extensive experimental evaluation of the accuracy of the synthetic datasets generated above, over workloads of linear and non-linear queries. In each case, we compare to prior methods specifically designed to optimize the accuracy for that type of workload. Our experiments show that PRIVBAYES is often *more* accurate than any prior method, even though it is not optimized for any specific type of query. When PRIVBAYES is less accurate than some prior method, the accuracy loss is small and, we believe, an acceptable tradeoff, since PRIVBAYES offers a generic solution that does not require prior knowledge of the workload and works well on many different types of queries.

2. PRELIMINARIES

This section reviews two concepts closely related to our work, namely, differential privacy and Bayesian networks.

2.1 Differential Privacy

Let D be a sensitive dataset to be published. Differential privacy requires that, prior to D's release, it should be modified using a randomized algorithm G, such that the output of G does not reveal much information about any particular tuple in D. The formal definition of differential privacy is as follows:

DEFINITION 1 (ε-DIFFERENTIAL PRIVACY [17]). *A randomized algorithm G satisfies ε-differential privacy, if for any two datasets D_1 and D_2 that differ only in one tuple, and for any possible output O of G, we have*

$$\Pr\left[G(D_1) = O\right] \le e^{\varepsilon} \cdot \Pr\left[G(D_2) = O\right], \qquad (1)$$

where $\Pr[\cdot]$ *denotes the probability of an event.*

In what follows, we say that two datasets are neighboring if they differ in only one tuple, i.e., the values of one tuple are changed while the rest are identifical. While there are many approaches to achieving differential privacy, we rely on the two best known and most-widely used, namely, the *Laplace mechanism* [17] and the *exponential mechanism* [31].

The Laplace mechanism releases the result of a function F that takes as input a dataset and outputs a set of numeric values. Given F, the Laplace mechanism transforms F into a differentially private algorithm, by adding i.i.d. noise (denoted as η) into each output value of F. The noise η is sampled from a *Laplace distribution* $\mathrm{Lap}(\lambda)$ with the following pdf: $\Pr[\eta = x] = \frac{1}{2\lambda}e^{-|x|/\lambda}$. Dwork et al. [17] prove that the Laplace mechanism ensures ε-differential privacy if $\lambda \ge S(F)/\varepsilon$, where $S(F)$ is the *sensitivity* of F:

Table 1: The attribute-parent pairs in $\mathcal{N}_1$

i	X_i	Π_i
1	*age*	$\emptyset$
2	*education*	{*age*}
3	*workclass*	{*age*}
4	*title*	{*age, education, workclass*}
5	*income*	{*workclass, title*}

DEFINITION 2 (SENSITIVITY [17]). *Let F be a function that maps a dataset into a fixed-size vector of real numbers. The* sensitivity *of F is defined as*

$$S(F) = \max_{D_1, D_2} \|F(D_1) - F(D_2)\|_1, \qquad (2)$$

where $\|\cdot\|_1$ denotes the L_1 norm, and D_1 and D_2 are any two neighboring datasets.

Intuitively, $S(F)$ measures the maximum possible change in F's output when we modify one arbitrary tuple in F's input.

When F's output is categorical instead of numeric, the Laplace mechanism does not apply, but the exponential mechanism [31] can be used instead. The exponential mechanism releases a differentially private version of F, by sampling from F's output domain Ω. The sampling probability for each $\omega \in \Omega$ is determined based on a user-specified *score function* f_s, which takes as input any dataset D and any element $\omega \in \Omega$, and outputs a numeric score $f_s(D, \omega)$ that measures the quality of ω: a larger score indicates that ω is a better output with respect to D. More specifically, given a dataset D, the exponential mechanism samples $\omega \in \Omega$ with a probability proportional to $\exp(f_s(D, \omega)/2\Delta)$, where Δ is a scaling factor that controls the degree of privacy protection. McSherry and Talwar [31] show that the exponential mechanism achieves ε-differential privacy if $\Delta \ge S(f_s)/\varepsilon$, where $S(f_s)$ is defined as:

$$S(f_s) = \max_{D_1, D_2, \omega'} \left| f_s(D_1, \omega') - f_s(D_2, \omega') \right|, \qquad (3)$$

for D_1 and D_2 any two neighboring datasets, and ω' any element in Ω. For convenience, we also refer to $S(f_s)$ as the *sensitivity* of f_s, as it is similar in form to sensitivity as defined above.

Both mechanisms can be applied quite generally; however, to be effective we seek to ensure that the noise introduced does not outweigh the signal in the data, and that it is computationally efficient to apply the mechanism. This requires a careful design of what functions to use in the mechanisms.

2.2 Bayesian Network

Let $\mathcal{A}$ be the set of attributes on a dataset D, and d be the size of $\mathcal{A}$. A *Bayesian network* on $\mathcal{A}$ is a way to compactly describe the (probability) distribution of the attributes in terms of other attributes. Formally, a Bayesian network is a directed acyclic graph (DAG) that (i) represents each attribute in $\mathcal{A}$ as a node, and (ii) models conditional independence among attributes in $\mathcal{A}$ using directed edges. As an example, Figure 1 shows a Bayesian network over a set $\mathcal{A}$ of five attributes, namely, *age*, *education*, *workclass*, *title*, and *income*. For any two attributes $X, Y \in \mathcal{A}$, there exist three possibilities for the relationship between X and Y:

Case 1: Direct dependence. There is an edge between X and Y, say, from Y to X. This indicates that for any tuple in D, its distribution on X is determined (in part) by its value on Y. We define Y as a *parent* of X, and refer to the set of all parents of X as its *parent set*. For example, in Figure 1, the edge from *workclass* to *income* indicates that the income distribution depends on the type of job (and also on title).

Table 2: Table of notations

Notation	Description
D	A sensitive dataset to be published
n	The number of tuples in D
$\mathcal{A}$	The set of attributes in D
d	The number of attributes in $\mathcal{A}$
$\mathcal{N}$	A Bayesian network over $\mathcal{A}$
$\Pr[\mathcal{A}]$	The distribution of tuples in D
$\Pr_{\mathcal{N}}[\mathcal{A}]$	An approximation of $\Pr[\mathcal{A}]$ defined by $\mathcal{N}$
$\mathrm{dom}(X)$	The domain of random variable X

Case 2: Weak conditional independence. There is a path (but no edge) between Y and X. Assume without loss of generality that the path goes from Y to X. Then, X and Y are *conditionally independent* given X's parent set. For instance, in Figure 1, there is a two-hop path from *age* to *income*, and the parent set of *income* is $\{workclass, title\}$. This indicates that, given workclass and job title of an individual, her income and age are conditionally independent.

Case 3: Strong conditional independence. There is no path between Y and X. Then, X and Y are conditionally independent given any of X's and Y's parent sets.

Formally, a Bayesian network $\mathcal{N}$ over $\mathcal{A}$ is defined as a set of d *attribute-parent (AP) pairs*, $(X_1, \Pi_1), \ldots, (X_d, \Pi_d)$, such that

1. Each X_i is a unique attribute in $\mathcal{A}$;

2. Each Π_i is a subset of the attributes in $\mathcal{A} \setminus \{X_i\}$. We say that Π_i is the parent set of X_i in $\mathcal{N}$;

3. For any $1 \le i < j \le d$, we have $X_j \notin \Pi_i$, i.e., there is no edge from X_j to X_i in $\mathcal{N}$. This ensures that the network is acyclic, namely, it is a DAG.

We define the *degree* of $\mathcal{N}$ as the maximum size of any parent set Π_i in $\mathcal{N}$. For example, Table 1 shows the AP pairs in the Bayesian network $\mathcal{N}_1$ in Figure 1; $\mathcal{N}_1$'s degree equals 3, since the parent set of any attribute in $\mathcal{N}_1$ has a size at most three.

Let $\Pr[\mathcal{A}]$ denote the full distribution of tuples in database D. The d AP pairs in $\mathcal{N}$ essentially define a way to approximate $\Pr[\mathcal{A}]$ with d conditional distributions $\Pr[X_1 \mid \Pi_1], \Pr[X_2 \mid \Pi_2], \ldots, \Pr[X_d \mid \Pi_d]$. In particular, under the assumption that any X_i and any $X_j \notin \Pi_i$ are conditionally independent given Π_i, we have

$$\begin{aligned}\Pr[\mathcal{A}] &= \Pr[X_1, X_2, \ldots, X_d] \\ &= \Pr[X_1] \cdot \Pr[X_2 \mid X_1] \cdot \Pr[X_3 \mid X_1, X_2] \ldots \Pr[X_d \mid X_1, \ldots X_{d-1}] \\ &= \prod_{i=1}^{d} \Pr[X_i \mid \Pi_i]. \qquad (4)\end{aligned}$$

Let $\Pr_{\mathcal{N}}[\mathcal{A}] = \prod_{i=1}^{d} \Pr[X_i \mid \Pi_i]$ be the above approximation of $\Pr[\mathcal{A}]$ defined by $\mathcal{N}$. Intuitively, if $\mathcal{N}$ accurately captures the conditional independence among the attributes in $\mathcal{A}$, then $\Pr_{\mathcal{N}}[\mathcal{A}]$ would be a good approximation of $\Pr[\mathcal{A}]$. In addition, if the degree of $\mathcal{N}$ is small, then the computation of $\Pr_{\mathcal{N}}[\mathcal{A}]$ is relatively simple as it requires only d low-dimensional distributions $\Pr[X_1 \mid \Pi_1], \Pr[X_2 \mid \Pi_2], \ldots, \Pr[X_d \mid \Pi_d]$. Low-degree Bayesian networks are the core of our solution to release high-dimensional data. Table 2 shows notation that will be frequently used in this paper.

3. SOLUTION OVERVIEW

This section presents an overview of PRIVBAYES, our solution for releasing a high-dimensional dataset D in an ε-differentially private manner. PRIVBAYES runs in three phases:

Algorithm 1 NoisyConditionals $(D, \mathcal{N}, k)$: returns $\mathcal{P}^*$

1: Initialize $\mathcal{P}^* = \emptyset$
2: **for** $i = k+1$ to d **do**
3: Materialize the joint distribution $\Pr[X_i, \Pi_i]$
4: Generate differentially private $\Pr^*[X_i, \Pi_i]$ by adding Laplace noise $\mathrm{Lap}\left(\frac{4\cdot(d-k)}{n\cdot\varepsilon}\right)$
5: Set negative values in $\Pr^*[X_i, \Pi_i]$ to 0 and normalize;
6: Derive $\Pr^*[X_i \mid \Pi_i]$ from $\Pr^*[X_i, \Pi_i]$; add it to $\mathcal{P}^*$
7: **for** $i = 1$ to k **do**
8: Derive $\Pr^*[X_i \mid \Pi_i]$ from $\Pr^*[X_{k+1}, \Pi_{k+1}]$; add it to $\mathcal{P}^*$
9: **return** $\mathcal{P}^*$

1. Construct a k-degree Bayesian network $\mathcal{N}$ over the attributes in D, using an $(\varepsilon/2)$-differentially private method. (k is a small value that can be chosen automatically by PRIVBAYES.)

2. Use an $(\varepsilon/2)$-differentially private algorithm to generate a set of *conditional distributions* of D, such that for each AP pair (X_i, Π_i) in $\mathcal{N}$, we have a noisy version of the conditional distribution $\Pr[X_i \mid \Pi_i]$. (We denote this noisy distribution as $\Pr^*[X_i \mid \Pi_i]$.)

3. Use the Bayesian network $\mathcal{N}$ (constructed in the first phase) and the d noisy conditional distributions (constructed in the second phase) to derive an approximate distribution of the tuples in D, and then sample tuples from the approximate distribution to generate a synthetic dataset D^*.

In short, PRIVBAYES utilizes a low-degree Bayesian network $\mathcal{N}$ to generate a synthetic dataset D^* that approximates the high dimensional input data D. The construction of $\mathcal{N}$ is highly nontrivial, as it requires carefully selecting AP pairs and the value of k to derive a close approximation of D without violating differential privacy. By contrast, the second and third phases of PRIVBAYES are relatively straightforward. In the following, we will clarify the details of these phases, and prove the privacy guarantee of PRIVBAYES; the algorithm for PRIVBAYES's first phase will be elaborated in Section 4.

Generation of Noisy Conditional Distributions. Suppose that we are given a k-degree Bayesian network $\mathcal{N}$. To construct the approximate distribution $\Pr_{\mathcal{N}}[\mathcal{A}]$, we need d conditional distributions $\Pr[X_i \mid \Pi_i]$ ($i \in [1, d]$), as shown in Equation (4). Algorithm 1 illustrates how the distributions specified by our algorithm can be derived in a differentially private manner. In particular, for any $i \in [k+1, d]$, the algorithm first materializes the joint distribution $\Pr[X_i, \Pi_i]$ (Line 3), and then injects Laplace noise into $\Pr[X_i, \Pi_i]$ to obtain a noisy distribution $\Pr^*[X_i, \Pi_i]$ (Line 4-5). To enforce the fact that these are probability distributions, all negative numbers in $\Pr^*[X_i, \Pi_i]$ are set to zero, then all values are normalized to maintain a total probability mass of 1 (Line 5).[1] After that, based on $\Pr^*[X_i, \Pi_i]$, the algorithm derives a noisy version of the conditional distribution $\Pr[X_i \mid \Pi_i]$, denoted as $\Pr^*[X_i \mid \Pi_i]$ (Line 6). The scale of the Laplace noise added to $\Pr[X_i, \Pi_i]$ is set to $4(d-k)/n\varepsilon$, which ensures that the generation of $\Pr^*[X_i, \Pi_i]$ satisfies $(\varepsilon/2(d-k))$-differential privacy, since $\Pr[X_i, \Pi_i]$ has sensitivity $2/n$. Meanwhile, the derivation of $\Pr^*[X_i \mid \Pi_i]$ from $\Pr^*[X_i, \Pi_i]$ does not incur any privacy cost, as it only relies on $\Pr^*[X_i, \Pi_i]$ instead of the input data D.

Overall, Lines 2-7 of Algorithm 1 construct $(d-k)$ noisy conditional distributions $\Pr^*[X_i \mid \Pi_i]$ ($i \in [k+1, d]$), and they satisfy $(\varepsilon/2)$-differential privacy, since each $\Pr^*[X_i \mid \Pi_i]$ is $(\varepsilon/2(d-k))$-differentially private. This is due to the composability property of

[1]More generally, we could apply additional post-processing of distributions, in the spirit of [5, 15, 21], to reflect the fact that lower degree distributions should be consistent. For simplicity and brevity, we omit such optimizations from this presentation.

differential privacy [16]. In particular, composability indicates that when a set of m algorithms satisfy differential privacy with parameters $\varepsilon_1, \varepsilon_2, \ldots, \varepsilon_m$, respectively, the set of algorithms as a whole satisfies $(\sum_i \varepsilon_i)$-differential privacy.

After $\Pr^*[X_{k+1} \mid \Pi_{k+1}], \ldots, \Pr^*[X_d \mid \Pi_d]$ are constructed, Algorithm 1 proceeds to generate $\Pr^*[X_i \mid \Pi_i]$ ($i \in [1,k]$). This generation, however, does not require any additional information from the input data D. Instead, we derive $\Pr^*[X_i \mid \Pi_i]$ ($i \in [1,k]$) directly from $\Pr^*[X_{k+1}, \Pi_{k+1}]$, which has been computed in Lines 2-7 of Algorithm 1. Such derivation is feasible, since our algorithm for constructing the Bayesian network $\mathcal{N}$ (to be clarified in Section 4) ensures that $X_i \in \Pi_{k+1}$ and $\Pi_i \subset \Pi_{k+1}$ for any $i \in [1,k]$. Since each $\Pr^*[X_i \mid \Pi_i]$ ($i \in [1,k]$) is derived from $\Pr^*[X_{k+1}, \Pi_{k+1}]$ without inspecting D, the construction of $\Pr^*[X_i \mid \Pi_i]$ does not incur any privacy overhead. Therefore, Algorithm 1 as a whole is $(\varepsilon/2)$-differentially private. Example 1 illustrates Algorithm 1.

EXAMPLE 1. *Suppose that we are given a 2-degree Bayesian network $\mathcal{N}$ over a set of four attributes $\{A,B,C,D\}$, with 4 AP pairs: $(A,\emptyset), (B,\{A\}), (C,\{A,B\})$, and $(D,\{A,C\})$. Given $\mathcal{N}$, Algorithm 1 constructs two noisy joint distributions $\Pr^*[A,B,C]$ and $\Pr^*[A,C,D]$. Based on $\Pr^*[A,C,D]$, Algorithm 1 derives a noisy conditional distribution $\Pr^*[D \mid A,C]$. In addition, the algorithm uses $\Pr^*[A,B,C]$ to derive three other conditional distributions $\Pr^*[A]$, $\Pr^*[B \mid A]$, and $\Pr^*[C \mid A,B]$. Given these four conditional distributions, the input tuple distribution is approximated as*

$$\Pr^*_{\mathcal{N}}[A,B,C,D] = \Pr^*[A] \cdot \Pr^*[B \mid A] \cdot \Pr^*[C \mid A,B] \cdot \Pr^*[D \mid A,C].$$

Generation of Synthetic Data. Even with the simple closed-form expression in Equation 4, it is still time and space consuming to directly sample from $\Pr^*_{\mathcal{N}}[\mathcal{A}]$ by computing the probability for each element in the domain of $\mathcal{A}$. Fortunately, the Bayesian network $\mathcal{N}$ provides a means to perform sampling efficiently without materializing $\Pr^*_{\mathcal{N}}[\mathcal{A}]$. As shown in Equation 4, we can sample each X_i from the conditional distribution $\Pr^*[X_i \mid \Pi_i]$ independently, without considering any attribute not in $\Pi_i \cup \{X_i\}$. Furthermore, the properties of $\mathcal{N}$ (discussed in Section 2.2) ensure that $X_j \notin \Pi_i$ for any $j > i$. Therefore, if we sample X_i ($i \in [1,d]$) in increasing order of i, then by the time X_j ($j \in [2,d]$) is to be sampled, we must have sampled all attributes in Π_j, i.e., we will be able to sample X_j from $\Pr^*[X_j \mid \Pi_j]$ given the previously sampled attributes. That is to say, the sampling of X_j does not require the full distribution $\Pr^*_{\mathcal{N}}[\mathcal{A}]$.

With the above sampling approach, we can generate an arbitrary number of tuples from $\Pr^*_{\mathcal{N}}[\mathcal{A}]$ to construct a synthetic database D^*. In this paper, we consider the size of D^* is set to n, i.e., the same as the number of tuples in the input data D.

Privacy Guarantee. The correctness of PRIVBAYES directly follows the composability property of differential privacy [16]. In particular, the first and second phases of PRIVBAYES require direct access to the input database, and each of them consumes $\varepsilon/2$ privacy budget. No access to the original database is invoked during the third (sampling) phase. The results of first two steps, i.e., the Bayesian network $\mathcal{N}$ and the set of noisy conditional distributions, are sufficient to generate the synthetic database D^*. Therefore, we have the following theorem.

THEOREM 1. PRIVBAYES *satisfies ε-differential privacy.*

4. PRIVATE BAYESIAN NETWORKS

This section presents our solution for constructing differentially private Bayesian networks. We will first introduce a non-private algorithm for Bayesian network construction (in Section 4.1), and then explain how the algorithm can be converted into a differentially private solution (in Sections 4.2 and 4.3).

Algorithm 2 GreedyBayes (D, k): returns $\mathcal{N}$

1: Initialize $\mathcal{N} = \emptyset$ and $V = \emptyset$
2: Randomly select an attribute X_1 from $\mathcal{A}$; add $(X_1, \emptyset)$ to $\mathcal{N}$; add X_1 to V
3: **for** $i = 2$ to d **do**
4: Initialize $\Omega = \emptyset$
5: For each $X \in \mathcal{A} \setminus V$ and each $\Pi \in \binom{V}{k}$, add (X, Π) to Ω
6: Select a pair (X_i, Π_i) from Ω with the maximal mutual information $I(X_i, \Pi_i)$
7: Add (X_i, Π_i) to $\mathcal{N}$; add X_i to V
8: **return** $\mathcal{N}$

4.1 Non-Private Methods

Suppose that we aim to construct a k-degree Bayesian network $\mathcal{N}$ on a dataset D containing a set $\mathcal{A}$ of attributes. Ideally, $\mathcal{N}$ should provide an accurate approximation of the tuple distribution in D, i.e., $\Pr_{\mathcal{N}}[\mathcal{A}]$ should be close to $\Pr[\mathcal{A}]$. A natural question is under what condition will $\Pr_{\mathcal{N}}[\mathcal{A}]$ closely approximate $\Pr[\mathcal{A}]$? We make use of standard notions from information theory to measure this. The *entropy* of a random variable X over its domain $\mathrm{dom}(X)$ is denoted by $H(X) = -\sum_{x \in \mathrm{dom}(X)} \Pr[X = x] \log \Pr[X = x]$,[2] and $I(\cdot,\cdot)$ denotes the *mutual information* between two variables as: $I(X, \Pi) =$

$$\sum_{x \in \mathrm{dom}(X)} \sum_{\pi \in \mathrm{dom}(\Pi)} \Pr[X = x, \Pi = \pi] \log \frac{\Pr[X = x, \Pi = \pi]}{\Pr[X = x] \Pr[\Pi = \pi]}, \quad (5)$$

where $\Pr[X, \Pi]$ is the joint distribution of X and Π, and $\Pr[X]$ and $\Pr[\Pi]$ are the marginal distributions of X and Π respectively. The *KL-divergence* [14] of $\Pr_{\mathcal{N}}[\mathcal{A}]$ from $\Pr[\mathcal{A}]$ measures the difference between the two probability distributions, and is defined by:

$$KL(\Pr[\mathcal{A}], \Pr_{\mathcal{N}}[\mathcal{A}]) = -\sum_{i=1}^{d} I(X_i, \Pi_i) + \sum_{i=1}^{d} H(X_i) - H(\mathcal{A}). \quad (6)$$

We seek a Bayesian network representation so that the KL-divergence between the original and the approximate distribution is small. In (6), the term $\sum_{i=1}^{d} H(X_i) - H(\mathcal{A})$ is solely decided by $\Pr[\mathcal{A}]$, which is fixed once the input database D is given. Hence, the KL-divergence of $\Pr_{\mathcal{N}}[\mathcal{A}]$ from $\Pr[\mathcal{A}]$ is small (in which case they closely approximate each other), if and only if $\sum_{i=1}^{d} I(X_i, \Pi_i)$ is maximized. Therefore, the construction of $\mathcal{N}$ can be modeled as an optimization problem, where we aim to choose a parent set Π_i for each attribute X_i in D to maximize $\sum_{i=1}^{d} I(X_i, \Pi_i)$.

For the case when $k = 1$, Chow and Liu show that greedily picking the next edge based on the maximum mutual information is optimal, leading to the celebrated notion of Chow-Liu trees [11]. However, as shown in [10], this optimization problem is NP-hard when $k > 1$. For this reason, heuristic algorithms (e.g., hill-climbing, genetic algorithms, and simulated annealing) are often employed in practice [28]. In the context of differential privacy, however, a different calculus applies: these methods incur a high cost in terms of sensitivity and so incur a large amount of noise. That is, these algorithms make many queries to the data, so that making them differentially private entails large perturbations which lead to poor overall accuracy. Therefore, we seek a new method that will imply less noise, and so give a better overall approximation when the noise is added. Thus we propose a greedy algorithm that makes fewer probes to the data, by extending the Chow-Liu approach to higher degrees, described in Algorithm 2.

In the beginning of the algorithm (Line 1), we initialize the Bayesian network $\mathcal{N}$ to an empty list of AP pairs. Let V be a set

[2] All logarithms used in this paper are to the base 2.

that contains all attributes whose parent sets have been fixed in the partial construction of $\mathcal{N}$. As a next step, the algorithm randomly selects an attribute (denoted as X_1) from $\mathcal{A}$, and sets its parent set Π_1 to $\emptyset$ (Line 2). The rest of the algorithm consists of $d-1$ iterations (Lines 3-7), in each of which we greedily add into $\mathcal{N}$ an AP pair with a large mutual information. Specifically, the AP pair in each iteration is selected from a candidate set Ω that contains every AP pair (X,Π) satisfying two requirements:

1. $|\Pi| \le k$, which ensures that $\mathcal{N}$ is a k-degree Bayesian network. This is ensured by choosing Π only from $\binom{V}{k}$, where $\binom{V}{k}$ denotes the set of all subsets of V with size $\min(k,|V|)$ (Lines 5-6).

2. $\mathcal{N}$ contains no edge from X_i to X_j for any $j<i$, which guarantees that $\mathcal{N}$ is a DAG. We ensure this condition by requiring that in the beginning of any iteration, V only contains the attributes whose parent sets have been decided in the previous iterations (Line 7). In other words, the parent set of X_i can only be a subset of $\{X_1, X_2, \ldots, X_{i-1}\}$, as a consequence of which $\mathcal{N}$ cannot contain any edge from X_i to X_j for any $j<i$.

Once the parent set of each attribute is decided, the algorithm terminates and returns the Bayesian network $\mathcal{N}$ (Line 9). The number of pairs considered in iteration i is $(d-i)\binom{i}{k}$, so summing over all iterations the cost is bounded by $d\sum_{i=1}^{d}\binom{i}{k} = d\binom{d+1}{k+1}$. This determines the asymptotic cost of the procedure. Note that when $k=1$, the above algorithm is equivalent to Chow and Liu's method [11] for constructing optimal 1-degree Bayesian networks.

4.2 A First-Cut Solution

Observe that in Algorithm 2, there is only one place where we interact directly with the input dataset D, namely, the greedy selection of an AP pair (X_i,Π_i) in each iteration of the algorithm (Line 6). Therefore, if we are to make Algorithm 2 differentially private, we only need to replace Line 6 of Algorithm 2 with a procedure that selects (X_i,Π_i) from Ω in a private manner. Such a procedure can be implemented with the exponential mechanism outlined in Section 2.1, using the mutual information function I as the score function. Specifically, we first inspect each AP pair $(X,\Pi)\in\Omega$, and calculate the mutual information $I(X,\Pi)$ between X and Π; After that, we sample an AP pair from Ω, such that the sampling probability of any pair (X,Π) is proportional to $\exp(I(X,\Pi)/2\Delta)$, where Δ is a scaling factor.

The value of Δ is set as follows. As mentioned in Section 3, PRIVBAYES requires that the construction of the Bayesian network $\mathcal{N}$ should satisfy $(\varepsilon/2)$-differential privacy. Accordingly, we set $\Delta = 2(d-1)S(I)/\varepsilon$, where $S(I)$ denotes the sensitivity of the mutual information function I (see Equation 3). This ensures that each invocation of the exponential mechanism satisfies $(\varepsilon/2(d-1))$-differential privacy. Given the composability property of differential privacy [16] and the fact that we only invoke the exponential mechanism $d-1$ times during the construction of $\mathcal{N}$, it can be verified that the overall process of constructing $\mathcal{N}$ is $(\varepsilon/2)$-differentially private.

Last, we calculate the sensitivity, $S(I)$.

LEMMA 1.

$$S(I(X,\Pi)) = \begin{cases} \frac{1}{n}\log n + \frac{n-1}{n}\log\frac{n}{n-1}, & \text{if } X \text{ or } \Pi \text{ is binary;} \\ \frac{2}{n}\log\frac{n+1}{2} + \frac{n-1}{n}\log\frac{n+1}{n-1}, & \text{otherwise,} \end{cases}$$

where n is the number of tuples in D.

This can be shown by considering the maximum change in mutual information based on its definition (5), as the various probabilities are changed by the alteration of one tuple. We omit the full proof for brevity, but the maximum difference in mutual information between binary variables is achieved by this example:

$X\backslash\Pi$	0	1
0	0	0
1	0	1

$X\backslash\Pi$	0	1
0	$\frac{1}{n}$	0
1	0	$\frac{n-1}{n}$

The mutual information of the left distribution is 0, and that of the right one is $\frac{1}{n}\log n + \frac{n-1}{n}\log\frac{n}{n-1}$.

4.3 An Improved Solution

The method in Section 4.2 is simple and intuitive, but may not achieve the best results: Observe that $S(I) > \log n/n$; this can be large compared to the range of I. For example, $\text{range}(I)=1$ for binary distributions. As a consequence, the scaling factor $\Delta = 2(d-1)S(I)/\varepsilon$ tends to be large, and so the exponential mechanism is still quite likely to sample (from Ω) an AP pair with a small mutual information. In that case, the Bayesian network $\mathcal{N}$ constructed using the exponential mechanism will offer a weak approximation of $\Pr[\mathcal{A}]$, resulting in a low-quality output from PRIVBAYES. To improve over this solution, we propose to avoid using I as the score function in the exponential mechanism. Instead, we define a novel function F that maps each AP pair $(X,\Pi)\in\Omega$ to a score, such that

1. F's sensitivity is small (with respect to the range of F).
2. If $F(X,\Pi)$ is large, then $I(X,\Pi)$ tends to be large.

The rationale is that since $S(F)$ is small with respect to range(F), the scaling factor $\Delta = 2(d-1)S(F)/\varepsilon$ will also be small, and hence, the exponential mechanism has a high probability to select an AP pair (X,Π) with a large $F(X,\Pi)$. In turn, such an AP pair tends to have a large mutual information between X and Π, which helps improve the quality of the Bayesian network $\mathcal{N}$.

In what follows, we will clarify our construction of F. To achieve property 2 above, we set F to its maximum value (i.e., 0) when I is greatest. To achieve property 1, we make $F(X,\Pi)$ decrease linearly in proportion to the L_1 distance from $\Pr[X,\Pi]$ to a distribution that maximizes F, since linear functions ensure that the sensitivity is controlled: the function does not change sharply anywhere in its domain. We first introduce the concept of *maximum joint distribution*, which will be used to define the peaks of F, and then characterize such distributions:

DEFINITION 3 (MAXIMUM JOINT DISTRIBUTION). *Given an AP pair (X,Π), a maximum joint distribution $\Pr^{\diamond}[X,\Pi]$ for X and Π is one that maximizes the mutual information between X and Π.*

LEMMA 2. *Assume that $|\text{dom}(X)| \le |\text{dom}(\Pi)|$. A distribution $\Pr^{\diamond}[X,\Pi]$ is a maximum joint distribution if and only if*

1. *$\Pr^{\diamond}[X=x] = 1/|\text{dom}(X)|$, for any $x\in\text{dom}(X)$;*
2. *For any $\pi\in\text{dom}(\Pi)$, there is at most one $x\in\text{dom}(X)$ with $\Pr^{\diamond}[X=x,\Pi=\pi]>0$.*

Proofs in this section are deferred to the appendix. We illustrate Definition 3 and Lemma 2 with an example:

EXAMPLE 2. *Consider a binary variable X with $\text{dom}(X) = \{0,1\}$ and a variable Π with $\text{dom}(\Pi) = \{a,b,c\}$. Consider two joint distributions between X and Π as follows:*

$X\backslash\Pi$	a	b	c
0	.5	0	0
1	0	.5	0

$X\backslash\Pi$	a	b	c
0	0	.2	.3
1	.5	0	0

By Lemma 2, both of the above distributions are maximum joint distributions, with $I(X,\Pi) = 1$.

Let (X,Π) be an AP pair, and $\mathcal{P}^\diamond[X,\Pi]$ be the set of all maximum joint distributions for X and Π. Our score function F (for evaluating the quality of (X,Π)) is defined as

$$F(X,\Pi) = -\frac{1}{2}\min_{\Pr^\diamond \in \mathcal{P}^\diamond} \left\| \Pr[X,\Pi] - \Pr^\diamond[X,\Pi] \right\|_1. \quad (7)$$

If $F(X,\Pi)$ is large, then $\Pr[X,\Pi]$ must have a small L_1 distance to one of the maximum joint distributions in $\mathcal{P}^\diamond[X,\Pi]$, and vice-versa. In turn, if $\Pr[X,\Pi]$ is close to a maximum joint distribution in $\mathcal{P}^\diamond[X,\Pi]$, then intuitively, $\Pr[X,\Pi]$ is likely to give a large mutual information between X and Π. In other words, the value of $F(X,\Pi)$ tends to be positively correlated with $I(X,\Pi)$. This explains why F could be a good score function to replace I. In addition, F has a much smaller sensitivity than I, as shown in the following theorem:

THEOREM 2. $S(F) = 1/n$.

This follows immediately from considering the L_1 distance between neighboring distributions. Observe that $S(F) < S(I)/\log n$, where n is the number of tuples in the input data. Meanwhile, the ranges of F and I are comparable; for example, range$(I) = 1$ and range$(F) = 0.5$ for binary domains. Therefore, when n is large (as is often the case), the sensitivity-to-range ratio of F is significantly smaller than that of I, which makes F a favorable score function over I for selecting AP pairs in the Bayesian network $\mathcal{N}$.

4.4 Computation of F

While (7) defines the function F, it still remains unclear how we can calculate $F(X,\Pi)$ given $\Pr[X,\Pi]$. In this subsection, we use dynamic programming to solve the problem for the case when all attributes in $\Pi \cup \{X\}$ have binary domains; we address the case of non-binary domains in Section 4.5.

Let (X,Π) be an AP pair where $|\Pi| = k$. Then, the joint distribution $\Pr[X,\Pi]$ can be represented by a 2×2^k matrix where the sum of all elements is 1. For example, Table 3(a) illustrates a joint distribution $\Pr[X,\Pi]$ with $|\Pi| = 2$. To compute $F(X,\Pi)$, we need to identify the minimum L_1 distance between $\Pr[X,\Pi]$ and a maximum joint distribution $\Pr^\diamond[X,\Pi] \in \mathcal{P}^\diamond[X,\Pi]$. Table 3(b) illustrates one such maximum joint distribution, whose L_1 distance to the distribution in Table 3(a) equals 0.4. To derive the minimum L_1 distance, a naive approach is to enumerate all maximum joint distributions in $\mathcal{P}^\diamond[X,\Pi]$; nevertheless, as $\mathcal{P}^\diamond[X,\Pi]$ may contain an infinite number of maximum joint distributions, a brute-force enumeration of $\mathcal{P}^\diamond$ is infeasible. To address this issue, we will first introduce an exponential-time algorithm for computing $F(X,\Pi)$, which will serve as the basis of our dynamic programming solution.

The basic idea of our exponential-time algorithm is to (i) partition the distributions in $\mathcal{P}^\diamond$ into a finite number of equivalence classes, and then (ii) compute $F(X,\Pi)$ by processing each equivalence class individually. By Lemma 2, any maximum joint distribution $\Pr^\diamond[X,\Pi]$ has the following property: for any $\pi \in \text{dom}(\Pi)$, either $\Pr^\diamond[X=0,\Pi=\pi] = 0$ or $\Pr^\diamond[X=1,\Pi=\pi] = 0$. In other words, for each column in the matrix representation of $\Pr^\diamond[X,\Pi]$ (where a column corresponds to a value in dom(Π)), there should be at most one non-zero entry. For example, the gray cells in Table 3(b) indicate the positions of non-zeros in the given maximum joint distribution.

For any two distributions in $\mathcal{P}^\diamond$, we say that they are *equivalent* if (i) their matrix representations have the same number of non-zero entries, and (ii) the positions of the non-zero entries are the same in the two matrices. Suppose that we divide the distributions in $\mathcal{P}^\diamond$ into equivalence classes, each of which contains a maximal subset of equivalent distributions. Then, totally there are $O(3^{2^k})$ equivalent classes. It turns out that we can easily calculate the minimum L_1 distance from $\Pr[X,\Pi]$ to each equivalence class.

Table 3: An example of joint distributions

$X \backslash \Pi$	00	01	10	11
0	.6	0	0	0
1	.1	.1	.1	.1

(a) input joint distribution

$X \backslash \Pi$	00	01	10	11
0	.5	0	0	0
1	0	.3	.1	.1

(b) maximum joint distribution

To explain, consider a particular equivalence class E. Let Z^- be the set of pairs (x,π), such that $\Pr^\diamond[X=x,\Pi=\pi] = 0$ for any $\Pr^\diamond[X,\Pi] \in E$. That is, Z^- captures the positions of all zero entries in the matrix representation of $\Pr^\diamond[X=x,\Pi=\pi]$. Similarly, we define the sets of non-zero entries in row $X=0$ and $X=1$ as

$$\begin{aligned} Z_0^+ &= \{(0,\pi) \mid \Pr^\diamond[X=0,\Pi=\pi] > 0\}, \text{and} \\ Z_1^+ &= \{(1,\pi) \mid \Pr^\diamond[X=1,\Pi=\pi] > 0\}. \end{aligned}$$

For convenience, we also abuse notation and define

$$\begin{aligned} \Pr[Z^-] &= \textstyle\sum_{(x,\pi)\in Z^-} \Pr[X=x,\Pi=\pi], \\ \Pr[Z_0^+] &= \textstyle\sum_{(x,\pi)\in Z_0^+} \Pr[X=x,\Pi=\pi], \\ \Pr[Z_1^+] &= \textstyle\sum_{(x,\pi)\in Z_1^+} \Pr[X=x,\Pi=\pi]. \end{aligned}$$

By Lemma 2, we have $\Pr^\diamond[Z^-] = 0$, $\Pr^\diamond[Z_0^+] = 1/2$, and $\Pr^\diamond[Z_1^+] = 1/2$ for any $\Pr^\diamond[X,\Pi] \in E$. Then, for any $\Pr[X,\Pi]$, its L_1 distance to a distribution $\Pr^\diamond[X,\Pi] \in E$ is bounded by:

$$\left\| \Pr[X,\Pi] - \Pr^\diamond[X,\Pi] \right\|_1 \geq \Pr[Z^-] + \left|\Pr[Z_0^+] - \frac{1}{2}\right| + \left|\Pr[Z_1^+] - \frac{1}{2}\right|.$$

Let $(x)_+$ denote $\max(0,x)$. Given that $\Pr[Z^-] + \Pr[Z_0^+] + \Pr[Z_1^+] = 1$, the above inequality can be simplified to

$$\left\| \Pr[X,\Pi] - \Pr^\diamond[X,\Pi] \right\|_1 \geq 2 \cdot \left[\left(\tfrac{1}{2} - \Pr[Z_0^+]\right)_+ + \left(\tfrac{1}{2} - \Pr[Z_1^+]\right)_+ \right]. \quad (8)$$

Furthermore, there always exists a $\Pr^\diamond[X,\Pi] \in E$ that makes the equality hold. In other words, once the positions of the non-zero entries in $\Pr^\diamond[X,\Pi]$ are fixed, we can use (8) to derive the minimum L_1 distance from any $\Pr[X,\Pi]$ to E, with a linear scan of the entries in the matrix representation of $\Pr[X,\Pi]$. By enumerating all $O(3^{2^k})$ equivalence classes of $\mathcal{P}^\diamond$, we can then derive $F(X,\Pi)$.

The above procedure for calculating F is impractical when $k \geq 4$, as the exhaustive search over all possible equivalence classes of $\mathcal{P}^\diamond$ is prohibitive. To tackle this problem, we propose a dynamic-programming-based optimization that reduces computation costs by taking advantage of the fact that the distributions are induced by n items.

Based on (8), our target is to find a combination of Z_0^+ and Z_1^+ (which therefore determine Z^-) that minimizes

$$\left(\frac{1}{2} - \Pr[Z_0^+]\right)_+ + \left(\frac{1}{2} - \Pr[Z_1^+]\right)_+.$$

We define the probability mass associated with Z_0^+ and Z_1^+ as K_0 and K_1 respectively. Initially, $K_0 = K_1 = 0$. For each $\pi \in \text{dom}(\Pi)$, we can either increase K_0 by $\Pr[X=0,\Pi=\pi]$ (by assigning $(0,\pi)$ to Z_0^+) or increase K_1 by $\Pr[X=1,\Pi=\pi]$ (by assigning $(1,\pi)$ to Z_1^+). We index $\pi \in \text{dom}(\Pi)$ as $\pi_1, \pi_2, \ldots, \pi_{2^k}$. We use $C(i,a,b)$ to indicate if $K_0 = a/n$ and $K_1 = b/n$ is reachable by using the first i π's, i.e., $\pi_1, \pi_2, \ldots, \pi_i$. It can be verified that (i) $C(i,a,b) = $ true if $i = a = b = 0$, (ii) $C(i,a,b) = $ false if $i < 0$ or $a < 0$ or $b < 0$, and

(iii) otherwise,

$$C(i,a,b) = C(i-1,a-n\Pr[X=0,\Pi=\pi_i],b) \vee C(i-1,a,b-n\Pr[X=1,\Pi=\pi_i]).$$

Given an input dataset D with n tuple, each cell in $\Pr[X,\Pi]$ must be a multiple of $1/n$. Thus, we only consider the case when a and b are integers in the range $[0,n]$. Thus, the total number of states $C(i,a,b)$ is $n^2 2^k$. A direct traversal of all states takes $O(n^2 2^k)$ time. To reduce this time complexity, we introduce the following concept:

DEFINITION 4 (DOMINATED STATE). *A state $C(i,a_1,b_1)$ is* dominated *by $C(i,a_2,b_2)$ if and only if $a_1 \leq a_2$ and $b_1 \leq b_2$.*

Note that a dominated state is always inferior to some other states, and hence, it can be ignored without affecting the correctness of final result. Consequently, we maintain the set of at most n non-dominated reachable states for each $i \in [1,2^k]$. The function F can be calculated by

$$F(X,\Pi) = -\min_{C(2^k,a,b)=\text{true}} \left(\frac{1}{2}-\frac{a}{n}\right)_+ + \left(\frac{1}{2}-\frac{b}{n}\right)_+.$$

As such, the total number of states that need to be traversed is $n2^k$, and thus the complexity of the algorithm is reduced to $O(n2^k)$. Note that k is small in practice, since we only need to consider low-degree Bayesian networks.

4.5 Extension to General Domains

The dynamic programming approach in Section 4.4 assumes that all attributes in the input data D are binary. In this section, we extend our solution to the case when D contains non-binary attributes.

Following the common practice in the literature [38], our first solution converts each non-binary attribute in the dataset into a set of binary attributes. In particular, for each categorical attribute X whose domain size equals ℓ, we first encode each value in X's domain into a binary representation with $\lceil \log \ell \rceil$ bits; after that, we convert X into $\lceil \log(l) \rceil$ binary attributes $X_1, X_2, \ldots, X_{\lceil \log \ell \rceil}$, such that X_i corresponds to the i-th bit in the binary representation. Meanwhile, for each continuous attribute Y, we first discretize the domain of Y into a fixed number b of equi-width bins (we use $b = 16$), and then convert Y into $\lceil \log b \rceil$ binary attributes, using a similar approach to the transformation of X. After the transformation, D can be encoded to form a new database D_b in the binary domain. After that, we apply PRIVBAYES on D_b to generate a synthetic dataset D_b^*, then decode it to get D^* in the original domain.

A second solution tries to preserve the semantics of (discrete) attributes more directly, via a more complex search. Following the outline for the binary case, we can model the computation of $F(X,\Pi)$ over non-binary attribute X and parent set Π as an optimization problem. Now the structure of X is more complex, the approach of dynamic programming does not apply. Instead, we can find a different combinatorial characterization of maximum distributions, and encode this with a set of (linear) constraints. The search for the minimum cost maximum distribution is the an optimization problem over these constraints, which can be solved by an integer program. We postpone details of this approach to the full version of this paper; in our experiments, we show results using the binary encoding, which is effective enough for our purposes.

4.6 Choice of k and θ-usefulness.

We have discussed how to build a k-degree Bayesian network under differential privacy, where k is considered as a given input to the algorithm. However, k is usually unknown in real applications and should be chosen carefully. The choice of k is non-trivial for PRIVBAYES. Intuitively, a Bayesian network with a larger k keeps more information from the full dimensional distribution $\Pr[\mathcal{A}]$, e.g., a $(d-1)$-degree Bayesian network approximates $\Pr[\mathcal{A}]$ perfectly without having any information loss. On the other hand, the downside of using large k is that it forces PRIVBAYES to anonymize a set of high-dimensional marginal distributions in the second phase, which are very vulnerable to noise due to their domains of large size. These noisy distributions are less useful after anonymization especially when the privacy budget ε is small, leading to a synthetic database full of random perturbation. With very small values of ε, the best choice may be to pick $k=0$, i.e. to model all attributes as independent. Hence, the choice of k should balance the informativeness of a Bayesian network and the robustness of marginal distributions. This balancing act is affected by three parameters: the total privacy budget ε, the total number of tuples in database n, and usefulness of each noisy marginal distribution in the second phase θ. We quantify this in the following definition.

DEFINITION 5 (θ-USEFULNESS). *A noisy distribution is θ-useful if the ratio of average scale of information to average scale of noise is no less than θ.*

LEMMA 3. *The noisy distributions in Algorithm 1 are $\left(\frac{n \cdot \varepsilon}{(d-k)\cdot 2^{k+3}}\right)$-useful.*

PROOF. In Algorithm 1, each marginal distribution is $(k+1)$-dimensional with a domain size 2^{k+1}. Therefore, the average scale of information in each cell is $1/2^{k+1}$.

For the scale of noise, we have $d-k$ marginal distributions to be anonymized and each of them consumes privacy budget $\varepsilon/2(d-k)$. The sensitivity of each marginal distribution is $2/n$. According to the Laplace mechanism, the Laplace noise N injected to each cell is drawn from distribution Lap $(4(d-k)/n\varepsilon)$ where the average scale of noise is $\mathrm{E}(|\eta|) = 4(d-k)/n\varepsilon$. □

The notion of θ-usefulness provides a more intuitive way to choose k automatically without closely studying the specific instance of the input database. Generally speaking, we believe a 0.5-useful noisy distribution is not good because the scale of noise is twice as that of information, while a 5-useful one is more reliable due to its large information to noise ratio. In practice, we set up a threshold θ, then choose the largest positive integer k that guarantees θ-usefulness in parameter learning (note, this is independent of the data, as it depends only on the non-private values ε, θ, n and d). If such a k does not exist, k is set to the minimum value, 0. In the experimental section, we will show that there is a wide range of θ to choose to train a PRIVBAYES model for good performance.

5. EXPERIMENTS

5.1 Experimental Settings

Datasets. We make use of four real databsets in our experiments: (i) Adult [4], which includes the information of 45,222 individuals extracted from the 1994 US Census, (ii) NLTCS [2], which contains records of 21,574 individuals participated in the National Long Term Care Survey, (iii) TPC-E [3], 40,000 tuples obtained by joining four tables in the TPC-E benchmark: "Trade", "Security", "Security status" and "Trade type", and (iv) BR2000 [1], which consists of 38,000 census records collected from Brazil in year 2000. Each of the four datasets contains both continuous and categorical attributes. Table 4 illustrates the properties of the datasets.

Tasks. We evaluate the performance of PRIVBAYES on two different tasks. The first task is to build all α-way marginals of a

Table 4: Dataset characteristics.

Dataset	Cardinality	Dimensionality	Domain size
Adult	45,222	15	$\approx 2^{52}$
NLTCS	21,574	16	$\approx 2^{16}$
TPC-E	40,000	24	$\approx 2^{77}$
BR2000	38,000	14	$\approx 2^{32}$

dataset [5]. For convenience, we use Q_α to denote the set of all α-way marginals. We evaluate Q_3 and Q_4 on NLTCS, but examine Q_2 and Q_3 instead on the remaining three datasets, since each of those datasets leads to a prohibitively large number of queries in Q_4. We measure the accuracy of each noisy marginal by the *total variation distance* [14] between itself and the noise-free marginal (i.e., half of the L_1 distance between the two marginals, when both of them are treated as probability distributions). We use the average accuracy over all marginals as the final error metric for Q_α.

The second task that we consider is to *simultaneously* train multiple SVM classifiers on a dataset, where each classifier predicts one attribute in the data based on all other attributes. Specifically, on Adult, we train four classifiers to predict whether an individual (i) is a female, (ii) holds a post-secondary degree, (iii) makes over $50K$ a year, and (iv) has never married, respectively. Meanwhile, on NLTCS, we construct four classifiers to predict whether a person (i) is unable to get outside, (ii) is unable to manage money, (iii) is unable to bathe, and (iv) is unable to travel, respectively. We omit the experiments on BR2000 and TCP-E for space reasons. For each classification task, we use 80% of the tuples in the data as the training set, and the other 20% as the testing set. We apply PRIVBAYES on the training data to generate a synthetic dataset, and then use the synthetic data to construct SVM classifiers. The quality of each classifier is measured by its *misclassification rate* on the testing set, i.e., the fraction of tuples in the testing data that are incorrectly classified.

For each of the aforementioned tasks, we repeat each experiment on each method 50 times, and we report the average measurements in our experimental results.

Baselines. For the task of answering count queries in Q_α, we compare PRIVBAYES with three approaches: (i) *Laplace* [17], which generates all α-way marginals of a dataset and then injects Laplace noise directly into each cell of the marginals, (ii) *Fourier* [5], which transforms the input data D into the Fourier domain, adds Laplace noise to a subset of Fourier coefficients and uses the noisy coefficients to construct α-way marginals, and (iii) *Contingency*, which first builds the noisy contingency table, and then projects it onto attribute subsets to compute marginals. However, *Contingency* is only applicable to NLTCS since its computational cost is proportional to the domain size of input data. We also considered several other existing approaches [15, 20, 24, 25, 39] for answering count queries under differential privacy, but find them inapplicable due to our datasets' large domain size. For fair comparison, we adopt two consistency techniques to boost the accuracies of baselines: (i) non-negativity, which rounds all negative counts in a noisy marginal to 0, and (ii) normalization, which linearly rescales the counts in a noisy marginal to make them sum to n.

For the task of training multiple SVM classifiers, we compare PRIVBAYES against four methods: *PrivateERM* [9], *PrivGene* [40], *NoPrivacy*, and *Majority*. In particular, *PrivateERM* and *PrivGene* are two state-of-the-art methods for SVM classification under differential privacy. *NoPrivacy* constructs classifiers directly on the input data without any privacy protection. *Majority* is a naive classification method under differential privacy that works as follows. Let $Y = \{0, 1\}$ be the attribute to be classified,

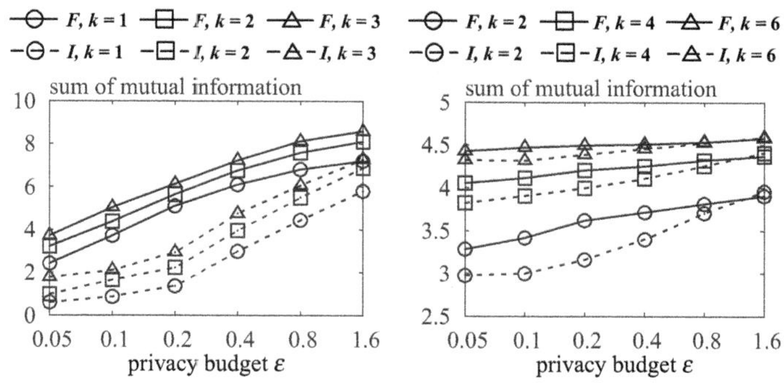

(a) Adult (b) NLTCS

Figure 2: Comparison between F and I

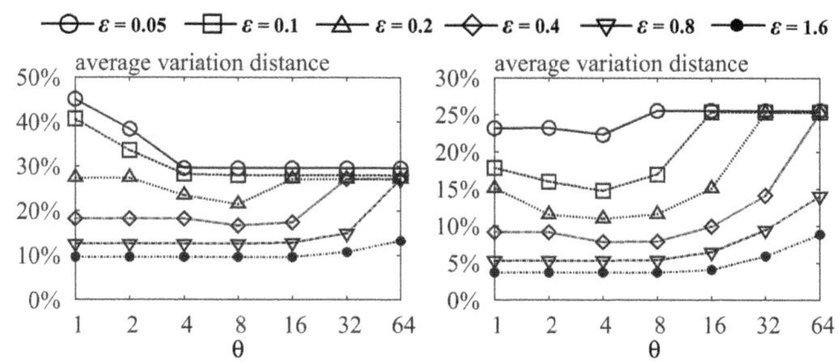

(a) Adult, Q_2 (b) NLTCS, Q_3

Figure 3: Choice of θ

and n be the number of tuples in the training data. *Majority* first counts the number of tuples in the training data with $Y = 1$, and then adds Laplace noise (with scale $1/\varepsilon$) into the count to ensure ε-differential privacy. If the noisy count is larger than $n/2$, then *Majority* predicts that all tuples in the testing data should have $Y = 1$; otherwise, *Majority* predicts $Y = 0$ for all tuples. For PRIVBAYES, *PrivGene*, and *NoPrivacy*, we adopt the standard hinge-loss C-SVM model [7] with $C = 1$; for *PrivateERM*, we adopt a slightly different SVM model with Huber loss [9], as it does not support the hinge-loss model.

5.2 Effect of Quality Function F

In the first set of experiments, we evaluate the effectiveness of score function F (in Section 4.2) against the mutual information function I. Figure 2 illustrates the performance of PRIVBAYES when combined with F and I, respectively, using Adult and NLTCS. The performance of each combination evaluated by the sum of the mutual information of every AP pair in the Bayesian network $\mathcal{N}$, i.e., $\sum_{i=1}^{d} I(X_i, \Pi_i)$. Observe that F significantly outperforms I in almost all cases. This is consistent with our analysis in Section 5.2 that F helps improve the quality of the Bayesian network constructed by PRIVBAYES.

For small k values (i.e., $k = 0, 1, 2$), the time taken to construct a Bayesian network with F is less than 1 minute and is negligible. For larger values of k, the time taken is typically higher (a few hours in the case of $k = 5$). Note that this is not a major concern, since data release is not considered a real-time problem, and the computation of F for different combinations of attributes can be easily parallelized.

5.3 Choice of θ

Recall that PRIVBAYES has only one internal parameter: the degree of Bayesian network k. As discussed in Section 4.6, we adopt the θ-usefulness criterion to automatically select an appropriate

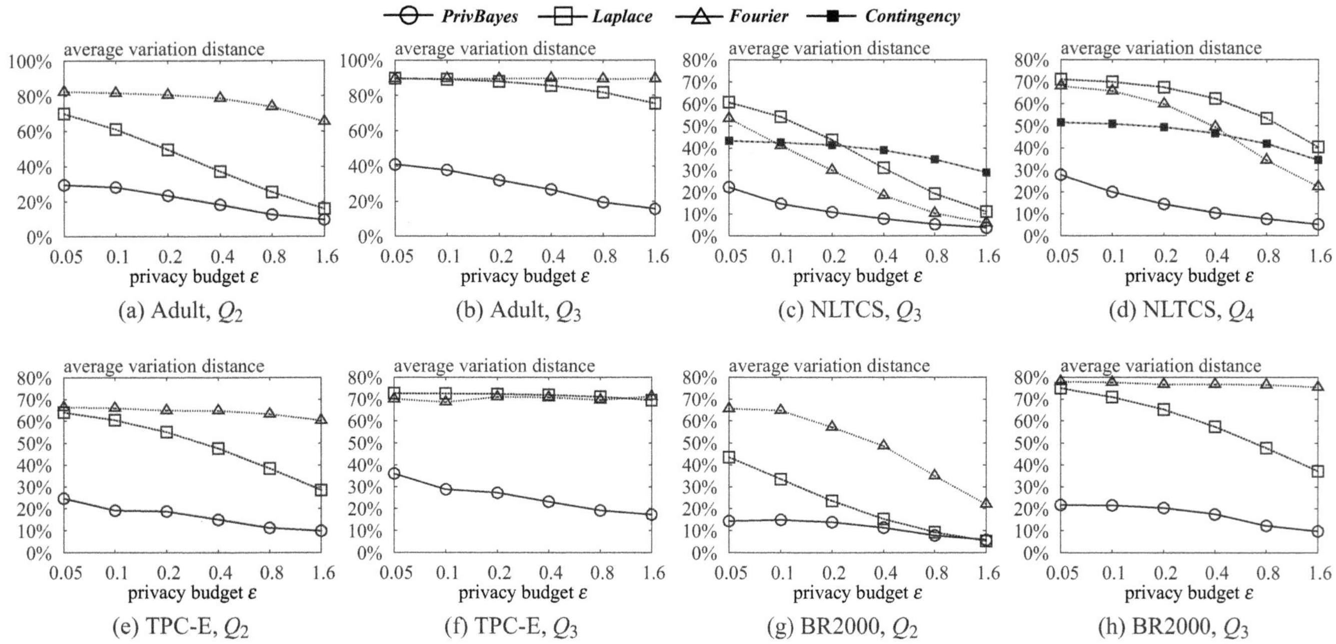

Figure 4: α-way marginals on four datasets

value for k, based on the number of tuples in the input data D as well as the domains of the attributes in D. To evaluate the effect of θ on PRIVBAYES, we use the Q_2 query set on Adult and the Q_3 query set on NLTCS, and examine the performance of PRIVBAYES in answering the queries, with varying θ and ε. Figures 3 illustrates the results. Observe that the average variation distance of the tested query set tends to be higher when θ is very small or very large. This is consistent with our analysis in Section 4.6 that (i) small θ leads to very noisy marginal distributions in the second phase of PRIVBAYES, which makes the synthetic dataset drastically different from the input data, and (ii) large θ makes it difficult for PRIVBAYES to construct a high quality Bayesian network in its first phase, which also leads to inferior synthetic data. Based on Figure 3, we infer that an appropriate value for θ should be in the range of $[2, 16]$. For all subsequent experiments, we set $\theta = 4$.

Note that our tuning of θ is only based on the Q_2 query set on Adult and the Q_3 query set on NLTCS, without inspecting other datasets or other tasks on Adult and NLTCS. Therefore, our choice of θ does not reveal any private information on TPC-E and BR2000, and it does not unfairly favor PRIVBAYES on the tasks of SVM classification on Adult and NLTCS.

5.4 α-way Marginals

This section compares PRIVBAYES with the *Laplace* and *Fourier* approaches on eight sets of marginals over four datasets, and *Contingency* on two sets over NLTCS. Figure 4 shows the average variation distance of each method for each query set Q_α, varying the privacy budget ε. PRIVBAYES clearly outperforms the other three methods in all cases. The relative superiority of PRIVBAYES is more pronounced when (i) ε decreases or (ii) the value of α increases. To explain, observe that when ε is small, PRIVBAYES chooses to construct a very low-degree Bayesian network (down to $k = 0$), due to the θ-usefulness criterion. As a consequence, the marginal distributions in the second phase of PRIVBAYES will be more robust against noise injection, which ensures the quality of the synthetic data will not degrade too significantly. In contrast, the performance of *Laplace* and *Fourier* is highly sensitive to ε, owing to which they incur considerable errors when ε decreases. *Contingency* also generates inaccurate marginals with low privacy budget, with performance improving slowly as ε increases.

Meanwhile, when α increases, the query set Q_α corresponds to a larger set of marginals, in which case the queries Q_α have a higher sensitivity. Therefore, *Laplace* needs to inject a larger amount of noise into Q_α for privacy protection, leading to higher query errors. *Fourier* also suffers from a similar issue. On the other hand, the error of PRIVBAYES is not sensitive to α, as the Bayesian network constructed (once) by PRIVBAYES enables it to nicely capture the correlations among attributes. Consequently, it can closely approximate the marginals pertinent to Q_α even when α increases.

5.5 Multiple SVM Classifiers

In the last set of experiments, we evaluate different methods for SVM classification. As explained in Section 5.1, on each of Adult and NLTCS, we train four SVM classifiers simultaneously. For PRIVBAYES, we apply it to generate only *one* synthetic dataset D^* from each training set, and then use D^* to train all four classifiers required. The other differentially private methods (i.e., *PrivateERM*, *PrivGene*, and *Majority*) can only produce one classifier at a time. Therefore, for each of those method, we evenly divide the privacy budget ε evenly into four parts, and use $\varepsilon/4$ budget to train each classifier. To illustrate the performance of *PrivateERM* when building a single classifier, we include an additional baseline referred to as *"PrivateERM (Single)"*. This baseline is identical to *PrivateERM*, expect that it uses a privacy budget of ε (instead of $\varepsilon/4$) in training each classifier.

Figure 5 shows the misclassification rate of each method as a function of the overall ε. The error of NoPrivacy remains unchanged for all ε, since it does not enforce ε-differential privacy—it represents the best case to aim for. The accuracy of Majority is insensitive to ε, since (i) it performs classification only by checking whether there exists more than 50% tuples in the training set with a certain label, and (ii) this check is quite robust against noise injection when the number of tuples in the training set is large (as is the case in our experiments).

As for the other methods, PRIVBAYES consistently outperforms *PrivateERM* and *PrivGene* on Adult, except for the case of $\varepsilon = 1.6$.

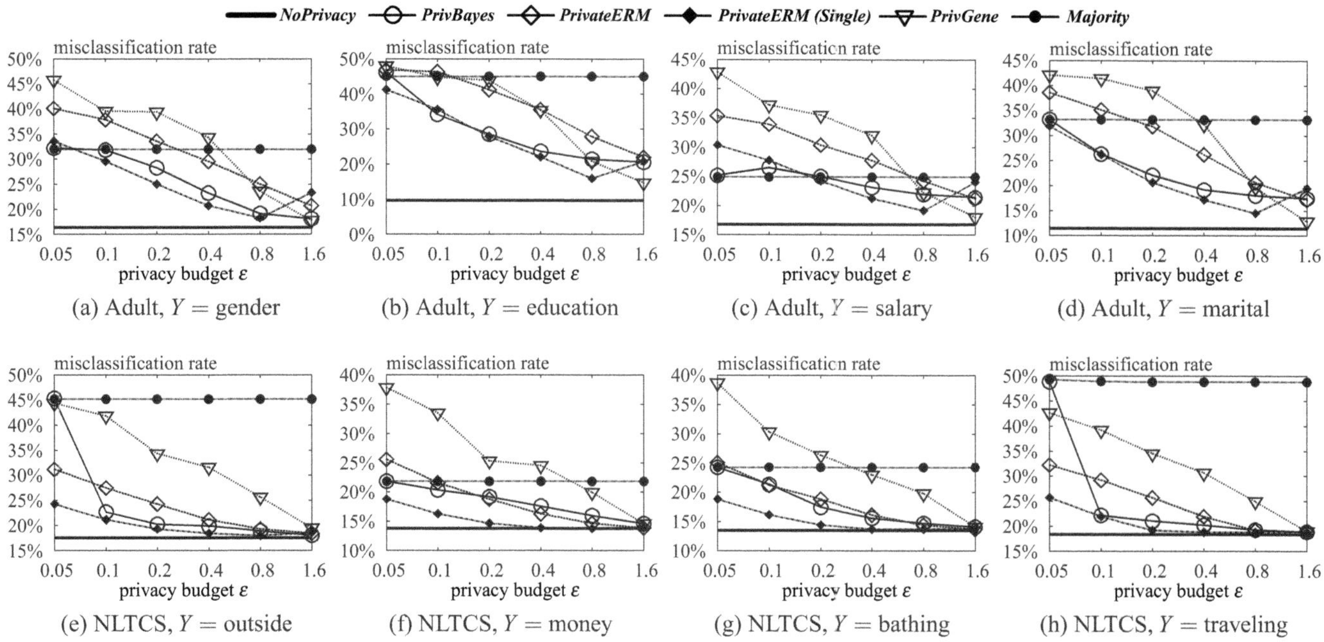

Figure 5: Multiple SVM classifiers on two datasets

Meanwhile, on NLTCS, PrivBayes and *PrivateERM* are comparable, and they both outperform *PrivGene*. Interestingly, in Figure 5(c), the misclassification rate of PrivBayes increases when ε changes from 0.05 to 0.1. The reason is that we have tuned the parameter θ for PrivBayes based on count queries on Adult and NLTCS, and hence, our choice of θ (and thus, the choise of k) does not always guarantee the best performance for PrivBayes on classification tasks. Overall, PrivBayes is superior to both *PrivateERM* and *PrivGene* on the this classification task.

On the other hand, PrivBayes is outperformed by *PrivateERM (Single)*[3] in most cases. This is reasonable given that *PrivateERM* is designed solely for SVM classification, whereas PrivBayes does not specifically optimize for SVM classification when it generates the synthetic data. In general, the fact that PrivBayes can support multiple analytical tasks (without incurring extra privacy overhead) makes it highly favorable in the common case when the user does not have a specific task in mind and would like to conduct *exploratory* data analysis by experimenting with various tasks.

6. CONCLUDING REMARKS

The model of Bayesian networks has proven a powerful way to represent correlated data approximately. We have seen that it is also highly effective as a model to release data while respecting privacy. We see that data released this way is is very accurate, and indeed offers better accuracy than customized mechanisms for particular objectives, such as classification. A crucial part of our approach is the crafting of a novel quality function F as a surrogate for mutual information, which dramatically improves the quality of the released data. This requires some effort in order to compute efficiently, although since this is part of the release process, we can afford to spend more time on this. Nevertheless, an open problem is to study functions which can substitute for mutual information and which are fast to compute.

The natural next step is to extend this work to databases over multiple tables. The approach of building a graphical model and releasing this privately applies here also. However, care is needed: in the examples we consider, each individual affects a single row of the initial database table. As we consider more complex schemas, the impact of an individual (and hence the scale of noise needed for privacy) may grow very large, and a more careful analysis is needed to ensure that noise does not outweigh the signal.

Acknowledgments. This work was supported by the Nanyang Technological University under SUG Grant M4080094.020, by the Microsoft Research Asia under a gift grant, and by the Ministry of Education (Singapore) under an AcRF Tier-2 grant.

7. REFERENCES

[1] Integrated public use microdata series international. https://international.ipums.org.
[2] Statlib. http://lib.stat.cmu.edu/.
[3] Transaction processing performance council. http://www.tpc.org.
[4] K. Bache and M. Lichman. UCI machine learning repository, 2013.
[5] B. Barak, K. Chaudhuri, C. Dwork, S. Kale, F. McSherry, and K. Talwar. Privacy, accuracy, and consistency too: a holistic solution to contingency table release. In *PODS*, pages 273–282, 2007.
[6] R. Bhaskar, S. Laxman, A. Smith, and A. Thakurta. Discovering frequent patterns in sensitive data. In *KDD*, pages 503–512, 2010.
[7] C.-C. Chang and C.-J. Lin. LIBSVM: A library for support vector machines. page 27, 2011.
[8] K. Chaudhuri and C. Monteleoni. Privacy-preserving logistic regression. In *NIPS*, pages 289–296, 2008.
[9] K. Chaudhuri, C. Monteleoni, and A. D. Sarwate. Differentially private empirical risk minimization. *Journal of Machine Learning Research*, 12:1069–1109, 2011.
[10] D. M. Chickering, D. Heckerman, and C. Meek. Large-sample learning of bayesian networks is NP-Hard. *Journal of Machine Learning Research*, 5:1287–1330, 2004.
[11] C. K. Chow and C. N. Liu. Approximating discrete probability distributions with dependence trees. *IEEE Transactions on Information Theory*, 14:462–467, 1968.
[12] G. Cormode, C. M. Procopiuc, E. Shen, D. Srivastava, and T. Yu. Differentially private spatial decompositions. In *ICDE*, 2012.

[3] The behavior of *PrivateERM (Single)* on Adult with $\varepsilon = 1.6$ is an artifact of the algorithm itself: it computes an internal parameter ε'_p as a function of ε, which yields a sub-optimal choice when $\varepsilon = 1.6$.

[13] G. Cormode, C. M. Procopiuc, D. Srivastava, and T. T. L. Tran. Differentially private publication of sparse data. In *ICDT*, 2012.
[14] A. B. Cybakov. *Introduction to nonparametric estimation*. Springer, 2009.
[15] B. Ding, M. Winslett, J. Han, and Z. Li. Differentially private data cubes: optimizing noise sources and consistency. In *SIGMOD*, pages 217–228, 2011.
[16] C. Dwork. Differential privacy. In *ICALP*, pages 1–12, 2006.
[17] C. Dwork, F. McSherry, K. Nissim, and A. Smith. Calibrating noise to sensitivity in private data analysis. In *TCC*, pages 265–284, 2006.
[18] D. Feldman, A. Fiat, H. Kaplan, and K. Nissim. Private coresets. In *STOC*, pages 361–370, 2009.
[19] A. Friedman and A. Schuster. Data mining with differential privacy. In *KDD*, pages 493–502, 2010.
[20] M. Hardt, K. Ligett, and F. McSherry. A simple and practical algorithm for differentially private data release. In *NIPS*, pages 2348–2356, 2012.
[21] M. Hay, V. Rastogi, G. Miklau, and D. Suciu. Boosting the accuracy of differentially private histograms through consistency. *PVLDB*, 3(1):1021–1032, 2010.
[22] D. Kifer, A. D. Smith, and A. Thakurta. Private convex optimization for empirical risk minimization with applications to high-dimensional regression. *Journal of Machine Learning Research - Proceedings Track*, 23:25.1–25.40, 2012.
[23] D. Koller and N. Friedman. *Probabilistic Graphical Models: Principles and Techniques*. MIT Press, 2009.
[24] C. Li, M. Hay, V. Rastogi, G. Miklau, and A. McGregor. Optimizing linear counting queries under differential privacy. In *PODS*, pages 123–134, 2010.
[25] C. Li and G. Miklau. An adaptive mechanism for accurate query answering under differential privacy. *PVLDB*, 5(6):514–525, 2012.
[26] C. Li and G. Miklau. Optimal error of query sets under the differentially-private matrix mechanism. In *ICDT*, pages 272–283, 2013.
[27] N. Li, W. Qardaji, D. Su, and J. Cao. Privbasis: Frequent itemset mining with differential privacy. *PVLDB*, 5(11):1340–1351, 2012.
[28] D. Margaritis. *Learning Bayesian Network Model Structure from Data*. PhD thesis, School of Computer Science, Carnegie-Mellon University, Pittsburgh, PA, May 2003.
[29] F. McSherry and R. Mahajan. Differentially-private network trace analysis. In *SIGCOMM*, pages 123–134, 2010.
[30] F. McSherry and I. Mironov. Differentially private recommender systems: Building privacy into the netflix prize contenders. In *KDD*, pages 627–636, 2009.
[31] F. McSherry and K. Talwar. Mechanism design via differential privacy. In *FOCS*, pages 94–103, 2007.
[32] P. Mohan, A. Thakurta, E. Shi, D. Song, and D. Culler. GUPT: privacy preserving data analysis made easy. In *SIGMOD*, pages 349–360, 2012.
[33] K. Nissim, S. Raskhodnikova, and A. Smith. Smooth sensitivity and sampling in private data analysis. In *STOC*, pages 75–84, 2007.
[34] V. Rastogi and S. Nath. Differentially private aggregation of distributed time-series with transformation and encryption. In *SIGMOD*, pages 735–746, 2010.
[35] B. I. P. Rubinstein, P. L. Bartlett, L. Huang, and N. Taft. Learning in a large function space: Privacy-preserving mechanisms for SVM learning. *Journal of Privacy and Confidentiality*, 4(1):65–100, 2012.
[36] A. Smith. Privacy-preserving statistical estimation with optimal convergence rate. In *STOC*, 2011.
[37] X. Xiao, G. Wang, and J. Gehrke. Differential privacy via wavelet transforms. In *ICDE*, pages 225–236, 2010.
[38] G. Yaroslavtsev, G. Cormode, C. M. Procopiuc, and D. Srivastava. Accurate and efficient private release of datacubes and contingency tables. In *ICDE*, pages 745–756, 2013.
[39] G. Yuan, Z. Zhang, M. Winslett, X. Xiao, Y. Yang, and Z. Hao. Low-rank mechanism: Optimizing batch queries under differential privacy. *PVLDB*, 5(11):1352–1363, 2012.
[40] J. Zhang, X. Xiao, Y. Yang, Z. Zhang, and M. Winslett. PrivGene: differentially private model fitting using genetic algorithms. In *SIGMOD*, pages 665–676, 2013.

APPENDIX

PROOF OF **Lemma 2**. The maximum mutual information between variables X and Π is

$$\max I(X,\Pi) = \min\{\max H(X), \max H(\Pi)\}$$
$$= \min\{\log|\mathrm{dom}(X)|, \log|\mathrm{dom}(\Pi)|\} = \log|\mathrm{dom}(X)|,$$

given that $|\mathrm{dom}(X)| \leq |\mathrm{dom}(\Pi)|$. Therefore, the maximum joint distribution for X and Π should be a joint distribution for X and Π with mutual information $\log|\mathrm{dom}(X)|$.

Suppose that $\Pr^\diamond(X,\Pi)$ is a joint distribution satisfying the two properties in Lemma 2. Given basic results in information theory, the two properties are equivalent to

1. $H(X) = \log|\mathrm{dom}(X)|$;
2. $H(X \mid \Pi) = 0$.

Thus, the mutual information of $\Pr^\diamond(X,\Pi)$ is

$$I(X,\Pi) = H(X) - H(X \mid \Pi) = \log|\mathrm{dom}(X)|.$$

By definition, $\Pr^\diamond(X,\Pi)$ is a maximum joint distribution.

On the other hand, suppose that $\Pr^\diamond(X,\Pi)$ is a maximum joint distribution with mutual information $\log|\mathrm{dom}(X)|$. The mutual information can be expressed as:

$$I(X,\Pi) = \log|\mathrm{dom}(X)| = H(X) - H(X \mid \Pi),$$

where $H(X) \leq \log|\mathrm{dom}(X)|$ and $H(X \mid \Pi) \geq 0$ always hold. Thus, we conclude that I is maximized in the (achievable) case that

1. $H(X) = \log|\mathrm{dom}(X)|$, which is achieved only by the uniform distribution over $\mathrm{dom}(X)$;
2. $H(X \mid \Pi) = 0$, which implies that there is an x for each π such that $\Pr[X = x \mid \Pi = \pi] = 1$.

The above two conditions are equivalent to the properties in the statement of Lemma 2. □

PROOF OF **Theorem 2**. Let $F_D(X,\Pi)$ be the F function for variable X and Π given input database D, i.e,

$$F_D(X,\Pi) = -\frac{1}{2}\min_{\Pr^\diamond \in \mathcal{P}^\diamond} \|\Pr_D[X,\Pi] - \Pr^\diamond[X,\Pi]\|_1.$$

Notice that $\mathcal{P}^\diamond[X,\Pi]$ is independent of the input database D. Now consider a pair of neighboring databases D_1 and D_2. We have

$$\|\Pr_{D_1}[X,\Pi] - \Pr_{D_2}[X,\Pi]\|_1 = 2/n. \tag{9}$$

Assume that $\Pr \in \mathcal{P}^\diamond[X,\Pi]$ is the closest maximum joint distribution to $\Pr_{D_1}[X,\Pi]$. We have

$$F_{D_1}(X,\Pi) = -1/2 \cdot \|\Pr_{D_1}[X,\Pi] - \Pr\|_1.$$

Combined with Equation 9, the L_1 distance between $\Pr_{D_2}[X,\Pi]$ and Pr can be upper bounded using the triangle inequality:

$$\|\Pr_{D_2}[X,\Pi] - \Pr\|_1$$
$$\leq \|\Pr_{D_1}[X,\Pi] - \Pr\|_1 + \|\Pr_{D_1}[X,\Pi] - \Pr_{D_2}[X,\Pi]\|_1$$
$$= -2 \cdot F_{D_1}(X,\Pi) + 2/n.$$

On the other hand, recall that Pr is a maximum joint distribution in $\mathcal{P}^\diamond[X,\Pi]$. Therefore,

$$F_{D_2}(X,\Pi) = -\frac{1}{2}\min_{\Pr^\diamond \in \mathcal{P}^\diamond} \|\Pr_{D_2}[X,\Pi] - \Pr^\diamond[X,\Pi]\|_1$$
$$\geq -\frac{1}{2}\|\Pr_{D_2}[X,\Pi] - \Pr\|_1$$
$$\geq -\frac{1}{2}\left(-2 \cdot F_{D_1}(X,\Pi) + \frac{2}{n}\right) = F_{D_1}(X,\Pi) - \frac{1}{n}.$$

Thus, $F_{D_1}(X,\Pi) - F_{D_2}(X,\Pi) \leq 1/n$. □

PriView: Practical Differentially Private Release of Marginal Contingency Tables

Wahbeh Qardaji
Dept. of Computer Science and CERIAS
Purdue University
wahbeh.qardaji@gmail.com

Weining Yang Ninghui Li
Dept. of Computer Science and CERIAS
Purdue University
{yang469,ninghui}@cs.purdue.edu

ABSTRACT

We consider the problem of publishing a differentially private synopsis of a d-dimensional dataset so that one can reconstruct any k-way marginal contingency tables from the synopsis. Marginal tables are the workhorses of categorical data analysis. Thus, the private release of such tables has attracted a lot of attention from the research community. However, for situations where d is moderate to large and k is beyond 3, no accurate and practical method exists. We introduce PriView, which computes marginal tables for a number of strategically chosen sets of attributes that we call views, and then use these view marginal tables to reconstruct any desired k-way marginal. In PriView, we apply maximum entropy optimization to reconstruct k-way marginals from views. We also develop a novel method to efficiently making all view marginals consistent while correcting negative entries to improve accuracy. For view selection, we borrow the concept of covering design from combinatorics theory. We conduct extensive experiments on real and synthetic datasets, and show that PriView reduces the error over existing approaches by 2 to 3 orders of magnitude.

Categories and Subject Descriptors

K.4.1 [**COMPUTERS AND SOCIETY**]: Privacy

Keywords

Differential Privacy; Marginal Table; Contingency Table

1. INTRODUCTION

In recent years, privacy-preserving data analysis has received a lot of attention in the research community, with the notion of differential privacy gradually becoming the de facto standard notion of privacy for this research area [10]. In this paper we consider the problem of computing a differentially private synopsis of a high-dimensional dataset so that one can reconstruct any low-dimensional marginal tables of the dataset. Marginal tables are the workhorses of categorical data analysis, e.g., data analysis in the medical, social and behavior sciences. In addition to being easy to interpret, they are sufficient statistics for popular classes of probabilistic models [5]. Because of this, they are the methods of choice for government agencies when releasing statistical summaries of categorical data. Marginal tables are essentially equivalent to OLAP (online analytical processing) cubes used in data management and analysis.

More specifically, we consider the following problem: Given a d-dimension binary dataset D, construct, in a differentially private way, a synopsis of D, so that one can relatively accurately compute the marginal table for any set of k attributes, referred to as k-way marginals. We assume that d, the number of dimensions, is large so that 2^d complexity is unfeasible. Given a k-way marginal obtained from the private synopsis, we measure its L_2 distance and Jensen-Shannon divergence from the true marginal, and aim at minimizing these error measures.

Marginal tables can be constructed directly by counting queries, which has been the center of focus for differentially private data analysis. Seminal work in differential privacy [6, 11] shows how to answer a set Q of counting queries when Q has at most on the order of $\sqrt{|D|}$ queries. Applying this approach, which we refer to as the Direct method, to our problem is to add independently generated noise to every k-way marginal table using $\epsilon/\binom{d}{k}$ as the privacy parameter. The L_2 error distance of the Direct method, however, is expected to be $O(d^k)$, which is large when d is not small (e.g., when $d \geq 32$) and k is beyond 3. A method of adding noise to Fourier coefficients is proposed in [4], which reduces the error slightly over the Direct method. The problem of generating marginals have been studied in a series papers in recent years [7, 15, 17, 16, 18, 28, 8, 22]; however, these methods do not scale when 2^d is large. In summary the current state of the art is that when 2^d-complexity is unfeasible, then the Fourier method in [4] is the best approach.

In this paper we improve this state of art by introducing PriView. There are two key insights behind PriView. First, rather than directly generating all $\binom{d}{k}$ marginal tables, one could do much better by generating marginal tables for a number of strategically chosen sets of attributes that we call *views*, and then use these views as a synopsis from which one can reconstruct any desired k-way marginals. Second, most datasets in practice define distributions that can be approximately factorized into the product of factors each of which contains only a few dimensions, which is the reason why graphical models are powerful tools to represent probability distributions encountered in practice. Thus it is unnecessary

SIGMOD'14, June 22–27, 2014, Snowbird, UT, USA.

ACM 978-1-4503-2376-5/14/06 ...$15.00.
http://dx.doi.org/10.1145/2588555.2588575.

to cover all k-way marginals when k is over 3. So long as the chosen views cover all, e.g., 2-way or 3-way marginals, we can reconstruct most k-way margainals with high accuracy for datasets in practice.

More specifically, our PriView approach has the following steps. One first chooses a set of views based on d, ϵ, and N (the number of data points). One then obtains noisy marginal tables for the views by adding Laplacian noise to these marginals. These views, however, may be overlapping. Thus the same information may be provided in multiple noisy views, each with independent noises added. This presents both a challenge and an opportunity. The challenge lies in how to reconcile potentially inconsistent information from different noisy views. The opportunity lies in the fact that by averaging results from different noisy views, one could obtain more accurate results. We thus post-process the noisy tables to make them mutually consistent. These consistent views form the synopsis from which one can compute any k-way marginal.

Our main contribution lies in developing these high-level ideas into an efficient and practical approach. More specifically, we propose to use the concept of covering design to generate sets of views, and introduce a method to select among them. We also introduce an efficient procedure to make noisy views mutually consistent. This step improves the accuracy of these views, and enables accurate reconstruction of k-way marginals. Furthermore, we introduce a Ripple Non-negativity approach to correct negative entries in noise views to improve accuracy. We also propose to apply the principle of maximum entropy for reconstructing k-way marginals. Finally, we experimentally evaluate our approach and show that PriView reduces the error distance by 2 to 3 orders of magnitude when compared with the state of the art. The PriView method also has the advantage that once the synopsis is generated, one can reconstruct k-way marginals for any k; thus one does not need to commit to a specific k value when constructing the noisy views.

The rest of the paper is organized as follows. We formalize our problem definition in Section 2. We then discuss existing approaches in Section 3. We introduce the PriView method in Section 4. We finally present related work in Section 6 and conclude in Section 7.

2. PROBLEM DEFINITION

We consider the following problem: **Given a d-dimensional binary dataset D, and a positive integer $k < d$, we want to differential privately construct a synopsis of D, so that any k-way *marginal contingency table* (marginal table for short) can be computed with reasonable accuracy.**

We now elaborate on this problem definition. D is a dataset that has d binary attributes; thus the set of all attributes can be defined as $\mathbf{A} = \{1, 2, \cdots, d\}$. Each tuple t in D is a binary string in $\{0,1\}^d$.

Information in D can be equivalently represented using the full contingency table, which has 2^d entries, one for each string $\{0,1\}^d$. Each entry gives the number of times the corresponding string occurs in D. When one wants to analyze the relationships among some of the attributes in $\mathbf{A}$, marginal tables can be constructed, by summing corresponding entries in the contingency table. More specifically, for any subset $A \subseteq \mathbf{A}$ of $k = |A|$ attributes, the marginal table for A has 2^k entries, one corresponding to each possible assignment of the k attributes in A. We call a marginal table for a set of k attributes a k-way marginal table.

Privacy Goal. The privacy requirement is such that the mechanism should satisfy differential privacy.

DEFINITION 1 (ϵ-DIFFERENTIAL PRIVACY [9, 11]). *A randomized mechanism $\mathcal{A}$ gives ϵ-differential privacy if for any pair of neighboring datasets D and D', and any $S \in Range(\mathcal{A})$,*

$$\Pr[\mathcal{A}(D) = S] \leq e^{\epsilon} \cdot \Pr[\mathcal{A}(D') = S].$$

In this paper we consider two datasets D and D' to be neighbors if one dataset equals the other dataset with one additional tuple added. We use $D \simeq D'$ to denote this.

One approach for computing a function g on dataset D while satisfying ϵ-differential privacy is to add to the output of $g(D)$ random noise following the Laplace distribution. The magnitude of the noise depends on the privacy budget ϵ, and GS_g, the *global sensitivity* or the L_1 sensitivity of g. This mechanism, denoted by $\mathcal{A}_g$, is given below:

$$\begin{array}{rrl} & \mathcal{A}_g(D) & = g(D) + \mathsf{Lap}\left(\frac{\mathsf{GS}_g}{\epsilon}\right) \\ \text{where} & \mathsf{GS}_g & = \max_{D \simeq D'} |g(D) - g(D')|, \\ \text{and} & \Pr[\mathsf{Lap}(\beta) = x] & = \frac{1}{2\beta} e^{-|x|/\beta} \end{array}$$

In the above, $\mathsf{Lap}(\beta)$ represents a random variable sampled from the Laplace distribution with scale parameter β.

Utility Goal. The utility goal is to generate k-way marginals that are close to the true values. Given a generated k-way marginal table $\tilde{\mathsf{T}}_A$ for a set A of attributes, we consider two error measures and aim at minimizing them.

The first is the L_2 distance between $\tilde{\mathsf{T}}_A$ and T_A, the k-way marginal table over A computed from the original dataset, when both are viewed as vectors consisting of 2^k elements. We call this the error distance. For a given method, the error distance is a random variable as its value depends on the noise added by the method. The expected value of the square of error distance is also the expected value of the sum of squared errors in each cell, and we call it the **Expected Squared Error (ESE)**. We often use the ESE to understand a method's utility.

The second is the Jensen-Shannon divergence between $\mathsf{norm}(\tilde{\mathsf{T}}_A)$ and $\mathsf{norm}(\mathsf{T}_A)$, where norm normalizes a marginal table by dividing each cell with the sum of all the cells, so that in the normalized table the sum of all cells equals 1. It is natural to use the Kullback-Leibler divergence between $\mathsf{norm}(\mathsf{T}_A)$ and $\mathsf{norm}(\tilde{\mathsf{T}}_A)$, since $D_{\mathsf{KL}}(P||Q)$ measures the information lost when Q is used to approximate P. However, $D_{\mathsf{KL}}(P||Q)$ is undefined when $Q(i) = 0$ and $P(i) \neq 0$ for some i, which can happen in our setting. We thus choose to use Jensen-Shannon divergence [25], which is a symmetrized and smoothed version of the Kullback-Leibler divergence:

$$D_{\mathsf{JS}}(P||Q) = \frac{1}{2} D_{KL}(P||M) + \frac{1}{2} D_{KL}(Q||M) \qquad (1)$$

where $M = \frac{P+Q}{2}$ and $D_{\mathsf{KL}(P||Q)} = \sum_i \ln\left(\frac{P(i)}{Q(i)}\right) P(i)$

Efficiency requirement. Let $N = |D|$ denote the number of tuples in the dataset. We assume that $N \ll 2^d$, and thus want to avoid $\Theta(2^d)$ computational complexity. According to result in [29], it is computationally unfeasible to output a new synthetic dataset that preserves accuracy for k-way marginals. As PriView generates a synopsis instead of a synthetic dataset, this result does not apply here. It only suggests that generating a synthetic dataset that is consistent with our synopsis may be computationally expensive.

Remarks. We assume that k is relatively small compared with d, that is, running time in low-degree polynomial in 2^k is acceptable. Note that a k-way marginal has 2^k entries, thus complexity linear in 2^k is unavoidable. In the experiments, we consider $k = 4, 6, 8$. However, our proposed PriView method easily extends to larger values of k. PriView consists of two stages. The first stage generates a synopsis of the dataset; and does not change its complexity when k increases. The second stage is to reconstruct any desired k-way marginal, which involves solving a convex optimization problem with 2^k variables.

In the experiments, we use three real datasets, one with $d = 9$ to compare our method against other methods that do not scale, the second with $d = 32$, and the third with $d = 45$. We also use Markov chain models to synthesize multiple datasets with $d = 64$.

3. ANALYZING EXISTING APPROACHES

In this section, we discuss existing approaches to the problem and analyze their effectiveness. Later we experimentally compare with all these methods whenever they can scale to the experimental setting.

3.1 The Flat Method

A basic approach, henceforth referred to as the Flat method, is to generate a noisy version of the full contingency table of D. In this method, one adds noise from distribution $\mathsf{Lap}\left(\frac{1}{\epsilon}\right)$ to all counts in the full contingency table of the dataset. This noisy full contingency table can then be used to compute any k-way marginal tables. This approach takes time $O(2^d)$.

To estimate the ESE, we observe that the noise added to each cell of the full contingency table has variance

$$V_u = \frac{2}{\epsilon^2} \tag{2}$$

We treat V_u as the unit of ESE. To reconstruct a k-way marginal table, one sums up the noisy counts for the corresponding cells in the contingency table. For each entry in the k-way marginal table, one sums up 2^{d-k} cells, and the marginal table has 2^k entries, each with independently generated noise. Thus, the ESE of the Flat method is

$$2^k \times 2^{d-k} V_u = 2^d V_u. \tag{3}$$

This approach works very well when d is small. See [21] for an analysis of its accuracy. However, when d is large it suffers from two problems. First, the time complexity and space complexity are both $\Theta(2^d)$, which is too large for larger values of d. Second, it will be highly inaccurate, as the ESE increases exponentially in d.

3.2 The Direct Method

Another method is to add independently generated Laplacian noise to each k-way marginal table [11]. To compute m marginal tables while satisfying ϵ-DP, one adds noise sampled from $\mathsf{Lap}\left(\frac{m}{\epsilon}\right)$ to each entry, resulting in a variance of $m^2 V_u$. As $m = \binom{d}{k}$ and each table has 2^k entries, this results in an ESE of

$$2^k \binom{d}{k}^2 V_u. \tag{4}$$

Comparing Equations (4) and (3), we can see that for smaller values of d, the Flat method is better. The Direct method starts outperforming the Flat method for larger d's. The exact values of d's for which the Direct method overtakes the Flat method depend on k and are given in the table below.

k	2	3	4	5
Condition for Direct better than Flat	$d \geq 16$	$d \geq 26$	$d \geq 36$	$d \geq 46$

Equations (3) and (4) may over-estimate the error, especially when the computed value is greater than 1. This is because large noises may result in negative values, which can be corrected. However, this over-estimation becomes significant only there are large negative values, in which case the error will remain large even after correcting tghem. For example, suppose that one noise entry is close to $-\frac{N}{2}$, then this means that the noise added to each entry is likely large enough to overwhelm the true counts in most cells.

The Direct method has time complexity $\Theta(\max(d^k, N))$ and space complexity of $\Theta(d^k)$; while the Flat method has time and space complexity of $\Theta(\max(2^d, N))$. When k is small, the Direct method scales much better than the Flat method when d increases.

3.3 Adding Noise in the Fourier Domain

Barak et al. [4] proposed the approach to add noises in the Fourier domain. Conceptually, each full contingency table corresponds to a set of 2^d Fourier coefficients, and each k-way marginal can be reconstructed using 2^k of these coefficients. To reconstruct all k-way marginals, one needs $1 + \binom{d}{1} + \binom{d}{2} + \cdots + \binom{d}{k}$ coefficients (corresponding to all binary strings with at most k 1's). One can publish noisy versions of these coefficients, which can be subsequently used to reconstruct any desired k-way marginal. The magnitude of noise added to the coefficients is similar to that in the Direct method. One advantage of this approach over the Direct method is that because there is a one-to-one correspondence between full contingency tables and the vectors of Fourier coefficients, the noisy marginals reconstructed from noisy Fourier coefficients are consistent in the sense that there exists a full contingency table that corresponds to the generated noisy marginals. However, the corresponding marginal table may contain negative entries. To avoid such negative entries, it is proposed to use linear programming to compute a full contingency table that does not contain any negative entries, while minimizing the largest error between the noisy Fourier coefficients and the Fourier coefficients computed from the contingency table.

Using linear programming to compute a full contingency table, which has 2^d entries, is unfeasible when d is large. When the linear programming step is not used, the method becomes adding noise to the Fourier coefficients, and then reconstruct the k-way marginal. Compared with the direct method, this reduces the ESE by a factor of 2^k.

3.4 Data Cubes

Ding et al. [8] tries to solve a very similar problem as PriView, namely how to reconstruct a set of marginals (query marginals) as accurately as possible. Their approach tries to find a set of marginals that together cover all query marginals, and then try to make them consistent. In the case of low-dimensional binary datasets, the principles in [8] will lead it to choose to publish the noisy version of the full contingency table, which is equivalent to the Flat method.

The main limitation of the approach in [8] is that the techniques, both for view selection and for view consistency, require time polynomial in 2^d, and is thus unfeasible in our setting. The techniques in [8] first organize all possible marginals in a lattice under the subset relation. With a d-dimensional binary dataset, there are 2^d marginals in the lattice. The method in [8] iteratively selects which marginals should be released. In each iteration, it traverses all 2^d marginals in the lattice and greedily selects one. The consistency techniques is also polynomial in 2^d because it constructs all marginals in the lattice that are above the chosen ones in order to achieve consistency.

Our approaches solve the same problem as in [8], but use different techniques in order to scale to larger d values. We are able to do this for the following reasons. First, unlike [8] we do not require all query marginals are covered by the views. Second, we use existing covering design, instead of greedily searching the lattice. Third, we develop a much more efficient consistency procedure.

3.5 The Matrix Mechanism

Proposed by Li et al. [22], the matrix mechanism is a method of answering a workload of predicate counting queries. Given some workload, the method finds an alternative set of queries, called a query strategy. Standard Laplace noise is then added to the strategy queries, the answers to which are used to give accurate answers to the original workload. A natural way to adapt the matrix mechanism to our purposes is to assume that the workload consists of all possible k-way marginal count queries.

Finding the best possible strategy queries is a semi-definite optimization problem. This requires a running time $O\left(2^{3d}(2^k\binom{d}{k})^3\right)$. An approximation presented in [23] runs in $O\left(2^{3d}\right)$, and another method in [31]. For all practical purposes, running the original optimization problem is unfeasible. Any approximation must be polynomial in 2^d, since there are 2^d basic queries one can use to form any strategy. We are able to run both approximation method for $d = 9$. We explore the accuracy of the approximations for small datasets in our experiments.

3.6 Multiplicative Weights Mechanism

Several approaches based on multiplicative updates were proposed in [17, 15, 16]. In these approaches, one maintains and improves a distribution approximating a given dataset for answering a set of counting queries. We consider the non-interactive version of the approach by Hartz et al. [16], which we use MWEM to denote. To release k-way marginals, the approach works as follows. The set of queries is the set of all k-way marginals. One starts with an initial full contingency table that is uniform, and then selects, using the exponential mechanism [26], a k-way marginal that is most incorrectly answered by the current distribution. One then obtains a noisy answer to the selected marginal, and updates the distribution to match the current state of knowledge. This process is repeated T times. Each round is allocated a privacy budget ϵ/T. Half of the privacy budget at each round is used to select a marginal that is most incorrectly answered, and the other half is used to get a noisy answer. The basic version of MWEM performs a single multiplicative update step in each round using the new query, and outputs the average from the distribution after each round. A theorem provides a utility bound for this method.

Experiments in [16] use the following two improvements over the basic version. In each round, one iterates over all existing query results 100 times to attempt to maximally benefit from the query results. Furthermore, queries are answered using the final distribution instead of using the average. While these improvements greatly improved the actual performance in practice, using them means that the theoretically proven utility bound no longer holds.

Maintaining a full contingency table requires time and space complexity $\Omega(2^d)$, and is unfeasible for larger d values. The largest d value used in [16] is $d = 16$. A technique is introduced in [16] to avoid explicitly storing the full contingency table. This technique, however, is limited to the case when the attributes can be partitioned into disjoint parts so that no query involves attributes from more than one part, which is not applicable to our problem.

3.7 Learning Based Approaches

The class of learning based approaches, first described in [15], with the current state of the art approach in this line of work, which is also the most practical, described in [28]. These approaches view the database as a function on queries, and aim to learn a good approximation of this function while satisfying differential privacy.

This approach in [28] runs in time $|D| \cdot d^{C\sqrt{k}\log(1/\gamma)}$, where γ is an accuracy parameter and C is a constant. While this is asymptotically appealing, it is impractical for the ranges of parameters that are of practical relevance. The complexity $d^{C\sqrt{k}\log(1/\gamma)}$ is asymptotically better than the $\binom{d}{k}2^k$ complexity of the Direct method; however, for smaller k's, this complexity is actually much worse. The utility bound suggests that when k is between 60 and 100, this method can start outperforming the Direct method; however, the method (and in fact all methods) will become computationally unfeasible long before k reaches that range, e.g., a k-way marginal requires $\Theta(2^k)$ storage.

4. THE PRIVIEW APPROACH

In this section, we describe our PriView approach for publishing k-way marginal tables from a d-dimensional dataset.

4.1 A Fruitful Middle Ground

Both the Direct method and the Flat method are unsuitable when d is large. They represent two extremes. The Flat method generates one huge contingency table, and the Direct method generates many tiny marginal tables. We observe that there is a fruitful middle ground between the two extremes: one could generate a small number of "mid-size" marginal tables that can be used to reconstruct k-way marginal tables with better accuracy.

To see the benefit of publishing these "mid-size" marginals, consider, for example, the case where $d = 16$ and $k = 2$. The Flat methods publishes 1 table with 2^{16} entries, resulting in ESE of $2^{16}\, V_u = 65536\, V_u$. The Direct method publishes $\binom{16}{2} = 120$ tables, resulting in ESE of $2^2\binom{16}{2}^2 V_u = 57600\, V_u$. However, one can publish six 8-way marginal tables, while ensuring that any 2-way marginal table can be reconstructed from one of the published 8-way marginal tables. This results in an ESE of $2^2 \cdot 6^2 \cdot 2^6 = 9126\, V_u$, a number significantly smaller than either extreme.

We call these "mid-size" marginals "views" of the dataset D. When we consider larger values of k, e.g., $k = 6$ or $k = 8$, trying to come up with views that cover all sets of k attributes may result in too many views, and too much noise to be added. Our method does not attempt to cover all such k-way marginals, and instead develop techniques to compute marginal tables when the k attributes are not fully contained in any single view.

Notation. We use T_A to denote the noisy marginal table over $A \subseteq \mathbf{A}$. Let Q_A denote the set of all possible counting queries by assigning each attribute in A a value of either 0 or 1. Then T_A can be viewed as a function $\mathsf{T}_A : Q_A \to \mathcal{R}$, where $\mathcal{R}$ is the set of real numbers. We use $\mathsf{T}_A \equiv \mathsf{T}'_A$ to denote that the two marginal tables over A are the same for every entry. And $\mathsf{T}_A(\cdot) \geq x$ to mean that every entry in the table is greater than x. Given T_A, and $A' \subseteq A$, we use $\mathsf{T}_A[A']$ to denote the marginal over A' constructed from T_A by summing the corresponding entries. In particular, $\mathsf{T}_A[\emptyset]$ gives the sum of all cells in T_A.

DEFINITION 2 (VIEW CONSISTENCY). *We say that two marginal tables T_{V_i} and T_{V_j} are* ***consistent*** *if and only if the marginal table over attributes in $V_i \cap V_j$ reconstructed from T_{V_i} is exactly the same as that reconstructed from T_{V_j}, that is, $\mathsf{T}_{V_i}[V_i \cap V_j] \equiv \mathsf{T}_{V_j}[V_i \cap V_j]$.*

4.2 Summary of The PriView Approach

We now give a summary of our PriView approach, which has the following steps.

1. **Choose the Set of Views.** The first step is to choose which marginal tables to generate. More specifically, we need to choose the set of views:
$$\mathbf{V} = \{V_1, V_2, \ldots, V_w\},$$
where each view $V_i \subseteq \mathbf{A}$ for $1 \leq i \leq w$ and $\bigcup_{i=1\ldots w} V_i = \mathbf{A}$. We choose these views so that each size-j marginal is covered by some V_i for some small values of j (often $j = 2$ or $j = 3$), and the resulting noise variance is relatively small. We describe the details for choosing $\mathbf{V}$ in Section 4.5.
2. **Generate Noisy Views.** In this step, for each view V_i we construct a differentially private marginal table, T_{V_i}, by adding Laplace noise $\mathsf{Lap}\left(\frac{w}{\epsilon}\right)$ to the counts specified by the table. This is the only step in the PriView approach that needs direct access to the dataset D. After this step, the dataset D is no longer accessed.
3. **Consistency Step.** In this step, we perform constrained inference on the marginal tables T_{V_i}'s. This step serves two purposes. First, by exploiting existing redundancy among views, it improves the accuracy of T_{V_i}'s. Second, it ensures that for any $i \neq j$, T_{V_i} and T_{V_j} are consistent. (See Definition 2 above.) This enables more accurate computation of marginals not fully covered by any view. We describe how this is performed in Section 4.4.
4. **Generating k-way Marginals.** Finally, we propose to use the maximum entropy method to generate an arbitrary k-way marginal table based on the T_{V_i}'s. In Section 4.3, we also discuss a few alternatives.

In the rest of this section, we present the steps of our PriView approach in the reverse order.

4.3 Computing k-way Marginals

Given a set of marginals produced from views in $\mathbf{V}$ that are mutually consistent, and a set A of attributes, where $|A| = k$, we want to compute the k-way marginal T_A. When all the attributes in A are "covered" by at least one view V_i, i.e. $A \subseteq V_i$, this step is trivial. We can construct T_A by summing over corresponding entries in T_{V_i}. However, when $A \not\subseteq V_i$ for each $V_i \in \mathbf{V}$, we need a method to return the marginal which best represents what we know about it.

Given A, for any view V_i, if $A \cap V_i = \emptyset$, then T_{V_i} provides no information. When $A \cap V_i$ contains j attributes, then T_{V_i} provides 2^j linear constraints on cells for T_A. Constraints obtained from different views, however, may not be linearly independent. Thus, we can extract all linearly independent constraints from all views. Unless A is fully contained in some view, the number of linearly independent constraints will always be less than 2^k. The combination of all constraints from all intersecting views results in an *under-specified* system of equations.

We now describe three approaches we have considered for the reconstruction step. The last approach is what we propose to use. We will experimentally compare the effectiveness of these four approaches.

Linear programming. One strategy is to adopt the linear programming approach proposed in [4], that is, to compute a marginal so that all the entries are non-negative, and the constraints are satisfied as much as possible.

$$\begin{array}{ll} \text{minimize} & \tau \\ \text{subject to} & \underset{a \in Q_A}{\forall}\ \mathsf{T}_A(a) \geq 0 \\ & \underset{V_i \in \mathbf{V}}{\forall}\ \underset{a' \in Q_{V_i \cap A}}{\forall}\ |\mathsf{T}_{V_i}(a') - \mathsf{T}_A(a')| \leq \tau \end{array}$$

In the above, τ is the maximum error for all constraints. This approach does not require the marginals for the views to be consistent.This approach is unsatisfying in that it considers consistency with regards to the constraints as the only factor in choosing a solution. Recall that we have under-specified constraints for the marginal table, and when they are consistent there are more than one solutions. The linear programming method has *no preference* among the set of consistent solutions. We thus consider other methods below. These methods all assume that all views are consistent.

Least Square Solution. One common approach to solving underdetermined systems of equations is to select the solution that has the least L_2 norm. We can thus express the problem of computing a k-way marginal as the following optimization

$$\begin{array}{ll} \text{minimize} & \sum_{a \in Q_A} \mathsf{T}_A(a)^2 \\ \text{subject to} & \underset{a \in Q_A}{\forall}\ \mathsf{T}_A(a) \geq 0 \\ & \underset{V_i \in \mathbf{V}}{\forall}\ \underset{a' \in Q_{V_i \cap A}}{\forall}\ \mathsf{T}_{V_i}(a') = \mathsf{T}_A(a') \end{array}$$

One can use standard quadratic programming approaches to solve the above optimization problem.

Maximum Entropy. The problem we have at hand is the estimation of a probability distribution with partial information. A common approach is to apply the Principle of Maximum Entropy. In Bayesian probability theory, the principle of maximum entropy states that, subject to precisely stated prior data (a set of precise constraints), the probability distribution which best represents the current state of knowledge is the one with largest information-theoretical entropy. We can thus express the problem of computing a k-way marginal as the following optimization

$$\begin{aligned} \text{maximize} \quad & -\sum_{a\in Q_A} \frac{\mathsf{T}_A(a)}{N_{\mathbf{V}}} \cdot \log\left(\frac{\mathsf{T}_A(a)}{N_{\mathbf{V}}}\right) \\ \text{subject to} \quad & \underset{a\in Q_A}{\forall}\ \mathsf{T}_A(a) \geq 0 \\ & \underset{V_i\in \mathbf{V}}{\forall}\ \underset{a'\in Q_{V_i\cap A}}{\forall}\ \mathsf{T}_{V_i}(a') = \mathsf{T}_A(a') \end{aligned}$$

In the above, $N_{\mathbf{V}}$ denotes the total count obtained from any $V_i \in \mathbf{V}$. Since all views are consistent, the value should be the same for any V_i.

We use an off-the-shelf convex optimization tool to solve the above optimization problem. In experiments, we found that sometimes convex optimization fails to find a solution after a fixed number of iterations. Since the constraints we have are noisy, we gradually relax the constraints by replacing each equality constraint as a pair of tight inequality constraints (using increasing larger toleration threshold) until the solver can find a solution.

4.4 Consistency between Noisy Views

The input to this step is a set of noisy marginal tables T_{V_i}, one for each set of attributes in the view set $\mathbf{V}$. The output is perturbed versions of these tables that are mutually consistent.

Mutual Consistency on a Set of Attributes. We first describe the method of ensuring that a set of view marginals are consistent on their common set of the attributes. Consider, wlog, views $V_1, \cdots, V_j$, let $A = V_1 \cap \ldots \cap V_j$. We want to ensure that $\mathsf{T}_{V_1}[A] \equiv \cdots \equiv \mathsf{T}_{V_j}[A]$. The goal is to make sure that $\mathsf{T}_{V_x}(a) = \mathsf{T}_{V_y}(a)$ for any two views $V_x, V_y \in \{V_1, V_2, \cdots, V_j\}$.

Here we apply the consistency techniques proposed in [19], and achieve consistency in two steps. The first step is to compute the best approximation for the marginal table T_A. Assuming that all $\mathsf{T}(V_i)$'s are constructed using the same privacy budget, and that $|V_1| = \cdots = |V_j|$, then for any $a \in Q_A$, the best approximation of $\mathsf{T}_A(a)$ that minimizes the variance of the noise is the arithmetic mean of the value from all views, i.e.:

$$\mathsf{T}_A(a) = \frac{1}{j}\sum_{i=1}^{j} \mathsf{T}_{V_i}(a)$$

The second step is to update all T_{V_i}'s to be consistent with T_A. One can view T_A as a set of $2^{|A|}$ mutually exclusive constraints on all the entries in T_{V_i}. For each constraint $c \in Q_A$, do

$$\mathsf{T}_{V_i}(c) \leftarrow \mathsf{T}_{V_i}(c) + \frac{\mathsf{T}_A(a) - \mathsf{T}_{V_i}(a)}{2^{|V_i|-|A|}},$$

where a is the query c restricted to attributes in A.

The following example illustrates mutual consistency between $\mathsf{T}_{V_1=\{a_1,a_2\}}$ and $\mathsf{T}_{V_2=\{a_1,a_3\}}$.

$\mathsf{T}_{V_1=\{a_1,a_2\}}$ before consistency	0.3	0.3	0.3	0.1
$\mathsf{T}_{V_2=\{a_1,a_3\}}$ before consistency	0.2	0.3	0.1	0.4
T_{V_1} projected on a_1	0.6		0.4	
T_{V_2} projected on a_1	0.5		0.5	
best estimat of $\mathsf{T}_{\{a_1\}}$	0.55		0.45	
$\mathsf{T}_{V_1=\{a_1,a_2\}}$ after consistency	0.275	0.275	0.325	0.125
$\mathsf{T}_{V_2=\{a_1,a_3\}}$ after consistency	0.225	0.325	0.075	0.375
T_{V_1} projected on a_2 is unchanged	0.6		0.4	
T_{V_2} projected on a_3 is unchanged	0.3		0.7	

Note that after mutual consistency, $\mathsf{T}_{V_1=\{a_1,a_2\}}$ and $\mathsf{T}_{V_2=\{a_1,a_3\}}$ agree on $\{a_1\}$ without changing the marginals of attributes not involved in the consistency.

Overall Consistency. We now describe how to ensure that all marginals are consistent on all subsets of attributes by performing a series of mutual consistency steps. The challenge here is to determine the order with which to perform the mutual consistency procedure. Suppose that we first make T_{V_1} and T_{V_2} consistent on the attribute set $V_1 \cap V_2 = \{a_1, a_2\}$, and then make T_{V_1} and T_{V_3} consistent on the attribute set $V_1 \cap V_3 = \{a_1, a_3\}$. This second step may make T_{V_1} and T_{V_2} inconsistent, because it may change the distribution of the attribute $\{a_1\}$. We note, however, if we have already made V_1, V_2, V_3 consistent on $\{a_1\}$, then the second step will not invalidate the consistency established in step 1. This is formalized in the following lemma.

LEMMA 1. *If T_{V_1} and T_{V_2} are already consistent on $A \subset V_1 \cap V_2$, then enforcing mutual consistency between T_{V_1} and T_{V_2} does not change the projection of T_{V_1} on any subset of $(V_1 \setminus V_2) \cup A$.*

PROOF. When updating T_{V_1} to affect the distribution of attributes in $V_1 \cap V_2$, increase to some cells in T_{V_1} must be balanced by equal amount of subtraction to other cells. When projecting T_{V_1} onto any subset of $(V_1 \setminus V_2) \cup A$, these changes cancel out. □

Utilizing Lemma 1, we propose the following procedure to ensure overall consistency. Take all sets of attributes that are the result of the intersection of some subset of $\mathbf{V}$; these sets form a partial order under the subset relation. One then obtain a topological sort of these sets, starting from the empty set. For each set A, one finds all views that include A, and ensures that these views are consistent on A. Note that consistency on the empty set of attributes ensures that the total counts in all marginals are the same, and this is done first. Following this order, a later consistency step will not invalidate consistency established in previous steps. Furthermore, following any topological order will result in the same result.

Accuracy through Ripple Non-Negativity. Noisy marginals may contain negative numbers. Since all entries in the true marginals are non-negative, one should change these negative numbers to 0. Intuitively this will improve the accuracy. However, experimental results have found that simply changing negative numbers to 0 dramatically increases the error. We believe that this is because the noisy answer for any query that includes cells that have low true counts is positively biased, because negative noises are partially removed, but positive noises remain. At the same time, the noisy answer for a query that does not include cells with low true counts does not have such a bias.

To avoid such bias, we introduced the following "Ripple" non-negativity method, which turns negative counts into 0 while decreasing the counts for its neighbors to maintain overall count unchanged. Given an ℓ-way marginal table, for any entry that has count $c < -\theta$ for some small value of θ, we set the entry to 0 and subtract $|c|/\ell$ from each of its ℓ neighboring cells (i.e., cells obtained by flipping one of the ℓ bits). As doing this may result in other cells to be below $-\theta$, this is iterated until no cell is below $-\theta$. As each iteration distributes a negative count into ℓ neighbors, it is guaranteed to terminate quickly.

Applying the ripple non-negativity step to the views, however, may make them inconsistent. We use Consistency + Non-negativity + Consistency. While the last consistency step may again introduce negative values, they tend to be very small. We tried adding more iterations of "Non-negativity + Consistency" and found that they produce negligible additional improvements.

4.5 Choosing a Set of Views

Finally, we need a method to choose the set $\mathbf{V}$ of views. Obviously it is desirable to have every attribute appear in at least one view; otherwise, information about that attribute is not present, and the estimation has to assume that it is equally likely to be 1 or 0, which may turn out to be very inaccurate. Going beyond covering every single attribute, it is natural to ensure that every pair of attributes are covered in some view, and then every triple of attributes, and so on. We thus take advantage of the following concept from combinatorics theory.

DEFINITION 3 (COVERING DESIGN [14, 13]). *A (w, ℓ, t)-covering design of a set P is a collection of w subsets of P, each of which contains ℓ elements and is called a block, such that any t-element subset of P is contained in at least one block. An* optimal *(w, ℓ, t)-covering design minimizes the number of blocks.*

Clearly, for a fixed P and t, the larger the ℓ, the smaller the w needs to be. We need a method to choose w, ℓ, t.

Setting $\ell = 8$. We recommend choosing $\ell = 8$ (or values close to it, such as between 7 and 11), and we now explain why. There are two sources of errors for any marginal generated by PriView: noise error, which is due to Laplacian noise added to satisfy differential privacy, and coverage error, which occurs when the marginal is not fully covered by any view.

To compute the noise error, we consider the result of reconstructing a pair of attributes. When choosing a set of w views of length ℓ each, reconstructing a pair from a single view that covers it has ESE of, $2^\ell w^2 \frac{2}{\epsilon^2}$. However, on average we expect a pair to be covered by $\frac{w\ell(\ell-1)}{d(d-1)}$ views, since there are $\frac{d(d-1)}{2}$ pairs, and these views include $\frac{w\ell(\ell-1)}{2}$ pairs. Averaging will reduce the ESE; thus the normalized error (after dividing N) is on the order of

$$err = \frac{1}{N}\sqrt{\frac{\frac{2^{\ell+1}w^2}{\epsilon^2}}{\frac{w\ell(\ell-1)}{d(d-1)}}} = \frac{2^{\frac{\ell+1}{2}}}{N\epsilon}\sqrt{\frac{wd(d-1)}{\ell(\ell-1)}} \quad (5)$$

We want to choose ℓ to minimize (5). We are given N, d, ϵ, and can choose w and ℓ. We observe that w and ℓ are interdependent. When we compare covering designs with similar coverage, we can assume that they have roughly the same number of pairs, and thus $w \propto \frac{1}{\ell(\ell-1)}$. Then choosing ℓ to minimize (5) can be achieved by minimizing $\frac{2^{\ell/2}}{\ell(\ell-1)}$. A similar analysis for noise error of reconstructing triples require minimizing $\frac{2^{\ell/2}}{\ell(\ell-1)(\ell-2)}$. Choosing $\ell = 8$ works well, as can be seen from the following table.

ℓ	$\frac{2^{\ell/2}}{\ell(\ell-1)}$	$\frac{2^{\ell/2}}{\ell(\ell-1)(\ell-2)}$	ℓ	$\frac{2^{\ell/2}}{\ell(\ell-1)}$	$\frac{2^{\ell/2}}{\ell(\ell-1)(\ell-2)}$
5	0.283	0.094	9	0.314	0.045
6	0.267	0.067	10	0.356	0.044
7	0.269	0.054	11	0.411	0.046
8	0.286	0.048	12	0.485	0.048

It is interesting to know that the choice of ℓ is independent from N, d, ϵ, thus $\ell = 8$ can be used cross all settings. We experimentally tested other choices of ℓ, and found that values close to 8 give quite close results.

Choosing t. Choosing the value for t does depend on N, d, ϵ. We observe that the overall error is affected by both the noise error and coverage error. Larger t provides better coverage, at the cost of higher noise error. We want to ensure that neither one is much larger than the other. The coverage error, however, cannot be analytically computed, as it depends on the nature of the dataset. It is high when there is high correlation among some attributes, which are not covered together. Empirically, we observe that choosing t so that the noise error falls in the range of 0.001 and 0.003 seems to work well.

Therefore, we find the best covering design with $\ell = 8$ for $t = 2, 3, 4$ and compute the error value from Equation (5). Many covering design solutions exist in online repositories such as [13], from which we look up the covering designs for the desired N, t, ℓ value and find the design as well as the value w. Computing the noise error using (5) also requires N, for which a rough estimate suffices. For example, one could use a very small privacy budget, say, $\epsilon = 0.001$ to obtain a noisy count for it.

As an example, consider the Kosarak dataset. The errors below are computed using the best known covering designs we found from [13], with $d = 32, N \approx 900,000, \epsilon = 1$.

	$t = 2$		$t = 3$		$t = 4$	
ℓ	w	err	w	err	w	err
8	20	0.00047	106	0.0011	620	0.0026

The noise error for $t = 2$ is 0.00045, which is significantly less than 0.001; that for $t = 3$ is 0.0011, and that for $t = 4$ is 0.0026, which is probably not worthwhile of the additional coverage improvement over $t = 3$. We thus would choose $t = 3$. However, for $\epsilon = 0.1$, these errors will be multiplied by a factor of 10, and we would need to choose $t = 2$. The other datasets we use have higher d values, and we will need to use $t = 2$ for them.

4.6 Space and Time Complexity

The space complexity of PriView approach is the set of views, i.e., $w2^\ell$, which is quite small.

The time complexity for publishing the synopsis consists of the following three steps: First, constructing noisy views takes time $O(wN + w2^\ell)$. Second, the time complexity of the consistency step is determined by how many mutual consistency steps are taken, and how many views are involved in

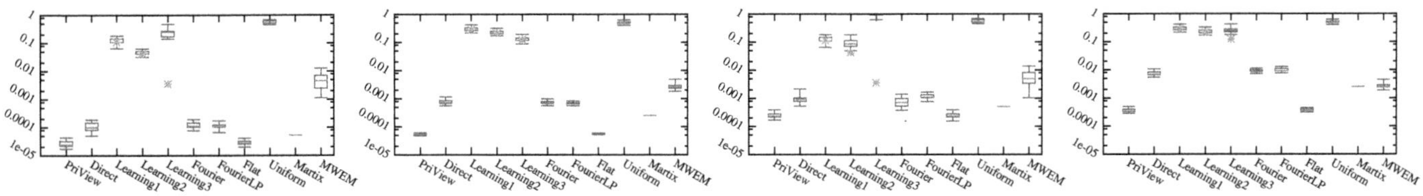

(a) $\epsilon = 1.0, k = 2$ (b) $\epsilon = 1.0, k = 4$ (c) $\epsilon = 0.1, k = 2$ (d) $\epsilon = 0.1, k = 4$

Figure 1: Comparing all approaches on the MSNBC dataset ($d = 9$). Results are L_2 error shown in log scale. PriView uses $C_2(6, 3)$.

each step. The non-negativity step has time complexity $O(w2^\ell)$. In our experiments, the total time for publishing a synopsis varies from several seconds to a few minutes.

The time to reconstruct one k-way marginal is determined by the convex optimization procedure with 2^k variables. Depending on k and the number of constrains, we've observed that it takes time between less a second and half a minute.

The following table shows the actual running time using a Python implementation and a 2.3GHZ processor. In the table, P denotes the time to construct the synopsis, including constructing noisy views, conduct ripple non-negativity on the views, and then the consistency step. The process of reconstructing a single 6-way marginal and a single 8-way marginal is represented by Q_6 and Q_8 correspondingly. The unit of time is second.

	$Kosarak : d = 32$		$AOL : d = 45$	
	$C_2(8, 20)$	$C_3(8, 106)$	$C_2(8, 42)$	$C_3(8, 326)$
P	$8.78s$	$90.81s$	$47.42s$	$593.27s$
Q_6	$0.16s$	$1.78s$	$2.71s$	$11.79s$
Q_8	$2.79s$	$35.96s$	$20.76s$	$77.54s$

Note that using covering design for $t = 2$ is quite fast on both datasets, and $C_3(8, 326)$ for AOL is not recommended and included here only for comparison purposes.

4.7 Extensions to Categorical Attributes

We focus on binary dataset, following the tradition in the literature on general methods for computing marginals [4, 15, 7, 18, 28]. This simplifies the presentation of the methods. However, PriView can be extended to datasets with categorical attributes that are not binary. The view consistency method in Section 4.4 and maximum entropy-based reconstruction method in Section 4.3 can be applied directly with non-binary categorical attributes. The only change is in the Ripple Non-negativity step, neighboring cells are obtained by changing only one value (as opposed to flipping one value). The view selection method, however, needs some modification. The same principles still apply. First, we want to limit the size (i.e., number of cells) in each view marginal. Let s denote the number of cells of each view, i.e., $s = 2^\ell$ when attributes are binary. For ease of analysis, assume that each attribute has b values, thus each view has $\log_b s$ attributes. To minimize the error, we want to minimize $\frac{\sqrt{s}}{\log_b s(\log_b s-1)}$ and $\frac{\sqrt{s}}{\log_b s(\log_b s-1)\log_b s(\log_b s-2)}$. As b increases, the optimal s values generally increases. Based on the minimization objective, as a rough guideline, we recommend the following ranges of s for different b values:

b	2	3	4	5
s	$100 - 1000$	$150 - 2000$	$200 - 3200$	$250 - 5000$

We also recommend choosing $t = 2$, since it apparently works well for a wide range of cases. One can then choose views to ensure that every pair of attributes are covered in some view. This step likely requires adapting existing covering design algorithms to the case where the number of attributes in each block depends on how many values these attributes have. Simple greedy algorithms can also be developed. Evaluating the performance of such methods is beyond the scope of this paper.

5. EXPERIMENTAL EVALUATION

In this section, we present the experimental results that demonstrate the efficacy of PriView.

Datasets. We use the following datasets in our experimental comparison

Kosarak [2]: This is a click-stream dataset from a Hungarian on-line news portal. We processed this dataset to include only the top 32 most popular pages. Each record thus has 32 binary attributes corresponding to whether a user visited the webpage. The total number of records in this dataset is 912,627.

AOL [1]: The AOL search log dataset includes the search keywords for 647,377 users. We used the WordNet [12] hypernyms corpus to generate a generalization taxonomy for the search keywords, which resulted in 45 categories. Each keyword was replaced by one of the 45 categories, resulting in 45 binary attributes.

MSNBC [3]: This is a click-stream dataset for msnbc.com, with 989,818 users. Each attribute indicates whether a user visited a particular pages in the msnbc portal. We preprocessed this dataset to include only 9 attributes.

MCHAIN: We synthesize several datasets using the markov chain model. We follow the approach of stationary binary sequence used in [30]. We vary the orders from 1 to 7, to examine the effectiveness of PriView with datasets with various degree of correlation among attributes. For order i, given the previous i bits, the probability of next bit being 1 is $0.5 + \left(1 - \frac{2s}{i}\right)/4$. Here s is number of 1's in the previous i bits. We treat each generated series of 64 bits as a record.

Evaluation Methodology. We use $\epsilon \in \{1.0, 0.1\}$ and $k \in \{4, 6, 8\}$ for our experiments. For each value of k, we randomly generate 200 sets of k attributes. For PriView with a set of views, we compute the average error of each query of five runs. In each run, we add noises to the views, and conduct consistency to compute the synopsis. We then plot the distribution of the 200 average errors. For comparison of PriView with other methods on the two large datasets, we also measure Jensen-Shannon divergence given in Equation 1. As results show that L_2 error distance and Jensen-Shannon divergence are similar, we do not show the Jensen-Shannon divergence for other experiments due to space limitation. When plotting L2 error, we normalize the value by dividing the error with N, so that the numbers are comparable across datasets.

To provide a clearer picture of an algorithm's behavior, we use candlesticks to plot the profile of errors for all query sizes. Each candlestick provides 5 pieces of information: the 25 percentile (the bottom of candlestick), the median (the bottom of the box), the 75 percentile (the top of the box), the 95 percentile (the top of the candlestick), and the arithmetic mean (the red bar). We use the notation $C_t(\ell, w)$ to denote a covering design that covers all t-sized subsets of attributes using w views with ℓ attributes in each view.

As a baseline comparison, we also plot the L_2 error for the Uniform method, which always returns a uniformly distributed marginal. If a method is no better than Uniform in a setting, then applying it in the setting is meaningless.

5.1 Comparisons on MSNBC

Figure 1 shows the results for comparing PriView against the existing methods we have discussed in Section 3 on the MSNBC dataset. We reduce the number of dimensions to 9 in order to be able to run the Learning-based approach [15] and the Matrix Mechanism [23]. These approaches have difficulty to scale to larger dimensions.

For such a small d value, most methods perform well. Our analysis would predict the Flat method to work quite well, and the Direct method to be slightly worse. We observe that PriView performs as well as Flat.

For the Fourier method [4], we present the results before and after the linear programming optimization, indicated by Fourier and FourierLP respectively. The results for both are comparable, and are essentially the same as that of the Direct method. The DataCube method in [8] would choose Flat, which performs very well. This method, however, cannot be used for large d values.

For the Matrix Mechanism, we plot the expected error variance by examining the strategy matrix. The result is better than direct, and worse than flat and PriView. This indicates that the approximation used in the Matrix Mechanism is not closer to optimal than the other methods.

The most interesting results in this figure are those for the learning-based approach. The algorithm requires choosing a γ value. Decreasing γ decreases approximation error, at the cost of increasing noise errors. We choose $\gamma = \{1/2, 1/4, 1/8\}$ which correspond to Learning1, Learning2, and Learning3 respectively in Figure 1. We also plot the result without adding the noise to satisfy differential privacy, indicted by the green stars on the graphs; this shows errors due to the approximation. We observe that the learning-based approach performs very poorly. Even without noises, the results are much worse than other methods. When $\gamma = 1/8$, noise error starts to dominate the approximation error; thus continuing decreasing γ will only make the accuracy worse. These learning-based approaches also do not scale well when d increases.

For the MWEM approach [16], an important parameter is T, the number of rounds. It is suggested in [16] that T should be greater than $4 \log d$. We use $T = \lceil 4 \log d \rceil + 2 = 15$, and note that the results are worse than Flat and Direct. We note that the error range is wide for $k = 2$, but narrower for $k = 4$. This is because obtaining 15 pairs is not quite enough to cover all 45 pairs, and pairs not covered may have large errors. On the other hand, obtaining 15 quadruples provides a better coverage.

5.2 Comparison on Kosarak and AOL.

The results for the Kosarak and AOL datasets are shown in Figure 2. The only methods that scale to such large datasets are those that do not require 2^d complexity; namely the Direct method and the Fourier method. We optimize their results by removing negative values and redistributing the difference evenly to all cells. This can sometimes make the L_2 error to be smaller than predicted by Equation (4). We show both the L_2 error and the Jensen-Shannon divergence for them. Since it is unfeasible to run the Flat method on 32 and 45 dimensions, we calculate and plot the expected normalized L_2 norm for Flat. In many situations, this calculated value is far greater than 1, which are most likely due to reconstructed marginals including large negative values. We cap it at 1 in order to simulate improvements from applying nonnegativity constraint. The results show the superiority of the PriView method, achieving 2 to 3 orders of magnitude of improvement over other approaches.

Our results show that the only case Direct outperforms Uniform is for the Kosarak dataset ($d = 32$) when $\epsilon = 1.0$ and $k = 4$. For all other settings, it essentially returns noise. The Flat method fares a little better in that when $d = 32$ and $\epsilon = 1.0$, its accuracy for $k = 6$ and $k = 8$ is an order of magnitude better than Uniform. For all other settings, it also returns noise. The Fourier method performs just slightly better than Direct.

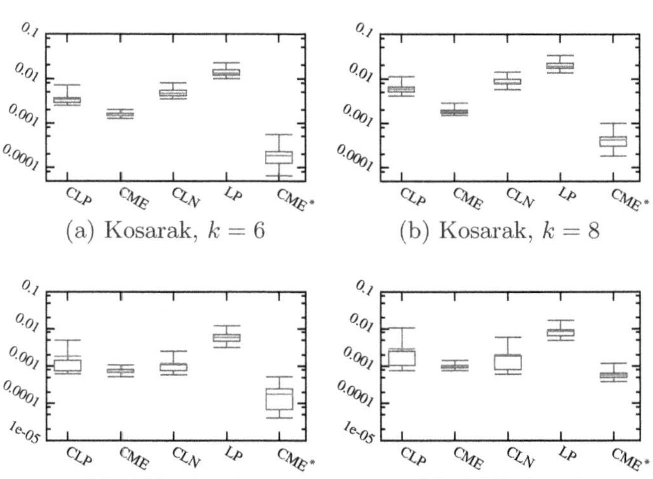

(a) Kosarak, $k = 6$ (b) Kosarak, $k = 8$

(c) AOL, $k = 6$ (d) AOL, $k = 8$

Figure 3: Comparing L_2 error for different reconstruction methods on the Kosarak dataset using $\mathbf{V} = C_3(8, 106)$ and on the AOL dataset using $\mathbf{V} = C_2(8, 42)$, all with $\epsilon = 1.0$. CME is the maximum entropy method, LP is the linear programming method, CLP is the linear programming method with a consistency preprocessing step, CLN is the least square method, and CME* is the maximum entropy method without adding noise.

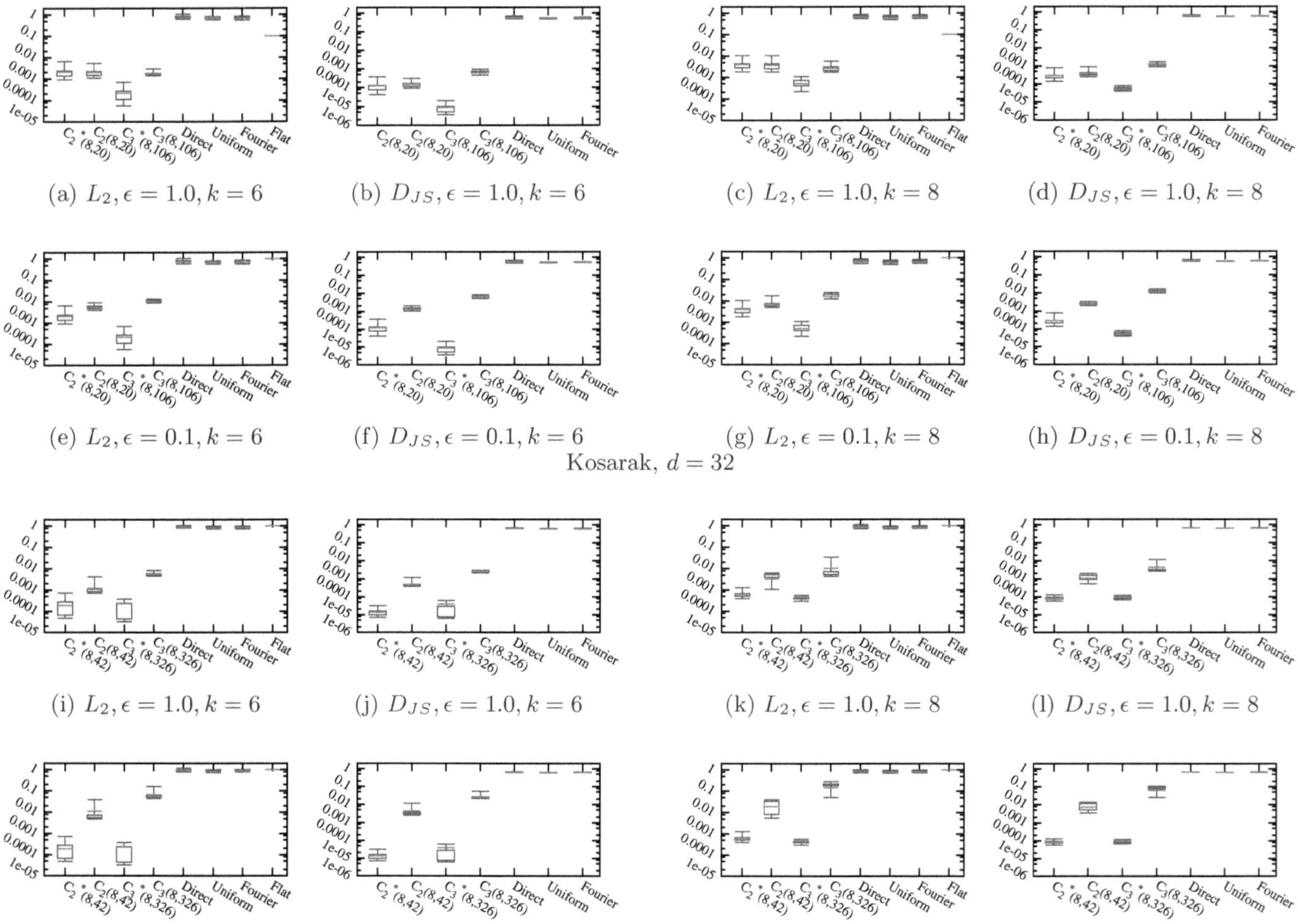

(a) $L_2, \epsilon = 1.0, k = 6$ (b) $D_{JS}, \epsilon = 1.0, k = 6$ (c) $L_2, \epsilon = 1.0, k = 8$ (d) $D_{JS}, \epsilon = 1.0, k = 8$

(e) $L_2, \epsilon = 0.1, k = 6$ (f) $D_{JS}, \epsilon = 0.1, k = 6$ (g) $L_2, \epsilon = 0.1, k = 8$ (h) $D_{JS}, \epsilon = 0.1, k = 8$

Kosarak, $d = 32$

(i) $L_2, \epsilon = 1.0, k = 6$ (j) $D_{JS}, \epsilon = 1.0, k = 6$ (k) $L_2, \epsilon = 1.0, k = 8$ (l) $D_{JS}, \epsilon = 1.0, k = 8$

(m) $L_2, \epsilon = 0.1, k = 6$ (n) $D_{JS}, \epsilon = 0.1, k = 6$ (o) $L_2, \epsilon = 0.1, k = 8$ (p) $D_{JS}, \epsilon = 0.1, k = 8$

AOL, $d = 45$

Figure 2: Comparing PriView with Flat and Direct on Kosarak and AOL. For Flat, only the expected average L_2 error is plotted. Results are shown in log scale. $C_t^*(l, w)$ uses covering design $\mathbf{V} = C_t(l, w)$ without adding noise.

5.3 Reconstruction & Non-negativity

Figure 3 shows the results from comparing the various reconstruction methods presented in Section 4.3. It is clear from the results that the maximum entropy method outperforms the alternatives.

The Linear Programming approach performs the worst. Recall that the Linear Programming approach does not require a consistency step. Instead, it tries to find a k-way marginal that is closest to all constraints. We conjecture that adding a consistency preprocessing step before applying the linear program will improve accuracy. To validate this claim, we ran the experiment again with the consistency step. This is shown as 'CLP' in the figures. As expected, the error substantially decreased. The result is most substantial with larger overlapping views for the AOL covering designs.

Figure 4 shows the impact of the performing the non-negativity step. Not using non-negativity ('None') has 2 to 4 times more error when compared with applying non-negativity. Simply change negative counts to zero(Simple) performs even worse, as this introduces systematic bias. Applying the naive non-negativity procedure of subtracting the same constant globally (Global) provide some improvement. Ripple method produces the best result. On the other hand, Consistency + Ripple + Consistency (Ripple_1) performs as well as repeating (Ripple + Consistency) 3 times after the initial Consistency step (Ripple_3).

5.4 Comparing Different Views

We now compare the accuracy due to choosing different views. The results for Kosarak are shown in Figure 6. Results for AOL are similar and are omitted due to space limitation. We use purple stars to denote the noise error computed from Equation 5. We can see that multiple covering designs with different ℓ values perform similarly. Choosing $\ell = 8$, while not optimal in all cases, perform reasonably well overall. We can also see that covering designs with $t = 3$ tend to have tighter band of errors than those covering only pairs. It also appears that choosing noise error to be around 0.002 would perform quite well.

5.5 Comparison on MCHAIN

Figure 5 illustrates the L_2 error on datasets generated by different order markov chain. For i'th order markov chain,

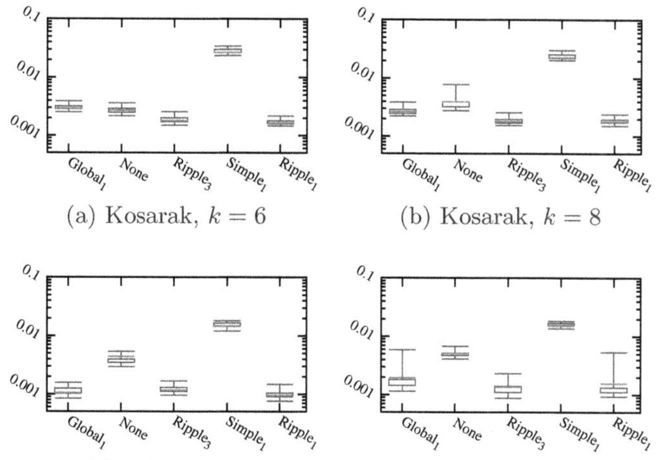

(a) Kosarak, $k = 6$ (b) Kosarak, $k = 8$

(c) AOL, $k = 6$ (d) AOL, $k = 8$

Figure 4: Comparing L_2 error for non-negativity methods on Kosarak using $\mathbf{V} = C_3(8, 106)$ and on AOL using $\mathbf{V} = C_2(8, 42)$, with $\epsilon = 1.0$. *Ripple*$_i$ applies the *Ripple* method i times. *None* keeps negative values unchanged. *Simple* changes all negative counts to zero. *Global* changes negative counts to zero, and then also subtracts a value from positive counts to maintain total count unchanged.

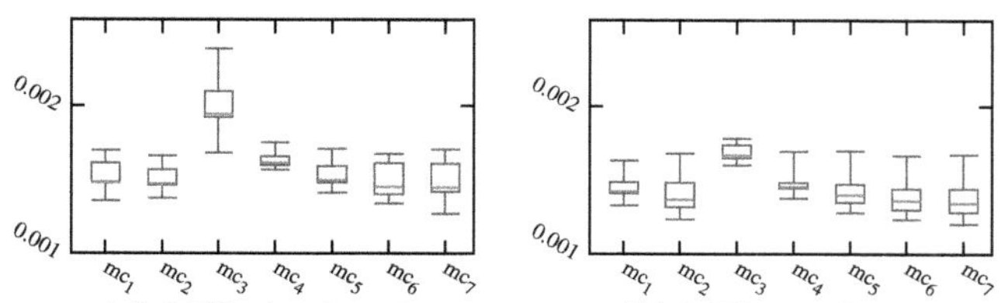

(a) MChain, $k = 6$ (b) MChain, $k = 8$

Figure 5: Comparing L_2 error on mc_i's, the i'th order markov chain datasets, using $\mathbf{V} = C_2(8, 72)$, with $\epsilon = 1.0$.

the value of current state is only denpendent on the previous i states. In the experiment, we are only using consecutive queries so that the queries demonstrate all interdependencies. We use $\mathbf{V} = C_2(8, 72)$. The results show that even though only pairs are covered, the results are quite accurate even for larger orders. Interestingly, the 3'rd order markov chain produces largest error. To understand this, observe that i'th order results in $i + 1$ attributes being highly correlated. For mc_1, all correlations are covered. For mc_2, while we do not guarantee that triples are covered, we guarantee that for any triple a_1, a_2, a_3, all three pairs are covered, and this seems to be sufficient to recover the joint distribution accurately. For mc_3, we have high correlation among 4 attributes, and covering only pairs results in noticeably larger (though still quite) errors. For even higher orders, the dependency among attributes weakens as each attribute is affected by the joint effect of more attributes, and the errors are quite small.

6. RELATED WORK

The notion of differential privacy was introduced in [6, 11, 9]. The method of adding Laplacian noise scaled with the sensitivity, which we use to generate view marginals, is proposed in [11]. Most closely related are previous approaches of releasing marginal tables with differential privacy. Several of these have been examined in detail in Section 3, including [4, 28, 22, 8, 15, 16].

There are a number of negative results regarding generating marginal tables. In [29], it is shown that it is computationally infeasible to construct a synthetic dataset that approximates 2-way marginals. Because we are constructing a synopsis, without trying to generate synthetic dataset from it, this negative result does not apply here. In [20], it is proven that when releasing all k-way marginals, if distortion is $o(\min\{\sqrt{n}/\log^{k^2+k+1} n, \sqrt{d^{k-1}}/\log^{k^2+3k-1} n\})$ per entry, then an adversary can reconstruct large fraction of the sensitive attribute entries, thus violating privacy. Note that the Direct method adds $O(\sqrt{d^k})$, and is thus "close to optimal", ignoring the inverse poly-logarithmic term. For $n \approx 2^{20}$, $d = 45$, $k = 6$, the above lowerbound becomes $\min\{2^{10}/20^{43}, 45^3/20^{53}\}$, which is about 10^{-64}. Thus the asymptotic lowerbound does not rule out the ability of accurately publishing k-way marginals in practice.

We use the concept of using constrained inference to post-process noisy results to improve accuracy introduced in [19], Qardaji and Li [27] present a method that employs recursive partitioning and summarization for multi-dimensional data publishing. This technique does not scale with larger d. Li et al. [24] use sets of attributes, similar to views, to release frequent itemsets in a differentially private manner. The views in that paper, however, are constructed using frequent items, require no consistency, and do not cover all attributes.

7. CONCLUSION

We have presented PriView: a practical method of computing marginal tables for datasets with more than a few dimensions. Instead of directly generating all k-way marginals, PriView generates marginals for a strategically chosen sets of attributes, which we call views. PriView combines existing ideas from different fields with new techniques developed in the paper. We have conducted extensive experiments on real and synthetic datasets, and shown that PriView advances the current sate of the art.

Acknowledgement. This paper is based upon work supported by the United States National Science Foundation under Grant No. 1116991. We would also like to thank the reviewers for their helpful comments.

8. REFERENCES

[1] AOL search log dataset. `http://www.gregsadetsky.com/aol-data/`.

[2] Frequent itemset mining dataset repository. `http://fimi.ua.ac.be/data/`.

[3] MSNBC.com anonymous web data data set. `http://archive.ics.uci.edu/ml/datasets/MSNBC.com+Anonymous+Web+Data`.

[4] B. Barak, K. Chaudhuri, C. Dwork, S. Kale, F. McSherry, and K. Talwar. Privacy, accuracy, and consistency too: a holistic solution to contingency table release. In *PODS'07*, pages 273–282, 2007.

[5] Y. M. Bishop, S. E. Fienberg, and P. W. Holl. *Discrete Multivariate Analysis: Theory and Practice.* Springer, 2007.

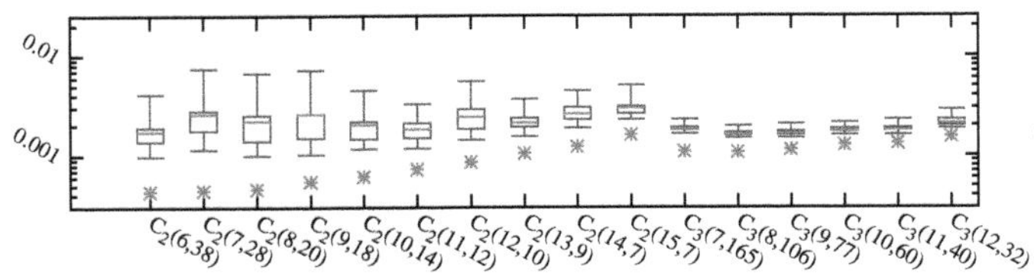

(a) Kosarak, $\epsilon = 1.0, k = 6$

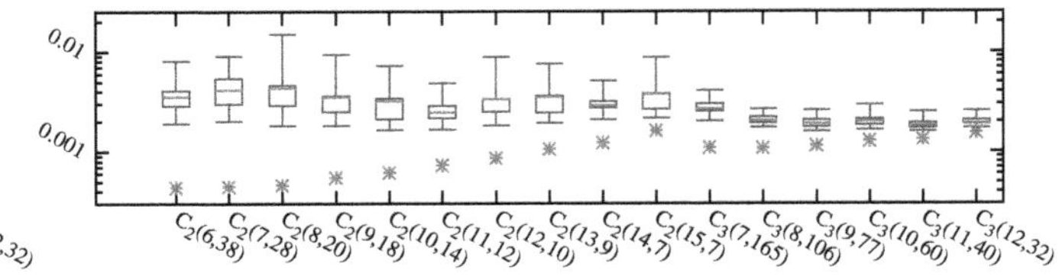

(b) Kosarak, $\epsilon = 1.0, k = 8$

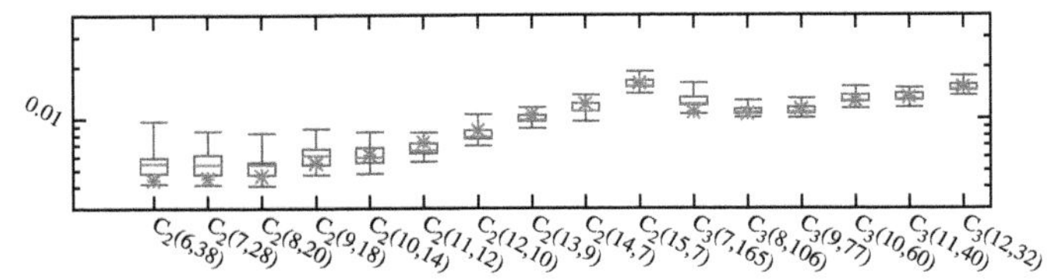

(c) Kosarak, $\epsilon = 0.1, k = 6$

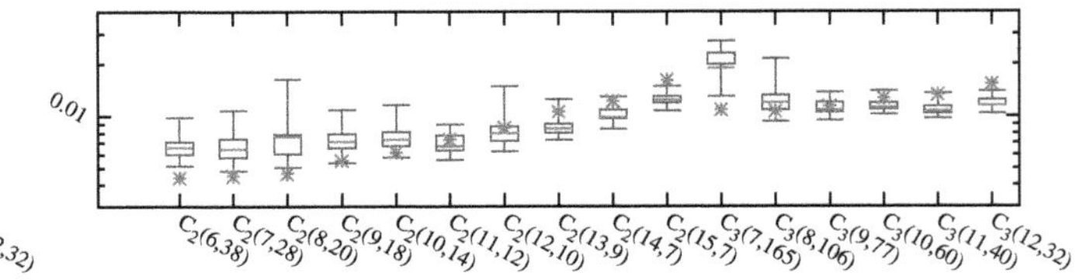

(d) Kosarak, $\epsilon = 0.1, k = 8$

Figure 6: Comparing L_2 error for different views on the Kosarak dataset

[6] A. Blum, C. Dwork, F. McSherry, and K. Nissim. Practical privacy: the SuLQ framework. In *PODS*, pages 128–138, 2005.

[7] M. Cheraghchi, A. Klivans, P. Kothari, and H. K. Lee. Submodular functions are noise stable. In *SODA*, pages 1586–1592, 2012.

[8] B. Ding, M. Winslett, J. Han, and Z. Li. Differentially private data cubes: optimizing noise sources and consistency. In *SIGMOD*, pages 217–228, 2011.

[9] C. Dwork. Differential privacy. In *ICALP*, pages 1–12, 2006.

[10] C. Dwork. A firm foundation for private data analysis. *Commun. ACM*, 54(1):86–95, 2011.

[11] C. Dwork, F. Mcsherry, K. Nissim, and A. Smith. Calibrating noise to sensitivity in private data analysis. In *TCC*, pages 265–284. Springer, 2006.

[12] C. Fellbaum. *WordNet: An Electronic Lexical Database*. Bradford Books, 1998.

[13] D. Gordon. La jolla covering repository, Nov. 2012. http://www.ccrwest.org/cover.html.

[14] D. M. Gordon, G. Kuperberg, and O. Patashnik. New constructions for covering designs. *J. Combin. Designs*, 3:269–284, 1995.

[15] A. Gupta, M. Hardt, A. Roth, and J. Ullman. Privately releasing conjunctions and the statistical query barrier. In *STOC*, pages 803–812, 2011.

[16] M. Hardt, K. Ligett, and F. McSherry. A simple and practical algorithm for differentially private data release. In *NIPS*, pages 2348–2356, 2012.

[17] M. Hardt and G. N. Rothblum. A multiplicative weights mechanism for privacy-preserving data analysis. In *FOCS*, pages 61–70. IEEE, 2010.

[18] M. Hardt, G. N. Rothblum, and R. A. Servedio. Private data release via learning thresholds. In *SODA*, pages 168–187, 2012.

[19] M. Hay, V. Rastogi, G. Miklau, and D. Suciu. Boosting the accuracy of differentially private histograms through consistency. *PVLDB*, 3:1021–1032, September 2010.

[20] S. P. Kasiviswanathan, M. Rudelson, A. Smith, and J. Ullman. The price of privately releasing contingency tables and the spectra of random matrices with correlated rows. In *STOC*, pages 775–784, 2010.

[21] J. Lei. Differentially private m-estimators. In *NIPS*, pages 361–369, 2011.

[22] C. Li, M. Hay, V. Rastogi, G. Miklau, and A. McGregor. Optimizing linear counting queries under differential privacy. In *PODS*, pages 123–134, New York, NY, USA, 2010. ACM.

[23] C. Li and G. Miklau. An adaptive mechanism for accurate query answering under differential privacy. *PVLDB*, 5(6):514–525, Feb. 2012.

[24] N. Li, W. H. Qardaji, D. Su, and J. Cao. PrivBasis: Frequent itemset mining with differential privacy. *PVLDB*, 5(11):1340–1351, 2012.

[25] J. Lin. Divergence measures based on the shannon entropy. *IEEE Trans. Inf. Theory*, 37(1):145–151, 1991.

[26] F. McSherry and K. Talwar. Mechanism design via differential privacy. In *FOCS*, pages 94–103, 2007.

[27] W. Qardaji and N. Li. Recursive partitioning and summarization: A practical framework for differential private data publishing. In *ASIACCS*, 2012.

[28] J. Thaler, J. Ullman, and S. Vadhan. Faster algorithms for privately releasing marginals. In *ICALP*, pages 810–821, 2012.

[29] J. Ullman and S. Vadhan. PCPs and the hardness of generating private synthetic data. In *TCC*, pages 400–416, 2011.

[30] O. V. Usatenko and V. A. Yampol'skii. Binary n-step markov chains and long-range correlated systems. *Phys. Rev. Lett.*, 90:110601, Mar 2003.

[31] G. Yuan, Z. Zhang, M. Winslett, X. Xiao, Y. Yang, and Z. Hao. Low-rank mechanism: Optimizing batch queries under differential privacy. *PVLDB*, 5(11):1352–1363, July 2012.

Blowfish Privacy: Tuning Privacy-Utility Trade-offs using Policies

Xi He
Duke University
Durham, NC, USA
hexi88@cs.duke.edu

Ashwin Machanavajjhala
Duke University
Durham, NC, USA
ashwin@cs.duke.edu

Bolin Ding
Microsoft Research
Redmond, WA, USA
bolin.ding@microsoft.com

ABSTRACT

Privacy definitions provide ways for trading-off the privacy of individuals in a statistical database for the utility of downstream analysis of the data. In this paper, we present *Blowfish*, a class of privacy definitions inspired by the Pufferfish framework, that provides a rich interface for this trade-off. In particular, we allow data publishers to extend differential privacy using a *policy*, which specifies (a) *secrets*, or information that must be kept secret, and (b) *constraints* that may be known about the data. While the secret specification allows increased utility by lessening protection for certain individual properties, the constraint specification provides added protection against an adversary who knows correlations in the data (arising from constraints). We formalize policies and present novel algorithms that can handle general specifications of sensitive information and certain count constraints. We show that there are reasonable policies under which our privacy mechanisms for k-means clustering, histograms and range queries introduce significantly lesser noise than their differentially private counterparts. We quantify the privacy-utility trade-offs for various policies analytically and empirically on real datasets.

Categories and Subject Descriptors

H.2.8 [**Database Applications**]: Statistical Databases; K.4.1 [**Computers and Society**]: Privacy

Keywords

privacy, differential privacy, Blowfish privacy

1. INTRODUCTION

With the increasing popularity of "big-data" applications which collect, analyze and disseminate individual level information in literally every aspect of our life, ensuring that these applications do not breach the privacy of individuals is an important problem. The last decade has seen the development of a number of privacy definitions and mechanisms that trade-off the privacy of individuals in these databases for the utility (or accuracy) of data analysis (see [4] for a survey). Differential privacy [6] has emerged as a gold standard not only because it is not susceptible to attacks that other definition can't tolerate, but also since it provides a simple knob, namely ϵ, for trading off privacy for utility.

While ϵ is intuitive, it does not sufficiently capture the diversity in the privacy-utility trade-off space. For instance, recent work has shown two seemingly contradictory results. In certain applications (e.g., social recommendations [17]) differential privacy is too strong and does not permit sufficient utility. Next, when data are correlated (e.g., when constraints are known publicly about the data, or in social network data) differentially private mechanisms may not limit the ability of an attacker to learn sensitive information [12]. Subsequently, Kifer and Machanavajjhala [13] proposed a semantic privacy framework, called Pufferfish, which helps clarify assumptions underlying privacy definitions – specifically, the information that is being kept secret, and the adversary's background knowledge. They showed that differential privacy is equivalent to a specific instantiation of the Pufferfish framework, where (a) every property about an individual's record in the data is kept secret, and (b) the adversary assumes that every individual is independent of the rest of the individuals in the data (no correlations). We believe that these shortcomings severely limit the applicability of differential privacy to real world scenarios that either require high utility, or deal with correlated data.

Inspired by Pufferfish, we seek to better explore the trade-off between privacy and utility by providing a richer set of "tuning knobs". We explore a class of definitions called *Blowfish privacy*. In addition to ϵ, which controls the amount of information disclosed, Blowfish definitions take as input a privacy *policy* that specifies two more parameters – which information must be kept secret about individuals, and what constraints may be known publicly about the data. By extending differential privacy using these policies, we can hope to develop mechanisms that permit more utility since not all properties of an individual need to be kept secret. Moreover, we also can limit adversarial attacks that leverage correlations due to publicly known constraints.

We make the following contributions in this paper:

- We introduce and formalize sensitive information specifications, constraints, policies and Blowfish privacy. We consider a number of realistic examples of sensitive information specification, and focus on count constraints.
- We show how to adapt well known differential privacy mechanisms to satisfy Blowfish privacy, and using the example of k-means clustering illustrate the gains in ac-

SIGMOD'14, June 22–27, 2014, Snowbird, UT, USA.
Copyright 2014 ACM 978-1-4503-2376-5/14/06 ...$15.00.
http://dx.doi.org/10.1145/2588555.2588581.

curacy for Blowfish policies having weaker sensitive information specifications.

- We propose the ordered mechanism, a novel strategy for releasing cumulative histograms and answering range queries. We show analytically and using experiments on real data that, for reasonable sensitive information specifications, the ordered hierarchical mechanism is more accurate than the best known differentially private mechanisms for these workloads.
- We study how to calibrate noise for policies expressing count constraints, and its applications in several practical scenarios.

Organization: Section 2 introduces the notation. Section 3 formalizes privacy policies. We define Blowfish privacy, and discuss composition properties and its relationship to prior work in Section 4. We define the policy specific global sensitivity of queries in Section 5. We describe mechanisms for kmeans clustering (Section 6), and releasing cumulative histograms & answering range queries (Section 7) under Blowfish policies without constraints and empirically evaluate the resulting privacy-utility trade-offs on real datasets. We show how to release histograms in the presence of count constraints in Section 8 and then conclude in Section 9.

2. NOTATION

We consider a dataset D consisting of n tuples. Each tuple t is considered to be drawn from a domain $\mathcal{T} = A_1 \times A_2 \times \ldots \times A_m$ constructed from the cross product of m categorical attributes. We assume that each tuple t corresponds to the data collected from a unique individual with identifier $t.\_id$. We will use the notation $x \in \mathcal{T}$ to denote a value in the domain, and $x.A_i$ to denote the ith attribute value in x.

Throughout this paper, we will make an assumption that the set of individuals in the dataset D is known in advance to the adversary and does not change. Hence we will use the indistinguishability notion of differential privacy [7]. We will denote the set of possible databases using $\mathcal{I}_n$, or the set of databases with $|D| = n$.[1]

DEFINITION 2.1 (DIFFERENTIAL PRIVACY [6]). *Two datasets D_1 and D_2 are neighbors, denoted by $(D_1, D_2) \in N$, if they differ in the value of one tuple. A randomized mechanism M satisfies ϵ-differential privacy if for every set of outputs $S \subseteq range(M)$, and every pair of neighboring datasets $(D_1, D_2) \in N$,*

$$Pr[M(D_1) \in S] \leq e^{\epsilon} Pr[M(D_2) \in S] \quad (1)$$

Many techniques that satisfy differential privacy use the following notion of *global sensitivity*:

DEFINITION 2.2 (GLOBAL SENSITIVITY). *The global sensitivity of a function $f : \mathcal{I}_n \to \mathbb{R}^d$, denoted by $S(f)$ is defined as the largest L1 difference $||f(D_1) - f(D_2)||_1$, where D_1 and D_2 are databases that differ in one tuple. More formally,*

$$S(f) = \max_{(D_1, D_2) \in N} ||f(D_1) - f(D_2)||_1 \quad (2)$$

A popular technique that satisfies ϵ-differential privacy is the Laplace mechanism [7] defined as follows:

[1]In Sec. 3 we briefly discuss how to generalize our results to other differential privacy notions by relaxing this assumption.

DEFINITION 2.3. *The Laplace mechanism, M^{Lap}, privately computes a function $f : \mathcal{I}_n \to \mathbb{R}^d$ by computing $f(D) + \eta$. $\eta \in \mathbb{R}^d$ is a vector of independent random variables, where each η_i is drawn from the Laplace distribution with parameter $S(f)/\epsilon$. That is, $P[\eta_i = z] \propto e^{-z \cdot \epsilon / S(f)}$.*

Given some partitioning of the domain $\mathcal{P} = (P_1, \ldots, P_k)$, we denote by $h_{\mathcal{P}} : \mathcal{I} \to Z^k$ the histogram query. $h_{\mathcal{P}}(D)$ outputs for each P_i the number of times values in P_i appears in D. $h_{\mathcal{T}}(\cdot)$ (or $h(\cdot)$ in short) is the *complete* histogram query that reports for each $x \in \mathcal{T}$ the number of times it appears in D. It is easy to see that $S(h_{\mathcal{P}}) = 2$ for all histogram queries, and the Laplace mechanism adds noise proportional to $Lap(2/\epsilon)$ to each component of the histogram. We will use Mean Squared Error as a measure of accuracy/error.

DEFINITION 2.4. *Let M be a randomized algorithm that privately computes a function $f : \mathcal{I}_n \to \mathbb{R}^d$. The expected mean squared error of M is given by:*

$$\mathcal{E}_M(D) = \sum_i \mathbb{E}(f_i(D) - \tilde{f}_i(D))^2 \quad (3)$$

where $f_i(\cdot)$ and $\tilde{f}_i(\cdot)$ denote the ith component of the true and noisy answers, respectively.

Under this definition the accuracy of the Laplace mechanism for histograms is given by $|\mathcal{T}| \cdot \mathbb{E}(Laplace(2/\epsilon))^2 = 8|\mathcal{T}|/\epsilon^2$.

3. POLICY DRIVEN PRIVACY

In this section, we describe an abstraction called a *policy* that helps specify which information has to be kept secret and what background knowledge an attacker may possess about the correlations in the data. We will use this policy specification as input in our privacy definition, called Blowfish, described in Section 4.

3.1 Sensitive Information

As indicated by the name, Blowfish[2] privacy is inspired by the Pufferfish privacy framework [13]. In fact, we will show later (in Section 4.2) that Blowfish privacy is equivalent to specific instantiations of semantic definitions arising from the Pufferfish framework.

Like Pufferfish, Blowfish privacy also uses the notions of secrets and discriminative pairs of secrets. We define a secret to be an arbitrary propositional statement over the values in the dataset. For instance, the secret $s : t.\_id =$ 'Bob' $\wedge$ $t.Disease =$ 'Cancer' is true in a dataset where Bob has Cancer. We denote by $\mathcal{S}$ a set of secrets that the data publisher would like to protect. As we will see in this section each individual may have multiple secrets. Secrets may also pertain to sets of individuals. For instance, the following secret $s : t_1.\_id =$ 'Alice' $\wedge$ $t_2.\_id =$ 'Bob' $\wedge$ $t_1.Disease = t_2.Disease$ is true when Alice and Bob have the same disease. However, in this paper, we focus on the case where each secret is about a single individual.

We call a pair of secrets $(s, s') \in \mathcal{S} \times \mathcal{S}$ *discriminative* if they are mutually exclusive. Each discriminative pair describes properties that an adversary must not be able to distinguish between. One input to a policy is a set of discriminative pairs of secrets $\mathcal{S}_{\text{pairs}}$.

We now present a few examples of sensitive information specified as a set of discriminative secrets.

[2]Pufferfish and Blowfish are common names of the same family of marine fish, Tetraodontidae.

- *Full Domain*: Let s^i_x be the secret $(t\_id = i \wedge t = x)$, for some $x \in \mathcal{T}$. We define $\mathcal{S}^{\text{full}}_{\text{pairs}}$ as:

$$\mathcal{S}^{\text{full}}_{\text{pairs}} = \{(s^i_x, s^i_y) | \forall i, \forall (x, y) \in \mathcal{T} \times \mathcal{T}\} \quad (4)$$

  This means that for every individual, an adversary should not be able to distinguish whether that individual's value is x or y, for all $x, y \in \mathcal{T}$.

- *Attributes*: Let $\mathbf{x} \in \mathcal{T}$ denote a multidimensional value. Let $\mathbf{x}[A]$ denote value of attribute A, and $\mathbf{x}[\bar{A}]$ the value for the other attributes. Then a second example of sensitive information is:

$$\mathcal{S}^{\text{attr}}_{\text{pairs}} = \{(s^i_{\mathbf{x}}, s^i_{\mathbf{y}}) | \forall i, \exists A, \mathbf{x}[A] \neq \mathbf{y}[A] \wedge \mathbf{x}[\bar{A}] = \mathbf{y}[\bar{A}]\} \quad (5)$$

  $\mathcal{S}^{attr}_{\text{pairs}}$ ensures that an adversary should not be able to sufficiently distinguish between any two values for each attribute of every individual's value.

- *Partitioned*: Let $\mathcal{P} = \{P_1, \ldots, P_p\}$ be a partition that divides the domain into p disjoint sets ($\cup_i P_i = \mathcal{T}$ and $\forall 1 \leq i, j \leq p, P_i \cap P_j = \emptyset$). We define partitioned sensitive information as:

$$\mathcal{S}^{\mathcal{P}}_{\text{pairs}} = \{(s^i_x, s^i_y) | \forall i, \exists j, (x, y) \in P_j \times P_j\} \quad (6)$$

  In this case, an adversary is allowed to deduce whether an individual is in one of two different partitions, but can't distinguish between two values within a single partition. This is a natural specification for location data – an individual may be OK with releasing his/her location at a coarse granularity (e.g., a coarse grid), but location within each grid cell must be hidden from the adversary.

- *Distance Threshold*: In many situations there is an inherent distance metric d associated with the points in the domain (e.g., L_1 distance on age or salary, or Manhattan distance on locations). Rather than requiring that an adversary should not be able to distinguish between any pairs of points x and y, one could require that each pair of points that are close are not distinguishable. So, for this purpose, the set of discriminative secrets is:

$$\mathcal{S}^{d,\theta}_{\text{pairs}} = \{(s^i_x, s^i_y) | \forall i, d(x, y) \leq \theta\} \quad (7)$$

  Under this policy, the adversary will not be able to distinguish any pair of values with certainty. However, the adversary may distinguish points that are farther apart better that points that are close.

All of the above specifications of sensitive information can be generalized using the *discriminative secret graph*, defined below. Consider a graph $G = (V, E)$, where $V = \mathcal{T}$ and the set of edges $E \subseteq \mathcal{T} \times \mathcal{T}$. The set of edges can be interpreted as values in the domain that an adversary must not distinguish between; i.e., the set of discriminative secrets is $\mathcal{S}^G_{\text{pairs}} = \{(s^i_x, s^i_y) \mid \forall i, \forall (x, y) \in E\}$. The above examples correspond to the following graphs: G^{full} corresponds to a complete graph on all the elements in $\mathcal{T}$. G^{attr} corresponds to a graph where two values are connected by an edge when only one attribute value changes. $G^{\mathcal{P}}$ has $|\mathcal{P}|$ connected components, where each component is a complete graph on vertices in P_i. Finally, in $G^{d,\theta}$, $(x, y) \in E$ iff $d(x, y) \leq \theta$.

We would like to note that a policy could have secrets and discriminative pairs about sets of individuals. However, throughout this paper, we only consider secrets pertaining to a single individual, and thus discriminative pairs refer to two secrets about the same individual. Additionally, the set of discriminative pairs is the same for all individuals. One can envision different individuals having different sets of discriminative pairs. For instance, we can model an individual who is privacy agnostic and does not mind disclosing his/her value exactly by having no discriminative pair involving that individual. Finally note that in all of the discussion in this section, the specification of what is sensitive information *does not depend on the original database* D. One could specify sensitive information that depends on D, but one must be wary that this might leak additional information to an adversary. In this paper, we focus on data-independent discriminative pairs, uniform secrets and secrets that only pertain to single individuals.

Throughout this paper, we will assume that the adversary knows the total number of tuples in the database (i.e., the set of possible instances is $\mathcal{I}_n$). Hence, we can limit ourselves to considering changes in tuples (and not additions or deletions). We can in principle relax this assumption about cardinality, by adding an additional set of secrets of the form $s^i_\perp$ which mean *"individual i is not in dataset"*. All of our definitions and algorithms can be modified to handle this case by adding $\perp$ to the domain and to the discriminative secret graph G. We defer these extensions to future work.

3.2 Auxiliary Knowledge

Recent work [12] showed that differentially private mechanisms could still lead to an inordinate disclosure of sensitive information when adversaries have access to publicly known constraints about the data that induce correlations across tuples. This can be illustrated by the following example. Consider a table D with one attribute R that takes values $r_1, \ldots, r_k$. Suppose, based on publicly released datasets the following $k-1$ constraints are already known: $c(r_1)+c(r_2) = a_1$, $c(r_2) + c(r_3) = a_2$, and so on, where $c(r_i)$ is the number of records with value r_i. This does not provide enough information to always reconstruct the counts in D (k unknowns but $k-1$ linear equations). However, if we knew the answer to some $c(r_i)$, then all counts can be reconstructed – in this way tuples are correlated.

Differential privacy allows answering all the count queries $c(r_i)$ by adding independent noise with variance $2/\epsilon^2$ to each count. While these noisy counts $\tilde{c}(r_i)$ themselves do not disclose information about any individual, they can be combined with the constraints to get very precise estimates of $c(r_i)$. That is, we can construct k independent estimators for each count as follow. For r_1, $\tilde{c}(r_1), a_1 - \tilde{c}(r_2), a_1 - a_2 + \tilde{c}(r_3), \ldots$ each equal $c(r_1)$ in expectation and have a variance of $2/\epsilon^2$. By averaging these estimators, we can predict the value of $c(r_i)$ with a variance of $2/(k\epsilon^2)$. For large k (e.g., when there are 2^d values in R), the variance is small so that the table D is reconstructed with very high probability, thus causing a complete breach of privacy.

Therefore, our policy specification also takes into account auxiliary knowledge that an adversary might know about the individuals in the private database. In Blowfish, we consider knowledge in the form of a set of deterministic constraints Q that are publicly known about the dataset. We believe these are easier to specify than probabilistic correlation functions for data publishers. The effect of the constraints in Q is to make only a subset of the possible database instances $\mathcal{I}_Q \subset \mathcal{I}_n$ possible; or equivalently, all instances in $\mathcal{I}_n \setminus \mathcal{I}_Q$ are impossible. For any database $D \in \mathcal{I}_n$, we denote by

$D \vdash Q$ if D satisfies the constraints in Q; i.e., $D \in \mathcal{I}_Q$. Examples of deterministic constraints include:

- *Count Query Constraints:* A count query on a database returns the number of tuples that satisfy a certain predicate. A count query constraints is a set of (count query, answer) pairs over the database that are publicly known.
- *Marginal Constraints:* A marginal is a projection of the database on a subset of attributes, and each row counts the number of tuples that agree on the subset of attributes. The auxiliary knowledge of marginals means these database marginals are known to the adversary.

3.3 Policy

DEFINITION 3.1 (POLICY). *A policy is a triple $P = (\mathcal{T}, G, \mathcal{I}_Q)$, where $G = (V, E)$ is a discriminative secret graph with $V \subseteq \mathcal{T}$. In P, the set of discriminative pairs $\mathcal{S}^G_{\text{pairs}}$ is defined as the set $\{(s^i_x, s^i_y) \mid \forall i \in \_id, \forall (x,y) \in E\}$, where s^i_x denotes the statement: $t.\_id = i \wedge t = x$. $\mathcal{I}_Q$ denotes the set of databases that are possible under the constraints Q that are known about the database.*

Note that the description of the policy can be exponential in the size of the input dataset. We will use shorthand to describe certain types of sensitive information (e.g., full domain, partition, etc), and specify the set of possible databases $\mathcal{I}_Q$ using the description of Q.

4. BLOWFISH PRIVACY

In this section, we present our new privacy definition, called Blowfish Privacy. Like differential privacy, Blowfish uses the notion of neighboring datasets. The key difference is that the set of neighbors in Blowfish depend on the policy P – both on the set of discriminative pairs as well as on the constraints known about the database.

DEFINITION 4.1 (NEIGHBORS). *Let $P = (\mathcal{T}, G, \mathcal{I}_Q)$ be a policy. For any pair of datasets D_1, D_2, let $T(D_1, D_2) \subseteq \mathcal{S}^G_{\text{pairs}}$ be the set of discriminative pairs (s^i_x, s^i_y) such that the ith tuples in D_1 and D_2 are x and y, resp. Let $\Delta(D_1, D_2) = D_1 \setminus D_2 \cup D_2 \setminus D_1$. D_1 and D_2 are neighbors with respect to a policy P, denoted by $(D_1, D_2) \in N(P)$, if:*

1. *$D_1, D_2 \in \mathcal{I}_Q$. (i.e., both the datasets satisfy Q).*
2. *$T \neq \emptyset$. (i.e., $\exists (s^i_x, s^i_y) \in \mathcal{S}^G_{\text{pairs}}$ such that the ith tuples in D_1 and D_2 are x and y, resp).*
3. *There is no database $D_3 \vdash Q$ such that $T(D_1, D_3) \subset T(D_1, D_2)$, or $(T(D_1, D_3) = T(D_1, D_2)$ & $\Delta(D_3, D_1) \subset \Delta(D_2, D_1))$.*

When $P = (\mathcal{T}, G, \mathcal{I}_n)$ (i.e., no constraints), D_1 and D_2 are neighbors if some individual tuples value is changed from x to y, where (x, y) is an edge in G. Note that $T(D_1, D_2)$ is non-empty and has the smallest size (of 1). Neighboring datasets in differential privacy correspond to neighbors when G is a complete graph.

For policies having constraints, conditions 1 and 2 ensure that neighbors satisfy the constraints (i.e., are in $\mathcal{I}_Q$), and that they differ in at least one discriminative pair of secrets. Condition 3 ensures that D_1 and D_2 are minimally different in terms of discriminative pairs and tuple changes.

DEFINITION 4.2 (BLOWFISH PRIVACY). *Let $\epsilon > 0$ be a real number and $P = (\mathcal{T}, G, \mathcal{I}_Q)$ be a policy. A randomized mechanism M satisfies (ϵ, P)-Blowfish privacy if for every pair of neighboring databases $(D_1, D_2) \in N(P)$, and every set of outputs $S \subseteq range(M)$, we have*

$$Pr[M(D_1) \in S] \leq e^{\epsilon} Pr[M(D_2) \in S] \tag{8}$$

Note that Blowfish privacy takes in the policy P in addition to ϵ as an input, and is different from differential privacy in only the set of neighboring databases $N(P)$. For $P = (\mathcal{T}, G, \mathcal{I}_n)$ (i.e., no constraints), it is easy to check that for any two databases that arbitrarily differ in one tuple ($D_1 = D \cup \{x\}, D_2 = D \cup \{y\}$), and any set of outputs S,

$$Pr[M(D_1) \in S] \leq e^{\epsilon \cdot d_G(x,y)} Pr[M(D_2) \in S] \tag{9}$$

where $d_G(x, y)$ is the shortest distance between x, y in G. This implies that an attacker may better distinguish pairs of points farther apart in the graph (e.g., values with many differing attributes in $\mathcal{S}^{\text{attr}}_{\text{pairs}}$), than those that are closer. Similarly, an attack can distinguish between x, y with probability 1, when x and y appear in different partitions under partitioned sensitive information $\mathcal{S}^{\mathcal{P}}_{\text{pairs}}$ ($d_G(x, y) = \infty$).

4.1 Composition

Composition [8] is an important property that any privacy notion should satisfy in order to be able to reason about independent data releases. We will study two kinds of composition for Blowfish privacy – sequential and parallel composition. Sequential composition ensures that a sequence of computations that each ensure privacy in isolation also ensures privacy. This allows breaking down computations into smaller building blocks. Parallel composition is crucial to ensure that too much error is not introduced on computations occurring on *disjoint* subsets of data. We can show that Blowfish satisfies sequential composition.

THEOREM 4.1 (SEQUENTIAL COMPOSITION). *Let $P = (\mathcal{T}, G, \mathcal{I}_Q)$ be a policy and $D \in \mathcal{I}_Q$ be an input database. Let $M_1(\cdot)$ and $M_2(\cdot, \cdot)$ be algorithms with independent sources of randomness that satisfy (ϵ_1, P) and (ϵ_2, P)-Blowfish privacy, resp. Then an algorithm that outputs both $M_1(D) = \omega_1$ and $M_2(\omega_1, D) = \omega_2$ satisfies $(\epsilon_1 + \epsilon_2, P)$-Blowfish privacy.*

We can also show that Blowfish satisfies a weak form of parallel composition in the presence of constraints. We refer the interested reader to the full version of the paper [10].

4.2 Relation to other definitions

In this section, we relate Blowfish privacy to existing notions of privacy. We discuss variants of differential privacy [6] (including restricted sensitivity [1]), the Pufferfish framework [13], privacy axioms [11], and a recent independent work on extending differential privacy with metrics [3].

Differential Privacy [6]: One can easily verify that a mechanism satisfies ϵ-differential privacy (Definition 2.1) if and only if it satisfies (ϵ, P)-Blowfish privacy, where $P = (\mathcal{T}, K, \mathcal{I}_n)$, and K is the complete graph on the domain. Thus, Blowfish privacy is a generalization of differential privacy that allows a data curator to trade-off privacy vs utility by controlling sensitive information G (instead of K) and auxiliary knowledge $\mathcal{I}_Q$ (instead of $\mathcal{I}_n$) in the policy.

Pufferfish Framework [13, 14]: Blowfish borrows the sensitive information specification from Pufferfish. Pufferfish defines adversarial knowledge using a set of data generating distributions, while Blowfish instantiates the same using publicly known constraints. We can show formal relationships between Blowfish and Pufferfish instantiations.

THEOREM 4.2. *Let $\mathcal{S}_{\text{pairs}}$ be the set of discriminative pairs corresponding to policy $P = (\mathcal{T}, G, \mathcal{I}_n)$. Let $\mathcal{D}$ denote the set of all product distributions $\{p_i(\cdot)\}_i$ over n tuples. $p_i(\cdot)$ denotes a probability distribution for tuple i over $\mathcal{T}$. Then a mechanism satisfies $(\epsilon, \mathcal{S}_{\text{pairs}}, \mathcal{D})$-Pufferfish privacy if and only if it satisfies (ϵ, P)-Blowfish privacy.*

THEOREM 4.3. *Consider a policy $P = (\mathcal{T}, G, \mathcal{I}_Q)$ corresponding to a set of constraints Q. Let $\mathcal{S}_{\text{pairs}}$ be defined as in Theorem 4.2. Let $\mathcal{D}_Q$ be the set of product distributions conditioned on the constraints in Q; i.e.,*

$$P[D = x_1, \ldots, x_k] \propto \begin{cases} \prod_i p_i(x_i) & \text{if } D \in \mathcal{I}_Q \\ 0 & \text{otherwise} \end{cases}$$

A mechanism M that satisfies $(\epsilon, \mathcal{S}_{\text{pairs}}, \mathcal{D}_Q)$-Pufferfish privacy also satisfies (ϵ, P)-Blowfish privacy.

Theorem 4.2 states that Blowfish policies without constraints are equivalent to Pufferfish instantiated using adversaries who believe tuples in D are independent (proof follows from Theorem 6.1 [14]). Theorem 4.3 states that when constraints are known, Blowfish is a necessary condition for any mechanism that satisfies a similar Pufferfish instantiation with constraints (we conjecture the sufficiency of Blowfish as well). Thus Blowfish privacy policies correspond to a subclass of privacy definitions that can be instantiated using Pufferfish.

Both Pufferfish and Blowfish aid the data publisher to customize privacy definitions by carefully defining sensitive information and adversarial knowledge. However, Blowfish improves over Pufferfish in three key aspects. First, there are no general algorithms known for Pufferfish instantiations. In this paper, we present of algorithms for various Blowfish policies. Thus, we can't compare Blowfish and Pufferfish experimentally. Second, all Blowfish privacy policies result in composable privacy definitions. This is not true for the Pufferfish framework. Finally, we believe Blowfish privacy is easier to understand and use than the Pufferfish framework for data publishers who are not privacy experts.[3] For instance, one needs to specify adversarial knowledge as sets of complex probability distributions in Pufferfish, while in Blowfish policies one only needs to specify conceptually simpler publicly known constraints.

Other Privacy Definitions: Kifer and Lin [11] stipulate that every "good" privacy definition should satisfy two axioms – transformation invariance, and convexity. We can show that Blowfish privacy satisfy both these axioms.

Recent papers have extended differential privacy to handle constraints. Induced neighbor privacy [12, 13] extends the notion of neighbors such that neighboring databases satisfy the constraints and are minimally far apart (in terms of tuple changes). Blowfish extends this notion of induced neighbors to take into account discriminative pairs of secrets and measures distance in terms of the set of different discriminative pairs. Restricted sensitivity [1] extends the notion of sensitivity to account for constraints. In particular, the restricted sensitivity of a function f given a set of constraints Q, or $RS_f(Q)$, is the maximum $|f(D_1) - f(D_2)|/d(D_1, D_2)$, over all $D_1, D_2 \in \mathcal{I}_Q$. However, tuning noise to $RS_f(Q)$ may not limit the ability of an attacker to learn sensitive information. For instance, if $\mathcal{I}_Q = \{0^n, 1^n\}$, then the restricted sensitivity of releasing the number of 1s is 1. Adding constant noise does not disallow the adversary from knowing whether the database was 0^n or 1^n.

A very recent independent work suggests extending differential privacy using a metric over all possible databases [3]. In particular, given a distance metric d over instances, they require an algorithm to ensure that $P[M(X) \subseteq S] \leq e^{\epsilon \cdot d(X,Y)} P[M(Y) \subseteq S]$, for all sets of outputs S and all instances X and Y. Thus differential privacy corresponds to a specific distance measure – Hamming distance. The sensitive information specification in Blowfish can also be thought of in terms of a distance metric over tuples. In addition we present novel algorithms (ordered mechanism) and allow incorporating knowledge of constraints. We defer a more detailed comparison to future work.

[3]We have some initial anecdotal evidence of this fact working with statisticians from the US Census.

5. BLOWFISH WITHOUT CONSTRAINTS

Given any query f that outputs a vector of reals, we can define a *policy specific sensitivity* of f. Thus, the Laplace mechanism with noise calibrated to the policy specific sensitivity ensures Blowfish privacy.

DEFINITION 5.1. (POLICY SPECIFIC GLOBAL SENSITIVITY). *Given a policy $(\mathcal{T}, G, \mathcal{I}_Q)$, $S(f, P)$ denotes the policy specific global sensitivity of a function f and is defined as* $\max_{(D_1,D_2)\in N(P)} ||f(D_1) - f(D_2)||_1$.

THEOREM 5.1. *Let $P = (\mathcal{T}, G, \mathcal{I}_Q)$ be a policy. Given a function $f : \mathcal{I}_Q \to \mathbb{R}^d$, outputting $f(D) + \eta$ ensures (ϵ, P)-Blowfish privacy if $\eta \in \mathbb{R}^d$ is a vector of independent random numbers drawn from $Lap(S(f, p)/\epsilon)$.*

When policies do not have constraints ($P = (\mathcal{T}, G, \mathcal{I}_n)$), (ϵ, P)-Blowfish differs from ϵ-differential privacy only in the specification of sensitive information. Note that every pair $(D_1, D_2) \in N(P)$ differ in only one tuple when P has no constraints. Therefore, the following result trivially holds.

LEMMA 5.2. *Any mechanism M that satisfies ϵ-differential privacy also satisfies $(\epsilon, (\mathcal{T}, G, \mathcal{I}_n))$-Blowfish privacy for all discriminative secret graphs G.*

The proof follows from the fact that ϵ-differential privacy is equivalent to $(\epsilon, (\mathcal{T}, K, \mathcal{I}_n))$-Blowfish privacy, where K is the complete graph.

In many cases, we can do better in terms of utility than differentially privacy mechanisms. It is easy to see that $S(f, P)$ is never larger than the global sensitivity $S(f)$. Therefore, just using the Laplace mechanism with $S(f, P)$ can provide better utility. For instance, consider a linear sum query $f_{\mathbf{w}} = \sum_{i=1}^n w_i x_i$, where $\mathbf{w} \in \mathbb{R}^n$ is a weight vector, and each value $x_i \in \mathcal{T} = [a, b]$. For G^{full}, the policy specific sensitivity is $(b - a) \cdot (\max_i w_i)$ the same as the global sensitivity. For $G^{d,\theta}$, where $d(x, y) = |x - y|$, the policy specific sensitivity is $\theta \cdot (\max_i w_i)$, which can be much smaller than the global sensitivity when $\theta \ll (b - a)$.

As a second example, suppose $\mathcal{P}$ is a partitioning of the domain. If the policy specifies sensitive information partitioned by $\mathcal{P}$ ($G^{\mathcal{P}}$), then the policy specific sensitivity of $h_{\mathcal{P}}$ is 0. That is, the histogram of $\mathcal{P}$ or any coarser partitioning can be released without any noise. We will show more examples of improved utility under Blowfish policies in Sec 5.

However, for histogram queries, the policy specific sensitivity for most reasonable policies (with no constraints) is 2, the same as global sensitivity.[4] Thus, it cannot significantly improve the accuracy for histogram queries.

Next, we present examples of two analysis tasks – k-means clustering (Section 6), and releasing cumulative histograms (Section 7)– for which we can design mechanisms for Blowfish policies without constraints with more utility (lesser error) than mechanisms that satisfy differential privacy. In k-means clustering we will see that using Blowfish policies helps reduce the sensitivity of intermediate queries on the data. In the case of the cumulative histogram workload, we can identify novel query answering strategies given a Blowfish policy that helps reduce the error.

6. K-MEANS CLUSTERING

K-means clustering is widely used in many applications such as classification and feature learning. It aims to cluster proximate data together and is formally defined below.

DEFINITION 6.1 (K-MEANS CLUSTERING). *Given a data set of n points $(t_1, ..., t_n) \in \mathcal{T}^n$, k-means clustering aims to partition the points into $k \leq n$ clusters $S = \{S_1, ..., S_k\}$ in order to minimize*

$$\sum_{i=1}^{k} \sum_{t_j \in S_i} ||t_j - \mu_i||^2, \tag{10}$$

where $\mu_i = \frac{1}{|S_i|} \sum_{t_j \in S_i} t_j$, and $||x - y||$ denotes L_2 distance.

The non-private version of k-means clustering initializes the means/centroids $(\mu_1, ..., \mu_k)$ (e.g. randomly) and updates them iteratively as follows: 1) assign each point to the nearest centroid; 2) recompute the centroid of each cluster, until reaching some convergence criterion or a fixed number of iterations.

The first differentially private k-means clustering algorithm was proposed by Blum et al. [2] as SuLQ k-means. Observe that only two queries are required explicitly: 1) the number of points in each new cluster, $q_{size} = (|S_1|, ..., |S_k|)$ and 2) the sum of the data points for each cluster, $q_{sum} = (\sum_{t_j \in S_1} t_j, ..., \sum_{t_j \in S_k} t_j)$, to compute the centroid. The sensitivity of q_{size} is 2 (same as a histogram query). Let $d(\mathcal{T})$ denote the diameter of the domain, or the largest L_1 distance ($||x - y||_1$) between any two points $x, y \in \mathcal{T}$. The sensitivity of q_{sum} could be as large as the diameter $2 \cdot d(\mathcal{T})$ since a tuple from x to y can only change the sums for two clusters by at most $d(\mathcal{T})$.

Under Blowfish privacy policies, the policy specific sensitivity of q_{sum} can be much smaller than $|\mathcal{T}|$ under Differential privacy (i.e. complete graph G^{full} for Blowfish policies). Since q_{size} is the histogram query, the sensitivity of q_{size} under Blowfish is also 2.

LEMMA 6.1. *Policy specific global sensitivities of q_{size} under the attribute G^{attr}, L_1-distance $G^{(L_1,\theta)}$, and partition $G^{\mathcal{P}}$ discriminative graphs (from Section 3) are smaller than the global sensitivity of q_{size} under differential privacy.*

PROOF. First, in the attribute discriminative graph G^{attr}, edges correspond to $(x, y) \in \mathcal{T} \times \mathcal{T}$ that differ only in any one attribute. Thus, if $|A|$ denotes maximum distance between two elements in A, then the policy specific sensitivity of q_{sum} under G^{attr} is $\max_A(2 \cdot |A|) < 2 \cdot d(\mathcal{T})$. Next, suppose we use $G^{L_1,\theta}$, where $x, y \in \mathcal{T}$ are connected by an edge if $||x - y||_1 \leq \theta$. Thus, policy specific sensitivity of q_{sum} is θ.

Finally, consider the policy specified using the partitioned sensitive graph $G^{\mathcal{P}}$, where $\mathcal{P} = \{P_1, P_2, \ldots, P_k\}$ is some data independent partitioning of the domain $\mathcal{T}$. Here, an adversary should not distinguish between an individual's tuple taking a pair of values $x, y \in \mathcal{T}$ only if x and y appear in the same partition P_i for some i. Under this policy the sensitivity of q_{sum} is at most $max_{P \in \mathcal{P}} 2 \cdot d(P) < 2 \cdot d(\mathcal{T})$. □

Thus, by Theorem 5.1, we can use the SULQ k-means mechanism with the appropriate policy specific sensitivity for q_{sum} (from Lemma 6.1) and thus satisfy privacy under the Blowfish policy while ensuring better accuracy.

6.1 Empirical Evaluation

We empirically evaluate the accuracy of k-means clustering for $(\epsilon, (\mathcal{T}, G, \mathcal{I}_n))$-Blowfish privacy on three data sets. The first two datasets are real-world datasets – TWITTER and SKIN SEGMENTATION[5]. The TWITTER data set consists of a total of 193563 tweets collected using Twitter API that all contained a latitude/longitude within a bounding box of $50N, 125W$ and $30N, 110W$ (western USA) – about 2222×1442 square km. By setting the precision of latitude/longitude coordinates to be 0.05, we obtain a 2D domain of size 400×300. The SKIN SEGMENTATION data set consists of 245057 instances. Three ordinal attributes are considered and they are B, G, R values from face images of different classes. Each of them has a range from 0 to 255. To understand the effect of Blowfish policies on datasets of different sizes, we consider the full dataset SKIN, as well as a 10% and 1% sub-sample (SKIN10, SKIN01) of the data.

The third dataset is a synthetic dataset where we generate 1000 points from $(0, 1)^4$ with k randomly chosen centers and a Gaussian noise with $\sigma(0, 0.2)$ in each direction.

In Figures 1(a)-1(d), we report the ratio of the mean of the objective value in Eqn. (10) between private clustering methods including Laplace mechanism and Blowfish privacy with $\mathcal{S}^{d,\theta}_{\text{pairs}}$, and the non-private k-means algorithm, for various values of $\epsilon = \{0.1, 0.2, ..., 0.9, 1.0\}$. For all datasets, $d(\cdot)$ is L_1 (or Manhattan) distance. The number of iterations is fixed to be 10 and the number of clusters is $k = 4$. Each experiment is repeated 5 times to find mean and variance. Figure 1(a) clusters according to latitude/longitude of each tweet. We consider five different policies: G^{full} (Laplace mechanism), $G^{d,2000km}$, $G^{d,1000km}$, $G^{d,500km}$, $G^{d,100km}$. Here, $\theta = 100$km means that the adversary cannot distinguish locations within a 20000 square km region. Figure 1(b) clusters the 1% subsample SKIN01 based on three attributes: B, G, R values and considers 5 policies as well: G^{full}, $G^{d,512}$, $G^{d,256}$, $G^{d,128}$, $G^{d,64}$ and $G^{d,32}$. Lastly, we also consider five policies for the synthetic dataset in Figure 1(c): G^{full}, $G^{d,1.0}$, $G^{d,0.5}$, $G^{d,0.25}$, $G^{d,0.1}$.

From Figures 1(a)-1(c), we observe that the objective value of Laplace mechanism could deviate up to 40 times away from non-private method, but under Blowfish policies objective values are no more than 5 times that for non-private k-means. Moreover, the error introduced by Laplace mechanism becomes larger with higher dimensionality – the ratio

[4]The one exception is partitioned sensitive information.

[5]`http://archive.ics.uci.edu/ml/datasets/Skin+Segmentation`

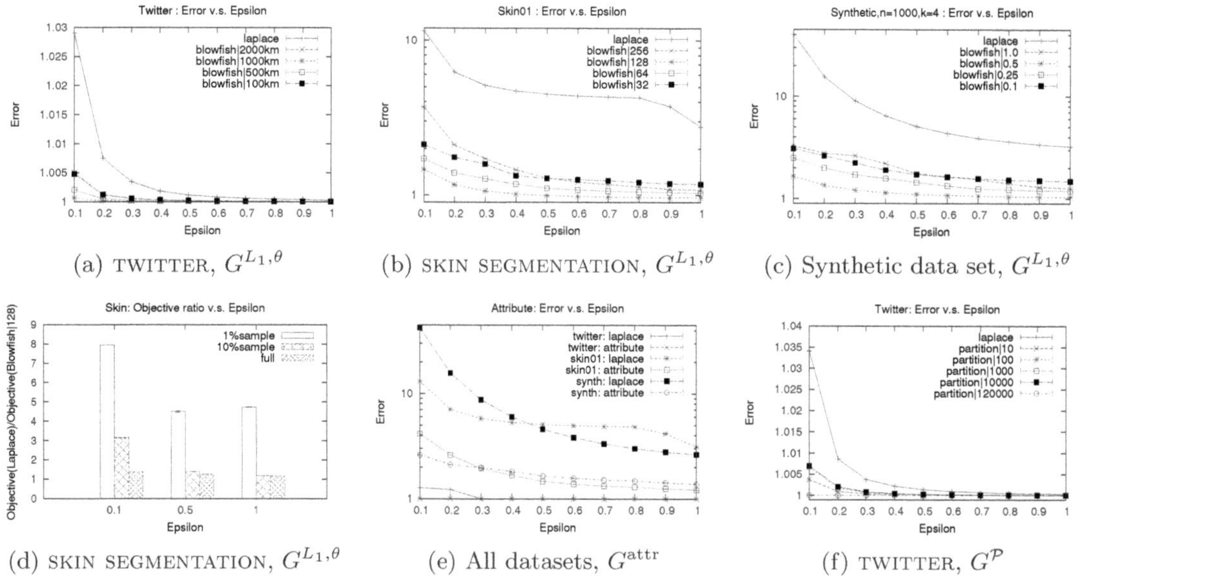

(a) TWITTER, $G^{L_1,\theta}$ (b) SKIN SEGMENTATION, $G^{L_1,\theta}$ (c) Synthetic data set, $G^{L_1,\theta}$

(d) SKIN SEGMENTATION, $G^{L_1,\theta}$ (e) All datasets, G^{attr} (f) TWITTER, $G^{\mathcal{P}}$

Figure 1: K-Means: Error under Laplace mechanism v.s Blowfish privacy for different discriminative graphs.

for Laplace mechanism in Figure Figure 1(c) and 1(b) (4 and 3 dimensional resp.) is much higher than that in the 2D TWITTER dataset in Figure 1(a). From Figure 1(b), we observe that the error introduced by private mechanisms do not necessarily reduce monotonically as we reduce Blowfish privacy protection (i.e. reduce θ). The same pattern is observed in Figure 1(a) and Figure 1(c). One possible explanation is that adding a sufficient amount of noise could be helpful to get out of local minima for clustering, but adding too much noise could lead to less accurate results.

To study the interplay between dataset size and Blowfish, we plot (Figure 1(d)) for SKIN, SKIN10 and SKIN01 the ratio of the objective value attained by the Laplace method to the objective value attained by one of the Blowfish policies: $G^{d,128}$. In all cases, we see an improvement in the objective under Blowfish. The improvement in the objective is smaller for larger ϵ and larger datasets (since the Laplace mechanism solution is close to the non-private solutions on SKIN).

Finally, Figures 1(e) and 1(f) summarize our results on the G^{attr} and $G^{\mathcal{P}}$ discriminative graphs. Figure 1(e) shows that under the G^{attr} Blowfish policy, the error decreases by an order of magnitude compared to the Laplace mechanism for SKIN01 and the synthetic dataset due to higher dimensionality and small dataset size. On the other hand, there is little gain by using G^{attr} for the larger 2D TWITTER dataset.

Figure 1(f) shows ratio of the objective attained by the private methods to that of the non-private k-means under $G^{\mathcal{P}}$, for partitions $\mathcal{P}$ of different sizes. In each case, the 300x400 grid is uniformly divided; e.g., in `partition|100`, we consider a uniform partitioning in 100 coarse cells, where each new cell contains 30x40 cells from the original grid. Thus an adversary will not be able to tell whether an individual's location was within an area spanned by the 30x40 cells (about 36,300 sq km). `partition|120000` corresponds to the original grid; thus we only protects pairs of locations within each cell in the original grid (about 30 sq km). We see that the objective value for Blowfish policies are smaller than the objective values under Laplace mechanisms, suggesting more accurate clustering. We also note that under `partition|120000`, we can do the clustering exactly, since the sensitivity of both q_{size} and q_{sum} are 0.

To summarize, Blowfish policies allow us to effectively improve utility by trading off privacy. In certain cases, we observe that Blowfish policies attain an objective value that is close to 10 times smaller than that for the Laplace mechanism. The gap between Laplace and Blowfish policies increases with dimensionality, and reduces with data size.

7. CUMULATIVE HISTOGRAMS

In this section, we develop novel query answering strategies for two workloads – cumulative histograms and range queries. Throughout this section, we will use Mean Squared Error as a measure of accuracy/error defined in Def 2.4.

DEFINITION 7.1 (CUMULATIVE HISTOGRAM). *Consider a domain $\mathcal{T} = \{x_1, ..., x_{|\mathcal{T}|}\}$ that has a total ordering $x_1 \leq ... \leq x_{|\mathcal{T}|}$. Let $c(x_i)$ denote the number of times x_i appears in the database D. Then, the cumulative histogram of $\mathcal{T}$, denoted by $S_{\mathcal{T}}(\cdot)$ is a sequence of cumulative counts*

$$\left\{ s_i \mid s_i = \sum_{j=1}^{i} c(x_j), \forall i = 1, ..., |\mathcal{T}| \right\} \tag{11}$$

Since we know the total size of the dataset $|D| = n$, dividing each cumulative count in $S_{\mathcal{T}}(\cdot)$ by n gives us the cumulative distribution function (CDF) over $\mathcal{T}$. Releasing the CDF has many applications including computing quantiles and histograms, answering range queries and constructing indexes (e.g. k-d tree). This motivates us to design a mechanism for releasing cumulative histograms.

The cumulative histogram has a global sensitivity of $|\mathcal{T}| - 1$ because all the counts in cumulative histogram except $s_{|\mathcal{T}|}$ will be reduced by 1 when a record in D changes from x_1 to $x_{|\mathcal{T}|}$. Similar to k-means clustering, we could reduce the sensitivity of cumulative histogram $S_{\mathcal{T}}(\cdot)$ by specifying the sensitive information, such as $\mathcal{S}^{\mathcal{P}}_{\text{pairs}}$ and $\mathcal{S}^{d,\theta}_{\text{pairs}}$. For this section, we focus on $\mathcal{S}^{d,\theta}_{\text{pairs}}$, where $d(\cdot)$ is the $L1$ distance on the domain and we assume that all the domains discussed here have a total ordering.

7.1 Ordered Mechanism

Let us first consider a policy $P_\theta = (\mathcal{T}, G^{d,\theta}, \mathcal{I}_n)$ with $\theta = 1$. The discriminative secret graph is a line graph, $G^{d,1} = (V, E)$, where $V = \mathcal{T}$ and $E = \{(x_i, x_{i+1}) | \forall i = 1, ..., |\mathcal{T}| - 1\}$. This means that only adjacent domain values $(x_i, x_{i+1}) \in \mathcal{T} \times \mathcal{T}$ can form a secret pair. Therefore, the policy specific sensitivity of $S_\mathcal{T}(\cdot)$ for a line graph is 1. Based on this small sensitivity, we propose a mechanism, named Ordered Mechanism $M^O_{G^{d,1}}$ to perturb cumulative histogram $S_\mathcal{T}(\cdot)$ over line graph $G^{d,1}$ in the following way. For each s_i, we add $\eta_i \sim Laplace(\frac{1}{\epsilon})$ to get $\tilde{s}_i$ to ensure (ϵ, P)-Blowfish privacy. Each $\tilde{s}_i$ has an error with an expectation equals to $\frac{2}{\epsilon^2}$. Note that Theorem 5.1 already ensures that releasing $\tilde{s}_i$'s satisfies (ϵ, P_1)-Blowfish privacy. Furthermore, observe that the counts in $S_\mathcal{T}(\cdot)$ are in ascending order. Hence, we can boost the accuracy of $\tilde{S}_\mathcal{T}(\cdot)$ using constrained inference proposed by Hay et al. in [9]. In this way, the new cumulative histogram, denoted by $\hat{S}_\mathcal{T}(\cdot)$, satisfies the ordering constraint and has an error $\mathcal{E}_{\hat{S}} = O(\frac{p \log^3 |\mathcal{T}|}{\epsilon^2})$, where p represents the number of distinct values in $\hat{S}_\mathcal{T}(\cdot)$ [9]. Note that, if we additionally enforce the constraint that $s_1 > 0$, then all the counts are also positive. In particular, when $p = 1$, $\mathcal{E}_{\hat{S}} = O(\frac{\log^3 |\mathcal{T}|}{\epsilon^2})$ and when $p = |\mathcal{T}|$, $\mathcal{E}_{\hat{S}} = O(\frac{|\mathcal{T}|}{\epsilon^2})$. Many real datasets are sparse, i.e. the majority of the domain values have zero counts, and hence have fewer distinct cumulative counts, i.e. $p \ll |\mathcal{T}|$. This leads to much smaller $\mathcal{E}_{\hat{S}}$ compared to $\mathcal{E}_{\tilde{S}}$. The best known strategy for releasing the cumulative histogram is using the hierarchical mechanism [9], which results in a total error of $O(\frac{|\mathcal{T}| \log^3 |\mathcal{T}|}{\epsilon^2})$. Moreover, the SVD bound [16] suggests that no strategy can release the cumulative histogram with $O(\frac{|\mathcal{T}|}{\epsilon^2})$ error. Thus under the line graph policy, the Ordered Mechanism is a much better strategy for cumulative histogram.

One important application of cumulative histogram is answering range query, defined as follows.

Definition 7.2 (Range Query). *Let D has domain $\mathcal{T} = \{x_1, ..., x_{|\mathcal{T}|}\}$, where $\mathcal{T}$ has a total ordering. A range query, denoted by $q[x_i, x_j]$ counts the number of tuples falling within the range $[x_i, x_j]$ where $x_i, x_j \in \mathcal{T}$ and $x_i \leq x_j$.*

Range queries can be directly answered using cumulative histogram $\hat{S}_\mathcal{T}(\cdot)$, $q[x_i, x_j] = \hat{s}_j - \hat{s}_{i-1}$. As each range query requires at most two noisy cumulative counts, it has an error smaller than $2 \cdot \frac{2}{\epsilon^2}$ (even without constrained inference). Hence, we have the following theorem.

Theorem 7.1. *Consider a policy $(\mathcal{T}, G^{d,1}, \mathcal{I}_n)$, where $G^{d,1}$ is a line graph. Then the expected error of a range query $q[x_i, x_j]$ for Ordered Mechanism is given by:*

$$\mathcal{E}_{q[x_i,x_j], M^O_{G^{d,1}}} \leq 4/\epsilon^2 \quad (12)$$

This error bound is independent of $|\mathcal{T}|$, much lower than the expected error using hierarchical structure with Laplace mechanism to answer range queries, $\mathcal{E}_{q[x_i,x_j],lap} = \frac{\log^3 |\mathcal{T}|}{\epsilon^2}$. Again, the SVD bound [16] suggests that no differentially private strategy can answer each range query with $O(\frac{1}{\epsilon^2})$ error. Other applications of $S_\mathcal{T}(\cdot)$ including computing quantiles and histograms and constructing indexes (e.g. k-d tree) could also use cumulative histogram in a similar manner as range query to obtain a much smaller error by trading utility with privacy under $G^{d,1}$. Next, we describe the *ordered hierarchical mechanism* that works for general graphs, $G^{d,\theta}$.

7.2 Ordered Hierarchical Mechanism

For a more general graph $G^{d,\theta} = (V, E)$, where $V = \mathcal{T}$ and $E = \{(x_i, x_{i\pm1}), .., (x_i, x_{i\pm\theta}) | \forall i = 1, ..., |\mathcal{T}|\}$, the sensitivity of releasing cumulative histogram $S_\mathcal{T}(\cdot)$ becomes θ. The Ordered Mechanism would add noise from $Lap(\frac{\theta}{\epsilon})$ to each cumulative counts s_i. The total error in the released cumulative histogram and range queries would still be asymptotically smaller than the error achieved by any differentially private mechanism for small θ. However, the errors become comparable as the θ reaches $\log |\mathcal{T}|$, and the Ordered Mechanism's error exceeds the error from the hierarchical mechanism when $\theta = O(\log^{3/2} |\mathcal{T}|)$. In this section, we present a hybrid strategy for releasing cumulative histograms (and hence range queries), called Ordered Hierarchical Mechanism, that always has an error less than or equal to the hierarchical mechanism for all θ.

Various hierarchical methods have been proposed in the literature [9, 19, 15, 20, 18]. A basic hierarchical structure is usually described as a tree with a regular fan-out f. The root records the total size of the dataset D, i.e. the answer to the range query $q[x_1, x_{|\mathcal{T}|}]$. This range is then partitioned into f intervals. If $\delta = \lceil \frac{|\mathcal{T}|}{f} \rceil$, the intervals are $[x_1, x_\delta]$, $[x_{\delta+1}, x_{2\delta}]$,..., $[x_{|\mathcal{T}|-\delta+1}, x_{|\mathcal{T}|}]$ and answers to the range queries over those intervals are recorded by the children of the root node. Recursively, the interval represented by the current node will be further divided into f subintervals. Leaf nodes correspond to unit length interval $q[x_i, x_i]$. The height of the tree is $h = \lceil \log_f |\mathcal{T}| \rceil$. In the above construction, the counts at level i are released using the Laplace mechanism with parameter $\frac{2}{\epsilon}$, and $\sum_i \epsilon_i = \epsilon$. Prior work has considered distributing the ϵ uniformly or geometrically [5]. We use uniform budgeting in our experiments.

Inspired by ordered mechanism for line graph, we propose a hybrid structure, called Ordered Hierarchical Structure OH for $(\epsilon, (\mathcal{T}, G^{d,\theta}, \mathcal{I}_n))$-Blowfish privacy. As shown in Figure 2(a), OH has two types of nodes, S nodes and H nodes. The number of S nodes is $k = \lceil \frac{n}{\theta} \rceil$, which is dependent on the threshold θ. In this way, we could guarantee a sensitivity of 1 among the S nodes. Let us represent S nodes as $s_1, ..., s_k$, where $s_1 = q[x_1, x_\theta]$,..., $s_{k-1} = q[x_1, x_{(k-1)\theta}]$, $s_k = q[x_1, x_{|\mathcal{T}|}]$. Note that the s_i nodes here are not the same as the count for cumulative histogram, so we will use range query $q[x_1, x_i]$ to represent the count s_i in a cumulative histogram. The first S node, s_1 is the root of a subtree consisting of H nodes. This subtree is denoted by H_1 and is used for answering all possible range queries within this interval $[x_1, x_\theta]$. For all $1 < i \leq k$, s_i has two children: s_{i-1} and the root of a subtree made of H nodes, denoted by H_i. Similarly, it also has a fan-out of f and represents counts for values $[(i-1)\theta + 1, i\theta]$. We denote the height of the subtree by $h = \lceil \log_f \theta \rceil$. Using this hybrid structure, we could release cumulative counts in this way: $q[x_1, x_{l\theta}] + q[x_{l\theta+1}, x_j]$, where $l\theta \leq j < (l+1)\theta$. Here $q[x_1, x_{l\theta}]$ is answered using s_l and $q[x_{l\theta+1}, x_j]$ is answered using H_l. Then any range query could be answered as $q[x_i, x_j] = q[x_1, x_j] - q[x_1, x_{i-1}]$.

Privacy Budgeting Strategy Given total privacy budget ϵ, we denote the privacy budget assigned to all the S nodes by ϵ_S and to all the H nodes by ϵ_H. When a tuple change

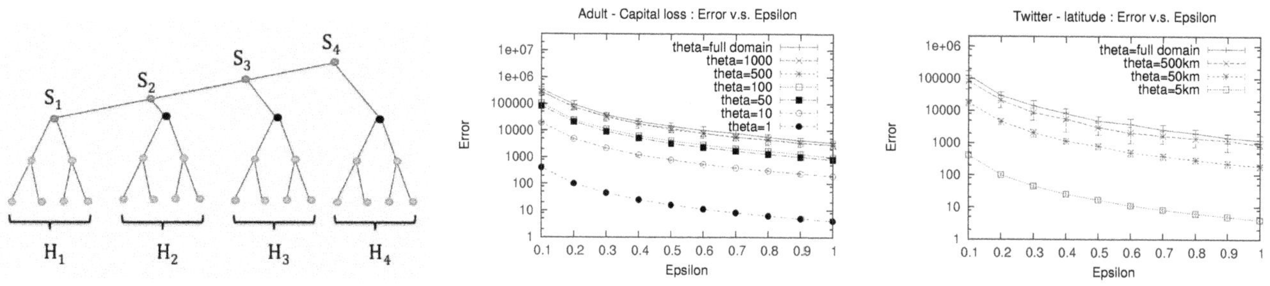

(a) Ordered Hierarchical Tree $\theta = 4$ (b) Adult - capital loss (c) Twitter - latitude

Figure 2: Ordered Hierarchical Mechanism. 2(a) gives an example of OH, where $\theta = 4$. 2(b) and 2(c) shows privacy-utility trade-offs for range query, using $G^{d,\theta}$ for sensitive information.

its value from x to y, where $d_G(x,y) \leq \theta$, at most one S node changes its count value and at most $2h$ H nodes change their count values. Hence, for $i = 2, ..., k$, we add Laplace noise drawn from $Lap(\frac{1}{\epsilon_S})$ to each s_i and we add Laplace noise drawn from $Lap(\frac{2h}{\epsilon_H})$ to each H node in the subtree H_i. As S_1 is the root of H_1, we assign $\epsilon = \epsilon_S + \epsilon_H$ to the tree H_1 and hence we add Laplace noise drawn from $Lap(\frac{2h}{\epsilon_H + \epsilon_S})$ to each H node in H_1, including s_1. In this way, we could claim that this OH tree satisfies $(\epsilon, (\mathcal{T}, G^{d,\theta}, \mathcal{I}_n))$-Blowfish privacy. When $\theta = |\mathcal{T}|$, H_1 is going to be the only tree to have all the privacy budget. This is equivalent to the hierarchical mechanism for differential privacy.

THEOREM 7.2. *Consider a policy $P = (\mathcal{T}, G^{d,\theta}, \mathcal{I}_n)$. (1) The Ordered Hierarchical structure satisfies (ϵ, P)-Blowfish privacy. (2) The expected error of releasing a single count in cumulative histogram or answering a range query this structure over $\mathcal{T}$ is ,*

$$\mathcal{E}_{q[x_i,x_j], M^{OH}_{G^{d,\theta}}} = O\left(\frac{|\mathcal{T}| - \theta}{|\mathcal{T}|\epsilon_S^2} + \frac{(f-1)\log_f^3 \theta}{\epsilon_H^2}\right) \quad (13)$$

PROOF. (sketch) 1) Increasing count of x by 1 and decreasing count of y by 1, where $d(x,y) < \theta$ only affect the counts of at most one S node and $2h$ H nodes. Since we draw noise from $Lap(\frac{1}{\epsilon_S})$ for S nodes and from $Lap(\frac{2h}{\epsilon_H})$ for H nodes (where $\epsilon = \epsilon_S + \epsilon_H$), we get (ϵ, P)-Blowfish privacy based on sequential composition.
2) Consider all the counts in cumulative histogram, and there are $|\mathcal{T}|$ of them, only $|\mathcal{T}| - \theta$ requires S nodes. Each S node has a error of $\frac{2}{\epsilon_S^2}$. This gives the first fraction in Eqn. (13). On average, the number of H nodes used for each count in cumulative histogram is bounded by the height of the H tree and each H node has an error of $\frac{8h^2}{\epsilon_H^2}$, which explains the second fraction in Eqn. (13). □

Each range query $q[x_i, x_j]$ requires at most 2 counts from cumulative histogram and its exact form of expected error is $\mathcal{E}_{q[x_i,x_j], M^{OH}_{G^{d,\theta}}} = c_1/\epsilon_S^2 + c_2/\epsilon_H^2$, where $c_1 = \frac{4(|\mathcal{T}| - \theta)}{|\mathcal{T}|+1}$ and $c_2 = \frac{8(f-1)\log_f \theta^3 |\mathcal{T}|}{|\mathcal{T}|+1}$. Given θ and f, at $\epsilon_S^* = \frac{c_1^{1/3}}{c_1^{1/3} + c_2^{1/3}}\epsilon$, we obtain the minimum

$$\mathcal{E}^*_{q[x_i,x_j], M^{OH}_{G^{d,\theta}}} = \frac{(c_1^{1/3} + c_2^{1/3})^3}{\epsilon^2} \quad (14)$$

In particular, when $\theta = |\mathcal{T}|$, $c_1 = 0$, this is equivalent to the classical hierarchical mechanism without S nodes and we have $\mathcal{E}_{q[x_i,x_j], M^{OH}_{G^{d,\theta}}} = O(\frac{\log^3 |\mathcal{T}|}{\epsilon^2})$. When $\theta = 1$, $c_2 = 0$, this is the pure Ordered Mechanism without using H nodes and $\mathcal{E}_{q[x_i,x_j], M^{OH}_{G^{d,\theta}}} = O(\frac{1}{\epsilon^2})$.

Complexity Analysis The complexity of construction of the hybrid tree OH and answering range query are $O(|\mathcal{T}|)$ and $O(\log \theta)$ respectively, where $\theta \leq |\mathcal{T}|$, which is not worse than the classical hierarchical methods.

7.3 Empirical Evaluation

We empirically evaluate the error of range queries for the Ordered Hierarchical Mechanism with $(\epsilon, (\mathcal{T}, G^{d,\theta}, \mathcal{I}_n))$-Blowfish privacy on two real-world datasets – ADULT and TWITTER. The ADULT data set[6] consists of Census records of 48842 individuals. We consider the ordinal attribute capital loss with a domain size of 4357. The TWITTER data set is the same dataset used for k-means clustering (Sec 6.1). Here, in order to have a total ordering for the dataset, we project the TWITTER data set on its latitude with a domain size of 400, around 2222 km. The fan-out f is set to be 16 and each experiment is repeated 50 times. Figure 2(b) shows the mean square error $\mathcal{E}$ of 10000 random range queries for various values of $\epsilon = \{0.1, 0.2, ..., 0.9, 1.0\}$. Seven threshold values $\theta = \{full, 1000, 500, 100, 50, 10, 1\}$ are considered. For ADULT, for example, $\theta = 100$ means the adversary cannot distinguish between values of capital loss within a range of 100 and $\theta = full$ means the adversary cannot distinguish between all the domain values (same as differential privacy). Figure 2(c) considers 4 threshold values $\theta = \{full, 500km, 50km, 5km\}$ for TWITTER. When $\theta = 1$ (ADULT) or $\theta = 5km$ (TWITTER), the ordered hierarchical mechanism is same as the ordered mechanism. From both figures, we see that as the θ increases, $\mathcal{E}$ decreases and orders of magnitude difference in error between $\theta = 1$ and $\theta = |\mathcal{T}|$.

8. BLOWFISH WITH CONSTRAINTS

In this section, we consider query answering under Blowfish policies with constraints $P = (\mathcal{T}, G, \mathcal{I}_Q)$, where $(\mathcal{I}_Q \subsetneq \mathcal{I}_n)$. In the presence of general deterministic constraints Q, pairs of neighboring databases can differ in any number of tuples, depending on structures of Q and the discriminative graph G. Computing the policy specific sensitivity in this general case is a hard problem, as shown next.

THEOREM 8.1. *Given a function f and a policy $P = (\mathcal{T}, G, \mathcal{I}_Q)$. Checking whether $S(f, P) > 0$ is NP-hard.*

[6] `http://mlr.cs.umass.edu/ml/datasets/Adult`

Theorem 8.1 implies that checking whether $S(f,P) \le z$ is co-NP-hard for general constraints Q. In fact, the hardness result holds even if we just consider the histogram query h and general *count query constraints.*

Hence, in the rest of this section, we will focus on releasing histograms under a large subclass of constraints called *sparse count query constraints.* In Section 8.1 we show that when the count query constraint is "sparse", we can efficiently compute $S(h,P)$, and thus we can use the Laplace mechanism to release the histogram. In Section 8.2, we will show that our general result about $S(h,P)$ subject to sparse count query constraints can be applied to several important practical scenarios.

8.1 Global Sensitivity for Sparse Constraints

A *count query* q_ϕ returns the number of tuples satisfying predicate ϕ in a database D, i.e., $\mathsf{q}_\phi(D) = \sum_{t\in D} \mathbf{1}_{\phi(t)=\text{true}}$. The auxiliary knowledge we consider here is a *count query constraint* Q, which can be expressed as a conjunction of query-answer pairs:

$$\mathsf{q}_{\phi_1}(D) = \mathsf{cnt}_1 \wedge \mathsf{q}_{\phi_2}(D) = \mathsf{cnt}_2 \wedge \ldots \wedge \mathsf{q}_{\phi_p}(D) = \mathsf{cnt}_p. \quad (15)$$

Since the answers $\mathsf{cnt}_1, \mathsf{cnt}_2, \ldots, \mathsf{cnt}_p$ do not affect our analysis, we denote the auxiliary knowledge or count query constraint as $Q = \{\mathsf{q}_{\phi_1}, \mathsf{q}_{\phi_2}, \ldots, \mathsf{q}_{\phi_p}\}$. Note that this class of auxiliary knowledge is already very general and commonly seen in practice. For example, marginals of contingency tables, range queries, and degree distributions of graphs can all be expressed in this form.

Even for this class of constraints, calculating $S(h,P)$ is still hard. In fact, the same hardness result in Theorem 8.1 holds for count query constraints (using a reduction from the Vertex Cover problem).

8.1.1 Sparse Auxiliary Knowledge

Consider a secret pair $(s_x^i, s_y^i) \in \mathcal{S}_{\text{pairs}}^G$ about a tuple t with $t.\_id = i$, and a count query $\mathsf{q}_\phi \in Q$. If the tuple $t \in D$ changes from x to y, there are three mutually exclusive cases about $\mathsf{q}_\phi(D)$: i) increases by one ($\neg\phi(x) \wedge \phi(y)$), ii) decreases by one ($\phi(x) \wedge \neg\phi(y)$), or iii) stays the same (otherwise).

Definition 8.1 (Lift and Lower). *A pair $(x,y) \in \mathcal{T} \times \mathcal{T}$ is said to lift a count query q_ϕ iff $\phi(x) = \text{false} \wedge \phi(y) = \text{true}$, or lower q_ϕ iff $\phi(x) = \text{true} \wedge \phi(y) = \text{false}$.*

Note that one pair may lift or lower many count queries simultaneously. We now define sparse auxiliary knowledge.

Definition 8.2 (Sparse Knowledge). *The auxiliary knowledge $Q = \{\mathsf{q}_{\phi_1}, \mathsf{q}_{\phi_2}, \ldots, \mathsf{q}_{\phi_p}\}$ is* sparse *w.r.t. the discriminative secret graph $G = (V,E)$, iff each pair $(x,y) \in E$ lifts at most one count query in Q and lowers at most one count query in Q.*

Example 8.1. (Lift, Lower, and Sparse Knowledge) *Consider databases from domain $\mathcal{T} = A_1 \times A_2 \times A_3$, where $A_1 = \{a_1, a_2\}$, $A_2 = \{b_1, b_2\}$, and $A_3 = \{c_1, c_2, c_3\}$ and count query constraint $Q = \{\mathsf{q}_1, \mathsf{q}_2, \mathsf{q}_3, \mathsf{q}_4\}$ as in Figure 3(a). With full-domain sensitive information, any pair in $\mathcal{T} \times \mathcal{T}$ is a discriminative secret and thus the discriminative secret graph G is a complete graph. A pair $((a_1,b_1,c_1),(a_2,b_2,c_2))$ lifts q_4 and lowers q_1; and a pair $((a_1,b_2,c_1),(a_1,b_2,c_2))$ neither lifts nor lowers a query. We can verify every pair either (i) lifts exactly one query in Q and lowers exactly one in Q, or (ii) lifts or lowers no query in Q. So Q is sparse w.r.t. the discriminative secret graph G.*

$\mathsf{q}_1: t.A_1 = a_1 \wedge t.A_2 = b_1$

$\mathsf{q}_2: t.A_1 = a_1 \wedge t.A_2 = b_2$

$\mathsf{q}_3: t.A_1 = a_2 \wedge t.A_2 = b_1$

$\mathsf{q}_4: t.A_1 = a_2 \wedge t.A_2 = b_2$

(a) $Q = \{\mathsf{q}_1, \mathsf{q}_2, \mathsf{q}_3, \mathsf{q}_4\}$

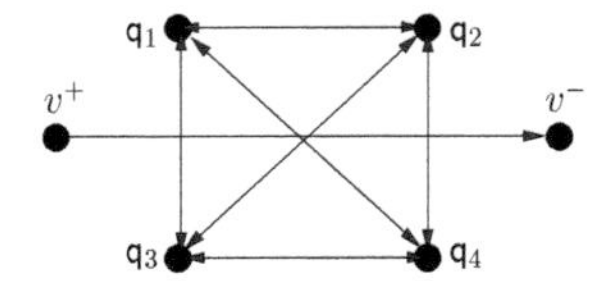

(b) $\mathcal{G}_P = (\mathcal{V}_P, \mathcal{E}_P)$

Figure 3: Policy graph $\mathcal{G}_P = (\mathcal{V}_P, \mathcal{E}_P)$ of databases with three attributes $A_1 = \{a_1, a_2\}$, $A_2 = \{b_1, b_2\}$, and $A_3 = \{c_1, c_2, c_3\}$ subject to count query constraint $Q = \{\mathsf{q}_1, \mathsf{q}_2, \mathsf{q}_3, \mathsf{q}_4\}$ and full-domain sensitive information

We will show that when the auxiliary knowledge Q is sparse w.r.t. the discriminative secret graph $G = (V,E)$ in a policy $P = (\mathcal{T}, G, \mathcal{I}_Q)$, it is *possible* to analytically bound the policy specific global sensitivity $S(h,P)$. To this end, let's first construct a directed graph called *policy graph* $\mathcal{G}_P = (\mathcal{V}_P, \mathcal{E}_P)$ from P, the count queries in Q forming the vertices, and the relationships between count queries and secret pairs forming edges.

Definition 8.3 (Policy Graph). *Given a policy $P = (\mathcal{T}, G(V,E), \mathcal{I}_Q)$, and a sparse count constraint Q, the policy graph $\mathcal{G}_P = (\mathcal{V}_P, \mathcal{E}_P)$ is a directed graph, where*

- *$\mathcal{V}_P = Q \cup \{v^+, v^-\}$: Create a vertex for each count query $\mathsf{q}_\phi \in Q$, and two additional special vertices v^+ and v^-.*
- *$\mathcal{E}_P$: i) add a directed edge $(\mathsf{q}_\phi, \mathsf{q}_{\phi'})$ iff there exists a secret pair $(x,y) \in E$ lifting $\mathsf{q}_{\phi'}$ and lowering q_ϕ; ii) add a directed edge (v^+, q_ϕ) iff there is a secret pair in E lifting q_ϕ but not lowering any other $\mathsf{q}_{\phi'}$; iii) add a directed edge (q_ϕ, v^-) iff there is a secret pair in E lowering q_ϕ but not lifting any other $\mathsf{q}_{\phi'}$; and iv) add edge (v^+, v^-).*

Let $\alpha(\mathcal{G}_P)$ denote the length (number of edges) of the longest simple cycle in $\mathcal{G}_P$. $\alpha(\mathcal{G}_P)$ is defined to be 0 if $\mathcal{G}_P$ has no directed cycle. Let $\xi(\mathcal{G}_P)$ be the length (number of edges) of a longest simple path from v^+ to v^- in $\mathcal{G}_P$.

Example 8.2. (Policy Graph) *Followed by Example 8.1, since the count query constraint Q is sparse w.r.t. the discriminative secret graph, we have its policy graph $\mathcal{G}_P = (\mathcal{V}_P, \mathcal{E}_P)$ as in Figure 3(b). For example, a pair $((a_1,b_1,c_1),(a_2,b_2,c_2))$ in $\mathcal{T} \times \mathcal{T}$ lifts q_4 and lowers q_1, so there is an edge $(\mathsf{q}_1, \mathsf{q}_4)$. There is no edge from v^+ or to v^-, except (v^+, v^-), because every pair in $\mathcal{T} \times \mathcal{T}$ either lifts one query and lowers one, or lifts/lowers no query. In this policy graph $\mathcal{G}_P$, we have $\alpha(\mathcal{G}_P) = 4$ and $\xi(\mathcal{G}_P) = 1$.*

Theorem 8.2. *Let h be the complete histogram query. In a policy $P = (\mathcal{T}, G, \mathcal{I}_Q)$, if the auxiliary knowledge Q is sparse w.r.t. G, then we have:*

$$S(h,P) \le 2\max\{\alpha(\mathcal{G}_P), \xi(\mathcal{G}_P)\},$$

If there exist two neighboring databases $(D_1, D_2) \in N(P)$ s.t. $\|h(D_1) - h(D_2)\|_1 = 2|T(D_1,D_2)|$ when $|T(D_1,D_2)| = \max_{(D',D'')\in N(P)} |T(D',D'')|$, then we have the equality:

$$S(h,P) = 2\max\{\alpha(\mathcal{G}_P), \xi(\mathcal{G}_P)\}.$$

See Appendix for a proof sketch. For a sparse count query constraint Q with respect to policy $P = (\mathcal{T}, G, \mathcal{I}_Q)$, we have the following immediate corollary about an upper bound.

COROLLARY 8.3. *In a policy $P = (\mathcal{T}, G, \mathcal{I}_Q)$, if Q is sparse w.r.t. G, then $S(h, P) \leq 2\max\{|Q|, 1\}$.*

Thus, drawing noise from Laplace($2\max\{|Q|, 1\}/\epsilon$) suffices (but may not be necessary) for releasing the complete histogram while ensuring (ϵ, P)-Blowfish privacy.

8.2 Applications

The problem of calculating $\alpha(\mathcal{G}_P)$ and $\xi(\mathcal{G}_P)$ exactly in a general policy graph $\mathcal{G}_P$ is still a hard problem, but becomes tractable in a number of practical scenarios. We give three such examples: i) the policy specific global sensitivity $S(h, P)$ subject to auxiliary knowledge of one marginal for full-domain sensitive information; ii) $S(h, P)$ subject to auxiliary knowledge of multiple marginals for attribute sensitive information; and iii) $S(h, P)$ subject to auxiliary knowledge of range queries for distance-threshold sensitive information.

8.2.1 Marginals and Full-domain Secrets

Marginals are also called *cuboids* in data cubes. Intuitively, in a marginal or a cuboid C, we project the database of tuples onto a subset of attributes $[C] \subseteq \{A_1, A_2, \ldots, A_k\}$ and count the number of tuples that have the same values on these attributes. Here, we consider the scenario when the adversaries have auxiliary knowledge about one or more marginals, i.e., the counts in some marginals are known.

DEFINITION 8.4 (MARGINAL). *Given a database D of n tuples from a k-dim domain $\mathcal{T} = A_1 \times A_2 \times \ldots \times A_k$, a d-dim marginal C is the (exact) answer to the query:*

SELECT A_{i_1}, A_{i_2}, ..., A_{i_d}, COUNT(*) FROM D
GROUP BY A_{i_1}, A_{i_2}, ..., A_{i_d}

Let $[C]$ denote the set of d attributes $\{A_{i_1}, A_{i_2}, \ldots, A_{i_d}\}$.

A marginal $[C] = \{A_{i_1}, A_{i_2}, \ldots, A_{i_d}\}$ is essentially a set of count queries $C^{\mathsf{q}} = \{\mathsf{q}_\phi\}$, where the predicate $\phi(t) := (t.A_{i_1} = a_{i_1}) \wedge (t.A_{i_2} = a_{i_2}) \wedge \ldots \wedge (t.A_{i_2} = a_{i_d})$, for all possible $(a_{i_1}, a_{i_2}, \ldots, a_{i_d}) \in A_{i_1} \times A_{i_2} \times \ldots \times A_{i_d}$.

Let $\mathcal{A} = \{A_1, A_2, \ldots, A_k\}$ be the set of all attributes. For a marginal C, define size$(C) = \prod_{A_i \in [C]} |A_i|$, where $|A_i|$ is the cardinality of an attribute A_i. So size(C) is the number of possible rows in the marginal C, or the number of the count queries in C^{q} constructed as above.

Suppose a marginal with $[C] \subsetneq \mathcal{A}$ is known to the adversary. Let $\mathcal{I}_{Q(C)}$ denote the set of databases with marginal C equal to certain value. Recall that we want to publish the complete histogram h of a database D from a domain $\mathcal{T} = A_1 \times A_2 \times \ldots \times A_k$. For the full-domain sensitive information, using Theorem 8.2, we have the global sensitivity equal to 2 size(C).

THEOREM 8.4. *Let h be the complete histogram. For a policy $P = (\mathcal{T}, G, \mathcal{I}_{Q(C)})$, where G represents the full-domain sensitive information $\mathcal{S}^{\text{full}}_{\text{pairs}}$ and $[C] \subsetneq \mathcal{A}$ is a marginal, we have $S(h, P) = 2$ size(C).*

PROOF. (sketch) Consider the set of count queries C^{q}. It is not hard to show that C^{q} is sparse w.r.t. the complete graph G. So we can construct a policy graph from $(\mathcal{T}, G, \mathcal{I}_{C^{\mathsf{q}}})$, which is a complete graph with vertex set C^{q}. From Theorem 8.2, we have $S(f, P) = 2|C^{\mathsf{q}}| = 2$ size(C). The upper bound $S(h, P) \leq 2|C^{\mathsf{q}}|$ is directly from Theorem 8.2, and it is not hard to construct two neighboring databases to match this upper bound as $[C] \subsetneq \mathcal{A}$. □

EXAMPLE 8.3. *Continuing with Example 8.2, note that the constraints in Figure 3(a) correspond to the marginal $[C] = \{A_1, A_2\}$. So from (i) in Theorem 8.2, we have $S(h, P) \leq 2 \times 4 = 8$. The worst case $S(h, P) = 8$ can be verified by considering the two neighboring databases D_1 and D_2, each with four rows: $a_1b_1c_1$ (in D_1)/$a_1b_2c_2$ (in D_2), $a_1b_2c_1/a_2b_1c_2$, $a_2b_1c_1/a_2b_2c_2$, and $a_2b_2c_1/a_1b_1c_2$.*

8.2.2 Marginals and Attribute Secrets

Now suppose a set of p marginals C_1, ..., C_p with $[C_1]$, ..., $[C_p] \subsetneq \{A_1, A_2, \ldots, A_k\}$ are auxiliary knowledge to the adversary. Let $\mathcal{I}_{Q(C_1, \ldots, C_p)}$ be the set of databases with these p marginals equal to certain values. For the attribute sensitive information, if the p marginals are disjoint, using Theorem 8.2 the global sensitivity is $2\max_{1 \leq i \leq p}$ size(C_i).

THEOREM 8.5. *Let h be the complete histogram. Consider a policy $P = (\mathcal{T}, G^{\text{attr}}, \mathcal{I}_{Q(C_1, \ldots, C_p)})$, where $[C_i] \subsetneq \mathcal{A}$ for any marginal C_i, and $[C_i] \cap [C_j] = \emptyset$ for any two C_i and C_j. Then we have $S(h, P) = 2\max_{1 \leq i \leq p}$ size(C_i).*

PROOF. (sketch) Consider the set of count queries $Q = C_1^{\mathsf{q}} \cup \ldots \cup C_p^{\mathsf{q}}$, it is not hard to show that Q is sparse w.r.t. G^{attr}. The policy graph from $(\mathcal{T}, G^{\text{attr}}, Q)$ is the union of p cliques with vertex sets C_1^{q}, ..., C_p^{q}. From Theorem 8.2, we have $S(h, P) = 2\max_i |C_i^{\mathsf{q}}| = 2\max_i$ size(C_i). The upper bound $S(h, P) \leq 2\max_i |C_i^{\mathsf{q}}|$ is directly from Theorem 8.2, and it is not hard to construct two neighboring databases to match this upper bound as $[C_i] \neq \mathcal{A}$. □

8.2.3 Grid and Distance-threshold Secrets

Our general theorem about $S(f, P)$ can be also applied to databases with geographical information.

Consider a domain $\mathcal{T} = [m]^k$, where $[m] = \{1, 2, \ldots, m\}$. When $k = 2$ or 3, $\mathcal{T}$ can be used to approximately encode a 2-dim plane or a 3-dim space. For two points $x, y \in \mathcal{T}$, we define *distance* $d(x, y)$ to be the L^p distance $||x - y||_p$. For two point sets $X, Y \subset \mathcal{T}$, we define $d(X, Y) = \min_{x \in X, y \in Y} d(x, y)$. A geographical database D consists of n points, each of which is drawn from the domain $\mathcal{T}$ and may represent the location of an object.

Define a rectangle $R = [l_1, u_1] \times [l_2, u_2] \times \ldots \times [l_k, u_k]$, where $l_i \in [m]$, $u_i \in [m]$, and $l_i \leq u_i$. A range count query q_R returns the number of tuples whose locations fall into the rectangle R. R is called a *point query* if $l_i = u_i$ for all i.

In this scenario, suppose the answers to a set of p range count queries are known to the adversary. So we can represent the auxiliary knowledge as $Q = \{\mathsf{q}_{R_1}, \mathsf{q}_{R_2}, \ldots, \mathsf{q}_{R_p}\}$. Also, suppose we aim to protect the distance-threshold sensitive information $\mathcal{S}^{d,\theta}_{\text{pairs}} = \{(s_x^i, s_y^i) \mid d(x, y) \leq \theta\}$ while the publishing complete histogram h.

Using Theorem 8.2, we can calculate the global sensitivity if all rectangles are disjoint, i.e., $R_i \cap R_j = \emptyset$ for any $i \neq j$, as follows. Construct a graph $\mathcal{G}_R(Q) = (\mathcal{V}_R, \mathcal{E}_R)$ on the set of rectangles in Q: i) create a vertex in $\mathcal{V}_R$ for rectangle R_i in each range count query q_{R_i} in Q; and ii) add an edge (R_i, R_j) into $\mathcal{E}_R$ iff $d(R_i, R_j) \leq \theta$. We can prove that the policy specific global sensitivity equals to 2(maxcomp(Q)+1) when there are no point query constraints, where maxcomp(Q) is the number of nodes in the largest connected component in $\mathcal{G}_R(Q)$. Note that maxcomp(Q) (and hence $S(h, P)$) can be computed efficiently.

THEOREM 8.6. *Let h be the complete histogram. For a policy $P = (\mathcal{T}, G, \mathcal{I}_Q)$, where $\mathcal{T} = [m]^k$, G represents the* *distance-threshold sensitive information* $\mathcal{S}^{d,\theta}_{\text{pairs}}$ $(\theta > 0)$*, and* Q *is a set of disjoint range count queries* $\{\mathsf{q}_{R_1}, \mathsf{q}_{R_2}, \ldots, \mathsf{q}_{R_p}\}$ *with* $R_i \cap R_j = \emptyset$ *for* $i \neq j$*. We have* $S(h, P) \leq 2(\text{maxcomp}(Q) + 1)$*. If none of the constraints are point queries, then* $S(h, P) = 2(\text{maxcomp}(Q) + 1)$*.*

9. CONCLUSIONS

We propose a new class of privacy definitions, called Blowfish privacy, with the goal of seeking better trade-off between privacy and utility. The key feature of Blowfish is a policy, where users can specify sensitive information that needs to be protected and knowledge about their databases which has been released to potential adversaries. Such a rich set of "tuning knobs" in the policy enable users to improve the utility by customizing sensitive information and to limit attacks from adversaries with auxiliary knowledge. Using examples of kmeans clustering, cumulative histograms and range queries, we show how to tune utility using reasonable policies with weaker specifications of privacy. For the latter, we develop strategies that are more accurate than any differentially private mechanism. Moreover, we study how to calibrate noise for Blowfish policies with count constraints when publishing histograms, and the general result we obtain can be applied in several practical scenarios.

Acknowledgements: We would like to thank Jiangwei Pan and the anonymous reviewers for their comments. This work was supported by the National Science Foundation under Grant # 1253327 and a gift from Google.

10. REFERENCES

[1] J. Blocki, A. Blum, A. Datta, and O. Sheffet. Differentially private data analysis of social networks via restricted sensitivity. In *ACM ITCS*, 2013.

[2] A. Blum, C. Dwork, F. McSherry, and K. Nissim. Practical privacy: the sulq framework. In *PODS*, 2005.

[3] K. Chatzikokolakis, M. AndrâĹŽÂl's, N. Bordenabe, and C. Palamidessi. Broadening the scope of differential privacy using metrics. In *Privacy Enhancing Technologies*. 2013.

[4] B.-C. Chen, D. Kifer, K. Lefevre, and A. Machanavajjhala. Privacy-preserving data publishing. *Foundations and Trends in Databases*, 2(1-2):1–167, 2009.

[5] G. Cormode, C. M. Procopiuc, D. Srivastava, E. Shen, and T. Yu. Differentially private spatial decompositions. In *ICDE*, pages 20–31, 2012.

[6] C. Dwork. Differential privacy. In *ICALP*, 2006.

[7] C. Dwork, F. McSherry, K. Nissim, and A. Smith. Calibrating noise to sensitivity in private data analysis. In *TCC*, pages 265–284, 2006.

[8] S. R. Ganta, S. P. Kasiviswanathan, and A. Smith. Composition attacks and auxiliary information in data privacy. In *KDD*, pages 265–273, 2008.

[9] M. Hay, V. Rastogi, G. Miklau, and D. Suciu. Boosting the accuracy of differentially-private queries through consistency. In *PVLDB*, pages 1021–1032, 2010.

[10] X. He, A. Machanavajjhala, and B. Ding. Blowfish privacy: Tuning privacy-utility trade-offs using policies. *CoRR*, abs/1312.3913, 2014.

[11] D. Kifer and B.-R. Lin. Towards an axiomatization of statistical privacy and utility. In *PODS*, 2010.

[12] D. Kifer and A. Machanavajjhala. No free lunch in data privacy. In *SIGMOD*, pages 193–204, 2011.

[13] D. Kifer and A. Machanavajjhala. A rigorous and customizable framework for privacy. In *PODS*, 2012.

[14] D. Kifer and A. Machanavajjhala. Pufferish: A framework for mathematical privacy definitions. *To appear ACM Transactions on Database Systems*, 39(1), 2014.

[15] C. Li, M. Hay, V. Rastogi, G. Miklau, and A. McGregor. Optimizing histogram queries under differential privacy. In *PODS*, pages 123–134, 2010.

[16] C. Li and G. Miklau. Optimal error of query sets under the differentially-private matrix mechanism. In *ICDT*, 2013.

[17] A. Machanavajjhala, A. Korolova, and A. D. Sarma. Personalized social recommendations - accurate or private? In *PVLDB*, volume 4, pages 440–450, 2011.

[18] W. Qardaji, W. Yang, and N. Li. Understanding hierarchical methods for differentially private histogram. In *PVLDB*, 2013.

[19] X. Xiao, G. Wang, and J. Gehrke. Differential privacy via wavelet transforms. In *ICDE*, pages 225–236, 2010.

[20] J. Xu, Z. Zhang, X. Xiao, Y. Yang, and G. Yu. Differentially private histogram publication. In *ICDE*, pages 32–43, 2012.

APPENDIX

Proof sketch of Theorem 8.2:
Recall that the policy specific global sensitivity is defined as

$$S(h, P) = \max_{(D_1, D_2) \in N(P)} ||h(D_1) - h(D_2)||_1.$$

We only show $S(h, P) \leq 2\max\{\alpha(\mathcal{G}_P), \xi(\mathcal{G}_P)\}$ here. We refer the reader to the full version of the paper [10] for the complete proof. It suffices to prove that for any two databases $D_1, D_2 \in \mathcal{I}_Q$, if $|T(D_1, D_2)| > \max\{\alpha(\mathcal{G}_P), \xi(\mathcal{G}_P)\}$, there must exist another database $D_3 \in \mathcal{I}_Q$ s.t. $T(D_1, D_3) \subsetneq T(D_1, D_2)$, i.e., $(D_1, D_2) \notin N(P)$; and thus for any two databases $(D_1, D_2) \in N(P)$, we have $||h(D_1) - h(D_2)||_1 \leq 2|T(D_1, D_2)| \leq 2\max\{\alpha(\mathcal{G}_P), \xi(\mathcal{G}_P)\}$ which implies $S(h, P) \leq 2\max\{\alpha(\mathcal{G}_P), \xi(\mathcal{G}_P)\}$.

To complete the proof, we consider two databases $D_1, D_2 \in \mathcal{I}_Q$ with $|T(D_1, D_2)| > \max\{\alpha(\mathcal{G}_P), \xi(\mathcal{G}_P)\}$, and show how to construct the D_3 defined above.

First of all, for any secret pair $(s^i_x, s^i_y) \in T(D_1, D_2)$, it must lift and/or lower some count query $\mathsf{q}_\phi \in Q$; otherwise, we can construct D_3 by changing the value of tuple t with $t.id = i$ in D_1 into its value in D_2.

To construct D_3, now let's consider a directed graph $\mathcal{G}_{D_1|D_2} = (\mathcal{V}_{D_1|D_2}, \mathcal{E}_{D_1|D_2})$, where $\mathcal{V}_{D_1|D_2} \subseteq \mathcal{V}_P$ and $\mathcal{E}_{D_1|D_2}$ is a multi-subset of $\mathcal{E}_P$ (i.e., an edge in $\mathcal{E}_P$ may appear multiple times in $\mathcal{E}_{D_1|D_2}$). $\mathcal{E}_{D_1|D_2}$ is constructed as follows: for each $(s^i_x, s^i_y) \in T(D_1, D_2)$, i) if (x, y) lifts $\mathsf{q}_{\phi'}$ and lowers q_ϕ, add a directed edge $(\mathsf{q}_\phi, \mathsf{q}_{\phi'})$ into $\mathcal{E}_{D_1|D_2}$; ii) if (x, y) lifts q_ϕ but not lowering any other $\mathsf{q}_{\phi'}$, add an edge (v^+, q_ϕ); and iii) if (x, y) lowers q_ϕ but not lifting any other $\mathsf{q}_{\phi'}$, add an edge (q_ϕ, v^-). $\mathcal{V}_{D_1|D_2}$ is the set of count queries involved in $\mathcal{E}_{D_1|D_2}$.

$\mathcal{G}_{D_1|D_2}$ is Eulerian, i.e., each vertex has the same in-degree as out-degree except v^+ and v^- (if existing in $\mathcal{G}_{D_1|D_2}$), because of the above construction and the fact that $D_1, D_2 \in \mathcal{I}_Q$. As $|\mathcal{E}_{D_1|D_2}| = |T(D_1, D_2)| > \max\{\alpha(\mathcal{G}_P), \xi(\mathcal{G}_P)\}$ (i.e., $\mathcal{G}_{D_1|D_2}$ is larger than any simple cycle or simple v^+-v^- path in $\mathcal{G}_P$) and $\mathcal{G}_{D_1|D_2}$ is Eulerian, $\mathcal{G}_{D_1|D_2}$ must have a proper subgraph which is either a simple cycle or a simple v^+-v^- path. Let $\mathcal{E}_{D_1 \to D_2}$ be the edge set of this simple cycle/path. Construct D_3 that is identical to D_1, except that for each secret pair (s^i_x, s^i_y) associated with each edge in $\mathcal{E}_{D_1 \to D_2}$, the value of tuple t with $t.id = i$ is changed from x to y. We can show that D_3 satisfies its definition, and thus $S(h, P) \leq 2\max\{\alpha(\mathcal{G}_P), \xi(\mathcal{G}_P)\}$.

Overlap Interval Partition Join

Anton Dignös
Department of Computer Science
University of Zürich, Switzerland
adignoes@ifi.uzh.ch

Michael H. Böhlen
Department of Computer Science
University of Zürich, Switzerland
boehlen@ifi.uzh.ch

Johann Gamper
Faculty of Computer Science
Free University of Bozen-Bolzano, Italy
gamper@inf.unibz.it

ABSTRACT

Each tuple in a valid-time relation includes an interval attribute T that represents the tuple's valid time. The overlap join between two valid-time relations determines all pairs of tuples with overlapping intervals. Although overlap joins are common, existing partitioning and indexing schemes are inefficient if the data includes long-lived tuples or if intervals intersect partition boundaries.

We propose *Overlap Interval Partitioning* ($\mathcal{OIP}$), a new partitioning approach for data with an interval. $\mathcal{OIP}$ divides the time range of a relation into k base granules and defines overlapping partitions for sequences of contiguous granules. $\mathcal{OIP}$ is the first partitioning method for interval data that gives a *constant clustering guarantee*: the difference in duration between the interval of a tuple and the interval of its partition is independent of the duration of the tuple's interval. We offer a detailed analysis of the *average false hit ratio* and the *average number of partition accesses* for queries with overlap predicates, and we prove that the average false hit ratio is independent of the number of short- and long-lived tuples. To compute the overlap join, we propose the *Overlap Interval Partition Join* (OIPJOIN), which uses $\mathcal{OIP}$ to partition the input relations on-the-fly. Only the tuples from overlapping partitions have to be joined to compute the result. We analytically derive the optimal number of granules, k, for partitioning the two input relations, from the size of the data, the cost of CPU operations, and the cost of main memory or disk IOs. Our experiments confirm the analytical results and show that the OIPJOIN outperforms state-of-the-art techniques for the overlap join.

Categories and Subject Descriptors

H.2 [**Database Management**]: Systems—*Query processing*

Keywords

Temporal databases; Overlap join; Interval partitioning

1. INTRODUCTION

A key operation in valid-time databases is the *overlap join* [11]: given two valid-time relations **r** and **s**, find all pairs of tuples $r \in \mathbf{r}$ and $s \in \mathbf{s}$ with overlapping intervals, i.e., $r.T \cap s.T$. The overlap join gives the query optimizer an efficient option if other predicates are absent, exhibit a poor selectivity, or must be evaluated after the overlapping interval has been computed. For instance, to find employees who are employed during at least 5 months when a project is ongoing, we first must determine the overlapping interval between an employee and a project, and then check that the duration of the overlapping interval is at least 5 months. Our goal is an efficient join for interval data that offers the query optimizer a viable option when other joins do not perform well.

Partitioning techniques for interval data associate each partition with a *partition interval*. Each tuple is stored in the best fitting partition, i.e., the partition interval must cover the interval of the tuple, and there may not exist a smaller partition interval that covers the interval of the tuple. As an example, consider a partition p with partition interval [2012-1, 2012-4] and a tuple s with interval [2012-2, 2012-3]. Tuple s can be stored in partition p since 2012-2 $\geq$ 2012-1 and 2012-3 $\leq$ 2012-4, and it is indeed stored in p if and only if there is no other partition with a smaller partition interval that covers the interval of s. Since a partition interval is usually larger than the intervals of the tuples in this partition, we get *false hits* when searching in a partition for tuples that overlap a query interval (a false hit is a tuple that is fetched with a partition but does not contribute to the result). False hits increase the number of IOs, since more data must be fetched, and the number of CPU operations, since false hits must be detected and discarded. In order to reduce the number of false hits, it is possible to create more partitions. Many partitions, however, increase the number of IOs since we get more partially filled blocks. This increases the number of CPU operations for *searching and navigating* in the access structure.

This paper proposes the OIPJOIN, together with *Overlap Interval Partitioning* ($\mathcal{OIP}$), to efficiently compute the overlap join. $\mathcal{OIP}$ partitions the time range of a relation uniformly at a granularity that is given by k temporally disjoint granules of duration d. We create partitions for all sequences of adjacent granules. This approach gives a *constant clustering guarantee*, i.e., the difference in duration between a tuple and its partition is less than $2d$, independent of the duration of the tuple. The access structure of $\mathcal{OIP}$, termed *lazy partition list*, omits empty partitions without sacrificing performance or functionality. The OIPJOIN is *self-adjusting*, i.e, it automatically determines the optimal number of granules, k, that minimizes the overhead costs of the OIPJOIN.

Example 1. Figure 1 illustrates $\mathcal{OIP}$ with $k = 4$ granules for two relations **r** and **s**. The time range of **r** is [2012-5, 2012-11], and the granules have a duration of $\lceil \frac{\text{2012-11} - \text{2012-5} + 1}{4} \rceil = \lceil \frac{7}{4} \rceil = 2$ months. This is the granularity at which relation **r** is partitioned. The partitions span 2, 4, 6, or 8 months. Similarly, relation **s** is par-

SIGMOD'14, June 22–27, 2014, Snowbird, UT, USA.

ACM 978-1-4503-2376-5/14/06 ...$15.00.
http://dx.doi.org/10.1145/2588555.2612175.

titioned over its time range [2012-1, 2012-12]. The granules have a duration of 3 months, and the partitions span 3, 6, 9, or 12 months. For the OIPJOIN, $\mathbf{r} \bowtie_{\mathbf{r}.T \cap \mathbf{s}.T} \mathbf{s}$, we process for each partition in $\mathbf{r}$ the overlapping (relevant) partitions in $\mathbf{s}$. For instance, for the partition that contains r_1 and r_2, three partitions in s are processed, yielding three false hits, namely $\{s_6\}$ for r_1 and $\{s_3, s_5\}$ for r_2. For the partition that contains r_3, two partitions in s are processed, and there are no false hits. Overall, five partitions of s are accessed with three false hits and eight result tuples.

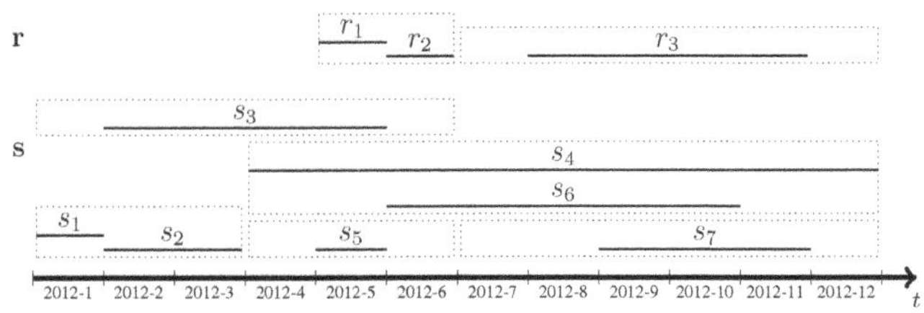

Figure 1: Sample Relations and $\mathcal{OIP}$.

False hits and partition accesses incur overhead costs for the OIPJOIN. The number of false hits and the number of partition accesses are inversely related. Increasing the number of granules k (i.e., shorter granules and more partitions) increases the number of partition accesses, but decreases the number of false hits, and vice versa. We analytically derive the k that minimizes the overhead costs by adapting to the size of the two relations, the cost of CPU operations, and the cost of IOs. Instead of assuming a dominating cost factor, we propose a cost model that accounts for CPU and IO costs. Note that IO costs can be memory IOs or disk IOs. A main memory IO is faster than a disk IO, but slower than a CPU operation [20]. Since data are transferred in chunks from the memory to the processor, it is favorable to store tuples in contiguous main memory blocks.

Summarizing, our technical contributions are as follows:

- We introduce $\mathcal{OIP}$ as partitioning strategy for the OIPJOIN. $\mathcal{OIP}$ offers a *constant clustering guarantee*, which ensures that the join does not deteriorate. The difference in duration between a tuple and its partition is less than two granules.
- We provide a detailed analysis of the *average false hit ratio* (AFR) and the *average number of partition accesses* (APA) for $\mathcal{OIP}$. We prove that AFR for uniformly distributed query intervals is smaller than $\frac{1}{k}$ and independent of the number of short- and long-lived tuples.
- The OIPJOIN is *self-adjusting*, i.e, it automatically determines the optimal number of granules k. We develop a cost function for the OIPJOIN and minimize this cost function to get the optimal number of granules k to partition the relations. k minimizes the overhead costs due to false hits and partition accesses for IO costs $c\_io \geq 0$ and CPU costs $c\_cpu \geq 0$.
- We describe an implementation of the OIPJOIN based on $\mathcal{OIP}$ and compare it with self-adjusting overlap joins based on quadtree, loose quadtree, segment tree, and relational interval tree. The experiments confirm that the OIPJOIN outperforms these approaches.

The rest of the paper is organized as follows. Section 2 discusses related work. Section 3 provides preliminaries. Section 4 describes overlap interval partitioning ($\mathcal{OIP}$) and its implementation. Section 5 analytically investigates the average false hit ratio (AFR) and the average number of partition accesses (APA) of $\mathcal{OIP}$. Section 6 describes the OIPJOIN and derives the optimal value for k. Section 7 reports the results of our empirical evaluation.

2. RELATED WORK

We describe, in turn, related work on (a) self-adjusting approaches that, as the OIPJOIN, adapt to the data and do not require user-specified parameters; (b) parameter-guided approaches that can/must be tuned with application-specific parameters; and (c) disk-based approaches that introduced some of the key concepts used in later works.

Self-Adjusting Approaches. The quadtree [10, 18] recursively subdivides the space into cells and places objects in the smallest enclosing cell.[1] Since split boundaries are propagated down the tree and objects are not allowed to overlap boundaries, small objects that overlap split boundaries end up high in the tree. Therefore the quadtree does not have a clustering guarantee. For instance, time range $[1, 32]$ is recursively split into $[1, 16]$ and $[17, 32]$ and so on, and a tuple with interval $[16, 17]$ is placed in the root. This yields many false hits for overlap predicates since all tree nodes that overlap the query interval need to be scanned. The quadtree relies on a hierarchical tree structure, and in order to navigate to nodes at lower levels, all parent nodes must be stored, even if they are empty. To avoid many partially filled blocks, density based splitting is used, which propagates tuples down the tree only when blocks are full. This, however, increases the number of false hits.

The loose quadtree [18, 19] addresses the limitations of the quadtree for small objects. It permits at each level partially overlapping cells. The amount of overlapping is determined by a user-specified cell expansion factor, $p > 0$, where $p = 1$ is widely accepted as the best value [23, 18]. An expanded cell has width $(1 + p) \cdot w$, where w is the width of a quadtree cell. For instance, time range $[1, 32]$ is recursively split into $[1, 24]$ and $[9, 32]$ and so on. A tuple with interval $[16, 17]$ is placed in either $[14, 17]$ or $[16, 19]$, which are the expanded quadtree cells for $[15, 16]$ and $[17, 18]$. The join performance deteriorates for long-lived tuples since the time ranges grow with a factor of two, i.e., the number of partitions for long-lived tuples is much lower than for small tuples. The loose quadtree provides a clustering guarantee that is not constant. The guarantee depends on the duration of a tuple and is weaker for longer tuples. For instance, for $p = 1$ and a relation that spans 2000 days, a tuple of duration 80 days can be in a partition that spans 250 days, yielding a difference of 170 days between the tuple and the associated partition. A tuple that spans 282 days can even be in a partition of 1000 days, which is a difference of 718 days.

The relational interval tree [14] implements Edelsbrunner's interval tree on top of a relational DBMS. The approach uses two B+-tree indices to index intervals according to a key and start point and end point. A query interval is first transformed into a key point list and a key range list, which in a second step are joined with the B+-tree indices. For instance, given an indexed time range of $[1, 64]$ and a query interval $[5, 7]$, the key point list is $\{32, 16, 8\}$ and the key range list $\{[4, 4], [5, 7]\}$. These lists are joined with the help of the two B+-tree indices to get the final result. Vari-

[1]In order to manage intervals with 2D access structures we omit the second dimension, which reduces 2D points and 2D rectangles to, respectively, 1D points and intervals.

ous join techniques based on the relational interval tree have been proposed [9], such as an Index-Based Loop Join and several partition based joins (Up-Down, Down-Down, Up-Up depending on tree traversal). In all these join techniques, long-lived tuples lead to many CPU operations since a large number of nodes must be joined. To get a better IO performance for block storage, the data can be clustered according to an index on either the start or the end points. Nevertheless, long-lived tuples deteriorate the performance since for long-lived tuples the clustering of the two indices varies more than for short-lived tuples.

The segment tree [4, 5] is an indexing technique for intervals. It builds disjoint segments (intervals) at the leaf level, using all start and end points in a relation. Internal nodes merge all segments of their children nodes. A tuple is associated with all sub-tree roots whose segment is completely covered by the tuple's interval. The segment tree efficiently retrieves all tuples that include a given time point. In order to compute an overlap join, possibly empty parent nodes must be scanned, and duplicated tuples that are assigned to multiple nodes must be fetched (IO cost) and identified (CPU cost). This is particularly expensive for long-lived tuples. For instance, for a relation with three tuples r_1, r_2, and r_3 with intervals $[1, 5]$, $[3, 9]$, and $[8, 9]$, respectively, we have at the leaf level (level 2) the four segments $[1, 2]$, $[3, 5]$, $[6, 7]$, and $[8, 9]$. At level 1, we have the segments $[1, 5]$ and $[6, 9]$, and at level 0 (root) the segment $[1, 9]$. Tuple r_2 is stored twice, namely in $[3, 5]$ and $[6, 9]$, and it must be read twice for the query interval $[5, 6]$.

Parameter-Guided Approaches. In [16], a spatially partitioned temporal join is proposed, where interval data is mapped to points in a two dimensional grid. Partitions are regions in the plane. Two relations are joined by determining for each partition of the outer relation the relevant partitions of the inner relation. Two implementations are proposed, namely to store partitions physically on disk blocks or to use spatial indices to index the regions of partitions. While existing spatial indices can be reused, long-lived tuples substantially increase the number of index nodes to scan. The number of partitions must be specified by the application.

The snapshot index [22] is an access method for disk resident transaction-time databases. Intervals in transaction-time databases are clustered since database modifications occur in increasing time order. Blocks are distinguished by usefulness according to an application parameter a that indicates the number of false hits a block is allowed to generate. Long-lived tuples are artificially deleted and re-inserted using controlled splits. Splitting is not a general solution for valid-time databases since it changes the meaning of tuples [8, 7]. Parameter a must be chosen as a tradeoff between artificial splits and false hits.

In [17], an approach is proposed for data that is stored in main memory. It is similar to the spatial hash join [15] and uses an R-Tree to group tuples into minimum bounding rectangles (MBRs). The tuples of one relation are stored in the leaf nodes, and the tuples of the other relation in the lowest internal node, where more than one child's MBR overlaps the tuple. The join is performed by joining leaf with internal nodes. The approach aims to reduce the number of CPU comparisons and requires three parameters: tree fanout, number of partitions, and cells per dimension.

Disk-Based Approaches. The size separation spatial join [13] is a partitioning strategy for the overlap join of disk resident spatial data and is similar to the quadtree. Instead of using a tree structure, the levels of the tree are mapped to sorted files. The join is then performed by a synchronized scan of two sorted files that represent the partitioned relations. The approach reduces IO and provides a good filling of blocks, but, due to the recursive space division, small objects are not guaranteed to be stored at a low level. Thus, the size separation spatial join has no clustering guarantee and may produce many false hits.

The grace partition join [21] is used for valid-time natural joins of disk resident data, i.e., overlap joins with additional equality predicates. It samples the relations to determine the partitions for the tuple intervals. A tuple is stored in the last partition it overlaps. Partitions are joined from the last to the first partition. Long-lived tuples that overlap several partitions are migrated to the next partition during join processing. The approach is only efficient for few long-lived tuples, where the overhead of migration is low.

The R*-tree [2, 3] uses MBRs to group nearby objects and stores object IDs in the leaf nodes. The internal nodes build an index on the leaf nodes using MBRs. MBRs of both leaf and internal nodes might overlap. The tree is expensive to construct due to the propagation of MBRs. Long-lived tuples increase the MBRs and produce more false hits (page faults). For overlap joins, it is necessary to follow multiple paths in the R*-tree.

3. PRELIMINARIES

We assume a discrete time domain, Ω^T, consisting of a linearly ordered set of time points. An interval T is a contiguous set of time points and is represented as a pair $[T_S, T_E]$, where T_S is the inclusive start point and T_E the inclusive end point. We use the following operations on time points and intervals: $x \in T$ if time point x is contained in interval T, i.e., $T_S \leq x \leq T_E$; $Q \cap T$ if Q and T intersect, i.e., there exists a time point x such that $x \in Q \wedge x \in T$; $T \subseteq U$ if interval T is contained in interval U, i.e., $\forall x \in T \Rightarrow x \in U$; $T_E - T_S$ determines the difference in number of time points between T_S and T_E; $T_S + x$ shifts time point T_S by x time points to the right, i.e., $T_E - T_S = x \Rightarrow T_S + x = T_E$; and $|T| = (T_E - T_S) + 1$ is the duration (length) of interval T.

We use tuple timestamping and associate each tuple with a single interval that represents the tuple's valid time. A temporal relation schema is represented as $R = (A_1, \dots A_m, T)$, where $A_1 \dots A_m$ are attributes with domain Ω_i and T is the interval attribute over $\Omega^T \times \Omega^T$. A tuple r over schema R is a finite set that contains for every A_i a value $v_i \in \Omega_i$ and for T an interval $[T_S, T_E] \in \Omega^T \times \Omega^T$. A temporal relation $\mathbf{r}$ over schema R is a finite set of tuples over R. A valid-time relation $\mathbf{r}$ spans time range $U = [U_S, U_E]$ if U_S is the smallest start time point of any tuple in $\mathbf{r}$ and U_E the largest end time point of any tuple in $\mathbf{r}$. We write l for the duration of the longest tuple in a relation $\mathbf{r}$, and λ for the duration of the longest tuple as a fraction of the time range, i.e., $\lambda = l/|U|$. We use indices r and s to distinguish between the outer and inner relation in joins, e.g., n_r and n_s are, respectively, the cardinality of the outer and inner relation in $\mathbf{r} \bowtie \mathbf{s}$.

4. OVERLAP INTERVAL PARTITIONING

In this section, we first define Overlap Interval Partitioning ($\mathcal{OIP}$) and show how the relevant partitions, i.e., partitions that overlap a query interval, are calculated. Second, we establish the constant clustering guarantee. Third, we show how to manage physical partitions of $\mathcal{OIP}$ with a lazy partition list that omits unused partitions.

4.1 Definition

$\mathcal{OIP}$ divides a time range U into k equally sized granules of duration d, which define the base granularity of the partitioning (we discuss in Section 6.2 how to derive k).

Definition 1. (*OIP Configuration*) Let $\mathbf{r}$ be a temporal relation with time range $U = [U_S, U_E]$. An *OIP configuration* for a given k is a triple (k, d, o), where $d = \lceil \frac{|U|}{k} \rceil$ is the duration of each granule and $o = U_S$ is the start point of the partitioned time range.

A partition interval spans a sequence of one or more adjacent granules. A tuple is assigned to the smallest partition whose partition interval completely covers the tuple's interval.

Definition 2. (*OIP Partition*) Let $\mathbf{r}$ be a temporal relation with $\mathcal{OIP}$ configuration (k, d, o). An *OIP partition*, $p_{i,j}$, with $0 \leq i \leq j < k$, spans all granules from i to j and has the partition interval $p_{i,j}.T = [o + i \cdot d, o + (j+1) \cdot d - 1]$. A tuple $r \in \mathbf{r}$ is placed in partition $p_{i,j}$ iff $\lfloor \frac{r.T_S - o}{d} \rfloor = i$ and $\lfloor \frac{r.T_E - o}{d} \rfloor = j$.

Example 2. Relation $\mathbf{s}$ in Figure 2 includes seven tuples and spans the time range $U = [2012\text{-}1, 2012\text{-}12]$. The $\mathcal{OIP}$ configuration with $k = 4$ granules is $(4, 3, 2012\text{-}1)$ with granule duration $d = \lceil \frac{|U|}{k} \rceil = \lceil \frac{12}{4} \rceil = 3$ months and start time point $o = U_S = 2012\text{-}1$. The partitions that span one granule are $p_{0,0}$, $p_{1,1}$, $p_{2,2}$, and $p_{3,3}$, each ranging over three months. The partitions $p_{0,1}$, $p_{0,2}$, $p_{0,3}$, $p_{1,2}$, $p_{1,3}$, and $p_{2,3}$ span more than one granule each, e.g., partition $p_{0,1}$ spans the range $[2012\text{-}1, 2012\text{-}6]$. Tuple s_1 is placed in partition $p_{0,0}$ since $\lfloor \frac{s_1.T_S - o}{d} \rfloor = \lfloor \frac{2012\text{-}1 - 2012\text{-}1}{3} \rfloor = \lfloor \frac{0}{3} \rfloor = 0$ and $\lfloor \frac{s_1.T_E - o}{d} \rfloor = \lfloor \frac{2012\text{-}1 - 2012\text{-}1}{3} \rfloor = \lfloor \frac{0}{3} \rfloor = 0$. Tuple s_6 is placed in partition $p_{1,3}$ since $\lfloor \frac{s_6.T_S - o}{d} \rfloor = \lfloor \frac{2012\text{-}6 - 2012\text{-}1}{3} \rfloor = \lfloor \frac{5}{3} \rfloor = 1$ and $\lfloor \frac{s_6.T_E - o}{d} \rfloor = \lfloor \frac{2012\text{-}10 - 2012\text{-}1}{3} \rfloor = \lfloor \frac{9}{3} \rfloor = 3$. Five out of ten partitions are empty, namely $p_{0,3}$, $p_{0,2}$, $p_{1,2}$, $p_{2,2}$, and $p_{3,3}$.

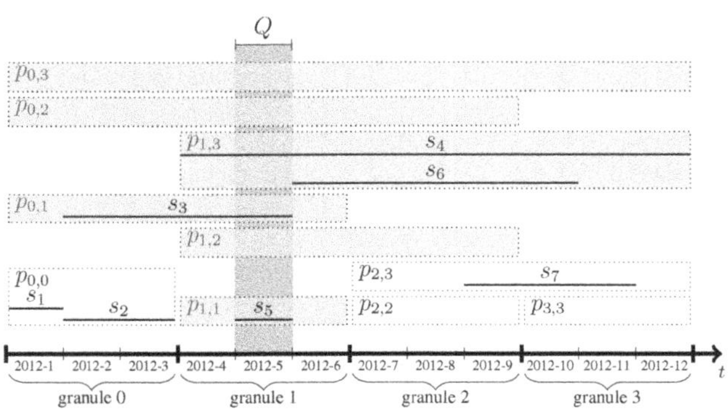

Figure 2: $\mathcal{OIP}$ with Configuration $(4, 3, 2012\text{-}1)$ for s.

LEMMA 1 ($\mathcal{OIP}$ OVERLAP QUERY) *Let (k, d, o) be an $\mathcal{OIP}$ configuration and $Q = [Q_S, Q_E]$ be a query interval. The candidate tuples that possibly overlap Q are in partitions $p_{i,j}$ for which $i \leq e = \lfloor \frac{Q_E - o}{d} \rfloor$ and $j \geq s = \lfloor \frac{Q_S - o}{d} \rfloor$. We term these partitions the* relevant partitions*; s is the start and e the end index of Q.*

PROOF. (By contradiction) Assume a partition $p_{i,j}$ with $j < s = \lfloor \frac{Q_S - o}{d} \rfloor$, which contains a tuple r that overlaps Q. According to Definition 2, tuple r is placed in a partition $p_{i,j}$ with $i = \lfloor \frac{r.T_S - o}{d} \rfloor$ and $j = \lfloor \frac{r.T_E - o}{d} \rfloor$. Since $j < s$, we get $r.T_E < Q_S$, i.e., $r.T$ and Q do not overlap, which contradicts our assumption. Similarly, a tuple in $p_{i,j}$ with $i > e = \lfloor \frac{Q_E - o}{d} \rfloor$ cannot overlap Q since $r.T_S > Q_E$. $\square$

Example 3. Consider Figure 2 with the $\mathcal{OIP}$ configuration $(4, 3, 2012\text{-}1)$ and the query interval $Q = [2012\text{-}5, 2012\text{-}5]$. For the relevant partitions, $p_{i,j}$, the following constraints hold: $i \leq e = \lfloor \frac{Q_E - o}{d} \rfloor = \lfloor \frac{2012\text{-}5 - 2012\text{-}1}{3} \rfloor = \lfloor \frac{4}{3} \rfloor = 1$ and $j \geq s = \lfloor \frac{Q_S - o}{d} \rfloor = \lfloor \frac{2012\text{-}5 - 2012\text{-}1}{3} \rfloor = \lfloor \frac{4}{3} \rfloor = 1$. This is satisfied for partitions $p_{0,3}$, $p_{0,2}$, $p_{0,1}$, $p_{1,3}$, $p_{1,2}$, and $p_{1,1}$ (gray boxes), which contain all candidate tuples for the query interval Q.

Next, we establish the *constant clustering guarantee* of $\mathcal{OIP}$: the difference in duration between a tuple and its partition is less than two granules, i.e., constant and independent of the duration of a tuple. Note that the number of time points per granule or the duration of a granule have no impact on our solution. The constant clustering guarantee ensures (a) an excellent partitioning since the difference in duration between a tuple and its partitions is less than two granules, (b) an average false hit ratio that is independent of the intervals of tuples (cf. Section 5.1), and (c) it allows to take advantage of empty partitions by increasing k (cf. Section 6.2).

LEMMA 2 (CONSTANT CLUSTERING GUARANTEE) *Let (k, d, o) be an $\mathcal{OIP}$ configuration for relation $\mathbf{r}$. The difference in duration between a tuple $r \in \mathbf{r}$ and its partition p is less than $2d$:*

$$\forall r \in \mathbf{r} (r \in p \Rightarrow |p.T| - |r.T| < 2d).$$

PROOF. We show that the difference in duration of the smallest tuple in a partition $p_{i,j}$ and $p_{i,j}$ is less than $2d$. A tuple r is placed in partition $p_{i,j}$ iff $i = \lfloor \frac{r.T_S - o}{d} \rfloor$ and $j = \lfloor \frac{r.T_E - o}{d} \rfloor$ (cf. Definition 2). Thus, we have $i \cdot d \leq r.T_S - o \leq (i+1)d - 1$ and $j \cdot d \leq r.T_E - o \leq (j+1)d - 1$. The smallest tuple in $p_{i,j}$ has duration $|[(i+1)d - 1, j \cdot d]| = j \cdot d - (i+1)d + 2$, and $p_{i,j}$ has duration $|[i \cdot d, (j+1)d - 1]| = (j+1)d - i \cdot d$. Hence, the difference in duration between the smallest tuple r in $p_{i,j}$ and $p_{i,j}$ is $2d - 2 < 2d$. $\square$

For instance, for a relation that spans 2000 days and with $k = 200$, we have $d = 10$ days. A tuple that spans 80 days can be in a partition that spans 90 days, which is a difference of 10 days. A tuple that spans 282 days can be in a partition that spans 300 days, which is a difference of 18 days. Note that the difference is always less than $2d = 20$ days.

4.2 Lazy Partitioning

We represent the $\mathcal{OIP}$ access structure as a triangle in a distance regular square grid graph [6], as illustrated in Figure 3(a) for the $\mathcal{OIP}$ in Figure 2. We call this a *triangular grid graph* with grid points (i, j) for $0 \leq i \leq j < k$. To find all relevant partitions for a query interval with start index s and end index e, we determine all partitions $p_{i,j}$ for which $j \geq s$ and $i \leq e$ (cf. Lemma 1). We start at the top-left corner of the grid (i.e., $i = 0, j = k-1 = 3$) and move along the path with decreasing j as long as $j \geq s$. At each node $p_{0,j}$, we follow the path with increasing i as long as $i \leq min(j, e)$. In Figure 3(a), the relevant partitions (gray) for query interval Q are on the paths $p_{0,3} \rightarrow p_{1,3}$, $p_{0,2} \rightarrow p_{1,2}$ and $p_{0,1} \rightarrow p_{1,1}$.

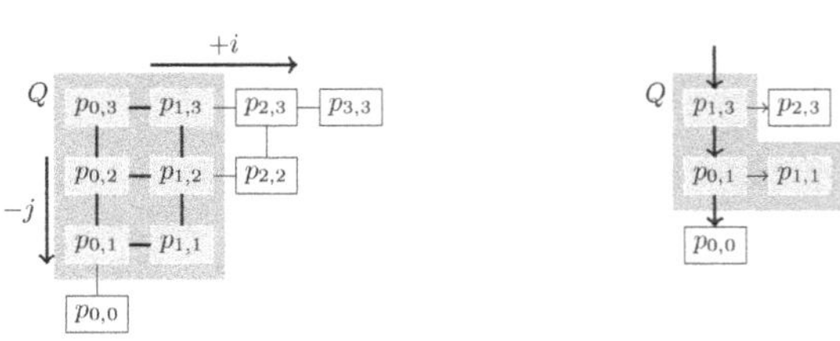

(a) Triangular Grid Graph. (b) Lazy Partition List.

Figure 3: Management of $\mathcal{OIP}$ Partitions.

The number of possible $\mathcal{OIP}$ partitions corresponds to the number of nodes in a triangular grid graph and grows quadratically with the number of granules k.

PROPOSITION 1 (NUMBER OF PARTITIONS) *For k granules, the number of possible partitions is $|\mathbf{p}| = \sum_{i=0}^{k-1}(k-i) = \frac{k^2+k}{2}$.*

The *lazy partition list* is a compressed triangular grid graph that includes only non-empty partitions. Figure 3(b) shows the lazy partition list of our example. It includes only the non-empty partitions and the directed edges that are needed for navigation. The *main list* starts at the upper-left corner and connects nodes with decreasing j from top to bottom. Each node of the main list starts a *branch list* that connects (from left to right) nodes with the same j-value and increasing i-value.

The lazy partition list has the following advantages: (a) the number of CPU operations is reduced since empty partitions do not appear in the access structure; (b) k can be increased if not all partitions are used (cf. Section 5.2 and Section 6.2); and (c) the number of partitions is upper bounded by the cardinality of the partitioned relation, independent of the value of k.

LEMMA 3 (NUMBER OF PARTITIONS WITH LAZY PARTITIONING) *Assume an $\mathcal{OIP}$ configuration (k, d, o) for a relation $\mathbf{r}$ with n tuples whose valid time duration is at most λ. The number of partitions, $|\mathbf{p}|$, of $\mathcal{OIP}$ for $\mathbf{r}$ is upper bounded by $min(k\lceil\lambda \cdot k\rceil + k - \frac{\lceil\lambda \cdot k\rceil^2}{2} - \frac{\lceil\lambda \cdot k\rceil}{2}, n)$.*

PROOF. Tuples in $\mathbf{r}$ span at most $\lceil\lambda \cdot k\rceil$ granules. From Lemma 2 we have that the difference in duration of a partition and its tuples is less than two granules. Thus, the longest used partition spans at most $\lceil\lambda \cdot k\rceil + 1$ granules, and we have $|\mathbf{p}| \leq \sum_{x=0}^{\lceil\lambda \cdot k\rceil+1-1}(k-x) = k\lceil\lambda \cdot k\rceil + k - \frac{\lceil\lambda \cdot k\rceil^2}{2} - \frac{\lceil\lambda \cdot k\rceil}{2}$. Since empty partitions are not created, $|\mathbf{p}|$ cannot exceed n. □

Example 4. Assume a relation with tuple durations up to 20% of the relation's time range, i.e., $\lambda = 0.2$. With $k = 200$, at most $200\lceil 0.2 \cdot 200\rceil + 200 - \frac{\lceil 0.2 \cdot 200\rceil^2}{2} - \frac{\lceil 0.2 \cdot 200\rceil}{2} = 7,380$ partitions out of $\frac{200^2+200}{2} = 20,100$ possible partitions are used, i.e., 37%, while 63% are empty.

4.3 Implementation of $\mathcal{OIP}$

Our implementation of $\mathcal{OIP}$ uses a lazy partition list, $\mathcal{L}$, to keep track of indices and storage blocks of partitions. Figure 4 shows the lazy partition list for our running example.

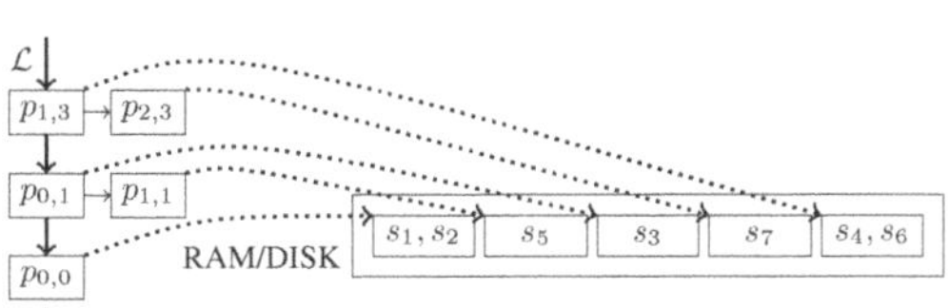

Figure 4: $\mathcal{OIP}$ Lazy Partition List $\mathcal{L}$ with Block Pointers.

Algorithm 1 creates the lazy partition list $\mathcal{L}$ for an input relation $\mathbf{r}$ with n tuples and an $\mathcal{OIP}$ configuration (k, d, o). After initializing an empty partition list, the relation is sorted according to the tuples' partition $p_{i,j}$ with j in ascending and i in descending order. The indices i and j of the partition to which a tuple r is assigned are computed according to Definition 2. The sorting ensures that tuples fall either into the first node of the list ($c = nil \vee c.j < j$) or into a new node that is prepended to $\mathcal{L}.head$ ($c.i > i$). The sorting reduces the complexity of insertions from $O(k)$ to $O(1)$ and gives a total runtime complexity for constructing $\mathcal{L}$ of $O(n \log n)$, which is independent of k and ensures that storage blocks are allocated sequentially.

Algorithm 1: OIPCREATE (r, (k,d,o))

Input: Relation $\mathbf{r}$ and $\mathcal{OIP}$ configuration (k, d, o)
Output: Partition list $\mathcal{L}$

$\mathcal{L}$:= empty partition list;
Sort $\mathbf{r}$ by $\lfloor\frac{r.T_E - o}{d}\rfloor$ ASC and $\lfloor\frac{r.T_S - o}{d}\rfloor$ DESC;
foreach $r \in \mathbf{r}$ **do**
  $i := \lfloor\frac{r.T_S - o}{d}\rfloor$;
  $j := \lfloor\frac{r.T_E - o}{d}\rfloor$;
  $c := \mathcal{L}.head$;
  if $c = nil \vee c.j < j$ **then**
    $\mathcal{L}.head :=$ new node with partition $p_{i,j}$;
    $\mathcal{L}.head.down := c$;
  else if $c.i > i$ **then**
    $\mathcal{L}.head :=$ new node with partition $p_{i,j}$;
    $\mathcal{L}.head.down := c.down$;
    $\mathcal{L}.head.right := c$;
  Add r to $\mathcal{L}.head$;
return $\mathcal{L}$;

Example 5. Consider relation $\mathbf{s}$ in Figure 2. The call of OIPCREATE (s, (4,3,2012-1)) constructs $\mathcal{L}$[2] as follows:

1. $\mathbf{r} = sort(\mathbf{s}) = \langle s_1, s_2, s_5, s_3, s_7, s_4, s_6\rangle$, $\mathcal{L} = \langle\rangle$
2. $r = s_1$, $i = \lfloor\frac{2012\text{-}1 - 2012\text{-}1}{3}\rfloor = 0$, $j = \lfloor\frac{2012\text{-}1 - 2012\text{-}1}{3}\rfloor = 0$, $\mathcal{L} = \langle\langle(0, 0, \{s_1\})\rangle\rangle$
3. $r = s_2$, $i = \lfloor\frac{2012\text{-}2 - 2012\text{-}1}{3}\rfloor = 0$, $j = \lfloor\frac{2012\text{-}3 - 2012\text{-}1}{3}\rfloor = 0$, $\mathcal{L} = \langle\langle(0, 0, \{s_1, s_2\})\rangle\rangle$
4. $r = s_5$, $i = \lfloor\frac{2012\text{-}5 - 2012\text{-}1}{3}\rfloor = 1$, $j = \lfloor\frac{2012\text{-}5 - 2012\text{-}1}{3}\rfloor = 1$, $\mathcal{L} = \langle\langle(1, 1, \{s_5\})\rangle, \langle(0, 0, \{s_1, s_2\})\rangle\rangle$
5. $r = s_3$, $i = \lfloor\frac{2012\text{-}2 - 2012\text{-}1}{3}\rfloor = 0$, $j = \lfloor\frac{2012\text{-}5 - 2012\text{-}1}{3}\rfloor = 1$, $\mathcal{L} = \langle\langle(0, 1, \{s_3\}), (1, 1, \{s_5\})\rangle, \langle(0, 0, \{s_1, s_2\})\rangle\rangle$

The algorithm terminates and returns the lazy partition list $\mathcal{L} = \langle\langle(1, 3, \{s_4, s_6\}), (2, 3, \{s_7\})\rangle, \langle(0, 1, \{s_3\}), (1, 1, \{s_5\})\rangle, \langle(0, 0, \{s_1, s_2\})\rangle\rangle$, which is illustrated in Figure 4.

5. ANALYTICAL RESULTS OF $\mathcal{OIP}$

In this section, we analyze the quality of $\mathcal{OIP}$ using two different measures. The *average false hit ratio*, AFR, measures the precision of a partitioning in terms of the average number of tuples that are retrieved for a query interval but do not contribute to the result. The *average number of partition accesses*, APA, quantifies the number of partitions that are fetched for a query.

5.1 Average False Hit Ratio

Definition 3. (*False Hits*) Let P be a partitioning of a valid-time relation $\mathbf{r}$ and Q be a query interval. The *false hits*, $\mathsf{F}(P, Q)$, are the tuples that are retrieved when fetching the relevant partitions, but are not part of the query result, i.e.,

$$\mathsf{F}(P, Q) = \{r \mid \exists p \in P(r \in p \wedge p.T \cap Q \wedge \neg(r.T \cap Q))\}.$$

Consider Figure 2. For the query interval $Q = [2012\text{-}5, 2012\text{-}5]$, only the relevant partitions are fetched (i.e., $p_{1,1}$, $p_{0,1}$, $p_{1,3}$). The false hits are $\mathsf{F}(\mathcal{OIP}, Q) = \{s_6\}$ since partition $p_{1,3}$ is fetched, but s_6 does not overlap Q. The result tuples are s_3, s_4, and s_5.

[2]We use nested lists as an abstract notation. For instance, $\mathcal{L} = \langle\langle a\rangle, \langle b, c\rangle\rangle$ has nodes a, b, c; $\mathcal{L}.head = a$; $a.down = b$; $b.right = c$; $a.right$, $b.down$, $c.down$, and $c.right$ are nil.

We proceed by defining the sum false hit ratio as the percentage of false hits over all possible point queries, i.e., the false hits produced by all queries over query intervals of duration 1 divided by the total number of tuples.

Definition 4. (*Sum False Hit Ratio*) Let P be a partitioning of a valid-time relation $\mathbf{r}$ with time range U. The *sum false hit ratio*, $\mathsf{SFR}(P)$, for all query intervals $[x, x]$ that overlap U is defined as

$$\mathsf{SFR}(P) = \frac{\sum_{x \in U} |\mathsf{F}(P, [x, x])|}{|\mathbf{r}|}.$$

For the $\mathcal{OIP}$ shown in Figure 2, we have $\mathsf{SFR}(\mathcal{OIP}) = \frac{|\mathsf{F}(\mathcal{OIP}, [2012\text{-}1, 2012\text{-}1])| + \dots + |\mathsf{F}(\mathcal{OIP}, [2012\text{-}12, 2012\text{-}12])|}{7} = \frac{14}{7} = 2$. Thus, for all query intervals of duration 1, two times the number of tuples in $\mathbf{s}$ are retrieved as false hits.

LEMMA 4. *The sum false hit ratio of a partitioning P over a time range U is independent of the query interval duration q, i.e., it is the same for all query intervals $[x, x+q-1]$ that overlap U for any value of q:*

$$\mathsf{SFR}(P) = \frac{\sum_{x \in U} |\mathsf{F}(P, [x, x])|}{|\mathbf{r}|} = \frac{\sum_{Q: Q \cap U \wedge |Q| = q} |\mathsf{F}(P, Q)|}{|\mathbf{r}|}.$$

PROOF. Consider a time point $x \in U$ and a partition $p \in P$. Query interval $[x, x]$ of duration 1 can produce false hits in p if there is a non-overlapping part before x (i.e., $p.T_S < x$) and/or a non-overlapping part after x (i.e., $x < p.T_E$). All tuples that start and end in one of the two non-overlapping parts are false hits. We consider now query intervals of duration $q > 1$. The query interval $[x, x+q-1]$ produces the same non-overlapping part before x, and the query interval $[x-q+1, x]$ the same non-overlapping part after x, yielding together exactly the same false hits for partition p as the point query with interval $[x, x]$. Since for each x there exists exactly one query interval of duration q that starts at x and one that ends at x, it is straightforward to generalize this result to the sum over all partitions and time points in U. This proves the lemma. □

Next, we define the average false hit ratio for an arbitrary query interval of duration $q \geq 1$.

Definition 5. (*Average False Hit Ratio*) Let P be a partitioning for a relation $\mathbf{r}$ with time range U. The *average false hit ratio*, $\mathsf{AFR}(P)$, for a query interval duration q is defined as

$$\mathsf{AFR}(P) = \frac{\mathsf{SFR}(P)}{|U| + q - 1}.$$

PROPOSITION 2. *The* $\mathsf{AFR}(P)$ *decreases monotonically with increasing query interval duration q.*

Example 6. Consider Figure 2 with the time range $U = [2012\text{-}1, 2012\text{-}12]$ and the sum false hit ratio $\mathsf{SFR}(\mathcal{OIP}) = 2$. The number of query intervals of duration $q = 1$ is $|U| + q - 1 = 12$, yielding an average false hit ratio $\mathsf{AFR}(\mathcal{OIP}) = 2 \cdot \frac{1}{12}$ $(= 16.7\%)$, i.e., on average 16.7% of the fetched tuples are false hits. The number of query intervals of duration $q = 5$ is $|U| + q - 1 = 16$, yielding an average false hit ratio $\mathsf{AFR}(\mathcal{OIP}) = 2 \cdot \frac{1}{16}$ $(= 12.5\%)$.

For the analysis of the average false hit ratio of $\mathcal{OIP}$ in the following Theorem 1, we use duration complete relations. A *duration complete relation*, $\mathbf{r}^l_U$, contains exactly one tuple for each interval up to a duration l in the time range U, i.e.,

$$\forall T \subseteq U(|T| \leq l \Rightarrow \exists r \in \mathbf{r}^l_U(r.T = T)),$$
$$\forall r \in \mathbf{r}^l_U(|r.T| \leq l),$$
$$\forall r, r' \in \mathbf{r}^l_U(r \neq r' \Rightarrow r.T \neq r'.T).$$

For instance, the duration complete relation $\mathbf{r}^2_{[0,3]}$ contains a total of seven tuples with intervals $[0, 0]$, $[1, 1]$, $[2, 2]$, $[3, 3]$, $[0, 1]$, $[1, 2]$, $[2, 3]$. Duration complete relations ensure that the AFR is calculated over tuples of all possible positions and durations in U.

THEOREM 1. *Assume an $\mathcal{OIP}$ with configuration (k, d, o). The average false hit ratio for duration complete relations is independent of the duration of the tuples and upper bounded by*

$$\mathsf{AFR}(\mathcal{OIP}) < \frac{1}{k}.$$

The proof of Theorem 1 is provided in the Appendix.

5.2 Average Number of Partition Accesses

The *average number of partition accesses*, APA, quantifies how many partitions are accessed on average to retrieve all tuples that overlap a query interval, i.e., how many relevant partitions exist.

LEMMA 5 (APA UPPER BOUND) *Assume an $\mathcal{OIP}$ with configuration (k, d, o), where all partitions are used. The average number of partition accesses for query intervals with uniformly distributed start and end time points is:*

$$\mathsf{APA}(\mathcal{OIP}) \leq \frac{k^2 + k + 1}{3}.$$

PROOF. For query intervals with uniformly distributed start and end time points, every query interval starting in granule s and ending in granule e has the same probability. Thus, we need to compute the number of partitions that a query interval accesses when starting in s and ending in e, which is the total number of partitions minus all partitions ending before s and all partitions starting after e as follows:

$$\#acc(s, e) = \frac{k^2 + k}{2} - \sum_{i=0}^{s-1}(s - i) - \sum_{i=0}^{k-e-1}(k - e - 1 - i)$$
$$= k + k \cdot e - \frac{s^2 + s}{2} - \frac{e^2 + e}{2}.$$

We sum the number of partition accesses, $\#acc(s, e)$, for all $s \leq e < k$ and divide the sum by the cardinality of $s \leq e < k$ to get:

$$\mathsf{APA}(\mathcal{OIP}) = \frac{\sum_{e=0}^{k-1} \sum_{s=0}^{e} (\#acc(s, e))}{\sum_{e=0}^{k-1} \sum_{s=0}^{e} (1)} = \frac{k^2 + k + 1}{3}.$$

□

Since empty partitions are not present in the $\mathcal{OIP}$ access structure, APA is reduced if not all partitions are used. We use a tightening factor to quantify the reduction of partitions with lazy partitioning. The *tightening factor*, τ, with $0 < \tau \leq 1$, is calculated as the ratio between the number of used partitions with lazy partitioning (Lemma 3) and the total number of partitions (Proposition 1). For instance, the tightening factor in Example 4 is $\tau = 1890/5050 = 0.37$.

THEOREM 2 (APA) *Assume an $\mathcal{OIP}$ configuration (k, d, o) for a relation with n tuples and a tightening factor τ with $0 < \tau \leq 1$. The average number of partition accesses is:*

$$\mathsf{APA}(\mathcal{OIP}) \leq min(\tau \cdot \frac{k^2 + k + 1}{3}, n).$$

PROOF. The proof follows from Lemma 5 and Lemma 3. The tightening factor τ is the ratio of the number of used and the number of possible partitions. The inequality holds since the multiplication with τ conservatively assumes that the longest partitions, which produce more partition accesses than shorter partitions, are omitted. □

6. THE OVERLAP JOIN OIPJOIN

This section presents the OIPJOIN algorithm, derives the optimal number of granules k, illustrates its calculation by an example, and analyzes the runtime complexity of the OIPJOIN.

6.1 The OIPJOIN Algorithm

Algorithm 2 computes the OIPJOIN for relations $\mathbf{r}$ and $\mathbf{s}$. First, k (cf. Section 6.2) and the $\mathcal{OIP}$ configurations of the two relations are determined. The partitions are created by calling OIPCREATE, and the result relation $\mathbf{z}$ is initialized. Then, the algorithm iterates over each outer partition in $\mathcal{L}_r$ and performs an overlap query (cf. Lemma 1) with the query interval $[Q_S, Q_E]$ of the outer partition (cf. Definition 2). If $[Q_S, Q_E]$ does not overlap the time range of the inner relation $\mathbf{s}$, the outer partition is skipped. Otherwise, the indices s and e of the query interval $[Q_S, Q_E]$ are determined. The relevant partitions of the inner relation that overlap with the query interval are fetched, and the tuples are joined with the tuples in the outer partition. The result tuples are collected in $\mathbf{z}$.

Algorithm 2: OIPJOIN $(\mathbf{r}, \mathbf{s})$

```
Input: Relation r and relation s
Output: z = {r ∘ s | r ∈ r ∧ s ∈ s ∧ r.T ∩ s.T}
Determine k for r and s for given IO and CPU costs;
Determine configurations (k, d_r, o_r) for r and (k, d_s, o_s) for s;
L_r ← OIPCREATE(r, (k, d_r, o_r));
L_s ← OIPCREATE(s, (k, d_s, o_s));
z := ∅;
foreach node c_r in L_r do
    Q_S := o_r + c_r.i · d_r;
    Q_E := o_r + (c_r.j + 1) · d_r − 1;
    if Q_E ≥ o_s ∧ Q_S < o_s + k · d_s then
        s := ⌊(Q_S − o_s) / d_s⌋;
        e := ⌊(Q_E − o_s) / d_s⌋;
        c_s := L_s.head;
        while c_s ≠ nil ∧ c_s.j ≥ s do
            x := c_s;
            while x ≠ nil ∧ x.i ≤ e do
                z := z ∪ { joined tuples from c_r and x};
                x := x.right;
            c_s := c_s.down;
return z;
```

Example 7. Consider Figure 1 with $k = 4$. We get the $\mathcal{OIP}$ configurations (4, 2, 2012-5) for $\mathbf{r}$ and (4, 3, 2012-1) for $\mathbf{s}$. OIPCREATE creates the lazy partition lists $\mathcal{L}_r = \langle\langle(1,3,\{r_3\})\rangle, \langle(0,0,\{r_1,r_2\})\rangle\rangle$ and $\mathcal{L}_s = \langle\langle(1,3,\{s_4,s_6\}),(2,3,\{s_7\})\rangle, \langle(0,1,\{s_3\}),(1,1,\{s_5\})\rangle, \langle(0,0,\{s_1,s_2\})\rangle\rangle$. The first outer partition is processed as follows:

$$
\begin{aligned}
c_r &= (1,3,\{r_3\})\\
&\quad Q_S = \text{2012-5} + 1\cdot 2 = \text{2012-7}\\
&\quad Q_E = \text{2012-5} + (3+1)\cdot 2 - 1 = \text{2012-12}\\
&\qquad s = \lfloor \tfrac{\text{2012-7}-\text{2012-1}}{3} \rfloor = \lfloor \tfrac{6}{3} \rfloor = 2\\
&\qquad e = \lfloor \tfrac{\text{2012-12}-\text{2012-1}}{3} \rfloor = \lfloor \tfrac{11}{3} \rfloor = 3\\
&\qquad c_s = \mathcal{L}_s.head = (1,3,\{s_4,s_6\})\\
&\qquad\quad x = c_s = (1,3,\{s_4,s_6\})\\
&\qquad\qquad \mathbf{z} = \{r_3 \circ s_4, r_3 \circ s_6\}\\
&\qquad\quad x = x.right = (2,3,\{s_7\})\\
&\qquad\qquad \mathbf{z} = \{r_3 \circ s_4, r_3 \circ s_6, r_3 \circ s_7\}\\
&\qquad c_s = c_s.down = (0,1,\{s_3\})
\end{aligned}
$$

The second (and last) outer partition, $c_r = (0,0,\{r_1,r_2\})$, is processed in a similar way, yielding the final result $\mathbf{z} = \{r_3 \circ s_4, r_3 \circ s_6, r_3 \circ s_7, r_1 \circ s_3, r_1 \circ s_4, r_1 \circ s_5, r_2 \circ s_4, r_2 \circ s_6\}$.

6.2 Number of Granules k

Choosing k (i.e., the number of granules) is the most important decision for the OIPJOIN. In order to derive k for the outer and the inner relation, we proceed in two steps. First, we provide a cost function for the OIPJOIN, and second, we minimize the cost function with respect to k.

Cost Function. The cost function considers the CPU cost of a comparison operation (*c_cpu*) and the cost of a block IO (*c_io*). A block IO can refer to either main memory or disk. The cost function models the *overhead* due to partition accesses and false hits. Recall that the cost for creating the partitioning is, due to sorting, independent of k and thus not included in the cost function.

Let k_r and k_s be the number of granules for the outer and inner relation, respectively. For the join we fetch, for each of the $O(k_r^2)$ outer partitions, $O(k_s^2)$ inner partitions, i.e., $O(k_r^2 \cdot k_s^2)$. Furthermore, for each outer and inner tuple we have, respectively, $O(\frac{n_s}{k_s})$ and $O(\frac{n_r}{k_r})$ false hits, i.e., $O(n_s \cdot \frac{n_r}{k_r} + n_r \cdot \frac{n_s}{k_s})$. Both, $O(k_r^2 \cdot k_s^2)$ and $O(n_s \cdot \frac{n_r}{k_r} + n_r \cdot \frac{n_s}{k_s})$ reach their minimum when $k_r = k_s$, i.e., outer and inner relation are partitioned using the same number of granules k. Thus, we have a cost function with $k = k_r = k_s$:

$$
\begin{aligned}
cost(k) &= |\mathbf{p}_r| \cdot \mathsf{APA} \cdot (c\_io + 2 \cdot c\_cpu) +\\
&\quad |\mathbf{p}_r| \cdot n_s \cdot \mathsf{AFR} \cdot (\frac{c\_io}{b} + 2 \cdot \frac{n_r}{|\mathbf{p}_r|} \cdot 2 \cdot c\_cpu) \qquad (1)\\
&= x \cdot \mathsf{APA} + y \cdot \mathsf{AFR}
\end{aligned}
$$

The first line is the cost for partition accesses. For each of the $|\mathbf{p}_r|$ outer partitions, the algorithm accesses APA inner partitions. Each partition access costs one extra *c_io* since an inner partition can have at most one partially filled block (remember we only measure the overhead) and two *c_cpu* (comparison i and j) for checking if this partition in the lazy partition list is relevant. The second line is the cost for false hits. For each of the $|\mathbf{p}_r|$ outer partitions, $n_s \cdot$ AFR false hits in the relevant inner partitions produce extra block transfers, where b is the average number of tuples per block of the inner relation. The costs for identifying false hits is two *c_cpu* (comparison T_S and T_E) for each false hit in the outer partition and each false hit in the relevant inner partitions.

Determining k. We derive k by minimizing the cost function using the partial derivative of $x \cdot \mathsf{APA} + y \cdot \mathsf{AFR}$. The terms quantify, respectively, the increase of the costs due to partition accesses and the decrease of the costs due to false hits. k can be increased as long as the costs for AFR decrease more than the costs for APA increase. The optimal k is the point where the cost for accessing partitions starts growing faster than the cost for false hits decreases, which is the minimum of the cost function.

Since the complexity of the cost function prevents an analytical solution of the minimization problem, we proceed in two steps to derive k. First, we keep $|\mathbf{p}_r|$ and τ constant and derive k as follows:

1. Compute the partial derivative of $x \cdot \mathsf{APA} + y \cdot \mathsf{AFR}$. We use APA and AFR from Theorems 1 and 2 to get $x \cdot \tau \cdot \frac{k^2+k+1}{3} + y \cdot \frac{1}{k}$. The partial derivative with respect to k is $\partial_k(x \cdot \tau \cdot \frac{k^2+k+1}{3} + y \cdot \frac{1}{k}) = x \cdot \tau \cdot (\frac{2}{3} \cdot k + \frac{1}{3}) - \frac{y}{k^2}$.
2. Solve $x \cdot \tau \cdot (\frac{2}{3} \cdot k + \frac{1}{3}) - \frac{y}{k^2} = 0$ to get the k that minimizes the cost function:

$$k = \frac{\sqrt[3]{(162 \cdot y - x \cdot \tau + 18 \cdot \sqrt{y \cdot (81 \cdot y - x \cdot \tau)}) \cdot (x \cdot \tau)^2}}{6 \cdot x \cdot \tau} + \frac{x \cdot \tau}{3(\sqrt[3]{(162 \cdot y - x \cdot \tau + 18 \cdot \sqrt{y \cdot (81 \cdot y - x \cdot \tau)}) \cdot (x \cdot \tau)^2}} - \frac{1}{6} \approx \sqrt[3]{\frac{3 \cdot y}{2 \cdot x \cdot \tau}}.$$

In the second step, we use an iterative process that refines $|\mathbf{p}_r|_n$ and τ_n in each step in order to determine k. More specifically, we calculate the number $|\mathbf{p}_r|_n$ of outer partitions and the tightening factor τ_n from the previously calculated k_n, starting with $k_0 = 1$. After substituting x and y (cf. Equation (1)) in the above equation for k, we obtain the recurrence:

$$k_{n+1} = \sqrt[3]{\frac{3 \cdot n_s}{2 \cdot (c\_io + 2 \cdot c\_cpu) \cdot \tau_n}} \cdot \left(\frac{c\_io}{b} + \frac{4 \cdot n_r \cdot c\_cpu}{|\mathbf{p}_r|_n}\right) \quad (2)$$

We start with $k_0 = 1$ and calculate the number of outer partitions, $|\mathbf{p}_r|_0$, according to Lemma 3, i.e.,

$$|\mathbf{p}_r|_n = min(k_n \lceil \lambda_r \cdot k_n \rceil + k_n - \frac{\lceil \lambda_r \cdot k_n \rceil^2}{2} - \frac{\lceil \lambda_r \cdot k_n \rceil}{2}, n_r),$$

and the tightening factor τ_0 as the number of inner partitions (cf. Lemma 3) divided by the number of possible partitions (cf. Proposition 1), i.e.,

$$\tau_n = \frac{min(k_n \lceil \lambda_s \cdot k_n \rceil + k_n - \frac{\lceil \lambda_s \cdot k_n \rceil^2}{2} - \frac{\lceil \lambda_s \cdot k_n \rceil}{2}, n_s)}{(k_n^2 + k_n)/2}.$$

We repeatedly calculate k_{n+1} from $|\mathbf{p}_r|_n$ and τ_n until k converges to the minimum cost.

Example 8. Consider two relations $\mathbf{r}$ and $\mathbf{s}$, each with a time range $|U| = 10\text{M}$. Relation $\mathbf{r}$ has $n_r = 10\text{M}$ tuples, and the maximum duration of tuples is $l_r = 1,000$, i.e., $\lambda_r = 0.0001$. Relation $\mathbf{s}$ has $n_s = 100\text{M}$ tuples, and the maximum duration of tuples is $l_s = 5,000$, i.e., $\lambda_s = 0.0005$. Both relations are stored in main memory in blocks of 512 bytes. With a tuple size of 35 bytes, $b = 14$ tuples fit into a block. The time of a CPU operation is 0.5 nsec (2GHz), and the time to fetch a block from main memory is 10 nsec, i.e., $c\_cpu = 0.5$ and $c\_io = 10$. Starting with $n = 0$ and $k_0 = 1$, we get the following values:

n	k_n	$\lvert\mathbf{p}_r\rvert_n$	τ_n
0	1	1	1
1	64,633	517,036	0.00105
2	7,967	15,933	0.00126
3	23,819	95,270	0.00109
4	13,761	41,280	0.00116
5	17,795	53,382	0.00112
6	16,522	49,563	0.00121
7	**16,521**	**49,560**	**0.00121**
8	**16,521**	**49,560**	**0.00121**

Thus, k converges to $k = 16,521$, which is the number of granules for the OIPJOIN.

Figure 5 illustrates the convergence of k for relations of different size. The iterative process to find k converges since at each step we reduce the power by $\frac{1}{3}$. Note that due to the ceiling function and integer calculus in $|\mathbf{p}_r|_n$ and τ_n, k may not converge to a single number, but oscillate between two. In this case the final k is the average between these two numbers.

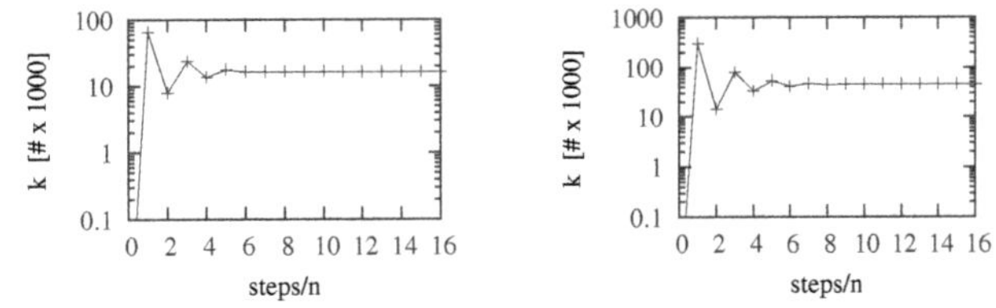

(a) $n_r = 10\text{M}$ and $n_s = 100\text{M}$ (b) $n_r = 100\text{M}$ and $n_s = 1\text{G}$

Figure 5: Convergence of k.

6.3 Complexity Analysis

The complexity of the OIPJOIN is composed of three parts: $O(|\mathbf{p}_r| \cdot \text{APA})$ partition fetches; $O(n_s \cdot n_r \cdot \text{AFR})$ false hits; and $O(n_z)$ for retrieving n_z result tuples. After substituting AFR and APA according to Theorem 1 and 2, we get the sum $O(|\mathbf{p}_r| \cdot \tau \cdot k^2) + O(n_s \cdot n_r \cdot \frac{1}{k}) + O(n_z)$. The asymptotic k according to Equation (2) is $k = O((\frac{n_s \cdot n_r}{|\mathbf{p}_r| \cdot \tau})^{1/3})$.

The *upper bound complexity* occurs with tightening factor $\tau = 1$ (no tightening). In this case we get a low k to keep the cost for partition accesses low. From $\tau = 1$ we get $|\mathbf{p}_r| = O(k^2)$ (cf. Section 5.2), i.e.,

$$k = O((\frac{n_s \cdot n_r}{k^2})^{1/3})$$
$$k^{5/3} = O((n_s \cdot n_r)^{1/3})$$
$$k = O((n_s \cdot n_r)^{1/5})$$

Inserting this into the above sum gives $O(n_r^{4/5} \cdot n_s^{4/5} + n_z)$.

The *lower bound complexity* occurs with tightening factor $\tau = O(\frac{1}{k})$ (maximal tightening). In this case we get a high k, since the cost for partition accesses is low. From $\tau = O(\frac{1}{k})$ we get $|\mathbf{p}_r| = O(k)$. Then k is:

$$k = O((\frac{n_s \cdot n_r}{k \cdot \frac{1}{k}})^{1/3}) = O((n_s \cdot n_r)^{1/3})$$

Inserting this into the sum gives $O(n_r^{2/3} \cdot n_s^{2/3} + n_z)$.

To illustrate the complexity, we performed an overlap join between two relations with 5M tuples each and between two relations with 10M tuples each. As a reference point, we also compare it with the lower and upper bound of a sort-merge join (SMJ) of the same relations. Table 1 shows the runtimes in seconds (as usual, the time to write result tuples is excluded). We can see that the runtime increased approximately by a factor of $2^{2/3} \cdot 2^{2/3} = 2.52$ for the lower bound and by a factor of $2^{4/5} \cdot 2^{4/5} = 3.03$ for the upper bound. The increase in runtime for the sort-merge join is 2.06 (linear) for the lower bound and 4.00 (quadratic) for the upper bound.

		5M	10M	increase
OIPJOIN:	LB ($\tau \approx 1/k$)	46	120	×2.61
	UB ($\tau = 1$)	2,028	6,655	×3.28
SMJ:	LB	3.2	6.6	×2.06
	UB	81,043	324,175	×4.00

Table 1: Runtime and Factor of Runtime Increase.

7. EMPIRICAL EVALUATION

This section evaluates the performance of the OIPJOIN and compares it empirically with the other self-adjusting approaches. The first set of experiments evaluates how k adapts to the cost of CPU operations and the cost of block IOs. We also verify our cost function by relating it to the actual runtime. The second set of experiments evaluates the performance of different approaches for a varying percentage and distribution of long-lived tuples. The ability to efficiently process data with long-lived tuples, i.e., tuples with a non-negligible temporal duration, is the most crucial aspect of algorithms and access methods for temporal data. The OIPJOIN outperforms related approaches by a large margin. The third set of experiments shows that the OIPJOIN scales better than the other approaches for real world datasets, coming from animal feed industry, personnel office, and open source software. Between $0.03\%-20\%$ of the tuples are larger than 8% of the data's time range, which already leads to significant differences. Finally, we show that the OIPJOIN scales better than the other approaches for disk resident data since it considers both CPU and IO costs.

Setup. For the experiments we use a 2 x Intel(R) Xeon(R) CPU E5-2440 0 @ 2.40GHz machine with 64GB main memory running CentOS 6.4. All algorithms have been implemented in C. We use a tuple size of 35 bytes. The block size is 512 bytes for relations stored in main memory (gives the best performance on our machine) and 4K bytes (physical disk block size) when stored on disk. We implemented all algorithms for both disk and main memory storage. The cost to perform a CPU operation (0.5 nsec) on our machine is about 20 times faster than fetching a main memory block (10 nsec). We use synthetic datasets with a time range of $[1, 2^{24}]$ as well as real world datasets (described below).

The OIPJOIN is compared against the following state-of-the-art approaches. *Loose quadtree (lqt)*: We implemented a partition-based algorithm that joins every node of the outer tree with all relevant nodes in the inner tree. We use a cell expansion factor $p = 1$, which is widely accepted as the best value [18, 23] and gave the best results in our experiments. We use density based splitting, i.e., tuples are propagated down the tree only if a block is full. Together with block storage, this gave a runtime improvement up to 400% compared to random access to single tuples. Since in all experiments the loose quadtree outperformed the quadtree, the latter is not shown in the plots. *Relational interval tree (rit)*: We implemented the RI-Tree Up-Down partition-based algorithm [9]. When data is stored in main memory, we do not use blocks to store tuples contiguously. The reason is that even for a clustering index, the time to fetch 512 bytes that contain only a few matching tuples outweighs the advantages of contiguous memory access. *Segment tree (sgt)*: We implemented the segment tree, where the index is build on the inner relation and the overlap join is computed by joining each tuple of the outer relation with the segment tree. Duplicates are identified during join processing by testing whether the intersecting interval starts before the currently joined segment; if so, it has already been joined in a previous segment. *Sort-merge join (smj)*: We implemented a sort-merge join that sorts the tuples of the outer relation by the end point and the tuples of the inner relation by the start point. The sort order of the inner relation is used to stop scanning when an inner tuple has a larger start point than the end point of the outer tuple. The sort order of the outer relation allows to limit the backtracking to the maximum duration of tuples in the relations. We implemented the join using blocks. In spite of more false hits, this increases the performance due to less backtracking. All runtime experiments include the time to create the indices. For all approaches, the index creation time is $\approx 1\%$ of the total runtime for data kept in memory and $\approx 5\%$ for disk resident data.

Number of Granules k. The first experiment shows how the OIPJOIN adapts to c_cpu and c_io. We use synthetic data: an outer relation with 10M tuples and an inner relation with 100M tuples, both with tuple durations up to 0.1% of the time range. Figure 6(a) shows k when varying the ratio $\frac{c\_cpu}{c\_io}$ from 0.001 to 100. When c_cpu gets more expensive, k increases so that more partitions are generated. Figure 6(b) and 6(c) show, respectively, the corresponding AFR (decreasing) and the number of block IOs (increasing). Figure 6(d) shows the runtime for main memory resident data. It illustrates that also for data that is stored in main memory the performance can be increased if the costs of memory IOs and the costs of CPU operations are considered for determining the optimal k.

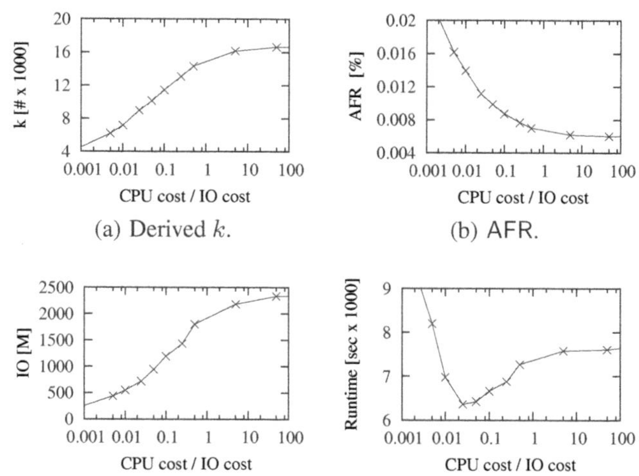

(a) Derived k. (b) AFR. (c) Block IOs. (d) Runtime (Main Memory).

Figure 6: Derived k with Varying c_cpu and c_io.

The next experiment compares the cost function of the OIPJOIN to the actual runtime. We use the same relations as in the previous experiment and vary k. Figure 7(a) shows the cost function for $c\_cpu = 0.5$ nsec and $c\_io = 10$ nsec. Figure 7(b) shows the actual runtime for the same setting. It is easy to see that both functions have the same shape with the minimum at $k = 10,130$.

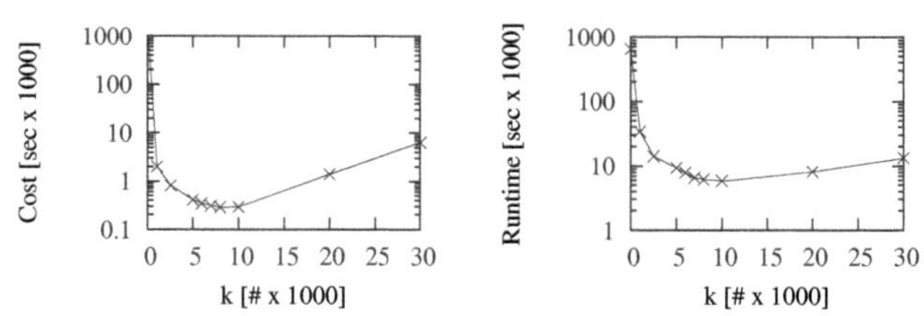

(a) Cost Function (Overhead). (b) Runtime.

Figure 7: Cost Function and Runtime.

Long-Lived Tuples. The next experiment compares the performance of the OIPJOIN (oip) with the loose quadtree (lqt), the relational interval tree (rit), the segment tree (sgt), and the sort-merge join (smj), by varying the number of long-lived tuples and the maximum duration of tuples. The two input relations have 10M tuples each, with long-lived tuples that have a duration up to 8% and an average duration of 4% of the relation's time range. Short-lived tuples have a maximum duration of 0.01% of the time range. Figure 8 shows the runtime and the AFR of the four algorithms. The AFR of the relational interval tree and segment tree are omitted since they produce no false hits. The OIPJOIN significantly outperforms the other approaches since it does not suffer from long-lived tuples and has a very small AFR (the curve is close to the x-axis). In contrast, the loose quadtree is very sensitive to long-lived tuples, and the AFR increases drastically. This yields much higher runtimes due to excessive comparison operations and the filtering of false hits. Although the relational interval tree does not produce false hits, its performance decreases with the increase of long-lived tuples since a higher number of index nodes need to be joined, which requires a high number of operations on the indices. The segment tree scales worse than the relational interval tree, since with longer tuple durations many duplicates need to be fetched and tested. In our experiments, the segment tree outperforms the relational interval tree only for tuple durations smaller than 0.001%. The performance of the sort-merge join is highly affected by the longest tuple in the dataset, but it scales better than the loose quadtree.

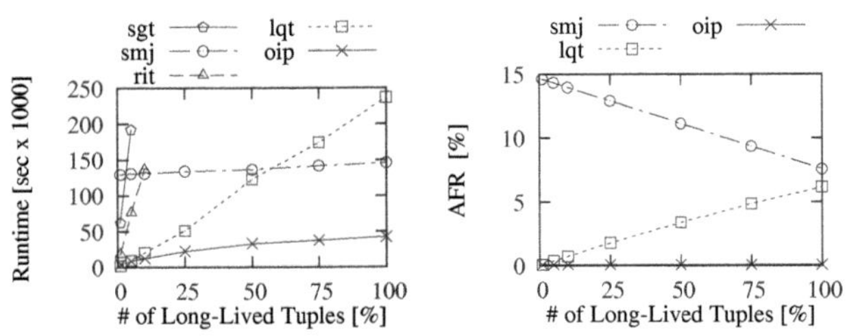

(a) Varying Number of Long-Lived Tuples.

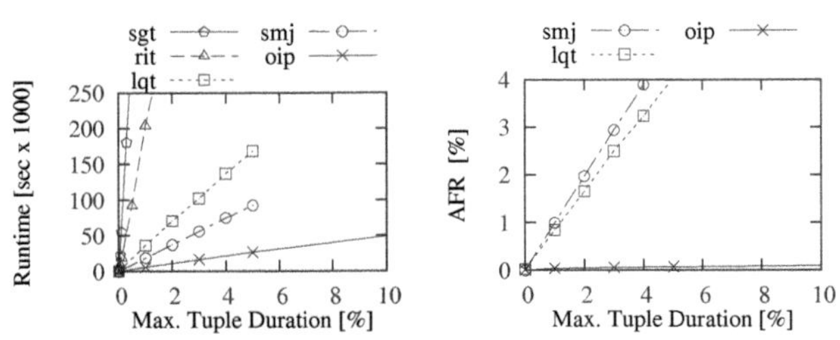

(b) Varying Maximum Duration of Tuples.

Figure 8: Long-Lived Tuples.

Real World Datasets. We use three real world datasets that differ in size and data distribution. The main properties of these datasets are summarized in Table 2. The Incumbent dataset [12] records the history of employees assigned to projects over a 16 year period at a granularity of days. The Feed dataset records the history of measured nutritive values of feeds over a 24 year period at a granularity of days; a measurement of a nutrient remains valid until a new measurement for the same nutritive value and feed becomes available. The Webkit dataset [1] records the history of files of the svn repository of the Webkit project over a 11 year period at a granularity of milliseconds. The valid times indicate the periods when a file did not change. Figure 9 shows the temporal distributions of the data (i.e., the number of overlapping tuple intervals at each time point) and the histograms of tuple durations.

	Incumbent	Feed	Webkit
Cardinality	$83,852$	$3,697,957$	$1,213,476$
Time Range	$5,895$	$8,610$	$\approx 2^{39}$
Min. Duration	1	1	$\approx 2^{10}$
Max. Duration	574	$8,589$	$\approx 2^{39}$
Avg. Duration	184	432	$\approx 2^{34}$
Distinct Points	$2,689$	$5,584$	$110,165$

Table 2: Properties of Real World Datasets.

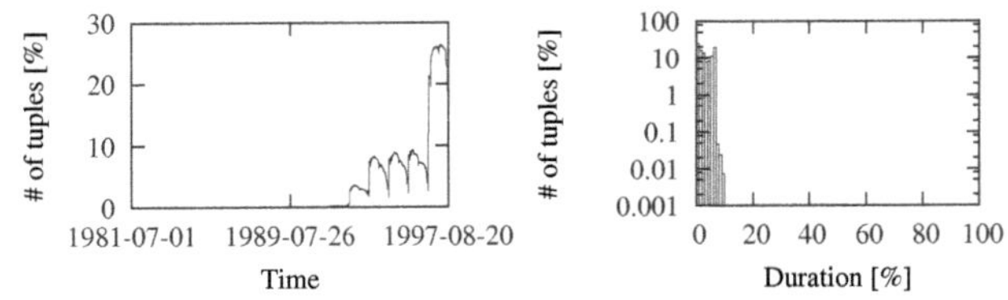

(a) Incumbent Dataset.

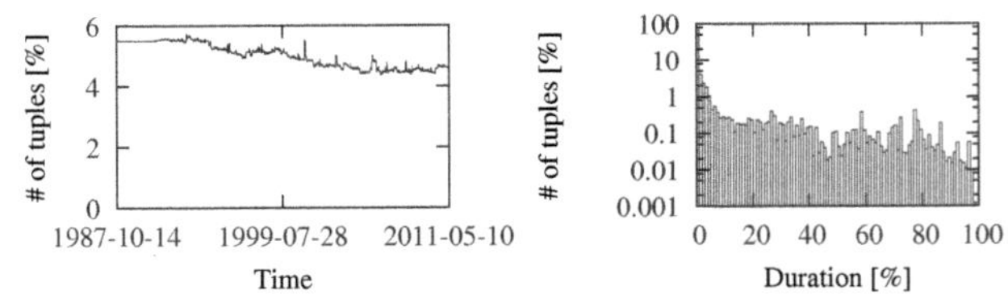

(b) Feed Dataset.

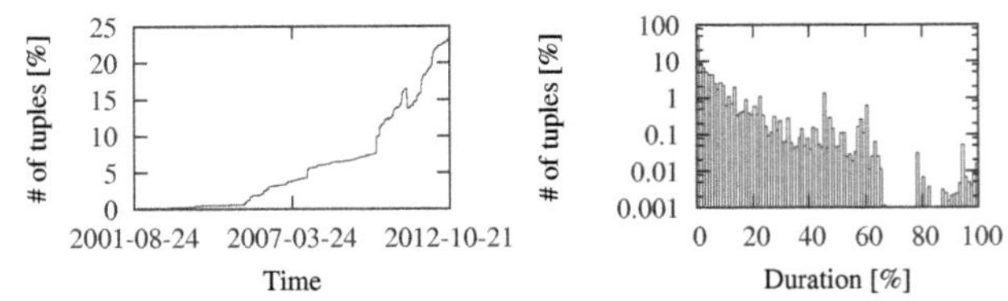

(c) Webkit Dataset.

Figure 9: Tuple Intervals per Time Point and Duration Histogram of Real World Datasets.

For all three datasets we perform an overlap join, using a subset of the dataset as the outer relation and the entire dataset as the inner relation. We use the smaller as the outer relation, since it typically has fewer partitions, and thus some partitions of the larger relation are not accessed at all during the join. Figure 10 shows the runtime and the AFR for the three datasets depending on the size of the outer relation. The OIPJOIN has the best performance in all three settings. The other approaches suffer from long-lived tuples, e.g., the AFR of the loose quadtree is much larger than the one of the OIPJOIN, and it does not adapt to the size of the dataset. The AFR of the sort-merge join is omitted since it reaches 30–50%.

Scalability on Disk. The last experiment shows the scalability of the algorithms for disk resident data. We vary the number of inner tuples from 100M to 1500M. The number of outer tuples is 1% of the inner relation. Both relations have tuple durations up to 0.1% of the time range. c_io is 200 times higher than c_cpu. Figures 11(a) and 11(b) show the number of block IOs and the AFR. Figure 11(c) shows the runtime behavior on a server with 64GB of main memory, where a large number of disk blocks is cached by the operating system. Although the loose quadtree, due to its density-based splitting strategy, is the best approach in terms of block IOs, it produces a large number of false hits. The OIPJOIN adapts to both the cost of block IOs and the cost of false hits, and thus outperforms all other approaches in terms of runtime. The segment tree performs worst, in particular in terms of IO (close to the y-axis), since for each outer tuple, duplicated inner tuples and thus disk blocks are fetched several times. We run the same experiment for the three best approaches on a different machine with a similar CPU but only 4GB main memory, that is, fewer disk blocks are cached by the operating system. The runtime behavior is shown in Figure 11(d) and is slower, as expected. The loose quadtree per-

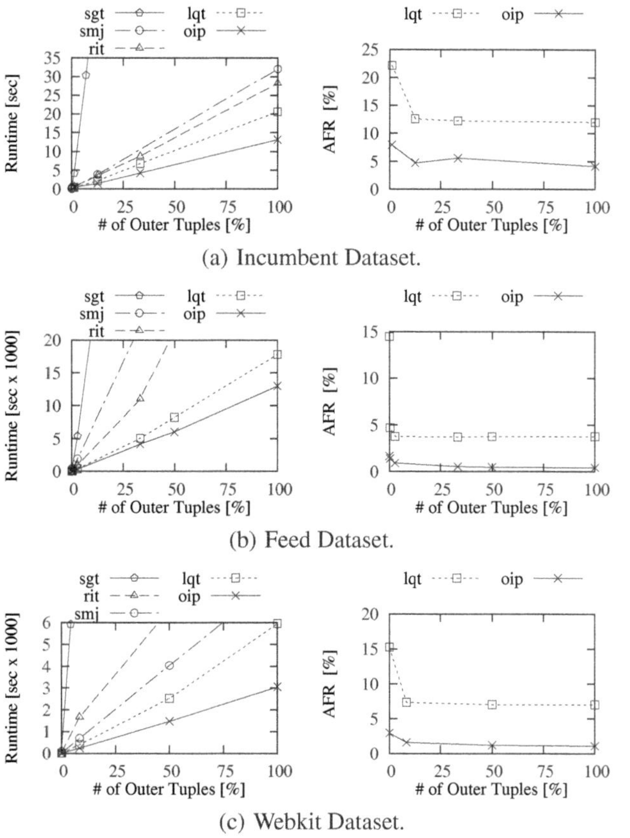

Figure 10: Runtime and AFR for Real World Datasets.

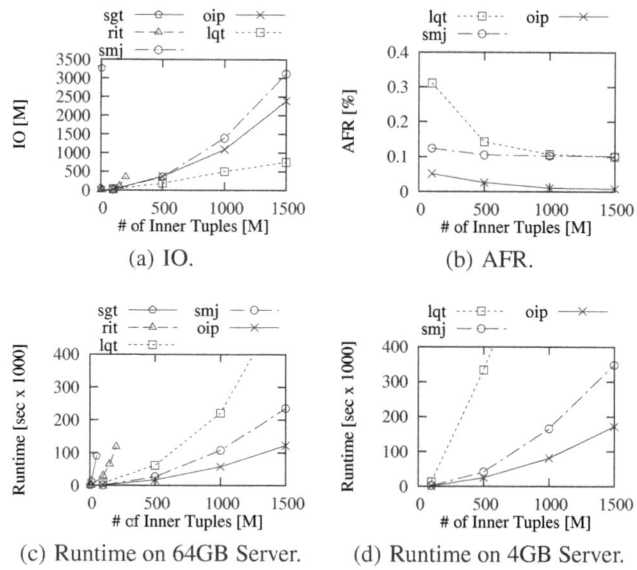

Figure 11: Varying Number of Tuples of Disk Resident Data.

forms much worse on this machine despite fewer IOs. The reason is that the OIPJOIN and the sort-merge join benefit from sequential reads due to sorting. The loose quadtree does not have sequential blocks on disk, hence the disk seek time deteriorates the performance of the loose quadtree.

Summary. The OIPJOIN is the most efficient and robust approach if the data includes long-lived tuples since it provides a constant clustering guarantee and adapts to both the cost for false hits and the cost for partition accesses. The loose quadtree and the relational interval tree are only competitive if the dataset contains a very low number of long-lived tuples. In all other cases, either the false hits or the navigation in the index structure incur high costs. For datasets with only very short tuples (or point data), the sort-merge join is the most efficient approach, but it deteriorates as soon as the dataset contains a few long-lived tuples.

8. CONCLUSION

In this paper, we have presented the overlap interval partition join (OIPJOIN) for valid-time relation together with *Overlap Interval Partitioning* ($\mathcal{OIP}$). $\mathcal{OIP}$ permits overlapping partitions that are not derived from a recursive hierarchical space division. In contrast to other approaches, the OIPJOIN does not deteriorate in the presence of long-lived tuples and adjusts the number of partitions based on the size of the dataset, the cost of CPU operations, and the cost of IOs. An in-depth empirical evaluation shows that the OIPJOIN outperforms state-of-the-art techniques for the overlap join.

Future work points in several directions. First, it is interesting to investigate how to update $\mathcal{OIP}$ incrementally if the relation changes, since the partitioning allows an expansion on both space boundaries by increasing k and maintaining an offset on the indices. For this the effects on k and the treatment of the ending variable "now" must be studied. Second, it is possible to refine the cost function for, e.g., different buffer replacement strategies. Third, we have planned to develop statistics to tighten k not only based on the maximum duration of tuples, but also on the data distribution.

9. REFERENCES

[1] The webkit open source project. http://www.webkit.org, 2012.

[2] N. Beckmann, H.-P. Kriegel, R. Schneider, and B. Seeger. The R*-tree: An efficient and robust access method for points and rectangles. In *SIGMOD*, pages 322–331, 1990.

[3] N. Beckmann and B. Seeger. A revised R*-tree in comparison with related index structures. In *SIGMOD*, pages 799–812, 2009.

[4] J. L. Bentley. Solutions to klee's rectangle problems. Technical report, Carnegie Mellon University, 1977.

[5] M. Berg, M. Kreveld, M. Overmars, and O. Schwarzkopf. More geometric data structures. In *Computational Geometry*, pages 211–233. Springer Berlin Heidelberg, 2000.

[6] A. E. Brouwer, A. M. Cohen, and A. Neumaier. *Distance Regular Graphs*. Springer-Verlag, 1989.

[7] A. Dignös, M. Böhlen, and J. Gamper. Query time scaling of attribute values in interval timestamped databases. In *ICDE*, pages 1304–1307, 2013.

[8] A. Dignös, M. H. Böhlen, and J. Gamper. Temporal alignment. In *SIGMOD*, pages 433–444, 2012.

[9] J. Enderle, M. Hampel, and T. Seidl. Joining interval data in relational databases. In *SIGMOD*, pages 683–694, 2004.

[10] R. A. Finkel and J. L. Bentley. Quad trees: A data structure for retrieval on composite keys. *Acta Inf.*, 4:1–9, 1974.

[11] D. Gao, C. S. Jensen, R. T. Snodgrass, and M. D. Soo. Join operations in temporal databases. *VLDB J.*, 14(1):2–29, 2005.

[12] J. A. G. Gendrano, R. Shah, R. T. Snodgrass, and J. Yang. University information system (uis) dataset. TimeCenter CD-1, 1998.

[13] N. Koudas and K. C. Sevcik. Size separation spatial join. In *SIGMOD*, pages 324–335, 1997.

[14] H.-P. Kriegel, M. Pötke, and T. Seidl. Managing intervals efficiently in object-relational databases. In *VLDB*, pages 407–418, 2000.

[15] M.-L. Lo and C. V. Ravishankar. Spatial hash-joins. In *SIGMOD*, pages 247–258, 1996.

[16] H. Lu, B. C. Ooi, and K.-L. Tan. On spatially partitioned temporal join. In *VLDB*, pages 546–557, 1994.

[17] S. Nobari, F. Tauheed, T. Heinis, P. Karras, S. Bressan, and A. Ailamaki. Touch: In-memory spatial join by hierarchical data-oriented partitioning. In *SIGMOD*, pages 701–712, 2013.

[18] H. Samet. *Foundations of Multidimensional and Metric Data Structures*. Morgan Kaufmann Publishers Inc., San Francisco, CA, USA, 2005.

[19] H. Samet, J. Sankaranarayanan, and M. Auerbach. Indexing methods for moving object databases: games and other applications. In *SIGMOD*, pages 169–180, 2013.

[20] A. Silberschatz, P. B. Galvin, and G. Gagne. *Operating System Concepts*. Wiley Publishing, 9th edition, 2012.

[21] M. D. Soo, R. T. Snodgrass, and C. S. Jensen. Efficient evaluation of the valid-time natural join. In *ICDE*, pages 282–292, 1994.

[22] V. J. Tsotras and N. Kangerlaris. The snapshot index: An i/o-optimal access method for timeslice queries. *Inf. Syst.*, 20(3):237–260, 1995.

[23] T. Ulrich. Loose octrees. In *Game Programming Gems*, pages 444–453. Charles River Media, 2000.

APPENDIX

A. PROOF OF THEOREM 1

PROOF. (Theorem 1) The proof is split into three parts. In Part 1 we compute the SFR of $\mathcal{OIP}$ for a duration complete relation $\mathbf{r}^l_{kd}$ and a query interval with duration q. In Part 2 we use the result of Part 1 to show that $\mathsf{AFR}(\mathcal{OIP}) < \frac{1}{k}$ for tuples of duration $l = 1$ and query intervals of duration $q = 1$. From Proposition 2 we have that the $\mathsf{AFR}(\mathcal{OIP})$ for $q > 1$ is smaller. In Part 3 we show that for tuples up to larger durations, i.e., $l > 1 \leq k \cdot d$, the SFR of $\mathcal{OIP}$ and the $\mathsf{AFR}(\mathcal{OIP})$ are smaller than for $l = 1$, thus $\mathsf{AFR}(\mathcal{OIP}) < \frac{1}{k}$.

Part 1: Assume $l \leq d$. We compute first the sum of false hits for partitions p that span one granule. Assume a query interval Q with $q = 1$ that overlaps p. Let $v \geq 0$ be the duration of the non-overlapping part of p before Q starts. If $v \leq l$, we have $\frac{v^2+v}{2}$ false hits in this part of the partition, i.e., all intervals in p that start and end before Q. If $v \geq l$, we have $\frac{v^2+v}{2} - \sum_{x=l}^{v}(v-x) = vl - \frac{l^2-l}{2}$ false hits in this part, i.e., all intervals in p up to duration l that start and end before Q. We sum the false hits of all query intervals of duration 1 and get $\sum_{v=0}^{l-1}(\frac{v^2+v}{2}) + \sum_{v=l}^{d-1}(vl - \frac{l^2-l}{2}) = \frac{l^3-l}{6} + \frac{ld^2-l^2d}{2}$. The same sum is obtained for false hits in the non-overlapping part after the query interval Q ends. Thus, for k granules we get a total of $k(\frac{l^3-l}{3} + ld^2 - l^2d)$ false hits.

Next, we compute the sum of false hits for partitions that span more than one granule. For $l \leq d$, only partitions of duration $2d$ contain tuples. Each of these partitions contains $\frac{l^2-l}{2}$ tuples, i.e., all tuples up to duration l that start in the first half and end in the second half of the partition. The total number of matching tuples for all query intervals of duration 1 is $2\sum_{p=1}^{l-1}\sum_{x=1}^{p}(x) = \frac{l^3-l}{3}$. Thus, for $k-1$ partitions of duration $2d$ there are $2d$ possible query intervals of duration $q = 1$ that overlap a partition with $\frac{l^2-l}{2}$ tuples. Subtracting from these tuples the $\frac{l^3-l}{3}$ matches gives a total of $(k-1)(2d\frac{l^2-l}{2} - \frac{l^3-l}{3})$ false hits.

Adding up the false hits for the partitions and dividing the sum by the number of tuples $|\mathbf{r}^l_{kd}| = kdl - \frac{l^2-l}{2}$ we get

$$\mathsf{SFR}(\mathcal{OIP}) = \frac{2(l^2 - 3dl + 3kd^2 - 3kd + 3d - 1)}{3(2kd - l + 1)} \text{ for } l \leq d. \quad (3)$$

Now assume $l > d$. Let l be a multiple of d and $h = l/d$. Partitions that span one granule are completely full. This yields a total of $k\frac{d^3-d}{3}$ false hits, by replacing l in the first case of the proof with d. Then we have $\sum_{x=1}^{h-1}(k-x)$ partitions that span more than one granule, are not longer than l, and are completely filled. Each of these partitions produces up to $d^3 - d^2$ false hits. The only partitions that are longer than l and contain tuples of duration $l = hd$ have duration $d(h+1)$, of which $(k-h)$ exist. Each of these partitions contains $\frac{d^2-d}{2}$ tuples up to size l. The total number of matching tuples for all query intervals of duration 1 is $2\sum_{p=1}^{d-1}\sum_{x=1}^{p}(x) = \frac{d^3-d}{3}$, and the total number of matches where no false hits are possible is $\frac{d(h-1)(d^2-d)}{2}$. Thus, for $k-h$ partitions we get $(k-h)\Big(d(h+1)\frac{d^2-d}{2} - (\frac{d^3-d}{3} + \frac{d(h-1)(d^2-d)}{2})\Big)$. Finally, we divide the sum by the number of tuples $|\mathbf{r}^l_{kd}| = kdl - \frac{l^2-l}{2}$ and get

$$\mathsf{SFR}(\mathcal{OIP}) = \frac{(d-1)(6kd - d + 2 - 3l)}{3(2kd - l + 1)} \text{ for } l > d. \quad (4)$$

Part 2: We show that $\mathsf{AFR}(\mathcal{OIP}) < \frac{1}{k}$ for tuples of duration $l = 1$ and query intervals of duration $q = 1$. We use the $\mathsf{SFR}(\mathcal{OIP})$ of Part 1 for $l \leq d$ (since d must be at least 1) and set $l = 1$ in Equation (3) to get:

$$\mathsf{SFR}(\mathcal{OIP}) = \frac{2(1^2 - 3d1 + 3kd^2 - 3kd + 3d - 1)}{3(2kd - 1 + 1)} = d - 1$$

Next, we set $q = 1$ and divide by the number of query intervals $kd + q - 1 = kd + q - 1 = kd$ (ref. Definition 5), and get

$$\mathsf{AFR}(\mathcal{OIP}) = \frac{\mathsf{SFR}(\mathcal{OIP})}{kd + q - 1} = \frac{d-1}{kd + 1 - 1} = \frac{1}{k} - \frac{1}{kd} < \frac{1}{k}.$$

Part 3: We show that for $l > 1 \leq kd$ the $\mathsf{SFR}(\mathcal{OIP})$ is smaller than for $l = 1$, i.e., smaller $d - 1$ and thus $\mathsf{AFR}(\mathcal{OIP}) < \frac{1}{k}$. Recall that the SFR is independent of the query interval duration q (ref. Lemma 4). First, we consider $1 < l \leq d$ and Equation (3):

$$d - 1 > \frac{2(l^2 - 3dl + 3kd^2 - 3kd + 3d - 1)}{3(2kd - l + 1)}$$

$$3(2kd - l + 1)(d - 1) > 2(l^2 - 3dl + 3kd^2 - 3kd + 3d - 1)$$

$$-2l^2 + (3 + 3d)l - 3d - 1 > 0$$

By solving the quadratic equation $-2l^2 + (3+3d)l - 3d - 1 = 0$ we get $l = \{1, \frac{3d+1}{2}\}$, since the quadratic term is negative we have an concave down parabola and thus the inequality we need to show for $1 < l \leq d$ holds for $1 < l < \frac{3d+1}{2}$.

Second, we consider $d < l \leq kd$ and Equation (4):

$$d - 1 > \frac{(d-1)(6kd - d + 2 - 3l)}{3(2kd - l + 1)}$$

$$3(2kd - l + 1)(d - 1) > (d - 1)(6kd - d + 2 - 3l)$$

$$6kd - 3l + 3 > 6kd - d + 2 - 3l$$

$$d > -1$$

Since $d \geq 1$, we have that the $\mathsf{SFR}(\mathcal{OIP})$ and the $\mathsf{AFR}(\mathcal{OIP})$ for $l > 1$ is smaller than for $l = 1$, thus $\mathsf{AFR}(\mathcal{OIP}) < \frac{1}{k}$. □

Similarity Joins for Uncertain Strings*

Manish Patil
Louisiana State University
USA
mpatil@csc.lsu.edu

Rahul Shah
Louisiana State University
USA
rahul@csc.lsu.edu

ABSTRACT

A string similarity join finds all similar string pairs between two input string collections. It is an essential operation in many applications, such as data integration and cleaning, and has been extensively studied for deterministic strings. Increasingly, many applications have to deal with imprecise strings or strings with fuzzy information in them. This work presents the first solution for answering similarity join queries over uncertain strings that implements possible-world semantics, using the edit distance as the measure of similarity. Given two collections of uncertain strings $\mathcal{R}$, $\mathcal{S}$, and input (k,τ), our task is to find string pairs (R,S) between collections such that $Pr(ed(R,S) \leq k) > \tau$ i.e., the probability of the edit distance between R and S being at most k is more than probability threshold τ. We can address the join problem by obtaining all strings in $\mathcal{S}$ that are similar to each string R in $\mathcal{R}$. However, existing solutions for answering such similarity search queries on uncertain string databases only support a deterministic string as input. Exploiting these solutions would require exponentially many possible worlds of R to be considered, which is not only ineffective but also prohibitively expensive. We propose various filtering techniques that give upper and (or) lower bound on $Pr(ed(R,S) \leq k)$ without instantiating possible worlds for either of the strings. We then incorporate these techniques into an indexing scheme and significantly reduce the filtering overhead. Further, we alleviate the verification cost of a string pair that survives pruning by using a trie structure which allows us to overlap the verification cost of exponentially many possible instances of the candidate string pair. Finally, we evaluate the effectiveness of the proposed approach by thorough practical experimentation.

Categories and Subject Descriptors

H.2 [**DATABASE MANAGEMENT**]: Systems—*Query processing*

*This work is supported in part by National Science Foundation (NSF) Grants CCF–1017623 and CCF–1218904.

SIGMOD/PODS'14, June 22 - 27 2014, Snowbird, UT, USA

Keywords

Uncertain strings; string joins; edit distance

1. INTRODUCTION

Strings form a fundamental data type in computer systems and string searching has been extensively studied since the inception of computer science. String similarity search takes a set of strings and a query string as input, and outputs all the strings in the set that are similar to the query string. A join extends the notion of similarity search further and require all similar string pairs between two input string sets to be reported. Both similarity search and similarity join are central to many applications such as data integration and cleaning. Edit distance is the most commonly used similarity measure for strings. The edit distance between two strings r and s, denoted by $ed(r,s)$, is the minimum number of single-character edit operations (insertion, deletion, and substitution) needed to transform r to s. Edit distance based string similarity search and join has been extensively studied in the literature for deterministic strings [7, 3, 2, 13, 18, 5]. However, due to the large number of applications where uncertainty or imprecision in values is either inherent or desirable, recent years have witnessed increasing attention devoted to managing uncertain data. Several probabilistic database management systems (PDBMS), which can represent and manage data with explicit probabilistic models of uncertainty, have been proposed to date [17, 16]. Imprecision in data introduces many challenges for similarity search and join in databases with probabilistic string attributes, which is the focus of this paper.

Uncertainty model: Analogous to the models of uncertain databases, two models - string-level and character-level - have been proposed recently by Jeffrey Jestes et al. [10] for uncertain strings. In the string-level uncertainty model all possible instances for the uncertain string are explicitly listed to form a probability distribution function (pdf). In contrast, the character-level model describes distributions over all characters in the alphabet for each uncertain position in the string. We focus on the character-level model as it is realistic and concise in representing the string uncertainty. Let $\Sigma = \{c_1, c_2, ..., c_\sigma\}$ be the alphabet. A character-level uncertain string is $S = S[1]S[2]...S[l]$, where $S[i]$ $(1 \leq i \leq l)$ is a random variable with discrete distribution over Σi.e., $S[i]$ is a set of pairs $(c_j, p_i(c_j))$, where $c_j \in \Sigma$ and $p_i(c_j)$ is the probability of having symbol c_j at position i. Formally $S[i] = \{(c_j, p_i(c_j)) | c_j \neq c_m$ for $j \neq m$, and $\sum_j p_i(c_j) = 1\}$. When the context of a string is unclear we represent $p_i(c_j)$

for string S by $Pr(S[i] = c_j)$. Throughout we use a lower case character to represent a deterministic string (s) against the uncertain string denoted by a upper case character (S). Let $|S|$ ($|s|$) be the length of string S (s). Then the possible worlds of S is a set of all possible instances s of S with probability $p(s)$, $\sum p(s) = 1$. S being a character-level uncertain string, $|S| = |s|$ for any of its possible instances.

Query semantics: In addition to capturing uncertainty in the data, one must define the semantics of queries over the data. In this regard, a powerful model of possible-world semantics has been the backbone of analyzing the correctness of database operations on uncertain data. For uncertain string attributes, Jestes et al. [10] made the first attempt to extend the notion of similarity. They used expected edit distance (*eed*) over all possible worlds of two uncertain strings. Given strings R and S, $eed(R, S) = \sum_{r_i,s_j} p(r_i)p(s_j)ed(r_i, s_j)$, where s_j (r_i) is an instance of S (R) with probability $p(s_j)$ ($p(r_i)$). Though *eed* seems like a natural extension of edit distance as a measure of similarity, it has been shown that it does not implement the possible-world semantics completely at the query level [6]. Consider a similarity search query on a collection of deterministic strings with input string r. Then, string s is an output only if $ed(r, s) \leq k$. For such a query R over an uncertain string collection, possible world semantics dictate that we apply the same predicate $ed(r, s) \leq k$ for each possible instance r of R, s of S and aggregate this over all worlds. Thus, a possible world with instances r, s can contribute in deciding whether S is similar to R only if s is within the desired edit distance of r. However, for the *eed* measure, all possible worlds (irrespective but weighted by edit distance) contribute towards the overall score that determines the similarity of S with R. To overcome this problem, in [6] the authors have proposed a (k,τ)-matching semantic scheme. Using this semantic, given a edit distance threshold k and probability threshold τ, R is similar to S if $Pr(ed(R, S) \leq k) > \tau$. We use this similarity definition in this paper for answering join queries.

Problem definition: Given two sets of uncertain strings $\mathcal{R}$ and $\mathcal{S}$, an edit-distance threshold k and a probability threshold τ, similarity join finds all similar string pairs $(R, S) \in \mathcal{R} \times \mathcal{S}$ such that $Pr(ed(R, S) \leq k) > \tau$. Without loss of generality, we focus on self join in this paper i.e. $\mathcal{R} = \mathcal{S}$.

Related work: Uncertain/Probabilistic strings have been the subject of study for the past several years. Efficient algorithms and data structures are known for the problem of string searching in uncertain text [8, 1, 9, 19]. In [6] authors have studied the approximate substring matching problem, where the goal is to report the positions of all substrings of uncertain text that are similar to the query string. Recently, the problem of similarity search on a collection of uncertain strings has been addressed in [4]. However, most of these works support only deterministic strings as query input. Utilizing these techniques for uncertain string as input would invariably need all its possible worlds to be enumerated, which may not be feasible to do taking into account the resultant exponential blowup in query cost. Though the problem of similarity join on uncertain strings has been studied in [10], it makes use of expected edit distance as a measure of similarity. We make an attempt to address some of the challenges involved in uncertain string processing by investigating similarity joins on them in this paper.

Our Contributions: In this paper, we present a comprehensive investigation on the problem of similarity joins for uncertain strings using (k,τ)-matching [6] as the similarity definition and make the following contributions:

- We propose a filtering scheme that integrates q-gram filtering with probabilistic pruning, and we present an indexing scheme to facilitate such filtering.
- We extend the frequency distance filtering introduced in [4] for an uncertain string pair and improve its performance while maintaining the same space requirement.
- We propose the use of a trie data structure to efficiently compute the exact similarity probability (as given by (k,τ)-matching) for a candidate pair (R, S) without explicitly comparing all possible string pairs.
- We conduct comprehensive experiments which demonstrate the effectiveness of all proposed techniques in answering similarity join queries.

2. PRELIMINARIES

In this section we briefly review filtering techniques for deterministic strings available in literature and extend them for uncertain strings later in the article. Let r, s be the two deterministic strings and k be the edit distance threshold.

2.1 q-gram Filtering

We partition s into $k+1$ disjoint segments $s^1, s^2, ..., s^{k+1}$. For simplicity let each segment be of length $q \geq 1$ i.e, $s^x = s[((x-1)q+1)..xq]$. Further, let $pos(s^x)$ represent the starting position of segment s^x in string s i.e, $pos(s^x) = (x-1)q+1$. Then using the pigeonhole principle, if r is similar to a string s, it should contain a substring that matches a segment in s. A naive method to achieve this is to obtain a set $q(r)$ enumerating all substrings of r of length q and for each substring check whether it matches s^x for $x = 1, 2, .., k+1$. However, in [14] authors have shown that we can obtain a set $q(r, x) \subseteq q(r)$ for each segment of s such that it is sufficient to test each substring $w \in q(r, x)$ for a match with s^x. Table 1 shows sets $q(r, x)$ populated for a sample string r. Using the proposed "position aware" substring selection, set $q(r, x)$ includes substrings of r with start positions in the range $[pos(s^x) - \lfloor (k-\Delta)/2 \rfloor, pos(s^x) + \lfloor (k+\Delta)/2 \rfloor]$ and with length q. The number of substrings in set $q(r, x)$ is thus bounded by $k+1$. In [14] authors prove that the substring selection satisfies "completeness" ensuring any similar pair (r, s) will be found as a candidate pair. We use a generalization of this filtering technique by partitioning s into $m > k$ partitions [14, 15] as summarized in the following lemma.

LEMMA 1. *Given a string r and s, with s partitioned into $m > k$ disjoint segments, if r is similar to s within an edit threshold k, r must contain substrings that match at-least $(m-k)$ segments of s.*

Once again by assuming each segment of s to be of length $q \geq 1$, we can compute the set $q(r, x)$ and attempt to match each $w \in q(r, x)$ with s^x as before to apply the above lemma.

2.2 Frequency Distance Filtering

Given a string s from the alphabetΣ , a frequency vector $f(s)$ is defined as $f(s) = [f(s)_1, f(s)_2, ..., f(s)_\sigma]$, where $f(s)_i$ is the count of the ith alphabet of Σi.e, c_i. Let $f(r)$ and $f(s)$ be the frequency vectors of r and s respectively. Then the frequency distance of r and s is defined as $fd(r, s) = max\{pD, nD\}$,

$$pD = \sum_{f(r)_i > f(s)_i} f(r)_i - f(s)_i, nD = \sum_{f(r)_i < f(s)_i} f(s)_i - f(r)_i$$

Frequency distance provides a lower bound for the edit distance between r and s i.e., $fd(r,s) \leq ed(r,s)$ and can be computed efficiently [12]. Thus, we can safely decide that s is not similar to r if $fd(r,s) > k$.

3. q-GRAM FILTERING

In this section we adopt and extend the ideas introduced for deterministic strings earlier in Section 2.1 to uncertain strings. We begin with the simpler case where either of the two uncertain strings R and S is deterministic. Let R be that string with r being its only possible instance. We try to achieve an upper bound on the probability of r and S being similar i.e., $Pr(ed(r,S) \leq k)$. We then build upon this result for the case when both strings are uncertain and obtain an upper bound on the probability of R and S being similar i.e., $Pr(ed(R,S) \leq k)$.

Before proceeding, we introduce some notation and definitions. A string w of length l matches a substring in T starting at position i with probability $Pr(w = T[i..i+l-1]) = \prod_{ps=1}^{l} p_{i+ps-1}(w[ps])$. A string w matches T with probability $Pr(w = T) = \prod_{ps=1}^{l} p_{ps}(w[ps])$ if $|w| = |T| = l$; otherwise it is 0. We simply say w matches with T (or vice versa) if $Pr(w = T) > 0$. The probability of string W matching T is given by $Pr(W = T) = \prod_{ps=1}^{l} \sum_{c_j \in \Sigma} Pr(W[ps] = c_j) \times Pr(T[ps] = c_j)$. Once again, we say W matches T if $Pr(W = T) > 0$ for simplicity.

3.1 Bounding $Pr(ed(r,S) \leq k)$

The possible worlds $\Omega$of S is the set of all possible instances of S. A possible world $pw_j \in \Omega$ is a pair $(s_j, p(s_j))$, where s_j is an instance of S with probability $p(s_j)$. Let $p(pw_j) = p(s_j)$ denote the probability of existence of a possible world pw_j. Note that s_j is a deterministic string and $\sum p(pw_j) = 1$. Then by definition, $Pr(ed(r,S) \leq k) = \sum_{ed(r,s_j) \leq k} p(pw_j)$. We first establish the necessary condition for r to be similar to S within an edit threshold k, i.e., $Pr(ed(r,S) \leq k) > 0$, and then try to provide an upper bound for the same.

Necessary condition for $Pr(ed(r,S) \leq k) > 0$:
We partition the string S into $m > k$ disjoint substrings. For simplicity, let q be the length of each partition. Note that each partition $S^1, S^2, ..., S^m$ is an uncertain string. Let r contain substrings matching $m' \leq m$ segments of S i.e., the number of segments of S with $Pr(w = S^x) > 0$ for any substring w of r is m'. Then it can be seen that for any $pw_j \in \Omega$, r contains substrings that match with at most m' segments from $s_j^1, s_j^2, ..., s_j^m$ that partition s_j. Based on this observation, the following lemma establishes the necessary condition for $Pr(ed(r,S) \leq k) > 0$.

LEMMA 2. *Given a string r and a string S partitioned into $m > k$ disjoint segments, for r to be similar to S i.e., $Pr(ed(r,S) \leq k) > 0$, r must contain substrings that match at-least $(m-k)$ segments of S.*

To apply the above lemma, we can obtain a set $q(r,x)$ using position aware selection as described earlier and use it to match against segment S^x. Table 1 shows the above lemma applied to a collection of uncertain strings. None of the segments of S_1 match any substring in r and hence they can not form a candidate pair. For S_2, even though the second segment matches some substring in r, we do not use it as we know by position aware substring selection that such an alignment can not lead to an instance of S that is similar to r. We can reject S_2 as well since it has only one matched segment. Strings S_3 and S_4 survive this pruning step and are taken forward.

Table 1: Application of q-gram Filtering

$m=3$, $q=2$, $k=1$, τ=0.25			
r	GGATCC		
$q(r,x)$	GG GA	GA AT TC	TC CC
S_1	A{(C,0.5),(G,0.5)}A{(C,0.5),(G,0.5)}AC		
	(AC,0.5) (AG,0.5)	(AC,0.5) (AG,0.5)	(AC,1)
S_2	AA{(G,0.9),(T,0.1)}G{(C,0.3),(G,0.2),(T,0.5)}C		
	(AA,1)	(GG,0.9) (TG,0.1)	(CC,0.3)✓ (GC,0.2) (TC,0.5)✓
S_3	G{(A,0.8),(G,0.2)}CT{(A,0.8),(C,0.1),(T,0.1)}C		
	(GA,0.8)✓ (GG,0.2)✓	(CT,1)	(AC,0.8) (CC,0.1)✓ (TC,0.1)✓
S_4	{(G,0.8),(T,0.2)}GA{(C,0.3),(G,0.2),(T,0.5)}CT		
	(GG,0.8)✓ (TG,0.2)	(AC,0.3) (AG,0.2) (AT,0.5)✓	(CT,1)

Computing upper bound for $Pr(ed(r,S) \leq k)$:
So far we were interested in knowing if there exists a substring $w \in q(r,x)$ that matches segment S^x. We now try to compute the probability that one or more substrings in $q(r,x)$ match S^x. Let E_x denote such an event with probability α_x. Then $\alpha_x = Pr(E_x) = \sum_{w \in q(r,x)} Pr(w = S^x)$. The correctness of α_x relies on the following observations:

- $q(r,x)$, being a set, contains all distinct substrings.
- Event of substring $w_i \in q(r,x)$ matching S^x is independent of substring $w_j \in q(r,x)$ matching S^x for $w_i \neq w_j$.

Next, our idea is to prune out the possible worlds of S which can not satisfy the edit-distance threshold k with r and obtain a set $\mathcal{C} \subseteq \Omega$ of candidate worlds. We can then use $Pr(\mathcal{C}) = \sum_{pw_j \in \mathcal{C}} p(pw_j)$ as the upper bound on $Pr(ed(r,S) \leq k)$. Consider a possible world pw_j in which s_j is the possible instance of S. s_j being the deterministic string, we can apply the process of q-gram filtering described in Section 2.1 to quickly assess if s_j can give edit distance within threshold k. If yes, pw_j is a candidate world and we include it in $\mathcal{C}$. This naive method requires all possible worlds of S to be instantiated and hence is too expensive to be used. Below we show how to achieve the desired upper bound i.e., $Pr(\mathcal{C})$ without explicitly listing set Ω or $\mathcal{C}$.

For ease of explanation, let $m = k+1$. We partition the possible worlds in Ω into sets$\Omega_0, \Omega_1, ..., \Omega_m$ such that:

- Ω_y includes any possible world pw_j where r contains substrings matching exactly y segments from $s_j^1, ..., s_j^m$ that partition s_j i.e., $y = |\{s_j^x | s_j^x \in q(r,x) \text{ for } x = 1,2,..,m\}|$.
- $\Omega = \Omega_0 \cup \Omega_1 \cup \Omega_2 \cup ... \cup \Omega_m$
- $\Omega_y \cap \Omega_z = \emptyset$ for $y \neq z$

With this partitioning ofΩ , we have following:

$$Pr(\mathcal{C}) = Pr(\Omega_1 \cup \Omega_2 \cup ... \cup \Omega_m) = Pr(\Omega \setminus \Omega_0)$$
$$= Pr(\Omega) - Pr(\Omega_0) = 1 - \prod_{x=1}^{m}(1 - \alpha_x)$$

In the above equation,Ω_0 denotes the event that none of the segments of S match substrings of r. By slight abuse of notation, we say S^x matches r (using position aware substring selection) if $\alpha_x > 0$. Then, the following lemma summarizes our result on the upper bound.

LEMMA 3. *Let r and S be the given strings with edit threshold k. If S is partitioned into $m = k + 1$ disjoint segments, $Pr(ed(r, S) \leq k)$ is upper bounded by $(1 - \prod_{x=1}^{m}(1 - \alpha_x))$, where α_x gives the probability that segment S^x matches r.*

Generalizing upper bound for $m > k$***:***
Finally, we turn our attention to compute $Pr(\mathcal{C})$ for the scenario where S is partitioned into $m > k$ segments. Once again considering the partitioning of Ω introduced above $Pr(\mathcal{C}) = Pr(\cup_{y=(m-k)}^{m}\Omega_y) = \sum_{y=m-k}^{m} Pr(\Omega_y)$. Then we observe that computing $Pr(\Omega_y)$ in this equation boils down to the following problem: There are m events E_x ($x = 1, 2, ..m$) and we are given $Pr(E_x) = \alpha_x$. What is the probability that exactly y events (among those m events) happen? Our solution is as follows. Let $Pr(i, j)$ denote the probability that, within the first i events, j of them happen. We then have the following recursive equation: $Pr(i, j) = Pr(E_i)Pr(i-1, j-1) + (1-Pr(E_i))Pr(i-1, j)$. By populating the $m \times m$ matrix using a dynamic programming algorithm based on the above recursion, we can lookup the last column to find out $Pr(\Omega_y)$ for $y = m - k, ..., m$. This recursion gives us an efficient ($O(m^2)$) way to compute $Pr(\mathcal{C})$. We note that it is possible to improve the running time to $O(m(m-k))$, but leave out the details for simplicity.

THEOREM 1. *Let r and S be the given strings with edit threshold k. Also assume S is partitioned into $m > k$ disjoint segments and α_x represents the probability that segment S^x matches r. Then $Pr(ed(r, S) \leq k)$ is upper bounded by the probability that at-least $(m - k)$ segments of S match r or in another words probability that r contains substrings matching at-least $(m - k)$ segments of S.*

Continuing the example in Table 1, we now try to apply the above theorem to strings S_3 and S_4. For S_3 we have $\alpha_1 = 1$, $\alpha_2 = 0$, and $\alpha_3 = 0.2$. Therefore the upper bound on S_3's similarity with r is $0.2 < \tau$ and S_3 can be rejected. Even though four out of six possible worlds of S_3 contribute to $\mathcal{C}$, the probability of each of them being small their collective contribution falls short of τ. Similarly the upper bound for S_4 can be computed as 0.4 and the pair (r, S_4) qualifies as a candidate pair. Thus Theorem 1 with an implicit requirement of Lemma 2 to be satisfied integrates q-gram filtering and probabilistic pruning.

Let string S be preprocessed such that each segment S^x is maintained as a list of pairs $(s_j^x, p(s_j^x))$, where s_j^x is an instance of S^x with probability $p(s_j^x)$. Also assume r is preprocessed and sets $q(r, x)$ are available to us for $x = 1, 2, .., m$ ($|q(r, x)| = k + 1$, $\sum_{x=1}^{m} |q(r, x)| = (k + 1)m$). Then the desired upper bound can be computed efficiently by applying the above theorem as it only adds the following computational overhead in comparison to its counterpart of deterministic strings: (1) computation cost for α_x of each segment is bounded by k and mk overall, (2) the cost of computing $Pr(\mathcal{C})$ using dynamic programming is bounded by $m(m-k)$.

3.2 Bounding $Pr(ed(R, S) \leq k)$

In this subsection, we follow the analysis from the earlier subsection taking into account the uncertainty introduced for string R. The possible worlds Ω of R and S is the set of all possible instances of $R \times S$. A possible world $pw_{i,j} \in \Omega$ is a pair $((r_i, s_j), p(r_i) * p(s_j))$, where s_j (r_i) is an instance of S (R) with probability $p(s_j)$ ($p(r_i)$). Also $p(r_i) * p(s_j)$ denote the probability of existence of a possible world $pw_{i,j}$ and $\sum p(pw_{i,j}) = 1$. Then by definition, $Pr(ed(R, S) \leq k) = \sum_{ed(r_i,s_j) \leq k} p(pw_{i,j})$.

Necessary condition for $Pr(ed(R, S) \leq k) > 0$***:***
We begin by partitioning the string S into $m > k$ disjoint substrings as before and assume q to be the length of each partition. Then the following lemma establishes the necessary condition for R to be similar to S within edit threshold.

LEMMA 4. *Given a string R and a string S partitioned into $m > k$ disjoint segments, for R to be similar to S i.e., $Pr(ed(R, S) \leq k) > 0$, R must contain substrings that match at-least $(m - k)$ segments of S.*

The correctness of the above lemma can be verified by extending the earlier observation as follows: Let R contain substrings matching $m' \leq m$ segments of S i.e., the number of segments of S with $Pr(W = S^x) > 0$ for any (uncertain) substring W of R is m'. Then for any $pw_{i,j} \in \Omega$, r_i contains substrings that match with at most m' segments from $s_j^1, s_j^2, ..., s_j^m$ that partition s_j. Next, we obtain a set $q(R, x)$ for each segment S^x of S using the position aware substring selection. This allows us to only test substrings $W \in q(R, x)$ for a match against S^x. We highlight that the substring selection mechanism only relies on the length of two strings R and S, start position of a substring W of R and that of S^x. Therefore following same arguments in [14], we can prove that any similar pair (R, S) will be reported as a candidate.

Computing α_x***:***
Let E_x denote an event that one or more substrings in set $q(R, x)$ match segment S^x and let α_x be its probability. Using a trivial extension of the earlier result in Section 3.1, we could perhaps compute $\alpha_x = Pr(E_x) = \sum_{W \in q(R,x)} Pr(W = S^x)$. However, we show that this leads to incorrect computation of α_x and requires a careful investigation. Let $R = A\{(A, 0.8), (C, 0.2)\}AATT$, $S = A\{(A, 0.8), (C, 0.2)\}AGCT$, $k = 1$ and $q = 3$. Then, we have $S^1 = A\{(A, 0.8), (C, 0.2)\}A$, $q(R, 1) = \{A\{(A, 0.8), (C, 0.2)\}A, \{(A, 0.8), (C, 0.2)\}AA\}$. Using the above formula $Pr(E_1) = 0.64+0.04+0.64 = 1.32$, which is definitely incorrect. To understand the scenario better, let's replace each substring $W \in q(R, x)$ by a list of pairs $(w_j, p(w_j))$, where w_j is an instance of W with probability $p(w_j)$. Note that it is only a different way of representing set $q(R, x)$ and both representations are equivalent. $q(R, 1) = \{(AAA, 0.8), (ACA, 0.2), (AAA, 0.8), (CAA, 0.2)\}$ and $Pr(E_1) = \sum_{w \in q(R,x)} p(w) \times Pr(w = S^x) = 1.32$ as before. However, this representation reveals that we have violated the second observation which requires matching of two substrings $w_i, w_j \in q(R, x)$ with S^x to be independent events. In the current example, both occurrences of a substring AAA in $q(R, 1)$ belong to same possible world and effectively its probability contributes twice to $Pr(E_1)$.

We overcome this issue by obtaining an equivalent set $q(r,x)$ of $q(R,x)$ that satisfies the substring uniqueness requirement i.e., $w_i \neq w_j$ for all $w_i, w_j \in q(r,x)$ with $i \neq j$, and implicitly make the matching of two of its substrings with S^x independent events. To achieve this we pick up all distinct (deterministic) substrings $w \in q(R,x)$ (think of a representation of set $q(R,x)$ consisting of $(w_j, p(w_j))$ pairs) to be part of $q(r,x)$. To distinguish between these two sets, let $p_R(w_j)$ represent the probability associated with substring w_j in $q(R,x)$ and $p_r(w_j)$ be the same for $q(r,x)$. Then, we maintain the equivalence of sets by following the two step process described below for each $w \in q(r,x)$ and obtain the probability to be associated with it i.e., $p_r(w)$.

Step 1: Sort all occurrences of w in $q(R,x)$ by their start positions in R. Group together all occurrences that overlap with each other in R to obtain groups $g_1, g_2, ...$ Then no two occurrences across the groups overlap each other. Such a grouping is required only when there is a suffix-prefix match for w (i.e., some suffix of w represents same string as its prefix), otherwise all its overlapping occurrences represent different possible worlds of R and hence are in a single group by themselves. We assign the probability $p(g_i)$ to each group g_i as described below. Let ps_j represent the start position of occurrence w_j in R for $j = 1, 2, .., |g_i|$. The region of overlap between an occurrence w_j of w and its previous occurrences in R is given by range $[y, z] = [ps_j, ps_{j-1} + q - 1]$. We define $\beta_j = \beta_{j-1} + pr_R(w_j) - Pr(w_j[1..(z - y + 1)] = R[y..z])$ with the initial condition $\beta_0 = 1$, $ps_0 = -1$. Then $p(g_i) = \beta_{|g_i|}$. In essence, we keep adding the probability of every occurrence while taking out the probability of its overlap.

Step 2: Assign $p_r(w) = 1 - \prod(1 - p(g_i))$.

The first step combines all overlapping occurrences into a single event and then we find out the probability that at-least one of these events takes place in second step. Now we can correctly compute the probability of event S^x matching substrings in $q(R,x)$ by using its equivalent set $q(r,x)$ as $\alpha_x = Pr(E_x) = \sum_{w \in q(r,x)} p_r(w) \times Pr(w = S^x)$. For the example under consideration, for a substring "AAA" we obtain a single group with its associated probability 0.8 using the process described above. Then $q(r,1) = \{(AAA, 0.8), (ACA, 0.2), (CAA, 0.2)\}$ and $Pr(E_1) = 0.68$ is correctly computed.

Computing upper bound for $Pr(ed(R,S) \leq k)$***:***
Finally, to obtain the upper bound on $Pr(ed(R,S) \leq k)$ we obtain set $\mathcal{C} \subseteq \Omega$ by pruning out those possible worlds which can not satisfy the edit-distance threshold k. Consider a possible world $pw_{i,j}$ in which s_j (r_i) is a possible instance of S (R). Both r_i and s_j being deterministic strings, we can quickly assess if r_i and s_j can be within edit distance k by applying the process of q-gram filtering described in Section 2.1. If affirmative, $pw_{i,j}$ is a candidate world and we include it in $\mathcal{C}$. However, our goal is to compute $Pr(\mathcal{C})$ without enumerating all possible worlds of $R \times S$. As before, we partition the possible worlds in Ω into sets$\Omega_0, \Omega_1, ..., \Omega_m$ such that $\Omega = \cup_{y=0}^{m} \Omega_y$ and$\Omega_y \cap \Omega_z = \emptyset$ for $y \neq z$. Moreover, Ω_y includes any possible world $pw_{i,j}$ where r_i contains substrings matching exactly y segments from $s_j^1, ..., s_j^m$ that partition s_j i.e, $y = |\{s_j^x | s_j^x \in q(r_i, x) \text{ for } x = 1, 2, .., m\}|$. Then $Pr(\mathcal{C}) = Pr(\cup_{y=(m-k)}^{m} \Omega_y) = \sum_{y=m-k}^{m} Pr(\Omega_y)$ and can be computed by following the same dynamic programming approach described earlier. Therefore the key difference in the current scenario (both R and S are uncertain) from the one in the previous subsection is the computation of α_x. After computing all α_x we can directly apply Lemma 2 and Theorem 1 and are rewritten as below. By slight abuse of notation as before, we say S^x matches R if $\alpha_x > 0$.

LEMMA 5. *Let R, S be the given strings with edit threshold k. If S is partitioned into $m = k+1$ disjoint segments, $Pr(ed(R,S) \leq k)$ is upper bounded by $(1 - \prod_{x=1}^{m}(1 - \alpha_x))$, where α_x gives the probability that segment S^x matches R.*

THEOREM 2. *Let R, S be the given strings with edit threshold k. Also assume S is partitioned into $m > k$ disjoint segments and α_x represents the probability that segment S^x matches R. Then $Pr(ed(R,S) \leq k)$ is upper bounded by the probability that at-least $(m - k)$ segments of S match R or, in another words the probability that R contains substrings matching at-least $(m - k)$ segments of S.*

It is evident that the cost of computing the upper bound in the above theorem is dominated by the set $q(r,x)$ computations. If this is assumed to be part of the preprocessing then the overhead involved is exactly the same as in the previous subsection. Let the fraction of uncertain characters in the strings be θ, and the average number of alternatives of an uncertain character be γ. For analysis of q-gram filtering, we assume uncertain character positions to be uniformly distributed from now onwards. Then $|q(r,x)| = (k+1)\gamma^{\theta \cdot q}$, and computing set $q(r,x)$ for each segment takes $q\gamma^{\theta \cdot q}$ times when string R is deterministic (previous subsection). Note that the multiplicative q appears only when substring w has a suffix-prefix match and its occurrences in set $q(R,x)$ overlap. Assuming typical values $\theta = 20\%$, $\gamma = 5$ and $q = 3$, it takes only two and half times longer to compute α_x when R is uncertain using $q(r,x)$.

4. INDEXING

Using Theorem 2 we observe that if a string R does not have substrings that match a sufficient number of segments of S, we can prune the pair (R, S). We use an indexing technique that facilitates the implementation of this feature to prune large numbers of dissimilar pairs. So far we assumed each string S is partitioned into m segments, each of which is of length q. In practice, we fix q as a system parameter and then divide S into as many disjoint segments as necessary i.e. $m = max(k+1, \lfloor |S|/q \rfloor)$. Without loss of generality let $m = \lfloor |S|/q \rfloor$. We use an even-partition scheme [14, 15] so that each segment has a length of q or $q+1$. Thus we partition S such that the last $|S| - \lfloor |S|/q \rfloor * q$ segments have length $q+1$ and length is q for the rest of them.

Let $\mathcal{S}_l$ denote the set of strings with length l and $\mathcal{S}_l^x$ denote the set of the x-th segments of strings in S_l. We build an inverted index for each $\mathcal{S}_l^x$ denoted by $\mathcal{L}_l^x$ as follows. Consider a string $S_i \in \mathcal{S}_l$. We instantiate all possibilities of its segment S_i^x and add them to $\mathcal{L}_l^x$ along with their probabilities. Thus $\mathcal{L}_l^x$ is a list of deterministic strings and for each string w, its inverted list $\mathcal{L}_l^x(w)$ is the set of uncertain strings whose x-th segment matches w tagged with probability of such a match. To be precise, $\mathcal{L}_l^x(w)$ is enumeration of pairs $(i, Pr(w = S_i^x))$ where i is the string-id. By design, each such inverted list $\mathcal{L}_l^x(w)$ is sorted by string-ids as described later. We emphasize that a string-id i appears at most once in any $\mathcal{L}_l^x(w)$ and in as many lists $\mathcal{L}_l^x(w)$ as the number of possible instances of S_i^x. We use these inverted indices to answer the similarity join query as follows.

We sort strings based on their lengths in ascending order and visit them in the same order. Consider the current string $R = S_i$. We find strings similar to R among the visited strings only using the inverted indices. This implies we maintain indices only for visited strings to avoid enumerating a string pair twice. It is clear that we need to look for similar strings in $\mathcal{S}_l$ by querying its associated index only if $|R| - k \leq l \leq |R|$. To find strings similar to R, we first obtain candidate strings using the proposed indexing as described in next paragraph. We then subject these candidate pairs to frequency distance filtering (Section 5). Candidate pairs that survive both these steps are evaluated with CDF bounds (Section 6.1) with the final verification step (Section 6.2) outputting only the strings that are similar to R. After finding similar strings for $R = S_i$, we partition S_i into $m > k$ (as dictated by q) segments and insert the segments into appropriate inverted index. Then we move on to the next string $R = S_{i+1}$ and iteratively find all similar pairs.

Finally, given a string R, we show how to query the index associated with $\mathcal{S}_l$ to find candidate pairs (R, S) such that $S \in \mathcal{S}_l$ and $Pr(ed(R,S) \leq k) > \tau$. We preprocess R to obtain $q(r,x)$ that can be used to query each inverted index $\mathcal{L}_l^x$. For each $w \in q(r,x)$ we obtain an inverted list $\mathcal{L}_l^x(w)$. Since all lists are sorted by string-id, we can scan them in parallel to produce a merged (union) list of all string-ids i along with the α_x computed for each of them. We maintain a *top* pointer in each $\mathcal{L}_l^x(w)$ list that initially points to its first element. At each step, we find out the minimum string-id i among the elements currently at the top of each list, compute α_x for a pair (R, S_i) using the probabilities associated with string-id i in all $\mathcal{L}_l^x(w)$ lists (if present). After outputting the string-id and its α_x as a pair in the merged list, we increment the *top* pointers for those $\mathcal{L}_l^x(w)$ lists which have the *top* currently pointing to the element with string-id i. Let the merged list be $\mathcal{L}\alpha_x$. Once again all $\mathcal{L}\alpha_x$ lists for $x = 1, 2, .., m$ are sorted by string-ids. Therefore by employing *top* pointers and scanning lists $\mathcal{L}\alpha_x$ in parallel, we can count the number of segments in S_i that matched with their respective $q(r,x)$ by counting the number of $\mathcal{L}\alpha_x$ lists that contain string-id i. If the count is less than $m-k$ we can safely prune out candidate pair (R, S_i) using Lemma 5. Otherwise, we can compute the upper bound on $Pr(ed(R, S_i) \leq k)$ by supplying the α_x values already computed to the dynamic programming algorithm. If the upper bound does not meet our probability threshold requirement, we can discard string S_i as it can not be similar to R by Theorem 2, otherwise (R, S_i) is a candidate pair.

Given a string R, the proposed indexing scheme allows us to obtain all strings $S \in \mathcal{S}$ that are likely to be similar to R without explicitly comparing R to each and every string in $\mathcal{S}$ as has been done for related problems in the area of uncertain strings [10, 6, 4]. For a string r in a deterministic strings collection, we need to consider $m(k+1)$ of its substrings while answering the join query using the procedure just described. In comparison, in the probabilistic setting we need to consider $m(k+1)\gamma^{\theta \cdot q}$ deterministic substrings of R. Moreover, a string-id can belong to at most $\gamma^{\theta \cdot q}$ inverted lists in $\mathcal{L}_l^x$ in probabilistic setting whereas inverted lists are disjoint for deterministic strings collection. Thus, the proposed indexing achieves competitive performance against its counterpart for answering a join query over deterministic strings. Further, indexing scheme uses disjoint q-grams of strings instead of overlapping ones as in [6, 4]. This allows us to use slightly larger q with same storage requirements.

5. FREQUENCY DISTANCE FILTERING

As noted in [4], frequency distance displays great variation with increase in the number of uncertain positions in a string and can be effective to prune out dissimilar string pairs. We first obtain a simple lower bound on $fd(R, S)$ and then show how to quickly compute the upper bound for the same. For each character $c_i \in \Sigma$, let $f(S)_i^c$, $f(S)_i^t$ denote the minimum and maximum possible number of its occurrences in S respectively. For brevity, we drop the function notations and denote these occurrences as fS_i^c and fS_i^t. Note that fS_i^c also represents the number of occurrences of c_i in S with probability 1 and fS_i^t represents the number of certain and uncertain positions of c_i. Thus $fS_i^u = fS_i^t - fS_i^c$ gives the uncertain positions of c_i in S. fR_i^c, fR_i^u and fR_i^t are defined similarly. We observe that, if $fR_i^t < fS_i^c$, any possible world pw of $R \times S$, will have a frequency distance at least $(fS_i^c - fR_i^t)$. By generalizing this observation, we can obtain a lower bound on $fd(R, S)$ as summarized below.

LEMMA 6. *Let R and S be two strings from the same alphabet Σ, the we have $fd(R,S) \geq max\{pD, nD\}$, where*

$$pD = \sum_{fS_i^t < fR_i^c} (fR_i^c - fS_i^t),\ nD = \sum_{fR_i^t < fS_i^c} (fS_i^c - fR_i^t)$$

Since the edit distance of a string pair is lower bounded by its frequency distance, we can prune out (R, S) if the minimum frequency distance obtained by above the lemma is more than the desired edit threshold k. To obtain the upper bound on the probability of $fd(R, S)$ being at most k, we use the technique introduced in [4] that relies on the expected value of all possible frequency distances. Using such an expectation for positive and negative frequency distance $(E[pD], E[nD])$, One-Sided Chebyshev Inequality and following the same analysis in [4], we obtain following theorem.

THEOREM 3. *Let R and S be two strings from the same alphabet Σ. Then we have,*

$$Pr(ed(R,S) \leq k) \leq Pr(fd(R,S) \leq k) \leq \frac{B^2}{B^2 + (A-k)^2}$$

$$where,\ A = \frac{||R| - |S||}{2} + \frac{E[pD] + E[nD]}{2}$$

$$B^2 = \frac{(|R| - |S|)^2}{2} + \frac{(||R| - |S||)(E[pD] + E[nD])}{2} + min(|R| \cdot E[nD], |S| \cdot E[pD]) - A^2$$

The main obstacle in using the above theorem is efficient computation of $E[pD] = \sum_{c_i} E(fR_i - fS_i)$, $E[nD] = \sum_{c_i} E(fS_i - fR_i)$. We focus on computing $E[nD]$ below as $E[pD]$ can be computed in a similar fashion. With frequency of c_i in S i.e. fS_i varying between fS_i^c and fS_i^t, let $Pr(fS_i = x)$ represents the probability that c_i appears exactly x times. Putting it an other way, $Pr(fS_i = x)$ represents the probability that c_i appears at exactly $(x - fS_i^c)$ uncertain positions from (fS_i^u) uncertain positions overall. This leads to a natural dynamic programming algorithm that can compute $Pr(fS_i = x)$ for all $x = fS_i^c, ..., fS_i^t$ by spending $O((fS_i^u)^2)$ time. Please refer to [4] more details. With the goal of efficiency in computing $E[nD]$, authors preprocess S and maintain these values in $O(fS_i^u)$ space. Without loss of generality, let $fR_i^c < fS_i^c \leq fR_i^t < fS_i^t$. Then by definition, $E[nD] = \sum_{c_i} E[nD_i]$ where,

$$E[nD_i] = \sum_{x=fR_i^c}^{fR_i^t} \sum_{\substack{y=max\\(x+1, fS_i^c)}}^{fS_i^t} Pr(fR_i = x) Pr(fS_i = y)(y - x)$$

In the above equation, $Pr(fR_i = x)$ and $Pr(fS_i = y)$ can be computed in constant time using precomputed answers. Therefore, a naive way of computing $E[nD_i]$ will take $O(fS_i^u fR_i^u)$. Below we speed up this computation and achieve $min(fS_i^u, fR_i^u)$ time. We maintain the following probability distributions for each c_i of S. For $0 \leq x \leq fS_i^u$,

$$S1_i[x] = Pr(fS_i = fS_i^c + x)$$

$$S2_i[x] = \sum_{y=x}^{fS_i^u} Pr(fS_i = fS_i^c + y)$$

$$S3_i[x] = \sum_{y=x}^{fS_i^u} (y - x + 1) Pr(fS_i = fS_i^c + y)$$

$$S4_i[x] = \sum_{y=0}^{x} (x - y) Pr(fS_i = fS_i^c + y)$$

$S1_i$ is simply a probability distribution of c_i appearing at uncertain positions in range $[0, fS_i^u]$ (precomputed using dynamic programming). $S2_i$ maintains the probability that c_i appears at at-least x uncertain positions i.e. $S2_i[x] = Pr(fS_i \geq fS_i^c + x)$. $S3_i$ maintains the same summation with elements in the summation series scaled by $1, 2, ...$ Finally $S4_i$ takes the summation series for $Pr(fS_i \leq fS_i^c + x)$, scales it by $0, 1, ...$ in reverse direction and maintains the output at index x. The intuition behind maintaining the scaled summations is that, given a particular frequency z of fR_i, the expectation of its frequency distance with $fS_i \in [fS_i^c, fS_i^t]$ resembles the summation series for $S3_i[x]$ or $S4_i[x]$. All the above distributions can be computed in $O(fS_i^u)$ time and occupy the same $O(fS_i^u)$ storage. Similar probability distributions are also maintained for R. We achieve the speed up without hurting preprocessing time and at no additional storage cost. $E[nD_i]$ can now be computed as follows:

$$E[nD_i] = \sum_{x=fR_i^c}^{fS_i^c - 1} \sum_{y=fS_i^c}^{fS_i^t} (...) + \sum_{x=fS_i^c}^{fR_i^t} \sum_{y=x+1}^{fS_i^t} (...)$$
$$= nD_i^1 + nD_i^2$$

$$nD_i^1 = \sum_{x=fR_i^c}^{fS_i^c - 1} Pr(fR_i = x) (\sum_{y=fS_i^c}^{fS_i^t} Pr(fS_i = y)(y - x))$$

$$= \sum_{x=fR_i^c}^{fS_i^c - 1} Pr(fR_i = x)(fS_i^c - x - 1) \sum_{y=fS_i^c}^{fS_i^t} Pr(fS_i = y)$$

$$+ \sum_{x=fR_i^c}^{fS_i^c - 1} Pr(fR_i = x) \sum_{y=fS_i^c}^{fS_i^t} Pr(fS_i = y)(y - fS_i^c + 1)$$

$$= R4_i[fS_i^c - fR_i^c - 1] \times S2_i[0]$$
$$+ (R2_i[0] - R2_i[fS_i^c - fR_i^c]) \times S3_i[0]$$

$$nD_i^2 = \sum_{x=fS_i^c}^{fR_i^t} Pr(fR_i = x) \sum_{y=x+1}^{fS_i^t} Pr(fS_i = y)(y - x)$$

$$= \sum_{x=fS_i^c}^{fS_i^t} R1_i[x - fR_i^c] \times S2_i[x - fS_i^c + 1]$$

If the fraction of uncertain characters in the strings is θ, frequency filtering summarized in Theorem 3 can be applied in $O(\sigma\theta(|R| + |S|))$. Typical alphabet size being constant, the efficiency of applying frequency filtering depends on the degree of uncertainty and string lengths. Therefore, with increase in length of input strings, improvement from $|R| \times |S|$ to $|R| + |S|$ provides substantial reduction in the filtering time. While answering the similarity join query, we preprocess $R = S_i \in \mathcal{S}_l$ to compute the arrays for each character in alphabet Σ and maintain them as a part of our index. All candidate pairs passing the q-gram filtering are then subjected to frequency distance filtering for further refinement before moving onto next string $R = S_{i+1} \in \mathcal{S}_l$.

6. VERIFICATION

The goal of verification is to conclude whether strings in the candidate pair (R, S) that has survived the above filters, are indeed similar i.e., $Pr(ed(R, S) \leq k) > \tau$. A straightforward solution is to instantiate each possible world of $R \times S$ and add up the probabilities of possible worlds where possible instances of R, S are within edit threshold k. Before resorting to such expensive verification, we make a last attempt to prune out a candidate pair, by extending the CDF bounds in [6]. If unsuccessful, we use the trie-based verification that exploits common prefixes shared by instances of an uncertain string.

6.1 Bound based on CDF

We briefly review the process in [6] and highlight the changes needed to compute the mentioned bounds correctly when both input strings are uncertain. We populate the matrix $|R| \times |S|$ using dynamic programming. In each cell $D = (x, y)$, we compute (at most) $k + 1$ pairs of values i.e., $\{(L[j], U[j]) | 0 \leq j \leq k\}$, where $L[j]$ and $U[j]$ are the lower and upper bounds of $Pr(ed(R[1..x], S[1..y]) \leq j)$ respectively. Then by checking the bounds in the cell $(|R|, |S|)$, we can accept or reject the candidate string pair (R, S), if possible. To fill in the DP table, consider a basic step of computing bounds of a cell $D = (x, y)$ from its neighboring cells - upper left: $D1 = (x-1, y-1)$, upper: $D2 = (x, y-1)$, and left: $D3 = (x-1, y)$. As noted in [6], when the $R[x]$ matches $S[y]$ (with probability $p_1 = \sum_{c_i} Pr(R[x] = c_i) Pr(S[y] = c_i)$), it is always optimal to take the distribution from the diagonal upper left neighbor. When $R[x]$ does not match $S[y]$ with probability $p_2 = 1 - p_1$, we use the relaxations suggested in [6]. Let $(argmin D_i)$ returns index i $(1 \leq i \leq 3)$ such that $L_{D_i}[0]$ is greatest; a tie is broken by selecting the greatest $L_{D_i}[1]$ and so on.

THEOREM 4. *At each cell $D = (x, y)$ of the DP table, $L[j] \leq Pr(ed(R[1..x], S[1..y]) \leq j) \leq U[j]$, where*

$$L[j] = max(p_1 L_{D_1}[j],\ p_2 L_{(argmin\ D_i)}[j-1])$$

$$U[j] = min(1,\ p_1 U_{D_1}[j] + p_2 U_{D_1}[j-1] + \sum_{i=2}^{3} U_{D_i}[j-1])$$

PROOF. We follow the analysis in [6] as follows. Consider a possible world $pw_{i,j}$ in which $r_i[x] = s_j[y]$. Let the distance values at cells D and D_i $(1 \leq i \leq 3)$ be v and v_i, respectively. Then we have $v = v_1$. This is because $v_2, v_3 \geq v_1 - 1$; thus, $v = min(v_1, v_2 + 1, v_3 + 1) = v_1$. Next, consider a possible world $pw_{i,j}$ in which $r_i[x] \neq s_j[y]$. Then, $v = min(v_i) + 1$. By using $(argmin\ D_i)$, we pick one fixed

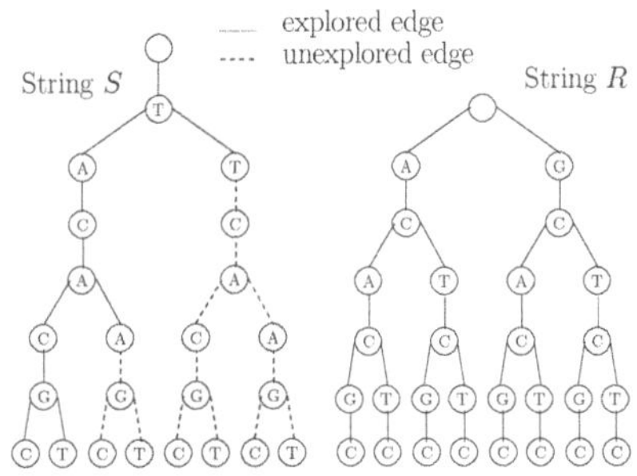

Figure 1: Trie-based Verification Example

neighbor cell (i.e., the one that has a small distance value with the highest probability) instead of accounting for all possible worlds in which $r_i[x] \neq s_j[y]$; and hence the true v value could be smaller than this one in some possible worlds. However, we observe that out of all possible worlds with distance v in the cell D, worlds with edit distance v in D_1 are not disjoint with worlds with distance $v-1$ for D_2. The same argument applies for worlds with $v-1$ as distance in D_3 as well. Therefore, we choose the maximum out of the two scenarios as our lower bound. For obtaining the upper bound, the case where $r_i[x]$ matches $s_j[y]$ remains the same. Possible world $pw_{i,j}$ with distance $v-1$ for D_2, can be extended by reading an addition character of R and we get distance v in cell D for all of them. Similarly, moving from distance $v-1$ in D_3 to distance v in D can be thought to be the case of inserting a character of S. Hence, we do not need to scale down the probability $U_{D_2}[v-1]$ as well $U_{D_3}[v-1]$ to obtain the upper bound for cell D. □

We note that the bounds summarized in the above theorem are different than the ones presented in [6], as they cannot be used directly for the current scenario[1]. Finally, the simple DP algorithm can be improved by computing $(L[j], U[j])$ only for those cells $D = (x, y)$ for which $|x-y| \leq k$, since $L[k] = U[k] = 0$ otherwise. Thus, we can apply the CDF bounds based filtering for a candidate pair (R, S) in $O(min(|R|, |S|)(k+1)max(k,\gamma))$ where γ is average number of alternatives of an uncertain character.

6.2 Trie-based Verification

Prefix-pruning has been a popular technique to expedite verification of a deterministic string pair (r, s) for edit threshold k. A naive approach for this verification would be to compute the dynamic programming matrix (DP) of size $|r| \times |s|$ such that cell (x, y) gives the edit distance between $r[1...x]$ and $s[1...y]$. Prefix-pruning observes that if all cells in row x i.e., $(x, *)$ do not meet threshold k, then the following rows can not have cells with edit distance k or less i.e., $DP[i > x, *] > k$. Even using such an early termination condition, verifying all-pairs (all possible of instance of $R \times S$) for a candidate pair (R, S) can be expensive. With the goal of avoiding naive all-pairs comparison, we propose trie-based verification. Let $\mathcal{T}_S$ be the trie of all possible instances of S and $\mathcal{T}_R$ be the same for string R. Let node u in $\mathcal{T}_S$ represents a string u (obtained by concatenating the edge labels from root to node u), then all possible instances of S with u as a prefix are leaves in the subtree rooted at u. We say a node $u \in \mathcal{T}_S$ is similar to node $v \in \mathcal{T}_R$ if $ed(u, v) \leq k$. Using prefix-pruning then we have following observation [5]:

- Given $u \in \mathcal{T}_S$, $v \in \mathcal{T}_R$: if u is not similar to any ancestor of v, and v is not similar to any ancestor of u, any possible instance s of S with prefix u can not be similar to a possible instance r of R with v as its prefix.

Using the technique in [11, 5], we can compute a set of similar nodes in $\mathcal{T}_R$ for each node $u \in \mathcal{T}_S$. Then, if $u = s_j$ is a leaf node, each node $v = r_i \in \mathcal{T}_R$ in its similar set that is also a leaf node, gives us a possible world $pw_{i,j}$ whose probability contributes to $Pr(ed(R, S) \leq k)$. However techniques in [5] implicitly assume both trie structures are available. Here we propose on-demand construction of trie which avoids all possible instances of S to be enumerated. Note that we still need to build the trie $\mathcal{T}_R$ completely. However its construction cost can be amortized as we build $\mathcal{T}_R$ once and use it for all candidate pairs $(R, *)$. As noted in [11], nodes in $\mathcal{T}_R$ that are similar to node $u \in \mathcal{T}_S$ can be computed efficiently only using such a similarity set already computed for its parent. This allows us to perform a (logical) depth first search on $\mathcal{T}_S$ and materialize the children of $u \in \mathcal{T}_S$ only if its similarity set is not empty. Figure 1 illustrates of this approach and reveals that on-demand trie construction can reduce the verification cost by avoiding instantiation and consequently comparison with a large fraction of possible worlds of S. In the figure, only the nodes linked with solid lines are explored and instantiated by the verification algorithm. Moreover, we do not display the similar node sets and the probabilities associated with trie nodes for simplicity.

7. EXPERIMENTS

We have implemented the proposed indexing scheme and filtering techniques in C++. The experiments are performed on a 64 bit machine with an Intel Core i5 CPU 3.33GHz processor and 8GB RAM running Ubuntu. We consider the following algorithms for comparisons which use only a subset of the filtering mechanisms. Algorithm QFCT makes use of all the filtering schemes listed in this article whereas QCT, QFT, FCT bypass frequency-distance filtering, filtering based on CDF bounds and q-gram filtering respectively.

Datasets: We use two synthetic datasets obtained from their real counterparts employing the technique used in [10, 4]. The first data source is the author names in dblp ($|\Sigma| = 27$). For each string s in the dblp dataset we first obtain a set $A(s)$ of strings that are within edit distance 4 to s. Then a character-level probabilistic string S for string s is generated such that, for a position i, the pdf of $S[i]$ is based on the normalized frequencies of the letters in the i-th position of all the strings in $A(s)$. The fraction of uncertain positions in a character-level probabilistic string i.e., θ is varied between 0.1 to 0.4 to generate strings with different degree of uncertainty. The string length distributions in this dataset follow approximately a normal distribution in the range of $[10, 35]$. For the second dataset we use a concatenated protein sequence of mouse and human ($|\Sigma| = 22$), and break it arbitrarily into shorter strings. Then uncertain strings are obtained by following the same procedure as that for the dblp data source. However, for this dataset we use slightly larger string lengths with less uncertainty i.e. string lengths roughly follow uniform distribution in the range $[20, 45]$ and θ ranges between 0.05 to 0.2. In both datasets, the average number of choices (γ) that each probabilistic character $S[i]$ may have is set to 5. The default values used for the dblp dataset are: the number of strings in collection $|\mathcal{S}| = 100$K,

[1]a) Lower bound violation: $r = ACC$, $S = A\{(C, 0.7), (G, 0.1), (T, 0.1)\}$ with $k = 1$. b) Upper bound violation: $r = DISC$, $S = DI\{(C, 0.4), (S, 0.5), (R = 0.1)\}$ with $k = 1$.

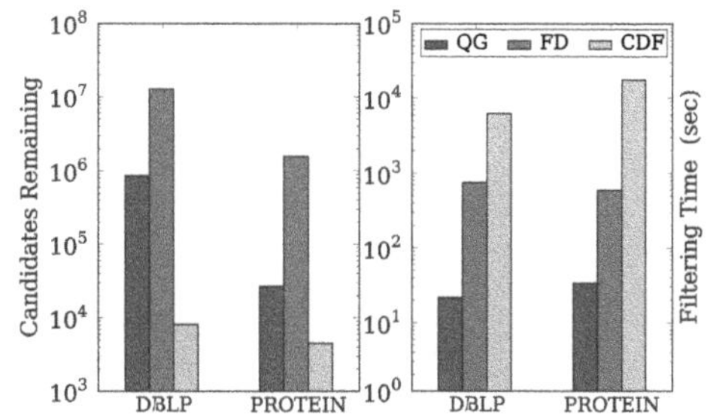

Figure 2: Effectiveness vs. Efficiency

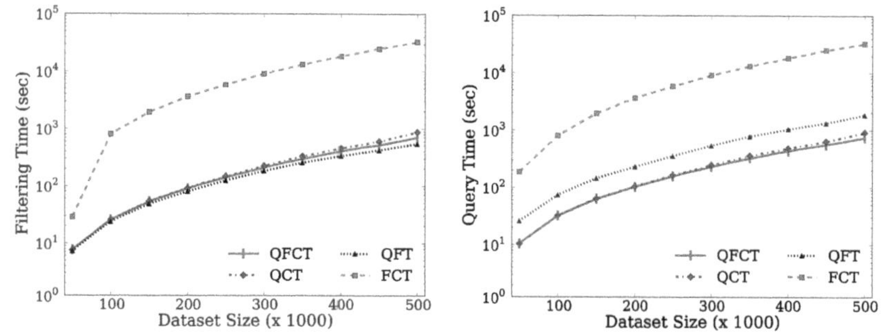

Figure 3: Effect of Dataset Size $|\mathcal{S}|$

average string length ≈ 19, $\theta = 0.2$, $k = 2$, $\tau = 0.1$, and $q = 3$. Similarly for protein dataset we use default setting with $|\mathcal{S}| = 100$K, average string length $= 32$, $\theta = 0.1$, $k = 4$, $\tau = 0.01$, and $q = 3$.

7.1 Effectiveness vs. Efficiency of Pruning

In this set of experiments, we compare the pruning ability of the filtering techniques and the overhead of applying them on both the datasets with $\theta = 0.2$, $k = 2$ and $\tau = 0.1$. Figure 2 shows the number of candidates remaining after applying each filtering scheme and reveals that CDF bounds provide the tightest filtering among the three. Effectiveness of the CDF follows from the fact that it uses upper as well as lower bounds to prune the strings. The upper bound obtained by q-gram filtering tends to be looser than the CDF as it depends on the partitioning based on q, whereas frequency distance based upper bound is sensitive to the length difference between two strings. However, the effectiveness of CDF comes at the cost of time. On the other hand, q-gram filtering is extremely fast and can still prune out a significant number of candidate pairs taking advantage of the indexing scheme. For the protein dataset, q-gram is close to CDF bounds in terms of effectiveness and is an order of magnitude faster than computing CDF bounds. Frequency distance filtering being dependent only on alphabet size and uncertain positions in the strings (against CDF's dependance on string length) can help to improve query performance by reducing the number of candidate pairs passed on to CDF for evaluation. Therefore, in the following experiments, algorithm variants use these filtering techniques in the increasing order of their overhead as suggested by their acronyms.

Figure 2 also reveals that applying q-gram filtering and the CDF bounds filtering takes longer for the protein dataset than for dblp data. Due to larger string length and fixed q, q-gram filtering needs to partition protein strings into a larger number of segments (i.e., m). Thus, there are more α_x probabilities to be computed and it takes longer to compute the desired upper bound in Theorem 2. Similarly, computing CDF bounds needs to populate a dynamic programming matrix whose size depends on the string lengths. However, frequency distance filtering benefits from smaller alphabet set and lower degree of uncertainty in protein sequences and shows better performance for the protein data.

7.2 Effects of Data Size $|\mathcal{S}|$

Figure 3 shows the scalability of various algorithms on the dblp dataset, where we vary $|\mathcal{S}|$ from 50K to 500K. With computationally inexpensive q-gram filtering as the first step, algorithms QFCT, QFT and QCT achieve efficient filtering even for the larger datasets. For the exceptional case of the algorithm FCT, the filtering overhead increases almost quadratically with increase in the input size as both filtering techniques (frequency distance and CDF bounds) need to explicitly compare the query string R with all possible strings $S \in \mathcal{S}$ ($|S| \geq |R| - k$). Also, the filtering time required for QFT and QCT closely follows that for QFCT. This confirms the ability of q-gram filtering to significantly reduce the filtering overhead, and highlights the advantages offered by the proposed indexing scheme incorporating it.

Figure 3 also shows the time required for answering the join query for these algorithms. FCT, lacking efficient filtering (though effective), takes the longest to output its answers. However, the query time for QFT, despite using efficient q-gram filtering, shows a rapid increase. In contrast to this, the good scalable behavior of QFCT and QCT emphasizes the need for using tight filtering conditions based on the lower and upper bounds of CDF. In the absence of these, exponentially more number of candidates need trie-based verification which results in quickly deteriorating query performance. Thus, a combination of q-gram filtering with CDF bounds in QFCT achieves the best of both worlds, allowing us to restrict the increase in both filtering time as well as the number of trie-based verifications. Though the number of outputs increased quadratically with data size, the increase in the number of false positives in the verification step of QFCT (i.e., the scenario where a candidate pair was not an output after verification) was found to be linear to the output size. An order of magnitude performance gain of QFCT over others seen in Figure 3 will be further extended for larger input collections. With algorithm QFT requiring a higher number of expensive verifications and QCT showing similar trends as that of QFCT, we use only the remaining two algorithms i.e., QFCT and FCT for the experiments to follow. We also append a character 'D' or 'P' to the algorithms acronym to distinguish between its query times on the dblp and protein datasets.

7.3 Effects of θ

An increase in the number of uncertain positions in the string has a detrimental effect on both algorithms QFCT and FCT as shown in Figure 4. This is due to the direct impact of θ on every step of the algorithm in answering join queries. Starting with the q-gram filtering, more uncertain positions for query string R imply more time required for populating the sets $q(r, x)$ as a preprocessing step, as well as for adding the string R to inverted indices after answering the query. Also the larger size of set $q(r, x)$ due to the increase in θ increases look up time in inverted indices and consequently

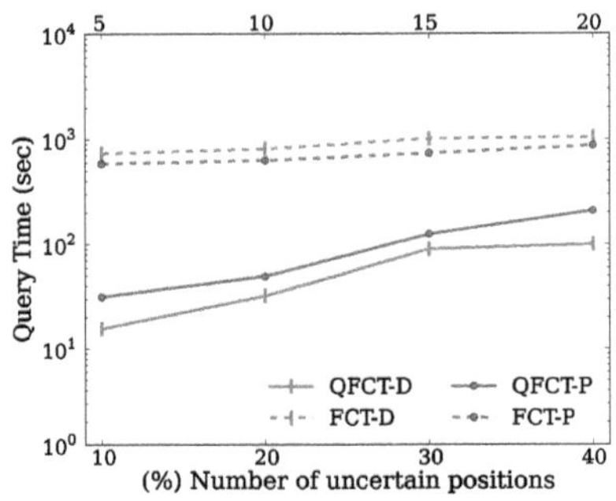

Figure 4: Effect of θ

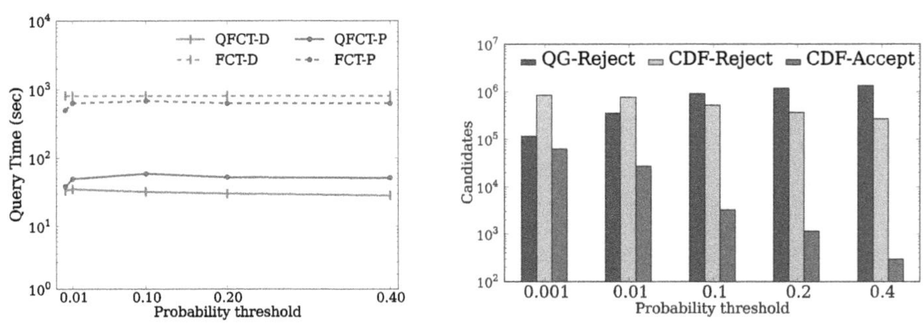

Figure 5: Effect of τ

increase the time required for computing α_x. Though size of a set $q(r,x)$ can increase exponentially with θ, its impact is limited due to the small fixed value of q. There is another subtle impact of θ on q-gram filtering. With more uncertain positions in query string R, more strings in the collection can be matched with substrings of R. We found this increase to be linear with $\approx 1.5\%$ of all join pairs evaluated by q-gram filtering for $\theta = 0.1$ to only $\approx 4\%$ evaluated for $\theta = 0.4$ on the dblp dataset. Thus, proposed q-gram filtering serves the purpose of efficient pruning even with the increased uncertainty.

The impact of θ on the computation of frequency distance and CDF bounds is more obvious. Computing the expected frequency distance of a character directly depends on the number of positions in input strings (R, S) where it appears probabilistically. Due to the probability computation of two positions matching in R and S ($R[x] = S[y]$), it takes longer to populate a dynamic programming matrix for CDF. Thus, the increase in filtering time of query algorithms is almost linear to θ. Finally, in the trie-based verification, more possible words need to be evaluated, increasing verification cost exponentially. In conclusion, the verification step is the worst affected among all due to large θ and is the primary contributor in increased time for answering join queries. We note that in most of the scenarios, algorithm QFCT takes longer to answer join queries for the protein data than for the dblp data because of the higher overhead of q-gram and CDF filtering, which we pointed out in Section 7.1. On the other hand, algorithm FCT performs better for the protein data by virtue of faster frequency filtering as seen earlier. This comparative behavior of QFCT and FCT is also evident in Figure 4.

7.4 Effects of τ

Figure 5 shows the results on the dblp and protein dataset for different values of τ from 0.001 to 0.4. Though the query times remain insensitive to τ for a large range, a gradual increase or decrease in probability threshold has a two fold effect on query algorithms. We analyze the scenario by looking at the number of candidate pairs pruned by CDF bounds either by accepting based on lower bound or rejecting based on upper bound. As τ increases, upper bound filter becomes more and more selective as it can reject more number of candidate pairs. On the contrary, filtering based on lower bound looses its effectiveness with increased τ as it can not accept as many strings as it can for smaller values of τ. Thus the relative increase and decrease in number of candidate pairs pruned by CDF upper and lower bound respectively determines the overall effect of varying τ. When upper bound filter can not compensate for the loss in effectiveness of lower bound, more candidate pairs require trie-based verification resulting in higher query time. Such a scenario is evident in Figure 5 for protein data for τ ranging from 0.001 to 0.1.

τ has an interesting effect on q-gram filtering. Figure 5 shows the number of candidates pairs rejected by q-gram filtering in QFCT. It also shows the count of accepted candidates using CDF lower bound and rejected by CDF upper bound in QFCT. Note that q-gram filtering only uses the upper bound and Figure 5 shows the reduced effectiveness of CDF lower bound filtering. As τ increases, probabilistic pruning (Theorem 2) becomes more effective and prunes out a significant number of candidate pairs that satisfy the necessary condition for two strings to be similar as described in Lemma 5 (shown in Figure 5). In effect, q-gram filtering reduces the overhead of applying CDF bounds and to some extent compensates for the increased verification cost, if any. This effect can be seen by gradual decrease in the number of candidates rejected by CDF even though an increased number of candidates are pruned using the upper bound overall. Finally, for large τ, the q-gram filtering advantage coupled with reduced output size due to more selective τ results in improved query time.

7.5 Effects of k

Figure 6 shows the time required for answering a join query on the dblp dataset when k changes from 1 to 4 and for the protein dataset with $k = 2, 4, 6, 8$. With increased k we can expect more string pairs to satisfy an edit threshold and hence an increase in query time. As we loosen the edit threshold requirement, the effectiveness of q-gram filtering begins to deteriorate since the requirement for Lemma 5 can be met with string S having less number of its partitions being matched with substrings in R. Therefore, even with probabilistic pruning, many false candidates pairs are passed on to frequency distance and CDF filtering routines. Also, the number of candidates removed by the upper bound of frequency distance and CDF decreases with an increase in k. Though lower bound filtering in CDF can accept more candidates with an increase in k, this benefit is easily offset by loose upper bounds resulting in net increase in verification cost. With increased k, the time required for algorithm QFCT approaches that of FCT but still manages to save up to 35% of FCT's query cost.

7.6 Effects of q

In this set of experiments we try to investigate the effect of q-gram length on the efficiency and effectiveness of q-gram filtering using input collections with 100K strings. As pointed out earlier, q-gram filtering incurs more filtering overhead for higher string lengths with fixed q. We can hope

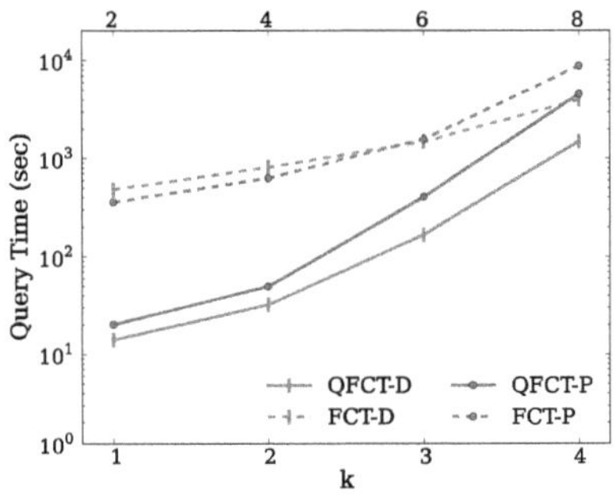

Figure 6: Effect of k

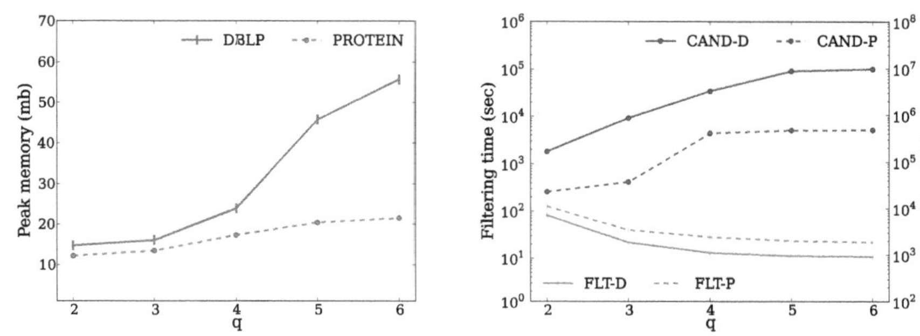

Figure 7: Effect of q

to reduce this overhead by increasing q, however such an increase has side-effects on the space-time tradeoffof q-gram filtering. Even though we will have fewer partitions for each string due to increased q, each segment now has more possible instances to be added to the inverted indices increasing the storage requirement as shown in Figure 7. The rate of increase is faster for the dblp dataset because of higher θ i.e., more uncertain positions and larger alphabet set. We note that we use peak memory usage as a measure that accounts for the indices maintained at any point during query answering based on the length of a string currently under consideration. Further, this also implies that query preprocessing that populates sets $q(r, x)$ needs more time offsetting the benefits of higher q to some extent. Figure 7 shows the improvement in the filtering time for q varying from 2 to 6. With size of $q(r, x)$ increasing exponentially with q, the improvement in filtering time achieved due to fewer segments also decreases exponentially.

For deterministic strings, increasing q makes it difficult for a segment of string s to match with substrings of query string r and implies potential improvement in pruning ability of q-gram filtering. For uncertain strings though, due to higher q, a segment may contain a larger number of uncertain positions. Hence there are more number of possible instances with increased chances for a segment to find a match in substrings of a query string. As a result, the effectiveness of q-gram filtering diminishes gradually for higher q as seen in Figure 7. We note that, though filtering time improves with q, time required for answering a join query shows uni-valley behavior as less effective filtering causes increased query time for higher q even with less filtering overhead. We found $q = 3$ or $q = 4$ offers the best combination of fast effective pruning with acceptable storage requirement. With peak memory usage of inverted indices less than the input data size itself for both $q = 3$ and 4, the space required for storing all indices as required for answering similarity search queries was found to be only ≈ 1.5 and ≈ 2 times the data size respectively.

7.7 Evaluating Trie-based Verification

We now analyze the performance benefits offered by the trie-based verification over a naive way of doing the same. Figure 8 shows the verification time required for answering join queries on the dblp and protein datasets with varying degree of uncertainty i.e., parameter θ. With an increase in the number of uncertain positions in the string, the number of possible worlds increases exponentially. This results in increased verification cost for both trie-based and naive verification. In naive verification, we need to enumerate possible worlds for each string in the dataset and also enumerate possible words for each of the candidate strings that may form a similar pair with it. In effect, we may enumerate all possible worlds for each string more than once. Additionally, given a candidate pair (R, S) it needs to compare every possible instance of R with that of S. In contrast, the trie-based verification enumerates all possible words for each string S only once and when it is selected as a candidate for some other string R in database, it enumerates and compares only those possible worlds which are highly likely to be similar to some instance of R. Thus the performance gains of trie-based verification increase with increasing θ as seen in Figure 8. We note that the cost of verification using trie-based approach also increases exponentially due to the requirement of having a complete trie in place for query string R. Moreover, trie-based verification can be more expensive than the naive method in scenarios where the majority of instances of $R \times S$ satisfy the edit threshold due to the overhead of building a trie and computing a set of similar nodes for each node in the trie. Though we obtained performance gains using trie-based verification on the protein data as well, they were less significant than for the dblp data due to higher string lengths, lower degree of uncertainty (θ) and smaller alphabet set.

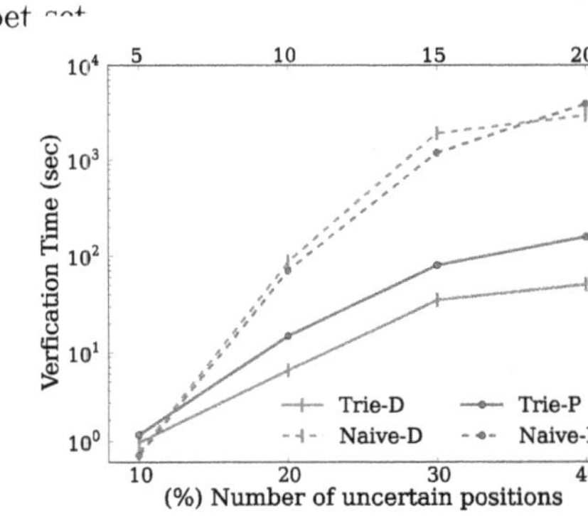

Figure 8: Trie-based Verification

7.8 Effects of String Length

In this final set of experiments, we test algorithms QFCT and FCT by varying the length of the probabilistic strings. For studying this effect, we use the 100K versions of the dblp and protein datasets, and append each probabilistic string to itself for 0,1,2 or 3 times. To ensure that the verification step does not get excessively expensive, we limit the number of probabilistic characters in a probabilistic string to be at most 8. Clearly, the costs of both algorithms increase with longer strings as seen in Figure 9. In terms of filtering time, computation of q-gram filtering and CDF bounds takes longer as string lengths increase, as described earlier in Section 7.1. However, frequency distance filtering being dependent only on the number of uncertain character positions remains unaffected. This allows algorithm FCT to close the performance gap with QFCT for higher string lengths by virtue of efficient frequency distance filtering. Additionally, verification cost begins to dominate the query time with the increase in string lengths. We note that even trie-based verification needs to instantiate all possible worlds for each probabilistic string once while answering a join query. With each possible world enumeration taking more time, higher string length adversely affects the verification step. For fixed k, τ, and uncertain character positions, the number of output pairs decreases with increase in string length. Despite this, the query time increases because of the aforementioned reasons. We emphasize that the proposed filtering techniques maintain their effectiveness with varying lengths as the fraction of the candidate pairs that undergo verification and are accepted as output remains almost constant.

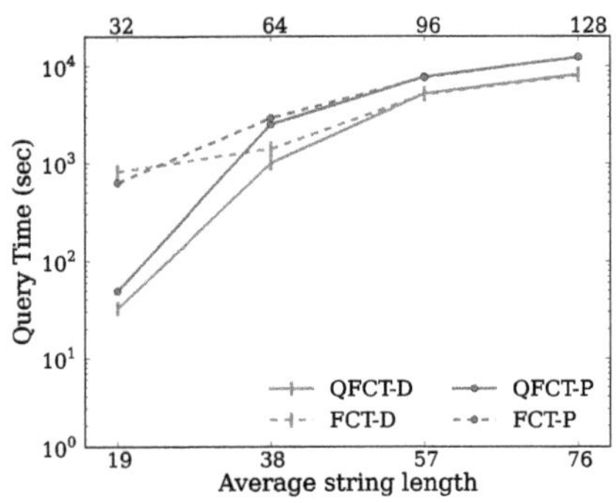

Figure 9: Effects of string length

7.9 Comparison with EED

In this subsection, we qualitatively compare the join query algorithm in [10] against algorithms presented in this work:

1. We partition each string in the collection based on q whereas q-gram filtering in [10] makes use of overlapping q-grams. This allows us to significantly reduce the space required for storing all q-grams ($\approx 5 \times$ *datasize* as reported in [10] against our index of twice the data size).
2. q-gram filtering presented in [10] requires each probabilistic string pair to be evaluated during query execution tasks like computation of frequency distance, CDF bounds computation. Algorithm QFCT employes indexing that incorporates q-gram filtering before applying expensive filters. Therefore, we can expect QFCT to offer benefits over the query algorithm in [10] similar to its advantages over algorithm FCT seen in Figure 3.
3. Computing the exact *eed* between two probabilistic strings requires all possible worlds for two strings to be instantiated in the same way as a naive verification method discussed in Section 7.7. On the other hand trie-based verification allows us to determine the similarity of a string pair efficiently (refer to Figure 8).

8. CONCLUSIONS

In this paper, we study the largely unexplored problem of answering similarity join queries on uncertain strings. We propose a novel q-gram filtering technique that integrates probabilistic pruning and extends frequency distance and CDF based filtering techniques. In future work, we plan to investigate tighter filtering conditions and improvements to the trie-based verification algorithm.

9. REFERENCES

[1] A. Amir, E. Chencinski, C. S. Iliopoulos, T. Kopelowitz, and H. Zhang. Property matching and weighted matching. In *CPM*, pages 188–199, 2006.

[2] A. Arasu, V. Ganti, and R. Kaushik. Efficient exact set-similarity joins. In *VLDB*, pages 918–929, 2006.

[3] S. Chaudhuri, V. Ganti, and R. Kaushik. A primitive operator for similarity joins in data cleaning. In *ICDE*, page 5, 2006.

[4] D. Dai, J. Xie, H. Zhang, and J. Dong. Efficient range queries over uncertain strings. In *SSDBM*, pages 75–95, 2012.

[5] J. Feng, J. Wang, and G. Li. Trie-join: a trie-based method for efficient string similarity joins. *VLDB J.*, 21(4):437–461, 2012.

[6] T. Ge and Z. Li. Approximate substring matching over uncertain strings. *PVLDB*, 4(11):772–782, 2011.

[7] L. Gravano, P. G. Ipeirotis, H. V. Jagadish, N. Koudas, S. Muthukrishnan, and D. Srivastava. Approximate string joins in a database (almost) for free. In *VLDB*, 2001.

[8] C. S. Iliopoulos, C. Makris, Y. Panagis, K. Perdikuri, E. Theodoridis, and A. Tsakalidis. The weighted suffix tree: An efficient data structure for handling molecular weighted sequences and its applications. *Fundam. Inf.*, 71:259–277, February 2006.

[9] C. S. Iliopoulos, K. Perdikuri, E. Theodoridis, A. K. Tsakalidis, and K. Tsichlas. Algorithms for extracting motifs from biological weighted sequences. *J. Discrete Algorithms*, 5(2):229–242, 2007.

[10] J. Jestes, F. Li, Z. Yan, and K. Yi. Probabilistic string similarity joins. In *SIGMOD Conference*, pages 327–338, 2010.

[11] S. Ji, G. Li, C. Li, and J. Feng. Efficient interactive fuzzy keyword search. In *WWW*, pages 371–380, 2009.

[12] T. Kahveci and A. K. Singh. Efficient index structures for string databases. In *VLDB*, pages 351–360, 2001.

[13] N. Koudas, S. Sarawagi, and D. Srivastava. Record linkage: similarity measures and algorithms. In *SIGMOD Conference*, pages 802–803, 2006.

[14] G. Li, D. Deng, J. Wang, and J. Feng. Pass-join: A partition-based method for similarity joins. *PVLDB*, 5(3):253–264, 2011.

[15] M. Patil, X. Cai, S. V. Thankachan, R. Shah, S.-J. Park, and D. Foltz. Approximate string matching by position restricted alignment. In *EDBT/ICDT Workshops*, pages 384–391, 2013.

[16] S. Singh, C. Mayfield, S. Mittal, S. Prabhakar, S. E. Hambrusch, and R. Shah. Orion 2.0: native support for uncertain data. In *SIGMOD*, pages 1239–1242, 2008.

[17] J. Widom. Trio: A system for integrated management of data, accuracy, and lineage. In *CIDR*, pages 262–276, 2005.

[18] C. Xiao, W. Wang, and X. Lin. Ed-join: an efficient algorithm for similarity joins with edit distance constraints. *PVLDB*, 1(1):933–944, 2008.

[19] H. Zhang, Q. Guo, and C. S. Iliopoulos. An algorithmic framework for motif discovery problems in weighted sequences. In *CIAC*, pages 335–346, 2010.

Track Join: Distributed Joins with Minimal Network Traffic

Orestis Polychroniou[*]
Columbia University
orestis@cs.columbia.edu

Rajkumar Sen
Oracle Labs
rajkumar.sen@oracle.com

Kenneth A. Ross[†]
Columbia University
kar@cs.columbia.edu

ABSTRACT

Network communication is the slowest component of many operators in distributed parallel databases deployed for large-scale analytics. Whereas considerable work has focused on speeding up databases on modern hardware, communication reduction has received less attention. Existing parallel DBMSs rely on algorithms designed for disks with minor modifications for networks. A more complicated algorithm may burden the CPUs, but could avoid redundant transfers of tuples across the network. We introduce *track join*, a novel distributed join algorithm that minimizes network traffic by generating an optimal transfer schedule for each distinct join key. Track join extends the trade-off options between CPU and network. Our evaluation based on real and synthetic data shows that track join adapts to diverse cases and degrees of locality. Considering both network traffic and execution time, even with no locality, track join outperforms hash join on the most expensive queries of real workloads.

1. INTRODUCTION

The processing power and storage capacity of a single machine can be large enough to fit small to medium scale databases. Nowadays, servers with memory capacity of more than a terabyte are common. Packing a few multi-core CPUs on top of shared non-uniform access (NUMA) RAM provides substantial parallelism, where we can run database operations (i.e. sort, join, and group-by) on RAM-resident data at rates of a few gigabytes per second [2, 3, 29, 34, 36].

Database research has also evolved to catch up to the hardware advances. Fundamental design rules of the past on how a DBMS should operate are now being revised due to their inability to scale and achieve good performance on modern hardware. Special purpose databases are now popular against the one-size-fits-all approach [32], while accelerators [26] are the implicit manifestation of the same concept.

[*]Work partly done when author was at the Oracle Labs.

[†]Work supported by National Science Foundation grant IIS-0915956 and a gift from Oracle Corporation.

SIGMOD'14, June 22–27, 2014, Snowbird, UT, USA.

http://dx.doi.org/10.1145/2588555.2610521.

The advances in database design for storage and execution on modern hardware have not been met by similar advances in distributed parallel database design. When the most fundamental work on distributed and parallel databases was published [5, 11, 20], hardware advances of today like multi-core parallelism had not yet occurred. Techniques to speed up short-lived distributed transactions [32] target distributed commit protocols, which suffer from network latencies rather than throughput. Queries where communication is inevitable are less popular research topics or are left for data-centric generic distributed systems for batch-processing [7, 24].

The latest network technologies may be slow relative to main-memory-resident processing. A 40 Gbps InfiniBand measured less than 3 GB/s real data rate per node during hash partitioning. If done in RAM, partitioning to a few thousand outputs runs close to the memory copy bandwidth [29, 34]. For instance, a server using 4X 8-core CPUs and 1333 MHz quad-channel DDR3 DRAM achieves a partition rate of 30–35 GB/s, more than an order of magnitude higher than the InfiniBand network. Recent work [3] achieves a hash join rate of 4.85 GB/s of 32-bit key, 32-bit payload tuples on 4X 8-core CPUs. Such high-end hardware is common in marketed configurations for large-scale analytics.

Network optimization is important for both low-end and high-end hardware. In low-end platforms where the network is relatively slow compared to local in-memory processing, we expect the execution time to be dominated by network transfers. Thus, any network traffic reduction directly translates to faster execution. In high-end platforms, given that the network still cannot be as fast as the RAM bandwidth, completion times are also reduced if the reduction in network traffic is comparable with the increase in CPU cycles.

In order to show how much time databases can spend on the network, we give an example of a real analytical workload from a large commercial vendor, using a market-leading commercial DBMS. Using 8 machines connected through 40 Gbps InfiniBand (see Section 4 for more details of the configuration), we found that the five most expensive queries spend $\approx$ 65–70% of their time transferring tuples on the network and account for 14.7% of the total time required to execute the entire analytical workload with more than 1500 queries. All five queries have a non-trivial query plan (4–6 joins), but spend 23%, 31%, 30%, 42%, and 43% of their total execution time on a single distributed hash join.

A sophisticated DBMS should have available options to optimize the trade-off between network and CPU utilization. One solution would be to apply network optimization at a higher level treating the network as a less desired route for data transfers, without modifying the underlying algorithms. These approaches are common in generic distributed processing systems [7]. A second solution would be to employ data compression before sending data over the network. This solution is orthogonal to any algorithm but can consume a lot of CPU resources without always yielding substantial compression. A third solution is to create novel algorithms for database operator evaluation that minimize network communication by incurring local processing cost. This approach is orthogonal and compatible with compression and other higher level network transfer optimizations.

Grace hash join [9, 17] (throughout the paper we will use the term *hash join* to refer to Grace hash join on network [9], rather than disk [17]) is the predominant method for executing distributed joins and uses hash partitioning to split the initial problem into shared-nothing sub-problems that can proceed locally per node. Partitioning both tables works almost independently of the table sizes. However, hash join is far from network-optimal because it transfers almost the full size of both tables over the network. Using pre-determined hash functions guarantees load balancing, but limits the probability that a hashed tuple will not be transferred over the network to $1/N$ on N nodes.

We introduce track join, a novel algorithm for distributed joins that minimizes transfers of tuples across the network. The main idea of track join is to decide where to send rows on a key by key basis. The decision uses information about where records of the given key are located. Track join has the following properties: it (i) is orthogonal to data-centric compression, (ii) can co-exist with semi-join optimizations, (iii) does not rely on favorable schema properties, such as foreign key joins, (iv) is compatible with both row-store and column-store organization, and (v) does not assume favorable pre-existing tuple placement. We implement track join to evaluate the most expensive join operator in the most expensive queries of real workloads. We found that track join reduces the network traffic significantly over known methods, even if pre-existing data locality is removed and all data are used in optimally compressed form throughout the join.

Section 2 describes the track join algorithm presenting three variants starting from the simplest. In Section 3, we discuss costs for query optimization, tracking-aware hash joins, and semi-join filtering. Section 4 presents our experimental evaluation using both synthetic datasets and real workloads. In Section 5 we briefly discuss future work. In Section 6 we discuss related work and conclude in Section 7.

2. ALGORITHMIC DESCRIPTION

Formally, the problem under study is the general distributed equi-join. The input consists of tables R and S split arbitrarily across N nodes. Every node can send data to all others and all links have the same performance. We present three versions of track join gradually evolving in complexity.

The first version discovers network locations that have at least one matching tuple for each unique key. We then pick one side of the join and broadcast each tuple to all locations that have matching tuples of the other table for the same join key. We use the term *selective broadcast* for this process.

The second version gathers not only an indicator whether a node has tuples of a specific join key or not, but also the number and total size of these tuples. We pick the cheapest side to be selectively broadcast independently for each key.

The third and full version of track join extends the second version by generating an optimal join schedule for each key achieving minimum payload transfers, without hashing or broadcasting. The schedule migrates tuples from one table to potentially fewer nodes than the original placement, before selectively broadcasting tuples from the other table.

The algorithm will be described in this section using a pipelined approach. We assume three processes (R, S operating on tables R and S, and T that generates schedules) running simultaneously on all nodes, but once per node. A non-pipelined approach is also possible (see Section 4).

The algorithmic display convention used throughout this paper intentionally shows types next to variables when their values are being assigned. Unless a new value assignment is explicitly written, the variable was previously assigned a value now used as an input parameter. $|x|$ denotes set size.

2.1 2-Phase Track Join

The 2-phase (or *single broadcast*) is the simplest version of track join. The first phase is the tracking phase, while the second phase is the selective broadcast phase.

In the first phase, both R and S are projected to their join key and sent over the network. The destination is determined by hashing the key, in the same way that hash join sends tuples. Duplicates are redundant and are eliminated. Every node receives unique keys and stores them alongside the id of the source node. In our display of the algorithm, this operation is done by a different process named T, which also generates the transfer schedules. The location of process$_T$ is determined by hashing the join key, thus, distributing the task of scheduling equally across all nodes.

Algorithm 2-phase track join: process$_R$ − R to S

```
T_R ← {}
for all <key_R|S k, payload_R p_R> in table R do
  if k not in T_R then
    send k to process_T (hash(k) mod N)
  end if
  T_R ← T_R + <k, p_R>
end for
barrier
while any process_T n_T sends do
  for all <key_R|S k, process_S n_S> from n_T do
    for all <k, payload_R p_R> in T_R do
      send <k, p_R> to n_S
    end for
  end for
end while
```

Algorithm 2-phase track join: process$_S$ − R to S

```
T_S ← {}
for all <key_R|S k, payload_S p_S> in table S do
  if k not in T_S then
    send k to process_T (hash(k) mod N)
  end if
  T_S ← T_S + <k, p_S>
end for
barrier
while any process_R n_R sends do
  for all <key_R|S k, payload_R p_R> from n_R do
    for all <k, payload_S p_S> in T_S do
      commit <k, p_R, p_S>
    end for
  end for
end while
```

Algorithm 2-phase track join: process_T − R to S

```
T_R|S ← {}
while any process_R or any process_S n_R|S sends do
  for all <key_R|S k> from n_R|S do
    T_R|S ← T_R|S + <k, n_R|S>
  end for
end while
barrier
for all distinct key_R|S k in T_R|S do
  for all <k, process_R n_R> in T_R|S do
    for all <k, process_S n_S> in T_R|S do
      send <k, n_S> to n_R
    end for
  end for
end for
```

In the second phase, we only transfer tuples from one table. Assuming we transfer R tuples, node T (process_T) sends messages to each location with matching R tuples, including the key and the set of S tuples' locations. Finally, R tuples are selectively broadcast to the tracked S locations, instead of all nodes in the network, and are joined locally.

Choosing whether to send R tuples to S tuple locations, or S tuples to R locations, has to be decided by the query optimizer before the query starts executing, similar to the traditional inner–outer relation distinction of hash join.

2-phase track join transfers payloads from one table only. If the input tables have mostly unique keys and the selectivity is high, the cost comprises of tracking plus $\min(|R|, |S|)$.

Algorithm 3-phase track join: process_T

```
barrier
T_R|S ← {}
while any process_R or any process_S n_R|S sends do
  for all <key_R|S k, count c> from n_R|S do
    T_R|S ← T_R|S + <k, n_R|S, c>
  end for
end while
barrier
for all distinct key_R|S k in T_R|S do
  R, S ← {}, {}
  for all k, process_R n_R, count c> in T_R|S do
    R ← R + <n_R, c · width_R>
  end for
  for all k, process_S n_S, count c> in T_R|S do
    S ← S + <n_S, c · width_S>
  end for
  RS_cost ← broadcast R to S
  SR_cost ← broadcast S to R
  if RS_cost < SR_cost then
    for all <k, process_R n_R> in T_R|S do
      for all <k, process_S n_S> in T_R|S do
        send <k, n_S> to n_R
      end for
    end for
  else
    for all <k, process_S n_S> in T_R|S do
      for all <k, process_R n_R> in T_R|S do
        send <k, n_R> to n_S
      end for
    end for
  end if
end for
```

Algorithm 3-phase track join: process_S

... symmetric with process_R of 3-phase track join ...

Algorithm 3-phase track join: process_R

```
T_R ← {}
for all <key_R|S k, payload_R p_R> in table R do
  T_R ← T_R + <k, p_R>
end for
barrier
for all distinct key_R|S k in T_R do
  c ← |k in T_R|
  send <k, c> to process_T (hash(k) mod N)
end for
barrier
while any process_S or any process_T sends do
  if source is process_T n_T then
    for all <key_R|S k, process_S n_S> from n_T do
      for all <k, payload_R p_R> in T_R do
        send <k, p_R> to n_S
      end for
    end for
  else if source is process_S n_S then
    for all <key_R|S k, payload_S p_S> from n_S do
      for all <k, payload_R p_R> in T_R do
        commit <k, p_R, p_S>
      end for
    end for
  end if
end while
```

2.2 3-Phase Track Join

In the 3-phase (or *double broadcast*) track join, we can decide whether to broadcast R tuples to the locations of S tuples, or vice versa. The decision is taken per distinct join key. In order to decide which selective broadcast direction is cheaper, we need to know how many tuples will be transferred in each case. Thus, instead of only tracking nodes with at least one matching tuple, we also track the number of matches. To generalize for variable lengths, we transfer the sum of matching tuple widths, rather than a count.

Bi-directional selective broadcast can distinguish cases in which moving S tuples would transfer fewer bytes than moving R tuples. The decision whether to selectively broadcast $R \rightarrow S$ or vice versa is taken for each distinct key independently and we do not rely on the optimizer to pick the least expensive direction overall for the entire join.

The cost estimation for one selective broadcast direction is shown below. In practice, we compute both directions and pick the cheapest. The complexity is $O(n)$, where n is the number of nodes with at least one matching tuple for the given join key. The total number of steps required is less than the number of tuples. Thus, the theoretical complexity is linear. The messages that carry location information, logically seen as key and node pairs, have size equal to M.

Algorithm track join: broadcast R to S

$R_{all} \leftarrow \sum_i |R_i|$
$R_{local} \leftarrow \sum_i |R_i|$, **where** $|S_i| > 0$
$R_{nodes} \leftarrow |i$, **where** $|R_i| > 0 \wedge i \neq self|$
$S_{nodes} \leftarrow |i$, **where** $|S_i| > 0|$
$RS_{cost} \leftarrow R_{all} \cdot S_{nodes} - R_{local} + R_{nodes} \cdot S_{nodes} \cdot M$
return RS_{cost}

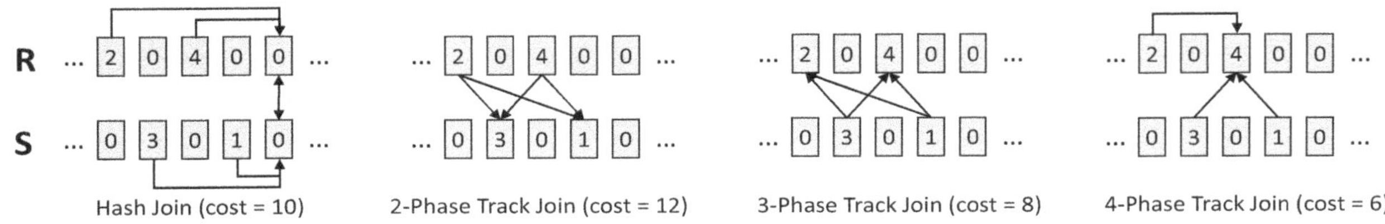

Figure 1: Example of network transfers in hash join and track join per distinct join key

2.3 4-Phase Track Join

In the full version of track join, the join is logically decomposed into single key (cartesian product) joins for each unique key. By minimizing the network cost of each cartesian product, we reduce the network cost of the entire join. If we omit the cost of tracking which we cannot optimize, 4-phase track join transfers the minimum amount of payload data possible for an early-materialized distributed join.

4-phase track join extends 3-phase track join by adding a more complicated scheduling algorithm and a migration phase. It ensures that when tuples from one table are selectively broadcast to matching tuple locations from the other table, we have already migrated tuples to a subset of nodes, minimizing the total network transfers. We will prove that optimal network traffic scheduling still takes linear time.

In Figure 1 we show an example of how the different algorithms behave for a single key join. In hash join, we assume the hash destination is the fifth node. In 2-phase track join we selectively broadcast R tuples to matching S tuple locations and in 3-phase track join we choose the opposite direction, since it is cheaper. The 4-phase track join first migrates R tuples, before selectively broadcasting S tuples.

The schedules by 4-phase track join sometimes exhibit behavior similar to that of hash join, where all tuples are sent into a single node to perform the join. Even in such a case, the node will be the one with the most pre-existing matching tuples, as seen in Figure 1, maximizing locality.

Algorithm 4-phase track join: process$_S$

```
... symmetric with processR of 4-phase track join ...
```

Algorithm 4-phase track join: process$_R$

```
... identical to the 1st phase of 3-phase track join ...
barrier
... identical to the 2nd phase of 3-phase track join ...
barrier
while any processT or any processR sends do
  if source is processT nT then
    for all <keyR|S k, processR nR> from nT do
      for all <k, payloadR pR> in TR do
        send <k, pR> to nR
        TR ← TR − <k, pR>
      end for
    end for
  else if source is processR nR then
    for all <keyR|S k, payloadR pR> from nR do
      TR ← TR + <k, pR>
    end for
  end if
end while
barrier
... identical to the 3rd phase of 3-phase track join ...
```

We formalize the problem of network traffic minimization for a single key (cartesian product) join, assuming for simplicity that the plan is known to every node and no location messages are sent. Assume that x_{ij} is the binary decision of sending R tuples from node i to node j, while y_{ij} is the binary decision of sending S tuples from j to i. $|R_i|$ represents the total size of R tuples residing in node i, while $|S_j|$ is the total size of S tuples in node j. Since each schedule is on a single key, we have to join every R_i data part with every S_j data part. One way is by sending R tuples from i to j, setting $x_{ij} = 1$. The second way is by sending S tuples from j to i, setting $y_{ij} = 1$. The last way is by sending both R_i and S_j to a common third node. In short, we need some node k, where $x_{ik} = 1$ and $y_{kj} = 1$. Local sends do not affect network traffic, thus, all x_{ii} and y_{jj} are ignored.

$$\text{min: } \sum_i \sum_{j \neq i} x_{ij} \cdot |R_i| + y_{ij} \cdot |S_j| \quad \text{s.t. } \forall i, j \sum_k x_{ik} \cdot y_{kj} \geq 1$$

Algorithm 4-phase track join: process$_T$

```
barrier
... identical to the 2nd phase of 3-phase track join ...
barrier
for all distinct keyR|S k in TR|S do
  R, S ← {}, {}
  for all <k, processR nR, count c> in TR|S do
    R ← R + <nR, c · widthR>
  end for
  for all <k, processS nS, count c> in TR|S do
    S ← S + <nS, c · widthS>
  end for
  RScost, Smigr ← migrate S & broadcast R
  SRcost, Rmigr ← migrate R & broadcast S
  if RScost < SRcost then
    for all <k, processS nS> in Smigr do
      dS ← any processS not in Smigr
      send <k, dS> to nS
      TR|S ← TR|S − <k, nS, count cmigr>
      TR|S ← TR|S − <k, dS, count cdest>
      TR|S ← TR|S + <k, dS, cmigr + cdest>
    end for
  else
    for all <k, processR nR> in Rmigr do
      dR ← any processR not in Rmigr
      send <k, dR> to nR
      TR|S ← TR|S − <k, nR, count cmigr>
      TR|S ← TR|S − <k, dR, count cdest>
      TR|S ← TR|S + <k, dR, cmigr + cdest>
    end for
  end if
end for
barrier
... identical to the 3rd phase of 3-phase track join ...
```

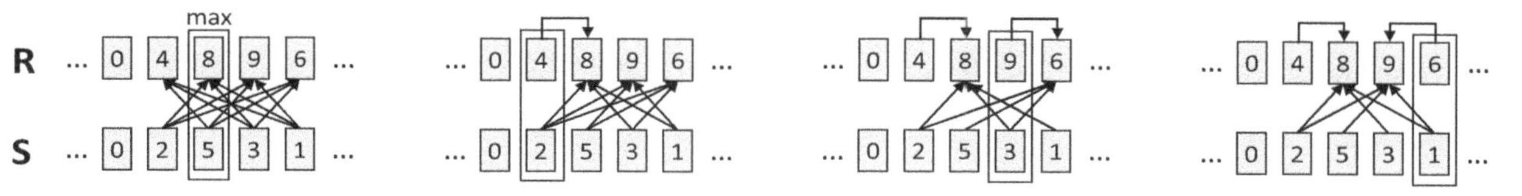

Selective Broadcast (cost = 0+33) Migrate 4? Yes (cost = 4+24) Migrate 9? No (cost = 13+16) Migrate 6? Yes (cost = 10+14)

Figure 2: Example of 4-phase track join optimal schedule generation per distinct join key

We solve the traffic minimization problem by optimizing selective broadcasts using migrations. Before the $R \rightarrow S$ selective broadcast, we migrate S tuples across nodes, depending on whether the cost of the later broadcast of R tuples is reduced. The mechanism allows only S tuples to be transferred, thus, we can easily decide whether the S tuples of some node should stay in place, or be transferred somewhere with more S tuples. We reduce the cost of the later selective broadcast also considering the migration cost. The algorithm shown below includes location messages of size M.

Algorithm track join: migrate S & broadcast R

$R_{all} \leftarrow \sum_i |R_i|$
$R_{local} \leftarrow \sum_i |R_i|$, **where** $|S_i| > 0$
$R_{nodes} \leftarrow |i$, **where** $|R_i| > 0 \wedge i \neq self|$
$S_{nodes} \leftarrow |i$, **where** $|S_i| > 0|$
$RS_{cost} \leftarrow R_{all} \cdot S_{nodes} - R_{local} + R_{nodes} \cdot S_{nodes} \cdot M$
$max_S \leftarrow i$, **where** $|S_i| > 0 \wedge \forall j : |R_i| + |S_i| \geq |R_j| + |S_j|$
$S_{migr} \leftarrow \{\}$
for $i \leftarrow 1$ **to** $|\{S_1, S_2, ...\}|$ **do**
  if $|S_i| > 0$ **and** $i \neq max_S$ **then**
    $\Delta \leftarrow |R_i| + |S_i| - R_{all} - R_{nodes} \cdot M$
    if $i \neq self$ **then**
      $\Delta \leftarrow \Delta + M$
    end if
    if $\Delta < 0$ **then**
      $RS_{cost} \leftarrow RS_{cost} + \Delta$
      $S_{migr} \leftarrow S_{migr} + \{i\}$
    end if
  end if
end for
return RS_{cost}, S_{migr}

THEOREM 1. *We can generate optimal selective broadcast schedules ($R \rightarrow S$) by allowing the migration of (S) tuples.*

PROOF. We want to compute a set of nodes $S_{migr} \subseteq S$, where any node i in S_{migr} migrates local matching tuples. Observe that the migration destination does not affect the network cost, thus, can be any node in $S - S_{migr}$. Let z_i be the binary decision whether node i keeps all local matching S tuples or migrates them ($z_i = 0 \Leftrightarrow i \in S_{migr}$). The cost of migrating selective broadcast from R to S is then:

$$(\sum |R_i|) \cdot (\sum z_i) - (\sum |R_i| \cdot z_i) + \sum |S_i| \cdot (1 - z_i)$$

The $\sum |R_i|$ term is the total size of R tuples, the $\sum z_i$ is the number of locations with S tuples, the $\sum |R_i| \cdot z_i$ are the R tuples that were local during broadcast and $\sum |S_i| \cdot (1 - z_i)$ is the cost of migrating S tuples. Since $\sum |R_i| (\equiv R)$ and $\sum |S_i| (\equiv S)$ are independent of all z_i, the formula can be minimized by checking each z_i independently. Finally, since S_{migr} cannot contain all nodes, we force the node with the largest $|R_i| + |S_i|$ and $|S_i| > 0$, out of S_{migr} ($z_i = 1$). □

THEOREM 2. *The minimum optimized selective broadcast direction ($R \rightarrow S$, or $S \rightarrow R$) is also the minimum network traffic schedule for single key (cartesian product) joins.*

PROOF. Given a computed S_{migr}, migrating any R_x to any R_y can only increase the cost. If $y \in S - S_{migr}$, the cost remains the same, as we moved R_x once, but now it is local to S_y and skip y during the selective broadcast. If $y \in S_{migr}$, we increase the cost of the migrating phase by $|R_x|$, but the cost of the selective broadcast remains the same. □

In Figure 2 we show an example of 4-phase track join schedule generation for a single key. We start from the cost of selective broadcast and check for each node whether migrating all matching tuples reduces the cost. As shown, nodes with no matching tuples are not considered at all.

The time to generate each schedule depends on the number of tuples per join key. The input is an array of triplets: key, node, and count (or size). If a node does not contain a key, the triplet is not considered at all. Thus, scheduling is in the worst case linear in the total number of input tuples.

Using multiple threads per process is allowed and is, of course, essential to achieve good performance on CPU intensive tasks. Track join allows all in-process operations across keys to be parallelized across threads freely, since all local operations combine tuples with the same join key only.

2.4 Traffic Compression

Track join, as described so far, makes absolutely no effort to reduce the data footprint by compression. Modern analytical database systems employ distinct column value dictionaries [26, 35]. The compression process can occur offline, and data are processed in compressed form throughout the join. In this section, we briefly discuss some techniques that can further reduce network traffic on top of track join.

The simplest case is delta encoding [18, 31]. With sufficient CPU power, we can sort all columns sent over the network. Track join imposes no specific message order for all types of messages, besides the barrier synchronization across phases. Thus, the potential compression rate increases.

A second technique is to perform partitioning at the source to create common prefixes. For instance, we can radix partition the first p bits and pack $(w-p)$-bit suffix with a common prefix. We can even tune the compression rate, by employing more partition passes to create wider prefixes. Each pass has been shown to be very efficient on memory-resident data, close to the RAM copy bandwidth [29, 34]. If the inputs retain dictionary encoding through the join, the number of distinct values using the same prefix is maximized.

A similar optimization we can use for track join is to avoid sending node locations alongside keys by partitioning in corresponding groups. We avoid sending the node part in messages containing key and node pairs by sending many keys with a single node label after partitioning by node.

3. QUERY OPTIMIZATION

The formal model of track join is used by the query optimizer to decide whether to use track join in favor of hash join or broadcast join. We prove track join superior to hash join, even after making the latter tracking-aware using globally unique record identifiers. Finally, we discuss how track join interacts with semi-join filtering on selective joins.

3.1 Network Cost Model

In this section, we assume a uniform distribution of tuples across nodes for simplicity. This is the worst case for track join since it precludes locality. Track join optimization is not limited to one distribution as we will explain shortly.

The network cost of the ubiquitous hash join, omitting the $1/N$ in place transfer probability on N nodes, is:

$$t_R \cdot (w_k + w_R) + t_S \cdot (w_k + w_S)$$

where t_R and t_S are the tuple counts of tables R and S, w_k is the total width of the join key columns used in conjunctive equality conditions, while w_R and w_S are the total width of relevant payload columns later used in the query.

To define the network cost of 2-phase track join, we first determine the cost of tracking. The number of nodes that contain matches for each key is upper bounded by N and is t/d, in the worst case when equal keys are randomly distributed across nodes, where t is the number of tuples and d is the number of distinct values. We refer to these quantities as $n_R \equiv \min(N, t_R/d_R)$ and $n_S \equiv \min(N, t_S/d_S)$.

We define the input selectivity (s_R and s_S) as the percentage of tuples of one table that have matches in the other table, after applying all other selective predicates. The number of distinct nodes with matching payloads also includes the input selectivity factor. We assume that the selective predicates do not use the key column and the number of distinct keys is unaffected. We refer to these quantities as $m_R \equiv \min(N, (t_R \cdot s_R)/d_R)$ and $m_S \equiv \min(N, (t_S \cdot s_S)/d_S)$.

Using the above terms, the cost of 2-phase track join is:

$$\begin{aligned} &(d_R \cdot n_R + d_S \cdot n_S) \cdot w_k && \text{(track R \& S keys)} \\ &+d_R \cdot m_S \cdot w_k && \text{(transfer S locations)} \\ &+t_R \cdot s_R \cdot m_S \cdot (w_k + w_R) && \text{(transfer R} \to \text{S tuples)} \end{aligned}$$

For 3-phase track join, we transfer counters during tracking. The $t/(d \cdot s)$ fraction gives the average repetition of keys on each node if the distribution and node placement is assumed to be uniform random. We use this metric to estimate how many bits to use for representing counters (or tuple widths). We refer to the counter lengths using $c_R \equiv \log(t_S/(d_S \cdot n_S))$ and $c_S \equiv \log(t_S/(d_S \cdot n_S))$. If some keys' repetitions exceed the maximum count, we can aggregate at the destination. The cost of 3-phase track join is:

$$\begin{aligned} &d_R \cdot n_R \cdot (w_k + c_R) + d_S \cdot n_S \cdot (w_k + c_S) && \text{(tracking)} \\ &+d_{R_1} \cdot m_{S_1} \cdot w_k + t_{R_1} \cdot s_{R_1} \cdot m_{S_1} \cdot (w_k + w_{R_1}) && (R_1 \to S_1) \\ &+d_{S_2} \cdot m_{R_2} \cdot w_k + t_{S_2} \cdot s_{S_2} \cdot m_{R_2} \cdot (w_k + w_{S_2}) && (S_2 \to R_2) \end{aligned}$$

In this formula, we assume the tuples are split into two separate classes R_1, S_1 and R_2, S_2. The tuples of R_1 are defined based on whether the $R \to S$ direction is less expensive than the $S \to R$ direction at distinct join key granularity. We briefly explain how these classes are estimated, shortly.

The query optimizer should pick 2-phase track join rather than 4-phase when both tables have almost entirely unique keys, which is enabled by the distinct values estimation. Simple broadcast join can be better if one table is very small.

If actual numbers are required, instead of relative comparison of available algorithms, we can estimate the network cost of track join using correlation classes. For example, the R_1 and R_2 classes used in the cost of 3-phase track join represent the percentages of tuples of R that are joined using the $R \to$ (for R_1), or the $S \to R$ (for R_2) selective broadcast direction. To populate the classes, we can use *correlated sampling* [37], a recently proposed technique that preserves the join relationships of tuples, is independent of the distribution, and can be generated off-line. The sample is augmented with initial placements of tuples. Besides computing the exact track join cost, we incrementally classify the keys to correlation classes based on traffic levels, and combine their cardinality and average traffic. A simplified version of 4-phase cost is shown below, using the classes that combine 3-phase track join (R_1, S_1, R_2, S_2) with hash join (R_3, S_3):

$$\begin{aligned} &d_R \cdot n_R \cdot (w_k + c_R) + d_S \cdot n_S \cdot (w_k + c_S) && \text{(tracking)} \\ &+d_{R_1} \cdot m_{S_1} \cdot w_k + t_{R_1} \cdot s_{R_1} \cdot m_{S_1} \cdot (w_k + w_{R_1}) && (R_1 \to S_1) \\ &+d_{S_2} \cdot m_{R_2} \cdot w_k + t_{S_2} \cdot s_{S_2} \cdot m_{R_2} \cdot (w_k + w_{S_2}) && (S_2 \to R_2) \\ &+d_{R_3} \cdot n_{R_3} \cdot w_k + t_{R_3} \cdot s_{R_3} \cdot (w_k + w_{R_3}) && (R_3 \to \text{h(k)}) \\ &+d_{S_3} \cdot n_{S_3} \cdot w_k + t_{S_3} \cdot s_{S_3} \cdot (w_k + w_{S_3}) && (S_3 \to \text{h(k)}) \end{aligned}$$

These three correlation classes merge hash join with 3-phase track join and are the most common in real queries. More classes can be defined by combining them in a step function.

A limitation of track join is that it invests significant time working with keys compared to hash join. When the payloads are small, we expect track join to perform worse than hash join, unless there is locality. For instance, if the joined tables have equal cardinality ($t_R = t_S$) and entirely unique keys, in order to not transfer more than hash join, we need:

$$\begin{aligned} 4 \cdot w_k + \min(w_R, w_S) &\leq 2 \cdot w_k + w_R + w_S \\ \Leftrightarrow \quad 2 \cdot w_k &\leq \max(w_R, w_S) \end{aligned}$$

i.e., the larger payload width must be two times bigger than the join key width, assuming there is no pre-existing locality.

3.2 Tracking-Aware Hash Join

Late materialization is a popular approach for designing main memory databases. The technique is typically used in column stores [26, 31], but can also be viewed as an optimizer decision, whether deferring column access and carrying record identifiers (rids) costs less than early materialization. An analysis of tuple reduction by interleaving late materializated operations is out of the scope of this paper.

In the simple case, keys are hashed, rids are implicitly generated, and payloads are fetched afterwards. The cost is:

$$(t_R + t_S) \cdot w_k + t_{RS} \cdot (w_R + w_S + \log t_R + \log t_S)$$

where t_{RS} is the number of output joined tuples.

When distributed, rids contain a local id and a node id. To use the implicit tracking information carried in a rid would be to migrate the result to the tuple location, instead of fetching the tuples where the rid pair is. For instance, assume a join of R and S, where fetching S payloads is costlier than R. Using the R rid, we migrate the R rid where the R tuple resides. The S tuple is sent to the location of the R tuple, after a request with the S rid and the R destination.

Assuming that no later operation precedes payload fetching, we can further elaborate the improvement by redoing the join on the final destination. In the above example, we send one local id to the R node and the local id to the S node, alongside the node id of the R node. Sending the node id can be avoided as in track join. The payload brought from the S node will be coupled with the join key. The R rid will access the tuple and rejoin it with the incoming tuple from the S node. The network cost of the resulting method is:

$$(t_R + t_S) \cdot w_k + t_{RS} \cdot (\min(w_R, w_S) + w_k + \log t_R + \log t_S)$$

We prove that this approach is less effective than track join. Initially, it transfers the key column without any duplicate elimination or reordering to allow implicit rid generation. In contrast, track join transfers either the distinct keys of each node only, or an aggregation of keys with short counts. Afterwards, track join performs optimal transfers overall. The rid-based hash join transfers payloads from the shorter side to all locations of the larger side where there is a match, the same schedule as 2-phase track join. Instead, track join resends keys, which, unless uncompressed, have shorter representation than rids. Thus, the simplest 2-phase track join subsumes the rid-based tracking-aware hash join.

The extra cost of transferring rids is non trivial. As shown in our experiments, real workloads may use less than 8 bytes of payload data while globally unique rids must be at least 4 bytes. The rids of both tables together may be wider than the smaller payloads, making late materialization less effective for distributed compared to local in-memory processing.

3.3 Semi-Join Filtering

When join operations are coupled with selections, we can prune tuples both individually per table and across tables. To that end, databases use semi-join [4, 22] implemented using Bloom filters [6], which are optimized towards network traffic. In our analysis, we assume a two-way semi-join.

When a false positive occurs, hash join transfers the whole tuple in vain. In track join, the matches are determined when the keys are tracked. All join keys with no matches are discarded up front using the key projection; no location or tuples are transferred thereafter. Whereas late materialized hash join reduces the penalty of filter errors by using key and rid pairs, track join sends less than the key column alone.

Assuming the length per qualifying tuple in the filter to be w_{bf}, the cost of filtered early materialized hash join is:

$$\begin{aligned}
&(t_R \cdot s_R + t_S \cdot s_S) \cdot N \cdot w_{bf} && \text{(broadcast filters)}\\
&+t_R \cdot (s_R + e) \cdot (w_k + w_R) && \text{(transfer S tuples)}\\
&+t_S \cdot (s_S + e) \cdot (w_k + w_S) && \text{(transfer R tuples)}
\end{aligned}$$

where e is the relative error of the Bloom filters.

The cost of filtered late materialized hash join, is:

$$\begin{aligned}
&(t_R \cdot s_R + t_S \cdot s_S) \cdot N \cdot w_{bf} && \text{(broadcast filters)}\\
&+t_R \cdot (s_R + e) \cdot (w_k + \log t_R) && \text{(transfer S pairs)}\\
&+t_S \cdot (s_S + e) \cdot (w_k + \log t_S) && \text{(transfer R pairs)}\\
&+t_{RS} \cdot (w_R + w_S + \log t_R + \log t_S) && \text{(fetch payloads)}
\end{aligned}$$

where t_{RS} includes the standard output selectivity factor.

The cost of 2-phase track join, using Bloom filtering, is:

$$\begin{aligned}
&(t_R \cdot s_R + t_S \cdot s_S) \cdot N \cdot w_{bf} && \text{(broadcast filters)}\\
&+d_R \cdot (s_R + e) \cdot me_R \cdot w_k && \text{(track filtered R)}\\
&+d_S \cdot (s_S + e) \cdot me_S \cdot w_k && \text{(track filtered S)}\\
&+d_R \cdot s_R \cdot m_S \cdot w_k && \text{(transfer S locations)}\\
&+t_R \cdot s_R \cdot m_S \cdot (w_k + w_R) && \text{(transfer R tuples)}
\end{aligned}$$

where $me_R \equiv \min(N, t_R \cdot (s_R + e)/d_R)$ and similarly for me_S.

The cost of broadcasting the filters can exceed the cost of sending a few columns for reasonable cluster size N. Track join does perfect semi-join filtering during tracking. Thus, it is more likely to subsume the Bloom filtering step compared to early materialized hash join, which sends all columns, and late materialized hash join, which sends keys and rids.

4. EXPERIMENTAL EVALUATION

Our evaluation is split into two parts. First, we simulate distributed joins to measure network traffic across encoding schemes (Section 4.1). Second, we implement and measure track join against hash join execution times (Section 4.2).

4.1 Simulations

In the simulations we assume 16 nodes and show 7 cases: broadcast $R \to S$ (BJ-R) and $S \to R$ (BJ-S), hash join (HJ), 2-phase track join $R \to S$ (2TJ-R) and $S \to R$ (2TJ-S), 3-phase track join (3TJ), and 4-phase track join (4TJ).

In the three experiments shown in Figure 3, the tuple width ratio of R and S are $1/3$, $2/3$, and $3/3$. The key width is included in the tuple width and is 4 bytes. The tables have equal cardinality (10^9) and almost entirely unique keys. Thus, track join selectively broadcasts tuples from the table with smaller payloads to the one matching tuple from the table with larger payloads and the 2-phase version suffices.

In the general case hash join has $1/N^k$ probability in order for all k matching tuples to be on the same node that was the result of hashing the key. For track join, this probability is $1/N^{k-1}$ because the collocation can occur in any node. When both tables have almost unique keys, the difference is maximized since $k \approx 2$ is the lower bound for equi-joins.

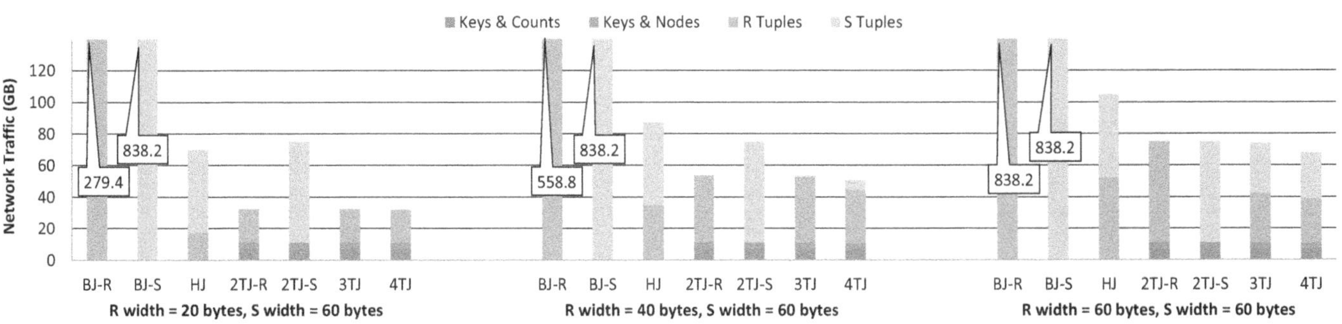

Figure 3: Synthetic dataset of 10^9 vs. 10^9 tuples with $\approx 10^9$ unique join keys

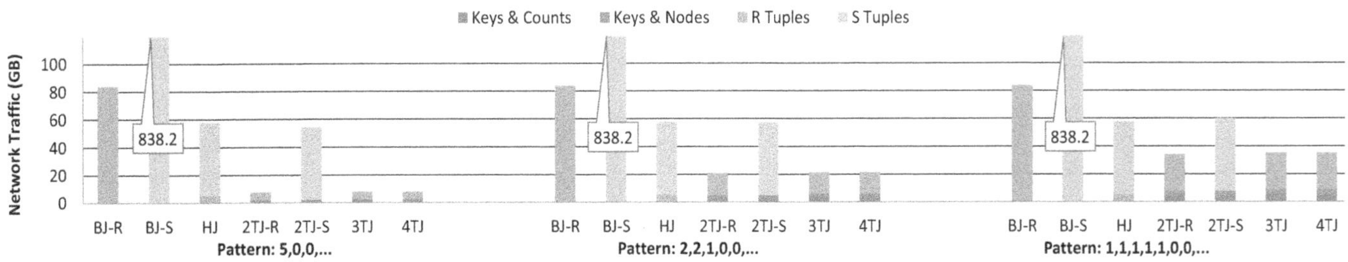

Figure 4: Synthetic dataset of $2 \cdot 10^8$ unique vs. 10^9 tuples (single side intra-table collocated)

In Figure 4, we show how locality can affect track join performance. We assume S to have 1 billion 60-byte tuples and R to have 200 million 30 byte tuples with unique keys. S repeats each key 5 times but key locations follow patterns specified below each chart. The pattern 5,0,0,... means all 5 key repeats are on a single node. The pattern 2,2,1,0,0,... represents 2 nodes with 2 repeats of the same key and 1 node with 1 repeat. The pattern 1,1,1,1,1,0,0,... means all repeats are on different nodes. This placement is artificially generated to represent different degrees of locality.

As shown in the left part of the result, when all repeats are collocated on the same node, regardless of which node that may be, track join will only transfer matching keys to a single location. When the tuple repeats follow the 2,2,1 pattern, still better than uniform placement, the traffic is still reduced compared to hash join. Note that random placement collocates repeats to some degree.

We do the same experiment using small tables for both inputs. Each table has 40 million tuples with unique keys and repeats each key 5 times. Since each key has 5 repeats on each table, we generate 25 output tuples per unique key. These numbers were picked so that the outputs on all figures of the current page are of the same size. In Figure 4 we produce 1 billion tuples as output. In Figures 5 and 6 we use 200 million tuples with 40 million distinct join keys for both tables, thus each key has 25 output tuples. The tuple widths are still 30 bytes for R and 60 bytes for S.

The difference between Figure 5 and Figure 6 is whether the tuples across tables are collocated. In the first, the 5,0,0,... configuration means all repeats from R are on a single node and all repeats from S are on a (different) single node. We term this case, shown on Figure 5, *intra-table* collocation. When same key tuples from across tables are collocated, locality is further increased. We term this case, shown on Figure 6, *inter-table* collocation. When all 10 repeats are collocated, track join eliminates all transfers of payloads. Messages used during the tracking phase can only be affected by the same case of locality as hash join.

Figures 4, 5, and 5 show the weakness of 2-phase and 3-phase track join to handle all possible equi-joins. If both tables have values with repeating keys shuffled randomly with no repeats in the same node, 4-phase track join is similar to hash join. However, track join sends far less data when matching tuples are collocated, inside or across tables.

In the rest of our experimental evaluation, for both simulation and our implementation of track join, we use queries from real analytical workloads. We did extensive profiling among real commercial workloads with one sophisticated commercial DBMS. The commercial bundle hardware of the DBMS is an 8-node cluster connected by 40 Gbps InfiniBand. Each node has 2X Intel Xeon E5-2690 (8-core with 2-way SMT) CPUs at 2.9 GHz, 256 GB of quad-channel DDR3 RAM at 1600 MHz, 1.6 TB flash storage with 7 GB/s bandwidth, and 4X 300 GB hard disks at 10,000 RPM.

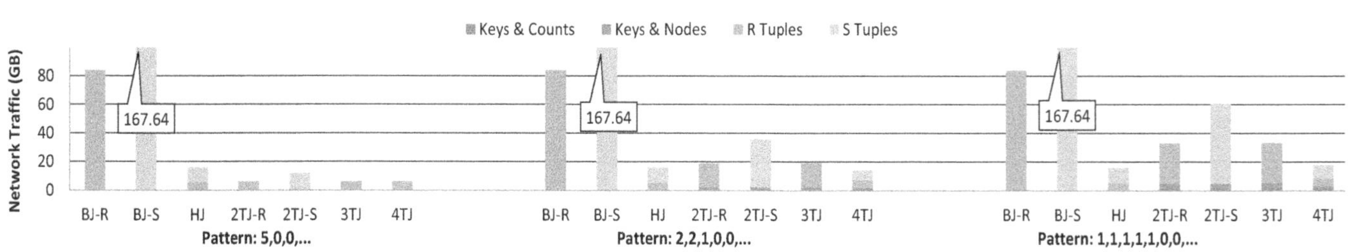

Figure 5: Synthetic dataset with $2 \cdot 10^8$ tuples per table with $4 \cdot 10^7$ unique keys (intra collocated)

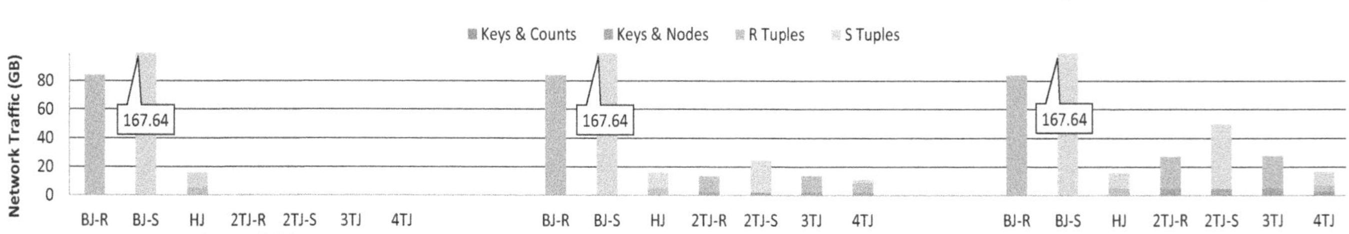

Figure 6: Synthetic dataset with $2 \cdot 10^8$ tuples per table with $4 \cdot 10^7$ unique keys (inter & intra collocated)

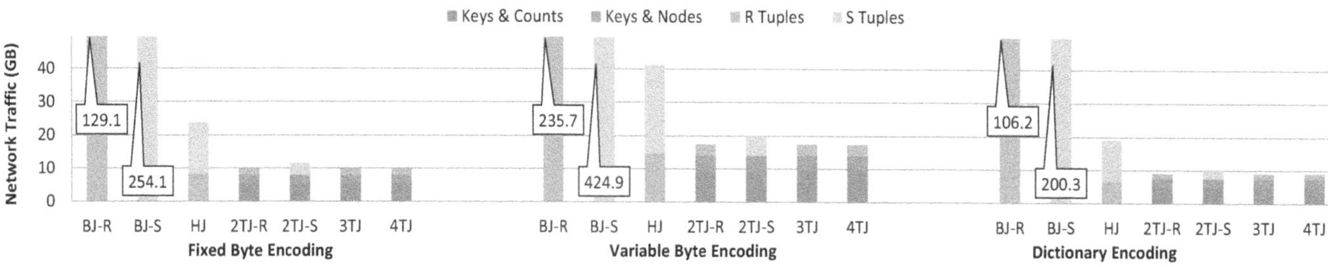

Figure 7: Slowest join sub-query of slowest query (Q1) of real workload X (original tuple ordering)

In the next experiment we use the slowest query (Q1) from a real workload (X). All query plans were generated by the same commercial DBMS. Q1 includes a hash join that we profiled to take 23% of the total execution time. The two join inputs, shown in table 1, are both intermediate relations and consist of 769,845,120 and 790,963,741 tuples. The join output has 730,073,001 tuples. Q1 joins 7 relations, after applying selections on 4, and performs one final aggregation.

	Column name	Distinct values	Bits
R	J.ID (key)	769,785,856	30
	T.ID	53	6
	J.T.AMT	9,824,256	24
	T.C.ID	297,952	19
S	J.ID (key)	788,463,616	30
	T.ID	53	6
	S.B.ID	95	7
	O.U.AMT	26,308,608	25
	C.ID	359	9
	T.B.C.ID	233,040	18
	S.C.AMT	11,278,336	24
	M.U.AMT	54,407,160	26

Table 1: R ($\approx$ 770M tuples) $\bowtie$ S ($\approx$ 791M tuples)

In Figure 7, we use 3 different encoding schemes, fixed byte (1, 2 or 4 byte) codes, fixed bit dictionary codes, and variable byte[1] encoding. The input displayed locality, since broadcasting R transferred $\approx 1/3$ of R tuples compared to hash join. We would expect both to transfer the whole R table. We shuffle and repeat the experiments in Figure 8.

Workload X contains more than 1500 queries and the same most expensive hash join appears in the five slowest queries, taking 23%, 31%, 30%, 42%, and 43% of their execution time. The slowest five queries require 14.7% of the total time required for all queries in the workload (> 1500) cumulatively and spend $\approx$ 65–70% of their time on the network. Time was measured by running the entire X workload on the commercial DBMS we use. The hash join in all five queries operates on the same intermediate result for the key columns, but each query uses different payloads. Queries Q2–Q5 are similar to Q1 and do 4–6 joins followed by aggregation. We study the same expensive join as in Q1.

All columns of the join are of number type and would use variable byte encoding if left uncompressed, which is expensive for network use. As shown in Figures 7 and 8, where we presented results for the most expensive query (Q1), using uncompressed keys increases the cost of track join. Since we cannot optimize the tracking phase, it is preferable to compress the key columns rather than the payload columns.

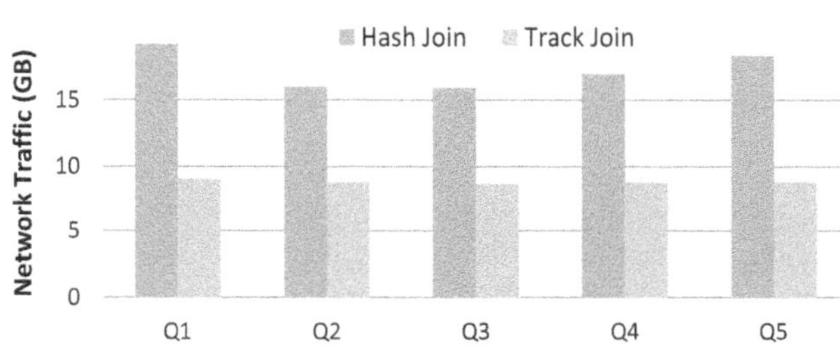

Figure 9: Common slowest join sub-query in slowest queries 1–5 of X (optimal dictionary compression)

In Figure 9, we compare hash and track join on the slowest five queries, using dictionary coding with the minimum number of bits, which is also the optimal compression scheme that we can apply here. The total bits per tuple for R:S are 79:145, 67:120, 60:126, 67:131, and 69:145 respectively. The network traffic reduction is 53%, 45%, 46%, 48%, and 52% respectively. Here, both inputs have almost entirely unique keys. Thus, assuming we pick the table with shorter tuples (R here) as the one we selective broadcast during 2-phase track join, all track join versions have similar performance, sending each tuple from table with shorter tuples to the single location of the match from the table with wider tuples.

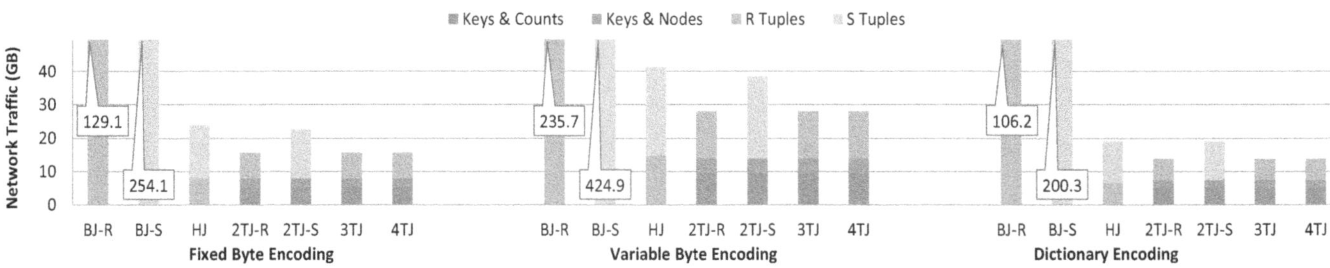

Figure 8: Slowest join sub-query of slowest query (Q1) of real workload X (shuffled tuple ordering)

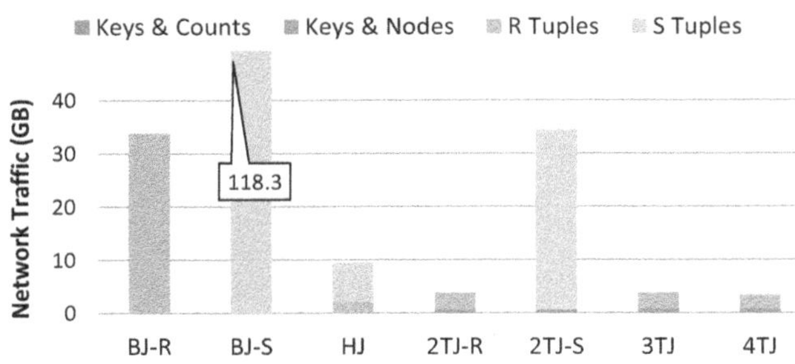

Figure 10: Slowest join in slowest query of uncompressed variable byte[1] Y (original tuple ordering)

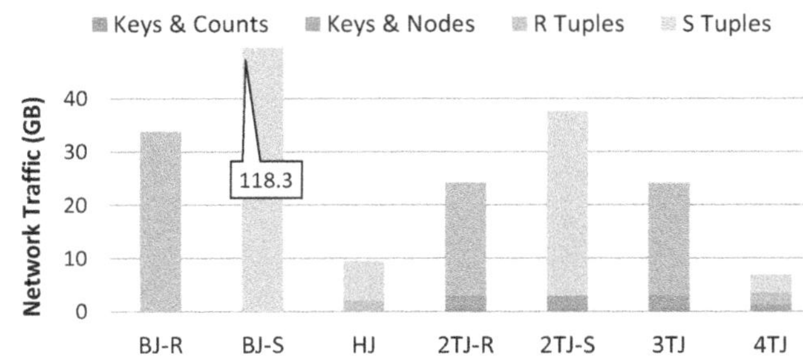

Figure 11: Slowest join in slowest query of uncompressed variable byte[1] Y (shuffled tuple ordering)

In the X workload, the key columns have less than 1 billion distinct values, and thus, fit in a 32-bit integer if dictionary encoded. However, the actual values do not fit in the 32-bit range. In some cases, we can effectively reduce the data width using simple compression schemes [18] that allow fast decompression and do not require accessing large dictionaries that are unlikely to remain CPU-cache-resident. On the other hand, dictionaries reduce the width of data types and, if sorted, can perform equality and ordering operations with the dictionary index. Decoding arbitrary n-bit dictionary indexes can be implemented efficiently [18, 35]. However, in many operations, including non-selective equi-joins, dictionary accesses are redundant. In our results for compressed workload X, we omit dictionary dereference traffic as the join can proceed solely on compressed data.

In all experiments we omit dictionary dereference traffic as the join can proceed solely on compressed data. Dictionaries are also compressed before the join using the minimum number of bits required to encode the distinct values of the intermediate relation. This is the optimal encoding scheme, when most keys are unique and have no specific value ordering. If the dictionaries are not compressed at runtime, we need to rely on the original dictionary that encodes all distinct values of original tables. Encoding to the optimal compression is not always the best choice as the total gain may be outweighed by the total time needed to re-compress. The decision to compact the dictionary and re-compress an intermediate relation, is taken by the query optimizer.

In our last simulation we use a second real workload (Y). We isolate the most expensive hash join out of 9 joins from the slowest query out of the $\approx$ 90 analytical queries in Y. According to our profiling, the top query takes 20% of the time required to run all queries cumulatively and the hash join takes about 36% of the total query execution time.

In Figure 10 we show the running time using the original data ordering. The R table has 57,119,489 rows and the S table has 141,312,688 rows. The join output consists of 1,068,159,117 rows. The data are uncompressed and use variable byte encoding. The tuples are 37 and 47 bytes wide, the largest part of which is due to a character 23-byte character column. The large output of the query makes it a good example of high join selectivity that has different characteristics from foreign and candidate key joins. Late materialization could cause this query to be excessively expensive, if payloads are fetched at the output tuple cardinality.

The last experiment is a good example of the adaptiveness of track join. We need many repeated keys since the output cardinality is 5.4 times the input cardinality which also applies per distinct join key. The naïve selective broadcast of 2-phase and 3-phase track join almost broadcasts R.

In Figure 11, we re-run the experiment on the same workload as Figure 10, but first we shuffle the input to remove all locality. The 4-phase version is better than hash join, while the other versions almost broadcast R due to key repetitions.

The 2-phase track join can be prohibitive if there is no locality and we choose to broadcast S tuples to R tuple locations. This is due to sending S tuples to too many nodes to match with R and is shown in Figure 11. The opposite broadcast direction is not as bad, but is still three times more expensive than hash join. 4-phase track join adapts to the shuffled case and transfers 28% less data than hash join.

4.2 Implementation

For the next set of experiments, we implement hash join and track join in C++ using system calls but no libraries. The network communication uses TCP and all local processing is done in RAM. We use four identical machines connected through 1 Gbit Ethernet, each with 2X Intel Xeon X5550 (4-core with 2-way SMT) CPUs at 2.67 GHz and 24 GB ECC RAM. The RAM bandwidth is 28.4 GB/s for reading data from RAM, 16 GB/s for writing data to RAM, and 12.4 GB/s for RAM to RAM copying. We compile with GCC 4.8 using `-O3` optimization, the OS is Linux 3.2, and we always use all 16 hardware threads on each machine.

In Table 2 we show the CPU and network use for hash join and all track join versions. Our platform is severely network bound since each edge can transfer 0.093 GB/s, if used exclusively. Although track join was presented using a pipelined approach in Section 2, we separate CPU and network utilization by de-pipelining all operations of track join. Thus, we can estimate performance on perfectly balanced and much faster networks by dividing the time of network transfers accordingly. We assume the data are initially on RAM and the join results are also materialized on RAM.[2]

Input		Time	HJ	2TJ[3]	3TJ	4TJ
X	Orig.	CPU	4.308	5.396	6.842	7.500
		Network	87.754	38.857	44.432	44.389
	Shuf.	CPU	4.598	6.457	7.601	8.290
		Network	87.828	61.961	67.117	67.518
Y	Orig.	CPU	2.301	2.279	3.355	2.400
		Network	30.097	10.800	11.145	10.476
	Shuf.	CPU	2.331	2.635	3.536	2.541
		Network	30.191	28.674	29.520	18.230

Table 2: CPU & network time (in seconds) on the slowest join of the most expensive query of X and Y

[1] The variable byte scheme of X, Y uses base 100 encoding.
[2] We materialize Y in chunks as it does not fit in RAM.
[3] 2TJ uses the $R \rightarrow S$ direction for selective broadcasts.

Step Description	Workload X		Workload Y	
	Orig.	Shuf.	Orig.	Shuf.
Hash partition R tuples	0.347	0.350	0.054	0.054
Hash partition S tuples	0.478	0.477	0.167	0.167
Transfer R tuples	29.464	29.925	7.197	7.392
Transfer S tuples	57.199	57.142	22.550	22.945
Local copy tuples	0.115	0.115	0.039	0.039
Sort received R tuples	1.145	1.288	0.176	0.179
Sort received S tuples	1.627	1.777	0.535	0.572
Final merge-join	0.601	0.602	1.322	1.321

Table 3: Distributed hash join steps (in seconds)

Our implementation supports fixed byte widths. For X, we use 4-byte keys, 7-byte payloads for R, and 18-byte payloads for S. For Y, we use 4-byte keys, 33-byte payloads for R, and 43-byte payloads for S. The node locations use 1 byte and the tracking counts use 1 byte for X and 2 for Y.

Using workload X in the original order, 2-phase track join increases the CPU time by 25%, but reduces the network time by 56% compared to hash join. 3-phase and 4-phase track join increases the CPU time by 59% and 74%, but do not reduce network more than 2-phase track join. If X is shuffled, 2-phase track join, the best version here, increase the CPU time by 40% reduces the network time by 29%.

Using Y in the original order, 2-phase track join suffices to reduce the network time by 64% compared to hash join without affecting the CPU time. If Y is shuffled, 2-phase and 3-phase track join increase the CPU time without saving network, due to key repetitions. In fact, we would transfer more data than hash join, as shown Figure 11, if we used more nodes. 4-phase track join, the only useful version here, increases the CPU time by 9% and reduces network by 40%.

We project track join performance on 10X faster network (10 Gbit Ethernet) by scaling the network time. For X, we project track join to be $\approx$ 29% faster than hash join. For Y, track join would be $\approx$ 37% faster. Note that the hardware bundle of the commercial DBMS uses both faster CPUs (2X 8-core CPUs at 2.9GHz) and network (40 Gbit InfiniBand).

Tables 3 and 4 show the times per step for hash join and 4-phase track join. We use sort-merge-join (MSB radix-sort) for local joins. Data movement is separated between remote and local transfers. For track join, we sort both tables and aggregate the keys. We shuffle keys and counts across the network and generate schedules by splitting pairs of nodes into four distinct parts for migrating and broadcasting R and S. The transferred pairs are merge-joined to translate nodes into payloads. The payloads are shuffled and the final join occurs. For X, scheduling takes half the time of local hash join, but is redundant since 2-phase track join suffices. For Y, scheduling is crucial and takes almost negligible time.

5. FUTURE WORK

The original ordering of tuples in X exhibits locality skew among nodes, reducing the potential for improvement over hash join. If some nodes exhibit more locality than others, we need to take into account the balancing of transfers among nodes and not only aim for minimal network traffic.

A pipelined implementation can reduce end-to-end time by overlapping CPU and network [16]. Track join is more complex than hash join, offering more choices for overlap. Thus, investigating alternative implementations that overlap CPU and network to minimize time is a crucial problem.

Step Description	Workload X		Workload Y	
	Orig.	Shuf.	Orig.	Shuf.
Sort local R tuples	0.979	1.300	0.182	0.182
Sort local S tuples	1.401	1.792	0.534	0.565
Aggregate keys	0.229	0.227	0.022	0.025
Hash part. keys, counts	0.373	0.372	0.011	0.018
Transfer key, count	26.800	27.339	0.977	1.378
Local copy key, count	0.034	0.034	0.093	0.001
Merge recv. key, count	0.506	0.507	0.015	0.022
Generate schedules and partition by node	1.627	1.650	0.035	0.047
Tran. $R \to S$ keys, nodes	7.277	10.913	0.346	0.532
Tran. $S \to R$ keys, nodes	6.046	1.562	0.135	0.247
Local copy keys, nodes	0.016	0.016	0.000	0.000
Merge rec. keys, nodes	0.237	0.235	0.007	0.012
Merge-join $R \to S$ keys, nodes $\Rightarrow$ payloads and partition by node	0.315	0.456	0.068	0.098
Merge-join $S \to R$ keys, nodes $\Rightarrow$ payloads and partition by node	0.355	0.204	0.067	0.082
Transfer $R \to S$ tuples	2.664	27.532	6.086	9.600
Transfer $S \to R$ tuples	0.001	0.001	3.235	6.462
Local copy $R \to S$ tuples	0.067	0.017	0.007	0.009
Local copy $S \to R$ tuples	0.138	0.037	0.021	0.008
Merge rec. $R \to S$ tuples	0.161	0.531	0.045	0.067
Merge rec. $S \to R$ tuples	0.141	0.066	0.043	0.045
Final merge-join $R \to S$	0.419	0.555	0.822	0.793
Final merge-join $S \to R$	0.342	0.161	0.518	0.556

Table 4: Track join (4-phase) steps (in seconds)

6. RELATED WORK

The foundations of distributed query processing and database implementation [5, 8, 10, 11, 20] have been laid some decades back. The baseline hash join algorithm we also use in our work is the version presented in the Grace database machine [17], later parallelized by the Gamma project [9]. Distributed algorithms that filter tuples to reduce network traffic have been extensively studied, namely semi-joins [4, 28, 30], Bloom-joins [22], and other approaches [19].

Contemporary databases, as mentioned, shift from the one-size-fits-all paradigm [32] and are designed as optimized programs for specific needs, the most important cases being analytical and transactional systems. Transactional distributed databases are targeting higher transaction throughput, by eliminating unnecessary network communication [32] due to latency induced delays of distributed commit protocols. Storage managers have also been improved since [13, 14] to keep up with the increasing speed. Analytical systems have evolved into column stores [26, 31] and query execution works primarily in RAM [21]. Using the latest hardware platforms, the network bandwidth remains an order of magnitude lower than the RAM bandwidth. There has also been significant work towards optimizing main-memory resident database operators, namely linear scans [18, 35], joins [2, 3, 15], group-by aggregations [36], and sorting [25, 29, 34].

In distributed sorting [16], CPU and network time can be overlapped by transferring keys and payloads separately. If the response time is important, a modified hash join has been proposed [33]. On faster networks, distributed joins have been evaluated [12], but the network was not the bottleneck for the algorithm used. Recent work discusses network time optimization [27] covering joins. The optimization is NP-complete and therefore cannot be applied per-key. In contrast, track join minimizes network volume using linear scheduling applied per key, achieving a finer granularity optimum. While completion time is not necessarily a better metric than network volume when partial results can be consumed as soon as they are generated, track join can utilize the temporal scheduling of [27] to reduce end-to-end time.

Popular generic distributed systems [7, 24] have been used for database operations such as joins [1, 23], minimizing network transfers by carefully mapping "map" and "reduce" operators to the most relevant data. However, "tracking" is still required to achieve high granularity collocation. Based on our non-pipelined implementation, track join can be re-implemented for MapReduce. Thus, network optimizations can occur both at a coarse-grain granularity by the framework and at a fine-grain granularity by using track join.

7. CONCLUSION

We presented track join, a novel algorithm for distributed joins that minimizes communication and therefore, network traffic. To minimize the number of tuples transferred across the network, track join generates an optimal transfer schedule for each distinct join key after tracking initial locations of tuples. Track join makes no assumptions about data organization in the DBMS and does not rely on schema properties or pre-existing favorable data placement to show its merits.

We described three versions of track join, studied cost estimation for query optimization, compared the interaction with semi-join filtering, and showed track join to be better than tracking-aware hash join. Our experimental evaluation shows the efficiency of track join at reducing network traffic and shows its adaptiveness on various cases and degrees of locality. Our evaluation shows that we can reduce both network traffic and total execution time. The workloads were extracted from a corpus of commercial analytical workloads and the queries were profiled as the most expensive out of all the queries in each workload using a market-leading DBMS.

8. ACKNOWLEDGMENTS

We thank John Kowtko, Nipun Agarwal, and Eric Sedlar of the Oracle Labs for their invaluable help and support.

9. REFERENCES

[1] F. N. Afrati and J. D. Ullman. Optimizing joins in a map-reduce environment. In *EDBT*, pages 99–110, 2010.

[2] M.-C. Albutiu, A. Kemper, and T. Neumann. Massively parallel sort-merge joins in main memory multi-core database systems. *PVLDB*, 5(10):1064–1075, June 2012.

[3] C. Balkesen et al. Multicore, main-memory joins: Sort vs. hash revisited. *PVLDB*, 7(1):85–96, Sept. 2013.

[4] P. A. Bernstein and D.-M. W. Chiu. Using semi-joins to solve relational queries. *J. ACM*, 28(1):25–40, Jan. 1981.

[5] P. A. Bernstein et al. Query processing in a system for distributed databases. *ACM Trans. Database Systems*, 6:602–625, 1981.

[6] B. H. Bloom. Space/time trade-offs in hash coding with allowable errors. *Comm. ACM*, 13(7):422–426, July 1970.

[7] J. Dean and S. Ghemawat. MapReduce: simplified data processing on large clusters. In *OSDI*, pages 137–150, 2004.

[8] D. J. DeWitt et al. Implementation techniques for main memory database systems. In *SIGMOD*, pages 1–8, 1984.

[9] D. J. DeWitt et al. The Gamma database machine project. *IEEE Trans. Knowl. Data Engin.*, 2(1):44–62, Mar. 1990.

[10] D. J. DeWitt and J. Gray. Parallel database systems: the future of high performance database systems. *Comm. ACM*, 35:85–98, 1992.

[11] R. Epstein, M. Stonebraker, and E. Wong. Distributed query processing in a relational data base system. In *SIGMOD*, pages 169–180, 1978.

[12] P. W. Frey, R. Goncalves, M. Kersten, and J. Teubner. Spinning relations: high-speed networks for distributed join processing. In *DaMoN*, pages 27–33, 2009.

[13] M. Grund et al. HYRISE: A main memory hybrid storage engine. *PVLDB*, 4(2):105–116, Nov. 2010.

[14] R. Johnson et al. Shore-MT: a scalable storage manager for the multicore era. In *EDBT*, pages 24–35, 2009.

[15] C. Kim et al. Sort vs. hash revisited: fast join implementation on modern multi-core CPUs. *PVLDB*, 2(2):1378–1389, Aug. 2009.

[16] C. Kim et al. CloudRAMsort: fast and efficient large-scale distributed RAM sort on shared-nothing cluster. In *SIGMOD*, pages 841–850, 2012.

[17] M. Kitsuregawa, H. Tanaka, and T. Moto-Oka. Application of hash to data base machine and its architecture. *New Generation Computing*, 1:63–74, 1983.

[18] D. Lemire et al. Decoding billions of integers per second through vectorization. *Software: Pract. Exper.*, May 2013.

[19] Z. Li and K. A. Ross. PERF join: an alternative to two-way semijoin and Bloomjoin. In *CIKM*, pages 137–144, 1995.

[20] L. F. Mackert and G. M. Lohman. R* optimizer validation and performance evaluation for distributed queries. In *VLDB*, pages 149–159, 1986.

[21] S. Manegold, P. A. Boncz, and M. L. Kersten. Optimizing database architecture for the new bottleneck: memory access. *VLDB J.*, 9(3):231–246, 2000.

[22] J. K. Mullin. Optimal semijoins for distributed database systems. *IEEE Trans. Software Engin.*, 16(5):558–560, May 1990.

[23] A. Okcan and M. Riedewald. Processing theta-joins using mapreduce. In *SIGMOD*, pages 949–960, 2011.

[24] A. Pavlo et al. A comparison of approaches to large-scale data analysis. In *SIGMOD*, pages 165–178, 2009.

[25] O. Polychroniou and K. A. Ross. A comprehensive study of main-memory partitioning and its application to large-scale comparison- and radix-sort. In *SIGMOD*, 2014.

[26] V. Raman et al. DB2 with BLU acceleration: So much more than just a column store. *PVLDB*, 6(11):1080–1091, Aug. 2013.

[27] W. Roediger et al. Locality-sensitive operators for parallel main-memory database clusters. In *ICDE*, 2014.

[28] N. Roussopoulos and H. Kang. A pipeline n-way join algorithm based on the 2-way semijoin program. *IEEE Trans. Knowl. Data Engin.*, 3(4):486–495, Dec. 1991.

[29] N. Satish et al. Fast sort on CPUs and GPUs: a case for bandwidth oblivious SIMD sort. In *SIGMOD*, pages 351–362, 2010.

[30] J. W. Stamos and H. C. Young. A symmetric fragment and replicate algorithm for distributed joins. *IEEE Trans. Parallel Distributed Systems*, 4(12):1345–1354, Dec. 1993.

[31] M. Stonebraker et al. C-store: a column-oriented DBMS. In *VLDB*, pages 553–564, 2005.

[32] M. Stonebraker et al. The end of an architectural era: (it's time for a complete rewrite). In *VLDB*, pages 1150–1160, 2007.

[33] T. Urhan and M. J. Franklin. XJoin: A reactively-scheduled pipelined join operator. *IEEE Data Engin. Bulletin*, 23:27–33, June 2000.

[34] J. Wassenberg and P. Sanders. Engineering a multi core radix sort. In *EuroPar*, pages 160–169, 2011.

[35] T. Willhalm et al. SIMD-scan: ultra fast in-memory table scan using on-chip vector processing units. *PVLDB*, 2(1):385–394, Aug. 2009.

[36] Y. Ye, K. A. Ross, and N. Vesdapunt. Scalable aggregation on multicore processors. In *DaMoN*, pages 1–9, 2011.

[37] F. Yu et al. CS2: a new database synopsis for query estimation. In *SIGMOD*, pages 469–480, 2013.

On-the-Fly Token Similarity Joins in Relational Databases

Nikolaus Augsten
University of Salzburg
Salzburg, Austria
nikolaus.augsten@sbg.ac.at

Armando Miraglia
VU University Amsterdam
Amsterdam, Netherlands
a.miraglia@student.vu.nl

Thomas Neumann
TU München
Munich, Germany
neumann@in.tum.de

Alfons Kemper
TU München
Munich, Germany
kemper@in.tum.de

ABSTRACT

Token similarity joins represent data items as sets of tokens, for example, strings are represented as sets of q-grams (substrings of length q). Two items are considered similar and match if their token sets have a large overlap. Previous work on similarity joins in databases mainly focuses on expressing the overlap computation with relational operators. The tokens are assumed to preexist in the database, and the token generation cannot be expressed as part of the query.

Our goal is to efficiently compute token similarity joins on-the-fly, i.e., without any precomputed tokens or indexes. We define *tokenize*, a new relational operator that generates tokens and allows the similarity join to be fully integrated into relational databases. This allows us to (1) optimize the token generation as part of the query plan, (2) provide the query optimizer with cardinality estimates for tokens, (3) choose efficient algorithms based on the query context. We discuss algebraic properties, cardinality estimates, and an efficient iterator algorithm for tokenize. We implemented our operator in the kernel of PostgreSQL and empirically evaluated its performance for similarity joins.

1. INTRODUCTION

The similarity join, which computes pairs of objects that are similar with respect to some similarity measure, is a fundamental operation in many application areas such as record linkage, data cleaning, and information retrieval. Many interesting similarity measures are based on so-called token sets. In a first phase, the objects of interest are represented as sets of tokens, for example, strings may be represented as the set of all their q-grams (overlapping substrings of length q). In the second phase, the overlap between the token sets is computed. Intuitively, two objects are similar if the overlap between their token sets is large.

Previous work has mainly focused on the second phase, the computation of the set overlap. Stand-alone applications [1, 5, 18, 23] based on inverted indexes and relational implementations [7, 9, 24] have been proposed for that purpose. The first phase, the representation of data items as tokens, has received little attention. The token generation is assumed to be an offline process that is not part of the query evaluation. In previous relational approaches, the tokens are stored in tables called token indexes, which are precomputed using external applications or user-defined functions (UDF).

The goal of our work is to compute token similarity joins in relational databases on-the-fly, i.e., without any precomputed index structure. This allows us to compute similarity queries on any attribute, whereas index approaches are limited to the indexed attributes. Further, we do not need to deal with index updates. Updating token indexes is cumbersome since they are stored as ordinary tables, and the update mechanism must be implemented manually, for example, using triggers and UDFs.

The corner stone of our work is the *tokenize operator*, a new relational operator that elegantly represents the token generation as part of the query plan and thus expresses the full token similarity join as a relational query. The integration of the token generation into the query plan opens new opportunities for query optimization. At the logical level, we discuss equivalence rules for reordering tokenize with all standard relational operators, for example, pushing down selection and projection beneath tokenize. We provide cardinality estimates for well-known token functions and a non-blocking iterator algorithm for tokenize. We design and implement an efficient algorithm for nested tokenize operators, which are a frequent pattern in filter/verify implementations of token similarity joins.

At the conceptual level, the tokenize operator replicates the tokenized tuple for each token. This is very convenient from the query point of view since all attributes of the tuple are still available after the tokenization process, for example, to verify candidates in a similarity join. However, replicating tuples is expensive and leads to large intermediate results. Implementations of the tokenize operator should not physically replicate tuples. We discuss two techniques to avoid the replication of tuples in practical query plans. Summarizing, our contributions are the following:

- We propose *tokenize*, a new relational operator that generates tokens. We discuss equivalence rules for reordering tokenize with all standard relational algebra operators, provide cardinality estimates, and a non-blocking iterator algorithm.
- Our *similarity selection* algorithm efficiently evaluates a frequent query pattern that combines nested tokenize operators with selection and grouping. Similarity se-

SIGMOD'14, June 22–27, 2014, Snowbird, UT, USA.
Copyright 2014 ACM 978-1-4503-2376-5/14/06 ...$15.00.
http://dx.doi.org/10.1145/2588555.2610530.

lection is used, for example, for conjunctive predicates and candidate verification in filtered joins.

- *Virtual tuple replication* is a new technique that solves the problem of large intermediate results due to tuple replication and is applicable if tokenize is directly followed by a grouping operator.
- We implemented tokenize in the kernel of PostgreSQL. We evaluate the performance of our techniques for generating tokens and for similarity joins on large synthetic and real world datasets.

This paper is structured as follows. We briefly introduce the notation in the next section and provide background material in Section 3. The tokenize operator, its algebraic properties, an iterator algorithm, and cardinality estimates are presented in Section 4. In Section 5 we discuss tokenize in the context of similarity queries. Our algorithms are empirically evaluated in Section 6 and related work is discussed in Section 7. We draw conclusions in Section 8.

2. PRELIMINARIES AND NOTATION

A relation is a *bag* of tuples. If R is a relation, then $\mathcal{R} = \langle r_1, r_2, \ldots, r_n \rangle$ is its schema. We write $R\langle r_1, r_2, \ldots, r_n \rangle$ to define the schema of table R. The set of attributes that appears in a tuple $t \in R$ or in a predicate θ is denoted as $attr(t)$ resp. $attr(\theta)$. The restriction of a tuple $t \in R$ to the attribute sequence $A \subseteq \mathcal{R}$ is denoted as $t.A$, the value of a single attribute $r \in \mathcal{R}$ is $t.r$, the concatenation of two tuples is $t_1 \circ t_2$. Given two attribute sequences, A and B, AB is the concatenation of the two sequences, and $A \cup B$ denotes the attributes of A followed by the attributes of $B \setminus A$, maintaining the order of both A and B.

The bag of elements $x_1, x_2, \ldots, x_n$ is denoted as $\{x_1, x_2, \ldots, x_n\}_b$. We adapt the set builder notation to bags such that $X = \{x \mid P(x)\}_b$ is the bag of all elements x that satisfy formula $P(x)$. If $P(x)$ is a predicate on $x \in Y$, where Y is a bag, then x is bound to every occurrence of an element in Y, even if it occurs multiple times. We also use expressions with multiple free variables $x_1, x_2, \ldots, x_n$ that are bound by $P(x_1, x_2, \ldots, x_n)$. For example, the duplicate preserving selection $\sigma_{r=1}(R)$ is defined as $\{t \mid t \in R, t.r = 1\}_b$, the join $R \bowtie_{R.r=S.s} S$ on bags is defined as $\{x \circ y \mid x \in R, y \in S, x.r = y.s\}_b$.

3. BACKGROUND: TOKEN SIMILARITY JOINS

Many similarity measures represent data objects by their tokens. The similarity between two data objects is computed as the similarity between their token sets (for example, using Jaccard similarity). Queries that use such similarity measures in their predicates are *token similarity queries*.

In this section we introduce token functions that decompose an object into its tokens, recap similarity measures between token sets, and define the token similarity join.

3.1 Token Functions

We abstract from the specific data type and look at the commonalities of token-based similarity measures. Token-based similarity measures decompose each object into multiple tokens that form a token set. The function that maps objects to tokens is the *token function*. Token functions were defined for a variety of data types, for example, strings (q-grams [21], positional q-grams [9], v-grams [11]), text documents (words and word shingles [6]), and XML documents or other trees (binary branches [25], pq-grams [4]).

We define token functions to operate on tuples. Token functions may produce duplicate tokens, i.e., the token function maps a tuple to a bag of tuples.

Definition 1. The *token function* $\alpha(.)$ maps a tuple t with schema A to a non-empty bag of token tuples t' with schema B, $A \cap B = \emptyset$,

$$\alpha(t) = \{t' \mid t' \text{ is a token of } t\}_b, \quad \alpha(t) \neq \emptyset. \qquad (1)$$

A token function that always produces a set, i.e., does not produce duplicates, is called *set producing function*. Any token function can be transformed into a set producing function by concatenating each tuple with a frequency counter. The counter is 1 for the first appearance of an element and is incremented for each further appearance of that element in the bag. Formally, bag $X = \{t_1^{m_1}, t_2^{m_2}, \ldots, t_n^{m_n}\}$, where $t_i^{m_i}$ is a tuple that appears m_i times in X, is transformed to the set $S = \bigcup_{1 \leq i \leq n} \bigcup_{1 \leq j \leq m_i} (t_i \circ \langle j \rangle)$. Under this transformation, the set operations on S ($\cup$, $\cap$, $\setminus$) give the same result as the corresponding bag operations on X [15].

Example 1. The q-gram tokens of a string s are all substrings of length q of the extended string $\#^{q-1} \circ s \circ \#^{q-1}$, for example, the q-gram token function ($q = 2$) maps the tuple $\langle \texttt{banana} \rangle$ to the bag $\{\langle \texttt{\#b} \rangle, \langle \texttt{ba} \rangle, \langle \texttt{an} \rangle, \langle \texttt{na} \rangle, \langle \texttt{an} \rangle, \langle \texttt{na} \rangle, \langle \texttt{a\#} \rangle\}_b$. Note that the q-grams an and na each appear twice. The corresponding set producing token function produces the set $\{\langle \texttt{\#b}, 1 \rangle, \langle \texttt{ba}, 1 \rangle, \langle \texttt{an}, 1 \rangle, \langle \texttt{na}, 1 \rangle, \langle \texttt{an}, 2 \rangle, \langle \texttt{na}, 2 \rangle, \langle \texttt{a\#}, 1 \rangle\}$.

Token functions are specific to types, similar to the aggregate functions SUM or AVG, which are defined for numeric types. A system that supports token queries must provide token functions for the types that allow similarity queries. Cardinality estimates for string and tree tokens are discussed in Section 4.5. All other results presented in this paper are independent of the data type.

3.2 Set Similarity Conditions

Token similarity queries are based on set similarity. Popular set similarity functions are overlap, $O(X,Y) = |X \cap Y|$, Jaccard, $J(X,Y) = |X \cap Y|/|X \cup Y|$, and Cosine similarity, $C(X,Y) = |X \cap Y|/\sqrt{|X||Y|}$. High values indicate high similarity. To simplify the discussion, we will henceforth consider similarity conditions of the form $O(X,Y) \geq k$, where k is an overlap threshold. Constraints using Jaccard or Cosine similarity are represented as overlap constraints as follows: $J(X,Y) \geq K \Rightarrow O(X,Y) \geq \frac{K}{1+K}(|X| + |Y|)$, $C(X,Y) \geq K \Rightarrow O(X,Y) \geq K\sqrt{|X||Y|}$.

The cardinality of the token sets is computed using a counter during the generation of the tokens. The core challenge is to compute the intersection between pairs of token sets efficiently, i.e., the overlap similarity. All set similarity conditions can be extended to the case of weighted token sets without changing the essence of the problem [7].

3.3 Token Similarity Joins

The token similarity join matches similar tuples from two relations. The similarity is computed as the overlap between the tokens of the join attributes.

Definition 2. Given relations R and S with schema $\mathcal{R}$ and $\mathcal{S}$, respectively, attribute sequences $A \subseteq \mathcal{R}$, $B \subseteq \mathcal{S}$, a token functions $\alpha(.)$ defined on A and B, and overlap threshold $k > 0$. The *token similarity join* $\tilde{\bowtie}_{A,B,\alpha,k}$ computes all tuples $x \circ y$, $x \in R$, $y \in S$, such that $O(\alpha(x.A), \alpha(y.B)) \geq k$.

$$R \tilde{\bowtie}_{A,B,\alpha,k} S = \\ \{x \circ y \mid x \in R, y \in S, O(\alpha(x.A), \alpha(y.B)) \geq k\}_b \qquad (2)$$

Different from exact predicates (e.g., $R.A = S.B$), the similarity predicate cannot be evaluated by simply inspecting the attribute values of a tuple. The predicate is formulated over the token sets, which are not stored in the relation. This requires new query evaluation techniques.

A brute force algorithm that evaluates the overlap similarities in a nested loop is too expensive. Efficient algorithms transform the similarity join on token sets to an equality join on tokens. Previous work [2, 7, 24] assumes the tokens to be pre-materialized in tables called *token indexes*, and the token similarity join is evaluated as an equality join on token indexes. The token index is defined as follows:

Definition 3. Given relation R with schema $\mathcal{R}$, $A \subseteq \mathcal{R}$, a set producing token function $\alpha(.)$ defined on A. The *token index* for $R.A$ is defined as

$$I^{R.A} = \{t \circ tk \mid t \in \pi^D(R), tk \in \alpha(t.A)\}, \qquad (3)$$

where π^D eliminates duplicates.

Example 2. Consider relation R and token index $I^{R.A}$ in Figure 1. The token index stores q-gram tokens with a frequency counter. To simplify the presentation, we concatenate q-gram and counter.

A
banana
orange

(a) Relation R.

A	token
banana	#b,1
banana	ba,1
banana	an,1
banana	na,1
banana	an,2
banana	na,2
banana	a#,1
...	...
...	...
orange	#o,1
orange	or,1
orange	ra,1
orange	an,1
orange	ng,1
orange	ge,1
orange	e#,1

(b) Token index $I^{R.A}$.

Figure 1: Tokens of relation R using q-grams.

Let $I^{R.A}\langle\mathcal{R}, token\rangle$ and $I^{S.B}\langle\mathcal{S}, token\rangle$ be token indexes for R and S, respectively, $\mathcal{R} \cap \mathcal{S} = \emptyset$. The token similarity join between R and S for a set producing token function $\alpha(.)$ is implemented as (γ is the grouping operator)

$$R \tilde{\bowtie}_{A,B,\alpha,k} S = \pi_{\mathcal{R},\mathcal{S}}(R \bowtie S \bowtie \\ \sigma_{olap \geq k}\gamma_{\mathcal{R},\mathcal{S};\text{COUNT}(*)\rightarrow olap}(I^{R.A} \bowtie I^{S.B})).$$

The join pairs tuples with identical tokens, grouping and counting compute the token overlap between two values A and B. Only value pairs that satisfy the overlap threshold k are returned. The final joins restore duplicates in R and S (which were removed in the token index), the projection removes the overlap attribute. In practical implementations, token indexes only store a key of R resp. S, not the entire tuple. Then, the join with R and S is also required to restore attributes missing in the index.

4. COMPUTING TOKENS

Our goal is to integrate the token similarity join in relational databases without any precomputed indexes. In this section we discuss the generation of tokens when no index is available. We start with a "poor man's" solution that uses table functions, a feature that is present in many systems. Unfortunately, table functions are inflexible and lead to poor query plans. The full-fledged solution is the *tokenize* operator. We define the operator, show equivalence rules to reorder tokenize with other relational operators, present a non-blocking iterator algorithm, and discuss cardinality estimates for different token functions.

4.1 Poor Man's Solutions

Off-the-shelf systems mainly offer two options to generate tokens: stand-alone client applications and table functions.

Stand-alone client. An external client application connects to the database, e.g., via ODBC or JDBC, reads the input table, computes the tokens, and inserts the token index as a new table into the database. This approach is only useful to precompute token indexes and is not applicable to on-the-fly similarity queries. Sending the input table to the client and writing the tokens back to the database creates substantial overhead. In this approach, generating the tokens is a one-time action and the token index is not maintained on updates.

Table function. A table function is a user-defined function that returns a table and is used in the `FROM` clause of SQL like a regular table. The input to the table function is the table to be tokenized, the output is the token index. We define a table function `tblfunc(R,A)` that computes the tokens for attribute A of relation R (cf. Figure 1). Table functions compute the token index on-the-fly and no index must be maintained. The data remains in the database, thus eliminating the overhead of sending it to a client application.

The main problem with table functions is that they are a black box to the query optimizer. In particular, no algebraic transformation rules are applicable to table functions, and the cardinality of the output is unknown, which leads to poor query plans. Consider the following query on two customer tables R and S with schema $\langle ssn, name, address, city\rangle$ that joins customers from New York based on the token similarity of their names (set producing token function assumed).

```
SELECT TR.ssn, TS.ssn
FROM tblfunc('R', 'name') TR, tblfunc('S', 'name') TS
WHERE TR.token = TS.token
  AND TR.city = 'New York' AND TS.city=TR.city
GROUP BY TR.ssn, TS.ssn
HAVING COUNT(*) >= k;
```

A good plan for this query produces tokens only for the customers from New York and projects the required columns before applying the table function. Unfortunately, the optimizer cannot push down selection and projection over the table function since the table function is a black box. Figure 2 shows the best query plan achievable with table functions. Clearly, this plan is suboptimal: (a) the tokens are produced for all tuples from R, and (b) name, city, and address attributes of both tables are replicated for each token.

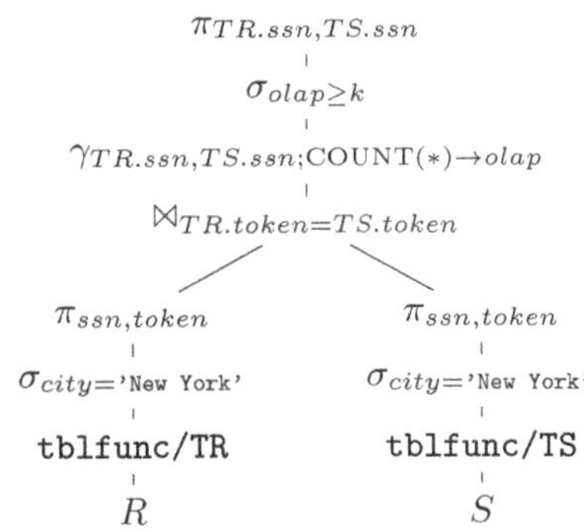

Figure 2: Logical query plan with table functions.

Another problem is the cardinality estimation. The query optimizer does not know the number of tuples that the table function produces. Some systems allow users to define a constant number of rows. Thus, in our example, the output cardinality of the table function is estimated with the same constant independently of the number of rows in R and the number of tokens per row. This leads to poor join orders and poor choices of join, grouping, and sorting algorithms.

In some cases it is possible to hand-craft better query plans, for example, by creating a view or temporary table that selects the customers from New York before applying the table function. For complex queries this is cumbersome or not possible at all. PostgreSQL allows token functions in the select clause (deprecated functionality) such that selections on non-tokenized attributes can be pushed down. None of these workarounds solves the problem of missing cardinality estimates.

4.2 Full Integration: Tokenize Operator

We introduce *tokenize*, a new relational operator that produces tokens. The tokenize operator is integrated into the kernel of the database system and solves the main issues of table functions. In particular, accurate cardinality estimates and rewrite rules for tokenize with all standard relational operators lead to efficient query plans.

The tokenize operator concatenates the tuples of a relation with the tokens produced for one or more attribute values of each tuple. Since a single tuple typically produces multiple tokens, the original tuple is replicated, and each copy is concatenated with one of the tokens. The tokenize operator abstracts from the data type of the tokenized attribute. The tokens are produced by the token function, which is a parameter of the tokenize operator, comparable to aggregation functions for the grouping operator.

Definition 4. Given relation R with schema $\mathcal{R}$ and token function $\alpha(.)$ that maps tuples with signature A, $A \subseteq \mathcal{R}$, to bags of token tuples, the *tokenize operator* is defined as

$$\tau_{\alpha(A)}(R) = \{t \circ t' \mid t \in R, t' \in \alpha(t.A)\}_b. \tag{4}$$

The tokenize operator extends schema $\mathcal{R}$ with token attributes. We write $\tau_{\alpha(A)\rightarrow A'}(R)$ to rename the new attributes to A', $A' \cap \mathcal{R} = \emptyset$, resulting in schema $\mathcal{R}A'$.

Example 3. We apply the tokenize operator to the string attribute A of relation R in Figure 1a: $\tau_{\alpha^q(A)\rightarrow token}(R)$. The token function $\alpha^q(.)$ produces unique q-grams ($q = 2$) using a frequency counter. The result is shown in Figure 1b.

Note that the tokenize operator only conceptually replicates all attribute values. When implementing the operator, the replication of the attribute values that are not tokenized can often be avoided as will be discussed in Section 4.6.

4.3 Equivalence Transformations

We provide equivalences for reordering tokenize with all standard relational operators. Tokenize has very pleasant algebraic properties: reordering rules for all operators exist and nested tokenize operators can be reordered as well. This is an important feature that allows the query optimizer to produce efficient query plans. All equivalences in this section are defined on bags. The duplicate eliminating projection $\pi^D(.)$ transforms bags to sets. Due to space constraints we omit the proofs in this section.

Union, intersection, and difference. The tokenize operator can be pushed down simultaneously on both sides below bag union, bag intersection, and bag difference. Since these operators do not increase the number of tuples, but tokenize does, the equivalence rules will typically be used from right to left, i.e., tokenize will be computed last.

LEMMA 1. *Given two relations R and S with schemas $\mathcal{R}$ and $\mathcal{S}$, respectively. If $\mathcal{R} = \mathcal{S}$ and $A \subseteq \mathcal{R}$, then*

$$\tau_{\alpha(A)}(R \cup S) = \tau_{\alpha(A)}(R) \cup \tau_{\alpha(A)}(S), \tag{5}$$
$$\tau_{\alpha(A)}(R \cap S) = \tau_{\alpha(A)}(R) \cap \tau_{\alpha(A)}(S), \tag{6}$$
$$\tau_{\alpha(A)}(R \setminus S) = \tau_{\alpha(A)}(R) \setminus \tau_{\alpha(A)}(S). \tag{7}$$

Selection. Selection can be pushed down beneath the tokenize operator. This allows us to use other (cheap and selective) predicates in the query to reduce the number of tokens that must be produced for the similarity predicates.

LEMMA 2. *Given relation R with schema $\mathcal{R}$. If $A \subseteq \mathcal{R}$ and $attr(\theta) \subseteq \mathcal{R}$, then*

$$\tau_{\alpha(A)}(\sigma_\theta(R)) = \sigma_\theta(\tau_{\alpha(A)}(R)). \tag{8}$$

Projection. We distinguish the duplicate preserving projection $\pi(R) = \{t.A \mid t \in R\}_b$ (Lemma 3) and the duplicate eliminating projection $\pi^D(R) = \{t.A \mid t \in R\}$ (Lemma 4).

LEMMA 3. *Given relation R with schema $\mathcal{R}$ and attribute sequences $A'' \subseteq A'$, $A' \cap \mathcal{R} = \emptyset$, $A \subseteq \mathcal{R}$, $A \neq \emptyset$, $B \subseteq \mathcal{R}$. For duplicate preserving projection the following holds:*

$$\pi_{BA''}(\tau_{\alpha(A)\rightarrow A'}(R)) = \pi_{BA''}(\tau_{\alpha(A)\rightarrow A'}(\pi_{B\cup A}(R))) \tag{9}$$

This equivalence rule allows us to push down projection beneath tokenize and remove unnecessary columns early in the query plan. The output attributes B exist in the input relation R, while A'' is a subset of the new token attributes. When all tokenized and all token attributes are returned, i.e., $A \subseteq B$ and $A' = A''$, the rule simplifies to

$$\pi_{BA'}(\tau_{\alpha(A)\rightarrow A'}(R)) = \tau_{\alpha(A)\rightarrow A'}(\pi_B(R)).$$

Lemma 4 shows our results for duplicate eliminating projection. Eq. (10) corresponds to Eq. (9) in the previous lemma. Eq. (11) states that tokens which do not appear in the final projection do not need to be produced. Note that this is not true for duplicate preserving projection since the tokenize operator introduces new duplicates. Eq. (12) treats the special case of set producing functions.

LEMMA 4. *Given relation R with schema $\mathcal{R}$ and attribute sequences $A'' \subseteq A'$, $A' \cap \mathcal{R} = \emptyset$, $A \subseteq \mathcal{R}$, $A \neq \emptyset$, $B \subseteq \mathcal{R}$. For duplicate eliminating projection the following holds:*

$$\pi^D_{BA''}(\tau_{\alpha(A)\to A'}(R)) = \pi^D_{BA''}(\tau_{\alpha(A)\to A'}(\pi_{B\cup A}(R))) \quad (10)$$

$$\pi^D_B(\tau_{\alpha(A)}(R)) = \pi^D_B(R) \quad (11)$$

If $A \subseteq B$ and the token function $\alpha(.)$ is set producing, then

$$\tau_{\alpha(A)\to A'}(\pi^D_B(R)) = \pi^D_{BA'}(\tau_{\alpha(A)\to A'}(R)). \quad (12)$$

Cross product and join. Tokenize can be pushed down beneath cross products and joins if all tokenized attributes belong to the same relation.

LEMMA 5. *Given two relations R and S with schemas $\mathcal{R}$ and $\mathcal{S}$, respectively. If $A \subseteq \mathcal{S}$, then*

$$\tau_{\alpha(A)}(R \times S) = R \times \tau_{\alpha(A)}(S), \quad (13)$$

$$\tau_{\alpha(A)}(R \bowtie_\theta S) = R \bowtie_\theta \tau_{\alpha(A)}(S). \quad (14)$$

Nested tokenize operators. The order of nested tokenize operators on a relation R can be reversed if both operators are applied to attributes of R, i.e., they do not access attributes produced by the other tokenize operator. Nested tokenize operators are used in token similarity selections. The duplicate preserving projection in the following lemma reorders the attributes in the output.

LEMMA 6. *Given a relation R with schema $\mathcal{R}$. If $A \subseteq \mathcal{R}$ and $B \subseteq \mathcal{R}$, then*

$$\tau_{\alpha(A)\to A'}(\tau_{\beta(B)\to B'}(R)) = \pi_{\mathcal{R},B',A'}(\tau_{\beta(B)\to B'}(\tau_{\alpha(A)\to A'}(R))). \quad (15)$$

4.4 Iterator Algorithm for Tokenize

The tokenize operator has an efficient iterator implementation. Independent of the token function, the tokenize operator is always implemented as a non-blocking iterator that requires only a single input tuple to produce the first output tuple. Algorithm 1 shows an iterator algorithm for tokenize. Only a single tuple is maintained at any time. Each call of *next* returns a tuple for one token. The tokens are produced by the token function $\alpha(.)$, which is an iterator as well.

Many useful token functions (q-grams, binary branches, pq-grams, word shingles, etc.) produce token bags of linear size and have non-blocking iterator algorithms. For example, the first q-gram can be produced before any other q-gram of the string is computed. Algorithm 2 shows an iterator implementation of the (bag producing) q-gram token function. The set producing version of this function maintains a hash map of ⟨*token*, *frequency*⟩ pairs. Each time a token is produced, it is looked up in the map. If it is there, its *frequency* is incremented, otherwise it is inserted with *frequency* = 1. Both versions are non-blocking: the first token of a tuple is returned before the tokens of any other tuple are produced.

Algorithm 1: Tokenize(R, A, α)

```
init:
  t ← nil;                                  // tuple with schema R
next:
  repeat
    if t = nil then
      t ← next tuple from R;
      if t = nil then return nil;
      α.init(t.A);
    token ← α.next();
    if token = nil then t ← nil else return t ∘ token;
  until true;
```

Algorithm 2: $\alpha^q(\langle s\rangle)$

```
init:
  s' ← #^(q−1) ∘ s ∘ #^(q−1);              // extended string
  pos ← 0;                                  // current position in s'
next:
  if pos ≤ |s'| − q then
    pos++;
    return ⟨s'[pos ... pos + q − 1]⟩;
  else return nil;
```

4.5 Cardinality Estimates

We utilize the catalog statistics to estimate the output cardinality of the tokenize operator. Accurate cardinality estimates are important for computing the cost of the tokenize operator and for generating efficient query plans. For example, the join order and the bucket size for hash based join and grouping algorithms depend on the size of the input tables. In similarity joins, tokenize is always followed by join and grouping operators.

The cardinality of tokenize is a function of the number of input tuples, n, and the attribute length, and is specific to the token function. We discuss the following token functions: q-grams for strings, binary branches, and pq-grams for trees. Trees are stored as XML or user-defined types. For (shredded) tree encodings that store one tree node per tuple, for example, the interval encoding, we use an aggregate function that produces a tree from a group of tuples [4].

q-Grams: The number of q-grams of string s with $|s|$ characters is $|\alpha^q(\langle s\rangle)| = |s| + q - 1$ [9]. For n input strings, the cardinality is $C^q = n * (\bar{s} + q - 1)$. n is provided by the input node of the tokenize operator in the query plan. The average string length $\bar{s}$ is estimated from the column width, which is available in the catalog. If the column width is available only as a byte value, $\bar{s}$ also depends on the encoding. For example, for the UTF-16 encoding, the number of characters in a string with b bytes is at most $b/2$.

Binary branches: A binary branch [25] is a token consisting of a tree node, its first child, and its right sibling. Dummy nodes are used if no children or right siblings are available. For a tree T with $|T|$ nodes, $|\alpha^{bb}(\langle t\rangle)| = |T|$ binary branches exist [25], thus the cardinality is $C^{bb} = n\bar{T}$, where $\bar{T}$ is the average tree size. If the tree is the result of a grouping operator, $\bar{T}$ is estimated as the number of nodes in all trees (cardinality of the tree node table) divided by the number of expected groups (each group produces one tree).

For XML and user-defined tree types there are two options: (a) The estimate for $\bar{T}$ is based on the column width; this requires an additional parameter with the average node size in bytes. (b) The catalog statistics are extended with size estimates for the tree data types.

pq-Grams: A *pq*-gram [4] token of a tree T consists of a node, its $p-1$ closest ancestors, and q consecutive children; like for binary branches, dummy nodes are used to substitute missing nodes. The number of *pq*-grams for a tree with $|T|$ nodes and L leaves is $|\alpha^{pq}(\langle t \rangle)| = 2L + q(|T| - L) - 1$ [4]. We use the upper bounds $2|T| \geq |\alpha^{pq}(\langle t \rangle)|$ for $q = 1$ and $q|T| \geq |\alpha^{pq}(\langle t \rangle)|$ for $q \geq 2$ such that the cardinality only depends on $|T|$. With the average tree size, $\bar{T}$, the cardinality estimates for n trees are $C^{pq}_{q=1} = 2n\bar{T}$ and $C^{pq}_{q\geq 2} = qn\bar{T}$

Summarizing, useful cardinality estimates for well-known token functions exist. Due to the linearity of these functions, the estimates are accurate also if the sizes of the tokenized objects vary and are not uniformly distributed. If tokenize is preceded by an operator that removes tuples, for example, selection, the average size of the remaining tuples may deviate from the overall average and render the cardinality estimate less accurate. The second factor, n, is not affected.

4.6 Avoiding Tuple Replication

The straightforward implementation of the tokenize operator replicates a tuple for each of its tokens. This is expensive since large intermediate tables are produced. A first step to reduce the intermediate result size is to push down projection beneath tokenize to limit the input tuples of the tokenize operator to the attributes that will be required later in the query (cf. Lemma 3). Unfortunately, this is often not enough, for example, when a query returns the tokenized values. We discuss two approaches to avoid the physical replication of tuples.

Virtual tuple replication. We observe that many queries produce tokens only as an intermediate step and a grouping operator removes the tokens in the final result. Consider, for example, the following query, which counts the number of tokens in each string A of relation $R\langle A \rangle$ (cf. Figure 1), where A is a key.

$$\gamma_{A;\text{COUNT}(*)\rightarrow cnt}(\tau_{\alpha(A)\rightarrow tk}(R)) \quad (16)$$

The tuples of each group have identical values on all attributes except the token attribute tk. Our approach is to store the replicated attribute values only once for each group, i.e., for one tuple of the group. In addition, we store a flag for each attribute that is set only if the corresponding attribute value is stored in the tuple. In order to restore the groups we add a new attribute, the *group identifier*, which uniquely identifies the tuples of the tokenized relation and has the same value for all tokens in a single group. We denote the tokenize operator that produces virtual tuples with $\tau_{\alpha(A);gid}(R)$, where *gid* is the group identifier.

Example 4. We produce the tokens for example relation R (cf. Figure 1) with virtual tuple replication. The virtual tuple bit array (VTBA) and the token table are shown in Figure 3. The symbol $\perp$ represents omitted values that are not physically stored and thus require no extra space. The name of the group identifier is *gid*.

The grouping operator restores the values using a special aggregation function, REST(A), that ignores all omitted values of attribute A and returns the first value of each group that is not omitted. We rewrite Eq. (16) as follows:

VTBA			$\tau_{\alpha^q(A)\rightarrow token;gid}(R)$		
			gid	*A*	*token*
1	1	1	1	banana	#b,1
1	0	1	1	$\perp$	ba,1
...	...	...	...	...	...
1	0	1	1	$\perp$	a#,1
1	1	1	2	orange	#o,1
1	0	1	2	$\perp$	or,1
...	...	...	...	...	...
1	0	1	2	$\perp$	e#,1

Figure 3: Virtual tuple replication.

$$\pi_{A,cnt}(\gamma_{gid;\text{REST}(A)\rightarrow A,\text{COUNT}(*)\rightarrow cnt}(\tau_{\alpha(A);gid}(R))) \quad (17)$$

Virtual tuple replication is very effective to reduce the size of the intermediate token tables. In main memory, we store one bit instead of a pointer to a memory address. The gain is even larger when the query writes intermediate results to disk since without virtual tuple replication the pointers must be dereferenced during materialization.

Virtual tuple replication is transparent to the user and is applied whenever the tokenize operator is directly followed by a grouping step on a key of the tokenized tuples. After virtual tuple replication and before restoring the attribute values we cannot access the omitted values. Any selection on omitted attributes is pushed down below the tokenize operator. Operations that remove tokenized tuples are not allowed on virtual tuples since they may remove the only tuple that contains the omitted values.

Temporal IDs. When virtual tuple replication is not applicable, we substitute the replicated attributes by a numeric key and restore them later using a join. Consider, for example, the following query that computes the relevance of the documents in relation $R\langle id, A \rangle$ to the keyword `'john'`; *id* is a numeric key, A stores unique documents.

$$\gamma_{A;\text{COUNT}(*)\rightarrow rel}(\sigma_{tk=\texttt{'john'}}(\tau_{\alpha(A)\rightarrow tk}(R))) \quad (18)$$

This is inefficient since the documents in A are replicated for each token. We rewrite the query using temporal IDs:

$$\pi_{A,rel}(R \bowtie \gamma_{id;\text{COUNT}(*)\rightarrow rel}(\sigma_{tk=\texttt{'john'}}(\pi_{id,tk}(\tau_{\alpha(A)\rightarrow tk}(R)))))$$

The inner projection is integrated into the tokenize operator, and attribute A is never physically replicated. The join restores attribute A. Since the tokenize operator produces a large number of tuples, but the final result of the query is at most $|R|$, the cost for the join is typically smaller than the cost for replicating A.

5. SIMILARITY JOINS WITH TOKENIZE

This section discusses the tokenize operator in the context of a well-known filter/verify framework for similarity joins. In particular, the efficient implementation of prefix filters, the verification of candidates, and the use of tokens in materialized views are discussed.

Token similarity join. Given two relations, R and S, $\mathcal{R} \cap \mathcal{S} = \emptyset$, $A \subseteq \mathcal{R}$, $B \subseteq \mathcal{S}$, a set producing token function $\alpha(.)$.

The token similarity join with tokenize is implemented as

$$R \tilde{\bowtie}_{A,B,\alpha,k} S = \pi_{\mathcal{R},\mathcal{S}}(R \bowtie S \bowtie \sigma_{olap \geq k} \quad (19)$$
$$\gamma_{\mathcal{R},\mathcal{S};\text{COUNT}(*) \to olap}(\tau_{\alpha(A) \to tk}\pi^D(R) \bowtie \tau_{\alpha(B) \to tk}\pi^D(S))).$$

The tokenize operator enriches the tuples of R and S with tokens. The tokenized tuples are joined, and for each pair of tuples from R and S the overlap is computed. Only tuples that satisfy the overlap threshold are returned. The deduplication (π^D) avoids double counting of tokens in the grouping step; the joins with R and S restore the duplicates.

5.1 Prefix Filtering

The equality join on tokens in the basic implementation of the token similarity join (Eq. (19)) produces large intermediate results if some of the tokens are frequent, i.e., appear in many token sets. A well-known approach to address this problem is the so-called prefix filter [7, 24]. The prefix of a token set is a small subsequence of the sorted token set. The length of the subsequence depends on the overlap threshold k and is $|X|-k+1$ for a token set X [7]. If two prefixes have no tokens in common, the similarity between the respective objects will not meet the threshold, thus the objects are not in the result set. The join on the prefixes produces candidate pairs with false positives, but no false negatives.

We define an operator $\text{topN}_{C;D;N}(T)$ that groups the tuples of relation T by the attributes $C \subseteq \mathcal{T}$ and returns the first N elements of each group in sort order of $D \subseteq \mathcal{T}$. In SQL, topN is implemented using window functions. Using topN and tokenize, the *prefix filter candidates*, C, for the similarity join $R \tilde{\bowtie}_{A,B,\alpha,k} S$ are computed as follows:

$$C \leftarrow \pi^D_{A,B}(topN_{A;tk;\text{COUNT}(*)-k+1}(\tau_{\alpha(A) \to tk}\pi^D_A(R)) \bowtie$$
$$topN_{B;tk;\text{COUNT}(*)-k+1}(\tau_{\alpha(B) \to tk}\pi^D_B(S))) \quad (20)$$

Since the filter produces false positives, a verification step is required. The verification step needs access to the complete token set for each item, which gets lost in the prefix filter. Thus, the token sets must be restored:

$$R \tilde{\bowtie}_{A,B,\alpha,k} S = \pi_{\mathcal{R},\mathcal{S}}(R \bowtie S \bowtie \sigma_{olap \geq k}$$
$$\gamma_{A,B;\text{COUNT}(*) \to olap}\sigma_{A'=B'}\tau_{\alpha(A) \to A'}\tau_{\alpha(B) \to B'}(C)) \quad (21)$$

The nested tokenize operators restore the tokens for all candidate pairs, the selection $A' = B'$ on the tokens and the grouping compute the overlap for each candidate pair.

5.2 Computing Effective Prefixes

We propose efficient algorithms for computing prefixes on-the-fly using the tokenize operator. A prefix of length N of set X consists of the first N elements of X in sort order. The filter condition is valid for any sort order (all token sets must follow the same order). A good sort order minimizes the candidate set. We distinguish prefix algorithms for uniform and skewed token distributions.

Uniform token distribution. All tokens appear with similar frequency, and all sort orders produce similar candidate numbers. Thus, we use the default sort order of the token type, e.g., alphanumeric sorting for string tokens. Algorithm 1 for the tokenize operator produces a single token on each call. Let $N = |X| - k + 1$ be the length of the prefix of token set X for threshold k. Then, the prefix can be computed very efficiently by piping the tokens into a top-N sort operator. Top-N sorting of all elements of the token set X requires only $O(|X| \log N)$ time and $O(N)$ memory (as opposed to $O(|X| \log |X|)$ time and $O(|X|)$ memory for sorting the full set). For high similarity thresholds, for which the prefix filter is effective, N is much smaller than $|X|$.

The length of the prefix, N, also depends on the cardinality of the token set, $|X|$, which is different for each token set. For many token functions, the cardinality of the token set can be predicted based on the length of the input (cf. Section 4.5). If the cardinality of the token set is not known, the tokens are cached before they are sent to the top-N sorting operator, which increases the memory complexity to $O(|X|)$.

Skewed token distribution. Frequent tokens can substantially increase the candidate set if they appear in the prefixes. A popular heuristics sorts the tokens by their document frequency in ascending order. The document frequency, *df*, of a token is the number of token sets in which the token appears. In previous work, the *df* values were assumed to be given. Using the tokenize operator, we compute the *df* values on-the-fly in a relational query:

$$DF \leftarrow \gamma_{tk;\text{COUNT}(*) \to df}\tau_{\alpha(A) \to tk}(\pi^D_A(R))$$

DF stores the document frequency, *df*, for each token, *tk*. In order to sort the tokens, we need to join with the *df* values, and the prefix is computed as

$$\text{topN}_{A;df;\text{COUNT}(*)-k+1}(\tau_{\alpha(A) \to tk}(\pi^D_A(R)) \bowtie DF).$$

The prefix computation is efficient: (a) The tokens in the index, $I^{R.A} = \tau_{\alpha(A) \to tk}(\pi^D_A(R))$, are foreign keys that reference DF. (b) DF is typically much smaller than the token index. If DF fits in main memory, efficient in-memory aggregation is used to compute the document frequencies, and the join scans the token index only once. Table 1 shows the overall number of tokens ($|I^{R.A}|$) vs. the number of distinct tokens ($|DF|$) for 107k author names from DBLP (q-grams with frequency counter). (c) topN groups by the tokenized attribute A. By using a join algorithm that preserves the order of the token index, no extra grouping is required. (d) The prefix is computed using efficient top-N sorting.

	$q=1$	$q=2$	$q=3$	$q=4$	$q=5$
$\|I^{R.A}\|$	2,961,769	3,171,769	3,381,769	3,591,769	3,801,769
$\|DF\|$	235	2,242	17,560	94,462	275,496

Table 1: Overall vs. distinct tokens for DBLP author names.

5.3 Efficient Candidate Verification

The candidate verification in Eq. (21) suffers from the following performance issues: (a) The nested tokenize operators produce the cross product of the two token sets for each tuple in R, leading to quadratic runtime in the number of tokens per tuple. (b) Tuples with matching tokens must be grouped; grouping is expensive.

Our solution is *token similarity selection*, $\tilde{\sigma}$, a new relational operator based on tokens. The selection predicate is an overlap constraint on the tokens of two attribute values.

Definition 5. Given relation R with schema $\mathcal{R}$, attribute sequences $A \subseteq \mathcal{R}$, $B \subseteq \mathcal{R}$, token function $\alpha(.)$ defined on A and B, threshold $k > 0$. *Token similarity selection* returns all tuples $t \in R$ such that $O(\alpha(t.A), \alpha(t.B)) \geq k$:

$$\tilde{\sigma}_{A,B,\alpha,k}(R) = \{t \mid t \in R, O(\alpha(t.A), \alpha(t.B)) \geq k\}_b \quad (22)$$

We implement token similarity selection as a non-blocking iterator (Algorithm 3), i.e., only a single tuple, t, is processed at any time. The algorithm hashes the tokens of $t.A$ and probes the tokens of $t.B$ until the threshold is reached. When all tuples of R are consumed, `nil` is returned. For a tuple with $n = \max(|\alpha(t.A)|, |\alpha(t.B)|)$ tokens, the overlap condition is verified in $O(n)$ time and space (if we assume $O(1)$ for probing the hash table of size $O(n)$).

Algorithm 3: TokenSimilaritySelection(R, A, B, α, k)

```
init:
olap : integer;
H : hash table of tokens;
t : tuple with schema R;
next:
repeat
    t ← next tuple from R;
    if t = nil then return nil;
    olap ← 0; H ← ∅;
    foreach a ∈ α(t.A) do              // building phase
        insert a into hash table H;
    if |H| ≥ k then
        foreach b ∈ α(t.B) do          // probing phase
            if b ∈ H then olap++;
            if olap ≥ k then return t;
until true;
```

Algorithm 3, which assumes a set producing token function, is easily extended to bags by maintaining a counter for each element in the hash table that keeps track of the multiplicity of the token in the building phase. In the probing phase, the counter is decremented on each successful probe.

Early termination. If the cardinality of the token sets is known upfront, the smaller token set should be used in the building phase. Further, we can stop after probing the i-th token of $\alpha(t.B)$ if $olap + |\alpha(t.B)| - i < k$, i.e., the remaining tokens in $\alpha(t.B)$ will not reach threshold k.

LEMMA 7. *Given relation R with schema $\mathcal{R}$, attribute sequences $A \subseteq \mathcal{R}$, $B \subseteq \mathcal{R}$, a set producing token function $\alpha(.)$ on A and B, overlap threshold $k > 0$. The following holds:*

$$\tilde{\sigma}_{A,B,\alpha,k}(R) = \pi_{\mathcal{R}}(R \bowtie \sigma_{olap \geq k} \gamma_{\mathcal{R};\mathrm{COUNT}(*) \to olap} \sigma_{A'=B'} \tau_{\alpha(A) \to A'} \tau_{\alpha(B) \to B'} \pi^D(R))$$

Relation R is de-duplicated to avoid double counting of tokens; the duplicates are restored in the final join with R. If R is duplicate free, π^D and the join with R are not required.

With Lemma 7, we substitute in Eq. (21) and rewrite the candidate verification to use Algorithm 3:

$$R \tilde{\bowtie}_{A,B,\alpha,k} S = R \bowtie S \bowtie \tilde{\sigma}_{A,B,\alpha,k}(C) \quad (23)$$

5.4 Token Indexes as Materialized Views

Previous work on token similarity joins [7, 24] requires precomputed token indexes, which are stored as regular tables in the database (cf. Section 3.3). When token indexes are available, it may be beneficial to use them in the query plan instead of producing the tokens on-the-fly.

Using the tokenize operator, token indexes are expressed as relational queries: $I^{R.A} = \tau_{\alpha(A) \to tk}(\pi^D(R))$. This allows us to store token indexes as materialized views, which has the following benefits: First, materialized views can be updated by the database system, thus alleviating the problem of outdated token indexes when the data changes. Incremental index updates have been studied, for example, for *pq*-grams [3]. Second, the query optimizer "understands" the contents of the materialized view and can substitute tokenize operators in the query plan where appropriate.

Candidate generation. When precomputed prefixes (called *prefix indexes*) with document frequency sorting are available for the required threshold k, it is typically beneficial to use them: scanning the (small) prefix index is always faster than computing it from scratch (cf. Section 5.2).

Care must be taken when the similarity join is preceded by selection operators, i.e., the join is performed on subsets of the relations for which the prefix index was computed. The token distribution in the joined subset may differ from the distribution in the overall relation. Since the prefixes depend on the token distribution, precomputed prefixes may lead to additional candidates compared to on-the-fly prefixes.

Another limitation is that the prefix size depends on the similarity threshold. Thus, a prefix index for threshold k cannot be used for thresholds $k' > k$. A fix for this problem was proposed by Xiao et al. [24]: for each token in the index, its position within the sorted token set and the cardinality of its token set are stored. The similarity join is then extended such that only the relevant token subsets are joined.

Candidate verification. In order to verify prefix filter candidates $C\langle A, B\rangle$, the token sets for A and B must be restored. When materialized token indexes, $I^{R.A} = \tau_{\alpha(A) \to tk}(\pi^D_A(R))$ and $I^{S.B} = \tau_{\alpha(B) \to tk}(\pi^D_B(S))$, are available, this is achieved by joining C with the token indexes:

$$R \tilde{\bowtie}_{A,B,\alpha,k} S = \pi_{\mathcal{R},\mathcal{S}}(R \bowtie S \bowtie \sigma_{olap \geq k} \gamma_{A,B;\mathrm{COUNT}(*) \to olap}(I^R \bowtie C \bowtie I^S)) \quad (24)$$

In practical implementations, attributes A and B in the indexes and in the candidate set are replaced by numeric IDs. Even then this approach is inefficient: to compute the overlap, i.e., verify the candidates, an expensive grouping step is required. Our experiments show that Algorithm 3, which computes the tokens on-the-fly, outperforms the index approach and should thus be used for candidate verification even when materialized views are available.

6. EXPERIMENTAL EVALUATION

We perform all tests on a virtual machine with 4 CPUs (x86, 64 bit, 2.6 GHz), 96 GB RAM, running Linux (kernel 3.11.0, 64-bit). Our operators are implemented in PostgreSQL 9.0.9, which we run with the default settings.

Implementation. We have integrated our tokenize and token similarity selection operators into the kernel of PostgreSQL. This required changes in the parser, the query optimizer, and the executor. The changes in the parser are straightforward. We had to extend the query optimizer to deal with the equivalences in Section 4.3 and provide cost estimates. In PostgreSQL, the overall cost is the sum of a cost per disk block and a CPU cost per tuple. The disk cost estimate is inherited from the underlying scan node, for the CPU cost we use the cardinality estimates in Section 4.5. We use a pessimistic cardinality estimate for token similarity selection and assume that no tuples are removed.

Datasets. We use three real world datasets that were used by previous work [24] to test the efficiency of similarity joins: DBLP[1] (bibliography data, 863.5k tuples, 117MB), ENRON[2] (email communication, 517.4k tuples, 701MB), and TREC[3] (references from the MEDLINE database, 348.0k tuples, 297MB). We generate q-gram tokens (without extending the string with dummy characters [24]) and word tokens (which split strings on white space and punctuation). The resulting token sets are **DBLP-5** (93.9M 5-grams of DBLP), **DBLP-W** (12.3M word tokens of DBLP), **ENRON-W** (133.9M word tokens of ENRON), and **TREC-8** (305.6M 8-grams of TREC).

6.1 Tokenize Operator

Generating tokens. The first step for token similarity queries is the generation of the tokens. We compare the efficiency of computing the tokens with four different approaches: (a) a stand-alone application that inserts the tokens into a database table (*stand-alone*), (b) a user-defined table function (*table function*, cf. Section 4.1), (c) a join query that uses the substring function to create tokens (*substring*), (d) our tokenize operator (*tokenize*). The *substring* approach was proposed by Gravano et al. [9] and is specific to q-grams for strings. In our tests, we configure also the other approaches to produce q-grams. We produce tables $R\langle id, s\rangle$, where id is an integer key and s is a random string. We vary the number of strings N, the string length $|s|$, and the token length q, and measure the time for producing the respective q-gram token index $I\langle id, token\rangle$.

The stand-alone application is written in Java 1.6 and uses a JDBC driver. It reads the strings from table R, computes the q-grams, and inserts them into the index table I. We use prepared insert statements that are sent to the database server in large batches (of 100k tuples). We also materialize the indexes for the other approaches to get a fair comparison. The *substring* approach uses a table $N\langle i\rangle$ that stores all integers in the range $[1..s_{max} - q + 1]$, where s_{max} is the maximum length over all input strings. The q-gram generation is expressed as a join query:

```
SELECT id, substring(R.s, N.i, q) AS tk
FROM R, N WHERE N.i = 1 OR N.i <= length(R.s) - q + 1;
```

This query produces duplicate tokens. We group by (id, tk) and use the window function `row_number()` of PostrgeSQL to number the duplicate tokens in each group.

The runtime results are shown in Figures 4a-c. The stand-alone approach is (almost) linear in all parameters, but the overhead for exporting the strings and importing the tokens into the database is large. The substring approach must use grouping to deduplicate the tokens, which is inefficient. The tokenize operator leverages the fact that the tokens are produced in groups and deduplicates without grouping overhead. The tokenize operator wins in all settings, followed by the table function approach, which shows similar performance. Figure 4d shows the runtime for tokenizing our real world datasets. The runtime is linear in the number of output tokens. The runtime per token varies between 0.94μsec for DBLP-5 and 1.05μsec for ENRON-W. Since the number of tokens per tuple varies, also the time for tokenizing a single tuple varies and ranges between 14.6μsec for DBLP-W and 854.7μsec for TREC-8.

[1] `http://dblp.uni-trier.de/`

[2] `http://www.cs.cmu.edu/~enron/`

[3] `http://trec.nist.gov/data/t9_filtering.html`

Tokenize vs. table function. We analyze the effect of pushing down selection beneath tokenize and use the example discussed in Section 4.1. We create two customer relations, R and S, with schema $\langle ssn, name, city\rangle$; ssn is a numeric key, $name$ and $city$ are random strings with 50 characters, except for 1,000 tuples of each relation, which have the value `New York` for the $city$ attribute. We join customers from New York with similar names using q-gram tokens ($q = 2$, Jaccard threshold $K = 0.9$) and measure the runtime for different sizes of the input tables using (i) a table function, (ii) the tokenize operator to generate tokens. The result is shown in Figure 5. The selection on the $city$ attributes cannot be pushed down over the table function, leading to slow runtimes for large tables. The tokenize operator generates tokens only for customers from New York and is fast also for large tables.

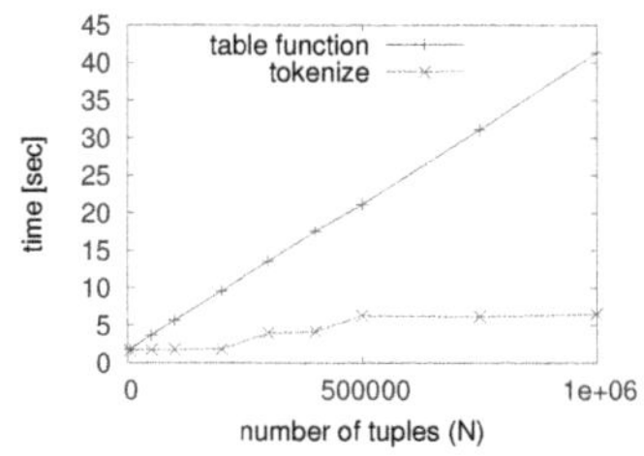

Figure 5: Tokenize vs. table function ($q = 2$, $K = 0.9$).

Avoiding tuple replication. We test the performance of virtual tuple replication (VTR, cf. Section 4.6) on relations $R\langle A_0, A_1, \ldots, A_{20}\rangle$ with $1M$ tuples; A_0 stores randomly selected DBLP author names, A_i, $1 \le i \le 20$, is a string of 50 characters. Figure 6a shows the runtime for computing tokens on A_0 when a different number of columns, $A_1, A_2, \ldots, A_i$, is replicated for each token. Without VTR, a pointer is stored for each replicated attribute value. VTR sets only a single bit per value, and its performance advantage increases with the number of replicated columns. In Figure 6b we materialize the tokens on disk. VTR produces much smaller indexes. If VTR is not used, the string values must be replicated on disk. Table 2 shows the runtime results for the token count query discussed in Section 4.6 (a) without VTR (Eq. (16)), (b) with VTR (Eq. (17)), and (c) with temporal IDs. VTR and temporal IDs perform similarly. Physically replicating the tuples is slow.

Dataset	(a) No VTR	(b) VTR	(c) Temp. ID
DBLP-5	819.3 sec	50.0 sec	46.7 sec
DBLP-W	113.6 sec	9.9 sec	10.4 sec
ENRON-W	> 1 hour	96.5 sec	88.7 sec
TREC-8	> 1 hour	162.9 sec	156.3 sec

Table 2: Avoiding tuple replication: token count query.

Full text search. We compare our tokenize operator with the full text search feature of PostgreSQL. Full text search ranks strings in a database according to a set of query keywords. Similar to our word tokens, the data strings are split on white space. Different from our approach, the tokens are stored in a single attribute value, which limits the number of tokens per tuple. We rank the top-10 strings in DBLP and ENRON using three keywords that appear in the respective datasets. We use the standard rank function for

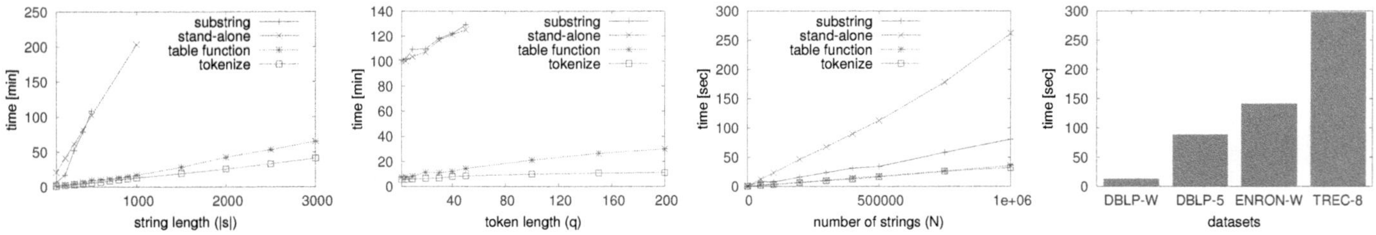

(a) $q = 5$, $N = 10^6$.
(b) $|s| = 500$, $N = 10^6$.
(c) $|s| = 10$, $q = 3$.
(d) Real world datasets.

Figure 4: Efficiency of token generation.

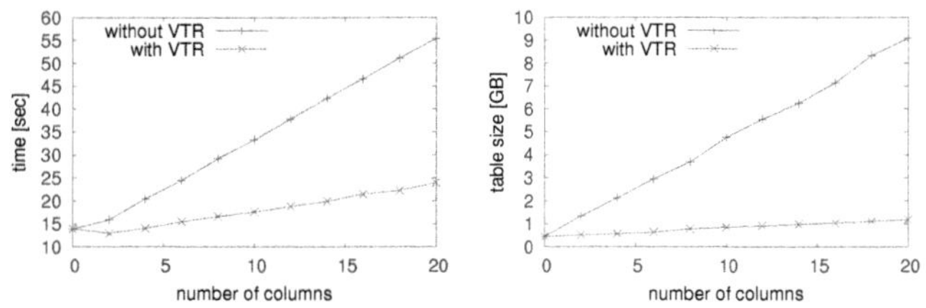

(a) $q = 5$, $N = 10^6$.
(b) $q = 5$, $N = 10^6$.

Figure 6: Virtual tuple replication: (a) generating tokens, (b) size of materialized tokens.

full text search in PostgreSQL, and rank by the number of matching keywords when using our tokenize operator. The runtimes are 25.2 sec for full text search on DBLP and 7.3 sec for the tokenize query. The runtime difference is due to the additional steps that are performed in full text search, for example, removing stop words, which cannot be switched off. On the ENRON dataset, full text ranking was not successful since the strings exceed the maximum allowed length of 1MB. The runtime for our tokenize operator is 8.1 sec.

6.2 Verifying Join Candidates

Token index. We test the efficiency of token similarity selection (Algorithm 3) for verifying candidates that result from prefix filtering and compare to the token index approach (cf. Section 5.4). We do not use early termination, i.e., the cardinalities of the token sets are not assumed to be known upfront. The dataset used in this experiment is a subset of DBLP consisting of the publications in major database venues[4], resulting in 12k records. The records have schema $\langle pid, title, venue\rangle$, where pid is an integer key. We create a q-gram token index for the title attribute, $I\langle pid, tk, len\rangle$, where tk is the token and len is the length of the tokenized title (avg. 59.2). We use $q = 5$ and create prefix indexes for the Jaccard thresholds $K \in \{0.95, 0.9, 0.8, 0.7, 0.6\}$; the tokens are ordered by increasing document frequency. We compute a similarity self join on the title strings using the prefix filter approach. A candidate set is computed by joining the prefix indexes on tokens. The number of candidates ranges from 1.99M ($K = 0.6$) to 24.1k ($K = 0.95$), the number of result tuples from 12.9k ($K = 0.6$) to 12.2k ($K = 0.95$).

The candidate pairs are verified using (i) *token similarity selection* (cf. Eq. (23)), (ii) *token index* (cf. Eq. (24)). Figure 7a shows the runtime results for varying thresholds. The similarity selection approach is up to 20 times faster than the token index approach (note the log scale on the y-axis), and the advantage increases for smaller thresholds, i.e., larger candidate sets. Figure 7b shows the verification time per tuple for both approaches. For the token index approach the verification time increases with the number of candidates since the tokens of all candidates must be grouped. Differently, the token similarity selection leverages the fact that the tokens are already grouped by candidate pairs when they are produced on-the-fly. No global grouping is required, and the verification time per tuple is independent of the overall number of candidates.

[4]SIGMOD, PVLDB/VLDB, ICDE, PODS, ICDT, TODS, VLDBJ

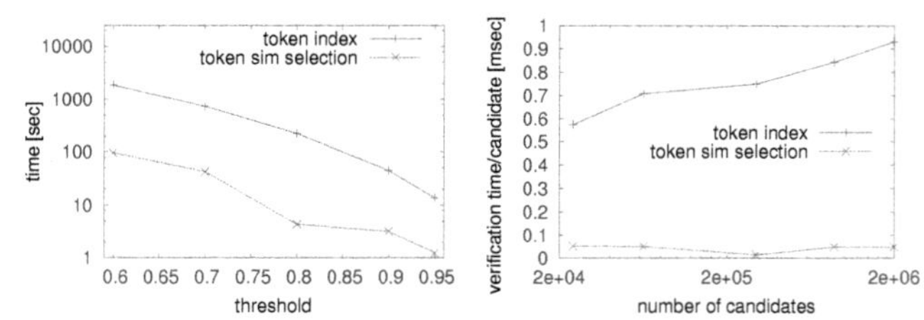

(a) Varying Jaccard threshold.
(b) Time per candidate.

Figure 7: Efficiency of token similarity selection.

Token similarity selection. We test the efficiency of token similarity selection (Algorithm 3) on a synthetic data set of random string pairs when the number of tuples N, the string length $|s|$, and the token size q vary. A subset of the results for Jaccard threshold $K = 0.9$ is shown in Table 3. The runtime t is linear for varying string lengths $|s|$ and varying numbers of tuples N: In all tested scenarios, the values t/N range between 0.009 and 0.011, the values $t/|s|$ between 5.64 and 6.74, where t is the runtime in milliseconds. For varying q values the ratio t/q decreases from 1225 for $q = 2$ to 174 for $q = 50$, and rises again to 283 for $q = 200$; we attribute the runtime difference to the hash map used in the similarity selection algorithm. Overall, token similarity selection is linear in the string length $|s|$, the number of tuples N, and remains efficient for varying token sizes q. Varying the similarity threshold has no visible effect on the runtime since we test without early termination. Further, the random strings in our test rarely match.

6.3 Similarity Join with Prefix Filter

We test the tokenize operator for similarity joins with prefix filter. The join proceeds in three steps: (1) prefix generation, (2) candidate set computation, (3) verification of the candidates. For the candidate set computation we use the disk-based *ppjoin* algorithm discussed by Xiao et al. [24]. We

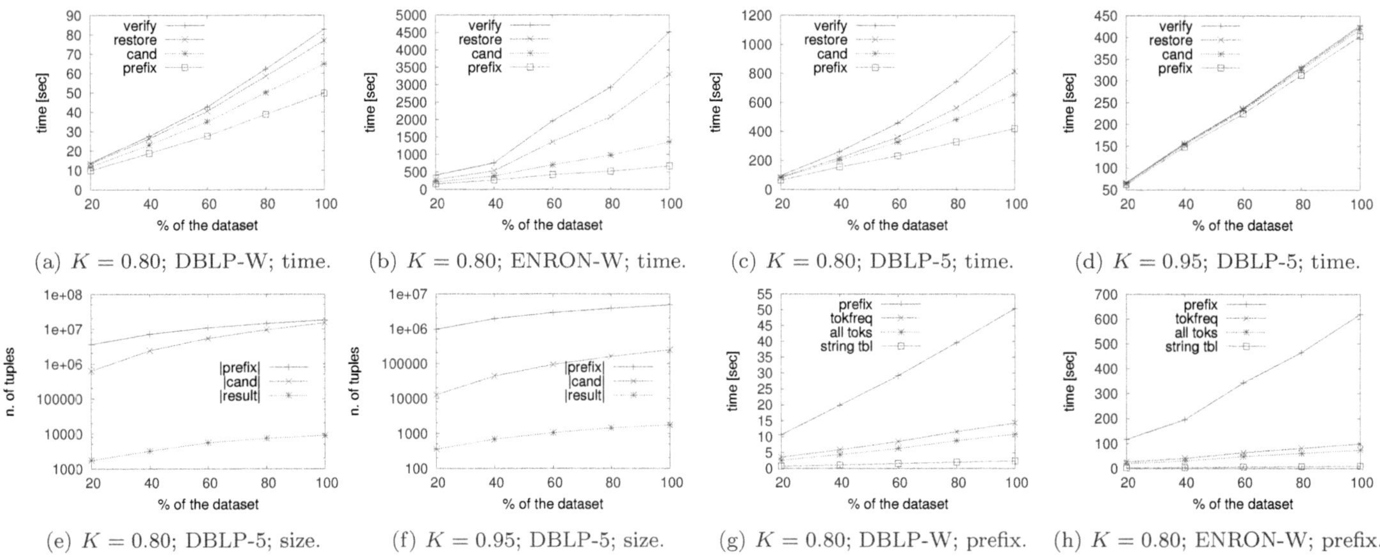

(a) $K = 0.80$; DBLP-W; time. (b) $K = 0.80$; ENRON-W; time. (c) $K = 0.80$; DBLP-5; time. (d) $K = 0.95$; DBLP-5; time.

(e) $K = 0.80$; DBLP-5; size. (f) $K = 0.95$; DBLP-5; size. (g) $K = 0.80$; DBLP-W; prefix. (h) $K = 0.80$; ENRON-W; prefix.

Figure 8: Similarity join with prefix filter.

$\|s\|$	100	500	1000	2500	5000
runtime [sec]	0.62	2.91	6.09	16.53	33.70

(a) $q = 5$, $N = 10000$.

q	2	10	50	100	200
runtime [sec]	2.45	3.47	8.73	18.72	56.65

(b) $|s| = 500$, $N = 10000$.

N	1000	10000	100000	1000000
runtime [sec]	0.011	0.094	0.916	9.252

(c) $q = 3$, $|s| = 10$.

Table 3: Efficiency of token similarity selection.

compute the required prefix tables and tokens on-the-fly using our tokenize operator. The candidates are verified using token similarity selection after restoring the original strings with a join. The runtime results are shown in Figure 8 as cumulative values over the different steps.

Prefix generation. The prefix generation (*prefix*) scales well with the size of the data (Figures 8a-d). The share in the overall runtime of the join increases with the similarity threshold since higher thresholds produce smaller candidate (|*cand*|) and result sets (|*result*|, Figures 8e-f). We break down the runtime of the prefix computation into (a) scanning the input tables (|*string tbl*|), (b) computing the tokens (*all toks*), (c) computing the document frequencies (*tokfreq*), and (d) joining the tokens with the document frequencies to produce the prefix tables (*prefix*, Figures 8g-h).

Candidate verification. We use temporal IDs for the similarity join (cf. Section 4.6) and restore the original strings before the candidate verification (*restore*, Figures 8a-d). Restoring the strings is fast for the short strings of DBLP and involves more overhead for the long strings of ENRON. The candidate verification with token similarity selection is efficient and scales to large datasets (*verify*).

7. RELATED WORK

Token-based similarity measures decompose data items into sets of tokens. Tokens were defined for plain string data [9, 11, 21, 26], text documents [6], and structured data types like XML [2], trees [4, 8, 25], and graphs [27, 28]. Our work is orthogonal to these works. We propose a new relational operator, tokenize, that abstracts from the specifics of data types and token shapes, and moves the token generation from stand-alone applications into the database kernel.

Joins with token-based similarities in the predicate are known as set similarity joins. Sarawagi and Kirpal [18] propose the MergeOpt algorithm, which uses inverted list indexes, Arasu et al. [1] use a signature-based approach. An important optimization is the so-called prefix filter [7]. Prefix filters can dramatically reduce the number of candidate pairs for which the similarity predicate must be evaluated. The fastest algorithms for set similarity joins, all-pairs [5], ppjoin [23], ppjoin+ [24], and mpjoin [16], are based on prefix filters. Wang et al. [22] show that larger prefixes can be beneficial and propose a cost model to select an appropriate prefix length. Chaudhuri et al. [7] propose the SSJoin as a relational operator for set similarity joins. Xiao et al. [24] provide SQL implementations for all-pairs and ppjoin/ppjoin+. Li et al. [12] study techniques to support search-as-you-type queries in SQL and propose an indexing method based on q-grams. In all these works, the token generation is assumed to be an offline process that is not further discussed.

Gravano et al. [9] generate q-grams using the substring function of SQL. We empirically compare our tokenize operator to this approach and show the superior efficiency of tokenize; further, tokenize is not specific to q-grams or strings.

Xiao et al. [24] propose a user-defined function to verify the candidates of the prefix filter step. This function is a black box for the query optimizer. Our token similarity selection operator breaks up the black box and expresses the candidate verification as a relational query.

Silva et al. [19, 20] propose a similarity join operator for relational databases and provide equivalence rules for their operator. Like in our work, their focus is on the integration of similarity queries into the database kernel. However, they do not consider token similarity joins, but propose different join paradigms for similarity joins on numeric values.

Finally, there are a number of database techniques that are related on a more technical level: Table functions [13] have been proposed to generate additional tuples on demand, which could also be used to produce token streams. The main limitation is that the optimizer usually does not understand the semantics, output cardinality, or other properties of the function, and treats it as a black box. Non-relational data models like NF^2 [17] or object-oriented databases could represent tokens as native sets associated with each input tuple. Mamoulis [14] proposes join strategies, Helmer et al. [10] study index structures based on set-valued attributes. We do not assume set-valued attributes, but store the tokens in first normal form.

8. CONCLUSION

In this paper, we have introduced the tokenize operator that allows the full similarity join, including the generation of tokens, to be executed within the database kernel. We provided equivalence rules for reordering our operator with all standard relational operators and proposed an efficient implementation as an iterator algorithm. To the best of our knowledge, this is the first work to allow the implementation of the full similarity join in the kernel of the database system.

Acknowledgments. This work was partially supported by the SyRA project of the Free University of Bozen-Bolzano and the Autonomous Province of Bolzano - South Tyrol, Italy, Promotion of Educational Policies, University and Research Department. We thank Willi Mann and Anton Dignös for their helpful suggestions.

9. REFERENCES

[1] A. Arasu, V. Ganti, and R. Kaushik. Efficient exact set-similarity joins. In *Proc. VLDB*, pages 918–929. ACM, 2006.

[2] N. Augsten, M. Böhlen, C. Dyreson, and J. Gamper. Windowed *pq*-grams for approximate joins of data-centric XML. *The VLDB J.*, 21(4):463–488, 2012.

[3] N. Augsten, M. Böhlen, and J. Gamper. An incrementally maintainable index for approximate lookups in hierarchical data. In *Proc. VLDB*, pages 247–258. ACM, 2006.

[4] N. Augsten, M. Böhlen, and J. Gamper. The *pq*-gram distance between ordered labeled trees. *ACM TODS*, 35(1):1–36, 2010.

[5] R. J. Bayardo, Y. Ma, and R. Srikant. Scaling up all pairs similarity search. In *Proc. WWW*. ACM, 2007.

[6] A. Z. Broder. On the resemblance and containment of documents. In *Proc. Compression and Complexity of Sequences (SEQUENCES)*, pages 21–29. IEEE Computer Society, 1997.

[7] S. Chaudhuri, V. Ganti, and R. Kaushik. A primitive operator for similarity joins in data cleaning. In *Proc. ICDE*. IEEE Computer Society, 2006.

[8] M. Garofalakis and A. Kumar. XML stream processing using tree-edit distance embeddings. *ACM TODS*, 30(1):279–332, 2005.

[9] L. Gravano, P. G. Ipeirotis, H. V. Jagadish, N. Koudas, S. Muthukrishnan, and D. Srivastava. Approximate string joins in a database (almost) for free. In *Proc. VLDB*, pages 491–500. Morgan Kaufmann, 2001.

[10] S. Helmer and G. Moerkotte. A performance study of four index structures for set-valued attributes of low cardinality. *The VLDB J.*, 12(3):244–261, 2003.

[11] C. Li, B. Wang, and X. Yang. VGRAM: Improving performance of approximate queries on string collections using variable-length grams. In *Proc. VLDB*, pages 303–314. ACM, 2007.

[12] G. Li, J. Feng, and C. Li. Supporting search-as-you-type using SQL in databases. *IEEE TKDE*, 25(2):461–475, 2013.

[13] D. Maier and D. S. Warren. Incorporating computed relations in relational databases. In *Proc. SIGMOD*, pages 176–187. ACM, 1981.

[14] N. Mamoulis. Efficient processing of joins on set-valued attributes. In *Proc. SIGMOD*, pages 157–168. ACM, 2003.

[15] A. Mazeika, M. H. Böhlen, N. Koudas, and D. Srivastava. Estimating the selectivity of approximate string queries. *ACM TODS*, 32, 2007.

[16] L. A. Ribeiro and T. Härder. Generalizing prefix filtering to improve set similarity joins. *Inf. Syst.*, 36(1):62–78, 2011.

[17] M. A. Roth, H. F. Korth, and A. Silberschatz. Extended algebra and calculus for nested relational databases. *ACM TODS*, 13(4):389–417, 1988.

[18] S. Sarawagi and A. Kirpal. Efficient set joins on similarity predicates. In *Proc. SIGMOD*, pages 743–754. ACM, 2004.

[19] Y. Silva, W. Aref, and M. Ali. The similarity join database operator. In *Proc. ICDE*, pages 892–903. IEEE Computer Society, 2010.

[20] Y. N. Silva, W. G. Aref, P.-Å. Larson, S. Pearson, and M. H. Ali. Similarity queries: their conceptual evaluation, transformations, and processing. *The VLDB J.*, 22(3):395–420, 2013.

[21] E. Ukkonen. Approximate string-matching with *q*-grams and maximal matches. *Theoretical Computer Science*, 92(1):191–211, 1992.

[22] J. Wang, G. Li, and J. Feng. Can we beat the prefix filtering? An adaptive framework for similarity join and search. In *Proc. SIGMOD*, pages 85–96. ACM, 2012.

[23] C. Xiao, W. Wang, X. Lin, and J. X. Yu. Efficient similarity joins for near duplicate detection. In *Proc. WWW*, pages 131–140. ACM, 2008.

[24] C. Xiao, W. Wang, X. Lin, J. X. Yu, and G. Wang. Efficient similarity joins for near-duplicate detection. *ACM TODS*, 36(3):15:1–15:41, 2011.

[25] R. Yang, P. Kalnis, and A. K. H. Tung. Similarity evaluation on tree-structured data. In *Proc. SIGMOD*, pages 754–765. ACM, 2005.

[26] X. Yang, B. Wang, and C. Li. Cost-based variable-length-gram selection for string collections to support approximate queries efficiently. In *Proc. SIGMOD*, pages 353–364. ACM, 2008.

[27] Z. Zeng, A. K. H. Tung, J. Wang, J. Feng, and L. Zhou. Comparing stars: On approximating graph edit distance. *PVLDB*, 2(1):25–36, 2009.

[28] X. Zhao, C. Xiao, X. Lin, and W. Wang. Efficient graph similarity joins with edit distance constraints. In *Proc. ICDE*, pages 834–845. IEEE Computer Society, 2012.

Tracking Set Correlations at Large Scale

Foteini Alvanaki
Saarland University
Saarbrücken, Germany
alvanaki@mmci.uni-saarland.de

Sebastian Michel
Saarland University
Saarbrücken, Germany
smichel@mmci.uni-saarland.de

ABSTRACT

In this work, we consider the continuous computation of correlations between co-occurring tags that appear in messages published in social media streams. The vast amount and pace these messages are created makes it necessary to parallelise the computation of correlations to various nodes in a computing cluster. The main challenge in this is to ensure that each node will compute a subset of the coefficients and every coefficient will be computed by some node. The core task is to continuously create and maintain partitions of the tags and forward the incoming messages based on them. Our approach proposes and evaluates several algorithms that partition the tags to the nodes while at the same time they minimise the replication of tags to the nodes and balance the load on them. The proposed framework is implemented in Java within the Storm stream processing platform. We evaluate the partitioning algorithms and validate the feasibility of our approach through a thorough experimental study performed using real data.

Categories and Subject Descriptors

C.2.4 [**Distributed Systems**]: Distributed applications; H.4 [**Information Systems Applications**]: Miscellaneous

Keywords

Distributed Stream Processing; Partitioning; Set Correlations

1. INTRODUCTION

In 2012, Twitter alone contributed over 200 million tweets a day and around 2.3 billion posts were shared on Facebook[1]. Such user generated content is usually carrying short textual annotations – so called tags – that specify the topic of a tweet, content of videos or images, locations and persons, or events. Analysing these massive and topically diverse streams of user generated content in real time is one of the dimensions of the big data challenge, with the ultimate goal to extract valuable information for business settings, political campaigns, disease outbreak warnings etc. One of the applications most prominently visible in recent research aims specifically at extracting trends out of Twitter tweets. Here, the choice of terms used as hashtags is not imposed by Twitter, which results in a wild use of such tags – person names, brands, locations, events, etc. Computing correlation measures between co-occurring tags proves to be challenging, due to high rate of arriving data together with the massive amounts of contained tags. In order to meet the needs of real-time applications, it is necessary to distribute the computations to multiple nodes (machines), where each node will be responsible to compute the measures of interest for a subset of all co-occurring tags. In this work, we specifically consider the computation of the Jaccard coefficient; for a set of tags it is defined as the ratio of the number of documents annotated with all of the set's tags to the number of documents annotated with any of the tags. This paper devises and evaluates algorithms and the necessary information processing topology within the Storm stream processing platform [19] to allow computing Jaccard coefficients for all co-occurring tags of a Twitter-scale data stream.

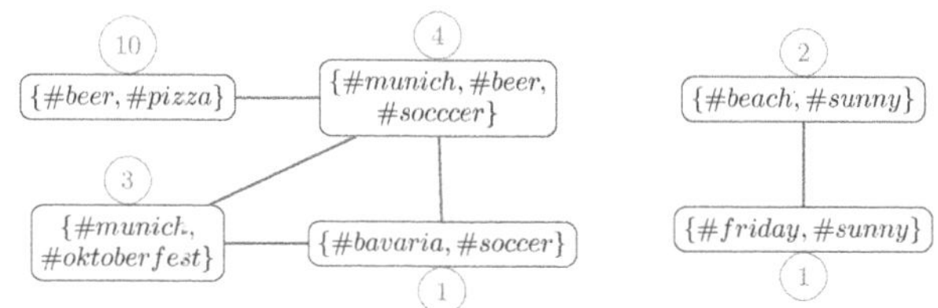

Figure 1: Example of a tagset graph with relations

Consider for instance the graph in Figure 1. Each vertex represents a set of co-occurring tags with a weight equal to the number of received documents that were annotated with the specific tagset. There is an edge between two vertices if the corresponding tagsets have common tags. A partition that assigns connected components of vastly different size to different nodes creates large load imbalances. Assuming that the ratio of incoming documents does not change over time, the node assigned the partition with tags {**#munich**, **#beer**, **#pizza**, **#socccer**, **#oktoberfest**, **#bavaria**} will receive and process 86% of the incoming documents, while the node assigned the partition with tags {**#beach**, **#sunny**, **#friday**} only the remaining 14%. On the other hand, a partition that cuts the large connected component creates replicated tags, which increases/causes the communication overhead. Assuming that the partitions are {**#munich**, **#beer**, **#socccer**, **#oktoberfest**, **#beach**, **#sunny**, **#friday**} and

[1]http://www.statisticbrain.com/social-networking-statistics

SIGMOD/PODS'14, June 22–27 2014, Snowbird, UT, USA.

http://dx.doi.org/10.1145/2588555.2610510.

{**#beer**, **#pizza**, **#socccer**, **#bavaria**} all documents containing either **#beer** or **#socccer** will have to be forwarded to both nodes.

1.1 Problem Statement

We consider a stream of documents $\mathcal{D}$ obtained through Twitter or other social media. Each document d_i in this stream is annotated with a set of tags (or hashtags) $s_i = \{t_1, t_2, \ldots, t_k\}$.

We use a time-based sliding window over the documents to limit the focus on the most recent of them. Before moving the window, we estimate the similarity of the tags in any subset of co-occurring tags currently in the window computing its Jaccard coefficient. Assuming a set $TG = \{t_1, t_2, \ldots\}$ of all tags in the window, we compute the Jaccard coefficient for all sets $\{t_i, t_j, \ldots\} \in 2^{TG}$ that *co-occur in at least one document.* While the consideration of all subsets in TG is computationally intractable in theory, in practice, the natural restriction to tags that actually co-occur in the observed data renders the computation feasible. This is due to the relatively low number of tags per tweet and the, in general, quite disperse use of hashtags in thematically unrelated communities.

We want to distribute the computation of the Jaccard coefficients to multiple nodes. For that, we want to assign a set of tags pr_i out of TG to each node n_i. Each node n_i will then be responsible to compute the Jaccard coefficient for all sets of co-occurring tags in 2^{pr_i}. The distribution of the tags to the nodes should ensure that

1. All co-occurring tags are assigned to some node, such that all Jaccard coefficients can be computed.
2. Assignment of the same tag to multiple nodes is avoided, so that the network traffic is kept low.
3. Assignment of popular tags is spread, such that the load in the nodes is balanced.

Formally: *For a set $\mathcal{S}$ of tagsets $s_i = \{t_1, t_2, \ldots\}$ annotating a set of documents $D = \{d_1, d_2, \ldots\}$ create k partitions $pr_1, \ldots, pr_k$ such that*

1. $\forall s_i \in \mathcal{S}\ \exists pr_j : s_i \subseteq pr_j$ *(i.e. coverage)*
2. $\sum_{t_i \in \{\bigcup_j s_j\}} (|\{pr_m \mid t_i \in pr_m\}|)$ *is minimised (i.e. little/no replication)*
3. *given $l_i = |\{d_m \mid s_j \subseteq pr_i \wedge s_j$ annotates $d_m\}|)$ to be the load of a node i; minimise the Gini coefficient, or in general the load variance, among the nodes (i.e., balanced load)*

1.2 Contributions and Outline

In this paper, we make the following contributions.

- We derive a data dissemination scheme that assigns tags to nodes considering their co-occurrences and using communication and computational load as optimisation criteria.
- We discuss a theoretic view on the performance of the presented partitioning algorithms.
- We describe a detailed operator topology that we implemented within the Storm distributed stream processing framework.
- We present the results of a carefully conducted experimental evaluation in a Storm cluster, using real Twitter data.

The remainder of this paper is organised as follows. Section 2 discusses the related work. Section 3 describes the key idea and framework. Section 4 presents algorithms to distribute tags to nodes. Section 5 estimates theoretically the expected performance of the presented partitioning algorithms. Section 6 describes in details the implementation of our system using the distributed data stream processing platform Storm. Section 7 addresses the problem of dynamically adapting partitions to evolving tag usage and Section 8 presents the results of our experimental evaluation and summarizes the lessons learned. Section 9 concludes the paper.

2. RELATED WORK

Analysing massive streams of user generated content in real time is one of the dimensions of the big data challenge, and most prominently visible in works specifically aiming at extracting trends out of Twitter tweets. Among the early works along these lines is the Twitter Monitor approach, by Mathioudakis and Koudas [15], which extracts bursty tags and then groups them to form meaningful descriptions of individual trends. Our own approach, enBlogue [2], computes the magnitude of a trend as the prediction error of the tagset correlation, where the Jaccard coefficient is computed for pairs of observed tags – or a subset of them.

There are many works on identifying topics on Twitter. For example Sriram et al. in [18] try to assign tweets in broad categories like News, Opinions etc. In [16] the authors limit the topics they identify to those containing known entities and in [20] to those happening at specific places. Weiler et al. in [21] identify topics using the inverse document frequency and Ritter et al. in [17] use more sophisticated NLP techniques and unsupervised clustering. All these works and many more focus on identifying qualitative topics over Twitter and overlook any performance issues. Similarly, in the work of Eftekhar et al. [7] the main focus is to identify high quality topics. The procedure is preformed offline over data gathered during a whole day. In this setting they also try to develop algorithms that can identify topics efficiently. In this work, we focus on continuously computing tag correlation statistics over multiple servers in a computing cluster. The computed statistics can serve as input to various works above. The task to compute tag correlations in a distributed fashion requires partitioning the incoming data stream. As we deal with set-valued data (i.e. Tweets and their hashtags), the problem is related to graph partitioning. The graph in our case has tagsets as nodes and edges between tagsets that share tags; we will review this in more detail in Section 4. Graph partitioning is a well studied problem and many algorithms on solving this problem exist. Among the best known is the Kernighan-Lin algorithm [12] and the algorithms based on spectral analysis [6]. The algorithms based on spectral analysis use the eigenvectors of the connection matrices to estimate the areas in the graph where the partitions should be performed. Given a set of partitions, the Kernighan-Lin algorithm transfers vertices from one partition to the other trying to minimise the edge-cut. The combination of these algorithms [11] has been shown to produce better partitions. The above and any other partitioning algorithm could be used in our setting to create the partitions of tag-sets. However, in a dynamic environment like ours all these techniques are deemed computationally expensive considering the observation that any partitioning computed will be valid/appropriate only for a short period. Additionally, there are algorithms that maintain graphs dynamically (e.g. [8]). Dynamic techniques are more appropriate for our setting. However, methods for dynamic graph maintenance

$\mathcal{TG}$, t_i	Global set of tags, A single tag
$\mathcal{D}, d_i$	A set of documents, A single document
T_i	The set of documents annotated with tag t_i
$\mathcal{T}$	A set of sets T_i
$\mathcal{S}, s_i$	A set of tagsets, A single tagset
$\mathcal{PR}, pr_i$	A set of tag partitions, A single tag partition
k	Number of partitions
$\mathcal{DS}, ds_i$	A set of disjoint sets, A disjoint set
l_i, c_i	Load of tagset s_i, Cost of tagset s_i
P	Number of Partitioners
thr	The threshold allowed before repartitions are requested
tps	Incoming tweets per second

Table 1: Notations used in the paper

are restricted to changes in the edges and cannot handle additions or deletions of vertices. Changes in vertices (e.g. new tagsets) are very common in our approach.

Using probabilistic sketching data structures like Bloom Filters [3] or Count-Min sketches [5] has been proposed to accelerate set operations like intersection of union. If we use them to represent the sets of documents annotated with each tag we will falsely consider tags to be co-occurring, due to "false positives" imposed by the sketches. In a setting as ours were most of the tags do in fact not co-occur, i.e. their sets of documents have an empty intersection, using sketches will pose a significant overhead forcing us to consider many non co-occurring tags.

An early version of this paper has been published in [1]; we refer to it for its modeling of the expected communication overhead of set-cover–based partitioning methods that we briefly pick up in this work.

3. IDEA AND FRAMEWORK

We consider a stream $\mathcal{D}$ of incoming documents d_i each one annotated with a set of tags $s_i = \{t_1, t_2, \dots\}$ from a global set of tags TG. We have at our disposal k machines that are independent from each other, i.e. they cannot communicate. We want to *assign* the tags in TG to the k machines (or nodes) in such a way that each machine can compute the Jaccard coefficient for a subset of the sets of co-occurring tags seen in the input. The tagsets for which a Jaccard coefficient is computed should equal the co-occurring tags found in the incoming stream of documents. After the assignment, each machine receives all documents annotated with tags it has been assigned.

Assume there are 2 machines and the received documents along with their tagsets are summarised by the graph in Figure 1. One of multiple possible partitions is the following

- pr_1={`#munich`, `#beer`, `#soccer`, `#oktoberfest`, `#beach`, `#sunny`, `#friday`}
- pr_2={`#beer`, `#pizza`, `#bavaria`, `#soccer`}

The node assigned partition pr_1 will compute the Jaccard coefficient for the sets of co-occurring tags in the following list

- {`#munich`, `#beer`}
- {`#munich`, `#soccer`}
- {`#beer`, `#soccer`}
- {`#munich`,`#beer`, `#soccer`}
- {`#munich`, `#oktoberfest`}
- {`#beach`, `#sunny`}
- {`#friday`, `#sunny`}

The node will not compute a Jaccard coefficient for {`#oktoberfest`,`#friday`}, for instance, since the two tags do not co-occur in any of the received documents. Similarly, the node assigned partition pr_2 will compute a Jaccard coefficient for the tagsets

- {`#bavaria`, `#soccer`}
- {`#beer`, `#soccer`}
- {`#beer`, `#pizza`}

In the above partitioning, the tags `#beer` and `#soccer` are assigned to both nodes, introducing *communication overhead* as any document containing either of these tags would be forwarded to both nodes. However, this cannot be avoided. Removing for example `#beer` from pr_2 will result in loosing the coefficient for the tagset {`#beer`, `#pizza`}, since there will be no node assigned both the tags.

Assuming that the relative number of documents annotated with each tagset remains the same through time, the expected load in each node is computed as the number of documents annotated with any of the tags the node has been assigned. In this example, the tags in pr_1 are found in 21 documents (the documents annotate with {`#beer`, `#pizza`}, {`#bavaria`, `#soccer`} or {`#munich`, `#beer`, `#soccer`}) and the tags in pr_2 in 15 (the documents annotated with {`#munich`, `#beer`, `#soccer`}, {`#munich`, `#oktoberfest`} or {`#beer`, `#soccer`}). Thus, the node assigned pr_1 will have a load of 58% and the node assigned pr_2 the remaining 42%.

Ideally, partitions are mutually disjoint and cause equal load to the nodes that are responsible for handling them. In practise, such an ideal partitioning does not necessarily exist due to the characteristics of the data. Algorithms aim at low mutual overlap for low communication overhead and, as much as possible, equally loaded nodes.

With evolving time, new tags and unseen tag combinations are introduced by users, and the relative popularity of the assigned tagsets changes deteriorating the quality of the partitions. We propose a practical online solution that

(i) computes partitions based on the recently observed tags and their co-occurrences,
(ii) introduces updates/additions to computed partitions to account for new tags and new tag co-occurrences
(iii) monitors the quality of the partitions and triggers their recomputation

The framework we propose consists of three main operators

Calculator: it counts occurrences of tagsets and computes the Jaccard coefficients for the co-occurring tags

Partitioner: it computes tag partitions that indicate which Calculator receives which documents

Disseminator: it forwards the documents to the Calculators according to the defined partitions and monitors the quality of the partitions

The implemented topology within the Storm framework is presented in Section 6. The next paragraphs give an introduction to the high-level task each individual operator is continuously performing.

3.1 Calculator Operator

Each Calculator is assigned a set of tags and is responsible to compute the Jaccard coefficients for all sets of co-occurring tags in this set. The Jaccard coefficient for a set of tags $s_i = \{t_1, t_2, \dots, t_n\}$ is computed as the ratio of the number of documents annotated with all tags in s_i to the number of documents annotated with any of the tags in s_i:

$$J(t_i|_{i=1}^{n}) = \frac{|\bigcap_j \{d_j\}|}{|\bigcup_j \{d_j\}|} \tag{1}$$

where d_j is a document annotated with any of the tags in s_i In order to compute this measure, the Calculator operator needs to be provided with all documents that contain any of the Calculator's partition of tags. For each set of co-occurring tags existing in the data, the Calculator maintains a simple counter for its occurrences, that is the count of documents that contain *all* of the tagset's tags. The count of documents that are annotated with *any* of the tagset's tags is given by the inclusion-exclusion principle:

$$\left|\bigcup_{i=1}^{n} a_i\right| = \sum_{k=1}^{n}(-1)^{k+1}\left(\sum_{1\leq i_1<\cdots<i_k\leq n} |a_{i_1}\cap\cdots\cap a_{i_k}|\right) \tag{2}$$

Still, Calculators have to receive all documents annotated with *any* of the tags they have been assigned. At first glance, this exact counting of occurrences of all subsets sounds prohibitively expensive due to the combinatorial explosion for large number of tags. However, since tags are used to indicate the topic of a document and the documents we consider in this work are posts in the Blogosphere, e.g. tweets (i) less than 10 tags are used per document (cf. e.g. [7]) and (ii) not all possible tag combinations are used.

3.2 Partitioner Operator

The Partitioner operator uses a set of recent documents and decides how the tags found in these should be partitioned to the Calculators. The partitioning algorithm, used by the Partitioner to split the tags to the Calculators, should take care to split them such that for any tagset seen in the input there is one Calculator assigned all tags comprising it. For any tagset which is not completely assigned to a Calculator the Jaccard coefficient cannot be computed. Section 4 discusses algorithms used for the partitioning.

3.3 Disseminator Operator

The Disseminator operator has a global view of the tags assigned to each Calculator. It receives the incoming documents and is responsible to forward them to the appropriate Calculators, i.e. those that have been assigned tags used for the annotation of the document. Finding efficiently the Calculators that should be informed about each document is important. The work [10] on indexing set-valued attributes suggests that using an inverted index is more efficient compared to other techniques. For each tag t_i a set $\{C|C \text{ is counting tag } t_i\}$ of Calculators is kept and indexed by key t_i, usually in a simple hash-based index. For a received document, an index lookup for each tag in the document is performed to obtain the Calculators that should receive this document.

4. PARTITIONING ALGORITHMS

Any partitioning algorithm used to split the tags to the partitions must ensure that for every set of co-occurring tags there is one partition containing *all* its tags – the Jaccard coefficient of a not completely captured tagset cannot be computed. Additionally, it should create partitions of equal load and minimise the communication overhead.

This problem can be modeled as a *graph partitioning problem*. Each vertex v_i in the graph corresponds to a tagset s_i and there is an edge $e_{(v_i,v_j)}$ between two vertices v_i, v_j if the corresponding tagsets s_i, s_j have common tags. The weight of a vertex v_i represents the number of documents that will be forwarded to the Calculator assigned the tagset s_i. The weight of an edge $e_{(v_i,v_j)}$ represents the reduction in the number of documents that will be forwarded to the Calculator assigned both tagsets s_i, s_j.

For the kind of data we consider in this work – tagsets of low cardinality occurring in social media messages like tweets – a graph constructed like this contains a large amount of small connected components. In the following, we present a partitioning algorithm that uses these connected components to create disjoint sets of tags, grouped afterwards into k partitions (Subsection 4.1). Additionally, we present algorithms based on the Set Cover [4] problem (Subsection 4.2).

4.1 Disjoint Sets Algorithm (DS)

In social media like Twitter users annotate their messages with tags that reflect the topics discussed on them. Tags describing the same topic are thus strongly connected, i.e. found in the same messages, while being completely disconnected from the other tags. Algorithm 1 is based on this observation.

Algorithm 1: Disjoint Sets Algorithm **(DS)**

Input: Integer k, Set $\mathcal{S}$ of tagsets s_i,
Set of tags $\mathcal{TG}$, Set $\mathcal{T}$ of sets of documents T_i
Output: Set $\mathcal{PR}$ of k tag partitions pr_i

1 $\mathcal{DS} = \{\}, \mathcal{PR} = \{\}$
2 **while** $\mathcal{TG} \neq \emptyset$ **do**
3   **find** $ds_j = \bigcup_i s_i$ disjoint set of tags
4     $l_j = |\bigcup_i T_i|,\ t_i \in ds_j$
5     $\mathcal{DS} = \mathcal{DS} \cup \{ds_j\}$
6     $\mathcal{TG} = \mathcal{TG} \setminus ds_j$
7 **end while**
8 **while** $\mathcal{DS} \neq \emptyset$ **do**
9     $ds_i = argmax_{ds_j} l_j$
10     $\mathcal{DS} = \mathcal{DS} \setminus \{ds_i\}$
11   **if** $k > 0$ **then**
12         $pr_k = ds_i$
13         $\mathcal{PR} = \mathcal{PR} \cup \{pr_k\}$
14         $k = k - 1$
15   **else**
16         $pr_i = argmin_{pr_j} \sum_{ds_k \in pr_j} l_k$
17         $pr_i = pr_i \cup ds_i$
18   **end if**
19 **end while**
20 **return** $\mathcal{PR}$

Initially the sets of tags that form connected components, *disjoint sets*, are identified (Algorithm 1, Lines 2-7). The identified disjoint sets are merged into k sets/partitions, where k is the number of available machines (Algorithm 1, Lines 8-19). Each disjoint set ds_j carries a load l_j equal to the number of documents annotated with any of the tags $t_i \in ds_j$ (Algorithm 1, Line 4). As long as there are more disjoint sets to be assigned the one with the biggest load is selected (Algorithm 1, Line 9) and assigned to the partition with the lowest current load (Algorithm 1, Line 16).

At the end of the algorithm there are k tag partitions with approximately the same load. Because of the initial phase where disjoint sets are identified and never split after that, the algorithm guarantees that for any set of co-occurring tags there is a single node that has been assigned all its tags. So, the Jaccard coefficient for any set of co-occurring tags can be computed.

In case there are not enough disjoint sets to create k partitions or there is a disjoint set that is very big, set-cover–based algorithms, presented below, can be used in combination with the disjoint sets algorithm to split this set (or these sets) to smaller ones.

4.2 Set-Cover–Based Algorithms

The following algorithms treat the creation of k partitions as a *Set cover problem* (SCP) over the input tagsets s_i. The general SCP assumes that all elements of the given sets are independent to each other. Therefore, a collection of sets $S = \{\{1,2,3\},\{2,4\},\{3,4\},\{4,5\}\}$ can be represented with less sets like $\{\{1,2,3\},\{4,5\}\}$ without losing information. Considering $\{1,2,3\}$ and $\{4,5\}$ to create two partitions there is one partition containing every single element in S.

In our setting, assigning each single element in a partition is not enough. Instead, every occurring tagset should be assigned as a whole to some partition as the Jaccard coefficient for non-assigned tagsets cannot be computed locally at the Calculator nodes. We use a greedy approach of the *Budgeted Maximum Coverage Problem* [13] to create k initial partitions and then assign to them all non-assigned tagsets.

In the *Budgeted Maximum Coverage Problem* there is a collection of sets $S = \{s_1, s_2, \ldots, s_n\}$ defined over a collection of elements $TG = \{t_1, t_2, \ldots, t_n\}$. Each set $s_i \in S$ has a cost c_i, each element $t_i \in TG$ has a weight w_i and there is a budget B. The goal is to find a collection of sets S' with total cost that does not exceed the budget B with maximised total weight of covered elements. In our setting, the sets s_i are the sets of co-occurring tags and the elements t_i are the tags. The weight of each single tag is equal to the unit, i.e. there are no tags more important than others.

In each iteration of the *Budgeted Maximum Coverage Problem* there is a subset $C \subset S$ of n sets s_i that have been selected to be part of the final set cover. The best set to be added in C is the one that covers the most elements not already covered by the sets in C, while at the same time the total cost does not exceed the budget B. We do not have a hard limit on the budget, but we want to minimise the final cost of the cover.

Algorithm 2 outlines the procedure followed for the selection of the k initial sets that will be later used as the basis for the k partitions. At each iteration the tagset s_i with the minimum cost that covers the most uncovered tags (Algorithm 2, Line 3) is added to the set of selected tagsets.

Algorithm 2: Set Cover Based Algorithms – Phase 1: Creation of initial partitions

Input: Integer k, Set $\mathcal{S}$ of tagsets s_i,
Set $\mathcal{T}$ of sets of documents T_i
Output: Set $\mathcal{PR}$ of k tag partitions pr_i

1 $CV = \{\}$ `// Set of already covered tags`
2 **while** $k > 0$ **and** $\mathcal{S} \neq \emptyset$ **do**
3 $\quad s_i = argmin_{s_j} c_j$ **and** $argmax_{s_j} |s_j \setminus CV|$
4 $\quad pr_k = s_i$
5 $\quad \mathcal{PR} = \mathcal{PR} \cup \{pr_k\}$
6 $\quad \mathcal{S} = \mathcal{S} \setminus \{s_i\}$
7 $\quad CV = CV \cup s_i$
8 $\quad k = k - 1$
9 **end while**
10 **return** $\mathcal{P}$

The cost of each set s_i differs depending on whether the algorithm optimises for the communication overhead or for the processing load. In case the measure of interest is the **communication overhead**, the cost c_i of each set s_i in each iteration is equal to the number of tags $t_j \in s_i$ that are already covered by the sets in C. When the measure of interest is the **processing load**, the cost c_i of each set s_i in each iteration is equal to the difference of the share this set has in the load to the optimal share. Each tag t_i has been found in a set of documents T_i. The cardinality of the union of these documents for all tags $t_i \in s_j$ is considered to be the load l_j of the tagset s_j. Assuming we are in the mth iteration of the algorithm, C contains $m - 1$ sets and we will select the mth set. The optimal share of load in this iteration is $pl_{op} = \frac{1}{m}$, i.e. the load is equally distributed to all nodes. The real share of load of a candidate set s_n is $pl_n = \frac{l_n}{\sum_i^{m-1} l_i + l_n}$ and the cost of s_n is define as $|pl_{op} - pl_n|$.

To the initial k partitions created using Algorithm 2 are added the remaining tagsets until there is no unassigned tagset. The best partition to assign a tagset depends again on the measure of interest. When optimising for the communication overhead (**SCC** algorithm shown in Algorithm 3), in each iteration the set with the most not covered tags having the least total tags is selected (Algorithm 3, Line 3). The selected tagset is added to the partition sharing with it the most tags having the least load (Algorithm 3, Line 4). When optimising for the load distribution (**SCL** algorithm shown in Algorithm 4) in each iteration the set with the most load having the least already covered tags is selected (Algorithm 4, Line 3). The selected tagset is added to the partition having the least load sharing the most tags with the selected tagset (Algorithm 4, Line 4).

Algorithm 3: Set Cover Based Algorithms – Phase 2: Assigning the remaining tagsets minimising the communication overhead **(SCC)**

Input: Set $\mathcal{PR}$ of k initial tag partitions pr_i,
Set $\mathcal{S}$ of tagsets s_i,
Set $\mathcal{T}$ of sets of documents T_i
Output: Set $\mathcal{PR}$ of k final tag partitions pr_i

1 $CV = \bigcup_i pr_i$ `// Set of already covered tags`
2 **while** $\mathcal{S} \neq \emptyset$ **do**
3 $\quad s_i = argmax_{s_j} |s_j \setminus CV|$ **and** $argmin_{s_j} |s_j|$
4 $\quad pr_i = argmax_{pr_j} |s_i \cap pr_j|$ **and** $argmin_{pr_j} \sum_{s_k \in pr_j} l_k$
5 $\quad pr_i = pr_i \cup s_i$
6 $\quad \mathcal{S} = \mathcal{S} \setminus \{s_i\}$
7 $\quad CV = CV \cup s_i$
8 **end while**
9 **return** $\mathcal{PR}$

In prior work [1], the partitioning problem is treated as a *Maximum Coverage Problem without budget* to select the k first tagsets. The assignment of the remaining tagsets to partitions is performed using the number of tags shared among the tagset and the partition. Algorithm 2 is used also in this case to select the k initial tagsets setting the cost of each tagset to zero. The second phase of this set cover based algorithm (called **SCI**) is described in Algorithm 5. In each iteration, a random set is selected (Algorithm 5, Line 2) and added to the partition with which it shares the most tags (Algorithm 5, Line 3)

Algorithm 4: Set Cover Based Algorithms – Phase 2: Assigning the remaining tagsets balancing the processing load **(SCL)**

Input: Set $\mathcal{PR}$ of k initial tag partitions pr_i,
Set $\mathcal{S}$ of tagsets s_i,
Set $\mathcal{T}$ of sets of documents T_i
Output: Set $\mathcal{PR}$ of k final tag partitions pr_i

```
CV = ⋃_i pr_i // Set of already covered tags
while S ≠ ∅ do
    s_i = argmax_{s_j} l_j and argmin_{s_j} |s_j ∩ CV|
    pr_i = argmin_{pr_j} Σ_{s_k ∈ pr_j} l_k and
           argmax_{pr_j} |s_i ∩ pr_j|
    pr_i = pr_i ∪ s_i
    S = S \ {s_i}
    CV = CV ∪ s_i
end while
return PR
```

Algorithm 5: Set Cover Based Algorithms – Phase 2: Assigning the remaining tagsets as described in [1] **(SCI)**

Input: Set $\mathcal{PR}$ of k initial tag partitions pr_i,
Set $\mathcal{S}$ of tagsets s_i,
Set $\mathcal{T}$ of sets of documents T_i
Output: Set $\mathcal{PR}$ of k final tag partitions pr_i

```
while S ≠ ∅ do
    s_i = S.random()
    pr_i = argmax_{pr_j} (s_i ∪ pr_j)
    pr_i = pr_i ∪ s_i
    S = S \ {s_i}
end while
return PR
```

5. THEORETIC PROPERTIES

The performance of the described algorithms depends on how well they can create similar-sized and non-overlapping partitions. We review these aspects by investigating the expected size of the biggest disjoint set of tags – which is crucial for the DS algorithm – and the expected degree of communication overhead for equally sized tag partitions. For additional details on the latter we refer to [1].

5.1 Number of Disjoint Sets

Assume a tagger that randomly annotates tweets with tags following uniform distribution. The derived graph G having one vertex for each tag and one edge for each pair of co-occurring tags can be described by the Erdős–Rényi graph model [9]. According to Erdős and Rényi's theory a graph G can be described either by the number of vertices n and the number of edges M, $G(n, M)$, or by the number of vertices n and the probability p than an edge between two vertices exists, $G(n, p)$. The number of edges M and the probability p are related with each other with $M = \binom{n}{2}p$.

Erdős and Rényi [9] derive properties of G, depending on the ratio between the number of vertices n and the edge probability p. For $np < 1$, the graph is expected to not have any connected component larger than $O(log(n))$, while for $np > 1$, it it likely to have one large component, and no other component contains more than $O(log(n))$ vertices (with a theoretical special case of $np = 1$, left out in the discussion).

We investigated the frequency of tweets with respect to the number of tags they contain using a sample of 15 million tweets received through Twitter's streaming API (on a randomly chosen day; Jan 28, 2012). The results showed that the number of tags used to annotated the tweets follows Zipf's law, i.e. no tags at all are the most popular case, one tag the second most popular case, and so on, with skew parameter $s = 0.25$.

A tweet annotated with m tags adds $\binom{m}{2}$ edges in the graph, one edge for each pair of co-occurring tags, and according to Zipf's law the frequency of tweets annotated with m tags, considering that a tweet can be annotated with m_{max} tags at most, is given by the formula $f(m, m_{max}, s) = \frac{\frac{1}{m^s}}{\sum_{i=1}^{m_{max}} \frac{1}{i^s}}$. The expected number of edges in $G(n, M)$ is computed as

$$E[M] := t \times \sum_{m=2}^{m_{max}} \left[f(m, m_{max}, s) \times \binom{m}{2} \right]$$

where t is the *distinct* number of tweets – as obviously duplicate tweets do not add any additional edges.

Out of the roughly 15 million tweets per day that we observed in the 10% sample obtained from Twitter, we observed around 600,000 distinct tags in roughly 700,000 distinct tweets. To have statistics about the full stream (100%), we assume the worst case for the DS algorithm: 600,000 distinct tags, as in the 10% sample stream, but 7 million distinct tweets. Considering a graph over a 5 minute window of tweets leads to an np value of 0.76, if a maximal value of $m_{max} = 8$ tags per tweet is assumed. For a 10 minute window, we get $np = 1.52$, for the same m_{max}, but $np = 0.85$ for $m_{max} = 6$.

This model assumed independence of tags. If we actually count the number of distinct tag pairs (i.e., edges) that we see per day in the Twitter data (assuming the 100% stream has 10 times more of them than our 10% sample), we have around 5.5 million distinct pairs per day, i.e., around 34,000 distinct tag pairs (edges) added per 10 minutes, which leads to $np = 0.11$ for the graph after 10 minutes, instead of $np = 1.52$ assuming independence of tag usages in the above model. We see that the above model is given a pessimistic behaviour of the expected disjoint sets, as the number of edges (tag pairs) is over estimated. On the other hand, it still describes pretty well how the various factors render the DS algorithm applicable or not – according to Erdős and Rényi's theory.

Further, as long as users select tags from topic-specific vocabularies, graph G falls apart in as many connected components as topics. This comes to rescue the DS algorithm to a large extent. However, if tags from multiple topic-specific vocabularies are mixed there is still the danger to have one large connected component. The existence of a large connected component is more likely when tweets from the more distant past are considered together with tweets from the more recent past since the content drift in tweets can cause mixing tags from different topics. Additionally, if tags from a joint vocabulary are used with probability $1 - \alpha$ a large connected component can develop for any $\alpha < 1$, with faster development for smaller values of α.

5.2 Communication

We presented the modeling of the expected communication overhead for equal-sized and randomly-created partitions in [1], where the expected number of partitions that are affected by a single tweet is studied. We call this the *communication load*, with a value of 1 indicating zero *com-*

munication overhead. Considering a vocabulary of v tags, n tweets over which the partitions are formed, k partitions and m tags per tweet, the expected communication load is given as

$$E[communication] := k \times \left(1 - \left[\frac{\binom{v-m}{m}}{\binom{v}{m}}\right]^{\frac{n}{k}}\right)$$

This means that for small vocabulary and large number of tags per tweet, each incoming tweet needs to be sent to (almost) all partitions; a knockout blow for any decentralised approach. For large vocabularies and few tags per tweet, as it is the case for Twitter data, the problem appears tractable. This is also verified by the experimental evaluation.

6. OPERATORS AND TOPOLOGY

For the implementation of our framework, we have used the distributed stream processing system Storm [19]. In this section, we briefly describe the basic characteristics of it and the specific implementation of our approach.

6.1 Storm

Storm is a framework that provides a fault-tolerant, distributed stream processing infrastructure, similar to what MapReduce/Hadoop is for batch processing. It can scale to big loads/rates of data by adding more machines for individual processing tasks running in parallel. Application developers have to *provide the implementation* of stream sources and operators, following the provided API.

Spouts, Bolts and Topologies.

Operators in Storm are organised in a graph, called topology. The nodes in the topology are connected to each other depending on how they communicate. The communication in Storm is performed following a push-based model. Storm distinguishes two kinds of nodes, **Spouts** and **Bolts**. Spouts are sources of streams. Bolts consume incoming streams, process them and emit new streams.

The application developer that defines a topology is specifying at the same time the number of instances for each operator. Storm creates that many threads for each operator to perform the processing across the cluster of machines. For each Bolt in the topology the developer should provide its functionality by implementing the *execute* method, which is invoked in every incoming tuple and, in general, outputs a new tuple to the consuming (subscribed) Bolts.

Data Flow Specification.

The operators in Storm work with tuples, i.e. simple lists of named values. Bolts consume data from Spouts or other Bolts by registering to their output streams. One of the key properties of Storm is to allow **multiple instances** of Spouts and Bolts. If multiple instances of a Bolt exist, Storm offers various rules that dictate how the tuples flow from producing Bolts or Spouts to the consuming multi-instance Bolt:

shuffle grouping: Tuples are distributed randomly over the various instances of the registered Bolt ensuring that each instance receives approximately the same number of tuples.

all grouping: Tuples are broadcasted, thus each instance gets all tuples.

fields grouping: Tuples are forwarded based on the values on one or multiple of their fields. It enables directing tuples based on their semantics/content.

local grouping: Tuples are forwarded on instances that reside on the same JVM.

direct grouping: Tuples are forwarded to specific instance (or instances) by using the instance's unique identifier.

6.2 Implemented Topology and Operators

The topology of our approach, implemented in Storm, is shown in Figure 2. It shows the basic operators – Source, Disseminator, Partitioner and Calculator – as introduced in Section 3 and a few more – Parser, Merger and Tracker. The numbers inside the circles indicate whether there is one (1) or multiple (n) instances/tasks created for each operator. In the following we describe in more details the implementation of all the operators.

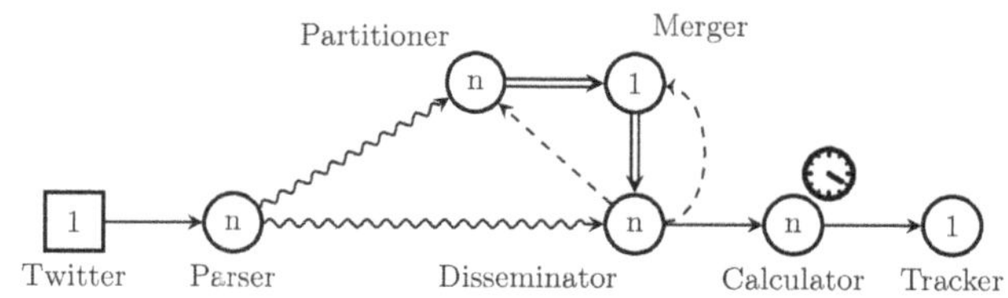

Figure 2: Topology

Parser.

The Source (Spout) in our implementation produces a stream of Twitter tweets, either based on live data through Twitter's streaming API or for repeatability of experiments read from a file. Tweets are sent using shuffle grouping to one of the multiple instances of the Parser Bolt. Parser Bolts are responsible to extract for each tweet d_i a set of tags s_i containing the hashtags used by the users to annotate it. This tagset can be enriched with named entities, location, or sentiment, extracted from the messages' body and interpreted as additional tags. For each incoming tweet d_i the Parser emits a tuple of the form $(timestamp_i, s_i)$, where $timestamp_i$ is the time of the arrival of d_i in the system. Disseminator and Partitioner both register to Parser.

Partitioner.

The Partitioner operator is responsible to create the tag partitions using one of the algorithms presented in Section 4. To accelerate the procedure of partitioning multiple instances of this operator can be created. Each Partitioner instance receives tuples from the Parser using *field grouping* on the whole tagset s_i. This way the same tagsets are forwarded always to the same Partitioner instances.

Partitioners maintain a sliding window (cf. e.g. [14]) of size W over the incoming tagsets. Conceptually, this window can be time-based (e.g. capturing 5 minutes of tweets) or count-based (e.g. 10000 tweets). When the Partitioners are asked to create partitions they use the tagsets currently in the window. The creation of new partitions is triggered by the Disseminator when the quality of the current partitions has deteriorated significantly.

Partitioners emit tuples of the form $(\{pr_1, pr_2, ..., pr_k\})$.

Merger.

With multiple Partitioners present, the final number of created partitions amounts to more than k, the requested number of partitions. This creates the need for an additional operator, the Merger, which takes the partitions from the Partitioners and creates the final k partitions.

The Merger can be viewed as another Partitioner. It receives tagsets and outputs tag partitions. The tagsets it receives are the tag partitions created by the Partitioners. Following this principle, the Merger creates the final partitions using the same algorithm the Partitioners use.

To preserve the general idea of the Disjoint Sets algorithm when executing it in the Merger, we make a slight change in the Disjoint Sets (DS) Algorithm executed in the Partitioners. Partitioners execute only the first part of it, i.e. they create *all* possible disjoint sets but do not merge them into k partitions. The Merger receiving these sets is thus able to combine them into bigger disjoint sets and merge them afterwards into k final partitions.

The Merger sends the final partitions to the Disseminator and waits for messages from it regarding tagsets seen in the input but not found in any of the partitions. For any such tagset, sent by the Disseminator, the Merger finds the best fitting partition and informs back the Disseminator about its decision. This procedure is described in detail in Section 7.

Disseminator.

The Disseminator receives the partitions from the Merger and uses them to create an index from tags to Calculators (Section 3). For every tagset s_i, sent by the Parser using *shuffle grouping*, the Disseminator searches this index for the Calculators that have been assigned any of the tags in s_i. It sends a tuple of the form (s_i^j) to each of the involved Calculators. s_i^j is a subset of s_i containing all tags assigned to Calculator j. For example, suppose that $s_i = \{a, b, c\}$ and Calculator 1 is assigned the tags a, b, c and Calculator 2 is assigned the tags a, c. The Disseminator will output the tuples $(\{a, b, c\})$ and $(\{a, c\})$, each one delivered to the appropriate Calculator using *direct grouping*. These messages are called *notifications*. To accelerate the notification of Calculators for the received tagsets multiple instances of the Disseminator operator can be created.

Apart from notifying the Calculators, the Disseminator is responsible to inform the Merger about the tagsets in the input that are not reflected in the partitions. Additionally, they monitor the partitions and trigger repartitions when the quality of them, with respect to communication overhead and processing load, is not any more acceptable. More details on this are provided in Section 7.

Calculator.

Calculators are responsible to compute the Jaccard coefficients for a set of co-occurring tags. They register to the Disseminators and receive from them tuples of the form $(\{t_1, t_2, \ldots, t_n\})$ using *direct grouping*.

Calculators are oblivious to the tags they have been assigned. They infer the information about the sets of co-occurring tags for which they should compute a Jaccard coefficient from the messages they receive from the Disseminators. Calculators compute the Jaccard coefficients as describe in Section 3. For this, each Calculator should know the cardinalities of the intersections of co-occurring tags and thus this is the information stored by them.

Consider for example that Calculator 1 receives the tuple $(\{a, b, c\})$. From that it infers that it should compute the Jaccard coefficient for the tagsets $\{a, b, c\}, \{b, c\}, \{a, b\}, \{a, c\}$ (i.e all subsets of tags included in the received tuple). For each of these tagsets it creates a counter. If the counter already exists it updates it increasing it by one.

Every y time units the Calculators use the counters to compute the maximum possible number of Jaccard coefficients. The coefficients are emitted and the counters are deleted.

Tracker.

The Tracker operator receives the Jaccard coefficients emitted by the Calculators and uses them to perform further computations. If the same tags are assigned to multiple partitions it might happen that multiple Calculators emit Jaccard coefficients for the same tagset simultaneously. In such a case, the Tracker should select one of them for further usage. We opted for the coefficient computed over data tracked for a longer period. For this reason, Calculators emit tuples of the form $(s_i, J(s_i), CN(s_i))$. $J(s_i)$ is the Jaccard coefficient for s_i and $CN(s_i)$ is the value of the counter used for s_i. When receiving multiple tuples for the tagset s_i, the Tracker keeps the one with the maximum $CN(s_i)$. This heuristic guarantees that at least all tagsets assigned to the partitions during the creation of them will have a correct Jaccard coefficient not mixed with a Jaccard coefficient computed in a Calculator as a result of the evolution of the partitions.

7. HANDLING DYNAMICS

Twitter is highly dynamic. Old topics evolve through time and new topics appear very frequently introducing new tags and tag combinations. These dynamics are even more acute when focusing on a small subset of the data, i.e. data obtained during the last 5 or 10 minutes. However, theory and real data show that it is not feasible to create partitions over large windows as the existence of a large number of tweets causes the DS algorithm to break due to a large connected component (Section 5.1), while the set-cover–based algorithms suffer from large amounts of redundant communication (Section 5.2). In our setting, we identify and handle the following two requirements:

Evolving Partitions: tags and tag co-occurrences not reflected in the partitions are continuously seen in the input. Triggering the recreation of partitions for each of them is clearly not feasible. Instead they are incrementally added to the existing partitions.

Partition Quality Monitoring: enriching partitions with additional tags affects the quality of them in terms of communication overhead and load balance. Identifying that the quality is not within acceptable limits anymore and creating new partitions is necessary.

As Disseminators connect the two logical parts of our approach, the creation of the partitions and the computation of the Jaccard coefficients, they have a central role in addressing the above two points.

7.1 Evolving Partitions

Disseminators directly notice when a tagset s_i is not found in any of the partitions since they cannot find a Calculator being assigned all tags in it. If s_i is seen in the input sn times without being found in any Calculator the Disseminator informs the Merger about it and the Merger adds it in the best possible partition. The best partition to add a tagset depends on the partitioning algorithm. For the DS, SCC and SCI algorithms the partition is selected so that the increase in communication is minimised. For the SCL algorithm the partition is selected so that the load in the Calculators remains as balanced as possible. The addition of a tagset to some partition is called *Single Addition*. The occurrence threshold sn is ideally small, not to miss important tagsets, but large enough to ignore spam or typos.

When a Single Addition is performed the Disseminators receive a message from the Merger telling them the Calculator that was assigned the tagset. Disseminators use this message to update their indices. All Disseminators receive the message independently of whether they asked for the addition or not.

7.2 Partition Quality Monitoring

Every time a new partition is created the Merger notifies the Disseminators about it sending to each of them a tuple of the form $(partitions, avgCom, maxLoad)$. Disseminators use *partitions* to create their index. *avgCom* and *maxLoad* contain the average communication and the maximum load of the created partitions as computed immediately after their creation. Disseminators use *avgCom* and *maxLoad* as *reference values* to ensure that the quality of the partitions through time remains within acceptable bounds.

In order to estimate the quality of the partitions at any time the Disseminators maintain some statistics representing the current average communication $avgCom'$ and maximum load $maxLoad'$ of the partitions. For each received tagset s_i the Disseminators store for each Calculator whether a notification was sent to it or not. Consider the example where $s_i = \{a, b, c\}$, Calculator C_1 is assigned $\{a, b, c\}$ and Calculator C_2 is assigned $\{a, c\}$. Assume there is one more Calculator C_3 not assigned any of the tags in s_i. Two of the Calculators, the Calculators C_1 and C_2, receive a notification and one Calculator, Calculator C_3 does not. Only tagsets for which there was at least one notification sent are considered in the statistics.

When z tagsets have been considered, the Disseminators compute the average sent notifications $avgCom'$ as the sum of all sent notification divided by z. $maxLoad'$ is computed as the percentage of the most notifications sent to a single Calculator. As long as both $avgCom'$ and $maxLoad'$ do not exceed $avgCom$ and $maxLoad$ respectively more than a threshold *thr* the Disseminators reset the statistics and continue using the existing partitions. Otherwise, the Disseminators ask from the Partitioners to create new partitions. Increasing *thr* decreases the number of repartitions allowing for worse performance with respect to communication overhead or processing load.

7.3 Topology Scaling

In the used version (v0.8.2) of Storm a reconfiguration of a running topology is not possible. Storm only allows to rebalance a topology creating more threads (executors) or workers but does not allow changing the number of instances (tasks) for each operator. In order to be able to adjust the number of Calculators to the observed load the necessary logic should be implemented in the operators. The maximum expected number of Calculators should be defined before submitting the topology. The Partitioners can specify the actual number of Calculators that are used at any time by adjusting the number of partitions they create. Only Calculators that are assigned a partition are indexed by the Disseminators, receive documents and compute Jaccard coefficients.

8. EXPERIMENTS

We have implemented the above operators in Java 1.7. For the experiments we used a cluster of 26 Linux (3.12.0) servers, each running Storm 0.8.2 (with Zookeeper 3.4.5). Each machine has an Intel quad-core i7-2600K CPU@3.4GHz and 16GB RAM.

The dataset we used consists of 6 hours of tweets obtained through the **Twitter's streaming API** on September 5, 2013. In all experiments, we compare four algorithms: Set Cover Based focusing on communication (**SCC**), Set Cover Based focusing on processing load (**SCL**), Disjoint Sets (**DS**) and the approach in [1] (**SCI**), which we described in detail in Section 4.

8.1 Parameters

Number of partitions k**:** We set the number of partitions (the number of calculators in the topology) to 5, 10 and 20. In general, keeping the communication low while maintaining the processing load equally distributed are contradicting goals. Keeping the load in each Calculator close to the average means that tagsets sharing tags have to be assigned to different partitions and keeping the communication low means that tagsets sharing tags should be assigned to the same partitions resulting in unbalanced partitions. The attempt to balance the two measures is becoming harder as the number of partitions increases.

Number of Partitioners P**:** We set the number of Partitioners that in parallel try to create the partitions to 3, 5 and 10.

Data arrival rate *tps***:** In real world 1300 tweets are created every second. For that we set the arrival rate of tweets on the system to 1300 and 2600 tweets per second.

Repartition Threshold *thr***:** Repartition threshold defines the maximum percentage of change that is considered acceptable by the Disseminators. When the processing load or the communication have changed more than the provided threshold the Disseminators ask for repartitioning. We set the repartition threshold to 0.5 and 0.2. A threshold of 0.5 means that the communication (or processing load) is 50% worse than the communication (processing load) when the partitions were computed.

8.2 Experimental Results

The results for the various parameters show the same trend. For this reason we decided to set the parameters to a specific value and show the corresponding results. More specifically, unless otherwise mentioned to be varied, we set the parameters to the following values *P=10, k=10, thr=0.5, tps=1300*. All configurations use one Parser and one Disseminator.

The Disseminator asks for a Single Addition when a tagset is seen in the input without being found in any Calculator 3 times. The statistics used to estimate the quality of the partitions (average communication and maximum load) are computed for every 1000 tweets for which there was a notification sent. Calculators report the Jaccard coefficients every 5 minutes. The Partitioners create the partitions using the set of tweets seen in the previous 5 minutes.

8.2.1 Communication

We define the Communication to be the average number of messages sent from the Disseminator to Calculators for each received tagset. We do not consider tagsets which are not found in any Calculator and, thus, do not cause any message to be sent. The plots in Figure 3 show how the change in each parameter affects the communication.

We see that the number of partitions plays the most important role in the communication (Figure 3c). Having more partitions makes it difficult to assign tags to them without making partitions overlap. This is not true for DS which creates the partitions using only disjoint sets. For this reason DS has in general the best performance with respect to communication. On the other hand, SCL which focuses mainly on balancing the processing load shows the worst performance with respect to communication. Surprisingly SCI performs significantly worse than SCC although the algorithms are very similar in principle. This justifies our choice to develop a new algorithm with the communication as its primary optimisation criterion.

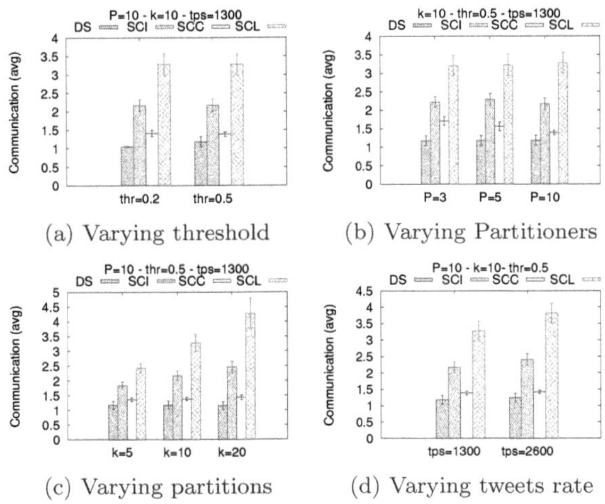

(a) Varying threshold (b) Varying Partitioners

(c) Varying partitions (d) Varying tweets rate

Figure 3: Communication

8.2.2 *Processing Load*

We define the Processing Load of a single Calculator C_i to be the percentage of notifications sent to C_i out of the total sent notifications. To measure the inequality of Processing Load in the various Calculators we use the Gini coefficient. The Gini coefficient is one of the most common measures of statistical dispersion and it is defined mathematically based on the Lorenz curve which depicts the cumulative proportion of ordered individuals mapped onto the corresponding cumulative proportion of their size. A small value of the Gini coefficient indicates a more balanced distribution.

The plots in Figure 4 show how the various parameters affect the load distribution. SCL with primary optimisation criterion the balanced processing load shows the best performance. The parameter that affects the load balance most is the number of partitions (Figure 4c). The reasoning is similar to that used for the communication. Having more partitions makes it more difficult to balance the load on them without increasing substantially the communication. Interestingly SCC, in contrast to SCI, is affected also by the number of Partitioners (Figure 4b). The difference between SCC and SCI is that SCI randomly chooses the next tagset to be added to some partition while SCC selects the more appropriate tagset to be added to some partition. The plot in Figure 4b suggests that the careful selection of the next tagset although keeps communication low (cf. Figure 3b) cannot help load balance.

8.2.3 *Jaccard Accuracy*

The Calculators can compute the Jaccard coefficient only for the tagsets they have been assigned. During the partitioning we make sure that all tagsets present in the data are assigned to some Calculator. However, as new documents are received new tag combinations arise. The Disseminator waits until it has seen such a tagset $sn = 3$ times before asking for a Single Addition. After the Single Addition is completed the tagset might or might not be seen in the input again. In case it is seen again, then a Jaccard coefficient will be reported that will deviate from the correct coefficient since until the addition is completed none of the Calculators tracks the counter needed for the tagset. In case it is not seen again, a Jaccard coefficient will not be computed at all

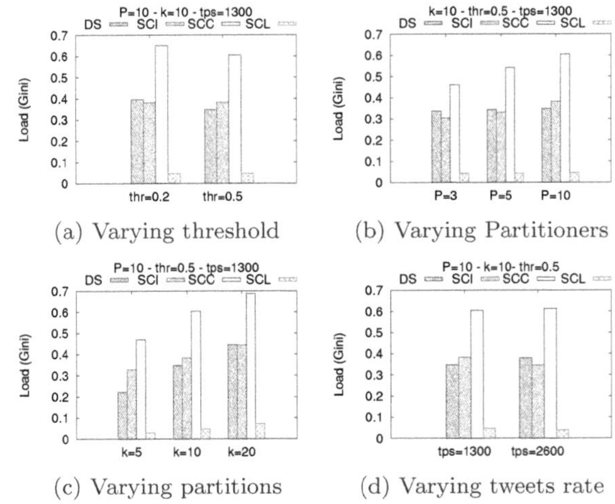

(a) Varying threshold (b) Varying Partitioners

(c) Varying partitions (d) Varying tweets rate

Figure 4: Processing Load

resulting in missing completely the information about this tagset. To measure the error in accuracy and the total loss of coefficients we implemented a centralised approach which gets all tagsets and computes their Jaccard coefficients. We use the centralised results as our baseline. Since a tagset is added when seen at least 3 times the centralised approach considers only tagsets appearing more than 3 times.

Our experiments showed that all algorithms manage to compute a Jaccard coefficient for more than 97% of the tagsets seen more than 3 times in the input. In Figure 5 we report on the average error of these Jaccard coefficients compared to the Jacacrd coefficients computed for the same tagsets by the centralised approach.

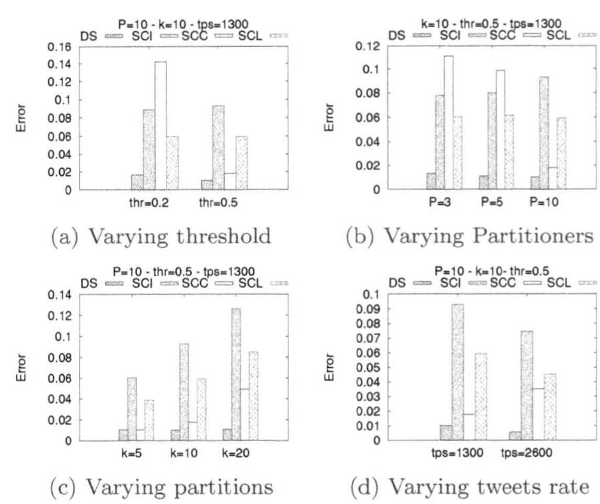

(a) Varying threshold (b) Varying Partitioners

(c) Varying partitions (d) Varying tweets rate

Figure 5: Error for tagsets seen more than 3 times

In general, DS is the algorithm computing the most accurate coefficients. It is interesting that an increase in the number of Partitioners causes a significant reduction in the error of SCC (Figure 5b). Additionally, an increase in the rate decreases the error in all algorithms but SCC (Figure 5d). Both these cases are related to the number of repartitions (see plots in Figure 6). When a repartition happens it might be the case that tagsets assigned to some Calculator before it are assigned to another Calculator after it. This causes multiple coefficients for the same tagsets being reported while none of them is accurate.

8.2.4 *Number of Repartitions*

The number of repartitions depicts how Single Additions affect the quality of the partitions. A repartition is triggered if either the communication or the processing load exceeds the threshold. In some cases both measures had been found to have exceeded the threshold. The plots in Figure 6 show the effect of the various parameters on the number of repartitions. As expected, DS does repartitions caused by load imbalance. SCC and SCI although focusing on communication, similarly to DS, have repartitions caused by big communication overhead. What is interesting is that SCL and SCI do not manage to drop the number of repartitions for bigger threshold (Figure 6a) . This contradicts our expectations and suggests that it is very difficult in general for these algorithms to maintain acceptable communication.

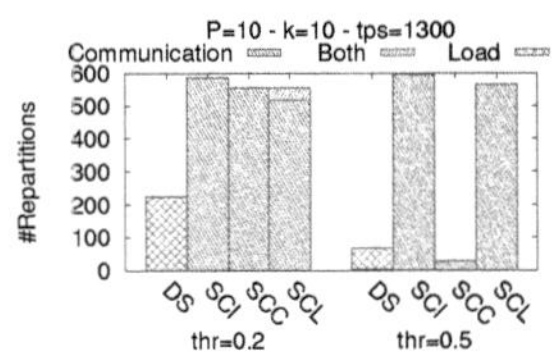

(a) Varying threshold

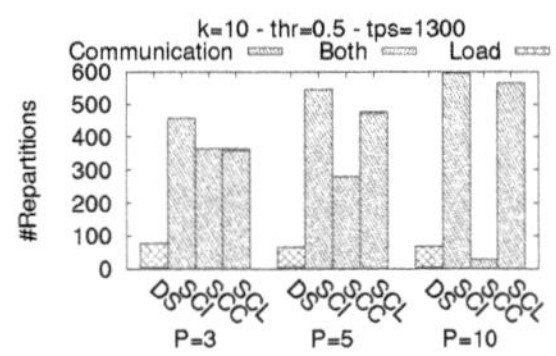

(b) Varying Partitioners

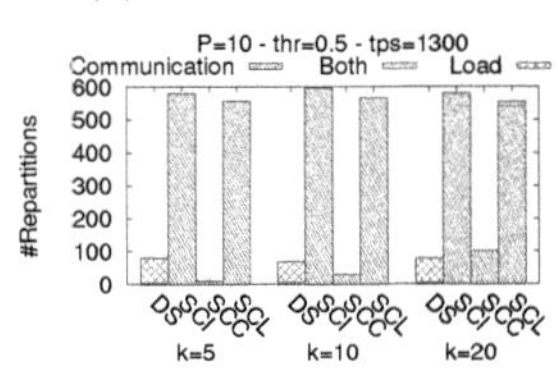

(c) Varying partitions

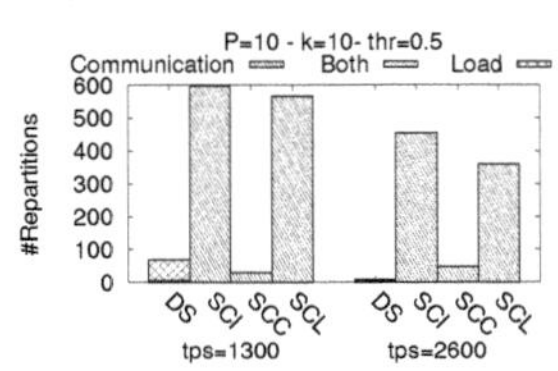

(d) Varying tweets rate

Figure 6: Number of Repartitions

8.2.5 *Evolution of Partition Quality*

The plots in Figures 8 and 9 show the changes in communication and processing load with evolving time. For the communication the average communication is used while for the processing load we show the detailed load in each Calculator. The processing load has been sorted so that one line has always the load of the most loaded Calculator, another line has the load of the second most loaded Calculator and so on. One vertical line has been drawn representing the points when a repartition was performed.

The plots regarding DS clearly show the effect of the Single Additions and the repartitions to the communication (Figure 8a) and processing load (Figure 9a). As long as there are repartitions happening the communication stays low while there is one Calculator having more load that the others. Between repartitions the communication increases and processing load tends to become more balanced, i.e. the load of the most loaded Calculator decreases, until the next repartition when communication decreases again and load becomes more unbalanced. Similar results are seen for SCC in Figures 8b and 9b. For SCL and SCI the results are not that clear since there are very many repartitions (there is approximately one repartition every 2750 processed documents). However, for SCL Figure 9c clearly shows that the processing load is balanced through the whole experiment.

8.2.6 *Connectivity of Tagsets*

In Figure 7, we report some statistics regarding the Twitter dataset as they are fundamentally related to the problem we consider in this work and, in particular, relevant for the performance of the DS algorithm. For the measurements, we used the same tweets we used for the experiments. Over them we defined non-overlapping sliding windows of 4 different sizes (2, 5, 10 and 20 minutes). Every time the window slides we measure the maximum percentage of tags contained in a single connected component of tags and the maximum number of documents related with a single connected component.

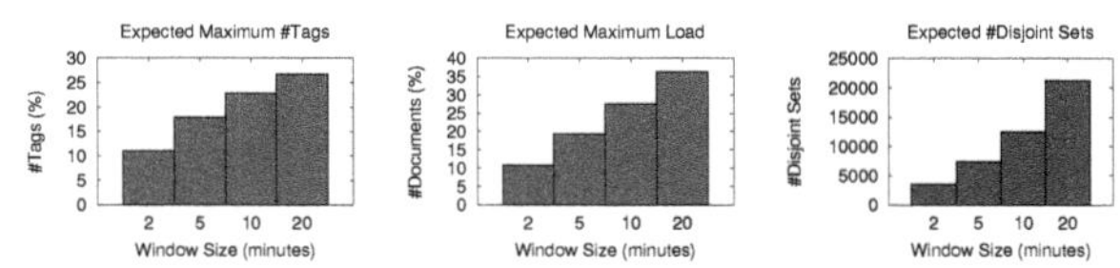

(a) Maximum size of connected tagset per round (b) Maximum load of connected tagset per round (c) Number of connected tagsets per round

Figure 7: Tagsets connectivity and load

8.3 Lessons Learned

We observe by the experimental evaluation, supported by the theoretic reasoning in Section 5, that our presented approach is feasible for Twitter-style data characteristics. It further has proven doable to tune the set-cover–based methods according to which cost (communication or processing) is most critical. The disjoint sets (DS) algorithm has by design optimal communication load (zero redundancy) but in practise and theory can reach scenarios where the load imbalances are too drastic, given one (or few) large evolving disjoint sets. If that happens, splitting the large disjoint sets is required, but current data characteristics did not exhibit such a case. Thus, as the rule of thumb, for current, Twitter-scale streams, DS is the method of choice, particularly since it reaches the most accurate results as fewer tagsets are assigned to multiple nodes, thus, there are fewer Jaccard coefficients reported multiple times. However, we did see that some partitions in the DS algorithm have higher load than others, so if balancing load is crucial and network cost is not critical, SCL should be used instead of DS. Ultimately, disjoint sets should form the basis of all partitioning algorithms, but large ones need to be split (to not impair the load balancing), for instance by applying set-cover–based algorithms like SCL.

9. CONCLUSION

Detecting shifts in correlation between annotations in social media content is a common technique to analyse streams of social media, most importantly Twitter. With data arriving at high rates is becomes computationally infeasible to compute co-occurrence statistics on a single machine or semantically too restrictive to impose a fixed, small tag vocabulary to focus on. In this work, we addressed the problem of computing correlation statistics for tagsets arriving in a massive data stream, involving the consideration of all subsets of co-occurring tags with no restriction on the used tags. The key idea was to spread the computation to multiple machines in a computing cluster by continuously defining partitions of tags according to which the data is spread to counting nodes. We implemented a prototype of our approach using the distributed stream processing engine Storm and evaluated several partitioning algorithms together with the generic behaviour of the system under realistic load, using data obtained through the Twitter streaming API. Overall, we showed in theory and practise that it is feasible to track the ocurrences/correlation of all existing tagsets in

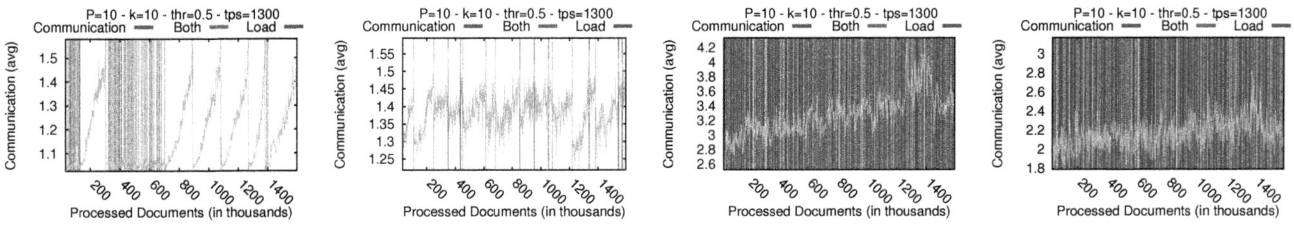

(a) DS Communication (b) SCC Communication (c) SCL Communication (d) SCI Communication

Figure 8: Communication over Time

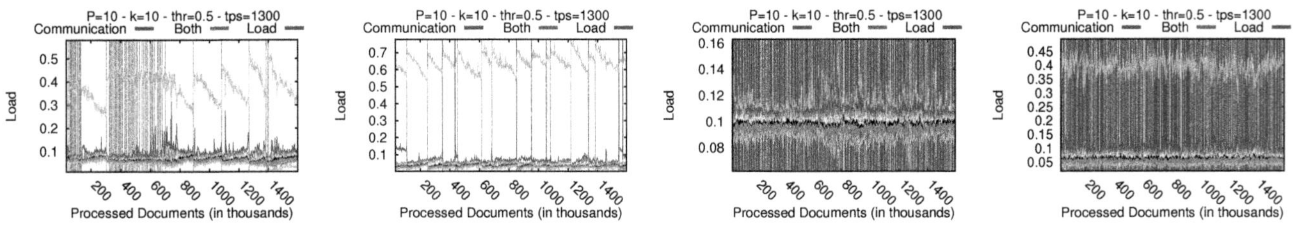

(a) DS Load (b) SCC Load (c) SCL Load (d) SCI Load

Figure 9: Processing Load over Time

Twitter-scale data streams. We believe this is an enabling step toward high-quality, large-scale social trend mining as no ad-hoc pruning of the tagset space is anymore required.

ACKNOWLEDGMENTS

We thank the anonymous reviewers at SIGMOD for their constructive feedback that helped improving this work and the Database Architectures group at CWI Amsterdam for providing access to their computing cluster. This work has been partially supported by the Excellence Cluster on Multimodal Computing and Interaction (MMCI) and the German Research Foundation (DFG) under grant MI 1794/1-1.

10. REFERENCES

[1] F. Alvanaki and S. Michel. Scalable, continuous tracking of tag co-occurrences between short sets using (almost) disjoint tag partitions. *DBSocial*, 2013.

[2] F. Alvanaki, S. Michel, K. Ramamritham, and G. Weikum. See what's enblogue: real-time emergent topic identification in social media. *EDBT*, 2012.

[3] B. H. Bloom. Space/time trade-offs in hash coding with allowable errors. *Commun. ACM*, 13(7), 1970.

[4] T. H. Cormen, C. E. Leiserson, R. L. Rivest, and C. Stein. *Introduction to Algorithms, Third Edition.* The MIT Press, 3rd edition, 2009.

[5] G. Cormode. Count-min sketch. *Encyclopedia of Database Systems*, 2009.

[6] W. Donath and A. Hoffman. Algorithms for partitioning graphs and computer logic based on eigenvectors of connection matrices. *IBM Technical Disclosure Bulletin*, 15(3), 1972.

[7] M. Eftekhar and N. Koudas. Partitioning and ranking tagged data sources. *PVLDB*, 6(4), 2013.

[8] D. Eppstein, Z. Galil, and G. F. Italiano. Dynamic graph algorithms. *Algorithms and Theory of Computation*, 1999.

[9] P. Erdős and A. Rényi. On the evolution of random graphs. In *Publication of the Mathematical Institute of the Hungarian Academy of Sciences*, 1960.

[10] S. Helmer and G. Moerkotte. A performance study of four index structures for set-valued attributes of low cardinality. *VLDB J.*, 12(3), 2003.

[11] B. Hendrickson and R. Leland. A multilevel algorithm for partitioning graphs. *Supercomputing*, 1995.

[12] B. Kernighan and S. Lin. An Efficient Heuristic Procedure for Partitioning Graphs. *The Bell Systems Technical Journal*, 49(2), 1970.

[13] S. Khuller, A. Moss, and J. Naor. The budgeted maximum coverage problem. *Inf. Process. Lett.*, 70(1), 1999.

[14] J. Krämer and B. Seeger. Semantics and implementation of continuous sliding window queries over data streams. *ACM Trans. Database Syst.*, 34(1), 2009.

[15] M. Mathioudakis and N. Koudas. Twittermonitor: trend detection over the twitter stream. *SIGMOD*, 2010.

[16] A.-M. Popescu, M. Pennacchiotti, and D. Paranjpe. Extracting events and event descriptions from twitter. *WWW (Companion Volume)*, 2011.

[17] A. Ritter, Mausam, O. Etzioni, and S. Clark. Open domain event extraction from twitter. *KDD*, 2012.

[18] B. Sriram, D. Fuhry, E. Demir, H. Ferhatosmanoglu, and M. Demirbas. Short text classification in twitter to improve information filtering. *SIGIR*, 2010.

[19] Storm: Distributed and fault-tolerant realtime computation. `http://storm-project.net/`.

[20] K. Watanabe, M. Ochi, M. Okabe, and R. Onai. Jasmine: a real-time local-event detection system based on geolocation information propagated to microblogs. *CIKM*, 2011.

[21] A. Weiler, S. Mansmann, and M. H. Scholl. Towards an advanced system for real-time event detection in high-volume data streams. *PIKM*, 2012.

Aggregate Estimation Over a Microblog Platform

Saravanan Thirumuruganathan[†], Nan Zhang[††], Vagelis Hristidis[‡], Gautam Das[†]
[†]University of Texas at Arlington [††]George Washington University [‡]University of California, Riverside
[†]{saravanan.thirumuruganathan@mavs, gdas@cse}.uta.edu [††]nzhang10@gwu.edu
[‡]vagelis@cs.ucr.edu

ABSTRACT

Microblogging platforms such as Twitter have experienced a phenomenal growth of popularity in recent years, making them attractive platforms for research in diverse fields from computer science to sociology. However, most microblogging platforms impose strict access restrictions (e.g., API rate limits) that prevent scientists with limited resources - e.g., who cannot afford microblog-data-access subscriptions offered by GNIP *et al.* - to leverage the wealth of microblogs for analytics. For example, Twitter allows only 180 queries per 15 minutes, and its search API only returns tweets posted within the last week. In this paper, we consider a novel problem of estimating aggregate queries over microblogs, e.g., "how many users mentioned the word 'privacy' in 2013?". We propose novel solutions exploiting the user-timeline information that is publicly available in most microblogging platforms. Theoretical analysis and extensive real-world experiments over Twitter, Google+ and Tumblr confirm the effectiveness of our proposed techniques.

Categories and Subject Descriptors

H.4 [**Information Systems Applications**]: Miscellaneous; H.2.8 [**Database Management**]: Database Applications—*Data Mining*

Keywords

Aggregate Estimation; Microblogs; Twitter; Random Walk

1. INTRODUCTION

The Microblogs Query Aggregation Problem: Online microblogging platforms have experienced a phenomenal growth of popularity in recent years, because they offer easy and compelling ways for millions of users to post content and interact with each other. In addition to providing attractive mediums for person-person interactions, microblogging platforms also offer unprecedented opportunities for microblog data analytics, i.e., big-picture views of what people are saying, because they contain a deluge of opinions, viewpoints, and conversations by millions of users, at a scale that would be otherwise impossible to gather using more traditional methods such as controlled surveys. In fact, microblog service providers such as Twitter and their partners are already attempting to analyze their data, ranging from public opinion to spatiotemporal popularity of topics, and using the results to build advertising campaigns or monitor the reputation of companies.

Although these are important applications for companies, microblogging platforms also provide free (but limited) public access to their data in the form of restricted APIs, which offer great opportunities for other, often non-commercial applications, such as the type of studies that would be most useful to a social scientist. For example, a social researcher may wish to analyze publicly available microblog conversations and postings to determine the change in general public's attitudes on individual privacy before and after the news of Edward Snowden's leakage of NSA surveillance became public. Other examples can include studies of the spread of obesity-promoting attitudes, the mechanisms of bullying in colleges or schools, and the early detection of suicidal discourse.

A core functionality to facilitate such analytics is to answer *aggregate queries* over publicly available microblog data, which is the focus of this paper. An example of aggregate query is "How many Twitter users used the keyword `privacy` in 2013?". We shall consider SUM, COUNT, AVG queries on various attributes of microblog users or posts (e.g., users' age or posts' length), with selection conditions on keywords and other attributes like time.

We emphasize that our techniques will necessarily generate approximate answers; exact answers are infeasible since they require access to the complete data (and are also often unnecessary in many applications, since approximate aggregates are usually sufficient for obtaining "big-picture" views of the data). Our methods should be efficient in the following sense - the number of API calls made to the microblogging service provider should be as few as possible in generating the approximate aggregate.

Limitations of Existing Microblog APIs: Many of the popular microblog sites like Twitter, Tumblr, Instagram, Yammer, Weibo, Identi.ca (and some other social networking sites like Google+ and Facebook that also offer microblogging features) offer search API calls, which allow retrieving posts containing query keywords, but the results are limited, e.g., past week in Twitter Search API [6]. Other microblogs limit the maximum number of search results one could retrieve to at most a few thousands.

A notable exception to such search APIs is Twitter's Streaming API, which allows retrieving large numbers of posts given keyword and other conditions[1]. Unfortunately, the streaming interface only allows retrieving Twitter postings *in the future*, and there is no way to obtain historical tweets. Thus, a a sociologist will never be able to study the origin of a trending keyword unless he/she is somehow

[1]If no condition is specified, the streaming API returns a $\sim 1\%$ sample of all tweets - a ratio too small to reliably compute many aggregates (e.g., those that are conditioned on a keyword).

SIGMOD'14, June 22–27, 2014, Snowbird, UT, USA.

ACM 978-1-4503-2376-5/14/06 ...$15.00.
http://dx.doi.org/10.1145/2588555.2610517 .

(magically) able to predict such a keyword ahead of time. Note that there are companies like GNIP [2] and Datasift [1] that sell historic microblog data; however the subscription fee is often rather high (e.g., $3,000 per month for Twitter alone at Datasift.com [1]) for a non-commercial setting such as social science research.

Limitations of Previous Research on Estimation of Aggregates on Social Networks: There has been work on estimating aggregate functions on social networks [13, 15, 17, 24]. These works generally use random walk-based sampling on the social graph, or adaptations of it like Metropolis-Hastings [12]. However, they are inefficient for the type of aggregate queries that we study for the following reasons: They only consider *broad aggregates*, that is, aggregates on the whole social network, and not constrained by keywords. Most of these techniques enable aggregate estimation by drawing a random sample of *all* microblog users, and extrapolating from the sample. For our purpose, however, aggregate queries have keyword selection conditions that match only an extremely small fraction of these users - e.g., the number of Twitter users who have used the keyword `privacy` in their postings is only 0.4% of all active users. A straighforward solution would be to only consider users who satisfy the selection condition during the sampling random walk. However, we found that this leads to a social subgraph with tightly connected communities that that significantly increase its convergence time (its *burn-in* period).

Outline of Our Results: We develop MICROBLOG-ANALYZER, an efficient platform to enable the accurate estimation of aggregate queries over an online microblogging service. Its design is based on a central and novel idea: to leverage the *user-timeline interface* (offered by most microblogging platforms) to bypass the above-described limitations on the search API. The user-timeline API inputs a user-id and returns all (for all practical purposes as discussed in §2) public posts generated by the user.

MICROBLOG-ANALYZER operates as follows: we start from a user who recently generated a post satisfying the aggregate query keyword condition (e.g., who is returned by the search API), and then traverse a carefully constructed *subgraph of the social graph*, where users are nodes and user connections are edges, according to the aggregate query, in order to sample (and retrieve through the user-timeline interface) a small number of user timelines based on which we generate our aggregate estimation. There are two main technical issues facing this design: (1) how to design the aggregate-dependent subgraph, and (2) how to traverse such a subgraph, in order to enable efficient and accurate aggregate estimations.

First, we propose a *level-by-level subgraph* to address the issue of subgraph design. Specifically, we introduce a novel taxonomy of user connections (i.e., edges) based on the aggregate being estimated and user timelines. A critical feature of this taxonomy is our finding that, while certain types of edges are beneficial to efficient sampling, others are detrimental to it and should be *removed* from the graph. We adjust the original social graph according to this taxonomy to produce the level-by-level subgraph and, by performing simple random walks [20] over it, develop MICROBLOG-ANALYZER-Simple Random Walk (MA-SRW), our first algorithm for aggregate estimations over a microblog platform. We present theoretical analysis and real-world experiments to demonstrate the superiority of MA-SRW over several baseline graph designs.

Then, to address the graph traversal issue, we develop a *topology aware random walk* over the level-by-level subgraph. Previous random walk techniques (e.g., as used in MA-SRW) are oblivious and therefore generic to the topology of the underlying graph. This often requires a large query cost for the so-called burn-in period [12] in order for the sampling probability of each node to converge to a stationary distribution, so that the sampled nodes can be used for aggregate estimations. We show that, by leveraging knowledge of the underlying graph topology - specifically, the level-by-level structure - our traversal algorithm removes the need of this burn-in period (and the associated query cost) - enabling a significantly more efficient and accurate aggregate estimation process. The execution of topology-aware random walk over the level-by-level graph forms our final algorithm, MICROBLOG-ANALYZER-Topology-Aware Random Walk (MA-TARW).

Summary of Contributions:

- We define the novel problem of aggregate estimation over historic microblog data (§2). We develop a novel idea leveraging the user-timeline access provided by online microblogs to bypass the limitations they place on the search API, and present a platform to tackle the aggregate estimation problem (§3).
- To effectively sample the social graph according to an aggregate query, we develop a level-by-level subgraph topology and demonstrate through theoretical analysis and experimental results its superiority over a number of baseline graph designs (§4).
- To efficiently sample a level-by-level graph, we develop a topology aware random walk which leverages the special properties of a level-by-level graph topology to significantly outperform baseline solutions such as traditional random walks (§5).
- We present comprehensive experiments on Twitter, Google+ and Tumblr that show the significant improvement our methods offer compared with the state-of-the-art (§6).

2. PROBLEM DEFINITION

In this section, we start with describing a data-access model that abstracts the API interfaces provided by most popular microblogs, and then define the problem of aggregate estimation.

Model of Microblog Data Access: In general, a microblogging platform offers three functionalities: (1) share concise updates in text (e.g., Twitter, Google+, Tumblr), image (e.g., Instagram), or video (e.g., Vine); (2) form social connections with each other (e.g., follower/followee in Twitter, Circles in Google+, Likes in Tumblr); and (3) search, subscribe to, and consume the updates posted by users. Correspondingly to these three functionalities, most microblogging platforms - e.g., Twitter, Tumblr, Instagram, Google+, Weibo, Yammer etc. allow the following three types of *queries*:

1. `SEARCH`: Given a keyword (or keywords) w, return *recent* microposts that contain w. Most microblog sites only return posts in recent weeks – e.g., the last weeks posts in Twitter API [6]. Other microblogs restrict search to top-k results where k could be in the low thousands. They do so for two main reasons: recent data are generally more interesting to users, and many microblog service providers consider selling access to historic data an important monetization channel [1, 2].
2. `USER CONNECTIONS`: Given a user u, return all other users "connected" with u. Note that "connections" here are loosely defined - they can be follower/followee relationships (as in Twitter), friendships (as in Friendfeed), etc. Almost all real-world microblogs, e.g., Twitter, Instagram, Tumblr, allow complete access to all user connections (unless a user sets it to private).
3. `USER TIMELINE`: Given a user u, return all posts published by u. To simplify the taxonomy, we assume that a user timeline query also returns the user's profile information (e.g., name, demographics). Like user connection queries, real-world microblogs seldomly limit the returned user timelines, with one

notable exception of Twitter which only publishes the most recent 3200 tweets published by a user. Nonetheless, according to recent studies, only a very small fraction of extremely prolific users - 5% [4] - have posted more that 3,200 tweets and even for these users only very old tweets are missing, in contrast to the search API that only goes back one week [6] (e.g., even Justin Bieber only posted 2,500 tweets between Apr and Dec 2013). Given that in this paper we focus on aggregate estimations, it is safe to assume that this small number of incomplete user timelines has little effect on the estimated aggregates.

Note that the above interfaces could alternatively be implemented through *web crawling* of the microblog site if an API is not available. However, web search interfaces often have unknown selection and ranking criteria that make them less desirable for aggregate estimations - e.g., in Twitter, posts may be missing from the web search but not from the search API results [6]; similarly Tumblr and other sites often perform unpredictable query expansion at their Web search interface. Further, many sites do not allow web-page scraping, e.g., as specified in Twitter (https://twitter.com/tos).

Another important interface limitation imposed by microblogging APIs is an upper bound on the number of queries a user can issue in a time period. For example, Twitter's search API [6] allows only 180 queries over a 15 minute window, and Reddit API allows no more than one request every two seconds.

Problem Definition: In this paper, we address the problem of aggregate estimations over microblogs by issuing queries through the above-described limited microblog interface. Specifically, we consider aggregate queries of the form `SELECT AGGR(`$f(u)$`) FROM` U `WHERE CONDITION` where U is the set of all users, $f(u)$ is any function that returns a numeric measure for each user u (e.g., age or #connections), `AGGR` is an aggregate function such as COUNT, SUM or AVG, and `CONDITION` determines whether a user u should be considered for (i.e., included in) the aggregate.

It is important to note that the above-described form covers not only aggregates over users, but also *aggregates over posts* as well. For example, the COUNT of posts containing keyword `privacy` can be specified as follows: `CONDITION` returns TRUE if a user has `privacy` appearing in its timeline, and FALSE otherwise; $f(u)$ returns the number of posts containing `privacy` in the user's timeline; and `AGGR` is SUM.

While many different predicates can be specified in `CONDITION`, we highlight two specific types: (a) *keyword predicates* - i.e., a user is included iff its timeline contains a pre-determined keyword (e.g., `privacy` in the above example); (b) *time window* - e.g., users who mentioned `privacy` from Jul to Dec 2013. Keyword predicates are prevalent in aggregates required by social science studies because most of these studies focus on one or a few topics specifiable as keywords. For this reason, in this paper we focus on aggregate queries with at least one keyword predicate, optionally a time window, as well as other other predicates on a user's profile attributes (e.g., gender, age, number of connections).

Performance Measures: The performance of an aggregate estimation algorithm is measured in terms of efficiency and accuracy. Given the query-rate limit enforced by most microblogging platforms, the efficiency is the *query cost* - i.e., the number of queries and/or API calls (on `SEARCH`, `USER CONNECTIONS`, and `USER TIMELINE`) the algorithm issues to the microblog.

For accuracy, given estimation $\tilde{\theta}$ of an aggregate θ, we apply the standard measure of *relative error* $|\tilde{\theta} - \theta|/\theta$. Note that the error is determined by two factors[2]: *bias*, i.e. $E(\tilde{\theta} - \theta)$, and *variance* of $\tilde{\theta}$.

[2]Specifically, the mean squared error MSE = bias^2 + variance.

Hence, given an aggregate query with keyword and other predicates, the objective of the *microblog aggregate estimation problem* studied in this paper is to produce an estimation while minimizing both query cost and relative error.

3. OVERVIEW OF MICROBLOG-ANALYZER

This section overviews MICROBLOG-ANALYZER, our system for enabling analytics over a microblog by issuing queries through its limited access interface. We start by presenting a key idea of MICROBLOG-ANALYZER: estimating aggregates by sampling user timelines. Then, we outline the design issues associated with two main components of MICROBLOG-ANALYZER: (1) GRAPH-BUILDER, i.e., the generation of a conceptual graph that connects user timelines together, and (2) GRAPH-WALKER, i.e., the design of an efficient sampling algorithm over such a graph. While §4 and §5 describe these two components in detail, we discuss at the end of this section how we prototyped MICROBLOG-ANALYZER over Twitter and collected ground-truth for its evaluation.

3.1 System Architecture

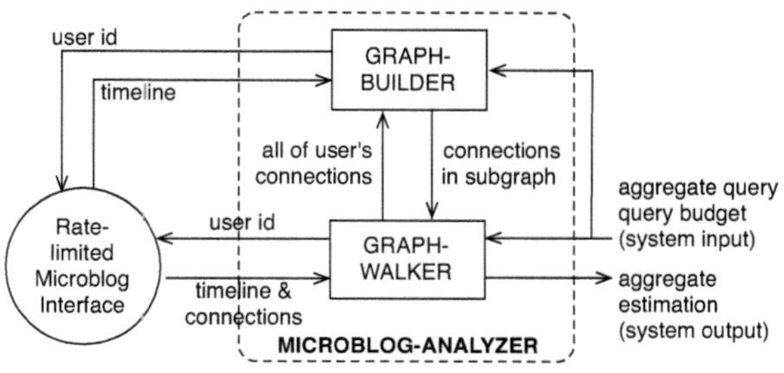

Figure 1: System Architecture

Figure 1 depicts the architecture for MICROBLOG-ANALYZER which has two main components: (1) GRAPH-BUILDER that builds a graph connecting users and (2) GRAPH-WALKER that performs a random walk over such a graph. The system works as follows:

- It receives as input an aggregate query to be estimated (as defined in §2), a query budget (i.e., the maximum number of queries MICROBLOG-ANALYZER can issue to the microblog), as well as one or a few "seed users" which have posted microblogs satisfying the selection condition of the aggregate. Note that such seed users can be easily identified through the limited search API (e.g., for Twitter, users who posted a keyword in the past week).
- Given a seed user, MICROBLOG-ANALYZER uses the GRAPH-BUILDER to determine which other users are its *neighbors*. As we shall show later, the design of GRAPH-BUILDER can range from simply using all social connections of the user to a carefully designed algorithm that takes into account the aggregate being estimated and certain user timeline information to select a subset of such social connections. We shall discuss the design of this component in the next subsection and then in detail in §4.
- Given the neighbors, GRAPH-WALKER determines the probability for MICROBLOG-ANALYZER to "transit to" and sample each neighbor for aggregate estimation. Once again, the design ranges from simply choosing each neighbor uniformly at random (i.e., simple random walk) to a carefully designed algorithm that takes into account certain topological properties of the graph produced by GRAPH-BUILDER. We shall discuss the design of this component in the next subsection and then in detail in §5.

Table 1: Components employed by proposed algorithms

	GRAPH-BUILDER	GRAPH-WALKER
MA-SRW	Level-by-Level (§4)	Level-by-Level (§4)
MA-TARW	Simple RW [20]	Topology-Aware RW (§5)

- The above process can be repeated multiple times until exhausting the query budget, so as to produce a more accurate aggregate estimation as the final output of MICROBLOG-ANALYZER.

3.2 Key Idea: User-Timeline Based Analytics

Feasibility of User-Timeline Based Analytics: To address the often stringent limit on search query interfaces, a key data source MICROBLOG-ANALYZER leverages is the user timeline - i.e., all historic posts published by a user - which, as discussed in §2, is readily accessible through the access interface of many microblogs.

To understand why user-timeline information can be used to answer aggregate queries (especially those with keyword predicates) defined in §2, we start by considering an extremely inefficient technique which nevertheless demonstrates the feasibility of this idea. Note that, as shown by many previous studies [13, 18, 24], the vast majority of users in a microblogging service are linked in a connected graph through social relationships revealed by the service - e.g., follower/followee in Twitter, Circles in Google+, blog followers in Tumblr, comments on same post in Reddit, etc. For the purpose of this paper, we consider such a *social graph* to be undirected. For directed relationships such as follower/followee on Twitter, one can easily convert them to undirected edges by considering two users to be connected if either follows the other.

Given the social graph, one can simply start with one user and recursively follow edges (using user connections API) to reach and crawl the timeline of most users - making it possible to answer aggregates based on the locally crawled data. While this brute-force method demonstrates the feasibility of acquiring sufficient information (for aggregate estimation) through user-timeline queries, it unfortunately requires a prohibitively high query cost given the access-rate limit discussed in §2. In addition, most crawled data would be completely useless for aggregate estimation - e.g., even for a broad query like the count of users who have tweeted `privacy` in 2013, the vast majority of user timelines would be irrelevant because only a very small percentage ($\approx$ 0.4% of its active users) of all Twitter users satisfies the selection condition - leading to a significant waste of resources.

To address this problem, MICROBLOG-ANALYZER only *samples* users who satisfy the keyword predicate specified in the aggregate query, and then produce aggregate estimations according to the collected sample. There are two design issues that are critical for enabling the sampling-based method:

Design Issue 1 (Subgraph Generation): A straightforward method to sample user timelines is to perform a *random walk* over the social graph - e.g., a simple random walk [20] recursively jumps from one user to one of its neighbors chosen uniformly at random - so timelines of sample users (taken after a sufficient number of "burn-in" transitions [12]) can be used for aggregate estimations. A problem with this method, however, is that topology of the social graph is very "*unfriendly*" for sampling and requires a high query cost for random walks to "burn-in". While we shall discuss this finding in detail in §4, an intuitive explanation here is that the social graph contains many "redundant" edges which may "trap" a random walk inside a tightly connected component - i.e., preventing the walk from efficiently sampling all nodes in the graph.

As such, to enable efficient sampling, the first design issue we must address is how to "on-the-fly" remove the redundant edges and find a *subgraph* that satisfies two conditions: (1) *high recall:* it still includes most if not all users who satisfy the selection condition of the aggregate to be estimated, and (2) *sampling-friendly:* the subgraph should have a "well-knit" [20, 26] topology and therefore facilitate an efficient random walk process. One can see that the high-recall requirement ensures the closeness of estimations generated from the subgraph to the ground truth, while the friendliness requirement ensures an efficient random walk process. We shall develop a novel technique for subgraph construction in §4.

Design Issue 2: Sampling Design: In the above discussions, we considered a direct application of traditional random walk techniques (e.g., simple random walk [20] or Metropolis-Hastings random walk [12]) over the user-timeline graph (or subgraph, once the above design issue is addressed). While there has been a large body of work on using these random walks for aggregate estimation over large graphs [13, 15, 17, 19, 20] a key deficiency of it is the significant query cost required by answering COUNT and SUM queries.

While samples collected by random walks can be directly used to estimate AVG queries (as a weighted average of all sample tuples), if one does not know the total number of nodes in the graph (which is often the case in practice), generating estimations for COUNT and SUM often needs to use a significantly more expensive mark-and-recapture [9] based technique (e.g., [15]). However, in this method $\Omega(\sqrt{n})$ samples are needed to produce just one collision over an n-node graph - an extremely high query cost even for a perfectly built subgraph containing only users satisfying the selection condition. For example, to estimate the COUNT of all users who tweeted `privacy` in 2013 (about 894,000), this means at least thousands of samples must be collected, incurring a very high query cost. To address this deficiency, the second design issue is how to efficiently traverse the graph to estimate AVG, COUNT and SUM aggregates. We shall develop a novel sampling algorithm to achieve these objectives in §5. Table 1 shows which subgraph generation (GRAPH-BUILDER) and graph sampling (GRAPH-WALKER) components are employed by the two key proposed algorithms of this paper.

Prototype Design for Twitter Experiments: Before presenting out detailed design of MICROBLOG-ANALYZER in §4 and §5, we would like to briefly discuss how we prototyped over Twitter, the preeminent micro-blogging platform. Note that while we focus the rest of the paper on this Twitter prototype, the adaption to other micro-blogging platforms is straightforward - e.g., we present experiments in §6 over Google+ and Tumblr.

Twitter's REST API [5] naturally fits into the data access model detailed in §2. The search API retrieves tweets matching the given keywords which were posted during the past week [6]. The user timeline API provides access to a user's historic tweets (up to the last 3200). Since Twitter allows asymmetric relationship between users, we have to use two APIs to retrieve all the users who follow user u and all users who are followed by u, in order to collect all user connections as defined in the undirected social graph. Each API call returns up to 5000 connections while the vast majority (upwards of 95% [4]) of users have fewer than 100.

We now briefly describe how we collected the ground truth for evaluating our prototype's effectiveness on estimating aggregates such as "COUNT of all users who tweeted about `privacy` in 2013". We used the streaming API to collect all public tweets mentioning a diverse set of keywords (such as cities, celebrities, organizations, etc.) between Jan 1, 2013 to Oct 31, 2013. Twitter ensures that the stream returns all relevant tweets as long as their frequency is less than about 1% of the entire Twitter Firehose (total volume) [7]. Our specified keywords were selective and did not receive any rate limit exception, which means that this is an accurate ground truth to evaluate aggregate estimation algorithms.

4. LEVEL-BY-LEVEL SUBGRAPH

Recall that GRAPH-BUILDER aims to construct a subgraph (of the social graph defined in §3) with two properties: (1) a high recall of (timelines of) users who satisfy the selection condition of the aggregate query to be estimated, and (2) a topology that enables efficient sampling of such users. In this section, we start by describing a baseline method that achieves (1) but fails (2). The deficiencies of this baseline motivate us to propose a novel *level-by-level* subgraph to satisfy both. At the end of this section, we present Algorithm MA-SRW which enables aggregate estimation by performing simple random walks over the level-by-level graph.

Running example: Throughout this section and the next, we consider as running example the estimation of the following aggregate query over our Twitter prototype: AVG(number of followers) of users who tweeted the keyword `privacy` in 2013.

4.1 Baseline Subgraphs and Their Deficiencies

We start with discussing *term-induced subgraph*, a straightforward subgraph construction which serves as a baseline for our study. Simply put, unlike the original graph which includes all user timelines, the term-induced graph consists of only users who satisfy the *keyword selection condition* of the aggregate query. In the running example, this leads to a subgraph consisting of all users who have tweeted `privacy` before. From a practical standpoint, this means that, during the random walk process, we always start with a user who has `privacy` in his/her timeline and only transit to users who satisfy the same criteria.

The rationale for this baseline approach is simple: Since nodes in the term-induced subgraph form a superset of those covered by the aggregate, the subgraph has a high recall as long as it remains connected or has a large connected component. On the other hand, the sampling efficiency is likely to be improved because of the reduced graph size. The design of the subgraph balances between the two objectives by filtering nodes only with keyword predicates (defined in §2) - which, as shown below, vastly reduces the subgraph size while keeping it connected - but not other conditions in the aggregate query - e.g., a time-interval condition which, when overly short, can result in a low recall.

Our experiments on Twitter confirmed the validity for the high-recall assumption - for all keywords and hashtags we tested (from popular ones such as `Fiscalcliff, New York, Superbowl` to more obscure ones such as `Tunisia, Simvastatin`), the largest connected component of the subgraph contains almost all (on average 94% - see Table 2 for details) nodes in the subgraph - demonstrating the high-recall of a term-induced subgraph. Intuitively, this is because of the strong correlation between social relationships and co-mentioning of keywords - i.e., not only are terms/hashtags likely propagated between followers and followees, but users who have similar interests tend to be connected *and* use the same keywords - leading to the high recall.

For sampling efficiency, our findings were mixed. While the query cost is indeed much lower than the original social graph, it is still very expensive. For the running example (average number of followers for users who tweeted `privacy`), this subgraph required close to 49,000 queries to obtain an estimate with less than 5% relative error. While this value is significantly less than than the 144,000 queries required for the original graph, it is still high considering Twitter's rate limit. Figures 2 and 3 how the term-induced subgraph performs on estimating AVG(number of followers) and COUNT for users who tweeted `privacy`, respectively.

Table 2: Statistics: Term Induced & Level-by-Level Subgraphs

Keyword	Recall	Avg#common neighbors	% of intra & cross-level
`FiscalCliff`	97%	16, 2	27%, 1%
`New York`	91%	49, 3	32%, 2%
`Super Bowl`	93%	34, 1	29%, 2%
`Obamacare`	96%	21, 5	22%, 1%
`Tunisia`	86%	11, 4	28%, 1%
`Simvastatin`	81%	19, 2	24%, 2%
`Oprah Winfrey`	91%	22, 4	29%, 3%

To understand why the efficiency problem remains with the term-induced subgraph, we note that even though users who tweeted `privacy` only represent a small percentage of all Twitter users, the number of *edges* connecting them in the term induced graph is still very large (e.g., close to 1 million edges connecting approximately 142 thousand nodes for the running example). With such a large and dense graph, the efficiency of sampling critically depends on whether the graph topology is carefully designed to enable efficient random walks.

Unfortunately, we found a special topological property of the term induced subgraph that is indeed very "unfriendly" for efficient sampling: Note that, exactly because of the same reason why the term-induced graph likely has a high recall, keywords are often propagated among users that form tightly connected communities (e.g., measured according to graph modularity [26]). This actually requires a random walk to have a long burn-in period because it is likely "trapped" inside a tightly connected community before having a sufficient probability to propagate to other parts of the graph. Our experiments on Twitter confirmed this finding. The burn-in period (with Geweke threshold [11] $Z <= 0.1$) for the entire Twitter graph and the term induced subgraph (for `privacy`) were approximately 700 and 610 respectively. Similar behavior was observed for other keywords also (see Figure 4 for details).

One can see from the above discussion that the straightforward design of a term-induced subgraph cannot adequately address the sampling-efficiency problem of the original social graph, mainly because of the long burn-in dictated by traversing between tightly connected communities. In the next subsection, we describe our proposed methods for constructing a "sampling-friendlier" subgraph topology - specifically, by exploiting *time dimension* of the term-induced subgraph - i.e., the time order with which users posted a specified term like `privacy`.

4.2 Level-by-Level Subgraph

4.2.1 Key Idea and Rationale

To develop our idea of a level-by-level subgraph, we start with introducing a taxonomy of edges in the term-induced subgraph and discuss how each type of edges affect the efficiency of random walks. Consider a simple organization of all nodes (users) into multiple *levels* according to the time when a user first qualified for the keyword predicate (i.e., tweeted `privacy` in the running example). Consider an arbitrary time interval, say 1 day. We partition all users in the term-induced subgraph into multiple segments according to the interval (e.g., users published `privacy` between Jan 1, 13 and Oct 31, 13 will be partitioned into 303 segments).

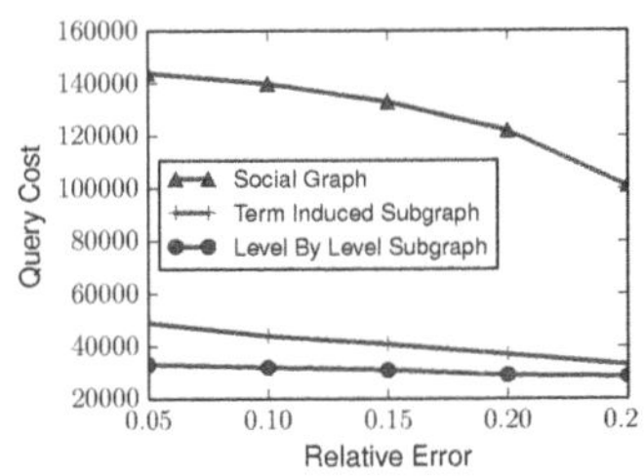

Figure 2: AVG(followers): Users who tweeted privacy

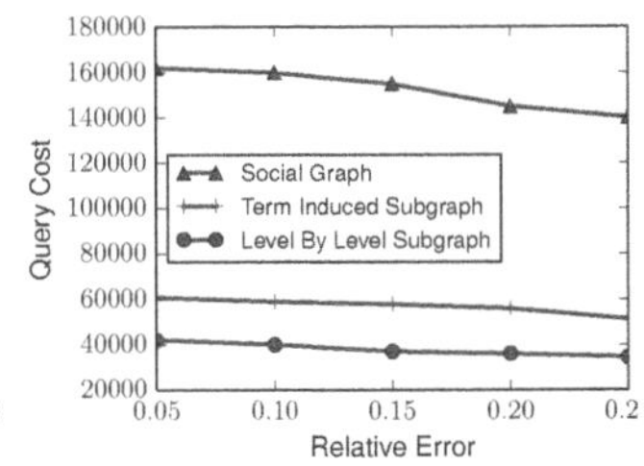

Figure 3: COUNT: Users who tweeted privacy

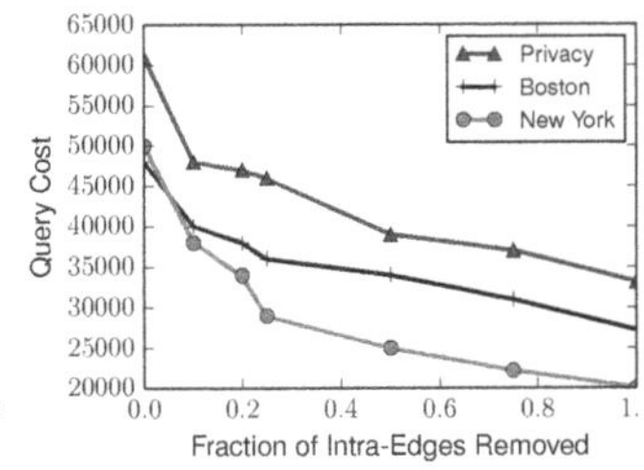

Figure 4: Impact of removing intra-edges on Query Cost

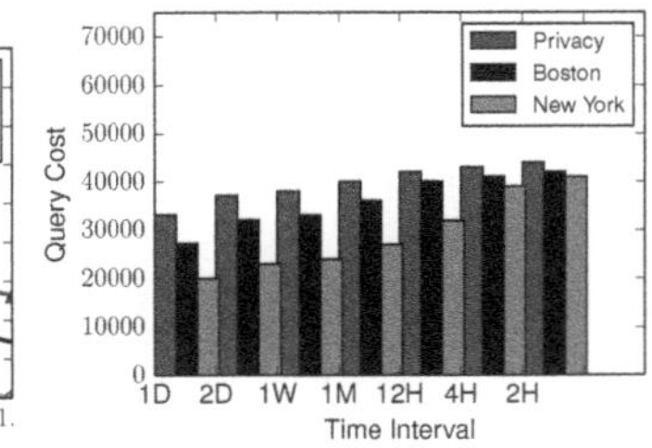

Figure 5: Impact of T on query cost (H=hours, D=days, W=weeks, M=months)

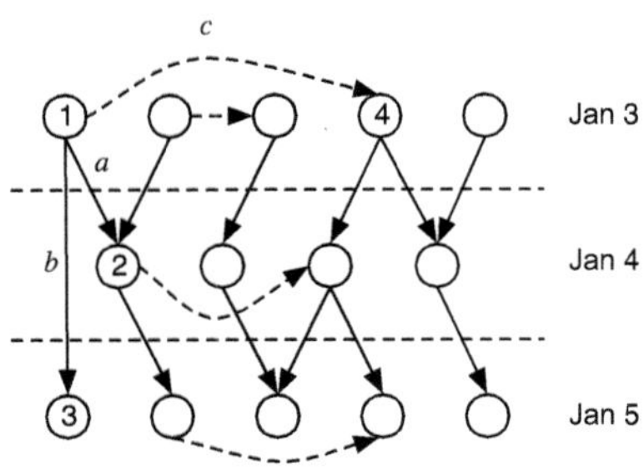

Figure 6: Level-by-Level View of term-induced Subgraph H.

If we draw each segment as a "virtual level" as in Figure 6, and place these levels from top to bottom in chronological order, then we can classify all edges in the subgraph into three categories: *(a) Adjacent-level edges* connect two users in adjacent levels - e.g., Edge a in Figure 6 connects User 1 who first tweeted `privacy` on Jan 3 and User 2 who did so on Jan 4. *(b) Cross-level Edges* connect two users in unequal and non-adjacent levels - e.g., Edge b in Figure 6. *(c) Intra-level Edges* connect two users in the same level - e.g., Edge c in Figure 6.

The reason why we introduce such a ternary classification is because, interestingly, these three types of edges serve different roles in facilitating or deterring the random walk process. Specifically, we found that, for a "reasonable" time interval (>1 hour), (more) intra-level edges are *detrimental* to the efficiency of random walks, while (more) adjacent-level edges are *beneficial* to it. Cross-level edges, on the other hand, contribute to more efficient random walks but are relatively rare in practice (e.g., less than 1% for `privacy`. See Table 2 for other keywords).

While we shall verify this finding both theoretically and experimentally in §4.2.2, we would like to start here with an intuitive explanation for the varying effects different types of edges have on sampling efficiency. Intuitively, intra-level edges usually exist between users in a tightly connected component (as described in §4.1), while adjacent- and cross-level edges are most often not. This has been observed before - e.g., it was found in [3] that 92% retweets produced by followers of a user occur within 1-hour of the original tweet, demonstrating that most followers "respond" within very short time, leading to intra-level edges between users in a tightly connected component. Our experiments confirmed this observation - e.g., Table 2 (column 2) contrasts, for various keywords, the average number of common neighbors shared by two users connected by an intra-level edge and those who are not. We can observe that, on average, one in four edges in the term induced subgraph is an intra-level edge. Further, the users connected by an intra level edges have significantly more common neighbors.

One can see from this explanation that, to "burn-in" to a stationary distribution, a random walk needs to cross adjacent- and/or cross-level edges and cannot get "stuck" inside a small group of users tightly connected by intra-level edges. Combine this with the fact that a substantial percentage of edges in a real-world term-induced graph are intra-level ones (e.g., even for a short interval of 1 hour, more than 28% of edges for keyword `privacy` are intra-level ones), a key idea for our subgraph design subgraph is to *remove all intra-level edges* from the term-induced graph. We refer to this subgraph as the *level-by-level subgraph* because it only contains edges between different levels. From a practical standpoint, this means that the random walk needs to follow a simple rule: transit from a user to its neighbor if and only if they did not first tweet `privacy` in the same day.

One can see that, to properly design a level-by-level subgraph, one needs to address two key issues. One is, of course, to verify that removing intra-level edges indeed improves the efficiency of random walks. We shall discuss this verification in §4.2.2. The other has to deal with the *time interval* used in defining intra-level edges. Note that an intra-level edge could be classified as adjacent- or even cross-level edge with a different time interval. We shall develop the proper setup of time interval for an aggregate in §4.2.3.

4.2.2 *Effect of Intra-Level Edges*

We now analyze the effect of intra-level edges on the efficiency of random walks in two steps. First, we present theoretical analysis on a simple example of level-by-level graph to illustrate how the removal of intra-level edges makes the graph more "well-knit" and more efficient for random walks. Then, we present experimental findings from our Twitter prototype to demonstrate the efficiency improvements achieved by removing intra-level edges.

For theoretical analysis, we consider the change of *graph conductance* [20] after the removal of intra-level edges. The *conductance* $\varphi(G)$ of a graph G measures how "well-knit" G is - i.e., how fast a random walk can converge to its stationary distribution. Specifically, we have

$$\varphi(G) = \min_{S \subsetneq V} \frac{\sum_{v_i \in S, v_j \in \overline{S}} a_{ij}}{\min\left(a(S), a(\overline{S})\right)} \tag{1}$$

where V is the set of vertices in G, S and $\overline{S} = V \backslash S$ form a partition of V into two disjoint subsets, $a_{ij} = 1$ if there is an edge connecting v_i and v_j in G and 0 otherwise, and $a(S) = \sum_{v_i \in S} \sum_{v_j \in V} a_{ij}$. In general, a simple random walk burns-in faster on graphs with higher conductance [21].

Given the complexity of analyzing the conductance of an arbitrary graph, for the purpose of this paper, we consider a simple example of a level-by-level subgraph G as follows. Let there be n nodes in the graph which are distributed evenly across h levels (so each level contains n/h nodes). The adjacent-level edges in the graph are constructed such that each node at Level i ($i \in [1, h-1]$) is connected with d nodes chosen uniformly at random from those at Level $i+1$. The intra-level edges, on the other hand, connect each node at Level i with d' other nodes chosen uniformly at random from Level i. While this simple model does not match real-world graph topologies, it nevertheless gives us an indication of how intra-level edges affect conductance, as demonstrated in the following theorem.

THEOREM 4.1. *The conductance for G is*

$$\varphi(G) = \begin{cases} \frac{h}{(k+d)(h-1)n} & \text{if } d \leq \frac{n}{2h},\ k \leq \frac{n}{2h} \\ \min\left(\frac{2kh-n}{kh+dn}, \frac{2d}{2d(h-1)+hk}\right) & \text{if } d \leq \frac{n}{2h},\ \frac{n}{2h} < k < \frac{n}{h} \\ \min\left(\frac{2dh-n}{kh+dn}, \frac{2d}{2d(h-1)+hk}\right) & \text{if } \frac{n}{2h} < d < \frac{n}{h},\ k \leq \frac{n}{2h} \\ \min\left(\left(k - \frac{n}{2h}\right)\frac{2dh-n}{kh+dn}, \frac{2d}{2d(h-1)+hk}\right) & \text{if } \frac{n}{2h} < d < \frac{n}{h},\ \frac{n}{2h} < k < \frac{n}{h} \end{cases} \quad (2)$$

After removing all intra-level edges, the conductance of G' is

$$\varphi(G') = \begin{cases} \frac{h}{nd(h-1)} & \text{if } d \leq \frac{n}{2h} \\ \min\left(\frac{2hd-n}{nd}, \frac{1}{h-1}\right) & \text{if } \frac{n}{2h} < d < \frac{n}{h} \end{cases} \quad (3)$$

PROOF. We give a proof sketch due to space limitations by showing *adding* intra level edges to a level by level graph actually decreases conductance. For simplicity, we consider a level-by-level graph (G') with h levels where each level has exactly n/h nodes. Each node is connected with $d(d \ll n/h)$ randomly chosen nodes in adjacent levels. In order to compute the conductance of this graph, we have to identify the cut that has the lowest conductance. There are two possible cuts - horizontal (where the cut disconnected two adjacent levels) or vertical (where the cut disconnects the graph into subgraphs, each with h levels).

After some algebraic manipulations, we can notice that the conductance of the horizontal cut is $\varphi(G')_{S_h} = \frac{1}{h-1}$. Similarly, the conductance of vertical cut is:

$$\varphi(G')_{S_v} = \begin{cases} \frac{h}{nd(h-1)} & \text{if } d \leq \frac{n}{2h} \\ min\left(\frac{2hd-n}{nd}, \frac{1}{h-1}\right) & \text{if } \frac{n}{2h} < d < \frac{n}{h}. \end{cases} \quad (4)$$

The conductance of the graph is $min(\varphi(G')_{S_h}, \varphi(G')_{S_v})$. In order to analyze the impact of intra level edges, we assume a simple model where each node has k randomly chosen intra-layer edges. We can see that the horizontal cut for this graph: $\phi(G)_{S_h} = 1/(h-1+hk/(2d))$. i.e. the horizontal cut with intra level edges decrease the conductance. There are four possible cases for vertical cut depending on the value of d and h. The second argument for min in Equation 2 provides the value for $\phi(G)_{S_v}$. Comparing the equations, we can notice that the additional factor of k (introduced due to intra level edges) actually reduces conductance. □

One can see from the theorem, specifically the comparison between (2) and (3) that the removal of intra-level edges significantly increases the graph conductance and thereby make the random walk process more efficient. Our experiments on the Twitter prototype verified this finding. Figure 4 shows, for various keywords , how the removal of 10% to 100% randomly chosen intra-level edges affect the query cost of simple random walks to achieve a relative error of $\leq 5\%$ on estimating the average number of followers for all users who tweeted the keyword in 2013. One can observe from the figure that as the query cost decreases dramatically when intra level edges are removed. Even removal of subset of such edges is actually helpful. We observed that this modification, on average, reduces the query cost for most keywords by at least 20%.

4.2.3 Time Interval in Level-by-Level Subgraph

We now address the second issue - how to properly set the time interval T which directly affects edge classification. Once again, we start with theoretical analysis on optimal T based on the simple example of level-by-level graph described in §4.2.2. Then, we verify the analysis with experimental findings over Twitter.

Theoretical Analysis: Note that the setting of T affects two parameters in this simple model: (1) the number of levels h - the longer T is, the smaller h, and (2) d, the number of (randomly chosen) Level $i+1$ nodes a Level i node is connected with. Here the relationship between T and d is not as clear: While a longer T will in general lead to more nodes on Level $i+1$, it *might* actually reduce d if most followers of the Level i node already responded within the time interval corresponding to Level i. The following corollary to Theorem 4.1 illustrates the relationship between h and d in order to maximize conductance of the level-by-level subgraph.

COROLLARY 4.1. *To maximize the conductance of G', there is*

$$d = \frac{(2h-1)(2h-2)}{h(2h-9)} \quad (5)$$

The proof follows directly from Theorem 4.1. Intuitively, this means that instead of setting the T to a fixed value, we should adjust it according to the propagation pattern of the query term or hashtag. Specifically, the average number of followers who "pick up" the hashtag after the current time interval should be close to its optimal value d as shown in (5). For example, if the average degree is around $d = 14$, then there should be around $h \approx 5$ levels in the lattice structure. Of course, the real-world scenario is more complex. For example, the average number of "pick ups" tends to decline over time - indicating that the time interval should be dynamically changed throughout the duration of propagation [3, 18].

Another interesting observation from the corollary is that the optimal value of d becomes very close to 2 (i.e., its limit when $h \to \infty$) when h is reasonably large. For example, we have $d = 2.13$ and 2.06 when $h = 50$ and 100, respectively. This means that when the keyword of interest has been propagated for a long time (e.g., `privacy`), we can set T according to a simple rule of $d = 2$.

Practical Design: Recall that GRAPH-BUILDER constructs the best subgraph *on-the-fly* during aggregate estimation. First, we discuss a simpler problem where we are given a set of candidate values for T and aim is to identify which is best for estimating an aggregate. Constructing the term-induced subgraph for each value and comparing them is not ideal as it would require a prohibitive query cost. Instead, we perform a *pilot* random walk using each of the time intervals. Each of the pilot random walks uses a smaller budget (e.g., 50 samples) and terminates quickly. Using the partial topology revealed by each walk, we compute h and d and estimate the value of conductance using (3). The time interval with the highest conductance is selected and used for the rest of the process.

We evaluated the effectiveness of this over Twitter. Specifically, we identified a set of diverse time intervals varying from 1-hour to 1-month. For each time interval, we estimated its efficacy in sampling as against the theoretical value of the conductance. In other words, we ordered the time intervals in the horizontal x axis based on their conductance. We then performed random walk for each of these time intervals and compared the query cost to achieve a relative error of less than 5%. Figure 5 shows the results for three keywords. One can see that the orders based on theoretical conductance and experimental performance are consistent.

Algorithm MA-SRW: Recall from §3 the two key components of MICROBLOG-ANALYZER: GRAPH-BUILDER and GRAPH-WALKER. In this section, we developed a level-by-level subgraph for GRAPH-BUILDER. We now combine it with simple random walk in GRAPH-BUILDER to produce Algorithm MICROBLOG-ANALYZER-Simple Random Walker (MA-SRW). The samples obtained are then used for aggregate estimation in the same way as simple random walk [20]. Algorithm 1 depicts the pseudocode for MA-SRW.

Algorithm 1 MA-SRW

1: Retrieve seed users
2: **while** Remaining query budget > 0 **do**
3: Retrieve samples using simple random walk. At each transition, only select from edges that belong to the level-by-level graph according to time interval T.
4: **end while**
5: Perform aggregate estimation as in simple random walk [20].

5. TOPOLOGY-AWARE RANDOM WALKS

To understand the key ideas of our Topology-Aware random walk algorithm, we start by briefly discussing the deficiencies of existing techniques, specifically the direct application of simple random walk or Metropolis-Hastings random walk to the level-by-level subgraph we constructed in Section 4. Then, we develop the key ideas for a novel topology-aware, level-by-level, random walk and present our MA-TARW algorithm.

5.1 Deficiencies of Traditional Random Walks

As mentioned in the introduction, the existing techniques have two main problems: (1) although they produce asymptotically unbiased (according to their respective stationary distributions) samples after a burn-in period, the number of transitions required for the burn-in is usually high [25]; and (2) while they can be combined with mark-and-recapture [9] to estimate SUM and COUNT queries based on the samples, the query cost often rises to a prohibitively high level for practical purposes.

We note here that the fundamental reason underlying these problems is the *inability* of traditional random walk techniques to estimate the probability for a node u to be chosen as a sample. Note that while simple random walk is known to have a stationary distribution that assigns probability proportional to a node's degree $d(u)$, it is still impossible to compute the exact probability for a node to be accessed (i.e., $d(u)/(2|E|)$ where E is the set of all edges) unless one knows the total number of edges in the graph. Similarly, to know the exact probability for a node to be accessed by Metropolis-Hastings random walk (i.e., $1/|V|$ where V is the set of all vertices), one has to know the total number of nodes in the graph. Clearly, neither piece of knowledge is available *a priori* in our case - and estimating them (e.g., by using mark-and-recapture) requires a very high query cost.

To understand the importance of knowing the exact probability for a node to be accessed, note that such knowledge indeed addresses both deficiencies outlined above. First, with knowledge of $p(u)$, the probability for a node to be taken as a sample, one can simply apply the Hansen-Hurwitz estimator [14] to generate an *unbiased* estimation for any SUM or COUNT query defined in §2 as $f(u)/p(u)$, where $f(u)$ is the result of applying the SUM or COUNT query over u itself[3]. This avoids the usage of mark-and-recapture and, as a result, significantly reduces the query cost required for answering SUM and COUNT queries[4].

Similarly, the efficiency problem - i.e., the long burn-in period required - is also (at least partially) caused by the lack of knowledge on the probability for a node to be sampled at a certain step of the random walk. Specifically, the lack of knowledge mandates a long burn-in period for the sampling probability to converge to its target stationary distribution. If one can compute $p(u)$ during each step of the random walk process, then an unbiased aggregate estimation can be generated as long as $p(u) > 0$ for all u in the graph[5] - potentially saving significant query cost for the sampling process.

Admittedly, if one has no knowledge of the global graph topology, it is impossible to compute or make any meaningful estimation[6] of $p(u)$ without incurring as high a query cost as mark-and-recapture [9, 15]. The reason is simple - without "recapturing" at least some nodes accessed before, it is impossible to determine the scale of the graph as, theoretically speaking, it is entirely possible that the access cost we have incurred so far is still smaller than the average pairwise distance between nodes in the graph (one can always construct such an extreme-case scenario), making it impossible to guarantee or even estimate the error of aggregate estimations.

Fortunately, the subgraph construction technique described in §4 affords us substantial knowledge of the graph topology - not the entire node/edge sets - but knowledge of the level-by-level structure all nodes and edges are organized by, and which level a node falls into. As we shall show in the following subsection, such knowledge gives us the ability to efficiently compute an unbiased estimation of $p(u)$, which in turns enables a significantly more efficient (topology-aware) sampling process than the traditional random walk techniques.

5.2 Key Idea: Level-by-Level Random Walk

In this section, we first develop a novel level-by-level random walk process by leveraging knowledge of the subgraph topology we constructed in §4. We also explain why this process requires far fewer queries than traditional (simple or Metropolis-Hastings) random walks. Then, we discuss how to estimate $p(u)$ in a level-by-level random walk - which in turn enables accurate aggregate estimations.

Description of Level-by-Level Random Walk: To understand the level-by-level random walk process, we start by considering a simple example where a level-by-level subgraph constructed for a given keyword has h levels and only edges between nodes of adjacent levels. As shown in Figure 6, the top level consists of users who mentioned the keyword earliest, while users at the bottom one or few levels are guaranteed to be returned by Twitter's search API (which has a time limit of about 1 week [6]) - i.e., our random walk process starts from these bottom levels. Note that every edge in the graph is directed from top to bottom.

Our topology-aware, level-by-level, random walk follows a bottom-top-bottom flow on the subgraph - i.e., a *random walk instance* starts from the bottom level and moves up one level at a time, by following the inverse direction of edges, until reaching a node with no incoming edge. Then, it reverses traversal direction and starts

[3]e.g., if the aggregate is the number of posts containing `privacy`, then $f(u)$ is the number of u's posts containing `privacy`.

[4]Note that AVG queries can be simply estimated as SUM/COUNT.

[5]Note that the requirement $p(u) > 0$ is here to ensure that the sampling process can reach all nodes covered by the aggregate.

[6]Here we use "meaningful" to refer to estimations with statistical guarantees on bias and/or variance.

following the original edge directions to transit down, again one level at a time, until it reaches a node with no outgoing edge - at which time (this instance of) the random walk terminates. At each transition during the random walk, a branch is chosen uniformly at random. Note that *all nodes* we pass through during a random walk will be used to generate one aggregate estimation - and one can execute multiple instances of the random walk and average out the results to produce more accurate estimations - the details of these issues shall be described in the next subsection.

Before discussing the probability for each node to be chosen by such a level-by-level random walk, we first note that the query cost required by each instance of the random walk is much smaller than that for traditional topology-oblivious random walks. Specifically, our walk instance requires at most $2(h-1)$ transitions, orders of magnitude fewer than simple and Metropolis-Hastings random walks, according to the results in §6.2.

There is a simple reason behind this advantage: by leveraging knowledge of the level-by-level topology, our random walk process is capable of transiting between different "clusters" of nodes much faster than traditional topology-oblivious random walks. Specifically, for a $2(h-1)$-step level-by-level random walk instance over the above-described h-level graph, each of the first (or last) $h-1$ steps is guaranteed to draw from mutually exclusive subsets of nodes. This makes the random walk process reach (with a positive probability) all nodes in the graph much faster than traditional random walks which, despite improved subgraph designs, still have a fairly high probability to return to their origin point after a small number of transition steps [10].

Unbiased Estimation of $p(u)$: We now consider the estimation of $p(u)$ - the probability for a level-by-level random walk instance to reach a node u in the subgraph. To do so, we first define some notation. We use $\acute{p}(u)$ and $\grave{p}(u)$ to represent the probability for a random walk to reach u during the bottom-top and top-bottom phases, respectively. Also, we use $\nabla(u)$ and $\Delta(u)$ to denote the set of neighbors of u on the levels above and below u, respectively. The key observation for estimating $\acute{p}(u)$ and $\grave{p}(u)$ is

$$\acute{p}(u) = \sum_{v\in\Delta(u)} \frac{\acute{p}(v)}{|\nabla(v)|}, \quad \grave{p}(u) = \sum_{v\in\nabla(u)} \frac{\grave{p}(v)}{|\Delta(v)|}, \tag{6}$$

which holds for all but two exceptions: (1) for a node u with no incoming edges - i.e., when $\nabla(u) = \varnothing$ - we have $\grave{p}(u) = \acute{p}(u)$, and (2) for a node u with no outgoing edges - i.e., when $\Delta(u) = \varnothing$ - it is either $\acute{p}(u) = 1/s$ - where s is the number of seed nodes[7] the random walk might start from - if u is one of the seed nodes, or $\acute{p}(u) = 0$ otherwise.

Equation 6 illustrates a simple recursive process for producing an unbiased estimation of $p(u)$: Note that if we choose a node v uniformly at random from $\Delta(u)$, then

$$\omega(\acute{p}(u)) = \frac{|\Delta(u)|\cdot\acute{p}(v)}{|\nabla(v)|} \tag{7}$$

is an unbiased estimation for $\acute{p}(u)$ (same[8] applies to $\grave{p}(u)$). In addition, if we replace $\acute{p}(v)$ in (7) with an unbiased estimation of it, say $\omega(\acute{p}(v))$, then $|\Delta(U)|\cdot\omega(\acute{p}(v))/|\nabla(v)|$ remains an unbiased estimation of $\acute{p}(u)$ as long as the random selection of v from $\nabla(u)$ is independent of the estimation of $\omega(\acute{p}(v))$.

[7]Recall from §3 that seed nodes consist of users returned by the limited search interface - e.g., for Twitter, those who tweeted the keyword within the last week and thus returned by the Search API.

[8]i.e., if we choose a node v uniformly at random from $\nabla(u)$, then $|\nabla(u)|\cdot\grave{p}(v)/|\Delta(v)|$ is an unbiased estimation for $\grave{p}(u)$.

Algorithm 2 ESTIMATE-$\acute{p}$

Input: u
if $\Delta(u) == \varnothing$ **then**
  //u is a bottom level node
  $\acute{p}(u) = \begin{cases} 1/s & \text{If } u \text{ is one of the } s \text{ seeds} \\ 0 & \text{Otherwise} \end{cases}$
else if $\nabla(u) == \varnothing$ **then**
  //u is a top level node
  $\acute{p}(u) = \grave{p}(u)$
else
  Pick a node v randomly from $\Delta(u)$
  $\acute{p}(v) =$ ESTIMATE-$\acute{p}$ (v)
  $\acute{p}(u) = \frac{|\Delta(U)|\cdot\acute{p}(v)}{|\nabla(v)|}$
end if

As such, the recursive process works as follows: After each instance of the level-by-level random walk terminates, we take $\acute{U}$ and $\grave{U}$, the sets of nodes the instance passes through during the bottom-top and top-bottom phases, respectively. Then, for each node $u \in \grave{U}$, we start a bottom-top, level-by-level random walk starting from u, this time for the sole purpose of recursively estimating $\grave{p}(u)$. On the other hand, for each node $u \in \acute{U}$, we start a top-bottom level-by-level random walk to estimate $\acute{p}(u)$ in a recursive fashion. Algorithm 2 depicts the pseudocode for estimating $\acute{p}(u)$ (the algorithm for $\grave{p}(u)$ is similar). One can see that this process can produce unbiased estimations of $\grave{p}(u)$ or $\acute{p}(u)$ for every node that the random walk instance passes through - i.e., every node that will be used in the aggregate estimation process, as explained in the next subsection.

Since the above discussions have established the unbiasedness of $f(u)/\grave{p}(u)$ on SUM and COUNT estimations as well as the unbiasedness of $\omega(\grave{p}(u))$ on estimating $\grave{p}(u)$, we now consider the other important factor affecting the error of aggregate estimation: *variance*. Specifically, the following theorem illustrates the estimation variance produced by topology aware random walk for SUM aggregates. Note that since COUNT can be considered as a special case of SUM (when $f(u) = 1$), estimation errors of COUNT and AVG (i.e., SUM/COUNT) aggregates can be derived accordingly.

THEOREM 5.1. *For aggregate $Q_{\rm A}$:* SELECT SUM($f(u)$) FROM U WHERE *cond, after r random walk instances, topology aware random walk generates an estimation variance*

$$\sigma^2 = \left(\sum_{u\in cond} \frac{(V+1)\cdot f(u)^2}{r\cdot\grave{p}(u)}\right) - \frac{Q_{\rm A}^2}{r}, \textit{ where} \tag{8}$$

$$V = \sum_{u\in cond}\sum_{\rho\in\mathcal{P}(u)} \grave{p}(u)\cdot p(\rho)\cdot\left(\frac{\grave{p}(u)}{\omega(\rho)} - 1\right)^2 \tag{9}$$

when r is sufficiently large, where $Q_{\rm A}$ is the real aggregate value, $\mathcal{P}(u)$ is the set of all bottom-top-bottom paths from u to one of the seed nodes, $\omega(\rho)$ is the estimation of $\grave{p}(u)$ produced by Algorithm 2 when path ρ is taken for estimating $\grave{p}(u)$, and $p(\rho)$ is the probability for ρ to be taken.

We do not include the proof here due to space limit. Note that an intuitive explanation for V in the theorem is the variance of $\grave{p}(u)/\omega(\grave{p}(u))$, where $\omega(\grave{p}(u))$ is the estimation of $\grave{p}(u)$ produced by our algorithm, taken over the randomness of $\omega(\grave{p}(u))$. One can observe from the theorem that a key factor determining the estimation variance is the values of $\grave{p}(u)$ for nodes in the subgraph. To understand why, note from (8) that, given V, σ^2 is in general inversely proportional to $\grave{p}(u)$. Thus, if the subgraph happens to be highly skewed so as to have a node u with an extremely small $\grave{p}(u)$, then the estimation variance σ^2 (and thereby the aggregate estimation error) can be very large. Fortunately, as we shall show in §6, the variance is indeed fairly small in practice for the wide variety of keywords we tested.

Before concluding this subsection, we would like to briefly discuss the additional query cost introduced by the probability estimation process. One can see that, in order to estimate $\grave{p}(\cdot)$ or $\acute{p}(\cdot)$ for the (at most) $2h-1$ nodes the random walk passes through, this process requires at most $(2h-1)\cdot(h-1)$ additional transitions. While such $O(h^2)$ query cost surpasses that required by the level-by-level random walk itself, it is unlikely to cause any efficiency concern in practice because of the following two reasons.

First, as one can see from the results in §6.2, even a query cost of $O(h^2)$ is still an order of magnitude lower than topology-oblivious random walks, and second, the real-world query cost for estimating $\grave{p}(\cdot)$ or $\acute{p}(\cdot)$ is often lower than the worst-case scenario. To understand why, consider a common scenario where the level-by-level subgraph has one or a small number of roots at the top. Let there be one root v_r. Note that once we produce an estimation of $\grave{p}(v_r)$ (which is equal to $\acute{p}(v_r)$), we can reuse it for estimating $\grave{p}(\cdot)$ for *all* nodes in the top-bottom phase of *all* random walk instances - i.e., for these nodes, the probability estimation process only needs to walk bottom-up and not top-bottom anymore - saving about half of the query cost because of a single cache.

5.3 Algorithm MA-TARW

In this subsection, we put together the previous discussions of level-by-level subgraph, topology aware random walk and the unbiased estimation of selection probability $\grave{p}(u)$ to develop Algorithm MA-TARW, which can be used to estimate SUM, COUNT and AVG aggregates with or without selection conditions.

Algorithm 3 depicts the pseudocode for MA-TARW. First, it uses a small number of bootstrapping transitions to identify the best time interval T for the level-by-level subgraph (see §4.2.3 for details). It randomly picks a bottom level node (a user who has recently tweeted about the hashtag) and performs a bottom-top-bottom random walk instance $\mathcal{R}_i$ as described in previous subsection. For each node u in the walk $\mathcal{R}_i$, it computes the selection probability ($\acute{p}(u)$ or $\grave{p}(u)$). All nodes in $\mathcal{R}_i$ are used in computing a single estimate of the aggregate query. This random walk process is then repeated for multiple times - with the average estimate being outputted as the final aggregate estimation.

Algorithm 3 MA-TARW

Estimate best value of T using bootstrapping transitions
while Remaining query budget > 0 **do**
  Perform a bottom-top-bottom random walk $\mathcal{R}_i$
  $\acute{p}(u)$ = ESTIMATE-$\acute{p}$ (u) $\forall\, u \in \acute{U}$ of $\mathcal{R}_i$
  $\grave{p}(u)$ = ESTIMATE-$\grave{p}$ (u) $\forall\, u \in \grave{U}$ of $\mathcal{R}_i$
  // Remove nodes from $\acute{U}, \grave{U}$ that does not match input query
  $\widetilde{f}(\mathcal{R}_i) = \frac{1}{|\mathcal{R}_i|}\left(\sum_{u\in\acute{U}}\frac{f(u)}{\acute{p}(u)} + \sum_{u\in\grave{U}}\frac{f(u)}{\grave{p}(u)}\right)$
end while
Return average of all previous estimates $\widetilde{f}(\mathcal{R}_i)$

6. EXPERIMENTAL EVALUATION

6.1 Experimental Setup

Hardware and Platform: All our experiments were conducted on a computer with Intel Core(TM) i5 2.50 GHz CPU with 8 GB of RAM. The algorithms were implemented in Python 2.7.

Datasets: We tested our algorithms on three real-world microblogging platforms - Twitter, Google+ and Tumblr. These were chosen due to their popularity and accessibility of their developer API. While the majority of our experiments were conducted over Twitter, we observed similar behavior on the other microblogs also.

Detailed discussion on how MICROBLOG-ANALYZER is instantiated for Twitter is found in §3.2. We now briefly describe how Google+ and Tumblr are instantiated. Google+ has an *Activity* API (equivalent to the Twitter search API) that allows us to search for posts that specify a particular keyword. It also has an API to retrieve user profile information, as allowed by the privacy setting of the user. However, some basic information such as display name are always available. Similar to Twitter, connections in Google+ are asymmetric. Connections are grouped into various groups, called *Circles*. Google+ has a *courtesy* rate limit of 10,000 queries per day and 5 per second. Due to the difficulty in retrieving connections (the API only provides the connections of an authenticated user), we define two users to be connected if they performed some activity together in last year, i.e., they liked, shared or commented the same post. Tumblr is another popular microblogging platform where users host multiple blogs and can follow blogs of other users. The posts in blogs correspond to tweets in Twitter which can then be liked or reblogged by other users. Tumblr has extensive API to retrieve various information about blogs. Requests are rate-limited to one every 10 seconds.

Aggregate Queries and Ground Truth: In our experiments, we focused on aggregate queries AVG, COUNT and SUM. We evaluated aggregate measures such as the number of followers, display name length, number of likes in the blog etc. For Twitter, we used the streaming API to collect all public tweets mentioning a diverse set of keywords (such as cities, celebrities, organizations etc) between Jan 1 - Nov 1, 2013. Since Twitter ensures that the stream returns all relevant tweets as long as their frequency is less than 1% of the Twitter Firehose and our keywords are not too frequent, this provides a reasonable ground truth over which aggregate estimation algorithms can be evaluated. Figure 7 shows the frequency of three keywords used in the evaluation over time - `privacy` (a relatively low frequency term with occasional spikes), `New York` (a perpetually popular and high frequency keyword) and `Boston` (keyword that has medium frequency but had a singular spike on Apr 15, 2013 when the Marathon Bombing occurred). For Google+ and Tumblr, no convenient way to collect ground truth exists. To get a reasonable approximation, we instantiated multiple samplers that performed simultaneous random walks until they converged to their stationary distribution (with Geweke threshold $Z \leq 0.05$). The average estimate from all the walks serves as ground truth.

Performance Measures: Our aggregate estimation algorithms were evaluated according to two measures. Efficiency was measured as the number of API interface calls. Notice that multiple API calls could be required to obtain the result of a single query. For example, Twitter's followers API returns 5000 users per call and hence multiple calls are required to retrieve all followers of a celebrity. To measure accuracy, we use the relative error (see §2).

Algorithms Evaluated: We evaluated MA-SRW, MA-TARW and the state-of-art baseline M&R described next. Recall from §4 that MA-SRW outperformed SRW on the original or the term-induced social graph. Hence, to keep the presentation clear, we do not present any experiments on the original or the term-induced social graph. To the best our knowledge, we have not found any research that performs general aggregate estimation over microblogs. The closest is [15] that performs size (COUNT) estimation for (entire) social networks and does not directly support keyword-specific size estimation. We adapted [15] to only consider nodes that match the

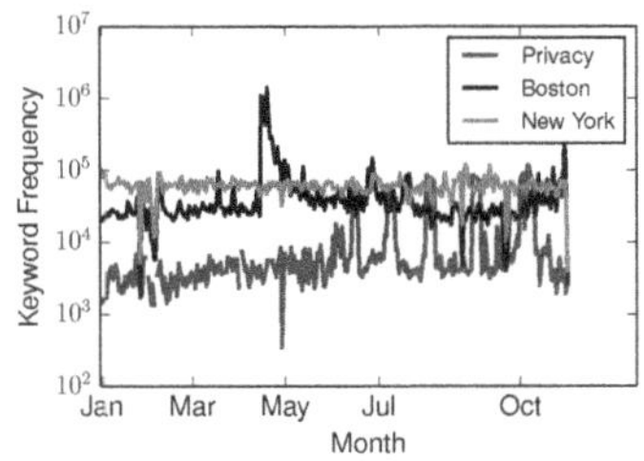

Figure 7: Frequencies of Chosen Keywords

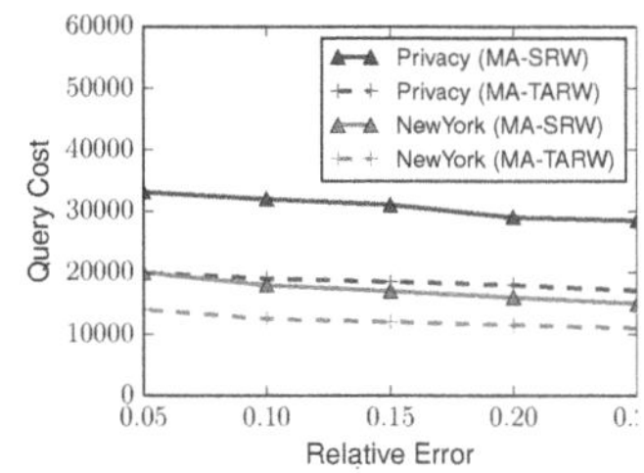

Figure 8: Twitter: AVG(followers)

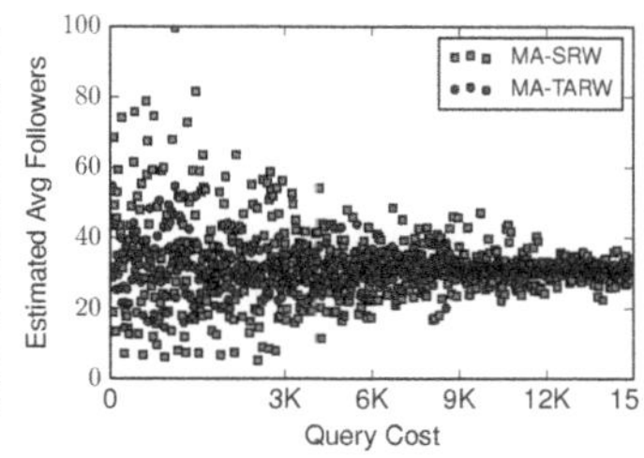

Figure 9: Twitter: Estimated AVG(followers)

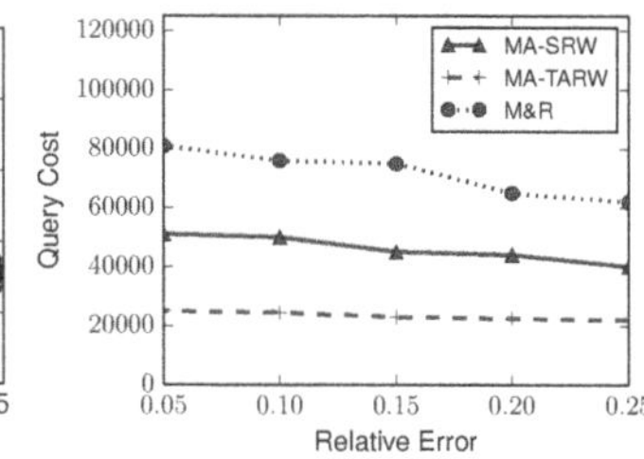

Figure 10: Twitter: Count(users)

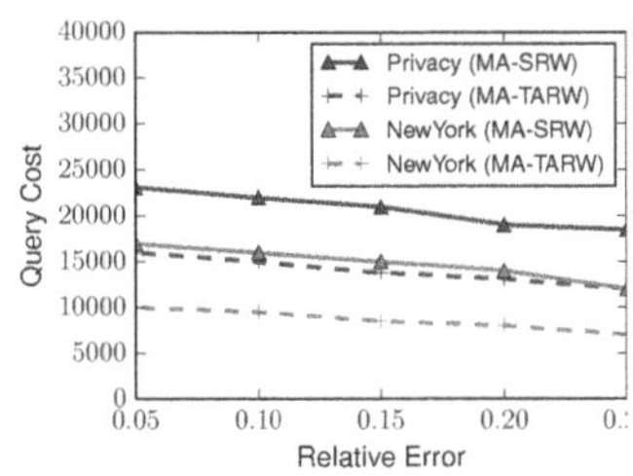

Figure 11: Twitter: AVG(Display Name)

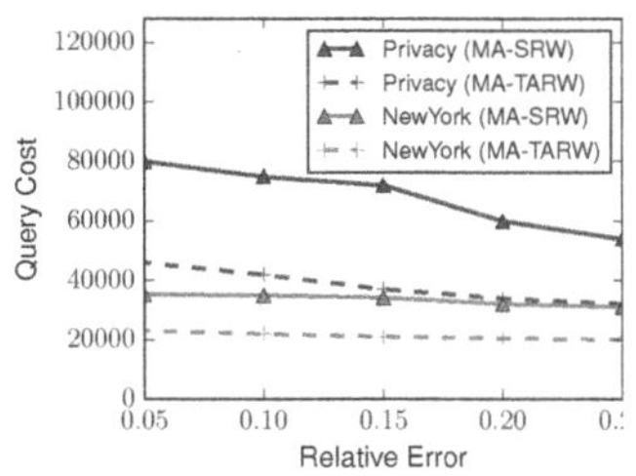

Figure 12: Google+: AVG(Display Name)

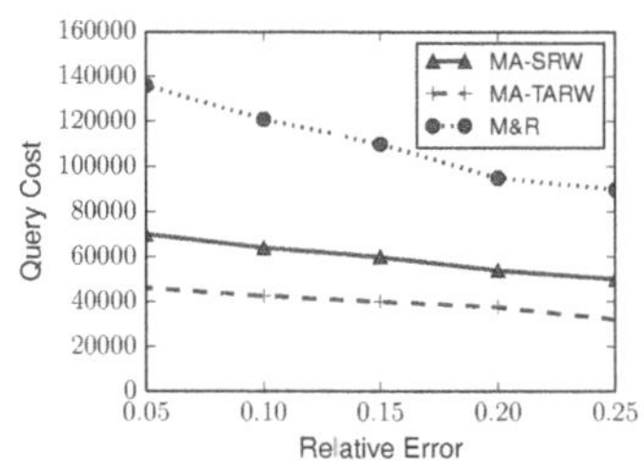

Figure 13: Google+: COUNT (male users who tweeted)

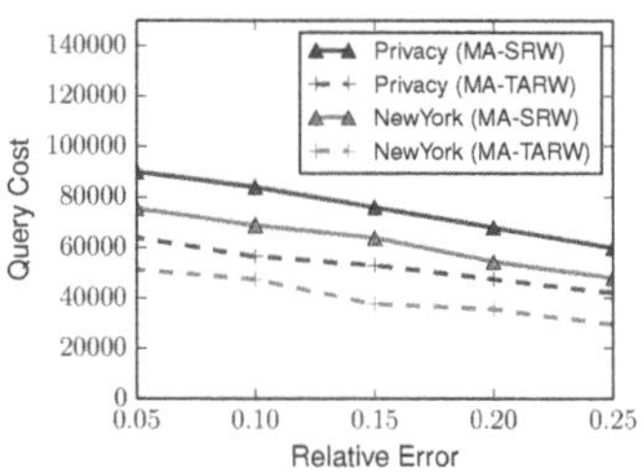

Figure 14: Tumblr: AVG(Likes)

Table 3: Average Percent Improvement of MA-TARW

KEYWORD	MA-SRW (AVG)	MA-SRW (COUNT)	M&R (COUNT)
`Boston`	39	44	72
`Oprah`	27	37	67
`Simvastatin`	29	41	74
`$WMT`	33	51	78
`Lipitor`	24	47	76
`Tunisia`	33	31	53
`Tahrir`	41	55	61

query and used it to measure the size of the term induced subgraph and refer this algorithm as M&R (for mark and recapture); we only include it for COUNT (as the algorithm was designed for).

6.2 Experimental Results

We start with Twitter. Table 3 shows the average percentage improvement in Twitter query cost achieved by MA-TARW over MA-SRW and M&R for AVG(followers) and COUNT(users) queries (from Jan 1, 2013 to Oct 31, 2013) involving diverse keyword conditions to achieve a relative accuracy error of 5%. The results show that MA-TARW outperforms both competing algorithms and confirm our theoretical analysis.

Next, we study in more detail specific aggregate queries. We use MA-TARW to estimate the average number of followers of all users who tweeted `privacy`. Figure 8 shows that MA-TARW significantly outperforms MA-SRW. Figure 9 also validates this conclusion by showing that MA-TARW converges to the true estimate and has a lower variance in its estimate within few thousand queries.

We then perform a COUNT estimate of all users who tweeted `privacy`. Figure 10 shows that MA-TARW outperforms both MA-SRW and baseline M&R. Recall from Figure 3 that M&R requires lower query cost when evaluated on the level-by-level subgraph than on term induced subgraph; this is why we execute M&R on the level-by-level subgraph to better evaluate our topology-aware navigation algorithm. We next consider an aggregate query to estimate the average display name length of Twitter users who tweeted `privacy`. In contrast to AVG(#followers) shown above, this requires substantially smaller number of queries as this measure has a lower variability than that of number of followers. Figure 11 shows that MA-TARW seems to leverage this aspect by essentially "skipping" such edges (which would have often been intra-level edges).

Next we evaluate our algorithms on Google+. Figures 12 and 13 show the performance of estimating the average display name length and count of male users (gender is generally missing from Twitter profiles, and hence we did not use it as a condition above) who posted `privacy` during the time period. We notice that MA-TARW outperforms the competing algorithms. It must be noted that the absolute query cost is much higher than in Twitter. This is to a large extent due to the fact that APIs of Google+ (such as Activity search) returns at most 20 results per invocation compared to 200 in Twitter's timeline API.

Finally, we evaluate our algorithms on Tumblr. Here, we evaluated the average number of likes obtained by posts with *textual* content containing the keyword `privacy`. Figure 14 shows that MA-TARW has the best performance.

7. RELATED WORK

Graph Sampling Through Random Walks: A number of existing papers have studied the problem on sampling large graphs [8, 17, 19, 20] while [13, 15, 25] specifically focus on online social networks. Sampling techniques and the ground truth definition vary depending on whether the global topology is known [13, 19] or unknown. For the latter, [13, 19] compared the efficiency of various sampling techniques such as simple random walk (SRW), Metropolis-Hastings (MHRW), BFS and DFS. [13] also studied the problem of running multiple, parallel random walks. We used SRW as the basis of MA-SRW as [13] reported that SRW is typically 1.5-8 times faster than MHRW, which was observation as well.

Analytics of Twitter and Other Microblogs: While there has been plethora of work on using social media data from Twitter and other microblogs on specific analytics tasks (typically over current and future data), our paper is the first to study the problem of aggregate estimation over historic data. [16] provides an high level overview of possible analytics tasks over Twitter. Other analytics tasks include monitoring trends [22], predicting stock prices [28], topical expertise [27], measure information propagation in Twitter [23], such as in the context of natural disasters. There has been a set of paid and free third party services such as Sysomos, Topsy, Trendsmap etc that allow you to perform simple analytics tasks (such as monitor popular trends, analyze your tweeting/retweeting behavior, visualize your social network etc). However, none of the free ones allow analytics over historic data and even the paid ones offer simple, canned analytic options.

Search Engine Analytics: Another category of related research is analytics over a search engine's corpus (e.g., [29]) - simply because a microblog service can be considered as a search engine (collecting, indexing and publishing documents posted by all users). However, search-engine-analytics techniques cannot be directly applied because of the limitation of search interface provided by microblogging services. Note that a key assumption made by all existing search-engine-analytics techniques is that the search interface can reveal *all* documents in the corpus (through answers to a very large set of search queries). This, unfortunately, is not the case for microblogging services. For example, Twitter search API is limited to tweets published in the last week [6]. These limitations prevent existing search-engine-analytics techniques from being applied.

8. CONCLUSIONS AND FUTURE WORK

We proposed novel solutions to perform aggregate query estimation on microblogging data that exploit the provided user timeline API calls. We showed how to define a conceptual level-by-level subgraph of the social graph that allows dramatically more efficient random walk-based sampling. Then, we further improved our solution by proposing a novel topology-aware navigation strategy on the level-by-level subgraph that significantly outperforms existing random walk sampling methods. Theoretical analysis and experiments over microblogs confirm the effectiveness of our solutions.

9. ACKNOWLEDGEMENTS

The work of Saravanan Thirumuruganathan and Gautam Das was partially supported by National Science Foundation under grants 0812601, 0915834, 1018865 and grants from Microsoft Research. Nan Zhang was supported in part by the National Science Foundation under grants 0852674, 0915834, 1117297, and 1343976. Vagelis Hristidis was partially supported by National Science Foundation grant 1216007 and a Samsung GRO grant. Any opinions, findings, conclusions, and/or recommendations expressed in this material, either expressed or implied, are those of the authors and do not necessarily reflect the views of the sponsors listed above.

10. REFERENCES

[1] Datasift pricing. In *http://datasift.com/pricing/*, 2013.

[2] Gnip. In *http://gnip.com*, 2013.

[3] Sysomos twitter retweet statistics. In *http://www.sysomos.com/insidetwitter/engagement/*, 2013.

[4] Sysomos twitter usage statistics. In *http://www.sysomos.com/insidetwitter/*, 2013.

[5] Twitter api. In *https://dev.twitter.com/docs/api/1.1*, 2013.

[6] Twitter search. In *https://dev.twitter.com/docs/using-search*, 2013.

[7] Twitter Streaming API. In *https://dev.twitter.com/docs/streaming-apis*, 2013.

[8] E. M. Airoldi and K. M. Carley. Sampling algorithms for pure network topologies: a study on the stability and the separability of metric embeddings. *ACM SIGKDD Explorations Newsletter*, 7(2):13–22, 2005.

[9] L. Cowen. Handbook of Capture-Recapture Analysis. *The Quarterly Review of Biology*, (3):310.

[10] C. Domb. On multiple returns in the random-walk problem. In *Proc. Cambridge Philos. Soc*, volume 50, pages 586–591. Cambridge Univ Press, 1954.

[11] J. Geweke et al. *Evaluating the accuracy of sampling-based approaches to the calculation of posterior moments*. Federal Reserve Bank of Minneapolis, Research Department, 1991.

[12] W. R. Gilks. *Markov Chain Monte Carlo In Practice*. Chapman and Hall/CRC, 1999.

[13] M. Gjoka, M. Kurant, C. T. Butts, and A. Markopoulou. Walking in facebook: a case study of unbiased sampling of osns. INFOCOM'10, pages 2498–2506, 2010.

[14] M. H. Hansen and W. N. Hurwitz. On the theory of sampling from finite populations. *AMS*, 14(4):333–362, 1943.

[15] L. Katzir, E. Liberty, and O. Somekh. Estimating sizes of social networks via biased sampling. WWW '11, 2011.

[16] S. Kumar, F. Morstatter, and H. Liu. Twitter data analytics, 2013.

[17] M. Kurant, M. Gjoka, C. T. Butts, and A. Markopoulou. Walking on a graph with a magnifying glass: stratified sampling via weighted random walks. SIGMETRICS '11.

[18] K. Lerman and R. Ghosh. Information contagion: An empirical study of the spread of news on digg and twitter social networks. *ICWSM*, 10:90–97, 2010.

[19] J. Leskovec and C. Faloutsos. Sampling from large graphs. KDD '06, pages 631–636, 2006.

[20] L. Lovász. Random walks on graphs: A survey. In *Combinatorics, Paul Erdős is Eighty*, volume 2. 1996.

[21] L. Lovasz and R. Kannan. Faster mixing via average conductance. In *STOC*, pages 282–287, 1999.

[22] M. Mathioudakis and N. Koudas. Twittermonitor: Trend detection over the twitter stream. SIGMOD '10.

[23] M. Mendoza, B. Poblete, and C. Castillo. Twitter under crisis: Can we trust what we rt? In *SOMA*, 2010.

[24] A. Mislove, M. Marcon, K. P. Gummadi, P. Druschel, and B. Bhattacharjee. Measurement and analysis of online social networks. SIGCOMM '07, pages 29–42, 2007.

[25] A. Mohaisen, A. Yun, and Y. Kim. Measuring the mixing time of social graphs. In *SIGCOMM '10*, 2010.

[26] M. E. J. Newman. Modularity and community structure in networks. *PNAS*, 103(23), 2006.

[27] A. Pal and S. Counts. Identifying topical authorities in microblogs. In *WSDM*, pages 45–54. ACM, 2011.

[28] E. J. Ruiz, V. Hristidis, C. Castillo, A. Gionis, and A. Jaimes. Correlating financial time series with micro-blogging activity. In *WSDM*, pages 513–522. ACM, 2012.

[29] M. Zhang, N. Zhang, and G. Das. Mining a search engine's corpus: Efficient yet unbiased sampling and aggregate estimation. SIGMOD '11.

Tripartite Graph Clustering for Dynamic Sentiment Analysis on Social Media

Linhong Zhu
Information Sciences Institute
University of Southern California
linhong@isi.edu

Aram Galstyan
Information Sciences Institute
University of Southern California
galstyan@isi.edu

James Cheng
Dept. of Computer Science & Engineering
The Chinese University of Hong Kong
jcheng@cse.cuhk.edu.hk

Kristina Lerman
Information Sciences Institute
University of Southern California
lerman@isi.edu

ABSTRACT

The growing popularity of social media (e.g., Twitter) allows users to easily share information with each other and influence others by expressing their own sentiments on various subjects. In this work, we propose an unsupervised *tri-clustering* framework, which analyzes both user-level and tweet-level sentiments through co-clustering of a tripartite graph. A compelling feature of the proposed framework is that the quality of sentiment clustering of tweets, users, and features can be mutually improved by joint clustering. We further investigate the evolution of user-level sentiments and latent feature vectors in an online framework and devise an efficient online algorithm to sequentially update the clustering of tweets, users and features with newly arrived data. The online framework not only provides better quality of both dynamic user-level and tweet-level sentiment analysis, but also improves the computational and storage efficiency. We verified the effectiveness and efficiency of the proposed approaches on the November 2012 California ballot Twitter data.

1. INTRODUCTION

Recently there has been a significant growth in the use of social media platforms such as Twitter. Spurred by that growth, companies, advertisers, and political campaigners are seeking ways to analyze the sentiments of users through the Twitter platform on their products, services and policies. For instance, a political group that is advocating a new policy for "labeling genetically modified organisms (GMO)", might want to know the positions of different users toward that policy, which requires accurate estimations of users' sentiments (i.e., whether a user has expressed a positive, negative or neutral attitude towards GMO labeling), and such information can be obtained from Twitter as shown in Figure 1.

SIGMOD'14, June 22–27, 2014, Snowbird, UT, USA.

http://dx.doi.org/10.1145/2588555.2593682.

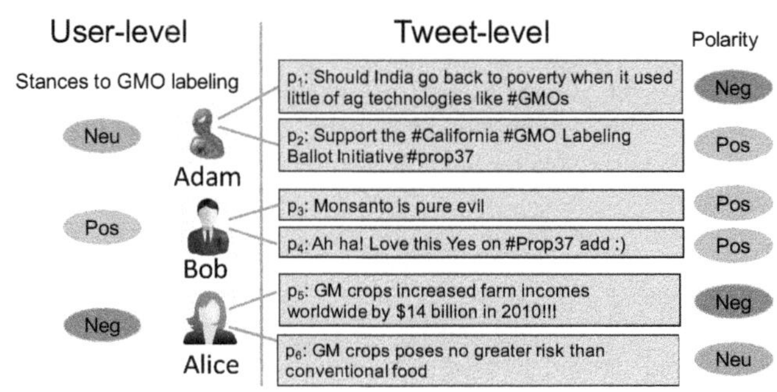

Figure 1: An example of both user-level and tweet-level sentiments toward the topic "labeling genetically modified organism (GMO)"

Most prior work on Twitter sentiment analysis has focused on understanding the sentiments of individual tweets [2, 11, 6, 31, 28, 15], although more recently some authors have addressed the problem of inferring user-level sentiments [29, 17]; see Section 6 for more details. Smith et al. [27] and Deng et al. [7] study both tweet-level and user-level sentiments, but they assume that a user's sentiment can be estimated by aggregating the sentiments of all his/her posts. Although the sentiments of users are correlated with the sentiments expressed in tweets, such simple aggregation can often produce incorrect results, in part because sentiment extracted from short texts such as tweets will generally be very noisy and error prone. For instance, in Figure 1, Bob is positive towards GMO labeling, however, tweet p_3 might be classified as "negative" due to the occurrence of word "evil" and simple aggregation of both p_3 and p_4 would produce incorrect sentiment for Bob. In contrast, inferring the sentiment of p_3 jointly with the sentiment of Bob's other tweets can potentially produce a more accurate classification for tweet p_3 and Bob's overall sentiment. This example motivates us to jointly analyze both tweet-level and user-level sentiments, by modeling the dependencies among users, tweets and words.

Another important challenge is understanding and characterizing the temporal evolution of user-level sentiment. For example, user Adam in Figure 1 seems to be against GMO labeling at first, but changes his mind in support of GMO labeling, perhaps due to interactions with other users. Another real-world example is provided

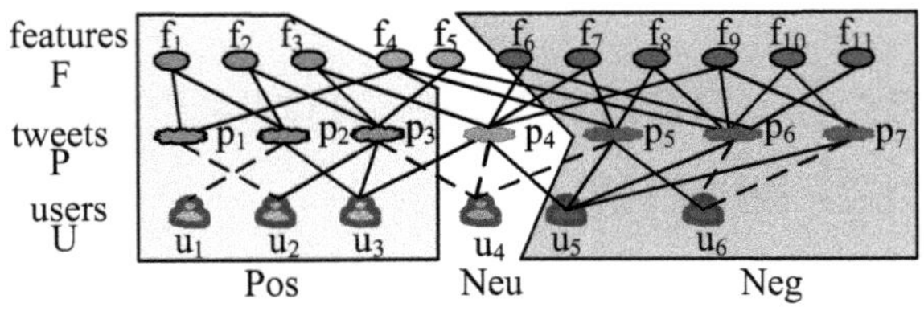

Figure 2: Co-clustering of a tripartite graph of features, users and tweets. The dashed/solid lines represent posting/re-tweeting relations between users and tweets.

by the recent release of iPhone5: While many users were tweeting positive comments prior to the release, several hours of limited sales and high price issues generated a wave of negative sentiments from users. Unfortunately, current offline approaches [2, 11, 6, 31, 28, 15] that focus on static data, might either miss those dynamic patterns in the temporal data by simply classifying users' sentiments as neutral, or become very time-consuming when applied repeatedly to temporal snapshots (e.g., each minute/hour) of the entire collection. While recent work has addressed sentiment dynamics [5, 24], those studies have mainly focused on understanding how the aggregate volume of positive/negative tweets changes with time, while discarding possible interesting dynamics on individual user level. Furthermore, due to the "long-tail" phenomenon, changes in tweet volume might be attributed to a relatively small fraction of super-active users, so that the dynamics of the aggregate sentiment might not be very representative of a typical user.

To address the above-mentioned challenges, we study the sentiment co-clustering problem, which aims to simultaneously cluster the sentiment of tweets and users. We propose a unified unsupervised *tri-clustering* framework, to solve the sentiment-clustering problem by solving its dual problem: co-cluster a tripartite graph which represents dependencies among tweets, users and features into sentiment class. We give an example of a tripartite graph co-clustering as follows.

EXAMPLE 1. *Figure 2 shows an example of a tripartite graph, which models the correlation among features (e.g., words), tweets and users. There are three layers of nodes (i.e., features F, users U, and tweets P), where a feature node $f \in F$ is connected with a tweet $p \in P$ if the tweet p contains the feature f; and a user $u \in U$ is connected with a tweet p if either u posts or re-tweets the tweet p. Therefore, if we can obtain a good clustering over the tripartite graph, for instance, we obtain three subsets $\{f_1, f_2, f_3, p_1, p_2, p_3, u_1, u_2, u_3\}$, $\{f_4, f_5, p_4, u_4\}$ and the remaining, then the users are clustered into positive users$\{u_1, u_2, u_3\}$, neutral users$\{u_4\}$ and negative users$\{u_5, u_6\}$, while the tweets are clustered into three subsets $\{p_1, p_2, p_3\}$, $\{p_4\}$ and $\{p_5, p_6, p_7\}$ simultaneously.*

This example reveals several advantages of the proposed tri-clustering framework. First, tri-clustering framework exploits the duality between sentiment clustering and tripartite graph co-clustering to perform both user-level and tweet-level sentiment analysis. Second, since co-clustering is an unsupervised approach, neither labeled data nor high quality of labels are required, though performance can be improved by including high quality labeled data or outputs of other sentiment analysis approaches. Finally, a useful feature of co-clustering is that it can utilize the intermediate clustering results of tweets to improve the clustering results of users, and vice versa.

We present a non-negative matrix co-factorization algorithm to obtain a good co-clustering of a tripartite graph. Since the cluster label corresponds to a special instance "sentiment", we adopt the emotion consistency regularization to make the clustering of features more relevant to the feature lexicon, and the clusters close to the sentiment classes. Motivated by prior observations that social relation information is highly correlated with sentiment [27], we incorporate graph regularization technique into matrix co-factorization, and use it to exploit social relationship information for better sentiment clustering. The graph regularization aims to incur a penalty if two users are close in social relation but have different sentiments.

Finally, we extend the tripartite graph co-clustering to an online setting. We leverage previous clustering results to obtain better clustering performance for newly arrived Twitter data. Furthermore, our online framework also uses the temporal regularization over smooth evolution of both features (i.e., vocabularies) and users: (i) sentiments of vocabularies evolve smoothly over a short period; (ii) considering the entire population, the majority of users rarely change their mind within a short time. By minimizing the temporal regularization, our framework is able to achieve high accuracy in both tweet-level and user-level dynamic sentiment analysis.

We summarize the main contributions of our work as follows:

- We propose an unsupervised unified tri-clustering framework for both tweet-level and user-level sentiment analysis. We then design an analytical multiplicative algorithm to solve sentiment clustering problem with the offline tri-clustering framework.
- We incorporate online setting into our framework, which allows us to study the dynamic factor of user-level sentiments, as well as the evolution of latent feature factors. Next, we also devise an online algorithm for dynamic tri-clustering problem, which is efficient in terms of both computation and storage, and effective in terms of clustering accuracy.
- We conduct a set of experiments on the November 2012 California ballot Twitter data, and verify that our approach is more effective than the state-of-the-art unsupervised method for sentiment analysis, ESSA [15], and is even comparable to supervised methods such as SVM [27] and Naïve Bayes [11], and semi-supervised methods such as Label propagation [12, 28, 29] and UserReg [7].

In the rest of the paper, we first introduce the notations and formally define our problem in Section 2. In Section 3 we propose an offline tri-clustering framework, and develop an analytical algorithm to solve the clustering problem in the offline framework. Next, in Section 4 we show how to extend the offline framework into the online setting by incorporating the temporal regularization. We also describe the proposed efficient online algorithm which updates the clustering of tweets, users and features with newly arrived data and partial previous results. The experimental studies are conducted in Section 5. We review the related works in Section 6 and finally conclude our work in Section 7.

2. PROBLEM DEFINITION

We first introduce the notations used in this paper, which are listed in Table 1 for quick reference. A tweet is represented as a triple p=$< x, u, t >$ where x is the feature vector representing the tweet p, u represents a user who posts p and t is the associated timestamp. The label of sentiment classes is denoted as $c \in \{\texttt{pos, neg, neu}\}$. For easy representation, we also use n to denote the number of tweets, m to denote the number of users, l to denote the number of features, and k to denote the number of clusters/classes.

Table 1: Notations and explanations

Notations	Explanations
n and m	number of tweets and users
l and k	number of features and clusters
P, U and F	a set of tweets, users, and features
X_p/X_u	tweet-feature/user-feature matrix
X_r/G_u	user-tweet/user-user matrix
$S_p/S_f/S_u$	tweet/feature/user cluster matrix
H_p/H_u	$k \times k$ association matrix
$M_{(i)}$	the ith row of matrix M
$\mathtt{tr}(M)/\|\|M\|\|_F$	trace/Frobenius norm of matrix M
D_u/L_u	Diagonal/Laplacian matrix of G_u
$M(t)$	matrix M at timestamp t
$n(t)/m(t)$	number of tweets/users at time t
X_{ud}/X_{un} $/X_{ue}$	user-feature matrix for disappeared users, new users, and evolving users

For each tweet p_i, its *tweet-level sentiment* can be represented as a vector $S_{p(i)} \in R_+^k$ where $S_{p(ij)}$ denotes the probability that tweet p_i is in sentiment class j. Similarly, for each user u_i, the *user-level temporal sentiment* at time t can also be represented as a vector $S_{u(i)}(t) \in R_+^k$, where $S_{u(ij)}(t)$ denotes the likelihood of user u_i's sentiment in class j at time t.

With the terminologies defined above, we now formally define our sentiment co-clustering problem as follows:

PROBLEM 1. *Given a series of temporal tweet data* $\{p_1, p_2, \cdots, p_t\}$ *that are related to the same topic, our purpose is to automatically and collectively infer the sentiments of all the observed tweets* $S_p \in R_+^{n\times k}$, *and the temporal sentiments of all the observed users* $\{S_u(1) \in R_+^{m\times k}, S_u(2), \cdots, S_u(t)\}$.

3. OFFLINE FRAMEWORK

As discussed briefly in Section 1, we formulate Problem 1 as the co-clustering problem of a tripartite graph as shown in Figure 2. To find a good clustering for a tripartite graph, Gao et al. [10] pointed out that the co-clustering over a tripartite graph X-Y-Z can be divided into the clusterings over two bipartite graphs X-Y and Y-Z. For instance, co-clustering over a tripartite graph shown in Figure 2 can be obtained by clustering over two bipartite graphs F-P and P-U separately. However, this formulation has the drawback that the dependence between features and users is ignored. Furthermore, the user-user social relation, which has been verified to be effective in sentiment analysis [27], has not been taken into consideration either.

To address this problem, we employ a two-level clustering for a given tripartite graph, when a tripartite graph is separated into three mutually related bipartite graphs, namely, tweet-feature bipartite graph (matrix representation $X_p \in R_+^{n\times l}$), user-feature bipartite graph (matrix representation $X_u \in R_+^{m\times l}$), and user-tweet bipartite graph (matrix representation $X_r \in R_+^{m\times n}$). At the inter-level, we deal with the mutual dependency among bipartite graphs, and show that the intermediate clustering results of a bipartite graph can be further applied to the clustering process of another bipartite graph. At the intra-level, we study the clustering for each single bipartite graph, and then formulate the bipartite graph clustering as a factorization problem for the non-negative matrix representation of the given bipartite graph. Finally, inter-level clustering and intra-level clustering are mutually performed.

Figure 3 illustrates the overall idea of the two-level clustering in our framework. Assume that tweets are clustered into three classes

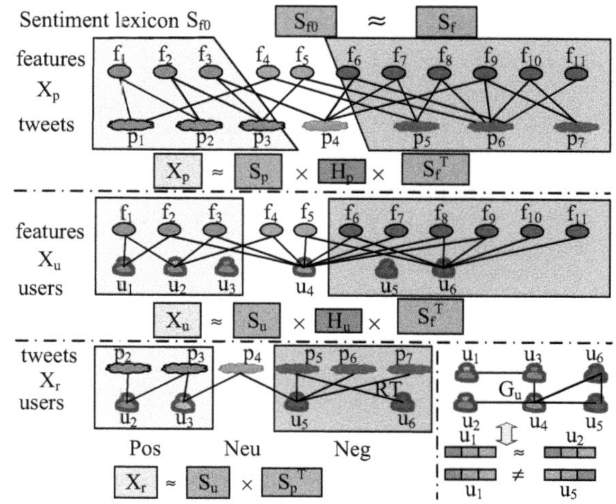

Figure 3: Offline tri-clustering framework overview (the figure is best viewed in color)

$\{p_1, p_2, p_3\}$, $\{p_4\}$ and $\{p_5, p_6, p_7\}$ by clustering the tweet-feature bipartite graph at the intra-level; their clustering results can then be utilized to improve the clustering of user-tweet bipartite graph at the inter-level and vise versa.

With the idea of the two-level clustering, now we propose a new Tri-clustering framework to perform both user-level and tweet-level sentiment analysis. The objective of our Tri-clustering framework is formulated as follows:

$$\begin{aligned} \arg\min_{\substack{S_f,S_u,S_p,\\ H_u,H_p\geq 0}} \{&\|X_p - S_pH_pS_f^T\|_F^2 + \|X_u - S_uH_uS_f^T\|_F^2 \\ &+ \|X_r - S_uS_p^T\|_F^2 \\ &+ \alpha\|S_f - S_{f0}\|_F^2 + \beta\mathtt{tr}(S_u^TL_uS_u)\} \\ \text{s.t. } &S_fS_f^T = I, S_pS_p^T = I, S_uS_u^T = I \end{aligned} \quad (1)$$

where each of the first three terms represents the intra-level bipartite graph clustering, and the aggregation of these three terms represents the inter-level bipartite graph clustering. We will discuss how simple aggregation captures the inter-level bipartite graph dependency later in Section 3.1. We suggest that these three bipartite graphs are equally important and hence no parameter is introduced to control their contributions. In addition, we also incorporate sentiment lexicon information (on the top of Figure 3) into the framework by adding regularization functions to features, and emotion correlation between users and re-tweeting users by using user-graph regularization (see right bottom of Figure 3). Although these two pieces of information are useful, they play a minor role in sentiment clustering. Therefore, we introduce two parameters, $\alpha, \beta \in [0, 1]$, to weigh the contributions of feature lexicon and user-graph regularization. In the following, we elaborate more details about each component.

- **co-clustering of tweets and features.**

$$\min_{S_f,H_p,S_p} \|X_p - S_pH_pS_f^T\|_F^2 \quad (2)$$

where $\|M\|_F$ denotes the Frobenius norm of a matrix M, $S_f \in R_+^{l\times k}$ denotes the feature cluster information with $S_{f(ij)}$ represents the probability that the i-th feature belongs to the j-th cluster, H_p represents the association between features and tweet classes.

- **co-clustering of users and features.**

$$\min_{S_f, H_u, S_u} ||X_u - S_u H_u S_f^T||_F^2 \quad (3)$$

where H_u denotes the the association between features and user classes. This is similar to tweet clustering: we argue that users can be characterized by the word features of their tweets and word features can be clustered according to their distribution among users.

- **co-clustering of re-tweeting users and tweets**

$$\min_{S_u, S_p} ||X_r - S_u S_p^T||_F^2 \quad (4)$$

where X_r is the user-retweet matrix and $X_{r(ij)}$ represents that the i-th user retweets the j-th tweet.

- **emotion consistence between clusters and sentiment classes.**

$$\min_{S_f} ||S_f - S_{f0}||_F^2 \quad (5)$$

where S_{f0} represents the sentiment information of features (e.g. sentiment lexicon), and $S_{f0(ij)}$ is the probability that the i-th feature belongs to the j-th sentiment class. In this component, we add a regularization to make the feature representation more relevant to the task of sentiment representation, and the clusters close to the sentiment classes.

- **emotion correlation between users and re-tweeting users.**

$$\min_{S_u, G_u} \frac{1}{2} \sum_i \sum_j ||S_{u(i)} - S_{u(j)}||_2^2 G_{u(i,j)} = \mathrm{tr}(S_u^T L_u S_u) \quad (6)$$

where G_u is a user-user graph of which each node is a user and each edge denotes the user-user re-tweeting relationship, $S_{u(i)}$ is a vector which represents the cluster association for user i, $L_u = D_u - G_u$ is the Laplacian matrix of the user-user re-tweeting graph, and tr represents the trace of a matrix. This expression incurs a penalty if two users are close in the user-user graph but have different sentiment labels.

3.1 Offline Optimization Algorithm

In the offline framework, we develop an analytical algorithm, which belongs to the category of traditional multiplicative update algorithm [19], to solve Eq. (1).

Updating $\mathbf{S_f}$.

Optimizing Eq. (1) with respect to S_f is equivalent to solving

$$\min_{S_f \geq 0} ||X_p - S_p H_p S_f^T||_F^2 + ||X_u - S_u H_u S_f^T||_F^2 + \alpha||S_f - S_{f0}||_F^2$$

$$\text{subject to } S_f S_f^T = I$$

We introduce the Largrangian multiplier $\mathcal{L}$ for non-negative constraint (i.e., $S_f \geq 0$) and Δ for orthogonal constraint (i.e., $S_f S_f^T$=I) to S_f in Eq. (1), which leads to the following Largrangian function $L(S_f)$:

$$L(S_f) = ||X_p - S_p H_p S_f^T||_F^2 + ||X_u - S_u H_u S_f^T||_F^2 + \alpha||S_f - S_{f0}||_F^2 - \mathrm{tr}[\mathcal{L}_{S_f} \cdot S_f^T] + \mathrm{tr}[\Delta_{S_f}(S_f S_f^T - I)]$$

The next step is to optimize the above terms w.r.t. S_f. We set $\frac{\partial L(S_f)}{\partial S_f}$=0, and obtain:

$$\mathcal{L}_{S_f} = -2X_p^T . S_p H_p + 2S_f H_p^T S_p^T S_p H_p - 2X_u^T S_u H_u + 2S_f H_u^T S_u^T S_u H_u + 2\alpha(S_f - S_{f0}) + 2S_f \Delta_{S_f}$$

Algorithm 1 offline algorithm for tri-clustering

Input: X_p, X_r, X_u, S_{f0}, user-user retweeting graph G_u, parameters: α and β
Output: S_u, S_p, S_f
1: initialize S_u, S_p, S_f, H_u, $H_p \geq 0$;
2: **while** it does not converge:
3: update S_p according to Eq. (10);
4: update H_p according to Eq. (9);
5: update S_u and H_u according to Eq. (11) and Eq. (8);
6: update S_f according to Eq. (7);
7: **return** S_u, S_p, S_f;

Using the KKT condition $\mathcal{L}_{S_f}(i,j) \cdot S_f(i,j)$=0 [18], we obtain:

$$[-X_p^T . S_p H_p + S_f H_p^T S_p^T S_p H_p - X_u^T S_u H_u + S_f H_u^T S_u^T S_u H_u + \alpha(S_f - S_{f0}) + S_f \Delta_{S_f}](i,j) S_f(i,j) = 0$$

where $\Delta_{S_f} = S_f^T X_u^T S_u H_u - H_u^T S_u^T S_u H_u + Sf^T X_p^T S_p H_p - H_p^T S_p^T S_p H_p - \alpha S_f^T (S_f - S_{f0})$.

Following the updating rules proposed and proved in [9], we have:

$$S_f \leftarrow S_f \circ \sqrt{\frac{X_u^T S_u H_u + X_p^T S_p H_p + \alpha S_{f0} + S_f \Delta_{S_f}^-}{S_f H_u^T S_u^T S_u H_u + S_f H_p^T S_p^T S_p H_p + \alpha S_f + S_f \Delta_{S_f}^+}} \quad (7)$$

where $\circ$ denotes element-wise multiplication operator, and $\Delta_{S_f}^+ = (|\Delta_{S_f}| + \Delta_{S_f})/2$ and $\Delta_{S_f}^- = (|\Delta_{S_f}| - \Delta_{S_f})/2$.

Updating other matrices.

Similar to the updating rule of S_f, the updating rules for the remaining matrices are as follows, where the detailed proofs are omitted here due to space limit but can be found in the technical report of this paper [35]:

$$H_u \leftarrow H_u \circ \sqrt{\frac{S_u^T X_u S_f}{S_u^T S_u H_u S_f^T S_f}} \quad (8)$$

$$H_p \leftarrow H_p \circ \sqrt{\frac{S_p^T X_p S_f}{S_p^T S_p H_p S_f^T S_f}} \quad (9)$$

$$S_p \leftarrow S_p \circ \sqrt{\frac{X_p S_f H_p^T + X_r^T S_u + S_p \Delta_{S_p}^-}{S_p H_p S_f^T S_f H_p^T + S_p S_u^T S_u + S_p \Delta_{S_p}^+}} \quad (10)$$

where $\Delta_{S_p} = S_p^T X_p S_f H_p^T - H_p S_f^T S_f H_p^T + S_p^T X_r^T S_u - S_u^T S_u$.

$$S_u \leftarrow S_u \circ \sqrt{\frac{X_u S_f H_u^T + X_r S_p + \beta G_u S_u + S_u \Delta_{S_u}^-}{S_u H_u S_f^T S_f H_u^T + S_u S_p^T S_p + \beta D_u S_u + S_u \Delta_{S_u}^+}} \quad (11)$$

where $\Delta_{S_u} = S_u^T X_u S_f H_u^T - H_u S_f^T S_f H_u^T + S_u^T X_r S_p - S_p^T S_p - \beta S_u^T L_u S_u$.

Algorithm 1 gives the offline optimization algorithm. From Algorithm 1, we can understand better why simple aggregation in Eq. (1) has taken advantage of the mutual relations among tweets, features and users. For example, in Line 5, updating sentiment clustering of users S_u requires the intermediate results of tweet clustering S_p and feature clustering S_f; while in Line 6 the feature-cluster matrix S_f is computed from these two matrices S_u and S_p.

Correctness and Convergence Analysis. We now analyze the correctness and convergence property of our offline algorithm. The objective function in Eq. (1) must be greater than or equal to zero.

To prove the convergence of Algorithm. 1, we need to show that Eq. (1) is non-increasing under the updating steps in Eq. (7), Eq. (8), Eq. (9), Eq. (10) and Eq. (11). In the following discussion, we show that Eq. (1) is non-increasing under the updating step in Eq. (7), while Eq. (1) is non-increasing under the updating steps in Eq. (10), Eq. (11), Eq. (8) and Eq. (9) can be proved similarly.

We follow a similar procedure described in [19]: We first find an auxiliary function which is a upper bound of the given objective function, and then show that updating rules can be obtained by minimizing the auxiliary function. We use $\mathcal{J}$ to denote the part of the objective function in Eq. (1) that is related to S_f:

$$\mathcal{J} = \|X_p - S_p H_p S_f^T\|_F^2 + \|X_u - S_u H_u S_f^T\|_F^2 + \alpha\|S_f - S_{f0}\|_F^2 + \mathrm{tr}[\Delta_{S_f}(S_f S_f^T - I)]$$

We first give the following lemma, where the proof can be found in the technical report of this paper [35].

LEMMA 1. *Function* $G(S_f, S_f^t) = \mathcal{J}(S_f^t) - 2AS_f^t(\log S_f - \log S_f^t) + 2B(\frac{S_f^2 + (S_f^t)^2}{2S_f^t} - S_f^t)$ *is an auxiliary function for* $\mathcal{J}$, *where* S_f^t *denotes the value of* S_f *derived from last iteration,* $A = X_p^T S_p H_p + X_u^T S_u H_u + \alpha S_{f0} + S_f^t \Delta_{S_f^t}^-$, *and* $B = S_f^t H_u^T S_u^T S_u H_u + S_f^t H_p^T S_p^T S_p H_p + \alpha S_f^t + S_f^t \Delta_{S_f^t}^+$.

With the auxiliary function $G(S_f, S_f^t)$, the minimum is achieved by setting $\frac{\partial G(S_f, S_f^t)}{\partial S_f} = 0$, which leads to

$$S_f^{t+1} \leftarrow S_f^t \circ \sqrt{\frac{X_u^T S_u H_u + X_p^T S_p H_p + \alpha S_{f0} + S_f^t \Delta_{S_f^t}^-}{S_f^t H_u^T S_u^T S_u H_u + S_f^t H_p^T S_p^T S_p H_p + \alpha S_f^t + S_f^t \Delta_{S_f^t}^+}}$$

This is identical to Eq. (7), which proves the correctness of the updating rule for S_f in Algorithm 1.

In addition, since $G(S_f, S_f^t)$ is an auxiliary function, $\mathcal{J}$ is non-increasing under this update rule and thus converges to local optimum [19].

Complexity Analysis. The running time for multiplying rectangular matrices (one $m \times p$-matrix with one $p \times n$-matrix), if performed naïvely, is $O(mnp)$. Therefore, the running time complexity of Algorithm 1 is $(rk(nl + ml + nm + m^2))$, where r is the total number of iterations, and n, m, l and k are described in Table 1. Note that both k and r are very small in our framework: k= 2 or 3 (positive, negative, and/or neutral), and r is around 10 to 100, which is also verified in our experiments. Furthermore, due to the sparsity of matrices and those fast matrix multiplication algorithms (e.g., two $n \times n$ matrix multiplication can be computed in $O(n^{2.3727})$), the exact computational cost can be much lower than the worst case theoretical result. For the space consumption, we need to store the four input matrices with complexity $O(nl + ml + nm + m^2)$.

4. ONLINE FRAMEWORK

We have introduced the offline Tri-clustering framework to handle static data. We now present our online framework, where the temporal data is coming in a streaming fashion. There are two naive ways to deal with temporal data: (1) applying the offline tri-clustering framework to the entire dataset whenever new data is added, or (2) applying tri-clustering only to new data independently at each time interval. The first approach gives high quality clustering but is too time-consuming, while the second one is efficient but leads to poor quality.

Table 2: Top-8 words with highest frequency.

Neg	corn (1463), farmer (1223), noprop37 (1211), crop (881) million (778), feed (380), India (380), seed (355)
Pos	yeson37 (23789), labelgmo (6485), monsanto (5809), stopmonsanto (1312), carighttoknow (1286), health (1094), safe (526), cancer (511)

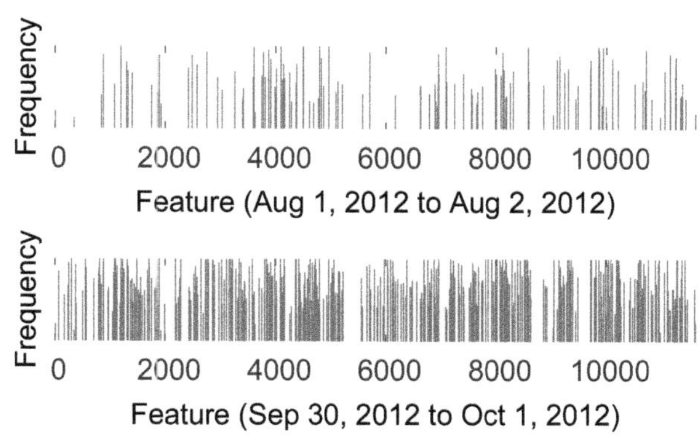

Figure 4: The evolution of features

Our online framework achieves a good tradeoff between the above two extremes and is able to study the evolution of sentiments. Before we present the online framework, we first introduce the following two observations: (1) The frequency distribution of vocabularies changes over time; however, the sentiments of vocabularies do not change or change slowly over time. (2) Considering the entire population, the majority of users rarely change their mind within a short time.

To verify Observation 1, we plot the frequency of vocabularies used by the same user in two different time periods in our dataset, as shown in Figure 4. We notice that there are significant differences between the distributions of features for these two time period (the same result can be found in other randomly selected users too). Then, we show the top-8 words with the highest frequency in each pos/neg class from our dataset, as listed in Table 2. And we found that the set of high-frequency words tend to be popular in the entire period of our data collection. In addition, their associated sentiments also do not change over time. Thus, this observation provides us the intuition to utilize the previous sentiment clustering results of features to improve the clustering quality of tweets/users.

Observation 2 has been shown in various existing works. For example, Smith et al [27] showed that the sentiments of users before election are highly correlated with the sentiments of users after election with Pearson correlated coefficient of 0.851. In addition, Deng et al. [7] reported that for several topics, two posts created by the same user have similar sentiments. This is understandable since information presented in the past sets up expectations for what the user expects in the future. This observation motivates us to improve the clustering quality of users based on their previous clustering results.

Thus, intuitively, for each emerging sub-collections of tweets at time t, the sentiment information can be naturally obtained through factorizing new data matrix $X_p(t)$, with reference to few previous sentiment clustering results of features according to Observation 1. In other words, instead of repeatedly accessing and analyzing the past data matrices $X_p(t-1), \cdots, X_p(1)$, we utilize intermediate sentiment clustering results of features obtained between time $[t - w, t)$, where w is the time window size, to achieve good results for tweet-level sentiment analysis at time t.

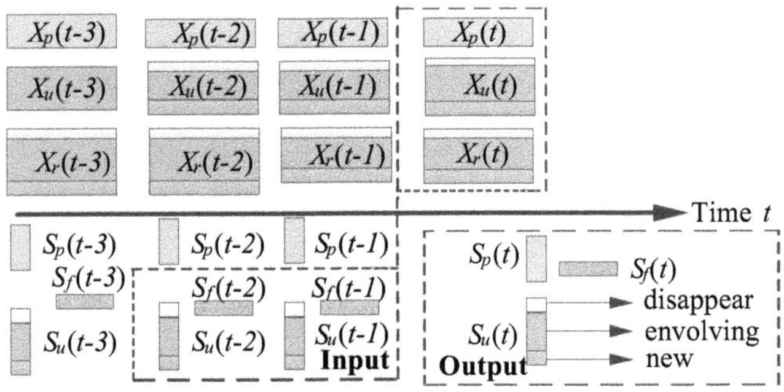

Figure 5: Online tri-clustering framework for dynamic sentiment clustering

Similarity, for each sub-collections of users at time t, we group users at time t into three categories: new users, disappeared users, and evolving users. For new users, we conduct sentiment analysis based on the current user and tweet information and past sentiment clustering results of features; while for evolving users, Observation 2 suggests that previous sentiment clustering results for these users are also very useful for current sentiment analysis.

Based on the above discussions, we design our online framework to make use of previous sentiment results for current sentiment analysis. Particularly, we adopt the temporal regularization technique to utilize the previous clustering results of both users and features, as suggested by the above two observations. We define the temporal regularization of a time-dependant matrix $M(t)$ to measure the smoothness of evolution as follows:

$$R(M(t)) = \sum_t ||M(t) - M_w(t)||_F^2 \tag{12}$$

where $M(t)$ denotes the matrix information at time t and $M_w(t)$ denotes the past information of matrix M within $[t-w, t)$. A larger value of Eq. (12) means less smoothness of evolution.

Now we address the unsolved question in Eq. (12), i.e., how to utilize the previous results for current sentiment analysis. $M_w(t)$ can be simply initialized as an aggregation of all the previous results within $[t-w,\ t)$. A natural modification is to give higher importance to more recent information. For example, sufficient results within $[t-w,\ t)$ are aggregated over time, and an exponential decay is used to forget out-of-date results. Thus, we define $S_{fw}(t)=\sum_{i=1}^{w-1}\tau^i S_f(t-i)$ and $S_{uw}(t)=\sum_{i=1}^{w-1}\tau^i S_f(t-i)$, where $\tau \in (0, 1]$ is the time-decaying factor.

The discussion above motivates the following objective function that is optimized at every time point t (Figure 5 depicts the overall online framework with w=2):

$$\begin{aligned}\arg \min_{\substack{S_f(t), S_u(t)\\ S_p(t), H_u(t),\\ H_p(t)\geq 0}} \{ & ||X_p(t) - S_p(t)H_p(t)S_f(t)^T||_F^2 \\ & + ||X_{u(e,n)}(t) - S_{u(e,n)}(t)H_u(t)S_f(t)^T||_F^2 \\ & + ||X_{r(e,n)}(t) - S_{u(e,n)}(t)S_p(t)^T||_F^2 \\ & + \alpha||S_f(t) - S_{fw}(t)||_F^2 \\ & + \beta \mathrm{tr}(S_u(t)^T L_u(t) S_u(t)) \\ & + \gamma||S_{u(d,e)}(t) - S_{uw}(t)||_F^2\} \\ \text{s.t. } & S_f(t)S_f(t)^T, S_p(t)S_p(t)^T, S_u(t)S_u(t)^T = I \end{aligned} \tag{13}$$

where $S_{u(d,e)}(t)$ denotes the sub matrix resulted by horizontally concatenating two blocks of users, α controls the contribution of temporal regularization for feature clustering, β weighs the temporal graph regularization, and γ controls the contribution of temporal regularization for user clustering.

4.1 Online Algorithm

We now present our online multiplicative update algorithm, which solves the objective function given by Eq. (13). Our algorithm is able to achieve the co-clustering for tweets, features, and users with one scan of the dataset, short response time and limited memory usage.

$\mathbf{H_u(t)}$, $\mathbf{H_p(t)}$, and New Tweets $\mathbf{S_p(t)}$. First, let us consider the updating rules for H_u and H_p. Since they are independent to the temporal regularization, we can naturally apply the same update rules in the offline framework to the subset data matrices at time t. Note that for simplicity, we just write $A(t)B(t)C(t)$ as $ABC(t)$.

$$H_u(t) \leftarrow H_u(t) \circ \sqrt{\frac{S^T_{u(e,n)} X_{u(e,n)} S_f}{S^T_{u(e,n)} S_{u(e,n)} H_u S_f^T S_f}(t)} \tag{14}$$

$$H_p(t) \leftarrow H_p(t) \circ \sqrt{\frac{S_p^T X_p S_f}{S_p^T S_p H_p S_f^T S_f}(t)} \tag{15}$$

Similarly, the tweet-level sentiments at current time, $S_p(t)$, can be updated using the following equation:

$$S_p(t) \leftarrow S_p(t) \circ \sqrt{\frac{X_p S_f H_p^T + X_r^T S_u + S_p \Delta^-_{S_p}}{S_p H_p S_f^T S_f H_p^T + S_p S_u^T S_u + S_p \Delta^+_{S_p}}(t)} \tag{16}$$

where $\Delta_{S_p} = S_p^T X_p S_f H_p^T(t) - H_p S_f^T S_f H_p^T(t) + S_p^T X_r^T S_u(t) - S_u^T S_u(t)$.

Evolving Features. According to Observation 1, temporal regularization is used to ensure a smooth evolution from $S_{fw}(t)$ to $S_f(t)$. Therefore, for the optimization of $S_f(t)$, we first need to pay attention to the computation of $S_{fw}(t)$, which is the time-decaying aggregation of previous sentiment clustering results of features. Thus, we derive the update rule for $S_f(t)$ as follows:

$$S_f(t) \leftarrow S_f(t) \circ \sqrt{\frac{X_u^T S_u H_u + X_p^T S_p H_p + \alpha S_{fw} + S_f \Delta^-_{S_f}}{S_f H_u^T S_u^T S_u H_u + S_f H_p^T S_p^T S_p H_p + \alpha S_f + S_f \Delta^+_{S_f}}(t)} \tag{17}$$

where $\Delta_{S_f}(t) = S_f(t)^T X_u(t)^T S_u(t) H_u(t) - H_u(t) S_u(t)^T S_u(t) H_u(t) + F(t)^T X_p(t)^T S_p(t) H_p(t) - H_p(t) S_p(t)^T S_p(t) H_p(t) - \alpha S_f(t)^T (S_f(t) - S_{fw}(t))$.

New Users. For a new user, we do not have the smooth constraint for temporal evolution, and the sentiment information $S_u(t)$ at time t can be obtained locally by factorizing the current data matrix $X_u(t)$ and $X_r(t)$. However, those new users might be connected to existing users through re-tweeting relations, and hence the optimization of $X_u(t)$ should be performed under the temporal graph regularization as well.

$$S_u(t) \leftarrow S_u(t) \circ \sqrt{\frac{X_u S_f H_u^T + X_r S_p + \beta G_u S_u + S_u \Delta^-_{S_{un}}}{S_u H_u S_f^T S_f H_u^T + S_u S_p^T S_p + \beta D_u S_u + S_u \Delta^+_{S_{un}}}(t)} \tag{18}$$

where $\Delta_{S_{un}}(t) = S_u(t)^T X_u(t) S_f(t) H_u(t)^T - H_u(t) S_f(t)^T S_f(t) H_u(t)^T + S_u(t)^T X_r(t) S_p(t) - S_p(t)^T S_p(t) - \beta S_u(t)^T L_u(t) S_u(t)$.

Evolving Users. The computation of $S_u(t)$ for evolving users is similar to the optimization for new users except that we also have the smooth constraint for evolution (i.e., the sentiment information

Algorithm 2 On-line algorithm for dynamic sentiment clustering

Input: New data $X_p(t)$, $X_r(t)$, $X_u(t)$, user-user re-tweeting graph $G_u(t)$, old clustering matrix $S_{fw}(t)$ and $S_{uw}(t)$, parameters: α, β, γ, w and τ
Output: $S_u(t)$, $S_p(t)$, $S_f(t)$, $H_u(t)$, and $H_p(t)$
1: initialize $S_f(t) = S_{fw}(t)$, $S_{u(d,e)}(t) = S_{uw}(t)$;
2: randomly initialize $S_p(t)$, $H_p(t)$, $H_u(t) \geq 0$;
3: **while** it does not converge:
4: update $S_f(t)$ according to Eq. (17);
5: update $S_p(t)$, $H_p(t)$ according to Eq. (16) and Eq. (15);
6: update $H_u(t)$ according to Eq. (14);
7: for new user: update according to Eq. (18);
8: for evolving user: update according to Eq. (19);
9: **return** $S_u(t)$, $S_p(t)$, $S_f(t)$;

of users $S_u(t)$ has a steady transmission from the past $S_{uw}(t)$), which leads to:

$$S_u(t) \leftarrow S_u(t) \circ \sqrt{\frac{X_u S_f H_u^T + X_r S_p + \gamma S_{uw}(t) + \beta G_u S_u + S_u \Delta^-_{S_{ue}}}{S_u H_u S_f^T S_f H_u^T + S_u S_p^T S_p + \gamma S_u + \beta D_u S_u + S_u \Delta^+_{S_{ue}}}(t)} \quad (19)$$

where $\Delta_{S_{ue}}(t) = S_u^T(t) X_u(t) S_f(t) H_u(t)^T - H_u(t) S_f(t)^T S_f(t) H_u(t)^T + S_u(t)^T X_r(t) S_p(t) - S_p(t)^T S_p(t) - \beta S_u(t)^T L_u(t) S_u(t) - \gamma S_u(t)^T (S_u(t) - S_{uw}(t))$.

Now we can present our on-line algorithm, as shown in Algorithm 2. The idea is similar to offline algorithm except that now we utilize the previous results for better initialization (line 1) and we have different update rules for $S_f(t)$ and $S_u(t)$ (Lines 4–8).

Correctness and Convergence Analysis. Although Eq. (13) contains the additional temporal regularization, Algorithm 2 still converges. We analyze the convergence by showing that Eq. (13) is non-increasing under the update step for evolving users $S_u(t)$ with temporal regularization. Specifically, let us use $\mathcal{J}$ to denote the part of the objective function in Eq. (13) that is related to S_u, then we show that the updating rule to S_u can be obtained by minimizing the following auxiliary function $G(S_u, S_u^t)$ for $\mathcal{J}(S_u)$. In addition, since $G(S_u, S_u^t)$ is an auxiliary function, $\mathcal{J}$ is non-increasing under this update rule and thus converges to local optimum.

LEMMA 2. *Function* $G(S_u, S_u^t) = \mathcal{J}(S_u^t) - 2AS_u^t(\log S_u - \log S_u^t) + 2B(\frac{S_u^2 + (S_u^t)^2}{2S_u^t} - S_u^t)$ *is an auxiliary function for* $\mathcal{J}(S_u)$, *where* $A = X_u S_f H_u^T + X_r S_p + \beta G_u S_u^t + S_u^t \Delta^-_{S_u^t} + \gamma S_{uw}^t$, *and* $B = S_u^t H_u S_f^T S_f H_u^T + S_u^t S_p^T S_p + \beta D_u S_u^t + S_u^t \Delta^+_{S_u^t} + \gamma S_u^t$.

The proof is given in the technical report of this paper [35].

Complexity Analysis. The computational complexity of Algorithm 2 is $O(rk(n(t)l + m(t)l + n(t)m(t) + m(t)^2))$ and the space complexity is $O(n(t)l + m(t)l + n(t)m(t) + m(t)^2 + lk + m(t-1)k)$, where $m(t)$ and $n(t)$ denote the number of new users and tweets at time t, respectively. We conclude that Algorithm 2 is efficient and requires little memory due to the small size of $n(t)$ and $m(t)$ on average, which is also verified in Figures 11(a) and 12(a) in our experiments.

5. EXPERIMENTS

We use real Twitter dataset about "California ballot initiatives" collected between August 2012 and December 2012 [27]. Specifically, we choose two popular ballot initiatives, Propositions 30 (Temporary Taxes to Fund Education) and 37 (Genetically Engineered Foods, Labeling), as the target topics, and test our proposed approaches over labeled data which is related to these two propositions. The statistics of labeled tweets and users are reported in Table 3 (note that not every user has label information). In addition, we use the automatically built sentiment lexicon "Yes" word lists and "No" word lists [27] to initialize the feature sentiment class matrix S_{f0}.

Table 3: Statistics of tweets and users

Prop	Tweet		User			
	Pos	Neg	Pos	Neg	Neu	unlabeled
30	8777	5014	146	100	98	493
37	34789	2587	294	61	8	1564

We quantitatively evaluate the performance of tri-clustering using the Normalized Mutual Information (NMI) and clustering accuracy to compare how well the discovered clusters reproduce the sentiment classes present in the data.

Clustering Accuracy. Given an outputted cluster $o \in C$ and with reference to a ground truth class $g \in G$, the clustering accuracy of the outputted clustering C on the ground truth clustering G evaluates the percentage of data with correct assignments.

$$A(C, G) = \frac{1}{n} \sum_{o \in C} \max_{g \in G} |o \cap g|$$

where n is the number of data samples.

Normalized Mutual Information (NMI). Given the outputted clustering C and ground truth clustering G, the NMI is defined as:

$$NMI(C, G) = \frac{2 \times I(C; G)}{H(C) + H(G)}$$

where $H(C)$ and $H(G)$ denotes the entropy, and $I(C; G)$ is the mutual information between C and G, which is defined as

$$I(C; G) = \frac{\sum_i \sum_j p(o_i \cap g_j) \log \frac{p(o_i \cap g_j)}{p(o_i) p(g_j)}}{\sum_i \sum_j \frac{|o_i \cap g_j|}{n} \log \frac{n |o_i \cap g_j|}{|o_i||g_j|}}$$

In our experiments, for NMI and clustering accuracy, we use the benchmark implementation from the work [3].

Existing Methods for Comparison. For tweet-level performance, we compare our offline tri-clustering approach with the state-of-the-art unsupervised method, ESSA [15], supervised methods, SVM [27] and Naïve Bayes (NB) [11], and semi-supervised methods, label propagation (LP) [12, 28] with 5% labels (LP-5) and 10% labels (LP-10) and UserReg [7] with 10% labels. ESSA has been shown in [15] to outperform a set of existing unsupervised approaches such as lexicon-based approach MPQA [32] and document-clustering approach ONMTF [9]. LP is a popular semi-supervised method, while UserReg is a very recent method and has been shown in [7] to outperform a set of existing semi-supervised approaches.

For user-level performance, we compare our approach with the recent unsupervised graph clustering method BACG [33, 34] which utilizes both structure (e.g., user-user graph) and content (e.g., feature representation for users) information, supervised methods SVM and Naïve Bayes, and semi-supervised methods LP [29] with 5% labels (LP-5) and 10% labels (LP-10) and UserReg with 10% labels. For BACG and LP, we built a user-user retweeting graph, where each node represents a user, and each edge denotes the user-user retweeting relation. We then apply BACG to this graph to obtain the clustering of users, and apply standard LP algorithm on this graph with partial labeled nodes to classify the unlabeled

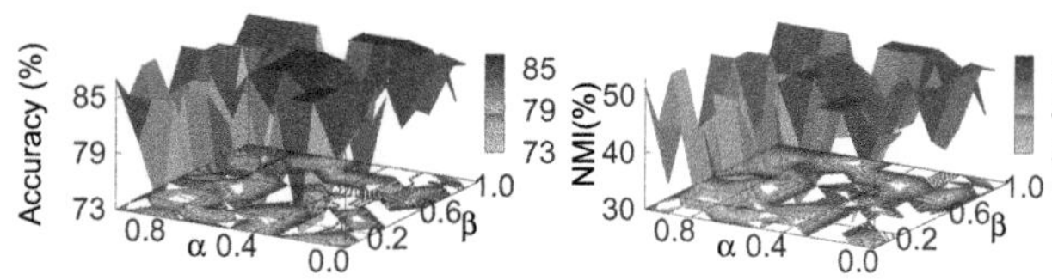

(a) Clustering accuracy (b) NMI

Figure 6: User-level quality comparison when varying α and β on Proposition 30 data (the figure is best viewed in color)

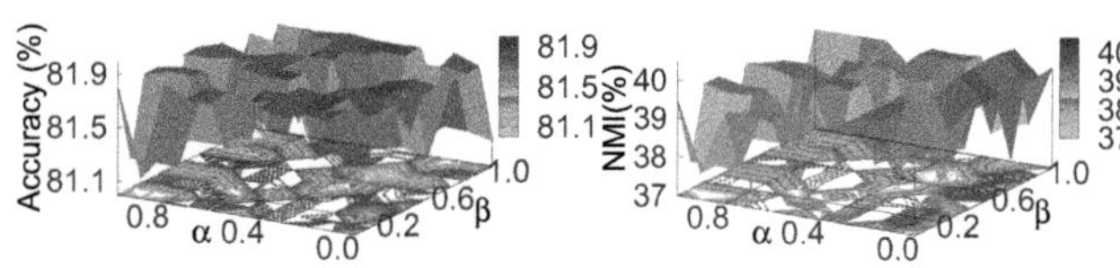

(a) Clustering accuracy (b) NMI

Figure 7: Tweet-level quality comparison when varying α and β on Proposition 30 data (the figure is best viewed in color)

nodes [29]. For UserReg, according to their paper, the sentiments of users are estimated by aggregating sentiments of related tweets [7].

For online framework, we compare our algorithm with two baseline algorithms, mini-batch and full-batch. The mini-batch algorithm, which applies our offline tri-clustering algorithm to each snapshot of new data matrices, can be considered as a simulation for the extreme design of online algorithm with high scalability but may sacrifice the quality. On the other hand, the full-batch algorithm, which applies the offline tri-clustering algorithm to the entire dataset whenever new data arrives at each timestamp, simulates another extreme with high quality but very time-consuming.

5.1 Offline Performance Evaluation

Varying Parameters. We first examine the effects of varying parameters on the performance of our approach. In the offline framework, we have two parameters, α and β, which control the contributions of feature lexicon information and the social relationship information, respectively. Since it is not clear whether these two parameters are independent or not, we vary these two parameters together, and then observe the change of both tweet-level and user-level performance.

Figure 6 compares the user-level performance of different parameters over the Proposition 30 dataset. First, we observe that the best accuracy (colored as dark blue in Figure 6) can be found within either α=0, $\beta = [0.5, 0.8]$, or $\alpha = [0.7, 1]$, $\beta = 1$; while the best NMI is achieved with parameters α=0, $\beta = [0.6, 0.9]$. Thus, the best parameters for user-level sentiment analysis can be set to α=0, $\beta = [0.5, 0.8]$. The combination indicates that lexicon-based regularization is inessential for user-level sentiment analysis, especially when it is compared to social relation-based graph regularization. Despite graph regularization is useful (e.g., when $\beta = [0.5, 0.8]$), heavy regularization (i.e., β=1) deteriorates the performance. The results verify our assumption that social relation is useful, but they cannot replace the roles of latent feature vectors (e.g, tf-idf term vector representation) and user-tweet relations.

Now let us turn our attention to the relation between tweet-level quality and parameters. We want to answer the following two questions: whether the best combination of parameters (α=0.0, β=[0.5, 0.8]) still holds, and whether the two regularizations are also needed for tweet-level analysis. Figure 7 depicts the tweet-level sentiment results. When α=0.1, β=0.9, tri-clustering obtains the best accuracy for Proposition 30; while α=0.1, β=0.8, it achieves the best performance in terms of NMI. Thus, we suggest that a combination of parameters (α=0.1, β=[0.8, 0.9]) might be a good choice. This differs from user-level sentiment analysis in that it prefers light lexicon-based regularization to no regularization (α=0). Another difference is that tweet-level sentiment analysis is less sensitive to parameters than user-level sentiment analysis. When varying parameters, the tweet-level accuracy only varies between 81% and 82%, while the user-level accuracy changes from 73% and 85%.

We also conducted this set of experiments with varying parameters on another topic Proposition 37 dataset, and we observed similar results and hence omit the details here due to space limit. Moreover, in order to balance between the tweet-level performance and user-level performance, in all the following offline experiments, we set α=0.05, β=0.8.

Convergence Analysis. Figure 8 examines how fast our algorithm converges. When the number of iterations is around 10, our algorithm tends to converge in terms of total error of Eq. (1). However, if we look at each single component, after 10 iterations, first the algorithm minimizes the loss for Eq. (3) at the cost of increasing the error of Eq. (2), and then vice versa. This is because our objective is to minimize all components (including regularization and co-factorization), instead of each single equation. Thus, the algorithm searches among each local optimum of the five components and finally finds the global balancing point.

Comparison with Existing Methods. Table 4 reports the tweet-level accuracy and NMI values of different methods. Although our tri-clustering method is worse than the supervised methods SVM and NB, it does not require any labeling, while the performance of a supervised method is highly related to the quality and sufficiency of labeled data. Compared with semi-supervised methods, our method is much better than LP with 5% labels (i.e., LP-5), and better than or comparable with LP with 10% labels (i.e., LP-10). Considering another state-of-the-art semi-supervised method UserReg, tri-clustering is worse than UserReg with 10% labels (i.e., UserReg-10) on dataset Prop 30 but better than UserReg-10 on dataset Prop 37. These results support our claim that tri-clustering has an advantage over supervised and semi-supervised methods when labeled data are either insufficient or with poor quality. In another unsupervised method ESSA, two virtual tweet-tweet graph and feature-feature graph are built to improve the tweet-level accuracy. Specifically, two tweets or features are linked if they are similar to each other. The computation of tweet-tweet graph and feature-feature graph is very time consuming. Comparing our method with ESSA, our method focuses more on user-level accuracy and does not require the tweet-tweet graph and feature-feature graph, but the results show that our method is consistently better than ESSA in terms of both clustering accuracy and NMI values.

We also report the user-level performance comparison in Table 5. The clustering accuracy of tri-clustering is very close to the supervised methods SVM and NB. Compared with the semi-supervised methods, our method is significantly better than LP-10 and even outperforms UserReg-10. The better performance over UserReg-10 also indicates that the estimation of users' sentiments by aggregating over tweet-level sentiments is biased. Finally, our method

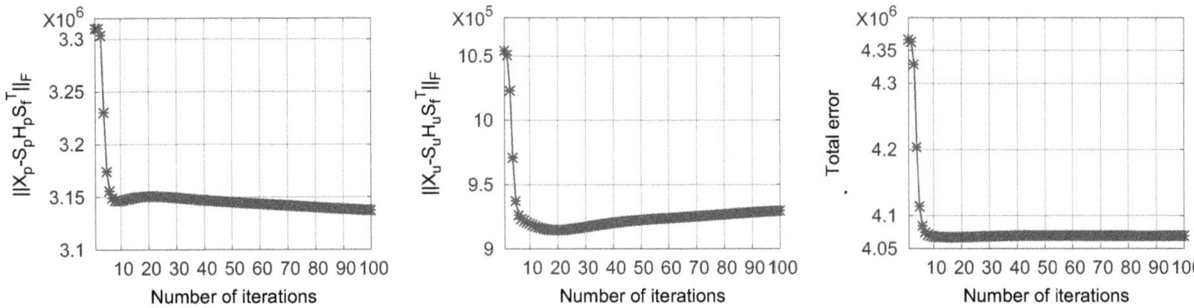

(a) Average loss for Eq. (2) (b) Average loss for Eq. (3) (c) Average loss for Eq. (1)

Figure 8: The average Frobenius loss of tweet-feature matrix approximation, user-feature matrix approximation and the objective function of tri-clustering on the Proposition 30 datasets

Table 4: Tweet-level sentiment analysis comparison

Metric	Accuracy		NMI	
Prop	30	37	30	37
Supervised				
SVM [27]	89.35	93.17	–	–
NB [11]	85.75	89.22		
Semi-supervised				
LP-5 [12, 28]	77.20	87.49	–	–
LP-10 [12, 28]	86.60	88.20	–	–
UserReg-10 [7]	86.76	90.08	–	–
Unsupervised				
ESSA [15]	81.69	85.87	38.71	15.88
Tri-clustering	81.87	92.15	40.24	18.93
Online tri-clustering	91.88	92.24	67.73	29.85

Table 5: User-level sentiment analysis comparison

Metric	Accuracy		NMI	
Prop	30	37	30	37
Supervised				
SVM [27]	89.81	87.84	–	–
NB [11]	88.69	83.8		
Semi-supervised				
LP-5 [29]	31.77	82.05	–	–
LP-10 [29]	77.45	84.25	–	–
UserReg-10 [7]	82.10	84.28	–	–
Unsupervised				
BACG [33]	75.37	70.51	33.70	53.70
Tri-clustering	86.88	86.17	52.47	71.98
Online tri-clustering	89.22	88.48	53.89	73.48

is also significantly better than another unsupervised clustering approach BACG which also incorporates both user-user relations and feature vector representation of users.

5.2 Online Performance Evaluation

Varying Parameters. We first evaluate the effects of varying the different parameters α, β, γ, τ, and time window size w, on the online performance of our algorithm. We notice that time window size w is related to the granularity of timestamp. For example, using each second as the unit of timestamp naturally leads to larger w than using each day as the unit. Consider the real scenario, in our experiments, we set the unit of timestamp as per day, and set

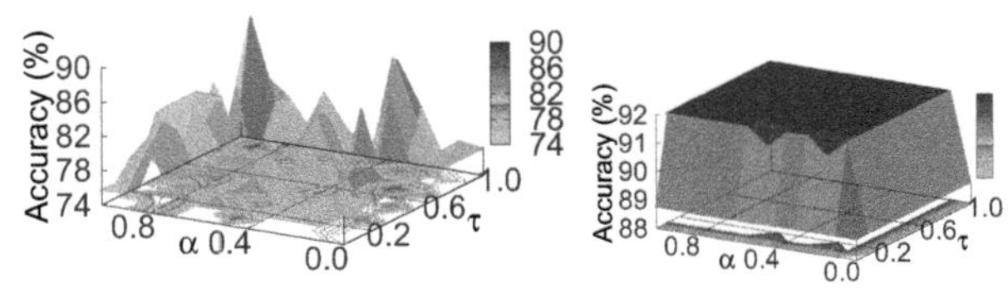

(a) User-level (b) Tweet-level

Figure 9: Clustering accuracy when varying α and τ on Proposition 30 data (the figure is best viewed in color)

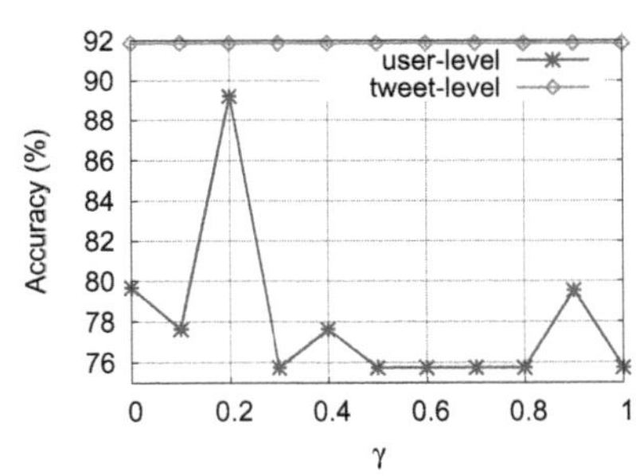

Figure 10: Clustering accuracy when varying γ for Proposition 30 data

$w = 2$. We still set β=0.8, the same as the offline experiments but we need to change α since now it is related to parameter τ as well. Therefore, we first evaluate the performance when varying both α and τ. The user-level accuracy and tweet-level accuracy are reported in Figure 9. In terms of user-level accuracy, it obtains the highest value when both α and τ are set to 0.9. In terms of tweet-level accuracy, similar to the offine experiments, it is much less sensitive unless both α and τ are greater than zero. We do not report the results of NMI values since we can draw similar conclusion as that from the accuracy values. Thus, we set α and τ as 0.9 for the online experiments.

The last step is to evaluate the effect of parameter γ when all of the other parameters are fixed. The results are shown in Figure 10. Clearly, the best result is obtained when γ=0.2. Meanwhile, parameter γ does not have any effect on the tweet-level accuracy. This is

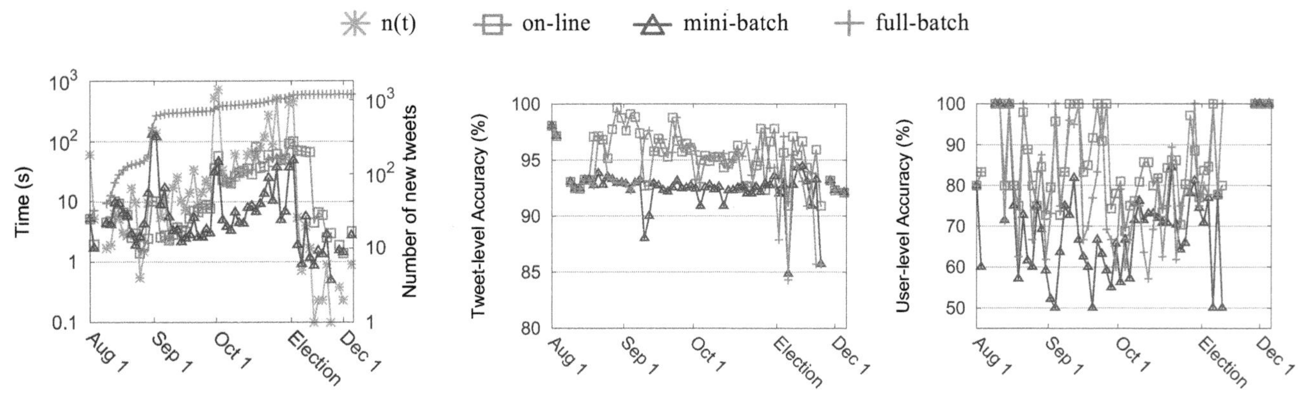

(a) Total running time (b) Tweet-level accuracy (c) User-level accuracy

Figure 11: Online performance results for Proposition 30 data (the figure is best viewed in color)

because γ controls the smooth evolution of user-level sentiment, which is relatively independent with the tweet-level sentiment.

The results on another topic Proposition 37 dataset are similar and hence omit the details here due to space limit.

Comparison with the Offline Algorithm. The last two rows of both Table 4 and Table 5 show that the online algorithm obtains much higher accuracy than the offline algorithm for both tweet-level and user-level performance, and sometimes even outperforms the supervised methods. This is not surprising since in the online framework, we have considered the evolution of latent feature vectors while in the offline framework, it simply assumes that the features are static. However, in real life, people may tend to use different vocabularies in different time period. Thus, our online algorithm, which subsumes the evolution of latent feature vectors, outperforms the offline algorithm in terms of clustering accuracy.

Performance Comparison of Online Algorithms. We also compare our online algorithm with the two baseline algorithms, mini-batch and full-batch, on both the Proposition 30 and Proposition 37 datasets. The results are reported in Figures 11 and 12. First, we verify whether our online algorithm is as efficient as the theoretical time complexity analysis. Figure 11(a) and Figure 12(a) plot the running time of the three algorithms. Note that the left y-axis represents the running time, and the right y-axis denotes the number of new tweets, $n(t)$, for each timestamp t. For Proposition 30, our online algorithm is much faster than the full-batch algorithm but slower than the mini-batch algorithm. This is because our online algorithm needs additional cost to access the previous clustering results (i.e., $S_{fw}(t)$, $S_u(t-1)$) and compute the temporal regularization. However, when they are tested on Proposition 37 data, the online algorithm is comparable to the mini-batch algorithm. The difference in performance for the different datasets is caused by the variation on the average number of new tweets per day (i.e., $n(t)$) between Proposition 30 and Proposition 37. Based on Figure 11(a) and Figure 12(a), we notice that the average number of new tweets per day on Proposition 37 is much larger than Proposition 30; and thus the cost to access the data matrices $X_p(t)$, $X_u(t)$ and $X_r(t)$ dominate the incurred overhead by the matrices $S_{fw}(t)$ and $S_u(t-1)$. When $n(t)$ is small such as on Proposition 30, though our online algorithm is slower than the mini-batch algorithm, it is less sensitive to the bursty of tweets than the mini-batch algorithm. For example, around Sep 1, there is a sudden rise in the volume of tweets and our online algorithm is much more efficient than the mini-batch algorithm due to its advantage in utilizing the previous clustering results.

Figures 11(b) and 12(b) compare the tweet-level accuracy of the three algorithms. The mini-batch algorithm, which is very efficient since it only needs to access a small set of newly arrived data at each timestamp, obtains the lowest accuracy. Our online algorithm, achieves an accuracy as good as the expensive full-batch algorithm on proposition 30 data and even outperforms the full-batch algorithm on proposition 37.

The user-level performance comparison on Proposition 30 and 37 is reported in Figures 11(c) and 12(c). The results are similar to the tweet-level accuracy, which show that our online algorithm is comparable to the full-batch algorithm, and both of them are significantly better than the mini-batch algorithm.

To conclude, the results verify that our online algorithm achieves a good trade-off between efficiency and clustering quality.

6. RELATED WORKS

We first discuss related work on sentiment analysis. We also discuss some related work on non-negative matrix factorization.

6.1 Sentiment Analysis

We summarize a set of representative (but by no means exhaustive) methods to sentiment analysis in Table 6, where we group existing approaches into three directions. First, we consider whether a method aims to identify positive or negative sentiment in a piece of text (tweet-level analysis) or to determine the sentiments of users (user-level analysis). A large amount of research in the area of sentiment analysis has focused on classifying text polarity [23, 2, 11, 6, 31, 14, 28, 24, 15, 36]. Smith et al. [27] and Deng et al. [7] analyzed the sentiments of users by aggregating the sentiments of their tweets. Tan et al. [29] directly analyzed the sentiments of users using a semi-supervised approach. Specifically, a semi-supervised label propagation algorithm is utilized to determine the sentiment of a user by the sentiments of his/her tweets and the sentiments of his/her immediate neighbor users in a heterogeneous graph built upon social relations. However, with insufficient labeled nodes or the labeled nodes are densely condensed in a small region of the entire graph, the performance of this approach is not encouraging. Another issue is that Smith et al. [27] have pointed out that the emotion correlation among users and following or @mention users (which are used in [29] to build heterogeneous graph), is relatively lower than users and re-tweeting users. Kim et al. [17] utilized the

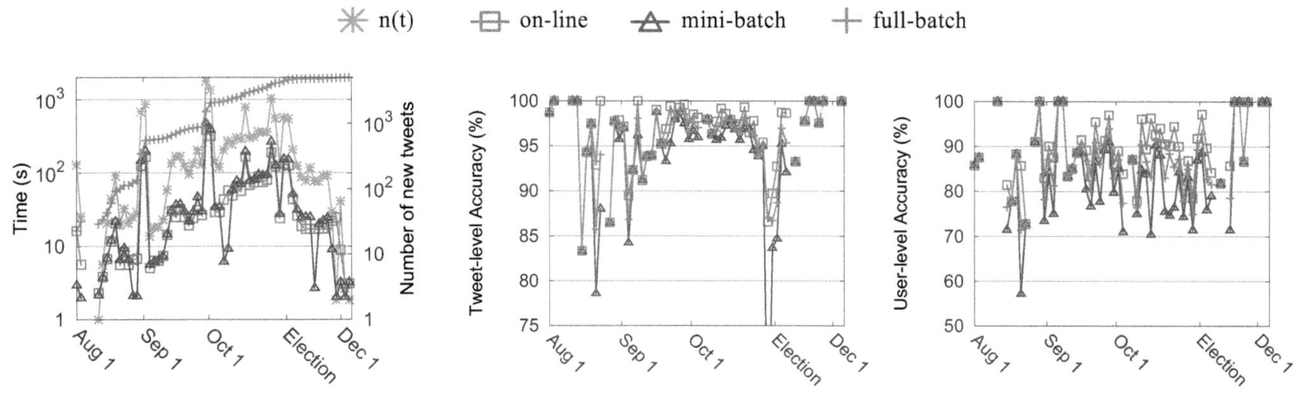

(a) Total running time (b) Tweet-level accuracy (c) User-level accuracy

Figure 12: Online performance results for Proposition 37 data (the figure is best viewed in color)

Table 6: Methods for sentiment analysis

methods	[2, 6] [11, 25] [31, 21]	[12] [28]	[27]	[17] [29]	[7]	[5] [24]	[14] [15]	this work
tweet	√	√	√		√	√	√	√
user			√	√	√			√
SL	√		√					
USL						√	√	√
SSL		√		√	√			
dynamic						√		√

collaborative filtering techniques to analyze the sentiments of users based on the sentiments of similar users. The similarity of two users are evaluated by whether they have expressed similar sentiments towards the same set of topics. This approach totally ignored the rich information of tweets and features, as well as social relationship such as user-user re-tweeting relation. Instead, in this work, we propose a tri-clustering framework, to obtain the sentiment clustering of both tweets and users simultaneously. Our approach utilizes the re-tweeting social relation and dependencies among users, tweets, and features, and is independent with the quality of labeled data.

Second, we focus on the requirement of labeled data by different methods. Many existing approaches [2, 11, 6, 31, 23, 27] are based on supervised learning (SL), where, give some labeled data, one trains and applies a standard classifiers to extract sentiment. Graph-based semi-supervised learning (SSL) algorithms, have been applied to the problem of sentiment analysis [12, 28, 29, 7], assuming that similar texts/users receive similar sentiment labels. Unfortunately, the above approaches either use some forms of linguistic processing [2, 6] or rely on large amounts of training data [11, 21, 27], both of which heavily involve the inputs from humans[1]. In contrast to previous approaches, unsupervised learning (USL) approaches, which do not require any labeling or input from human, are inadequately studied. Some approaches[14, 24] used linguistic models or some other form of knowledge to categorize the sentiment of documents. A more recent approach ESSA [15] studied the problem of unsupervised sentiment analysis with emotional signals. In this work, we establish the duality between sentiment clustering and co-clustering of a tripartite graph with the unified tri-clustering framework, which belongs to the category of unsupervised methods.

Finally, we focus on the ability of different methods to perform dynamic sentiment analysis. Most of the existing approaches discussed above either just perform static sentiment analysis or simply report how the number of positive/negative tweets are changing over time [5, 24]. Instead, our framework is able to identify the evolution of both features and sentiments of users, which distinguishes our work from existing sentiment analysis works.

[1]Human labeling is very difficult even with the help of Crowdsourcing.

6.2 Non-negative Matrix Factorization

Due to its wide application in various areas such as text mining [37, 15], pattern recognition [3], machine learning [13, 22] and bioinformatics [8], nonnegative matrix factorization (NMF) has attracted much interest from researchers. Generally, nonnegative matrix factorization aims to factor a matrix X, into two [19, 3] (or three [9, 37, 15]) lower-dimension matrices and minimizes the square error/divergence between X and the approximation of X using those lower-dimension matrices. There are several algorithms that are proposed to find the sub-optimal solution of those lower-dimension matrices, for instance, Lee and Seung [19] proposed two different multiplicative algorithms to update the matrices. Other more recent approaches include using the projected gradient descent methods [20], the active-set method and the block principal pivoting [16] to update the matrices. If one of the factors (lower dimension matrices) satisfies the separability condition, Arora et al. [1] also proposed a polynomial-time algorithm to find the exact NMF solution.

In this work, we explored the feasibility of applying NMF to Twitter sentiment analysis domain. We further developed an online framework with several temporal and graph regularization for both user-level and tweet-level sentiment analysis. Both our online objective function and optimization algorithm are different from the existing online NMF algorithms [4, 30, 26].

7. CONCLUSIONS

We studied both user-level and tweet-level dynamic sentiment analysis on social media data. We proposed a novel tri-clustering framework, making use of mutual dependency among features, tweets and users. We developed an analytical algorithm with fast convergence to solve the proposed objective function in the offline tri-clustering framework. We further investigated how the proposed framework can be extended to online setting by considering the dynamic evolution of features and sentiments of users. We proposed an online algorithm, which is efficient in terms of both running time and storage size, to achieve a good clustering for both tweets and users in a dynamic setting. We also extensively evaluated our algorithms on real Twitter data about November 2012 California ballot initiatives.

For future work, we consider to propose a unified tripartite graph co-clustering framework, with a set of optional regularizations which include graph regularization, sparsity regularization, diversity regularization, temporal regularization, and guided regularization (semi-supervised regularization). This framework can be applied to many different domains such as community detection, transfer learning and node role mining, without the restriction to only sentiment analysis.

Acknowledgment

We thank Xia Hu for providing the implementation of ESSA [15]. This research was supported in part by DARPA grant No. W911NF–12–1–0034.

8. REFERENCES

[1] S. Arora, R. Ge, R. Kannan, and A. Moitra. Computing a nonnegative matrix factorization – provably. In *STOC Conference*, pages 145–162. ACM, 2012.

[2] L. Barbosa and J. Feng. Robust sentiment detection on twitter from biased and noisy data. In *COLING Conference*, pages 36–44. Association for Computational Linguistics, 2010.

[3] D. Cai, X. He, J. Han, and T. S. Huang. Graph regularized nonnegative matrix factorization for data representation. *IEEE Trans. Pattern Anal. Mach. Intell.*, 33(8):1548–1560, 2011.

[4] B. Cao, D. Shen, J.-T. Sun, X. Wang, Q. Yang, and Z. Chen. Detect and track latent factors with online nonnegative matrix factorization. In *IJCAI Conference*, pages 2689–2694. Morgan Kaufmann Publishers Inc., 2007.

[5] M. Castellanos, U. Dayal, M. Hsu, R. Ghosh, M. Dekhil, Y. Lu, L. Zhang, and M. Schreiman. Lci: a social channel analysis platform for live customer intelligence. In *SIGMOD Conference*, pages 1049–1058, New York, NY, USA, 2011. ACM.

[6] D. Davidov, O. Tsur, and A. Rappoport. Enhanced sentiment learning using twitter hashtags and smileys. In *COLING Conference*, pages 241–249, Stroudsburg, PA, USA, 2010. Association for Computational Linguistics.

[7] H. Deng, J. Han, H. Ji, H. Li, Y. Lu, and H. Wang. Exploring and inferring user-user pseudo-friendship for sentiment analysis with heterogeneous networks. In *SDM*, pages 378–386. SIAM, 2013.

[8] K. Devarajan. Nonnegative matrix factorization: an analytical and interpretive tool in computational biology. *PLoS Comput Biol*, 4(7):e1000029, 2008.

[9] C. Ding, T. Li, W. Peng, and H. Park. Orthogonal nonnegative matrix t-factorizations for clustering. In *SIGKDD Conference*, pages 126–135. ACM, 2006.

[10] B. Gao, T.-Y. Liu, X. Zheng, Q.-S. Cheng, and W.-Y. Ma. Consistent bipartite graph co-partitioning for star-structured high-order heterogeneous data co-clustering. In *SIGKDD Conference*, pages 41–50. ACM, 2005.

[11] A. Go, R. Bhayani, and L. Huang. Twitter sentiment classification using distant supervision. *Technical report*, pages 1–6, 2009.

[12] A. B. Goldberg and X. Zhu. Seeing stars when there aren't many stars: Graph-based semi-supervised learning for sentiment categorization. In *TextGraphs WorkShop*, pages 45–52. Association for Computational Linguistics, 2006.

[13] Q. Gu and J. Zhou. Co-clustering on manifolds. In *SIGKDD Conference*, pages 359–368. ACM, 2009.

[14] V. Hatzivassiloglou and K. R. McKeown. Predicting the semantic orientation of adjectives. In *COLING/EACL Conference*, pages 174–181, Morristown, NJ, USA, 1997. Association for Computational Linguistics.

[15] X. Hu, J. Tang, H. Gao, and H. Liu. Unsupervised sentiment analysis with emotional signals. In *World Wide Web Conference*. ACM, 2013.

[16] J. Kim and H. Park. Fast nonnegative matrix factorization: An active-set-like method and comparisons. *SIAM J. Sci. Comput.*, 33(6):3261–3281, 2011.

[17] J. Kim, J. Yoo, H. Lim, H. Qiu, Z. Kozareva, and A. Galstyan. Sentiment prediction using collaborative filtering. In *ICWSM'13*, 2013.

[18] H. W. Kuhn and A. W. Tucker. Nonlinear programming. In *Proceedings of the 2nd Berkeley Symposium on Mathematical Statistics and Probability*, pages 481–492. University of California Press, Berkeley, CA, USA, 1950.

[19] D. D. Lee and H. S. Seung. Algorithms for non-negative matrix factorization. In *NIPS Conference*, pages 556–562. MIT Press, 2000.

[20] C.-J. Lin. Projected gradient methods for nonnegative matrix factorization. *Neural Comput.*, 19(10):2756–2779, 2007.

[21] J. Lin and A. Kolcz. Large-scale machine learning at twitter. In *SIGMOD Conference*, pages 793–804. ACM, 2012.

[22] M. Long, J. Wang, G. Ding, D. Shen, and Q. Yang. Transfer learning with graph co-regularization. In *AAAI Conference*, 2012.

[23] P. Melville, W. Gryc, and R. D. Lawrence. Sentiment analysis of blogs by combining lexical knowledge with text classification. In *SIGKDD Conference*, pages 1275–1284, New York, NY, USA, 2009. ACM.

[24] L. T. Nguyen, P. Wu, W. Chan, W. Peng, and Y. Zhang. Predicting collective sentiment dynamics from time-series social media. In *WSDM Workshop*, pages 6:1–6:8. ACM, 2012.

[25] B. Pang, L. Lee, and S. Vaithyanathan. Thumbs up?: sentiment classification using machine learning techniques. In *EMNLP Conference*, pages 79–86, Stroudsburg, PA, USA, 2002. Association for Computational Linguistics.

[26] A. Saha and V. Sindhwani. Learning evolving and emerging topics in social media: a dynamic nmf approach with temporal regularization. In *WSDM Conference*, pages 693–702. ACM, 2012.

[27] L. Smith, L. Zhu, K. Lerman, and Z. Kozareva. The role of social media in the discussion of controversial topics. In *SocialCom/PASSAT Conference*, 2013.

[28] M. Speriosu, N. Sudan, S. Upadhyay, and J. Baldridge. Twitter polarity classification with label propagation over lexical links and the follower graph. In *Workshop on Unsupervised Learning in NLP*, pages 53–63. Association for Computational Linguistics, 2011.

[29] C. Tan, L. Lee, J. Tang, L. Jiang, M. Zhou, and P. Li. User-level sentiment analysis incorporating social networks. In *SIGKDD Conference*, pages 1397–1405, New York, NY, USA, 2011. ACM.

[30] F. Wang, P. Li, and A. C. Knig. Efficient document clustering via online nonnegative matrix factorizations. In *SDM Conference*, pages 908–919, 2011.

[31] X. Wang, F. Wei, X. Liu, M. Zhou, and M. Zhang. Topic sentiment analysis in twitter: a graph-based hashtag sentiment classification approach. In *CIKM Conference*, pages 1031–1040, New York, NY, USA, 2011. ACM.

[32] T. Wilson, J. Wiebe, and P. Hoffmann. Recognizing contextual polarity in phrase-level sentiment analysis. In *HLT/EMNLP Conference*, pages 347–354. Association for Computational Linguistics, 2005.

[33] Z. Xu, Y. Ke, Y. Wang, H. Cheng, and J. Cheng. A model-based approach to attributed graph clustering. In *SIGMOD Conference*, pages 505–516, 2012.

[34] Z. Xu, Y. Ke, Y. Wang, H. Cheng, and J. Cheng. Gbagc: A general bayesian framework for attributed graph clustering. *To appear in TKDD*, 2014.

[35] L. Zhu, A. Galstyan, J. Cheng, and K. Lerman. Tripartite graph clustering for dynamic sentiment analysis on social media. *Technical Report (arXiv:1402.6010v2 [cs.SI])*, 2014.

[36] L. Zhu, S. Gao, S. J. Pan, H. Li, D. Deng, and C. Shahabi. Graph-based informative-sentence selection for opinion summarization. In *ASONAM Conference*, pages 408–412, 2013.

[37] F. Zhuang, P. Luo, H. Xiong, Q. He, Y. Xiong, and Z. Shi. Exploiting associations between word clusters and document classes for cross-domain text categorization. *Stat. Anal. Data Min.*, 4(1):100–114, 2011.

A Temporal Context-Aware Model for User Behavior Modeling in Social Media Systems

Hongzhi Yin[†] Bin Cui[†] Ling Chen[‡] Zhiting Hu[†] Zi Huang[§]
[†]Key Lab of High Confidence Software Technologies (MOE), School of EECS, Peking University
[‡]QCIS, University of Technology, Sydney
[§]School of Information Technology Electrical Engineering, University of Queensland
[†]{bestzhi, bin.cui, huzhiting}@pku.edu.cn [‡]ling.chen@uts.edu.au [§]huang@itee.uq.edu.au

ABSTRACT

Social media provides valuable resources to analyze user behaviors and capture user preferences. This paper focuses on analyzing user behaviors in social media systems and designing a latent class statistical mixture model, named *temporal context-aware mixture model* (TCAM), to account for the intentions and preferences behind user behaviors. Based on the observation that the behaviors of a user in social media systems are generally influenced by *intrinsic interest* as well as the *temporal context* (e.g., the public's attention at that time), TCAM simultaneously models the topics related to users' intrinsic interests and the topics related to temporal context and then combines the influences from the two factors to model user behaviors in a unified way. To further improve the performance of TCAM, an item-weighting scheme is proposed to enable TCAM to favor items that better represent topics related to user interests and topics related to temporal context, respectively. Based on TCAM, we design an efficient query processing technique to support fast online recommendation for large social media data. Extensive experiments have been conducted to evaluate the performance of TCAM on four real-world datasets crawled from different social media sites. The experimental results demonstrate the superiority of the TCAM models, compared with the state-of-the-art competitor methods, by modeling user behaviors more precisely and making more effective and efficient recommendations.

Categories and Subject Descriptors

H.3.3 [**Information Search and Retrieval**]: Information filtering; H.2.8 [**Database Applications**]: Data mining

Keywords

User Behavior Modeling; Temporal Recommender system; Probabilistic generative model; Social Media Mining

1. INTRODUCTION

With the rising popularity of social media, a better understanding of users' rating behaviors[1] is of great importance for the design of many applications, such as personalized recommendation, information filtering, behavioral targeting and computational advertising. Research efforts [21, 24] have been undertaken to model users' interests to help them find interesting items by analyzing their historical behaviors. However, existing work [21, 24, 27] simply assumes that users prefer items based on their intrinsic interests, which may not be accurate in many social application scenarios. For example, when choosing a book to read or a movie to watch, the users are likely to prefer books/movies that interest them. In contrast, when selecting news to read or users to follow in a social network (e.g., Twitter), it is most likely that users will be attracted respectively by breaking news or famous users who are followed by the general public [30, 18, 5]. Therefore, users' rating behaviors on items may not necessarily indicate users' intrinsic interests. New models are desired to better account for user behaviors in social medias to learn user preferences more precisely.

After investigating multiple social media systems, we observe that user rating behaviors are generally influenced by two factors: *the intrinsic interest of the user* and *the attention of the general public*. While the user's intrinsic interest is relatively stable, the attention of the general public changes from time to time; for example, the hot topics on a microblogging site evolve over time. Hence, in our work, we refer to the attention of the public during a particular time period as *temporal context*.

The two factors have different degrees of influence on user rating behaviors for different types of social media platforms as a result of the different characteristics (e.g., life cycles and updating rates) of various types of social media items. For instance, news is a type of time-sensitive item with a short life cycle – few people want to read outdated news; while the life cycle of movies is relatively longer, with many classic old movies being highly ranked in the popularity list. For time-sensitive social media items, users are more easily influenced by the temporal context, whereas they tend to make decisions based on their intrinsic interests when choosing less time-sensitive items such as books and movies.

To model user rating behaviors in social media systems, therefore, it is critical to identify users' intrinsic interests as well as the temporal context (i.e., the attention of the general public during a particular time period). Moreover, it is essential to model the influence degrees of the two factors in different social media systems.

To this end, we propose a temporal context-aware mixture model (TCAM) to mimic user rating behaviors in a process of decision making. As shown in Figure 1, TCAM is a latent class statistical mixture model that simultaneously models the topics [13, 3] related to users' intrinsic interests and the topics related to temporal context, and then combines the influences from the user interest and the temporal context to model user behaviors in a unified manner. Specifically, the model discovers (1) users' personal interest distri-

[1]We use the term "rating behavior" to denote general user actions on items in social media systems, such as rating and viewing.

SIGMOD/PODS'14, June 22–27, 2014, Snowbird, UT, USA.
Copyright 2014 ACM 978-1-4503-2376-5/14/06 ...$15.00.
http://dx.doi.org/10.1145/2588555.2593685.

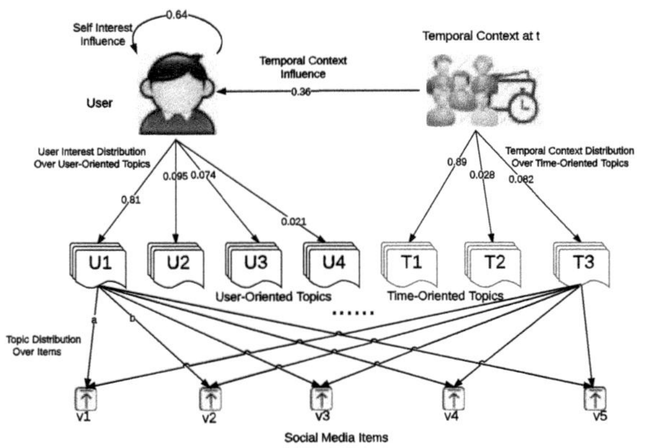

Figure 1: An Example of TCAM Model

bution over a set of latent topics; (2) the temporal context distribution over a set of latent topics; (3) an item generative distribution for each latent topic; and (4) the mixing weights that represent the influence probabilities of users' personal interest and the temporal context. It is worth mentioning that the set of latent topics used to model user interest is different from the topics used to model the temporal context. The former are called *user-oriented topics* and the latter are referred to as *time-oriented topics*.

The generative process of user rating behaviors in TCAM is briefly illustrated as follows. Suppose a user u selects an item v in a time interval t. TCAM first tosses a coin, based on the influence probabilities of the two factors, to decide whether this behavior results from the influence of the user's personal interest or the influence of the temporal context. If it results from the influence of the user's personal interest, TCAM chooses a *user-oriented topic* for u based on the user's intrinsic interest (with a certain probability). The selected topic in turn generates an item v following on from the topic's item generative distribution. Otherwise, if the influence from the temporal context is sampled, TCAM chooses a *time-oriented topic* according to the general public's interest during t, which in turn generates an item v.

Similar to traditional topic models where popular words in a document corpus are usually ranked high in each topic [5, 4], popular social media items tend to be estimated as having high generation probability by TCAM, which impairs the quality of the discovered user-oriented topics and time-oriented topics. User-oriented topics are supposed to capture user intrinsic interests, but a popular item favored by many users conveys less information about a user's intrinsic interest than an item favored by few users (i.e., a salient item) [32]. Similarly, a popular item constantly favored by users cannot well represent a time-oriented topic because the public's attentions change over time. Hence, to improve the performance of TCAM, we devise an item-weighting scheme to promote the importance of salient items and bursty items, which enhances the quality of the underlying topics detected by TCAM.

To demonstrate the applicability of our proposed TCAM model, we investigate how TCAM can be deployed to facilitate temporal recommendation in social media systems, i.e., making recommendations based on not only user interests but also temporal context. To speed up the process of online recommendation for large social media data, we design an efficient query-processing technique by extending the Threshold Algorithm (TA) [10]. Briefly, we precompute K sorted lists of items according to the K latent topics learned by TCAM. In each list, items are sorted based on their generative probabilities with respect to the corresponding topic. At query time, we access items from the K sorted lists and compute top-k items by extending the TA algorithm. The algorithm has the nice property of terminating early without scanning all items. Specifically, it terminates when the ranking score of the k-th item in the result list is higher than the threshold score. This TA-based scheme allows us to efficiently return the top-k recommendations by examining the minimum number of items.

The main contributions of our work are summarized as follows.

- We design a novel temporal context-aware mixture model (TCAM) to model user rating behaviors in social media systems which considers the influences of both user interest and temporal context in item selection process.
- We distinguish between user-oriented topics and time-oriented topics, which enables the precise identification of user personal interest and the temporal context.
- We propose an item-weighting scheme to enhance the performance of TCAM by exploiting the frequency distribution and temporal distribution of social items.
- To enhance the performance of TCAM in temporal recommendation for large social media data, we design an efficient query-processing technique.
- We conduct extensive experiments to evaluate the performance of the proposed models based on four sets of real-life data from different social media systems. The experimental results demonstrate the superiority of TCAM over existing approaches.

The remainder of the paper is organized as follows. Section 2 reviews the existing work related to our research. Section 3 details the temporal context-aware mixture model (TCAM). We deploy TCAM model to facilitate temporal recommendation in Section 4. We carry out extensive experiments and report the experimental results in Section 5 and conclude the paper in Section 6.

2. RELATED WORK

In this section, we review related research from the following two areas: topic modeling and temporal recommendation techniques.

Topic Model. Topic models provide a useful means to discover topic structures from large document collections. While traditional topic models, such as LDA [3] and PLSA [13], do not address the temporal information in a document corpus, a number of temporal topic models have been proposed to consider topic evolution over time. Mei and Zhai [20, 26] studied mining evolutionary topics from texts by comparing topics modeled in consecutive time intervals. Wang and McCallum [25] designed the TOT model that treats time stamps of documents as an observed continuous variable generated by topics. This model is designed to capture temporal features with beta distribution, confining each topic into a narrow time distribution. Some other models, such as Dynamic Topic Model (DTM) [2], MAP-PLSA [12] and Online LDA [1], are also proposed to study topic changes over time.

The TimeUserLDA model proposed by Diao et al. [9] is designed for finding bursty topics from microblogs. Although this model assumes that user posting behaviors are influenced by both user interest and global topic trends, there is only one shared set of underlying topics in TimeUserLDA, i.e., there is no distinction between underlying user-oriented topics and time-oriented topics. Thus, the topics detected by their models look confusing and noisy since they conflate both user interest and temporal context. To improve the topic discovery process, Yin et al. [33] recently proposed a unified model to detect both stable and temporal topics simultaneously from social media data.

Recently, topic models have been applied to collaborative filtering. X. Jin et al. [14] proposed an approach based on LDA to discover the hidden semantic relationships among items for recommendation. In [6], a hard-constraint-based LDA method was used to deal with user-community data, in which each user is viewed as a document and the communities that this user joins are viewed as words in the document. In contrast, Y. Kang et al. [15] proposed a soft-constraint-based LDA method for community recommendations. We refer to these topic model-based CF methods as "traditional" recommendation techniques which simply assume that items rated by users represent their intrinsic interests and ignore the influence from other factors. Recently, Yin et al. [34] proposed a location-content-aware topic model to produce location-based recommendation. Xu et al. [30] and Mao et al. [31] assumed that user behaviors are influenced by both user interests and the behaviors of their social friends, and proposed mixture latent topic models to capture these factors. Again, these models make use of one set of shared topics to model two factors. The estimated topics are confusing and difficult to interpret, which causes the recommendation results to degenerate. Moreover, these models do not exploit the temporal information.

Temporal Recommendation. Many successful temporal collaborative filtering methods are based on latent factor models. For example, the Netflix award winning algorithm *timeSVD++* [16] assumes that the latent features consist of components that evolve over time and a dedicated bias for each user at each specific time point. This model can effectively capture local changes to user preferences which the authors claim to be vital for improving performance. Xiong et al. proposed a Bayesian probabilistic tensor factorization model (BPTF) in [29]. BPTF represents users, items and time in a shared low-dimensional space, and predicts the rating score that a user u will assign to item v at time t using the inner product of their latent representations. Demonstrated by the experimental results on Netflix data, both BPTF and timeSVD++ perform well on the rating prediction task because they incorporate time effects into models. One main disadvantage with these models is that the learnt latent low-dimensional space is difficult to interpret. Recently, Liu et al. [19] addressed a new problem - online evolutionary collaborative filtering, which tracks user interests over time for the purpose of making timely recommendations. They extended the widely used neighborhood based algorithms by incorporating temporal information and developed an incremental algorithm for updating neighborhood similarities with new data. However, most of the existing temporal recommendation models [16, 29, 19] are designed for the task of rating prediction rather than top-k recommendation.

3. USER RATING BEHAVIOR MODELING

In this section, we first introduce relevant definitions and notations used throughout this paper. We then present the novel temporal context-aware mixture model for modeling user rating behaviors in social media systems.

3.1 Notations and Definitions

The notations used in this paper are summarized in Table 1.

Definition 1. **(User Rating)** A user rating is a triple $(u,\ t,\ v)$ that denotes a rating behavior (e.g., purchasing, clicking and tagging) made by user u on item v during time interval t.

Definition 2. **(User Document)** Given a user u, the user document, D_u, is a set of pairs $\{(v,\ t)\}$ representing the rating behaviors on items during different time intervals made by u.

Definition 3. **(Rating Cuboid)** A rating cuboid $\boldsymbol{C}$ is an $N \times T \times V$ cuboid, where N is the number of users, T is the number of time intervals and V is the number of items. A cell indexed by $(u,\ t,\ v)$ stores the rating score that user u assigned to item v during time interval t.

User actions on items, such as tagging, downloading, purchasing and clicking, can be represented as a user rating. Either explicit feedback or implicit feedback can be used to compute the value of rating score. For example, given a user u who frequently uses a tag v during time interval t, the usage frequency can be used as the rating score to reflect the user's preference on the tag during that time period.

Definition 4. **(Topic)** Given a collection of items $\boldsymbol{I} = \{v_i\}_{i=1}^{V}$, a topic z is represented by a topic model $\boldsymbol{\phi}_z$, which is a multinomial distribution over items $\boldsymbol{\phi}_z = \{P(v_i|\boldsymbol{\phi}_z) \text{ or } \phi_{zv_i}\}_{i=1}^{V}$.

To illustrate the semantic meaning of a topic, we choose top-k items that have the highest probability under the topic, as shown in Figure 2. In our work, we distinguish between **user-oriented topics** $\boldsymbol{\phi}_z$ and **time-oriented topics** $\boldsymbol{\phi}'_x$ although both of them are represented by a multinomial distribution over items. User-oriented topics are used to model user interest, which is assumed to be generally stable over time. In contrast, time-oriented topics are used to model the temporal context (i.e., the public's attention during a particular time), which has a clear temporal feature. For example, the popularity of the topics may increase or decrease over time and reach a peak during a certain period of time, as shown in Figure 2.

Definition 5. **(User Interest)** Given a user u, her/his intrinsic interest, denoted as $\boldsymbol{\theta}_u$, is a multinomial distribution over user-oriented topics.

Definition 6. **(Temporal Context)** Given a time interval t, the temporal context during t, denoted as $\boldsymbol{\theta}'_t$, is a multinomial distribution over time-oriented topics or items.

SYMBOL	DESCRIPTION
u, t, v	user u, time interval t, item v
N, T, V	number of users, time intervals, and items
M_u	number of items rated by user u
λ_u	the mixing weight specific to user u
K_1	number of user-oriented topics
θ_{uz}	probability that user-oriented topic z is chosen by user u
$\boldsymbol{\theta}_u$	intrinsic interest of user u denoted by $\boldsymbol{\theta}_u = \{\theta_{uz}\}_{z=1}^{K_1}$
$\boldsymbol{\phi}_z$	item proportions of user-oriented topic z, denoted by $\boldsymbol{\phi}_z = \{\phi_{zv}\}_{v=1}^{V}$
ϕ_{zv}	probability that item v is generated by user-oriented topic z
K_2	number of time-oriented topics
$\boldsymbol{\theta}'_t$	the temporal context during time interval t denoted by $\boldsymbol{\theta}'_t = \{\theta'_{tx}\}_{x=1}^{K_2}$
θ'_{tx}	probability that time-oriented topic x is generated by time interval t
$\boldsymbol{\phi}'_x$	item proportions of time-oriented topic x, denoted by $\boldsymbol{\phi}'_x = \{\phi'_{xv}\}_{v=1}^{V}$
ϕ'_{xv}	probability that item v is generated by time-oriented topic x

Table 1: Notations used in this model

3.2 Temporal Context-Aware Mixture Model

Given a rating cuboid $\boldsymbol{C}$ which stores users' rating histories, we aim to model user rating behaviors by exploiting the information captured in $\boldsymbol{C}$. Before presenting the devised model, we first describe an example to illustrate the motivation of our design.

As mentioned before, users' rating behaviors in social media systems are influenced by not only intrinsic interest but also the

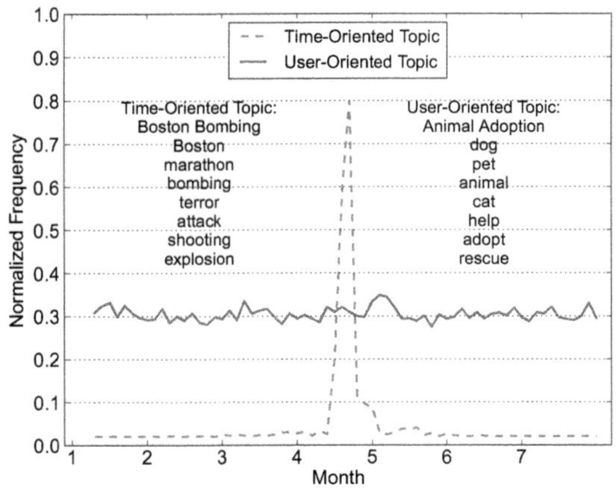

Figure 2: An Example of Two Types of Topics in Delicious

temporal context. It is crucial to distinguish between user-oriented topics and time-oriented topics, because the two have very different characteristics. For example, Figure 2 shows an example of a user-oriented topic and a time-oriented topic detected by TCAM model from Delicious. For demonstration, we present only the top eight tags that have the highest probability under each topic. We can easily tell the difference between the two topics from both their temporal distributions and the content descriptions. For the time-oriented topic, the items (i.e., tags) are related to a certain event (e.g.,"Boston Marathon bombings"). The popularity of the topic experiences a sharp increase during a particular time interval (e.g., in April 2013). For the user-oriented topic, the items are about the user's regular interest (e.g., "Pet Adoption"). The temporal distribution of the topic does not show any spike-like fluctuation. Hence, our TCAM models the user-oriented topics and the time-oriented topics simultaneously.

To consider the influence of the user intrinsic interest and the temporal context in a unified manner, TCAM computes the likelihood that a user u will rate an item v during a time interval t as follows.

$$P(v|u, t, \boldsymbol{\Psi}) = \lambda_u P(v|\boldsymbol{\theta}_u) + (1 - \lambda_u) P(v|\boldsymbol{\theta}'_t) \tag{1}$$

where $\boldsymbol{\Psi}$ denotes the model parameter set, $P(v|\boldsymbol{\theta}_u)$ is the probability that item v is generated from u's intrinsic interest, denoted as $\boldsymbol{\theta}_u$, and $P(v|\boldsymbol{\theta}'_t)$ denotes the probability that item v is generated from the temporal context during time interval t, i.e., $\boldsymbol{\theta}'_t$. The parameter λ_u is the mixing weight which represents the influence probability of the user interest. That is, user u is influenced by personal interest $\boldsymbol{\theta}_u$ with probability λ_u, and is influenced by the temporal context $\boldsymbol{\theta}'_t$ with probability $1 - \lambda_u$, for decision making. It is worth mentioning that TCAM holds personalized mixing weights for individual users, considering the differences between users in personalities (e.g., openness and agreeableness).

The user interest component $\boldsymbol{\theta}_u$ is modeled by a multinomial distribution over user-oriented topics, and each item is generated from a user-oriented topic z. Thus, $P(v|\boldsymbol{\theta}_u)$ is computed as follows.

$$P(v|\boldsymbol{\theta_u}) = \sum_{z=1}^{K_1} P(v|\boldsymbol{\phi}_z) P(z|\boldsymbol{\theta}_u) \tag{2}$$

As for the temporal context component $\boldsymbol{\theta}'_t$, we design two alternative methods to model it, which leads to two variations of TCAM: Item-based TCAM (ITCAM) and Topic-based TCAM (TTCAM). For the former, we model each temporal context $\boldsymbol{\theta}'_t$ as a time-oriented topic which is a multinomial distribution over all items during time interval t. For the latter, we model each temporal

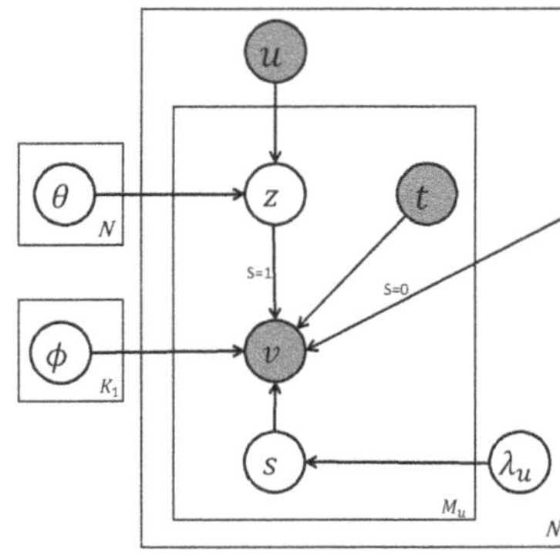

Figure 3: The Graphical Representation of ITCAM

context $\boldsymbol{\theta}'_t$ as a multinomial distribution over latent time-oriented topics. As a running example in Figure 1, the user is influenced by personal interest and the temporal context with probabilities 0.64 and 0.36, respectively. Four user-oriented topics and three time-oriented topics are also shown respectively, where the weights representing the user's interest distribution over the user-oriented topics as well as the temporal context distribution over the time-oriented topics are labeled in the corresponding edges. We can see that user-oriented topic U1 dominates the user's interest, and time-oriented topic T1 attracts most attentions from the general public at time t. The probabilities of topic generating items are also labeled in the corresponding edges. For example, the weight b on the edge linking topic U1 and item v2 represents the probability of U1 generating item v2.

Below, we will describe the details of the two variations of TCAM model and compare their performance in Section 5.

3.2.1 Item-based TCAM

Figure 3 illustrates the generative process of ITCAM with a graph model. The structure of ITCAM is similar to the PLSA model, but ITCAM has additional machinery to handle the mixing weight λ_u. In particular, a latent random variable s, associated with each item, is adopted as a switch to determine whether the item is generated according to the temporal context $\boldsymbol{\theta}'_t$ or the user's interest $\boldsymbol{\theta}_u$. s is sampled from a user-specific Bernoulli distribution with the mean λ_u. N indicates the number of users; K_1 is the number of user-oriented topics; T is the number of time intervals and M_u is the number of items rated by u. Figure 3 shows that each temporal context $\boldsymbol{\theta}'_t$ is modeled as a multinomial distribution over items. The generative process of ITCAM is summarized as follows.

For each item v rated by u during time interval t:

1. Sample s from $Bernoulli(\lambda_u)$
2. If $s = 1$
   (a) Sample topic z from $Multinomial(\boldsymbol{\theta}_u)$
   (b) Sample item v from $Multinomial(\boldsymbol{\phi}_z)$
3. Else
   (a) Sample item v from $Multinomial(\boldsymbol{\theta}'_t)$

Model Inference. Given a rating cuboid $\boldsymbol{C}$, the learning procedure of our model is to estimate the unknown model parameter set $\boldsymbol{\Psi} = \{\boldsymbol{\theta}, \boldsymbol{\phi}, \boldsymbol{\theta}', \boldsymbol{\lambda}\}$. The log likelihood is derived as follows:

$$L(\boldsymbol{\Psi}|\boldsymbol{C}) = \sum_{u=1}^{N} \sum_{t=1}^{T} \sum_{v=1}^{V} C[u, t, v] \log P(v|u, t, \boldsymbol{\Psi}) \tag{3}$$

where $P(v|u, t, \boldsymbol{\Psi})$ is defined in Equation (1).

The goal of parameter estimation is to maximize the log likelihood in Equation (3). As this equation cannot be solved directly by applying Maximum Likelihood Estimation (MLE), we apply an EM approach instead. In an expectation (E) step of the EM approach, we introduce $P(s|u,t,v;\widehat{\mathbf{\Psi}})$ which is the posterior probability of choosing personal interest $\boldsymbol{\theta}_u$ (i.e., $s=1$) or temporal context $\boldsymbol{\theta}'_t$ (i.e., $s=0$) respectively given user rating behavior (u,t,v) and the current estimations of the parameters $\widehat{\mathbf{\Psi}}$. In a maximization (M) step, parameters are updated by maximizing the expected complete data log-likelihood $Q(\mathbf{\Psi}|\widehat{\mathbf{\Psi}})$ based on the posterior probability computed in the E-step.

In the **E-step**, $P(s|u,t,v;\widehat{\mathbf{\Psi}})$ is updated according to Bayes formulas as follows,

$$P(s|u,t,v;\widehat{\mathbf{\Psi}}) = \frac{s\lambda_u P(v|\boldsymbol{\theta}_u) + (1-s)(1-\lambda_u)P(v|\boldsymbol{\theta}'_t)}{\lambda_u P(v|\boldsymbol{\theta}_u) + (1-\lambda_u)P(v|\boldsymbol{\theta_t}')} \tag{4}$$

where $P(v|\boldsymbol{\theta}_u)$ is defined as in Equation (2). To obtain the updated parameters $P(z|\boldsymbol{\theta}_u)$ and $P(v|\boldsymbol{\phi}_z)$, another posterior probability $P(z|s=1,u,t,v;\widehat{\mathbf{\Psi}})$ is computed as follows:

$$P(z|s=1,u,t,v;\widehat{\mathbf{\Psi}}) = \frac{P(v|\boldsymbol{\phi}_z)P(z|\boldsymbol{\theta}_u)}{\sum_{z'=1}^{K_1} P(v|\boldsymbol{\phi}_{z'})P(z'|\boldsymbol{\theta}_u)} \tag{5}$$

Based on $P(z|s=1,u,t,v;\widehat{\mathbf{\Psi}})$ and $P(s=1|u,t,v;\widehat{\mathbf{\Psi}})$, we introduce the notation $P(z|u,t,v;\widehat{\mathbf{\Psi}})$ as follows,

$$P(z|u,t,v;\widehat{\mathbf{\Psi}}) = P(z|s=1,u,t,v;\widehat{\mathbf{\Psi}})P(s=1|u,t,v;\widehat{\mathbf{\Psi}}) \tag{6}$$

With simple derivations [13], we can obtain the expectation of complete data log-likelihood for ITCAM:

$$\begin{aligned} Q(\mathbf{\Psi}|\widehat{\mathbf{\Psi}}) = &\sum_{u=1}^{N}\sum_{v=1}^{V}\sum_{t=1}^{T} C[u,t,v]\{P(s=1|u,t,v;\widehat{\mathbf{\Psi}}) \\ &\sum_{z=1}^{K_1} P(z|s=1,u,t,v;\widehat{\mathbf{\Psi}})\log[\lambda_u P(v|\boldsymbol{\phi}_z)P(z|\boldsymbol{\theta}_u)] \\ &+ P(s=0|u,t,v;\widehat{\mathbf{\Psi}})\log[(1-\lambda_u)P(v|\boldsymbol{\theta}'_t)]\} \end{aligned} \tag{7}$$

In the **M-step**, we find the estimation $\mathbf{\Psi}$ that maximizes the expectation of the complete data log-likelihood $Q(\mathbf{\Psi}|\widehat{\mathbf{\Psi}})$ with the constraints $\sum_{v=1}^{V} P(v|\boldsymbol{\phi}_z)=1$, $\sum_{v=1}^{V} P(v|\boldsymbol{\theta}'_t)=1$ and $\sum_{z=1}^{K_1} P(z|\boldsymbol{\theta}_u)=1$ using the following updating formulas.

$$P(z|\boldsymbol{\theta}_u) = \frac{\sum_{v=1}^{V}\sum_{t=1}^{T} C[u,t,v]P(z|u,t,v;\widehat{\mathbf{\Psi}})}{\sum_{z'=1}^{K_1}\sum_{v=1}^{V}\sum_{t=1}^{T} C[u,t,v]P(z'|u,t,v;\widehat{\mathbf{\Psi}})} \tag{8}$$

$$P(v|\boldsymbol{\phi}_z) = \frac{\sum_{t=1}^{T}\sum_{u=1}^{N} C[u,t,v]P(z|u,t,v;\widehat{\mathbf{\Psi}})}{\sum_{v'=1}^{V}\sum_{t=1}^{T}\sum_{u=1}^{N} C[u,t,v']P(z|u,t,v';\widehat{\mathbf{\Psi}})} \tag{9}$$

$$P(v|\boldsymbol{\theta}'_t) = \frac{\sum_{u=1}^{N} C[u,t,v]P(s=0|u,t,v;\widehat{\mathbf{\Psi}})}{\sum_{v'=1}^{V}\sum_{u=1}^{N} C[u,t,v']P(s=0|u,t,v';\widehat{\mathbf{\Psi}})} \tag{10}$$

With an initial random guess of $\mathbf{\Psi}$, we alternately apply the E-step and M-step until a termination condition is met. To adapt to different users, we estimate the parameter λ_u in M-step, instead of picking a fixed λ value for all users. This personalized treatment can automatically adapt the model parameter estimation to various users. Specifically, λ_u is estimated as follows.

$$\lambda_u = \frac{\sum_{t=1}^{T}\sum_{v=1}^{V} C[u,t,v]P(s=1|u,t,v;\widehat{\mathbf{\Psi}})}{\sum_{t=1}^{T}\sum_{v=1}^{V}\sum_{s=0}^{1} C[u,t,v]P(s|u,t,v;\widehat{\mathbf{\Psi}})} \tag{11}$$

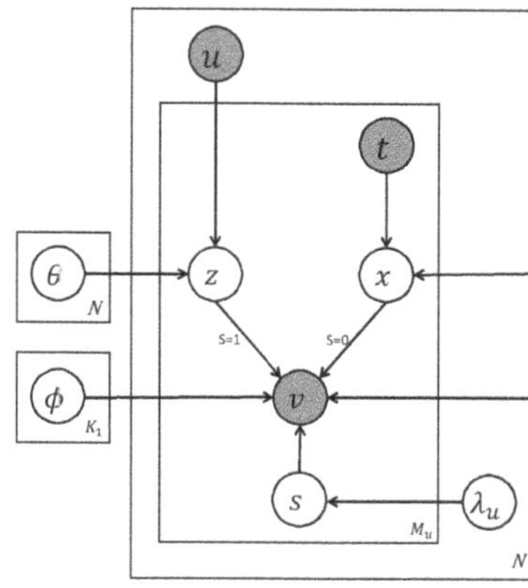

Figure 4: The Graphical Representation of TTCAM

3.2.2 *Topic-based TCAM*

Figure 4 illustrates the generative process of TTCAM with a graph model. In particular, the temporal context $\boldsymbol{\theta}'_t$ is modeled as a multinomial distribution over a set of time-oriented topics instead of a set of items. Thus, the computation of $P(v|\boldsymbol{\theta}'_t)$ is reformulated as in Equation (12).

$$P(v|\boldsymbol{\theta}'_t) = \sum_{x=1}^{K_2} P(v|\boldsymbol{\phi}'_x)P(x|\boldsymbol{\theta}'_t) \tag{12}$$

The generative process is summarized as follows. For each item v rated by u during time interval t:

1. Sample s from $Bernoulli(\lambda_u)$
2. If $s=1$
   (a) Sample topic z from $Multinomial(\boldsymbol{\theta}_u)$
   (b) Sample item v from $Multinomial(\boldsymbol{\phi}_z)$
3. Else
   (a) Sample topic x from $Multinomial(\boldsymbol{\theta}'_t)$
   (b) Sample item v from $Multinomial(\boldsymbol{\phi}'_x)$

Model Inference. To estimate model parameters in TTCAM, we apply an EM approach similarly.

In the **E-step**, similar to the parameter estimation in ITCAM, $P(s|u,t,v;\widehat{\mathbf{\Psi}})$ and $P(z|s=1,u,t,v;\widehat{\mathbf{\Psi}})$ are updated according to Equations (4, 5) where $P(v|\boldsymbol{\theta}'_t)$ is defined as in Equation (12) and $P(v|\boldsymbol{\theta}_u)$ is defined as in Equation (2). To obtain the updated parameters $P(x|\boldsymbol{\theta}'_t)$ and $P(v|\boldsymbol{\phi}'_x)$, we introduce the posterior probability $P(x|s=0,u,t,v;\widehat{\mathbf{\Psi}})$, defined as follows:

$$P(x|s=0,u,t,v;\widehat{\mathbf{\Psi}}) = \frac{P(v|\boldsymbol{\phi}'_x)P(x|\boldsymbol{\theta}'_t)}{\sum_{x'=1}^{K_2} P(v|\boldsymbol{\phi}'_{x'})P(x'|\boldsymbol{\theta}'_t)} \tag{13}$$

Based on $P(x|s=0,u,t,v;\widehat{\mathbf{\Psi}})$ and $P(s=0|u,t,v;\widehat{\mathbf{\Psi}})$, we introduce the notation $P(x|u,t,v;\widehat{\mathbf{\Psi}})$ as follows.

$$P(x|u,t,v;\widehat{\mathbf{\Psi}}) = P(x|s=0,u,t,v;\widehat{\mathbf{\Psi}})P(s=0|u,t,v;\widehat{\mathbf{\Psi}}) \tag{14}$$

In the **M-step**, the model parameters $P(z|\boldsymbol{\theta}_u)$, $P(v|\boldsymbol{\phi}_z)$, and λ_u are estimated according to Equations (8, 9, 11). $P(x|\boldsymbol{\theta}'_t)$ and $P(v|\boldsymbol{\phi}'_x)$ are inferred using the following formulas.

$$P(x|\boldsymbol{\theta}'_t) = \frac{\sum_{v=1}^{V}\sum_{u=1}^{N} C[u,t,v]P(x|u,t,v;\widehat{\mathbf{\Psi}})}{\sum_{x'=1}^{K_2}\sum_{v=1}^{V}\sum_{u=1}^{N} C[u,t,v]P(x'|u,t,v;\widehat{\mathbf{\Psi}})} \tag{15}$$

$$P(v|\boldsymbol{\phi}'_x) = \frac{\sum_{t=1}^{T}\sum_{u=1}^{N} C[u,t,v]P(x|u,t,v;\widehat{\mathbf{\Psi}})}{\sum_{v'=1}^{V}\sum_{t=1}^{T}\sum_{u=1}^{N} C[u,t,v']P(x|u,t,v';\widehat{\mathbf{\Psi}})} \tag{16}$$

3.2.3 Discussion about Parameter setting

In our model, we still have four hyper-parameters to tune manually, including the number of user-oriented topics K_1, the number of time-oriented topics K_2, the number of time intervals T and the number of EM iterations. K_1 and K_2 are the desired numbers of user-oriented topics and time-oriented topics respectively, which need to be tuned empirically. T is the number of time intervals used in our model for generating time-oriented topics, which provides users with the flexibility to adjust the granularity/length of time interval. The larger T is, the more fine-grained time intervals are. Regarding the number of EM iterations, we observe that convergence can be achieved in a few iterations (e.g., 50) because the model inference procedure using the EM approach is fast. It is worth mentioning that EM algorithms can be easily expressed in MapReduce [8, 28], so the inference procedure of TCAM can be naturally decomposed for parallel processing, which is scalable to large-scale datasets.

3.3 Enhancement of TCAM

In this section, we first introduce the challenge, arising from popular items, encountered by TCAM, and then propose an item weighting scheme to improve our proposed models.

Similar to traditional topic models, both ITCAM and TTCAM assume that all items are equally important in computing generation probabilities. As a result, popular items with more ratings tend to be estimated with high generation probability and ranked in top positions in each topic, which impairs the quality of both the user-oriented topics and the time-oriented topics.

For user-oriented topics, popular items are not good indicators of user intrinsic interests. A popular item rated by many users conveys less information about a user's interest than an item rated by few users. For time-oriented topics, it is expected that items representing the public's attention at a given time should be ranked high, such as items with bursty temporal distributions, since bursts of items are generally triggered by breaking news or events that attract the public's attention. Unfortunately, bursty items are most likely to be overwhelmed by long-standing popular items. Figure 5 shows the temporal frequency of the top six tags of a sample time-oriented topic discovered from Delicious. It can be observed that the topic concerns swine flu. The temporal distributions of three bursty tags, "flu", "mexico" and "swineflu", experience sharp spikes. Although the trends of the three tags do not always synchronize, they each go through a drastic increase and reach a peak in July 2009. The bursts in these curves are triggered by a real-world event, i.e., the swine flu outbreak in Mexico. The other three tags, "news", "health" and "death", maintain high frequency throughout the year. However, they convey little information about the event. Although they are relevant to the event, they are related to many other topics as well. Hence, it is desirable to rank bursty items higher than popular item when representing time-oriented topics.

To address the challenge posed by the popular items, we propose an item-weighting scheme to reduce the importance of popular items while promoting weights for salient (i.e., infrequent) and bursty items in computing generation probability. From the viewpoint of information theory [7], the entropy of an item v is defined as follows:

$$E(v) = -\sum_{u} P(u|v)\log P(u|v)$$

Suppose that the item v is preferred by users with equal probability $P(u|v) = \frac{1}{N(v)}$, the maximum entropy is,

$$E(v) = \log N(v)$$

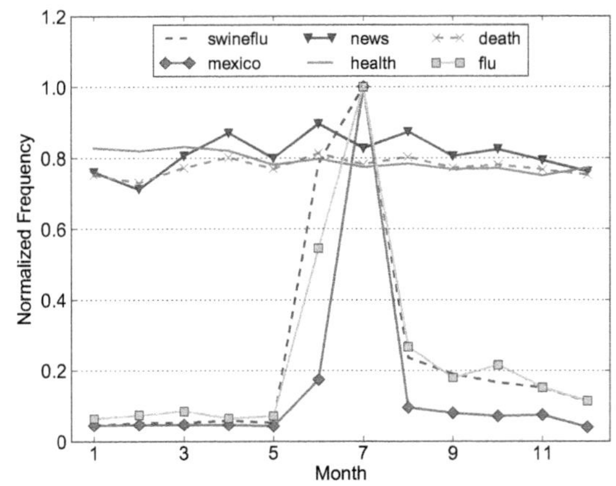

Figure 5: An Example of Bursty Tags and Popular Tags.

Generally, the entropy of an item tends to be proportional to its frequency/popularity $N(v)$. Hence, in the following analysis, we use the maximum entropy to approximate the exact entropy to simplify the calculation.

To allow salient items to be ranked higher in user-oriented topics, the weights of items should be inversely proportional to the entropy, as discussed above. Hence, we propose a concept called *inverse user frequency* to measure the ability of items to represent salient information. Let N be the total number of users in the entire data set; the *inverse user frequency* for the item v is defined as follows:

$$iuf(v) = \log N - \log N(v) = \log \frac{N}{N(v)} \quad (17)$$

which is similar to the inverse document frequency for a term in text mining.

To take into account the bursty information of items, we propose to compute the *bursty degree* of an item v using the following equation:

$$B(v,t) = \frac{N_t(v)}{N_t}\frac{N}{N(v)} \quad (18)$$

where $N_t(v)$ represents the popularity of item v during time interval t, i.e., the number of users who rate item v during time interval t, N_t is the number of active users during time interval t, $N(v)$ is the overall popularity of v across all time intervals, and N is the total number of users in the data set.

Combining the inverse user frequency and the bursty degree of items, we assign weight to the item v as follows.

$$w(v,t) = iuf(v) \times B(v,t) \quad (19)$$

Integrating the weights of items defined in Equation (19), we obtain the weighted user-time-item cuboid $\bar{\boldsymbol{C}}$ from the original $\boldsymbol{C}$ as follows:

$$\bar{C}[u,t,v] = C[u,t,v]w(v,t) \quad (20)$$

which can be used in both variations of the TCAM model.

4. TEMPORAL RECOMMENDATION

The conventional top-k recommendation task can be stated as follows: given a user, the recommender system should recommend a small number, say k, of items from all the available items. Note that the conventional top-k recommendation task does not consider the temporal information. However, in reality, user rating behaviors, influenced by both user interests and the temporal context, are dynamic. For example, user u rating item v in time interval

t does not mean that u still favors v in time interval $t+1$. Besides, each item has its own lifespan, especially for time-sensitive items such as news. It is undesirable to recommend outdated news. Hence, an ideal recommender system is expected to have the ability to recommend the right item v to user u in the right time interval t, rather than in other time intervals. In this paper, we propose the task of temporal top-k recommendation as follows: given a query $q = (u, t)$, i.e., a querying user u with a time interval t, the recommender model recommends k items which match u's interests and the temporal context at t.

Below, we will present how to deploy TCAM to facilitate temporal recommendations.

4.1 Computation of Ranking Score

Once we have inferred model parameters of TCAM, such as user interest $\boldsymbol{\theta}$, temporal context $\boldsymbol{\theta}'$, user-oriented topics $\boldsymbol{\phi}$, time-oriented topics $\boldsymbol{\phi}'$ and mixing weights $\boldsymbol{\lambda}$, given a query $q = (u, t)$, a ranking score $S(u,t,v)$ for each item v can be computed according to Equation (22), and then the top-k items with highest ranking score will be returned. Specifically, when receiving a query $q = (u, t)$, a new multinomial distribution for the query, $\boldsymbol{\vartheta}_q$, is first constructed by combining $\boldsymbol{\theta}_u$ and $\boldsymbol{\theta}'_t$. More specifically, we expand the user interest and temporal context spaces to be of the same dimension. For example, if there are K_1 user-oriented topics and K_2 time-oriented topics, the expanded topic space will have $K = K_1 + K_2$ topics. The expanded user interest distribution is defined as $\widetilde{\boldsymbol{\theta}}_u =< \boldsymbol{\theta}_u, 0, \cdots, 0 >$, where we set 0 on the time-oriented topics. Similarly, we define the expanded temporal context distribution to be $\widetilde{\boldsymbol{\theta}}'_t =< 0, \cdots, 0, \boldsymbol{\theta}'_t >$. The new distribution is defined as $\boldsymbol{\vartheta}_q = \lambda_u \widetilde{\boldsymbol{\theta}}_u + (1-\lambda_u)\widetilde{\boldsymbol{\theta}}'_t$. Correspondingly, we renumber the time-oriented topic x and change its range from $[1, \cdots, K_2]$ to $[K_1+1, \cdots, K]$. Then, we use $\varphi_{\tilde{z}v}$ to denote the weight of item v on dimension $\tilde{z}$ that corresponds to user-oriented topic z or time-oriented topic x, which depends on the value of $\tilde{z}$, as shown in Equation (21).

$$\varphi_{\tilde{z}v} = \begin{cases} \phi_{zv} & \tilde{z} \le K1 \\ \phi'_{xv} & \tilde{z} > K1 \end{cases} \tag{21}$$

$$S(u,t,v) = \sum_{\tilde{z}=1}^{K} \vartheta_{q\tilde{z}} \varphi_{\tilde{z}v} \tag{22}$$

4.2 Fast Top-k Recommendation

The straightforward method of generating the top-k items needs to compute the ranking scores for all items according to Equation (22), which is computationally inefficient, especially when the number of items becomes large. To speed up the online process of producing recommendations, we extend the Threshold-based Algorithm (TA) [10], which is capable of finding the top-k results by examining the minimum number of items.

We first pre-compute ordered lists of items, where each list corresponds to a latent topic learned by TCAM model. For example, given K topics (K_1 user-oriented topics plus K_2 time-oriented topics), we will compute K lists of sorted items, $L_{\tilde{z}}$, $\tilde{z} \in \{1, 2, ..., K\}$, where items in each list $L_{\tilde{z}}$ are sorted according to $\varphi_{\tilde{z}v}$ as defined in Equation (21). Given a query $q = (u, t)$, we run Algorithm 1 to compute the top-k items from the K sorted lists and return them in the priority list L. As shown in Algorithm 1, we first maintain a priority list PL for the K lists where the priority of a list $L_{\tilde{z}}$ is the ranking score (i.e., $S(u,t,v)$) of the first item v in $L_{\tilde{z}}$ (Lines 2-6). In each iteration, we select the most promising item (i.e., the first item) from the list that has the highest priority in PL and add it to the result list L (Lines 9-16). When the size of L is no less than k, we will examine the k-th item in the result list L. If the ranking score of the k-th item is higher than the *threshold score* (i.e., S_{Ta}), the algorithm terminates early without checking any subsequent items (Lines 18-21). Otherwise, the k-th item v' in L is replaced by the current item v if v's ranking score is higher than that of v' (Lines 22-25). In the end of each iteration, we update the priority of current list as well as the threshold score (lines 28-33).

Algorithm 1: Threshold-based algorithm

Input: A query $q = (u, t)$; inferred model parameters $\boldsymbol{\theta}_u$, $\boldsymbol{\theta}'_t$ and λ_u; ranked lists $(L_1, ..., L_K)$;
Output: List L with all the k highest ranked items;

1 Initialize priority lists PQ, L and the threshold score S_{Ta};
2 **for** $\tilde{z} = 1$ *to* K **do**
3    $v = L_{\tilde{z}}.getfirst()$;
4   Compute $S(u,t,v)$ according to Equation (23);
5    $PQ.insert(\tilde{z}, S(u,t,v))$;
6 **end**
7 Compute S_{Ta} according to Equation (24);
8 **while** *true* **do**
9    $nextListToCheck = PQ.getfirst()$;
10    $PQ.removefirst()$;
11    $v = L_{nextListToCheck}.getfirst()$;
12    $L_{nextListToCheck}.removefirst()$;
13   **if** $v \notin L$ **then**
14   **if** $L.size() < k$ **then**
15        $L.insert(v, S(u,t,v))$;
16   **end**
17   **else**
18        $v' = L.get(k)$;
19   **if** $S(u,t,v') > S_{Ta}$ **then**
20   break;
21   **end**
22   **if** $S(u,t,v') < S(u,t,v)$ **then**
23          $L.remove(k)$;
24          $L.insert(v, S(u,t,v))$;
25   **end**
26   **end**
27   **end**
28   **if** $L_{nextListToCheck}.hasMore()$ **then**
29      $v = L_{nextListToCheck}.getfirst()$;
30   Compute $S(u,t,v)$ according to Equation (23);
31      $PQ.insert(nextListToCheck, S(u,t,v))$;
32   Compute S_{Ta} according to Equation (24);
33   **end**
34   **else**
35   break;
36   **end**
37 **end**

Equation (23) illustrates the computation of the threshold score, which is obtained by aggregating the maximum $\varphi_{\tilde{z}v}$ represented by the first item in each list $L_{\tilde{z}}$ (i.e., $\max_{v \in L_{\tilde{z}}} \varphi_{\tilde{z}v}$). Consequently, it is the maximum possible ranking score that can be achieved by remaining unexamined items. Hence, if the ranking score of the k-th item in the result list L is higher than the threshold score, L can be returned immediately because no remaining item will have a higher ranking score than the k-th item.

$$S_{Ta} = \sum_{\tilde{z}=1}^{K} \vartheta_{q\tilde{z}} \max_{v \in L_{\tilde{z}}} \varphi_{\tilde{z}v} \tag{23}$$

5. EXPERIMENTS

In this section, we experimentally evaluate the performance of our proposed TCAM models.

5.1 Data Sets

Our experiments are conducted on four real data sets: Digg, MovieLens, Douban Movie and Delicious. The basic statistics of the four data sets are shown in Table 2.

- **Digg:** Digg is a popular social news aggregator, which allows users to vote news stories up or down, called *digging* or

	Digg	MovieLens
# of users	139,409	71,567
# of items	3,553	10,681
# of ratings	3,018,197	10,000,054
time span(year)	2009-2010	1998-2009
	Douban Movie	Delicious
# of users	50,885	201,663
# of items	69,908	2,828,304
# of ratings	52,604,958	36,966,661
time span(year)	2005-2010	2008-2009

Table 2: Basic statistics of the four data sets

burying, respectively. The Digg data set used in our experiment is Digg2009 [17], a publicly available data set containing 3,018,197 votes on 3553 popular stories cast by 139,409 distinct users. Although this data set contains only the IDs of news stories (the titles and the contents of stories are excluded), it is sufficient to evaluate the effectiveness of user behavior modeling in our work.

- **Douban Movie:** Douban[2] is the largest movie review website in China. In total, we crawled $50,885$ unique users and $69,908$ unique movies with $52,604,958$ movie ratings.
- **MovieLens:** MovieLens is a publicly available movie data set from the web-based recommender system MovieLens. The data set contains $10M$ ratings on a scale from 1 to 5 made by 71567 users on 10681 movies. We selected users who had rated at least 20 movies.
- **Delicious:** Delicious is a collaborative tagging system where users can upload and tag web pages. We collected 201,663 users and their tagging behaviors during the period Feb. 2008 - Dec. 2009. The data set contains 2,828,304 tags. Topics on technology and electronics account for about half of all web pages. Most of the other web pages are about breaking news with strong temporal features.

5.2 Comparisons

The temporal context-aware mixture model (TCAM) has two variants: **ITCAM** (Section 3.2.1) and **TTCAM** (Section 3.2.2). Both models can be enhanced by the item-weighting scheme, which leads to two optimized versions: *W-ITCAM* and *W-TTCAM*. We compare them with four categories of competitor approaches.

- **User-Topic Model (UT)**: We implemented a user-topic model following the previous works [21, 24]. This model is similar to the classic author-topic model (AT model) [23] which assumes that topics are generated according to user interests. The probabilistic formula of the user topic model is presented as follows, where θ_B is a background for smoothing.

$$P(v|u;\mathbf{\Psi}) = \lambda_B P(v|\boldsymbol{\theta}_B) + (1-\lambda_B)\sum_z P(z|\boldsymbol{\theta}_u)P(v|\boldsymbol{\phi}_z)$$

- **Time-Topic Model (TT)**: Following previous works [20, 26], we implemented a time-topic model. This model considers only the temporal information and ignores user interests. TT assumes that topics are generated by the temporal context, and that user behaviors are influenced by the temporal context. The probabilistic formula of the time-topic model is presented as follows.

$$P(v|t;\mathbf{\Psi}) = \lambda_B P(v|\boldsymbol{\theta}_B) + (1-\lambda_B)\sum_x P(x|\boldsymbol{\theta}'_t)P(v|\boldsymbol{\phi}'_x)$$

[2]http://douban.com

- **BPRMF**: This is a state-of-the-art matrix factorization model for item ranking optimized using BPR [22]. This model outperforms most of the existing recommender models in the task of top-k item recommendation. We used the BPRMF implementation provided by MyMediaLite, a free software recommender system library [11].
- **BPTF**: This is a state-of-the-art recommender model for rating prediction which uses a probabilistic tensor factorization technique by introducing additional factors for time [29]. This model outperforms most of the existing recommender models that consider time information.

5.3 Performance on Recommendation

In this section, we evaluate both the effectiveness of the suggested recommendations and the efficiency of generating top-k recommendations. Below, we first introduce the evaluation methods.

5.3.1 Evaluation Methods

Recommendation Effectiveness. For each user u, we randomly split her rated items during time interval t, $S_t(u)$, into 80% training items $S_t^{train}(u)$, and 20% test items $S_t^{test}(u)$. Given a querying user u in time interval t, if a recommended item is in the test set $S_t^{test}(u)$, it's a "hit" item, otherwise it's a "miss". A five-fold cross validation is employed to ensure the validity of the experimental results. To make the experimental results comparable, we use multiple well-known metrics to measure the ranked results. Similar to evaluations in information retrieval, we first use Precision@k to assess the quality of the top-k recommended items as follows:

$$Precision@k = \frac{\#hits}{k}$$

where $\#hits$ is the number of "hit" items in the top-k recommended items. We also consider NDCG, a widely used metric for a ranked list. NDCG@k is defined as:

$$NDCG@k = \frac{1}{IDCG} \times \sum_{i=1}^{k} \frac{2^{r_i}-1}{\log(i+1)}$$

where r_i is 1 if the item at position i is a "hit" item and 0 otherwise. IDCG is chosen for the purpose of normalization so that the perfect ranking has an NDCG value of 1. Considering that some users may have a large number of items in the test data while some have just a few, we also adopt the $F1$ score as our metric.

Recommendation Efficiency. The efficiency of the online recommendation mainly depends on 1) the number of items in the dataset and 2) the number of items recommended. Therefore, we test the efficiency of our proposed methods over these two factors.

5.3.2 Effectiveness of Temporal Recommendations

Figures 6 and 7 report the performance of the proposed models and other competitors in terms of Precision@k, NDCG@k and F1@k on Digg and MovieLens data sets, respectively. From the reported results, we observe that: (1) Our proposed models ITCAM, TTCAM, W-ITCAM and W-TTCAM, outperform other competitors such as UT, TT and BPRMF consistently on both data sets. This observation shows that recommendation accuracy, especially temporal recommendation accuracy, can be improved by considering both user intrinsic interests and the temporal context simultaneously. Note that, although BPTF performs almost as well as our proposed ITCAM model since it also exploits the temporal context information when recommending items, our W-ITCAM, TTCAM and W-TTCAM consistently outperform it. (2) W-ITCAM and W-TTCAM achieve higher temporal recommendation accuracy than

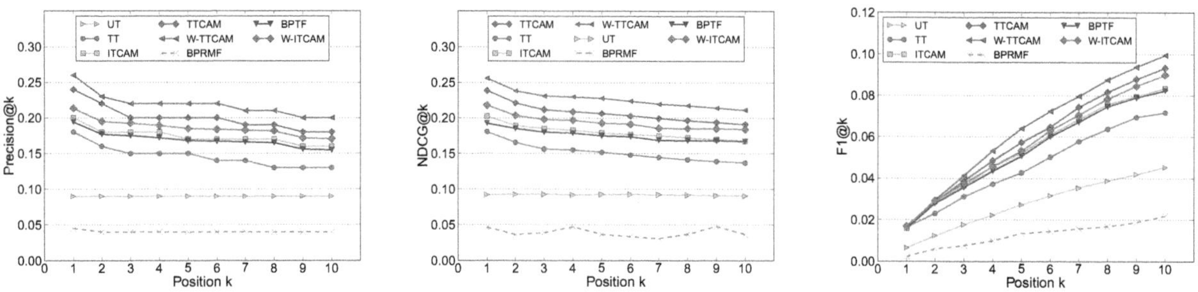

Figure 6: Temporal Accuracy on Digg Data Set

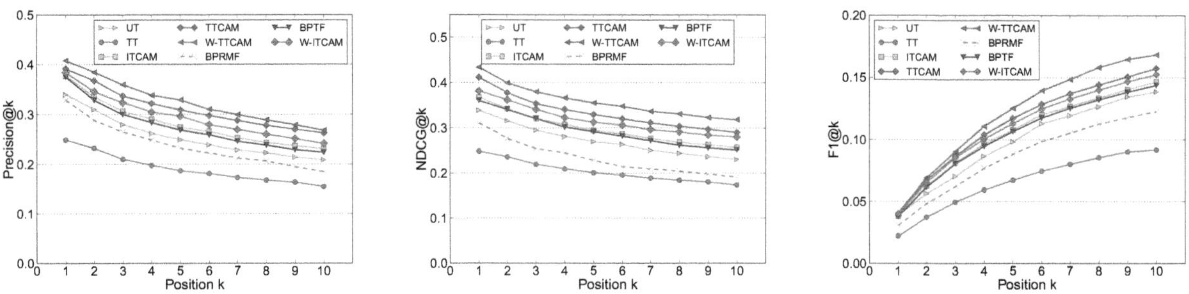

Figure 7: Temporal Accuracy on MovieLens Data Set

ITCAM and TTCAM, respectively, which shows the benefits brought by the item weighting scheme. Comparing TTCAM (W-TTCAM) with ITCAM (W-ITCAM), TTCAM (W-TTCAM) consistently performs better than ITCAM (W-ITCAM), verifying the advantage of modeling temporal context as a distribution over latent topics. (3) Comparing UT and TT on the two data sets, we find that UT performs better than TT on the MovieLens data set, while TT beats UT on the Digg data set. This is because news is a type of time-sensitive item while a movie is less time-sensitive. UT exploiting user interests works better in recommending less time-sensitive items while TT exploiting the temporal context is superior in recommending time-sensitive items.

There are three parameters in our models, namely, the length of time interval, the number of user-oriented topics (K1) and the number of time-oriented topics (K2). Tuning these model parameters is critical to the model performance. The experimental results presented above are obtained with the optimal parameter settings: (1) the optimal time intervals are one month for MovieLens and Douban Movie datasets, and three days for the Digg dataset, respectively; (2) the default values for K1 and K2 are 60 and 40 in TTCAM and W-TTCAM. We study the impacts of varying the three parameters below in details.

5.3.3 *Effect of the Length of Time Interval*

This experiment is to study the effect of the length of time interval. The length of time interval controls the time granularity of temporal recommendations. A larger length of time interval implies that the recommendation results will be less time-aware. To focus on the impact of the length of time interval, we only consider the models which utilize temporal influence. We report NDCG@5 on the Digg data set in Table 3. We also tune the length of time interval on other datasets and similar trends are observed, which are omitted due to space constraints. From the table, we have the following two observations.

- The first observation is that as the length of time interval increases, the NDCG values of all methods first increase, and then decrease. One possible reason for early increasing NDCG is that increasing the length makes the data in a time interval denser. Later on, NDCG decreases as the length of time interval gets larger, because increasing the length of time interval reduces the temporal influence. All methods achieve their best performance when the length of time interval is set to three days on this dataset, which could be a tradeoff of aforementioned two factors.
- Another important observation is that, for all lengths of time intervals, our proposed methods outperform other comparison methods. Among our proposed methods, W-TTCAM and W-ITCAM outperform TTCAM and ITCAM, respectively, showing the benefits brought by our proposed item-weighting technology.

5.3.4 *Effect of the Number of Topics*

This experiment is to study the effect of number of user-oriented topics (K1) and number of time-oriented topics (K2) on Digg dataset. Figure 9 reports the results of varying K1 from 10 to 100 when fixing K2 to 20, 40, 60 and 80, respectively. For example, W-TTCAM-40 represents the model W-TTCAM with 40 time-oriented topics. From the figure, we observe that the performance of our proposed model W-TTCAM first increases with the increasing number of user-oriented topics (K1), and remains nearly stable when K1 is larger than 60. By comparing W-TTCAM-20, W-TTCAM-40, W-TTCAM-60 and W-TTCAM-80, we find that W-TTCAM-20 performs worst while other three almost perform equally well and their curves almost overlap. For this dataset, the performance of W-TTCAM does not change much when the number of time-oriented topics (K2) is larger than 40.

5.3.5 *Efficiency of Recommendations*

We next proceed to perform an efficiency comparison of different temporal recommendation algorithms on Douban Movie and Movielens datasets. It is worth mentioning that there is different number of movies in these two datasets, i.e., 69,908 and 10,681, respectively. All the recommendation algorithms are implemented

Length of time interval	TT	ITCAM	TTCAM	W-TTCAM	BPTF	W-ITCAM
1 day	0.1062	0.1254	0.1444	0.1594	0.1226	0.1287
2 days	0.1365	0.1612	0.1857	0.2050	0.1576	0.1655
3 days	**0.1517**	**0.1791**	**0.2063**	**0.2278**	**0.1751**	**0.1839**
4 days	0.1426	0.1684	0.1939	0.2141	0.1646	0.1729
5 days	0.1274	0.1505	0.1733	0.1913	0.1471	0.1545
6 days	0.1153	0.1361	0.1568	0.1731	0.1331	0.1397
7 days	0.1123	0.1325	0.1527	0.1685	0.1296	0.1361
8 days	0.1092	0.1290	0.1485	0.1640	0.1261	0.1324
9 days	0.1077	0.1272	0.1465	0.1617	0.1243	0.1306
10 days	0.1059	0.1253	0.1443	0.1589	0.1230	0.1283

Table 3: Performance of varying length of time interval on Digg dataset

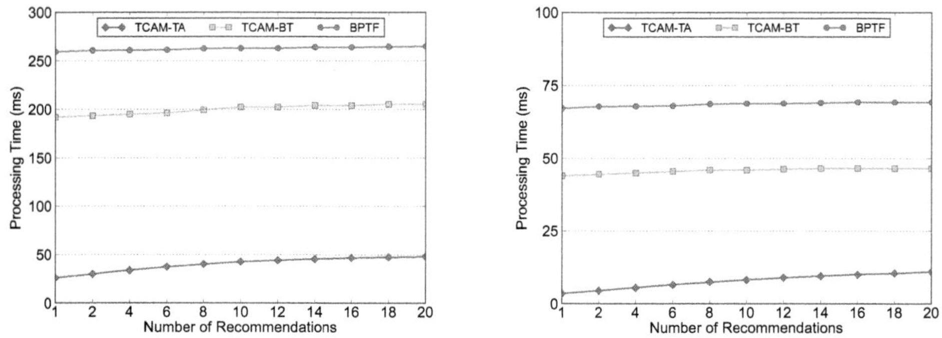

(a) Douban Movie dataset

(b) Movielens dataset

Figure 8: Efficiency w.r.t Online Recommendations

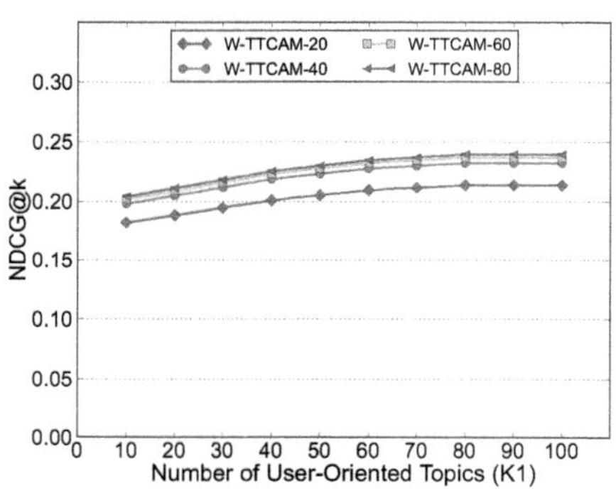

Figure 9: Performance of varying number of topics

in Java (JDK 1.6) and run on a Linux Server with 32G RAM. In this section, we first report their online recommendation time costs, and then present their offline training time.

Efficiency of Online Recommendations. In the efficiency study , we adopt two methods to utilize the knowledge learnt by TCAM to produce online recommendations. The first is called TCAM-TA and uses the proposed TA-based query processing technique in Section 4.2 to produce top-k recommendations. The second is called TCAM-BF and uses brute-force algorithm to produce top-k recommendations. In TCAM-BF, we scan all items within the dataset and compute their ranking scores, and then recommend k items with the highest scores. It should be noted that the state-of-the-art temporal recommender model BPTF also needs to scan all items to produce top-k recommendations because the ranking function in BPTF does not have the nice property of monotonicity which is required by TA algorithm [10].

Figures 8(a)-8(b) present the average online time costs of different methods with a varying number of recommendations for datasets Douban Movie and MovieLens respectively. For example, on average our proposed TCAM-TA can find top-10 items (that could most interest a user) from the Douban Movie dataset in 46ms, from the Movielens dataset in 9 ms. From the figures, we can observe that 1) TCAM-TA outperforms TCAM-BF and BPTF significantly in both datasets, justifying the benefits brought by the proposed TA-based query processing technique; 2) TCAM-BF is more efficient than BPTF in both datasets because BPTF computes the rating score that a user u will assign to item v at time t using the inner product of three vectors (i.e., user, item and time latent representations in a shared low-dimensional space) [29] while TCAM computes the ranking score using the inner product of two vectors (i.e., the query and item latent representations), as shown in Equation (22); 3) the time cost of TCAM-TA increases with the increasing number of recommendations because TCAM-TA needs to scan more items to find the k items with highest ranking scores, but TCAM-TA is still much more efficient than TCAM-BF and BPTF since the number of recommendations (i.e., k) is often constrained in a small range (e.g., $[1 \cdots 20]$); 4) the time cost (TC) of each algorithm in Douban Movie is more expensive than that in Movielens, showing that if a dataset has more items available, it requires more processing time to produce top-k recommendations.

Douban Movie			Movielens		
BPRMF	TCAM	BPTF	BPRMF	TCAM	BPTF
84.32	110.87	940.46	14.76	22.40	170.88

Table 4: Comparison on Model Training Time (Minute)

Efficiency of Offline Model Training. Table 4 shows the training time of three models on two datasets. From the table, we observe that our proposed TCAM model achieves comparable efficiency performance with BPRMF. As is expected, the training of BPTF is much slower than our TCAM and BPRMF. Note that although BPRMF achieves best efficiency performance, its recommendation accuracy value is much lower than our TCAM model because it does not exploit the temporal information, as is shown and analyzed in Section 5.3.2.

5.4 Temporal Context Influence Study

In this section, we study the influence degrees of users' personal interests and the temporal context on users' decision making. The user interest influence probability λ_u and the temporal context influence probability $1 - \lambda_u$ are learnt automatically in TCAM models. Due to space constraints, we focus on W-TTCAM. We are interested in how significantly the temporal context influences the user's decisions on different social media platforms.

Since different people have different mixing weights, we plot the distributions of both the personal interest and the temporal context influence probabilities across all users. The results on the MovieLens data set are shown in Figure 10, where Figure 10 (a) plots the cumulative distribution of personal interest influence probabilities, and Figure 10(b) shows the temporal context influence probabilities. It can be observed that, in general, people's personal interest influence is significantly higher than the influence of the temporal context. For example, Figure 10(a) shows that the personal interest influence probability of more than 76% of users is higher than the 0.82. This observation indicates that most movies consumed by users are selected in accordance with their interests and tastes.

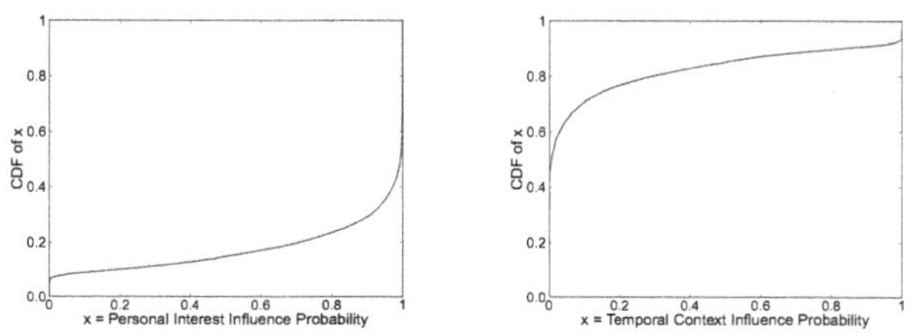

(a) Personal Interest Influence (b) Temporal Context Influence

Figure 10: Temporal Context Influence Result (MovieLens)

Figures 11(a) and 11(b) show respectively the personal interest influence probabilities and temporal context influence probabilities learnt from the Digg data. As shown in Figure 11(a), the personal interest influence probability is smaller than the temporal context influence probability. For example, the temporal context influence probability of more than 70% of users is higher than 0.5. The implication of this finding is that people are mainly influenced by the temporal context when choosing news to read. By comparing the analysis results obtained from the two datasets, we can observe that the temporal context influence on users' choice of news to read is much more significant than it is on the selection of movies to watch. This is probably because news is a time-sensitive item which is driven by offline social events, while movies are less time-sensitive.

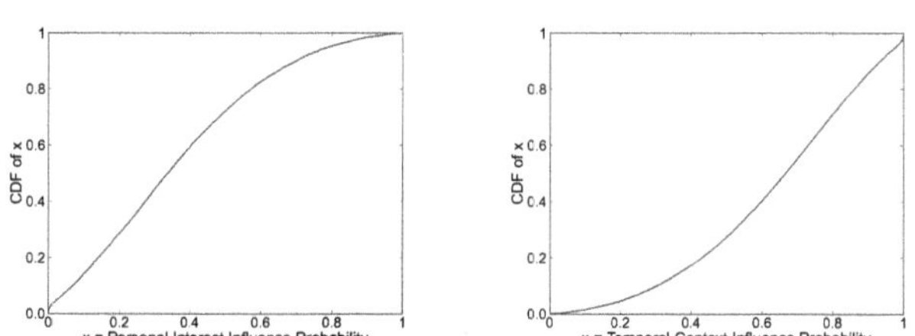

(a) Personal Interest Influence (b) Temporal Context Influence

Figure 11: Temporal Context Influence Result (Digg)

5.5 Analyzing Latent Topics

To analyze the topics detected by our TCAM models, we note that Table 5 and Table 6 respectively present two time-oriented

TT	TTCAM	W-TTCAM
latest	news	michaeljackson
headline	world	mj
news	death	moonwalk
investigative	jackson	death
michaeljackson	michaeljackson	investigative
event	headline	news

Table 5: Time-Oriented Topic "Michael Jackson" Detected by Different Models on Delicious

TTCAM	W-TTCAM
Forrest Gump (1994)	Transformers (2007)
Zodiac (2007)	Tau ming chong (2007)
Transformers (2007)	Zodiac (2007)
Roman Holiday (1953)	Becoming Jane (2007)
Tau ming chong (2007)	Kidnap (2007)
Edward Scissorhands (1990)	Secret (2007)
Kidnap (2007)	I Am Legend(2007)

Table 6: Time-Oriented Topic T2007 Detected by Different Models on Douban Movie

topics detected by different models on the datasets of Delicious and Douban Movie. We can make the following observations from the tables: (1) On the Delicious dataset, the time-oriented topics of "michael jackson's death", detected by TT and TTCAM, rank popular tags with abstract semantics like "event", "headline", and "world" in the top positions because of their high frequencies. As a matter of fact, these tags are of little value in describing the event and users may not be interested in them. In contrast, our proposed W-TTCAM clearly promotes concrete words like "moonwalk" because of the tight co-burst relationship with the word "Michael Jackson", which shows that W-TTCAM can cluster correlated bursty tags into a time-oriented topic, enabling the time-oriented topic to be represented by tags that are more relevant to the real event. (2) On the Douban Movie data set, the time-oriented topic T2007, detected by TTCAM, ranks popular movies like "Forrest Gump", "Roman Holiday" and "Edward Scissorhands" in the top positions as a result of their high popularity. In contrast, the top movies in T2007 detected by W-TTCAM were all released in the year 2007, which shows that W-TTCAM can accurately cluster movies released around the same time into a time-oriented topic by promoting bursty movies such as "Becoming Jane" and "Secret". Based on the above observations, we conclude that the time-oriented topics can be better modeled with the item weighting scheme.

To examine whether the user-oriented topics and time-oriented topics detected by the TCAM models can really capture user interest and temporal context, we present both user-oriented and time-oriented topics detected by W-TTCAM on Douban Movie dataset in Table 7. From the table, we can easily tell the difference between the user-oriented and time-oriented topics on movies. Specifically, the user-oriented topics capture the genres of films by clustering similar-taste movies into a topic, while movies under each time-oriented topic share a similar release time and the popularity of the corresponding time-oriented topic also reaches its peak during that period. The movie types and release time which are respectively captured by the user-oriented and time-oriented topics are shown in the second row of the table.

6. CONCLUSION AND FUTURE WORK

In this paper, we proposed a temporal context-aware mixture model (TCAM) to model user rating behaviors in social media systems, by taking into account two factors, user intrinsic interests as an internal factor, and temporal context as an external factor.

U1	U15	T2010	T2009
Same-Sex	Horror/Thriller	2010	2009
Shelter (2007)	Eden Lake (2008)	Salt (2010)	District 9 (2009)
Starcrossed (2005)	Dead Silence (2007)	Inception (2010)	The Boat That Rocked (2009)
Get Real (1999)	See prang (2008)	The Expendables (2010)	The Founding of A Republic (2009)
Maurice (1987)	The Hills Have Eyes (2006)	The Twilight Saga: Eclipse (2010)	Sophie's Revenge (2009)
For a Lost Soldier (1992)	Dawn of the Dead (2004)	Temple Grandin (2010)	Eternal Beloved (2009)
The Trip (2002)	Silent Hill (2006)	Sex and the City 2 (2010)	Empire of Silver (2009)
Lucky Blue (2007)	The Last House on the Left (2009)	Sherlock Season 1 (2010)	Overheard (2009)

Table 7: Comparison between User-Oriented and Time-Oriented Topics Detected on Douban Movie

We introduced two different types of topics to model user interests and temporal context, respectively. We designed two methods to model the temporal context, and an item-weighting scheme was developed to enhance the TCAM models by exploiting the frequency distribution and temporal distribution information of items. To demonstrate the applicability of TCAM, we deployed this model to facilitate temporal recommendation. We also designed an efficient query processing technique to speed up the process of online recommendation. We demonstrated the superiority of the proposed TCAM models on four popular social media datasets.

There are several directions for future research. First, we would like to explore enhancements to our models by exploiting the effect of user social network on user rating behaviors, e.g., to study how a user's friends affect her/his rating behaviors. Second, it would be an interesting future direction to consider time-evolving user interests which generally change over time. Third, since the user generated data in social media is very noisy, it would be interesting to incorporate a background distribution to filter the noise in social media data.

7. ACKNOWLEDGMENTS

This research is supported by the National Natural Science Foundation of China under Grant No. 61272155. This work is also supported, in part, by the Australian Research Council (ARC) Discovery Project under Grant No. DP140100545.

8. REFERENCES

[1] L. AlSumait, D. Barbara, and C. Domeniconi. On-line lda: Adaptive topic models for mining text streams with applications to topic detection and tracking. In *IEEE Conf. on Data Mining*, pages 993–1022, 2008.

[2] D. M. Blei and J. D. Lafferty. Dynamic topic models. In *ICML*, pages 113–120, 2006.

[3] D. M. Blei, A. Y. Ng, and M. I. Jordan. Latent dirichlet allocation. In *Journal of Machine Learning Research*, pages 993–1022, 2003.

[4] Y. Cha, B. Bi, C.-C. Hsieh, and J. Cho. Incorporating popularity in topic models for social network analysis. In *SIGIR*, pages 223–232, 2013.

[5] Y. Cha and J. Cho. Social-network analysis using topic models. In *SIGIR*, pages 565–574, 2012.

[6] W. Y. Chen, J. C. Chu, J. Luan, H. Bai, Y. Wang, and E. Y. Chang. Collaborative filtering for orkut communities: discovery of user latent behavior. In *WWW*, pages 681–690, 2009.

[7] T. M. Cover and J. A. Thomas. *Elements of information theory*. Wiley-Interscience, 1991.

[8] A. S. Das, M. Datar, A. Garg, and S. Rajaram. Google news personalization: Scalable online collaborative filtering. In *WWW*, pages 271–280, 2007.

[9] Q. Diao, J. Jiang, F. Zhu, and E. P. Lim. Finding bursty topics from microblogs. In *ACL*, pages 536–544, 2012.

[10] R. Fagin, A. Lotem, and M. Naor. Optimal aggregation algorithms for middleware. In *PODS*, pages 102–113, 2001.

[11] Z. Gantner, S. Rendle, C. Freudenthaler, and L. Schmidt Thieme. Mymedialite: a free recommender system library. In *RecSys*, pages 305–308, 2011.

[12] A. Gohr and A. Hinneburg. Topic evlolution in a stream of documents. In *SIAM*, 2009.

[13] T. Hofmann. Probabilistic latent semantic analysis. In *UAI*, 1999.

[14] X. Jin, Y. Zhou, and B. Mobasher. A maximum entropy web recommendation system: combining collaborative and content features. In *KDD*, pages 612–617, 2005.

[15] Y. Kang and N. Yu. Soft-constraint based online lda for community recommendation. In *PCM*, pages 494–505, 2010.

[16] Y. Koren. Collaborative filtering with temporal dynamics. In *KDD*, pages 447–456, 2009.

[17] K. Lerman and R. Ghosh. Information contagion: An empirical study of the spread of news on digg and twitter social networks. In *ICWSM*, 2010.

[18] J. Liu, P. Dolan, and E. R. Pedersen. Personalized news recommendation based on click behavior. In *IUI*, pages 31–40, 2010.

[19] N. N. Liu, M. Zhao, E. Xiang, and Q. Yang. Online evolutionary collaborative filtering. In *RecSys*, pages 95–102, 2010.

[20] Q. Mei and C. Zhai. Discovering evolutionary theme patterns from text: An exploration of temporal text mining. In *KDD*, pages 198–207, 2005.

[21] M. Michelson and S. A. Macskassy. Discovering users' topics of interest on twitter: a first look. In *AND*, pages 73–80, 2010.

[22] S. Rendle, C. Freudenthaler, Z. Gantner, and L. Schmidt Thieme. Bpr: Bayesian personalized ranking from implicit feedback. In *UAI*, pages 452–461, 2009.

[23] M. Rosen Zvi, T. Griffiths, M. Steyvers, and P. Smyth. The author-topic model for authors and documents. In *UAI*, pages 487–494, 2004.

[24] J. Stoyanovich, S. Amer Yahia, C. Marlow, and C. Yu. Leveraging tagging to model user interests in del.icio.us. In *AAAI*, 2008.

[25] X. Wang and A. McCallum. Topics over time: A non-markov continueous-time model of topical trends. In *KDD*, pages 424–433, 2006.

[26] X. Wang, C. Zhai, X. Hu, and R. Sproat. Mining correlated bursty topic patterns from coordinated text streams. In *KDD*, pages 784–793, 2007.

[27] Z. Wen and C. Y. Lin. On the quality of inferring interests from social neighbors. In *KDD*, pages 373–382, 2010.

[28] J. Wolfe, A. Haghighi, and D. Klein. Fully distributed em for very large datasets. In *ICML*, pages 1184–1191, 2008.

[29] L. Xiong, X. Chen, T. K. Huang, J. G. Schneider, and J. G. Carbonell. Temporal collaborative filtering with bayesian probabilistic tensor factorization. In *SDM*, pages 211–222, 2010.

[30] Z. Xu, Y. Zhang, Y. Wu, and Q. Yang. Modeling user posting behavior on social media. In *SIGIR*, pages 545–554, 2012.

[31] M. Ye, X. Liu, and W. C. Lee. Exploring social influence for recommendation: a generative model approach. In *SIGIR*, pages 671–680, 2012.

[32] H. Yin, B. Cui, J. Li, J. Yao, and C. Chen. Challenging the long tail recommendation. *Proc. VLDB Endow.*, 5(9):896–907, 2012.

[33] H. Yin, B. Cui, H. Lu, Y. Huang, and J. Yao. A unified model for stable and temporal topic detection on social platform. In *ICDE*, pages 661–672, 2013.

[34] H. Yin, Y. Sun, B. Cui, Z. Hu, and L. Chen. Lcars: A location-content-aware recommender system. In *KDD*, pages 221–229, 2013.

Indexing for Interactive Exploration of Big Data Series

Kostas Zoumpatianos
University of Trento
zoumpatianos@disi.unitn.it

Stratos Idreos
Harvard University
stratos@seas.harvard.edu

Themis Palpanas
Paris Descartes University
themis@mi.parisdescartes.fr

ABSTRACT

Numerous applications continuously produce big amounts of data series, and in several time critical scenarios analysts need to be able to query these data as soon as they become available, which is not currently possible with the state-of-the-art indexing methods and for very large data series collections. In this paper, we present the first adaptive indexing mechanism, specifically tailored to solve the problem of indexing and querying very large data series collections. The main idea is that instead of building the complete index over the complete data set up-front and querying only later, we interactively and adaptively build parts of the index, only for the parts of the data on which the users pose queries. The net effect is that instead of waiting for extended periods of time for the index creation, users can immediately start exploring the data series. We present a detailed design and evaluation of adaptive data series indexing over both synthetic data and real-world workloads. The results show that our approach can gracefully handle large data series collections, while drastically reducing the data to query delay: by the time state-of-the-art indexing techniques finish indexing 1 billion data series (and before answering even a single query), adaptive data series indexing has already answered $3*10^5$ queries.

1. INTRODUCTION

Big Data Series. Recent advances in sensing, networking, data processing and storage technologies have significantly eased the process of generating and collecting tremendous amounts of data series at extremely high rates and volumes. Formally, a data series $T=(p_1,...p_n)$ is defined as a sequence of points $p_i=(v_i,t_i)$ where each point is associated with a value v_i and a time t_i in which this recording was made. A common characteristic is that analysts need to examine the sequence of values (i.e., the data series) rather than the individual points independently. Such data can be networking information, web usage data, scientific data (e.g., electrocardiograms, weather data, etc.) as well as financial data (e.g., stock market data), to practically any kind of data series. In this way, there has been a significant interest in the data management community towards analyzing data series in real time with the minimum possible processing and storage overhead.

SIGMOD'14, June 22–27, 2014, Snowbird, UT, USA.

ACM 978-1-4503-2376-5/14/06 ...$15.00.
http://dx.doi.org/10.1145/2588555.2610498 .

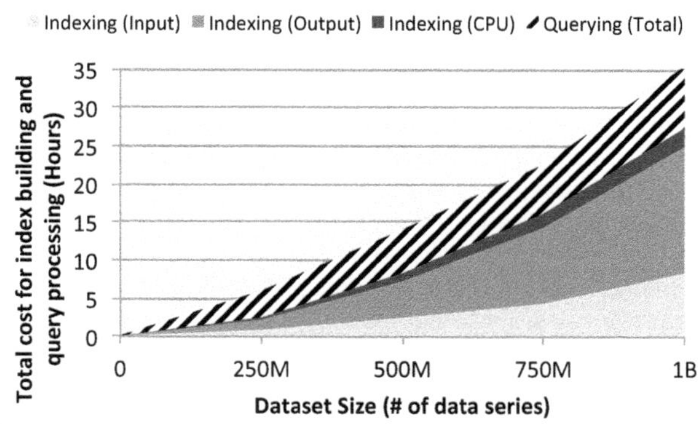

Figure 1: The data to query gap: building a state-of-the-art index and answering 10^5 queries for big data series collections.

The Data to Query Gap. For big data exploration, it is prohibitive to rely to full sequential scans for every single query, and therefore, indexing is required. The target of indexing techniques is to make query processing efficient enough, such that the analysts can repeatedly fire several exploratory queries with quick response times. However, we show in this paper that the amount of time required to build a data series index can be a significant bottleneck; Figure 1 shows that it takes more than a full day to build a state-of-the-art index (iSAX 2.0 [6]) over a data set of 1 billion data series in a modern server machine. The main cost components of indexing are reading the data to be indexed, spilling the indexed data and structures to disk, as well as incurring the computation costs of figuring out where each new data entry belongs to (in the index structure). As the data size grows, the total indexing cost increases dramatically, to a degree where it creates a big and disruptive gap between the time when the data is available and the time when one can actually have access to the data. In fact, as the data grows, the query processing cost (10^5 queries in the case of Figure 1) increasingly becomes a smaller fraction of the total cost (indexing + querying). We will discuss this experiment and its set-up in more detail later on, but for now it is interesting to note that the performance shown in Figure 1 is actually the optimal one as we have chosen a leaf size which enables a quick index build time. As Figure 2 shows (for a 500 million data series set), the smaller the leaf size is the harder it becomes to build an index, while the bigger the leaf size is, the more we penalize query answering times (10^5 queries in this case). Thus, simply choosing a large leaf size does not resolve the data to query problem.

Data Exploration. As data sizes grow even bigger, waiting for several days before posing the first queries can be a major show-stopper for many applications both in businesses and in sciences. In addition, firing exploratory queries, i.e., queries which are not known a priori, is becoming quickly a common scenario. That is, in many cases, analysts and scientists need to explore the data before they can figure out what the next query is, or even which experiment to perform next; the output of one query inspires the formulation of the next query, and drives the experimental process. In such cases, performing tuning and initialization actions up-front suffers from the fact that we do not have enough knowledge about which data parts are of interest, e.g., [15, 19]. Similarly, in many applications, predefined queries are beneficial only if they can track data patterns or events within a given time limit; e.g., traffic monitoring applications for advertisement need to quickly determine user positions and interests.

Adaptive Data Series Indexing. We propose an adaptive indexing solution which minimizes the index creation time allowing users to query the data soon after its generation and several times faster compared to state-of-the-art indexing approaches. As more queries are posed, the index is continuously refined and subsequent queries enjoy even better execution times. Although the concept of adaptive indexing has been studied in the context of column-store databases, there the main goal is to incrementally sort individual arrays (i.e., columns) for point or range queries over 1-dimensional points. In contrast, a data series index is a tree-based index that is tailored to answer similarity search queries over data series collections, thus requiring very different techniques, able to simultaneously index multiple arrays (i.e., data series).

Contributions. Our contributions are summarized as follows.

- We demonstrate the inability of state-of-the-art indexing to cope with exploratory analysis of very large data series collections. We show that the index creation time is a major bottleneck which becomes exponentially worse as data grows.
- We introduce the first adaptive data series index. Adaptive data series indexing minimizes the data to query gap by delaying actions until they are absolutely necessary. Initialization cost is kept at very low levels; only a minimal tree structure based on a summary of the data is built initially. Then, the index structure is continuously enriched as more data and queries arrive and only for the hot part of the data. Each query that is not covered by the current contents of the index, triggers a sequence of actions that have as a side-effect more data to be brought inside the index.
- Furthermore, we demonstrate that no special set-up is required regarding critical low-level details such as leaf size and tree depth. We propose adaptive data series indexing algorithms that start with a rather big leaf size and a shallow tree in order to minimize initialization costs for new data, but then as queries arrive and focus to specific data areas, they adaptively and automatically expand hot subtrees and adjust leaf sizes in the hot branches of the index to minimize querying costs.
- Through a detailed experimental evaluation with both synthetic and diverse real-world workloads, we show that it is possible to drastically reduce the data to query time, being able to handle several hundreds of thousands of queries by the time that state-of-the-art data series (iSAX 2.0 [6]) and multi-dimensional (R-trees [13], X-trees [4], KD-Trees [3]) techniques are still in the index creation phase.

2. RELATED WORK

In this section, we briefly discuss related work and we introduce the necessary background knowledge on adaptive indexing and on state-of-the-art data series indexing.

Similarity Search in Data Series. One of the most basic data mining tasks is that of finding similar data series in a database [1]. The query comes in the form of a data series X and it says "find me

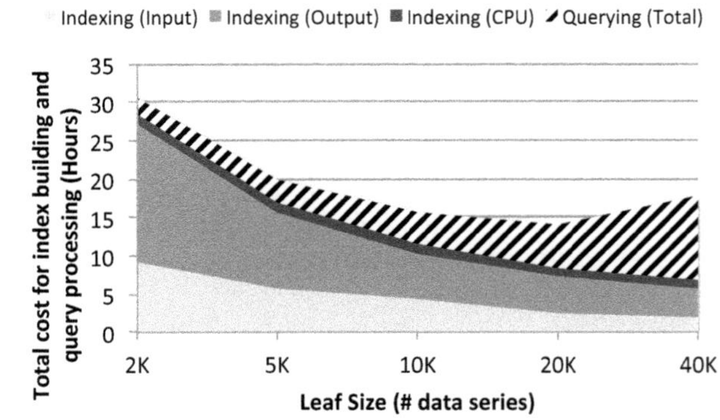

Figure 2: The indexing to querying trade-off: bigger leaf sizes improve indexing speed, but penalize query answering times.

the data series in the database which is most similar to X". Similarity search is an integral part of most data mining procedures, such as clustering [33], classification and deviation detection [5, 9]. A common approach for answering such queries is to perform a dimensionality reduction technique (the particular choice is of small importance [24]) such as *Discrete Fourier Transforms (DFT) [1]*, *Discrete Wavelet Transforms (DWT)* [8], *Discrete Haar Wavelet Transforms (DHWT)*, *Piecewise Aggregate Approximation (PAA)* [22, 34], or *Symbolic Aggregate approXimation (SAX)* [23] and then use this representation for indexing. At the same time, a large set of indexing methods have been proposed for this kind of representations, including traditional multidimensional [13, 4] and specialized [29, 30, 6, 2, 32, 7] indices. Moreover, various distance measures have been presented that work on top of such indexes, e.g., Discrete Time Warping (DTW) and Euclidean Distance (ED).

Our work follows the same high level principles, but it is the first to introduce an adaptive indexing mechanism for data series in order to assist exploratory similarity search in big data sets. In all previous work, the data series index is built in one step a priori and no queries may be processed until the index is ready. On the contrary, in our work, query processing and index building are interleaved, resulting in a drastically reduced data to query time.

Adaptive Indexing. The concept of adaptive indexing was recently introduced in the context of column-store databases [17, 16, 18, 20, 14, 28, 11, 12]. The intuition is that instead of building database indexes up-front, indexes are built during query processing, adapting to the workload. In particular, the algorithms are focused on how to incrementally sort columns in main-memory column-stores. The query predicates are used as pivots during the index refinement steps. Each index refinement step performed during a single query can be seen as a single step of an incremental quick-sort action. As more queries touch a column, this given column reaches closer to a sorted state. The benefit is that adaptive indexing avoids fully sorting columns up front at a high initialization cost, especially when there is no idle time to do so, or no reliable workload knowledge that this is indeed needed. These ideas have also been extended lately for Hadoop-based environments [27].

Even though in this paper we follow the same philosophy, our work is the first to design an adaptive index for data series processing and similarity search queries. Contrary to working with arrays as in column-store relational databases in the case of cracking, our work is based on tree-structures, which are suited for data series indexing, where we index more than one columns at a time (since each data series can be considered an array) via reduced resolutions. One could also consider storing a data series as a row in a column-store, i.e., each point being a separate attribute and then use adaptive indexing. However, then we lose the locality property as accessing one data series would require accessing several different files. Sideways cracking [18] has been proposed in order to handle multiple columns in a column-store, but this is a completely different paradigm, indexing a single relational table across one dimension at a time, and essentially relying in replication to align columns. In addition, contrary to indexing relational data where a global ordering can be imposed, i.e., incrementally creating a range index, in our case a global ordering is not possible and we are answering nearest neighbor queries. Our index introduces several novel techniques for adaptive data series indexing such as creating only a partial tree structure deep enough to not penalize the first queries with a lot of splits, and filling it on demand, as well as adapting leaf sizes on-the-fly and with varying leaf sizes across the index. Some concepts that have appeared in past adaptive indexing work apply here as well, but only as concepts, as the design of the algorithms and data structures is tailored for data series. For example, like in [20, 28] we start with a lightweight preparatory step, but without having a global unique ordering of the data. In addition, the notion of adaptively bringing the data inside the index is conceptually similar to partial sideways cracking [18].

Data Series Representations and the iSAX Index. We now discuss the state-of-art data series indexing schemes. In 2000, Yi and Faloutsos [34], as well as Keogh et al. [22], both independently presented the idea of segmented means [34] or Piecewise Aggregate Approximation (PAA) representation [22]. This representation allows for dimensionality reduction in the time domain, by segmenting the data series in equal parts and calculating the average value for each segment. An example of PAA representations can be seen in Figure 3; in this case the original data series is divided into 4 equal parts. Based on PAA, Lin et al. [23] introduced the Symbolic Aggregate approXimation (SAX) representation. It works by partitioning the value space in segments of sizes that follow the normal distribution. Each PAA value can then be represented by a character (or a small number of bits) that corresponds to the segment that it falls into. This leads to a representation with a very small memory footprint, an important requirement for managing very large data series collections. A segmentation of size 3 can be seen in Figure 3, where the data series is represented with the SAX word "10 10 11".

The SAX representation was later extended to indexable SAX (iSAX) [29]; it considers variable cardinality for each character of a SAX representation, and as a result variable degrees of precision. An iSAX representation is composed of a set of characters that form a word. Each word represents a data series available in the dataset. Each character in a word is accompanied by a number that denotes its cardinality (the number of bits that describe this character). In the case of a binary alphabet, with a word size of 3 characters and a maximum cardinality of 2 bits, we could have a set of data series (two in the following example) represented with the following words: $00_2 10_2 01_2$, $00_2 11_2 01_2$, where each character has a full cardinality of 2 bits and each word corresponds to one data series. If we now reduce the cardinality of the second character in each word, we could represent both of them with a single iSAX representation: $00_2 1_1 01_2$. That is because 1_1 corresponds to both 10 and 11, since the last bit is trailed when the cardinality is reduced. By starting with a cardinality of 1 for each character in the root node and by gradually performing splits by increasing the cardinality by one character at a time, one can build a tree index [29, 30]. Such cardinality reductions can be efficiently calculated with bit mask operations.

The state-of-the-art iSAX 2.0 index is also based on this property [6]; it is a data series index that implements fast bulk loading. Figure 3 depicts an example where each iSAX word has 3 segments and each segment a maximum cardinality of 4 (2 bits). The root node has 2^w children (2^3 in Figure 3) while each child node forms a binary sub-tree. Each leaf node corresponds to a split in one dimension and points to a single area of the domain.

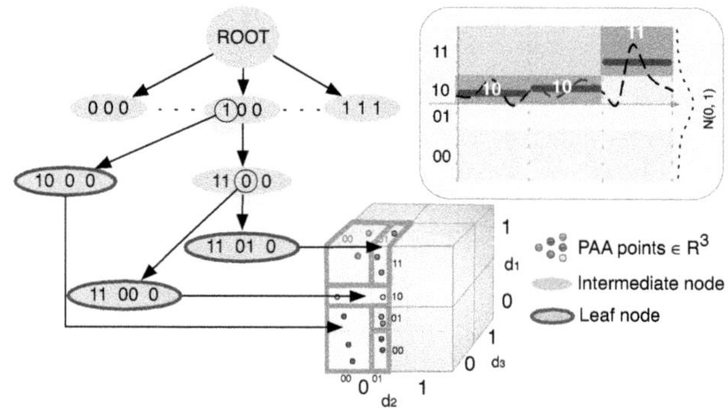

Figure 3: An example of iSAX and SAX representations.

Our contributions build on top of this line of work by enabling adaptive indexing using the state-of-the-art iSAX representations. Contrary to past work, our new adaptive index allows for incremental, continuous and adaptive index creation during query time. Initialization cost is kept low, bringing the ability to query the data set much sooner than in past work. We show both the significant bottleneck faced by state-of-the-art indexing as we grow to large data, as well as the drastic improvement that adaptive indexing brings.

Scans Vs Indexing. Even though recent studies have shown that in certain cases sequential scans can be performed very efficiently [26], such techniques are only applicable when the database consists of a single, long data series, and queries are looking for potential matches in small subsequences of this long data series. Such approaches, however, do not bring benefit to the general case of querying a mixed database of several data series, which is the focus of this study. Therefore, indexing is required in order to efficiently support data exploration tasks, which involve ad-hoc queries, i.e., the query workload is not known in advance.

3. THE ADAPTIVE DATA SERIES INDEX

In this section, we present adaptive data series indexing in detail, and describe how it can reduce the data to query gap by *shifting costly index creation steps from the initialization time to the query processing time*. For ease of presentation, we discuss adaptive data series indexing in two steps; initially we present ADS, a design which introduces the concept of adaptively and incrementally loading data series in the index. Then, we discuss ADS+ which introduces the concept of adaptive splits and adaptive leaf sizes. Finally, we present PADS+, an aggressive variation of ADS+, which is tailored for even better performance in skewed workloads.

3.1 The ADS Index

In order to increase the exploration ability we need to decrease the data to query time. That is, we need to decrease the amount of time needed until a user can access and query new data with good response time. The main bottleneck is the index construction overhead. ADS attacks the index construction bottleneck by shifting the construction of the leaf nodes of the index (the only nodes that can carry raw values for the data series, and have to be stored on disk) to query time. During the index creation phase, ADS creates a tree which contains only the iSAX representation for each data series; the actual data series remain in the raw files and are only loaded in an adaptive way if a relevant query arrives. On the contrary, state-of-the-art indexes, such as iSAX 2.0, a priori load all raw data series in the index at the leaves of the tree (in order to reduce random I/O during query processing). The analysis of the performance of iSAX

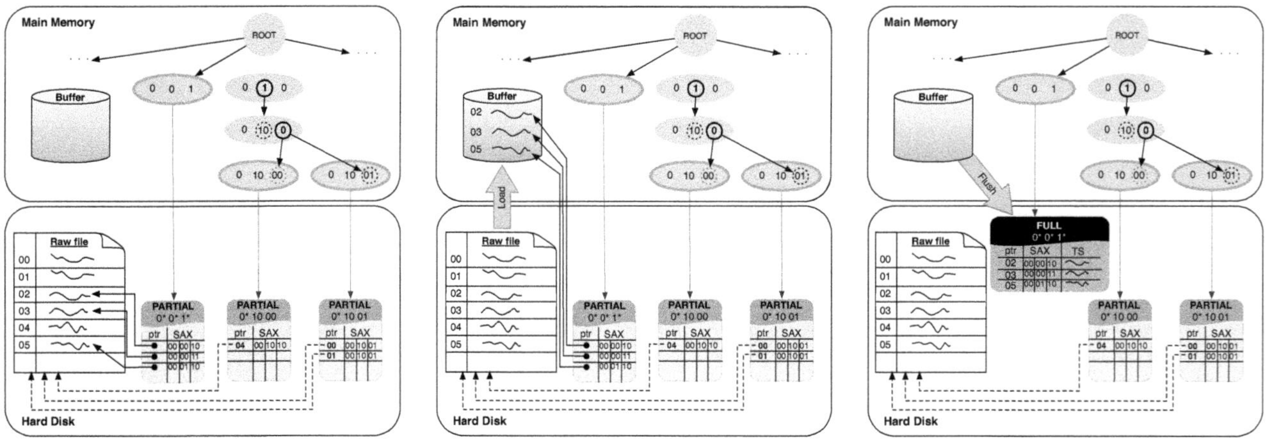

(a) Initial state (b) Buffered leaf state (c) Flushed leaf state

Figure 4: The ADS index states.

2.0 in Figure 1 motivates our design choice for ADS; it shows that reading from and writing to disk is the main cost component during the indexing phase of iSAX 2.0. The results show that a big part of these read and write costs is due to reading the raw data series from disk and to writing the leaves of the index tree back to disk (after insertions). Motivated by data exploration scenarios where we do not know a priori which data series are interesting and relevant for our analysis, ADS avoids these costs completely at initialization time; it pays such costs at query time, only when absolutely necessary, and only for the data parts which are relevant to the workload. Below we describe ADS in detail.

3.1.1 Index Creation

The index creation phase takes place before queries can be processed but it is kept very lightweight. The process can be seen in Algorithm 1. The input is a raw file which contains all data series in ASCII form. ADS builds a minimal tree during this phase, i.e., a tree which does not contain any data series. The tree contains only iSAX representations. The process starts with a full scan on the raw file to create an iSAX representation for each data series entry. This can be seen in lines 2-5 of Algorithm 1. For data series we also record its offset in the raw data file so future queries can easily retrieve the raw values. To minimize random memory access and random I/O we use a set of buffers in main memory (line 6) to temporarily hold data to be added in the index. When these buffers are full (line 7), we move the data to the appropriate leaf buffer in the index (see discussion in Buffering later on). If necessary, we perform split operations on the way (lines 12-15). The split operation is described in detail in Algorithm 2. Then we sequentially flush each leaf buffer to the disk (Algorithm 1, line 19), set each leaf to be in PARTIAL mode which means that we do not store any raw data series in this leaf (line 20). This process continues until we have indexed all raw data series. We will discuss how we handle new data (updates) later on.

Delaying Leaf Construction. The actual data series are only necessary during query time, i.e., in order to give a complete and correct answer. During the index creation time, the iSAX representations are sufficient to build the index tree. In addition, not all data series are needed to answer a particular set of queries. In this way, ADS first creates all necessary iSAX representations and builds the index tree without inserting any data series and only adaptively inserts data series during query processing (to be discussed later on). There are numerous benefits that come with such a design decision, the most important being the significantly reduced cost to build the index. While it is clear that materializing leaves on demand will

Algorithm 1: createIndex(**file, index, n**)

```
1  while not reached end of file do
2      position = current file position;
3      dataSeries = read data series of size n from file;
4      isax = convert dataSeries to iSAX;
5      Move file pointer n points;
6      Add the (isax, position) pair in the index's FBL buffer;
7      if the main memory is full then
8          // Move data from the First Buffers (FBL layer)
9          // to the appropriate Leaf Buffer (LBL layer)
10         for every (isax, position) pair ∈ FBL buffer do
11             targetLeaf = Leaf of index for putting (isax, position);
12             while targetLeaf is full do
13                 Split(targetLeaf, isax);
14                 targetLeaf = New leaf for putting (isax, position);
15             Insert (isax, position) in targetLeaf's LBL buffer;
16         // Flush all Leaf Buffers containing (isax, position) pairs to
17         // the disk, and set them in PARTIAL mode (no raw data)
18         for every leaf in index do
19             Flush the LBL buffer of this leaf to the disk;
20             Set leaf to be in PARTIAL mode;
21         clear buffers;
```

incur a large random I/O cost, the main benefit comes from the fact that (a) ADS avoids dealing with the raw data series (i.e., other than the single scan on the raw file to create the iSAX representations), (b) it does not move the raw data series through the tree, and it (c) it does not place the raw data series into the leaf nodes. The data series simply stay in the raw file. This brings benefits in terms of I/O and memory bandwidth used during indexing. Especially when ADS comes to the point of spilling leaf nodes to disk (i.e., all leaves when there is no more free memory), it has a big advantage in that its leaf nodes are very lightweight, containing only iSAX representations, which can be orders of magnitude smaller than the data series themselves. For example, a data series of 256 points with a float precision of 4 bytes, can be efficiently summarized with 16 characters of 1 byte each. Moreover, by not inserting the data series in the index, we significantly reduce the cost of splits at the leaf level during the indexing phase; the I/O cost is minimized as only iSAX representations are shuffled between index nodes. All ADS variations maintain the main index tree in memory, while leaf nodes are kept on disk.

Buffering. ADS improves locality when inserting data by buffering data at two levels of the index. Buffering amortizes random access (both in memory and on disk) and is a common practice

Algorithm 2: Split(**leaf**)

```
1 diskData = get data from leaf's disk pages;
2 Insert diskData in leaf's buffer (LBL buffer);
3 Split leaf in the best point and create two new children leaves;
4 Set leaf as an intermediate node;
5 Set leaf.leftChild in PARTIAL mode;
6 Set leaf.right in PARTIAL mode;
7 for every (isax, position) pair ∈ leaf's LBL buffer do
8 |   Insert (isax, position) pair in the appropriate child leaf;
```

to improve locality in tree-based indexes, e.g., [35, 6], or even in database query plans (which typically have a tree shape) [36]. During index creation, instead of pushing iSAX representations through the index one at a time, ADS initially keeps those in the First Buffer Layer (FBL), a set of buffers corresponding to the children nodes of the index root. Once the FBL is full (i.e., all free memory is consumed), these representations are then passed through the tree and moved to the second layer of buffers corresponding to the leaf nodes of the index, called Leaf Buffer Layer (LBL). Data is then flushed to disk one leaf at a time, ensuring sequential writes. Additionally, every time that a leaf needs to be split and iSAX representations need to be read from disk, we keep them in the LBL, until we run out of space (Algorithm 2, lines 1-2). The leaves are flushed again when there is no more free memory.

Mapping on the Raw File. ADS reduces the index creation costs by not keeping around the data series. However, the raw data series is needed when queries arrive. For this reason, ADS needs an efficient way to quickly access a given data series entry. To achieve this, ADS maintains a single pointer for each data series entry X in the leaf node where data series X would normally reside. This is a pointer to the raw data file that provides direct access to the raw data series. (As we will discuss later on, the first time the leaf is accessed by a query all pointers are dropped and the corresponding raw data series are loaded.)

Example. An example of ADS is shown in Figure 4; the figure depicts the state of the index after certain events. An index is built on top of a set of iSAX words with a word size of 3 characters and a maximum cardinality for each character of 2 bits. The leaf nodes are depicted as oval shapes with border lines and the intermediate nodes without any border lines. Each intermediate node is split on a single character; the one surrounded by a bold cycle. Each leaf node is connected to a file on disk, where the full cardinality iSAX representations and the corresponding pointers to the raw file are stored. Figure 4(a) shows how the index looks like immediately after the initialization phase and before any query has been processed. In this case, all leaf nodes are in PARTIAL mode, i.e., they do not contain any data series, since no query has been executed yet. Figure 4(b) and Figure 4(c) show what happens when a query arrives and we discuss that in the next subsection.

3.1.2 Querying and Refining ADS

We continue our discussion by describing the process of query answering using ADS. Contrary to static indexes, the querying process in ADS contains a few extra steps. In addition to answering a query q, the query process refines the index during the processing steps of q. These extra index refinement steps do not take place after the query is answered; they develop completely on-the-fly and are necessary in order to answer q. At any given time, ADS contains just enough information in order to handle the current workload. Thus, when new queries arrive, which do not follow the patterns in previous requests, ADS needs to enrich the index with more information.

Searching the Index. When a query arrives (in the form of a data series), it is first converted to an iSAX representation. Then, the index tree is traversed searching for a leaf with an iSAX representation similar to that of the query. Whether such a leaf exists already or not, depends not only on the data, but also on past queries. In the case that the leaf node where the search ends is in PARTIAL mode, i.e., it contains only iSAX representations but not any data series, then all missing data series are fetched from the raw file.

Enriching the Index. To enrich a partial leaf, ADS fetches the partial leaf from disk and reads all the positions in the raw file of the data series that belong in this leaf. (A partial leaf holds the iSAX representation for each data series and also its position in the raw file.) Then, it sorts those positions (to ensure sequential access to the raw file) and fetches the raw data series. The new data series are assigned to leaf nodes and kept in memory in the LBL buffers (Figure 4(b)). The corresponding leaf node contains pointers to the buffered data. When there is no more free memory, the LBL buffers are flushed to disk (as seen in Figure 4(c)). The corresponding leaf is then marked as FULL. At this point the leaf data is fully materialized and future queries that need to access the data series for this leaf node, need to fetch the binary leaf data from disk or from the LBL buffer.

Creating the Answer. Once the data series that match the current query are available (either being fetched from the raw file, from the buffer, or from disk) then the real distance from the query is calculated. The minimum distance found in the leaf is used as the Best So Far (BSF) answer. If the BSF is not 0, which means that we did not get an exact match, then the node with potentially the best possible answer has to be identified. This is done in a recursive way as in the original iSAX index using the MinDistPaaToiSAX as described in [29] and until we are not able to improve BSF anymore. The difference is that if a new leaf is needed which is in partial mode, ADS will enrich this leaf on-the-fly.

Example. Continuing the example of Figure 4, Figure 4(b) and Figure 4(c) show what happens when a query arrives. Figure 4(b) depicts the case when a query reaches a non materialized leaf. The raw data series are fetched in main memory buffers, and the leaf now points to them. If the buffers become full, the raw data series for each leaf are flushed to disk, thus converting them into fully materialized leaves. This can be seen in Figure 4(c); the full leaf contains both the iSAX representations and the raw data series.

3.2 The ADS+ Index (Adaptive Leaf Size)

ADS drastically reduces the index creation time by avoiding the insertion of raw data series in the index until a relevant query arrives. However, there is opportunity for significant further optimizations; by studying the operations that get executed during adaptive index building and refinement we found that the time spent during split operations in the index tree is a major cost component.

Leaf Size and Splits. Splits are expensive as they cause data transfer to and from disk (to update node data). The main parameter that affects split costs is the leaf size, i.e., a tree with a big leaf size has a smaller number of nodes overall, causing less splits. Thus, a big leaf size reduces index creation time. However, as we have shown in Figure 2, big leaves also penalize query costs and vice versa: when reaching a big leaf during a search, we have to scan more data series than with a small leaf. State-of-the-art indexes rely on a fixed leaf size which needs to be set up front, during index creation time, and typically represents a compromise between index creation cost and query cost.

Adaptive Leaf Size. To further optimize the data to query time, we introduce a lightweight variation of ADS, *ADS+*, with a more transparent initialization step. The main intuition is that one can quickly build the index tree using a large leaf size, saving time from very expensive split operations, and rely on queries that are then go-

Algorithm 3: SplitADS+(**leaf**, **targetLeafSize**)

```
1 /* If the leaf size is bigger than the target leaf size, split node. */
2 if leaf's leaf size > targetLeafSize then
3 |   Split(node);
4 |   SplitADS+(node.leftChild, targetLeafSize);
5 |   SplitADS+(node.rightChild, targetLeafSize);
```

Algorithm 4: approxSearchADS+(**dataSeries**, **isax**, **index**, **queryTimeLeafSize**)

```
1 targetLeaf = leaf of index where this isax should be inserted;
2 if targetLeaf's leaf size > queryTimeLeafSize then
3 |   // It can be additionally split
4 |   SplitADS+(targetLeaf, queryTimeLeafSize);
5 |   targetLeaf = targetLeaf's descendant where this isax should be
  |   inserted;
6 // Calculate the real leaf distance between the dataSeries
7 // and the raw data series that this leaf refers to or contains.
8 bsf = calculateRealLeafDistance(targetLeaf, dataSeries);
9 return bsf;
```

Algorithm 5: exactSearchADS+(**dataSeries**, **index**, **queryTimeLeafSize**)

```
1  isax = convert dataSeries to iSAX;
2  bsf = approxSearchADS+(dataSeries, isax, index,
   queryTimeLeafSize);
3  bsfDist = Infinite;
4  queue = Initialize a priority queue with the root nodes of the index;
5  while node = pop next node from queue do
6  |   if node is a leaf and MinDist(dataSeries, node) < bsfDist then
7  |   |   if node's leaf size > queryTimeLeafSize then
8  |   |   |   // Need to split this leaf more
9  |   |   |   SplitADS+(node, queryTimeLeafSize);
10 |   |   |   Re-Insert node in queue;
11 |   |   else
12 |   |   |   // No need to split any more
13 |   |   |   dist = calculateRealLeafDistance(dataSeries, node);
14 |   |   |   if dist < bsfDist then
15 |   |   |   |   bsf = node;
16 |   |   |   |   bsfDist = dist;
17 |   else if MinDist(dataSeries, node) >= bsfDist then
18 |   |   // Found the nearest neighbor, break the loop
19 |   |   break;
20 |   else
21 |   |   // It is an intermediate node: push children to the queue.
22 |   |   minDLeft = MinDist+(dataSeries, node.leftChild);
23 |   |   minDRight = MinDist+(dataSeries, node.rightChild);
24 |   |   if minDLeft < bsfDist then
25 |   |   |   Put node.leftChild in queue with priority minDLeft;
26 |   |   if minDRight < bsfDist then
27 |   |   |   Put node.rightChild in queue with priority minDRight;
28 return bsf;
```

Algorithm 6: MinDist+(**dataSeries**, **leaf**)

```
1  if leaf is in FULL mode then
2  |   /* Use the coarse SAX representation of all the data series and
   |   calculate the minimum distance .*/
3  |   return MinDist(dataSeries, leaf);
4  else
5  |   /* The node is not materialized yet. We can load the small iSAX
   |   representations file and calculate a tighter minimum distance
   |   using the iSAX representations of all the data series. */
6  |   isaxValues = Get all isax representations from disk and LBL;
7  |   maxMinDist = 0;
8  |   for isax ∈ isaxValues do
9  |   |   minDist = MinDist(dataSeries, isax);
10 |   |   if minDist > maxMinDist then
11 |   |   |   maxMinDist = minDist;
12 |   return maxMinDist;
```

ing to force splits in order to reduce the leaf sizes in the hot areas of the index. ADS+ uses two different leaf sizes: a big build-time leaf size for optimal index construction, and a small query-time leaf size for optimal access costs. This allows us to make future queries benefit from every split operation performed, finding the relevant data by traversing the tree, and not by scanning larger leaves. Initially, the index tree is built as in plain ADS (Algorithm 1), with a constant leaf size, equal to build-time leaf size. In traditional indexes, this leaf size remains the same across the life-time of the index. In our case, when a query that needs to search a partial leaf arrives, ADS+ refines its index structure on-the-fly by recursively splitting the target leaf, until the target sub-leaf becomes smaller or equal to the query-time leaf size. This can be seen in Algorithm 3. Additionally both Approximate and Exact search have been modified to use this policy, a shown in Algorithm 4 (lines 2-5) and Algorithm 5 (lines 7-10), respectively.

Intuitively what happens is that the target leaf is split until it becomes small enough, while all leaves created due to split actions but are not needed for this query are then left untouched and thus with a leaf size which is between the big construction-time leaf size and the small query-time leaf size. If and only if the workload shifts and future queries need to query those leaves, then ADS+ automatically splits those leaves even further to reach a leaf size that gives good query processing times.

Example. An example of this process is shown in Figures 5(a) and 5(b). Figure 5(a) depicts the state of ADS+ after initialization and before any query has arrived, while Figure 5(b) shows how a single query results in adaptive splits of the right sub-tree until the target leaf node is fully materialized; intermediate nodes remain in partial mode and with a variable leaf size.

Adaptive and on demand leaf splitting allow ADS+ to have both fast index building and fast query processing. It does not waste time on creating fine-grained versions of each sub-tree of the index, but rather concentrates on the parts that are related to the current workload. When queries focus to a subset of the dataset, ADS+ does not need to exhaustively index and optimize all data; it rather concentrates on the most related sub-trees of the index. When the workload shifts and a new area of the index becomes relevant, then the first few queries adaptively optimize the index for the new area as well by expanding the proper sub-trees and adjusting leaf sizes.

Delaying Leaf Materialization. Another optimization that gives ADS+ a lightweight behavior is that it delays leaf materialization even further. In particular, when traversing the tree for query processing, which leads to adaptive leaf splitting, ADS+ does not materialize the initial big leaf, nor all the leaves it creates on its way to the target small leaf. For example, when ADS+ needs to split big leaf X and this results in X being split recursively into n new nodes until we reach the target leaf Z with a small leaf size, ADS+ fully materializes only leaf Z. For the rest of the leaves it uses the partial information contained in the leaves to perform the splits, i.e., the iSAX representations. This results in (a) less computation as opposed to having to split based on raw data, (b) less I/O as SAX representations are much smaller, and (c) it enhances the adaptive behavior of ADS+ as it materializes only the truly interesting data that the queries are targeting.

3.3 Partial ADS+ (PADS+)

Although the ADS variations described above help to reduce the indexing cost by omitting the raw data from the index creation process, ADS and ADS+ still need to spend time for creating the basic index structure. This means that users still have to wait until this

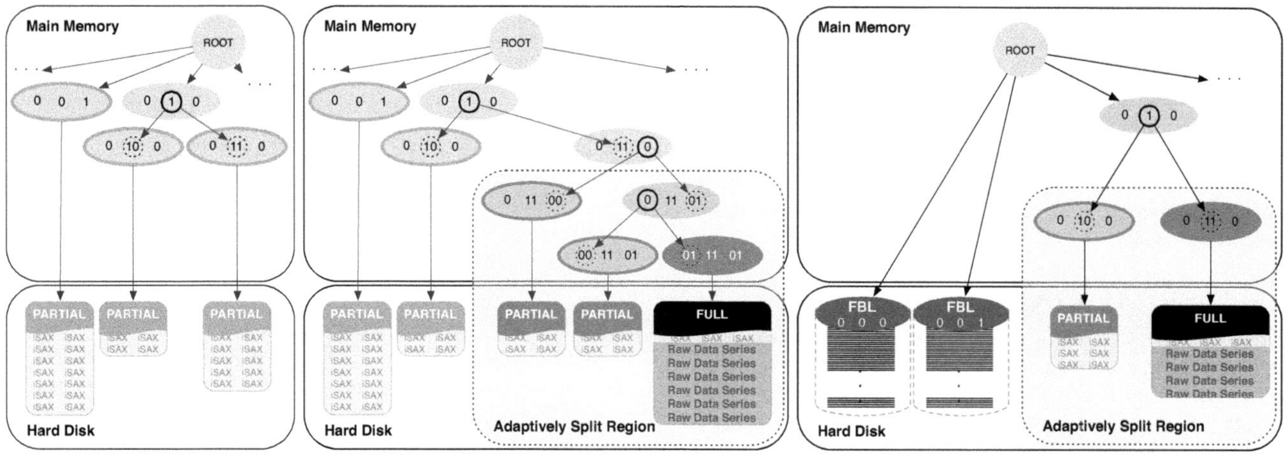

(a) ADS+ after index building. (b) ADS+ index after a query. (c) PADS+ index after a query.

Figure 5: Examples of ADS+ and PADS+.

process finishes, and even though it is a much faster process than full indexing, still certain applications may want *even faster* access to their data. To further optimize the data to query time, we introduce a more lightweight technique which extends ADS+ with an even more transparent initialization step. It is tailored for scenarios where users may want to fire just a few approximate queries, as well as for scenarios with high query workload skew. The new approach is named *Partial ADS+ (PADS+)* and its main intuition is to gradually build parts of the index tree, and only for small subsets of the data as queries arrive. The concept is similar to the idea of partial indexes [31] with the difference that the index is not static, i.e., it is not defined for a pre-decided set of the data; instead it continuously evolves to fit the workload.

Index Initialization. The initialization step of PADS+ is kept as lightweight as possible. PADS+ does not build an index tree at all; there is only a root node with a set of FBL buffers that contain only the iSAX representations. The only step which takes place during the initialization phase is that PADS+ creates the iSAX representations based on the raw data (as in ADS+). This requires a complete scan of the raw data. But then, instead of spending a significant effort using the SAX representations to create a tree as ADS+ does, PADS+ stops at this point and is ready to process queries. The iSAX representations are first kept in in-memory FBL buffers and then (contrary to ADS and ADS+) spilled to disk when the buffers are full. All these steps are similar to a subset of the initialization effort that takes place for ADS+. This approach allows PADS+ to significantly reduce the data-to-query time.

Adapting to Queries. PADS+ continuously and incrementally is refined as queries arrive. As the workload shifts and requires new data areas, the nodes in the index tree are adaptively and recursively split to smaller nodes that contain the required data. It follows the same procedure as with ADS+ with the difference that the starting point is an index with a just single root node with no children nodes. In this way, only the parts of the index which are truly relevant for the workload are further developed as queries arrive.

Skewed Workloads. Such an adaptive design favors scenarios where there is high skew in the workload, i.e., only part of the dataset is interesting, or when there is periodical skew in the sense that queries focus on a single area of the domain for a given time before the focus shifts to another area.

Querying. When a query is issued, PADS+ converts the query to its iSAX representation and finds the corresponding FBL buffer stored on disk. It then loads the iSAX representations found in this bucket and adaptively splits it, until the query-time leaf size is reached. It loads the raw time series for the corresponding leaf and answers the query using the approximate search of iSAX [29, 30, 6]. If an approximate answer is not good enough, it follows the regular ADS+ Exact Search algorithm, performing adaptive splits every time that the distance to a leaf node that has not yet been split to the query-time leaf size has to be calculated.

Every time that a query needs data which might be missing from the tree, it needs to scan the appropriate FBL buffer iSAX file and perform an adaptive split operation on it. To optimize this, the initial leaf size is set to infinite; thus adaptive split operations can be performed by splitting the large buffers and creating large leaf files, which are split again, only if there is a query that asks for them. Further on, using 16 PAA segments (which is common in practice), we initially have 2^{16} FBL buffers. As a result, given a dataset of 1 billion data series, each one of the 65536 FBL buffers will on average contain around 15 thousand iSAX representations. Using a 1 byte representation for each iSAX character (i.e., cardinality 256), and given the fact that we have 16 segments, we would need 16 bytes for representing each data-series. This means that the average FBL size would be around 235 KB: a file size that makes it trivial to perform split operations on.

Example. An illustration of the PADS+ index can be seen in Figure 5(c). It represents a random instance after a few queries have arrived. The index is not fully built; only a small part of the index is created and only some of the leaves are materialized, following the workload. For example, the two leftmost children of the root point directly to FBL buffers on disk; no query has gone through this path. On the contrary, the rightmost child of the root is split, leading to a subtree which reaches down to two leaf nodes. This subtree is created as a side-effect of a query requesting for data series that belong in the leaf that is now marked as FULL in Figure 5(c).

3.4 Updates

Updates are also handled in an adaptive way.

Inserts. Insertions is the main scenario of interest in data exploration environments, i.e., in a scientific database new data is continuously created, but past data is not discarded. Handling inserts in all ADS variations is done by simply appending the new data series in the raw file, while only its iSAX representation and its position in the raw file is pushed through the index tree. If the new data series belongs in a leaf which is already in FULL mode, then we simply flip a bit in this leaf so that future queries know that more data exists. In either case, no further actions are needed for partial leaves. If a future query reaches a FULL leave with pending inserts, then it fetches the new inserts on-the-fly and it merges them in the leaf in the same way it is done for PARTIAL leaves (as we discussed earlier).

Deletes. When a data series needs to be deleted, we simply mark the data series as deleted in its corresponding leaf (via an in-memory per-leaf bit-vector). Whether the leaf is partial or full does not make a difference. Future queries ignore deleted data series, while future insertions can exploit the space created in this leaf by these ghost entries.

4. EXPERIMENTAL EVALUATION

In this section, we present a detailed experimental evaluation. We demonstrate that adaptive data series indexing for an initialization time that is significantly lower than state-of-the-art approaches, drastically reducing the data-to-query time by one order of magnitude. We show that our algorithms enable users to perform hundreds of thousands of queries faster, while the index creation cost is spread across multiple queries.

Algorithms. We benchmark all indexing methods presented in this paper and we compare all our adaptive indexing variations against the state-of-the-art iSAX 2.0 index [6] that supports bulk loading, as well as against sequential scans and state-of-the-art multi-dimensional indexes such as R-Trees [13] and X-Trees [4]. In addition, we performed certain memory usage optimizations for iSAX 2.0; we use an LRU buffer for recently queried nodes and also after loading we maintain its last loading buffer in memory.

Infrastructure. All the data structures and algorithms presented, as well as an optimized version of iSAX 2.0, are built from scratch in C and compiled with GCC 4.6.3 under Ubuntu Linux 12.04.2. We used an Intel Xeon machine with 64GB of RAM and 4x 2TB, SATA, 7.2K RPM Hard Drives in RAID0. All algorithms are set such as they make maximum use of all available memory.

Benchmarks. We use synthetic benchmarks for a fine grained analysis as well as real-life benchmarks to demonstrate the usefulness of adaptive data series indexing. We generate synthetic datasets using a random walk data series generator. This is a generator, where a random number is drawn from a Gaussian distribution $N(0,1)$, then at each time point a new number is drawn from this distribution and added to the value of the last number. This kind of data generation has been extensively used in the past [1, 10, 25, 2, 29, 30, 6], and has been shown to effectively model real-world financial data [10]. Each dataset is z-normalized before being indexed. Unless mentioned otherwise, each data series consists of 256 points and each point has a float precision of 4 bytes, while the query workload is random. Each query is given in the form of a data series q and the index is trying to locate if this data series or a similar one exist in the database. We study both query intensive workloads as well as updates and various workload patterns including skewed workloads.

4.1 Reducing the Data to Query Time

Motivation. In our motivation discussion in the introduction section of the paper, we discussed Figure 1 as an example that demonstrates the limits of state-of-the-art indexing techniques. For this experiment, we used a synthetic data set of up to 1 billion data series and 10^5 random queries (73% of which need to fetch new data from the raw file). The main observation is that as we try to index more and more data, the initialization time to build a state-of-the-art data series index becomes a prohibitive factor. With 1 billion data series it takes more than a full day in order to index all data using the state-of-the-art iSAX 2.0 index even when a preferable leaf size is used (Figure 1).

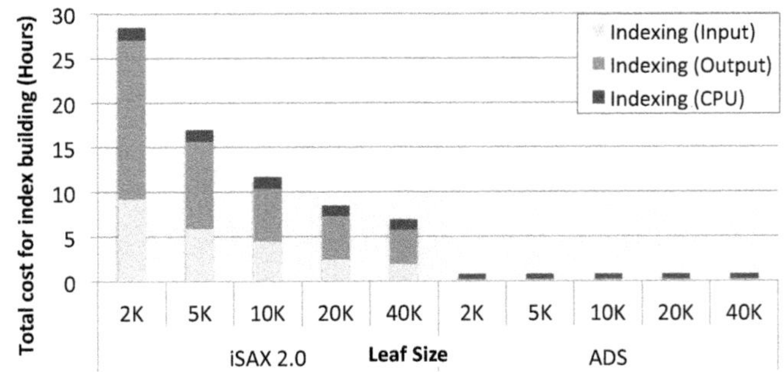

Figure 6: Reducing indexing costs.

Minimizing Indexing Costs. Let us now see how the adaptive data series indexing ideas can help in reducing the index building costs. In this experiment, we use the same set-up as before, but we now use a constant data size of 500 million data series and we vary the leaf size. We test iSAX 2.0 against ADS.

Figure 6 depicts the results, where we show the total time needed to index all data. ADS drastically reduces the index build time compared to iSAX 2.0 regardless of the leaf size. For example, for the case of a leaf size of 20K data series, which is the best case for iSAX 2.0 (we elaborate on this choice in the following paragraphs), ADS builds the index in only half an hour, while iSAX 2.0 needs 8 hours.

The breakdown of the indexing costs in Figure 6 explains this behavior. *Input* is the time spent reading data from disk. *Output* is the time spent writing data to disk. *CPU* is the time spent doing any kind of computation during indexing. ADS avoids the expensive steps of placing each data series in its corresponding leaf node. The net result is that the Input and Output costs, i.e., the I/O costs, drop drastically compared to iSAX 2.0. At the same time, also the CPU cost drops as ADS does not have to go through the index to place each data series. Overall, reducing the I/O and CPU costs results in a major benefit for ADS during the indexing phase.

The Query Processing Bottleneck of Plain ADS. Having seen that ADS can reduce the indexing costs, let us now see the effect on query processing. Figure 7 shows the results. Using the same set-up as in the previous experiment, it depicts the total time to build the index and to process all 10^5 queries. There are two observations from the behavior seen in Figure 7. First, ADS allows its first few queries to access the data faster than iSAX 2.0. For example, if we take the best leaf size case for ADS (2K) and the best leaf size case for iSAX 2.0 (20K), we see (marked with the red arrow) that ADS can answer 12,700 queries by the time iSAX 2.0 is still indexing and has not answered a single query (9 hours). In this way, ADS provides a quick gateway to the data as it was the original intention and motivation. However, as we process more and more queries and regardless of the leaf size, ADS looses its initial advantage; queries take too long to process and overall ADS does not present a feasible solution.

The main reason why ADS suffers is that even a single query might result in fetching a significant amount of raw data series. For example, if a query reaches a leaf which is not yet materialized and the leaf size is set to 2K, then ADS needs to fetch 2K raw data series in order to materialize the leaf. Such costs, significantly penalize queries and in the case of random workloads, as in the example of Figure 7, where each query may hit a completely different area of the index, this brings a significant overall cost. In a more focused workload, i.e., where queries focus on a given part of the index, the overall performance is drastically different as we do not reach the point where we need to fetch extra raw data very often. We discuss such examples later on.

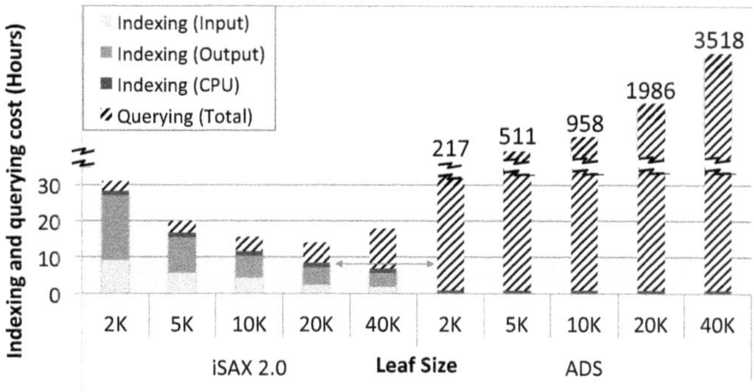

Figure 7: The query processing bottleneck.

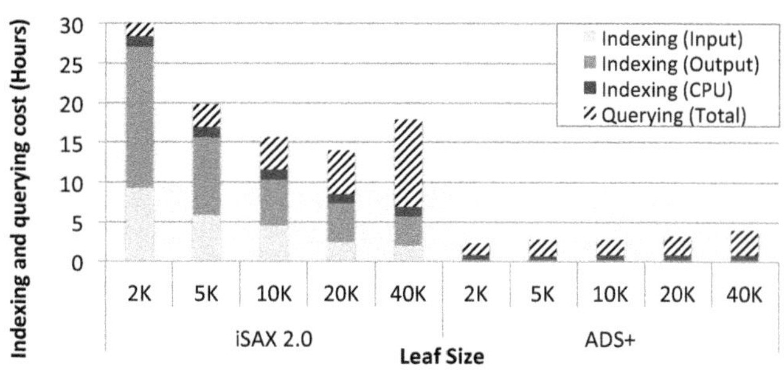

Figure 8: Reducing the data-to-query time with ADS+.

Still though, ADS does not represent a robust solution, i.e., a solution that would be globally applicable in arbitrary workloads.

Robustness with ADS+. This is exactly the motivation for ADS+. ADS+ maintains the adaptive properties of ADS but it is also robust and scalable. To demonstrate this behavior, we repeat the previous experiment, this time using also ADS+. Figure 8 shows that ADS+ significantly outperforms iSAX 2.0 not only during the index building phase but also during the query processing phase. For example, for the best case of iSAX 2.0, i.e., with leaf size 20K, ADS+ can create the index and process all 10^5 queries in only 3 hours while iSAX 2.0 needs roughly 15 hours. In fact, ADS+ can process the queries even faster as it may use even smaller leaf sizes.

Next, we show that ADS+ is robust even when in inferior set-up. Using the same set-up (data and queries) as before, we vary the available memory the algorithms can exploit. In addition, for iSAX 2.0 we use a buffer pool with an LRU policy so that it can hold recently visited nodes in memory. In Figure 9, it can be seen that even if we use 10% of the main memory for ADS+, it can still answer all of the 10^5 queries before iSAX 2.0 has finished indexing using 100% of the main memory.

The main novelty in ADS+ is that it can maintain a lightweight index-building step due to only partially building the index but also due to using a large leaf size during this phase. Then, as queries arrive, it adaptively splits leaves in hot areas of the index such that queries in this area may be processed at a smaller cost. In this way, ADS+ solves the robustness and scalability problem of ADS by introducing adaptive node splits, i.e., by being able to adjust the shape of the index based on the workload and only for the areas which are hot and may cause expensive steps for individual queries.

Choosing the Query-Time Leaf Size. The query-time leaf size indicates the finest granularity in which we will split a node with ADS+, and consequently it is directly related to the amount of raw data that we store on disk under each leaf. We have experimented with various query-time leaf sizes ranging from 1 data-series to 1000 data-series, and measured the average page utilization for 3 different page sizes, as well as the average query answering time. We did this by running 10^5 queries on a dataset of 500 million data-

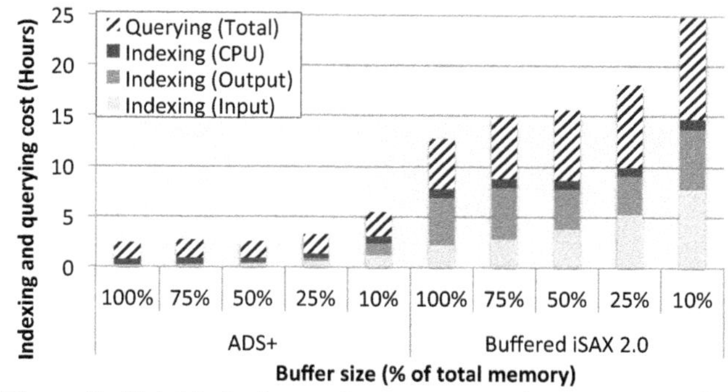

Figure 9: Total indexing and query answering cost as we increase the buffer size for ADS+ and iSAX 2.0.

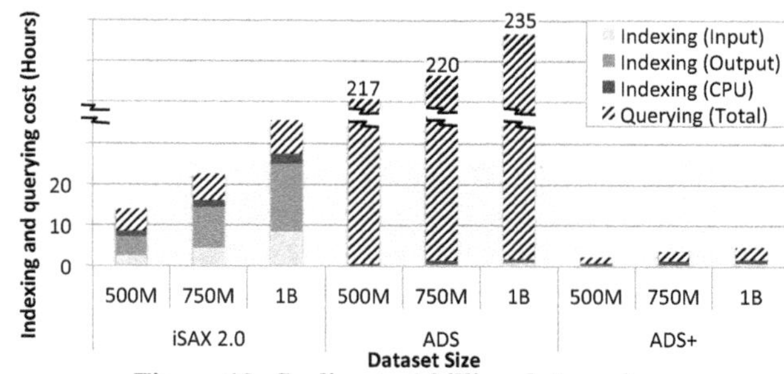

Figure 10: Scaling to 1 billion data series.

series. As we can see in Table 1, the smaller the query-time leaf size is, the less data we have to fetch from the raw data file, and the faster the materialization of the leaf node is. On the other hand, very small values of query-time leaf size adversely affect space utilization, since page occupancy will be small. As a result, it is important to choose a leaf size that will allow for the maximum page utilization while at the same time offers an acceptable query answering time. For the rest of our experiments we use 10, since when using a page size of 8KB, we maximize page occupancy at around 89% (Table 1 in bold) and the average query answering time remains relatively low at 69 milliseconds.

Query-time leaf size	1	10	100	1000
Query time (millisecond)	11.27	67.64	499.95	4031.68
Number of 4KB pages	0.25	1.79	17.23	171.48
Number of 8KB pages	0.12	**0.89**	8.61	85.74
Number of 16KB pages	0.06	0.45	4.30	42.87

Table 1: Varying query-time leaf size.

Scaling to 1 Billion Data Series. Next, we stress all indexing strategies to study how they can cope with an increasing data set size. We study the behavior up to 1 billion data series and with 10^5 random queries. Regarding leaf sizes, we use the optimal leaf size observed for each index strategy, i.e., 20K for iSAX 2.0, 2K for ADS, and for ADS+ 2K build-time and 10 query-time leaf size. Figure 10 shows the total time to build the index and answer all queries. Across all data sizes, ADS+ consistently outperforms all other strategies by a big margin.

For 1 billion data series, ADS+ answers all 10^5 *queries in less than 5 hours, while iSAX 2.0 needs more than 35 hours.*

By adaptively expanding the tree and adjusting leaf sizes only for the hot workload parts, ADS+ enjoys a 7*x* gain over full indexing in iSAX 2.0. In addition, ADS+ significantly outperforms ADS; even though ADS can significantly reduce indexing costs for all data sizes, as we process more and more queries it suffers due to the high cost of fetching unindexed data series for large leaves during query processing. ADS+ avoids this problem by adaptively

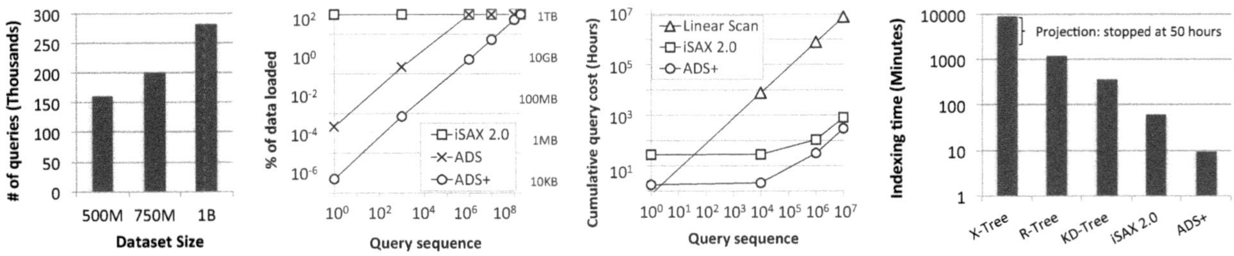

(a) Queries answered by ADS+ while iSAX 2.0 is still indexing. (b) Percentage of data indexed. (c) Per query response time. (d) ADS+ against spatial indexes.

Figure 11: Reducing the data-to-query time with ADS+ as we scale to big data.

splitting its leaves. Also, the rate at which the cost of ADS+ grows is significantly smaller than that of iSAX 2.0; For example, going from 500M to 1B data series, iSAX 2.0 needs more than twice the time, while ADS+ enjoys a sub-linear cost increase.

Figure 11 provides further insights. Figure 11(a) depicts the number of queries that ADS+ can answer within the time that iSAX 2.0 is still indexing. The bigger the data set, the more queries ADS+ can answer before iSAX 2.0 answers even a single query; for the case of 1 Billion data series ADS+ manages to answer nearly $3*10^5$ queries while iSAX 2.0 is still indexing. this verifies the fact that ADS+ is more suited towards very large data sets compared to traditional non-adaptive indexing approaches.

Data Touched. In addition, Figure 11(b) shows the amount of data actually touched (indexed) as the query sequence evolves. To see the long term effect, we let a big number of queries run, i.e., 10^7 queries. For iSAX 2.0 the behavior in Figure 11(b) is a flat curve as everything is indexed blindly up front. With ADS and ADS+ though, we index a much smaller percentage of the data; as more queries are processed, more data is indexed and only when needed. While ADS indexes all data by the time it processes 10^6 queries, ADS+ manages to touch even less data; since it splits leaves adaptively to much smaller sizes it needs to materialize much smaller leaves and thus it touches less data overall. In this way, even after 10^7 queries it has touched only 10% of the data, while it needs more than 190M queries in order to touch all the data (i.e., completely build the index). In fact, since this is a random workload, this is the worst case for adaptive indexing as most queries lead to fetching raw data series and enriching the index. This is why ADS has touched all data by query 10^6; most queries will need to materialize a partial leaf and thus they need to fetch $2*10^3$ new data series (its leaf size); $2*10^3*10^6$ adds up to well above 10^9 (the data set size). On the contrary, ADS+ uses a query-time adjustable leaf size of only 10 data series; thus even if all queries need to fetch new data, by query 10^7 we would have fetched at most 10^8 data series which is about the 10% (of the original 10^9 data set) we see in Figure 11(b). By doing less work and only when necessary, ADS+ allows users to have quick access to their data.

Per Query Performance. We continue our study with a discussion that focuses on the individual query performance based on the previous 1 Billion data series experiment and 10 Million random queries. Here we also include the scan strategy, i.e., when we do not build an index; instead, every query performs a complete scan over all data series. We will not use ADS from now on as ADS+ consistently outperforms ADS.

Figure 11(c) shows the cumulative per query response time as the query sequence evolves. The scan strategy has a constant but slow response time; every query adds the same cost to the total cumulative costs. Eventually, the scan strategy becomes prohibitive if we want to repeatedly query the same big data; it takes close to 10^5 hours to handle all queries. iSAX 2.0 pays a big cost to build the index (this is included in the cost of Query 1) but then queries are very fast, i.e., the cumulative cost curve is flat as every query adds very little cost. Once the index is built, every iSAX 2.0 query incurs a constant cost; still though there is a big bottleneck to access the data due to the high indexing costs which means that the first query needs to wait for several hours. On the contrary, ADS+ enjoys quick data access time; it finishes building the index and answering all queries by the time iSAX 2.0 is still indexing and has not answered a single query.

In fact, while the crossover point of the scan strategy with iSAX 2.0 is at about 35 queries, for ADS+ it is only at 2 queries. This means that for iSAX 2.0 to be useful we need to fire at least 35 queries while ADS+ starts bringing gains already after the first 2 queries. Moreover, while the average query answering time for ADS+ is about 50 milliseconds, that of iSAX 2.0 is 200 milliseconds. In other words, iSAX 2.0 is never going to amortize its initialization overhead over ADS+ and thus it is always beneficial to use adaptive indexing as opposed to full a priori indexing. This is because of the larger leaf size that is used by iSAX 2.0, in order to reduce the index building time by compromising query times a bit. On the other hand, ADS+ adaptively splits leaves for the hot part of the data and thus it can reduce access times even further. Furthermore, the cost of query answering for ADS+ (essentially, materializing the data of the leaf) increases linearly with leaf utilization. This cost ranges from 20ms when the leaf is already materialized to 160ms when the leaf contains all 10 data-series that need to be loaded from the raw file. When ADS+ needs to perform splits, the query answering times are 129ms for 1-10 splits, 138ms for 10-20 splits, 148ms for 20-30 splits, and 160ms for 30-40 splits. All these times are significantly smaller than the required time to answer a query using serial scan (more than 46min).

4.2 ADS+ Vs. Multi-dimensional Indexes

One interesting question is how indexes which are tailored for data series search compare against state-of-the-art spatial indexes. In this experiment, we compare ADS+ and iSAX 2.0 against KD-Tree [3], R-Tree [13], and X-Tree [4], a state-of-the-art adaptive version of R-Tree. X-Tree creates a tree with minimal overlap between nodes and it allows for variable sized nodes in order to accommodate minimum overlapping. Such spatial indexes can be used for indexing data series and performing similarity search; the main idea is that we can use the PAA representations of data series to create a KD-Tree, an R-Tree, or an X-Tree.

Here, we use a set of 100 million data series. In all the cases, the amount of dimensions for the reduced dimensionality PAA representation is set to 16 while the original size of each data series is 256 points. Figure 11(d) depicts the time needed to complete the index building phase for each index. Overall, both data series

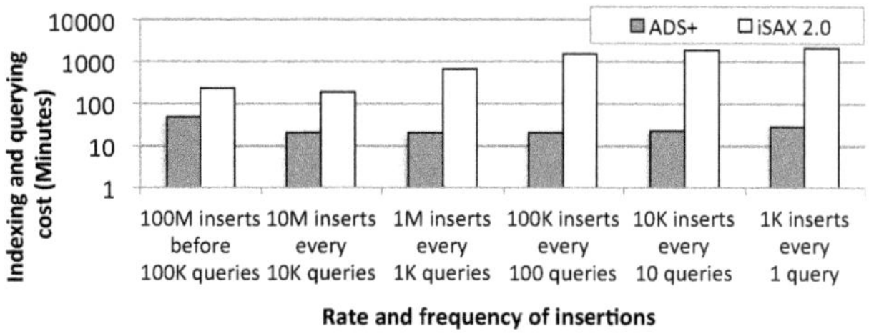

Figure 12: Robust ADS+ performance in update workloads.

tailored indexes, iSAX 2.0 and ADS+, significantly outperform the more generic spatial indexes. For example, iSAX 2.0 is one order of magnitude faster than R-Tree while ADS+ is two orders of magnitude faster, and more than an order of magnitude faster than KD-Tree. The raw benefit comes from the fact iSAX 2.0 and ADS+ are tailored to perform efficient comparisons of SAX representations (with bitwise operations). ADS+ being adaptive enjoys further benefits as we discuss in previous experiments as well. X-Tree is significantly slower as a result of its more expensive index building phase which focuses on minimizing overlap between nodes. Naturally, this helps query processing times as less overlap allows queries to focus faster on data of interest. However, as we scale to big data, index building is the main bottleneck and thus X-Tree is prohibitively expensive.

4.3 Adaptive Behavior under Updates

In our next experiment we study the behavior of ADS+ and iSAX 2.0 with updates. We use a synthetic data set of 100 million data series and 10^5 random queries. This time, queries are interleaved with updates. In particular, we perform the experiment in 6 steps. Each time a varying number of new data series arrive and at different query intervals. Figure 12 shows the results. The first set of bars represents the case where all data has arrived up front and all queries run afterwards. The second set of bars (10M inserts every 10K queries) represents a scenario where every 10^4 queries 10^7 new data series arrive until we reach a total of 10^8 data series (i.e., the complete data set) and a total of 10^5 queries (i.e, the complete query workload). Similarly, the rest of the bars vary the frequency and the rate of incoming data until the extreme case where we get 1000 new insertions after every single query.

In all cases, ADS+ maintains its drastic performance advantage over iSAX 2.0. When all data arrives up front, the cost is naturally higher; more data has to be queried. For the rest of the cases where data arrives incrementally, interleaving with queries, we observe that when data arrives more frequently the overall cost increases slightly. This is a result of both the fact that merging of updates needs to happen more often and of the fact that more queries need to be processed against more data. However, even in the extreme case where we receive 1000 new data series after every query, ADS+ maintains its adaptive behavior and good performance being able to outperform static iSAX 2.0 by 2 orders of magnitude.

The behavior under deletions is similar. For example in experiments with a data set of 100 million data series, ADS+ performs deletions with an average deletion time of only 0.2 milliseconds.

4.4 Real-life Workloads

Here, we demonstrate the ability of ADS+ to drastically reduce the data-to-query time in real-life scenarios. In all cases, we use the optimal settings found in the synthetic benchmarks: for iSAX 2.0 uses a leaf size of 20K data series, while ADS+ uses a build time leaf size of 2K data series which adaptively drops down to 10.

Texmex Corpus. The first real-life scenario is an image analysis scenario from the Texmex corpus [21]. This dataset contains 1 Billion images which are translated into a set of 1 Billion data series

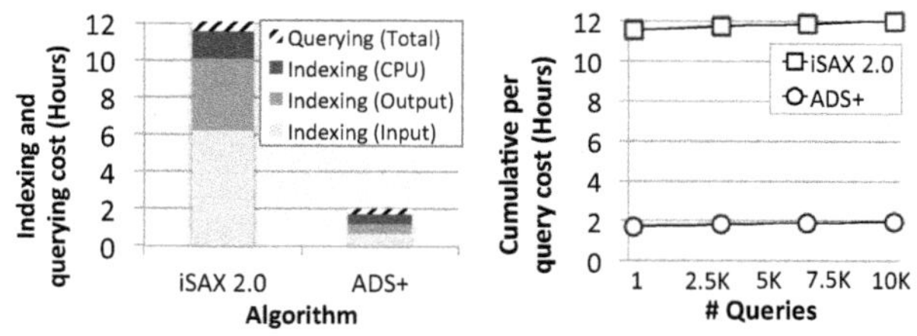

(a) Total costs. (b) Cumulative per query costs (Query 1 includes indexing).

Figure 13: Indexing 1 Billion images (SIFT vectors) and answering 10^4 queries.

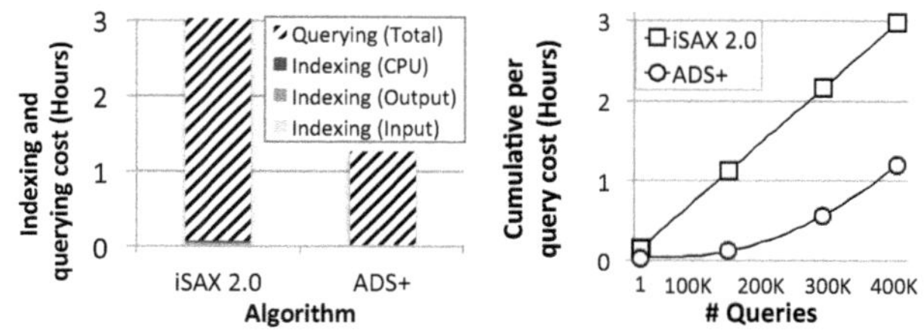

(a) Total costs. (b) Cumulative Per query costs (Query 1 includes indexing).

Figure 14: Indexing 20 Million DNA subsequences from the Homo Sapiens genome and answering $4 * 10^5$ queries.

(SIFT feature vectors) of 128 points each. The scenario is that a user is searching the corpus for images similar to an existing image that they already have. The corpus also contains 10^4 such example queries together with information about which image in the corpus is the nearest neighbor, i.e., the most similar one, for each query.

Figure 13 shows the results. Figure 13(a) shows the total cost to go through the indexing phase and to process all queries. ADS+ maintains its drastic gains as we have seen in the synthetic benchmarks study. Overall, ADS+ finishes answering all queries 6 times faster compared to iSAX 2.0. It is interesting to mention that ADS+ gains not only during the indexing phase but also during the query processing phase, i.e., the time it takes to answer all 10^4 queries is smaller with ADS+. This is because these real-life queries are not completely random, i.e., the workload focuses in specific areas of the index. In such cases, ADS+ has the benefit of working on an index which essentially contains less data; it has loaded only the data which are relevant for the hot workload set.

Figure 13(b) helps to understand this behavior even more by demonstrating the evolution of the query processing costs, i.e., the graph shows how the indexing and query processing costs evolve through the query sequence for each indexing strategy. For iSAX 2.0 the first query needs to wait until the whole index is built which takes almost 12 hours. From there on, each query can be processed quite fast. On the contrary, ADS+ allows the first query to access the data in less than 2 hours, while by the time we reach the 2 hours mark all 10^4 queries have been processed. Overall, ADS+ process all queries in just 2 hours, while iSAX 2.0 needs more than 11 hours just for the indexing phase and without processing a single query.

DNA Data. The second real-life scenario comes from the biology domain. This dataset contains the full genome of the Homo Sapiens (human) which is translated into 20 Million data series of 640 points each, obtained using a sliding window of size 16000, down-sampled by a factor of 25. The scenario is that a user is trying to identify subsequences of the human genome that match subsequences in other genomes. In this way, we create our queries from the genome of the Rhesus Macaque ape which is also translated into 20 Million data series of 640 points each, obtained in the same manner, and each one of these data series can be used as a query against the human genome in search for similar patterns.

Workload	Cross-over point (PADS+ over ADS+)
Random	2899 queries
Low skew	2970 queries
Medium skew	3097 queries
High skew	3825 queries

Table 2: Fast access with PADS+ with varying skew.

Figure 14 shows the results. Similarly to previous experiments, ADS+ brings a significant benefit both in terms of total costs and in terms of per query costs. With ADS+ we can index the data and process all queries 3 times faster, i.e., only after one hour, while with iSAX 2.0 we need to wait for 3 hours. Compared to previous performance examples, it is interesting to note that in this experiment we have a very different data to queries ratio, i.e., we have a relatively small data set of 20 Million data series and a relatively big query set of $4 * 10^5$ queries. Thus, the indexing cost is a much smaller factor of the total cost compared to previous experiments. Still though, ADS+ brings a major benefit and shows a scalable behavior, mainly due to its ability to adapt its shape to workload patterns, by expanding sub-trees and adjusting leaf sizes on-the-fly.

4.5 Providing Fast Insight with PADS+

Having shown that it is possible to reduce the user waiting time, without excessively penalizing the query answering time, we now show that we can achieve even faster access to the data for skewed workloads. In this experiment we analyze the performance of ADS+, PADS+ and iSAX 2.0 over a dataset of 1 billion data series and a varying set of query workloads, ranging from completely skewed to completely random queries. In total, we run 10^4 queries. For low skew, 60% of the queries are picked from 40% of the domain. In the medium skew workload, 80% of the queries are picked from 20% of the domain, while for the high skew workload 99.99% of the queries are picked from 0.01% of the domain.

For all workloads both ADS+ and PADS+ significantly outperform iSAX 2.0 being 10 to 20 times faster. iSAX 2.0 needs about 28 hours to index all data and process all queries with the bulk of the time spent in indexing (included in the cost of Query 1). Both ADS+ and PADS+ can do so in less than 1.5 hours for 10^3 queries, and less than 3 hours for 10^4 queries. ADS+ improves slightly as skew increases; less data has to be fetched from outside the index. PADS+, though, as seen in Table 2, manages to improve performance even more as skew increases, being faster than ADS+ and iSAX 2.0 for all skewness levels for the first 2000 queries and for almost 4000 queries in the case of high skewness. When the workload is skewed, this means that PADS+ can focus on certain parts of the index tree and avoid node splits and disk spilling once it optimizes the index for the hot part.

While ADS+ provides the best overall solution being both fast and robust, PADS+ provides an attractive solution when we know we want to fire only a few thousands of queries.

5. CONCLUSIONS

We show that state-of-the-art data series indexing approaches cannot cope with the data deluge. The time needed to build a data series index becomes prohibitive as the data grows, and may take more than 24 hours to index a collection of 1 billion data series. We propose an adaptive indexing approach, where the index is built incrementally and adaptively. Both the shape of the tree index and the leaf sizes are tuned adaptively and automatically to fit the workload on-the-fly. Using both synthetic and diverse real-life data, we show that our new adaptive indexing approach copes significantly better with the ever growing data series collections, and can answer several thousands of queries in the time that state-of-the-art indexing approaches are still in the indexing phase.

6. REFERENCES

[1] R. Agrawal, C. Faloutsos, and A. N. Swami. Efficient similarity search in sequence databases. In *FODO*, pages 69–84, 1993.

[2] I. Assent, R. Krieger, F. Afschari, and T. Seidl. The TS-tree: efficient time series search and retrieval. In *EDBT*, pages 252–263, 2008.

[3] J. L. Bentley. Multidimensional Binary Search Trees Used for Associative Searching. *Commun. ACM*, 18(9):509–517, Sept. 1975.

[4] S. Berchtold, D. A. Keim, and H.-P. Kriegel. The X-tree: An index structure for high-dimensional data. In *VLDB*, pages 28–39, 1996.

[5] Y. Bu, T. wing Leung, A. W. chee Fu, E. Keogh, J. Pei, and S. Meshkin. Wat: Finding top-k discords in time series database. In *SDM*, pages 449–454, 2007.

[6] A. Camerra, T. Palpanas, J. Shieh, and E. Keogh. iSAX 2.0: Indexing and mining one billion time series. In *ICDM*, pages 58–67, 2010.

[7] A. Camerra, J. Shieh, T. Palpanas, T. Rakthanmanon, and E. Keogh. Beyond One Billion Time Series: Indexing and Mining Very Large Time Series Collections with iSAX2+. *KAIS*, 39(1):123–151, 2014.

[8] K.-P. Chan and A.-C. Fu. Efficient time series matching by wavelets. In *ICDE*, pages 126–133, 1999.

[9] V. Chandola, A. Banerjee, and V. Kumar. Anomaly detection: a survey. *ACM Computing Surveys*, 41(3):1–58, 2009.

[10] C. Faloutsos, M. Ranganathan, and Y. Manolopoulos. Fast subsequence matching in time-series databases. In *SIGMOD*, pages 419–429, 1994.

[11] G. Graefe, F. Halim, S. Idreos, H. A. Kuno, and S. Manegold. Concurrency control for adaptive indexing. *PVLDB*, 5(7):656–667, 2012.

[12] G. Graefe, F. Halim, S. Idreos, H. A. Kuno, S. Manegold, and B. Seeger. Transactional support for adaptive indexing. *VLDB J.*, 23(2):303–328, 2014.

[13] A. Guttman. R-Trees A Dynamic Structure for Spatial Searching. In *SIGMOD*, pages 47–57, 1984.

[14] F. Halim, S. Idreos, P. Karras, and R. H. C. Yap. Stochastic database cracking: Towards robust adaptive indexing in main-memory column-stores. *PVLDB*, 5(6):502–513, 2012.

[15] S. Idreos, I. Alagiannis, R. Johnson, and A. Ailamaki. Here are my Data Files. Here are my Queries. Where are my Results? In *CIDR*, pages 57–68, 2011.

[16] S. Idreos, M. L. Kersten, and S. Manegold. Updating a Cracked Database. In *SIGMOD*, pages 413–424, 2007.

[17] S. Idreos, M. L. Kersten, and S. Manegold. Database Cracking. In *CIDR*, pages 68–78, 2007.

[18] S. Idreos, M. L. Kersten, and S. Manegold. Self-organizing Tuple Reconstruction in Column-stores. In *SIGMOD*, pages 297–308, 2009.

[19] S. Idreos and E. Liarou. dbtouch: Analytics at your fingertips. In *CIDR*, 2013.

[20] S. Idreos, S. Manegold, H. A. Kuno, and G. Graefe. Merging what's cracked, cracking what's merged: Adaptive indexing in main-memory column-stores. *PVLDB*, 4(9):585–597, 2011.

[21] H. Jegou, M. Douze, and C. Schmid. Product quantization for nearest neighbor search. *TPAMI*, 33(1):117–128, 2011.

[22] E. Keogh, K. Chakrabarti, and M. Pazzani. Dimensionality reduction for fast similarity search in large time series databases. *KAIS*, 3(3):263–286, 2000.

[23] J. Lin, E. Keogh, and S. Lonardi. A symbolic representation of time series, with implications for streaming algorithms. In *DMKD*, pages 2–11, 2003.

[24] T. Palpanas, M. Vlachos, E. J. Keogh, and D. Gunopulos. Streaming time series summarization using user-defined amnesic functions. *TKDE*, 20(7):992–1006, 2008.

[25] D. Rafiei and A. Mendelzon. Similarity-based queries for time series data. In *SIGMOD*, pages 13–25, 1997.

[26] T. Rakthanmanon, B. Campana, A. Mueen, G. Batista, B. Westover, Q. Zhu, J. Zakaria, and E. Keogh. Searching and mining trillions of time series subsequences under dynamic time warping. In *SIGKDD*, pages 262–270, 2012.

[27] S. Richter, J.-A. Quiane-Ruiz, S. Schuh, and J. Dittrich. Towards zero-overhead static and adaptive indexing in hadoop. *VLDBJ*, 2013.

[28] F. M. Schuhknecht, A. Jindal, and J. Dittrich. The Uncracked Pieces in Database Cracking. *PVLDB*, 7(2):97–108, 2013.

[29] J. Shieh and E. Keogh. iSAX: Indexing and Mining Terabyte Sized Time Series. In *SIGKDD*, pages 623–631, 2008.

[30] J. Shieh and E. Keogh. iSAX: disk-aware mining and indexing of massive time series datasets. *DMKD*, 19(1):24–57, 2009.

[31] M. Stonebraker. The case for partial indexes. *SIGMOD Rec.*, 18(4):4–11, 1989.

[32] Y. Wang, P. Wang, J. Pei, W. Wang, and S. Huang. A data-adaptive and dynamic segmentation index for whole matching on time series. *PVLDB*, 6(10):793–804, 2013.

[33] T. Warren Liao. Clustering of time series data - a survey. *Pattern Recognition*, 38(11):1857–1874, 2005.

[34] B. Yi and C. Faloutsos. Fast time sequence indexing for arbitrary lp norms. In *VLDB*, pages 385–394, 2000.

[35] J. Zhou and K. A. Ross. Buffering accesses to memory-resident index structures. In *VLDB*, pages 405–416, 2003.

[36] J. Zhou and K. A. Ross. Buffering database operations for enhanced instruction cache performance. In *SIGMOD*, pages 191–202, 2004.

Histograms as a Side Effect of Data Movement for Big Data

Zsolt István Louis Woods Gustavo Alonso
Systems Group, Dept. of Computer Science
ETH Zürich, Switzerland
{firstname.lastname}@inf.ethz.ch

ABSTRACT

Histograms are a crucial part of database query planning but their computation is resource-intensive. As a consequence, generating histograms on database tables is typically performed as a batch job, separately from query processing. In this paper, we show how to calculate statistics as a *side effect* of data movement within a DBMS using a hardware accelerator in the data path. This accelerator analyzes tables as they are transmitted from storage to the processing unit, and provides histograms on the data retrieved for queries at virtually no extra performance cost. To evaluate our approach, we implemented this accelerator on an FPGA. This prototype calculates histograms faster and with similar or better accuracy than commercial databases. Moreover, the FPGA can provide various types of histograms such as *Equi-depth*, *Compressed*, or *Max-diff* on the same input data in parallel, without additional overhead.

Categories and Subject Descriptors

H.2 [**Database Management**]: Systems

Keywords

FPGA, Statistics, Histogram, Query Optimization

1. INTRODUCTION

Statistics such as histograms play an important role in modern databases. They have been long used for query optimization, where they influence, *e.g.*, how the data is accessed or what join algorithm is used. Furthermore, now that we have entered the era of big data, histograms and statistics in general are becoming even more important: besides standard query optimization decisions, knowing the data distribution could also influence the choice between different types of CPU cores, the amount of data moved between different computing nodes, etc. One important property of histograms is that they are useful only when accurate enough and up-to-date, but updating them takes processing power away from query processing. As a result, histograms are mostly calculated in maintenance windows, and often with sampling, to reduce their impact on response time [37]. However, the sheer amount of data that needs to be processed means that the traditional techniques for statistical analysis and histogram creation will be increasingly difficult to apply. Take for instance the previously mentioned case of sampling: in order to balance execution time and accuracy, most modern databases do not calculate the histograms on the full data but on a small sample. While this approach provides good results if the sample is representative [5], when the time budget for statistical computation is small, the sampling rate could become so low that reasonable accuracy can not be guaranteed for the resulting histogram.

In this paper, we introduce the idea of *statistics calculated on the data path*. By moving the task of calculating histograms to a specialized hardware device, we can obtain them virtually for 'free' every time we retrieve a table from any form of storage, *i.e.*, without throttling throughput and by only adding negligible latency. Apart from the obvious benefit of off-loading the calculation of histograms to an accelerator, which frees computing cycles on the CPU, there is also a second benefit: If histograms can be refreshed every time a table is scanned, the global freshness of statistics will be higher than that of current systems.

As a proof of concept, we have implemented a statistical accelerator using a field-programmable gate array (FPGA) that, to our knowledge, is the first of its kind. With this prototype we show that not only the histograms are calculated faster than on a CPU but also that we can provide many different types of histograms (Equi-depth, Compressed, and Max-diff) at no additional performance cost. The main benefit of using FPGAs is that due to their inherent parallelism they can stream the data through, minimizing the added latency, and calculate the histogram in parallel at the same time. In future systems, the FPGA could be replaced with an application-specific integrated circuit (ASIC), which has the same advantages but consumes less power, or with a small specialized processor attached directly to storage [10].

Contribution. In this paper, we revisit the state-of-the-art in histograms for databases and propose an accelerator in the data path for building histograms as a side effect to data movement. We implement a prototype of such an accelerator using an FPGA. We show that the FPGA can handle high throughput and very large table sizes – both crucial for processing *big data*. By implementing canonically accepted histogram types we can also guarantee accuracy on the statistics derived by the accelerator.

SIGMOD/PODS'14, June 22 - 27 2014, Snowbird, UT, USA.
Copyright 2014 ACM 978-1-4503-2376-5/14/06 ...$15.00.
http://dx.doi.org/10.1145/2588555.2612174.

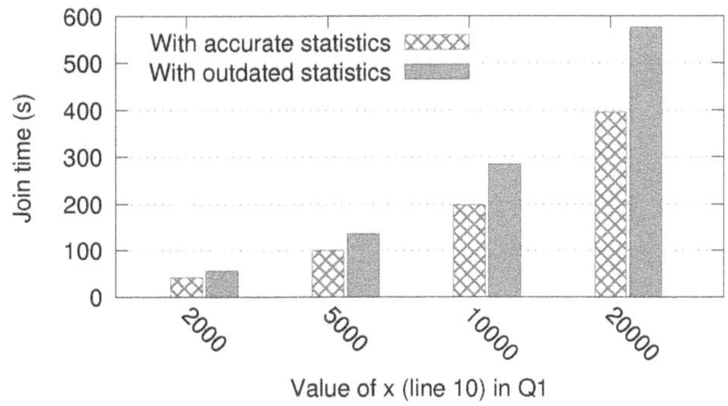

Figure 1: Effect of fresh statistics on query plans

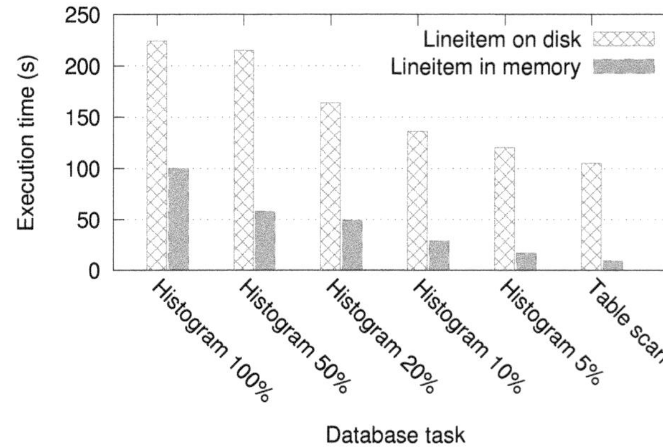

Figure 2: Even with sampling, analysis is more expensive than a full table scan in databases

Outline. The rest of this paper is structured as follows: We motivate our work with an example, and then relate to other work in Section 2. Section 3 discusses the most common histograms used in modern databases. In Section 4, we present the architecture of our system on a high level before covering the implementation details in Section 5. We evaluate our approach in Section 6, discuss ideas for future work in Section 7, and conclude in Section 8.

2. MOTIVATION AND RELATED WORK

In this paper, we propose a hardware accelerator for calculating accurate histograms on tables retrieved in full table scans, at no additional CPU cost. To understand the importance of accurate histograms, consider an example query on two TPC-H [8] tables, *lineitem* and *customer*, that highlights how the query planner decisions are influenced by statistical information in commercial databases. The query calculates a derived final price for items that have some base price, and then counts the number of such entries per client that have a balance larger than the final price:

```
1  with somelines as
2  (
3   select (l_tax*l_extendedprice) as val
4   from lineitem
5   where l_extendedprice=2001 --skewed value
6  )                                              (Q1)
7  select customer.c_custkey, count(*) as cnt
8   from customer, somelines
9   where somelines.val<customer.c_acctbal
10    and customer.c_custkey<x --parameter
11   group by customer.c_custkey;
```

We ran this query on a widely used commercial database, and observed that the number of lines matching the base price changes the optimal query plan. To demonstrate this effect we generated *lineitem* with 60 million rows (scale factor 10), then increased the number of records with price "2001" to 120,000. When we ran Q_1 after updating these lines, without refreshing statistics, the database was operating under the assumption that the value "2001" appears less than fifty times in the *l_extendedprice* column, as the initial statistics on *lineitem* suggested.

Since statistics gathering needs to be explicitly triggered in databases[1], even after running the query multiple times, the query planner was producing the same sub-optimal plan. Figure 1 shows that after updating the statistics on the column, the query planner correctly adjusted the plan, which resulted in better query performance. The main difference between the two query plans is the order in which the tables are joined with Sort Merge Join; and that when running with outdated statistics, the database underestimates the size of one of the join tables by almost four orders of magnitude. As Figure 1 also illustrates, by increasing the number of matching items in the *customer* relation, the effect can be further amplified – this highlights that even for simple queries fresh statistics are very important.

In the case of this particular example, the query planner error can be easily avoided by updating the histogram on the *l_extendedprice* column. In commercial databases however, even with sampling, statistics collection is an expensive process. Figure 2 illustrates how long it takes for the database to update the histogram with different levels of sampling on one column of the TPC-H *lineitem* table (scale factor 10) residing on disk and in memory. Additionally, we included in the figure the time it takes to perform a very simple query with a full table scan on the same data. This is to show how much more work the database performs to build a histogram even from only a 5% sample compared to answering a query with a full table scan. While not discussed here, in Section 6.2 we show that sampling may also negatively affect query planning. This is why providing histograms built from the complete data, delivered with no performance penalty as a by-product of full table scans, is a valuable addition to modern database systems.

Related Work. In this paper we propose a statistics accelerator that *passively* operates on the data that is moved to the processor for query processing. A similar idea, though using conventional CPUs, was first proposed by Zhu et al [37]. The key idea is what Zhu et al. call the *piggyback method*, that collects statistics by piggybacking additional data retrievals during the processing of a user query in order to update existing statistics. While this method improves the *freshness* of histograms, the CPU still has to process the data and derive the statistics. The authors admit that as a consequence their method may slow down query processing in favor of more up-to-date statistics.

Using an accelerator to compute statistics was previously suggested by Heimel et al. [13]. In this work, a GPU was

[1]For instance, in Oracle this can be done with the following command: DBMS_STATS.GATHER_TABLE_STATS. The columns to analyze, the number of buckets in the histogram, and the sampling rate can be specified as parameters.

Figure 3: Equi-width

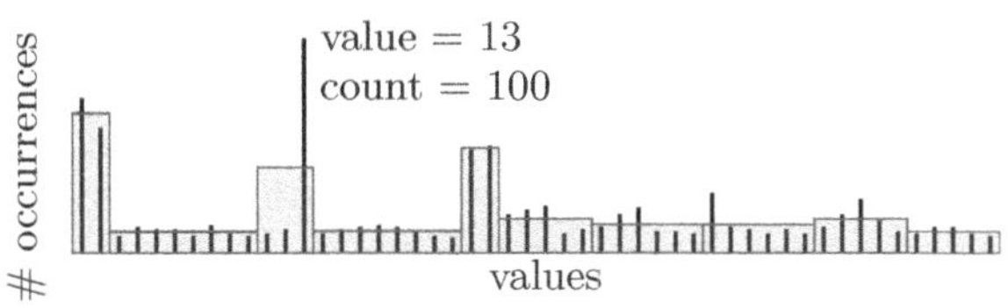

Figure 4: Equi-depth

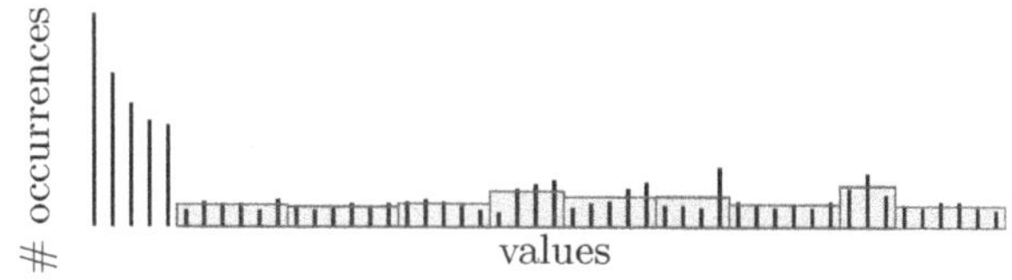

Figure 5: Compressed

Figure 6: Max-diff

used to provide the query optimizer with statistics such as range selectivity estimations. However, the authors observe that copying whole tables to the GPU quickly becomes a bottleneck, and therefore they rely on sampling for larger tables. This means that even though the parallel resources on the GPU provide the estimates much faster than the CPU, the solution still suffers from all the drawbacks of sampling.

Utilizing specialized hardware in the data path to compute statistics as a side effect does not suffer from these shortcomings, and the existence of such accelerators is reasonable since many systems are already using similar accelerators today to improve query performance. For instance, IBM/Netezza's data warehouse appliance [15] uses FPGAs close to storage to which it pushes simple SQL operators. The work in [4] explores FPGAs as accelerators for join operations in columnar main-memory databases; in Cipherbase [2] they are used for encrypted SQL query processing, and in [9, 35] for partial SQL query execution. Furthermore, smart SSDs [10] and flash stores [18] have been proposed, which exploit the processing elements inside storage devices to off-load different database operators.

In the bigger picture, specialized hardware, and FPGAs in particular, have been successfully used in many areas of data processing, *e.g.*, for pattern matching and XML filtering [21, 34, 32], network intrusion detection [36], traffic control information processing [33], algorithmic trading [29], streaming query execution [24, 30, 23]. Furthermore, FPGAs have been recently used even for accelerating main-memory distributed hash tables [1, 6, 17].

3. HISTOGRAMS IN DATABASES

In this section, we revisit the most common types of histograms used in databases today [16]. It is important to understand the high-level differences between these histograms before we discuss the hardware implementation of each of them (Section 5). To illustrate these differences, we consider an arbitrary data distribution, which we use for Figures 3 through 6. These figures have on the x-axis the different values and on the y-axis their count as bars. The histogram buckets are blue rectangles. The area of every rectangle corresponds to the total count of a bucket. Within a bucket, uniform distribution is assumed, *i.e.*, the height of the rectangle corresponds to the estimated count of each value within the respective bucket.

Equi-width Histogram. The simplest histogram is the so-called *equi-width* histogram, displayed in Figure 3. It divides the value range into n buckets and then counts the number of occurrences in each bucket. In Figure 3, the value range is divided into $n = 10$ buckets. Each bucket counts the number of occurrences of five consecutive values in this range. This type of histogram is easy to construct in linear time using *bucket sort* [7] (sometimes referred to as *bin sort*). However, as can be seen in Figure 3, this histogram does not represent *skewed* data very well, which is why equi-width histograms are seldom used in databases.

Equi-depth Histogram. A more common histogram used in databases is the *equi-depth* histogram, which represents skewed data more accurately. PostgreSQL, Oracle and DB2 all use some version of this histogram. In an equi-depth histogram, all buckets have an equal or close to equal count but the value range that a bucket spans is no longer fixed. A common way to generate an equi-depth histogram is to first sort the data. The bucket boundaries are then given by the values found at every $^{\#occurrences}/_{n}$ position in the sorted data. Figure 4 displays an equi-depth histogram constructed from the same data used to generate the equi-width histogram in Figure 3.

Compressed Histogram. While the equi-depth histogram handles skewed data better than the equi-width histogram, heavy hitters are still a problem. For instance, in Figure 4, a single value (the annotated bar) appears more often than any other item, but its count is not high enough to occupy a full bucket – when estimating the values belonging to this bucket some of them will be overestimated, and the peak will be underestimated. The so-called *Compressed* histogram mitigates this effect by counting the most frequent values separately and then generating an equi-depth histogram on the remaining values. Figure 5 shows a Compressed histogram, where the five most frequent values are counted separately.

V-Optimal and Max-diff Histogram. Poosala et al. [27] proved that from all possible histograms, the so-called *v-optimal* histogram provides the best approximation on the real data distribution. In this type of histogram the bucket boundaries are chosen such that the variance within every bucket is minimized. However, computing a v-optimal histogram is prohibitively expensive [27], which is why these histograms are not used in practice. A heuristic that is easier to compute and approximates a v-optimal histogram is the *Max-diff* histogram, which is implemented in Microsoft's

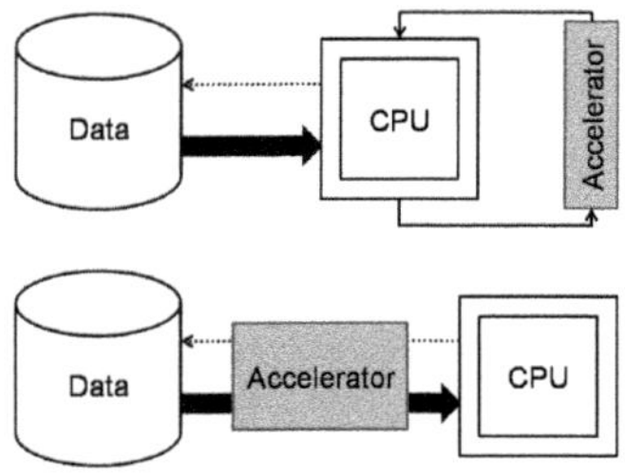

Figure 7: Explicit (top) vs. implicit (bottom) accelerator

SQL Server [20]. In a Max-diff histogram the bucket boundaries are positioned where the difference in occurrence count are maximal between adjacent pairs of values. This is a much easier optimization problem than minimizing the variance within buckets, as in the v-optimal histogram. In Figure 6, a Max-diff histogram is depicted, representing the same data as the other histograms in this section.

Automated Statistics. Since histogram calculation and statistic gathering is a costly operation, with many parameters, most modern database engines offer automated statistic gathering on the tables. Oracle [26], IBM DB2 [14] and Microsoft SQL Server [19] all will decide based on the table contents and workloads which tables need statistics, which columns need more detailed statistics such as histograms, and when to update the statistics for different tables. While these methods are effective, they operate under a very strict time budget, meaning that statistics and histograms cannot be refreshed as often as they should be. This is why using accelerators is highly beneficial: the automated tools could operate at higher efficiency, and refresh statistics more frequently than before.

4. SYSTEM OVERVIEW

An accelerator can be integrated into a system either as an explicit accelerator located on the side of the host system, or as an implicit accelerator, one that is on the data path (Figure 7). The fundamental difference between the two is that while the former needs to be accessed explicitly, and data needs to be copied to it, the latter is active every time data is streaming through it. In our case this means that histograms can be calculated *every time* data is retrieved for processing, as opposed to *on demand*, when the host decides to send data to the accelerator. Copying data from the CPU to the accelerator might not even be feasible without disrupting query processing if the tables are very large. By contrast, the only important requirement of an accelerator on the data path is that it must not introduce significant latency into the data stream. In this paper, we show that it is possible to offer sophisticated histograms and still guarantee only a negligible delay in the data stream.

FPGAs. We chose to implement our prototype system using an FPGA because FPGAs are well suited for dataflow type applications [22, 36], and can handle stream processing very well [29, 30, 23]. This makes them an ideal candidate for statistical accelerators, because we can dedicate hardware circuits to forward the incoming data, and use other parallel parts of the chip for calculating histograms. This way, the only cost of calculating histograms on the FPGA from the point of view of the host is the time it takes to stream the original data through the FPGA.

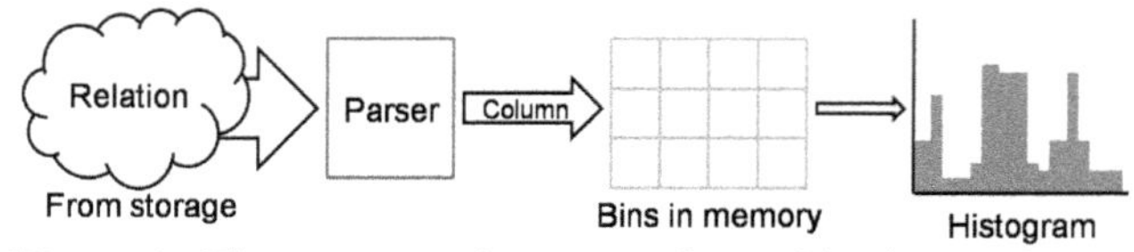

Figure 8: The conceptual steps performed in the accelerator

Figure 8 depicts the main steps that need to be carried out to produce histograms, and Figure 9 shows the implementation on the FPGA, consisting of the corresponding three modules: Parser, Binner and Histogram creation. In the following we will refer to the collection of these three as the *statistical circuit*. The role of the *Parser* is to parse the input data (database pages), and to keep only the column that will be processed by the rest of the circuit. The choice of the column is communicated by the host, with a metadata packet piggybacked on the original command to the data storage. To this end, the logic to filter the column of interest is a simple counting state machine. The second stage in the global pipeline is the *Binner* module, which calculates the in-memory sorted representation of the data on the streaming input. Finally, the *Histogram* module reads this representation from memory and uses it to build various histograms – Equi-depth, Max-diff and Compressed. These two modules are decoupled in their operation, since they only interact through regions in memory. This means that while for some data the histogram is calculated in the Histogram module, another input table can be already processed and binned at a different region in memory.

Histograms in linear time. Even though FPGAs excel at pipeline processing, the available on-chip memory (to keep state) is very limited, and the off-chip high-capacity memory is much slower to access. As a result, we were looking for ways to minimize the state required for performing the steps depicted in Figure 8. Parsing can be done in constant space and time with a simple finite-state machine (FSM). More challenging is the binning step, in which the data is radix sorted and aggregated in memory. For this we use an algorithm that runs in linear time, requires constant state and the amount of memory depends not on the size of the dataset but its cardinality. Inspired by the *bin sort* algorithm [7], the FPGA will associate a memory range with the range of values in the column. Assuming that the data in the column is of integer or fixed-point type, its corresponding count aggregate in memory can be updated directly on every appearance. Once the whole dataset has streamed by, the memory will hold a sorted view of the data. As later explained, the histogram creation step can also be carried out in linear time on the binned data. Since the cardinality is always smaller or equal than the input data set, the whole circuit will run in linear time, and require linear memory to store the sorted view.

Histograms as a side effect. As already mentioned, an accelerator in the data path is most useful if it never slows down the regular flow of data to the host. To fulfill this goal, our design, shown in Figure 9, has a dedicated cut-through path for the data going from storage to host. The actual statistical calculation is performed on a copy of the input, obtained by introducing a *Splitter* in the data path that duplicates the data flow. In terms of throughput, the FPGA can easily implement complex logic at 10 Gbps or even 100 Gbps throughput [17, 11, 3], so a cut-through path

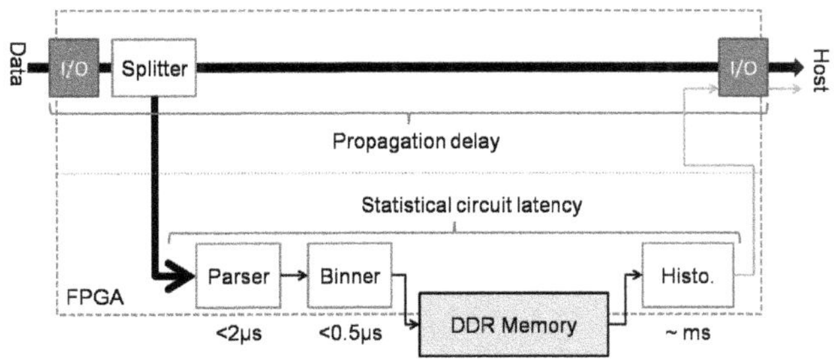

Figure 9: The FPGA implements cut-through logic for the data stream, and performs statistical operations on the side

should never be the bottleneck. As for latency, the delay introduced by the FPGA on the data is the combination of the Splitter and the I/O logic of the FPGA. The latency of the Splitter is in the order of nanoseconds, as it only needs to replicate the data, and the I/O logic's latency usually is in the order of microseconds, depending almost exclusively on the transmission medium and protocol. When compared to the retrieval time of large database tables, these latencies become negligible.

The latency of the core statistics circuit, which operates asynchronously and in parallel to the cut-through logic, can be broken down to 1) parsing, 2) binning and 3) histogram building. The time it takes for the Parser to extract the relevant information from the input rows depends on the data source type, but based on the current state of the art for FPGAs and with a conservative estimate, it can be performed with an FSM below $2\mu s$ for all data source types. The Binner module's latency is dominated by the memory access latency, which in our development platform was measured to be on average around $0.4\mu s$ (60 cycles at 150 MHz). The latency added by the Histogram module is the only latency in the millisecond range, and is not constant but grows with the number of bins residing in memory. A detailed discussion on the latency of different operations in this module is presented in Section 6.3.

Memory acts as a decoupling element between the Binner and the Histogram module, as they interact in a producer-consumer-like manner. As a result of this separation, only the throughput of the Binner module needs to be large enough to handle all input data without dropping rows. As we discuss in Section 6, in our prototype the bottleneck is the memory access rate, but even so we can handle sufficiently high input rates.

Based on the above analysis it is safe to say that the FPGA indeed is just a "bump in the wire", and that it will not degrade the read/write performance of the system. Since the histogram calculation happens in parallel to data transmission, and does not interfere with it.

5. IMPLEMENTATION

In this section, we focus on the implementation of the two most important modules of the statistical circuit: the Binner and the Histogram module.

5.1 Binner Module

Figure 10 shows the high-level view of the Binner module, composed of a preprocessor and a pipeline that interacts with off-chip memory. It is configured and fed with data by

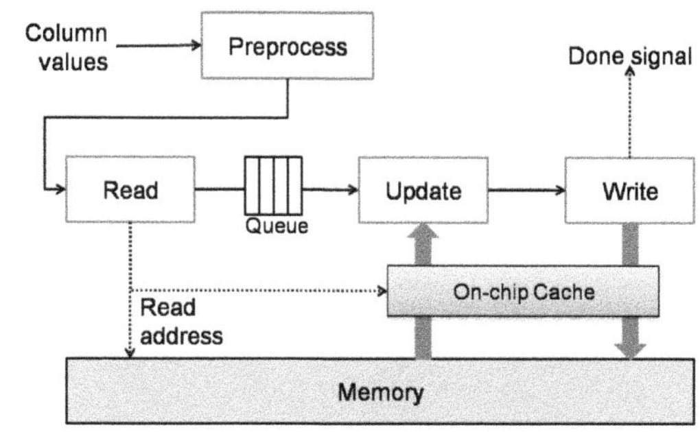

Figure 10: Binner: Module that processes the input stream into bins in memory

the Parser module, and its control output is connected to the Histogram module.

5.1.1 *Preprocessor*

Before the bins can be updated in memory, the input values need to be translated into actual memory addresses. The transformation from value space (contents of the column) to address space (the corresponding memory location) is the simplest for integer-type columns: for these it is enough to subtract the minimum value in the column from all values, and use the difference as an address. It is also possible to divide the values by some constant to assign multiple values to the same bin. This is useful when the granularity of interest is higher than that of the underlying data type. As an example, a column could store date values that change with the granularity of days, but the representation could be a second-based timestamp in the database. Additionally, databases often store data using their proprietary formats. For instance Oracle stores date objects not as a single epoch number, but unpacked, encoding the year, month, day, etc., explicitly [25]. The preprocessor can be used to convert a handful of predefined unpacked types to integers. This way, even if the internal representation is not a single integer, it is possible to calculate histograms on the column.

5.1.2 *Pipeline*

The Binner performs a bin-sort [7] operation, where values of the column are mapped to bins, and the counter in the bin is incremented on every appearance of the value. In software, this logic would be implemented as a tight loop:

```
for all input items {
  index = preprocess(input)
  array[index]++
}
```

The above representation however hides some of the complexity of interfacing with memory. In order to increment a bin count multiple operations have to be performed on the memory, which means that every iteration of the loop will take time in terms of memory latency. To hide this latency, we can break the loop up into a pipeline. We annotated each operation with the name of the pipeline stage that performs it below:

```
pipeline input items {
  index = preprocess(input)     [PREPROCESS]
  count = array[index]          [READ]
  newcount = count + 1          [UPDATE]
  array[index] = newcount       [WRITE]
}
```

These stages can be performed in parallel for different items, which means that we are not bound anymore by the memory

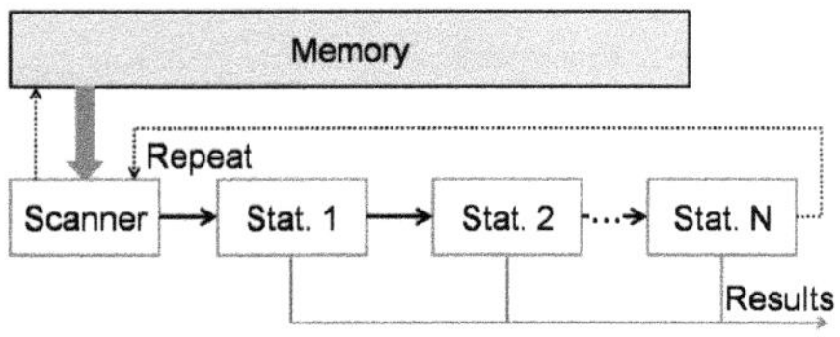

Figure 11: Histogram module: built from a series of statistic blocks which process the bins in a pipeline

access latency, but simply by the number of access operations the memory can handle per second, *i.e.* the pipeline can take full advantage of the memory.

The implementation of each pipeline stage follows intuitively from the pseudocode description. The *read* stage takes the addresses created by the preprocessor, and converts them into read commands to the memory. The physical read address in the memory may differ from the logical index of items because memory lines pack multiple bins (in our implementation eight). Once a read command has been issued, the logical address is put into the FIFO queue between the read and update stages. It is necessary to buffer the logical address so that the read stage can issue multiple commands to the memory while the *update* stage is waiting for the read data. When the memory provides the requested data, the *update* stage will pop an item from the queue, and increment the bin corresponding to the logical address and pass the updated memory line and the address to the next stage. The *write* stage will write back the memory line, and increment an internal counter that keeps track of the total number of items processed, which will be used in the histogram building phase. When the last input item reaches the write stage, the Binner module will send the total count to the Histogram module, signaling that it finished.

5.1.3 On-chip Caching

One issue with the pipeline presented above is that when two identical values follow each other, so called "read after write" conflicts can occur. Due to the high latency of the off-chip memory, it can happen that the second value will cause a read from memory before the incremented bin from the previous value could be stored back to memory. To overcome this issue, an often utilized technique for FPGAs is to simply stall the pipeline until it is certain that the first write was finished [12]. In our case this behavior is not acceptable, because it would mean that the processing speed of the circuit is dependent on the contents of a column. We want to guarantee same performance for the Binner module, regardless of the amount of skew in the data distribution.

To ensure that the circuit can always process items at the maximum speed allowed by the memory, we dedicate a small amount of on-chip memory to be used as a cache (1KB), which in essence forwards the values of recently accessed bins between the pipeline stages. The cache is a write-through cache whose size is adjusted to be able to store the maximum number of items that can arrive in the fixed time-frame defined by the memory access latency. The memory lines are stored on a small on-chip block RAM (BRAM), and this BRAM is indexed with the help of a lookup table that stores the memory addresses belonging to the items currently in the pipeline. Whenever a new item enters the pipeline, its data is either served from memory, or if fresher data is available, it is retrieved directly from the cache. The

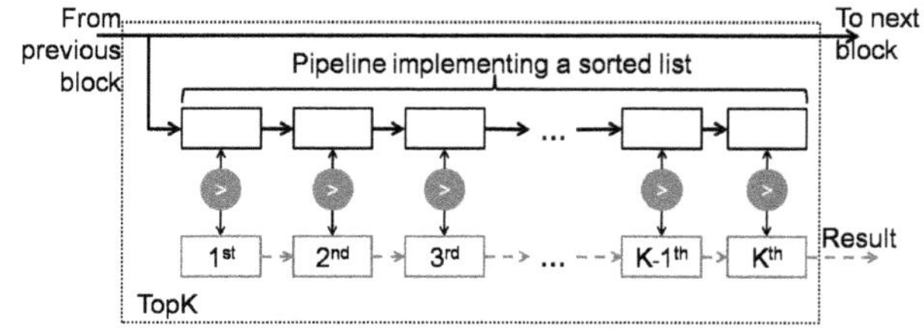

Figure 12: The TopK block implements a sorted list that stores the largest frequencies seen so far

architecture of this cache is highly scalable, and it can be easily ported to other memory types with higher or lower latency.

5.2 Histogram Creation and Statistics

The histogram building step begins once all the values in a column are binned in memory. The histogram building is carried out by the Histogram module, which is a pipeline internally. As shown in Figure 11, the first block in the pipeline is the *Scanner* block that scans the area of memory that contains the bins associated with the processed column. The start address and the amount of memory to read is provided by the Binner module after it completed processing the last input item.

As soon as the Scanner block starts receiving data from memory, it passes on the bin counts to a daisy-chain of statistical blocks. These blocks implement different histogram types or calculate different statistical properties on the input data. What they have in common is that they always relay the input unchanged to the next block. As we will show later, there are some blocks that need multiple scans of the bins – these blocks can tell the scanner through a feedback channel (*repeat*) to read and stream the bins again if necessary. Apart from the input and output ports used for streaming the bin data, these blocks also have a "result output", a port on which they communicate the histograms to the host.

For the Histogram module we have implemented four different types of statistics algorithms (and as a consequence, there can be up to four different types of statistical blocks in the chain). These are: a list of the most frequent items (TopK), as well as histograms of type equi-depth, Max-diff and Compressed. In the following we will explain first how the TopK block and the equi-depth histogram work, and then show how, by simple modifications to these two, we can build blocks that calculate the other two types of histograms.

5.2.1 Basic Blocks

Some operations on the sorted bin data can be performed in linear time, with only one scan of the data. We have implemented two such operations: maintaining the list of K most frequent items (TopK) and an equi-depth histogram.

Equi-depth Histograms. The block that calculates the equi-depth histogram is initialized with the number of histogram buckets to create, and the total number of items as counted by the Binner module. The number of buckets to create is a parameter of this block that is stored in a small on-chip memory. As a consequence, it is possible to change this value when a read request is sent. This gives the host flexibility of choosing the granularity of the histogram.

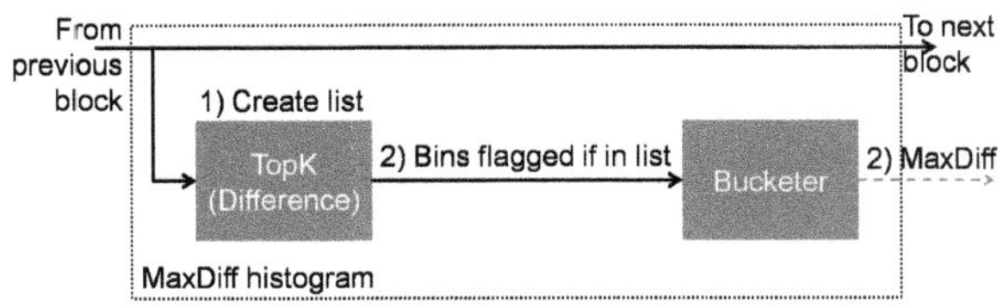

Figure 13: The Max-diff histogram is calculated in two scans, using modified TopK and equi-depth blocks

In an equi-depth histogram the sum of frequencies in each bucket should be equal to the total sum of frequencies divided by the number of buckets. Therefore, as a first step, this block will divide the total count of items (provided by the Binner module) by the number of buckets this block is configured to produce, and store the result in an internal memory. When bins are streamed through this block, both a running sum and the count of bins are maintained. When the sum is larger or equal than the limit, a new bucket is created. While the buckets might be larger than the limit, they will always contain all appearances of the same item in one bucket. This behavior is identical to Oracle's *hybrid equi-depth* histograms. The final output of this block consists of the aggregate sum in the bucket and the number of bins in it.

TopK. One way of finding the bins with the highest count is to sort them by their count. To carry out this operation in software most likely an algorithm such as quick-sort would be chosen, but on the FPGA there is not enough on-chip memory to act as intermediary storage for all bins while being sorted (accessing the off-chip DRAM for sorting purposes is not an option due to the very high access latency). Our solution is to use a sorting method inspired by insertion sort (like in [31]) that can be implemented using a pipeline structure. The role of the TopK block is to provide only the K highest ranking elements, so the list used for the insertion sort can be bounded at K. The pipeline, shown in Figure 12, consists of items entering on the left side and propagating through all elements of the list. If an item reaches the position where it should be in the sorted list, and this location is still empty, it is stored there. On the other hand, if the location is already occupied by a smaller item, the two will be swapped, with the smaller item traveling further in the pipeline. This means that instead of shifting the whole list right for insertions (as one would do in software), the swapping is done in the pipeline. This design decision is important because it allows for a continuous flow of items without the need to stall the input while the list is being shifted. A consequence of the pipelined design is that the number of logical elements needed for implementing this block are a linear function of the length of the list. In our experiments, we synthesized the circuit with a list size of 64, but larger sizes are also possible. They are not necessarily needed, however, because the role of this block is not to sort the entire data, but to find the set of K highest-ranking values.

5.2.2 *Composite Blocks*

Based on the previous two blocks we can build more elaborate histograms. These composite blocks need two scans of the binned data in memory. On the first scan they preprocess the data using a modified TopK block. The histogram is created on the second scan, using a modified equi-depth block.

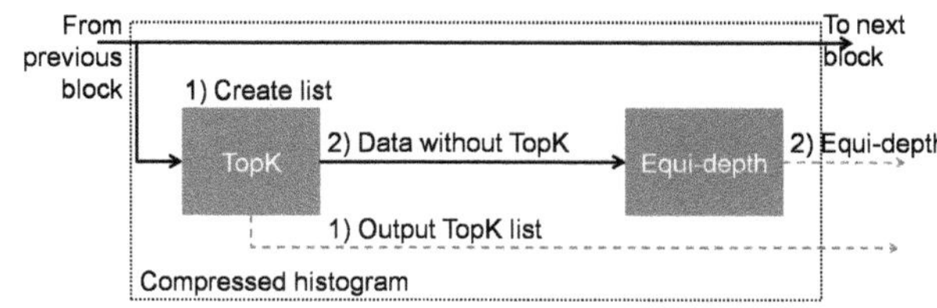

Figure 14: The Compressed histogram is calculated in two scans, using a modified TopK and an equi-depth block

Max-diff. In order to calculate the Max-diff histogram, first the K largest differences between bins need to be determined. For this, we can use a modified TopK block which instead of looking at the size of the bins looks at the difference between two consecutive bins. This is achieved by putting a subtract logic at the entry to said block that will replace the count of a bin with the difference between consecutive bins. When the first scan has finished, the list of top K differences is kept in the TopK circuitry. As Figure 13 shows, on the second scan bins are compared to the elements of this list, and flagged when found (that is, the bins that created the K biggest differences are flagged). A modified equi-depth block will use the flag as a bucket-creation condition instead of comparing the current count to some threshold value. The output of this block has the same format as the original equi-depth histogram block's output.

Compressed Histograms. The Compressed histogram is even easier to obtain from the two building blocks we have (Figure 14). On the first scan the top K frequent items are determined and kept in the list of the modified TopK block. They are output at the end of the scan, just as the regular top frequency list would be but their values are not removed from the registers. On the second scan, the modified TopK block filters out all bins that appear in the frequent list (flagging them as invalid data), and forwards the rest of the data to an instance of the equi-depth block that then constructs an equi-depth histogram of the less frequent values.

6. EVALUATION

Our evaluation setup is a Maxeler workstation[2], which has a quad-core Intel I7 2600S processor and 32 GB of main memory, running CentOS 6. The FPGA is a *Xilinx Virtex-6 SXT475* chip on a PCIe card (8 lanes, Gen1). As shown in Figure 15, the FPGA has its own dedicated 24 GBs of DDR3 memory, accessible directly from the chip. Our custom circuit was clocked at 150 MHz for all experiments. While the platform at our disposal did not allow for using the FPGA directly as an "implicit accelerator", as we show in this section the performance of the statistical circuit can be accu-

[2] http://www.maxeler.com/products/desktop/

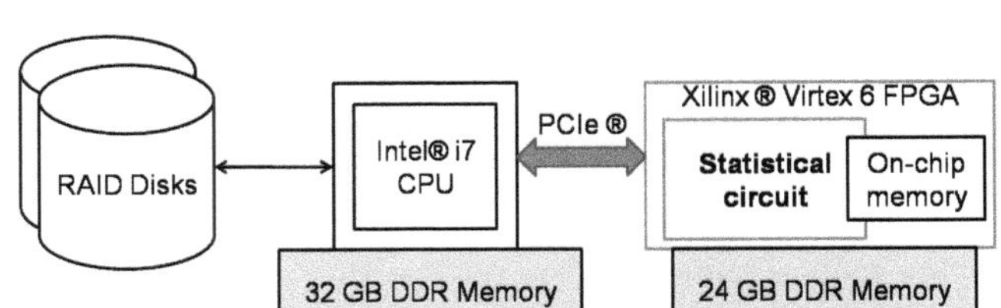

Figure 15: The Maxeler Box we used for our experimental evaluation has a Xilinx FPGA attached via PCIe

	Binner performance (values/second)	Equiv. rate for 1 column table	Equiv. rate for *lineitem*
Cache never hit (Worst)	20Million/s	80MB/s	2.9GB/s
Cache always hit (Best)	50Million/s	200MB/s	7.4GB/s
Pipeline (Ideal)	75Million/s	300MB/s	11.1GB/s

Table 1: Measured and ideal performance of the Binner module

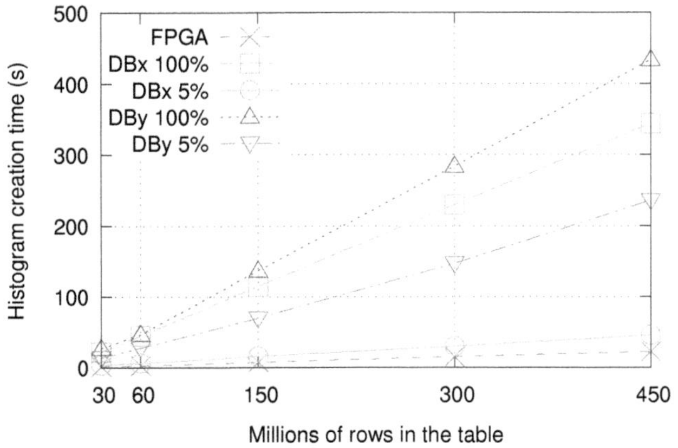

Figure 16: Effect of sampling on database histogram calculation

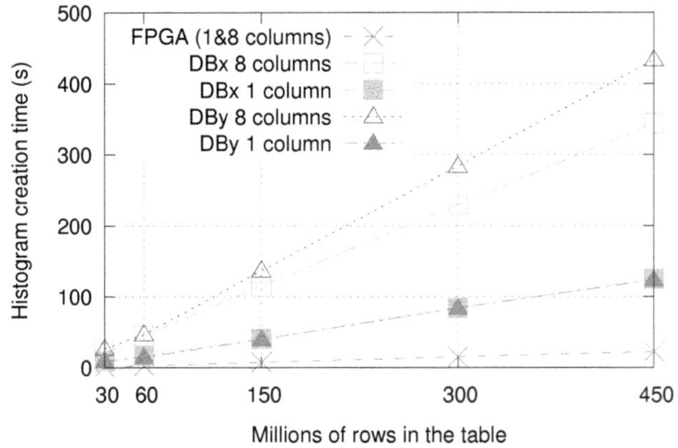

Figure 17: Reducing the number of columns in the table makes analysis faster

rately evaluated nonetheless. We compare the performance of the FPGA with two common commercial databases, referred to as *DBx* and *DBy* in the rest of this evaluation section.

6.1 Memory Access Rate

As explained in Section 5.1.2, the performance of the Binner module is determined by the off-chip memory: The maximum rate at which the Binner can handle input items is bound by the number of operations the memory controller can perform per second. We measured this number on our development system, and observed that it is relatively low because in the Maxeler workstation the memory attached to the FPGA is optimized for high bandwidth scans, not random access on small data chunks. Even so, as Table 1 summarizes, in the worst case, the memory can sustain 20 million updates to the bins per second, which translates to processing a one column table at 80 MB/s[3]. When processing a column of a table that has wider rows, such as *lineitem* from TPC-H , the rate that can be sustained for the table as a whole is significantly higher.

In case the data is heavily skewed, and therefore similar items often follow each other in bursts, it is possible to perform a higher number of updates per second. This is because in our implementation we do not issue read commands for items that are already in the cache. Consequently, the average number of memory accesses per bin update decreases, which in turn increases throughput. Additionally, when accessing rows in a less random manner, the memory also exhibits a higher access speed. Since the performance increase depends on the data distribution, we decided to conduct all our experiments with data that does not take advantage of the cache. In addition to the two measured values in Table 1, we also show the maximum throughput the statistical pipeline can achieve with sufficiently fast memory.

6.2 Histograms Building Speed

The goal of the following experiments is to show that our prototype accelerator can provide the same histograms as DBx and DBy at a fraction of the cost. The type of the histogram calculated on all three systems was equi-depth, left at the default bucket size for the databases, and set to 256 in the case of the FPGA. The tables we used for the experiments were cached in memory, and are derived from the *lineitem* table of the TPC-H benchmark. For the first measurements we created an eight column version of *lineitem* using the first eight numeric columns of the original table – this was achieved by truncating the output of the data generator. We used this setup to increase the number of rows that fit in memory.

Baseline. As a first experiment we measure a baseline on how much time it takes for the two commercial databases to calculate histograms on the eight column table created with TPC-H scale factors 5, 10, 25, 50 and 75. On the CPU we report the times to calculate the histogram on *l_quantity* as the execution time of the stored procedures which perform the statistical analysis; and for the FPGA we defined as runtime the time it takes from sending the first byte of the data through PCIe, until all result bytes from the FPGA were received. There is no delay inside the FPGA between receiving the first byte of the data and the start of the binning pipeline. Also, the FPGA is always processing the full input data, sampling is only done in case of the DBMSs.

Figure 16 shows that the FPGA performs much better than either of the databases, even when they use sampling. An interesting artifact of the graph is that the runtime of DBy does not decrease proportionally with the decrease in sampling rate – this means that for very large tables DBy

[3]This number is derived from the fact that the memory controller can handle 40 million read or write accesses per second in the worst case, and each bin update requires a read and a write operation. Assuming the input to be 32 bit numbers the 1 column throughput is 4B*20M/s=80MB/s

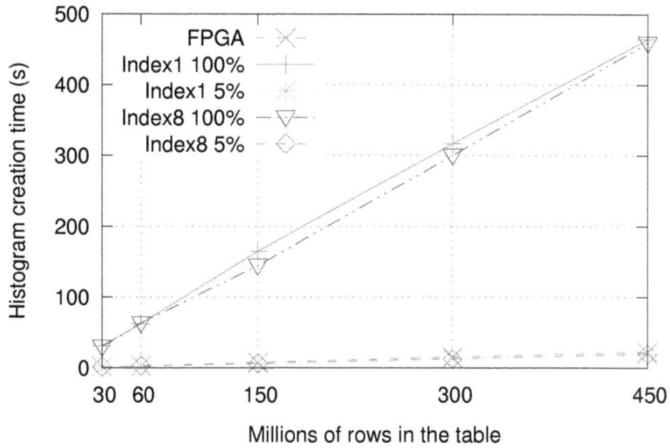

Figure 18: Calculating histograms on indexed tables in DBx

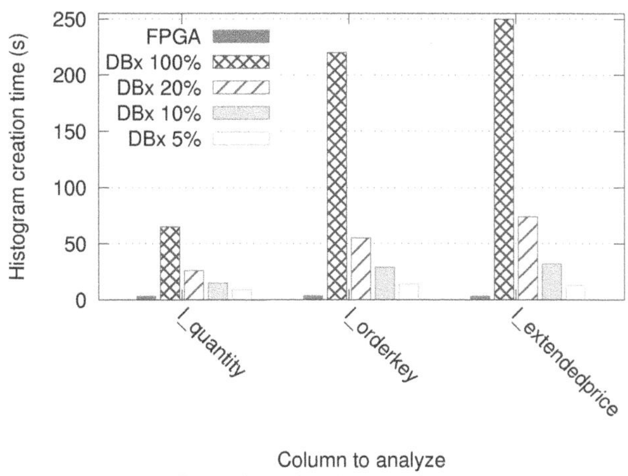

Figure 19: Effect of cardinality on histogram creation

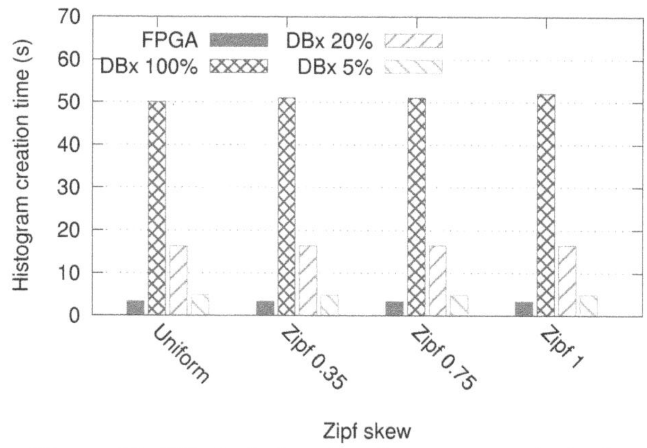

Figure 20: Effect of skew in columns on analysis time

might not be able to provide any sophisticated statistics if the time limit for acquiring them is too small.

As a follow up experiment, we reduced the *lineitem* table to a one column version, and repeated the previous measurements without sampling on this table. By having only one column, the runtimes for the databases should reflect the true CPU time needed to analyze a single column without other overheads. Figure 17 shows that even in this best-case scenario for DBx and DBy performing analysis without sampling will still take almost an order of magnitude longer than on the FPGA.

Indexed column. The third set of experiments that we show targets only DBx because it has the functionality of calculating histograms on indexes, whereas DBy does not. We created an index both on the 8 column *lineitem* (Index8) and the 1 column variant (Index1). Figure 18 shows how the performance of DBx improves when dealing with indexed columns – independent of the width of the rows the index was created on. This is most likely due to the fact that the index is a sorted representation of the underlying data, and hides the width of the original rows. Actually, with 5% sampling DBx is so fast that it catches up with the FPGA. The FPGA, however, is doing full table scans in this time. It is also important to note that 1) the creation and maintenance of the index introduces high costs, which are not represented at all in this graph, and 2) the histograms created are not equivalent because the FPGA version is built on the complete view of the data and the other only on a small sample of it.

Skew and Cardinality. As further exploration of histogram calculation costs, we compared the times for different columns of the *lineitem* table (scale factor 10), having different cardinalities and data types. Figure 19 shows that low-cardinality columns (like *l_quantity* with less than 100 different values) are cheaper to analyze than very high cardinality columns (such as *l_extendedprice* and *l_orderkey*). These results suggest that dealing with fixed-point arithmetic instead of integers introduces further overheads in DBx. The FPGA on the other hand is not noticeably influenced by the cardinality of the input dataset. A detailed discussion on the exact cost for the histogram building phase in the FPGA is presented in Section 6.3, but for tables with millions of rows or more, these costs are negligible.

Figure 20 shows that, as opposed to cardinality, skew has little effect on runtimes. The table we built for this experiment is populated with synthetic data (8 columns), with a cardinality of 2048 and Zipf distribution.

Automatic choice of sampling rate. While it is true that sampling can yield very accurate approximations of the actual data distributions [5], it can also happen that if the data is under-sampled important features are lost. What is even worse is that randomly, some features do not always show up in the histogram, which in turn leads to oscillations in the query plan. To illustrate how even very small errors in the histogram can lead to inadequate query plans, we revisited the query Q_1 from Section 2 using PostgreSQL. We chose PostgreSQL for this experiment because it is open-source and by modifying the analyzer's source code it is possible to force results into the histogram data structure.

We made a few changes to the query[4] and introduced small spikes at random in the data distribution of the *lineitem* table (scale factor 1): for a handful of prices we increased their occurrences to 2000 each, which is a very small skew given that there are six million rows in the table. PostgreSQL's automatic sampling detects these spikes only with roughly 50% probability each, and this leads to an oscilla-

[4]We introduced an ORDER BY clause in the first part and are joining on equality; This is needed so that PostgreSQL will consider not only Nested Loops Join in the optimizer

Block	Resource Usage	Resource Scaling	Result Latency	Result Size	Scans	Max. Freq.
TopK	2.5% (T=64)	$\mathcal{O}(T)$	$2\Delta+2T$	T * 8bytes	1	170MHz
Equi-depth	<1%	$\mathcal{O}(1)$	$2\Delta/B$	B * 8bytes	1	240MHz
Max-diff	<3% (B=64)	$\mathcal{O}(B)$	$(2\Delta+2B) + 2\Delta/B$	B * 8bytes	2	170MHz
Compressed	<3% (T=64)	$\mathcal{O}(T)$	$(2\Delta+2T) + 2\Delta/B$	(T+B) * 8bytes	2	170MHz

Table 2: Summary of properties and resource consumption on a Virtex6 FPGA of the four statistical blocks

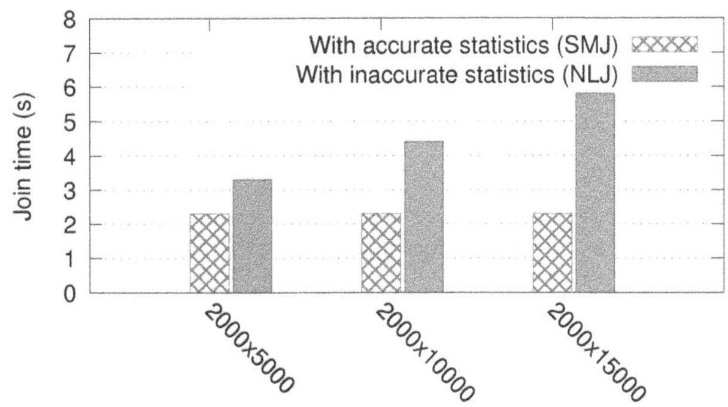

Figure 21: In PostgreSQL wrongly chosen query plans can lead to significant performance differences

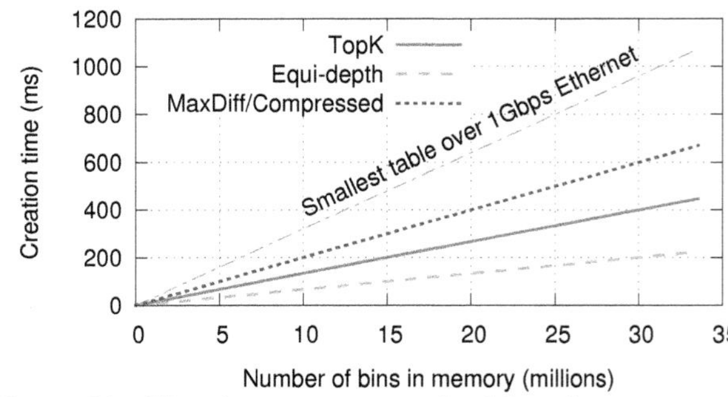

Figure 22: The time to process the binned representation grows linearly with the bucket count for every block

tion between a Nested Loops (NLJ) and a Sort Merge Join (SMJ) based query plan every time the table is analyzed. As Figure 21 shows, the runtimes are very different for the same data depending on the accuracy of the histograms. Furthermore, as the number of records participating in the join is increased, the more significant the difference becomes. When forced to use accurate histograms, PostgreSQL will correctly use Sort Merge Join.

6.3 Statistics Blocks

In addition to evaluating the accelerator as a whole, we present the different properties of the four statistical blocks (TopK, Equi-depth, Max-diff and Compressed) that were implemented for this paper. The most important input parameters to the Histogram module are:

- T : Number of top frequencies (exact counts) to maintain, and number of frequencies to remove in Compressed histograms
- B : Number of buckets to create for the equi-depth, Max-diff and the Compressed histogram
- Δ : The number of bins in memory that have to be read out for histogram creation

The most important properties of the four blocks are:

- Resource consumption : This property shows how much real estate each block is occupying. We express this as a percentage of the total resources on our FPGA.
- Resource scaling : This property shows how the block scales in terms of logic resource usage with increased bucket/frequency counts. This is an important metric because it shows how large each block can be made on a given FPGA.
- Result latency : This is the amount of time it takes for the block to produce the first result byte from the moment the first bin is retrieved from memory. This is expressed in number of clock cycles, which at 150 MHz last for 6.6 ns.
- Result size : The size of data in bytes that is output as a result of the statistical algorithm. Since each bucket is output as a pair of 32-bit integers, each bucket needs 8 bytes.
- Scans : How many times the block needs to scan the bins in order to finish its respective algorithm.
- Maximum frequency : The maximum frequency at which the given block can be clocked on the chip. This number is important, because in an FPGA design the final clock rate has to be chosen to be lower or equal than the minimum of all blocks.

Table 2 summarizes these properties for the four blocks we have implemented. Apart from the Equi-depth block all the others need logic resources relative to the number of buckets they produce. Consequently, these should always be scaled to a number of buckets that ensures good quality histograms but still fits on the FPGA. In terms of result latency, again the Equi-depth block will return the first bucket as soon as the threshold has been reached, but the other blocks take longer to create their results. The TopK block needs to read all bins before the top-list can be finalized. Similarly, both the Max-diff and Compressed histograms will start outputting buckets only once the data has been read in its entirety. With respect to pass-through latency, each block adds a constant number of cycles, which are necessary for copying the data into the internal logic. In our implementation this latency is 2 cycles per block. This means that with all four blocks on the chip, the last one will receive the contents of the first bin only 40ns (6*6.66ns) later than the first one.

To quantify the cost of creating histograms from the binned representation in our implementation we measured the time it takes for each block from the first retrieved bin, to the last result bucket output. As can be seen in Figure 22, this time increases linearly for each type of block, and the Max-diff and Compressed take as long as the TopK and equi-depth combined. This is not surprising, because these are a combination of the latter two. The reason for the TopK block to take longer than the equi-depth is that depending on the contents of the top-list, it can take two cycles to process a single input item, while the equi-depth always takes one cycle per input. The times in the graph are not additive, that is, if more blocks are chained together, their completion times will still be as shown in the graph. As a point of reference, Figure 22 also includes the minimum time it would take to stream a 1 column table over 1 Gbps Ethernet. Since we are targeting big data use-cases, it is very likely that the total number of rows in a table is orders of magnitudes higher than the cardinality of the column – making the cost of these histograms negligible.

Histogram variety. While we showed in the previous subsections that the FPGA can calculate histograms faster than software databases, we did not compare their feature set yet. In the following, we compare the types of statistics that four popular databases use with what the FPGA can offer. The Oracle database engine creates either equi-depth histograms (end-balanced or simple) or TopK representation on the data [26]. IBM DB2 and PostgreSQL gather both simple equi-depth histograms and TopK statistic [14, 28] on the data. Microsoft SQL Server calculates only Max-diff histograms [20]. The FPGA can provide TopK and equi-depth together with no additional cost. This means that as long as the FPGA processes at least as much of the data as the databases it will always provide the same, or more accurate, histograms as the databases. However, on top of this standard set of statistics, for no added cost, the FPGA can also create Max-diff and Compressed histograms.

7. FUTURE WORK

A next step for our prototype would be to scale it up to be able to handle single columns arriving at 10 Gbps line rate. Since in our architecture the memory is the immediate bottleneck, the first step would be to move the prototype to an FPGA board with faster memory than our current development board. Then the Parser and Binner modules would become the next bottleneck. However, these modules could easily be replicated to provide the aggregated throughput of 10 Gbps (Figure 23) – in fact, achieving higher data rates by replication is a common practice in FPGA development. The input items copied from the pass-through line can be distributed in a round-robin fashion to the different copies of the Binner module, which will calculate the partial counts in their memories.

The histogram module would not need to be modified even if the circuit is targeting higher input rates because it is completely decoupled from the input stream through the memory. If there are multiple memory chips used in the system, the partial counts can be aggregated in constant time before they are fed into the statistical blocks.

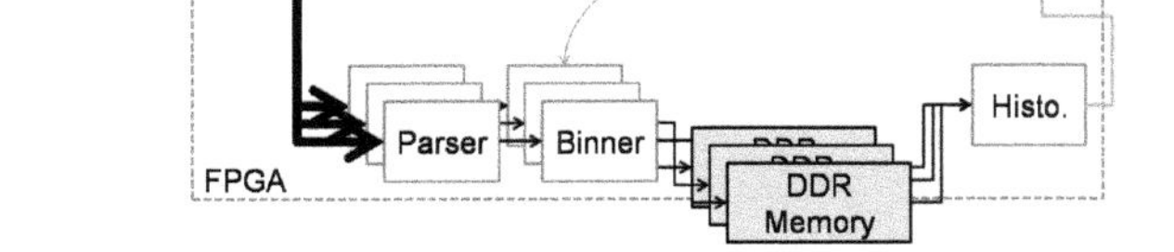

Figure 23: Higher data rates can be achieved by scaling up on future platforms

8. CONCLUSION

In the era of big data, data processing happens in increasingly distributed and heterogeneous environments. As a result, the choice of the best processing platform for a particular data processing task is crucial. As the state of the art in database design shows, statistics are successfully used to derive the right execution plans, but unfortunately obtaining these statistics is becoming increasingly difficult. In this paper, we propose an approach to change the traditional way of calculating histograms in batches, to an always-on statistical accelerator. This accelerator, which sits in the data path, acts as a bump in the wire and creates histograms for the data that it relays.

We have implemented the proposed idea on an FPGA to show the feasibility of moving the statistical logic into small dedicated circuits. We show both a speedup for the histogram calculation as well as the potential increase in accuracy when compared to two commercial databases. We also discuss the current platform limitations and propose ways of removing them.

Acknowledgements

This work is funded in part by grants from Xilinx, as part of the Enterprise Computing Center (www.ecc.ethz.ch), and Microsoft Research, as part of the Joint Research Center MSR-ETHZ-EPFL. The FPGA equipment used in the paper was acquired under the Maxeler University Program.

9. REFERENCES

[1] H. Angepat, D. Chiou, et al. An FPGA-based in-line accelerator for Memcached. *IEEE Computer Architecture Letters*, 99, 2013.

[2] A. Arasu, S. Blanas, K. Eguro, R. Kaushik, D. Kossmann, R. Ramamurthy, and R. Venkatesan. Orthogonal security with Cipherbase. *Proc. of the 6th CIDR, Asilomar, CA*, 2013.

[3] M. Bando, N. S. Artan, and H. J. Chao. Flashlook: 100Gbps hash-tuned route lookup architecture. In *High Performance Switching and Routing, 2009. HPSR 2009. International Conference on*, pages 1–8. IEEE, 2009.

[4] J. Casper and K. Olukotun. Hardware acceleration of database operations. In *Proceedings of the 2014 ACM/SIGDA international symposium on Field-programmable gate arrays*, pages 151–160. ACM, 2014.

[5] S. Chaudhuri, R. Motwani, and V. Narasayya. Random sampling for histogram construction: How much is enough? In *ACM SIGMOD Record*, volume 27, pages 436–447. ACM, 1998.

[6] Convey. Memcached with hybrid-core computing white paper. http://www.conveycomputer.com/files/6113/7998/5068/CONV-13-047_MCD_whitepaper.pdf, 2013.

[7] T. H. Cormen, C. Stein, R. L. Rivest, and C. E. Leiserson. *Introduction to Algorithms*. McGraw-Hill Higher Education, 2nd edition, 2001.

[8] T. P. P. Council. TPC-H benchmark specification, 2008. http://www.tcp.org/hspec.html.

[9] C. Dennl, D. Ziener, and J. Teich. Acceleration of SQL restrictions and aggregations through FPGA-based dynamic partial reconfiguration. In *Field-Programmable Custom Computing Machines (FCCM), 2013 IEEE 21st Annual International Symposium on*, pages 25–28. IEEE, 2013.

[10] J. Do, Y.-S. Kee, J. M. Patel, C. Park, K. Park, and D. J. DeWitt. Query processing on Smart SSDs: Opportunities and challenges. In *Proc. of the 2013 ACM SIGMOD Conference on Management of Data*, pages 1221–1230, New York, NY, USA, 2013.

[11] J. J. Garnica, S. Lopez-Buedo, V. Lopez, J. Aracil, and J. M. G. Hidalgo. A FPGA-based scalable architecture for URL legal filtering in 100GbE networks. In *Reconfigurable Computing and FPGAs (ReConFig), 2012 International Conference on*, pages 1–6. IEEE, 2012.

[12] R. J. Halstead, B. Sukhwani, H. Min, M. Thoennes, P. Dube, S. Asaad, and B. Iyer. Accelerating join operation for relational databases with FPGAs. In *Field-Programmable Custom Computing Machines (FCCM), 2013 IEEE 21st Annual International Symposium on*, pages 17–20. IEEE, 2013.

[13] M. Heimel and V. Markl. A first step towards GPU-assisted query optimization. In *The Third International Workshop on Accelerating Data Management Systems using Modern Processor and Storage Architectures, Istanbul, Turkey*, 2012.

[14] IBM. DB2 Version 10.1 for Linux, UNIX, and Windows. http://pic.dhe.ibm.com/infocenter/db2luw/v10r1/index.jsp.

[15] IBM/Netezza. The Netezza data appliance architecture: A platform for high performance data warehousing and analytics, 2011. http://www.redbooks.ibm.com/abstracts/redp4725.html.

[16] Y. Ioannidis. The history of histograms (abridged). In *Proceedings of the 29th international conference on Very large data bases-Volume 29*, pages 19–30. VLDB Endowment, 2003.

[17] Z. Istvan, G. Alonso, M. Blott, and K. Vissers. A flexible hash table design for 10Gbps key-value stores on FPGAs. In *Field Programmable Logic and Applications (FPL), 2013 23rd International Conference on*, pages 1–8. IEEE, 2013.

[18] S.-W. Jun, M. Liu, K. E. Fleming, et al. Scalable multi-access flash store for big data analytics. In *Proceedings of the 2014 ACM/SIGDA international symposium on Field-programmable gate arrays*, pages 55–64. ACM, 2014.

[19] Microsoft. SQL Server Autostat Functionality. http://support.microsoft.com/kb/195565.

[20] Microsoft. SQL Server Documentation: Statistics. http://technet.microsoft.com/en-us/library/ms174384.aspx.

[21] R. Moussalli et al. Accelerating XML query matching through custom stack generation on FPGAs. In *HiPEAC'10*, Pisa, Italy, Jan. 2010.

[22] R. Mueller, J. Teubner, and G. Alonso. Data processing on fpgas. *Proceedings of the VLDB Endowment*, 2(1):910–921, 2009.

[23] R. Mueller, J. Teubner, and G. Alonso. Streams on wires: a query compiler for fpgas. *Proceedings of the VLDB Endowment*, 2(1):229–240, 2009.

[24] M. Najafi, M. Sadoghi, and H.-A. Jacobsen. Flexible query processor on FPGAs. *Proceedings of the VLDB Endowment*, 6(12):1310–1313, 2013.

[25] Oracle. Call Interface Programmer's Guide. http://docs.oracle.com/cd/B28359_01/appdev.111/b28395/oci03typ.htm#g467721.

[26] Oracle. White Paper on Understanding Optimizer Statistics, 2012. http://www.oracle.com/technetwork/database/focus-areas/bi-datawarehousing/twp-optimizer-stats-concepts-110711-1354477.pdf.

[27] V. Poosala, P. J. Haas, Y. E. Ioannidis, and E. J. Shekita. Improved histograms for selectivity estimation of range predicates. *ACM SIGMOD Record*, 25(2):294–305, 1996.

[28] PostgreSQL. 9.3 On-line Documentation: Statistics. http://www.postgresql.org/docs/9.3/static/view-pg-stats.html.

[29] M. Sadoghi et al. Efficient event processing through reconfigurable hardware for algorithmic trading. *VLDB'10*, Sept. 2010.

[30] M. Sadoghi, R. Javed, N. Tarafdar, H. Singh, R. Palaniappan, and H.-A. Jacobsen. Multi-query stream processing on fpgas. In *Data Engineering (ICDE), 2012 IEEE 28th International Conference on*, pages 1229–1232. IEEE, 2012.

[31] J. Teubner, R. Mueller, and G. Alonso. FPGA acceleration for the frequent item problem. In *Data Engineering (ICDE), 2010 IEEE 26th International Conference on*, pages 669–680. IEEE, 2010.

[32] J. Teubner, L. Woods, and C. Nie. Skeleton automata for fpgas: reconfiguring without reconstructing. In *Proceedings of the 2012 ACM SIGMOD International Conference on Management of Data*, pages 229–240. ACM, 2012.

[33] P. Vaidya et al. Symbiote: A reconfigurable logic assisted data stream management system (rladsms). In *SIGMOD'10*, Indianapolis, IN, USA, June 2010.

[34] L. Woods, J. Teubner, and G. Alonso. Complex event detection at wire speed with FPGAs. *Proceedings of the VLDB Endowment*, 3(1-2):660–669, 2010.

[35] L. Woods, J. Teubner, and G. Alonso. Less watts, more performance: an intelligent storage engine for data appliances. In *Proceedings of the 2013 international conference on Management of data*, pages 1073–1076. ACM, 2013.

[36] Y.-H. E. Yang, W. Jiang, and V. K. Prasanna. Compact architecture for high-throughput regular expression matching on FPGA. In *ANCS'08*, San Jose, CA, USA, Nov. 2008.

[37] Q. Zhu, B. Dunkel, N. Soparkar, S. Chen, B. Schiefer, and T. Lai. A piggyback method to collect statistics for query optimization in database management systems. In *Proceedings of the 1998 conference of the Centre for Advanced Studies on Collaborative research*, page 25. IBM Press, 1998.

A Formal Approach to Finding Explanations for Database Queries*

Sudeepa Roy
University of Washington
Seattle, WA, USA
sudeepa@cs.washington.edu

Dan Suciu
University of Washington
Seattle, WA, USA
suciu@cs.washington.edu

ABSTRACT

As a consequence of the popularity of *big data*, many users with a variety of backgrounds seek to extract high level information from datasets collected from various sources and combined using data integration techniques. A major challenge for research in data management is to develop tools to assist users in explaining observed query outputs. In this paper we introduce a principled approach to provide explanations for answers to SQL queries based on *intervention*: removal of tuples from the database that significantly affect the query answers. We provide a formal definition of intervention in the presence of multiple relations which can interact with each other through foreign keys. First we give a set of recursive rules to compute the intervention for any given explanation in polynomial time (data complexity). Then we give simple and efficient algorithms based on SQL queries that can compute the top-K explanations by using standard database management systems under certain conditions. We evaluate the quality and performance of our approach by experiments on real datasets.

Categories and Subject Descriptors

H.1.0 [**Models and Principles**]: General; H.2.8 [**Database Management**]: Database Applications

Keywords

Explanations; Causality; Intervention; Recursion; Data cube

1. INTRODUCTION

As a consequence of the popularity of "big data", many users with a variety of backgrounds seek to extract high level information from datasets. The typical scenario is this. A user integrates a number of data sets, computes some statistics, then seeks an explanation for what she sees. Why are these data values outliers? Or why are they *not* outliers? Why are two graphs similar (or dissimilar)? Why is this value so high (low)? A major challenge for research in both data management and AI is to develop tools to assist users in explaining observed query outputs.

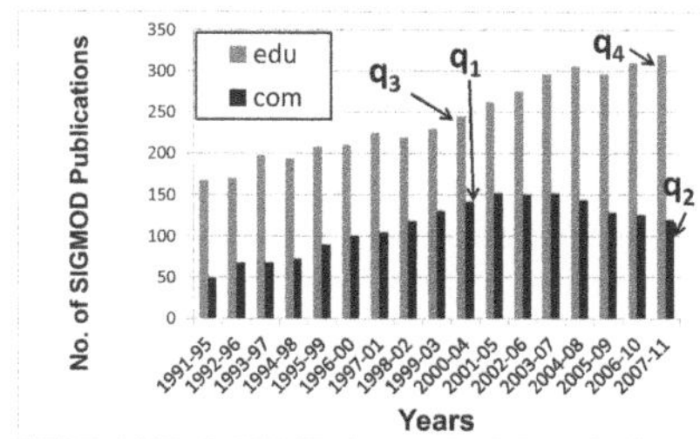

Figure 1: Number of SIGMOD publications in a five years windows, broken down into papers from industry ('com') and academia ('edu'). While both increase until 2000-2007, afterward the number of papers from academia continue to increase while that from industry decreases.

Consider the following example. Figure 1 shows the number of publications in SIGMOD during a moving five years window, broken down into papers published by authors from industry and papers published by authors from academia. The graph was generated using a three-way-join SQL query over the DBLP dataset integrated with an affiliation table[1]. Around 2000-2007 one can notice an interesting bump: while before that period both the number of academic and industrial papers increase over time, after that period the number of academic papers continues to increase, but that of industrial papers decreases. This is clearly an interesting phenomenon. For certain users (say, the director of a government funding agency), it is important to find explanations for this phenomenon, by digging deeper into the data.

The golden standard for an explanation is the *actual cause* of the observed outcome. Causality has been studied and defined algorithmically by Judea Pearl, in a highly influential work [11]. At the core, causality is defined in terms of intervention: an input is said to be a cause if we can affect the output by changing just the value of that input, while keeping all others unchanged. Causality can only be established in a controlled physical experiment, and cannot be derived solely from data. (Pearl, and others, circumvent that by assuming that causal paths are already known, allowing the

*This research was partially supported by NSF Awards IIS-0911036 and IIS-1115188.

SIGMOD'14, June 22–27, 2014, Snowbird, UT, USA.

ACM 978-1-4503-2376-5/14/06 ...$15.00.
http://dx.doi.org/10.1145/2588555.2588578.

[1]The affiliation information was available only for some authors, therefore the graph does not include all papers; papers with authors from both industry and academia are included in both bars.

rank	explanation
1	[affiliation = ibm.com]
2	[affiliation = bell-labs.com]
3	[author = Rajeev Rastogi]
4	[affiliation = ucla.edu]
5	[author = Hamid Pirahesh]
6	[affiliation = asu.edu]
7	[author = Rakesh Agrawal]
8	[affiliation = utah.edu]
9	[affiliation = gwu.edu]

Figure 2: Top explanations for the observation in Figure 1.

controlled experiment to be simulated algorithmically.) In contrast, an *explanation* lowers the bar of causality, and only requires that a change in the input affects the output [6, 9]: the more it affects the output, the better the explanation. All previous work on explanations have adopted the principle of intervention either explicitly or implicitly (for example, by using *influence* as a metric for explanation [19]).

In the context of databases, a major challenge in finding explanations is the difficulty of defining and computing interventions for complex datasets and queries. Users often examine multiple datasets, and the query is complex, involving joins and aggregates; often the question is the relationship of several queries rather than a single query. The challenge is to define an intervention, and compute all interventions in real time. Previous work on explaining data outcomes have been restricted to single table only, and to queries without joins [15, 2, 6, 19]. However, many interesting observations in data are made when we integrate multiple data sets and run complex queries, including joins. Any single dataset may be uninteresting, but once we join them we make interesting observations, which we wish to explain.

In this paper we introduce a principled approach to query explanation that applies to SQL queries. Our definition is based on intervention: an explanation is a predicate with the property that, when we remove from the database all tuples satisfying that predicate, then we affect significantly the outcome that we want to explain. For an illustration we show in Figure 2 the top explanations for the observation made in Figure 1. For example, `bell-labs` had a very active database groups in the mid 90's: if we intervene by removing `bell-labs` from the data then we flatten to some extent the bump in industrial publications in the late 90's (prior to 2000-2007) thus "explaining" the bump; similar explanations come from top researchers in industrial labs who published intensively in the 90's. A different kind of explanations are for the increase in academic publications: a large chunk comes from some highly prolific academic database groups established or increased during the 2000's, such as `asu.edu`, `utah.edu`, `gwu.edu`. Notice that all these are simply "explanations" and we do not claim to establish causality: in this particular example, the only way to prove causality would be to repeat the history. However, good explanations can go a long way in helping the user dig deeper in search for the ultimate cause[2]

In this paper we make the following contributions:

Framework In Section 2 we define a formal framework for explaining the outputs to SQL queries based on the notion of intervention. A key novel feature of our approach is to use foreign keys to model causal paths. We observe that SQL's cascade-delete rule already encodes a causal path: a record with a key `pk` is a cause for all records whose foreign key is `fk` = `pk`. We introduce a novel constraint that captures the reverse causal path, which often occurs in data, namely when the latter record causes the former record: we call this a back-and-forth foreign key, and show that it models naturally causal paths in databases. For example an author is cause for all her papers, hence if the intervention removes the author then it must also remove all her papers; in contrast the author is not a cause of her institution, hence an intervention may remove the author without removing her institution. In our framework, such causal paths can be modeled through a simple extension of foreign keys.

Theory In Section 3 we show that the minimal intervention associated to an explanation is uniquely defined. This is a key property for our framework, which allows us to measure the degree of explanation based on its unique minimal intervention. We further show that it can be defined as the minimal fixpoint of a recursive program that is monotone in its IDBs (hence has a unique minimal fixpoint), yet non-monotone in the input database (the intervention is not monotone in the input). We show some important properties of the recursive program: in particular we identify restrictions on the input schema under which the fixpoint is obtained in a constant number of iterations, thus eliminating the need for recursion.

Implementation and Optimization In Section 4 we show that, under certain restrictions, one can use SQL's data-cube operation to compute the degree of *all* candidate explanations, then return the top k to the user. While this technique works only under certain restrictions on the query and the database schema, when it can be applied, then it can compute and rank all explanations in real time. Furthermore, the entire computation can be pushed inside the database engine and, therefore, exploit all optimizations available for the data cube. Notice that, in contrast to our approach, the technique proposed recently by Wu and Madden [19] is based on a search algorithm on decision trees, which needs to be performed outside of the DBMS.

Experiments In Section 5 we run experiments on two real datasets. We show that explanations returned by our framework are interesting, and that they can be computed and returned in real time.

Related Work.

Pearl and others have explored various definitions of causality primarily using the concept of *counterfactuals* (see, e.g., [11, 12]); Meliou et al. adapted these notions to database queries [7, 8]. Silverstein et al. [15] study causal relationship in data mining settings for market basket data. Various approaches to explanations exists in the AI literature [10, 20]. In databases, Khoussainova et al. [6] proposed the system PerfXplain that explains systems performance. Fabbri and LeFevre studied explanation-based auditing of access log [3]. Das et al. [2] studied the problem of "Meaningful Ratings Interpretation (MRI)" based on the idea of data cube. Kanagal et al. [5] studied the problem of computing top-k influential variables and top-k explanations (to answer, *e.g.*, "why a tuple is in the output", "why the probability of an output tuple is greater than another one") in probabilistic databases. In recent work, Wu and Madden [19] discussed a

[2]We believe that the cause for the phenomenon observed in our example is a combination of a strategic hires by several Computer Science Departments of strong database faculty, combined with a hiring slowdown or even decline of database groups at some major industrial research labs.

framework for finding explanations for aggregate queries on a single relation based on the notion of influence. Related to explanation are Sarawagi and Sathe's techniques for efficient and automated data analysis in OLAP cubes (by RELAX, DIFF, and SURPRISE operators) [13, 14]. Our framework for explanation shares the same common philosophy of previous systems (measuring explanation by some sort of intervention or influence), but is the first comprehensive approach that can handle complex SQL queries over complex database schemas.

2. FRAMEWORK OF EXPLANATIONS

Let D be a database consisting of relations $R_1, \cdots, R_k$. For all[3] $i \in [k]$ we denote A_i the set of attributes of R_i. We assume that each relation R_i has a primary key, $\mathtt{pk} \subseteq A_i$. A *numerical query* is an expression of the form:

$$Q = E(q_1, \ldots, q_m) \tag{1}$$

Here each q_j is any SQL query where the `select` clause contains a single aggregate operator (q_j = `select agg(...) ...`), and E is an arithmetic expression, consisting of any numerical operators legal in SQL $(+, -, *, /, \log, \exp$ etc).

DEFINITION 2.1. *A* user question *is a pair (Q, dir), where (i) Q is a numerical query, and (ii) $dir \in \{high, low\}$ is a direction specifying whether the user thinks Q is higher or lower than the expected value on D.*

EXAMPLE 2.2. *Our running example is a simplified version of the DBLP database[17] and has the following schema:*
`Author(id, name, inst, dom)`
`Authored(id, pubid)`
`Publication(pubid, year, venue)`
A small instance is in Figure 3. The "bump" around 2000-07 in Figure 1 is expressed as the following numerical query

$$Q = \frac{q_1}{q_2} / \frac{q_3}{q_4} = \frac{q_1}{q_2} \times \frac{q_4}{q_3}$$

which compares the ratios of SIGMOD publications from dom =' *com' and* dom =' *edu' in 2000-04 to that in 2007-11. The user question is $(Q, high)$. Here*

```
q1: select count(distinct z.pubid)
    from Author x, Authored y, Publication z
    where x.id = y.id and y.pubid = z.pubid
        and z.venue = 'SIGMOD' and x.dom = 'com'
        and 2000 <= z.year and z.year <= 2004
```

Similar queries can be written for

```
q2:    (2007 <= z.year <= 2011, x.dom = 'com'),
q3:    (2000 <= z.year <= 2004, x.dom = 'edu'), and
q4:    (2007 <= z.year <= 2011, x.dom = 'edu').
```

The bars for these four queries are indicated in Figure 1.

We envision a user interface[4] where the user would interact with the system by generating a graph (like Figure 1) using a group-by SQL query with one or several aggregates: each aggregate value represents a point in the graph. Using a graphical interface the user would select some points on the graph (like the four bars in Figure 1) and ask why a certain relationship holds; the system would convert this into a user question (Q, dir), as illustrated in our example. In this paper we assume that input to the system is the user question (Q, dir).

Author

id	name	inst	dom	
A1	JG	C.edu	edu	r_1
A2	RR	M.com	com	r_2
A3	CM	I.com	com	r_3

Publication

pubid	year	venue	
P1	2001	SIGMOD	t_1
P2	2011	VLDB	t_2
P3	2001	SIGMOD	t_3

Authored

id	pubid	
A1	P1	s_1
A2	P1	s_2
A1	P2	s_3
A3	P2	s_4
A2	P3	s_5
A3	P3	s_6

Figure 3: Tables for the running example, identifiers are shown next to the tuples for easy reference.

Given a database instance $D = (R_1, \ldots, R_k)$, we denote by $U(D) = R_1 \bowtie \ldots \bowtie R_k$ the universal relation, obtained by joining all tables on all foreign key constraints. The universal table for our running example in Figure 3 is shown in Figure 4. We assume that all relations are *semijoin-reduced*[5]; in other words, for every i, $R_i = \Pi_{A_i}(U(D))$, i.e. R_i can be obtained by projecting the universal relation on its attributes; if this does not hold, we simply replace R_i with $\Pi_{A_i}(U(D))$. In our running example, this means that every author has published at least one paper, and every paper has at least one author. All relations in Figure 3 are semijoin-reduced. We also assume that the schema is acyclic for simplicity[6].

2.1 Explanations

In response to a user question (Q, dir), the system returns a list of candidate explanations.

DEFINITION 2.3. *A* candidate explanation *ϕ is a conjunction of predicates on attributes: $\phi = \bigwedge_j \phi_j$, where each ϕ_j is an atomic predicate of the form $\phi_j = [R_i.A \ \mathtt{op} \ c]$, where A is an attribute of R_i, c is a constant, and* $\mathtt{op} \in \{=, <, \leq, >, \geq\}$.

We note that our choice of defining explanations as predicates is similar to other frameworks for explanations [9, 19, 6], and is unlike frameworks for causality, where a cause is defined to consist of a single tuple [7, 8] (not predicates).

A simple example is ϕ = [`Author.name` = `JG`]; another example is ϕ = [`Author.name` = `JG` ∧ `Publication.year` = `2001`]. The intuition is that the tuples in the database that satisfy the predicates in the explanation are major contributors to the value of Q being too high or too low. The system will rank the candidate explanations in *decreasing order* of their *degree of explanation*, which measures of how well ϕ explains the observed phenomenon. We will define two such degrees. The first one, called *degree of explanation by aggravation*, is simple but more limited: it simply measures the value of Q on the subset of the database that satisfies ϕ. Let $U = U(D)$ be the universal table, and denote $U_\phi = \sigma_\phi(U)$. Let D_ϕ be the database whose relations are $\Pi_{A_1}(U_\phi), \ldots, \Pi_{A_k}(U_\phi)$. Then:

DEFINITION 2.4. *Given database D and a user question (Q, dir), the* degree of a candidate explanation ϕ by aggra-

[3]For two integers $a \leq b$, $[a, b]$ denotes the set $\{a, a+1, \cdots, b-1, b\}$ and $[b] = [1, b]$.
[4]We are currently developing the user interface.

[5]They are called *globally consistent* in [1]
[6]We can handle cyclic schemas but with the standard restrictions for the universal relation [16], sec 17.8, page 1056.

vation *is defined as:*

$$\mu_{aggr(D,Q,dir)}(\phi) = \begin{cases} -Q(D_\phi) & \textit{if } dir = low \\ Q(D_\phi) & \textit{if } dir = high \end{cases}$$

We will omit D, Q, dir in the subscript where they are clear from the context. Intuitively, if we restrict the database to tuples that satisfy the explanation predicate, it will further *aggravate* the situation by changing the answer to Q in the same direction as dir (*e.g.*, if $dir = low$, explanations with even lower values of $Q(D_\phi)$ will have top ranks).

The explanation by aggravation is appealing through its simplicity, but it ignores any causality path. Our second definition is called *degree of explanation by intervention* and is based on causality relations in the data, which we define next.

2.2 Causal Paths and Foreign Keys

An *intervention* is a set of tuples to be deleted from D. If $\Delta_i \subseteq R_i$ for $i \in [k]$, then we denote the intervention as $\Delta = (\Delta_1, \ldots, \Delta_k)$ and write $D' = D - \Delta$ for the residual database instance after deleting all tuples in Δ. Each candidate explanation ϕ defines a certain intervention Δ^ϕ; its *degree of explanation by intervention* is the amount by which the query on the residual database $Q(D')$ moves in the direction expected by the user. Unlike aggravation, intervention Δ^ϕ includes all tuples reachable through a *causal path* (discussed further in Section 3.3). Intuitively, there exists a causal path from a tuple t to another tuple t' if t is a necessary cause for t'. In other words, if we delete t from the database then the semantics of the data is such that we must delete t' as well. Pearl defines causal paths in terms of causal networks [10]. In this paper we propose a simpler definition of a causal path by exploiting the foreign-key relationships in the database.

A standard foreign key constraint $R_j.\mathtt{fk} \to R_i.\mathtt{pk}$ means that for every tuple $t_j \in R_j$ there exists a tuple $t_i \in R_i$ such that $t_j.\mathtt{fk} = t_i.\mathtt{pk}$. For a simple example, in Figure 3 we have the foreign key `Authored.id` → `Author.id`. Every foreign key automatically induces a causal relation between the two tuples, which we denote $t_i \to t_j$. The precise meaning that we give to this causal relation is that, whenever we delete t_i from the database, we must delete t_j as well. We call this causal relation a *cascade* causal relation, because it corresponds precisely to the cascade rule in SQL.

In some datasets, however, the reverse causal relation holds too, $t_j \to t_i$. This happens when every member of a collection is necessary for the existence of the collection; for example, every author is necessary for the existence of a paper, every part is needed for the existence of an electronic gadget. In that case we denote the foreign key constraint as $R_j.\mathtt{fk} \hookrightarrow R_i.\mathtt{pk}$. The meaning is that we have two causal relations, a cascade relation $t_i \to t_j$ and *backward cascade* relation, which we denote by $t_j \dashrightarrow t_i$: if either t_i or t_j is deleted then the other tuple must be deleted as well. We say that $R_j.\mathtt{fk} \hookrightarrow R_i.\mathtt{pk}$ is a *back-and-forth* foreign key.

Definition 2.5. *Let $D = (R_1, \ldots, R_k)$ be a database with a set of foreign keys (standard and back-and-forth). Let $\Delta = (\Delta_1, \ldots, \Delta_k)$, where $\Delta_i \subseteq R_i$ for all $i \in [k]$. We call Δ* closed *if it satisfies the following conditions:*

- *For every standard foreign key $R_j.\mathtt{fk} \to R_i.\mathtt{pk}$ and for all tuples $t_i \in R_i, t_j \in R_j$ such that $t_j.\mathtt{fk} = t_i.\mathtt{pk}$, if $t_i \in \Delta_i$ then $t_j \in \Delta_j$.*
- *For every back-and-forth foreign key $R_j.\mathtt{fk} \hookrightarrow R_i.\mathtt{pk}$ and for all tuples $t_i \in R_i, t_j \in R_j$ such that $t_j.\mathtt{fk} = t_i.\mathtt{pk}$ (a) if $t_i \in \Delta_i$ then $t_j \in \Delta_j$ (forth), and (b) if $t_j \in \Delta_j$ then $t_i \in \Delta_i$ (back).*

id	pubid	name	inst	dom	year	venue	
A1	P1	JG	C.edu	edu	2001	SIGMOD	u_1
A2	P1	RR	M.com	com	2001	SIGMOD	u_2
A1	P2	JG	C.edu	edu	2011	VLDB	u_3
A3	P2	CM	I.com	com	2011	VLDB	u_4
A2	P3	RR	M.com	com	2001	SIGMOD	u_5
A3	P3	CM	I.com	com	2001	SIGMOD	u_6

Figure 4: Universal table $U(D)$ for the running example.

We illustrate on our running example Figure 3. Here we have a natural causal path from authors to papers: the presence of an author is necessary for their papers. In other words, if we delete an author from the database, then we should delete all her papers too. By contrast, there exists no causal path from papers to authors: we can delete a paper without deleting its authors. This is captured by a standard foreign key and a back-and-forth foreign key:

$$\begin{aligned} &\mathtt{Authored.id} \to \mathtt{Author.id} \\ &\mathtt{Authored.pubid} \hookrightarrow \mathtt{Publication.pubid} \end{aligned} \qquad (2)$$

Referring to the tuples in Figure 3, we have the causal relations $r_1 \to s_1 \dashrightarrow t_1$ and also $r_1 \to s_3 \dashrightarrow t_2$. This means that if we delete the author r_1 then we must also delete s_1, s_3, t_1, t_3, then also delete s_2 and s_4 by the standard cascade rule.

The *intervention* associated to a candidate explanation ϕ is a set of tuples Δ^ϕ to be deleted.

Definition 2.6. *Let $D = (R_1, \cdots, R_k)$ be a database and ϕ be a candidate explanation. A set $\Delta = (\Delta_1, \cdots, \Delta_k) \subseteq D$ is called a* valid intervention *for ϕ if:*

1. *Δ is closed (Definition 2.5).*
2. *The residual database $D - \Delta$ is semi-join reduced.*
3. *For each tuple t in the residual universal relation $U(D-\Delta)$, $\phi(t) = \mathtt{false}$.*

The intervention associated to ϕ, denoted Δ^ϕ, is the minimal valid intervention for ϕ, in the sense that, for every valid Δ' we have $\Delta^\phi \subseteq \Delta'$.

The trivial intervention $\Delta = D$ is always valid, but in general, is not minimal. We show in the next section that there always exists a unique minimal intervention. Our second (and main) definition of degree of explanation is based on intervention:

Definition 2.7. *Given database D and a user question (Q, dir), the* degree of a candidate explanation ϕ by intervention *is defined as:*

$$\mu_{interv(D,Q,dir)}(\phi) = \begin{cases} Q(D - \Delta^\phi) & \textit{if } dir = low \\ -Q(D - \Delta^\phi) & \textit{if } dir = high \end{cases}$$

Note that the sign for μ_{interv} is opposite to that for μ_{aggr} (Definition 2.4), since unlike μ_{aggr} here we want to intervene or inhibit the situation by changing the value of Q in the opposite direction of dir.

Example 2.8. *For our running example, consider the explanation ϕ = [`Author.name` = `JG` ∧ `Publication.year` = `2001`]. The associated intervention is:*

$$\Delta_{\mathtt{Author}} = \emptyset \qquad \Delta_{\mathtt{Authored}} = \{s_1, s_2\} \qquad \Delta_{\mathtt{Publication}} = \{t_1\}$$

To see this, note that we must delete s_1. If we don't then any residual database $D' \subseteq D$ that contains s_1 must contain r_1, t_1, and therefore its universal relation contains (r_1, s_1, t_1), which satisfies ϕ; but this violates item 3 of Definition 2.6. But once we delete s_1 we must also delete t_1 (because of the back-and-forth `Authored.pubid` ↪ `Publication.pubid`*), then cascade delete s_2. Notice how the causal path from* `Author` *to* `Publication` *lead to an asymmetric intervention Δ^ϕ, where we delete the paper with* `Publication.year` = 2001 *but do not delete the author with* `Author.name` = `JG`.

In contrast, if both foreign keys in Eq.(2) were standard, then intervention Δ^ϕ will be symmetric for the same ϕ:

$$\Delta_{\texttt{Author}} = \emptyset \qquad \Delta_{\texttt{Authored}} = \{s_1\} \qquad \Delta_{\texttt{Publication}} = \emptyset$$

because if we delete only s_1 then all foreign keys still hold, and no tuple in the universal relation satisfies ϕ.

We explain now the critical role of item (2) of Definition 2.6, requiring the residual database $D - \Delta^\phi$ to be semijoin reduced. This is necessary in order to ensure that every explanation has a unique, minimal, and valid intervention. To see why the condition is necessary, consider this example:

EXAMPLE 2.9. *The schema is $R_1(\underline{x})$, $S_1(x,y)$, $R_2(\underline{y})$, $S_2(y,z)$, $R_3(\underline{z})$. There are four standard FK's (from S_1 to R_1, R_2, and from S_2 to R_2, R_3), the database instance is*

$$D = \{R_1(a), S_1(a,b), R_2(b), S_2(b,c), R_3(c)\} \qquad (3)$$

and the explanation $\phi = [R_1.x = a \wedge R_2.y = b \wedge R_3.z = c]$. If we don't require the residual database to be semi-join reduced, then there are two minimal interventions, $\Delta = \{S_1(a,b)\}$ and $\Delta = \{S_2(b,c)\}$: in both cases the residual database $D - \Delta$ has dangling tuples and its universal relation is empty, thus satisfying all conditions in Definition 2.6, except item (2).

Since we require $D - \Delta$ to be semijoin reduced, there is always a unique minimal intervention Δ^ϕ (we prove this in the next section), and this is an important property that makes our framework work, since we can rank explanations based on degree of their *unique* minimal intervention[7]. Continuing Example 2.9, the minimal intervention is $\Delta^\phi = D$, because after semijoin reduction the residual database becomes $\emptyset$.

Finally, our last remark is that the minimal intervention Δ^ϕ is a non-monotone function of the input database[8]. We show this by continuing Example 2.9 further:

EXAMPLE 2.10. *Suppose we insert the tuples $S_1(a,b')$, $R_2(b')$, $S_2(b',c)$ into D (Eq.(3)): the minimal intervention decreases to $\Delta^\phi = \{S_1(a,b), R_1(b), S_2(b,c)\}$, in other words the tuples $R_1(a)$, $R_3(c)$ remain in the residual database. Notice that this is a valid intervention – the universal table of the residual database has a single tuple $(R_1(a), S_1(a,b'), R_2(b'), S_2(b',c), R_3(c))$, which does not satisfy ϕ.)*

We show in Section 3 how to compute Δ^ϕ efficiently, then discuss in Section 4 how to compute efficiently *all* degrees of intervention $\mu(D, Q, dir, \phi)$, for all candidate explanations ϕ, using SQL's data cube feature.

[7]For simple aggregate (SPJA) queries this is not a limitation (the dangling tuples do not contribute to the query answer). But for more complex nested aggregate queries this constraint is needed to have a unique minimal intervention.

[8]This is somewhat surprising, since, in contrast, D_ϕ, is a monotone function in the database.

3. COMPUTATION OF INTERVENTION

In this section we show how to compute the intervention Δ^ϕ associated to a candidate explanation ϕ. We show that Definition 2.6 is equivalent to the minimal fixpoint of a monotone query; in particular, it follows that the minimal valid intervention is well defined and unique. We also discuss convergence properties of this recursive query.

3.1 Rules for Intervention

Given a database D, consider the following recursive program $\mathbf{P}$, computing k sets $\Delta = (\Delta_1, \Delta_2, \cdots, \Delta_k)$:

$$\Delta_i = R_i - \Pi_{A_i}\sigma_{\neg\phi}[R_1 \bowtie \cdots \bowtie R_k] \qquad \forall i \in [k] \qquad \text{(i)}$$
$$\Delta_i = R_i - \Pi_{A_i}[(R_1 - \Delta_1) \bowtie \cdots \bowtie (R_k - \Delta_k)] \qquad \forall i \in [k] \qquad \text{(ii)}$$
$$\Delta_i = R_i \ltimes_{\texttt{pk=fk}} \Delta_j \qquad \text{(iii)}$$
$$(\forall \text{ back-and-forth } R_j.\texttt{fk} \hookrightarrow R_i.\texttt{pk})$$

The body of each rule in $\mathbf{P}$ is a relational algebra expression; multiple rules with the same head predicate Δ_i are interpreted as a union. The join operators in Rules (i) and (ii) are on all foreign key constraints: that is, both compute the universal relation. We explain the program next. Rule (i) computes Δ_i that represent a minimum set of tuples to be deleted from each R_i to ensure that no tuples in the universal relation satisfy ϕ. In general, this Δ_i is a strict subset of $\Pi_{A_i}\sigma_\phi[R_1 \bowtie \cdots \bowtie R_k]$; in our running example for the candidate explanation ϕ : [`Author.name` = `JG` ∧ `Publication.year` = 2001], we do not want to delete the tuple r_1 with [`Author.name` = `JG`] from the `Author` relation since he is a coauthor of another publication that does not satisfy the predicate ϕ (tuple t_2 with `year` = 2011). Rule (ii) performs a semijoin reduction on $R_1 - \Delta_1, \ldots, R_k - \Delta_k$; in particular this rule also enforces the cascade semantics for every foreign key dependency. There is one instance of Rule (iii) for every back-and-forth foreign key, which simply enforces the backwards cascade semantics for that foreign key. Recall that the *semi-join* operation is defined as $R \ltimes S = \Pi_{Attr(R)}(R \bowtie S)$; Rule (iii) simply removes from R_i (by inserting into Δ_i) all tuples t_i for which there exists some $t_j \in \Delta_j$ with $t_j.\texttt{fk} = t_i.\texttt{pk}$.

PROPOSITION 3.1. *The program $\mathbf{P}$ is monotone in $\Delta_1, \cdots, \Delta_k$, but is* not *monotone in the input database $R_1, \ldots, R_k$ (and therefore is not equivalent to any datalog program).*

To see that $\mathbf{P}$ is monotone in $\Delta_1, \cdots, \Delta_k$, note that in Rule (ii) all Δ_i's occur under two set difference operators, hence all three rules are monotone in Δ. Therefore, $\mathbf{P}$ has a unique minimal fixpoint, which can be computed in the normal fashion, by starting with $\Delta^0 = (\emptyset, \ldots, \emptyset)$, then computing iteratively $\Delta^0 \subseteq \Delta^1 \subseteq \Delta^2 \subseteq \ldots$ until we reach a fixpoint $\Delta^\ell = \Delta^{\ell+1}$; we denote $\mathbf{P}(D) = \Delta^\ell$ the minimal fixpoint. Interestingly, the program is *not* monotone in the input database; in Example 2.10, Δ^ϕ decreased when D increased. Nevertheless,

PROPOSITION 3.2. *The program $\mathbf{P}$ can be expressed in datalog$^\neg$ by a straightforward rewriting.*

Below, $\mathbf{x_i}$ denote the set of variables used in R_i, all $\mathbf{x_i}$ use the same variable for the same attribute, and $\mathbf{x} = \cup_i \mathbf{x_i}$:

$$S_i(\mathbf{x}_i) \ :- \ R_1(\mathbf{x_1}), \cdots, R_k(\mathbf{x_k}), \neg\phi(\mathbf{x}) \qquad \forall i \in [k]$$

$$\begin{array}{lll} \Delta_i(\mathbf{x}_i) & :- & R_i(\mathbf{x}_i), \neg S_i(\mathbf{x}_i) \quad \forall i \in [k] \quad \text{(Rule (i))} \\ T_i(\mathbf{x}_i) & :- & R_1(\mathbf{x_1}), \neg\Delta_1(\mathbf{x_1}), \cdots, R_k(\mathbf{x_k}), \neg\Delta_k(\mathbf{x_k}) \\ & & \qquad\qquad\qquad\qquad \forall i \in [k] \\ \Delta_i(\mathbf{x}_i) & :- & R_i(\mathbf{x}_i), \neg T_i(\mathbf{x}_i) \quad \forall i \in [k] \quad \text{(Rule (ii))} \\ \Delta_i(\mathbf{x}_i) & :- & R_i(\mathbf{x}_i), \Delta_j(\mathbf{x}_j) \quad \text{for } R_j.\mathtt{fk} \hookrightarrow R_i.\mathtt{pk} \text{ (Rule (iii))} \end{array}$$

Rule (i) is not recursive and is applied only in the first iteration. We will refer to the tuples collected after the first iteration $\Delta^1 = \{\Delta_1^1, \cdots, \Delta_k^1\}$ as the *seed tuples*. The following theorem shows that P computes the (unique) intervention Δ^ϕ for a given ϕ.

THEOREM 3.3. *The unique minimal fixpoint* $\mathbf{P}(D)$ *is equal to the intervention* Δ^ϕ *associated to an explanation* ϕ *(Definition 2.6).*

PROOF. $U(D - \Delta^1) = (R_1 - \Delta_1^1) \bowtie \cdots \bowtie (R_1 - \Delta_1^1)$ is exactly the subset of $U(D)$ that does not satisfy ϕ, where Δ^1 denotes the seed tuples collected in the first iteration by Rule (i). Hence any minimal $\Delta^\phi = (\Delta_1, \cdots, \Delta_k)$ satisfying the third condition of Definition 2.6 satisfies that

$$U(D - \Delta^\phi) \subseteq U(D - \Delta^1) \tag{4}$$

Rules (ii) and (iii) ensure the first and second conditions of Definition 2.6 that Δ^ϕ is closed and $D - \Delta^\phi$ is semijoin-reduced. Hence it suffices to show that any such valid $\Delta^\phi \supseteq \Delta^1$. Then it immediately follows that a minimal Δ^ϕ is the unique least minimal fixpoint of the program $\mathbf{P}(D)$.

Suppose $\Delta^\phi \not\supseteq \Delta^1$. Assume, without loss of generality, that $\Delta_1 \not\supseteq \Delta_1^1$. Then, there exists $y \in \Delta_1^1 - \Delta_1$ Then, $y \in \Delta_1^1 \Rightarrow y \notin R_1 - \Delta_1^1$, which implies that

$$\nexists \quad t \in U(D - \Delta^1) \text{ such that } \Pi_{A_i} t = y \tag{5}$$

Also, $y \notin \Delta_1 \Rightarrow y \in R_1 - \Delta_1$. Since $D - \Delta^\phi$ is semijoin-reduced,

$$\exists \quad t \in U(D - \Delta^\phi) \text{ such that } \Pi_{A_i} t = y \tag{6}$$

(5) and (6) together contradict (4). Hence $\Delta^\phi \supseteq \Delta^1$ and the theorem holds. ☐

3.2 Convergence Properties of the Rule Set

Since the program $\mathbf{P}$ is monotone, the polynomial data complexity is immediate:

PROPOSITION 3.4. *The Rules (i)-(iii) converge in* $\leq n$ *iterations where* $n = \sum_{i=1}^k |R_i|$.

Further, if there are no back-and-forth foreign keys (only standard cascade delete holds), we have a much faster convergence:

PROPOSITION 3.5. *If the input database has no back-and-forth foreign keys, then Rules (i)-(iii) in program* $\mathbf{P}$ *converge in only two steps,* i.e., $\Delta_i^2 = \Delta_i^3$ *for all* $i \in [k]$.

PROOF SKETCH. After iteration 1, the seed tuples (if any) are computed applying Rule (i), so possibly some $\Delta_i^1 \supsetneq \Delta_i^0$. After iteration 2 (if needed), relations are again semijoin-reduced by applying Rule (ii), so possibly some $\Delta_i^2 \supsetneq \Delta_i^1$. Rule (iii) cannot be applied since there are no back-and-forth foreign keys. By Rule (ii), all $R_i - \Delta_i^2$ are semijoin-reduced relations. Therefore, $R_i - \Delta_i^2 = \Pi_{A_i}[(R_1 - \Delta_1^2) \bowtie \cdots \bowtie (R_k - \Delta_k^2)]$; *i.e.*, $\Delta_i^3 = R_i - (R_i - \Delta_i^2) = \Delta_i^2$. ☐

Table R_1

a	
a_1	r_1
a_2	r_2

Table R_3

c	a	b	
c_1	a_1	b_0	s_{1a}
c_2	a_1	b_1	s_{1b}
c_3	a_2	b_1	s_{2a}
c_4	a_2	b_2	s_{2b}

Table R_2

b	
b_0	t_0
b_1	t_1
b_2	t_2

(a) Individual relations

R_1.a	R_3.c	R_3.a	R_3.b	R_2.b
a_1	c_1	a_1	b_0	b_0
a_1	c_2	a_1	b_1	b_1
a_2	c_3	a_2	b_1	b_1
a_2	c_4	a_2	b_2	b_2

(b) Universal relation

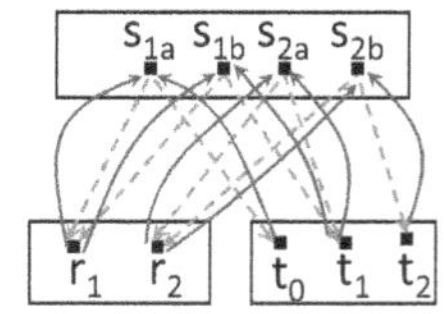

(c) Data causal graph

Figure 5: Example where program $\mathbf{P}$ needs $n - 1$ iterations. For general $n = 2p + 1$, R_1, R_2, R_3 will have tuples $(r_1, \cdots, r_p)$, $(t_0, \cdots, t_p)$, and $(s_{1a}, s_{1b}, \cdots, s_{pa}, s_{pb})$ respectively, and the rules converge in $2p$ steps.

For no back-and-forth foreign keys, the following corollary also holds. This will be useful to efficiently compute the degree of explanations in the next section.

COROLLARY 3.6. *If there are no back-and-forth foreign keys, then*

$$(R_1 - \Delta_1) \bowtie \cdots \bowtie (R_k - \Delta_k) = \sigma_{\neg\phi}(R_1 \bowtie \cdots \bowtie R_k)$$

PROOF SKETCH. By Proposition 3.5, $\Delta = \Delta^2$. After the first iteration, by Rule (i), $U(D - \Delta^1) = \sigma_{\neg\phi}(R_1 \bowtie \cdots \bowtie R_k)$. Since $\Delta^2 \supseteq \Delta^1$, $U(D - \Delta^1) \supseteq U(D - \Delta^2)$. We claim that $U(D - \Delta^1) = U(D - \Delta^2)$, which will prove the lemma.

Suppose not. Then there exists $t \in U(D - \Delta^1) - U(D - \Delta^2)$. Since $t \notin U(D - \Delta^2)$, there exists $i \in [k]$ such that $\Pi_{A_i} t \notin R_i - \Delta_i^2$. Then $\Pi_{A_i} t \in \Delta_i^2$. Hence $\Pi_{A_i} t \in R_i - \Pi_{A_i} U(D - \Delta^1)$. Hence $\Pi_{A_i} t \notin \Pi_{A_i} U(D - \Delta^1)$, which implies that $t \notin U(D - \Delta^1)$. This is a contradiction since we assumed that $t \in U(D - \Delta^1) - U(D - \Delta^2)$. ☐

On the other hand, the following example shows that, if we have a very simple schema with three relations $R_1(\underline{a})$, $R_2(\underline{b})$, $R_3(\underline{c}, a, b)$, and two back-and-forth foreign keys $R_3.a \hookrightarrow R_1.a$ and $R_3.b \hookrightarrow R_2.b$, then Rules (i)-(iii) take $n - 1$ iterations to converge, which also shows that the upper bound in Proposition 3.4 is essentially tight.

EXAMPLE 3.7. *We illustrate for* $n = 9$. *The three relations and the initial universal relation are shown in Figure 5, where every tuple is assigned an identifier for easy reference. Our candidate explanation is* $\phi : (\mathtt{c} = c_1)$. *Initially all* $\Delta_i^0 = \varnothing$, *for* $i \in [1, 3]$. *In iteration 1, only* Δ_3^1 *changes to* $\{s_{1a}\}$. *In iteration 2,* $\Delta_1^2 = \{r_1\}, \Delta_2^2 = \{t_0\}$ *by Rule (iii),* $\Delta_3^2 = \Delta_3^1$. *In iteration 3,* $\Delta_1^3 = \Delta_1^2, \Delta_2^3 = \Delta_2^2$, *but* $\Delta_3^3 = \Delta_3^2 \cup \{s_{1b}\}$ *by Rule (ii). In iteration 4, only* Δ_2^4 *changes:* $\Delta_2^4 = \Delta_2^3 \cup \{t_1\}$ *by Rule (iii). The same process is repeated through iterations 4 to 8, and the tuples* s_{2a}, r_2, s_{2b}, t_2 *are acquired in their respective* Δ_i*s.*

3.3 Avoiding Recursion in Special Cases

In general we need a recursive query to compute Δ^ϕ (Example 3.7), while Proposition 3.5 shows that in a very simple case recursion can be avoided completely. Here we generalize Proposition 3.5 and show that for a class of acyclic causal

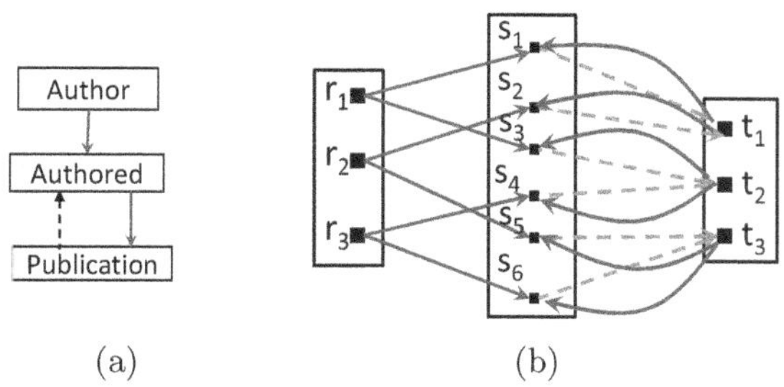

Figure 6: (a) Schema causal graph, (b) Data causal graph

graphs recursion can be avoided and be replaced by an iterative query with a bounded number of steps[9].

DEFINITION 3.8. *Fix a database schema. The* schema causal graph*, G, has one node for each relation $R_1, \cdots, R_k$; for every standard foreign key R_j*.fk $\rightarrow$ *R_i*.pk *there is an edge from R_i to R_j; for every back-and-forth foreign key R_j*.fk $\hookrightarrow$ *R_i*.pk *there is an edge from R_i to R_j, and a dotted edge from R_j to R_i.*

Let D be a database. The data causal graph*, G_D, has one node for each tuple in D and the following edges:*

1. *There is a directed solid edge from $t_i \in R_i$ to $t_j \in R_j$ if $\forall\ u \in U(D),\ \Pi_{A_j} u = t_j \ \Rightarrow \Pi_{A_i} u = t_i$.*
2. *There is a directed dotted edge from $t_j \in R_j$ to $t_i \in R_i$ if there is a dotted edge (R_j, R_i) in G and t_j*.fk = *t_i*.pk.

Intuitively, both graphs depict the standard and back-and-forth causal relations through solid and dotted edges, at the schema and at the data level respectively. However, at the data level, the definition is more involved because it also needs to account for semi-join reduction. First, note that for every standard foreign key R_j.fk $\rightarrow$ R_i.pk and two tuples t_i, t_j s.t. t_i.pk = t_j.fk there is a solid edge $t_i \rightarrow t_j$, because every universal tuple u for which $\Pi_{A_j} = t_j$ must have $t_i = \Pi_{A_i}(u)$. However, suppose that t_j is the only tuple in R_j with the property t_j.fk = t_i.pk: then if we delete t_j we end up deleting t_i too when doing the semi-join reduction. The definition ensures that in the latter case we also have a solid edge $t_j \rightarrow t_i$.

In figures we show the relations R_i as *supernodes* containing data nodes; also if there is both a solid edge and a dotted edge between two nodes, we omit the solid edge. The schema causal graph and the data causal graph of our running example (Example 2.2) is shown in Figure 6, whereas Figure 5c shows the data causal graph for Example 3.7. Recall that a path in a graph is called *simple* if every node is visited at most once.

DEFINITION 3.9. *A causal path P is a simple, directed path in G_D. The* causal-length *of P is the number of directed dotted edges in P.*

For instance, in Figure 6, $P = r_1 \rightarrow s_1 \dashrightarrow t_1 \rightarrow s_2$ is a causal path from r_1, of causal length 1. Further, P is *maximal*.

Recall that Δ^1 denotes the set of the seed tuples, defined by Rule (i). The following proposition gives a tighter convergence property of program **P** in terms of the maximum causal length of the causal paths from the seed tuples.

[9]Note that (i) our general framework does not require the causal graph to be acyclic, and (ii) causal graphs can have cycles even if the schema is acyclic, as is the case with our running example.

PROPOSITION 3.10. *The program **P** converges in $\leq 2q + 2$ steps, where q is the maximum causal-length over all causal paths P starting at a seed tuple.*

We get Proposition 3.5 as a corollary of Proposition 3.10 when there are no back-and-forth foreign keys (*i.e.*, no dotted edges in G_D, or $q = 0$). It can also be verified that there is a causal path in Example 3.7 of length $q = |R_3| = (n-1)/2$ (n is odd), and therefore it takes $n - 1 \leq 2q + 2$ steps to converge.

PROOF. The proof is an immediate extension of the proof of Proposition 3.5. It suffices to note that Rule (ii) in isolation can fire at most once, because after one application all relations $R_i - \Delta_i$ are semi-join reduced. Therefore, progress is made only as long as Rule (iii) can discover new facts, and this happens at most q times. The factor 2 accounts for possible alternation between the rules (ii) and (iii), while the additive term +2 is for applying Rule (i) in the first iteration, and for the final semi-join reduction in the last iteration. □

Proposition 3.10 tightens Proposition 3.4. As we saw in Example 3.7, if some relation R_j has two back-and-forth foreign keys R_j.fk $\hookrightarrow$ R_i.pk and R_j.fk $\hookrightarrow$ R_p.pk, then recursion is required. However, we use the proposition to show that, in an acyclic schema, if no relation R_j has two back-and-forth foreign keys, then recursion can be avoided (in this case the maximum number of back-and-forth foreign keys $\leq k$).

PROPOSITION 3.11. *Suppose the schema causal graph is simple[10] and acyclic. Furthermore, suppose that every relation R_j has at most one back-and-forth foreign key. Then the program **P** converges in $2s + 2$ steps where s = the total number of back-and-forth foreign keys in the schema. As a consequence, Δ^ϕ can be computed by a non-recursive query.*

PROOF. We show that the causal length of any causal path is bounded by s. Then the proposition follows from Proposition 3.10. In particular, we show that for any causal path P and any relation R_i, there can be at most one tuple $t \in R_i$ on P with a dotted outgoing edge on P.

Suppose not. Then there is a relation R_i, a database D, a causal path $P = u_0 \rightarrow \ldots t \dashrightarrow v \rightarrow \ldots t' \dashrightarrow v' \rightarrow \ldots u_\ell$ in G_D, where t, t' are two distinct tuples in R_i (note that a causal path is simple and the schema causal graph is acyclic), and both outgoing edges (t, v) and (t', v') are dotted edges. Note that v, v' must belong to the same relation R_j since there is at most one outgoing dotted edge from R_i. Further, $v \neq v'$ since the causal path is simple.

By Definition 3.8, if there is a directed path from $x \in R_i$ to $y \in R_j$ in G_D, then there is a tuple $u \in U(D)$ such that $\Pi_{A_i} u = x$ and $\Pi_{A_j} u = y$. Then the causal path $P_{v \rightsquigarrow t'}$, which is a sub-path of P from v to t', indicates that there is a tuple $u \in U(D)$ with $\Pi_{A_j} u = v$ and $\Pi_{A_i} u = t'$. This is a contradiction since there is a back-and-forth foreign key R_j.fk $\hookrightarrow$ R_i.pk, and therefore $t \in R_i$ can only join with $v \in R_j$ whereas $v \neq v'$. Hence the proposition follows. □

As an application, consider our running example in Figure 3, whose schema has the two foreign keys in Eq.(2). Only one is a back-and-forth foreign key, therefore the program **P** terminates in at most 4 iterations. Concretely, it can be unfolded into four steps: Rule (i) computes the seeds, Rule (ii) performs semi-join reduction, Rule (iii) does backwards cascade, and finally Rule (ii) performs the final semi-join reduction.

[10]There is at most one foreign key between any two relations.

4. FINDING TOP EXPLANATIONS

Given a user question (Q, dir), the system needs to iterate over all candidate explanations $\phi_1, \phi_2, \ldots$, compute their degrees, and rank them accordingly (either by aggravation μ_{aggrv} or by intervention μ_{interv}). To compute μ_{interv}, we have shown in Section 3 that each intervention $\Delta^{\phi_1}, \Delta^{\phi_2}, \ldots$, can be computed in polynomial time in the size of the database; however, a naive approach that computes sequentially $\mu_{interv}(\Delta^{\phi_1}), \mu_{interv}(\Delta^{\phi_2}), \ldots$ is too inefficient to be used interactively. In this section we show that, under certain conditions, the top-K explanations can be found efficiently using existing DBMS systems that support *data cube* operations. Throughout this section we only consider candidate explanations where the predicate is an equality operator.

The data cube operation is supported in most of the commercial database management systems (SQLServer, DB2, Oracle). It can find the value of an aggregate query for all combinations of values of the attributes specified in the GROUP BY clause, where the 'dont-care' attributes take `null` value. We illustrate the cube operation below:

EXAMPLE 4.1. *The following query computes a cube over the data in Figure 3.*

```
select x.name, z.year, count(*)
from Author x, Authored y,
              Publication z
where x.id = y.id
   and y.pubid = z.pubid
group by x.name, z.year
with cube
```

name	year	
JG	2001	1
JG	2011	1
RR	2001	2
CM	2001	1
CM	2011	1
JG	null	2
RR	null	2
CM	null	2
null	2001	4
null	2011	2
null	null	6

Each row in the cube corresponds to an explanation: e.g., *the row* $(null, 2001, 4)$ *corresponds to* z.year = 2001*, while the row* $(CM, 2011, 1)$ *to* [x.name = CM $\wedge$ z.year = 2001].

4.1 Degrees of Explanation using Data-Cube

We start by showing how to compute μ_{aggr} using data-cube. Recall from Eq.(1) that Q is an arithmetic expression on several aggregate queries $Q = E(q_1, \ldots, q_m)$. $U = U(D) = R_1 \bowtie \ldots \bowtie R_k$ is the universal relation, and D_ϕ is the database whose relations are $\Pi_{A_1}(\sigma_\phi(U)), \ldots, \Pi_{A_k}(\sigma_\phi(U))$. Recall: $\mu_{aggr}(\phi) = Q(D_\phi) = E[q_1(D_\phi), \cdots, q_m(D_\phi)]$.

For each aggregate query q_j compute a data-cube where each row contains the values $q_j(\sigma_\phi(U)) = q_j(D_\phi)$ for some candidate explanation ϕ. Next, join these m cubes, and compute the expression E on the values $q_1(D_\phi), \ldots, q_m(D_\phi)$. The join is a *full outer join* so that we do not lose explanations ϕ which do not appear in some of these m cubes; in those cubes they are considered to have zero value. Finally, return the explanations with the top K values of E.

Next, we show how to compute μ_{interv} using data-cube, under certain restrictions. For presentation purposes we assume that the degree of explanation (Definition 2.7) is given by $\mu_{interv}(\phi) = Q(D - \Delta^\phi)$; the case when the sign is negative is similar and omitted.

DEFINITION 4.2. *An aggregate query q is* intervention-additive *if for all input databases D and candidate explanation ϕ, we have $q(D - \Delta^\phi) = q(D) - q(D_\phi)$, where Δ^ϕ is the intervention defined in Definition 2.6.*

A numerical query $Q = E(q_1, \cdots, q_m)$ is intervention-additive *if all $q_j, j \in [m]$ are intervention-additive.*

When the numerical query Q is intervention-additive, we can compute $\mu_{interv}(\phi)$ for all ϕ using data-cube operations. For each query q_j, start by computing a data-cube where each row contains $q_j(\sigma_\phi(U)) = q_j(D_\phi)$ for some candidate explanations ϕ; derive $q_j(D - \Delta^\phi) = q_j(D) - q_j(D_\phi)$. Next, we join these m cubes, and in each row compute the expression E on the values $q_1(D - \Delta^\phi), \ldots, q_m(D - \Delta^\phi)$. Finally, we return the explanations with the top-K values of E.

In general, note that, $U(D - \Delta^\phi) \subseteq U(D - \Delta^1) = U_{\neg\phi} = U - U_\phi$ (see the proof of Theorem 3.3), where Δ^1 is the set computed by the first iteration of program **P** by Rule (i). So, in general, $q(D - \Delta^\phi) = q(D) - q(D_\phi)$ does not hold. We give two sufficient conditions for the query to be intervention-additive.

Count(∗). If q is a `count(*)` aggregate over the universal relation $R_1 \bowtie \ldots \bowtie R_k$ where there are no back-and-forth foreign keys, then it is intervention-additive. This follows from Corollary 3.6 which shows that $U(D - \Delta^\phi) = U - U_\phi$, and due to the additive property of `count(*)` queries.

Count(distinct R_i.pk). If q is a `count(distinct` R_i`.pk)` aggregate over the universal relation $R_1 \bowtie \ldots \bowtie R_k$, and there exists some back-and-forth foreign key R_j.fk $\hookrightarrow R_i$.pk such that every row in $U(D)$ contains a unique tuple from R_j, then q_j is intervention-additive. For instance, our running DBLP example with the foreign keys given in Eq.(2), a query with an aggregate of the form `count(distinct pubid)` is intervention-additive for any explanation ϕ, since every row of $U(D)$ contains a unique entry from the `Authored` table, although $U(D - \Delta^\phi)$ may be a strict subset of $U - U_\phi$. [11]

In the presence of back-and-forth foreign keys the intervention-additive property does not hold in general (*e.g.*, `count(*)` queries on our running example are not intervention-additive). However, we can sometimes transform the database into an equivalent database (meaning that it has the same causal paths) where each back-and-forth foreign key is replaced with several standard foreign keys. We illustrate this on our running example in Figure 3; a formal argument is deferred to the full version of this paper. Assume that every paper in the database has at most 3 authors. Then we make three copies of the `Author` and `Authored` tables: $\texttt{Author}_i(\underline{\texttt{id}_i}, \texttt{name}_i, \texttt{inst}_i, \texttt{dom}_i)$ and $\texttt{Authored}_i(\underline{\texttt{kad}_i}, \texttt{id}_i, \texttt{pubid})$, where kad_i is the primary key of $\texttt{Authored}_i$. Then we convert `Publication` to

$$\texttt{Publication}'(\texttt{kad}_1, \texttt{kad}_2, \texttt{kad}_3, \underline{\texttt{pubid}}, \texttt{year}, \texttt{venue}).$$

[11] To see this, consider the subset U_ϕ of U which are removed by Rule (i) to find the initial set Δ^1. Since every entry of `Authored` appears in exactly one row of U, $[\Pi_{Attr(\texttt{Authored})} U_\phi = \Delta^1_{\texttt{Authored}}]$ and $[\Pi_{Attr(\texttt{Authored})} U_{\neg\phi} = \texttt{Authored} - \Delta^1_{\texttt{Authored}}]$. By backwards cascade, Rule (iii) will include entries in $\Delta^2_{\texttt{Publication}}$ that tuples in $\Delta^1_{\texttt{Authored}}$ refer to. Then Rule (ii) will further include tuples in $\Delta^3_{\texttt{Authored}}$ (if any) that join with $\Delta^2_{\texttt{Publication}}$. As a result, $U(D - \Delta^\phi)$ will not have any publication from $\Delta^2_{\texttt{Publication}}$, and will have all the publications from $\texttt{Publication} - \Delta^2_{\texttt{Publication}}$. The `count(distinct pubid)` query q on $D_\phi \equiv U_\phi$ will exactly count the publications from $\Delta^2_{\texttt{Publication}}$. The `count(distinct pubid)` query q on $(D - \Delta^\phi)$ counts the publications in $\texttt{Publication} - \Delta^2_{\texttt{Publication}}$, which is exactly the same as $q(D) - q(D_\phi)$.

Then, the foreign keys given in Eq.(2) are replaced by the following standard foreign keys:

- $\texttt{Authored}_\texttt{i}.\texttt{id}_\texttt{i} \to \texttt{Author}_\texttt{i}.\texttt{id}_\texttt{i}$, $i \in [3]$
- $\texttt{Publication.kad}_\texttt{i} \to \texttt{Authored}_\texttt{i}.\texttt{kad}_\texttt{i}$,$i \in [3]$

The entries `Author` and `Authored` tables are replicated in their three instances, and a dummy value is added to every table to allow for < 3 authors for a publication. The (at most) three authors are assigned arbitrarily to $kad_1, \cdots, kad_3$, for < 3 authors, they take the dummy value. It is not hard to see that now there will be exactly one entry per distinct `pubid` in the universal table. Then `count(*)` is run on the universal table (the predicate on the `Author` table changes to a disjunction of the condition on three authors), and the results are grouped by a post-processing step.

4.2 Algorithm

We now describe briefly our algorithm that computes degrees of all explanations (both μ_{interv} and μ_{aggr}). The input is an intervention-additive numerical query $Q = E(q_1, \cdots, q_m)$ (Definition 4.2), and a subset of attributes A' on which explanations are being thought; the subset A' helps both in focusing the search and improving performance and can be set by the user.

Algorithm 1 Computes $\mu_{interv}(\phi)$ and $\mu_{aggr}(\phi)$ for all ϕ.

1: Let $u_1, \cdots, u_m$ be the values of all aggregate queries $q_1, \cdots, q_m$ on the original database D.
2: Let $C_1, \cdots, C_m$ be the data cubes for $q_1, \cdots, q_m$; store the aggregate values as attributes $v_1, \cdots, v_m$ in $C_1, \cdots, C_m$ respectively (*i.e.*, for any row ϕ, $v_j(\phi) = q_j(D_\phi)$).
3: Let M = the full outer join on the cubes $C_1, \cdots, C_m$.
4: Add a column in M for μ_{interv}; set it as $\mu_{interv}(\phi) = sign \times E(u_1 - v_1(\phi), \cdots, u_m - v_m(\phi))$ for each row ϕ ($sign = +1$ if $dir = low$, $sign = -1$ if $dir = high$).
5: Add a column in M for μ_{aggr}; set it as $\mu_{aggr}(\phi) = sign \times E(v_1(\phi), \cdots, v_m(\phi))$ for each row ϕ ($sign = +1$ if $dir = high$, $sign = -1$ if $dir = low$).

Optimizations. We employed several optimizations. The individual cubes $C_1, \cdots, C_m$ are materialized before they were joined to compute M. As illustrated in Example 4.1, the rows in the cubes will have `null` values for 'dont-care' attributes, which prevents us from using equi-join, because if both attribute A and B are null, then the equality $A = B$ fails. A naive solution will be to check for all combinations of null or not null, as in (`isnull A and isnull B`) `or` (`A = B`). To use equi-join, we replaced all `null` values in all the m cubes with a dummy value before performing the join.

4.3 Finding Minimal and Top Explanations

Once the table M is materialized by Algorithm 1, we can run top-K SQL queries to find explanations with high degrees (μ_{interv} or μ_{aggr}). However, blindly looking at the top-K outputs may result in some redundant answers. Consider Example 4.1, and assume that $Q = q_1$. Here all the explanations will have the same value for both μ_{interv}, μ_{aggr}. Although $\phi_1 = [\texttt{name} = RR, \texttt{inst} = \texttt{null}]$ and $\phi_2 = [\texttt{name} = \texttt{null}, \texttt{inst} = MS]$ denote two "minimal" explanations both having the same value for μ_{interv}, the explanation $\phi_3 = [\texttt{name} = RR, \texttt{inst} = MS]$ is dominated by both ϕ_1, ϕ_2 and therefore is redundant. Formally, we call an explanation ϕ *minimal* if there are no other explanation ϕ' such that $\mu_{interv}(\phi) \leq \mu_{interv}(\phi')$, and the $(attribute, value)$ pairs with $value \neq \texttt{null}$ for ϕ' is a subset of such pairs for ϕ (similarly for μ_{aggr}). We ignore the trivial explanation where all attributes take `null` value.

We implemented two strategies for finding minimal top-K explanations[12], which we empirically evaluated.

1. **Minimal-self join:** while outputting the top-K explanations, use a self-join on M to find the minimal explanations that are not dominated by others (the actual query is simple and is omitted).
2. **Minimal-append:** A dummy value is chosen such that it is > all valid values. Then a Top-1 query is run for K steps, that outputs explanations in decreasing order of μ_{interv} (or μ_{aggr}) which will give preference to shorter explanations having the same degree. To eliminate the non-minimal explanations, all explanations $\phi_1, \cdots, \phi_{i-1}$ output in the first $i-1$ steps are appended to the Top-1 query in the i-th iteration in the `WHERE` clause as $(\neg\phi_1) \wedge \cdots \wedge (\neg\phi_{i-1})$.

5. EXPERIMENTS

We present our experimental results in this section. We describe qualitative and performance evaluation on the natality dataset in Section 5.1, and on the DBLP dataset in Section 5.2. The prototype of our system was built in Java with JDK 6.0 over Microsoft SQLServer 2012. All experiments were run locally on a 64-bit Windows 7 machine with Intel(R) Core^{TM} i7-2600 processor (4 GB RAM, 3.40 GHz).

5.1 Natality Dataset

The *natality dataset* contains all the births registered in the United States in 2010, and is a public dataset available from the National Center for Health Statistics (NCHS) through the Centers for Disease Control and Prevention (CDC), `http://www.cdc.gov/nchs/data_access/ftp_data.htm`. The dataset has 233 attributes, 4,007,106 anonymized entries, and 2.89GB size. The attributes are about the mother (age, race, marital status, education, smoking habit, disease information during pregnancy, etc), about the father, about the delivery process (in hospital or not, caesarian or not, time and type of prenatal care received during pregnancy), and about the health of the baby after birth (as *APGAR* score[18]). The APGAR score (`AP`) is an integer between 0 and 10; we define `AP` = `good` if `AP` $\in [7, 10]$, and `poor` if $\in [0, 6]$ [18]. Our goal is to "explain" the APGAR score (`AP`) in terms of the other attributes, and we report here two such experiments for qualitative and performance evaluation[13]:

(i) **APGAR Score vs. race (R) of the mother ($\mathbf{Q_{Race}}$)**: Figure 8 (details in Figure 7) shows that for $R = Asian$,

[12] Our definition of minimality prefers 'general' explanations with less conditions that a larger number of tuples satisfy. An alternative meaning of minimality can prefer 'specific' explanations with more conditions that a smaller number of tuples satisfy. Our techniques can support both definitions and the user will be able to specify her choice in our system.

[13] Our goal in these experiments was to efficiently visualize different conditions that characterize the predicates in the questions asked by the user, and not to establish any social, medical, or scientific claims.

AP	Race			
	White	Black	Am. Ind.	Asian
poor	49873	19600	1037	3058
good	3012046	613464	45580	242593

AP	Marital status	
	married	unmarried
poor	35961	35491
good	2322404	1591279

Figure 7: No. of tuples for Q_{Race} and $Q_{Marital}$

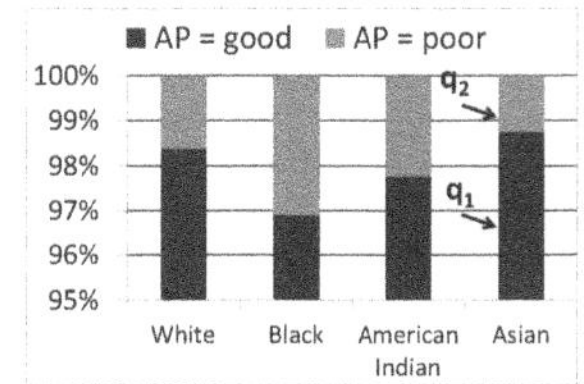

Figure 8: Plot for Q_{Race}

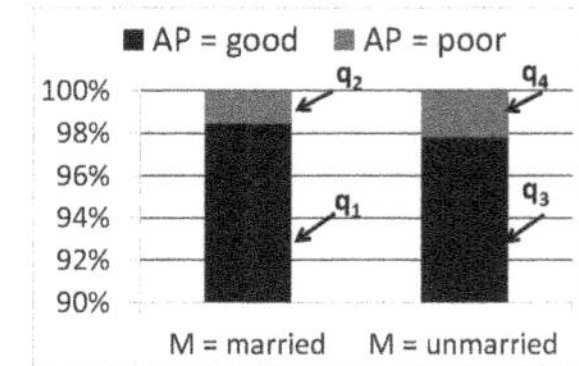

Figure 9: Plot for $Q_{Marital}$

the percentage of babies with AP = good is higher than the percentage of babies with AP = poor. For this observation, the user question is $(Q_{Race}, high)$, where $Q_{Race} = \frac{q_1}{q_2}$; q_1, q_2 are count(*) queries for [AP = good, $R = Asian$] and [AP = poor, $R = Asian$]. A more interesting question may be why this ratio (AP = good vs. poor) is higher for $R = Asian$ than for $R = Black$, which can be easily captured as another question $(Q'_{Race}, high)$, $Q'_{Race} = (\frac{q_1}{q_2})/(\frac{q_3}{q_4})$, here q_3, q_4 are count(*) queries similar to q_1, q_2.

(ii) APGAR Score vs. marital status (M) of the mother ($Q_{Marital}$): Figure 9 (with details in Figure 7) shows that the ratio of AP = good to AP = poor is higher for M = married, than for M = unmarried. For this observation, the user question is $(Q_{Marital}, high)$, where $Q_{Marital} = \frac{q_1}{q_2} / \frac{q_3}{q_4}$; q_1, q_2, q_3, q_4 respectively count the entries in the database that satisfy (i) M =married, AP = good, (ii) M =married, AP = poor, (iii) M =unmarried, AP = good, and (iv) M =unmarried, AP = poor.

5.1.1 Qualitative Evaluation

We restricted the search space of candidate explanations to five attributes (recoded in groups): (1) Age (A), (2) whether the mother used tobacco during pregnancy (T), (3) the month when prenatal care began (1st/2nd/3rd trimester or none) (PN), (4) level of education (Edu), (5) marital status of the mother (M) for Q_{Race} and race (R) for $Q_{Marital}$. We chose a threshold such that at least one of the aggregate queries q_j has value ≥ 1000. We also added a small threshold of 0.0001 to all counts to avoid any division by zero error in the calculation of the ratios.

Q_{Race}

	explanation	μ_{interv}
1	M=married	-62.3
2	PN=1st trim.	-75.1
3	T=non smoking	-75.3
4	Edu>=16 yrs.	-75.6
5	A=30-34 yrs.	-75.8

$Q_{Marital}$

	explanation	μ_{interv}
1	Edu> 16yrs	-1.381
2	A=30-34 yrs	-1.387
3	PN=1st. trim, T=non smoking	-1.396
4	A= 15-19 yrs	-1.397
5	PN=1st. trim	-1.405

Figure 10: Top-5 (minimal) explanations by intervention for Q_{Race} and $Q_{Marital}$.

Explanation by intervention for Q_{Race} and $Q_{Marital}$. The top-5 (minimal) explanations are shown in Figure 10. They are very general containing only one or two attribute, and therefore have high support (high counts for $q_1, q_2, \cdots$). By removing the intervention Δ, the value of $Q_{Race}(D - \Delta^{\phi})$ becomes smaller than the original value $Q_{Race}(D) = 79.3$. Intuitively, the top-5 answers say that the query's output can be explained by the fact that Asian mothers are not too young, married, non-smoking, received higher education, and received early prenatal care; because, if they were removed from the population, the value of Q_{Race} becomes smaller. Similarly, the original value of $Q_{Marital}(D)$ was 1.46, and the top explanations lower this value either by decreasing $\frac{q_1}{q_2}$ more (removing older, educated, non-smoking mothers reduces this fraction), or by increasing $\frac{q_3}{q_4}$ more (removing younger mothers will affect the unmarried population more than the married population). We get similar observations for Q'_{Race}, the details are omitted due to lack of space.

Explanation by aggravation for Q_{Race} and $Q_{Marital}$. Figure 11 shows the top-3 explanations by aggravation. Similar to explanations by intervention, for Q_{Race}, mothers who are not too young, do not smoke, highly educated, married, and received early prenatal care appear in the top explanations. However, these explanations are more specific (conjunction of multiple attributes), and therefore their support (counts) are smaller (a few thousands). If the queries q_1, q_2 are restricted to these sub-populations, the value of Q_{Race} becomes much higher than the original value of 79.3. On the other hand, for $Q_{Marital}$, the two top explanations make the value of $\frac{q_1}{q_2}$ infinity (∞) since $q_2 = 0$.

5.1.2 Performance Evaluation

Our framework to output top explanations consists of two main steps: (i) compute the degrees of explanations for all candidate explanations and store them in a table M (ref. Section 4.2), and (ii) given M, compute the *minimal* top-k explanations (ref. Section 4.3). In this section we evaluate different approaches for these two steps varying the following parameters: (a) *the size of input data* – to vary input data size, we selected and stored $x\%$ entries from the natality table at random and varied x from 0.01 (only ~400 rows) to 50 (2M rows); (b) *the number of attributes used in explanation predicates* – the attributes are multi-valued (with 2-9 distinct values), more attributes lead to more candidate explanations; and (c) *complexity of the user question* – this is number of select-aggregate queries $q_1, q_2, \cdots$ used in the questions. We considered Q_{Race} and $Q_{Marital}$, which involve two (q_1, q_2) and four $(q_1, \cdots, q_4)$ such queries respectively. In addition, for (ii), we vary k to evaluate the approaches to output minimal explanations discussed in Section 4.3.

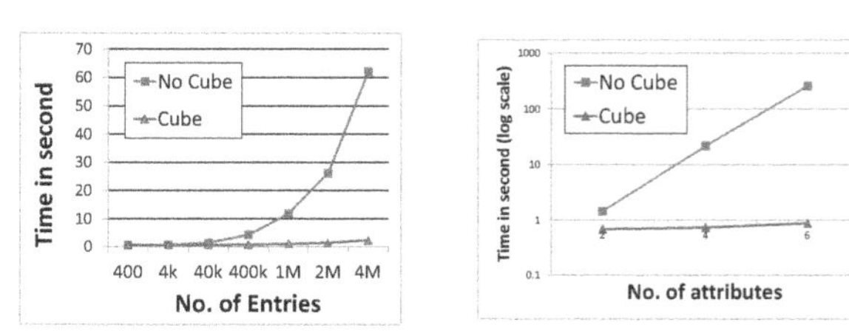

Figure 12: Benefits of data cube optimization for Q_{Race}: (a) Data size vs. time (with two attributes), (b) No. of attributes vs. time (with 1% entries)

Benefits of data cube optimization. Figure 12 compares the naive evaluation that iterates over all combinations

Q_{Race}

	explanation	μ_{aggr}
1	M=married, Edu≥16 yrs, PN=2nd trim.	174
2	M=married, A=40–44 yrs, Edu≥ 16 yrs, PN=1st trim.	173
3	Edu≥16 yrs, PN=2nd trim., T=non smoking	172

$Q_{Marital}$

	explanation	μ_{aggr}
1	A=15–19 yrs, Edu=9–11 yrs, PN=3rd trim.	$1.36 \times 10^4 (\infty)$
2	A<15 yrs	$1.23 \times 10^4 (\infty)$
3	Edu = 9–11 yrs, PN=no prenatal care, T=non smoking	3.2

Figure 11: Top-3 (minimal) explanations by aggravation for Q_{Race} and $Q_{Marital}$.

of attributes used in the explanations (referred to as 'No Cube'), v.s. Algorithm 1 (referred to as 'Cube'), for the query Q_{Race}. In the first graph we vary the input data size (the number of entries on the horizontal axis are approximate), whereas in the second graph we vary the number of attributes used in the explanations. Both the graphs show that the benefit from the data cube is dramatic. In the remaining experiments we only discuss the data cube implementation.

Size of the data vs. time. Figure 13a shows the time required to compute the degrees for all candidate explanations (*i.e.*, table M) for Q_{Race} and $Q_{Marital}$ as a function of the size of the input database. The same four attributes A, T, PN, BP were used as relevant attributes in the explanations for both the queries. As expected, the time taken by the queries increases with the database size. Recall that to compute table M, Algorithm 1 first computes the cubes $C_1, C_2, \cdots$ for $q_1, q_2, \cdots$, and then computes M by doing full outer joins on $C_1, C_2, \cdots$. Hence $Q_{Marital}$ requires more time, because compared to two queries q_1, q_2 in Q_{Race}, $Q_{Marital}$ has four such queries. However, the time taken by both queries is only < 4 seconds even for the entire dataset, making it suitable for an interactive setting.

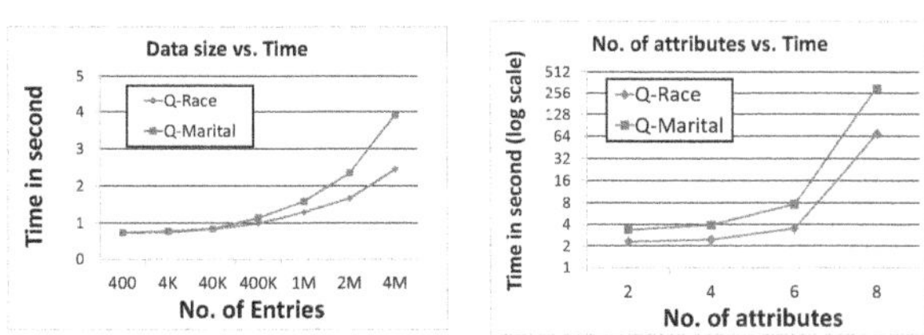

(a) Data size vs. time (b) No. of attributes vs. time

Figure 13: Time to compute degrees for all explanations

Number of attributes in explanation predicates vs. time. Figure 13b shows the time to compute the degrees of explanations as a function of the number of attributes used in the explanations. Here we used the entire dataset (4M entries) and added four other attributes to A, T, BN, BP (mother's education, sex of the infant born, whether the mother had hypertension/diabetes). The time is shown in log-scale; as expected, the time increases rapidly with the number of attributes. The cube algorithm can run up to six attributes within a few seconds, afterward the time increases due to increase in the number of candidate explanations. For eight attributes there are > $71K$ candidate explanations for Q_{Race} and > $192K$ candidate explanations for $Q_{Marital}$ joining (resp. two and four) cubes with $33k$ – $78K$ rows. The cubes $C_1, C_2, \cdots$ and the table M that contains all explanations and their degrees are small (< 3.8 MB for Q_{Race} and < 11.32 MB for $Q_{Marital}$).

Outputting 'minimal' top-K explanations. Figure 14 shows the time taken to compute the top-K explanations by μ_{interv} for Q_{Race} on the entire natality dataset

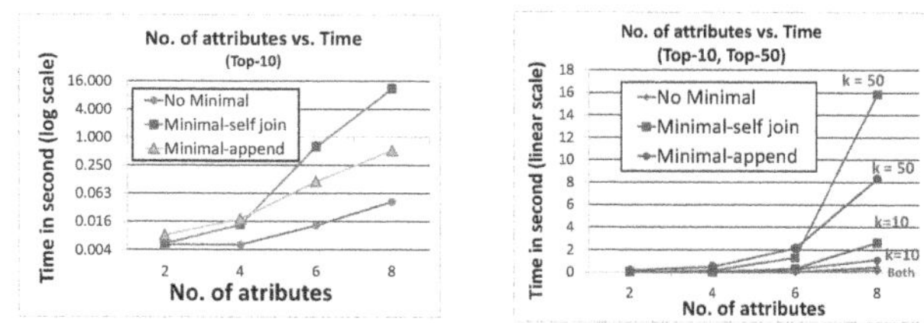

Figure 14: Time to compute *minimal* top-K explanations

where we again vary the number of attributes on the horizontal axis (since this is run on the stored table M, the behavior for $Q_{Marital}$ and μ_{aggr} is similar). The plots compare three top-K strategies, (i) **No Minimal:** simply output the top-K answers sorted by μ_{interv} by a SQL top-K query, (ii) **Minimal-self join**, and (iii) **Minimal-append**, as discussed in Section 4.3. Clearly, the *No Minimal* approach takes the least time, but can output redundant explanations (the explanation ranked 5 in Figure 10 is the 14th explanation if we do not enforce minimality). *Minimal-self join* performs slightly better than *Minimal-append* when the number of relevant attributes is small (since computing the self-join on M is less expensive than running a top-1 query K times). However, for larger value of the number of relevant attributes *Minimal-append* performs much better (takes < 1 sec for K = 10 even with eight attributes).

5.2 DBLP Dataset

We also experimented on a database obtained by integrating the popular DBLP data [17], from which we extracted the tables Author (1.095M entries), Authored (5.127M entries), and (conference) Publication (1.088M entries), with Geo-DBLP, a research project from another research group [4], which includes affiliation information (affiliation, city, and country) for every publication obtained by crawling ACM[14] Our goal was to validate our system's ability to explain queries over integrated datasets. We have already described one such query in Section 1 (Figures 1 and 2); here we discuss another experiment.

The graph Figure 15a shows the percentage of SIGMOD and PODS publications by country, between 2001 and 2011 (note that the country information is not available from all publications). As expected, there are fewer PODS papers than SIGMOD papers from most countries: however, surprisingly, more than 50% of the papers from the UK are in PODS. We used our system to search for explanations.

We express this as a user question (Q, low), where $Q = \frac{q_1}{q_2}$, and q_1, q_2 respectively count the number of distinct SIGMOD and PODS publications from UK between 2001 and 2011. Due to limited availability of the country information, we express publications from UK as [`domain` =' *uk*' ∨ `country` =' *United Kingdom*'], where *domain* is extracted

[14]The affiliation in Geo-DBLP is not normalized, and may contain several formats like 'Univ.', 'U.' or 'University' for the same institute as well as joint affiliation using 'and'.

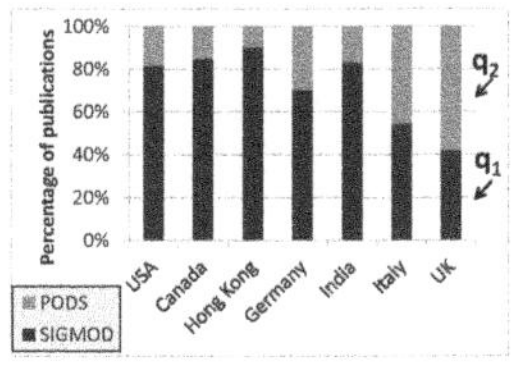

(a)

	explanation	μ
1	name=L. Libkin	1.04
2	name= G. Gottlob	0.81
3	name= F. Geerts	0.74
4	name= M. Benedikt	0.74
5	city= Edinburgh	0.73
6	city= Oxford	0.72
7	inst= Oxford Univ.	0.69

(b)

Figure 15: (a) Plot for percentage of SIGMOD and PODS publications in different countries between 2001 and 2011, (b) Top explanations by intervention μ_{interv}

from homepage urls in DBLP, and *country* is from Geo-DBLP. Therefore both q_1, q_2 involve equi-join of eight tables (three from DBLP and five from Geo-DBLP). The relevant attributes considered are *Author.name*, *Author$_G$.inst*, *Affiliation$_G$.city* (*Author* is from DBLP, whereas *Author$_G$ and Affiliation$_G$ are from Geo-DBLP*).

The top explanations by intervention are shown in Figure 15b which shows researchers from UK who published a lot more in PODS in 2001-2011 than in SIGMOD, and the universities in UK (researchers who published both in SIGMOD and PODS do not appear in the top explanations). The explanations [`city` = $Oxford$] has higher value of μ_{interv} than [`inst` = $Oxford\, Univ.$] due to the presence of [`inst` = *Semmle Ltd.*] in Oxford city, and different format of the university in the database ('Oxford', 'University of Oxford' etc.). The top explanations by aggravation are similar and therefore omitted. With three relevant attributes, the time taken to compute and materialize the table M (ref. Algorithm 1) is 2.176 seconds; although eight tables were joined in the cube operation, three having $> 1M$ rows, the time taken is small possibly due to low selectivity of the queries q_1, q_2 and use of indexes on the primary keys of all the tables. The time taken to top-50 answers by *Minimal -self join* is < 4 ms (the joined table M has < 1000 entries).

6. DISCUSSIONS

We proposed a formal framework for finding explanations for database queries. Our approach is based on the notion of intervention from the causality literature, and exploits foreign key constraints in a novel way in order to describe causal paths in the data. We proved a key property, that every explanation has a unique minimal intervention, and gave a recursive query that can compute this intervention; we further showed that, under certain conditions, recursion can be avoided and the degrees of all candidate explanations can be efficiently computed using SQL's data cube operation. We evaluated our approach on two real datasets, showing that our techniques find interesting explanations and can find them efficiently.

Some extensions are required to expand the applicability of explanations, and we incorporate some of these in the system that we are currently developing. (i) **Beyond data cube:** The data cube optimization is highly effective when it applies, but when it fails to apply then naive iterative algorithm is too slow. We are currently investigating optimizations to the iterative algorithm that can be deployed for general queries. **(ii) Explanations with inequalities, and disjunctions:** In some applications meaningful explanations include inequalities (e.g. papers with `year` > 1977 $\wedge$ `year` < 1982) and disjunctions (e.g. `author` = `Levy` $\vee$ `author` = `Halevy`) Conceptually, our framework can support such explanations, but adding them would increase the search space of explanations, making query evaluation and ranking more challenging. **(iii) Intervention vs. aggravation:** Unlike explanation by intervention, explanation by aggravation can always be computed using the data cube, without any restrictions. However, they completely ignore causal path, hence they are useful only in simple schemas that have few, or no foreign keys. In future work we consider a hybrid definition between intervention and aggravation that uses some, but not all causal path,a nd can always be evaluated by the data cube. (iv) **Beyond count queries** and **`more complex user questions`:** Complex questions are supported in our framework, and we are currently implementing them in our prototype. For example, *why is this sequence of bars increasing(decreasing)*, translates into *why is the slope of the linear regression of these datapoints positive(negative)?*, which can easily converted into a numerical query as in Eq.(1). A challenge, however, is designing a effective user interface that allows users to ask such complex questions.

7. REFERENCES

[1] S. Abiteboul, R. Hull, and V. Vianu. *Foundations of Databases.* Addison-Wesley, 1995.

[2] M. Das, S. Amer-Yahia, G. Das, and C. Yu. Mri: Meaningful interpretations of collaborative ratings. *PVLDB*, 4(11):1063–1074, 2011.

[3] D. Fabbri and K. LeFevre. Explanation-based auditing. *Proc. VLDB Endow.*, 5(1):1–12, Sept. 2011.

[4] F. Hadiji, K. Kersting, C. Bauckhage, and B. Ahmadi. Geodblp: Geo-tagging dblp for mining the sociology of computer science. *CoRR*, abs/1304.7984, 2013.

[5] B. Kanagal, J. Li, and A. Deshpande. Sensitivity analysis and explanations for robust query evaluation in probabilistic databases. In *Proceedings of the 2011 ACM SIGMOD International Conference on Management of data*, SIGMOD '11, pages 841–852, New York, NY, USA, 2011. ACM.

[6] N. Khoussainova, M. Balazinska, and D. Suciu. Perfxplain: debugging mapreduce job performance. *Proc. VLDB Endow.*, 5(7):598–609, Mar. 2012.

[7] A. Meliou, W. Gatterbauer, K. F. Moore, and D. Suciu. The complexity of causality and responsibility for query answers and non-answers. *PVLDB*, 4(1):34–45, 2010.

[8] A. Meliou, W. Gatterbauer, S. Nath, and D. Suciu. Tracing data errors with view-conditioned causality. In *SIGMOD Conference*, pages 505–516, 2011.

[9] M. Pacer, T. Lombrozo, T. Griffiths, J. Williams, and X. Chen. Evaluating computational models of explanation using human judgments. In *UAI*, 2013.

[10] J. Pearl. *Probabilistic reasoning in intelligent systems: networks of plausible inference.* Morgan Kaufmann Publishers Inc., San Francisco, CA, USA, 1988.

[11] J. Pearl. *Causality: models, reasoning, and inference.* Cambridge University Press, 2000.

[12] J. Pearl. An introduction to causal inference. *The International Journal of Biostatistics*, 6, 2010.

[13] S. Sarawagi and G. Sathe. i3: intelligent, interactive investigation of olap data cubes. In *SIGMOD*, 2000.

[14] G. Sathe and S. Sarawagi. Intelligent rollups in multidimensional olap data. In *VLDB*, 2001.

[15] C. Silverstein, S. Brin, R. Motwani, and J. Ullman. Scalable techniques for mining causal structures. *Data Min. Knowl. Discov.*, 4(2-3):163–192, July 2000.

[16] J. D. Ullman. *Principles of Database and Knowledge-Base Systems: Volume II: The New Technologies.* W. H. Freeman & Co., New York, NY, USA, 1990.

[17] `http://dblp.uni-trier.de/xml`.

[18] `http://en.wikipedia.org/wiki/Apgar_score`.

[19] E. Wu and S. Madden. Scorpion: Explaining away outliers in aggregate queries. *PVLDB*, 6(8), 2013.

[20] C. Yuan, H. Lim, and M. L. Littman. Most relevant explanation: computational complexity and approximation methods. *Ann. Math. Artif. Intell.*, 61(3):159–183, 2011.

MISO: Souping Up Big Data Query Processing with a Multistore System

Jeff LeFevre[+†] Jagan Sankaranarayanan[*] Hakan Hacıgümüş[*]
Junichi Tatemura[*] Neoklis Polyzotis[+] Michael J. Carey[%]

[*]NEC Labs America, Cupertino, CA [+]University of California, Santa Cruz [%]University of California, Irvine

{jlefevre,alkis}@cs.ucsc.edu, {jagan,hakan,tatemura}@nec-labs.com, mjcarey@ics.uci.edu

ABSTRACT

Multistore systems utilize multiple distinct data stores such as Hadoop's HDFS and an RDBMS for query processing by allowing a query to access data and computation in both stores. Current approaches to multistore query processing fail to achieve the full potential benefits of utilizing both systems due to the high cost of data movement and loading between the stores. Tuning the physical design of a multistore, i.e., deciding what data resides in which store, can reduce the amount of data movement during query processing, which is crucial for good multistore performance. In this work, we provide what we believe to be the first method to tune the physical design of a multistore system, by focusing on which store to place data. Our method, called MISO for MultISstore Online tuning, is adaptive, lightweight, and works in an online fashion utilizing only the by-products of query processing, which we term as *opportunistic views*. We show that MISO significantly improves the performance of ad-hoc big data query processing by leveraging the specific characteristics of the individual stores while incurring little additional overhead on the stores.

1. INTRODUCTION

Parallel relational database management systems (RDBMS) have long been the "work horse" storage and query processing engine of choice for data warehousing applications. Recently there has been a substantial move toward "Big Data" systems for massive data storage and analysis; HDFS with Hive is perhaps the most common example of such a system. The arrival of big data stores has set off a flurry of research and development, initially dealing with questions such as which store is best suited for which purpose; however, the growing consensus is that both stores have their place, and many organizations simultaneously deploy instances of each. Currently these stores have different roles – the big data store for exploratory queries to find business insights and the RDBMS for business reporting queries, as depicted in Figure 1(a).

Having both a parallel RDBMS and a big data store inevitably raises questions about combining the two into a "multistore" system, either for performance reasons or for analysis of data sets that span both stores. There have been a number of interesting proposals for this

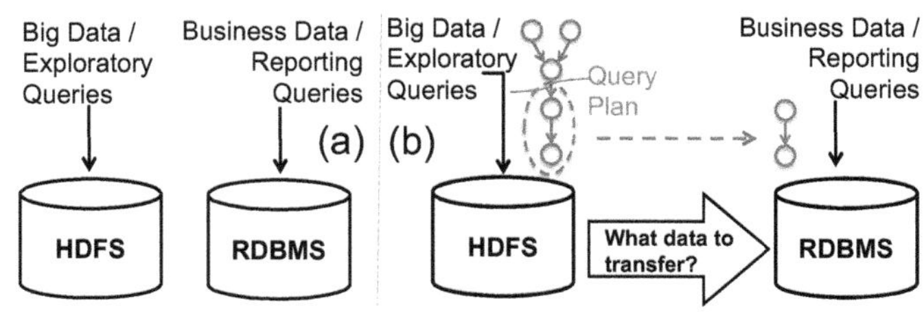

Figure 1: Typical setup in today's organizations showing (a) two independent stores and (b) multistore system utilizing both stores.

combination [2,9,11,22]. In this paper we explore a simple yet powerful and ubiquitous opportunity: using the parallel RDBMS as an accelerator for big data queries, while preserving the above-mentioned roles for both stores.

Multistore systems represent a natural evolution for big data analytics, where query processing may span both stores, transferring data and computation as depicted in Figure 1(b). One approach to multistore processing is to transfer and load all of the big data into the RDBMS (i.e., up-front data loading) in order to take advantage of its superior query processing performance [17] relative to the big data store. However, the large size of big data and the high cost of an ETL process (Extract-Transform-Load) may make this approach impractical [17,21]. Another approach is to utilize both stores during query processing by enabling a query to transfer data on-the-fly (i.e., on-demand data loading). However, this results in redundant work if the big data workload has some overlap across queries, as the same data may be repeatedly transferred between the stores.

A more effective strategy for multistore processing is to make a tradeoff between up-front and on-demand data loading. This is challenging since exploratory queries are ad-hoc in nature and the relevant data is changing over time. A crucial problem for a multistore system is determining *what* data to materialize in *which* store at *what* time. We refer to this problem as tuning the physical design of a multistore system.

In this paper we present the first method to tune the physical design of a multistore system. While physical design tuning is a well-known problem for a conventional RDBMS, it acquires a unique flavor in the context of multistore systems. Specifically, tuning the physical design of a multistore system has two decision components: *what* data to materialize (i.e., which materialized views) and *where* to materialize the data (i.e., which store). Our primary focus in this paper is on the *where* part since this is critical to good multistore query performance. Furthermore, since the different stores are coupled together by a multistore execution engine, the decision of where to place the data creates a technically interesting problem that has not been addressed in the existing literature. Beyond its technical merits, we argue that the problem actually lies at the core of multistore system design — regardless of how multistore systems are setup (i.e., tightly versus loosely coupled) or the way they are used (i.e., enabling data analysis spanning

[†]Work done when the author was at NEC Labs America

SIGMOD'14, June 22–27, 2014, Snowbird, UT, USA.

http://dx.doi.org/10.1145/2588555.2588568 .

stores versus query acceleration). Without a well-tuned design, a multistore system will be forced to split query processing between the big data store and the RDBMS in a way that does not leverage the full capabilities of each system.

We introduce *MISO*, a MultIStore Online tuning algorithm, to "soup up" big data query processing by tuning the set of materialized views in each store. MISO maximizes the utilization of the existing high-performance RDBMS resources, employing some of its spare capacity for processing big data queries. Given that the RDBMS holds business data that is very important to an organization, DBAs are naturally protective of RDBMS resources. To be sensitive to this concern, it is important that our approach achieves this speedup with little impact on the RDBMS reporting queries. MISO is an adaptive and lightweight method to tune data placement in a multistore system, and it has the following unique combination of features:

- It works online. The considered workload is ad-hoc as the analysts continuously pose and revise their queries. The multistore design automatically adapts to the dynamically changing workload.
- It uses materialized views as the basic element of physical design. The benefits of utilizing materialized views are that views encapsulate prior computation, and the placement of views across the stores can obviate the need to do costly data movement on-the-fly during query processing. Having the right views in the right store at the right time creates beneficial physical designs for the stores.
- It relies solely on the by-products of query processing. Query processing using HDFS (e.g., Hadoop jobs) materializes intermediate results for fault-tolerance. Similarly, query processing in multistore systems moves intermediate results between the stores. In both cases we treat these intermediate results as *opportunistic* materialized views, which can be strategically placed in the underlying stores to optimize the evaluation of subsequent queries. These views represent the current relevant data and provide a way to tune the physical design almost for free, without the need to issue separate costly requests to build materialized views.

Online physical design tuning has been well-studied, but previous works have not considered the multistore setting. Other previous work has studied query optimization for multistore systems in the context of a single query accessing data in different stores. In contrast, our proposed technique allows the multistore system to tailor its physical design to the current query workload in a low-overhead, "organic" fashion, moving data between the stores depending on common patterns in the workload. A key metric for evaluating big data queries is the time-to-insight (TTI) [13], since this metric represents the total time to get answers from data — which includes more than query execution time. TTI includes data-arrival-to-query time (the time until new data is queryable), the time to tune the physical design, *and* the query execution time. TTI represents a holistic time metric for ad-hoc workloads over big data, and our approach results in significant improvements for TTI compared to other multistore approaches.

In the following sections we describe the MISO approach to speeding up big data queries by utilizing the spare capacity available in the RDBMS, performing lightweight online tuning of the physical design of the stores. In Section 2 we provide an overview of the related work, and we describe our multistore system architecture in Section 3. We describe the problem of multistore design and its unique challenges in Section 4. In the remainder of the section we present MISO, which solves the multistore design problem by tuning both stores. Since we take an online approach, the design adapts to changing workloads. Furthermore, as the design is opportunistic, MISO imposes little additional overhead. In Section 5 we provide experimental results showing the benefits of MISO in improving TTI, up to $3.1\times$, and further analyze where the improvements come from. Then in Section 5.4, we show that MISO has very little impact on an RDBMS that is already executing a workload of reporting queries. Finally, we summarize our findings in Section 6.

2. RELATED WORK

Multistore query processing. Earlier work from Teradata [25] and HadoopDB [2] tightly integrates Hadoop and a parallel data warehouse, allowing a query to access data in both stores by moving (or storing) data (i.e., the working set of a query) between each store as needed. These approaches are based on having corresponding data partitions in each store co-located on the same physical node. The purpose of co-locating data partitions is to reduce network transfers and improve locality for data access and loading between the stores. However, this requires a mechanism whereby each system is aware of the other system's partitioning strategy; the partitioning is fixed, and determined up-front. More recent work [9,22] presents multistore query optimizers for Hadoop and a parallel RDBMS store. These systems "split" a query execution plan across multiple stores. Data is accessed either in its native store, or via an external table declaration. A single query is executed across both systems by moving the working set between stores during query processing. These systems represent "connector approaches" between Hadoop and an RDBMS, using a data transfer mechanism such as Sqoop [4] (or their own in-house equivalent).

Recent work on Invisible Loading [1] addresses the high up-front cost of loading raw files (Hadoop data) into a DBMS (column-store). In the spirit of database cracking [12], data is incrementally loaded and reorganized in the DBMS by leveraging the parsing and tuple extraction done by MR jobs, and a small fraction of the extracted data is silently loaded by each MapReduce query. The data loaded represents horizontal and vertical sub-partitions of the Hadoop base data. This approach also represents opportunistic design tuning, but the views belong to a very specific class, i.e., horizontal and vertical fragments of base data. Furthermore, this approach requires the corresponding processing nodes of each store to be co-located on the same physical node (similar to the Teradata work). In this approach, the query acceleration obtained is primarily due to the improved data access times for HadoopDB since data is stored as structured relations in an RDBMS rather than flat files in HDFS. In contrast, our approach supports a more general class of materialized views, which essentially allows us to share computation across queries instead of only improving access to base data. Moreover, we allow the big data system and the RDBMS to remain separate without modifying either system or requiring them to be tightly integrated.

Finally, multistore systems share some similarities with federated databases in that both use multiple databases working together to answer a single query. However, with a federated system there is typically a strong sense of data and system ownership, and queries are sent to the location that owns the data to answer the query. With our multistore scenario, the roles of the stores are different — queries are posed on the base data in HDFS, while the RDBMS is only used as a query accelerator.

Reusing MapReduce computations. Previous work has shown that intermediate results materialized during query processing in Hadoop can be cached and reused to improve query performance [10, 15]. The work in [10] reuses these results at the syntactic level. This means that a new query's execution plan must have an identical subplan (operations and data files) to a previous query in order to reuse the previous results. Some recent work [15] utilizes Hadoop intermediate results as opportunistic materialized views at the semantic level and reuses them by a query rewriting method. These methods all focus on a single system and it is not straightforward to extend these approaches to a multistore setup. In MISO we treat both the intermediate materializations in Hadoop and the working sets transferred during multistore query processing as opportunistic materialized views, and we reuse

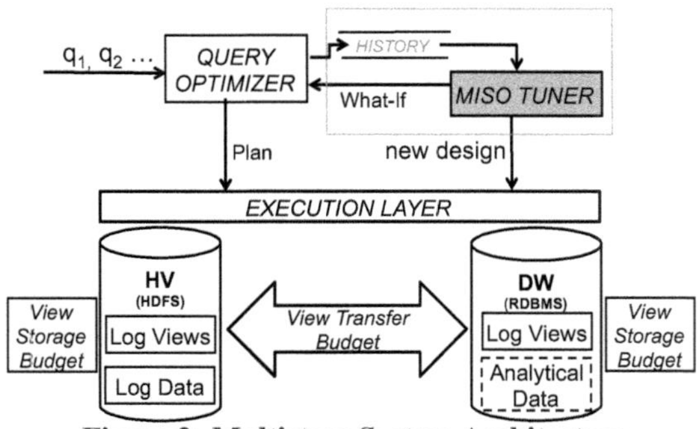

Figure 2: Multistore System Architecture

them at a semantic level. We then use these views to tune the physical design of both stores together.

Physical design tuning. Much previous work [5, 18, 19] has been done on online physical design tuning for centralized RDBMS systems. The objective of online tuning is to minimize the execution cost of a dynamically changing workload, including the cost to tune (reconfigure) the physical design. New designs may be materialized in parallel with query execution or during a reconfiguration phase. A reconfiguration phase may be time-constrained. For example, a new design may be materialized during a period of low system activity. Each of these prior works considers a single database system and uses indexes as the elements of the design. Our work considers a multistore system and utilizes opportunistic materialized views as the design elements. Tuning a multistore system adds interesting dimensions to the online tuning problem, particularly since data is being transferred between stores (similar to reconfiguration) during query processing. Obtaining good performance hinges upon a well-tuned design that leverages the unique characteristics of the two systems.

Other recent work on tuning has addressed physical design for replicated databases [8] where each RDBMS is identical and the workload is provided offline. In contrast, our work addresses online workloads and the data management systems in a multistore scenario are not identical. Moreover, with multistore processing the systems are not standalone replicas but rather data (i.e., views) and computation may move fluidly between the stores during query processing.

Recent work [16] has shown how to apply multi-query optimization (MQO) methods to identify common sub-expressions in order to produce a beneficial scheduling policy for a batch of concurrently executing queries. Due to the materialization behavior of MapReduce, these approaches can be thought of as a form of view selection, since the common sub-expressions identified are effectively beneficial views for a set of in-flight queries. However, MQO approaches require that the queries are provided up-front as a batch, which is very different from our online case with ad-hoc big data queries; hence, MQO approaches are not directly applicable to our scenario.

To summarize, all previous work has focused on either multistore processing for a single query or tuning a single type of data store. By dynamically tuning the multistore physical design, our approach utilizes the combination of these two stores to speed up a big data query workload.

3. SYSTEM ARCHITECTURE AND MULTISTORE TUNING

In a multistore scenario there are two data stores, the big data store and the RDBMS. In our system, the big data store is Hive (HV) and the RDBMS is a commercial parallel data warehouse (DW) as depicted in Figure 2. HV contains the big data log files, and DW contains analytical business data. While some multistore systems enable a single query to access data that spans both stores, MISO accelerates big data exploratory queries in HV by utilizing some limited spare capacity in DW and tuning the physical design of the stores for a workload of queries. In this way, MISO makes use of existing resources to benefit big data queries. With this approach, DW acts as an *accelerator* in order to improve the performance of queries in HV; later we show that MISO achieves this speedup with very little impact on DW.

Figure 2 depicts our system architecture, containing the *MISO Tuner*, the *Query Optimizer*, the *Execution Layer*, and the two stores HV and DW. In our system, each store resides on an independent cluster. HV contains log data while DW contains analytical data, but in this work our focus is on accelerating big data queries posed only on the log data. As indicated in the figure, each store has a set of materialized *views* of the base data (i.e., logs) stored in HV, and together these views comprise the multistore physical design.

For fault-tolerance, Hadoop-based systems (e.g., HV) materialize intermediate results during query execution, and we retain these by-products as *opportunistic* materialized views. On the other hand, DW products generally do not provide access to their intermediate materialized results. However, if those results become available, then they can also be used for tuning. In our system, we consider the class of opportunistic materialized views when tuning the physical design. It is MISO Tuner's job to determine the placement of these views across the stores to improve workload performance. When placing these views, each store has a view storage budget as indicated in the figure, and there is also a transfer budget when moving views across the stores. These budgets limit the total size of views that can be stored and transferred.

3.1 System Components

Data sets. The primary data source in our system is large log files. Here we expect social media data drawn from sites such as Twitter, Foursquare, Instagram, Yelp, etc. This type of data is largely text-based with little structure. Logs are stored as flat HDFS files in HV in a text-based format such as JSON or XML.

Queries. The input to the system is a stream of queries $q_1, q_2, \cdots$ as indicated in Figure 2. The query language is HiveQL, which represents a subset of SQL implemented by Hive (HV). Queries are declarative and posed directly over the log data, such that the log schema of interest is specified within the query itself and is extracted during query execution. In HV, extracting flat data from text files is accomplished by a SerDe (serialize/deserialize) function that understands how to extract data fields from a particular flat file format (e.g., JSON). A query q may contain both relational operations and arbitrary code denoting user-defined functions (UDFs). UDFs are arbitrary user code, which may be provided in several languages (e.g., Perl, Python); the UDFs are executed as Hadoop jobs in HV. Queries directly reference the logs and are written in HiveQL, the system automatically translates query sub-expressions to a DW-compliant query when executing query sub-expressions in DW. The processing location (DW or HV) is hidden from the end user, who has the impression of querying a single store.

Execution Layer. This component is responsible for forwarding each component of the execution plan generated by the *Query Optimizer* to the appropriate store. A multistore execution plan may contain "split points", denoting a cut in the plan graph whereby data and computation is migrated from one store to the other.

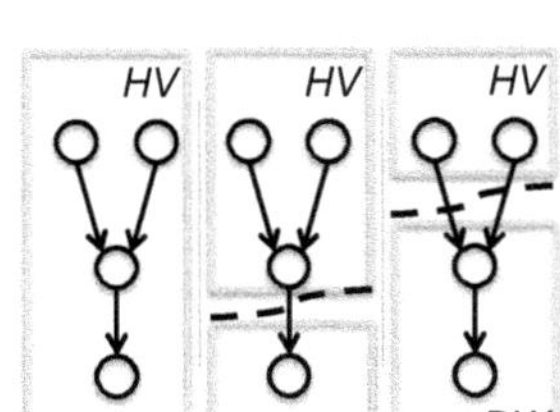

Since DW is used as a accelerator for HV queries, the splits in a plan move data and computation in one direction: from HV to DW. It is the multistore query optimizer's job (described next) to select the split points for the plan. As an example, the figure alongside has three panels, showing an execution plan (represented as a DAG) and then two possible split points indicated by the cuts. At each split point, the execution layer migrates the intermediate data (i.e., the working set corresponding to the output of the operators above the cut) and resumes executing the plan on the new store. Note that in the second panel, one intermediate data set needs to be migrated by the execution layer, while in the third panel two intermediate data sets need to be migrated. When intermediate data sets are migrated during query execution, they are stored in temporary DW table space (i.e., not catalogued) and discarded at the end of the query. The execution layer is also responsible for orchestrating the view movements when changes to the physical design are requested by the tuner. When views are migrated during tuning, they are stored in permanent DW table space and become part of the physical design until the next tuning phase.

Multistore Query Optimizer. This component takes a query q as input, and computes a multistore execution plan for query q. The plan may span multiple stores, moving data and computation as needed, and utilizes the physical design of each store. Multistore query optimizers are presented in [9, 22], and our implementation is similar to that in [22]. As noted in [22,23], the design of an optimizer that spans multiple stores must be based on common cost units (expected execution time) between stores, thus some unit normalization is required for each specific store. Our multistore cost function considers three components: the cost in HV, the cost to transfer the working set across the stores, and the cost in DW, expressed in normalized units. For HV we use the cost model given in [16] and for DW we use its own cost optimizer units obtained from its "what-if" interface. We performed experiments to calibrate each system's cost units to query execution time, similar to the empirical method used in [22]. As it turns out, when the necessary data for q was present in DW, it was always faster to execute q in DW by a very wide margin. Because the stores have very asymmetric performance, the HV units completely dominate the DW units, making a rough calibration/normalization of units sufficient for our purposes.

Because the choice of a split point affects query execution time, it is important to choose the right split points. The multistore query optimizer chooses the split points based on the logical execution plan and then delegates the resulting sub-plans to the store-specific optimizers. The store in which query sub-expressions are executed depends on the materialized views present in each store. Furthermore when determining split points the optimizer must also consider valid operations for each store, such as a UDF that can only be executed in HV. Moving a query sub-expression from one store to another is immediately beneficial only when the cost to transfer and load data from one store to another plus the cost of executing the sub-expression in the other store is *less than* continuing execution in the current store. Furthermore, due to the asymmetric performance between the stores we observed that when the data (views) required by the sub-expression was already present in DW, the execution cost of the sub-expression was always lower in DW. The primary challenge for the multistore query optimizer is determining the point in an execution plan at which the data size of a query's working set is "small enough" to transfer and load it into DW rather than continue executing in HV.

In our implementation, we have added a "what-if" mode to the optimizer, which can evaluate the cost of a multistore plan given a hypothetical physical design for each store. The optimizer uses the rewriting algorithm from [15] in order to evaluate hypothetical physical designs being considered by the MISO Tuner.

MISO Tuner. This componentis invoked periodically to reorganize the materialized views in each store based on the "latest traits" of the workload. The tuner examines several candidate designs and analyzes their benefit on a sliding window of recent queries (*History* in Figure 2) using the what-if optimizer. The selected design is then forwarded to the execution layer, which then moves views from HV to DW and from DW to HV (indicated in Figure 2) as per the newly computed design. The invocation of the MISO tuner, which we term a *reorganization phase*, can be time-based (e.g., every 1h), query-based (e.g., every n queries), activity-based (e.g., when the system is idle), or a combination of the above. In our system, reorganizations are query-based.

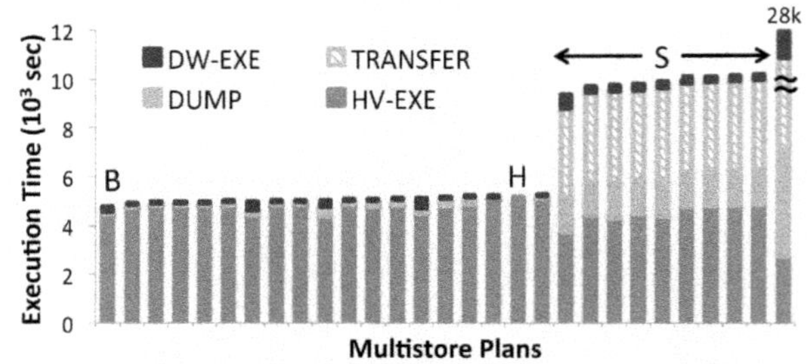

Figure 3: Execution time profile of all multistore plans for a single query. Plans are ordered by increasing execution time.

The *View Transfer Budget* is indicated in Figure 2 by the arrow between the stores. This represents the total size of views in GB transferred between the stores during a reorganization phase and is provided as a constraint to the tuner. The HV *View Storage Budget* and the DW *View Storage Budget* are also indicated in the figure and similarly provided as constraints to the tuner. These represent the total storage allotted in GB for the views in each store. While DW represents a tightly-managed store, HV deployments are typically less tightly-managed and may have more spare capacity than DW. For these reasons, new opportunistic views created in HV between reconfigurations are retained until the next time the MISO tuner is invoked, while the set of views in DW is not altered except during reorganization phases. In any Hadoop configuration, there must be enough temporary storage space to retain these materializations during normal operation, we only propose to keep them a little while longer – until the next reorganization phase. Since the HV view storage budget is only enforced at tuning time, a few simple policies can be considered if the system has limited temporary space: Reorganizations could be done more frequently, a simple LRU policy could be applied to the temporary space, or a small percentage of the HV view storage budget could be reserved as additional temporary space.

3.2 Overview of Multistore Tuning

Tuning the physical design of a multistore system is important to obtaining good query performance. In a multistore system, the query optimizer can choose many different split points at which to migrate computation from one store to the other during query evaluation. The overall execution time of a query is dependent on the existing physical design of each store, and varies depending on which portion of the query is evaluated in which store. A well-tuned physical design enables query execution plans to migrate to the DW sooner rather than later, thus making more extensive use of the DW's superior query-processing capabilities. In contrast, without a good physical design, the high cost of data movement will cause a query to spend more time in the slower HV store, which in turn provides limited opportunities for optimization. We demonstrate this point with the following simple experiment.

Figure 3 provides the execution time profiles (ordered from lowest to highest) for all possible plans of a single query, where each plan represents a unique split. The query is a complex query from [14] (query A_1v_1), that accesses social media data (e.g., Twitter, Foursquare), has multiple joins, computes several aggregates, and contains UDFs. These queries relate to marketing scenarios for a new product, and they try to identify potential customers based on their interests as identified in social media data. While the figure only shows one query, the trends observed were typical of all queries that we tested. Each plan begins execution in HV, and for each split point, the intermediate data is migrated to DW where the remainder of the plan is executed. For each plan, the stacked bar indicates the time spent executing in HV (red), the time spent to DUMP (green) and then TRANSFER/LOAD (yellow) the intermediate data over the network into DW, and finally the time spent executing in DW (blue).

The plan with the lowest execution time is on the far left of the figure, marked B. This plan is only 10% faster than the HV-only execution plan marked H. The worst plan in the figure is on the far right, at 28,000 seconds, and the bar is truncated here for display purposes. This plan represents the earliest possible split point, using HV only as an ETL engine to load all data into DW and then execute the query. From these observations it is clear that multistore execution offers little benefit for a single query (10% in the best case), and many multistore plans (those marked S) are *far more* expensive than the HV-only plan. This is due to the very high cost to transfer and load data from HV to DW, as can be seen in the yellow and green portions of the plans marked S. Additionally, there is a clear delineation between "good" plans (those to the left of S) and "bad" plans (those marked S).

We have found that the good plans all dump, transfer and then load much smaller data sets into DW than the bad plans, as shown in Figure 3. Good plans represent splits where the size of the intermediate data is small enough to offset the transfer and load costs. Unfortunately, we typically observed that the working set size does not shrink significantly until near the end of the query. This effect was also observed in Bing MapReduce workflows [3] (i.e., "little data" case). Another recent paper [22] examines a related experimental setup with two stores, and their optimizer considers ping-ponging a query (multiple sync/merges) back and forth across both stores. An examination of their experimental results reveals that the queries with the best performance are those that remain in Hadoop until the working set is small before spilling their remaining computation to the DW; effectively degenerating into the single-split multistore plans that we consider here. Hence, a query is only able to utilize DW for a small amount of processing, not benefiting much from DW's superior performance.

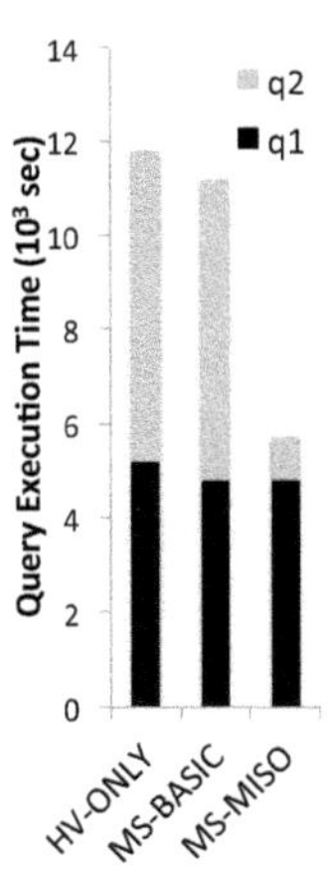

Tuning the physical design of HV and DW can facilitate earlier split points for multistore query plans. Better still, when the right views are present a query can bypass HV and execute directly in DW, thus taking advantage of DW's superior performance. The role of the tuner is to move the "right views" into the "right store". Again, we illustrate this point with another experiment on the same multistore system. In the figure alongside, we consider a workload of two exploratory queries, q_1 and q_2, that correspond to A_1v_2 and A_1v_3 from the workload in [14]. These are subsequent queries issued by the same data analyst, and thus have some overlap. Query q_1 is executed first, followed by q_2, and each query produces some opportunistic views when executed in HV.

The figure reports the total execution time for q_1 followed by q_2 using three different system variants. HV-ONLY represents an HV system that executes both queries in their entirety and does not utilize DW at all. MS-BASIC represents a basic multistore system without tuning, and is the same as the setting in Figure 3. This system does not make use of opportunistic views to speed up query processing. MS-MISO represents our multistore system using the MISO Tuner. To produce the MS-MISO result in the figure, we triggered a reorganization phase after q_1 but before q_2 executed. During reorganization, the Tuner transfers views between the stores in order to create beneficial designs for q_2. In the figure, MS-BASIC is only about 8% faster than HV-ONLY; while MS-MISO is about 2× faster than both HV-ONLY and MS-BASIC. While this result is for 2 related queries, for a larger workload MS-MISO results in up to 3.1× improvement later in Section 5. MS-MISO's improvement over MS-BASIC is because the tuner created a new multistore physical design after q_1, which enabled q_2 to take advantage of DW performance since the "right" views were present in DW.

4. MISO TUNER

In this section we describe the details of the MISO Tuner component shown in Figure 2. Because we address the online case where new multistore designs will be computed periodically, we desire a solution that is lightweight with low-overhead. This is achieved in the following ways. Since we utilize opportunistic views, the elements of our design are almost free, thus the tuner does not incur an initial materialization cost for a view. The reorganization time is controlled by the view transfer budget and view storage budgets for HV and DW. The values for these constraints can be kept small, in order to restrict the total tuning time. At the beginning of each reorganization phase, the tuner considers migrating views between the stores based on the recent workload history (indicated in Figure 2) and computes the new physical designs for HV and DW, subject to the view storage budget constraints and the view transfer budget.

Multistore systems notwithstanding, solving even a single physical design problem is computationally hard [6] because the elements of the design can interact with one another. Commercial tools (e.g., IBM DB2 Design Advisor [24]) take a heuristic approach to the physical design problem for a single store by treating it as a variant of the knapsack problem with a storage budget constraint. We similarly treat the multistore design problem as a variant of a knapsack problem. Our scenario is different in that we have two physical designs to solve, where each is dependent on the other, and each design has multiple dimensions — a view storage budget constraint and a view transfer budget constraint — that are consumed at different rates depending on the current design of each store. Due to the hardness of the problem, an optimal solution is impractical thus we take a heuristic approach. In order to keep our approach lightweight, we develop an efficient dynamic programming based knapsack solution.

4.1 Basic Definitions and Problem Statement

The elements of our design are materialized views and the universe of views is denoted as V. The physical design of each store is denoted as V_h for HV, and V_d for DW, where $V_h, V_d \subseteq V$. The values B_h, B_d denote the view storage budget constraints for HV and DW respectively, and the view transfer budget for a reorganization phase is denoted as B_t. As mentioned previously, reorganization phases occur periodically (e.g., after j queries are observed by the system), at which point views may be transferred between the stores. The constraints B_h, B_d, and B_t are specified in GB.

Let $\mathcal{M} = \langle V_h, V_d \rangle$ be a *multistore design*. $\mathcal{M}$ is a pair where the first component represents the views in HV, and the second component represents the views in DW. In this work we restrict the definition to include only two stores, but the definition may be extended to include addition stores in the more general case.

We denote the most recent n queries of the input stream as workload W. A query q_i represents the ith query in W. The cost of a query q given multistore design $\mathcal{M}$, denoted by $cost(q, \mathcal{M})$, is the sum of the cost in HV, the cost to transfer the working set of q to DW and the cost in DW under a hypothetical design $\mathcal{M}$. The evaluation metric we use for a multistore design $\mathcal{M}$ is the total workload cost, defined as:

$$TotalCost(W, \mathcal{M}) = \sum_{i=1}^{n} cost(q_i, \mathcal{M}). \quad (1)$$

Intuitively, this metric represents the sum of the total time to process all queries in the workload. This is a reasonable metric, although others are possible. Note that the metric does not include the reorganization constraint B_t since it is provided as an input to the problem.

V_h, V_d	Design of HV and DW before reorg
V_{cands}	Candidate views for M-KNAPSACK packing
V_h^{new}, V_d^{new}	Design of HV and DW after reorg
V_d^-	Views evicted from DW ($= V_d - V_d^{new}$)
B_h, B_d, B_t	View storage and transfer budgets
B_t^{rem}	Transfer budget remaining after DW design
$sz(v), bn(v)$	Size and benefit of view $v \in V_{cands}$

Table 1: MISO Tuner variables.

The *benefit* of a view $v \in V$ for a q query is loosely defined as the change in cost of q evaluated with and without view v present in the multistore design. Formally, $benefit(q, v) = cost(q, \mathcal{M} \cup v) - cost(q, \mathcal{M})$, where $\mathcal{M} \cup v$ means that v is added to both stores in $\mathcal{M}$.

For a query q, a pair of views (a, b) may interact with one another with respect to their benefit for q. The interaction occurs when the benefit of a for q changes when b is present. We employ the *degree of interaction* (*doi*) as defined in [20], which is a measure of the magnitude of the benefit change. Furthermore, the type of interaction for a view a with respect to b may be positive or negative. A positive interaction occurs when the benefit of a increases when b is present. Specifically, a and b are said to interact positively when the benefit of using both is higher than the sum of their individual benefits. In this case, we want to pack both a and b in the knapsack. A negative interaction occurs when the benefit of a decreases when b is present. As an example, suppose that either a or b can be used to answer q. Hence both are individually beneficial for q, but suppose that a offers slightly greater benefit. When both views are present, the optimizer will always prefer a and thus never use b, in which case the benefit of b becomes zero. In this case packing both a and b in the knapsack results in an inefficient use of the view storage budget. We will utilize both the *doi* and the type of interaction between views when formulating our solution later.

Given our definitions of multistore design, the constraints, cost metric, and workload, we can define the multistore design problem.

Multistore Design Problem. Given an observed query stream, a multistore design $\mathcal{M} = \langle V_h, V_d \rangle$, and a set of design constraints B_h, B_d, B_t, compute a new multistore design $\mathcal{M}^{new} = \langle V_h^{new}, V_d^{new} \rangle$, where $V_h^{new}, V_d^{new} \subseteq V_h \cup V_d$, that satisfies the constraints and minimizes future workload cost.

4.2 MISO Tuner Algorithm

Because we desire a practical solution to the multistore design problem, we adopt a heuristic approach in the way we handle view interactions and solve the physical design of both stores. In this section we motivate and develop our heuristics and then later in the experimental section we show that our approach results in significant benefits compared to simpler tuning approaches.

The workload we address is online in nature, hence reorganization is done periodically in order to tune the design to reflect the recent workload. Our approach is to obtain a good multistore design by periodically solving a static optimization problem where the workload is given. At each reorganization phase, the tuner computes a new multistore design $\mathcal{M}^{new} = \langle V_h^{new}, V_d^{new} \rangle$ that minimizes total workload cost, as computed by our cost metric $TotalCost(W, \mathcal{M}^{new})$. Note that minimizing the total workload cost here is equivalent to maximizing the benefit of $\mathcal{M}^{new}$ for the representative workload W. The MISO Tuner algorithm is given in Algorithm 1, and its variables are defined in Table 1. We next give a high-level overview of the algorithm's steps and then provide the details in the following sections.

The first two steps given in lines 3 and 4 handle interactions between views as a pre-processing step before computing the new designs. The tuner algorithm begins by grouping all views in the current designs V_h and V_d into interacting sets (line 3). The goal of this step is to identify views that have strong positive or negative interactions with other views in V. At the end of this step, there are multiple sets of views,

Algorithm 1 MISO Tuner algorithm

1: **function** MISO_TUNE($\langle V_h, V_d \rangle, W, B_h, B_d, B_t$)
2: $\quad V \leftarrow V_h \cup V_d$
3: $\quad P \leftarrow$ COMPUTEINTERACTINGSETS(V)
4: $\quad V_{cands} \leftarrow$ SPARSIFYSETS(P)
5: $\quad V_d^{new} \leftarrow$ M-KNAPSACK(V_{cands}, B_d, B_t)
6: $\quad B_t^{rem} \leftarrow B_t - \sum_{v \in V_h \cap V_d^{new}} sz(v)$
7: $\quad V_h^{new} \leftarrow$ M-KNAPSACK($V_{cands} - V_d^{new}, B_h, B_t^{rem}$)
8: $\quad \mathcal{M}^{new} \leftarrow \langle V_h^{new}, V_d^{new} \rangle$
9: $\quad$ **return** $\mathcal{M}^{new}$
10: **end function**

where views within a set strongly interact with each other, and views belonging to different sets do not. We sparsify each set by retaining some of the views and discarding the others (line 4). To sparsify a set, we consider if the nature of the interacting views within a set is positive or negative. If the nature of the interacting views is strongly positive, then as a heuristic, those views should always be considered together since they provide additional benefit when they are all present. Among those views, we treat them all as a *single* candidate. If the nature of the interacting views is strongly negative, those views should not be considered together for $\mathcal{M}^{new}$ since there is little additional benefit when all of them are present. Among those views, we choose a representative view as a candidate and discard the rest. We describe these steps in detail in Section 4.3.

After the pre-processing step is complete, the resulting set of candidate views V_{cands} contains views that may be considered independently when computing the new multistore design, which is done by solving two multidimensional knapsack problems in sequence (lines 5 and 7). The dimensions of each knapsack are the storage budget and the transfer budget constraints. First on line 5, we solve an instance of a knapsack for DW, using view storage budget B_d and view transfer budget B_t. The output of this step is the new DW design, V_d^{new}. Then on line 7, we solve an instance of a knapsack for HV, using view storage budget B_h and any view transfer budget remaining (B_t^{rem}) after solving the DW design. The output of this step is the new HV design, V_h^{new}. The reason we solve the DW design first is because it can offer superior execution performance when the right views are present. With a good DW design, query processing can migrate to DW sooner thus taking advantage of its query processing power. For this reason, we focus on DW design as the primary goal and solve this in the first phase. After the DW design is chosen, the HV design is solved in the second phase. In this two-phase approach, the design of HV and DW can be viewed as complimentary, yet formulated to give DW greater importance than HV as a heuristic. We describe the two knapsack packings in detail in Section 4.4.

4.3 Handling View Interactions

Here we describe our heuristic solution to consider view interactions since they can affect knapsack packing. For example if a view v_a is already packed, and a view v_b is added, then if an interaction exists between v_a and v_b, the benefit of v_a will change when v_b is added. Our heuristic approach only considers the strongest interactions among views in V, producing a set of candidate views whereby we can treat each view's benefit as independent when solving the knapsack problems. This is because a dynamic programming formulation requires that the benefit of items already present in the knapsack does not change when a new item is added. We use a two-step approach to produce the candidate views V_{cands} that will be used during knapsack packing, described below.

Before computing the interacting sets, we first compute the expected benefit of each view by utilizing the predicted future benefit function from [18]. The benefit function divides W into a series of non-overlapping epochs, each a fraction of the total length of W. This represents the recent query history. In this method, the predicted future benefit of each view is computed by applying a decay on the view's benefit per epoch — for each $q \in W$, the benefit of a view v for query q is weighted less as q appears farther in the past. The outcome of the computation is a smoothed averaging of v's benefit over multiple windows of the past. In this way, the benefit computation captures a longer workload history but prefers the recent history as more representative of the benefit for the immediate future workload.

Compute Interacting Sets. To find the interacting sets, we use the method from [19] to produce a *stable partition* $P = \{P_1, P_2, \ldots, P_m\}$ of the candidate views V, meaning views within a part P_i do not interact with views in another part P_j. In this method, the magnitude of the interaction (i.e., change in benefit) between views within each part P_i is captured by *doi* [20]. When computing *doi*, we slightly modify the computation to retain the sign of the benefit change, where the sign indicates if the interaction is positive or negative. For a pair of views that have both positive and negative interactions, the magnitude is the sum of the interactions, and the sign of the sum indicates if it is a net positive or negative interaction. The partitioning procedure preserves only the most significant view interactions, those with magnitude above some chosen threshold. The threshold has the effect of ignoring weak interactions. The value of the threshold is system and workload dependent, but should be sufficiently large enough to result in parts with a small number (e.g., 4 in our case) of views thus only retaining the strongest interactions.

Since the parts are non-overlapping (i.e., views do not interact across parts), each part may be considered independently when packing M-KNAPSACK. This is because the benefit of a view in part P_i is not affected by the benefit of any view in part P_j, where $P_i \neq P_j$. At this point however, some parts may have a cardinality greater than one, so we next describe a method to choose a representative view among views within the same part.

Sparsify Sets. To sparsify the parts, we first take account of positively interacting views, then negatively interacting views. We exploit positive interactions by applying a heuristic to ensure that views that have a large positive interaction are packed together in the knapsack. Within each part, view pairs with positive interactions are "merged" into a single knapsack item, since they offer significant additional benefit when used together. The new item has a weight equal to the sum of the size of both views, and the benefit is the total benefit when both views are used together. This merge procedure is applied recursively to all positively interacting pairs within each part, in decreasing order of edge weight. Merging continues until there are no more positively interacting pairs of views within the part.

After applying the merge procedure, all parts with cardinality greater than 1 contain only strongly negative interacting views. Our next heuristic is to not pack these views together in the knapsack, but select one of them as a representative of the part. This is because packing these views together is an inefficient use of knapsack capacity. To choose the representative, we order items in the part by decreasing benefit per unit of weight and only retain the top item as a representative of the part. This greedy heuristic is commonly used for knapsack approaches to physical design [7, 24] and we use it here for choosing among those views with strong negative interactions within a part. The procedure is applied to each part until all parts have a single representative view. After these steps, the resultant partition P contains only singleton parts. These parts form V_{cands} and are treated as independent by M-KNAPSACK.

4.4 MISO Knapsack Packing

During each reorganization window, the MISO Tuner solves two instances of a 0-1 multidimensional knapsack problem (M-KNAPSACK henceforward); the first instance for DW and the second instance for HV. Each instance is solved using a dynamic programming formulation. At the beginning of each reorganization window, note that V_h includes all views added to the HV design by the MISO tuner during the previous reorganization window as well as any new opportunistic views in HV created since the last reorganization. During reorganization, the MISO tuner computes the new designs V_h^{new} and V_d^{new} for HV and DW respectively. Since the DW has better query performance, as a first heuristic MISO solves the DW instance first resulting in the best views being added to the DW design. Furthermore, we ensure $V_h \cap V_d = \emptyset$ to prevent duplicating views across the stores. Although this is also a heuristic, our rationale is it potentially results in a more "diverse" set of materialized views and hence better utilization of the limited storage budgets in preparation for an unknown future workload. If desired, this property could be relaxed by including all views in V_{cands} when packing both HV and DW.

As an additional heuristic we do not limit the fraction of B_t that can be consumed when solving the DW design in the first phase. Any remaining transfer budget B_t^{rem} can then be used to transfer views evicted from DW to HV. This means that all of the transfer budget could potentially be consumed during the first phase when transferring views to DW. Alternatively, we could reserve a fraction of B_t for transfers in each direction, although this too would be a heuristic.

4.4.1 Packing DW M-Knapsack

In this phase, the target design is V_d^{new}, and the M-KNAPSACK dimensions are B_d and B_t. There are two cases to consider when packing DW. Views in HV (V_h) will consume the transfer budget B_t (Case 1), while views in DW (V_d) will not (Case 2). The candidate views are $V_{cands} = V_h \cup V_d$. The variable k denotes the kth element in V_{cands} (i.e.,view v_k), the order of elements is irrelevant. The recurrence relation C is given by the following two cases.

Case 1: $v_k \in V_h$ applies when view v_k is present in HV.

$$C(k, B_d, B_t) = \begin{cases} C(k-1, B_d, B_t) & ; sz(v_k) > B_t \\ \max \begin{cases} C(k-1, B_d, B_t), \\ C(k-1, B_d - sz(v_k), B_t - sz(v_k)) + bn(v_k) \end{cases} & ; sz(v_k) \leqslant B_t, sz(v_k) \leqslant B_d \end{cases}$$

In this case, either element k does not fit in B_t (since $sz(v_k) > B_t$), and if so, skip element k and continue. Otherwise, k does fit in B_t and B_d (since $sz(v_k) \leqslant B_t$, and $sz(v_k) \leqslant B_d$), and if so take the max value of either (a) skip element k and continue, or (b) add element k to M-KNAPSACK, subtract its size from B_t and B_d, accumulate its benefit ($bn(v_k)$), and continue.

Case 2: $v_k \notin V_h$ applies when view v_k is not in HV.

$$C(k, B_d, B_t) = \begin{cases} C(k-1, B_d, B_t) & ; sz(v_k) > B_d \\ \max \begin{cases} C(k-1, B_d, B_t), \\ C(k-1, B_d - sz(v_k), B_t) + bn(v_k) \end{cases} & ; sz(v_k) \leqslant B_d \end{cases}$$

In this case, either element k does not fit in B_d (since $sz(v_k) > B_d$), and if so, skip element k and continue. Otherwise, k does fit in B_d (since $sz(v_k) \leqslant B_d$), and if so take the max value of either (a) skip element k and continue, or (b) add element k to M-KNAPSACK, subtract its size from B_d, accumulate its benefit ($bn(v_k)$), and continue. At the end of this first phase the design of DW, V_d^{new}, is complete.

4.4.2 Packing HV M-Knapsack

In this phase, the target design is V_h^{new}, and the M-KNAPSACK dimensions are B_d and B_t^{rem}, and V_d^- represents the views evicted from the DW which are now available for transfer back to HV. The solution is symmetric to Phase 1, with modified inputs. The value B_t is initialized to B_t^{rem}. The candidate views are those remaining in V_h and those evicted from DW (V_d^-); therefore $V_{cands} = (V_h \cup V_d) - V_d^{new}$. We similarly have 2 cases, defined in Phase 2 as:

- Case 1: $v_k \in V_d^-$ applies when view v_k was evicted from DW.
- Case 2: $v_k \notin V_d^-$ applies when view v_k was not evicted from DW.

As before, these cases indicate whether a view needs to be moved or not. The recurrence relations from Phase 1 can now be used with these modified cases.

The complexity of our knapsack approach is $O(|V| \cdot \frac{B_t}{d} \cdot \frac{B_d}{d} + |V| \cdot \frac{B_t}{d} \cdot \frac{B_h}{d})$, where d represents the discretization factor (e.g., 1 GB). By discretizing the storage and transfer budgets, this approach can be made efficient in practice and suitable for our scenario that requires periodically recomputing new designs.

5. EXPERIMENTAL STUDY

In this section we present an experimental evaluation of the effectiveness of MISO for speeding up multistore queries. First we evaluate MISO in a multistore system in the absence of any other workload on DW in order to better understand the performance of our tuning techniques. Later we perform a more realistic evaluation of MISO by using a DW with limited spare capacity by running a background workload on DW. We then measure the impact of the multistore queries on the DW background workload and vice-versa. In Section 5.1 we describe the experimental methodology. In Section 5.2 we compare MS-MISO to several other system variants to highlight its benefit for multistore query processing. Then in Section 5.3 we compare the behavior MS-MISO to several possible multistore tuning algorithms. Lastly in Section 5.4, to evaluate MS-MISO in a realistic scenario we model a DW with an existing business workload and show the impact of executing multistore queries on the DW.

5.1 Methodology

Data sets and workloads. Our evaluation utilizes three data sets: a 1 TB Twitter data stream of user "tweets", a 1 TB Foursquare data stream of user "check-ins", and a 12 GB Landmarks data set represent static data containing geographical information about locations of popular interest. The identity of the user is common across Twitter and Foursquare logs, while the checkin location is common across the Foursquare and Landmarks logs. The data sets are stored in their native JSON format as logs in HDFS.

Our workload consists of 32 complex analytical queries given in [14] that access social media data and static historical data, for restaurant marketing scenarios. The queries model eight data analysts, each posing and iteratively refining a query multiple times during their data exploration. Each analyst (referred to as A_i for Analyst i) evolves a query through four versions denoted as $A_iv_1, A_iv_2, A_iv_3, A_iv_4$. An evolved query version A_iv_2 represents a mutation of the previous version A_iv_1, as described in [14], thus there is some overlap between queries. The queries contain relational operators as well as UDFs, and the queries are written in HiveQL with UDFs included via the Hive-CLI.

Stores. We utilize two distinct data stores: a Hive store (HV) and a parallel data warehouse (DW). Each store is a cluster of nodes, and the clusters are independent. The clusters are connected via 1GbE network and reside on adjacent racks. Each node has the same hardware: 2 Xeon 2.4GHz CPUs (8 cores), 16 GB of RAM, and exclusive access to its own disk (2TB SATA 2012 model). Additionally, the head nodes each have another directly attached 2 TB disk for data staging (used for data transfers and loading between the stores). HV runs Hive version 0.7.1 and Hadoop version 0.20.2, while DW runs the latest version of a widely-used, mature commercial parallel database (row-store) with horizontal data partitioning across all nodes. The HV cluster has 15 machines and the DW cluster has 9 machines. The HV cluster is 1.5× the size of the DW cluster since HV is less expensive than DW and thus in a realistic setting would typically be larger.

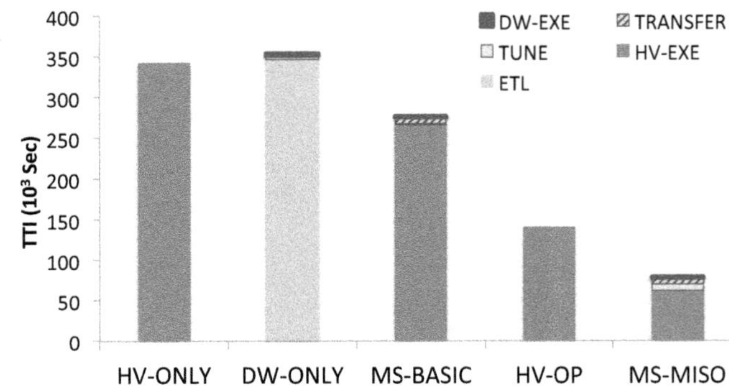

Figure 4: Performance results for 5 system variants.

Experimental parameters. For some experiments we vary the view storage budgets B_h, B_d and the view transfer budget B_t. B_h, B_d are varied as a fraction of the base data size in each store. Because the log data is stored in HV, we consider its base data size to be 2TB corresponding to the size of the logs. Because there is no log data stored in DW, we consider its "base data" size to be 200 GB corresponding to the relevant portion of the log data accessed by the queries. For example, $B_h = 2\times$ is 4TB, whereas $B_d = 2\times$ is 400GB. B_t is expressed in GB representing the size of the data transferred between the stores during each reorganization phase.

System variants. We evaluate the workload on several system variants described below. Note that all base data (logs) is stored in HV.

- HV-ONLY is the Hive store. Queries complete their entire execution in the 15 node HV store only.
- DW-ONLY is the data warehouse store. Queries complete their entire execution in the 9 node DW store only. Prior to query execution, we ETL the subset of the log data accessed by the queries using HV as an ETL engine. Note that using Hive or Pig for ETL is becoming a common industry practice (e.g., Netflix, Yahoo, Intel). [1] Any UDFs that do not execute in DW are applied as part of the ETL process in HV, before loading into DW.
- HV-OP is an HV store that retains opportunistic views and rewrites queries using these views, with the method from [15]. When views exceed the view storage budget, they are evicted using an LRU replacement policy. Queries complete their entire execution in the 15 node HV store only.
- MS-BASIC is a basic multistore system, that does not make use of opportunistic views. Queries may execute in part on both the 15 node HV store and the 9 node DW store as determined by the optimizer.
- MS-MISO is our multistore system that uses the MISO Tuner, which determines the placement of views in each store. Queries may execute in part on both the 15 node HV store and 9 node DW store, as determined by the optimizer which takes into account the current placement of views in each store. Reorganization phases (R) occur every 1/10 of the full workload, which in this case is after every 3 queries. When computing the expected future benefit (Section 4.3), we use a query history length of 6 and epoch length of 3 queries. During reorganizations, no queries are executed and MISO completes all view movements, after which time query execution begins again.

[1] http://techblog.netflix.com/2013/01/hadoop-platform-as-service-in-cloud.html, http://developer.yahoo.com/blogs/hadoop/pig-hive-yahoo-464.html, http://hadoop.intel.com/pdfs/ETL-Using-Hadoop-on-Intel-Arch.pdf

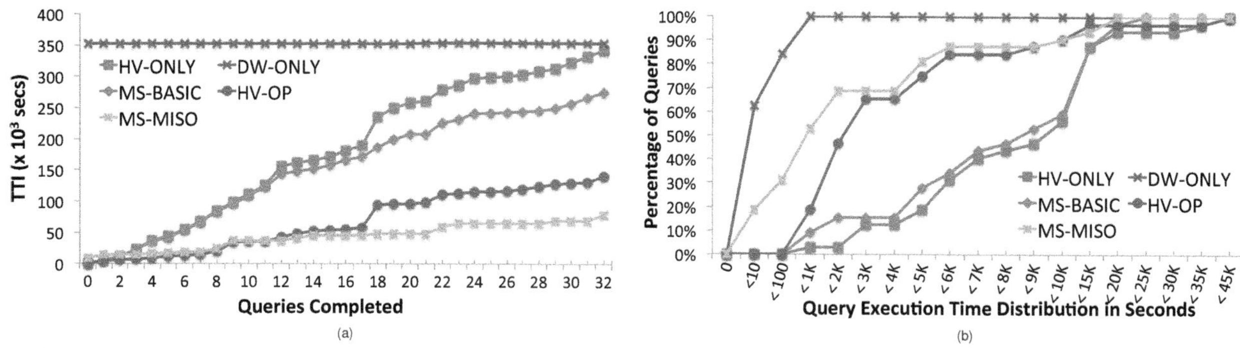

Figure 5: CDF plots as a function of percent workload complete for (a) TTI and (b) query execution time distribution.

Metrics. Our primary metric is TTI, representing the total elapsed time from workload submission to workload completion. TTI is defined as the cumulative time of loading data, transferring data during query execution, tuning the systems, and executing the queries. Wherever relevant, we break down TTI into the following components.

1. HV-EXE is the cumulative time spent executing queries in HV.
2. DW-EXE is the cumulative time spent executing queries in DW.
3. TRANSFER is the cumulative time for transferring (and loading) data between the stores during multistore query execution.
4. TUNE is the cumulative time spent computing new designs by a tuning algorithm, moving views between stores, and creating any recommended indexes for the views in DW.
5. ETL is the time spent loading the relevant data into DW using HV as an ETL engine before executing the workload. ETL time is only applicable to the DW-ONLY system variant.

5.2 Main Results

We first summarize the main results showing how MS-MISO outperforms other system variants. Figure 4 compares MS-MISO with the 4 other system variants – HV-ONLY, DW-ONLY, MS-BASIC, and HV-OP. In this experiment, HV-OP has a view storage budget of 2× on HV, and views are retained in HV within the storage budget using a simple LRU caching policy. MS-MISO has storage budgets B_h and B_d of 2× and B_t of 10GB. The systems variants are shown along the x-axis, and the y-axis reports TTI in seconds. For MS-MISO, TTI also includes time to compute new designs as well as the time spent moving views during reorganization phases. HV-ONLY represents the native system for our Hive queries, thus we use it as the baseline for comparing the other system variants.

Figure 4 shows MS-MISO has the best performance in terms of TTI, and DW-ONLY has the worst performance. DW-ONLY is actually 3% slower than HV-ONLY. This is because the vast majority of TTI for DW-ONLY is spent in the ETL phase, while the query execution time (DW-EXE) only constitutes a small fraction of the TTI. Although ETL is very expensive, it is a one-time process in our system and the cost is amortized by the benefit DW provides for all the queries in the workload. Clearly DW-ONLY would provide greater benefit for a longer workload. However, making this high up-front time investment to ETL all of the data is difficult to justify due to the exploratory nature of the queries. MS-BASIC offers limited performance improvement over HV-ONLY, only 19%, or a 1.2× speedup. This is due to the high cost of repeatedly transferring data between the stores for each query. Since the data transferred and loaded is not retained after a query completes, subsequent queries do not benefit from this effort. HV-OP shows a 59% improvement over HV-ONLY, representing a 2.4× speedup. This improvement is attributable to opportunistic views retained during query processing in HV. MS-MISO has a 77% improvement over HV-ONLY, representing a speedup of 4.3×. MS-MISO also results in a 68% improvement over MS-BASIC (3.1×), and a 44% improvement over HV-OP (1.8×). These results show that MS-MISO is able to utilize both the opportunistic views and DW effectively to speed up query processing.

The improvement of MS-MISO over HV-OP and MS-BASIC can be attributed to the following two reasons. First, it is able to load the right views into the right store during its reorganization phases. The reorganization phases allow MS-MISO to tune both stores periodically as the workload changes dynamically. This is especially important for exploratory queries on big data, since the queries and the data they access are not known up-front. Second, by performing lightweight periodic reorganization, MS-MISO is able to benefit from DW's superior query processing power. Furthermore, these two factors are relevant even with small storage budgets. For example, when we repeat this experiment using B_h and B_d equal to 0.125×, MS-MISO still results in 59% improvement over HV-ONLY (2.4× speedup). Next we provide a breakdown of the performance of MS-MISO to offer insights into how the combination of these two factors results in better performance.

5.2.1 *Breakdown of TTI*

To further breakdown the previous results from Figure 4, Figure 5 reports the cumulative distribution plots (CDF) for (a) TTI, and (b) query execution time for the five system variants. Figure 5(a) shows TTI along the y-axis, and the number of queries completed on the x-axis. A point (x, y) in this figure indicates that x queries had a total TTI of no more than y seconds. DW-ONLY has the worst TTI due to its significant delay before any query can begin execution – the first query can only start after the ETL completes at 348,000 seconds. In contrast, HV-ONLY, HV-OP, MS-BASIC, and MS-MISO allow users to start querying right away, although with varying performance. MS-BASIC and HV-ONLY have similar performance, again indicating that MS-BASIC is not able to make effective use of DW because it only considers a single query at a time and does not perform any tuning. HV-OP has the second best TTI due to its effective use of opportunistic views. MS-MISO has the fastest TTI among all system variants while still offering the benefits of immediate querying.

Figure 5(b) shows the percent of queries with execution time less than 10, 100, 1,000, 2,000 and so on until 45,000 seconds. To gain insight on how the queries perform, we report query execution time only, which does not include any ETL time or tuning time. Clearly DW-ONLY has the best query performance (top-most curve) with 84% of queries completing in less than 100 seconds and all the queries finishing within 1,000 seconds. Furthermore, the DW-ONLY curve shows that nearly 65% of queries complete within 10 seconds, and 90% within 100 seconds. In contrast, HV-ONLY performs worst (bottom-most curve) with less than 3% of queries completing within 1,000 seconds. The systems near the bottom of the graph, HV-ONLY, MS-BASIC, and HV-OP, have no queries that execute in less than 100 seconds. The systems near the top of the graph, DW-ONLY and MS-MISO, complete at least 30% of their queries in less than 100 seconds. While it is not surprising that DW-ONLY outperforms MS-

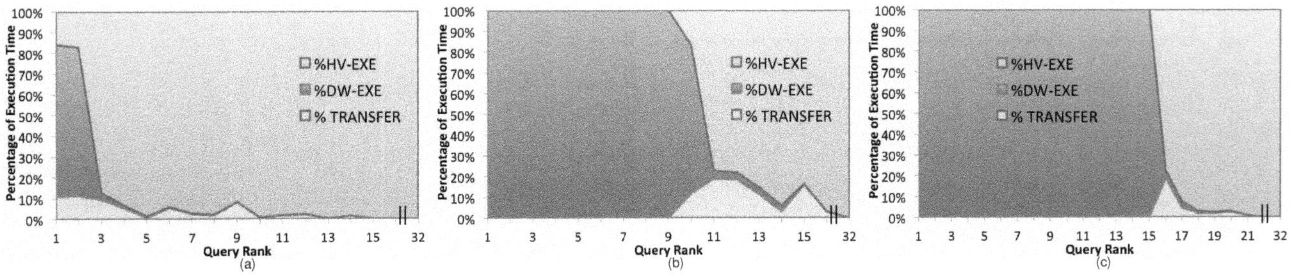

Figure 6: Breakdown of execution time into DW-EXE, HV-EXE and Transfer time components for queries from Figure 5(b); (a) MS-BASIC, (b) MS-MISO for $0.125\times$ storage budget, and (c) MS-MISO for $2\times$ storage budget.

MISO in terms of its *post-ETL* query performance, DW-ONLY is no longer competitive when ETL time is included. This shows that the lightweight adaptive tuning approach of MS-MISO is able to utilize the query processing power of DW without incurring the high up front cost of the ETL process.

5.2.2 Breakdown of Store Utilization

Next we highlight why MS-MISO performs better than MS-BASIC by examining the amount of time queries spend in each store. For each system in Figure 6, the y-axis indicates the fraction of time each query spends in HV, DW, or transferring data. For each system we rank the 32 queries by their DW utilization percent, and assign query rank 1 to the query that has the highest DW utilization, and rank 2 to the query with the next highest DW utilization; the x-axis indicates the query rank. Because the utilization trends stabilize after 15–20 queries, we truncate the x-axis in each figure.

Figure 6 shows this breakdown for three system variants – MS-BASIC in (a), MS-MISO with $0.125\times$ view storage budget in (b), and MS-MISO with $2\times$ view storage budget in (c). For MS-BASIC, only 2 queries spend the majority of their execution time in DW. In contrast, 9 of the queries in MS-MISO with the $0.125\times$ storage budget spend the majority of their total execution time in DW. This increases to 14 queries when the MS-MISO storage budget is increased to $2\times$.

Another way of quantifying DW utilization for each system is to consider the total execution time spent in HV versus DW for the first fastest queries in the workload, i.e., query ranks 1–16 in each figure. For queries ranked beyond 16, the HV-EXE component dominates most of a query's execution time, which does not illuminate DW utilization at all. With MS-BASIC in Figure 6(a), for every second spent in DW the queries spend 55 seconds in HV. With MS-MISO in Figure 6(b), for every 1 second spent in DW the queries only spend 1.6 seconds in HV. With MS-MISO in Figure 6(c), for every 1 second spent in DW the queries only spend 0.12 seconds in HV. This breakdown shows that MS-MISO is able to utilize DW more effectively than MS-BASIC, and increasing the storage budget for MS-MISO further increases DW utilization.

Finally, a different way to to examine store utilization is by reporting the ratio of plan operators executed by each store for each of the 32 queries. For MS-BASIC the best splits for all 32 queries were typically about 2/3 of the operators in HV and 1/3 in DW. For MS-MISO, an overview of the 32 splits is roughly as follows. For the fastest 9 queries, the split was 0/3 HV and 3/3 DW. For the next-fastest 20 queries, the average split was 1/3 HV and 2/3 DW. For the remaining 3 queries the average split was around 2/3 HV and 1/3 DW. Note that splits do not correlate exactly with plan execution times in Figure 6(b) due to the asymmetric performance of the stores.

5.3 Tuning Algorithm Comparisons

In this section we evaluate MS-MISO against four other possible tuning techniques for multistore physical design.

- MS-BASIC: Performs no tuning (i.e., does not use views).

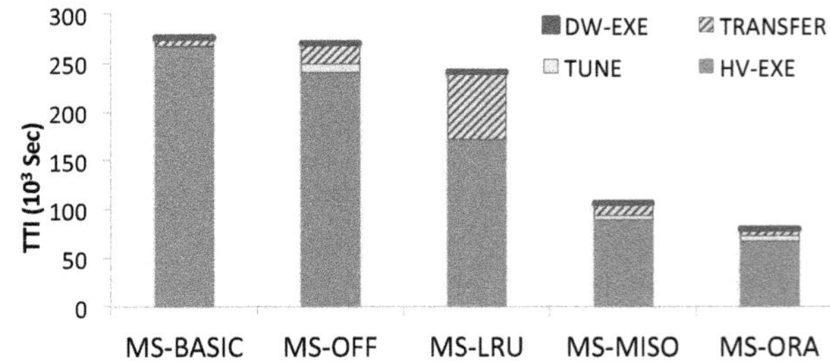

Figure 7: *TTI* Comparison of multistore tuning techniques.

- MS-OFF: Performs offline tuning, where it is given the entire workload up-front and tunes the stores one time by choosing the most useful set of views for the workload. This approach represents what is possible with current design tools and is provided only as a point of reference to show the performance trends.
- MS-LRU: Performs "passive" tuning by retaining working sets transferred between the stores during query execution as "views." LRU and its many variants are access-based approaches and provide a simple way of deciding which views to retain within a limited storage budget.
- MS-MISO: Performs online tuning using our MISO Tuner.
- MS-ORA: Performs online tuning using our MISO Tuner also, but the *actual* future workload is provided rather than predicted. This technique ("oracle") is just provided as a point of reference as the best performance possible for the MISO Tuner.

Tuning parameters for MS-OFF, MS-LRU, MS-MISO, and MS-ORA are set to $B_h = 0.125\times$, $B_d = 0.125\times$, and $B_t = 10$ GB since these budgets represent a more constrained environment.

Figure 7 compares the performance of the tuning techniques described above. Among all techniques, MS-BASIC performs the worst. This shows that multistore query processing without tuning does not perform as well as any of the other tuning techniques. Among the techniques that perform tuning, MS-OFF has the worst performance because the small storage budgets are insufficient to store all beneficial views for the entire workload. MS-MISO provides a 60% improvement over MS-OFF since it is able to adapt the physical design to the changing workload. Furthermore, MS-MISO results in a 56% improvement over MS-LRU because MS-LRU does not explicitly consider view benefits or interactions. This is because MS-LRU is an access-based approach whereas MS-MISO is a cost-benefit based approach that considers view benefits and interactions. Notice there is a large transfer time for MS-LRU, indicating that this method does not do a good job of retaining beneficial views. Finally, MS-MISO is 32% worse than MS-ORA, since the actual future workload is unknown to MS-MISO.

5.3.1 Varying the Tuning Parameters

Next, we analyze the performance of MS-MISO, MS-OFF, and MS-LRU under varying tuning constraints. Figure 8 shows the performance of MS-OFF, MS-LRU, and MS-MISO as we vary the storage

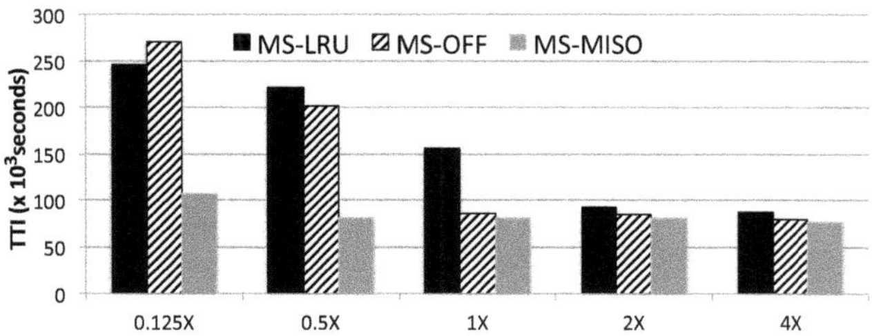

Figure 8: Varying the view storage budgets B_h and B_d, while transfer budget B_t is held constant at 10GB.

budget parameters B_h and B_d from $0.125\times$ to $4.0\times$. B_t was kept fixed at 10 GB. The y-axis reports TTI, and the x-axis shows the storage budgets on each store.

MS-MISO performs the best for all storage budgets, including the larger storage budgets. Among the smaller budgets of $0.125\times$ and $0.5\times$, both MS-OFF and MS-LRU perform significantly worse than MS-MISO. However, the performance of MS-OFF and MS-LRU improves with increasing storage budgets. For example, at $1\times$ budget, MS-MISO is 50% better than MS-LRU but only 7% better than MS-OFF, while with larger budgets the performance of all three methods begins to converge. The tuning techniques begin to have similar performance with larger storage budgets (2–4$\times$) since there is plenty of available storage space to retain many views in support of the recent workload.

5.4 Utilizing DW with Limited Spare Capacity

Now that we have shown the basic performance tradeoffs with MS-MISO, we evaluate MS-MISO in a realistic scenario with a DW that has limited spare capacity – that is, a DW that is executing a workload of reporting queries. As DW is a tightly-controlled resource, it is important to understand how our method affects the DW. To do this, we measure the impact of the multistore query workload on the DW reporting queries as well as the impact of the DW queries on the multistore query workload. These experiments are important because they model a realistic deployment scenario for a multistore System where an organization has two classes of stores and may want to utilize their existing DW resources to speed up the big data queries in HV.

To model a running DW, we consider varying amounts of spare IO and CPU capacity by executing a reporting query workload in DW. We examine four cases: A DW with 20% spare IO capacity, 20% spare CPU capacity, 40% spare IO capacity, and 40% spare CPU capacity. The spare capacities are measured as the amount of unused resources as reported by Linux IOstat; for example, 60% CPU consumption indicates a 40% spare CPU capacity. We measure these values for each of the 9 machines in the DW cluster every 10 seconds, and report the average value. In this scenario, we execute a background DW workload on the DW cluster that consumes a fixed proportion of IO or CPU resources. Below, we present the results for one case: a DW with 40% spare IO capacity. The remaining three cases showed very similar trends and hence are omitted. However, Table 2 below summarizes all of the results.

The multistore query workload is then executed as a single stream of 32 queries. As the multistore query workload is executed, we measure its impact on the background DW queries by the amount of slowdown of the background queries, representing the impact that the multistore workload has on the reporting queries running in DW. Conversely, we also measure the impact of the DW queries on the multistore workload.

To create a DW environment with limited IO or CPU resources, we use a single TPC-DS query and run multiple parameterized versions of the query in parallel in order to consume a fixed amount of each resource. The queries are used to control the amount of spare IO or CPU capacity. To do this, we first load a 1TB scale TPC-DS dataset into DW. We then selected 2 queries, query templates q3 and q83, since query q3 is IO intensive and query q83 is CPU intensive. To obtain 40% spare IO capacity in DW, we continuously execute one instance of q3 (which consumes 60% of the IO resources). To obtain 20% spare IO capacity, we continuously execute three instances of q3. Similarly, to obtain 40% spare CPU capacity in DW, we continuously execute two instances of q83 (which consumes 60% of the CPU resources). To obtain 20% spare CPU capacity, we continuously execute three instances of q83. All views transferred during multistore query execution are kept in a temporary table space, whereas views transferred by MS-MISO during reorganization are stored in permanent table space.

Figure 9(a) reports the CPU and IO load for the DW cluster with 40% spare IO capacity. The x-axis corresponds to time steps during experiment, and the y-axis indicates CPU and IO resource consumption. Initially, the IO is stable at 60% and the CPU consumption is at about 20%, then the multistore queries begin executing. Multistore queries may spend a lot of their execution time in HV, during which time DW continues executing only its background workload.

The peaks in Figure 9(a) (e.g., marked R, T) correspond to periods of either view transfers during reorganization (R) by MS-MISO or working set transfers during query processing (T), while the flatter areas (e.g., marked Q) correspond to periods of multistore query execution. For both R and T cases, the data transfers put heavy demands on the IO resources, in some instances consuming 100% of the IO resources. In Figure 9(a), view transfers during (R) and (T) phases consume a lot of the available spare capacity of DW, while multistore query execution (Q) has little impact on the spare capacity. This results in brief instances of high resource impact, but long time periods with low impact. Next, we show how the resource consumption by the multistore queries impacts the execution of the running DW queries.

Figure 9(b) shows the average execution time of the DW background queries as Multistore queries are executed for the same experiment. The x-axis again reports the timesteps during the experiment and the y-axis reports the average execution time of q3 during the entire experiment. The average execution time of q3 when no Multistore queries are executing is 1.06 seconds. Over the course of the entire experiment, the average execution time of q3 increased to 1.09 seconds, representing an overall slowdown of 2.5% for q3. The peaks in this figure correspond similarly to working set transfers during query execution (T), or view transfers during reorganization (R). This figure shows that these events briefly impacting the average execution time of q3, which increases to over 5 seconds several times. The regions Q again correspond to Multistore query execution in DW. This figure shows that the impact on the average execution time of DW background queries is very small in spite of brief periods of high impact.

Table 2: Impact of multistore workload on DW queries and vice-versa.

DW Spare Capacity		Percent Slowdown of	
		DW Queries	Multistore Workload
IO	40%	1.1%	2.5%
	20%	1.7%	4.0%
CPU	40%	0.3%	4.2%
	20%	0.8%	5.0%

In order to quantify the impact of an active DW versus an empty DW, Table 2 reports the impact of the multistore workload and the DW queries on each other. For the DW queries, we report the slowdown in their average execution time with versus without the multistore queries running. For the multistore queries, we report the slowdown in the TTI with and without the DW queries executing. The slowdown of the DW queries due to the Multistore queries less than 2%. Similarly, the slowdown of the multistore workload is no more than 5% versus an empty DW. This shows that the impact of the workloads on each other is actually quite minimal, indicating MS-MISO is indeed beneficial when there is limited spare capacity in DW.

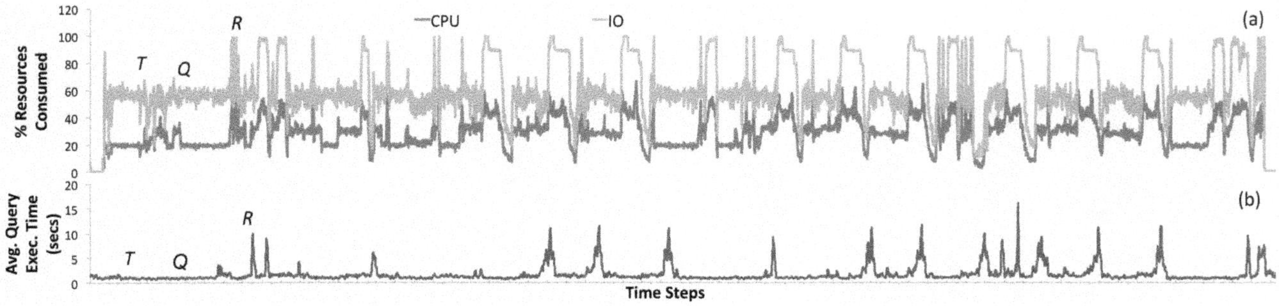

Figure 9: Impact of multistore workload on DW with 40% spare IO capacity showing (a) IO/CPU resources consumed and (b) average query execution time of the DW queries.

6. DISCUSSION AND CONCLUSION

The previous work on multistore systems has considered optimizing queries over data sets that span multiple stores. In this work we showed how a DW can be used as an accelerator for big data queries. Our main insight was that tuning the multistore system's physical design is key to achieving good performance. For a multistore system to be effective, it should use both stores toward their strengths: HV is best used for sifting through massive volumes of big data and extracting a small yet relevant subset of the data; DW is best used for processing this small subset of data efficiently since it can be loaded quickly with a short-term impact on the DW queries. In this paper, we argued that identifying this changing subset and determining where to store it is at the core of the concept of multistore systems. Our lightweight adaptive tuning method realizes the benefits of multistore processing by leveraging the strengths of each store to ensure that the current relevant subset of data (i.e., opportunistic views) is present in the "best" store based on the observed workload which is changing dynamically.

In this paper, we kept the transfer budget, B_t, small since a larger value has several undesirable consequences: a larger impact to DW during reorganization phases (slowing down DW queries), tuning consumes a large portion of TTI, and each reorganization moves more data across the network. However, there is a trade-off between how frequently one reorganizes the system versus the size of B_t. For instance, a small transfer budget value would allow more frequent reorganizations, each with a short-term impact on DW. An appropriate setting for B_t is dependent upon the nature of the workload and choosing a balance between the desired speed up for exploratory queries with the tolerable impact on DW reporting queries.

Our multistore approach combines the scalability of HV with the query performance of DW to leverage their unique strengths. There are several emerging big data systems such as Impala, Spark, Asterix, Stinger, and Hadoop 2.0 that make interesting design trade-offs to deliver good performance. An interesting area of future work is to explore ways of combining these emerging systems into multistores in a way that leverages their different strengths.

Although we do not address updates in this work, for future work there are several interesting considerations for maintaining opportunistic views; primarily due to the nature of the query domain (i.e., exploratory analysis), the way views are created (i.e., opportunistically), and the append-only nature of the updates in HDFS.

Acknowledgement: We thank Jeffrey Naughton and Hector Garcia-Molina for their insightful comments on the earlier versions of the paper. We also thank the anonymous SIGMOD reviewers for their useful feedback. J. LeFevre and N. Polyzotis were partially supported by NSF grant IIS-0447966 and a research grant from NEC labs.

7. REFERENCES

[1] A. Abouzeid, D. J. Abadi, and A. Silberschatz. Invisible loading: access-driven data transfer from raw files into database systems. In *EDBT*, 2013.

[2] A. Abouzeid, K. Bajda-Pawlikowski, D. Abadi, A. Silberschatz, and A. Rasin. HadoopDB: an architectural hybrid of MapReduce and DBMS technologies for analytical workloads. *PVLDB*, 2(1), 2009.

[3] S. Agarwal, S. Kandula, N. Bruno, M.-C. Wu, I. Stoica, and J. Zhou. Re-optimizing data-parallel computing. In *NSDI*, 2012.

[4] Apache Sqoop. http://sqoop.apache.org/, 2013.

[5] N. Bruno and S. Chaudhuri. An online approach to physical design tuning. In *ICDE*, 2007.

[6] S. Chaudhuri, M. Datar, and V. Narasayya. Index selection for databases: A hardness study and a principled heuristic solution. *TKDE*, 16(11), 2004.

[7] S. Chaudhuri and V. Narasayya. An efficient, cost-driven index selection tool for Microsoft SQL Server. In *VLDB*, 1997.

[8] M. P. Consens, K. Ioannidou, J. LeFevre, and N. Polyzotis. Divergent physical design tuning for replicated databases. In *SIGMOD*, 2012.

[9] D. J. DeWitt, A. Halverson, R. Nehme, S. Shankar, J. Aguilar-Saborit, A. Avanes, M. Flasza, and J. Gramling. Split query processing in Polybase. In *SIGMOD*, 2013.

[10] I. Elghandour and A. Aboulnaga. ReStore: Reusing results of MapReduce jobs. *PVLDB*, 5(6), 2012.

[11] H. Hacigümüs, J. Sankaranarayanan, J. Tatemura, J. LeFevre, and N. Polyzotis. Odyssey: A multi-store system for evolutionary analytics. *PVLDB*, 6(11), 2013.

[12] S. Idreos, M. L. Kersten, and S. Manegold. Database cracking. In *CIDR*, 2007.

[13] S. LaValle, E. Lesser, R. Shockley, M. Hopkins, and N. Kruschwitz. Big data, analytics and the path from insights to value. *MIT Sloan Management Review*, 52(2), 2011.

[14] J. LeFevre, J. Sankaranarayanan, H. Hacıgümüş, J. Tatemura, and N. Polyzotis. Towards a workload for evolutionary analytics. In *SIGMOD Workshop on Data Analytics in the Cloud (DanaC)*, 2013. Extended version *CoRR abs/1304.1838*.

[15] J. LeFevre, J. Sankaranarayanan, H. Hacıgümüş, J. Tatemura, N. Polyzotis, and M. J. Carey. Opportunistic physical design for big data analytics. In *SIGMOD*, 2014.

[16] T. Nykiel, M. Potamias, C. Mishra, G. Kollios, and N. Koudas. MRShare: sharing across multiple queries in MapReduce. *PVLDB*, 3(1–2), 2010.

[17] A. Pavlo, E. Paulson, A. Rasin, D. J. Abadi, D. J. DeWitt, S. Madden, and M. Stonebraker. A comparison of approaches to large-scale data analysis. In *SIGMOD*, 2009.

[18] K. Schnaitter, S. Abiteboul, T. Milo, and N. Polyzotis. On-line index selection for shifting workloads. In *ICDE*, 2007.

[19] K. Schnaitter and N. Polyzotis. Semi-automatic index tuning: keeping DBAs in the loop. *PVLDB*, 5(5), 2012.

[20] K. Schnaitter, N. Polyzotis, and L. Getoor. Index interactions in physical design tuning: modeling, analysis, and applications. *PVLDB*, 2(1), 2009.

[21] A. Simitsis, K. Wilkinson, M. Castellanos, and U. Dayal. QoX-driven ETL design: Reducing the cost of ETL consulting engagements. In *SIGMOD*, 2009.

[22] A. Simitsis, K. Wilkinson, M. Castellanos, and U. Dayal. Optimizing analytic data flows for multiple execution engines. In *SIGMOD*, 2012.

[23] A. A. Soror, U. F. Minhas, A. Aboulnaga, K. Salem, P. Kokosielis, and S. Kamath. Automatic virtual machine configuration for database workloads. *TODS*, 35(1), 2010.

[24] G. Valentin, M. Zuliani, D. C. Zilio, G. Lohman, and A. Skelley. DB2 advisor: An optimizer smart enough to recommend its own indexes. In *ICDE*, 2000.

[25] Y. Xu, P. Kostamaa, and L. Gao. Integrating Hadoop and parallel DBMS. In *SIGMOD*, 2010.

Efficient Top-K SimRank-based Similarity Join

Wenbo Tao
Department of Computer Science, Tsinghua University, Beijing, China
twb11@mails.tsinghua.edu.cn

ABSTRACT

SimRank is an effective and widely adopted measure to quantify the structural similarity between pairs of nodes in a graph. In this paper we study the problem of top-k SimRank-based similarity join, which finds k pairs of nodes with the largest SimRank values. To the best of our knowledge, this is the first attempt to address this problem. We propose a random-walk-based method to efficiently identify top-k pairs. Experiment results on real datasets show that our method significantly outperforms baseline approaches.

1. MOTIVATION

SimRank is a widely-adopted measure to evaluate the structural similarity between pairs of nodes in a graph. The SimRank-based similarity join problem [1] aims to find similar node pairs from a graph which have many real-world applications, such as link prediction and friend recommendation in social networks. However traditional SimRank-based similarity join requires users to input a threshold t manually and finds all pairs of objects x and y whose similarity scores exceed the threshold t. Nevertheless, it is rather hard to select an appropriate threshold because a large threshold leads to large numbers of irrelevant results while a small threshold causes small numbers of results (even empty). In practice, users only want to know a relatively small number of similar pairs, e.g, the 10 most similar pairs. Under such circumstance, users have to try different thresholds to meet their needs, which is a tedious task. To alleviate this problem, we study the top-k all pair similarity join problem which computes the most similar pairs without a given threshold.

2. PROBLEM STATEMENT

DEFINITION 1 (TOP-k SIMRANK-BASED SIMILARITY JOIN). *Given a graph with n nodes and e edges, the top-k SimRank-based similarity join problem aims to find the k pairs of nodes with the largest SimRank values where the SimRank value between two nodes a and b, denoted by $S(a,b)$, is recursively defined as below:*

$$S(a,b) = \begin{cases} 1 & a = b \\ \frac{C}{|I(a)||I(b)|} \sum_{i=1}^{|I(a)|} \sum_{j=1}^{|I(b)|} S(I_i(a), I_j(b)) & a \neq b \end{cases} \tag{1}$$

where C is a decay factor between 0 and 1, $I(a)$ is the neighbor set of a and $I_i(a)$ is the i-th neighbor of a.

3. ALL-PAIR SIMRANK

Conventional methods compute the all-pair SimRank array by using Eq.(1) in an iterative manner:

$$R_k(a,b) = \frac{C}{|I(a)||I(b)|} \sum_{i=1}^{|I(a)|} \sum_{j=1}^{|I(b)|} R_{k-1}(I_i(a), I_j(b)) \tag{2}$$

where $R_k(a,b)$ denotes the SimRank score on the kth iteration. According to [2], SimRank score converges fast and by mathematical induction, we have (see [2] for the proof):

$$s(a,b) - R_k(a,b) \leq C^{k+1} \tag{3}$$

Thus, a few iteration steps are enough to get adequate accuracy. For example, with $C = 0.3$ and the accuracy requirement $\delta = 0.001$, the total iteration steps ξ satisfies:

$$0.3^{\xi+1} \leq 0.001 \quad \Rightarrow \quad \xi \geq \lceil \log_{0.3} 0.001 \rceil - 1 = 5 \tag{4}$$

The time complexity of this iterative approach is $O(\xi D^2 n^2)$ where D is the average degree of all n nodes, and will degenerate into $O(\xi n^4)$ in the worst case. Even though many works such as [3] have been proposed to speed up `all-pair` SimRank computation, any methods using Eq.(1) explicitly are not suitable for top-k SimRank-based similarity join, because they have to access all pairs of nodes in each iteration even for identifying a small number of most similar pairs.

4. OUR METHOD

To improve the time and space complexity of `all-pair` SimRank calculation, we adopt the random surfer-pairs model proposed in [4] to improve efficiency. The basic idea is to transform Eq.(1) to an equivalent model using parallel random walk paths. Formally, Eq.(1) can be transformed to[1]

$$S(a,b) = \begin{cases} 1 & a = b \\ \sum_{t:(a,b)\to(x,x)} P[t] C^{l(t)} & a \neq b \end{cases} \tag{5}$$

SIGMOD'14, June 22–27, 2014, Snowbird, UT, USA.
ACM 978-1-4503-2376-5/14/06.
http://dx.doi.org/10.1145/2588555.2612662.

*This work is supervised by Prof. Guoliang Li at Department of Computer Science, Tsinghua University, Beijing, China.

[1] See [4] for details.

where t is a two-way path $a \rightarrow x$ and $b \rightarrow x$ on which two surfers starting from a and b respectively walk equal number of steps along the edges, with x as their **first meeting location**. $P[t] = \prod_{x \in t} \frac{1}{|I(x)|}$ is the probability of this two-way path and $l(t)$ denotes the number of steps.

Apart from an abstract math equation, this model describes an equivalent method by computing the summation of the probabilities of random walk paths. It is a good starting point in that we can reconsider the top-k SimRank-based similarity join problem from a new perspective of view which is more concise. Moreover, as we can see in the following discussions, for each node, this model only accesses a small portion of nodes.

In Eq.(4), the threshold ξ is also the longest length of the paths we need to consider [4]. Existing work shows that it only needs to enumerate paths within five steps without loss of too much accuracy [4]. However, the simple method of enumerating all pairs and then sorting the random walks has the time complexity of $O(n^2 D^{\xi})$. That is still uncomputable for large graphs even optimized by extensive sharing computation. Rather than tracing the two surfers at the same time, we partition this simultaneous procedure into two independent processes where each surfer walks on their own:

DEFINITION 2 (SUMMATION OF ONE WAY PATHS). *$Sim(a, x, l)$ is the sum of the probabilities of all one-way paths with starting node a, destination x and length l.*

This array can be computed efficiently by dynamic programming because $Sim(a, x, l)$ can be recursively computed with increasing l. A more insightful observation reveals that, by multiplying $Sim(a, x, l)$ and $Sim(b, x, l)$, we can easily get the summation of the probabilities of all l-step two-way paths whose starting points are a and b respectively and ending point is x.

Note that the random walk model summarizes all first meeting two-way paths, so we ought to subtract extra multi-meeting paths from the multiplication of $Sim(a, x, l)$ and $Sim(b, x, l)$. We use $\Delta(x, l)$ to denote the possibility that two surfers both start at x and meet again within $\xi - l$ steps. This array can be easily calculated by utilizing including and excluding principle for each paths starting from x. Then, it directly follows:

$$R_{\xi}(a, b) = \sum_{l=1}^{\xi} \sum_{x=1}^{n} Sim(a, x, l) \cdot Sim(b, x, l) \cdot (1 - \Delta(x, l)) \quad (6)$$

For further discussions, we transform Eq.(6) into :

$$S(a, b) \approx R_{\xi}(a, b) = \sum_{l=1}^{\xi} \sum_{x=1}^{n} Sim'(a, x, l) \cdot Sim'(b, x, l) \quad (7)$$

where $Sim'(a, x, l) = Sim(a, x, l) \cdot \sqrt{1 - \Delta(x, l)}$.

The simplicity of Eq.(7) motivates us to model $Sim'(a, *, *)$ as a vector in $n\xi$-dimension space, and then computing $S(a, b)$ is simply equivalent to calculating the inner products between the two vectors. Thus, the top-k SimRank-based similarity join problem can be solved by identifying k pairs of vectors with the largest inner product values. This is a classical problem, and we extend the matrix compression method proposed in [5] to address this problem. The overall time complexity is $O(nD^{\xi})$.

5. EXPERIMENTAL STUDY

Data sets. We conducted experiments on three real data sets. *YeastS*[2] is an interaction network between proteins. It has 2.3K nodes and 7.2K edges. Each node characterizes a protein and each edge represents an interaction between two proteins detected by modern detection methods.

Cit-HepPh[3] is a citation graph that covers all the citations within 34.5K papers with 421K edges in the period from January 1993 to April 2003.

BerkStan[4] is a Berkeley-Stanford web page graph with 685K pages and 7.6M edges. The edges represent hyperlinks between web pages.

Evaluation setup. We implement our algorithm using C++ language. The compilation is GCC 4.8.1 with -O2 flag. The experiments were conducted on a Ubuntu server with two Intel Xeon E5420 CPUs (8 cores, 2.5GHz) and 128GB memory. Each experiment was run 3 times, the average metrics are reported below.

Parameter choosing. We choose the decay factor $C = 0.3$ in all experiments. When we evaluate running time, for each three data sets we set $k = 20$, i.e, requiring the algorithm to return the 20 most similar node pairs, and set $\xi = 5$.

Competitor approach. We compare our method's performance with `SRJ Query` [1] which has a parameter – threshold t and returns all pairs of nodes whose SimRank values are larger than t. To adapt `SRJ Query` to solve the top-k SimRank-based similarity join problem, we dynamically tune t and for each t, we call the `SRJ Query` and then adjust search bounds according to the number of returned pairs.

Main Results. The vector matrix was actually very sparse and the ratio of the number of non-zero elements to n^2 was very small as shown in Figure 1. We also compare our running time with `SRJ Query`. `SRJ Query` has a very time consuming off-line phase for creating indices, so we discarded the runtime of this part and compare our total running time only with its online query time. Figure 2 shows that our method outperformed `SRJ Query` greatly.

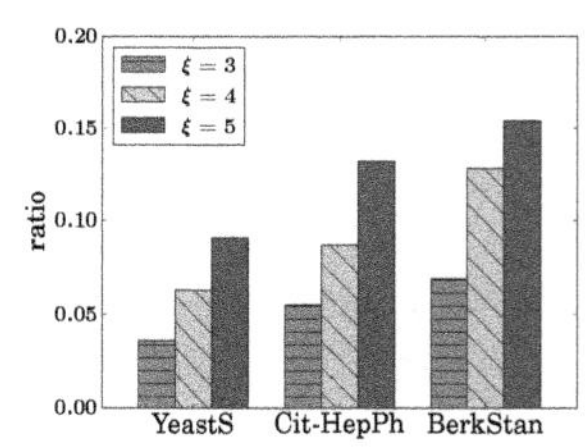

Figure 1: #Non-Zero/Size(n^2)

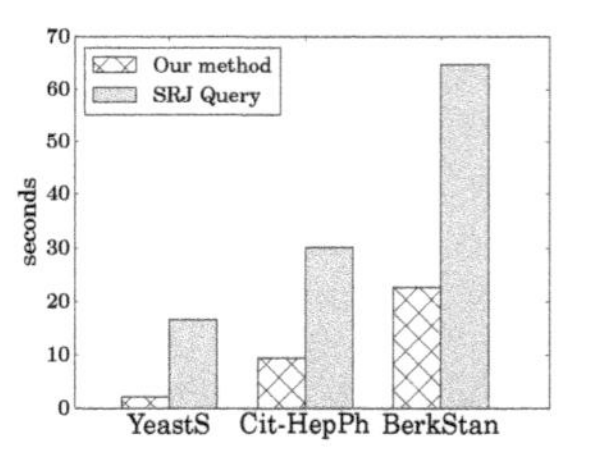

Figure 2: Comparision with Baselines

6. REFERENCES

[1] W. Zheng, L. Zou, Y. Feng, L. Chen, and D. Zhao, "Efficient simrank-based similarity join over large graphs," *PVLDB*, vol. 6, no. 7, pp. 493–504, 2013.

[2] D. Lizorkin, P. Velikhov, M. N. Grinev, and D. Turdakov, "Accuracy estimate and optimization techniques for simrank computation," *VLDB J.*, vol. 19, no. 1, pp. 45–66, 2010.

[3] W. Yu, X. Lin, and W. Zhang, "Towards efficient simrank computation on large networks," in *ICDE*, pp. 601–612, 2013.

[4] G. Jeh and J. Widom, "Simrank: a measure of structural-context similarity," in *KDD*, pp. 538–543, 2002.

[5] Y. Low and A. X. Zheng, "Fast top-k similarity queries via matrix compression," in *CIKM*, pp. 2070–2074, 2012.

[2] http://vlado.fmf.uni-lj.si/pub/networks/data/bio/Yeast/Yeast.htm

[3] http://snap.stanford.edu/data/cit-HepPh.html

[4] http://snap.stanford.edu/data/web-BerkStan.html

Multi-dimensional Data Statistics for Columnar In-Memory Databases

Curtis Kroetsch*
David R. Cheriton School of Computer Science
Faculty of Mathematics
University of Waterloo
Waterloo, Ontario, Canada
cckroets@uwaterloo.ca

ABSTRACT

The research presented here studies the multi-dimensional data statistics in the context of columnar in-memory database systems. Such systems, for example SAP HANA [4], SQL Server Apollo, or IBM BLU, use an order-preserving dictionary with dense encoding on the read-optimized storage which encodes the values of a single column in an ordered, dense-domain dictionary. The dictionary maps variable-length domain values to fixed-size dictionary entries. This encoding reduces memory consumption as dictionary values can be represented with fewer bits than the original values, and allows queries to be evaluated efficiently on the encoded data. The main characteristics of the dictionary encoding is that it results in a dense domain of values which can be exploited for building efficient data statistics objects.

Categories and Subject Descriptors

H.2.4 [**Database Management**]: Systems—*Query Processing*

Keywords

Multi-dimensional data statistics, Histograms

1. INTRODUCTION

Columnar in-memory databases divide its data into two storages: one read-optimized storage, aka *main storage*, and one write-optimized storage, aka *delta storage*. The delta storage is merged into main storage in a process known as *delta-merge* operation. During a delta-merge operation, for a specific column, the column dictionary will be rebuilt to reflect the data in the new main storage. Hence, any structure built using the main's dictionary has to be rebuilt after a delta-merge operation. For example indexes, materialized views, or data statistics built on main storage have to be rebuilt after a delta-merge operation. In this context, the requirements for data statistics objects to be fast to (re)build, space efficient, and precise are more stringent than in a classical database system, as the benefit for using dense-domain dictionaries must be balanced to the requirement for rebuild after each delta-merge operation.

The work presented in ACM SIGMOD 2014 in [3], in the context of SAP HANA, shows how ordered dictionaries are exploited for the efficient construction of precise and concise one-dimensional histograms. One-dimensional data statistics built for dictionary-encoded columns can be made very efficient from point of view of space, built time, and quality of estimates [3].

In contrast, we study here if multi-dimensional histograms can also be made space-efficient, built-time efficient, and have good quality of estimates when built on ordered dictionary encoded data, hence on dense domains of values.

In this paper we present some preliminary results on building and using multi-dimensional histograms based on r-trees [1], similar to rK-Hist proposed in [2]. The main focus is to improve the construction algorithms, from point of view of build-time, space efficiency, and the quality of the estimates for range queries. The proposed design and implementation proved so far to provide very accurate cardinality estimates for the data points with dense integer domains while its space and build time is comparable to previous work.

The purpose of a multi-dimensional histogram is to summarize a dataset over d dimensions. A dataset consists of N distinct points, each with d values and a measure. A point p has the form $p = (v_1, \cdots, v_d)$ where v_i represents the value of dimension i in p. Each point in the dataset also has an associated measure equal to $f(p) \in \mathbb{Z}^+$ which is the number of occurrences of the point p in the dataset. For a dataset with N distinct points, there are $M = \sum_{i=1}^{N} f(p_i)$ non-distinct points. A histogram for a dataset is a collection of buckets, where each bucket stores some information about a hyper-space it represents. Given a range query Q over d dimensions, the histogram estimates the number of points in the dataset that intersect with Q.

We designed a series of improvements to the original rK-Hist algorithms presented in [2], the most important are described below.

*The student author and the adviser, Dr. Anisoara Nica, SAP AG, Waterloo, Ontario, Canada, Anisoara.Nica@sap.com, worked on this project during the student's co-op term in Summer 2013.

SIGMOD'14, June 22–27, 2014, Snowbird, UT, USA.
Copyright 2014 ACM 978-1-4503-2376-5/14/06 ...$15.00.
http://dx.doi.org/10.1145/2588555.2612663 .

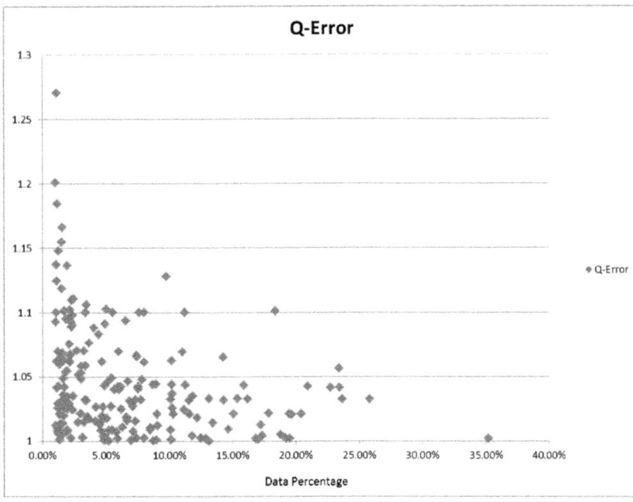

Figure 1: Cardinality Estimate Accuracy:
6-dimension points;
10 million distinct points;
516896321 non-distinct points;
200 range queries;
q-error = $max\{$ (actual cardinality / estimated cardinality), (estimated cardinality / actual cardinality) $\}$
q-error: Average: 1.0449, Maximum: 1.2702, Minimum: 1.0000

Improvement to Bucket Decomposition Method: The initial bucketing scheme may produce sub-optimal, non-uniform buckets which can lead to poor cardinality estimations. Bucket decomposition is one of the optimizations the rK-Hist uses to produce better results. Consequently, the rK-Hist uses a cost function to evaluate the uniformity of a bucket to determine if the points inside should be re-bucketed. Specifically, instead of creating the desired number of buckets initially, only 90% are created. The cost function is applied to each bucket and 5% of the absolutely worst buckets are considered for decomposition. Then a "sliding window" [2] approach is used to decompose each of the worst buckets into two buckets of greater quality if possible. These newly created buckets are also considered for further decomposition. Decomposition continues until enough buckets are created or the buckets can no longer decompose.

For the bucket decomposition algorithm, we observed that once a bucket ω becomes decomposed into ω_1 and ω_2, these new buckets are likely to be more uniform than those outside of the 5% decomposition list. This is because the 'sliding window' technique is typically very affective in removing dead space from the bucket. Decomposing further ω_1 and ω_2 is a waste if there are worse buckets to consider. So instead of initially moving the worst buckets to a separate list, we store all buckets in a priority queue Υ, according to their cost. When decomposing, the worst bucket, which appears at the top of Υ, is processed. Newly created buckets are also inserted back into Υ, hence the best bucket to be considered for decomposition is the bucket with the worst quality according to the cost function. Algorithm 1 describes the procedure in more detail.

Improvement to cost function C: The original cost function C in Algorithm 1 is calculated based on the K-Uniformity metric of a bucket. This metric aims to assess the relative emptiness of a bounding box. This is done by recursively partitioning the points in a bucket into their own box, via a k-d-tree. The K-Uniformity is the standard deviation of the volumes of each box. The higher this metric, the worse the distribution is inside the bucket.

The complexity of calculating this metric for a bucket ω, where $n = |\omega|$ is $O(n \lg n)$. This computation also requires that the original points be read again (potentially bring back into main memory) which is very expensive. We use instead $C(\omega)$ = Volume(minimum bounding box (ω)) [1] which is much cheaper to compute. The main advantage is that it doesn't require revisiting the raw data again and has a much smaller complexity, $O(d)$ for a d-dimensional dataset.

Algorithm 1 Improved Bucket Decomposition

Input: A set B of I initial buckets, a cost function C, and the total buckets to be produced α.
Output: A set Υ of α buckets.
$\Upsilon \leftarrow PriorityQueue(B, C)$
while $size(\Upsilon) < \alpha$ **do**
$\omega \leftarrow ExtractMax(\Upsilon)$
$(\omega_1, \omega_2) \leftarrow Decompose(\omega)$
$Push(\Upsilon, \omega_1)$
$Push(\Upsilon, \omega_2)$
end while

Figure 1 shows the cardinality estimate accuracy for randomly generated range queries, on large datasets of 516896321 non-distinct points. We measure the q-error metrics as introduced in [3]. The x-axis represents the actual cardinality (in percentage) of the generated queries.

2. CONCLUSION

We studied a certain type of multi-dimensional data statistics for dense domains which naturally characterize the dictionary encoded columns in a columnar in-memory databases. We plan to further exploit the properties that characterize such systems in building and maintaining different types of data statistics objects which are efficient and accurate.

3. REFERENCES

[1] Daniar Achakeev and Bernhard Seeger. A class of r-tree histograms for spatial databases. In *SIGSPATIAL/GIS*, pages 450–453, 2012.
[2] Todd Eavis and Alex Lopez. Rk-hist: an r-tree based histogram for multi-dimensional selectivity estimation. In *ACM CIKM*, pages 475–484, 2007.
[3] Guido Moerkotte, Dave DeHaan, Anisoara Nica, Norman May, and Alexander Boehm. Exploiting ordered dictionaries to efficiently construct histograms with q-error guarantees in SAP HANA. In *ACM SIGMOD*, 2014.
[4] Vishal Sikka, Franz Färber, and Anil Goel andWolfgang Lehner. SAP HANA: The evolution from a modern main-memory data platform to an enterprise application platform. In *PVLDB*, volume 6, pages 1184–1185, 2013.

A User Interaction Based Community Detection Algorithm for Online Social Networks

Himel Dev *
Department of Computer Science and Engineering
Bangladesh University of Engineering and Technology, Dhaka, Bangladesh
himeldev@gmail.com

ABSTRACT

Existing community detection techniques either rely on content analysis or only consider the underlying structure of the social network graph, while identifying communities in online social networks (OSNs). As a result, these approaches fail to identify *active communities*, i.e., communities based on actual interactions rather than mere friendship. To alleviate the limitations of existing approaches, we propose a novel solution of community detection in OSNs.

Categories and Subject Descriptors

H.2.8 [**Database Management**]: Database Applications—*Data Mining*

Keywords

Community Detection, Social Networks

1. INTRODUCTION

The community detection involves grouping of similar users into clusters, where users in a group are strongly bonded with each other than the other members in the network. We propose a novel community detection technique that considers the structure of the social network and interactions among the users while detecting the communities. The key idea of our approach comes from the following observations: (i) the degree of interaction between each pair of users can widely vary, which we term as *the strength of ties*, and (ii) for each pair of users, the degree of interactions with common neighbors (e.g., mutual friends in Facebook), which we term the *group behavior*, play an important role to determine their belongingness to the same community. Based on these two observations, we propose an efficient solution to detect communities in OSNs. The detailed experimental study shows that our proposed algorithm significantly outperforms state-of-the-art techniques for both real and synthetic datasets.

*Under supervision of Dr. Mohammed Eunus Ali and Dr. Tanzima Hashem from CSE, BUET

SIGMOD/PODS'14, June 22–27, 2014, Snowbird, UT, USA.
ACM 978-1-4503-2376-5/14/06.
http://dx.doi.org/10.1145/2588555.2612664.

2. RELATED WORK

SCAN [3] and Truss [1] use the neighborhood concept of common neighbors, which has similarity with our group interaction concept for un-weighted graphs. However, these are pure link-based methods based on topological structures. They focus only on the information regarding the linkage behavior (connection) for the purposes of community prediction and clustering. They do not utilize different attributes present in networks, and as a result, their performance degrades in networks with rich contents, e.g., OSNs.

3. METHODOLOGY

The proposed community detection algorithm has four phases. In the first phase, the algorithm quantifies the degree of interaction between every connected pair of users in the OSNs and based on these interactions, in the second phase, the algorithm quantifies the group behavior for every pair of users who are connected via common neighbors. In the third phase, the algorithm determines the probability of two users belonging to the same community using the impact of interaction between them and their group behavior. Finally, in the fourth phase, the algorithm applies hierarchical clustering to detect communities based on the computed probabilistic measure.

3.1 Quantifying the Interaction

Given a social graph $G(V, E)$ and user interaction data, the algorithm constructs an *Interaction Graph*, $G_I(V, E, W)$, where each weight $w_{uv} \in W$ quantifies the degree of interaction between two users u and v. We have considered the following three factors to quantify interaction between two users: interaction type, average number of interactions for a particular interaction type, and relative interaction.

Interaction Type: Now-a-days OSNs involve interactions of different types. For example, Facebook users can interact via personal messages, wall posts, photo tags, page likes etc. To quantify the degree of interaction between two users, it is necessary to consider all interaction types. In addition, we observe that, some of these interaction types indicate stronger bonding than the others. Thus, it is important to prioritize the interaction types in an order. Prioritizing the interaction types in terms of bonding is especially useful for applications such as friend recommendation, and influence analysis. We prioritize different interaction types using weights.

In addition, in an OSN, there could be both active and passive users. Sometimes there is no interaction involved in a link established by a passive user. This can also happen for newly joined users of an OSN. To determine the community in which a passive/new user belongs to, we consider the establishment of friendship between two users as a special type of interaction and to incorporate this special type of interaction, our communication detection algorithm provides a threshold value for each established friendship link.

Average Number of Interactions for a Particular Interaction Type: Another important factor to consider is the average number of interactions for a particular interaction type, which is not same for all interaction types. To address this issue, we normalize the number of interactions for each type using the average value corresponding to the type. Otherwise, interaction types with higher average values eliminate the effect of type prioritization.

Relative Interaction: We observe that the importance of an interaction can vary among users based on their activities. To incorporate this issue in quantifying the interaction between users for our community detection algorithm, we take relative interaction into account. To quantify the impact of relative interaction, we normalize each interaction in terms of total interaction of the involved users.

Quantification: Let $\{I^1, I^2, ..., I^t\}$ represent t interaction types in an OSN. Assume that weights $W^1, W^2, ..., W^t$ are associated with $I^1, I^2, ..., I^t$, respectively, where $W^i > W^j$, if I^i represents stronger bonding between users than that of I^j. We first quantify interaction between users based on $\{I^1, I^2, ..., I^t\}$, and then to incorporate the impact of links without interaction, we add an additional threshold value, ϵ, to the quantified interaction.

Let i^t_{uv} represent the number of interactions of type t between users u and v, and n is the number of users in the social graph $G(V, E)$. The average number of interactions for a particular type t, $\bar{I}^t$, is computed as $\sum_{u \in V} \sum_{v \in V \wedge u \neq v} i^t_{uv}/n$. The normalized number of interactions of type t between u and v, I^t_{uv}, is computed as $i^t_{uv}/\bar{I}^t$.

Considering prioritized interaction types, links without interaction, and the average number of interactions for each interaction type, the algorithm quantifies interaction between two users u and v as $\hat{w_{uv}}$ using the following equations:

$$\hat{w_{uv}} = I^1_{uv} \times W^1 + I^2_{uv} \times W^2 + ... + I^t_{uv} \times W^t + \epsilon \quad (1)$$

Finally, to incorporate the impact of the relative importance of an interaction between users u and v, the algorithm considers the quantified interactions of u and v with their neighbors $N(u)$ and $N(v)$, respectively, using Equation 1 and modifies $\hat{w_{uv}}$ as w_{uv} using the following equation:

$$w_{uv} = \frac{1}{2}\left(\frac{\hat{w_{uv}}}{\sum_{x \in N(u)} \hat{w_{ux}}} + \frac{\hat{w_{uv}}}{\sum_{y \in N(v)} \hat{w_{yv}}}\right) \quad (2)$$

3.2 Quantifying Group Behavior

Given an interaction graph, $G_I(V, E, W)$, the algorithm constructs a *Group Interaction Graph*, $G_{GI}(V, E', W')$, where there is an edge, $e'_{uv} \in E'$ between two users u and v, if they have at least a common neighbor. W' is a set of weights, where each weight quantifies the group behavior between two users with respect to common neighbors. Let $M_{uv} = \{m_1, m_2, ..., m_h\}$ represent h common neighbors (mutual friends) of u and v, where $m_1, m_2, ..., m_h, u, v \in V$. The interaction with a common neighbor $m_i \in M_{uv}$, $w^{m_i}_{uv}$ is quantified as $w^{m_i}_{uv} = \min(w_{um_i}, w_{vm_i})$.

The proposed algorithm computes the interaction of every pair of users who are connected via one or more common neighbor with respect to each of their common neighbors and then quantifies the group behavior for pair of users, $w_{M_{uv}} \in W'$ as follows:

$$w_{M_{uv}} = \sum_{i=1}^{h} w^{m_i}_{uv} \quad (3)$$

3.3 Computing the Probabilities

Given an interaction graph, $G_I(V, E, W)$, and a group interaction graph, $G_{GI}(V, E', W')$, the algorithm constructs a *Probability Graph*, $G_p(V, E \cup E', P)$, where each weight $p_{uv} \in P$ represents a probability between two vertices u and v to belong in the same community.

DEFINITION 3.1. ***(Probability of belonging to the same community)*** *Let w_{uv} and $w_{M_{uv}}$ represent the weight of interaction between u and v and their group behavior, respectively, and α be a parameter used to combine the impact of w_{uv} and $w_{M_{uv}}$, where $0 \leq \alpha \leq 1$. The probability of u and v to belong to the same community, p_{uv}, is defined as follows:*

$$p_{uv} = \alpha * w_{uv} + (1 - \alpha) * w_{M_{uv}} \quad (4)$$

We use the parameter α to control the impact of w_{uv} and $w_{M_{uv}}$ on probability for users u and v. We experimentally find the appropriate value of α that identifies the communities with a high accuracy.

3.4 Hierarchical Clustering

The final phase of the proposed algorithm involves identifying communities by applying hierarchical clustering in the probability graph $G_p(V, E \bigcup E', P)$.

Distance Measure: In our approach, the probability $p_{uv} \in P$ of u and v to belong to the same community serves as the similarity measure, $(1 - p_{uv})$ serves as distance.

Linkage Criterion: To estimate the distance between two clusters C_i and C_j, we have used 'Unweighted Pair Group Method with Arithmetic Mean (UPGMA)'as the linkage criterion.

4. EXPERIMENTAL EVALUATION

We have observed that for a real Facebook user interaction dataset, our algorithm achieves the *highest* normalized mutual information (NMI) and pairwise F-measure (PWF) values, (0.79, 0.79), which are significantly higher than the NMI and PWF values achieved by other competitive methods such as Girvan-Newman (0.49, 0.38), Walktrap (0.78, 0.77), Leading Eigenvector (0.73, 0.75), Infomap (0.35, 0.3), Multilevel (0.63, 0.56) [2]. Moreover, our algorithm performs reasonably well for different benchmark datasets, for both weighted and un-weighted social graphs.

5. REFERENCES

[1] J. Cohen. Trusses: Cohesive subgraphs for social network analysis. 2008.

[2] H. Dev, M. E. Ali, and T. Hashem. User interaction based community detection in online social networks. In *Database Systems for Advanced Applications*, volume 8422, pages 296–310. 2014.

[3] X. Xu, N. Yuruk, Z. Feng, and T. A. J. Schweiger. Scan: a structural clustering algorithm for networks. In *ACM SIGKDD*, pages 824–833, 2007.

EDS: A Segment-based Distance Measure for Sub-trajectory Similarity Search

Min Xie *
The Hong Kong University of Science and Technology
mxieaa@ust.hk

ABSTRACT

In this paper, we study a *sub-trajectory similarity search* problem which returns for a query trajectory some trajectories from the trajectory database each of which contains a *sub-trajectory* similar to the query trajectory. We show the insufficiency of the *distance measures* that are originally designed for *trajectory similarity search* where each trajectory *as a whole* is compared with the query trajectory, and thus we introduce a new *segment-based* distance measure called *EDS* (Edit Distance on Segment) for sub-trajectory similarity search. We conducted experiments on a real data set showing the superiority of our EDS distance measure.

Categories and Subject Descriptors

H.2.8 [**Database Management**]: Database Applications—*spatial databases and GIS*

Keywords

Sub-trajectory; Similarity search

1. INTRODUCTION

Due to the popularity of location-tracking devices trajectory data is ubiquitous nowadays. *Trajectory similarity search* which returns for a query trajectory some trajectories from the trajectory database each of which *as a whole* is similar to the query trajectory is a popular query on trajectory data [1–3, 5, 6]. In some cases, a trajectory that is *not similar* to the query trajectory *as a whole* might contain a *sub-trajectory* (a portion of the trajectory) that is *similar* to the query trajectory, and finding the similar sub-trajectories is useful in many applications. To illustrate, consider the following scenario.

Suppose that we as a taxi company received a complaint from a passenger that one of our taxi drivers drove along an unnecessarily long route for a higher charge. Apart from checking whether this fooling behavior happened, we also want to check whether some other taxi drivers have cheated passengers by driving along a similar route. Using the traditional trajectory similarity search techniques might give us the conclusion that no trajectories are similar to the query trajectory. This, however, is usually not the real case since we might have some taxi trajectories which contain *sub-trajectories* that are similar to the query trajectory and thus the corresponding drivers are bad citizens and should be figured out.

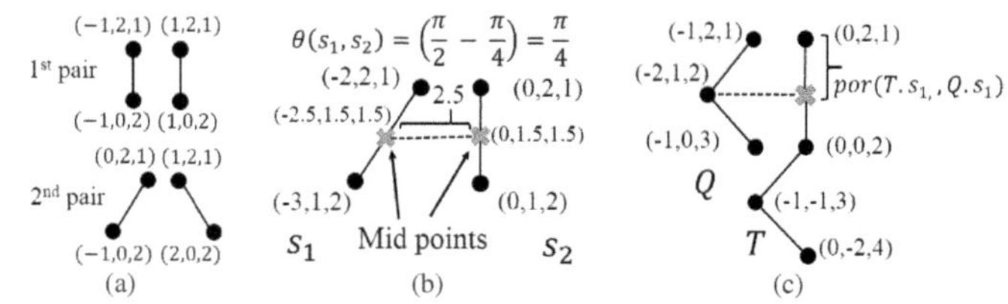

Figure 1: (a) Point-based distance and segment-based distance (b) Segment transformation cost (c) Computational example

For the sub-trajectory search problem, one may think of the approach that computes the distance between *each possible sub-trajectory* of a trajectory and the query trajectory by using one of the existing trajectory distance measures [1–3, 5, 6], which, however, has an expensive computation cost since a trajectory consisting of n sampled points simply has $O(n^2)$ possible sub-trajectories. In this paper, we design a distance measure called *EDS* (Edit Distance on Segment) which avoids the costly enumeration of all possible sub-trajectories for a trajectory. Instead, EDS only enumerates all possible *suffixes* of the trajectory (note that a trajectory consisting of n sampled points has $O(n)$ possible suffixes only). Another related work is [4] which defines a distance measure based on two segments, instead of two trajectories (or sub-trajectories).

Besides, the existing trajectory distance measures [1–3, 5, 6] are all *point-based* which means that only the information about the sampled points of the trajectory is utilized which sometimes is not sufficient enough. To illustrate, consider Figure 1(a) where we have four trajectories each of which has two points and each point is associated with a triplet (x, y, t) indicating that the point has its location at (x, y) and its timestamp of t. According to these existing distance measures, the distance between the first pair of two trajectories (the two at the top) is the same as the distance between the second pair of two trajectories (the two at the bottom), which, makes little sense since obviously the two trajectories in the second pair are more dissimilar than the two in the first pair. Our EDS distance measure is more robust in these cases, since it is *segment-based*, meaning that the information of the segments, including not only the information of points but also the other information such as direction and length, is utilized for measuring the similarity.

Contribution. We identify the problem of sub-trajectory similarity search, design a new distance measure EDS for the problem, and conducted experiments which verified our new measure EDS.

2. DISTANCE MEASURE: EDS

Let T be a trajectory of n segments, $(s_1, s_2, ..., s_n)$. Each segment s_i $(1 \leq i \leq n)$ has a start point denoted by $s_i.p_1$ and an end point denoted by $s_i.p_2$. Besides, we denote by $T.s_i$ the ith segment

*The author would like to thank Cheng Long and Raymond Chi-Wing Wong for their helpful suggestions for improving the presentation in this paper.

SIGMOD/PODS'14, Jun 22-27 2014, Snowbird, UT, USA
ACM 978-1-4503-2376-5/14/06.
http://dx.doi.org/10.1145/2588555.2612665.

of T. Given two points p_1 and p_2, $d(p_1, p_2)$ denotes the Euclidean distance between p_1 and p_2.

The major idea of our distance measure EDS is to define the distance between two trajectories to be the minimum cost of a series of *segment-wise* transformations each of which changes one segment to the other. Before we introduce EDS, we define the cost of a segment-wise transformation, i.e., the cost of changing a segment to another one. The intuition we use is that given two segments s and s', we can transform s to s' by *displacing*, *stretching* and *rotating* s properly. Thus, we capture the cost of the segment-wise transformation by using the cost of each of these three operations.

Definition 1. Given two segments s and s', the cost of the segment-wise transformation between s and s', denoted by $cost(s, s')$, is defined to be

$$w_{dis} \cdot c_{dis}(s, s') + w_{str} \cdot c_{str}(s, s') + w_{rot} \cdot c_{rot}(s, s') \quad (1)$$

where w_{dis}, w_{str} and w_{rot} are three weights, $c_{dis}(s, s') = d(mid(s), mid(s'))/d_{max}$ is the displacing cost ($mid(s)$ is the mid-point of s and d_{max} is a large distance such as the maximum distance between two points in the trajectory database), $c_{str} = 1 - \min\{|s|, |s'|\}/max\{|s|, |s'|\}$ is the stretching cost ($|e| = d(s.q_1, s.p_2)$), and $c_{rot} = \theta(s, s')/\pi$ is the rotating cost ($\theta(s, s')$ is the angle between the vector from $s.p_1$ to $s.p_2$ and that from $s'.p_1$ to $s'.p_2$).

To illustrate, consider Figure 1(b). Suppose that d_{max} is 3.16 (the maximum distance between two points). $c_{dis}(s_1, s_2) = d(mid(s_1), mid(s_2))/d_{max} = 2.5/d_{max} = 0.791$, $c_{str}(s_1, s_2) = 1 - \frac{|s_2|}{|s_1|} = 1 - \frac{1}{\sqrt{2}} = 0.293$ and $c_{rot}(s_1, s_2) = \theta(s_1, s_2)/\pi = (\frac{\pi}{2} - \frac{\pi}{4})/\pi = 0.25$. Then, $cost(s_1, s_2) = 0.791 + 0.293 + 0.25 = 1.334$ if all weights are 1.

With the segment-wise transformation cost defined, we explain our distance measure EDS as follows. Let T be a trajectory and Q be the query trajectory. We denote the distance between T and Q under the EDS distance measure by $EDS(T, Q)$. We transform between T and Q with two operators, namely *insertion* and *replacement*. We start from $T.s_1$ on T and $Q.s_1$ on Q. We have three options.

- We *insert* $T.s_1$ into $Q.s_1$ which means that $T.s_1$ is transformed to the *portion* of $Q.s_1$ that begins from the start point of $Q.s_1$ and stops at the point along $Q.s_1$ which is nearest to the end point of $T.s_1$. We denote this portion of $Q.s_1$ by $por(Q.s_1, T.s_1)$. In this case, $EDS(T, Q)$ corresponds to $cost(T.s_1, por(Q.s_1, T.s_1))$ plus the EDS distance between T excluding $T.s_1$ and Q excluding $por(Q.s_1, T.s_1)$ (which is defined recursively).
- We *insert* $Q.s_1$ into $T.s_1$ which has an analogous meaning as the first option and we define $EDS(T, Q)$ accordingly.
- We *replace* $T.s_1$ with $Q.s_1$ which means that $T.s_1$ is transformed to $Q.s_1$. Then, $EDS(T, Q)$ is $cost(T.s_1, Q.s_1)$ plus the EDS distance between T excluding $T.s_1$ and Q excluding $Q.s_1$ (which is defined recursively).

Then, the minimum one among these three costs corresponds to $EDS(T, Q)$. Formally, we have $EDS(T, Q) =$

$$\begin{cases} 0 & \text{if } |Q| = 0 \\ \infty & \text{if } |T| = 0 \text{ and } |Q| \neq 0 \\ min\{ & otherwise \\ cost(T.s_1, por(Q.s_1, T.s_1)) + EDS(T \backslash T.s_1, Q \backslash por(Q.s_1, T.s_1)) \\ cost(por(T.s_1, Q.s_1), Q.s_1) + EDS(T \backslash por(T.s_1, Q.s_1), Q \backslash Q.s_1), \\ cost(T.s_1, Q.s_1) + EDS(T \backslash T.s_1, Q \backslash Q.s_1)\} \end{cases}$$

where $T \backslash s$ denotes the resulting trajectory of T by excluding s. (2)

Compared with the existing distance measures [1–3, 5, 6], our EDS distance measure has two advantages. First, in order to do sub-trajectory similarity search (i.e., finding the most similar sub-trajectory to the query trajectory), with EDS, it is enough to enumerate all possible *suffixes* of the trajectory (which has order $O(n)$) while with one of the existing distance measures, it has to enumerate all possible *sub-trajectories* of the trajectory (which has order $O(n^2)$). This is because our definition of EDS already traverses all possible *prefixes* (See the case of "$|Q| = 0$"). Second, EDS is a *segment-based* distance measure which by its nature is better than a *point-based* distance measure (adopted by existing distance measures) since segments capture more information than points.

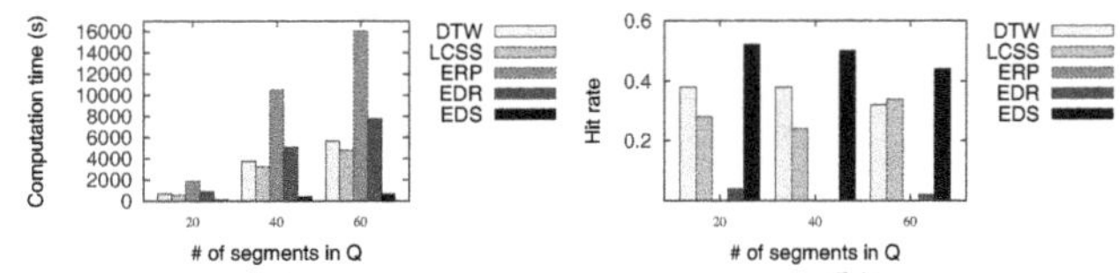

(a) (b)

Figure 2: Comparison with Existing Distance Measurements

In Figure 1(c), we compute the EDS distance between trajectory Q and T. To obtain the best sub-trajectory in T, we compute the EDS distance between Q and all the suffixes of T, namely $T_1 = T[1, 3]$, $T_2 = T[2, 3]$ and $T_3 = T[3, 3]$ where $T[i, 3]$ is the trajectory from segment s_i to s_3. When computing $EDS(T_1, Q)$, we first insert $Q.s_1$ to $T.s_1$ by creating $por(T.s_1, Q.s_1)$ and compute $cost(por(T.s_1, Q.s_1), Q.s_1)$. $Q.s_2$ is then replaced with the remaining half of $T.s_1$ (i.e. $T.s_1 \backslash por(T.s_1, Q.s_1)$). After these two transformations, there are no remaining segments in Q and therefore all the remaining segments in T are skipped. Similarly, we compute $EDS(T_2, Q)$ and $EDS(T_3, Q)$. Finally, $EDS(T_2, Q)$ turns out to be the smallest cost, corresponding to the final answer.

3. EXPERIMENTS AND CONCLUSION

We conducted our experiments on a benchmark dataset "Athens trucks" (http://www.chorochronos.org/?q=node/5) which contains 1100 trajectories of various lengths. Our query trajectory Q was generated by first randomly selecting a trajectory from the data set, second randomly sampling a sub-trajectory of the selected trajectory, and third slightly adjusting the sampled sub-trajectory. We say that an answer is returned correctly by a query Q if the sampled sub-trajectory is returned. We vary the number of the segments in Q for our experiments and use two measures, namely "computation time" and "hit rate". The "computation time" means the time cost of computing the distance measure and the "hit rate" means the percentage of the queries that return answers correctly. The results are shown in Figure 2. According to Figure 2(a), the computation cost based on our EDS distance measure is significantly smaller than that based on other distance measures (the efficiency gap is about 10 times faster). According to Figure 2(b), the hit rate based on our EDS distance measure is higher than that based on other distance measures (the effectiveness gap is about 1.5 to 10 times better).

In conclusion, we propose a new and better measure EDS for sub-trajectory similarity search. An interesting direction is to design some indexing techniques for EDS distance measure.

4. REFERENCES

[1] L. Chen and R. Ng. On the marriage of lp-norms and edit distance. In *VLDB*, 2004.

[2] L. Chen, M. T. Özsu, and V. Oria. Robust and fast similarity search for moving object trajectories. In *SIGMOD, pages 491-502*, 2005.

[3] E. Frentzos, K. Gratsias, and Y. Theodoridis. Index-based most similar trajectory search. In *ICDE, pages 816-825*, 2007.

[4] J. G. Lee, J. Han, , and K. Y. Whang. Trajectory clustering: a partition-and-group framework. In *SIGMOD*, 2007.

[5] M. Vlachos, G.kollios, and D. Gunopulos. Discovering similar multidimensional trajectories. In *ICDE*, 2002.

[6] B.K. Yi, H.V. Jagadish, and C. Faloutsos. Efficient retrieval for similar time sequences under time warping. In *ICDE, pages 201-208*, 1998.

Spatio-temporal Visual Analysis for Event-Specific Tweets

Mashaal Musleh[§]
KACST GIS Technology Innovation Center, Umm Al-Qura University, Makkah, KSA
mmusleh@gistic.org

1. INTRODUCTION

Twitter is one of the most popular social networks where people use to tweet about their opinions, feelings, desires, ...etc. One of the most important and consistent behaviors of Twitter users is posting a plethora of tweets about *events* of different types, e.g., Oscars celebration, soccer games, and natural disasters. For such kind of event-specific tweets, geotagged tweets grab the biggest attention because all events by nature have a spatial extent. For example, while Boston Marathon explosions were going on, in April 2013, users rush to Twitter seeking tweets from the marathon location [2]. Thus, within a large project called Taghreed for comprehensive real-time and offline analysis and visualization for Twitter data (see www.gistic.org/taghreed), we are working on a module that aims to semi-automate the task of visually analyzing event-specific tweets, for arbitrary events, over the spatial and temporal dimensions. In this poster, we present our on-going work on this module and discuss three of its use cases. We also discuss our future plans to extend the module for larger data sizes and make it interactive while the events are going-on.

2. PROBLEM STATEMENT

Input: A set of tweets that are related to a specific event.
Output: A web-based application that facilitates visual spatio-temporal analysis of the input tweets.
Constraints: The application should enable:

- Interactivity, so that any operation's response time should not exceed fractions of a second.
- Spatial analysis at any granularity level within the event spatial extent.
- Temporal analysis at two levels: single point of time and time range within the event period.

With our problem statement constraints, our ultimate vision is to provide an easy tool to create an *efficient* and detailed *visual* analysis tool for a large number of tweets, overcoming the existing limitations of visualization tools. For example, in Oscars 2014 night, the famous Bradley Cooper selfie is retweeted 3+ Million times making a new retweet record. The previous record, of 750K+, was achieved by Barack Obama's "four more years" tweet which is also related to the event of USA presidential elections.

§The author is mentored by Amr Magdy and Mohamed F. Mokbel who are affiliated to both University of Minnesota and KACST GIS Technology Innovation Center at the time this poster is published.

SIGMOD'14, June 22–27, 2014, Snowbird, UT, USA.
ACM 978-1-4503-2376-5/14/06.
http://dx.doi.org/10.1145/2588555.2612666.

3. RELATED WORK

The majority of work on events in Twitter community lies in the category of event detection through conducting spatio-temporal analysis on incoming tweets, few examples are [1, 4, 5]. The only work that addresses automating event analysis is [3]. However, this work mainly targets the problem of automating the analysis of users' responses to identify the segments and topics of the event that got praise or criticism. Both types of work are inherently different from our goal to automate producing visual analysis user interface. In fact, the output of both can be an input to our module to automatically generate the visual analysis interface.

4. SOLUTION OVERVIEW

As we highlighted before, our module aims to *semi-automate* the visual analysis task for a specific event. That points to existence of non-automated steps in the whole process. In this section, we give a brief overview of the whole process. First, we describe the non-automated data collection step for a specific event. Then, we describe how the current module takes this data and produces the corresponding web application per the problem statement in Section 2. Finally, we discuss the future plans for this module to handle larger data sizes and being interactive while the event is going-on.

Before running our module, we manually collect geotagged tweets, through Twitter public streaming APIs, that are related to the target event. In this context, events data are classified into three categories based on event type: (1) Event data that is defined only with certain hashtags, e.g., Oscars, with no certain spatial extent as many people tweet about it globally, (2) Event data that is defined only with certain spatial extent, e.g., Hajj which is a Mulsim religious trip that happens annually only in certain regions in city of Makkah, Saudi Arabia, and (3) Event data that is defined with both certain hashtags and spatial extent, e.g., local sports games. Around the clock, Taghreed, the project that our module is part of, is drinking from Twitter streaming APIs and archiving the tweets in a secondary storage. We extract the event data from either the archive or the streaming APIs directly if we know ahead about the event.

After collecting the event-specific tweets, they are stored in files and fed as an input to our module. The module is producing a simple web application that currently consists of a single HTML file and a single JavaScript file. The web application interface has two mandatory components and two optional components. The two mandatory components are: (1) A geographical map, currently based on Google Maps APIs, that display the spatial distribution of the tweets, and (2) A timeline that allows to move from a time slice to another. The geographical map has two modes of operation: it either presents the individual tweets along with their text content or a heatmap that shows the relative density of the tweets over the space. The timeline has three modes of operation: selecting tweets at either one point of time, a temporal range, or play the tweets changes over time to show the changes in a chronological order. The two optional components are: (1) A check-box set that optionally exclude tweets of certain areas, e.g., cities, and (2) A statistics panel that is used only in what called *two-side events*, where the event involves tweets about two competitor entities, e.g., sports games or elections, to display statistics about tweets of each side. The module takes a configuration file that determines the input tweet files, the included optional components along with its configuration, and the temporal granularity of the timeline. The spatial and temporal extents are automatically detected from the tweets and Google Maps by default allow the zooming functionality to explore the data on different levels of spatial granularity. Section 5 is discussing actual use cases with different examples for the produced web interface.

The future plans for this module lies in two folds: (1) Handling larger sizes of data, and (2) Producing interactive web applications that changes while the event is going-on. Currently, we are using Twitter public streaming APIs to collect data which gives a small percentage of the whole firehose. Thus, the largest number of event-specific tweets we collected so far is 40K tweets. Currently, we handle tweets in main memory for interactive response with the users. However, if we want to scale for the whole firehose size, we can get an extreme example like Oscar 2014 celebration where more than 3 Million tweets are related. For such number, additional challenges are imposed in both using the main memory of web browsers and for rendering the data on the geographical map layers. Our plan is to extend this to use a sort of secondary storage that renders data on geotagged images in the back end. Then, we send those images to the front end to be aligned with the geographical map tiles. This should keep the interactivity requirement satisfied.

As we are using live streaming APIs for data collection, a possible and interesting extension for our module is to produce a visual analysis interface for future events where the data collection is running live while the event is going-on and fed to the web application periodically, e.g., in hourly basis, so that the analysis changes online. Once the event comes to an end, the analysis interface would remain stable as if it is produced with the current version of the module. This may be interesting for some events like USA presidential elections where the whole nation, and probably the whole World, is sitting in front of screens following and tweeting the results.

5. SUMMARY OF MAJOR RESULTS

We applied our module to three major events: (1) Oscars 2014 celebration, (2) Saudi final cup soccer game, and

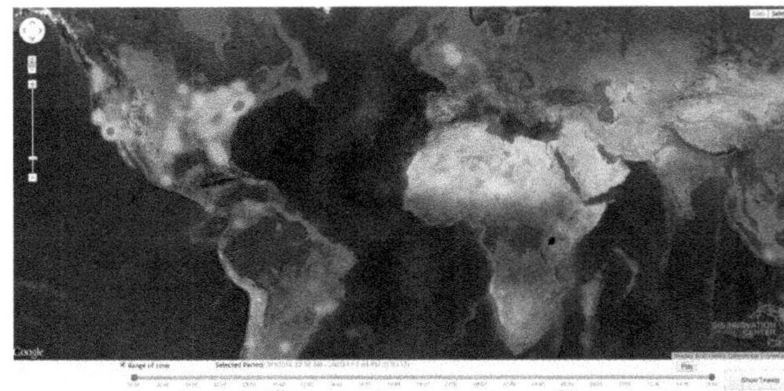

Figure 1: Oscars 2014 tweets

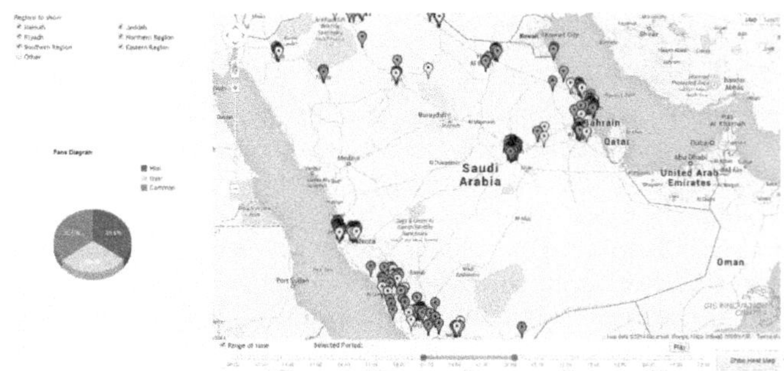

Figure 2: Saudi final cup soccer game tweets

(3) Hajj, which is the largest gathering of Muslim people worldwide annually in city of Makkah, Saudi Arabia. Figures 1 and 2 show two examples of the produced interface. We can see the difference between a two-side event like the soccer game and a normal event like Oscars 2014. In a two-side event, the statistics panel is used to show ratio of tweets of each side over time. Also, the soccer game is a local event that make sense to use check-boxes to include/exclude tweets from certain cities in Saudi Arabia. The three produced interfaces are available online on www.gistic.org/oscars2014,
www.gistic.org/hilal_vs_nasr, and www.gistic.org/hajj-tweets.

The provided spatio-temporal visual analysis is helpful in showing the users behavior during the event. For our use cases, in Hajj tweets, our interface tells something about the flow of pedestrians during Hajj days in Makkah regions and people opinions about the provided services, through showing individual tweets, which is important for the administrative authorities. In the local soccer game, one can visually measure the popularity of each team by city and over time. This is useful for sports analysis broadcasts.

6. REFERENCES

[1] H. Abdelhaq, C. Sengstock, and M. Gertz. EvenTweet: Online Localized Event Detection from Twitter. In *VLDB*, 2013.

[2] http://www.latimes.com/business/technology/la-fi-tn-after-boston-explosions-people-rush-to-twitter-for-breaking-news-20130415,0,3729783.story,2013.

[3] Y. Hu, F. Wang, and S. Kambhampati. Listening to the Crowd: Automated Analysis of Events via Aggregated Twitter Sentiment. In *Proceedings of the International Joint Conference on Artificial Intelligence*, pages 2640–2646, 2013.

[4] R. Li, K. H. Lei, R. Khadiwala, and K. C.-C. Chang. TEDAS: A Twitter-based Event Detection and Analysis System. In *ICDE*, 2012.

[5] T. Sakaki, M. Okazaki, and Y. Matsuo. Earthquake shakes twitter users: Real-time event detection by social sensors. In *WWW*, 2010.

PackageBuilder: Querying for packages of tuples

Kevin Fernandes*
University of Massachusetts
Amherst, USA
kevinf@umass.edu

additional authors:
Matteo Brucato Rahul Ramakrishna Azza Abouzied Alexandra Meliou

ABSTRACT

PACKAGEBUILDER is a system that extends query engines to support package generation. A package is a collection of tuples with certain global properties defined on the collection as a whole. In contrast to traditional query answers where each answer tuple needs to satisfy the query predicates, each answer package needs to satisfy global constraints on the collection of tuples: e.g., a package of recipes that collectively do not exceed 2,200 calories. PACKAGEBUILDER introduces simple extensions to the SQL language to support package-level predicates, and includes a simple interface that allows users to load datasets and interactively specify package queries. Our system allows users to interactively navigate through the result packages, and to provide feedback by fixing tuples within a package. PACKAGEBUILDER automatically processes this feedback to refine the package queries, and generate new sets of results.

Categories and Subject Descriptors:
H.2.3 [Languages]: Query languages
Keywords: PACKAGEBUILDER, package queries, constraint optimization

1. INTRODUCTION

Traditional database queries define selection predicates that each tuple in the result needs to satisfy. For example, it is easy to query a database of recipes to retrieve all the gluten-free meals, assuming that the amount of gluten is reported as an attribute for each recipe. Traditional SQL queries fall short in scenarios that require a set of answer tuples to satisfy constraints collectively. Such scenarios arise in a variety of applications.

EXAMPLE 1.1 (MEAL PLANNER). *An athlete needs to put together a dietary plan in preparation for a race. She wants a high-protein set of three meals for the day, that are between 2000 and 2500 calories in total. All meals should be gluten-free.*

This example cannot be expressed in traditional SQL: SQL queries can easily check conditions that apply to each tuple individually (e.g., no gluten), but they do not offer ways to specify constraints that need to be verified collectively over a set of answer tuples (e.g., enforce a limit on the total number of calories).

We present PACKAGEBUILDER, a system that augments database functionality to support the creation of *packages*. A *package* is a collection of tuples that individually satisfy *base constraints* and collectively satisfy *global constraints*. The base constraints are equivalent to regular selection predicates. For example, in the meal planner application, the gluten-free restriction is a base constraint, as it can be verified independently on each meal. In contrast, the requirement that total calories should be within 2,000 to 2,500 calories needs to be assessed over a collection of meals.

2. A QUERY LANGUAGE FOR PACKAGES

We designed PaQL, a SQL-based package query language for PACKAGEBUILDER, which allows for the declarative specification of packages. We use the meal planner scenario (Example 1.1) to highlight PaQL's key features. The following query builds the athlete's daily meal package:

```
SELECT      PACKAGE(R) AS P
FROM        Recipes R
WHERE       R.gluten = 'free'
SUCH THAT   count(*) =3 AND
            sum(calories) BETWEEN 2000 and 2500
MAXIMIZE    sum(protein)
```

The introduction of the keyword PACKAGE differentiates PaQL queries from relational SQL queries. Semantically, PACKAGE, constructs *bags* from the tuples of the base relations listed in the FROM clause. With no further constraints, there are infinitely many packages that can be built from non-empty base relations[1].

The *objective* clause MAXIMIZE is unique to packages as well: it specifies that out of all packages that satisfy the base and global constraints, the ones with larger values in the MAXIMIZE clause are preferable. The objective clause can

*Kevin Fernades is a senior undergraduate student, and active contributor to the development of the meal-planner application MealBot within the PACKAGEBUILDER framework. The other contributors are listed as additional authors.

[1] A package can have duplicate items within it. For example a recipe can repeat multiple times.

SIGMOD'14, June 22–27, 2014, Snowbird, UT, USA.
ACM 978-1-4503-2376-5/14/06.
http://dx.doi.org/10.1145/2588555.2612667.

list more than one objective, e.g., MAXIMIZE sum(protein), sum(carbs).

A package query defines two kinds of constraints. *Base constraints* are defined in the WHERE clause, and they are equivalent to selection predicates: any tuple in the package needs to satisfy all base constraints. In the example query, the base constraint R.gluten = 'free' specifies that each meal in the package should be gluten-free. *Global constraints* are defined in the SUCH THAT clause: each global constraint needs to be satisfied collectively in the whole package. For example, count(*)=3 specifies that the entire package should have exactly 3 meals.

3. COMPUTING PACKAGE RESULTS

Evaluating package queries is nontrivial: even if packages do not allow duplicate tuples, the number of possible packages is in the worst case exponential in the number of base tuples. In contrast to preference queries [6, 3], PACKAGEBUILDER does not define preferences across constraints, and relies on different evaluation methods that combine the use of constraint optimization solvers, heuristic pruning, and local search. PACKAGEBUILDER uses and extends the TIRESIAS query engine [4] to evaluate PaQL queries. The evaluation engine translates package queries to constraint optimization problems, and employs state-of-the-art constraint solvers to derive valid packages. Even though PACKAGEBUILDER uses the TIRESIAS query engine it has several differences:

- Package queries specify tuple collections (packages), whereas the how-to queries in TIRESIAS specify modifications (updates) to underlying datasets.
- The PACKAGEBUILDER engine allows a tuple to appear multiple times in a package result; this feature does not map to any operation in TIRESIAS.
- PaQL is SQL-based whereas TIRESIAS uses a variant of Datalog.
- PACKAGEBUILDER supports arbitrary boolean formulas in the SUCH THAT clause, whereas TIRESIAS only supports conjunctive how-to queries.
- PACKAGEBUILDER employs additional heuristic and pruning techniques to increase the efficiency of package queries.

4. UNDERGRADUATE INVOLVEMENT

The undergraduate author is developing the MealBot application as a demonstration of the PACKAGEBUILDER framework. MealBot allows users to seamlessly create meal plans that are customized to their nutritional needs. For example, children struggling with obesity are often prescribed a diet that includes 5 meals a day such that each meal is between 300 and 450 calories and the meal plan itself maximizes protein intake and minimizes fat intake. A child's parent can use MealBot to specify complex constraints and retrieve suitable meal plans. MealBot provides different interaction methods to specify and refine meal plans, both using PaQL as well as allowing users to enter constraints through a visual interface.

We list here the major efforts that involved the undergraduate author:

Backend support (ongoing). Interactions with MealBot are translated behind the scenes to PaQL queries. This layer, developed in Python, transforms PaQL queries to constraint optimization problems and invokes CPLEX [2] to evaluate them. This is a team effort that focuses on different evaluation strategies and design of optimization heuristics for PaQL queries. The undergraduate author is involved in the implementation of greedy heuristics that explore package solutions in a random-walk fashion. The undergraduate author is also heavily involved in testing and modifying components of the system.

Front-end development (ongoing). The MealBot interface is also a team effort, aiming to support various forms of package representations and query interactions. The undergraduate author is involved in various components of the interface support, including the development of a *suggestion* interface: when a user of MealBot selects an attribute, tuple, or value, the interface provides intelligent suggestions for possible constraints.

Data collection (completed). For the purposes of MealBot, we collected a rich dataset of recipes, including detailed nutritional data from two web sources: Yummly [5] and allrecipes.com [1]. Our web crawler used the Cheerio and PG modules of the Node.js platform. All of the collected data contains absolute nutritional information, such as calorie count, and each attribute's daily percentage value based on a 2000 calorie diet. MealBot uses PostgreSQL as the backend data management system, and all collected recipes are stored in a single table.

5. RESEARCH DIRECTIONS

We are currently exploring several interesting research directions within the PACKAGEBUILDER project. Package queries are strictly more complex than regular SQL queries, and their evaluation is not feasible with exhaustive search. We are exploring solutions that reduce that search space prior to the execution of package predicates, and we are experimenting with different greedy heuristics.

On the interaction front, we are developing smart filters that allow users to navigate the solution space more efficiently. The challenge is that typically there is a large number of valid package solutions, and each package in itself can be large. As a result, users are overwhelmed by the results, and have a hard time understanding them. Our goal is to find meaningful summarizations of the solution space, for example, grouping similar packages together and quickly finding related packages with each user selection.

6. REFERENCES

[1] Allrecipes. http://allrecipes.com.

[2] IBM ILOG. CPLEX: High-performance software for mathematical programming and optimization. http://www.ilog.com/products/cplex.

[3] W. Kießling, M. Endres, and F. Wenzel. The preference sql system - an overview. *IEEE Data Engineering Bulletin*, 34(2):11–18, 2011.

[4] A. Meliou and D. Suciu. Tiresias: The database oracle for how-to queries. In *Proceedings of the ACM SIGMOD International Conference on Management of Data (SIGMOD)*, pages 337–348, Scottsdale, AZ, May 2012.

[5] Yummly. http://www.yummly.com.

[6] X. Zhang and J. Chomicki. Preference queries over sets. *2013 IEEE 29th International Conference on Data Engineering (ICDE)*, 0:1019–1030, 2011.

Privacy Preserving Social Graphs for High Precision Community Detection

Himel Dev *
Department of Computer Science and Engineering
Bangladesh University of Engineering and Technology, Dhaka, Bangladesh
himeldev@gmail.com

ABSTRACT

Discovering communities from a social network requires publishing the social network's data. However, community detection from raw data of a social network may reveal many sensitive information of the involved parties, e.g., how much a user is involved in which communities. An individual may not want to reveal such sensitive information. To resolve this issue, we address the problem of privacy preserving community detection in social networks. More specifically, we want to ensure that community detection is possible from the published social graph/data but the identity of users involved in a community should not be disclosed.

Categories and Subject Descriptors

H.2.8 [**Database Management**]: Database Applications—*Data Mining*

Keywords

Social Networks, Community Detection, Privacy

1. PROBLEM FORMULATION

Community Detection: The community detection in a social graph $G(V, E)$ involves grouping vertices into clusters $C = \{C_1, C_2, C_3, ...\}$, where C_i contains vertices from V that are closely related, and hence forms a community.

Privacy Preserving Community Detection: Our objective is to detect original communities from the published social graph, but the identity of the users involved in a community should not be disclosed.

2. RELATED WORK

Several anonymization methods have been proposed to battle the privacy attacks on social network data [5, 3, 4]. A popular class of these methods involves graph modification, i.e., anonymizing a graph by modifying (i.e, inserting and/or deleting) edges and vertices. However, none of these works strongly consider preserving *community structure* while developing privacy protection techniques. As a result, the developed graph modification techniques lead to indiscriminate modification of edges without focusing on the underlying community structure. Such indiscriminate modification of edges may disfigure the community structure and lead to misleading communities which highly deviate from the communities in the original social graph. Thus, state-of-the art graph modification approaches fail to serve our purpose of high precision community detection from privacy preserving social graphs.

3. METHODOLOGY

Our solution is based on a probability graph, where each edge is assigned a probability denoting the likelihood of two users to belong to the same community. We use the likelihood information from the probability graph to construct a privacy-preserving version of the original social graph which is highly accurate in terms of community detection queries. In particular, we greedily modify the original social graph focusing on the community structure preservation, using the likelihood information from the probability graph.

Probability Graph: Given a weighted/un-weighted social graph G, we construct a *Probability Graph* (weighted) G_p, where each weight p_{uv} represents a probability between two vertices u and v to belong in the same community [1]. The vertices of G_p are similar to those in G, but the number of edges in G_p is higher. Note that, an edge with weight p_{uv} exists in G_p, when u and v are either directly connected or connected via one or more common neighbors in G.

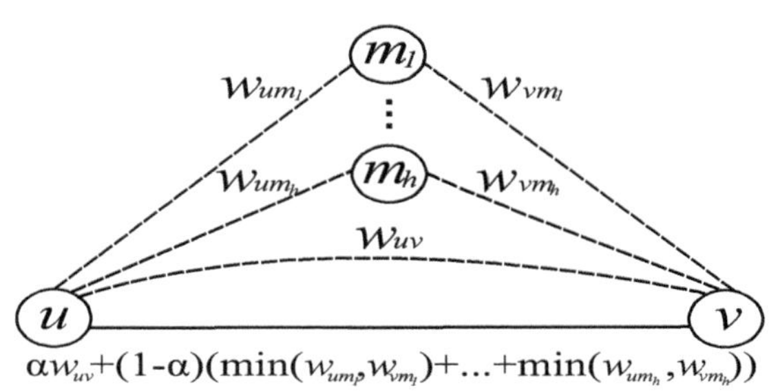

Figure 1: Probability (p_{uv}) Calculation

Let, the degree of interaction between two users u and v in the original social graph G be w_{uv}. Also assume that in

*Under supervision of Dr. Mohammed Eunus Ali and Dr. Tanzima Hashem from CSE, BUET

SIGMOD/PODS'14, June 22–27, 2014, Snowbird, UT, USA.
ACM 978-1-4503-2376-5/14/06.
http://dx.doi.org/10.1145/2588555.2612668.

the original social graph G, u and v have h common neighbors (mutual friends) $\{m_1, m_2, ..., m_h\}$, and the degree of interaction of u and v with any common neighbor m_i be w_{um_i} and w_{vm_i} respectively. Then, in the probability graph G_p, we define the *probability* p_{uv} of two users u and v to belong to the same community as $p_{uv} = \alpha * w_{uv} + (1 - \alpha) * \sum_{i=1}^{h} min(w_{um_i}, w_{vm_i})$.

Privacy Preserving Social Graph: We construct privacy preserving version of social graph which can be used to identify communities analogous to the communities in the original social graph. We construct the privacy graph by greedily modifying the original graph using likelihood information from the probability graph. The key idea of this greedy modification is to replace the random edge deletion-addition scheme of state-of-the-art graph modification approaches with a biased random scheme that favors the existing inter-community edges during edge deletion and the non-existing inner-community edges during edge addition.

Biased Random Scheme: Under the biased random scheme, (i) an existing potential inter-community edge has higher probability of being deleted and (ii) a non-existing potential inner-community edge has higher probability of being added, during the modification of the social graph to construct a privacy preserving version of it. The scheme identifies the potential inter and inner community edges based on the likelihood information from the probability graph G_p. Note that, a high weighted edge in the probability graph is a potential inner-community edge, and a low weighted edge in the probability graph is a potential inter-community edge. The scheme works as follows:

1. Split the edge set of probability graph G_p into two disjoint sets E (analogous to the edge set in G) and E' (potential inner-community edges non-existent in G). Note that, each edge e_{uv} that belongs to one of these sets, has an associated probability value p_{uv}.

2. Create an edge set E^p for the privacy graph and initialize it with the edges from the set E.

3. (i) For each edge $e_{uv} \in E$, calculate its probability of being deleted from the privacy graph as: $\frac{f(1-p_{uv})}{\sum_{e_{ij} \in E} f(1-p_{ij})}$.
(ii) For each edge $e_{uv} \in E'$, calculate its probability of being added to the privacy graph as: $\frac{f(p_{uv})}{\sum_{e_{ij} \in E'} f(p_{ij})}$.
Here, $f()$ is a monotonic function which defines the degree of bias during privacy graph construction. For example, an exponential $f()$ function implies a highly biased graph modification technique, which is most likely to delete only the existing inter-community edges and add only the non-existing inner-community edges during edge modification. However, such a function makes the process relatively deterministic, which is not preferred in case of privacy preserving techniques.

4. Calculate the cumulative deletion/addition probabilities (cp) for edge set E/E'.

5. To delete/add an edge, (i) generate a random number $U(0, 1)$, (ii) if the number is within the range $cp_{(i-1)}$ and cp_i, delete/add the ith edge of the set E/E' from/to the edge set E^p. Note that, cp_0 is 1.

6. For consecutive m edge deletion or addition, repeat step 3 to step 5 for m times.

During edge addition, one can also allow edges that are not in the set E' by preserving their slot. For example, to probabilistically allow $x\%$ edges barring the set E', we need to calculate the addition probability of an edge $e_{uv} \in E'$ (associated with step 3) as: $(1 - \frac{x}{100}) * \frac{f(p_{uv})}{\sum_{e_{ij} \in E'} f(p_{ij})}$.

Further, for the edges outside E', we need to distribute the remaining probability $(\frac{x}{100})$ uniformly among the edges.

The biased random scheme can also be used with weighted graphs. In case of weighted graphs, we assign weights to the newly added edges by generating random numbers using the probability distribution corresponding to the current edge weights.

4. EXPERIMENTAL EVALUATION

We evaluate the performance of our proposed privacy graph construction method by comparing it with the state-of-the-art random m edge deletion-insertion method backed up by many approaches [2]. We compare these two methods in terms of the degree to which these privacy preserving methods preserve the underlying community structure of the original social graph. More specifically, for each of these privacy preserving methods, we determine the relevance/similarity of identified communities from the original social graph and the privacy graph constructed via the corresponding method. We use normalized mutual information (NMI) and pairwise F-measure (PWF) to compare the similarity of identified communities from the original social graph and corresponding privacy graph. Then, we compare the NMI and PWF values (degree of relevance) attained by each method to identify the superior method in terms of community structure preservation. We can see that, for two networks (Karate and Jazz) our algorithm achieves significantly higher NMI and PWF values compared to the competing random m edge deletion-insertion method.

Algorithm ↓	Karate		Jazz	
	NMI	PWF	NMI	PWF
Proposed	0.8283	0.8551	0.8643	0.8539
Random m del-add	0.4759	0.4454	0.6753	0.5257

5. REFERENCES

[1] H. Dev, M. E. Ali, and T. Hashem. User interaction based community detection in online social networks. In *Database Systems for Advanced Applications*, volume 8422, pages 296–310. 2014.

[2] M. Hay, G. Miklau, D. Jensen, P. Weis, and S. Srivastava. Anonymizing social networks. Technical Report 07-19, University of Massachusetts Amherst, March 2007.

[3] X. Wu, X. Ying, K. Liu, and L. Chen. A survey of privacy-preservation of graphs and social networks. In *Managing and Mining Graph Data*, volume 40, pages 421–453. 2010.

[4] E. Zheleva and L. Getoor. Privacy in social networks: A survey. In *Social Network Data Analytics*, pages 277–306. 2011.

[5] B. Zhou, J. Pei, and W. Luk. A brief survey on anonymization techniques for privacy preserving publishing of social network data. *SIGKDD Explor. Newsl.*, 10(2):12–22, December 2008.

Author Index

www.ingramcontent.com/pod-product-compliance
Ingram Content Group UK Ltd.
Pitfield, Milton Keynes, MK11 3LW, UK
UKHW051420290926
15471UKWH00009B/1707